FOCUS ON EDUCATIONAL RESEARCH IN THE UNITED KINGDOM
1997 – 1999

Volume 1: The Research

Edited by

Janet May-Bowles

Alison Evans

Alison Jones

63108303

INVESTOR IN PEOPLE

Published in December 1999
by the National Foundation for Educational Research,
The Mere, Upton Park, Slough, Berkshire SL1 2DQ

ISBN 0 7005 3000 2

CONTENTS

FOREWORD

We would like to thank all the researchers who sent in details of their work for inclusion in the database. For this publication we have included all the items received in the period 1997 – 1999. Items are arranged alphabetically by the name of the institution where the research is being carried out; within each institution, the entries are arranged alphabetically by department and within the department by researcher. Each entry is listed against all of its keywords. Whilst every effort has been made to check the accuracy of the information, there may be inconsistencies and errors for which we apologise. A linked service operated by the NFER's Library and Information Service backs up *Focus on Educational Research* (see below).

EDUCATIONAL RESEARCH SERVICE

If there is a project on which you would like to have more information please check if there are any publications. If there are, we are likely to be able to supply photocopies for you (within the terms of the Copyright Act). We may also be able to supply a list of bibliographic references to additional items for you to read.

You can contact us by letter:

> Educational Research Service
> National Foundation for Educational Research
> The Mere
> Upton Park
> Slough
> Berkshire
> SL1 2DQ

Telephone: 01753 574123

Fax: 01753 747193

E-mail: enquiries@nfer.ac.uk **or** j.may-bowles@nfer.ac.uk.

ACKNOWLEDGEMENTS

The editors would like to thank the secretarial staff and other staff in the various institutions who distributed the questionnaires and ensured that they were completed and returned.

We are also grateful to Enver Carim, Mary Hargreaves, Richard Downing and Hilary Hosier for their assistance with the production of this book.

Aberdeen University

0001

Centre for Educational Research, Department of Sociology, Edward Wright
Building, Dunbar Street, Aberdeen AB24 3QY
01224 272000

Aberdeen University, Department of Postgraduate Medicine, Postgraduate Centre,
Polwarth Building, Foresterhill, Aberdeen AB25 2ZD
01224 681818

French,F.Ms; *Supervisor*: Kiger, A. Dr

A study of continuing medical education for general practitioners in Grampian region, Orkney and Shetland in the 1990s

ABSTRACT: All General Practitioners (GPs) practising in North-East Scotland, Orkney and Shetland in 1995 were offered the opportunity to draw up a personal learning plan (PLP) aided by a continuing medical examination (CME) adviser. This project had been initiated by Dr Malcolm J. Valentine, Associate Adviser in General Practice. Within this context, the following research aims were identified: 1) to set modern general practice in its historical, political, economic and social contexts; 2) to study the divisions within general practice, particularly gender divisions; 3) to explore attempts by Government and the profession to control the work of general practice and the CME of GPs; 4) to identify the obstacles faced by GPs when trying to identify and/or meet their CME needs; and 5) to explore differences in approach to CME by individual GPs. The following surveys were conducted: a) a pilot survey of all 390 GP principals in Grampian, Orkney and Shetland; b) a survey of 242 participants in the PLPs project and 89 non-participants; c) and a survey of non-principals in Grampian region only. Records of CME attendances by principals were scrutinised and 36 interviews conducted with randomly selected GPs. The results indicate that: 1) GPs are working under increased pressure due to Government reforms and increased patient demand; 2)general practice is internally divided by type of practice (fundholding and non-fundholding), by gender and occupational status (male, full-time principals versus female, part-time principals and non-principals); 3) lack of time was the main obstacle to participation in CME; 4) GPs approaches to CME ranged from the 'passiveaccepter' to the 'active seeker'.

PUBLISHED MATERIAL: FRENCH, F.H. & VALENTINE, M.J. 'An evaluation of personal learning plans for general practitioners in Grampian region (North-East Scotland)', British Journal of General Practice. (in press).; FRENCH, F.H. & VALENTINE, M.J. 'The introduction of personal learning plans forgeneral practitioners in Grampian region, Orkney and Shetland', Education in General Practice. (in press).

STATUS: Individual research

DATE OF RESEARCH: 1996-continuing

KEYWORDS: **medical education; physicians; professional continuing education**

0002

Department of Education, Regent Walk, Aberdeen AB9 1FX
01224 272000

Darling, J. Dr; Glendinning, A. Mr

Gender and subject choice amongst pupils

ABSTRACT: This project aimed to establish a baseline picture for further study using data on presentation and performance in national examinations. At S4 (age = 15) there are marked variations in the proportions of males and females across the curriculum, although there is equality in Mathematics and English. The polarisation is even more marked at S5. Aggregating performance across all subjects, females clearly do better than males at Standard Grade (S4). There is little or no overall difference at Higher Grade (S5), but there is greater diversity of performance according to subject.

STATUS: Sponsored project

SOURCE OF GRANT: Grampian Region TVE £1,500

DATE OF RESEARCH: 1993-1993

KEYWORDS: **academic achievement; choice of subjects; sex differences**

0003

Department of Education, Regent Walk, Aberdeen AB9 1FX
01224 272000

Darling, J. Dr; Glendinning, A. Mr

Gender and promotion amongst teaching staff in Grampian

ABSTRACT: This project used existing data to explore the promotion patterns amongst teaching staff in the Grampian Region. A research report has been generated, indicating, amongst other findings, that in secondary schools men are more likely to be in promoted posts even within departments numerically dominated by women (e.g. English). In the primary sector, size of school is a major determinant of whether women achieve promotion to headship.

STATUS: Sponsored project

SOURCE OF GRANT: Grampian Region TVE £1,500

DATE OF RESEARCH: 1993-1993

KEYWORDS: **equal opportunities - jobs; gender equality; promotion -occupational; teaching profession; women teachers; womens employment**

0004

Department of Education, Regent Walk, Aberdeen AB9 1FX 0
1224 272000

Shucksmith, J. Mrs; Kiger, A. Dr; Glendinning, A. Mr

Expanding education: the expansion of further and higher education and young people's welfare

ABSTRACT: The expansion of the tertiary sector will raise problems for student welfare. The project examines the well-being and progress of approximately 2,500 students in 3 higher education establishments in Scotland. The study has 2 major strands: a quantitative survey of a cohort of students entering the tertiary sector, involving a clustered random sample stratified across sectors; and a qualitative study of some 20 students involving indepth interviews and keeping a diary. The intention is to explore the different needs for student support in an era when a broader cohort of students is being drawn into the system.

STATUS: Sponsored project

SOURCE OF GRANT: Aberdeen University £17,000

DATE OF RESEARCH: 1992-1993

KEYWORDS: **further education; higher education; sixteen to nineteen education; student health and welfare; student needs**

0005

Department of Management Studies, Edward Wright Building, Dunbar Street, Old Aberdeen AB24 3QY 01224 272000

Aberdeen University, Arkleton Centre for Rural Development Research, St Mary's, King's College, Aberdeen AB24 3UF

McKee, L. Dr; Maclean, C. Dr; Mauthner, N. Dr

Children, family, community and work: an ethnography of the oil and gas industry in Scotland

ABSTRACT: The research explores inter-relationships between parental employment, workplace policies and family life, in the context of the dramatic changes in labour market structure, culture and policies seen in the last decade. Key questions include: 1) Has the changing nature of work offered positive opportunities for some parents and their children? 2) Are some employment arrangements disadvantaging parents and/or children, socially, physically or emotionally? 3) How do children experience, construct and understand both parental working patterns and the wider labour market? 4) How do chldren perceive oil work and the oil industry, and what are their future work aspirations? 5) To what extent are parental work decisions influenced by children, both directly and indirectly? 6) What occupational health and employment policies related to work-family issues are in place across the oil industry, and how are these developing? 7) What are the policy implications of taking into account the expressed views, needs and interests of children and parents with regard to work-family issues? The research questions are being addressed through an indepth case study of 50 families living in communities in the Grampian area. The families have children aged 8-12 and a parent employed in the oil and gas industry. Companies in the oil and gas sector are at the forefront of changes which are beginning to affect many organisations worldwide (e.g. internationalisation, outsourcing, casualisation). Issues arising from these changes include protracted absences from home, long distance commuting, flexibility, lengthening working hours, and job mobility and insecurity. The project is taking a mixed-methods approach. Focus groups with children are being conducted in primary schools, including the use of vignette, discussion and drawing techniques. Parents of focus group children then complete a postal questionnaire, which provides detailed work-family information before follow-up interviews with all family members are conducted in the home or workplace. In order to give a holistic picture of the lives of families employed within the oil and gas industry, the data from children and parents are set within broader community and industrial contexts. Interviews are being carried out with key community figures including teachers, social workers, doctors, educational psychologists, councillors and ministers. Interviews are also being conducted with members of oil industry related organisations (including trades unions and women/family support groups) and with occupational health and mental health professionals. Human resources personnel in operator and contractor companies are being interviewed about employment, family-friendly, and occupational health policy and practice. The project aims to formulate policy recommendations in partnership with the oil industry, occupational and community health services and agencies acting on behalf of children. The findings will add to European Union debate about 'the reconciliation of work and home life' and help develop and promote child-sensitive employment practices and policies. The research findings will be of interest to a wide range of groups including: children, parents, carers, schools and educational bodies, oil companies, voluntary sector agencies, occupational and community medical services, and local and national government.

STATUS: Sponsored project

SOURCE OF GRANT: Economic and Social Research Council £120,412

DATE OF RESEARCH: 1997-continuing

KEYWORDS: childhood attitudes; children; community; employed parents; employment patterns; family life; fathers; home environment; petroleum industry; scotland

Anglia Polytechnic University

0006

Anglia Business School, Danbury Park Conference Centre, Danbury, Chelmsford CM3 4AT
01245 225511

Marchant, J. Mr; Trafford, V. Dr

The management of income generation in secondary schools

ABSTRACT: The Education Reform Act 1988 has provided schools with opportunities to manage its site and premises beyond the school day. Schools may also, now, supplement their budgets by lettings, the hire of facilities and other activities which raise funds. Income generating activities have thus developed beyond the traditional support provided by Parent Teacher Associations to something quite central to a school's financial base. Evidence shows that secondary schools which seek to generate additional income are likely – initially – to exhibit: (1) development plans which do not refer to this financial activity; (2) staff role statements which seldom include responsibility for this activity; (3) a general staff awareness of the need for this activity; (4) the absence of planned staff development for this activity; and (5) alterations being made to the traditional roles of teachers who are involved in this activity. This evidence also suggests that schools' dependence on self-generated funds will bring about internal structural change thereby consolidating the activity of income generation within the institutional management system of schools. The current research is testing the extent to which formal structural change has been introduced by secondary schools which have adopted strategic income generating policies. Follow-up questionnaires, and selective interviews, are being undertaken with twenty-five secondary schools in one local education authority. The findings will illuminate current management practices in schools which generate additional income from their own efforts.

PUBLISHED MATERIAL: SMITH, M. (Ed). (1993). Managing institutional development. Loughborough: Loughborough University Press.

STATUS: Sponsored project

SOURCE OF GRANT: Anglia Polytechnic University £500

DATE OF RESEARCH: 1992-1993

KEYWORDS: educational finance; fund raising; income; money management; school funds; secondary education

0007

Anglia Business School, Danbury Park Conference Centre, Danbury, Chelmsford CM3 4AT
01245 225511

Trafford, V. Dr; Evans, D. Mr

The Technical and Vocational Education Initiative (TVEI) in Essex schools and colleges: capitalising on the investment

ABSTRACT: The Technical and Vocational Education Initiative (TVEI) extension is now four years through its seven year lifespan in the Essex Local Education Authority (LEA). The research is focused upon the schools and colleges who are participating in Phase One of the project and whose funding ceased in March 1993. The aim of the research is to identify how institutional management and curriculum practices have determined the effective delivery of TVEI. The investigation is based on responses from all 44 schools and colleges involved in Phase One (1988-93), for which purpose a questionnaire has been designed, piloted and administered with a 5% return. Interviews were also conducted in nine schools, randomly selected. The data gathered from these schools, which includes school documentation, institutional plans, inspectors' reports etc., will provide material for case studies. Note has been taken of the literature which details how institutions respond to, adopt and then implement developmental change. This has been supplemented by drawing on information from national publications, consultants' reports and other publicly available TVEI documentation. An interim report suggests that there is strong evidence of assimilation of TVEI practices in mainstream curriculum and TVEI processes (e.g. monitoring and evaluation) in institutional management procedures. It is also evident that there is a high level of integration in those case study schools with whom good practice is associated. The final report will be published in April 1993.

STATUS: Sponsored project

SOURCE OF GRANT: Essex County Council £8,000

DATE OF RESEARCH: 1992-1993

KEYWORDS: institutional administration; tvei

0008

Anglia Business School, Danbury Park Conference Centre, Danbury, Chelmsford CM3 4AT
01245 225511

Davies, J. Prof.

Devolution in universities: a study of the devolvement of authority to faculties

ABSTRACT: Many universities in Europe and Australia are currently engaged in devolving budgetary, academic and administrative authority to faculties, for various reasons: creation of large clusters to secure academic excellence; simplification of administrative processes; empowerment; creation of an entrepreneurial ethic; and effective management of financial reduction. The study attempts to explore: 1) reasons for devolution in various sample universities in Australia, New Zealand, Netherlands and UK; 2) manifestations of devolution in budget, academic and administrative terms and its scope in eleven major areas of university administration. 3) consequences for faculty management. 4) consequences for the central management of the university. 5) effects in academic, administration and budgeting terms. The study is based on a number of institutional case studies which are assessed against several templates of organisational development.

The results are intended to be: principles for the conception of devolution; classification of manifestations of devolution; and a template for the assessment of the effectiveness of devolution.

STATUS: Sponsored project

SOURCE OF GRANT: Three Australian Universities ; Australian Committee of Vice Chancellors

DATE OF RESEARCH: 1992-1997

KEYWORDS: educational administration; universities; university administration

0009

Anglia Business School, Danbury Park Conference Centre, Danbury, Chelmsford CM3 4AT
01245 225511

Lung, M. M; *Supervisors*: Trafford, V. Dr; Evans, D. Mr

Nursing education: the integration of an emergent discipline into the academic community

ABSTRACT: The early and mid 1990s represent a period of significant organisational transition for nursing education in England. The colleges of nursing which move into the national higher education sector both face and, in their turn, create specific issues of academic, organisational and managerial integration. Previous research findings (Lung 1993) posited that the process of amalgamation for colleges with universities exhibited the three stages of affiliation, accreditation and coalition of integration. The proposed research concerns itself with this final stage. It sets out to test integration, as defined in the final stage, by the value sets of the academic community towards the emergence of nursing as a new, and young, discipline. A representative sample of universities and their respective amalgamating schools of nursing, will form the study area. Evidence will be accessed from documentary sources, questionnaire surveys and interviews to provide triangulations upon perceptions of integration. Use will be made of interviews with key personnel to identify and catalogue the micropolitical influences during the period of transition in certain amalgamations. This evidence will be presented through case studies from which models will be advanced to explain the mutual dynamics of institutional transition and reception.

STATUS: Individual research

DATE OF RESEARCH: 1993-1997

KEYWORDS: **higher education; nurse education**

0010

Anglia Business School, Danbury Park Conference Centre, Danbury, Chelmsford CM3 4AT 01245 225511

Boddington, G. Mr; *Supervisors*: Jenkins, H. Prof. ; Trafford, V. Dr

Transition from public service to market place: staff experiences in one local education authority, 1992-1995

ABSTRACT: The research will be undertaken within one local education authority (LEA) during the period April 1992 to April 1995. The focus for the research is to trace the behaviours adopted by a group of education advisors attempting to come to terms with a a major change in their working environment. The context will be the staff response to, and handling of the change-over from, the traditional LEA public service role to one where entrepreneurial values dominate. Thus the research will document, interpret and explain what happened and what can be learned from the experience of a single LEA during this unique transition in a field of study where at present no research based literature exists. The researcher is a member of the organisation to be investigated. As a result, an ethnographic approach will be used to understand the meanings and significances which staff in the LEA place upon their own behaviour and that of others. This evidence will be supplemented by the analysis of documentary materials and chronological interviews with both advisory service staff and other key members of the LEA. A triangulation of these staff perspectives on the emergent themes will provide internal and theoretical empirical validity. Findings will be presented through case studies of an incident and multiple concept nature. Systems mapping will be used to illustrate, and then to analyse, the changing role relationships within these episodic case studies over the period of the research. This data will be rich in real life experiences, thereby enabling grounded theory propositions to be advanced. Thus the case studies will not be offered as a model from which generalities may be drawn, rather they will provide an illumination which will relate to other local authority organisations as they move towards market orientation. Thus as a consequence of these findings the research will: 1) map the micropolitics and staff interactions during the above period, thereby identifying conjunctions of criticality in the life of the LEA and its advisory service; 2) create models which explain the phases through which the above change processes appear to pass, noting how specific situation variables can be related together; and 3) offer a concluding commentary upon the way(s) by which one LEA prepared itself to operate in a more entrepreneurial manner in its advisory service.

STATUS: Individual research

DATE OF RESEARCH: 1993-1997

KEYWORDS: educational administration; local education authorities

0011

Anglia Business School, Danbury Park Conference Centre, Danbury, Chelmsford CM3 4AT 01245 225511

Fenton, M. Mr; *Supervisors*: Trafford, V. Dr ; Evans, D. Mr

The role of corporate image in parental choice: a study of parental and institutional perceptions

ABSTRACT: This research investigates the role of institutional image in the process of parental choice of secondary school. The focus of the research will be on the nature and evolution of the decision-making process which families undertake and the impact of the corporate identity of schools on that process. It will also examine the process by which schools seek to project their image in the market place. The Education Reform Act 1988 provides the essential context of the research. In the climate of this and subsequent legislation, schools have become dependent on pupil numbers for the allocation of resources (the Local Management of Schools). Reinforced by demographic trends, many areas have been characterised by surplus capacity in terms of school places and this has led to greatly increased competition between schools for pupils. In this market oriented climate, it has become increasingly important for schools to develop strategies designed to gain maximum market advantage. From the parental standpoint, families in many areas have been bombarded with promotional literature produced by schools and have invested very considerable amounts of time and emotional capital in their choice of school. Likewise, schools have devoted considerable resources into marketing activities. It is the interface of this process that this research will explore. If a market-oriented approach to education is to be a successful weapon in the raising of educational standards, then the interface between parents and schools takes on a critical significance. Parents must be seen to be making rational choices based on an accurate image of the quality of provision offered by the school. The way in which the process of choice develops and responds to the marketing activities of schools is an area where literature currently exists. In order to chart the influence of schools' marketing activities on the complex decision-making process it is necessary to base the research on a group of adjacent secondary schools and their associated primary schools. The group of families selected have children in primary school Year 5 going into Year 6. This 12-month period is the crucial one for decision-making as final secondary school choices are made by the end of the Autumn term of Year 6. The attitudes of this group will be tracked over time to establish the most important influences on the decision-making process and how attitudes are influenced by the marketing activities of secondary schools. The method is predominantly ethnographic, incorporating interviews with teachers, parents, prospective and current pupils. Focus groups will be used to explore common issues, whilst participant and observatory methods will supplement documentary analysis. Analysis of the data will establish how parents perceive the image of different schools, and how far that perception of image affects their decision-making process.This data will allow a comparison to be made between the image of the secondary school as seen by parents and the intended image as developed by school managers. The data will then be used to generate models to describe and explain the interaction between the marketing activities of secondary schools and the corporate image as perceived by parents.

STATUS: Individual research

DATE OF RESEARCH: 1994-1997

KEYWORDS: **corporate identity; marketing; parent attitudes; parent choice; school brochures; school image; secondary education**

0012

Anglia Business School, Victoria Road South, Chelmsford CM1 1LL
01245 493131

Hughes, S. Mrs; *Supervisors*: McNay, I. Prof. ; Wisker, G. Dr

Academic staff strategies and institutional response in higher education to high student numbers and the diversification of student type

ABSTRACT: Higher education institutions have experienced and are continuing to experience a period of marked change. The pressure for these changes has mainly come from a growth in student numbers, leading to a more diverse student population; financial cutbacks, leading to resource constraints; and the pressure to improve and maintain quality. All these factors appear to have influenced the role of teachers in higher education and have impacted on their relationship with their students and how they approach the teaching and assessment of those students. At the present time the expansion in student numbers has been halted and higher education is experiencing a period of consolidation. Although future provision is now under review, it would appear that this period of consolidation offers an opportunity to investigate what teachers are doing and to determine successful coping strategies that have been adopted by academic staff and to collect examples of good practice. The objectives of the research are as follows: 1) To determine what teaching and coping strategies academic staff have developed or adopted to deal with large student numbers and the increasing diversity of students. 2) To determine the extent and the form of support that academic staff have received from their institution to help them cope, in order to highlight areas that need attention. 3) To identify training and development needs in order to influence the objectives and content of future staff development within higher education. Research is being undertaken in 3 higher education institutions (i.e. Anglia Polytechnic University and 2 other universities which were previously polytechnics). The primary research methods include the use of questionnaries, interviews and teaching observation.

STATUS: ndividual research

DATE OF RESEARCH: 1996-continuing

KEYWORDS: change strategies; educational change; higher education; nontraditional students; student numbers; student recruitment; teaching methods

0013

Anglia Business School, Centre for Higher Education Management, Danbury Park Conference Centre, Danbury, Chelmsford CM3 4AT
01245 225511

Bell, M. Ms; *Supervisors*: McNay, I. Prof.; Trafford, V. Dr

Shifting patterns of student choice and their implications for university strategic planning

ABSTRACT: The aim of the study is to establish key factors influencing student choice in relation to higher education and to determine the implications for university strategic planning. It will focus particularly on factors affecting women's choices and determine which cognisance there is of this in institutional strategic planning. Since November 1992 higher education has shifted from large scale expansion to a period of 'consolidation'. Other indicators of the significant changes in higher education include: the diminution in student financial support; regional planning at further education level; incorporation and expansion of further education; abolition of the binary divide; unified admissions to a single university sector; and funding of courses designed to promote science enrolments. Institutional planning is now a firmly established university activity. The research will focus on the planning 'machinery' and process within institutions and determine whether it is capable of accommodating short and long term shifts in student choice. A questionnaire survey will be used to elicit the factors influencing student choice. A case study approach employing a triangulation of methods will be used for the institutional research. The research will be undertaken in a three-year period in two regional samples of schools, sixth form colleges and further education colleges, plus one major university within each of the corresponding regions.

STATUS: Individual research

DATE OF RESEARCH: 1994-1997

KEYWORDS: educational planning; higher education; student recruitment; university administration; university choice

0014

Anglia Business School, Department of Management, East Road, Cambridge CB1 1PT
01223 363271

Evans, R. Mr; *Supervisors*: Jenkins, H. Prof.; Trafford, V. Dr

Organisational architecture in colleges of further education: case studies in organisational change

ABSTRACT: Colleges of further education have, particularly in the last 10 years, been faced with an increasingly complex and turbulent environment. To meet these challenges a number of further education colleges have been making radical and innovative changes to their management structures and processes. For example, a small number of colleges have made far reaching changes from traditional hierarchical systems to new systems such as matrix and networking systems. Certainly, many colleges are seeking to move to new more responsive structures and to implement more flexible systems which can respond quickly to rapid changes in the environment. Organisational architecture is not only to do with structures and roles, but with processes, issues, leadership policies and politics which reflect the organisational culture. This research is based on the belief that there is a need to make a thorough and comparative assessment of the range of different approaches to organisational architecture and design in further education colleges. The research will examine a range of structures and processes adopted by further education colleges to seek out: 1) How structures and processes are being changed. 2) The rationales for the varying structures and processes. 3) The effectiveness of the different approaches to organisational architecture. The work will include: 1) A review of the management literature with special reference to issues related to organisational architecture and its underpinning concepts. 2) An identification of different approaches to organisational architecture within further education colleges. 3) An indepth and comprehensive analysis of the design and operation of management structures and processes employed in further education colleges by examining a number of key structural indicators and processes, e.g. vision and environmental fit; division of authority; leadership approaches and devolved power; creation and use of self-managing teams; coordination and collaboration processes; business/ academic strategies; resource allocation and budgetary arrangements; information systems; patterns and policies for staff development; systems for dealing with students; quality systems. An assessment will be made of factors underlying any change in structures such as the linkage between structural and cultural changes.

STATUS: Individual research

DATE OF RESEARCH: 1993-1997

KEYWORDS: college administration; colleges of further education; educational administration; further education; institutional administration; organisational change

0015

Anglia Business School, Department of Management, East Road, Cambridge CB1 1PT
01223 363271

Billinton, J. Mr; *Supervisors*: Jenkins, H. Prof.; McNay, I. Prof.; Evans, D. Mr

A policy analysis of the issues of accessibility to baccalaureate level studies in the Province of Saskatchewan

ABSTRACT: The purpose of the study is to conduct a prospective policy analysis, to determine if there is an acceptable policy solution to accommodate the perceived need of extending baccalaureate level studies in Saskatchewan. In addition, the investigation, using the same policy analysis techniques, will study issues and options related to providing more educational opportunities at the university level for Aboriginal and Metis residents of the Province. The research will be a qualitative case study of the position of key policy stakeholders, in the post-secondary education system in Saskatchewan, regarding the extension of baccalaureate level studies in the Province. The study will describe the major factors perceived to affect the need to increase accessibility and whether it is desirable and/ or feasible to provide university level education at institutions other than the two universities and their associated colleges. In addition, the desirability and/or feasibility of other models or policies to increase accessibility will be described. The most acceptable policy solution will be identified and recommendations for policy formation will be developed from the findings.

STATUS: Individual research

DATE OF RESEARCH: 1993-1998

KEYWORDS: access to education; canada natives; educational policy; qualifications

0016

Anglia Business School, Department of Management, East Road, Cambridge CB1 1PT
01223 363271

Elsmore, P. Dr;Supervisor: Jenkins, H. Prof.; Trafford, V. Dr

Leadership style and the management of cultural change: an investigation into the realities of organisational culture

ABSTRACT: The purpose of the work is to: 1) explore the relationships between leadership style and changes in organisational culture; 2) analyse how new cultures are created through leadership activity and how this culture is enacted within the organisation. Particular attention will be paid to Schein's concept of primary/secondary mechanisms in creating culture and to blocks to organisational change; 3) test out the realities of changes in organisational culture as perceived by middle-level staff compared with the intra-organisational marketed messages on culture transmitted by leaders within the organisation; 4) examine the benefits of culture change in terms of quality enhancement and improvements in organisational performance. There has been considerable publicity given to a number of major organisations in the UK which have made radical changes to their culture during the last five years. Entry is now being sought to up to 6 large organisations such as British Telecom and Metropolitan Police which can offer rich data on cultural change. The research approach will be mainly ethnographic and interpretive - involving detailed studies of a small number of influential organisations. The main research instruments will be semi-structured interviews, non-participant observation together with a limited use of questionnaires. Some use of quantitative data will be made in looking at organisational performance.

STATUS: Individual research

DATE OF RESEARCH: 1992-1997

KEYWORDS: **leadership; management studies; organisational change**

0017

Anglia Centre for Educational Development, Bishop Hall Lane, Chelmsford CM1 1SQ
01245 483131

Badley, G. Prof.

An analysis of the role of educational development centres in modern universities in the UK and abroad

ABSTRACT: The overall aim of the research is to inquire into the ways in which educational development centres may or should contribute to the life of a modern university, especially in a climate where universities may be perceived as having moved from a (relatively comfortable) culture of collegiality to a (relatively harsh) culture of managerialism. The project will examine current concepts of collegiality, managerialism and development (especially staff and educational development) in the UK and US universities and will focus on the range of values, understandings and practices that these concepts are perceived to embody by senior managers and by educational developers. The research will attempt to discover similarities and differences between the perceptions of the 2 groups and will also attempt to generate a model of good practice in educational development in higher education.

PUBLISHED MATERIAL: BADLEY, G. (1996). 'Educational development in the managerial university', Journal of Education Through Partnership, Vol 1, No 1, pp.53-70. ; BADLEY, G. 'Educational development in times of drift and shift', Quality Assurance in Education. (in press).

STATUS: Sponsored project

SOURCE OF GRANT: Anglia Polytechnic University £2,500 ; RAE (1996) Fund £1,000

DATE OF RESEARCH: 1995-continuing

KEYWORDS: **comparative education; higher education; professional development; teacher development; united states of america; universities**

0018

Department of Education, Sawyers Hall Lane, Brentwood CM15 9BT
01227 264504
Suffolk Local Education Authority, St Andrew House, County Hall, Ipswich IP4 1LJ 0

1473 230000

Bash, L. Dr; Curran, C. Mr; Leming, E. Mrs

Parents and special educational needs

Abstract: The aims are to: 1) gain a greater insight into the range of experiences of parents of children with special educational needs who have been statutorily assessed by one local education authority; and 2) identify the support and information needs of parents during the assessment process. A subsidiary aim is an examination of parental empowerment in an area of educational decision-making. The eventual sample size was approximately 300 sets of parents who have been interviewed, using a structured schedule. The results are in the process of being analysed.

STATUS: Sponsored project

SOURCE OF GRANT: Suffolk Local Education Authority £5,000

DATE OF RESEARCH: 1995-1997

KEYWORDS: **parent attitudes; parent participation; special educational needs; statements - special educational needs**

0019

Graduate School, Victoria Road South, Chelmsford CM1 1LL
01245 493131

Davies, J. Prof.

Agendas for higher education in 21st century

ABSTRACT: The research was commissioned by UNESCO and the European Rectors' Conference to assist both organisations to prepare their strategic policy agendas for the first 2 decades of the next century. These, in turn, will strongly condition the policies of national governments and institutions. A particular feature of the research is the perceptions of higher education (HE) agendas from the standpoint of external stakeholders: industry; clusters of commerce; public sector; students. The study is framed along 4 main dimensions: agendas and contributory factors in relation to: 1) teaching and learning; 2) preparation for the world of work; 3) advancement of knowledge and research; 4) transmission of cultural values in a European context. 20 case study institutions form the sample for the research, encompassing a variety of national settings across Europe; types of HE systems; types of institutional traditions; sizes; profiles etc. Case study institutions have provided strategic predictions in each of the 4 above areas, and also in relation to Mission and Positioning, and Strategies of Organisational Development. The resultant analysis thus provides conclusions on the 4 main agenda clusters; institutional types; regional tendencies; as well as changing patterns of organisational development.

The findings form a substantial element in UNESCO's World Conference on Higher Education (Paris 1998), which is being directed by the Principal Investigator – Professor J. Davies, and is in association with 20 colleagues in various European universities.

PUBLISHED MATERIAL: DAVIES, J.L. (1997). Agendas for higher education in the 21st century. Paper presented at the UNESCO European Regional Conference, Palermo, 24-26 September 1997. ; DAVIES, J.L. Agendas for higher education in the 21st century. Paris: UNESCO. (in press).

STATUS: Sponsored project

SOURCE OF GRANT: UNESCO (Higher Education Division ; Association of European Universities (European Rectors Conference), jointly £150,000

DATE OF RESEARCH: 1996-1997

KEYWORDS: **educational planning; educational policy; educational strategies; europe; higher education; universities**

0020

Graduate School, Victoria Road South, Chelmsford CM1 1LL
01345 493131

Davies, J. Prof.

Articulation of universities with their stakeholders in a regional context

Abstract: The project is designed to further the European Union's (EU) interests in the contribution of universities to the social, economic and cultural development of their regions, through cooperative programmes of activity with stakeholders of various types. It attempts to explore the perceptions of stakeholders of universities and vice-versa in an action setting, and to identify the range and effectiveness of various interactive mechanisms in terms of contributions to: 1) cultural development; 2) vocational education and training; 3) regional economic development; 4) regional impact; and 5) built environment. 20 'university clusters' have been identified as the basis of the study, each cluster comprising a focal university, associated university and a range of stakeholder partners. These are selected on the basis of 3 regional categories: 1) universities in peripheral regions of their country; 2) universities in regions of economic revival; 3) universities in regions of strong and concentrated economic development. These categories may well be modified as the study proceeds taking account of regional wealth-poverty and regional growth potential and nationality.

Each 'cluster' will embark on an action research project and the results monitored and reported initially to a major EU conference in Berlin in 1998

STATUS: Sponsored project

SOURCE OF GRANT: European Community DG XXII European Rectors Conference

DATE OF RESEARCH: 1997-1998

KEYWORDS: educational planning; europe; higher education; universities

0021

School of Applied Sciences, Department of Computer Science, East Road, Cambridge CB1 1PT
01223 363271

Davies, C. Dr

Validation of entrance tests for applicants to degree level courses in computer science

ABSTRACT: The profile of entrants to higher education in the UK has changed dramatically in recent years. The increase in student numbers has come not only from school leavers with A levels but from those with other, vocational qualifications such as National Vocational Qualification (NVQ) and Business and Technician Education Council (BTEC) Diplomas. Additionally, Anglia Polytechnic University operates an open admissions policy, welcoming mature students, many of whom do not have the educational qualifications that would be required of school leavers. As a result, it is becoming increasingly difficult to predict success or, more importantly for the potential student, failure. Preliminary work here examining Polytechnics and Colleges Admissions Service forms was unable to find good predictors of failure in the data collected by such forms. Middlesex University School of Psychology has developed it own entrance tests for applicants to their degree course who have completed an Access course. As with Computer Science, applicants to Psychology courses are not required to have studied the subject before applying to university and often have no formal qualifications in their chosen subject. Psychology departments therefore have similar problems to Computer Science departments. Additionally, both subjects require a level of numeracy in students. Middlesex University School of Psychology is allowing Anglia to use their entrance tests in an attempt to validate them for use on Computer Science students. The tests were given to all of this year's intake (about 90 students) and will be marked blind. Test results will be compared with students' performance on the course throughout their career. The first results will be available in September 1997.

STATUS: Sponsored project

SOURCE OF GRANT: Anglia Polytechnic University

DATE OF RESEARCH: 1996-continuing

KEYWORDS: access to education; admission criteria; computer science; higher education; tests

0022

School of Applied Sciences, Department of Computer Science, East Road, Cambridge CB1 1PT
01223 363271

Wilkes, J. Dr

Aspects of recruitment to university courses in computer science

ABSTRACT: The aims of the project are to discover the origins of recruits to computer science courses and, in particular, the ways, if any, by which they have come into contact with the culture of computer science and the effects, if any, of cultural stereotypes of the 'computer scientist' on

recruitment. The study pays special attention to women entrants. Investigation is by questionnaire and selected follow-up interviews. The final sample will be approximately 400, consisting of 6th formers and entrants to computer science courses over 2 years at 2 universities in the Cambridge area. The work is ongoing, but preliminary results suggest that cultural stereotypes are not significant in either encouraging or inhibiting recruitment.

PUBLISHED MATERIAL: WILKES, J. (1996). 'Stereotypes, young people and computing'. In: MYERS, C. et al. (Eds). The responsible software engineer. Godalming: Springer-Verlag.

STATUS: Sponsored project

SOURCE OF GRANT: Anglia Polytechnic University £1,550

DATE OF RESEARCH: 996-1997

KEYWORDS: choice of subjects; computer science; course selection - students; higher education; stereotypes; student recruitment; students

0023

School of Arts and Letters, Department of Music, East Road, Cambridge CB1 1PT 01223 363271 London University, Institute of Education, 20 Bedford Way, London WC1H 0AL
0171 580 1122

Sear, G. Ms; Supervisor: Plummeridge, C. Dr

Music and the National Curriculum: a study of teachers and teaching

ABSTRACT: The researcher's Masters degree dissertation was: Perception and Response: Pupil and Teacher Attitudes to Listening and Appraising in the National Curriculum for Music. The research indicated that whilst the school environment and National Curriculum requirements appeared to have relatively little effect on the content of what was taught, teacher influence, and in turn, what influenced the teacher were vital. Furthermore, the individual and personal judgements of the teacher, based on their own skills, personal music interests and their view of listening, derived from training or personal conviction, were most influential in determining the choice of repertoire. Based on the evidence currently available, the judgement made by the Music Working Group and others that specialist secondary music teachers would easily incorporate and synthesise the requirements of the National Curriculum into their existing practice appears to be too simplistic and optimistic. A music teacher's specialist training is only 'one part' of an intricate web of determinants which affect how an individual responds to and implements curriculum change. The focus of this PhD research is on 10 individual secondary music teachers. It considers the scope and nature of the various determinants on their philosophy and practice of music education. In order to best explore how the potential variables affect a teacher's attitude to change, the researcher has chosen to employ 'life history' methodology in this research as being best suited to discover why music teachers react in many and diverse ways to the imposition of the National Curriculum for Music.

Published Material: SEAR, G.L. (1996). 'Music teachers' response to change and control: implications for teachers and curriculum development', British Journal of Curriculum and Assessment, Vol 6, No 2, pp.38-41.

STATUS: Individual research

DATE OF RESEARCH: 1995-continuing

KEYWORDS: music; music teachers; national curriculum

0024

School of Community Health and Social Studies, East Road, Cambridge CB1 1PT
01223 363271

Winter, R. Prof.; Sobiechowska, P. Ms; Buck, A. Ms

Professional learning through reflective writing

Abstract: The research project is an extension of an aspect of a PhD thesis on the philosophical basis for "action research". It explores the process of experiential learning by examining how experience may be focused and analysed through the writing process. It draws on theories of writing, symbolism and ideology. The aim of the study is to identify a range of modes of writing which embody challenging intellectual processes, other than the conventional "academic report". The process of the research project consists of a series of taught courses in which students from a range of professional backgrounds undertake a professional writing project. By the time the study is written up, a total of 50 students will have undertaken the course. A variety of methods are being explored to develop the effectiveness of the course process, and the students' work is being collected, together with notes on the methods and illustrative examples used. The outcomes of the study will be a descriptive analysis of the process, illustrated by examples of students' writing.

PUBLISHED MATERIAL: WINTER, R. (1991). 'Interviewers, interviewees and the exercise of power (fictional-critical writing as a method for educational research)', British Educational Research Journal, Vol 17, No 3, pp.251-262. ; WINTER, R., PLUMMER, G. & NEWMAN, K. (1993). 'Exchanging letters: a format for collaborative action research', Educational Action Research, Vol 1, No 2, pp.305-314. ; WINTER, R. (1993). 'Action research, practice and theory', Educational Action Research, Vol 1, No 2, pp.315-316. ; WINTER, R. & LANDGREBE, B. (1994). '"Reflective" writing on practice-professional support for the dying?', Educational Action Research, Vol 1, No 4, pp.83-94.

STATUS: Individual research

DATE OF RESEARCH: 1991-1998

KEYWORDS: experiential learning; professional personnel; writing - composition; writing exercises

0025

School of Languages and Social Sciences, Department of Geography, East Road, Cambridge CB1 1PT
01223 363271

Fitzgerald, M. Ms

The contribution of geography to environmental education

ABSTRACT: The aim is to evaluate geography's contribution to education for sustainable development. The proposed method is an analysis of school syllabuses and assessment procedures in the United Kingdom and California. Initial research suggests that geography's separation of the 'human' and the 'physical' undermines its potential to synthesise ecology and environment in the ways needed to bring about new environmental ethics.

PUBLISHED MATERIAL: FITZGERALD, M. (1990). 'Education for sustainable development: decision-making for environmental education in Ethiopia', The International Journal of Educational Development, Vol 10, No 4, pp.289-302. ; FITZGERALD, M. (1990). 'Environmental education in Ethiopia: the sources of decision-making'. In: BANDHU, D., SINGH, H. & MAITRA, A.K. Environmental education and sustainable development. New Delhi: Indian Environmental Society. ; FITZGERALD, M. (1990). 'Education for sustainable development: a long-term strategy for famine prevention in Ethiopia', Occasional Paper No 9 in Rural Studies. Anglia Polytechnic, Division of Geography.

STATUS: Individual research

DATE OF RESEARCH: 1991-1993

KEYWORDS: environmental education; geography

0026

School of Languages and Social Sciences, Department of Geography, East Road, Cambridge CB1 1PT
01223 363271

Fitzgerald, M. Ms

Education for sustainable development in the Third World: education's potential to reduce vulnerability to disaster

ABSTRACT: Agenda 21, signed at the Earth Summit in Rio de Janeiro in 1992, offered an holistic, interdisciplinary and politically-aware model of environmental education (EE) for sustainable development. The aims of this research are two-fold. The first is to evaluate this model alongside other more traditional models of EE. The second is to examine the contribution that EE can make to reducing the vulnerability of specific groups of people, such as women, to disasters like famines.

PUBLISHED MATERIAL: FITZGERALD, M. (1994). 'Environmental education in Ethopia: a strategy to reduce vulnerability to famine'. In: VARLEY, A. (Ed). Disasters, Development and Environment. Chichester: Wiley.

STATUS: Individual research

DATE OF RESEARCH: 1995-1997

KEYWORDS: developing countries; development education; environmental education

0027

School of Languages and Social Sciences, Department of Sociology, East Road, Cambridge CB1 1PT
01223 363271

Newcastle upon Tyne University, Centre for Urban Regional Development Studies, Newcastle upon Tyne NE1 7RU
0191 222 6000

Webster, A. Dr ; Rappert, B. Mr ; Charles, D. Dr

University spin-offs, small and medium enterprises, and the science base: the effective use of intellectual property

ABSTRACT: The desire to exploit intellectual property (IP) in the public sector research base (PSRB) has been an ongoing concern of those within, as well as outside of, government. In this project, the researchers will compare the regional success of university spin-off firms (USOs) and small and medium size enterprises (SMEs) in managing the exploitation of IP through both informal and formal linkages with the PSRB (primarily universities). Little analysis has been done in terms of informal PSRB linkages and a wider range of IP arrangements for smaller enterprises, and almost none for USO's. Yet universities must accommodate both types of organisations to facilitate effective linkages and the exploitation of IP. Differences between USOs and SMEs in their formal and informal institutional ties and their different cultural familiarity with universities provide for an informative point of comparison. At the same time, despite these variations, a comparison of USOs and SMEs should also enable each to learn from the other's practices. This project, then, will identify best practice models for universities with regard to formal and informal IP agreements with smaller enterprises, while taking into account necessary variations in this practice.

STATUS: Collaborative

SOURCE OF GRANT: Economic and Social Research Council £ 88,000

DATE OF RESEARCH: 1995-1998

KEYWORDS: copyright; industry higher education relationship; intellectual property; research; science policy; scientific research; small businesses; universities

0028

Science and Technology Studies Unit, East Road, Cambridge CB1 1PT
01223 363271

Skinner, D. Dr; Rosen, P. Dr; McLaughlin, J. Dr; Supervisor: Webster, A. Dr

Negotiating needs and negotiating uses: technology acquisition as a process of consumption

ABSTRACT: This project explores the acquisition and use of new information technology (IT) based systems across 3 contrasting sectors: clinical, retailing and higher education. The investigation of higher education was focused on the MAC initiative at one of the universities involved. The objective is to determine how users respond to these systems, how they come to define their value over time and how these evaluations are reflected, if at all, in system designers' and purchasers' assumptions about user needs. The sectors chosen allow for comparability in their shared concern with issues such as design quality, usability, training and product reliability, whilst at the same time providing variability in the kinds of systems being introduced. Qualitative semi-structured interviews were carried out with a range of users and with management and IT staff behind the purchase and design of the system. Since one of the researchers' contentions is that acquisition happens over time, the sites were returned to and key respondents interviewed twice more. All the inteviews were transcribed and placed with NUD 1ST software for analysis. Theoretically, the project aims to interrogate existing literatures in technology acquisition and in consumption theory, with the objective of developing a new model of how organisations undergo the process of acquiring new technology. The project examines the mediating factors which influence the direction of change and the shape of technology. These mediating factors include identities in organisations and in technology; organisational cultures; and professional boundaries within organisations.

PUBLISHED MATERIAL: MCLAUGHLIN, J., ROSEN, P., SKINNER, D. & WEBSTER, A. Valuing technology: organisations, culture and change.

London: Routledge. (in press).

STATUS: Sponsored project

SOURCE OF GRANT: Economic and Social Research Council £80,000

DATE OF RESEARCH: 1995-1998

KEYWORDS: computer system design; higher education; human computer interaction; information technology; organisational climate

Associated Examining Board

0029

Stag Hill House, Guildford GU2 5XJ   01483 506506

Baird, J. Ms; Eason, S. Mr; Pinot de Moira, A. Ms ; Meyer, L. Ms ; Taylor, M. Mr; *Supervisor*: Cresswell, M. Dr

Examinations research programme

ABSTRACT: The Associated Examining Board Research and Statistics Group carries out a continuing programme of research into fundamental problems associated with educational measurement together with work on specific examinations. Particular areas of study being pursued in 1997, 1998 and 1999 are: standard setting; marking reliability; mark scaling and aggregation. A further aspect of the work involves collaborative studies with other United Kingdom examining boards and groups to investigate the extent to which all the General Certificate of Secondary Education (GCSE) and General Certificate of Education (GCE) examinations are set, marked and graded to comparable standards.

PUBLISHED MATERIAL: CRESSWELL, M.J. (1996). 'Defining, setting and maintaining standards in curriculum embedded examinations'. In: GOLDSTEIN, H. & LEWIS, T. Assessment problems, developments and statistical issues. Chichester: Wiley. ; NEWTON, P.E. (1996). 'The reliability of marking of General Certificate of Secondary Education scripts: Mathematics and English', British Educational Research Journal, Vol 22, No 4, pp.405-420. ; GOLDSTEIN, H. & CRESSWELL, M.J. (1996). 'The comparability of different subjects in public examinations: a theoretical and practical critique', Oxford Review of Education, Vol 22, No 4, pp.435-442. ; NEWTON, P. (1997). 'Measuring comparability of standards between subjects: why our statistical techniques do not make the grade', British Educational Research Journal, Vol 23, No 4, pp.433-449. ; CRESSWELL, M.J. (1998). 'What are examination standards? The role of values in large scale assessment'. Proceedings of the 22nd IAEA Conference on The Effects and Related Problems of Large Scale Testing in Educational Assessment, Beijing, 1998.

STATUS: Sponsored project

SOURCE OF GRANT: Associated Examining Board

DATE OF RESEARCH: 1983-continuing

KEYWORDS: assessment; bias; evaluation; examinations; general certificate of education; general certificate of secondary education; moderation - marking; reliability; standards

Association for Science Education

0030

College Lane, Hatfield AL10 9AA   01707 267411

London University, King's College, School of Education, Cornwall House, Waterloo Road, London SE1 8WA   0171 836 5454

Goldsworthy, A. Mrs; Wood-Robinson, V. Mrs; *Supervisor*: Watson, R. Dr

Association for Science Education – King's Science Investigations in Schools project

ABSTRACT: The project aims to: 1) report how teachers currently implement attainment target 1 of the National Curriculum for Science (Sc1), and to explore the influence of the orders on the nature of the investigative work done; 2) identify successful practice and its benefits to pupils; 3) identify problems faced by teachers in using investigative work and ways of overcoming them; 4) review the National Curriculum orders for Sc1 in order to identify both positive and negative aspects of the orders and to make recommendations for their revision. The project began in September

1996 and is due to be completed before the new millenium in December 1999. the project involves working with consultative groups of teachers of children aged 8 to 14. A national questionnaire study and detailed case study work in schools, as well as a dissemination phase.

PUBLISHED MATERIAL: GOLDSWORTHY, A. & WATSON, J.R. (1997). 'In the know', Times Educational Supplement, 3 January, Science Extra, pp.VII-IX ; WATSON, J.R. (1997). 'ASE-King's Science Investigations in Schools project', Education in Science, No 171, pp.22-23.

STATUS: Sponsored project

SOURCE OF GRANT: Wellcome Trust £150,000

DATE OF RESEARCH: 1996-continuing

KEYWORDS: national curriculum; primary education; science activities; science education; secondary education

Aston University

0031

Aston Triangle, Birmingham B4 7ET   0121 359 3611

Khan, M. Mr; *Supervisors*: Wright, S. Dr; Ager, D. Prof.

A study of current practices in heritage/mother tongue language teaching with special reference to Pakistanis

ABSTRACT: Birmingham has become a place of settlement for a number of groups originating from the Indian sub-continent. Now, according to the 1991 census, one-third of Birmingham's population consists of these groups. These people have brought with them a range of cultures, languages and dialects. Birmingham is now a multilingual and multicultural city. In view of this it would be useful to update information on one particular group of which the researcher has intimate knowledge - a significant population is from Pakistan and Kashmir. Patterns of immigration were such that male workers arrived first, and children followed later. These children were placed in special centres to learn English, and then moved to mainstream education. A parallel system of mother tongue teaching was set up, due to concerns in the community. This system has strengths and weaknesses; there is room for improvement. Improvement is normally made from a position of knowledge and understanding. The research project proposes to specifically answer the following questions: 1) Are these communities in a situation of language shift or not? If so, why? If not, why not? What is likely to happen in the future? 2) What evidence is there that it would be beneficial for the communities either to: a) make that language shift in cultural, religious and economic terms; or b) fight the language shift? A successful outcome can be piloted and a policy framework proposed for these communities.

STATUS: Individual research

DATE OF RESEARCH: 1995-continuing

KEYWORDS: bilingualism; cultural background; ethnic groups; language maintenance; mother tongue; pakistanis

0032

Aston Triangle, Birmingham B4 7ET   0121 359 3611

Khan, M. Mr; *Supervisors*: Wright, S. Dr ; Ager, D. Prof.

Language shift in the Kashmiri-English speaking bilinguals of Birmingham: attitudes, practices and educational implications

ABSTRACT: A study of current practices in heritage/mother tongue language teaching in the UK with special reference to the Birmingham based communities originating in Pakistan and Azad Kashmir. The research questions are as follows: 1) Are these communities in a situation of language shift or not? If not, why not? 2) What evidence is there that it would be beneficial (in cultural, religious, economic terms) for them either to: a) make that language shift; or b) fight the language shift? 3) Do the language maintenance programmes already in existence appear successful? If so, why? If not, why not? 4) What are the institutional structures? How does education interact with religion in this situation? 5) Are there attitudinal problems? Are these linked to generation, sex or class? Who wants to maintain the mother tongue and why? 6) What are the practices in pedagogy? Are they good, bad or indifferent? 7) If the research concludes that language maintenance is beneficial, what could be a model for a successful language maintenance programme? The sample will be the community formed by immigration from Azad Kashmir – 14-15 year olds in full-time secondary education (at an 11-16 comprehensive) and 16-18 year olds in full-time secondary education (at a 6th form college).

STATUS: Individual research

DATE OF RESEARCH: 1995-continuing

KEYWORDS: asians; bilingual pupils; bilingualism; ethnic groups; language maintenance; language usage; mother tongue

0033

Aston Business School, Aston Triangle, Birmingham B4 7ET
0121 359 3611

Miller, H. Mr; Higson, H. Dr

Research into university secretaries and administrators

Abstract: This work focuses on the work and social relationships of female administrative and senior secretarial workers in universities. This group was chosen because there had been little concentration on this group of workers and more senior university staff had been studied more extensively already. It involved an analysis of interviews with more than 20 secretarial and administrative personnel working in departments and in the centre of a university. By means of these and by contextualisation in an account of the work, management control and conflict within an English university, it explores issues such as the relationship between formal job descriptions and actual work peformed, and whether or not working is becoming more demanding, intense and complex, and the reasons why. Areas discussed include the use of technology, the importance of formal qualifications versus on-the-job experience, motivation and remuneration, and social relationships between different groups of staff. The study confirms that university secretarial and administrative staff have been affected by changes in higher education practice as much as senior management and other academic colleagues. The support staff interviewed had come to terms with increasing workloads, the reduction of their colleagues, the consequent changes in their roles and responsibilities. This put a great deal of pressure on these staff and there were clear signs of stress. However, there was a strong commitment to the institution and a surprising satisfaction from the extra responsibility and in doing a good job.

STATUS: Team research

DATE OF RESEARCH: 1996-continuing

KEYWORDS: **administrative change; administrators; educational administration; higher education; secretaries; universities**

0034

Aston Business School, Aston Triangle, Birmingham B4 7ET
0121 359 3611

Higson, H. Dr

A critique of the operation of an activity database in the management of academics

ABSTRACT: Aston Business School has run an activity database for many years in order to facilitate the management of the School. The School's interest in its own load model has been widened to a study of the use of load models generally. It recently hosted a seminar to examine the use of load models in higher education and to foster the exchange of ideas. The published paper discusses the use of Aston's model and its uses as a flexible tool which can be used for informing both day-to-day managerial and longer term strategic decisions. It gives a brief outline of the model and discusses the factors which were taken into account when setting it up. Particular attention was paid to the uses made of the model and the problems encountered in developing it. The paper concludes with an appraisal of the model's impact and of additional developments which are now being considered. These include the introduction of a financial contribution model, based on the load data, which was introduced in 1998/99. The researchers conclude that load models are a useful tool to aid operational and strategic planning, and that they can have a profound effect on the management of the School. It is, however, a very time consuming process and care must be taken that the data is as accurate as possible and that the system introduced is not over complex. The research continues and the proceedings of the seminar and the effects of the contribution model on the School will be published

PUBLISHED MATERIAL: HIGSON, H., FILBY, J. & GOLDER, V. (1998).

'A critique of a model for an academic staff activity database developed to aid a department in strategic and operational decision-making', Perspectives, Vol 2, No 1.

STATUS: Team research

DATE OF RESEARCH: 1994-continuing

KEYWORDS: **higher education; management information systems**

Avon and Somerset Constabulary

0035

Criminal Investigation Department, Police Headquarters, PO Box 37, Valley Road, Portishead, Bristol BS20 8QJ
01275 816463

Gould, C. DCI; Jones, K. DC; McKiernan, P. Mrs; Sanders, D. Ms

Holiday snapshots: protecting young people on European exchanges from abuse

ABSTRACT: Detective Chief Inspector Chris Gould is a 1998 national recipient of a Home Office, Police Research, grant. Together with Detective Constable Kaye Jones, they have uncovered numerous examples of abuse throughout the European Union, where foreign students have been placed in the care of host families. Such visits have been organised via school exchanges, twinning associations, language schools or other specialist businesses. The abuse ranges from organised sexual assaults with known paedophiles, to episodes of emotional abuse and neglect. Examples include the placement of a 13 year-old child into squat conditions in Germany where he was exposed to drug and alcohol abuse, a 14 year-old girl placed with a London family where she witnessed daily beatings given by the alcoholic father to his wife, a girl who was made to sleep in a cupboard under the stairs, another who had to bathe in a bathroom without a door, and a young Spanish boy placed with a Schedule 1 sex offender in Bath. The officers are now gathering best practices from around the globe in an effort to influence Governments and, particularly, European legislators. They are currently writing a book, identifying the loopholes and weaknesses and suggesting sensible, practical solutions for parents, host families and organisations, whilst at the same time trying to influence legislative changes and industry regulation. Publications detailing the content and findings of the research, and also offering practical and sensible advice are to become available following the conclusion of the research project.

STATUS: Sponsored project

SOURCE OF GRANT: Home Office £19,300

DATE OF RESEARCH: 1998-continuing

KEYWORDS: **child abuse; children at risk; exchange programmes**

Banstead Mobility Centre

0036

Damson Way, Orchard Hill, Queen Mary's Avenue, Carshalton SM5 4NR 0181 770 1151

Ponsford, A-S. Mrs; *Supervisor*: Simms, B. Dr

Learner drivers with cerebral palsy

ABSTRACT: Many individuals with Cerebral Palsy (CP) are unable, or find it too exhausting, to use public transport. Being able to drive, therefore, can help them to achieve independence and enhance the opportunities for both employment and social life. This is confirmed by the results of the current study which considers CP learners and drivers of average cognitive ability. The majority of those who drove were also in employment. Although it is the case that some CP individuals may not be aware of the facilities available for driving ability assessment, it is disappointing that a 1990 report found that only a small number of those who had been assessed had begun tuition. These studies have suggested that the reasons for not beginning tuition include a reluctance to buy a suitable (often adapted) car before tuition and the lack of local experienced driving instructors. The results indicate two areas which need further investigation. The first concerns awareness of facilities for driving assessment amongst the CP population. The second centres on those who are assessed as able to drive, but who do not do so. The proposed study investigates the availability of information regarding driving assessment units, experienced driving instructors and adapted cars based at educational establishments. To obtain a measure of awareness of driving potential, a nationwide survey of 100 young people (16-20 years) with Cerebral Palsy, in further education or vocational training, will be made. The difficulties some potential drivers experience following driving assessment will be explored by face-to-face, semi-structured interviews with 20-30 CP individuals, previously assessed at the Banstead Mobility Centre. By identifying areas of need in relation to driving, it is hoped that the provision of support or facilities in local areas will increase the chances of CP individuals becoming safe and competent drivers.

STATUS: Sponsored project

SOURCE OF GRANT: Spastics Society £13,255

DATE OF RESEARCH: 1991-1993

KEYWORDS: **cerebral palsy; driver education**

0037

Damson Way, Fountain Drive, Carshalton SM5 4NR
0181 770 1151

O'Toole, L. Mrs

The development of a procedure to reduce the road accident involvement of drivers following traumatic brain injury

ABSTRACT: This study attempted to develop assessment procedures which will reduce the road accident involvement of drivers who return to driving, or learn to drive, following a Traumatic Brain Injury (TBI), by screening out drivers who appear to demonstrate impaired processes likely to affect safety on the road. 75 clients who had completed 'driving ability' assessments at the Banstead Mobility Centre were monitored following assessment. The correlation between cognitive and visual assessment to in-car performance, advice on assessment, current driver status and accident and incident involvement was examined. Group results demonstrated a significant relationship between tests of executive functioning, new learning (memory), visual perception, visual deficit and in-car performance, general advice on assessment and current driving status. Furthermore, cognitive deficit, particularly frontal-executive deficit, meory and visual-peceptual deficit in combination with visual deficit appears more likely to prevent driving. Assessment procedures require further refining, with continued evaluation of their predictive validity for driving following TBI.

STATUS: Sponsored project

SOURCE OF GRANT: Eagle Star Insurance Company £5,000

DATE OF RESEARCH: 1994-1997

KEYWORDS: accident prevention; cognitive measurement; driving skills; injuries; neurological impairments; traffic safety

Bath Spa University College

0038

Newton Park, Newton St Loe, Bath BA2 9BN   01225 875875
Bristol University, Graduate School of Education, Centre for Curriculum and Assessment Studies, 22 Berkeley Square, Bristol BS8 1JA   01179 289000

Towler, L. Ms; *Supervisor*: Broadfoot, P. Prof.

Profiling in the primary school: extension of self-assessment in primary schools 1989-1991 – collaborative approach to assessment

ABSTRACT: This project investigates the background and issues surrounding the introduction of Records of Achievement, or profiles, to the primary school and, in particular, the principle of involving children and parents as partners, with teachers, in the assessment process. It explores the contribution made by the literature and research into Records of Achievement in the secondary context, in order to develop both a rationale for, and a critique of, self-assessment and examines ways in which these may prove applicable to primary children. The issues examined include the development of skills necessary for effective review and analysis of achievement and the extent to which young children may be empowered through ownership of their profile. The effect of individual differences in

respect of age, gender, attainment and culture are also explored, and the implications for school policy on assessment considered. A qualitative case study of the introduction of profiling in one primary school was carried out in order to determine the extent to which children of ten and eleven years may be capable of taking responsibility for their own learning and benefit from involvement in their own self-assessment. The research also included using questionnaires and interviews, to gain the reaction and response of parents to the introduction of profiles as a method of reporting on achievement and to the request for their involvement in the process.

The conclusions drawn indicate that a coherent school policy for assessment, which is supported by the commitment of teachers and parents, can ensure that the principle of assessment as first and foremost the responsibility of the learner is both valid and can be realistically applied in education from the early years.

PUBLISHED MATERIAL: BROADFOOT, P., et al (1991). 'Implementing National Assessment: issues for primary teachers', Cambridge Journal of Education, Vol 21, No 2, pp.153-168. ; TOWLER, L. & BROADFOOT, P. (1992). 'Self-assessment in the primary school', Educational Review, Vol 44, No 2, pp.137-151.

STATUS: Individual research

DATE OF RESEARCH: 1993-continuing

KEYWORDS: **assessment; primary education; profiles; pupil responsibility; records of achievement; school reports; self evaluation – individuals**

0039

Newton Park, Newton St Loe, Bath BA2 9BN   01225 875875
Warwick University, Institute of Education, Coventry CV4 7AL
01203 523523

Pegg, J. Mr; Supervisor: Grozier, G. Dr ; Halpin, D. Dr

Parents and schools: towards public accountability

ABSTRACT: The Conservative Government has introduced various mechanisms into the education system to give parents a more central role in school accountability. The introduction of parental choice - to be informed by specific "performance indicators", the provisions for the increased representation of parents on school governing bodies, and the requirements for schools to provide certain information for parents are all part of the process of making schools more accountable to parents. But what impact are these changes having in practice on the actions and perceptions of the parents themselves? The research is therefore essentially concerned with looking at the role parents actually play in school accountability, within the context of recent educational reforms, and the factors and experiences that may influence this. The research will attempt to discover what form(s) of accountability parents are operating in practice, through their involvement and interaction with schools and teachers. The aims of the research are based on attempting to provide answers to the following questions: 1) What role do parents play in school accountability? 2) What factors and experiences may influence that role? 3) What form of accountability are parents operating in their relationship with their children's school? The research is concerned primarily with parents' interpretations of the way they interact with schools to identify the ways in which they define certain situations and to discover how they see their role in the accountability process. The research will therefore be grounded in an interpretive paradigm with mainly qualitative research methods being used in data collection.

STATUS: Individual research

DATE OF RESEARCH: 1994-1997

KEYWORDS: **accountability; parent attitudes; parent choice; parent participation; parent school relationship**

Bath University

0040

School of Education, Claverton Down, Bath BA2 7AY
01225 826826

Ritchie, R. Mr; *Supervisor*: Denley, P. Dr

Evaluating the effectiveness of a practitioner's use of a constructivist

approach for developing scientific knowledge and understanding in primary students during their initial training and primary teachers on inservice courses

ABSTRACT: Implementing the National Curriculum for Science requires primary teachers to develop pupils' knowledge and understanding in science, particularly through exploration and investigation, and assess their progress. For many teachers this is proving difficult because they lack appropriate background knowledge and understanding in science themselves. Recent research (Kruger & Summers, 1989) has confirmed that many primary teachers have no formal qualifications in science. Present recruits to teacher training are not required to have a qualification in science and existing cohorts in institutions include many students with limited scientific backgrounds. Consequently, the training of teachers and successful inservice education of teachers (INSET) requires trainers to adopt approaches that will develop scientific knowledge and understanding in teachers. Considerable research in the secondary sector, and limited research in the primary sector have shown the importance of adopting a constructivist approach to science education. The purpose of the research is to examine the effectiveness with adult learners of the use of such an approach. Focused observation and analysis of personal practice results in modifications to teaching and evaluation of changes. Effectiveness is assessed in terms of improved knowledge and understanding of scientific ideas. The project will look for evidence of improved understanding and the impact of this on the learning opportunities provided for children in the classroom. Formal and informal methods have been used to validate the research.

STATUS: Individual research

DATE OF RESEARCH: 1989-1993

KEYWORDS: **inservice teacher education; preservice teacher education; primary education; science education; student teachers**

0041

School of Education, Claverton Down, Bath BA2 7AY
01225 826826

Jamieson, I. Prof.

Models of progression in teacher placements in industry

Abstract:This is a study of the role of industrial placements in the professional development of student teachers and teachers. A sample of 50 teachers and student teachers at various stages in their careers/courses are being studied in three different locations via qualitative interviewing.

STATUS: Sponsored project

SOURCE OF GRANT: Department of Employment ú 16,000

DATE OF RESEARCH: 1992-1993

KEYWORDS: **industrial secondments; industry education relationship; preservice teacher education; teacher development**

0042

School of Education, Claverton Down, Bath BA2 7AY
01225 826826

Sweeney, S. Mr; *Supervisor*: Thompson, J. Prof.

Music in the National Curriculum: implications of assessment for pupils, teachers and schools

ABSTRACT: The implementation of a National Curriculum for Music in schools will have significant implications for a subject that is characterised by a wide diversity of practice in relation to teaching and learning styles, and assessement. Assessment being a central feature of the new legislation, this at present is one of the less well developed areas of practice in music education. The research identifies and evaluates, on the basis of materials provided to schools, some of the pertinent issues relating to the assessment of music Learning across the five to sixteen age-range. The research includes a review of the relevant literature, and a survey of existing practice in music education within sixty-three schools in the south and south-west of England. A trial and evaluation of some of the proposed material for the National Curriculum for Music was carried out in eight schools, using case study techniques, involving pupils from across the five to sixteen age-range, with particular reference to composing and notation. Evidence collected during the period of research supports the existence of a wide diversity of practice in schools and it confirms that assessment of pupils'

musical development, via the quality of their classwork, is an underdeveloped area of practice. The research suggests that teachers in schools, via the class activities of performing, composing, listening and appraising, should reinforce children's understanding of musical skills and concepts. Assessment will serve as an invaluable vehicle for monitoring and evaluation in this respect.

Status: Individual research

Date of Research: 1989-1993

KEYWORDS: assessment; music; national curriculum

0043

School of Education, Claverton Down, Bath BA2 7AY
01225 826826

Harris, A. Ms

Experiential learning in higher education

ABSTRACT: In 1991 Universities Funding Council (UFC) funding was obtained to conduct a research project into experiential learning in higher education. The project was initially envisaged as a three year research programme which focused upon the ways in which experiential learning was conceptualised and realised within the specific context of professional training. In the first year it was intended to explore the perceptions of students, tutors and supervisors about the role and purpose of experiential learning in training. It was decided to compare two different areas of professional training which were similar in their professional demands. The areas of teaching and social work were chosen because of the fact that teachers and social workers have to deal continually with unfamiliar, new and complex situations with pupils and clients. The emphasis in both professions is very much upon individual responsiveness to a situation which is immediate and has important repercussions for the learner and the client. The training processes in the courses of teachers and social workers and the understanding of that development by tutors and supervisors comprise the core of this research. Central to this investigation is an examination of the role experience plays in professional learning and development. Consequently, students, supervisors and tutors have been interviewed about their understanding of learning from experience. The first year of the project has mainly focused upon students' pre-experience perceptions and understanding of the training process. In particular it has investigated the types of experiences students' expect to encounter in their professional training and how they think they might learn from these experiences. The relationship between theory and practice has also been explored with students, tutors and supervisors as well as their views on what experiences might assist in the process of professional development.

STATUS: Sponsored project

SOURCE OF GRANT: Universities Funding Council £84,000

DATE OF RESEARCH: 1991-1993

KEYWORDS: **experiential learning; preservice teacher education; prior learning; social work studies**

0044

School of Education, Claverton Down, Bath BA2 7AY
01225 826826

Jamieson, I. Prof.; Harris, A. Dr; Chambers, J. Ms

Development of education – business policy and structures

ABSTRACT: Research in schools, colleges and businesses about the most appropriate structures for education-business liaison. The focus is on student learning and cost as two key variables. Data gathering will be via a structured interviewing programme.

STATUS: Sponsored project

SOURCE OF GRANT: Lancashire Local Education Authority; East Lancashire Training and Enterprise Council; Lancashire Area West Training and Enterprise Council, jointly £18,500

DATE OF RESEARCH: 1993-1993

KEYWORDS: **industry education relationship; training and enterprise councils**

0045

School of Education, Claverton Down, Bath BA2 7AY
01225 826826

Reid, A. Dr; *Supervisor:* Scott, W. Dr ; Oulton, C. Mr

How might the geography teacher effectively use the study of local issues to contribute to pupils' environmental education?

Abstract: The aims of the research are: 1) To investigate geography teachers' conceptualisation of environmental education. This will concentrate on theoretical and ideological frameworks, principles of pedagogy and the practice thereof. 2) To investigate how the dispositions of schools and the practices found within them can affect the provision of environmental education. This will focus on a school's context, planning and implementation of environmental education (from policy to practice), and make particular reference to the study of local issues in geography classes. 3) To identify how the issues investigated in aims (1) and (2) are related to practices found within contrasting schools. This will concentrate on how aims and objectives are implemented in the provision of environmental education, and will examine the position of education for the environment in the study of local issues. 4) To discover how the outcomes of aim (3) might inhibit or maximise the effectiveness of using the study of local issues to contribute to pupils' environmental education, and improve our understanding of the relationship between theory and practice in this area. The research is aimed at qualified secondary school teachers of geography in England and Wales who teach environmental geography courses. The method will include: 1) A survey and investigation of previous research and literature, focusing on ideology, objectives and the implementation of environmental education within schools in England and Wales. 2) Research instruments to be identified and shaped to meet aims (1) and (2) (policy and practice), for example, questionnaires, document analysis, interviews and observation schedules. 3) The identified sample (10-15) will be followed-up with research instruments designed to achieve aims (3) and (4) above. 4) The results of the research will be analysed, with conclusions drawn where appropriate. Particular emphasis will be placed on the effectiveness of strategies and how inhibitory factors may be overcome.

STATUS: Individual research

DATE OF RESEARCH: 1994-1998

KEYWORDS: environmental education; geography; local issues

0046

School of Education, Claverton Down, Bath BA2 7AY
01225 826826

Azizi, N. Mr; *Supervisor*: Jamieson, I. Prof.

A search for the work-related curriculum relationship between education and employment in Iran

ABSTRACT: Renewal of the structure, aims and principles of education in Iran has started during the last three decades. Although the system of education in this country has been restructured, it is far from the desired condition and has been faced with some problems, possibly caused by unsuitable curriculum planning. One of the most important problems in this system is the lack of a clear relationship between schooling and work. The result of this system is the problem of unemployment among increasing numbers of high school graduates. The researcher is looking for a model of curriculum which emphasises factors such as transition, adaptability, differentiation, work and problem-solving. Therefore the main questions in this research are: why, what and how should the education system include work in the curriculum? The research aims are: 1) To study the nature of the relationship between schooling and employment in Iran. 2) To determine the factors which affect young people's employment. 3) To investigate appropriate models of the work-related schooling. The research will include the systematic collection of data from four groups of people: high-school students (n=200); high-school teachers (n=100); curriculum policy makers (n=20) and employers (n=40). The research will be a descriptive study which will involve the following stages: 1) review of the published literature and identification of the major reasons which affect employment and unemployment of high-school graduates; 2) development of research instruments to be shaped to meet the aims of research; 3) analysis of the recorded data with specific reference to research purposes; 4) evaluation of the results of the research, drawing conclusions where appropriate, and formulating recommendations and suggestions for further research.

STATUS: Individual research

DATE OF RESEARCH: 1994-1997

KEYWORDS: **iran; school to work transition; work education relationship; youth employment**

0047

School of Education, Claverton Down, Bath BA2 7AY
01225 826826

Stables, A. Dr; Wikeley, F. Ms

Pupils' approaches to subject option choices

ABSTRACT: The research will investigate the subject preferences, perceptions of subject importance and approaches to Year 9 subject choices of school pupils aged 13/14 in the South West of England. In Phase 1 of the project, approximately 1500 pupils will be given a questionnaire investigating their subject preferences and perceptions of subject importance. In Phase 2, a stratified sample of pupils in 4 schools will be interviewed about their approaches to option choices and their perceptions of the curriculum generally. They will be interviewed again in Year 10, one year later. The results gained will be compared with those of a similar project in the mid-1980s.

PUBLISHED MATERIAL: STABLES, A. (1990). 'Differences between pupils from mixed and single-sex schools in their enjoyment of school subjects and in their attitudes to science and to school', Educational Review, Vol 42, No 3, pp.221-230. ; STABLES, A. (1996). Subjects of choice: the process and management of pupil and student choice. London: Cassell. ; STABLES, A. (1996). 'Paradox in compound educational policy slogans: evaluating equal opportunities in subject choice', British Journal of Educational Studies, Vol 44, No 2, pp.159-167.; STABLES, A. 'Perspectives on subject choice: the case for a humane liberalism in curriculum planning', Journal of Curriculum Studies. (in press).

STATUS: Sponsored project

SOURCE OF GRANT: Economic and Social Research Council £17,422

DATE OF RESEARCH: 1995-1997

KEYWORDS: **choice of subjects; key stage 3; key stage 4; pupil attitudes; pupil interests; secondary education; sex differences**

0048

School of Education, Claverton Down, Bath BA2 7AY
01225 826826

Fletcher, S. Ms; *Supervisor*: Calderhead, J. Prof.

Involvement in initial teacher education (ITE): the school's perspective

ABSTRACT: The research involved a literature survey of schools' increasing role in initial teacher training (ITE) since the Department for Education and Employment (DfEE) Circular 9/92 which shifted the responsibility for ITE from higher education (HE) towards teaching staff in schools. Papers published/submitted so far in these research areas include: Mentoring and the Role of Form Tutoring; Mentoring in an international context in schools; School-based as against HE based mentoring: a personal perspective; and Gender issues in relation to mentoring. The present research involves 2 case studies of schools' involvement in ITE. One school has 3 partnerships with different higher education institutions (HEIs), and the other school has no involvement in partnership with HE but is the lead school in a School Centred Initial Teacher Training Consortium (SCITT).

PUBLISHED MATERIAL: CALVERT, M. & FLETCHER, S. (1994). Working with your student teacher. Cheltenham: Mary Glasgow Publications. ; FLETCHER, S. (1997). 'Essay - review of modelling reflective practice among pre-service teachers', Teaching and Teacher Education, Vol 13, No 2, pp.237-243. ; FLETCHER, S. (1997). 'ITE and form tutoring: a question of responsibility', Mentoring and Tutoring, Vol 5, No 1, pp.45-51.

STATUS: Individual research

DATE OF RESEARCH: 1995-1998

KEYWORDS: **preservice teacher education; school based teacher education**

0049

School of Education, Claverton Down, Bath BA2 7AY
01225 826826

Gough, S. Mr; *Supervisor*: Scott, W. Dr ; Oulton, C. Mr

An exploration of environmental education approaches to management training in a context of rapid economic development

ABSTRACT: Environmental education (EE) is widely agreed to have had, as yet, little impact in the prevention of environmental degradation or the achievement of sustainability. Economic development and environmental management, by contrast, have had and continue to have large impacts, mostly to the detriment of the environment. Development and environmental management practitioners have made numerous appeals to education as a necessary means to make their practice sustainable. The research seeks to explore a mechanism (adaptive concepts or AdCs) by which EE might both respond to these appeals while simultaneously promoting its own goals. The research aims are: 1) To identify AdCs within the shared context of EE, environmental management and economic development. 2) To use two such AdCs to develop EE interventions in a management education programme instigated as part of a national development strategy in a developing country. 3) To evaluate these interventions in terms of the effectiveness of teaching and learning, and make a preliminary evaluation of the usefulness of AdCs as a way of introducing EE components into such management education programmes. The research began with a literature review which is well-developed and extensive. A first case study has been completed using the AdC 'quality'. Two further case studies are in hand.

PUBLISHED MATERIAL: GOUGH, S. (1995). 'Environmental education a region of rapid development: the case of Sarawak', Environmental Education Research, Vol 1, No 3, pp.327-336. ; GOUGH, S. (1997). 'Adding value: an environmental education approach for business and management training', Environmental Education Research, Vol 3, No 1, pp.5-16.

STATUS: Individual research

DATE OF RESEARCH: 1994-1998

KEYWORDS: developing countries; economic development; environment; environmental education; management development

0050

School of Education, Claverton Down, Bath BA2 7AY
01225 826826

Cambridge, J. Mr; *Supervisor*: Thompson, J. Prof.

An inquiry into values dissonance in international education

ABSTRACT: Experience shows that the participants in education in an international context frequently hold a range of different values concerning the aims and purposes of education. Teachers and learners bring prior experience from their own national education systems into the international school which influence their views on, and expectations of, the teaching-learning process. School administrators and governors also bring their own educational values into the international school, which is itself located in a host country whose cultural values may contrast with those of the school itself. There is a developing literature which documents the demands upon business managers in a culturally diverse environment; how can this body of knowledge, skills and attitudes be transferred to the theory and practice of education in an international context? Sources of data will be: an opportunity sample of teachers attending the International Summer School at the University of Bath School of Education, and teachers, administrators and students in a sample of international schools (sample composition yet to be finalised). Data collection will be by a variety of quantitative and qualitative methods, including questionnaire, semistructured interview, observation and collection of artifacts.

STATUS: Individual research

DATE OF RESEARCH: 1996-continuing

KEYWORDS: comparative education; cross cultural studies; educational objectives; educational principles; international schools; values

0051

School of Education, Claverton Down, Bath BA2 7AY
01225 826826

Drake, B. Mr; *Supervisor*: Thompson, J. Prof.

The development of a pastoral system within the framework of a new international school

Abstract: This research investigates: a) the development of a pastoral care system for an international college from the pre-planning stage, through implementation, in the first 2 years together with evaluation and refinement for continued institutional use; b) how such factors as the expectations of the host country students, parents and the board of governors affect the planning and implementation process, and how other factors such as physical strictures, financial constraints and the range of cultural expectations represented in the student body as a whole will be involved; c) with respect to the first year of introduction, the impact of staff selection on the expectations of staff, students and parents, as part of the whole process.

STATUS: Individual research

DATE OF RESEARCH: 1993-1998

KEYWORDS: international schools; overseas students; pastoral care –education

0052

School of Education, Claverton Down, Bath BA2 7AY
01225 826826

Crosland, M. Miss; *Supervisor*: Jamieson, I. Prof.

What makes an effective subject department in secondary schools?

Abstract: The research is rooted in the school effectiveness movement, and is focused on the unit of organisation in a secondary school most closely associated with the management and delivery of teaching and learning, i.e. the subject department. It aims to: a) identify what 'effective' means in the context of a subject department; b) what factors contribute to this effectiveness; c) to explore the differences among effective English, mathematics and science departments. Research is in 29 departments in 13 schools in rural and suburban areas. Questionnaires have been given to 2,300 pupils in Years 7, 8 and 11 and to 170 teachers; interviews have been held with 65 teachers, 29 heads of department and 18 senior managers. Departments were identified by value added data to give a selection of those effective in General Certificate of Secondary Education (GCSE) performance (using value added), average and ineffective. Results have been analysed and conclusions drawn that 'effective' means effective in examination performance, promoting the subject, teaching and learning, person management, use of resources, mentoring/evaluation, in the whole school context. The factors for effectiveness are: the right person for the job of head of department, a clear vision of the subject, common aims, suitable schemes of work, common approach to teaching and learning, team work, friendship, ability to deal with problems, supportive but 'hands off' senior management. The differences among English, mathematics and science are to do with teaching styles and the pupils' perception of the subject.

STATUS: Individual research

DATE OF RESEARCH: 1996-continuing

KEYWORDS:departments; educational quality; english; mathematics; school effectiveness; science education; secondary education

0053

School of Education, Claverton Down, Bath BA2 7AY 01225 826826

Bullock, K. Mrs; Wikeley, F. Ms

Evaluation of personal learning plans

ABSTRACT: Cambridgeshire Careers Guidance Limited (CCG) is working with all schools in the county to enhance pupil learning, careers education and guidance, assessment and recording of achievement through personal learning planning (PLP) in Year 9. The evaluation of this project is collecting data in order to investigate the quality, strengths, weakenesses and added value of the models of personal learning planning in the schools. The evaluation model is longitudinal with data gathering, judgement and feedback at several key stages. Qualitative and quantitative data is being gathered to identify: a) the views of CCG providers, PLP development officers and careers advisers on the implementation and running of the project; b) pupils' perceptions of the PLP process and of their own developing knowledge, skills and attitudes; and c) tutors' perceptions of the effectiveness of the PLP process, the implications for the school and the personal, educational and vocational development of their tutees. The sample has been constructed from all 30 schools taking part in the PLP project from September 1996. Data collection strategies have been designed for each of the groups with a stake in the initiative. The main research method follows two Year 9 tutor groups in the 1996/97 academic year from all 30 institutions taking part in the PLP project. Each group has been given a short questionnaire which focuses on key aspects of PLPs and largely take the form of a semantic differential. These questions will be repeated at later stages and attitude changes which can be related to PLPs will be monitored. A simplified version of the questionnaire will be developed for use in special schools. A control group of Year 11 students in Summer 1997 will also be identified. A sample of tutors has been drawn from all those concerned with PLPs in the 30 schools, and a representative from each school will be interviewed by telephone once each year. This allows ongoing issues to be identified, analysed and followed up. Data is being triangulated by asking the tutors and students a similar set of questions about key elements of the PLP process. Consultation with providers is a key feature at all stages of the research.

STATUS: Sponsored project

SOURCE OF GRANT: Department for Education and Employment

DATE OF RESEARCH: 1996-1998

KEYWORDS: key stage 3; key stage 4; learner educational objectives; learning; pupil development; records of achievement; secondary education; secondary school pupils

0054

School of Education, Claverton Down, Bath BA2 7AY
01225 826826

Cunningham, J. Br; *Supervisor*: Whitehead, J. Mr

Supporting teachers and other action researchers in improving the quality of education for themselves and their students

ABSTRACT: For the purposes of this study the researcher will be exploring, with a number of teacher researchers from different disciplines (some within the context of whole-school development), the significance of spiritual, religious, moral, social and cultural values within their educative relationships with their pupils and within a whole-school context. In pursuance of these ends, and within these relationships, the researcher will also be seeking to utilise teacher and pupil memories, existential experiences and understandings and knowledge. Evidence will be asked from the teachers which can be used to judge the quality and effectiveness of the teachers' actions with the pupils, within a whole-school context. The researcher will also be exploring the significance of an educational journey for the political and economic context in which the enquiries are located.

STATUS: Individual research

DATE OF RESEARCH: 1993-1998

KEYWORDS: action research; cultural awareness; moral development; spiritual development; teacher pupil relationship; teacher researchers; teacher role

0055

School of Education, Claverton Down, Bath BA2 7AY
01225 826826

Coyle, A. Ms; *Supervisor*: Jamieson, I. Prof.

Career breaks taken by women teachers in primary education

ABSTRACT: Taking a holistic view of women's lives, the research is focusing upon the phenomenon of the career break – where/when it occurs in the life history and what kinds of activities are undertaken in this period. Possible outcomes of the investigation are that there may be clearly identifiable stages of a woman's life and career, for example, a 'two-stage' career, i.e. before and after a career break, or that there are no clearly definable 'stages' as such, more a richly interwoven fabric of life experiences.

STATUS: Individual research

DATE OF RESEARCH: 1993-1998

KEYWORDS: career break; teaching profession; women teachers; womens employment

0056

School of Education, Claverton Down, Bath BA2 7AY
01225 826826

Chronaki, A. Ms; *Supervisor*: Calderhead, J. Prof.

Case studies in the implementation of art-based activities for the teaching of mathematics

ABSTRACT: This work explores how three teachers use a series of art-based activities in teaching mathematics. For the research, a series of activities were devised, including slides and worksheets provided for teachers' use in their classes. The study involves classroom research, specifically the ways teachers implement the materials, as well as their associated beliefs, views and motivations. Research methodology is qualitative, involving methods for data collection such as classroom observation, informal interviewing and videotaping of lessons. Analysis is based mainly on interpretative inquiry using triangulation and respondent validation for verification. Theorising emerges through the data and is related with and reflected upon a constructivist theoretical perspective. Data, their analysis and findings, are presented in three case studies. The research is seen to have implications for the teaching of mathematics, such as what significance mathematics teachers place on the artistic aspects of the activities and how they relate this to the teaching of a particular mathematics topic.

STATUS: Individual research

DATE OF RESEARCH: 1990-1997

KEYWORDS: art activities; classroom research; mathematics; mathematics materials

0057

School of Education, Claverton Down, Bath BA2 7AY
01225 826826

Augerinou, M. Ms; *Supervisor*: Ericson, J. Mr

Visual literacy: its anatomy and diagnosis

ABSTRACT: This research concentrates on the concept of visual literacy, its interpretation and definition. There are two major themes to the research plan, the first of which is to attempt to define a shared meaning of the term amongst groups of people who have a vested interest in the subject; and secondly, to work towards an operational definition of visual literacy, an aspect which has proved especially problematic for both practitioners and previous researchers. The research will involve continuing work on the development of tests using Debe's Hierarchy as the theoretical framework. These tests will then be employed as an interview schedule with a target audience. Those with vested interest in visual literacy include: architects, graphic artists, interior designers, media studies, educational technologists. Although it is likely that perceptions will differ both between and within each of these groups, the research will be attempting to identify those aspects which are deemed to be fundamental to their understanding of the concept.

STATUS: Individual research

DATE OF RESEARCH: 1993-1998

KEYWORDS: visual literacy; visual perception

0058

School of Education, Claverton Down, Bath BA2 7AY
01225 826826

Abdullah, S. Ms; *Supervisor*: Calderhead, J. Prof.

Malaysian home economics teachers' understanding and views of home economics as a field of study

ABSTRACT: The study will examine: 1) Malaysian teachers' understanding and views of the subject in terms of its definitions including the orientation and relevance of home economics as a field of study, roles and functions, component areas and its integrated nature internally and externally; 2) their ideas of factors contributing to these understandings and views, including the problems faced by home economics and the present curriculum and approaches used to teach the subject and professional prospects; and 3) if there is any relationship between these understandings and views, and certain demographic factors as well as content and approaches to classroom or laboratory activities. There will be two parts to the study. The first part will be a general survey of a sample of the teachers, both college and university trained. The second part will be case studies of four selected teachers based on the findings of the survey. The survey will attempt to examine the overall understanding and view of teachers of home economics;

whereas the case studies will attempt to explore if there is any implication of their understandings and views on their educational activities including classroom and laboratory activities.

STATUS: Individual research

DATE OF RESEARCH: 1994-1997

KEYWORDS: home economics; malaysia; teacher attitudes

0059

School of Education, Claverton Down, Bath BA2 7AY
01225 826826

Graystone, J. Mr; *Supervisor*: Jamieson, I. Prof.

The governance of further education colleges in Britain with reference to other selected countries

ABSTRACT: The purpose of this research is to investigate, through a comparative study: 1) how governing bodies in further education (FE) are carrying out the responsibilities set out in recent legislation; 2) to trace the development of governing bodies before and after the Education Reform Act 1988 and the Further and Higher Education Act 1992; 3) to examine whether governing bodies are being run 'on business' lines and the meaning of this phrase in an educational context; 4) to examine how governing bodies operate and their relationship with college management; 5) how they measure performance; 6) how they tackle challenges; 7) how they train and develop their members; 8) how they measure their own performance. The research will also investigate the impact on governing bodies of external bodies such as Training and Enterprise Councils and to trace the development of national bodies representing the interests of governing bodies and to consider issues arising from the governance of other public sector institutions and of public companies.

STATUS: Individual research

DATE OF RESEARCH: 1996-continuing

KEYWORDS: colleges of further education; comparative education; educational administration; further education; governance; governing bodies; management in education; training and enterprise councils

0060

School of Education, Claverton Down, Bath BA2 7AY 01225 826826
Spouse, J. Miss; *Supervisor*: Calderhead, J. Prof.

A study of the development of professional knowledge, skills and attitudes in pre-registration nursing students and the influence of peer support mechanisms

ABSTRACT: This study aims to: 1) investigate how student nurses believe they learn their clinical practice craft knowledge; 2) explore the use and value of peer support mechanisms to students, in the development of their craft knowledge; 3) compare the students' perceived value of the mentor (qualified nurse) with that of the peer (student) in helping them to learn; 4) identify the specific variables between the two support systems; 5) investigate the relationship of verbal and written debriefing activities to the students' perception of their increase in skill; 6) consider whether journal keeping is a useful adjunct to promoting learning and whether the activity is complementary to verbal interaction and learning.

STATUS: Individual research

DATE OF RESEARCH: 1991-1997

KEYWORDS: clinical experience; mentors; nurse education; nurses; peer teaching

0061

School of Education, Claverton Down, Bath BA2 7AY
01225 826826

Monaghan, P. Mrs; *Supervisor*: Jamieson, I. Prof.

School development planning processes and the approaches used in their implementation

ABSTRACT: This study aims to: 1) describe the development processes, tools and approaches used in schools and the rationale for their introduction; 2) investigate whether the introduction of these approaches has actually resulted in school improvement; 3) compare the outcomes of this research with those of previous studies into school improvement and increasing school effectiveness; and 4) identify the key factors which appear to have

enabled or inhibited school improvement.

STATUS: Individual research

DATE OF RESEARCH: 1992-1997

KEYWORDS: educational quality; planning; school development planning; school effectiveness; school improvement

0062

School of Education, Claverton Down, Bath BA2 7AY
01225 826826

Parfitt, A. Mr; *Supervisor*: Jamieson, I. Prof.

Distinctive qualities and features of Church of England (CE), Voluntary Controlled (VC) and Voluntary Aided (VA) primary schools in the Diocese of Bath and Wells, and Salisbury

ABSTRACT: This research would provide evidence of which Church schools exercise a distinctive role in the primary phase of education, and indicators of that individuality. The research has the potential to make a significant contribution to Church schools in planning their own development, and is of interest to the Church authorities in determining their own policies in relation to education.

STATUS: Individual research

DATE OF RESEARCH: 1994-continuing

KEYWORDS: church and education; primary education; voluntary schools

0063

School of Education, Claverton Down, Bath BA2 7AY
01225 826826

Taylor, K. Ms; *Supervisor*: Calderhead, J. Prof.

An investigation into the role and potential of social skills training in the mainstreaming of pupils with special educational needs

ABSTRACT: This research will investigate how well a sample of mainstreamed primary special needs children are coping with the social demands of school. It will analyse the nature and adequacy of the children's social skills and their interactions with others and will construct a social skills training package in order to evaluate its effects in helping pupils adjust to the school environment. The study will involve a survey of teachers in local primary schools and a series of 12 case studies of children with special educational needs. Particular attention will be given to identifying strengths and weaknesses in social skills and their possible contribution to the intergration problem. An interaction analysis schedule will be used as part of the observation. It is expected that the study will lead to a fuller appreciation of the role of social skills in the integration of special needs children and an understanding of how social skills difficulties might be catered for in the social context.

STATUS: Individual research

DATE OF RESEARCH: 1990-1997

KEYWORDS: interpersonal competence; mainstreaming; primary education; primary school pupils; pupil behaviour; social skills; special educational needs

0064

School of Education, Claverton Down, Bath BA2 7AY
01225 826826

Sylvester, R. Mr; *Supervisor*: Thompson, J. Prof.

Development stages in the early life of characteristically international schools in Africa

ABSTRACT: This study will seek to define development stages in the early life of characteristically international schools in Africa and seek to identify: 1) what is the relationship between a characteristically international school and the presence/absence of a dominant minority sub-culture within the school community; 2) to what degree is it important for parents to display a strong identification with the school's mission and actively understand and support its key aspects in these schools; 3) to what extent is the goal of preparing children to re-enter their home schools system a prominent or deciding feature in the total mission of these schools; 4) to what extent is the treatment of issues of diversity a central feature of these schools as seen in both mission articulation and programme definition; 5) if it can be found that these schools adopt an increasingly consultative model of decision-making as their international character emerges.

STATUS: Individual research

DATE OF RESEARCH: 1995-continuing

KEYWORDS: africa; international schools

0065

School of Education, Claverton Down, Bath BA2 7AY
01225 826826

Donnabhain, D. Mr; *Supervisor*: Jamieson, I. Prof.

Cross-curricular tasks in pre-vocational education

ABSTRACT: The research is based on a pre-vocational course that was introduced to schools in the Republic of Ireland in 1995. The aim of the research is to investigate the impact of cross-curricular tasks on a work-related curriculum from the perspective of students. The implications for teachers, school administrators, teacher educators and policymakers are explored. The research investigates the extent to which cross-curricular tasks, based on self-perceived needs and interests of students, lead to integrated learning. The role of cross-curricular tasks in giving students access to a broad base of knowledge and to the development of abilities for economic life is explored. It examines the manner in which self-directed learning helps participants to cope with the low status of pre-vocational courses. A case study of the implementation of the pre-vocational course in 3 different schools was based on interviews with 27 students, 11 teachers, 1 vice-principal and 3 principals. Data analysis was in accordance with Grounded Theory procedures and techniques. The available evidence suggests that cross-curricular tasks create a learning environment, based on the experiences of the learner, that is conducive to structural and possibly functional integration.

STATUS: Individual research

DATE OF RESEARCH: 1996-continuing

KEYWORDS: cross curricular approach; ireland; school leavers; vocational education; work education relationship; work related curriculum

0066

School of Education, Claverton Down, Bath BA2 7AY
01225 826826

Woods, J. Mr; *Supervisor*: Thompson, J. Prof.

An investigation into the pastoral care in international schools

ABSTRACT: Over the past few years, with the increased mobility of people from all parts of the world and different cultures, international schools have found themselves dealing with situations that can benefit from a pastoral curriculum incorporated into its institution. The purpose of this research is therefore to examine the advantages a school and its students can receive from a pastoral care programme; to see what limitations are needed in a pastoral care programme; to examine the budgeting for pastoral care programmes – will the money spent be of value for the school and its students? The research will begin with one school. A close examination of its pastoral programmes will result in a questionnaire being sent to several international schools to gather further responses to the content and structure of their pastoral curriculum. Interviews with the same questions will take place in a few schools worldwide to further this investigation.

STATUS: Individual research

DATE OF RESEARCH: 1994-continuing

KEYWORDS: international schools; overseas students; pastoral care –education

0067

School of Education, Claverton Down, Bath BA2 7AY
01225 826826

Harrison, J. Ms; *Supervisor*: Stables, A. Dr

An investigation into reading habits and preferences of National Curriculum key stage 3 learners

ABSTRACT: The research intends to focus on the reading habits of National Curriculum key stage 3 learners across a range of abilities. It will attempt to identify preferences of boys and girls and possible courses for and

outcomes of those preferences. Recent research shows clearly the implication 'that greater attention paid to harnessing and developing boys' and girls' reading interests .... would have positive effects in further improving attitudes to English generally'. Evidence for and against promoting various reading material to key stage 3 learners as a means of encouraging and stimulating both pleasure and advancement will be presented. Initial data will be collected by means of a stratified sample across the West of England answering closed questions on a questionnaire sent to schools. The questionnaire will yield both quantitative and qualitative data and will be analysed according to established methods. A case study will then be undertaken, involving a small number of pupils whose reading habits will be investigated over 2 years, using a variety of data collection techniques.

STATUS: Individual research

DATE OF RESEARCH: 1996-continuing

KEYWORDS: key stage 3; reading; reading habits; recreational reading; secondary education; secondary school pupils; sex differences

0068

School of Education, Claverton Down, Bath BA2 7AY
01225 826826

Austin, T. Ms; *Supervisor*: Whitehead, J. Mr

Uncovering community: treasures in the snow

ABSTRACT: Using an action research approach, this thesis describes and explains the researcher's learning as a professional educator as she examines her professional life. The focus of this work is on the process of defining, expressing and communicating those values which are used as standards of practice and judgement as well as finding an appropriate form in which to represent her learning. This process may make a distinctive and original contribution to educational knowledge. Through the use of story, personal and professional lives are blended to document a 10-year study. Beginning with a focus on a classroom of 12-year old students, the researcher seeks to facilitate a community of students. She then moves outward to begin to initiate communities with the parents of the students, the teaching peers within the school, and the teacher researcher colleagues across the state of Alaska, and other educators and researchers on a local, state, national and international level. It is through the analysis of interactions with these communities that the researcher came to understand her own values and their role in practice as a professional educator and in life.

STATUS: Individual research

DATE OF RESEARCH: 1992-1998

KEYWORDS: teacher development; teaching profession; values

0069

School of Education, Claverton Down, Bath BA2 7AY
01225 826826

Clarke, B. Mrs; *Supervisor*: Jamieson, I. Prof.

A study of flexible learning in post-registration nurse education

ABSTRACT: Changes in the organisation of the National Health Service have had a significant impact on the demand for continuing professional development in nursing. These changes have led to a multiplicity of modes of professional education for the post-registration nurse. Distance and open learning are becoming more widespread with the emergence of flexible learning. Although this term is in common use, the meaning of the term may not be adequately shared. In addition, the nature of flexible learning and the parameters of flexibility offered within nurse education remain unclear. This study seeks to address these issues with the aid of questionnaire-based surveys and case studies of questionnaires whose continuing professional development programmes were deemed to use flexible modes of learning

STATUS: Individual research

DATE OF RESEARCH: 1994-1998

KEYWORDS: flexible learning; nurse education; nurses; professional continuing education

0070

School of Education, Claverton Down, Bath BA2 7AY
01225 826826

Brown, G. Mr

The matching examinations data to the Youth Cohort Study

ABSTRACT: The aim of the project was to improve the quality of information from Cohort 7 Sweep 2 of the Youth Cohort Study (YCS) on qualifications. This is done by the matching of individuals with GCE A/AS-level examination achievement data, for England only. Cohort 7 Sweep 2 of the YCS was carried out in Spring 1996 for young people who were academic age 18. The information collected in the YCS includes self-reported educational attainment but in this sweep the data on GCE A/AS levels was not asked of all respondents. The project matched the A/AS-level data, for England, held by the University of Bath with a file from the YCS. The output was sent to the Social Community and Planning Research (SCPR) to incorporate into the main YCS database and update existing analyses.

STATUS: Sponsored project

SOURCE OF GRANT: Department for Education and Employment £8,027

DATE OF RESEARCH: 1998-1998

KEYWORDS: **a level examinations; cohort analysis; examination results; general certificate of secondary education; youth cohort study**

0071

School of Education, Claverton Down, Bath BA2 7AY
01225 826826

Reid, A. Dr; *Supervisor*: Martin, S. Dr ; Bullock, K. Ms ; Bishop, K. Mr

Learning from GCSE coursework

ABSTRACT: The aim of this project is to conduct an analysis of the potential of coursework within the General Certificate of Secondary Education (GCSE) to identify teaching and learning strategies that foster independent learning, critical thinking and creativity, constructs which are ill-defined but apparently highly valued and invoked as a basis for individuals to develop a capacity and a passion for lifelong learning. In order to define and establish descriptors of these constructs, the study will involve researching in partnership with teachers. The investigation will scrutinise current practice in GCSE coursework, probe students' understanding of their own organisation of, and approaches to, learning through coursework and examine how teaching and learning styles are influenced by the coursework assessment framework.

STATUS: Sponsored project

SOURCE OF GRANT: Economic and Social Research Council £35,682

DATE OF RESEARCH: 999-continuing

KEYWORDS: **coursework; general certificate of secondary education; learning strategies; lifelong learning; secondary education**

0072

School of Education, Claverton Down, Bath BA2 7AY
01225 826826

Omar, M. Ms; *Supervisor*: Ericson, J. Mr

An evaluation of the skills needed by teachers to make better and more appropriate use of visual materials in their teaching

ABSTRACT: Visuals have always had a role in education. However, since the invention of the printing press in the 15th century, and the ensuing rise in literacy, visuals such as pictures have taken a less important role in education. As a teacher, the researcher had been aware for a long time of the huge importance of teaching visual literacy. However, visual literacy was taken for granted – one assumes that children and adults understand most pictures. The researcher now realises the complexity of visual literacy. Many researchers have stressed the importance of developing skills in visual literacy and the researcher is now aware of the developments which are taking place in this field. However, evidence from literature and from previous research has made her realise that there appears to be an unbridged gulf between the classroom teacher and the educational researcher. This research aims to investigate the skills needed and problems faced by teachers to make better and more appropriate use of visuals in the classroom. The research questions are: 1) What categories of visuals do teachers employ in primary schools? 2) What learning purposes do teachers have when employing visuals? 3) What level of interpretative skills do teachers demonstrate? 4) What categories and classification of visual materials can be identified from the literature? 5) What are the different learning purposes

associated with different categories of visual? 6) What are the skills of interpreting visual material? (2-dimensional, still, non-projected pictures). 7) Given that we can identify a number of different skills of interpreting visual material, how can we develop these skills in teachers who do not possess them? The research will focus on primary school teachers in Bath and Bristol. The sample includes teachers from across the range of age and experience, and teaching various subjects. The study will be confined to Years 3 and 4 because the children have learned to read but generally still rely heavily on pictures for understanding. The research will involve structured observation, analysis of lesson plans and visual materials, and semi-structured interviews. It will identify specific respondents and will develop case studies of good/or distinctive practice. The researcher will draw up practical guidelines for teachers and teacher trainers which will narrow the gap between theory and practice of visual interpretation. In this way, it is hoped that teachers will be able to make fuller use of the power of visual messages in a positive and informed manner.

STATUS: Individual research

DATE OF RESEARCH: 1997-continuing

KEYWORDS: teaching methods; visual aids; visual literacy

0073

School of Education, Claverton Down, Bath BA2 7AY
01225 826826

Sahin, C. Miss; *Supervisor*: Stables, A. Dr ; Bullock, K. Ms

Teachers' beliefs and practices in relation to the use of questions in the teaching of literacy and numeracy at key stage 2

ABSTRACT: he Rt. Hon. David Blunkett MP, Secretary of State for Education and Employment was cited in the National Literacy Strategy 1998 quoting "All our children deserve to leave school equipped to enter a fulfilling adult life. But if children do not master the basic skills of literacy and numeracy while they are at primary school, they will be seriously disadvantaged later". Many people including politicians and educators believe that standards in mathematics and English are getting lower (Times Educational Supplement, 23 January 1998). To prevent this, two projects, the National Literacy Strategy (NLS) and the National Numeracy Project (NNP) were set up in 1996 by the Department for Education and Employment (DfEE). The researcher chose English and mathematics for this study because they are fundamental subjects of the curriculum. It will investigate the differences between teachers' beliefs and their practices when they use questioning methods in English and mathematics. (The interest is in what are the links between the questioning method and effective learning?). It will also investigate the effects of the NNP and NLS on teachers' beliefs and their practices about questioning methods. The research aims are: 1) To understand teachers' beliefs such as: a) what are the links between the questioning method and effective learning?; b) what are the alternatives to questioning?; c) how often are questions asked?; d) what kinds of questions are used in different lessons? 2) To investigate the differences and similarities between teachers' beliefs and their practices in relation to the use of questions in the teaching of literacy and numeracy at key stage 2. 3) In addition, the research will probe teachers' beliefs about effects of NLS and NNP on questioning. The researcher will use qualitative research methods and will be aimed at key stage 2 teachers in Bath and Wiltshire for the initial survey of about 20 teachers.

STATUS: Individual research

DATE OF RESEARCH: 1997-continuing

KEYWORDS: **key stage 2; literacy; mathematics education; numeracy; primary education; reading; teaching methods**

0074

School of Education, Claverton Down, Bath BA2 7AY
01225 826826

Stables, A. Dr ; Bishop, K. Mr; Lencastre, M. Dr; Stoer, S. Prof.; Soetaert, R. Prof.

The development of environmental awareness through literature and media education

ABSTRACT: Despite being identified as a "cross-curricular theme" in various national curricula across the European Union environmental education in schools has often been handled largely by teachers of science and of geography. There are, however, both theoretical and pragmatic reasons for also embedding environmental education more firmly within the arts and humanities. In theoretical terms, there is widespread agreement that the environment is partly shaped by human hands, and that what happens to it is dependent on human cultural and value systems. The project involves networks of practising teachers, in conjunction with academics from three European countries, in developing, trialling and evaluating exemplar materials for schoolteachers to use across Europe in order to stimulate further work in the areas referred to in the above paragraphs. The aim is to raise the level of awareness of environmental issues, and to empower students to take more effective action in relation to these issues, while also providing stimulating and useful materials for the teaching of literary and media studies, thus, in turn, enabling environmental education to become truly "cross-curricular".

STATUS: Sponsored project

SOURCE OF GRANT: European Commission DGXI ú 27,000

DATE OF RESEARCH: 1997-1998

KEYWORDS: comparative education; cross curricular approach; environmental education; europe; literature studies; media studies

0075

School of Education, Claverton Down, Bath BA2 7AY
01225 826826

Yonge, C. Dr; *Supervisor*: Stables, A. Dr

An investigation into the ways in which children use collaborative talk to develop their response to text

Abstract: The thesis attempts to answer the question of how children make sense of literary text through collaborative reading tasks in a primary classroom, and what implications are raised for teachers. It will present a case study carried out on a small group following a collaborative reading procedure in which the teacher uses a mix of whole class and small group communication, and makes the ground rules for speaking and listening explicit as part of the set tasks. As part of the school collaborative reading programme, the pupils are given clear instructions and preparation in answering task questions and following a systematic process-oriented approach to planning and monitoring their own work. The selected mixed group were observed over three terms using a wide range of ethnographic methods of data collection and analysis, in which the researcher role was that of participant observer. The study suggests that the learning process is much more sophisticated than is generally assumed by teachers, and that teachers need to be enabled to generate process indicators for collaborative talk and task performance, with which to monitor and assess individual learning, rather than relying on predetermined definitions of 'on' task talk and learning outcomes. The thesis is built around data that have been collected while leaving the normal classroom activities relatively uninterrupted by the research process, in contrast to other research into collaborative learning which has tended to either isolate the target groups physically from the classroom or use researcher designed tasks. The implications raised are therefore grounded in naturalistic data from the daily activities of a large classroom, and the thesis thus aims to address issues of classroom teaching by highlighting the intercontextual nature of children's learning talk and the importance of aspects of the teacher's role such as task design and identifying process indicators.

PUBLISHED MATERIAL: YONGE, C.J. & STABLES, A. (1998). 'I am it the clown: problematising the distinction between "off task" and "on task" talk, Language and Education, Vol 12, No 1, pp.55-70.

STATUS: Individual research

DATE OF RESEARCH: 1994-1998

KEYWORDS: classroom communication; group work; learning processes

0076

School of Education, Claverton Down, Bath BA2 7AY
01225 826826

Inland Revenue Board of Malaysia, Block 11, Floor 16, Government Complex, Jalan Duta, 50600 Kuala Lumpur, Malaysia

Yahya, M. Ms; *Supervisor*: Lauder, H. Prof.

The creation of government agencies as learning organisations – a case study of the Malaysian Inland Revenue Board

ABSTRACT: The research investigates the possibility of creating a learning organisation in government agencies, with reference to the Malaysian Inland Revenue Board (MIRB) as a case study. The research focuses on learning in MIRB and the potential where 'learning' might ultimately take the development of the organisation. The fast growing external environment, new technology, intricate issues of tax avoidance and evasion promotes a strong challenge to MIRB, stimulating it to keep up to date with knowledge. Specifically the objectives of the research are to: 1) identify the kind of learning most appropriate for MIRB; 2) investigate the factors that promote or impede learning in the organisation; 3) relate learning to the career structure and incentives for the staff; 4) generate a theory of learning organisation for government agencies; 5) make practical recommendation to MIRB on how to improve learning and keep up with knowledge. The methods used in this research are predominantly qualitative. Instruments employed for this research are interviews; questionnaires, document analysis; and observation. The research is currently at the stage of data collection.

STATUS: Individual research

DATE OF RESEARCH: 1997-continuing

KEYWORDS: learning; learning organisation; malaysia

0077

School of Education, Claverton Down, Bath BA2 7AY
01225 826826
London University, Institute of Education, 20 Bedford Way, London WC1H 0AL   0171 580 1122
Cardiff University, School of Education, Senghennydd Road, Cardiff CF2 4YG   01222 874000

Lauder, H. Prof.; Green, A. Dr; Brown, P. Prof.

High skills project

ABSTRACT: The aims of the research are to: 1) conduct a comparative analysis of the different national routes to a 'high skills' economy; 2) develop a comparative theory of skills formation and the conditions within which the upgrading of the labour supply is most effectively utilised; 3) develop an interdisciplinary and dynamic approach to the study of skills formation within different national economies, using a combination of qualitative and quantitative research methods; 4) enhance the comparative richness of data by using multinational corporations with sites in 2 or more different countries under investigation as a way of contrasting approaches to training and human capital resource policies and practices; 5) contribute to the enhancement of post-compulsory education and training (PCET) and labour market policies in Britain through a critical evaluation of the ways in which British skills formation can be improved through policy importation.

STATUS: Sponsored project

SOURCE OF GRANT: Economic and Social Research Council

DATE OF RESEARCH: 1997-continuing

KEYWORDS: comparative education; germany; korea; labour market; singapore; skilled workers; skills; training; vocational education

Benchmark Research Limited

0078

8 White Oak Square, London Road, Swanley BR8 7AG
01322 614050

Hales, J. Ms

The Enterprise in Higher Education graduate follow-up survey

ABSTRACT: A 3-phase postal survey was used to track a cohort of final year undergraduates through their first 12 months following graduation. The survey covers graduates from Enterprise in Higher Education (EHE) funded courses and those who did not benefit from EHE funding and includes data on job search techniques, subsequent labour market status, level of job and salary. The study considers whether the EHE objective of developing graduates who are more employable and more able to meet employer needs has been successfully achieved.

STATUS: Sponsored project

SOURCE OF GRANT: Department for Education and Employment £128,200

DATE OF RESEARCH: 1994-1997

KEYWORDS: **enterprise in higher education; graduate employment; graduate surveys; salaries**

Berkshire County Council

0079

Education Department, Strategic Planning and Information Systems, Shire Hall, Shinfield Park, Reading RG2 9XE   01734 233425

Lawrance, R. Mr

Analysis of examination results

ABSTRACT: Information is received from National Consortium for Examination Results (NCER) and examination results are analysed by subject, sex and school and a combination of the three. These are in the form of detailed tabulations and summary measures of performance. Results for examinations taken at different times are matched together to produce overall summaries of attainment. Information on the ethnic origin of candidates is added to the results, which are also analysed by ethnicity. Work on contextualising the results with socio-economic data is underway.

STATUS: Sponsored project

SOURCE OF GRANT: Berkshire County Council

DATE OF RESEARCH: 1981-1998

KEYWORDS: **examination results; institutional evaluation; performance indicators**

0080

Education Department, Strategic Planning and Information Systems, Shire Hall, Shinfield Park, Reading RG2 9XE   01734 233425

Lawrance, R. Mr

Berkshire school pupil forecasting system

ABSTRACT: The objective of the Berkshire school pupil forecasting system is to predict numbers of pupils of each age group in every Berkshire school, for up to 10 years ahead. The basic approach in forecasting is the 'cohort trend' method, where changes observed to cohorts of pupils over previous years are applied in the future. Recent enhancements to the system include: (1) the prediction of primary school entry (i.e. 5 year old) age pupils by relating intakes to the past and predicted resident population of the school catchment area, using data from the Research and Intelligence Unit's Population Estimation and Projection Models; and (2) prediction of intakes to secondary schools by using data from the Education Department's computerised Secondary School Allocation System. Forecasts are produced annually using pupil numbers in January.

STATUS: Sponsored project

SOURCE OF GRANT: Berkshire County Council

DATE OF RESEARCH: 1976-continuing

KEYWORDS: **educational planning; local education authorities; long range planning; prediction; pupil numbers; regional planning**

0081

Education Department, Strategic Planning and Information Systems, Shire Hall, Shinfield Park, Reading RG2 9XE   01734 233425

Eno, R. Mr; Symonds, G. Mr

Survey of ethnic origin, first language and religion

ABSTRACT: A survey of pupils of specified ages in all schools in Berkshire to identify the ethnic origin, first language and religion of each pupil.

STATUS: Sponsored project

SOURCE OF GRANT: Berkshire County Council

DATE OF RESEARCH: 1990-continuing

KEYWORDS: **ethnic groups; mother tongue; pupils; religion; surveys**

0082

Education Department, Strategic Planning and Information Systems, Shire Hall, Shinfield Park, Reading RG2 9XE   01734 233425

Lawrance, R. Mr

Survey of disruptive children in Year 1

ABSTRACT: An annual survey of Year 1 pupils to monitor severe disruptive or non-conforming behaviour. The results are used to identify trends and to contribute to the development of effective strategies for dealing with such children.

STATUS: Sponsored project

SOURCE OF GRANT: Berkshire County Council

DATE OF RESEARCH: 1993-continuing

KEYWORDS: **behaviour problems; discipline problems; disruptive pupils; emotional and behavioural difficulties; infant school pupils; primary school pupils; problem children; surveys**

Birmingham University

0083

School of Continuing Studies, Edgbaston, Birmingham B15 2TT 0121 414 3344

Seeley, M. Rev.; Supervisor: Tann, J. Prof.

How clergy learn: a study of formal and informal continuing education of clergy in the Church of England

ABSTRACT: In the past decade there has been a substantial increase in the provision of continuing education courses for Church of England clergy. This has happened with little apparent awareness of the effectiveness of such an approach, or understanding of the nature of clergy learning. The aim of this study is to investigate the factors which facilitate and inhibit clergy learning using the insights of learning organisation theory. The study will consider the nature of formal and informal education among clergy, the role of the structure of the Church of England in relation to patterns of power and value within the Church, the continuing role of social class, the function of theological models, and the changing social profile of clergy.

STATUS: Individual research

DATE OF RESEARCH: 1993-continuing

KEYWORDS: **clergy; continuing education; learning processes; professional education; religious education; theological education**

0084

School of Continuing Studies, Edgbaston, Birmingham B15 2TT 0121 414 3344

Ross, K. Dr; Bowl, R. Mr

The education and training needs of users of adult services and their carers

ABSTRACT: The aims of this research project were, broadly, to investigate the reality behind the rhetoric of user involvement as outlined in recent legislation such as the Citizen's Charter and the National Health Service and Community Care Act. Explicitly, the project aimed to explore the extent to which users of adult services are encouraged to have a voice in the services they receive, particularly in day centre settings. In addition, the project intended to look at the development of user forums and their effectiveness. The study wanted to identify what education and training needs existed amongst user groups which, if met, would enable users (and carers) to take a more proactive role in the planning and delivery of services. A total of 300 individuals took part in the study and care staff were also contacted for their views relating to user participation. Informal discussions took place with groups of users about their particular experiences in day – care settings, using informal methods of note-taking, but focusing on the issues concerning users rather than imposing the researcher's own agenda. The project focused on people with physical disabilities, people with learning difficulties and people experiencing mental distress, across three local authority areas in the West Midlands. Key findings include the fact that irrespective of client group or location, by far the most pertinent influence on user empowerment was the specific culture of the day-centre they attended and, more importantly, the management style of the senior staff group. Recommendations of the research include the desirability of providing training opportunities to adult users to encourage greater confidence in participating in decision-making processes.

STATUS: Sponsored project

SOURCE OF GRANT: Universities Funding Council

DATE OF RESEARCH: 1992-1993

KEYWORDS: adult day centres; caregivers; educational needs; services; special educational needs

0085

School of Continuing Studies, Edgbaston, Birmingham B15 2TT
0121 414 3344

Tann, J. Prof.

Evaluation of a programme of interventions on clinical pharmacy for community pharmacists

ABSTRACT: The project arose out of the recognition that clinical training is needed for community pharmacists to be able, effectively, to extend working relationships with general practitioners (GPs) and to participate in joint liaison groups. It was believed that post-registration clinical pharmacy training, modelled on suitably modified programmes run for hospital pharmacists, was needed. The project commenced with a training needs analysis using a diagnostic workshop technique validated by a telephone survey. This was followed by phase 2 during which training materials on six topics were produced. The evaluation project was designed to: 1) review the appropriateness of the methodology of training needs analysis; 2) review participants' use of and reactions to distance learning materials prepared on two topics; and 3) make recommendations to the project team for subsequent distance learning materials and to assess the overall intervention. The methodology included observation, team meetings, an interim survey and a final telephone survey of all community pharmacists who had participated at some stage in the programme. The evaluation identified important content and process outcomes of the clinical pharmacy interventions. Feedback during the course of the project contributed to increasingly well produced distance learning materials, to effective tutor manuals, and to case studies.

The process outcomes included: 1) the development of staff who had been involved in the project; 2) greater confidence and a more proactive approach to clinical practice amongst the participants, together with improved relationships with GPs; and 3) lateral networking with group members. The most important longer term outcome of the intervention was the clinical orientation of the participants.

STATUS: Sponsored project

SOURCE OF GRANT: Centre for Pharmacy Postgraduate Education

DATE OF RESEARCH: 1991-1993

KEYWORDS: clinical experience; distance education; pharmaceutical education; pharmacists; professional training; programme evaluation

0086

School of Continuing Studies, Edgbaston, Birmingham B15 2TT
0121 414 3344

Rubienska, A. Ms; Supervisor: Tann, J. Prof.

Organisation learning in the training function of some overseas government offices

ABSTRACT: The introduction of Western management practices is often a condition of donor agencies to third world countries. With reference to UK comparitors, the research will investigate intended and attempted transformations of training organisations in a selection of developing countries. The study will be located within the theorising and literature on learning organisations.

STATUS: Individual research

DATE OF RESEARCH: 1995-continuing

KEYWORDS: developing countries; development aid; organisational theories; training

0087

School of Continuing Studies, Edgbaston, Birmingham B15 2TT
0121 414 3344

Nolan, M. Ms; Supervisor: Hicks, C. Dr

Antenatal education post 'Changing Childbirth': does it help parents make informed choices?

ABSTRACT: The literature of childbirth education suggests that attending parentcraft classes does not improve the outcome of childbirth, either in obstetric terms or in terms of satisfaction with the birth experience. This study is informed by the ethos of 'Changing Childbirth' (Great Britain. Department of Health. (1993). Changing childbirth. London: HMSO) and aims to compare antenatal classes provided by The National Childbirth Trust (NCT) and by the Parentcraft Department of a large teaching hospital. Techniques of quantitative analysis are used to assess whether classes improve parents' knowledge-base, their ability to make informed choices and participate actively in their own care, and their confidence to look after their babies. The sample comprises 100 primiparous couples attending NCT classes and 100 attending hospital classes. A small preliminary study established demographic details about couples attending classes at the hospital and with the NCT (Nolan, 1995). The second part of the study involves semi-structured interviews with providers and consumers of antenatal education: parents; NCT teachers and teacher trainers; midwives and midwifery tutors; maternity unit managers and NCT policy-makers; and women such as Kitzinger and Flint who have been influential in the development of antenatal education. A grounded theory (Strauss & Corbin, 1990) approach is used for interview analysis.

The evidence from the quantiative and qualitative wings of the study will be used to suggest new directions for antenatal education so that it is better able to maximise health education opportunities for the childbearing population. The study also has implications for effective use of financial and manpower resources within the voluntary and statutory sectors.

Published Material: NOLAN, M. (1994). 'Effectiveness of antenatal education', British Journal of Midwifery, Vol 2, No 11, pp.534-538. ; NOLAN, M. (1995). 'A comparison of attenders at antenatal classes in the voluntary and statutory sectors: educational and organisational implications', Midwifery, Vol 11, pp.138-145.

STATUS: Individual research

DATE OF RESEARCH: 1994-1997

KEYWORDS: antenatal education; birth; parent education; parenting skills; pregnancy

0088

School of Continuing Studies, Edgbaston, Birmingham B15 2TT
0121 414 3344

Price, P. Ms; Supervisor: Hicks, C. Dr

Children's nurses: are they educated to meet the needs of children?

ABSTRACT: Government reports, recommendations, nursing syllabuses and course guidelines published over the last 45 years have all agreed that children in hospital have special needs. There is also agreement that such children should be nursed by specially trained nurses. The initial selection of students for the child branch will be surveyed to determine if there are any particular characteristics that are expected of children's nurses. Students of adult and children's nursing will then be compared at various points in their education to determine their knowledge, understanding and attitudes towards the needs of children. These tests will involve the development of attitude scales. It is anticipated that children's nurses will have a better understanding of the needs of children when they have been admitted to hospital, than any other group. This should demonstrate that nurses who have undertaken such courses are the most appropriately qualified to nurse children in hospital.

Conclusions drawn from the proposed study will enable the development of courses which will equip students of children's nursing with the skills and knowledge to meet the needs of children more appropriately. Post-registration training courses could also be developed to enable qualified nurses to develop their own knowledge and meet the requirements of the United Kingdom Central Council for Nursing, Midwifery and Health Visiting (UKCC) that registered nurses demonstrate that they have kept themselves up-to-date with current practice.

STATUS: Individual research

DATE OF RESEARCH: 1994-1998

KEYWORDS: hospital personnel; hospitalised children; nurse education; nurses

0089

School of Continuing Studies, Edgbaston, Birmingham B15 2TT
0121 414 3344

Weir, R. Mr; Supervisor: Tann, J. Prof.

The principles of the learning organisation as a model for recovery and renewal in the methodist church

ABSTRACT: Declining support for the Christian churches in England is well known. The Methodist church in England has lost half its members since 1945. Presiding over a diminishing support base the Church has remained relatively isolated from change forces which have operated on virtually every other institution. While commercial enterprises have been forced to change in order to remain competitive and change has generally been accompanied by new approaches to leadership, less bureaucracy, leaner structures and empowerment, as well as new organisational structures, the churches have remained isolated. The project will consider the applicability of the principles of the learning organisation to the Methodist church. The methodology will involve a largely qualitative approach, the project being located within a larger ecumenical study of Christian mission, the researcher thereby having access to a wider database. The study will be partly longitudinal and will seek benchmark change in parish communities.

STATUS: Individual research

DATE OF RESEARCH: 1996-continuing

KEYWORDS: **change strategies; methodist church; organisational change**

0090

School of Continuing Studies, Edgbaston, Birmingham B15 2TT
0121 414 3344

McGrath, S. Ms

Evaluation of training re: domestic violence, delivered by Children's Society project

ABSTRACT: Wymeley Birch Family Centre has developed a training module built around a role play of a child and her mother entering a hostel for women suffering from abuse. The research aims to evaluate the effectiveness of the training in changing attitudes, practices and behaviours of the workers, in the personal social services (PSS). The investigation is designed to test out pre-and post-training attitudes, via questionnaires administered before and 3 weeks after training. This is followed-up by semi-structured interviews conducted 3 months after training with 2 randomly selected participants from each course. Courses have been delivered to Diploma in Social Work students, probation workers, social service department workers, magistrates, hostel workers, police, Women's Aid and Relate.

STATUS: Sponsored project

SOURCE OF GRANT: Children's Society £5,000

DATE OF RESEARCH: 1997-1998

KEYWORDS: **battered women; family violence; social services; staff development; training**

0091

School of Continuing Studies, Edgbaston, Birmingham B15 2TT
0121 414 3344

Duffell, S. Ms; *Supervisor*: Hicks, C. Dr; Wheeler, S. Ms

The impact of anxiety on school Tasks and Tests performance

ABSTRACT: Since the introduction of school league tables teachers have been under increased pressure to push their pupils to achieve ever higher results in the Tasks and Tests. It is hypothesised that this results in greater pressure being placed upon children resulting in high levels of anxiety, which for many may have a detrimental affect upon their performance. The research data is based on Year 6 pupils in 6 primary schools in North Birmingham and is spread over a 4-year period. Every pupil in each Year 6 school group is tested for trait levels of anxiety. After this they are tested for state levels of anxiety which are measured using the Spielberger 'State-Trait Anxiety Inventory for Children'. This takes place one month prior to the assessment tasks, during the week of the Tasks and a few weeks after the Tasks. The data is recorded along with the teacher assessments and the final externally produced test scores. The research aims to show a correlation between levels of anxiety and pupil performance in anxiety inducing situations such as national testing. During the third and fourth years of the research, interventions will be designed to attempt to reduce levels of teacher and pupil anxiety. These interventions will be available in three of the schools, and not in the other three. The results of these interventions will be monitored and conclusions drawn.

STATUS: Individual research

DATE OF RESEARCH: 1996-continuing

KEYWORDS: **assessment; primary education; stress - psychological; tasks and tests; test anxiety; tests**

0092

School of Continuing Studies, Edgbaston, Birmingham B15 2TT
0121 414 3344

Manchester University, Department of Pharmacy, Oxford Road, Manchester M13 9PL   0161 275 2000

Tann, J. Prof.; Blenkinsopp, A. Dr

Learning by star performers in community pharmacy

ABSTRACT: A pilot study in three family health service authorities (FHSAs) was undertaken to test the methodology and basic assumptions. On the basis of the results the full project was designed. The main hypothesis is that star performers can be identified by key stakeholders in service provision and that the learning styles of star performers differ from those of the occupational norm. It is thought that networking will have a key part to play in the informal learning methodologies that star performers use in acquiring information on innovation.

STATUS: Sponsored project

SOURCE OF GRANT: National Health Service Executive

DATE OF RESEARCH: 1995-1997

KEYWORDS: **cognitive style; health personnel; learning strategies; pharmacists; pharmacy**

0093

School of Continuing Studies, Edgbaston, Birmingham B15 2TT
0121 414 3344

Queen Elizabeth Medical Centre, School of Physiotherapy, Edgbaston, Birmingham B15 2TH   0121 472 1311

Cross, V. Mrs; *Supervisor*: Hicks, C. Dr

Predictors of student learning outcomes in clinical education and their effects on clinical and academic staff/student development programmes

ABSTRACT: For academic institutions involved with education in medicine and allied health professions, clinical education presents the most problematical component of courses. Inconsistency and inequity in the quality of students' learning experiences, lack of validity and reliability in assessment of students' clinical performance, poor standards of clinical teaching and low levels of motivation amongst clinical educators and lack of time and staff devoted to clinical education by clinical managers, all give rise to continuing concern within academic institutions. Central to their concern is the detrimental effect of such findings on student learning outcomes. These outcomes may take the form of performance assessment grades, clinical examination results, patient satisfaction ratings etc. Five groups of individuals exert an influence on clinical education: academic staff; clinical managers; clinical educators; students; and patients. However, development programmes have focused on the assumption that improving the quality of clinical teaching by changing the attitudes and developing the facilitation and teaching skills of clinical educators is the key to improving learning outcomes. The proposed research will investigate the validity of this assumption in relation to undergraduate physiotherapy education. Are the actions and attitudes of clinical educators as pivotal as they have been made to appear? Are other factors equally or more influential in ensuring successful student learning outcomes from clinical education? The aims of the research are to formulate, implement and evaluate a staff/student development programme designed to optimise student learning in clinical education, on the basis of identified best predictors of student learning outcomes.

STATUS: Individual research

DATE OF RESEARCH: 1993-1997

KEYWORDS: **clinical experience; medical education; outcomes of education**

0094

School of Education, Edgbaston, Birmingham B15 2TT
0121 414 3344

Thomas, H. Prof.; Bullock, A. Dr

The funding of schools after the Education Reform Act 1988

ABSTRACT: The principal aims of this study are to: 1) describe and analyse the pattern of resource distribution in local education authorities; 2) examine the change in priorities as the system moves from one method of funding to another; 3) investigate the relationship between the resource priorities of the local education authority and those of the school; and 4) inquire into the rationale of resource decisions. The methods used are: quantitative analysis of local education authority budgetary data; and school level budgetary data.

PUBLISHED MATERIAL: BULLOCK, A.D. & THOMAS, H. (1992). Pupil numbers and school budgets: an exmination of formula allocations to schools of different size. Birmingham: University of Birmingham, School of Education. ; THOMAS, H. & BULLOCK, A.D. (1992). 'Local management funding formulae and LEA discretion'. In: SIMKINS, T., ELLISON, L. & GARRETT, V. (Eds). Implemeting educational reform: the early lessons. Harlow: Longmans. ; BULLOCK, A.D. & THOMAS, H. (1993). 'Comparing school formula allocations: an exploration of some problems'. In: WALLACE, G. (Ed). Local management, central control: schools in the market place. Bournemouth: Hyde Publications. ; BULLOCK, A.D,. & THOMAS, H. (1993). 'Pupil-led funding and local management funding formulae'. In: SMITH, M. & BUSHER, H. (Eds). Managing schools in an uncertain environment: resources, marketing and power. Sheffield: Sheffield Hallam University. ; THOMAS, H. (1994). 'Markets, collectivities and management', Oxford Review of Education, Vol 20, No 1, pp.41-56.

STATUS: Sponsored project

SOURCE OF GRANT: Leverhulme Trust £42,000

DATE OF RESEARCH: 1990-1993

KEYWORDS: educational finance; financial policy; financial support; local management of schools

0095

School of Education, Edgbaston, Birmingham B15 2TT
0121 414 3344

Thomas, H. Prof. ; Arnott, M. Ms ; Bullock, A. Dr

The impact of Local Management of Schools

ABSTRACT: The project aims to describe and analyse the impact of Local Management of Schools (LMS). From a national questionnaire, two follow-up surveys and visits to 40 schools, data have been gathered on a range of issues including: 1) headteachers' perceptions of their changing role, and the benefits and unwelcome consequences of LMS; 2) impact on learning; 3) workload; 4) changes in staffing patterns; 5) changing pupil numbers; 6) formula, finance and budgets; 7) management and planning; and 8) the role of local education authorities and governing bodies.

PUBLISHED MATERIAL: ARNOTT, M., BULLOCK, A.D. & THOMAS, H. (1992). The impact of local management on schools: a source book. Birmingham: University of Birmingham, School of Education. ; BULLOCK, A.D., THOMAS, H. & ARNOTT, M. (1993). 'The impact of local management on schools: a view from head teachers', Local Government Policy Making, Vol 19, No 5, pp.57-61. ; ARNOTT, M., BULLOCK, A.D. & THOMAS, H. (1993). 'The potential for both disaster and success is great: issues arising from head teachers' attitudes to local management of schools'. In: WALLACE, G. (Ed). Local management, central control: schools in the market place. Bournemouth: Hyde Publications. ; BULLOCK, A.D. & THOMAS, H. (1994). The impact of local management on schools: final report. Birmingham: University of Birmingham, School of Education.

STATUS: Sponsored project

SOURCE OF GRANT: National Association of Head Teachers £62,000

DATE OF RESEARCH: 1991-1993

KEYWORDS: educational change; head teachers; local management of schools; school based management

0096

School of Education, Edgbaston, Birmingham B15 2TT
0121 414 3344

Shepherson, D. Mr; *Supervisor*: Thomas, H. Dr

Economic decision-making models on non-advanced further education

ABSTRACT: An investigation of the relationship between resource decisions and curriculum decision processes will be examined in the context created by the local authority role in creating a framework for strategic planning, as influenced by the Local Authority Act and the Education Reform Act 1988. At the centre of the analysis will be an opportunity cost model of decision making. It is expected that quantitative data will be collected reflecting commonly used performance indicators. This will be analysed in the context of qualitative data, based upon interviews, relating to the perceptions of individuals on their valuations of resource and curriculum alternatives.

STATUS: Individual research

DATE OF RESEARCH: 1989-1993

KEYWORDS: educational finance; educational planning; local education authorities

0097

School of Education, Edgbaston, Birmingham B15 2TT
0121 414 3344

Richmond, J. Mr; *Supervisor*: Thomas, H. Dr

Problems and possibilities of managing small secondary schools (circa 400) as a result of the Education Reform Act 1988

ABSTRACT: The Education Reform Act 1988 has implications for the management and size of schools within a local authority, Her Majesty's Inspectorate having suggested that four-form entry schools may be the minimum under Local Management of Schools yet many secondary schools fall below this minimum. In order to examine the problems and possibilities for the management of such schools, the proposed research will be both qualititative and quantitative in approach. Key issues of the 1988 Act will be reviewed and consideration given to the requirements of the Government through the Department for Education and Science, those of the local education authority as well as the needs of small schools themselves.

STATUS: Individual research

DATE OF RESEARCH: 1990-1993

KEYWORDS: education reform act 1988; local management of schools; school size; small schools

0098

School of Education, Edgbaston, Birmingham B15 2TT
0121 414 3344

Upton, C. Dr

Transcription and analysis of the domestic accounts of Merton College, Oxford, for the Tudor period

ABSTRACT: College domestic accounts remain as one of the last largely unexplored sources of university academic, social, political and economic history for the Tudor period. Those of Merton College are particularly full for this century. The project will transcribe and publish these accounts. At the same time, a series of articles will describe and evaluate the material they contain and, where possible, link it with that available from other similar educational institutions. The work is expected to show in detail the various problems that Oxford colleges met at this period in their relations with secular and ecclesiastical authorities and to provide some insight into the management of college finance. Since Merton College was an establishment of middle size, with a stable position and well established links with the outside world, this study will also throw light on the role of the educated elite in Tudor society and the reactions of that society to problems of the provision and control of higher education in a world affected by changes of the Renaissance and Reformation. The first two volumes of the transcripts, covering the period 1482-1494 and 1495-1507, are being prepared for publication by the Oxford Historical Society.

PUBLISHED MATERIAL: FLETCHER, J.M. & UPTON, C.A. (1983). 'Destruction, repair and removal: an Oxford college chapel during the Reformation', Oxoniensia, No 48, pp.119-130. ; FLETCHER, J.M. & UPTON, C.A. (1984). 'A short description of the sixteenth century domestic accounts of Merton College, Oxford'. In: Die Geschichte der Universitaten un ihre Erforschung, Leipzig, pp.54-67. ; FLETCHER, J.M. & UPTON, C.A. (1987). 'Monastic enclave' or 'open society'? A consideration of the role of women in the life of an Oxford college community in the early Tudor period', History of Education, No 16, pp.1-9. ; FLETCHER, J.M. & UPTON, C.A. (Eds). (1996). The domestic accounts of Merton College, Oxford. Volume 1: 1 August 1482-1 August 1494. Oxford Historical Society New Series Vol 34. Oxford: Oxford Historical Society.

STATUS: Sponsored project

SOURCE OF GRANT: Economic and Social Research Council ; Merton College ; British Academy – jointly £5,000

DATE OF RESEARCH: 1980-continuing

KEYWORDS: educational history; institutional administration; universities

0099

School of Education, Edgbaston, Birmingham B15 2TT
0121 414 3344

Martin, J. Ms; *Supervisor*: Thomas, H. Dr

The effectiveness of schooling and educational resource management

ABSTRACT: This is a national survey of 18 sample scondary schools (both Locally Managed and Grant Maintained) to illuminate aspects of good practice in terms of the relationship between resource management and school effectiveness. This will be followed by selection of 3 case study schools which exemplify good practice in the relationship and where the changed responsibilities and contexts of the school are being used to secure improvement. A concluding analysis will interpret field study material in relation to the characteristics of school reform in England and Wales.

STATUS: Sponsored project

SOURCE OF GRANT: Department for Education ú 45,000

DATE OF RESEARCH: 1992-1993

KEYWORDS: educational administration; educational finance; educational software; resource allocation; school effectiveness

0100

School of Education, Edgbaston, Birmingham B15 2TT
0121 414 3344

Hammersley, P. Rev.; *Supervisor*: Hull, J. Prof.

Adult learning problems and the experience of loss: a study of religious rigidity

ABSTRACT: The study into the nature of religious rigidity drew upon the work of M.H. Spero and the object relations tradition of psychoanalytic theory. 135 participants were recruited from trainees for the lay ministry of reader in the Church of England. Participants were tested for rigidity of adaptability using the Cattell 16PF questionnaire, the Schutz Firo-B self awareness test, and a 'coping with loss sitautions' test and religious attitudes (rigidity) test. 36 participants were selected on the basis of their high or low rigidity score, and were interviewed in a tape-recorded semi-structured interview. These were transcribed to provide narrative texts which were analysed for the variables anxiety, grandiosity, splitting, emotional detachment and lack of autonomy. Results indicated an association between unresolved loss, particularly in early life, and rigid patterns of religious belief and practice, inhibiting the capacity to be self reflective and to integrate faith with like experience in response to the training received.

PUBLISHED MATERIAL: HAMMERSLEY, P. (1997). 'Rigidity and loss in adult theological learners'. Proceedings of the Canadian Conference of Catholic Bishops (CARAVAN), Ottawa, Canada, 1997.

STATUS: Sponsored project

SOURCE OF GRANT: YAPP Educational Trust £1,000

DATE OF RESEARCH: 1991-1997

KEYWORDS: church and education; religious education; theological education

0101

School of Education, Edgbaston, Birmingham B15 2TT
0121 414 3344

Wade, B. Prof.; Moore, M. Dr

Babies into books

ABSTRACT: The pilot 'Bookstart' project (Wade and Moore 1993) showed the benefit of early exposure to books. The 'Babies into Books' project investigates home activities, with a focus on book-sharing. Home-visits, observation, intonational analysis and questionnaire methods seek to discover what differences (if any) there are between a sample (30) of families who received Bookstart packs and a control group (30) who did not.

PUBLISHED MATERIAL: WADE, B. & MOORE, M. (1993). Bookstart in Birmingham. London: Book Trust.

STATUS: Individual research

DATE OF RESEARCH: 1993-1993

KEYWORDS: books; early childhood education; early experience; early reading; infants; parent participation

0102

School of Education, Edgbaston, Birmingham B15 2TT
0121 414 3344

Wade, B. Dr; Moore, M. Dr; Pastor, C. Prof.; Berdousi, E. Ms

European perspectives on viewpoints of pupils with special educational needs

ABSTRACT: Published work (Wade, B. and Moore, M. (1993). The experience of special education. Milton Keynes: Open University) reports the views of a sample of New Zealand and British school children with special educational needs. It is argued that information provided by clients on such topics as teachers, lessons, peer groups, parents, and feeling different, is important for providing for pupils with special educational needs using the original questionnaires and sentence completion instruments in translation. Comparative studies are being made in Greece (Corinthus) and Spain (Sevilla) with samples of children (80 in each country) in special schools and mainstream classrooms.

PUBLISHED MATERIAL: WADE, B. & MOORE, M. (1993). The experience of special education. Milton Keynes: Open University.

STATUS: ndividual research

DATE OF RESEARCH: 1993-continuing

KEYWORDS: comparative education; disabilities; mainstreaming; pupil attitudes; special educational needs; special schools

0103

School of Education, Edgbaston, Birmingham B15 2TT
0121 414 3344

Belfield, C. Dr ; Rikowski, G. Dr; Marr, A. Dr ; *Supervisor*: Thomas, H. Prof.

An evaluation of continuing vocational education in higher education institutions in England

ABSTRACT: This is an evaluation of development funding for continuing vocational education in English higher education institutions (HEIs). It will involve evaluation of the process, provision and performance, including an economic impact study and a study of cost-effectiveness. The research will include visits to 20 HEIs for data collection (documents and interviews) and visits to 6 HEIs for detailed evaluation of continuing vocational education. The results will be available in 1998.

STATUS: Sponsored project

SOURCE OF GRANT: Higher Education Funding Council for England

DATE OF RESEARCH: 1997-1998

KEYWORDS: continuing education; cost effectiveness; economics education relationship; higher education; vocational education

0104

School of Education, Edgbaston, Birmingham B15 2TT
0121 414 3344

Mills, R. Mr; *Supervisor*: Wade, B. Prof.

Adult perspectives of childhood

ABSTRACT: Using a combination of quantitative and qualitative approaches, with data gained from 474 questionnaires, 170 prose testimonies and 20 interviews, the views of childhood held by 5 groups are analysed: teachers; educational professionals other than teachers; students in teacher training; other students; parents. 6 main perspectives are identified from the reading and matched with the target groups: child as animal; child as apprentice; child as innocent; child as member of a distinct group; children as persons in their own right; child as victim/ vulnerable. Substantial, differential evidence is found to support all but the first listed perspective (child as animal), with child as victim/vulnerable receiving a great deal of coverage, particularly in the prose testimonies. Quantitative and qualitative data is seen to be mutually supportive, with life history material providing insights of great depth and particularity.

PUBLISHED MATERIAL: MILLS, R.W. (1997). 'Childhood - when did it end?', Primary Practice, No 10, pp.43-46. ; MILLS, R.W. & MILLS, R.M. Child of our time. Variations in adult views of childhood with age', International Journal of Early Years Education, Vol 6, No 1. (in press).

STATUS: Individual research

DATE OF RESEARCH: 1994-1998

KEYWORDS: **attitudes; childhood; children; parent attitudes; student attitudes; teacher attitudes**

0105

School of Education, Edgbaston, Birmingham B15 2TT
0121 414 3344

Osler, A. Dr

Human rights and democracy in schools

ABSTRACT: The project aims to strengthen and develop collaboration between educational researchers concerned with democracy and human rights in education and those working in the fields of human rights law, social policy, political science and international relations. It considers the potential of a human rights framework as the basis for research and policy development in promoting equity and social justice – for example, through initiatives to promote race and gender equality in schools. The study will examine the implications of incorporating the European Convention on Human Rights into UK domestic law on the education of teachers and children. It will also consider how the Convention on the Rights of the Child might be implemented in schools and local education authorities.

STATUS: Sponsored project

SOURCE OF GRANT: Economic and Social Research Council £11,650; Council of Europe

DATE OF RESEARCH: 1998-continuing

KEYWORDS: **childrens rights; democracy; human rights**

0106

School of Education, Edgbaston, Birmingham B15 2TT
0121 414 3344

Williams, E. Dr; Soares, A. Dr

The changing role of higher education in secondary initial teacher training

ABSTRACT: A survey of views of higher education staff, school teachers and student teachers on the role of higher education in initial teacher training. Anticipated sample size in excess of 4,000.

STATUS: Sponsored project

SOURCE OF GRANT: Association of Teachers and Lecturers £11,000

DATE OF RESEARCH: 1998-continuing

KEYWORDS: **attitudes; higher education; preservice teacher education; student teacher attitudes; teacher attitudes**

0107

School of Education, Edgbaston, Birmingham B15 2TT 0121 414 3344

Cole, T. Mr; *Supervisor*: Visser, J. Mr

Effective special school provision for pupils with emotional and behavioural difficulties

ABSTRACT: This research established a database of all special schools whose main intake were pupils with emotional and behavioural difficulties (EBD). These schools were surveyed by questionnaire, with a 56% response rate. The questionnaire elicited data on education practice and policy, care work and the Children's Act 1989 in relation to effectively meeting the

needs of pupils with EBD. 18 schools were visited and interviews with key players conducted. An analysis of published Office for Standards in Education (OFSTED) inspection reports was conducted. A detailed review of the literature was compiled. The results when published will indicate factors which affect 'good practice' in meeting the needs of pupils with emotional and behavioural difficulties who are placed in special schools.

PUBLISHED MATERIAL: VISSER, J. & COLE, T. (1996). 'An overview of English special schools provision for children with emotional and behavioural difficulties', Emotional and Behavioural Difficulties, Vol 1, No 3, pp.11-16. ; COLE, T., VISSER, J. & UPTON, G. Effective schooling for pupils with emotional and behavioural difficulties. London: David Fulton.; COLE, T. & VISSER, J. 'How should effectiveness of schools for pupils with EBD be assessed', Emotional and Behavioural Difficulties, Vol 3, No 1. (in press).

STATUS: Sponsored project

SOURCE OF GRANT: Shotton Hall Trust £46,000

DATE OF RESEARCH: 1996-1998

KEYWORDS: **educational quality; emotional and behavioural difficulties; school effectiveness; special educational needs; special schools**

0108

School of Education, Edgbaston, Birmingham B15 2TT
0121 414 3344

Bibby, R. Mr; *Supervisor*: Wade, B. Prof.

Changing English: paradigm lost or paradigm regained?

ABSTRACT: The purpose of the study was to examine curricular and pedagogical change in the subject of English in secondary schools between the school years 1993/94 and 1996/97. The questions posed at the start of the research concerned how changes in English teaching are brought about by external agents, i.e. the implementation of the National Curriculum, the implementation of new assessment procedures, the implementation of 4-yearly school inspections, and how changes are brought about by internal agents, i.e. school and/or department management, teachers' inservice training, teachers' own reading and thinking. It also sought to find whether those changes provided a better English curriculum for pupils. A longitudinal multiple case study was conducted over a 4-year period in 5 schools: 11-18 urban grant-maintained girls grammar school; 11-18 rural comprehensive school; 11-18 urban comprehensive school; 11-16 county town grant-maintained denominational school; 9-13 new town grant-maintained middle school. The conclusions of the research are that change has not brought about identifiable improvement in pupil achievement but has produced greater commonality in pupils' experience of English and that a quasi-paradigm shift has taken place in the English curriculum but not a true paradigm shift.

STATUS: Individual research

DATE OF RESEARCH: 1994-1998

KEYWORDS: **curriculum development; educational change; english; english studies curriculum; national curriculum; secondary education**

0109

School of Education, Edgbaston, Birmingham B15 2TT
0121 414 3344

Hull, J. Prof.

Money and education

ABSTRACT: The study of money cannot be confined to economics since in advanced contemporary money-cultures human relations, values and attitudes are profoundly affected by money. Because it functions both at the ideological level, influencing the structure and purposes of institution, and at the individual level, influencing self-esteem, identity and ambition, money undoubtedly generates its own spirituality. From the theological point of view, when money is taken to be an end in itself instead of the most general means to most ends, it may be regarded as an idol, a distorted form of the God-image and of God-consciousness. This enquiry studies the history of the growth of money as a spiritual force, culminating in the globalisation of today. The educational implications of the problem of the money-spirituality are explored, with special reference to the education of Christian adults and new understandings of the mission of the church. Special attention is paid to self-deception, both individual, ecclesial and societal as one of the principal coping strategies used by both children and adults to justify life as lived in a world of injustice and suffering caused by the gloablisatiion of money in its present forms. The place of values and of spirituality in the school curriculum is studied in the light of this cultural, psychological and theological understanding of money. Spiritual education is interpreted not as the cultivation of aesthetic sensibility, nor as the intensification of inner life, but as taking place when children and young people are inspired to live for others.

PUBLISHED MATERIAL: HULL, J.M. (1995). 'Spiritual education, religion and the money culture', Briefing: Education. (The official documentation service of the Catholic Bishops' Conference of England and Wales and of Scotland). Special Issue, June 1995. ; HULL, J.M. (1996). 'Christian education in a capitalist society: money and God'. In: FORD, D. & STAMPS, D.L. (Eds). Essentials of Christian community: for Daniel W. Hardy on his 65th birthday. Edinburgh: T & T Clark. ; HULL, J.M. (1997). 'Christian education: sufficient or necessary? Part 1', The Epworth Review, Vol 24, No 1, pp.40-48 January, pp.40-48 and Vol 24, April, pp.38-46. ; HULL, J.M. (1997). 'Christian education: sufficient or necessary? Part 2', The Epworth Review, Vol 24, No 2, pp.38-46.

STATUS: Sponsored project

SOURCE OF GRANT: St Peter's College Saltley Trust £18,270

DATE OF RESEARCH: 1994-continuing

KEYWORDS: economics; money; religious education; spiritual development; values

0110

School of Education, Edgbaston, Birmingham B15 2TT
0121 414 3344

Ng, S. Mr; *Supervisor*: Hull, J. Prof.

Death, dying and bereavement in British education: a study of attitudes and practices, with special reference to Chinese beliefs and customs

ABSTRACT: The British Education Reform Act 1988 set education within the context of the spiritual, moral, cultural, mental and physical development of pupils and of society. Spiritual education helps us search for meaning and purpose in life, for values by which we live and respond to challenging experiences, such as loss, grief and suffering. Education about death, dying and bereavement for children, especially in the context of a multi-faith religious education (including Chinese religions and beliefs) can contribute significantly to the spiritual and humanistic areas of the curriculum. Although the United States has some good models for teaching in this context, Britain lags behind. Having examined the need for education about death for children and for teachers, and the need to teach these topics in religious education, this study uses quantitative and qualitative methods (questionnaires and content analysis) to investigate the attitudes of teachers and pupils towards teaching the topics of death and dying. A random sample of Birmingham primary and secondary teachers (n=99) and pupils (Year 6 and Year 8, n=619) completed the questionnaires (including the closed and open-ended questions). All these questionnaires were examined by descriptive analysis and inferential analysis. Furthermore, in order to explore ways in which to include the topics of death, dying and bereavement in the religious curriculum, the researcher used a content analysis of 20 Agreed Syllabuses for Religious Education (from different local education authorities) from 1995 to 1996. This analysis will include some enquiry into the presence of teaching about Confucian, Taoist, and Buddhist concepts of death from Chinese Culture. In the light of this, the researcher makes recommendations to improve both curriculum and method.

STATUS: Individual research

DATE OF RESEARCH: 1994-1998

KEYWORDS: **bereavement; chinese culture; death; religious education**

0111

School of Education, Edgbaston, Birmingham B15 2TT
0121 414 3344

Hull, J. Prof.

Religious education and religionism

ABSTRACT: Religionism is the form taken by religion when individual or collective identity is fostered by negative images or beliefs about people from other religions. This enquiry studies the history, sociology, psychology and theology of religionism, asserting that description such as 'fundamentalism' and 'sectarianism' do not adequately describe the phenomenon. The appearance of religionism in recent British official educational policy is studied and the profile of beliefs typical of religionism is outlined. Religionism is compared and contrasted with communalism, tribalism, fundamentalism, evangelism and theological debate. A central question is whether, to what extent and under what conditions a religious doctrine or belief may lead to religionism. The Christian doctrine of the Holy Trinity is examined with this question in view. It is argued that religious education should combat religionism, and this is described as a proposal for an anti-religionist religious education, modelled upon anti-racist and anti-sexist education. This would involve the de-construction of major religious belief systems, in so far as these have developed so as to express or imply religionism. The various methods currently in use in religious education are examined in order to assess their potential contribution to this enterprise, and the educational and theological implications of an anti-religionist religious education are explored.

PUBLISHED MATERIAL: HULL, J.M. (1992). 'The transmission of religious prejudice', British Journal of Religious Education, Vol 14, No 2, pp.69-72. ; THOMPSON, P. (1993). 'Religionism: a response to John Hull', British Journal of Religious Education, Vol 16, No 1, pp.47-50. ; HULL, J.M. (1995). 'The Holy Trinity and Christian education in a pluralist world. London: National Society. ; HULL, J.M. (1996). 'A critique of Christian religionism in recent British education'. In: ASTLEY, J. & FRANCIS, L.J. (Eds). Christian theology and religious education. London: SPCK.

STATUS: Sponsored project

SOURCE OF GRANT: St Peter's College Saltley Trust £18,270

DATE OF RESEARCH: 1992-continuing

KEYWORDS: **religious differences; religious discrimination; religious education**

0112

School of Education, Edgbaston, Birmingham B15 2TT 0121 414 3344

Evans, L. Mrs; *Supervisor*: Wade, B. Prof.

Evaluation of initiatives for raising standards

ABSTRACT: This study is an illuminative evaluation of initiatives for raising standards of teaching and learning in one Midlands local education authority. It evaluates 3 major strands of the project - Reading Recovery, Parental Involvement and Learning Opportunities (homework clubs) and describes the intentions, contexts, processes and outcomes of the initiatives employed. The main body of research is based on 3 schools, 2 primary and 1 secondary with a further 30 providing data on the Reading Recovery programme. Both quantitative and qualitative data are used to support findings, involving an approximate total of 500 children, 40 teachers and 40 parents. Results show varying degrees of success in the different initiatives and how each impacts on whole-school improvement. The comparison between short term gains and longer term trends demonstrates the limitations of 'quick fix' projects and emphasises the effectiveness of initiatives which are adequately planned, supported and resourced over a reasonable period of time. The study concludes by addressing the cost effectiveness of initiatives when considered alongside various measures of success.

STATUS: Individual research

DATE OF RESEARCH: 1992-1998

KEYWORDS: **educational quality; intervention; local education authorities; parent participation; parent school relationship; primary education; reading; reading improvement; school effectiveness; school improvement; secondary education; standards**

0113

School of Education, Edgbaston, Birmingham B15 2TT
0121 414 3344

Bullock, A. Dr; Thomas, H. Prof.

An evaluation of Paul Hamlyn teacher fellowships with the University of the First Age

ABSTRACT: Funding is for an evaluation of the First Age Teacher Fellowships as funded by the Paul Hamlyn Foundation. The University of the First Age is a Birmingham Local Education Authority initiative. The total number of Fellowships over the 4 year period (1996-2000) is 64. The monitoring and evaluation procedures combine the work of the teacher fellows themselves in their study for postgraduate diploma and the University of Birmingham research team. The evaluation will explore: 1) the impact of the fellowships on their approach to teaching; 2) the impact on host schools as organisations; 3) the impact on learners using key stage 3 and 4 data and pre-test and post-test attitude surveys; 4) the impact on young people in the host schools who do not attend the University of the First Age; 5) the impact on teaching and learning styles across the City of Birmingham; 6) the impact on achievement levels city wide. The culmination of the evaluation process will be a major report on the impact of the University of the First Age teacher fellowships on school improvement and effectiveness in a major urban area.

STATUS: Sponsored project

SOURCE OF GRANT: Paul Hamlyn Foundation via the University of the First Age

DATE OF RESEARCH: 1996-continuing

KEYWORDS: action research; learning activities; local education authorities; pupil improvement; school effectiveness; school improvement; secondary education; teacher development; teacher fellowships; teaching methods

0114

School of Education, Edgbaston, Birmingham B15 2TT
0121 414 3344

Bedward, J. Ms; *Supervisor*: Williams, E. Dr

Games for the girls: the impact of recent policy on the provision of physical education and sporting opportunities for adolescent females

ABSTRACT: A study aiming to: 1) improve understanding of female pupils' attitudes to National Curriculum physical education activity areas; 2) assess the effect of female pupils' curriculum experience upon disposition to participate in activities outside school; 3) make recommendations for policy and practice. This is a qualitative study following up issues arising from earlier quantitative work. Three schools were used as research sites. The methods used include lesson observations and interviews with staff and pupils.

STATUS: Sponsored project

SOURCE OF GRANT: Nuffield Foundation £28,000

DATE OF RESEARCH: 1996-1998

KEYWORDS: attitudes; games; girls; national curriculum; physical education; pupil attitudes; sex differences; sports; womens education

0115

School of Education, Edgbaston, Birmingham B15 2TT
0121 414 3344

Daniels, H. Prof.; Miller, C. Dr ; Smith, C. Mr ; Sharples, M. Prof.

The development of a pilot Internet mediated teacher education programme for special educational needs coordinators in primary and secondary schools

ABSTRACT: The intended course participants of the Internet inservice teacher education (INSET) module are professionals with a wide variety of experiences and needs - the teaching of the course will have to reflect this. Thus the course should be flexible and should draw on the students' experiences, for example through case-based tutoring or action learning. There should also be provision for peer interaction, for exchange of case experience and for support. Technology can support this through structured tutor mediated computer conferencing to address specific problems and through a problem-oriented database where students can access case report and frequently asked questions. The course will draw on the content of current Birmingham University courses on special educational needs: Policy, Practice and Provision; Improving Classroom Achievement; and on newly produced material drawn from other special educational needs (SEN) modules informing special educational needs coordinators (SENCOs) about the range of difficulties in learning and disabilities which hinder educational progress. The course participants will also be made aware of the range of differences in development and learning style (whether or not they arise through developmental disabilities) and strategies for responding to individual educational needs that may prevent them from becoming 'special'.

STATUS: Sponsored project

SOURCE OF GRANT: British Telecom £10,000

DATE OF RESEARCH: 1998-1998

KEYWORDS: computer uses in education; information technology; inservice teacher education; internet; special educational needs; special educational needs coordinators; teleconferencing

0116

School of Education, Edgbaston, Birmingham B15 2TT
0121 414 3344

Cole, T. Mr; *Supervisor*: Daniels, H. Prof.; Visser, J. Mr

A study of the effects of local education authority arrangements in relation to pupils with behavioural problems

ABSTRACT: This project is concerned with two areas of the Nuffield Foundation's interest in the field of children with special needs: 1) Provision for the education of children with emotional and behavioural difficulties, including those excluded from mainstream schooling. 2) Critical studies of the implementation of the legislation and statutory arrangements for dealing with the education of children with special needs. The proposed research seeks to answer the following questions: 1) What patterns of educational provision are maintained by local education authorities (LEAs) for pupils with emotional and behavioural difficulties, including those excluded from mainstream schooling who are at risk of becoming marginalised? 2) Are there LEA arrangements which are associated with low mean rates of marginalisation across schools within LEAs and low variation in rates of marginalisation between schools within LEAs? 3) Is there an association between teacher and pupil perceptions of the meaning and function of schooling and the arrangements made by LEAs for pupils with problems?

STATUS: Sponsored project

SOURCE OF GRANT: Nuffield Foundation £27,000

DATE OF RESEARCH: 1998-continuing

KEYWORDS: disruptive pupils; emotional and behavioural difficulties; local education authorities; special educational needs; suspension

0117

School of Education, Edgbaston, Birmingham B15 2TT
0121 414 3344

Cole, T. Mr; *Supervisor*: Daniels, H. Prof.; Visser, J. Mr

Children with emotional and behavioural difficulties in mainstream schools

ABSTRACT: The research will focus on the means by which this effective practice may be achieved in mainstream schools. The distinction between pupil behaviour and discipline (DFE Circular 8/94) and children with emotional and behavioural difficulties (DFE Circular 9/94) will be a concern of this project. Mainstream schools that have been recognised by the Office for Standards in Education (OFSTED) as sites of good practice with respect to behaviour and discipline will be scrutinised for their approaches to pupils with emotional and behavioural difficulties (EBD). Case studies which embody good practice in both respects will be used to provide notes of guidance on the implementation and development of such practice in mainstream primary and secondary schools. The research aims to: 1) identify how effective practice in relation to assessment, provision and evaluation for pupils with emotional and behavioural difficulties in mainstream schools is achieved; and 2) establish a knowledge base upon which further work could be built. This knowledge base would be comprised of information relating selected social, behavioural and educational outcomes to aspects of mainstream school organisation, policy development and implementation strategy at sites of good practice. Further work could provide detailed ethnographies of development and change over time at selected sites. The overall research objectives are outlined below and budget limitations will constrain the extent to which these are achievable: 1) To define the characteristics of good local education authority (LEA) and mainstream school behavioural and special educational needs (SEN) policies. 2) To detail the specific assessment arrangements within mainstream schools and outside agencies (e.g. school psychological services, behaviour support services, social services and health services) that identify pupils with EBD. 3) To define the factors necessary for consistent implementation of assessment arrangements. 4) To examine the processes by which mainstream school behaviour policy, as portrayed in documentation, is realised in observable effective practice. 5) To identify the extent to which curricular and organisational factors promote positive behaviour and the high achievement of pupils. 6) To analyse the evaluative strategies used by mainstream schools and LEAs to ensure that policy is fully implemented. 7) To identify the means by which mainstream schools communicate and collaborate with interested/involved agencies (e.g. school psychological services, behaviour support services, social services and health services). 8) To identify the characteristics of an effective teacher of EBD children.

STATUS: Sponsored project

SOURCE OF GRANT: Department for Education and Employment £75,000

DATE OF RESEARCH: 1997-1998

KEYWORDS: **behaviour management; classroom management; discipline; disruptive pupils; emotional and behavioural difficulties; mainstreaming; special educational needs**

0118

School of Education, Edgbaston, Birmingham B15 2TT
0121 414 3344

Harris, J. Dr ; Cole, T. Mr ; *Supervisor*: Daniels, H. Prof.; Cumella, S. Dr; Visser, J. Mr

Educational support for children with mental health issues including the emotionally vulnerable

ABSTRACT: This research project has 3 objectives: Objective 1 - to review the research literature relating to the mental health issues experienced by emotionally vulnerable young people aged 0-19 years. As indicated in the specification the literature survey will include: 1) government guidance pertinent to the primary research aim; and 2) any previous surveys of this group carried out in the City of Birmingham. The survey will also include the following areas: 1) the mental health issues experienced by emotionally vulnerable young people; 2) examples of good practice in relation to the organisation of such services and the provision made; and 3) the means by which the nature and extent of mental health issues of the type described above might be identified. The review will focus on the evidence available which illustrates the effect that mental health problems have on the educational and social functioning of children and young people and ways in which provision can be made to overcome these difficulties. Objective 2 – under guidance from the coordinating/steering group, researchers will gather information using agreed survey techniques in order to identify any mental health difficulties which significantly impair the educational and/ or social functioning of emotionally vulnerable young people within a defined area of the city. Objective 3 – to seek to describe the range of educational provision made available by agencies working with emotionally vulnerable young people within the defined area and identify the shortfall of provision and current need.

STATUS: Sponsored project

SOURCE OF GRANT: Birmingham City Council Children's Joint Planning Group Funding Initiative ú 24,784

DATE OF RESEARCH: 1998-continuing

KEYWORDS: **emotional and behavioural difficulties; special educational needs; support services**

0119

School of Education, Edgbaston, Birmingham B15 2TT
0121 414 3344

Birmingham University, School of Dentistry, St Chad's, Queensway, Birmingham B4 6NN

Bullock, A. Dr; Frame, J. Prof.; Ribbins, P. Prof.; Butterfield, S. Dr; Belfield, C. Dr

Evaluation of short courses in dentistry

ABSTRACT: The aim of this study is to examine how the short course aspect of postgraduate dental education is currently monitored and evaluated at all levels within the West Midlands region. The focus of the study is Section 63 courses. The main outcome of the 5-part study is a set of guidelines on evaluation methods along with draft instruments. An audit of existing approaches to the evaluation of short courses at the regional

level and across all local centres in the West Midlands was conducted as Part 1. Interviews were held with the regional director and deputy director of postgraduate dental education and the 11 local clinical tutors in the West Midlands. Documents relating to course provision and cost data were also collected and examined. Part 2 examined existing approaches in practice in 3 local centres in the West Midlands. Questionnaires were administered to general dental practitioners attending Section 63 courses in the Autumn of 1996 in these centres. This provided a sample of 194 dentists. The course lecturers (9 in total) were also sent questionnaires. in Part 3, a revised evaluation framework was developed which was piloted in Part 4. The new procedure was trailed with all short courses running in October in the 3 centres (21 in total). It included immediate post-course questionnaires for participants, lecturers' self-evaluation forms, clinical tutors' evaluation forms and delayed impact-on-practice questionnaires. In Part 5, results and recommendations will be written into a final report and presentations made.

STATUS: Sponsored project

SOURCE OF GRANT: Department of Health £60,000

DATE OF RESEARCH: 1996-1997

KEYWORDS: **cost effectiveness; course evaluation; dentistry; dentists; professional continuing education**

0120

School of Education, Edgbaston, Birmingham B15 2TT
0121 414 3344

Birmingham University, School of Dentistry, St Chad's, Queensway, Birmingham B4 6NN

Bullock, A. Dr; Frame, J. Prof.; Butterfield, S. Dr; Belfield, C. Dr; Ribbins, P. Prof.

An evaluation of assessment methods during post-registration dental education

ABSTRACT: This study will evaluate how post-registration dental eduation is currently assessed. Formative and summative assessment methods for generic and specialist courses in the primary and secondary care settings will be evaluated. Ways in which assessment procedures might be modified to ensure consistently high standards across a range of educational experience, relevance and cost-effectiveness will be identified. The aims are to: 1) describe the overall strengths and weaknesses of existing assessment systems; 2) determine if existing systems are relevant, cost-effective and consistent; 3) suggest how systems for the assessment of postgraduate dental education could, if necessary, be modified to ensure that consistently high standards, which are relevant to patients' needs are universally achieved in a cost-effective manner. The aims will be met in a four-staged study. In the first, the scope and purpose of different modes of assessment in vocational, basic and specialist education will be described. Assessment types will then be mapped and evaluated. In Phase 2, a detailed study of the policy and practice of assessment in two centres will be undertaken. It will include an assessment of the nature and quality of the supervised practical experience. Phase 3 will provide a managerial perspective on assessment: how is cost-effectiveness, consistency and comparability established and managed? The final phase will provide an evaluation of assessment methods and recommendations for the implications of an improved assessment system.

STATUS: Sponsored project

SOURCE OF GRANT: Department of Health £65,010

DATE OF RESEARCH: 1998-continuing

KEYWORDS: **assessment; dentistry; dentists; professional continuing education**

0121

School of Education, Edgbaston, Birmingham B15 2TT
0121 414 3344

British Institute of Learning Disabilities, Wolverhampton Road, Kidderminster DY10 3PP   01902 850251

Cook, M. Mrs; *Supervisor*: Upton, G. Prof.; Harris, J. Dr

Developing school-based services for children with severe learning difficulties and challenging behaviour

ABSTRACT: The general aim of the project is to improve the quality of school-based services for children with severe learning difficulties who present various forms of challenging behaviour. More specifically it involves: a) collaboration with teachers and care staff in special schools for children with severe learning difficulties in the design and implementation of a range of strategies for the management and amelioration of challenging behaviour in schools; b) monitoring and evaluating different intervention strategies to identify those which can be most effectively employed in schools; and c)developing an in-service training programme which will assist teachers and other staff in working more effectively with children with challenging behaviour. The study is being carried out in two phases. In the first phase five schools are involved in the development of the intervention strategies which will be evaluated in phase two in a further five schools.

STATUS: Sponsored project

SOURCE OF GRANT: Mental Health Foundation £62,000

DATE OF RESEARCH: 1992-1993

KEYWORDS: **emotional and behavioural difficulties; learning disabilities; special education teachers; special educational needs; special schools**

0122

School of Education, Edgbaston, Birmingham B15 2TT
0121 414 3344

Cardiff University, School of Social Policy and Social Administration, PO Box 920, Cardiff CF1 3XP   01222 874000

Osler, A. Dr; Williamson, H. Dr; Haahr, J. Dr; Kazepov, Y. Dr; Blanc, M. Dr; Veldhuis, R. Dr

The contribution of European Commission community action programmes in the fields of education, training and youth to the development of citizenship with a European dimension

ABSTRACT: This research is being carried out in collaboration with colleagues in PLS Consult, Copenhagen; IARD Instituto di Recera, Milan; CUES -Universities de Nancy; and the Instituut Voor Publiek en Politiek, Amsterdam. Research examines the contribution of community action programmes in the fields of education, training and youth to the development of active citizenship with a European dimension. It draws on case studies of good practice across 18 European countries, including all of the Member States of the European Union. Since Europe is based on a shared political culture of democracy, education for active citizenship implies that new ways need to be found of enabling individuals and groups to play a fuller part as European citizens and develop a new European identity which can exist alongside existing local, national ethnic and religious identities. The project examines how this has been achieved in a range of transnational European Commission funded projects in general and vocational education, highlighting good practice.

PUBLISHED MATERIAL: OSLER, A. & STARKEY, H. 'Rights, identities and inclusion: European action programmes as political education', Oxford Review of Education. (in press).

STATUS: Sponsored project

SOURCE OF GRANT: European Commission DGXXII

DATE OF RESEARCH: 1997-1997

KEYWORDS: **citizenship; comparative education; europe; european citizenship; european dimension; european union; human rights**

0123

School of Education, Centre for Religious Education Development and Research, Edgbaston, Birmingham B15 2TT   0121 414 3344

Hull, J. Prof.; Reeve, J. Miss

Cathedrals through touch and hearing

ABSTRACT: The aim of the project is to explore the problems of presenting architecture to visually handicapped people. Cathedrals in England are being equipped with special facilites including wooden models, ground plans, tactile illustrations, cassette recordings and braille guides. The project was mainly confined to West Midlands cathedrals during 1988/89 but will work in more than 20 cathedrals nationwide during the following years. The work is sponsored by the Archbishop of York.

PUBLISHED MATERIAL: HULL, J.M. (1990). Touching the rock: an experience of blindness. London: SPCK (Society for the Promotion of

Christian Knowledge). ; HULL, J.M. (1990). 'On being a whole body seer: an epistemic condition for the education of the blind', British Journal of Visual Impairment, pp.62-63. ; HULL, J.M. (1990). 'The God of the blind', The New Beacon, Vol 74, No 877, pp.200-204. ; REEVE, J. (1991). 'Keeping in touch with cathedrals', British Journal of Visual Impairment, Autumn.

STATUS: Sponsored project

SOURCE OF GRANT: Industrial and charitable sources £162,179

DATE OF RESEARCH: 1986-1993

KEYWORDS: **architectural education; blindness; educational equipment; special educational needs; visual impairments**

0124

School of Education, Edgbaston, Birmingham B15 2TT
0121 414 3344

Glasgow University, Department of English, Glasgow G12 8QQ
0141 339 8855

Dhesi, K. Mrs; Stuart-Smith, J. Dr; *Supervisor*: Martin, D. Dr

Phonological processing and literacy skills in bilingual/biliterate children

ABSTRACT: The research was conducted in a national climate of concern about academic achievement of linguistic minority learners. Literacy, an important vehicle for learning, was the focus of the study. The aims of the research were to: 1) develop assessment procedures of phonological processing and literacy skills (reading, spelling and writing) in English and one other widely spoken minority language, Panjabi; 2) extend current theoretical frameworks of phonological processing; 3) contribute to the growing body of knowledge on giving pupils a 'voice', particularly linguistic minority pupils with special needs, by collecting a new body of information on specific bilingual/biliteracy needs from linguistic minority pupils with literacy difficulties; 4) evaluate the need for qualified bilingual personnel in the field of bilingual/literacy needs. Phonological processing and literacy skills were assessed in both languages of 65 children (35 boys, 30 girls), aged 6-7 years, fluent in Panjabi and English, from schools in West Birmingham and Smethwick, West Midlands, UK, and a small cohort (5) with alleged literacy difficulties. They were interviewed in both languages about their perceptions of being bilingual and biliterate. Issues around working in a bilingual skill-mix team were monitored throughout. Bilingual phonological processing is influenced by the phonological features of the language, development of literacy and to some extent by gender. Children's feelings about being bilingual and biliterate are influenced by language of interview and gender. A minority of children were dissatisfied with their identity. Children with literacy difficulties showed no significant differences. Working in a skill-mix team due to lack of recruitment of a bilingual researcher, has implications for bilingual research.

PUBLISHED MATERIAL: STUART-SMITH, J. & MARTIN, D. (1997). 'Investigating literacy and pre-literacy skills in Panjabi/English schoolchildren', Educational Review, Vol 49, No 2, pp.181-197.; MARTIN, D., STUART-SMITH, J. & DHESI, K.K. 'Insiders and outsiders: translating in a bilingual research project'. In: FRANCIS, G. & HUNSTON, S. (Eds). Language at work. Clevedon: BAAL/Multilingual Matters. (in press). ; MARTIN, D. & STUART-SMITH, J. 'Exploring bilingual children's perceptions of being bilingual and biliterate: implications for educational provision', British Journal of Sociology of Education, Special Issue. (in press). ; MARTIN, D. & STUART-SMITH, J. 'Investigating perceptions of literacy in bilingual children'. In: MARTIN-JONES, M. & JONES, K. (Eds). Multilingual literacies: comparative perspectives on research and practice. London: John Benjamins. (in press).

STATUS: Sponsored project

SOURCE OF GRANT: Economic and Social Research Council £30,000

DATE OF RESEARCH: 1996-1997

KEYWORDS: **bilingual pupils; bilingualism; ethnic groups; language skills; literacy; phonology; primary education; primary school pupils; pupil attitudes; reading skills; young children**

0125

School of Education, Edgbaston, Birmingham B15 2TT
0121 414 3344

Liverpool Local Non-stipendary Ministry, Gesterfield Farmhouse, Halsall Road, Halsall L39 8RN   01704 841202

Leslie, D. Rev.; *Supervisor*: Hull, J. Prof.

Education for ministerial transformation: a study of training for local non-stipendary ministry in the Church of England

ABSTRACT: Local non-stipendary ministry (LNSM) participants need to learn how to understand, interpret and communicate their faith contextually. This LNSM course is designed to enable them to reflect critically as individuals and as a group on what they experience on their learning journey. The aim is to analyse the extent to which the Liverpool course enables participants to manage the transition from a private and pietistic understanding of religious faith to one which is public and emancipatory. Evidence will be sought to show the extent to which transformative learning takes place for each individual participant and collectively as a group. Evidence will be sought to show which elements of the course trigger transformative learning. Individual and group research will be carried out using descriptors drawn from the 8 learning outcomes set for the course. Those recognised by the participants to be the most significant triggers for transformative learning will be analysed using the 'salmon line' method to measure the extent of transformative learning for each participant and the group. The exercise will be repeated to show which elements of the course best facilitated the process of transformation. Sample -2 cohorts: 10 persons and 9 persons.

STATUS: Individual research

DATE OF RESEARCH: 1994-continuing

KEYWORDS: **clergy; theological education**

0126

School of Education, Edgbaston, Birmingham B15 2TT
0121 414 3344
London University, Institute of Education, 20 Bedford Way, London WC1H 0AL

Fielding, S. Mr; Hey, V. Dr; Creese, A. Dr; *Supervisor*: Daniels, H. Prof.; Leonard, D. Dr

Gender and learning: a study of underachievement in junior schools

ABSTRACT: The research aims to study the giving and taking of support for learning by pupils from their peers and teachers. It will focus upon gender, race and class in order to investigate the relation between school culture, patterns of interpersonal relations, and learning and achievement. There has been widespread concern about boys' level of achievement especially the reading levels of African-Caribbean and white working class boys in junior schools. The structuring of learning in the schools has been seen as a principal reason for boys' lower literacy levels. However, there is little to support this empirically. The project will investigate the extent to which learning is a gendered activity and also which schools, and which practices within schools, are capable of enabling the majority of boys to be successful. The preliminary hypothesis is that boys experience a contradiction between cultural messages and practices associated with forms of masculinity and those teaching practices considered optimal learning activities. Involved autonomy, for example, may not easily sit within a school centred around group and team work. In order to shed light on these interactive practices, the team will re-engage with girls' experiences of learning to cast more light on why boys appear to be adopting less effective strategies. To guide this investigation, the researchers will be drawing on the ideas of Vygotsky and feminist and anti-racist work on classroom interaction to learning.

STATUS: Sponsored project

SOURCE OF GRANT: Economic and Social Research Council £208,755

DATE OF RESEARCH: 1997-continuing

KEYWORDS: **academic achievement; achievement; boys; educational environment; ethnic groups; junior schools; learning; peer influence; primary education; sex differences; social class; underachievement**

0127

School of Education, Research Centre for the Education of the Visually Handicapped, Edgbaston, Birmingham B15 2TT   0121 414 3344

Hull, T. Mr; *Supervisor*: Humphreys, G. Prof.; Riddoch, M. Dr

The nature and development of spatial processing in blind children and

young adults: an approach based on the use of tactile maps

ABSTRACT: This project has examined the ability of blind children and young adults to perceive and process spatial information derived from tactile maps and graphics. It consists of seven experimental studies, covering the basic skills necessary for map reading, an examination of subjects' mental models of the layout of a map, and tests of both spatial and verbal short term memory (STM). The concept of tactile-spatial STM, for which a new test is developed, is explored in terms of its development with age, the effects of mental rotation and possible representational systems which might underlie it. A successful attempt is made to improve STM by the use of mnemonics. The results of this project have implications both for theory and for the practice of designing tactile maps.

PUBLISHED MATERIAL: HULL, T. (1992). 'Children's understanding of tactile maps'. Proceedings of the Ninth Quinquennial Conference of the International Council for the Education of the Visually Handicapped. Bangkok, Thailand, 1992. ; HULL, T. & MASON, H.L. 'The development of short term memory in blind children', Journal of Visual Impairment and Blindness. (in press).

STATUS: Individual research

DATE OF RESEARCH: 1990-1993

KEYWORDS: **blindness; maps; memory; raised line drawings; spatial ability; tactile adaptation; visual impairments**

0128

School of Education, Research Centre for the Education of the Visually Handicapped, Edgbaston, Birmingham B15 2TT   0121 414 3344

Tobin, M. Prof; Hill, E. Mrs; Greaney, J. Dr

Standardisation of a braille version of the Neale analysis of reading ability test

ABSTRACT: Given the dearth of objective measures of measuring reading attainment among school-age readers of braille, the aim has been to develop an assessment tool that will allow teachers to measure, simultaneously, braille reading speed, accuracy, and comprehension skills, and to use the resulting information for devising appropriate remedial programmes. Over 300 learners in the age-range 6-18 years were tested, and it is estimated that this represents over 40% of the relevant population. One of the most significant findings relates to the massive disparity in speed of reading by touch-readers as compared with their fully-sighted peers. A teachers' handbook is in the course of preparation.

PUBLISHED MATERIAL: GREANEY, J., HILL, E., MASON, H. & ARTER, C. (1994). 'The development of a new test of children's braille-reading ability', British Journal of Visual Impairment, Vol 12, No 2, pp.54-56. ; TOBIN, M.J., WHITTAKER, J.R., GREANEY, J. & HILL, E.W. (1997). 'The issue of braille capitalisation in the UK: the BAUK survey', British Journal of Visual Impairment, Vol 15, No 1, pp.5-9. ; GREANEY, J. (1997). 'The development of a new standardized test of children's braille reading abilities in Britain', Journal of Visual Impairment and Blindness, Vol 90, No 3, pp.265-266.

STATUS: Sponsored project

SOURCE OF GRANT: Royal National Institute for the Blind

DATE OF RESEARCH: 1994-1997

KEYWORDS: **assessment; blindness; braille; reading achievement; reading tests; special educational needs; standardised tests; tests; visual impairments**

0129

School of Education, Research Centre for the Education of the Visually Handicapped, Edgbaston, Birmingham B15 2TT   0121 414 3344

Minett, S. Dr; *Supervisor*: Tobin, M. Prof.

An approach to science for pupils with a visual impairment

ABSTRACT: This thesis reviews the literature on the teaching of science to visually impaired pupils at secondary school level and then describes a particular approach to teaching physics in the 6th form of a special school. The approach is based on a structured system of technical skills and the necessary psycho-motor skills which give access to the apparatus and procedures used in experimental, laboratory work. The approach: provides opportunities for mastery of the technical skills; supports the theoretical parts of the A-level course by providing experiences which give a feeling for basic phenomena; develops skills that are transferable to other subject areas of higher education; and motivates, stimulates interest, and promotes self-esteem. The approach is evaluated in terms of these factors, using data from observational studies made as practical work is being carried out, and from interviews with past and present pupils.

PUBLISHED MATERIAL: MINETT, S. (1997). 'Science', In: MASON, H., MCCALL, S., ARTER, C., MCLINDEN, M. & STONE, J. (Eds), Visual impairment: access to education for children and young people. London: David Fulton.

STATUS: Individual research

DATE OF RESEARCH: 1994-1997

KEYWORDS: **blindness; mainstreaming; physics; science education; secondary education; special educational needs; special schools; visual impairments**

0130

School of Education, Research Centre for the Education of the Visually Handicapped, Edgbaston, Birmingham B15 2TT   0121 414 3344

Stone, J. Mrs; *Supervisor*: Tobin, M. Prof.

The self-concept and realisation of their blindness of young blind children

ABSTRACT: It is hypothesized that the course of the normal development of the concept of 'self' among fully-sighted children is likely to be similar in most respects among blind children, but with some divergencies in relation to actual time-span and to the intensity of external factors that impinge upon development. The phenomenon is also affected by the blind child's growing awareness of his/her own blindness and of how this may make him/her different from other children. This process is being explored by means of a critical review of current theories, by face-to-face interviews with blind children in special and mainstream schools, by observational methodologies, by questionnaires, and by intensive case histories.

PUBLISHED MATERIAL: STONE, J. (1997). 'The pre-school child'. In: MASON, H., MCCALL, S., ARTER, C., MCLINDEN, M. & STONE, J. (Eds). Visual impairment: access to education for children and young people. London: David Fulton.

STATUS: Individual research

DATE OF RESEARCH: 1994-continuing

KEYWORDS: **blindness; self concept; special educational needs; visual impairments; young children**

0131

School of Education, Research Centre for the Education of the Visually Handicapped, Edgbaston, Birmingham B15 2TT   0121 414 3344

Simkiss, P. Mrs

Accessible information systems for visually impaired adults seeking employment

ABSTRACT: This project is concerned with the development of accessible information systems for visually impaired students in higher and further education who are seeking employment. The system(s) are computer-based and offer users the opportunity to explore options for themselves, and there is a World Wide Web site. This was preceded by a review of existing information and guidance systems, and an investigation of primary user requirements, involving over 200 blind and partially sighted people. The prototype system has now been pilot-tested and is now being offered with speech and magnification access options. A bulletin describing the service (now known as GROW - Gateway to Reaching Opportunities for Work) has been currently sent out to over 1000 libraries and other agencies.

PUBLISHED MATERIAL: SIMKISS, P.H. (1996). 'Surf to opportunity with RNIB', Individual Commitment News, November 1996. ; SIMKISS, P.H. (1997). 'The redeployment of blind and partially sighted staff in the banking industry', Work: A Journal of Prevention, Assessment and Rehabilitation, Vol 8, pp.197-200.

STATUS: Sponsored project

SOURCE OF GRANT: Royal National Institute for the Blind

DATE OF RESEARCH: 1997-continuing

KEYWORDS: **blindness; computer uses in education; employment opportunities; further education; higher education; information systems; information technology; internet; partial vision; special**

educational needs; visual impairments

0132

School of Education, Research Centre for the Education of the Visually Handicapped, Edgbaston, Birmingham B15 2TT 0121 414 3344

Tobin, M. Prof.

Formative evaluation of the Forest House Assessment Centre

ABSTRACT: This is an ongoing formative evaluation of the Forest House Assessment Centre, which is a unit where multi-handicapped, visually impaired children can go, with their parents, for an extended residential assessment. Interviews are being conducted with parents to ascertain their opinions about the service and to obtain their recommendations for improving it. Staff members are also being interviewed jointly and separately to determine the nature of their input and to obtain their ideas and recommendations for how the assessment process can be made more effective. Information from the interviews are then being fed back to the Centre's administrators and the staff as a whole. @#Published Material:#@ TOBIN, M.J., HILL, E.W., WOOD, D., BARANYOVITS, P., BOX, J., FINCH, V. & KNIGHT, C. (1994). 'Assessing multi-handicapped visually impaired children: an interim evaluation of an assessment centre, Part 1', New Beacon, Vol 924, pp.4-9. ; TOBIN, M.J., HILL, E.W., WOOD, D., BARANYOVITS, P., BOX, J., FINCH, V. & KNIGHT, C. (1994). 'Assessing multi-handicapped visually impaired children: an interim evaluation of an assessment centre, Part 2', New Beacon, Vol 925, pp.8-12.

STATUS: Sponsored project

SOURCE OF GRANT: Royal National Institute for the Blind ; Birmingham University

DATE OF RESEARCH: 1994-continuing

KEYWORDS: **assessment; blindness; evaluation; multiple disabilities; observation and assessment centres; special educational needs; visual impairments**

0133

School of Education, Research Centre for the Education of the Visually Handicapped, Edgbaston, Birmingham B15 2TT   0121 414 3344

McLinden, M. Mr; *Supervisor*: Tobin, M. Prof.

Tactile symbolic communication systems: strategies of tactual information processing by multiply-disabled visual impairment learners

ABSTRACT: Through a series of case studies, involving the use of formal observation techniques (time and event sampling) and small-scale experimental methods, the issue is addressed of how learners in the age range 0-19 years, who are blind and functioning at an early stage of development, use their hands and mouths to explore objects. One of the major problems is how to design a structured observation framework for categorising, coding, and analysing the haptic and oral manipulation/exploration activities and strategies. It is hypothesised that these severely multi-handicapped learners may be using inefficient haptic manipulation and other investigative strategies which then yield imprecise information about the world. In turn it is argued that objective knowledge and concept formation are delayed. The observational and experimental methodologies will, it is hoped, generate information that can be used for structuring haptic intervention programmes for this group of learners.

STATUS: Individual research

DATE OF RESEARCH: 1995-1998

KEYWORDS: **blindness; exploratory behaviour; multiple disabilities; special educational needs; tactual perception; visual impairments**

0134

School of Education, Research Centre for the Education of the Visually Handicapped, Edgbaston, Birmingham B15 2TT   0121 414 3344

Lorimer, P. Dr; *Supervisor*: Tobin, M. Prof.

A critical evaluation of the historical development of the tactile modes of reading and an analysis and evaluation of researches carried out in endeavours to make the braille code easier to read and to write

ABSTRACT: Part 1 is an evaluative history of the various embossed codes evolved so that blind people could become literate, from 1786 when the first embossed book was produced. The early codes used in France, Britain, and America are described, reasons given for the need to review the code from time to time and the ongoing need for cooperation between English speaking peoples to maintain uniformity in the use of braille. Evaluation has taken account not only of the conditions of the times during which the codes were used, but also of the findings of research carried out during the present century. Part 2 includes evaluations of some of the major works included in the mass of research that has been carried out in braille reading. An introduction to the psychophysical aspects of the tactile system is followed by an account of the effect of elements of the braille code on accuracy, comprehension and rate of reading and attempts to increase the slow rate of braille reading. The final chapter gives information concerning ongoing research, and reasons are given for the continuing value of the use of braille which is now being helped and challenged by technological invention.

STATUS: Individual research

DATE OF RESEARCH: 1993-1997

KEYWORDS: blindness; braille; literacy; raised line drawings; sensory aids; tactile adaptation; tactual perception; visual impairments

0135

School of Education, Research Centre for the Education of the Visually Handicapped, Edgbaston, Birmingham B15 2TT   0121 414 3344

McCall, S. Mr; *Supervisor*: Tobin, M. Prof.

Moon as a route to literacy

ABSTRACT: This is an analytical and evaluative investigation into the development of language and literacy in blind children who have additional learning difficulties. The history of the various tactile codes that have been designed over the past century is outlined, and the relevance of these systems to the abilities and needs of multi-handicapped visually impaired learners is discussed with comparisons being made with the problems encountered in achieving literacy by sighted children who also have learning difficulties. The methodology of the research includes surveys of the beliefs and practices of teachers, of observations of new interventional procedures being used (especially in relation to non-braille alternatives such as Moon script), and measurements of the cognitive and tactual perception abilities/skills of learners and the demands made upon them by the Moon script. Given the small numbers of the target group, combined nevertheless with great heterogeneity, then one of the principal methods of enquiry and report will be indepth case studies.

PUBLISHED MATERIAL: MCCALL, S. (1994). 'Communication - options and issues'. In: ETHERIDGE, D. & MASON, H.L. (Eds). Visually impaired: curricular access and entitlement in further education. London: David Fulton. ; MCCALL, S., MCLINDEN, M. & STONE, J. (1996). Moon Cats teaching guide: Guide to teaching Moon to pupils with a visual impairment. London: Royal National Institute for the Blind. ; MCCALL, S. (1997). 'The development of literacy through touch'. In: MASON, H., MCCALL, S., ARTER, C., MCLINDEN, M. & STONE, J. Visual impairment: access to education for children and young people. London: David Fulton.

STATUS: Individual research

DATE OF RESEARCH: 1992-continuing

KEYWORDS: blindness; braille; learning disabilities; literacy education; moon; multiple disabilities; raised line drawings; sensory aids; special educational needs; tactile adaptation; visual impairments

0136

School of Education, Research Centre for the Education of the Visually Handicapped, Edgbaston, Birmingham B15 2TT   0121 414 3344

Franks, J. Mrs; *Supervisor*: Tobin, M. Prof.

The future of rehabilitation training in the UK

ABSTRACT: The purpose of this research is to discover what are the full support and special training needs of visually impaired people. This is being affected by means of questionnaires and face-to-face interviews with rehabilitation workers and their employers. Some of the issues being addressed are to do with the relative emphasis on literacy and communication, mobility, self-help, and other traditional 'skills' of the rehabilitation professionals, as against counselling, improving residual vision, and what are called 'holistic' approaches. The intention is an outcome that will help to shape the strategies for training rehabilitation

staff. Some 330 subjects have participated in the questionnaire phase of the enquiry, and it is believed that so large a sample will give credence to the inferences drawn from the data and to the recommendations that will be fed back to respondents, training agencies and employers.

PUBLISHED MATERIAL: FRANKS, J. 'To braille or not to braille', British Journal of Visual Impairment. (in press).

STATUS: Individual research

DATE OF RESEARCH: 1995-1998

KEYWORDS: blindness; life skills; literacy; rehabilitation; special educational needs; training; visual impairments

0137

School of Education, Research Centre for the Education of the Visually Handicapped, Edgbaston, Birmingham B15 2TT   0121 414 3344

Arter, C. Mrs; *Supervisor*: Tobin, M. Prof.

The reading difficulties of braillists of average and above-average intelligence

ABSTRACT: This investigation focuses upon a group of braille readers who are thought to be of at least average intelligence and who are performing well in many areas of the curriculum, but who also seem to be experiencing considerable difficulties with the reading of braille. The enquiry is seeking to determine (by means of a questionnaire to teachers) whether there is indeed such a group of children, and then to measure the nature and extent of difficulties by means of reading, intelligence, and mathematics tests. Much of the data will come, therefore, from this formal testing of abilities and skills, but also from examination of the school records of the children's educational progress. Comparisons between achievements/scores on these tests are to be made to identify any common patternings in skills and in the types of errors being made. The principal method of analysing and reporting will be through individual, indepth case histories of some 20 subjects. Among the expected outcomes are descriptions and evaluations of teaching methods used to overcome difficulties, and the notion of braille dyslexia will be examined as a possible explanation of the observed difficulties.

PUBLISHED MATERIAL: ARTER, C. & MASON, H.L. (1994). 'Spelling for the visually impaired child', British Journal of Visual Impairment, Vol 12, No 2, pp.8-21. ; ARTER, C. (1997). 'Listening skills'. In: MASON, H., MCCALL, S., ARTER, C., MCLINDEN, M. & STONE, J. Visual impairment: access to education for children and young people. London: David Fulton.

STATUS:Individual research

DATE OF RESEARCH:#@ 1994-continuing

KEYWORDS: blindness; braille; raised line drawings; reading difficulties; special educational needs; visual impairments

0138

School of Education, Research Centre for the Education of the Visually Handicapped, Edgbaston, Birmingham B15 2TT   0121 414 3344

London University, Imperial College of Science, Technology and Medicine, Academic Unit, Western Eye Hospital, Marylebone Road, London NW1 5YE   0171 886 6666

Oxford University, National Perinatal Epidmology Unit, Radcliffe Infirmary, Oxford OX2 6HE   01865 224875

Nottingham University, Academic Division of Child Health, School of Human Development, University Hospital, Nottingham NG7 2UH

Tobin, M. Prof.; Fielder, A. Prof.; Johnson, A. Dr; Stephenson, T. Prof.

Retinopathy of prematurity

ABSTRACT: This collaborative project, involving 4 universities, is a follow-up investigation of a group of over 400 children now entering upon the secondary school phase of their education. All were diagnosed at birth as affected by some degree of retinopathy of prematurity. As many as possible of the cohort are being contacted with a view to being assessed in terms of their educational progress and of their visual status. This is a unique investigation in that considerable information is available about their perinatal well-being, and this will be correlated with information about their progress in school, about behaviour, and about other educational and psychological variables.

STATUS: Sponsored project

SOURCE OF GRANT: National Health Service ; Action Research, jointly £200,000

DATE OF RESEARCH: 1996-continuing

KEYWORDS: **child development; followup studies; premature infants; secondary education; special educational needs; visual impairments**

0139

School of Education, Research Centre for the Education of the Visually Handicapped, Edgbaston, Birmingham B15 2TT   0121 414 3344

Tobin, M. Prof.; Hill, E. Mrs

Cognitive development and school achievement in visually impaired children

ABSTRACT: This is an investigation into the cognitive development and school achievement of blind and partially sighted learners. One part of the enquiry, which is an ongoing project, comprised a group of 120 children who were aged 5 in the school year 1973 and who were tested then on at least an annual basis as they proceeded through the years of their formal school education. This core group has been supplemented by groups of other children of various ages who have been tested on a one-off basis, with a view to increasing/checking the validity and reliability of the data. In addition to the use of conventional (and adapted) cognitive and perceptual tests, tests of braille and print reading are administered. The overall purpose is to determine whether and if so how blindness and severe visual disability may influence educational development.

PUBLISHED MATERIAL: TOBIN, M.J., BOZIC, N., DOUGLAS, G. & GREANEY, J. (1996). 'How non-visual modalities can help the young visually impaired child to succeed in visual and other tasks', British Journal of Visual Impairment, Vol 14, No 1, pp.11-17. ; TOBIN, M.J. (1996). 'Optimising the use of sensory information'. In: BOZIC, N. & MURDOCH, H. (Eds). Learning through interaction: technology and children with multiple disabilities. London: David Fulton. ; TOBIN, M.J. (1997). 'Psychological assessment'. In: MASON, H., ARTER, C., MCCALL, S., MCLINDEN, M. & STONE, J. (Eds). Visual impairment: access to education for children and young people. London: David Fulton. ; TOBIN, M.J., BOZIC, N., DOUGLAS, G., GREANEY, J. & ROSS, S. (1997). 'Visually impaired children: development and implications for education', European Journal of Psychology of Education, Vol XII, No 4, pp.431-447.

STATUS: Sponsored project

SOURCE OF GRANT: Royal National Institute for the Blind

DATE OF RESEARCH: 1996-continuing

KEYWORDS: **academic achievement; achievement; blindness; cognitive development; longitudinal studies; special educational needs; visual impairments**

0140

School of Education, Research Centre for the Education of the Visually Handicapped, Edgbaston, Birmingham B15 2TT   0121 414 3344

Tobin, M. Prof.; Douglas, G. Dr

Centre software development

ABSTRACT: This ongoing project is concerned with the design and evaluation of microcomputer software for use by visually impaired children, older students, and adults. The aims are to teach basic literacy skills to very young blind and partially sighted children, to increase accessibility to the National Curriculum, and to facilitate job employment of blind and visually impaired adults in the 'computer age'. The software is designed and developed in collaboration with teachers specifically qualified and experienced in the education of learners who have severe visual disabilities.

PUBLISHED MATERIAL:#@ DOUGLAS, G. & MCLINDEN, M. (1996). 'The Apple Macintosh and users with a visual impairment', Open Learning Systems News, Vol 58, pp.10-11. ; MURNION, S. (1996). 'Internet: Update on World Wide Web access', Visability, Vol 17, p.28. ; DOUGLAS, G. (1996). 'The use of touch typing software', Visability, Vol 17, pp.29-31. ; BOZIC, N. (1997). 'Educational technology'. In: MASON, H., ARTER, C., MCCALL, S., MCLINDEN, M. & STONE, J. (Eds). Visual impairment: access to education for children and young people. London: David Fulton.

STATUS: Sponsored project

SOURCE OF GRANT: Blatchington Court Trust £130,000

DATE OF RESEARCH: 1994-continuing

KEYWORDS: **blindness; computer software; computer uses in education; educational software; information technology; special educational needs; visual impairments**

0141

School of Education, Research Centre for the Education of the Visually Handicapped, Edgbaston, Birmingham B15 2TT   0121 414 3344

Yakubu, A. Dr; *Supervisor*: Tobin, M. Prof.

An investigation of the effectiveness of mathematics teaching to students with visual impairment in Nigeria: attitudes and resources

ABSTRACT: Mathematics teaching and learning is considered to be a problem area in relation to those who are blind. The difficulties are, as shown in this thesis, not related solely to conceptual matters or to the means of communication (materials, equipment, conversion of visual illustrations to tactile formats), but also to the attitudes of teachers and the population at large towards blindness. The 'means' used in Nigeria are described and are compared to those in use in countries that are better resourced. Particular areas of conceptual difficulty, viz: fractions, are explored, mainly through formal testing of blind students in a selected region of Nigeria. Attitudes (of the students themselves, of their sighted peers, and of their teachers (in special and mainstream settings) are measured by means of questionnaires, face-to-face interviewing, and observations in classrooms and elsewhere. The main conclusions and recommendations are to do with the need for teacher training, for the use of cheaply available indigenous materials, and for a programme to increase understanding of blind people's abilities and needs.

STATUS: Individual research

DATE OF RESEARCH: 1994-1997

KEYWORDS: **blindness; mathematics education; nigeria; visual impairments**

0142

School of Education, Research Centre for the Education of the Visually Handicapped, Edgbaston, Birmingham B15 2TT   0121 414 3344

Tobin, M. Prof.

Assessing preschool blind and partially sighted children

ABSTRACT: The educational importance of early identification of children with potentially handicapping disabilities is now taken for granted. One of the difficulties with the very young visually impaired child is that there are few well-standardised procedures designed specifically for assessing the development of such children. In the Research Centre for the Education of the Visually Handicapped, a preschool playgroup has been set up. In addition to the direct support it provides for the families, it offers the Centre's researchers the opportunity to observe behaviour in open-play settings as the children interact with their peers and with adult carers and with visitors, and as they learn to use materials and equipment (including computers). These informal assessments are supplemented by information from various checklists and developmental scales, thus enabling the researchers to develop their own expertise which can then be passed on to students at Birmingham University on courses for would-be teachers of visually impaired children.

PUBLISHED MATERIAL: TOBIN, M.J. (1994). Assessing visually handicapped people: an introduction to test procedures. London: David Fulton. ; TOBIN, M.J. (1997). 'Psychological assessment'. In: MASON, H., ARTER, C., MCCALL, S., MCLINDEN, M. & STONE, J. (Eds). Visual impairment: access to education for children and young people. London: David Fulton. ; ROSS, S. & TOBIN, M. (1997). 'Object permanence, reaching and locomotion in infants who are blind', Journal of Visual Impairment and Blindness, Vol 91, No 1, pp.25-32.

STATUS: Sponsored project

SOURCE OF GRANT: Royal National Institute for the Blind; Birmingham University; Birmingham Royal Institution for the Blind; Birmingham City Education Department

DATE OF RESEARCH: 1990-continuing

KEYWORDS: **assessment; blindness; partial vision; preschool children; special educational needs; visual impairments; young children**

0143

School of Education, Research Centre for the Education of the Visually Handicapped, Edgbaston, Birmingham B15 2TT   0121 414 3344

Tobin, M. Prof.; Hill, E. Mrs

Silent and oral reading speeds in cognitive and adventitiously blinded students and adults

ABSTRACT: The investigation into oral and silent reading speeds has continued throughout 1998, and 100 subjects have so far participated in the project. As would be expected, silent reading is proving to be quicker than oral reading, and the congenitally blind people are more skilled than those with a later onset of blindness. Gender differences are, if present, not yet discernible, or at least statistically significantly different. The work is continuing, with support from the Royal National Institute for the Blind and the charity Blindness: Research for Learning, Work and Leisure.

STATUS: Sponsored project

SOURCE OF GRANT: Royal National Institute for the Blind ; Blindness: Research for Learning, Work and Leisure

DATE OF RESEARCH: 1997-continuing

KEYWORDS: blindness; braille; reading rate; visual impairments

0144

School of Education, Edgbaston, Birmingham B15 2TT
0121 414 3344
Sandwell Metropolitan Borough Council, Child Guidance Centre, 12 Grange Road, West Bromwich, West Midlands B70 8PD
0121 553 7411

Bovair, K. Mr ; Smith, C. Mr; Watts, P. Mr; *Supervisor*: Upton, G. Prof.

Disruptive behaviour in schools: post Elton Project Sandwell Initiative

ABSTRACT: The aim of this project is to collect quantitative and qualitative data, in order to further illuminate the nature, causes and consequences of disruptive behaviour in schools. An assessment will be made of the impact of the Elton Report (Discipline in schools: the report of the Committee of Enquiry chaired by Lord Elton. Department of Education and Science, 1989) on responses to disruptive behaviour in schools. A detailed examination of developments in one local education authority over a period of one school year will be carried out. The study will combine survey and case study analyses. The consequences of disruption will be examined in terms of school/local education authority responses and subsequent pupil placements.

STATUS: Sponsored project

SOURCE OF GRANT: Birmingham University ú 2,000

DATE OF RESEARCH: 1991-1993

KEYWORDS: antisocial behaviour; discipline; disruptive pupils; pupil behaviour; pupil placement

0145

School of Education, Edgbaston, Birmingham B15 2TT
0121 414 3344
The Birmingham Initiative, Christian Education Office, Ladywood Methodist Church, St Vincent Street West, Ladywood, Birmingham B16 8RW   0121 454 8154

Reddie, A. Mr; *Supervisor*: Hull, J. Prof.

Christian education and black cultures in Britain: equipping black children in the Church, as a worked example

ABSTRACT: The background to this research lies in the question of the Christian education of black children in Britain. Anecdotal evidence has always suggested that present methods of Christian education, and the curriculum materials used in churches in Britain, are inadequate for the affective and cognitive development of African Caribbean (black) children and young people. This action research project, through the development of an 'African-centred' Christian education curriculum, written by the researcher (and informed by the literature in this area) is attempting to see how this cultural specific, enculturation approach, can improve the practice of Christian education in a specific number of churches in Birmingham. 26 churches form a central component in the project, coming from Methodist, Anglican, Baptist and United Reformed traditions. The churches are predominantly comprised of black people: black children and young people form the greater preponderance of those attending traditional 'Sunday schools' on a Sunday morning. This action-reflection intervention, through semi-structured interviews and participant observations, is seeking to investigate and assess the impact of this new form of pedagogy upon the practice of Christian education and upon the self-concept and affirmatory sense of selfhood amongst black children and young people. Approximately 200 children and young people are involved in the research project, although, for indepth qualitative accounts, a smaller sample of around 40 children are being investigated. The results to date have indicated very clearly how this culturally specific 'Afrocentric' pedagogy is having beneficial effects upon the children and young people. The project aims to tentatively point towards a new epistemology for the Christian education of (black) African Caribbean children and young people in Britain. A two-volume book will be published in June 1998. This is a Christian education curriculum, that has been piloted at the heart of the research project. The material is informed by the discipline of black theology, the educational work of Paulo Frieire and historical development of Black Christian education, principally in the United States.

PUBLISHED MATERIAL: REDDIE, A.G. Growing into hope. Peterborough: Methodist Publishing House. (in press).

STATUS: Individual research

DATE OF RESEARCH: 1995-continuing

KEYWORDS: black culture; black youth; church and education; ethnic groups; religious education; sunday schools

0146

School of Education, Edgbaston, Birmingham B15 2TT
0121 414 3344
Warwick University, Institute of Education, Coventry CV4 7AL
01203 523523

Ranson, S. Prof.; Martin, J. Ms; Vincent, C. Dr

Little polities: schooling, governance and parental participation

ABSTRACT: This research seeks to investigate the ways in which parents formulate and express their views and opinions concerning the school and the extent and manner to which the school recognises and incorporates those views. It suggests parental involvement in school governance is an exemplar of citizenship as enacted and experienced in relation to a public sector institution. Through case studies of 6 urban schools (2 secondary and 4 primary) 2 of which (1 secondary and 1 primary) will be the focus for indepth study, the efficacy of the school structures which exist for encouraging parental involvement will be considered. The differential involvement of parents with the school, and specifically the effects of ethnicity, gender and class on this, will be a major focus for study. A survey and indepth interviewing of a sample of parents will explore how parents express a voice within a school, what form that voice takes, which issues generate voice, what reactions and responses they have received and occasions when they feel unable to speak.

STATUS: Sponsored project

SOURCE OF GRANT: Economic and Social Research Council

DATE OF RESEARCH: 1997-continuing

KEYWORDS: parent control; parent participation; parent school relationship

0147

School of Psychology, Edgbaston, Birmingham B15 2TT
0121 414 3344

Stones, E. Prof.

Psychology and pedagogy: investigations into the relationships between principles of psychology of human learning and practical teaching and the supervision of practical teaching in teacher training

ABSTRACT: The work comprises a variety of investigations by experienced teachers into different aspects of pedagogy and employing different approaches. Qualitative as well as quantitative data are sought for. Surveys of current practice are complemented by empirical work exploring the effects of theory based practical pedagogical intervention into the teaching of a wide variety of subjects. Experiments are predominantly naturalistic, clinical, learning based and outcome-oriented case studies involving small groups of teachers or student teachers and their pupils.

PUBLISHED MATERIAL: STONES, E. (1987). 'Teaching practice supervision: bridge between theory and practice', European Journal of Teacher Education, Vol 10, No 1, pp.67-69. ; STONES, E. (1989). 'Pedagogical studies in the theory and practice of teacher education', Oxford Review of Education, Vol 15, No 1, pp.3-15. ; STONES, E. (1993). Teaching and learning: the shadow and the substance. Occasional Paper No 6. Birmingham: University of Birmingham, Institute for Advanced Research in the Humanities. ; STONES, E. (1994). Quality teaching: a sample of cases. London: Routledge. ; STONES, E. (1994). 'Reform in teacher education: the power and the pedagogy', Journal of Teacher Education, Vol 45, No 4, pp.1-9. A full list of publications is available from the researcher.

STATUS: Individual research

DATE OF RESEARCH: 1983-continuing

KEYWORDS: **educational theories; learning theories; psychology; teacher education; teaching experience; teaching practice; teaching process**

0148

School of Psychology, Edgbaston, Birmingham B15 2TT
0121 414 3344

Beck, S. Ms; Riggs, K. Dr; *SupervisorS*: Robinson, E. Prof. ; Peterson, D. Dr

Counterfactual reasoning in young children: when do realist errors occur?

ABSTRACT: People's ability to imagine how things might realistically be, or how things would have been under different circumstances, frees them from the constraints of their immediate environment and underlies the idealism and moral philosophies which enrich our culture. This research is in the development of this counterfactual reasoning ability. The researchers are examining the counterfactual reasoning skills of children aged 3-5 years, using a variety of specially developed tasks which require the child to imagine how things might be had some event not occurred, or had something different happened. Comparisons will be made with standard 'false belief' tasks in which children are asked to infer the belief of someone who was absent when some relevant event (such as the moving of a desired object) took place. Acknowledgement of false belief in children requires the ability to handle a counterfactual situation: something which the child knows to be false is held to be true by the other person. The results so far show correlations between performance in false belief tasks and tasks which require counterfactual reasoning about the physical world, and are consistent with the possibility that chldren find counterfactual situations difficult to handle irrespective of their mental or physical content. The results also suggest that making current reality less salient does not help children acknowledge a counterfactual situation.

STATUS: Sponsored project

SOURCE OF GRANT: Economic and Social Research Council £61,000

DATE OF RESEARCH: 1995-1998

KEYWORDS: **hypothetical situations; imagination; logical thinking; preschool children; reasoning; young children**

Bishop Grosseteste College

0149

Newport, Lincoln LN1 3DY   01522 527347

Bentley, S. Ms; *Supervisor*: Stoneham, P. Ms

Children's literature and linguistic theory

ABSTRACT: The research explores language play within a wide range of children's literature. Firstly, it establishes that children's authors have been fascinated for the last two hundred years with language and its workings. The thesis will briefly cite a wide range of authors to demonstrate that this is the case. It then moves on to ask why this is so, using textual, cultural, psychological, linguistic, philosophical and biographical approaches. The authors who are explored in most detail are Lewis Carroll, Enid Blyton, and Russell Hoban. The theories of Mikhail Bakhtin (dialogism and polyphony) and Jacques Derrida (deconstruction and the play of the trace) are particularly crucial to the analysis. The thesis concludes by considering how this analysis can help us to understand better the nature and importance of children's literature.

STATUS: Individual research

DATE OF RESEARCH: 1995-1998

KEYWORDS: **books; childrens literature; language; linguistics**

0150

Newport, Lincoln LN1 3DY   01522 527347
Edinburgh University, Department of Divinity, Old College, South Bridge, Edinburgh EH8 9YL   0131 650 1000

Chater, M. Dr; *Supervisor*: McDonald, J. Dr

A new vision for religious education: the evolution from divergent models of religious education towards a convergence based upon new metaphors

ABSTRACT: This thesis re-examines the philosophical bases of religious education (RE). It explores the historical assumption that the two models of RE, confessional and non-confessional, exist in opposition to each other. This assumption is questioned and found unsatisfactory by means of a critical review and development of selected theorists, among them Hull, Grimmitt, Groome and Noran. It is argued that the two models can be more convergent and consistent with each other than previously envisaged. The possibilities of further convergence are tested in two ways. First, there is a discussion of the work of the confessionalist, Thomas Groome, alongside two non-confessionalists, Michael Grimmitt and Alex Rodger. This discussion yields substantial items of agreement but also some areas of important difference. Next, there is a documentary and statistical analysis of the extent to which confessional (denominational) RE has participated in non-confessional courses, structures and course development documents in the Scottish system between 1988 and 1993. Both tests reveal substantial agreement between the models together with some theoretical and practical factors which will impede any full convergence, both now and in future. The thesis offers a new vision for the subject, based on sources not usually associated with it, namely psychotherapy and liberation theology. These sources are taken as metaphors and are applied to RE's internal dynamics between pupils, teacher, religious text (in its broadest sense), faith communities, and the wider society. At the conclusion, some unresolved issues and remaining tasks are identified.

PUBLISHED MATERIAL: CHATER, M. (1995). 'A healing model of religious education', British Journal of Religious Education, Vol 17, No 2, pp.121-128.

STATUS: Individual research

DATE OF RESEARCH: 1993-1997

KEYWORDS: religious education; spiritual development

BMRB International

0151

Hadley House, 79 Uxbridge Road, Ealing, London W5 5SU
0181 280 8351

Rigg, M. Mr

Evaluation of Modern Apprenticeships: survey of apprentices

ABSTRACT: This is the Department for Education and Employment (DfEE) second survey of young people participating in Modern Apprenticeship (MA) and a comparison group of young people doing A-levels or Advanced General National Vocational Qualifications (GNVQs). It is a postal questionnaire survey of 3,000 apprentices and a comparison group of some 1,500 young people, covering England and Wales. In addition, there will be a small number of focus groups to explore particular issues with young people. An earlier study along similar lines was published by the DfEE (RS51). This was done in the very early stages of the initiative. The current study is being carried out to obtain the views of young people now that the initiative is well established. It covers a wide range of issues, including activity before MA; awareness of MA among the comparison group; the importance of factors such as school, careers, parents/friends in making choices, the quality of the experience; and their career plans.

Published Material: SAUNDERS, L., LINES, A., MACDONALD, A. & SCHAGEN, I. (1997). Modern Apprenticeships: a survey of young people. DFEE Research Studies RS51. London: the Stationery Office.

STATUS: Sponsored project

SOURCE OF GRANT: Department for Education and Employment £55,951

DATE OF RESEARCH: 1997-1998

KEYWORDS: **a level examinations; apprenticeships; employment; general national vocational qualifications; modern apprenticeships; sixteen to nineteen education; youth attitudes; youth employment**

Bolton Institute

0152

Department of Psychology, Deane Road, Bolton BL3 5AB
01204 528851

Pressler, S. Ms; *Supervisor*: Williamson, J. Dr

Analogical reasoning and problem solving: modelling and instruction *@

ABSTRACT: The research evaluates the psychological validity of models of analogical problem-solving, mainly with 10 and 11-year-old children. In particular, traditional and contemporary approaches to analogical problem-solving are considered. Traditional, or structural, approaches to analogical reasoning are challenged. Models incorporating assumptions emanating from theories of development are revised in accordance with findings, both those in the current study and those seen in the literature. Initially a structural model of analogical reasoning was investigated and revised. More latterly a study involving instruction was carried out upon the basis of the findings of the study to date and other work seen in the literature, namely that of Goswami. However, the training study , as well as intermediary studies, also incorporated investigations relating to a 'pragmatic' 'intensional' verbal analogy relation type distinction after Bejar *et al* 1991. Initial investigations used analogical problems to investigate Gentner's structural approach to analogical problem-solving. Problem solutions and causal reasoning were investigated. The results from various conditions involving paired problems did not lend direct support to Gentner. Further investigations examined performance on verbal analogies, both with respect to relational understanding and performance on the analogy problems devised earlier in the study. On the basis of these findings, in agreement with the work of Goswami, a training study was devised. The training study focused on the training of certain types of relations between pairs of words, later embedded within verbal analogies subsequently tested. Results suggested that whilst near transfer of training occurred, transfer and generalisation of training did not occur. Children receiving training on relational focus showed a higher awareness of such, subsequent to completion of all measures taken during the course of the training study. Analysis investigating incorrect choice alternatives was also undertaken. Conclusions from the training study, including incorrect verbal analogy choices, are in agreement with the work of Goswami.

PUBLISHED MATERIAL: PRESSLER, S.J. (1993). 'Can 10-11 year old children solve the tumour problem via analogy?', The Psychology Postgraduate Affairs Group Newsletter, Spring, pp.20-21. ; PRESSLER, S.J. (1995). 'The relationship between children's relational understanding and passing and failing verbal analogy items'. Proceedings of the British Psychological Society Conference, February 1995.

STATUS: Individual research

DATE OF RESEARCH:1990-continuing

KEYWORDS: **analogy; cognitive processes; logic; models; problem solving; reasoning**

0153

Department of Psychology, Deane Road, Bolton BL3 5AB
01204 528851

Charlton, J. Dr; *Supervisor*: Birkett, P. Dr

The development and nature of computer engagement, addiction and anxiety, and their influence upon computing performance during educational courses

ABSTRACT: In the project's first phase, the concept of computer engagement was developed as a construct of particular relevance to individuals with highly positive computing attitudes. A psychometric measure of both engagement and computer anxiety was constructed (the Computer Apathy and Anxiety Scale (CAAS). Use of the CAAS Apathy - Engagement Scale with computing students in higher education showed greater engagement for programming-oriented students than for students on more applications-oriented courses. Level of engagement also predicted the course performance of programming-oriented students within a multivariate context. Preliminary evidence suggests that depth of computer engagement, but not differences in masculine personality characteristics such as independence and tough-poise, can help explain why a minority of females opt to study programming-oriented, rather than applications-oriented, computing. This observation is relevant to redressing the particularly marked gender asymmetries on the former types of course. The recently begun second phase of the project extends into the realm of pathological computing behaviour. The issue of whether 'computer addiction' is a bona fide behavioural addiction will be addressed, with the CAAS Apathy – Engagement Scale being adapted in an attempt to measure addiction. The resulting scale will be used to select possibly computer addicted individuals for closer examination of their computing behaviour. In parallel, the behaviour of computer anxious individuals will also be examined. Developmental antecedents of addiction and anxiety will be considered and comparisons made between highly computer engaged, computer addicted and computer anxious individuals with respect to psychological factors, perceptions of computers and computing performance.

PUBLISHED MATERIAL: CHARLTON, J.P. & BIRKETT, P.E. (1995). 'The development and validation of the Computer Apathy and Anxiety Scale', Journal of Educational Computing Research, Vol 13, No 1, pp.41-59. ; CHARLTON, J.P. & BIRKETT, P.E. 'Psychological characteristics of students on programming-oriented and applications-oriented computing courses', Journal of Educational Computing Research. (in press). ; CHARLTON, J.P. & BIRKETT, P.E. 'An integrative model of factors related to computing course performance', Journal of Educational Computing Research. (in press).

STATUS: Individual research

DATE OF RESEARCH:#@ 1992-continuing

KEYWORDS: **anxiety; attitudes; computer literacy; computers; higher education; human computer interaction; personality; student attitudes**

0154

School of Education and Health Studies, Chadwick Campus, Chadwick Street, Bolton BL2 1JW   01204 528851

Phillips, T. Dr; Farrell, V. Mr; Ross, R. Ms; Norman, M. Ms

Patterns of teaching and learning in the post-compulsory sector of education in the 1990's

ABSTRACT: Over the past ten years there have been some very basic changes in the curriculum for the post-compulsory sector of education. One immediate consequence of this is a need for some examination to be made of the kinds of teaching that may now be found in this sector, these may be new or a development on what has gone before. The issue comes into sharp focus when teacher trainers are engaged in supervising teaching practice and find their students engaged in many activiites in the name of teaching which traditional notions of teaching has not prepared them for. This project will seek to open up this area for conceptualising with observational studies playing and important role. The proposal is for an initial study at Bolton which might hopefully pave the way for a larger project later with other providers of post-compulsory education teacher training. The aims are: (1) to carry out a small scale survey of patterns of teaching and learning characteristics of work in contemporary post-compulsory education; and (2) to review literature on conceptions of teaching and learning that may be adequate to describe such patterns.

STATUS: Sponsored project

SOURCE OF GRANT: Bolton Institute of Higher Education £5,000

DATE OF RESEARCH: 1991-1993

KEYWORDS: **further education; open education; teaching methods**

0155

School of Education and Health Studies, Chadwick Campus, Chadwick Street, Bolton BL2 1JW   01204 528851

Ross, R. Ms

Case study of Accreditation of Prior Learning (APL) in further education

ABSTRACT: One of the objectives of the National Council for Vocational Qualifications (NCVQ) is to encourage and enable previous learning to be accredited against national standards. This process is known as Accreditation of Prior Learning (APL). The aim of the project is to look at current practices within a small cross section of further education institutions, compare their various systems and contrast these with traditional methods of assessment and accreditation. The research will be conducted through interviews and observation. It is envisaged that the results will help to: (1) identify good practice; (2) highlight any problem areas; and (3) determine the effect of APL procedures on the role of the tutor.

STATUS: Sponsored project

SOURCE OF GRANT: Bolton Institute of Higher Education £1,200

DATE OF RESEARCH:#@ 1992-1993

KEYWORDS: **achievement; assessment; experiential learning; further education; national vocational qualifications; prior learning**

0156

School of Education and Health Studies, Chadwick Campus, Chadwick Street, Bolton BL2 1JW   01204 528851

King, J. Mr ; Kenny, C. Ms

The use of CD ROM in the curriculum in further and higher education: students attitudes and perceptions

ABSTRACT: CD ROM applications are increasingly being used in further and higher education institutions to enable students to research material for assignments. This initial study aims to identify the attitudes of students to using this method of investigation and also to elicit from the students whether they use different search strategies with CD ROM applications than they do with paper based material. A sample of 200 students on further education and higher education courses will be used in the initial study. For the initial investigation a free response questionnaire will be used to elicit differences in search strategies and a variation of Osgood's semantic differential table will be used to ascertain attitudes to CD ROM use. Following the initial study it is intended to extend the work to other sample groups to ascertain whether there are differences according to the course being followed. In addition, the research will examine to what extent staff setting assignments are taking expected differences in search strategies into account when deciding on assessment criteria.

STATUS: Sponsored project

SOURCE OF GRANT: National Council for Educational Technology £1,500

DATE OF RESEARCH: 1992-1993

KEYWORDS: **cd roms; further education; higher education; information retrieval; information systems; search strategies; student attitudes**

Bradford University

0157

Centre for Continuing Education, 12 Claremont, Bradford BD7 1DP 01274 733466

Field, J. Dr

Lifestyle, values and educational participation among adults

ABSTRACT: Most studies of participation in adult education focus upon socio-economic and demographic factors, such as social class, age or gender. However, participation rates also vary widely within categories, and this study is concerned to discover whether lifestyle patterns can be related to educational participation among the adult population. Two major methods will be used to explore the extent to which educational participation can be explained with reference to life cycle patterns. They are: (a) surveys of adult learners in personal development courses and in craft-based courses, using an established lifestyle analysis; and (b) semi-structured interviews to explore the degree of inner-directedness within adult learners' value systems, and to investigate the role of material factors in influencing decisions to participate. Outcomes will be analysed using a conceptual framework that will draw upon the work of Pierre Bourdieu as well as of market research theorists and critics of post-modernist sociology.

PUBLISHED MATERIAL: FIELD, J. (1991). 'Out of the adult hut: Institutionalisation, individuality and new values in the education of adults'. In: RAGGATT, P. & UNWIN, L. (Eds). Change and intervention: vocational education and training. London: Falmer Press.

STATUS: Individual research

DATE OF RESEARCH: 1992-1993

KEYWORDS: **adult education; life style; participation**

0158

Centre for Continuing Education, 12 Claremont, Bradford BD7 1DP 01274 733466

Jowitt, J. Mr

Lifelong learning – the cultural constraints on the development of a learning society in the UK

ABSTRACT: This study will analyse the role that business, the public sector and other institutions are playing in the development of learning situations, in particular the development of support for non-vocational education and training. The analysis will rest on a series of qualitative interviews with firms and the public sector in two regions of the UK (Yorkshire – Humberside and East Anglia) with a small amount of comparative work in other member states of the European Community.

PUBLISHED MATERIAL: JOWITT, A. (1992). 'Science parks, academic research and economic regeneration'. In: HILPERT, U. (Ed). Regional innovation and decentralisation. London: Routledge.

STATUS: Sponsored project

SOURCE OF GRANT: Universities Funding Council £30,000

DATE OF RESEARCH: 1992-1993

KEYWORDS: **access to education; adult education; continuing education; lifelong learning**

0159

Centre for Continuing Education, 12 Claremont, Bradford BD7 1DP 01274 733466

Allen, S. Prof.; Mitchell, G. Dr

The role of the personal tutor in relation to the needs of students from non-traditional backgrounds

ABSTRACT: The University of Bradford aims to widen access to its full-time and part-time courses. To this end, a number of support services for students are provided, including the allocation of a personal tutor for all undergraduates. This study concentrates upon the roles and responsibilities of such tutors, particularly in relation to full-time and part-time studies from groups normally under represented in higher education. It focuses selectively upon departments drawn from the Boards of Studies in Engineering, Social Sciences and Natural and Applied Sciences. Data was collected from questionnaires sent to 90 personal tutors and a proportion of student views were elicitied by the same means

STATUS: Sponsored project

SOURCE OF GRANT: Bradford University £2,125

DATE OF RESEARCH: 1991-1993

KEYWORDS: **access to education; higher education; nontraditional education; student counselling; student health and welfare**

0160

Management Centre, Emm Lane, Bradford BD9 4JL   01274 733466

McClements, R. Mr; Helm, P. Mr; Woods, M. Dr; *Supervisor*: Gilding, D. Dr

Multimedia business training

ABSTRACT: This project will develop and evaluate different forms of flexible delivery of management education, that allow structured self-learning. A pilot 'Learning Resource Centre' will be established with an industrial partner. The project will study: (1) the place of student centred learning in the management development process; (2) the design and production of suitable modules of learning material; (3) the 'learning and technology' required; (4) the physical facilities needed; (5) the management of learning resource centres; (6) effectiveness of multimedia.

STATUS: Sponsored project

SOURCE OF GRANT: Bradford University £60,000

DATE OF RESEARCH: 1991-continuing

KEYWORDS: **educational media; learner centred methods; learning resources centres; management development; management studies; multimedia**

0161

Management Centre, Emm Lane, Bradford BD9 4JL   01274 733466

Morgan, P. Dr ; Broadfield, A. Mrs ; *Supervisor*: Randell, G. Prof.

The micro-skills of management

ABSTRACT: This is a long-term project which is studying the actual skills that are required for the effective management of people at work. Early studies concentrated on verbal skills and showed how they can be used for bringing about behavioural and organisational change using 'staff appraisal' as the vehicle for interaction at work. This research was mainly based on the analysis of audio and videotapes, and direct observation of appraisal interviews. Again using videotapes the skills of leading small groups have been studied, where it was discovered that keeping in balance, 'participation', 'problem-solving', 'goal-setting' and 'supportiveness' was crucial for effective work-teams. Recent work has investigated the nature of managerial concern and its relationship to the personality characteristics of a manager. Also the determinants of successful written communication, through distributed memoranda, for bringing about organisational change. This has produced detailed findings of how to write memos to staff which help them to 'feel communicated'.

PUBLISHED MATERIAL: RANDELL, G.A. (1979). 'The skills of staff development'. In: SINGLETON, W.T. et al. (Eds). The analysis of social skills. New York: Plenum. ; RANDELL, G.A. (1981). 'Management education and training'. In: SINGLETON, W.T. (Ed). Management skills: Vol 3 in the study of real skills. Lancaster: MTP. ; RANDELL, G.A. (1981). 'Employee appraisal'. In: SISSON, K. (Ed). Personnel management in Britain. Oxford: Blackwell.

STATUS: Team research

DATE OF RESEARCH: 1980-1998

KEYWORDS: **change strategies; interpersonal competence; leadership; management; organisational change; personnel management**

0162

Management Centre, Emm Lane, Bradford BD9 4JL   01274 733466

Callaghan, C. Dr; Baverstock, S. Dr; *Supervisor*: Wright, P. Dr

Influencing behaviour and emotion at work

ABSTRACT: Two studies were carried out into the specific behaviours associated with influencing behaviour and handling emotion at work. Dr Callaghan developed a 6-category system for classifying verbal behaviour in 2 person interactions. One hundred and twelve role-played appraisal interviews lasting 10-30 minutes were video-recorded. Immediately following the interviews, interviewees assessed how successful they had been on an 8-item questionnaire. Eighteen interviews (6 successful, 6 moderately successful and 6 unsuccessful) were selected for detailed analysis. It was found that high scoring interviewers enquired and attended more; medium scoring interviewers guided and informed more, with low scoring interviewers coming second; and low scoring managers rewarded and deterred more, with medium scoring interviewers coming second. Sequential analysis of interviewer and interviewee behaviour suggests reasons for the above findings, e.g. high scoring interviewers used guidance less, but such guidance was more likely to be accepted by interviewees. In Dr Baverstock's research, 61 role-played interviews lasting 8-35 minutes were video-recorded. Interviewees were briefed to portray someone who was angry, anxious or depressed. The interviewer's success in handling the emotion in question was assessed by the interviewee immediately following the interview. Interviewer and interviewee behaviour during the interview was categorised according to Stiles' Verbal Response Mode Taxonomy. It was found that successful interviewers used advice more than unsuccessful interviewers; moderately successful interviewers used reflections more than unsuccessful interviewers; and unsuccessful interviewers used more confirmations than moderately successful interviewers. These findings suggest that the precepts of Rogers' non-directive counselling are not universally applicable in the work environment.

PUBLISHED MATERIAL: WRIGHT, P.L. (1993). 'Interpersonal skills training: interactions between research and practice'. Paper presented at the 6th European Congress on Work and Organizational Psychology, Alicante, April, 1993. ; WRIGHT, P.L. (1994). 'Intercultural communication: the case for the systematic study of verbal behaviour'. Paper presented at the 23rd International Congress of Applied Psychology,

Madrid, July, 1994. ; WRIGHT, P.L. & TAYLOR, D.S. (Eds). (1994). Improving leadership performance: an interpersonal skills approach to developing leadership effectiveness. London: Prentice-Hall. ; CALLAGHAN, C.A. & WRIGHT, P.L. (1994). 'Verbal leader behaviour in appraisal interviews: an observational study'. Paper presented at the British Psychological Society Occupational Psychology Conference, Birmingham, January, 1994. ; WRIGHT, P.L. & BAVERSTOCK, S.M.A. (1997). 'Effective emotion-handling at work: research and practice'. Paper presented at the 8th European Congress on Work and Organizational Psychology, Verona, 2-5 April, 1997.

STATUS: Team research

DATE OF RESEARCH: 1987-1997

KEYWORDS: **appraisal interviews; interpersonal competence; personnel management**

0163

Management Centre, Emm Lane, Bradford BD9 4JL   01274 733466
Dalhousie University, Halifax, Nova Scotia, Canada B3H 4H6

Curri, G. Ms; *Supervisor*: Randell, G. Prof.

Organisational change in universities

ABSTRACT: This thesis argues that restructuring, leadership, or managing relationships between individuals and groups (i.e. the primary elements of change) are not sufficient on their own to achieve major organisational change in universities. Moreover, the findings suggest that change does not occur unless external forces demanding change are stronger than internal forces wishing to maintain the status quo. The triad model of change illustrates the symbiotic relationships between the primary elements of change and the internal and external forces that determine whether the institutional equilibrium remains unchanged. The model presents a holistic approach to an increase in efficiency and effectiveness in universities, the stated reason for restructuring by government. The model recognises the importance of organizational development theory by placing it at the centre. The model was developed as the result of observations from two case studies in restructuring of tertiary systems and personal perception. In addition to analysing and scoring interview data, ranking was used to compare and then to test results using qualitative research methods. The findings suggest that the model could be used to assess the probability of implementing restructuring successfully. Whether the model would be applicable for organizational change without external forces should be the topic for further research.

STATUS: Individual research

DATE OF RESEARCH: 1992-1997

KEYWORDS: **educational administration; higher education; institutional administration; organisational change; universities; university administration**

0164

Management Centres, Emm Lane, Bradford BD9 4JL
01274 733466

Prescott, K. Miss

Curriculum development for business and management education

ABSTRACT: Despite strives to build better links between business schools and industry, research still points to a mismatch between curriculum provision and management needs. The research being undertaken sets out to explore the nature and scope of this mismatch and ways in which it can be overcome. The research is mostly based on secondary sources and a questionnaire sent out to over 1,000 individuals who have graduated from Bradford University Management Centre and who are now working in a diverse array of business and management roles. Their knowledge of educational institutions and the needs of industry/management make them ideal commentators. The research highlights the problems of adapting to the dynamic demands of industry, in particular the constraints imposed by the Centre's own internal organisational structures and practices.

STATUS: Individual research

DATE OF RESEARCH: 1997-1998

KEYWORDS: **business education; curriculum development; followup studies; graduate surveys; industry; industry higher education relationship; management studies; organisational development**

Brighton University

0165

Chelsea School Research Centre, Gaudick Road, Eastbourne BN20 7SR
01273 600900

Whitehead, J. Dr

The generalizability of achievement orientations across young people's success and failure experiences in sport

ABSTRACT:The first study of subjective achievement orientations in sport (Ewing, 1981) employed the critical incident method, in which subjects recall a subjective success experience, in order to avoid experimenter bias in defining success. Subjective achievement orientations were then determined by factor analysis of Likert items, which subjects responded to with reference to the critical incidents they had selected. However, Ewing did not report the correspondence between the critical incidents and the Likert ratings, and it is unclear to what extent a subject-selected meaningful incident relates to a goal perspective which generalizes across different sporting experiences. The present study, conducted with 890 subjects in middle and upper schools, explores the relationship between Ewing's ability, mastery, social approval and sportventure orientations, and subjects' critical incidents and attributions for success and failure. Differences in age and gender sub-groups are reported, and recommendations made for improved methodology and further research.

PUBLISHED MATERIAL: WHITEHEAD, J. (1993). 'Why children choose to do sports or stop'. In: LEE, M.J. (Ed). Watching children in sport: principles and practices. London: E. & F.N. Spon. ; WHITEHEAD, J. 'Multiple achievement orientations and participation in youth sport: a cultural and developmental perspective', International Journal of Sports Psychology. (in press).

STATUS: Individual research

DATE OF RESEARCH: 1992-1993

KEYWORDS: achievement; failure; motivation; sports

0166

Chelsea School Research Centre, Gaudick Road, Eastbourne BN20 7SR 01273 600900

Wood, S. Mrs; *Supervisors*: Fleming, S. Dr ; Tomlinson, A. Prof.

The physical education curriculum in higher education: a study of the gender dimensions of socialisation in the physical education profession

ABSTRACT:The study will analyse the socialisation processes in the gender relations of the professional practice of physical education (PE) teacher's educators. Part of the investigation will be of the socialisation into sport that physical education/sports students experience prior to their entry into higher education, and the way in which these experiences affect students' abilities to recognise and challenge gender stereotyping in their own sports experiences. A further consideration will be the impact of coeducational training upon physical education professional practice, particularly for women and physical education students in initial teacher education. Information will be gathered through: questionnaires to a cohort of first year students entering teacher training in physical education; through interviews with selected women students and school physical education teachers; and participant observation in coeducational and physical practice and in informal interaction.

STATUS: Individual research

DATE OF RESEARCH: 1993-1997

KEYWORDS: physical education teachers; preservice teacher education; socialisation; teacher educators

0167

Chelsea School Research Centre, Gaudick Road, Eastbourne BN20 7SR 01273 600900

Liverpool John Moores University, School of Education and Community Studies, I M Marsh Campus, Barkhill Road, Liverpool L17 6BD 0151 231 2121

Murdoch, E. Prof.; Hudson, J. Ms ; Latham, A-M. Miss ; Shenton, P. Miss; Phillips, C. Mrs; Yau, K. Miss

School based teacher education partnerships: issues in physical education

ABSTRACT: Legislation in Department for Education Circular 9/92 has led to the formation of partnerships between schools and higher education institutions(HEI's) in the initial training of teachers. Greater emphasis has been placed on schools, consequently there have been changes in the role of both school and HEI personnel. This project is investigating the impact of partnerships on the initial training of prospective physical education and dance teachers, both to include the impact of those involved in postgraduate and undergraduate courses. Key foci include: 1) the student/ mentor relationship; 2) mechanisms of quality assurance; and 3) models of teaching competence. Samples consist of HEI-based personnel (link tutors, who oversee the scheme and liaison between schools and HEI); school-based personnel (professional tutors responsible for providing a whole school approach to training mentors and responsible for students during school placements, and headteachers); and students. Methods of investigation include case studies of: individual student/mentor dyads; observation of group meetings; individual interviews; and questionnaires. Subject samples vary according to the methodology in current use. Results thus far, from interviews with postgraduate students, indicate the importance of the mentor as an educator, a support mechanism, a counsellor, and an information base for the student. Results from interviews conducted with mentors and link tutors will provide reflective and prospective perspectives of the partnership scheme. Implications of the research will be to inform and improve current initial teacher training within the partnership scheme.

STATUS: Sponsored project

SOURCE OF GRANT: Brighton University Chelsea School Research Centre ; Liverpool John Moores University

DATE OF RESEARCH: 1993-1997

KEYWORDS: institutional cooperation; mentors; partnerships; physical education teachers; preservice teacher education; school based teacher education; student teachers

0168

Faculty of Education, Sport and Leisure, Falmer, Brighton BN1 9PH 01273 600900

Austin, S. Mr; *Supervisors*: Fox, C. Dr; Laing, S. Dr

Collaborative narrative discourse in children's writing at key stage 1

ABSTRACT: The thesis aims to describe and analyse the processes and outcomes of collaborative writing, in narrative form, in infant classrooms. Selected groups of children were recorded during the writing process. Their interactions and written texts were transcribed and analysed at the level of the word, sentence and text. The reported and analysed sample which forms the main text of the thesis is a series of case studies. However, the researcher collected background data from hundreds of children in National Curriculum key stages 1, 2 and 3, aiming originally to complete a much broader project. Comparisons were made between the same pupils' individual and independent writing and their group creations. The research is naturalistic and ethnographic, conducted by a practising teacher acting as participant-observer, and charts the journey that each piece of writing takes from initial idea to a product which the group or individual feels is finished. The hypothesis is that there are distinct educational benefits for children and teachers in the use of contexts for collaborative writing in the primary school classroom. It was discovered that collaborative writing increases motivation, especially in reluctant writers. Group and paired writing scaffolds the emerging writer and enhances the children's knowledge about language. Collaborative skills can improve over time and with appropriate teacher intervention. Children benefit from opportunities to write independently and collaboratively. Collaborative writing develops children's thinking skills and allows the teacher opportunities to listen to the thought processes of hypothesis, metacognition, metalinguistics and metanarrative.

PUBLISHED MATERIAL: AUSTIN, S. (1992). 'George's story'. In: Storytelling. West Sussex Language Papers 1. Chichester: West Sussex County Council. ; AUSTIN, S. (1993). 'Remembrance of things past'. In: SOUTER, I. Stories to read aloud. Leamington Spa: Scholastic.

STATUS: Individual research

DATE OF RESEARCH: 1991-1997

KEYWORDS: children as writers; group work; narration; primary school pupils; story telling; writing - composition

Bristol University

0169

Centre for Deaf Studies, 22 Berkeley Square, Bristol BS8 1HP
01179 289000

Callaway, A. Dr; *Supervisor*: Kyle, J. Dr

Deaf children and their families in China: a cross-cultural study

ABSTRACT: The aim of this study is to investigate the attitudes and experiences of Chinese parents of deaf children so that appropriate and effective pre-school programmes that depend on parental participation can be developed. The parents of deaf children attending a pre-school for deaf children in Nanjing were interviewed, as well as a sample of parents of deaf children living in the countryside in a poor area in north Jiangsu Province (October – December 1994). Preliminary results indicate that diagnosis is often delayed, especially in the countryside; parents spend much time and money going to different hospitals and doctors to find a 'cure'; hearing aids are acquired late and are often poorly maintained; parents want their children to learn to speak rather than use sign language, although simple sign is usually used at home. Some parents of profoundly deaf children feel stigmatised; most parents express anxiety about their child's future, especially their job status and economic security. Most parents say they will not have a second child as the deaf child will not get enough attention. The present policy of the Chinese government is to emphasise the role of parents in educating their deaf children: this study intends to outline the factors which will contribute or detract from this aim, and suggest ways in which parents can be supported in this role.

PUBLISHED MATERIAL: CALLAWAY, A.C. (1984). 'The children's hospital in Chongqing', China Now, No 108, pp.14-16. ; CALLAWAY, A.C. (1986). 'Educating deaf children', China Now, No 116, pp.17-18. ; CALLAWAY, A.C. (1987). 'Employing the disabled', China Now, No 121, pp.32-34.

STATUS: Individual research

DATE OF RESEARCH: 1993-1997

KEYWORDS: **china; deafness**

0170

Centre for Deaf Studies, 22 Berkeley Square, Bristol BS8 1HP
01179 289000

Morgan, G. Mr; *Supervisor*: Woll, B. Dr

Aspect development in British Sign Language

ABSTRACT: This work will attempt to describe the important linguistic feature of 'aspect' in British Sign Language (BSL) and its development in young children. A longitudinal observation of children interacting with deaf parents using BSL will attempt to trace the interactional origins of aspect and its later development in the process of becoming a competent user of BSL. Video-recording of naturalistic situations will provide the data. The expected conclusions are of similar chronological development as in hearing children's use of verbal aspect. However the differences described in BSL aspect may provide evidence for different learning strategies in BSL than with spoken language.

Status: Individual research

Date of Research: 1994-1997

KEYWORDS: **deafness; manual communication; sign language**

0171

Centre for Deaf Studies, 22 Berkeley Square, Bristol BS8 1HP
01179 289000
Allsop, L. Ms;Kyle, J. Dr; Day, L. M; Sutton-Spence, R. Dr

The distribution, use and lexical, grammatical features of mouth pattern in British Sign Language

ABSTRACT: This project will select samples of British Sign Language from archives of signed material to classify and encode different mouth pattern (non-manual marker). The results will demonstrate the different features of mouth patterns in the Syntax of British Sign Language.

STATUS: Sponsored project

SOURCE OF GRANT: Economic and Social Research Council £28,420

DATE OF RESEARCH:#@ 1996-1997

KEYWORDS: **deafness; hearing impairments; manual communication; sign language**

0172

Department for Continuing Education, 8-10 Berkeley Square, Bristol BS8 1HH　　　01179 289000

Thomas, E. Prof.

Innovation and effective training and management methods for language training

ABSTRACT: This project involves the collaboration of the research with 17 partners in European countries. The objectives of the programme are to: 1) improve the quality and innovation capacity of language training systems and arrangements in Europe; 2) promote cooperation on language skill requirements and training needs for employees in business and industry; 3) promote the incorporation into language training of the results of recent research and development; and 4) identify and encourage the use of innovative training methods and good management practices to aid the development of linguistic skills. Language trainers and managers will undertake visits to study the training and management methods used by other training organisations; visit reports will be disseminated to all the partners via the World Wide Web (WWW); and an overall report of the programme will be circulated to all the partners at the end of the project. This report will be available to others interested via WWW.

STATUS: Sponsored project

SOURCE OF GRANT: European Union ú 88,300

DATE OF RESEARCH: 1995-1997

KEYWORDS: **europe; international educational exchange; languages for specific purposes; modern language studies; second language teaching; training**

0173

Graduate School of Education, 35 Berkeley Square, Bristol BS8 1JA
01179 289000

Crossley, M. Dr ; Bennett, A. Mr

The impact of the Belize Primary Education Development Project: case studies

ABSTRACT: This is essentially a qualitative study of the impact of the Belize Primary Education Development Project (BPEDP) in selected schools. Case studies involving collaboration between school and external personnel (from both Belize and the University of Bristol) will be conducted, focusing upon the documentation of the nature and quality of teaching and learning. Nine to twelve schools will be involved and the development of local research capacity will also be included through research training workshops. Phase 2 will be a contribution to the evaluation of the BPEDP through case studies of participating schools and a number of related statistical studies.

Published Material: CROSSLEY, M. & BENNETT, J.A. (1997). 'Planning for case study evaluation in Belize, Central America'. In: CROSSLEY, M. & VULLIAMY, G. (Eds). Qualitative educational research in developing countries. New York: Garland.

STATUS: Sponsored project

SOURCE OF GRANT: Belize Primary Education Development Project

DATE OF RESEARCH: 1994-1997

KEYWORDS: **belize; developing countries; development education; educational quality; primary education**

0174

Graduate School of Education, 35 Berkeley Square, Bristol BS8 1JA
01179 289000

Marangou, A. Mrs; *Supervisors*: Meadows, S. Dr; Webster, A. Dr

The transition from home to school: a study of social, cultural and emotional factors in Greek children

ABSTRACT: The transition from the pre-school to the actual school years in Greece is not, at present, considered as a period during which children deserve special treatment or provision. Many demands are placed upon the children with serious consequences on their school performance, relationships and emotional development. The research will primarily look at the quality and quantity of time spent on selected teacher/pupil verbal and non-verbal interactions, pupils' activities and pupils' physical movements while at school, during the transitional period (i.e. the 5 1/2 to 6 1/2 year old age group). The aim of this research is to draw attention to a period of children's lives which, the researcher believes, is crucial, but which has not received adequate attention. Hopefully, the conclusions will be used as recommendations to teachers and adults responsible for children's lives at this delicate stage

STATUS: Individual research

DATE OF RESEARCH: 1994-1997

KEYWORDS: **early childhood education; greece; preschool to primary transition; primary school pupils; school readiness**

0175

Graduate School of Education, 35 Berkeley Square, Bristol BS8 1JA
01179 289000

Moschovaki, E. Miss; *Supervisor*: Meadows, S. Dr

Classroom story reading with young children

ABSTRACT: Although it is generally accepted that classroom story reading is important, nevertheless research on reading stories with young children is still limited and mainly descriptive. Thus an indepth study is needed on how story reading styles influence young children's cognition in a classroom context. The research questions of this project are mainly concerned with the following areas: 1) Are there significant differences among teachers' strategies when reading aloud different books (i.e. information/narrative/familiar/unfamiliar) for identifying distinctive story reading styles? 2) What is the relationship between the affective and cognitive dimensions of story reading for empowering children to demonstrate higher cognitive demand thinking and more complex verbal behaviour? 3) What assists children in taking initiatives during the process of reading stories which lead story reading interaction from being teacher-regulated to becoming group-regulated? 4) Is there a relationship between teachers' story reading styles and children's emergent behaviour in the classroom library? One hundred and forty story readings will be collected from thirty schools, and classroom observations of children's behaviour will take place as well as interviews of teachers. Hopefully, the research outcomes will identify effective ways for classroom story reading and better understanding of teaching styles. Moreover, it may clarify the effects on children's interest towards books and their literacy development. This will assist teachers in becoming aware of the significance of their own behaviour when interacting with children, in modelling specific linguistic and literacy patterns, and how they can complement family literacy in order to achieve successful transition to primary school.

STATUS: Individual research

DATE OF RESEARCH: 1993-1997

KEYWORDS: **childrens literature; early childhood education; reading aloud to others; story reading; teacher pupil relationship**

0176

Graduate School of Education, 35 Berkeley Square, Bristol BS8 1JA
01179 289000

Deakin Crick, R. Ms; *Supervisor*: Hill, T. Mr

The Grant Maintained status policy self management and diversity: limits and possibilities

ABSTRACT: The policy of Grant Maintained status is perhaps the most extreme example of a move by a Western government towards self management of schools. The accompanying policy of diversity and choice within a quasi-market system of provision brings to the fore the question of whose vision and whose values are shaping schools. This project explores the teaching and learning world views of leaders in two self-managing schools through the use of personal construct methodology and analyses them in the light of a Habermasian orientation towards strategic, hermeneutical and emancipatory rationality. It then critically analyses the discourse in which the school people and certain key policy-makers participate, seeking to identify the knowledge/power components which influence schooling. It concludes that profound diversity in schools can only occur where there is a strong orientation towards hermeneutical self-management which is inspired by a communal desire for professional

responsibility and autonomy and which is served by strategic rationality. Without such hermeneutical self-management, strategic rationality becomes either an end in itself or it works in the service of external ideologies, de-professionalising teachers and depressing the ability of schools to respond to their own communities. The dominant discourse of the market, underpinned by a liberal ideology, works in the service of capital, individual consumerism and political power and does not address the macro-question of difference, nor the micro-question of critique. The development of profound diversity in schools in a condition of postmodernity requires fresh understanding of the formation of the self, and the development of virtue in the context of community and tradition. It also requires the re-professionalisation of teachers and a focus on the ethics of educational leadership.

STATUS: Individual research

DATE OF RESEARCH: 1994-1997

KEYWORDS: **grant maintained schools; school based management**

0177

Graduate School of Education, 35 Berkeley Square, Bristol BS8 1JA
01179 289000

Krespi, A. Ms; *Supervisor*: Osborn, M. Dr

Teachers and the National Curriculum: a comparative study of primary school teachers in England and Greece

ABSTRACT: The research project is a comparative study of primary school teachers' attitudes towards the National Curriculum of two European countries, England and Greece. In the proposed study, teachers' attitudes towards the content, implementation and delivery of the curriculum will be examined through interviews, questionnaires and classroom observations. Closely related to the above issues is the issue of control, which governments, educationists and other agents exercise over the teachers, through the National Curriculum. The relative autonomy of the teachers in the two countries to negotiate the curriculum, to intervene in its delivery and possibly in its content will be considered. The study will also investigate the teachers' perceptions in relation to their professionalism and the National Curriculum in each country.

STATUS: Individual research

DATE OF RESEARCH: 1995-1997

KEYWORDS: **comparative education; greece; national curriculum; primary school teachers; teacher attitudes**

0178

Graduate School of Education, 35 Berkeley Square, Bristol BS8 1JA
01179 289000

Roe, J. Mrs; *Supervisor*: Webster, A. Dr

Peer relationships, play and language of visually impaired children

ABSTRACT: Visually impaired children have been integrated in mainstream schools, but little attention has been given to the way in which visually impaired children interact with other children. This research aims to: 1) analyse the development of language and play in visually impaired children; and 2) analyse how the relationships with peers affect the play and language of this group of children. Twenty children between the ages of 3 and 8 are participating in the research. The researcher will observe free play which occurs in natural settings and look at the kind of social contact visually impaired children and other children establish between themselves. Therefore, aspects such as level of interaction, forms of play, verbal and non-verbal behaviours and their social functions will be analysed. The findings of the research will hopefully contribute towards an understanding of effective strategies for the integration of visually impaired children. @#Status:#@ Individual research @#Date of Research:#@ 1993-1997 @#KEYWORDS: mainstreaming; peer relationship; play; pupil behaviour; social behaviour; special educational needs; verbal communication; visual impairments #@ @*/0179*@ Graduate School of Education, 35 Berkeley Square, Bristol BS8 1JA 01179 289000 Cinemre, Y. Mr ; @#Supervisor:#@ Gilpin, A. Ms ; Osborn, A. Dr @*Word guessing strategies of poor and good Turkish English as a foreign language (EFL) readers when comprehending a familiar and unfamiliar text *@ @#Abstract:#@ This study aims to investigate the vocabulary guessing strategies of poor and good Turkish English as a foreign language (EFL) readers when they are comprehending a familiar and unfamiliar text. The design is a cross-sectional single sample design in which information has been obtained by using a self-completion questionnaire and think-aloud protocols. Research in this focus has been based on schemata (Bartlett, 1932/1967), discourse domain hypothesis (Douglas and Selinker, 1985), and Stanovich's (1980-84) interactive compensatory hypothesis. Schouten van Parraren's (1985) theory is also relevant to the study. Thirty subjects have been selected out of 394 English readers by using English Language Battery (ELBA). They read and thought-aloud when trying to guess the meaning of words unknown to them in a familiar and unfamiliar text. The two texts were selected using Fry's (1977), Mugford's (1970) and Flesch's (1948) readability formulas. Text familiarity was defined using a questionnaire. In the analysis of the protocols, the frequency distribution of strategy types used by the subjects tend to be very skewed and there were many cases in single categories. So, non-parametric tests were used. One of the most suitable ones was Wilcoxon Matched-pairs Singled Ranks Test, this was used to see whether there was a signficant (statistical) difference in mean rank between frequency of strategy use when reading familair against unfamiliar text. The analysis is still continuing.

STATUS: Individual research

DATE OF RESEARCH: 1994-1997

KEYWORDS: english – second language; reading comprehension; turkey

0180

Graduate School of Education, 35 Berkeley Square, Bristol BS8 1JA
01179 289000

Arslan, R. Mr; *Supervisor*: Gilpin, A. Ms

Ongoing development of Teaching English as a Foreign Language (TEFL) teachers at Turkish universities

ABSTRACT: Ongoing development of foreign language teachers of English at Turkish universities will be analysed. Teachers' attitudes toward development processes will be identified. The study will attempt to find out what deficiencies the present inservice training programmes have, what strengths will exist, and what other ways can be presented to those undergoing staff development activities. Out of 57 Turkish universities some samples will be chosen, and questionnaires distributed to collect data. The data will be analysed both quantitatively and qualitatively. The study might contribute to the development of foreign language teachers in Turkey and in other countries with similar programmes.

STATUS: Individual research

DATE OF RESEARCH: 1994-1997

KEYWORDS: english – second language; language teachers; turkey

0181

Graduate School of Education, 35 Berkeley Square, Bristol BS8 1JA
01179 289000

Watson, G. Mr; *Supervisor*: Hoyle, E. Prof.

Strategic management and the incorporation of further education

ABSTRACT: This on-going research is attempting to investigate the issue of the management of strategy and change in the post-incorporation college of further education. It is particularly interested in how the process of incorporation has changed management. The area for investigation is not only the process, content and outcomes of change, but also its context. Thus the significance of the role of the 'enterprise culture' is also being researched. Four colleges were initially chosen from which to gather information and perspectives about the change prior to Vesting Day and afterwards and this has involved: a) semi-structured interviews with members of the senior management teams of the colleges; b) the issuing of a questionnaire to all other college members - administration, teaching and technical. Following the completion of the analysis of the returns and the interviews, it is intended to return to the colleges to begin to undertake further research using primary documentary evidence, observation of meetings and interviews with key players in the strategic management process.

STATUS: Individual research

DATE OF RESEARCH: 1993-1998

KEYWORDS: change strategies; colleges of further education; educational change; further education; management in education

0182

Graduate School of Education, 35 Berkeley Square, Bristol BS8 1JA
01179 289000

Crow, S. Mrs; *Supervisor*: Furlong, J. Prof.

Evaluation of integration of nursing education within higher education: analysis of organisational and cultural change

ABSTRACT: Nursing education has changed radically in the last decade. Students, formerly National Health Service (NHS) employees are now full-time students following diploma or degree courses in the university sector. Nurse teachers, formerly employed by the NHS, have now become lecturers in higher education. The aim of this study is to explore the perceptions of nurse lecturers of the impact of organisational and cultural change on working conditions following integration. A case-study approach is being adopted; subjects being interviewed in context of characteristics of the organisation of which they are a part. The samples used are: 1) 3 case-study sites, 6 subjects per case-study organisation; 2) focus groups n=5, total sample n=60 subjects, with the purpose of studying the impact of integration in relation to research culture. Data analysis will involve: content analysis of qualitative data; literature process of deconstruction, categorisation and reconstruction. The research is still progressing.

STATUS: Individual research

DATE OF RESEARCH: 1995-1997

KEYWORDS: higher education; nurse education; nurses; organisational change

0183

Graduate School of Education, 35 Berkeley Square, Bristol BS8 1JA
01179 289000

Le Var, R. Mrs; *Supervisor*: McMahon, A. Ms

An investigation of the development of professional standards concerned with resourcing nursing, midwifery and health visiting programmes of education for English National Board for approval of institutions and programmes

ABSTRACT: The English National Board for Nursing, Midwifery and Health Visiting is replacing its regulations and guidelines for the approval of educational institutions and programmes with standard statements. The investigation will focus on the development of professional standards concerned with resourcing nursing, midwifery and health visiting programmes. The views of key stakeholders on the draft standards and how they shape their development will be identified. The investigation will also identify factors influencing the Board's final decisions regarding the standards. The aims of the study are to identify and compare the views of Board officers, Board members and other key stakeholders on the potential effectiveness of the draft standards to ensure adequate and appropriate resourcing of nursing, midwifery and health visiting programmes and their potential to replace the staff:student ratio statements within the Board's requirements; to identify how the key stakeholders' views shape the development of the standards; to identify the factors influencing the Board's final decisions regarding the standards; and to critically review relevant literature. The issues addressed by the research are not clear-cut but complex and relative involving views of diverse groups of people, representing value judgements and perceptions. They will require conceptual analyses. The methodology chosen for the study is qualitative research, with quantitative elements. To obtain answers to the research questions, the following methods will be used: 1) participant observation; 2) documentary analysis; 3) consultations on the draft standards with key stakeholders; and 4) semi-structured individual and group interviews with Board officers and members, education providers and other stakeholders.

STATUS: Individual research

DATE OF RESEARCH: 1996-1998

KEYWORDS: accreditation - courses; higher education; nurse education; nurses; standards

0184

Graduate School of Education, 35 Berkeley Square, Bristol BS8 1JA
01179 289000

Shanyinde, P. Mr; *Supervisors*: Sutherland, R. Prof.; Molyneux, S. Dr

To investigate pupil-pupil scaffolding as a learning strategy using microcomputer-based laboratories in chemistry

ABSTRACT: The use of computers in science learning and teaching is the general theme of the investigation. The researcher will draw on both Piaget's and Vygotskian Perspective as a theoretical framework. The aim is to document and analyse the questions pupils ask each other while working on tasks in a computer environment (datalogging in particular). The research design will be basically qualitative and will involve observation, interviews and document analysis. The sample will be based on criteria related to computer use and maximum variation sampling, ie. categorised pupil questions and meanings.

STATUS: Individual research

DATE OF RESEARCH: 1996-continuing

KEYWORDS: chemistry; classroom communication; computer uses in education; information technology; scaffolding; science education

0185

Graduate School of Education, 35 Berkeley Square, Bristol BS8 1JA
01179 289000

Matoti, S. Mrs; *Supervisor*: Garrett, R. Dr

The roles and responsibilities of the science head of department in colleges of education in South Africa

ABSTRACT: The roles and responsibilities of heads of department in South African schools and colleges in some former education departments were not well defined. The study looks/investigates the perceptions of rectors, heads of department and lecturers about the role of the science head of department. The aim is to improve the effectiveness of the science head of department. The study is confined to the Eastern Province of the Republic of South Africa. All twenty colleges in the province were sampled. Science heads of department (biology, physical science, general science and agricultural science) and lecturers and rectors and vice-rectors were used (sample approximately 100). Methods of collecting data include: postal questionnaires and indepth semi-structured interviews.

STATUS: Individual research

DATE OF RESEARCH: 1995-1997

KEYWORDS: department heads; science education; south africa #@

0186

Graduate School of Education, 35 Berkeley Square, Bristol BS8 1JA
01179 289000

Greenfield, C. Dr; *Supervisor*: John, P. Mr

Teaching and learning citizenship in an English comprehensive school

ABSTRACT: While much has been written on the theory and practice of education for citizenship, there appears to be relatively little published work on the outcomes of this aspect of education. After a review of the historical context of education for citizenship, and a review of the relevant literature, the dissertation describes a small ethnographic research project. The project was located in a typical English comprehensive school and aimed at describing education for citizenship from three distinct perspectives: a) the policies and aims drawn up by the school as an organisation; b) the views and practice of teachers; and c) the experience and opinions of pupils. The study found that whilst there was coherence in the central policies of the school, this clarity was lost mainly through the inconsistent interpretation and implementation of these policies by teachers. The resulting picture of citizenship attitudes being transmitted to pupils is therefore somewhat confused. Nonetheless the research indicates a weak conception of community responsibilities amongst 13-year-olds, and a generally narrow world view. The dissertation concludes by offering some suggestions as to how the research project could have been strengthened, and also how the practice of education for citizenship at the school in question could be made more effective.

PUBLISHED MATERIAL: GREENFIELD, C.J. (1993). 'Public-spirited pieces of paper', Education, Vol 182, No 10, pp.170-171. ; GREENFIELD, C.J. (1995). 'Citizenship, school and the spirit', Friends Quarterly, Vol 28, No 5, pp.218-222. ; JOHN, P. & GREENFIELD, C. (1996). 'Tomorrow's citizens'. In: TIMMER, V. & VELDHUIS, R. (Eds). Political education - towards a European democracy. Netherlands: Institute for Public Policy/ Germany: Bundeszentrale fur politische bildung.

STATUS: Individual research

DATE OF RESEARCH: 1992-1997

KEYWORDS: citizenship education; moral education; secondary education; values education

0187

Graduate School of Education, 35 Berkeley Square, Bristol BS8 1JA
01179 289000

Yadeta, M. Mr; *Supervisor*: Hoyle, E. Prof.

Educational accountability in Ethiopia

ABSTRACT: A change from a highly centralised Marxist System to a decentralised democratic system requires re-drawing of the line of accountability relationships. Drawing on the perceptions of 10 policy architects, 8 principals and 24 senior secondary school teachers, as well as one group of a parents' committee, the research intends to identify the existing and potential modes of accountability in the Ethiopian education system with the aim of making realistic recommendations for accountability policy to improve the quality of educational provision. In addition to the interviews with the above mentioned groups, the research will review and analyse educational policy documents relevant to accountability. Because of its potential for researching into the meaning subjects give to the realities in their context, a qualitative approach is employed.

STATUS: Individual research

DATE OF RESEARCH: 1996-1998

KEYWORDS: accountability; educational policy; ethiopia

0188

Graduate School of Education, 35 Berkeley Square, Bristol BS8 1JA
01179 289000

Lau, P. Mr; *Supervisor*: Furlong, J. Prof.

Quality teaching in Personal, Social and Moral Education: a study of teacher professional learning

ABSTRACT: The main aim of the study is to investigate the natural learning processes of teachers after they have been exposed to an inservice training programme. An attempt is made in this study to determine how teachers' learning takes place and what produces successful learning. In this particular study, the researcher will be engaged in working with a group of teachers to examine what goes on after they are exposed to a programme of training in pedagogy. A form of action research is involved in this process. Participants in this study will actively engage themselves in self-examination of how they learn to improve the quality of their teaching in the curriculum area of Personal Social and Moral Education (PSME). The researcher will facilitate the reflective processes. The study is carried out within the framework of a qualitative approach. Essentially, open-ended interviews will be carried out with the subjects to elicit their perceptions and views concerning their learning. The purpose is to elicit personal narratives or stories about concrete events and experiences. It involves an attempt to describe the lived experiences of a group of secondary school teachers who are actively engaged in improving their practice in the curriculum area of PSME. Six teachers will be tracked for a period of two academic terms in order to determine the learning processes they go through in planning a course on PSME and turning the curriculum into lessons and learning activities.

STATUS: Individual research

DATE OF RESEARCH: 1996-1998

KEYWORDS: inservice teacher education; learning; moral education; personal and social education; teacher development; teacher effectiveness

0189

Graduate School of Education, 35 Berkeley Square, Bristol BS8 1JA
01179 289000

Wells, J. Mr; *Supervisor*: John, P. Dr

Factors influencing the choice of post-registration health and nursing degrees and their utility in professional practice

ABSTRACT: The large increase in availability of post-registration degrees for nurses over the last few years has led to nurses having to make a choice about which, if any, degree to take. The research investigates the influences that may be brought to bear and that result in the choice of course. The research sample is drawn from nurses taking two alternative degrees in one institution, a BSc (Hons) in Nursing Studies and a BSc (Hons) in Health Studies. Both degrees are modular with a large choice of modules on each course, many of which are common to both. The Nursing Studies degree is more focal than the wider 'generic' Health Studies degree. The latter is chosen by twice as many as the former. The research population consists of all who graduated in 1995 and 1996 and all students registered in December 1996 from/on both courses. The first, quantitative element of the research determines the personal and professional characteristics and enables the population to be categorised into groups and sub-groups. The data are dervied from the institution's database, supplemented by a postal questionnaire. This data will establish profiles and distinguish variations of interest and enable a selection of subjects to be made for the qualitative element of the research. The second and main element of the research will be qualitative and will consist of indepth interviews of a selective sample of 30-40 individuals chosen to 'represent' clearly distinguishable sub-groups identified from the quantitative element. The research aims to identify and understand differences in the influences of degree choice and the extent to which the choices of course and modules relate to the individuals' professional practice.

STATUS: Individual research

DATE OF RESEARCH: 1996-1997

KEYWORDS: degrees – academic; nurse education; nurses

0190

Graduate School of Education, 35 Berkeley Square, Bristol BS8 1JA
01179 289000

Newton, S. Mr; *Supervisor*: Osborn, A. Dr

An investigation of the factors which influence the GCSE performance of secondary school pupils

ABSTRACT: A group of 600 Year 9 pupils (in 6 schools on the edge of a large city) were tested in 1994 using: a) National Curriculum tests in English, mathematics and science; and b) cognitive ability tests (CAT) - verbal and non-verbal. The peformance of each of these pupils in GCSE examinations in 1996 was recorded for each pupil. Other data was recorded - gender, ethnicity, attendance in Years 10 and 11, eligibility for free school meals, and a variety of other indicators of socio-economic status (based upon postal code data). A statistical analysis was carried out (using minitab) to determine which factors were the most significant in predicting a pupil's GCSE performance. Preliminary results suggest that one of the most powerful predictors of GCSE performance is the CAT verbal test result. Once that has been taken into account, socio-economic data add little. Standard assessment tasks (SATs) data is of limited use. SATs mathematics and science results have some value in prediction, whilst SATs English results appeared to have no value - even in predicting GCSE English results.

STATUS: Individual research

DATE OF RESEARCH: 1994-1998

KEYWORDS: academic achievement; achievement; assessment; examination results; general certificate of education; performance factors; secondary education; secondary school pupils; standard assessment tasks; tasks and tests; test results

0191

Graduate School of Education, 35 Berkeley Square, Bristol BS8 1JA
01179 289000

Matoti, S. Dr; *Supervisor*: McMahon, A. Ms

Teacher evaluation in the Eastern Cape Province of South Africa: a review of policy and practice in the primary school sector (1985-1995)

ABSTRACT: This study examined the teacher perceptions of the policy and practice of teacher evaluation in primary schools in the Eastern Cape Province of South Africa between 1985 and 1995. It focused on the formal evaluation of teachers by heads of department, deputy principals, principals and school inspectors. The final aim of the study was to make proposals, in the light of the findings of research, for a teacher evaluation scheme that would be acceptable to the teachers and which would contribute to the restoration and maintenance of the culture of teaching and learning. The researcher's basic assumption was that teachers were not opposed to teacher evaluation per se but to the way in which it was done. The other assumptions were that teachers were likely to find evaluation conducted within the school (internal evaluation) more acceptable than that done by inspectors (external evaluation), and that the link between teacher evaluation and inservice support to teachers was tenuous and weak. The research was conducted by a survey questionnaire on a sample of 145 teachers, 21 heads of department and deputy principals and 8 inspectors, and by interviews with 12 principals, 3 deputy principals, 5 teachers, 3 inspectors and 2 representatives of teacher organisations, all selected from a cross-section of schools according to former departments of education. Questionnaires and interviews were used to collect data. The samples were drawn from the Northern Region (Queenstown), the biggest region in the Eastern Cape. The practices and schemes of teacher evaluation were examined in the light of the characteristics of what research in other countries has shown to be effective teacher evaluation schemes. The research results showed that around 95% of the respondents saw teacher evaluation as necessary. The following are the weaknesses they pointed out in the scheme that is still in use: 1) Evaluators did not always give teachers feedback on their peformance; did not always give them an opportunity to express their views on the evaluation; and did not always follow up on the evaluations. 2) Evaluations were infrequent and limited mainly to classroom observation. 3) The evaluation criteria were not always made explicit. Although a Chi square test showed no significant differences in the perception of teachers across departments, the actual percentages did show some difference. The results showed that the link between teacher evaluation and inservice training was weak. They showed that the evaluation model that was followed was the control model. The following are the recommendations: 1) A new system of teacher evaluation that is a school-based and continuous process. 2) Strong resource support for teacher evaluation and teacher development. 3) Special training for teacher evaluators. 4) Involvement of teachers in evaluation and use of evaluation by teams in the case of evaluation for merit pay and promotion.

STATUS: Individual research

DATE OF RESEARCH: 1994-1997

KEYWORDS: south africa; teacher evaluation

0192

Graduate School of Education, 35 Berkeley Square, Bristol BS8 1JA
01179 289000

Obeidat, M. Mr; *Supervisor*: Furlong, J. Prof.

An evaluation of an English as a foreign language (EFL) inservice training programme in Jordan

ABSTRACT: This research aims at investigating the English as a Foreign Language (EFL) teachers' views on certain practical and pedagogical issues related to the programme. It also aims at examining whether or not the teachers' views about the methods of training activities match their classroom performance. The instruments and samples used are: 1) questionnaires/closed and open-ended questions (n=100); 2) interviews (n=12); 3) classroom observation (n=6) using notes and events as indicatives of actual classroom practices. Each teacher was observed during five successive sessions. @#Status:#@ Individual research

Date of Research: 1994-1997

KEYWORDS: english - second language; jordan; programme evaluation; second language teaching

0193

Graduate School of Education, 35 Berkeley Square, Bristol BS8 1JA
01179 289000

Woodd, M. Ms; *Supervisor*: John, P. Mr

Learning to leap from a peer: a qualitative case study of mentoring practice in the induction of new teachers in further education

ABSTRACT: The study was conducted in a large mixed institution, where a mentoring scheme was set up to help the induction of over 60 new staff. The aims of the study were to determine the styles of mentoring practice applicable to mentors of new staff, in order to facilitate a comprehensive and acceptable training programme for both mentors and mentees, which will lead to continuing professional development. The need to manage this change in practice was recognised, as was the intention of introducing full scale indepth mentoring rather than the common practice of 'buddying'.

The methodological design uses a questionnaire to identify scheme participants, who will take part in qualitative interviews, in order to explore key issues of understanding and practice in depth. The place of case study is argued from the position of the writer who is a mentor and hence, a participant observer in the study. Focus groups are used to explore 'group think' around the issues and to triangulate the data. This is presented through data displays to examine key themes which emerge from the data analysis. New definitions and models of mentoring are presented, together with a range of mentoring styles which could apply. Recommendations for improving practice within the specific context are made, and issues such as the possibility of a culture change through mentoring are recognised. Methodological constructs are examined to explore the context in which the qualitative data collection is made, and recommendations for future research are made.

STATUS: Individual research

DATE OF RESEARCH: 1995-1997

KEYWORDS: **colleges of further education; further education; further education teachers; mentors; teacher induction; teaching profession**

0194

Graduate School of Education, 35 Berkeley Square, Bristol BS8 1JA
01179 289000

Sutherland, R. Prof.; Molyneux, S. Dr

Mathematical competencies of GNVQ science students: the role of computers

ABSTRACT: The research has three main aims: 1) characterise the mathematical practices of General National Vocational Qualification (GNVQ) science students; 2) to investigate the advantages and disadvantages of the GNVQ approach to mathematics; 3) to study the role of computers in providing support for students' mathematical practices.

STATUS: Sponsored project

SOURCE OF GRANT: Leverhulme Trust £68,980

DATE OF RESEARCH: 1995-1997

KEYWORDS: **computer uses in education; general national vocational qualifications; information technology; mathematics skills; science education**

0195

Graduate School of Education, 35 Berkeley Square, Bristol BS8 1JA
01179 2789000

Power, S. Dr; Clark, A. Ms

The right to know - parents and school reports: research and information in State education (RISE)

ABSTRACT: The research will explore the accessibility and appropriateness of school-parent reporting procedures in the light of recent government policy. Against the backdrop of a national survey, the research will investigate perceptions of and reactions to school reports across different communities of parents within selected case study secondary schools. It will draw on these various experiences to identify and disseminate examples of good practice.

STATUS: Sponsored project

SOURCE OF GRANT: Nuffield Foundation £29,802

DATE OF RESEARCH: 1996-1997

KEYWORDS: **parent participation; parent school relationship; school reports; secondary education**

0196

Graduate School of Education, 35 Berkeley Square, Bristol BS8 1JA
01179 289000

Johnson, D. Dr; Broadfoot, P. Prof. ; Hayter, J. Mr

Assessing the quality of learning and teaching in developing countries

ABSTRACT: This study seeks to place teachers' assessments of children's learning at the centre of the teaching and learning process. Through a broadly participatory methodology, a framework for classroom-based assessments and a system for collecting evidence of primary school children's work is being developed in Malawi and Sri Lanka. Through an analysis of children's work in languages (English and national languages) and mathematics, the study will contribute to our understanding of children's learning in developing countries. Further, by involving teachers in the process of task setting and assessment, the study will enhance their capacity to make explicit and principled judgements of children's achievements and to use the knowledge derived from assessments to inform their teaching.

STATUS: Sponsored project

SOURCE OF GRANT: Overseas Development Administration Research Scheme £81,000

DATE OF RESEARCH: 1995-1997

KEYWORDS: **assessment; developing countries; development education; learning; malawi; primary education; sri lanka**

0197

Graduate School of Education, 35 Berkeley Square, Bristol BS8 1JA
01179 289000

Hill, T. Mr; Oldroyd, D. Mr; Hall, V. Dr

Development of structured learning materials for award-bearing courses in primary school management for international use

ABSTRACT: The aims of the research are to: 1) expand the Graduate School of Education's provision of award-bearing courses in educational management for primary schools in the international market by means of structured learning, workplace-based self-development units, specially designed for developing countries; and 2) design two units with the 'Management Self-development for Primary Schools - International Edition' as the basis for an indigenised study package for use in current and future in-country Graduate School of Education courses.

STATUS: Sponsored project

SOURCE OF GRANT: Bristol University £10,000

DATE OF RESEARCH: 1996-1998

KEYWORDS: **developing countries; educational administration; educational materials; international educational exchange; management in education; material development; primary education**

0198

Graduate School of Education, 35 Berkeley Square, Bristol BS8 1JA
01179 289000

Shareef, A. Mr; *Supervisor*: Hoyle, E. Prof.

Stakeholder perspectives on improving the quality of education in the Maldive Islands

ABSTRACT: The study is aimed at providing some research guidance and grounding to quality improvement effects in education in the Maldives, as well as developing some strategies for use in this effort. Mostly qualitative methods are being used. Data has been collected and analysed, but conclusions have not yet been reached.

STATUS: Individual research

DATE OF RESEARCH: 1994-1997

KEYWORDS: **educational quality; maldives**

0199

Graduate School of Education, 35 Berkeley Square, Bristol BS8 1JA
01179 289000

Hall, V. Dr

Workplace-based Supported Individual Study (SIS) Units and dissertation research in advanced study courses

ABSTRACT: The project will develop and pilot an approach to tutoring distance learners, both overseas and in the UK, engaged in workplace-based investigation and research as part of continuing professional development (CPD) for accreditation in mixed-mode advanced study courses from certificate to doctoral levels. It will also produce a tutors' guide and students' support package to enhance the implementation of Supported Individual Study (SIS) units and dissertation research by students who are distant from their tutors and rely on the post, e-mail, exchange of tape-recorded commentaries and telephone tutoring.

STATUS: Sponsored project

SOURCE OF GRANT: Higher Education Funding Council for England £11,500

DATE OF RESEARCH: 1996-1997

KEYWORDS: **dissertations; distance education; independent study; nontraditional education; professional continuing education; teaching methods; work based learning**

0200

Graduate School of Education, 35 Berkeley Square, Bristol BS8 1JA
01179 289000

Kington, A. Miss ; *Supervisors*: Osborn, M. Dr; Pollard, A. Prof.

Teacher-pupil relationships at National Curriculum key stage 2: two case studies

ABSTRACT: This study aims to examine teacher-pupil relationships in the primary school, focusing specifically on National Curriculum key stage 2 children, and has concentrated on classes at the top and bottom of this age range. It looks at the relationship of the class teacher with the pupils and pays particular attention to possible variations in this relationship, such as age, gender, social class and culture. The objective of this study is to throw light on this area by undertaking: 1) a critical scrutiny of the context within which the study is placed; 2) an examination of the theories of symbolic interactionism, teacher-pupil relationships, and teacher and pupil expectation and typification; 3) an analysis of data gathered from practising teachers and pupils on their perceptions of classroom relationships. These representations of the teacher-pupil relationship will be linked with the theoretical analysis to make an informed judgement about the possible implications of teacher-pupil relationships. The analysis will focus on: 1) What types of relationships exist in the primary school? 2) What is it about these relationships that may produce more effective learning? 3) How can relationships effectively benefit the child's educational development? 4) How do the expectations of the teacher and pupils affect the teacher-pupil relationship? 5) Are there certain variables that can affect the relationship, such as age, gender, social class and culture? The research design consists of mainly qualitative research instruments inspired by the models of the Primary Assessment, Curriculum and Assessment (PACE) Study (Pollard et al, 1994). There will be a 3 week pilot study in one school to test out all research instruments. The main study will involve: 1) school documents, e.g. prospectus, school policies, class information; 2) field notes, taken at beginning and end of each term in each of the target classrooms; 3) systematic observations of each target child; 4) pupil diaries completed by each target child over 3 terms; 5) interviews with each target teacher; 6) interviews with each target child; and 7) follow-up interviews with each target teacher. The sample consisted of 2 schools in constrasting socio-economic areas. Within each school, research was with a Year 3 and a Year 6 class (therefore, 2 teachers in each school) and targeted 8 children (4 girls and 4 boys) in each class. This gave a contrast in age range and social class, and also provided another relevant question. Does the teacher-pupil relationship change from key stage 1 - key stage 2, and from primary school to secondary school?

STATUS: Individual research

DATE OF RESEARCH: 1994-continuing

KEYWORDS: **key stage 2; primary education; primary school pupils; teacher pupil relationship**

0201

Graduate School of Education, 35 Berkeley Square, Bristol BS8 1JA 01179 289000

Wilson, K. Ms; *Supervisor*: Grant, M. Dr

Participation within the health promoting school award scheme in Somerset

ABSTRACT: The researcher is an advisory teacher for health related education, supporting schools involved in Somerset's Health Promoting School Award project. The purpose behind this PhD study is to enable the researcher to be more effective in her work and therefore improve support for these schools. A literary review will explore aspects of school health promotion, and the introduction of such an initiative into a school. The investigation will draw on the researcher's experience of working with over 40 schools, which have taken part to date. Fieldwork will be in 2 phases, each phase based in 1 primary and 1 secondary school. The first phase (completed in July 1996) involved semi-structured interviews with the health education coordinator, headteacher and a group of students, in both schools, who had completed the award. This data was triangulated against documentary evidence obtained from the schools, and the researchers' own perceptions of what happened in the schools. The investigations were approached in a broadly phenomenological fashion, with the findings influencing the content and focus of future fieldwork. The second phase (September 1996-December 1997) will repeat this fieldwork, narrowing the focus, but extending the number of interviewees within each school. There will be more observations of meetings and work, relating to the award scheme, as it takes place in the classroom or elsewhere in school. It is hoped that the data and a diary of how the researcher has changed her professional practice will be informative to other colleagues in similar roles, and stimulate reflection on their own work.

STATUS: Individual research

DATE OF RESEARCH: 1995-continuing

KEYWORDS: **health education; health promoting schools; health promotion; primary education; secondary education**

0202

Graduate School of Education, 35 Berkeley Square, Bristol BS8 1JA
01179 289000

Simmonds, M. Mrs; *Supervisors*: Gillibrand, E. Mrs ; Meadows, S. Dr

Getting a life: a study of the coping strategies and support needs of young people in Year 11

ABSTRACT: This study is intended to explore the concerns and coping strategies of young people in Year 11, who are facing public examinations and the end of compulsory schooling. The participants are drawn from a part of England designated an area of rural deprivation. Pupils in one tutor group from each of 3 state schools, and individuals from independent schools, have been interviewed during each term of Year 11, a cycle which is currently being repeated with a new cohort. The methods are drawn from qualitative research, in particular unstructured and semi-structured interviews with individuals and small groups, and the approach collaborative. The lifestyles of the particpants and the concept of postponed gratification seem to be relevant as do health issues. The interviews have also raised ethical questions to do with confidentiality. It is hoped that a grounded and rich picture will emerge which will have implications for professionals working with adolescents.

STATUS: Individual research

DATE OF RESEARCH: 1994-1998

KEYWORDS: **adolescent attitudes; adolescents; coping; life style; school leavers; secondary education; secondary school pupils; stress - psychological; youth**

0203

Graduate School of Education, 35 Berkeley Square, Bristol BS8 1JA
01179 289000

Smith, B. Dr

An evaluation of Norwegian aid to education in Pakistan

ABSTRACT: An evaluation of the impact at classroom level of 5 educational projects in Pakistan funded by Norwegian Aid to Education in Pakistan (NORAD). The initiatives to be evaluated are concerned with: 1) teacher education by distance learning; 2) free textbooks for girls; 3) scholarships for girls (to encourage enrolment); 4) supply of annotated textbooks to primary school teachers; 5) supply of supplementary readers to primary schools; 6) development of a magazine for teachers. From the research findings it is expected that future aid projects will be designed and implemented more effectively.

STATUS: Sponsored project

SOURCE OF GRANT: Norwegian Aid to International Development (NORAD) £150,000

DATE OF RESEARCH: 1996-1997

KEYWORDS: **developing countries; development aid; development education; norway; pakistan; programme evaluation**

0204

Graduate School of Education, 35 Berkeley Square, Bristol BS8 1JA
01179 289000

Pollard, A. Prof.; Broadfoot, P. Prof.; Osborn, M. Dr

Primary assessment, curriculum and experience (PACE): phase 3

ABSTRACT: This project is the final part of a unique, longitudinal study of teacher and pupil experiences and practices in primary schools in England. It is concerned with teachers' conceptions of professionalism and with pupil perspectives of primary schooling, in the context of observed classroom behaviour and practices related to curriculum, pedagogy and assessment. Additionally, this analysis will be related to the social contexts of government policies over the period of study since 1989, thus enabling a consideration of both intended and unintended consequences and associated processes of school and classroom mediation.

Published Material BROADFOOT, P., MCNESS, E., POLLARD, A., OSBORN, M. & TRIGGS, P. (1996). 'It's no use to anyone: perspectives on the 1996 key stage 2 SATS'. In: PACE Working Paper No 24. Paper presented at the British Educational Research Association Annual Conference, Lancaster University, 12-15 September 1996. ; BROADFOOT, P., MCNESS, E., POLLARD, A., OSBORN, M. & TRIGGS, P. (1996). 'Assessment discourse: a study of Year 4 and Year 6 teachers'. In: PACE Working Paper No 25. Paper presented at the British Educational Research Association Annual Conference, Lancaster University, 12-15 September 1996. ; BROADFOOT, P., MCNESS, E., POLLARD, A., OSBORN, M. & TRIGGS, P. (1996). 'Statutory teacher assessment: a teacher's dilemma'. In: PACE Working Paper No 26. Paper presented at the British Educational Research Association Annual Conference, Lancaster University, 12-15 September 1996. ; OSBORN, M., CROLL, P., BROADFOOT, P., POLLARD, A., MCNESS, E. & TRIGGS, P. (1997). 'Policy into practice and practice into policy: creative mediation in the primary classroom'. In: HELSBY, G. & MCCULLOCH, G. (Eds). Teachers and the National Curriculum. London: Cassell.

STATUS: Sponsored project

SOURCE OF GRANT: Economic and Social Research Council £200,000

DATE OF RESEARCH: 1995-1997

KEYWORDS: **assessment; curriculum development; national curriculum; primary education; primary school pupils; primary school teachers; teaching methods**

0205

Graduate School of Education, 35 Berkeley Square, Bristol BS8 1JA
01179 289000

Kapsalis, G. Mr; *Supervisors*: Pollard, A. Prof.; Garrett, R. Dr

Multigrade and non-multigrade Greek primary schools: the quality of pupils' learning experiences

ABSTRACT: Recent statistics have shown that the majority (61-88%) of primary schools in Greece are small, in the sense that at least 2 grades have to be combined in the same classroom. Low birth rates and the rapid urbanisation of the last decades are among the reasons being given for the lack of sufficient number of pupils. Although the majority of schools are small, yet no special provision has been made to accommodate their needs, since decisions concerning the curriculum, materials and the content of subjects, are based on the realities and necessities of big urban schools, where combination of grades is non-existent. Therefore, among the issues that need to be examined are: 1) The problems small multigrade schools confront. 2) The content of the curriculum that is prescribed for teachers. 3) The amount and type of pupils' task engagement in both multigrade and non-multigrade primary schools. 4) The quality of pupils' learning experiences in both institutions. The methodology followed for this research will be based on 2 methods: 1) questionnaires will be delivered to teachers of both multigrade and non-multigrade schools; and 2) classroom observation of a representative sample of children in both types of schools will take place. Special attention will be given to select a representative sample of schools from both the mainland and the islands. The major outcomes of this research will be: 1) To describe the existing situation in both types of schools. 2) To identify the existing problems. 3) To examine pupils' learning experiences in multigrade and non-multigrade Greek primary schools and suggest lessons that can be learnt from both types of schools.

STATUS: Individual research

DATE OF RESEARCH: 1996-continuing

KEYWORDS: **greece; primary education; small schools**

0206

Graduate School of Education, 35 Berkeley Square, Bristol BS8 1JA
01179 289000

Counsell, C. Ms; *Supervisors*: Furlong, J. Prof.; John, P. Mr

Investigating history teachers' understandings of progression in pupils' learning

ABSTRACT: The research aims to investigate secondary school history teachers' implicit understandings of progression in pupils' learning of history by examining the ways in which teachers' perspectives on progression relate to their practice. School history has been heavily influenced by explicit, received models of progression. Earlier models were challenged in the 1970s by notions less related to knowledge and more related to the methods by which that knowledge can be acquired. Some emphasis upon historical processes (e.g. enquiry) and historical concepts (e.g. cause, consequence) has now become the accepted norm. This has generated a research tradition which attempts to indicate paths of progression by exploring children's ideas about historical concepts and evidence. This 'skills' approach has been enormously influential. The whole structure of the 1991 National Curriculum for history was deemed to embody progress in concepts and skills. Links with knowledge or 'content' were stressed but the exact relationship with skills was left obscure. History teachers were left to implement the model. Their response was illuminating. The skill-centred 10-level structure for history was judged frustratingly artificial and impossible to implement without becoming mechanistic and reductionist. In 1995 the National Curriculum was further revised, yet difficulties continue because 2 central problems are unresolved: 1) Does an hierarchy of 'skill' have any validity in history? and 2) How can teachers conceptualise the relationship between 'knowledge' and 'skill'? Current research into progression attempts to address these issues by constructing models of 'children's ideas' and testing these on pupils. It seeks yet more valid models of 'children's understanding', using quasi-experimental approaches outside of the normal classroom setting. Although this may prove to be helpful in some ways, it does not relate to how teachers think and act. The methodology is external to what history teachers habitually do in helping pupils to 'get better' at history. It is very likely that history teachers have rich, well-developed notions of progression which they rarely articulate as such. The proposed research will therefore investigate the mix of subject-based factors and pedagogical criteria which teachers call up and define when structuring programmes of learning. It will examine the ways in which teachers' models of progression manifest themselves at the level of their practice and identify any dissonance which exists between their 'theories-in-use', 'espoused theories' and received models of progression. The study uses 3 types of data - lesson observation, open-ended interviews and planning documentation. The research will utilise a methodology in which short sequences of consecutive lessons (typically 2) are videoed. The videoed material is analysed in its own right, and also used as cues in open-ended follow-up interviews so as to uncover the implicit links which teachers secure with prior and future learning. This concrete, small-scale focus has so far proved successful as a way of helping teachers to articulate, and to characterise in their own terms, their choice and sequence of detailed subject matter. This is important if the study is to illuminate perspectives which may be tacit or embedded at the level of practice.

STATUS: Individual research

DATE OF RESEARCH: 1996-continuing

KEYWORDS: **history; history teachers; learning; secondary education; teaching methods**

0207

Graduate School of Education, 35 Berkeley Square, Bristol BS8 1JA
01179 289000

Simpson, I. Mr; *Supervisor*: Broadfoot, P. Prof.

German teacher assessment

ABSTRACT: Recent focus on teacher assessment in Britain has led the researcher to examine the German experience of teacher assessment in an (unpublished) MSc dissertation at Oxford University Department of Educational Studies. The aim of the current research is to examine the German teacher assessment system in detail. It is hoped that some of the lessons learned by German research into teacher assessment can be brought into the discussion on the subject in England and Wales.

STATUS: Individual research

DATE OF RESEARCH: 1996-continuing

KEYWORDS: **assessment; assessment by teachers; comparative education; germany**

0208

Graduate School of Education, 35 Berkeley Square, Bristol BS8 1JA
01179 289000

Cromey-Hawke, N. Mr; *Supervisor*: Furlong, J. Prof.

Effects of national inspection on school improvement: 1994-99 the Office for Standards in Education's (OFSTED) first cycle

ABSTRACT: The project will investigate the impact of the first cycle of the Office for Standards in Education (OFSTED) inspections on a cross-section of secondary schools, with particular emphasis on: 1) their influence on definitions and perceptions of performance at teacher, faculty and whole-school levels; 2) the response of school senior and middle managers to the inspection report in their re-formulation of school development plans; 3) the extent to which teachers/managers have a shared understanding (or an increased understanding) of 'quality' in education as a result of the inspection itself and subsequent changes in the establishment of school policies. The research is based on the following rationale and questions: 1) Public and professional awareness of issues of 'quality' in education have been raised during the last decade. 2) Schools have become more accountable through a variety of new structures and processes, notably a national inspection system based upon a throughput model. 3) School effectiveness studies are now giving a far clearer picture of the factors and forces that contribute towards what constitutes 'quality' and how it can be defined and assessed. 4) What relationship this new inspection system has to such thinking, and to the achievement of that quality is, however, uncertain. 5) Strong political agendas have existed overtly or, just as importantly perhaps, been suspected - this has contributed to a climate of uncertainty and suspicion amongst differing sections of the educational world. The initial outcomes of a pilot M.Ed study were in response to the inspections themselves. Redefinition of the aims and targeting of a smaller sample is now intended, to investigate a range of questions such as: 1) What evidence is there of how schools respond to an imposed agenda for change, such as the OFSTED process provides? 2) What strategies for the management of change have been found most useful following such 'benchmarking'? 3) Has the initial empowerment felt in particular by middle managers increased or drifted away once the 'threat' of inspection has gone? 4) Has the much publicised 'trauma' of inspection had long-term effects? 5) How has school development planning responded to the challenges and how has inspection impacted upon internal review and development procedures? Together these form the main focus: 1) Have these inspections contributed to genuine school development? 2) Have they either provoked or assisted in a wider sense of organic growth in schools? 3) If not, if OFSTED is seen by schools as merely an end in itself, what then are teachers', managers' and governors' perceptions of school development and improvement? What impact has the OFSTED inspection had over a period of 6 years in contributing to teachers' own learning attitudes and the improvement (or not) of the schools? It is intended to target 20 schools from the pilot study. The selection criteria will be: a) willingness to contribute; b) key stages 3 and 4; c) a balance of school type/size, single sex and co-educational and geographical distribution (minimum 3 local education authorities) + Grant Maintained Schools); d) those which the pilot revealed had already acted upon their inspection reports by the time of the pilot surveying (6 months post-inspection); and e) those which the pilot revealed as being dissatisfied with OFSTED's findings. Questionnaire based investigation of 1) their progress in meeting OFSTED's original areas for development, and 2) any other school improvement action, will be made of these 20 schools over the academic year 1995/96. This target group will then be refined to a sub-sample of 10 schools, using the same criteria and balance as the original 20, but also dependent on their questionnaire responses. This sub-sample will form case studies to be investigated throughout 1996/97. A second questionnaire surveying the 20 school target group in 1997/98 and a further round of case study visits of the 10 school sub-group in 1998/99 will take place. From 1997 the composition of the 20 school target group will remain open to the influence of change, in particular being responsive to the reinspection of any of the original pilot cohort of schools. The likelihood that the existence and relevance of the original OFSTED inspection model may have changed is acknowledged and adds another potential dimension, i.e. how do OFSTED's and schools' perceptions of school improvement now relate to each other?

STATUS:#@ Individual research

DATE OF RESEARCH: 1995-continuing

KEYWORDS: **educational quality; inspection; inspectors - of schools; ofsted; school development planning; school effectiveness; school improvement**

0209

Graduate School of Education, 35 Berkeley Square, Bristol BS8 1JA
01179 289000

Gilchrist, I. Mr; *Supervisor*: Webster, A. Dr

The professional judgement of headteachers

ABSTRACT: The study will concentrate on the decision-making characteristics and processes of these professional thinkers in secondary schools and will focus on the individual psychological processes involved, together with organisational issues and how these inter-relate. The research will analyse the cognitive processes that headteachers demonstrate with the aim of constructing a conceptualised model of headteachers' professional judgement. At an organisational level, headteachers' decisions will be examined in their institutional setting. Particular attention will be paid to the centrality and influence that headteachers' judgements are assumed to have on the growth, development and effectiveness of their institutions, both in organisational and human terms.

STATUS: Individual research

DATE OF RESEARCH: 1996-continuing

KEYWORDS: **decision making; head teachers; judgment; teaching profession**

0210

Graduate School of Education, 35 Berkeley Square, Bristol BS8 1JA
01179 289000

Planel, C. Ms; *Supervisors*: Broadfoot, P. Prof.; Osborn, M. Dr

A comparative ethnographic study of pupil perceptions in English and French primary schools

ABSTRACT: The research explores educational and cultural values as revealed by pupil perceptions in 2 contrasting educational systems. National cultural values in education needed first to be identified before positing their effects on children's learning. Theoretically the study follows an interpretevist and social constructivist framework. The study has been taken up and expanded into an Economic and Social Research Council (ESRC) funded project (R000235960) Quality and Experience of Schooling Transnationally (QUEST). The sample consisted of 4 primary schools, 2 English schools were socio-economically matched from 2 French schools. Two classes from each of these schools were observed for a total of 9 weeks, the pupil perceptions were gathered from 240 children who were interviewed in groups of 2 or 3 children. The study has shown how children interpret pedagogy through their cultural values, that it is cultural values which underpin educational processes. The more authoritarian pedagogy and emphasis on rigour and method in learning of the French system was made meaningful to French pupils because they were more extrinsically motivated, they had a clearer view of the role of education in their careers, and they were clearer about how to achieve educational goals. French pupil culture included a stronger work ethic and an assumption that effort was more important than ability. @#Published Material:#@ PLANEL, C. (1996). 'Children's experience of learning', EERA Bulletin, Vol 2, No 1, pp.13-20. ; PLANEL, C. 'National cultural values and their role in learning: a comparative ethnographic study of state primary schooling in England and in France', Comparative Education. (in press).

STATUS: Individual research

DATE OF RESEARCH: 1992-continuing

KEYWORDS: **comparative education; educational experience; france; primary education; primary school pupils; pupil attitudes**

0211

Graduate School of Education, 35 Berkeley Square, Bristol BS8 1JA
01179 289000

Hean, S. Ms ; *Supervisor*: Garrett, R. Dr

Investigation of teaching strategies in science in Chile

ABSTRACT: Large differences exist between the national examination scores achieved by students in private and state schools in Chile. This study hopes to investigate factors, teaching strategies in particular, that may contribute to differences in science scores of students in secondary education. More specifically, this study hopes to compare and contrast teaching practices amongst secondary science teachers in state and private schools in Chile, compare and contrast the level of motivation of science students in these different schools, and to investigate the associations that may exist between certain teaching practices, student motivation, science achievement and school types. Samples of teachers and students of private, privately subsidised and municipal schools will be surveyed using questionnaires administered to teachers and students. The student and teacher population are from the La Serena region in Chile. Students are 14-16 years of age, presently in the second year of the first cycle of secondary education. They will write national examinations at the end of this year. The aim of these questionnaires will be to determine teaching strategies employed and the level of motivation of students. The study sample will also write standardised tests aimed at measuring their level of science achievement. The survey will be followed by a more in-depth case study analysis of a high and a low achieving school.

STATUS: Individual research

DATE OF RESEARCH: 1996-continuing

KEYWORDS: **chile; science education**

0212

Graduate School of Education, 35 Berkeley Square, Bristol BS8 1JA
01179 289000

Walker, B. Ms; *Supervisors*: Hoyle, E. Prof.; Bird, E. Dr

The impact of maternity on women teachers' employment patterns

ABSTRACT: The research aims to explore the factors affecting individual women teachers' decisions regarding their patterns of employment in relation to motherhood. Under scrutiny are the teacher-mother's decision to remain in service/take a career-break after the birth of her child(ren) and the timing and mode of her return to teaching. The study focuses on both macro and micro-level influences on teacher-mothers' employment pattern decisions, including the state of teacher supply and demand and prevailing education and employment policy at the time; personal economic and career circumstances and orientations; and individuals' perception and experience of teacher and mother roles. The research design incorporates both quantitative and qualitative methods. A survey by questionnaire of women teachers drawn from a cross-section of local education authority (LEA) primary and secondary schools provides data on actual teacher-mother employment behaviour, whilst follow-up interviews with 20-30 respondents explore individuals' decision-making processes, subsequent employment patterns and satisfaction levels. (Interviewees had their first child after the 1975 legislation which led to the introduction of statutory maternity leave provision). Respondents imply their decisions regarding motherhood and employment were freely chosen. However the preliminary findings show a trend, suggesting that individual behaviours are strongly shaped by the social, economic and political context in which they are made. Continuous employment has become the norm during the last decade, though some re-negotiate their full-time contracts to part-time. An earlier generation displayed more varied patterns than the expected continuous employment or career-break, with some adopting different patterns in respect of each child

STATUS: Individual research

DATE OF RESEARCH: 1990-continuing

KEYWORDS: **career break; employment patterns; maternity; mothers; teaching profession; women teachers; womens employment**

0213

Graduate School of Education, 35 Berkeley Square, Bristol BS8 1JA
01179 289000

Mann, C. Ms; *Supervisor*: Claxton, G. Prof.

The role of meditation in education

ABSTRACT: The small scale qualitative research project that was undertaken as part of the researcher's M.Ed degree (1995) highlighted certain crucial implications which are now pursued with further research. The turning point of the 10-week research project was when the researcher introduced Guided Visualisation into the group. It achieved in a short time what the groupwork, games and exercises had only begun to do, i.e. develop the supportive group needed to form the 'scaffolding' for learning to take place. The PhD study will take this research further and test the hypothesis that Guided Visualisation and Meditation have a vital role in creating the foundation for learning to take place. Industry and sport already use the technique of visualisation to promote excellence, commitment and success. Education needs to become aware of its vital role in schools in the following ways: 1) To stimulate imagery and imagination. All research into the brain and accelerated learning attests to the vital link between imagery, emotion and the long-term memory. 'Whole' brained learning involves the logical sequential left with the artistic, intuitive, effective gestalt of the right in releasing the true potential of the brain learning how to learn, learning how to be fluid, flexible, adaptable and autonomous. 2) As a means of 'stilling'; promoting relaxation and awareness it can help children to locate their inner strengths; regain the locus of control, promote goal setting, personal responsibilities and autonomy. This time for reflection forms the platform for learning. The paradox exists that to be truly part of society and altruistic, one must first be introspective and egoistic. Children can learn to be centred; self-disciplining; setting and achieving goals. It is hoped that the research will contribute both to theory and practice and hopefully broaden our knowledge of the importance of establishing the foundations pre-requisite to learning at any time of life.

STATUS: Individual research

DATE OF RESEARCH: 1996-continuing

KEYWORDS: **attention control; imagery; learning; learning strategies; meditation; scaffolding; visualisation**

0214

Graduate School of Education, 35 Berkeley Square, Bristol BS8 1JA
01179 289000

Broadfoot, P. Prof.; Thomas, J. Ms; Hinett, K. Ms; Stanton, K. Prof.; Taylor, I. Ms

Self-assessment in professional and higher education (SAPHE)

ABSTRACT: The project is concerned with developing student learning to help them plan, monitor and evaluate their work. The researchers aim to: 1) develop, pilot and evaluate a variety of self- and peer-assessment tools; 2) explore the relationship between self-assessment techniques and course content; and 3) develop staff and student skills of self-reflection and self-monitoring. This is a collaborative project based on 4 sites and within the disciplines of Law and Social Work. The 4 sites are: the Universities of Bristol, Bath and the West of England (UWE) and Southampton Institute. The University of Bristol is the lead site with the project management based in, and drawing on the expertise of the Graduate School of Education.

STATUS: Sponsored project

SOURCE OF GRANT: Higher Education Funding Council for England

DATE OF RESEARCH: 1996-continuing

KEYWORDS: **higher education; learning processes; learning strategies; legal education – professions; professional education; reflection; self evaluation -individuals; social work; students #@**

0215

Graduate School of Education, 35 Berkeley Square, Bristol BS8 1JA
01179 289000

Brown, L. Ms; Sutherland, R. Prof.

Curriculum materials available to support courses bridging the gap between GCSE and A-level mathematics

ABSTRACT: The project will review the range of curriculum materials available in secondary schools to support courses to bridge the gap between GCSE and A-level and, if necessary, stimulate the development of additional materials.

PUBLISHED MATERIAL: WINTER, J. (1997). A study of curriculum materials available to support courses bridging the gap between GCSE and A-level mathematics. Bristol: University of Bristol, Graduate School of Education.

STATUS: Sponsored project

SOURCE OF GRANT: Qualifications and Curriculum Authority

DATE OF RESEARCH: 1996-1997

KEYWORDS: a level examinations; curriculum development; educational materials; general certificate of secondary education; mathematics education; secondary education

0216

Graduate School of Education, 35 Berkeley Square, Bristol BS8 1JA
01179 289000

Dawson, N. Dr

Education and occupational training for teenage mothers in Europe

ABSTRACT: The aim of this study is to identify education and occupational training for teenage mothers throughout Europe by identifying current practice and structures which affect access. The research is to be carried out in the UK, Italy, Ireland, Norway and Poland.

STATUS: Sponsored project

SOURCE OF GRANT: European Commission: Leonardo da Vinci programme

DATE OF RESEARCH: 1998-continuing

KEYWORDS: access to education; comparative education; europe; ireland; italy; norway; poland; teenage mothers; training; unmarried mothers; vocational education

0217

Graduate School of Education, 35 Berkeley Square, Bristol BS8 1JA
01179 289000

Huckman, L. Dr

Collaborative resource management in small primary schools

ABSTRACT: The research will identify effective resource management strategies employed by headteachers and staff of clusters of small primary schools who are sharing resources. It will aim to provide practical guidance to headteachers, governors and external agents who provide support for small schools. Interviews will be conducted with those directly involved in organising, implementing and evaluating collaborative activities to record their perspectives. Cluster meetings and joint activities involving the schools will be observed and relevant documentation will be studied. The research findings will be disseminated in articles and professional journals via a dissemination conference for academic and non-academic users.

STATUS: Sponsored project

SOURCE OF GRANT: Leverhulme Trust

DATE OF RESEARCH: 1997-1998

KEYWORDS: educational administration; institutional cooperation; primary education; school federations; shared resources and services; small schools

0218

Graduate School of Education, 35 Berkeley Square, Bristol BS8 1JA
01179 289000

Molyneux, S. Dr

Mathematical experiences and mathematical practices in the higher education science

ABSTRACT: This project will contribute to the development of a theoretical framework for understanding the ways in which learners conduct the practice of mathematics in settings where the main focus is the learning of another domain. The particular focus is to investigate the ways in which mathematics is presented to, and represented by, students following science-related courses in higher education, drawing on situated- and distributed-cognition theoretical ideas.

STATUS: Sponsored project

SOURCE OF GRANT: Economic and Social Research Council

DATE OF RESEARCH: 1998-continuing

KEYWORDS: higher education; mathematical applications; mathematics education; science education

0219

Graduate School of Education, 35 Berkeley Square, Bristol BS8 1JA
01179 289000

Mosley, J. Ms; Dawson, N. Dr; McNess, E. Ms

Research and evaluation on the impact of Circle Time

ABSTRACT: The project will describe and explain the impacts of Circle Time in primary schools in one local education authority. Specific objectives are: 1) to investigate professional perspectives on the impacts, value and constraints of introducing Circle Time in primary schools; and 2) to analyse the processes involved in Circle Time and its implementation and to locate these in terms of significant literature on personal, social and moral development within primary schools and the creation of effective learning communities.

STATUS: Sponsored project

SOURCE OF GRANT: Wiltshire Local Education Authority

DATE OF RESEARCH: 1997-1997

KEYWORDS: circle time; class organisation; classroom management; grouping -teaching purposes; primary education; teaching methods

0220

Graduate School of Education, 35 Berkeley Square, Bristol BS8 1JA
01179 289000

Osborn, A. Dr

Research and evaluation of a secondary schools inservice training education (INSET) project in Uganda

ABSTRACT: A survey has been carried out to provide baseline information about teaching practices in English, mathematics and science in Ugandan secondary schools. An inservice teacher education (INSET) programme and the establishment of Teacher Resource Centres (TRCs) has been implemented by the Centre for British Teachers (CfBT) in Uganda funded by an Overseas Development Administration grant. A quasi-experimental research design is planned to assess the impact of the INSET programme and TRCs on teacher practice. This longitudinal study will focus on changes occurring in a sample of 60 schools.

STATUS: Sponsored project

SOURCE OF GRANT: Overseas Development Administration

DATE OF RESEARCH: 1996-1997

KEYWORDS: developing countries; development education; inservice teacher education; secondary education; teacher centres; uganda

0221

Graduate School of Education, 35 Berkeley Square, Bristol BS8 1JA
01179 289000

Broadfoot, P. Prof.; Osborn, M. Dr; Planel, C. Ms

The Quality in Experiences of Schooling Transnationally (QUEST) learning strategies study: a comparative study of children's learning strategies in mathematics and language

ABSTRACT: This is a further analysis of the QUEST data focusing on the similarities and differences in pupils' learning strategies in England and France which underpin their respective profiles of performance on common assessments in mathematics and language. The findings will provide an indication of the relative strengths and weaknesses of English pupils as compared to similar pupils in a comparable European country. Furthermore, the study will illuminate the source of these strengths and weaknesses in terms of curriculum content and teachers' classroom practice, as well as the more general national cultural context.

PUBLISHED MATERIAL: OSBORN, M. (1997). 'Children's experience of schooling in England and France: some lessons from a comparative study', Education Review, Vol 11, No 1, pp.46-52. ; OSBORN, M. (1997). 'When being top is not seen as best', Times Educational Supplement, No 10, p.14, January 1997.

STATUS: Sponsored project

SOURCE OF GRANT: Qualifications and Curriculum Authority

DATE OF RESEARCH: 1997-1998

KEYWORDS: assessment; comparative education; educational experience; france; language; mathematics education; outcomes of

education; primary education; primary school pupils; pupil attitudes; teaching methods

0222

Graduate School of Education, 35 Berkeley Square, Bristol BS8 1JA
01179 289000

Osborn, M. Dr; Broadfoot, P. Prof

National culture: educational goals and pupil experience of secondary schooling: a comparative European study

ABSTRACT: The project will compare the educational experience, attitudes to schooling and approaches to learning of secondary school children in England, France and Denmark in the light of differing cultural traditions at national institutional and classroom level.

STATUS: Sponsored project

SOURCE OF GRANT: Economic and Social Research Council

DATE OF RESEARCH: 1998-continuing

KEYWORDS: **comparative education; cultural differences; denmark; educational objectives; france; pupil attitudes; pupil experience; secondary education**

0223

Graduate School of Education, 35 Berkeley Square, Bristol BS8 1JA
01179 289000

Pollard, A. Prof.; Filer, A. Dr; Furlong, J. Prof.

Identity and secondary schooling: a longitudinal ethnography of pupil careers, phase 5

ABSTRACT: This project will provide a detailed analysis of the development of secondary pupils' identities, patterns of strategic action, learning and careers in relation to social contexts and influences during adolescence. It will build on existing ethnographic data sets, analysis and theoretical models on pupils from the age of 4 in primary schools and it will culminate in an analysis of pupil performance in GCSE examinations. The research will complete a unique ethnographic record of identity development and pupil careers throughout the years of compulsory schooling and will contribute to sociological understanding of processes of social and cultural reproduction.

STATUS: Sponsored project

*SOURCE OF GRAN*t: Economic and Social Research Council

DATE OF RESEARCH: 1996-continuing

KEYWORDS: **adolescents; ethnography; examination results; general certificate of secondary education; identity; longitudinal studies; primary secondary education; pupil development; pupil performance; secondary education; secondary school pupils; socioeconomic background**

0224

Graduate School of Education, 35 Berkeley Square, Bristol BS8 1JA
01179 289000

Webster, A. Dr; Roe, J. Ms

Schooling and the visually impaired child: patterns of teaching and experience which promote competence

ABSTRACT: This study aims to analyse critical functions of play, languuae, social competence, mobility, exploration, problem solving, in relation to the patterns of socio-interactive experience observed at visually impaired children school. Main outcomes of the study will be information on which factors promote or hinder development when selecting or designing educational settings for visually impaired children.

STATUS: Sponsored project

SOURCE OF GRANT: Guide Dogs for the Blind Association

DATE OF RESEARCH: 1996-1998

KEYWORDS: **mainstreaming; peer relationship; play; pupil behaviour; social behaviour; special educational needs; verbal communication; visual impairments**

0225

Graduate School of Education, 35 Berkeley Square, Bristol BS8 1JA
01179 289000

Thomas, E. Prof.

Innovative language training and management methods

ABSTRACT: This programme is a development of the Leonardo da Vinci-funded language exchange programme LE2/3664. That programme included exchanges of language trainers from 7 Member States. This project adds visits from a further 6 countries (of which 4 are new) and builds upon the results from the first programme taking into account the experience gained from it. The aims are to: 1) improve language training in Europe by incorporating the results of recent research and development on language training through cooperation between university and non-university language training providers; 2) identify and encourage the use of innovative training methods (including self-training in the workplace, open and distance learning, hypermedia and multimedia methods) and good management practices (including effective methods of clients' needs analysis and increased access to training) to aid the development of linguistic skills as part of vocational training measures; 3) improve the quality and innovation capacity of language training systems and arrangements in the Member States, particularly in Belgium, France, Finland, Portugal and the United Kingdom, together with Switzerland; 4) promote cooperation on language skill requirements for employees in business and industry to enable the freer movement of people within the Common Market; and 5) promote the development of an open European vocational training area through the investigation of the need for and possible involvement in the development of European language qualifications. The need for two training modules for language trainers was indicated by the results of the first Programme and plans have been made by the members of the earlier partnerships to develop these; the need for further training modules will be investigated by the partners in this project.

STATUS: Sponsored project

SOURCE OF GRANT: European Union Leonardo Project £44,768

DATE OF RESEARCH: 1997-1998

KEYWORDS: **europe; language teachers; modern language studies**

0226

Graduate School of Education, 35 Berkeley Square, Bristol BS8 1JA
01179 289000

Bath Spa University College, Newton Park, Newton St Loe, Bath BA2 9BN   01225 875875

Sutherland, R. Prof.; Harries, T. Mr

A comparison of primary mathematics textbooks from 5 countries with a particular focus on the treatment of number

ABSTRACT: Mathematics textbooks are likely to reflect the school mathematics culture of a particular country. Although they can be used by teachers in a range of different ways they will emerge from beliefs about mathematics, learning and the role of the teacher. The overall aim of this project is to compare and contrast primary mathematics textbooks from England, France, Hungary, Singapore and the USA.

STATUS: Sponsored project

DATE OF RESEARCH: 1997-1998

KEYWORDS: **comparative education; france; hungary; mathematics education; numbers; primary education; singapore; textbooks; united states of america**

0227

Graduate School of Education, 35 Berkeley Square, Bristol BS8 1JA
01179 289000

Bristol University, Department of Computing Service, Tyndall Avenue, Bristol BS8 1UD

Barnes, S. Dr; Grant, A. Mr; Lewis, D. Mr; Ford, K. Ms

Transferable information technology (IT) skills for undergraduate and taught postgraduate students

ABSTRACT: The project will carry out a university wide needs analysis of information technology (IT) skills required and provision available; evaluate learning materials and methods to acquire IT skills; develop programme to deliver IT skills; and pilot the programme.

STATUS: Sponsored project

SOURCE OF GRANT: Bristol University £26,000

DATE OF RESEARCH: 1995-1997

KEYWORDS: computer literacy; computer uses in education; higher education; information technology; skills; transfer of learning

0228

Graduate School of Education, 35 Berkeley Square, Bristol BS8 1JA 01179 289000

Bristol University, Department of Psychology, 8 Woodland Road, Bristol BS8 1TN

Gillibrand, E. Mrs; Osborn, A. Prof.; Robinson, P. Prof.

Single sex classes, pupils' confidence, motivation and achievement

ABSTRACT: This is a longitudinal study to examine the effects of being in a single sex class on pupils' confidence, motivation and achievement in science. Pupils in Year 9 have been allocated to single sex teaching groups for science lessons and the research will monitor the progress and performance of pupils in science up to GCSE. This will be compared with pupils' achievement in previous year cohorts.

STATUS: Team research

DATE OF RESEARCH: 1997-1998

KEYWORDS: academic achievement; achievement; motivation; science education; secondary education; secondary school pupils; self esteem; single sex classes

0229

Graduate School of Education, 35 Berkeley Square, Bristol BS8 1JA 01179 289000

Bristol University, Department of Psychology, 8 Woodland Road, Bristol BS8 1TN

Gilpin, A. Mrs; Robinson, P. Prof.

Constructive discussion as a means of developing competence in problem-solving and evaluation skills in the context of essay and dissertation

ABSTRACT: The focus will be on how one should set about planning and executing a dissertation or empirical project, and evaluating it both at process and product levels. While the evaluative criteria for assignment assessment can be applied to each phase of a dissertation, and to the finished product, the particular criteria for evaluation and the kind of evidence relevant to each phase differ, and differ according to the nature of the project.

STATUS: Sponsored project

SOURCE OF GRANT: Bristol University

DATE OF RESEARCH: 1996-1997

KEYWORDS: discussion; dissertations; essays; higher education; problem solving; writing – composition

0230

Graduate School of Education, 35 Berkeley Square, Bristol BS8 1JA 01179 289000

Bristol University, Faculty of Engineering, Senate House, Bristol BS8 1TH

Barnes, S. Dr; Hale, R. Mr

Electronic conferencing to support postgradutae students working at a distance

ABSTRACT: The project will explore the use of electronic conferencing within well-established programmes in the Graduate School of Education and Faculty of Engineering at the University of Bristol. Postgraduate students based in the UK and overseas are disadvantaged during the individual project phase of their studies by being at a distance. Using electronic conferencing the researchers hope to develop new techniques for supporting these students and helping them develop collaborative support systems among themselves. Feasibility studies on different techniques available through electronic conferencing (e.g. bulletin boards, discussion groups, chat sessions, usenet news) will be central to the project to explore how students and tutors can make best use of the system and how their use affects the learning that occurs.

STATUS: Sponsored project

SOURCE OF GRANT: Bristol University

DATE OF RESEARCH: 1997-1998

KEYWORDS: computer uses in education; distance education; graduate study; higher education; information technology; teleconferencing

0231

Graduate School of Education, 35 Berkeley Square, Bristol BS8 1JA 01179 289000

Bristol University, Institute of Child Health, Children's Hospital, St Michael's Hill, Bristol BS2 8VJ   01179 215411

Meadows, S. Dr; Osborn, A. Dr; Dawson, N. Dr; Golding, J. Prof.; Greenwood, R. Ms

Teenage mothers and their children: factors affecting their health and development

ABSTRACT: This is an examination of the factors affecting the health and development of teenage mothers and their children through analysis of the Avon Longitudinal Study of Pregnancy and Childhood (ALSPAC) database, comparing younger and older teenage mothers (under 16/16-19) and their children with other maternal age groups. The objectives are to: 1) identify the particular factors occurring in pregnancy and the early stages of which increase the risk of subsequent developmental problems in babies born to teenage mothers; 2) identify compensatory factors in the lives of teenage mothers which reduce the developmental risks to the children; 3) examine the interaction of risk variables in the development of the child and the psychological health of the mother; 4) draw out policy implications for the prevention of unwanted pregnancies in very young mothers, for education, health and care of such mothers and their children, and for support of parenting under conditions of risk.

STATUS: Sponsored project

SOURCE OF GRANT: NHS Executive: Research and Development Programme £22,535

DATE OF RESEARCH: 1996-1997

KEYWORDS: child rearing; children at risk; health; mother child relationship; parenting skills; teenage mothers; unmarried mothers

0232

Graduate School of Education, 35 Berkeley Square, Bristol BS8 1JA 01179 289000

Bristol University, Institute of Learning and Research Technology, 8 Woodland Road, Bristol BS8 1TN

Webb, J. Mr; *Supervisors*: Sutherland, R. Prof.; Squires, J. Dr

Study skills and learning to learn: a deconstructive catalysis of the language used in Internet-based induction students to British higher education

ABSTRACT: Notions of higher education, learning, study etc. have changed rapidly in recent years. Particularly with the advent of the Worldwide Web (www). However, little research has taken place on the changed relationships and assumptions this entails. (CF: Peter Scott's (1995) 'Meaning of mass H.E.). This research will examine the language, or more broadly, 'text(s)' through which the notion of the 'student' is constructed within online tuition in general study skills. It will use the approach of 'deconstruction' as expounded by the contemporary French philosopher Jacques Derrida. Rather than on explicit intentions, this approach focuses on unspoken, undecideable and possibly unthinkable origins and assumptions (claims to knowledge, power, authority etc). The samples will comprise wording, images, and the appearance and behaviour of software-for-students, taken from several study skills packages and online services. The results will be a 'catalysis' – a creative and lateral perspective on the positioning of students (as consumers, workers, inheritors etc), embedded in those practices. It is hoped that the research will show the value of deconstruction as a 'tool for thought' in the meta-discourse of higher education.

STATUS: Individual research

DATE OF RESEARCH: 1995-continuing

KEYWORDS: computer uses in education; higher education; information technology; internet; learning strategies; study skills

0233

Graduate School of Education, 35 Berkeley Square, Bristol BS8 1JA
01179 289000

Canterbury Christ Church College, North Holmes Road, Canterbury
CT1 1QU　　　01227 767700

Broadfoot, P. Prof.; Osborn, M. Dr; Sharpe, K. Dr

Quality in experiences of schooling transnationally (QUEST): children's experiences of schooling in England and France

ABSTRACT: This project is comparing the educational experience, attitudes to school, and learning outcomes of primary school children in England and France in the light of differing teaching approaches and curriculum content in the two countries.

PUBLISHED MATERIAL: OSBORN, M. (1997). 'Children's experience of schooling in England and France: some lessons from a comparative study', Education Review, Vol 11, No 1, pp.46-52.

STATUS: Sponsored project

SOURCE OF GRANT: Economic and Social Research Council ú 92,560

DATE OF RESEARCH: 1995-1997

KEYWORDS: **assessment; comparative education; educational experience; france; language; mathematics education; outcomes of education; primary education; primary school pupils; pupil attitudes; teaching methods**

0234

Graduate School of Education, 35 Berkeley Square, Bristol BS8 1JA
01179 289000

Cardiff University, School of Education, Senghennydd Road, Cardiff
CF2 4YG　　　01222 874000

Rutgers University, New Jersey, USA

Broadfoot, P. Prof.; Winter, J. Ms; Davies, B. Prof.; Firestone, W. Prof.

Assessment Bristol Cardiff (ABC): a comparative study of the impact of assessment policy on teaching in secondary schools

ABSTRACT: Data will be collected from two matched secondary schools in Bristol and Cardiff from classes in Years 8 and 9 concerning mathematics teachers' assessment practice and the sources of influences on it. The study extends work already carried out by Professor Firestone in two US States and uses partly the same instruments adapted for the UK. Methods include interviews and classroom observation.

STATUS: Sponsored project

SOURCE OF GRANT: Spencer Foundation

DATE OF RESEARCH:#@ 1997-1997

KEYWORDS: **assessment; comparative education; mathematics education; secondary education; united states of america**

0235

Graduate School of Education, 35 Berkeley Square, Bristol BS8 1JA
01179 289000

Centre for British Teachers, Quality House, Gyosei College, London
Road, Reading　　　01189 756200

Crossley, M. Dr; Osborn, A. Dr; Waudo, J. Dr; Juma, M. Dr

Research and evaluation of a primary school management project in Kenya

ABSTRACT: The research consists of a survey of 1,200 Kenyan primary schools to provide baseline data on the management practices of headteachers in order to assess the impact on such practices of a development programme designed to improve headteacher management skills. Qualitative school and community studies are also being carried out to complement the quantitative approach of the baseline survey.

STATUS: Sponsored project

SOURCE OF GRANT: Overseas Development Administration £20,400

DATE OF RESEARCH: 1996-1998

KEYWORDS: **developing countries; development education; educational administration; head teachers; kenya; management development; primary education**

0236

Graduate School of Education, Centre for International Studies in Education, 35 Berkeley Square, Bristol BS8 1JA　　　01179 289000

Harrop, B. Mr; *Supervisor*: Garrett, R. Dr

The role of cultural difference in the work of international education consultants

ABSTRACT: The researcher had worked as an expatriate lecturer in higher education for 6 years in South East Asia. His personal and professional experience in cross-cultural educational environments led him to question the nature and degree of effectiveness of cross-cultural education consultancy. This study aims to undertake a qualitative study of how culture impacts upon the work of key players in the consultancy process and assist the researcher to reflect on and improve his professional practice. In-depth interviews were carried out with consultants, agents/donors and recipients of cross-cultural consultancy. Verbatim transcripts of those interviews form the raw data of the study. By undertaking interviews in different modes and with differing aims, the researcher hopes to contribute to this rapidly growing methodology.

STATUS: Individual research

DATE OF RESEARCH: 1996-1997

KEYWORDS: **consultancy; cultural differences; education consultants; international educational exchange**

0237

Graduate School of Education, 35 Berkeley Square, Bristol BS8 1JA
01179 289000

Glamorgan University, Business School, Pontypridd CF37 1DL
01443 480480

Whiting, D. Ms; *Supervisor*: Hoyle, E. Prof.

Professional ethics and teaching

Abstract: Professional ethics in teaching is an exploratory study of secondary school teachers' conception of professional ethics, professional behaviour, professional codes of conduct, and how teachers may be adequately prepared to resolve the ethical issues they face in practice. The research aims to: 1) conduct an exploratory study in two local education authorities (LEAs) in England and Wales, which may provide the basis for continued study on professional ethics in teaching; 2) analyse the response of a sample of novice, expert and headteachers in secondary schools to: a) the concept of professional ethics; b) behaving professionally; c) a constructed code of conduct; d) socialisation in professional ethics. A body of knowledge surrounding the professionalisation of teachers in England and Wales already exists which provides a valuable insight into the concepts of the professionalisation, de-professionalisation and new professionalism of teachers. However, there is a gap where little research has been undertaken which explicity examines the professionality of teachers, in particular their understanding of and perceptive response to behaving professionally. To forward both knowledge and practice this study will explore the concept of professional ethics in teaching: what teachers understand by the term; what it is to behave professionally; and how teachers are socialised into specific ethics which govern their behaviour in practice. Further, at a time when the General Teaching Council (England and Wales) is exploring a statement of ethics which make its implicit values explicit (GENERAL TEACHING COUNCIL (England and Wales). (1996). Draft statement of ethical principals for the teaching profession), it is apposite to research teacher responses to this statement and how they perceive they might be socialised appropriately to meet the demands of the statement. Essentially the researcher will seek to uncover a number of assumptions which surround the professionality of teachers in relation to professional ethics. The analysis of the teachers' responses will cover both description and theory, as well as implications for practice. The descriptive elements will focus on how much commonality and/or variation exists within differing groups of secondary school teachers' conception of professional ethics and behaving professionally, plus the adequacy of the main sources of influence in socialising them in this area, as well as the implications and sufficiency of a code of conduct. The theoretical consideration will be to build on this analysis to contemplate normative ethics in teaching. It is anticipated that the practical implications of the study will inform the need, or otherwise, to develop a model of professional education in ethics for teachers. The research design will be a cross-sectional focused interview in a parallel-sample design (n=24).

STATUS: Individual research

DATE OF RESEARCH: 1996-1997

KEYWORDS: **code of conduct; professional ethics; teacher behaviour; teachers; teaching profession**

0238

Graduate School of Education, 35 Berkeley Square, Bristol BS8 1JA
01179 289000
King Alfred's College of Higher Education, Sparkford Road, Winchester SO22 4NR   01962 841515

Blanc, P. Mr; *Supervisor*: Sutherland R. Prof.

A study of students' heuristics and external representations in the solution of investigative mathematics problems

ABSTRACT: Changes to the mathematics curriculum that followed from the Cockroft Report (Great Britain. Department for Education and Science. (1982). Mathematics counts: Report of the Committee of Inquiry into the Teaching of Mathematics in Schools under the Chairmanship of Dr. W.H. Cockcroft. London: HMSO), led to 'Investigations' becoming part of assessed coursework for GCSE, ensuring that they become common occurrences in UK schools. The mathematics education literature has questioned the effectiveness of how these are practised in mathematics classrooms suggesting routinisation as an unwelcome consequence. The specific concerns of this research are how students' strategies are characterised by types of external representation (ER) chosen and how these are influenced by learnt heuristics. Major influences on the study are mathematics problem-solving literature, ERs (from cognitive psychology) and the work of Guy Brousseau. The setting for Phase 1 was an initial teacher education course working with 30 first year students (mature students and recent school leavers). Methodology is largely qualitative including protocol analysis and semi-structured interviews. Phase 1 has reported on approaches to a range of such problems. The main findings suggest that, whilst nearly all students use diagrammatic ERs, more successful students interact with their written workings in an iterative as opposed to a linear way. Some ERs are used mechanistically and unproductively as separators of activity. Phase 2 will examine similar phenomena using a smaller sample in a controlled experimental setting.

PUBLISHED MATERIAL: BLANC, P. (1995). 'Investigating the mathematics learning of student teachers: explorations and discoveries?'. Proceedings of the British Society for Research in Learning Mathematics, Birmingham, March, 1995. ; BLANC, P. & SUTHERLAND, R. (1996). 'Student teachers' approaches to investigative mathematics: iterative engagement or disjointed mechanisms?'. Proceedings of the 20th International Conference on Psychology of Mathematics Education, Valencia, Spain, 1996.

STATUS: Individual research

DATE OF RESEARCH: 1994-continuing

KEYWORDS: **mathematics education; mathematics teachers; preservice teacher education; problem solving; student teachers**

0239

Graduate School of Education, Language Centre, 30/32 Tyndall's Park Road, Bristol BS8 1PY   01179 289000

Lockett, A. Mr; *Supervisor*: Beveridge, M. Prof.

The theoretical foundations of the construct of general academic discourse and its implications for English for academic purposes (EAP) writing pedagogy

ABSTRACT: The research is aimed at exploring the nature, theoretical ramifications, and pedagogical implications of the construct of 'general academic discourse'. The study involves discourse and text analysis related to academic language data across disciplines. A survey-based research methodology is also employed to establish some basic principles with regard to the composition of written academic discourse from both writer and reader perspectives. It is anticipated that the results will yield insights assisting English for academic purposes (EAP) tutors in achieving better-informed practice in assisting non-native English-using university students in develoing academic writing skills.

STATUS: Individual research

DATE OF RESEARCH: 1994-continuing

KEYWORDS: **english – second language; english for academic purposes; english for specific purposes; overseas students; second language teaching; writing -composition; writing skills**

0240

Graduate School of Education, 35 Berkeley Square, Bristol BS8 1JA
01179 289000
Leeds Metropolitan University, School of Information Management, The Grange, Beckett Park Campus, Leeds LS6 3QS   01132 832600

Gibbs, S. Ms; *Supervisor*: Claxton, G. Prof.

Learning to learn the hard way: learning styles and approaches to doctoral (PhD) research

ABSTRACT: The aim is to try and identify whether a person's learning style has an affect on the way they approach a PhD. The low completion rate of doctoral research suggests that how a person approaches such research may be crucial to their ability to complete. Learning style may be one variable in this. The learning style (and subsequent supervision style) of the supervisor may also be important. It is hoped to use the Honey and Mumford Learning Styles Inventory (LSI) to survey 20-30 doctoral students in each major area of arts, sciences and social sciences. Five to six students (and their supervisors) will be interviewed, identified from the LSI. Two new universities and two old universities in the Yorkshire region will be surveyed.

STATUS: Individual research

DATE OF RESEARCH: 1996-continuing

KEYWORDS: **cognitive style; doctoral degrees; learning strategies; research projects; student research**

0241

Graduate School of Education, 35 Berkeley Square, Bristol BS8 1JA
01179 289000
London University, Institute of Education, 20 Bedford Way, London WC1H 0AL   0171 580 1122

Sutherland, R. Prof.; Wolf, A. Prof.

Geometrical modelling and industrial statistics for engineering students

ABSTRACT: The aims of the project are to: carry out indepth analysis, over a range of industries and contexts, of the ways geometry/trigonometry are being used in the workplace; develop new approaches to teaching both these areas of mathematics, based on extensive use of computers; and analyse existing curriculum specifications for geometry/trigonometry and statistics and make recommendations for future syllabuses and curriculum development.

STATUS: Sponsored project

SOURCE OF GRANT: Nuffield Foundation £39,501

DATE OF RESEARCH: 1995-1998

KEYWORDS: **curriculum development; engineering education; geometry; higher education; mathematics education; statistics**

0242

Graduate School of Education, 35 Berkeley Square, Bristol BS8 1JA
01179 289000
London University, Institute of Education, 20 Bedford Way, London WC1H 0AL   0171 580 1122

Sutherland, R. Prof.; Dewhurst, H. Ms; Wolf, A. Prof.

Computer-based mathematics in the formation of European engineers: training materials for transnational use

ABSTRACT: The application of mathematics to practical problems is a defining characteristic of modern industrial society yet creates major difficulties for many young and adult workers. Engineering is a highly competitive, rapidly changing industry, and engineering employers have a strong expressed interest in the mathematics component of engineering training. Given this background the aims of the project are: 1) to examine engineering companies' requirements in terms of mathematical competencies of engineering technicians, and the similarities and differences between training provisions in France, UK and Sweden; 2) development of computer-based materials for teaching mathematics; 3) development of distance teaching scenarios for the training of engineering technicians.

STATUS: Sponsored project

SOURCE OF GRANT: European Commission : Leonardo da Vinci project

DATE OF RESEARCH: 1996-continuing

KEYWORDS: comparative education; computer uses in education; engineering education; engineers; europe; france; information technology; international educational exchange; mathematics education; sweden; training

0243

Graduate School of Education, 35 Berkeley Square, Bristol BS8 1JA
01179 289000

Newcastle upon Tyne University, Department of Education, St Thomas Street, Newcastle upon Tyne NE1 7RU   0191 222 6000

London University, Institute of Education, 20 Bedford Way, London WC1H 0AL   0171 580 1122

Power, S. Dr; Edwards, A. Prof.; Wigfall, V. Ms

Destined for success? Educational biographies of academically able children

ABSTRACT: This research project is investigating the careers of a previously identified and researched group of 'academically able' pupils. Based on autobiographical accounts, the research explores the extent to which these 600 children have realised their early educational promise and the various routes by which they have been able to translate their achievements into further educational opportunities and occupational locations. It is also exploring the ways in which their diverse educational experiences have influenced their relationships with family and friends.

PUBLISHED MATERIAL: POWER, S., WHITTY, G. & EDWARDS, T. (1996). 'Destined for success: analysing the educational trajectories of 24 academically able girls'. In: Proceedings of the CEDAR Conference, University of Warwick, April 1996. ; POWER, S., WHITTY, G. & EDWARDS, T. (1996). 'The role of the assisted places scheme in privatisation and marketisation'. In: Proceedings of the ECER Conference, Seville, Spain, September 1996. ; POWER, S., EDWARDS, T. & WHITTY, G. (1996). 'Selected for success? State sponsorship of academically able children'. In: Proceedings of the ECER Conference, Seville, Spain, September 1996.

STATUS: Sponsored project

SOURCE OF GRANT: Economic and Social Research Council £126,140

DATE OF RESEARCH: 1994-1997

KEYWORDS: ability; academic aspiration; access to education; gifted; opportunities; outcomes of education; private education; state schools

0244

Graduate School of Education, 35 Berkeley Square, Bristol BS8 1JA
01179 289000

Payam-E-Noor University, Distance Education, Lashkarak Road, PO Box 19395-4697, Tehran, Iran   010 98 212441511

Ebrahimzadeh, I. Mr; *Supervisor*:Crossley, M. Dr; Oldroyd, D. Mr

The development of distance education in Iran with special reference to the planning and management of Payam-E-Noor University (PNU)

ABSTRACT:#@ Iranian higher education policymakers have decided to estabish a distance education university under the name of Payam-E-Noor University (PNU). PNU's initial progress has shown that distance education (DE) holds great potential in Iran for the expansion of higher education opportunities to a wider range of people. It is also believed to be more cost effective than conventional provision. As the only higher level DE university in the country and one of the eleven mega-universities in the world, the future of the PNU is important to the whole higher education system in Iran. The aims of the project are to: 1) document the development of DE in Iran from an historical perspective; 2) develop a detailed case study of PNU as a mega-university; 3) conduct a critical analysis of the planning and management of PNU in the light of the related international literature; 4) draw out implications from the study for the future improvement of DE policy and practice in Iran; 5) relate the findings of the PNU case study to the broader theoretical literature on DE. The research design is adapted from a model provided by Yin (1994), and further structured by reference to industrial theory (Peters, 1967) and policy-making and policy-implementation components, based on Hodgkinson's (1991) model of leadership applied to the PNU. The management process of PNU is analysed in the light of four of Bush's (1994) management theories to clarify the nature of policy implementation at the university. Since a main goal of this study involves the documentation of PNU's missions, and the analysis of its planning and management process and theoretical underpinnings, a largely qualitative case study strategy was developed. The case study of PNU has applied three main techniques for collecting varied data and documeting institutional aspects of PNU with regard to political, economic and cultural forces that modelled it over time. These three techniques are: 1) indepth interview; 2) documentary analysis; 3) observation and reflection of experiential knowledge. The study of the only DE university in Iran (PNU) reveals that the perceptions, perspectives and problems of policymakers and planners have much to offer the international DE community eager to learn about the experiences of rare mega-universities. This case study also tests Peters (1967) industrial theory in action in one mega-university in an Islamic industrial/transitional developing country. In this respect the study makes an original and challenging contribution to Iranian studies. In documenting the development of PNU and its planning and management processes, the research makes a further original contribution to the existing literature about the management and planning of DE in Iran from which policymakers and planners, both within the country and in the wider internationl community, can draw for improved policy-making and policy implementation.

STATUS: Individual research

DATE OF RESEARCH: 1994-1997

KEYWORDS: distance education; higher education; iran; universities

0245

Graduate School of Education, 35 Berkeley Square, Bristol BS8 1JA
01179 289000

University of Wales College, Newport, Caerleon Campus, PO Box 179, Newport NP6 1YG   01633 430088

Furlong, J. Prof.; Sutherland, R. Prof.; Furlong, R. Ms

Screen play: an exploratory study of children in 'techno-popular culture

ABSTRACT: The project will make a detailed study of the engagement of young people with different aspects of 'techno-popular culture': television, video, computers, computer games, CD-Rom, the Internet etc. It will explore how, when and where young people use such technologies, the role of such technologies in their lives more generally and the forms of thinking and learning they facilitate.

STATUS: Sponsored project

SOURCE OF GRANT: Economic and Social Research Council

DATE OF RESEARCH: 1997-continuing

KEYWORDS: adolescents; cd roms; children; computer games; computer uses at home; computers; home computers; information technology; internet; popular culture; television; videotape recordings

0246

School of Education, 35 Berkeley Square, Bristol BS8 1JA
01179 303030

Grant, M. Dr; Came, F. Mr; Bowker, P. Mr; Noble, J. Mrs

Special educational needs and the GCSE

ABSTRACT: The programme of research and development work reviewed the efficacy of existing General Certificate of Secondary Education (GCSE) provision for pupils with special educational needs and low-attaining pupils, and showed how better access to assessment and certification could be achieved. In September 1991, the project was expanded to include approaches adopted by a sample of examining bodies, other than GCSE examining groups, to provision made for pupils with special educational needs. Methods used included a questionnaire survey of 55 mainstream schools in England and Wales; interviews in 30 special schools; interviews with a range of representatives of examining groups, examining bodies, special educational needs (SEN) interest groups/interested parties and indepth research and development work in two case study local education authorities (LEAs). The research report identified developments in practice which have improved opportunities for pupils with special educational needs to gain accreditation at 16+. The report was accompanied by support materials designed to provide techniques and procedures through which teachers and examiners could monitor and improve aspects of their assessment strategies. The project centred upon five National Curriculum subjects: English; mathematics; science; technology; and geography.

Status: Sponsored project

SOURCE OF GRANT: School Examinations and Assessment Council £340,000

DATE OF RESEARCH: 1991-1993

KEYWORDS: **assessment; examinations; general certificate of secondary education; low achievement; secondary education; special educational needs**

0247

School of Education, 35 Berkeley Square, Bristol BS8 1JA
01179 289000

Filer, A. Dr; *Supervisors*: Pollard, A. Prof.; Broadfoot, P. Prof.

Classroom contexts of assessment in a primary school

ABSTRACT: The research is concerned with the provision for assessment related to the National Curriculum for England and Wales (Education Reform Act 1988). Through it, is presented a critique of some aspects of the provision with respect to teacher assessment. The focus of the study concerns the extent to which such assessments can be viewed as objective and comparable statements of the achievements of individuals and schools. An examination has been made of both formal, National Curriculum related, and informal assessments for a cohort of white, predominantly working class children as they moved through Years 1 to 3 of an English primary school. Data was collected from the three teaching environments using ethnographic methods. These included participant observation, teacher and pupil interviews and the use of documentary evidence. The research sets assessments in the context in which they were made. It examines the notion of assessment as a product of a teacher-created classroom context that is complex in its origins. Principal findings of the study are as follows: 1) There are fundamental and persistent differences between teachers in their classroom strategies that have an impact upon pupil responses and hence upon assessments made. 2) These fundamental differences between teachers are not addressed by governmental concerns for systematising teacher assessment in the pursuit of comparability across sites of assessment. 3) Teacher assessments which appear 'objective' are the outcome of differentiating processes and contain within them a range of other pupil skills and attributes. 4) Teacher assessments are inevitably context-related.

PUBLISHED MATERIAL:#@ FILER, A. (1993). 'Contexts of assessment in a primary school classroom', British Educational Research Journal, Vol 19, No 1, pp.95-107. ; FILER, A. (1993). 'The assessment of classroom language: challenging the rhetoric of 'objectivity',' International Studies in Sociology of Education, Vol 2, No 2. ; FILER, A. (1993). 'Teacher assessment: a sociological perspective'. Paper given at British Educational Research Association, Liverpool, 1993. ; FILER, A. (1993). Classroom contexts of assessment in a primary school. Unpublished PhD thesis. Bristol: University of the West of England.

STATUS: Individual research

DATE OF RESEARCH: 1989-1993

KEYWORDS: **assessment; national curriculum; primary education; school based assessment**

0248

School of Education, 35 Berkeley Square, Bristol BS8 1JA
01179 289000

Osborn, M. Dr; Black, E. Dr

Delivering the National Curriculum at key stage 2: the implications for primary schools

ABSTRACT: The general aim of the study is to explore the implications for primary schools of delivering the National Curriculum at key stage 2. More particularly, the research has four main elements: 1) Curriculum-led staffing and its implications for teachers: The study will explore the extent to which schools are moving towards a curriculum-led staffing model and the implications of pressures to move towards more specialist subject teaching for the work of the classroom teacher. 2) Whole-school strategies for changes: The study will investigate developments in whole-school

approaches to curriculum planning, strategies used for the implementation of institutional development plans, and the role of curriculum coordinators/subject specialists. 3) Collegiality and collaboration amongst primary school teachers: The study will explore the impact of current changes on teachers' working relationships with colleagues both within and beyond the classroom. 4) The impact of assessment at key stage 2: The study will examine the changes made by Years 5 and 6 teachers to their working patterns in preparation for the first national assessment of eleven year olds. The study will be conducted in two parts. The first will consist of interviews with headteachers and teachers of pupils in Years 5 and 6 in primary schools in Avon, Somerset and the West Midlands. The second part will consist of a wider survey based on a postal questionnaire. @#Published Material:#@ OSBORN, M. & BLACK, E. (1994). Delivering the National Curriculum at key stage 2: the changing nature of teachers' work. Final Report to the National Association of Schoolmasters/Union of Women Teachers (NAS/UWT). Birmingham: NAS/UWT, Hillscourt Education Centre, Rednal, Birmingham.

STATUS: Sponsored project

SOURCE OF GRANT: National Association of Schoolmasters/Union of Women Teachers £15,000

DATE OF RESEARCH: 1992-1993

KEYWORDS: **curriculum development; educational change; national curriculum; primary education; primary school teachers; teacher role; teacher workload**

0249

School of Education, 35 Berkeley Square, Bristol BS8 1JA
01179 289000

Crossley, M. Dr; Thomas, H. Mr; Clarke, G. Ms; Tabi, T. Mr

Modularisation in higher education: trans-national issues

ABSTRACT: The implementation of modularisation at two universities (Bristol and Ghana) is compared through two detailed, qualitative, case studies. Focus is placed upon the administrative perspective and motivating factors, both internal and external. External pressures for modularisation in Ghana resulted in rapid change, but the results of this has not been empirically evaluated. The University of Bristol has adopted a more cautious strategy and involved academic staff more fully in the planning and implementation process. The views of academic staff in both contexts requires further documentation and analysis.

PUBLISHED MATERIAL: CROSSLEY, M., CLARKE, G., TABI, T. & THOMAS, H. (1993). 'Implementing the process of modularisation in higher education: some trans-national issues', Higher Education Quarterly, Vol 47, No 4, pp.334-356.

STATUS: Sponsored project

SOURCE OF GRANT: British Council

DATE OF RESEARCH: 1992-1993

KEYWORDS: **comparative education; ghana; higher education; modular courses; universities**

0250

School of Education, 35 Berkeley Square, Bristol BS8 1JA
01179 303030

Barnes, S. Dr; *Supervisor*: Satterly, D. Dr

Individual differences in learning to use word processing systems

ABSTRACT: The efficient use of a word processing system can be viewed as a combination of four factors: factors common to all types of learning; factors specific to word processing tasks; factors specific to the sample being studied; and factors or individual differences that were not measured in the present study. Previous research on the acquisition of word procesing skills has focused on the limitations of the systems under investigation or the training strategies used. This study departs from previous research and focuses on how the personal characteristics of the users affect their use of the word processing system. Learning to use a word processing system is viewed within the framework of an information processing approach to learning. This study describes a short-term longitudinal investigation of university secretaries learning to use Microsoft Word 5. Thirty-one secretaries participated in a four week study which included the carrying out of editing tasks using Microsoft Word 5. Background characteristics, approaches to learning, conditions for learning, and scores on the Eysenck Personality Questionnnaire were also elicited from the subjects. Statistical analyses (including repeated measures ANOVAs, factor analyses, and cluster analysis) were carried out to explore individual differences in efficient use of the word processing system and to investigate styles of word processing use. The results suggest that although all secretaries made progress through the course of this investigation, none of them had reached a level of expert use of Microsoft Word 5 and the majority were still 'finding their way'. Styles of word processing use were related to characteristics of the individuals' personal backgrounds and personality. There was no evidence to support the notion of the need for optimal conditions for learning as proposed by adult learning theories.

STATUS: Individual research

DATE OF RESEARCH: 1986-1993

KEYWORDS: **adult learning; human computer interaction; learning strategies; secretaries; word processing**

0251

School of Education, 35 Berkeley Square, Bristol BS8 1JA
01179 303030
Cardiff University, School of Education, Senghennydd Road, Cardiff CF2 4YG   01222 874000
Create Consultants, 109 West End Lane, London NW6 4SY
0171 328 8619

Bolam, R. Prof.; McMahon, A. Ms; Pocklington, K. Mr; Weindling, R. Mr

National evaluation of the headteacher mentoring pilot schemes

ABSTRACT: The broad aim of the research was to carry out a formative evaluation of the Department for Education (DFE) funded national mentor support programme for new headteachers, during its initial period of operation up to March 1993. The focus of the evaluation was upon: 1) the overall organisation and management of the schemes; 2) the organisation, content, methods, implementation and effectiveness of training; and 3) the roles and tasks of mentors and the effectiveness of the mentoring process in helping new headteachers adapt to their role. Data were collected through: initial visits to 12 consortia organising schemes and interviews with key personnel; a questionnaire to mentors and new headteachers, which had a response rate of 303 mentors (68%) and 238 (65%) new headteachers; a questionnaire to regional organisers with a response rate of 68 (51.5%); and interviews with 16 pairs of successful mentors and new headteachers. The participants concluded that mentoring was of practical benefit to new headteachers and that it should be continued and made more widely available. Other recommendations were that the arrangements for organisation and funding needed to be improved, and that preparatory training for mentors was necessary. Specific conclusions were drawn about the nature of the mentoring process.

Published Material: BOLAM, R., McMAHON, A., POCKLINGTON, K. & WEINDLING, D. (1993). National evaluation of headteacher mentoring pilot schemes. London: Department for Education.

STATUS: Sponsored project

SOURCE OF GRANT: Department for Education

DATE OF RESEARCH: 1992-1993

KEYWORDS: **head teachers; mentors; programme evaluation; teaching profession**

0252

School of Education, National Development Centre for Educational Management & Policy, 35 Berkeley Square, Bristol BS8 1JA
01179 303030
University of Wales, Cardiff, School of Education, Senghennydd Road, Cardiff CF2 4YG   01222 874000

Wallace, M. Dr; *Supervisor*: Bolam, R. Prof.

The role of the senior management team in secondary schools

ABSTRACT: The aim of this research is to examine how senior management teams manage secondary schools within a context of educational reform and to identify approaches to teamwork which appear to be effective. Senior managers in secondary schools may face a greater need than hitherto to co-ordinate their work so as to effectively orchestrate the implementation of multiple innovations. The research will be conducted in two local

education authorities (LEAs). In each LEA, case studies will be carried out during the summer of 1991 in three schools where all members of the senior management team express a strong commitment to teamwork. A longitudinal case study will be undertaken in one of these schools.

STATUS: Sponsored project

SOURCE OF GRANT: Economic and Social Research Council £57,000

DATE OF RESEARCH: 1991-1993

KEYWORDS: **educational administration; educational change; management teams; school based management; secondary education**

0253

School of Education, 35 Berkeley Square, Bristol BS8 1JA
01179 289000
University of the West of England, Faculty of Education, Redland Campus, Redland Hill, Bristol BS6 6UZ   01179 741251

Broadfoot, P. Prof.; Pollard, A. Prof.; Osborn, M. Dr; Abbott, D. Ms; *Supervisor*: Croll, P. Prof.

Primary assessment, curriculum and experience (PACE): phase 1

ABSTRACT: The project aims to describe and analyse the responses of pupils and teachers in infant schools and infant departments to the National Curriculum and related innovations. This includes a consideration of the views of headteachers and teachers of the new reforms and their impact on the school and, in particular, an analysis and evaluation of the development of strategies for change. The study aims to contribute to theoretical perspectives on teacher professionalism and on the control and impact of educational change. It is designed too to consider the impact of the National Curriculum on the curriculum and pedagogy of the infant school. Issues of teacher aims and expectations, curriculum content and time allocation, teaching methods and pupil classroom experience, are being addressed. As well as considering the impact of the National Curriculum on teachers and pupils, the study will provide baseline data on contemporary infant practice. The project will also evaluate materials in action and their impact on pupils. The operation of the assessments in classrooms will be studied and pupil responses to the assessment tasks considered. Conflicting claims about pupil perceptions of and reactions to being tested are being considered. The research involves interviews with 150 teachers drawn from 48 schools in 8 local education authorities plus four rounds of detailed classroom studies in a sub-sample of nine classrooms to study curriculum change and pupil experience in more depth. Classroom studies are also being conducted during the implementation of the first unreported and reported Standard Assessment Tasks in these nine schools.

STATUS: Sponsored project

SOURCE OF GRANT: Economic and Social Research Council £149,973

DATE OF RESEARCH: 1989-1993

KEYWORDS: **assessment; educational change; infant school curriculum; infant school education; national curriculum; primary school teachers; pupil attitudes**

British Educational Communications and Technology Agency

0254

Milburn Hill Road, Science Park, Coventry CV4 7JJ
01203 416994

Stevens, C. Mr; Thomas, M. Mr

An investigation into the use of voice recognition systems with pupils with special educational needs

ABSTRACT: As recently as 3 years ago voice recognition was a little known and even less understood option for disabled people. It was expensive and problematic. Now the scene has changed and systems are cheaper, faster and can produce better results. The question is, do they really work and, if they do, how can they work for pupils with special educational needs (SEN)? In order to produce this advice it is necessary to investigate: 1) work which has already been done in this field; 2) the use of the systems in as many situations of learners with SEN as possible; 3) teachers' and users' reaction to the benefits offered by the systems; and 4) how use of the systems enables learners to demonstrate what they know, understand and can do and how they could raise standards. Information will be gathered from a wide range of sources to answer the research questions outlined above. Centres will be identified through the British Educational Communications and Technology Agency (BECTA) networks. They will be set tasks at the beginning of the work, and may also be requested to undertake further investigations as a result of issues arising from information being gathered. The views of teachers, therapists and users will be sought. The 12 centres identified will include mainstream and special schools, be geographically spread and enable the systems to be used by learners with physical disabilities, visual impairment, specific learning difficulties and severe learning difficulties. The Centres will be working over 2 financial years, although the bulk of the funding would be available in year 1. While advice and support resulting from this investigation would focus on the needs of learners with SEN in school situations, its impact would be to exemplify good practice for all learners where voice recognition systems are being used. The final report from the work will define the fitness for purpose of all the systems and describe the circumstances under which they can be used to the maximum effect for a range of learners with SEN.

STATUS: Sponsored project

SOURCE OF GRANT: Department for Education and Employment

DATE OF RESEARCH: 1998-continuing

KEYWORDS: computer uses in education; information technology; special educational needs; voice recognition technology

0255

Milburn Hill Road, Science Park, Coventry CV4 7JJ   01203 416994
Leicester University, School of Education, 21 University Road, Leicester LE1 7RF   01162 522522

Avis, P. Dr; Underwood, J. Dr; Cavendish, S. Dr; Dowling, S. Mrs ; Lawson, A. Mr; Fogelman, K. Prof.

Integrated learning systems in UK schools

ABSTRACT: The overall aims of the project were to evaluate the use of integrated learning systems (ILS) in UK schools and to define the conditions of use which were most effective. It focused, in the first phase, on measuring learning gains of pupils in 12 UK schools: 4 primary and 8 secondary. Two software packages were used: 1) SuccessMaker - an American system produced by the Computer Curriculum Corporation and marketed in the UK by Research Machines. 2) Global Learning Systems - a British system produced by Systems Integrated Research. A formal evaluation of learning gains was carried out by Leicester University, School of Education, managed by the National Council for Educational Technology (NCET) and funded by the 4 UK education departments. The first phase evaluation found that the American system, SuccessMaker, produced significant learning gains in numeracy, but no significant difference in literacy results. The data for the British system, Global, were inconclusive. The second phase of the evaluation followed-up some of the questions raised in phase 1, such as: 1) Which group of pupils will ILS suit? 2) What are the conditions of use that create the most effective learning gains? 3) Will gains in literacy emerge over a longer period of time? 4) Are the learning gains found for numeracy in phase 1 repeatable and sustainable? 5) Will learning gains be achieved with Global Learning Systems in a second phase? The results of phase 2 showed that ILS is more suitable for some groups of pupils than others. Those groups looked at included: pupils for whom English is a second language; pupils with special educational needs; underachieving pupils; and able students. It also showed that the learning gains achieved in numeracy for SuccessMaker in phase 1 were repeatable and that those pupils who made learning gains in phase 1 maintained their advantage over their peers in phase 2. The evaluation also showed that, amongst other factors, the level of teacher involvement in the implementation of ILS directly affects the results achieved with the system. The more involved the teacher, the better the learning gains. No learning gains were detected for those pupils using Global Learning Systems compared to their peers. However, a separate study of GCSE results by Prof. Carol Fitz-gibbon at Newcastle University, as part of the Year 11 information system, showed that these pupils achieved almost one grade higher using Global mathematics than would normally be expected. Some conclusions from the research indicate: 1) There is considerable evidence that pupils do learn from integrated learning systems. The main issues is

not if pupils learn but what and how they learn. 2) The use of ILS has a marked and positive effect on pupils' attitudes, motivation and behaviour. As yet evidence is inconclusive as to whether these positive impacts generalise beyond experience with ILS to influence more general attitudes towards schooling or school subjects. 3) Where the use of ILS at least matches what can be achieved with conventional teaching, these systems offer a stimulating means of extending the range of learning opportunities open to pupils. However, the results suggest that exclusive reliance on ILS for preparation for key stage 3 tests and GCSE examinations may have a negative impact, and imply that teaching by other methods is pedagogically necessary during the period of immediate preparation for these examinations. 4) Although teachers and headteachers were generally positive in their attitudes towards integrated learning systems and their educational impact, there are issues to address concerning the apparent gap between the acquisition and evaluation of core skills and the wider knowledge and skills tested in examination performance. 5) There was evidence from all 3 phases of evaluation that ILS can help to enhance teachers' confidence in IT and contribute to the development of their knowledge and skills in the management and use of educational technology.

PUBLISHED MATERIAL: UNDERWOOD, J., CAVENDISH, S. & LAWSON, T. (1997). Embedding integrated learning systems in the curriculum: final report. Coventry: British Educational Communications and Technology Agency. ; UNDERWOOD, J., CAVENDISH, S. & LAWSON, T. (1997). The sustainability of learning gains: an investigation of the medium-term impact of integrated learning systems on pupil performance: final report. Coventry: British Educational Communications and Technology Agency. ; SIZMUR, S., WHETTON, C. & HARMAN, J. (1998). Integrated learning systems evaluation project. Phase III: final report. Coventry: British Educational Communications and Technology Agency. ; LEWIS, A. & COSTLEY, D. (1998). ILS evaluation: phase III autoskills (Academy of Reading). Coventry: British Educational Communications and Technology Agency. ; WOOD, D. (1998). The UK ILS evaluations: final report. Coventry: British Educational Communications and Technology Agency.

STATUS: Sponsored project

SOURCE OF GRANT: National Council for Educational Technology ; Department for Education and Employment ; Welsh Office Education Department ; Department of Education Northern Ireland ; Scottish Office Education Department

DATE OF RESEARCH: 1993-1998

KEYWORDS: computer assisted learning; computer uses in education; educational software; information technology; integrated learning systems; primary education; secondary education

British Institute of Traffic Education Research

0256

Kent House, Kent Street, Birmingham B5 6QF   0121 622 2402

Platt, C. Mrs; Lee, T. Mrs

Road safety materials for General National Vocational Qualifications (GNVQ) courses

ABSTRACT: The research has 3 specific objectives: 1) To identify opportunities for disseminating road safety knowledge within specific General National Vocational Qualification (GNVQ) units. 2) To identify suitable road safety resources to meet these opportunities. 3) To ensure that the resources are accepted by the National Council for Vocational Qualifications. The tasks involved include: 1) map the current range of GNVQs at each level and identify the areas relevant to road safety development; 2) review current GNVQ teaching materials to identify approaches that can be adapted for road safety education activities; 3) assess the suitability of existing road safety resources for GNVQ courses and identify gaps; 4) develop and evaluate appropriate guidance material for teachers related to the identified GNVQ units; 5) propose how the national, regional and local support services for road safety education and GNVQ courses may be harnessed to promote dissemination.

STATUS: Sponsored project

SOURCE OF GRANT: Department of Transport £135,000

DATE OF RESEARCH: 1996-continuing

KEYWORDS: **educational materials; general national vocational qualifications; material development; safety education; secondary education; traffic safety**

0257

Kent House, Kent Street, Birmingham B5 6QF   0121 622 2402

Platt, C. Mrs

Road safety education for children transferring from primary to secondary schools

ABSTRACT: The project will develop and evaluate a training pack or programme aimed at improving the safety of children in the 10-12 year age group, that is, those transferring from primary to secondary school. The research will consist of 4 stages: 1) A review of existing road safety materials and programmes targeted at this age group, via schools and home, aimed at enlisting active involvement of parents/carers and the identification of educational and other objectives of any road safety training for this age group. 2) The identification of the best approaches for this age group, including school-based training and parent/carer participation. 3) The development of an agreed resource and/or programme. 4) An independent evaluation of the resource and/or programme.

STATUS: Sponsored project

SOURCE OF GRANT: Department of Transport £180,000

DATE OF RESEARCH: 1996-1998

KEYWORDS: **educational materials; material development; primary education; safety education; secondary education; traffic safety**

0258

Kent House, Kent Street, Birmingham B5 6QF   0121 622 2402
Transport Research Laboratory, Crowthorne RG45 6AU
01344 770467

Clayton, A. Dr; Harland, G. Mr

Review of provision of road safety education in schools: a 10-year follow-up

ABSTRACT: A study by Reading University (SPEAR, M., SINGH, A. & DOWNING, C.S. (1987). The current state of road safety education in primary and middle schools. Crowthorne: Transport Research Laboratory) reviewed the state of road safety education (RSE) in schools and colleges throughout the UK in the mid 1980s. The present study is a follow-up to that research. It involves: 1) The assessment of the current provision of RSE in schools and further education (FE) colleges in England, Wales and Northern Ireland and in FE colleges in Scotland. (The state of RSE in Scottish schools was reported earlier in separate research by the British Institute of Traffic Education Research (BITER). 2) An assessment of the role of police and health professionals in RSE provision throughout the UK. 3) A comparison of the current provision of RSE with that identified in the Reading University study. 4) An assessment of the current usage of RSE resources developed through Department of Transport funding. 5) The identification and dissemination of examples of good practice in RSE. 6) Recommendations as to methods to improve the content and delivery of RSE in schools. @#Published Material:#@ MENZIES, I.M. & CLAYTON, A.B. (1995). A national survey of road user education in Scottish secondary schools. A report to the Scottish Office. Birmingham: British Institute of Traffic Education Research. ; PLATT, C.V., PRINGLE, S. & CLAYTON, A.B. (1996). A national survey of road user education in Scottish primary schools. A report to the Scottish Office. Birmingham: British Institute of Traffic Education Research.

STATUS: Sponsored project

SOURCE OF GRANT: Department of Transport £208,000

DATE OF RESEARCH: 1996-1998

KEYWORDS: **further education; primary education; safety education; secondary education; traffic safety**

Brunel University

0259

Department of Continuing Education, Uxbridge UB8 3PH
01895 274000

Sheddick, A. Ms; Jones, S. Ms

Grant maintained schools survey

ABSTRACT: Survey of all grant maintained schools covering headteachers' views of the effect of being grant maintained in all aspects of the schools' functioning.

STATUS: Sponsored project

SOURCE OF GRANT: Brunel University £7,000

DATE OF RESEARCH: 1995-continuing

KEYWORDS: **educational administration; educational finance; grant maintained schools; head teachers; school based management**

0260

Department of Government, Centre for the Evaluation of Public Policy and Practice, Uxbridge UB8 3PH   01895 274000

Kogan, M. Prof.; Cordingley, P. Ms

Governing the reformed system of education

ABSTRACT: An analysis of the range of governing patterns set in train by the legislation of 1988 and 1993. The research analyses these models against intended outcomes of values, needs and functions. The research was conducted in three local education authority areas and through a series of consultations at which emerging conceptualisations were tested and developed.

PUBLISHED MATERIAL: CORDINGLEY, P. & KOGAN, M. (1993). In support of education: the functioning of local Government. London: Jessica Kingsley Publishers.

STATUS: Sponsored project

SOURCE OF GRANT: Joseph Rowntree Foundation £70,000

DATE OF RESEARCH: 1991-1993

KEYWORDS: **educational administration; educational change; educational policy; governance; governing bodies; local education authorities; management in education**

0261

Department of Government, Centre for the Evaluation of Public Policy and Practice, Uxbridge UB8 3PH   01895 274000
Sussex University, Institute of Education, Education Development Building, Falmer, Brighton BN1 9RG   01273 606755

Becher, T. Prof.; Henkel, M. Ms; Kogan, M. Prof

Graduate education in Britain

ABSTRACT: The research followed six disciplines in eighteen departments in twelve institutions through interviews and study of documentation. It analysed research, graduate education, funding and policies at the national level, and the processes of recruiting, training and assessing graduate students.

PUBLISHED MATERIAL: BECHER, T., HENKEL, M. & KOGAN, M. (1993). Graduate education in Britain. London: Jessica Kingsley Publishers.

STATUS: Sponsored project

SOURCE OF GRANT: Nuffield Foundation £5,000

DATE OF RESEARCH: 1990-1993

KEYWORDS: **graduate study; higher education; student recruitment**

0262

Department of Government, Centre for the Evaluation of Public Policy and Practice, Uxbridge UB8 3PH   01895 274000

Hanney, S. Dr; Lansbury, A. Dr; Vaux, J. Ms; Laing, D. Mrs; *Supervisors*: Henkel, M. Ms; Kogan, M. Prof.

Evaluation of foresight programme

ABSTRACT: The project is evaluating academic responses to the UK Foresight Programme. It is examining how far members of the academic community at different levels have supported and responded to the Programme, what patterns of response emerge and whether they are changing. The study is being undertaken in 2 case areas: health and life sciences, and materials. It is based on documentary materials, a survey and interviews with key policymakers, members of the relevant committees and panels and a sample of academics within the subject areas.

STATUS: Sponsored project

SOURCE OF GRANT: Nuffield Foundation £52,000

DATE OF RESEARCH: 1997-1998

KEYWORDS: futures - of society; health; higher education; industry; resources; technology transfer

0263

Department of Government, Centre for the Evaluation of Public Policy and Practice, Uxbridge UB8 3PH 01895 274000

Healy, C. Ms; Hanney, S. Dr; Jones, S. Ms; *Supervisors*: Henkel, M. Ms; Kogan, M. Prof.

International study of higher education reforms

ABSTRACT: The study is a free-standing part of a research programme being conducted collaboratively by an English, a Swedish and a Norwegian research team. The aim is to study the changing role of government in the 3 countries in the creation and execution of higher education policy from the 1970s to the present time; to examine how higher education reforms have been received and implemented or counteracted by academic faculty and academic leaders, and to analyse how reform policies and structural changes have affected the working lives, values, identities, and productivity of academics in higher education institutions. It is thus a study of relationships between macro and micro level change. An overarching aim is to compare the 3 countries in these dimensions. An attempt will be made to construct a general comparative framework, using common organising themes and enlisting salient theories in the descriptive analysis and comparison of key political and academic phenomena. The English study incorporates extensive studies of quality assurance, the Enterprise Initiative and the role of interest groups and elites in policy formation. Much of the emphasis of the whole study is on the impact of reforms on curriculum and its delivery and on research agendas and epistemologies.

PUBLISHED MATERIAL: HENKEL, M. (1997). 'Academic values and the university as corporate enterprise', Higher Education Quarterly, Vol 51, No 2, pp.134-143. ; HENKEL, M. (1997). 'Teaching quality assessments: public accountability and academic autonomy in higher education', Evaluation, Vol 3, No 1, pp.9-23.

STATUS: Sponsored project

SOURCE OF GRANT: Swedish Council for Higher Education Studies ; Spence Foundation

DATE OF RESEARCH: 1994-1998

KEYWORDS: comparative education; educational change; educational policy; higher education; norway; sweden

0264

Department of Government, Centre for the Evaluation of Public Policy and Practice, Uxbridge UB8 3PH   01895 274000
Keele University, Department of Education, Keele ST5 5BG 01782 621111

Kogan, M. Prof.; Maden, M. Prof.; Jones, S. Dr

A review of the OFSTED system of school inspection

ABSTRACT: The review will evaluate the following: 1) The impact of inspections on individual schools and those directly concerned with them. 2) The extent to which a range of stakeholders, including schools, parents, local authorities, inspectors, teacher associations and key subject associations, have confidence in the current inspection process and consider that it stimulates a culture of improvement and better achievement. 3) The extent to which the inspection process is perceived to be appropriate to all types of schools. 4) The extent to which the methods, process and outcomes of inspection are considered to be appropriate and thereby provide valid and reliable evidence from which to make both individual and national judgements about school and teacher performance. 5) Whether or not inspection is considered to provide accountability to directly involved

professional groups and policymakers and, more informally, to parents as direct users of the system. 6) The way in which the Office for Standards in Education (OFSTED) inspections form part of a range of other inspectorial and audit activities which bear on schools and the impacts and relationships between these. 7) The real costs of inspection and the extent to which it represents value for money.

STATUS: Sponsored project

SOURCE OF GRANT: Joseph Rowntree Charitable Trust to OFTSTIN (Office for Standards in Education) £62,000

DATE OF RESEARCH: 1998-1998

KEYWORDS: educational quality; inspection; inspectors - of schools; ofsted; school effectiveness; school improvement; standards

0265

Department of Government, Centre for the Evaluation of Public Policy and Practice, Uxbridge UB8 3PH   01895 274000

Henkel, M. Ms; Healy, C. Ms; *Supervisors*: Tsaosis, D. Prof.; Kogan, M. Prof.

Lifelong learning: the implications for the universities in the European Union

ABSTRACT: The object of the project is to analyse the structural and functional implications of lifelong learning in the European Union (EU). The British project is part of a larger project convened by the Pantheion University, Athens, and includes contributions from France, Germany, Greece, Norway, Spain and Sweden. The objectives of the research are: a) To identify, measure and analyse the extent and nature of the actual involvement of the universities in lifelong learning. This will involve addressing the general question of the reformulation of educational goals and examining the actual and potential strategies of the universities concerning lifelong learning. b) To examine, describe and analyse the implications which lifelong learning educational practices and programmes are having, or are anticipated to have, on traditional power structures and traditional forms of knowledge within the universities. c) To describe, compare and analyse actual and potential policies of universities in this area with corresponding policies, explicitly or implicitly stated, in various EU educational documents and programmes as well as in documents of various international organisations. This will also involve examining case studies and literature on lifelong learning at a European and international level. d) Examine the actual and potential links which the universities have with employers and other stakeholders as a consequence of adopting lifelong learning educational programmes. This will involve examining models of lifelong learning and problems of quality assurance and certification. The research will attempt to identify and analyse changes in knowledge and shifts from traditional discipline-based domains to non-traditional lifelong learning domains and will analyse changes in power relationships and structures as a consequence of involvement in lifelong learning. It will identify structural and attitudinal obstacles and explore potential points of growth. It will explore changes in certification and quality assurance related to lifelong learning and methods of disseminating it within the universities.

PUBLISHED MATERIAL: CAVE, M., HANNEY, S. & HENKEL, M. & KOGAN, M. (1997). The use of performance indicators in higher education: the challenge of the quality movement. London: Jessica Kingsley Publishers, 3rd Edition. ; HENKEL, M. (1997). 'Academic values and the university as corporate enterprise', Higher Education Quarterly, Vol 51, No 2, pp.134-143. ; HENKEL, M. & LITTLE, B. (Ed). (1998). Changing relationships between higher education and the state. London: Jessica Kingsley Publishers. ; HENKEL, M. (1998). 'Higher education'. In: LAFFIN, M. (Ed). Beyond bureaucracy? New approaches in public management. Aldershot: Ashgate.

STATUS: Sponsored project

SOURCE OF GRANT: European Union; Brunel University

DATE OF RESEARCH: 1998-continuing

KEYWORDS: continuing education; higher education; lifelong learning

0266

Department of Human Sciences, Uxbridge UB8 3PH 01895 274000

King, E. Ms ; Supervisor:Richardson, J. Prof.

Shifting identities: older students' interaction with higher education - exploring the researcher and the researched

ABSTRACT: This thesis sets out to explore two inter-related but distinct research areas: the constructions of older students as learners at university; and the positionings of the researcher and the researched. Represented here is a longitudinal cyclical study, which employs a grounded analysis of 21 female and 4 male students, aged 22-25, at their point of entry into higher education, with 13 self-identified as having come from a working class background, and 18 having entered higher education via an Access course. Initial life-story interviews were carried out close to the end of particpants' first semester in higher education, followed by 19 follow-up interviews close to the end of the second year. The final cycle with the participants involved a focus group with 6 women and 1 man who, at the same university, were in the final year of their degree course. Interviewees were invited to respond to the patterns and themes arising from transcripts and papers for publications. Using a grounded analysis, the core strategy emerging from the life-story narratives, affecting all but 2 of these individuals' sense of self, and their resultant identities as learners, is summarised as discontinuity or conflict in childhood, indicated by a number of constituents relating to: parental characteristics, personal and family trauma, and environmental change. In the context of preparing for and entering higher education as older students, the research explores the themes associated with time, especially the concept of the 'right time'. The researcher focuses on how core concepts such as self-worth, esteem and confidnece, not necessarily restricted to one chronological period, are highlighted when confronted with the challenge posed by the institution. Identifying points of similarity and difference in the data, the researcher proposes a conception of learner identity that is often in flux, one that, affected by temporal dimensions, entails a multiplicity of overlapping and shifting constituents. In emphasising the affective aspect of reflexivity, the aim is to complement what is perceived as the shifting conceptual terrain associated with a post-structuralist notion of the self and recognise that there is no essentialist 'blueprint' to enable researchers to understand better how to use themselves as researchers. The researcher relates an appraisal of her own performance to a broader, theoretical consideration of the interviewing context, contributing to what she considers to be a much neglected area of methodology within psychology. A number of issues and ethical concerns relating to researcher responsibility are discussed, and in relation to this, a comparison is made between pertinent aspects of the counselling interview and the research interview. Extrapolating from a particular feminist standpoint, representation of the self and others that are represented through the processes of the research are discussed to develop an analytical framework that extends beyond a language of experience.

PUBLISHED MATERIAL: RICHARDSON, J.T.E. & KING, E. (1991). 'Gender differences in the experience of higher education: quantitative and qualitative approaches', Educational Psychology, Vol 11, Nos 3 & 4, pp.363-382. ; KING, E. (1996). 'The use of the self in qualitative research'. In: RICHARDSON, J.T.E. (Ed). The handbook of qualitative research methods for psychologists and social scientists. Leicester: BPS Books. ; HAYES, K., KING, E. & RICHARDSON, J.T.E. (1997). 'Mature students in higher education 111: approaches to studying in Access students', Studies in Higher Education Education, Vol 22, No 1, pp.19-31. ; KING, E. (1998). 'Entering higher education: older students' constructions of self as learners'. In: RADFORD, J. (Ed). Gender and choice in education and occupation. London: Routledge. ; BOLA, B., DREW, C., GILL, R., HARDING, S., KING, E. & SEI, I.B. (1998). 'Representing ourselves and representing others: a response', Feminism and Psychology, Vol 8, No 1.

STATUS: Individual research

DATE OF RESEARCH: 1992-1998

KEYWORDS: higher education; learning experience; mature students; nontraditional students; student experience

0267

Department of Human Sciences, Uxbridge UB8 3PH
01895 274000

Green, A. Dr

Item context effects on children's mathematical problem-solving performance

ABSTRACT: This experiment set out to examine the impact of different forms of contextualisation on problem-solving performance of children from 2 age groups (Year 4 and Year 6). The amount and type of context used in setting mathematical items was varied. The study was a mixed 2 (age groups) x 2 (gender) x 3 (mathematical content) x 4 (context) design. Four items from each of the categories number, algebra, and shape and space were constructed, yielding 12 different items. The items were produced in each of the following 4 contexts - no context, visual information redundant, verbal information redundant, and visual and verbal information relevant, yielding a total of 48 items for each age group. The researcher then constructed 4 booklets of 12 items, mixing type of context within each booklet and ensuring that each item appeared in just one context in each booklet. Children of both sexes (n=148) from 3 schools participated in the experiment. Mathematical ability was denoted as below average, average or above average on the basis of objective assessments and teacher observations. Children worked on the 4 booklets over 4 45-minute sessions, each session separated by a break of 3 or 4 days. Preliminary analyses indicate the following: a repeated measures ANOVA showed large main effects for context, as well as the predicted effects for mathematical content and ability; there were significant interactions between mathematical content and context, mathematical content, context and ability, and mathematical content, context and gender. These results suggest that performance in some content areas is influenced by the context in which an item is presented, and that context can hamper performance. Further, children of different abilities appear to be differentially influenced by the way in which an item is contextualised. Finally, results are largely consistent across the 2 age groups, the effects of context more pronounced with the younger children.

STATUS: Sponsored project

SOURCE OF GRANT: Brunel University £3,500

DATE OF RESEARCH: 1996-1998

KEYWORDS: mathematics education; problem solving

0268

Department of PE and Sport, Osterley Campus, Borough Road, Isleworth TW7 5DU   0181 891 0121

Armour, K. Mrs

The ecology of physical education: an investigation into the 'life' of a physical education department

ABSTRACT: Within an ethnographic, case study framework, this research uses observations, interviews and life history reflections to investigate the 'life' of a physical education department in a secondary school. The central focus is upon the four physical education teachers in the department, charting how they develop their personal understanding of the nature and purpose of physical education. These understandings are located in the broader context of the school and the conflicting perspectives of senior teachers, parents and pupils. In the final analysis, the ecological metaphor is found wanting and the dramatic nature of 'interacting scripts' for education and physical education is highlighted in the framework of the agent/structure debate.

STATUS: Individual research

DATE OF RESEARCH: 1988-1993

KEYWORDS: physical education; physical education teachers

0269

School of Education, Twickenham Campus, 300 St Margaret's Road, Twickenham TW1 1PT   0181 891 0121

Hilliman, P. Mrs; *Supervisor*: Sandow, S. Dr

An investigation into the management of change in a local education authority, with particular reference to special educational needs

ABSTRACT: This study aims to elucidate the processes underlying a failed innovation and to identify the contributing factors. The analysis includes an examination of the interaction between the identification of the need for change, and the role of the education department. Interviews, reports and public documents provide sources for analysis.

STATUS: Individual research

DATE OF RESEARCH: 1991-1993

KEYWORDS: educational change; educational innovation; local education authorities; special educational needs

0270

School of Education, Twickenham Campus, 300 St Margaret's Road, Twickenham TW1 1PT   0181 891 0121

Wiles, N. Mr; *Supervisors*: Wright, D. Dr; Cleminson, A. Dr

Development of a hypermedia system to teach scientific concepts

ABSTRACT: The research will: 1) establish the knowledge and understanding of electricity among primary school teachers; 2) develop an interactive hypermedia system, based on constructivist learning theory, to allow learners to master concepts relating to electricity; and 3) evaluate the effectiveness of the system developed.

STATUS: Individual research

DATE OF RESEARCH: 1994-1998

KEYWORDS: **computer uses in education; electricity; hypermedia; information technology; science education; scientific concepts**

0271

School of Education, Twickenham Campus, 300 St Margaret's Road, Twickenham TW1 1PT   0181 891 0121

Marris, C. Mr; *Supervisors*: Hinchcliffe, V. Dr; Sandow, S. Dr

Representation and theory of mind in children with autism

ABSTRACT: A previous study investigated the 'intellectual to visual realism shift' across drawing tasks - cylinders, cubes, houses, mugs, self-portraits. Meta-representation was investigated using a puppet-play false belief task. Findings of the study indicated that children with autism were able to represent 'non-mental' representations: graphic representation followed a similar developmental pattern to the mainstream peer group whilst the capacity for meta-representation appeared markedly delayed in the group of children with autism. However there was some evidence that the ability for mentalistic representation may be present in a small number of children with autism. The present study will investigate the development of representation in children with autism with particular reference to graphic representation and representation of mental states.

STATUS: Individual research

DATE OF RESEARCH: 1995-1998

KEYWORDS: **autism; representation**

0272

School of Education, Twickenham Campus, 300 St Margaret's Road, Twickenham TW1 1PT   0181 891 0121

Male, T. Mr; Allen, F. Mrs; Norton, A. Mr; Lyons, T. Mr

Meanwhile back at the ranch: a study of deputy headteachers in UK secondary schools

ABSTRACT: The aim is to undertake an observational and interactive study of the role and tasks of deputy headteacher in UK secondary schools. Approximately 10 deputies will be tracked across the entire academic year of 1995-96. It is anticipated that the researchers will visit each deputy once a month, a total of 10 visits, each of a minimum of half-day's duration. This observation will be supplemented by semi-structured interviews of each subject at the outset, mid-term and conclusion of the year. In addition, the subjects will be invited to joint sessions sponsored by the research team to exchange and compare experiences. It is anticipated that the final report will give a clearer picture of the nature of a deputy headteacher's role in schools than is currently available.

STATUS: Sponsored project

SOURCE OF GRANT: Brunel University College

DATE OF RESEARCH: 1995-1997

KEYWORDS: **deputy head teachers; secondary education; teacher role; teaching profession**

0273

School of Education, Twickenham Campus, 300 St Margaret's Road, Twickenham TW1 1PT   0181 891 0121

Williams, M. Dr; *Supervisors*: Thomas, L. Prof.; Gregory, G. Dr

The impact of the English National Curriculum (1990) on the work of teachers at key stage 2

ABSTRACT: A longitudinal study which exlores the impact of the English National Curriculum (1990) on the work of teachers at key stage 2 based on teachers' experiernces viewed in relation to a theoretical template of questions. The questions - refined during a process of iteration throughout the research - provided a conceptual framework which kept it focused and manageable. Data - obtained from interviews, document study and observation -derived from five cases were subject to qualitative analysis which involved progressive reflection, the use of matrices to sort and sift and the identification of similar phrases, patterns, themes and differences, both between and across the range of participants, and across the various cases. Key patterns and differences emerged which were then cross matched with each subsequent case in a process of refocusing and refinement. Several issues emerged prompting questions about teachers' experience of: (1) subject knowledge across all four language modes of English; (2) the complexities involved in teaching pupils to read; (3) process approaches to teaching writing; (4) the part that metatextual and metalinguistic understanding plays in learning; (5) teaching techniques which support the teaching of speaking and listening; (6) the relationship between standard English and language variation. These were viewed within the context of the National Literacy Strategy (March, 1998) in order to reach conclusions and frame recommendations for theory, practice and policy.

Published Material: WILLIAMS, M. (1993). 'The English National Curriculum at key stage 2', Reading, Vol 27, No 3, pp.9-14.

STATUS: Individual research

DATE OF RESEARCH: 1995-1998

KEYWORDS: **curriculum development; educational change; english; english studies curriculum; english studies teachers; key stage 2; literacy education; national curriculum; national literacy strategy; primary education; teacher attitudes**

0274

School of Education, Twickenham Campus, 300 St Margaret's Road, Twickenham TW1 1PT   0181 891 0121

Liptai, S. Ms; *Supervisors*: Thomas, L. Prof.; Fisher, R. Dr

Thinking about music: developing children's musical thinking through discussion in primary classrooms

ABSTRACT: The 'community of enquiry', as defined by American philosopher Matthew Lipman, is a powerful structure for generating discussion in a group. By exchanging their views and ideas about a stimulus, the members of the group participate in a cooperative, self-governing and democratic community. By listening to, evaluating, criticising and building on each other's ideas, the participants develop a range of thinking and collaborative skills which they are known to transfer to other areas of learning. The researcher is investigating the use of music as the stimulus - either on its own or in combination with works of art - in 'communities of enquiry' with primary school age children. The main questions are: 1) Which kinds of musical stimuli and what kinds of presentation of these stimuli generate the richest and most philosophical discussions? 2) What aspects of music can be most usefully investigated in this way? 3) What are the learning outcomes? (e.g. do the children come to appreciate the syntactic and non-syntactic features of works of music? Do they understand the socio-cultural embeddedness of musical works? Does their learning influence their own musical acitivities, e.g. performing, improvising, composing?).

PUBLISHED MATERIAL: LIPTAI, S. (1996). A case for an aesethetic community of enquiry if ..... then', Journal of Philosophical Enquiry in Education, Issue 2.

STATUS: Individual research

DATE OF RESEARCH: 1995-1998

KEYWORDS: **classroom communication; discussion - teaching technique; learning strategies; music; primary education; primary school pupils; teaching methods; thinking skills**

0275

School of Education, Twickenham Campus, 300 St Margaret's Road, Twickenham TW1 1PT   0181 891 0121

Rask, H. Ms; Williams, M. Ms

Raising literacy standards at National Curriculum key stage 1

ABSTRACT: The investigation is within the ethnographic, interpretive paradigm. It aims to identify factors which enable the most able Year 1 pupils to extend and develop their literacy during National Curriculum key stage 1 and beyond. It aims to provide a research-based contribution to the current debate on the teaching of reading, and the interrelationship between reading and writing development in the early years. The focus on particularly able young readers and writers aims to illuminate factors which will promote early achievement in literacy. The research methodology will involve small scale studies in 4 schools. Data will be collected through teacher interviews, parent interviews and child conferences. The researchers will adopt both participant and non-participant roles whilst undertaking fieldwork in these schools. Interrogation and factor analysis of the data will be conducted and written-up. The intended outcomes of this research are joint articles in both professional and refereed journals with the dissemination of the findings at a suitably focused international conference.

STATUS: Sponsored project

SOURCE OF GRANT: Brunel University £5,130

DATE OF RESEARCH: 1996-1998

KEYWORDS: **able pupils; key stage 1; literacy education; primary education; reading teaching; teaching methods; writing teaching**

0276

School of Education, Twickenham Campus, 300 St Margaret's Road, Twickenham TW1 1PT   0181 891 0121

Hodkinson, S. Prof.; Catt, R. Mr; Cleminson, A. Mr; Humble, M. Mr

Keys: achievement in mathematics, English and science at National Curriculum key stage 3

ABSTRACT: This project aims to monitor and evaluate the achievements of a sample of pupils in 3 schools at National Curriculum key stage 3 in mathematics, science and English. Planned interventions to provide baseline information on achievements, feedback on teacher and pupil actions, information on pupil work outputs, and comment on subject and school organisation/processes, are intended to identify and ameliorate barriers to raising achievement. The extent to which the processes identified are implemented in the schools, and achievement in key stage tests, are being used to evaluate the effectiveness of the interventions.

STATUS: Sponsored project

SOURCE OF GRANT: Kensington and Chelsea Local Education Authority £24,000

DATE OF RESEARCH: 1996-continuing

KEYWORDS: **academic achievement; assessment; english; key stage 3; mathematics education; national curriculum; science education; secondary education**

0277

School of Education, Twickenham Campus, 300 St Margaret's Road, Twickenham TW1 1PT   0181 891 0121

Thomas, L. Prof.; Wood, K. Dr

Teachers' views of their role in developing professional competence

ABSTRACT: Classroom teachers' involvement in initial teacher education (ITE) as mentors provides an opportunity to study their understanding of their role in the development of professional competence. This study uses a method of contextual analysis called phenomenography to map teachers' developing views of competence as their involvement in an ITE programme deepens. Expected outcomes include a set of conceptions of professional competence and case studies of ITE mentor development.

STATUS: Team research

DATE OF RESEARCH: 1996-1998

KEYWORDS: **mentors; preservice teacher education; teaching profession**

0278

School of Education, Twickenham Campus, 300 St Margaret's Road, Twickenham TW1 1PT   0181 891 0121

Noor, N. Ms; *Supervisor*: Hodkinson, S. Prof.

Secretarial training in Malaysia and the needs of the business community

ABSTRACT: The fast developing economy of Malaysia is imposing new demands for employment skills. This study considers the case of secretarial skills and new entrants to the labour market. It aims to provide insights into the nature of a secretarial training curriculum which will meet the demands of employers. The principal research instruments are a survey of comparative curricula in the UK and Malaysia, questionnaire surveys of principal newspaper advertisements for secretarial employment over a 6 month period, questionnaire surveys of past students of a large institute and their employers (on the functions, perceived effectiveness and training of secretaries), and exemplar experiment in curriculum innovation in the large institute. The findings will inform curriculum development.

STATUS: Individual research

DATE OF RESEARCH: 1994-1997

KEYWORDS: **malaysia; office occupations education; secretaries; vocational education**

0279

School of Education, Twickenham Campus, 300 St Margaret's Road, Twickenham TW1 1PT   0181 891 0121

Hodkinson, S. Prof.

Target teaching: service personnel into teaching

ABSTRACT: The need for 50% more secondary school teachers in National Curriculum subjects by the year 2000 has been identified by the Department for Education and Employment. Some 10,000 personnel leave the armed services annually, many of whom have the necessary qualifications and subject skills for entry into teacher training. Despite this, very few currently choose teaching as a further career. This project aims to identify service personnel who are considering teaching as a career, to assess the perceived barriers to entry and to monitor final destinations. Interventions designed by the Teacher Training Agency to target this group will be taken into account. Survey instruments include interviews at career briefings, and a postal questionnaire of enquirers to a dedicated information service. The outcomes are intended to inform policy on schemes for mature entrants to the profession.

STATUS: Sponsored project

SOURCE OF GRANT: Teacher Training Agency £10,000

DATE OF RESEARCH: 1996-1998

KEYWORDS: **armed forces; preservice teacher education; student recruitment; teacher employment; teacher recruitment; teacher supply and demand; teaching profession**

0280

School of Education, Twickenham Campus, 300 St Margaret's Road, Twickenham TW1 1PT   0181 8910121

Wood, K. Dr; Thomas, L. Prof.

Learning to teach: a phenomenographic perspective

ABSTRACT: It has been established in empirical and theoretical studies around the world in a broad range of learning contexts that the outcome of learning is logically related to the learner's approach to learning. It can be argued that this is also true of learning to teach particular subject matter - beginning teachers who adopt a surface approach to learning to teach achieve restricted outcomes, while those who adopt a deep approach achieve an understanding of what is required for meaningful pupil learning of their subject. Research to date has shown, with reference to the development of an initial teacher education (ITE) curriculum programme, how it is possible to teach beginning teachers so that they adopt a deep approach to learning to teach their subject. This is done by focusing their attention on the variation in their pupils' learning and understanding of subject matter. The results of a year-long action research study of beginning teachers' experience of this teacher education programme are available. A set of qualitatively different conceptions of teaching was produced which allowed the outcomes of the programme - beginning teachers' developing conceptions of teaching their subject - to be related through detailed case studies to qualitative differences in approach to learning to teach (deep or surface). This has subsequently allowed for the development of a new framework for testing the quality of teacher learning and for evaluating specific models of teacher education, e.g. those based on statements of competence or National Curriculum attainment targets.

PUBLISHED MATERIAL: WOOD, K. (1996). 'The teacher as learner in teaching economics and business'. In: HODKINSON, S.R. & JEPHCOTE, M. (Eds). Teaching economics and business. Oxford: Heinemann. ; WOOD, K. (1996). 'Competence, awareness and the education of teachers', Economic Awareness, Vol 8, No 1, pp.17-23. ; WOOD, K. (1997). 'Learning to teach economics - a phenomenographic perspective'. In: WALSTAD, W. (Ed). Secondary economics and business education: new developments in the United Kingdom, United States of America and other nations. Hassocks: Economics and Business Education Association.

STATUS: Team research

DATE OF RESEARCH: 1991-1998

KEYWORDS: learning theories; preservice teacher education; student teachers

0281

School of Education, Twickenham Campus, 300 St Margaret's Road, Twickenham TW1 1PT   0181 891 0121

Murray, J. Ms ; *Supervisors*: Green, T. Dr ; Brown, A. Mr

Between the chalk face and the ivory towers: a study of primary initial teacher educators in the university sector

ABSTRACT: The research study looks at the impact of the Department of Education and Science Circular 3/84 (which required all initial teacher educators to have 'recent and relevant' school experience) on primary initial teacher education (ITE). The empirical work includes a study of the career development of 15 teacher educators in 3 UK universities. The empirical work is related to an analysis of institutional cultures in the developing schools of education within established and 'new' universities. The findings of the study have yet to be formalised.

PUBLISHED MATERIAL: MURRAY, J. (1996). 'Recent experience of teacher educators in the UK'. Paper given at the British Educational Management and Administration Society International Conference, 1996. ; MURRAY, J. (1996). 'Teacher educators, teaching and research'. Paper given at the British Educational Research Association Annual Conference, Lancaster University, Lancaster, September 1996. ; MURRAY, J. Integration or dichotomy of teaching and research? A case of primary initial teacher educators', Teachers and Teaching. (in press).

STATUS: Individual research

DATE OF RESEARCH: 1994-continuing

KEYWORDS: higher education; preservice teacher education; teacher educators; universities

0282

School of Education, Twickenham Campus, 300 St Margaret's Road, Twickenham TW1 1PT   0181 891 0121

White, P. Mr; *Supervisors*: Thomas, L. Prof.; Hodkinson, S. Prof.

Young people and the lottery

ABSTRACT: The National Lottery has had a huge impact on individuals' economic choices since its launch in November 1994. The extent to which the Lottery has had an impact on people's lives can be measured by the fact that over 400 prizes of 1 million pounds or more have been won, in addition to over 95% of the adult population claiming to have played the lottery at some point and around 70% claiming to play on a regular basis (National Council for Voluntary Organisations 1997). What these statistics clearly show is that the Lottery is a fact of life in the world of today's young people. What is not shown is what young people make of it. The main objective of this study is to examine the development of the National Lottery, since it was introduced in November 1994, from the perspective of young people. The setting up of a national survey (to be based on interviews with a sample of young people) will explore how young people would like the Lottery to be organised and run as we approach the expiry date of the current operator's licence in 2001. The research will have implications for policy and practice and the accounts of young people's experience will also be used to illuminate theory.

STATUS: Individual research

DATE OF RESEARCH: 1997-continuing

KEYWORDS: adolescents; economics; gambling; national lottery; youth

0283

School of Education, Twickenham Campus, St Margaret's Road, Twickenham TW1 1PT   0181 891 0121

Exeter University, Northcote House, The Queen's Drive, Exeter EX4 4QJ 01392 263263

Koshy, V. Dr; *Supervisors*: Ernest, P. Dr; Radnor, H. Dr

The impact of the National Curriculum on the teaching and learning of mathematics

ABSTRACT: The study investigates, based on a selected sample of primary school teachers teaching key stage 2 pupils, the impact of a centrally imposed National Curriculum on the teaching and learning of mathematics. Empirically, it looks at teachers' perceptions of what changes have been brought about by the introduction of the National Curriculum and how these perceptions matched what was happening in classrooms. Within an ethnographic, interpretive paradigm the study was conducted using a mixture of methodologies. Data was collected in 2 phases, using questionnaires and interviews in the first phase and further interviews and case studies in the second. The first phase of the study showed that teachers felt a number of changes had taken place in their mathematics teaching as a result of the introduction of the National Curriculum. Many of these changes were amongst the 'recommended good practices' which have evolved from curriculum development initiatives over the last few decades. The second phase of the study which focused on the nature of the classroom practices and how the 'perceived' changes were actually translated into classroom practice, highlighted some mismatch between 'perceptions' and actual 'practices'. For implementing the National Curriculum, teachers relied heavily on their own interpretations of the programmes of study and commercially produced materials. The overloaded content and perceived lack of subject knowledge caused much stress and anxiety for teachers who took part in the study.

PUBLISHED MATERIAL: MITCHELL, C. & KOSHY, V. (1995). Effective teacher assessment. London: Hodder & Stoughton.

STATUS: Individual research

DATE OF RESEARCH: 1991-1997

KEYWORDS: key stage 2; mathematics education; national curriculum; primary education; teaching methods

0284

School of Education, Twickenham Campus, 300 St Margaret's Road, Twickenham TW1 1PT   0181 891 0121

Exeter University, School of Education, St Luke's, Heavitree Road, Exeter EX1 2LU   01392 263263

Casey, R. Mr; Supervisor: Ernest, P. Dr

Language – games and rules in learning mathematics

ABSTRACT: The thesis has as its purpose the formulation of a model of a reader of mathematical text and the roles of natural language, symbolism and diagrams in the processes of interpretation of such text. It has arisen out of a concern with the distinction between the development of rationality and the encouragement of creativity produced by years of working with, and delivering strategies for, higher ability children. The thesis is very inter-disciplinary, using concepts from linguistics, semantics, artificial intelligence and philosophy. The model produced incorporates the notions of parallel distributed processing and lifeworld and is set in the context of developments in hermeneutics so as to give indications of means of encouraging a creative attitude in a learner of mathematics.

STATUS: Individual research

DATE OF RESEARCH: 1992-1998

KEYWORDS: able pupils; language; mathematical vocabulary; mathematics education; text structure; textbooks

0285

School of Education, Twickenham Campus, 300 St Margaret's Road, Twickenham TW1 1PT   0181 891 0121

Exeter University, School of Education, St Luke's, Heavitree Road, Exeter EX1 2LU   01392 263263

Koshy, V. Dr; Casey, R. Mr; Ernest, P. Dr

Raising achievement in mathematics

ABSTRACT: During recent years British pupils' lack of numeracy skills has been highlighted in international comparisons and in Office for Standards in Education (OFSTED) inspections. The project aims to raise pupils' mathematical achievement by developing their numerical skills through an intervention programme and evaluate the effectiveness of the programme. The sample will be 50 pupils from Years 5 and 6 who are performing at Level 3/4 according to Teacher Assessment. All 50 children have been pre-tested using National Curriculum Tasks and Tests; a subset of the 50 has been interviewed. A control group has also been set up. After the intervention programme, all 50 will be post-tested and interviewed to assess the effect of the programme. Conclusions will be drawn and a major project will be set up based on the results; using a larger sample.

PUBLISHED MATERIAL: HENLEY, J. (1998). Mental maths. Level 1. London: Collins Educational. ; HENLEY, J. (1998). Mental maths. Level 2. London: Collins Educational. ; HENLEY, J. (1998). Mental Maths. Level 3. London: Collins Educational.

STATUS: Sponsored project

SOURCE OF GRANT: Wandsworth Local Education Authority

DATE OF RESEARCH: 1997-continuing

KEYWORDS: **achievement; intervention; mathematics achievement; mathematics education; numeracy; primary education; pupil improvement**

0286

School of Education, Twickenham Campus, 300 St Margaret's Road, Twickenham TW1 1PT   0181 891 0121

Hammersmith and Fulham Local Education Authority, Town Hall, King Street, London W6 9JU   0181 748 3020

Fisher, R. Dr; McCarthy, M. Ms

School improvement through thinking skills project

ABSTRACT: This project involves 15 schools: 12 primary and 3 secondary (one of which is a special school designated for students with moderate learning difficulties). The project is unique in the UK not only because of its focus on creating Thinking Schools, but also because of the range of personnel involved which include headteachers and classroom teachers from each school, together with their link local education authority (LEA) inspectors and educational psychologists, as well as with trainee psychologists attached to each school. The rationale underpinning of the project is that of developing the school as a learning organisation. The key strands of enhancing the effectiveness of school leadership and management, enhancing the quality of teaching and learning, and enhancing the development of pupils as effective thinkers and learners are woven together in a management and development strategy. This involves headteachers and senior management teams in the planning, implementing and evaluation of strategies for improving the portfolio of teaching skills and techniques which they identify as relevant for their school. Headteachers are being supported by link inspector and psychologists in evaluating the results of the project, developing further the systematic collection of evidence and the ability of schools to identify the value added benefits of the project. The project will aim to show evidence of school improvement that will build on the developing body of research about school improvement, as well as making its own positive contribution to our growing understanding of ways of developing pupils' thinking and learning, and of improving schools as communities for thinking and learning.

Published Material: FISHER, R. (1995). Teaching children to think. Cheltenham: Stanley Thornes. ; FISHER, R. (1995). Teaching children to learn. Cheltenham: Stanley Thornes. ; FISHER, R. Teaching philosophy for children. London: Cassell

STATUS: Sponsored project

SOURCE OF GRANT: Hammersmith and Fulham Local Education Authority ; Department for Education and Employment, jointly £10,000

DATE OF RESEARCH: 1996-1997

KEYWORDS: **learning strategies; primary education; school improvement; secondary education; teaching methods; thinking skills**

0287

School of Education, Twickenham Campus, 300 St Margaret's Road,

Twickenham TW1 1PT   0181 891 0121

Hammersmith and Fulham Local Education Authority, Town Hall, King Street, London W6 9JU   0181 748 3020

Fisher, R. Mr; Stoker, R. Mr

Thinking and learning skills project 1997/98

ABSTRACT: The aims of the project address the teaching and learning of higher order, metacognitive skills to improve the academic achievement of primary-age children. 6 primary and 1 nursery school in the London Borough of Hammersmith and Fulham are involved in the project. Project development, management and review within each school is the responsibility of the headteacher and senior management, assisted by educational psychologists and project directors. The school improvement project through Developing Thinking and Learning Skills 1997/98 with its focus on metacognition builds on the success of the 1996/97 project and aims to make a major contribution to the study of metacognitive development in the primary years.

PUBLISHED MATERIAL: FISHER, R. Teaching philosophy for children. London: Cassell. (in press). ; FISHER, R. Thinking about thinking. Oxford: Nash Pollock. (in press).

STATUS: Sponsored project

SOURCE OF GRANT: Hammersmith and Fulham Local Education Authority £2,000

DATE OF RESEARCH: 1997-1998

KEYWORDS: **learning strategies; metacognition; primary education; school improvement; teaching methods; thinking skills**

0288

School of Education, Twickenham Campus, 300 St Margaret's Road, Twickenham TW1 1PT   0181 891 0121

London University, Institute of Education, Department of Education and International Development, 20 Bedford Way, London WC1H OAL 0171 580 1122

Garner, P. Dr; *Supervisor*: Jones, C. Mr

Disruptive behaviour in United Kingdom and United States schools: a comparative study

ABSTRACT: This research uses 'pupil reality' to investigate disruptive behaviour in the UK and USA. Such a response is at the heart of a paradigm which might be best described as 'ecological', where the pupil is viewed as central to the microsystem. The research focuses upon two case studies (one each in the USA and UK). Pupils and their teachers are interviewed (unstructured) and other instruments include critical biographies, diaries, and gathering formal documentary evidence. The research hopes to point to cross-cultural differences in the responses of disruptive pupils to their schooling.

STATUS: Individual research

DATE OF RESEARCH: 1988-1993

KEYWORDS: **antisocial behaviour; comparative education; discipline problems; disruptive pupils; united states of america**

0289

School of Education, Twickenham Campus, 300 St Margaret's Road, Twickenham TW1   1PT 0181 891 0121

University of Kent at Canterbury, Canterbury CT2 7NZ 01227 764000

Hinchcliffe, V. Dr; *Supervisor*: Forrester, M. Dr

The social cognitive development of children with severe learning difficulties

ABSTRACT: This research involves questionnaires, observation and intervention studies to compare the social cognitive development of non-learning impaired and learning impaired children. Children's metalinguistic abilities and their use of mental state language is investigated. The research aims to point to useful teaching procedures for teachers of children with severe learning difficulties.

STATUS: Individual research

DATE OF RESEARCH: 1988-1993

KEYWORDS: **cognitive development; learning disabilities; social cognition; special educational needs**

Cambridge University

0290

Department of Applied Economics, The Old Schools, Trinity Lane, Cambridge CB2 1YN   01223 337733

Pratten, C. Mr

Methods of projecting further education and training

ABSTRACT: The Department of Applied Economics at Cambridge University were asked to prepare econometric models of the participation of 16 and 17 year-olds in full-time education and training, to explain past changes and forecast future changes. The report highlights a number of factors which have affected the participation in education and training significantly since 1954, these include prior attainment, wage differentials and unemployment.

STATUS: Sponsored project

SOURCE OF GRANT: Department for Education and Employment £15,446

DATE OF RESEARCH: 1996-1997

KEYWORDS: further education; school leavers; sixteen to nineteen education; training; vocational education

0291

Department of Experimental Psychology, Downing Site, Downing Street, Cambridge CB2 3EB   01223 333550

Goswami, U. Dr

Orthographic and phonological factors in reading development

ABSTRACT: A series of experiments examining the contribution of orthographic and phonological knowledge to reading development in children are proposed, based on the interactive analogy model of learning to read proposed by Goswami, 1993. Studies will examine both single word and prose reading, and will include both monosyllabic and bi-syllabic words. The methodology depends on contrasting children's reading accuracy and speed for different lists of real and nonsense words, or on contrasting their recognition or learning of the spelling patterns of such words after reading controlled story texts. Pilot data has shown that this methodology is viable with young children. A clearer specification of the role of orthographic and phonological factors in normal reading will clarify the sources of pathology in developmental dyslexia, and will also have implications for neural network (PDP) models of reading that attempt to characterise the relationship between brain and behaviour.

STATUS: Sponsored project

SOURCE OF GRANT: Medical Research Council £86,125

DATE OF RESEARCH: 1994-1998

KEYWORDS: beginning reading; reading skills

0292

Department of Experimental Psychology, Downing Site, Downing Street, Cambridge CB2 3EB   01223 333550

Mackintosh, N. Prof.; Mascie-Taylor, C. Dr

Cognitive and educational attainment in different ethnic groups

ABSTRACT: Ever since the performance of children from ethnic minorities in British schools first became a public issue some 25 years ago, the received wisdom has been that children from the Indian sub-continent might find some initial difficulties in adapting, but would typically emerge from school with qualifications at least as good as those of whites. The problem, it was assumed, was that children of West Indian or African origin did not succeed so well. This wisdom is challenged by the result of a large national survey of 10 year-olds in 1980 - where West Indian children outperformed those of Pakistani or Bangladeshi origin, and did just about as well as those of Indian origin, on a variety of educational and cognitive measures. It is planned to analyse the data of a follow-up survey when these children were 16 to see whether this pattern of differences stayed constant.

PUBLISHED MATERIAL: WEST, A.M., MACKINTOSH, N.J. & MASCIE-TAYLOR, C.G.N. (1992). 'Cognitive and educational attainment in different ethnic groups', Journal of Biosocial Science, Vol 24, No 4, pp.539-554.

STATUS: Sponsored project

SOURCE OF GRANT: Economic and Social Research Council

DATE OF RESEARCH: 1996-1998

KEYWORDS: academic achievement; achievement; cognitive ability; ethnic groups; primary school pupils; secondary school pupils

0293

Department of Experimental Psychology, Downing Site, Downing Street, Cambridge CB2 3EB   01223 333550

Mackintosh, N. Prof.

What do IQ tests measure and do not measure?

ABSTRACT: What do IQ tests measure? Do they really measure all aspects of intelligence? What is intelligence? Is it one thing or many? Although IQ testers have established that their tests have many desirable statistical properties, all of which one would want to see in a good measure of intelligence, and although IQ test scores do predict many other things of importance about people, IQ testers either remain uncomfortable when asked these seemingly fundamental questions, or bluster about the ubiquity and importance of (g) the general factor revealed by factor analysis. The research project will make a start at answering some of these questions. It will first test the idea that IQ tests do not pick up differences in the way people learn incidentally, unreflectively, or unintentionally, and that differences in such 'implicit' learning ability are important for understanding differences in skill or success in many spheres of life (including such traditional validators of IQ as school achievement). A second set of experiments will try to ascertain the extent to which a variety of quite different psychological processes underlie performance on different types of IQ test (verbal, non-verbal, spatial etc) and therefore test the hypothesis that the general factor (g), common to all IQ tests, cannot be reduced to a single psychological process.

STATUS: Sponsored project

SOURCE OF GRANT: Economic and Social Research Council

DATE OF RESEARCH: 1997-continuing

KEYWORDS: assessment; intelligence; intelligence quotient; intelligence tests; tests

0294

Department of Geography, Downing Place, Cambridge CB2 3EN 01223 339957

Bennett, R. Prof.

Education-Business Partnerships (EBP's): targets and stocktake

ABSTRACT: The objective of the report is to provide a stocktake of the current development of Education-Business Partnerships (EBP's). This has the purpose of providing a quality assessment of the current level of development in EBP's in different local education authorities (LEA's). The purpose of the stocktake is to provide a measure of the current development of EBP's against which future evolution and progress can be judged. It is intended that this will encourage existing effective EBP's whilst setting clear targets for the LEA's which have not yet developed full EBP's, and that further assessments will be made annually to stimulate the development of EBP's.

PUBLISHED MATERIAL: BENNETT, R.J., MCCOSHAN, A. & SELLGREN, J. (1989). 'The organisation of business-education links: further findings from the CBI schools questionnaire. Department of Geography Research Papers. London: London University, London School of Economics and Political Science, Department of Geography. ; CONFEDERATION OF BRITISH INDUSTRY. (1992). Education-business partnerships: the learning so far. London: Confederation of British Industry. ; CONFEDERATION OF BRITISH INDUSTRY. (1994). Creating a learning community: a CBI review of education-business links. London: Confederation of British Industry. ; BENNETT, R.J. (1995). 'School-business links: clarifying objectives and processes', Policy Studies, Vol 16, No 1, pp.23-48.

STATUS: Sponsored project

SOURCE OF GRANT: Shell UK; Confederation of British Industry £14,000

DATE OF RESEARCH: 1988-continuing

KEYWORDS: education business partnerships; industry education relationship; local education authorities; partnerships; school to work transition; vocational education

0295

Faculty of Social and Political Sciences, Sociological Research Group, Free School Lane, Cambridge CB2 3RQ   01223 334549

Blackburn, R. Dr; Jarman, J. Dr

Class and gender inequality in access to higher education

ABSTRACT: The last fifty years have seen fundamental changes in education throughout the industrial world, including the United Kingdom. While these changes have affected education at all levels, they have been most dramatic in higher education. There has been massive expansion of provision which has transformed its character and social significance. This research examines, and attempts to explain, the changing patterns of class and gender inequalities in UK higher education. The focus is on access to what may be regarded as the top segment of higher education, full-time university degree courses. Sources include British Labour Force Surveys, and the sample for the Oxford Mobility Study, as well as various forms of published data, mainly from UK government publications.

PUBLISHED MATERIAL: BLACKBURN, R.M. & JARMAN, J. (1992). 'Changing inequalities in access to higher education', Working Paper 12. Cambridge: Cambridge University Sociological Research Group. ; BLACKBURN, R.M. & JARMAN, J. (1993). 'Changing inequalities in access to British universities', Oxford Review of Education, Vol 19, No 2, pp.197-215.

STATUS: Individual research

DATE OF RESEARCH: 1992-1993

KEYWORDS: **access to education; equal education; gender equality; higher education; social class**

0296

Homerton College, Hills Road, Cambridge CB2 2PH
01223 507111

Nottingham University, School of Education, University Park, Nottingham NG7 2RD   01159 515151

Whitebread, D. Mr; *Supervisor*: Youngman, M. Dr

An investigation of cognitive factors involved in the development of problem-solving strategies by young children

ABSTRACT: The study explores the development of young children's problem-solving abilities, and the cognitive factors which might be related to this. Such development is conceptualised in terms of the emergence of increasingly sophisticated and powerful cognitive strategies. Children's performance on an inductive reasoning task (the multidimensional discrimination learning (MDL) task was examined. The sample consisted of 72 Leicestershire primary school children, comprising three equal groups of 24 children aged 6, 8 and 10 years. The children were also tested on a number of cognitive factors theoretically predicted to influence performance on reasoning and problem-solving tasks. These predictors included working memory capacity, metacognitive awareness and control, style of attribution, and two measures of cognitive style (cognitive tempo and field dependence-independence). Cluster analysis of strategic components revealed a pattern of 7 clusters of increasingly complex strategic behaviours used by the children on the MDL task. These strategy clusters appeared to be principally differentiated by an increasing ability to integrate information gained from different trials. Two stylistic variations were also identified which were related to the number of hypotheses verbalised on each trial. Further investigation involving multiple regression analyses revealed that the major factor which predicted strategic behaviour and performance on the MDL task was metacognitive awareness and control. However, correlational analyses of subgroups revealed interactions between predictors, and between predictors and strategies, in relation to performance. No significant effects were revealed relating to gender, but age effects in relation to predictors, strategies and performance were indicated. The implications for future research and for the development of children's thinking and problem-solving skills within educational contexts are discussed.

STATUS: Individual research

DATE OF RESEARCH: 1985-1993

KEYWORDS: **cognitive processes; cognitive style; learning strategies; problem solving**

0297

Research Centre for English and Applied Linguistics, Trumpington Street, Cambridge CB2 1QA   01223 332340

Williams, J. Dr

Bilingual lexical processing

ABSTRACT: The project examines two aspects of lexical processing in non-fluent bilinguals (first year undergraduates studying French, and upper intermediate and advanced foreign learners of English from various language backgrounds): (i) the content of the semantic representations automatically activated by words, and whether words in the bilingual's two languages have representational elements in common; (ii) the mechanisms by which the bilingual controls of language is accessed by a written word, and whether there are circumstances under which no such control can be exercised. Both sets of studies employ experimental methodologies and theoretical models from psycholinguistic research on monolingual lexical processing. Preliminary results show that (i) words in the two languages share 'core semantic' features (e.g. those determining the relations between SUITCASE and BAG), whereas the information supporting 'schematic' relations (e.g. KING - CROWN) is either not automatically activated (even in the monolingual) or is not shared by words in different languages; and (ii) even when performing a task entirely in one language a bilingual's semantic knowledge of the other language is still active (e.g. when a French-English bilingual is performing a reading task entirely in English the word PAIN can be shown to automatically and unconsciously activate the concept BREAD. Current experiments are investigating whether language selective-processing is influenced by language dominance and the degree of phonological processing involved in the task.

STATUS: Individual research

DATE OF RESEARCH: 1993-1993

KEYWORDS: **bilingualism; lexicology; word recognition**

0298

Research Centre for English and Applied Linguistics, Keynes House, Trumpington Street, Cambridge CB2 1QA   01223 332340

Brown, G. Prof.

Inferences in spatial and temporal tasks

ABSTRACT: The study will investigate the nature of inferences constructed, mentioned and/or acted upon by participants in cooperative spatially and temporally structured tasks. The data consists of conversations between 14-16 year olds and undergraduates as they work together to achieve a task. The investigation will build upon the analysis of this data reported in Speakers, Listeners and Communication, 1995.

PUBLISHED MATERIAL: BROWN, G. (1995). Speakers, listeners and communication. Cambridge: Cambridge University Press.

STATUS: Individual research

DATE OF RESEARCH: 1995-continuing

KEYWORDS: **communication skills; conversation; discourse analysis; group work; inferences; secondary education; speech communication**

0299

Research Centre for English and Applied Linguistics, Keynes House, Trumpington Street, Cambridge CB2 1QA   01223 332340

Ketabi, S. Mr; Supervisor: Brown, E. Prof.; Brown, G. Prof.

An investigation into the acquisition of modality by Persian learners of English

ABSTRACT: The main aim of this study is to investigate the acquisition of modality by Persian learners of English. Modality is defined as grammaticalization or lexicalization of speaker's attitude towards what is said (uncertainty, etc). This study investigates the acquisition of modality by 3 groups of Persian learners of English at 3 consecutive 'levels' of studying English at university, by using 4 different types of data elicitation techniques i.e. a) 'free-production', b) 'paraphrase', c) 'translation', and d) 'scale'. The following questions are asked: 1) What are the similarities and differences between a group of English native speakers and 3 groups of Persian learners of English as far as comprehension and production of some modal meanings are concerned? 2) What is the role of the first language (L1), Persian, transfer as one of the possible factors contributing to the differences observed? 3) Are there general patterns or regularities in the interlanguage grammar of Persian learners with regard to the acquisition of modality in English? Do they pass through certain developmental stages in their acquisition? If there are found to be some patterns, do they correspond with the patterns found in L1 acquisition?

STATUS: Individual research

DATE OF RESEARCH: 1993-1997

KEYWORDS: english - second language; grammar; second language learning

0300

Research Centre for English and Applied Linguistics, Keynes House, Trumpington Street, Cambridge CB2 1QA   01223 332340

Lee, B. Mr; *Supervisor*: Brown, G. Prof.

Establishing common ground in written correspondence

ABSTRACT: The purpose of this dissertation is to throw light on the processes involved in establishing shared beliefs between interactants involved in authentic written correspondence of a transactional nature. A case study comprising 8 consecutive letters is analysed to investigate the processes. In order to do this, 3 layers of analyses are made. Firstly, how the reader interprets the key utterances by generating the necessary inferences in accordance with his perception of what his writer's intentions and reasoning schema may be. This interpretative process is further demonstrated to be influenced by the expanding context and by the reader's intention in reading. Secondly, how the writer packages her referring expressions and utterances in order to establish new/given information. Information status is anlaysed at 2 levels: entity and propositional. The interaction of the 2 levels of information is represented graphically, making it possible to offer new insights on the relationship between attenuation of linguistic forms, propositional content, information status and the discourse context. Thirdly, realising that the assumptions made by the writer and reader in packaging and inferring respectively are embedded, a new technique is developed to configure their evolving shared beliefs/doubts, showing how common ground is/is not established. The results of this configuration make it possible to characterise the nature of common ground, particularly in terms of a taxonomy. The conclusion for the dissertation is to suggest what a cognitive model of the process of establishing common ground may look like.

STATUS: Individual research

DATE OF RESEARCH: 1994-1997

KEYWORDS: communication research; letters - correspondence; mutual intelligibility

0301

Research Centre for English and Applied Linguistics, Keynes House, Trumpington Street, Cambridge CB2 1QA   01223 332340

Walter, H. Ms; *Supervisor*: Williams, J. Dr

What is the involvement of working memory in reading in a foreign language?

ABSTRACT: Working memory has been and continues to be extensively studied, as has its involvement in the development and operation of the skill of reading texts in a first language (L1). Much work has also been done on the higher levels of processing that take place when some sort of mental representation of the text is constructed in skilled first-language reading. However, little has been done to apply these models to the process of reading in a foreign language (L2). At the same time, there is a body of commonly used but unverified methodology in the teaching of L2 reading. This project involves applying L1 models to the examination of working memory involvement in L2 reading, in the hope of a) informing practice in L2 teaching and b) throwing more light on reading processes in L1, since the same subjects will be studied in their L1 and L2 reading. To reduce variables, all subjects will be French-L1 learners of English. Three groups will be studied: 14 year-olds who have studied in English for approximately 3 years; 17 year-olds with approximately 6 years of English; and advanced bilinguals.

STATUS: Individual research

DATE OF RESEARCH: 1996-continuing

KEYWORDS: memory; reading; reading comprehension; second language learning

0302

Research Centre for English and Applied Linguistics, Keynes House, Trumpington Street, Cambridge CB2 1QA   01223 332340

Elston, K. Ms; *Supervisors*: Williams, J. Dr; Brown, G. Prof.; Malmkjaer, K. Dr

An enquiry into cross-language differences in lexical-conceptual relationships and their effect on L2 lexical processing

ABSTRACT: The thesis will address how cross-language differences in lexical-conceptual relationships affect second language lexical processing. The notion of one-to-one first language (L1) to second language (L2) equivalence often presupposed by empirical researchers is challenged. The work is composed of background material which outlines the many ways in which an L1 and L2 can differ with regard to the ways concepts are represented by word forms (with examples comparing English and German). The psychological processing of the following are then considered: 1) L2 words which correspond to homonyms in L1. 2) L2 words which correspond to polysemous words in L1. 3) L2 words which represent a conceptual distinction not 'lexicalized' in the L1. 4) L2 polysemous words which share some meanings with the L1 but that differ in their polysemous 'extensions' (cognates and non-cognates will be investigated). 5) L2 words which are false friends with an L1 word. 6) L2 words which correspond closely to the L1 but which have different collocational and use patterns (i.e. bleached verbs). A composite of experiments using priming (lexical decision tasks), eye fixation times, anaphora resolution, and picture size judgements will be carried out by German learners of English (at least 20 intermediate, upper-intermediate, and advanced subjects for all experiments). It is anticipated that results will show carry-over of an L1 word's 'semantic space', even for advanced learners, while the more novice learners are, the transfer effects will increase. Hopefully the project will shed light on areas of difficulty in vocabulary learning and the psychological processes that underline such problems.

PUBLISHED MATERIAL: ELSTON, K, (1996). 'Processing L1 homonyms, polysemous nouns and cognates in the L2: evidence of L1 lexical-conceptual relationships as an influential factor in L2 lexical processing', Working Papers in English and Applied Linguistics, Vol 3, pp.58-78.

STATUS: Individual research

DATE OF RESEARCH: 1997-continuing

KEYWORDS: language research; second language learning; vocabulary

0303

Research Centre for English and Applied Linguistics, Keynes House, Trumpington Street, Cambridge CB2 1QA   01223 332340

Trenkic, D. Ms; *Supervisor*: Brown, G. Prof.

Reference, definiteness and presupposition of existence in English and Serbo-Croatian

ABSTRACT: In discourse, the speaker's assumptions about the hearer's knowledge and beliefs are reflected in the linguistic forms used for information packaging. These forms, in turn, serve to provoke the hearer to infer presuppositions. One of the presupposition-indicating devices in English is the definite article. The present research explores how these aspects are managed in Serbo-Croatian (which has no overt definite-indefinite marking) and which linguistic devices Serbian learners of English use when trying to refer and to make a distinction between new-known-given entities. Problems in communication are expected when a learner uses a form which inappropriately indicates the presupposition of information which the hearer does not share, or when he/she fails to recognise the presupposition generated by a certain form. For data elicitation the map task (a co-operative task where subjects exchange information which is only partially shared) will be used. The results should be relevant to a general theory of definiteness in natural languages, as well as to the more practical purposes of language teaching and translator training.

STATUS: Individual research

DATE OF RESEARCH: 1996-continuing

KEYWORDS: discourse; english - second language; language research; language variation; second language learning; serbocroatian

0304

Research Centre for English and Applied Linguistics, Keynes House, Trumpington Street, Cambridge CB2 1QA   01223 332340

Field, J. Mr; *Supervisor*: Williams, J. Dr

Lexical segmentation in first and foreign language listening

ABSTRACT: In connected speech, there are few clues to indicate where one word ends and the next begins. English listeners therefore appear to rely upon a strategy which assumes that each stressed syllable initiates a new word. This research aims to extend knowledge of this type of metrical segmentation strategy by: 1) examining the segmentation of weak rather than strong syllables; 2) examining the segmentation of several words rather than single ones; 3) examining the segmentation strategies employed by those who are in the process of acquiring English as a foreign language. Its approach differs in 3 ways from those of earlier studies. Firstly, it focuses upon the outcomes of segmentation rather than the process, seeking to show not how segmentation occurs but what segmentation decisions are made and the extent to which they differ as between native and non-native speakers. Secondly, there is a phonological slant to the way the research questions are phrased and the evidence is interpreted. One consideration is the tension which exists between syntactic structure and surface prosodic features. Thirdly, the research has a pedagogical dimension. Metrical segmentation theory carries important implications for the teaching of languages. It is useful to discover how the segmentation decisions of listeners in the process of acquiring English differ from those of native listeners. Such information could materially assist the teaching of second language listening skills.

PUBLISHED MATERIAL: FIELD, J. (1996). 'Retrieving the functor', Working Papers in English and Applied Linguistics, Vol 2, pp.55-73.

STATUS: Individual research

DATE OF RESEARCH: 1993-1998

KEYWORDS: lexicology; linguistics; second language teaching; speech communication

0305

Research Centre for English and Applied Linguistics, Keynes House, Trumpington Street, Cambridge CB2 1QA   01223 332340

Zevgoli, S. Ms; *Supervisors*: Isimpli, I. Dr; Parodio, T. Dr ; Blevins, J. Dr

The parameter of reflexive anaphors: evidence from second language acquisition

ABSTRACT: One of the ways reflexivity can be expressed in Modern Greek (MG) is with the reflexive 'o eaftos mu'. The above anaphor constitutes an exceptional case with respect to its morphosyntactic structure: unlike the Russian monomorphemic reflexive sebe 'self' and the English bimorphemic reflexive myself, the MG reflexive is a full noun phrase consisting of the determiner o ('the'), the head eaftos ('self'), and a possessive pronoun mu ('my'). This research will be twofold. The first part will attempt to account for the following distributional peculiarities of MG reflexives: 1) MG reflexives can appear in subject position; 2) they can appear in subject position of certain types of psychological predicates only; and 3) in the appropriate context (i.e. that specified in (2), they must be co-indexed with an object clitic. Having formulated the parameter that distinguishes the simple, complex and 'full NP' reflexives, as in Russian, English and MG respectively, the second part of the research will investigate the acquisition of reflexives by adult second language (L2) learners, in cases where the parameter has a different value in the first language (L1) and the L2. To this end the researcher will devise a set of experiments consisting in grammaticality judgement tasks, which will be distributed among the following groups of learners at intermediate and advanced levels: a) Russian, Polish, Serbian and Croatian learners of MG; b) MG learners of Russian, Polish, Serbian and Croatian; c) Russian, Polish, Serbian and Croatian learners of English; and d) English learners of Russian, Polish, Serbian and Croatian. Data obtained from the grammaticality judgement tests will serve as a basis for determining the case in which the degree of difficulty in acquiring reflexives in an L2 is greater.

PUBLISHED MATERIAL: ZEVGOLI, S. 'The parameter of reflexive anaphors: the case of Modern Greek', Working Papers in English and Applied Linguistics, Vol 4. (in press).

STATUS: Individual research

DATE OF RESEARCH: 1996-continuing

KEYWORDS: greek; language research; second language learning

0306

Research Centre for English and Applied Linguistics, Keynes House, Trumpington Street, Cambridge CB2 1QA   01223 332340

Ishikawa, L. Ms; *Supervisors*: Brown, G. Prof.; Malmkjaer, K. Dr; Parodi, T. Dr

Explicitation in the output of simultaneous interpreting

ABSTRACT: Explicitation (the technique of making explicit in the target text information that is implicit in the source text) is crucial to cross-linguistic, cross-cultural communication for the sake of grammaticality, coherence and appropriacy in the target text (TT) culture. The explicitation hypothesis states that explicitation is universally inherent in the translation process because of the necessity to reformulate ideas in the target language. Various attempts have been made to identify the actual components and the cause of explicitation. For example, a greater concentration of cohesive devices are found in the TT, irrespective of differences between the sources language (SL) and the target language (TL), while editorial-type explicitation was found to be prominent, lexical manipulation was uncommon in the TT given the institutional and time constraints. This is in line with the claim that the translated text shows: 1) lexical impoverishment and 2) improvement of logic, etc. Other types of explicitation concern cultural issues. The explicitation hypothesis is not generally believed to be relevant to simultaneous interpreting, however. Any type of addition is said to be rare (1% to 5% at most of the TT) because of the time constraints involved in the discipline. However, the researcher's pilot study exhibited an overwhelming amount of addition (76% of the TT). Considering the linguistic and typological differences between Japanese and English, an extremely detailed analysis was carried out at morphological, semantic and syntactic levels to reveal 48% of non-obligatory addition (out of which 42% was explicitation) in the TT. This is still a significant amount of explicitation. Further analysis of the data revealed a new dimension to the explicitation hypothesis: a psychological operation on coherence which involves processing dynamics of anaphoric references.

PUBLISHED MATERIAL: ISHIKAWA, L. (1996). 'An empirical study of Japanese time indicators in relation to the analysis of time in Japanese narrative', Working Papers in English and Applied Linguistics, Vol 3, pp.99-125. ; ISHIKAWA, L. 'Discourse processing dynamics of explicitation in Japanese into English simultaneous interpreting', Working Papers in English and Applied Linguistics, Vol 4. (in press).

STATUS: Individual research

DATE OF RESEARCH: 1996-1998

KEYWORDS: applied linguistics; english; japanese; language research; translation

0307

Research Centre for English and Applied Linguistics, Keynes House, Trumpington Street, Cambridge CB2 1QA   01223 332340

Brown, G. Prof.; Hendriks, H. Dr; Breheny, R. Mr

Selecting the relevant context

ABSTRACT: The study will consider how relevant aspects of context become activated in the hearer's mind during the interpretation of an utterance.

PUBLISHED MATERIAL: BROWN, G. (1998). 'Selecting context'. In: MALMKJAER, K. & WILLIAMS, J. Context in language learning and language understanding. Cambridge: Cambridge University Press.

STATUS: Team research

DATE OF RESEARCH: 1998-continuing

KEYWORDS: communication research; discourse analysis; inferences

0308

School of Education, Shaftesbury Road, Cambridge CB2 2BX
01223 369631

McLaughlin, C. Ms

Evaluation of teacher appraisal in Havering

ABSTRACT: The project aims to evaluate the training and implementation of teacher appraisal in a London Borough. The schools in the Borough were divided into 2 cohorts and the evaluation covers both cohorts. Headteacher appraisal was also evaluated. The methods used were as follows: Questionnaires to all participants and then interviews in the sample schools. In Cohort 2 sample schools volunteers also kept diaries of the process. In Cohort 1 the interviewed sample was 4 out of a total of 20 primary schools, 1 special school and 2 out of a total of 4 secondary schools. The same sample was in Cohort 2. The evaluation is now completed and a report published.

STATUS: Sponsored project

SOURCE OF GRANT: Havering Borough Council

DATE OF RESEARCH: 1992-1993

KEYWORDS: **teacher effectiveness; teacher evaluation**

0309

School of Education, Shaftesbury Road, Cambridge CB2 2BX
01223 369631

McIntyre, D. Prof.; Cooper, P. Dr

Teachers' and pupils' perceptions on effective teaching and learning at National Curriculum key stage 3

ABSTRACT: This research seeks to understand the craft knowledge of teachers and pupils as they engage in classroom activity of a kind which they perceive to be effective teaching and learning. It is set in the context of National Curriculum English and History teaching at key stage 3 and follows up earlier work (BROWN, S. & MCINTYRE, D. (1993). Making sense of teaching. Buckingham: Open University Press) aimed at making explicit the thinking underlying what is usually taken for granted professional teaching by teachers. It focuses especially on the subject-related aspects of teaching and on ways in which teachers take account of differences among their pupils; and it seeks to reveal pupils' ways of traying to learn effectively in classrooms and what they see their teachers as doing to facilitate that learning. The focus is on specific observed teaching and learning episodes. The current final phase of the work is concerned with analysing data on Year 9 teaching.

PUBLISHED MATERIAL: COOPER, P. & MCINTYRE, D. (1993). 'Commonality in teachers' and pupils' perceptions of effective classroom learning', British Journal of Educational Psychology, Vol 63, No 3, pp.381-399. ; COOPER, P. & MCINTYRE, D. (1996). Effective teaching and learning: teachers' and students' perspectives. Buckingham: Open University Press. ; COOPER, P. & MCINTYRE, D. (1996). 'The importance of power sharing in classrooms'. In: HUGHES, M. (Ed.) Teaching and learning in changing times. Oxford: Blackwell.

STATUS: Sponsored project

SOURCE OF GRANT: Economic and Social Research Council £100,000

DATE OF RESEARCH: 1991-1997

KEYWORDS: **english; history; key stage 3; learning strategies; national curriculum; pupil attitudes; secondary education; teacher attitudes; teacher effectiveness; teaching methods**

0310

School of Education, 17 Trumpington Street, Cambridge CB2 1QA
01223 332888

Wells, R. Dr; *Supervisor*: Hunt, M. Dr

An investigation into representations of girlhood in girls' popular magazines and school textbooks, 1900-1930.

ABSTRACT: Education plays a crucial role in transmitting ideologies of gender, and its prescriptions and practices are indications of how society views girls and women. Although classroom practice enables us to identify some changes in the conceptualisation of girlhood, an historical record of that practice cannot easily be reconstructed. However, an examination of school textbooks can provide some account, since they represent evidence of what authority believed ought to be taught in classrooms. Through their prescriptions, textbooks provide a commentary on how girlhood was viewed and what assumptions about feminine characteristics surrounded it. They can tell us how the content of girls' education was changing, and which commonly held beliefs about their schooling had a particular effect on that education. They are also highly revealing about the ways in which the education of girls differed from that of boys. Finally, they give some account of the purposes for which girls were being educated and the adult roles for

which they were being prepared. A concentrated analysis of the experience of girlhood through educational resources produces only a partial picture since it excludes other important sites of socialisation. It is therefore necessary to investigate other areas where representations of girlhood are to be found. Magazines for girls are one such site in which adult characterisations of girlhood are implicit in production and, like textbooks, they are highly prescriptive in nature. The magazines examined show how prescriptions and advice were offered to readers on behaviour, appearance, activities, employment prospects and adult destinies. Their broad scope gives an account of who adolescent girls were thought to be, and who they were expected to become in adult life. An examination of English, mathematics and science and domestic-science textbooks used in elementary and secondary schools between 1900-1910 and 1920-1930 will be compared with an analysis of the content of magazines published for adolescent girls during the same period, 1900 to 1930. The magazines examined are: Girls' Realm and Girl's Own Paper (issues between 1900 and 1910) and School Friend, Schoolgirls' Weekly, The Schoolgirl, Girl's Own Paper and Every Girl's Paper (issues between 1920 and 1930).

STATUS: Individual research

DATE OF RESEARCH: 1988-1993

KEYWORDS: **childrens literature; comics - publications; educational history; girls; popular culture; sex role; textbooks; womens education**

0311

School of Education, 17 Trumpington Street, Cambridge CB2 1QA
01223 332888

Booth, M. Dr; Matthews, R. Mr; Larsson, Y. Dr

History teaching in Japanese and English secondary schools

ABSTRACT: This project will explore: a) the beliefs of Japanese and English history teachers about the nature and teaching of history and how far these beliefs influence their teaching styles; b) the reactions to the teaching of history in each other's countries; c) the Japanese and English pupils' attitudes to the teaching and learning of history; d) how Japanese and English pupils create an historical narrative which both evaluates and explains photographic source-based issues from 20th century world history; e) the influence of the media on the acquisition by the Japanese and English pupils of historical knowledge and understanding.

PUBLISHED MATERIAL: BOOTH, M., SATO, M. & MATTHEWS, R. (1995). 'Case studies of history teaching in Japanese junior high schools and English comprehensive secondary schools', Compare, Vol 25, No 3, pp.279-301. ; LARSSON, Y., BOOTH, M. & MATTHEWS, R. (1998). 'Attitudes to the teaching of history and the use of creative skills in Japan and England: a comparative study', Compare, Vol 28, No 3, pp.305-314.

STATUS: Sponsored project

SOURCE OF GRANT: Daiwa Anglo-Japanese Foundation

DATE OF RESEARCH: 1995-1997

KEYWORDS: **comparative education; history; japan; secondary education**

0312

School of Education, 17 Trumpington Street, Cambridge CB2 1QA
01223 332888

Arizpe, E. Dr; *Supervisor*: Arnot, M. Dr

Arianne

ABSTRACT: Project Arianne is a European Commission funded project involving Denmark, France, Germany, Greece, Italy, Portugal, Spain and the UK. It aims to: 1) identify effective strategies to broaden traditional assumptions underlying masculinity in participating countries; 2) develop the ability of secondary schools to investigate masculinity as a gender issue, and assess the school's role in relation to differences in the behaviour of girls and boys and the promotion of particular concepts of masculinity; 3) develop effective teaching and evaluation strategies; 4) encourage the sharing of common resources, research methodologies and school reform techniques. The expected outcomes are: 1) a change in attitudes, behaviour, aspirations or achievement of adolescent male pupils in the consortium of pilot schools in the participating member states; 2) a change in the knowledge, experience and understanding of masculinity amongst the staff, parents and pupils in the pilot schools; 3) the production of guidelines/

good practice for secondary schools; and 4) networking and collaboration between academics, teachers and administrators/advisors across the participating member states.

STATUS: Sponsored project

SOURCE OF GRANT: European Commission

DATE OF RESEARCH: 1996-1997

KEYWORDS: adolescents; boys; comparative education; international educational exchange; masculinity; secondary education; sex differences

0313

School of Education, Shaftesbury Road, Cambridge CB2 2BX
01223 369631

Bage, G. Dr

Pilot evaluation of selected English Heritage materials

ABSTRACT: This is a pilot evaluation which focused upon a restricted range of English Heritage teachers' booklets and video materials and is restricted to a limited geographical area. It asked a series of questions which looked at: the way teachers and children use the materials; which parts are most helpful and why; are the materials the ones teachers say they want and need; how could they be improved; how helpful are the different formats; and what sort of materials would it be most helpful for English Heritage to produce in the future etc. To try to get some answers to these questions, existing English Heritage documentation and other relevant research were reviewed; interviews were held with members of English Heritage staff; questionnaires were issued to users; and interviews held with a user sample. A written report summarised the main findings of the research conducted, which offered preliminary answers to questions posed and advice on areas specified by English Heritage.

STATUS: Sponsored project

SOURCE OF GRANT: English Heritage

DATE OF RESEARCH: 1996-1997

KEYWORDS: cultural education; educational materials; resource materials; teaching guides; videotape recordings

0314

School of Education, Shaftesbury Road, Cambridge CB2 2BX
01223 369631

Collins, F. Ms; *Supervisor*: Bage, G. Dr

Teaching as Story Telling (TASTE)

Abstract: The project will harness teaching and storytelling to the task of improving schools and will result in the telling and writing of 'real stories' for schools and other heritage bodies to teach through. It aims to make the National Curriculum more accessible, relevant, local and interesting by encouraging teachers to use storied content and methods in their practice. It promotes arts across the curriculum by showing that pedagogy that is well established in the teaching of English can enhance any subject. It will seek to make school curricula more culturally diverse by drawing in particular upon the storied skills and knowledge of different cultural traditions. Initially the project is focusing on the London Borough of Greenwich and Norfolk Local Education Authority.

STATUS: Sponsored project

SOURCE OF GRANT: Sir John Cass's Foundation; The Calouste Gulbenkian Foundation; Cambridge University

DATE OF RESEARCH: 1997-continuing

KEYWORDS: oral history; school improvement; story telling; teaching methods

0315

School of Education, Shaftesbury Road, Cambridge CB2 2BX
01223 369631

Fielding, M. Mr ; Sebba, J. Ms

Essex primary school improvement and research and development programme

ABSTRACT: The principal aim of the project, which has a primary focus, is to enable schools to develop strategies for improving the quality of

teaching and learning provided for all pupils. Alongside this there are two other aims: 1) to increase the capacity of Essex Local Education Authority (LEA) to support schools; and 2) to increase understanding of the process and outcomes of school improvement across the LEA and beyond. Progress reports will be produced during the course of the project and a final report at the end.

STATUS: Sponsored project

SOURCE OF GRANT: Essex Local Education Authority

DATE OF RESEARCH: 1995-1998

KEYWORDS: educational quality; local education authorities; primary education; school effectiveness; school improvement

0316

School of Education, 17 Trumpington Street, Cambridge CB2 1QA
01223 332888

Walford, R. Mr

Views and visions of the environment of school pupils in the UK

ABSTRACT: This project follows on from the Land Use-UK project and concentrates on the material collected on pupils' perceptions of their contemporary environment. The data collected will be investigated and will lead to a major, comprehensive report being prepared and disseminated to interested environmental and educational agencies and the national press. The project will provide for the first time an insight into the environmental attitudes and opinions of a cross-section of young people in the UK.

STATUS: Sponsored project

SOURCE OF GRANT: Dennis Curry Charitable Trust; Cambridge University

DATE OF RESEARCH: 1997-1998

KEYWORDS: environment; environmental education; pupil attitudes

0317

School of Education, Shaftesbury Road, Cambridge CB2 2BX
01223 369631

Creese, M. Dr; McIntyre, D. Prof

The impact of governors on school effectiveness

ABSTRACT: This was a follow-up externally-funded project which drew on and extended the findings of an internally-funded pilot study. The researchers were involved in studying a number of schools in which the governing body was making, or appeared to be making, a significant contribution towards school improvement in terms of pupils' learning and behaviour. A headteacher and chair of governors of each participating school identified one issue which had been resolved recently in their school and one which was just emerging. In the case of the former, a time line will be constructed of the signficant events, written comments sought from the headteacher and chair of governors, and interviews held to provide data. In the case of the issue of current concern, teachers and governors were invited to keep diaries of the main events as the issue develops, a follow-up interview took place on the way they felt the issue had progressed. Office for Standards in Education (OFSTED) reports were used as an independent view of the overall effectiveness of the schools and data was gathered on the effectiveness of the governing body. When all the data had been collected for each school, a report was written and presented to the governors and staff involved for comment/amendment. At the end of the project, the project directors disseminated their findings at a conference.

STATUS: Sponsored project

SOURCE OF GRANT: Unilever PLC; Royal Mail; Cambridge University

DATE OF RESEARCH: 1997-1998

KEYWORDS: educational administration; educational quality; governing bodies; learning; pupil behaviour; school effectiveness; school governors; school improvement

0318

School of Education, Shaftesbury Road, Cambridge CB2 2BX
01223 369631

Rouse, M. Mr

School reform and the involvement of pupils with disabilities in England

and Wales: the lessons for the United States

ABSTRACT: This research involved a cross-cultural comparison of the extensive special eduational needs reforms being implemented in the UK and the movement towards school-based reform in the US. The strong parallels between the two movements provided an opportunity for special education policymakers and practitioners in the US to examine the feasibility as well as the issues related to implementing specific reforms. Conferences in the US and the UK have provided and will continue to provide opportunities for dissemination. This was phase 1 of a longer-term international project.

STATUS: Sponsored project

SOURCE OF GRANT: University of Maryland, USA

DATE OF RESEARCH: 1996-1997

KEYWORDS: comparative education; disabilities; educational change; educational policy; international educational exchange; mainstreaming; special educational needs; united states of america

0319

School of Education, 17 Trumpington Street, Cambridge CB2 1QA
01223 332888

Beardon, T. Mrs; Krishna, S. Dr

Mathematics enrichment project

Abstract: The project aims to: 1) advance the development of mathematical thinking and language; 2) promote an interest in mathematics, to raise the standards of achievement in school mathematics, to assist the mathematical development of children who have the potential to go on to study mathematical subjects at university, and to support the special educational needs of exceptionally able children; 3) promote and support the setting up of locally organised user groups and mathematics clubs by providing resources on the Internet, and offering advice and inservice training for teachers; 4) conduct research into the effect of communication technology and peer assistance on the quality of learning for very able pupils, on the quality of teaching offered by schools, on the cognitive gains for peer teachers and learners, and on the development of increased usage of information technology (IT) in mathematics teaching.

STATUS: Sponsored project

Source of Grant: University of Cambridge Local Examinations Syndicate; Royal Society Committee on the Public Understanding of Science; The London Mathematical Society

DATE OF RESEARCH: 1996-continuing

KEYWORDS: able pupils; computer uses in education; gifted; information technology; mathematical ability; mathematics education

0320

School of Education, Shaftesbury Road, Cambridge CB2 2BX
01223 369631

Bowers, T. Dr; Dee, L. Ms; West, M. Mr; Wilkinson, D. Mr

Evaluation of the user-friendliness of the Special Needs Code of Practice

ABSTRACT: The main aims of this research project are to illuminate the views of the 3 principal user groups - local education authority (LEA) officers and professional personnel, school staff and governors, and parents and parent representative groups - concerning its format and content. Elements of the Code's content which may be seen by some or all users as ambiguous, deficient, or otherwise in need of modification or amendment will be identified. Users's views will be sought concerning the practical utility of actions, criteria, time-frames etc laid out in the Code and those of the Code's guidelines which are not being generally adhered to, with reasons, will be identified. The project team will also suggest modifications which might be made to the Code in the light of the above. Three major outcomes are envisaged: a substantial report of main findings, a 'good practice' guide, illustrated by case studies and examples, and a short, critically annotated review of relevant literature and research findings.

STATUS: Sponsored project

SOURCE OF GRANT: Department for Education and Employment

DATE OF RESEARCH: 1997-1998

KEYWORDS: code of practice; special educational needs

0321

School of Education, Shaftesbury Road, Cambridge CB2 2BX
01223 369631

McLaughlin, C. Ms; Ebbutt, D. Mr

Anglia drugs and alcohol evaluation

ABSTRACT: The evaluation reported on the extent that the project, sponsored by the Drug Action Teams of East Anglia, has met its stated aims within the time period it has set itself. In particular it will report on the effectiveness and 'worthwhileness' of the range of strategies adopted with respect to the target audience. These strategies refer to television commercials, roadshows and other ways of promoting public awareness of drug misuse across East Anglia. The innovatory element of roadshows in prison was also commented on. Issues raised about drug education in general were also reported.

STATUS: Sponsored project

SOURCE OF GRANT: Drug Action Teams of East Anglia £8,000

DATE OF RESEARCH: 1997-1998

KEYWORDS: alcohol abuse; alcohol education; drug abuse; drug education; health education

0322

School of Education, Shaftesbury Road, Cambridge CB2 2BX
01223 369631

Wharton, M. Mr; Supervisor: Adams, A. Mr

Understanding the dynamics of successful collaboration: an evaluation of Comenius 1 European Education Projects in 3 European Union countries

ABSTRACT: The project is intended to conduct a tri-national investigation of Comenius Action 1 multilateral school-based European Education Projects (EEPs) in order to ascertain their effectiveness, the conditions that lead to successful partnerships, and the degree of innovation that results in the schools as a consequence of such partnerships. This will be achieved by working with the coordinating schools in 3 European Union (EU) countries, as well as with a sample of their partner schools, in order to investigate the similarities and differences that may be observed. The instruments that will be employed have already been developed in an initial Cambridge-based study in 1995-96, which acted as a pilot project and on which a report has already been prepared and lodged with the European Commission. The project will be undertaken through the administration and analysis of questionnaires distributed to the coordinating schools in the 3 partner countries to be followed by indepth interviews in a selected 15-20% sample of schools in those countries. Further evidence will be obtained by the distribution of further questionnaires to the partner schools in the other countries with which the coordinating schools have worked. The study seeks to investigate organisational, curriculum, and attitudinal and cultural issues and their contribution to innovation in the partner schools.

STATUS: Sponsored project

SOURCE OF GRANT: European Commission

DATE OF RESEARCH: 1999-continuing

KEYWORDS: europe; institutional cooperation; international educational exchange; partnerships

0323

School of Education, Shaftesbury Road, Cambridge CB2 2BX
01223 369631

Dee, L. Ms

Guide to transition planning during the final years of schooling for young people with special educational needs

ABSTRACT: The 1993 Code of Practice gave guidance to schools on the conduct of 14+ and subsequent annual reviews as part of the process of supporting young people with statements of special educational needs during their transition from school to the next stage of their lives. The purpose of this guide is to support special educational needs coordinators (SENCOs) and those in special schools responsible for transition planning to interpret the guidance and to move transition planning practice towards a dynamic and supportive process. The guidance will be based on data drawn from two research studies. The first, carried out on behalf of the

Department for Education and Employment (DfEE) by the University of Cambridge School of Education, surveyed the views of professionals and parents on the user-friendliness of the Code of Practice including the guidance on transition. The second is a three year long study of the experiences of parents and young people with special educational needs during the final years of schooling. The database consists of interviews conducted annually with students, parents and teachers, observations of annual reviews, documentation and questionnaire data from a range of professionals on the perceived usefulness of the review meetings. Thus access is possible to information about both the views and experiences of the main stakeholders in the decision-making process gathered over three years.

STATUS: Sponsored project

SOURCE OF GRANT: Department for Education and Employment

DATE OF RESEARCH: 1999-continuing

KEYWORDS: school leavers; special educational needs; special educational needs coordinators; transition education

0324

School of Education, Shaftesbury Road, Cambridge CB2 2BX
01223 369631

Bage, G. Dr; Grisdale, R. Mr; *Supervisor*: Lister, B. Mr

Evaluation of key stage 2 history classical elements

ABSTRACT: This project aims to establish current practice in the planning and implementation of the classical elements of key stage 2 (KS2) history in the hope of making a significant contribution both to the forthcoming review of the National Curriculum and to the wider debate about the place of classics in schools. The project will involve: 1) analysing the central legislation and advice 1988-1997 to establish the effect of changes in policy in this period on the classical elements of the primary curriculum; 2) examining the position and influence of subject associations, local education authorities (LEAs), researchers, publishers and other advisory bodies to ascertain what advice is currently offered to schools and teachers by these bodies and how their approaches compare; 3) gathering data from a range of LEAs to establish a general picture of the provision of the classical elements of KS2 history; 4) visiting a small number of schools to seek the views of teachers on the value of teaching the classical world at KS2, to identify examples of good practice in the planning and teaching of the classical elements of KS2 history, to ascertain the range of resources used both inside and outside school (including information technology (IT) resources) and the level of inservice teacher education (INSET) or other specialist training received by teachers to help them teach unfamiliar aspects of the Greeks and Romans. The research will have 3 major outcomes: 1) a substantial report on the main findings, with recommendations, where appropriate, for future policy and delivery; 2) the dissemination of the main findings through conferences for teachers and other interested parties; 3) the development of new teaching materials which take into account the findings of the research.

STATUS: Sponsored project

SOURCE OF GRANT: School Curriculum and Assessment Authority

DATE OF RESEARCH: 1997-continuing

KEYWORDS: classics education; history; national curriculum; primary education

0325

School of Education, Shaftesbury Road, Cambridge CB2 2BX
01223 369631

Boyd, E. Mrs; Arnold, R. Mr; *Supervisor*: Cooper, P. Dr

The promotion and evaluation of nurture groups

ABSTRACT: The project has 5 clear objectives: 1) to establish the distribution of nurture groups in England and Wales; 2) to define the nature of nurture groups in terms of practical and organisational arrangements; 3) to generate and pilot evaluation techniques to assess the effectiveness of nurture groups; 4) to contribute to the development of nurture groups through the dissemination of information, consultancy and advice; 5) to secure funding for the continuation of the programme. The initial phase of the project will focus on the first objective. Ten representative local education authorities (LEAs) have been contacted to identify the current

incidence and provision for children with emotional and behavioural difficulties, including nurture group provision and subsequently all LEAs were sent a questionnaire. The intention is to establish a dialogue about children's needs and to offer support and information to anyone interested. As the project progresses, other issues and provision may arise which need follow up and dissemination.

STATUS: Sponsored project

SOURCE OF GRANT: Department for Education and Employment; Calouste Gulbenkian Foundation; Cambridge University School of Education

DATE OF RESEARCH: 1998-continuing

KEYWORDS: emotional and behavioural difficulties; intervention; nurture groups; special educational needs; support services

0326

School of Education, Shaftesbury Road, Cambridge CB2 2BX
01223 369631

McLaughlin, C. Ms; Gubb, J. Ms

Developmental counselling and guidance - an action research project

ABSTRACT: This project aims to investigate the development of skills and processes commonly associated with counselling and guidance, or pastoral care, in the classroom and other locations of the teacher's work. The intention is to discover how best to develop these skills in all teachers, not just specialists, to support and facilitate learning in its widest sense. An action research approach has been chosen in order to pursue research and development simultaneously. Work is already underway in 3 secondary schools and these will provide sites for detailed case studies. A cross-case data collection and analysis will aim to map the development of guidance content and processes in these schools and examine the blocks, barriers and facilitating factors which promote or hinder development. The project is also international. Three related projects are underway in Holland, Russia and the USA. There is very close cooperation with the Dutch arm of the project. Findings will be shared and will lead to national and international studies, as well as informing the Dutch government's policy in teacher education. The first year of the project has already been completed and the project will run until the year 2000. School-based research will finish in October 1999. All 3 schools are working collaboratively.

STATUS: Sponsored project

SOURCE OF GRANT: Cambridge University £39,500

DATE OF RESEARCH: 1997-continuing

KEYWORDS: comparative education; counselling; guidance; pastoral care -education; teacher development

0327

School of Education, Shaftesbury Road, Cambridge CB2 2BX
01223 369631

Adams, A. Mr

Pupil underachievement: training for school improvement

ABSTRACT: The aims of the project over a 2-year period are to: 1) identify and describe patterns of underachievement in pupils aged 12-19 in the partner regions; 2) collect data relating to underachievement, especially case study materials of successful strategies of improving pupils achievement, for comparison on an international scale; 3) use the data collection and case studies as a basis for locally based seminars leading to a course on school improvement specifically to help teachers develop strategies leading to greater differentiation of teaching methods and more flexible teaching strategies so as to respond to the different learning styles of pupils; 4) run an international catalogue course on school improvement; 5) develop materials from the courses which can be used as a basis for dissemination and a resource pack for teachers; and 6) disseminate the end results of the programme through publications and linked series of national conferences.

STATUS: Sponsored project

SOURCE OF GRANT: European Commission ; Partner institutions

DATE OF RESEARCH: 1999-continuing

KEYWORDS: academic achievement; achievement; school improvement; secondary education; underachievement

0328

School of Education, Shaftesbury Road, Cambridge CB2 2BX
01223 369631

Rouse, M. Dr; Florian, L. Dr

Investigating effective classroom practice in inclusive education

ABSTRACT: Inclusive education has been given a high profile by the Labour Government in its education consultation process, yet relatively little is known about how to make it work, particularly at the classroom level. A major challenge for research is to produce evidence about the strategies available to teachers wishing to create the conditions for inclusive learning in their classrooms. Although there is some agreement in the literature about the general strategies that might be used by teachers, such as cooperative learning, peer-mediated instruction, multi-age grouping and collaborative teaching, relatively little is known about the ways in which these techniques work (or do not work) in the context of the secondary schools National Curriculum and the demand for higher standards in classrooms which include children with a wide range of needs. The main purpose of this research is to identify and evaluate the classroom strategies and techniques currently being utilised in a series of case study secondary schools with a commitment to inclusion. A variety of methods are being used to collect evidence for this project including: 1) a survey of all teachers in case study schools to ascertain the extent to which they are familiar with and use the strategies and techniques that are thought to promote inclusive classroom practice; 2) classroom observations to investigate what teachers actually do to include all learners in the lesson; 3) 'inclusion journals' kept by volunteer teachers for a period of 5 weeks; and 4) follow-up interviews and group discussions with teachers who have kept journals and have been observed, to clarify and check researchers' understandings. To date, 8 teachers in 6 different subject areas have been observed teaching across Years 7-11. These teachers have also been keeping inclusion journals from October half-term. A questionnaire designed to obtain information about mainstream classroom teacher familiarity and use of teaching strategies thought to promote inclusive practice has been developed and administered in 3 schools. Results of the project are due out in May 1999.

STATUS: Sponsored project

SOURCE OF GRANT: Cambridge University

DATE OF RESEARCH: 1998-continuing

KEYWORDS: classroom observation techniques; mainstreaming; secondary education; special educational needs; teaching methods

0329

School of Education, 17 Trumpington Street, Cambridge CB2 1QA
01223 332888
Cambridge University, Homerton College, Hills Road, Cambridge CB2 2PH
01223 507111

Ruthven, K. Dr; Rousham, L. Mr; Chaplin, D. Ms

The calculator as a cognitive tool in mathematics education

ABSTRACT: This project examined the long-term influence of a 'calculator-aware' approach to the teaching of number, which encouraged pupils to develop informal methods of calculation, and to use calculators to explore number and execute demanding computations. Data was gathered in 6 neighbouring primary schools, of which 3 had participated in the pioneering project which developed this curriculum. The influence of national reforms on the experiences of pupils was explored through interviews with their teachers. The approach to number in the former project schools had remained distinctive during the earlier stage of primary education, but there had been substantial convergence during the later stage. A 'macro study' examined the mathematical attainment and attitudes of 162 pupils who had remained in the same school throughout their primary education. At age 7, the calculator-aware approach was associated with a wider range of attainment, but at age 11 there was no treatment effect related to attainment. The calculator-aware approach was, however, associated with more positive attitudes to mental calculation. A 'micro study' examined the computational strategies used by a structured sub-sample of 56 pupils. Pupils who had followed the calculator-aware approach made more use of mental calculation in solving number problems. In tackling a challenging realistic problem, the calculator helped some pupils to work with unusual problem representations and to concentrate on planning and monitoring computations. However, there were important dissonances between pupils' conceptions and the calculator's operation. Equally, important limitations arose from the transience of the calculator's record of operations and results.

PUBLISHED MATERIAL: RUTHVEN, K., ROUSHAM, L. & CHAPLIN, D. (1997). 'The long-term influence of a 'calculator-aware' number curriculum on pupils' mathematical attainments and attitudes in the primary phase', Research Papers in Education, Vol 12, No 3, pp.249-281. ; RUTHVEN, K. & CHAPLIN, D. (1998). 'The calculator as a cognitive tool: upper-primary pupils tackling a realistic number problem', International Journal of Computers for Mathematical Learning, Vol 2, No 3, pp.93-124. ; RUTHVEN, K. (1998). 'The use of mental, written and calculator strategies of numerical computation by upper-primary pupils within a 'calculator-aware' number curriculum', British Educational Research Journal, Vol 24, No 1, pp.21-42.

STATUS: Sponsored project

SOURCE OF GRANT: Economic and Social Research Council £25,690

DATE OF RESEARCH: 1995-1997

KEYWORDS: calculators; cognitive development; mathematics education; numbers; primary education

0330

School of Education, 17 Trumpington Street, Cambridge CB2 1QA
01223 332888
Cambridge University, Homerton College, Hills Road, Cambridge CB2 2PH
01223 507111

Sebba, J. Ms; Gray, J. Prof; West, M. Mr; Wilcox, B. Prof.; Wilkin, M. Ms

School effectiveness GEST: education and good practice

ABSTRACT: This project aims to: 1) map the detailed patterns of expenditure on School Effectiveness Grants for Education Support and Training (SE GEST) across local education authorities (LEAs) and schools; 2) provide a clear picture of the criteria being applied to determine the distribution of SE GEST and the rationales underlying such criteria; 3) assess the impact of SE GEST on school and LEA practice in relation to the development of school improvement strategies; and 4) identify schools and LEAs in which particularly effective practices appear to have been adopted and to provide information about these, primarily through case studies. The report 'Sharpening the Focus: SEGEST, Improvement and Raising Standards' was published by the Department for Education and Employment (DfEE) in March 1998 and informed the subsequent revisions to the Standards Fund.

STATUS: Sponsored project

SOURCE OF GRANT: Department for Education and Employment

DATE OF RESEARCH: 1997-1998

KEYWORDS: education support grants; educational finance; educational quality; grants; local education authorities; school effectiveness; school improvement

0331

School of Education, 17 Trumpington Street, Cambridge CB2 1QA
01223 332888
Cambridge University, Homerton College, Hills Road, Cambridge CB2 2PH 01223 507111

Arnot, M. Dr; James, M. Dr; Gray, J. Prof.; Rudduck, J. Prof.

Gender and educational performance: a review of recent research

ABSTRACT: This project was commissioned by the Office for Standards in Education (OFSTED) to provide teachers and others with a summary review and critique of recent studies in an area of current concern and interest. The intention was to identify the patterns of performance that are indicated in reliable research studies, then to evaluate the strengths of the most persuasive explanations of differential performance. The project team reviewed studies related to male/female development and school careers; pupil participation in curriculum and assessment; school culture and organisation; and labour market issues.

STATUS: Sponsored project

SOURCE OF GRANT: Office for Standards in Education

DATE OF RESEARCH: 1996-1997

KEYWORDS: academic achievement; achievement; differential performance; performance; pupil development; sex differences

0332

School of Education, 17 Trumpington Street, Cambridge CB2 1QA
01223 332888
Cambridge University, Homerton College, Hills Road, Cambridge CB2 2PH
01223 507111

Gardner, P. Dr; Cunningham, P. Dr ; Starns, P. Dr

The impact of wartime evacuation upon teacher attitude and practice

ABSTRACT: The research will investigate one of the greatest social upheavals in the 20th century domestic history of Great Britain: the programme of mass evacuation of school children from the great cities to safer reception areas during the Second World War. Evacuation has been studied from a number of historical perspectives, but never has the role played by the thousands of school teachers who accompanied their pupils to safety been systematically explored. This is what the research will endeavour to do. The research is designed particularly to examine how the experience of evacuation impacted collectively upon the professional sensibilities and the pedagogical practices of classroom teachers. The central consideration here is how the enforced closeness of teacher and pupil throughout the period of evacuation may have led to a reformulation of the idealised pupil-teacher relationship upon which teachers built their professional expectations and practices. A further significant question turns on how any such reformulation, should it have occurred among individual practitioners, might have been transmitted into a more general currency throughout the teaching profession. The research proposes to examine two distinct historical periods: the short-term moment of evacuation itself and the longer-term post-war period in which the ramifications of what was an intense and unprecedented professional experience were played out. In each period, the research is designed particularly to focus upon teachers' professional attitudes and classroom practices. The methods the research will employ include oral history interview, life history interview and focus group discussion, together with archival and documentary analysis.

STATUS: Sponsored project

SOURCE OF GRANT: Economic and Social Research Council

DATE OF RESEARCH: 1998-continuing

KEYWORDS: **educational history; evacuation; teacher attitudes; teaching profession; war**

0333

School of Education, 17 Trumpington Street, Cambridge CB2 1QA
01223 332888
Cambridge University, School of Education, Shaftesbury Road, Cambridge CB2 2BX   01223 369631

Booth, M. Dr; Bradley, H. Mr; Hargreaves, D. Prof.; Southworth, G. Dr; Stanley, P. Ms

Training of doctors in hospitals

ABSTRACT: The project, in partnership with hospital staff, aims to: 1) develop a programme to help senior doctors to train junior colleagues more effectively and efficiently, with special reference to on-the-job training and coaching; 2) identify, develop and disseminate good practice in a range of specialities in making the most effective use of coaching without impairing service delivery; 3) clarify and describe the coaching skills that are generic to all postgraduate medical education and to characterise those which are specific to a range of specialities clinical settings (clinics, wards, theatres, GP surgeries); 4) develop a range of training resources for senior and junior doctors which will help them to implement and benefit from such coaching practices; 5) examine how coaching and on-the-job training can be developed within protected training time; 6) investigate how formal and informal training may be better inter-related; 7) provide assistance to doctors with ways of talking about, analysing and improving such training; 8) enhance the role of registrars in on-the-job training of senior house officers (SHO's); 9) identify how doctors can provide and obtain higher quality feedback for one another during training; 10) undertake the research essential to the development of the training programme and resources; 11) assist in the acceptance of the 12) changed practices and in the generation of an enhanced culture of training; devise a system for disseminating the outcomes of the project beyond the particular people and hospitals participating in the project.

PUBLISHED MATERIAL: BOOTH, M., BRADLEY, H., HARGREAVES, D.H. & SOUTHWORTH, G. (1995). 'Training of doctors in hospitals: a comparison with teacher education', Journal of Education for Teaching, Vol 21, No 2, pp.145-161. ; HARGREAVES, D.H. (1996). 'Transforming the apprenticeship model of training', British Journal of Hospital Medicine, Vol 55, No 6, pp.342-343. ; HARGREAVES, D.H., BOWDITCH, M. & GRIFFIN, D. (1997). On-the-job training for surgeons. London: Royal Society of Medicine. ; HARGREAVES, D.H., SOUTHWORTH, G., STANLEY, P. & WARD, S. (1997). On-the-job training for physicians. London: Royal Society of Medicine. ; BOOTH, M.B. (1998). 'Teaching and learning in a neonatal intensive care unit', Archive of Disease in Childhood, Vol 78, No 3, pp.275-277.

STATUS: Sponsored project

SOURCE OF GRANT: Anglia and Oxford Postgraduate Medical & Dental Education Committee £209,207

DATE OF RESEARCH: 1995-1997

KEYWORDS: **clinical experience; hospital personnel; hospitals; medical education; on the job training; physicians**

0334

School of Education, Shaftesbury Road, Cambridge CB2 2BX
01223 369631
Greenwich University, School of Social Sciences, Wellington Street, London SE18 6PF   0181 331 8000
London University, Institute of Education, 20 Bedford Way, London WC1H 0AL   0171 580 1122

Cooper, P. Dr; Maras, P. Dr; Norwich, B. Prof.

Effects of adults' attributions on pupils with attention and activity problems

ABSTRACT: The project aims to identify children in primary and secondary schools who show emotional and behavioural difficulties with the focus on attentional and activity difficulties. It then aims to discover whether these children have been identified in different services (education, health and social services) and the effects of these differing systems on their treatment and provision.

STATUS: Sponsored project

SOURCE OF GRANT: Economic and Social Research Council £45,953

DATE OF RESEARCH: 1998-continuing

KEYWORDS: **attention deficit disorders; diagnostic assessment; discipline problems; disruptive pupils; emotional and behavioural difficulties; hyperactivity; pupil evaluation; special educational needs**

0335

School of Education, Shaftesbury Road, Cambridge CB2 2BX
01223 369631
London University, King's College, School of Education, Cornwall House, Waterloo Road, London SE1 8WA   0171 836 5454

Walsh, A. Ms; *Supervisor*: Brown, M. Prof.

The calculator as a catalyst for change - children and number

ABSTRACT: Although the electronic calculator is well accepted as a tool in society and with young children, very little is known about the possible potential of the effective use of a calculator to support the learning of number within mathematics for children in the primary years, and thus also its possible potential as a 'catalyst for change'. This research study uses an ethnographic methodology to follow the development of four schools in their attempts to integrate the calculator into the teaching and learning of number with children from 6/7 years upwards, which began as part of the work of Primary Initiatives in Mathematics Education project in which the research played a leading role. The study will cover a five year period of development. Some evidence presented to date calls into question the general perception of how and when children acquire particular number concepts and skills and their ability to deal with them. The research study involves a detailed analysis of these findings with particular reference to the development of place value and further research focusing on the children's understanding of and ability to use and apply number. It is intended to address issues related to implications for teaching.

STATUS: Individual research

DATE OF RESEARCH: 1987-1993

KEYWORDS: **arithmetic and number education; calculators; mathematics education; primary education**

0336

School of Education, Shaftesbury Road, Cambridge CB2 2BX
01223 369631

National Council of Educational Research and Training, Sri Aurobindo Marg, New Delhi, India

Ainscow, M. Prof.; Jangira, N. Prof.; Ahuja, A. Mrs

Effective schools for all: a multi-site action research project in India

ABSTRACT: This initiative grew out of the United Nations Economic, Scientific and Cultural Organisation (UNESCO) international project 'Special Needs in the Classroom'. It involves representation of 22 teacher education institutions from different regions of India and explores the use of active learning approaches in teacher education as a means of encouraging teaching for diversity. Data is being collected using a variety of instruments. The intention is that the findings will be used as a basis for wider dissemination activities involving some further 400 training institutions. Additional indepth studies are also being carried out in a small number of primary schools in the Delhi area.

STATUS: Sponsored project

SOURCE OF GRANT: United Nations Economic, Scientific and Cultural Organisation; UNESCO); United Nations International Children's Emergency Fund (UNICEF)

DATE OF RESEARCH: 1991-1993

KEYWORDS: **india; mainstreaming; special educational needs; teacher education**

0337

School of Education, Shaftesbury Road, Cambridge CB2 2BX
01223 369631

Nottingham University, School of Education, University Park, Nottingham NG7 2RD   01159 515151

Hopkins, D. Prof.; Ainscow, M. Prof. ; Southworth, G. Dr; West, M. Mr; Fielding, M. Mr; Beresford, J. Mr; Sebba, J.Ms

Developing classroom conditions that improve the quality of education for all (CCIQEA)

ABSTRACT: During the past three years the project has established a close working relationship between the research team and some 25 schools from 6 local education authorities (LEA's). The overall aim of the project has been to strengthen each school's ability to provide quality education for all its pupils by building upon existing good practice. In so doing, the researchers will produce and evaluate a model of school development, and a programme of support. There is an assumption that schools are most likely to strengthen their ability to provide enhanced outcomes for all pupils when they adopt ways of working that are consistent with their own aspirations as well as the current reform agenda. The schools were asked to identify and to work on their own projects and priorities, but to do so in a way which embodied a set of 'core' values about school improvement. These values relate to shared vision, opportunity provided by external pressures, the creation and maintenance of learning conditions for the whole school community, the development of structures encouraging collaboration and empowerment, and the shared responsibility of monitoring and evaluation. To date, the thrust of this work has focused on the identification of those conditions which relate to the management arrangements in the school. However, the researchers are conscious of pressures both from our project schools, and from the wider school improvement community, to develop the model further by addressing classroom arrangements in a similar way.

PUBLISHED MATERIAL: AINSCOW, M. & HOPKINS, D. (1993). 'Making sense of school improvement: an interim account of the "Improving the quality of education for all" project', Cambridge Journal of Education, Vol 23, No 3, pp.287-304. ; AINSCOW, M. & HOPKINS, D. (1993). 'No room for hit squads', Education, Vol 182, No 3, p.50. ; HOPKINS, D. (1994). 'Yellow brick road', Managing Schools Today, Vol 3, No 6, pp.14-17. ; AINSCOW, M. et al. (1994). Creating the conditions for school improvement: a handbook of staff development activities. London: David Fulton Publishers. ; HOPKINS, D. et al. (1994). School improvement in an era of change. School Development Series. London: Cassell. A full list of publications is available from the researchers.

STATUS: Sponsored project

SOURCE OF GRANT: Participating Schools £20,000; Cambridge University Institute of Education £25,000

DATE OF RESEARCH: 1994-1998

KEYWORDS: **classroom environment; educational improvement; educational quality; school effectiveness**

0338

School of Education, Shaftesbury Road, Cambridge CB2 2BX
01223 369631

Nottingham University, School of Education, University Park, Nottingham NG7 2RD   01159 515151

West, M. Mr; Hopkins, D. Prof

Evaluation at the local level

ABSTRACT: This project was set up to study the phenomena of local school evaluation and, following re-analysis of a number of recent evaluations, comparisons will be made between evaluations carried out in the UK and in Scandinavian countries. Further data gathering needs and areas requiring conceptual elaboration will be identified. Progress with other partners in the research will be discussed to produce further conceptual clarity. Outcomes will be disseminated at international conferences and case study reports will be produced.

STATUS: Sponsored project

SOURCE OF GRANT: Swedish National Agency; British Council; Cambridge University

DATE OF RESEARCH: 1995-1998

KEYWORDS: **comparative education; educational quality; evaluation; institutional evaluation; scandinavia; school effectiveness; school improvement**

0339

School of Education, Shaftesbury Road, Cambridge CB2 2BX
01223 369631

University of East Anglia, School of Education and Professional Development, Norwich NR4 7TJ   01603 456161

Southworth, G. Dr; *Supervisors*: Nias, J. Prof.; MacDonald, B. Prof.

Primary school headship: an analysis derived from an ethnographic study of a single headteacher

ABSTRACT: An ethnographic study was conducted into the work of a single, male headteacher. Using participant observation and interviews over the course of a school year (one day per week) data were collected and then analysed and written-up as a case study. The case study offers a portrait of the headteacher at work. Whilst a number of themes emerge from the study the main issue centres upon the power of the headteacher. The researcher is critical of the headteacher's power in the school and analyses why the headteacher is powerful and how this might be altered and headship reconceptualised.

PUBLISHED MATERIAL: SOUTHWORTH, G. (1995). Looking into primary headship: a research based interpretation. Basingstoke: Falmer Press Ltd.

STATUS: Individual research

DATE OF RESEARCH: 1987-1993

KEYWORDS: **head teachers; primary education; school organisation; teaching profession**

0340

School of Education, Shaftesbury Road, Cambridge CB2 2BX
01223 369631

University of Utah, Department of Special Education, Milton Bennion Hall, Salt Lake City, Utah 84112, USA   0101 801 581 8122

University of Maryland, College Park, Department of Special Education, Maryland 20742, USA   0101 301 405100

Rouse, M. Mr; Hardman, M. Dr; Florian, L. Dr

Towards the effective inclusive school

ABSTRACT: The State of Utah (USA) has been committed for a number of years to the development of inclusive schools in which all pupils, regardless of disability will be educated. This evaluation and research project by the

State investigated the outcomes of the initiative and the progress made to full inclusion. Initial findings indicate progress in a range of significant areas in certain parts of the State. Barriers to change, as well as an account of innovative practice, are included in the final report.

PUBLISHED MATERIAL: FLORIAN, L. & ROUSE, M. (1993). 'Utah's inclusive schools': a report to the Utah State Department of Education, Salt Lake City, Utah.

STATUS: Sponsored project

SOURCE OF GRANT: State of Utah £8,451 @#Date of Research: 1992-1993

KEYWORDS: **institutional evaluation; mainstreaming; special educational needs; united states of america; whole school approach**

Canterbury Christ Church College

0341

North Holmes Road, Canterbury CT1 1QU　　　01227 767700

Clift, S. Dr; Stears, D. Mr; Forrest, S. Mr; Black, P. Ms

Travel, lifestyles and health project

ABSTRACT: The project is engaged in a variety of studies to explore the connections between travel, tourism and health risks (particularly risks of human immunodeficiency syndrome (HIV) infection and sexually transmitted diseases associated with sexual behaviour), and to consider the role of health promotion and health education in this area. Specific studies currently underway include: 1) An investigation (in association with Luton University) of health preparations and risks among British tourists to the Gambia. 2) A study of sexual behaviour abroad among attenders at genito-urinary medicine clinics in South East England. 3) An investigation of the sexual behaviour of gay men in the context of holidays abroad. The project has also coordinated the Europe Against Aids Summer Campaign in the UK for two years and produced educational resources to support the work of the Campaign with young people in secondary schools.

PUBLISHED MATERIAL: STEARS, D. (1993). Travel health promotion: a survey of the work of district health promotion units in the UK. Canterbury: Canterbury Christ Church College, Centre for Health Education and Research. ; CLIFT, S. & CLARK, N. (1995). Dimensions of holiday experience and their implications for health: study of British tourists in Malta. Canterbury: Canterbury Christ Church College, Centre for Health Education and Research. ; CLIFT, S. & PAGE, S. (Eds). (1995). Health and the international tourist. London: Routledge. ; CLIFT, S. & WILKINS, J. (1995). 'Travel, sexual behaviour and gay men'. In: AGGLETON, P. et al. (Eds). Aids: safety, sexuality and risk. London: Taylor and Francis. ; CLIFT, S. & THOMAS, L. (1995). Europe against aids: summer campaign 1995. Schools Resource Pack. Canterbury: Canterbury Christ Church College, Centre for Health Education and Research.

STATUS: Sponsored project

SOURCE OF GRANT: South Thames Regional Health Authority £26,000

DATE OF RESEARCH: 1992-1997

KEYWORDS: **acquired immune deficiency syndrome; health education; health promotion; sexuality; sexually transmitted diseases; tourism; travel**

0342

North Holmes Road, Canterbury CT1 1QU　　　01227 767700

Holliday, A. Dr; Hyde, M. Mr ; Taylor, R. Mr; Bax, S. Mr; Kyeyune, R. Mr

Cultural transferability of British approaches to international contexts in English language education

ABSTRACT: English language education in both foreign and second language contexts throughout the world is dominated by technologies originating in Britain, North America and Australasia. The research project investigates the appropriacy of this technology transfer in a variety of activities in which British teachers, teacher educators, curriculum developers or curriculum project managers work with students, teachers and educational administrators from other countries. Data is being collected through observation of classroom and other events, and interviews with

and reports from students, teachers and administrators. Sources include English teaching and teacher education within the Department of Language Studies at Canterbury Christ Church College of Higher Education, projects with which the Department is involved in Cyprus, South Africa, Mexico, Malaysia and Syria, and professional contacts in a range of other countries. Students within the Department are also encouraged to carry out small-scale research in this area. A main focus is the investigation of what happens at the interface between different regional, professional-academic, institution, classroom and educational cultures. The research methodology is interpretive, sometimes employing applied ethnography.

PUBLISHED MATERIAL: HOLLIDAY, A.R. (1991). 'From materials development to staff development: an informed change in direction in an EFL project', System, Vol 19, No 3. ; HOLLIDAY, A.R. (1992). 'Intercompetence: sources of conflict between local and expatriate ELT personnel', System, Vol 20, No 2. ; HOLLIDAY, A.R. (1992). 'Tissue rejection and informal orders in ELT projects: collecting the right information', Applied Linguistics, Vol 13, No 4, pp.404-24. ; TAYLOR, R. (1992). 'The production of training packs in in-service teacher training', ELT Journal, Vol 46, No 4, pp.356-61. ; HOLLIDAY, A.R. (1994). 'The house of TESEP and the communicative approach', ELT Journal, Vol 14, No 1, pp.3-11. A full list of publications is available from the researcher.

STATUS: Individual research

DATE OF RESEARCH: 1991-continuing

KEYWORDS: **comparative education; english - second language; international educational exchange; second language teaching**

0343

North Holmes Road, Canterbury CT1 1QU　　　01227 767700

Sharpe, K. Dr

French primary schooling in action

ABSTRACT: This research project focuses on the operation of France's national curriculum in primary schools in a northern French town. In particular, two contrasting schools were selected for long-term ethnographic study, one located in an affluent area near the centre and the other situated on a run down municipal housing estate on the outskirts in an officially designated educational priority zone. During the period of the fieldwork (1989-1992) a variety of methodological strategies was used to assemble a diverse array of evidence to investigate the extent of educational homogenity existing between the two schools. Through the examination of official and unofficial documentation, observation in the classroom and around the schools, and interviews, discussions and conversations with teachers and pupils, it became clear that, despite their widely divergent economic and cultural situations, the two schools provided largely homogeneous educational experience for two socially heterogeneous populations. It is contended in the latter part of the study that theoretical analysis of the data gathered indicates that this educational homogeneity arises not from the mere existence of national programmes of study designed to ensure a basic curricular entitlement, but rather out of the whole 'national context' in which French primary schooling is embedded.

PUBLISHED MATERIAL: SHARPE, K. (1991). 'Coming off a strict diet', Times Educational Supplement, 6 December 1991, p.22. ; SHARPE, K. (1992). 'Catechistic teaching style in French primary education: analysis of a grammar lesson with seven year olds', Comparative Education, Vol 28, No 3, pp.249-268. ; SHARPE, K. (1992). 'Educational homogeneity in French primary education: a double case study', British Journal of Sociology of Education, Vol 13, No 3, pp.329-348. ; SHARPE, K. (1992). 'French recipes', Times Educational Supplement, 25 September 1992.

STATUS: Sponsored project

SOURCE OF GRANT: Economic and Social Research Council £9,000

DATE OF RESEARCH: 1989-1993

KEYWORDS: **comparative education; france; primary education**

0344

North Holmes Road, Canterbury CT1 1QU　　　01227 767700

Harrington, V. Ms; *Supervisors*: Hay, A. Prof.; Thomas, P. Mr

Aspects of the geography of rural primary school provision

ABSTRACT: The rationalisation of rural primary school provision is part of the broader problem of service provision and viability in rural communities. Both 'the problem' and possible responses to it embody a spatial component, and it is on this that the project focuses. Census data will be used to establish a typology of English rural areas, on the basis of population migration characteristics and other socio-economic variables. This will be linked with a similar typology, in which rural areas are grouped according to patterns of primary school provision. Sample case studies will be used to examine the relationship between the social geography of particular areas and relevant aspects of educational policy.

STATUS: Individual research

DATE OF RESEARCH: 1995-continuing

KEYWORDS: **educational planning; educational policy; population trends; primary education; rural areas; rural schools**

0345

North Holmes Road, Canterbury CT1 1QU   01227 767700
David, T. Prof.

Researching early childhood education: methodological and ethical issues

ABSTRACT: This is a survey of methods and the issues in current early childhood education research, in preparation for the publication of a book. It will include interviews with well-known researchers in the field.

STATUS: Individual research

DATE OF RESEARCH: 1996-1998

KEYWORDS: **early childhood education; educational research; nursery education; preschool education**

0346

North Holmes Road, Canterbury CT1 1QU   01227 767700
Fletcher, M. Mr

Identifying probability concepts in games

ABSTRACT: The aims of this research are: 1) to identify the probability ideas in television game shows, quizzes etc; 2) to show how children's/students'/adults' misconceptions about probability lead them to adopt inappropriate strategies. The research looks at game shows such as 'Play Your Cards Right', 'Strike it Lucky', 'Family Fortunes'. The research analyses people's strategies on these game shows. 60 shows have been taped and analysed, i.e. a sample of 120 people. The results/conclusions are published in 'Teaching Statistics' and 'Teaching Mathematics and its Applications'.

PUBLISHED MATERIAL: FLETCHER, M. (1994). 'Odds that don't add up', Teaching Statistics, Vol 16, No 2. ; FLETCHER, M. (1995). 'Rankings that don't add up', Teaching Mathematics and its Applications, Vol 14, No 2. ; FLETCHER, M. (1995). 'Play your cards right', Teaching Statistics, Vol 17, No 2. ; FLETCHER, M. (1996). 'Quiz night at the local', Teaching Statistics, Vol 18, No 1. ; FLETCHER, M. 'A model for a game of pool', Teaching Mathematics and its Applications. (in press).

STATUS: Individual research

DATE OF RESEARCH: 1994-continuing

KEYWORDS: **game theory; mathematics education; probability; statistics**

0347

North Holmes Road, Canterbury CT1 1QU   01227 767700
Brunel University, School of Education, Twickenham Campus, 300 St Margaret's Road, Twickenham TW1 1PT   0181 891 0121

Dunnill, R. Mr; *Supervisors*: Wood, K. Dr; Hodkinson, S. Prof.

Learning to learn in economics: a phenomengraphic perspective

ABSTRACT: Amongst all the debates about education, one vital issue seems all too often to be forgotten - whatever else it is about, education must be about student learning. But what is learning? For many, including policymakers, it seems to be a given, often referred to as standards, something about which a clear consensus is assumed to exist. The learner seems to play a passive and almost incidental part in the whole process. The proposed research will take a different stance, that of phenomenography. This argues that learning involes the learner developing qualitatively different conceptions of that which is being learnt. The learner is placed at the heart of the education process. Economics will provide the

context for the research. This involves huge numbers of post-16 students in a variety of different courses which might be described as 'academic', 'applied' and 'vocational'. The research will, therefore, examine and discuss what it means to learn economics through researching learners' understandings of their own learning in different conceptions of the subject. Drawing on those elements of the subject which are common to different kinds of course, it will identify and discuss the qualitative differences between students' understandings of what it means to learn in economics. To date, no previous research has been carried out in this area.

STATUS: Individual research

DATE OF RESEARCH:#@ 1996-continuing

KEYWORDS: **economics; learning; learning theories; sixteen to nineteen education**

0348

North Holmes Road, Canterbury CT1 1QU   01227 767700
Chichester Institute of Higher Education, Bognor Regis Campus, Upper Bognor Road, Bognor Regis PO21 1HR   01243 816000
University College of St Martin, Bowerham Road, Lancaster LA1 3JD 01524 384384

Tod, J. Mrs; Blamires, M. Mr; Preston, M. Mrs; Jacques, K. Ms

Code of Practice: individual education plans for Special Educational Needs

ABSTRACT: The Department for Education and Employment (DfEE), conscious of the demands imposed by the Code of Practice for the Assessment and Identification of Special Educational Needs issued to mainstream schools in September 1994, funded two projects during 1995/96 'The Role of the SENCO' (Special Educational Needs Coordinator) and Individual Action Plans (IEPs). This project has been funded as a collaborative project between two higher education institutes (HEIs) and four local education authorities (LEAs) in the South East of England region. The aim of the project is to develop guidance to schools to help them produce IEPs which: 'provide effective help; allow for efficient use of resources; relate to curricular assessment of work, identify clear targets and result in plans which are comprehensible and simple for schools to deliver'. Data collection, involving the use of conferencing, questionnaire, interview and observation, seeks to identify best of good practice in a range of primary and secondary mainstream settings. Administrative and educational functions of IEPs will be identified and software developed to assist schools with effective implementation and evaluation of IEPs. Dissemination will be via four national conferences, written guidance, and software publication.

STATUS: Sponsored project

SOURCE OF GRANT: Department for Education and Employment £65,700

DATE OF RESEARCH: 1995-1997

KEYWORDS: **code of practice; individual education plans; individualised methods; mainstreaming; special educational needs**

0349

North Holmes Road, Canterbury CT1 1QU   01227 767700
Lancaster University, Department of Educational Research, Cartmel College, Bailrigg, Lancaster LA1 4YW   01524 65201

Jones, A. Dr; *Supervisor*: Smith, L. Dr

Field dependence revisited: an evaluation for psychology and education

ABSTRACT: Field dependence was developed by Herman Witkin and refers to the extent to which a person is dependent versus independent of the organisation of the surrounding perceptual field. A principal measure of field dependence is the Embedded Figures Test (EFT) where individuals must locate a previously seen figure within a larger, complex figure. Wide-reaching empirical claims have been made for field dependence. The resulting typology was heralded for its simplicity of measurement, and became the focus of more researches than any other cognitive style. This popularity, however, was a two-edged sword. A neglect of some central problems led to its rapid decline in the 1980s. This study has 3 parts. The first reviews the way the theory developed. Key problems that contributed to its decline are identified. Six problems are selected for the conceptual and empirical investigation in the second part. A main problem is that field dependence measures have been unable to display discriminant validity with conventional intelligence tests. Field-independence has frequently been associated with higher spatial and overall intelligence. This, with too much reliance on gaining correlates with other tests, rather than theories, has left the theory confused, and badly structured. This study re-evaluates the relationship that field dependence (using the EFT) has with 5 topics both conceptually and empirically. Field dependence is measured using the EFT and the Cognitive Styles Analysis (CSA) which may be a more value-free measure: 1) psychometric intelligence; 2) the triarchic theory of intelligence; 3) achievement motivation; 4) Jung's personality types; 5) school performance. The aims of the project are: 1) to investigate the pattern of associations between field dependence and the 5 topics selected (using the EFT); 2) to compare the possibly different patterns of relationships when the CSA is used; and 3) to evaluate whether the CSA can identify the cognitive attributes of both styles. The sample comprised 67, 11 year-old children from 2 Lancashire schools. Each topic is presented in individual chapters. In each case the topic is reviewed, specific hypotheses are made, the method of investigation is described and the data analyses are reported. In all topics except motivation, the EFT was unable to identify most field-dependent attributes, but able to identify those associated with the field-independent style: the EFT was unable to show discriminant validity with the WISC-R intelligence tests, or the Richmond Test of Basic Skills (RTBS). It was also only able to show partial convergent validity with Sternberg's Triarchic Theory of Intelligence, by an association between the field-independent style and higher scores or an investigative task designed to measure selective encoding. This one-sidedness of the EFT also appeared in the topic of school performance, where the test was only found to identify the higher subject performances of field-independent children and their subject preferences - failing to identify the higher performances and subject preferences of field-dependents. By contrast, the CSA displayed a greater degree of discriminant validity by its divergence with intelligence test scores and RTBS performance It also had higher convergent validity with the investigative tasks of Sternberg's Triarchic Theory of Intelligence and the subject performances and preferences. The conclusion was made that the EFT is a less successful reflection of field dependence theory as described by Witkin, than the CSA. The theoretical and methodological implications are described in the final part, with suggestions for future research.

STATUS: Individual research

DATE OF RESEARCH: 1994-1997

KEYWORDS: **cognitive style; field dependence independence; psychology**

0350

North Holmes Road, Canterbury CT1 1QU   01227 767700
Nene College of Higher Education, Park Campus, Boughton Green Road, Northampton NN2 7AL   01604 735500

Bridge, C. Mr; *Supervisors*: Thomas, P. Mr; Matthews, M. Dr

The development of geographical understanding in the primary school child

ABSTRACT: The National Curriculum has raised the profile of geography teaching in the primary classroom. Both teachers and children are faced with a geographical vocabulary which fronts an understanding of concepts and processes with which most are unfamiliar. Research into children's understanding of maps or places has illustrated the slow and partial development of holistic views plus the high level of abstraction and generalisation required. This study will: review the range of conclusions drawn in recent research into environmental perception; make comparisons with current curricular demands in geography in the primary school; and consider desirable outcomes of young children's learning in geography. It is hoped that this preliminary investigation will reveal the range of conceptual demand being made on young children. The focus will be on aspects of physical and human geography which are within the child's own experience. The data collection aspect of the study will seek to involve two to three hundred children. It will investigate the quality of children's responses to key geographical concepts and processes across significant age bands in the primary school.

STATUS: Individual research

DATE OF RESEARCH: 1993-continuing

KEYWORDS: **geographic concepts; geography; primary education**

0351

North Holmes Road, Canterbury CT1 1QU   01227 767700
University of Ljubljana, 61000 Ljubljana, Kongresni trg 12, Slovenia

Aubrey, C. Prof.; Kavkler, M. Mrs; Tancig, S. Dr; Magajna, L. Dr

School children's acquisition, use and maintenance of quantitative thinking in mathematics (for ages 6-12 years)

ABSTRACT: The Third International Mathematics and Science Study (TIMSS) has placed Slovene 9 year-olds significantly above the international average and English 9 year-olds sigificantly below average, although the Second International Assessment of Educational Progress (IAEP) in mathematics and science showed performance of both countries to be 'middling'. The overall goals of the project were to investigate the development of children's arithmetic knowledge, problem-solving and calculation strategies in 2 cultural contexts in relation to existing curricula. 40 children at each age were drawn from elementary schools in each country and several standardized and non-standardized instruments were applied. 12 children at each level were selected for individual assessment of calculation strategies. Slovene and English pupils' scores for word problem-solving were similar at 9, 10 and 11 years but these findings masked wide differences in numerical abilities and performance in arithmetical calculation between high and low attainers at each age level and between countries. Whilst performance of English pupils at 6 years was superior to Slovene preschoolers of the same age, at 7 years Slovene pupils had caught up and between 8 and 11 years forged ahead. The broad and balanced National Curriculum in mathematics including algebra, shape and space and data handling which English pupils follow may be at the cost of achieving accuracy and fluency in arithmetic calculation which Slovene pupils clearly demonstrate. Improvement in mathematical problem-solving in both countries would be desirable, however, and this will be the goal of the next stage of the collaboration.

PUBLISHED MATERIAL: AUBREY, C. (1996). 'How in the world do children develop mental methods of calculation?', The School Field, Cognition, Learning and Instruction, Vol VII, No 3/4, pp.120-152/

STATUS: Sponsored project

SOURCE OF GRANT: British Council £8,000; Ministry of Education and Sport, Slovenia £5,200; Ministry of Science and Technology, Slovenia £6,760

DATE OF RESEARCH: 1994-1998

KEYWORDS: **arithmetic; comparative education; computation; curriculum development; mathematical ability; mathematics education; primary education; slovenia**

Cardiff University

0352

Department of Continuing Education and Professional Development, PO Box 920, Cardiff CF1 3XP   01222 874000

Newcombe, L. Mrs; *Supervisor*: Awbery, G. Dr

Intensive Welsh courses (WLPAN) and the wider social environment

ABSTRACT: This project will examine the factors influencing the extent to which adults who have learnt Welsh on an intensive Welsh course (WLPAN) actually succeed in using the Welsh language in their social environment after completing the course.

STATUS: Individual research

DATE OF RESEARCH: 1996-continuing

KEYWORDS: **adult education; adult students; second language learning; welsh**

0353

School of Education, Senghennydd Road, Cardiff CF2 4YG
01222 874000

Obeid, S. Mr; *Supervisor*: Nolan, R. Dr

Curriculum development in technical and vocational education in Saudi Arabia related to students' needs, perceptions and expectation

ABSTRACT: This is a study that aims to determine the cause of student wastage in technical and vocational education institutes in Saudi Arabia as a basis of the need for curriculum development.

STATUS: Sponsored project

SOURCE OF GRANT: Saudia Arabia Ministry of Education

DATE OF RESEARCH: 1991-1993

KEYWORDS: arab states; dropout research; student wastage; technical education; vocational education

0354

School of Education, Senghennydd Road, Cardiff CF2 4YG
01222 874000

Loudon, M. Mrs; *Supervisor*: Allsobrook, D. Dr

Cardiff Collegiate Faculty of Education: provision of routes to graduate status for certificated teachers

ABSTRACT: The research examines the significance of attainment of graduate status for participants - both providers and students.

STATUS: Individual research

DATE OF RESEARCH: 1985-1993

KEYWORDS: b ed degrees; graduates; student teachers; teacher certification; teacher education

0355

School of Education, Senghennydd Road, Cardiff CF2 4YG
01222 874000

Loudon, M. Mrs; Williamson, H. Dr; *Supervisor*: Davies, B. Prof.

Youth work curriculum in Wales

ABSTRACT: The aim of this project is to inform the debate on the youth work curriculum in Wales. Twenty-five youth work settings were visited to elicit the views of youth workers and young people on current and future provision.

STATUS: Sponsored project

*SOURCE OF GRAN*t: Welsh Office £27,000

DATE OF RESEARCH: 1992-1993

KEYWORDS: community organisations; youth; youth leaders; youth service

0356

School of Education, Senghennydd Road, Cardiff CF2 4YG
01222 874000

Howells, M. Miss; *Supervisor*: Donald, A. Dr

Training for the part-time youth service

ABSTRACT: Most of the face-to-face work in the youth service is carried out by part-time workers. Therefore one way of ensuring good youth work is through the training of the part-time work force. This study describes the development of training for part-time youth work from the Albemarle report to the present, and sets it in the context of the aims of the youth service. Common elements in training are analysed. The social, economic and geographic background of Mid Glamorgan as an example, and the relationship of this with youth service provision are outlined. An investigation, based on a questionnaire and follow-up interview, of the perceptions of their training of 101 participants in the initial training course provided by the county over a period of four years is described. Issues such as the relationship between training and policies and practices; equal opportunities; and communications are discussed. Main findings were that for many of the respondents, the training increased self-confidence and paved the way to new opportunities in employment or in personal life; that the part-time workers concerned brought into the youth service a wide variety of skills which were not always used as fully as they might have been; and that, although there are interesting developments in new forms of training, course-based provision still has a valuable place.

PUBLISHED MATERIAL: HOWELLS, M.J. & DONALD, A. (1992). The contribution made to the youth service by the interests and activities of part-time youth workers. Wales Youth Agency, Occasional Paper, March.

STATUS: Individual research

DATE OF RESEARCH: 1990-1993

KEYWORDS: part time employment; training; youth service

0357

School of Education, Senghennydd Road, Cardiff CF2 4YG
01222 874000

Edwards, M. Mr; *Supervisor*: Donald, A. Dr

The development, monitoring and evaluation of an advanced training course for part-time community education workers

ABSTRACT: This action research/case study concerns the development, monitoring and evaluation of an advanced training course for part-time youth and community workers in South East Wales. The study is designed to reflect on the participants' individual experiences in terms of personal and professional development in the circumstance of a Stage II training course. It attempts to place this innovative and unique course within the context of past and current local education authority training policy and practice. Qualitative data were gathered through participant observation; an analysis of student course journals; evaluation sheets; questionnaires; and tutor/participant meetings. The thesis concludes that there is a need for Welsh statutory youth services to consider the development of progressive training models based on consultation, negotiation and an acceptance of part-time youth worker training needs.

PUBLISHED MATERIAL: LOUDON, M. & EDWARDS, M. (1989). 'The identification of inservice needs of part-time community education workers - a case study', Researching INSET, pp.104-109, September.

STATUS: Individual research

DATE OF RESEARCH: 1989-1993

KEYWORDS: community organisations; training; youth leaders; youth service

0358

School of Education, Senghennydd Road, Cardiff CF2 4YG
01222 874000

Rose, J. Mr; *Supervisor*: Donald, A. Dr

Youth work management policy to practice

ABSTRACT: This study is an investigation into how youth work managers and full- and part-time youth workers within an identified local education authority translate their organisation's youth work policy into practice. It will be concerned with examining the consistency of practice throughout the organisation by trying to determine how quality standards are established and maintained for core elements of the youth work curriculum. It attempts to do this by identifying the political process by which policy is developed and then follows the interpretation of that policy through to the point of delivery with young people. Data are being collected from historical documents relating to policy discussion by the education sub-committee responsible for youth work; and through interviews with the chair of the relevant education sub-committee, assistant director of youth work, county adviser, part-time youth worker and young people. Questionnaires will also be used to obtain data from area youth workers, full-time youth workers, part-time youth workers and young people.

STATUS: Individual research

DATE OF RESEARCH: 1991-1993

KEYWORDS: community organisations; policy; youth service

0359

School of Education, Senghennydd Road, Cardiff CF2 4YG
01222 874000

Gukhool, P. Ms; *Supervisor*: Aspinall, M. Ms

Social and psychological adjustment of educated married women in Mauritius

ABSTRACT: The work concerns a study of the attitudes towards, and difficulties encountered by, educated working women in Mauritius. The investigation involved participatory observation, questionnaire and indepth questioning of some of the 120 respondents. These were women representing the different racial groups in Mauritius with the emphasis being upon those whose ancestors came from the Indian Sub-Continent, as for historic reasons family attitudes towards their participation in professional work has been slowest to change. Whilst it is being established that attitudes are changing, women are still meeting family and male hostility. However the actual results are not yet available.

STATUS: Individual research

DATE OF RESEARCH: 1987-1993

KEYWORDS: **gender equality; mauritius; womens education; womens employment**

0360

School of Education, Senghennydd Road, Cardiff CF2 4YG
01222 874000

Saunders, K. Ms; *Supervisor*: Aspinall, M. Ms

Women and education in Nepal

ABSTRACT: The study examines teacher education and the structure of education in Nepal and questions whether policies will lead to equality in education and employment opportunities for girls and women. The research, spanning the years 1988-90, investigates the situation of female teachers living in Karnali Zone, a remote mountainous region of Mid-West Nepal. In addition, the lives of young girls from the Karnali area are highlighted. Restrictions in attendance at full-time formal school and the introduction of non-formal classes to meet the educational needs of 'out-of-school' girls are discussed. The researcher argues that traditional structures can obstruct equality and suggests that development agencies and educational policy makers sometimes perpetuate the status quo of inequality.

STATUS: Individual research

DATE OF RESEARCH: 1988-1993

KEYWORDS: **educational policy; equal education; gender equality; nepal; womens education**

0361

School of Education, Senghennydd Road, Cardiff CF2 4YG
01222 874000

Nolan, R. Dr

Effectiveness of nurse teacher training related to experience since qualifying

ABSTRACT: This project aims to determine how effective nurse teacher training at University of Wales College of Cardiff and elsewhere was in relation to experience. The sample comprises a random selection of nurse/midwifery teachers who qualified over the past four years taken from college records and via contacts from other centres.

STATUS: Individual research

DATE OF RESEARCH: 1992-1993

KEYWORDS: **nurse education; nurse teachers; programme effectiveness**

0362

School of Education, Senghennydd Road, Cardiff CF2 4YG
01222 874000

Kandeh, F. Mr; *Supervisor*: Sutton, R. Dr

Teaching, learning and educational technology: a case study of a sample of secondary schools in Sierra Leone

ABSTRACT: Like most developing countries, Sierra Leone views a literate population with appropriate skills and relevant specialisms as a pre-requisite for national development. However, rapid population growth and a phenomenal expansion of both primary and secondary sectors, have in recent years continued to impose insurmountable strains on the weak and sick economy. Therefore much needs to be done to improve the efficiency and effectiveness of the teaching-learning process to justify government expenditure on education. This study finds that a growing level of inadequacies and constraints restricting the teaching-learning process in general and in particular, the secondary sector of the educational system. Specific problems include: a) a growing degree of failure among candidates to satisfy examination requirements in primary and secondary examinations; b) the high rate of repeaters and dropouts - about 40% of pupils repeat or drop out before reaching form three of the secondary school system; c) a general dissatisfaction with secondary school products by employers. Using questionnaire and observation methods and a sample of form three secondary school pupils and teachers the research aims to determine: 1) the professional background, experience and qualification of teachers; 2) the attitudes of pupils towards learning; 3) to what extent availability of

and in what ways audio-visual media are being used; 4) to what extent teachers employ the principles of educational technology in lesson planning and in the selection of appropriate teaching methodologies; 5) to what extent teachers in the sample have experience or have been trained in the use of various audio-visual media and attitudes towards its use; 6) the attitudes of teachers towards the application of a systematic approach to the design and development of lessons; and also their attitudes towards training for this.

STATUS: Individual research

DATE OF RESEARCH: 1989-1993

KEYWORDS: **developing countries; educational improvement; secondary education; sierra leone**

0363

School of Education, Senghennydd Road, Cardiff CF2 4YG
01222 874000

Rees, G. Prof.; Fevre, R. Prof.; Furlong, J. Prof.; Gorard, S. Dr

Patterns of participation in post-compulsory education and training: a regional study

ABSTRACT: This is a study of participation and non-participation in education and training throughout adult life. It identifies typical patterns and examines their variation in terms of time and place. One purpose is to produce a clearer conception of the purpose and meaning of and progress towards a learning society. The study is based on a survey of 1,100 local householders (selected by repeated selective systematic sampling) which gathered retrospective learning histories dating back to 1944. This was followed by 200 indepth interviews of a sub-sample and analysis of the changes in adult training provision over the same period. Working papers by Gorard, S.A.C. on 'Patterns of participation in adult education and training' are available from the University of Wales, Cardiff, School of Education.

PUBLISHED MATERIAL: REES, G. 'Making a learning society', Welsh Journal of Education, Vol 6. (in press).

STATUS: Sponsored project

SOURCE OF GRANT: Economic and Social Research Council Learning Society Programme £107,000 ; West Wales Training and Enterprise Council; Gwent Training and Enterprise Council; Mid Glamorgan Training and Enterprise Council

DATE OF RESEARCH: 1996-1998

KEYWORDS: **adult education; adult learning; adults; learning society; lifelong learning; participation; training**

0364

School of Education, Senghennydd Road, Cardiff CF2 4YG
01222 874000

Pugsley, L. Ms; *Supervisor*: Fitz, J. Dr

Higher education markets: how do students choose a university?

ABSTRACT: The research project is midway to completion. Adopting a qualitative focus it combines a number of methods in order to identify the ways in which potential undergraduates 'choose' a university. A cohort of students entering A-level/National Vocational Qualification courses in September 1995 have been tracked over 2 years in order to identify how and when choices are made. The study combines questionnaire surveys, focus groups, semi-structured and one to one interviews with pupils, teachers and family units to determine: 1) how students 'choose'; 2) who facilitates the choosing; 3) how market trends have impacted on universities and what their responses have been; 4) how are schools responding to the higher education market, is the response different between schools and, if so, how. Using 10 case study schools, differing in type and average A-level points per pupil, the research aims to address these questions and to determine the impact of social class on the choosing process. Given the 'freeze' on student grants and the shift to a system of loans, the project also aims to determine patterns of application and location to identify any trends towards a localised market.

STATUS: Individual research

DATE OF RESEARCH: 1995-1998

KEYWORDS: **educational markets; higher education; school to higher education transition; students; universities; university choice**

0365

School of Education, Senghennydd Road, Cardiff CF2 4YG
01222 874000

Pocklington, K. Mr; *Supervisor*: Wallace, M. Prof.

Managing large scale reorganisation of schooling

ABSTRACT: An investigation of 2 large scale initiatives to reorganise schooling focusing on managing implementation at local education authority (LEA) and school levels. Interviews are being conducted in the 2 LEAs and 14 of their schools beween February 1996 and October 1997. Reorganisation for these schools entails either closure, merger or a change in the pupil age range.

PUBLISHED MATERIAL: WALLACE, M. & POCKLINGTON, K. (1998). 'Realising the potential of large scale reorganisation for promoting school improvement', Educational Management and Administration, Vol 26, No 3, pp.229-241. ; WALLACE, M. & POCKLINGTON, K. 'Large scale reorganisation: a route to school improvement?', School Effectiveness and School Improvement. (in press).

STATUS: Sponsored project

SOURCE OF GRANT: Economic and Social Research Council

DATE OF RESEARCH: 1996-1998

KEYWORDS: **closures; educational administration; educational planning; educational policy; educational reorganisation; local education authorities; mergers**

0366

School of Education, Senghennydd Road, Cardiff CF2 4YG
01222 874000

Selwyn, N. Mr; *Supervisor*: Moss, G. Dr

The permeation of information technology into 16-19 education

ABSTRACT: This project aims to investigate the levels of integration of information technology (IT) in the 16-19 educational setting (i.e. school based 6th forms, tertiary and further education colleges). Research is taking place in 5 secondary schools and 3 tertiary/further education colleges and involves a range of quantitative methods (i.e. questionnaires, attitude scaling) and qualitative methods (i.e. individual ability tests, focus group and individual interviews). The project aims to investigate how use of IT differs in terms of subject areas, courses of study, type of institution and individual factors such as gender, previous experiences of IT, etc. As well as concentrating on student and teacher variables, the study will also examine the role and influence of the IT coordinator and institutional management on IT use as well as the effectiveness of pre and inservice teacher training for the 16-19 sector.

PUBLISHED MATERIAL: SELWYN, N. (1997). 'Assessing students' ability to use computers: theoretical considerations for practical research', British Educational Research Journal, Vol 23, No 1, pp.47-59. ; SELWYN, N. 'Students' attitudes towards computers: validation of a computer attitude scale for 16-19 education', Computers and Education. (in press). ; SELWYN, N. 'Teaching IT to the "computer shy"', Journal of Vocational and Educational Training. (in press).

STATUS: Individual research

DATE OF RESEARCH: 1995-1998

KEYWORDS: **computer uses in education; further education; information technology; sixteen to nineteen education; sixth forms; tertiary colleges**

0367

School of Education, Senghennydd Road, Cardiff CF2 4YG
01222 874000

Salvidge, P. Mrs; *Supervisors*: Davies, B. Prof.; Neary, M. Dr

Community care for people with learning disabilities: who should provide the care

ABSTRACT: This research asks the question - who should be the main service providers for people with a learning disability, living in the community? It will evaluate special education; health and social services for people with a learning disability. The research methodology will include: content analyses of the curriculum for social workers and nursing students; semi-structured interviews with clients and relatives; and questionnaires.

The basis for this research is the All Wales Strategy (GREAT BRITAIN. WELSH OFFICE (1983). All Wales Strategy for the development of services for mentally handicapped people. Cardiff: Welsh Office) which recommends the closing of mental handicap hospitals in Wales, and the main service provider to be social services as opposed to the National Health Service.

STATUS: Individual research

DATE OF RESEARCH: 1996-continuing

KEYWORDS: **adults; community services; health services; learning disabilities; social services; special educational needs; training**

0368

School of Education, Senghennydd Road, Cardiff CF2 4YG
01222 874000

Heath, R. Miss; *Supervisors*: Rees, G. Prof.; Salisbury, J. Dr

Language, culture and markets in further education

ABSTRACT: This is a PhD research project. The proposed research aims to investigate Welsh educational markets, to document how Welsh school students engage in choosing further education (FE) institutions and programmes of study. It will closely examine the factors that influence decision-making, in what has become a highly competitive and complex market place. The research will particularly focus on documenting the impact of cultural and linguistic factors upon economic consumer behaviour in the market place. The research strategies employed will largely be qualitative in nature allowing for fieldwork to be carried out in school and FE colleges in two contrasting regions of Wales. One, a largely anglophone, urban area, with the second area selected for its predominantly Welsh language school provision. Fieldwork will include semi-structured interviews with staff, school pupils and FE college students. Documentary analysis of marketing materials and media will explore the strategies used by institutions to compete in their markets. Senior staff and marketing managers in schools and colleges will be interviewed to elicit institutional responses, strategies and perceptions to their market. Year 11 pupils who are actively making choices in the term before their GCSEs will be interviewed to explore the reasons behind their decisions. Year 12 students in Welsh 6th form schools and FE colleges will also form part of the sample, to document responses to their new trajectories in FE.

STATUS: Individual research

DATE OF RESEARCH: 1997-continuing

KEYWORDS: **educational markets; school leavers; school to further education transition; sixteen to nineteen education; wales; welsh**

0369

School of Education, Senghennydd Road, Cardiff CF2 4YG
01222 874000

Stroud, D. Mr; *Supervisors*: Rees, G. Prof.; Fevre, R. Prof.

Higher education students' social construction of labour markets

ABSTRACT: The aim of this study is to examine how students enrolled at institutes of higher education to develop their social construction of the labour market. The study will attempt to establish empirically, in terms of careers information, rationality of decision-making etc, how undergraduates construct their perception of the labour market from which they then act upon. The focus of this study will be on the processes that influence and inform an individual in defining labour market expectations. A particular concern will be upon notions of individualised private investment within higher education and students' expected rates of return. Students face growing demands for personal financial contributions in an increasingly marketised education system, e.g. tuition fees, student loans, etc. The theoretical background, in light of this, falls upon theories of human capital, investment, consumerism and rights of citizenship. The proposed method of research for this study is the qualitative analysis of semi-structured interviews. In focusing on undergraduates, the research sample will be selected from the University of Cardiff, University of Glamorgan, and the Welsh College of Music and Drama. 60 students will be interviewed. Interviews will be conducted over a 2-year period - pre and post the implementation of tutorial fees. The study will attempt to draw some implications from gender, the institution attended and discipline studied, although this will be difficult given the small number of students. However, this study will be able to ascertain an understanding of the outlook that students have of the labour market.

STATUS: Individual research

DATE OF RESEARCH: 1997-continuing

KEYWORDS: higher education; labour market; students

0370

School of Education, Senghennydd Road, Cardiff CF2 4YG 01222 874000

White, P. Mr; *Supervisors*: Rees, G. Prof.; Salisbury, J. Dr

Guidance and destination: the transition from school to post-16 education and training

ABSTRACT: The aim of the research is to investigate the influence of formal careers education and guidance (CEG) on students' perceptions of educational and labour market opportunities post-16 and explore how they position themselves in relation to these options. Set against a background of the recent and continuing expansion of the further and higher education sector and training initiatives, and competition between local providers, the study also seeks to illuminate the perspectives of staff currently active in CEG. Based in a specific geographical locale chosen for its particular diversity of educational institutions (EIs), the sample is drawn from a total of 10 schools and colleges. Staff involved in CEG provision as well as the headteacher or principal were interviewed in all institutions and 10 students were interviewed in each of the 6 institutions offering 11-16 education. Student samples were balanced for gender and ability. A selected number of students will be interviewed in the first term of the academic year after their compulsory schooling has ended. All fieldwork was conducted using 'reflexive interviewing' (Hammersley and Atkinson, 1995) with interviews lasting between 20 and 60 minutes for students and between 30 and 90 minutes for staff. Data from the interviews will be analysed with the help of Q.R.S NUD IST software.

STATUS: Individual research

DATE OF RESEARCH: 1996-continuing

KEYWORDS: career education; school leavers; school to further education transition; sixteen to nineteen education; training; vocational education; vocational guidance

0371

School of Education, Senghennydd Road, Cardiff CF2 4YG 01222 874000

Rees, G. Prof.; Gorard, S. Dr; Fitz, J. Dr; Salisbury, J. Dr

The comparative performance of boys and girls at school in Wales

ABSTRACT: The project is to a specification from the Qualifications, Curriculum and Assessment Authority for Wales (ACCAC): 1) to describe the patterns of school performance of boys and girls in Wales over time via secondary analysis of key stage 1 to A-level data for all pupils in Wales from 1992 to 1997; 2) to identify those factors likely to explain these patterns on the basis of a review of previous studies; 3) to make recommendations for further work in this area. In summary, the method of analysing difference in attainment by gender was based on the proportionate gender gap at each grade of an assessment. This led to a more complex pattern than that which is widely portrayed. Therefore much previous published work in this area was found to be addressing a situation that does not occur in Wales (nor by implication in England). This means that a much wider-ranging study is required of the determinants of the specific patterns encountered here. Whatever gaps occur in any assessment, they are 'in favour of girls'. In terms of aggregate measures of individual performance, the gap between boys and girls has fallen since 1992. There are no gaps at all in some subjects such as mathematics, sciences and computing. The largest gaps are in English and Welsh. The gaps in favour of girls increase with every grade or level, so that girls appear over-represented in the highest grades at any assessment, while boys appear over-represented in mid to low grades. The 'gaps' at the lowest level in any assessment are among the smallest. Therefore the apparent under-achievement of boys is not uniformly distributed along the attainment scale, nor clustered at the lowest end.

STATUS: Sponsored project

SOURCE OF GRANT: Qualifications, Curriculum and Assessment Authority for Wales £8,000

DATE OF RESEARCH: 1997-1998

KEYWORDS: academic achievement; achievement; boys; girls; primary education; pupil performance; secondary education; sex differences; wales

0372

School of Education, Senghennydd Road, Cardiff CF2 4YG 01222 874000

Renold, E. Ms; *Supervisor*: Fitz, J. Dr

Presumed innocence: an ethnographic investigation into the production of gender/sexual identities in the primary school

ABSTRACT: This study explores the salience of gender and sexuality in children's lives during their final year at primary school. It focuses on 10/11 year old boys and girls through an ethnographic study across two small town primary schools in the East of England of white ethnicity and mixed social class. Alongside detailed observations, indepth unstructured and some focused group interviews were conducted to foreground children's own experiences and subjective constructions of their gendered and sexualised identities. Appropriating Butler's (1990) thesis that gender is routinely constructed through a heterosexual matrix, this study locates the primary school as a key arena for the production of hetero/sexualities, thus deconstructing and challenging 'childhood innocent' discourses (Walkerdine 1990). Following a feminist poststructuralist framework also allows for an appreciation of gender identities as power-laden, relational, fluid, multiple and contextually contingent. The discursive production of masculinities, femininities and heterosexualities organises the structure of the thesis where gender/sexual discourses and discursive practices make available various subject positions which boys and girls differently take-up, try on, invest in, resist and reproduce. The social, emotional and educational consequences that can arise from particular subordinated and marginalised gender identities are also central to the study.

PUBLISHED MATERIAL: RENOLD, E. (1997). 'All they've got on their brains is football: sport, masculinity and the gendered practices of playground relations', Sport, Education and Society, Vol 2, No 1, pp.5-23.

STATUS: Individual research

DATE OF RESEARCH: 1994-1998

KEYWORDS: primary education; sex differences; sexual identity; sexuality

0373

School of Education, Senghennydd Road, Cardiff CF2 4YG 01222 874000

Hesketh, A. Dr

Invested or vested interests? Parental perceptions of student finance

ABSTRACT: Building on previous research into student finance by the author, this research will examine the perceptions and reactions of students' parents to the recent changes to student support announced in the recent National Inquiry into Higher Education by Sir Ron Dearing. Financial support from the Research Initiative Fund will provide the foundation for the completion of one self-standing research project and nurture a second stage for which external funding from the research councils will be sought (see below). Central to the philosophy underpinning the introduction fo the new student loan scheme in 1990 was the belief that, where possible, students should be viewed as financially independent from their parents who were perceived to be shouldering too great a proportion of the required private investment in their son's or daughter's higher education. Now, under the new post-Dearing arrangements which advocate the principle that 'those with the means to do so (should) make a fair contribution to the costs of their higher education' (Dearing, 1997), all this is set to change once again. Crucially, the new Labour Government is pressing ahead with their implementation without, as yet, substantive evidence stemming from empirical research, and in the face of growing concern among policy analysts as to how both users and providers of university education will react to the new arrangements. The research proposed here will empirically address these concerns. The objectives of the research are to examine: 1) the variations in how the parents of prospective and actual undergraduates perceive the incoming policy of financial support for students in general and their role within it in particular; 2) the extent to which the incoming policy will shape the perceptions of the costs and benefits of higher education held by the parents, and how these perceptions ultimately shape the educational choices and experiences of their children; 3) the possible and actual effects of the new financial system upon different social groups (e.g. class, gender and ethnicity) orientation to participation within the upper reaches of a learning society in general and within higher education in particular.

PUBLISHED MATERIAL: HESKETH, A.J. (1998). Invested or vested interests? Parental perceptions of student finance. Working Paper No 1. Cardiff: Cardiff University, School of Education.

STATUS: Sponsored project

SOURCE OF GRANT: University of Wales £10,000

DATE OF RESEARCH: 1998-continuing

KEYWORDS: educational finance; financial needs; higher education; parent attitudes; parent financial contribution; private financial support; student financial aid; student loans; students

0374

School of Education, Senghennydd Road, Cardiff CF2 4YG
01222 874000

Melhuish, E. Prof.

Education for travellers' children in Wales

ABSTRACT: The study of the education provision for traveller children in Wales aims to obtain accurate data of numbers and ages of traveller children entitled to receive services from local education authorities. The researchers believe that the numbers of children counted officially and the existing information on their needs under-represent the true picture for a number of reasons. It is also felt that the existing support provided by central government under the Education Reform Act 1988 Section 210 funding through the Department for Education and Employment (DfEE) under-funds Wales in proportion to England. There is, therefore, a case for increased funding to local authorities in Wales. Travellers residing in or resorting to Wales are targets for the study, defined by Welsh Office Circular 79/94 as 'persons of nomadic habit of life', further amended by the Court of Appeal to include also 'persons who wander or travel for the purpose of making or seeking their livelihood not including persons who move from place to place without any connection between their movement and their means of livelihood'.

STATUS: Sponsored project

SOURCE OF GRANT: Save the Children Fund £15,000; Welsh Office

DATE OF RESEARCH: 1998-1998

KEYWORDS: educational needs; educationally disadvantaged; transient children; travellers - itinerants; wales

0375

School of Education, Senghennydd Road, Cardiff CF2 4YG
01222 874000

Trojanowska, L. Ms; Gilden, R. Ms; *Supervisor*: Melhuish, E. Prof.

The role of close and diverse relationships in early literacy development

ABSTRACT: The researchers will describe the ways in which specific dimensions of social context support young children's development. Specifically, the ways in which one dimension of social context, peer interaction, supports early literacy learning in the first year of formal schooling (kindergarten) will be examined in three studies. Literacy learning for young children is defined on two levels: children's use of 'literate language' (a variant of oral language explicates meaning and linguistic processes, often in narrative form) and in terms of standardised measures of reading and writing. Guided by equilibration theory the researchers suggest that two aspects of the peer context (diverse social networks and friendships) may afford literate language and more formal aspects of literacy. Equilibration theory states that cognitive conflict and resolution drive cognitive development. It is proposed that diversity of social networks maximises the use of literate language because of the varied perspectives to which children must accommodate. It is also suggested that the interactions between familiar peers and friends may support this form of language because of the varied perspectives to which children must accommodate. It is further suggested that the interactions between familiar peers and friends may support this form of language because of the emotional support of trust. Studies 1 and 2 will experimentally manipulate

peer familiarity, friendship, and diversity and their effects on literate language and literacy. In addition to basic scientific information, this project should be useful for policymakers and educators to minimise the risks of school failure for disadvantaged children.

STATUS: Sponsored project

SOURCE OF GRANT: Economic and Social Research Council £40,000

DATE OF RESEARCH: 1997-continuing

KEYWORDS: child development; early childhood education; literacy; social networks; young children

0376

School of Education, Senghennydd Road, Cardiff CF1 4YG
01222 874000

Crozier, R. Dr

Shyness and self-consciousness in childhood

ABSTRACT: This research project investigates shyness and self-consciousness in childhood, with an interest in its educational implications. The first stage in the research involved the construction of a self-report questionnaire to assess shyness in the age range 8 to 12 years. A second study found that shyness was significantly correlated with self-esteem. This project continues in two areas: assessing the relationship between shyness and children's performance on tests of language development; examining age-related changes in children's understanding of shyness. This second strand is guided by theories which suggest a distinction between two forms of shyness, fearful and self-conscious, with the second form appearing later than the first. Results support this thesis.

PUBLISHED MATERIAL: CROZIER, W.R. (1995). 'Shyness and self-esteem in middle childhood', British Journal of Educational Psychology, Vol 65, No 1, pp.85-95. ; CROZIER, W.R. (1997). Individual learners: personality differences in education. London: Routledge. ; CROZIER, W.R. (1998). 'Self-consciousness in shame: the role of the "other"', Journal for the Theory of Social Behaviour, Vol 28, pp.101-114.

STATUS: Individual research

DATE OF RESEARCH: 1994-continuing

KEYWORDS: childhood; self esteem; shyness

0377

School of Education, Senghennydd Road, Cardiff CF2 4YG
01222 874000

Bristol University, Graduate School of Education, 35 Berkeley Square, Bristol BS8 1JA   01179 289000

Fitz, J. Dr; Davies, W. Prof.; Broadfoot, P. Prof.; Winter, J. Ms; Firestone, W. Prof.

A study of local response to national assessment in England and Wales

ABSTRACT: This study focused on the assessment of National Curriculum key stage 3 (KS3) mathematics and how it impacts on teaching. The study employed research instruments developed in a study of grade 8 mathematics teaching and assessment in Maine and Maryland (USA) and these were adapted for use in 4 schools in the UK, 2 each in Cardiff and Bristol, by a research team which included an American scholar. Research included interviews with headteachers, curriculum directors, heads of mathematics departments and 16 mathematics teachers and also classroom observations of mathematics teaching. In the exploration of school responses to national assessment the study found that: a) considerable responsibilities for the interpretation of the National Curriculum and assessment framework had been devolved to heads of department; b) alignment of topics to ensure relevant topics had been covered prior to KS3 tests; c) setting was a common response to the challenges posed by 'tiered' papers; and d) teachers tended to organise lessons around instruction followed by individualised exercises rather than collaborative problem solving.

STATUS: Sponsored project *SOURCE OF GRANT*: Spencer Foundation (USA) £3,500

DATE OF RESEARCH: 1997-1998

KEYWORDS: assessment; key stage 3; mathematics education; national curriculum; secondary education

0378

School of Education, Senghennydd Road, Cardiff CF2 4YG
01222 874000

London University, Institute of Education, 20 Bedford Way, London
WC1H 0AL   0171 580 1122

Oxford University, Department of Educational Studies, 15 Norham
Gardens, Oxford OX2 6PY   01865 274024

Siraj-Blatchford, I. Dr; Sylva, K. Prof.; Sammons, P. Dr; *Supervisor*:
Melhuish, E. Prof

Studying the effects of innovations in nursery school provision

ABSTRACT: This study addresses the characteristics of preschool education
associated with educational achievement in primary school and social
development. It investigates the effectiveness of different forms, both
traditional and innovative, of nursery education. These forms are also
compared with other forms of preschool provision being studied in a parallel
project. Multilevel modelling is the chosen analysis strategy to disaggregate
the differential effects of different provisions and of preschool from
primary school effects. The project is targeted on guiding future government policy.

STATUS: Sponsored project

SOURCE OF GRANT: Department for Education and Employment
£333,000

DATE OF RESEARCH: 1998-continuing

KEYWORDS: **academic achievement; achievement; early childhood
education; nursery education; preschool education**

0379

School of Education, Senghennydd Road, Cardiff CF2 4YG
01222 874000

Oxford University, Department of Educational Studies, 15 Norham
Gardens, Oxford OX2 6PY   01865 274024

London University, Institute of Education, 20 Bedford Way, London
WC1H 0AL   0171 580 1122

Sylva, K. Prof.; Siraj-Blatchford, I. Dr; Sammons, P. Dr; McSherry, K. Ms;
Supervisor: Melhuish, E. Prof.

The effectiveness of preschool provision in Northern Ireland

ABSTRACT: This is a prospective study of 750 children from 3-7 years of
age as they move through preschool provision to the end of key stage 1 in
Northern Ireland. Recent research evidence on the benefits of pre-school
experience and new government policy point to the need for robust evidence
on the long-term effects of different types of provision. The research will
consider whether different types of preschool provision lead to different
benefits. This study investigates four types of preschool provision attended
by the majority of 3-4 year olds in Northern Ireland: playgroups, nursery
schools/classes, private day nurseries, and social services/voluntary centres.
It also investigates early entry to Reception class as a form of preschool
provision. Because preschool centres differ in various characteristics which
cut across type of centre, the study considers which characteristics of centres
are associated with medium-term benefits irrespective of type of centre.
Initially, 650 children will be selected from 80 centres in the 5 library
boards of Northern Ireland. Somewhat later 100 'home' children who have
not attended formal preschool will be recruited to the study at the start of
Reception class in primary school. At the start of primary school and end
of key stage 1 the children's academic and behavioural competence will
be related to family, community, preschool centre, location characteristics
using the multilevel modelling techniques already established in school
effectiveness research. The results of this study will have relevance for
educational policy, planning and practice. The research project has the
advantage of team experts in preschool education and care, child
development, qualitative and quantitative methods as well as school
effectiveness. The proposed study allows for comparison to be made with
a parallel study underway in England. Hence the quality of preschool
provision, and children's needs and progress throughout preschool and
early primary school can be compared between Northern Ireland and
England and related to National Curriculum considerations. There is the
added advantage that the combination of data from Northern Ireland and
England can be used to better guide interpretations of results and to better
inform policy, for Northern Ireland, England and the UK.

STATUS: Sponsored project

SOURCE OF GRANT: Northern Ireland Office £468,000

DATE OF RESEARCH: 1998-continuing

KEYWORDS: **child development; early childhood education; northern
ireland; preschool education**

0380

School of Education, Senghennydd Road, Cardiff CF2 4YG
01222 874000

University of Wales, Cardiff, Centre for Advanced Studies in Social
Sciences, 35 Corbett Road, Cardiff CF1 EB

Cooke, P. Prof.; Davies, B. Prof.; Fitz, J. Dr ; Cockrill, A. Dr; Scott, P. Dr

Training for multi-skilling: a comparison of British and German experience

ABSTRACT: The project investigates difficulties in the delivery of
vocational education and training in multi-skilling for employees in the
caring professions, construction and engineering industries in Britain and
Germany. It has 4 main objectives. Firstly, it aims to contribute to the
definition of the key elements of a learning society. In particular, it looks
at the extent to which networks of cooperation between different institutions
may assist the development of a culture favourable to learning. Secondly,
it examines the extent to which the training problem in Britain is caused
by shortcomings in the training system. Thirdly, it investigates the possible
impacts of specific programmes such as the Modern Apprenticeship
Scheme, National Vocational Qualifications, General National Vocational
Qualifications, National Targets for Education and Training, and Investors
in People on the British training system, and how these programmes and
initiatives compare with German schemes for meeting changing skills
requirements. Finally, it seeks to establish if changes (including the
programmes and initiatives mentioned above) in the British vocational
training system can provide employers with better qualified, multi-skilled
trainees. The success of these programmes and initiatives will be evaluated
and compared with equivalent schemes in Germany.

STATUS: Sponsored project

SOURCE OF GRANT: Economic and Social Research Council £110,000

DATE OF RESEARCH: 1995-1997

KEYWORDS: **comparative education; construction industry;
engineering; germany; health services; inservice education; on the job
training; skill development; social services; staff development;
training; vocational education**

0381

School of Education, Senghennydd Road, Cardiff CF2 4YG
01222 874000

University of Wales Institute, Cardiff, Department of Education,
Cyncoed Centre, Cyncoed Road, Cardiff CF2 6XD   01222 551111

Rowlands, M. Mr; *Supervisor*: Sutton, R. Dr

Student teachers' conception of the nature of science and learning

ABSTRACT: The aim of this research is to investigate any interrelationship
between the construction of primary school student teachers' conceptions
of the nature of science and the construction of their conceptions of teaching
and learning. Case studies will be carried out of a small number of primary
school student teachers during the period of their four-year teacher training
course. Triangulation will be achieved by employing several techniques,
including: observation of classroom interactions; interviews; and analysis
of journals and teaching materials. Results will generate theories grounded
in the data and illuminated by developments in the history, philosophy and
sociology of science and science education.

STATUS: Individual research

DATE OF RESEARCH: 1992-1997

KEYWORDS: **philosophy of science; preservice teacher education;
science education; scientific literacy; student teachers**

Cheltenham and Gloucester College of Higher Education

0382

Department of Professional Education, The Park, Cheltenham
GL50 2QF   01242 532700

Hockey, J. Dr; Collinson, J. Ms

Careers and identities of contract researchers (social science) in higher education

ABSTRACT: Little is known about contract researchers in higher education (HE) and what is known tends to eminate from survey data. To put flesh on the bones, a qualitative project was initiated in 1994. Focusing on contract researchers' identities, careers, relationships and adjustment to their role, during 1994-95 61 qualitative interviews were completed at 11 sites of HE with social science researchers. Data analysis is presently being completed. The output is expected to be published in 1997.

STATUS: Individual research

DATE OF RESEARCH: 1994-1997

KEYWORDS: **careers; contracts; higher education; researchers; social scientists**

0383

Department of Professional Education, The Park, Cheltenham
GL50 2QF   01242 532700

Hockey, J. Dr; Collinson, J. Ms

Research students and their supervisors in art and design practice based research

ABSTRACT: There is little empirical literature on research degree study in art and design and its supervision. Moreover, there has been zero research on projects which combine the traditional thesis with creative objects (paintings, sculpture, photographs, holography etc). The latter kind of research project is developing rapidly in art and design. To remedy this lacuna, a qualitative interview project, covering research students/ supervisors at 25 higher education (HE) sites was initiated in 1995. Data collection is in progress. Expected published output is 1997/1998.

STATUS: Individual research

DATE OF RESEARCH: 1995-1997

KEYWORDS: **art education; design; higher education; student research; supervisors**

0384

Department of Professional Education, The Park, Cheltenham
GL50 2QF   01242 532700

Littledyke, M. Dr; Ross, K. Dr; Robertson, J. Ms

Perceptions and practices in primary science and environmental education

ABSTRACT: The project phases include: 1) Single school case study analysis and questionnaire/interview analysis of a range of primary schools (n=15) to assess the impact of National Curriculum science. 2) Questionnaire survey of teachers and Year 6 children in a sample of schools (n=35) to assess attitudes and practices in science and environmental education. 3) Interviews with classes of children (Year 1 to Year 6) to examine attitudes and values. 4) Action research programme (2 classes of children with parallel groups for comparison) to explore values and attitudes in environmental and social issues within National Curriculum science.

*PUBLISHED MATERIA*l: LITTLEDYKE, M. (1994). 'Primary teacher responses to the National Curriculum for science', School Science Review, Vol 75, No 273, pp.106-116. ; LITTLEDYKE, M. (1996). 'Ideology, epistemology and pedagogy and the National Curriculum for science: the influence on primary science', Curriculum Studies, Vol 4, No 1, pp.119-139. ; LITTLEDYKE, M. (1996). 'Science education for environmental awareness in a postmodern world', Environmental Education Research, Vol 2, No 2, pp.197-214.

STATUS: Sponsored project

SOURCE OF GRANT: Teaching Training Agency £2,000; Cheltenham and Gloucester College of Higher Education

DATE OF RESEARCH: 1992-continuing

KEYWORDS: **environmental education; key stage 1; key stage 2; national curriculum; primary education; primary school pupils; primary school teachers; pupil attitudes; science education**

0385

Faculty of Education and Health, The Park, Cheltenham
GL50 2QF   01242 532700

Charlton, A. Dr ; Leo, E. Ms ; Indoe, D. Mr ; James, J. Ms

Evaluation of a teacher training package designed to enhance pupils' self-image

ABSTRACT: The research involves an evaluation of an inservice teacher training package constructed by the researchers. The package - EASI Teaching Package (Enhancement Approaches with the Self-Image) - is designed to assist teachers to improve the self-image of their pupils. Evaluation will incorporate a pre-/post intervention design. Seventy-two teachers (drawn from nine primary schools) are to constitute the intervention group. They will receive the EASI Teaching Programme (4 one and a half hour meetings) over a 4 week period. A comparison group (similar size/ type to the intervention group) will receive no special treatment. Pre-/post evaluations will utilise indices of teachers' classroom behaviour, and pupils' self-image reports and behavioural functioning.

STATUS: Individual research

DATE OF RESEARCH: 1990-1993

KEYWORDS: **inservice teacher education; programme evaluation; pupil development; self concept**

0386

Faculty of Education and Health, The Park, Cheltenham
GL50 2QF   01242 532700

Huxford, L. Dr; *Supervisors*: Terrell, C. Prof.; Bradley, L. Dr

The development of phonemic strategies in spelling and in reading

ABSTRACT: This research examined young children's developing phonemic strategies in spelling and reading and the effect of training in using a phonemic strategy to spell on children's ability to use a phonemic strategy to read. On the basis of existing research data tests were devised which enabled a comparison to be made between children's use of phonemic strategy in spelling and their use of such a strategy in reading. Forty-six children aged between 45 and 85 months took part in a longitudinal study. Tests in spelling, reading and their component subskills were administered at approximately 8-week intervals. Results suggested that children were able to use a phonemic strategy for spelling earlier than for reading and the children scored on the subtests associated with spelling earlier than those associated with reading. There was a strong relationship between phonemic spelling and its component subskills. The relationship between phonemic reading and its component subskills was weak. A causal relationship between spelling and reading was explored in a 5-month training study involving 45 children aged between 60 and 75 months. Children's spelling improved as a result of phonemic, but not logographic, training in spelling. However, over the period of the study, neither form of spelling training appeared to have an effect on children's ability to read.

PUBLISHED MATERIAL: HUXFORD, L., TERRELL, C. & BRADLEY, L. (1991). 'The relationship between the phonological strategies employed in reading and spelling', Journal of Research in Reading, Vol 14, Part 2, pp.99-105. ; HUXFORD, L., TERRELL, C. & BRADLEY, L. (1992). 'Invented spelling and learning to read'. In: STERLING, C. & ROBSON, C. Psychology, spelling and education. Clevedon: Multilingual Matters. ; HUXFORD, L.M. & TERRELL, C. (1992). 'The development of phonemic strategies in early literacy'. In: HORNSBY, B. Literacy 2000: Proceedings of the 1992 International Conference on Dyslexia. London Hornsby Centre.

STATUS: Individual research

DATE OF RESEARCH: 1987-1993

KEYWORDS: **early reading; phonemics; phonology; primary education; primary school pupils; reading; reading teaching; spelling; young children**

0387

Graduate School, Pittville Research Centre, Pittville Campus, Albert Road, Cheltenham GL52 3JG   01242 532210

MacLennan, H. Ms; Ross, K. Dr

Action research into the evaluation of student perceptions of professional studies in fine art programmes

ABSTRACT: The research arose from an evaluation of a new professional studies programme for Fine Art. Needing to know more about student perceptions about the role of work placements (and their understanding of learning outcomes) a qualitative research study was designed, based on group and one-to-one interviews, using a small sample. Initial results showed a series of contradictions and anxieties among students but revealed that learning outcomes were well designed. New work focuses on students' mixed feelings about 'graduate' skills and their approach to their subject-based studies in Fine Art. Using recorded interviews from a larger sample of 65 students, and discourse analysis, the researchers hope to uncover the cause of anxiety, and in the analysis, propose ways forward for improving student motivation and experience.

PUBLISHED MATERIAl: A full list of publications is available from the researchers.

STATUS: Sponsored project

SOURCE OF GRANT: Enterprise in Higher Education £5,000; European Union £5,000; ELIA £78,875

DATE OF RESEARCH: 1995-1998

KEYWORDS: **art education; arts; fine arts; higher education; professional education; student attitudes; student placement; work experience**

0388

Graduate School, Pittville Research Centre, Pittville Campus, Albert Road, Cheltenham GL52 3JG   01242 532210

Reading University, School of Education, Bulmershe Court, Woodlands Avenue, Earley, Reading RG6 1HY   01189 875123

Fuller, M. Prof.; Dooley, P. Ms; Ayles, R. Mrs

Girls in former boys' schools

ABSTRACT: The overriding aim is to document the experiences of girls in former boys' schools, where girls are in a small minority. The schools are fee-paying (but not only 'public' schools) in England only. Within that aim, the researchers are also interested to document parents' reasons for making such a choice for their daughters; how the initiative is viewed by male pupils; teachers' perceptions of the initiative to admit girls. The research is contextualised within an equal opportunities remit. The methods used are: analysis of prospectuses; and interviews (with pupils, staff and parents). The results from an early analysis of prospectuses show that: 1) equal opportunities do not appear to be on the public agenda of these schools; 2) co-education is treated unproblematically; 3) schools appear to be still boys' schools which happen to have girls in them.

STATUS: Collaborative

DATE OF RESEARCH: 1994-continuing

KEYWORDS: **boys; coeducation; girls; independent schools; single sex schools**

Chichester Institute of Higher Education

0389

Bishop Otter College, College Lane, Chichester PO19 4PE
01243 816000

Sylvester, C. Ms; *Supervisor*: Gaine, C. Dr

A critical examination of practices that support the integration of care and education services in residential establishments for children

ABSTRACT: The primary aim of this research is to develop a theoretical understanding of the relationship between care and education with direct reference to practice in residential childcare establishments. The sub-aims are to: 1) explore areas of professional 'overlap' between social work and education; 2) examine the impact of grounded practice initiatives on the relationship between care and education providers; 3) examine the impact of grounded practice initiatives on young people's responses to learning; 4) contribute to methodological considerations of applied action research.

The research will be based on an action research model underpinned by the researcher as 'reflective practitioner' (McNiff, 1988). Researcher involvement will also be developed through a participant observation role. Qualitative methods will be the dominant methodological tools of this research, supporting a grounded theory approach to the task (Glaser & Straus, 1967). The anticipated outcomes of the research are: a) the identification of practices that facilitate and inhibit the integration of care and education services; b) clarification of shared practice areas between teachers and social workers; and c) an increased awareness of the impact of establishment research in supporting service development.

STATUS: Individual research

DATE OF RESEARCH: 997-continuing

KEYWORDS: **agency cooperation; child caregivers; educational cooperation; residential care; social work**

0390

Bognor Regis Campus, Upper Bognor Road, Bognor Regis PO21 1HR
01243 816000

Ferguson, J. Ms ; Davies, R. Dr

Teacher professionalism: the role of initial training in the professional development of teachers

ABSTRACT: The lack of any recent research on the competences and notions of professionalism held by practising teachers means that the construction of competences for the beginning teacher - and our understanding of their links with induction and continuing professional development - is being conducted on the basis of limited information. The project will provide important data about teacher perceptions of their professionalism; the role of initial teacher education in their professional development; and the sequencing of their training. The key research issues are: 1) How do teachers define 'teacher professionalism'? 2) What contribution did their initial training make to their professionalism? 3) How do they draw on their experiences as beginning and experienced teachers when mentoring trainee teachers? The research will be conducted in two phases and will incorporate quantitative and qualitative research methods. A survey questionnaire will be administered to a sample of 150 teachers at the beginning and end of the reserch project. The sample will be drawn from partnership schools across West Sussex and will include teachers from both school phases and a variety of school types. A sample of 75 teachers, with varying lengths of professional experience, will be drawn from the survey respondents. Qualitative research techniques (focus groups and interviews) will be used to gather data on teacher perceptions of professionalism (phase 1) and professional development (phase 2) from the sample of 75 teachers.

PUBLISHED MATERIAL: DAVIES, R. & FERGUSON, J. (1996). 'Teachers as learners project: teachers' views of the role of initial teacher education in developing their professionalism', Journal of Education for Teaching, Vol 23, No 1, pp.39-56.

STATUS: Sponsored project

SOURCE OF GRANT: Chichester Institute of Higher Education £9,430

DATE OF RESEARCH: 1994-1998

KEYWORDS: **preservice teacher education; professional development; teacher attitudes; teacher development; teaching profession**

0391

Bognor Regis Campus, Upper Bognor Road, Bognor Regis PO21 1HR
01243 816000

Batho, R. Mr; *Supervisor*: Benton, M. Prof.

Teaching Shakespeare at National Curriculum key stage 3

ABSTRACT: This investigation has arisen out of the introduction, for the first time, of the compulsory study and examination of Shakespeare for all 13/14 year olds. Its aims are to: 1) identify the different perceptions of teachers and pupils to the teaching of Shakespeare; 2) investigate the range of teaching of Shakespeare at National Curriculum key stage 3; and 3) investigate whether the introduction of the compulsory testing of Shakespeare at key stage 3 has altered teachers' approaches and practices. The first stage was a survey of Shakespeare in English departments in 50 secondary schools, conducted by a postal questionnaire sent to English teachers in those schools. This was followed up in the second stage with the observation of Shakespeare being taught to Year 9 pupils in 5 of the schools. The third stage involved the interviewing of pupils and teachers in those 5 schools.

PUBLISHED MATERIAL: BATHO, R. (1998). 'Shakespeare in secondary schools', Educational Review, Vol 50, No 2, pp.163-172.

STATUS: Individual research

DATE OF RESEARCH: 1993-continuing

KEYWORDS: **english; english literature; english studies curriculum; key stage 3; literature; secondary education**

0392

Bognor Regis Campus, Upper Bognor Road, Bognor Regis PO21 1HR
01243 816000

Blake, D. Mr; Hanley, V. Dr; Jennings, M. Mr

Change in teacher education: interpreting and experiencing new professional roles

ABSTRACT: The project aims to investigate ways in which changes in teacher education are being interpreted. In its first year (1993-94) the project focused on the implementation and evaluation of a school-based Postgraduate Certificate in Education (PGCE) secondary course operating under the arrangements set in train by the Department for Education Circular 9/92. The research surveyed the views of students, mentors, teachers and college tutors on the operation of school-based initial teacher education. Interviews were conducted with a sample of respondents in twenty-four school locations. In the second phase of the project (1994-96) attention was switched to school-based and school-centred training arrangements in the primary (PGCE) programme. The research focused on mentoring in four case study schools by investigating philosophies and strategies, by observing mentoring 'in action' at different stages of the process, and by interviewing mentors, students and link tutors. In 1996-98 the research team is focusing on the perceptions of ITT held by newly qualified teachers in schools.

PUBLISHED MATERIAL: BLAKE, D., HANLEY, V., JENNINGS, M. & LLOYD, M. (Eds). (1995). Researching school-based teacher education. Aldershot: Avebury. ; BLAKE, D., HANLEY, V., JENNINGS, M. & LLOYD, M. (1995). 'School-based teacher training: the view from higher education', Education Today, Vol 45, No 1, pp.40-42. ; BLAKE, D. (1995). 'Change in teacher education: interpreting and experiencing new professional roles', Collected Original Resources in Education, Vol 19, No 2. Microfiche IC02-IF04. ; BLAKE, D., HANLEY, V., JENNINGS, M. & LLOYD, M. 'Primary tutors' attitudes to school-based training', Journal of Teacher Development, Vol 5, No 3, pp.23-29.

STATUS: Sponsored project

*SOURCE OF GRAN*t: Chichester Institute of Higher Education £6,690

DATE OF RESEARCH: 1993-1998

KEYWORDS: **mentors; postgraduate certificate in education; preservice teacher education; school based teacher education; student teacher attitudes; teacher attitudes**

0393

Bognor Regis Campus, Upper Bognor Road, Bognor Regis PO21 1HR
01243 816000

Lansdell, J. Ms

A longitudinal study into the nature of progression in mathematical learning and the role of language in that progression

ABSTRACT: There seems to be no clearly articulated and widely used theoretical framework for understanding the incremental learning processes in which children engage. This project aims to further develop the theory of complex learning originated by Norman and Rumelhart in 1978 in order to assist teachers in matching tasks more effectively to children's learning needs. This indepth longitudinal study of six children's learning in mathematics is qualitative. Using mathematical tasks, observation, informal and structured interviews, baseline information was obtained about the children's existing knowledge and understanding of particular aspects of mathematics. Mathematical activities were then designed and introduced to promote progression in the children's learning. The data collected as they worked through the tasks indicated which learning processes were in operation. Primary sources for data collection were the teaching activities themselves and the diagnosis of the children's learning. Data collection techniques included observation (participant and non-participant) and

interviews (informal and structured). Recording the data will involve use of field notes, audio and video tapes, children's drawings and written evidence. Preliminary findings indicate that children's progression in the learning of mathematics is dependent upon: 1) the learning experiences on offer; 2) the opportunity to verbalise existing learning; 3) effective diagnosis and task matching; and 4) recognition of children's difficulties and a constructive response to them.

PUBLISHED MATERIAL: GATRELL, M. & LANSDELL, J. (1993). 'A small-scale study into the nature of progression in the mathematical learning of three six-year old children'. Conference Paper presented at British Educational Research Conference, Liverpool, September 1993. ; GATRELL, M. & LANSDELL, J. (1994). 'A small-scale study of the nature of progression in children's learning in mathematics', Research in Education, No 51, pp.85-86.

STATUS: Sponsored project

SOURCE OF GRANT: Chichester Institute of Higher Education £4,000 ; Leverhulme Trust £4,100

DATE OF RESEARCH: 1993-1998

KEYWORDS: **learning activities; learning processes; mathematics education**

0394

Bognor Regis Campus, Upper Bognor Road, Bognor Regis PO21 1HR
01243 816000

Gilbert, S. Ms; Gardner, J. Ms; Hanley, V. Dr

Effective support at National Curriculum key stage 1: interpreting new training and roles for specialist teacher assistants

ABSTRACT: The context of the research is the Government's concern to support learning at National Curriculum key stage 1 by introducing specialist teacher assistants. The local context is the Institute's own specialist teacher assistants pilot course approved by the Department for Education in September 1994. The training of specialist teacher assistants is attracting support and criticism, but claim and counter claim are not yet rooted in research. The researchers believe that the research will contribute to national and local debate. The aims of the research are to: a) investigate how the new training is being interpreted in different higher education institutions; b) compare different models of training; c) discover expectations raised by the advent of specialist teacher assistant training; d) investigate the effectiveness of training as judged by headteachers, students and tutors; and e) contribute to the wider debate on specialist teacher assistant training. The research involves: gathering data for comparative course analyses/survey; questionnaires administered to specialist teacher assistants; questionnaires to be sent to headteachers; interviewing headteachers in schools; and follow-up fieldwork (gathering data on the perceived effectiveness of specialist teacher assistants).

STATUS: Sponsored project

SOURCE OF GRANT: Chichester Institute of Higher Education £1,500

DATE OF RESEARCH: 1994-1998

KEYWORDS: **specialists; support staff; training**

0395

Bognor Regis Campus, Upper Bognor Road, Bognor Regis PO21 1HR
01243 816000

Preston, M. Mrs

Students with dyslexia in higher education

ABSTRACT: The 'laboratory' for this research is the newly-established learning support unit which has been set up to extend and enhance the support currently on offer to students at the Chichester Institute of Higher Education with dyslexia and associated learning difficulties. Careful assessment and monitoring procedures are being put in place in order to evaluate the success of the support and remediation offered. The research project will take the form of a series of case studies of six very disparate students who have availed themselves of the services of the unit.

STATUS: Sponsored project

SOURCE OF GRANT: Higher Education Funding Council £40,000 ; Chichester Institute of Higher Education £20,000

DATE OF RESEARCH: 1995-continuing

KEYWORDS: **dyslexia; higher education; learning disabilities; learning support; special educational needs; student needs; students; support services**

0396

Bognor Regis Campus, Upper Bognor Road, Bognor Regis PO21 1HR
01243 816000

Player, K. Ms; *Supervisors*: Hanley, V. Dr; Blake, D. Mr

Class size and use of space at National Curriculum key stage 2

ABSTRACT: The primary aim of the project is to investigate the interconnections between class size and available space in National Curriculum key stage 2 classrooms. Additional aims include: investigating the management of space as a key resource at school level; tracing National Curriculum demands on space at key stage 2; and examining how these demands are being met by teachers. The project is informed by the ongoing debate on the relationship between class size and pupil attainment and will seek to define available space as an important factor in the class size debate. Using a variety of research methods, perceived and observed responses to available space will be investigated, with a particular focus on the implications for National Curriculum delivery at key stage 2. Research findings will provide an account of the physical setting and limits within which teachers work, together with their responses. Objectives for the study include the mapping of school wide management strategies and participant perceptions of their impact. Research methods will include a survey of schools by questionnaire to be followed up by a series of case studies. Data will be collected in the case study schools by means of participant observation, semi-structured interviews with staff and group discussions with pupils. Data will also be gathered as to the architectural plans and history of the school buildings, and adaptions in their use and constitution.

STATUS: Individual research

DATE OF RESEARCH: 1996-continuing

KEYWORDS: **class size; classroom management; classrooms; key stage 2; primary education; pupil numbers; school buildings; space utilisation**

0397

Bognor Regis Campus, Upper Bognor Road, Bognor Regis PO21 1HR
01243 816000

Greenland, P. Mr; *Supervisors*: Ahmed, A. Prof.; Williams, H. Ms

Conceptualising an 'expert system' to support primary teachers in mathematics

ABSTRACT: The research seeks to identify the components which might form part of a future 'expert system' to support primary teachers in their delivery of the mathematics curriculum. Through using the Delphi technique to identify the relative importance of such components, the research endeavours to focus on areas of teachers' knowledge necessary to the efficient teaching of primary mathematics. This research utilises Shulman's 1986 model of teaching knowledge as a basis to provide the elements of Professional Content Knowledge (PCK) for the first round of questionnaires.

PUBLISHED MATERIAL: GREENLAND, P.J. (1996). 'The Delphi method: a description of the technique and an exemplar of its use in educational research'. Paper presented to the British Educational Research Association Conference, Lancaster, 12-15 September 1996.

STATUS: Individual research

DATE OF RESEARCH: 1994-1998

KEYWORDS: **computer uses in education; expert systems; information technology; mathematics education; primary school teachers**

0398

Bognor Regis Campus, Upper Bognor Road, Bognor Regis PO21 1HR
01243 816000

Gaine, C. Dr

Educational outcomes – new developments in inequality *@

ABSTRACT: New findings about inequal outcomes with respect to race, gender and class – showing some differences with previous patterns – are being explored. The intention is to provide a coherent summary of trends and developments. The outcome will be published in book form by Falmer Press.

STATUS: Individual research

DATE OF RESEARCH: 1996-1997

KEYWORDS: **academic achievement; equal education; outcomes of education; racial differences; sex differences; social class #@**

0399

Bognor Regis Campus, Upper Bognor Road, Bognor Regis PO21 1HR
01243 816000

Davies, R. Dr; Jennings, M. Mr; Tatham, T. Mr; Thompson, B. Ms

Impact of mentor training on teachers' practice

ABSTRACT: With substantial numbers of teachers on Mentor Training courses (over 120 in 1995-96 and 275 in 1996-97, including both primary and secondary teachers), the Chichester Institute of Higher Education is a major national provider of this training and therefore in a position to derive research evidence on its impact. The project is designed to assess the impact of a 30-hour Mentor Training (Primary) course on the practice of course participants. The course took place over the academic year 1995-96 with a total of 75 participants completing the course. The impact of the course will be assessed with reference to participants: 1) practice as mentors of students, Newly Qualified Teachers (NQTs) or other colleagues; 2) own classroom practice; 3) own management practice. The course was evaluated (on completion, in July 1996) with a standard evaluation instrument and with a questionnaire designed to elicit information more specifically on participants' own practice. Therefore, substantial information was available for analysis from 40 respondents, 83% of whom indicated that the course had had an impact on their mentoring practice, and a similar proportion who indicated that it had affected their classroom/management practice. This has been supplemented by interviews with a sample (12), approximately 6 months after completion of the course. Although participants readily affirm the benefits of the course on their practice as mentors supporting students, NQTs or other colleagues, it is believed that a course of this nature leads participants to examine, analyse and re-evaluate their own practice in the classroom and, if appropriate, as a manager of other staff (teaching or non-teaching). This study is designed to gauge the nature and extent of the impact of training on such practice.

STATUS: Sponsored project

SOURCE OF GRANT: Chichester Institute of Higher Education £2,000

DATE OF RESEARCH: 1997-1998

KEYWORDS: **mentor training; mentors; teacher development**

0400

Bognor Regis Campus, Upper Bognor Road, Bognor Regis PO21 1HR
01243 816000

Harber, D. Ms; *Supervisors*: Ahmed, A. Prof.; Williams, H. Ms

A study of one group of reception pupils and their teacher in relation to the pupils' growth of mathematical understanding

ABSTRACT: The primary aim of the research is to investigate the mathematical knowledge, concepts and competencies of a group of children when they enter school and to document the outcomes of a programme of work in which 3 inter-related elements are considered significant. These are: 1) pupils having opportunities to talk to teachers and non-teaching assistants about their strategies for solving mathematical problems; 2) the use of analyses of responses to tasks and problems to determine subsequent learning objectives; 3) making the mathematics in everyday situations explicit to children through questions, explanations or descriptions. Implicit within the project is the intention to generate a profile of behavioural evidence from which inferences can be made about types of experience which have a positive effect on the development of young children.

STATUS: Individual research

DATE OF RESEARCH: 1997-continuing

KEYWORDS: **baseline assessment; mathematical ability; mathematics education; primary education; primary school pupils; reception classes; teacher pupil relationship; young children**

0401

Bognor Regis Campus, Upper Bognor Road, Bognor Regis PO21 1HR
01243 816000

Gaine, C. Dr

Anti-racism and the Internet

ABSTRACT: A website will be on-line by April 1998 with the facility to 'track' users' pathways through it. This tracking will be used to explore the pattern of assumptions and ideas about 'race' and ways of engaging with them in ways which are educationally useful.

STATUS: Sponsored project

SOURCE OF GRANT: European Union £10,000; Comic Relief £5,000

DATE OF RESEARCH: 1998-continuing

KEYWORDS: information technology; internet; racial attitudes

0402

Bishop Otter College, College Lane, Chichester PO19 4PE
01243 816000

Keyworth, S. Mr; *Supervisors*: Briginshaw, V. Ms; Clarke, G. Ms

An examination of the ways in which dance and physical education are gendered and the impact of this on male physical education teacher trainees with reference to their experiences of dance and physical education as revealed in their lifestories

ABSTRACT: The aim of this study is to generate spaces for the development of new ways of theorising and understanding male physical education teacher education (PETE) experiences of dance. Feminist scholarship considering the role PETE plays in the reproduction of patriarchal gender relations has only recently focused on the way male trainees are shaped and constrained by the creation of regulatory sexual categories, and dominant ideologies of hegemonic masculinity. This is worthy of further investigation as gender largely represents a blind spot in male thought. With experiences of embodiment central to ideologies of masculinity and sexuality, this study proposes to examine 'why' physical education's heterosexual imperative enables certain sexed identities while repressing others. Manifesting itself as a binary relation, masculinity becomes valued over and accomplished through distancing from femininity. Recent research reveals the majority of male PETE programmes marginalise dance, as it represents a 'feminizing practice'. This study seeks to address this by demonstrating that both physical education and dance reflect to a certain extent the social construction and historical specificity of gender. Further, consideration of Butler (1990) suggests gender is a cultural performance fashioning the illusion of an inner gender core. Theorised life stories will be collected from 8 male PETE trainees within a single institution. It is anticipated these will highlight how contemporary PETE training both privileges and oppresses the males it has been designed to serve. In so doing it will be argued that it is necessary to construct a new more liberal framework in PETE.

STATUS: Individual research

DATE OF RESEARCH: 1998-continuing

KEYWORDS: dance; masculinity; men; physical education; physical education teachers; sexuality

0403

Bishop Otter College, College Lane, Chichester PO19 4PE
01243 816000

Bath Spa University College, Newton Park, Newton St Loe, Bath
BA2 9BN   01225 875875

Connolly, P. Dr; Waterhouse, H. Dr; Bowman, M. Ms

The religious beliefs of scientists

ABSTRACT: After commenting on some of the American research on the religious beliefs of scientists (Leuba, 1916, 1933; Larson and Witham, 1996) this pilot study will employ the questions used by the above-mentioned researchers, along with a relevant selection from the European Values Survey, to ascertain the nature and extent of scientists' religious beliefs in one British university. It is intended (assuming the availability of funding) to extend the pilot work into a national survey.

STATUS: Collaborative

DATE OF RESEARCH: 1997-continuing

KEYWORDS: **beliefs; higher education; religion; religious attitudes; science teachers; scientists; universities**

0404

Bishop Otter College, College Lane, Chichester PO19 4PE
01243 816000

Taylor, V. Ms; *Supervisors*:Briginshaw, V. Ms; Gray, W. Dr

Girls' experience of classical ballet: contemporary feminine subjectivity, engaging with women's art, practice and stereotypical social role

ABSTRACT: Recent dance scholarship has established classical ballet as a patriarchal model of idealised femininity. The researcher proposes that such a thesis cannot explain the dancer's whole experience, and is itself a product of the dominance of the visual in western culture. The project will examine possible relationships of a fantasy femininity to a lived one, and the interchange of both of these with patriarchy, by focusing on the experience of pre-pubescent girls, who are often drawn to ballet as part of their fantasy life. Interviewing using, an ethnographic approach and methodology, 9-11 year-old girls, the researcher expects to assemble testimony which reveals multiple and shifting meanings, reflecting complex and ambiguous positions, conscious and unconscious, of the young subject in formation. The dancer's experience will be examined through psycho-analysis, phenomenology, and theories of performativity. Analysing the ballet class leads to a consideration of mimicry, its ritual and magical implications, and its insertion into psycho-analytic discourse through the visual. By comparing the findings with sociological investigations into the schooling of girls (particularly in relation to social class), the researcher will parallel Walkerdine's (1990) analysis of the valuing of 'true understanding' over rote learning in the classroom with questioning the superiority of 'creative' dance over a culturally received form. The researcher will examine ballerina/fairytale princess fantasies in relation to fairytale scholarship, in particular to its studies of gender formation. The research will add to knowledge concerning the formation of feminine subjectivity in contemporary British society, to dance scholarship, and to a growing oral history of girls' experience.

STATUS: Individual research

DATE OF RESEARCH: 1997-continuing

KEYWORDS: **arts; ballet; dance; fantasy; femininity; girls**

0405

Bishop Otter College, College Lane, Chichester PO19 4PE
01243 816000
Southampton University, Faculty of Educational Studies, Highfield, Southampton SO9 5NH   02380 595000

Laws, C. Mr; *Supervisor*: Evans, J. Dr

Individualism and curriculum development in physical education

ABSTRACT: The word individualism is often used by educational writers and teachers without conscious precision as to its meaning. The research project attempts to discover whether teachers' commitment to individualism is expressed in their practice of teaching. Data have been utilized from a four year case study at one secondary school. The emphasis of the research focuses on the interpretative paradigm adopting the qualitative principles associated with ethnography. Initial analysis of data indicates that while individualistic approaches are expressed in the formal intended curriculum, they are not always evident in the practice of teaching. Issues of equality of opportunity, equal worth, and value were recognised by teachers but their practice did not express their commitment to these issues. The capacity of teachers to achieve an individualistic approach in their practice was also related to the distribution of power in schools and the limits inherent in the philosophy of individualism.

PUBLISHED MATERIAL: 2AWS, C.J. (1990). 'Individualism and teaching games: a contradiction of terms?', British Journal of Physical Education, Vol 21, No 4. Research supplement, No 8, pp.2-6. ; LAWS, C.J. (1994). 'The process of recontextualisation and transformation of P.E.knowledge'. Proceedings of 10th Commonwealth and International Scientific Congress, University of Victoria, August 1994. ; LAWS, C.J. (1994). 'Rhetorical justification for new approaches to teaching games - are physical education teachers deluding themselves?'. Proceedings of 10th Commonwealth and International Scientific Congress, University of Victoria, August 1994.

STATUS: Individual research

DATE OF RESEARCH: 1986-1993

KEYWORDS: **curriculum development; individualism; physical education; teaching methods; theory practice relationship**

0406

Bishop Otter College, College Lane, Chichester PO19 4PE
01243 816000

Sussex University, Institute of Education, Education Development Building, Falmer, Brighton BN1 9RG   01273 606755

Paton, R. Mr; *Supervisor*: Cooper, B. Dr

Renewal in music and education

ABSTRACT: This is a theoretical and empirical study of musical learning and its role in the changing nature of musical functions and forms. It includes epistemology of music, psychological aspects of musical learning, improvisation and "holding forms" (containment structures for improvised musical acts). There will be empirical back-up from workshops with students, children and people with learning disabilities, also study of new-style methods and courses elsewhere.

STATUS: Individual research

DATE OF RESEARCH: 1986-1993

KEYWORDS: **learning; music**

0407

Bognor Regis Campus, Upper Bognor Road, Bognor Regis PO21 1HR
01243 816000

Southampton University, Faculty of Educational Studies, Research and Graduate School of Education, Highfield, Southampton SO9 5NH 02380 595000

Mirador, J Ms; *Supervisors*: Randall, M. Dr; Grenfell, M. Dr; Gaine, C. Dr

An investigation of written feedback, tutor interaction and student interactions on Master of Arts programmes

ABSTRACT: This study has two major aims: 1) to investigate the genre of written feedback through an analysis of discourse structure and linguistic features in feedback forms; 2) to examine how such feedback is interpreted by students. This study also has the following sub-aims: 1) to identify the specific types of information (e.g. aspects of academic development versus formal literacy skills) and the ways by which they are organised in written feedback; 2) to identify which expressions are used to signal specific types of information; 3) to identify the cognitive-pedagogical or socio-cultural factors that bear on: a) tutor choice of discourse structure and linguistic forms in written feedback; b) student interpretation of the feedback; 4) to determine the level of congruence between tutor intended messages in feedback forms and student interpretation of such messages. The proposed study differs from other genre-based investigations as it focuses on analysing the discourse structure and linguistic features in written feedback as a springboard to reveal intentions proposed by tutors against intentions perceived by students.

STATUS: Individual research

DATE OF RESEARCH: 1998-continuing

KEYWORDS: **feedback; higher education**

0408

Bognor Regis Campus, Upper Bognor Road, Bognor Regis PO21 1HR
01243 816000

Southampton University, Faculty of Educational Studies, Research and Graduate School of Education, Highfield, Southampton SO9 5NH 02380 595000

Barnard, R. Mr; *Supervisors*: Randall, M. Dr; Mitchell, R. Dr

An investigation of the interaction patterns between some non-English speaking learners and their teachers and their classroom peers in a New Zealand intermediate school

ABSTRACT: The study uses concepts derived from language socialisation theory to illuminate a specific learning context, and open up for reflective discussion some of the cultural and sociolinguistic factors which may promote or constrain effective learning and teaching within that situation. Extensive background reading of theoretical discussions and empirical studies, both in New Zealand and elsewhere, suggests that the learners in focus in this study are entering a zone of proximal development within a complex linguistic and cultural setting - the mainstream classroom of a New Zealand school. They are assisted in closing the gap between actual and potential achievement within that zone by English as a second or other language (ESOL) teachers, mainstream teachers, and fellow-learners within the mainstream class. Some of that assistance may be considered to be scaffolding. Through such scaffolding and other help in the classroom, these learners will come to terms with the complexities of classroom discourse. Their understanding and appropriation of different aspects of the discourse will be manifest in verbal interaction between these learners and their teachers and fellow-students in the classroom.

STATUS: Individual research

DATE OF RESEARCH: 1997-continuing

KEYWORDS: **bilingualism; english - second language; ethnic groups; integration studies; new zealand; verbal communication**

0409

Centre for International Education and Management, Bognor Regis Campus, Upper Bognor Road, Bognor Regis PO21 1HR
01243 816000

Randall, M. Dr; Lavender, S. Ms

Investigating group interaction of international and British students following modular degree programmes

ABSTRACT: The aim of the project is to examine the possible effects which task type, national background and personality may have on the patterns of interaction observed in group work. This work is part of an umbrella project researching into overseas student experience in UK higher education. This particular part of the project involves a study of group interactions of Malaysian students following a degree programme in the UK. The students are undergraduate English language teacher trainees and their studies include modules in which they are taught as a closed group (i.e. Malaysian students only), and modules which they follow alongside British home students.

STATUS: Sponsored project

SOURCE OF GRANT: Chichester Institute of Higher Education

DATE OF RESEARCH: 1997-continuing

KEYWORDS: **group dynamics; group work; higher education; intercultural communication; overseas students; student experience; students**

0410

Centre for International Education and Management, Bognor Regis Campus, Upper Bognor Road, Bognor Regis PO21 1HR
01243 816000

Escola Superior de Educacao, Nucleo de Linguas, IPS De Setubal, Estefanilha, 2910 Setubal, Portugal

Naysmith, J. Mr; Palma, A. Ms

Attitudes of post-primary foreign language teachers towards pupils with primary foreign language experience

ABSTRACT: A comparative survey has been undertaken in both West Sussex and Setubal, Portugal, by means of questionnaires issued to all foreign language teachers in each region in post-primary stage schools. The questionnaire is designed to seek the views of such teachers on pupils' experience of foreign language learning. It seeks to establish the extent of primary foreign language learning in each region and to discover attitudes of teachers in receiving post-primary school pupils with language experience. It aims to discover attitudes towards the value of primary foreign language learning for later foreign language learning and to examine questions raised about the coordination of such experience across school levels. Analysis of questionnaires will be undertaken during 1997-98 and key areas followed up with focus groups of teachers in each region. A follow-up study will be undertaken during 1998-1999 to establish the comparative views of primary teachers of foreign languages.

STATUS: Sponsored project

SOURCE OF GRANT: British Council; JNICT

DATE OF RESEARCH: 1997-continuing

KEYWORDS: **comparative education; language teachers; modern language studies; portugal; primary education; primary to secondary**

transition; secondary education; secondary school teachers; teacher attitudes; transfer pupils

0411

Centre for International Education and Management, Bognor Regis Campus, Upper Bognor Road, Bognor Regis PO21 1HR
01243 816000

Escola 4, Mern Martins, Portugal Centre for Inservice Training for Special Education, Guinir Road, Brussels 1040, Belgium

Preston, M. Ms; Stephenson, H. Ms; Olivera, E. Ms; Wuastanberg, A. Ms

Intercultural reading project in 3 European countries

ABSTRACT: The purpose of this intercultural reading project is to prepare children for a society where people's diversity is respected and to help children to cope with that diversity. The project will encompass not only ethnic diversity, but also socio-economic differences, gender relationships and the disabled. Thus, the concept of 'culture' is used broadly. Through the vehicle of stories and picture books, children can be made aware of their own cultural values and standards which will in turn help them to be more aware of behaviour, values and institutions from other cultures. More specifically, the project will facilitate an exchange of fairy tales, fables, legends and folk tales from the various linguistic areas. The project will also consider picture books which deal with universal psychological themes such as being and feeling different, and fear, loneliness and jealousy.

STATUS: Collaborative

DATE OF RESEARCH: 1997-continuing

KEYWORDS: **childrens literature; europe; intercultural programmes; reading; story reading**

0412

Centre for International Education and Management, Bognor Regis Campus, Upper Bognor Road, Bognor Regis PO21 1HR
01243 816000

Exeter University, School of Education, St Luke's, Heavitree Road, Exeter EX1 2LU 01392 263263

Randles, M. Ms; *Supervisors*: Taylor, W. Dr; Wright, T. Dr

Teachers' voices in inservice teacher education (INSET): perceptions from a Malaysian world

ABSTRACT: An ethnographic account of teachers' perceptions and understandings of the nature of inservice teacher education (INSET) by means of analysis of their original stories. The study aims to contribute new ideas to the field of INSET especially with reference to teachers in Malaysia. The design of the investigation is derived from the data; a series of stories collected and recorded on audio-tape, interviews, written accounts, researcher's diary together with documents. This is a qualitative study which is currently concerned with a small number of indepth interviews from the 104 interviews carried out to date. The study will present the participants' and the researchers' responses to the analysis of the data, insights into teacher thinking and personal and professional development in teachers' stories.

STATUS: Individual research

DATE OF RESEARCH: 1994-1998

KEYWORDS: **inservice teacher education; malaysia; teacher attitudes; teacher development**

0413

Centre for International Education and Management, Bognor Regis Campus, Upper Bognor Road, Bognor Regis PO21 1HR
01243 816000

Southampton University, Faculty of Educational Studies, Research and Graduate School of Education, Highfield, Southampton S09 5NH
02380 595000

Lavender, S. Ms; *Supervisors*: Naysmith, J. Mr; Brumfit, C. Prof.

Individual responses to cross-cultural English language inservice teacher education

ABSTRACT: This study examines patterns of response of experienced non-native speaker teachers of English and trainers of English teachers from Korea and Thailand to short, intensive in-service programmes at the Chichester Institute of Higher Education. The participants of these programmes are required not only to function during their courses in a different educational culture, but also to consider ideas from that culture in the light of their own educational systems. In order not to pre-judge responses a grounded theory and progressive focusing, approach is adopted. A variety of instruments including questionnaire, ranking, visual metaphor, group consultation, individual interviews, group diaries, tutor interviews, researcher diary, on-going correspondence and feedback on training ideas, is used to explore responses. The focus is mainly on a case study approach to individual participants although small group, whole group and in-country data are used to illuminate responses. Preliminary outcomes suggest that differences in cultural context have important implications for participants. The outcomes also suggest that particpants have a skills model of training and teaching to which they aspire only at certain levels depending on how they view their own language, teaching and training skills. They may thus seek to improve these skills at the levels they deem appropriate, irrespective of the overall aims of a course.

STATUS: Individual research

DATE OF RESEARCH:#@ 1995-1998

KEYWORDS: **cultural differences; english - second language; inservice teacher education; language teachers; overseas students; second language teaching**

0414

Centre for International Education and Management, Bognor Regis Campus, Upper Bognor Road, Bognor Regis PO21 1HR
01243 816000

Sussex University, Institute of Education, Education Development Building, Falmer, Brighton BN1 9RG   01273 606755

Hurst, R. Ms; *Supervisors*:Leach, F. Dr; Stephens, D. Dr

The impact of changes to the design and delivery of preservice teacher training programmes following the introduction of school syllabus reform in the English language syllabus

ABSTRACT: The research enquiry will focus on teacher training institutions which do not currently have degree awarding status. A major objective of donor policy is the provision of 'education for all' which in turn has brought focus on the quality of teaching and learning in the primary sector. Although the teacher training colleges are the major training agencies for qualifying teachers, they are ignored as a research base in favour of Curriculum Design Centres or the education faculties of the university sector. The aims of this research are to: 1) assess the actual impact of reforms in the school syllabus on both the specialist (English language) and core curriculum departments; 2) examine whether the teaching/learning activities which may be an integral part of schools is adopted or reflected in the teaching/learning activities of the colleges; 3) investigate what advantages (professional or financial) may be identified by college teaching staff in the reform of their programmes; and 4) assess the impact of reforms on the newly 'graduating' teachers emerging from the colleges.

STATUS: Individual research

DATE OF RESEARCH: 1996-continuing

KEYWORDS: **curriculum development; english; english studies curriculum; preservice teacher education**

0415

Bognor Regis Campus, Upper Bognor Road, Bognor Regis PO21 1HR
01243 816000

Fordwater School, Summersdale Road, Chichester PO19 4PL
01243 782475

Preston, M. Mrs; Seach, D. Ms

The education of children with autistic spectrum disorder in mainstream schools

ABSTRACT: The aim of this research is to examine and evaluate current educational provision for children with autistic spectrum disorder in mainstream schools. The researchers will consider the diversity of provision, which ranges from fairly segregated units attached to mainstream schools, to complete integration. Other issues arising from the research are: 1) specialist teaching methods for 'tuning into autism'; 2) the transfer to secondary schooling; 3) the effect in the classroom of integrating a child with autistic spectrum disorder; 4) the role of parents.

STATUS: Team research

DATE OF RESEARCH: 1996-1997

KEYWORDS: **autism; mainstreaming; special educational needs**

0416

Bishop Otter College, College Lane, Chichester PO19 4PE
01243 816000
Hat Hill Sculpture Foundation, Hat Hill, Goodwood, Chichester
PO18 0QP   01243 538449

Parfitt, D. Mr; *Supervisors*: Sandys-Renton, T. Mr; Chubb, S. Ms

Materials for sculpture research at Goodwood

ABSTRACT: This is a collaborative project in conjunction with Goodwood Sculpture Park and Chichester Institute of Higher Education. The aim of this research project is to create an Internet based resource that provides information relevant to sculptors concerning materials and processes. Both the form of the resource and the content of the database aim to integrate the lateral nature of creative enquiry with the quantitative focus of materials science and engineering. Besides being the first resource of its kind, it is anticipated that the new insights gained from this research will provide sculptors with a bridge to initiatives being undertaken in the field of materials science. The research project has full access to the sculpture, resources and contacts of Goodwood sculpture park, an organisation of international importance for British sculpture. Sculpture at Goodwood will also house the Internet resource and provide the infrastructure for artist liaison and publication through CD Rom and print. The Internet site is: www.sculpture.org.uk

STATUS: Sponsored project

SOURCE OF GRANT: Chichester Institute of Higher Education £7,250; Hat Hill Sculpture Foundation £7,250

DATE OF RESEARCH: 1998-continuing

KEYWORDS: **art activities; arts; cd roms; computer uses in education; design; information technology; institutional cooperation; internet; sculpture**

0417

Bishop Otter College, College Lane, Chichester PO19 4PE
01243 816000
Hertfordshire University, School of Social Work, Learning Difficulties and Mental Health, Meridian House, 32-36 The Common, Hatfield AL10 0NZ   01707 284000

Hayes, J. Ms; *Supervisors*: Briginshaw, V. Ms; Payne, H. Dr; Brown, D. Prof.

Personal growth through the creative arts: significance for students of dance (performance and choreography)

ABSTRACT: This research aims to examine how personal growth through the creative arts impacts upon the creative process of students of dance in higher education. It provides a qualitative analysis of the experience of 3 cohorts of students participating in a creative arts therapies personal development group. Data is taken from semi-structured interviews (group and individual) and reference is made to students' writing in a weekly diary where permission is granted. The results of the research will inform future practice and will be of interest to creative arts therapists and teachers of dance performance and choreography.

PUBLISHED MATERIAL: HAYES, J. (1996). 'Dance therapy: process and performance', Studies in Theatre Production, Issue 13, pp.29-37. ; HAYES, J. (1997). 'Dance movement therapy: its significance for dancer training'. Proceedings of the 30th Annual Conference Congress on Research in Dance, 31 October-2 November, 1997.

STATUS: ndividual research

DATE OF RESEARCH:#@ 1996-continuing

KEYWORDS: **art therapy; creative art; dance; higher education**

0418

Bishop Otter College, College Lane, Chichester PO19 4PE 01243 816000 King Alfred's College of Higher Education, Sparkford Road, Winchester SO22 4NR 01962 841515

Erricker, C. Mr; Erricker, J. Mrs; Ota, C. Mrs

Children and Worldviews Project: Phases 1 and 2

ABSTRACT: The Children and Worldviews Project is an ongoing project investigating the nature and development of children's thinking in relation to significant events and relationships in their lives. It has interviewed over 150 chldren between the ages of 5 and 11 using qualitative research methods: semi-structured and focused interviews. Children have, in particular, addressed issues concerning death, loss, conflict and the environment. The researchers have also examined children's use of religious and scientific concepts in the construction of their explanations. The project has developed the strategy of taking children's stories to other children as a research and pedagogical method, and is now engaged in taking children's stories to adults and developing a narrative method of pedagogy in selected schools which also addresses emotional literacy. The findings of the research, so far, indicate an underestimation of children's conceptual development and a lack of school provision and educational policy with regard to holistic development. The project is investigating these issues in relation to the current debate on spiritual and moral education and the initiatives of the School Curriclum and Assessment Authority (now Qualifications and Curriculum Authority). The basis of the project's approach is narrative theory. An account of the first 3 years of the project's research is given in The Education of the Whole Child (1997). In particular, the project is concerned with the use of narrative, genre and metaphor in the way that children and adults communicate their understandings and the way in which this can enable development.

PUBLISHED MATERIAL: ERRICKER, C. & ERRICKER, J. (1994). 'Metaphorical awareness and the methodology of religious education', British Journal of Religious Education, Vol 16, No 3, pp.174-184. ; ERRICKER, C. & ERRICKER, J. (1995). 'Children speaking their minds', Panorama, Vol 7, No 1, pp.96-109. ; OTA, C., ERRICKER, C. & ERRICKER, J. (1997). 'The secrets of the playground', Pastoral Care in Education, Vol 15, No 1, pp.19-24. ; ERRICKER, C., ERRICKER, J, SULLIVAN, D. & OTA, C. (1997). The education of the whole child. London: Cassell. ; ERRICKER, C. (1998). 'Journeys through the heart: the effect of death loss and conflict on children's worldviews', Journal of Beliefs and Values, Vol 19, No 1, pp.107-118. A full list of publications is available from the researchers.

STATUS: Sponsored project

SOURCE OF GRANT: Collaborating Colleges £39,800

DATE OF RESEARCH: 1994-continuing

KEYWORDS: **child development; emotional development; moral development; religious education; spiritual development; story telling**

0419

Bishop Otter College, College Lane, Chichester PO19 4PE
01243 816000
King Alfred's College of Higher Education, Sparkford Road, Winchester SO22 4NR   01962 841515

Ota, C. Mrs; *Supervisors*: Cole, O. Dr; Erricker, C. Mr; Erricker, J. Mrs

The place of religious education in children's worldviews

ABSTRACT: In the context of this study religious education takes account of social, moral, cultural and spiritual education and the influence of the ethos of schools with a religious foundation. The aims are to investigate the change in the worldviews of children as a result of encountering specific religious concepts as well as establishing the nature of children's worldviews. This is a piece of qualitative research which draws on data collected from 4 parallel classes in 2 Roman Catholic and 2 Anglian schools. In each class interviews have been conducted with small groups of children, and concept maps and drawings from the same children also form part of the data. At present the data is being analysed and it would seem that the school environment can have a fundamental influence on the way children are either encouraged or limited in their development of a worldview. Although other factors such as family and media are important, initial work with the data would seem to suggest that the school has a key role in the way children respond to religious education -either concepts are incorporated into their personal worldviews, changed to be in line with an alternative framework or alternatively rejected as irrelevant. The data suggests that children respond favourably to situations where they are allowed to explore a variety of concepts and ideas in their emerging sense of identity and understanding of the world.

PUBLISHED MATERIAL: ERRICKER, C., ERRICKER, J., SULLIVAN, D. & OTA, C. (1997). The education of the whole child. London: Cassell. ; A full list of publications is available from the researchers.

STATUS: Individual research

DATE OF RESEARCH: 1996-1998

KEYWORDS: **child development; moral development; religious education; spiritual development**

0420

Bishop Otter College, College Lane, Chichester PO19 4PE
01243 816000 King Alfred's College of Higher Education, Sparkford Road, Winchester SO22 4NR   01962 841515

Randall, L. Ms; *Supervisors*: @ Cole, O. Dr; Erricker, C. Mr; Erricker, J. Mrs

A narrative approach towards children's understanding of death and loss

ABSTRACT: Taking as its focus one of the emergent themes from data generated by the Children and Worldviews Project, this research aims to investigate the ways in which children experience and gain their understanding of death and loss within the context that these concepts tend to be ignored within social and educational discourse. The first stage of this research involved identifying and evaluating current literature and complementary studies. This has shown a growing interest in children's responses to death and an increased awareness of the need to recognise the signficance of events of death and loss within childhood. It has also highlighted the need for more systematic research to be conducted within this area. Using qualitative methodology, the researcher will work with a sample of approximately 50 children within the National Curriculum key stage 2 age group to gain an overview of the nature and scope of events which children have perceived as a signficant loss. The aim will then be to conduct an indepth study of a smaller group, taken from the original sample, to identify how the children have gained understanding of these experiences. The role which narrative has played within the understanding process will also be analysed. It is hoped that the findings of this study can be used to explore ways in which the concepts of death and loss could be presented within the primary classroom to enable children to gain positive undestandings of these concepts.

STATUS: Individual research

DATE OF RESEARCH: 1996-continuing

KEYWORDS: **bereavement; death; key stage 2; primary education**

0421

Bognor Regis Campus, Upper Bognor Road, Bognor Regis PO21 1HR
01243 816000

Plymouth University, Faculty of Arts and Education, Rolle School of Education, Douglas Avenue, Exmouth EX8 2AT   01395 255309

Lansdell, J. Ms; Gatrell, M. Ms

A small-scale study into the role of language in young children's understanding of mathematical concepts

ABSTRACT: How can children's learning of mathematics be enhanced? This project aimed to further develop the theory of complex learning originated by Norman and Rumelhart in 1978 in order to assist teachers in matching tasks more effectively to children's learning needs. This indepth study of six 4 to 6 year-old children's learning in mathematics over 2 years was qualitative. Using mathematical tasks, observation, informal and structured interviews, baseline information was obtained about the children's existing knowledge and understanding of particular aspects of mathematics. Mathematical activities were then designed and introduced to promote progression in the children's learning. Data collection techniques included observation (participant and non-participant) and interviews (informal and structured). Data was recorded using field notes, audio and video tapes, children's drawings and written evidence. Interim findings indicated that these children's progression in the learning of mathematics was dependent upon the learning experiences on offer, effective diagnosis and task matching, recognition of the children's difficulties and a constructive response to them, and the opportunity to verbalise their existing learning. The next phase of the research focused upon: whether progression was linear or in the form of a network, and how the teacher's use of language influenced the children's progression in learning. Preliminary analysis of the findings suggest that teachers need to be aware that certain mathematical words are likely to cause children problems because they have a different meaning in every day usage. There is a need to take note of the way children use such words in order to assess their understanding, and to focus as appropriate either on the mathematical meaning of these particular words, or on the mathematics.

PUBLISHED MATERIAL: GATRELL, M. & LANSDELL, J. (1994). 'A small-scale study of the nature of progression in children's learning in mathematics', Research in Education, No 51, pp.85-86. ; LANSDELL, J. (1997). 'Introducing young children to the language of mathematics', Language and Learning. (in press)

STATUS: Sponsored project

SOURCE OF GRANT: Leverhulme Fellowship £4,100

DATE OF RESEARCH: 1993-1997

KEYWORDS: **mathematical concepts; mathematical vocabulary; mathematics education; primary education; primary school pupils; young children**

0422

Bognor Regis Campus, Upper Bognor Road, Bognor Regis PO21 1HR
01243 816000

Southampton University, Faculty of Educational Studies, Highfield, Southampton SO9 5NH   02380 595000

Pinel, A. Mr; *Supervisor*: Evans, J. Dr

Embedded teacher development

ABSTRACT: The central interest 'embedded teacher development' refers to processes through which teachers develop perceptions of their task, while continuing as classroom practitioners. The major concerns are how they learn more about the capabilities and powers of their pupils and how they attempt to provide more opportunities for the release of these powers through reflecting on and re-structuring their approaches to them and to their teaching material. The medium is (mainly) mathematics. The teachers are primary teachers.

STATUS: Individual research

DATE OF RESEARCH: 1987-1993

KEYWORDS: **primary school teachers; teacher behaviour; teacher development; teacher role; teaching methods**

0423

Bishop Otter College, College Lane, Chichester PO19 4PE
01243 816000

Southampton University, School of Theology and Religion, Highfield, Southampton SO0 5NH   02380 595000

Mantin, R. Ms; *Supervisors*: Grey, M. Prof.; Long, A. Ms

The role of goddess symbolism in feminist spirituality

ABSTRACT: There has been a resurgence of interest over the last 25 years in ancient and contemporary goddess religion. This research examines the use of goddess language in new forms of spiritual feminism. An interest in the implications of goddess symbolism for theology, thealogy and spirituality, and for feminist strategies and alliances, has led to a focus on the work of Carol Christ. This exploration has also necessitated a consideration of post-modern and post-structural challenges to the use of 'women's experience' as a means of spirituality. Research into feminist critiques and reconstructions of religious language has implications for religious education. This research has contributed to publications on the role of feminist studies of religion in promoting an education for equality.

STATUS: Individual research

DATE OF RESEARCH: 1997-1998

KEYWORDS: **feminism; gender equality; religious education; spiritual development**

0424

Bognor Regis Campus, Upper Bognor Road, Bognor Regis PO21 1HR
01243 816000

Sussex University, Institute of Education, Education Development Building, Falmer, Brighton BN1 9RG   01273 606755

Lloyd, M. Ms; *Supervisors*: Hanley, V. Dr; George, R. Ms; Lacey, C. Prof.

Student teachers' experiences of a secondary Postgraduate Certificate in Education: a case study at the Chichester Institute

ABSTRACT: Recent government policy has located more initial teacher education in schools, thereby reducing the role of higher education. This research examines the impact of the shift towards school-based teacher training and the implications it poses for race, gender and social class issues within training programmes. To gain some insight into the views and experiences of student teachers undertaking a one-year school-based Secondary Postgraduate Certificate in Education (PGCE) course, research was conducted with two consecutive cohorts of students at a college of higher education. Each cohort totalled around 70 students. Data were gathered through formal participant observations of college-based sessions; informal contact with students and college tutors; beginning- and end-of-course questionnaires with students; semi-structured interviews with 24 students and 10 college tutors; tracking 12 individual students in school for one day; and observations of PGCE programme meetings at college. Preliminary analysis of data reveals that women students consistently ascribe greater importance than their male colleagues to equality issues addressed within their training course. With students spending two-thirds of their training year in school, the researcher looked at how student teachers generally give precedence to the school-based components of the PGCE programme over the college-based courses. The research also explores how the college-based component of the PGCE on Thursdays and Fridays, during students' serial school experience, comes to be conceptualised by some students as 'a long weekend'.

PUBLISHED MATERIAL: LLOYD, M. (1996). '"A long weekend": student teachers' experiences of a secondary PGCE course'. Paper presented to the British Educational Research Association Annual Conference, Lancaster University, 11-15 September 1996.

STATUS: Individual research

DATE OF RESEARCH:#@ 1994-1998

KEYWORDS: **equal education; postgraduate certificate in education; preservice teacher education; school based teacher education; student teacher attitudes; student teachers**

City University

0425

Department of Continuing Education, Continuing Education Research Unit, Northampton Square, London EC1V OHB   0171 477 8000

Carter, J. Ms; Webb, S. Ms; *Supervisor*: Davies, P. Dr

Wider participation for adults and the role of professional bodies in the finance sector

ABSTRACT: The project has mapped the education and training routes to professional qualifications and membership across the finance sector and has identified the scale and scope of the involvement of professional bodies and associations particularly in relation to the control of qualifications and the recognition of courses and establishments. It has reviewed opportunities for adult learners and returners to pursue professional qualifications at initial level and considered the impact of national frameworks for vocational qualifications and of European developments.

PUBLISHED MATERIAL: CARTER, J. & WEBB, S. (1993). Professional education in the finance sector: open to all? London: City University. @#*STATUS*: Sponsored project

SOURCE OF GRANT: Universities Funding Council £25,000

DATE OF RESEARCH: 1992-1993

KEYWORDS: **access to education; finance occupations; mature students; professional education**

0426

Department of Continuing Education, Continuing Education Research Unit, Northampton Square, London EC1V OHB 0171 477 8000

Wilkinson, D. Mr; *Supervisors*: Davies, P. Dr; Roberts, P. Prof.

Cost benefit analysis of quality assurance mechanisms in education

ABSTRACT: The background to this project is the growth of quality assurance mechanisms and procedures in further and higher education. The aims of the project are to identify the costs and benefits of quality assurance arrangements, and to develop ways of measuring those which can be measured and of accounting for those which cannot. From this work, developed in the context of the national framework for quality assurance in Access courses, a working model to evaluate arrangements in other contexts will be developed and tested in a range of situations. It is also

hoped to develop an interactive, multi-media working model from the paper-based and spreadsheet versions.

PUBLISHED MATERIAL: WILKINSON, D. (1997). 'Assuring quality in Access courses: the authorised version', Quality Assurance in Education, Vol 5, No 1, pp.32-39. ; WILKINSON, D. (1997). 'AVAs - adding value to Access? A cost-benefit analysis of Access quality assurance', Quality Assurance in Education, Vol 5, No 2, pp.80-84.

STATUS: Individual research

DATE OF RESEARCH: 1994-1998

KEYWORDS: **access programmes; cost effectiveness; educational quality; quality assurance**

0427

Department of Continuing Education, Continuing Education Research Unit, Northampton Square, London EC1V 0HB   0171 477 8000

Capizzi, E. Ms

An evaluation of the impact of the National Open College Network accreditation of Trades Union Congress courses

ABSTRACT: The aim of the project is to assess the impact of National Open College Network accreditation of the Trades Union Congress (TUC) Health and Safety and Voluntary Officers courses on: a) specific aspects of participation patterns; b) delivery of curriculum and working culture of the group; c) union representatives' expectations and use of credit. It will also identify 'good practice' in facilitating TUC broad educational and union aims in this programme. The methods will include semi-structured interviews and survey questionnaires with union representatives and tutors. A full list of publications is available from the researcher.

STATUS: Sponsored project

SOURCE OF GRANT: Trades Union Congress Education Department

DATE OF RESEARCH: 1998-1998

KEYWORDS: **adult education; continuing education; credits; labour education; open colleges; trade union education**

0428

Department of Continuing Education, Continuing Education Research Unit, Northampton Square, London EC1V 0HB   0171 477 8000

Capizzi, E. Ms; Heycock, T. Ms

Credit for volunteers

ABSTRACT: This small study is a 'satellite' of a larger Learning Society project on credit. Volunteering is sometimes seen as a possible route to employment or education at a higher level. Some voluntary organisations run courses which can earn credits from the Open College Network, and a small number of these courses are mainly or solely for volunteers. The research aims to study 4 or 5 such courses to see how and why credit is being used, and in particular whether students wish or are able to use these credits to progress to employment or more education. A full list of publications is available from the researchers.

STATUS: Individual research

DATE OF RESEARCH: 997-1998

KEYWORDS: **accreditation of prior learning; adult education; continuing education; credits; volunteers**

0429

Department of Continuing Education, Continuing Education Research Unit, Northampton Square, London EC1V 0HB   0171 477 8000

Carter, J. Ms; *Supervisors*: Davies, P. Dr; Capizzi, E. Ms

Credit-based learning in prison education: learning within walls

ABSTRACT: The research aims to explore the use of credit-based learning within prison education departments. In particular, to identify reasons for the adoption of credit-based systems; their impact on student motivation and on the curriculum, including informal learning opportunities and behavioural change. Interviews with managers of education departments in 3 prisons, interviews with educational staff and students (inmates). The research arises out of a larger Economic and Social Research Council study into credit-based learning.

STATUS: Individual research

DATE OF RESEARCH: 1997-1998

KEYWORDS: **credits; prison education; prisoners; teaching methods**

0430

Department of Continuing Education, Continuing Education Research Unit, Northampton Square, London EC1V 0HB   0171 477 8000

Hillier, Y. Dr

Higher level NVQs: the candidates' experiences

ABSTRACT: Little research has been conducted into the experience of candidates undertaking National Vocational Qualifications (NVQs) from the perspective of the candidates. The case study analyses the impact of Learning Development and Human Resource Management NVQs Level 4 for 16 candidates drawn from two groups: associate lecturers who teach adults in higher education; and trainers who work in the public, private and voluntary sectors. It identifies the cost and benefit to candidates who have been working towards or successfully completed the NVQ. The case study tests the claims of NVQ rhetoric by analysing candidates' perceptions. Candidates were highly skilled professionals who all possessed traditional academic or vocational qualifications. This provided an opportunity to ask them to compare their experiences of undertaking the NVQ with their previous qualifications. The study shows that despite the scathing criticisms of the competence based NVQs, there are gains for the stakeholders. The consumption and investment benefits for individuals can be demonstrated. Individuals can see the benefits for their organisation. Their professional practice has characteristics of flexibility needed by a workforce ready to meet challenges of the next century. However, the exchange value and use value of the NVQ award is problematic. The question remains, can higher level NVQs be used effectively as a mechanism for continuing professional development and more importantly, will they be valued?

PUBLISHED MATERIAL: HILLIER, Y. (1997). 'Competence based qualifications in training, development and management', Journal of Further and Higher Education, Vol 21, No 1, pp.33-41. ; HILLIER, Y. (1998). 'Candidates' experience of high level NVQs'. Proceedings from Third International Conference on Education of Adults, University of Exeter, July 1998. ; HILLIER, Y. (1999). 'Higher level NVQs: the candidates' experience', Journal of Vocational Education and Training, Spring. (in press).

STATUS: Individual research

DATE OF RESEARCH: 1997-1998

KEYWORDS: **competency based education; national vocational qualifications; professional education; vocational education**

0431

Department of Continuing Education, Continuing Education Research Unit, Northampton Square, London EC1V 0HB   0171 477 8000

Hillier, Y. Dr

Research capability in further education

ABSTRACT: The pilot study aimed to develop an analytical tool for self-audit of research capability in further education colleges. It is an example of collaboration and cooperation between colleges in the sector and considers how a regional research network can develop its research capability and responsiveness to research initiatives. The two aims of the pilot were to use an audit tool and evaluate its effectiveness in establishing the research capability of the participating further education college and to use the self-audit tool to foster research capability within the further education sector. The study identified that the staff within further education colleges have enormous potential for conducting research but are hampered by a variety of institutional and perceptual barriers. More colleges are being sought to further test the audit tool.

PUBLISHED MATERIAL: HILLIER, Y. 'Research capability in further education: a proposed methodology for use in the sector', College Research. (in press).

STATUS: Individual research

DATE OF RESEARCH: 1998-continuing

KEYWORDS: **colleges of further education; further education; research**

0432

Department of Continuing Education, Continuing Education Research Unit, Northampton Square, London EC1V 0HB   0171 477 8000

Australian Council for Educational Research, Private Bag 55, Camberwell, Victoria 3124, Australia   01707 284000

Hertfordshire University, Faculty of Information Sciences, College Lane, Hatfield AL10 9AB

Haines, C. Prof.; Izard, J. Prof; Crouch, R. Mrs

Assessment of complex mathematical tasks

ABSTRACT: The researchers are working on the assessment of complex mathematical tasks using a rating scale methodology to measure student achievement. This is based on the work of Griffin and Forwood in relation to Adult Literacy and Numeracy. The work has been extended to look at peer, self and group assessment issues and considers the performance of the judges, students and the test instrument itself. The rating scales are derived from focus group interactions and have shown themselves to be robust, although further research is required. Data has come from various sources in higher education, with distinct applications and outcomes.

PUBLISHED MATERIAL: HAINES, C.R., IZARD, J.F. & LE MASURIER, D.W. (1994). 'Modelling intentions realised: assessing the full range of developed skills'. In: BREITEIG, T., HUNTLEY, I.D. & KAISER-MESSMER, G. (Eds). Teaching and learning mathematics in context. US: P-H. ; HAINES, C.R. & IZARD, J.F. (1994). 'Assessing mathematical communications about projects and investigations', Educational Studies in Mathematics, Vol 27, No 4, pp.373-386. ; CROUCH, R.M. & HAINES, C.R. (1995). 'Understanding self, peer and tutor marking in mathematical tasks: analysing oral communications'. In BURTON, L. & IZARD, J.F. (Eds). Using FACETS to investigate innovative mathematics assessments. Birmingham: University of Birmingham. ; HAINES, C.R. & IZARD, J.F. (1995). 'Assessment in context for mathematical modelling'. In: HUNTLEY, I.D. & BLUM, W. (Eds). Advances and perspectives in the teaching of mathematical modelling and applications. Yorklyn, Delaware, USA: Water Street Mathematics.

STATUS: Collaborative

DATE OF RESEARCH: 1989-continuing

KEYWORDS: **assessment; higher education; mathematical applications; mathematics achievement; mathematics education**

0433

Department of Continuing Education, Continuing Education Research Unit, Northampton Square, London EC1V 0HB   0171 477 8000

London University, Institute of Education, Centre for Longitudinal Studies, 20 Bedford Way, London WC1H 0AL   0171 612 6900

Capizzi, E. Ms; Carter, J. Ms; *Supervisors*: Davies, P. Dr; Bynner, J. Prof.

The impact of credit based systems of learning on learning cultures

ABSTRACT: Many of the features or effects claimed for credit based systems of post-compulsory learning are also those identified as features of a learning society: equity and equal opportunities; the promotion of participation and progression and a culture of achievement rather than of failure; the valuing of learning inside and outside formal institutions of education; support for individual responsibility for learning; student centred learning and reflective practitioners; a community of learners. This study seeks to examine those claims. The study has 4 objectives: 1) To investigate the impact of credit based systems of learning on: a) the learning values and behaviour of students; b) the values, policies and practices of training providers; c) the recruitment and training policies of employers; d) the learning culture of the organisational settings in which learning occurs; e) the development of learning communities. 2) To assess the extent to which a credit framework increases participation in education and training and aids progression among traditionally non-participating groups in a range of formal and informal settings (college, workplace, hospital, prison, voluntary organisation, home). 3) To investigate the processes of learning and assessment under credit based system through which changes in values and practices occur. 4) To compare the motives, attitudes, behaviour and patterns of participation and progression of: a) learners registered for the Credit Accumulation and Transfer (CAT) scheme in the London region (London Open College Federation - LOCF); b) learners enrolled in CAT and non-CAT based programmes in a further education (FE) college (Waltham Forest College); c) participants and non-participants in education and training in a national longitudinal dataset (the National Child Development Study - NCDS); d) learners registered in credit based systems in France (SUDES, Universite de Lille I and the Academie of the Nord Pas de Calais region). In addition to the insitutions indicated above, J. Sainsbury PLC and, through their membership of LOCF, a number of other employers and the London Training and Enterprise Councils (TECs) are collaborating in the study. The methods are: 1) quantitative analysis of the NCDS data and student records for learners registered with LOCF, Waltham Forest College, Sainsbury, SUDES and the Nord Pas de Calais GRETA; 2) documentary analysis of relevant papers and publications; 3) interviews with teachers, learners, employers and managers; 4) learning diaries kept by a small sample of learners; 5) workshops and seminars with partners and participants.

PUBLISHED MATERIAL: A full list of publications is available from the researchers.

STATUS: Sponsored project

SOURCE OF GRANT: Economic and Social Research Council

DATE OF RESEARCH: 1995-1998

KEYWORDS: adult education; adult learning; comparative education; continuing education; credit transfer; credits; flexible learning; mature students; open education; training

0434

Department of Continuing Education, Continuing Education Research Unit, Northampton Square, London EC1V 0HB   0171 477 8000

University of Queensland, Graduate School of Education, Brisbane, Queensland 4072, Australia

Haines, C. Prof.; Hillier, Y. Dr; Tofaridou, I. Miss; Galbraith, P. Dr

Mathematical characteristics of students on entry to higher education

ABSTRACT: The researchers are trying to understand the mathematical characteristics of students on entry to higher education in terms of their mechanical, interpretive and constructive skills. Secondly, they are looking at the way in which computers may be used to affect students' perceptions of mathematics, computing and their interaction. Test instruments in each of these areas have enabled a deeper understanding of these issues. Data from the application of 2 test instruments to 3 cohorts of students (n=500) forms the basis for the research analysis. This research has recently been extended to include comparative studies in Cyprus.

PUBLISHED MATERIAL: GALBRAITH, P.L. & HAINES, C.R. (1995). 'Students' mathematical characteristics: some developmental skills for engineering and mathematics', IMA Bulletin, Vol 31, No 11/12, pp.175-179. ; GALBRAITH, P.L., PEMBERTON, M. & HAINES, C.R. (1996). 'Testing to a purpose: assessing the mathematical knowledge of entering undergraduates'. In: CLARKSON, P.C. (Ed), Technology in mathematics education. Melbourne: The Mathematics Education Research Group of Australasia, Deakin University Press. ; GALBRAITH, P.L. & HAINES, C.R. (1997). 'Some meathematical characteristics of students entering applied mathematics degree courses'. In: HOUSTON, S.K., BLUM, W., HUNTLEY, I.& NEILL, N.T. (Eds). Teaching and learning mathematical modelling: innovation, investigation and applications. Chichester: Horwood Publishing. ; GALBRAITH, P.L. & HAINES, C.R. (1998). 'Disentangling the nexus: attitudes to mathematics and technology in a computer learning environment', Educational Studies in Mathematics. (in press).

STATUS: Collaborative

DATE OF RESEARCH: 1994-continuing

KEYWORDS: australia; comparative education; computer uses in education; greece; higher education; mathematics education; mathematics skills; students

Cleveland County Council

0435

Research and Intelligence Unit, PO Box 17, Melrose House, 1 Melrose Street, Middlesbrough TS1 2YW   01642 248155

Rollings, G. Ms; Kicks, P. Mr; Smith, M. Mr

Local Management of Schools: resource allocation formula

ABSTRACT: The construction, maintenance and reformulation of a formula designed to allocate the aggregated schools budget to primary and secondary schools, both mainstream and special.

STATUS: Sponsored project

SOURCE OF GRANT: Cleveland County Council

DATE OF RESEARCH: 1988-1998

KEYWORDS: educational administration; educational finance; educational planning; local education authorities; local management of schools; resource allocation

0436

Research and Intelligence Unit, PO Box 17, Melrose House, 1 Melrose Street, Middlesbrough TS1 2YW   01624 248155

Elliott, K. Mr; Turner, S. Mr

Analysis of GCSE results

ABSTRACT: Analysing GCSE results for each school by relating the results to each pupil's background as defined by the level of disadvantage of the 1991 census enumeration district in which each pupil lives.

STATUS: Sponsored project

SOURCE OF GRANT: Cleveland County Council

DATE OF RESEARCH: 1988-1998

KEYWORDS: disadvantaged; examination results; general certificate of secondary education; institutional evaluation; performance indicators

0437

Research and Intelligence Unit, PO Box 17, Melrose House, 1 Melrose Street, Middlesbrough TS1 2YW   01642 248155

Wilson, P. Mr; Kicks, P. Mr

Allocation of school bus contracts

ABSTRACT: computerised method based on linear programming has been developed to help the annual allocation of school transport routes to contractors. The routes are mainly home to school, but also include some school to swimming baths routes. The process is designed to give a minimum cost allocation, coping with the fact that contractors bid for more routes than they have vehicles, discounts and other complexities. The process is also designed to be less resource intensive than previous manual processes.

PUBLISHED MATERIAL: WILSON, P. (1994). 'The methodology of allocating school bus contracts'. Cleveland R & I Unit Report CR866. Middlesborough: Cleveland County Council.

STATUS: Sponsored project

SOURCE OF GRANT: Cleveland County Council

DATE OF RESEARCH: 1994-1998

KEYWORDS: bus transport; local education authorities; school buses; transport; travel

0438

Research and Intelligence Unit, PO Box 17, Melrose House, 1 Melrose Street, Middlesbrough TS1 2YW   01642 248155

Elias, P. Mr; Turner, S. Mr

Pupil projections by school

ABSTRACT: Projections are produced for every school in the county. These are used for budgeting purposes and for determining the need for, and timing of, changes in the number of places at schools, and changes in the number of schools. The projections take into account the number and type of houses being built, and cleared, the effect of new houses, and the transition to established housing.

STATUS: Sponsored project

SOURCE OF GRANT: Cleveland County Council

DATE OF RESEARCH: 1980-1998

KEYWORDS: educational planning; local education authorities; long range planning; prediction; pupil numbers; regional planning

0439

Research and Intelligence Unit, PO Box 17, Melrose House, 1 Melrose Street, Middlesbrough TS1 2YW   01642 248155

Lofthouse, M. Mr

Education adviser scheduling

ABSTRACT: The development of a computer-aided system to schedule activities of education advisers. This encompasses Office for Standards in Education (OFSTED) inspections won by Cleveland's Advisory Service, pilot inspections, headteacher appraisals, and in-house professional development courses for teachers run by advisers (around 200 per year). The appraisal of a headteacher is done by a fellow headteacher, as well as the adviser for the school. The system is designed to allocate the headteacher to appraise each headteacher, satisfying a given list of criteria. The system attempts to produce a level adviser workload, and includes monitoring and updating routines.

PUBLISHED MATERIAL: LOFTHOUSE, M. (1994). 'How operational research is helping the education department's advisory service'. Cleveland R & I Unit Report CR869. Middlesborough: Cleveland County Council.

STATUS: Sponsored project

SOURCE OF GRANT: Cleveland County Council

DATE OF RESEARCH: 1991-1998

KEYWORDS: **advisers; head teachers; inspection; inspectors - of schools; local education authorities; ofsted; scheduling; teacher evaluation**

0440

Research and Intelligence Unit, PO Box 17, Melrose House, 1 Melrose Street, Middlesbrough TS1 2YW   01642 248155

Turner, S. Mr; Elliott, K. Mr

School profiles

ABSTRACT: Information is being produced for use by schools as management tools. It enables the school, and the local education authority as a 'critical friend', to compare itself with all other schools within the authority as an aid in determining relative performance. The information covers GCSE examination and other test results, socio-economic data and mapping of pupil home addresses to show the effect of parental preference.

STATUS: Sponsored project

SOURCE OF GRANT: Cleveland County Council

DATE OF RESEARCH: 1994-1998

KEYWORDS: **educational administration; educational planning; local education authorities; parent choice; profiles; school effectiveness**

0441

Research and Intelligence Unit, PO Box 17, Melrose House, 1 Melrose Street, Middlesbrough TS1 2YW 01642 248155

Peace, D. Mr

Local Management of Schools: directed activities (lettings)

ABSTRACT: Development and maintenance of a scheme to reimburse schools for the out-of-hours use of their premises by the local education authority - e.g. night classes, youth and community activities, scouts etc.

STATUS: Sponsored project

SOURCE OF GRANT: Cleveland County Council

DATE OF RESEARCH: 1989-1998

KEYWORDS: **educational facilities; educational finance; local education authorities; local management of schools; school buildings; school community relationship**

Coopers and Lybrand Associates

0442

1 Embankment Place, London WC2N 6NN   0171 213 2892

Thompson, Q. Mr; *Supervisor*: D'Armenia, M. Ms

Investment appraisal of Education Support Grant XXX for the training of youth leaders in the inner cities in England and in the valleys in Wales

ABSTRACT: The Department of Education and Science commissioned Coopers and Lybrand to carry out an investment appraisal of Education Support Grant (ESG) XXX for the training of youth leaders in the inner cities in England and in the Valleys in Wales. The appraisal estimated the total investment in the local scheme; assessed the extent of support from other sources; compared costs with those of other forms of youth worker training; assessed the costs and benefits of the schemes; and evaluated the efficiency of the ESG mechanism. This was one of a number of evaluation exercises of the ESG, the combined results of which will allow the Department to assess the overall value of the programme and its viability as a model for future youth training.

STATUS: Sponsored project

SOURCE OF GRANT: Department of Education and Science £53,500

DATE OF RESEARCH: 1991-1993

KEYWORDS: **financial support; inner city; investment; training; youth leaders; youth service**

0443

1 Embankment Place, London WC2N 6NN 0171 213 2892

Lakin, J. Mr; *Supervisor*: Thompson, Q. Mr

Local Management of Schools (LMS) and small schools

ABSTRACT: The study was to produce a good management guide for small schools operating under Local Management of Schools (LMS). Research was carried out in four local education authorities (LEAs) with samples of schools with less than 200 pupils. Schools were visited and headteachers, governors and non-teaching staff interviewed. LEA officers were also consulted. A good management guide was then produced and circulated to all small schools in England and Wales

STATUS: Sponsored project

SOURCE OF GRANT: Department for Education £56,000

DATE OF RESEARCH: 1993-1993

KEYWORDS: **educational administration; local management of schools; school based management; small schools**

0444

1 Embankment Place, London WC2N 6NN   0171 583 5000

Snell, C. Mr

Reducing bureaucratic burdens on teachers

ABSTRACT: Coopers and Lybrand were asked to report to the Department for Education and Employment (DfEE) Working Group on Reducing the Bureaucratic Burden on Teachers. Their task was to identify sources of bureaucracy, where the burden falls in schools and what improvements could be made. Fieldwork for the study took place between 1 September and 30 October. It included interviews with the relevant Government and national bodies, as well as visits to 14 schools, where discussions were held with senior and middle managers and classroom teachers. 4 main sources of burdens were identified: external demands for information; internal organisational demands; new demands arising from new approaches to teaching and learning; and the working style of teachers in responding to these. A number of recommendations were made, most of which were included in the Working Group's final report to Ministers. Those recommendations included: 1) better signposting of documents to enable headteachers to assess quickly their relevance and importance and who should be dealing with them; 2) making more use of sampling when consulting schools; 3) streamlining and reducing the need for bid-based funding; 4) measures to encourage headteachers and senior managers to ensure that teachers' time is well spent.

PUBLISHED MATERIAL: COOPERS and LYBRAND (1997). Reducing the bureaucratic burden on teachers. DFEE Research Report RR41. London: HMSO.

STATUS: Sponsored project

SOURCE OF GRANT: Department for Education and Employment £60,500

DATE OF RESEARCH: 1997-1997

KEYWORDS: **bureaucracy; educational administration; nonteaching duties; school organisation; teacher workload; time management**

Council for Environmental Education

0445

94 London Street, Reading RG1 4SJ   01189 502550

Midgley, C. Ms

Building support for environmental education (Phase II)

ABSTRACT: The overall aim is to develop a coherent strategy for the development of information provision in the field of environmental education. Specific objectives are to: 1) support the formation of local structures and networks for information provision, distribution and communication; 2) develop communication and cooperative working between environmental education information providers; 3) provide training and support for information providers; 4) support users by increasing their awareness of available sources of information; 5) develop criteria for the evaluation of materials and to apply these as appropriate; 6) provide comprehensive information on training opportunities for environmental education; and 7) strengthen and enhance the Council for Environmental Education (CEE's) information services into a National Information Centre for Environmental Education.

PUBLISHED MATERIAL: MIDGLEY, C. (1994). 'Environmental education: are we meeting the needs?', Environmental Information Forum News, No 1, p.3.

STATUS: Sponsored project

SOURCE OF GRANT: Department of the Environment £21,000; Esso UK plc £15,000

DATE OF RESEARCH: 1994-1997

KEYWORDS: educational resources; environmental education; information needs; information sources

0446

94 London Street, Reading RG1 4SJ   01189 502550

Elcome, D. Mr

Guidelines for biodiversity education

ABSTRACT: The aim of the project is to research and produce a guidance document on delivering effective biodiversity education. The document will target a range of providers, such as countryside rangers, reserve wardens, conservation staff and volunteers, and those working in zoos, museums and field centres. The objectives are to: 1) identify and document examples of 'hands on' biodiversity education practice; 2) ensure the case studies cover a range of sites, represent different levels of provision and reflect the range of approaches to biodiversity education in England; 3) draw from these examples recommendations and ideas for those involved in the delivery of biodiversity education; and 4) encourage the inclusion of values, benefits and wise use as aspects of biodiversity education. A detailed questionnaire was sent to a wide range of sites and organisations throughout the country in January 1997. Some of the responses to this will be followed up by telephone interviews, and a selected number of sites will be visited by the consultant to look at their work in more depth. These sites will feature as case studies in the final document. The research findings will be published as a guideline document which is scheduled for publication in September 1997.

PUBLISHED MATERIAL: MCLEISH, E. (1997). Educating for life: guidelines for biodiversity education. Reading: Council for Environmental Education.

STATUS: Sponsored project

SOURCE OF GRANT: Department of the Environment; Biodiversity Education Working Group; Hobsons Publishing

DATE OF RESEARCH: 1996-1997

KEYWORDS: biodiversity; environmental education

0447

94 London Street, Reading RG1 4SJ   01189 502550
Reading University, School of Education, Bulmershe Court, Woodlands Avenue, Earley, Reading RG6 1HY   01189 875123 ;

Gayford, C. Dr; Simpkin, B. Mr

Youth participation in decision-making processes with an emphasis on the environment

ABSTRACT: In Rio de Janeiro in July 1992, 180 Heads of State met to discuss the problems facing the world and its 5 billion inhabitants. One result of this Summit was an action plan for the 21st century called Agenda 21. Amongst a plethora of other environmental and developmental considerations, Agenda 21 calls for the participation of today's young people in environmental and developmental decision-making. It recognises that their involvement is critical in moving towards more sustainable ways of life. In April 1996 the Council for Environmental Education's Youth Unit embarked on a 3-year programme partly funded by the Department for Education and Employment working in partnership with youth and environmental agencies. The programme will develop a series of regional fora which will empower young people to establish their own peer education activities and events aimed at raising environmental awareness. A major survey, 'Young People in the 80s', commissioned by the Department of Education and Science concluded that young people had largely rejected their own involvement in politics as a means to bring about improvements in society. In 1990 a MORI poll identified that, whilst young people have indicated a strong interest in all things environmental, there is little evidence to suggest that they are prepared to get involved with existing environmental agencies to convert their concerns to action. On 12 July 1995 Peter Kilfoyle MP talked to Parliament about the alienation of youth from the political process. He pointed out that in the 1992 general election 2.5 million young people, 47% of the total eligible to vote, did not bother to exercise their franchise. Given the lack of youth participation both in political decision-making processes and environmental agencies, it is difficult to see how the Agenda 21 aims for youth participation will be satisfied. The Council for Environmental Education National Young People's Environmental Network (NYPEN) project aims to increase the opportunities for consultation with young people and in return promote their participation in decision-making processes with regard to the environment. The research will rigorously examine the development of NYPEN. It will adopt the regional fora and ensuing national conferences as case studies for youth participation. From these case studies a series of indicators of participation by young people, specifically in environmental decision-making processes, will be established. It is anticipated that this 5-year research project will provide a comprehensive and reliable set of indicators for youth participation in decision-making processes. The youth work world and especially the environmental youth work world is bereft of reliable research into this most fundamental area of its work. The conclusions reached will support and inform a range of initiatives including those linked to the Agenda 21 process in securing an increased level of youth participation in decision-making processes.

STATUS: Collaborative

DATE OF RESEARCH: 1996-continuing

KEYWORDS: attitudes; decision making; environment; environmental education; participation; youth

Coventry University

0448

School of Art and Design, Priory Street, Coventry CV1 5FB
01203 631313

Flynn, S. Ms ; *Supervisors*: Richards, C. Prof.; Miles, T. Prof.; Hinton, P. Dr

The design of a multimedia calculator and its use in teaching numeracy to those with learning difficulties

ABSTRACT: The aim of this study was to investigate the potential of multimedia systems for the teaching of numeracy to a range of pupils and learners with learning difficulties. This potential was established through the original design of an interactive learning package which, through evaluation, was demonstrated to be effective for this purpose. The interactive multimedia learning package, the Multimedia Interactive Calculator (MIC), which combines simulated learning materials with a calculator interface, has been designed as result of classroom-based studies together with iterative prototype evaluation. The visual styling of its interface and operation is the consequence of design decisions made in response to classroom observations, literature surveys, and other evaluations carried out as part of this research. The MIC mediates between the concrete concepts of learning number and the abstract sense of mathematics, a transition which is difficult for many pupils, particularly dyslexics. The evaluations of the MIC have been successful in demonstrating its use for teaching pupils the concepts of number and the routines of addition and subtraction, thus indicating the potential of multimedia for this purpose. The interactive multiplication tables, incorporated into the design of the MIC, seemed to be effective in helping pupils to discover number patterns and in aiding their recall of number facts, thus demonstrating its usefulness for teaching mathematics to those with learning difficulties. The visual display of the MIC has been designed to overcome the particular problem of poor short-term memory and other difficulties displayed by dyslexics, for example: symbol recognition; directional and spatial difficulties; language and labelling; notational aspects; and the concepts of number and arithmetic. All calculations carried out with the MIC are displayed as a vertical algorithm, reinforcing the place value of each digit. The vertical algorithm is the layout generally taught and used in the primary classroom. The MIC has been developed using the software 'Macromedia Director 4.0' on an Apple Macintosh computer, allowing the easy development of working prototypes and changes to be made in response to evaluations and users' needs. The MIC has been developed into an interactive CD-Rom that will run on both Apple Macintosh and PC platforms which is published by Inclusive Technology, UK.

PUBLISHED MATERIAL: RICHARDS, C.J. & FLYNN, S.J. (1994). The design of a multimedia calculator and its use in teaching numeracy: technical report 26. Loughborough: Advisory Group on Computer Graphics (AGOCG). ; FLYNN, S.J. (1995). 'Prototyping learning tools for special needs using multimedia digital creativity, CADE '95. Proceedings from CADE '95 Conference, Brighton, 1995. ; FLYNN, S.J. (1996). 'An evaluation of two calculator keypad designs for pupils with mathematics difficulties, Postgraduate Conference Papers, CADE 96. Proceedings from CADE '96 Postgraduate Conference, Coventry, 1996. ; FLYNN, S.J., DEKKER, K. & RICHARDS, C.J. (1996). 'The design and evaluation of an interactive calculator for children'. Proceedings of Eurographics UK Chapter, 14th Annual Conference, Imperial College, London, 1996.

STATUS: Sponsored project

SOURCE OF GRANT: Coventry University £42,000

DATE OF RESEARCH: 1992-1997

KEYWORDS: **calculators; computer uses in education; dyslexia; educational software; information technology; learning disabilities; mathematics education; multimedia; numeracy; special educational needs**

0449

School of Health and Social Sciences, Priory Street, Coventry CV1 5FB
01203 631313

Heames, R. Mrs; Green, M. Mrs

Investigation into course evaluation (module)

ABSTRACT: A course evaluation programme has been tested, modified and used with some success in the B.Sc Occupational Therapy course at Coventry University. The aims of the present small study are to: (1) review present provision; (2) produce a scheme of evaluation which might be generally useful (across different disciplines); (3) investigate the most effective and efficient method of data analysis. Letters of enquiry have initially been sent to all seven higher education institutions linked in the Midlands through staff development programmes. Two other institutions (known to have been involved in course evaluation) have also been contacted. Information collected from these sources and within Coventry University will determine visits to be made to clarify the areas/topics evaluated, the methodology used, the method of processing data and subsequent action taken. A pilot evaluation will be produced and tested, followed by a final version. Systems of data handling will be considered from the beginning and will, to some extent determine the design.

STATUS: Sponsored project

SOURCE OF GRANT: Coventry University: Learning Systems Development Fund£2,244

DATE OF RESEARCH: 1992-1993

KEYWORDS: **course evaluation; educational quality**

0450

School of Health and Social Sciences, Priory Street, Coventry CV1 5FB
01203 631313

Nene College of Higher Education, Park Campus, Boughton Green Road, Northampton NN2 7AL   01604 735500

Leicester University, School of Education, 21 University Road, Leicester LE1 7RF   01162 522522

Merriman, L. Mrs; *Supervisors*: Winch, C. Prof.; Field, D. Dr

Changing by degrees: a study of the transition from diploma to degree in chiropody, occupational therapy and radiography

ABSTRACT: The aims of this research are two-fold. Firstly, to explore the impact of degree status on the initial education and training of chiropodists, occupational therapists and radiographers. Secondly, to explore how changes to initial education and training, as a result of the transition from diploma to degree, contribute to the professional project of the 3 para-professions. The research is based on a case study approach and involves one school from each para-profession. A combined qualitative-quantitative methodology has been used. The use of a comparative approach (one case study school from each para-profession) strengthens the ability to make generalisations from the research findings. Early findings reveal the reduced influence of the professional bodies and increased influence and control of the higher education institutions over the new degrees. The aims of the degree courses are very different from the diploma courses. There is a desire to develop a different, better practitioner who will contribute to the development of these three para-professions. The emphasis is on the development of autonomous, independent practitioners equipped with research skills which can be used to inform and enhance the professional knowledge base.

STATUS: Individual research

DATE OF RESEARCH: 1993-1997

KEYWORDS: **degrees - academic; medicine; professional education; students**

0451

School of Health and Social Sciences, Priory Street, Coventry CV1 5FB
01203 631313

Warwick University, Department of Continuing Education, Continuing Education Research Centre, Coventry CV4 7AL   01203 523523

Clouder, D. Ms; *Supervisor*: Hughes, C. Dr

Personal and professional development through continuing education and its impact on affective relationships

ABSTRACT: The research adopts a qualitative approach to the exploration of development and change in self and identity over a period of continuing education. In addition, the aim is to consider the effect of development on affective relationships making connnections between education and adult life. The study will take the form of a semi-longitudinal study which will monitor change in 12 occupational therapy students over the 3 years of their honours degree course, the focus being on both personal and professional development. Methods used include indepth interviews, discourse analysis and participant observation.

PUBLISHED MATERIAL: CLOUDER, D.L. (1997). 'Women's ways of coping with continuing education', Adults Learning, Vol 8, No 6, pp.146-148. ; HARRISON, K. & CLOUDER, D.L. (1998). 'A focus on quality: hearing the student voice from a professional curriculum in higher education', The New Academic: The Journal of Learning and Teaching in Higher Education, Vol 7, No 1, pp.11-14. ; CLOUDER, D.L. (1998). 'Getting the "right" answers: student education as a reflection of intellectual development', Teaching in Higher Education, Vol 3, No 2, pp.185-195. ; CLOUDER, D.L. (1998). 'Reflective practice: is it happening in the workplace? Proceedings of the Conference on Emergent Fields in Management: Connecting Learning and Critique, University of Leeds, Leeds, July 1998.

STATUS: Individual research

DATE OF RESEARCH: 1996-continuing

KEYWORDS: **continuing education; higher education; individual development; occupational therapists; professional education**

De Montfort University

0452

37 Lansdowne Road, Bedford MK40 2BZ   01234 351966

Whitehead, M. Dr; Lockwood, A. Ms

The contribution of Physical Education to National Curriculum cross-curricular themes, dimensions and skills

ABSTRACT: Bedford College is supporting a research project looking at the role of Physical Education in National Curriculum cross-curricular themes, dimensions and skills. The initial stimulus to the project was the result of a perceived mismatch between the potential Physical Education has to make a significant contribution to cross-curricular work and the lack of recognition of this potential in National Curriculum documentation. The research has three strands: (a) a literature search of references outside the National Curriculum; (b) a detailed examination of National Curriculum documentation; and (c) an investigation to ascertain how far schools already acknowledge the potential for Physical Education in this area. The first of the strands is still in process while the second and third are complete.

STATUS: Sponsored project

SOURCE OF GRANT: Bedford College of Higher Education

DATE OF RESEARCH: 1992-1993

KEYWORDS: cross curricular approach; national curriculum; physical education

0453

Polhill Avenue, Bedford MK41 9EA   01234 351671

Sampson, J. Mr; Stephenson, H. Ms; Wooldridge, I. Mrs; *Supervisor*: Yeomans, R. Mr

Teacher education and mentorship

ABSTRACT: The aims of the research are: to clarify the nature of mentorship and the skills mentors use in working with students; to identify similarities and differences within various systems; and to suggest the conditions which are conducive to successful mentoring outcomes in primary teacher education. The project uses case studies of twelve mentors across three forms of primary teacher education with Bedford College programmes: Postgraduate Certificate in Education(PGCE); Articled teachers scheme; and year three of the Bachelor of Education (B.Ed) course. Each researcher has acted as participant observer within one or more of the schools over a period of at least seven months (with the exception of B.Ed. four week school experience). Case studies are in the process of being written, using field diaries, documentary sources, and semi-structured interviews. The whole is subject to an ethical code governing participant rights. Once draft data has been cleared with participants, issues will be generated across case studies. The scheme has now been extended to include secondary schools.

PUBLISHED MATERIAL: SAMPSON, J.S. & YEOMANS, R.M. (1994). Primary school mentorship in action. Lewes: Falmer Press.

STATUS: Sponsored project

Source of Grant: Paul Hamlyn Foundation £7,500; Bedford College of Higher Education £7,500

DATE OF RESEARCH: 1991-1993

KEYWORDS: mentors; preservice teacher education; primary school teachers; secondary school teachers

0454

37 Lansdowne Road, Bedford MK40 2BZ   01234 351966

Leask, M. Ms

Teaching and learning with new technologies

ABSTRACT: Advances in technology require teachers to review their notions of how they should teach, how students can learn effectively and what resources are required to support both activities. The Internet and Multimedia poses the latest challenge. Multimedia is defined by the National Council for Educational Technology as "the mixing of words, pictures, motion, video, sound, animation and photographic images on a computer". The rapid proliferation of commercially produced multimedia compositions (i.e. packages) has meant that in many compositions, pedagogical issues appear to have taken second place in the race to get products to the market place. However, a pedagogical framework for the use of the Internet and multimedia compositions in education is yet to be developed. Considerable research is needed if we are to fill in this pedagogical framework with 'grounded' knowledge about teaching and learning styles which lead to the achievement of planned learning outcomes. In this work, the researchers evaluate a range of projects which have been undertaken with student (undergraduate) teachers at De Montfort University in the UK and in Australian schools.

STATUS: Sponsored project

SOURCE OF GRANT: British Council

DATE OF RESEARCH: 1994-continuing

KEYWORDS: computer assisted learning; computer uses in education; information networks; information technology; learning processes; multimedia; teaching methods; telecommunications

0455

Polhill Avenue, Bedford MK41 9EA   01234 351671
De Montfort University, Scraptoft Campus, Scraptoft, Leicester LE7 9SU
01162 577866

Wilcockson, D. Mr; *Supervisor*: Rowley, D. Mr

The causes of underachievement: a school study

ABSTRACT: This is a study of underachievement in a middle school. It begins by focusing on the concerns expressed by teachers regarding the apparent mismatch between children's potential (as expressed by intelligence tests) and actual level of functioning (as measured by a reading test). Using data gathered over 11 years and obtaining a sample population of 3,326 children, the researcher was able to identify underachieving children within the school and compare this population with the wider local and national populations. By using the Social Adjustment Guides (Stott) it should be possible to correlate this with the underachieving population to investigate the relationship between underachievement and behaviour, and to look at gender and cultural issues. Further studies are designed to sample the perspectives of children, teachers and parents with regard to their views about the causes of underachievement. Surveys, questionnaires and discourse analysis will be used to obtain this information. The research is designed to involve the teachers in an active way in order to raise awareness of the causes of underachievement, to relate the research to the inservice teacher education (INSET) requirements of the school and to develop a programme of intervention.

PUBLISHED MATERIAL: WILCOCKSON, D. (1994). 'Children's perspectives on underachievement'. Proceedings of CARN Conference, Birmingham University, 22-24 April 1994. ; WILCOCKSON, D. (1994). 'Underachievement in a middle school'. Proceedings of the British Education Research Association Conference, Oxford University, 10 September 1994. ; WILCOCKSON, D. (1994). 'Teachers' perspectives on underachievement', Education Today: Journal of the College of Preceptors, Vol 44, No 4, pp.41-54. ; WILCOCKSON, D. (1995). 'Understanding underachievement in schools'. Proceedings of the CARN Conference, Nottingham University, 8-10 September 1995. ; A full list of publications is available from the researcher.

STATUS: Individual research

DATE OF RESEARCH: 1994-1997

KEYWORDS: achievement; behaviour; low achievement; middle schools; sex differences; underachievement

0456

School of Arts and Humanities, Centre for Postgraduate Teacher Education, The Gateway, Leicester LE1 9BH   01162 551551

Rice, J. Mrs; O'Sullivan, T. Mr; Saunders, C. Ms

Communication and professional competencies in a modular humanities programme

ABSTRACT: The Communication and Professional Studies (CPS) programme plays a key role in the degree scheme in arts and humanities (DSAH) at De Montford University. In brief, its function is two-fold: (1) it is designed to equip students with the core skills necessary to participate effectively within a flexible, modular arts degree; and (2) it begins to develop in students some of the key vocational and future career skills relevant to their undergraduate studies. This project was completed in

August 1993. A summary of the aims include open learning packages; developing tutoring and student-centred delivery skills for staff; research on teaching and learning requirements generated by DSAH and staff development to support these needs; provide a model for development for open learning packages on the Level 1 DSAH programme. The conclusions reached by the project team were that the diversity of student needs can be best accommodated by offering a variety of teaching and learning experiences. There was a marked difference between mature students and 'traditional' post A-level entrants. The former were keen on the flexibility that open learning offered them but were concerned about their study skills; the latter were less inclined to open learning but were confident in their study skills abilities which were fresh to them from recent studying. The majority of students preferred learning in a context of practical, applied situations rather than lectures. The open learning packages were welcomed but students also wanted staff support in conjunction with them. Staff's responses to the idea of open learning packages were favourable if guarded. There was a recognition of the amount of time needed to assemble a successful package. Some staff took the opportunity to attend staff development sessions on the application of computer aided learning.

STATUS: Sponsored project

SOURCE OF GRANT: De Montfort University £19,000

DATE OF RESEARCH: 1991-1993

KEYWORDS: communication skills; competency based education; humanities; minimum competencies; modular courses; open education

0457

School of Arts and Humanities, Centre for Postgraduate Teacher Education, The Gateway, Leicester LE1 9BH   01162 551551

Mason, R. Prof.; Maughan, C. Mr

The artists-in-education training project

ABSTRACT: This pilot project was set up in 1990 by the Arts Council working conjunction with three regional arts associations and Leicester Polytechnic (now De Montfort University). It aims were 'to provide performing artists, visual artists, craftspeople, writers and composers with the skills they need to work with confidence in education today'. The programme implemented in 1991 covered a ten day period and included residential training weekends staffed by a combination of artists, teachers and educators and six day placements in primary or secondary schools. The progress of the project was systematically documented and evaluated by a project officer specifically appointed for this purpose. The evaluation report identified strengths and weaknesses of the programme of training and of the residencies in terms of the contribution they made to arts learning in schools.

PUBLISHED MATERIAL: ILLSLEY, R. (1991). Artists-in-education training project: external summative evaluation. Leicester: Leicester Polytechnic. ; THOMAS, S. (1991). Artists-in-education training project: artists' report I. Leicester: Leicester Polytechnic. ; THOMAS, S. (1992). Artists-in-education training project: artists' report II. Leicester: De Montfort University. ; MASON, R. (1993). Artists-in-education training project: final report. Leicester: De Montfort University.

STATUS: Sponsored project

SOURCE OF GRANT: Arts Council of Great Britain ú 30,000

DATE OF RESEARCH: 1990-1993

KEYWORDS: artists; peripatetic teachers; training

0458

School of Arts and Humanities, Centre for Postgraduate Teacher Education, The Gateway, Leicester LE1 9BH   01162 551551

Tyers, J. Mr; *Supervisor*: Allison, B. Prof.

A study of personality and other attributes, qualities and opinions of 'A' level design students

ABSTRACT: Recent research identified subjective claims that students studying 'A' level design possessed certain qualities, attributes and abilities not found in students who studied other academic 'A' level examination subjects. The principle aim of the research was to objectively: (1) Identify and quantify the differences between the structure and content of the 'A' level design examination course and other 'A' level examination courses. (2) Identify and compare the personality characteristics, attributes, abilities and opinions of 'A' level design students with those who study other 'A' level subjects. (3) Identify and compare the personality characteristics, attributes and abilities of potential 'A' level design students with those who chose to study the subject. (4) Determine the relationship between the personality characteristics, attributes and abilities of 'A' level design students and: (a) success in the final examination; (b) general intelligence; (c) arts/science bias; (d) gender. (5) Determine the extent to which, if any, an 'A' level design examination course develops certain personal qualities, attributes, abilities and opinions in students. (6) Determine the validity of teacher assessment of those personal qualities which lead to success in the final examination. The following methodologies were used: (a) descriptive studies; (b) causal-comparative cross-sectional studies; (c) quasi-experimental longitudinal studies. The instruments used included: (a) descriptive questionnaires; (b) unstandardised single pole 'designing' attributes rating scale; (c) AH4 and AH6 general ability tests; (d) Cattell's 16 Personality Factor Questionnaire. The subjects included: (a) cluster sample of 200 'A' level design students; (b) sample of 100 other 'A' level students; (c) sample of 30 'A' level design teachers; (d) sample of 5 other 'A' level teachers. The data was subjected to statistical analysis based on: (a) differences between means; (b) analysis of variance; (c) correlation. A number of significant differences were objectively shown to exist between the groups of students and teachers which provides a firmer basis for the understanding of the effects on students of specialised study in design. The data also provided standardised 16PF norms for British 'A' level students.

STATUS: Individual research

DATE OF RESEARCH: 1988-1993

KEYWORDS: a level examinations; design; learner characteristics; student attitudes

0459

School of Arts and Humanities, Centre for Postgraduate Teacher Education, The Gateway, Leicester LE1 9BH   01162 551551

Bruntlett, S. Mr; *Supervisor*: Allison, B. Prof.

The use of computer based technology in the development of teaching and learning strategies in art and design education

ABSTRACT: The action research project will begin with a preliminary survey of existing practice in Computer Aided Art and Design (CAAD) teaching and learning. This qualitative research project will be accomplished by a series of visits and a search of the literature. Teachers' narratives (experienced or beginners in terms of CAAD), will be gathered from taped or otherwise documented interviews and conversations with a dozen art educators from a wide variety of art and design backgrounds. Hard copy relating to 'best methods', curricula or schemes of work for CAAD will be compiled, analysed and interpreted. These will be compared with schemes of work in National Curriculum (Art) and differences or similarities accounted for. Examples of work will be collected to show what is currently being achieved using teaching and learning strategies. This will lead to a structured critical analysis of CAAD practice and form the basis of a specific CAAD curriculum which may be based on competence, objectives, process or other models. Such a curriculum will be tested by both experienced and inexperienced teachers to see if there is a demonstrable need for a separate curriculum, or whether existing art and design curricula can accommodate new technologies as they develop as is claimed by some theories of art. The results of such testing will determine the best use of new technology in art and design education which will be formulated in a series of recommendations relating to the appropriateness or otherwise of new technology across art and design experience in secondary education.

PUBLISHED MATERIAL:#@ A full list of publications is available from the researcher.

STATUS: Individual research

DATE OF RESEARCH: 1994-1997

KEYWORDS: art education; computer assisted design; computer uses in education; design; information technology

0460

School of Arts and Humanities, Centre for Postgraduate Teacher Education, The Gateway, Leicester LE1 9BH   01162 551551

Leicester University, School of Education, 21 University Road, Leicester LE1 7RF   01162 522522

Stuart, J. Mrs; *Supervisors*: Allison, B. Prof.; Merry, R. Dr

Art critical abilities: modes of reasoning and intellectual development

ABSTRACT: The present study seeks to continue an enquiry into the nature of the relationship between artistic and intellectual development, through the vehicle of art criticism in art and design education. The intention is to extend the findings of a replication of Hickey's (1975) enquiry which established such a relationship through a study of art critical abilities both in Hickey's terms of cognitive and perceptual functions and also through modes of reasoning measure. Therefore the present aim is to elaborate the modes of concrete and formal reasoning measure in conjunction with a programme of study to promote modes of reasoning through art critical development in secondary education. The theoretical framework to examine cognition-perception and modes of reasoning was derived from educational psychology and critical studies in art education. Theories of cognitive development were derived from Piaget's model of logical operations (Inhelder and Piaget, 1964), modified by Bruner's (1967) theory of instruction; and perception from Arnheim's (1954) theory of visual perception. Feldman's (1971) theoretical art critical strategy of Description, Analysis, Interpretation and Evaluation, interpreted as art critical abilities, examined the role of cognition-perception through an hypothetical model of reasoned explanation. The modes of reasoning measure combined the theories of Peel's (1971) transference of the Piagetian model to concrete and formal judgements with Bernstein's (1961) theory of language as an indicator of cognitive development, to provide a measure in art critical terms. The measure allows analysis of critical thinking in a subject specific area (McPeck, 1981). The research methodology involves the provision, testing and evaluation of the contribution of the critical strategy programme of study, to cognitive development through modes of reasoning. The programme will be tested with two samples of pupils aged twelve years and sixth-formers, with tests for operational levels; critical abilities and modes of reasoning for statistical analysis of data. The educational advantages will be: (a) an empirically tested programme which promotes and objectively measures artistic development in terms of concrete and 'higher' level cognitive thinking through modes of reasoning; and (b) a contribution to the debate about the nature and merits of critical thinking in specific subject areas.

STATUS: Individual research

DATE OF RESEARCH: 1989-1997

KEYWORDS: art education; criticism; intellectual development; reasoning

0461

School of Arts and Humanities, Centre for Postgraduate Teacher Education, The Gateway, Leicester LE1 9BH   01162 551551
London University, Imperial College of Science, Technology and Medicine, Department of Mechanical Engineering, Exhibition Road, London SW7 2AZ   0171 589 5111

Nagata, T. Mr ; *Supervisors*: Allison, B. Prof.; Coe, B. Mr; Kennaway, A. Prof.

An investigation into the spatial visualisation ability and psychopedagogical strategies for training designers

ABSTRACT: This project includes: (1) A review of literature relating to spatial abilities to determine indicators of maturity in terms of developmental level and susceptibility for training in visual spatial representation. Critical review of strategies for the development of abilities to represent visual spatial form from a cognitive viewpoint. Critical review of the potential effect of related factors including the visual/haptic (Lowenfeld, 1964) and field-dependency/independency (Witkin et al 1949) dichotomies. (2) The development of a pedagogical strategy designed to develop visualisation and representational skills and the generation of aptitude measures applicable to higher education students in the design fields. (3) The validation of the strategy and aptitude measures with a pilot sample of higher education design students. It is hypothesised that the anticipated variations in the students' performances on pre-test and post-test criterial tasks will be due, in particular, to differences in spatial abilities. (4) Experimental design, in particular: (a) development of test battery - spatial abilities and representational skills; (b) instructional treatments - traditional drawing methods and experimental drawing methods; (c) selection of experimental and control groups drawn from graphic design,

industrial design and engineering students. (5) Implementation of research design. Pre-tests; experimental teaching programmes; post-tests. Protocol analysis on the basis of comparison of psychopedagogic strategies. (6) Analysis of data and conclusions.

STATUS: Individual research

DATE OF RESEARCH: 1992-1997

KEYWORDS: design; designers; spatial ability

0462

School of Arts and Humanities, Centre for Postgraduate Teacher Education, The Gateway, Leicester LE1 9BH   01162 551551
Roehampton Institute London, Roehampton Lane, London SW15 5PU   0181 392 3000

Kypreou, I. Ms; *Supervisors*: Allison, B. Prof.; Mason, R. Dr

Assessment in fine art at first degree level: a comparative study of the principles and methods underlying assessment of fine art students in Athens and Leicester

ABSTRACT: Evaluation of worth in art historically has been a contentious issue, particularly when affected by fashion or taste. Nonetheless, assessment of quality or worth has been a necessary element in national competitions and central in education at all levels. In undergraduate and postgraduate fine art courses, assessment is a central element in determining levels of award. Two degree courses in fine art, in Britain and in Greece are compared in terms of the procedures and criteria employed for the assessment of students' work. In both institutions the assessment of students at first degree level is based principally on their practical work. A major difference between the two institutions is that whilst in Greece the final assessment is made by tutors in discussion without written or specified criteria, in Britain the assessment is based on explicit documented criteria. However, in both institutions there is no doubt that underpinning all assessment is the consideration of the extent to which the individual students are able to demonstrate their capability as professional artists and it is likely that, implicitly, the assessment in both institutions is based on commonly held concepts of fine art activity and shared beliefs about the nature of artistic production. The study aims to determine: (i) the role theories of art play in the assessment of fine art students at first degree level; (ii) whether the assessment procedures in two fine art institutions in Britain and in Greece respectively, can be described relative to theories of art and art criticism; and (iii) the extent to which the differing procedures of assessment utilised in the two institutions are subject to or affected by the theoretical positions adopted by individual tutors. In order to achieve this, a triangulation model is pursued to determine the relationships between explicated criteria, assessors'/tutors' theoretical positions and students' perceptions of assessment. More specifically, the objectives of the study are to determine: (iv) the tutors' perspectives of teaching in fine art, of curriculum, assessment procedures and criteria and whether their personal artistic inclinations affect the above; (v) the students' perspectives of teaching in fine art, curriculum, assessment procedures and criteria and whether these perceptions are affected by factors such as achievement or gender; (vi) the researcher's perspective of the structure, teaching and curricula of the fine art courses, the procedures and criteria for assessment and the level of objectivity operating in the assessment of painting students. Some of the methodological problems and concerns and a sample of the findings of this ongoing research as well as a selection of visual examples of students' work from both institutions will be presented.

STATUS: Individual research

DATE OF RESEARCH: 1989-1997

KEYWORDS: art education; arts; assessment; comparative education; degrees -academic; greece

Derby University

0463

Western Road, Mickleover, Derby DE3 5GX   01332 622222

Parker-Jenkins, M. Prof.

What do Muslim children need from the education system?

ABSTRACT: This case study of a Muslim girls' school in the Midlands will provide an insight into an unexplored area which has recently provoked educational debate here and abroad: the lack of understanding between the State educational system and the Muslim community. Adopting an ethnographic approach, the aim of the study is to examine educational provision in non-maintained Muslim schools and to consider the extent to which the maintained school sector is able to accommodate Muslim needs. The study involves 6 Muslim and 6 non-Muslim schools and is conducted by a small team comprising both Muslims and non-Muslims. Initial research of the Islamic Academy, Leicester; visits to other Muslim schools in Britain to provide comparative analysis; and to state schools with high numbers of Muslim children, followed by indepth interviewing of interested parties; educationalists; clergy; academics; and community leaders. Finally, the production of a report, study guide and articles for publication, offering practical solutions to the problems of educating Muslim children within State schools and in accordance with parents' religious convictions. The education system is presently being criticised by 'Muslims' who see an incompatibility between values taught at home and those at school. Although voluntary aided status may be granted to Muslim schools in the future, there will still be a large element of Muslim children who remain in regular maintained schools. Accommodating their educational needs will continue to be a pressing concern for educationalists and this research will provide a direct contribution to knowledge in the field of cultural diversity.

PUBLISHED MATERIAL: PARKER-JENKINS, M. (1990). 'Muslin needs won't disappear', New Era in Education, Vol 17, No 1. ; PARKER-JENKINS, M. (1990). 'Muslim educational needs', Multicultural Education Journal, (U.S.A.), Vol 8, No 2. ; PARKER-JENKINS, M. (1990). 'Multiculturalism in British schools: lessons for Canada', Canadian School Executive', Vol 10, No 5. ; PARKER-JENKINS, M. (1991). 'Muslim matters: exploring the educational needs of the Muslim child', New Community, Vol 17, No 4.

STATUS: Sponsored project

SOURCE OF GRANT: Nottingham University Administered Funding Body £5,048

DATE OF RESEARCH: 1991-1993

KEYWORDS: **islamic education; muslims; religion and education; religious cultural groups; womens education**

0464

Western Road, Mickleover, Derby DE3 5GX   01332 622222

Ibbotson, J. Mrs; *Supervisors*: Young, D. Dr; Wallace, G. Prof.

Gender differences in management communication in secondary schools

ABSTRACT: The research project arises from the recognition of a statistically significant shortfall of female managers in education at middle management level and above. It is concerned with possible sociolinguistic barriers for women in reflecting the 'valued' management style in secondary schools. The aims are: 1) to elucidate, within the real managerial transactions of middle managers, gender differences in the strategic use of language in interactions; 2) to evaluate the extent to which, as a result, females might be negatively valued as managers at different levels; 3) to explore senior managers' perceptions of middle management communications which might be seen to affect promotion prospects. The literature suggests the concept of an identifiable 'feminine' style of management with linguistic usage employed by women in managerial transactions identified as interpersonal, interactive, participative, unifying as opposed to the 'masculine' assertive, status-engrossed, dominating style. Little research has been published on gender differences in communication styles within real managerial transactions. This research explores these and considers whether any 'feminine' speech repertoires disadvantage women as managers. It considers how language works as part of the management process. The fieldwork consists of observations of formal team meetings led by 2 male and 2 female middle managers in 4 secondary schools (16 meetings in all), which have been recorded and transcribed for discourse analysis. The study therefore utilises quantitative data (occurrence of specific speech traits) and an interpretive approach in its analysis. Additionally, headteachers in structured interviews were asked to rank order features of communication skills and strategies in order to consider how far they evaluate these skills in middle managers when making decisions about promotion. The study investigates whether there is any relationship between these evaluations and gender-based communicative performance and whether female managers' strategies are negatively valued.

PUBLISHED MATERIAL: ADAMS, J. (1995). 'Cracking the glass?

Balancing your management team', Management in Education, Vol 9, No 5, pp.27-28.

STATUS: Individual research

DATE OF RESEARCH: 1994-1998

KEYWORDS: **communication skills; educational administration; management; management in education; sex differences; verbal communication; women; women teachers; womens education**

0465

Western Road, Mickleover, Derby DE3 5GX   01332 622222

Al-Daami, K. Mr; *Supervisors*: Wallace, G. Prof.; Weller, P. Dr

Curriculum change and development in Jordan

ABSTRACT: This research describes the role of elementary school teachers in Jordan in connection with curriculum change and development. It identifies the ways in which professional teachers have been faced with increased central control and concludes by responding directly to the Ministry of Education. A survey involving interviews and questionnaires was conducted with elementary school teachers of different school location, age, gender, experience of teaching, qualifications and subjects taught, and in various school locations. Headteachers and education officials were also interviewed to establish the degree of involvement of elementary school teachers in their curriculum planning process. The fieldwork focuses on the specific case of Jordan where involving the teacher in curriculum development and change is seen a increasingly important but where there has been little research into curriculum change. Jordan is going through immense social, economic and political changes, not the least of which is an influx of refugees mainly from Iraq. It has a highly centralised and prescriptive education system. Although there are channels for feeding back curriculum issues to the Ministry of Education, there is little or no legitimised process for using teachers' professional skills in meeting local needs.

PUBLISHED MATERIAL: AL-DAAMI, K. & STANLEY, J. (1998). 'The contribution of primary school teacher to curriculum planning and development', The Curriculum Journal, Vol 9, No 3, pp.357-376.

STATUS: Individual research

DATE OF RESEARCH: 1995-continuing

KEYWORDS: **curriculum development; jordan**

0466

Western Road, Mickleover, Derby DE3 5GX   01332 622222

Greatorex, J. Ms; *Supervisors*: Nyatanga, L. Mr; Wallace, G. Prof.

Educational levels in a healthcare context

ABSTRACT: In this thesis the undergraduate levels 1, 2, 3 and the postgraduate level M are investigated. The investigation is based on the concept of levels in higher education as introduced by the Council for National Academic Awards (CNAA). Many higher education institutes use or are planning to use a Credit Accumulation and Transfer (CAT) scheme. Within CAT it is assumed that consistent standards are applied at each level in all higher education institutes. The assumption behind CAT suggests that the concept of levels should be investigated in order to establish whether educators do or do not agree on 'descriptors'. Descriptors are descriptions of the attributes required of learners at levels 1, 2, 3 and M. This issue is tackled using the example of education in the healthcare professions. In order to identify whether educators can agree on descriptors for the healthcare profession, the Delphi Technique was used. The educators individually allocated levels to a series of descriptors. Educators came to a consensus on the appropriate level for some descriptors. These descriptors were summarised. This summary gave a description of the attributes required for each level that healthcare educators could agree upon. The results of this thesis suggest that there is some agreement about required attributes, however, levels also serve a purpose as a management or bureaucratic tool, there are still some inconsistencies in the notion of levels, and therefore there are still problems with the notions of equivalence and transfer.

STATUS:Individual research

DATE OF RESEARCH: 1992-1997

KEYWORDS: academic achievement; accreditation of prior learning; credit transfer; health personnel; higher education; professional education

0467

Western Road, Mickleover, Derby DE3 5GX   01332 622222

Cordingley, A. Ms; *Supervisors*: Dolan, J. Mr; Sharma, U. Prof.; Wallace, G. Prof.

Parental access to choice in schooling: a European perspective

ABSTRACT: The rhetoric of parental choice and parental involvement in decision-making for schooling assumes increasing strength in Britain and other European nations. However the factors affecting parental access to such choice and decisions are intricate and complex, and operate at structural as well as personal levels. Through review of educational policies with regard to the enhanced involvement of parents in schooling processes and structures in a selected range of European countries, it is expected that a loosely structured interview schedule will be generated, this is intended to illuminate the motivations and experiences of parents who elect to send their children to schools having distinctive educational ethos and pedagogies. These methodologies will form the basis for a critical evaluation of the degree of genuine access to choice and decision-making for parents on a comparative basis.

STATUS: Individual research

DATE OF RESEARCH: 1996-continuing

KEYWORDS: access to education; comparative education; parent choice

0468

Western Road, Mickleover, Derby DE3 5GX   01332 622222

Harcourt, K. Mr; *Supervisors*: Wallace, G. Prof.; Young, D. Dr ; Roberts, B. Dr

Newspapers in education' - curriculum enhancement through education-business partnership

ABSTRACT: Since the mid 1970s, government policies have sought to encourage education/business relations. The two main reasons for this come from different rationales. At one level, the policy appears designed to bring education and training curricula closer to the needs of industry (POLLARD, A., PURVIS, J., WALFORD, G. (Eds). (1988). Education, training and the new vocationalism: experience and policy. Milton Keynes: Open University Press). At another, the policy fits with a general attempt to get more private finance into public services. Newspapers in Education (NIE) fulfils the objective of bringing private finance into schools, but little evaluative work has been done on the relationship between such initiatives and curriculum enhancement. Nor have the costs and benefits to the business partner been assessed. NIE began in the UK in 1980, influenced initially by established practice in the USA and Scandinavia. Local and regional newspapers were encouraged to make their links with education formal by employing or releasing staff to interact with schools. The commercial incentive was, and remains, that whilst newspapers' readerships are decreasing, an exposure to newspapers at school might encourage readers for the future. The educational incentive for schools to participate has been seen as the curriculum enhancement arising from the provision of educational resources. However, to date, only one substantive study has addressed the educational benefits for pupils of NIE in the UK. At a broader level, Ball (BALL, S. (1990). The micro-politics of the school: towards a theory of social organisation. London: Routledge) and Ross (ROSS, A. (Ed). (1990). Economic and industrial awareness in the primary school. London: PNL Press) and Fullan (FULLAN, M. (1991). The new meaning of educational change. London: Cassell) have explored something of the different interplay of interests and tensions in recent schooling policy. This research will review a 3-year NIE partnership project between 164 schools in Humberside and their local newspaper, the Hull Daily Mail (a Northcliffe enterprise). The approach is that of the case-study using a selected group of 5 primary schools of varying organisation styles, recruiting pupils from a range of socioeconomic backgrounds. Data will be gathered using observations, semi-structured interviews, documentation, pupils' work and self-reports. The focus is both on the perceptions of and engagement with the materials, and the tensions in the education/business partnership (e.g. COOPER, P. & MCINTYRE, D. (1993). 'Commonality in teachers, and pupils' perceptions of effective classroom learning', British Journal of Educational Psychology, Vol 63, No 3, pp.381-399; and WOODS, P. (1993). Critical events in teaching and learning. Lewes: Falmer Press). This is an ethnographic approach to understanding the way political initiatives are attempting to bring education and industry into closer 'partnership'. At PhD level, the study will illuminate the micropolitical, professional and cultural issues relevant to the debates generated by such changes.

PUBLISHED MATERIAL: HARCOURT, K., ROBERTS, B. & YOUNG, D. (1995). 'Accrediting professional reflection'. Paper presented at the Towards a Learning Workforce Conference, Lancaster University, 1995. ; HARCOURT, K. (1996). 'Newspapers and readers, research and practice'. In NEALE, B. (Ed). Literacy saves lives. Shepreth: United Kingdom Reading Association.

STATUS: Sponsored project

SOURCE OF GRANT: Northcliffe Newspaper Group Ltd

DATE OF RESEARCH: 1995-1998

KEYWORDS: education business partnerships; literacy; newspapers; partnerships; primary education; teaching methods

0469

Western Road, Mickleover, Derby DE3 5GX   01332 622222

Parker-Jenkins, M. Prof.; Hartas, D. Dr; Irving, B. Mr

The Careers Service: gate-keepers to careers' opportunities for Muslim women

ABSTRACT: The aim of the study is to investigate the extent to which the Careers Service staff are able to meet the career needs of Muslim women (in the 14-18 year age group) through an examination of their understanding of this particular client group and the practices they employ. As a major gate-keeper to benefits and access to employment and training opportunities, Careers Services occupy a pivotal position. The inquiry draws on the research team's experience of Muslim communities in Britain which has spanned over a decade. In this study the methodology is two-fold: a survey of careers companies in England, Scotland and Wales to identify good practice, using questionnaires and telephone follow-up; and semi-structured interviews of personnel in five of these organisations to provide indepth case study analysis. Overall, the research explores the interface between gender, religion and ethnicity, and the extent to which career services facilitate career advancement of minority women with special reference to those of a Muslim background. A Good Practice Guide will be produced for the Department for Education and Employment (DfEE) in 1999.

STATUS: Sponsored project

SOURCE OF GRANT: Department for Education and Employment £20,000

DATE OF RESEARCH: 1998-continuing

KEYWORDS: career choice; careers service; labour market; muslims; vocational guidance; women; womens employment

0470

Western Road, Mickleover, Derby DE3 5GX 01332 622222

Revill, P. Mr ;*Supervisors*: Wallace, G. Prof.; Parker-Jenkins, M. Prof.

Assessment of cognition in competence based education and training

ABSTRACT: Current competence based education and training methods do not yet relate performance with knowledge and understanding (cognition) explicitly. Rather knowledge and understanding are regarded as implicit in the behaviours that are assessed as competent. Research will focus on developing methods and techniques linking explicitly competent performance with underpinning cognition. Evaluation of current assessment practice will be undertaken through observation of up to 15 qualified and experienced assessors of management occupational standards. All assessments will be videoed to provide a record of the activity and a basis for review, feedback and analysis. In the first tranche of observations, commonalities of practice, methods of confirming cognition and competence will be identified. Assessors will use 'think aloud' as described by Ericsson and Simon (1993) and Lloyd, Lawson and Scott (1996) whilst assessing documentary evidence. A number of summative assessment interviews of candidates will also be observed and recorded. Data emerging will be used to identify interesting practice and areas of concern within the assessment process. This information will be used to assist in the definition of guidelines and development of alternative assessment techniques. These will be shared with the original tranche of assessors, who will be asked to use them in a second round of observed and recorded assessments, using different, but similar standardised materials. The initial review process will be repeated to obtain feedback from assessors and their candidates.

From this critical evaluation of the methods and techniques of assessment, the ways assessors understand the relationship between cognition and competency will be elucidated.

STATUS: Individual research

DATE OF RESEARCH: 1998-continuing

KEYWORDS: assessment; cognitive ability; competency based education; skills; training; vocational education

0471

Western Road, Mickleover, Derby DE3 5GX   01332 622222
Charles University, Education Faculty, Mathematics Department, MD Rettigove 4, 11636 Prague, Czech Republic   01042 2449 1111

Koman, M. Prof.; Littler, G. Prof.

Teaching units to promote mathematical thinking

ABSTRACT: 'Teaching units' has become a phrase with a multiplicity of meanings from the ideas of 'programmed learning' to the structure of a series of lessons. This research is aimed at developing 'teaching units' which will involve both pupil and teacher in solving problems in applicable mathematics, some of which are closed and others open. The aim will be to develop work which allows pupils to apply their mathematical knowledge, to show their understanding of or lack of understanding of mathematics, to develop mathematical thinking, the ability to conjecture and the ability to develop strategies to help solve the problem. The teaching units will be piloted in schools and the effect on the pupils' mathematical ability evaluated.

STATUS: Collaborative

DATE OF RESEARCH: 1996-continuing

KEYWORDS: mathematical applications; mathematics education; problem solving; teaching methods

0472

Western Road, Mickleover, Derby DE3 5GX   01332 622222
Charles University, Education Faculty, Mathematics Department, MD Rettigove 4, 11636 Prague, Czech Republic   0044 133 262 2222

Littler, G. Prof.; Hejny, M. Prof.

Photoalgebra

ABSTRACT: Many pupils find great difficulty understanding algebra and this research is targeted at the very first period of algebraic thinking. The researchers hope to show that much of the work in number and measures in elementary/primary schools can be harnessed to help pupil's understanding of algebra. For instance, it is hoped to show that the way in which young pupils are introduced to the symbolism of number in arithmetic can influence their attitude towards the learning of algebra. Pre-algebraic thinking will be analysed and show how the world of algebra emerges from the world of arithmetic. Developmental models will be constructed to show the progression in mathematics from arithmetic to algebra and pupils thinking as they approach the solution of problems during these stages. Examples of pupil's work will be used to illustrate the issues raised. Papers will be published in mathematical teacher's journals to enable teachers to use the research in developing constructivist teaching strategies for the development of the teaching of algebra.

STATUS: Collaborative

DATE OF RESEARCH: 1997-continuing

KEYWORDS: algebra; arithmetic; mathematical concepts; mathematics education; models; primary education; teaching methods

0473

Western Road, Mickleover, Derby DE3 5GX   01332 622222
Czech Republic Academy of Sciences, Mathematical Institute, Zitna 25, 115 67 Prague, Czech Republic

Ticha, M. Dr ; Kurina, F. Prof.; Littler, G. Prof.

Spatial awareness of children starting school compared with their teachers' pre-conceived ideas

ABSTRACT: Children are asked to complete 6 tasks which test their ability to copy diagrams, perceive 3-dimensional objects drawn in 2 dimensions, halve a shape, complete a reflection, differentiate heights and a particular shape. All the children tested must have less than 3 weeks formal schooling. Prior to the children being given the tests, their teachers are asked to state what percentage of their children would be successful in each test. The researchers hope to show that teachers under-estimate children's spatial ability on entering school. If the tests are successful in showing a discrepancy, their use will be promulgated through papers in relevant mathematical journals.

STATUS: Collaborative

DATE OF RESEARCH: 1996-continuing

KEYWORDS: geometry; mathematics education; primary education; reception classes; spatial ability; teacher expectations; young children

0474

Western Road, Mickleover, Derby DE3 5GX   01332 622222
Leicestershire Careers and Guidance Service, Pocklingtons Walk, Leicester LE1 6BT   01162 627254

Parker-Jenkins, M. Prof.; Haw, K. Dr ; Irving, B. Mr

Muslim girls: career destinations and labour market implications

ABSTRACT: Muslim women presently constitute an unknown percentage of the workforce in Britain, and we know very little about their career patterns, choices of employment or career destinations. They are often perceived as an 'invisible' and unobtrusive element of the labour market and are under-utilised in terms of their potential as human resources and their contribution to the economy. The central objectives of this research are: 1) To develop a fuller understanding of the intersections between gender, class, ethnicity, racism and religion, and how such a multiplicity of factors inscribe the position of Muslim women in the labour market. 2) To analyse the role that educational and career institutions play in encouraging or discouraging young Muslim women along certain paths of education and employment, and thus the reasons for their career destinations and advancement in the United Kingdom. The significance of this research is that it aims to study Muslim women post-16, within identified geographical areas. Further, within the framework of analysis, the research seeks to explore issues behind the under-representation of Muslim women in their perceptions and experiences of paid employment and educational institutions, and proposes new approaches to policy and practice.

PUBLISHED MATERIAL: PARKER-JENKINS, M. (1990). 'Why Muslim needs won't disappear', New Era in Education, Vol 71, No 1, pp.14-16. ; PARKER-JENKINS, M. (1991). 'Muslim matters: the educational needs of the Muslim child', New Community, Vol 17, No 4, pp.569-582. ; PARKER-JENKINS, M. (1992). Educating Muslim children. Nottingham: Nottingham University, School of Education. ; PARKER-JENKINS, M. (1995). Children of Islam: teacher's guide to meeting the needs of Muslim pupils. Stoke-on-Trent: Trentham Books Ltd.

STATUS: Sponsored project

SOURCE OF GRANT: Leverhulme Trust

DATE OF RESEARCH: 1995-1998

KEYWORDS: career choice; careers; ethnic groups; labour market; muslims; religious cultural groups; womens education; womens employment

Dundee University

0475

Centre for Medical Education, Ninewells Hospital and Medical School, Dundee DD1 9SY   01382 660111

Roff, S. Mrs; McAleer, J. Dr; Stewart, A. Dr; *Supervisor*: Harden, R. Prof.

Staff development for further improvement of medical education in Bangladesh medical schools

ABSTRACT: A multi-year training programme in staff development for medical education is being conducted and will be evaluated for its sustainability beyond the life of the international funding.

STATUS: Sponsored project

SOURCE OF GRANT: Overseas Development Administration

DATE OF RESEARCH: 1994-continuing

KEYWORDS: bangladesh; medical education

0476

Centre for Medical Education, Ninewells Hospital and Medical School, Dundee DD1 9SY   01382 660111

Mulholland, H. Dr

Assessment of competence in general practice

ABSTRACT: The research was designed to improve the reliability and validity of the Membership Examination of the Royal College of General Practitioners (RCGP). Results of the last five years were analysed (for approximately 2,000 candidates each year) and recommendations made as to changes in numbers and types of questions in the existing papers. Two new types of test were developed: (1) The Critical Reading Paper in which candidates have to read, critically evaluate and discuss applications of scientific journal articles and of printed material of a variety of forms. (2) The simulated surgery in which candidates are placed in conditions which simulate as far as possible real surgery conditions and are assessed on their competence in consultation. This part of the research is now being continued with funding from the European Community.

PUBLISHED MATERIAL: LOCKIE, C. (1990). (Ed). 'The MRCGP Examination', Occasional Paper, No 46. London Royal College of General Practitioners.

STATUS: Sponsored project

SOURCE OF GRANT: Royal College of General Practitioners; Department of Health; European Community

DATE OF RESEARCH: 1988-1993

KEYWORDS: **assessment; competence; examinations; medical education; medicine; physicians**

0477

Centre for Medical Education, Ninewells Hospital and Medical School, Dundee DD1 9SY   01382 660111

McAleer, J. Dr; *Supervisors*: Harden, R. Prof.; Laidlaw, J. Miss

A programme to encourage and facilitate doctors' participation in clinical audit

ABSTRACT: The need for audit as one aspect of clinical practice is now generally accepted throughout the medical profession. Its adoption requires a change in behaviour of doctors - one which will be successful and long lasting. This distance learning programme intends to provide a more indepth training about audit by using a 5 stage approach - awareness, interest, appraisal, trial and adoption. The programme will be designed to relate audit to the doctor's (both hospital and community) day to day practice and encourage further learning about audit on-the-job. It comprises a resource book which contains key information about audit. In addition participants will receive a series of 'doctors' diaries' in which audit activities will be described in a problem based format. Responses to these problems will be collected and feedback provided - using comparisons between decisions made and those of colleagues. There will also be a number of practical audit activities linked to the diaries. The programme will be offered on a national basis. The wealth of information collected as part of the distance learning programme will be analysed with the key findings published in report form. Another feature of the study is concerned with an evaluation of the complete package.

PUBLISHED MATERIAL: ARNOLD, C. et al (1992). Moving to audit: what every doctor needs to know about audit. Dundee: University of Dundee; The Postgraduate Office.

STATUS: Sponsored project

SOURCE OF GRANT: Scottish Office Home and Health Department

DATE OF RESEARCH: 1991-1993

KEYWORDS: **distance education; institutional evaluation; medical services; professional continuing education**

0478

Centre for Medical Education, Ninewells Hospital and Medical School, Dundee DD1 9SY   01382 660111

Horton, P. Ms; Rogerson, E. Mrs; *Supervisor*: Harden, R. Prof.

Diploma in Advanced Nursing Studies/Bachelor of Nursing, Bachelor of Midwifery

ABSTRACT: The Diploma and Degree courses aim to equip the individual with the knowledge and ability necessary to provide a high standard of individualised nursing care which is research based and reinforces individual accountability of the practitioner. Furthermore, the course aims to embrace the dynamics of change, link theory to practice and emphasise the necessity for continuing professional updating and educational development.

PUBLISHED MATERIAL: ROGERSON, E. et al (1992). Nursing in the 90's. Dundee: University of Dundee, Centre for Medical Education.

STATUS: Sponsored project

SOURCE OF GRANT: University of Dundee ; Tayside Health Board

DATE OF RESEARCH: 1990-continuing

KEYWORDS: **nurse education; nurses; obstetrics; qualifications**

0479

Centre for Medical Education, Ninewells Hospital and Medical School, Dundee DD1 9SY   01382 660111

Mulholland, H. Dr

Evaluation of interactive video tutorials in anatomy

ABSTRACT: The project consists of qualitative and quantitative evaluation of the effectiveness of interactive video tutorials in Anatomy. Methods used are pre- and post-tests, interaction analysis and questionnaire. Individual and group use of the tutorials are being evaluated.

STATUS: Sponsored project

SOURCE OF GRANT: Rheumatism and Arthritis Council £3,000

DATE OF RESEARCH: 1991-1993

KEYWORDS: **human computer interaction; interactive video; medical education**

0480

Centre for Medical Education, Ninewells Hospital and Medical School, Dundee DD1 9SY   01382 660111

Mulholland, H. Dr

Assessment of vocational training in general practice

ABSTRACT: The project consists of a survey of methods of assessment currently in use in the Northern Region in the Vocational Training Schemes for General Practice.

STATUS: Sponsored project

SOURCE OF GRANT: Regional Adviser in General Practice, Northern Region

DATE OF RESEARCH: 1992-1993

KEYWORDS: **medical services; training**

0481

Centre for Medical Education, Ninewells Hospital and Medical School, Dundee DD1 9SY   01382 660111

McAleer, S. Dr; Roff, S. Mrs; *Supervisor*: Harden, R. Prof.

Course development for health professions education

Abstract: The development and evaluation of face-to-face and distance learning formats for health professions education/medical education.

STATUS: Sponsored project

SOURCE OF GRANT: Overseas Development Administration

DATE OF RESEARCH: 1988-continuing

KEYWORDS: **courses; distance education; health personnel; medical education**

0482

Centre for Medical Education, Ninewells Hospital and Medical School, Dundee DD1 9SY   01382 660111

Kindlen, M. Miss; Finegan, W. Dr; *Supervisor*: Harden, R. Prof.

Diploma in palliative care

ABSTRACT: The development and piloting of a multiprofessional distance learning programme in palliative care will be evaluated as an example of interprofessional learning.

STATUS: Sponsored project

SOURCE OF GRANT: Macmillan Cancer Relief Fund

DATE OF RESEARCH: 1990-continuing

KEYWORDS: **distance education; health personnel; hospices - terminal care; medical education; nurse education; qualifications**

0483

Centre for Medical Education, Ninewells Hospital and Medical School, Dundee DD1 9SY   01382 660111

Davis, M. Dr; *Supervisor*: Harden, R. Prof.

Design of staff development training for South America

ABSTRACT: The design, implementation and evaluation of distance learning staff development programme in health/medical education for 23 multiprofessional campuses in South America.

STATUS: Sponsored project

SOURCE OF GRANT: Kellogg Foundation

DATE OF RESEARCH: 1995-continuing

KEYWORDS: **health personnel; medical education; south america; staff development**

0484

Centre for Medical Education, Ninewells Hospital and Medical School, Dundee DD1 9SY   01382 660111

Stewart, A. Dr; *Supervisor*: Harden, R. Prof.

Design of staff development programmes for India and Nepal

ABSTRACT: The design, delivery and evaluation of varying programmes for staff development for health professionals in India and Nepal.

STATUS: Sponsored project

SOURCE OF GRANT: Overseas Development Agency ; British Council

DATE OF RESEARCH: 1994-continuing

KEYWORDS: **health personnel; india; nepal; programme development; staff development**

0485

Centre for Medical Education, Ninewells Hospital and Medical School, Dundee DD1 9SY   01382 660111

Dunkley, P. Dr; *Supervisor*: Harden, R. Prof.

Development of surgical skills training programmes in laparoscopic surgery

ABSTRACT: Design and development of a surgical skills unit offering training at various levels, and its evaluation over a five year period.

STATUS: Sponsored project

SOURCE OF GRANT: Consortium of commercial companies

DATE OF RESEARCH: 1992-continuing

KEYWORDS: **medical education; medicine; surgery**

0486

Centre for Medical Education, Ninewells Hospital and Medical School, Dundee DD1 9SY   01382 660111

Mitchell, H. Miss; *Supervisor*: Harden, R. Prof.

Task-based learning project for senior house officers

ABSTRACT: The development and evaluation of structured training for senior house officers on the principles of task-based learning and managed learning through the development of study guides and feedback systems.

STATUS: Sponsored project

SOURCE OF GRANT: Scottish Office

DATE OF RESEARCH: 1994-1997

KEYWORDS: **health personnel; learning activities; medical education**

0487

Centre for Medical Education, Ninewells Hospital and Medical School, Dundee DD1 9SY   01382 660111

Davis, M. Dr ; Crosby, J. Mrs; *Supervisor*: Harden, R. Prof.

Development and evaluation of the Medical School curriculum

ABSTRACT: An evaluation of the change process in the development of the new Medical School curriculum at Dundee University.

STATUS: Sponsored project

SOURCE OF GRANT: Scottish Higher Education Funding Council

DATE OF RESEARCH: 1993-continuing

KEYWORDS: **medical education**

0488

Centre for Medical Education, Ninewells Hospital and Medical School, Dundee DD1 9SY   01382 660111

Leicester University, Department of General Practice, Leicester General Hospital, Gwendolen Road, Leicester LE5 4PW   01162 584873

Mulholland, H. Dr; Fraser, R. Prof.; *Supervisor*: McKinlay, R. Dr

Assessment of consultation competence in general practice

ABSTRACT: This is the second stage of the 'Assessment of competence in general practice' project. The project consists of a series of studies into the validity and reliability of the Leicester Assessment Package. The criteria on which assessment is to be based were validated by submission to 100 course organisers. An experiment was undertaken in which five doctors carried out six standardised patient consultations and were assessed by six markers. Another study investigated the correlation between scores based on video and those based on live consultations. A further study will investigate the effects on scores if assessors are allowed to question candidates about the reasons for their actions.

PUBLISHED MATERIAL: HARDEN, R.M. et al (Eds). (1992). Approaches to the assessment of clinical competence. Dundee: University of Dundee; Centre for Medical Education.

STATUS: Sponsored project

SOURCE OF GRANT: Department of Health ; Royal College of General Practitioners

DATE OF RESEARCH: 1991-1993

KEYWORDS: **assessment; competence; examinations; medical education; medicine; physicians**

0489

Department of Applied Computing, Nethergate, Dundee DD1 4HN   01382 223181

Rowe, G. Dr; Thorburn, G. Mr

Automated computer program marking system

ABSTRACT: A package allowing tutors to specify a design for a computer program, which will then evaluate a student's program, checking for modular structure, dynamic correctness, etc.

STATUS: Individual research

DATE OF RESEARCH: 1994-1997

KEYWORDS: **assessment; computer assisted testing; computer uses in education; information technology**

0490

Department of Psychology, Centre for Paired Learning, Dundee DD1 4HN   01382 223181

Topping, K. Dr; Bremner, W. Mr; Holmes, E. Ms

Promoting social competence

ABSTRACT: A survey and review of the literature on the effectiveness of programmes to promote social competence in children of school age has led to the creation of a searchable database of over 700 items. A survey of good practice in Scotland has yielded over 100 case studies, embodied in the 'Practical Guide'. A survey of relevant resource and training packages is embodied in the 'Resources Guide'. These are fronted by a brief guide to conducting a whole-school social competence audit. Links with related research in the USA and Australia have been made.

STATUS: Sponsored project

SOURCE OF GRANT: Scottish Office Education and Industry Department £30,000

DATE OF RESEARCH: 1996-1998

KEYWORDS: **social behaviour; social skills**

0491

Department of Social Work, Dundee DD1 4HN   01382 223181

Kendrick, A. Dr; Fraser, A. Dr

An examination of the factors that promote the development of an integrated child care strategy

ABSTRACT: This is an overview study of current policies and developments in Scottish Social Work Departments which relate to the integration of residential and community child care services between agencies (particularly Social Work and Education) and with Social Work Departments. The study will be carried out by content analysis of policy and planning documents and by interviews with key social work personnel. In three selected local authorities the nature of the integration of child care services will be studied in more detail over two years. A cohort study will look at career patterns of children in care and will focus on the outcomes of particular social work placements. Collection of data will be by questionnaire, analysis of case files and interviews with children and young people. Interviews will be carried out with personnel involved with the cohort of children to examine the relationship between organisational structures policies and practice as perceived by social work staff, Children's Panel Members and Reporters to the Children's Panel. To provide information about the level of inter-agency integration, educational staff will be interviewed.

STATUS: Sponsored project

SOURCE OF GRANT: Social Work Services Group £200,000

DATE OF RESEARCH: 1990-1993

KEYWORDS: **child welfare; community services; residential care; scotland; social services; social work**

0492

Institute for Education and Lifelong Learning, Dundee DD1 4HN
01382 223181

Hartley, D. Prof.

An analysis of government policy for teachers' professional development in Scotland: 1979-1990

ABSTRACT: An analysis of government documentation and research on teachers' continuing professional development, informed by critical theory.

PUBLISHED MATERIAL: HARTLEY, J.D. (1986). 'Structural isomorphism and the management of consent in education', Journal of Education Policy, Vol 1, No 3, pp.229-237. ; HARTLEY, J.D. (1990). 'Tests, tasks and Taylorism: a model T approach to the management of education', Journal of Education Policy, Vol 5, No 1, pp.67-76. ; HARTLEY, J.D. (1989). 'Beyond collaboration: the management of professional development in Scotland', British Journal of Education for Teaching, Vol 10, No 2, pp.253-261. ; HARTLEY, J.D. (1990). 'Beyond competency: a socio-technical model of continuing professional education', British Journal of Inservice Education, Vol 16, No 1, pp.66-70.

STATUS: Individual research

DATE OF RESEARCH: 1986-1998

KEYWORDS: **educational policy; inservice teacher education; professional development; scotland; teacher development**

0493

Institute for Education and Lifelong Learning, Dundee DD1 4HN
01382 223181

Murray, R. Mr; Supervisor: Hartley, D. Prof.

The development of managerialism in Scottish education since 1945

ABSTRACT: The study examines the increasing tendency in Scottish education to use industrial and corporate modes of management in education since 1945.

STATUS: Individual research

DATE OF RESEARCH: 1988-1993

KEYWORDS: **educational history; management in education; scotland**

0494

Institute for Education and Lifelong Learning, Dundee DD1 4HN
01382 223181

Watt, S. Dr; Hutchinson, A. Ms

Special entry initiative and guide to good practice

ABSTRACT: This project aims to promote the collaboration between higher education institutions in the promotion and evolvement of special entry initiatives to higher education. In particular, to encourage the wider participation of nontraditional groups of young people in higher education, and in science and engineering. In addition, the project aims to produce a guide to good practice which will better prepare 5th and 6th formers for life in higher education.

PUBLISHED MATERIAL: WATT, S. (1995). 'Special entry summer schools'. BP Aiming for a College Education Series of Briefings. Poole: BP Educational Service.

STATUS: Sponsored project

SOURCE OF GRANT: Paul Hamlyn Trust £71,000

DATE OF RESEARCH: 1994-1998

KEYWORDS: **access programmes; access to education; engineering; higher education; nontraditional students; science education; student recruitment; university admission**

0495

Institute for Education and Lifelong Learning, Dundee DD1 4HN
01382 223181

Watt, S. Dr; Blicharski, J. Dr

Opportunities and obstacles: a pilot study of the subsequent progress of students who attended the University of Dundee Access Summer School

ABSTRACT: This study is following the progress of students who completed the University of Dundee Access Summer School. As well as recording their academic progress, the study will also identify any academic and non-academic problems that students encounter. Both qualitative and quantitative data is being collected, allowing the target cohort to be compared to control groups of traditional and borderline university entrants (n=around 100 for each group). Data will be obtained from university student records and through questionnaires. The findings of the study are likely to lead to better preparation of students for higher education.

STATUS: Sponsored project

SOURCE OF GRANT: Scottish Enterprise Tayside £4,000; Scottish Office Education Department £1,000; Mitchell Trust £3,000; Tayside Regional Council £4,000

DATE OF RESEARCH: 1995-1997

KEYWORDS: **access programmes; access to education; followup studies; higher education; mature students; nontraditional students; summer schools; university administration**

0496

Institute for Education and Lifelong Learning, Dundee DD1 4HN
01382 223181

Watt, S. Dr; Cullen, M. Ms

The bridge between school and university

ABSTRACT: This research is intended to provide two publications aimed: 1) at university senior management; and 2) at the Director of Education to ensure the success and importance of special entry initiative for young people to access higher education is firmly portrayed and publicised. Two journal articles are planned, targeted at academics which: a) chart the successful programme of students who have progressed through university summer school; and b) compare and contrast the programme of young Access students with mature Access students.

STATUS: Sponsored project

SOURCE OF GRANT: An anonymous educational trust £11,500

DATE OF RESEARCH: 1996-1997

KEYWORDS: **access programmes; access to education; higher education; nontraditional students; student recruitment; summer schools; university admission**

0497

Institute for Education and Lifelong Learning, Dundee DD1 4HN
01382 223181

Watt, S. Dr; Collins, C. Ms

Personal transferable skills in non traditional-students

ABSTRACT: By means of questionnaire and diary study, this project will investigate which kinds of extra-curricular activities undergraduates undertake will best enhance certain types of personal transferable skills. The undergraduates targeted are those from nontraditional backgrounds who are often in most need of increased transferable skills to enhance their employment prospects.

STATUS: Sponsored project

SOURCE OF GRANT: Carnegie Trust £12,000

DATE OF RESEARCH: 1996-1997

KEYWORDS: **employment potential; higher education; nontraditional students; skills; students; transfer of learning**

0498

Institute for Education and Lifelong Learning, Dundee DD1 4HN 01382 223181

Stocks, J. Mr

Mental testing in Scotland 1920-1950

ABSTRACT: The aim is to discover the reasons for the use in the 1930s and 1940s of intelligence tests as part of the selection procedure for secondary education in Scotland; and the reasons why, in spite of their availability and the widespread enthusiasm for such tests among key figures in the Scottish education system, they were not adopted earlier. Comparison will be made with the development of intelligence testing in England, as described by Gillian Sutherland (SUTHERLAND, G. (1984). Ability, merit and measurement: mental testing and English education, 1880-1940. Oxford: Clarendon Press) and Adrian Wooldridge (WOOLDRIDGE, A. (1994). Measuring the mind: education and psychology in England, c1860-c1990. Cambridge: Cambridge University Press). Sources being used include the records of the Scottish Education Department and of a number of education authorities, national newspapers, and the Scottish Educational Journal.

STATUS: Individual research

DATE OF RESEARCH: 1995-1998

KEYWORDS: **educational history; intelligence tests; scotland; selective admission; tests**

0499

Institute for Education and Lifelong Learning, Dundee DD1 4HN 01382 223181

Cooke, A. Mr

James Stuart and the origins of English university extension

ABSTRACT: James Stuart (1843-1913) was the key figure in the development of the University extension movement at Cambridge in the late 1860s and 1870s. Recent research by Goldman (1995) on Oxford university extension has challenged the concept of Stuart as a 'pioneer', setting him in the context of social and institutional changes taking place both inside and outside the university system for at least a generation before Stuart came on the scene. Although this is true, Stuart remains an important figure. Themes will include Stuart's involvement in the movement for women's access to higher education through the North of England Council for Promoting the Higher Education of Women. Another major theme will be his involvement in the education of working class men through the auspices of the Co-operative movement and Mechanics' Institutes. From these experiences came his idea of a 'peripatetic university' financed by the profits of the Co-operative societies and bringing together an alliance of middle class women and working class men. Stuart brought with him the more 'democratic' traditions of Scottish universities into the elitist atmosphere of Cambridge He exemplifies the role of the outsider as an educational innovator. As a Scot, a Congregationalist and an applied scientist, Stuart was outside the mainstream of Cambridge University life in this period, although as a Fellow of Trinity College, Cambridge, he was in a position to press for change. Comparisons will be made with Nicholay Grundtvig, another influential 19th century educator.

PUBLISHED MATERIAL: COOKE, A. (1998). 'James Stuart and the origins of English university extension'. In: MARTIN-FRIEDENTHAL, Y. (Ed) Proceedings of the VI International Conference on the History of

Adult Education. Frankfurt: Peter Lang.

STATUS: Individual research

DATE OF RESEARCH: 1996-1997

KEYWORDS: **adult education; continuing education; educational history; extension education; universities; womens education; working class**

0500

Institute for Education and Lifelong Learning, Dundee DD1 4HN 01382 223181

Siann, G. Prof.; Findlay, G. Mr

Students' perceptions of their first year of study on science and engineering courses with particular reference to gender issues

ABSTRACT: Students entering their second year on science and engineering courses will be asked to fill out a questionnaire. In order to maximise the response rate, participants will be able to take part in a lottery. Items on the questionnaire explore their satisfaction with aspects of teaching and assessment in their first year, their reasons for choosing their course and university, their expectation of employment, their experience of assistance in the university with problems, their stress level during the first year, whether they had part-time jobs during term time and, if they did, if they thought this affected their performance. Embedded in these questions are items relating specifically to gender - for example, whether they consider science to have a masculine or feminine image, their views of the gender balance on their courses of both staff and students, whether they think gender balance is important.

STATUS: Team research

DATE OF RESEARCH: 1996-1997

KEYWORDS: **engineering; higher education; science education; sex differences; student attitudes; students**

0501

Institute for Education and Lifelong Learning, Dundee DD1 4HN 01382 223181

Cooke, A. Mr

Scotland and the 1919 Report

ABSTRACT: The Final Report of the Adult Education Committee of the Ministry of Reconstruction in 1919 is rightly regarded as a key document in the history and ideology of British adult education. Waller (1956) described it as 'probably the most important contribution ever made to the literature of adult education' and later writers such as Wiltshire (1980), Goldman (1995) and Fieldhouse (1996), although more restrained, have all recognised its importance. The Report's subtitle 'A design for democracy' reflects the context of the period when the growing power of the labour movement was making itself felt across all spheres of British life including the universities. However, in Scotland, both the labour movement and the education system, including the universities, were distinctively different from their equivalents south of the border. This was the era of 'Red Clydeside' when the activities of John Maclean and independent working class educational organisations such as the Labour College and the Plebs League commanded much more support in the west of Scotland than the activities of WEA. On the other side of the coin, the Scottish universities were seen as more 'democratic' than the older English universities with a wider social mix, whilst the School Boards exercised tight control over all forms of adult education, unlike the system in England and Wales where voluntary bodies and university joint committees could be funded directly through central government. In the Scottish context, the 1919 Report provides an interesting model of the interaction between emerging social movements and existing educational institutions.

PUBLISHED MATERIAL: COOKE, A. (1998). 'Scotland and the 1919 Report'. In: COOKE, A.J. and MACSWEEN, A. (Eds). Proceedings of the VII International Conference on the History of Adult Education. Frankfurt: Peter Lang. (in press).

STATUS: Individual research

DATE OF RESEARCH: 1998-continuing

KEYWORDS: **adult education; continuing education; educational history; scotland**

0502

Institute for Education and Lifelong Learning, Dundee DD1 4HN
01382 223181

Allardice, M. Mr; *Supervisor*: Blicharski, J. Dr

Learning their lessons

ABSTRACT: This project tracks the destinations and progress of students who attend the University of Dundee Access Summer School and Aspire courses (approximately 140 per year). Building up a significant database will allow many comparisons to be made, in particular, the effects of disadvantage, the relationship between entry qualifications and progression, the role of intensive entry initiative courses and barriers to lifelong learning. By the end of the project, which follows on from a pilot study which ran from 1995 to 1997, over 600 students will have been followed from school, through university and into employment.

STATUS: Sponsored project

SOURCE OF GRANT: Dundee University; Scottish Enterprise Tayside, jointly £12,000; Dundee City Council £12,000

DATE OF RESEARCH: 1998-continuing

KEYWORDS: **access programmes; access to education; followup studies; higher education; nontraditional students; student destinations; summer schools**

0503

Institute for Education and Lifelong Learning, Dundee DD1 4HN
01382 223181

Hartley, D. Prof.

Education and social change: curriculum, pedagogy, assessment and management

Abstract: The study has 3 main purposes: 1) To describe and explain the uncertainties that beset us as '2000' approaches. 2) To point out the many transitions taking place in education during the current post-modern phase of late capitalism, and to do so by referring to notions of curriculum, pedagogy, assessment and organisation in education. 3) To consider attempts made so far by policymakers to structure the education system so that, on the one hand, it comes to terms with rapid cultural and social changes whilst, at the same time, coping with the economic imperatives of meeting the growing 'challenge' of the emergent Pacific-rim nations.

PUBLISHED MATERIAL: HARTLEY, D. (1997). Re-schooling society. London: Falmer Press. ; HARTLEY, D. (1997). 'The new managerialism in education: a mission impossible?', Cambridge Journal of Education, Vol 27, No 1, pp.47-57. ; HARTLEY, D. (1997). 'Values added: some sociological interpretations of values in education', Scottish Educational Review, Vol 29, No 2, pp.163-173. ; HARTLEY, D. (1998). 'Repeat prescription: national curriculum for initial teacher training education, 1987-1997', British Journal of Educational Studies, Vol 46, No 1, pp.68-83.

STATUS: Individual research

DATE OF RESEARCH: 1996-1998

KEYWORDS: **assessment; curriculum development; educational change; educational policy; management in education; social change**

0504

Institute for Education and Lifelong Learning, Dundee DD1 4HN
01382 223181
St Andrews University, School of Management, Kinnesburn, St Andrews KY16 9DJ
01334 462808

Siann, G. Prof.; Wilson, F. Dr

Students' views on gender issues

ABSTRACT: All students, undergraduate and postgraduate, are being asked to complete an anonymous questionnaire as they matriculate in the 1996-97 session at the University of Dundee. In order to maximise the response rate, participants will be able to take part in a lottery. The questionnaire comprises fixed and open-ended items and also uses vignettes. Issues covered concern gender roles, working mothers, childcare issues, masculinity, and attitudes to feminism. Analyses will utilise the independent variables of age, gender, faculty and year of study.

STATUS: Collaborative

DATE OF RESEARCH: 1996-1997

KEYWORDS: **child rearing; feminism; higher education; masculinity; men; sex differences; student attitudes; students; universities; women**

0505

Institute for Education and Lifelong Learning, Dundee DD1 4HN
01382 223181
Stirling University, Department of Biological and Molecular Sciences, Stirling FK9 4LA
01786 473171

Watt, S. Dr; Roger, A. Ms; Cooper, M. Dr; Cronin, C. Ms; Duffield, J. Mrs

Women's access to, participation in, and career progression through science, engineering and technology

ABSTRACT: This project will produce three guides to good practice in the promotion of access to participation in and career progression through science, engineering and technology. Methods involve a literature search to ascertain existing good practice over a six month period. The guide will be piloted for six months and reviewed for global publication in September 1997.

STATUS: Sponsored project

SOURCE OF GRANT: Scottish Higher Education Funding Council £105,000

DATE OF RESEARCH: 1995-1997

KEYWORDS: **access to education; career choice; engineering; science based occupations; science education; student recruitment; technology; university admission; womens education; womens employment**

Durham University

0506

School of Education, Leazes Road, Durham DH1 1TA
0191 374 2000

Breet, F. Ms; *Supervisors*: Byram, M. Prof.; Thompson, L. Ms

Verbal interaction in mathematics lessons in four secondary schools in Anglophone Cameroon

ABSTRACT: The study examines the role of classroom language in the learning mathematics through English as a second language. Teachers of English and mathematics will be trained to work together and change classroom practices. Consequences for children's learning will be monitored.

STATUS: Sponsored project

SOURCE OF GRANT: Overseas Development Administration

DATE OF RESEARCH: 1990-1993

KEYWORDS: **cameroon; cross curricular approach; english - second language; language of instruction; mathematics education**

0507

School of Education, Leazes Road, Durham DH1 1TA
0191 374 2000

Abu-Jalala, F. Mrs; *Supervisor*: Byram, M. Prof.

The cultural dimension of English as a Foreign Language in the Arabian Gulf States

ABSTRACT: The research aims to examine the possibility of introducing English as a foreign language (EFL) together with its western culture in an Arabic/Islamic culture, and to what extent. The study falls into two branches. Firstly, investigating the experts' (university staff, English language Inspectors, the curriculum planning department and teachers) opinion using the 'Delphi Technique', questionnaire method. Secondly, pupils at the secondary stage are involved in interviews and questionnaires to give their opinions about the same issue. The size of the sample is governed by the size of the population of teachers and pupils - this will include English language staff in secondary schools and the University of Qatar, and secondary school pupils.

STATUS: Sponsored project

SOURCE OF GRANT: British Council in Doha £1,700

DATE OF RESEARCH: 1989-1993

KEYWORDS: arab states; english - second language; second language teaching

0508

School of Education, Leazes Road, Durham DH1 1TA
0191 374 2000

Byram, M. Prof.

Culture and civilisation studies for advanced language learners - an experiment in French and English schools

ABSTRACT: The purpose of the research is to develop curricula, teaching and assessment methods for advanced language learning with reference to cultural studies, i.e. acquiring knowledge and understanding of the way of life and thinking of a foreign people and country. The research takes place in England and France and is based on existing approaches to teaching culture at GCE 'A' level and Baccalaureat. The design involves, in both countries, a team of teachers and researchers who develop, operate and evaluate an experimental curriculum and assessment. The curriculum has two main emphases: that learners should acquire knowledge and understanding of selected dimension of French/English culture (defined as above); and that learners should acquire the research tools - largely those of ethnography - to carry out their own investigations of a foreign culture. The cooperation of teams working in parallels in France (at the institut National de Recherche Pedagogique) and in England provides for mutual information on research and development methods, on teaching techniques and on evaluation. The report will include, as well as a description of the research process, a specimen curriculum and materials to illustrate the principles underpinning the experiment.

STATUS: Sponsored project

SOURCE OF GRANT: Leverhulme Trust £90,700

DATE OF RESEARCH: 1990-1993

KEYWORDS: comparative education; cultural education; educational materials; second language learning; teaching methods

0509

School of Education, Leazes Road, Durham DH1 1TA
0191 374 2000

Qattous, K. Mr; *Supervisor*: Byram, M. Prof.

English language teaching - an evaluation of an industrial training programme

ABSTRACT: The English for Specific Purposes (ESP) course for workers in the Aramco petroleum company will be analysed and evaluated as an example of programme development and ESP in industrial settings.

STATUS: Individual research

DATE OF RESEARCH: 1988-1993

KEYWORDS: arab states; english - second language; english for specific purposes; programme evaluation

0510

School of Education, Leazes Road, Durham DH1 1TA
0191 374 2000

Byram, M. Prof.

Education for international understanding through foreign language teaching: a German - British collaborative project

ABSTRACT: The purpose of the project is to investigate the contribution of foreign language teaching to international understanding through the images of a country purveyed in language teaching. The focus is on the images purveyed by textbooks for teaching English in Germany and German in England. The design involves a team of teachers and researchers at the Universities of Durham and Braunschweig (Germany). Working in German-English pairs, the teams analyse the images of German-English life portrayed in textbooks for secondary schools according to criteria including representativity, accuracy, realism and appropriateness to learners. Each textbook analysis includes a detailed account of the content of the book as well as an evaluation. The project also involves theoretical development of

criteria for evaluation and discussion of the relationship between language teaching and teaching for international understanding or 'politische Erziehurig'.

PUBLISHED MATERIAL: DOYE, P. (Ed). (1990). Grossbritannien: seine Darstellung in duetschen Schulbuchern fur den Englischunterricht. Frankfurt: Deisterweg.

STATUS: Sponsored project

SOURCE OF GRANT: Durham University £2,000; British Council £2,800

DATE OF RESEARCH: 1990-1993

KEYWORDS: cultural awareness; english - second language; german; modern language studies; textbook evaluation

0511

School of Education, Leazes Road, Durham DH1 1TA
0191 374 2000

Stockdale, C. Mr; *Supervisor*: French, M. Mr

The Mechanics Institution movement in the North East of England

ABSTRACT: This research looks at the history of the development of the Mechanics Institutions in the North East of England between 1820 and 1902. It includes comparisons of contemporary and recent literature about the Movement. The Movement's activities will be evaluated within the context of the social and economic climate of the period, together with the legacy of educational, literary and social development in terms of failure and success. The research includes consultation of contemporary records existing within the region and also those of institutions in other parts of the country. Standard texts have been used to support the political, social, economic and cultural background against which the Movement evolved.

STATUS: Individual research

DATE OF RESEARCH: 1990-1993

KEYWORDS: adult education; educational history; mechanics institutes

0512

School of Education, Leazes Road, Durham DH1 1TA
0191 374 2000

Morrison, K. Mr; *Supervisor*: Gilliland, J. Mr

Developing emancipatory curricula in primary schools

ABSTRACT: The study critiques the work of Jurgen Habermas and indicates how it may be used to inform a debate on developing emancipation through primary school curricula. Issues in the sociology of knowledge are addressed which bridge the gap between Habermasian theory and school curricula. A case study of the National Curriculum of England and Wales is undertaken, focussing particularly on cross-curricular issues. A short empirical research is undertaken to attempt to complete an analysis of the contribution of Habermas to curriculum theory and practice.

PUBLISHED MATERIAL: MORRISON, K. (1989). 'Bringing progressivism into a critical theory of education', British Journal of Sociology of Education, Vol 10, No 1, pp.3-18.

STATUS: Individual research

DATE OF RESEARCH: 1990-1993

KEYWORDS: educational theories; primary school curriculum

0513

School of Education, Leazes Road, Durham DH1 1TA
0191 374 2000

Mahmoud, T. Mr; *Supervisor*: Galloway, D. Prof.

Making efficient use of microcomputers in teaching mathematics to gifted children in the Jordanian primary schools

ABSTRACT: The study offers a critical examination of concepts of giftedness, in the context of mathematics. It presents a framework for the development of computer based programmes of individualized education for the mathematically gifted. It tests the framework by pilot studies in a sample of schools in Jordan.

STATUS: Individual research

DATE OF RESEARCH: 1989-1993

KEYWORDS: computer uses in education; gifted; individualised methods; information technology; jordan; mathematics; primary education

0514

School of Education, Leazes Road, Durham DH1 1TA
0191 374 2000

Aubrey, C. Ms

An investigation of teachers' mathematical subject knowledge and the processes of instruction in reception classes (phase 2)

ABSTRACT: Using the applicants' existing data on children's informal mathematical knowledge as the basis of a framework for analysing teachers' pedagogical subject knowledge, the aim is to explore the coordination and utilisation of teacher and pupil knowledge in the complexities of reception classrooms. The project will follow a cohort of children through their first year in school to investigate the learning and teaching. Classroom processes will be documented by recording discourse occurring during activities and by observing teachers' structure and management of mathematical content, children's behaviour and response, and roles of teacher and pupil as learning progresses. By these means it is hoped to establish goals and processes associated with teaching and learning early years mathematics.

PUBLISHED MATERIAL: AUBREY, C. (1993). 'An investigation of the mathematical knowledge and competencies which young children bring into school', British Educational Research Journal, Vol 19, No 1, pp.27-41. A full list of publications is available from the researcher.

STATUS: Sponsored project

SOURCE OF GRANT: Economic and Social Research Council £34,690

DATE OF RESEARCH: 1992-1993

KEYWORDS: early childhood education; infant school teachers; mathematics education; reception classes

0515

School of Education, Leazes Road, Durham DH1 1TA
0191 374 2000

Benna, I. Mrs; Supervisors: Byram, M. Prof.; Davies, C. Dr

Motivation of women to higher education in northern Nigeria

ABSTRACT: The level of education attained by a society is an important indicator of its degree of development. In most societies, educational policies are designed to give all citizens the right and opportunity to education regardless of sex, social status, religion or ethnic origin. Despite this equal right, in Nigeria, the proportion of educated women when compared to their male counterparts is significantly lower. This situation is even worse at the level of higher education. Some of the reasons for this are socio-economic and others are cultural. The main focus of this study is to find out the extent to which the female population of northern Nigeria has attained education higher than the secondary school level, and what factors motivate them to acquire such education. The study also aims to identify those areas of specialisation which tend to attract women when they opt for higher education and why these areas more than others are attractive to them. The main instruments for the collection of data for the study are indepth interview and structured questionnaire which will be administered to sample respondents from among women graduates, and students of institutions of higher learning in northern Nigeria. It is hoped that the results of this study will make some useful input, not only at the policy formulation level, but also at the policy implementation level. The findings could also be used to enhance those factors that encourage women to go for higher education, and could suggest measures that would encourage them to study areas which have, so far, proved unattractive to them.

STATUS: Individual research

DATE OF RESEARCH: 1994-continuing

KEYWORDS: higher education; nigeria; womens education

0516

School of Education, Leazes Road, Durham DH1 1TA
0191 374 2000

Makinde, S. Mr; Supervisors: McGuinness, J. Mr; Grace, G. Prof.

Black supplementary schools as alternative educational provision: a study in community response to racism

ABSTRACT: The majority of black children in Britain attend mainstream schools that have their background, development and structures based on class, status and power. These are characterised by the inequalities that exist when addressing the issues that relate to black children, and in the schools' relationships with black children and the community. The aim of this study is to investigate the perceptions of black children, parents, teachers and the community and the nature of relationship that exists between them. British education has used the inequalities that exist within the system to categorise black children as underachievers, and disruptive. These categorisations have been blamed on the background of the children (i.e. home, language, attitude to school, low self-image etc). Series of educational programmes such as multicultural education, and supports, have been developed within the mainstream school to address the issue. This thesis will argue that racism (i.e. inequality in the treatment of black children) is the major factor contributing to the children remaining underachievers and that black supplementary schools is the way forward. The thesis will examine the features, origin, mission, curriculum contents and the relationships that exist within black supplementary schools in the London area. The research data will be a collection of headteachers, teachers, pupils, parents, and community accounts. Semi-structured and open-ended questions will be used through a collaborative method of questioning. The researcher will adopt his own method of analysis. The research will examine if there are any inadequacies in the provision, and explore how counselling could be used to maximise outcomes within existing limited resources.

STATUS: Individual research

DATE OF RESEARCH: 1993-1998

KEYWORDS: black achievement; black pupils; equal education; ethnic groups; racial attitudes; supplementary education

0517

School of Education, Leazes Road, Durham DH1 1TA
0191 374 2000

Morahan, M. Ms; Supervisor: Alred, G. Dr

Bullying behaviours in pre-school children

ABSTRACT: Bullying in schools has become a widely recognised problem in recent years. The problems of unreported bullying can have serious long term consequences for both the bully and the victim. Currently, research has begun to address the problem of bullying amongst very young children. Bullying behaviours have been observed in nursery children, there is evidence of unprovoked aggression in preschool children towards their peers, with no obvious reward. However, little is known about the amount or type of bullying that occurs in the nursery, and the relationship, if any, to school bullying behaviours. The aims of the research are to: 1) examine whether bullying behaviours are present in children under five; 2) assess the nature of these behaviours using systematic observation methods; and 3) evaluate the research in relation to current perspectives on bullying in schools. In order to identify the extent of bullying in preschool children, a questionnaire will be administered to the staff on their knowledge of bullying in a representative sample of local education authority (LEA) run nursery schools/units in the North East of England. To examine the nature of bullying behaviours, observations and video recordings will be made of children in a selection of nursery school settings. These observations will be categorised on the child's intent, i.e. friendly, annoying etc.

STATUS: Individual research

DATE OF RESEARCH: 1994-1997

KEYWORDS: aggression; antisocial behaviour; behaviour problems; bullying; nursery schools; preschool children; young children

0518

School of Education, Leazes Road, Durham DH1 1TA
0191 374 2000

Meng-ching, H. Miss; Supervisor: Byram, M. Prof.

Teaching English as a foreign language in the cultural dimension

ABSTRACT: The background to this project is the teaching of English as a foreign language in Taiwan's junior high school. The aims are to: 1) investigate the effect of cultural contact on the pupils' self/national identities;

2) investigate whether cultural introduction can enhance the pupils' learning interests.

STATUS: Individual research

DATE OF RESEARCH: 1994-continuing

KEYWORDS: english - second language; second language learning; taiwan

0519

School of Education, Leazes Road, Durham DH1 1TA
0191 374 2000

Merrell, C. Mrs; Henderson, B. Mr; Fraser, J. Mr; Albone, S. Mr; Jones, P. Mr; *Supervisor*: Tymms, P. Dr

Performance indicators in primary schools

ABSTRACT: The Performance Indicators in Primary Schools (PIPS) project is one of the family of information systems offered by the Curriculum, Evaluation and Management Centre (CEM Centre) at the University of Durham. The PIPS Project is designed to monitor the attainment, attitudes and progress (value-added) of children as they move through primary school. It begins with a 15-minute baseline assessment of early reading and mathematics skills conducted on an individual basis within the first seven weeks of a child entering school. Attainment in reading, mathematics (and science at Year 6) are monitored at regular intervals throughout the child's primary school years, and value-added scores are calculated. The standardised results are fed back directly into schools. They are available for monitoring progress at individual, class and school levels over annual or key stage intervals. The PIPS project has grown dramatically since it began in 1993. There are currently 4,500 schools taking part in the United Kingdom and overseas. In addition to providing valuable information to schools, the extensive amount of data which is gathered enables researchers at the CEM Centre to conduct further research. The results from some of this research are available from the CEM Centre.

PUBLISHED MATERIAL: TYMMS, P. (1997). 'Science in Primary Schools: an investigation into differences in the attainment and attitudes of pupils across schools', Research in Science & Technologies Education, Vol 15, No 2, pp.149-159. ; TYMMS, P., MERRELL, C. & HENDERSON, B. (1997). 'The first year at school: a quantitative invetigation of the attainment and progress of pupils', Educational Research and Evaluation 1997, Vol 3, No 2, pp.101-118. ; TYMMS, P. (1998). 'Baseline assessment, value-added and the prediction of reading', Journal of Research in Reading, Vol 22, No 1, pp.27-36. ; TYMMS, P. (1998). 'Accountability and quality assurance'. In: RICHARDS, C. & TAYLOR, P. (Eds). How shall we school our children?: Future of Primary Education. London: Falmer Press. ; TYMMS, P. (1999). Baseline assessment and monitoring in primary schools: achievements, attitudes and value-added indicators. London: David Fulton.

STATUS: Sponsored project

SOURCE OF GRANT: participating schools

DATE OF RESEARCH: 1993-continuing

KEYWORDS: academic achievement; baseline assessment; educational quality; mathematics achievement; performance indicators; primary education; reading achievement; school effectiveness; value added

0520

School of Education, Leazes Road, Durham DH1 1TA
0191 374 2000
Durham University, Business School, Mill Hill Lane, Durham DH1 3LB
0191 374 2268

Iredale, N. Mrs; *Supervisor*: Palmer, J. Dr

A comparative study of the values, attitudes and beliefs held by primary school teachers and industry in the area of work-related education

ABSTRACT: Over the last decade there has been an enormous growth of work-related initiatives in education. The thrust has been substantially upon secondary schools but a number of programmes have targeted primary schools. There is, however, no clear evidence as to the impact which has been made although there are indications that certain pressures upon schools have proved influential. Casual observation would suggest, however, that work-related education remains peripheral in many schools and appears to be fragmented even when visible. A better understanding of attitudes to, and values placed upon this work by teachers and industrialists alike would enable schools and industry to respond in a considered and useful fashion to these external pressures. The proposed study aims to provide: 1) insight into the attitudes and beliefs of teachers engaged in work-related education and the impact this might have on their approach; 2) an analysis of influencing factors on the formation of these beliefs (external and internal to school); 3) insight into the views of those who in the corporate business sector are charged with developing strategies toward the education sector; 4) understanding of the process by which the work-related initiatives are developed; 5) understanding of the specific outcomes sought from work in the primary school by both sides. A preliminary review of the literature to date reveals the paucity of knowledge in this area. It is hoped that this thesis will provide original information not only to attitudes, values and beliefs, but to the processes which influence them.

STATUS: Individual research

DATE OF RESEARCH: 1997-continuing

KEYWORDS: business; industry and education; primary education; primary school teachers; teacher attitudes; work related curriculum

0521

School of Education, Leazes Road, Durham DH1 1TA
0191 374 2000
Hull University, Department of Education, Hull HU6 7RX
01482 346311

Warburton, P. Mr; Sleap, M. Mr; Cale, L. Mrs

Physical activity patterns of primary school children

ABSTRACT: There is now wide recognition of the positive effect regular exercise can have on our health. The main aim of this observation study is to monitor the exercise activity levels of children aged between 5 and 11 years. This observation study forms part of a wider evaluation of the Happy Heart Resource Materials which was undertaken between February 1991 and June 1992. The method of observation to be used will be based on a paper presented by O'Hara and Colleagues (1988) which validated a minute by minute observation procedure against heart rate. Between 60 and 70 children were observed in the spring of 1991 and again during the same period in 1992. Half of the children will act as a control group whilst the other half will receive regular input from the Happy Heart Resource Materials. The children will be observed both in school and at home. The results from the study will be used to assess the impact of the Happy Heart Resource Materials with regard to possible changes in children's activity patterns.

STATUS: Sponsored project

SOURCE OF GRANT: Health Education Authority £16,000

DATE OF RESEARCH: 1990-1993

KEYWORDS: educational materials; exercise; health activities; health promotion; heart rate; physical activities; primary school pupils

0522

School of Education, Leazes Road, Durham DT1 1TA
0191 374 2000
University of Qatar, Doha, PO Box 2713, Qatar
974 83-2222

Hassan, F. Mr; *Supervisor*: Byram, M. Prof.

Sociocultural aspects of teaching English to Arabic speaking students

ABSTRACT: In foreign language learning the learner's affective variables seem to be playing a very crucial role. For example, the learner's own attitude towards learning the target language can be influenced by his/her attitudes towards the native speakers of this language and their culture. There is accumulating evidence that prejudice or active dislike diminishes motivation and interferes with learning. The attitudes of the Arab students in the Gulf towards the English language people and culture have never been investigated before. In doing so, the present research aims to find out: (a) if these students come into the English language class with already acquired perceptions of the target language, people and culture and what these perceptions are; (b) what the students' attitudes towards the English people and culture are and whether these tend to be stereotypical; (c) if there is an association between these perceptions and attitudes and if the association is significant; and (d) investigate the relationship between the students' attitudes and perceptions on the one hand, and the learners' achievement in the target language on the other. the study sample consists of 60 male and 120 female students starting their first year in Qatar University. The research tools are: self-report writing, questionnaires, interviews, semantic differential tests and results of final achievement examinations kept in the university records.

STATUS: Individual research

DATE OF RESEARCH: 1989-1993

KEYWORDS: **arab states; cultural awareness; english - second language; foreign culture; native speakers; second language learning**

Economic Research Services

0523

Crestina House, Archbold Terrace, Newcastle upon Tyne NE2 1DB
01912 121010

Burge, K. Mr

Evaluation of Modern Apprenticeships: survey of employers

ABSTRACT: This project is evaluating the impact of Modern Apprenticeships (MA) on employers, including the effect on their recruitment and training practices and their views on the operation of MAs. A similar survey was undertaken early in the life of MAs (published as RS 53); a new survey was required to examine the impact on employers once MAs had been extended to new sectors and bedded down. A telephone survey of 1500 employers is being carried out, together with face-to-face interviews with 200 employers to explore issues in more detail. In addition, telephone interviews will be carried out with 100 employers not involved in the initiative. The study will look at what difference MA makes to the employers, and will explore issues relating to implementing the frameworks. It will examine the extent to which MA has increased the supply and quality of intermediate level skills.

PUBLISHED MATERIAL: HASLUCK, C., HOGARTH, T., MAGUIRE, M. & PITCHER, J. (1997). Modern apprenticeships: a survey of employers. The effect of Modern Apprenticeships on employers' training practices and the availability of NVQ Level 3 training. DFEE Research Studies RS53. London: The Stationery Office.

STATUS: Sponsored project

SOURCE OF GRANT: Department for Education and Employment £67,380

DATE OF RESEARCH: 1998-1998

KEYWORDS: **apprenticeships; employer attitudes; employers; employment; modern apprenticeships; youth employment**

Edinburgh University

0524

Centre for Educational Sociology, 7 Buccleuch Place, Edinburgh EH8 9LW
0131 650 4186

Paterson, L. Dr; *Supervisor*: McPherson, A. Prof.

The efficient use of talent in the expansion of Scottish higher education

ABSTRACT: The object of the research is to investigate the scope for exploiting untapped talent among young people (aged under 20) as a result of the fundamental changes affecting Scottish higher education.

PUBLISHED MATERIAL: A full list of publications is available from the Research Administrator

STATUS: Sponsored project

SOURCE OF GRANT: The Leverhulme Trust £25,632

DATE OF RESEARCH: 1992-1993

KEYWORDS: **access to education; educational change; further education; higher education; sixteen to nineteen education**

0525

Centre for Educational Sociology, 7 Buccleuch Place, Edinburgh EH8 9LW
0131 650 4186

Raffe, D. Prof.; Howieson, C. Ms

The effectiveness of new curriculum models for initial vocational training: Phase 2 - Partnership on modularisation

ABSTRACT: To provide information and analysis to support policy makers in European Community member states who seek to pursue policy objectives in initial vocational training through modularisation.

PUBLISHED MATERIAL: A full list of publications is available from the Research Administrator.

STATUS: Sponsored project

SOURCE OF GRANT: European Community: Petra Programme £74

DATE OF RESEARCH: 1992-1993

KEYWORDS: **comparative education; curriculum development; european union; modular courses; vocational education**

0526

Centre for Educational Sociology, 7 Buccleuch Place, Edinburgh EH8 9LW
0131 650 4186

McPherson, A. Prof.; Raffe, D. Prof.; Bagnall, G. Dr; Lamb, J. Dr; Middleton, L. Ms

A survey of young people in the Central Region

ABSTRACT: To conduct a 10% survey of young people in the Scottish Central Region.

PUBLISHED MATERIAL: A full list of publications is available from the Research Administrator.

STATUS: Sponsored project

SOURCE OF GRANT: Central Regional Council £8,365

DATE OF RESEARCH: 1992-1993

KEYWORDS: **school leavers; school to work transition; sixteen to nineteen education; surveys; youth**

0527

Centre for Educational Sociology, 7 Buccleuch Place, Edinburgh EH8 9LW
0131 650 4186

McPherson, A. Prof.; Raffe, D. Prof.; Bagnall, G. Dr; Lamb, J. Dr; Middleton, L. Ms

A survey of Strathclyde 16-19 year olds

ABSTRACT: To conduct a survey of a 10% sample of school leavers from Strathclyde Region secondary schools.

PUBLISHED MATERIAL: A full list of publications is available from the Research Administrator.

STATUS: Sponsored project

SOURCE OF GRANT: Strathclyde Regional Council £30,000

DATE OF RESEARCH: 1992-1993

KEYWORDS: **school leavers; school to work transition; sixteen to nineteen education; surveys; youth**

0528

Centre for Educational Sociology, 7 Buccleuch Place, Edinburgh EH8 9LW
0131 650 4186

Lamb, J. Dr; Smart, C. Mr; Inder, R. Dr

Access to distributed data for statistical information and analysis

ABSTRACT: This is a collaborative project with: University of Edinburgh; the Office for National Statistics; DESAN Market Research, Amsterdam; University of Ulster; Central Statistics Office, Cork, Ireland; Statistics Finland and Athens University. At National Statistical Institutes (NSIs), statistical information is held in a variety of ways and it is not practical to convert existing practice to the latest technology. This project aims to use distributed database techniques and World Wide Web (WWW) technology in order to facilitate more effective access to statistical data by Europe's research and policy community. The project aims to provide a facility that allows an NSI to make available with minimum effort, whatever data and metadata it currently has, under its own control. The central model exploits developments in statistical theory to construct a client/server architecture in which computation is carried out at a local level, and partially processed statistical queries are passed to a global model which combines them. The project also exploits Web technology, particularly the indexing of free text metadata, and the use of 'active agents' (such as the program Java) to interface with users. It uses data from the Dutch and Scottish school leavers surveys to test the feasibility of comparable educational data from 2 different countries in an open environment such as the Web.

PUBLISHED MATERIAL: LAMB, J.M., BELL, D., MCCLEAN, S., MURTAGH, F., BURNHILL, P., HATZOPOULOS, M. & RUTJES, J.J. (1997). 'Using the Internet to analyse statistical data in a distributed environment'. In: EUROSTAT. (Eds). New techniques and technologies for statistics II. Oxford: IOS Press.

STATUS: Sponsored project

SOURCE OF GRANT: European Union (ESPRIT) £1,388,000

DATE OF RESEARCH: 1997-continuing

KEYWORDS: comparative analysis; databases; information systems; information systems; international educational exchange; internet; netherlands; school leavers; school to work transition; scotland; sixteen to nineteen education; statistical data; statistics; surveys

0529

Centre for Educational Sociology, 7 buccleuch Place, Edinburgh EH8 9LW
0131 650 4186

Lamb, J. Dr; Brannen, K. Mrs; Fairgrieve, J. Mrs

Integrated documentation and retrieval environment for statistical aggregates

ABSTRACT: This is a collaborative project with: University of Edinburgh; Vienna University; Athens University; University of Ulster and DESAN Market Research, Amsterdam. The objective is to design and implement an integrated statistical information and data processing system targeted at the practical needs of National Statistics Institutes and similar offices. The main emphasis will be put on easy and powerful data dissemination capabilities as well as on support in data retrieval, data aggregation and export of data to third party systems. The project uses advanced meta-information methodologies for processing data descriptions for both primary (observation) data and secondary (aggregated) data. The research will focus on the development of a unified metadata language supporting harmonisation of national data at supranational level, and a formalised description of statistical information processing over the whole life cycle of statistical data. It uses data and metadata (complementary information about the raw data) from the Dutch and Scottish school leavers surveys to test the feasibility of developing a harmonised and accurate view of school leavers in a European setting.

PUBLISHED MATERIAL: FROESCHL, K.A. (1997). Metadata management in statistical information processing. Vienna: Springer Computer Science. ; LAMB, J.M., BRANNEN, K., PAGRACH, K. & RUTJES, H. (1997). 'Quality frames for a European survey: a new approach to modelling transitions in youth'. In: WERQUIN, P., BREEN, R. & PLANAS, J. (Eds). Youth transitions in Europe: themes and evidence. Marseilles: Centre d'Etudes et de Researches sur les Qualifications (CEREQ).

STATUS: Sponsored project

SOURCE OF GRANT: European Union (ESPRIT) £1,500,000

DATE OF RESEARCH: 1996-continuing

KEYWORDS: comparative education; databases; europe; international educational exchange; netherlands; school leavers; school to work transition; scotland; sixteen to nineteen education; statistical data; statistics; surveys

0530

Centre for Educational Sociology, 7 Buccleuch Place, Edinburgh EH8 9LW
0131 650 4186

Raffe, D. Prof.; Croxford, L. Dr; Martin, C. Mr; Brannen, K. Mrs

A 'home international' comparison of 14-19 education and training systems in the UK

ABSTRACT: UK education and training policy has increasingly tried to learn from overseas experience, but other countries' education systems, and their economic and social contexts, are often too different for lessons to be easily drawn. Several commentators have argued that UK policymakers

may learn more by comparing the 4 territories of the UK, where the differences in education systems and their contexts are much smaller. For such learning to take place, we need to understand both the differences and the similarities among these systems. However, our comparative knowledge of the UK education and training systems owes more to myth and political rhetoric than to rigorous empirical analysis. There has been only limited and fragmentary research comparing the 4 UK systems, and most of this has been descriptive rather than analytical or explanatory. Cross-national research in education and training has focused on nation-states, especially large ones, and has seldom addressed the issues posed by comparisons of different national systems within a state. The project will fill a gap in the research by conducting a systematic comparison of England, Scotland, and (as far as the data permit) Wales and Northern Ireland. It will focus on the pathways followed by young people from 14 to 19 years, and on the ways these pathways interact with the institutional context of education and training. It will construct and analyse an integrated dataset from existing youth cohort surveys.

STATUS: Sponsored project

SOURCE OF GRANT: Economic and Social Research Council £133,975

DATE OF RESEARCH: 1997-continuing

KEYWORDS: cohort analysis; comparative education; educational administration; educational policy; school leavers; school to work transition; secondary education; sixteen to nineteen education; training; vocational education

0531

Centre for Educational Sociology, 7 Buccleuch Place, Edinburgh EH8 9LW
0131 650 4186

Martin, C. Mr; Raffe, D. Prof.

Vocational training and labour market transitions

ABSTRACT: This research is in association with 3 other European research institutes led by the Economic and Social Research Institute, Dublin. The study will link data from 4 national surveys of school leavers in order to compare processes of labour market entry, with particular attention to early leavers and those at greatest risk of exclusion. Its main objectives are to: 1) devise a conceptual framework which describes the nature of the institutional relationships between education/training and labour market entry among young people in Ireland, Scotland, the Netherlands and France; 2) construct a comparative database on labour market transitions among young people one year after leaving full-time education in Ireland, Scotland, the Netherlands and France; 3) generate and test hypotheses about the likely effects (and effectiveness) of varying institutional mechanisms on processes of labour market exclusion among young people.

STATUS: Sponsored project

SOURCE OF GRANT: European Union (LEONARDO programme)

DATE OF RESEARCH: 1996-1998

KEYWORDS: comparative education; employment; france; ireland; labour market; netherlands; school leavers; school to work transition; scotland; training; unemployment; vocational education; youth employment; youth unemployment

0532

Centre for Educational Sociology, 7 Buccleuch Place, Edinburgh EH8 9LW
0131 650 4186

Howieson, C. Ms; Raffe, D. Prof.

Strategies for post-16 education in Europe

ABSTRACT: This research by the Centre for Educational Sociology at Edinburgh University is in association with 10 other European research institutes led by the University of Jyvaskyla, Finland. The project aims at promoting the parity of esteem for initial vocational education by finding new strategies linking vocational and academic/general education and working life in post-16 education and training. The analyses cover the upper secondary level of educational systems, encompassing study programmes and teaching/learning arrangements in 8 European education systems (Austria, England, Finland, France, Germany, Norway, Scotland and Sweden). The purposes of the project are to: 1) analyse the different European strategies for combining vocational and academic/general studies and working life; 2) describe models of linking school-based and on-the-job training; and 3) promote new experiments and exchange programmes in Europe. Data will be gathered and summarised by means of: comparative analyses of national strategies; local networking and evaluating the experiences of pilot schools; and collaborative writing processes. The results and recommendations of the project will be published and disseminated to policymakers, researchers, teachers, headteachers and social partners internationally.

PUBLISHED MATERIAL: LASONEN, J. (Ed). (1996). Reforming upper-secondary education in Europe. Publications Series B, No 92. Finland: University of Jyvaskyla, Institute for Educational Research. ; RAFFE, D. (1997). 'Higher still in European perspective', Scottish Educational Review, Vol 29, No 2, pp. 121-133. ; LASONEN, J. & YOUNG, M. (1998). Parity of esteem in European post 16 education. Finland: University of Jyvaskyla, Institute for Educational Research.

STATUS: Sponsored project

SOURCE OF GRANT: European Union (LEONARDO programme) £17,262

DATE OF RESEARCH: 1995-1997

KEYWORDS: **academic education; academic vocational divide; comparative education; europe; international educational exchange; sixteen to nineteen education; training; vocational education**

0533

Centre for Educational Sociology, 7 Buccleuch Place, Edinburgh EH8 9LW
0131 650 4186

Raffe, D. Prof.; Brannen, K. Mrs; Biggart, A. Mr

A comparative analysis of transitions from education to work in Europe (CATEWE)

ABSTRACT: Comparative analysis of transitions from education to work in Europe (CATEWE) will analyse the transition from education to work in a comparative European perspective. The objective of this research is to develop a more satisfactory framework for understanding transitions in different European systems and to use this framework to analyse the factors affecting success and failure in education/training outcomes and labour market integration. There will be a major focus on delineating the institutional embeddedness of these transition processes, thus enhancing comparative knowledge on the operation of different linkages between the education and training system and the labour market. The research will have a dynamic perspective, analysing changes in transition processes over time and their relationship to changes in institutional and labour market conditions. The main data source for the project will be the school leavers' surveys in Ireland, Scotland, France and the Netherlands. These analyses will be enriched and extended by comparative analyses of the Labour Force Surveys for a wider range of European countries. Together, comparative analyses of these two sources of data will provide a strong empirical basis for studying the process of initial labour market entry, the factors influencing successful integration or exclusion, and the interaction of these factors with institutional and societal variables. CATEWE will have a direct input into policy development on transitions through its contribution to the Organisation for Economic Co-operation and Development's (OECD) Thematic Review of the Transition from Initial Education to Working Life, and through national and European Union (EU)-level policy channels.

STATUS: Sponsored project

SOURCE OF GRANT: European Commission (TSER Programme) £1.2 million

DATE OF RESEARCH: 1998-continuing

KEYWORDS: **comparative education; europe; school leavers; school to work transition; training; vocational education**

0534

Centre for Educational Sociology, 7 Buccleuch Place, Edinburgh EH8 9LW
0131 650 4186

Lamb, J. Dr; Slack, R. Dr; Van Der Kuyl, T. Mr

Educational multimedia in compulsory school: from pedagogical assessment to product assessment

ABSTRACT: This project aims to map the dynamics of multimedia use in an educational context and to generate an on-line database of multimedia applications for use by teachers and suppliers of educational multimedia.

The project brings together teachers, students, teacher trainers and developers across Europe in an investigation of the potentialities of multimedia products to inform practice both within the classroom and in the development of materials. The project is carried out in conjunction with the Research Centre of Social Sciences in the Faculty of Social Sciences and the Scottish Interactive Technology Centre in the Faculty of Education. This project is a new area for the Centre of Educational Sociology (CES), and provides an excellent opportunity to pursue the study of the use of Information and Communication Technology (ICT) in teaching and learning, and of collaborating with colleagues in the Faculty of Education.

STATUS: Sponsored research

SOURCE OF GRANT: European Union Educational Multimedia Taskforce £724,482

DATE OF RESEARCH: 1998-continuing

KEYWORDS: **computer uses in education; information technology; multimedia**

0535

Centre for Educational Sociology, 7 Buccleuch Place, Edinburgh EH8 9LW
0131 650 4186

Raffe, D. Prof.; Biggart, A. Mr; Croxford, L. Dr; Howieson, C. Ms; Fairgrieve, J. Ms

OECD thematic review: the transition from initial education to working life: UK background report

ABSTRACT: The UK is one of 14 countries participating in the Organisation for Economic Cooperation and Development's (OECD) Thematic Review of the Transition from Initial Education to Working Life. The Centre for Educational Sociology was commissioned to write the Background Report for the UK, which served as the main source document for the OECD's review team which visited the UK in September 1998. The report was prepared in collaboration with York Consulting Limited, and is expected to be published on the internet. @#Status:#@ Sponsored project

SOURCE OF GRANT: Department of Education and Employment £10,000

DATE OF RESEARCH: 1998-1998

KEYWORDS: **school leavers; school to work transition; youth employment**

0536

Centre for Educational Sociology, 7 Buccleuch Place, Edinburgh EH8 9LW
0131 650 4186

Tinklin, T. Ms; Raffe, D. Prof.; Croxford, L. Dr; Biggart, A. Mr; Howieson, C. Ms; Brannen, K. Mrs; Fairgrieve, J.Ms

Scottish school leavers' survey: special studies

ABSTRACT: These studies will focus on five areas: 1) entrants to higher education; 2) high-achieving females; 3) low-achieving males; 4) entrants to government training programmes; 5) early entrants to employment. A report will be produced on the results of each study. The studies will be conducted mainly using secondary analysis of the Scottish School Leavers Surveys (SSLS) (conducted by Social and Community Planning Research (SCPR) since 1993). The SSLS is a nationally-representative survey of young people who have attended Scottish schools. Information from the surveys includes young people's family background, qualifications, experiences at school from the age of 14, routes to further education and training, and labour market destinations. They will also draw on data from the Scottish Young People's Surveys (conducted bi-annually by Centre for Educational Sociology 1977-1991), allowing analyses of trends over time in each area studied.

STATUS: Sponsored project

SOURCE OF GRANT: Scottish Office Education and Industry Department £123,486

DATE OF RESEARCH: 1998-continuing

KEYWORDS: **achievement; cohort analysis; further education; higher education; school to work transition; sex differences; sixteen to nineteen education; training; underachievement; youth employment**

0537

Centre for Educational Sociology, 7 Buccleuch Place, Edinburgh EH8 9LW
0131 650 4186
London University, Institute of Education, 20 Bedford Way, London
WC1H 0AL
0171 580 1122

Howieson, C. Ms; Raffe, D. Prof.; Spours, K. Prof.; Young, M. Prof.

Unifying academic and vocational learning: Scottish and English/Welsh approaches

ABSTRACT: Many commentators argue that the UK needs a more unified system of post-compulsory education and training which would end divisions between academic and vocational learning. In Scotland, the government's Higher Still reforms will bring existing academic and vocational courses into a unified system at 16-plus. In England and Wales the Dearing Review confirmed the importance of a 3-track system based on A-levels, General National Vocational Qualifications (GNVQs), and National Vocational Qualifications (NVQs), but proposed a number of ways to increase student choice and provide more coherence for the system as a whole. The project aims to: 1) compare approaches to unifiying academic and vocational learning in post-compulsory education and training in Scotland and in England and Wales; 2) develop the concept of a unified system; to clarify its relationship with the concept of a learning society; to explore issues in the design of unified systems; 3) develop complementary concepts and understandings of the process of unifying academic and vocational learning; and 4) engage with and reinforce the 'learning process' of policy development and implementation. Its activities include: 1) a review of research and policy debates in the UK and selected overseas countries; 2) mapping unifying initiatives and other developmetns within the context of the contrasting approaches to national policy in Scotland and in England and Wales; 3) carrying out a number of case studies to investigate responses to national policy at different levels and the resolution of issues likely to be critical to implementing a unified system; and 4) preparing seminars and working papers for participants and other users of the research.

PUBLISHED MATERIAL: HOWIESON, C. (1997). 'Unifying academic and vocational learning: the state of the debate in England and Scotland', Journal of Education and Work, Vol 10, No 1, pp.5-35. ; YOUNG, M., SPOURS, K., HOWIESON, C. & RAFFE, D. (1997). 'Unifying academic and vocational learning and the idea of a learning society', Journal of Education Policy, Vol 12, No 6, pp.527-537. ; RAFFE, D., SPOURS, K., YOUNG, M. & HOWIESON, C. (1998). 'The unification of post-compulsory education: towards a conceptual framework', British Journal of Educational Studies, Vol 46, No 2, pp.169-187. ; SPOURS, K. & YOUNG, M. (1998). '14-19 education: the legacy opportunities and challenges', Oxford Review of Education, Vol 24, No 1, pp.83-97. ; RAFFE, D., HOWIESON, C., SPOURS, K, & YOUNG, M. 'Issues in a 'home international' comparison of policy strategies: the experience of the unified learning project'. In: COFFIELD, F.J. (Ed), Why's the beer always stronger up north? The pleasures and pains of comparative research. Bristol: Policy Press.

STATUS: Sponsored project

SOURCE OF GRANT: ESRC The Learning Society Programme £154,760

DATE OF RESEARCH: 1996-1998

KEYWORDS: **academic education; academic vocational divide; qualifications; sixteen to nineteen education; unified learning; vocational education**

0538

Centre for Educational Sociology, 7 Buccleuch Place, Edinburgh EH8 9LW
0131 650 4186
Strathclyde University, Centre for Careers Education and Guidance, Jordanhill Campus, Southbrae Drive, Glasgow G13 1PP
0141 950 3000

Howieson, C. Ms; Semple, S. Ms

The effectiveness of Careers Services

ABSTRACT: The research will map Careers Service provision across Scotland and develop a typology of Careers Services with which to analyse variation in provision. It will assess the effectiveness of different methods in meeting the needs of young people, parents, employers and training providers and consider the extent to which Careers Service provision is integrated with other provision. It will analyse the outcomes of Careers Service inputs for young people, develop and apply measures of impact, utility and service effectiveness and identify ways in which Careers Services can improve provision. A sample of 5 careers companies will be selected for further study. Within these areas surveys will be conducted with young people, employers, and training providers. A programme of interviews will be carried out with Careers Service staff, teachers, college staff, parents, local enterprise companies, education authority and Careers Service Board representatives, and national employers/training organisations.

STATUS: Sponsored project

SOURCE OF GRANT: Scottish Office Education and Industry Department £105,623

DATE OF RESEARCH: 1997-continuing

KEYWORDS: **careers service; scotland; vocational guidance**

0539

Centre for Educational Sociology, 7 Buccleuch Place, Edinburgh EH8 9LW
0131 650 4186
Strathclyde University, Department of Statistics and Modelling Science, Glasgow G1 1XQ
0141 552 4400

McPherson, A. Prof.; Robertson, C. Dr

Schools' effects on attainment in school and higher education

ABSTRACT: The project will show whether attainment in higher education is influenced by the student's school, and whether any such effect can be explained by characteristics of that school, including the school's effectiveness at secondary level.

PUBLISHED MATERIAL: A full list of publications is available from the Research Administrator.

STATUS: Sponsored project

SOURCE OF GRANT: Economic and Social Research Council £26,665

DATE OF RESEARCH: 1992-1993

KEYWORDS: **academic achievement; higher education; school effectiveness; secondary education**

0540

Department of Mathematics and Statistics, James Clerk Maxwell Building, The King's Buildings, Mayfield Road, Edinburgh EH9 3JZ
0131 650 1000

Jackman, S. Mrs; *Supervisor*: Searl, J. Dr

Extended exercises in undergraduate mathematics education for non-specialists

ABSTRACT: The often-reported failure of students to apply their mathematical knowledge in contextualised problems will be addressed. A series of tasks will be devised (together with assessment schemes) and evaluated. A mixture of illuminative and survey evaluation will be used. The project will involve some 1,500 first year students at three Scottish universities.

STATUS: Sponsored project

SOURCE OF GRANT: Enterprise in Higher Education

DATE OF RESEARCH: 1994-1997

KEYWORDS: **higher education; mathematical applications; mathematics education**

0541

Department of Social Anthropology, Old College, South Bridge, Edinburgh EH8 9YL
0131 650 1000
Cambridge University, Department of Social Anthropology, New Museum Site, Free School Lane, Cambridge
01223 334599

De La Gorgendiere, L. Dr; *Supervisor*: Hart, J. Dr

Education and development in Ghana (an Asante village study, linked to education and development more generally in Ghana)

ABSTRACT: The aim of the research was to examine the link between education and the process of development in Ghana. The research covered developmental issues in contemporary Ghana and sought to understand the link between education and the process of development. Through an indepth village study, the research concluded that the effects of out-migration for the purposes of seeking further education, employment, and/or extending networks tended to have a negative effect on rural development. Education becomes a means of 'individual' development and advancement, not a means of 'mobilization of the collectivity' for development. The problems of the educational system in Ghana are vast and not readily explainable outside the context of the current socio-political situation. The policies for education that have been shaped by the implementation of structural reforms to the economy (International Monetary Fund/World Bank) have served to push formal education out of the reach of many through the institution of 'cost-recovery measures', thus widening the gap between those who can or cannot afford to educate their children.

STATUS: Individual research

DATE OF RESEARCH: 1990-1993

KEYWORDS: **developing countries; development education; ghana**

0542

Equity Studies and Special Education, Patterson Land, Holyrood Road, Edinburgh EH8 8AO
0131 650 1000

Nisbet, P. Mr; Spooner, R. Dr; Millar, S. Ms; Aitken, S. Dr; Wilson, A Mr; Arthur, E. Ms; Whittaker, E.Mr

Supportive writing technology

ABSTRACT: Information technology has much to offer children with writing difficulties. There are a wide range of different tools available and this project is comparing word processors and computer-based systems providing speech output, spell-checking, word bank and word prediction, and voice recognition. Spell-checker performance was evaluated using a set of 150 mis-spelled words, representing the type of errors made by writers with spelling difficulties. Word prediction programs were tested using three sample texts. The outcome of the research is a book, entitled "Supportive writing technology" which gives the results of the analysis and advice on using the tools within classroom situations.

STATUS: Sponsored project

SOURCE OF GRANT: Scottish Office Education and Industry Department £16,252

DATE OF RESEARCH: 1997-continuing

KEYWORDS: **computer uses in education; dyslexia; information technology; spellchecker; word processing; writing difficulties**

0543

Equity Studies and Special Education, Patterson Land, Holyrood Road, Edinburgh EH8 8AO
0131 650 1000

Nisbet, P. Mr; Spooner, R. Dr; MacFarlane, P. Mr; Millar, S. Ms; Aitken, S. Dr

Development of word prediction and phonetic spellchecker software

ABSTRACT: This project will research and develop a word prediction and phonetic spell-checker for low-cost 'Windows CE' portable computers, designed for use in schools. The word prediction component is based upon an existing system already available for desktop computers. The spellchecker will investigate a novel algorithm developed by Roger Spooner, which involves converting the written error into component phonemes, and then comparing probabilities of possible phonetic errors.

STATUS: Sponsored project

SOURCE OF GRANT: Scottish Office Education and Industry Department

DATE OF RESEARCH: 1999-continuing

KEYWORDS: **computer uses in education; dyslexia; information technology; spellchecker; word processing; writing difficulties**

0544

Equity Studies and Special Education, Patterson Land, Holyrood Road, Edinburgh EH8 8AO
0131 650 1000

Millar, S. Ms; Larcher, J. Dr

'Freestyle' communication application development

ABSTRACT: This project will develop a powerful dynamic screen based communication application for primary-school aged children with severe communication and physical impairments. The system will utilise both text (with word prediction) and symbol based storage strategies, and will be implemented with 'Freestyle' portable Macintosh computer. In order to integrate communication with the device into the classroom environment, the application will provide both functional communication content, and curriculum appropriate vocabulary. The system will be evaluated by pupils and teachers in schools in Scotland.

STATUS: Sponsored project

SOURCE OF GRANT: Scottish Office Education and Industry Department £16,160

DATE OF RESEARCH: 1999-continuing

KEYWORDS: **communication aids - for disabled; communication problems; computer uses in education; information technology; special educational needs**

0545

Faculty of Education, Moray House, Holyrood Campus, Holyrood Road, Edinburgh EH8 8AQ
0131 651 6296

Morris, J. Mr; *Supervisors*: Entwistle, N. Prof.; McPherson, A. Prof.

The work of the Scottish Council for Research in Education 1928-1993

ABSTRACT: This is a study of the Scottish Council for Research in Education which was one of the earliest research councils to be found in Europe. Its history is traced from total independence relying on voluntary but professional labour, to that of a group of professional researchers still having independence but within the bounds of a market economy. The main themes will be testing shading into assessment; outreach i.e. dissemination of findings to the teaching force and in international activity; policy where customer-contractor and even negotiated research works within a range of constraints. The methodology will be that of archive search with the Founder Institutions, the Education Institute of Scotland and the Association of Directors of Education, Scotland, and other appropriate bodies such as the Scottish Office Education Department, the Public Record Office, West Register House, Edinburgh and the archive of the Council itself. It will include taped interviews with leading Council Members and officials, past and present. Four of its five Directors and all its Chairmen for the past 40 years are still alive. The researcher has had an association with the Council, first as a subject in one of its projects in 1932 and subsequently in a variety of roles including that of assessor.

STATUS: Individual research

DATE OF RESEARCH: 1991-1993

KEYWORDS: **educational history; educational research; scotland**

0546

Faculty of Education, Moray House, Holyrood Campus, Holyrood Road, Edinburgh EH8 8AQ
0131 651 6296

Francis, E. Mrs; *Supervisor*: Perfect, H. Mr

Research on values education (ROVE)

ABSTRACT: The project is concerned with the identification of approaches to teaching and learning which are beneficial to the development of values education for students over the age of 16 years. The aim of the project is to highlight the philosophical and methodological issues which should be addressed whenever the development of a values curriculum is contemplated. The focus will be the language currently used by educationalists in curriculum guidelines and educational settings which conveys a sense of values and approaches to teaching and learning which enable values education. The enquiry is being conducted with: teachers; lecturers in teacher education and other academic disciplines; curriculum developers; and educational administrators in central and local government. A network committed to the study of values in education will be created to enhance discussion of values education in Scotland for the 16+ age group. A number of unpublished working papers are available on request from the project team.

STATUS: Sponsored project

SOURCE OF GRANT: Gordon Cook Foundation £40,000

DATE OF RESEARCH: 1991-1993

KEYWORDS: **curriculum development; sixteen to nineteen education; values education**

0547

Faculty of Education, Moray House, Holyrood Campus, Holyrood Road, Edinburgh EH8 8AQ
0131 651 6296

Diniz, F. Mr; Reid, G. Dr

Specific learning difficulties (Dyslexia) project

ABSTRACT: The aims of the research are to investigate the potential for developments in teacher education to meet the needs of those concerned about the education of children with specific learning difficulties associated with dyslexia.

STATUS: Sponsored project

SOURCE OF GRANT: Scottish Dyslexia Trust

DATE OF RESEARCH: 1990-1993

KEYWORDS: **dyslexia; learning disabilities; reading difficulties; special educational needs; teacher education**

0548

Faculty of Education, Moray House, Holyrood Campus, Holyrood Road, Edinburgh EH8 8AQ
0131 651 6296

Hamilton, J. Dr

Language medium teaching

ABSTRACT: The aim of the research is to examine the effects of language medium teaching on learner motivation and foreign language proficiency within the Scottish context.

STATUS: Sponsored project

SOURCE OF GRANT: Moray House Institute of Education

DATE OF RESEARCH: 1990-1993

KEYWORDS: **learning motivation; modern language studies; scotland; second language teaching**

0549

Faculty of Education, Moray House, Holyrood Campus, Holyrood Road, Edinburgh EH8 8AQ
0131 651 6296

Dyer, C. Dr; *Supervisors*: King, K. Prof.; Donn, G. Dr

Operation Blackboard: policy implementation in Indian elementary education

ABSTRACT: In the search to achieve universal elementary education, India's 1986 National Policy on Education initiated a qualitative improvement in elementary education. A major strategy was Operation Blackboard, a programme for upgrading physical facilities in small Indian elementary schools, which this thesis takes as a case study. This examination of public policy implementation in India's complex federal polity contextualises Operation Blackboard within the historical development of the elementary sector. It draws on policy science based implementation research and educational innovations literature to develop a theoretical framework, but finds they cannot fully explain the dichotomy between 'appearance', or policy rhetoric, and the 'reality' of contexts beyond the policy making environment. A critical analysis of Indian policy documents straddles that gap by revealing their implicit and explicit rationales, which may conflict once policy moves into 'reality', where implementors operate in the domain of this unresolved conflict. The methodology of 'backwards mapping' starts from three case study sites in Gujarat and works backwards through local administrations, to New Delhi. The study finds that centralised national policy does not allow for the varying capacity of teachers in different socio-economic contexts to absorb an innovation, while bureaucrats attach greater importance to operating norms than outcomes of their actions. The centrality of teachers to the education process is acknowledged but not acted upon; education policy is used as a lever in centre State relations. For universal elementary education to be achieved, the State must reappropriate its own educational policy arena; and struggles for control must be replaced by

centre State dialogue.

PUBLISHED MATERIAL: DYER, C. (1992). 'Networking: a possible approach to Centre-State policy dialogue in India', Norrag News, No 13, pp.72-73.

STATUS: Individual research

DATE OF RESEARCH: 1989-1993

KEYWORDS: **educational policy; india; primary education**

0550

Faculty of Education, Moray House, Holyrood Campus, Holyrood Road, Edinburgh EH8 8AQ
0131 651 6296

Dyer, C. Dr

British resource on international training and education (BRITE) inventory

ABSTRACT: The inventory of the British Resource on International Training and Education (BRITE) is intended as a document that summarises the varied nature and scope of Britain's institutional expertise in that area. The principal beneficiaries will be research and training institutes and agencies, and private and non-governmental organisations. BRITE points towards the location of expertise, and subject and area-wise specialisations in a format that can be regularly updated.

STATUS: Sponsored project

SOURCE OF GRANT: British Council £4,000

DATE OF RESEARCH: 1993-1993

KEYWORDS: **information sources; international education**

0551

Faculty of Education, Moray House, Holyrood Campus, Holyrood Road, Edinburgh EH8 8AQ
0131 651 6296

Mongiello, A. Ms; *Supervisors*: Donn, G. Dr; Anderson, C. Mr

A comparative study of transition from nursery to infant school in England and Scotland

ABSTRACT: The issue of continuity is not new, it has been recognised as being vitally important in early education for many years. More recently, the issues of continuity and progression have come to the forefront of educational discussion, mainly due to the introduction of the National Curriculum in England and Wales and the 5-14 Curriculum Guidelines in Scotland, and the increasing diversity of nursery provision in the UK as a whole, while it may appear that the UK offers a wide range of early childhood services, this does not necessarily mean that all parents have a wide choice. Due mainly to financial constraints on local authorities, most preschool places are in services in the private market and depend on parents' ability to pay, taking no account of family income or circumstances. In the last 10 years the number of places in private nurseries has increased by 259%. Research has shown that the nature and quality of early learning outside the home affects a child's development. Those children who receive high quality preschool education programmes have shown a wide range of positive personal, social and educational outcomes. There is a real concern that as commercial ventures, private nurseries may well not prioritise the issue of quality in terms of good educational practice, whilst the demand for places is so high. Although there is a large body of research in the USA, very little has taken place in the UK which looks specifically at the quality of nursery provision in the private sector. This is mainly due to the fact that private nurseries have only come into existence in the past 5 to 10 years. In researching this area there would be a desire to adopt the use of qualitative rather than quantitative techniques, i.e. semi-structured interviews, open-ended questionnaires and extensive observations. There would be little intention to produce any statistical analysis of the findings. The researcher would be far more interested in gaining an 'insight' to the processes taking place during the transition period.

STATUS: Individual research

DATE OF RESEARCH: 1996-continuing

KEYWORDS: **early childhood education; educational quality; infant education; nursery education; outcomes of education; preschool education; preschool to primary transition; primary education; private education**

0552

Faculty of Education, Moray House, Holyrood Campus, Holyrood Road, Edinburgh EH8 8AQ
0131 651 6296

Amyes, D. Mrs; *Supervisors*: Donn, G. Dr; Black, M. Dr

An analysis of the influences on rural land use in the Scottish curriculum

ABSTRACT: From an examination of the influences on the role of rural land use in the Scottish curriculum (especially in light of the current curriculum innovations which include the 5-14 Curriclum Guidelines and assessment), this research will: 1) outline the historical, political and social background to the inclusion of rural land use within the curriculum; 2) analyse the relevance of theoretical writings on the curriculum and culture to the current inclusion of rural land use in the curriculum; and 3) through this analysis provide an understanding of the influences on current curriculum development for rural land use, particularly in relation to the 5-14 Environmental Studies Curriculum Guidelines.

STATUS: Individual research

DATE OF RESEARCH: 1994-1997

KEYWORDS: **curriculum development; environmental education; land use; rural areas; rural studies; scotland**

0553

Faculty of Education, Moray House, Holyrood Campus, Holyrood Road, Edinburgh EH8 8AQ
0131 651 6296

Jordan, E. Mrs; *Supervisors*: Sharp, S. Dr; Kidd, J. Dr

Travellers in Scottish education in the 1990s

ABSTRACT: Gypsies and travellers are officially recognised as the most marginalised group in state education, yet there are few statistics available in Scotland to make any clear statements or on which to base policy and action. The Scottish Office provides a grant on an annual, recurring, basis to Moray House to maintain an initiative in this area. This research builds on that basis. The aim is to carry out research in schools over a 4-year period in order to build up a national statistical databank of travellers in Scottish schools. It also aims to get a traveller perspective on schooling and to seek to compare current experiences with those recorded from earlier dates, both written and oral, to see if there is any qualitative shift in perceptions. Methodology is varied and linked to the data being sought. Statistics from schools are sought through written questionnaires annually. Perceptions of schools' experiences are sought through case studies of a variety of schools, in size, stage and setting. Historical data is gleaned from a review of the existing literature, including audio cassette recordings of face-to-face interviews with travellers. Present day experiences are drawn from face-to-face interviews with a range of travellers, in grouping and age range. Views of other professionals, such as workers employed by voluntary organisations and site managers, are also recorded as they help to flesh out the picture, based on their closer and much longer involvement with traveller families. The results, so far, indicate that there continues to be a serious problem in low attendance and achievement levels, despite intensive input by some education authorities to redress the situation. Travellers do express a concern at diminishing life chances and see education as an opportunity for improvement, yet there has been little significant change in uptake of schooling. While not all results are yet available, an analysis of work so far indicates that the conclusions are likely to be that Scotland has not provided equality of opportunity in education for this most marginalised group, and that there will be a need for some institutional change if progress is to be made before the end of this century.

STATUS: Individual research

DATE OF RESEARCH: 1992-1997

KEYWORDS: **access to education; educationally disadvantaged; gypsies; transient children; travellers - itinerants**

0554

Faculty of Education, Moray House, Holyrood Campus, Holyrood Road, Edinburgh EH8 8AQ
0131 651 6296

McCulloch, K. Mr; Ducklin, A. Mr

Placement as a predictor of career direction: a longitudinal study of community education BA students

ABSTRACT: The purpose of the current research relates to consideration of the approach used at Moray House in identifying community education placement opportunities and allocating students. The relationship hypothesised 'that a choice of pupil placement is a consistent predictive indicator of preferred and actual first professional employment setting' has been demonstrated satisfactorily, but has also been shown to provide an inadequate explanation of the phenomenon under consideration. A systematic framework for the description of professional settings has been developed in the first phase of the research, and is being used as the basis for data collection in the longitudinal study. A report of the first phase is being prepared for publication. Improved understanding of the nature of students' experience and its consequences will be important, not only at an institutional level, but in the wider context of professional education for community education. Improvements in the understanding of the processes examined in the project will also be of interest to the regulatory body - Community Education Validation and Endorsement (CeVe) Scotland.

STATUS: Sponsored project

SOURCE OF GRANT: Heriot-Watt University, Moray House Institute of Education

DATE OF RESEARCH: 1994-1998

KEYWORDS: **careers; community education; followup studies; placement**

0555

Faculty of Education, Moray House, Holyrood Campus, Holyrood Road, Edinburgh EH8 8AQ
0131 651 6296

Crawford, E. Dr

A methodology for placement preparation (initial teacher training students)

ABSTRACT: This is an action-research project involving all students and some staff within a four-year initial teacher training in technology. A teaching methodology, 'Reflective Analysis of Experience', has been adapted from the methods of psychodynamic consultancy and brief intervention is made with each year of the undergraduate course. This teaching considers technology as a social, psychological and physical reality and reflectiveness is taken to be the process of being aware of links between one's subjectivity and the environment. The supposition which the research explores is that, via this teaching, students will have a more explicit understanding of the subjective elements in learning/teaching situations, both their own and their pupils', and will be better enabled to modify their reactions towards realistic value-based responses to the needs of the school and classroom context. The research aims are to: 1) clarify and communicate the nature of the facilitating behaviours and skills used in a 'reflective analysis' methodology; 2) relate description of the methodology to the theoretical understanding of human development from which it derives; 3) identify criteria indicating professional development of this nature, i.e. capacity to be reflective and in touch with personal authority to effect appropriate influence; 4) design and apply evaluative tests for these criteria; 5) assess the general effects of the placement preparation over the four-year period for a cohort of students. The methods used are mainly qualitative: discourse analysis, from students, supervising tutors and teachers; structured interviews; analysis of normal reports and grades of the student's work on teaching practice. A standard psychological 'Personal Profile Inventory' is being used with the cohort when entering and leaving their course, and also with a sample of students from other comparable courses; the numbers involved in these samples are necessarily small.

PUBLISHED MATERIAL: CRAWFORD, E. (1995). 'Reflective analysis of experience: trainee teachers on placement in schools'. Proceedings of the Third International Conference on History, Philosophy and Science Teaching, University of Minnesota, October 28-November 1, 1995.

STATUS: Sponsored project

SOURCE OF GRANT: Heriot-Watt University, Moray House Institute of Education

DATE OF RESEARCH: 1993-1997

KEYWORDS: **preservice teacher education; reflection; student teachers; teaching experience; teaching practice**

0556

Faculty of Education, Moray House, Holyrood Campus, Holyrood Road, Edinburgh EH8 8AQ
0131 651 6296

Conlon, T. Dr; McKendree, J. Dr; Stenning, K. Prof.; Lee, J. Dr; Cox, R. Dr; Oberlander, J. Dr

Integrating social and representational aspects of problem-solving across the high school curriculum

ABSTRACT: Cognitive science has developed deep semantic and computational understandings about representations, notably how they can be selected and adapted to fit novel problems; the role they play in solitary reasoning; and how they function in dialogical communication. This proposal is to put these theories to use in designing curriculum interventions at high school level which bridge between the formal understandings of representations taught in mathematics and science, and social understandings traditionally taught in the humanities. These interventions will aim at student grasp of generalisations both about social relations in communication, and about representations across domains of their application. The researchers propose a theory about how to integrate and develop existing materials, rather than the reinvention of many excellent curriculum resources which address parts of the problem.

STATUS: Sponsored project

SOURCE OF GRANT: McDonnel Foundation, Cognitive Studies for Educational Practice Program £259,000

DATE OF RESEARCH: 1995-continuing

KEYWORDS: **mathematics; problem solving; reasoning; science education**

0557

Faculty of Education, Moray House, Holyrood Campus, Holyrood Road, Edinburgh EH8 8AQ
0131 651 6296

Mahmoud, H. Mr

Action research in reflective teaching

ABSTRACT: The thesis reports the findings of an ethno-cognitive study into an action research (AR) approach in the context of the experienced teacher of English to speakers of other languages (TESOL). The prime intent of the study, which incorporated the methods of interviews, observation, journal logs and 3 teachers' AR reports, was to investigate teachers' attitudes towards the AR, their perceptions of it, the impacts of the approach and to what extent they perceived the approach to be congruent with their normal practice. The findings of the study supported the expectations of the research and provided some implications to TESOL teacher education.

STATUS: Individual research

DATE OF RESEARCH: 1994-continuing

KEYWORDS: **action research; english - second language; reflective teaching; second language teaching**

0558

Faculty of Education, Moray House, Holyrood Campus, Holyrood Road, Edinburgh EH8 8AQ
0131 651 6296

Kraipipadh, P. Mr

An analysis of basic education for all in Thailand: a model for a 12 year basic educational provision

ABSTRACT: This thesis concerns educational policy management in Thailand. The Thai government expects to provide equal access to free 12 year basic education for all by the year 2001. The study uses mix-methodology, both qualitative and quantitative enquiries, in order to investigate deeply in this area mainly for clarifications in its requirements, capacity, feasibility and implementation, in respect of the core concept of the contingency approach. Finally an alternative model for the educational provision is suggested.

STATUS: Individual research

DATE OF RESEARCH: 1994-continuing

KEYWORDS: **educational policy; thailand**

0559

Faculty of Education, Moray House, Holyrood Campus, Holyrood Road, Edinburgh EH8 8AQ
0131 651 6296

Cross, A. Ms

The story-strategy interface: a cross-cultural exploration of developing learner identities

ABSTRACT: A cross-cultural comparison of story telling environments and their impact in learning strategies of two groups of 9-11 year-olds in Scotland and South Africa, modelled on ethnographic work by Shirley Bryce Heath and cultural psychology and child development studies in Africa by Robert Serpell and Daniel Wagner.

STATUS: Individual research

DATE OF RESEARCH: 1998-continuing

KEYWORDS: **comparative education; learning strategies; scotland; south africa**

0560

Faculty of Education, Moray House, Holyrood Campus, Holyrood Road, Edinburgh EH8 8AQ
0131 651 6296

Closs, A. Ms; Arshad, R. Ms; Stead, J. Dr

The school experience of refugee children in Scotland

ABSTRACT: The overall aim of this qualitative research is to identify educational responses which are perceived as constructive, empathic and practicable by refugee pupils, their families and school staff in the context of Scottish schools (other previous and concurrent studies have been undertaken only with large English conurbations). Indepth interviews were conducted with 18 parents, 14 children/young people and 24 teaching staff from 4 schools. A full report and a summary account with recommendations for schools will be produced.

STATUS: Team research

DATE OF RESEARCH: 1997-continuing

KEYWORDS: **educational experience; immigrants; refugees; scotland; transient children**

0561

Faculty of Education, Moray House, Holyrood Campus, Holyrood Road, Edinburgh EH8 8AQ
0131 651 6296

Ravenscroft, J. Mr; Buultjens, M. Mrs; Aitken, S. Dr; Carey, K. Mr

An investigation to determine best practice for visually impaired students using personal computers without additional access software

ABSTRACT: To establish criteria for a protocol to enable people with visual impairment to access and use commercial word processing packages and other software without additional specialist programmes.

STATUS: Sponsored project

SOURCE OF GRANT: Royal National Institute for the Blind £30,000

DATE OF RESEARCH: 1999-continuing

KEYWORDS: **blindness; information technology; special educational needs; visual impairments; word processing**

0562

Faculty of Education, Moray House, Holyrood Campus, Holyrood Road, Edinburgh EH8 8AQ
0131 651 6296

Millar, G. Mr

Does the self-managing primary school provide a better quality of teaching and learning than its council-run counterpart and is it a model that is applicable to all socio-economic areas?

ABSTRACT: This study is about whether self-management works and if it does work is it only in some contexts? Areas to be explored will be: central policymaking background; what the model of self-management is; how such schools can justify their existence in terms of providing 'better' quality teaching and learning; is it only schools in affluent areas that can be self-managed; quality assurance; and the ethical dimension.

STATUS: Individual research

DATE OF RESEARCH: 1998-continuing

KEYWORDS: **educational administration; management in education; primary education; school based management**

0563

Faculty of Education, Moray House, Holyrood Campus, Holyrood Road, Edinburgh EH8 8AQ
0131 651 6296

Abdalla, M. Mr

The role of background knowledge on English as a second language (ESL) reading comprehension

ABSTRACT: Considerable attention has been given to the role of background knowledge in second language reading comprehension. Schema theorists believe that the comprehension process is an interaction between the reader and the text. The text alone does not carry meaning. It is not enough to rely on one's linguistic competence which is actually considered part of one's total background knowledge. The current research reports an empirical study of the effect of cultural background knowledge on reading comprehension. Two experiments have been conducted. The first study consists of 100 subjects: 50 Egyptian and 50 Danish. Two reading passages were used, one reflects the content domain of the reader's background of the Egyptian group and the other reflects the content domain of the reader's background of the Danish group. The students' recall protocols and answers on the cloze test were analysed and corrected. In the second experiment, a think-aloud technique was used. Six students representing the 2 cultures participated in the activity. Their responses to the reading passages were recorded, transcribed and then analysed. The findings will be discussed in terms of the schema-theoretic approaches to English as a second language (ESL) reading. This will be followed by a pedagogical section in which suggestions for teaching reading will be provided.

STATUS: Individual research

DATE OF RESEARCH: 1991-continuing

KEYWORDS: **english - second language; reading comprehension; second language learning**

0564

Faculty of Education, Moray House, Holyrood Campus, Holyrood Road, Edinburgh EH8 8AQ
0131 651 6296

Reid, G. Dr; Kirk, J. Mrs; Mullin, K. Ms; Hui, D. Ms

Identifying good practice in dyslexia assessments

ABSTRACT: This research will identify best practices in relation to assessment and supporting dyslexic adults in employment. This involves both a national survey and workshops throughout the UK collaborating with a number of professional groups and voluntary organisations, including occupational psychologists, careers staff, employment disability advisers, employers' organisations, and dyslexia organisations from the voluntary sector. The outcome will be a report indicating how the Employment Service should proceed in relation to assessing and supporting dyslexic adults.

STATUS: Sponsored project

SOURCE OF GRANT: Employment Service

DATE OF RESEARCH: 1999-continuing

KEYWORDS: **dyslexia; employment**

0565

Faculty of Education, Moray House, Holyrood Campus, Holyrood Road, Edinburgh EH8 8AQ
0131 651 6296

Wishart, J. Prof.; Pitcairn, T. Dr

Psychological development in children with learning disabilities

ABSTRACT: This research is looking at psychological factors influencing developmental outcome in children with learning disabilities, with a major focus on Down's syndrome. The psychological environment in which children with learning difficulties grow and learn is inevitably very different from that experienced by ordinary children and expectations in teachers and parents, the children's learning partners, are often unnecessarily low. Differences in the nature, course and stability of cognitive development in children with developmental disabilities are being monitored and motivation and task engagement examined at different ages/developmental stages with a view to identifying more effective intervention strategies.

PUBLISHED MATERIAL: FRANCO, F. & WISHART, J.G. (1995). 'The use of pointing and other gestures by young children with Down's syndrome', American Journal on Mental Retardation, Vol 100, No 2, pp.160-182. ; WISHART, J.G. (1996). 'Avoidant learning styles and cognitive development in young children with Down syndrome'. In: STRATFORD, B. & GUNN, P. (Eds). New approaches to Down's syndrome. London: Cassell. ; WISHART, J.G. & MANNING, G. (1996). 'Trainee teachers' attitudes to inclusive education for children with Down's syndrome', Journal of Intellectual Disability Research, Vol 40, pp.56-65. ; WISHART, J.G. (1996). 'Early intervention'. In: FRASER, W.I., MACGILLVRA, R. & GREEN, A. (Eds). Hallas' caring for people with intellectual disabilities. 9th Edition. Oxford: Butterworth-Heinemann.

STATUS: Team research

DATE OF RESEARCH: 1995-continuing

KEYWORDS: **child development; cognitive development; downs syndrome; learning disabilities; special educational needs**

0566

Faculty of Education, Moray House, Holyrood Campus, Holyrood Road, Edinburgh EH8 8AQ
0131 651 6296

Leslie, M. Ms

Early intervention in the teaching of reading

ABSTRACT: In Scotland, since the mid-1990s, there has been a marked increase in interest from policymakers in the setting up of early intervention projects. These projects have been aimed at preventing early reading failure and have been targeted at children attending schools situated in areas of socio-economic disadvantage. This research project gathered both quantitative assessment data and qualitative interview, diary and questionnaire data from a cluster of 6 primary schools and 4 nursery schools taking part in a self-initiated and self-funded project.

PUBLISHED MATERIAL: MCMILLAN, G. & LESLIE, M. (1998). The early intervention handbook: intervention in literacy. Edinburgh: The City of Edinburgh Council. ; LESLIE, M. & MCMILLAN, G. 'Early intervention in the teaching of reading: the Edinburgh projects', Educational and Child Psychology, Vol 16, No 1. (in press).

STATUS: Sponsored project

SOURCE OF GRANT: Local Education Authorities

DATE OF RESEARCH: 1996-continuing

KEYWORDS: **intervention; literacy education; reading; reading difficulties; reading teaching**

0567

Faculty of Education, Moray House, Holyrood Campus, Holyrood Road, Edinburgh EH8 8AQ
0131 651 6296

Ferguson, R. Mr

The relationship between play behaviour and development in young blind and sighted children

ABSTRACT: The purpose of this research is to: 1) investigate the relationship between play behaviour and development in young blind children; 2) compare the play behaviour of blind preschool children with the play behaviour of sighted preschool children; 3) evaluate implications of the above findings in relation to differences in play behaviour; and 4) set the findings in the context of current educational practice.

STATUS: Individual research

DATE OF RESEARCH: 1997-continuing

KEYWORDS: **blindness; child development; play; special educational needs; visual impairments; young children**

0568

Faculty of Education, Moray House, Holyrood Campus, Holyrood Road, Edinburgh EH8 8AQ
0131 651 6296

Burford, B. Dr; Katsavras, J. Ms

Social work students' perceptions of gender styles in interpersonal communication: implications for practice

ABSTRACT: Gender differences in styles of interpersonal communication is a common theme running through a wide range of research. It is essential that those training for vocational professions have an understanding of the communication styles of men and women and an awareness of their own and each other's mode of communicating. The purpose of this research is to develop an interview schedule and questionnaire that will enable information to be gathered about social work students' perceptions of interpersonal communication. Information will also be collected about students' preferred styles of learning in relation to interpersonal communication and its role in social work practice. In order to achieve these objectives, questionnaire and interview schedules will be developed and tested for validity and reliability with 10 students. Following design modifications, indepth interviews will be conducted with a further 20 students. When all interviews are completed these 20 interviewees and a further 30 students will complete questionnaires.

STATUS: Sponsored project

SOURCE OF GRANT: Edinburgh University

DATE OF RESEARCH: 1997-continuing

KEYWORDS: interpersonal communication; professional education; sex differences; social workers

0569

Faculty of Education, Moray House, Holyrood Campus, Holyrood Road, Edinburgh EH8 8AQ
0131 651 6296

Sangster, P. Mrs

What do student teachers know and believe about language

ABSTRACT: To research knowledge and beliefs about language held by teachers in training. The focus will be on the preservice cohorts for primary education and on the English and foreign language Postgraduate Certificate in Education (PGCE) groups. The team will report its initial findings in July/August.

STATUS: Team research

DATE OF RESEARCH: 1997-continuing

KEYWORDS: language; preservice teacher education; student teachers

0570

Faculty of Education, Moray House, Holyrood Campus, Holyrood Road, Edinburgh EH8 8AQ
0131 651 6296

Williams, K. Mr

The Son-Rise program for autism: issues for parents and professionals

ABSTRACT: The purpose of the research is to: 1) examine how common home-based approaches for autism (including the Son-Rise program) are in the Lothian region; 2) investigate how parents' use of the Son-Rise program techniques with their children changes over time, and how their children respond to these changes; 3) document the experience of UK families using the Son-Rise program, including effects on family relationships, resolution of issues involved in combining the approach with traditional schooling, and any difficulties met in applying the techniques and running the program.

STATUS: Individual research

DATE OF RESEARCH: 1997-continuing

KEYWORDS: autism; special educational needs; therapy

0571

Faculty of Education, Moray House, Holyrood Campus, Holyrood Road, Edinburgh EH8 8AQ
0131 651 6296

Entwistle, N. Prof.; Tait, H. Dr; McCune, V. Ms; Orr, S. Mrs

University students' approaches to studying

ABSTRACT: Over many years, an inventory of approaches to studying has been refined both conceptually and psychometrically to try to identify students with ways of studying likely to lead to poor academic performance. The most recent study examined the factor structure of the current version of the inventory (ASSIST) and used cluster analysis to identify a group of students whose pattern of scores were atypical, and whose attainment levels were also low. This phenomenon has been identified in other studies and is called 'dissonance'. In 1998-9, students are being asked to complete two versions of the inventory - the original inventory, Approaches to Studying Inventory (ASI) and the current one. Comparisons will be made between the two versions and produced as a handbook describing the inventory and its use.

PUBLISHED MATERIAL: TAIT, H. & ENTWISTLE, N.J. (1996). 'Identifying students at risk through ineffective study strategies', Higher Education, Vol 31, No 1, pp.97-116. ; TAIT, H., ENTWISTLE, N.J. & MCCUNE, V. (1998). 'ASSIST: a reconceptualisation of the approaches to studying inventory'. In: RUST, C. (Ed). Improving student learning: improving students as learners. Oxford: Oxford Brookes University, The Oxford Centre for Staff and Learning Development ; ENTWISTLE, N.J., TAIT, H. & MCCUNE, V. 'Patterns of response to an approach to studying inventory across contrasting groups and contexts', European Journal of the Psychology of Education. (in press).

STATUS: Sponsored project

SOURCE OF GRANT: Godfrey Thomson Trust Fund

DATE OF RESEARCH: 1996-continuing

KEYWORDS: higher education; learning strategies; students; study skills; underachievement

0572

Faculty of Education, Moray House, Holyrood Campus, Holyrood Road, Edinburgh EH8 8AQ
0131 651 6296

Crowther, J. Mr; Tett, L. Ms

Ways in which practitioners conceptualise critical literacy and their implications for policy and practice

ABSTRACT: Political and public debate about literacy standards is taking place in a context where practitioners of adult literacy are raising questions about what literacy is and whose standards are used. The purpose of this study is to explore alternative ways in which practitioners conceptualise critical literacy and to examine their implications for the development of policy and practice.

PUBLISHED MATERIAL: CROWTHER, J. & TETT, L. (1998). 'Families at a disadvantage: class, culture and literacies', British Educational Research Journal, Vol 24, pp.449-460. ; CROWTHER, J. & TETT, L. (1998). 'Developing critical literacy'. In: BENN, R. (Ed). Research, teaching and learning: making connections in the education of adults. Proceedings of the SCUTREA 28th Conference, 1998. ; CROWTHER, J., TETT, L. with GALLOWAY, V. 'Cultural politics and adult literacy practice in the new Scotland', Studies in the Education of Adults. (in press).

STATUS: Sponsored project

SOURCE OF GRANT: Edinburgh University

DATE OF RESEARCH: 1997-continuing

KEYWORDS: adult education; critical reading; literacy

0573

Faculty of Education, Moray House, Holyrood Campus, Holyrood Road, Edinburgh EH8 8AQ
0131 651 6296

Reid, G. Dr; Weedon, C. Dr; Mullin, K. Ms

Assessment of emerging literacy skills: Group Test

ABSTRACT: This research will produce a Group Test to be used by teachers to identify literacy difficulties in the early stages of primary school. It will consist of 3 packages: a Users Manual; a Screening Battery and a Diagnostic Profiling Battery. The key feature of the batteries is that they allow collection of data in large group settings that has been more usually collected in 1:1 settings. Development is currently at the third stage of piloting and the indication is that a robust and effective group test will be the outcome. Publication of the complete batteries is currently under consideration by a major test publisher.

PUBLISHED MATERIAL: REID, G. (1997). Dyslexia: a practitioners handbook. Chichester: Wiley.

STATUS: Sponsored project

SOURCE OF GRANT: Edinburgh University

DATE OF RESEARCH: 1998-continuing

KEYWORDS: diagnostic tests; literacy; reading difficulties

0574

Faculty of Education, Moray House, Holyrood Campus, Holyrood Road, Edinburgh EH8 8AQ
0131 651 6296

Closs, A. Ms

Outlook still uncertain: enabling the continuing education of young people with chronic and/or deteriorating conditions

ABSTRACT: The qualitative study is investigating the post-school formal and informal education and social lives of young people in Scotland who have chronic and/or deteriorating conditions. The emphasis of the research is on evaluating the extent to which the education offers: 1) continuity and progression from their school experience; 2) sufficient flexibility and support to enable optimal outcomes; and 3) a quality of life which meets with the students' aspirations for social activities and peer companionship. Prominence is given to the students' voices although the policies and practices of their providing educational establishments/services are also examined. The publication draws on both an earlier study of children and some early pilot work carried out for the current project.

PUBLISHED MATERIAL: CLOSS, A. (1998). 'The quality of life of young people with life-threatening conditions'. In: ROBINSON, C. & STALKER, K. (Eds). Growing up with disability. London: Jessica Kingsley.

STATUS: Individual research

DATE OF RESEARCH: 1998-continuing

KEYWORDS: individual needs; pupil needs; sick children; special educational needs

0575

Faculty of Education, Moray House, Holyrood Campus, Holyrood Road, Edinburgh EH8 8AQ
0131 651 6296

Entwistle, N. Prof.; Skinner, D. Mr; Entwistle, D. Dr; Orr, S. Mrs

Student teachers' conceptions of teaching

ABSTRACT: Students taking a Postgraduate Certificate in Education (PGCE) Primary course in Edinburgh and in Vasa, Finland, have been involved in a study designed to investigate their conceptions of 'good teaching'. In 1998, 55 students completed an inventory of their approaches to studying (ASSIST). As part of their course, they were subsequently asked to write a short essay on 'What makes good teaching', and were provided with 10 short extracts which presented deliberately contrasting views. On completion of the essays, students completed a questionnaire on how they carried out this assignment. Based on the inventory scores and the questionnaires, 33 students at Edinburgh were chosen for interview. 24 of the interviews were transcribed (based on the judgement of the interviewer) and preliminary analyses have been written up. These focused on the students' reactions to the extracts, the form of the more elaborated conceptions, and examples of possible influences on those conceptions. Early in 1999, the year group has been asked to carry out the same assignment, more firmly integrated into their study programme, and with a developed form of questionnaire which will be the main source of data, together with the essay. The data collected in Finland have yet to be analysed.

PUBLISHED MATERIAL: ENTWISTLE, N.J., SKINNER, D.,

ENTWISTLE, D.M. & ORR, S. 'Conceptions of "good teaching" as learning outcomes'. In' RUST, C. (Ed). Improving student learning outcomes. Oxford: Oxford Brookes University, The Oxford Centre for Staff and Learning Development. (in press).

STATUS: Sponsored project

SOURCE OF GRANT: Godfrey Thomson Trust Fund £2,500

DATE OF RESEARCH: 1997-continuing

KEYWORDS: preservice teacher education; student teacher attitudes; student teachers; teacher effectiveness; teaching practice; teaching process

0576

Faculty of Education, Moray House, Holyrood Campus, Holyrood Road, Edinburgh EH8 8AQ
0131 651 6296

Crowther, J. Mr; Martin, I. Mr

Learning through struggles for social justice in a changing policy environment

ABSTRACT: This research focuses on the conflicts, compromises and contradictions involved in struggles for social justice and is concerned with how and what people learn in the process. It connects with an historical tradition in adult and community education which is concerned with non-institutionalised, collective forms of learning allied to social action through a curriculum which reflects and furthers the complex and often contradictory concerns and interests of exploited and oppressed groups.

PUBLISHED MATERIAL: CROWTHER, J. & MARTIN, I. (1997). 'Popular education in Scotland today', Concept, Vol 7, No 2. ; CROWTHER, J., MARTIN, I. & SHAW, M. (1997). 'Critical culture in Scottish adult and community education', Adults Learning, Vol 8, No 8, pp.203-206. ; CROWTHER, J. (1998). 'Popular education and the struggle for democracy'. In: CROWTHER, J., MARTIN, I. & SHAW, M. (Eds). Popular education and social movements in Scotland today. Leicester: National Institute of Adult and Continuing Education. ; MARTIN, I. (1998). 'Introductory essay: popular education and social movements in Scotland today'. In: CROWTHER, J., MARTIN, I. & SHAW, M. (Eds). Popular education and social movements in Scotland today. Leicester: National Institute of Adult and Continuing Education.

STATUS: Sponsored project

SOURCE OF GRANT: Edinburgh University £3,250

DATE OF RESEARCH: 1997-continuing

KEYWORDS: adult education; social change

0577

Faculty of Education, Moray House, Holyrood Campus, Holyrood Road, Edinburgh EH8 8AQ
0131 651 6296

Conlon, T. Dr

Classroom tools for knowledge-based modelling and knowledge acquisition

ABSTRACT: The technology of knowledge-based systems undoubtedly offers potential for educational modelling, yet its practical impact on today's school classrooms is very limited. To an extent this is because the tools presently used in schools are EMYCIN-type expert system shells. The main premise of this research is that these shells make knowledge-based modelling unnecessarily difficult and that tools which exploit knowledge acquisition technologies empower learners to build better models. The researcher is investigating how such tools can be designed and has built some prototypes. To evaluate their usability, a model building course has been conducted in 5 secondary schools. During the course pupils built hundreds of models in a common range of domains. Some of the models were built with an EMYCIN-type shell whilst others were built with a variety of prototype knowledge acquisition systems. The knowledge acquisition systems emerged as superior in important respects.

PUBLISHED MATERIAL: CONLON, T. (1995). 'Expert systems, shells and schools: present practice, future prospects', Instructional Science, Vol 23, No 1, pp.111-131. ; CONLON, T. (1995). 'AI tools and the classroom: theory into practice (papers from the Scottish International PEG Conference)', Instructional Science, Vol 23, Nos 1-3. ; CONLON, T. (1995).

'Persistent collaboration: a methodology for applied AIED', Journal of Artificial Intelligence in Education, Vol 7, No 3/4. ; CONLON, T. (1997). Beyond rules: the development and evaluation of knowledge acquisition tools for educational knowledge based modelling. Unpublished PhD thesis. Edinburgh: University of Edinburgh, Department of Artificial Intelligence. ; CONLON, T. (1998). 'Alternatives to rules for knowledge-based modelling', Instructional Science. (in press).

STATUS: Individual research

DATE OF RESEARCH: 1995-continuing

KEYWORDS: **computer uses in education; expert systems; information technology**

0578

Faculty of Education, Moray House, Holyrood Campus, Holyrood Road, Edinburgh EH8 8AQ
0131 651 6296

Martin, I. Mr; Shaw, M. Ms

Sustaining social purpose education in the current policy context

ABSTRACT: The project is focused on a number of individual workers who are at the leading edge of critical practice in the broad field of community-based education. The researchers interest is in what attracts workers to a field of practice that is still characterised by relatively low professional status, modest levels of remuneration, and insecurity as a consequence of precarious and unpredictable funding. The research focuses in particular on the attitudes and motivation of these workers in a rapidly changing policy context.

PUBLISHED MATERIAL: MARTIN, I. & SHAW, M. (1997). 'Sustaining social purpose in the current policy context'. In: ARMSTRONG, P., MILLER, N. & ZUKAS, M. (Eds). Crossing borders, breaking boundaries: research in the education of adults. London: University of London, Birkbeck College. ; CROWTHER, J., MARTIN, I. & SHAW, M. (1997). 'Critical culture in Scottish adult and community education', Adults Learning, Vol 8, No 8, pp.203-206. ; CROWTHER, J., MARTIN, I. & SHAW, N. (Eds). (1999). Popular education and social movements in Scotland today. Leicester: National Institute of Adult and Continuing Education.

STATUS: Sponsored project

SOURCE OF GRANT: Edinburgh University £1,500

DATE OF RESEARCH: 1996-continuing

KEYWORDS: **adult education; adult educators; community education; social values**

0579

Faculty of Education, Moray House, Holyrood Campus, Holyrood Road, Edinburgh EH8 8AQ
0131 551 6296

Fraser, H. Ms; MacDougall, A. Ms; Pirrie, A. Dr; Croxford, L. Dr

National evaluation of early intervention

ABSTRACT: This research is evaluating the major Scottish initiative in all local education authorities on early intervention in literacy and numeracy at the early stages of the primary school. There are three major strands of the research: an analysis of value for money; the assessment of effectiveness in raising attainment; and an analysis of the perspectives of the various stakeholders

STATUS: Sponsored project

SOURCE OF GRANT: Scottish Office Education and Industry Department £165,000

DATE OF RESEARCH: 1998-continuing

KEYWORDS: **intervention; literacy; local education authorities; numeracy; primary education; reading difficulties; scotland; young children**

0580

Faculty of Education, Moray House, Holyrood Campus, Holyrood Road, Edinburgh EH8 8AQ
0131 651 6296

Maciver, M. Mr

Gaelic medium education as a policy issue

ABSTRACT: An examination of Gaelic medium education in the context of a devolving Scotland. Are policies for Gaelic medium education important in the relationship between a language and emerging 'nationhood'? Is there a relationship between Gaelic and nationhood? Is all of this located in a political discord?

STATUS: Individual research

DATE OF RESEARCH: 1999-continuing

KEYWORDS: **gaelic medium education; scotland**

0581

Faculty of Education, Moray House, Holyrood Campus, Holyrood Road, Edinburgh EH8 8AQ
0131 651 6296

Maia de Paiva, B. Mrs

Problems of interaction in learning

ABSTRACT: The focus of the current project is the conception of interaction in the learning process. Two aspects are to be examined. Firstly, an initial analysis of existing interaction models in the epistemological and social theories of Piaget, Vygostsky and Habermas, and secondly the relationship between interaction and cognition in the context of institutional learning.

STATUS: Individual research

DATE OF RESEARCH: 1999-continuing

KEYWORDS: **cognitive processes; interaction; learning**

0582

Faculty of Education, Moray House, Holyrood Campus, Holyrood Road, Edinburgh EH8 8AQ
0131 651 6296

Draper, J. Mrs; Fraser, H. Ms; Taylor, W. Mr; Sharp, S. Dr

Teachers at work in Scotland: a 10 year follow-up study based on the probationer study sample

ABSTRACT: This research builds on 10 years of work on teacher careers, beginning with a study of probationer teachers (1988-91), with a follow-up at the 5-year stage. Those teachers are now in their tenth year of teaching and this project will revisit them to study their career paths and future intentions and their current views of teaching.

PUBLISHED MATERIAL: FRASER, H., TAYLOR, W. & DRAPER, J. (1997). 'Teachers at work: early experience of professional development', British Journal of In-Service education', Vol 23, No 2, pp.283-295. ; DRAPER, J. (1997). 'Converting from secondary to primary: strategic or magnetic decisions?', School Leadership and Management, Vol 17, No 3, pp.345-355. ; DRAPER, J., FRASER, H., RAAB, A., SHARP, S. & TAYLOR, W. (1997). Routes into primary teaching. Research Report for Scottish Office Education and Industry Department and General Teaching Council. ; DRAPER, J., FRASER, H., RAAB, A. & TAYLOR, W. (1997). Probationers on supply. Research report for the General Teaching Council. ; DRAPER, J., FRASER, H. & TAYLOR, W. 'Teachers' careers: accident or design?', Teacher Development, Vol 2, No 3. (in press).

STATUS: Sponsored project

SOURCE OF GRANT: General Teaching Council £3,500

DATE OF RESEARCH: 1999-continuing

KEYWORDS: **career development; followup studies; scotland; teacher attitudes; teacher development; teachers; teaching profession**

0583

Faculty of Education, Moray House, Holyrood Campus, Holyrood Road, Edinburgh EH8 8AQ
0131 651 6296

Goodall, K. Ms

Collaborative learning in young children with Down's syndrome

ABSTRACT: The research will examine the socio-cognitive interactions of young children with Down's syndrome, children with non-specific learning difficulties and typically-developing children when collaborating with partners on a task. The research aims to identify any inter-group differences in interactive styles and to examine specifically whether experience of collaborative learning is beneficial to the child with Down's syndrome.

STATUS: Individual research

DATE OF RESEARCH: 1997-continuing

KEYWORDS: **downs syndrome; group work; learning disabilities; special educational needs**

0584

Faculty of Education, Moray House, Holyrood Campus, Holyrood Road, Edinburgh EH8 8AQ
0131 651 6296

Kite, A. Mrs

A guide to better thinking

ABSTRACT: The purpose of the research is to advance our understanding of and make an original contribution to the development of children's thinking. The main focus of the research is: a) production of 'A Guide to Better Thinking', an innovative resource designed to help upper primary school children becoming more effective thinkers and learners and promote the teaching of 'good thinking' in our schools; b) piloting new materials; c) evaluation of programme. These research activities have been enabled by: 1) an analytical review of Thinking skills, exploring different methodologies/approaches/current debates; 2) selecting effective strategies for the development of Thinking Skills from existing materials and approaches; 3) identifying features of the learning environment which promote Thinking Skills. The aim is to develop a programme capable of making a unique contribution to Teaching Thinking and help children achieve a new sense of identity as thinkers and learners.

STATUS: Individual research

DATE OF RESEARCH: 1997-continuing

KEYWORDS: **learning strategies; primary education; thinking skills**

0585

Faculty of Education, Moray House, Holyrood Campus, Holyrood Road, Edinburgh EH8 8AQ
0131 651 6296
Birmingham University, School of Education, Edgbaston, Birmingham B15 2TT
0121 414 3344

Tett, L. Ms; Martin, I. Mr; Kay, H. Ms; Munn, P. Prof.; Ranson, S. Prof.; Martin, J. Ms

Schools and community education

ABSTRACT: The study reviews the current links between schools and community education and describes a variety of collaborative initiatives. It analyses these links in terms of the values, purposes, tasks and conditions under which collaborative activity takes place, and generates a framework to describe and compare the diversity of relevant educational practice. It argues that the great diversity of learning needs can only be addressed through collaboration between institutions using a variety of professional skills and that, although schools and community education have different kinds of core business, the potential of both can only be realised when they are both seen as essential elements of a community education system.

PUBLISHED MATERIAL: BLAIR, A., TETT, L., MARTIN, I., MUNN, P. & RANSON, S. (1998). School and community education: the mapping study. Edinburgh: University of Edinburgh, Moray House Institute of Education. ; TETT, L., RANSON, S., MARTIN, I., MUNN, P., KAY, H. & MARTIN, J. (1998). Schools and community education for the learning age. Edinburgh: University of Edinburgh, Moray House Institute of Education.

STATUS: Sponsored project

SOURCE OF GRANT: Scottish Office Education and Industry Department £74,540

DATE OF RESEARCH: 1996-continuing

KEYWORDS: **community education; school college relationship**

0586

Faculty of Education, Moray House, Holyrood Campus, Holyrood Road, Edinburgh EH8 8AQ
0131 651 6296

Birmingham University, School of Education, Research Centre for the Education of the Visually Handicapped, Edgbaston, Birmingham B15 2TT
0121 414 3344

Buultjens, M. Mrs; Mason, H. Dr; Odor, P. Mr

Improving the accessibility of video and multimedia to students with visual impairment

ABSTRACT: Rapidly changing methodologies in traditional campus-based education and in distance learning have resulted in video and multimedia technology being increasingly used in individual and group work to access primary sources of information. This change from text to image-based learning poses serious problems of access to students with a visual impairment. This project set out to survey current students on access strategies and difficulties; to identify non-technological supports and solutions; and to explore the potential of the change of new video and multimedia technologies in providing in-built access alternatives. Questionnaires were prepared for teachers and students, and after piloting were targeted at 2 distinct groups of respondents. The first and most important was a traditional survey of places of learning within the UK. The researchers undertook to provide these with large print (tick-box), text-file on disk, tape or braille versions of the questionnaire, and took care to ensure that the text-file versions of questionnaires were easy to read and complete using a screen reader. The survey size was defined in part by the resources available to produce and mark these diverse formats. The second data gathering exercise was aimed at interested World Wide Web (WWW) and e-mail contacts using the most straightforward versions of the questionnaire - those which were simple to distribute, and which could be automatically marked but which were broader in its scope than the questionnaires. As well as personal contacts, descriptions of the project and requests for information were sent to Web sites and Newsgroups with an interest in disability generally, visual impairment, video, new generation TV, multimedia, education and special education, and distance learning. It was hoped to discover aspects of production or design which had not been thought of. The appeal for information was broadcast on selected Web Newsgroups; via the Scottish Sensory Centre's home pages; and to selected colleagues via e-mail. The main results of the survey are contained in the paper delivered at the International Council for the Education of the Visually Impaired (ICEVI) Conference in Sao Paulo, Brazil, in August 1997. The potential for enhancing video, broadcast and multimedia for visually impaired viewers has expanded greatly over the last few years. It became clear during the pilot work that although the title of the project focused on traditional VHS video, both technologies and other issues were much broader. The conclusion was to cover perceptual issues and design trade-offs; the technology; legislative regimes and their influences; available tools and techniques; economics of production; and barriers to international exchange of materials. The ambitions for the technology awareness sections expanded beyond present day analogue broadcasting and video (VHS) and current audio subtitling techniques and systems to include multi-track compression techniques as used in digital broadcasting; multimedia with video components; CD-ROMS; and digitial video disk. Initially the aim had been to produce a booklet and accompanying video, the latter being to show some of the techniques and issues. After looking at the range of topics, especially to expose aspects of multimedia and future TV, it was decided to show some of the more complex elements on CD-ROM. Of course, not everyone has access to multimedia PCs, so a printed version is still provided. HTML and WWW standards of production are used, such pages can then be viewed on any computer-operating system platform using standard Web browsers like Netscape and Microsoft Internet Explorer. Quicktime was used for the video components. The researchers also offer advice on what video and, especially, what multimedia video can be developed without normal studio settings, and for what programme makers will need professional help. The situation is like that for print materials at the introduction of desktop publishing: desktop video suites at reasonable cost will enable local developers to do in-house what has only been possible in full editing suites in studios.

PUBLISHED MATERIAL: SCOTTISH SENSORY CENTRE. (1998). Video for visually impaired learners CD-Rom: a guide for teachers, students, designers of educational materials and programme producers. Edinburgh: Heriot-Watt University, Moray House Institute of Education. (CD-ROM available from the Scottish Sensory Centre, Moray House Institute of Education, Holyrood Road, Edinburgh EH8 8AQ).

STATUS: Sponsored project

SOURCE OF GRANT: Viscount Nuffield Auxilliary Fund £22,735

DATE OF RESEARCH: 1996-1998

KEYWORDS: cd roms; computer uses in education; educational materials; information technology; low vision aids; material development; multimedia; videodiscs; visual impairments

0587

Faculty of Education, Moray House, Holyrood Campus, Holyrood Road, Edinburgh EH8 8AQ
0131 651 6296
Birmingham University, School of Education, Research Centre for the Education of the Visually Handicapped, Edgbaston, Birmingham B15 2TT
0121 414 3344

Buultjens, M. Mrs; Odor, J. Mr; Mason, H. Dr

Case studies in staff development and video/multimedia design to improve access for students with visual impairment

ABSTRACT: This project extend work done for a previous Viscount Nuffield Auxiliary Fund project which, after surveying visually impaired students and lecturing staff on access difficulties and strategies, produced a CD-Rom and Web-based advice pack (Video for Visually Impaired Learners) describing technological and non-technological solutions as well as outlining the potential of digital technologies for providing in-built access alternatives. Current research will provide practical examples of real-world implementation strategies and the resources needed. An enhanced second edition of the CD-Rom will be produced and again mounted as an open access Web resource.

STATUS: Sponsored project

SOURCE OF GRANT: Viscount Nuffield Auxiliary Fund £24,200

DATE OF RESEARCH: 1998-continuing

KEYWORDS: cd roms; computer uses in education; educational materials; information technology; low vision aids; material development; multimedia; videodiscs; visual impairments

0588

Faculty of Education, Moray House, Holyrood Campus, Holyrood Road, Edinburgh EH8 8AQ
0131 651 6296
Glasgow University, Department of Psychology, Glasgow G12 8QQ
0141 339 8855

Reid, G. Dr; *Supervisor*: Hinton, J. Dr

School organisation, teachers' work stress and the effect of an intervention programme

ABSTRACT: Many studies have recognised the prevalence of stress in teaching and the multi-faceted nature of teacher stress, some have highlighted the importance of school organisational factors. This aspect has increased in importance due to the pace and extent of curricula and organisational changes within the teaching profession. This research has focused on examining organisational factors and particularly their relationship with other stress factors. The stress model used throughout this research has been the theoretical model of processes involved in psychological stress causation, continuation and change 'Psystress' (Hinton and Burton, 1992). Four studies were conducted for this research with a total of 212 teachers from both the primary and secondary school sectors. A principal aim of the research was to develop and evaluate a whole-school stress management package focusing on issues arising from organisational factors and particularly organisational and curricular change. The studies examined: the relationship between stress factors in teaching; the roles of perceived organisational change; personal planning; responsibility and concern; and the relationship between stress variables and dimensions of the school organisational climate. A further study examined the effects of an intervention programme using 3 different treatment conditions - whole school, individual counselling and one dealing with an aspect of the curriculum. The results showed statistically significant relationships between the stress factors within the 'Psystress' model indicating its suitability for stress research with the teaching profession. The results also highlighted the relationship between organisational climate and work stress. A factor analysis with organisational climate and the 'Psystress' model identified 3 factors which were named 'leadership insight', 'workplace ethos' and 'innovatory climate'. The results of the evaluation of the intervention programme showed that all three factors - organisational, curriculum and individual counselling - should be considered within a comprehensive package for stress management in schools as no one particular method was significantly more effective, in all the measures used in the evaluation, than any other. Each method showed merits in specific areas. An applied model of dealing with teacher stress in the workplace was developed 'a reciprocal model for intervention' - this model highlights the interaction between the different factors all of which need to be addressed if work stress in teaching is to be effectively addressed.

STATUS: Individual research

DATE OF RESEARCH: 1991-1997

KEYWORDS: organisational climate; school organisation; stress psychological; teachers; teaching profession

0589

Faculty of Education, Moray House, Holyrood Campus, Holyrood Road, Edinburgh EH8 8AQ
0131 651 6296
London University, University College London, Gower Street, London WC1E 6BT
0171 387 7050
Napier University, 219 Colinton Road, Edinburgh EH14 1DJ
0131 444 2266

Entwistle, N. Prof.; Anderson, C. Dr; Walker, P. Dr; Tait, H. Dr

University lecturers' conceptions of teaching

ABSTRACT: As part of a more general evaluation study in 1997, lecturers from 6 departments were interviewed. Heads of department were asked to identify 2 colleagues who were particularly enthusiastic about their teaching and 2 who were not. 24 lecturers were identified, of whom interviews could be arranged with 20. One section of the interview focused on the lecturers' conceptions of learning and teaching, and their approaches to lecturing. Analysis of the transcripts confirmed the wide variety of conceptions held by academic staff identified in recent Australian studies, but suggested that the more sophisticated conceptions were themselves more variable than the previous literature suggested. Based on these findings, a concept map has been developed which relates conceptions of learning to conceptions of teaching, while ongoing work is looking in depth at how conceptions of teaching may change over time, and the relationships between experiential and research-based descriptions of conceptions of teaching. Part of this work is being carried out collaboratively with colleagues in Australia.

PUBLISHED MATERIAL: ENTWISTLE, N.J. (1998). 'Motivation and approaches to studying: motivating and conceptions of teaching'. In: BROWN, S., ARMSTRONG, S. & THOMPSON, G. Motivating students. London: Kogan Page. ; ENTWISTLE, N.J. (1998). 'Conceptions of teaching for academic staff development: the role of research'. In: GREGORY, K.J. (Ed) Development training for academic staff: proceedings of a conference held by Goldsmith's College, University of London, in association with IBM (UK) on 26 March 1998. London: Goldsmith's College, University of London. ; ENTWISTLE, N.J. 'Approaches to studying and levels of understanding: the influences of teaching and assessment'. In: SMART, J.C. (Eds). Higher education: handbook of theory and practice, Vol X. New York: Agathon Press. (in press). ; ENTWISTLE, N.J. & WALKER, P. 'Conceptions of teaching and levels of understanding: emerging structures and shifting awareness'. In: RUST, C. (Ed) Improving student learning outcomes. Oxford: Oxford Brookes University, The Oxford Centre for Staff and Learning Development. (in press).

STATUS: Sponsored project

SOURCE OF GRANT: Godfrey Thomson Trust Fund £1,500

DATE OF RESEARCH: 1997-continuing

KEYWORDS: higher education; lecturers; teacher attitudes; teaching practice; teaching process

0590

Faculty of Education, Scottish Centre for Education Overseas, Moray House, Holyrood Campus, Holyrood Road, Edinburgh EH8 8AQ
0131 651 6296
Ahrens, P. Mrs

An investigation into the difficulties of introducing innovation in English language teaching in developing countries

ABSTRACT: This research grew out of work for a presentation at the British Council Dunford House Conference in 1990 on the topic of sustainability in the design of English language teaching projects. A database of difficulties was compiled in consultation with overseas Master of Arts (MA) students and used at the conference. This will be expanded and put into a hierarchy, in consultation with current overseas students, to form a questionnaire which will be sent to previous students, now seeking to introduce various innovative practices in their home systems. The results will be an ordered list of difficulties actually encountered by practitioners in the field. Later research might seek to identify ways of coping with these difficulties.

STATUS: Sponsored project

SOURCE OF GRANT: Moray House Institute of Education £250

DATE OF RESEARCH: 1992-1993

KEYWORDS: **developing countries; english - second language; second language teaching**

0591

Faculty of Education, Scottish Centre for Education Overseas, Moray House, Holyrood Campus, Holyrood Road, Edinburgh EH8 8AQ
0131 651 6296

Ahrens, P. Mrs; Dickinson, N. Ms

Teaching foreign languages at primary level

ABSTRACT: This piece of research looks at English language teaching in Europe and at the teaching of foreign languages in Scotland at the primary level. It relates to the increased interest in and demand for foreign language learning at primary level. Data has been collected and is still in the process of being collected on the problems teachers of a foreign language at primary level face. From existing data a checklist of common difficulties has been designed. This has been trialled and refined. Copies of this checklist have been sent to contacts in various countries. The data from the checklists will be analysed. Visits have been made within Edinburgh to selected primary schools where a foreign language is being taught. A report will be written on the different models of teaching a foreign language at primary level in use and teachers will be asked to fill in a checklist about their specific problems. The analysis of the data should show the main areas that cause problems to teachers at this level. Further research will set out to identify and collect teachers' coping strategies.

STATUS: Sponsored project

SOURCE OF GRANT: Moray House Institute of Education £500

DATE OF RESEARCH: 1991-1993

KEYWORDS: **modern language studies; primary education; problems; second language teaching; teaching methods**

Education for Development

0592

Building 33, Reading University, London Road, Reading RG1 5AQ
01189 316317

Street, B. Prof.; Millican, J. Ms; Holland, D. Ms; Robinson, A. Dr; Newell-Jones, K. Dr; Maddox, B. Mr; *Supervisor*: Rogers, A. Prof.

Post-literacy: a survey of current trends and future development

ABSTRACT: This is a comparative study of current trends in post-literacy in the developing countries programmes. Case studies of Kenya, Nepal, India and other countries. Some visits will be made and a literature search carried out. It is based on the research report on post-literacy published by the Overseas Development Administration (ODA) in 1994 entitled 'Using literacy: a new approach to post-literacy materials'.

PUBLISHED MATERIAL: ROGERS, A. (1994). Using literacy: a new approach to post-literacy materials. London: Overseas Development Administration.

STATUS: Sponsored project

SOURCE OF GRANT: Department for International Development

DATE OF RESEARCH: 1997-1998

KEYWORDS: **adult education; continuing education; developing countries; literacy**

Exeter University
0593

School of Education, St Luke's, Heavitree Road, Exeter EX1 2LU
01392 263263

Somers, J. Mr

The nature of learning in educational drama

ABSTRACT: Very little evidence exists about the nature of learning in educational drama. Given the current status of drama in the National Curriculum, it is timely that we attempt to prove that, in addition to aesthetic learning, drama also permits participants to engage with, and change their attitudes towards, the issues and concepts which form the content of the drama. The research team, which included 4 secondary drama teachers, has devised, piloted and evaluated a research lesson pack which is now in use in 74 schools nationally. Data is being sent to Exeter for analysis and it is expected that early results will be available by Spring 1995. The data collection includes the use of attitude and social distance scales and teacher and pupil observation and evaluation. It is hoped that the work may pave the way for a more focused qualitative project. Research lessons deal with attitudes of mental handicap; old age and gender stereotyping as well as the use of photographs as a stimulus for making drama and children's awareness of story form.

STATUS: Sponsored project

SOURCE OF GRANT: Exeter University Research Fund £3,000

DATE OF RESEARCH: 1989-1993

KEYWORDS: **curriculum development; drama; educational materials; learning experience**

0594

School of Education, St Luke's, Heavitree Road, Exeter EX1 2LU
01392 263263

Preece, P. Prof.

Student attitudes regarding effective teaching behaviours - a teaching practice study

ABSTRACT: An Anglicized version of the Teaching Behaviours Questionnaire was given to Postgraduate Certificate in Education (PGCE) secondary students before teaching practice (TP). After TP, quantitative ratings on each student for each category on the standard assessment schedule were obtained. This permitted the investigation of the factorial structure of the instrument and provided TP performance scores for correlating with scores on the attitude inventory. In a related intervention exercise, half of the science student group received feedback on the research evidence concerning teaching behaviour covered in the inventory. By using the other half of the group as a control, the effect of the intervention on TP performance was investigated.

PUBLISHED MATERIAL: PREECE, P.F.W. (1994). 'The classroom competence and attitudes towards pedagogical principles of beginning teachers', British Journal of Educational Psychology, Vol 64, No 2, pp.295-299. ; PREECE, P.F.W. (1994). 'A little knowledge is a dangerous thing', Science Teacher Education, No 12, p.11. ; PREECE, P.F.W. (1994). '"Knowing that" and "knowing how": general pedagogical knowledge and teaching competence', Research in Education, No 52, pp.42-50.

STATUS: Sponsored project

SOURCE OF GRANT: Exeter University

DATE OF RESEARCH: 1991-continuing

KEYWORDS: **postgraduate certificate in education; preservice teacher education; student attitudes; student teacher evaluation; teacher behaviour; teaching practice**

0595

School of Education, St Luke's, Heavitree Road, Exeter EX1 2LU
01392 263263

Biddle, S. Dr; Fox, K. Dr; Armstrong, N. Prof.

Psychological aspects of children and physical activity

ABSTRACT: Children aged 11-12 years (N=250) have been tested on physical activity and psychological constructs to see if activity levels and choices can be related to the psychology of the child. Preliminary evidence indicated that more active boys were intrinsically motivated towards physical education and sport, whereas girls required more extrinsic motivation. Active and less active children could also be discriminated on the basis of motivational orientations and physical self-perceptions. Ongoing research is following up these findings and is investigating achievement cognitions and self-perceptions.

PUBLISHED MATERIAL: BIDDLE, S. & ARMSTRONG, N. (1992). 'Children's physical activity: An exploratory study of psychological correlates', Social Science and Medicine, Vol 34, No 3, pp.325-331.

STATUS: Sponsored project

SOURCE OF GRANT: Exeter University £4,000; Northcott Medical Foundation £14,000

DATE OF RESEARCH: 1990-1993

KEYWORDS: **child psychology; exercise; health; physical activities; physical activity level**

0596

School of Education, St Luke's, Heavitree Road, Exeter EX1 2LU
01392 263263

Hazlewood, P. Dr; *Supervisor*: Wragg, E. Prof.

The influence of teacher appraisal on secondary school management

ABSTRACT: The imminent introduction of formal teacher appraisal into schools based on the premises that appraisal would monitor teacher performance, improve practice and enhance the overall management of schools provides a platform for considerable debate. The principal aim of this investigation is to consider the influence that teacher appraisal has on the management of secondary schools. A range of hypotheses relating to management of schools are being tested. Based on case studies of four similar sized secondary schools (for 11-16 age group) in similar localities, the research used unstructured interview as the primary methodology. Validity is currently being established through group discussion and other methods. A detailed questionnaire is being utilized to test hypotheses arising from the interviews. Approximately 45 teachers in various management positions were interviewed and questionnaires were sent to a range of 198 teachers in six schools.

STATUS: Sponsored project

SOURCE OF GRANT: Wiltshire Local Education Authority; Pool School

DATE OF RESEARCH: 1989-1993

KEYWORDS: **educational administration; secondary education; teacher evaluation**

0597

School of Education, St Luke's, Heavitree Road, Exeter EX1 2LU
01392 263263

Watson-Broughton, A. Mrs; *Supervisors*: Copley, T. Prof.; John, M. Prof.

Spiritual development through the medium of art

ABSTRACT: The aim of this research is to discover the most relevant way to deliver the aims of the Education Reform Act 1988 with reference to daily acts of worship. To promote the spiritual aspects of a balanced curriculum in the secondary school, a working definition of 'spiritual' needs to be drawn. This needs to address the current secular nature of society. Since symbols have always played an important role in worship, background research in aesthetics was undertaken along with a study of National Curriculum art documents. Particular artists from history were highlighted and their ideas, aims and aspirations related to recent legislation on acts of worship in schools. A distinction was drawn at all times between worship in a religious community and worship in an educational community.

STATUS: Individual research

DATE OF RESEARCH: 1991-1997

KEYWORDS: **education reform act 1988; religion and education; school worship; spiritual development**

0598

School of Education, St Luke's, Heavitree Road, Exeter EX1 2LU
01392 263263

Desforges, C. Prof.; Hughes, M. Prof.

Parents and assessment at National Curriculum key stage 1

ABSTRACT: The aim of the proposed research is to study the effect that parents' conceptions of teaching, learning and assessment may have on the assessment and reporting procedures currently being introduced into schools, and to study the effect that these procedures may in turn have on parents. It is hypothesised that two important mediating factors could be the accuracy of teachers' perceptions of parents' views, and the extent to which parents are directly involved in the assessment process. The specific research questions to be addressed are: (1) What are parents' conceptions of teaching, learning and assessment? (2) How accurately are these conceptions perceived by teachers? (3) How far do teachers' perceptions of parents influence their actual assessment behaviour? (4) How far do teachers actually involve parents in the assessment process, and to what effect? (5) What do teachers select to report to parents at the end of the assessment process? (6) What do parents make of these reports, and what effects do they have on their conceptions of teaching, learning and assessment, and on their relationship to the school? (7) What effects do the assessment and reporting processes have on teachers' perceptions of parents' conceptions, and on teachers' classroom practice?

STATUS: Sponsored project

SOURCE OF GRANT: Economic and Social Research Council £55,943

DATE OF RESEARCH: 1991-1993

KEYWORDS: **academic records; parent aspiration; parent school relationship; school based assessment**

0599

School of Education, St Luke's, Heavitree Road, Exeter EX1 2LU
01392 263263

Trotter, A. Mrs; *Supervisor*: Bennett, S. Prof.

Differential provision for children with special educational needs in ordinary schools

ABSTRACT: The aim of the study is to investigate the effects of various kinds of provision made for children with special educational needs at secondary level. Three main systems were investigated - the support base, withdrawal, and in-class support. Children were selected at primary level who were deemed to be in need of special educational needs provision at secondary school. Their entry into secondary school and subsequent performance was closely monitored. Along with details of their academic performance, the research includes the views of their parents and the children themselves.

PUBLISHED MATERIAL: BENNETT, N. & CASS, A. (1989). From special to ordinary schools: case studies in integration. London: Cassell.

STATUS: Individual research

DATE OF RESEARCH: 1986-1988

KEYWORDS: **mainstreaming; secondary education; special educational needs; support services**

0600

School of Education, St Luke's, Heavitree Road, Exeter EX1 2LU
01392 263263

Al-Seaidy, H. Mr; *Supervisors*: Burghes, D. Prof.; Hughes, M. Prof.

Interactive video: an evaluative study

ABSTRACT: The aim of this study is twofold, firstly to evaluate a mathematics based interactive video package called School Disco. The evaluation process has followed flexible lines which falls within both the traditional 'measurement oriented evaluation' and the newly developed 'cognitive oriented approach'. The second aim of the study is to assess secondary school teachers' awareness of interactive video and its development in the British schools. The study is divided into six chapters: Chapter 1 reviews the problem of the research and provides the research aims; Chapter 2 focuses on the developments in instrumental media and also discusses the developments of interactive video implementation in British schools; Chapter 3 focuses on the learning theories applied in an interactive video context; Chapter 4 reviews the methodology of the research and explains the statistical tools used; Chapter 5 presents the results and findings of both studies as well as discussion of these findings in relation to the research literature; Chapter 6 sums up the research final findings and conclusions.

STATUS: Individual research

DATE OF RESEARCH: 1990-1997

KEYWORDS: **computer uses in education; information technology; interactive video; mathematics education; multimedia**

0601

School of Education, St Luke's, Heavitree Road, Exeter EX1 2LU
01392 263263

Greenhough, P. Ms; *Supervisors*: Hughes, M. Dr; Preece, P. Prof.

The inter-relationship of cognitive abilities, attitudes, social interaction and performance in early logo learning

ABSTRACT: This research investigates the inter-relationship of cognitive abilities, attitudinal factors, social interaction and performance in young children. The context of the research is paired learning with a computer and in the first instance focuses on early Logo activities. Seventy-two, Year 3 children worked either in same-sex or mixed pairs for five sessions with the floor Turtle on drawing or driving activities. They also worked for two sessions individually. Prior to the work with the Turtle, the children were assessed on five British Abilities Scales. Prior, during and after the sessions their attitudes to the task, their partner, and gender stereotypes were assessed. All sessions were videotaped and the social interaction transcribed.

STATUS: Sponsored project

SOURCE OF GRANT: Nuffield Foundation £25,000

DATE OF RESEARCH: 1990-1993

KEYWORDS: **cognitive ability; computer assisted learning; interaction; logo; turtles - robots**

0602

School of Education, St Luke's, Heavitree Road, Exeter EX1 2LU
01392 263263

Peacock, A. Dr

Parents' understanding of science in the National Curriculum

ABSTRACT: The research is a longitudinal study of parents of children entering school in Autumn 1989 in 11 representative primary schools in one local authority. The sample is identical to that being used for a larger study (Parents and the National Curriculum, sponsored by Leverhulme Trust, director Dr M. Hughes) and the current study works closely with Dr Hughes' team. The study uses semi-structured interviews on a serial basis with parents, teachers and head teachers, to ascertain the flow of information to parents about their children's science work at National Curriculum key stage 1, and to evaluate parents' understanding of the information received. The study has so far highlighted clear differences of perception between parents and teachers about what parents know and need to know; and is currently investigating parents' interpretations of the reports received after the 1991 Standard Assessment Tasks.

PUBLISHED MATERIAL: PEACOCK, A. & BOULTON, A. (1991). 'Parents' understanding of science at key stage 1', Education 3-13, Vol 19, No 3, pp.26-29. ; PEACOCK, A. & BOULTON, A. 'Teacher-parent communication about science at key stage 1', Education 3-13, Vol 23. (in press).

STATUS: Sponsored project

SOURCE OF GRANT: Exeter University Research Committee Grant £5,000

DATE OF RESEARCH: 1990-1993

KEYWORDS: **national curriculum; parent attitudes; parent school relationship; primary education; science education**

0603

School of Education, St Luke's, Heavitree Road, Exeter EX1 2LU
01392 263263

Cousins, J. Ms; *Supervisors*: Desforges, C. Prof.; Hughes, M. Dr

The place of reflection in teachers' processes of change

ABSTRACT: This is an ethnographic study of teachers' theories about the language of young children when they start school and how these influence their classroom practice. It is based on a piece of action research carried out with 10 reception teachers for a year and examines the development of their own theories and the courses of change.

STATUS: Individual research

DATE OF RESEARCH: 1986-1993

KEYWORDS: **change; child language; classroom management; teacher attitudes**

0604

School of Education, St Luke's, Heavitree Road, Exeter EX1 2LU
01392 263263

Neather, E. Mr

Foreign language training for initial teacher training (ITT) students

ABSTRACT: The aim of this project is to: (1) establish a detailed register of current language experience and competence amongst all undergraduate and Postgraduate Certificate in Education (PGCE) students at the School of Education; (2) enquire into the aspirations and wishes of students in terms of foreign language learning, and their perception of the place of foreign languages in their careers, and in the future lives of the children they teach; (3) relate the pattern of such wishes and aspirations to the pattern of main subject courses followed by students with a view to establishing what language courses could best be offered to which groups of students; (4) investigate the resources and timetabling of access courses for students wishing to pursue individual programmes of less common languages, such as Greek and Portuguese, for which class tuition might not be available; (5) discuss with course tutors the role and function of foreign languages in the course profile of students with a view to integrating foreign language modules into the overall course structure on a rational and planned basis; (6) investigate the practice followed by other institutions of teacher training, and to make comparisons with foreign languages in teacher training establishments in other countries of the European Community; and (7) explore the needs and aims of foreign languages teaching in primary and middle schools in Devon. It is proposed that the project should last three terms from October 1992. This would give time to carry out surveys and put in place a carefully considered pilot scheme at the start of the new academic year in October 1993. Proposals and recommendations would then be made in December 1993 for possible implementation of a full programme in October 1994. The research will involve questionnaire surveys and interviews with students (sample=420 postgraduate students and 917 undergraduate students) and staff colleagues; visits to other institutions and attendance at European conferences.

STATUS: Sponsored project

SOURCE OF GRANT: Department for Education £4,590

DATE OF RESEARCH: 1992-1993

KEYWORDS: **modern language studies; preservice teacher education; student teachers**

0605

School of Education, St Luke's, Heavitree Road, Exeter EX1 2LU
01392 263263

Vosloo, M. Mr; *Supervisor*: Davis, N. Prof.

Beyond the fantasy are the rules: mental models and computer games

ABSTRACT: Computer games are motivating but why and what are the users doing? This research looks at the mental models of novice and experienced game players in education.

STATUS: Individual research

DATE OF RESEARCH: 1990-1993

KEYWORDS: **cognitive processes; computer games**

0606

School of Education, St Luke's, Heavitree Road, Exeter EX1 2LU
01392 263263

Owen, G. Mr; *Supervisors*: Davis, N. Prof.; Sparkes, A. Dr

The implementation of information technology (IT) in the UK state secondary school sector: case study into social reality and influence

ABSTRACT: The research originated from a belief that the management of information technology within schools was more than the information technology (IT) teacher being a resource manager. The stance was that schools, where IT was used by staff, was due to an effective IT coordinator. An effective coordinator had a written IT policy that staff carried out. The stance has evolved due to a paradigm shift. The researcher's thesis is that the implementation of IT is determined by the culture and micro-political climate of the institution, the power and authority - formal and informal - of the IT coordinator and their communication and advocacy skills. The paradigm shift has caused the research to fall into two distinct phases. The first phase followed a positivistic design with data collected by questionnaire using structured questions. The variables were informed by business and educational management theories. Correlation was sought between formal status of the IT coordinator, policy production, resource organisation and management style with rank order rating of school use by members of the local education authority information technology advisory team. Acceptance of the coordinators' perceptions confirmed the hypothesis. Field observations, as a participant observer, indicated that reality did not match the statements. Adopting a critical stance that contextualised the innovation and questioned influence resulted in the second phase. A re-interpretation of the findings according to context and key factor influencing strategies is ongoing from illustrative institutions. Data is collected and analysed from interview dialogues. The case study findings suggest that where an IT coordinator is utilising people management skills, powers of negotiation and advocacy at all organisational levels rather than technical skills, then the innovation is more accepted into the staff and pedagogic culture.

PUBLISHED MATERIAL: DAVIS, N., KIRKMAN, C. & OWEN, G. (1992). 'Changing pedagogy with information technology in the UK National Curriculum'. In: Proceedings of the 9th International Conference of Technology and Education, Paris, 1992. ; OWEN, G.D. (1992). 'Whole school management of information technology', School Organisation, Vol 12, No 1, pp.29-40. ; SPARKES, A.C. & OWEN, G. (1994). 'Physical education and information technology: cross curricular alliances?', British Journal of Physical Education, Vol 25, No 2, pp.23-28. ; OWEN, D.G. (1994). Implementing IT provision in secondary schools: an excursion into influence and social reality. In: Proceedings of the 11th International Conference on Technology of Education, London, 1994.

STATUS: Individual research

DATE OF RESEARCH: 1989-1997

KEYWORDS: computer uses in education; coordinators; information technology; secondary education

0607

School of Education, St Luke's, Heavitree Road, Exeter EX1 2LU
01392 263263

Chedzoy, S. Ms; Mitchell, R. Mr; Supervisors: Green, L. Ms; Rolfe, L. Ms ; Hennessy, S. Ms

The readiness of primary teachers to train students in teaching the arts in schools

ABSTRACT: In the light of recent UK government policy to shift a greater proportion of the responsibility for teacher education into schools the team of researchers are concerned about the quality of experience currently being offered by teachers training students in Art, Dance, Drama and Music. An initial study was set up to enquire into the education and training of primary undergraduate student teachers in the Arts in schools. The research was undertaken by a team of education lecturers from Exeter University, School of Education, who work in the fields of Art, Dance, Drama and Music. This team asked fundamental questions about what students were learning from teachers in preparation for teaching these subjects and the level of readiness of teachers to undertake their role. The strategy for data collection and analysis combined qualitative and quantitative methods. A sample of second year undergraduate student teachers completed a questionnaire on their experience of teaching the Arts in schools. A small sub-sample of students were then interviewed by the research team. This process was repeated with the same students in year four of their undergraduate programme. There were a number of important findings which have implications for school-based teacher training, for example, that the number of students able to learn from teachers in the Arts was significantly low. This suggests

that existing expertise in these subjects is lacking and raises issues regarding inservice training and school-based initial teacher education. The second phase of the research is now underway and it is monitoring the experiences of students in schools during their second year and final teaching practices. The research methodology remains the same with the addition of interviews with classroom teachers which will both broaden the research data, and yield a more informed view of teachers' readiness to train students in these 4 subjects.

STATUS: Sponsored project

SOURCE OF GRANT: Exeter University

DATE OF RESEARCH: 1994-1998

KEYWORDS: art education; arts; dance; design and technology; music; preservice teacher education; school based teacher education

0608

School of Education, St Luke's, Heavitree Road, Exeter EX1 2LU
01392 263263

Preece, P. Prof.

Stage theory models of cognitive development

ABSTRACT: Mathematical models of the proportions of the population at various stages of cognitive development as a function of age have been developed. These account well for empirical data for the age range 13-18 years.

PUBLISHED MATERIAL: PREECE, P.F.W. (1993). 'Comment: modelling the stages of cognitive development', Journal of Research in Science Teaching, Vol 30, pp.1013-1014. ; PREECE, P.F.W. & READ, K.L.Q. (1995). A stage-theory model of cognitive development', British Journal of Mathematical and Statistical Psychology, Vol 48, pp.1-7. ; PREECE, P.F.W. & READ, K.L.Q. A classical IQ model of the stages of cognitive development', Intelligence. (in press).

STATUS: Individual research

DATE OF RESEARCH: 1993-continuing

KEYWORDS: age differences; cognitive development; developmental stages; mathematical models

0609

School of Education, St Luke's, Heavitree Road, Exeter EX1 2LU
01392 263263

Copley, T. Prof.; Savini, H. Mrs

BIBLOS: teaching the Bible

ABSTRACT: The aim of the research is to investigate whether the Bible can be taught in a way which is educationally meaningful in a society categorised as plural and/or secular. The methods will include: consultation with theologians and educationalists on criteria for selection of biblical material; trialling of materials in selected schools in each National Curriculum key stage in two local education authorities (LEA's) (one urban, one rural); evaluation of results in project report; and publication of classroom materials. A first report on the project entitled 'Echo of Angels' is available from the Biblos Office, Exeter University, School of Education.

STATUS: Sponsored project

SOURCE OF GRANT: St Luke's College Foundation Trust; The London Bible House Fund

DATE OF RESEARCH: 1996-continuing

KEYWORDS: biblical literature; primary education; religion and education; religious education; secondary education

0610

School of Education, St Luke's, Heavitree Road, Exeter EX1 2LU
01392 263263

Chamberlin, R. Dr; Haynes, G. Ms; Wragg, C. Dr; Supervisor: Wragg, E. Prof.

Leverhulme primary improvement project

ABSTRACT: Improving the way in which children learn, especially in a vital field like literacy, has become a major challenge for teachers and others working in education. The aim of this research was to focus on schools over one complete academic year to find out, both by observation of lessons and by interviews, what strategies different primary schools adopt to improve standards of literacy, with particular emphasis on reading: what happens in lessons; which factors seem to facilitate and which seem to hinder progress in reading; and what progress is made by individual children. The research had three main strands. Study One involved interviews with a sample of primary headteachers, language coordinators, local education authority advisers and other professionals. Study Two comprised intensive case studies of 18 primary schools, 35 class teachers and 236 individual pupils. These schools are located in three English Regions: the Midlands, South East England, and South West England. In Study Three a questionnaire survey of a sample of 1395 primary headteachers was undertaken. This findings reveal a great deal about the nature of classroom and school practice, and provides valuable information for schools themselves, local authorities, inspectors and advisers, teacher training institutions and other bodies responsible for literacy, primary education or devising training programmes for teachers.

PUBLISHED MATERIAL: WRAGG, C. et al. (1998). Improving literacy in the primary school. London: Routledge.

STATUS: Sponsored project

SOURCE OF GRANT: Leverhulme Trust £143,570

DATE OF RESEARCH: 1994-1997

KEYWORDS: **literacy; literacy education; primary education; reading; reading teaching; school effectiveness; school improvement**

0611

School of Education, St Luke's, Heavitree Road, Exeter EX1 2LU
01392 263263

Ernest, P. Dr; Almeida, D. Mr; Poulson, L. Ms

Mathematical texts: a semiotic analysis of mathematical texts and their classroom use

ABSTRACT: The aim of the project is to develop a theoretical perspective on the nature of mathematical texts (in school, university and professional mathematics). Central to this is the theory of how the learner or reader is constructed as a mathematical subject through reading/writing mathematical text. An important influence is: ROTMAN, B. (1993). Ad infinitum ... the ghost in Turing's machine: taking God out of mathematics and putting the body back in - an essay in corporeal semiotics. Stanford CA: Stanford UP. Secondary and tertiary students will be observed working through mathematical texts, and interviewed in depth. Sample texts will be analysed linguistically.

PUBLISHED MATERIAL: ERNEST, P. (1993). 'Mathematical activity and rhetorical: a social constructivist account'. Proceedings of International Psychology of Mathematics Education Conference, Tsukuba University, Tokyo, Japan, July 1993.

STATUS: Sponsored project

SOURCE OF GRANT: Exeter University £6,000

DATE OF RESEARCH: 1994-1997

KEYWORDS: **mathematical linguistics; mathematics education; semiotics; textbooks**

0612

School of Education, St Luke's, Heavitree Road, Exeter EX1 2LU
01392 263263

Fox, K. Dr; Biddle, S. Dr

Achievement goal theory in sport and physical education

ABSTRACT: Achievement goal theory is applied to motivation in sport and physical education. Samples include children, adolescents, elite athletes.

PUBLISHED MATERIAL: DUDA, J.L., FOX, K.R., BIDDLE, S.J. & ARMSTRONG, N. (1992). 'Children's achievement goals and beliefs about success in sport', British Journal of Educational Psychology, Vol 62, No 3, pp.313-323. ; FOX, K.R., GOUDAS, M., BIDDLE, S., DUDA, J.L. & ARMSTRONG, N. (1994). 'Children's task and ego goal profiles in sport', British Journal of Educational Psychology, Vol 64, No 2, pp.253-261. ; FOX, K.R. (1994). 'Research perspectives on children's competence and achievement in physical education and sport', British Journal of Physical Education, Vol 25, No 2, pp.20-22. ; GOUDAS, M., BIDDLE, S. & FOX, K. (1994). 'Perceived locus of causality, goal orientations, and perceived competence in school physical education classes', British Journal of

Educational Psychology, Vol 64, No 3, pp.453-463.

STATUS: Individual research

DATE OF RESEARCH: 1990-continuing

KEYWORDS: **motivation; objectives; physical education; sports**

0613

School of Education, St Luke's, Heavitree Road, Exeter EX1 2LU
01392 263263

Osorio, A. Mr; *Supervisors*: Davis, N. Prof.; Hughes, M. Prof.

Telematics in educational environments

ABSTRACT: This project consists of a study of the educational potential of telematics and its implication for teacher education. A study to find out how telematics, as an educational tool or resource, can support teachers' development or adaptation in response to previewed continuous change in their professional activity. The project constitutes a multiple case study of a contemporary event in multiple site location in order to allow the collection of evidence from the use of technology by student teachers and teachers in various stages of their careers. Two cases are being followed: Study 1 Telematics in initial teacher education, investigating a case of using telematics (e-mail, computer conferencing, desktop and videoconferencing) in initial teacher education at the Exeter University School of Education Postgraduate Certificate in Education (PGCE) course during the academic years of 1994/95 and 1995/96. Study 2 - Telematics in inservice teacher education, investigating a case of using telematics (e-mail, computer conferencing and similar text information handling tools) in inservice teacher education. This study follows teachers from small rural primary schools in the Peneda-Geres National Park in Portugal, during the year of 1995. Data collection includes a range of techniques to assure different perspectives from participants and to allow triangulation when doing the analysis of the data; questionnaires at various stages of the process, semi structured interviews; observation of activities, electronic mail messages and computer conferencing articles; documents and field notes.

PUBLISHED MATERIAL: OSORIO, A. (1995). 'Telematics for teacher education: issues from a European Conference', Journal of Information Technology for Teacher Education, Vol 4, No 2, pp.183-195.

STATUS: Individual research

DATE OF RESEARCH: 1994-1997

KEYWORDS: **computer uses in education; electronic mail; information networks; information technology; inservice teacher education; preservice teacher education; telecommunications; teleconferencing**

0614

School of Education, St Luke's, Heavitree Road, Exeter EX1 2LU
01392 263263

Miles, P. Mr; *Supervisors*: Davis, N. Prof.; Burden, R. Dr

The talking computer project: an intervention for children experiencing dyslexia and other literacy difficulties

ABSTRACT: The use of a talking computer supported by structure, effective mediation and giving the child the locus of control, predicted that children experiencing dyslexic and other literacy difficulties should make significant progress. These predictions proved to be true with average gains of 9 months in reading being achieved with just 20 minutes per day for 29 days. Spelling showed significant increases and memory skills improved by 2 years. Follow-up assessment showed not only maintenance, but also further gains, without additional access to the talking word-processor. Teachers and parents have reported increased interest in books, greater on-task behaviour, more written work, improved behaviour and a more positive self-esteem. Accompanying the development of the project materials was the development of a training schedule. Trainees, even those with no previous computing experience, learn the minimal computing skills and the important educational skills in a day. It is new technology joining up with traditional remedial methods and has proved accessible to parents wanting to work with their own children. The method, materials and training were continually revised to reflect feedback from users. The progress was measured by way of a pre-test - post-test design and involved a pilot study (12 children), a wider pilot study (24 children) and a main study (74 children). The children were aged from 7 to 15 and were experiencing specific and general learning difficulties. The final work will include case studies, questionnaire analysis and quantitative data.

PUBLISHED MATERIAL: CLIFFORD, V. & MILES, M. (1993). 'Talk back', Special Children, No 68, pp.23-25. ; MILES, M. & CLIFFORD, V. (1994). 'A way with words', Special Children, No 74, pp.29-32. ; MILES, M. (1994). 'The Somerset talking computer project'. In: SINGLETON, C. (Ed). Computers and dyslexia. Hull: The Dyslexia Computer Resources Centre. ; CLIFFORD, V. & MILES, M. (1995). AcceleRead AcceleWrite: a guide to using talking computers to help your children learn to read and write. London: Iansyst.

STATUS: Individual research

DATE OF RESEARCH: 1993-continuing

KEYWORDS: **computer assisted reading; computer uses in education; dyslexia; information technology; intervention; reading difficulties; talking computers**

0615

School of Education, St Luke's, Heavitree Road, Exeter EX1 2LU
01392 263263

Preece, P. Prof.

Subject-matter knowledge of secondary science teachers

ABSTRACT: The language used by secondary science teachers to describe forces is being investigated, as well as their understanding of forces and motion.

PUBLISHED MATERIAL: PREECE, P.F.W. 'Force and motion: pre-service and practising secondary science teachers' language and understanding', Research in Science and Technological Education. (in press).

STATUS: Sponsored project

SOURCE OF GRANT: Exeter University

DATE OF RESEARCH: 1994-continuing

KEYWORDS: **force; motion; physics; science education; science teachers; scientific literacy; secondary education**

0616

School of Education, St Luke's, Heavitree Road, Exeter EX1 2LU
02392 263263

Baxter, J. Dr ; Preece, P. Prof.

Computers and multimedia technology in science education

ABSTRACT: The effectiveness of multimedia learning materials for the delivery of parts of the Science National Curriculum is being investigated using an experimental/control groups design.

STATUS: Sponsored project

SOURCE OF GRANT: Exeter University

DATE OF RESEARCH: 1995-continuing

KEYWORDS: **computer uses in education; information technology; multimedia; science education**

0617

School of Education, St Luke's, Heavitree Road, Exeter EX1 2LU
01392 263263

Davis, N. Prof.; Wright, B. Mr; Still, M. Mr

Bristol educational online network

ABSTRACT: The education online network (EON) project involves 11 schools in South Bristol in a pilot of a national broadband network model. It will provide an affordable desktop managed network that enables the delivery of online interactive educational services and curriculum applications. The provision of specialist courses, inservice teacher training, sharing of resources and cross-phase collaboration will also be features of the project. Research staff will perform 3 key roles: 1) new modes of teacher training; 2) acceleration of the process of innovation; 3) assessment of the educational benefits. Each school will use desktop videoconferencing systems to link to Exeter University for tailor-made professional development. Although the video window may be used for teachers and university tutors to see each other, more importantly video will be derived

from videotape, videodisc, still video camera, document scanner or an additional camera. A teacher and a tutor will also be able to share the software applications on the workstation. This enables the university tutor to demonstrate ways in which the integrated learning system or any other application, can be integrated within the curriculum. This intensive and tailor-made professional development will speed the process of innovation, benefiting the schools, to enable them to adapt and adopt new technologies with speed and minimal disruption. The university team will collect case studies which illustrate the educational value. The multimedia resources and communications opportunities offered through the EON project will be an important trial in preparation for an education system which will be suited to the information society.

STATUS: Sponsored project

SOURCE OF GRANT: International Computers Limited; British Telecom, jointly £110,925

DATE OF RESEARCH: 1995-1997

KEYWORDS: **computer uses in education; information networks; information technology; inservice teacher education; multimedia; preservice teacher education; telecommunications; teleconferencing**

0618

School of Education, St Luke's, Heavitree Road, Exeter EX1 2LU
01392 263263

Davis, N. Prof.; Tearle, P. Mrs ; Baggott, L. Dr; Twyford, J. Mr; Jennings, S. Mrs

Telematics for teacher training

ABSTRACT: This is a European Commission sponsored project in association with: Dublin City University; Institut Universitaire De Formation Des Maitres De L'Academie De Grenoble, France; Universsudade Di Minho, Portugal; Oulu University, Finland; International Computers Limited, London; Utrecht University, Netherlands; the Istituto Technologie Didattiche, Italy; and University of Gwent, Belgium. The Telematics for Teacher Training project (T3) has encouraged over 4,000 teachers to adopt telecommunications and new technologies in schools and universities across the European Union. It will establish courses for teachers within a growing consortium of universities and commercial services, which will continue to develop beyond the millennium. Primary and secondary teachers, their teacher trainers and library staff, will develop new practices together, enhancing the quality of learning and knowledge of Europe within the curriculum. Best practice will be refined for teachers of mathematics, languages, science and technology in several European languages and many cultures. T3 will focus on supporting the new approach to education and training within the European Union: lifelong learning. Teachers will model this practice in front of their students. Teachers' skills in both telematics applications and in tutoring students how to learn for themselves will be available, even in remote rural areas, with the use of new technologies. Universities in Belgium, Finland, France, Ireland, Italy, The Netherlands, Portugal and the UK form the consortium with support from partners which include telecommunication companies. These universities across Europe will design and develop courses for both staff and students. For example, 'Telematics for teachers of mathematics'. Other courses will use telematics naturally within their delivery, such as in school based teacher training and in the tutoring of teachers studying for Masters of Education. Commercial partners and ministries will use the experience to develop policies, services and marketing strategies appropriate to education. The three year project will commence in January 1996 and within two months, the 'T3 Centrum' will provide a meeting place for teachers on the Internet. There they will find resources, information and opportunities for team teaching and collaborative development across Europe. International desk top videoconferencing through dial-up ISDN will provide further opportunities. The project will also refine a European core curriculum in telematics for teacher trainers and provide guidelines for library staff in their support of teachers. These will be validated with European professional associations and education ministries.

STATUS: Sponsored project

SOURCE OF GRANT: European Commission £1,584,766

DATE OF RESEARCH: 1996-continuing

KEYWORDS: **electronic mail; international educational exchange; preservice teacher education; telecommunications; teleconferencing**

0619

School of Education, St Luke's, Heavitree Road, Exeter EX1 2LU
01392 263263

Cousins, J. Ms; *Supervisors*: Desforges, C. Prof.; Hughes, M. Prof.

Teachers talking: theorising from their experiences

ABSTRACT: This empirical research fits into the broad area of teachers' professional development and research into teachers' thought processes. The perspective is humanistic constructivist. To enhance understanding of the part played by 'talk' in theory generation, the researcher draws upon socio-cultural and cognitive psychology in Bruner (BRUNER, J. (1990). Acts of meaning. Cambridge, MA: Harvard University Press). The researcher questions how ten reception teachers use language (talk) to theorise from their classroom experiences. This action research with participant observation and a case study approach, was carried out in collaboration with the ten teachers for a year. The research vehicle was the oral language of young children. Tape recordings were made of the ten teachers' half-termly research discussions about their experiences of children who did not appear to talk at school and the classroom practice they used to encourage such children. These six focused, and purposeful, professional discussions allowed adequate time for depth, expansion, challenge and presentation of alternative stances. Evidence provided by the tape recordings illuminates the part which the communicative process plays in theory generation and in the changes (or lack of changes) in teachers' theories. The following five categories of teachers' professional talk were identified: 1) to reassure each other; 2) to reinforce theories; 3) to challenge theories; 4) to realise the possibility of an alternative theory for the same phenomenon; 5) to reconstruct theories. The results show that initially the predominant talk of the ten teachers fell into categories (1) and (2) which reflect either no theorising of experience, or theorising to confirm or to reinforce a point of view. In the course of their research, the teachers' talk deepened to (3) the challenge of a theory, followed by (4) the presentation or realisation of an equally valid theory which, in turn, sometimes resulted in (5) theory construction. The research is small-scale but nevertheless gives evidence of how teachers' professional discussions can provide the 'deep' process experience needed for intellectual growth and the reconstruction of their theories. When related to the work of Chinn and Brewer (CHINN, C. & BREWER, W. (1993). 'The role of anomalous data in knowledge acquisition: a theoretical framework and implications for science instruction', Review of Educational Research, Vol 63, No 1, pp.1-49), and that of Desforges (DESFORGES, C. (1995). How does experience affect theoretical knowledge for teaching?. Exeter: University of Exeter Research Publication), teacher challenge (3) is a key element which creates a state of intellectual disequilibrium necessary for change. In their subconscious search for a new equilibrium, teachers may consider another theory. The researcher's evidence shows, however, that such theory reconstruction is complex. Teachers' theories have also to match their experiences and to work for them in practice.

STATUS: Individual research

DATE OF RESEARCH: 1987-1998

KEYWORDS: **discussion; educational theories; teacher attitudes; teaching experience**

0620

School of Education, St Luke's, Heavitree Road, Exeter EX1 2LU
01392 263263

Harvey, P. Mr; Birbeck, N. Mr; Holbrook, A. Mr; *Supervisors*: Davis, N. Prof.; Williams, M. Dr

The COPERNICUS project and MATEN project

ABSTRACT: The COPERNICUS project is sponsored by the European Commission under DG XIII. Coordinated by the Faculty of Educational Science and Technology at the University of Twente in the Netherlands, the COPERNICUS project is devoted to investigation into the methods and techniques for flexible and distance learning. The University of Exeter, under the supervision of Professor Niki Davis, has been involved in the project since its inception in January 1995, together with universities in Lithuania (Kaunas University of Technology), Ukraine (Glushkov Institute of Cybernetics) and Bulgaria (Sofia University). The project will run until December 1997. The growth of distance education is taking place at a rapid pace. This has generated a number of issues regarding the challenges faced by learners who are studying alone and are often in remote locations. The main goal of the COPERNICUS project is to develop a pedagogical framework for teleteaching using telematics networks which can be applied to both individual learners and groups. This will involve the development of a conceptual model for a flexible and distance learning system (FDLS) that will enable the project team to create methods and techniques for courseware development. The project is now at the stage of developing courses on Communication and Information Technologies (CIT) and English teaching. The MATEN project is building upon this adding multimedia on the Web and a course in multimedia. It is also researching the organisation of distance learning centres.

STATUS: Collaborative

SOURCE OF GRANT: European Commission £38,000

DATE OF RESEARCH: 1997-continuing

KEYWORDS: **computer assisted learning; computer uses in education; distance education; flexible learning; information technology; international educational exchange; telecommunications; telecourses**

0621

School of Education, St Luke's, Heavitree Road, Exeter EX1 2LU
01392 263263

Bennett, N. Prof.; Dunne, E. Mrs; Carre, C. Dr

The acquisition and development of core skills in higher education and employment

ABSTRACT: The overarching aim of the project is to achieve improvements in the acquisition and development of core skills in both higher education and employment. Research objectives are to ascertain: 1) university teachers' understandings of their role, purposes and priorities, and how those relate to practice; 2) an understanding of what core skills are taught, with which approaches and with what quality of outcomes, in both university and employment settings; 3) students' conceptions of teaching and learning in universities, including attitudes towards the acquisition of core skills; 4) employers' perspectives on the need for core skills in different types of employment; 5) descriptions of the core skills used, for what purposes and in what contexts, during the first year of graduate employment; 6) provision of models of good practice, including guidance on implementation, derived from both higher education and employment settings. The design has been planned in three stages. In Stage 1, policy and practice in four universities will be ascertained prior to the study of examples of innovatory practice in the teaching of core skills. In Stage 2, the focus will be on graduates in their first year of employment, in particular on their expectations and experiences, the skill demand in their different work or task contexts, and the opportunities for, and quality of, training in core skills. In Stage 3, the focus will be on ways of improving core skills provision either side of the higher education/employment interface, including development work on implementation. Data will be collected from 32 staff in 16 departments in 4 universities. Data in employment settings will be acquired from national, and small and medium sized enterprises, chosen to represent the range of graduate employment. A range of research methods will be used, including interview, observation, and narrative techniques.

STATUS: Sponsored project

SOURCE OF GRANT: Economic and Social Research Council £143,000

DATE OF RESEARCH: 1995-1998

KEYWORDS: **basic skills; graduate employment; higher education; skill development; skills; transfer of learning**

0622

School of Education, St Luke's, Heavitree Road, Exeter EX1 2LU
01392 263263

Altun, E. Mr; *Supervisors*: Davis, N. Prof.; Preece, P. Prof.

Interactive multimedia systems in teaching and learning: a study of interactive video with special reference to learner attitudes, anxiety and learning preferences

ABSTRACT: The theme of the research is based on evaluating one of the latest multimedia technologies, interactive video, in regard to students' attitudes, anxieties and learning preferences. For this purpose, a review of the literature has been carried out which articulates interactivity and interactive learning concepts, theories of learning and their implications for multimedia applications, student anxiety and instructional technologies as well as attitudes to various learning settings. The gathering of data includes: observations, filming, questionnaires and interviews. A total of 139 students from a college in Taunton have participated in the data collection for the study over a period of two years. Qualitative and quantitative data analysis has been applied.

STATUS: Individual research

DATE OF RESEARCH: 1993-1997

KEYWORDS: anxiety; computer assisted learning; computer uses in education; human computer interaction; information technology; interactive video; multimedia; student attitudes

0623

School of Education, St Luke's, Heavitree Road, Exeter EX1 2LU
01392 263263

Greenhough, P. Ms; *Supervisors*: Hughes, M. Prof.; Preece, P. Prof.

The effects of gender and status on social interaction and learning in young children

ABSTRACT: This research examines the social interaction taking place in 36 similar ability dyads as they use simple logo commands to control a turtle robot. The children (aged 7-8 years) worked in same-sex pairs (12 girl-girl, 12 boy-boy) or mixed pairs (12 boy-girl) over a period of time and on different tasks. Central research questions concern how the gender of the child and the gender of the partner effect interaction and outcomes. A particular focus is the extent to which pairs vary in terms of equality and mutuality and whether these vary over time or according to task. The research also considers how the observed interactions relate to the children's judgements of self and partner efficacy. Statistical analyses of the data are, as yet, incomplete.

STATUS: Individual research

DATE OF RESEARCH: 1991-1997

KEYWORDS: group work; interaction; interpersonal relationship; learning; peer relationship; primary education; pupil behaviour; sex differences

0624

School of Education, St Luke's, Heavitree Road, Exeter EX1 2LU
01392 263263

Burghes, D. Prof.; Blum, W. Prof.

Kassel project

ABSTRACT: The Kassel project is an international comparative project on the teaching and learning of mathematics. To enable comparisons to be made between the ways in which mathematics is taught in each of the participating countries, the researchers are undertaking large scale testing and observation of mathematics classes, measuring the progress of individual pupils aged 14-16, over 2 or 3 years, looking at a variety of influences on teaching and learning for each participating class. These include school type, schemes of work, teaching time, and mathematical curriculum. The information is obtained through the use of questionnaires. Three countries, England, Scotland and Germany, were involved in the first phase of the project, starting in 1994. Since then, another 14 countries worldwide have joined. Progress is measured by yearly 40 minute tests in the topics - Number, Shape and Space, Algebra and Handling Data. Exact translations of the tests are used. Comparisons are made relative to a yardstick of potential ability in mathematics measured through a Potential Test, taken by each pupil at the beginning of their participation in the project. Data is processed using a statistical software package, to enable analysis, comparison and correlation of progress with a variety of influencing factors. Schools receive full information about the progress of their own participating pupils; the complete analysis of test results will be available to all for comparison. Reports based on the data and its analysis will not name individual schools. The aim of the project is to make recommendations about good practice in the teaching and learning of mathematics, based on sound research evidence. The researchers hope to be able to provide relevant information on aspects such as: 1) comparison in attainment across topics in the participating countries; 2) changes in numerical competence with increasing use of calculators; 3) effectiveness of self-paced schemes; and 4) problem solving and investigational aspects in the teaching of mathematics. The final project report is due in the Summer of 1999.

STATUS: Sponsored project

SOURCE OF GRANT: The Gatsby Charitable Foundation; Exeter University; Kassel University; The Post Office; The British Council

DATE OF RESEARCH: 1993-1997

KEYWORDS: comparative education; international educational exchange; mathematics achievement; mathematics education; secondary education

0625

School of Education, St Luke's, Heavitree Road, Exeter EX1 2LU
01392 263263

Burghes, D. Prof.

Mathematics enhancement programme: demonstration project

ABSTRACT: The mathematics enhancement programme, demonstration project, is being set up to implement the main recommendations resulting from the Kassel project, which has been comparing attainment in secondary school mathematics in 17 countries worldwide and attempting to identify factors which give rise to enhanced progress. The recommendations cover areas including the mathematics curriculum and the way in which mathematics is taught and assessed. From Summer 1996, the researchers at the Centre for Innovation in Mathematics Teaching (CIMT) will be working with a number of schools with the objective of raising mathematical attainment in pupils across all ability levels. They are following the Year 10 cohorts through to General Certificate in Secondary Education (GCSE) examinations in about 95 schols in the Summers of 1998 and 1999. Mathematics staff in each project school will work closely with support staff at CIMT in order to implement the recommendations. The first year of the project will be used to foster strong links between CIMT and its project schools, with inservice courses designed to clarify the researchers' objectives and to give guidance on how to put into practice recommendations for Year 9 classes. The main implementation will be in the following two years as the pupils study for their GCSE examinations. Schemes of work will be based on top sets reaching Level 10, middle sets reaching Level 8 and lower sets reaching Level 6, of the National Curriculum. It is expected that schools will continue to use some of their current resources, but these will be supplemented, and in some cases replaced, by material provided by CIMT, including suitable tests linked to the schemes of work. Inservice and extra resource material will be provided free to project schools, although only limited central funds will be available to schools for supply cover or other relevant support. The project is being extended in 1998/99 by working with Year 7 cohorts in about 90 schools (and continuing into Years 8 and 9 in subsequent years) and by working with Reception and Year 1 pupils in the feeder primary schools to some of the secondary project schools.

STATUS: Sponsored project

SOURCE OF GRANT: The Gatsby Charitable Foundation; The Post Office; British Steel; Esso

DATE OF RESEARCH: 1995-continuing

KEYWORDS: curriculum development; educational improvement; improvement programmes; mathematics education; secondary education

0626

School of Education, St Luke's, Heavitree Road, Exeter EX1 2LU
01392 263263

Lings, P. Ms; *Supervisor*: Desforges, C. Prof.

Subject differences in applying knowledge to learn: towards a theory of constraints and modularity

ABSTRACT: The view that children apply their knowledge to learn in different ways according to the academic subject underpins current perspectives on learning and teaching. The structure of the National Curriculum, for instance, with its insistence on the learning and teaching of discrete academic subjects, has evolved from deep-rooted epistemological beliefs in subject differences. This study investigates whether children engage differently with different subjects in the classroom. A theoretical perspective is taken which is informed by a view which sees knowledge building as both a personal in-the-head process and also as dependent on the socio-cultural setting. Key studies are evaluated in the area of children as curriculum theorists. A major contribution to ways of understanding knowledge application is then described: the theory of constraints and modularity. The study reviews the literature that illustrates how this theory has been applied in infant research and in classroom learning. In the current study, primary children were given tasks in which they had the opportunity to learn in mathematics, English and science. Using thinking-aloud protocols, data was collected on their thoughts and actions while they were engaged with these subjects and trying to learn. To develop the theory of constraints and modularity, twelve of these case studies were analysed using qualitative data analysis methods. The results support the view that, contrary to current assumptions, children do not differentiate between subjects, but are constrained, rather, by their expereince in the context of the classroom.

STATUS: Individual research

DATE OF RESEARCH: 1991-1997

KEYWORDS: **cognitive processes; intellectual disciplines; learning processes**

0627

School of Education, St Luke's, Heavitree Road, Exeter EX1 2LU
01392 263263

Roberts, A. Ms; *Supervisors*: Desforges, C. Prof.; Harvard, G. Mr

The cognitive skills of experienced occupational therapists and their development

ABSTRACT: This research study aims to identify the cognitive skills that experienced therapists use in practice. It also aims to explore to what extent these skills develop during a period of continuing education. The participants are all therapists, about to start the first or second year of an advanced course or one year post course. The total population of 54 students were asked to participate; 41 gave their consent. This study is naturalistic and employs a cross-sectional and longitudinal design. It is cross-sectional in that it gathers data from different year groups on 2 occasions a year apart and longitudinal in that it follows individuals as case studies across 2 years of their development. Written facsimile materials were used to elicit therapists' thinking about the tasks of the profession. Analysis of the content and process of thinking is currently taking place. Preliminary findings suggest that thinking processes and development are idiosyncratic and therefore a semi-structured interview was carried out with all participants in order to examine factors which may have affected their development.

STATUS: Individual research

DATE OF RESEARCH: 1993-1997

KEYWORDS: **cognitive development; occupational therapists; professional continuing education; professional development; thinking skills**

0628

School of Education, St Luke's, Heavitree Road, Exeter EX1 2LU
01392 263263

Ursell, S. Mrs; *Supervisor*: Desforges, C. Prof.

Secondary teachers' models of knowledge application in mathematics

ABSTRACT: The purpose of the research is to identify the mental models that mathematics teachers have of knowledge use and application, and the relationship of these models to teaching and learning in the National Curriculum in key stages 3 and 4. The issue of knowledge application is significant in education and is identified as such in National Curriculum mathematics. It is expected that children will be taught to use and apply the skills and concepts they meet. However, there is a mountain of evidence showing that this objective is proving very difficult to attain. The researcher's view is that the teacher is the key mediator of mathematics experience in the classroom and that teachers' activities are themselves mediated by the models of instruction which they operate. The objective of the research is to identify teachers' models of mathematics application for teaching and learning and to relate these to children's modes of engagement with the curriculum. A sample of teachers, willing to collaborate in the project, has been recruited. Data will be collected using a range of interview and systematic classroom observation methods as appropriate. Data will be required on teachers' planning, thinking, objectives, evaluations and activities in the classroom as they present and monitor work for children. Data will also be required on the nature and level of children's engagement in the tasks. Data collection will focus on tasks and activities specifically

designed to promote applications. Analysis will relate thinking to planning, provision and pupil engagement. It is anticipated that the research will explore models of teacher planning which, to smaller or greater degrees, support pupils' engagement in applications work. It is expected that a model of professional development will be identified in this domain.

STATUS: Individual research

DATE OF RESEARCH: 1995-continuing

KEYWORDS: **key stage 3; key stage 4; mathematics education; mathematics teachers; secondary education; teaching methods; teaching process**

0629

School of Education, St Luke's, Heavitree Road, Exeter EX1 2LU
01392 263263

Haynes, G. Ms; Wragg, C. Dr; Chamberlain, R. Dr; *Supervisor*: Wragg, E. Prof.

Teaching competence project

ABSTRACT: Most teachers are found to be competent at their job, but a small number are alleged to be incompetent. This is the largest study ever undertaken in the UK of teachers who are said to be incompetent. The research uses interviews and questionnaires to elicit the perceptions and experiences of over a thousand people, including headteachers, teachers, local authority officers, trade union officials, parents, governors and pupils. A large-scale national survey produced 654 responses from primary and secondary headteachers, each describing in detail the case of a teacher alleged to be incompetent in which they had been personally involved. There have also been interviews with 70 headteachers. 70 teachers against whom allegations have been made have also been studied, as has a sample of teachers who have worked alongside teachers said not to be competent. Interviews with local authority officers and officials from all the major teacher and headteacher unions who have been involved in competence proceedings show in detail what transpires when action is taken. Lay constituencies are also included, and questionnaires from and interviews with chairs of governing bodies and parents have given a picture of their experiences and perceptions. The pupil perspective is also included and 500 interviews with children of both primary and secondary age have been carried out.

PUBLISHED MATERIAL: WRAGG, E.C., HAYNES, G.S., WRAGG, C.M. & CHAMBERLAIN, R.P. Failing teachers. London: Routledge. (in press).

STATUS: Sponsored project

SOURCE OF GRANT: Gatsby Foundation £139,157

DATE OF RESEARCH: 1997-continuing

KEYWORDS: **incompetent teachers; teacher effectiveness; teaching profession**

0630

School of Education, St Luke's, Heavitree Road, Exeter EX1 2LU
01392 263263

Desforges, C. Prof.; Green, L. Ms; Chedzoy, S. Ms; Hennessy, S. Ms; Rolfe, L. Ms; Naughton, C. Mr; Stanton, W. Mr

Researching the base-line skills primary teachers need to train students in teaching the arts in schools

ABSTRACT: Recent government requirements for teacher education have changed the balance of school-based training of students giving teachers greater responsibility for training students. This research involves systematic enquiry into both the effectiveness of the university-based courses and the support given by primary teachers to students in teaching the arts in schools. The Gulbenkian Report (1982) identified that primary teachers lacked confidence in teaching the arts. Nevertheless, the National Curriculum has now made it a statutory requirement for primary teachers to teach Art, Dance, Drama and Music. This being the case, under the new arrangements in which teacher training is substantially undertaken by teachers in schools, what effect does this lack of confidence have on their effectiveness in training students and what are the components of confidence? There has been no recent national research into the teaching of the arts but Whitehead and Menter (1996) report that teachers generally perceive themselves as lacking in professional expertise and confidence. This is an issue of national not just local concern. We are researching teachers' confidence and competence to help students plan, teach and assess the four subjects. Our research attempts to establish what teachers do that contributes most usefully to the students' approaches to teaching the subjects. It will also lead to greater insights and understanding of the nature of teacher 'confidence'. Analysis of the findings will generate ideas that will both inform initial teacher training and allow the development of strategies and procedures to better support student learning in schools.

PUBLISHED MATERIAL: ROLFE, L. & CHEDZOY, S. (1997). 'A study of student teachers' perceptions of teaching dance in primary schools', European Journal of Physical Education, Vol 2, No 2, pp.218-227. ; STANTON, W. (1997). 'Teacher education or on-the-job training? The position of drama', National Association for Drama in Education Journal (Australia), Vol 21, No 2, pp.61-73. ; GREEN, L., CHEDZOY, S., HARRIS, W., MITCHELL, R., NAUGHTON, C., ROLFE, L. & STANTON, W. (1998), 'A study of student teachers' perceptions of teaching the arts in primary schools', British Educational Research Journal, Vol 24, No 1, pp.95-107. ; GREEN, L. & MITCHELL, R. 'Student teachers' perceptions of art teaching in primary schools', Journal of Art & Design Education. (in press).

STATUS: Sponsored research

SOURCE OF GRANT: University of Exeter Research Fund £5,000

DATE OF RESEARCH: 1996-continuing

KEYWORDS: art education; arts; dance; drama; music; preservice teacher education; primary education; primary school teachers; school based teacher education; student teachers; teacher confidence

0631

School of Education, St Luke's, Heavitree Road, Exeter EX1 2LU
01392 263263

Preece, P. Prof.; *Supervisor*: Baxter, J. Dr

Telecommunications in Primary Science (TIPS)

ABSTRACT: In this project, set up jointly by Exeter University and British Telecom, the aim is to investigate the sharing of good practice in primary science teaching among schools through the medium of telematics.

STATUS: Sponsored project

DATE OF RESEARCH: 1996-continuing

KEYWORDS: computer uses in education; information technology; primary education; science education; telecommunications; teleconferencing

0632

School of Education, St Luke's, Heavitree Road, Exeter EX1 2LU
Kenyatta University, Nairobi, Kenya

Peacock, A. Dr; Murila, B. Ms

Primary science text material for second language learners in developing countries

ABSTRACT: The project is investigating the difficulties which science textbooks pose for children when they are required to learn in a language which is not their mother tongue. It is being developed jointly with staff from Kenyatta University, Nairobi, and universities in South Africa. Initially, a research method is being refined for observing how teachers and children use science material in primary classrooms. Simultaneously, detailed textual and meta-textual analyses are being made of material used in classrooms, based on a wide range of recently developed methods for such analysis, particularly in South Africa and Canada.

PUBLISHED MATERIAL: PEACOCK, A. (1995). 'The use of primary science schemes with second language learners', Primary Science Review, Vol 38, pp.14-15. ; PEACOCK, A. (1996). 'An agenda for research on text material in primary science for second language learners of English in developing countries', Journal of Multilingual and Multicultural Development, Vol 16, No 5, pp.389-402.

STATUS: Sponsored project

SOURCE OF GRANT: University of Exeter Research Fund; British Council
DATE OF RESEARCH: 1994-continuing

KEYWORDS: developing countries; english - second language; language of instruction; science education; textbooks

0633

School of Education, St Luke's, Heavitree Road, Exeter EX1 2LU
01392 263263
Plymouth University, Faculty of Arts and Education, Rolle School of Education, Douglas Avenue, Exmouth EX8 2AT
01395 255309

Savage, J. Ms; *Supervisor*: Desforges, C. Prof.

The role of informal assessment in teachers' practical action

ABSTRACT: Claims for the value of assessment in learning are extensive. These claims are advanced more on rhetoric than evidence. If there are conceptual or empirical links between teacher assessment and future action taken in classrooms, studies establishing these are hard to find. If the focus is on the relationship between assessment and its ability to promote learning, a better understanding of classroom practice seems essential. This classroom based research is intended to inform two questions: 1) In what ways do teachers distinguish between children; and 2) How do these perceived differences relate to the provision for learning made for children in practice in classrooms? A sample of 9 teachers of 5-7 year olds had their classroom action videotaped. The technique of stimulated recall was used to collect data on teacher thinking on action as taped. To date, a detailed analysis of the data with regard to 3 of the 9 teachers has been carried out. Findings so far are that the 3 teachers made considerable distinctions at the conceptual level between the children. They did not make distinctions at the level of planning activities and in providing materials, nor were there signficicant differences in interaction patterns between each teacher and their target children. The study raises a number of questions relevant to understanding life in classrooms and to the improvement of practice.

PUBLISHED MATERIAL: SAVAGE, J. & DESFORGES, C. (1995). 'The role of informal assessment in teachers' practical action', Educational Studies, Vol 21, No 3, pp.433-446.

STATUS: Individual research

DATE OF RESEARCH: 1989-1997

KEYWORDS: assessment; assessment by teachers; informal assessment; primary education; teacher behaviour; teacher pupil relationship

0634

School of Education, St Luke's, Heavitree Road, Exeter EX1 2LU
01392 263263
Reading University, Faculty of Education and Community Studies, Department of Science and Technology Education, Bulmershe Court, Earley, Reading RG6 1HY
01189 875123
Sheffield Hallam University, Multimedia Centre for Education, 36 Collegiate Crescent, Sheffield S10 2BP
01142 720911
University of Northumbria at Newcastle, Educational Development Service, Ellison Building, Ellison Place, Newcastle upon Tyne NE1 8ST
0191 232 60

Davis, N. Prof.; Tearle, P. Ms; Hart, D. Ms; Dillon, P. Dr; Hudson, A. Ms; Edwards, A. Mr

Images for teaching education: a teaching and learning technology programme project

ABSTRACT: The 3-year Teaching and Learning Technology Programme: Images for Teaching Education, was led by the University of Exeter in collaboration with the University of Reading, Sheffield Hallam University and the University of Northumbria at Newcastle. The project has created and is disseminating and implementing a range of multimedia resources which will enhance and extend initial teacher education (ITE) throughout the UK. The resources address issues and practice relevant to every student teacher across all subject disciplines. The resources include: 1) Critical Encounters in Secondary Education videodisc, videotape and support materials; 2) Multimedia in the Learning Environment - videodisc, videotape and support materials; 3) English Chalklands - Photo CD Portfolio and support materials; 4) Design and Technology - Photo CD and support materials. It is anticipated that the materials will reinforce and enhance current courses, as well as extending teaching and learning styles. Some of the resources will also be applicable to other students in higher education, as well as being useful for inservice teacher education, staff development in schools and universities, and use in other establishments such as libraries, museums and other educational institutions. Alongside the materials, the project has developed a flexible learning framework which responds to the need to integrate the materials into an appropriate self-study framework. The development of versions of the resources on other formats is under review. In addition to this, new approaches are being explored which incorporate multimedia communications.

PUBLISHED MATERIAL: TEARLE, P. (1995). Critical encounters in secondary education: interactive videodisk and related materials. Exeter: University of Exeter, TLTP ITE Consortium. ; HUDSON, A. & POUNTNEY, R. (1995). Multimedia in the learning environment: interactive videodisk and related materials. Exeter: University of Exeter, TLTP ITE Consortium. ; DILLON, P. (1995). English Chalklands: Photo CD Portfolio and related materials. Exeter: University of Exeter, TLTP ITE Consortium. ; DILLON, P. (1995). Design and Technology: Photo CD and related materials. Exeter: University of Exeter, TLTP ITE Consortium.

STATUS: Sponsored project

SOURCE OF GRANT: Higher Education Funding Council for England; Scottish Higher Education Funding Council; Higher Education Funding Council for Wales; Department of Education Northern Ireland; Participating Universities, jointly £300,000

DATE OF RESEARCH: 1993-1998

KEYWORDS: **computer uses in education; educational materials; information technology; material development; multimedia; preservice teacher education**

0635

School of Education, St Luke's, Heavitree Road, Exeter EX1 2LU
01392 263263
University College of St Mark and St John, Derriford Road, Plymouth PL6 8BH
01752 777188

Wray, D. Prof.; Medwell, J. Ms; Poulson, L. Ms

The effective teachers of literacy project

ABSTRACT: The aim of this research is to explore the question of how teachers of literacy become effective, by identifying how and when this effectiveness is acquired. Key questions of the research include the following: 1) What do effective teachers know about literacy and how to teach it; how was this knowledge gained and developed? 2) How do teachers become effective at organising literacy work in their classrooms? 3) What are the specific opportunities for, and experience of, inservice training or curriculum development which have helped teachers become more effective at teaching literacy? 4) What are the key change points in literacy teacher development? 5) What specific forms of support and leadership in schools have encouraged and supported effective teachers of literacy? A sample of 300 teachers deemed to be effective teachers of literacy will be identified. Criteria used in identification of the sample will include Office for Standards in Education (OFSTED) reports, local education authority (LEA) personnel recommendations and value added test data. A questionnaire will be completed to establish the key features of the teachers' backgrounds, experience, literacy knowledge and teaching strategies. A sub-sample of 30 teachers will be interviewed and observed twice whilst teaching literacy. Interviews will focus on these teachers' beliefs about and attitudes towards literacy and its teaching. A parallel study will investigate the literacy knowledge, attitudes and beliefs of a sample of 50 teachers in training and 50 newly qualified teachers. Similar research techniques will be used. This study will enable the researchers to make comparisons between expert and novice teachers of literacy.

STATUS: Sponsored project

SOURCE OF GRANT: Teacher Training Agency £75,000

DATE OF RESEARCH: 1995-1997

KEYWORDS: **literacy education; reading teaching; teacher development; teacher effectiveness; writing teaching**

0636

School of Postgraduate Medicine and Health Sciences, St Luke's, Heavitree Road, Exeter EX1 2LU
01392 263263

Armstrong, N. Prof.

Children's health and well-being

ABSTRACT: The Children's Health and Exercise Research Centre, under the direction of Professor Armstrong and colleagues, has been devoted to the study of children's health and well-being since its development from the coronary prevention in children project in 1987. Initial research focused on the prevalence in children of factors known to be associated with coronary heart disease in adults, i.e. adverse lipid profiles, high blood pressure, obesity, cigarette smoking, low levels of physical fitness and sedentary lifestyles. Subsequent work has focused on developmental aspects of aerobic fitness, body composition and physical activity patterns; challenged conventional means of assessing and interpreting young people's body composition, fitness and physical activity; examined the effects of exercise training on children's health and fitness; and explored the implications of the data for school health education and physical education programmes. A series of intergrated cross-sectional studies have involved 1,500 children aged 9 to 18 years. In addition, a 4 year longitudinal study of 270 children, aged 10 years at onset, has been completed. The data have described the prevalence of coronary risk factors in children and in particular, the low level of young people's habitual physical activity. The results of recent and ongoing studies have demonstrated that there is little evidence to suggest that the current generation of children and adolescents are less fit than their predecessors.

PUBLISHED MATERIAL: ARMSTRONG, N., BALDING, J., GENTLE, P. & KIRBY, B. (1990). 'Patterns of physical activity among 11 to 16 year-old British children', British Medical Journal, Vol 301, pp.203-205. ; ARMSTRONG, N., KIRBY, B., MCMANUS, A. & WELSMAN, J. (1995). 'Aerobic fitness of prepubescent children', Annals of Human Biology, Vol 22, pp.427-441. ; ARMSTRONG, N., KIRBY, B., MCMANUS, A. & WELSMAN, J.R. (1997). 'Prepubescents' ventilatory responses to exercise with reference to sex and body size', Chest, Vol 112, pp.1554-1560. ; ARMSTRONG, N. & WELSMAN, J. (1997). Young people and physical activity. Oxford: Oxford University Press.

STATUS: Sponsored project

SOURCE OF GRANT: British Heart Foundation; Healthy Heart Research Trust; Northcott Devon Medical Foundation; Physical Education Association; Sports Council; Reebok PLC

DATE OF RESEARCH: 1985-continuing

KEYWORDS: **children; health; human body; physical activities; physical activity level; well being**

Further Education Development Agency

0637

Coombe Lodge, Blagdon, Bristol BS18 6RG
01761 462503

Civil, J. Mrs; *Supervisor*: Fineman, S. Dr

Effects of emotion and sexuality in the organizational processes of management

ABSTRACT: This research will look at the effect of emotions and sexuality in the organizational processes of management. Particularly, appraisal, management, structures, interviews, promotions and divisions of labour.

STATUS: Individual research

DATE OF RESEARCH: 1990-1993

KEYWORDS: **administration; emotions; employment practices; sex differences; sexuality**

0638

Coombe Lodge, Blagdon, Bristol BS18 6RG
01761 462503

Davies, P. Mr

Choice of further studies at the end of compulsory education

ABSTRACT: The research was based around focus groups and telephone interviews with 396 young people who took GCSEs during 1992, concerning the significant demographic and attitudinal factors which influenced their choice of further studies.

STATUS: Sponsored project

SOURCE OF GRANT: Commercial contract

DATE OF RESEARCH: 1992-1993

KEYWORDS: choice of subjects; demography; further education; pupil attitudes; sixteen to nineteen education

0639

Coombe Lodge, Blagdon, Bristol BS18 6RG
01761 462503

Warrender, A-M. Mrs; Havard, R. Mr

Investors in People in post-16 institutions

ABSTRACT: The aim of this research is to identify: the extent to which post-16 institutions are committed to Investors in People; perceptions of connection with total quality management and British Standard 5750; and perceptions of support institutions have or are likely to receive from Training and Enterprise Councils. A survey report will be available from March 1993.

STATUS: Sponsored project

SOURCE OF GRANT: The Staff College

DATE OF RESEARCH: 1992-1993

KEYWORDS: colleges of further education; management in education; quality control; sixteen to nineteen education; staff development

0640

Citadel Place, Tinworth Street, London SE11 5EH
0171 840 5400

Clift-Harris, J. Ms

Inclusive colleges

ABSTRACT: This project will debate and define the concept of inclusiveness in different contexts, collect existing quality standards and performance indicators, identify gaps and issues to be addressed, and decide the next steps forward in re-defining the vision.

STATUS: Sponsored project

SOURCE OF GRANT: Further Education Development Agency

DATE OF RESEARCH: 1997-1997

KEYWORDS: colleges of further education; further education; mainstreaming; special educational needs

0641

Citadel Place, Tinworth Street, London SE11 5EH
0171 840 5400

Faraday, S. Ms

Positive approaches to challenging behaviour

ABSTRACT: In response to concerns within the further education (FE) sector about a range of challenging behaviours, this project will develop practical guidance and training in formulating and implementing college policy on challenging behaviour; the legal aspects of challenging behaviour; and strategies for promoting appropriate behaviour.

STATUS: Sponsored project

SOURCE OF GRANT: Further Education Development Agency

DATE OF RESEARCH: 1997-1997

KEYWORDS: colleges of further education; discipline problems; emotional and behavioural difficulties; further education; mainstreaming; special educational needs

0642

Citadel Place, Tinworth Street, London SE11 5EH
0171 840 5400

Gray, S. Ms

New products and services for consultancy

ABSTRACT: This project aims to produce professionally presented audit and planning tools, to enable colleges to assess their current capacity to contribute to local and regional economic development activities and to

plan their future involvement.

STATUS: Sponsored project

SOURCE OF GRANT: Further Education Development Agency

DATE OF RESEARCH: 1997-1998

KEYWORDS: college community relationship; colleges of further education; consultancy; further education

0643

Citadel Place, Tinworth Street, London SE11 5EH
0171 840 5400

Faraday, S. Ms

Whole college approaches to key skills

ABSTRACT: This project will support the implementation of a whole college approach to key skills delivery in college and in work-based programmes, and will examine the issues arising from Sir Ron Dearing's review of 16-19 qualifications.

STATUS: Sponsored project

SOURCE OF GRANT: Further Education Development Agency

DATE OF RESEARCH: 1996-1998

KEYWORDS: basic skills; colleges of further education; further education; qualifications; sixteen to nineteen education; skill development

0644

Citadel Place, Tinworth Street, London SE11 5EH
0171 840 5400

O'Kane, J. Mr

Contextualisation of GNVQs for the printing industry

ABSTRACT: This project, now in its second phase, is identifying the feasibility of contextualising the newly devised General National Vocational Qualifications (GNVQs) for the printing industry in order to ensure that the qualifications meet the industry's training needs.

STATUS: Sponsored project

SOURCE OF GRANT: British Printing Industries Federation

DATE OF RESEARCH: 1997-1998

KEYWORDS: general national vocational qualifications; industry further education relationship; printing; publishing industry; qualifications; training; vocational education; work education relationship

0645

Citadel Place, Tinworth Street, London SE11 5EH
0171 840 5400

Hughes, M. Ms

Developing vocational education and training for the 21st century

ABSTRACT: This project will examine the extent to which current proposals for post-16 vocational qualifications, and the underpinning educative processes, arising from the Dearing and Beaumont reviews, will result in an adequate and sufficient range of vocational qualifications to meet current and predicted future socio-economic demands.

STATUS: Sponsored project

SOURCE OF GRANT: Further Education Development Agency

DATE OF RESEARCH: 1997-1997

KEYWORDS: qualifications; sixteen to nineteen education; training; vocational education

0646

Citadel Place, Tinworth Street, London SE11 5EH
0171 840 5400

Hull, L. Ms

Work related curriculum for 14-16 year olds in colleges

ABSTRACT: This project seeks to identify examples of current good practice by colleges of integrated and collaborative partnerships for work related education for 14-16 year olds. It will address those issues which have a direct bearing on the implementation of good practice and develop models for the future in the light of changes in the 14-19 vocational offering. Clear links are made with the project on progression from National Curriculum key stage 4 to ensure a holistic approach to handling this age group in order to achieve a seamless progression from school to college.

STATUS: Sponsored project

SOURCE OF GRANT: Further Education Development Agency

DATE OF RESEARCH: 1997-1998

KEYWORDS: **colleges of further education; curriculum development; fourteen to nineteen education; further education; institutional cooperation; key stage 4; partnerships; school college relationship; school to further education transition; secondary education; sixteen to nineteen education; vocational education; work education relationship; work related curriculum**

0647

Citadel Place, Tinworth Street, London SE11 5EH
0171 840 5400

Sparkes, P. Ms

Planning the 14-19 curriculum

ABSTRACT: The impact on post-16 institutions of the increasing use of vocational qualifications at National Curriculum key stage 4 cannot be under-estimated. Schools and colleges will find it increasingly important to enter into collaborative arrangements in order to ensure the appropriate progression of students at 16.

STATUS: Sponsored project

SOURCE OF GRANT: Further Education Development Agency

DATE OF RESEARCH: 1997-1998

KEYWORDS: **colleges of further education; fourteen to nineteen education; further education; institutional cooperation; key stage 4; qualifications; school college relationship; school to further education transition; secondary education; sixteen to nineteen education; vocational education; vocational qualifications**

0648

Citadel Place, Tinworth Street, London SE11 5EH
0171 840 5400

Davies, P. Mr

Non-completion of GNVQs

ABSTRACT: The Department for Education and Employment has funded a major survey research project which will establish accurate measures of retention and drop-out in General National Vocational Qualifications (GNVQs), completion of courses, and time taken to complete, and the attainment of GNVQ qualifications, in full or in part. It will examine and quantify the reasons for drop-out and failure to finish courses, failure to obtain the qualification, having finished the course, and the varying time periods taken to complete and to qualify.

STATUS: Sponsored project

SOURCE OF GRANT: Department for Education and Employment

DATE OF RESEARCH: 1997-1997

KEYWORDS: **course completion rate; dropouts; further education; general national vocational qualifications; qualifications; sixteen to nineteen education; student wastage; vocational education; vocational qualifications**

0649

Citadel Place, Tinworth Street, London SE11 5EH
0171 840 5400

Kypri, P. Mr

New learning for new work

ABSTRACT: The Further Education Development Agency is engaged with a number of college, company and university representatives in a research and development consortium called 'New Learning for New Work'. The consortium has developed a series of work packages aimed at identifying the overarching skills and capabilities that will be required in workplaces in the medium term future (5-20 years ahead). From these it will investigate the kinds of learning processes and curricula that will be required to meet these requirements. Research data is being drawn from existing examples of best practice in organisations in the public, private and voluntary sectors.

STATUS: Sponsored project

SOURCE OF GRANT: Further Education Development Agency

DATE OF RESEARCH: 1997-1998

KEYWORDS: **curriculum development; further education; industry further education relationship; labour force development; learning activities; skill development; training; vocational education; work education relationship; work related curriculum**

0650

Citadel House, Tinworth Street, London SE11 5EH
0171 840 5400

Barwuah, A. Mr

Access to education and training: high density residential estates

ABSTRACT: There are indications that in spite of the need to improve on employability through education and training, and college efforts at widening participation notwithstanding, participation rates in socio-economically deprived areas are generally low. This study examines the issues as they apply to inner-city high density residential areas.

STATUS: Sponsored project

SOURCE OF GRANT: Further Education Development Agency

DATE OF RESEARCH: 1997-1997

KEYWORDS: **access to education; disadvantaged environment; further education; participation rate; training; urban areas; vocational education**

0651

Citadel Place, Tinworth Street, London SE11 5EH
0171 840 5400

Barwuah, A. Mr

Further education student profiles and college catchment areas

ABSTRACT: Further education colleges need detailed information about the populations of their catchment areas to aid marketing and other strategic activities. This study demonstrates how the information can be obtained and how it can be used to widen participation.

STATUS: Sponsored project

SOURCE OF GRANT: Further Education Development Agency

DATE OF RESEARCH: 1997-1997

KEYWORDS: **college community relationship; colleges of further education; further education; marketing; student recruitment**

0652

Citadel Place, Tinworth Street, London SE11 5EH
0171 840 5400

Martinez, P. Mr

Information and quality systems to promote student retention

ABSTRACT: Colleges already gather large volumes of data for a variety of internal and external purposes. Large scale investigations into student retention and drop-out are beyond the means of most colleges and are, in any case, impractical as routine sources of managerial information. This project will provide consultancy to a group of representative colleges to: a) determine the causes of student completion and drop-out; and b) create robust information and quality systems to promote student retention.

STATUS: Sponsored project

SOURCE OF GRANT: Further Education Development Agency

DATE OF RESEARCH: 1996-1997

KEYWORDS: **colleges of further education; course completion rate; dropouts; further education; student wastage**

0653

Citadel Place, Tinworth Street, London SE11 5EH
0171 840 5400

Barwuah, A. Mr

Urban student drop-out on different courses and programmes

ABSTRACT: This project will work with a sample of students from different programmes (subject areas) with high or low retention rates to examine what features cause such variations and what strategies can be undertaken to address student non-completion.

STATUS: Sponsored project

SOURCE OF GRANT: Further Education Development Agency

DATE OF RESEARCH: 1997-1997

KEYWORDS: **colleges of further education; course completion rate; dropouts; further education; student wastage; urban areas**

0654

Citadel Place, Tinworth Street, London SE11 5EH
0171 840 5400

Green, M. Ms

Guidance and progression at 17+

ABSTRACT: This focuses on young people who leave after one year of full-time post-school education, either because their GCSE/Intermediate General National Vocational Qualification (GNVQ) etc. is completed or they have dropped out of a 2-year programme. The emphasis is on improving destination data, guidance and progression opportunities.

STATUS: Sponsored project

SOURCE OF GRANT: Further Education Development Agency

DATE OF RESEARCH: 1997-1997

KEYWORDS: **dropouts; further education; guidance; sixteen to nineteen education; student destinations; vocational guidance**

0655

Citadel Place, Tinworth Street, London SE11 5EH
0171 840 5400

Davies, P. Mr

Factors affecting take-up of 16+ educational provision

ABSTRACT: The main outcome of this research will be a report outlining the main factors which affect students' post-16 intentions. In particular, it will highlight the factors which impact on young people in inner city areas. It will also provide examples of good practice in the provision of information and advice to young people on careers and post-16 options. The reasons for students choosing particular types of provision will be discussed.

STATUS: Sponsored project

SOURCE OF GRANT: Further Education Development Agency

DATE OF RESEARCH: 1996-1998

KEYWORDS: **career awareness; further education; guidance; pupil destinations; school leavers; school to work transition; sixteen to nineteen education; urban areas; vocational guidance**

0656

Citadel Place, Tinworth Street, London SE11 5EH
0171 840 5400

Davies, P. Mr

What makes for a satisfied student?

ABSTRACT: The Further Education Development Agency (FEDA) Survey Research Unit has considerable experience in conducting surveys of students on behalf of national bodies and individual colleges. This project will draw together the key findings arising from this work, so as to summarise the factors that are most and least associated with student satisfaction.

STATUS: Sponsored project

SOURCE OF GRANT: Further Education Development Agency

DATE OF RESEARCH: 1997-1998

KEYWORDS: **further education; participant satisfaction; student attitudes; students**

0657

Citadel Place, Tinworth Street, London SE11 5EH
0171 840 5400

Caskie, H. Ms

Counteracting gender bias in management development

ABSTRACT: This project aims to develop a framework for management development and assessment which promotes the inclusion of female experience and expertise in norms of management theory and practice. It will ascertain whether the existing Management Charter Initative (MCI) Senior Management Standards provide a framework which adequately reflects the style, values and culture of female senior managers in further education.

STATUS: Sponsored project

SOURCE OF GRANT: Further Education Development Agency

DATE OF RESEARCH: 1995-1998

KEYWORDS: **colleges of further education; further education; management development; management in education; sex differences; women; womens employment**

0658

Citadel Place, Tinworth Street, London SE11 5EH
0171 840 5400

Gray, M. Mr

Human resource planning

ABSTRACT: This project highlights colleges' needs to find, develop and retain people who can deliver their mission and targets. The Further Education Development Agency (FEDA) is producing practical guidance on how to plan qualitatively and quantitatively for the staff a college needs, using expertise and creative ideas from the further education sector and elsewhere.

STATUS: Sponsored project

SOURCE OF GRANT: Further Education Development Agency

DATE OF RESEARCH: 1996-1998

KEYWORDS: **academic staff recruitment; colleges of further education; further education; further education teachers; personnel management; professional development; recruitment; staff development**

0659

Citadel Place, Tinworth Street, London SE11 5EH
0171 840 8400

Lawson, L. Ms; Hull, L. Ms

Defining good practice: seminars and research projects

ABSTRACT: One of the Further Education Development Agency (FEDA) priorities is to help improve the quality of the learning experience of students in the further education sector. This particular project is designed to give direct and positive support to the classroom teachers by enabling: 1) practitioners to be actively involved in the drawing up of good practice criteria in their own subject areas; 2) FEDA to gather information about where good teaching practice exists, so that it can be recognised and celebrated through publications and training events.

STATUS: Sponsored project

SOURCE OF GRANT: Further Education Development Agency

DATE OF RESEARCH: 1996-1998

KEYWORDS: **colleges of further education; educational quality; further education; further education teachers; teacher effectiveness**

0660

Citadel Place, Tinworth Street, London SE11 5EH
0171 840 5400

Dixon, S. Ms

The development of self-critical improvement cultures

ABSTRACT: This project is designed to develop strategies for the development of self-critical and improving course/programme teams.

STATUS: Sponsored project

SOURCE OF GRANT: Further Education Development Agency

DATE OF RESEARCH: 1996-1998

KEYWORDS: colleges of further education; criticism; educational quality; further education; self evaluation - groups

0661

Citadel Place, Tinworth Street, London SE11 5EH
0171 840 5400

Dixon, S. Ms

Performance indicators for self-assessment

ABSTRACT: This project will devise performance indicators relating to the headings of the new inspection framework and guidance on how to use these performance indicators in order to assist colleges in their self-assessment.

STATUS: Sponsored project

SOURCE OF GRANT: Further Education Development Agency

DATE OF RESEARCH: 1997-1997

KEYWORDS: colleges of further education; educational quality; further education; institutional evaluation; performance indicators; quality control; self evaluation - groups

0662

Citadel Place, Tinworth Street, London SE11 5EH
0171 840 5400

Brownlow, S. Ms

The nature of higher and further education sub-contractual partnerships

ABSTRACT: The Further Education Funding Council (FEDA), in partnership with the Centre for Policy Studies in Education at the University of Leeds, University of Surrey and JM Consulting, have been commissioned by the Higher Education Funding Council for England (HEFCE) to investigate concerns surrounding franchising schemes. This will be both in terms of the motivation for their development, and about the standard and specification of franchised arrangements as expressed in contractual agreements and operationalised practice.

STATUS: Sponsored project

SOURCE OF GRANT: Higher Education Funding Council for England

DATE OF RESEARCH: 1998-1998

KEYWORDS: colleges of further education; contracts; cooperative programmes; educational cooperation; franchising; further education; higher education; institutional cooperation; partnerships

0663

Citadel Place, Tinworth Street, London SE11 5EH
0171 840 5400

Reisenberger, A. Ms

Good practice in access and support strategies

ABSTRACT: This project will seek to identify the range and scope of access and support strategies for young people in further education (FE) sector colleges; provide baseline data ont he management, planning, resourcing and curriculum models currently in use; identify the views of staff and student; identify case studies of good practice; make recommendations for the development of access and support strategies and disseminate the findings through a report and event targeted at the sector.

STATUS: Sponsored project

SOURCE OF GRANT: Department for Education and Employment

DATE OF RESEARCH: 1996-1998

KEYWORDS: access to education; further education

0664

Citadel Place, Tinworth Street, London SE11 5EH
0171 840 5400

Green, M. Ms

Trialling the new ProFile in further and continuing education

ABSTRACT: The Department for Education and Employment (DfEE) have commissioned the Further Education Development Agency to pilot and trial a new national record of achievement in the further education sector (ProFile). A combination of projects will cover the use of ProFile by all client groups in further education, recording progress and achievement of key skills, assessment and certification of skills gained, the role of careers and guidance staff, and its use of teaching and non-teaching staff.

STATUS: Sponsored project

SOURCE OF GRANT: Department for Education and Employment

DATE OF RESEARCH: 1997-1998

KEYWORDS: colleges of further education; continuing education; further education; profiles; records of achievement; student records; students

0665

Citadel Place, Tinworth Street, London SE11 5EH
0171 840 5400

Walker, L. Ms

Professional Code of Conduct for further education teachers

ABSTRACT: This project aims to produce a professional Code of Conduct for further education teachers, through consultation with professional bodies and trialling with potential users.

STATUS: Sponsored project

SOURCE OF GRANT: Further Education Development Agency

DATE OF RESEARCH: 1997-1997

KEYWORDS: code of practice; further education; further education teachers; teacher behaviour; teaching profession

0666

Dumbarton House, 68 Oxford Street, London W1N 0DA
0171 436 0020

Kypri, P. Mr

Training and Enterprise Council bulletins

ABSTRACT: This project will produce a series of bulletins focusing on the Training and Enterprise Council (TEC)/further education (FE) interface and targeted at TEC learning development managers and FE business development managers.

STATUS: Sponsored project

SOURCE OF GRANT: Further Education Development Agency

DATE OF RESEARCH: 1997-1997

KEYWORDS: further education; information dissemination; training and enterprise councils

0667

Citadel Place, Tinworth Street, London SE11 5EH
0171 840 5400

Kypri, P. Ms

Employee development schemes

ABSTRACT: The key purpose of this project is to examine the role of employee development schemes in promoting lifetime learning and economic development. The research will provide examples of good practice and provide quality criteria for measuring effectiveness.

STATUS: Sponsored project

SOURCE OF GRANT: Further Education Development Agency

DATE OF RESEARCH: 1997-1998

KEYWORDS: employee development schemes; employees; further education; lifelong learning; staff development

0668

Citadel Place, Tinworth Street, London SE11 5EH
0171 840 5400

Reisenberger, A. Ms

The experience of the learner in further education

ABSTRACT: This project follows the learning careers of 36 young people from their final year of schooling, through further education, and into work, higher education or other destination.

STATUS: Sponsored project

SOURCE OF GRANT: Further Education Development Agency

DATE OF RESEARCH: 1998-1998

KEYWORDS: **followup studies; further education; higher education; learning; longitudinal studies; school leavers; school to work transition; sixteen to nineteen education; student destinations; students**

0669

Citadel Place, Tinworth Street, London SE11 5EH
0171 840 5400

Morris, A. Mr

Funding further education - work package 1

ABSTRACT: The Further Education Development Agency (FEDA) aims to evaluate the impact of the Further Education Funding Council (FEFC) funding on provision in colleges and on management practice. It intends to assess how the current methodologies might service the development of post-school education over the coming decade. Before it embarks on this, FEDA wish to consult with the sector to design and agree the objectives and scope of the main study.

STATUS: Sponsored project

SOURCE OF GRANT: Further Education Development Agency

DATE OF RESEARCH: 1998-1998

KEYWORDS: **colleges of further education; educational administration; educational finance; further education; sixteen to nineteen education**

0670

Citadel Place, Tinworth Street, London SE11 5EH
0171 840 5400

Tait, T. Mr

Learning with information technology

ABSTRACT: This project will research the 'leap of faith' which some claim further education has made by investing in information technology (IT) by undertaking some fundamental research on the potential of IT to improve the learning process. The project will investigate and disseminate good practice and offer advice to teachers and institutions.

STATUS: Sponsored project

SOURCE OF GRANT: Further Education Development Agency

DATE OF RESEARCH: 1996-1998

KEYWORDS: **computer uses in education; further education; information technology; learning activities**

0671

Citadel Place, Tinworth Street, London SE11 5EH
0171 840 5400

James, S. Mr

Furthering local economies - phase 1

ABSTRACT: A project to determine the range, extent and potential for expansion of the role of English and Welsh further education colleges in local economic development and national competitiveness.

STATUS: Sponsored project

SOURCE OF GRANT: Further Education Development Agency

DATE OF RESEARCH: 1997-1998

KEYWORDS: **college community relationship; colleges of further education; economic development; further education**

0672

Citadel Place, Tinworth Street, London SE11 5EH
0171 840 5400

Mager, C. Ms

A curriculum vision for further education

ABSTRACT: This project will seek to establish a Further Education Development Agency (FEDA) lecture series, providing a forum for the sector to think beyond the here and now, and speculate creatively and broadly about future possibilities, roles and responsibilities in relation to learning. It will facilitate high profile debate, aimed at the education policy community, which raises alternative perspectives and thinking about the curriculum and its context in the future.

STATUS: Sponsored project

SOURCE OF GRANT: Further Education Development Agency

DATE OF RESEARCH: 1998-1998

KEYWORDS: **curriculum development; further education**

0673

Citadel Place, Tinworth Street, London SE11 5EH
0171 840 5400

Mager, C. Ms

Qualifications support contract

ABSTRACT: To secure a basis for continuity in planning and support for the implementation of a unitised credit framework and to provide support for sector secondees to the Qualifications and Curriculum Authority (QCA).

STATUS: Sponsored project

SOURCE OF GRANT: Further Education Funding Council

DATE OF RESEARCH: 1998-1998

KEYWORDS: **credits; further education; qualifications; sixteen to nineteen education**

0674

Citadel Place, Tinworth Street, London SE11 5EH
0171 840 5400

Tait, T. Mr

National credit framework network development project 1997/98

ABSTRACT: This project will continue to improve the services provided to the sector linking colleges and informing them about the applications and opportunities surrounding the use of unitisation and credit for institutional, local and national developments.

STATUS: Sponsored project

SOURCE OF GRANT: Further Education Development Agency

DATE OF RESEARCH: 1997-1998

KEYWORDS: **credits; further education; units of study**

0675

Citadel Place, Tinworth Street, London SE11 5EH
0171 840 5400

Tait, T. Mr

Credit framework: strategic development activities and advice

ABSTRACT: This project aims to build a wider consensus of support for utilisation and credit and to steer the Further Education Development Agency's (FEDA) work in this area, drawing on the expertise of key individuals and organisations supporting credit based developments within education training and the policy community.

STATUS: Sponsored project

SOURCE OF GRANT: Further Education Development Agency

DATE OF RESEARCH: 1997-1998

KEYWORDS: **credits; further education; units of study**

0676

Citadel Place, Tinworth Street, London SE11 5EH
0171 840 5400

Tait, T. Mr

Quality systems in unitised credit-based qualifications

ABSTRACT: The project will review a range of established unitised credit-based programmes and qualifications to examine the approaches to quality assurance. The work will inform Qualifications and Curriculum Authority's (QCA) advice to Government about the feasibility of developing a unitised credit-based system of qualifications.

STATUS: Sponsored project

SOURCE OF GRANT: Further Education Development Agency

DATE OF RESEARCH: 1998-1998

KEYWORDS: **credits; further education; qualifications; units of study**

0677

Citadel Place, Tinworth Street, London SE11 5EH
0171 840 5400

Bone, M. Mr

The effective staff and student governor

ABSTRACT: Staff/student governors are concerned about their effectiveness. This project will explore their perspectives and prepare an action plan to improve effectiveness. It has the support of NATFHE (University and College Lecturers Union), National Union of Students and UNISON.

STATUS: Sponsored project

SOURCE OF GRANT: Further Education Development Agency

DATE OF RESEARCH: 1997-1998

KEYWORDS: **colleges of further education; further education; governing bodies**

0678

Citadel Place, Tinworth Street, London SE11 5EH
0171 840 5400

Field, M. Mr; Peeke, G. Mr

Spotlight on management

ABSTRACT: This project will identify and record the components of good college management practices as exemplified by those colleges who received a Grade 1 for management in their Further Education Funding Council inspection reports. Good Practice Guides will be produced based on case studies.

STATUS: Sponsored project

SOURCE OF GRANT: Further Education Development Agency

DATE OF RESEARCH: 1997-1998

KEYWORDS: **colleges of higher education; educational administration; further education; management in education**

0679

Citadel Place, Tinworth Street, London SE11 5EH
0171 840 5400

Walker, L. Ms

Effective management of part-time lecturing staff

ABSTRACT: In recent years, many colleges have increased their use of part-time lecturing staff and some have changed the basis on which these staff are employed, through the use of teaching agencies. Claims are made, on the one hand, that this practice offers financial advantages to colleges, and, on the other, that there is a negative impact on the quality of provision. This project will seek to investigate and evaluate approaches to the management of part-time lecturing staff, and to identify good practice.

STATUS: Sponsored project

SOURCE OF GRANT: Further Education Development Agency

DATE OF RESEARCH: 1998-1998

KEYWORDS: **colleges of further education; further education; part time academic staff; part time employment**

0680

Citadel Place, Tinworth Street, London SE11 5EH
0171 840 5400

Brownlow, S. Ms; Reisenberger, A. Ms

Improving college effectiveness: scoping

ABSTRACT: Improving college effectiveness is central to all sector institutions and to the agencies which support and regulate them. This project seeks to establish the scope and focus for future development work to improve college effectiveness, learning from current sector experience and from other sectors (such as the school improvement movement). The Further Education Development Agency (FEDA) will take forward the recommendations of this project in a further set of development project during 1998/99.

STATUS: Sponsored project

SOURCE OF GRANT: Further Education Development Agency

DATE OF RESEARCH: 1998-1998

KEYWORDS: **college effectiveness; colleges of further education; educational quality; further education**

0681

Citadel Place, Tinworth Street, London SE11 5EH
0171 840 5400

Brownlow, S. Ms; Stott, C. Ms

Improving college effectiveness: effective college leadership

ABSTRACT: This project aims to identify effective approaches to the leadership of further education (FE) colleges. It takes as its definition of effectiveness the concepts of sustainedly high and/or sustained improvement in student achievement. Case studies from 8 colleges will be compared which demonstrate either significant improvements in student achievement or sustainedly high student achievement, and will look at the leadership of those colleges through qualitative and quantitative data.

STATUS: Sponsored project

SOURCE OF GRANT: Further Education Development Agency

DATE OF RESEARCH: 1998-1998

KEYWORDS: **college effectiveness; colleges of further education; educational quality; further education**

0682

Citadel Place, Tinworth Street, London SE11 5EH
0171 840 5400

Brownlow, S. Ms

Good practice in management development

ABSTRACT: Eight college based projects will address different aspects of college management development and will produce materials, programmes and other practical resources for colleges to use. Topics to be addressed include: using assessment centres for management development; developing modular, accredited programmes; transferring people management skills from classroom to staffroom; work-based learning approaches to management development; evaluating different forms of management development. The projects will run throughout 1998/99 with more than 50 colleges involved, and the resulting materials will be made available to other colleges in early 1999/2000.

STATUS: Sponsored project

SOURCE OF GRANT: Further Education Development Agency

DATE OF RESEARCH: 1998-1998

KEYWORDS: **colleges of further education; educational administration; further education; management development; management in education**

0683

Citadel Place, Tinworth Street, London SE11 5EH
0171 840 5400

Stott, C. Ms

Implementing college mergers

ABSTRACT: Colleges are being encouraged to consider merger as a possible strategy to improve the curriculum offer in an area and reduce costs. Evidence from other sectors suggests that the way the people issues are handled during and after the merger process are critical to the ultimate success of a merger. This project will examine experience of merger in the further education (FE) sector, seek reference to mergers' experience in other service sector organisations, and develop checklists of key issues and good practice guidance and examples.

STATUS: Sponsored project

SOURCE OF GRANT: Further Education Development Agency

DATE OF RESEARCH: 1998-1998

KEYWORDS: colleges of further education; educational administration; further education; mergers

0684

Citadel Place, Tinworth Street, London SE11 5EH
0171 840 5400

Brownlow, S. Ms

Standards for management in further education

ABSTRACT: This project will develop national occupational standards for further education managers in the UK. It will draw on the existing Management Charter Initiative (MCI) management standards together with other important sources including further education (FE) specific standards (in UK and Scotland), the funding councils' inspection frameworks for college management and standards for headteachers and subject leaders in the schools sector. The work will be overseen by a Steering Group on behalf of the FE Staff Development Forum, and will refer to a Task Group of sector representatives for practical advice on the standards as they develop. Drafting aims to complete by January 1999 and subsequent work packages will engage in extensive consultation with the sector followed by formal trials of the standards in use, and implementation planning, including preparation of a framework for any associated management qualifications for FE. The Further Education Development Agency (FEDA) is carrying out this project in partnership with the Scottish Further Education Unit.

STATUS: Sponsored project

SOURCE OF GRANT: Qualifications and Curriculum Authority ; Scottish Qualifications Authority

DATE OF RESEARCH: 1998-1998

KEYWORDS: colleges of further education; educational administration; further education; management; management in education; standards

0685

Citadel Place, Tinworth Street, London SE11 5EH
0171 840 5400

Gidney, M. Ms

Financial portrait of Vocational Education and Training (VET) in UK

ABSTRACT: The project will develop a descriptive portrait of the financing structures and mechanisms for vocational education and training in the UK. It will complement the existing monograph on Vocational Education and Training (VET) in the UK. These two documents in combination will provide an invaluable introduction to UK VET systems and their financing for a range of audiences, including policymakers, researchers, practitioners and planners. It will offer a comprehensive but clear outline of financing of VET in the UK to those from within and beyond the UK.

STATUS: Sponsored project

SOURCE OF GRANT: CEDEFOP

DATE OF RESEARCH: 1997-1998

KEYWORDS: educational finance; training; vocational education

0686

Citadel Place, Tinworth Street, London SE11 5EH
0171 840 5400

Fletcher, M. Mr

Assessing the impact of student financial support

ABSTRACT: Local authority discretionary awards have become significantly less common in recent years. There is also substantial variation between local authorities in the exercise of their powers to grant financial support. Variation of practice between local authorities, though a matter of concern on grounds of equity, presents a real research opportunity to identify whether access, retention and achievement might be correlated with the availability

or scale of financial support.

STATUS: Sponsored project

SOURCE OF GRANT: Further Education Development Agency

DATE OF RESEARCH: 1998-1998

KEYWORDS: educational finance; grants; local education authorities; student financial aid

0687

Citadel Place, Tinworth Street, London SE11 5EH
0171 840 5400

Faraday, S. Ms

Evaluation of the Further Education Funding Council additional support mechanism

ABSTRACT: The project is intended to investigate how colleges use the additional support element of the funding mechanism, identify where there are differences in college practice and where further guidance might be needed. Working in collaboration with officers of the Council and sector colleges, the Further Education Development Agency (FEDA) will draft, consult on, amend and disseminate a guidance document drawing on good practice from colleges.

STATUS: Sponsored project

SOURCE OF GRANT: Further Education Funding Council

DATE OF RESEARCH: 1998-1998

KEYWORDS: colleges of further education; educational finance; further education

0688

Citadel Place, Tinworth Street, London SE11 5EH
0171 840 5400

Kypri, P. Mr

Developing an implementation kit

ABSTRACT: The aim of this project is to promote college involvement in work-based employee development schemes through the development of corporate learning centres, the introduction of individual learning account for the University for Industry. Colleges will be able to work effectively with business to enhance the learning employability of their staff.

STATUS: Sponsored project

SOURCE OF GRANT: Further Education Development Agency

DATE OF RESEARCH: 1997-1998

KEYWORDS: colleges of further education; further education; staff development; work based learning

0689

Citadel Place, Tinworth Street, London SE11 5EH
0171 840 5400

Kypri, P. Mr

Adult training programmes

ABSTRACT: Workskills pilots for adult training are to be launched in April 1997. This project will provide information on the pilot programme for the unemployed and guidance on the operation of the schemes.

STATUS: Sponsored project

SOURCE OF GRANT: Further Education Development Agency

DATE OF RESEARCH: 1997-1998

KEYWORDS: adult education; skills; training; unemployment

0690

Citadel Place, Tinworth Street, London SE11 5EH
0171 840 5400

James, S. Mr

Europartnerships

ABSTRACT: A strategic research project to compare the experience of the UK further education (FE) sector in economic development with that of similar tertiary institutions in Europe.

STATUS: Sponsored project

SOURCE OF GRANT: Further Education Development Agency

DATE OF RESEARCH: 1998-1998

KEYWORDS: **comparative education; europe; further education; sixteen to nineteen education; tertiary education**

0691

Citadel Place, Tinworth Street, London SE11 5EH
0171 840 5400

Hughes, M. Ms

Examining the college's role in Education Business Partnerships

ABSTRACT: This project will investigate the extent to which Education Business Partnerships assist the development of effective links between further education (FE) colleges and employers.

STATUS: Sponsored project

SOURCE OF GRANT: Further Education Development Agency

DATE OF RESEARCH: 1998-1998

KEYWORDS: **colleges of further education; education business partnerships; further education**

0692

Citadel Place, Tinworth Street, London SE11 5EH
0171 840 5400

Hughes, M. Ms

Investing in training for the 21st century

ABSTRACT: While employers are constantly exhorted to invest in training, methods employed to determine the value of this are not well developed. This project will analyse the current methods used by British Aerospace to develop its Virtual University and how the business case for this investment is produced.

STATUS: Sponsored project

SOURCE OF GRANT: Further Education Development Agency

DATE OF RESEARCH: 1997-1998

KEYWORDS: **financial support; industry further education relationship; investment; training**

0693

Citadel Place, Tinworth Street, London SE11 5EH
0171 840 5400

Kypri, P. Mr

New Deal implementation kit

ABSTRACT: The key purpose of the New Deal is to enhance the employability of the long-term unemployed. Colleges therefore have a central role to play in the effective implementation of the New Deal. Colleges committed to the New Deal will be important not only on the full-time education and training strand, but on all the options so that education and training are offered to all learners. The purpose of this project is to support colleges in the implementation of the New Deal through the production of a viewpoints and implementation guide aimed at senior managers and New Deal coordinators in colleges.

STATUS: Sponsored project

SOURCE OF GRANT: Further Education Development Agency

DATE OF RESEARCH: 1997-1998

KEYWORDS: **colleges of further education; further education; new deal; training; unemployment**

0694

Citadel Place, Tinworth Street, London SE11 5EH
0171 840 5400

Hughes, M. Ms

The use of realistic working environments in skills development

ABSTRACT: This project will attempt to quantify the numbers and types of realistic working environments in further education (FE) colleges and the extent to which they can be used to develop the skills required to support the economic development of the local/regional workforce.

STATUS: Sponsored project

SOURCE OF GRANT: Further Education Development Agency

DATE OF RESEARCH: 1997-1998

KEYWORDS: **colleges of further education; further education; skill development; skills; work environment**

0695

Citadel Place, Tinworth Street, London SE11 5EH
0171 840 5400

James, S. Mr

Economic impact of further education

ABSTRACT: This work package, part of the project 'Furthering local economies' involves a seminar of experts on local and regional economic development. It will assess the models, approaches, usefulness and viability of students on the economic impact of further education (FE) colleges.

STATUS: Sponsored project

SOURCE OF GRANT: Further Education Development Agency

DATE OF RESEARCH: 1998-1998

KEYWORDS: **college community relationship; colleges of further education; economic development; further education**

0696

Citadel Place, Tinworth Street, London SE11 5EH
0171 840 5400

Cowham, T. Mr

Implementation of the National Traineeships

ABSTRACT: To develop and produce an implementation and development kit to support colleges in the introduction and development of National Traineeships programmes.

STATUS: Sponsored project

SOURCE OF GRANT: Further Education Development Agency

DATE OF RESEARCH: 1997-1998

KEYWORDS: **adults; national traineeship; training**

0697

Citadel Place, Tinworth Street, London SE11 5EH
0171 840 5400

James, S. Mr

Models of good partnership practice in vocational education and training (VET) delivery

ABSTRACT: To analyse and compare local networks of vocational education and training (VET) providers in 5 different European member states. The study aims at identifying different models of introducing quality criteria into a local or regional vocational training system through a networking approach.

STATUS: Sponsored project

SOURCE OF GRANT: CEDEFOP

DATE OF RESEARCH: 1998-1998

KEYWORDS: **comparative education; europe; training; vocational education**

0698

Citadel Place, Tinworth Street, London SE11 5EH
0171 840 5400

Hughes, M. Ms; Barwuah, A. Mr

Supporting local small business development

ABSTRACT: This project will pilot a partnership approach to supporting small business developments, involving further education (FE) colleges, training and enterprise councils (TECs), business links, and other local players who are also envisaged in promoting small and medium enterprises (SMEs) development etc.

STATUS: Sponsored project

SOURCE OF GRANT: Further Education Development Agency

DATE OF RESEARCH: 1997-1998

KEYWORDS: **business; colleges of further education; further education; industry further education relationship; partnerships; small businesses; training and enterprise councils**

0699

Citadel Place, Tinworth Street, London SE11 5EH
0171 840 5400

Clift-Harris, J. Ms

Inclusive learning

ABSTRACT: This project will debate and define the concept of inclusiveness in different contexts, collect existing quality standards and performance indicators, identify gaps and issues to be addressed, and decide the next steps forward in redefining the vision.

STATUS: Sponsored project

SOURCE OF GRANT: Further Education Development Agency

DATE OF RESEARCH: 1997-1998

KEYWORDS: **colleges of further education; educational quality; further education; learning disabilities; mainstreaming; performance indicators; special educational needs; standards**

0700

Citadel Place, Tinworth Street, London SE11 5EH
0171 840 5400

Faraday, S. Ms

Towards inclusive learning

ABSTRACT: The report of the Further Education Funding Council's (FEFC's) committee for learning difficulties and disabilities, 'Inclusive learning', identifies the Further Education Development Agency's (FEDA's) key role in supporting the sector to implement the recommendations in inclusive learning. In order to achieve this, FEDA has carried out an extensive consultation with college managers and practitioners to identify the priority areas for development and has agreed these with FEFC staff. This research project has a series of components, each of which addresses key areas for investigation and development. The components are structured to inform each other where appropriate and to offer cross fertilisation of ideas and development.

STATUS: Sponsored project

SOURCE OF GRANT: Further Education Development Agency

DATE OF RESEARCH: 1997-1998

KEYWORDS: **colleges of further education; further education; learning disabilities; mainstreaming; special educational needs**

0701

Citadel Place, Tinworth Street, London SE11 5EH
0171 840 5400

Faraday, S. Ms

Developing learning plans that secure 'the match'

ABSTRACT: This project will identify the components of and processes involved in the production and use of effective individual learning plans. It will result in a publication offering guidance and exemplars.

STATUS: Sponsored project

SOURCE OF GRANT: Further Education Development Agency

DATE OF RESEARCH: 1997-1998

KEYWORDS: **colleges of further education; further education; individual learning plans**

0702

Citadel Place, Tinworth Street, London SE11 5EH
0171 840 5400

Faraday, S. Ms

National Qualifications Framework: developing entry level

ABSTRACT: This project will examine effective practice at entry level, define 'progression templates' and identify effective learning programmes, accreditation and means of recognising achievement.

STATUS: Sponsored project

SOURCE OF GRANT: Further Education Development Agency

DATE OF RESEARCH: 1997-1998

KEYWORDS: **access to education; colleges of further education; further education; student improvement**

0703

Citadel Place, Tinworth Street, London SE11 5EH
0171 840 5400

Faraday, S. Ms

College-based development projects

ABSTRACT: This project is designed to promote inclusive learning through college based development activities and to produce a directory of useful documentation.

STATUS: Sponsored project

SOURCE OF GRANT: Department for Education and Employment

DATE OF RESEARCH: 1997-1998

KEYWORDS: **colleges of further education; development plans; further education; mainstreaming; special educational needs**

0704

Citadel Place, Tinworth Street, London SE11 5EH
0171 840 5400

Faraday, S. Ms

Technical survey - support for students with disabilities

ABSTRACT: To devise and test out survey instrument, to be used to carry out a national survey of technical support to enable students to learn effectively.

STATUS: Sponsored project

SOURCE OF GRANT: Further Education Development Agency

DATE OF RESEARCH: 1998-1998

KEYWORDS: **disabilities; further education; information technology; special educational needs; support services**

0705

Citadel Place, Tinworth Street, London SE11 5EH
0171 840 5400

Faraday, S. Ms

Quality and provision for students with learning difficulties/disabilities in Wales

ABSTRACT: To produce an audit instrument to enable further education (FE) institutions in Wales to self-assess inclusive learning/provision for students with learning difficulties and/or disabilities. The outcome will be a published audit instrument with guidance notes.

STATUS: Sponsored project

SOURCE OF GRANT: Further Education Development Agency

DATE OF RESEARCH: 1998-1998

KEYWORDS: **college effectiveness; colleges of education; educational quality; further education; mainstreaming; self evaluation - groups; special educational needs**

0706

Citadel Place, Tinworth Street, London SE11 5EH
0171 840 5400

Faraday, S. Ms

College-based research networks 1998/99

ABSTRACT: The project is designed to promote inclusive learning through college-based research networks and to produce a directory of project documentation.

STATUS: Sponsored project

SOURCE OF GRANT: Further Education Development Agency

DATE OF RESEARCH: 1998-1998

KEYWORDS: **colleges of further education; educational research; further education; mainstreaming**

0707

Citadel Place, Tinworth Street, London SE11 5EH
0171 840 5400

Clift-Harris, J. Ms

Sector/specialist college collaboration

ABSTRACT: In the Further Education Funding Council (FEFC) report 'Inclusive learning', one of the recommendations was to encourage collaboration between specialist/sector colleges. There is evidence of emerging models of effective collaboration, yet this is not common across the sector. This research aims to develop effective practice where it exists and use this to inform the development of models which could then be used by colleges in order to develop collaborative practice.

STATUS: Sponsored project

SOURCE OF GRANT: Further Education Development Agency

DATE OF RESEARCH: 1998-1998

KEYWORDS: **colleges of further education; further education; mainstreaming; special educational needs**

0708

Citadel Place, Tinworth Street, London SE11 5EH
0171 840 5400

Davies, V. Ms

English as a Foreign Language in colleges

ABSTRACT: A research project carried out in partnership with the British Council to look at the extent and range of English as a Foreign Language (EFL) provision in further education (FE) colleges. Good practice will be identified and the results disseminated to Heads of EFL at a summer conference.

STATUS: Sponsored project

SOURCE OF GRANT: Further Education Development Agency; British Council

DATE OF RESEARCH: 1997-1998

KEYWORDS: **colleges of further education; english - second language; further education; second language teaching**

0709

Citadel Place, Tinworth Street, London SE11 5EH
0171 840 5400

Peeke, G. Mr

Developing standards for lecturers

ABSTRACT: Funded by the Department for Education and Employment, and run in conjunction with the Further Education Development Agency's (FEDA's) Further Education Staff Development Forum, this project aims to develop and promote standards, which are widely accepted within the further education (FE) sector, for teachers/learners support.

STATUS: Sponsored project

SOURCE OF GRANT: Department for Education and Employment

DATE OF RESEARCH: 1997-1998

KEYWORDS: **further education; further education teachers; lecturers; standards**

0710

Citadel Place, Tinworth Street, London SE11 5EH
0171 840 5400

Kypri, P. Mr

Key skills kit

ABSTRACT: The implementation of effective key skills strategies to support college students and learners in the workplace is a priority for the further

education (FE) sector. The purpose of this research is to develop a key skills implementation kit, support the delivery of key skills in FE and workplace contexts.

STATUS: Sponsored project

SOURCE OF GRANT: Further Education Development Agency

DATE OF RESEARCH: 1997-1998

KEYWORDS: **core skills; further education; key skills**

0711

Citadel Place, Tinworth Street, London SE11 5EH
0171 840 5400

Mager, C. Ms

Key skills in A-levels - subject specific materials

ABSTRACT: This project will develop a range of activities, assignments and materials to support the development of key skills through A-level Sociology, and pilot a model for developing such materials which can be applied in other A-level subjects.

STATUS: Sponsored project

SOURCE OF GRANT: Further Education Development Agency

DATE OF RESEARCH: 1997-1998

KEYWORDS: **a level examinations; core skills; key skills**

0712

Citadel Place, Tinworth Street, London SE11 5EH
0171 840 5400

Green, M. Ms

Initial assessment of key skills

ABSTRACT: Colleges are placing great importance on the need to make early and informed judgement about learners' skills in order to guide them toward and select them for the most appropriate learning programme. This project, funded through the National Council for Vocational Qualifications (NCVQ), aims to agree and implement good practice criteria and guidance for the development of initial assessment tools for key skills. It will produce and publish such tools for national dissemination, and establish procedures which support valid and reliable initial assessment of key skills.

STATUS: Sponsored project

SOURCE OF GRANT: Qualifications and Curriculum Authority

DATE OF RESEARCH: 1997-1998

KEYWORDS: **assessment; colleges of further education; core skills; further education; key skills**

0713

Citadel Place, Tinworth Street, London SE11 5EH
0171 840 5400

Mager, M. Ms

Specifying qualifications - developing a common language and template

ABSTRACT: A joint project with the Association of Colleges and Institute of Education to explore with representatives of key national bodies, the need and process for developing a common language and template for qualification specifications, and to make proposals for further work.

STATUS: Sponsored project

SOURCE OF GRANT: Further Education Development Agency; Association of Colleges

DATE OF RESEARCH: 1997-1998

KEYWORDS: **further education; qualifications**

0714

Citadel Place, Tinworth Street, London SE11 5EH
0171 840 5400

Hughes, M. Ms

Good practice in the delivery of vocational education and training

ABSTRACT: This project will suggest a common set of guiding principles for quality in Vocational Education and Training (VET), against which qualifications and the learning programmes which lead to these, can be assessed. It will also suggest effective teaching and learning strategies to promote achievement and excellence in VET. It will do this through extensive consultation with employers; national bodies and college practitioners. A Good Practice Guide will be published at the end of the project.

STATUS: Sponsored project

SOURCE OF GRANT: Further Education Development Agency

DATE OF RESEARCH: 1997-1998

KEYWORDS: learning strategies; teaching methods; training; vocational education

0715

Citadel Place, Tinworth Street, London SE11 5EH
0171 840 5400

Pierce, J. Ms; Mager, C. Ms

Uses of unitised pathways

ABSTRACT: This project will review a range of unitised and credit related pathways of assessment to evaluate the rationale for their development, funding and delivery issues, and the implementation of these findings for the national framework. The term 'pathway' is used to refer to the way in which groups of units of assessment are arranged into learning progrmmes to assist the progression of particular groups of students towards their learning goals. Through the Kennedy Report much interest has been generated in the need to widen participation through unitised credit related pathways. There has been no systematic collection and evaluation of why practitioners have gone to the trouble of devising these new pathways, what gaps they fill and how learners and employers benefit from them. In order to provide sound advice to colleges and policymakers, the Further Education Development Agency (FEDA) needs up-to-date data about why such pathways are developed. This may relate to new areas of learning, better accessibility for particular target groups of learners, better retention and completion, more reasonable costs of delivery and accreditation. This study wil help FEDA to understand better the nature and implications of this for qualifications and funding systems. Colleges have argued strongly over recent years that a unitised and credit based framework is essential to support them in widening participation and delivering an inclusive curriculum. This project aims to generate detailed evidence about why colleges and others are developing such programmes. It will examine examples of such programmes in detail to establish their key features. The researchers hope that this work will also generate examples of unitised pathways designed to help to include formerly excluded learners, and to help employers. The outcomes will also be of interest to Qualifications and Curriculum Authority (QCA) as it considers the nature of a new post-compulsory qualifications system, and prepared advice to ministers on the possible development of a unit-based credit framework.

STATUS: Sponsored project

SOURCE OF GRANT: Further Education Development Agency

DATE OF RESEARCH: 1998-1998

KEYWORDS: assessment; further education; student improvement

0716

Citadel Place, Tinworth Street, London SE11 5EH
0171 840 5400

Morris, A. Mr

The Science Museum - a resource for 16+ education

ABSTRACT: An analysis of the resources of the Science Museum will be analysed in relation to the needs of different types of courses in further education (FE). Case studies will be carried out on actual museum usage. A report containing advice to teachers, examples of good practice, and information on current usage by the 16+ age group will be produced. It is expected that the outcome will be of interest to users of other museums.

STATUS: Sponsored project

SOURCE OF GRANT: Science Museum

DATE OF RESEARCH: 1998-1998

KEYWORDS: further education; museums; science education; sixteen to nineteen education

0717

Citadel Place, Tinworth Street, London SE11 5EH
0171 840 5400

Hull, L. Ms

Achieving coherence of vocational provision and student experience in schools and colleges - establishing guidelines

ABSTRACT: This project will identify and test factors in good practice in achieving vocational coherence. It will produce implementation guidelines and tools designed to encourage vocational coherence in the 14-19 curriculum within schools and colleges.

STATUS: Sponsored project

SOURCE OF GRANT: Further Education Development Agency

DATE OF RESEARCH: 1998-1998

KEYWORDS: coherence; curriculum development; fourteen to nineteen education; further education; secondary education; sixteen to nineteen education; vocational education

0718

Citadel Place, Tinworth Street, London SE11 5EH
0171 840 5400

Hull, L. Ms

Achieving coherence of vocational provision and student experience in schools and colleges

ABSTRACT: This project will develop and trial multi-agency models for the delivery of an inclusive work related/vocational curriculum for 14-19 year-old learners.

STATUS: Sponsored project

SOURCE OF GRANT: Further Education Development Agency

DATE OF RESEARCH: 1998-1998

KEYWORDS: coherence; curriculum development; fourteen to nineteen education; further education; secondary education; sixteen to nineteen education; vocational education

0719

Citadel Place, Tinworth Street, London SE11 5EH
0171 840 5400

Mager, C. Ms; Morris, A. Mr

A signature qualification for further education

ABSTRACT: There have been a number of calls for a 'signature qualification' for further education (FE). This project will critically evaluate the purpose, design and feasibility of such a qualification.

STATUS: Sponsored project

SOURCE OF GRANT: Further Education Development Agency

DATE OF RESEARCH: 1998-1998

KEYWORDS: further education; qualifications

0720

Citadel Place, Tinworth Street, London SE11 5EH
0171 840 5400

Hull, L. Ms

Heritage crafts: scoping

ABSTRACT: A scoping project into heritage craft training provision in further education (FE) institutions in order to inform further research and investigation opportunities. It will address regeneration, conservation and heritage appreciation and lifelong learning agendas in the context of heritage crafts and the role of FE.

STATUS: Sponsored project

SOURCE OF GRANT: Further Education Development Agency

DATE OF RESEARCH: 1998-1998

KEYWORDS: colleges of further education; cultural background; further education; handicrafts; lifelong learning

0721

Citadel Place, Tinworth Street, London SE11 5EH
0171 840 5400

Dixon, S. Ms

Self-assessment of colleges: preparing for accreditation

ABSTRACT: College accreditation can be seen as a logical extension of the development of self-assessment. Many mature, self-critical and improving colleges will want to move rapidly towards college accreditation. This project will provide guidance on how to do so.

STATUS: Sponsored project

SOURCE OF GRANT: Further Education Development Agency

DATE OF RESEARCH: 1997-1998

KEYWORDS: **accreditation - institutions; colleges of further education; further education; institutional evaluation; self evaluation - groups**

0722

Citadel Place, Tinworth Street, London SE11 5EH
0171 840 5400

Dixon, S. Ms

Classroom observation for self-assessment and appraisal purposes

ABSTRACT: A project to develop a protocol and guidance to enable classroom observations to be used for both self-assessment and appraisal purposes in colleges.

STATUS: Sponsored project

SOURCE OF GRANT: Further Education Development Agency

DATE OF RESEARCH: 1997-1998

KEYWORDS: **classroom observation techniques; colleges of further education; further education; institutional evaluation; self evaluation - groups**

0723

Citadel Place, Tinworth Street, London SE11 5EH
0171 840 5400

Edwards, J. Ms

Validating college self-assessment reports

ABSTRACT: A project to help colleges to develop appropriate procedures for validating the evidence and judgements in their self-assessment reports.

STATUS: Sponsored project

SOURCE OF GRANT: Further Education Development Agency

DATE OF RESEARCH: 1997-1998

KEYWORDS: **colleges of further education; further education; institutional evaluation; self evaluation - groups**

0724

Citadel Place, Tinworth Street, London SE11 5EH
0171 840 5400

Clift-Harris, J. Ms

Self-assessment in specialist colleges

ABSTRACT: This project aims to identify the development and support needs of specialist residential colleges in relation to developing appropriate self-assessment processes which meet Further Education Funding Council (FEFC) requirements and provide rigorous data which are manageable in the specialist residential context.

STATUS: Sponsored project

SOURCE OF GRANT: Further Education Funding Council

DATE OF RESEARCH: 1998-1998

KEYWORDS: **adult residential colleges; colleges of further education; further education; institutional evaluation; self evaluation - groups**

0725

Citadel Place, Tinworth Street, London SE11 5EH
0171 840 5400

Edwards, J. Ms; Walker, L. Ms

Self-assessment of support areas

ABSTRACT: This project has been designed to develop guidance on the self-assessment and improvement of quality standards in college support areas. It will draw from and build on best practice in industry/other public services and colleges.

STATUS: Sponsored project

SOURCE OF GRANT: Further Education Development Agency

DATE OF RESEARCH: 1998-continuing

KEYWORDS: **colleges of further education; educational quality; further education; institutional evaluation; self evaluation - groups; standards; support services**

0726

Citadel Place, Tinworth Street, London SE11 5EH
0171 840 5400

Dixon, S. Ms

Self-assessment for different inspection frameworks

ABSTRACT: This project will examine published material on different inspection frameworks and the experience of colleges which have been subject to the requirements of more than one framework. From this it will develop guidance which will enable colleges to streamline their self-assessment processes and documentation.

STATUS: Sponsored project

SOURCE OF GRANT: Further Education Development Agency

DATE OF RESEARCH: 1998-continuing

KEYWORDS: **colleges of further education; inspection**

0727

Citadel Place, Tinworth, London SE11 5EH
0171 840 5400

Dixon, S. Ms

Self-assessment of quality assurance and governance

ABSTRACT: This project will explore the characteristics of colleges which have achieved high inspection grades for quality assurance (QA) and have had their self-assessment report validated by the Inspectorate. It will culminate in guidance for the achievement of QA systems which encourage rigorous self-assessment and action for improvement.

STATUS: Sponsored project

SOURCE OF GRANT: Further Education Development Agency

DATE OF RESEARCH: 1998-continuing

KEYWORDS: **educational quality; further education; governance; quality assurance**

0728

Citadel Place, Tinworth Street, London SE11 5EH
0171 840 5400

Dixon, S. Ms

A college code of practice for inspection

ABSTRACT: This project will involve the Further Education Development Agency (FEDA) in working collaboratively with colleges and the Association of Colleges to develop a code of practice for colleges being inspected, complementary to that recently published by the Further Education Funding Council (FEFC) for inspectors.

STATUS: Sponsored project

SOURCE OF GRANT: Further Education Development Agency

DATE OF RESEARCH: 1998-continuing

KEYWORDS: **colleges of further education; educational quality; further education; inspection**

0729

Citadel Place, Tinworth Street, London SE11 5EH
0171 840 5400

Tait, T. Mr

Telematics (education superhighways)

ABSTRACT: Further Education Development Agency (FEDA) is participating in a number of superhighways projects in the UK and will contribute its own experience as well as use information and evaluation of the projects to offer information and guidance to the further education (FE) sector at large.

STATUS: Sponsored project

SOURCE OF GRANT: Further Education Development Agency

DATE OF RESEARCH: 1996-1998

KEYWORDS: computer networks; computer uses in education; further education; information technology; internet

0730

Citadel Place, Tinworth Street, London SE11 5EH
0171 840 5400

Lawson, L. Ms; Hull, L. Ms

Spotlight on learning 1997/98

ABSTRACT: Spotlight on learning aims to define, locate and describe good practice in the teaching and learning of specific subjects in further education (FE). It is designed for subject teachers and curriculum leaders. The benefits are: a good practice framework, which can be customised by teaching teams and their managers to support the development of a reflective, self-assessing culture; a series of one day events in different parts of the country, offering teachers the chance to hear about examples of good practice and share materials and ideas; a manual containing the good practice framework and 10 articles by practising FE teachers, all on disc for customising to context.

STATUS: Sponsored project

SOURCE OF GRANT: Further Education Development Agency

DATE OF RESEARCH: 1997-1998

KEYWORDS: colleges of further education; further education; learning strategies; teaching methods

0731

Citadel Place, Tinworth Street, London SE11 5EH
0171 840 5400

Reisenberger, A. Ms

Enhancing training for careers education and guidance

ABSTRACT: Further Education Development Agency (FEDA) is providing a training directory of opportunities for staff in further education (FE) colleges on careers education and guidance, together with guidelines on case studies for briefing non-specialist managers.

STATUS: Sponsored project

SOURCE OF GRANT: Department for Education and Employment

DATE OF RESEARCH: 1997-1998

KEYWORDS: careers advisers; colleges of further education; further education; teacher development; vocational guidance

0732

Citadel Place, Tinworth Street, London SE11 5EH
0171 840 5400

Wright, W. Mr

More than just customers: promoting active student participation and influence in college life

ABSTRACT: This project will be undertaken in collaboration with the National Youth Agency and other related agencies. It will investigate the activities which exist in further education (FE) colleges to promote active student participation in college life, particularly in governance and decision-making. The project will seek to disseminate good practice and analyse the benefits of these activities to students and to colleges.

STATUS: Sponsored project

SOURCE OF GRANT: National Youth Agency

DATE OF RESEARCH: 1999-continuing

KEYWORDS: colleges of further education; decision making; further education; governance; student participation; students

0733

Citadel Place, Tinworth Street, London SE11 5EH
0171 840 5400

Wright, W. Mr; Stott, C. Ms

New approaches to student counselling

ABSTRACT: This project will seek to describe the various models which exist in colleges for counselling and guidance support, analyse student and staff perceptions of the service and suggest quality indicators for colleges seeking to improve their provision.

STATUS: Sponsored project

SOURCE OF GRANT: Further Education Development Agency

DATE OF RESEARCH: 1998-continuing

KEYWORDS: colleges of further education; further education; student counselling

0734

Citadel Place, Tinworth Street, London SE11 5EH
0171 840 5400

Lockitt, B. Mr

Multimedia bilingual materials via the Internet

ABSTRACT: This project, commissioned by the Further Education Funding Council (FEFC), aims to produce a range of bilingual learning materials in a number of identified curriculum areas, and to utilise the Internet as a project management tool. It will publish all learning materials via the World Wide Web to raise awareness of bilingualism within the Welsh further education (FE) sector, maximise learners' and developers' potential by using the FE-NET 96 infrastructure. It will also produce a range of bilingual learning material in identified European languages.

STATUS: Sponsored project

SOURCE OF GRANT: Further Education Funding Council

DATE OF RESEARCH: 1997-1998

KEYWORDS: bilingualism; educational materials; internet; welsh

0735

Citadel Place, Tinworth Street, London SE11 5EH
0171 840 5400

Donovan, K. Mr

Learning technologies research programme

ABSTRACT: Following Council News 40, the Further Education Funding Council (FEFC) has released funding to move forward on the outstanding recommendations of the Learning and Technology Committee. The research and development work, commissioned as a result of the Higginson Report, involves related themes of efficiency/effectiveness and cost effectiveness with respect to: use of information technology (IT) for learning; college use of Intranets and sector use of the Internet.

STATUS: Sponsored project

SOURCE OF GRANT: Further Education Funding Council

DATE OF RESEARCH: 1998-continuing

KEYWORDS: colleges of further education; computer uses in education; further education; information technology; internet

0736

Citadel Place, Tinworth Street, London SE11 5EH
0171 840 5400

Attewell, J. Ms

Benchmarking information and learning technology

ABSTRACT: An electronic survey will be used to maximise responses as well as to save time and printing and postage costs. An electronic form will be e-mailed to college Quality in Information and Learning Technology (QUILT) coordinators and Information and Learning Technology (ILT)/ college information systems (CIS) management who will be requested to e-mail completed forms to the Further Education Development Agency (FEDA). The survey results will be added to data previously collected by the Further Education Funding Council (FEFC) and RM Consulting. Desk research will collect information about total cost of ownership (TCO) and information technology (IT) resourcing strategies in the private and public sectors.

STATUS: Sponsored project

SOURCE OF GRANT: Further Education Development Agency

DATE OF RESEARCH: 1998-continuing

KEYWORDS: **colleges of further education; further education; information technology; quality control**

0737

Citadel Place, Tinworth Street, London SE11 5EH
0171 840 5400

Edwards, J. Ms

Committed learners

ABSTRACT: The BBC has started a 'Committed Learners Service' offering opportunities for guidance, learning and accreditation to viewers of the BBC Summer Nights, Learning Zone and Daytime programmes, working with 130 education centres. The Further Education Development Agency (FEDA) has been commissioned by the BBC to conduct an evaluation of the service in 1997/98 with learners and providers, to see whether the scheme is succeeding in its goal of turning passive viewers into active learners.

STATUS: Sponsored project

SOURCE OF GRANT: Further Education Development Agency

DATE OF RESEARCH: 1997-1998

KEYWORDS: **adult education; educational television; television**

0738

Citadel Place, Tinworth Street, London SE11 5EH
0171 840 5400

Martinez, P. Mr

Raising achievement in further and adult education

ABSTRACT: This project will help to raise student achievement by sharing good practice from colleges and adult education services.

STATUS: Sponsored project

SOURCE OF GRANT: Further Education Development Agency

DATE OF RESEARCH: 1997-1998

KEYWORDS: **achievement; adult education; colleges of further education; further education; student improvement**

0739

Citadel Place, Tinworth Street, London SE11 5EH
0171 840 5400

Barwuah, A. Mr; Wright, W. Mr

Differential completion and achievement

ABSTRACT: The project aims to determine the different rates of recruitment and achievement of disadvantaged students in various further education (FE) colleges, identify good practice and provide guidance to other colleges.

STATUS: Sponsored project

SOURCE OF GRANT: Further Education Development Agency

DATE OF RESEARCH: 1997-1998

KEYWORDS: **achievement; colleges of further education; disadvantaged; educationally disadvantaged; further education; student recruitment**

0740

Citadel Place, Tinworth Street, London SE11 5EH
0171 840 5400

Davies, P. Mr

Impact of further education deprived areas

ABSTRACT: A survey of the impact of further education (FE) sector colleges on the range of deprived populations within their catchment areas, so as to identify and disseminate the characteristics of effective practice.

STATUS: Sponsored project

SOURCE OF GRANT: Further Education Funding Council

DATE OF RESEARCH: 1998-continuing

KEYWORDS: **colleges of further education; disadvantaged; disadvantaged environment; further education**

0741

Citadel Place, Tinworth Street, London SE11 5EH
0171 840 5400

Johnson, M. Mr

The experience of the learner in further education

ABSTRACT: This project follows the learning careers of 36 young people from their final year of schooling, through further education, and into work, higher education or other destination.

STATUS: Sponsored project

SOURCE OF GRANT: Further Education Development Agency

DATE OF RESEARCH: 1994-continuing

KEYWORDS: **further education; further education to higher education transition; further education to work transition; higher education; school to work transition; sixteen to nineteen education; student destinations**

0742

Citadel Place, Tinworth Street, London SE11 5EH
0171 840 5400

Fletcher, M. Mr

The impact of the funding methodology

ABSTRACT: The project intended to provide an objective assessment of the impact of the Further Education Funding Council (FEFC) funding methodology. Working with Further Education Development Agency (FEDA) staff and a research specialist, selected colleges will help identify key hypotheses and test them using both national statistical data and local records.

STATUS: Sponsored project

SOURCE OF GRANT: Further Education Development Agency

DATE OF RESEARCH: 1998-continuing

KEYWORDS: **colleges of further education; educational finance; further education**

0743

Citadel Place, Tinworth Street, London SE11 5EH
0171 840 5400

Fletcher, M. Mr

Assembling the evidence

ABSTRACT: Further Education Development Agency (FEDA) is seeking to identify all current research into funding vocational education and training (VET) in the UK and develop a specialist research network to support and promote researchers. The project will also develop a full and simple summary of key further education (FE) statistics to help promote informed discussion on policy and practice in vocational education.

STATUS: Sponsored project

SOURCE OF GRANT: Further Education Development Agency

DATE OF RESEARCH: 1998-continuing

KEYWORDS: **educational finance; educational research; further education; training; vocational education**

0744

Citadel Place, Tinworth Street, London SE11 5EH
0171 840 5400

Fletcher, M. Mr

Funding models

ABSTRACT: Further Education Development Agency (FEDA) is carrying out research into alternative approaches to funding further education (FE) to help identify the most effective ways of implementing lifelong learning agenda.

STATUS: Sponsored project

SOURCE OF GRANT: Further Education Development Agency

DATE OF RESEARCH: 1998-continuing

KEYWORDS: educational finance; further education; lifelong learning

0745

Citadel Place, Tinworth Street, London SE11 5EH
0171 840 5400

Fletcher, M. Mr

Rates of return in further education

ABSTRACT: Further Education Development Agency (FEDA) is commissioning research to identify the financial benefits to individuals from investing their time and money in acquiring further education (FE) qualifications. It will help learners make better informed choices about how and what we learn, and help policymakers and providers organise learning opportunities better.

STATUS: Sponsored project

SOURCE OF GRANT: Further Education Development Agency

DATE OF RESEARCH: 1998-continuing

KEYWORDS: further education; outcomes of education; rewards; students

0746

Citadel Place, Tinworth Street, London SE11 5EH
0171 840 5400

Fletcher, M. Mr

Unitisation shadow pilot project

ABSTRACT: The Further Education Funding Council (FEFC) have accepted a recommendation of their Fundamental Review Group that they should explore the implications of developing the funding methodology by linking it to a unit based credit framework. The intention is to run a shadow pilot in a limited number of institutions during 1998/99 which will enable a more detailed assessment of the technical issues involved in such a development, the likely benefits and the costs of a full-scale implementation.

STATUS: Sponsored project

SOURCE OF GRANT: Further Education Development Agency

DATE OF RESEARCH: 1998-continuing

KEYWORDS: credits; educational finance; further education

0747

Citadel Place, Tinworth Street, London SE11 5EH
0171 840 5400

Mager, C. Ms

Tomorrow's colleges

ABSTRACT: This project will seek to establish a Further Education Development Agency (FEDA) lecture series, providing a forum for the sector to think beyond the here and now, and speculate creatively and broadly about future possibilities, roles, responsibilities in relation to learning. It will facilitate high profile debate, aimed at the education policy community, which raises alternative perspectives and thinking about the curriculum and its context in the future.

STATUS: Sponsored project

SOURCE OF GRANT: Further Education Development Agency

DATE OF RESEARCH: 1997-1998

KEYWORDS: curriculum development; further education

0748

Citadel Place, Tinworth Street, London SE11 5EH
0171 840 5400

Kypri, P. Mr

Skills and capabilities for the 21st century

ABSTRACT: The citizens of the future will require skills for life in a rapidly changing, technologically advanced, global environment. Two papers have been commissioned, between Further Education Development Agency (FEDA) and the Association of Colleges, in preparation for a major project on investigating key skills and capabilities for the 21st century. Their purpose is to inform the implementation of a range of college-based development projects on this theme.

STATUS: Sponsored project

SOURCE OF GRANT: Further Education Development Agency; Association of Colleges

DATE OF RESEARCH: 1997-1998

KEYWORDS: colleges of further education; core skills; further education; key skills

0749

Citadel Place, Tinworth Street, London SE11 5EH
0171 840 5400

Pierce, J. Ms

The further education curriculum: how are colleges shaping the curriculum they offer?

ABSTRACT: The project is intended to monitor and evaluate the changes that colleges are making to the curriculum in further education (FE) and its delivery to reach funding projects.

STATUS: Sponsored project

SOURCE OF GRANT: Further Education Development Agency

DATE OF RESEARCH: 1998-continuing

KEYWORDS: curriculum development; educational finance; further education

0750

Citadel Place, Tinworth Street, London SE11 5EH
0171 840 5400

Hayward, A. Ms

Investigating FEDA projects

ABSTRACT: This project is an internal investigation of the way Further Education Development Agency (FEDA) carries out its research. It is intended to develop a self-critical culture in order to ensure quality of service.

STATUS: Sponsored project

SOURCE OF GRANT: Further Education Development Agency

DATE OF RESEARCH: 1998-continuing

KEYWORDS: colleges of further education; educational research; further education

0751

Citadel Place, Tinworth Street, London SE11 5EH
0171 840 5400

Mager, C. Ms; Morris, A. Mr

Statistical information I and II

ABSTRACT: This project will assist Further Education Development Agency (FEDA) in identifying and presenting key statistical information for the sector. It will also enhance the statistical basis of a number of FEDA research projects.

STATUS: Sponsored project

SOURCE OF GRANT: Further Education Development Agency

DATE OF RESEARCH: 1998-continuing

KEYWORDS: colleges of further education; further education; statistical data; statistics

0752

Coombe Lodge, Blagdon, Bristol BS18 6RG
01761 462503

Further Education Unit, Spring Gardens, Citadel Place, Tinworth Street, London SE11 5EH
0171 962 1280

Graystone, J. Mr; Reece, I. Mr; Bayliss, J. Ms; Evans, S. Ms; Warrender, A-M. Mrs; *Supervisor:* Coleman, J. Mrs

Further education governing bodies and their contribution to a quality learning service

ABSTRACT: This project for the Further Education Unit (RP 716): (1) maps the current composition and characteristics of governing bodies in further education, with particular interest in their potential for an impact on curriculum issues; (2) identifies governors' current (a) expertise and experience, relevant to further education governance; and (b) individual commitment to curriculum issues and ways of working which contribute to the effectiveness of the college as a learning service; and (3) makes recommendations to further education (FE) colleges for incorporation, having regard for the wider responsibilities of governing bodies in the future. A short literature search was carried out, followed by a questionnaire completed by 214 FE colleges in England and Wales. Interviews were then held with over 50 governors from selected colleges, and five governing body meetings were observed.

STATUS: Sponsored project

SOURCE OF GRANT: Further Education Unit; The Staff College

DATE OF RESEARCH: 1992-1993

KEYWORDS: **colleges of further education; educational quality; governing bodies**

Further Education Funding Council

0753
Cheylsmore House, Quinton Road, Coventry CV1 2WT
01203 863000

Stock, M. Mr

Summary measures of student activity

ABSTRACT: It is customary to indicate the size of an educational institution or sector by a summary measure such as full-time equivalent; part-time students are given less weight than those who are full-time. Changes to data sources meant that the former measure for further education (FE) in England could no longer be applied. The report examines the principles underlying judgements of the throughput and efficiency of a sector, and explores some alternative formulations of a summary measure.

STATUS: Sponsored project

SOURCE OF GRANT: Department for Education and Employment £14,000

DATE OF RESEARCH: 1997-1997

KEYWORDS: **colleges of further education; educational quality; further education; performance indicators; student numbers**

GHK Economics and Management

0754
30 St Pauls Square, Birmingham B3 1QZ
0121 212 2800

Mackie, I. Mr

Evaluation of New Start project

ABSTRACT: 17 New Start partnership projects have been funded by the Department for Education and Employment (DfEE) focusing on young people aged 14 to 17 who are currently not in learning or at risk of leaving learning prematurely. The national study will evaluate the effectiveness of the first phase of the projects in identifying the nature and scale of the problem at the local area and will draw out key lessons on developing a partnership approach to tackling disaffection. Once action plans have been agreed, the evaluation will examine the progress of the action against

objectives and ultimately try to assess the overall added value of the whole set of projects. A series of interviews will be carried out with key partners and with young people themselves.

STATUS: Sponsored project

SOURCE OF GRANT: Department for Education and Employment £98,301

DATE OF RESEARCH: 1997-continuing

KEYWORDS: **disaffection; investing in young people; new start; partnerships; secondary education**

Glamorgan University

0755
Business School, Pontpridd CF37 1DL
01443 480480

Jones, J. Ms; *Supervisor:* Farrell, C. Dr

The role of parents in education in schools

ABSTRACT: The aim of the research is to analyse the role of parents in compulsory education with particular reference to different models of involvement. It will explore the response of the system in relation to the different models. Data will be collected by means of questionnaires and interviews with parents, educational managers, governors and local education authority personnel principally in South Wales.

STATUS: Individual research

DATE OF RESEARCH: 1997-continuing

KEYWORDS: **parent participation; parent school relationship**

0756
Business School, Pontypridd CF37 1DL
01443 480480

Connolly, U. Mrs; *Supervisor:* James, C. Prof.

The improving schools project

ABSTRACT: The project aims: 1) to identify schools which have substantially changed their practice for the purpose of improving pupil achievement; 2) to explore, analyse and document the change in practice; and 3) to facilitate the sharing of successful practice. Data will be collected from 32 schools primary and secondary schools. Special schools and Welsh medium schools are also included in the sample. 10 schools will be the subject of indepth case study. Data will be collected by means of interview and documentary analysis. In a second phase of the project, development initiatives will be established in order to further improve practice. These will also be the subject of indepth study by means of case study.

PUBLISHED MATERIAL: CONNOLLY, U. & JAMES, C. (1997). 'Achieving school improvement by integrating research and development: a collaboration between schools, local authorities and higher education'. Paper presented to the Annual Conference of the In-service and Professional Development Association, Dunchurch, Warwickshire, 28-30 November 1997.

STATUS: Sponsored project

SOURCE OF GRANT: Glamorgan University £22,000; Bridgend LEA £5,500; Caerphilly LEA £5,500; Merthyr Tydfil LEA £5,500; Rhonnda-Cynon-Taff LEA £5,500

DATE OF RESEARCH: 1996-1998

KEYWORDS: **educational quality; primary education; school effectiveness; school improvement; secondary education**

0757
Business School, Pontypridd CF37 1DL
01443 480480

James, C. Prof.; Whiting, D. Dr

The career anchorage of deputy headteachers

ABSTRACT: Although there is a body of knowledge surrounding the promotion and career patterns of teachers in England and Wales, it provides little insight into the career anchorage perspective of deputy headteachers, i.e. the point against which future occupational positions may be evaluated.

Further, there is a scarcity of literature and empirical data which definitively investigates the lack of promotion to headship. The research aims are to conduct an exploratory study of deputy headteachers in a sample of primary and secondary schools in one local education authority in England and Wales, to provide the basis for continued study and improved understanding of the career progression of deputy headteachers; to identify factors against which deputy headteachers present and future occupational positions are evaluated, explicitly in relation to headship; and to study the response of deputy headteachers perceptions of lack of promotion to headship. Data will be collected by means of questionnaires and semi-structured interviews.

PUBLISHED MATERIAL: JAMES, C.R. & WHITING, D. (1997). 'Headship inclinations: researching the career perspectives of deputy headteachers'. Paper presented to the British Educational Management and Administration Society Annual Conference, Robinson College, Cambridge, 19-21 September 1997.

STATUS: Sponsored project

SOURCE OF GRANT: Glamorgan University £3,000

DATE OF RESEARCH: 1996-1997

KEYWORDS: **career development; deputy head teachers; head teachers; primary education; promotion - occupational; secondary education; teaching profession**

0758

Business School, Pontypridd CF37 1DL
01443 480480

Farrell, C. Dr; Law, J. Ms

The role of school governors in Wales

ABSTRACT: The role of the school governor is a crucial one but remains under-explored particularly in respect of the accountability of governing bodies. Simultaneously, the ways in which schools themselves discharge their accountability is under-researched. This project seeks to explore the ways in which governors discharge their accountability and the ways in which schools manage their accountability. Data will be collected by means of semi-structured interviews with parents, governors and headteachers.

PUBLISHED MATERIAL: FARRELL, C.M. & LAW, J. (1997). 'The accountability of governing bodies'. Paper presented to the Annual Conference of the British Educational Research Association, University of York, York, 11-14 September 1997.

STATUS: Sponsored project

SOURCE OF GRANT: Glamorgan University £3,000

DATE OF RESEARCH: 1996-1997

KEYWORDS: **accountability; governing bodies; school governing bodies; school governors; wales**

0759

Business School, Pontypridd CF37 1DL
01443 480480

Hutchings, T. Mr; *Supervisor*: James, C. Prof.

A case study of curriculum development in higher education

ABSTRACT: The nature of the professional knowledge of university lecturers remains significantly under-researched in relation to the professional knowledge of school teachers, for example. Very little is known about how those who teach in higher education plan, prepare and evaluate their teaching nor upon what kinds of personal education theories they base their actual teaching practice. On a broader scale, very little is known about the process of curriculum development in higher education. The study sets out to explore the practice of curriculum development in higher education through a case study of the development of a Higher National Diploma course in computing. In the longitudinal study, data will be collected from those engaged in the development in order to explicate and analyse the theories on which their curriculum development practice is founded.

STATUS: Individual research

DATE OF RESEARCH: 1995-continuing

KEYWORDS: **computer literacy; curriculum development; higher education**

0760

Business School, Pontypridd CF37 1DL
01443 480480

Kontra, E. Mr; *Supervisor*: James, C. Prof.

The need for a culture sensitive approach to teacher training in English foreign language teaching

ABSTRACT: This project looks at two related aspects of the teaching of English as a foreign language in Hungary. The first project looks at the needs and expectations of learners of English in Hungary, the second examines the different ways in which Hungarian students approach the learning of English. The first project uses questionnaires and interviews with teachers and learners of English as a second language to look at the expectations of those teachers and learners of native English-speaking teachers. In the second project a variety of data collection methods (observation, interviews and questionnaires) are used to collect and categorise the language learning strategies of Hungarian secondary school pupils.

STATUS: Individual research

DATE OF RESEARCH: 1995-1998

KEYWORDS: **english - second language; hungary; language teachers; second language learning**

0761

Business School, Pontypridd CF37 1DL
01443 480480

Pritchard, A. Mr; *Supervisors*: Jones, N. Dr ; James, C. Prof.

Managing change in a school context: case studies of change

ABSTRACT: The policies ushered in by the Education Reform Act 1988 set in train considerable changes within schools. In grant-maintained schools, the transition required those schools to change their practice, particularly in relation to the management of external relationships and their customer/ market led orientation. This action research-based study explores the role of the leader of the grant-maintained school as manager of change; the management of change of particular aspects of curricular provision with reference to changes in post-16 provision in particular, and managing the development of staff particularly in response to the changes wrought by grant-maintained status.

STATUS: Individual research

DATE OF RESEARCH: 1996-continuing

KEYWORDS: **change strategies; educational administration; educational change; grant maintained schools; school based management**

0762

Business School, Pontypridd CF37 1DL
01443 480480

Weddell, M. Mr; *Supervisor*: James, C. Prof.

English language teacher education project in East and Central Europe 1990-97: using the present to inform the future

ABSTRACT: Up until the enormous political changes which took place throughout Eastern Europe in 1989-90, the study of Russian had been compulsory in Hungarian schools and the study of western languages had been strictly limited. The changes resulted in two immediate needs: the requirement to retrain the teachers of Russian whose expertise in the teaching of Russian was no longer to become teachers of other (mostly language) teachers; and to produce a large number of western foreign language teachers as quickly as possible to teach western languages in place of Russian in schools all over Hungary. In response, many universities implemented new 3-year programmes of teacher education designed to emphasise the more practical aspects of language teacher education. The general aim of the research is to explore and analyse the change in language teacher training in Hungary during this period. Data will be collected from a variety of stakeholders in the change process by means of questionnaires and semi-structured interviews.

STATUS: Individual research

DATE OF RESEARCH: 1996-continuing

KEYWORDS: **english - second language; hungary; language teachers**

0763

Business School, Pontypridd CF37 1DL
01443 480480

Turner, D. Dr

A study of changes in funding arrangements on the behaviour of institutions of higher education

ABSTRACT: The project originated in concerns about the use of funding formulae to provide central, policy-guided 'steer' to an autonomous system of higher education institutions. It started from detailed study of the funding of teaching by the Polytechnics and Colleges Funding Council and the Higher Education Funding Council for England. Subsequently it has been extended to cover international comparisons and the funding of research. Techniques from operational research have been employed to describe and evaluate the direction and effectiveness of 'policy steer' provided by funding mechanisms, and to evaluate the extent to which funding policy is in line with explicit national policy. In many cases a dysfunction between intended policy direction and the steer provided by funding mechanisms can be seen, and the mechanisms of the funding steer can be illuminated.

PUBLISHED MATERIAL: TURNER, D.A. (1994). 'Formula funding of higher education in the Czech Republic: creating an open system', Studies in Higher Education, Vol 19, No 2, pp.139-50. ; TURNER, D.A. (1997). 'University funding'. In: GOKULSING, K. & DACOSTA, C. Usable Knowledges as the goal of higher education. Lampeter: Edwin Mellen Press. ; TURNER, D.A. (1997). 'Formula funding in higher education: neither centralised nor decentralised'. In: WATSON, K., MODGIL, C. & MODGIL, S. (Eds). Educational dilemmas: debate and diversity. Volume 2: Reforms in higher education. London: Cassell. ; TURNER, D.A. (1997). 'Formula funding of higher education in the Czech Republic: creating an open system'. In: DARVAS, P. (Ed). Higher education in Europe. New York; London: Garland.

STATUS: Individual research

DATE OF RESEARCH: 1990-continuing

KEYWORDS: comparative education; economics education; educational finance; educational policy; higher education; relationship; universities

0764

Department of Property and Development Studies, Pontypridd CF37 1DL
01443 480480

Williams, T. Mr; *Supervisors*: Hughes, T. Mr; Hibberd, P. Prof.; Gronow, S. Mr

The application of quality management principles to learning

ABSTRACT: In vocational courses there are two principle customers whose needs are to be satisfied; the students and the employers. Research has shown that these needs are difficult to define and equally difficult to satisfy. The aims of the research are therefore to: (1) identify the key personal and technical skills necessary in professional quantity surveying practice; (2) develop a simulation based teaching vehicle on the basis of (1) above; and (3) use quality management principles to monitor and improve the learning experience.

PUBLISHED MATERIAL: HUGHES, T. & WILLIAMS, T. (1991). Quality Assurance, a Framework to Build on. Oxford: Blackwell Scientific Publications. ; HUGHES, T. & WILLIAMS, T. (1991). 'Learning by experience: integrated learning materials based on a construction project', Building Technology and Management, Vol 18, pp.56-64, Kuala Lumpur, Building Technology Society.

STATUS: Sponsored project

SOURCE OF GRANT: Department of Employment: Enterprise in Higher Education Initiative £9,000

DATE OF RESEARCH: 1991-1993

KEYWORDS: educational quality; industry higher education relationship; quality control; vocational education; work education relationship

0765

Educational Development Unit, Pontypridd CF37 1DL
01443 480480

Saunders, D. Prof.

Developing a portfolio of personal development

ABSTRACT: A cross-section of students is engaged in a longitudinal study involving self-assessment of study and transferable skills. Academic and personal achievement are also recorded, and the final stage of the project involves the preparation of one-page profile sheets for use with curriculum vitae.

PUBLISHED MATERIAL: SAUNDERS, D. (1990). 'The assessment of prior experiential learning', Simulation Games for Learning, Vol 20, No 1, pp.76-85. ; SAUNDERS, D. (1992). 'Profiling in higher education', Journal of the National Association for Staff Development, No 26, pp.51-57.

STATUS: Sponsored project

SOURCE OF GRANT: Department of Employment: Enterprise in Higher Education Initiative

DATE OF RESEARCH: 1990-1993

KEYWORDS: higher education; profiles; records of achievement; resumes personal; self evaluation - individuals; skill development

0766

Educational Development Unit, Pontypridd CF37 1DL
01443 480480

Rogers, S. Ms; *Supervisors*: Hawkins, P. Prof.; Gornal, L. Ms

Attitudes towards women in the management of schools

ABSTRACT: This study attempts to explore the nature of organisations by comparing two management styles, 'transformational' and 'transactional'. Using a 'prescriptive model' it explores the relationship between management theory and management practice. The male nature of the organisational world provides the major lens through which females are viewed - serving at one level to suggest the absence of women from positions of responsibility in senior management teams; while at another level to cast images of females in management positions in a contradictory light. The study explores the link between gender-related stereotyping and attitudes towards women in school management. It recognises that cultural dimensions of organisational life through positive affirmative action play a vital part in creating equal opportunities for the upward mobility of female staff into senior management teams in today's schools in the UK.

STATUS: Individual research

DATE OF RESEARCH: 1993-continuing

KEYWORDS: educational administration; head teachers; management in education; sex differences; teaching profession; womens employment

0767

Educational Development Unit, Pontypridd CF37 1DL
01443 480480

Gaston, K. Miss; King, L. Miss; *Supervisors*: Saunders, D. Prof.; Race, P. Prof.

Investigating student experiences

ABSTRACT: In October 1994 the first cohort of students to have been involved in the National Record of Achievement will arrive at the University. One of the proposed aims is to evaluate the actual and perceived benefits of recording achievement in schools and colleges, and associated expectations of higher education. A second aim is to investigate the effects of the recording achievement process on university students' social, personal and academic development - including the monitoring of any associated difficulties or problems. A particular interest is in tracing improving, as well as deteriorating performance for cohorts of students as they move through levels 1 and 2 of a modular system. A third and final aim involves the use of summative profiles in the final year of study, when students are going for interviews and meeting employers. The project hopes to compare students' expectations and capabilities, based on their recording of achievement experience, with interview and job application experience.

PUBLISHED MATERIAL: SAUNDERS, D. (1992). 'Profiling in higher education', Journal of the National Association for Staff Development, Vol 26, pp.51-57.

STATUS: Sponsored project

SOURCE OF GRANT: Higher Education Funding Council for Wales £75,000

DATE OF RESEARCH: 1994-1997

KEYWORDS: achievement; higher education; profiles; records of achievement; student development; student experience; student records

0768

Educational Development Unit, Pontypridd CF37 1DL
01443 480480

Smalley, N. Ms; *Supervisor*: Saunders, D. Prof.

Simulation gaming in higher education

ABSTRACT: The Media Simulation for Universities and Schools (MESUS) investigates the development of school pupils' skills and attitudes toward technology and communication. The project involves teams of 14 year-old school pupils who write news stories and then edit a simulated electronic newspaper which is located on the internet. In so doing, vocational opportunities associated with careers in journalism, public relations and information services are explored through experiential learning. The MESUS activity evaluates the benefits of simulation gaming within this cross-educational sector partnership, and makes comparisons with pupils' baseline measures as reported through self-assessment and teacher-assessed inventories.

PUBLISHED MATERIAL: POWELL, T., SAUNDERS, D. & ROLFE, J. (Eds). The international simulation and gaming research yearbook. London: Kogan Page (in press). ; SAUNDERS, D. & POWELL, T. (1998). 'Developing a European media simulation through new information and communication technologies'. In: ROLFE, J. et al. The international simulation and gaming research yearbook. London: Kogan Page.

STATUS: Sponsored project

SOURCE OF GRANT: European Union: Socrates £126,000

DATE OF RESEARCH: 1997-continuing

KEYWORDS: access to education; adult education; adult learning; computer uses in education; higher education; information technology; journalism; mature students; newspapers; simulation

0769

Educational Development Unit, Pontypridd CF37 1DL
01443 480480

Rogers, A. Mr; *Supervisor*: Saunders, D. Prof.

Investigating staff-student relationships in higher education

ABSTRACT: This project traces the emergence and development of student-staff relationships as undergraduates move from level one (first year) to level three (final year) studies within the BA and BSc (Hons) Combined Studies programme at the University of Glamorgan. Through using interviews and questionnaires a series of 'critical incidents' linked to assessment, feedback and specific teaching styles are being identified. An additional consideration and the difference in expectations that students and staff have about learner-teacher relationships.

STATUS: Individual research

DATE OF RESEARCH: 1995-continuing

KEYWORDS: assessment; feedback; higher education; lecturers; students; teacher student relationship; teaching methods

0770

Educational Development Unit, Pontypridd, Glamorgan CF37 1DL
01443 480480

Richards, L. Ms; *Supervisor*: Saunders, D. Prof.

Developing an information strategy within higher education

ABSTRACT: The evolution of an entire information strategy for a new university is monitored and critically evaluated whilst being compared with other information strategy initiatives linked with national policy as well as the Joint Information Systems Committee (JISC). The strategy involves indepth interviews with lecturers and support staff as well as focus groups and brainstorming workshops which in particular identify developments in information technology. A special interest lies with the development of open and flexible learning, along with staff development methods and concerns.

STATUS: Sponsored project

DATE OF RESEARCH: 1998-continuing

KEYWORDS: access to education; higher education; information systems; information technology; information transfer; universities; widening participation

0771

Educational Development Unit, Pontypridd CF37 1DL
01443 480480

Edwards, R. Dr

Helping students to learn

ABSTRACT: Many of today's students have difficulties in higher education arising from lack of confidence, lack of support, or circumstantial difficulties. This research will attempt to clarify these, and suggest methods for overcoming them, including the teaching of modules from a personal and professional development field.

STATUS: Sponsored project

SOURCE OF GRANT: Glamorgan University

DATE OF RESEARCH: 1998-continuing

KEYWORDS: higher education; learning; learning strategies; students

0772

Educational Development Unit, Pontypridd CF37 1DL
01443 480480

Edwards, R. Dr

Improving teaching through observation

ABSTRACT: Pilot projects will be established in selected departments of the University of Glamorgan in an attempt to demonstrate that the observation of teaching sessions can benefit both the observers and the observed.

STATUS: Sponsored project

SOURCE OF GRANT: Glamorgan University

DATE OF RESEARCH: 1998-continuing

KEYWORDS: classroom observation techniques; higher education; observation; teacher effectiveness; teaching methods; teaching process

0773

Educational Development Unit, Pontypridd CF37 1DL
01443 480480

Edwards, R. Dr

Assessment through multiple choice questions

ABSTRACT: This developmental project is aimed at encouraging teaching staff to develop their use of computer assisted assessment and multiple choice questions to assess deep learning.

STATUS: Sponsored project

SOURCE OF GRANT: Glamorgan University

DATE OF RESEARCH: 1998-continuing

KEYWORDS: assessment; computer assisted testing; higher education; multiple choice tests

0774

School of Computer Studies, Pontypridd CF37 1DL
01443 480480

Edwards, R. Dr

Community projects in student learning

ABSTRACT: A computer based database of 100 local voluntary or non-profit making organisations is held and maintained. These organisations are sources of student group or individual projects, and teaching staff are encouraged to use these projects in their teaching.

PUBLISHED MATERIAL: EDWARDS, R.M. (1993). 'Community Enterprise at the University of Glamorgan'. In: BUCKINGHAM-HATFIELD, S. (Ed). Community enterprise in higher education in the 1990s'. London: Community Service Volunteers.

STATUS: Sponsored project

SOURCE OF GRANT: Glamorgan University: Enterprise Unit ; Department of Employment: Enterprise in Higher Education Unit

DATE OF RESEARCH: 1989-continuing

KEYWORDS: **community organisations; databases; student projects**

0775

School of Computer Studies, Pontypridd CF37 1DL
01443 480480

Edwards, R. Dr

Student centred learning

ABSTRACT: Currently, teaching methods are being investigated through a totally self-assessed course (PAD1) in the Department of Business and Administrative Studies at Glamorgan University. Publication of this work is in preparation. Also in connection with the research field, a workshop on simulation and role playing was presented in Glasgow in December 1989.

PUBLISHED MATERIAL: EDWARDS, R.M. & WARE, A.J. (1989). 'Case study: an approach to the teaching and assessment of introductory computing', Education and Training Technology International, Vol 26, No 1, pp.68. ; EDWARDS, R.M. (1989). 'An experiment in student self assessment', British Journal of Educational Technology, Vol 20, No 1, p.5. ; EDWARDS, R.M. & SUTTON, R.A. (1992). 'A practical approach to student centred learning', British Journal of Educational Technology, Vol 23, No 1, p.4.

STATUS: Individual research

DATE OF RESEARCH: 1989-continuing

KEYWORDS: **assessment; higher education; learner centred methods; self evaluation - individuals; teaching methods**

0776

School of Computer Studies, Pontypridd CF37 1DL
01443 480480

Farthing, D. Mr

Using multiple choice questions to assess final year honours degree students: assessing high-order thinking

ABSTRACT: Despite the attractive characteristics of multiple-choice questions - efficient to mark, not subjective, etc. - they are rarely considered a suitable substitute for traditional essay-type questions. This is especially true for final year honours degree examinations. This research introduces a new form of assessment: the Permutational Multiple-Choice Question (PMCQ). Results of trials in final year degree examinations indicate that these questions are as good as essay-type questions at discriminating among candidates. They also offer many benefits: 1) consistency and reliability in marking; 2) reduced need for cross checking among assessment teams, or between franchised institutions; 3) objective and reproducible results; 4) efficiency in marking; 6) quicker to mark; 7) can be automated; 7) broad coverage of syllabus. Unlike traditional multiple-choice questions, PMCQs are not susceptible to candidates guessing the correct answer. Candidates who guessed the answers in a PMCQ test could expect a mark of only 3% (compared with 25% in a 'choose one from four' test), and the likelihood of gaining a 40% pass mark in a test of ten PMCQs would be only 1:4500 (rather than approximately 1:5).

PUBLISHED MATERIAL: FARTHING, D.W., JONES, D.M. & MCPHEE, D. (1998). 'Permutational multiple-choice questions: an objective and efficient alternative to essay-type examination questions'. Proceedings of the 3rd Annual Conference on Integrating IT into Computer Science Education, Dublin City University, Dublin, 17-21 August 1998.

STATUS: Individual research

DATE OF RESEARCH: 1997-continuing

KEYWORDS: **assessment; multiple choice tests**

Glasgow Caledonian University

0777

Department of Psychology, City Campus, Cowcaddens Road, Glasgow G4 0BA
0141 331 3000

Siann, G. Prof.

Vocational guidance: with special reference to the needs of ethnic minorities

ABSTRACT: The research study is concerned with identifying, instituting and evaluating measures designed to meet the vocational needs of secondary school pupils in two target groups: a) ethnic minority pupils, particularly females; and b) pupils from socially disadvantaged backgrounds in schools to be identified by equal opportunities advisors. The aims of the study over three years are to: 1) compare the take up of vocational guidance services by ethnic minority and ethnic majority pupils in the selected schools; 2) identify possible modifications in vocational guidance within these schools in order to improve the service to the target groups; 3) identify channels of communication with parents of pupils in the target groups in such a way as to increase parents' knowledge of the educational opportunities on offer to pupils after the completion of secondary school; 4) help institute and monitor changes in vocational guidance practice based on the findings in the selected schools; and 5) evaluate the changes in vocational guidance instituted in the selected schools.

STATUS: Sponsored project

SOURCE OF GRANT: Project schools £5,000; Glasgow Caledonian University £60,000

DATE OF RESEARCH: 1993-1997

KEYWORDS: **career counselling; ethnic groups; minority groups; secondary school pupils; vocational guidance**

Glasgow University

0778

Centre for Science Education, Glasgow G12 8QQ
0141 339 8855

Otis, K. Mr; *Supervisors*: Johnstone, A. Prof.; Reid, N. Dr

Integrated learning in biology

ABSTRACT: This work is concentrating on undergraduate students who have come to university with 'adequate qualifications' but who are making 'heavy weather' of an undergraduate course. The underlying hypothesis is that the learning methods which proved successful at school are no longer adequate for tertiary education, and particularly for a course which is driving students to autonomous learning. The work is being done in small group 'clinics' and is based upon mind-mapping and other knowledge integrating techniques, reporting and recording of progress is by case study in the first phase of the study. This has now been extended to include medical students on a problem-based learning course.

STATUS: Individual research

DATE OF RESEARCH: 1997-continuing

KEYWORDS: **biology; higher education; learning processes; school to higher education transition; science education; teaching methods**

0779

Centre for Science Education, Glasgow G12 8QQ
0141 339 8855

Yang, M-J. Miss; *Supervisors*: Reid, N. Dr; Webb, G. Prof.

Problem solving in chemistry through group work

ABSTRACT: This project is based on previous work on the effectiveness of group problem solving. The project will investigate the types of problem most amenable to this approach and seek to measure 'gain' in both cognitive and affective domains.

STATUS: Individual research

DATE OF RESEARCH: 1998-continuing

KEYWORDS: **chemistry; group work; problem solving; science education; secondary education**

0780

Centre for Science Education, Glasgow G12 8QQ
0141 339 8855

Sirhan, G. Mr; *Supervisors*: Reid, N. Dr; Webb, G. Prof.; Johnstone, A. Prof.

A study of an undergraduate chemistry course designed on educational principles and less on content

ABSTRACT: A course designed on educational principles to cater for the influx of chemistry students with differing entrance qualifications (from H grade to no previous chemistry), proved very successful in its first 2 years. Since then, the indications are that it has lost its way. This research project is studying the factors behind the 'success' and attempting to isolate the factors behind its 'slipping'. The student sample is about 250. Comparisons with a conventional course (running in parallel) are being carried out. Following a survey, new supplementary course material has been developed and will be evaluated.

STATUS: Individual research

DATE OF RESEARCH: 1997-continuing

KEYWORDS: chemistry; course evaluation; higher education; nontraditional students; science education; teaching methods

0781

Centre for Science Education, Glasgow G12 8QQ
0141 339 8855

Skryabina, E. Mrs; *Supervisors*: Reid, N. Dr; Webb, G. Prof.

Decision nodes on the way to a physics degree

Abstract: Data is being gathered by interview and questionnaire from pupils in primary schools, pupils in secondary schools at each stage where decisions are made which affect career direction, and from undergraduates at each decision stage leading to a physics degree. The questionnaires have been piloted and modified before being applied to large groups. The ultimate aim is to provide information to schools and universities about the factors (including the curriculum) which affect the directions taken by students.

STATUS: Individual research

DATE OF RESEARCH: 1997-continuing

KEYWORDS: attitudes; choice of subjects; decision making; higher education; physics; primary school pupils; pupil attitudes; pupil destinations; science education; secondary school pupils; student attitudes; students

0782

Centre for Science Education, Glasgow G12 8QQ
0141 339 8855

Al-Sheili, A. Mr; *Supervisors*: Johnstone, A. Prof.; Reid, N. Dr; Webb, G. Prof.

The effectiveness of 'projected' practical work in Omani schools

ABSTRACT: This researcher comes from a situation where large classes in secondary school preclude the possibility of laboratory practical or even conventional demonstration work. The research embraces the development of overhead projection techniques to enable at least demonstration to be a possibility. The development will be evaluated in the UK and Oman in terms of learning and attitude development among pupils and teachers.

STATUS: Individual research

DATE OF RESEARCH: 1998-continuing

KEYWORDS: audiovisual aids; demonstrations - educational; laboratory procedures; large classes; oman; overhead projectors; projection equipment; science education

0783

Centre for Science Education, Glasgow G12 8QQ
0141 339 8855

Ambusaidi, A. Mr; *Supervisors*: Johnstone, A. Prof.; Leonard, E. Dr

Testing fixed response assessment tools in secondary and tertiary science courses

ABSTRACT: The effect of structure upon the reliability and validity of fixed response questions is under study. The design and evaluation of new methods to overcome the shortcomings are revealed by the first part of the study. The overall aim is to produce valid and reliable methods for measuring connected learning which are machine markable.

STATUS: Individual research

DATE OF RESEARCH: 1997-continuing

KEYWORDS: assessment; fixed response questions; marking - scholastic; science education

0784

Centre for Science Education, Glasgow G12 8QQ
0141 339 8855

Badcock, K. Dr; *Supervisors*: Johnstone, A. Prof.; Doughty, G. Dr

Attitudes to learning among Honours level engineers

ABSTRACT: This work had its origins in an advanced computer assisted learning (CAL) package for aerospace engineering. The CAL package was in two forms, visual and mathematical (conceptual). A study of student preferences led to the present work which investigates the attitudes of senior students to what they regard as 'university approved' learning.

STATUS: Individual research

DATE OF RESEARCH: 1996-continuing

KEYWORDS: attitudes; engineering education; engineers; higher education; learning; student attitudes

0785

Centre for Science Education, Glasgow G12 8QQ
0141 339 8855

Bahar, M. Mr; *Supervisors*: Johnstone, A. Prof.; Hansell, M. Dr

Techniques for exploring the structures in long-term memory of undergraduate biologists

ABSTRACT: The aims are to construct, test and intercorrelate various methods of exploring how undergraduates lay down information in long-term memory and relate the findings to various teaching/learning environments. The test body is 800 undergraduates per year. The techniques used so far are the familiar word association tests, concept maps and structural communication. In addition, measurements have been made on learning styles.

STATUS: Individual research

DATE OF RESEARCH: 1996-continuing

KEYWORDS: biology; cognitive structures; higher education; learning processes; memory; science education; students

0786

Centre for Science Education, Glasgow G12 8QQ
0141 339 8855

Doherty, M. Mr; *Supervisors*: Johnstone, A. Prof.; Al-Naeme, F. Dr; Pollock, M. Dr

A study of learning problems in technology at secondary school level

ABSTRACT: This work has attempted to investigate some areas of the technology courses taught in schools which present difficulties for pupils. They have been examined in terms of learning styles and cognitive load and clear pointers are emerging. Material has been re-written in the light of the findings and trial results are awaited.

STATUS: Individual research

DATE OF RESEARCH: 1996-1998

KEYWORDS: learning processes; science education; technology education

0787

Centre for Science Education, Glasgow G12 8QQ
0141 339 8855

Selepeng, D. Ms; *Supervisors*: Johnstone, A. Prof.; Hansell, M. Dr

Attitude changes in undergraduate biologists

ABSTRACT: This research arises from a problem in the University of Botswana in which students, doing a combined degree in science and education, are failing in science while doing well in education. To arrive at agreed aims between the courses, both have to have common aspirations and standards. Student attitudes are an important strand in this. The present study is devising and using modified test instruments based upon Perry's work (1970s). So far instruments have been designed, evaluated and modified in readiness for a study following students through 3 years of study and relating attitude change to curriculum change.

STATUS: Individual research

DATE OF RESEARCH: 1997-continuing

KEYWORDS: **biology; botswana; student attitudes**

0788

Centre for Science Education, Glasgow G12 8QQ
0141 339 8855

Androga, R. Mr; *Supervisors*: Reid, N. Dr; Johnstone, A. Prof.

Attitude development with 14-16 year-old school pupils

ABSTRACT: This research arises from a problem in Sudanese science education at secondary school level. Pupils are taught in very large groups by traditional approaches. There is little opportunity for pupils to look at the implication of science for their society, culture and economy. The project seeks to develop new curriculum materials, of direct relevance in the Sudanese curriculum, which allow pupils to develop informed awareness of the implications of science in their communities. Topics like industrial development, pollution, and health are covered. Full evaluation is proposed with 14-16 year-old Sudanese school pupils. The work follows previous work which has demonstrated significant attitude development with Scottish secondary pupils and university students, following the use of curriculum materials which demand high levels of learner interaction.

STATUS: Individual research

DATE OF RESEARCH: 1998-continuing

KEYWORDS: **pupil attitudes; science education; sudan**

0789

Centre for Science Education, Glasgow G12 8QQ
0141 339 8855
Glasgow University, Department of Adult and Continuing Education, Glasgow G12 8QQ
Glasgow University, Department of Psychology, Glasgow G12 8QQ

Mackenzie, A. Ms; *Supervisors*: Johnstone, A. Prof.; Brown, R. Mr

The learning experience of medical undergraduates in traditional and problem-based courses

ABSTRACT: Considerable research - mostly American - into students' patterns of thinking has been carried out within the theoretical framework of cognitive development proposed by Perry (1970, 1981). Many of the studies have drawn on this framework in an attempt to design undergraduate courses (in a range of disciplines) which will challenge students' conceptions of knowledge and learning and encourage pluralism, critical thinking and self-determination on the part of learners. The general aim of this study is to investigate the learning experience of 2 cohorts of medical undergraduates (n=480), one studying within a traditional curriculum, the other in the revised, problem-based curriculum. Specifically, the study will focus on the students' conceptions of 1) 'learning'; 2) the nature of knowledge; 3) the student's role; 4) the lecturer's role at different stages during the first 2 undergraduate years. The study will also involve comparisons of the conceptions of the 2 cohorts of students, made within the framework of cognitive development proposed by Perry. Methods will include questionnaire and interview.

STATUS: Individual research

DATE OF RESEARCH: 1995-continuing

KEYWORDS: **cognitive development; higher education; learning processes; learning strategies; medical education; medical students; students**

0790

Dental School, 378 Sauchiehall Street, Glasgow G2 3JZ
0141 339 8855
Glasgow University, Laboratory of Human Anatomy, Glasgow G12 8QQ
0141 211 9854
West of Scotland Centre for Postgraduate Dental Education, 378 Sauchiehall Street, Glasgow G2 3JZ

Watt, M. Dr; McDonald, S. Dr; Sanders, C. Mr

Computer applications in Applied BioDental Sciences teaching

Abstract: Areas of study which require an appreciation of progressive changes of appearances and relationships can take full advantage of the facilities provided by computer imaging techniques. The researchers are using self-instructional computer-assisted learning (CAL) programs and also teacher-led computer presentations in the laboratory, either in place of microscopic work or in support of it in the Applied BioDental Sciences course in the dental undergraduate course. Clinical, radiological, diagrammatic and histological images are combined in presentations to help the students to integrate histological studies into a more overall view than can be gained by traditional histology laboratory work. The difficulties associated with the mechanics of use of the microscope are removed, leaving only those concerned with interpretation of the sections. Distracting artefacts can be removed by retouching, different magnifications viewed simultaneously, labels applied when appropriate, and questions asked. The development of spatial awareness skills is necessary to understand most topics in embryology. Scanning electron micrographs (SEMs) at the same magnification and orientation of similarly sectioned sheep embryos of various ages are used to prepare morphing sequences showing development of various structures in the head. These sequences form the core of CAL programs and video presentations, supplemented by still images and additional sequences based on diagrams. The efficiency and effectiveness of these products is being assessed. Students have consistently commented favourably on the programs. Typical comments have been 'I never understood that before' and 'that was a complete revelation', suggesting that the program clarified concepts which previously eluded their understanding.

PUBLISHED MATERIAL: WATT, M.E., MCDONALD, S.W. & WATT, A. (1995). 'Computer animations: a new way of presenting development of the face and palate to dental students', Clinical Anatomy, Vol 8, p.372. ; WATT, M.E., MCDONALD, S.W. & WATT, A. (1996). 'A computer morphing of scanning electron micrographs: an adjunct to embryology teaching' Surgical and Radiological Anatomy, Vol 18, pp.329-33.

STATUS: Collaborative

DATE OF RESEARCH: 1995-continuing

KEYWORDS: **computer assisted learning; computer uses in education; dental education; dentistry; dentists; information technology; multimedia**

0791

Department of Adult and Continuing Education, Glasgow G12 8QQ
0141 339 8855

Kane, L. Mr

Popular education in Latin America

ABSTRACT: A study of non-governmental 'popular' education in Latin America, particularly in relation to adults involved in popular (social) movements (such as the Landless People's Movement in Brazil). One of the aims is to consider how the Latin American experience could enlighten radical adult education practice in the UK. Areas under examination include: a) the relationship between popular education and the state; b) the role of ideology in popular education; c) the methodology of popular education. Currently, the research is related to publishing articles but eventually the aim is to produce a book giving a comprehensive guide to the subject.

STATUS: Individual research

DATE OF RESEARCH: 1996-continuing

KEYWORDS: **adult education; community education; comparative education; latin america**

0792

Department of Adult and Continuing Education, Glasgow G12 8QQ
0141 339 8855

MacKinnon, A. Dr; Mackenzie, A. Ms

Strategies for introducing adults to rigorous science study

ABSTRACT: Access courses are one of the options available to adults planning to return to full-time study in science or engineering. The researchers take the view that modular structures are limited in their scope for cognitive development, and that they cause problems of 'functional fixity' in e.g. the application of mathematical skills in physical or life sciences. Adults with specific vocational aims may be deterred by material that is abstract, and strategies for introducing such material and motivating its study must be devised. The researchers have designed a Science Access course which aims at developing generic problem-solving skills, and 'mental flexibility', as well as basic knowledge of mathematics, physics and chemistry, while engaging students' interest. The progress of students in their subsequent academic careers will be followed, as a test (the only valid test) of the strategies and thinking embodied in this course.

STATUS: Team research

DATE OF RESEARCH: 1995-1998

KEYWORDS: **access programmes; access to education; mature students; science education**

0793

Department of Adult and Continuing Education, Glasgow G12 8QQ
0141 339 8855

Clayton, P. Dr

Ethnic minorities in Greater Glasgow: exploratory research into issues of access for adult learners

ABSTRACT: The aim of this policy-oriented research was an initial exploration of the barriers to participation in adult education and training faced by ethnic minorities, including refugees, in Greater Glasgow. Although research is carried out on the general issue of Scotland's ethnic minorities, very little has been done so far on adult education. The main, but not exclusive, focus was on women. Census data was used to quantify and map ethnic minority members in the area. Interviews were carried out with two community education workers in areas with large Chinese and Asian populations; the director of the Ethnic Minority Enterprise Centre; an employment counsellor of the Scottish Refugee Council; and a development worker at the Meridian Information and Resource Centre for Black and Ethnic Minority Women. The main conclusions were predictable: the major barrier is language, followed by finance. Women, however, faced the special difficulty of fearing to use public transport to reach courses of higher levels than those provided by the Community Education Service. Not only is provision for non-native speakers of English held to be wholly inadequate, it is also too far from the areas of ethnic minority concentration.

PUBLISHED MATERIAL: CLAYTON, P. (1995). 'Ethnic minorities and adult education in Greater Glasgow - some developments'. In: MARK, R. (Ed). Report of a Conference on Adult Education for a Multicultural Society. Belfast: Queen's University of Belfast, Institute of Continuing Education.

STATUS: Individual research

DATE OF RESEARCH: 1995-1998

KEYWORDS: **access to education; adult education; adult students; community education; ethnic groups; womens education**

0794

Department of Adult and Continuing Education, Glasgow G12 8QQ
0141 339 8855

Clayton, P. Dr; Slowey, M. Prof.; Friese, M. Dr; Crete, N. Mme.; Ward, M. Ms; de Elejabeitia, C. Dr

Vocational guidance and counselling for women returners

ABSTRACT: This is a collaborative research project between: Glasgow University, Department of Adult and Continuing Education; Institut fur angewandte Biographie und Lebensweltforschung, FB 12, Universitat Bremen, Germany; Delegation a la Formation, Ministere du Travail, de l'Emploi et de la Formation Professionannelle, Paris, France; Centre for Training Policy, Department of Management, University of Cork; and Equipo de Estudios, Calle Puerto Rico 5-6, Madrid, Spain. Good quality, impartial educational guidance and employment counselling for adults (henceforth referred to as vocational guidance and counselling) are essential for many people attempting to negotiate the complexities of modern labour markets - yet statutory adult guidance services are not universal in the European Union. Women, particularly those who are attempting to enter the labour market as adults, face particular difficulties in gaining well-paid employment with a career structure. The researchers aimed to discover what provision exists for the group known as 'women returners' (which effectively means almost all women, excluding only those with an unbroken employment history since ending continuous full-time education). The countries concerned were the United Kingdom, France, Germany, Ireland

and Spain. Some of the services surveyed were national, others local. Having gained some perception of the amount and quality of existing services, the researchers then interviewed experts in each country in order to make recommendations for improvement. Although the focus was entirely on women, it became clear that many of the innovative practices discovered would equally benefit 'men returners', such as the long-term unemployed.

PUBLISHED MATERIAL: CLAYTON, P.M. (1996). 'A transnational study of vocational guidance and counselling provision for women returners', Adults Learning, Vol 8, No 2, pp.40-41. ; CHISHOLM, L. (1997). Getting in, climbing up and breaking through. Bristol: Policy Press.

STATUS: Sponsored project

SOURCE OF GRANT: European Commission £69,410

DATE OF RESEARCH: 1994-1998

KEYWORDS: **career counselling; comparative education; europe; vocational guidance; womens education; womens employment**

0795

Department of Adult and Continuing Education, Glasgow G12 8QQ
0141 339 8855

Turner, R. Mr

Feasibility of and participation in credit bearing programmes by part-time adult students

ABSTRACT: This research has its origins in a new development, based in the Department of Adult and Continuing Education, to promote part-time and mixed study opportunities in the University of Glasgow. In the pilot year of operation (1995-96), over 1,000 students were registered for the credit bearing programme offered by the Department and the focus of the research is to investigate the characteristics of those who are participating, their motivations for taking courses and their future plans. Methods used will include questionnaire surveys and individual interviews with both students and tutors with a specific focus on reactions to the use of various assessment strategies in the programme.

STATUS: Individual research

DATE OF RESEARCH: 1995-1997

KEYWORDS: **adult education; adult students; continuing education; credits; mature students; part time students**

0796

Department of Adult and Continuing Education, Glasgow G12 8QQ
0141 339 8855

Slowey, M. Prof.; Clayton, P. Dr

Long-term personal, social and economic outcomes of learning in the West of Scotland

ABSTRACT: Although there has been a great deal of analysis of adult participation in education and training, there is a paucity of research into the long-term outcomes of such participation. The research aims to discover the personal, social and economic outcomes for adults in the West of Scotland who had taken part about five years previously in the following types of learning: the Adults in Schools Programme; Scottish Wider Access Programme (SWAP) courses in colleges and Access courses at the University of Glasgow; community education through a variety of outreach initiatives, including the Community Education Service; open and continuing education; and vocational learning and training. Individual interviews are given, lasting around one hour, taped and transcribed verbatim. Questions cover childhood background, initial education, labour market history, motivation to enter and experience of the relevant course and the outcomes from participation. The research is still ongoing. So far 84 interviews have been carried out and some analysis has been done, yielding 2 articles so far. Conclusions so far tend to bear out the findings of a large-scale quantitative survey of Swedish men: that initial disadvantage is not easily compensated for by adult education in employment terms, and that those who benefit most from adult education are those with prior advantages. As regards personal outcomes, however, the benefits are much more evenly spread.

PUBLISHED MATERIAL: CLAYTON, P.M. (1995). 'Learning workers in two organisations in the West of Scotland: social, economic and personal outcomes of training'. In: Proceedings of Towards a Learning Workforce Conference, Lancaster University, Department of Continuing Education, September 12-13, 1995. ; CLAYTON, P.M. & SLOWEY, M. (1996).

'Towards the 'flexible' workforce? Implications for gender and the education and training of adults', Scottish Journal of Adult and Continuing Education, Vol 3, No 2, pp.45-62.

STATUS: Sponsored project

SOURCE OF GRANT: Scottish Office Education Funding Council £20,000

DATE OF RESEARCH: 1993-1997

KEYWORDS: access programmes; access to education; adult education; adult students; followup studies; higher education; mature students; outcomes of education

0797

Department of Adult and Continuing Education, Glasgow G12 8QQ
0141 339 8855

Clayton, P. Dr; Ward, M. Ms; Maiello, M. Dr; Lonn, H. Ms; Slowey, M. Prof.; Pia, A. Mrs

Access to vocational guidance and counselling for socially excluded groups

ABSTRACT: This is a collaborative project between: Glasgow University, Department of Adult and Continuing Education; Fondazione Seveso, Milan, Italy; Centre for Public Policy, University College, Cork, Ireland; and Vantaa Institute of Continuing Education, University of Helsinki, Finland. In view of the increased complexity of adult education/training and the labour market, vocational guidance and counselling can play a vital role in facilitating eventual labour market entry. For certain groups, however, there is a problem of access to such services. This study concerns facilitating access to services for groups in danger of social exclusion.

STATUS: Sponsored project

SOURCE OF GRANT: European Commission Leonardo programme £186,776

DATE OF RESEARCH: 1996-1998

KEYWORDS: access to information; career awareness; disadvantaged; europe; information needs; international programmes; labour market; training; vocational education; vocational guidance

0798

Department of Adult and Continuing Education, Glasgow G12 8QQ
0141 339 8855

Hamilton, R. Dr

The educational vision of Jane Addams

ABSTRACT: The research considers the social and political agenda of Jane Addams as reflected in her adult education work during the early years of her Social Settlement, Hull House, established in Chicago in 1889. Primary and secondary source material are consulted, including the writings of Addams herself, course programmes and related documentation, and newspaper articles from the period.

STATUS: Individual research

DATE OF RESEARCH: 1994-1997

KEYWORDS: adult education; educational history

0799

Department of Adult and Continuing Education, Glasgow G12 8QQ
0141 339 8855

Karkalas, A. Mrs; Mackenzie, A. Ms

Access, university and post-university experience of adult students from the Access course run by Glasgow University's Department of Adult and Continuing Education: final phase

ABSTRACT: This project, reported in the last Register in respect of most of the findings, followed up all students who had completed the Department's Access course 1979-1991. The final part of this wide-ranging survey by questionnaire focuses on the post-university careers and experiences of the 67 students who had graduated at the time of the survey. Some respondents perceived a mismatch between their university qualifications and their subsequent careers, with a substantial minority (30%) regarding their job as failing to reflect their qualifications. About a quarter also considered their university education had little impact on gaining employment, developing a career, or increasing job satisfaction. Difficulty in finding employment was not gender-related but was particularly marked among

those who both were over 40 on gaining their first degree and had graduated less than 2 years before the date of the survey. On the other hand, few commented on this lack of vocational 'fit' and almost all claimed to have derived deep personal satisfaction from their higher education. The unusually high proportion (just over half) of respondents entering postgraduate study may support this, though it is likely that vocational reasons were also operative. The study clearly relates to recent concerns about higher education being viewed in largely instrumental terms.

PUBLISHED MATERIAL: MACKENZIE, A. & KARKALAS, A. (1997). '"Was it all worthwhile?" Access students' experience of postgraduate study and employment', International Journal of University Adult Education, Vol 37, No 1, pp.40-57.

STATUS: Team research

DATE OF RESEARCH: 1991-1997

KEYWORDS: access programmes; access to education; followup studies; graduate employment; higher education; mature students; students

0800

Department of Adult and Continuing Education, Glasgow G12 8QQ
0141 339 8855

Hamilton, R. Dr

Chicago and Glasgow - a comparative study of the settlement movement

ABSTRACT: The research examines the early years, 1889-1910, of two settlements, Hull House in Chicago, and the Queen Margaret Settlement Association in Glasgow. The development of both settlements are compared and contrasted and parallels identified. Both can be regarded as among the leading settlements in their respective countries, both offered routes for educated women into specialised types of charity work and later social work, and both provide impulses for reform in wider society. Primary source material is consulted, in particular newspapers from the period 1889-1910, annual reports, course programmes, and the writings of the women involved.

STATUS: Individual research

DATE OF RESEARCH: 1996-1998

KEYWORDS: adult education; educational history; womens education

0801

Department of Adult and Continuing Education, Glasgow G12 8QQ
0141 339 8855

Maclachlan, K. Ms

The individual and organisational impact of Employee Development Schemes in both the University of Glasgow and areas of regeneration within the city

ABSTRACT: The research aims to evaluate the impact of several Employee Development Schemes in Glasgow. The first and largest, 'Learning Works', was established in the University of Glasgow for targeted categories of staff employed by the University, and the second, 'Learning Works in Govan', aims to replicate the model within small and medium sized enterprises in an area of regeneration in the city. It then spread using staff from the original dissemination area throughout other parts of Glasgow. The research is looking at change at an individual and organisational level that has occurred as a result of the schemes, and also at key features and processes that have contributed to the success, or otherwise, of the initiatives. A variety of research tools are being used in order to gauge short and longer term impact, and to draw comparisons between the different schemes. They include interviews, questionnaires, focus groups and case studies with learners, work supervisors and organisational managers. As the University scheme only started in September 1997, and the Govan one in December 1997, evaluative data from the learners is only beginning to emerge, but the initial response rates from staff are very encouraging, with the University having 870 registered learners from a staff group of 2025, and the Govan scheme having 70 from only small businesses in the area.

PUBLISHED MATERIAL: MACLACHLAN, K. (1997). 'Learning works in Glasgow', Higher Education Digest (Supplement), Issue 27, Spring.

STATUS: Individual research

DATE OF RESEARCH: 1997-continuing

KEYWORDS: adult education; continuing education; employee development schemes; employees; lifelong learning; staff development; work based learning

0802

Department of Adult and Continuing Education, Glasgow G12 8QQ
0141 339 8855

MacKenzie, A. Ms; Davies, J. Ms

Initial training in counselling: personal, educational and vocational outcomes

ABSTRACT: The aim of the study is to follow-up participants in part-time first-level training in counselling to determine the extent to which such training has been used as a means of career change, career enhancement, or possibly as a trigger for further study in related or unrelated fields. All those participants who completed a year-long certificate course (n=80) over a 5-year period will be included in a questionnaire survey.

STATUS: Team research

DATE OF RESEARCH: 1997-1998

KEYWORDS: counselling; counsellor training; followup studies

0803

Department of Adult and Continuing Education, Glasgow G12 8QQ
0141 339 8855

Steele, T. Dr

European popular education movements 1850-1950: the interface between popular knowledge(s) and academic disciplines and the role of the adult educator

ABSTRACT: This study draws on work undertaken since 1990 in part with Professor Stuart Marriott at the University of Leeds as a Universities Funding Council funded project on university extension in Europe in the 19th century and extended subsequently in ESREA cross-cultural seminars. It aims to discriminate between the various forms of adult education - university extension, universites populaires, folk high schools etc. - and the social movements associated with them. The study will analyse the nature of these movements for popular education, the forms of popular knowledge owned by them, the demand for 'relevance' and what they expected of 'university' and other forms of formal education. It will then consider the connections between these and emergent academic disciplines such as English studies, sociology, geography and other social sciences and how this relation was affected by the creation of specialist knowledges. Finally it will look at the role of the intellectuals engaged in adult education and the question of public intellectuals.

PUBLISHED MATERIAL: STEELE, T. (1991). 'Metropolitan extensions: comparisons of two moments in the export of British university adult education'. In: MARRIOTT, J.S. (Ed). British-Dutch-German relationships in adult education, 1880-1930: studies in the theory and history of cross-cultural communication in adult education. Leeds: University of Leeds, School of Education, Study of Continuing Education Unit. ; STEELE, T. (1993). 'A science for democracy: the growth of university extension in Europe 1890-1920'. In: HAKE, B.J. & MARRIOTT, S. (Eds). Adult education between cultures, encounters and identities in European adult education since 1890. Leeds: University of Leeds, School of Education, Study of Continuing Education Unit. ; STEELE, T. (1994). 'The colonial metaphor and the mission of Englishness: adult education and the origins of English studies'. In: MARRIOTT, S.& HAKE, B.J. (Eds). Cultural intercultural experiences in European adult education: essays on popular and higher education since 1890. Leeds: University of Leeds, School of Education, Study of Continuing Education Unit. ; STEELE, T. (1996). 'Karl Mannheim, an emigre intellectual and the 'sociological turn' in British adult education'. In: HAKE, B.J., STEELE, T. & TIANA-FERRER, A. Masters, missionaries and militants: studies of social movements and popular adult education 1890-1939. Leeds: University of Leeds, School of Education, Study of Continuing Education Unit.

STATUS: Individual research

DATE OF RESEARCH: 1990-continuing

KEYWORDS: adult education; comparative education; educational history; europe; extension education

0804

Department of Education, Glasgow G12 8QQ
0141 339 8855

Kirk, R. Ms; *Supervisors*: Wilkinson, J. Dr; Hill, M. Prof.

Day care in Tayside: its impact on family relationships and well-being

ABSTRACT: Based on a sample of 100 families using social work day care in Tayside, the study is an indepth investigation of the impact of the day care on children and families. The study is using instrumentation (reliable and valid schedules) to examine parents social support networks and children's development. The study is an attempt to cast light on the extent to which day care can help families with a child 'at risk' or the subject of abuse.

PUBLISHED MATERIAL: KIRK, R. (1990). Parents and their perceptions of family centres on Tayside. Dundee: Tayside Regional Council.

STATUS: Individual research

DATE OF RESEARCH: 1991-1998

KEYWORDS: children at risk; community services; day care; family life; family problems; social networks

0805

Department of Education, Glasgow G12 8QQ
0141 339 8855

Wilkinson, J. Prof.

A research and evaluation study of community nurseries in Strathclyde Region 1989-1992

ABSTRACT: The study is a research and evaluation study into the strengths and weaknesses of new types of establishments (community nurseries) for families with young children set up in Strathclyde Region following publication of the Member/Officer Group Report, Under Fives (1985). Based on two pilot community nurseries and a conventional nursery school, the evaluation was conducted at a number of levels: (1) achievement of aims and objectives with explanations for successes and failures; (2) assessment of quality of the nursery environment; (3) children's developmental progress; (4) development of the nurseries; (5) effects of the nurseries on families; (6) inter-agency liaison; (7) applications and admissions. Methods used were: interview; observation; children's assessments and analysis of documents. The study shows that quality in the community nurseries is high; most children and families are benefiting and that the nurseries are targeted at the most needy.

PUBLISHED MATERIAL: WILKINSON, J.E. & KELLY, B., & BRADY, J. (1990). 'Pre-five evaluation: research in Scotland', Forum on Educational Research in Scotland, No 6, The school in its community. Edinburgh: SCRE. ; WILKINSON, J.E. & STEPHEN, C. (1992). Evaluating ourselves. Glasgow: University of Glasgow, Department of Education. ; WILKINSON, J.E., KELLY, B. & STEPHEN, C. (1993). Flagships: an evaluation/research study of community nurseries in Strathclyde 1989-1992. Glasgow: University of Glasgow, Department of Education.

STATUS: Sponsored project

SOURCE OF GRANT: Strathclyde Regional Council £85,000

DATE OF RESEARCH: 1989-1993

KEYWORDS: agency cooperation; child caregivers; community services; day care centres; early childhood education; programme evaluation; quality control

0806

Department of Education, Glasgow G12 8QQ
0141 339 8855

Grant, N. Prof.

Multicultural education

ABSTRACT: This project is based on several publications and on a previous course, now being reorganised into a book. It deals with identity, cultural identity, language and cultural demands on education, at home and abroad. It also deals with the persistence of racism, and the best ways of combating it, in Scotland and abroad, both the 'immigrant' - descended populations and the various native Scottish populations and the positions of their languages, Punjabi, Urdu, Cantonese, Gaelic and Scots. The position of all their languages in education will also be explored.

PUBLISHED MATERIAL: GRANT, N. (1992). '"Scientific" racism: what price objectivity?', Scottish Educational Review, Vol 21, No 1, pp.24-31. ; GRANT, N. (1993). 'Multicultural societies in the European community - the odd case of Scotland', European Journal of Intercultural Studies, Vol 5, No 1, pp.51-59. ; GRANT, N. (1997). 'Some problems of cultural identity: a comparative examination of multicultural education', Comparative Education, Vol 33, No 1, pp.9-28. ; GRANT, N. (1997). 'Multicultural education in Scotland: ourselves and others', Scottish Educational Review, Vol 29, No 2, pp.134-144.

STATUS: Individual research

DATE OF RESEARCH: 1986-continuing

KEYWORDS: **antiracism education; bilingual education; ethnic groups; identity; multicultural education; multiculturalism; scotland**

0807

Department of Education, Glasgow G12 8QQ
0141 339 8855

MacKenzie, M. Mr

The thoughts of Parker Palmer with specific reference to the teaching of religious education in Scotland

ABSTRACT: The research will: (1) analayse Palmer's thoughts, specifically as explained in his book 'The company of strangers: Christians and the renewal of America's public life' (New York: Crossroad 1990); and (2) compare this thinking with Scottish politics, education systems and the thinking emanating from the Association of Teachers of Religious Education in Scotland (ATRES) a body of which the researcher is a member. The aim is a synthesis of political, educational and religious thought in Scotland based on a comparison with the United States, focused on the work of that country's foremost religious thinkers.

STATUS: Individual research

DATE OF RESEARCH: 1992-1993

KEYWORDS: **religion and education; scotland**

0808

Department of Education, Glasgow G12 8QQ
0141 339 8855

Humes, W. Dr

Partnership: a conceptual analysis

ABSTRACT: The concept of partnership is frequently invoked in educational discourse. This study attempts to disentangle its various meanings using a range of examples covering home/school relations, education/industry links and central/local government responsibilities. The question of whether it is simply a rhetorical device designed to disguise differential power will be considered.

STATUS: Individual research

DATE OF RESEARCH: 1992-1993

KEYWORDS: **government - administrative body; home school relationship; industry education relationship; partnerships**

0809

Department of Education, Glasgow G12 8QQ
0141 339 8855

Grant, N. Prof.; Humes, W. Dr

Scottish education after the 1696 Education Act

ABSTRACT: This study is part of a larger project for publication entitled 'Scotland: a concise cultural history'. The project as a whole will cover literature, science, the law, the arts and religion as well as education. The chapter on education will deal with legislation, access and expansion, democracy and equality, and the changing nature of the policy process. Several recurring myths about Scottish education will be challenged.

STATUS: Individual research

DATE OF RESEARCH: 1992-1993

KEYWORDS: **educational history; scotland**

0810

Department of Education, Glasgow G12 8QQ
0141 339 8855

Humes, W. Dr

The management of morale

ABSTRACT: This is a small scale project which attempts to review recent research on teacher morale and to consider its implications for educational managers. Among the topics to be considered are communication systems, decision making processes, promotion, innovation and professional autonomy. The question of whether central and local government are expecting educational managers to do an impossible job will be addressed.

PUBLISHED MATERIAL: HUMES, W. (1993). 'Scottish ideas for managing morale', Management in Education, Vol 7, No 3, pp.9-10.

STATUS: Individual research

DATE OF RESEARCH: 1992-1993

KEYWORDS: **educational administration; teacher morale; teaching profession**

0811

Department of Education, Glasgow G12 8QQ
0141 339 8855

Kirkham, J. Mr; *Supervisor*: MacKenzie, M. Mr

A critical analysis of Thomas Greenfield's subjective approach to the field of educational administration in the context of an interdisciplinary initiative to the field, drawing on sociology of education, anthropology, philosophy and organisation theory in general

ABSTRACT: This project includes: (1) an analysis of all relevant documentation following Greenfield's paper to the 1974 International Intervisitation Programme in Bristol; (2) an examination of the resulting subjective/systems debates; (3) a detailed review of the relevant literature; (4) an exploration of the justificatory philosophical sources used by Greenfield and his critics; (5) comparison of Greenfield's 'new perspective' with the 'new directions' movement in the sociology of education; (6) an examination of the importance of anthropological and ethnographic research methods in educational administration; (7) an examination of ambiguity models in relation to systems and subjective approaches; (8) the relevance of the Inlogou Report; (9) a critical examination of the possibility of resolving the subjective/systems debate.

STATUS: Individual research

DATE OF RESEARCH: 1988-1993

KEYWORDS: **educational administration; organisational theories**

0812

Department of Education, Glasgow G12 8QQ
0141 339 8855

Marker, W. Mr; *Supervisor*: MacKenzie, M. Mr

Policy making in teacher education in Scotland 1959-1981

ABSTRACT: This project includes: (1) a study of the policy process, involving interviews and analysis of original documentation; (2) a UK analysis which compares policy in England with that of Scotland; (3) examination of demographic and economic factors, as well as political and pressure group considerations with regard to major decisions such as college closure. Conclusions and analysis takes place within a theoretical framework. The research illuminates key issues and processes concerning teacher education in Scotland during the period studied.

STATUS: Individual research

DATE OF RESEARCH: 1987-1993

KEYWORDS: **comparative education; educational history; educational policy; scotland; teacher education**

0813

Department of Education, Glasgow G12 8QQ
0141 339 8855

Boyd, B. Dr; *Supervisor*: MacKenzie, M. Mr

'Let a hundred flowers blossom...': a study of educational policy making in

Scotland in the 1970's, 1980's and early 1990's: formulation, implementation and dissemination, using the 10-14 report as a case study

ABSTRACT: This project includes: (1) an examination of the primary and secondary scene in Scotland by means of a case study of the 10-14 initiative; (2) a study of local government reorganisation; (3) a look at the School as an important element in the policy implementation process and a consideration of why the 10-14 initiative failed to be implemented as a policy and was instead replaced by the Government's 5-14 Development Programme. Data is used from the 10-14 Committee. In addition, interviews with members of the policy community are presented as commentary both on the 10-14 initiative and on the policy making process generally. Various papers, including memos and letters from participants in the 10-14 initiative are examined. Thus 10-14 is offered as a case study of the Scottish educational policy making process. The influence of 'New Light' ideology is also examined.

STATUS: Individual research

DATE OF RESEARCH: 1988-1993

KEYWORDS: **educational innovation; educational policy; middle school education; scotland**

0814

Department of Education, Glasgow G12 8QQ
0141 339 8855

Tikly, L. Mr; *Supervisor*: Humes, W. Dr

Education policy in South Africa since 1948

ABSTRACT: This study examines the changing nature of educational policy in South Africa since 1948. It shows how the orthodoxies of apartheid were challenged and transformed by major economic forces. Debates both within the National Party and the African National Congress are examined critically. Interviews with leading political and educational figures are used to explain the context and recommendations of key documents (such as the De Lange Report). The implications of the reform process for future policy are considered.

STATUS: Individual research

DATE OF RESEARCH: 1990-1993

KEYWORDS: **educational history; educational policy; politics education relationship; south africa**

0815

Department of Education, Glasgow G12 8QQ
0141 339 8855

Ariffin, S. Mrs; *Supervisors*: Grant, N. Prof.; Barr, A. Mr

Characteristics of secondary schools in Pulau Penang, Malaysia

ABSTRACT: This project examines the implementation of a scheme for the teaching of English in Malaysian schools, recently introduced by the Government, and the effectiveness of this implementation. Field studies have been carried out in Malaysia with questionnaires on teachers' experience of inservice training for the purpose, and their attitudes towards it.

STATUS: Individual research

DATE OF RESEARCH: 1990-1993

KEYWORDS: **english - second language; malaysia; secondary education**

0816

Department of Education, Glasgow G12 8QQ
0141 339 8855

Emara, H. Mrs; *Supervisors*: Grant, N. Prof.; Barr, A. Mr

The effects of language difficulties on the achievements of Arab students

ABSTRACT: Many higher education courses (e.g. medicine) in Saudi Arabia are taught in English, and difficulties have emerged in students' performance. This project examines the psycholinguistic issues that arise in the course of studying through a language not native to either the teacher or the learner, and some of the difficulties that emerge in the particular circumstances of Saudi universities. Documentary and fieldwork has been used in this project.

STATUS: Individual research

DATE OF RESEARCH: 1988-1993

KEYWORDS: **english - second language; higher education; language of instruction; saudi arabia**

0817

Department of Education, Glasgow G12 8QQ
0141 339 8855

Sarkar, R. Mrs; *Supervisor*: Wilkinson, J. Dr

The teaching of community languages in Scotland

ABSTRACT: This is a study of the teaching of community languages in Scotland, especially among the Asian community. The problem of policy and practice will be addressed and likely future developments will be considered.

STATUS: Individual research

DATE OF RESEARCH: 1993-continuing

KEYWORDS: **asians; bilingualism; ethnic groups; language maintenance; language policy; mother tongue**

0818

Department of Education, Glasgow G12 8QQ
0141 339 8855

Campbell, P. Mr; *Supervisor*: MacKenzie, M. Mr

Nordic folk high schools and their possible application to Scotland

ABSTRACT: This is a study of the development and function of the Folk High Schools in Denmark, Norway, Sweden and elsewhere in Scandinavia, examining the different patterns in the various countries.

STATUS: Individual research

DATE OF RESEARCH: 1993-1998

KEYWORDS: **adult education; comparative education; lifelong learning; mature students; peoples universities; scandinavia**

0819

Department of Education, Glasgow G12 8QQ
0141 339 8855

Limond, D. Mr; *Supervisors*: Paterson, H. Mr; Maver, I. Dr

A history of girls' education in Scotland 1872-1945

ABSTRACT: There is no Scottish equivalent to Kamm's work on the education of girls in England. This investigation seeks to fill that part of the gap by constructing a history of girls' education in Scotland from 1872 to the end of the 2nd World War. The main methodologies employed are: a) archival research, including school archives; b) ethnographic research; and c) oral records.

STATUS: Individual research

DATE OF RESEARCH: 1993-1997

KEYWORDS: **educational history; girls; scotland; womens education**

0820

Department of Education, Glasgow G12 8QQ
0141 339 8855

Kane, H-M. Ms; *Supervisor*: MacKenzie, M. Mr

The school as a learning organisation

ABSTRACT: Drawing on an extensive international literature, the research analyses spirituality, metaphor and myth in organisations and in organisational theory with particular reference to the concept of the learning organisation. The implications for school management, teaching and learning will be examined and recommendations made.

STATUS: Individual research

DATE OF RESEARCH: 1994-continuing

KEYWORDS: **educational principles; institutional environment; learning; organisational climate**

0821

Department of Education, Glasgow G12 8QQ
0141 339 8855

Kerr, T. Mr; *Supervisors*: Paterson, H. Mr; Green, M. Dr

Quintilian on moral education - a re-evaluation

ABSTRACT: Quintilian's reputation as a mediocre teacher of oratory and rhetoric is in need of revision. By returning to original sources, and by surveying appropriate research in Britain and Europe, this investigation seeks to rehabilitate an important Roman educator.

STATUS: Individual research

DATE OF RESEARCH: 1994-1998

KEYWORDS: **educational history; roman history**

0822

Department of Education, Glasgow G12 8QQ
0141 339 8855

Kirkwood, M. Dr; *Supervisors*: Paterson, H. Mr; Jeacocke, J. Dr

Embedding problem solving, higher order thinking and metacognition into an introductory computer programming course

ABSTRACT: Courses in computer programming can be so designed as to enhance the transferable problem solving skills of students. This investigation involves the design, delivery and evaluation of such a course to secondary school pupils (n=48), by participant observation and interviews. Initial results indicate that such courses appear to enhance the problem solving skills of students.

STATUS: Individual research

DATE OF RESEARCH: 1991-1997

KEYWORDS: **cognitive processes; computer programming; computer uses in education; information technology; metacognition; problem solving**

0823

Department of Education, Glasgow G12 8QQ
0141 339 8855

O'Hagan, F. Mr; *Supervisor*: Paterson, H. Mr

The influence of the religious orders on Catholic education in Glasgow during the 19th and 20th centuries

ABSTRACT: The important role of male and female religious orders in setting up and promoting schools and colleges for the education of Roman Catholics in the city has only been partially explored. This research aims to write a fuller history, by: a) archival research; and b) compiling an oral record of participants.

STATUS: Individual research

DATE OF RESEARCH: 1995-continuing

KEYWORDS: **catholic educators; catholic schools; church and education; educational history; religion and education; roman catholic church**

0824

Department of Education, Glasgow G12 8QQ
0141 339 8855

McKernan, G. Mr; *Supervisors*: McGonigal, J. Dr; MacKenzie, M. Mr

The monster and the teddy bear: the construction of children and childhood in picture books 1945-1995

ABSTRACT: The proposed research project will attempt a critical evaluation of trends in representations of childhood presented in picture books and infant reading schemes. It will seek to expose the ideological assumptions underlying texts. Since the study covers an extended period of time, a time during which much social change has taken place, a concern of the study will be to identify the nature and direction of ideological shift over the period. Through such texts children may be being presented with images of 'the family' which do not at all match their own lived experience, or which represented 'stereotypical' gender roles, or social inequalities as inevitable, 'normal' or desirable. Similarly, such images have the potential to reinforce or challenge racial stereotypes. In the light of initiatives such as Strathclyde Regional's Social Strategy and MCARE programme, it must be a concern of teachers and others to be aware of the ideological content of the picture books and infant reading schemes which are so much a part of the infant classroom. The study seeks to contribute to this awareness. The study is influenced by: daily experience of reading with and to infant school children in a Glasgow school; and recent writing on ideology and children's fiction by John Stephens, Peter Hollindale and others. There is little related research; the bulk of related work has been concerned with children's fiction in general and not specifically with picture books. The researcher will use the collection of the National Library of Scotland, and the library and resource centre of Jordanhill campus. The overall aim is to explore the relationship between trends in representations of the family in picture books and infant reading schemes and social change. The research will ask: 1) How has the family been represented in picture books and infant reading schemes in the period of the study? 2) To what extent have changes in patterns of family life been accurately reflected in picture book representations? 3) To what extent have changes in patterns of family life been reflected in family representations in infant reading schemes? The study will include: a) review and assessment of modern theoretical perspectives on the family; b) review of changes in the related areas of marriage, parenthood and gender divisions - assessing the nature and direction of change in the post-war period; c) review and evaluation of popular images of children and understandings of childhood in the period; d) assessment and refinement of interrogative techniques for locating ideology in texts and pictures; and e) application of arguments and critical approaches to as wide as possible a range of texts.

STATUS: Individual research

DATE OF RESEARCH: 1994-1998

KEYWORDS: **books; childrens literature; ideology; picture books; stereotypes**

0825

Department of Education, Glasgow G12 8QQ
0141 339 8855

Wilkins, N. Ms; *Supervisor*: Paterson, H. Mr

Educational responses to adolescent disaffection

ABSTRACT: Following on the work of Feuerstein and others, the plan is to: a) investigate the reasons for adolescent disaffection in a Scottish island community; b) design and implement a curriculum in a college of further education based on ideas of 'cognitive enrichment'; and c) evaluate the effectiveness of such a curriculum.

STATUS: Individual research

DATE OF RESEARCH: 1994-1998

KEYWORDS: **adolescent attitudes; adolescents; behaviour modification; cognitive restructuring; curriculum development; further education; youth problems**

0826

Department of Education, Glasgow G12 8QQ
0141 339 8855

Winters, J. Mr; *Supervisor*: Paterson, H. Mr

Continuing education for nurses with particular reference to clinical skills

ABSTRACT: This research deals with the design, delivery and evaluation of skills training programmes for nurses in clinical practice. Such practice will be analysed in terms of competences, skills and attitudes in an attempt to construct an articulated model of the practice and investigate the effectiveness of programmes based on such a model.

STATUS: Individual research

DATE OF RESEARCH: 1994-continuing

KEYWORDS: **clinical experience; nurse education; nurses; professional continuing education**

0827

Department of Education, Glasgow G12 8QQ
0141 339 8855

Drennan, L. Ms; *Supervisor*: MacKenzie, M. Mr

Total quality management in higher education

ABSTRACT: A critique of literature governing total quality management (TQM) and its applicability to higher education. A case study of one (perhaps two) universities using archival material, interviews and public documents. The aim is to analyse how TQM has been used in higher education to identify its potential, highlight its weaknesses and to make conclusions and recommendations with respect to higher education policy.

STATUS: Individual research

DATE OF RESEARCH: 1993-continuing

KEYWORDS: educational administration; higher education; quality control; universities

0828

Department of Education, Glasgow G12 8QQ
0141 339 8855

Pignatelli, F. Prof.; *Supervisor*: MacKenzie, M. Mr

The development of Strathclyde Region's Education Service (1975-1996)

ABSTRACT: An analysis of the managerial and education thinking leading to the creation of Strathclyde Region with particular emphasis on the theories of corporate management and planning. By interview with key personnel and examination of both internal and external documentation to cast light on the management of Strathclyde Region's Education Service during the period of its existence. The aims are: 1) to investigate the thinking behind, and the impact of, key management documents such as the reports by the Institute of Local Government Studies (INLOGOV); 2) To relate the management of education to the forces and developments leading to the ultimate demise of Strathclyde Region; and 3) To draw conclusions of significance and help to researchers in the fields of local government, educational management and administration, management theory and the policy process.

STATUS: Individual research

DATE OF RESEARCH: 1995-continuing

KEYWORDS: educational administration; local education authorities; management in education

0829

Department of Education, Glasgow G12 8QQ
0141 339 8855

Creechan, G. Mr; *Supervisor*: Paterson, H. Mr

A history of maritime education in the Glasgow area

ABSTRACT: This important area of educational history in the area has yet to be investigated. The aim is to trace the history of nautical and maritime education in the Glasgow area. This will be done by: a) accumulating an oral and video record of the memories and views of merchant seamen, master mariners, teachers and lecturers; and b) archival research.

STATUS: Individual research

DATE OF RESEARCH: 1994-1998

KEYWORDS: educational history; nautical education

0830

Department of Education, Glasgow G12 8QQ
0141 339 8855

Dordi, R. Ms; *Supervisor*: Wilkinson, J. Dr

Efficacy of educational strategies in intervention programmes for young offenders in Scotland

ABSTRACT: The study will be a formative evaluation of the project, examining the mechanisms by which its stated aims and objectives are being implemented, by focusing on the process of intervention. Using appropriate methodology and research tools, the study will attempt to address the issues raised by the research questions: 1) What are the perceptions, both in terms of consensus and differences of the various stakeholders involved, of the functioning of the intervention process? 2) Is there an 'information coordination - communication linkage' between programme users linking planning, implementation and evaluation of the programmes? 3) What is the quality of the treatment strategies, methods and initiatives used, particularly with regard to effective and relevant presentation with both clarity and depth regarding users? 4) How do the various stakeholders perceive these programmes and how in the implementation of these programmes is the treatment of conflicting goals and conflicting interest groups resolved? 5) How effectively designed are these programmes in meeting the needs, interests and problems of the participants, and are they worth the cost both in time and resources? The dominant methodology and research tools employed by the study will be: a) documentary evidence and official statistics; b) non-participant observation; c) structured interviews using audio-tape recording and questionnaires with programme administrators or the project staff, project administrators or project managers, social workers, project evaluators both internal and external, participants, ex-participants, law enforcers - fiscals and sherriffs, other agencies, cooperating community and other stakeholders.

STATUS: Individual research

DATE OF RESEARCH: 1994-1998

KEYWORDS: educational strategies; intervention; offenders; probation; programme evaluation; youth problems

0831

Department of Education, Glasgow G12 8QQ
0141 339 8855

Martin, A. Mr; *Supervisor*: Paterson, H. Mr

Information technology literacy in higher education: the role and effectiveness of central course provision

ABSTRACT: Many universities are now providing, centrally, information technology courses for students. This research aims to evaluate the effectiveness of such provision by comparing the situation in two UK universities.

STATUS: Individual research

DATE OF RESEARCH: 1996-continuing

KEYWORDS: computer literacy; computer uses in education; higher education; information technology; universities

0832

Department of Education, Glasgow G12 8QQ
0141 339 8855

McGlone, C. Ms; *Supervisor*: Wilkinson, J. Dr

Evaluation of the effectiveness of Solution Focused Brief Therapy for children 5-12 years

ABSTRACT: The study will be based upon 8-12 cases referred to the Behaviour Support Team in Lanarkshire. The referrals come through Psychological Services and therefore there exists a formal system whereby an initial assessment has been carried out, a variety of strategies have been tried and the need for further intervention in the form of support has been granted. Support usually takes the form of a support teacher working with the child, the teacher and the parent to achieve a manageable solution to the problem. In Lanarkshire one of the approaches used is that of Solution Focused Brief Therapy which is essentially a positive problem solving approach to the management of disruptive pupils. The study will include various sections: 1) Emotionally and behaviourally disruptive pupils - who are they? A 1990s perspective. This section deals with the labelling of pupils and the relationship between social factors and the phenomena of challenging behaviours. 2) Inclusion versus exclusion. The management of behaviourally disruptive pupils concerns every school and there has been an emphasis upon excluding the pupil from school. 3) The legal framework (Scotland). The implications of The Children Act 1989 in relation to the exclusion procedures. The responsibilities of schools and local authorities. 4) Behaviour support system - a divisional response to the problem of disruptive behaviour in mainstream primary schools. 5) The referral system. 6) The role of the behaviour support teacher. 7) The role of the educational psychologist. The pupil is referred by the psychologist and it is their assessment which shall be used as the baseline for measuring any changes over time. There is a review held every 8 weeks, or more frequently if necessary. Thus the psychologist has a monitoring role as well as assisting in the evaluation of an intervention. 8) The responsibility of the school system towards the referred pupil, the class teacher, the parents and the other pupils.

STATUS: Individual research

DATE OF RESEARCH: 1995-continuing

KEYWORDS: behaviour modification; disruptive pupils; emotional and behavioural difficulties; exclusion; learning support; mainstreaming; problem children; special educational needs; support services; support teachers; suspension; therapy #@

0833

Department of Education, Glasgow G12 8QQ
0141 339 8855

Dumbleton, P. Mr; Baron, S. Mr

Construing and constraining

ABSTRACT: A critique and reformulation of how those with 'learning difficulties' have been construed and constrained by professional knowledge and common sense and how, reciprocally, this has construed and constrained the professionals and the competent.

STATUS: Individual research

DATE OF RESEARCH: 1997-continuing

KEYWORDS: **learning disabilities; special educational needs**

0834

Department of Education, Glasgow G12 8QQ
0141 339 8855

Wilkinson, J. Prof.; Stephen, C. Dr

Development of a quality assurance scheme for Scottish independent nurseries

ABSTRACT: The aims of the project are to: 1) investigate and compare a range of existing literature on quality for early years services; 2) compile a quality assurance (QA) manual for use by independent nurseries providing early years services (0-5 years) and after-school care; 3) scrutinise QA submissions from Scottish Independent Nurseries Association (SINA) nurseries; 4) report back to each nursery and to SINA; and 5) advise on development planning.

PUBLISHED MATERIAL: STEPHEN,. C. & WILKINSON, J.E. (1996). The SINA quality assurance scheme: a manual. Glasgow: University of Glasgow.

STATUS: Sponsored project

SOURCE OF GRANT: Scottish Independent Nurseries Association (SINA) £28,708

DATE OF RESEARCH: 1997-1998

KEYWORDS: **after school care; day care; early childhood education; nursery schools; quality assurance; quality control; scotland**

0835

Department of Education, Glasgow G12 8QQ
0141 339 8855

Paterson, H. Mr

Ethnographic study of secondary education in Scotland

ABSTRACT: The study attempts to explain the psychic, social and cultural significance of secondary schooling in Scotland.

STATUS: Individual research

DATE OF RESEARCH: 1997-1997

KEYWORDS: **ethnography; scotland; secondary education**

0836

Department of Education, Glasgow G12 8QQ
0141 339 8855

Watson, D. Mr; *Supervisor*: Paterson, H. Mr

History of educational use of computers in Scottish schools

ABSTRACT: This research aims to analyse reasons for the partial use of computers for teaching in Scottish primary and secondary schools - they are used extensively in some areas but hardly at all in others. The main method is historical using: a) document analysis, and b) oral history involving interviews with leading participants.

STATUS: Individual research

DATE OF RESEARCH: 1997-continuing

KEYWORDS: **computer uses in education; information technology; primary education; scotland; secondary education**

0837

Department of Education, Glasgow G12 8QQ
0141 339 8855

Androga, R. Mr; *Supervisor*: Paterson, H. Mr

Education in the Sudan from 1956: a study in Islamization

ABSTRACT: There were signs of the Islamization of Sudanese education before independence in 1956 but the processes have increased markedly since then, especially recently with a fundamentalist government in power. These developments are part of an aggressive movement to create a pan-Arab-Islamic sphere of influence. The objectives of the research are: 1) to analyse these processes in Sudanese education since 1956; 2) to determine their effects and implications in the country, and in Africa as a whole; 3) to compile an archive of government and opposition documentation; 4) to propose a curriculum model for a multi-cultural Sudan.

STATUS: Individual research

DATE OF RESEARCH: 1997-continuing

KEYWORDS: **africa; educational history; islamic education; sudan**

0838

Department of Education, Glasgow G12 8QQ
0141 339 8855

Biko, S. Ms; *Supervisor*: Mackenzie, M. Mr

Educational management: the competencies required in the role of principal in an incorporated further education college

ABSTRACT: The research investigates the changed management role of principal of Scottish further education colleges since the process of incorporation removed the colleges from local authority control. Using case-study, interview, data and records analysis the researcher will map out the competencies now required of principals in the context of modern management theory. The findings will have implications for management selection and training and will also, it is hoped, make a contribution to theory.

STATUS: Individual research

DATE OF RESEARCH: 1997-continuing

KEYWORDS: **colleges of further education; competence; educational administration; further education; management in education; principals**

0839

Department of Education, Glasgow G12 8QQ
0141 339 8855

Campbell, R. Ms; *Supervisor*: Baron, S. Mr

Children and their communities

ABSTRACT: An investigation into how children construct their relationship to the community and how it constructs them, with particular reference to an ethnographic study of a deprived area.

STATUS: Individual research

DATE OF RESEARCH: 1997-continuing

KEYWORDS: **children; community**

0840

Department of Education, Glasgow G12 8QQ
0141 339 8855

Conroy, J. Mr; *Supervisor*: MacKenzie, M. Mr

The politics of value and the value of politics

ABSTRACT: This is a theoretical/philosophical analysis of values in education with specific reference to the values which underpin educational policy. The analysis draws on a wide range of literature - ethical, sociological, political and literary - in an attempt to illuminate the decision-making processes which govern contemporary education.

STATUS: Individual research

DATE OF RESEARCH: 1997-continuing

KEYWORDS: **educational philosophy; educational policy; ethics; politics education relationship; values**

0841

Department of Education, Glasgow G12 8QQ
0141 339 8855

Hannah, K. Ms; *Supervisor*: MacKenzie, M. Mr

Support for learning: staff development issues in mainstream secondary schools

ABSTRACT: The research analyses the concept of 'special educational needs' in the context of organisational pathologies. In terms of policy, it analyses the impact of the Warnock Report in the Scottish situation. Examination is made of the policy of integration, its theory and its effects. By extensive interviewing and questionnaire techniques a profile of practice will be created leading to recommendations in respect of future policy pertaining to staff development.

STATUS: Individual research

DATE OF RESEARCH: 1996-continuing

KEYWORDS: **mainstreaming; scotland; secondary education; special educational needs; staff development; teacher development**

0842

Department of Education, Glasgow G12 8QQ
0141 339 8855

McEachern, C. Ms; *Supervisor*: Baron, S. Mr

Modern foreign languages and children with special needs

ABSTRACT: A European comparative study of approaches to integrating children with special needs into the modern foreign language classroom.

STATUS: Individual research

DATE OF RESEARCH: 1997-continuing

KEYWORDS: **comparative education; europe; mainstreaming; modern language studies; special educational needs**

0843

Department of Education, Glasgow G12 8QQ
0141 339 8855

Phillips, A. Ms; *Supervisor*: Baron, S. Mr

Conductive education and the transition to mainstream school

ABSTRACT: A study of the transition of pupils from the Craighabbert Centre to mainstream, or other primary schools, including a comparison with other forms of preschool provision for the child with cerebral palsy.

STATUS: Individual research

DATE OF RESEARCH: 1997-continuing

KEYWORDS: **cerebral palsy; conductive education; mainstreaming; special educational needs**

0844

Department of Education, Glasgow G12 8QQ
0141 339 8855

Turner, R. Mr; McGill, P. Mr

Impact and effectiveness of educational guidance for part-time adult students

ABSTRACT: The study aims to monitor the effectiveness of a dedicated advice and guidance service for adults considering the possibility of part-time study towards a university award. There has been a survey of those who have received face-to-face guidance from the service to ascertain why advice has been sought; its impact upon individuals' educational plans and motivations for study. Data is still being collected for analysis.

STATUS: Team research

DATE OF RESEARCH: 1997-continuing

KEYWORDS: **adult counselling; educational guidance; guidance; higher education; mature students; part time degrees**

0845

Department of Education, Glasgow G12 8QQ
0141 339 8855

Walker, M. Dr; Wilkinson, J. Dr; Phipps, A. Dr; Gonzalez, M. Mr; Warhurst, C. Dr

Collaborative action research studies - higher education

ABSTRACT: In action research the focus of the research process and its outcomes is improving and understanding the practice of teaching, learning and professional development, as well as the generation of situated and contextual knowledge about higher education practices. A key assumption here is that practice is more likely to be improved if lecturers themselves have been involved in addressing the conditions, theories and principles for improvement, through their own practice. Besides, as the ones living the experience of teaching with all its twists and turns and dilemmas, lecturers are arguably best placed to describe and analyse their practices. Moreover, projects across multiple sites might in time contribute to more generalised theories and theorising about higher education practice. Collaborative and scholarly action research serves to challenge technocratic approaches to educational understanding, innovation and improvement. Such technocratic approaches ('tips for teachers', or skills acquired and 'reproduced') are akin to the 'surface' learning strategies we wish to discourage on the part of our students. In active and creative learning situations, informed by evidence and its rigorous and scholarly analysis and interpretation, theoretical knowledge and practical understanding is generated 'from the ground up' by practitioners. Thus academics might on the one hand create and advance knowledge in higher education on the basis of their concrete practical experience; and on the other hand actively improve that practice, their understanding of practice, and where possible the context of that practice in a creative process of professional development under their own control and direction.

STATUS: Sponsored project

SOURCE OF GRANT: Glasgow University £10,000

DATE OF RESEARCH: 1998-continuing

KEYWORDS: **action research; higher education; lecturers; teacher researchers**

0846

Department of Education, Glasgow G12 8QQ
0141 339 8855

Wilkinson, J. Dr

Engineering identities: class and gender in becoming and being electrical engineers

ABSTRACT: There is now an extensive literature which explores issues and problems on the exclusion of women from careers in electrical engineering. This study articulates with these studies but poses further questions in terms of social class and identity formation. The issue is how to identify commonalities and differences in the experiences of men and women who have studied electrical engineering (and hence who are 'successful'), and to understand the extent to which these commonalities and differences can be accounted for in terms of social class, gender and cultural patterns. What are the patterns of recognition and exclusion from becoming and being an electrical engineer? The project takes the view that identity is affected by the politics of class and gender (amongst other factors), but at the same time individuals try to shape and control their own personal identities. Thus the shaping of our identities by gender and class as sites of struggle and oppression are not absolute, fixed or pre-determined. Central to this exploration is the use of 'critical autobiography' and life history narratives in which autobiographical material is used to reflect on and critique patterns of class and gender formation. In this the identities we construct are in continual construction and reconstruction (which is not to say they are incoherent or fragmentary).

STATUS: Sponsored project

SOURCE OF GRANT: Glasgow University £8,000

DATE OF RESEARCH: 1998-continuing

KEYWORDS: **career choice; electrical engineering; identity; sex differences; social class**

0847

Department of Education, Glasgow G12 8QQ
0141 339 8855
Aberdeen University, Department of Sociology, King's College, Aberdeen AB9 2UB
01224 272000

Edinburgh University, Faculty of Education, Moray House, Holyrood Campus, Holyrood Road, Edinburgh EH8 8Q
0131 651 6296

Wilkinson, J. Prof.; Watt, J. Dr; Napuk, A. Ms; Normand, B. Ms

Record keeping in the preschool year in Scotland

ABSTRACT: In order to inform the process of compiling appropriate baseline assessment of children in their first year of primary school in Scotland, a national survey of current record-keeping/assessment practices in Scottish preschool centres was recently conducted. The fundamental purpose of the survey was to ascertain current practice and procedures in local authority, voluntary sector and independent sector provision. This report outlines the results and implications of the survey. A questionnaire was issued to a 25% sample of Scottish preschool centres with a return rate of 57%. Follow-up interviews were conducted with a sub-sample on the basis of innovative practice. The main findings are as follows: 1) Nearly one-third of centres did not maintain written records on children's progress. This was a more common feature of playgroups than other types of centre. 2) The most common aspect of development recorded is language/literacy/reading (65.8%) with social/personal development second (65.2%) and physical/ motor third (58.2%). 3) The most common method of compiling the records was by observation. 4) Most centres use an ad hoc instrument (77%) which is a feature across all types of centres. 5) The vast majority of centres share the record with parents either through written information or through a meeting with parents. 6) The purpose of record-keeping considered least important were to assist quality assurance and accountability and to inform the next stage of a child's education. A very high proportion of centres did not regard passing information to the primary school teacher as important and in over half of the centres such transfer did not take place.

PUBLISHED MATERIAL: WILKINSON, J.E., WATT, J., NAPUK, A., & NORMAND, B. (1998). Record keeping in the pre-school year in Scotland: A report to the Scottish Office. Edinburgh: Scottish Office Education and Industry Department.

STATUS: Sponsored project

SOURCE OF GRANT: Scottish Office Education and Industry Department £20,000

DATE OF RESEARCH: 1997-1998

KEYWORDS: **assessment; baseline assessment; child development; early childhood education; preschool education; profiles; recordkeeping; scotland; young children**

0848

Department of Education, Glasgow G12 8QQ
0141 339 8855
Aberdeen University, Department of Sociology, King's College, Aberdeen AB9 2UB
01224 272000
Edinburgh University, Faculty of Education, Moray House, Holyrood Campus, Holyrood Road, Edinburgh EH8 8AQ
0131 651 6296

Wilkinson, J. Prof.; Watt, J. Dr; Napuk, A. Ms; Normand, B. Ms

Baseline assessment in Scotland - evaluation of pilot procedures

ABSTRACT: The purpose of the research is to evaluate the implementation of pilot procedures for baseline assessment of children in their first year of Scottish primary schooling. A sample of 27 schools has been identified in which to carry out the pilot work. The schools are selected to be representative of a wide range of primary schools in Scotland. The methods used to evaluate the procedures are: teacher diaries; questionnaires and follow-up interviews. Issues identified for the evaluation are: 1) the overall approach to the assessment; 2) teacher involvement; 3) content of the assessment form; 4) process of assessment; 6) support available to teachers; and 6) value of the outcome. On the basis of the results from the pilot, the Minister of Education for Scotland will decide on the next stage of implementation.

STATUS: Sponsored project

SOURCE OF GRANT: Scottish Office Education and Industry Department £20,000

DATE OF RESEARCH: 1997-continuing

KEYWORDS: **assessment; baseline assessment; primary education;**
programme evaluation; reception classes; school entrance age; scotland; value added; young children

0849

Department of Education, Glasgow G12 8QQ
0141 339 8855
Bradford University, School of Health Studies, Richmond Road, Bradford BD7 1DP
01274 733466

Dearnley, C. Ms; *Supervisors*: Matthew, R. Dr; Whitemoss, B. Ms

Impact of open learning on the personal and professional development of health care professionals

ABSTRACT: This study aims to consider the concept of change in relation to personal and professional development among qualified nurses studying an open learning programme of higher education. There are numerous references in the literature which indicate that Enrolled Nurses (ENs) traditionally feel undervalued and professionally disadvantaged. There is, however, little discussion how this impacts on their development when exposed to education. A qualitative approach is to be used to examine individual experiences and feelings in an attempt to explain a number of inter-related phenomena. Semi-structured interviews along with standard questionnaires, e.g. learning styles will be used on an initial pilot study of up to 10 selected ENs on open learning programmes. The pilot study commenced in March 1998.

STATUS: Individual research

DATE OF RESEARCH: 1997-continuing

KEYWORDS: **nurse education; nurses; open education; professional continuing education; professional development**

0850

Department of Education, Glasgow G12 8QQ
0141 339 8855
Edinburgh University, Faculty of Education, Moray House, Holyrood Campus, Holyrood Road, Edinburgh EH8 8AQ
0131 651 6296

Wilkinson, J. Prof.; Napuk, A. Ms

Review of baseline assessment

ABSTRACT: A number of countries have recently identified the need to develop schemes for assessment of children's broad educational achievements on entry to school, commonly referred to as baseline assessments. The UK is at the forefront of these developments. Baseline assessments are now part of legislation (Education Act 1997) in England and Wales. A review of literature and relevant baseline assessment schemes was commissioned by the Research and Intelligence Unit of the Scottish Office Education and Industry Department from the authors of this report. Key policy decisions are now required to be taken in Scotland with regard to the establishment of Scottish baseline assessments in the light of lessons to be learned from similar developments in other countries. The purpose of this report is to inform that decision-making process. The report begins with a brief examination of the relationship between the type of assessment used in education and the purpose of such assessments. It then locates these matters in the context of current developments in early childhood education. The review then examines current developments in a number of countries, beginning with an outline of such developments in different parts of the United Kingdom. A range of baseline assessment schemes currently in use is examined with the salient features of each scheme highlighted. A number of critical issues which need to be addressed in the development of baseline assessment schemes are then examined. Finally, a brief comparative analysis is undertaken, and some conclusions and recommendations are drawn.

STATUS: Sponsored project

SOURCE OF GRANT: Scottish Office Education and Industry Department £6,000

DATE OF RESEARCH: 1997-1997

KEYWORDS: **assessment; baseline assessment; comparative education; literature reviews; primary education; reception classes; school entrance age; value added; young children**

0851

Department of Education, Glasgow G12 8QQ
0141 339 8855
Glasgow Caledonian University, Stobhill Hospital, 300 Balgray Hill Road, Glasgow G21 3UR
0141 331 3000

Quirk, E. Mr; *Supervisor*: Baron, S. Mr

Role of life sciences in initial nurse education

ABSTRACT: An investigation into the role of life sciences in initial nurse education in the context of the structural reform of the profession and the National Health Service

STATUS: Individual research

DATE OF RESEARCH: 1996-continuing

KEYWORDS: **biological sciences; nurse education; nurses; science education**

0852

Department of Education, Glasgow G12 8QQ
0141 339 8855
Glasgow University, Royal Infirmary, Centre for Rheumatic Diseases, Glasgow G4 0SF
0141 211 4687
Department of Rheumatology, King's Mill Centre, Mansfield Road, Nottingham NG17 4JL
01623 672377

Hamilton, D. Dr; Kane, D. Mr; Lim, K. Mr; Sturrock, R. Mr

Multimedia computer challenges in rheumatology for undergraduates

ABSTRACT: An inter-disciplinary team from the Department of Education, the Centre for Rheumatic Diseases at the University of Glasgow, together with the Department of Rheumatology, King's Mill Centre, Nottingham, is developing a multimedia package of 6 cases in rheumatology for use by undergraduates and also by clinicians. The package, available for computers running Windows 95 or Windows NT 4.0, would also be intended for assessment purposes in medical schools and could be made available on a commercial basis globally. In a text-only version it is intended to be placed on the World Wide Web. The aim of the package is to improve undergraduates' and clinicians' rheumatology skills.

STATUS: Sponsored project

SOURCE OF GRANT: Arthritis and Rheumatism Council £82,169

DATE OF RESEARCH: 1997-continuing

KEYWORDS: **computer uses in education; information technology; medical education; multimedia; rheumatology**

0853

Department of Education, Glasgow G12 8QQ
0141 339 8855
Glasgow University, Strathclyde Centre for Disability Research, Glasgow G12 8QQ

Baron, S. Mr; Riddell, S. Prof.

The meaning of 'The Learning Society' for adults with learning difficulties

ABSTRACT: The project has the following objectives: 1) to illuminate the nature and possibility of a Learning Society for adults with learning difficulties by mapping the services provided by education, training, employment and community care agencies throughout Scotland; 2) to assess the experiences of adults with learning difficulties at different points in their life cycle; 3) to develop key theoretical debates about choice, barriers to full social participation and the attainment of adult status by people with learning difficulties; 4) to develop ways of involving adults with learning difficulties in the research process and to contribute to the development of good policy and practice in the field of learning difficulties. The first phase of the research (6 months) is devoted to an analysis of current policies and debates about disability, learning and choice for people with learning difficulties in the fields of education, training and employment. Key informant interviews will be used to map patterns of provision in Scotland. On the basis of this survey, further research will be conducted in 2 of the new Scottish authorities, one predominantly urban and one predominantly rural. The second phase of the research focuses on case studies of adults with learning difficulties in these 2 authorities. Three age groups have been identified for the study: people from 16-23 years of age who are making the transition from statutory schooling to adult status; people from 23-35 years of age who have moved beyond the initial transition stage and people above the age of 40 who are making the transition to middle and later life. Within each of these age groups the research will identify differences in experience linked to gender, ethnicity and types of barriers faced. In particular, the research seeks to draw out contrasts between people who have little contact with formal services and those who have access to innovative services.

PUBLISHED MATERIAL: RIDDELL, S., BARON, S., STALKER, K. & WILKINSON, H. (1997). 'The concept of the learning society for adults with learning difficulties: human and social capital perspectives', Journal of Education Policy, Vol 12, No 6, pp.473-483. ; BARON, S., STALKER, K., RIDDELL, S. & WILKINSON, H. 'The learning society: the highest stage of human capitalism'. In: COFFIELD, F. (Ed). Skills formation. Bristol: Policy Press. (in press). ; BARON, S., RIDDELL, S. & WILKINSON, H. 'The best burgers: the person with learning difficulties as worker'. In: SHAKESPEARE, T. (Ed). The disability reader. London: Cassell. (in press). ; RIDDELL, S., BARON, S. & WILKINSON, H. 'Training from cradle to grave: social justice and training for people with learning difficulties', Journal of Education Policy. (in press).

STATUS: Sponsored project

SOURCE OF GRANT: Economic and Social Research Council Learning Society Programme £107,000

DATE OF RESEARCH: 1996-continuing

KEYWORDS: **adult education; learning disabilities; learning society; special educational needs; training**

0854

Department of Education, Glasgow G12 8QQ
0141 339 8855
Nene College of Higher Education, Park Campus, Boughton Green Road, Northampton NN2 7AL
01604 735500
Reid Kerr College, Renfrew Road, Paisley PA3 4DA
0141 889 4225

Grant, N. Prof.; Matheson, D. Dr; Docherty, J. Mr

Comparative education - educating the world

ABSTRACT: This project draws on much work done already and is now being put together in book form. It is intended to bring together work already being done in comparative education, thus: 1) methods and uses of comparative education, particularly for our own system; 2) study of areas: Europe, North America, South America, developing countries, the Pacific rim; 3) national case studies: the British Isles, France and Germany, Spain, Denmark, Mexico and Latin America, Japan, the United States, the USSR to the Commonwealth of Independent States. (In every case, these are countries with which at least one of the researchers has personal experience); 4) cross-cultural themes: the education of minorities, the curriculum, education for work, the interaction of educational systems, etc.

PUBLISHED MATERIAL: GRANT, N. & BELL, R.E. (1995). Unit 1: models of education: block 7, education in Europe. Milton Keynes: Open University Press. ; GRANT, N. (1996). 'European and cultural identity at the European, national and regional levels'. In: WINTHER-JENSEN, Th. (Ed). Challenges to European education: cultural values, national identities and global responsibilities. Frankfurt am Main: Peter Lang GmbH. ; GRANT, N. (1997). 'Democracy and cultural pluralism: towards the 21st century'. In: WATTS, R.J. & SMOLICZ, J.J. (Eds). Cultural democracy and ethnic pluralism. Frankfurt am Main: Peter Lang GmbH. ; GRANT, N. (1997). 'Scandinavia as a unit of study in comparative education'. In: KNUT, T. (Ed). Streiftog i historisk og komparativ pedagogikk. Oslo: Universitete i Oslo, Pedagogisk forskningsinstitutt.

STATUS: Team research

DATE OF RESEARCH: 1997-1998

KEYWORDS: **comparative education; education systems; educational policy; educational practices; international education**

0855

Department of Education, Glasgow G12 8QQ
0141 339 8855
St Andrew's College of Education, Duntocher Road, Bearsden, Glasgow
G61 4QA 0141 943 1424

Smith, C. Ms; *Supervisors*: Wilkinson, J. Dr; Hayward, L. Ms

The effectiveness of peripatetic teaching services to hearing impaired children in Scotland

ABSTRACT: The research focuses on peripatetic services supporting pupils with hearing impairment in mainstream secondary schools in Scotland. The investigation will cover the historical development of such services; the range of policies adopted by central and local government and an indepth study of practices in one Region, i.e. Strathclyde. Longitudinal case studies are being set up of two different support systems and compared with provision for hearing impaired children in a special school. Aspects such as: social integration; staff deployment; parental and pupil perspective; and resources will be examined in detail. Based on the data, an attempt will be made to evaluate the effectiveness of peripatetic services.

STATUS: Individual research

DATE OF RESEARCH: 1993-1997

KEYWORDS: educational quality; hearing impairments; mainstreaming; peripatetic teachers; special educational needs; support teachers; teacher effectiveness

0856

Department of Electronics and Electrical Engineering, Robert Clark Centre for Technological Education, 66 Oakfield Avenue, Glasgow G12 8LS
0141 330 4976

Brown, M. Dr; Draper, S. Dr; Henderson, F. Ms; McAteer, E. Dr; Turner, I. Mr; *Supervisors*: Doughty, G. Dr; Pollock, M. Dr

Teaching with independent learning technologies

ABSTRACT: The project studied how a higher education institution increased its application of technology for teaching. The project utilised many change management methods, and action research revealed many conclusions of how to make social and technological changes towards the use of information technology (IT) in teaching and learning. Not-invented-here resistance was overcome so that externally-produced packages were imported. Much effort was spent on refining and applying evaluation instruments - illuminative, formative, integrative, summative - for software, learning processes and their outcomes. The project used questionnaires and focus groups, confidence logs and diaries, and diagnostic and summative assessment. This information was able to specify implications for activities, materials and evaluation required for successful integration. Work is continuing on a main objective to identify techniques to improve value-for-money in delivering courses. Three issues have emerged: 1) Courses can gain efficiency and cost-effectiveness - the same learning at lower cost. Students become more independent learners, their performance - the benefit - remains 'good enough'. Many hours of lecturer's time can be freed each year, some for individual student attention, some for research. Alternatives are regarded as of equal benefit, so evaluation is of costs alone, in terms of time. 2) Benefits can be evaluated in terms of the quality of learning, such as assessment results and pass rates. In many courses benefits can be gained with no change in cost. 3) Learning technology can be applied to gain benefit: cost ratio, e.g. improve or restore learning quality for an increased student:staff ratio.

PUBLISHED MATERIAL: DOUGHTY, G. et al. (1995). Using learning technologies: interim conclusions from the TILT project. Glasgow: University of Glasgow. ; BROWN, M.I. (1996). 'Measuring learning resource use', Computers and Education, Vol 27, No 2, pp.103-113. ; DOUGHTY, G. (1996). 'Computers for teaching and learning'. In: TAIT, J. & KNIGHT, P. (Eds). The management of independent learning. London: Kogan Page and Staff and Educational Development Association. ; DOUGHTY, G., POLLOCK, M., MCATEER, E. & TURNER, I. (1997). 'Conversion of a mathematics course to tutor-supported computer-assisted flexible learning'. In: BROWN, S. (Ed). Open and distance learning: case studies from industry and education. London: Kogan Page.

STATUS: Team research

DATE OF RESEARCH: 1993-continuing

KEYWORDS: computer assisted learning; computer uses in education; higher education; independent study; information technology; multimedia; teaching methods

0857

Department of Electronics and Electrical Engineering, Robert Clark Centre for Technological Education, 66 Oakfield Avenue, Glasgow G12 8LS
0141 330 4976

Canavan, B. Mr; *Supervisor*: Doughty, G. Dr

Improving the delivery of learning technology for engineering education

ABSTRACT: Following work in the Joint Funding Council's Teaching and Learning Technology Programme, this PhD project focuses on education leading towards electronics professionals. It investigates how the application of cost-effective cross-platform learning technology influences the progression from school to university and from university to continuing professional development. It includes Scottish factors such as the value of Higher Technological Studies as an entrance qualification to engineering courses.

STATUS: Individual research

DATE OF RESEARCH: 1997-continuing

KEYWORDS: computer assisted learning; computer uses in education; engineering education; higher education; information technology; multimedia; professional continuing education

0858

Department of Electronics and Electrical Engineering, Robert Clark Centre for Technological Education, Glasgow G12 8LS
0141 330 4976

Zavogli, Z. Dr; *Supervisor*: Doughty, G. Dr

Design and evaluation of a teaching package using HyperCard techniques and multimedia for first year university students learning basic electrical concepts with models and analogies

ABSTRACT: This project indicates that well-designed computer-based environments with models and analogies can provide advantages over approaches using other media. Such environments can be exploited to promote cognitive conflict, confronting students with the inconsistencies entailed by their own (mis)conceptions, which is believed to be beneficial for learning. Using models and analogies the project explored: the nature of students' beliefs about electrical concepts which are in conflict with scientific beliefs; the prerequisites required of computer-based environments which can promote learning of these concepts through models and analogies; issues related to educational theory and practice, students' learning and teaching; the design of software using HyperCard techniques and multimedia for the creation of models and analogies. A software package was constructed to reveal misconceptions to the student by comparing their predictions with simulated circuits, then asking them to describe their conceptions through the computer, and enter into dialogue with other students and the teacher. Classes were studied by observation with the learning package, assessments, interviews and questionnaires. Implications of the results from using models and analogies, in the area of education, were analysed. The advantages and disadvantages of these kinds of computational environments for the improvement of students' learning were discovered in detail, mainly with emphasis on the nature of students' (mis)conceptions which are deeply seated and persistent. Recommendations are made on how such environments can be designed and constructed in the near future in order to create suitable mental models for a better understanding of electrical concepts and phenomena.

STATUS: Individual research

DATE OF RESEARCH: 1992-continuing

KEYWORDS: computer assisted learning; computer uses in education; electricity; higher education; hypermedia; information technology; multimedia

0859

Department of Electronics and Electrical Engineering, Robert Clark Centre for Technological Education, 66 Oakfield Avenue, Glasgow G12 8LS
0141 330 4976

Henderson, F. Ms; *Supervisor*: Doughty, G. Dr

Towards a standardized multi-application methodology for the evaluation of computer assisted learning (CAL) episodes and materials

ABSTRACT: This work started as part of a wider team project, and is being completed individually. The project investigates methods for evaluating the use of computers in teaching and learning in higher education, especially in improving students' learning by formative evaluation of how interventions are affected by the whole teaching and learning process. It requires work with academic teams delivering learning, others producing courseware, and students of all ages and experience, using computer-based courseware in classroom settings. The evaluation provides formative information to the teachers, partly to suggest improvement to the courseware, but mainly to adjust their teaching methods to make the best use of the technology to maximise student learning. Techniques have been developed with several classes, including teaching mathematics to engineers, fracture mechanics and electronic seminars for music students.

PUBLISHED MATERIAL: DRAPER, S., BROWN, M., EDGERTON, E., HENDERSON, F., MCATEER, E., SMITH, E. & WATT, H. (1994). Observing and measuring the performance of educational technology: report by the University of Glasgow's Institutional Project in the Teaching and Learning Technology Programme (TILT). Glasgow: University of Glasgow. ; CREANOR, L., DURNDELL, H., HENDERSON, F.P., PRIMROSE, C., BROWN, M.I., DRAPER, S.W. & MCATEER, E. (1995). A hypertext approach to information skills: development and evaluation. Glasgow: University of Glasgow. ; BROWN, M.I. (1996). 'Measuring learning resource use', Computers and Education, Vol 27, No 2, pp.103-113. ; DRAPER, S.W. (1996). 'Integrative evaluation: an emerging role for classroom studies of CAL', Computers and Education, Vol 26, Nos 1-9, pp.17-32.

STATUS: Individual research

DATE OF RESEARCH: 1995-continuing

KEYWORDS: **computer assisted learning; computer uses in education; higher education; information technology; multimedia**

Glasgow University

0860

Centre for Science Education, Glasgow G12 8QQ
0141 339 8855

Selepeng, D. Ms; *Supervisors*: Johnstone, A. Prof.; Sutcliffe, R. Dr; Hansell, M. Dr

Using a variation on the Perry model to track developments in student thinking in biology

ABSTRACT: Students' attitudes to learning condition the learning which takes place. This research, based upon a simplified Perry model, is seeking to follow students' attitudes to learning from the end of secondary school to the end of a degree course in biology. The monitoring is being done by questionnaires based upon a 'Perry Semantic Differential' and a more open-ended one. These are supplemented by interviews. The aim is to relate attitude changes to forms of teaching, particularly methods tending towards autonomous learning.

STATUS: Individual research

DATE OF RESEARCH: 1997-continuing

KEYWORDS: **attitudes; biology; higher education; learning; learning activities; learning strategies; school to higher education transition; science education; student attitudes; students; teaching methods**

Greenwich University

0861

School of Education, Avery Hill Campus, Mansion Site, Bexley Road, Eltham, London SE9 2PQ
0181 331 8000

Lloyd, C. Dr; Draper, M. Mr; Farmer, G. Mr

Learning interactively at a distance (LID)

ABSTRACT: Increasingly the needs of students in training, and of the trainers themselves, will need to be met through a variety of learning experiences, much of it at a distance. Multimedia technology can make a contribution to this process. A network of schools, in partnership with the University of Greenwich, and with teachers on inservice programmes of training, was convened in July 1994 and connected to the University through a telecommunications conference network CIX. Ongoing work is concerned with developing networks to support students in schools on initial teaching practice and their mentors. Evaluation mechanisms established at the outset as an integral part of the project proposals are already being used to: 1) explore the nature of the conference dialogue between all teachers and lecturers in the network; 2) explore the appropriateness, flexibility, ease of use and cost of the technology; 3) extend the network with other UK partners and into a wider range of content areas of training; 4) investigate the links which might be extended to European partners in Sweden and the Netherlands. The project is ongoing and is now seeking further funding.

STATUS: Sponsored project

SOURCE OF GRANT: Enterprise in Higher Education £10,000; Greenwich University

DATE OF RESEARCH: 1994-continuing

KEYWORDS: **computer networks; computer uses in education; distance education; information technology; multimedia; preservice teacher education**

0862

School of Education, Avery Hill Campus, Mansion Site, Bexley Road, Eltham, London SE9 2PQ
0181 331 8000

Hui, S. Mr; *Supervisors*: Brook, D. Mr; Browne, G. Mr

Family and school socialisations, and the identity structure of Chinese adolescents in Britain: a comparative study

ABSTRACT: This research will include questionnaire and interview methods, with samples of Chinese children, their parents and their teachers.

STATUS: Individual research

DATE OF RESEARCH: 1995-1998

KEYWORDS: **chinese; ethnic groups; ethnicity; identity; parent school relationship; socialisation**

0863

School of Education, Avery Hill Campus, Mansion Site, Bexley Road, Eltham, London SE9 2PQ
0181 331 8000

Levy, R. Mr; *Supervisors*: Hacker, G. Mr; Wykes, C. Miss

School partnership in initial teacher training

ABSTRACT: This research will include survey and interview methods with teacher trainers and selected school personnel.

STATUS: Individual research

DATE OF RESEARCH: 1995-1998

KEYWORDS: **institutional cooperation; partnerships; preservice teacher education; school based teacher education**

0864

School of Education, Avery Hill Campus, Mansion Site, Bexley Road, Eltham, London SE9 2PQ
0181 331 8000

Bricheno, P. Mrs; *Supervisors*: Clegg, C. Dr; Austin, R. Mr

Science teaching: the transition from primary to secondary school

ABSTRACT: This research will include survey and interview methods with primary and secondary school teachers.

STATUS: Individual research

DATE OF RESEARCH: 1995-1998

KEYWORDS: **primary to secondary transition; science education; science teachers**

0865

School of Education, Avery Hill Campus, Mansion Site, Bexley Road, Eltham, London SE9 2PQ
0181 331 8000

Jones, L. Ms; *Supervisors*: Craft, M. Prof.; Ingham, A. Dr

Human factors influencing safety in school science and the home: an investigation into children's (11-16 years) safety attitudes, knowledge and perception of risk

ABSTRACT: Accident statistics appear to indicate that children aged 11-16 years significantly vary in their accident risk potential in different environments when presented with comparable type hazards. It is a phenomenon that requires investigation. Injuries caused by accidents represent a significant public health problem throughout the world. Children and adolescents are particularly vulnerable. However, despite their importance in terms of both health and socio-economic impact, the World Health Organisation reported recently that research into the causation and prevention of accidents has received little attention at national or international level. Previous work in this area has tended to attempt to identify factors contributing to childhood accidents by addressing specific situations (e.g. road safety etc), specific types of accident/injury (e.g. poisonings, scalds, falls etc) or specific personal factors (e.g. personality, age, gender, socio-economic status etc). However, these identified factors are unlikely to act independently of each other as suggested by the limits of these studies and a more complete analysis is required. Adults' attitudes, risk perceptions and knowledge in regard to matters of health and safety have been found to be highly influential in accident causation. The aim of this thesis is to determine children's attitudes, risk perception and knowledge in regard to hazards/hazardous activities commonly encountered within the home (statistically a high risk environment) and compare them with those, in regard to comparable hazards/hazardous activities, encountered within a secondary school science learning context (statistically a low risk environment). In addition, this study will attempt to identify factors prompting good safety attitudes, risk perception and safety knowledge and as a result, propose strategies for the improved transferability of safety concepts in children, thereby lowering their potential for accidents in high risk environments.

PUBLISHED MATERIAL: JONES, L. & TOWLER, I. (1995). Risk assessment and risk perception: Proceedings of the 1995 ASET Conference. University of Greenwich Occasional Paper. London: University of Greenwich.

STATUS: Individual research

DATE OF RESEARCH: 1994-1998

KEYWORDS: **accidents; danger; home environment; laboratory safety; pupil attitudes; risk; safety; science education**

0866

School of Education, Avery Hill Campus, Mansion Site, Bexley Road, Eltham, London SE9 2PQ
0181 331 8000

Gravelle, M. Ms

Partnerships in effective teacher training

ABSTRACT: Changes in the role of schools in initial teacher training have resulted in new definitions of partnership. Schools, and the mentors and class teachers within them, are under pressures, both internal and external, which may limit their wish or ability to become involved in teacher education. Link tutors from institutes of higher education could find that their role with respect to school experience has changed and that the balance between the support and assessment elements has altered. Student teachers, the third member of the partnership, can experience a divorce of theory from practice which has implications for their attitude toward the different elements of their training. Students are in a similar situation to many support teachers who work in mainstream classrooms where they are at once highly visible and have low status. A model that has been successful for staff development and effective learning is collaborative teaching. The focus is on pupils' learning rather than on the teacher and the effect is, often, to clarify what constitutes effective teaching. The research consists of a case study (the researcher is working in a school for half day per week) which investigates the effects and effectiveness of a partnership and collaborative model of teacher training. Evidence of pupil learning provides the starting point for reflecting on the effectiveness of the trainee teacher. The responses of members of the partnership will be evaluated.

PUBLISHED MATERIAL: GRAVELLE, M. (1996). 'Training the effective teacher: developing partnerships in initial teacher training'. National

Association for Language Development in the Curriculum (NALDIC) Occasional Paper, Spring 1996. Watford: National Association for Language Development in the Curriculum.

STATUS: Individual research

DATE OF RESEARCH: 1996-1997

KEYWORDS: **cooperation; mentors; partnerships; preservice teacher education; school based teacher education; student teacher supervisors; student teachers**

0867

School of Education, Avery Hill Campus, Mansion Site, Bexley Road, Eltham, London SE9 2PQ
0181 331 8000

Dolden, R. Mr; Goddard, W. Mr; Rose, C. Ms; *Supervisor*: Ingham, A. Dr

Health and safety in schools: the role and function of a health and safety coordinator: a European study

ABSTRACT: Health and safety in schools is an issue of increasing concern and importance, not only in the UK but also in Europe. The influence of European and national legislation has resulted in schools formalising structures for the implementation of health and safety policies. In many schools coordinators will be 'appointed' and have a delegated role. There is considerable variation in the roles of such coordinators both with respect to the interpretation of the term 'health and safety', and also the level of responsibility of the coordinator within the school management structure. Educationalists from the University of Greenwich, London and the Hogeschool van Utrecht, Netherlands have worked together for a number of years on a European wide curriculum development project to design and implement a training programme for a health and safety coordinator in school. The underlying philosophy of the development is that of the Health Promoting School, but with the concept of health broadened to include a whole-school approach to health, safety and environmental care (HSE). This development has formed the basis for research in the area of health and safety. This comparative research analyses roles and functions of school HSE-coordinators in Europe and compares professional training programmes in health and safety. An evaluation of the HSE coordinator training programme is being carried out within a European context and in particular the effectiveness of alternative teaching and learning modes such as information technology (IT) based distance learning

STATUS: Team research

DATE OF RESEARCH: 1996-continuing

KEYWORDS: **comparative education; coordinators; environment; europe; health education; health promoting schools; health promotion; international educational exchange; safety; safety education**

0868

School of Education, Avery Hill Campus, Mansion Site, Bexley Road, Eltham, London SE9 2PQ
0181 331 8000

Mayes, J. Ms; Barron, P. Mr; Doggett, A. Ms

Science evaluation project

ABSTRACT: This project involves a targeted evaluation of the Science component of the B.Ed (Hons) Degree in the light of recent changes in the requirements for the science curriculum in schools (through the National Curriculum) and for the training of primary school teachers in sciences.

STATUS: Sponsored project

SOURCE OF GRANT: Greenwich University £2,000

DATE OF RESEARCH: 1991-1993

KEYWORDS: **b ed degrees; preservice teacher education; science curriculum; science education**

0869

School of Education, Avery Hill Campus, Mansion Site, Bexley Road, Eltham, London SE9 2PQ
0181 331 8000

Harland, L. Ms; Taylor, P. Ms; Townsend, R. Ms; Brook, D. Mr

Seminar leadership: the development of performance indicators

ABSTRACT: This project is exploring the possibilities and limitations of formulating performance indicators in the area of seminar leadership skills. It will look at the process of small/group tutors interactions, widening its scope to involvement in other departments of the University. The research methodology is twofold: (i) in the form of collaborative action research; (ii) in the form of observation and feedback or collaborative evaluation. The collaboration is between the research and the seminar leader.

STATUS: Sponsored project

SOURCE OF GRANT: Greenwich University £2,000

DATE OF RESEARCH: 1991-1993

KEYWORDS: leadership; performance indicators; seminars; small group teaching; teacher effectiveness; teaching methods; university teaching

0870

School of Education, Avery Hill Campus, Mansion Site, Bexley Road, Eltham, London SE9 2PQ
0181 331 8000
Sussex University, Institute of Education, Education Development Building, Falmer, Brighton BN1 9RG
01273 606755

Goddard, W. Mr; *Supervisor*: Cooper, B. Dr

Redefinitions and reconstructions of technical education in secondary schools in England and Wales 1944-1989

ABSTRACT: This research investigates the influences and developments which have caused curriculum development to take place in the secondary school subject area which represents Technical. Attention is given to key actors in the field as well as to subject associations, research projects and government initiatives. The project will show how the interaction between these various segments have fostered new developments in the subject area.

STATUS: Individual research

DATE OF RESEARCH: 1985-1993

KEYWORDS: curriculum development; educational history; secondary education; technical education

0871

School of Post Compulsory Education and Training, Avery Hill Campus, Southwood Site, Avery Hill Road, Eltham, London SE9 2HB
0181 331 8000

Ainley, P. Dr; Bailey, B. Mr

The business of learning: staff and student experiences of further education in the 1990s

ABSTRACT: A comparison of the effects of the Further Education Funding Council (FEFC) funding methodology upon two representative further education colleges (a large generalist college in a mainly black and inner-city area of London, and a tertiary college in the home counties attended by mainly younger (16-18) students. By interviewing students at Foundation, Intermediate and Advanced levels of learning in classroom, work-based and work-shop provision, along with their teachers, those teachers' line or middle managers, as well as the senior management team at both colleges the book, published by Cassell in Autumn 1997, gives readers a feeling of what it is like to teach and study in further education in England today. It also shows how apparently very different colleges are affected in markedly similar ways by the new funding method. The book begins with a history of the origins of further education and its recent history. It ends with recommendations for future policy.

PUBLISHED MATERIAL: AINLEY, P. & BAILEY, B. (1997). The business of learning. London: Cassell. ; AINLEY, P. (1997). 'Crisis of the colleges', Education Today and Tomorrow, Vol 29, No 2. ; AINLEY, P. (1997). 'Towards a learning or a certified society, students in Britain', Youth and Policy, No 56, pp.4-13. ; AINLEY, P. (1997). 'Towards a learning society or towards learning fare', Social Policy Review, No 9, pp.50-86.

STATUS: Sponsored project

SOURCE OF GRANT: Greenwich University; Lewes Tertiary College; Lewisham College

DATE OF RESEARCH: 1995-1997

KEYWORDS: colleges of further education; economics education relationship; educational finance; further education; marketing

0872

School of Post Compulsory Education and Training, Avery Hill Campus, Southwood Site, Avery Hill Road, Eltham, London SE9 2HB
0181 331 8000

Jones, D. Dr

The foundations of modern vocationalism - relationships between religion, work and vocational education

ABSTRACT: The research arises from a doctoral thesis entitled: 'The relationship between religion, work and education and the influence of 18th and 19th century Nonconformist entrepreneurs' in which Weber's hypothesis regarding the relationship between ascetic Protestantism and the emergence of modern capitalism was re-examined. Using a prosopographical approach, empirical evidence was presented in support of Weber's theory that Protestant ethics were a significant factor in the development of a modern rationalised capitalistic society. Justification for the research lay predominantly in Weber's own limited recourse to biographical evidence concerning the attitudes and activities of neo-Calvinistic capitalist entrepreneurs. Three pivotal themes religion, work and vocational education - provided the central focus for 9 detailed case studies, through which the lives of 23 representative Nonconformist entrepreneurs, variously active in business between the years 1780-1900 were examined. Evidence was presented in support of the view that the ethics of ascetic Protestantism extensively influenced, not only the personal behaviour of this representative group in relation to economic activity, but also their various successes in establishing a work discipline among the labouring classes and system of education through which attitudes and behaviour patterns conducive, not to say essential, for a burgeoning industrial society, were effectively developed. While, as argued in the thesis, evidence strongly supported Weber's theory of an 'elective affinity' between Protestant ethics and the spirit of modern capitalism, that research has led to further socio-historical questions related to the development of modern rationalised capitalist society. Is there evidence which might suggest that the lives of successful businessmen from other religious group were similarly imbued with an ethic of work conducive to accumulating wealth? Can it be argued that a comparable 'elective affinity' existed between the religious ideals and enterprising spirit of other distinctive groups within an expanding industrial elite, e.g. 18th and 19th century Jewish capitalists? If so, what was its genesis? How might it differ from the ideals of Protestant asceticism? Is there evidence to support/refute a proposition that other prominent social elites played an equally significant role in the establishment of an ethic of work and system of education, suitable for an industrialising society? To answer these questions, this project will examine the lives of a selected group of Jewish entrepreneurs active in business between the years 1780-1900. The data will be juxtaposed against findings previously scrutinised in relation to the lives of neo-Calvinistic capitalists. Using a prosopographical approach, a uniform set of questions will be addressed in order to establish: a) the degree of uniformity within the 2 groups, and b) the degree of perceived congruence and dissonance between the groups, in relation to the fundamental question under consideration, i.e. the extent, or otherwise, to which the religious ethics of these 2 clearly defined industrial elites were instrumental in universally changing social attitudes and behaviour patterns in relation to work and vocational education throughout the period of industrialisation?

PUBLISHED MATERIAL: JONES, D.K. (1992). 'Prosopography - background and application', Auto/Biography: Bulletin of the British Sociological Association Study Group on Auto/Biography, Sources and Selves, Vol 1, No 1, pp.3-7. ; JONES, D.K. (1993). 'Towards Victorian values', Reformed Quarterly, Vol 3, No 4, pp.2-6. ; JONES, D.K. (1993). 'Religion and lives in the 19th century', Auto/Biography: Bulletin of the British Sociological Assocation Study Group on Auto/Biography, Vol 2, No 2, pp.59-73. ; JONES, D.K. (1994). 'The juxtaposition of lives: Benjamin Franklin (1706-1790) and Edward Baines (1774-1848)', Auto-Biography Bulletin of the British Sociological Association Study Group on Auto-Biography, Vol 3, No 1.1, pp.105-113.

STATUS: Individual research

DATE OF RESEARCH: 1996-continuing

KEYWORDS: educational history; religion and education

0873

School of Post Compulsory Education and Training, Avery Hill Campus, Southwood Site, Avery Hill Road, Eltham, London SE9 2HB
0181 331 8000

Francis, B. Dr; *Supervisor*: Humphreys, J. Prof.

The arrangements for nurse education

ABSTRACT: The research examines the statutory arrangements for nurse education, and the development in policy in this area since the mid-1980s. In particular, the way in which the quasi-market for nurse education is managed, in terms of the level of coordination of educational supply with demand for newly qualified nurses in the labour market. The research aims to analyse and comment on these arrangements, and to identify areas of inefficiency. The impact of these arrangements on professionalisation of the nursing profession is also examined. The research has mainly involved policy analysis, though qualitative methods are also being developed. Specific aspects of investigation have included: an examination and evaluation of the consortia mechanism for commissioning nurse education, and monitoring the system's development; the different arrangements for the commissioning of nurse education in the various UK nations and in Australia; the impacts of marketisation and professionalisation movements on nurse education; the impact of professionalisation on nursing's hegemonic authority over the notion of 'care'; and the different level of demand for nurse education amongst various social groups.

PUBLISHED MATERIAL: FRANCIS, B. & HUMPHREYS, J. (1998). 'Commissioning nurse education', Nursing Standard, Vol 12, No 23, pp.45-47. ; FRANCIS, B. & HUMPHREYS, J. (1998). 'Devolvement or centralisation? Differences in the development of nurse education commissioning policy between the UK nations', Nurse Education Today, Vol 18, No 6, pp.427-516. ; FRANCIS, B. & HUMPHREYS, J. (1998). 'Regulating non-nursing healthcare workers', Nursing Standard, Vol 12, No 47, pp.35-37. ; FRANCIS, B. & HUMPHREYS, J. (1998). 'The commissioning of nurse education by consortia: a quasi-market analysis', Journal of Advanvced Nursing, Vol 28,No 3, pp.517-523. ; FRANCIS, B. & HUMPHREYS, J. 'Enrolled nurses and the professionalisation of nursing: a comparison of nurse education and skill-mix in Australia and the UK', International Journal of Nursing Studies. (in press).

STATUS: Sponsored project

SOURCE OF GRANT: Higher Education Funding Council

DATE OF RESEARCH: 1993-continuing

KEYWORDS: **nurse education; nurses**

0874

School of Post Compulsory Education and Training, Avery Hill Campus, Southwood Site, Avery Hill Road, Eltham, London SE9 3HB
0181 331 8000

Jones, D. Dr

Relationships between religion, work and vocational education: a comparative study of the influence of 18th and 19th century Nonconformist and Jewish entrepeneurs

ABSTRACT: The research arises directly from doctoral research completed in 1996, in which Max Weber's hypothesis regarding the relationship between ascetic Protestantism and the emergence of modern capitalism was re-examined. Using a prosopographical (collective biographical) approach, the attitudes and actions of a selected group (23) of 18th/19th century Nonconformist businessmen were scrutinised. While resultant evidence gave support to Weber's thesis, not least in the related development of a work ethic and system of vocational education essential for a burgeoning industrial society, further socio-historical questions were inevitably raised. For example, is there corresponding evidence to support, or alternatively refute, a proposition that other prominent social elites (say, 18th/19th century Anglo-Jewish capitalists) played an equal or, indeed, more significant role than their Nonconformist counterparts, in the development of modern capitalism, in establishing an ethic of work and system of education suitable for an industrialising society? A collective biographical approach is again being utilised, to examine the lives of a similarly sized group of Anglo-Jewish entrepeneurs, active in business between the years 1780-1900. Resultant data will be compared and contrasted with previous findings, in order to establish: a) the degree of uniformity within the two groups, and b) the degree of perceived congruence and dissonance between the groups in relation to the fundamental question, the extent, or otherwise, to which the religious ethics of these two clearly defined industrial elites were instrumental in universally changing social attitudes and behaviour patterns in relation to work and vocational education, throughout the period of industrialisation?

PUBLISHED MATERIAL: JONES, D.K. (1992). 'Prosopography - background and application', Auto/Biography, Bulletin of the British Sociological Association Study Group on Auto-Biography, Vol 1, No 1, pp.3-7. ; JONES, D.K. (1993). 'Towards Victorian values', Reformed Quarterly, Vol 3, No 4, pp.2-6. ; JONES, D.K. (1993). 'Religion and lives in the 19th century - examining the Protestant ethic thesis through group biography', Auto/Biography, Bulletin of the British Sociological Association Study Group on Auto-Biography, Vol 2, No 2, pp.59-73. ; JONES, D.K. (1995). 'The juxtaposition of lives: Benjamin Franklin (1706-1790) and Edward Baines (1774-1848)', Auto/Biography, Bulletin of the British Sociological Association Study Group on Auto-Biography, pp.105-113.

STATUS: Individual research

DATE OF RESEARCH: 1996-continuing

KEYWORDS: **educational history; employment; religion and education; social history; vocational education**

0875

School of Post Compulsory Education and Training, Avery Hill Campus, Southwood Site, Avery Hill Road, London SE9 2HB
0181 331 8000

Ainley, P. Dr; Watson, J. Ms

New learning pathways: stratification and progression in post-compulsory education and training

ABSTRACT: This pilot study is a collaboration between the School of Post Compulsory Education and Training at Greenwich University and the Centre for Policy Studies in Education at Leeds University. It builds on previous comparisons of further education colleges in Lewes and Lewisham and work on the further education (FE)/higher education (HE) interface at Leeds. The new study will contrast patterns of provision by sixth forms, FE, HE and training agents in the contrasted sub-regions of SE London, East Sussex and Leeds - each area being of comparable size and containing two HE institutions, but having very different patterns of post-16 participation. Using new data sets, such as the Further Education Funding Council's (FEFC's) Individual Student Record, the research will map numbers of learners progressing along different 'pathways' within and between school sixth forms, training schemes, colleges and on to university. The 'maps' will allow easy comparison between areas and show whether new patterns of participation are emerging. The research relates to new policy developments, such as the involvement of regional development agencies in post compulsory education and training, the introduction of tuition fees for HE, widening participation in FE, equalising funding between sixth forms, training and FE, and the effects of Welfare to Work

PUBLISHED MATERIAL: AINLEY, P. & BAILEY, B. (1997). 'The business of learning: staff and student experiences of further education in the 1990's. London: Cassell.

STATUS: Sponsored project

SOURCE OF GRANT: Economic and Social Research Council

DATE OF RESEARCH: 1999-continuing

KEYWORDS: **further education; higher education; individualised student record; school to further education transition; sixteen to nineteen education; training**

0876

School of Post Compulsory Education and Training, Avery Hill Campus, Southwood Site, Avery Hill Road, Eltham, London SE9 2HB
9171 331 8000

Francis, B. Dr

The impact of gender construction on pupils' learning and educational choices

ABSTRACT: The aim of the proposed study is to investigate the ways in which constructions of gender may impact on approaches to education at post-14. Particularly, it would explore how symbolic gender cultures, constructed and taken up in the classroom by girls and boys to delineate their gender identity, impact on pupils' approaches to education and potentially on their consequent examination achievement. It would also examine how these gender constructions impact upon pupils' post-14 subject and educational provision choices.

STATUS: Sponsored project

SOURCE OF GRANT: Economics and Social Research Council (ESRC)

DATE OF RESEARCH: 1998-continuing

KEYWORDS: academic achievement; choice of subjects; pupil attitudes; pupil performance; secondary education; secondary school pupils; sex differences; sex stereotypes; sexual identity

0877

School of Post Compulsory Education and Training, Avery Hill Campus, Southwood Site, Avery Hill Road, Eltham, London SE9 2HB
0181 331 8000

Supervisors: Francis, B. Dr; Robson, J. Dr

Gendered patterns in class of first degree award

ABSTRACT: The study seeks to investigate and analyse gender differences in writing style amongst undergraduate students, and to analyse these according to their constructions of gender. It is hoped that the findings may also shed light on the gendered pattern of first degree levels awarded to undergraduate students.

STATUS: Sponsored project

SOURCE OF GRANT: Social Science Research Centre, University of Greenwich

DATE OF RESEARCH: 1999-continuing

KEYWORDS: academic achievement; higher education; sex differences; writing evaluation

0878

School of Post compulsory Education and Training, Avery Hill Campus, Southwood Site, Avery Hill Road, Eltham, London SE9 2HB
0181 331 8000

Watson, J. Ms; Williams, E. Ms; Jones, A. Mr

Education audit for London

ABSTRACT: A comprehensive review of education and training in London, creating a baseline for the London Skills Strategy. Three measures were used: expenditure, numbers participating, and outcomes. The sectors covered included secondary schools, further education colleges, government-funded training (including the European Social Fund (ESF) and Single Regeneration Budget (SRD)), employer-funded training, and higher education. Analysis for the further education sector made use of the individualised student record (ISR) kept for each student. The conclusions were that education and training in London is diverse and polarised. The curriculum in colleges is chaotic, and most students are outside the national qualifications framework. Statistics are kept in different ways in each sector, so that comparability is difficult. There are no records of trainees funded by ESEF or SRB. There are particular problems with monitoring outcomes, for example in surveying destinations of students, where there is no exchange of good practice across sectors. Recommendations were made for the improvement of data collection and for a partnership-based approach to educational planning in London. The full project report and a summary are available from Focus Central London TEC. The research will be further disseminated in a series of papers to be submitted to education, local economy and social policy journals.

STATUS: Sponsored project

SOURCE OF GRANT: Focus Central London TEC

DATE OF RESEARCH: 1998-continuing

KEYWORDS: education systems; further education; london; secondary education; training

Guildford Educational Services Limited

0879

32 Castle Street, Guildford GU1 3UW
01483 579454
Scienter Scrl, Via Val D'Aposa 3, 1-40123 Bologna, Italy
Infotel, C Orense 68, Madrid 28020
ORAVEP, 6 Boulevard Saint-Denis, Paris 75010

Ward, C. Mrs; Pokorny, S. Ms; Carbajo, J. Mr; Quesnel, O. Ms

Computer assisted assessment in the workplace

ABSTRACT: The objectives of the project are: 1) to encourage the use of valid and reliable computer-based testing in the workplace, both for formative assessment of trainees' progress and, where appropriate, to contribute to the award of vocational qualifications; and 2) transfer to appropriate groups throughout Europe. The key activities will be: 1) creation and evaluation of guidance on the implementation of computer assisted assessment and distance learning materials on the preparation of valid and reliable tests; 2) a directory of available products to accompany the guidance; 3) creation and field testing of item banks for small and medium enterprises (SMEs) - topics are Foundry work and the use of the Internet; 4) dissemination of guidance and distance learning materials; and 5) dissemination of item banks. This project will involve research into available tools for computer assisted assessment and their practical applications. The outcomes of the project will be: 1) guidance on the use of computer assisted assessment in the workplace; 2) a directory of available products (on disc); 3) distance learning materials on the creation of valid and reliable tests; and 4) banks of objective test items.

PUBLISHED MATERIAL: A full list of publications is available from the researchers.

STATUS: Sponsored project

SOURCE OF GRANT: European Commission; Department for Education and Employment: Technologies for Training

DATE OF RESEARCH: 1996-1998

KEYWORDS: assessment; computer assisted testing; distance education; information technology; internet; on the job training; tests; training

0880

32 Castle Street, Guildford GU1 3UW
01483 579454

Ward, C. Mrs

Review of the use of information and communications technology in examinations

ABSTRACT: The objectives of the project were to: 1) review current uses of information and communications technology (ICT) in the processes of examining in the United Kingdom and internationally; 2) provide advice on the practical implications and potential for improving the quality of public examinations in England through the use of ICT developments; 3) identify those areas of the GCSE and GCE examining process where value would be added through the greater use of ICT; 4) where appropriate, make recommendations about the development programme that would be required to trial, implement and evaluate the greater use of ICT. Methodology included bibliographic and other information sources, review of software, discussions with examining boards and questionnaire to a sample of examiners. The range of techniques investigated were: objective testing; item banking (objective questions); optical mark reading and optical character reading (objective questions); computer-delivered objective questions; adaptive testing; computer-delivered information technology tests; computer-delivered simulations; computerised item-generation; computer marking of free-response questions; item banking (non-objective questions); optical mark reading and optical character reading (examiner mark sheets); use of computers for written answers; on-line transmission of assessment material; on-line testing. The main conclusion was that lack of hardware in schools precludes use of ICT in fixed-date examinations in the short-term, but that there is scope for development of computer-delivered testing in the medium term. Computer-delivered tests are already used in a range of other contexts, e.g. UK higher education and in the United States.

STATUS: Sponsored project

SOURCE OF GRANT: Qualifications and Curriculum Authority

DATE OF RESEARCH: 1997-1998

KEYWORDS: assessment; computer assisted testing; computer uses in education; examinations; information technology

Harris City Technology College

0881

The Dyslexia Centre, 9 Maberley Road, Upper Norwood, London SE19 2JH
0181 771 2261
Canterbury Christ Church College, North Holmes Road, Canterbury CT1 1QU
01227 767700

Tod, J. Ms; *Supervisors*: Jones, L. Mr; Abbott, P. Mr

Dyslexia research project

ABSTRACT: A three year research project has been set up at the Dyslexia Centre of Harris City Technology College in Upper Norwood, South London. The research body is Harris City Technology College in conjunction with Christchurch College, Canterbury. The aim of the new centre is the development of best practice in the teaching of dyslexic students. The provision of special teacher training in this area of learning difficulty and the undertaking of research and development in the use of technology and materials appropriate to the teaching of dyslexic students. The aims of the project are: (1) to measure the progress over three academic years of a group of pupils entering the Harris CTC in September 1990, diagnosed as having the specific learning difficulty known as dyslexia, using a range of approaches designed to enable these pupils to participate fully and effectively in the City Technology College curriculum which includes access to the National Curriculum; (2) to devise new approaches and resource materials in order to test their value for pupils in the Harris CTC and to enable the Centre to develop resource materials for a wide use with the CTC age group (11-18); (3) to develop the use of information technology and work with dyslexic pupils in the Harris CTC and to disseminate good practice in this respect. The project runs from 1 November 1990 to 31 October 1993.

STATUS: Sponsored project

SOURCE OF GRANT: Department for Education £250,000

DATE OF RESEARCH: 1990-1993

KEYWORDS: city technology colleges; dyslexia; educational materials; special educational needs; teaching methods

Health Promotion Wales

0882

Research and Development Division, Ffynnon-las, Ty Glas Avenue, Llanishen, Cardiff CF4 5DZ
01222 752222

Tudor-Smith, C. Mr; Frankland, J. Ms; Playle, R. Ms; Moore, L. Dr

An evaluation of Life Education Centres

ABSTRACT: Life Education Centres (LECs) were established in Australia in 1979 as a drug education/prevention project for young schoolchildren. The project aim was to develop skills and build self-esteem which would enable children to make responsible decisions concerning themselves and their bodies. The Centres are mobile classrooms staffed by trained educators which visit schools for several days at a time. They contain sophisticated audio-visual aids, including illuminated models of body systems and organs. They also use more traditional educational methods such as games, films and role play. The lessons which last between 30 and 60 minutes are primarily for children aged between 5 and 11 years. Since June 1990 Health Promotion Wales has coordinated a pilot project of LECs in the Principality. This includes an evaluation of the effects of LECs visits to primary schools. The study will examine any changes in school curriculum content, changes in pupils' knowledge, attitudes or skills and school policy development. A multi-stage evaluation design has been adopted involving teachers, pupils and parents. In the first stage of this design, a sample of 171 teachers and 509 pupils were asked to complete pre and two post test questionnaires. Primary findings suggest that both teachers and pupils have favourable views on participating in an LEC visit, and that attendance at an LEC was a predictor of greater drug knowledge and understanding of techniques used in advertising cigarettes.

STATUS: Sponsored project

SOURCE OF GRANT: Health Promotion Wales

DATE OF RESEARCH: 1993-1997

KEYWORDS: health education; health promotion; primary education

0883

Research and Development Division, Ffynnon-las, Ty Glas Avenue, Llanishen, Cardiff CF4 5DZ
01222 752222
Bristol University, Department of Social Medicine, Canynge Hall, Whiteladies Road, Bristol BS8 2PR
01179 289000

Tudor-Smith, C. Mr; Roberts, C. Mr; Playle, R. Ms; Moore, L. Dr

Welsh Youth Health Survey

ABSTRACT: The overall goal of the Welsh Youth Health Survey is to gain new insights into and increase our understanding of health behaviours, lifestyles and their context in young people. In addition, the surveys have become the major source of information for the development and direction of health promotion action in Wales. In each of the 5 surveys to date (1 every 2 years since 1986), a two-stage sampling procedure has been used to recruit respondents. For the first stage, a stratified random sample of secondary schools were selected from lists of the 8 local education authorities (LEA's) in Wales. For the second stage, schools were asked to randomly select from the school registers 30 pupils each from Years 7, 9 and 11. The use of specific subject classes or streamed classes is not permitted as these might not consist of a representative sample of pupils. The number of 11-16 year olds participating and returning usable data in 1986, 1988, 1990, 1992 and 1994 were 6203, 4580, 6549, 5503 and 3930, respectively. Data are gathered anonymously through a self-completion questionnaire focusing on key health areas such as smoking, diet, physical activity and alcohol use. In recent years questions have been added on drug use, safety related behaviours and attitudes and the school setting. Key findings from the 5 surveys indicate that drug use has increased among both sexes and that consumption of alcohol and tobacco has grown among teenage girls in particular. In terms of the school setting, data indicate a relationship between 'alienation' from school and health compromising behaviours. The Welsh Youth Survey is part of a wider World Health Organisation (WHO) coordinated Health Behaviour in School Aged Children (HBSC) study.

PUBLISHED MATERIAL: SMITH, C. (1991). 'Smoking among young people: some recent developments in Wales', Health Education Journal, Vol 50, pp.8-11. ; NUTBEAM, D. & AARO, Leif E. (1991). 'Smoking and pupil attitudes towards school: the implications for health education with young people: results from the WHO Study of Health Behaviour Among Schoolchildren', Health Education Research, Vol 6, No 4, pp.415-421. ; SMITH, C., WOLD, B. & MOORE, L. (1992). 'Health behaviour research with adolescents: a perspective from the WHO health behaviour in school-aged children study', Health Promotion Journal of Australia, Vol 2, pp.41-44. ; SMITH, C. & NUTBEAM, D. (1992). 'Adolescent drug use in Wales', British Journal of Addiction, Vol 87, No 2, pp.227-233. ; SMITH, C., NUTBEAM, D., ROBERTS, C., MOORE, L. & CATFORD, J. (1994). 'Current changes in smoking attitudes and behaviours among adolescents in Wales, 1986-1992', Journal of Public Health Medicine, Vol 16, pp.165-171. A full list of publications is available from the researchers.

STATUS: Sponsored project

SOURCE OF GRANT: Welsh Office

DATE OF RESEARCH: 1986-continuing

KEYWORDS: adolescent attitudes; adolescents; health; life style; pupil attitudes; pupil behaviour; secondary education; secondary school pupils; wales

Helen Arkell Dyslexia Centre

0884

Frensham, Farnham GU10 3BW
01252 792400

Smith, P. Mr

To provide teachers with teaching strategies for dyslexic children

ABSTRACT: The research is to provide teachers with teaching strategies for dyslexic children that have been demonstrated to be effective under individual, group and and classroom conditions. The project consists of 5 stages and commenced in September 1995. Work has started on Stage 5 which involves field trials in 4 schools: 3 local education authority (LEA) maintained and 1 independent. Various teaching strategies will be used including 3 methods found to be effective during earlier stages of the research. Reports on the results of the first 4 stages are available from the Helen Arkell Dyslexia Centre.

STATUS: Sponsored project

SOURCE OF GRANT: Department for Education and Employment £55,203

DATE OF RESEARCH: 1995-1998

KEYWORDS: dyslexia; mainstreaming; primary education; special educational needs; teaching methods

Heriot-Watt University

0885

Department of Business Organisation, Riccarton Campus, Currie, Edinburgh EH14 4AS
0131 449 5111

Lumsden, K. Prof.; Scott, A. Prof.

The determinants of achievement for distance learning MBA students: the relative efficacy of MBA by distance learning

ABSTRACT: This is part of a long term research programme on efficiency in education which has focused on the determinants of student performance in economics and student opinion of teaching techniques. Edinburgh Business School (EBS) has run a distance learning Masters in Business Administration (MBA) course since 1990, and currently has over 8,000 students worldwide. Since launching the MBA, a research database has been maintained which contains the results of all aspects of student performance in all MBA subjects for students on EBS distance learning and taught MBA courses. The examinations themselves are carefully constructed and comprise multiple choice, cases and essays; students have no choice of question. Students have also been surveyed regularly to provide their opinion of faculty members and teaching techniques. This very large database makes it possible to investigate the relationships among different measures of student performance, the connection between student characteristics and performance, the relative efficacy of different teaching modes and the determinants of student opinion of courses, faculty members and teaching approaches. The research will use multiple regression techniques to estimate relationships of the general form - Performance = F (Student characteristics, teaching techniques).

PUBLISHED MATERIAL: LUMSDEN, K.G., SCOTT, A. & CUTHBERT, M. (1986). 'A comparison between multiple regression and log linear analyses as applied to educational data'. In: HODKINSON, S. & WHITEHEAD, R. (Eds). Economics education: research and development issues. London and New York: Longman. ; LUMSDEN, K.G. & SCOTT, A. (1987). 'The economics student reexamined: male and female differences in comprehension', Journal of Economic Education, Vol 18, No 4, pp.365-375. ; LUMSDEN, K.G. & SCOTT, A. (1995). 'Evaluating faculty performance on executive programmes', Education Economics, Vol 3, No 1, pp.19-32. ; LUMSDEN, K.G. & SCOTT, A. (1995). 'Economics performance on multiple choice and essay exams: a large scale study of accounting students', Accounting Education, Vol 4, No 2, pp.34-42.

STATUS: Sponsored project

DATE OF RESEARCH: 1998-continuing

KEYWORDS: achievement; assessment; business administration education; distance education; higher education; masters degrees; performance; students

Hertfordshire University

0886

School of Humanities and Education, Watford Campus, Wall Hall, Aldenham, Watford WD2 8AT
01707 284000

Campbell, R. Prof.

Hearing children read

ABSTRACT: Now in its second phase, this study aims to explore the effectiveness of various teacher responses to the mistakes of early beginning readers. An indepth case study of two children reading to their teacher throughout a school year has been conducted. Interactions were audio-recorded and subsequently transcribed. Results have suggested that a word cueing strategy was particularly helpful to the reader. However, effectiveness needs to be explored at various levels and recent articles have debated this topic. Differences between infant and junior school teachers are being explored. The study has been extended into nursery classrooms.

PUBLISHED MATERIAL: CAMPBELL, R. (1988). Hearing children read. London: Routledge. ; CAMPBELL, R. (1990). Reading together. Milton Keynes: Open University Press. ; CAMPBELL, R. (1992). Reading real books. Milton Keynes: Open University Press. ; CAMPBELL, R. (1992). Reading in the early years handbook. Milton Keynes: Open University Press.; CAMPBELL, R. (Ed). (1998). Facilitating preschool literacy. Newark, Delaware, USA: International Reading Association. A full list of publications is available from the researcher.

STATUS: Individual research

DATE OF RESEARCH: 1980-continuing

KEYWORDS: beginning reading; early reading; oral reading; reading skills; teacher pupil relationship

0887

School of Humanities and Education, Watford Campus, Wall Hall, Aldenham, Watford WD2 8AT
01707 284000

Thornton, M. Dr

The educational division of labour as it relates to subject specialism and gender in primary schools

ABSTRACT: This study followed-up Ph.D research work on specialisation and the primary curriculum. It aimed to explore, map and explain gender differences across areas of subject responsibility and management in primary schools. The study involved data collection from over 200 schools. Data relating to male/female teachers' careers in primary teaching has been published. Follow-up work continues in the area of male/female teaching careers, subject specialism and initial teacher education entry and outcomes, through statistical analysis and interview data.

PUBLISHED MATERIAL: THORNTON, M. (1990). 'Primary specialism', Early Years, Vol 11, No 1, pp.34-38. ; THORNTON, M. (1995). 'When is a specialist not a specialist? When she/he teaches younger children the whole curriculum', Early Years, Vol 16, No 1, pp.5-8. ; THORNTON, M. (1995). 'Primary teachers and the primary curriculum', New Era in Education, Vol 76, No 3, pp.78-83. ; THORNTON, M. (1996). 'Subject specialism, gender and status: the example of primary school mathematics', Education 3-13, Vol 24, No 3, pp.52-54.

STATUS: Individual research

DATE OF RESEARCH: 1992-1998

KEYWORDS: men teachers; preservice teacher education; primary education; primary school teachers; sex differences; teacher role; teaching profession

0888

School of Humanities and Education, Watford Campus, Wall Hall, Aldenham, Watford WD2 8AT
01707 284000

Miller, L. Ms; *Supervisors*: Campbell, R. Prof.; Powell, S. Dr

Literacy development in the preschool years

ABSTRACT: The main focus of the research is literacy development in the preschool years. The research will raise questions about a number of key issues: 1) How is environmental print used with preschool children at home, and in preschool settings, such as nursery schools, nursery classes, reception classes and playgroups? 2) In what ways do preschool settings provide for and support children's literacy development? 3) In what ways do adults support children's literacy development, with particular reference to developing children's knowledge about books and print? Methods used will include: audio tape recordings of parents and their preschool children sharing books together; observations of children and adults in a range of preschool settings; and collection and analysis of literacy related children's work.

PUBLISHED MATERIAL: MILLER, L. (1995). Towards reading: literacy development in the pre-school years. Buckingham: Open University Press.; MILLER, L. (1995). "'I can read that. It says 'happy shopper'" - the role of environmental print in early literacy development', Early Years, Vol 16, No 1, pp.20-26. ; MILLER, L. (1997). 'A vision for the early years curriculum in the United Kingdom', International Journal of Early Childhood, Vol 29, No 11, pp.34-41. ; MILLER, L. (1998). 'Literacy interactions through environmental print'. In: CAMPBELL, R. (Ed). Facilitating preschool literacy. Newark, Delaware USA: International Reading Association.

STATUS: Individual research

DATE OF RESEARCH: 1994-continuing

KEYWORDS: **early childhood education; early reading; literacy education; nursery education; parent participation; prereading experience; preschool education**

0889

School of Humanities and Education, Watford Campus, Wall Hall, Aldenham, Watford WD2 8AT
01707 284000

Thornton, M. Dr; Bricheno, P. Mrs
Primary teachers' career patterns
ABSTRACT: This research builds on and further develops previous work on the educational division of labour as it relates to subject specialism and gender in primary schools. A national survey has been undertaken using postal questionnaires to teachers in a random sample of local education authorities (LEAs) across all types of state primary school provision. A positive response rate of 25% has been achieved from a sample of 400 schools. The objectives are to identify career patterns and teachers' views about promotion in relation to gender, qualifications, age, inservice education, full and part-time work patterns, and length of experience. The research aims, overall, to improve our understanding and knowledge of differing career structures and opportunities for men and women in primary teaching from the perspectives of the teachers with a long-term view to enhancing the status of primary teaching as a chosen career, increasing male recruitment and making more equitable male and female opportunity for career advancement. The postal questionnaire survey will be followed by selected follow-up interviews.

STATUS: Individual research

DATE OF RESEARCH: 1998-continuing

KEYWORDS: **career development; men teachers; primary school teachers; sex differences; teachers; teaching profession; women teachers**

0890

School of Humanities and Education, Watford Campus, Wall Hall, Aldenham, Watford WD2 8AT
01707 284000
Loughborough University of Technology, Department of Education, Loughborough LE11 3TU
01509 263171

Thornton, M. Dr; Reid, I. Prof.; Bricheno, P. Mrs
Primary students' reasons for choosing teaching as a career
ABSTRACT: This research is based on a questionnaire survey of 2000+ first year undergraduate and 1-year Postgraduate Certificate in Education (PGCE) primary students across 15 teacher training institutions. It aims to establish students' reasons for choosing primary teaching as a career and what influenced their choice. These reasons will be mapped against face data relating to gender, age on entry, present accommodation arrangements, post work experience and prior length and type of employment. Follow-up interviews will be conducted with a selection of student respondents who have indicated their willingness to participate further.

STATUS: Collaborative

DATE OF RESEARCH: 1998-continuing

KEYWORDS: **career choice; preservice teacher education; primary school teachers; sex differences; student teacher attitudes; student teachers; teaching profession**

Higher Education Statistics Agency
0891

18 Royal Crescent, Cheltenham GL50 3DA
01242 255577

Benfield, C. Ms
Performance indicators in higher education
ABSTRACT: Institutional performance indicators on teaching (e.g. student progression, exit qualifications, employment destinations) which take account of the characteristics of the students and institutions, to enable more equitable comparisons. This information is needed to provide data for employers and prospective students on the comparative performance of difference courses at different higher education (HE) institutions.

STATUS: Sponsored project

SOURCE OF GRANT: Department for Education and Employment £27,611

DATE OF RESEARCH: 1997-1998

KEYWORDS: **educational quality; higher education; performance indicators; universities**

Hospitality Training Foundation
0892

International House, High Street, Ealing, London W5 5DB
0181 579 2400

Murphy, N. Ms; Milne, W. Ms; *Supervisor*: Ervin, J. Ms
Cost benefit analysis
ABSTRACT: A unique piece of research aiming to provide tangible evidence of the business benefits resulting from sound training strategies and investment produced from case studies across a sample of organisations in different sectors of the industry. The specific aims will be to: a) identify appropriate measures to gauge the effect of training on business performance; b) identify a number of organisations in different sectors of the industry who will participate in a longitudinal study; c) provide practical results which any type of organisation in any sector of the hospitality industry will be able to relate to; d) provide results which address the particular training issues relating to small, medium and large organisations; e) publish and widely disseminate the results of the study in an appealing format which will have impact but which relies on hard evidence rather than anecdote.

STATUS: Sponsored project

SOURCE OF GRANT: Department for Education and Employment

DATE OF RESEARCH: 1996-continuing

KEYWORDS: **cost effectiveness; hospitality industry; training; vocational education**

0893

International House, High Street, Ealing, London W5 5DB
0181 579 2400

Barnett, P. Mr; Kenny, J. Ms; Davie, S. Ms; *Supervisor*: Ervin, J. Ms
International skills benchmarking for public houses and restaurants
ABSTRACT: The project aims to identify the key competitiveness issues which relate to skills acquisition and competence in the public house and restaurant sector of the hospitality industry. To this effect, a comparative study is being carried out between the UK and a number of its key international competitors, e.g. US, France, Germany, Ireland, Italy and Spain. The study involves carrying out skills benchmarking visits to companies in the UK and overseas with a view to providing practical evidence of the relative success of company training strategies and establishing examples of best practice. In addition, it aims to provide

evidence of how skills and training outcome are linked to company and sector performance and can put firms ahead of their competitors.

STATUS: Sponsored project

SOURCE OF GRANT: Department of Education and Employment

DATE OF RESEARCH: 1997-continuing

KEYWORDS: comparative education; competence; hospitality industry; skill development; skills; training

0894

International House, High Street, Ealing, London W5 5DB
0181 579 2400

Barnett, P. Mr; Hollowood, N. Ms; *Supervisor*: Ervin, J. Ms

Skills shortages, labour turnover and recruitment practices in the hospitality industry

ABSTRACT: Many vacancies in the hospitality industry are being left unfilled. This problem will be further compounded by the industry's forecast growth put at 310,000 new jobs by the year 2004. Research by the Hospitality Training Foundation has shown signficant rates of labour turnover up to 200% in some sectors of the hospitality industry. This research aims to produce an up-to-date report on skills shortages, labour turnover and recruitment practices by region, sector and occupation. It also intends to produce recommendations to form effective recruitment and retention policies.

STATUS: Sponsored project

SOURCE OF GRANT: Department for Education and Employment

DATE OF RESEARCH: 1997-1998

KEYWORDS: employment opportunities; hospitality industry; labour market; labour needs; labour turnover; recruitment; skills; skills shortages

Huddersfield University

0895

School of Education and Professional Development, Holly Bank Road, Lindley, Huddersfield HD3 3BP
01484 422288

Smith, V. Miss; *Supervisors*: Tizard, J. Ms; Breckin, M. Dr; McKenzie, P. Mr

General National Vocational Qualifications (GNVQ's): the relationship between liberal, general and vocational education, with special reference to business studies for 16-19 year olds

ABSTRACT: General National Vocational Qualifications (GNVQs) represent a response to the perceived imbalance in British education, whereby vocational and academic subjects do not enjoy parity of esteem. It is the aim of the GNVQs, seen as the vocational A-level, to transcend the academic/vocational divide. It is the aim of this project to examine their ability to do so. To date this has involved the researcher conducting a series of interviews with those concerned with GNVQ business courses. This information was analysed and used to formulate national survey questionnaires for staff and students concerned with GNVQ business. GNVQs have been compared to other curricular models via 'ideal-type' analysis (e.g. the liberal, the general and the vocational), and 'curriculum criticism' (e.g. A-levels, Business and Technology Education Council (BTEC), City and Guilds of London Institute (CGLI), Royal Society of Arts (RSA), National Vocational Qualifications (NVQ's) and GNVQ's), the aim being to compare the traditional approaches to the 16-19 curricula with new vocational approaches. Ultimately the question of whether a liberal education is relevant today will be raised. Explorations of a more relevant and valid approach to a liberal education will ensue and alternatives will be suggested where necessary. This will be conducted in the light of GNVQs. To complete this phase of the project, interviews are to be conducted with specialists from the fields of both education and business. These interviews will be concerned with how the interviewees perceive liberal, general and vocational education; which approach, and/or characteristics of a stated approach, are deemed relevant for the current education environment; and whether GNVQs can fulfil such requirements.

PUBLISHED MATERIAL: SMITH, V. (1994). 'The transition to GNVQ's in business studies', Educa, No 47, pp.8-9. ; SMITH, V. & TIZARD, J.

(1995). 'General National Vocational Qualifications: the relationship between liberal, general and vocational education', Research in Education, No 53, pp.89-91.

STATUS: Individual research

DATE OF RESEARCH: 1993-1997

KEYWORDS: academic education; business education; liberal education; national vocational qualifications; qualifications; secondary education; sixteen to nineteen education; vocational education; vocational qualifications

0896

School of Education and Professional Development, Holly Bank Road, Lindley, Huddersfield HD3 3BP
01484 422288

Jones, A. Mr; *Supervisors*: Newbold, D. Prof.; Lemon, W. Prof.; Bennet, Y. Dr

Engineering, science and technology: an exploration of pre-GCSE pupils' perceptions and aspirations

ABSTRACT: This study is concerned with the appraisal and evaluation of 'technological' school-industry links and initiatives. The underlying purpose of most such projects and initiatives is to encourage favourable conceptualisation of engineering, science and technology. However, the evaluation of such links has typically been characterised by the relation of highly subjective 'feel good' factors by the adults involved with such projects. An easily applied, objective, instrument capable of measuring the conceptual change that such initiatives endeavour to bring about would provide useful assistance in the evaluation of school-industry engineering, science and technology enhancement programmes and projects. The research has a number of discrete but complementary purposes: 1) To gain a picture of how contemporary pupils conceptualise engineers, scientists and technology. 2) To develop an evaluation instrument for school-industry links in regard of science, technology and engineering initiatives. 3) To consider the appropriateness of current engineering, science and technology school-industry initiatives and propose constructive alternative strategies. A survey instrument based mainly on the 'semantic differential' has been developed, piloted and administered to some 500 Year 9 pupils in 4 secondary schools. Data exploration has yielded some significant findings using a variety of statistical techniques, including factor analysis. Sub-group comparisons of pupils' perceptions of engineers, scientists and technology have been made. Significant differences (and similarities) in perception have been observed. Sub-groups so far studied include groups based on: gender; school; and 'technological awareness' level. To add depth to the understanding being gained (and to help refine the survey instrument) projective interview techniques have been developed and piloted. Twelve small group interviews have taken place in 3 schools with pupils selected from their survey scores. The projective technique used has proved itself able to get pupils freely talking about their views of engineers, scientists and technology. Although analysis of the interview data obtained is at an early stage, it is clear that it will help in the refinement of the survey instrument and make contributions to other areas of research. For example, pupils' poor awareness of the range of careers that involve engineering and/or science, their notions about the low level of mathematical understanding needed to do engineering, and their views about women in science, that will challenge the basis of many positive discrimination initiatives. The research is now moving towards the development of an objective evaluation instrument for use in assessing the effectiveness of technological school-industry links in producing 'desired' conceptual shift.

STATUS: Individual research

DATE OF RESEARCH: 1994-1998

KEYWORDS: attitudes; engineering; industry education relationship; pupil attitudes; science based occupations; science technology and society; secondary education; technology; work education relationship

0897

School of Education and Professional Development, Holly Bank Road, Lindley, Huddersfield HD3 3BP
01484 422288

Williamson, I. Mr; *Supervisors*: Cullingford, C. Prof.; Oliver, P. Dr; Harris, A. Mrs

Experiences of alienation during early adolescence

ABSTRACT: This thesis is attempting to synthesise American models of alienation (after Seeman) with the qualitative tradition of school disaffection in Britain. Alienation is defined as both process and state and an attempt is being made to reconstruct the concept whilst relating this explicitly to processes within the school context. This study has involved the use of both quantitative and qualitative methods. 254 students in Years 9 and 10 completed a series of personality inventories and attitude scales to assess the extent, nature, correlates and consequences of school alienation. This has included a detailed analysis of cultural variables. Current research is of a more ethnographic nature and involves the use of semi-structured interviews which ask young offenders to retrospect upon their experiences in and around school life.

PUBLISHED MATERIAL: WILLIAMSON, I. & CULLINGFORD, C. (1997). 'The uses and misuses of "alienation" in the social sciences and education', British Journal of Educational Studies, Vol 45, No 3, pp.263-275.

STATUS: Individual research

DATE OF RESEARCH: 1995-1998

KEYWORDS: alienation; cultural background; culture; ethnic groups; pupil alienation; pupil behaviour; social behaviour; truancy

0898

School of Education and Professional Development, Holly Bank Road, Lindley, Huddersfield HD3 3BP
01484 422288

Webb, C. Ms; *Supervisors*: Cullingford, C. Prof.; Oliver, P. Dr; Jarvis, C. Mrs

Young children's perceptions of acceptable and unacceptable behaviour

ABSTRACT: Previous work on bullying has tended to quantify the problem and offer solutions to it. Few have analysed why unacceptable behaviour takes place, what the motivations are, and the influences that are brought to bear. This research seeks to find out how attitudes towards behaviour, moral factors and rules develop. It is planned to analyse the thought processes of 9 year old and 6 year old children to trace the difference, and, in particular the attitudes expressed, towards parents and peers, as well as school. Semi-structured interviews are being tested.

STATUS: Individual research

DATE OF RESEARCH: 1995-1998

KEYWORDS: antisocial behaviour; behaviour problems; behaviour standards; bullying; childhood attitudes; moral values; pupil attitudes

0899

School of Education and Professional Development, Holly Bank Road, Lindley, Huddersfield HD3 3BP
01484 422288

Laurenson, M. Mrs; *Supervisors*: Harris, G. Dr; Sheehan, J. Dr

The GNVQ paradigm: vocational versus academic in health and social care

ABSTRACT: The aims of this research are to look at the dilemmas faced by General National Vocational Qualification (GNVQ) Advanced Health and Social Care students nearing completion of their course and the choices open to them in employment opportunity, or in gaining access into higher education. This will be undertaken by comparing attitudes from: GNVQ students following a vocational course in health and social care; 'A' level students following an academic course and seeking a career in the health and social care sector; employers in health and social care sectors; and universities offering higher education courses in the health and social care fields. It will address the question of National Standards by comparing the North/South divide. It will address class issues by looking at the number of working/middle class students applying for the vocational GNVQ route and comparing this with the number of working/middle class applying from the traditional 'A' level route. This will highlight if the changes in educational provision have led to equality of opportunity, or if it is a way of dividing academia and promoting exclusivity through emphasis on the 'A' level route by the old established universities, or by employers. The research will look into the recent changes in educational and training provision brought about by legislation in 1991 and 1994 and the response through policy and practice issues. The Conservative Government policy of creating a highly trained workforce, in line with Europe, has led to an increase in the number of students undertaking further and higher education, and an increase in the number of new universities by the elevation of the old polytechnics and by allowing some further education colleges to offer higher education courses. These institutions offer students a selection of both vocational and academic courses, many of which now have an increased vocational content. If, as the Prime Minister John Major suggests, we now live in a classless society, then students gaining a qualification through the non-traditional route should be able to gain access to the same employment opportunities and the same universities as their counterparts. However, in reality, do vocational students have equal access in employment opportunity and in gaining access to the old established universities? Are they penalised by undertaking the vocationally led GNVQ route, or considered second in line after their 'A' level counterparts? Do more GNVQ students, than the 'A' level students, apply to the new universities rather than the old established universities and, if so, why? To carry out this research, questionnaires will be sent to students currently studying on the GNVQ Advanced Health and Social Care course in 8 further education colleges; 4 based in the North of England and 4 in the South of England. Students currently undertaking the more traditional 'A' level route through 8 schools and expecting a career in the health and social care field will also be sent questionnaires using the same demographic criteria. Questionnaires will be sent to 8 universities in total. These will consist of 2 old universities and 2 new universities in both the North and South of England. An employers' perspective will be gained by sending questionnaires to 8 major teaching hospitals, and 8 social service departments; 4 to each in the North and 4 to each in the South of England asking about their recruitment policies. This will help to highlight if the GNVQ qualification has parity with the gold standard of the 'A' level in the eyes of universities and employers.

STATUS: Individual research

DATE OF RESEARCH: 1995-1998

KEYWORDS: a level examinations; access to education; further education; health services; higher education; national vocational qualifications; social services; university admission

0900

School of Education and Professional Development, Holly Bank Road, Lindley, Huddersfield HD3 3BP
01484 422288

Cuthell, J. Mr; *Supervisors*: Cullingford, C. Prof.; Crawford, R. Mr

Interactions between learners and information technology

ABSTRACT: This is a pupil based research project with 5 main themes: what young people do when learning and working with information technology; their perceptions of the learning process and the language they use to describe it; the transactions that take place during work, both individually and within groups; ways in which learners adapt prior learning strategies and devise new ones, and ways in which learning and work strategies can be correlated with pupils' experience and use of new technology. Research data covering the 1800 pupils (11-18) of Boston Spa Comprehensive School, West Yorkshire, is drawn from 3 surveys (average sample size 1200) in 1995, 96 and 97 (comparative survey in 1997 with an inner-city comprehensive school in Leeds) which measured the level of home ownership of computers. Uses and Gratifications analyses of pupil responses have been undertaken, and surveys across the National Curriculum key stage 3 and 4 cohorts have examined perceived benefits of computer use for coursework. Investigations of teacher computer ownership have included analysis levels of improvement seen in the work of pupils who utilise computers. Most recent findings show 59% of pupils in the school have access to a home computer. This rises through 62% at Year 10, 67% Year 11 to 72% in Year 12/13. 80% of teachers surveyed felt that pupil work was improved by computer use: some by up to 25%.

PUBLISHED MATERIAL: CUTHELL, J. (1996). 'Teachers lag behind students', Times Educational Supplement, 29 November 1996. ; CUTHELL, J. (1997). 'Patterns of computer ownership', Computer Education 86, June 1997, pp.13-23.

STATUS: Individual research

DATE OF RESEARCH: 1994-continuing

KEYWORDS: computer ownership; computer uses in education; computers; information technology; learning strategies; secondary education; secondary school pupils

0901

School of Education and Professional Development, Holly Bank Road, Lindley, Huddersfield HD3 3BP
01484 422288

Butroyd, R. Mr; *Supervisors*: Cullingford, C. Prof.; McKenzie, P. Mr; Sanderson, P. Mr

The formation, role and effects of secondary teachers' beliefs in the context of increased accountability and reduced autonomy

ABSTRACT: There are many reasons for the current concern with the values of society. Education has become a focus for this concern. This study would explore the notion of 'values' amongst teachers and pupils in the secondary sector of education. At the same time, this work would investigate the role of human agency within the structure of a centrally imposed National Curriculum. Teachers' values are a public, as well as a personal, matter. With the development of centralised initiatives, such as the National Curriculum and the changes flowing from the Education Reform Act 1988, it is important to investigate the notion of a shared value system. The aims of the research are to: 1) identify origins of teacher motivation to teach; 2) examine the role of teachers' values in the prevention, mitigation, or development of key features of the teachers' career life cycle; 3) examine the relationship between teachers' values and pupil experience; 4) explore teachers' values, motivation and practice in the context of recent changes in the labour market; 5) consider the teachers' role as an agent of change. Sample A will be 100 teachers in 10 schools - this sample will take account of the gender, ethnic, age, responsibility and subject profile of the school staff. The schools will be from a cross section of the state secondary sector. Sample B will be 100 pupils from 2 sixth form colleges - this sample will have had experience of teachers who operate within the frameworks created by, and subsequent to, the Education Reform Act 1988

PUBLISHED MATERIAL: BUTROYD, R. (1997). Teacher appraisal: the connection between teaching quality and legislation'. In: CULLINGFORD, C. (Ed). Assessment versus evaluation. London: Cassell. ; BUTROYD, R. (1997). 'Are the values of secondary school teachers really in decline?', Educational Review, Vol 49, No 3, pp.251-258.

STATUS: Individual research

DATE OF RESEARCH: 1996-continuing

KEYWORDS: **attitudes; secondary education; secondary school teachers; teacher attitudes; teacher role; teaching profession; values**

0902

School of Education and Professional Development, Holly Bank Road, Lindley, Huddersfield HD3 3BP
01484 422288

Fisher, R. Mr; *Supervisors*: Cullingford, C. Prof.; Newbold, D. Prof.

The vocational curriculum in England and Wales: a socio-historical study of the Business and Technology Education Council's National Diploma in Business and Finance

ABSTRACT: This socio-historical study of the vocational curriculum in England and Wales focuses on the Business and Technology Education Council's (BTEC) National level programmes in Business and Finance. The study provides an account of the inception and development of the BTEC National curriculum. Vocationalism, as a cultural and ideological phenomenon within education, is theoretically contextualised with particular reference to the work of Gramsci, Althusser, Foucault and Lyotard. The study is underpinned by empirical research based on course documentation, participant observation in a further education college, and a questionnaire survey of lecturers, employers, students and other parties (sample size 381).

STATUS: Individual research

DATE OF RESEARCH: 1993-continuing

KEYWORDS: **business and technology education council; educational history; vocational education**

0903

School of Education and Professional Development, Holly Bank Road, Lindley, Huddersfield HD3 3BP
01484 422288

Mitchell, P. Mr; *Supervisors*: Evans, B. Prof.; Stafford, W. Prof.

Academic freedom and responsibility in higher education, including higher education provision in colleges of further education

ABSTRACT: The broad aim of the study is to explore the extent to which academic freedom continues to have meaning and relevance in relation to the current political and financial environment. The study will include reference to the applicability of academic freedom to degree programmes outside the universities as such.

PUBLISHED MATERIAL: MITCHELL, P. (1998). 'Beyond the universities: academic freedom and responsibility'. In: MITCHELL, P. (Ed). Beyond the universities: the new higher education. Aldershot: Arena.

STATUS: Individual research

DATE OF RESEARCH: 1997-continuing

KEYWORDS: **academic freedom; higher education**

0904

School of Education and Professional Development, Holly Bank Road, Lindley, Huddersfield HD3 3BP
01484 422288

Gossman, P. Mr; *Supervisors*: Herrick, C. Dr; Cullingford, C. Prof.; Trorey, G. Dr

Does geography A-level coursework achieve its aims?

ABSTRACT: A-level geography syllabuses contain an element of coursework, often representing a significant proportion of the final result. Most coursework takes the form of one, personal individualised study. The research will investigate the types of objective that individual studies are designed to promote and will assess their relevance and validity in A-level geography. A series of recent publications have stressed the need for the inclusion of 'hard' and 'soft' key skills in the curriculum. The study will examine the extent to which individual studies are perceived by both teachers and students to promote the development of these key skills. A mixture of quantitative and qualitative methods will be used including a national survey of heads of geography in Sixth Form colleges and indepth case studies of 4 Sixth Form colleges with regard to the perceptions of both staff and students through interviewing. The 4 colleges will be selected on the basis of their size and the nature of the catchment area in order to obtain data from a range of students with broad socio-economic characteristics. Students' experiences will be collected prior to their coursework and after its completion in order to compare their experiences. A random sample of students will be used at each college. Staff interviews in these locations will be used at each college. Staff interviews in these locations will be used in order to gain a broader picture of the relevance of coursework. Staff will be asked about the aims for the individual studies in terms of the Qualifications and Curriculum Authority (QCA) criteria and as a vehicle for developing key skills.

STATUS: Individual research

DATE OF RESEARCH: 1997-continuing

KEYWORDS: **a level examinations; core skills; coursework; geography; key skills; learning strategies**

Hull University

0905

Department of Education, Hull HU6 7RX
01482 346311

McClelland, V. Prof.

History of the Roman Catholic involvement in education in England and Wales since 1935. (Within a general history of the Roman Catholic church in England and Wales since 1935)

ABSTRACT: The project re-evaluates the origins of the dual system in education since 1944 and locates educational policy in the Roman Catholic church in England and Wales within the general ecclesiastical development of the period since 1935. The work will estimate the effect of the Second Vatican Council upon educational development and will examine the social upheaval within the Catholic community since 1965. It will also provide indications of the future of the current partnership between church and state in educational provision.

PUBLISHED MATERIAL: McCLELLAND, V. (1988). 'Sensus Fidelium': the developing concept of Roman Catholic effort in education in England

and Wales'. In: TULASIEWICZ, W. & BROCK, C. (Eds). Christianity and educational provision. London: Routledge. ; McCLELLAND, V. (1991). 'The effect of the Council on Catholicism: Great Britain and Ireland'. In: HASTINGS, A. (Ed). Modern Catholicism: Vatican II and after. London: SPCK. ; McCLELLAND, V. (1991). 'Gravissimum Educationis'. In: HASTINGS, A. (Ed). Modern Catholicism: Vatican II and after. London: SPCK.

STATUS: Sponsored project

SOURCE OF GRANT: The National Catholic Fund

DATE OF RESEARCH: 1989-1998

KEYWORDS: catholic schools; church and education; church state relationship; educational history; educational policy; roman catholic church

0906

Department of Education, Hull HU6 7RX
01482 346311

Pereiro, J. Rev.; *Supervisor*: McClelland, V. Prof.

The teaching office of the church

ABSTRACT: H.E. Manning's years as Archbishop of Westminster coincided with a renewed interest in the 'Education Question'. The civilizing value of education, the social and economic benefits which would follow from its wider extension, were themes dear to Victorian England. The interest in education and the rapid nationwide development of the educational structures soon led to an all important debate about the respective roles of the individual, the Church and the State in this area. H.E. Manning played a prominent part in the 'Education Question'. On the one hand, he made a considerable contribution to the setting up of the Catholic Educational System. He also intervened quite decisively in the above-mentioned debate through his connections with men in power and his involvement in the official commissions set up to examine present policy and to offer solutions to the educational problems of the times. The research concentrates on the philosophical principles from which he draws his suggestions to solve the problems and tensions of the age, as well as for the setting up of the educational system on a proper basis to assure its greater effectiveness.

STATUS: Individual research

DATE OF RESEARCH: 1990-1993

KEYWORDS: church education relationship; educational history; educational philosophy

0907

Department of Education, Hull HU6 7RX
01482 346311

Gonzalez, B. Mr; *Supervisor*: Gorwood, B. Dr

The teaching and learning of geography in schools in Gibraltar

ABSTRACT: Examination results over the last 10 years have given much concern in Gibraltar with regard to geography. There have been several visible trends which suggest a decrease in importance and status of the subject in the school curriculum. The research aims to identify the factors which have been responsible for this downward trend. In British schools geography is one of the more popular subjects and the results obtained compare quite favourably with the results obtained in other diciplines. Why is there such a marked contrast with the results obtained in Gibraltar? The research will concentrate on the learning of the subject and the importance of environmental stimulus or lack of it, and an indepth analysis of the existing geographical curriculum taught in schools at all levels.

STATUS: Individual research

DATE OF RESEARCH: 1989-1993

KEYWORDS: geography; gibraltar

0908

Department of Education, Hull HU6 7RX
01482 346311

Douglas, F. Mr; *Supervisor*: McClelland, V. Prof.

A study of pre-school education in the Republic of Ireland with particular reference to those pre-schools which are listed by the Irish Pre-School Playgroups Association in Cork City and County

ABSTRACT: This study was undertaken in order to investigate the activities which took place in Irish pre-schools other than those within the formal school system. The principle focus of the research concerned the degree to which pre-school children were being 'cognitively stretched' by the curriculum in which they were engaged. The social, linguistic, physical and creative development of these children was also considered. Twenty-three pre-schools were taken at random from the membership list in Cork City and County of the Irish Pre-School Playgroups Association. One pre-school which was not a member was added. This study, which took place between 1986 and 1990 was eclectic in nature, employing a multi-faceted approach encompassing a target child observational schedule, interviews, a study of classrooms, a questionnaire, and an interaction and analysis system. Among other things, the results showed that the 157 children engaged in this study were being 'cognitively stretched' for approximately one-quarter of the time if they were in a playgroup and approximately one half of the time if they were in a Montessori setting.

STATUS: Individual research

DATE OF RESEARCH: 1989-1993

KEYWORDS: early childhood education; ireland; montessori method; nursery education; play groups; preschool education

0909

Department of Education, Hull HU6 7RX
01482 346311

Waugh, D. Mr; *Supervisor*: Gorwood, B. Dr

Implementing educational changes in primary schools with particular reference to small schools

ABSTRACT: The research takes the form of questionnaire and survey work on the methods used, and problems encountered, when primary schools attempt to meet the requirements of the Education Reform Act 1988. A survey of around 200 schools has been undertaken and a number of case studies made. The aim of the research is to determine whether school size affects the ability to implement change. It is hoped that recommendations can be made, which will draw upon examples of 'good practice', to enable schools to fulfil legal requirements in an educationally acceptable way.

STATUS: Individual research

DATE OF RESEARCH: 1990-1993

KEYWORDS: education reform act 1988; educational change; educational legislation; educational planning; primary education; school size; small schools

0910

Department of Education, Hull HU6 7RX
01482 346311

Clifford, J. Ms; *Supervisor*: McClelland, V. Prof.

The religious education of young adults attending university

ABSTRACT: This research will look at: 1) the relationship between the secular university and religion; 2) the place and relationship of the Church in an academic community; 3) the role of institutionally appointed professional religious leadership in a modern university; 4) the organisational aspects of a campus ministry; 5) the aims of religious education for the university student; 6) a survey of religious experiences, attitudes and expectations of university students; and 7) a programme of religious ministry to university students.

STATUS: Individual research

DATE OF RESEARCH: 1993-1998

KEYWORDS: higher education; religion and education; religious education; universities

0911

Department of Education, Hull HU6 7RX
01482 346311

Bates, E. Mr ; @#Supervisor:#@ Bottery, M. Dr

The National Curriculum in England and Wales: a philosophical examination of the development of the National Curriculum

ABSTRACT: This is a philosophical thesis examining the varied faces: educational; social; political et al, which have been involved in the evolution and continuing development of the National Curriculum.

STATUS: Individual research

DATE OF RESEARCH: 1993-1998

KEYWORDS: **curriculum development; educational philosophy; national curriculum; primary education; secondary education**

0912

Department of Education, Hull HU6 7RX
01482 346311

Kalve, P. Mr; *Supervisor*: McClelland, V. Prof.

Bridging the divide? The aims, objectives and assumptions of religious education in present-day Catholic and secular traditions: a comparison

ABSTRACT: The purpose of this study is to: 1) analyse the aims, objectives and assumptions of religious education in present-day Catholic and secular traditions; and 2) examine comparatively the similarities and dissimilarities of approach to religious education by each tradition. It is the underlying thesis of this study that it is in comparing the approaches in understanding of each tradition to religious education that it becomes possible to reach a fuller understanding of what religious education is, both in itself, and also in the approaches of the two traditions which are here examined. The research of these two traditions' approaches to religious education centres around the generic philosophical and educational epistemologies of each tradition. In particular, three areas of study are considered: 1) The philosophical and epistemological background for the Catholic and secular traditions' concepts of knowledge. 2) The implications of these respective philosophical and epistemological approaches for religious education in each tradition. 3) The deeper understanding of the processes of religious education provided through a comparative analysis of the two traditions' approaches.

STATUS: Individual research

DATE OF RESEARCH: 1994-1998

KEYWORDS: **catholics; religion and education; religious education; secularisation**

0913

Department of Education, Hull HU6 7RX
01482 346311

Henworth, A. Mr; *Supervisor*: Squires, G. Dr

Quality and quality assurance of land-based further education and training

ABSTRACT: Quality and quality assurance became a major issue for post-compulsory education in the late 1980's. Institutions within the education service are now under considerable and increasing pressure to demonstrate to a wide range of groups and bodies that they are able to meet certain quality criteria. The issue of quality raises two crucial questions for providers of land-based further education and training: what is quality provision in vocational education and training in this sector?; and how is this quality demonstrated? The purposes of this study are therefore firstly to examine the development of the quality issue with reference to further education and training; secondly to identify how quality is perceived by the many stakeholders of land-based further education and training; thirdly to clarify the wide-ranging implications which quality and quality assurance have for the future of land-based further education and training; and fourthly to investigate and recommend strategies for the continued provision of land-based further education and training which encompass the demands of the quality issue.

STATUS: Individual research

DATE OF RESEARCH: 1993-1997

KEYWORDS: **agricultural education; educational quality; further education; land use; quality assurance; vocational education**

Institute for Employment Studies

0914

Mantell Building, University of Sussex, Falmer, Brighton BN1 9RF
01273 686751

Jagger, N. Mr; Connor, H. Mrs; Court, G. Dr

Institute for Employment Studies graduate review

ABSTRACT: An annual review of the graduate labour market, intended to inform employers and other policymakers about current trends in higher education, the supply of graduates, and the recruitment market. This is mainly desk-based research, using published data from the Department For Education (DFE) and other sources, and from Institute for Employment Studies (IES) database. A report provides key facts and figures with commentary.

PUBLISHED MATERIAL: A full list of publications is available from the researchers.

STATUS: Sponsored project

SOURCE OF GRANT: Institute for Employment Studies Corporate Research Fund (20 employers)

DATE OF RESEARCH: 1995-continuing

KEYWORDS: **employment opportunities; graduate employment; graduates; labour market; work education relationship**

0915

Mantell Building, Sussex University, Falmer, Brighton BN1 9RF
01273 686751

Hillage, J. Mr; Pearson, R. Mr; Anderson, A. Mr; Tamkin, P. Ms

Review of educational research relating to schools

ABSTRACT: A review has been commissioned to examine the direction, organisation, funding, quality and impact of educational research, primarily in the schools field, in order to produce recommendations for its future development. It involves literature review, face-to-face interviews and group discussions with researchers, funders, policymakers and practitioners, and a 'call for evidence'.

PUBLISHED MATERIAL: HILLAGE, J., PEARSON, R., ANDERSON, A. & TAMKIN, P. (1998). Excellence in research in schools. DFEE Research Brief No 74. London: Department for Education and Employment.

STATUS: Sponsored project

SOURCE OF GRANT: Department for Education and Employment £54,950

DATE OF RESEARCH: 1998-1998

KEYWORDS: **educational research; literature reviews**

Institute of Child Health

0916

The Wolfson Centre, Great Ormond Street Hospital, Mecklenburgh Square, London WC1N 2AP
0171 837 7618

Pennington, L. Ms; *Supervisors*: McConachie, H. Dr; Jolleff, N. Ms; Wisbeach, A. Ms

Putting training into practice: evaluating 'My Turn to Speak'

ABSTRACT: The current project has two parts to it. Firstly, the development team for 'My Turn to Speak' will run study days to familiarise speech therapists, teachers and others who might wish to use the published training package. The study days will include some of the activities of the workshop, and discussion on how best to implement the approach in various schools and with children who have various levels of severity of physical disorder. The second part of the current project involves evaluating the workshops that have been run by the development team, and comparing their process and outcome with workshops run by new tutors, often past participants. One aim of the package is to facilitate the setting up of a rolling programme of training throughout a school. In addition a multiple baseline, single case study is being undertaken to look at the implementation of the team approach to communication with one child.

PUBLISHED MATERIAL: PENNINGTON, L., JOLLEFF, N., McCONACHIE, H., WISBEACH, A. & PRICE, K. (1993). My Turn to Speak: A Team Approach to Augmentative Communication. London: Institute of Child Health, distributed by Winslow Press.

STATUS: Sponsored project

SOURCE OF GRANT: The Viscount Nuffield Auxiliary Fund £11,683

DATE OF RESEARCH: 1993-1993

KEYWORDS: **communication aids - for disabled; communication disorders; programme evaluation; special educational needs; workshops**

0917

The Wolfson Centre, Great Ormond Street Hospital, Mecklenburgh Square, London WC1N 2AP
0171 837 7618

Sonksen, P. Dr; Dale, N. Dr

Developmental outcome in young severely visually impaired children: risk factors and management

ABSTRACT: Developmental deceleration or regression-developmental setback (DS) amongst visually impaired (VI) preschool children are more common than in sighted children. In the setting of the Wolfson Centre's Developmental Vision Clinic for babies and preschool children with VI, a retrospective study of 102 VI babies with documented normal early development revealed that 31% of the profoundly visually impaired (PVI) and 5% of those with some 'form' vision (SVI) underwent DS. The children showed 2 patterns of disorder: either a severe slowing down and plateauing in acquisition of language and cognitive skills (with loss of skills in some cases) or an increasing disorder in communication and social interaction skills but with continuing development of language and cognitive skills. The developmental regression emerged at a vulnerable stage in the development of attention control and behavioural independence (between 16 to 27 months) and adverse social factors were present in 60% of the families. The contributions of psychosocial/environmental factors, organic disorder of the nervous system and degree of visual impairment to this serious developmental outcome are not known. The project will study the environmental, behavioural and neurological factors contributing to developmental outcome and setback . 200 children will be recruited for the study who are aged less than 16 months when first seen, are profoundly or severely visually impaired, with no additional physical or hearing impairment. A longitudinal prospective investigation of the target clinical population will be pursued. Multiple measures will be taken at regular intervals between infancy and 48 months of age. Standard demographic data will be complemented by the findings of paediatric neurological, hearing and opthalmological examination, including an MRI scan. The visual protocol will include diagnostic evaluation, standard and functional measures. Developmental and psychological measures include Reynell Zinkin Cognitive and Language Scales, a Social-Communication Parent Questionnaire (SCPQ) (which has been specially designed for the study), inventory measures of maternal mental health and adjustment to child disability, familial resources and stress levels and adverse life events. Videotaped observations of parent-child interaction and child attention behaviours will be coded. Initially, and at interim assessments, children will be allocated to categories of current outcome (normal, delayed, severely delayed) and at the age of 4 years also to trend outcome (normal, deceleration, acceleration, disorder/setback) on the basis of ratings on the SCPQ and the Child Autism Rating Scale (CARS). These groupings will be used in multivariate analysis to look for variables (including type of disorder, adverse social and medical factors, social and communicative developmental factors) which are predictive of adequate and poor outcome. The summary variables will be derived from the set of measures described previously.

PUBLISHED MATERIAL: SONKSEN, P.M., PETRIE, A. & DREW, K.J. (1992). 'Promotion of visual development of severely visually impaired babies: evaluation of a developmentally based programme', Developmental Medicine and Child Neurology, Vol 33, pp.330-335. ; CASS, H.D., SONKSEN, P.M. & MCCONACHIE, H. (1994). 'Developmental setback in severe visual impairment', Archives of Disease in Childhood, Vol 70, pp.192-196.

STATUS: Sponsored project

SOURCE OF GRANT: Child Health Research Appeal Trust £1,500; Mary Kitzinger Trust £2,500

DATE OF RESEARCH: 1995-continuing

KEYWORDS: **blindness; cognitive development; communication disorders; developmental disabilities; infants; learning disabilities; preschool children; special educational needs; visual impairments; young children**

0918

The Wolfson Centre, Great Ormond Street Hospital, Mecklenburgh Square, London WC1N 2AP
0171 837 7618

Clarke, M. Mr; Wood, P. Ms; Price, K. Ms; *Supervisor*: McConachie, H. Dr

Evaluation of speech and language therapy for children using communication aids

ABSTRACT: Follow-up studies of the introduction of communication aids have shown that the potential for such systems is often not recognised. Factors suggested by parents as inhibiting the use of communication aids include lack of speech and language therapy support. At present the pattern of speech and language therapy provision and its relationship to the development of functional communication skills is unknown. 24 children who use a communication aid involving at least 20 symbols/pictures have been recruited. Children with rapidly progressive degenerative neurological conditions have been excluded. The measures used are: 1) Input variables - a) the pattern of delivery of speech and language therapy in schools; b) the child's day of attendance at school during the year. 2) Outcome measures - a) change in amount of communication aid observed in school; b) staff perceptions of progress on specific therapy objectives; c) change in assessed functional communication skills. 3) Interview measures - a) communication aid users and a school friend, chosen by the communication aid user, will be interviewed concerning their views on communication aid use; b) teachers will be interviewed concerning their perceptions of augmentative and alternative communication, and their strategies in the classroom to encourage communication aid use. Quantitative analysis will relate child and input variables to outcome measures. The findings will be illustrated by reference to qualitatitve information gained in interview. The study will suggest predictors of progress in children's communicative behaviour, including the value of support gained from speech and language therapy intervention. It will also identify potential barriers to communicative progress.

STATUS: Sponsored project

SOURCE OF GRANT: National Health Service Research and Development Programme £140,214

DATE OF RESEARCH: 1997-continuing

KEYWORDS: **communication aids - for disabled; language handicaps; special educational needs; speech handicaps; speech therapy**

Keele University

0919

Department of Education, Keele ST5 5BG
01782 621111

Wakelin, M. Mrs; *Supervisor*: Wringe, C. Dr

The use of performance indicators in the evaluation of educational institutions

ABSTRACT: Current use of performance indicators is to be surveyed and evaluated in relation to currently proposed educational aims. Their validity as a measure of educational effectiveness and their effect on the performance of teachers and institutions will be assessed.

STATUS: Individual research

DATE OF RESEARCH: 1989-continuing

KEYWORDS: **educational objectives; educational quality; institutional evaluation; performance indicators; school effectiveness**

0920

Department of Education, Keele ST5 5BG
01782 621111

Burgess, R. Mr; *Supervisor*: Gleeson, D. Prof.

Research and evaluation of Cheshire LEA's Technical and Vocational Education Initiative (TVEI), Inservice Education of Teachers (INSET) & Education Support Grant (ESG) programmes

ABSTRACT: The aim is to provide an up-to-date case study analysis of a small group of schools (secondary, primary and special) and a further education institution, in order to evaluate the impact of Technical and Vocational Education Initiative (TVEI), Inservice Education of Teachers

(INSET) and Education Support Grant (ESG) initiatives on staff development and teaching and learning processes.

STATUS: Sponsored project

SOURCE OF GRANT: Cheshire Local Education Authority £35,000

DATE OF RESEARCH: 1989-1993

KEYWORDS: education support grants; inservice teacher education; programme evaluation; tvei

0921

Department of Education, Keele ST5 5BG
01782 621111

Powell, G. Mr

The order of knowledge

ABSTRACT: The study will offer a radical re-assessment of the development of education, especially since the Renaissance. It will involve a new interpretation of the significance of Plato's analysis of the classical conceptual system which has dominated our education.

STATUS: Individual research

DATE OF RESEARCH: 1988-1993

KEYWORDS: educational history; educational theories; philosophy

0922

Department of Education, Keele ST5 5BG
01782 621111

Thompson, D. Mr

The history and promotion of geological and earth-science education in the United Kingdom and elsewhere in the world

ABSTRACT: The history of geological and earth science education in the United Kingdom reveals the important part that geology, geologists and the geological profession played in the early days of the growth of science education from 1830 to 1900 in both schools and vocational courses, e.g. of the Department of Science and Arts. The wives of geologists were in the van of women's education and extra mural education. A decline to a nadir in the 1930s has been followed by a steady rise in the growth of interest, culminating in the formation of the Association of Teachers of Geology (1967) (now the Earth Science Teachers' Association (1988), and the acceptance of Earth Science in Science in the national curriculum of the UK and many other countries.

PUBLISHED MATERIAL: THOMPSON, D.B. (1993). 'Highlights from the history of the geological curriculum in schools, colleges and universities', Teaching Earth Sciences, Vol 18, No 3, p.113. ; THOMPSON, D.B. (1993). Geoscience education in schools worldwide - a summary report on the presentations at the International Geoscience Education Conference, Southampton', Teaching Earth Sciences, Vol 18, No 4, pp.123-129. ; THOMPSON, D.B. & KING, C.J.H. (1996). 'Geoeducation in schools worldwide: an overview'. In: STOW, D.A.V. & MCCALL, G.J.H. (Eds). Geoscience education and training in schools and universities for industry and public awareness. Rotherdam: Balkema. ; THOMPSON, D.B. (1998). 'From a physical geology - geography education for a few aged 11-16 to an earth-environmental science education for all aged 4-16'. In: FORTHER, R.W. & MEYER, V.J. (Eds). Learning about the earth as a system. Proceedings of the Second International Conference on Geoscience Education, University of Hawaii at Hilo. Columbus, Ohio: Ohio State University.

STATUS: Individual research

DATE OF RESEARCH: 1970-continuing

KEYWORDS: earth science; educational history; geology; physical sciences; science education

0923

Department of Education, Keele ST5 5BG
01782 621111

Marques, L. Mr; *Supervisor*: Thompson, D. Mr

Children's alternative ideas about earth-science concepts, e.g. continental drift and plate tectonics

ABSTRACT: Children's alternative ideas relating to earth-science concepts have been only modestly researched. Following work in 1988 on children's ideas of the origin of the earth, the origin of life and the nature and origin of volcanoes, the research has now turned to children's views of the origin of continents, oceans and the possible wandering of the former. Following a pilot study with pupils and teachers and indepth interviews with pupils, a questionnaire survey of the views of 300 Portuguese children has been administered. It is conjectured that the many garbled ideas of students accrue from watching television, reading newspapers and attempting to use ideas drawn from science and geography lessons at school. So far 30 or so alternative ideas have been noted and curriculum strategies which challenge many of them been developed and trialled. An historical epistemological approach to teaching these topics has been successfully trialled in schools at ages 13-14 and 16-17.

PUBLISHED MATERIAL: THOMPSON, D.B. (1996). 'Portuguese and English students' ideas on the nature and origin of earth, life, volcanoes, earthquakes and soil'. In: STOW, D.A.V. & MCCALL, G.J.H. (Eds). Geoscience education and training in schools and universities for industry and public awareness. Rotherdam: Balkema. ; MARQUES, L. & THOMPSON, D.B. (1996). 'The alternative ideas and misconceptions of Portuguese students (aged 15-17)'. In: STOW, D.A.V. & MCCALL, G.J.H. (Eds). Geoscience education and training in schools and universities for industry and public awareness. Rotherdam: Balkema. ; MARQUES, L. & THOMPSON, D.B. (1997). 'Portuguese students' understanding at ages 10-11 and 14-15 or the origin and nature of the earth and the development of life', Research in Science and Technological Education, Vol 15, No 1, pp.29-51. ; MARQUES, L. & THOMPSON, D.B. (1997). 'Misconceptions and conceptual changes concerning continental drift and plate tectonics amongst Portuguese students aged 16-17', Research in Science and Technological Education, Vol 15, No 2, pp.195-222.

STATUS: Individual research

DATE OF RESEARCH: 1989-1998

KEYWORDS: comprehension; earth science; oceanography; physical sciences; plate tectonics

0924

Department of Education, Keele ST5 5BG
01782 621111

Thompson, D. Mr

Curriculum materials for earth-science teaching in the National Curriculum and elsewhere

ABSTRACT: Earth Science is new to the science curriculum in the United Kingdom. Curriculum materials need to be written, trialled and published quickly. Trials are to be carried out on whole classes of 20-30 pupils. Materials are designed for variety and balance of approach and a concentration on pupil activity including practical experimental work. Publication is via the Earth Science Teachers' Association 'Science of the Earth' and 'Project Earth'. A list of Earth Science Teachers Association publications is available from Geo Supplies Ltd, 11 Station Road, Chapeltown, Sheffield S30 4XH.

PUBLISHED MATERIAL: THOMPSON, D.B. (1995). 'A guide to the history and geology of quarrying at localities along the natural history trail in Corbet Wood, Grinshill, North Shropshire. Wem: Clive & Grinshill Conservation Committee. ; THOMPSON, D.B. (1997). Excursion to the permo-jurassic rocks of the Cheshire and East Irish sea and basins in the area of the Wirral. Liverpool: Liverpool University, Earth Science Department. ; THOMPSON, D.B. (1998). A geological excavation guide to Alderley Education. Manchester: Manchester University Museum.

STATUS: Individual research

DATE OF RESEARCH: 1988-continuing

KEYWORDS: earth science; educational materials; material development; national curriculum; physical sciences; science education

0925

Department of Education, Keele ST5 5BG
01782 621111

Maden, M. Prof.; Gough, G. Dr; Johnson, M. Mr; Glover, D. Dr *Successful

Successful schooling

ABSTRACT: The project aims to establish further information and knowledge about 'successful schooling', by means of questionnaires and indepth interviews with pupils, parents and teachers.

STATUS: Sponsored project

SOURCE OF GRANT: Local Education Authorities £25,000

DATE OF RESEARCH: 1990-continuing

KEYWORDS: **educational quality; outcomes of education; parent school relationship; school effectiveness**

0926

Department of Education, Keele ST5 5BG
01782 621111

Parkhouse, P. Mr

Undergraduate physicists' and post-graduate scientists' (undergoing teacher training) understanding of the nature of science

ABSTRACT: The current research is concerned with students' understanding of the nature of science. It is in two principal parts: one concerned with undergraduate physicists and the other with post-graduate science students undergoing a course of training for teaching at Keele University. Some of the post-graduate science students will be followed during their teaching practice to see if their teaching exemplifies their beliefs and whether the researcher is able to influence this by heightening their awareness through prolonged contact with them. The approach is ethnographic and the stimulus of a free-response questionnaire followed by recorded interviews elucidating their responses has been adopted. In addition both samples have to interact with specially prepared practical materials designed to reveal further their philosophical standpoints.

STATUS: Individual research

DATE OF RESEARCH: 1991-1998

KEYWORDS: **comprehension; philosophy of science; science education; scientific concepts; student attitudes**

0927

Department of Education, Keele ST5 5BG
01782 621111

Miller, D. Mr

Mathematics and pupils and information technology (MAPIT)

ABSTRACT: The aim of this research is to improve secondary school pupils' learning and understanding of mathematics by developing strategies which will enable mathematics departments to exploit more fully the potential of information technology within the mathematics classroom. The research is concerned with all aspects of computer use in mathematics classrooms, however, one area of particular interest is the use of notebook computers. The nature of the research is to: (1) provide appropriate training for teachers involved in the research; (2) collect case study data at regular intervals from the schools; and (3) provide formative and summative reports for the schools. In addition, information has been collected from Postgraduate Certificate in Education (PGCE) mathematics students on teaching practice. The interim reports and final results will be detailed in appropriate journals.

STATUS: Sponsored project

SOURCE OF GRANT: Keele University: Department of Education £1,500

DATE OF RESEARCH: 1992-continuing

KEYWORDS: **computer uses in education; information technology; mathematics education; microcomputers; secondary education**

0928

Department of Education, Keele ST5 5BG
01782 621111

Miller, D. Mr

The use of computers in mathematics lessons

ABSTRACT: The aim of this research is to examine the use of computers in secondary school mathematics lessons. Information has been collected by questionnaire from 100 secondary schools in England and Wales. The survey requested information about the computer equipment in school; the time spent by pupils using computers in mathematics; the programs in use in the school; the views of the head of mathematics on the use of computers; and the training needs of the mathematics department. The results will be detailed in appropriate journals.

STATUS: Individual research

DATE OF RESEARCH: 1992-1993

KEYWORDS: **computer uses in education; information technology; mathematics education; secondary education**

0929

Department of Education, Keele ST5 5BG
01782 621111

Powell, G. Mr

Educating the educators

ABSTRACT: At a time when teacher education has given way to the exclusive claims of training, the study will set out to construct an educational scheme to prepare future educators. In particular, it will explore the nature of the specific knowledge needed by educators to respond to individual differences.

STATUS: Individual research

DATE OF RESEARCH: 1994-1998

KEYWORDS: **preservice teacher education; teacher educators**

0930

Department of Education, Keele ST5 5BG
01782 621111

Ozga, J. Prof.

Women managers in higher and further education

ABSTRACT: The aim of the project is to build on work completed for the publication 'Women in Education Management' (Ozga, 1993) in order to provide detailed case studies of women in management in higher and further education. A small sample of senior managers has been selected for work shadowing, and the study will develop detailed accounts of their work practices over a six month period. It will also make use of life history methods to develop detailed accounts of women's experience of management and of their experience of 'careers'. The data will be analysed in order to explore the extent to which they support claims of productive gender-related difference in management styles.

PUBLISHED MATERIAL: OZGA, J. (Ed). (1993). Women in Education Management. Buckingham: Open University Press.

STATUS: Individual research

DATE OF RESEARCH: 1993-continuing

KEYWORDS: **administrators; educational administration; further education; higher education; management in education; women; womens employment**

0931

Department of Education, Keele ST5 5BG
01782 621111

Wringe, C. Dr

Evaluation of: Formation Autonome des Professeurs des Langues Etrangers lors des visites dans des Institutions Scolaires Etrangeres. (Continuing professional development for language teachers during visits to foreign schools)

ABSTRACT: The project linked national language teaching associations in 12 European Union countries. It involved brief visits by 230 established language teachers to institutions in other countries where either their teaching language is spoken or where they may observe that language being taught by foreign colleagues. In addition to the inservice training value of the project to the participants involved, it is also intended to develop and evaluate appropriate procedures, administrative frameworks and learning materials. Formative evaluation of the project is by a series of questionnaires, extensive interviews and on-site visits. The project is directed by Professor Michel Chandelier of the Universite Rene Descartes, Paris, on behalf of the Federation Internationale des Professeau des Langues Vivantes.

STATUS: Sponsored project

SOURCE OF GRANT: European Union (Lingua) £126,200

DATE OF RESEARCH: 1993-1998

KEYWORDS: **europe; international educational exchange; language teachers; modern language studies**

0932

Department of Education, Keele ST5 5BG
01782 621111

Gunter, H. Mrs; *Supervisor*: Ozga, J. Prof.

A critical history of the origins of educational administration and its development into educational management 1960-1990

ABSTRACT: Since the Education Reform Act, 1988, there has been an explosion in education management text, journals, and courses in the UK. Education management has taken on the concepts and tools of business literature and there is an emphasis on 'How to do it' manuals and courses. This is in direct contrast to the late 1960s. Today the literature is about educational administration which is rooted in the social sciences, whereas in the late 1960s it differed considerably in relation to concepts, language, and tone. The aims of the research are: 1) To compare and contrast the theoretical references and frameworks on which educational administration (1960s-1990s) and educational management respectively draw. 2) To identify the key figures in the construction and dissemination of the 'disciplines' of educational administration, and educational management, and to interrogate their accounts of the factors that contributed to the changing nature of the area. The methods used are: 1) The development of a historical and thematic framework through a literature search of key events, issues, and ideologies pertinent to educational administration and management. This is linked to the political, economic, social and technological context from the 1960s. 2) Review of the literature in relation to: the theoretical origins, and development of educational administration as an academic area of study; the current text on educational administration and management; learned journals; the growth in professional organisations and networks. 3) Identify key writers and actors in educational management and administration from late 1960s and present day. Interviews with a sample of these people. The doctoral dissertation will chart the history of the development and definition of a major area of educational practice. It will contribute to an understanding of the link between the social and political context, and the development and definition of a significant area of professional practice. Very little work has been done on the development of education management in the UK, or on its antecedents, and this research will both document the process of development and investigate the factors that contribute to the particular form of its development and current configuration.

STATUS: Individual research

DATE OF RESEARCH: 1994-continuing

KEYWORDS: **literature reviews; management in education**

0933

Department of Education, Keele ST5 5BG
01782 621111

King, C. Mr

What are the most effective ways of developing the teaching of new subject matter brought into a curriculum for the first time through a National Curriculum: a case study of the new Earth science component in the national science curriculum

ABSTRACT: It is only rarely that teachers are asked to teach a new and unfamiliar area of content through the requirements of a National Curriculum but this has happened to many teachers faced with the Earth science component of the national science curriculum in England and Wales. The main aims of the research are to identify those factors that teachers have found most helpful in the teaching of this new material, and then to provide more of these, if possible, whilst evaluating their continuing effectiveness. A pilot project will be carried out through use of the Keele Partnership mentor network. Teachers will be questioned on the factors they have found most helpful in teaching the new Earth science component of the national science curriculum. These might include commonly available broad science textbooks, specially published Earth science materials, help from colleagues in the science or geography departments, inservice teacher education (INSET) delivered in house, within local education authorities (LEAs), from outside centres or nationally, etc. The questioning will involve meetings with teachers as well as use of questionnaires. If this approach is successful,

the questionnaire approach will be extended to teachers in other mentor networks in the country. The conclusions will be published and the findings acted upon, where possible, to develop the understanding of the Earth science component of the national science curriculum amongst those teachers involved in its delivery. This should result in the more effective teaching of this material in schools.

STATUS: Individual research

DATE OF RESEARCH: 1997-continuing

KEYWORDS: **curriculum development; earth science; educational materials; inservice teacher education; national curriculum; science education; teacher development**

0934

Department of Education, Keele ST5 5BG
01782 621111

Fleming, D. Mr; Coles, M. Mr

Development of understanding in chemistry

ABSTRACT: The project arises from a growing concern about standards in Chemistry at General Certificate of Secondary Education (GCSE) level. The aim is to try to find evidence about changes in standards, if any, over the period 1988-1996 through a detailed survey of examination papers, syllabuses and mark schemes. If possible this will be supported by a review of candidates' scripts in these examinations in the Grades A-C range. The analysis of examination papers will consider breadth and depth of subject matter covered, types of questions asked, mark allocations, and in particular quantitative tasks. A common analysis document is being used by a group of experienced chief examiners. The results of this analysis are being entered into a common database from which the changes in standards, if any, will be identified. Examination papers from all 4 GCSE boards in England in both Sciences Doubled Award and Chemistry are included in the survey. Most syllabuses are being sampled at 2-year intervals between 1988 and 1996. The outcome is a report to the Royal Society of Chemistry, this will be used by the Society to inform their thinking or revision of the Science National Curriculum early in the 21st century. A paper and/or articles may also be written for publication.

STATUS: Sponsored project

SOURCE OF GRANT: Royal Society of Chemistry £7,100

DATE OF RESEARCH: 1996-continuing

KEYWORDS: **chemistry; educational quality; examination papers; examination syllabuses; examinations; general certificate of secondary education; science education; secondary education; standards**

0935

Department of Education, Keele ST5 5BG
01782 621111

Glover, D. Dr; Johnson, M. Mr; Gough, G. Dr; *Supervisor*: Gleeson, D. Prof.

Middle management and school improvement project

ABSTRACT: The focus of the project will be on the changing role of middle management in raising levels of achievement, learning and school effectiveness. Little is known about this strategic group which mediates national and local policy at the school level. At a time when schools are looking to change their management and staffing structures, this project represents a timely intervention in the movement towards successful schooling. It also has important implications for staff and career development, including raised levels of pupil-staff motivation and achievement in schools, linked with wider education targets. The aims are to: 1) increase awareness of the strategic role of middle management in improving school effectiveness, curriculum, learning and achievement; and 2) to focus on middle management as a change agent in secondary education in the Central England region. The objectives are to: 1) analyse the changing role of middle management; 2) promote better understanding of the contribution of middle management in raising levels of achievement and learning; and 3) provide models of 'good practice' and dissemination relevant both to a consortia of case study schools, and a wider audience of institutions in the region. A key feature of the project will be to define the target group: who middle management are, and what they do and can do. Currently, middle management is seen to constitute heads of department, heads of year, coordinators, curriculum managers and team leaders. This may be too limited or too broad a definition. A working hypothesis of this project is that current definitions will need revisiting and revising. A further question concerns whether the lines between senior management, middle management and teachers are becoming more distinct or blurred. This study will shed light on this including strategies for the future. The methodology will involve: using a combination of formative and summative approaches; a tripartite approach, linking schools, local education authorities (LEAs) and Central England Training and Enterprise Council (CENTEC); initial case studies of 5/6 schools in the Reditch/Bromsgrove area, involving feedback to individual schools and consortia as a whole; and a distillation report and pack/guide relevant to all schools in the region. The outcomes of the research will be to: a) disseminate 'best practice' through case studies, to a wider audience through promoting school improvement; b) provide insight and evidence of the changing role of middle management in raising levels of achievement in schools; c) enhance school/LEA/Training and Enterprise Council (TEC) partnerships in meeting local, regional and national education targets; and d) initiate formative and summative feedback, involving reports and a pack (or guide) of relevant materials for all schools in the region.

STATUS: Sponsored project

SOURCE OF GRANT: Central England Training and Enterprise Council £12,000

DATE OF RESEARCH: 1996-1997

KEYWORDS: **achievement; educational administration; local education authorities; management in education; middle management; motivation; school effectiveness; school improvement; secondary education; training and enterprise councils**

0936

Department of Education, Keele ST5 5BG
01782 621111

Shain, F. Dr; *Supervisor*: Gleeson, D. Prof.

Changing teaching and managerial cultures in further education

ABSTRACT: Following the introduction of the Further and Higher Education Act 1992, the project examines the changing professional culture of further education (FE) at local level. Its wider purpose is also to analyse the policy connections underpinning changing FE and State relations, and to study the new forms of teaching and managerial cultures which relate to such change. The study will consider the effects of funding government policy, markets, student composition, staffing and labour markets on colleges and their responses to such influences. The local focus is the way teachers and managers in FE define and construct the professional meaning of their work. More broadly, the research is interested in new professional knowledge created in the changing context of FE, and how such knowledge will affect the future of the sector. In so doing, the study will address two inter-connected issues concerning the impact of incorporation and markets on FE institutions. The first concerns how market influence translates into tension and innovation in the way teachers and managers approach their work. The second analyses the increasingly strong impact of human resources strategies in FE, and their impact on manager/teacher relations. In response, the study will pay particular attention to the part teacher/manager relations plays in defining new cultures of FE, in 3/4 designated case study institutions. The approach is based mainly on interviews and observations with teachers and managers, including documentary and policy analysis in the institutions involved.

STATUS: Sponsored project

SOURCE OF GRANT: Economic and Social Research Council £82,468

DATE OF RESEARCH: 1997-continuing

KEYWORDS: **change strategies; colleges of further education; educational administration; educational change; educational markets; further education; management in education; teaching methods**

0937

Department of Education, Keele ST5 5BG
01782 621111

Evans, T. Mrs; *Supervisor*: Ozga, J. Prof.

Perceptions of effectiveness in the governance of small primary schools

ABSTRACT: This research focuses upon an examination of the hypothesis that, while there are skills, values and responsibilities (perceived and statutory) which unite all school governing bodies, distinctions can be drawn between the practice, values etc of governance of small primary schools and those of larger schools in England. Through examination of the governance of a representative range of urban, suburban and rural small primary schools, the research seeks to disclose the extent to which these schools are distinctive and the extent to which they share values, perceptions and practice. The research is undertaken through questionnaires, structured interviews and observations.

STATUS: Individual research

DATE OF RESEARCH: 1997-continuing

KEYWORDS: **educational administration; governance; governing bodies; primary education; school governors**

0938

Department of Education, Keele ST5 5BG
01782 621111

Maden, M. Prof.; Sharp, S. Mr

Role of local education authorities in raising educational achievement/school improvement

ABSTRACT: The Audit Commission has a statutory role in the inspection and review of local authorities in England and Wales. More recently it is working in collaboration with the Office for Standards in Education (OFSTED) in the inspection of local education authorities (LEAs) in relation to school improvement. This research investigated 5 local education authorities where 'good practice' re: their impact on school improvement was believed to exist. Visits were made to the local education authorities. Interviews were conducted with the chief education officer, chief inspector or advisor and 2 or 3 headteachers of schools which had 'markedly improved' over recent years (based on objective performance data and LEA assessments). The main findings indicated that: 1) the role of the Chief Education Officer (CEO) is crucial in raising expectations and setting priorities across schools and the LEA itself; 2) new skills and knowledge amongst inspectors/advisors were identified, as well as their professional development/skills updating programmes; 3) 'research conscious' LEAs are ahead of the game and schools are aware of this and expect LEAs to 'add value' by being well-informed and capable of mediating 'top-down' requirements/value systems etc.

STATUS: Sponsored project

SOURCE OF GRANT: Audit Commission £12,000

DATE OF RESEARCH: 1997-1997

KEYWORDS: **educational quality; local education authorities; school effectiveness; school improvement**

0939

Department of Education, Keele ST5 5BG
01782 621111

Whitehead, S. Dr

Examination of changing organisational cultures in further education

ABSTRACT: This ongoing research focuses on the changing work culture of further education (FE), in particular the managers of FE colleges and their attempts to control the effects of incorporation after 1993. The research draws on the narratives of men and women managers: their discursive positions; self-identities; and association with dominant managerialism. To date, 30 managers have been interviewed in over 25 FE colleges across the Midlands and North of England. The work will continue over the next few years, and is expected to expand to include the opinions and perceptions of lecturer level employees. Theoretically, the work is informed by critical organisational analysis which draws on feminist, post-structuralist and post-modern (neo-Fordist) understandings of self, identity, masculinity, work and organisational life. Results so far indicate a shift in dominant gender discourse in FE; the emergence of an 'inhman resource management'. A possible emergence of a 'critical mass' of women managers; and covert patterns of resistance by managers to externally imposed 'rationalities'.

PUBLISHED MATERIAL: WHITEHEAD, S. (1996). 'Men, managers and the shifting discourses of post-compulsory education', Research in Post-Compulsory Education, Vol 1, No 2, pp.151-168. ; WHITEHEAD, S.

(1998). 'Disrupted selves', Gender and Education, Vol 10, No 2, pp.199-215. ; WHITEHEAD, S. 'From paternalism to entrepreneuralism', Discourse: Studies in the Cultural Politics of Education. (in press). ; WHITEHEAD, S. 'Contingent masculinities'. In: ROSENEIL, S. & SEYMOUR, J. (Eds). Practising identities. London: Macmillan.

STATUS: Individual research

DATE OF RESEARCH: 1994-continuing

KEYWORDS: **administrators; colleges of further education; educational administration; further education; management in education; management of change; organisational change**

0940

Department of Education, Keele ST5 5BG
01782 621111

Johnson, M. Mr; Gough, G. Dr

Homework club and study support project

ABSTRACT: This is a self-standing piece of research carried out for the Department for Education and Employment (DfEE) on pupils'/parents' perceptions of extra curricular learning opportunities provided in 12 schools nationally. Although a discreet piece of research, it is in support of work carried out by Education Extra which also did a broad evaluation of the work, and separate reports were presented to the DfEE. Work included preparation and distribution of 24 different questionnaires to pupils and parents, the analysis of same, and a final report on the data.

STATUS: Sponsored project

SOURCE OF GRANT: Department for Education and Employment £8,719

DATE OF RESEARCH: 1997-1998

KEYWORDS: **extracurricular activities; homework; parent attitudes; pupil attitudes; study support centres**

0941

Department of Education, Keele ST5 5BG
01782 621111

Johnson, M. Mr; Gough, G. Dr; Watson, R. Mr; Glover, D. Dr

Raising achievement, enhancing employability

ABSTRACT: Two separate research projects to determine the effectiveness of strategies put in place by the project group in 26 schools in Lancashire: 1) Construction, distribution and analysis of questionnaires to headteachers leading to a first report in Summer 1997 (26 schools included in sample). 2) Case studies conducted in 8 of the 26 schools to be written as a report in Summer 1998.

STATUS: Sponsored project

SOURCE OF GRANT: Lancashire County Council £13,870

DATE OF RESEARCH: 1997-1998

KEYWORDS: **achievement; educational quality; pupil performance; school effectiveness; school improvement**

0942

Department of Education, Keele ST5 5BG
01782 621111

Johnson, M. Mr; Watson, R. Mr; Spencer, P. Mrs; *Supervisor*: Gleeson, D. Prof.

Key skills project

ABSTRACT: This research is carried out on behalf of the Staffordshire Training and Enterprise Council and the Staffordshire Education Authority. The project's focus is upon the ways in which schools in socially deprived areas of Stoke-on-Trent and Staffordshire are seeking to deliver a 'key skills' curriculum to pupils in primary (Stoke-on-Trent) and secondary (Staffordshire) schools. The work involves qualitative research conducted by means of interviews in the following areas: 1) the rationale for the school's participation in the project; 2) the way(s) in which the target group of pupils are chosen; 3) the strategies schools are initiating to implement the project; 5) the ways in which baseline assessment is being used to inform this process; 6) the deployment of resources; 7) the evidence of appropriate activity being initiated in response to the needs of the project; 8) the progress being made in the development of appropriate recording, tracking and

monitoring systems; 9) the extent and effectiveness of support from the representatives of the Stoke-on-Trent LEA; and 10) the perceived outcomes of the strategies adopted to date. A final report is to be written on the findings.

STATUS: Sponsored project

SOURCE OF GRANT: Staffordshire Training and Enterprise Council £12,000

DATE OF RESEARCH: 1998-continuing

KEYWORDS: **core skills; educational improvement; key skills; secondary education; sixteen to nineteen education; skill development; skills; transfer of learning**

0943

Department of Education, Keele ST5 5BG
01782 621111

Parkhouse, P. Mr

Pupils changing attitudes towards secondary science

ABSTRACT: The work, initiated by the Successful Schools Project at Keele University, has been developed into a separate core subject study which is looking at secondary pupils' changing attitudes to Science as they move up through the school. It is well known that many children seem to be turned away from science during the Year 7-Year 11 period and it is hoped to unravel factors which may be contributing to this. A pilot phase has been followed by a large scale study of some 7,500 pupils aged 11-16 from 11 different schools. In this phase, a third of the pupils were randomly chosen to answer a science questionnaire, another third a mathematics one and the final third one on the school subject of English. All questionnaires had 60 questions, 40 of which were common to the 3 questionnaires and 20 were subject specific. A statistical analysis of the science specific questionnaire has been completed and will be ready for presentation for publication early in 1999. A presentation of results from the pilot and early interpretation of the main study is to be published in the Proceedings of the Association of Science Education Tutors. The main study included an opportunity for all the pupils to give free responses within a given framework and analysis of the 20,000 responses received is currently being undertaken.

STATUS: Sponsored project

SOURCE OF GRANT: Keele University

DATE OF RESEARCH: 1998-continuing

KEYWORDS: **pupil attitudes; science education; secondary education**

0944

Department of Education, Keele ST5 5BG
01782 621111

Parkhouse, P. Mr

Students' impressions of transition from university education department to school-based teaching practice

ABSTRACT: Work is in progress which has analysed Postgraduate Certificate in Education (PGCE) students' positive impressions of their transition from a university education department into the partnership with school-based teaching practice. School-based factors which positively help the continued development of the necessary teaching attributes are being looked for. In the first phase, weekly diaries were kept by the students learning to teach one of the three secondary school core subjects, viz. English, Mathematics and Science. The work is continuing for another year with a second science cohort. A second phase followed in which, at the end of their school experience in the training year, students reflected on the characteristics which had been most important in their initial training. A paper produced for the Association of Science Education Tutors is to be published in the Proceedings of the Association of Science Education Tutors. A paper comparing the experiences of students in training from the 3 core subjects of English, mathematics and science is to be published with co-author Tricia Evans early in 1999.

STATUS: Sponsored project

SOURCE OF GRANT: Keele University

DATE OF RESEARCH: 1998-continuing

KEYWORDS: **preservice teacher education; school based teacher education; student teacher attitudes; student teachers; teaching practice**

0945

Department of Education, Keele SL5 5BG
01782 621111

Alexiadou, N. Miss; *Supervisor*: Ozga, J. Prof.

Education governance and social integration and exclusion in Europe

ABSTRACT: New ways to govern education are necessary in order to obtain a more fair, sensitive and efficient educational system which is necessary in order to get a more developed society who will be able to fight exclusion. New ways to govern education will lead to increased segregation and decreased equity and equality in education as well as in society and will increase the amount of social exclusion. The aims of the project are to (1) review and analyse current research on education governance and social integration and exclusion among youth; (2) describe and analyse different national/regional systems of education in the context of educational traditions and governance strategies in different European countries; (3) describe and analyse the discourse on education governance in international organisations and the potential impact of this on national discourses; (4) analyse experiences of and strategies to deal with new governance structures in education among politicians and administrators as well as teachers and head-teachers in different European countries; (5) analyse national and international statistics on social integration and exclusion related to education; (6) describe and analyse implications of education governance for the social integration and exclusion of youth; (7) compare different national cases in Europe with a focus on relations between education governance and social integration and exclusion; and (8) inform and discuss results and conclusions of the studies with education actors in different contexts.

STATUS: Sponsored project

SOURCE OF GRANT: European Commission: Targeted Socio-economic Research, European Union £36,667

DATE OF RESEARCH: 1998-continuing

KEYWORDS: **comparative education; educational policy; equal education; europe; governance; social exclusion; social integration**

0946

Department of Education, Keele ST5 5BG
01782 621111

Pye, D Mr; *Supervisors*: Ozga, J. Prof.; Jones, K. Mr; Lawn, M. Dr

Education action zones

ABSTRACT: The issue that needs investigation is the Education Action Zones (EAZ) 'project': what it means for the future governance of education, how the public/private partnerships will work, and its potential as a model for 'third way' policy making. These are very large questions, and require work in this proposed pilot phase in order to refine them as topics for research, and to establish the feasibility of data collection in some areas. It is felt that these large issues should be researched, as it is in these areas that the EAZs are breaking new ground. Thus the ways in which they are established, and the ground rules they develop for effective operation, will rapidly become significant for policy-making across the education service, and possibly in other arenas. It can also be argued that, while their impact on educational effectiveness in terms of raising classroom performance will require careful evaluation, it is equally important to investigate their impact on the structures and processes of the education service, and on relationships within it. The aim is to: (1) test the feasibility and usefulness of data collection in the areas identified above; (2) have a research presence in the start-up phase in a reasonable sample of the 25 approved EAZs; (3) be closely involved from the beginning in two EAZs that the researchers intend to follow through from inception, namely Birmingham and Sheffield; and (4) keep up-to-date with rapidly changing developments.

STATUS: Sponsored project

SOURCE OF GRANT: Nuffield Foundation £8,053

DATE OF RESEARCH: 1998-continuing

KEYWORDS: **disadvantaged environment; education action zones; educational improvement; educational policy; school improvement**

0947

Department of Education, Keele ST5 5BG
01782 621111

Thomas, E. Dr; Jones, R. Mr; Spencer, P. Mrs; Johnson, M. Mr; *Supervisors*: Gleeson, D. Prof.; Jary, D. Prof.; Pike, C. Dr

Widening Participation Project - evaluation

ABSTRACT: This research is carried out on behalf of the Further Education Funding Council Staffordshire Strategic Partnership. The project's focus is upon the ways in which post16 providers in eight socially deprived areas of Staffordshire are seeking to provide greater access to education and extend the numbers of students engaging in study beyond the age of 16. The work involves the preparation, distribution and analysis of monthly diaries for completion by the community link workers who are to be the principal agents in putting into effect the work of the project. Case studies will be carried out in the post-16 institutions in each of the eight areas concerned and interviews will be conducted with link workers and their line managers. An evaluative report will be written on the findings.

STATUS: Sponsored project

SOURCE OF GRANT: FEFC (Further Education Funding Council) Staffordshire Strategic Partnership £10,000

DATE OF RESEARCH: 1998-continuing

KEYWORDS: **access to education; disadvantaged environment; further education; sixteen to nineteen education; widening participation**

0948

Department of Education, Keele ST5 5BG
01782 621111

Johnson, M. Mr; Gough, G. Dr; Graham, J. Mr; *Supervisor*: Maden, M. Prof.

Improving learning: the use and availability of books in schools

ABSTRACT: This research is carried out on behalf of the Educational Publishers Council. The project's focus is upon the provision of course and/or text books for use in class in secondary schools in England and Wales, and for use in extra-curricular and homework situations. Its purpose is to establish patterns of usage in different curriculum areas and to distinguish between the use and availability of text/course books in lessons and for the purposes of study outside the classroom and at home. From headteachers and subject leaders will be learned how the schools' resourcing and pedagogical policies impact on book availability and usage, and from parents will be gained a perception of the importance they attach to text/course books in respect of work that pupils do outside the classroom. The work involves the preparation, distribution and analysis of questionnaires to pupils, headteachers, subject leaders and parents in a random and representative sample of 50 schools selected by Office for Standards in Education (Ofsted) from their database, the collection and analysis of qualitative data from focus groups of pupils and teachers from the same schools, and a final report on the findings.

STATUS: Sponsored project

SOURCE OF GRANT: Educational Publishers Council

DATE OF RESEARCH: 1998-continuing

KEYWORDS: **books; educational materials; textbooks**

0949

Department of Education, Keele ST5 5BG
01782 621111

Supervisor: King, C. Mr

How well do science teachers understand the Earth science they teach? A case study of teacher understanding of the plate tectonics theory

ABSTRACT: Earth science has been a component of the National Science Curriculum in England and Wales for some 10 years and so teachers have generally had ample opportunity to develop their understanding of this 'new' component in their science teaching. A test sheet has been devised to test current misconceptions and understanding of the theory of plate tectonics, focusing particularly on the understanding of the evidence for plate tectonics. This instrument has been applied at a number of inservice teacher education (INSET) sessions, which have been attended by science teachers seeking to develop their understanding of plate tectonics. It will also be used on PGCE students from a variety of backgrounds to test their understanding and to provide a comparison with practising science teachers. Identification of the misconceptions and problems will allow the development of more effective INSET in the future.

STATUS: Individual research

DATE OF RESEARCH: 1998-continuing

KEYWORDS: earth science; science education; science teachers; subject knowledge

0950

Department of Education, Keele ST5 5BG
01782 621111
Cambridge University, Homerton College, Hills Road, Cambridge CB2 2PH
01223 507111

Maden, M. Prof.; Johnson, M. Mr; Rudduck, J. Prof.; Flutter, J. Ms; Doddington, C. Ms

Improving learning: the pupils' agenda

ABSTRACT: The Improving Learning Project is supported by the Nuffield Foundation and is being undertaken jointly by teams of researchers based at Cambridge and Keele. Recent research carried out by the two teams has highlighted a number of aspects of schooling where change could, according to pupils, make a difference to their engagement with learning and, ultimately, to their levels of achievement. There is growing evidence to suggest that pupils' agenda for school improvement are often different from those that are constructed by policymakers. For example, recent research in Australia looks at differences in the way that school principals, teachers, parents and pupils judge effective teaching and learning in schools. The study concludes that not all schools are responding to the perceived desires of pupils and suggests that schools build better opportunities for pupils to voice their concerns. The project aims to support both primary and secondary schools in enhancing pupils' achievement by documenting and disseminating examples of good practice in relation to three aspects: 1) Creating a positive learning culture: the researchers will look for schools which have changed pupils' attitudes to learning in significant ways, i.e. schools where there has been concern about pupils' motivation and engagement; where a strong anti-work culture has developed and been held in place by members of the peer group; and where teachers have managed to change that culture, legitimating a commitment to school work so that pupils no longer feel that working and talking about work is 'non-cool'. The strategies may have depended on developing a school-wide language of achievement (a 'can-do' culture), or a new system of support and/or rewards for effort as well as achievement. 2) Catching and keeping up: the researchers will look for schools which have decided to give attention to two issues: the issue of 'keeping up' for pupils who are finding learning a struggle in particular subjects; and the issue of 'catching up' for pupils who have missed work, whether an odd day or longer periods, whether through illness or choice. From earlier work it is known that pupils do not always understand the longer term significance of 'continuities' in learning and they may think that missing the odd lesson doesn't matter. Pupils may want to 'keep up' and 'catch up' but they do not always understand what is entailed, and some find it easier, in the end, to give up rather than catch up. It is also known that it is very time-consuming for teachers to give close individual support to such pupils and the researchers are interested in the strategies schools are developing to respond to these issues. 3) Pupils helping other pupils in their learning: the researchers want to identify schools that provide opportunities for pupils to support other pupils in their learning. This may be in relation to particular tasks, like paired reading schemes, or it may be in relation to other aspects of work. The strategy may even be used in some schools of designating particular pupils who are known to be good at a subject or topic to help pupils who have difficulty, or who have missed lessons (as in the second theme). The learning 'partnerships' may be long-term or short-term, they may involve older and younger pupils working together or pupils in the same year group; they may be about regular school work or they may be about homework (or 'extension' work). The Project also responds to the needs of teachers, expressed at meetings throughout the country, for studies that will help them to understand and take account of what pupils have to say about things that support their learning and things that get in the way of their learning. The methodology involves making contact with schools which are developing strategies in one (or more) of the three themes and which would be willing to provide us with some information about their work. Local education authorities will be asked if they know of schools which have been developing the strategies the researchers wish to study. Questionnaries to schools, followed by visits and interviews with teachers and pupils in selected schools, will form the basic approach.

STATUS: Sponsored project

SOURCE OF GRANT: Nuffield Foundation £9,892

DATE OF RESEARCH: 1998-continuing

KEYWORDS: educational quality; learning; organisational climate; peer teaching; pupil attitudes; pupil motivation; pupil participation; pupil performance; school effectiveness; school improvement

0951

Department of Education, Keele ST5 5BG
01782 621111
London University, Institute of Education, 20 Bedford Way, London WC1H 0AL
0171 580 1122

Jones, K. Mr; Gunther, K. Prof.; Buckingham, D. Dr; Kelley, P. Mr; Davies, H. Ms

Children's media culture: education, entertainment and the public sphere

ABSTRACT: This research project is looking at the ways in which children are targeted and defined as a specific audience for television and related media. It focuses specifically on the changing relationship between education and entertainment in children's media culture. The research combines three dimensions. First, it considers policy and professional practice in media production for children. This aspect of the project will be based on the historical analysis of policy documents, interviews with key media personnel, and case studies of the uses of audience research in the production process. Second, the research will analyse media texts - television programmes, magazines, computer games and so on - which are produced specifically for the child audience. This will include a quantitative survey of trends in television programming over the past 3 decades; and qualitative analysis of texts drawn from a similar historical range. Third, the research will consider how children themselves perceive and negotiate these definitions. This will combine an analysis of existing statistical data about the child audience, seeking to identify the distinctiveness and diversity of their uses of media; and qualitative research with children, using small-group interviews and activities.

PUBLISHED MATERIAL: JONES, K. (1996). 'Children's schooling and children's television'. Paper presented at the Symposium on Post-Conservative Education Policy, British Education Research Association Conference, Lancaster University, September 1996. ; JONES, K. (1997). 'Children's television in the 1950s: the BBC, competition and cultural change'. Paper presented at the Manchester Broadcasting Symposium, University of Manchester, April 1997. ; JONES, K. (1998). 'Children's television in the 1950s: the BBC, competition and cultural change'. In: RALPH, S., LEES, T. & LANGHAM-BROWN, J. (Eds). What price creativity? Luton: John Libby Media. ; JONES, K., BUCKINGHAM, D., DAVIES, H. & KELLEY, P. Children's television: history, discourse and practice. London: British Film Institute. (in press).

STATUS: Sponsored project

SOURCE OF GRANT: Economic and Social Research Council £160,000

DATE OF RESEARCH: 1996-1998

KEYWORDS: childhood interests; childrens literature; childrens television; comics - publications; computer games; mass media

0952

Department of Education, Keele ST5 5BG
01782 621111
Open University, School of Education, Walton Hall, Milton Keynes MK7 6AA
01908 274066

Ozga, J. Prof.

Elites in education policy making

ABSTRACT: The aim of the project was to explore the nature of policy making in education in England in the post-war period and to use that exploration as the basis for interrogation of major theoretical approaches to the study of policy making, especially pluralism and Marxism. A further aim was to ensure that the role of permanent officials in policy making was recorded and discussed, and to do this through the use of life history methods. The study was undertaken using a variety of methods, including documentary analysis, exploration of archives, and extended interviews with members of the policy elite. The identification of this group was a considerable part of the project, and included the tracing of connections among them. The interim conclusions of the project indicated the strong influence exerted on policy by permanent officials at the centre and in the localities, and indicated their interconnectedness and their adherence to particular forms of provision. This in turn suggested that some modification of conventional pluralist approaches to education policy making was necessary.

PUBLISHED MATERIAL: GEWIRTZ, S. & OZGA, J. (1990). 'Partnership, pluralism and education policy: a reassessment', Journal of Education Policy, Vol 5, No 1, pp.37-48. ; OZGA, J. (1990). 'Policy research and policy theory: a comment on Fitz and Halpin', Journal of Education Policy, Vol 5, No 4, pp.359-362. ; GEWIRTZ, S. & OZGA, J. (1994). 'Interviewing the education policy elite'. In: WALFORD, G. (Ed). Doing research on the powerful in education. London: University College London Press. ; OZGA, J. & GEWIRTZ, S. (1994). 'Sex, lies and audiotape'. In: HALPIN, D. & TROYNA, B. (Eds). Researching education policy: ethical and methodological issues. Basingstoke: Falmer Press.

STATUS: Sponsored project

SOURCE OF GRANT: Open University Research Committee £30,000

DATE OF RESEARCH: 1988-1997

KEYWORDS: **educational planning; educational policy; policy formation**

0953

Department of Psychology, Keele ST5 5BG
01782 621111

Afzalnia, M. Mr; *Supervisor*: Hartley, J. Prof.

Reading, listening and television viewing: a study in children's cognition

ABSTRACT: This research is concerned with the relationships between children's television viewing and their school performance with an emphasis on their reading, listening and viewing comprehension skills. Seventy eight 9-10 year olds were selected from a local school to take part. Tests of reading, intelligence and listening skills, together with questionnaires, were used to collect information about the children's abilities and their parents' and teachers' attitudes towards their reading and listening habits. While the results of the test studies supported the assumption that predicted that children's general reading and listening skills would relate to their viewing comprehension, the obtained data did not produce much support for the hypothesis that assumed a positive relationship between children's sensitivity to the audio channel of television and their verbal receptive achievements. The assumption that there would be a positive relationship between children's background variables and their reading, listening and viewing skills was mostly supported. However, the data indicated that some variables (such as library membership) were more important than the others. It was found that children with low achievements in reading and listening also had some difficulty with their overall cognition which was shown in their difficulty in general learning.

PUBLISHED MATERIAL: AFZALNIA, M.R. (1993). 'Television literacy and young children's promotion of mental health'. In: TRENT, D. (Ed). Promotion of mental health, Aldershot: Avebury. ; A full list of proposed publications is available from the researcher.

STATUS: Sponsored project

SOURCE OF GRANT: Government of Iran

DATE OF RESEARCH: 1988-1993

KEYWORDS: **academic achievement; cognitive ability; listening skills; reading achievement; television research; television viewing**

0954

Department of Psychology, Keele ST5 5BG
01782 621111

Hartley, J. Prof.

Designing instructional text

ABSTRACT: This research focuses on the design of instructional text mainly in the form of printed materials - which enables the reader to do or to understand something. The research covers three areas: (1) the layout of such materials; (2) the language of such materials; and (3) the use of structural devices which enable people to find their way about a piece of text. Work with layout stresses the importance of using the 'white-space'

systematically in order to convey the underlying structure of text. Work with language suggests the importance of simpler wording. Work with 'access structures' indicates how devices such as headings and summaries can aid recall. Recently the research has broadened its focus of interest to include work with braille, audio-taped instruction, and electronic text.

PUBLISHED MATERIAL: HARTLEY, J. (1990). 'Author, printer, reader, listener: four sources of confusion when listening to tabular/diagrammatic information', British Journal of Visual Impairment, Vol VIII, pp.51-53. ; HARTLEY, J. (Ed). (1992). Technology and writing: readings in the psychology of written communication. London: Jessica Kingsley Publishers.; HARTLEY, J. (1994). Designing instructional text. 3rd edition. London: Kogan Page. ; HARTLEY, J. (1994). 'Designing instructional text for older readers: a literature review', British Journal of Educational Technology, Vol 25, No 3, pp.172-188. ; HARTLEY, J. (1997). 'Applying psychology to text design: a case history', International Forum for Information and Documentation, Vol 22, No 1, pp.3-10.

STATUS: Individual research

DATE OF RESEARCH: 1970-continuing

KEYWORDS: **educational materials; educational media; low vision aids; printing; textbooks**

0955

Department of Psychology, Keele ST5 5BG
01782 621111

Loumidis, K. Mr; *Supervisor*: Hill, A. Dr

Social problem solving and learning disabilities (mental handicap): evaluation of a therapeutic training programme

ABSTRACT: There is evidence to suggest that Social Problem Solving Training can help people with learning disabilities (Loumidis, 1992). The study reported here had three parts. In the first part, 22 people with learning disabilities living at a residential hospital and 24 people who lived in the community were assessed to establish baseline measures of intellectual, adaptive and maladaptive functioning. Social problem solving skills were assessed on the basis of people's ability to solve hypothetical but personally relevant social and interpersonal problems. The responses obtained from this measure were rated on the basis of eleven scoring criteria, providing a rigorous and detailed analysis of people's abilities. During the second part of the study, 29 people were selected for training and these were assigned to two residential groups and two community groups, each group receiving an average of 15 hours of training. While maintaining the traditional components of social problem solving programmes, significant modifications in the process of training were required. The remaining 17 people of the sample formed two control groups. At the end of training the measures initially used to establish baseline performance were re-administered to obtain post treatment-scores. In the third part of the study the effects of training were assessed by comparing performance on the measures of problem solving and adaptive/maladaptive behaviour.

PUBLISHED MATERIAL: LOUMIDIS, K.S. (1992). 'Can "Social Problem Solving Training" help people with learning difficulties?'. In: TRENT, D.R. (Ed). The promotion of mental health: Volume 1. Aldershot: Avebury Press.; LOUMIDIS, K.S. (1992). 'Evaluating social problem solving groups for people with learning disabilities'. In: LOUMIDIS, K.S. (Chair): Cognitive behavioural approaches for people with learning disabilities. Symposium presented at the British Psychological Society Conference, London.

STATUS: Individual research

DATE OF RESEARCH: 1990-1993

KEYWORDS: **learning disabilities; life skills; problem solving; social skills; special educational needs**

0956

Department of Psychology, Keele ST5 5BG
01782 621111

Hartley, J. Prof.

Structured abstracts in the social sciences: presentation, readability and recall

ABSTRACT: The information explosion continues unabated. In education, as in other sectors, more and more learned articles are published every year.

Readers, researchers and users of information need assistance in finding out, quickly and easily, what information there is in their field and its relevance for them. This study investigates how the careful design of abstracts for articles published in the social sciences can improve information transfer and recall. The research examines how to write structured abstracts - popular in the medical literature - which contain subheadings, such as aims, methods, results and conclusions. It looks to see if such abstracts are easier to read, search and recall, and it looks at readers' preferences for the typographic settings of such abstracts.

PUBLISHED MATERIAL: HARTLEY, J. & SYDES, M. (1996). 'Which layout do you prefer? An analysis of readers' preferences for different typographic layouts of structured abstracts', Journal of Information Science, Vol 22, No 1, pp.27-37. ; HARTLEY, J., SYDES, M. & BLURTON, A. (1996). 'Obtaining information accurately and quickly: are structured abstracts more efficient?', Journal of Information Science, Vol 22, No 5, pp.349-356. ; HARTLEY, J. & SYDES, M. (1996). 'Are structured abstracts easier to read than traditional ones?', Journal of Research in Reading, Vol 20, No 2, pp.122-136. ; HARTLEY, J. (1997). 'Is it appropriate to use structured abstracts in social science journals?', Learned Publishing, Vol 10, No 4, pp.313-317.

STATUS: Individual research

DATE OF RESEARCH: 1994-continuing

KEYWORDS: abstracts; information sources; periodicals; writing for publication

0957

Department of Psychology, Keele ST5 5BG
01782 621111

Hudson, W. Ms; *Supervisors*: Cullen, C. Prof.; Hogg, J. Mr

Evaluation of the effectiveness of open learning training on sexual abuse in services for people with learning disabilities

ABSTRACT: Sexual abuse in services for people with learning disabilities is a major issue. This research will provide an open-learning training package and protocol, based on best available practice, and will evaluate its effects on staff in a range of health and social service settings.

STATUS: Sponsored project

SOURCE OF GRANT: Health Services and Public Health Research Board; Scottish Office, jointly £134,350

DATE OF RESEARCH: 1995-continuing

KEYWORDS: health services; learning disabilities; open education; sexual abuse; social services; staff development

0958

Department of Psychology, Keele ST5 5BG
01782 621111

Hawker, D. Mr; *Supervisor*: Boulton, M. Dr

An investigation of the effects of different types of bullying and low peer acceptance in junior and secondary school children

ABSTRACT: This project looks at the effects of different types of peer relationship problems on internalising difficulties in British schoolchildren. It is hypothesised that subordination will lead to depression, and that exclusion will lead to anxiety. A longitudinal series of quantitative interviews will be carried out with one hundred and seventy four children in three Year 4 classes (8-9 year olds) and three Year 7 classes (11-12 year olds). These interviews will record self-reported outcomes of depression (measured with the Children's Depression Inventory (CDI), anxiety (measured with the Revised Children's Manifest Anxiety Scale (RCMAS), and loneliness (measured on Asher and Wheeler's Loneliness and Social Dissatisfaction Questionnaire). These outcomes will also be predicted by clusters of measures related to exclusion and subordination. These measures include: self-reported and peer-reported bullying behaviour; peer-and self-reported sociometric profiles; peer-reported dominance hierarchies; and an adapted version of Gilbert's Social Comparison Rating Scale. Harter's Self-Perceived Competence Scale will be used to take into account the effects of low self-esteem on depression. Using a multiple regression model, results will be interpreted with respect to the previous work mentioned above.

STATUS: Individual research

DATE OF RESEARCH: 1993-continuing

KEYWORDS: anxiety; behaviour problems; bullying; depression - psychology; peer acceptance; peer relationship; primary education; primary school pupils; secondary education; secondary school pupils; self esteem

0959

Department of Psychology, Keele ST5 5BG
01782 621111

Supervisor: Hegarty, J. Dr

CASE: computer applications to special education

ABSTRACT: CASE is a unit to support users of microcomputers in special education, particularly those who work with adults who have severe learning difficulties. The work of the unit combines research, development of software and hardware devices, consultancy and staff training.

PUBLISHED MATERIAL: HEGARTY, J.R. (1991). Into the 1990's: the present and future of microcomputers for people with learning difficulties. Market Drayton: Change Publications. ; HARTVELD, A. & HEGARTY, J.R. (1996). 'Augmented feedback and physiotheraphy practice', Physiotherapy, Vol 82, No 8, pp.480-490.

STATUS: Sponsored project

SOURCE OF GRANT: Various public and charitable sources

DATE OF RESEARCH: 1985-continuing

KEYWORDS: computer system design; computer uses in education; information technology; learning disabilities; microcomputers; special educational needs

0960

Department of Psychology, Keele ST5 5BG
01782 621111

Trueman, M. Dr; Hartley, J. Prof.

The time management skills of university students

ABSTRACT: Time-management skills are thought to be important in the academic performance of university students. However, there has been little research into whether or not this is the case. At Keele University, a British version of Britton and Tesser's American time-management scale has been developed and used with the students. In the study, the students were divided into three age groups: traditional entry students aged less than 21 years (n=172); borderline mature students aged 21-25 (n=50); and older mature students aged more than 25 years (n=71). The analyses indicated: a) that women students in general reported significantly better time-management skills than did men students; and b) that the older mature students reported significantly better time-management skills than did the other two groups. Academic performance, however, was only modestly predicted by age and scores on one component of the time-management scale.

PUBLISHED MATERIAL: TRUEMAN, M. & HARTLEY, J. (1994). 'Measuring the time-management skills of university students'. Paper presented to the Society for Research in Higher Education Annual Conference, University of York, December, 1994. ; TRUEMAN, M. & HARTLEY, J. (1994). 'Time-management skills in traditional entry and mature students'. Paper presented to the London Conference of the British Psychological Society, December, 1994.

STATUS: Individual research

DATE OF RESEARCH: 1994-continuing

KEYWORDS: higher education; mature students; students; time management; universities

0961

Department of Psychology, Keele ST5 5BG
01782 621111

Hartley, J. Prof.; Trueman, M. Dr

Older learners at university: academic performance and study skills

ABSTRACT: This research concentrates on the academic performance and study skills of mature students. Three studies have been carried out. The first of these - using 'archival' data - compared the academic performance of 324 mature and 324 traditional-entry students at Keele, matched in terms of sex and subjects studied. The final year degree classes obtained by these

2 groups matched almost perfectly, and there were no significant differences between them. The second study compared the academic performance of 56 mature and 56 traditional-entry psychology students completing first-year modules in psychology at Keele. There were no significant differences in performance on essays and examinations, but the mature students had greater difficulties with writing laboratory reports in the first semester. However, this difference had disappeared by the end of the second semester. The third study examined the scores of 293 first-year psychology students at Keele on an Anglicised version of an American time-management scale. The students were divided into 3 groups: traditional-entry students - aged less than 21 years; borderline mature students - aged 21-25 years; and older mature students - aged more than 25 years. Analyses indicated: 1) that the women students in general reported significantly greater time-management skills than did men students; and 2) that the older mature students reported significantly better time-management skills than did the other 2 groups. Academic performance, however, was only modestly predicted by age and scores on one component of the time-management scale.

PUBLISHED MATERIAL: TRUEMAN, M. & HARTLEY, J. (1996). 'A comparison between the time-management skills and academic performance of mature and traditional-entry students', Higher Education, Vol 32, pp.199-215. ; HARTLEY, J. & TRUEMAN, M. (1997). 'What's the bottom line? how well do mature students do at university'. In: SUTHERLAND, P. (Ed). Adult learning: a reader. London: Kogan Page. ; HARTLEY, J., TRUEMAN, M. & LAPPING, C. 'The performance of mature and younger students at Keele University: an analysis of archival data', Journal of Access Studies. (in press).

STATUS: Team research

DATE OF RESEARCH: 1990-continuing

KEYWORDS: academic achievement; higher education; mature students; nontraditional students; performance; students; study skills; universities

0962

Department of Psychology, Keele ST5 5BG
01782 621111

Boulton, M. Dr; O'Neill, S. Ms

Links between children's participation in music and peer relationships

ABSTRACT: This investigation is examining the links between the type of musical instrument children choose to play and peers' perceptions of, and behaviour towards, them. Prior research had shown that many instruments are viewed as being appropriate for only one sex by adults (e.g. the flute is seen as a feminine instrument and the drum as a masculine instrument). That similar stereotypes exists for children was confirmed in Study 1. The researchers hypothesised that the gender stereotypes associated with specific musical instruments would influence participants' beliefs concerning the likely reactions of peers towards targets who played them. In line with this prediction, Study 2 showed that participants expected hypothetical targets who played what were generally expected to be 'gender-inappropriate' instruments. They would be treated more negatively by classmates (liked less and bullied more) than targets who played 'gender-appropriate' instruments. This result suggests that some children may eschew certain instruments in order to avoid negative peer reactions. Study 3 will extend this research by interviewing children about their own direct experiences of peer reactions that arose out of their involvement with specific musical instruments.

PUBLISHED MATERIAL: O'NEILL, S. & BOULTON, M.J. (1995). 'His 'n' hers? Is there a gender bias towards musical instruments', Music Journal, Vol 60, No 11, pp.358-359. ; O'NEILL, S. & BOULTON, M.J. 'Boys' and girls' preferences for musical instruments: a function of gender?', Psychology of Music. (in press).

STATUS: Individual research

DATE OF RESEARCH: 1994-1997

KEYWORDS: bullying; music; musical instruments; peer acceptance; peer relationship; sex differences; stereotypes

0963

Department of Psychology, Keele ST5 5BG
01782 621111

Boulton, M. Dr; Chau, C. Mr

Predicting children's feelings of loneliness, levels of depression, and school adjustment from friendship quality and levels of peer victimization

ABSTRACT: This study comprises a short-term longitudinal investigation of the concurrent and predictive links between 2 aspects of junior school children's relationships with peers (friendship quality and levels of victimization) and measures of their psychological adjustment (feelings of loneliness, depression and school adjustment). Phase 1 and phase 2 data will be collected at the start and end of a school year, respectively. Standardised measures of the variables of interest will be administered in individual interviews. Although the study will enable several theoretically driven hypotheses to be tested, one key prediction that will be assessed is that the negative effects of peer victimization will be attenuated for those children who have good quality friendships.

STATUS: Individual research

DATE OF RESEARCH: 1996-1998

KEYWORDS: depression - psychology; friendship; loneliness; peer relationship; primary education; primary school pupils; pupil adjustment; victimization

0964

Department of Psychology, Keele ST5 5BG
01782 621111

Hartley, J. Prof.

Learning and studying in higher education

ABSTRACT: The research spans many aspects of learning and studying in higher education over several years. Specific issues are listed in the publications below, and are brought together in the 1998 text. Of particular concern has been an interest in note-taking, academic writing, and mature students.

@#Published Material:#@ TRUEMAN, M. & HARTLEY, J. (1996). 'A comparison between the time-management skills and academic performance of mature and traditional-entry students', Higher Education, Vol 32, No 2, pp.199-215. ; HARTLEY, J. & TRUEMAN, M. (1997). 'What's the bottom line? How well do mature students do at university?'. In: SUTHERLAND, P. (Ed). Adult learning: a reader. London: Kogan Page. ; HARTLEY, J. (1998). Learning and studying: a research perspective. London: Routledge.; HARTLEY, J. 'Why shouldn't students write their own textbooks? A case-history in authentic learning'. In: VAN LAAR, D., RADFORD, J. & ROSE, D. (Eds). Innovations in teaching psychology. Birmingham: Staff and Educational Development Association (SEDA). (in press).

STATUS: Individual research

DATE OF RESEARCH: 1964-continuing

KEYWORDS: higher education; learning strategies; mature students; study skills; time management

0965

Department of Psychology, Keele ST5 5BG
01782 621111

Sloboda, J. Prof.; O'Neill, S. Dr; Boulton, M. Dr

Social and motivational factors influencing young people's participation and achievement in music

ABSTRACT: Music is one of the most important ways in which young people define and express their social identity. Parents, policymakers and providers of music services recognise that involving children and adolescents with music and music training has high value in terms of artistic experience, personal fulfilment, and educational development. It is, therefore, somewhat surprising to find that many young people who are offered opportunities to learn instruments either refuse them, or engage for a brief period before abandoning them. Systematic investigation of the socio-cultural barriers to acquisition of musical competence is in its infancy, and the proposed study aims to further our understanding of the reasons why many young people are not learning instruments, and, in particular, why those who begin to learn so often give up after a relatively short period. A piecemeal approach which considers isolated factors, which is characteristic of previous research in this area, is of limited value in capturing the complex processes and inter-relationships between the many factors that are likely to impinge upon children's decisions to take up, sustain, avoid or abandon musical activities. In the researcher's view, insufficient attention has been paid to the way in which young people's social and educational support may function as critical intervening factors between individuals' belief systems and their levels of musical participation. Thus, the researchers have proposed a multidimensional model that will enable them to test complex relationships. The project will begin with a large-scale survey of young people's attitudes towards, and involvement in, music. This will provide a broad picture of the current state of participation in music among young people aged 11-16. A one-year longitudinal interview study will then be carried out focusing on two important transition periods in young people's lives: a) the change between junior and secondary school as there is limited evidence to suggest that many children give up instruments following this transition; and b) during the latter part of secondary school when music is no longer a requirement of the National Curriculum and young people begin working towards GCSEs and other formal qualifications. Finally, the most detailed information will be obtained through a number of indepth case studies. The research will assess: a) whether an elevated drop-out rate exists during the two transition periods; b) the extent to which social and motivational factors influence young people's decisions to participate in or abandon musical study; and c) how young people actively construct their lives in relation to music.

STATUS: Sponsored project

SOURCE OF GRANT: Economic and Social Research Council £128,000

DATE OF RESEARCH: 1998-continuing

KEYWORDS: **achievement; adolescent attitudes; attitudes; motivation; music; music activities; participation; pupil attitudes; social influences; youth**

King Alfred's College of Higher Education

0966

Sparkford Road, Winchester SO22 4NR
01962 841515

Shillor, I. Ms; *Supervisors*: Reis, S. Prof.; Knight, D. Dr

Thought processes of mathematically gifted children

ABSTRACT: Children who are mathematically gifted seem to manifest different ways of thinking. This research aims to identify some of these thought processes, and relate them to a measure of giftedness, which is to be identified. The research is based on case studies, where children who have been identified as gifted are given a variety of tasks, and their responses recorded. At the moment some preliminary research is taking place, to identify the tasks suitable for this research. As a result it is hoped to create a bank of tasks in a variety of mathematical areas, which can be used for the main research. A number of the tasks identified so far have given rise to some very interesting work with children, which has been reported at a variety of conferences.

PUBLISHED MATERIAL: SHILLOR, I. & EGAN, B. (1993). 'Maths game: problem solving and mathematical activity', Educational Studies in Mathematics, Vol 24, No 3, pp.313-317.

STATUS: Individual research

DATE OF RESEARCH: 1993-1998

KEYWORDS: **cognitive processes; gifted; mathematical ability**

0967

Sparkford Road, Winchester SO22 4NR
01962 841515

Brown, W. Mr; *Supervisors*: Penny, A. Prof.; Wardle, W. Prof.

A critical study of the degree of match (and mismatch) between educational and business philosophies and needs within the proprietary school sector

ABSTRACT: The aims of the research are to: 1) undertake a critical analysis of business and educational philosophies in the proprietary school sector; 2) develop appropriate management models to address the needs of schools

in this sector; 3) evaluate the appropriateness of these models in a group of case study schools.

STATUS: Individual research

DATE OF RESEARCH: 1995-1997

KEYWORDS: **business philosophy; educational philosophy; management in education; private education; school based management**

0968

Sparkford Road, Winchester SO22 4NR
01962 841515

Scaife, M. Dr; Van Duuren, M. Dr

Children's representations of artificially intelligent devices

ABSTRACT: Artificially intelligent devices such as computers and robots are complex artefacts with an increasing presence in everyday life taking many different forms including media representations, general conversations and actual hands-on experience. Such devices can be viewed both from psychological and philosophical vantage points to be intriguingly positioned somewhere between more traditional inanimate objects and animate objects. Much of the child computer interaction literature however has focused on the how-to-benefit-best aspects of computer usage within specific domains of utility. Very little literature appears to exist on how children conceptualise 'smart machines' at a more general level. This research examines, from a developmental perspective, common-sense representations of computers and robots, not from the more limited perspective of a particular usage but rather by investigating how these devices have entered the conceptual worlds of children (aged from 5 to 12) and adults as 'encultured goods'. Three different methodological approaches formed the basis of an empirical programme which is presented in the form of 5 studies. In the first study a series of more spontaneously occurring representations of intelligent devices were investigated using a story writing exercise and role-play format. In the second and the third studies, subjects were asked to judge and justify whether a number of target objects, including a computer and a robot as well as more traditional inanimate objects, had a (sort of) brain and whether these objects were capable of accomplishing various brain related activities such as thinking and remembering. In the fourth and fifth studies subject were confronted with a computer and robot which had been made to behave counter-factually, similar to ways in which such devices are (mis)represented in the media. These (mis)representations included situations in which a computer/robot exhibited apparent abilities to sustain an everyday dialogue and situations where a robot was seemingly capable of autonomous movement. The findings from the different research approaches were in part compatible and in part complementary and were interpreted in the light of a domain-specific rather than a stage-general account of cognitive development. It was found that the generally opaque ways of funtioning of these devices, specifically the particularities arising from their programmed nature, often were not part of the representations of such devices, especially where the youngest children were concerned. It is suggested that even very young children may benefit considerably from engaging in philosphically orientated discussions in a classroom setting, resulting in an increased understanding of both natural and artificial intelligence.

PUBLISHED MATERIAL: VAN DUUREN, M.A. (1994). 'The use of intelligent technology at home and at school: what do parents think?', British Journal of Educational Technology, Vol 25, No 3, pp.231-233. ; VAN DUUREN, M.A. & SCAIFE, M. (1995). 'How do children represent intelligent technology?', European Journal of Psychology of Education, Vol 10, No 3, pp.289-301. ; SCAIFE, M. & VAN DUUREN, M.A. (1995). 'Do computers have brains? What children believe about intelligent artefacts', British Journal of Developmental Psychology, Vol 13, No 4, pp.367-377. ; VAN DUUREN, M. & SCAIFE, M. (1996). '"A robot's brain controls itself, because a brain hasn't got a brain, so it just controls itself" - young children's attributions of brain related behaviour to intelligent artefacts', European Journal of Psychology of Education, Vol 11, No 4, pp.365-376.

STATUS: Collaborative

DATE OF RESEARCH: 1990-continuing

KEYWORDS: **artificial intelligence; computer uses in education; computers; human computer interaction; information technology; pupil attitudes; robotics**

0969

Sparkford Road, Winchester SO22 4NR
01962 841515
University of Natal, Department of Education, Pietermaritzburg, South Africa 3201

Penny, A. Prof.; Wardle, W. Prof.; Harley, K. Prof.; Jessop, T. Ms

An investigation into the development of a collaborative approach to inservice teacher education in primary schools in Kwa-Zula Natal, South Africa

ABSTRACT: The study is investigating the development of a collaborative model of inservice teacher education (INSET) in Kwa-Zula Natal, South Africa. In Phase One, a critical analysis of the rationales underpinning traditional approaches to INSET in developing contexts is being undertaken. The potential for teacher biographies to inform models of INSET is being explored. In Phase Two, a refined narrative approach will be used to elicit teacher biographies, leading in Phase Three to the development of a programme of action-research based INSET.

STATUS: Collaborative

DATE OF RESEARCH: 1995-1998

KEYWORDS: developing countries; inservice teacher education; south africa; teacher development

Kingston University

0970

Faculty of Education, Kingston Hill Centre, Kingston Hill, Kingston upon Thames KT2 7LB
0181 547 2000

Cremin, M. Mr; Jones, S. Mr; Kearney, L. Ms

Investigating primary school children's use of the imagination in classroom drama

ABSTRACT: Assessing drama within the classroom has received some attention recently, but this has not included the central process of the imagination. There is a need to develop a language about the imagination arising from conceptual clarity, which has its roots in actual practice. This will enable teachers to assess the imagination and to develop teaching objectives and strategies, which deliberately address the imagination rather than the existing 'laissez-faire' expectation of its untutored development. A qualitative methodology has been used, using triangulation consisting of teachers, as participant observers, and also as critical commentators, as well as researchers from the wider community, through presentation and discussion of papers at research conferences. The pupils as participants in both action and reflection, as well as some of their parents, have given their assessment of the processes. All these discussions and comments have been placed within the context of accepted classroom drama practice and its underpinning theory. This theory has come from the arts, language, theatre practice, education, sociology and hermeneutics. The data has been collected from semi-structured interviews, audio and video-tape recordings of the children, as well as visual and written outcomes. These have been collected from a series of different lessons in several schools as part of the normal teaching programme for classes. The published outcomes to date are formative statements which consider the nature of the imagination, its processes, forms, functions and sources, as it is used in classroom drama. The significance of both the individuals' and social context are factors which are anticipated to be important variables to be investigated further.

PUBLISHED MATERIAL: CREMIN, M. & JONES, S. (1996). 'Some aspects of the imagination in classroom drama', Drama: The Journal of National Drama, Vol 4, No 3/Vol 5, No 1, pp.6-11. ; CREMIN, M. 'The imagination and originality in English and classroom drama', English in Education, Vol 32, No 2. (in press).; CREMIN, M. 'Identifying some imaginative processes in the drama work of primary school children as they use three different kinds of drama structures for learning', Research in Drama Education, Vol 3, No 2. (in press).

STATUS: Sponsored project

SOURCE OF GRANT: Kingston University £3,800

DATE OF RESEARCH: 1995-continuing

KEYWORDS: drama; imagination; primary education

0971

Faculty of Education, Kingston Hill Centre, Kingston Hill, Kingston upon Thames KT2 7LB
0181 547 2000

Gibson, M. Prof.

A history of Kingston University

ABSTRACT: The history traces the evolution of Kingston University from its beginnings in approximately 1870 to the present day in relationship to other local and national educational developments. It includes studies of its role as a Technical Institute, Technical College, College of Technology, Polytechnic and University. As Kingston University emerged from a series of mergers and recessions, the history of the constituent bodies, including Gipsy Hill Teacher Training College, the Kingston Art College, the College of Further Education, the Day Commercial School, the Junior and Secondary Technical Schools and the Junior Arts School are studied. An attempt has been made to place the institution within its politico-economic-social framework. The history will be published by Kingston University in the first instance.

STATUS: Sponsored project

SOURCE OF GRANT: Kingston University

DATE OF RESEARCH: 1996-1998

KEYWORDS: educational history; further education; higher education; universities

0972

Faculty of Education, Kingston Hill Centre, Kingston Hill, Kingston upon Thames KT2 7LB
0181 547 2000
Reading University, School of Education, Bulmershe Court, Woodlands Avenue, Earley, Reading RG6 1HY
01189 875123

Parker, Z. Ms; Supervisors: Lomax, P. Prof.; Denicolo, P. Dr

An action research approach to the experience of studying for a research degree

ABSTRACT: This doctoral study uses an educational action research perspective to explore the experience of studying for a research degree. A small number of central case studies look at the experience of doctoral study within two different institutions and within five different faculties of the one institution. The study aims to explore what it is like to do a PhD in different settings, using different research paradigms. Questions asked include: 1) What kind of learning is research? 2) How does doctoral research fit with the rest of one's life as a learner? 3) What kind of support do part-time researchers benefit from? 4) How can small-scale qualitative research capture the diverse experience of individuals studying for the same award? 5) How do research students fit into the culture of a new university? Using a variety of qualitative methods (including repertory grid technique, concept mapping, indepth loosely structured interviews, 'snake' technique) to build indepth case-studies, these questions are explored with the aim of improving supervision/support provision procedures in the future. Findings so far indicate the need for better provision of support for part-time students and for structures within institutions which recognise the diversity of needs and abilities of students pursuing doctoral study.

PUBLISHED MATERIAL: LOMAX, P. & PARKER, Z. 'Accounting for ourselves: the problematic of representing action research', Cambridge Journal of Education, Vol 25, No 3. (in press).

STATUS: Individual research

DATE OF RESEARCH: 1993-1997

KEYWORDS: doctoral degrees; graduate study; higher education; student research

0973

School of Humanities, Penrhyn Road, Kingston upon Thames KT1 2EE
0181 547 2000
Nene College of Higher Education, Park Campus, Boughton Green Road, Northampton NN2 7AL
01604 735500

Perkins, G. Ms; Supervisor: Griffin, G. Prof.

Issues of identity for contemporary women artists

ABSTRACT: A major focus of the PhD project was the impact of art education on women artists' self image and work. Over 40 professional women artists from the East Midlands Arts Register who had been in higher education (HE) fine art education after 1975 (introduction of degrees) and at least 3 years in practice since the completion of their degrees were interviewed. The results showed that fine art degrees offer women students very little by way of appropriate role models (few, if any, women artists are presented); little is done to encourage work across media (although most women work in general media); there are major biases in 'acceptable' themes in art which are majorly male-focused; virtually nothing is done to encourage knowledge of professional practice; and no account is taken in the perpetuation of the myth of the romantic artist image of women's students' lived reality. The thesis is a serious indictment of fine art education in HE as currently practised in Britain.

STATUS: Individual research

DATE OF RESEARCH: 1995-1998

KEYWORDS: **art education; fine arts; higher education; women**

Lancaster University

0974

Department of Educational Research, Cartmel College, Bailrigg, Lancaster LA1 4YW
01524 65201

Tinkler, P. Dr

Young women and leisure, 1920-1950

ABSTRACT: This research has two aims. Firstly it explores the structural and ideological context within which young women's leisure was situated in terms of the social and economic conditions in which girls grew up and the influences which young women were exposed to through the family, schooling, paid work, formal leisure provision, media and popular culture. Secondly, it aims to uncover the actual leisure practices of young women during the period 1920-50. The research is structured in two parts reflecting these dual aims. The first part of this research addresses the social, economic and ideological context of young women's leisure activity. It draws upon a range of sources including official documentation, academic and popular literature; census material and Board/Ministry of Education statistics; a range of data relating to the conditions of life of young women including that pertaining to schooling, paid work, housing and home conditions, health, courtship and sexuality. Three main themes structure this part of the research - access to leisure, the temporal dimensions of leisure, and the question of suitable leisure activity. The second part of the research explores young women's experience and understanding of leisure using oral history sources as well as autobiographies, diaries, contemporary studies and material from the Mass Observation Archive (Sussex University).

STATUS: Sponsored project

SOURCE OF GRANT: British Academy

DATE OF RESEARCH: 1990-1993

KEYWORDS: **girls; leisure time; recreational activities; womens studies**

0975

Department of Educational Research, Cartmel College, Bailrigg, Lancaster LA1 4YW
01524 65201

Rimmershaw, R. Dr

Collaborative writing

ABSTRACT: This is a study of the collaborative writing practices of writers in the academic community. The main focus is on why they are involved, how they manage the collaboration, and how they deal with issues of identity and power in collaborating. The sample comprises 20 academic writers from eight disciplines, and from undergraduate to professional status. The main source of data is indepth interviews. Additional sources used are observation and tape-recordings of collaborations in progress, and written reports by collaborators on the production of specific pieces of writing.

PUBLISHED MATERIAL: RIMMERSHAW, R.E. (1992). 'Collaborative writing practices and writing support technologies'. In: SHARPLES, M. (Ed). Computers and Writing: Issues and Implementations. Dordrecht: Kluwer Academic Publishers.

STATUS: Individual research

DATE OF RESEARCH: 1990-1993

KEYWORDS: **authors; cooperation; writing - composition**

0976

Department of Educational Research, Cartmel College, Bailrigg, Lancaster LA1 4YW
01524 65201

Serafingos, J. Mr; *Supervisor*: Rogers, C. Dr

Teachers planning and evaluation of mathematics in Greek high schools

ABSTRACT: This project is an examination of the ways in which a sample of Greek mathematics teachers think about their subject and their teaching, and how these understandings influence the kinds of experiences that are selected and presented to children in the mathematics curriculum. This is of particular interest in Greek education because of the high emphasis that is placed upon high school teachers' subject degree studies and the lack of any significant professional training for high school teaching.

STATUS: Sponsored project

SOURCE OF GRANT: Greek Ministry of Education scholarship

DATE OF RESEARCH: 1988-1993

KEYWORDS: **greece; mathematics education; mathematics teachers; teacher education**

0977

Department of Educational Research, Cartmel College, Bailrigg, Lancaster LA1 4YW
01524 65201

Fulton, O. Prof.

Enterprise in higher education: evaluation

ABSTRACT: This is a rolling evaluation of enterprise in higher education at Lancaster University. The first year investigated organisational and implementation issues, using interviews with staff. The second year focused on student experiences, using interviews with students. The third year looked at institutional diffusion and impact using staff and student interviews and student questionnaires.

STATUS: Sponsored project

SOURCE OF GRANT: Training, Enterprise and Education Directorate £35,000

DATE OF RESEARCH: 1988-1993

KEYWORDS: **enterprise in higher education; higher education; programme evaluation; work education relationship**

0978

Department of Educational Research, Cartmel College, Bailrigg, Lancaster LA1 4YW
01524 65201

Knight, P. Dr

A comparative study of outcomes and process in English higher education

ABSTRACT: This is a comparative study of the outcomes of higher education institutions and universities. Although there has been plentiful research into student learning in higher education, and consequent recommendations for effective teaching, it does not readily allow explanation of the performance of public sector institutions in the 1980s. In a decade where student expenditure has remained below that of the university sector (allowing for research funding), when public sector student numbers have burgeoned, and when staff-student ratios have become less favourable, the number and proportion of 2:1 and 1st class degrees have also grown on a sector-wide basis as compared to universities. The study attempts to find out why this should be. The focus is upon academic departments teaching the same subject. The usual forms of input and process data are to be collected, but close attention is being given also to the structure of courses; to observation of teaching; and to the assessment of student performance leading to degree classification. The working hypothesis is that there are general, distinct differences in the teaching/learning processes in the two sectors (university:public).

STATUS: Individual research

DATE OF RESEARCH: 1991-1993

KEYWORDS: college effectiveness; higher education; outcomes of education; universities and colleges

0979

Department of Educational Research, Cartmel College, Bailrigg, Lancaster LA1 4YW
01524 65201

Machell, J. Ms; *Supervisor*: Saunders, M. Dr

The reconstruction and transfer of learning: teaching for effective learning in higher education

ABSTRACT: 'Transfer of learning' is a much used but misused phrase. 'Transfer' represents a facile, inflexible and surface approach to learning which has limited use value. In contrast 'reconstructing learning' - applying previous learning creatively in new contexts - offers far more potential benefits and it is this ability, rather than simple transfer, which instructional strategies should aim to develop. The research will (1) identify the key differences between transfer and reconstruction; (2) establish connections between current educational concerns and reconstruction; (3) examine key theories of learning which contribute to an understanding of reconstruction; (4) explore the ways in which teaching in higher education facilitate reconstruction; (5) discuss the implications of reconstructions for teaching methods in higher education.

STATUS: Individual research

DATE OF RESEARCH: 1989-1993

KEYWORDS: higher education; prior learning; transfer of learning

0980

Department of Educational Research, Cartmel College, Bailrigg, Lancaster LA1 4YW
01524 65201

Rogers, C. Dr; *Supervisors*: Rogers, C. Dr; Galloway, D. Prof.

Learned helplessness and self-worth motivation in children with special educational needs

ABSTRACT: The project aims to identify: (1) the prevalence of the motivational styles of mastery orientation, self-worth motive and learned helplessness in pupils in two secondary schools and their feeder primary schools; (2) the degree to which the distribution of styles varies in children with special needs contrasted to whole populations; (3) changes in prevalence of style over time in a longitudinal sample; (4) changes in prevalence across year groups with cross-sectional samples; (5) differences between curriculum areas with regard to the prevalence of motivational styles; and (6) to examine the degree to which factors associated with school (e.g. school attended, teacher) influence the prevalence of each style. Theoretical developments by Weiner, Nicholls and Covington provide a general background to the research. The sample consists of all children in the final year of 12 primary schools who are followed into years seven and eight in two secondary schools. Further cross-sectional samples are obtained with pupils in years nine and eleven in the secondary schools. Information about motivational style is obtained from analysis of children's performance on curriculum related tasks in mathematics and English. Additional information is obtained from questionnaires completed by pupils and teachers. Pupil attainment data is used to identify children with special needs and also to allow comparisons between motivational style and achievement levels. A sub-sample of children have been interviewed. Data analysis has been, largely, completed. Initial results suggest increases in maladaptive motivational styles consequent upon transfer to secondary schools, and differences in proportion of pupils showing maladaptive styles as a function of the curriculum subject.

STATUS: Sponsored project

SOURCE OF GRANT: Economic and Social Research Council £84,280

DATE OF RESEARCH: 1991-1993

KEYWORDS: helplessness; motivation; self esteem; special educational needs

0981

Department of Educational Research, Cartmel College, Bailrigg, Lancaster LA1 4YW
01524 65201

Armstrong, D. Mr; *Supervisor*: Galloway, D. Prof.

The assessment and statementing of children with emotional and behavioural difficulties: child and parent perspectives

ABSTRACT: A sample of 29 children, who were being assessed under the Education Act 1981 because of emotional and behavioural difficulties, was identified for an indepth case study of the assessment procedures. The research focused in particular on the perspectives of the children and their parents. The research had 3 aims: (1) to examine the perspectives of children and their parents on the procedures for assessing special educational needs; (2) to describe and provide a theoretical account of the concept of emotional and behavioural difficulties informed by the perspectives of children and their parents; (3) to describe and provide a theoretical analysis of sources of conflict and agreement between clients and professionals and to consider the implications of these for conceptualisations of the client-professional relationship.

PUBLISHED MATERIAL: ARMSTRONG, D., GALLOWAY, D. & TOMLINSON, S. (1991). 'Decision-making in psychologists' professional interviews', Educational Psychology in Practice, Vol 7, No 2, pp.82-87. ; ARMSTRONG, D. & GALLOWAY, D. (1992). 'On being a client: conflicting persectives on assessment'. In: BOOTH, T., SWANN, W., MASTERSON, M. & POTTS, P. (Eds). Policies for diversity in education. London: Routledge/Open University. ; ARMSTRONG, D. & GALLOWAY, D. 'Who is the child psychologist's client? Responsibilities and Options for psychologists in educational settings', Association for Child Psychology and Psychiatry Newsletter. (forthcoming). ; Details of proposed publications are available from the researcher.

STATUS: Individual research

DATE OF RESEARCH: 1989-1993

KEYWORDS: emotional and behavioural difficulties; special educational needs; statements - special educational needs

0982

Department of Educational Research, Cartmel College, Bailrigg, Lancaster LA1 4YW
01524 65201

Ding, D. Mr; *Supervisor*: Fulton, O. Prof.

Enterprising higher education: links between higher education institutions and industrial, commercial sectors

ABSTRACT: As a comparative study, this research focuses on mapping out the main trends over the past decade of higher education institutions (HEIs) links with industrial and commercial sectors in Britain and China, examining the rationales and attempting to find appropriate models for each. Through interviews with a selective sample of personnel numbering nearly 60 in HEIs in both countries; together with documentation review, this qualitative study illustrates a diversified picture of the present links respectively, where some interesting similarities are found. Meanwhile, differences of the links are also paid attention and probed, as obvious gaps remain between the two nations' fundamental social structures as well as educational systems. In sum, the current linkage at all levels would, against resistance, continue to exist since there is a growing recognition that this link is not only a channel eventually generating funds for the much needed HEI pool, particularly in a time when its main, central funding sources are dwindling in real terms, but also a vitality which animates higher education progress. However, at present the links have formulated a challenge in both HE frameworks, since its behaviours are generally alien, unfamiliar to many, and still on a trial base. This controversy has inevitably confronted traditional ethos long established in higher education. Currently found issues show that unless some all-round strategies and policies are available and in effect, the links for some HEIs would cause quality problems and put the health of those linking institutions in jeopardy.

STATUS: Sponsored project

SOURCE OF GRANT: Overseas research studentship; Lancaster University studentship

DATE OF RESEARCH: 1989-1993

KEYWORDS: enterprise education; industry higher education relationship; institutes of higher education

0983

Department of Educational Research, Cartmel College, Bailrigg, Lancaster LA1 4YW
01524 65201

Nwaokolo, P. Mr; *Supervisor*: Saunders, M. Dr

Public construction of the status of teachers and teaching in Nigeria with special interest in vocational teachers: a case study of the Delta and Edo States of Nigeria

ABSTRACT: This study arose following complaints as evidenced in the literature about poor public image and poor status of teachers in Nigeria. Its aim is to ascertain the extent of the problem, explore its nature and why it exists, with a view to proffering suggestions for the solution of the problem. The enquiry was carried out as a case study of the Edo and Delta States of Nigeria between January 1991 and September 1992. A total of 171 teachers, student-teachers, educational administrators, business and public administrators, professionals, clerks/artisans and typical village peasant farmers were interviewed in 9 major towns of Edo and Delta States. A questionnaire was also administered on 150 subjects, mainly to teachers and student-teachers. Its principal aim was to locate the teacher and the teaching profession on an occupational prestige ladder. Secondly, it aimed at identifying the social standing of the vocational teacher among colleagues in the same secondary school system. Data on the subject matter was also generated through documents, and more unobtrusive means such as monitoring radio commentaries and casual discussion with members of the public. The data is now being analysed but it is already clear that the poor status of teachers in Nigeria is traceable to unattractive conditions of service such as poor pay; salary irregularity; the unhelpful attitude of civil servants implementing policies that favour teachers; poor working environment; presence of a large number of unqualified teachers in the system; poor promotion, denial and/or delayed fringe-benefits; and non-professionalisation of teaching. Other factors which are a consequence of the earlier ones include poor teacher dedication to duty and unimpressive appearance and attitude that portray teaching as synonymous with poverty.

STATUS: Sponsored project

SOURCE OF GRANT: European Community

DATE OF RESEARCH: 1990-1993

KEYWORDS: nigeria; professional recognition; status need; teacher attitudes; teachers; teaching profession

0984

Department of Educational Research, Cartmel College, Bailrigg, Lancaster LA1 4YW
01524 65201

McHugh, G. Mrs; *Supervisor*: Saunders, M. Dr

Evaluation of the Lancashire Licensed Teachers Scheme

ABSTRACT: This is a brief evaluation of the Lancashire Licensed Teachers Scheme which has been jointly delivered by Lancashire Local Education Authority and the two collaborating colleges of education, which has been running since September 1991.

STATUS: Sponsored project

SOURCE OF GRANT: Lancashire Local Education Authority £37,000

DATE OF RESEARCH: 1992-1993

KEYWORDS: licensed teachers; preservice teacher education; programme evaluation; teacher qualifications; teaching profession

0985

Department of Educational Research, Cartmel College, Bailrigg, Lancaster LA1 4YW
01524 65201

Sambili, H. Dr; *Supervisor*: Saunders, M. Dr

Do school based vocational programmes work? a case study of employment related experiences of Kenya's 8-4-4 graduates

ABSTRACT: Unemployment in Kenya was seen to be rising the fastest among school leavers; those most affected being from poor socio-economic backgrounds as they faced high parental expectations. The study sets out to investigate the employment related experiences of the first cohort of Kenya's recently adopted 8-4-4 vocationalised school curriculum. Three specific questions addressed were: (1) How did the value attribution tendency to their educational qualifications and experiences vary with time? (2) What were the relative roles of economic and cultural support factors (enabling factors) in the attempted application of the acquired functional skills by the school leavers? (3) What is the school leavers' perspective of the new system's potential in solving the unemployment problem? More than three hundred school leavers from a representative number of schools in one of Kenya's eight Provinces were contacted by postal questionnaires, using their home addresses (17 months after leaving school). Two hundred questionnaires were returned. Thirty four leavers were later interviewed (27 months after leaving school) in the field during the second phase of fieldwork. The conclusion of the research is that the new system was shown to be popular amongst most of the leavers but the application of any acquired skills was greatly constrained by the lack of economic and cultural support and that student behaviour is strongly influenced by socio-cultural factors such as the cultural stigmatisation against self-employment.

STATUS: Sponsored project

SOURCE OF GRANT: Kenyan Ministry of Education £30,000

DATE OF RESEARCH: 1990-1993

KEYWORDS: kenya; school leavers; school to work transition; unemployment; vocational education; youth employment

0986

Department of Educational Research, Cartmel College, Bailrigg, Lancaster LA1 4YW
01524 65201

Frank, F. Ms; Hamilton, M. Dr; McHugh, G. Mrs

Evaluation of European funded initiatives, at Knowsley Community College, Merseyside

ABSTRACT: This project is a rolling programme of evaluation for Knowsley Community College, covering European Community funded courses in progress at the College. Evaluation is formative and built into development of the courses so as to provide feedback at every stage. Methods include interviews, group discussions and questionnaires with students, tutors and management, collecting documentation of course outcomes and aims. The first phase of the project will be completed by the end of March 1994 and covers 4 courses - 2 Horizon courses, 1 new opportunities for women and 1 Euroform course. Approximately 50 students are covered by these courses.

STATUS: Sponsored project

SOURCE OF GRANT: Knowsley Community College £10,000

DATE OF RESEARCH: 1994-continuing

KEYWORDS: colleges of further education; community colleges; course evaluation; european union; international programmes

0987

Department of Educational Research, Cartmel College, Bailrigg, Lancaster LA1 4YW
01524 65201

Warin, J. Ms; *Supervisor*: Rogers, C. Dr

Gender self-typification and self-esteem

ABSTRACT: The entry into formal schooling at age five provides the context within which young children's developing sense of self-awareness will be developed. In relation to this, particular interest lies in the child's self-typification along gendered lines.

STATUS: Sponsored project

SOURCE OF GRANT: Economic and Social Research Council

DATE OF RESEARCH: 1991-1998

KEYWORDS: infant school pupils; reception classes; self concept; self esteem; sex differences; sexual identity; young children

0988

Department of Educational Research, Cartmel College, Bailrigg, Lancaster LA1 4YW
01524 65201

Ford, M. Mr; *Supervisor*: Rogers, C. Dr

Anxiety and learning styles

ABSTRACT: Interest in the assessment of anxiety levels in school pupils and its impact upon their learning strategies has waned over recent years, nevertheless, current changes in education systems suggest that the time is right for a re-examination of the ways in which these factors relate to each other. A variety of measures of anxiety and learning styles will be employed with an emphasis upon signs of compulsive behaviour.

STATUS: Individual research

DATE OF RESEARCH: 1992-1998

KEYWORDS: **anxiety; cognitive style; learning processes; pupil behaviour**

0989

Department of Educational Research, Cartmel College, Bailrigg, Lancaster LA1 4YW
01524 65201

O'Brien, R. Mr; *Supervisor*: Saunders, M. Dr

The learner and learning context within NVQs

ABSTRACT: The National Vocational Qualification (NVQ) movement in the UK really got underway in 1986 following the review of vocational qualifications by Oscar Deville. Subsequently, the National Council for Vocational Qualifications (NCVQ) was established with a remit to rationalise the post-16 qualification 'jungle' and to introduce a single qualification framework, based on five levels, that could incorporate all post-16 qualifications. Qualifications that are submitted (by awarding bodies) for inclusion within this new framework, have to be accredited by NCVQ. As part of the accreditation process, a qualification has to be based on the NCVQ notion of 'competence' and designed in such a way as to fulfil the criteria for acceptance. The qualification must also fall within the functional approach to the current view of competence based education and training. The number of voices critical of this movement has begun to rise. The Smithers report (SMITHERS, A. (1993). All our futures, Britain's education revolution: a Dispatches report. Manchester: Channel Four Television) focused national attention on the shortcomings of NVQs when compared with previous awards and existing European qualifications. Terry Hyland (1994) in 'Silk Purses and Sows Ears' indicates that the NVQ framework is "ill equipped to provide the necessary foundation for post-16 curriculum reform". Claire Callender in 'Will NVQs Work - Evidence from the Construction Industry' states that construction trainers believe NVQs are 'undermining' their professional and craft skills. Her conclusion also expressed concern that vocational training should not be at the expense of pedagogic concerns or based on limiting and narrowly defined competences. Are these criticisms justified, and are the identified concerns really to be found in the implementation of NVQs? This research will examine the theoretical underpinning to NVQs, its impact on pedagogic performance and the consequences for the experiences of learners. Research will be conducted through a literature review, and data collected using questionnaires and interviews with both lecturers and students in further education colleges.

STATUS: Individual research

DATE OF RESEARCH: 1994-continuing

KEYWORDS: **competency based education; national vocational qualifications; qualifications; vocational education**

0990

Department of Educational Research, Cartmel College, Bailrigg, Lancaster LA1 4YW
01524 65201

Jones, A. Dr; *Supervisor*: Smith, L. Dr

The reality and utility of learning styles

ABSTRACT: The subject of 'learning styles' has suffered a dramatic decline in popularity over recent years. Why? Is it worth reviving? If so, how? The first, and theoretical, part of this study addresses these questions in 2 ways. It emphasises one cause for its decline; that the overzealous production of quantifiable 'tests', and the almost lethargic attitude towards theoretical development, has left the domain fragmented, diluted, and unable to answer key questions concerning the underlying nature of style. Until recently, the many 'uses' of learning styles (i.e. the different uses) have either been ignored or categorised (on the basis of their suspect measures), leaving the construct with little established 'reality' or 'utility' for education and psychology. The second part suggests that in order to move beyond the present fragmentation and reliance upon doubtful measures, we need to return to a more exploratory approach, where the 'core' features of styles behaviours are examined in terms of the relationship with school performance and inter-relationships. It is argued that grounded theory is a useful methodology in this pursuit. The empirical part of the research uses the techniques associated with grounded theory to build a substantive theory of styles. The study mainly uses 90, 10-11 year olds, but some younger children may also be used.

STATUS: Individual research

DATE OF RESEARCH: 1994-1997

KEYWORDS: **cognitive style; learning processes; primary education**

0991

Department of Educational Research, Cartmel College, Bailrigg, Lancaster LA1 4YW
01524 65201

Soloman, Y. Dr; Lewis, C. Dr; Penn, R. Dr

Fathers, work and family life: the construction of paternal roles in families with teenagers

ABSTRACT: This project looks at a selection of families in Rochdale who participated in an Economic and Social Research Council (ESRC) funded project in 1987, and to add to the already existing data about fathers' domestic involvement in those families in the sample who now have teenage children. This means that this forms an instant longitudinal study which also includes information on the fathers' involvement in the families when the children were younger. The researchers are particularly interested in asking questions regarding the impact of employment patterns on these families: 1) What sort of domestic involvement unemployed fathers have when mothers go out to work? 2) What about dual earner households? 3) What does everybody in the family say about the sort of roles that fathers (and mothers) actually have and what they ought to have? 4) How do family members describe their relationships and do they see employment patterns as having an effect on these? 5) How do teenage children and their parents differ in terms of their views on fathers' actual and ideal roles? 6) How do teenage boys and girls perceive their own employment and parenting futures? Most of the data will be qualitative, but some will be survey-type data, as was the original ESRC data. The project will run for three years, with a possible extension to take in the extra dimension of a large number of families of Punjabi origin who participated in the original sample.

STATUS: Sponsored project

SOURCE OF GRANT: Joseph Rowntree Foundation £78,968

DATE OF RESEARCH: 1995-continuing

KEYWORDS: **adolescents; attitudes; employment; family life; fathers; parents**

0992

Department of Educational Research, Cartmel College, Bailrigg, Lancaster LA1 4YW
01524 65201

Johnson, A. Mr; *Supervisor*: Hamilton, M. Dr

Adult literacy and students with special needs

ABSTRACT: The aims of the research are to: 1) chart the change in the treatment of students with special needs in adult literacy classes; and 2) explain why this change is happening and what its implications are for adults with special needs.

PUBLISHED MATERIAL: JOHNSON, A. & BERGIN, S. (1994). Learning difficulties and the power of labelling in further education. Mendip Paper MP071. Blagdon: Staff College. ; JOHNSON, A. (1995). 'Learning difficulties and the power of labelling', Adults Learning, Vol 6, No 8, pp.

STATUS: Individual research

DATE OF RESEARCH: 1992-continuing

KEYWORDS: adult education; adult literacy; adult students; learning disabilities; literacy education; special educational needs

0993

Department of Educational Research, Cartmel College, Bailrigg, Lancaster LA1 4YW
01524 65201

Black, L. Ms; *Supervisor*: Solomon, Y. Dr

Ethnic education: differential processes of classroom communication

ABSTRACT: A substantial body of theory and research emphasises the role of communication in the transmission of social and cultural ideas, whereby skilled adults enable children to appropriate and use knowledge in a process of guided participation (Vygotsky 1978; Bruner 1985). Transferring this idea into the classroom suggests that effective communcation between teacher and pupil is an essential part of learning (Mercer 1995), particularly if it is to foster principled as opposed to ritual knowledge (Edwards and Mercer 1987). An examination of the classroom communication processes in which minority ethnic pupils take part may indicate problems of social integration and exclusion. Biggs and Edwards (1991) analysis of classroom communication strongly suggests that there are differences in teacher-pupil communication patterns involving Punjabi pupils and those involving white pupils, while Brah and Minhas (1988) found that there are widespread assumptions amongst teachers that Muslim and Sikh girls are more passive and make fewer demands on teachers than white children. The proposed research will consider the origins, processes and qualitative nature of differential communication patterns and their influence on pupils' understanding of lesson content and the perceptions of their teachers' expectations. Video-recordings of a single multi-ethnic classroom will be made, observing teacher-pupil interactions. Interviews with pupils and teachers will ascertain a more accurate interpretation of the observed data. The proposed research will both extend current theory on classroom interaction and provide an important insight into the teaching of minorty ethnic pupils which can be used in initial teacher training, inservice teacher training and curriculum design.

STATUS: Individual research

DATE OF RESEARCH: 1996-continuing

KEYWORDS: classroom communication; communication; comprehension; ethnic groups; teacher pupil relationship; teaching methods; verbal communication

0994

Department of Educational Research, Cartmel College, Bailrigg, Lancaster LA1 4YW
01524 65201

Smith, L. Dr

Reasoning by recurrence in children's arithmetic

ABSTRACT: The ability to count is an important accomplishment of early childhood. Another important ability is reasoning by recurrence, which requires the realisation that any number has a successor N+1 in the same number series. This research will investigate reasoning by recurrence in children's arithmetic. One objective is to replicate a pioneering study due to Inhelder and Piaget (1963). A second is to adapt their design with 3 specific controls: one is relevant to children's ability to count; a second concerns children's ability to make deductive inferences; a third concerns children's knowledge of necessity in mathematical reasoning. These objectives will be investigated in 2 studies in which both quantitative and qualitative evidence will be collected. The findings will be discussed with special attention to: the claim made by Inhelder and Piaget (1963) that reasoning precedes mathematical deduction; whether reasoning by recurrence is deductive, argued, or non-deductive; providing better evidence for the development of necessary (or modal) knowledge; National Curriculum mathematics (School Curriculum and Assessment Authority (SCAA) 1994) and baseline assessment (SCAA 1996) and the tighter specification of the contribution of counting and reasoning in this part of the curriculum up to key stage 1.

STATUS: Sponsored project

SOURCE OF GRANT: Leverhulme Trust £14,000

DATE OF RESEARCH: 1998-1998

KEYWORDS: arithmetic; key stage 1; mathematics education; primary education; reasoning

0995

Department of Educational Research, Cartmel College, Bailrigg, Lancaster LA1 4YW
01524 65201

Quinn, J. Ms; *Supervisors*: Deem, R. Prof.; Skeggs, B. Dr

Marginalised in the mainstream? Women students in higher education

ABSTRACT: The research examines whether, in the light of the mass entry of women students into higher education (HE) and the growth of women's studies, the mainstream higher education curriculum is now 'women friendly'. It focuses on 3 inter-disciplinary subjects and conducts a case study of 3 HE institutions. Existing research on women students focuses on specific groups such as women returners. Curriculum concerns focus on courses designed by women, or on women in non-traditional areas. The debate which saw women's studies as an attack on the 'malestream' has not been developed in terms of how the mainstream curriculum in HE should change. Existing research on the implications of gender and subject choice focuses on traditional subjects, and the intersection between gender, race, sexuality or disability is not explored. This research looks at women students in the mainstream and explores their experience and diversity and how the curriculum impacts on them. The research methodology is feminist and qualitative, paying attention to reflexivity, power, paradox and contradiction. 9 focus groups will be conducted in 1998 with first year students, followed by interviews with 45 students in their second year (1999). These students will be asked to write diaries for a month before interview. Some seminar observation and examination of course material will take place, plus interviews with staff. Results will be written up in 1999/2000.

STATUS: Individual research

DATE OF RESEARCH: 1997-continuing

KEYWORDS: higher education; students; women; womens education

0996

Department of Educational Research, Cartmel College, Bailrigg, Lancaster LA1 4YW
01524 65201

Deem, R. Prof.

What factors influence the supposed underachievement of secondary school age boys?

ABSTRACT: This research hopes to investigate issues surrounding boys' underachievement at GCSE level, with particular reference to class. Behavioural and disciplinary problems may affect boys' development and are possibly related to their images of masculinity. Willis (1977) examined the effect of social factors on working class boys' schooling, but little work has been carried out covering the aspirations of middle class boys, and their perception of schooling and education. The researcher hopes to use action research/focus groups on 3 groups of 10 boys in different schools between Years 9 and 11, with a mixed group to serve as a control group. The aim is to follow each group through an academic year monitoring changes in attitudes, motivation, self-awareness (esteem/ego), and also to interview these boys with their parents. It is hoped that teachers will also be interviewed. The project intends to draw attention to the underlying causes of inequality in examination results and where real problems are identified, to give recommendations as to potential improvements in policy and/or the National Curriculum/teacher training. It would serve to illustrate the inhomogenity of the major groupings of pupils with the intention of further guiding policymakings in avoidance of generalisation

STATUS: Sponsored project

SOURCE OF GRANT: Economic and Social Research Council

DATE OF RESEARCH: 1997-continuing

KEYWORDS: academic achievement; achievement; boys; masculinity; motivation; pupil attitudes; secondary education; self concept; self esteem; sex differences; underachievement

0997

Department of Educational Research, Cartmel College, Bailrigg, Lancaster LA1 4YW
01524 65201

Steeples, C. Mrs; *Supervisors*: Goodyear, P. Prof.; Parkes, A. Dr

Voice annotations for collaborative distance learning and reflections on practice in networked learning environments

ABSTRACT: The advances made in the power and multimedia capabilities of personal computers alongside their use in supporting distributed forms of human-human communication have been exponential in recent years. In particular, the uses and perceived value of networked computer-based learning environments in the field of education have seen dramatic growth over the last 5 years. All areas of education, not only formal areas such as schools, post-compulsory and higher education, but also less formal work-based and professional development learning, offer important application areas for networked communications technologies. This research fits within this context of networked learning (or computer-mediated learning environments) for professional development learning. The specific focus is using stored voice annotations (voice messages) within computer-mediated learning environments for supporting collaborative processes. This includes the sharing of multiple viewpoints among distributed adult learners. The researcher is interested, in specific ways, in whether the annotations help learners with collaborative tasks, and their role in learners' subsequent learning and professional development from taking part in the task. Voice annotations will be used to help learners refine their own views, and from this to assess whether the annotations help them in learning from the collaborative process, in reflective activities particularly about practice. From the research, informed suggestions will be made for the future design of networked environments, used for collaborative learning tasks and for reflective activity. Most importantly the researcher will be able to comment in particular on the applicability of voice annotations.

STATUS: Individual research

DATE OF RESEARCH: 1992-continuing

KEYWORDS: **computer networks; computer uses in education; cooperative learning; distance education; information technology; multimedia**

0998

Department of Educational Research, Cartmel College, Bailrigg, Lancaster LA1 4YW
01524 65201

Steeples, C. Mrs

Voice annotation of multimedia artefacts: reflective learning on group practice

ABSTRACT: This project is situated within the multidisciplinary field of networked multimedia learning systems. It further concerns the domain of professional learning. It is concerned with how multimedia communication technologies (especially using digital auditory information) can support reflective learning by professionals, that follows their participation in group-based tasks. It will do this by analysing the uses made and the support given to collaborating practitioners from stored voice annotations. The annotations will allow participants to give explanation and to create elaborations upon multimedia artefacts. The artefacts will include video clips that represent critical incidents from participants' actions and decisions when engaged in collaborative problem-solving tasks (e.g. in design tasks). As the multimedia artefacts are reviewed by participants, the project will look critically at the value of the attached voice annotations, to both speakers and to listeners for reflective learning. This project will contribute to research on learning in online, distributed multimedia group-based systems. In particular it will report on the pedagogical value of persistent representations of practice (the elaborated multimedia artefacts). It will add to knowledge about reflective learning: on group-based cognitive and communication processes. Dissemination activities will include sharing the research-based accounts (e.g. in publications and in workshops) of effective learning support with multimedia resources. The project will also make recommendations for the design of future online learning systems in which learners elaborate and reflect upon their practice (and the knowledge tied to that practice). This is highly applicable to a wide range of professional practitioner communities such as professional learning in medicine or teaching.

STATUS: Sponsored project

SOURCE OF GRANT: Economic and Social Research Council £19,000
DATE OF RESEARCH: 1998-continuing

KEYWORDS: **computer uses in education; cooperative learning; information technology; multimedia; professional development; reflection**

0999

Department of Educational Research, Cartmel College, Bailrigg, Lancaster LA1 4YW
01524 65201

O'Donoghue, M. Mr; *Supervisor*: Goodyear, P. Prof.

Children, learning and electronic mail

ABSTRACT: The use of electronic mail and online communication as a learning tool has been the subject of a number of studies and nationally funded projects in the UK over the last 10 years. Electronic mail project work has been applied to almost every school curriculum subject area at every phase of compulsory education with various outcomes and degrees of success indicated by project managers, evaluators and coordinators. With rare exception, reports and evaluations conclude with details of how to plan and develop e-mail project work in schools following questionnaires, interviews and case studies. They also provide links to National Curriculum targets, and suggest what children and staff participating in similar project work can expect to gain in terms of knowledge, awareness or skills development. This thesis examines a number of the resulting claims from previous studies, and explores how the ideas, concepts and understanding children bring to electronic mail curriculum project work are developed by participation, experience and involvement, sometimes resulting in a number of misconceptions and misunderstandings which can pass undetected by project coordinators or classroom teachers. Comparison to related studies on children's misconceptions in other subject areas are made. Background and discussion on qualitative, quantitative and phenomenographic research methodologies in this work are provided, and details and reference to learning theory surrounding schemata are also included and brought into discussion. Following a summary and researcher reflection on the ideas and materials presented from the research findings, the thesis concludes with recommendations and issues for those concerned with developing learning, using electronic mail project work and outlines areas for further research and examination.

STATUS: Individual research

DATE OF RESEARCH: 1993-1998

KEYWORDS: **computer uses in education; electronic mail; information technology; learning activities**

1000

Department of Educational Research, Cartmel College, Bailrigg, Lancaster LA1 4YW
01524

Deem, R. Prof.; Fulton, O. Prof.; Reed, M. Prof.; Watson, S. Prof.

'New managerialism' and the management of UK universities

ABSTRACT: The research aims to explore the extent to which recent theories about 'new managerialism' in public sector organisations are borne out by an analysis of current perceptions of and narratives about management, organisational forms and management practices/mechanisms in UK universities, in the light of the many changes made to higher education in the last two decades. The research objectives are four-fold: to acquire new knowledge about how university academic managers perceive current/recent university management and to develop theories about 'new managerialism' which are consistent with these perceptions; to describe and explain some current organisational forms of universities in a number of case study institutions; to demonstrate the range of management practices and mechanisms currently found in different UK higher education institutions; to use our analysis of the data collected to improve our understanding of the most effective ways in which universities with different missions may be organised and managed to make a contribution to future policy on the selection and training of higher education academic managers (e.g. vice chancellors, pro-vice chancellors, deans, heads of departments). It will then move on to indepth interviews with a range of academic managers and those they manage in 12 universities. Finally, 4 universities with contrasting missions will be selected for more intensive study of their management, organisational forms and cultures, using observation, documentary analysis, focus groups and interviews.

STATUS: Sponsored project

SOURCE OF GRANT: Economic and Social Research Council £120,000

DATE OF RESEARCH: 1998-continuing

KEYWORDS: educational administration; higher education; management; management in education; universities

1001

Department of Educational Research, Cartmel College, Bailrigg, Lancaster LA1 4YW
01524 65201

Tyler, C. Ms; *Supervisor*: Reynolds, J. Mr

Key skills in realisation of key skills policy: a study in curriculum design, negotiation and implementation in further education

ABSTRACT: This study will relate current management and professional activities associated with key skills in further education (FE) to past and present policy. The research will trace the development of core/key skills over the past 20 years and will analyse the influence of national policy related to core skills to the way in which the further education curriculum has been designed and delivered. Having established the position of core/key skills with respect to the current development of teaching and learning in FE, it will use a case study approach to demonstrate current practice in one college. From this, some conclusions on the effectiveness of a whole college approach to key skills and its wider implications for curriculum design will be drawn and other issues will be analysed as they emerge. The aim of this study is to produce a clear picture of successful practice in a further education setting, and to identify less successful approaches, thus informing future plans for curriculum development. It is intended that this research will contribute to STENHURST, L. (1979). 'A theory of education and training which is accessible to other teachers', What is Action Research?

STATUS: Individual research

DATE OF RESEARCH: 1995-continuing

KEYWORDS: core skills; further education; key skills; skill development; skills

1002

Department of Educational Research, Cartmel College, Bailrigg, Lancaster LA1 4YW
01524 65201

Wang, S-Y. Mr; *Supervisor*: Saunders, M. Dr

The role of science teacher and teaching in national development: a case study of Taiwan

ABSTRACT: Since 1946 the importance of teaching science has been the object of curricular emphasis in Taiwan. One of the main objectives for the stress on science education is the hope that one day Taiwan will catch up with the world's advanced levels. Yet in the reality of science classrooms in Taiwanese junior high schools, whole class lecturing is the most common scene. It is shown that science teachers care more about how to teach all the contents in a required period of time, than how to make their pupils understand. This was blamed for hampering the curricular demand and for rigidifing pupils' cognitive development. This study intends to investigate the factors that make Taiwanese science teachers teach in this way. It aims to address what changes are necessary to modify current training programmes for Taiwanese science teachers. Documentary survey and interview were the main research instruments. Semi-structured interviews triangulated with field notes were conducted in Taiwan. The subjects were from different institutions across the island - 80 science teachers; 12 managerial personnel; 15 teacher training educators; and 7 members of the council on education reform. Data was analysed with qualitative methods and supplemented with quantitative methods. The characteristics of 'passivity' were found in Taiwanese science teaching. The 'authority adoration' culture, combining central controlled educational systems, were found to have helped shape these science teachers teaching in captive states.

PUBLISHED MATERIAL: WANG, S-Y. (1995). 'Seeking a remedy: a critique of training programme for science teachers in Taiwan'. Paper presented at the International Conference on Problem-based Learning in Higher Education, Linkoping, Sweden, 24-27 September 1995. ; WANG, S-Y. (1997). 'On considerations of Taiwan's educational problems', Taiwan Church News Express, 2 November 1997, p.16. (in Chinese).

STATUS: Individual research

DATE OF RESEARCH: 1994-1998

KEYWORDS: science education; taiwan

1003

Department of Educational Research, Cartmel College, Bailrigg, Lancaster LA1 4YW
01524 65201

Frank, F. Ms; Hamilton, M. Dr

Impact of European partnership on workplace basic skills projects

ABSTRACT: This is a collaborative project between the University of Lancaster; Derbyshire Community Education Department; University of Amsterdam; Comite de Liaison d'Associations en Mediterranee, France; Par Azur Immeuble 'Le Pingouin', France; Kek Kronos Ltd, Greece; and Centre for Working Life Research and Development, Halmstad University, Sweden. This research is linked to a Leonardo funded project which brings together workplace basic skills providers in 5 European countries. Several of the project partners are members of other European project partnerships. The aim of the research is to evaluate the impact of the project partnership itself on the ongoing work of each partner. The design and scope of the project is that each partner institution is to be involved in the design of evaluation instruments and data collection methods at the project's first full partner meeting in May 1998. These could be in the form of: responding monthly to a series of evaluation indicators charting impact of the partnership on their work; reflective diaries; video and other evidence; data to be collected by correspondence, by telephone and personal interview, and by examination of other types of evidence submitted by partners. At least 7 of the 13 project partners will be included in the survey. The results will be published in the form of a report comparing the impact of the partnership on the different partners. The conclusions will be brought out of the data and will be relevant for other institutions embarking on European collaborations.

STATUS: Sponsored project

SOURCE OF GRANT: European Commission (Leonardo) £100,000

DATE OF RESEARCH: 1998-continuing

KEYWORDS: basic skills; cooperative programmes; europe; international educational exchange; literacy; partnerships; work based learning

1004

Department of Educational Research, Centre for the Study of Education and Training, Cartmel College, Bailrigg, Lancaster LA1 4YW
01524 65201

Davies, H. Ms; *SUPERVISOR*: Saunders, M. Dr

Restructuring further education: a case study in cultural realignment

ABSTRACT: This is a case study of large further education colleges faced with incorporation. The research includes: 1) participant observation and discourse analysis; 2) considering different levels of analysis - at political, organisational, and practice levels; and 3) looking at the imposition of an emergent/dominant culture, and resistance.

STATUS: Individual research

DATE OF RESEARCH: 1993-1998

KEYWORDS: colleges of further education; educational administration; further education

1005

Department of Educational Research, Centre for the Study of Education and Training, Cartmel College, Bailrigg, Lancaster LA1 4YW
01524 65201

Frank, F. Ms

Developing good practice in Employee Development Schemes

ABSTRACT: This research aims to: 1) encourage the inclusion of basic skills training within existing and new Employee Development (ED) Schemes; and 2) set up 3 pilot projects integrating basic skills training within different types of ED scheme, building on and strengthening existing networks between workplace basic skills training providers and other actors involved in employee development schemes. Accredited staff development activities for basic skills professionals will be run to raise awareness of issues around workplace needs and changing priorities, including the role of employee development schemes. Information learned from the pilot projects and the experience of the consultancy will be disseminated to a wide audience with the view to setting the pilots up as a self-managing model.

STATUS: Sponsored project

SOURCE OF GRANT: Department for Education and Employment £17,000

DATE OF RESEARCH: 1996-1998

KEYWORDS: **adult basic education; basic skills; employee development schemes; employees; on the job training; staff development**

1006

Department of Educational Research, Centre for the Study of Education and Training, Cartmel College, Bailrigg, Lancaster LA1 4YW
01524 65201

Fulton, O. Prof.

Governmental policies and programmes for strengthening the relationship beween higher education institutions and the economy

ABSTRACT: This is a collaborative project between the University of Lancaster; University of Twente, the Netherlands; Institut fur Interdisziplinaire Forschung und Fortbildung, Austria; Katholieke Universiteit Leuven, Belgium; University of Joensuy, Finland; A.F. Forum, Rome; Norwegian Institute for Studies in Research and Higher Education, Norway; and Universidade do Porto, Portugal. The background to this project is the question: 'What are the main factors that have determined the success or failure of recent governmental attempts at the national or supranational level to strengthen the relationship between higher education institutions and the economy, nationally as well as internationally? This project will examine, at institutional level, the effects of governmental attempts on strengthening the relationship between higher education institutions and the economy in 8 countries. The theoretical framework to guide the national studies, the institutional case studies and the comparative analysis is based on theories and approaches derived from the neo-institutional, the resource dependence and innovation literature, as well as literature on governmental steering model and policy implementation. For examining comparatively the basic conceptualisations included in the framework, 3 analytical categories are distinguished: the intensity of market orientation of higher education institutions; the relevance of society orientation of higher education curricula; and the level of international orientation of higher education institutions. The basic assumption is that governmental policies and programmes for strengthening the relationship between higher education and economy, in order to be successful, should have an effect on higher education institutions in such a way that the market orientation of universities and colleges will be enlarged. In other words, success and failure of governmental policies and programmes at the national and supranational (European) level is dependent on the conversion of these policies and programmes by the institutions for higher education. Consequently, the conversion processes within the institutions for higher education will be examined in detail in all the 8 country reports.

STATUS: Sponsored project

SOURCE OF GRANT: European Commission, DGXII Targeted Socio-Economic Research Initiative £138,670

DATE OF RESEARCH: 1997-continuing

KEYWORDS: **comparative education; economics education relationship; educational policy; government intervention; higher education; universities**

1007

Department of Educational Research, Cartmel College, Bailrigg, Lancaster LA1 4YW
01524 65201
Liverpool University, Department of Occupational Therapy, Brownlow Hill, Liverpool L69 3GB
0151 794 2000

Martin, J. Mrs; *Supervisor*: Saunders, M. Dr

The rhetoric and practice of interprofessional education in health care

ABSTRACT: In health-care education the current discourse revolves around promoting inter-professional shared learning as key politicians, employers, practitioners and educationalists believe it is the panacea for solving some of the problems abounding in the UK health service. Changes have been taking place in the last decade to remove some of the barriers and to establish the infrastructure in higher education to facilitate opportunities for interprofessional health-care education at registration level. The University of Liverpool provides an ideal context to study the implementation of such educational reforms from the perspectives of one of the key stakeholders: the students (undergraduates). A qualitative research design has been chosen for this small-scale study to: 1) identify current discourse for interprofessional health-care education in the Faculty of Medicine; 2) obtain evidence of actual practice of interprofessional learning; 3) determine factors which promote or inhibit the reconstruction of policy into practice. A case study approach will be used in the investigation and data will be collected through: 1) documentation analysis - course succession documents, policy papers, minutes of meetings, curriculum guidelines and assessment forms; 2) 8 focus groups - 4 with first year students and 4 with third year students of 4 professional groups: doctors, nurses, occupational therapists, physiotherapists; 3) observation of 4 students (1 from each of 4 professional groups) during a working day in a clinical learning environment; 4) individual interview with these students at the end of observation. Data will be analysed thematically and compared with implementation theory for educational change.

STATUS: Individual research

DATE OF RESEARCH: 1997-continuing

KEYWORDS: **health personnel; interprofessional education; nurses; occupational therapists; physical therapists; physicians; professional education**

1008

Department of Educational Research, Cartmel College, Bailrigg, Lancaster LA1 4YW
01524 65201
Oxford Brookes University, School of Education, Wheatley Campus, Wheatley, Oxford OX33 1HX
01865 485930

Gaunt, D. Ms; *Supervisors*: Fulton, O. Prof.; Saunders, M. Dr

Continuing professional development provision in universities

ABSTRACT: Continuing professional development (CPD) provision is experiencing the fastest growth across all higher education. The majority of students on these programmes are part-time. Very little research has been undertaken on how well universities provide for them. An analysis of Higher Education Statistics Agency (HESA) figures will estimate the size and characteristics of the population in English higher education institutions. A measure of continuing professional development activity in one new university (Oxford Brookes) followed by questionnaire to a sample of CPD students at Oxford Brookes and interviews with heads of registry, finance, learning resources, student services, catering, site management and the vice-chancellor, will form the basis of a case study.

STATUS: Individual research

DATE OF RESEARCH: 1995-continuing

KEYWORDS: **higher education; professional continuing education; universities**

1009

Department of Educational Research, Cartmel College, Bailrigg, Lancaster LA1 4YW
01524 65201
Reading University, Faculty of Education and Community Studies, Department of Education Studies and Management, Bulmershe Court, Earley, Reading RG6 1HY
01189 875123

Deem, R. Prof.; Brehony, K. Dr; New, S. Ms

Reforming school governing bodies: a sociological investigation

ABSTRACT: School governing bodies in England and Wales were reshaped in the autumn of 1988 as a result of the 1986 (No 2) Education Act, with greater parental representation and more co-opted governors (including those from the business community). The 1986 Act and the 1988 Education Act have also given governors more power over schools than previously. The project is an indepth study of ten school governing bodies (four primary and six secondary) in two local education authorities. A pilot study ran from October 1988 to January 1990. The research has monitored what coping strategies governing bodies are using to deal with the tasks and responsibilities given to them by the new educational legislation and has also focused on the identification of power relations (including gender and race/ethnicity), decision making processes and networks of influence operating in the eight governing bodies. The project also, in addition, seeks to discover whether co-opted governors and parent governors (widely described as 'consumer') come to predominate over those sometimes termed 'producer' governors (teacher and local education authority representative) and headteachers. The work has been done through observation of formal, informal and sub-committee meetings, questionnaires and interviews.

PUBLISHED MATERIAL: DEEM, R. (1993). 'Education reform and school governing bodies in England: old dogs, new tricks or new dogs, new tricks?'. In: PREEDY, M. & GLATTER, R. (Eds). Managing the effective school. London: Paul Chapman.; DEEM, R. & BREHONY, K.J. (1993). 'Governing bodies and local education authorities: who shall inherit the earth?', Local Government Studies, Vol 19, No 1, pp.56-76. ; DEEM, R. & BREHONY, K.J. (1993). 'Consumers and education professionals in the organisation and administration of schools: partnership or conflict?', Educational Studies, Vol 19, No 3, pp.339-355. ; DEEM, R., BREHONY, K.J. & NEW, S. (1993). 'Education for all? Three schools go to market'. In: WALLACE, G. (Ed). Decentralised management in education. Bournemouth: Hyde Publications.; NEW, S. (1993). 'The token teacher: school governing bodies and teacher representation', International Studies in the Sociology of Education, Vol 3, No 1, pp.69-90.

STATUS: Sponsored project

SOURCE OF GRANT: Economic and Social Research Council £56,720

DATE OF RESEARCH: 1990-1993

KEYWORDS: **governing bodies; local management of schools; parent participation; participative decision making; school based management; school governors**

1010

Department of Educational Research, Cartmel College, Bailrigg, Lancaster LA1 4YW
01524 65201
Sunderland University, School of Engineering and Advanced Technology, Edinburgh Building, Chester Road, Sunderland SR1 3SD
0191 515 2000

Brown, K. Mr; *Supervisors*: Saunders, M. Dr; Knight, P. Dr

An investigation into the discontinuities between different post-16 routes into engineering higher education

ABSTRACT: The aims of the project are to: 1) determine whether there are major differences in knowledge of physical science principles between new entrants to engineering higher education (HE); 2) determine whether this is affected by pre-HE route. Four routes being examined are: A-level; General National Vocational Qualification (GNVQ) advanced engineering; National Diploma; Access/Foundation. A survey of new students at a number of higher education institutions (HEI) will be undertaken in September/October 1998. This will consist of 3 tests: 1) Questions about instances which will present students with everyday physical instances and ask them to comment true/false/don't know/not sure; 2) Ask students to mark, on diagrams, names and direction of forces; and 3) Simple calculation based tests. In addition, demographic information will be collected. The results of these tests will be analysed and inferences drawn in relation to route followed pre-university. Each of these routes will also be analysed in terms of the official documents and by a series of interviews with local further education colleges and schools.

PUBLISHED MATERIAL: BROWN, K.B. (1998). 'SARTOR 97: the background and the looming shake-out for university engineering departments', Engineering, Science and Education Journal, Vol 7, No 1, pp.41-48.

STATUS: Individual research

DATE OF RESEARCH: 1995-continuing

KEYWORDS: **engineering; higher education; nontraditional students; physical sciences**

1011

Department of Educational Research, Cartmel College, Bailrigg, Lancaster LA1 4YW
01524 65201
Thames Valley University, Wellington Street, Slough SL1 1YG
01753 534585

Hazell, R. Mr; *Supervisor*: Fulton, O. Prof.

Global tendencies in UK higher education

ABSTRACT: The State has been taking an increasingly centralised approach to the structure of higher education (HE). This research is investigating and summarising the main government policy that has led to a homogenised and commodified UK HE. From the outside it appears that UK HE is a brand in itself, rather than a series of different qualifications offered by different universities' departments, and is marketed as one brand by the British Council. UK universities have needed to diversify sources of income to improve autonomy as UK government funding has been constrained. Fee-paying overseas students are a small, but significant and growing income. Less significant is the emergent market for the overseas student who will study in an overseas franchise. This research will focus on the impact of franchising on the university; the nature of academic work; and student experience. Case studies will be used to support details from survey data, which will be built on unstructured interviews with diverse participants. The findings will have relevance for stakeholders, promoting and regulating such links, policymakers and implementers.

PUBLISHED MATERIAL: HAZELL, R. (1997). 'Exporting higher education: the Polish Open University', European Journal of Education, Vol 32, No 4, pp.397-410.

STATUS: Individual research

DATE OF RESEARCH: 1995-continuing

KEYWORDS: **economics education relationship; educational finance; educational markets; fees; franchising; higher education; overseas students; universities**

1012

Department of Educational Research, Cartmel College, Bailrigg, Lancaster LA1 4YW
01524 65201
University of Central Lancashire, Department of Education Studies, Preston PR1 2HE
01772 201201

Knight, P. Dr; Trowler, P. Dr

Entering the small and different worlds: new academics' experiences of higher education

ABSTRACT: This project aims to map the experiences of academics in their first years of teaching in 4 areas of study: teacher education; engineering; history and women's studies. The research questions centre around the attitudes, values, expectations and normative patterns they bring with them and the reciprocal effects produced as they encounter the multiple cultural configurations present in higher education contexts. The implications for personal identity, the implementation of curriculum policy and for staff development are a particular concern. Qualitative data collection techniques will be used in the 1997/98 academic year and around 30 academics in approximately 6 institutions will be involved.

PUBLISHED MATERIAL: TROWLER, P. (1996). 'Implementing modularity in a resource-depleted environment'. In: HIGHER EDUCATION QUALITY COUNCIL. Modular higher education in focus. London: HEQC.; HARVEY, L. & KNIGHT, P. (1996). Transforming higher education. Buckingham: Society for Research into Higher Education and Open University Press. ; TROWLER, P. Academics, work and change. Buckingham: Open University Press. (in press). ; A full list of publications is available from the researchers.

STATUS: Collaborative

DATE OF RESEARCH: 1997-continuing

KEYWORDS: **academic staff; higher education; organisational climate; teacher attitudes; teacher development; teaching profession**

1013

Department of Educational Research, Cartmel College, Bailrigg, Lancaster LA1 4YW
01524 65201
Westminster College, North Hinksey, Oxford OX2 9AT
01865 247644

Cox, E. Mrs; *Supervisor*: Saunders, M. Dr

Mentors: born or made?

ABSTRACT: Mentoring is now a regular induction and fast track management tool practised in many business and professional settings. This study looks at mentoring in the community and the increasing number of projects for the disadvantaged which rely on mentoring to some extent. The project considers the need for mentors as a feature of late modernity, and examines the need for mentors to be trained in order to focus their knowledge and skills for the task in hand. This research is based around two community mentoring schemes in Oxford. Interviews have been conducted to support the hypothesis that mentor training is essential, and student diaries and reports from one of the schemes give added weight to the arguments.

STATUS: Individual research

DATE OF RESEARCH: 1995-continuing

KEYWORDS: mentor training; mentors

1014

Department of Inservice Education and Training, Charlotte Mason College, Ambleside LA22 9BB
01539 433066

Alker, D. Mr; *Supervisor*: Postle, M. Dr

The identification of prerequisites for effective teacher mobility between Germany and the United Kingdom

ABSTRACT: The project will develop, implement, monitor and evaluate a training programme in consultation with local education authorities (LEAs) for the induction and transfer training of European Community (EC) trained teachers. The aims of the training programme are: (1) to introduce an appropriate range of teaching methods and styles to obtain a better match in teaching approaches; (2) to familiarise EC teachers with the National Curriculum; (3) provide support in meeting the language demands in both general communication skills and the language of the classroom; (4) develop confidence in coping with the demands of cultural and social difference. A major focus of the training programme will be school-based training in association with participating schools and LEAs

STATUS: Sponsored project

SOURCE OF GRANT: Department of Education and Science £20,000

DATE OF RESEARCH: 1989-1993

KEYWORDS: european union; germany; teacher mobility; teacher transfer; training

1015

Department of Management Learning, Gillow House, Bailrigg, Lancaster LA1 4YX
01524 65201

Lauriano, F. Mr; *Supervisor*: Easterby-Smith, M. Prof.

The management of knowledge for innovation in value-creating organisations

ABSTRACT: The study starts with the premise that the success of an organisation that competes through knowledge and innovation depends upon the effectiveness with which it can identify, apply and develop its distinctive knowledge base as situations change. The research, which is company-based, explores the types of knowledge available within the organisation, analyses those factors and processes which facilitate or hinder the transfer of knowledge; examines how new knowledge is created, and sheds light upon the kinds of relationships which exist between the organisation's knowledge-base and knowledge creation in their practice within specific field of activities. The methodology employed includes: 1) an initial analysis of case histories about main innovative ideas produced in the past, which allows generalisation to the process of knowledge creation and development within the organisation; 2) a subsequent implementation of activity theory, applied to specific communities of practice within the organisation (design engineers, research and development specialists, etc), that provides an analysis of how knowledge is created, developed and transmitted within the company. A final model which describes the management of knowledge of the organisation is proposed. The results of the research will be of value both to the academic community, because the research should add new insight to the complex field of study of organisational innovation, and to the company itself, because the work tends to increase awareness within the organisation of its learning capability and knowledge management to build new competencies for the present and future marketplace competition.

STATUS: Sponsored project

SOURCE OF GRANT: Economic and Social Research Council £9,300; Ford of Europe £9,000

DATE OF RESEARCH: 1998-continuing

KEYWORDS: business administration; knowledge management

1016

Department of Teacher and Education Studies, Charlotte Mason College, Ambleside LA22 9BB
01539 433066

Hegarty, P. Dr; Hegarty, P. Mrs

The Two Degrees - a comparative study of former students and first post headteacher satisfaction with initial teacher education at Charlotte Mason College

ABSTRACT: The Council for the Accreditation of Teacher Education (CATE) criteria for primary initial teacher education have occasioned very significant changes in B.Ed applied teacher education courses. This study aims to illuninate the levels of student and first post headteacher satisfaction with students' initial training. The methods include surveys of the whole output from Charlotte Mason College of the last two cohorts of Applied B.Ed and the first two cohorts of Subject Studies B.Ed, and observations and interviews with a small sample each year.

STATUS: Sponsored project

SOURCE OF GRANT: Charlotte Mason College £300

DATE OF RESEARCH: 1989-1993

KEYWORDS: b ed degrees; participant satisfaction; preservice teacher education; probationary teachers; student teachers; teaching experience

1017

Departmental of Educational Research, Cartmel College, Bailrigg, Lancaster LA1 4YW
01524 65201

Furlong, L. Mrs; *Supervisors*: Summerfield, P. Prof.; Deem, R. Prof.

Grammar school girls 1920-1960

ABSTRACT: The research uses oral history data detailing the experiences of a small group of women, working and middle class, scholarship and fee payers, who were pupils at single-sex grammar and high schools 1920-1960, to consider the discursive construction of individual schoolgirl subjectivities as a response to a selective, classed and gendered education.

STATUS: Individual research

DATE OF RESEARCH: 1992-continuing

KEYWORDS: educational history; girls; grammar schools; secondary education; single sex schools; womens education

Leeds Metropolitan University

1018

Faculty of Cultural and Education Studies, School of Teaching and Education Studies, Beckett Park, Leeds LS6 3QS
01132 832600

Welch, S. Ms; *Supervisors*: Roper, E. Mr; Sharp, A. Dr; Hall, A. Dr

Student teachers' learning about teaching and learning: the roles of reflection and personal theories

ABSTRACT: The study seeks to investigate the relationship between students' approaches to learning and the process of reflecting on personal and public theories of teaching and learning. Of particular interest is the area of possible conflict between public and private theories and how students react to this conflict. Monitoring a group of nine B.Ed. primary students over the four years of their course will provide data relating to influences on their learning and ways they make sense of public and private theories. Methods of eliciting and analysing data will be within a personal construct theory framework.

STATUS: Individual research

DATE OF RESEARCH: 1993-1998

KEYWORDS: learning strategies; learning theories; preservice teacher education; student teachers

1019

Faculty of Cultural and Education Studies, School of Teaching and Education Studies, Beckett Park, Leeds LS6 3QS
01132 832600

Bramwell, A. Mrs; *Supervisors*: Bennett, H. Mr; Roper, E. Mr; Sharp, A. Dr

Teacher appraisal: comparative school case studies in one small, urban local education authority

ABSTRACT: All the teachers within the particular local education authority have undergone a two-day training programme to be both appraisers and appraisees. The programme has been run by the same team from a university's department of education. The process for the two yearly cycle is laid down by the local authority (in line with the nationally agreed framework) and has been agreed with the local teaching unions. The hypothesis to be tested is that attitudes to appraisal, and the climate for a successful appraisal system, depend upon the management of the process within each school, and that despite a common framework there will be a vast range of experiences of appraisal amongst the teachers in the authority. The study will identify the differences in attitudes to appraisal, the differences in the management of the appraisal process and, where possible, the differences in the outcomes of the appraisal process in six different institutions within the authority. Selection of the schools is based on the broad variable of phase in addition to the narrower variables of size and culture. Questionnaires and interviews will be used in this naturalistic research and an executive summary of the six case studies will constitute the results of the enquiry.

STATUS: Individual research

DATE OF RESEARCH: 1994-1998

KEYWORDS: teacher development; teacher effectiveness; teacher evaluation; teaching profession

1020

Faculty of Cultural and Education Studies, School of Teaching and Education Studies, Beckett Park, Leeds LS6 3QS
01132 832600

Hall, K. Prof.

Level descriptions of National Curriculum assessment: an empirical study at key stage 1

ABSTRACT: 'Level descriptions' are summary, prose statements that describe the types of performance which pupils working towards particular levels of the National Curriculum, characteristically demonstrate. Teachers judge which level description best fits the pupil's performance. This study seeks to evaluate teachers' understanding and use of these statements as a means of assessing, recording and reporting attainments of 7 year-olds in 2 core subjects, English and mathematics. Key areas of investigation are: 1) how practitioners apply the level descriptions; 2) how they use them in communication with parents, pupils and colleagues; 3) how practice varies across teachers, schools and local education authorities (LEAs), and between subject areas; 4) how level descriptions relate to the subject content that teachers are obliged to teach; and 5) what the implications of the use of these level descriptions might be for the nature of teaching and learning in infant classes. Year 2 teachers, schools' assessment coordinators and senior LEA assessment officers will be interviewed each year of the project and assessment sessions will be observed. Documentary evidence in the form of National Curriculum statements, school/LEA assessment policy documents will be collected and analysed.

STATUS: Sponsored project

SOURCE OF GRANT: Economic and Social Research Council £33,266

DATE OF RESEARCH: 1998-continuing

KEYWORDS: assessment; assessment by teachers; key stage 1; national curriculum; primary education; pupil performance

1021

Faculty of Cultural and Education Studies, School of Teaching and Education Studies, Beckett Park, Leeds LS6 3QS
01132 832600

Hall, K. Prof.; Nuttall, W. Ms

Class size and infant classes

ABSTRACT: The study examines and compares the beliefs, attitudes and pedagogical practices of teachers of large and small infant classes in the North of England regarding class size. The research methodology is a combination of telephone survey (to identify small and large classes) and postal questionnaire survey to obtain information from the teachers about their views and their practices. 133 infant teachers, from state and independent schools, completed the questionnaire. In general, large and small class teachers share similar perspectives about class size and its impact on teaching and learning. The findings show that infant teachers, regardless of class size, strive to implement a particular type of pedagogy - one that values differentiation, individual contact, small group work and practical experiences, and that class size influences the degree to which they can obtain a fit between their pedagogical philosophy and their practice; that class size cannot be treated as undimensional in its impact on the quality of teaching and learning.

PUBLISHED MATERIAL: HALL, K. & NUTTALL, W. (1988). A survey of small and large class infant teachers. Leeds: Leeds Metropolitan University.

STATUS: Sponsored project

SOURCE OF GRANT: Leeds Metropolitan University £3,000

DATE OF RESEARCH: 1996-1998

KEYWORDS: class size; infant education; large classes; primary education; pupil numbers; small classes; teacher attitudes; teaching methods

1022

Faculty of Cultural and Education Studies, School of Teaching and Education Studies, Beckett Park, Leeds LS6 3QS
01132 832600

Myers, J. Ms; Bowman, H. Mr; *Supervisor*: Hall, K. Prof.

The teaching and learning of reading in English and Irish primary schools

ABSTRACT: The theme of the study is how teachers' teaching practices are influenced by their conceptions, values and teaching situation. The researchers are also interested in how pupils' reading practices are influenced by their knowledge, values and learning situation. In the latter regard, the notion of metacognition, or more specifically, children's metacomprehension strategies, is a key focus of the study. The extent and nature of children's use of metacognitive reading strategies and ipsative assessment would appear to be important factors in their success as readers. The study explores these aspects in relation to teachers' conceptions of reading and their expectations for and attitudes towards their pupils' reading progress. The overall aim is to examine how, in the case of reading, teaching and learning practices vary with different conceptions of reading (knowledge and values) different attitudes and expectations (values) different curriculum and assessment policies (teaching context) and different material resources (context); and to explore the inter-relationship between these processes. The research design consists of cross-cultural study of 2 countries, namely, Ireland and England with the teaching of reading to 9 year-olds in 2 inner cities/economically-disadvantaged urban areas being the focus. The 2 cities are Dublin and Leeds. 6 teachers in each city are participating. Data gathering consists of: teacher interviews; task-based conversations with 5 pupils in each class; 4 lesson observations in each class; and documentary data in the form of a) pupils' work, b) reading policies, c) resources/learning materials.

STATUS: Sponsored project

SOURCE OF GRANT: Leeds Metropolitan University £25,000

DATE OF RESEARCH: 1996-continuing

KEYWORDS: **comparative education; ireland; metacognition; primary education; reading; reading teaching; urban schools**

Leeds University

1023

Adult Education Centre, 37 Harrow Road, Middlesbrough, Cleveland TS5 5NT
01642 814987

O'Rourke, R. Ms; *Supervisor*: Croft, A. Dr

Creative writing in adult education

ABSTRACT: This project is to compile an evaluative survey of creative writing activity in the Cleveland, North Yorkshire and West Yorkshire regions. The main point of contact is with the existing writers groups and WRITEAROUND, Cleveland's festival for readers and writers. A small scale survey of random responses to elicit how much local knowledge there is about creative writing opportunities has also been planned. The research is concerned with the experience of teaching and learning within creative writing and explores the different sites within which such activity takes place, and what its value is to participants. The research is exploring the extent to which creative writing activity can best be understood and evaluated as an arts or an educational activity. The research methods include interviews, group discussions, participant observation, and a literature search

STATUS: Sponsored project

SOURCE OF GRANT: Universities Funding Council £32,103

DATE OF RESEARCH: 1992-1993

KEYWORDS: **adult education; creative writing**

1024

Adult Education Centre, 37 Harrow Road, Middlesbrough TS5 5NT
01642 814987
Birmingham University, School of Social Sciences, Centre for Contemporary Cultural Studies, Edgbaston, Birmingham B15 2TT
0121 414 3344

O'Rourke, R. Ms; *Supervisor*: Green, M. Mr

Creative writing: experiencing changing policy in education, arts and community development

ABSTRACT: The research focuses on changes in arts, education and community development between the 1970s and 1990s which resulted in the democratisation of literature through writing development. Its purpose is to evaluate whether greater participation in literature/writing has resulted from these policy changes; and whether access is appropriate/achievable in the cultural sector, as it has been in the wider educational area. It does so partly through a critical review/discussion of the changing policies towards literature, arts development and arts education and partly through mapping in detail the culture of writing in specific localities. This involves a qualitative, quasi-ethnographic approach to the experience of writing from people engaged with writing in a range of contexts, and at different levels on the amateur/professional continuum. It concludes that educational ideologies and practices have supplanted aesthetic ideologies and practices, but disputes that this equates with democracy.

STATUS: Individual research

DATE OF RESEARCH: 1990-continuing

KEYWORDS: **adult education; creative writing; cultural activities**

1025

Business School, Leeds LS2 9JT
01132 431751

Baker, M. Dr

Charity school provision in the UK

ABSTRACT: The aims of the project are to: 1) evaluate the contribution of Lady Hastings within the context of educational provision at the time; 2) examine the nature of charity school education with particular reference to gender; 3) examine the financial provision for charity schools; 4) examine

the nature of the accounting and financial control systems employed over time. The methods will involve using archival records of schools and educational trusts.

PUBLISHED MATERIAL: BAKER, M. (1997). 'The Lady Hastings' charity schools: accounting for eighteenth century rural philanthropy', History of Education, Vol 26, No 3, pp.255-265.

STATUS: Individual research

DATE OF RESEARCH: 1996-continuing

KEYWORDS: **charity schools; educational history**

1026

Centre for Studies in Science and Mathematics Education, Leeds LS2 9JT
01132 431751

Bassett, J. Mr; *Supervisor*: Wain, G. Mr

Key stage 1 of the National Curriculum in mathematics as it relates to infant schools in Huddersfield

ABSTRACT: This research study will investigate the mathematics curriculum of 70 schools engaged in key stage 1 of the National Curriculum in Huddersfield. It will cover the background to the setting up of the National Curriculum and the philosophy which underpins it. It will involve looking at infant/first school models of the curriculum and, in particular, the mathematics curriculum and to relate these to the National Curriculum. The content of key stage 1 of the National Curriculum will be analysed and compared with the pre National Curriculum mathematics curriculum. Similarly the assessment component will be analysed in terms of assessment theory and pre National Curriculum assessment procedures in school. The influence of the Standard Assessment Tasks of school internal curriculum assessments and approaches to teaching methods will be ascertained. The results of the first unreported Standard Assessment Tasks and the first reported Standard Assessment Tasks will be analysed in terms of what they mean in themselves and the affect on schools. The effects of the National Curriculum on the content of the mathematics curriculum in schools, internal assessment, and approaches to mathematics teaching will be assessed by means of a teacher questionnaire. This will be sent to all teachers involved in Key Stage 1 in 70 Huddersfield schools. A separate questionnaire will be sent to mathematics co-ordinators in the same schools. Selective interviews in a sample of the schools will be used to support the questionnaires. The questionnaires cover teacher opinions on effectiveness of National Curriculum INSET (Inservice Education of Teachers), areas where further training is needed, areas in which teachers feel confident/lacking confidence and resource needs to implement National Curriculum Mathematics.

STATUS: Individual research

DATE OF RESEARCH: 1989-1993

KEYWORDS: **assessment; first schools; infant schools; mathematics curriculum; mathematics teachers; standard assessment tasks**

1027

Centre for Studies in Science and Mathematics Education, Leeds LS2 9JT
01132 431751
York University, Department of Educational Studies, Heslington, York YO1 5DD
01904 430000

Driver, R. Prof.; Scott, P. Mr; Millar, R. Prof.; Leach, J. Dr

The development of children's understanding of the nature of science from 9 to 16

ABSTRACT: Concern has been expressed about the growing gap in understanding and awareness between scientists on the one hand and the general public on the other. The aim of this study was to investigate the ways in which students of school age understood the workings of the scientific community and its relationship to society, and the nature and status of scientific knowledge. The study focused on the ways in which students represented various features of science. Five interview tasks were designed in which 30 pairs of students at ages 9, 12 and 16 discussed various features of science in familiar school science contexts. Groups of 16 year old students worked on tasks in which information about scientists was presented and discussed, as part of science lessons. Data analysis involved three stages: (i) identification of particular representations of science used in particular contexts; (ii) identification of age-related trends; (iii) identification of broader trends across a range of contexts. We identified a number of portrayals of scientific knowledge and enquiry, ranging from naive realism through correlational modelling to theoretical modelling. The most common view at each age tended to be correlational modelling (knowledge emerges from finding correlations between variables and phenomena). These views of scientific knowledge and enquiry influenced students' interpretations of the functioning of the scientific community. Findings from this study can inform curriculum decisions about sequencing and the nature of curricular interventions, as well as theoretical issues about the nature of progression in learning and the purposes of the science curriculum.

PUBLISHED MATERIAL: Various publications are available from the Leeds University/York University Science Education Group.

STATUS: Sponsored project

SOURCE OF GRANT: Economic and Social Research Council £70,000

DATE OF RESEARCH: 1991-1993

KEYWORDS: **comprehension; primary education; science education; scientific concepts; scientific literacy; secondary education**

1028

Department of Social Policy and Sociology, Leeds LS2 9JT
01132 431751

Harrison, M. Dr; Law, I. Dr

Ethnic monitoring of undergraduate admissions processes and performance

ABSTRACT: This research involved statistical analysis and interviews focused on entry to case study degree schemes at Leeds University. A paper has been produced for the University's Department of Social Policy and Sociology Working Papers series and is available, price four pounds fifty pence (including postage and packing).

STATUS: Sponsored project

SOURCE OF GRANT: Leeds University

DATE OF RESEARCH: 1992-1993

KEYWORDS: **equal education; ethnic groups; student recruitment; university admission**

1029

Department of Sociology and Social Policy, Leeds LS2 9JT
01132 431751

Reuss, A. Ms; *Supervisor*: Pawson, R. Dr

Higher education and personal change in prisoners

ABSTRACT: An ethnographic study is being conducted as both teacher and researcher which involves 10 male inmates at Her Majesty's Prison Full Sutton. The inmate-students attend a course which parallels the 1st year B.A. course in Social Policy and Sociology at Leeds University. Individual and group informal interviewing techniques are being used with inmates and prison tutors together with secondary source information. A 'data-diary' recording classroom experiences is being kept and data is written up in the form of a 'tale from the field' with continuous analysis, assessment and evaluation taking place. The research will examine the effects of education on rehabilitation and habilitation, in so far as it focuses on the mechanisms of change experienced by inmates undergoing a substantial course in higher education within a maximum security dispersal prison. Education within the prison system tends to remain fragmentary, isolated from mainstream provision, and differs widely across the range of penal institutions in Britain. The opportunity to carry out research in what amounts to a massively under-researched area, presented itself with the establishment four years ago, of the Leeds University Full Sutton programme. This programme of research is closely associated with detailed work undertaken over many years at Simon Fraser University in Canada. The researcher's interest stems from practical and academic concerns relating to the 'transformative capacity' of Sociology, grounded in the teaching of mature students over several years.

STATUS: Individual research

DATE OF RESEARCH: 1993-continuing

KEYWORDS: **prison education; prisoners; rehabilitation**

1030

School of Continuing Education, Leeds LS2 9JT
01132 431751

Payne, J. Dr; *Supervisors*: Ward, K. Mr; Forrester, K. Dr

The Leeds adult learners at work project

ABSTRACT: The aims of the project are to study work-based learning to: (1) identify existing schemes and facilities by which employers cater for the continuing general education and training of their employees; (2) determine the factors that affect the success of such schemes; (3) explore the theoretical issues emerging which relate to adult learning at the workplace; (4) examine the policy issues relating to the development of lifelong learning; and (5) make international comparisons. In practical terms this will involve: gathering information about existing schemes; visiting existing schemes, together with interested individuals and organisations; and selecting a number of schemes in different kinds of enterprise for more detailed evaluation. Journal articles and a final report will be produced. An international conference on this topic will be held in Leeds from July 13-15 1993.

STATUS: Sponsored project

SOURCE OF GRANT: Universities Funding Council

DATE OF RESEARCH: 1991-1993

KEYWORDS: **adult education; labour force development; works schools**

1031

School of Continuing Education, Leeds LS2 9JT
01132 431751

Woodward, G. Ms; *Supervisors*: Taylor, R. Prof.; Butcher, V. Mrs

Guidance and empowerment for non-standard students in the new mass higher education institution: case study at the University of Leeds

ABSTRACT: The new mass higher education (HE) system urgently requires the development of a sophisticated information and guidance system. There are two principal reasons: 1) the influx of large numbers of 'non-standard' students who have special needs in terms of acquainting themselves with the world of HE, and devising learning packages which fulfil their personal and professional objectives; and 2) the high level of complexity of the new modular structures (for example, the University of Leeds now has 3,000 individual modules at undergraduate and taught postgraduate levels). The research investigates the inadequacies of the present system, the perceived needs of students (not least in terms of providing 'empowerment strategies'), and will suggest ways in which new structures can be developed.

STATUS: Sponsored project

SOURCE OF GRANT: Leeds Training and Enterprise Council

DATE OF RESEARCH: 1995-1997

KEYWORDS: **access to education; educational guidance; higher education; learning modules; mature students; modular courses; student needs; students**

1032

School of Continuing Education, Leeds LS2 9JT
01132 431751

Hutton-Jarvis, C. Ms; *Supervisors*: Zukas, M. Ms; Spencer, L. Mr

The educational potential of romantic fiction

ABSTRACT: The research takes the form of a case study exploring how critical thinking develops in mature women students on an Access to Higher Education course. The case study is in 2 sections. Section One is an ethnographic study of 2 groups of women students studying literature/cultural studies, including the popular romance, on an Access course. The methodology is located within an intepretive paradigm rooted in phenomenology and hermeneutics and consists of the analysis of students' learning journal, of participant observation notes on 210 hours of classroom contact, and of 60 interview transcripts. Section Two is a study of romantic fiction to illustrate its applicability as a tool for the development of critical thinking in a classroom setting. The approach followed is influenced by the reader response theory which acknowledges the importance of intertextuality and the active nature of the reading process, and by deconstructive techniques which show how it is possible to read against the grain, identifying the contradictions, absences and tensions which may challenge more obvious readings. In this way the research aims to show how romantic fiction can be used as the focus for analyses which interrogate some key personal and social concerns of the women in the case study groups.

PUBLISHED MATERIAL: JARVIS, C. (1994). Research and practice: a romantic relationship?'. In: ARMSTRONG, P., BRIGHT, B. & ZUKAS, M. (Eds). Reflecting on changing practices, contexts and identities. Proceedings of the 24th Annual Conference of SCUTREA, University of Hull, July 12-14, 1994.

STATUS: Individual research

DATE OF RESEARCH: 1993-1997

KEYWORDS: **access programmes; critical thinking; fiction; learning activities; literature; mature students; women**

1033

School of Continuing Education, Leeds LS2 9JT
01132 431751

Fraser, L. Ms; Kollontai, P. Ms; *Supervisor*: Ward, K. Mr

Widened provision: universities and disadvantaged communities

ABSTRACT: This action-research project aims to explore the possibility of creating more systematic pathways and progression routes between disadvantaged communities and individuals and the University of Leeds. The action research also includes an exploration of the potential and effectiveness of Accreditation of Prior Experiential Learning (APEL) and guidance structures both in the institution and the community.

STATUS: Sponsored project

SOURCE OF GRANT: Higher Education Funding Council for England

DATE OF RESEARCH: 1995-continuing

KEYWORDS: **access to education; accreditation of prior learning; admission criteria; disadvantaged; higher education; student recruitment; universities**

1034

School of Continuing Education, Leeds LS2 9JT
01132 431751

Taylor, R. Prof.; Ward, K. Mr

Workbased learning: project development at the University of Leeds

ABSTRACT: Workbased learning (WBL) is seen as a major area of development at the University of Leeds with a target of recruiting 10,000 WBL students at undergraduate and postgraduate level over the next few years. Partnerships arrangements with companies, and the accreditation of in-company training schemes are integrated parts of the project. Accreditation of Prior Experiential Learning (APEL) systems, including the provision of APEL modules, are being developed and the WBL programme is also based on electronic online learning and on the principles of distance and open learning. A range of curricula is being developed, concentrating upon a core of generic areas (e.g. computing, business studies) with a series of specialist provision for particular client groups. The proper development, supported by both Higher Education Funding Council for England (HEFCE) and University of Leeds funds, is being closely monitored and an evaluation report will be written in 1998-99.

STATUS: Team research

DATE OF RESEARCH: 1996-continuing

KEYWORDS: **experiential learning; higher education; industry higher education relationship; universities; work based learning**

1035

School of Continuing Education, Leeds LS2 9JT
01132 431751

Taylor, R. Prof.

The case for a revitalised liberal approach to post-compulsory education

ABSTRACT: In the post-Dearing context, and in the broader policy agenda of the new Labour Government's education plans, lifelong learning is a key concept. Both the Kennedy report on further education and the Dearing report on higher education give pride of place to this concept and to the accompanying imperatives for accessibility and relevance. Underlying these

powerful policy commitments are two linked motivating factors: the perceived needs of an increasing sophisticated economy for a more skilled and educated workforce, and the desire within the context of great accessibility for wider participation. This research is concerned with the moral and ideological bases of this ambitious policy agenda and in particular of the question of whether this liberal tradition has relevance and validity for post-compulsory education and training in the new environment. The analysis reviews critically the 'liberal tradition' and examines the shortcomings of the prevalent post-modernist alternatives. The analysis concludes with advocacy of a revitalised and radical liberal tradition as a basis for a new post-compulsory education and training agenda.

STATUS: Individual research

DATE OF RESEARCH: 1997-1997

KEYWORDS: **adult education; continuing education; educational change; liberal education; lifelong learning**

1036

School of Continuing Education, Leeds LS2 9JT
01132 431751
Brighton University, Mithras House, Lewes Road, Brighton BN2 4AT
01273 600900

Watson, D. Prof.; Taylor, R. Prof.

Lifelong learning and the university: a post-Dearing agenda

ABSTRACT: The university system is in the process of transformation from an elite to a mass model. One key aspect of this process is the rapid development of part-time, mature student cohorts, and, linked to this, the change in universities' cultures and curriculum approaches to a 'lifelong learning' perspective. The Dearing report (DEARING, R. (1997). Higher education in the learning society. London: National Committee of Inquiry into Higher Education) is likely to give organisational and financial confirmation of this transition. This study, co-authored by the Chair and Secretary of the Universities Association for Continuing Education, analyses the nature of this transition and the impact of the Dearing report upon the 'lifelong learning' concept. (David Watson, one of the authors, is a member of the Dearing Committee).

STATUS: Team research

DATE OF RESEARCH: 1996-1997

KEYWORDS: **continuing education; educational change; higher education; learning society; lifelong learning; mature students; nontraditional education; part time students; universities**

1037

School of Education, Leeds LS2 9JT
01132 431751

de Medeiros, C. Mrs; *Supervisor*: Orton, A. Dr

An investigation into errors made in attempts to solve mathematical problems

ABSTRACT: The study aims to investigate teacher perceptions of pupils' errors in elementary arithmetic with a view to developing teacher training techniques which will enable teachers to improve their teaching methods. Selected groups of young pupils have been tested using simple problems and their errors have been classified by teachers in training, in a preparatory study aimed at clarifying the issues and problems. A further study of pupils' problem solving has yielded data which is currently being analyzed.

STATUS: Sponsored project

SOURCE OF GRANT: Brazilian Government

DATE OF RESEARCH: 1988-1993

KEYWORDS: **arithmetic; mathematical ability; mathematics education; problem solving; teacher education; teaching methods**

1038

School of Education, Leeds LS2 9JT
01132 431751

McAuley, J. Mr; *Supervisors*: Roper, T. Mr; Orton, A. Dr

Cognitive style and learning mathematics

ABSTRACT: The implications of cognitive styles such as field dependence and field independence in learning mathematics have not been widely investigated. This study aims to focus on such styles and the implications in learning matrices. It is expected that pupils will be assessed and classified on a field dependence/field independence spectrum and the effects of different teaching styles will be measured.

STATUS: Individual research

DATE OF RESEARCH: 1989-continuing

KEYWORDS: **cognitive processes; cognitive style; field dependence independence; learning; mathematics education**

1039

School of Education, Leeds LS2 9JT
01132 431751

Child, D. Prof.; Baker, R. Mr

Survey of communication practices in schools for the hearing impaired in the United Kingdom

ABSTRACT: In 1987 a survey was carried out with a number of schools for the hearing impaired in England and Scotland using a total communication approach. When the findings were circulated, suggestions were made by several headteachers for a further study to explore in more detail the ways in which different modes of communication are used, demand for resource materials, training of staff and parents in communication skills and the roles of deaf people in the schools. It has subsequently been suggested that a new survey be carried out to establish exactly what range of approaches are used throughout all the schools at the present time. A questionnaire was designed which asks for communication approaches in use, in order to provide a base of information for planning for future needs. At the same time, it goes more deeply into aspects of practices in schools using a total communication approach, in response to the requests already made by headteachers. The questionnaire has now been circulated and a 100% return obtained. The data have been analysed and the findings circulated to all participants. Two papers have appeared in the Journal of The British Association of Teachers of the Deaf.

STATUS: Sponsored project

SOURCE OF GRANT: Northern Counties School for the Deaf £4,000

DATE OF RESEARCH: 1990-1993

KEYWORDS: **communication skills; deafness; hearing impairments; hearing therapy; special schools; total communication**

1040

School of Education, Leeds LS2 9JT
01132 431751

Lewis, I. Mr; *Supervisor*: Jenkins, E. Prof.; Donnelly, J. Dr

A study of technological capability as manifest in secondary school pupils' project work

ABSTRACT: The study is an exploration of 'the technology project' with particular attention being given to its origination, development and closure. An attempt is made to establish the criteria used by pupils in, for example, choosing one solution/design criteria in preference to another, evaluating/appraising their project as it develops. The work is based on an ethnographic study of pupils in classes in five Sheffield schools. Three schools are likely to be involved.

STATUS: Sponsored project

SOURCE OF GRANT: Leeds University: School of Education; Sheffield Local Education Authority

DATE OF RESEARCH: 1989-1993

KEYWORDS: **ability; projects - learning activities; pupil projects; secondary education; technology education**

1041

School of Education, Leeds LS2 9JT
01132 431751

Moncur, D. Mr; *Supervisor*: Orton, A. Dr

Students' understanding of literal algebraic equations and formulae

ABSTRACT: This research has been devised to compare the ability of pupils and students to solve numerical and literal equations in order to analyze why many learners find the step from numerical to literal so difficult. A preliminary study based on group testing was carried out using pupils from four schools in different parts of Britain. In some schools the literal equations were placed before the numerical. The main part of the research is based on individual interviews with a large sample of pupils, and transcription of this data is currently taking place.

STATUS: Individual research

DATE OF RESEARCH: 1987-1993

KEYWORDS: **algebra; cognitive processes; comprehension; mathematical formulas; mathematics education**

1042

School of Education, Leeds LS2 9JT
01132 431751

Marriott, S. Prof.; Coles, J. Mrs

'University extension' across the English-speaking world, 1867-1914

ABSTRACT: The project is a contribution to a larger research programme in the University of Leeds on inter-cultural influences in the field of adult education. It complements previous work on Anglo-German relations in adult education and on the significance of the English model of 'university extension' for the development of 'popular universities' in continental Europe. This project investigates the export of ideas and practices in university extension to the USA, Canada, Australia, New Zealand and South Africa. It considers why the English model attracted attention, and what happened to it after transplantation to a different social and cultural environment.

PUBLISHED MATERIAL: COLES, J. (1992). 'University extension in the United States'. In: HAKE, B.J. & MARRIOTT, S. (Eds). Adult education between cultures. Leeds: University of Leeds, Studies in Cross Cultural Communication in the Education of Adults, No 2.

STATUS: Sponsored project

SOURCE OF GRANT: Leverhulme Trust £18,750

DATE OF RESEARCH: 1991-1993

KEYWORDS: **adult education; comparative education; educational history; extension education**

1043

School of Education, Leeds LS2 9JT
01132 431751

Chambers, G. Mr

Diversification of first foreign language in Leeds schools

ABSTRACT: Traditionally French has been dominant as the first foreign language in Leeds secondary schools. German, as a second foreign language has been squeezed into as few as 5 terms in years 10 and 11. In line with recommendations of the National Curriculum, up to 20 Leeds schools have plans to introduce German as either first foreign language or first equal foreign language with French from year 7, as part of a diversification scheme. The purpose of the research is to examine the problems posed by this major change in policy and to seek some tentative solutions, insofar as this is possible, given the constraints of circumstances within individual schools. Interviews will be conducted with the local education authority (LEA) adviser for modern languages to establish the LEA approach to presenting diversification to schools, problems of resourcing and the implications of the reorganisation of secondary education in Leeds. Interviews will also be conducted in 15-20 schools committed to diversification as well as those which are delaying reform and those which have determined to retain the status quo of French as the first foreign language. The views of headteachers, heads of modern languages and class teachers are being sought on reasons for diversifying, staffing implications, training issues, resourcing and problems of transfer and continuity and other related matters. Outcomes of the research will be published in an extensive report in July 1993.

STATUS: Sponsored project

SOURCE OF GRANT: Leeds University: School of Education £8,300

DATE OF RESEARCH: 1992-1993

KEYWORDS: **french; german; modern language studies; national curriculum**

1044

School of Education, Leeds LS2 9JT
01132 431751

Demsetz, E. Ms; *Supervisors*: Tomlinson, P. Dr; Scott, P. Mr

Developing and evaluating a characterization of thought in a microanalysis of students' learning in science

ABSTRACT: A theory of learning is developed using the basic principles of network modelling, and the usefulness of the theory in analyzing science education research data is evaluated. The theory portrays learning as a structuring of knowledge occurring through two processes, termed 'conceptualization' and 'symbolization'. The structured knowledge is capable of supporting three types of thought, termed 'conceptual reasoning', 'intuitive thought', and 'procedural thought'. This characterization of thought is operationalized to allow the theory of learning to be 'trialled' in analyzing science education data. Data for this trial analysis is obtained using a 'non-comparative', open-interview methodology to probe the understandings of two sixth-form physics students learning about electricity. The usefulness of the theory is evaluated by examining the results of the trial analysis to identify issues which the analysis did and did not address. A set of guidelines is developed to allow the science education researcher to characterize research questions in terms of these issues, thereby determining whether the theory of learning will be useful to a particular research study.

STATUS: Individual research

DATE OF RESEARCH: 1991-1993

KEYWORDS: **electricity; learning processes; physics; science education; sixth form education**

1045

School of Education, Leeds LS2 9JT
01132 431751

Wain, G. Mr; Monaghan, J. Dr; Roper, T. Mr

The use of symbol manipulators in teaching algebra to year 10 pupils in secondary schools

ABSTRACT: The development of new systems for computers and calculators which manipulate algebraic symbols and perform calculus procedures have enormous potential for the teaching of algebra and calculus in secondary schools. This research project is aiming to explore the use of symbol manipulators with year 10 students in local secondary schools. The project is a pilot for a larger project which is hoped to be mounted in the future and will be concerned with middle ability and high ability pupils in two comprehensive schools. Each class will be taught a section of the algebra curriculum with the use of symbol manipulators either on hand-held calculators or on computers, and at the same time control groups will be taught the same material without the use of the technology. The pupils will be given a pre-test of the material, and a post-test shortly after the teaching and again after about six weeks. A number of the pupils involved will also be interviewed to find out some of the processes by which they had come to their solutions. The teaching will be observed by one person other than the teacher, and, for the classes that use the technology, a video recording will be made of the display on the screens. The observer will keep a diary about the teaching process and together with the videos an overview of the way that the teaching has been conducted will be compiled. This will be compared with the results of the tests on the pupils and interview material.

STATUS: Sponsored project

SOURCE OF GRANT: University of Leeds: Academic Development Fund £20,000

DATE OF RESEARCH: 1992-1993

KEYWORDS: **algebra; calculators; computer uses in education; information technology; mathematics education; secondary education**

1046

School of Education, Leeds LS2 9JT
01132 431751

Walton, R. Dr; *Supervisors*: Jenkins, E. Prof.; Rayner, M. Mr

Interactive science centres: some psychological and philosophical perspectives

ABSTRACT: This Ph.D. study explored a number of psychological and philosophical perspectives on the 'informal' learning associated with interactive science centres.

STATUS: Individual research

DATE OF RESEARCH: 1992-1998

KEYWORDS: **force; museums; science activities; science education; science teaching centres; scientific concepts**

1047

School of Education, Leeds LS2 9JT
01132 431751

Garrick, R. Mrs; *Supervisors*: Threlfall, J. Dr; Orton, A. Dr

A study of the pattern-making elements and early concepts of pattern evidenced in 3 and 4 year-olds play with nursery materials

ABSTRACT: The development of young children's abilities to perceive and create patterns will be studied, with particular relation to progression through the early years of learning mathematics.

STATUS: Individual research

DATE OF RESEARCH: 1992-continuing

KEYWORDS: **early childhood education; mathematics education; pattern recognition; play; young children**

1048

School of Education, Leeds LS2 9JT
01132 431751

Healy, M. Ms

An examination of the process of appraisal of headteachers in phase one of its implementation in one local education authority

ABSTRACT: The programme of headteacher appraisal is part of a national statutory programme involving all teachers. This research project involves a close consideration of the process as it affects a core group of ten headteachers. It is complemented by a study of the support offered by the local education authority (LEA) together with a survey of the larger cohort of headteachers in a LEA undertaking the process for the first time. Methods used involve: direct observation of the process of appraisal in the case of the core study; interviews with core study headteachers, peer appraisers and LEA appraisers; and a questionnaire to other headteachers in the cohort. Results are still emerging. Present indications suggest that important insights are to be gained as to the following issues: (1) the role of the LEA in appraisal; and (2) the headteachers' understanding of issues of accountability and their concept of the task of management.

STATUS: Sponsored project

SOURCE OF GRANT: Leeds University Research Fund £2,350

DATE OF RESEARCH: 1992-1993

KEYWORDS: **head teachers; teacher evaluation**

1049

School of Education, Leeds LS2 9JT
01132 431751

Jenkins, E. Prof.

School science education in England and Wales, 1960-1990

ABSTRACT: The study seeks to take forward a full length account of science education in schools in England and Wales completed in 1960. It will explore the social history and politics of the school science curriculum from the introduction of the Nuffield Science Teaching Projects in the early 1960s to the advent of the National Curriculum of the late 1980s.

PUBLISHED MATERIAL: JENKINS, E.W. (1989). 'Processes in science education: an historical perspective'. In: WELLINGTON, J. (Ed). Skills and processes in science education: a critical analysis. London: Routledge.; JENKINS, E.W. (1992). 'School science education: towards a reconstruction', Journal of Curriculum Studies, Vol 24, No 3, pp.229-246.

STATUS: Individual research

DATE OF RESEARCH: 1992-continuing

KEYWORDS: **educational history; science education**

1050

School of Education, Leeds LS2 9JT
01132 431751

Stephens, W. Dr

Education in Britain in its economic setting, 1780-1902

ABSTRACT: The aim of this project is to provide a survey of education in England, Scotland and Wales, 1780-1902 in its social and economic setting, stressing inter-relationship of educational change and socio-economic development.

PUBLISHED MATERIAL: STEPHENS, W.B. (1998). Education in Britain 1750-1914. London: Macmillan.

STATUS: Individual research

DATE OF RESEARCH: 1993-1997

KEYWORDS: **educational history**

1051

School of Education, Leeds LS2 9JT
01132 431751

Alexopolou, E. Miss; *Supervisors*: Driver, R. Prof.; Tomlinson, P. Dr

Small group discussion in physics: interaction and development of students' physics ideas

ABSTRACT: The study investigates the effect of group discussion on secondary students' understanding in three physics domains. The discussion processes are analysed in terms of social interaction as well as argument construction. The dynamics of change in students' physics reasoning are investigated. The results show that gender, group size, the forms of argument used as well as the type of social confrontation between group members all affect both the course and the outcomes of the discussion in terms of individual conceptual change.

PUBLISHED MATERIAL: ALEXOPOLOU, E., DRIVER, R. & TOMLINSON, P. (1992). 'Small group discussion in physics: interaction and development of students' physics understanding': Psychological and educational foundations of technology-based learning environments, Proceedings of the NATO Advanced Study Institute, Crete.

STATUS: Individual research

DATE OF RESEARCH: 1989-1993

KEYWORDS: **group discussion; group work; physics; science education**

1052

School of Education, Leeds LS2 9JT
01132 431751

Willcocks, J. Mr; *Supervisor*: Shorrocks-Taylor, D. Dr

Aspects of linguistic influence of primary school teachers on their pupils

ABSTRACT: The aim of the study is to investigate differing levels of articulacy among primary teachers, and to explore the relationship between teachers' articulacy and the developing articulacy of their pupils. The study includes the development of a schedule for the analysis of classroom syntax, and a phenomenological study of teachers' and trainee teachers' understanding of the nature of articulacy. Transcript data are derived from the classroom interactions of five Year 3 teachers in an English junior school, recorded via radio microphones during the first and last weeks of a school year.

STATUS: Individual research

DATE OF RESEARCH: 1991-1998

KEYWORDS: **articulation - speech; classroom communication; primary school teachers; teacher behaviour; teacher pupil relationship; verbal communication**

1053

School of Education, Leeds LS2 9JT
01132 431751

Sugden, D. Prof.; Utley, A. Ms

Manual skills in children with hemiplegic cerebral palsy

ABSTRACT: The overall aim of this project is to improve manual functions in children with hemiplegic cerebral palsy (CP) so that they can have total access to the National Curriculum. This includes: 1) providing a 'vocabulary' of grips that CP children use and adaptations they make; 2) describing reaching and grasping in CP children; 3) analysing the effect of the lesser involved side on the hemiplegic limb (interlimb coupling); and 4) analysing how this interlimb coupling is best achieved. The methods used in the study include: normal real live video analysis; and three dimensional kinematic analysis.

PUBLISHED MATERIAL: SUGDEN, D.A., & UTLEY, A. (1993). Manual skills in children with hemiplegic cerebal palsy. Report to the Spastics Society.

STATUS: Sponsored project

SOURCE OF GRANT: Spastics Society £21,000; Action Research £37,000; Leeds University

DATE OF RESEARCH: 1992-1993

KEYWORDS: **cerebral palsy; mobility aids; neurological impairments; psychomotor skills; special educational needs**

1054

School of Education, Leeds LS2 9JT
01132 431751

Sugden, D. Prof.; Beveridge, S. Dr; Whitelaw, S. Ms

Curricular entitlement at National Curriculum key stages 2 and 3 for children with special educational needs

ABSTRACT: This project investigates the assessment and delivery of National Curriculum key stages 2 and 3 to children with special educational needs. Examples of 'good practice' are being identified by 6 local authorities in primary, secondary and special schools. Initially headteachers and special needs coordinators are being interviewed; the second part involves observation in schools to examine the stated policies in practice.

STATUS: Sponsored project

SOURCE OF GRANT: Leeds University £44,000

DATE OF RESEARCH: 1993-1998

KEYWORDS: **mainstreaming; pupil needs; school effectiveness; special educational needs**

1055

School of Education, Leeds LS2 9JT
01132 431751

Higham, J. Mr; Sharp, R. Dr; Yeomans, D. Dr

Constructing a new curriculum: the rise of General National Vocational Qualifications

ABSTRACT: The aims of the research are to: 1) examine the educational and policy contexts from which General National Vocational Qualifications (GNVQ's) are emerging and the evolving principles and concepts which underpin the intended GNVQ curriculum; 2) investigate the recruitment procedures for GNVQ's in colleges and schools and their influence on curriculum practice; 3) investigate the ways in which the GNVQ curriculum is constructed in practice by teachers and students in colleges and schools and the nature of this effective curriculum; 4) investigate the broader institutional contexts in which the GNVQ curriculum is negotiated and realised; 5) use existing accounts and models of policy formulation and realisation, the management of innovation and curriculum construction to interrogate the empirical data on the GNVQ curriculum; and 6) use the empirical study to inform, modify and extend existing theoretical knowledge. While the specific focus of the research is upon the GNVQ curriculum, the over-arching objective is to increase knowledge and understanding of the ways in which education policies are realised and curricula are constructed. These research methods involve an analysis of a range of GNVQ documentation and intensive case study fieldwork in secondary schools, sixth form colleges, further education/tertiary colleges. The principal focus will be on the five vocational areas piloted in 1992/93 and introduced nationally in 1993/94 (Art and Design, Business, Health and Social Care, Leisure and Tourism and Manufacturing).

STATUS: Sponsored project

SOURCE OF GRANT: Economic and Social Research Council

DATE OF RESEARCH: 1995-1997

KEYWORDS: curriculum development; further education; general national vocational qualifications; secondary education; sixteen to nineteen education; sixth form colleges; vocational education; vocational qualifications

1056

School of Education, Leeds LS2 9JT
01132 431751

Laws, P. Mr; Supervisors: Jenkins, E. Prof.; Donnelly, J. Dr

Conceptions of teaching: their development in student teachers of English and science

ABSTRACT: The project is an attempt to investigate one element in the developing professional work of student teachers: their conceptions of teaching. Inevitably for secondary-sector teachers, such an investigation requires substantial reference to the students' subject knowledge which, for many, wil be the foundation on which they will begin to construct a teaching practice. The research is looking at how conceptions of teaching change as students become socialised into teaching, accustomed to the aptitudes and proclivities of school children and to the imperatives and constraints of schooling. The investigation followed 20 student teachers through their Postgraduate Certificate in Education (PGCE) year (which actually amounts to little more than 9 months). 11 of the students were taking the science-teaching course, 9 the English). Each student was interviewed 4 times at regular intervals during the course. The interviews were tape-recorded, transcribed and checked by the students for their accuracy. Qualitative analysis of these transcript data is underway at present. Initial findings suggest that the subject is indeed a vital part of the students' conceptions of what teaching is and that it determines to a significant extent their conceptions of pedagogical practice, i.e. how teaching should be done.

STATUS: Individual research

DATE OF RESEARCH: 1994-continuing

KEYWORDS: english; english studies teachers; preservice teacher education; science teachers; student teachers; teacher development; teaching methods; teaching practice

1057

School of Education, Leeds LS2 9JT
01132 431751

Garvey, B. Dr

A study of the professional and bureaucratic influences on those involved in the school inspection operations of the Office for Standards in Education

ABSTRACT: A sample will be made of officials and teachers who have recently been involved in Office for Standards in Education (OFSTED) school inspections. From this, sample structured interviews will be devised to determine the nature and mixture of the bureaucratic and professional elements involved in the inspectoral processes. The sample will be limited to the Yorkshire area.

STATUS: Sponsored project

SOURCE OF GRANT: Leeds University

DATE OF RESEARCH: 1994-1997

KEYWORDS: inspection; inspectors - of schools; ofsted; quality control

1058

School of Education, Leeds LS2 9JT
01132 431751

Cooke, L. Mrs; Supervisor: Jenkins, E. Prof.

Outdoor education since 1944 with particular reference to the West Riding of Yorkshire

ABSTRACT: Following a review of the range of activities encompassed by 'outdoor education', attention is focused on the development of such education after 1944 with reference to the former West Riding of Yorkshire. Documentary sources, published and unpublished, will be augmented by interview and oral history techniques. The intention is to produce a study of the factors that have shaped outdoor education since 1944.

STATUS: Individual research

DATE OF RESEARCH: 1993-1998

KEYWORDS: educational history; outdoor pursuits

1059

School of Education, Leeds LS2 9JT
01132 431751

Waring, S. Dr; Supervisors: Orton, A. Dr; Roper, T. Mr

Learning and teaching proof in mathematics through pattern

ABSTRACT: The aim was to investigate the extent to which the idea of proof in mathematics can be learned and taught by appealing to pattern. Students were pre-tested and post-tested using test items which required proofs, and interviews were used to probe understanding of proof and attitudes to proof. A specially prepared teaching programme was applied between pre- and post-test. Data from both group testing and individual interviewing were used to try to answer a set of detailed questions.

STATUS: Individual research

DATE OF RESEARCH: 1993-1997

KEYWORDS: mathematics education; proof - mathematics

1060

School of Education, Leeds LS2 9JT
01132 431751

Driver, R. Prof.; Leach, J. Dr; Lewis, J. Dr; Ryder, J. Dr; Wood, E. Dr; Radford, A.Dr

Undergraduate learning in science project

ABSTRACT: The Undergraduate Learning in Science Project is an interdepartmental collaboration at the University of Leeds which has carried out a number of research studies into teaching and learning science at university. Studies have involved the Departments of Biochemistry and Molecular Biology, Chemistry, Earth Sciences and Genetics, together with the School of Education. A major study was undertaken into the experiences of 12 students duringm their final year investigative projects. Longitudinal interviews and end of project surveys, examined the the influence of project supervision, workload, progress on the project, assessment and preparation of the final report on the students' experiences. A particular focus was on students' developing ideas about the nature of science. The students in the sample tended to talk aabout scientific knowledge as provable using empirical data alone. A minority of students felt that there may be more than one legitimate knowledge claim arising from a single data set. Aspects of the sociology of science were under-represented in our sample. Other studies have used case studies of tutorials, or laboratory work, to investigate the development of students' ideas about the nature of science during university science education.

PUBLISHED MATERIAL: RYDER, J. & LEACH, J. (1996). 'Learning what it means to be a biochemist: case study of a tutorial on glycolysis', Biochemical Education, Vol 24, No 1, pp.21-25. ; RYDER, J. & LEACH, J. (1997). 'Research projects in the undergraduate science course: students learning about science through enculturation'. Proceedings of the 4th International Student Learning Symposium, 1997. ; KEE, T.P. & RYDER, J. (1997). 'Developing communication and critical skills in undergraduates', University Chemistry Education, Vol 1, pp.1-4. ; RYDER, J., LEACH, J. & DRIVER, R. 'Undergraduate science students' images of the nature of science', Journal of Research in Science Teaching. (in press).

STATUS: Sponsored project

SOURCE OF GRANT: Leeds University £62,500

DATE OF RESEARCH: 1994-1998

KEYWORDS: higher education; learning; science education; scientific literacy; students

1061

School of Education, Leeds LS2 9JT
01132 431751

Noah, M. Mr; Garber, J. Mrs; Supervisors: Gibbs, W. Mr; Orton, J. Mrs

Sierra Leone square project

ABSTRACT: The project is a collaborative venture between students from Sierra Leone who have studied at Leeds and Hull, and members of the

International Education Group in the University of Leeds. The project aims to develop teaching materials and methods for improving the active learning of mathematics through the use of squared boards and squared books. The project group has produced materials (squared boards and books) and distributed them to ten pilot schools in Sierra Leone. The team has also produced teaching materials and run workshops in Freetown for both primary and secondary teachers. An interim evaluation of the project was carried out in 1994.

PUBLISHED MATERIAL: GIBBS, W. (1993). 'The Sierra Leone squared book and board project', Science Education Newsletter, No 108, pp.1-3.

STATUS: Sponsored project

SOURCE OF GRANT: British Council £3,000; Morel Trust £300

DATE OF RESEARCH: 1993-continuing

KEYWORDS: educational materials; international educational exchange; mathematics education; sierra leone

1062

School of Education, Leeds LS2 9JT
01332 431751

Anning, A. Prof.

An evaluation of 'Let's Get it Right': a self-evaluation system for those working with young children in group settings

ABSTRACT: Leeds Local Education Authority (LEA) introduced a self-evaluation framework for those working with young children in group settings in 1996. Professor Anning was commissioned to evaluate its impact on a range of settings: educational, early childhood centres and the independent/private and voluntary sectors. The design of the evaluation included: distribution of questionnaires to all recorded users/purchasers; follow-up interviews to a sample of 'negative' and 'positive' respondents; analysis of LEA documents relating to the initiative; focus group discussions. A full report was be submitted in March 1998.

PUBLISHED MATERIAL: ANNING, A. (1998). An evaluation of Let's Get it Right. Leeds: University of Leeds, School of Education.

STATUS: Sponsored project

SOURCE OF GRANT: Leeds Local Education Authority £5,000

DATE OF RESEARCH: 1996-1998

KEYWORDS: child caregivers; day care; local education authorities; preschool education; primary education; self evaluation - individuals; young children

1063

School of Education, Leeds LS2 9JT
01132 431751

Jenkins, E. Prof.; Shorrocks-Taylor, D. Prof.

Pupils' performance in science and mathematics in National Curriculum and Third International Study tests

ABSTRACT: Pupils in England and Wales (aged 9 and 13) formed two populations whose achievement in science and mathematics was assessed in the Third International Mathematics and Science Study (TIMSS). The research explores this performance at item level and compares it with pupil performance on the relevant National Curriculum tests. The comparison sheds more light on the detail of pupil performance and generates data of use in revising the science and mathematics component of the National Curriculum in England and Wales.

STATUS: Sponsored project

SOURCE OF GRANT: Qualifications and Curriculum Authority £24,000

DATE OF RESEARCH: 1997-1998

KEYWORDS: academic achievement; achievement; assessment; comparative education; mathematics achievement; mathematics education; national curriculum; primary education; pupil performance; science education; secondary education; tasks and tests; tests

1064

School of Education, Leeds LS2 9JT
01132 431751

Coleman, H. Dr

Measuring project impact in a primary English language project in Sri Lanka

ABSTRACT: This research aims to measure the impact of the Primary English Language Project (PELP) in Sri Lanka. This is a project funded by the Department for International Development (DfID). It attempts to examine project impact at 3 levels: Level 1 - teacher trainers working in the Regional English Support Centres (RESCs) throughout Sri Lanka; Level 2 - teachers teaching English in primary schools throughout the country; Level 3 - school pupils throughout the country. At Level 1, impact is measured through an attitudinal questionnaire annually and through an observation schedule. At Level 2, impact is measured through an attitudinal questionnaire and 2 observation schedules. At Level 3, impact is measured through: a test of listening and speaking in English; a test of reading in English; a test of writing in English; and an instrument to measure children's confidence in English. All the instruments are to be administered annually throughout the life of the Project, starting in 1997. So far, one administration has been carried out and the Level 2 data from 49 teachers have been analysed. These indicate that teachers who have attended inservice training activities in the RESCs spend more time paying attention to individuals and groups than teachers who have had no contact with the RESCs. Those who have attended inservice activities also spend less classroom time on administrative matters. However, both groups spend approximately the same amount of lesson time on evaluation.

STATUS: Sponsored project

SOURCE OF GRANT: Department for International Development

DATE OF RESEARCH: 1997-continuing

KEYWORDS: english - second language; primary education; programme evaluation; second language teaching; sri lanka

1065

School of Education, Leeds LS2 9JT
01132 431751

Cuckle, P. Dr; Broadhead, P. Dr; Hodgson, J. Ms

The relationship between OFSTED inspections and school development planning

ABSTRACT: This research arose from an earlier project on school development planning processes. It was thought that School Development Plans (SDPs) and Key Issues (KIs) in Office for Standards in Education (OFSTED) inspection reports might not be compatible and might undermine ongoing plans for development. The project investigated compatibility between existing SDPs and KIs, and factors influencing the implementation of post-OFSTED action plans in primary schools. The research used a questionnaire survey of 124 schools recently inspected, telephone interviews with 47 of the schools' headteachers and examination of supporting documentation (SDPs, copies of KIs and action plans based on the KIs). Headteachers generally found their KIs appropriate and considered them compatible with their SDPs; they were optimistic about implementing action plans despite considerable complexities evident in some KIs and despite apparent difficulties in choosing appropriate success criteria.

PUBLISHED MATERIAL: CUCKLE, P., HODGSON, J. & BROADHEAD, P. (1998). 'Investigating the relationship between OFSTED inspections and school development planning', School Leadership and Management, Vol 18, No 2, pp.271-283.

STATUS: Sponsored project

SOURCE OF GRANT: Nuffield Foundation £8,470

DATE OF RESEARCH: 1997-1997

KEYWORDS: development plans; inspection; ofsted; primary education; school development planning

1066

School of Education, Leeds LS2 9JT
01132 431751

Beard, R. Dr; Willcocks, J. Mr

Professional support for the Phonic Elements in Reading (PROSPERO)

ABSTRACT: The revised National Curriculum for English gives greater attention to the teaching of 'phonic knowledge' than its predecessor. Teachers may need to draw upon various kinds of professional support (e.g. courses, colleagues, teaching materials or self-organised study) in order to implement this revised curriculum. The research aims are: 1) to explore what primary school teachers are doing to implement the phonic knowledge elements of the revised National Curriculum for English at key stage 1 (5-7 year olds); 2) to investigate the increased demands which this implementation has made on teachers' knowledge, understanding and classroom practice; 3) to identify and describe teachers' views on the most supportive influences on their teaching of phonic knowledge at key stage 1; 4) to report the implications of the findings from this investigation for teacher education school development plans. A sample of teachers was interviewed to explore the demands which the revised National Curriculum has made on their knowledge, understanding and classroom practice in relation to teaching phonic knowledge. Some of their responses were incorporated into a questionnaire which was sent to: 1) all schools with key stage 1 classes in the West Yorkshire conurbation; and 2) a national sample of schools with key stage 1 classes. Questionnaire responses were analysed to illuminate the relationships between the key factors which teachers perceive to influence their practice, knowledge and understanding. The practice of a subsample of 10 teachers has been currently observed, and their knowledge and understanding of reading have been investigated in greater depth by interview. This subsample will be observed and interviewed again in 1999 to investigate the influence of the National Literacy Strategy on their knowledge, understanding and classroom practice in relation to teaching phonic knowledge.

STATUS: Sponsored project

SOURCE OF GRANT: Leeds University £1,000

DATE OF RESEARCH: 1996-continuing

KEYWORDS: **beginning reading; key stage 1; phonics; primary education; reading; reading teaching**

1067

School of Education, Leeds LS2 9JT
01132 431751

Hargraves, G. Mr; *Supervisors*: Bates, I. Prof.; Sharp, P. Dr

The origins of the National Vocational Qualification

ABSTRACT: This research is an historical account of the origins of the National Vocational Qualification (NVQ). It argues that the fundamental theoretical principles of the NVQ are derived from behavioural science, especially job analysis methods and criterion-referenced assessment of performance theories, developed from the 1950s, for the American military, by psychologists. The evolution of the NVQ from the Manpower Services Commission's development of the new training initiative is identified as the most signficant site, during the 1980s, in the emergence of British competence-based education and training. The concept of NVQ was invented by the 1985 to 1986 Review of Vocational Qualifications. The internal debates of the review are analysed.

PUBLISHED MATERIAL: HARGRAVES, G. (1995). 'The influence of the European Communities on the emergence of competence-based models of vocational training in England and Wales', British Journal of Education and Work, Vol 8, No 2, pp.28-40.

STATUS: Individual research

DATE OF RESEARCH: 1994-1998

KEYWORDS: **competency based education; educational history; national vocational qualifications; training; vocational education; vocational qualifications**

1068

School of Education, Leeds LS2 9JT
01132 431751

Jenkins, E. Prof.; Laws, P. Mr

Double Award science and subsequent performance at A-level in science

ABSTRACT: The research draws upon a literature search, a national questionnaire to 460 schools, and correspondence with local education authorities (LEAs) to examine what institutions do, if anything, to prepare pupils who have followed Double Award courses in science at GCSE, for work in A-level. The nature of any problems of transition is also described.

STATUS: Sponsored project

SOURCE OF GRANT: Qualifications and Curriculum Authority £4,000

DATE OF RESEARCH: 1997-1998

KEYWORDS: **a level examinations; general certificate of secondary education; science education; sixteen to nineteen education**

1069

School of Education, Leeds LS2 9JT
01132 431751

Anning, A. Prof.; Edwards, A. Prof.

The quality of literacy and numeracy curricula in preschool (including non-school) settings

ABSTRACT: The aim of the project was to draw on the expertise of practitioners and researchers to develop and articulate a curriculum model for effective education in literacy and numeracy for 0-5 year-old children in a range of preschool settings. Over a 2-year period practitioners were encouraged to use cycles of observation, reflection, action in their workplaces to investigate: 1) strategies currently used by educarers to promote children's learning; 2) how parents are effectively involved as partners in educating their children; 3) the organisational features that promote good quality teacning/learning episodes. Exemplar materials have been produced for training others to promote good quality literacy and numeracy learning for children in preschool settings.

PUBLISHED MATERIAL: ANNING, A. & EDWARDS, A. Promoting children's learning from birth to five: developing the new early years professional. Milton Keynes: Open University Press. (in press).

STATUS: Sponsored project

SOURCE OF GRANT: Leeds Local Education Authority; Kirklees Local Education Authority; Sheffield Local Education Authority, jointly £22,000

DATE OF RESEARCH: 1996-1998

KEYWORDS: **babies; child caregivers; early childhood education; educational quality; literacy education; numeracy; nursery education; parent participation; preschool education; young children**

1070

School of Education, Leeds LS2 9JT
01132 431751

Anning, A. Prof.

An evaluation of the pilot scheme Early Years Units in Kirklees Local Education Authority

ABSTRACT: In 1997/98 Kirklees Early Years Service pioneered early years units combining nursery and reception class education for 3-5 year-olds in 7 schools. The evaluation was designed to investigate whether the pilot phase was: a) providing access to early years education that suited family needs; and b) offered good quality educational experiences to children at the 'non-statutory' phase. The evaluation design included: 1) a questionnaire distributed to nursery, reception staff, National Curriculum key stage 1 coordinators, headteachers and deputy headteachers and the parents of children attending the units; 2) follow-up 2-day visits to the units to track children through sessions; 3) interviews with staff of the units and a sample of parents; 4) conversations with the children; 5) review of documentation relating to the initiative; 6) focus group discussions. A report was submitted in June 1998.

PUBLISHED MATERIAL: ANNING, A. (1998). An evaluation of the Kirklees Early Years Unit Pilot Programme. Leeds: University of Leeds, School of Education.

STATUS: Sponsored project

SOURCE OF GRANT: Kirklees Early Years Service £8,000

DATE OF RESEARCH: 1998-1998

KEYWORDS: **early childhood education; educational quality; nursery education; reception classes; young children**

1071

School of Education, Leeds LS2 9JT
01132 431751

Bocock, J. Ms; *Supervisors*: Smith, D. Dr; Scott, P. Prof.

Standard systems, non-standard students: experiences of progression from further to higher education

ABSTRACT: The research focuses on students following alternative qualification routes to traditional A-levels and their experiences of progression from further to higher education. It investigates whether and in what ways these students are disadvantaged by the route they choose. The study follows 4 cohorts of 'non-standard' students in different colleges of further education; 2 groups on one-year Access courses and 2 other groups taking vocational qualifications, the Advanced General National Vocational Qualification (GNVQ) and the Business and Technician Education Council (BTEC) National. Major themes covered by the research include reasons for choosing courses, initial plans for the future; problems of study; encounters with the higher education admissions system; institutional influences; and final decisions. Narratives of student experiences are supplemented by interviews with the students' principal tutors and a sample of admissions tutors in higher education. The research offers a series of conclusions about the nature of the student progression experience, problems facing such students in the task of looking for direction and of finding a place in higher education. It also identifies a number of priority areas for policymakers engaged in developing strategies for widening access to higher education in the future.

PUBLISHED MATERIAL: SMITH, D., BOCOCK, J. & SCOTT, P. (1996). Standard systems, non-standard students: experiences of progression from further to higher education. Leeds: University of Leeds, School of Education.

STATUS: Sponsored project

SOURCE OF GRANT: Esmee Fairbairn Charitable Trust £43,381

DATE OF RESEARCH: 1995-1997

KEYWORDS: **access to education; further education to higher education transition; higher education; nontraditional students; student experience; widening participation**

1072

School of Education, Leeds LS2 9JT
01132 431751

Jenkins, E. Prof.; Swinnerton, B. Dr

Primary/elementary school science in England and Wales since 1902

ABSTRACT: The research is a detailed historical study of science teaching in elementary and primary schools in England and Wales in the 20th century. It draws upon published and archival sources of oral history and explores how primary science was structured by reference to theories of how young children learn.

PUBLISHED MATERIAL: JENKINS, E.W. & SWINNERTON, B. (1998). From steps to stages: studies in twentieth century junior school science. London: Woburn Press.

STATUS: Sponsored project

SOURCE OF GRANT: Leeds University £42,000

DATE OF RESEARCH: 1995-1998

KEYWORDS: **educational history; primary education; science education**

1073

School of Education, Leeds LS2 9JT
01132 431751

Scott, P. Prof.; Smith, D. Dr

New leadership styles in mass higher education systems

ABSTRACT: The research focuses on the changing role of university vice-chancellors. It explores two broad hypotheses. First, that new forms of executive leadership in UK higher education have emerged based on managerial expertise rather than collegial or charismatic authority. Second, that there has been a power shift in universities with vice-chancellors becoming the dominant figures in defining their cultures and determining their institutional missions and performance. The research has four main elements. First, it explores the changing career experiences and backgrounds of vice-chancellors since 1960. Second, it explores the attitudes, opinions and expectations of vice-chancellors with reference to shifting institutional priorities, leadership 'styles' or aproaches and relations between the executive, lay and bureaucratic facets of university leadership. Third, it reviews developments in university leadership in other European and North American states in order to establish convergence/divergence from the pattern of evolution in the UK. Fourth, it relates empirical evidence on the changing role of vice-chancellors to models of leadership in order to develop more refined concepts of leadership in creative knowledge-based environments. The research uses a combination of desk and field-based methods including literature reviews, construction of databases of biographical information about UK vice-chancellors appointed since 1960, semi-structured interviews of a sample of serving vice-chancellors and other senior managers, extended periods of non-participant observation and questionnaire surveys of university rectors and presidents in selected European and North American states.

PUBLISHED MATERIAL: SMITH, D., SCOTT, P., BOCOCK, J. & BAROH, C. (1998).'Vice-chancellors and executive leadership in UK universities: new roles and relationships'. In: LITTLE, B. & HENKEL, M. (Eds). Changing relationships between higher education and the state. London: Jessica Kingsley. ; BAROH, C., BOCOCK, J., SCOTT, P. & SMITH, D. University leadership: the role of the chief executive. Buckingham: Open University Press.

STATUS: Sponsored project

SOURCE OF GRANT: Leverhulme Trust £69,000

DATE OF RESEARCH: 1995-1998

KEYWORDS: **educational administration; higher education; leadership styles; management in education; universities; vice chancellors**

1074

School of Education, Leeds LS2 9JT
01132 431751

Knight, P. Mrs

Linguistic and learning experience of emerging bilingual deaf children in a mainstream nursery

ABSTRACT: Central to this project is the goal of an effective bilingual support programme for a particular group of nursery-age deaf children (3-5 years) with emerging bilingual skills. In the context of this research project the term bilingual is used to refer to the development and use of 2 languages in different modalities, i.e. a signed and a spoken language. The term sign bilingualism has been coined to distinguish this particular form of bilingualism. As a result of one local education authority's (namely the Leeds LEA) policy of 'inclusion' for all children with special educational needs, this particular group of deaf children are in a nursery setting within a mainstream school. As part of the bilingual support programme they spend 50% of the time in the mainstream hearing nursery. This is a unique setting as currently Leeds is the only LEA to have a communication policy of Total Communication (TC) with bilingual support and a policy of inclusion for all deaf children. The focus of this research is the nature of the experience for these young deaf children in the maintream nursery setting in terms of: the potential for continuing to develop their linguistic skills; and equality or 'sameness' of access to the nursery curriculum as hearing peers.

PUBLISHED MATERIAL: KNIGHT, P. (1996). 'Deaf children's choice of activities in a BSL nursery', Laserbeam, No 25, pp.8-14. ; KNIGHT, P.A. (1996). 'Deaf children in a nursery setting'. In: KNIGHT, P. & SWANWICK, R. (Eds). Bilingualism and the education of deaf children - advances in practice. Leeds: Leeds University Press. ; KNIGHT, P. & SWANWICK, R. (Eds). (1996). Bilingualism and the education of deaf children - advances in practice. Leeds: University Press. ; KNIGHT, P. (1997). 'Bilingual nursery education - a challenging start', Deafness and Education, Vol 21, No 3, pp.20-30.

STATUS: Individual research

DATE OF RESEARCH: 1996-continuing

KEYWORDS: **deafness; early childhood education; hearing impairments; mainstreaming; nursery education; preschool education; sign language; special educational needs; total communication; young children**

1075

School of Education, Leeds LS2 9JT
01132 431751

Baker, R. Mrs; Knight, P. Ms

Total communication - current policy and practice

ABSTRACT: The aim of this project was to establish current definition of the term total communication (TC) as used within the education of deaf children. Data was collected from all schools and units who had registered a policy of TC with the National Deaf Children's Society register. A questionnaire was used to gather data on a preferred definition of TC (from a choice of three definitions). There was an option to reword the definition. Also schools and units were asked to quantify, impressionistically, the extent of their use of four different communication options with the deaf and hearing impaired pupils in their schools and units. The findings suggested that the trend towards TC, as a stated communication policy, continues in schools and units. The preference for a more philosophical and explicitly child centred definition was significant. Schools for the deaf were more likely to use British Sign Language (BSL) without voice regularly and less likely to use spoken English without sign regularly. Units reflected a mirror image. The data collected also suggested a growing trend towards more sign based approaches and less English based approaches than before. Both of these issues had been previously addressed in a research study by Baker and Child, 1993.

PUBLISHED MATERIAL: BAKER, R. & CHILD, D. (1993). 'Communication approaches used in school for the deaf in the UK', Journal of British Association of the Teachers of the Deaf, Vol 17, No 2, pp.36-47.; BAKER, P. & KNIGHT, P. (1998). 'Total communication - current policy and practice'. In: GREGORY, S., KNIGHT, P., MCCRAKEN, W., POWERS, S. & WATSON, L. (Eds). Issues in deaf education. London: David Fulton.

STATUS: Team research

DATE OF RESEARCH: 1997-1998

KEYWORDS: **deafness; hearing impairments; special educational needs; total communication**

1076

School of Education, Leeds LS2 9JT
01132 431751

Zukas, M. Ms; Malcolm, J. Ms

Models of the educator in higher education

ABSTRACT: The purpose of the project is to map, both bibliographically and conceptually, the models of the educator implicit in the literature of the education of higher education teachers; to relate and compare the development of these models with those evident in the literature of related fields; to locate the development of higher education teacher training within a broader theoretical and ideological context and develop a contribution to the theory and critique of practice in the field.

STATUS: Sponsored project

SOURCE OF GRANT: Economic and Social Research Council £37,000

DATE OF RESEARCH: 1998-continuing

KEYWORDS: **higher education; preservice teacher education; teacher educators**

1077

School of Education, Leeds LS2 9JT
01132 431751

Jenkins, E. Prof.; Donnelly, J. Dr

Controlling science teachers' work

ABSTRACT: The research is directed towards the production of a book that explores changes in, and control over, secondary school science teachers' work in the second half of the 20th century. It draws upon historical and empirical data, the former obtained from two Economic and Social Research Council (ESRC) funded projects, the latter concerned with the influence of the National Curriculum on science teachers' practice in England and Wales. It explores science teachers' own sense of ownership of the work and offers insights into the limitations of earlier and current attempts at science curriculum reform.

STATUS: Sponsored project

SOURCE OF GRANT: Higher Education Funding Council

DATE OF RESEARCH: 1998-continuing

KEYWORDS: **science education; science teachers**

1078

School of Education, Leeds LS2 9JT
01132 431751

Chambers, G. Dr; Roper, T. Mr

Reasons for students withdrawing from secondary initial teacher training

ABSTRACT: From the University of Leeds 1996-97 PGCE course (secondary) of 450 students, 50 students either withdrew or failed their school experience. This number was unusually large and prompted the question 'Why?' A research exercise was carried out and repeated in 1997-98. The findings for both years were very similar and related broadly to: (1) the level of commitment demanded; (2) the mismatch between students' perception and reality of the school experience; (3) (in a few cases) ambiguity in feedback provided by schools. To what extent are these findings representative of the experience of initial teacher training (ITT) providers? Research questions are: (1) What reasons do students give for withdrawing from the course? (2) What do schools understand to be the reasons for students withdrawing? (3) Do schools make changes to provision and practice in the light of the above? (4) What implications do the findings have for ITT providers? The research design and methodology will include: (1) analysis of data relating to the numbers of students withdrawing from the 1999/00 courses in a representative sample of 10 ITT providers; (2) analysis of PGCE interview report forms and standards profiles; (3) questionnaires sent to students, school coordinators and teacher-tutors, replicating the Leeds practice of 1996/97 and 1997/98; (4) analysis of school documentation (eg lesson reports, action plans etc); (5) interviewing a 10% sample of students and school-based tutors.

STATUS: Sponsored project

SOURCE OF GRANT: University of Leeds DIRF funding £600; Teacher Training Agency £14,470

DATE OF RESEARCH: 1997-continuing

KEYWORDS: **course completion rate; dropout research; preservice teacher training; student teachers; student wastage; teaching practice**

1079

School of Education, Leeds LS2 9JT
01132 431751
Bradford & Ilkley Community College, Great Horton Road, Bradford BD1 1AY
01274 753166

Robinson, P. Mr; *Supervisor*: Marriott, S. Prof.

Attitudes towards 'economic course' provision in the public further education sector

ABSTRACT: During the 1980s the further education (FE) sector has come under increasing pressure to operate within the context of a 'New Right Market Economy'. The purpose of this research is to enquire into and collect information about people's perceptions of how economic course provision within FE can be developed more effectively. Given a context of increasing competitiveness from other public and private agencies, the research aims to examine the attitudes of staff in terms of their willingness to embrace this current entrepreneurial philosophy, as well as to further consider present management and administrative structures in order to assess the degree to which these existing structures may hinder or facilitate flexible responses to commercial demands. The research has an ethnographic base and will aim to interview respondents from four sample areas: college managers and administrators; college staff academic and technical, other local training providers; and industrial managers. An initial pilot project took place within Bradford & Ilkley Community College during the academic year 1989/90 and five subsequent research projects were developed during the following 18 months.

STATUS: Sponsored project

SOURCE OF GRANT: Bradford & Ilkley Community College £4,800

DATE OF RESEARCH: 1989-1993

KEYWORDS: **course evaluation; economics education relationship; educational administration; educational economics; entrepreneurship; further education**

1080

School of Education, Centre for Studies in Science and Mathematics, Leeds LS2 9JT
01132 431751
University of Botswana, Department of Mathematics and Science Education, Postbag 0022, Gaborone, Botswana

Towse, P. Mr; Prophet, R. Mr

Language in the learning of science

ABSTRACT: The study developed out of observations of Forms 1 and 2 (Years 7 and 8) of classrooms in Botswana. Teachers in their extensive talk use the specialised vocabulary of science linked by large amounts of non-technical language, but the lack of student participation in classroom talk makes it impossible to assess whether the students understand what they are being taught. Through test instruments, the study explored some of the problems of learning science in a second language and concentrated on the understanding of non-technical words in science used both in and independent of context. Data was collected from 271 secondary students in Botswana, 136 students of Asian origin in the Leeds/BRadford area, and 216 first language English speakers from the same area of the UK. Gender appears to play no significant role in this understanding, but level of schooling does. Comparisons with previous studies show that there has been little improvement in the understanding of non-technical words in science over the past two decades, and considerable concerns remain about the way teachers use words in science. The study indicates that the problems are greatest for second language students in the UK and the results should be of concern not only to science teachers but to teachers of all subjects.

PUBLISHED MATERIAL: PROPHET, R. & TOWSE, P. (1995). 'Non-technical words in science: a comparative study', Southern Africa Journal of Mathematics and Science Education, Vol 2, Nos 1 & 2, pp.19-31.

STATUS: Team research

DATE OF RESEARCH: 1992-1998

KEYWORDS: **botswana; language of instruction; languages for specific purposes; science education; scientific vocabulary; second language learning**

1081

School of Education, Centre for Studies in Science and Mathematics Education, Leeds LS2 9JT
01132 431751

Twigger, D. Mr; *Supervisors*: Scott, P. Dr; Leach, J. Dr

A longitudinal study of the development of selected science concepts by pupils

ABSTRACT: The physical science conceptions of a cohort of thirty secondary school pupils in one high school are being studied at yearly intervals. The longitudinal data will be analysed in order to describe patterns in the ways pupils' basic science conceptions evolve.

STATUS: Individual research

DATE OF RESEARCH: 1993-1998

KEYWORDS: **concept formation; science education; scientific concepts**

1082

School of Education, Centre for Studies in Science and Mathematics Education, Leeds LS2 9JT
01132 431751

Kent, D. Mr; Towse, P. Mr

Perceptions of science and technology

ABSTRACT: The effects of science and technology have permeated all facets of our current socio-economic life and this study focuses on various aspects of that impact as judged by student teachers, secondary pupils and members of the public. Initially, from the data collected by administering a questionnaire to the whole of a Postgraduate Certificate of Education (PGCE) cohort (269 students), it was clear that the plethora of initiatives to foster more positive attitudes to science and technology in schools in the UK over the past two decades have largely failed. The evidence pointed towards a preference among most student teachers for education to be seen in liberal humanist terms rather than in pragmatic terms. On the other hand, the responses to mainly open-ended questions of 500 junior secondary pupils in Botswana and Lesotho revealed that they perceived science and technology in broad socio-economic terms, enabling people to cope in the modern world, gain employment (in both the formal and the informal sectors) and contribute

PUBLISHED MATERIAL: KENT, D. & TOWSE, P. (1996). 'Pupil-centred aims and objectives for technology education in Botswana and Lesotho'. In: BEUTE, N. (Ed). Technology education for development in South Africa. Proceedings of a Conference at Cape Technikon, Cape Town, 1996. ; KENT, D.W. & TOWSE, P.J. (1997). 'The attitudes and values of PGCE student teachers in relation to their capacity to promote enterprise and initiatives in their future pupils'. In: RAAT, J., DE VRIES, M. & MOTTIER, I. (Eds). Teaching technology for entrepreneurship and employment. Proceedings of the PATT-7 Conference, Pedagogical Technical College, Eindhoven, 1997.; KENT, D. & TOWSE, P. (1997). 'Students' perceptions of science and technology in Botswana and Lesotho', Research in Science and Technology Education, Vol 15, No 2, pp.161-172.

STATUS: Team research

DATE OF RESEARCH: 1995-continuing

KEYWORDS: **public opinion; pupil attitudes; science education; secondary education; student teacher attitudes; technology**

1083

School of Education, Centre for Studies in Science and Mathematics Education, Leeds LS2 9JT
01132 431751

Driver, R. Prof.; Wood-Robinson, C. Mr; Leach, J. Dr; Lewis, J. Dr

Young people's understanding of, and attitudes to, the new genetics

ABSTRACT: Current advances in gene technology mean that most young people will be faced with decisions relating to genetics at some time in their adult life. This study was designed to produce baseline data on the understanding of genetics, awareness of gene technology and opinions and attitudes towards gene technology of young people nearing the end of their compulsory science education. The focus was on their understanding of genetics rather than their recall of factual knowledge and on the issues which they considered and the knowledge which they drew on, in coming to a view about different uses of gene technology, rather than their actual opinions or attitudes. Understanding of genetics was investigated through the use of written questions requiring indvidual written responses and through a series of audio-taped group interviews. The development of attitudes/opinions was investigated through written questions (which provided information about the context and the opportunity to discuss points of view before giving a written response) and audio-taped group discussions, focusing on prenatal screening and genetic engineering. Analysis of the data wass predominantly qualitative. In total over 700 key stage 4 school pupils of all abilities, drawn from 12 different schools, took part in the main study. Results showed that many young people have only a very limited understanding of basic genetic concepts at the end of their compulsory science education. Despite this they could, if provided with appropriate information, discuss social issues within a science context and come to a reasoned view which they could justify.

PUBLISHED MATERIAL: LEACH, J., LEWIS, J., DRIVER, R. & WOOD-ROBINSON, C. (1996). Opinions on and attitudes towards genetic screening; A: Pre-natal screening (cystic fibrosis). Working Paper 5. Leeds: University of Leeds, School of Education, Centre for Studies in Science and Mathematics Education. ; LEWIS, J., DRIVER, R., LEACH, J. & WOOD-ROBINSON, C. (1997). Understanding genetics: materials for investigating students understanding, with some suggestions for their use in teaching. Leeds: University of Leeds, School of Education, Centre for Studies in Science and Mathematics Education. ; LEWIS, J., DRIVER, R., LEACH, J. & WOOD-ROBINSON, C. (1997). Understanding of basic genetics and DNA technology. Working Paper 2 of the 'Young People's understanding of, and attitudes to, the new genetics' project. Leeds: University of Leeds, School of Education, Centre for Studies in Science and Mathematics Education. ; LEWIS, J., DRIVER, R., LEACH, J. & WOOD-ROBINSON, C. (1997). Opinions on and attitudes towards genetic engineering: acceptable limits; A: The discussion task; Working Paper 7 of the 'young people's understanding of, and attitudes to, the new genetics' project. Leeds: University of Leeds, School of Education, Centre for Studies in Science and Mathematics Education. ; LEWIS, J., DRIVER, R., LEACH, J. & WOOD-ROBINSON, C. (1998). 'Students' attitudes to the new genetics: pre-natal screeding for cystic fibrosis'. In: BAYRHUBER, H. & BRINKMAN, F. (Eds). "What-why-how? Research in Didaktik of Biology. Proceedings of the First Conference of European Research in the Didactics of Biology, Kiel, 1998.

STATUS: Sponsored project

SOURCE OF GRANT: Wellcome Trust £75,000

DATE OF RESEARCH: 1994-1997

KEYWORDS: controversial issues - course content; genetics; key stage 4; pupil attitudes; science education; secondary education; secondary school pupils

1084

School of Education, Centre for Studies in Science and Mathematics Education, Leeds LS2 9JT
01132 431751

Donnelly, J. Dr; Jenkins, E. Prof.; Jenkins, I. Mrs

Change and continuity in classrooms

ABSTRACT: The aim of this study is to examine the institutional, epistemological and material influences on teachers' practice. The study is using history and science as comparators. These two subjects have been chosen because, despite their obvious differences, they are both grounded in the aim of creating understanding based on evidence, but history is an archetypal humanity. There is also some evidence that history is more buoyant in attracting pupils to study it beyond the end of compulsory schooling, despite its somewhat marginal position. The study is based primarily on interviews and observations of teachers in whole departments in 6 schools. However, this is complemented by a questionnaire-based study of teachers, focusing on such issues as their motivations for entering teaching, their aims in the classrooms and their normal classroom practices. The project also involves an interview-based study of student teachers of history and science. A total of 8 questionnaires has been deployed focusing on teaching activities, evaluation, the impact of policy and teachers' working environment. The project is currently in a data analysis phase. There is also some evidence that teachers enter teaching for largely serendipitous reasons (or at least without planning to do so). This unexpected finding is being followed up by a further study.

PUBLISHED MATERIAL: JENKINS, E. (1997). 'First choice instead of last resort', Times Educational Supplement, 7 November, 1997, p.7. ; JENKINS, E. (1998). 'On becoming a secondary science teacher in England', International Journal of Science Education, Vol 20, No 7, pp.873-881. ; DONNELLY, J.F. (1998). 'The place of the laboratory in secondary science teaching', International Journal of Science Education, Vol 20, No 5, pp.585-596. ; DONNELLY, J.F. 'Interpreting differences: comparing the aims of science and history teachers', Journal of Curriculum Studies. (in press).

STATUS: Sponsored project

SOURCE OF GRANT: Economic and Social Research Council £97,000

DATE OF RESEARCH: 1996-continuing

KEYWORDS: classroom observation techniques; history; history teachers; science education; science teachers; secondary education; teacher attitudes; teacher motivation; teaching methods; teaching process; teaching profession; teaching styles

1085

School of Education, Centre for Studies in Science and Mathematics Education, Leeds LS2 9JT
01132 431751

Kent, D. Mr; Towse, P. Mr

Assessment in design and technology

ABSTRACT: The study will consider how monitoring and assessing design and technology capability can be used to raise the standards of performance of students, teachers and departments. The study arises out of a series of interviews, conducted in 1997 in a number of local schools, which sought to identify the reasons for success and failure in the Office for Standards in Education (OFSTED) inspection reports. The purpose of the study is threefold: to build on the work of Kimbell and others in defining the process of pupil assessment by examining classroom practice; to consider the assessment hierarchy referred to by Black and Atkin, which links directly

to the concept of progression, a central tenet of the National Curriculum philosophy; and finally to identify and compare the models of best practice of teaching and learning of teacher performance and of departmental organisation and management suggested by OFSTED reports of secondary school inspections. It is intended initially to conduct the study in the 10 partnership schools used.

PUBLISHED MATERIAL: KENT, D. & TOWSE, P. 'Assessment of design and technology in secondary schools: sticks, hoops and carrots'. In: MOTTIER, I. & DE VRIES, M. (Eds). Assessing technology education. Proceedings of the PATT-8 Conference, Eindhoven: Pedagogical Technological College, 1998.

STATUS: Team research

DATE OF RESEARCH: 1998-continuing

KEYWORDS: assessment; design and technology; secondary education

1086

School of Education, Centre for Studies in Science and Mathematics Education, Leeds LS2 9JT
01132 431751
York University, Department of Educational Studies, York YO1 5DD
01904 430000

Leach, J. Dr; Lewis, J. Dr; Ryder, J. Dr; Millar, R. Prof.; Driver, R. Prof.

Improving labwork in science education

ABSTRACT: This project has been carried out in collaboration with researchers in Denmark, France, Germany, Greece and Italy. The coordinator is Professor Marie-Genevieve Sere, University of Paris XI. The focus of the project is upon student learning during labwork in upper secondary schools (i.e. age 16-18) and the first two years of undergraduate science education (i.e. age 18-20). The aims of the project include: 1) documentation of the place of labwork in the educational systems of the participating countries; 2) investigation of students' images of science within this age range, with particular emphasis upon how these images of science might influence learning during labwork; 3) investigation of teachers' purposes for using different kinds of labwork; 4) investigation of students' learning during various labwork activities. The first three aims were investigated through surveys, conducted under the responsibility of Dr A. Tiberghien (COAST, Lyon), Dr J. Leach (Leeds University) and Dr M. Welzel (University of Bremen) respectively. Students' learning during labwork has been investigated through a number of case studies of labwork carried out in each country, under the coordination of Prof. D. Psillos (University of Thessaloniki) and Prof. H. Niedderer (University of Bremen). In addition, a typology of labwork has been produced under the responsibility of Prof. R. Millar (University of York). Written products from the study are available at http://edu.leeds.ac.uk/projects/lis/labwork.htm

PUBLISHED MATERIAL: LEWIS, J. 'The use of mini-projects in preparing students for independent open-ended investigative labwork', Biochemical Education. (in press).

STATUS: Sponsored project

SOURCE OF GRANT: European Commission £100,000

DATE OF RESEARCH: 1996-1998

KEYWORDS: comparative education; higher education; laboratory experiments; practical science; science activities; science education; secondary education; sixteen to nineteen education

1087

School of Education, Centre for Studies in Science Research Group, Leeds LS2 9JT
01132 431751

Carson, E. Mrs; *Supervisors*: Driver, R. Prof.; Donnelly, J. Dr

A study of first year undergraduate students' learning in physical chemistry

ABSTRACT: The project aims to identify prior conceptions of undergraduate students beginning a course in classical chemical thermodynamics, and their conceptions after a course of instruction. Changes in conceptions will be identified as well as problems that students may have in conceptualizing and learning new material. This information will also be used to inform the University Chemistry Department regarding the extent to which their teaching aims have been realised. A pilot study, now in progress, will be used to develop and refine the instrument to be used in the main study. The pilot sample consists of six students (two female, four male of whom two are Asian). Questions and problems have been devised to probe understanding of specific concepts. Students have been interviewed individually and the interviews tape-recorded and then transcribed.

STATUS: Individual research

DATE OF RESEARCH: 1993-1997

KEYWORDS: **chemistry; higher education; learning; science education; scientific concepts; students**

1088

School of Education, Computer Based Learning Unit, Leeds LS2 9JT
01132 431751
CHALCS (Computer Assisted Learning School) TECHNORTH, 9 Harrogate Road, Leeds LS7 3NB
01132 623892

Hartley, R. Prof.; Pilkington, R. Dr

Computer support for collaborative models of learning and teaching

ABSTRACT: The aim is to develop and examine models of collaborative learning, supported by computer mediated communication, and aimed particularly at the development of conceptual understanding and skills of argumentation, explanation giving and problem-solving. The research is utilising and extending software tools (e.g. e-mail bulletin boards, conferencing and knowledge tree software and Internet/Web-based tools) which relate to the functional and support requirements of the learning tasks and the models of collaborative working. A principal context is with CHALCS - a community-based institution set in the multi-cultural university that provides support for several hundred students out-of-school hours and at the weekend. Its work makes extensive use of computers and this project will establish broad-based network links between the University and CHALCS so that learning support can be delivered electronically (synchronously and asynchronously) as well as in face-to-face meetings. Much attention will be given to the recording and analysis of the developing models of collaboration and the functions and effects of computer support. The research projects are set in science, the humanities, and working/literacy skills. The work is being extended to other inner city schools and to the local community in association with the Leeds Authority (funding has been obtained from the Single Regeneration Budget and The Prince's Trust, and two rsearch students with Economic and Social Research Council (ESRC) linked awards are part of the project team).

PUBLISHED MATERIAL: HARTLEY, J.R. (1996). 'Managing models of collaborative learning', Computers and Education, Vol 26, Nos 1-3, pp.163-170.

STATUS: Sponsored project

SOURCE OF GRANT: Leverhulme Trust £12,000; Single Regneration Budget (SRD) £50,000

DATE OF RESEARCH: 1997-continuing

KEYWORDS: **computer networks; computer uses in education; cooperative learning; electronic communication; higher education; information technology**

1089

School of Education, Leeds LS2 9JT
01132 431751
Kristianstad University, Kristianstad, Sweden

Ryder, J. Dr; Redfors, A. Dr

University science students' explanations of phenomena involving the interaction between matter and radiation

ABSTRACT: This project aims to develop an understanding of the ways in which university science students use models of the structure of matter to explain phenomena involving the interaction of matter and electromagnetic radiation. The project will design and pilot a written survey instrument and an interview schedule. Following piloting, these instruments will be used to gather data from a small sample of students in the UK and Sweden. Analysis of this data will identify typical models of the structure of matter deployed by students in their explanations of phenomena involving the interaction between matter and electromagnetic radiation. If necessary, the original research instruments will then be modified for use with a larger sample of students. Key research questions for this project are: 1) Do students

draw on appropriate scientific models to explain phenomena involving the interaction between matter and electromagnetic radiation? 2) Do individual students deploy models consistently across a range of matter/electromagnetic radiation interaction contexts? 3) What are students' views about the relationship between the world of models and the world of phenomena, in the context of matter and electromagnetic radiation interaction? 4) What epistemological and ontological status do these models have for students?

STATUS: Sponsored project

SOURCE OF GRANT: British Council £1,600

DATE OF RESEARCH: 1998-continuing

KEYWORDS: **higher education; matter; physics; radiation; science education**

1090

School of Education, Leeds LS2 9JT
01132 431751
London University, Institute of Education, 20 Bedford Way, London WC1H OAL
0171 580 1122

Cameron, L. Dr; *Supervisor*: Cook, G. Dr

Metaphor in educational discourse: a theoretical and empirical investigation

ABSTRACT: This thesis investigates metaphor used by teachers and textbook writers, and the impact on children. The theoretical investigation clarifies definitions and descriptions of metaphor, to establish a valid, adequate framework for analysis of metaphor in ordinary, contextualised interaction. A 'prosaics of metaphor' is developed, including metaphor identification procedures, a set of graded descriptors of metaphor, and interactional units of analysis to investigate metaphor in talk. Theoretical issues of the coherence of the category 'prosaic metaphor', and its relation with poetic metaphor, are discussed. Two empirical investigations centre around a 10 year-old child's discourse experience in a UK primary classroom. The first analyses transcribed talk, collected across different lessons, for use of metaphor in relation to teaching/learning goals. Results include information on the frequency, distribution and nature of metaphor in use, and insights into how metaphor is signalled and supported in teacher-pupil interaction. Metaphor use is explained in terms of contextual demands, and the set of graded descriptors is refined. The second investigation uses a variation of Think Aloud methodology to explore understanding of metaphors in scientific texts. Analysis shows how knowledge brought to a text, selection of metaphors, the place of metaphor in text structure, and mediation can influence understanding and learning. The study reveals how metaphor choice can oversimplify concepts and skills which children need to acquire in the middle years of education. Interaction is shown as central in providing access to new ideas through metaphor. These results carry implications for textbook writers, teachers, and others who may mediate content through metaphor. The thesis contributes to the field of metaphor studies through links found between child and adult use, and through development of tools for analysing metaphor in interaction.

PUBLISHED MATERIAL: CAMERON, L. (1993). 'Off the beaten track: implications for teachers of recent developments in the study of metaphor', English in Education, Vol 25, No 2, pp.4-15. ; CAMERON, L. (1996). 'Discourse context and the development of metaphor in children', Current Issues in Language and Society, Vol 3, No 1, pp.49-64. ; CAMERON, L. & LOW, G. (Eds). (1999). Researching and applying metaphor. Cambridge: Cambridge University Press.

STATUS: Individual research

DATE OF RESEARCH: 1990-1997

KEYWORDS: **child language; figurative language; metaphors**

1091

School of Education, Leeds LS2 9JT
01132 431751
Open University, School of Education, Centre for Language and Communication, Walton Hall, Milton Keynes MK7 6AA
01908 274066

Swanwick, R. Ms; *Supervisors*: Gregory, S. Dr; Swann, J. Dr

The language development of sign bilingual deaf children

ABSTRACT: This is an exploratory study into the sign language and English language development of deaf children who are being educated in a bilingual setting. Little is known about the process of sign bilingual language development in deaf children and the existing educational programmes are endorsed by principles rather than research outcomes. There is a need to know more about deaf children's approaches to learning English and the extent to which their knowledge of the visual-gestural language of sign language supports or influences this process. This study seeks to identify what types of language learning strategies the children are deploying and it is hypothesised that the children's enhanced metalinguistic awareness will play a significant part in the development of these strategies. A case study approach is taken with 6 sign bilingual deaf children. The children's individual responses to learning activities which require a certain level of metalinguistic awareness are video-recorded and analysed.

PUBLISHED MATERIAL: SWANWICK, R.A. (1996). 'Deaf children's strategies for learning English'. In: KNIGHT, P. & SWANWICK, R.A. (Eds). Bilingualism and the education of deaf children: advances in practice. Conference Proceedings. Leeds: University of Leeds. ; SWANWICK, R.A. (1998). 'English as a second language for deaf children: opportunities and challenges', Deafness and Education, Vol 22, No 2, pp.3-9. ; SWANWICK, R.A. (1998). 'The teaching and learning of literacy within a sign bilingual approach'. In GREGORY, S., KNIGHT, P., MCCRACKEN, W., POWERS, S. & WATSON, L. (Eds). Issues in deaf education. London: Fulton Press.

STATUS: Individual research

DATE OF RESEARCH: 1994-continuing

KEYWORDS: **bilingualism; deafness; english - second language; hearing impairments; sign language; special educational needs**

1092

School of Social Policy and Sociology, Leeds LS2 9JT
01132 431751

Wade, A. Ms; *Supervisors*: Smart, C. Prof.; Neale, B. Dr

New childhoods? children and co-parenting after divorce

ABSTRACT: Family policy has in recent years actively encouraged divorcing parents to negotiate shared parenting arrangements to ensure that, despite the separation, children retain close links with each parent throughout their childhood. This policy has been framed in terms of the children's welfare, but no research has yet been carried out in the UK on how children actually experience dividing their time between 2 separate households. This study seeks to explore children's experiences of co-parenting and will ask what, from the children's perspective, are the advantages and disadvantages of co-parenting; how children make the emotional and practical transitions from one household to another, particularly where lifestyles or expectations of children are dissimilar; and to what extent children are able to influence the post-divorce arrangements to which they are subject. The research will be conducted from a sociological perspective and is concerned with the way in which childhood can be said to be changing in relation to new styles of parenting. Thus we will ask, for example, if co-parenting is contributing to childhood becoming increasingly constrained as a result of expectations that children meet the parenting needs of separated adults or, alternatively, whether it allows children to experience greater freedom and responsibility through enlarged opportunities to negotiate with their parents. The researchers propose to carry out indepth interviews with 80 children aged between 6 and 16 years. The sample will be theoretically driven, children being selected on the basis of their age, gender and class to ensure equal representation across these categories.

STATUS: Sponsored project

SOURCE OF GRANT: Economic and Social Research Council £100,000

DATE OF RESEARCH: 1997-continuing

KEYWORDS: **child custody; child rearing; childhood needs; children; cooperative parenting; divorce; family life; family role; home environment; parent child relationship; parent role; parents**

Leicester University

1093

Department of Adult Education, 128 Regent Road, Leicester LE1 7PA
01162 522522

Clarke, J. Ms; *Supervisor*: Colls, R. Dr

The experience of part-time higher education for students from minority ethnic communities

ABSTRACT: This research is closely associated with the Higher Education Funding Council (HEFCE) widening provision initiative at the Department of Adult Education, University of Leicester. The student profile of the Department of Adult Education is very different to the profile of the population of Leicester. Approximately 5% of students are from minority ethnic communities whereas 30% of the population of Leicester are from the Asian or African Caribbean/African communities. The aims of the PhD research are threefold. The primary aim is to discover how a sample of students from minority ethnic groups experience part-time higher education and to examine what prevents and what facilitates their progress from Access, through progression, results and after course destination. In order to understand these processes Layder's (1993,1997) theory of social domains will be used as a conceptual framework. Layder (1997) argues that there are 4 distinct yet interconnected levels of social reality: the psychobiography of individuals (for example, their experiences of education); the situated activity (for example, classroom encounters); the setting (for example, the Department of Adult Education, community centre, classroom); the broader context (for example, education policy, structural racism). Secondly a realist epistemology is being adopted (Layder 1990) and the task is to uncover previously hidden processes at work which affect student experiences. The empirical data generated will allow deeper exploration of the interconnections between the different domains in order to develop grounded theory as advocated by Glaser and Strauss (1967). Lastly, this is action research which will help change practices so that a larger proportion of people from minority ethnic communities can benefit from the instrinsic and extrinsic rewards of part-time higher education.

STATUS: Individual research

DATE OF RESEARCH: 1996-continuing

KEYWORDS: **adult education; continuing education; educational experience; ethnic groups; higher education; mature students; part time students; students**

1094

Department of Adult Education, 128 Regent Road, Leicester LE1 7PA
01162 522522

Berryman, J. Dr; Windridge, K. Dr

Later motherhood: psychological health and adjustment in the children

ABSTRACT: There is ample evidence to indicate that there are important psychological differences between children born to older mothers compared with those of younger mothers. The current study is an extension of a longitudinal study of women's experience of pregnancy, birth and motherhood as a function of maternal age. The sample of over 100 women in this study comprises participants from the original sample (n=72, mothers in 2 age groups: 20-29 years and 35 and over at childbirth; and 2 parity groups: primiparous and multiparous mothers) plus an additional sample of 29 families recruited for this study (on the same basis as above). Children are assessed in their fifth year of life on a range of measures (to explore differences reported in earlier research) of psychological development. Mothers' perceptions of their children are assessed in open-ended interviews and standardised questionnaires.

PUBLISHED MATERIAL: BERRYMAN, J.C., WINDRIDGE, K.C. & THORPE, K. (1995). Older mothers: conception, pregnancy and birth after 35. London: Pandora. ; BERRYMAN, J.C. & WINDRIDGE, K.C. (1996). 'Pregnancy after 35 and attachment to the foetus', Journal of Reproductive and Infant Psychology, Vol 14, pp.133-143. ; WINDRIDGE, K.C. & BERRYMAN, J.C. (1996). 'Maternal adjustment and maternal attitudes during pregnancy and early motherhood in women of 35 and over', Journal of Reproductive and Infant Psychology, Vol 14, pp.45-55. ; BERRYMAN, J.C. & WINDRIDGE, K.C. (1997). 'Maternal age and employment in pregnancy and after childbirth', Journal of Reproductive and Infant Psychology, Vol 15, pp.287-302.

STATUS: Sponsored project

SOURCE OF GRANT: Nestle UK Ltd £72,768

DATE OF RESEARCH: 1995-1998

KEYWORDS: **birth; late parenthood; mother child relationship; mothers; pregnancy**

1095

Department of Psychology, University Road, Leicester LE1 7RH
01162 522522

Sluckin, A. Mrs; Foreman, N. Dr; Milloy, N. Dr

The aetiology and treatment of selective mutism (children who do not talk in school)

ABSTRACT: This research is undertaken by members of the Leicester Selective Muslim Information and Research Association (SMIRA). The research analyses the phenomenon of the child who does not talk in school despite having age-appropriate speech at home. Data on 25 such cases, including details of home background, exposure to more than one language, age at referral and number of school terms spent mute, has been accumulated. The research also involves scrutinisation of the treatment programmes to which children were exposed, in particular the extent to which behavioural treatment methods were incorporated. Statistical analysis revealed that those children having made little progress at follow-up were those having a clinical psychopathology in the immediate family (often maternal depression), and those having been given standard remedial programmes in school without a behavioural component. The results suggest that a subgroup of selective mute children can be identified that is likely to persist in selectivity of speaking, and that would benefit from the early application of treatment methods having a behavioural content. Current research is aimed at extending the data to a larger sample, analysing more closely the quality of speech shown by selective mute children in the home environment, and assessing quality of speech in the school environment on recovery. It is hoped to develop procedures for assessing the possible role of behavioural inhibition in the aetiology of the condition. The research group is linked to a registered charity devoted to researching selective mutism and offering support to the parents, teachers and other professionals currently having to deal with selectively mute children. The group is currently producing a video that will be distributed to parents and professionals throughout the UK on request. The work of this group may have special relevance to the difficulties of children who are difficult to test under National Curriculum arrangements due to their reluctance to speak. The group has links with Norway and the USA.

PUBLISHED MATERIAL: SLUCKIN, A., FOREMAN, N. & HERBERT, M. (1991). 'Behavioural treatment programmes and selectivity of speaking at follow-up in a sample of twenty-five selective mutes', Australian Psychologist, Vol 26, pp.132-137.

STATUS: Team research

DATE OF RESEARCH: 1975-continuing

KEYWORDS: **elective mutism; emotional and behavioural difficulties; inhibition; psychopathology; special educational needs; speech communication**

1096

Department of Psychology, University Road, Leicester LE1 7RH
01162 522522

Foreman, N. Dr; Wilson, P. Dr

The development of spatial awareness in children with physical handicaps, particularly those integrated in mainstream schools

ABSTRACT: Children's spatial awareness has been tested using a variety of paradigms, and the development of cognitive mapping skills charted across the preschool and primary school age-range. Using search tasks with groups of 10-20 infants, it has been shown that spatial awareness develops especially rapidly between 2 and 5 years (Foreman et al, 1984), and that reference memory develops in advance of working memory for visited places (Foreman, Warry & Murray, 1990). The research has also found, in groups of 30-40 able-bodied children, that independent spatial choice is necessary for the development of spatial awareness (Foreman, Foreman et al, 1990). In disabled children integrated in mainstream schools (N=10) it was found that mobility status determined accuracy in using cognitive spatial representations of the classroom and school campus compared with a matched control group (Foreman et al, 1989; Foreman & Gell, 1990). This work was carried out collaboratively between the Psychology Department of Leicester University and the Advisory Service for Physically Impaired Pupils in Mainstream Schools, based at Westbrook Special School, Long Eaton, Derbyshire. Current research is extending the earlier work, investigating whether locomotion in space and/or spatial choice in able-bodied pupils specifically affects working or reference components of spatial memory, and whether spatial skill relates to other areas of intellectual development such as reading, mathematical or technical ability. The research attempts to develop desk-top procedures and computerised tasks which measure spatial development. This will enable schools to identify spatial disabilities and offer appropriate remedial help. Within special education, the researchers are currently exploring the use of 'virtual reality' computerised environments as a possible means of remediating spatial difficulties in more severely disabled pupils, and in relating spatial difficulties to particular forms of cerebral dysfunction. The research currently focuses upon the use of computer-simulated spatial environments (3-D Virtual Reality) to enhance and assess spatial skills in disabled children, using a variety of interface devices.

PUBLISHED MATERIAL: FOREMAN, N., ORENCAS, C., NICHOLAS, E., MORTON, P. & GELL, M. (1989). 'Spatial awareness in 7 to 11-year old physically handicapped children in mainstream schools', European Journal of Special Needs Education, Vol 4, No 3, pp.171-80. ; FOREMAN, N., FOREMAN, D., CUMMINGS, A. & OWNES, S. (1990). 'Locomotion, active choice, and spatial memory in children', Journal of General Psychology, Vol. 117, pp.215-232. ; FOREMAN, N., WARRY, R. & MURRAY, P. (1990). 'Development of reference and working spatial memory in preschool children', Journal of General Psychology, Vol 177, pp.267-276. ; FOREMAN, N. (Ed). (1993). 'Virtual reality', Special Children, No 68, pp.26-27. ; A full list of publications is available from the researchers.

STATUS: Team research

DATE OF RESEARCH: 1983-continuing

KEYWORDS: **cognitive processes; mainstreaming; spatial ability; special educational needs**

1097

Department of Psychology, University Road, Leicester LE1 7RH
01162 522522

Colley, A. Dr; *Supervisor*: Hargreaves, D. Dr

Gender differences in educational computing in the humanities

ABSTRACT: Although Information Technology (IT) has become an important part of education at all levels, there is clear evidence that girls receive less benefit from IT. Research shows that boys are more interested in computers, and that they use them more at home and at school. Computers are widely used in the male-dominated areas of science and technology but they are now making a significant impact in the arts, in subject areas which traditionally have attracted girls. This project uses a large scale survey method (N=1,500) to investigate secondary school boys' and girls' interest in, attitudes towards and use of IT in English and music in which new technologies are increasingly being used. Previous research has found that girls are likely to perform better in science and technology subjects in single-sex schools, where they do not feel in competition with their male peers. A comparison will therefore be made between pupils in co-educational and single sex schools. Gender stereotyping has prevented many girls from developing an interest in science and technology. The project will provide valuable information which can be used to ensure that girls do not miss out on technological advancements in the humanities.

STATUS: Sponsored project

SOURCE OF GRANT: Leverhulme Trust £41,593.12

DATE OF RESEARCH: 1991-1993

KEYWORDS: **computer uses in education; gender equality; humanities; information technology; sex differences**

1098

School of Education, 21 University Road, Leicester LE1 7RF
01162 522522

Fogelman, K. Prof.; Reeder, D. Dr; Crook, D. Mr

Processes and outcomes of the introduction of comprehensive schools in England and Wales

ABSTRACT: This research looks at the processes and outcomes of the introduction of comprehensive schools in England and Wales. Ten representative authorities are being studied and Duke University, North Carolina (collaborating in the project) is working on data gathered by the National Child Development Study.

STATUS: Sponsored project
SOURCE OF GRANT: Spenser Foundation
DATE OF RESEARCH: 1991-1993

KEYWORDS: comprehensive schools; educational change; educational history; secondary education

1099

School of Education, 21 University Road, Leicester LE1 7RF
01162 522522

Dobson, N. Mr; *Supervisors*: Aplin, R. Mr; Wortley, A. Mrs

The development of outdoor adventurous pursuits and education in England and France from the mid-19th century to the 1970s

ABSTRACT: The aim of this research was to compare the development of adventurous outdoor pursuits in education in England and in France from the mid-19th century to the 1970s. The work involved visiting a number of centres, library searches, and interviewing general secretaries of voluntary organisations. For the wealthy, English public schools provided team games to occupy the boys and, later, for personal development. In France physical activity hardly existed in schools, except that a few prestigious lycees took boys on mountain treks from the 1860s. Drill/physical training/physical education were of low status and usually neglected. Philanthropic agencies took poor city children to the open air for therapeutic reasons from the mid-1800s in England and in France. Outdoor pursuits gained ground among the middle-classes; voluntary agencies such as the Scouts and Young Men's Christian Association (YMCA) were active on both sides of the Channel. After World War 2 outdoor pursuits increased in the educational domain. In England local education authorities (LEAs) and voluntary bodies experimented; in France the government directed experimentation but the popularity of outdoor activities increased in both societies. 'New education' has had a considerable influence, especially in France. Outdoor pursuits do not carry the stigma that physical education has long borne so public schoolmasters and professeurs were prepared to initiate work in this field.

STATUS: Individual research
DATE OF RESEARCH: 1991-1997

KEYWORDS: comparative education; educational history; france; outdoor pursuits; physical education; recreational activities; sports; youth movements; youth work

1100

School of Education, 21 University Road, Leicester LE1 7RF
01162 522522

Brown, M. Mrs; *Supervisors*: Wright, C. Dr; Fogelman, K. Prof.

Multicultural education: images at primary level

ABSTRACT: Is concern about minority pupils a worthy matter or are there more pressing problems in education? What does multicultural education mean in terms of actual school practice? Who is referred to when we use the term 'ethnic minority'? In this study an observational research will be conducted, with the aim of analysing attitudes and views of teachers and pupils of given primary schools. Three types of schools will be researched and formal and informal interviews with individuals and groups of teachers and pupils will be conducted. Records and reports will also be assessed in order to discover views on multicultural education and to ascertain if school experiences of ethnic minority pupils in the various schools are similar. It will also be decided whether the internal system of the schools and their teaching methods have differential effects on the pupils of ethnic minority. The three different types of school examined are: (a) large primary schools in inner city areas (Birmingham and London) where there exists a high percentage of pupils from ethnic minority backgrounds. In these schools multicultural educational techniques are used to an extreme to cater for 'supposed needs' especially in the area of language development; (b) primary schools in developing towns (Northampton and Cambridge) where pupils of multiethnic backgrounds attend on a smaller scale, and multicultural teaching methods and practices are incorporated in the curriculum successfully; (c) rural primary schools where heads and teachers alike believe that multicultural education is not needed in their school as no pupils of multiethnic backgrounds attend and they find multicultural education baffling, misleading and foreign. The study prompts questions in relation to the degree of multicultural awareness and practices observed in schools.

STATUS: Sponsored project
SOURCE OF GRANT: Overstone Park Kindergarten & Preparatory School
DATE OF RESEARCH: 1988-1993

KEYWORDS: ethnic groups; multicultural education; primary education

1101

School of Education, 21 University Road, Leicester LE1 7RF
01162 522522

Martin, J. Mrs; *Supervisor*: Lofthouse, M. Dr

Management and development of teacher education in Jamaica (the Caribbean) and England 1938-1988

ABSTRACT: This research will take an historical look at teacher training in the Caribbean and in Jamaica, in particular. Some indicators will be pointed up to present policy. The level is all through ages 5-16, but emphasis is upon adolescence and the tailoring of initial teacher training (ITT) towards it.

STATUS: Individual research
DATE OF RESEARCH: 1989-1993

KEYWORDS: educational history; jamaica; preservice teacher education

1102

School of Education, 21 University Road, Leicester LE1 7RF
01162 522522

Watkins, G. Ms; *Supervisor*: Hunter-Carsch, C. Mrs

Prompt Spelling: a practical approach to the teaching and learning of spelling at secondary level

ABSTRACT: The aim of the research was to generate, trial, develop and evaluate a practical approach to the teaching and learning of spelling in the secondary school. The desired focus was on developing the pupils' own skills in identifying and correcting spelling errors through working in partnership with a skilled speller and with the aid of a handheld electronic spellchecker. The development of the approach, 'prompt spelling', involved a series of investigations and 5 systematic studies with a total of over 60 pupils and 20 teachers. Research methods within the framework of action research included observation and interviews, interaction analysis and library based investigations. The foci of the studies included: 1) the role of the designer/field researcher and the impact of the originator on the prompters and promptees; 2) the communication of the approach without the direct intervention of the originator; 3) the process of peer tutoring; 4) a comparison of the effects of a phonic based approach and prompt spelling approach on spelling achievement; and 5) the effects of the approach on reading behaviour and achievement. The results of the exploratory investigations and studies cumulatively go beyond the generation and refinement of the approach to endorse its efficacy in raising pupils' spelling ages on standardised tests of spelling (Blackwell Spelling Test). The conclusions are that the approach is viable as a teaching and learning method and was found to be more effective than other methods in use in all of the participating schools and through correspondence extending the action research with over 25 schools nationwide.

PUBLISHED MATERIAL: WATKINS, G.A. & HUNTER-CARSCH, C.M. (1995). Prompt spelling: a practical approach to paired spelling', Support for Learning, Vol 10, No 3, pp.133-137. ; WATKINS, G.A. (1996). 'A teacher's guide to prompt spelling: using the Franklin electronic spellmaster. Franklin Electronic Publisher.
STATUS: Individual research
DATE OF RESEARCH: 1995-1997

KEYWORDS: achievement; literacy; peer teaching; reading achievement; secondary education; spellchecker; spelling; teaching methods

1103

School of Education, 21 University Road, Leicester LE1 7RF
01162 522522

Rappaport, J. Mrs; *Supervisor*: Hunter-Carsch, C. Mrs

An exploratory study of assessment and teaching of children with phonological awareness difficulties

ABSTRACT: The background to this study relates to concern about the seeming failure of a sample of children with specific language disorders and moderate learning difficulties to progress in literacy development. Their observed 'plateau' and its relationship to the need to develop phonological awareness is explored in one of two main strands of the study. The other strand concerns multidiscipline aspects of specific learning difficulties, the perceptions of roles of speech and language therapists, teachers and educational psychologists working with children in mainstream and special school contexts. The design of the investigation involves close study of ten language disordered children in special schools and the views of multidiscipline staff working with more than ten children in mainstream schools. Methods include: observation; analysis of the researchers' fieldnotes and professional reflective accounts; structured questionnaires using a triangulation approach; and a clinical study involving pre- and post-testing in the context of studying the effects of a structured teaching programme. Data collection is completed and analysis is in progress. Products include a test of rhyming ability (TORA), a specialised teaching programme and findings related to effective multidiscipline approaches to management and teaching of children with such difficulties.

STATUS: Individual research

DATE OF RESEARCH: 1993-continuing

KEYWORDS: **language handicaps; learning disabilities; mainstreaming; phonology; special educational needs; special schools**

1104

School of Education, 21 University Road, Leicester LE1 7RF
01162 522522

Aplin, R. Mr

Cultural awareness in French language teaching materials

ABSTRACT: An analytical examination of the cultural images contained within the new range of materials for French teaching in British schools, designed specifically for the National Curriculum. The texts, illustrations, core linguistic material of exercises, learner activities, teachers' support material, and extension material specifically produced for cultural information and awareness raising are analysed. Sample units are selected from each work subjected to analysis, and examples drawn from the varied media used to make up the overall package. The criteria against which they are analysed are the extent to which consideration and/or the presentation of the culture of the target community: a) is influenced by stereotypical views; b) is likely to reduce problems of motivation among learners; c) presents a factually authoritative aspect; and d) is susceptible to use within currently accepted principles of good practice.

STATUS: Sponsored project

SOURCE OF GRANT: Leicester University £1,400

DATE OF RESEARCH: 1997-continuing

KEYWORDS: **cultural awareness; educational materials; french; modern language studies; national curriculum**

1105

School of Education, 21 University Road, Leicester LE1 7RF
01162 522522

Aplin, R. Mr

Language awareness/knowledge about language: annotated bibliography

ABSTRACT: A bibliographical investigation of the materials available in the fields of language awareness and knowledge about language, related to the worlds of linguistics and the National Curriculum. The annotations provided in this listing of almost 600 titles will enable teachers, teacher educators, curriculum developers and researchers to select appropriate texts for their own needs.

PUBLISHED MATERIAL: APLIN, R. (1993). 'Language awareness bibliography, part 1', Language Awareness, Vol 2, No 2, pp.115-123. ; APLIN, R. (1993). 'Language awareness bibliography, part 2', Language Awareness, Vol 2, No 3, pp.175-185. ; APLIN, R. (1997). Language awareness/knowledge about language: an annotated bibliography. Leicester: Association for Language Awareness.

STATUS: Individual research

DATE OF RESEARCH: 1992-continuing

KEYWORDS: **bibliographies; english; language; language research; linguistics; national curriculum**

1106

School of Education, 21 University Road, Leicester LE1 7RF
01162 522522

Hall, B. Mrs; *Supervisor*: Cortazzi, M. Dr

Conceptual language barriers in bilingual learners

ABSTRACT: This research project aims to examine linguistic, cultural and social factors affecting the progress of bilingual learners in the English primary education system. There is a special focus on perceived conceptual language barriers. The study encompasses semi-structured interviews with teachers; pupil vocabulary testing; and analysis of classroom discourse. It is based in schools across Leicestershire. The results and conclusions will be used to inform future practice.

PUBLISHED MATERIAL: HALL, B. (1996). 'A review of action research'. In: CORTAZZI, M., GALEA, & HALL, B. (Eds). 'Aspects of language teaching and learning'. Proceedings of the University of Leicester Research Students Conference, 1996.

STATUS: Individual research

DATE OF RESEARCH: 1992-1998

KEYWORDS: **achievement; bilingual pupils; english - second language; primary education; primary school pupils; second language learning**

1107

School of Education, 21 University Roaed, Leicester LE1 7RF
01162 522522

Dowling, S. Mrs

Monitoring National Curriculum art: access to the curriculum for pupils with particular needs

ABSTRACT: Part of the School Curriculum and Assessment Authority's (SCAA) corporate plan for 1995-98 involves monitoring all aspects of the National Curriculum with a view to identifying areas where development work might be needed. This small project relates to art. It aims to investigate how teachers build access into their schemes of work in every aspect of the programme of study. The focus is largely on key stages 1 and 2. Approximately 9 schools will be visited across Buckinghamshire, Leicestershire and Northamptonshire, selected to provide balance in terms of special needs provision and quality of art practice in special and mainstream schools. The investigation will be carried out by means of a questionnaire, semi-structured interviews based on a teaching model and observation of classroom practice. Outcomes will include a critique of this model, findings from the investigation, identification of aspects of the programmes of study where teachers need support and recommendations for further work.

STATUS: Sponsored project

SOURCE OF GRANT: Schools Curriculum and Assessment Authority £1,500

DATE OF RESEARCH: 1996-1997

KEYWORDS: **art education; key stage 1; key stage 2; national curriculum; primary education; special educational needs**

1108

School of Education, 21 University Road, Leicester LE1 7RF
01162 522522

Dowling, S. Mrs; *Supervisor*: Fogelman, K. Prof.

The educational implications of low birth weight

ABSTRACT: This educational survey of a cohort of 200 very low birth weight babies at 7 years should be considered in the context of the 2 preceding geographically defined medical studies. The first study at 18 months (Graham et al 1987) showed that severe cases of cerebral palsy could be accurately predicted by ultrasound brain scans. In the second at school entry, the surviving 155 children were traced and matched for age, sex and race. All except 4 were in mainstream but quantitative results showed motor and intellectual abilities were significantly lower than their peers and risk of motor impairment was closely related to low birth weight (Levene et al 1992). Qualitative data indicated that many teachers did not know of the children's early history but were concerned regarding their emotional development and the parents' level of anxiety. The aim of the survey is to investigate the impact of this situation on learning in the classroom. The children were traced through the schools identified in the previous study. A response rate of 77% produced a cohort of 111 matched pairs. A teacher questionnaire covered National Curriculum key stage 1 attainments and perceptions of the children's and parents' behaviour. Findings show the attainment of children of very low birth weight are significantly lower in English and mathematics, and there is significant risk of behavioural disorder. A high level of parental concern is associated with the latter. Educational implications relate to the need for: 1) a low birth weight policy at government level; 2) inter-professional collaboration; 3) improved identification procedures; 4) teacher development; 5) classroom-based research; 6) support for parents and resources for intervention.

STATUS: Sponsored project

SOURCE OF GRANT: University of Leicester

DATE OF RESEARCH: 1992-1998

KEYWORDS: **academic achievement; achievement; birth weight; child development; parent needs; performance; premature infants; special educational needs**

1109

School of Education, 21 University Road, Leicester LE1 7RF
01162 522522

Nemati, M. Mr; *Supervisor*: Cortazzi, M. Dr

Mode of discourse effects on English as a foreign language (EFL) writing performance

ABSTRACT: It has been known for a long time that first language (L1) writers perform differently in different modes of discourse. Despite the importance of this, there has been no conclusive evidence to shed light on the issue of how English as a second language (ESL)/English as a foreign language (EF) learners' writing performance varies across discourse types. Therefore, this research study is designed to investigate the differences resulting from the effect of writing in 4 discourse modes: narrative, description, explanation, and argument. The probable differences were evaluated using the 3 dimensions of production (through eliciting compositions), recognition (through Cloze tests derived from compositions written in different discourse modes), and the learners' and teachers' attitudes towards these types of writing (through questionnaires). The pilot study as well as some parts of the main study completed so far, show a statistically significant difference among these discourse types, ranking descriptive and narrative writing as the easiest and argumentative as the most demanding type of writing.

STATUS: Individual research

DATE OF RESEARCH: 1994-1997

KEYWORDS: **discourse; english - second language; writing - composition**

1110

School of Education, 21 University Road, Leicester LE1 7RF
01162 522522

Wu, C. Ms; *Supervisor*: Robertson, D. Dr

The management of teaching Mandarin Chinese in British Chinese schools

ABSTRACT: How to teach Mandarin Chinese to speakers of other languages has become an important issue as the 'Chinese-speaking population' grows and 'learning Chinese' has become of more practical value. Chinese schools in the UK and throughout the world have been set up to educate people overseas in their own language and to maintain culture links with their country of origin. With the opening of Mainland China's huge market and the take-over of Hong Kong, Chinese schools, especially those in the UK, are facing new demands of organising Mandarin Chinese courses to keep up with the need. The aims of this study are: 1) to collect data from British Chinese schools about their current situation; 2) to find out from schools which offer Mandarin Chinese classes especially those which also offer

Cantonese classes - what kind of difficulties they are facing; 3) to compare the difficulties and methods which have been used to solve similar situations; and 4) hopefully to make recommendations for schools which are facing difficulties or which are considering organising courses in the future. Methods to be used for collecting information will include classroom observations, interviews (with headteachers, course organisers, Mandarin Chinese teachers, students and parents), as well as a field diary.

STATUS: Individual research

DATE OF RESEARCH: 1996-continuing

KEYWORDS: **chinese; language acquisition; language teachers; mandarin chinese; mother tongue**

1111

School of Education, 21 University Road, Leicester LE1 7RF
01162 522522

Barker, B. Mr; *Supervisor*: Galton, M. Prof.

Investigation of school effectiveness variables

ABSTRACT: School effectiveness research, often funded by government institutions in many countries, has shaped an educational agenda where individual schools are expected to transform their students' lives, in terms of GCSE (and other scores) and career prospects. The investigation challenges the assumptions and methodology of effectiveness research and proposes a qualitative approach with greater attention to the underlying experience of pupils and teachers. Fieldwork entails observing 2 schools (one deemed effective, another not so) for an extended period to compare and contrast institutional variables in the context of a critical ethnographic perspective.

STATUS: Individual research

DATE OF RESEARCH: 1996-continuing

KEYWORDS: **educational quality; performance indicators; school effectiveness; secondary education**

1112

School of Education, 21 University Road, Leicester LE1 7RF
01162 522522

Colls, R. Dr

Fulfilling the part-time higher educational needs for students from minority ethnic communities

ABSTRACT: This research and development work is part of the Higher Education Funding council (HEFCE) widening provision initiative. The student profile of the Department of Adult Education is very different to the profile of the population of Leicester. Approximately 5% of students are from minority ethnic communities whereas 30% of the population of Leicester are from the Asian or African Caribbean/African communities. The aim of the project is to develop contact with and establish the educational needs of adult members of minority ethnic communities, and to adjust and develop identified curriculum areas to meet these needs. In order to understand these processes Layder's (1993, 1997) theory of social domains will be used as a conceptual framework. Layder (1997) argues that there are 4 distinct yet interconnected levels of social reality: the psychobiography of individuals - (for example their experiences of education); the situated activity - (for example classroom encounters); the setting - (for example the Department of Adult Education, community centre, classroom encounters; the broader context - (for example education policy, structural racism). Needs have been surveyed through focus groups and indepth interviews. In the first phase, focus groups were drawn from the community centre users; Access students, overseas graduates on language courses and participants in a voluntary project. Indepth interviews were conducted with prospective, current and past students of the Department of Adult Education and undergraduate students studying part-time at another local institution. A black tutors' advisory group meets termly to reflect on the progress of the project and was involved in a Saturday school taster course. A number of these tutors are now teaching for the Department. Curriuculum development has taken place in the community through the development of the Certificate in Advice Work, the Certificate in Managing Voluntary and Community Groups, Certificates for Classroom Assistants and on mainstream programmes in the Department, in particular the BA Humanities, which now has a BA World Humanities option. Lastly the culture and ethos of the Department is being considered in order to work towards implementing and embedding change in the longer term. In the second phase of the research, the associational life of Leicester's black and Asian community will be surveyed. The researcher will be looking, in particular, at different forms of education, of all types, at all levels.

PUBLISHED MATERIAL: CLARKE, J. (1998). 'Leicester case study'. In: MCNAIR, S. (Ed). Widening provision. Bristol: Higher Education Funding Council for England.

STATUS: Sponsored project

SOURCE OF GRANT: Higher Education Funding Council for England £30,343

DATE OF RESEARCH: 1996-continuing

KEYWORDS: **access to education; adult education; continuing education; educational needs; ethnic groups; higher education; mature students; part time students; students; widening participation**

1113

School of Education, 21 University Road, Leicester LE1 7RF
01162 522522

Allen, T. Ms; *Supervisor*: Lawson, A. Mr

Exploration of relationships between ethnicity and reactions to transfer from school to further education (FE) college at 16

ABSTRACT: The main aims of the project are: 1) to look at the experience of school leavers as they develop throughout their first year of college; 2) to investigate how this choice and experience may be affected by ethnic influences on self-esteem, attitudes, aspirations and motivation; and 3) to identify gender differences, particularly those related to ethnicity and any combined impact on this phase of transfer. Observation, interviewing and questionnaires will all be used. Pupils currently in Year 11 will also complete an end of year questionnaire indicating transfer intentions and motivations. Teaching staff in colleges and schools will also be interviewed. Fieldwork is based in Nottingham and Leicester city areas.

STATUS: Sponsored project

SOURCE OF GRANT: University of Leicester £15,600

DATE OF RESEARCH: 1996-continuing

KEYWORDS: **ethnic groups; further education; motivation; pupil attitudes; school to further education transition; school to work transition; secondary education; self esteem; sex differences; sixteen to nineteen education; training; transfer pupils**

1114

School of Education, 21 University Road, Leicester LE1 7RF
01162 522522

Edwards, J. Mrs; *Supervisor*: Fogelman, K. Prof.

Centre for citizenship studies in education

ABSTRACT: The Centre for Citizenship Studies was established in 1991 to undertake research and development to promote and support citizenship education in schools. Its output includes a broadsheet series for schools, packs to support inservice education for schools and classroom materials, as well as books and journal articles. Recent research includes a survey of 144 primary schools throughout England. Main findings revealed positive attitudes to citizenship education, but variable practice constrained by lack of time, support and resources (see Kerr, 1996).

PUBLISHED MATERIAL: EDWARDS, J. & TROTT, C. (1995). 'Education for citizenship in key stages 1 and 2', Curriculum Journal, Vol 6, No 3, pp.395-408. ; KERR, D. (1996). Citizenship in primary schools. London: Institute for Citizenship Studies. ; FOGELMAN, K. (1996). 'Education for citizenship and the national curriculum'. In: DEMAINE, J. & ENTWISTLE, H. (Eds). Beyond communitarianism: citizenship, politics and education. London: MacMillan. ; FOGELMAN, K. (1996). 'European citizenship: a challenge for education'. In: TIMMER, J. & VELDHUIS, R. (Eds). Political education - towards a European democracy. Amsterdam: Instituut voor Politiek en Publiesk.

STATUS: Sponsored project

SOURCE OF GRANT: Barclaycard and Esso jointly £350,000

DATE OF RESEARCH: 1991-continuing

KEYWORDS: **citizenship education; cross curricular approach; primary education; secondary education; values education**

1115

School of Education, 21 University Road, Leicester LE1 7RF
01162 522522

Underwood, J. Dr

TEEODE - assessment and evaluation in open and distance learning

ABSTRACT: This is a collaborative project with Antonio Bartolome, Univesitat de Barcelona; Karl Steffens, Universitat zu Koln; Brigitte Denis, Service de Technologie de l'Education, Univeriste de Liege; Luciano Cecconi, Terza Universita degli Studi di Roma, Ordinario di Pedagogia sperimentale; and Lidia Graves, Universidade Aberta, Lisboa. Distance learning courses are an important way of meeting society's needs for more flexible ways of educating and training a modern workforce. Supporting students at a distance raises new and interesting questions. Of particular interest to the TEEODE project are the methods of assessment and evaluation employed by the various suppliers of distance learning courses. The aim of the TEEODE project is to develop a representative survey of the models of assessment and evaluation used by institutions supporting distance learning. This survey will cover all 15 member states of the European Union. For each of the member countries it is hoped to survey up to 10 institutions on their formal procedures or framework for assessment and evaluation; and up to 10 tutors on individual courses within those institutions on how they conduct their assessment and evaluation. This survey will be in 3 parts: 1) A questionnaire on the formal framework of procedures for assessment and evaluation of distance learning within each institution. 2) In selected cases, follow-up telephnoe interviews. 3) A second questionnaire to be answered by up to 10 course tutors on their assessment and evaluation of students on their distance learning courses.

STATUS: Sponsored project

SOURCE OF GRANT: European Union

DATE OF RESEARCH: 1996-1998

KEYWORDS: **assessment; comparative education; continuing education; distance education; europe; open education**

1116

School of Education, 21 University Road, Leicester LE1 7RF
01162 522522

Galton, M. Prof.; Hargreaves, L. Dr; Comber, C. Mr; Wall, D. Ms

The effects of school transfer on pupils at National Curriculum key stages 2 and 3

ABSTRACT: The project is a replication of part of the ORACLE project carried out in the late 1970s. It is examining the effects of transfer from primary to secondary school on pupils' classroom behaviour, achievement and attitudes to school, measures which showed a hiatus on transfer for a significant proportion of children in the previous study. The present study is interested in the extent to which the National Curriculum and emphasis on cross-phase continuity may reduce this effect. The main research methods are: systematic observation of children during their final year of primary/lower school and first year of secondary/middle phase; short achievement tests, self-esteem and attitudes to school measures; and semi-projective questionnaires using cartoons administered before and after transfer. Ethnographic observation was carried out of the children's 'induction day' experiences of their new schools, and of their first 4 days in the new school. Parents meetings, open nights and cross-phase teachers' meetings have been observed. Preliminary results of the observational data from primary classrooms suggest children spending less time off task, and teachers making more use of whole class audience at certain times and in certain curriculum areas. Results of the social measures and achievement tests are not yet available. There has been a considerable increase in cross-phase liaison between primary and secondary schools.

PUBLISHED MATERIAL: GALTON, M. (1983). 'Problems in transition'. In: GALTON, M. & WILLCOCKS, J. (Eds). Moving from the primary classroom. London: Routledge & Kegan Paul.

STATUS: Sponsored project

SOURCE OF GRANT: Economic and Social Research Council £51,000

DATE OF RESEARCH: 1995-1997

KEYWORDS: **developmental continuity; key stage 2; key stage 3; national curriculum; primary education; primary to secondary transition; pupil attitudes; pupil behaviour; secondary education; transfer pupils**

1117

School of Education, 21 University Road, Leicester LE1 7RF
01162 522522

Cavendish, S. Dr; Cavendish, N. Mr

Impact of Integrated Learning Systems on children

ABSTRACT: Research studies have shown that primary children show a weak understanding of the concepts underlying conventional arithmetic algorithms. They rely on learning procedures which result in numerous errors and slow progress (Van Lehn, 1986). One innovation which might be effective in eleminating certain types of errors is that of the use of computer systems called Integrated Learning Sytems (ILS). The first part of the present study focuses on pupils' errors in computation. Responses to a mathematics test are analysed for errors in basic arithmetic. The performance of pupils who used ILS over a period of 6 to 18 months is being compared to that of control groups. Pre- and post-test scripts were obtained from 260 pupils (520 scripts). The second focus of this study is the impact of ILS on pupils' motivation. There is a wealth of evidence that use of computers can be motivating to pupils. For the present study motivation was investigated using sentence completion items in response to cartoon drawings of a mathematics or English lesson. A small sample of this data has been analysed providing tentative findings that ILS pupils appear to have developed an independent way of working, and ILS pupils changed their view of the teacher from one of 'disciplinarian' to one of a 'helper'. The sample was very small and analysis of the whole sample is now underway.

STATUS: Sponsored project

SOURCE OF GRANT: Leicester University £3,902

DATE OF RESEARCH: 1997-1997

KEYWORDS: **computer assisted learning; computer uses in education; information technology; integrated learning systems; mathematics education; motivation; primary education; primary school pupils; pupil attitudes**

1118

School of Education, 21 University Road, Leicester LE1 7RF
01162 522522

Thornton, B. Mrs; *Supervisor:* Fogelman, K. Prof.

Language anxiety among 14-15 year-old learners in Britain

ABSTRACT: This study examines the existence of language anxiety among 14-15 year-old modern language learners in British secondary schools. A questionnaire was administered to 607 learners of French, German and Italian focusing on attitudinal and affective factors in language learning. Findings showed that anxiety was a factor in language learning, that it was related to other variables and that it did have a generally debilitating effect on language learning. An exception, however, was test anxiety which was reported as a positive motivator to learning by pupils within the study. The second phase of the project involved a detailed study of a smaller group of 52 Year 10 learners across the ability range to look at the effects of anxiety on the learning process and gain some insights as to the possible causes and ways in which it might be alleviated. This stage included a series of observations, interviews with students and teachers, semi-structured discussions and questionnaires. The data analysis relating to this stage is still ongoing.

STATUS: Individual research

DATE OF RESEARCH: 1994-continuing

KEYWORDS: **anxiety; modern language studies; secondary education; secondary school pupils**

1119

School of Education, 21 University Road, Leicester LE1 7RF
01162 522522

Moyles, J. Mrs; Adams, S. Mrs

Too busy to play? An intervention study to enhance and develop play practices for early years teachers and nursery nurses

ABSTRACT: The aims of this project are to: 1) analyse and evaluate play practices; generate and facilitate interactive practical play sessions; develop practitioners' capabilities to articulate their own constructs and rationales for play and to disseminate effective strategies; 2) learn how best to support early years practitioners to efficiently and effectively utilise play as a teaching and learning tool and process; and 3) produce a series of 'activity packs' on play and learning for practitioners, grounded in high quality practices and theoretically sound. The research entails: 1) conducting an investigation into how practitioners perceive play and, more importantly, the development of their own thorough, working constructs of play as part of developmentally appropriate learning processes for children; 2) undertaking practical play support sessions with selected practitioners in partnership with researchers to convert practitioners' known rhetoric about play into practical experiences which they define and articulate; 3) supporting practitioners in an interactive way in developing play and learning activities in which they themselves will be play partners; 4) enabling practitioners to convert their growing knowledge into ways and means of planning play within the early years curriculum in their own schools and match teaching through play to learning intentions and outcomes; and 5) conducting a thorough analysis and evaluation of practitioners' and researchers' emerging knowledge achieved as a result of the project. The project will include case studies of the main participants and their partnerships. It involves a purposive sample of selected participants drawn from a range of schools, initially in the Leicester area, who are already identified as 'quality' practitioners. The sample group will meet over Terms 1, 2 and 3 of the research period in order to develop and extend the basis of their knowledge and ideas for practice. They will keep journals, analyse videos of play situations in their own classrooms and evaluate the role of the adults.

STATUS: Sponsored project

SOURCE OF GRANT: Esmee Fairbairn Charitable Trust £45,000

DATE OF RESEARCH: 1997-continuing

KEYWORDS: **early childhood education; infant school teachers; nursery nurses; nursery school teachers; play; preschool education; young children**

1120

School of Education, 21 University Road, Leicester LE1 7RF
01162 522522

Galton, M. Prof.; Fogelman, K. Prof.

The use of discretionary time in the primary school

ABSTRACT: The Dearing report on the National Curriculum recommended slimming down, partly in order to free some 20% of the teaching time for use at the discretion of schools. The aims of this study were to clarify issues relating to this discretionary time in primary schools, such as how it is allocated, what it is used for and how these decisions are reached, and to explore primary teachers' attitudes to further changes in the curriculum. Information has been obtained in two ways. Unstructured interviews were undertaken with 8 headteachers in the Midlands in order to identify concerns and other factors affecting the allocation of discretionary time, and also to inform the design and explicate the results of a questionnaire survey. The survey entailed the distribution of 350 questionnaires, through the National Association of Primary Education. 161 (46%) were returned, representing a range of schools of different sizes, age ranges of pupils and proportions of full and part-time teaching staff. Results are reported in the publications listed below.

PUBLISHED MATERIAL: GALTON, M. & FOGELMAN, K. (1997). The use of discretionary time in primary schools. Leicester: University of Leicester, School of Education.; GALTON, M. & FOGELMAN, K. (1997/8). 'Discretionary time: a phantom concept', Education Review, Vol 11, No 2, pp.26-34.; GALTON, M. & FOGELMAN, K. 'The use of discretionary time in primary schools', Research Papers in Education. (in press).

STATUS: Sponsored project

SOURCE OF GRANT: National Union of Teachers £18,369

DATE OF RESEARCH: 1997-1997

KEYWORDS: curriculum development; discretionary time; primary education; primary school curriculum; school organisation; teacher attitudes; time management

1121

School of Education, 21 University Road, Leicester LE1 7RF
01162 522522

Cajkler, W. Mr; Busher, H. Dr

Approaches by teachers to staff development programmes in primary and secondary schools

ABSTRACT: This project sets out the working patterns preferred by teachers in primary and secondary schools when they are undertaking continuing professional development on both award-bearing and non-award bearing courses, and through school-based activities. Part of this investigation is also to discover the range of topics on which and in which teachers think they need to develop their professional skills and knowledge. In the first place the investigation is to be carried out through a large-scale survey of teachers' views in the Midlands. It is intended to follow-up the survey with a conference, both to present the findings to teachers in the Leicester area and to engage in group interviews with them on the matters under review, in particular exploring why they make the choices they do. Subsequent work is likely to take the form of case studies of teachers in particular schools.

STATUS: Team research

DATE OF RESEARCH: 1998-continuing

KEYWORDS: inservice teacher education; primary school teachers; secondary school teachers; teacher attitudes; teacher development

1122

School of Education, 21 University Road, Leicester LE1 7RF
01162 522522

Busher, H. Dr; Wortley, A. Mrs

The impact of a new headteacher on the culture and performance of a school

ABSTRACT: There is widespread acknowledgement in both the literature and in government reports in the UK that the impact of a headteacher on a school is great, and that the leadership he or she offers is a major factor in the direction which a school takes. This study focuses on recent key events as a new headteacher takes office in a school and begins to develop and helps the school to develop during the first 18 months of his/her term in office. To get a view on the culture and the micro-political processes of change, the headteacher and a number of other staff and governors are interviewed, using tape-recorded semi-structured interview about their views on particular critical incidents in the schools and the headteacher's development. Views are sought from these key witnesses roughly once every 6 weeks or every half-term. As schools as institutions are historically and socio-politically located, the interviews, especially the first ones, will explore these parameters within which the school's action is located.

STATUS: Team research

DATE OF RESEARCH: 1997-continuing

KEYWORDS: head teachers; organisational climate; school effectiveness

1123

School of Education, 21 University Road, Leicester LE1 7RF
01162 522522

Moyles, J. Mrs; Suschitzky, W. Mrs

Nursery teachers and nursery nurses comparative roles study

ABSTRACT: Teamwork in early years settings: how effectively do differentially trained adults work together to support the education of 3-7 year-olds? With current moves to increase educational provision for under-fives, the question of the level of training required for people who work with young children is under scrutiny. Early years personnel increasingly work alongside one another, apparently undertaking similar roles, and questions have been raised at government level regarding the type of training required by people specialising in the education of 3-7 year-olds. There is a dearth of research into beliefs, practices and knowledge, both curricular and pedagogic, of these differentially qualified adults. This research has investigated the working roles and relationships of these early years teams and their effectiveness in providing high quality learning experiences for children. An initial questionnaire survey of around 400 teachers, nursery nurses and classroom assistants, followed-up by structured interviews and observations with a 10% sample of differentially trained respondents drawn from a range of local education authorities in England, has highlighted widely differing roles and responsibilities and examined comparative training needs.

PUBLISHED MATERIAL: MOYLES, J. & SUSCHITZKY, W. (1995). 'A matter of difference: nursery teachers and nursery nurses working together', Education 3-13, Vol 23, No 3, pp.41-46. ; MOYLES, J. & SUSCHITZKY, W. (1997). 'The buck stops here ...! Nursery teachers and nursery nurses working together'. A report on an investigation into the working roles and relationships of nursery teachers and nursery nurses and their perceptions of each other's contribution to children's early learning. Leicester: University of Leicester and Esmee Fairbairn Foundation. ; MOYLES, J. & SUSCHITZKY, W. (1997). 'Jills of all trades ...? Classroom assistants in KS1 classes'. A report on an investigation into the working roles and relationships of KS1 teachers and classroom assistants, including those training as specialist teaching assistants, and their perceptions of each others' contribution to children's core curriculum learning. Leicester: University of Leicester and Association of Teachers and Lecturers. ; MOYLES, J. & SUSCHITZKY, W. (1997). 'The employment and deployment of classroom support staff - headteachers' perspectives', Research in Education, Vol 58, pp.22-34. ; MOYLES, J. & SUSCHITZKY, W. 'Painting the cabbages red? Training for support staff in early years classrooms'. In: ABBOTT, L. & PUGH, G. (Eds). Training issues in the early years. Milton Keynes: Open University Press.

STATUS: Sponsored project

SOURCE OF GRANT: Esmee Fairbairn Charitable Trust £25,000; Association of Teachers and Lecturers £12,000

DATE OF RESEARCH: 1995-1997

KEYWORDS: child care occupations; child caregivers; classroom assistants; early childhood education; infant school teachers; nursery education; nursery nurses; nursery school teachers; preschool education; teaching profession; training

1124

School of Education, 21 University Road, Leicester LE1 7RF
01162 522522

Griffiths, R. Mrs; Aldgate, J. Prof.; Ward, H. Dr

'Each day counts': raising achievement in numeracy and literacy with vulnerable children (looked after, older adopted, and at risk)

ABSTRACT: Many studies have established that the educational standards achieved by children who are looked after by local authorities are lower than should be expected (SSI/OFSTED 1997; Fletcher-Campbell 1997; House of Commons Health Committee Report 1998). The Health Committee Report says 'There should be a new emphasis on the duty of the whole local authority to ensure not only that children receive a full-time education suitable to their age, but also special help and attention to overcome their defects'. This proposal aims to develop effective ways of improving the children's educational achievement through work with the adults most closely involved in their day-to-day care. A study will look at foster carers', social workers', and teachers' views of their roles in overseeing and promoting the education of children who are looked after, and will aim to identify ways of improving carers and teachers; success as educational advocates. Children's and young people's views will also be sought wherever possible. The study will be linked to 3 action research projects which focus on supporting carers in improving children's numeracy, literacy and self-esteem. These projects will examine ways in which children's attainment can be raised, even when a carer only has a short period of time looking after a child. Two of the projects will concentrate on direct work with carers (through an education handbook, and through training sessions). The third project (a postal club) will use materials sent to looked after children themselves, and will evaluate the effects of this on carer' confidence and skills in helping children achieve educational aims.

STATUS: Sponsored project

DATE OF RESEARCH: 1999-continuing

KEYWORDS: achievement; adoption; child caregivers; foster children; literacy; looked after children; numeracy; pupil improvement; social workers

1125

School of Education, 21 University Road, Leicester LE1 7RF
01162 522522

Rogers, L. Mr

National Curriculum software project

ABSTRACT: This project has developed software and curriculum materials for supporting the use of information technology (IT) in practical science. So far, the main products have been the Insight and Junior Insight data-logging software accompanied by a range of documentation providing ideas of laboratory applications suited to science in the National Curriculum at key stages 2, 3 and 4. Currently the project is in the third phase of revising and upgrading all the existing materials for publication in September 1999.

STATUS: Individual research

DATE OF RESEARCH: 1998-continuing

KEYWORDS: computer uses in education; educational software; information technology; laboratory experiments; practical science; primary education; science education; secondary education

1126

School of Education, 21 University Road, Leicester LE1 7RF
01162 522522

Busher, H. Dr; Harris, A. Dr; Wise, C. Ms

Subject leaders and decision-making in secondary school departments

ABSTRACT: This research project explores what might be effective training processes for subject leaders in secondary schools. In doing so it has tried to gauge the range of current training provision in England and Wales, through a large scale survey, as well as exploring through case study, particular approaches to training. As part of finding out about effective training processes requires understanding what is involved in being an effective subject leader in a secondary school, part of the interview-based research explores that question too.

STATUS: Sponsored project

SOURCE OF GRANT: Teacher Training Agency £10,000

DATE OF RESEARCH: 1998-continuing

KEYWORDS: intellectual development; secondary education; subject leaders; teacher development

1127

School of Education, 21 University Road, Leicester LE1 7RF
01162 522522

Comber, C. Mr; Vlaeminke, V. Dr; Supervisors: Comber, C. Mr ; Vlaeminke, V. Dr

Boys' underachievement at key stage 3

ABSTRACT: Small-scale, school-commissioned study examining factors contributing to male underachievement. The study sought to explore the general attitudes of teachers to gender issues and of pupils to school and self, as well as evaluate a school-initiated intervention strategy aimed at raising achievement. These aims were achieved by: 1) detailed analysis of performance and other relevant data; 2) a questionnaire survey of Year 10 (first year) students: attitudes to school, self-ratings of behaviour, sex-role inventory; 3) semi-structured interviews with selected staff and students. The student survey sample comprised all Year 10 students. Interviews were conducted with 4 groups (2 single sex, 2 mixed) of 6 students selected to represent a range of abilities and attitudes to school, and with 8 teachers involved in the raising achievement scheme. Year 10 boys significantly underperformed in English but not in science or mathematics. However, in both questionnaire and interview, boys expressed the highest levels of academic confidence and self-esteem, but also saw themselves as erroneously perceived by teachers as disruptive or 'troublemakers'. High achievement in boys was positively associated with academic aspiration, confidence and self-ratings of behaviour, but in girls with academic confidence only. Neither masculinity nor femininity were related to achievement for either sex. In interview, teachers expressed general satisfaction with the existing intervention, but also offered suggestions for improvement and extension of the scheme. On male underachievement, teachers identified a form of masculinity which positioned learning as 'uncool', and emphasised the effect of a relatively small group of disruptive boys. Boys in general were perceived to be more disorganised and less conscientious than girls.

STATUS: Sponsored project

SOURCE OF GRANT: Leicester University

DATE OF RESEARCH: 1998-1998

KEYWORDS: academic achievement; achievement; boys; key stage 3; masculinity; pupil attitudes; secondary education; self esteem; sex differences; underachievement

1128

School of Education, 21 University Road, Leicester LE1 7RF
01162 522522

Hunter-Carsch, M. Mrs

Literacy at 11: Leicester Summer Literacy Schools Evaluation Report

ABSTRACT: The study aimed to investigate the impact of the 6 Summer Literacy Schools (SLS) in Leicester in 1998 on pupils' literacy achievement, training/experience of SLS on staff, participation of parents and contributing staff groups, and the attitudes of pupils and of parents, NFER (Group) Reading Test and the Vernon Spelling Test and qualitative assessment involving questionnaires, structured interviews, informal discussion and observation visits with pupils, staff and parents. Findings of testing 162 pupils are reported in terms of gains in reading and spelling age, story recall, attitudes and self-esteem. Staff were all deeply committed to encouraging learning and building pupils' self-esteem, and parents were generally very positive towards SLSs; many recommended that it be extended to more youngsters with literacy needs. Follow-up studies are being planned to include development of assessment procedures and intervention through drama.

STATUS: Sponsored project

SOURCE OF GRANT: Leicester City Education Authority £7,200

DATE OF RESEARCH: 1998-1998

KEYWORDS: literacy; primary to secondary transition; reading; spelling; summer literacy schools; summer schools

1129

School of Education, 21 University Road, Leicester LE1 7RF
01162 522522

Hislam, J. Mrs; Hargreaves, L. Dr

The National Literacy Project: an investigation into the effectiveness of guided reading at key stage 2

ABSTRACT: The National Literacy Strategy has the explicit aim of raising standards in reading and writing such that, by 2002, 80% of 11 year-olds will attain Level 4 in the end of key stage tests. The research project looks at a single but significant element of the hour, known as guided reading, and attempts to monitor its development and implementation at key stage 2 in a small number of local primary schools in which initial teacher trainees are placed.

STATUS: Sponsored project

SOURCE OF GRANT: Leicester University £2,200

DATE OF RESEARCH: 1998-continuing

KEYWORDS: directed reading activity; guided reading; key stage 2; literacy hours; national literacy project; national literacy strategy; primary education; reading; reading teaching

1130

School of Education, 21 University Road, Leicester LE1 7RF
01162 522522

Rogers, L. Mr

Control software project

ABSTRACT: This is a curriculum development project for use in primary and secondary schools. The aim is to develop a software package which will allow pupils to design and test computer control systems. It will address the needs of the National Curriculum for information technology under the attainment targets for monitoring and control. A new medium for representing such problems is envisaged, featuring graphical objects on the computer screen. The concept builds on the 'systems' approach to electronics developed in the past two decades and now widely used in schools. The program will break new ground by providing exciting new ways of engaging with the three stages for successful control activities: designing a solution to a problem; testing it by simulation on the screen; and then building a functional model controlled by the computer. There will be different layers of working to accommodate the needs of the youngest pupils at key stage 2 but also allow the development of more sophisticated systems up to key stage 4.

STATUS: Sponsored project

SOURCE OF GRANT: Addison, Wesley Longman £36,000

DATE OF RESEARCH: 1998-continuing

KEYWORDS: **computer uses in education; design and technology; educational software; information technology; primary education; secondary education**

1131

> School of Education, 21 University Road, Leicester LE1 7RF
> 01162 522522

Rogers, L. Mr; Jarvis, T. Ms; Holmes, K. Mr; Buzzard, B. Dr; Cooke, B. Dr; Barstow, M. Dr

Challenger Learning Materials project

ABSTRACT: The objective is to edit the curriculum support materials for the Challenger Learning Centre for Leicester which will open in Leicester in October 1999. The Centre is a major component of the Millennium Landmark Project to build the National Space Science Centre in Leicester due for completion in 2001. The original Challenger materials are from the USA and the main task is to adapt them to meet the requirements of the National Curriculum for England and Wales. The materials consist of teachers' guides for preparing pupils in the 10-14 age range for simulated space missions at the Centre. The practical activities for pupils give practice in basic science skills, communication and teamwork. There are also follow-up activities for use in schools after the mission.

STATUS: Sponsored project

SOURCE OF GRANT: National Space Science Centre £23,000

DATE OF RESEARCH: 1998-continuing

KEYWORDS: **science education; space exploration**

1132

> School of Education, 21 University Road, Leicester LE1 7RF
> 01162 522522
> Cambridge University, Homerton College, Hills Road, Cambridge CB2 2PH
> 01223 507111

Jarvis, T. Mrs; McKeon, F. Ms; Stephenson, P. Mr

SCIcentre: a national centre for initial teacher training in primary school science

ABSTRACT: The SCIcentre aims to increase the number of newly qualified primary teachers with accurate understanding of science concepts and skills, who can also provide appropriate stimulating scientific learning experiences for children. The centre intends to achieve this by promoting mutually beneficial collaboration between initial teacher training institutions in the UK by identifying, supporting and sharing innovative and effective approaches in primary school science. A report on ways of directing student science activity in schools, approaches to support teacher mentors in science and specialist primary science courses has been produced. The report was based on data collected from questionnaires supported by over 50 indepth interviews at different higher education institutions in the UK. A second report on science in the early years and related literacy and numeracy in science based on further data from 35 higher education institutions and SCITTs, has also been completed. Several other projects have been completed: namely videos on classroom organisation in science; broadsheet on developing citizenship in primary science and mentoring in primary science; booklets on using CD Roms and data logging in primary science; a booklet in promoting voluntary work by science undergraduates effectively in the primary classroom; a booklet on mentoring in primary science, as well as a report on experiences of teachers and researchers in science

activities. Other publications in hand include booklets on widening children's views of science and scientists; use of data processing, sensing and information technology (IT) graphics in primary science. Research is ongoing into the area of mentoring students, approaches for teaching chemical concepts such as melting, dissolving and evaporation and approaches used in key stage 2/3 courses. The data will form the basis for further publications.

PUBLISHED MATERIAL: BEARDON, T. & STEPHENSON, P. (1998). The science PAL resource pack: Leicester: University of Leicester School of Education, SCIcentre and Homerton College, Cambridge. ; DICKINSON, D. (1998). Using CD Roms in primary science. Leicester: University of Leicester School of Education, SCIcentre. ; JARVIS, T., MCKEON, F. & SHEARS, J. (1998). Report into course design in primary science initial teacher training. Leicester: University of Leicester School of Education, SCIcentre. ; JARVIS, T., MCKEON, F. & SHEARS, J. (1998). Video on organising primary science. Leicester: University of Leicester School of Education, SCIcentre and Leicester University Audio Visual Services. ; MCKEON, F., JARVIS, T., STEPHENSON, C. & WILKINS, C. (1998). Practice in primary science initial teacher training. Leicester: University of Leicester School of Education, SCIcentre. A full list of publications is available from the researchers.

STATUS: Sponsored project

SOURCE OF GRANT: Society of Chemical Industry £400,000

DATE OF RESEARCH: 1996-continuing

KEYWORDS: **preservice teacher education; primary education; primary school teachers; science education; science teachers; student teachers**

1133

> School of Education, 21 University Road, Leicester LE1 7RF
> 01162 522522
> Cambridge University, Research Centre for English and Applied Linguistics, Keynes House, Trumpington Street, Cambridge CB2 1QA
> 01223 332340

Norton, J. Ms; *Supervisor*: Malmkjaer, K. Dr

University of Cambridge: the English oral proficiency of Japanese learners

ABSTRACT: This study examines the performance of Japanese candidates in the Cambridge Speaking Tests (First Certificate in English; Certificate in Advanced English and Proficiency in English). Japanese candidates are shown to under-perform compared to European candidates and this is linked to cultural differences in communication styles. The data sample includes 33 candidates and consists of transcriptions of the Speaking Tests. A qualitative analysis of the transcriptions, which draws upon the theoretical frameworks of conversation analysis and discourse analysis, establishes linguistic and discoursal features in the respective performances which result in the awarding of particular marks on the various assessment scales of the tests. Quantitative analysis of certain aspects of the interview data offers a complementary perspective on the oral proficiency of the candidates. The findings of the analysis suggest that the Cambridge Speaking Tests provide an accurate indication of a candidate's oral proficiency with regard to the performance descriptors. The study refines the researcher's understanding of the assessment process and how this impacts upon rating outcomes. The oral proficiency interview is viewed as an example of cross-cultural communication. This study contrasts conversational interaction in Japanese and English and demonstrates that cultural communication style influences the oral testing situation. The issue of culture and communication styles and the cultural appropriacy of the Speaking Tests for Japanese candidates is of central interest to this study. Based upon the findings of the analysis and a discussion of the cultural and educational background of Japanese candidates, pedagogical recommendations are offered which suggest how the oral proficiency of Japanese candidates may be improved in preparation for the Speaking Tests. Other issues such as test standardisation and task effect receive brief consideration and indicate fruitful directions for future research in oral testing.

STATUS: Individual research

DATE OF RESEARCH: 1995-1997

KEYWORDS: **communication research; conversation; english - second language; japanese people; language styles; second language learning; speech communication**

1134

School of Education, Educational Management Development Unit, University Centre, Barrack Road, Northampton NN2 6AF
01604 630180

Bush, T. Prof.; Coleman, M. Dr; Glover, D. Dr

The management of grant-maintained schools

ABSTRACT: Research focused on the experience of the first one hundred schools to become grant maintained. Five questionnaires were sent to each of these schools to be completed by the headteacher, the chair of governors, a parent governor, a teacher governor and a teacher union representative. Detailed case studies were undertaken at five of the schools, one selective, three comprehensive and one primary. Both survey and case studies investigated the reasons for opting out and also considered the benefits and disadvantages perceived by the individuals within the schools. The research investigated management of admissions policies, finance, staff, curriculum, external relations and the relationship with governors. The conclusions were that grant maintained status has been efffective in raising morale within the schools studied. Three major weaknesses were identified, relating to preferential financing, the opportunity for grant maintained schools to introduce selection and the lack of accountability of the governors to the local community.

PUBLISHED MATERIAL: BUSH, T. & COLEMAN, M. (1992). The financial implications of mass opting out. Leicester: University of Leicester.; BUSH, T., COLEMAN, M. & GLOVER, D. (1993). Managing autonomous schools: the grant maintained experience. London: Paul Chapman Publishing. ; BUSH, T., COLEMAN, M. & GLOVER, D. (1993). 'Managing grant maintained primary schools', Educational Management and Administration, Vol 21, No 2, pp.69-78. ; COLEMAN, M., BUSH, T. & GLOVER, D. (1993). 'Researching autonomous schools: a survey of the first 100 GM schools', Educational Research, Vol 35, No 2, pp.107-126. ; GLOVER, D., BUSH, T. & COLEMAN, M. (1993). 'The early experience of grant maintained Church schools', Research in Education, No 50, pp.27-37.

STATUS: Sponsored project

SOURCE OF GRANT: Leverhulme Trust

DATE OF RESEARCH: 1992-1993

KEYWORDS: educational administration; educational change; grant maintained schools; management in education; school based management

1135

School of Education, Educational Management Development Unit, University Centre, Barrack Road, Northampton NN2 6AF
01604 630180

Bush, T. Prof.; Coleman, M. Dr; Moyles, J. Mrs; Merry, R. Dr; Lumby, J. Ms; Ryan, P. Mr

Comparative research on educational management: China and England

ABSTRACT: The link between the Shaanxi Teachers' University, Xi'an, and the University of Leicester has led to the development of this project, which involves visits to China by staff from Leicester and visits to England by Chinese colleagues. The aims of the research are: 1) To assess the effectiveness of management structures and processes in both countries. All types of schools to be included in the research covering the age range from 3-20. 2) To make recommendations to modify management structures and processes in order to facilitate school improvement and to advance teaching and learning. 3) To assess the role of women in school management, investigate barriers to their career development and make recommendations to advance their role. 4) To promote the development of academic staff in both China and United Kingdom with particular reference to the position of women. The main method used in China is case studies of 14 schools in the Province. The research has been matched by case studies in the East Midlands region of England. The findings of the research have been published in 7 articles in a special issue of the 'Compare' journal in 1998.

PUBLISHED MATERIAL: BUSH, T., QIANG, H. & FANG, J. (1998). 'Educational management in China: an overview', Compare, Vol 28, No 2, pp.133-140. ; COLEMAN, M., QIANG, H. & LI, Y. (1998). Women in educational management in China: experience in Shaanxi province, Compare, Vol 28, No 2, pp.141-154. ; MOYLES, J. & LIU, H. (1998).

'Kindergarten education in China: reflections on a qualitative comparison of management processes and perceptions', Compare, Vol 28, No 2, pp.155-169. ; RYAN, P., CHEN, X. & MERRY, R. (1998). 'In search of understanding: a qualitative comparison of primary school management in the Shaanxi region of China and England, Compare, Vol 28, No 2, pp.171-182. ; MERRY, R. & ZHAO, W. (1998). 'Managing special needs provision in China: a qualitative comparison of special needs provision in the Shaanxi region of China and England', Compare, Vol 28, No 2, pp.207-218.

STATUS: Sponsored project

SOURCE OF GRANT: British Council Beijing £15,000; State Education Commission of China £2,000

DATE OF RESEARCH: 1995-1998

KEYWORDS: china; comparative education; educational administration; international educational exchange; management in education

1136

School of Education, Educational Management Development Unit, University Centre, Barrack Road, Northampton NN2 6AF
01604 630180

Wise, C. Mrs; *Supervisor*: Bush, T. Prof.

Role of academic middle managers in secondary schools

ABSTRACT: Evidence from literature has shown that academic middle managers in secondary schools were having difficulty fulfilling their role as perceived by others prior to the Education Reform Act 1988. In particular, many were avoiding their personnel management responsibilities. This study hopes to look at some of the changes in expectations of middle managers after the 1988 Act and how they have accommodated these expectations.

STATUS: Individual research

DATE OF RESEARCH: 1995-1998

KEYWORDS: department heads; educational administration; management in education; middle management; secondary education

1137

School of Education, Educational Management Development Unit, University Centre, Barrack Road, Northampton NN2 6AF
01604 630180

Ryan, P. Mr; *Supervisor*: Bush, T. Prof.

The same but different: an investigation into the implementation of the National Curriculum in inner city and non-inner city primary schools

ABSTRACT: The background to this study is an interest in urban education and urban primary schools in particular. The literature base with reference to urban schools is small and concentrates, in the main, on issues of race or gender. This investigation is an attempt to highlight differences or similarities in practice in urban and non-urban schools, due to contextual factors. There is also an attempt to identify effective practices in urban schools that could serve as a model to other schools. Essentially the study aims to argue that urban schools are not necessarily 'failing' but engaging in something 'different'. The study is an investigation into differences in managing the implementation of the National Curriculum in English primary schools with particular reference to urban and non-urban schools. It is a qualitative study using case study methodology. Empirical data will be collected from a total of six schools, three urban and three non-urban.

PUBLISHED MATERIAL: RYAN, P. (1997). 'Managing primary schools: facilitating the learning relationship'. In: KITSON, N. & MERRY, R. (Eds). Teaching in the primary school: a learning relationship. London: Routledge.; RYAN, P. (1997). 'Developing the primary school curriculum: valuing subjects or children's learning?'. Paper presented to the Values and Curriculum Conference at the Institute of Education, University of London, 10-11 April 1997. ; RYAN, P. (1997). 'Managing the curriculum in the primary school: coordination or leadership?', Management in Education, Vol 11, No 3, pp.7-9. ; RYAN, P. 'The primary National Curriculum in England: a sociological perspective'. In: MOYLES, J. & HARGREAVES, L. (Eds). The primary classroom: learning from international perspectives. London: Routledge. (in press).

STATUS: Individual research

DATE OF RESEARCH: 1995-continuing

KEYWORDS: curriculum development; national curriculum; primary education; urban schools

1138

School of Education, Educational Management Development Unit, University Centre, Barrack Road, Northampton NN2 6AF
01604 630180

Coleman, M. Dr; *Supervisor*: Bush, T. Prof.

Women in educational management: the career progress and leadership style of female headteachers in England and Wales

ABSTRACT: A minority of senior managers in education are female. This disproportion is evident amongst headteachers of secondary schools in England and Wales, of whom approximately 23% are women. Reasons for the disproportionate under-representation of women in management may be related to overt and covert discrimination, obstacles to career progress within the work situation, the limitations imposed by domestic responsibilities and cultural stereotypes which identify leadership and management with males. Despite the masculine stereotype of leadership, research has identified 'feminine' styles of management with effective and successful leadership. Such 'people centred' management stresses caring and concern and promotes consultation and teamwork. This research is concerned with the career patterns and management style of those women who have been successful in becoming headteachers. There is a complex interplay of factors that may have influenced their success in reaching a position of authority. Amongst these are an expectation of 'masculine' leadership style. Drawing on a wide literature base of British and American research, the research seeks to analyse the complex factors that relate to the position of women in a senior educational leadership and management role. The methodology includes a qualitative element consisting of indepth interviews with female headteachers, and a quantitative element - a questionnaire to all the female headteachers of secondary schools in England and Wales.

PUBLISHED MATERIAL: COLEMAN, M. (1996). 'The management style of female headteachers', Educational Management and Administration', Vol 24, No 2, pp.163-174. ; COLEMAN, M. (1996). 'Barriers to career progress for women in education: the perceptions of female headteachers', Educational Research, Vol 38, No 3, pp.317-332. ; COLEMAN, M. (1997). 'Overcoming barriers to career progress: the female headteacher', Topic, Issue 18. Slough: National Foundation for Educational Research.

STATUS: Individual research

DATE OF RESEARCH: 1995-1998

KEYWORDS: careers; educational administration; head teachers; leadership styles; management; management in education; secondary education; teaching profession; women teachers; womens employment

1139

School of Education, Educational Management Development Unit, University Centre, Barrack Road, Northampton NN2 6AF
01604 630180

McFarlane, G. Mr; *Supervisor*: Lofthouse, M. Dr

British government policy on funding education for racial equality, with particular focus on Section 11 of the Local Government Act 1966

ABSTRACT: This research will focus on an historical review of British government policy on funding for race equality in education from the Education Act 1944 to the present day. The research will identify the major factors affecting policies on funding for race equality at governmental levels, including general political and educational decision-making departments; local education authority levels; key education unions and national organisations with dedicated views on race equality in education levels; school and community levels. This research will investigate policy papers, national and local guidelines and perceptions of the key stakeholders in the provision of resources and delivery of services by structured interviews with those stakeholders. A specific focus within this overview will be the impact of Section 11 of the Local Government Act 1966 on the above analysis. A multi-method approach will be adopted for the research, including a scrutiny of all relevant policy documentation; a focus on one particular local education authority, i.e. Bedfordshire LEA (to March 1997) and then Luton LEA (from April 1997 as it becomes a unitary authority). Data will be both qualitative and quantitative. The qualitative data collection

will be through structured interviews with key stakeholders across government, local education authority, union-national organisation representatives; schools' personnel (including parents) and the wider local community. The quantitative data will focus on an analysis of the 1995-96 survey on Section 11 in Bedfordshire schools. The study will make recommendations for future developments incorporating the key perceptions from all the stakeholders involved.

STATUS: Individual research

DATE OF RESEARCH: 1996-continuing

KEYWORDS: educational finance; educational history; educational legislation; educational policy; equal education; local education authorities; race

1140

School of Education, Educational Management Development Unit, University Centre, Barrack Road, Northampton NN2 6AF
01604 630180

Bush, T. Prof.

Redefining educational management

ABSTRACT: This project aims to redefine educational management in the light of momentous changes in the subject during the past 10 years. These include: 1) The international trend towards self-managing schools. 2) The intervention of the Teacher Training Agency in management development of schools. 3) Continuing debate about the relationship between general management and management in education.

PUBLISHED MATERIAL: BUSH, T., BELL, L., BOLAM, R. & RIBBINS, P. Redefining educational management. London: Paul Chapman Publishing. (in press). ; BUSH, T. 'Redefining educational management', Educational Management and Administration, Vol 27, No 3. Special Edition. (in press).

STATUS: Individual research

DATE OF RESEARCH: 1997-continuing

KEYWORDS: educational administration; management in education; school based management

1141

School of Education, Educational Management Development Unit, University Centre, Barrack Road, Northampton NN2 6AF
01604 630180

Bush, T. Prof.; Coleman, M. Dr; Lumby, J. Ms; Middlewood, D. Mr

Research and development in educational management - South Africa

ABSTRACT: The education system in South Africa is undergoing rapid and multiple changes following the demise of the former apartheid regime. This project examines the management of schools in one province (Kwa Zulu-Natal) in this dramatic context. Research is being conducted in primary and secondary schools in both urban and rural areas.

STATUS: Sponsored project

SOURCE OF GRANT: British Council; Private Sponsors, jointly £18,000

DATE OF RESEARCH: 1997-continuing

KEYWORDS: educational change; educational development; south africa

1142

School of Education, Educational Management Development Unit, University Centre, Barrack Road, Northampton NN2 6AF
01604 630180

Middlewood, D. Mr; Coleman, M. Dr; Lumby, J. Ms

The impact of in-house practitioner research upon organisational and individual improvement

ABSTRACT: The research explores the shifts in thinking and practice which individuals believe resulted from research projects in a wide range of schools and colleges in the UK and abroad, and how far those involved believe that the research approach used was valuable. Areas investigated include: curriculum management; structures; roles; the effects of multiple research projects on a school; school ethos and culture; links with school improvement; conditions for effective site-based research.

STATUS: Sponsored project

SOURCE OF GRANT: Leicester University £2,500

DATE OF RESEARCH: 1998-continuing

***KEYWORDS*: educational research; school improvement; teacher researchers**

1143

School of Education, 21 University Road, Leicester LE1 7RF
01162 522522

Liverpool John Moores University, Centre for Psychology, Trueman Building, 15-21 Webster Street, Liverpool L3 2ET
0151 231 2121

Smith, H. Ms; *Supervisor*: Merry, R. Dr

An exploration of primary teacher thinking about children's reading using personal construct psychology

ABSTRACT: The research sets out to examine primary teachers' personal beliefs and theories about the teaching of reading. After pilot studies with National Curriculum key stage 1 and 2 (KS1 & KS2) teachers using observation, semi-structured interviews and questionnaires, a repertory grid methodology was adopted. The main study followed 20 experienced KS1 and KS2 teachers from 8 Leicestershire schools over 1 year. At 3 points at approximately 6 monthly intervals these participants were interviewed in depth using an adapted form of Kelly's repertory grid technique to elicit their personal theories about reading. Analysis of these quantitatively revealed remarkable consistency in individual teachers' patterns of beliefs. This is unusual for this methodology which is usually seen as capturing a snapshot of the personal views of the participant. Qualitative analysis also revealed great consistency in teachers' beliefs. Taken as a whole, teachers were concerned with variables about individual children and made virtually no mention of theoretical orientations to reading.

STATUS: Individual research

DATE OF RESEARCH: 1993-1997

***KEYWORDS*: personal construct psychology; primary education; primary school teachers; reading teaching; teacher attitudes**

1144

School of Education, 21 University Road, Leicester LE1 7RF
01162 522522

Management Development Centre of Hong Kong, Vocational Training Council of Hong Kong, 11/F VCT Tower, 27 Wood Road, Wanchai, Hong Kong

Chung Leung, L. Mr; *Supervisor*: Busher, H. Dr

Developing managers: the interaction of competence approaches and Chinese culture in Hong Kong

ABSTRACT: This research investigates how managers can be educated and their skills and knowledge developed through a competence-based programme. It further investigates the effectiveness of this programme through structured questionnaires and interviews with participants on the programme and the supervisors in the workplace of these participants. One key area of concern is the extent of match/mismatch between a competence-based approach to learning and the demands and learning style of the Hong Kong education system, which most of the managers have gone through, and the social outlooks enshrined in Chinese culture. These perspectives are explored through the same methods. The sample is about 60 managers as students and their line supervisors.

STATUS: Individual research

DATE OF RESEARCH: 1996-continuing

***KEYWORDS*: china; competency based education; hong kong; management development**

1145

School of Education, 21 University Road, Leicester LE1 7RF
01162 522522

Nottingham University, School of Education, University Park, Nottingham NG7 2RD
01159 515151

Watling, R. Dr; Hopkins, D. Prof.; Harris, A. Dr; Haines, L. Ms

Longitudinal evaluation of the Derbyshire 'Quality Development Dialogue' (QDD)

ABSTRACT: This ongoing study of the Derbyshire Quality Development Dialogue is a summative and formative account of the project's development and its ability to impact at different levels of the education service throughout the country.

STATUS: Sponsored project

SOURCE OF GRANT: Derbyshire County Council £33,000

DATE OF RESEARCH: 1998-continuing

***KEYWORDS*: educational quality; local education authorities; school effectiveness; school improvement**

1146

School of Education, 21 University Road, Leicester LE1 7RF
01162 522522

University of Wales, Aberystwyth, Department of Education, PO Box 2, Aberystwyth SY23 2AX
01970 623111

Galton, M. Prof.; Fogelman, K. Prof.; Hargreaves, L. Dr; Comber, C. Mr ; Lawson, A. Mr; Thorpe, R. Mr; Roberts-Young, D.Mr

National evaluation of the Education Department's Superhighways Initiative (EDSI): Group A projects: curriculum projects based mainly in primary and secondary sectors in England and Wales

ABSTRACT: This evaluation concerns seven projects which are using 'superhighways' communications technology, i.e. channels capable of carrying graphic information, of supporting two-way interaction, Internet access and videoconferencing between users, between schools and with other remote sources. Five projects are based in England and two in Wales. Three involve primary phase schools, and four, secondary phase schools. The evaluation aims to identify the extent to which the projects meet their aims and objectives which include: 1) the development of children's communication skills via e-mail and videoconferencing; 2) promotion of children's awareness of themselves and their histories through graphic media; 3) increase in children's research skills using information technology (IT) and the Internet; and 4) providing on-line access to archives as resources for schools. The evaluation will focus on the appropriateness of the technology for its educational purposes, the training of teachers to use it, and its cost-effectiveness. All the projects involve partnerships between suppliers of hardware, software or cabling, and educational institutions, although the balance of industrial to educational commitment varies from large scale projects in which considerable hardware has been supplied to schools to be trialled, to small scale projects, in which a small number of schools have sought industrial partners in information technology to support particular projects or curriculum areas. Evaluation methods include regular on-site observations of children's use of the technology; interviews with teachers, children, project coordinators and industrial partners; and logging of children's IT activities during set periods. The evaluations of these seven projects and eighteen other 'superhighways' projects will be completed by April 1997.

STATUS: Sponsored project

SOURCE OF GRANT: National Council for Educational Technology for the DfEE, Welsh Office, Scottish Office, DENI £100,317

DATE OF RESEARCH: 1996-1997

***KEYWORDS*: communications; computer uses in education; electronic mail; information technology; internet; primary education; secondary education; telecommunications; teleconferencing**

Liverpool Hope University College

1147

Department of Enterprise and Business Development Department, Hope Park, Liverpool L16 9JD
0151 291 3000

Donert, K. Mr

Geography and the World Wide Web

ABSTRACT: This research investigates the use of the World Wide Web in teaching and learning geography. The work focuses on several aspects of the Web, including communication systems, multimedia, databases and information provision. The issues and benefits of using the Web are core to the research, which is being developed at higher education and school level.

STATUS: Sponsored project

DATE OF RESEARCH: 1998-continuing

KEYWORDS: **computer uses in education; geography; information technology; internet; multimedia**

1148

Department of Environmental and Biological Studies, Hope Park, Liverpool L16 9JD
0151 291 3000

Speake, J. Dr; Street, C. Ms

The use of journals by new undergraduates in biology, environmental studies and geography

ABSTRACT: This research project aims to investigate the use of journals by new undergraduate students. Research interest in this field has been partly generated by the Geography for the New Undergraduate (GNU) Higher Education Funding Council for England (HEFCE) Teaching and Learning Project currently being developed within the Environmental and Biological Studies Department at Liverpool Hope University College. First year students of biology, environmental studies and geography at Liverpool Hope University College provide the target sample. These students were surveyed, by questionnaire, at the end of their first semester courses. Questions set were devised to examine their use of journals within the different subject areas in terms of, for example, journals used, frequency of use, constraints and advantages of journal use, perceived values of using journals, and approaches to accessing journal information. Results are to be processed using OMR techniques and analysis of the data is to be conducted during early 1998.

STATUS: Sponsored project

SOURCE OF GRANT: Liverpool Hope University College

DATE OF RESEARCH: 1997-1998

KEYWORDS: **educational materials; higher education; information sources; periodicals; students; study skills**

1149

Department of Environmental and Biological Studies, Hope Park, Liverpool L16 9JD
0151 291 3000

Chambers, W. Dr; Gayton, E. Dr; Garner, W. Ms; Asquith, S. Mr; Donert, K. Mr; Hodgkinson, K. Ms

Literacy in undergraduates

ABSTRACT: The aims of the project are to: 1) identify levels and surface literacy on undergraduate students; 2) identify common literacy weaknesses and problems; 3) compare the performance of students following different subjects; 4) ascertain if literacy levels change during the first year of study; 5) ascertain if literacy levels change from the start of the first year to the end of the third year; 6) see if the use of personal computers have any effects on the level of literacy after being played; 7) ascertain the effectiveness of a grammar, punctuation and spelling intervention programme; 8) improve staff and student awareness of literacy problems and improve the performance of students. 36 first and 36 first and final year undergraduate students reading geography, environmental studies, biology and education were tracked at the start of Year 1, the end of Year 1, and the end of Year 3 for 42 aspects on literacy. The results are currently being analysed.

STATUS: Sponsored project

SOURCE OF GRANT: Liverpool Hope University College £2,000

DATE OF RESEARCH: 1997-1998

KEYWORDS: **higher education; literacy**

1150

Department of Environmental and Biological Studies, Hope Park, Liverpool L16 9JD
0151 291 3000

Garner, W. Ms; *Supervisor*: Chambers, W. Dr

Planning for primary geography: background of coordinator, planning processes and models - good practice based on OFSTED reports

ABSTRACT: The aims of the research are to explore the background/inservice experience of the coordinator, the range of planning models and the processes through which they were developed, and to relate the findings to Office for Standards in Education (OFSTED) reports with a view to identifying good practice. Senior advisers from 6 authorities will choose 5 schools (total sample size = 30 schools) and each adviser will choose schools on the basis of length of time the coordinator is in the role, inservice education (INSET) attendance, socio-economic and geographical context. Each school will be visited once, with a view to collecting curriculum documentation relating to primary geography. This will include key stage plans and schemes of work for the whole school. The geography coordinator will also be asked to complete a questionnaire, which will aim to measure academic background in terms of geography and any other relevant experiences, for example, attendance on extended inservice training or membership of the Geographical Association. The questionnaire will also elicit the process by which the curriculum documentation was developed, for example, with support from educational advisers and/or development in consultation with the whole staff. The first stage of data handling will be sorting and classifying the range of curriculum models. The second stage will be to summarise responses to the questionnaire and to relate these responses to types of curriculum planning models. Therefore the relationship between background of coordinator, process of development and planning models will be explored. The research will be extended, using the same data collected from schools and relating it to OFSTED documentation. This will be achieved through the use of a scale devised for the purpose of quantifying the content of OFSTED reports, with a view to identifying good practice.

STATUS: Sponsored project

SOURCE OF GRANT: Higher Education Funding Council £1,050

DATE OF RESEARCH: 1997-1998

KEYWORDS: **geography; ofsted; primary education; primary school curriculum; subject coordinators**

1151

Department of History, Hope Park, Liverpool L16 9JD
0151 291 3000

Lowden, K. Ms; *Supervisors*: Davies, J. Mr; Hollinshead, J. Dr

The training of women teachers during the 19th century, with particular reference to denominational provision

ABSTRACT: This study is an investigation into the denominational provision for the training of women teachers from the period c.1840 to 1900. The national context will be established and the North West of England will be used as a case study. In particular the provision by the Anglican diocese of Chester at Warrington Training College and by the Catholic diocese of Liverpool at Notre Dame College will be examined through the surviving archives of these two institutions. The scale of operation, the background of recruits, the nature of the curriculum, and the distinctive religious ethos will be examined.

STATUS: Individual research

DATE OF RESEARCH: 1996-continuing

KEYWORDS: **educational history; teacher education; women teachers**

1152

Department of Information Management and Communication, Hope Park, Liverpool L16 9JD
0151 291 3000
Leeds University, School of Education, Computer Based Learning Unit, Leeds LS2 9JT
01132 431751

Waraich, A. Mr; *Supervisor*: Brna, P. Dr

The role of narrative in intelligent tutoring systems (ITS)

ABSTRACT: The use of a distinct narrative in educational hypermedia systems has been shown to be useful for a number of reasons: 1) narrative structure can affect a learner's comprehension; 2) the use of narrative is a familiar and established method of structuring texts; 3) the structure of a narrative can be used by learners to assist in navigating a hypermedia environment; 4) the narrative itself can act as a motivating factor. The aim of this project is to review the use of narrative and other motivational strategies in intelligent tutoring systems and then develop and describe an architecture and narrative structure for a game based simulation to teach tertiary level students about the domain of computer architecture. Computer architecture courses involve abstract concepts and procedural knowledge. The problem faced by the tutor is devising suitable practical activities. A game-based simulation designed to teach the domain of computer architecture is currently under development as the computer architecture tutor (CAT). The design incorporates a strong sense of narrative using a fantasy environment that allows direct manipulation of animated graphical objects. The use of a strong narrative structure within a hypermedia based ITS is an area that has not been closely investigated. Several workers have commented on the relationship between good storytelling and good teaching. The aim of this project is to investigate the role of narrative in a hypermedia game based ITS for tertiary level students.

STATUS: Individual research

DATE OF RESEARCH: 1996-continuing

KEYWORDS: computer assisted learning; computer uses in education; hypermedia; information technology; narration

1153

Department of Information Technology, Hope Park, Liverpool L16 9JD
0151 291 3000

McKenna, P. Mr; *Supervisor*: Strivens, J. Ms

Gender and the language of the computer: a deconstruction of gender stereotyping within computer programming

ABSTRACT: The research arises at a general level from the under-representation of women in computing, and from responses to this, including academic research and public action plans. Programming has been perceived as one of the most problematic aspects of the computing curriculum, and as a high-status computing job. Approaches to program design and implementation have been characterised as 'masculine' and 'feminine' on the basis of broad analogies with gender analyses in other fields. This has resulted in a possibly self-fulfilling stereotyping of abilities that has potentially serious consequences for the position of women in computing. The research attempts to develop a new gender analysis for computer programming. A detailed critique of the work of Sherry Turkle and Seymour Papert is presented, eliciting inherent contradictions in what is a broadly accepted view of gender and programming. Practical studies are made of students programming and of their attitudes to approaches to programming, including abstraction and black boxes. Different programming paradigms, including object oriented and visual programming, are examined in the light of gender and semiotic analyses.

PUBLISHED MATERIAL: MCKENNA, P. (1996). 'De-sexing computing - gender, myths and stereotypes'. Proceedings of the 4th Annual Conference on the Teaching of Computing, Dublin City University, 1996.

STATUS: Individual research

DATE OF RESEARCH: 1996-continuing

KEYWORDS: computers; information technology; sex differences; stereotypes

1154

Department of Mathematics, Hope Park, Liverpool L16 9JD
0151 291 3000

Kahn, P. Dr

Enhancing advanced mathematical thinking

ABSTRACT: Developing basic mathematical skills, alongside the teaching of mathematical content, is considered in introductory undergraduate mathematics courses. Well publicised concerns and changes to undergraduate degrees indicate that students are now less well prepared for some aspects of university mathematics. With mass higher education and a broader school curriculum, it can no longer be assumed that many students have thoroughly grasped some of the skills needed to study mathematics at university: problem-solving; understanding of proof; improving own learning of mathematics and ability to transfer knowledge between topics. The project looks at the effectiveness of ways to develop these skills in first year undergraduates which involve both giving a basic theory of the skill itself and by providing opportunities for practice with standard content. This approach may also aid students' motivation for their study of mathematics and the retention of material. The role of reflection in developing the skills of advanced mathematical thinking is well established, but implementations in the UK have concentrated on third year courses, providing little opportunity to improve skill development during the degree as a whole. Such early implementation can further be expected to influence the theory itself. Whether and how such an approach aids the students involved will be considered. A standard instrument will determine changes in levels of confidence and motivation and examination results will be analysed, with the previous intake for comparison. Regular feedback will be sought from the students, who will each complete detailed course evaluation schedules.

PUBLISHED MATERIAL: KAHN, P.E. (1997). 'Building skill development into the undergraduate mathematics curriculum'. Proceedings of the 5th International Symposium on Improving Student Learning, Glasgow, September 1997.

STATUS: Sponsored project

SOURCE OF GRANT: Liverpool Hope University College £5,960

DATE OF RESEARCH: 1996-continuing

KEYWORDS: higher education; mathematical ability; mathematics; mathematics skills; students

1155

Department of Pscyhology, Hope Park, Liverpool L16 9JD
0151 291 3000

Norton, L. Dr; Thomas, S. Ms; Morgan, K. Mr

Full-time studying and long-term relationships: make or break

ABSTRACT: This research is a three year longitudinal study designed to investigate what happens when one of the partners in a stable, long-term interpersonal relationship, becomes a full-time student in higher education. Indepth interviews with a small sample of six students identified four major areas which were investigated with a larger sample. These were: 'marital' satisfaction; perceived support from partner; student stress; and student self-esteem. Questionnaires were sent out to over 200 mature students in their first year of an undergraduate degree at a university college. Ninety-three questionnaires were completed and returned. Correlation of the variables showed that there were significantly positive relationships between partner support and student marital satisfaction and self-esteem. At the same time, there were significantly negative relationships between partner support and student stress, as well as between student stress and self-esteem. Years two and three of the study will send out the same questionnaires to those students who responded in the first year to establish whether there is a change in the relationships between the variables over time. It is also intended to carry out indepth interviews (probably in the third year) with a small sample of students whose relationships have broken down and students who are extremely satisfied with their relationships. The findings from the second year of the study have been published (NORTON, L.s., THOMAS, S., MORGAN, K., TILLEY, A. & DICKINS, T.E. (1998). 'Full-time studying and long-term relationships: make or break for mature students?', British Journal of Guidance and Counselling, Vol 26, No 1, pp.75-88). These findings confirm those of the first year that there are particular stresses for students with domestic responsibilities and that the single most buffering effect was support from the student's partner. The second year analysis also found, however, that students experienced a decrease in the amount of partner support. Data have been collected from the third year of the questionnaire study and from the interviews carried out and are currently awaiting analysis.

PUBLISHED MATERIAL: NORTON, L.S., THOMAS, S., MORGAN, K., TILLEY, A. & DICKINS, T.E. (1998). 'Full-time studying and long-term relationships: make or break for mature students', British Journal of Guidance and Counselling, Vol 26, No 1, pp.75-88.

STATUS: Sponsored project

SOURCE OF GRANT: Liverpool Hope University College £200

DATE OF RESEARCH: 1994-1997

KEYWORDS: **family life; higher education; interpersonal relationship; mature students; spouses; students**

1156

Department of Psychology, Hope Park, Liverpool L16 9JD
0151 291 3000
Cheltenham and Gloucester College of Higher Education, Department of Professional Education, The Park, Cheltenham GL50 2QF
01242 532700

Norton, L. Dr; Ross, K. Dr; Atkinson, H. Ms; Carson, G. Ms

Student teachers: the factors affecting their conceptions of teaching and learning

ABSTRACT: 208 student teachers have taken part in a questionnaire study designed to find out to what extent their own prior learning experience will determine their conceptions of teaching and learning. Student teachers from two institutions and from B.Ed and Postgraduate Certificate in Education (PGCE) courses have taken part in this research which is investigating a number of different influences: 1) B.Ed or PGCE; 2) English or science; 3) prior experience of being taught at school. It is hypothesised that: 1) student teachers who are on a PGCE course are more likely than B.Ed students to hold a conception of teaching as learning facilitation and a learning conception allied to a deep rather than a surface approach; 2) student teachers from a science background are more likely to hold a constructivist conception of teaching and learning; and 3) prior learning experience will be more influential in determining student teacher conceptions than their learning experiences at university level. The data for this study are currently being analysed.

STATUS: Sponsored project

SOURCE OF GRANT: Liverpool Hope University College £883

DATE OF RESEARCH: 1900-continuing

KEYWORDS: **learning; preservice teacher education; student teacher attitudes; student teachers; teaching process**

1157

Department of Psychology, Hope Park, Liverpool L16 9JD
0151 291 3000
Keele University, Department of Psychology, Keele ST5 5BG
01782 621111
Plymouth University, Department of Psychology, Drake Circus, Plymouth PL4 8AA
01752 600600
Brunel University, Department of Human Sciences, Uxbridge UB8 3PH

Norton, L. Dr; Hartley, J. Prof.; Newstead,S. Prof.; Richardson, J. Prof.; Mayes, J. Ms; Mazuro, C. Ms

Lecturers' beliefs and behaviours

ABSTRACT: Over 600 university lecturers from different disciplines representing sciences, arts and social sciences in 4 university institutions took part in a questionnaire study designed to see if there was a match between lecturers' beliefs (or teaching conceptions) and their behaviours (or teaching and assessment practices). The data from this study are currently being analysed but initial findings suggest: 1) the two conceptions of teaching widely accepted in the research literature are confirmed as 'teaching as knowledge transmission' and 'teaching as learning facilitation'; 2) overall there was a match between beliefs and behaviours; and 3) some differences were found according to discipline, teaching experience and gender.

STATUS: Sponsored project

SOURCE OF GRANT: Liverpool Hope University College £4,549

DATE OF RESEARCH: 1997-continuing

KEYWORDS: **academic staff; higher education; lecturers; teacher behaviour; teaching methods**

1158

Department of Psychology, Hope Park, Liverpool L16 9JD
0151 291 3000
Liverpool University, Department of Psychology, PO Box 147, Liverpool L69 3BX
0151 794 2000

Brunas-Wagstaff, J. Dr; Norton, L. Dr; Wagstaff, G. Dr

The effects of student perceptions of the fairness of assessment on their learning strategies

ABSTRACT: This research was designed to investigate students' perceptions of the way tutors rewarded ability (defined as a deep approach) as opposed to effort (defined as strategies linked to use of sources) in coursework. In a previous study, Brunas-Wagstaff and Norton (1998) found that students believed that tutors rewarded ability rather than effort, but what that study did not take into account was what tutors actually did. This research addresses that question by asking both students and tutors about one specific coursework essay in psychology. 106 students and 8 tutors took part in the study. Students were asked about the strategies they had used, how much effort they had put into their essays and how much they thought the essay demonstrated their ability. Tutors were asked to estimate after they had marked the essay how much ability and how much effort they thought it demonstrated. Results indicated that students did not use many journal articles when preparing their essays in spite of believing that such a strategy was related to essay grade. They also believed that ability counted for more in essays than effort but this perception was inaccurate as tutors in this study actually rewarded students almost equally for both ability and effort.

PUBLISHED MATERIAL: BRUNAS-WAGSTAFF, J. & NORTON, L. (1998). 'Perceptions of justice in assessment: a neglected factor in improving students as learners'. In: RUST, C. (Ed). Improving student learning: improving students as learners. Oxford: The Oxford Centre for Staff Development. ; NORTON, L., BRUNAS-WAGSTAFF, J. & LOCKLEY, S. 'Learning outcomes in the traditional coursework essay: do students and tutors agree?'. In: RUST, C. (Ed). Improving student learning: improving student learning outcomes. Oxford: The Oxford Centre for Staff Development. (in press).

STATUS: Sponsored project

SOURCE OF GRANT: Liverpool Hope University College £937

DATE OF RESEARCH: 1997-continuing

KEYWORDS: **assessment; essays; higher education; justice; marking scholastic; student attitudes; student evaluation**

1159

Education Deanery, Hope Park, Liverpool L16 9JD
0151 291 3000

Bell, D. Dr

Subject leadership in primary schools: managing subject leaders effectively

ABSTRACT: The role of the subject leader/coordinator in primary schools has increased in importance in recent years but, despite the fact that there appears to be general agreement as to the nature of the role, there are many outstanding questions which need to be addressed. This study is part of a project which aims to examine the role of the curriculum coordinator/leader in primary schools and how it has changed in recent years; identify good practice and the factors which contribute to this; consider ways of assessing the effectiveness of coordinators/leaders; examine ways of supporting them to improve their contribution to the overall management of the school and the learning that takes place. This study focuses on the ways in which subject leaders/coordinators from a number of schools are managed by their headteachers in order to analyse the way in which they are part of the overall management structure and culture of the school. In particular the study attempts to identify ways in which the subject leaders/coordinators are enabled to carry out their role effectively. The project involves working with teachers in schools through questionnaires, diaries, interviews, observations in classrooms and group meetings.

STATUS: Sponsored project

SOURCE OF GRANT: Liverpool Hope University £10,000

DATE OF RESEARCH: 1996-continuing

KEYWORDS: **primary education; subject coordinators**

1160

Education Deanery, Hope Park, Liverpool L16 9JD
0151 291 3000

Fletcher, L. Ms; *Supervisor*: Bell, D. Dr

Subject leadership in primary schools: tasks and responsibilities of subject leaders

ABSTRACT: The role of the subject leader/coordinator in primary schools has increased in importance in recent years but, despite the fact that there appears to be general agreement as to the nature of the role, there are many outstanding questions which need to be addressed. This study is part of a project which aims to examine the role of the curriculum coordinator/leader in primary schools and how it has changed in recent years; identify good practice and the factors which contribute to this; consider ways of assessing the effectiveness of coordinators/leaders; examine ways of supporting them to improve their contribution to the overall management of the school and the learning that takes place. In particular, this study focuses on the subject leaders/coordinators from a number of schools in order to analyse the way in which they carry out their role and overcome the challenges they face. The project involves working with teachers in schools through questionnaires, diaries, interviews, observations in classrooms and group meetings.

STATUS: Individual research

DATE OF RESEARCH: 1996-continuing

KEYWORDS: **primary education; subject coordinators**

1161

Education Deanery, Hope Park, Liverpool L16 9JD
0151 291 3000

Bell, D. Dr

Accessing science for children with learning difficulties

ABSTRACT: This project aims to extend the understanding and effectiveness of teaching and learning in science for primary school children with learning difficulties and attempts to address a specific need of teachers who wish to access, assess and develop the scientific understanding of children with moderate to severe learning difficulties. The project is being carried out in partnership with practising teachers in primary schools for special educational needs. A range of elicitation and intervention activities are being explored in order to establish ways of helping children with moderate to severe learning difficulties express and extend their ideas in relation to selected science concepts. It is anticipated that, on completion of the project, it will be possible to give specific examples of the kinds of ideas that children with moderate to severe learning difficulties hold in relation to the science concepts; and provide guidance as to ways in which teachers can help these children express their ideas and develop a better scientific understanding. The findings of the project would also make a contribution to the wider debate about widening access to the curriculum for children with learning difficulties in relation to science and other areas of the curriculum.

PUBLISHED MATERIAL: BELL, D. (1998). 'Accessing science: challenges faced by teachers of children with learning difficulties in primary schools', Support for Learning, Vol 13, No 1, pp.26-31.

STATUS: Sponsored project

SOURCE OF GRANT: Nuffield Foundation £34,950

DATE OF RESEARCH: 1996-1998

KEYWORDS: **learning disabilities; primary education; science education; special educational needs**

1162

Education Deanery, Hope Park, Liverpool L16 9JD
0151 291 3000
Liverpool University, Department of Architecture and Building Engineering, PO Box 147, Liverpool L69 3BX
0151 794 2000

Wilson, K. Miss; *Supervisor*: Pepper, S. Prof.

High Wycombe as a centre of excellence in the cabinet making industry

ABSTRACT: The study examines the phenomenon of High Wycombe as a centre of excellence in the cabinet making and furniture industry, both in production of goods and the training of designers and makers. The study covers 100 years from the 1890s to the present day and looks at the rise (and fall) of industry and technical training in the town. The views and conceptions of these are examined from within and without the establishment in High Wycombe.

STATUS: Individual research

DATE OF RESEARCH: 1996-continuing

KEYWORDS: **furniture; training**

1163

Education Deanery, Hope Park, Liverpool L16 9JD
0151 291 3000
Liverpool University, Department of Education, PO Box 147, Liverpool L69 3BX
0151 794 2000

Clarkson, J. Mrs; *Supervisors*: Hamilton, D. Prof.; Johnston, K. Ms

A review of appraisal and the role of the local education authority 1991-1996

ABSTRACT: The study investigates the history and development of teacher appraisal since its introduction in 1991. It will seek to trace the call for teacher accountability from the Ruskin Speech to the White Paper 'Choice and Diversity 1992' and make links with the appraisal initiative. Consideration will be given to the role of the unions in the introduction of appraisal and the increasing demands for performance related pay, first suggested by Sir Keith Joseph in 1985 and based on appraisal procedures. Performance indicators, thought to provide empirical evidence of accountability and set in the appraisal procedure, will be examined. The study will then focus on the role of the local education authority (LEA) in the appraisal process using data collected from structured interviews and questionnaires given to LEA representatives in the North West of England. The political content of appraisal as a means of teacher accountability linked to performance rewards will be discussed.

PUBLISHED MATERIAL: CLARKSON, J. (1997). 'Teacher appraisal - is the torch about to scorch?'. Paper presented at the British Educational Research Association Annual Conference, University of York, 11-14 September 1997.

STATUS: Individual research

DATE OF RESEARCH: 1993-1998

KEYWORDS: **local education authorities; teacher development; teacher effectiveness; teacher employment benefits; teacher evaluation; teaching profession**

1164

Enterprise and Business Development Department, Hope Park, Liverpool L16 9JD
0151 291 3000

Donert, K. Mr; Brady, S. Mr

Use of computers in education

ABSTRACT: This research has been established to evaluate the use and development of modern information and communications technology (MICT) in education and specifically in the training and professional development of teachers. The projects have focused on open, multimedia-based applications, based on a range of themes. They include the generation of network-based learning environments and the implications for pedagogic delivery of teaching materials and the learning outcomes which results. The research initially looked at the use made of bulletin boards, e-mail and computer-mediated conferencing, but more recently it has looked at the protocols necessary for videoconferencing to be effectively used in education and the impact of 'dialogue' on generating effective World Wide Web based learning environments.

PUBLISHED MATERIAL: DONERT, K. (1997). A geographers guide to the internet. Sheffield: Geographical Association. ; DONERT, K. 'Using technology to create autonomous learning', Journal of Geography in Higher Education. (in press). ; DONERT, K., BRADY, S. & CLARKSON, J. 'Mass conferencing: coping with technology, a case of large audience videoconferencing', ALT-J. (in press).

STATUS: Sponsored project

SOURCE OF GRANT: Liverpool Hope University College

DATE OF RESEARCH: 1997-continuing

KEYWORDS: **computer uses in education; information technology; internet; preservice teacher education; teleconferencing**

Liverpool John Moores University

1165

School of Education and Community Studies, I M Marsh Campus, Barkhill Road, Liverpool L17 6BD
0151 231 2121

MacLeod, M. Mr; *Supervisors*: Huddart, D. Prof.; Griffiths, T. Mr

Strategies for the wider implementation of environmental education in higher education

ABSTRACT: The aims of this research are: 1) A 'cross-curricular greening' of the students' curriculum and the establishment of an Environmental Education entitlement in all teacher training courses. 2) A development policy for Environmental Education across the curriculum and an action plan for its implementation. 3) The development of a wider strategy for the development of Environmental Education within the Institution and the development of excellent environmental practices. 4) The adoption of a comprehensive environmental policy statement, an action plan for its implementation, and the adoption of a policy for the development of Environmental Education within this Institution. The project will involve: action research; questionnaire surveying; discussions; curriculum development; and evaluation.

STATUS: Individual research

DATE OF RESEARCH: 1993-1997

KEYWORDS: **curriculum development; environmental education; higher education**

1166

School of Education and Community Studies, I M Marsh Campus, Barkhill Road, Liverpool L17 6BD
0151 231 2121

Martin, D. Mr; *Supervisors*: Huddart, D. Prof.; Griffiths, T. Mr

An evaluation of earth education programmes as alternative methods of environmental education in schools and outdoor centres

ABSTRACT: Earth Education developed from Acclimatization which was a special introductory programme of carefully crafted, structured learning experiences based on discovery and experiential learning. This was based around structured programmes using a wide variety of activities. These programmes could be an important alternative method of Environmental Education but their success in imparting knowledge, giving an accurate view of ecological concepts, and in changing attitudes and behaviour has not been evaluated. The project includes: action research; questionnaire surveying; discussions; and curriculum evaluation in schools and centres which run Earth Education programmes. Short (a few days to a month) and longer term (1, 2 and 3 year) evaluations of the programme's success will be undertaken.

STATUS: Individual research

DATE OF RESEARCH: 1993-1998

KEYWORDS: **earth science; environmental education; learning activities**

1167

School of Education and Community Studies, I M Marsh Campus, Barkhill Road, Liverpool L17 6BD
0151 231 2121

Stanley, N. Mr; Mason, M. Mrs

CD-ROM in education: effective use

ABSTRACT: Experience in the classroom has indicated that when children are presented with a large amount of information, they find difficulty in extracting the relevant subset that will enable them to solve a problem, describe a characteristic or answer a question. This can also be observed to some extent in students at a different level. Working with children, and observing student teachers working with children, has shown that particular skills and strategies are necessary to extract the relevant information from written sources such as reference books. There is a tendency to attempt to present all the information which is offered, rather than to use, analyse and distill that which is relevant. Many children given a reference book will simply try to copy the contents. Students are encouraged to help children to develop strategies to overcome this when working with written materials. The research will focus on identifying strategies for the intelligent use of CD-ROM and investigating ways in which such strategies could be developed in learners at all stages of education. Obviously a small scale project such as this can only use a limited amount of research time and resources. In the light of this it is planned to utilise opportunities already scheduled to facilitate the enquiry. In addition, the research will try to identify what makes a 'good' CD-ROM.

STATUS: Sponsored project

SOURCE OF GRANT: National Council for Educational Technology £1,500

DATE OF RESEARCH: 1992-1993

KEYWORDS: **cd roms; computer uses in education; information technology**

1168

School of Education and Community Studies, I M Marsh Campus, Barkhill Road, Liverpool L17 6BD
0151 231 2121

Maxwell, S. Dr; McGuiness, P. Mr; Bilton, R. Prof.; Young, A. Dr

The influence of reducing diets on biochemical parameters and their implications on the health of young women

ABSTRACT: At any one time, a large proportion (30-40%) of the female population are trying to lose weight, although the majority are not overweight. This may have significant adverse physical and psychological health consequences. Teenagers face tremendous pressures regarding body image at a time in their life when nutritional needs are high, and choices made profoundly affect health, both at this time and in the future. It has been suggested that, while children may be well nourished in terms of protein and some vitamins, the functioning of the brain may be sensitive to borderline deficiency states of many other nutrients. Iron deficiency has been shown to play a key role in behaviour, mood, attention span and learning ability. There is no evidence on the effect of weight loss regimes on the biochemical parameters of the non-obese. The aim of the project is to determine the biochemical changes induced by reducing diets in young non-obese women. The research will include: 1) A questionnaire used to determine the frequency and type of dietary regimes used; 2) Volunteers (aged 18-24 years) who will be studied before, during and after a specific dietary regime. Anthropometric measurements, biochemical profiles and dietary intake will be assessed; 3) A dietary study of schoolgirls (aged 12-14 years). Volunteers will be studied in a similar manner to the older women. The results will be analysed using various computer statistical packages.

STATUS: Team research

DATE OF RESEARCH: 1996-continuing

KEYWORDS: **body composition; eating habits; girls; health; human body; women**

1169

School of Education and Community Studies, I M Marsh Campus, Barkhill Road, Liverpool L17 6BD
0151 231 2121

Peel, J. Dr; James, P. Dr; Daniels, M. Dr; Hart, N. Dr; O'Carroll, P. Mr; Dossor, D. Ms

The psychological health of trainee counsellors

ABSTRACT: The question of counsellors' motivation is a serious ethical issue. While at first glance counsellors may appear simply to be people who find job and personal satisfaction in helping others, on closer scrutiny the shadow side of counsellors' motivation may provoke concern. It is legitimate to suspect that many would-be counsellors embark upon training at best in order to understand their current and past emotional, social and psychological disease, at worst in order to improve their current mental health. If this is so, then it may be reasonable to suggest that people attracted to counselling training may not only show emotional and psychological disequilibrium, they may even represent a more disturbed group than people attracted to other forms of vocational training. Any indication that this is the case would be a serious matter for concern, for it is clear that the effectiveness of counselling is strongly influenced by the psychological health of the therapist. However, while it is clear that counsellors are less effective if they are themselves psychologically distressed, it is often claimed that those who have experienced and resolved distress make better counsellors. This would seem to imply that, although it is unethical for professionals to act as counsellors during periods of emotional difficulty, it is both acceptable and laudable to recruit students who show some degree of psychological vulnerability and then to seek to improve their psychological health during training. The question then arises as to whether counselling training can or does achieve this end. The purpose of this research project is to investigate these matters.

STATUS: Team research

DATE OF RESEARCH: 1996-continuing

KEYWORDS: **counsellor characteristics; counsellor training; counsellors; mental health; psychological services**

1170

School of Education and Community Studies, I M Marsh Campus, Barkhill Road, Liverpool L17 6BD
0151 231 2121

Moore, D. Ms; *Supervisors*: Clemson, D. Mr; Mason, M. Ms; Denton, B. Mr

The classification of children's mental arithmetic strategies for addition and subtraction at National Curriculum key stage 2

ABSTRACT: The purpose of this study is to develop a classification of the mental arithmetic strategies for addition and subtraction at National Curriculum key stage 2. The study is confined to these two operations because they are the first to be mainipulated mentally in school and they are closely linked. Children have been interviewed using a pre-determined set of questions designed to elicit as wide a range of strategies as possible. Questions are not presented in problem or story form but as calculations. To date, the research indicates that children's approaches may vary according to age and ability level so the sampling has taken these two factors into account. Children have been drawn from two primary schools and each year from Year 3 to Year 6 inclusive. The interviews are video-recorded and on the basis of researcher observations and tape analysis children's methods are being classified. Outcomes will include a set of test items which will allow the identification of individual children's mental arithmetic strategies.

PUBLISHED MATERIAL: MOORE, D. et al. (1996). 'Children's own mental arithmetic strategies for adding and subtracting at KS2: the development and application of a set of test items'. Paper presented at the British Educational Research Association Annual Conference, Lancaster University, September 1996.

STATUS: Individual research

DATE OF RESEARCH: 1993-1997

KEYWORDS: **addition; arithmetic; key stage 2; learning strategies; mathematics education; mental arithmetic; primary education; subtraction; tests**

1171

School of Education and Community Studies, I M Marsh Campus, Barkhill Road, Liverpool L17 6BD
0151 231 2121

Richards, K. Ms; *Supervisors*: Peel, J. Dr; Jones, P. Dr; Huddart, D. Prof.

An evaluation of the effectiveness of using outdoor education in the treatment of anorexia nervosa

ABSTRACT: Outdoor education and adventurous activities are a well established part of many therapeutic treatment regimes. This is widely recognised under the notion of adventure therapy. Current practice and research shows that adventure therapy makes a positive contribution to the treatment of substance abuse, post-traumatic stress disorder, juvenile delinquency and emotional and behavioural difficulties. Studies have examined the effectiveness of therapeutic applications of adventure in custodial settings of psychiatric hospitals as well as in the education sector. The body of knowledge available in relation to adventure therapy needs to be drawn upon and applied to include a greater variety of client groups. For example, adventure therapy may provide the medium to achieve therapeutic change with clients suffering from eating disorders. However, at present it is not clear whether adventure therapy can lead to improvement for such a client group. The purpose of this research is to focus upon the treatment of

anorexia nervosa. This research will provide an evaluation of the effectiveness of using an outdoor education programme for the treatment of anorexia nervosa.

STATUS: Individual research

DATE OF RESEARCH: 1997-continuing

KEYWORDS: **adventure education; anorexia nervosa; eating habits; therapy**

1172

School of Education and Community Studies, I M Marsh Campus, Barkhill Road, Liverpool L17 6BD
0151 231 2121

Edwards, E. Ms; *Supervisors*: Clemson, D. Mr; Burns, D. Mr; Bell, L. Prof.

The development and implementation of the Specialist Teacher Assistant (STA) initiative in the North West of England: an evaluation

ABSTRACT: From the 1970s onwards there has been an increase in the number of classroom assistants and volunteers in school. Successive reports and commentaries have encouraged this development. In 1994 the Department of Education invited further and higher education institutions to tender for the provision of courses for new assistants called Specialist Teacher Assistants (STAs). This initiative was greeted with mixed reactions and teaching unions were concerned that the STA courses might be a 'back door' entry to teaching. This research has, and continues to, track the STA initiative as it has developed. The research is case study based looking at experiences of STAs, schools and institutions mainly in the North West of England. Using interviews, questionnaires and observation, a range of issues have been identified and explored. These include STA deployment, recognition and job satisfaction, and issues relating to school and classroom organisation and management.

STATUS: Individual research

DATE OF RESEARCH: 1995-1998

KEYWORDS: **classroom assistants; key stage 1; primary education; specialist teacher assistant; teaching profession**

1173

School of Education and Community Studies, I M Marsh Campus, Barkhill Road, Liverpool L17 6BD
0151 231 2121

Meadow, M. Mr; *Supervisors*: Grant, D. Dr; Hackett, A. Dr; Jepson, M. Ms

An investigation into the perceptions, attitudes and experiences and lifestyle of lone parents

ABSTRACT: Current literature indicates that mothers and children from single parent households are disadvantaged in terms of their educational attainment, nutritional status and access to paid employment. A strong characteristic in favour of a child's school success is the educational attainment of the parents (Dronkers 1994). According to the Kennedy report "learning parents create learning families" (Kennedy 1997). Arguably higher attainment in education and training would increase employability eventually lifting poor households out of poverty. In the Health and Lifestyle Survey, Blaxter (1992) found that women on low incomes were much more likely, than those with higher incomes, to have fewer 'good' dietary habits, despite Government attempts to educate the public into choosing a more healthy diet. Low income families face particular difficulties in making healthier choices, and the reasons include: 1) insufficiency of income and knowledge (Stitt and Grant 1993 and 1996); 2) lone parents are characterised by low energy and low iron intakes (Gibney and Lee 1993). Current Government proposals for single parents (New Deal) are aimed at enabling women to gain a foothold in the labour market. This will help lone parents, who are ready to do so, move off benefits and into work. Successful community based interventions have highlighted that voluntary schemes can have quite dramatic results in helping lone parents become less dependent and more confident in their abilities to improve their life chances (Moore 1996). The aim is to investigate the attitude, perceptions and experiences of lone parents pre- and post-interventions in education/training within a deprived area of Liverpool. The objectives are: 1) using case study, determine skills, knowledge and attitudes of 10 lone parents pre- and post-interventions and compare with control group; 2) develop a core of measures which would indicate improvement in well-being, self esteem, confidence and changes in lifestyle, i.e. nutritional change, budgeting strategies etc.

STATUS: Sponsored project

SOURCE OF GRANT: Liverpool John Moores University £20,000

DATE OF RESEARCH: 1998-continuing

KEYWORDS: disadvantaged; educationally disadvantaged; one parent family

1174

School of Education and Community Studies, I M Marsh Campus, Barkhill Road, Liverpool L17 6BD
0151 231 2121

Mullins, P. Ms *Supervisors*: Walters, B. Dr; Peel, J. Dr

Differentiation: meeting diverse need

ABSTRACT: Over the past few years there has been an increasing concern about the level of exclusion and underachievement in the British school system - an awareness that schools have been failing an increasingly significant proportion of their children (Audit Commission 1992; Sebba, Byers and Rose 1993; King 1995; Potts et al 1995; Dwyfor and Garner 1997; Hornby et al 1997). The learners who are marginalised by the school system include children with additional educational needs, children who are excluded, disaffected and truant, looked after children, low attainers, and children with low literacy levels. The research aims to investigate the use of differentiated approaches on the engagement of marginalised pupils. The research takes place in 4 comprehensive schools. The methodology is a consultancy approach that focuses on process factors in changing practice to enhance levels of differentiation and their outcomes in terms of teaching and learning. Data collection is based on classroom observation, teacher interview and feedback, and process field notes. Results are being presented as case reports with cross case analysis. Conclusions will focus on the effectiveness of differentiation at a spread of levels outlined as descriptors of good practice. Inclusion in the learning process will be discussed in the light of findings that relate to engagement, level of understanding, pupil teacher interaction, challenge and progression, and match between teaching and learning.

STATUS: Team research

DATE OF RESEARCH: 1994-continuing

KEYWORDS: additional educational needs; comprehensive schools; differentiated curriculum; disaffection; exclusion; low achievement

1175

School of Education and Community Studies, I M Marsh Campus, Barkhill Road, Liverpool L17 6BD
0151 231 2121
Deeside College, Department of Art and Design, Kelsterton Road, Connah's Quay, Deeside CH5 4BR
01224 831531

Aiello, M. Mr; *Supervisors*: Leaman, O. Prof.; Clarke, J. Mr; Parkinson, F. Ms

The work related further education needs of Deeside, Clwyd: training requirements, funding and marketing

ABSTRACT: As a result of the Government's White Paper in May 1991, further education colleges and sixth form colleges have been granted autonomy from local education authorities (LEAs). These independent colleges are now responsible for designing and creating relevant and attractive courses to entice a range of clients to their college rather than their rival college. Funding will come via the Funding Councils and the Training and Enterprise Councils (TECs) which will hold funds for work related further education (WRFE) programmes. The TECs' objectives are to link vocational education to the local labour market needs. In an effort to promote retraining in the changing market place, the Government launched the Professional, Industrial and Commercial Update (PICKUP) Programme in 1982. The PICKUP Programme is designed to help increase, improve and meet the updating, retraining and educational needs of adults at work. Colleges need to define areas of retraining and skills updating, compile suitable and relevant WRFE courses, locate the funding, and sell the benefits of such training to employers using effective marketing strategies and printed marketing material. This thesis will research the training needs of five employers on Deeside, Clwyd, with the view to: establishing the present training levels of their workforce; defining the companies' short and long term objectives; and analysing the training needs of tomorrow's employees.

An investigation will be undertaken into WRFE training providers and funding opportunities; model courses will be put forward for pilot schemes; suitable marketing strategies will be compiled; and promotional material will be designed and produced and their effectiveness evaluated. The outcomes of the research will include: a definition of the historical and demographic characteristics of Deeside; a description of local WRFE training providers; a definition of the training needs; recognition of the need for skills updating; the accreditation of prior learning for experienced staff; establishment of training levels of the current workforce; feasibility studies of funding opportunities for pilot courses; an evaluation of present WRFE courses and, as a result, a framework for future WRFE courses; a definition of the specific marketing strategies; and sample marketing material required for the promotion of WRFE. The methods will include: 1) An investigation of the historical and demographic characteristics of Deeside. 2) Case studies of five major employers. 3) A survey in the form of (anonymous) postal questionnaires to all employees to ascertain their present skills levels. 4) Feasibility studies carried out into the content of current WRFE courses and an evaluation of their effectiveness in the form of face-to-face questionnaires. 5) Interviews with TEC officials, PICKUP agents, Welsh Office representatives, trade union representatives, and employees. 6) Model WRFE courses piloted and their effectiveness evaluated - via confidential opinion questionnaires to employers, employees, course providers, trade union representatives, and funding bodies. Sample marketing material specifically for the promotion of WRFE will be designed and produced, including an evaluation of their effectiveness.

STATUS: Individual research

DATE OF RESEARCH: 1993-1997

KEYWORDS: further education; industry further education relationship; training; vocational education

1176

School of Education and Community Studies, I M Marsh Campus, Barkhill Road, Liverpool L17 6BD
0151 231 2121
Surrey University, School of Educational Studies, Guildford GU2 5XH
01483 300800

Low, M. Mrs; Nicholls, G. Dr; *Supervisor*: Bell, L. Prof.

The development of teacher professional identity: the case of key stages 2 and 3 students and teachers

ABSTRACT: The research will examine 10 ways in which teacher's professional identity is developed and sustained in groups of National Curriculum key stages 2 and 3 students and newly qualified teachers. The sample will include students and teachers from 3 communities and it will track them from entry to the second year of teaching using interviews and focus groups.

STATUS: Sponsored project

SOURCE OF GRANT: Liverpool John Moores University

DATE OF RESEARCH: 1998-continuing

KEYWORDS: newly qualified teachers; professional development; student teachers; teacher development; teaching profession

1177

School of Health, Tithebarn Street, Liverpool L2 2ER
0151 231 2121
Liverpool John Moores University, School of Education and Community Studies, I M Marsh Campus, Barkhill Road, Liverpool L17 6BD

Simms, C. Ms; *Supervisors*: Clemson, D. Mr; Hawtin, A. Ms; Cunningham, C. Prof.

The perceptions of a range of professionals working with children and childhood

ABSTRACT: The aims of this project are to identify models of the child and childhood operated by specific professional groups. This will lead to descriptive and analytical models and the consistency with which each group uses the models. Children's lives are shared by a variety of influences and, in the UK, there have grown a range of professional groups, over many years, with a particular concern for children. In respect of social and economic policies there are three main sectors of professional contribution that have a major impact on children's lives. These are concerned with education, health, law and social welfare. Within these groups there are a number of sub-groups which can clearly be identified. These range from primary teachers, health visitors, to social workers and lawyers. This research project will identify a matrix of groups and sub-groups and sample from that matrix in order to start to develop a picture of the similarities and differences between the identified professional groups.

STATUS: Individual research

DATE OF RESEARCH: 1997-continuing

KEYWORDS: **children; professional personnel**

Liverpool University

1178

Department of Education, PO Box 147, Liverpool L69 3BX
0151 794 2000

Beattie, N. Dr

The Freinet Movement in its international context

ABSTRACT: The aim is to explore the Freinet Movement, which has been central to most 'progressive' developments in French education, over the period 1920 to the present day and to describe and discuss its cross-national impact. This has been considerable in some areas (e.g. Italy post-1945, Portugal post-1974) and nil in others (e.g. United Kingdom). By placing a very broad movement of opinion and practice in its cultural and historical context, this long-term enquiry should produce some clarification of elusive culture-bound ideas such as 'progressive' and 'international' dissemination.

STATUS: Individual research

DATE OF RESEARCH: 1987-1993

KEYWORDS: **comparative education; educational history; educational theories; progressive education**

1179

Department of Education, PO Box 147, Liverpool L69 3BX
0151 794 2000

Beattie, N. Dr

The educational impact of Celestin Freinet in France, and internationally (especially Italy, Germany and the United Kingdom)

ABSTRACT: Celestin Freinet (1896-1966) was an important innovator in French education, especially primary education, over the period from 1920 until his death. His work continues through an Institute he founded in Cannes. He had wide international contacts and influence, and he was politically active on the left. Research will be conducted by library work and interviews. It will place Freinet against his French background and explore the extent and significance of his international outreach, especially in Italy and Germany, and his failure to have any impact in the English speaking world. There is thus a comparative dimension to the work. A book is planned.

STATUS: Individual research

DATE OF RESEARCH: 1994-1997

KEYWORDS: **comparative education; educational history; educational theories; progressive education**

1180

Department of Education, PO Box 147, Liverpool L69 3BX
0151 794 2000

McGuigan, L. Mrs; Roberts, D. Mr; Hughes, A. Mr; *Supervisor*: Russell, T. Prof.

Development of National Curriculum standard tests in science for key stage 2

ABSTRACT: The project team at the Centre for Research in Primary Science and Technology will undertake the design and production of standard tests in science for 11 year olds in England and Wales. Assessment items will be developed using a network of practising primary teachers. The core team will coordinate informal trials and national pre-testing arrangements. Analysis of children's performance in the formal pre-testing, together with structured expert review, will lead to the production of tests covering levels 1-6 of the National Curriculum in science for 1996, 1997, 1998 and 1999. Test materials, evaluation reports and non-statutory materials are published with a Qualifications and Curriculum Authority (QCA) copyright.

STATUS: Sponsored project

SOURCE OF GRANT: School Curriculum and Assessment Authority

DATE OF RESEARCH: 1995-1998

KEYWORDS: **assessment; science education; science tests; tasks and tests; tests**

1181

Department of Education, PO Box 147, Liverpool L69 3BX
0151 794 2000

Hamilton, D. Prof.

Modernism and schooling

ABSTRACT: A study of European schooling in the period 1400-1700.

STATUS: Individual research

DATE OF RESEARCH: 1993-continuing

KEYWORDS: **educational history**

1182

Department of Education, PO Box 147, Liverpool L69 3BX
0151 794 2000

Skidmore, P. Ms; *Supervisors*: Harrop, S. Dr; Woodcock, G. Dr

Local radio and adult education

ABSTRACT: This study examines the use of local radio for educational work with adults. It tests the view that local radio is able to cater for an adult audience in a way which is different from other media, being able to focus on the involvement of the local community. Included in the research is the emergence of local radio in the history of radio broadcasting; the development of educational broadcasting in general; and the specific contribution of local radio to the education of adults. Methods used include: a documentary study; interviews with key personnel in national and local radio, and in adult education; and a case study of the policies and programmes of Radio Merseyside from the 1970s to the early 1990s, with an evaluation of their effectiveness. Provisional conclusions are as follows: i) Local radio has a unique contribution to make to adult education; ii) The demands made by involving members of the local community in programming are very heavy; iii) Personalities play a key role in the success or otherwise of educational policy.

STATUS: Sponsored project

SOURCE OF GRANT: Universities Funding Council £20,000

DATE OF RESEARCH: 1991-1993

KEYWORDS: **adult education; educational broadcasting; educational radio; local radio; mass media; radio**

1183

Department of Education, PO Box 147, Liverpool L69 3BX
0151 794 2000

Walsh, S. Ms; *Supervisor*: Martland, J. Mr

Developing navigational skills project: phase II

ABSTRACT: The research is conducted on behalf of the British Orienteering Federation. The sport involves the use of maps to find a series of control points in forests or moorland terrain. At the elite level it is a demanding physical and mental challenge. A major problem is that the athlete chooses where and when to run and is not in contact with the coach during competition and training activities. The research is investigating the use of self-report/think-aloud verbal data, in conjunction with structured interviews, to provide coaches with appropriate sets of technique specific questions to improve post performance feedback. More specifically, it aims to develop a cueing model for training by investigating the cues and prompts given to the athlete prior to training and to establish the efficacy of such cues and prompts in the subsequent performance of the athlete. The sample of coaches and athletes is drawn from the British National Squad, 15-17 years of age. The analyses of the verbal data will use a variety of qualitative and quantitative methods. This in turn will be validated with post-event recall, structured interviews and video analysis. Phase II commenced April 1994 and results are not available at present.

PUBLISHED MATERIAL: MCNEILL, C., MARTLAND, J.R. & PALMER, P. (1992). Orienteering in the National Curriculum: a practical guide for teachers. Doune: Harvey Map Services. ; MARTLAND, J.R. & WALSH, S.E. (1993). Developing navigational skills: using the Silva 7DNS Compass. Leeds: Sports Council, National Coaching Foundation. ; WALSH, S.E. & MARTLAND, J.R. (1993). 'The orientation and navigational skills of young children: the application of two intervention strategies', Journal of Navigation, Vol 146, No 1, pp.63-68. ; MARTLAND, J.R. (1994). 'New thinking in mapping skills'. In: MARSDEN, W.E. & HUGHES, J. (Eds). Primary school geography. London: David Fulton.

STATUS: Sponsored project

SOURCE OF GRANT: Sports Council: Sports Science Education Programme £116,000

DATE OF RESEARCH: 1994-1998

KEYWORDS: **navigation; orientation; orienteering; outdoor pursuits; sports**

1184

Department of Education, PO Box 147, Liverpool L69 3BX
0151 794 2000

Marsden, W. Prof.

The school textbook: theory and practice in geography, history and social studies

ABSTRACT: This is a comparative, historical study of theory and practice related to the nature and use of school textbooks in geography, history and social studies, from the early nineteenth century to the present. No overall scholarly monograph has been undertaken by a British writer on the topic, which draws heavily for intellectual sustenance on the extensively documented American experience. While there is a range of writing on specific aspects, such as racist and sexist bias, readability and historical elements, there appears to have been no major empirical project sponsored on the school textbook. A British anti-textbook ideology among educational elites is identified, and its nature and causes explored. After investigating comparative and historical perspectives, the study will cover issues of bias, stereotyping, censorship, in relation to race, class, gender, age and national identity. The final section will focus on writing and publishing, choosing and using textbooks, and the current situation in relation to the national curriculum.

PUBLISHED MATERIAL: MARSDEN, W. 'European textbooks and cross-national misunderstandings: some historical background'. In: FERREIRA, M. et al (Eds). Culture, geography and geographical education. Lisbon: IGU Commission on geographical education/Universidade Aberta. ; MARSDEN, W. (1998). 'Writing a book about textbooks: some preliminary considerations'. In: KENT, W. (Ed). Issues for research in geographical education: textbooks. University of London, Institute of Education. ; MARSDEN, W. 'Geography textbooks and educational reform: historical and comparative perspectives on the English situation'. In: BEDNARZ, S. et al (Eds). Textbooks and educational reform: an international perspective. (forthcoming).

STATUS: Individual research

SOURCE OF GRANT: Nuffield Foundation, Social Sciences Small Grants Scheme £2,880

DATE OF RESEARCH: 1998-continuing

KEYWORDS: **educational history; educational materials; geography; history; social sciences; textbook research; textbooks**

1185

Department of Education, Centre for Research in Primary Science & Technology, PO Box 147, Liverpool L69 3BX
0151 794 2000

Russell, T. Prof.; Qualter, A. Dr

Evaluation of the implementation of science in the National Curriculum

ABSTRACT: The evaluation rests on a number of issues which have been raised by Her Majesty's Inspectorate, the National Curriculum Council, and by others. There are three main ones: (1) coverage,; (2) progression; and (3) differentiation. In relation to coverage, it has been observed that teachers are to some extent failing to cover certain aspects of the National Curriculum in science; they may be overlooking them; or they may be deferring them. The reasons why this is the case are being explored with a

focus on planning for teaching science. The second study, on progression, involves a consideration of the match between the levels in the National Curriculum intended to represent progression in learning, and the order in which pupils develop their understanding in science. The third issue involves the study of the appropriateness of the order for less able, and more able and talented pupils. A mixture of individual interviews of teachers and pupils, national questionnaire, group interviews and classroom observation is used in meeting the not inconsiderable challenges of this project.

STATUS: Sponsored project

SOURCE OF GRANT: National Curriculum Council £345,000

DATE OF RESEARCH: 1991-1993

KEYWORDS: **curriculum development; national curriculum; science education**

1186

Department of Education, Environmental Education Research Unit, PO Box 147, Liverpool L69 3BX
0151 794 2000

Boyes, E. Dr; Stanisstreet, M. Dr

Development of the ideas of secondary school children concerning the ozone layer

ABSTRACT: The understanding of pupils between the ages of 11 and 16 about the ozone layer - what it is, what will damage it, and what will be the likely result of such damage - has been studied. Following the use of a preliminary open-form questionnaire, the ideas of a large cohort of children (over 1700) have been probed by closed-form questionnaire and by interviews with a subset of this group. Children seem aware that the ozone layer is a layer of gas around the earth, but less sure what that gas is. They also know that it protects the earth from ultra-violet rays from the sun, and that further depletion will allow more ultra-violet to earth and cause more skin cancer. Most also know that one cause of depletion is the use of chloroflurocarbons (CFCs), but may confuse the depletion of the ozone layer with the greenhouse effect and other forms of atmospheric pollution. The research provides evidence to suggest that such confusion between ideas is strongly held and that, even with this relatively new and abstract phenomenon as far as the children are concerned, ideas are held in a consistent and similar framework by most pupils. Similar research is being conducted in Greece and in the USA.

STATUS: Individual research

DATE OF RESEARCH: 1992-1993

KEYWORDS: **air pollution; conservation - environment; environmental education; misconceptions; scientific concepts; secondary school pupils**

1187

Department of Psychology, PO Box 147, Liverpool L69 3BX
0151 794 2000

Faber, D. Dr; *Supervisor*: Lovie, A. Dr

Binet's work and achievement: the first intelligence scales of 1905

ABSTRACT: The area of this research is the history of psychology. Although Binet is recognised as the pioneer of intelligence testing and his influence has been very great, the genesis of his scales is often misrepresented. The researcher's aim is to explain the achievement of Alfred Binet (1857-1911) with reference to his Intelligence Scales of 1905, the first 'true' tests of intelligence. The research involves identifying Binet's changing conceptions of intelligence and its developmental aspects, and tracing the origins of the test items in his experimental work in the 20 years preceding 1905. This also necessitates an examination of Binet's view of psychology as a science, his conception of a psychological experiment and the nature and role of introspections. The social and cultural contexts are important contributing factors to Binet's achievement, and are explained with reference to testing in other countries. In France, political forces and an immediate educational problem led to the Minister of Education's decision to have Paris school children tested or screened for ineducability. Binet's work, particularly that in association with the 'Sociate Libre pour L'Etude Psychologique de l'Enfant', was known by the authorities in 1904. The commission was entrusted to Binet; his earlier work and later collaboration with Simon resulted in the finally produced Scales of 1905, amply justifying their trust in the psychological work of Binet.

STATUS: Individual research

DATE OF RESEARCH: 1988-1993

KEYWORDS: **educational history; france; intelligence tests; psychological testing; psychology**

1188

Department of Sociology, Social Policy and Social Work Studies, PO Box 147, Liverpool L69 3BX
0151 794 2000

Roberts, K. Prof.

Young people in Armenia, Georgia and Ukraine

ABSTRACT: A set of investigations into the impact of economic and political changes among selected groups of young people.

STATUS: Sponsored project

SOURCE OF GRANT: International association for the promotion of cooperation with scientists from the independent state of the former Soviet Union (INTAS) £31,262

DATE OF RESEARCH: 1994-continuing

KEYWORDS: **armenia; eastern europe; georgia; political issues; social change; ukraine; youth**

1189

Department of Sociology, Social Policy and Social Work Studies, PO Box 147, Liverpool L69 3BX
0151 794 2000

Roberts, K. Prof.

Self-employment and unemployment among young people in East-Central Europe

ABSTRACT: Studies of samples of self-employed and unemployed young people in selected regions in Bulgaria, Hungary, Poland and Slovakia.

STATUS: Sponsored project

SOURCE OF GRANT: Advisory Centre for Education; Overseas Development Administration

DATE OF RESEARCH: 1996-1998

KEYWORDS: **eastern europe; youth employment; youth unemployment**

1190

Department of Sociology, Social Policy and Social Work Studies, PO Box 147, Liverpool L69 3BX
0151 794 2000

Roberts, K. Prof.

Young adults in the Russian Federation

ABSTRACT: A study of transitions from education to adulthood of young people in contrasting regions in the Russian Federation.

STATUS: Sponsored project

SOURCE OF GRANT: INTAS £49,000

DATE OF RESEARCH: 1998-continuing

KEYWORDS: **russia; school to work transition; young adults; youth**

London Borough of Wandsworth

1191

Education Department, Franciscan Road, Tooting, London SW17 8HE
0181 682 3759

Strand, S. Dr

The use of performance indicators for school improvement

ABSTRACT: The research investigates the development and application of performance indicators (PI) for Wandsworth schools. The development and operation of the key performance indicators (KPI) scheme is described. It was assumed that simply providing performance indicators (PIs) to schools would not of itself lead to school improvement: measurement of performance does not necessarily lead to improvement in performance. The research evaluates the way in which the KPI scheme is used to promote school improvement through: 1) a research programme explicitly investigating the relationships between PIs in order to generate targets for schools' achievements appropriate to their particular contexts; and 2) the use of the PIs in the context of a programme of annual school reviews (ASR) completed by the Inspectorate. Preliminary results indicate that PIs can enhance the quality of education where they are embedded in a wider evaluative context and are viewed as a vehicle for raising questions rather than providing answers.

PUBLISHED MATERIAL: STRAND, S. (1995). 'Key performance indicators for primary schools'. Paper presented to the European Conference on Educational Research, Bath, 14-17 September 1995.

STATUS: Sponsored project

SOURCE OF GRANT: London Borough of Wandsworth

DATE OF RESEARCH: 1994-1997

KEYWORDS: **educational improvement; educational quality; performance indicators; school effectiveness**

London University

1192

Goldsmiths College, Department of Educational Studies, New Cross, London SE14 6NW
0171 919 7171

Hurst, V. Ms; Blenkin, G. Ms

Monitoring and evaluation in workplace nurseries

ABSTRACT: The project aims to gain an insight into the evaluation procedures used by workplace nurseries, in particular the role of the 'outsider'. Ethnographic action research, based on two nursery centres, will investigate how staff may be supported in the monitoring and evaluation of their practice.

PUBLISHED MATERIAL: BLENKIN, G.M. & KELLY, A.V. (1992). (Eds). Assessment in early childhood education. London: Paul Chapman.

STATUS: Sponsored project

SOURCE OF GRANT: London University: Goldsmiths' College £3,700

DATE OF RESEARCH: 1990-1993

KEYWORDS: **employer supported day care; evaluation methods; institutional evaluation; self evaluation - groups**

1193

Goldsmiths College, Department of Educational Studies, New Cross, London SE14 6NW
0171 919 7171

Clyne, P. Mr; *Supervisor*: Coben, D. Dr

Professional development of adult educators in south east London

ABSTRACT: This project seeks to research the need for professional development of adult educators in south east London. This will be done through consultation with other providers of adult and continuing education in a range of settings including the new local education authorities, health authorities; social services and others. The aim will be to develop the curriculum and appropriate accreditation and transferability and to begin to provide short courses.

STATUS: Sponsored project

SOURCE OF GRANT: Universities Funding Coucil £15,000

DATE OF RESEARCH: 1991-1993

KEYWORDS: **adult education teachers; adult educators; professional development**

1194

Goldsmiths College, Department of Educational Studies, New Cross, London SE14 6NW
0171 919 7171

Gibbs, L. Ms

Research into the professional development and training of private music teachers

ABSTRACT: An initial survey of private music teachers, qualified and unqualified, to examine kinds of training/preparation teachers may or may not have received. Data from almost 600 questionnaires has been analysed, together with 60 follow-up interviews. Musical training is shown to be variable and lacking strongly on improvisation, composing and aural training. Training for teaching is also variable and external qualifications for teaching do not actually endorse teaching expertise. Teachers generally teach what they themselves have been taught. Survey interviews include information on private music teachers' perceptions of their effectiveness and their recommendations for further training and accreditation.

PUBLISHED MATERIAL: GIBBS, L. (1990). 'Private lives', Music Teacher, Vol 69, No 8, pp.11,13. ; GIBBS, L. (1990). 'How good are private music teachers', Journal of the Incorporated Society of Musicians, Vol 53, No 3, pp.78. ; GIBBS, L. (1991). 'Research into the professional development and training of private music teachers', Journal of the European Piano Teachers Association, Vol 12, No 36, pp.36. ; GIBBS, L. (1993). Private lives: report on the survey of private music teachers and their professional development and training. London: University of London, Goldsmiths' College. ; GIBBS, L. (1993). 'Private life and work: getting inside private music teaching', ISM Music Journal, August, pp.92-93.

STATUS: Sponsored project

SOURCE OF GRANT: Universities Funding Council £20,000

DATE OF RESEARCH: 1991-1993

KEYWORDS: **music; music teachers; professional development; professional training; teacher education**

1195

Goldsmiths College, Department of Educational Studies, New Cross, London SE14 6NW
0171 919 7171

Adams, T. Dr

Investigation into what factors pre-dispose students to seek counselling with special reference to: subject bias, special categories of college entry and history of mental instability

ABSTRACT: Data collected by Goldsmiths' Counselling Service over the last three years profiles a number of factors which the case-load presents. With regard to strategies of resourcing and academic pastoral support the data moves beyond an equation of student numbers and counselling hours. Relevant factors so far identified are that subject bias can appear to influence student stability; that special categories of students (e.g. mature) can cause considerable stress on the counselling provision; and that aspects of the psychological backgrounds of vulnerable students can lead to the service responding to problems that are reactivated through study. In order to address then the essential responsibilities of the Counselling Service provision the present study aims to evaluate students' specific needs by investigating what factors pre-dispose students to seek counselling. By appropriating the preliminary data, special reference is given in the study to subject bias, categories of college entry and history of mental instability. Research on student counselling services has been largely conducted by practising counsellors upon their own services. Such relatively small-scale research has resulted in a dearth of comparative studies across services. The present study is a comparative study made of the case-loads of counselling services in three institutions in the first instance. On identifying the small sample of services, students' specific needs are accessed by means of a semi-structured interview schedule, through which a base of information evolves and from which the final field work questions can be structured. The design of the pilot questionnaires will incorporate attitudes to and expectations of the counselling service, i.e. how the perception of student counselling consumerism affect the service provision. As a pilot study this research initiative will be broadened in scope at a national level.

STATUS: Sponsored project

SOURCE OF GRANT: London University: Goldsmiths' College £1,600

DATE OF RESEARCH: 1991-1993

KEYWORDS: **counselling services; higher education; pastoral care - education; student counselling; student needs**

1196

Goldsmiths College, Department of Educational Studies, New Cross, London SE14 6NW
0171 919 7171

Tomlinson, S. Prof.

Alternatives policies in education

ABSTRACT: The research stemmed from the view that post 1988 educational reforms could lead to a divided and divisive education system based on competitive individualism and on inappropriate market ideology. The project analysed the policy and ideological base of reforms, and attempted to suggest alternative policies based on consensus and cooperation which would still serve both individual development and economic needs. The methodology was library work and participatory action research in policy making left-of-centre groups.

PUBLISHED MATERIAL: TOMLINSON, S. (1991). 'Teaching by numbers', Fabian Review, Vol 103, No 2. ; TOMLINSON, S. (1992). 'Back to the future: streaming and selection', ACE Bulletin, No 45, pp.6-7. ; TOMLINSON, S. (1993). 'Education: vision, principles and policies', Renewal, No 1, pp.47-56. ; TOMLINSON, S. (1993). 'A nationalistic curriculum for white superiority?', ACE Bulletin, No 51, pp.10-11. ; TOMLINSON, S. (1994). Educational reform and its consequences. London: Rivers Oram Press.

STATUS: Sponsored project

SOURCE OF GRANT: Leverhulme Trust £20,500

DATE OF RESEARCH: 1990-1993

KEYWORDS: **education reform act 1988; educational change; educational policy; politics education relationship**

1197

Goldsmiths College, Department of Educational Studies, New Cross, London SE14 6NW
0171 919 7171

Mace, J. Ms; Gregory, E. Ms

Literacy at home and at school: the relationship between literacy practices in the households of children in two inner city primary schools and those of their classroom

ABSTRACT: The aims of this project were to: (1) investigate and report on the literacy practices in the households of children in two inner city primary schools; (2) compare these with those used by teachers in the schools; (3) test out a home-school event which would bring the two together. This was a pilot six month project, jointly supervised by two academics with, respectively, expertise in adult and primary literacy, and employing two part-time research assistants, working in two East London schools. A total sample of 10-12 households will have been used; half of the sample are bilingual Sylheti-speaking households; the other half, speakers of English as a first language. Parents in both groups include some with expressed literacy difficulties. The methods used included interviews, observations, and particpatory events. So far the results show evidence of under-expectation by school of children from Sylheti households; and interest in the role of television as a barrier to or inspiration for children's literacy. A successful grant application to the Economic and Social Research Council will mean a further one-year sequel to this study (1994-95).

STATUS: Sponsored project

SOURCE OF GRANT: Goldsmiths College research grant £4,195

DATE OF RESEARCH: 1992-1993

KEYWORDS: **adult literacy; home school relationship; literacy; literacy education; mother tongue; native speakers; primary education; teaching methods**

1198

Goldsmiths College, Department of Educational Studies, New Cross, London SE14 6NW
0171 919 7171

Mace, J. Ms

Reminiscence and the uses of literacy: transitions between oral and written narrative in reminiscence work with elderly people

ABSTRACT: The project (1) used oral history techniques with a community of pensioners sharing a common work history; and (2) explored the writing development issues of reminiscence work. This was a one-year study, commissioned by the Cottage Homes Charity, which provides accommodation on an estate in Mill Hill for 250+ retired staff from the retail trade. The research project involved a total of 50 of these residents. The methods used include tape-recorded individual interviews; group meetings; editorial individual/group meetings based on the tape transcripts; and publication of an anthology by the participants, documenting recollected life in department stores (1910 - 1985).

PUBLISHED MATERIAL: MACE, J. (Ed). (1993). Call yourself a draper: memories of life in the trade. London: Cottage Homes.

STATUS: Sponsored project

DATE OF RESEARCH: 1993-1993

KEYWORDS: **literacy; memory; older adults; oral history; personal narratives**

1199

Goldsmiths College, Department of Educational Studies, New Cross, London SE14 6NW
0171 919 7171

Jones, L. Ms

Continuity in curriculum learning experience (CICLE)

ABSTRACT: This project is monitoring the progress of a group of children from Year 6 through to Year 7, focusing on mathematics, science and design technology. The children were selected from a number of 'feeder' primary schools, feeding into the comprehensive school which they presently attend. They keep a weekly diary, recording their curriculum experience and their personal observations. Teachers and children have been interviewed. The content of the curriculum experience will be analysed and categorised using a content analysis schedule. Record keeping systems will be analysed and data collected about the curriculum materials used in each school.

PUBLISHED MATERIAL: JONES, L. & JONES, L.P. (1992). 'Spiralling upwards: progression across the interface', British Journal of Curriculum and Assessment, Vol 3, No 1, pp.10-12. ; JONES, L.P. & JONES, L. (1993). 'Keeping up the momentum: improving continuity', Education 3-13, Vol 21, No 3, pp.46-50. ; GRIFFITHS, J. & JONES, L. (1994). 'And you have to dissect frogs!', Forum, Vol 36, No 3, pp.83-84. ; JONES, L. (1995). 'Continuity in the curriculum', Forum, Vol 37, No 2, pp.44-46.

STATUS: Sponsored project

SOURCE OF GRANT: University of London Central Research Fund

DATE OF RESEARCH: 1991-1997

KEYWORDS: **curriculum development; developmental continuity; primary secondary education; primary to secondary transition**

1200

Goldsmiths College, Department of Educational Studies, New Cross, London SE14 6NW
0171 919 7171

Blenkin, G. Ms; Hurst, V. Ms; Hutchin, C. Ms; Miranda, K. Ms

Principles into practice: improving the quality of children's early learning

ABSTRACT: The project is concerned with improving the quality of children's early learning in schools, nurseries and other group settings. This is being achieved by focusing on the professional development of practitioners who are working with children under 8. It aims, firstly, to identify key aspects of professional ability crucial to the quality of children's early learning; secondly, to generate guidelines for improving professional practice in the early years; and thirdly, to disseminate these guidelines and other findings to practitioners, trainers and policy-makers. The project is divided into three phases. Phase One was a major national survey which has produced information concerning both the nature and the quality of provision, the level of resourcing and the qualifications of those professionals and others who are working with young children in group settings. It has also elicited the views of early years practitioners concerning quality provision. In Phase Two, a series of case studies has been conducted to explore with practitioners their effectiveness in implementing what they regard as a high quality curriculum. This is involving the practitioners in action research to enable them to investigate and critically reflect upon aspects of their own practice. In Phase Three, research findings and guidelines will be disseminated to a variety of audiences and the effectiveness of these different strategies will be evaluated. The strategies include presentations, publications and inservice training. The project is now in its third phase.

PUBLISHED MATERIAL: BLENKIN, G.M. & PAFFARD, F. (1994). 'Telling Verona's story: a search for principles in practice', Early Years, Vol 15, No 1, pp.30-36. ; BLENKIN, G.M. & YUE, N.Y.L. (1994). 'Profiling early years practitioners: some first impressions from a national survey', Early Years, Vol 15, No 1, pp.13-22. ; EDWARDS, G. & ROSE, J. (1994). 'Promoting a quality curriuclum in the early years through action research: a case study', Early Years, Vol 15, No 1, pp.42-47. ; BLENKIN, G.M. & YUE, N.Y.L. (1994). Principles into practice: improving the quality of children's early learning (year 1: June 1993-May 1994): interim report. London: London University, Goldsmiths College. ; BLENKIN, G.M. (1996). 'Lifelong professional development: an early years perspective', Education Today and Tomorrow, Vol 48, No 1, pp.6-8.

STATUS: Sponsored project

SOURCE OF GRANT: Esmee Fairbairn Charitable Trust £260,000; London Borough of Croydon £19,960; London Borough of Hounslow £19,980; London Borough of Southwark £9,980; London Borough of Hillingdon £9,980; London Borough of Lewisham £5,000; London Borough of Lambeth £15,000; Hertfordshire County Council £9,980

DATE OF RESEARCH: 1993-1997

KEYWORDS: **early childhood education; nursery education; preschool education**

1201

Goldsmiths College, Department of Educational Studies, New Cross, London SE14 6NW
0171 919 7171

Barlow, C. Ms

Black teachers' mentoring scheme

ABSTRACT: The aims of the Goldsmiths' Black Teachers' Mentoring Scheme, supported by British Telecom PLC, under that body's University Development Award Scheme, are to: 1) improve the take up of places in initial teacher training (ITT) from the black communities, especially school leavers, and thus to address under-representation of these communities in higher education (HE) in general and ITT in particular; 2) improve, via participation in the Scheme, the retention of black students, irrespective of entry route to HE; 3) address under-representation of black teachers; 4) improve retention rates of serving black teachers and enhance their opportunities for promotion; 5) create a support network of mentors/mentees to facilitate these aims; 6) evaluate these aims and foster good practice. The Scheme is divided into five phases: 1) information and consultation (including formation of steering and advisory groups); 2) development and implementation (including formation of networks); 3) evaluation and adaptation; 4) dissemination and information; 5) evaluation of phases 1 to 5. As it develops, the Scheme will make links with analogous, albeit different, conceptions of mentoring, e.g. school experience. Employing action research as the basic methodology, data collection, both qualitative and quantitative, will explore: issues relating to professional learning; the quality of mentor/mentee relations; good practice in the development of a mentoring scheme; the roles of steering and advisory committees; the roles of coordinators; issues relating to race in the professions; and the proportion of year cohorts entering higher education. The research also concerns itself with the efficacy of such schemes.

STATUS: Sponsored project

SOURCE OF GRANT: British Telecom; Deptford City Challenge; London University, Goldsmiths College

DATE OF RESEARCH: 1995-1997

KEYWORDS: **black teachers; mentors; preservice teacher education; teacher employment; teacher recruitment; teaching profession**

1202

Goldsmiths College, Department of Educational Studies, New Cross, London SE14 6NW
0171 919 7171

Mallett, M. Dr

Reflective writing from non-fiction: primary years

ABSTRACT: This is a 12 month, small scale, action research project in which the director teaches two different primary school classes alongside the class teacher for part of the school year. The aim is to identify some successful strategies in supporting children's writing from secondary sources. Discussion, drama and visual material will be used to enrich children's written accounts. The final report will either be in the form of an article or a short work.

STATUS: Sponsored project

SOURCE OF GRANT: London University, Goldsmiths College £1,077

DATE OF RESEARCH: 1994-1997

KEYWORDS: **nonfiction; primary education; writing - composition; writing exercises**

1203

Goldsmiths College, Department of Educational Studies, New Cross, London SE14 6NW
0171 919 7171

Coben, D. Dr; Thumpston, G. Ms

An investigation of mature students' mathematical experiences: the influence of these on career and learning opportunities

ABSTRACT: The project explores the 'mathematical life histories' of some mature students at Goldsmiths College, in order to gauge the influence of their experiences of mathematics on their perceptions of their career choices and learning opportunities.

PUBLISHED MATERIAL: COBEN, D. & THUMPSTON, D. (1995). 'Getting personal: adults' maths life histories'. Proceedings of Adults Learning Maths - A Research Forum Inaugural Conference, ALM-1, University of London, Goldsmiths College, 1995.

STATUS: Sponsored project

SOURCE OF GRANT: Goldsmiths College Research Committee £1,700

DATE OF RESEARCH: 1994-1997

KEYWORDS: **access to education; career choice; educational experience; higher education; mathematical ability; mathematics education; mature students; numeracy**

1204

Goldsmiths College, Department of Educational Studies, New Cross, London SE14 6NW
0171 919 771

Gregory, E. Dr; Mace, J. Ms; Williams, A. Dr; Rashid, N. Ms

Family literacy history and children's learning strategies at home and at school

ABSTRACT: In the UK, considerable evidence points to the poor reading achievement of children from both indigenous and ethnic minority disadvantaged families. At the same time, data on the relationship between illiteracy in the adult population and unsatisfactory school experience suggests a mismatch between school literacy and uses of literacy outside the school environment. This research investigates literacy activities in the lives of 5 year old children from indigenous and Bangladeshi origin families living in East London. It also examines the histories of the families in learning to read in school, as well as the teachers' own current literacy practices and reading histories. The second part of the project will focus particularly on the interaction over time between caregivers, teachers and children during different types of reading activities in the home and classroom. Analyses will be made using ethnographic (participant observation, interviews, case histories etc) and ethnomethodological (discourse analysis) approaches to identify and compare the reading progress of children from different cultural and literacy backgrounds in both in and out-of-school reading activities. Patterns of continuity and discontinuity between home and school practices, interaction between teacher or caregivers and children, and children's interpretation of the reading task in different domains will be uncovered.

PUBLISHED MATERIAL: GREGORY, E. (1993). 'Sweet and sour: learning to read in a British and Chinese school', English and Education, Vol 27, No 3, pp.53-59. ; GREGORY, E. (1993). 'Reading between the lines', Times Educational Supplement, No 4033, 15 September 1993, p.4. ; GREGORY, E. (1994). 'Cultural assumptions and early years' pedagogy: the effect of the home culture on minority children's interpretation of reading in school', Language, Culture and Curriculum, Vol 7, No 2, pp.111-124.

STATUS: Sponsored project

SOURCE OF GRANT: Economic and Social Research Council £29,860

DATE OF RESEARCH: 1994-1997

KEYWORDS: **adult literacy; disadvantaged environment; ethnic groups; home school relationship; literacy; parent participation; reading ability; reading teaching**

1205

Goldsmiths College, Department of Educational Studies, New Cross, London SE14 6NW
0171 919 7171

Davies, D. Mr; Rogers, M. Ms; *Supervisor*: Kimbell, R. Prof.

Primary teacher education in science, design and technology: experience, perceptions and classroom practice

ABSTRACT: The purpose of this research is to study the relationship between the scientific and technological learning experiences of new entrants to primary teacher training, the views concerning the relationship between science, design and technology expressed by these student teachers, and their subsequent approaches to classroom lesson planning. The sample consists of new entrants to the BA (Ed) Primary Education course at Goldsmiths College over a period of 3 years (pilot sample of 20 in 1996-97, samples of 90 in 1997-98 and 1998-99). Qualitative and quantitative data are collected using questionnaires and personal written statements to clarify prior experience and understanding, before the students are offered a choice of pedagogical models to inform their curriculum planning. Text analysis of subsequent classroom planning documents and semi-structured interviews after the students' first school experience are being conducted. Correlations have been drawn between these categories of data, both quantitatively (using SPSS software package) and qualitatively (using NUD 1ST software package). The results to date reveal that a simple, linear relationship between students' experience, views and planning approach must be rejected in favour of a more sophisticated model which allows for other important variables in their influence upon student's practice. The researchers will develop such a model to act as a framework for students' learning in this area, enabling them to locate themselves within the debate surrounding design, technology and science in the curriculum, and make informed pedagogical decisions. The results of this research will be of interest to teacher educators, inservice providers, and primary teacher trainees who will be able to use the instrument developed as a self-diagnostic tool.

PUBLISHED MATERIAL: DAVIES, D. (1997). 'The relationship between science and technology in the primary curriculum: alternative perspectives', Journal of Design and Technology Education, Vol 2, No 2, pp.101-111. ; DAVIES, D. & ROGERS, M. (1997). 'Different views, different outcomes: how the views of science and design and technology gained develop and support in effective classroom practice'. In: SMITH, J.S. (Ed). Proceedings of IDATER 97, Loughborough University, Loughborough, 1997.

STATUS: Individual research

DATE OF RESEARCH: 1996-continuing

KEYWORDS: **design and technology; preservice teacher education; science education; scientific literacy; student teachers; teaching practice**

1206

Goldsmiths College, Department of Educational Studies, New Cross, London SE14 6NW
0171 919 7171

Davies, M. Mr; *Supervisor*: Kwami, R. Dr

The impact of change upon music curriculum practice in schools: a comparative study of developments in England and Scotland between 1976-1998

ABSTRACT: The aims are: 1) to consider the way in which 'change' has impacted upon the school music curriculum in England and Scotland between 1976 and 1998; and 2) to suggest possible causes and effects for such 'change' and to provide reasons as to why the outcomes may have been different in each country. The investigation will: 1) examine the question of 'change' especially in the light of both pre- and post-1992 curriculum developments in schools; 2) examine the way in which teachers have reacted to the idea of 'change' and to the level of consultation involved in bringing about such developments; 3) highlight and review issues linked to the question of teacher response to change and control and of the implications for professional input into curriculum development. The research techniques are: a) questionnaire (including 'pilot' paper) for completion by teachers in both primary (30) and secondary schools (30) in both countries (sample size 60 x 2); b) conducting classroom observations in 2 local education authorities involving 4 secondary and 4 primary schools (i.e. 8 x 2 establishments) with follow-up use of semi-structured interviews; c) examining regional and national subject documentation to inform above discussions; d) undertaking interviews with key figures from the field of music education providing commentaries as to the impact of 'change' in both countries drawing comparisons with the views expressed by classroom practitioners and other recent research evidence.

STATUS: Individual research

DATE OF RESEARCH: 1996-continuing

KEYWORDS: **comparative education; music; music curriculum**

1207

Goldsmiths College, Department of Educational Studies, New Cross, London SE14 6NW
0171 919 7171
Bradford and Ilkley Community College, Department of Teacher Education, McMillan Building, Great Horton Road, Bradford BD7 1AY
01274 753189

Conteh, J. Ms; *Supervisor*: Gregory, E. Dr

The negotiation of meaning in multilingual classrooms

ABSTRACT: The aim of the study is to elicit the factors which seem to support successful learning for bilingual children of 8-10 years. The study is longitudinal, following the progress of a small group of children from Year 3 Year 5 and as they make the transition from first to middle school. The methodological approach is predominantly ethnographic, with the researcher (a qualified teacher with extensive experience of working in multilingual contexts) taking a participant-observer role. Data are being collected through tape recordings and field notes. For the initial 18 months (January 1996 - June 1997) regular visits were made to the classroom where the group of children worked. Since then, visits have been made once a term to the schools to which the children transferred. Home visits have also been made. So far, informal discussions have been held with teachers and these will be followed up by more formal interviews. The planned form for the thesis is a series of inter-related case studies which will seek to highlight the key issues. The conclusion will discuss the implications for professional development and classroom practice.

STATUS: Individual research

DATE OF RESEARCH: 1995-continuing

KEYWORDS: **bilingual pupils; learning processes; primary education**

1208

Goldsmiths College, Department of Educational Studies, New Cross, London SE14 6NW
0171 919 7171
Hong Kong Institute of Education, Special Education Department, 10 Lo Ping Road, Tai Po, Hong Kong

Hui, L. Ms; *Supervisor*: Tomlinson, S. Prof.

Policy and practice in Hong Kong for the education of children whose academic achievement is ranked in the bottom 10%

ABSTRACT: The number of children who are achieving poorly in academic achievement in Hong Kong is increasingly gradually and in 1990 the Education Department estimated that 4.3% of children at school would require intensive remedial services (Education Commission Report, 1990). The Education Commission of Hong Kong suggested that additional services should be implemented in the form of School-based Remedial Support Programme for the bottom 10% of secondary school pupils in mainstream schools. For children who are unmotivated to learn and young offenders, 3

practical schools to be established. For children who have severe learning difficulties, 7 Skills Opportunity Schools to be established (Education Commission Report, 1990). It is the major aim of this research to study the current practices with reference to the policies and needs of children whose academic achievement ranked in the bottom 10%. This research adopted a qualitative and case study approach in investigation. The sample included 6 schools with Resource Classes, 3 schools with School-based Remedial Support Programme, 3 practical schools, 3 skills opportunity schools, 2 resource teaching centres and 8 members of the Board of Education Sub-committee on Special Education. Interviews were conducted to collect viewpoints from school headteachers, teachers, parents, pupils, government officials and policymakers. Questionnaires will also be sent to school headteachers, teachers, parents and pupils, other than the samples. As the research is still in the stage of data collection therefore no results and conclusions have been reached.

STATUS: Sponsored project

SOURCE OF GRANT: Hong Kong Institute of Education

DATE OF RESEARCH: 1995-continuing

KEYWORDS: **achievement; hong kong; remedial education; underachievement**

1209

Goldsmiths College, Department of Educational Studies, New Cross, London SE14 6NW
0171 919 7171
Oxford Brookes University, School of Education, Wheatley Campus, Wheatley, Oxford OX33 1HX
01865 485930

Stiasny, M. Ms; *Supervisor*: Tomlinson, S. Prof.

The academic/vocational divide: education of 14-19 year olds in the UK

ABSTRACT: The education of 14-19 year olds in the UK is in a state of development and change; examinations are changing. The research will examine, using a survey of schools and pupils, the question of the academic/vocational divide. Has there been a fundamental shift, or is there still the traditional gap? This will be given a comparative dimension with research on Europe.

STATUS: Individual research

DATE OF RESEARCH: 1993-1997

KEYWORDS: **academic education; comparative education; educational change; examinations; secondary education; vocational education**

1210

Goldsmiths College, Department of Educational Studies, New Cross, London SE14 6NW
0171 919 7171
University of Hong Kong, Department of Education, Pokfulam Road, Hong Kong
010852 2859 2111

Au, M-L. Ms; *Supervisor*: Tomlinson, S. Prof.

The relationship beween policy and practice in the implementation of the target oriented curriculum in special schools for children with mental handicap in Hong Kong

ABSTRACT: In Hong Kong, children with mental handicap have been cared for and/or educated in separate institutions using a different curriculum from that used in mainstream schools for a long time. The emphasis in teaching and learning is very different in the mainstream and special school settings. A number of the initiatives promoted by the Hong Kong Education Department are regraded as for mainstream schools only. Recently, the curriculum reform initiative known as the Target Oriented Curriculum (TOC), which has been introduced in mainstream primary schools, has allowed special schools to join in as well. As this initiative was not originally planned for special schools, consequently the implications of the TOC initiative on the curriculum for children with mental handicap have not been clearly articulated. The main concerns of this study are: 1) on the genesis of the policy, and the interaction between policy and schools; 2) how TOC emerges as a policy for special school sectors; 3) how schools interpret and operationalise it; 4) how it is interpreted in different ways in schools. The above requires the curriculum be analysed at 3 levels, incorporating systematic/policy, school/organisation, and subject/classroom. At the policy level, documentary analyses and interviews of policy change agents are involved. At the school level, 7 multi-site case study schools are involved with interviews of principals and teachers. At the classroom level, classroom observations are conducted in the 7 multi-site case study schools. (Note: There are 41 schools for children with mental handicap in Hong Kong).

PUBLISHED MATERIAL: MORRIS, P., ADAMSON, R. AU, M-L. et al. (1996). Target oriented curriculum evaluation project: interim report. Hong Kong: University of Hong Kong, INSTEP, Faculty of Education.

STATUS: Individual research

DATE OF RESEARCH: 1994-continuing

KEYWORDS: **hong kong; learning disabilities; special educational needs; special schools**

1211

Goldsmiths College, Department of Psychology, New Cross, London
SE14 6NW
0171 919 7171

Myron-Wilson, R. Ms; *Supervisor*: Smith, P. Prof.

Bullying: a family perspective. Transgenerational patterns of attachment and attitudes to bullying

ABSTRACT: This research investigates the possible links between parental influence and children's social behaviour in school. There were four main areas of investigation: attachment, parental style, attitudes to bullying and family structure. Data was gathered from 196 school children aged 7-11. Each child completed the parental styles questionnaire (a measure of how children perceive their parenting), the family systems test (a representative measure of cohesion and power in the family), the separation anxiety test (a measure of attachment security) and the Provictim Scale (a measure of attitudes to bullying). Analyses show that insecurely attached children are more likely to have a high bully score (be nominated more for bullying behaviour). Analysis is now underway to explore the data collected from a smaller sub-sample of 41 parents of the above children. Transgenerational patterns of attachment and attitudes will be explored.

PUBLISHED MATERIAL: SMITH, P.K. & MYRON-WILSON, R. 'Parenting and school bullying', Journal of Clinical and Psychology and Psychiatry. (in press).

STATUS: Individual research

DATE OF RESEARCH: 1995-1998

KEYWORDS: **antisocial behaviour; attachment behaviour; attitudes; behaviour problems; bullying; family environment; parent attitudes; pupil attitudes**

1212

Goldsmiths College, Department of Psychology, New Cross, London
SE14 6NW
0171 919 7171

Sutton, J. Mr; *Supervisors*: Smith, P. Prof.; Swettenham, J. Dr

Bullying and social cognitive skills in middle childhood

ABSTRACT: In contrast to the popular stereotype and research tradition of the 'oafish' bully lacking in social skills and understanding, the bully may be a cold, manipulative expert in social situations, organising gangs and using subtle, indirect methods. Performance on a set of stories designed to assess understanding of cognitions and emotions was investigated in 193 7-10 year-olds in relation to role in bullying. Ringleader bullies scored higher than 'follower' bullies (those who helped or supported the bully), victims, and defenders of the victim. Results are discussed in terms of the need for further research into cognitive skills and emotion understanding in children who bully, the possible developmental pathway of social cognition in bullying, and important implications for intervention strategies.

PUBLISHED MATERIAL: SUTTON, J., SMITH, P.K. & SWETTENHAM, J. 'Bullying and theory of mind: a critique of the social skills deficit view of anti-social behaviour', Social Development. (in press). ; SUTTON, J. & SMITH, P.K. 'Bullying as a group process: an adaptation of the participant role scale approach', Aggressive Behaviour. (in press).

STATUS: Individual research

DATE OF RESEARCH: 1995-1998

KEYWORDS: **antisocial behaviour; behaviour problems; bullying; cognitive processes; pupil attitudes; social behaviour; social cognition**

1213

Goldsmiths College, Department of Psychology, New Cross, London
SE14 6NW
0171 919 7171

Dixon, R. Ms; *Supervisors*: Smith, P. Prof.; Jenks, C. Prof.

Deafness and bullying in childhood

ABSTRACT: The aim of this research is to explore and describe systems which support bullying of deaf children and systems which prevent and manage the bullying of deaf children in schools. It aims to explore the effect of intervention on the system, in particular to explore how the system uses new resources and information. Finally it aims to outline the long-term effects of bullying on individual deaf adults. The first study will look retrospectively at the experiences of 36 deaf adults, through semi-structured interviews. Subjects will be drawn from both deaf clubs and an audiology centre within the National Health Service. Both aural and signing (sign supported English and British Sign Language) subjects will be sought. The second study will look at bullying in up to 5 school systems. Children, staff and parents will be interviewed using a systematic framework. Each school will receive feedback on the findings within that school. If bullying is found to be encouraged or ignored by the system, recommendations will be offered and help implementing change will be made available. The researcher will return to each school 9 months later to reassess bullying within the school and how the system understands and responds to bullying, and to explore the uptake of resources by the school.

STATUS: Individual research

DATE OF RESEARCH: 1996-continuing

KEYWORDS: **behaviour management; bullying; deafness; discipline policy; hearing impairments; mainstreaming; special educational needs**

1214

Goldsmiths College, Department of Psychology, New Cross, London
SE14 6NW
0171 919 7171

Monks, C. Ms; *Supervisors*: Smith, P. Prof.; Swettenham, J., Dr

The role of attachment and social cognition in bullying during early childhood

ABSTRACT: Most research on bullying has concentrated on children aged 8 and above. To understand the origins of bullying behaviour we need to look earlier than 8 years. What factors make some children more at risk of being involved in bullying, either as the victim or the perpetrator? Attachment theory may provide useful insights into the influence of home background factors. There is some indication that bullies and victims are insecurely attached (Smith, Sutton & Myron-Wilson 1997). Traditionally bullies were thought to lack social skills, an alternative view is that at least some bullies, who use skills of manipulation and deception, have high social skills and well developed theory of mind abilities. Some evidence for this was reported by Sutton, Smith and Swettenham (1996) in a sample of 8-10 year-olds. However, this was limited to cognitive not emotional understanding, resulting in a 'cold, effective bully'. It would be useful to examine these findings with a younger group of children during their first years in school, from 4 to 6 years. A sample of approximately 200 children will be assessed. The researcher will obtain data on involvement in bullying behaviour (either as perpetrator, victim, reinforcer or outsider) using peer nomination (possibly adapted for younger children from the Salmivalli et al 1996 questionnaire), methods of bullying behaviour that they have witnessed (using a pictorial questionnaire, Smith and Levan 1995), attachment classification (SAT), family structure (FAST) and understanding of mind (including false belief, deception and recognition of emotions).

STATUS: Individual research

DATE OF RESEARCH: 1997-continuing

KEYWORDS: **antisocial behaviour; attachment behaviour; bullying; family structure; home environment; social skills; young children**

1215

Goldsmiths College, Department of Psychology, New Cross, London SE14 6NW
0171 919 7171

Shu, S. Ms; *Supervisor*: Smith, P. Prof.

International survey of bullying problems

ABSTRACT: This international study has 2 parts: 1) A report on the nature of bullying problems in different countries, and action taken to prevent it. This is being published in book form and comprises reports from about 20 countries. 2) A cross-national survey, using a standard self-report questionnaire, from samples of children aged 11-15 years in 6 countries: England, Japan, Netherlands, Norway, USA and Australia, with approximately 3,000 pupils in each country. Surveys were done in 1997 and are currently being analysed.

PUBLISHED MATERIAL: SMITH, P.K., MORITA, Y., JUNGES-TOS, J., OLWENS, D., CATALONO, R. & SLEE, P. (Eds). (1998). The nature of school bullying: a cross-national perspective. London: Routledge.

STATUS: Sponsored project

SOURCE OF GRANT: Japanese Ministry of Education £20,000

DATE OF RESEARCH: 1996-continuing

KEYWORDS: antisocial behaviour; bullying; comparative education; cross national studies

1216

Goldsmiths College, Faculty of Education, New Cross, London SE14 6NW
0171 919 7171

Jones, L. Ms; Allebone, B. Ms; Hirsi, M. Mr

Parental involvement in children's acquisition of numeracy: a home school numeracy project with Somali families in Greenwich

ABSTRACT: The project was developed with the intention of finding evidence about the ways in which children's home lives can support their development in school. In the area of mathematics in education, children in the UK appear to perform at a lower level than their peers in other comparable countries. There are also significant differences in attainment between ethnic groups in the UK. Findings from a previous funded project suggested that children in Somali families had considerable support from the family in their acquisition of numeracy on entry to school (JONES, L. & FARAH, R. (1995). Linking school and community practices. London: London University, Goldsmiths College, Department of Educational Studies). However, the families themselves expressed concern about their ability to continue to provide this support at the stage of transfer between National Curriculum key stages 2 and 3. The project aims to work with a small sample of parents, schools and teachers to identify good practice, generalisable to other contexts. It further aims to promote partnership between parents and teachers in which different approaches to numeracy are recognised. 13 children have been identified from Year 7 of 2 Greenwich schools (7 boys, 6 girls). Data is being gathered through participant observation in schools and semi-structured interviews with parents and children at home. The project is ongoing and results are not yet available, but interesting methodological issues are arising about working with a researcher/interpreter.

PUBLISHED MATERIAL: JONES, L. & FARAH, R. (1995). Linking school and community practices. London: London University, Goldsmiths College, Department of Educational Studies. ; JONES, L. & ALLEBONE, B. (1998). 'Researching "hard to reach" groups. Some methodological issues'. Proceedings of the First International Mathematics Education and Society Conference, Nottingham University, 6-11 September 1998. ; JONES, L. (1998). 'Home and school numeracy experiences for young Somali pupils in Britain', European Early Childhood Education Research Journal, Vol 6, No 1.

STATUS: Sponsored project

SOURCE OF GRANT: Paul Hamlyn Foundation £1,900

DATE OF RESEARCH: 1997-1998

KEYWORDS: ethnic groups; mathematics education; numeracy; parent participation

1217

Imperial College of Science, Technology and Medicine, Humanities Programme, Mechanical Engineering Building, Exhibition Road, London SW7 3BX
0171 589 5111

Hughes, J. Mr; *Supervisor*: Goodlad, S. Dr

Tutoring from colleges to schools

ABSTRACT: The aim of the project is to promote peer tutoring schemes, similar to Imperial College's 'Pimlico Connection', around the United Kingdom. This is when volunteer students from further or higher education act as tutors in local primary and secondary schools often in science, mathematics and technology lessons. The professional teacher uses them as an extra, and valuable, teaching resource. The student tutors provide positive role models to the school pupils and in doing so it is hoped to increase the aspiration for them to stay on in education and training beyond age 16. Students acquire communication, organisational and problem-solving skills as well as self-confidence. Student tutoring involves volunteer students going into local primary and secondary schools on a sustained and systematic basis. From the original Pimlico Connection Scheme the number has risen to 96 similar programmes.

PUBLISHED MATERIAL: GOODLAD, S. & HIRST, B. (1989). Peer tutoring: a guide to learning by teaching. London: Kogan Page. ; GOODLAD, S. & HIRST, B. (1990). Explorations in peer tutoring. Oxford: Blackwell. ; HUGHES, J.C. (1992). Tutoring: students as tutors in school. London: BP Educational Service. ; HUGHES, J.C. (1991) (Ed). Tutoring Resource Pack. London: BP Educational Service.

STATUS: Sponsored project

SOURCE OF GRANT: British Petroleum (BP) Aiming for a College Education Initiative £300,000

DATE OF RESEARCH: 1990-1993

KEYWORDS: mathematics education; peer influence; peer teaching; science education; student volunteers; technology education

1218

Imperial College of Science, Technology and Medicine, Humanities Programme, Mechanical Engineering Building, Exhibition Road, London SW7 3AZ
0171 589 5111
Science Museum, Exhibition Road, London SW7 5BD
0171 938 8234

McIvor, S. Ms; *Supervisor*: Goodlad, S. Prof.

Science interpretation project

ABSTRACT: Study Service gives students the opportunity to carry out work of direct practical social utility as part of their curriculum. As one form of study service, Imperial College students have, since 1975, acted as tutors in local schools, assisting teachers with the delivery of lessons in science, technology and mathematics. In 1994, with funding from the Nuffield Foundation, Imperial College started a joint project with the Science Museum to extend this idea, specifically to experiment with students as interpreters of science on the museum galleries. This project, which will enrich the education of students by encouraging them to make use of knowledge as they acquire it, has two primary objects: 1) To develop a programme of volunteer interpreters as a basis for assessing the feasibility of deploying volunteers in the interpretation and dissemination of science and technology in museums and heritage sites; 2) To help other museums and heritage sites set up schemes using models, procedures, and materials generated and tested in the project.

PUBLISHED MATERIAL: GOODLAD, S. & MCIVOR, S. (1998). Museum volunteers. London: Routledge.

STATUS: Sponsored project

SOURCE OF GRANT: Nuffield Foundation £50,000

DATE OF RESEARCH: 1994-1998

KEYWORDS: museums; science teaching centres; volunteers

1219

Institute of Education, 20 Bedford Way, London WC1H 0AL
0171 580 1122

Lawton, D. Prof.; Coles, M. Mr

National Council for Vocational Qualifications (NCVQ) Fellowship

ABSTRACT: This project is to examine impact and take-up of the new framework for National Vocational Qualifications (NVQs); it examines and supports the technical processes required to develop and implement NVQs as well as providing a critique of policy and strategy formation in vocational qualifications in the United Kingdom.

PUBLISHED MATERIAL: LAWTON, D. (1992). Education and politics in the 1990s: conflict or consensus? London: Falmer Press.

STATUS: Sponsored project

SOURCE OF GRANT: National Council for Vocational Qualifications £216,669

DATE OF RESEARCH: 1990-1997

KEYWORDS: **national vocational qualifications; qualifications; vocational education**

1220

Institute of Education, 20 Bedford Way, London WC1H 0AL
0171 580 1122

Swanwick, K. Prof.

Voices/Menuhin project

ABSTRACT: This project is an evaluation of a three year curriculum intervention in music in a primary school. A broad, sequenced and progressive music course will be supported by inservice work starting in September 1994. Two classes will be under observation in Oxford Gardens Primary School: Years 1 and 3. There are two main research questions: 1) What are the social and academic effects of this programme on the children taking part? 2) Does the programme result in the observable development of musical understanding?

STATUS: Sponsored project

SOURCE OF GRANT: Voices Foundation £7,100

DATE OF RESEARCH: 1994-1997

KEYWORDS: **music; music activities; primary education; singing**

1221

Institute of Education, 20 Bedford Way, London WC1H 0AL
0171 580 1122

Noss, R. Prof.; Hoyles, C. Prof.

Understanding the mathematics of banking

ABSTRACT: To understand how mathematical knowledge is mobilised in investment banking, and to produce materials which address the underlying mathematical concepts involved.

PUBLISHED MATERIAL: NOSS, R. & HOYLES, C. (1995). 'The mathematics of banking: an approach through computational modelling'. In: Proceedings of the First European Conference for Research on the Psychology of Mathematics Education, Osnabruck, 1995.

STATUS: Sponsored project

SOURCE OF GRANT: Swiss Bank Corporation £33,600

DATE OF RESEARCH: 1994-1998

KEYWORDS: **banking; mathematical applications**

1222

Institute of Education, 20 Bedford Way, London WC1H 0AL
0171 580 1122

Penn, H. Dr

Making change happen: an action research programme to into how nursery provision can be developed and supported

ABSTRACT: Five case studies of nurseries which have integrated childcare and education in early years. Four case studies of local authorities in the process of setting up nurseries which combine childcare and education in the early years. Seminar programme for policymakers on integration of care and education in the early years.

STATUS: Sponsored project

SOURCE OF GRANT: Baring Foundation £200,000

DATE OF RESEARCH: 1994-1997

KEYWORDS: **child caregivers; day care; early childhood education; nursery education; preschool education**

1223

Institute of Education, 20 Bedford Way, London WC1H 0AL
0171 580 1122

Job, D. Mr; Slater, F. Dr

Schools network on air pollution

ABSTRACT: The Geography Section at the Institute of Education is coordinating a schools based investigation of air quality across London. Sixteen schools are monitoring nitrogen dioxide, carbon monoxide and acid rain.

PUBLISHED MATERIAL: JOB, D. & SLATER, F. (1996). Schools network on air pollution: a school based monitoring project on London's air quality. Report of Findings. London: London University, Institute of Education.

STATUS: Sponsored project

SOURCE OF GRANT: The Sainsbury Family Charitable Trusts £21,000

DATE OF RESEARCH: 1994-1997

KEYWORDS: **air pollution; environmental education; field studies; geography; pollution**

1224

Institute of Education, 20 Bedford Way, London WC1H 0AL
0171 580 1122

Thomas, S. Dr

Analysis and presentation of 1997 and 1998 GCSE data

ABSTRACT: This is an extension of the Lancashire value added project which started in 1992 and aims to provide Lancashire secondary schools with ongoing feedback to assist school self evaluation and improvement processes.

PUBLISHED MATERIAL: THOMAS, S. (1995). 'Considering primary school effectiveness: an analysis of 1992 key stage 1 results', The Curriculum Journal, Vol 6, No 3, pp.279-295. ; THOMAS, S. & MORTIMORE, P. (1996). 'Comparison of value-added models for secondary school effectiveness', Research Papers in Education, Vol 11, No 1, pp.5-33.

STATUS: Sponsored project

SOURCE OF GRANT: Lancashire County Council £33,540

DATE OF RESEARCH: 1998-continuing

KEYWORDS: **examination results; examinations; general certificate of secondary education; school effectiveness; secondary education**

1225

Institute of Education, 20 Bedford Way, London WC1H 0AL
0171 580 1122

Thomas, S. Dr

Optimal multilevel models of school effectiveness: comparative analysis across regions

ABSTRACT: The project investigates three issues crucial to the development of school effectiveness research: 1) the specificiation of the optimal multilevel models for measuring secondary school effectiveness using a value added approach; 2) the extent of local area, regional and national differences in the size, consistency and stability of school effects and the impact of different student and school background factors on student outcomes; and 3) the nature of the underlying dimensions of school effectiveness.

STATUS: Sponsored project

SOURCE OF GRANT: Economic and Social Research Council £72,030

DATE OF RESEARCH: 1995-1998

KEYWORDS: **comparative analysis; educational quality; performance indicators; school effectiveness; secondary education; value added**

1226

Institute of Education, 20 Bedford Way, London WC1H 0AL
0171 580 1122

Swanwick, K. Prof.

South Bank Centre project

ABSTRACT: The project will study the effects of work at South Bank Centre on classes throughout National Curriculum key stage 3.

STATUS: Sponsored project

SOURCE OF GRANT: Esmee Fairbairn Charitable Trust £6,000

DATE OF RESEARCH: 1995-1997

KEYWORDS: **music**

1227

Institute of Education, 20 Bedford Way, London WC1H 0AL
0171 580 1122

Dockrell, J. Dr

Sources of word finding problems in language impaired children

ABSTRACT: The project concerns language impaired children who experience word finding difficulties (WFDs). Despite our detailed knowledge of individual factors that influence normal lexical acquisition, little is known about how these factors interact during acquisition, or of the effects of different types of experiences during the recall of words. A number of explanations of WFDs exist, but there has been no attempt to: 1) contrast these competing explanations in children experiencing language problems alone; 2) compare the patterns of deficit experienced by the children; or 3) develop a model of lexical production that acknowledges the types of deficits experienced by these children which the project will address. Experiments will be undertaken which will serve as an important step in defining the nature of the difficulties experienced by these children and lead to the development of intervention techniques. These studies will contribute to a fuller model and understanding of lexical production in children.

STATUS: Sponsored project

SOURCE OF GRANT: Wellcome Trust £51,209

DATE OF RESEARCH: 1996-1997

KEYWORDS: **child language; language acquisition; language handicaps; vocabulary development**

1228

Institute of Education, 20 Bedford Way, London WC1H 0AL
0171 580 1122

Kress, G. Prof.; Ogborn, J. Prof.

Visual communication in the learning of science

ABSTRACT: To analyse and document the variety of roles of visual communication used in science classrooms to provide a typology of kinds and functions of such images; to identify roles which form the grammar of such images; and to investigate methods of accessing knowledge and understanding in which visual imagery plays an essential role.

STATUS: Sponsored project

SOURCE OF GRANT: Economic and Social Research Council £124,700

DATE OF RESEARCH: 1995-1997

KEYWORDS: **imagery; science education; visual learning**

1229

Institute of Education, 20 Bedford Way, London WC1H 0AL
0171 580 1122

Porter, J. Ms

Curriculum access for deaf-blind children

ABSTRACT: The aim of this project is to investigate the strategies used by teachers with pupils who are deaf-blind to access the curriculum. The term 'strategies' is used here to include the communication modes and methods, teaching approaches, use of the environment, use of specialist resources, task presentation and organisation and any related aspects concerning the management of learning. The design of the study includes teacher questionnaire and log, completed over a one week period. The national

sample of 50 teachers will include teachers with deaf-blind pupils in mainstream, in specialist sensory provision and in severe learning difficulties (SLD) schools. The sample is skewed to represent the proportion of children to be found in each of the three settings. Information will be collated on teachers' decision-making to draw together information on teachers' experience of the effectiveness of different strategies and the conditions of use.

STATUS: Sponsored project

SOURCE OF GRANT: Department for Education and Employment £42,082

DATE OF RESEARCH: 1995-1997

KEYWORDS: **deaf blind; learning disabilities; special educational needs; teaching methods**

1230

Institute of Education, 20 Bedford Way, London WC1H 0AL
0171 580 1122

Oakley, A. Prof.

Randomised controlled trial of peer-led sex education in schools in North Thames

ABSTRACT: The risk of sexually transmitted disease and unwanted pregnancy are greatest in people aged 16-24 years. The need to reduce these unwanted sexual outcomes is emphasised in the government's strategy for health in England. Peer-led sex education is an increasingly popular intervention that has been successfully implemented in a number of different secondary schools, but without long-term outcome evaluation. This project will be a pilot study of a randomised controlled trial of peer-led sex education in schools. The aims are to reduce sexual risk taking and the incidence of unwanted sexual outcomes and to promote health. Four schools will be sampled, two intervention and two control. The intervention, developed through extensive practical experience, will be delivered by trained 16 year old "peers" to 13 year olds over two terms. A survey will be conducted at baseline and outcome assessment at three months post-intervention will include knowledge and attitudes about sexual behaviour and safer sex.

STATUS: Sponsored project

SOURCE OF GRANT: Department of Health £51,675

DATE OF RESEARCH: 1995-1997

KEYWORDS: **health education; peer teaching; secondary education; sex education**

1231

Institute of Education, 20 Bedford Way, London WC1H 0AL
0171 580 1122

Hoyles, C. Prof.; Healy, S. Ms

Justifying and proving in school mathematics

ABSTRACT: This project will survey conceptions amongst high-attaining students of the validity of a range of modes of justification in geometry and in algebra, including formal mathematical proof. Following this survey, the researchers will design computer-integrated teaching experiments in these two areas of the mathematics curriculum and evaluate their influence on students' conceptions of proof and the proving process.

STATUS: Sponsored project

SOURCE OF GRANT: Economic and Social Research Council £199,390

DATE OF RESEARCH: 1995-1998

KEYWORDS: **algebra; computer uses in education; geometry; information technology; mathematics education; proof - mathematics**

1232

Institute of Education, 20 Bedford Way, London WC1H 0AL
0171 580 1122

Leonard, D. Dr

Gender and schooling: are boys now under-achieving?

ABSTRACT: This is a series of seminars which will aim to map the field in debates about gender-related school achievement, with particular emphasis on the achievement of boys.

STATUS: Sponsored project

SOURCE OF GRANT: Economic and Social Research Council £7,040

DATE OF RESEARCH: 1995-1997

KEYWORDS: achievement; boys; sex differences; underachievement

1233

Institute of Education, 20 Bedford Way, London WC1H 0AL
0171 580 1122

Norwich, B. Prof.

Provision of a teacher centred strategy for implementing the Special Educational Needs Code of Practice

ABSTRACT: This study investigates the processes and outcomes of teacher support teams (TSTs) in secondary schools. In particular, it considers how a school's culture and support systems affect the implementation and outcomes of a TST. Moreover, the research looks at ways at TST can contribute to improving a school's provision for special educational needs and its implementation of the Code of Practice.

STATUS: Sponsored project

SOURCE OF GRANT: Department for Education and Employment £44,800

DATE OF RESEARCH: 1995-1997

KEYWORDS: educational policy; mainstreaming; secondary education; special educational needs; support services; support staff

1234

Institute of Education, 20 Bedford Way, London WC1H 0AL
0171 580 1122

Noss, R. Prof.; Hoyles, C. Prof.

Towards a mathematical orientation through computational modelling

ABSTRACT: Every aspect of personal or professional life is becoming increasingly mathematised. A primary aim of this research is to analyse a broad range of mathematical situations as described by adults on the basis of their personal or professional functionality. Research suggests that for learners to mathematise successfully, they must do so in the context of situations which are meaningful to them, and that they must build their own mathematical models, which can happen in computational settings. The research will involve the design and construction of activities based on computational modelling, in which individuals have to express their understandings on the form of formal yet meaningful computer "programs". These activities will serve simultaneously as a context in which to study the individual's construction of mathematical meanings, and as a setting in which individuals might come to coordinate more effectively everyday and mathematical approaches.

STATUS: Sponsored project

SOURCE OF GRANT: Economic and Social Research Council £89,520

DATE OF RESEARCH: 1996-1998

KEYWORDS: computer programming; mathematical models; mathematics achievement; mathematics education

1235

Institute of Education, 20 Bedford Way, London WC1H 0AL
0171 580 1122

Cowan, R. Dr; O'Connor, N. Dr

Calendrical calculation: talent and intelligence

ABSTRACT: The purpose of the projected studies is to verify and extend the studies of calendrical calculation among subjects of limited intelligence who are talented for this kind of performance. These investigations have been made predominantly by O'Connor and Hermelin (1986). These authors suggested that day-date calculations were in part rule-governed and did not depend solely on episodic memory. The project will aim to verify the independence of talent from intelligence as apparently shown by the subjects of the experiment and to clarify the degree to which the talent is independent of standard operations in arithmetical procedures.

STATUS: Sponsored project

SOURCE OF GRANT: University of London, FBT Charitable Fund

DATE OF RESEARCH: 1996-1998

KEYWORDS: cognitive processes; intelligence; learning disabilities; memory; special educational needs

1236

Institute of Education, 20 Bedford Way, London WC1H 0AL
0171 580 1122

Ouston, J. Dr

Secondary schools use of OFSTED inspections as a basis for school development

ABSTRACT: An investigation of how secondary schools might make effective use of Office for Standards in Education (OFSTED) inspection for their own development.

STATUS: Sponsored project

SOURCE OF GRANT: Nuffield Foundation

DATE OF RESEARCH: 1996-1997

KEYWORDS: inspection; ofsted; school improvement; secondary education

1237

Institute of Education, 20 Bedford Way, London WC1H 0AL
0171 580 1122

Williams, G. Prof.

Comparisons of higher education systems

ABSTRACT: Assembly of national indicators of higher education performance as part of a European project to compare university systems across Europe.

STATUS: Sponsored project

SOURCE OF GRANT: Hochshul-Information-Systems GmbH

DATE OF RESEARCH: 1995-1997

KEYWORDS: comparative education; education systems; educational quality; europe; higher education; performance indicators

1238

Institute of Education, 20 Bedford Way, London WC1H 0AL
0171 580 1122

Lines, D. Mr

Business and economics education

ABSTRACT: The purpose of this project is: 1) to create an entirely new General Certificate of Secondary Education (GCSE) which combines business studies and economics; 2) to provide published materials including computer software for both students and teachers; and 3) to provide inservice teacher education (INSET) and other support for teachers starting the course.

STATUS: Sponsored project

SOURCE OF GRANT: Nuffield Foundation £121,393

DATE OF RESEARCH: 1996-continuing

KEYWORDS: business education; curriculum development; economics education; examinations; general certificate of secondary education; secondary education

1239

Institute of Education, 20 Bedford Way, London WC1H 0AL
0171 580 1122

Hood, S. Ms; Mayall, B. Dr

Children's centre: a feasibility study

ABSTRACT: This 1-year project will explore with local people and agency staff the feasibility of establishing a Children's Centre in their area of inner London, and will identify their views on its aims, functions and character. If successful, the project may be funded for a further 2 years, to establish and monitor such a centre.

STATUS: Sponsored project

SOURCE OF GRANT: The Glass-House Trust

DATE OF RESEARCH: 1996-1997

KEYWORDS: child caregivers; day care centres

1240

Institute of Education, 20 Bedford Way, London WC1H 0AL
0171 580 1122

Penn, H. Dr

Childcare as a gendered occupation

ABSTRACT: An exploratory project which will focus on 2 London colleges of further education offering National Nursery Examination Board/National Vocational Qualification courses in childcare, to explore who accesses the courses and why and what the outcomes are for those who qualify. The project will use a multi-method approach, using focus groups, interview schedules and analysis of documentation.

PUBLISHED MATERIAL: PENN, H. (1997). Childcare as a gendered occupation. Research Report No 23. London: Department for Education and Employment.

STATUS: Sponsored project

SOURCE OF GRANT: Department for Education and Employment

DATE OF RESEARCH: 1996-1997

KEYWORDS: **child care occupations; child caregivers; further education; nursery nurses; sex differences**

1241

Institute of Education, 20 Bedford Way, London WC1H 0AL
0171 580 1122

Roberts, I. Dr; Oakley, A. Prof.

Effects of out of home day care on maternal and child health: a feasibility study for a randomised controlled trial

ABSTRACT: This study will prepare the ground for a randomised controlled trial (RCT) of out of home child care provision for lone parent families in areas of social and maternal deprivation. The aim is to undertake a systematic review of RCTs and to collect data from mothers on their attitudes to day care and to the proposed trial, to consult with health and welfare professionals and service providers and to develop full protocol for the trial.

STATUS: Sponsored project

SOURCE OF GRANT: NHS Executive

DATE OF RESEARCH: 1996-1997

KEYWORDS: **child caregivers; child minding; day care; health; mothers; one parent family; unmarried mothers; young children**

1242

Institute of Education, 20 Bedford Way, London WC1H 0AL
0171 580 1122

Wolf, A. Prof.

Evolution of General National Vocational Qualifications: final phase

ABSTRACT: Completes a national longitudinal survey of the evolution of General National Vocational Qualifications, including pupil/student destinations, management and classroom processes.

STATUS: Sponsored project

DATE OF RESEARCH: 1996-1997

KEYWORDS: **curriculum development; employment qualifications; followup studies; further education; general national vocational qualifications; secondary education; sixteen to nineteen education; student destinations; vocational education; work education relationship**

1243

Institute of Education, 20 Bedford Way, London WC1H 0AL
0171 580 1122

Thomas, S. Dr; Sammons, P. Dr

Evaluation of the Raising School Standards Initiative

ABSTRACT: This project will evaluate the impact of the implementation of the Raising School Standards Initiative. It is funded by the Belfast Education and Library Board and is part of the Making Belfast Work programme. A total of 4 secndary and 10 primary schools are involved. These are all schools in highly socio-economically disadvantaged areas with low levels of pupil attainment.

STATUS: Sponsored project

SOURCE OF GRANT: Belfast Education and Library Board

DATE OF RESEARCH: 1996-1997

KEYWORDS: **disadvantaged; educational quality; northern ireland; primary education; school effectiveness; school improvement; secondary education**

1244

Institute of Education, 20 Bedford Way, London WC1H 0AL
0171 580 1122

Sammons, P. Dr

Value-added analysis

ABSTRACT: Analysis of survey databases for infant and primary schools to explore the issue of value-added using baseline assessment and national assessment data at National Curriculum key stage 1.

STATUS: Sponsored project

SOURCE OF GRANT: Surrey County Council

DATE OF RESEARCH: 1996-1997

KEYWORDS: **assessment; baseline assessment; key stage 1; primary education; value added; young children**

1245

Institute of Education, 20 Bedford Way, London WC1H 0AL
0171 580 1122

Sammons, P. Dr; Thomas, S. Dr

The development of baseline and value-added measures for the Department of Education Northern Ireland Raising School Standards project

ABSTRACT: The development of baseline and value-added measures for Department of Education Northern Ireland Raising School Standards Initiative involves the collection, analysis and feedback to schools of individual pupil attainment data. A value-added approach is adopted for prior attainment and other pupil background characteristics.

STATUS: Sponsored project

SOURCE OF GRANT: Department of Education Northern Ireland £118,225

DATE OF RESEARCH: 1996-continuing

KEYWORDS: **baseline assessment; educational quality; northern ireland; primary education; school effectiveness; school improvement; value added**

1246

Institute of Education, 20 Bedford Way, London WC1H 0AL
0171 580 1122

Lines, D. Mr

Pass rates in accountancy examinations

ABSTRACT: An investigation into the pass rates for professional accountancy examinations set by the Institute of Chartered Accountants for England and Wales.

STATUS: Sponsored project

SOURCE OF GRANT: Institute of Chartered Accountants in England and Wales

DATE OF RESEARCH: 1996-1997

KEYWORDS: **accountancy education; accountants; examinations; pass rates; professional education**

1247

Institute of Education, 20 Bedford Way, London WC1H 0AL
0171 580 1122

Warwick, I. Mr; Whitty, G. Prof.

Vital youth evaluation

ABSTRACT: To evaluate the perceived effectiveness of Vital Youth - a 'young people's health empowerment project'. The evaluation is both informative and summative in nature. Information will be collected on the perceived effectiveness of a series of health promotion interventions undertaken with young people and intermediates in and out of school settings across the Brixton City Challenge area. Opportunities will be provided to vital youth workers, advisory group members and commissioners to reflect on the development of the project.

STATUS: Sponsored project

SOURCE OF GRANT: West Lambeth Community Care Trust

DATE OF RESEARCH: 1996-1998

KEYWORDS: adolescents; health education; health promotion; youth

1248

Institute of Education, 20 Bedford Way, London WC1H 0AL
0171 580 1122

Whitty, G. Prof.; Warwick, I. Mr

Perceived effects of Section 28 on addressing lesbian and gay issues in schools and HIV prevention education

ABSTRACT: The aims of the project are to: 1) examine, via a survey of 1000 randomly selected schools in England, ways in which schools are addressing bullying, support, and human immunodeficiency virus (HIV) education in relation to lesbian and gay pupils; 2) note the perceived effects of Section 28.

STATUS: Sponsored project

SOURCE OF GRANT: Terence Higgins Trust

DATE OF RESEARCH: 1996-1997

KEYWORDS: acquired immune deficiency syndrome; homosexuality; lesbianism; secondary education; sex education

1249

Institute of Education, 20 Bedford Way, London WC1H 0AL
0171 580 1122

Gillborn, D. Dr

Pupils' perspectives on exclusions from school

ABSTRACT: An analysis of pupil perspectives on discipline, behaviour, teaching and learning in secondary schools which historically have excluded a disproportionate number of black African Caribbean children.

STATUS: Sponsored project

SOURCE OF GRANT: London Borough of Islington £3,274

DATE OF RESEARCH: 1996-continuing

KEYWORDS: discipline; ethnic groups; exclusion; pupil attitudes; secondary education

1250

Institute of Education, 20 Bedford Way, London WC1H 0AL
0171 580 1122

Clarke, S. Ms; Gipps, C. Prof.

Monitoring consistency in teacher assessment

ABSTRACT: Evaluation of the use of School Curriculum and Assessment Authority (SCAA) teacher assessment (TA) publications and consistency in general TA practice in National Curriculum key stages 1, 2 and 3. The project involves questionnaire and case studies across England. The purpose of the project is to inform SCAA of teachers' needs in terms of future TA publications and to give a general guide to the future of teacher assessment.

STATUS: Sponsored project

SOURCE OF GRANT: School Curriculum and Assessment Authority

DATE OF RESEARCH: 1996-1997

KEYWORDS: assessment; assessment by teachers; educational materials; key stage 1; key stage 2; key stage 3; national curriculum

1251

Institute of Education, 20 Bedford Way, London WC1H 0AL
0171 580 1122

Barber, M. Prof.

Admissions policies in city technology colleges and technology colleges

ABSTRACT: The project will examine the admissions policies of the 15 city technology colleges and a sample of 15 technology colleges. It will examine the basic principles underpinning their policies and the extent to which the reality adheres to the principles.

STATUS: Sponsored project

SOURCE OF GRANT: City Technology Colleges Trust Ltd

DATE OF RESEARCH: 1996-1997

KEYWORDS: admission criteria; city technology colleges; secondary education; selection; selective admission; technology colleges

1252

Institute of Education, 20 Bedford Way, London WC1H 0AL
0171 580 1122

Stoll, L. Dr

Charting the progress of the new local education authority

ABSTRACT: Findings of studies of school improvement highlight the importance of the school participating in external partnerships, that includes the school district or local education authority (LEA). In April 1996, 13 new English LEAs were established as a result of local government reorganisation. 4 new LEAs are being followed for 2.5 years to chart their progress, to see to what extent they achieve their aims, and determine the extent to which they appear to influence and enhance improvement in their schools. These LEAs are located in different parts of England, cover rural, suburban and urban areas, and represent a range of sizes - with different numbers of schools. This action research study will include annual interviews with a variety of people, examination of key documents, and surveys of satisfaction with the LEAs. Feedback will be given during the study to the LEAs to help them with their planning. A final report will be provided for each LEA at the end of the project.

STATUS: Sponsored project

SOURCE OF GRANT: Various Local Education Authorities £44,937

DATE OF RESEARCH: 1996-1998

KEYWORDS: cooperation; educational administration; educational quality; local education authorities; partnerships; school effectiveness; school improvement

1253

Institute of Education, 20 Bedford Way, London WC1H 0AL
0171 580 1122

Barber, M. Prof.

Raising educational achievement in Downham Single Regeneration Budget Scheme

ABSTRACT: Evaluation of Single Regeneration Budget strategy on the Downham Estate.

STATUS: Sponsored project

SOURCE OF GRANT: Lewisham Education Authority

DATE OF RESEARCH: 1996-1997

KEYWORDS: disadvantaged; educational improvement; local education authorities; urban education; urban improvement

1254

Institute of Education, 20 Bedford Way, London WC1H 0AL
0171 580 1122

Siraj-Blatchford, J. Mr; Siraj-Blatchford, I. Dr

Learning through making in the early years

ABSTRACT: This project aims to establish the precise nature of the cognitive and affective benefits to be gained by encouraging young children (4 to 6 year olds) to make things. While the pioneers of the kindergarten movement extolled the benefits of such activities, and both preschool and infant educators have often promoted making, we still have very little knowledge or understanding of the child development processes or cognitive implications that are involved. This proposal argues that George Kelly's (1955) Personal Constructs Theory offers both a powerful conceptual framework and an appropriate methodological apparatus which may be employed to undertake this analysis.

STATUS: Sponsored project

SOURCE OF GRANT: Esmee Fairbairn Charitable Trust

DATE OF RESEARCH: 1996-1997

KEYWORDS: **cognitive development; creative activities; early childhood education; handicrafts; learning activities; personal construct theory; primary education; technology education; young children**

1255

Institute of Education, 20 Bedford Way, London WC1H 0AL
0171 580 1122

Siraj-Blatchford, I. Dr

Parent involvement in promoting the academic achievement of bilingual pupils in Brent primary schools

ABSTRACT: The aim of the research is to promote pupil achievement, special attention will be given to the needs of bilingual children, through improved home-school collaboration. The project will develop an adaptable model of strategies and materials; and examine the process which promotes home-school collaboration. The purpose of the model is to enable primary schools in Brent Local Education Authority (LEA), or other inner-city areas, to replicate this work. The project will provide, indepth analysis, insight and evidence on the impact on school change through the process of parent involvement. It will contribute towards an understanding of which strategies are most conducive to inner-city schools. The research aims are to be generalisable in the sense that it will provide illuminative insights to those who find themselves in similar contexts as the rest of the LEA. It will help staff to understand the diverse roles parents can play in school improvement.

STATUS: Sponsored project

SOURCE OF GRANT: London Borough of Brent

DATE OF RESEARCH: 1996-1997

KEYWORDS: **achievement; bilingual pupils; ethnic groups; home school relationship; parent participation; parent pupil relationship; parent school relationship; primary education; primary school pupils; pupil performance**

1256

Institute of Education, 20 Bedford Way, London WC1H 0AL
0171 580 1122

Buckingham D. Dr

Television news and the development of political understanding

ABSTRACT: The project proposes to investigate the relationship between education and entertainment in children's media culture through: 1) the study of policy and professional practice in media production for children; 2) through the analysis of texts produced specifically for children; and 3) through the study of children as an audience.

STATUS: Sponsored project

SOURCE OF GRANT: Nuffield Foundation

DATE OF RESEARCH: 1997-1997

KEYWORDS: **childrens television; mass media; news media; politics; television**

1257

Institute of Education, 20 Bedford Way, London WC1H 0AL
0171 580 1122

Scott, D. Dr

Evaluation of the Docklands Learning Acceleration project

ABSTRACT: This is an evaluation of the National Literacy Association Docklands Learning Acceleration Project which involves 14 junior schools and 1 special school in 3 local education authorities (LEAs): Tower Hamlets, Southwark and Newham. It aims to improve the standards of literacy and basic skills, concentrating for 2 years on the cohort of Year 3 children. The evaluation will last for 18 months.

STATUS: Sponsored project

SOURCE OF GRANT: National Literacy Association; Docklands Acceleration Project

DATE OF RESEARCH: 1996-1997

KEYWORDS: **accelerated learning; basic skills; computer uses in education; information technology; intervention; literacy; primary education; reading; writing skills**

1258

Institute of Education, 20 Bedford Way, London WC1H 0AL
0171 580 1122

Stuart, M. Dr

Getting ready for reading

ABSTRACT: The project aims to implement and evaluate 2 short programmes aiming to prepare rising fives for reading. Four schools in Tower Hamlets will take part. In two schools, a structured programme of Big Book reading will take place; in the other two, a structured phonics programme 'Jolly Phonics', designed for this age group, will take place. Schools will be matched across interventions for social and ethnic characteristics. Children in both interventions will be pretested on a variety of language and literacy measures; these will be measured again on programme completion. Immediate effects on reading and writing will be measured in the Summer of 1997, and longer-term results in the Summer of 1998.

STATUS: Sponsored project

SOURCE OF GRANT: London Docklands Development Corporation; St Katharine and Shadwell Trust; Canary Wharf Ltd; The Mercers' Company

DATE OF RESEARCH: 1997-1998

KEYWORDS: **beginning reading; phonics; prereading experience; primary education; reading readiness; reception classes; young children**

1259

Institute of Education, 20 Bedford Way, London WC1H 0AL
0171 580 1122

Hoyles, C. Prof.; Noss, R. Prof.

Intercultural microworld courseware for exploratory learning

ABSTRACT: The project explores: a) the need for the design of educationally focused and meaningful (for the pupils) learning environments for collaborative project work. There is a growing concern for the relevance of school activity to meaningful and applicable understandings for pupils. Changes in societies, abundance of information, the need to communicate and the influence of cultural diversity in personal life and work are posing new demanding challenges to education; b) the need to introduce the computer as an 'expressive medium' to pupils. The advent of computers in the school, instead of 'delivering' education to all, often enhances the lack of personal meaning for pupil activity since nuggets of computer use have begun to appear in curriculum subjects, which pre-suppose a computer culture which does not exist; c) the need to devise methods of using the technology in the actual process of 'learning how to learn'.

STATUS: Sponsored project

SOURCE OF GRANT: European Commission £17,330

DATE OF RESEARCH: 1996-1998

KEYWORDS: **computation; computer uses in education; educational software; information technology**

1260

Institute of Education, 20 Bedford Way, London WC1H 0AL
0171 580 1122

Rasbash, J. Mr

Extending multilevel modelling software using heterogeneous cluster and parallel computing technologies

ABSTRACT: Designing and implementing a parallel processing version of the multilevel software.

STATUS: Sponsored project

SOURCE OF GRANT: Higher Education Funding Council for England £77,209

DATE OF RESEARCH: 1996-continuing

KEYWORDS: **computer software; information technology; multilevel modelling**

1261

Institute of Education, 20 Bedford Way, London WC1H 0AL
0171 580 1122

Henderson, S. Dr

The value of early and sequential magnetic resonance imaging in predicting neurodevelopmental status in term infants with Hypoxic-Ischaemic Encephalopathy

ABSTRACT: This project is part of a much larger programme of research concerned with understanding the development of children who experience various types of trauma before or around the time of birth. It is a collaborative programme in which the researcher investigates medical, psychological and educational aspects of children's development. In this particular project, the researchers are concerned with the value of magnetic resonance imaging (MRI) as a predictor of the severity of a child's motor disability as well as the effect of any disability on educational attainment.

STATUS: Sponsored project

SOURCE OF GRANT: SCOPE

DATE OF RESEARCH: 1996-1998

KEYWORDS: **birth; child development; motor development; neurological impairments; special educational needs**

1262

Institute of Education, 20 Bedford Way, London WC1H 0AL
0171 580 1122

Lunt, I. Ms; Norwich, B. Prof.

Secondary school development project

ABSTRACT: Curriculum review and development project focusing on curriculum differentiation in Essex secondary schools with reference to special educational needs.

STATUS: Sponsored project

SOURCE OF GRANT: Essex County Council

DATE OF RESEARCH: 1996-1997

KEYWORDS: **differentiated curriculum; mainstreaming; secondary education; special educational needs**

1263

Institute of Education, 20 Bedford Way, London WC1H 0AL
0171 580 1122

Goldstein, H. Prof.

Hampshire baseline assessment and value-added project

ABSTRACT: The aims of the project are to provide: 1) advice to Hampshire Local Education Authority (LEA) concerning the ongoing collection of pupil and school data to feed into the baseline and value-added measures of primary school performance; 2) a pilot value-added analysis of the 1996 National Curriculum key stage 1 assessment results matched to the baseline assessments (administered to Reception class pupils in a sample of Hampshire primary schools; 3) advice and recommendations to Hampshire LEA concerning: a) the possibility for developing the Hampshire baseline assessment for all primary schools in order to provide a broader base of comparison; and b) the possibilities for developing/extending the pupil/class/school background information collected by Hampshire primary schools.

STATUS: Sponsored project

SOURCE OF GRANT: Hampshire County Council £34,970

DATE OF RESEARCH: 1996-1998

KEYWORDS: **achievement; assessment; baseline assessment; educational quality; key stage 1; performance; primary education; tasks and tests; value added**

1264

Institute of Education, 20 Bedford Way, London WC1H 0AL
0171 580 1122

Williams, G. Prof.; Parry, G. Mr; Barnett, R. Prof.

National Committee of Inquiry into Higher Education: analysis of evidence and commentary

ABSTRACT: Analysis of a commentary on evidence submitted in response to public consultation conducted by the National Committee of Inquiry into Higher Education (Dearing Committee); production of report for possible inclusion with the Report to be published in 1997 by the Committee itself.

STATUS: Sponsored project

SOURCE OF GRANT: Department for Education and Employment

DATE OF RESEARCH: 1996-1997

KEYWORDS: **educational change; educational finance; educational policy; higher education**

1265

Institute of Education, 20 Bedford Way, London WC1H 0AL
0171 580 1122

Gillborn, D. Dr

Achievement and experience in GCSE English and Mathematics: setting and selection project

ABSTRACT: The project will examine the importance of ethnic background as a factor in pupils' experience of, and performance in, General Certificate of Secondary Education (GCSE) English and Mathematics. Specifically, it aims to: 1) investigate whether ethnic origin is related to pupils' placement in teaching sets and differentiated (tiered) entry schemes; and 2) explore the significance of race as a factor in the school-based processes of teacher/pupil and pupil/pupil interaction that shape experience in teaching sets and influence final decisions about the most 'appropriate' level for GCSE entry.

STATUS: Sponsored project

DATE OF RESEARCH: 1995-1997

KEYWORDS: **academic ability; english; ethnic groups; examinations; general certificate of secondary education; mathematics education; race; secondary education; setting; streaming**

1266

Institute of Education, 20 Bedford Way, London WC1H 0AL
0171 580 1122

Alderson, P. Dr

Civil rights in school

ABSTRACT: The aim of the project is to conduct a questionnaire survey of the views of 3,000 school pupils, aged 8-16, about the United Nations Convention on the Rights of the Child 1989, and their civil rights in schools. The area involved is the UK and Northern Ireland, with all types of schools to be included. The project will include: a) group interviews in 20 schools; b) a brief survey of 300 teachers' views; c) development of methods for obtaining young people's views in large-scale research; d) a literature review about school pupils' rights; and e) collection of examples of good and new practices in schools. There are plans to expand this into an international project, and to set up information on a web site.

STATUS: Sponsored project

SOURCE OF GRANT: Economic and Social Research Council £81,021

DATE OF RESEARCH: 1996-1998

KEYWORDS: **childrens rights; civil rights; primary education; primary school pupils; pupil attitudes; school policy; secondary education; secondary school pupils; teacher attitudes**

1267

Institute of Education, 20 Bedford Way, London WC1H 0AL
0171 580 1122

Brosnan, T. Dr

Explanations of material change

ABSTRACT: The principal aim of this project is to delineate the range of explanations and explanation types that children will accept as valid accounts of some common changes in materials - ice-melting; iron rusting; sugar dissolving; and candles burning. Achieving the principal aim involves the further development and validation of an existing 'grammar' of explanations of material change. Essential contributory aims are the production of a computer programme, based on this grammar, to generate the sets of explanations, and the development of an associated methodology to elicit which explanations are acceptable to each of the children interviewed.

STATUS: Sponsored project

SOURCE OF GRANT: Economic and Social Research Council

DATE OF RESEARCH: 1997-1997

KEYWORDS: **chemistry; science education; secondary education**

1268

Institute of Education, 20 Bedford Way, London WC1H 0AL
0171 580 1122

Lunt, I. Ms; Cowen, R. Dr; Wolf, A. Prof.; Green, A. Dr

Convergence and divergence in European education systems

ABSTRACT: The aim of the project is to analyse trends in relation to a number of aspects of secondary and post-secondary education and training in the European member states to determine patterns of convergence and divergence.

STATUS: Sponsored project

SOURCE OF GRANT: European Commission

DATE OF RESEARCH: 1996-1997

KEYWORDS: **comparative education; education systems; educational policy; europe; further education; secondary education; sixteen to nineteen education; training**

1269

Institute of Education, 20 Bedford Way, London WC1H 0AL
0171 580 1122

Mortimore, P. Prof.; Goldstein, H. Prof.; Blatchford, P. Dr

Class size project

ABSTRACT: The project has 2 aims: 1) to examine connections between size of class on school and pupils progress; and 2) to examine connections between size of class and classroom processes. It involves 8 local education authorities (LEAs) and around 250 schools and will study pupils for 2 years after entry to school.

STATUS: Sponsored project

SOURCE OF GRANT: Various Local Education Authorities; Avon County Council, jointly £260,000

DATE OF RESEARCH: 1996-continuing

KEYWORDS: **achievement; class organisation; class size; classroom management; key stage 1; primary education; primary school pupils; pupil performance; teaching methods**

1270

Institute of Education, 20 Bedford Way, London WC1H 0AL
0171 580 1122

Goodey, C. Mr; Oakley, A. Prof.

Project inclusion

ABSTRACT: A full-time teacher seconded and paid by London Borough of Newham, together with the project director, will identify and extend good practice in making pupils with complex learning needs and attendant behaviour difficulties welcome and included in the ordinary life of mainstream classes. The method will involve class teachers, classroom assistants and pupil peers in action research, encouraging them to suggest and implement their own ideas.

STATUS: Sponsored project

SOURCE OF GRANT: London Borough of Newham

DATE OF RESEARCH: 1996-1997

KEYWORDS: **action research; emotional and behavioural difficulties; mainstreaming; special educational needs**

1271

Institute of Education, 20 Bedford Way, London WC1H 0AL
0171 580 1122

Moreno, C. Ms; Nunes, T. Dr

Addressing the communication needs of deaf children in the mathematics classroom

ABSTRACT: Deaf children are delayed in mathematics learning but hearing loss itself does not explain this delay. The researchers hypothesise that this delay results from their specific communications difficulties involving time, the representations of actions, and the use of written language in the mathematics classroom. They propose to carry out an intervention to support communications about mathematics through drawings and diagrams in the teaching of 4 core mathematics concepts. The interventions will be carried out by teachers of the deaf in special lessons during one year; the teachers will continue to implement the teaching of the National Curriculum through their chosen schemes in their regular lessons. The programme will be considered successful if: a) the gap between deaf children's mathematics achievement and their peers is reduced; and b) the children in the programme perform significantly better than an unseen control group.

STATUS: Sponsored project

SOURCE OF GRANT: Nuffield Foundation £43,570

DATE OF RESEARCH: 1998-continuing

KEYWORDS: **communication; deafness; mainstreaming; mathematics education; special educational needs**

1272

Institute of Education, 20 Bedford Way, London WC1H 0AL
0171 580 1122

Youdell, D. Ms

Evaluation of the school exclusion project

ABSTRACT: Evaluation of joint voluntary sector and local education authority (LEA) initiative aimed at preventing exclusions from school of primary pupils in the 4-7 age range. This will involve analysis and exclusion statistics and records and draw upon interview, observation and case study data with key professionals, teachers, parents/carers and pupils.

STATUS: Sponsored project

SOURCE OF GRANT: Royal Philanthropic Society £9,998

DATE OF RESEARCH: 1997-1998

KEYWORDS: **exclusion; primary education**

1273

Institute of Education, 20 Bedford Way, London WC1H 0AL
0171 580 1122

Noss, R. Prof.

Probability and risk: a research review

ABSTRACT: This project aims to map those sections of the mathematics education literature which bear on the problem of children's understanding of risk, with a view to specifying areas for further research.

STATUS: Sponsored project

SOURCE OF GRANT: Royal Society for the Prevention of Accidents

DATE OF RESEARCH: 1997-1997

KEYWORDS: **mathematics education; probability; risk**

1274

Institute of Education, 20 Bedford Way, London WC1H 0AL
0171 580 1122

Goldstein, H. Prof.

Advanced training workshops in multilevel modelling

ABSTRACT: To carry out advanced training in multilevel modelling, consisting of 5 workshops in the following areas: education, demography, political science, health services, spatial analysis.

STATUS: Sponsored project

SOURCE OF GRANT: Economic and Social Research Council £15,606

DATE OF RESEARCH: 1997-1998

KEYWORDS: **multilevel modelling; statistical analysis**

1275

Institute of Education, 20 Bedford Way, London WC1H 0AL
0171 580 1122

Thompson, S. Prof.; Yang, M. Dr; Goldstein, H. Prof.

Multilevel frameworks for specifying general meta-analysis

ABSTRACT: The project will extend current procedures for meta-analysis by viewing it as a particular case of the general hierarchical data model. This will extend the flexibility and explanatory power of meta-analysis. The project will look specifically at the issues of explaining between-study heterogeneity modelling multiple types of outcomes and dealing with measurements made at both study level and the individual, within study level. It will re-analyse some existing meta-analysis data sets.

STATUS: Sponsored project

SOURCE OF GRANT: Economic and Social Research Council £41,738

DATE OF RESEARCH: 1997-1998

KEYWORDS: **meta analysis; multilevel modelling; statistical analysis**

1276

Institute of Education, 20 Bedford Way, London WC1H 0AL
0171 580 1122

Woodhouse, G. Mr; Yang, M. Dr; Thomas, S. Dr; Goldstein, H. Prof.

Application of advanced multilevel modelling methods for the analysis of examination data

ABSTRACT: The project aims to: 1) extend multilevel modelling techniques to analyse institutional performance data where the response is a set of ordered categories, where there is a measurement error, where there are several responses not all of which are present; 2) provide important substantive information about the gender differences in different subjects in A-level examinations, adjusting for GCSE performance; 3) study institutional differences in terms of A-level performance, especially differential performance by subjects and student characteristics.

STATUS: Sponsored project

SOURCE OF GRANT: Economic and Social Research Council £177,462

DATE OF RESEARCH: 1998-continuing

KEYWORDS: **a level examinations; examination results; general certificate of secondary education; multilevel modelling; sex differences; statistical analysis**

1277

Institute of Education, 20 Bedford Way, London WC1H 0AL
0171 580 1122

Norwich, B. Prof.

Developing an assessment for monitoring learning progression in special schools in Southwark

ABSTRACT: This project aims to develop a systematic assessment scheme to monitor pupils' learning outcomes in special schools related to National Curriculum attainment targets.

STATUS: Sponsored project

SOURCE OF GRANT: Southwark Council £22,956

DATE OF RESEARCH: 1997-1998

KEYWORDS: **assessment; outcomes of education; special educational needs; special schools**

1278

Institute of Education, 20 Bedford Way, London WC1H 0AL
0171 580 1122

Miller, O. Ms; Porter, J. Ms

Improving provision for children with visual impairment and multiple disabilities placed in schools for severe learning or physical disability

ABSTRACT: The project aims to draw on the expertise of teachers working as specialists in the field of visual impairment and those whose areas of expertise lie within the field of learning and multiple disabilities. By combining this expertise it should be possible to examine the specific needs of the specific learning difficulty (SLD) sector in relation to the quality of provision available to children with severe visual loss. The project objectives are to link school policy development with training initiatives and thereby to enhance both the quality of information schools receive and their approaches to staff development.

STATUS: Sponsored will

SOURCE OF GRANT: Royal National Institute for the Blind

DATE OF RESEARCH: 1997-1997

KEYWORDS: **disabilities; learning disabilities; special educational needs; special schools; visual impairments**

1279

Institute of Education, 20 Bedford Way, London WC1H 0AL
0171 580 1122

Johnson, A. Prof.; Brodala, A. Ms; Stephenson, J. Dr; Oakley, A. Prof.

The effectiveness of peer-led sex education in school

ABSTRACT: This project is planned as a 5-year randomised controlled trial to test the effectiveness in promoting sexual health of a programme of sex education delivered by 16-17 year-olds to 13-14 year-olds including knowledge and attitudes, as well as intended and actual sexual behaviour.

STATUS: Sponsored project

SOURCE OF GRANT: Medical Research Council £663,015

DATE OF RESEARCH: 1997-continuing

KEYWORDS: **health education; peer teaching; sex education**

1280

Institute of Education, 20 Bedford Way, London WC1H 0AL
0171 580 1122

Hood, S. Ms; Mayall, B. Dr

Kingsland children's centre project

ABSTRACT: This study comprises a process evaluation of the development of an innovative children's centre, which offers education, leisure and health/welfare services to children aged 8-14 attending a secondary school in inner London and 3 of its feeder primary schools. The centre will run outside school hours, and will have 4 core staff. Children will participate in developing services in accordance with their own wishes. The study will run for 18 months and output will include guidelines for the development of similar services.

STATUS: Sponsored project

SOURCE OF GRANT: Sainsbury Family Charitable Trusts £43,150

DATE OF RESEARCH: 1997-continuing

KEYWORDS: **childrens centres; extracurricular activities**

1281

Institute of Education, 20 Bedford Way, London WC1H 0AL
0171 580 1122

Alderson, P. Dr

Enabling education: disabled pupils views about school

ABSTRACT: The aim is to write a book and related papers on special and mainstream schooling for children with disabilities and learning and behaviour difficulties in 2 contrasting local education authorities (LEAs).

STATUS: Sponsored project

SOURCE OF GRANT: Gatsby Charitable Foundation

DATE OF RESEARCH: 1997-1997

KEYWORDS: **mainstreaming; pupil attitudes; special educational needs**

1282

Institute of Education, 20 Bedford Way, London WC1H 0AL
0171 580 1122

Parry, G. Mr; Barnett, R. Prof.

Changing patterns of undergraduate curricula

ABSTRACT: The research will examine changes in the undergraduate curriculum in English higher education over the past 10 years and into the immediate future. Since the mid-1980s, participation by young people and adults has increased significantly, reaching levels associated with a mass system of higher education. The undergraduate curriculum has a key part in this expansion, but it has largely been neglected as a subject of recent research. As a result, higher education policy is being developed without an informed understanding of one of its key components. This project will identify the dominant components of contemporary undergraduate curricula and will assess patterns and directions of change.

STATUS: Sponsored project

SOURCE OF GRANT: Economic and Social Research Council £74,061

DATE OF RESEARCH: 1997-continuing

KEYWORDS: curriculum development; higher education

1283

Institute of Education, 20 Bedford Way, London WC1H 0AL
0171 580 1122

Davies, J. Mr; Earley, P. Mr; Fidler, B. Prof.; Ouston, J. Dr

The re-inspection of secondary schools: how do schools respond the second time around

ABSTRACT: This research project will explore the impact of re-inspection on secondary schools. The researchers have already undertaken national studies of secondary schools first inspected by OFSTED from 1993 to 1997. This phase of the research will include 10 schools which are to be re-inspected in 1997-1998. These schools were first inspected in 1993. Headteachers completed questionnaires about the impact of the inspection in 1994 and 1995, and staff were interviewed in 1996-97. In 1997-98 staff will be interviewed at each school before, and after, their second inspection to evaluate the impact on their development of the second inspection compared to the first, and the ways in which their experience of the first inspection has influenced their preparation for, and attitudes towards, the second inspection. New features of the inspection process (such as reports on individual teachers) will also be reviewed.

STATUS: Sponsored project

SOURCE OF GRANT: Nuffield Foundation

DATE OF RESEARCH: 1997-1998

KEYWORDS: inspection; ofsted; school development planning; school improvement; secondary education

1284

Institute of Education, 20 Bedford Way, London WC1H 0AL
0171 580 1122

Young, M. Dr

Post-16 education strategies

ABSTRACT: The Post-16 Centre is one of 8 national partners in this project. The overall theme is Post-16 education strategies, and together with European partners, the Institute is contrasting the experience of different countries in relation to 6 issues including: labour market contexts, reform and educational systems, networking and skills for the future, teacher cooperation, and qualifications and the flexibility of student programmes.

STATUS: Sponsored project

SOURCE OF GRANT: European Commission (Leonardo Programme) £75,120

DATE OF RESEARCH: 1995-continuing

KEYWORDS: comparative education; europe; sixteen to nineteen education

1285

Institute of Education, 20 Bedford Way, London WC1H 0AL
0171 580 1122

Youdell, D. Ms

African Caribbean excluded pupils: evaluation of the Grants for Education Support and Training (GEST)

ABSTRACT: Evaluation of a Grants for Education Support and Training (GEST) funded project in one inner London Borough. The GEST project aims to reduce exclusions (fixed term and permanent) from secondary schools, with a particular emphasis on addressing the over-representation of African Caribbean pupils in these exclusions. The evaluation draws on interview data and relevant documentation and includes key professionals within schools, the local education authority (LEA) and community organisations as well as pupils and parents.

STATUS: Sponsored project

SOURCE OF GRANT: London Borough of Islington

DATE OF RESEARCH: 1997-1998

KEYWORDS: afro caribbean youth; ethnic groups; exclusion

1286

Institute of Education, 20 Bedford Way, London WC1H 0AL
0171 580 1122

Watkins, C. Mr; Whitty, G. Prof.

External evaluation of healthier school partnership project 1997-1999

ABSTRACT: To provide evaluation support to a healthier schools partnership in South London, through feedback style evaluation with schools, project team and other stakeholders over a period of 3 years.

STATUS: Sponsored project

SOURCE OF GRANT: Lewisham Education Authority £20,000

DATE OF RESEARCH: 1997-continuing

KEYWORDS: health education; health promoting schools; partnerships; school health services

1287

Institute of Education, 20 Bedford Way, London WC1H 0AL
0171 580 1122

Hey, V. Dr; Leonard, D. Dr

Learning and gender: a study of underachievement in junior schools

ABSTRACT: This project aims to study the giving and taking of support for learning by pupils from their peers and teachers. It will focus on gender (by race and class) in order to investigate the relationship between school culture, patterns of interpersonal relations and learning, and achievement.

STATUS: Sponsored project

SOURCE OF GRANT: Economic and Social Research Council £104,432

DATE OF RESEARCH: 1997-continuing

KEYWORDS: academic achievement; achievement; learning; primary education; sex differences; underachievement

1288

Institute of Education, 20 Bedford Way, London WC1H 0AL
0171 580 1122

Donoughue, C. Ms

Evaluation of educational establishments

ABSTRACT: An analytical reflection on particular types of evaluation: external school evaluation and school self-evaluation. A comparative study of systems in Italy, Holland, Spain and England. The main activities of the project will be to analyse the political context and the particular emphasis on evaluation given in each country; to evaluate the success of the procedures for external and self-evaluation; and to describe the trends and innovations in this area of evaluation in each country.

STATUS: Sponsored project

SOURCE OF GRANT: European Commission

DATE OF RESEARCH: 1996-1998

KEYWORDS: educational quality; inspection; institutional evaluation; school effectiveness; self evaluation - groups

1289

Institute of Education, 20 Bedford Way, London WC1H 0AL
0171 580 1122

Leo, E. Dr; Stoll, L. Dr

Raising achievement in Island Schools project

ABSTRACT: This is the first phase of this project and includes data gathering, analysis and feedback related to pupil, teacher and parental attitudes in all Isle of Wight schools. From analysis of this information in relation to other Island information, a second phase will be developed to involve specific targeted and evaluated projects.

STATUS: Sponsored project

SOURCE OF GRANT: Isle of Wight Council

DATE OF RESEARCH: 1997-1998
KEYWORDS: **achievement; attitudes; pupil improvement**

1290

Institute of Education, 20 Bedford Way, London WC1H 0AL
0171 580 1122

McCallum, B. Dr; Gipps, C. Prof.

Primary teaching strategies, assessment and feedback

ABSTRACT: The aim of this study is to describe a range of teaching, assessment and feedback strategies used by 'expert' teachers in Year 2 and Year 6. The research will describe the teaching and assessment strategies that these teachers use with different groups of children and for different key subjects of the curriculum. It will articulate key differences between infant and junior school practices and, rather than simply reflecting what teachers say they do and are observed to do, bring this together with what research tells us about learning. The outcomes will be twofold: descriptions of effective primary practice will be produced; and the research will contribute to the theoretical understandings of pedagogy and the relationship among teaching, assessment and feedback.

STATUS: Sponsored project

SOURCE OF GRANT: Economic and Social Research Council £130,001

DATE OF RESEARCH: 1997-continuing

KEYWORDS: **assessment; feedback; primary education; teaching methods**

1291

Institute of Education, 20 Bedford Way, London WC1H 0AL
0171 580 1122

Clarke, S. Ms; Gipps, C. Prof.

Evaluation of statutory assessment at the end of key stage 1

ABSTRACT: This study is an evaluation of the 1997 national assessment programme at National Curriculum key stage 1. The evaluation involved questionnaires to 400 schools in England for both headteachers and Year 2 teachers, and case studies of teachers in a sample of 20 schools. The data presents information about specific issues relating to the actual tasks and tests; the administration of the tasks and tests; general issues around testing of 7 year-olds and teacher assessment at this age; and proposals for the future of key stage 1 assessment.

STATUS: Sponsored project

SOURCE OF GRANT: School Curriculum and Assessment Authority

DATE OF RESEARCH: 1997-1997

KEYWORDS: **assessment; assessment by teachers; key stage 1; national curriculum; primary education; tasks and tests**

1292

Institute of Education, 20 Bedford Way, London WC1H 0AL
0171 580 1122

Barber, M. Prof.

Nottingham primary achievement book

ABSTRACT: The research evaluates an inner city project to raise achievement of primary pupils. It examines initiatives in the areas of target grouping, behaviour management and home-school links, developed by 10 Nottingham schools. The methods used were: interview (including focus group interview), classroom observations and document analysis (including test results). A book is planned which will describe the outcomes of the research.

STATUS: Sponsored project

SOURCE OF GRANT: Nottingham Local Education Authority

DATE OF RESEARCH: 1997-1997

KEYWORDS: **achievement; behaviour management; grouping - teaching purposes; home school relationship; primary education; pupil improvement; school improvement; urban schools**

1293

Institute of Education, 20 Bedford Way, London WC1H 0AL
0171 580 1122

Aikman, S. Ms

Contradictions of intercultural education in the Peruvian Amazon

ABSTRACT: The study investigates the nature of interculturality and the conceptual basis and practice of intercultural education in order to elucidate areas of miscommunication between governments and indigenous peoples, and suggest fertile directions of the development of intercultural education. The research is carried out at the Institute of Education and the Peruvian Amazon, with a comparative focus on Peru, Bolivia and Ecuador.

STATUS: Sponsored project

SOURCE OF GRANT: National Academy of Education Spencer Foundation £25,000

DATE OF RESEARCH: 1997-continuing

KEYWORDS: **multicultural education; south america**

1294

Institute of Education, 20 Bedford Way, London WC1H 0AL
0171 580 1122

Hopkins, M., Mr; Riddell, A. Dr; Carr-Hill, R. Prof.

Performance indicators on education

ABSTRACT: The purpose of this research is to evaluate the potential ability of developing a set of performance indicators for aid to education. This involves: 1) detailed examination of the literature on performance indicators; 2) review of how performance indicators and other statistical systems are being used elsewhere; 3) analysis of 3 country case studies (Andhra Pradesh in India, Kenya and South Africa); 4) making recommendations.

STATUS: Sponsored project

SOURCE OF GRANT: Overseas Development Administration

DATE OF RESEARCH: 1997-1997

KEYWORDS: **comparative education; educational quality; performance indicators**

1295

Institute of Education, 20 Bedford Way, London WC1H 0AL
0171 580 1122

Walsh, P. Dr

An analysis of the status and attractiveness of initial vocational education and training

ABSTRACT: This project aims to survey a wide range of interest groups educational and training organisations, employers, trade unions, students, trainees, parents and the general public, to examine ways in which the status and attractiveness of initial vocational education and training can be enhanced.

STATUS: Sponsored project

SOURCE OF GRANT: European Commission (Leonardo Programme) £15,807

DATE OF RESEARCH: 1997-continuing

KEYWORDS: **training; vocational education**

1296

Institute of Education, 20 Bedford Way, London WC1H 0AL
0171 580 1122

Crook, D. Dr; Aldrich, R. Prof.

The Department for Education and Employment: a cultural and historical study

ABSTRACT: The relationship between education and employment is an issue of vital national and international importance. Its centrality was recognised in 1995 by the creation of the Department for Education and Employment (DfEE). Current investigations of the relationship, however, focus upon specific concerns such as curriculum, qualifications and skills, or demonstrate, for example, that the unemployed want jobs rather than training. This research will be located within broader cultural and historical frames of explanation, for the two cultures of education and employment have often been competing and antagonistic. The principle outcome of the research will be a major book, to be published in the centenary year of the foundation of the Board of Education in 1899.

STATUS: Sponsored project

SOURCE OF GRANT: Nuffield Foundation £46,509

DATE OF RESEARCH: 1997-continuing

KEYWORDS: educational history; employment; work education relationship

1297

Institute of Education, 20 Bedford Way, London WC1H 0AL
0171 580 1122

Kent, W. Mr

Eurogame project

ABSTRACT: The aim of the 'Eurogame' project is to create game-oriented, multilingual, multimedia curriculum resources for teaching and learning the geography of Europe. The resources will be designed, implemented and tested by a consortium of academics, school book publishers and multimedia experts in close association with teachers and students in 4 European countries. There are 4 committees with representatives from 5 different European countries which are working together on the project. Dr Ashley Kent is the coordinator for the user group which is responsible for liaising with the teachers and students in the countries.

STATUS: Sponsored project

SOURCE OF GRANT: European Commission £152,958

DATE OF RESEARCH: 1998-continuing

KEYWORDS: computer games; computer uses in education; europe; european dimension; european studies; geography; information technology; multimedia

1298

Institute of Education, 20 Bedford Way, London WC1H 0AL
0171 580 1122

Mortimore, P. Prof.; Hallam, S. Dr

Pilot pupil behaviour and discipline projects 1996-99 funded under the Grants for Education Support and Training (GEST) programme

ABSTRACT: The project aims to examine the effectiveness of the Grants for Education Support and Training (GEST) which were provided under the truancy, disruptive and disaffected pupils programme for a 3-year programme of pilot projects to help raise standards of behaviour and discipline in schools.

STATUS: Sponsored project

SOURCE OF GRANT: Department for Education and Employment £83,664

DATE OF RESEARCH: 1998-continuing

KEYWORDS: behaviour problems; disaffection; disruptive pupils; educational finance; grants; truancy

1299

Institute of Education, 20 Bedford Way, London WC1H 0AL
0171 580 1122

Mortimore, P. Prof.; Hallam, S. Dr; Ireson, J. Dr

Ability grouping in schools: practices and consequences

ABSTRACT: The project will explore the relationships between different kinds of ability grouping in the lower secondary phase of state comprehensive schools and academic, social and personal outcomes for pupils. Information will be gathered about the school ethos, school procedures for placing and moving pupils between groups, resource allocation, teacher attitudes and classroom practices.

STATUS: Sponsored project

SOURCE OF GRANT: Economic and Social Research Council £131,167

DATE OF RESEARCH: 1997-continuing

KEYWORDS: class organisation; grouping - teaching purposes; outcomes of education; secondary education; setting; streaming

1300

Institute of Education, 20 Bedford Way, London WC1H 0AL
0171 580 1122

Kutnick, P. Dr; Blatchford, P. Dr

The nature and use of classroom groups in primary schools

ABSTRACT: Placing pupils into various groups is a common organisational feature of all primary classrooms. However, too little is known about the nature of these groups and what functions they are designed to serve in the classroom in terms of pupils' learning. The two central aims of the proposed study are, firstly, to provide good descriptive data on the nature of groups used in a sample of UK primary classrooms and, secondly, to investigate their intended functions and how they are perceived by teachers and pupils. To explore these aims a two-phase investigation will be conducted: 1) a large scale survey of primary school teachers to ascertain the pedagogical principles on which pupils are grouped and whether these principles are derived from personal experience of the teacher, the school, the local education authority teaching, learning and support policies; and 2) once these principles are established, to explore their usage by teachers and their effects on pupils, in a number of classrooms.

STATUS: Sponsored project

SOURCE OF GRANT: Economic and Social Research Council £28,766

DATE OF RESEARCH: 1997-1998

KEYWORDS: class organisation; grouping - teaching purposes; primary education

1301

Institute of Education, 20 Bedford Way, London WC1H 0AL
0171 580 1122

Mortimore, P. Prof.; Leo, E. Dr

The role of parents in helping schools prepare young people for employment

ABSTRACT: This project will investigate the ways in which parents influence their children's attitudes and aspirations to work, as well as the differential impact of school and home on young people's understanding of employability. The researchers will examine a number of factors such as educational achievement, motivation, attitudes and aspirations, outlook, inter- and intra-personal skills and personal qualities, as well as ability to seek and overcome challenges. The research team will be led by a researcher and will comprise both educationalists and industrialists. The team will interview a wide range of young people, their parents, teachers and, where appropriate, their employers. The findings from the project will inform a future and potentially more extensive research project and will form the basis of a report for publication by Industry in Education

STATUS: Sponsored project

SOURCE OF GRANT: Industry in Education

DATE OF RESEARCH: 1997-1998

KEYWORDS: employment; parent participation; pupil attitudes; school to work transition; work attitudes

1302

Institute of Education, 20 Bedford Way, London WC1H 0AL
0171 580 1122

Warwick, I. Mr

HIV and schooling: an assessment of needs in 5 major states - European forum

ABSTRACT: To assess the needs of children and families affected by human immunodeficiency virus (HIV)/acquired immune deficiency syndrome (AIDS) in relation to current school-based policies, practices and problems in France, Italy, Portugal, Spain and the UK.

STATUS: Sponsored project

SOURCE OF GRANT: European Commission £35,683

DATE OF RESEARCH: 1996-1998

KEYWORDS: acquired immune deficiency syndrome; comparative education; educational policy; europe; pupil needs

1303

Institute of Education, 20 Bedford Way, London WC1H 0AL
0171 580 1122

Redman, P. Mr; Mac an Ghail, M. Prof.; Epstein, D. Dr

Children's 'relationship cultures' in Years 5 and 6

ABSTRACT: This project aims to investigate: 1) how children in schools aged 9-11 talk about emotional caring and family relationships; 2) the ways that children's understandings of such relationships appear in their play and talk with other children; 3) what children think about the portrayal of such relationships in TV and other popular media. The research will be carried out by observing children's behaviours in schools, recording their talk with each other and focus groups and interviews.

STATUS: Sponsored project

SOURCE OF GRANT: Economic and Social Research Council £118,496

DATE OF RESEARCH: 1998-continuing

KEYWORDS: **family relationship; pupil attitudes**

1304

Institute of Education, 20 Bedford Way, London WC1H 0AL
0171 580 1122

Ireson, J. Dr

Innovative grouping practices in secondary schools

ABSTRACT: This study is an indepth qualitative study of pupil grouping in 6 schools where innovative approaches have been adopted. The schools were identified as a result of the ESRC project which is a national project looking at the relative effectiveness of different forms of pupil grouping. The case studies have involved interviews with staff and pupils, analysis of documentation, observation and scrutiny of performance data. The report describes how schools have explored different forms of grouping and attempted to link them to outcome data. The descriptions will provide the basis for practical guidance to schools and local education authorities (LEAs) on pupil grouping to be published in Autumn 1998.

STATUS: Sponsored project

SOURCE OF GRANT: Department for Education and Employment £9,996

DATE OF RESEARCH: 1998-1998

KEYWORDS: **grouping - teaching purposes; mixed ability; pupil placement; school organisation; secondary education; setting**

1305

Institute of Education, 20 Bedford Way, London WC1H 0AL
0171 580 1122

Watkins, C. Mr; Leonard, D. Dr; Epstein, D. Dr

The violence-resilient school: a comparative study of schools and their environments

ABSTRACT: This project will investigate 6 London schools which appear to be more or less successful in managing violence of all kinds given similar levels of neighbourhood violence. The researchers are interested in tracing the difference made by institutional cultures and forms of management to levels of violence in and around the school.

STATUS: Sponsored project

SOURCE OF GRANT: Economic and Social Research Council £99,507

DATE OF RESEARCH: 1998-continuing

KEYWORDS: **antisocial behaviour; behaviour problems; discipline; violence**

1306

Institute of Education, 20 Bedford Way, London WC1H 0AL
0171 580 1122

Buckingham, D. Dr

Media arts in education

ABSTRACT: The research project will investigate ways in which young people's 'informal' competencies as cultural producers can be developed within the more 'formal' context of community arts work and education. It will focus on 2 key aspects of this process: the relationship between individual and group creativity; and the role of the audience for young people's productions. Its central emphasis will be on vocational potential such as work with young people in the 16-19 age group. The project will use case study, participant observation and action research methods.

STATUS: Sponsored project

SOURCE OF GRANT: Arts Council £85,300

DATE OF RESEARCH: 1998-continuing

KEYWORDS: **arts; community arts; media studies; popular culture; sixteen to nineteen education**

1307

Institute of Education, 20 Bedford Way, London WC1H 0AL
0171 580 1122

Williams, C. Dr

Disseminating environmental research to young people

ABSTRACT: UNESCO has expressed a concern that environmental education is often based on information that is out of date. The project will address this problem by developing methods for disseminating recent environmental research from the Economic and Social Research Council (ESRC) Global Environment Change Programme, direct to young people through a range of media.

STATUS: Sponsored project

SOURCE OF GRANT: Economic and Social Research Council £4,081

DATE OF RESEARCH: 1998-continuing

KEYWORDS: **environmental education; environmental research**

1308

Institute of Education, 20 Bedford Way, London WC1H 0AL
0171 580 1122

Little, A. Prof.

Globalisation, livelihoods and education

ABSTRACT: The research will generate a state-of-the-art review of the reciprocal effects of globalisation and education, with special reference to the role of educational qualifications in mediating the transition from education to livelihoods among the poorest groups in 'developing' countries society. The research will lead to the preparation of further research proposals for funding.

STATUS: Sponsored project

SOURCE OF GRANT: Department for International Development £19,664

DATE OF RESEARCH: 1998-continuing

KEYWORDS: **developing countries; development education; globalization**

1309

Institute of Education, 20 Bedford Way, London WC1H 0AL
0171 580 1122

Watson, D. Mr; Aldrich, R. Prof.; Williams, A. Dr

An historical study of London's education welfare services

ABSTRACT: The planned research will trace and analyse the evolution of education welfare services in London over the major part of the 20th century. These services emerged in the late 19th century to enforce regular attendance at school and were then broadened to include social work functions. Through its central focus on the services that were developed in London by the London County Council (LCC) and the Inner London Education Authority (ILEA), the research will produce a discrete case study that is of historical importance. Almost no research into the history of education welfare services has so far been undertaken and the planned study will produce a new body of information. It will also provide an historical perspective on current policy debates concerning truancy and non-attendance. In addition, the research will lay the basis for a larger, indepth study that will investigate the historical development of education welfare policy and practice in the UK as a whole. The methodology used will involve the detailed analysis of untapped archive material and other primary sources, as well as the collection of oral testimony from practitioners and children who were involved with the services at different times.

STATUS: Sponsored project

SOURCE OF GRANT: Economic and Social Research Council £42,626

DATE OF RESEARCH: 1999-continuing

KEYWORDS: **educational history; educational welfare**

1310

Institute of Education, 20 Bedford Way, London WC1H 0AL
0171 580 1122

Whitty, G. Prof.

History of HMI

ABSTRACT: A working group of former Her Majesty's Inspectors (HMI) with the general support of the Association of Her Majesty's Inspectors, intends to commission the publication of the post-war history of the Inspectorate of England and Wales. The book will incorporate two interwoven narratives: HMI's role and functions, relating to all parts of the education system, in responding to ministers and officials and in encouraging development; and, as the context of HMI's work, and account of that system in transformation.

STATUS: Sponsored project

SOURCE OF GRANT: Nuffield Foundation £60,470

DATE OF RESEARCH: 1998-continuing

KEYWORDS: **educational history; inspection; inspectors - of schools**

1311

Institute of Education, 20 Bedford Way, London WC1H 0AL
0171 580 1122

Guile, D. Mr; Griffiths, T. Ms

Work experience as an education and training strategy: new approaches for the 21st century

ABSTRACT: The project will analyse work experience as an education and training strategy, focusing on the 16-19 age group with the aim of developing transferable, innovative models relevant to changes in nature of work and to future learning. These will be case studies within and between European partners. The first stage focuses on literature reviews and policy studies. Partners are Kristianstad University (Sweden), Dublin City University, University of Valencia, Copenhagen Business School and National Institute of Vocational Education (Hungary).

STATUS: Sponsored project

SOURCE OF GRANT: European Commission £145,064

DATE OF RESEARCH: 1998-continuing

KEYWORDS: **comparative education; school to work transition; sixteen to nineteen education; training; vocational education**

1312

Institute of Education, 20 Bedford Way, London WC1H 0AL
0171 580 1122

Kress, G. Prof.

Rhetorics of the science classroom: a multi-modal approach

ABSTRACT: The aim of the project, starting from the language of description of explanations in the science classroom developed in the applicant's previous work, is to re-think the teaching and learning of science as part of a dynamic process in which teachers shape ideas to be learned through a plurality of devices and strategies, to make them suitable for and 'convincing' to pupils, describing these both from the perspective of the teacher and from the pupil. Through detailed analysis of classroom recordings, pupils responses and texts, the project will offer a carefully thought out and well-founded way of talking and thinking about communicating science. The project will produce arguments and evidence that the previous heavy reliance of communication studies on language as the 'primary' means of communication is simply not good enough. The project looks at communication as orchestrating a variety of modes, of which language is just one. The researcher will produce a theoretical framework, rooted in social semiotics, to move towards a new understanding of teaching as an act of communication; a framework exemplified richly from actual classroom practice.

STATUS: Sponsored project

SOURCE OF GRANT: Economic and Social Research Council £148,858

DATE OF RESEARCH: 1997-continuing

KEYWORDS: **classroom communication; rhetoric; science education**

1313

Institute of Education, 20 Bedford Way, London WC1H 0AL
0171 580 1122

Thomas, S. Dr

Innovative approaches in school evaluation

ABSTRACT: The primary objective of the project is to develop a framework that can be used in all the countries of the European Union as a common reference point, a way of understanding school evaluation, and a tool that can be used for gathering, analysing and interpreting information. The second objective is to examine different evaluation procedures, in the form of national case studies. The third objective is to provide some contextual interpretation with the national case studies and to use these for an international comparison. Finally the fourth objective is to disseminate the results of the project in a report to be used as a handbook on school evaluation for policymakers and school leaders.

STATUS: Sponsored project

SOURCE OF GRANT: European Union Socrates £43,500

DATE OF RESEARCH: 1997-1998

KEYWORDS: **comparative education; educational quality; europe; institutional evaluation; school effectiveness**

1314

Institute of Education, 20 Bedford Way, London WC1H 0AL
0171 580 1122

Clarke, S. Ms; Gipps, C. Prof.

Evaluation of statutory assessment key stage 1

ABSTRACT: This study is an evaluation of the 1998 national assessment programme at key stage 1. The evaluation involved questionnaires to 400 schools in England for both headteachers and Year 2 teachers, and case studies of teachers in a sample of 20 schools. The data presents information about: specific issues relating to the actual tasks and tests; the administration of the tasks and tests; general issues around testing of 7 year-olds and teacher assessment (TA) at this age; and proposals for the future of key stage 1 assessment.

STATUS: Sponsored project

SOURCE OF GRANT: Qualifications and Curriculum Authority £32,150

DATE OF RESEARCH: 1998-1998

KEYWORDS: **assessment; key stage 1; primary education; tasks and tests**

1315

Institute of Education, 20 Bedford Way, London WC1H 0AL
0171 580 1122

Griffiths, T. Ms

Education business partnership in Europe

ABSTRACT: The project aims to conduct a study of European education business partnership and its relation to social cohesion and to involve businesses working with schools, focusing on students up to the age of 16 but including older students, in European Union (EU) member states. The study will assist companies in developing realistic and innovative partnership strategies which help address the social and economic challenges of the 21st century.

STATUS: Sponsored project

SOURCE OF GRANT: European Business Network for Social Cohesion £26,875

DATE OF RESEARCH: 1998-1998

KEYWORDS: **education business partnerships; europe; industry education relationship**

1316

Institute of Education, 20 Bedford Way, London WC1H 0AL
0171 580 1122

Leney, T. Mr; Green, A. Dr

TACIS - Russia

ABSTRACT: This is a joint project with the University of Paris regarding reform of the educational system of the Russian Federation. It will look at: 1) the division of competences between federal, regional and local levels of the management of education; 2) the financial structures of the educational system and their relationships with decision-making at all levels (problems of elasticity of resources, efficiency and equity); 3) the adaptation of the supply of educational services to the present and foreseeable demands of the economy; 4) the elaboration of alternative long and short-term scenarios for the future of educational policy according to economic and social perspectives.

STATUS: Sponsored project

SOURCE OF GRANT: University of Paris £21,673

DATE OF RESEARCH: 1998-continuing

KEYWORDS: educational change; russia

1317

Institute of Education, 20 Bedford Way, London WC1H 0AL
0171 580 1122

Turner, S. Dr

Mapping access to health food in deprived areas: a pilot study in Brent

ABSTRACT: The project will develop indices of access to healthy food in a deprived area of inner London using systematic and qualitative survey instruments with Geographic Information Systems (GIS) software. The project will use participatory techniques to involve the local community, including schools, in data collection and analysis. The project will support curriculum and policy development in nutrition education in primary schools: information technology and other resources will be trialled and evaluated.

STATUS: Sponsored project

SOURCE OF GRANT: North Thames NHS Executive £39,217

DATE OF RESEARCH: 1997-continuing

KEYWORDS: food; nutrition; primary education

1318

Institute of Education, 20 Bedford Way, London WC1H 0AL
0171 580 1122

Mayall, B. Dr

Negotiating childhoods

ABSTRACT: A small-scale qualitative study of the daily lives of children (aged 9-13) living in a range of family types, with a focus on the division of labour for organising their days, and their dependence and independence.

STATUS: Sponsored project

SOURCE OF GRANT: Economic and Social Research Council £70,293

DATE OF RESEARCH: 1997-continuing

KEYWORDS: childhood; children; family life

1319

Institute of Education, 20 Bedford Way, London WC1H 0AL
0171 580 1122

Mortimore, P. Prof.; Ireson, J. Dr; Hallam, S. Dr

Ability grouping practices in the primary school

ABSTRACT: This project aims to establish: 1) the degree of ability grouping currently being utilised in schools for children aged 7-11; 2) whether there are any differences in the level of ability grouping used for different subject areas, with particular reference to mathematics, English and science; 3) whether ability grouping practices have changed since the introduction of: a) the National Curriculum; b) testing at key stage 1 and 2; c) the publication of test results at key stage 2. It is proposed to obtain information, when ability groupings are structured between rather than within classes, about school policy and practice in relation to resource allocation (staff, equipment and materials), teaching practices (pace, curriculum, teaching strategies, pupil activities) allocation to and movement of pupils between groups and the perceived advantages and disadvantages of different kinds of ability grouping.

STATUS: Sponsored project

SOURCE OF GRANT: Economic and Social Research Council £32,188

DATE OF RESEARCH: 1998-continuing

KEYWORDS: grouping - teaching purposes; key stage 1; key stage 2; primary education

1320

Institute of Education, 20 Bedford Way, London WC1H 0AL
0171 580 1122

Alderson, P. Dr

Cleeves school book

ABSTRACT: The aim is to write a book with a primary school on their unusual learning and inclusive methods. The book will be written by the pupils and staff, and published by David Fulton publishers for pupils and staff to use together in other schools.

STATUS: Sponsored project

SOURCE OF GRANT: Gatsby Charitable Foundation £9,140

DATE OF RESEARCH: 1998-1998

KEYWORDS: childrens rights; learning strategies; mainstreaming; primary education; teaching methods

1321

Institute of Education, 20 Bedford Way, London WC1H 0AL
0171 580 1122

Evans, J. Ms; Earley, P. Dr

Improving the effectiveness of school governing bodies

ABSTRACT: The project will document examples of effective governing bodies and collect data, via 2 linked questionnaire surveys, on governing body composition and factors affecting effectiveness. A central focus will be on how governing body effectiveness can be improved.

STATUS: Sponsored project

SOURCE OF GRANT: Department for Education and Employment £85,007

DATE OF RESEARCH: 1997-1998

KEYWORDS: educational administration; governing bodies; school governing bodies; school governors

1322

Institute of Education, 20 Bedford Way, London WC1H 0AL
0171 580 1122

Pan, H. Dr

Young people in transition

ABSTRACT: The research is being carried out jointly with the Institute of Employment Research at the University of Warwick. It involves secondary analysis of a number of longitudinal datasets in a study of transition to adulthood in a number of life domains. The part of the work carried out by the Institute of Education will involve use of the National Child Development Study (NCDS) and the 1970 British Cohort Study (BCS 70).

STATUS: Sponsored project

SOURCE OF GRANT: Joseph Rowntree Foundation £17,833

DATE OF RESEARCH: 1998-continuing

KEYWORDS: adolescents; cohort analysis; longitudinal studies; school to work transition; sixteen to nineteen education; training; youth

1323

Institute of Education, 20 Bedford Way, London WC1H 0AL
0171 580 1122

MacDonald, J. Ms; Ryszkowski, Y. Ms; Thomas, C. Ms

Work experience: learning framework - impact research

ABSTRACT: Focus Central London is registered for the distribution and dissemination of the 'Learning Frameworks' a series of tools devised by the University of Warwick to enable students undertaking pre- and post-16 work experience to develop individual learning objectives for their placements. The aims of the research are to: 1) examine the ways in which schools are using the frameworks in the classroom and at the workplace; 2) assess the impact of using the framework on pupils' learning from work experience with particular reference to their key skills, other work-related skills and employability; 3) explore the views of employers on the Framework and its impact on the structuring and processes of planning and reviewing placements.

STATUS: Sponsored project

SOURCE OF GRANT: FOCUS Central London TEC £10,000

DATE OF RESEARCH: 1998-1998

KEYWORDS: core skills; key skills; learning strategies; secondary education; work experience

1324

Institute of Education, 20 Bedford Way, London WC1H 0AL
0171 580 1122

Hayton, A. Ms; Corbett, J. Dr

Study visit to investigate the transition of young people with learning difficulties to paid employment

ABSTRACT: The project explores training programmes and practice in preparing young people with learning disabilities for employment in Cyprus and in Paris.

STATUS: Sponsored project

SOURCE OF GRANT: European Commission £1,622

DATE OF RESEARCH: 1998-continuing

KEYWORDS: cyprus; france; learning disabilities; special educational needs; training

1325

Institute of Education, 20 Bedford Way, London WC1H 0AL
0171 580 1122

Young, M. Dr

SPES-NET - sharpening the post-16 educational strategies by horizontal and vertical networking

ABSTRACT: This is a multiplier project to follow up the Leonardo da Vinci Post-16 strategies project funded by the European Union. It extends the comparisons from the original 8 countries to a further 6.

STATUS: Sponsored project

SOURCE OF GRANT: European Commission (Leonardo Programme) £7,415

DATE OF RESEARCH: 1998-continuing

KEYWORDS: comparative education; europe; sixteen to nineteen education; vocational education

1326

Institute of Education, 20 Bedford Way, London WC1H 0AL
0171 580 1122

Griffiths, T. Ms; Guile, D. Mr; Young, M. Dr

Distributed learning community (Future Learning Centre Demonstration Project 2)

ABSTRACT: A pilot project to explore the potential of developing a distributed learning community among further education (FE) college staff responsible for information technology (IT) promotion.

STATUS: Sponsored project

SOURCE OF GRANT: Arthur Andersen £30,000

DATE OF RESEARCH: 1998-continuing

KEYWORDS: computer uses in education; further education; information technology

1327

Institute of Education, 20 Bedford Way, London WC1H 0AL
0171 580 1122

MacDonald, G. Dr; Fowler, C. Dr; Griffiths, T. Ms

Schools' Internet project (Future Learning Centre Demonstration Project 2)

ABSTRACT: The Institute of Education will work with an intranet of schools from 3 London boroughs which have been technically equipped by Focus

Central London TEC. The Institute will assess needs, provide relevant training, develop a website and on-line education discussion and evaluate the results.

STATUS: Sponsored project

SOURCE OF GRANT: Arthur Andersen £30,000

DATE OF RESEARCH: 1998-continuing

KEYWORDS: computer networks; computer uses in education; information technology; internet

1328

Institute of Education, 20 Bedford Way, London WC1H 0AL
0171 580 1122

Petrie, P. Dr

Raising the quality of learning beyond the classroom technology assessment

ABSTRACT: A study of homework. Six European case studies of local authority and school practice and how these affect parents and children.

STATUS: Sponsored project

SOURCE OF GRANT: European Commission £17,411

DATE OF RESEARCH: 1998-continuing

KEYWORDS: homework; school effectiveness

1329

Institute of Education, 20 Bedford Way, London WC1H 0AL
0171 580 1122
Bath University, School of Education, Claverton Down, Bath BA2 7AY
01225 826826

Wikeley, F. Ms; Bullock, K. Ms

Personal learning planning for Cambridgeshire careers guidance

ABSTRACT: The project is a longitudinal evaluation of a process and personal learning planning by which it is hoped to raise pupil attainment. It involves the administration of an attitudinal questionnaire to Years 9 and 10 pupils in 30 schools involved in the process and 5 schools not participating. It also involves interviews with school coordinators and careers guidance staff.

STATUS: Sponsored project

SOURCE OF GRANT: Department for Education and Employment £3,763

DATE OF RESEARCH: 1998-1998

KEYWORDS: career awareness; pupil attitudes; secondary education; vocational guidance

1330

Institute of Education, 20 Bedford Way, London WC1H 0AL
0171 580 1122
Bristol University, Graduate School of Education, 35 Berkeley Square, Bristol BS8 1JA
01179 289000

Hunt, A. Mr; Wake, G. Mr; Wolf, A. Prof.; Sutherland, R. Prof.

Mathematics for all post-16

ABSTRACT: The overall project is evaluating the appropriateness of new free-standing mathematics units being made available for post-compulsory students; developing information technology-based teaching/support materials for some units; and examining classroom process. The Institute component focuses on the first of these.

STATUS: Sponsored project

SOURCE OF GRANT: Nuffield Foundation £18,110

DATE OF RESEARCH: 1998-continuing

KEYWORDS: mathematics education; sixteen to nineteen education

1331

Institute of Education, 20 Bedford Way, London WC1H 0AL
0171 580 1122
Cardiff University, School of Education, Senghennydd Road, Cardiff CF2 4YG
01222 874000

Pellegrini, A. Prof.; Blatchford, P. Dr

Playground games: their social context in junior school

ABSTRACT: This project builds on previous work on school recess/breaktime behaviour and management, which has shown the importance of recess as a context for social relations between children. A focused study of the social contexts of playground games will contribute to a better understanding of peer relations, and in particular friendships and popularity: better understanding of processes involved in school adjustment and difficulties faced by some children; and will contribute to school policies on behaviour and recess/breaktime in schools. The study has 3 objectives: 1) to investigate the development of and interconnections between games, friendships and social networks after entry to elementary (US - 6 years)/ junior school (England - 7 years); 2) to investigate differences between children and factors explaining involvement in playground games; and 3) to investigate differences between the UK and US in these areas.

STATUS: Sponsored project

SOURCE OF GRANT: Spencer Foundation £57,646

DATE OF RESEARCH: 1998-continuing

KEYWORDS: **childrens games; comparative education; friendship; peer relationship; play; playground activities; primary education; united states of america**

1332

Institute of Education, Centre for Longitudinal Studies, 20 Bedford Way, London WC1H 0AL
0171 612 6900

Parsons, S. Ms; *Supervisor*: Bynner, J. Prof.

Further analysis of Social Statistics Research Unit Birth Cohort Studies Basic Skills data

ABSTRACT: Within the time frame of the previous contract, two additional pieces of work are being undertaken: 1) the re-analysis of the Welsh data involving reconciliation of the methods for measuring basic skills performance with that in the birth cohort studies; 2) the analysis of the data collected from further education colleges relating to the effects on participation and the progress of basic skills remedial training. These displace two of the projects from the present programme: A) the antecedents of basic skills difficulties up to age 37 (National Child Development Study (NCDS) data); B) inter-generational transmission of basic skills difficulties (NCDS data). On the assumption that work on revisions to the present report, Adult Life and Basic Skills, due to be published in May, can be completed in the timescale for the present project, the two projects (A and B) will be undertaken within the first six months of the new contract, i.e. from April to September 1997. This work will then be followed by two new projects (C and D) to be undertaken over the period October 1997 to March 1998. The first new project (C), Basic Skills Deterioration, will be an investigation of the factors in employment and personal life associated with basic skills deterioration from 16-37. It will involve comparison of those cohort members whose basic skills had deteriorated, with those whose skills had improved or remained the same, drawing on the full longitudinal data set back to birth to take account of prior abilities and circumstances. The proposed timescale for this project is three months. The final project (D), Social Exclusion and Basic Skills, will be an examination of the role of basic skills difficulties in social exclusion. This will extend the initial work on this topic based on NCDS data (as reported in Adult Life and Basic Skills) to cover both cohort studies, with the aim of uncovering 'cohort differences' brought about by societal changes. The process of marginalisation of the cohort members with basic skills difficulties will be traced back to age 16 where data on public examinations will be used to pinpoint individuals with basic skills problems. The post-16 educational and employment record of these individuals in the two cohorts will be compared, taking account of basic skills changes as identified at 21 (Birth Cohort Study 70) and 37 (NCDS). The analysis will also extend to outcomes in personal and family life and public and social participation. For this latter purpose the researchers will be able draw on some of the data collected in the new Birth Cohort Study 70 postal survey carried out at age 26, which will be available for secondary analysis by then. The proposed timescale for this project is 3 months.

STATUS: Sponsored project

SOURCE OF GRANT: Basic Skills Agency £58,745

DATE OF RESEARCH: 1997-1998

KEYWORDS: **adult literacy; basic skills; cohort analysis; numeracy**

1333

Institute of Education, Centre for Longitudinal Studies, 20 Bedford Way, London WC1H 0AL
0171 612 6900

Shepherd, P. Mr; Parsons, S. Ms; Steedman, J. Ms; *Supervisor*: Bynner, J. Prof.

Further analysis and data collection on basic skills in the 1958 and 1970 British Cohort Studies (NCDS and BCS70)

ABSTRACT: Since 1991, the Social Statistics Research Unit has been engaged in a programme of research for the Basic Skills Agency. A sub-sample survey of the British Cohort Studies (BCS70) cohort in 1991 at age 21 involved an interview with cohort members, followed by an assessment of their basic literacy and numeracy skills through specially devised tests. The main thrust of the analysis of this cross-sectional data was concerned with the relationship between basic skills difficulties and transition to employment, and other matters relating to employment and family formation. Another project undertaken in the Social Statistics Research Unit utilised the full longitudinal record back to birth of cohort members, to try to unravel the sequence of conditions and experiences at home and at school, which led to the development of basic skills difficulties. The testing of cohort members' basic literacy and numeracy skills has been repeated in a similar sub-sample survey of 10% of National Child Development Study (NCDS) members at age 37, with new tests specially designed by the National Foundation for Educational Research. The NCDS sample was matched, in terms of the broad characteristics covered, with the sample used in the BCS70 survey. The first analysis project utilising the new data is described below. Approximately 12% of adults in the UK report have a basic skill problem. This figure was initially established from analysis of data from the fourth sweep of the NCDS undertaken in 1981 when cohort members were 23 years of age. The data identified by self-report a group of adults who felt the negative effects of poor literacy and numeracy skills in their everyday lives. Part of the current project builds on this earlier information and uses data collected for the fifth sweep of NCDS in 1991, when cohort members were 33. Adults who reported basic skills difficulties were found to under-achieve as a group, to have disproportionate numbers out of the paid workforce, to have low status occupations, and to lack many work-related skills. Essentially, a basic skill problem created a somewhat marginalised existence, restricting access to, and attainment of, many aims and activities. This was particularly likely to be the case when a basic skill difficulty was reported at both 23 and 33, rather than at one age only. Given the restrictions of self-reported measures of basic skills difficulties, the representative 10% sub-sample of NCDS cohort members provided much needed objective data on literacy and numeracy at age 37 (n=1714). 6% of the sample had very poor literacy and 23% had very poor numeracy. Most cohort members who performed poorly in the literacy tests also performed poorly in the numeracy tests. A comprehensive profile of cohort members with poor basic skill abilities is currently underway, with later work providing further insights into the antecedents of literacy and numeracy difficulties in adulthood.

PUBLISHED MATERIAL: EKINSMYTH, C. & BYNNER, J. (1994). The basic skills of young adults. London: Basic Skills Agency. ; BYNNER, J. & STEEDMAN, J. (1995). Difficulties with basic skills. London: Basic Skills Agency. ; BYNNER, J. & PARSONS, S. (1997). Does numeracy matter? London: Basic Skills Agency.

STATUS: Sponsored project

SOURCE OF GRANT: Basic Skills Agency £334,225

DATE OF RESEARCH: 1994-1997

KEYWORDS: **adult literacy; basic skills; cohort analysis; numeracy**

1334

Institute of Education, Centre for Longitudinal Studies, 20 Bedford Way, London WC1H 0AL
0171 612 6900

Bynner, J. Prof.

British born cohort studies: change and development in the British population

ABSTRACT: The Economic and Social Research Council (ESRC) has provided funding for the team working on the design of the planned 1999 surveys in the two national longitudinal birth cohort studies for which CLS is responsible the National Child Development Study (NCDS) and the 1970 British Cohort Study (BCS 70). The work entails extensive consultation with past and future users of the data set, and a major tracing operation (involving 7 temporary staff currently) to identify the present whereabouts of cohort members. The cohort members will be aged 29 in the case of BCS 70 and 41 in the case of NCDS. The research on them is interdisciplinary ranging from medicine through social science to education. Funding is being actively sought to support studies of the children of the cohort members to include medical measurements in the survey interview.

STATUS: Sponsored project

SOURCE OF GRANT: Economic and Social Research Council

DATE OF RESEARCH: 1998-continuing

KEYWORDS: **adults; cohort analysis; longitudinal studies**

1335

Institute of Education, Centre for Longitudinal Studies, 20 Bedford Way, London WC1H 0AL
0171 612 6900

Bynner, J. Prof.

Childhood educational problems

ABSTRACT: The main purpose of the project is to develop a coding frame for the analysis of writing samples collected in the birth cohort studies as part of the Basic Skills Agency funded work. Earlier coding frames have been developed in connection with the studies of children's writing and most recently in the 21-year survey of the BCS 70. This study will focus on the 37-year survey in the NCDS. A preliminary analysis will be undertaken with a view to developing a proposal for a comprehensive research project to go with the Basic Skills Agency in March 1999.

STATUS: Sponsored project

SOURCE OF GRANT: International Centre for Childhood Studies £10,500

DATE OF RESEARCH: 1998-continuing

KEYWORDS: **cohort analysis; writing skills**

1336

Institute of Education, Centre for Longitudinal Studies, 20 Bedford Way, London WC1H 0AL
0171 612 6900

Bynner, J. Prof.

Basic Skills Agency

ABSTRACT: The project is the latest stage of a programme of research conducted first for the Adult Literacy and Basic Skills Unit and currently for the Basic Skills Agency. Work involves secondary analysis of information about basic skills collected in specially commissioned surveys at age 21 in the 1970 British Cohort Study (BCS 70) and at age 37 in the National Child Development Study (NCDS). The current work funded under the grant includes an analysis of the relationship between basic skills difficulty and social exclusion, the effects of unemployment on literacy and numeracy.

STATUS: Sponsored project

SOURCE OF GRANT: Basic Skills Agency

DATE OF RESEARCH: 1998-continuing

KEYWORDS: **adult literacy; basic skills; cohort analysis; numeracy; social exclusion; unemployment**

1337

Institute of Education, Centre for Multicultural Education, 20 Bedford Way, London WC1H 0AL
0171 580 1122

Gundara, J. Dr

Diversity of expectations and influences on educational achievement of young gypsies/travellers aged 14-18

ABSTRACT: To examine the nature of such expectations and influences via exchanges with young people themselves, their parents, teachers and other practitioners concerned.

STATUS: Sponsored project

SOURCE OF GRANT: Centre de Recherches Tsiganes £2,783

DATE OF RESEARCH: 1993-1993

KEYWORDS: **cultural influences; gypsies; minority group children; performance factors; travellers - itinerants**

1338

Institute of Education, Centre for Multicultural Education, 20 Bedford Way, London WC1H 0AL
0171 580 1122

Gundara, J. Dr; Bourne, R. Mr

Commonwealth values in education

ABSTRACT: A three-year research and development project in human rights education at the secondary level, working with experimental schools in Botswana, India, Zimbabwe and Northern Ireland. The project is designed to provide teaching strategies and materials which can be used in more than one Commonwealth country.

STATUS: Sponsored project

SOURCE OF GRANT: Overseas Development Administration £75,000

DATE OF RESEARCH: 1995-1998

KEYWORDS: **botswana; civil rights; human rights; india; moral education; northern ireland; values education; zimbabwe**

1339

Institute of Education, 20 Bedford Way, London WC1H 0AL
0171 477 8000
City University, Department of Sociology, Northampton Square, London EC1V 0HB

Joshi, H. Prof.; Clarke, L. Dr; Wiggins, R. Dr

The changing home: outcomes for children

ABSTRACT: The project, in the Children 5-16 Programme, asks how children fare in the face of family disruption. Outcomes in cognitive development and behavioural adjustment are related to change in the home: departure (and arrival) of parents and residential mobility. The children and members of the 1958 cohort study, National Child Development Study, provide evidence for multivariate multilevel modelling. The Office for National Statistics Longitudinal Study provides a statistical backdrop on the child population. The NCD55 dataset is enhanced by our coding of migration. International comparisons are drawn with research in Scandinavia and USA.

STATUS: Sponsored project

SOURCE OF GRANT: Economic and Social Research Council

DATE OF RESEARCH: 1998-continuing

KEYWORDS: **child development; child welfare; childhood; family environment; family life; family structure; stepfamily**

1340

Institute of Education, Department of Child Development and Learning, 20 Bedford Way, London WC1H 0AL
0171 580 1122

Nunes, T. Dr

Children's understanding of the concept of area

ABSTRACT: An analysis of the effects of different tools for measuring on children's understanding of area.

PUBLISHED MATERIAL: NUNES, T., LIGHT, P., MASON, J. & ALLERTON, M. (1994). 'The role of symbols in structuring reasoning: studies about the concept of area'. Annual Meeting of the International Group for the Study of the Psychology of Mathematics Education, Lisbon, 1994.

STATUS: Sponsored project

SOURCE OF GRANT: Economic and Social Research Council £24,530

DATE OF RESEARCH: 1992-1993

KEYWORDS: **area; concept formation; mathematics education; measurement equipment**

1341

Institute of Education, Department of Child Development and Learning, 20 Bedford Way, London WC1H 0AL
0171 580 1122

Nunes, T. Dr

The role of feedback and collaboration in learning

ABSTRACT: A comparison between 9/10 year olds solving mathematics problems individually and in pairs.

STATUS: Sponsored project

SOURCE OF GRANT: Nuffield Foundation £3,000

DATE OF RESEARCH: 1993-1993

KEYWORDS: **feedback; group work; mathematics education; problem solving**

1342

Institute of Education, Department of Curriculum Studies, 20 Bedford Way, London WC1H 0AL
0171 580 1122

Hull, B. Mrs; *Supervisor*: Gipps, C. Prof.

The effects of the National Curriculum on infant teachers and their practice

ABSTRACT: The research aims to investigate the extent to which infant teachers respond to change, in particular the requirements of the National Curriculum. Case studies involving six teachers in two schools were carried out, employing techniques of participant observation and interviewing over a two year period. The results have been written up for submission as a Ph.D thesis which examines the image of teachers of young children through history and literature. This theme is developed into an examination of the growth of professionalism with regard to infant teachers, and with particular reference to gender inequalities in education, posing the hypothesis that infant teaching has suffered from low status because of its relationship to the education of girls and the social position of women in society.

PUBLISHED MATERIAL: HULL, B. (1990). 'The National Curriculum: its effects on infant teachers and their practice', Early Years, Vol 2, No 1, pp.39-44.

STATUS: Individual Research

DATE OF RESEARCH: 1989-1993

KEYWORDS: **infant education; infant school teachers; national curriculum; professional recognition; teaching profession**

1343

Institute of Education, Department of Curriculum Studies, 20 Bedford Way, London WC1H 0AL
0171 580 1122

Gipps, C. Prof.

Towards a theory of educational assessment

ABSTRACT: This is an attempt to draw together developments and writing in educational assessment to re-work the theoretical and conceptual underpinnings.

STATUS: Sponsored project

SOURCE OF GRANT: Nuffield Foundation £21,441

DATE OF RESEARCH: 1992-1993

KEYWORDS: **assessment**

1344

Institute of Education, Department of Curriculum Studies, 20 Bedford Way, London WC1H 0AL
0171 580 1122

Thomas, S. Dr; Mortimore, P. Prof.

National Curriculum key stage 1 analysis

ABSTRACT: The major aim of the project is to analyse the National Curriculum assessment results at key stage 1 of all schools in the Lancashire Local Education Authority, against a variety of background variables, to identify schools doing particularly well or badly.

STATUS: Sponsored project

SOURCE OF GRANT: Lancashire County Council £32,340

DATE OF RESEARCH: 1992-1993

KEYWORDS: **assessment; educational quality; national curriculum; school effectiveness**

1345

Institute of Education, Department of Curriculum Studies, 20 Bedford Way, London WC1H 0AL
0171 580 1122
Greenwich University, School of Education, Avery Hill Campus, Mansion Site, Bexley Road, Eltham, London SE9 2PQ
0181 331 8000

Harland, L. Ms; *Supervisor*: Gipps, C. Prof.

Supporting teachers, supporting children with special educational needs: an exploration of the partnership between class teachers and support teachers

ABSTRACT: The role of the support teacher is changing extensively. It is assumed that the move from withdrawing children with special educational needs from the classroom, towards working within the classroom, with the accompanying need to advise/consult the class teacher, has resulted in a qualitative improvement of educational provisions for these children. Questions are proposed which will explore the nature of the partnership between support teacher and class teachers. It is intended to uncover some of the tensions which accompany the work of the support teacher. So far there has been little evaluation of any possible improvement in educational provision for children with special educational needs which may have been accounted for by support teacher/class teacher collaboration.

STATUS: Individual research

DATE OF RESEARCH: 1986-1993

KEYWORDS: **partnerships; special educational needs; support teachers; teachers**

1346

Institute of Education, Department of Economics, Geography and Business Education, 20 Bedford Way, London WC1H 0AL
0171 580 1122

Thomas, L. Dr

Tower Hamlets College

ABSTRACT: This project will use Tower Hamlets College as a case study for an investigation of the implications of industry and work related activities for staff development and training needs.

PUBLISHED MATERIAL: CLARKE, P. (1993). The implications of work experience programmes for staff development and training. A case study: Tower Hamlets College. London: Institute of Education, The Economic Awareness Teacher Training Programme.

STATUS: Sponsored project

SOURCE OF GRANT: London East Training and Enterprise Council £2,500

DATE OF RESEARCH: 1992-1993

KEYWORDS: **colleges of further education; industry further education relationship; staff development; work experience programmes**

1347

Institute of Education, Department of Economics, Geography and Business Education, 20 Bedford Way, London WC1H 0AL
0171 580 1122

Thomas, L. Dr

The contribution of staff in industry and education to the success of work related activities

ABSTRACT: The overall aim of the study was to conduct a case study of Tower Hamlets College to investigate the implications of industry and work related activities for staff development and training needs.

STATUS: Sponsored project

SOURCE OF GRANT: London East Training and Enterprise Council; Unilever; Grand Metropolitan, jointly £2,500

DATE OF RESEARCH: 1992-1993

KEYWORDS: **industry education relationship; teacher development; work experience programmes**

1348

Institute of Education, Department of Educational Psychology and Special Educational Needs, 20 Bedford Way, London WC1H 0AL
0171 580 1122

Henderson, S. Dr; Dubowitz, L. Dr

Motor and perceptual competence in prematurely born children

ABSTRACT: The focus of this study, which is being carried out jointly with the Royal Postgraduate Medical School, is on children who were born prematurely, both with and without brain damage. The study has two distinct objectives; the first is to investigate the progress of these children in school. The second is to investigate the specific perceptual and motor difficulties which many of the children experience.

STATUS: Sponsored project

SOURCE OF GRANT: Medical Research Council £87,326; Nuffield Foundation £5,000

DATE OF RESEARCH: 1989-1993

KEYWORDS: **child development; motor development; neurological impairments; perceptual handicaps; premature infants; special educational needs**

1349

Institute of Education, Department of Educational Psychology and Special Educational Needs, 20 Bedford Way, London WC1H 0AL
0171 580 1122

Wedell, K. Prof.; Norwich, B. Prof.; Lunt, I. Ms; Evans, J. Ms

Clusters project

ABSTRACT: The project will describe the functioning of the cluster from an organisational point of view and look at the impact of the cluster organisation on special educational needs provision. Clusters of schools will be visited in four LEAs (local education authorities) and interviews of headteachers, teachers, educational psychologists (EPs) and other LEA personnel will be carried out.

STATUS: Sponsored project

SOURCE OF GRANT: Economic and Social Research Council £46,760

DATE OF RESEARCH: 1991-1993

KEYWORDS: **cluster grouping; educational cooperation; special educational needs; special schools**

1350

Institute of Education, Department of Educational Psychology and Special Educational Needs, 20 Bedford Way, London WC1H 0AL
0171 580 1122

Henderson, S. Dr

A new look at perceptuo-motor disorders in cerebral palsied children

ABSTRACT: The focus of the project is on children who find it difficult to negotiate their way around in the environment i.e. children who cannot judge the size of doorways, who cannot perceive distances accurately etc. Such children are handicapped in a school setting because they need so much help from others with their wheelchairs, in PE lessons, on the way to school etc. The aim of the study will be to try to establish what causes these problems lack of motor experience, visual disorders such as squints which lead to absence of stereopsis and types of brain disorder will be investigated.

STATUS: Sponsored project

SOURCE OF GRANT: Spastics Society £29,683

DATE OF RESEARCH: 1991-1993

KEYWORDS: **cerebral palsy; disabilities; motor reactions; perceptual handicaps; perceptual motor coordination; special educational needs**

1351

Institute of Education, Department of Educational Psychology and Special Educational Needs, 20 Bedford Way, London WC1H 0AL
0171 580 1122

Kambouri, M. Dr; Supervisor: Francis, H. Prof.

Dropout and progression in basic skills

ABSTRACT: The study aims to focus on the extent and reasons for dropout and progression from basic skills programmes and the level and nature of progression from programmes. It utilises questionnaires to tutors and students who have moved on or out of basic skills. In addition registers and patterns of attendance are monitored and data accumulated, coded and analysed. A final report will be published in 1993.

PUBLISHED MATERIAL: KAMBOURI, M. & FRANCIS, H. (1993). Research into progression and drop out in basic skills programmes. London: Adult Literacy and Basic Skills Unit. ; KAMBOURI, M. & FRANCIS, H. (1994). Time to leave: progression and drop out in basic skills programmes. London: Adult Literacy and Basic Skills Unit.

STATUS: Sponsored project

SOURCE OF GRANT: Adult Literacy and Basic Skills Unit £49,943

DATE OF RESEARCH: 1992-1993

KEYWORDS: **achievement; adult basic education; adult dropouts; basic skills; dropout research**

1352

Institute of Education, Department of Educational Psychology and Special Educational Needs, 20 Bedford Way, London WC1H 0AL
0171 580 1122

Dee, L. Ms

Assessment of students with disabilities or learning difficulties

ABSTRACT: An investigation into current assessment procedures used by colleges of further education (FE) to identify the learning support needs of young people and adults with disabilities or learning difficulties, with a view to producing guidelines for good practice.

STATUS: Sponsored project

SOURCE OF GRANT: Further Education Unit £20,000

DATE OF RESEARCH: 1992-1993

KEYWORDS: **assessment; colleges of further education; diagnostic assessment; further education; learning disabilities; special educational needs**

1353

Institute of Education, Department of Educational Psychology and Special Educational Needs, 20 Bedford Way, London WC1H 0AL
0171 580 1122

Wolf, A. Prof.

A bibliography and digest of basic skills in industrialised countries

ABSTRACT: The project will utilise existing database information to compile a digest of research into basic skills (in industrialised countries) undertaken since 1973. The project will produce a full bibliography and digest of research relevant to basic skills. It will concentrate on work undertaken in English speaking countries but reference to other relevant research will be made.

STATUS: Sponsored project

SOURCE OF GRANT: Adult Literacy and Basic Skills Unit (ALBSU) £31,000

DATE OF RESEARCH: 1993-1993

KEYWORDS: **basic skills; educational research**

1354

Institute of Education, Department of Educational Psychology and Special Educational Needs, 20 Bedford Way, London WC1H 0AL
0171 580 1122

Henderson, S. Dr; Demetre, J. Dr

Perceptuo-motor difficulties in prematurely born children

ABSTRACT: Perceptuo-motor difficulties in prematurely born children - do these problems affect the children's self-concept and do teachers notice? The focus of this study is on children with perceptuo-motor difficulties, a group whose special educational needs are often neglected. The aim of the study is twofold. The first objective is to investigate the way six year old children with such difficulties perceive themselves. The second objective is to determine whether infant school teachers recognise and are sensitive to these difficulties at such a young age. The investigation forms part of a much larger study of 200 prematurely born children whose development has been extensively documented over a six year period.

PUBLISHED MATERIAL: JONGMANS, M., HENDERSON, S.E., DE VRIES, L. & DUBOWITZ, L. (1993). 'Duration of periventricular densities in pre-term infants and neurological outcome at six years', Archives of Diseases in Childhood, Vol 69, pp.9-13.

STATUS: Sponsored project

SOURCE OF GRANT: Nuffield Foundation £4,820

DATE OF RESEARCH: 1993-1993

KEYWORDS: perceptual motor coordination; self concept; special educational needs

1355

Institute of Education, Department of English for Speakers of Other Languages, 20 Bedford Way, London WC1H 0AL
0171 580 1122

Flavell, R. Dr

The Radio English Direct Project

ABSTRACT: Radio English Direct is a series of programmes for English Language Teaching, devised and produced by English by Radio, part of BBC's World Service. The series is distinctive in that it is based on workshops carried out in the UK and in several sub-Saharan countries. The topics and voices of the 50 programmes are largely those of African teachers. The research project has provided formative and summative evaluation of the series, and of its integration into local language-learning contexts throughout Africa.

STATUS: Sponsored project

SOURCE OF GRANT: British Broadcasting Corporation £33,418

DATE OF RESEARCH: 1994-1998

KEYWORDS: educational radio; radio

1356

Institute of Education, Department of History, Humanities and Philosophy, 20 Bedford Way, London WC1H 0AL
0171 580 1122

Silto, W. Mr; *Supervisor*: Gordon, P. Prof.

The origins, development and failure of the Day Continuation School Movement in England and Wales

ABSTRACT: This research deals with the background behind the rise of Continuation Schools following the First World War. The importance of the 1918 Education Act and the Oxford school of idealist philosophers are described. The development and failure of the movement are traced in examination of local records of the seven LEAs which implemented Day Continuation Schools: this will also involve a study of Public Record Office files in order to ascertain the views of the Board of Education as well as the political papers of the main supporters of the movement and other interest groups.

STATUS: Individual research

DATE OF RESEARCH: 1990-1993

KEYWORDS: adult education; continuing education; educational history

1357

Institute of Education, Department of Mathematical Sciences, 20 Bedford Way, London WC1H 0AL
0171 580 1122

Sutherland, R. Prof.

Algebraic processes and the role of symbolism

ABSTRACT: A seminar group to coordinate and synthesise the United Kingdom work on algebraic thinking in school mathematics. The group has produced a set of clear questions and working hypotheses for future research collaboration with European colleagues.

STATUS: Sponsored project

SOURCE OF GRANT: Economic and Social Research Council £4,950

DATE OF RESEARCH: 1992-1993

KEYWORDS: algebra; computer uses in education; mathematics education; symbols - mathematics

1358

Institute of Education, Department of Mathematical Sciences, 20 Bedford Way, London WC1H 0AL
0171 580 1122

Pozzi, S. Mr

Mathematics learning and computer algebra systems

ABSTRACT: The aim of this study is to identify the influences of computer algebra systems (CAS) on A-level students' algebraic problem solving strategies. Case studies of eight students will be developed, each one consisting of a process and a background profile. The process profile will focus on students' strategies and approaches and how these are structured by the CAS environment, while the background profile will focus on students' competencies in algebra and attitudes to CAS.

PUBLISHED MATERIAL: POZZI, S. (1993). 'Computer algebra systems', Micromath, Vol 9, No 1, pp.26-27.

STATUS: Sponsored project

SOURCE OF GRANT: Economic and Social Research Council £31,150

DATE OF RESEARCH: 1992-1993

KEYWORDS: algebra education; computer uses in education; information technology; mathematics education; problem solving

1359

Institute of Education, Department of Mathematical Sciences, 20 Bedford Way, London WC1H OAL
0171 580 1122

Sutherland, R. Prof.

Exploiting mental imagery with computers, in mathematics education

ABSTRACT: The aim of this NATO advanced research workshop is to bring teachers in several disciplines together to explore the role of mental images in mathematics, particularly those stimulated by computer generated graphics and to chart directions for further research.

STATUS: Sponsored project

SOURCE OF GRANT: North Atlantic Treaty Organisation £19,417

DATE OF RESEARCH: 1993-1993

KEYWORDS: computer uses in education; imagery; information technology; mathematics education

1360

Institute of Education, Department of Mathematical Sciences, 20 Bedford Way, London WC1H OAL
0171 580 1122

Wolf, A. Prof.

Evaluation of the TEC Access to Assessment Initiative

ABSTRACT: An evaluation of a government funded special programme which gives Training and Enterprise Councils (TECs) earmarked funds designed to: (1) create networks of assessors who can provide assessment services for National Vocational Qualification (NVQ) candidates; and (2) promote Accreditation of Prior Learning.

PUBLISHED MATERIAL: CROWLEY-BAINTON, T. & WOLF, A. (1994). Access to assessment initiative. Sheffield: Department of Employment.

STATUS: Sponsored project

SOURCE OF GRANT: Department of Employment £22,915

DATE OF RESEARCH: 1992-1993

KEYWORDS: accreditation of prior learning; assessment; national vocational qualifications; training and enterprise councils; vocational education

1361

Institute of Education, Department of Music and Drama, 20 Bedford Way, London WC1H OAL
0171 580 1122

Swanwick, K. Prof.

Resources for music at key stage 2

ABSTRACT: Matching existing teaching and other resources against the National Curriculum Music specification.

STATUS: Sponsored project

SOURCE OF GRANT: Calouste Gulbenkian Foundation £ 10,000; Paul Hamlyn Foundation £5,000

DATE OF RESEARCH: 1993-1993

KEYWORDS: **educational resources; music; national curriculum**

1362

Institute of Education, Department of Music and Drama, 20 Bedford Way, London WC1H OAL
0171 580 1122

Shiobara, M. Dr; *Supervisor*: Swanwick, K. Prof.

The effect of movement on musical comprehension

ABSTRACT: The researcher examines the effect of movement on younger children's musical comprehension with special reference to the quality of their perception of music. Different approaches to the use of movement in the music curriculum are examined and it is shown that many of the aims and practices of the various methods have at one time or another entered the mainstream of the music curriculum. The approach of Jacques-Dalcroze in music education is discussed as a basis for the further theoretical development of this thesis. A theoretical framework for the examination of the crucial role of physical movement for musical comprehension is constructed. Background aesthetic theory is presented, and accounts are given by Piaget and others of the role of action or physical movement in the development of children's representational thought are discussed. An empirical investigation into the effect of movement on musical comprehension, and various problems associated with measurement of the child's ability to perceive and comprehend music, are discussed, and an experimental method for assessing the effect of movement on the musical perception of 7-8 year old children is proposed by the researcher. The experiments which were carried out in England and Japan are reported in detail and the results are presented. The findings indicate that movement appears to have a positive effect on the detail of musical perception. There are implications of the research for the development of the music curriculum and for further research work.

STATUS: Individual research

DATE OF RESEARCH: 1989-1993

KEYWORDS: **movement education; music; psychomotor skills**

1363

Institute of Education, Department of Music and Drama, 20 Bedford Way, London WC1H OAL
0171 580 1122

Hentschke, L. Dr; *Supervisor*: Swanwick, K. Prof.

The effect of movement on musical development

ABSTRACT: An investigation to see if responses made through listening in audience can be mapped according to the Swanwick and Tillman Spiral of Musical Development. The work includes a review of previous studies in the field of musical abilities, aptitudes, musical development and the assessment of listening in audience and a critical outline of the Spiral Theory of Musical development and its assessment criteria. This is analysed by employing five general developmental characteristics named as Temporality, Cumulativity, Directionality, New Mode of Organisation and Increased Capacity for Self Control. The terms in which musical development have been conceived are seen as being analogical to Piaget's Theory on Play Development in early childhood. This generalisation of the analogical process to the remaining activities of performing and listening in audience is discussed along with methods employed to assess listening in audience responses, which consisted of interviewing a total of 105 children in 2 field studies (in Brazil and England) by using 2 kinds of interview - structured and semi-structured. Results suggest that the proposed development sequence can be successfully mapped on to data gained centred on response to music as audience-listener. There are implications for music education, including consideration of the positive effect of a structured music curriculum.

STATUS: Individual research

DATE OF RESEARCH: 1989-1993

KEYWORDS: **music; music appreciation**

1364

Institute of Education, Department of Policy Studies, 20 Bedford Way, London WC1H 0AL
0171 580 1122

Williams, G. Prof.; Loder, C. Ms

Study of independent further and higher education

ABSTRACT: The Centre for Higher Education Studies is undertaking a survey of independent further and higher education in Great Britain in order to provide information on: (1) number and type of institutions; (2) number and characteristics of students (including age, sex, mode of study and domicile); (3) range of courses offered; (4) number and range of qualifications obtained by students; and (5) sources of financial support for students (e.g. grants under PICKUP, sponsorship by employers, mandatory and discretionary awards from local education authorities and training vouchers.

PUBLISHED MATERIAL: GOVERNMENT STATISTICAL SERVICE. (1993). 'Participation in independent sector further and higher education in Great Britain', DFE Statistical Bulletin, No 25, 1993.

STATUS: Sponsored project

SOURCE OF GRANT: Department of Education and Science £79,075

DATE OF RESEARCH: 1991-1993

KEYWORDS: **further education; higher education; independent colleges; private education; private universities**

1365

Institute of Education, Department of Policy Studies, 20 Bedford Way, London WC1H 0AL
0171 580 1122

Williams, G. Prof.

Identifying and developing a quality ethos for teaching in higher education

ABSTRACT: The primary aim of the project is to increase understanding of quality in higher education teaching by a systematic series of surveys of students, academics, administrators and employers of graduates.

STATUS: Sponsored project

SOURCE OF GRANT: Leverhulme Trust £137,879

DATE OF RESEARCH: 1991-1993

KEYWORDS: **educational quality; higher education; teacher effectiveness**

1366

Institute of Education, Department of Policy Studies, 20 Bedford Way, London WC1H 0AL
0171 580 1122

Oakley, A. Prof.; Fullerton, D. Ms

Establishing a social science database of controlled interventions in education and social welfare

ABSTRACT: The aims of the project are to review and classify the methodology of interventions in education and social welfare, to set up a computer database and compare the findings derived from different research designs.

STATUS: Sponsored project

SOURCE OF GRANT: Economic and Social Research Council £28,650

DATE OF RESEARCH: 1993-1993

KEYWORDS: **databases; intervention; pupil welfare**

1367

Institute of Education, Department of Policy Studies, 20 Bedford Way, London WC1H 0AL
0171 580 1122

Young, M. Dr; Barnett, M. Prof.

Evaluation of the technological Baccalaureate

ABSTRACT: The aims of this project are to investigate how pilot schools are using the Technological Baccalaureate and what the problems are of using the pilot scheme booklet. This will lead to an interim report for City & Guilds and the City Technology Colleges Trust with recommendations; a series of consultancy visits to the schools and colleges; and a final report.

STATUS: Sponsored project

SOURCE OF GRANT: City Technology Colleges Trust £15,000

DATE OF RESEARCH: 1992-1993

KEYWORDS: **qualifications; technology education**

1368

Institute of Education, Department of Policy Studies, 20 Bedford Way, London WC1H OAL
0171 580 1122

Williams, G. Prof.

Long term study of British universities

ABSTRACT: Statistical projections and systematic assembly of expert opinions to produce senarios of possible developments in British higher education by the early years of the next century.

STATUS: Sponsored project

SOURCE OF GRANT: Committee of Vice-Chancellors and Principals of the Universities of the United Kingdom £23,011

DATE OF RESEARCH: 1993-1993

KEYWORDS: **educational development; higher education; prediction; universities**

1369

Institute of Education, Department of Policy Studies, Health and Education Research Unit, 20 Bedford Way, London WC1H OAL
0171 580 1122

Aggleton, P. Prof.; Whitty, G. Prof.

South East Thames regional HIV education and training evaluation project

ABSTRACT: This is a project to evaluate the implementation of the South East Thames Regional Human Immunodeficiency Virus (HIV) Education and Training Strategy at district level. It will seek to identify via interviews with Human Immunodeficiency Virus/Acquired Immune Deficiency Syndrome (HIV/AIDS) prevention coordinators, trainers, training providers, workers in relevant non-statutory agencies and other key informants. The aims of the project are to discover (1) awareness of South East Thames Regional HIV Education and Training Strategy; (2) perceptions of its appropriateness and inclusiveness in meeting the HIV/AIDS training needs of relevant health authority personnel; (3) perceptions of the effectiveness and inclusiveness of this strategy in meeting the needs of clients and carers, for appropriate priorities for future HIV education and training; (4) appropriate ways in which the South East Thames Regional Health Authority might promote and support such work and (5) appropriate strategies by which such education and training might be monitored and evaluated on an ongoing basis.

STATUS: Sponsored project

SOURCE OF GRANT: South East Thames Regional Health Authority £15,865

DATE OF RESEARCH: 1991-1993

KEYWORDS: **acquired immune deficiency syndrome; evaluation; health education; training**

1370

Institute of Education, Department of Policy Studies, Health and Education Research Unit, 20 Bedford Way, London WC1H OAL
0171 580 1122

Whitty, G. Prof.; Aggleton, P. Prof.

AVERT AIDS: working with young people project

ABSTRACT: This project extends earlier work which researched the Human Immunodeficiency Virus/Acquired Immune Deficiency Syndrome (HIV/AIDS) training needs of adults who work with young people in youth service settings. A number of needs were identified. These ranged from information on social and medical issues to ways in which young people may be helped to learn about HIV infection and AIDS. The findings were disseminated via a resource for youth workers. The current project aims to develop the work to include the needs of teachers in secondary schools. It will : (1) research the needs of teachers in relation to classroom-based activity on HIV and AIDS; (2) compare these needs with those of workers in youth service settings; (3) identify ways in which teachers might best support and enable pupils in learning about the medical and social issues associated with HIV and AIDS. The projects findings will be disseminated via an updated resource package which emphasises participatory training within a clearly defined equal opportunities framework.

PUBLISHED MATERIAL: AGGLETON P. et al. (1993). AIDS: working with young people. Second Edition. Horsham: AVERT.

STATUS: Sponsored project

SOURCE OF GRANT: AIDS Education and Research Trust (AVERT) £38,299

DATE OF RESEARCH: 1992-1993

KEYWORDS: **acquired immune deficiency syndrome; health education; secondary education**

1371

Institute of Education, Department of Policy Studies, Health and Education Research Unit, 20 Bedford Way, London WC1H OAL
0171 580 1122

Aggleton, P. Prof.; Whitty, G. Prof.

Health Education Authority 'Men who have sex with men' project: selected examples of good practice in HIV/AIDS health promotion

ABSTRACT: This project seeks to identify and document instances of good practice in local Human Immunodeficiency Virus/Acquired Immune Deficiency Syndrome (HIV/AIDS) education work with men who have sex with men, with a view to making this information more widely available. The aims are to identify: (1) the range of activities currently underway to prevent HIV transmission amongst men who have sex with men; (2) projects and activities that have proved most appropriate, innovative and effective within specific local contexts; (3) factors which facilitate such work; (4) factors which hinder such work. Interviews will be carried out with relevant project personnel so as to lay the foundations for a number of case studies documenting good practice in this field. The case studies will be written up and made available through two project reports.

PUBLISHED MATERIAL: McKEVITT, C., WARWICK, I. & AGGLETON, P. (1994). Towards good practice: selective examples of HIV and AIDS health promotion with gay, bisexual and other men who have sex with men. London: Health Education Authority.

STATUS: Sponsored project

SOURCE OF GRANT: Health Education Authority £24,700

DATE OF RESEARCH: 1992-1993

KEYWORDS: **acquired immune deficiency syndrome; health education; homosexuality; sex education; sexuality; sexually transmitted diseases**

1372

Institute of Education, Department of Policy Studies, Health and Education Research Unit, 20 Bedford Way, London WC1H OAL
0171 580 1122

Whitty, G. Prof.; Aggleton, P. Prof.

Assessing quality in cross-curricular contexts: a case study

ABSTRACT: This project is exploring changing approaches to cross-curricular work in key stages 3 and 4 in the context of the National Curriculum. Particular attention is being paid to work relating to the National Curriculum Council's five designated cross-curricular themes. Baseline data from an earlier project conducted in 1988/1989 is being compared with a new survey of policy and practice in a sample of 1 in 4 secondary schools in England and Wales. Intensive observation and interviewing is being conducted in a sub-sample of 8 schools.

PUBLISHED MATERIAL: ROWE, G. & WHITTY, G. (1993). 'Five themes remain in the shadows', Times Educational Supplement, 9 April 1993. ;

ROWE, G., AGGLETON, P. & WHITTY, G. (1993). 'Cross-curricular work in secondary schools: the place of careers education and guidance', Careers Education and Guidance, June, pp.2-6. ; WHITTY, G., ROWE, G. & AGGLETON, P. (1994). 'Subjects and themes in the secondary school curriculum', Research Papers in Education, Vol 9, No 2, pp.159-181.

STATUS: Sponsored project

SOURCE OF GRANT: Economic and Social Research Council £49,711

DATE OF RESEARCH: 1992-1993

KEYWORDS: **cross curricular approach; curriculum development; educational quality; national curriculum**

1373

Institute of Education, Department of Policy Studies, Health and Education Research Unit, 20 Bedford Way, London WC1H 0AL
0171 580 1122

Whitty, G. Prof.

Cross-curricular work in post-primary schools in Northern Ireland

ABSTRACT: A national survey and detailed observation in a small sample of post-primary schools were used to compare the implementation of the educational themes specified in Northern Ireland's Education Reform Order 1989, with earlier findings about the implementation of the cross-curricular themes in England and Wales.

PUBLISHED MATERIAL: WHITTY, G., ROWE, G. & AGGLETON, P. (1994). 'Subjects and themes in the secondary-school curriculum', Research Papers in Education, Vol 9, No 2, pp.159-181.

STATUS: Sponsored project

SOURCE OF GRANT: Department of Education Northern Ireland £4,335

DATE OF RESEARCH: 1993-1993

KEYWORDS: **cross curricular approach; curriculum development; northern ireland**

1374

Institute of Education, Department of Science and Technology, 20 Bedford Way, London WC1H 0AL
0171 580 1122

MaCaskill, C. Mrs

Initial teacher training CD-ROM Scheme

ABSTRACT: This is an investigation of how CD-ROMs can be usefully employed by teachers and pupils in National Curriculum Technology. The aim is to explore the potential of using CD-ROM in National Curriculum Technology specifically for supporting attainment targets (AT) 1 and 2 for which pupils are required to research and investigate the context of their study and also to support AT 5, Information Technology. Two questions were posed: (1) how can CD-ROM be used to support pupils independent researching? (2) what researching strategies are normally employed by technology teachers, both in and out of the classroom, do they consider the use of CD-ROMs to be beneficial to this process.

STATUS: Sponsored project

SOURCE OF GRANT: National Council for Educational Technology £1,000

DATE OF RESEARCH: 1992-1993

KEYWORDS: **cd roms; computer uses in education; information seeking; information technology; national curriculum; technology education**

1375

Institute of Education, Department of Science and Technology, 20 Bedford Way, London WC1H 0AL
0171 580 1122

Ogborn, J. Prof.

Commonsense understanding of science

ABSTRACT: The project is concerned with the description of fundamental dimensions of commonsense or everyday reasoning about processes and events in the natural world, and the relation of these to scientific accounts of similar processes.

PUBLISHED MATERIAL: MARIANI, M. & OGBORN, J. (1990).

'Commonsense reasoning about conservation: the role of action', International Journal of Science Education, Vol 12, No 1, pp.51-66. ; MARIANI, M. & OGBORN, J. (1991). 'Towards an ontology of commonsense reasoning', International Journal of Science Education, Vol 13, No 1, pp.69-85. ; OGBORN, J. (1992). 'Fundamental dimensions of thought about reality: object, action, cause, movement, space and time'. In: Teaching about reference frames: from Copernicus to Einstein. Proceedings of GIREP Conference, Torun, Poland, August 1991. Torun: Nicholas Copernicus University Press. ; OGBORN, J. (1992). 'Basic structures underlying some mental models'. In: Mental models and everyday activities, Proceedings of Second Interdisciplinary Workshop on Mental Models, March 23-25, 1992, Cambridge.

STATUS: Sponsored project

SOURCE OF GRANT: Leverhulme Trust £43,567

DATE OF RESEARCH: 1992-1993

KEYWORDS: **explanation; physical environment; public opinion; reasoning; scientific attitudes; scientific literacy**

1376

Institute of Education, 20 Bedford Way, London WC1H 0AL
0171 580 1122
London University, Institute of Education, Thomas Coram Research Unit, 27-28 Woburn Square, London WC1H 0AA
0171 612 6957

Warwick, I. Mr; Whitty, G. Prof.; Aggleton, P. Prof.

Young people's database project

ABSTRACT: To develop an information database for those with a professional interest in health education and health promotion with young people, with particular reference to the provision of information on sensitive issues and for young people from under-served communities.

STATUS: Sponsored project

SOURCE OF GRANT: Health Education Authority

DATE OF RESEARCH: 1997-1998

KEYWORDS: **databases; health education; health promotion**

1377

Institute of Education, 20 Bedford Way, London WC1H 0AL
0171 580 1122
London University, Institute of Education, Thomas Coram Research Unit, 27-28 Woburn Square, London WC1H 0AA
0171 612 6957

Whitty, G. Prof.; Aggleton, P. Prof.

Mapping of health promotion education and training provision for health promotion specialists

ABSTRACT: The principal aim of the study is to map, describe and analyse current education and training in health promotion for health promotion specialists in England.

STATUS: Sponsored project

SOURCE OF GRANT: Health Education Authority

DATE OF RESEARCH: 1997-1998

KEYWORDS: **health education; health personnel; health promotion; training**

1378

Institute of Education, 20 Bedford Way, London WC1H 0AL
0171 580 1122
Nottingham University, School of Education, University Park, Nottingham NG7 2RD
01159 515151

Leo, E. Dr; Adey, K. Dr

Cognitive acceleration in the early years

ABSTRACT: To investigate cognitive acceleration strategies in primary school classrooms and motivational process; teaching and learning, knowledge transfer.

STATUS: Sponsored project

SOURCE OF GRANT: London Borough of Hammersmith and Fulham £69,881

DATE OF RESEARCH: 1998-continuing

KEYWORDS: cognitive ability; primary education; teaching methods

1379

Institute of Education, 20 Bedford Way, London WC1H 0AL
0171 580 1122
Oxford University, Department of Educational Studies, 15 Norham Gardens, Oxford OX2 6PY
01865 274024

Sylva, K. Prof.; Sammons, P. Dr

Baseline assessment: what do they measure and what do they predict?

ABSTRACT: This project is designed to examine the relationship between different forms of baseline assessment conducted at entry to school for children in 3 different regions. As part of a wide 5-year project 'Effective provision of preschool education' (funded by the Department for Education and Employment) baseline assessments of phonological awareness, social and behaviour development and children's scores on selected British Ability Sub-Scales are being conducted on a one-to-one basis by trained field workers. These results will be compared to data from teachers' reception baseline assessments of the same children. The relationships with children's characteristics (gender, ethnicity, age, socio-economic background) will be explored.

STATUS: Sponsored project

SOURCE OF GRANT: Qualifications and Curriculum Authority £25,676

DATE OF RESEARCH: 1998-continuing

KEYWORDS: baseline assessment; primary education; reception classes; young children

1380

Institute of Education, 20 Bedford Way, London WC1H 0AL
0171 580 1122
Oxford University, Department of Experimental Psychology, South Parks Road, Oxford OX1 3UD
01865 270360

Nunes, T. Dr; Bryant, P. Prof.

How do the phonological and lexical routes in reading and spelling develop

ABSTRACT: This investigation examines the independence of two sets of reading and spelling processes, one based on sounds and the other on grammar. Children's learning of grammatical spellings (e.g. 'ed' in past verbs, apostrophes) correlates with their grammatical awareness. This study tests the casual link between grammatical awareness and spelling development. Participants will be assigned to four groups, assessed in a pre-, a post-, and a delay post-test. Two groups will receive instruction on grammatical awareness; one of these also receives instruction on awareness of sounds; one of these also receives instruction on the connection between phonology and spelling. Predictions are that the groups' progress will be specific to the type of instruction received: those instructed in grammatical awareness will improve more in the use of grammatical spelling patterns than those instructed on awareness of sound.

STATUS: Sponsored project

SOURCE OF GRANT: Economic and Social Research Council £99,599

DATE OF RESEARCH: 1998-continuing

KEYWORDS: grammar; language acquisition; reading; spelling

1381

Institute of Education, Social Science Research Unit, 20 Bedford Way, London WC1H 0AL
0171 580 1122

Hewitt, R. Dr

Effects of teaching 'speaking and listening' in the National Curriculum

ABSTRACT: This is an examination of how the explicit teaching of 'speaking and listening' affects the performance of pupils' communicative skills and the conduct of collaboration in oral group work. The aims are to investigate: (1) how, at key stage 2 of the National Curriculum, the foregrounding of

talk as a subject of pedagogic activity in its own right affects: (a) how pupils communicate with each other in oral group work; (b) how their talk influences their group collaborations, and (2) how teachers' objectives in teaching and creating opportunities for the development of speaking and listening skills are realised or changed in practice.

STATUS: Sponsored project

SOURCE OF GRANT: Economic and Social Research Council £29,530

DATE OF RESEARCH: 1991-1993

KEYWORDS: communication skills; listening skills; national curriculum; speech communication

1382

Institute of Education, 20 Bedford Way, London WC1H 0AL
0171 580 1122
Strathclyde University, Centre for Research in Quality in Education, Jordanhill Campus, Southbrae Drive, Glasgow G13 1PP
0141 950 3000

Mortimore, P. Prof.; Thomas, S. Dr; Sammons, P. Dr; Macbeath, J. Prof.

Improving school effectiveness

ABSTRACT: The project covers three related action research projects concerning school development planning, ethos, and teaching and learning. Sixty Scottish schools (twenty-four intervention, thirty-six comparison) will be involved. The project is a collaborative venture conducted with the University of Strathclyde and combines the traditions of school effectiveness and school improvement research. Two age cohorts (one primary, one secondary) will form the focus of a study of student outcomes over a two year period. Value added analyses using multilevel modelling techniques will be used to examine progress/change in academic and social/affective outcomes. In addition, detailed qualitative analyses of school and classroom process data will be conducted to investigate the improvement process.

PUBLISHED MATERIAL: MORTIMORE, P., BUDGE, D. & MACBEATH, J. (1994). 'Quest for the secrets of success', Times Educational Supplement, No 4056, March 25, p.14. ; MACBEATH, J. & MORTIMORE, P. (1994). 'Improving school effectiveness: a Scottish approach'. Paper presented at the British Educational Research Association, Oxford, September 1994.

STATUS: Sponsored project

SOURCE OF GRANT: The Scottish Office Education Department £266,395

DATE OF RESEARCH: 1994-1997

KEYWORDS: development plans; educational improvement; educational quality; performance indicators; primary education; school effectiveness; secondary education; value added

1383

Institute of Education, Technology and Education Unit, 20 Bedford Way, London WC1H 0AL
0171 580 1122

Barnett, M. Prof.; Kent, A. Mr

Remote sensing in the Geography National Curriculum

ABSTRACT: This project involves the development of teacher education materials for remote sensing in the Geography National Curriculum. The geography order specifically requires that satellite images of the earth and aerial photographs should be used as resources. There are also many points where delivery would be much enhanced by the use of such images. The project aims to develop materials which will enable teachers to make wider use of all forms of remotely sensed images by illustrating how images can be integrated into the geography curriculum.

STATUS: Sponsored project

SOURCE OF GRANT: National Council for Educational Technology £77,296

DATE OF RESEARCH: 1992-1993

KEYWORDS: earth science; geography; inservice teacher education; national curriculum

1384

Institute of Education, Thomas Coram Research Unit, 20 Bedford Way, London WC1H 0AL
0171 580 1122

Petrie, P. Dr; Poland, G. Ms

Out of school services survey and evaluation

ABSTRACT: Twelve case studies of playschemes, using a consultative approach with providers and staff, followed by a survey of 100 schemes looking at objectives and their realisation; organisation and resources.

STATUS: Sponsored project

SOURCE OF GRANT: Department of Health £181,827

DATE OF RESEARCH: 1990-1993

KEYWORDS: **child care givers; community services; play; play centres; recreational activities**

1385

Institute of Education, Thomas Coram Research Unit, 27-28 Woburn Square, London WC1H 0AA
0171 612 6957

McGurk, H. Prof.; Hurry, J. Dr

Evaluation of Project Charlie: a drug prevention programme for primary school children

ABSTRACT: Project Charlie is a drug prevention programme for primary school children, developed in 1976 in the USA and now widely implemented there. Currently being piloted in London, The Home Office requested an evaluation of the programme. The impact of Project Charlie in two Hackney primary schools is being investigated on the basis of: (a) its objectives to improve children's 'life-skills'; decision making, peer-pressure resistance, self-esteem and making relationships; and (b) its goals, to inform on drug abuse and to alter drug-related behaviour and drug use. The degree to which this programme is acceptable and workable in these Hackney schools is also being established. Approximately 200 children aged between 7 and 11 years were tested on a battery of paper and pencil measures relating to their 'life-skills' and verbal competence. The majority of these children, 175, attending one school were tested, prior to receiving Project Charlie lessons for one period weekly. Half were randomly assigned to the Project Charlie group and half to the control group. After one year of the programme both the experimental and control groups are currently being re-tested.

STATUS: Sponsored project

SOURCE OF GRANT: Home Office £32,870

DATE OF RESEARCH: 1990-1993

KEYWORDS: **drug education; health education; life skills; primary school pupils**

1386

Institute of Education, Thomas Coram Research Unit, 27-28 Woburn Square, London WC1H 0AA
0171 612 6957

Hurry, J. Dr

Deliberate self-harm among young people

ABSTRACT: The aims of the project are to identify: 1) on a national basis, hospital policy, guidelines and staff training for the treatment of adolescents and young adults who have made a suicide attempt; 2) in a sub-sample, the range of procedures employed, with regard to assessment and referral/disposition for this patient group and the availability of specially trained staff in hospital accident and emergency departments; 3) the relationship between the treatment of a sub-sample of adolescents and: a) local policy and service provision and b) characteristics of the individual; 4) the factors involved in the adoption of service provision of a high standard (or the lack of such provision) for this group of patients.

STATUS: Sponsored project

SOURCE OF GRANT: Department of Health £36,163

DATE OF RESEARCH: 1995-1997

KEYWORDS: **emotional and behavioural difficulties; hospitals; self mutilation; suicide**

1387

Institute of Education, Thomas Coram Research Unit, 27-28 Woburn Square, London WC1H 0AA
0171 612 6957

Mooney, A. Ms; McGurk, H. Prof.

Anglo-Hungarian day care project

ABSTRACT: This collaboration will capitalise on the similarities and differences in the promotion of child and family welfare in the UK and Hungary by means of day care services, and make it possible to test new instruments and procedures for assessing quality in day care, being developed in the Thomas Coram Research Unit, in a wider range of settings than those available in the UK.

STATUS: Sponsored project

SOURCE OF GRANT: British Council £14,480

DATE OF RESEARCH: 1992-1997

KEYWORDS: **child caregivers; day care; hungary**

1388

Institute of Education, Thomas Coram Research Unit, 27-28 Woburn Square, London WC1H 0AA
0171 612 6957

Petrie, P. Dr

Users satisfaction with play and care services out-of-school

ABSTRACT: Two projects which are jointly funded. One looks at parents' and children's satisfaction with services and how this compares with the meaning they give to 'childhood'. It includes children with disability and children from different ethnic groups. The second draws on this and involves the production of an evaluation instrument.

STATUS: Sponsored project

SOURCE OF GRANT: Department of Health £245,472

DATE OF RESEARCH: 1994-1997

KEYWORDS: **child caregivers; clubs; holidays; parent attitudes; play; pupil attitudes; recreation; recreational activities**

1389

Institute of Education, Thomas Coram Research Unit, 27-28 Woburn Square, London WC1H 0AA
0171 612 6957

Petrie, P. Dr

The satisfaction of young people aged 10-13, and of their parents with out-of-school care and recreational provision

ABSTRACT: The aim of this project is to study the satisfaction of the users of care and recreational facilities such as after-school clubs and holiday play schemes known as School-age Childcare on out-of-school provision. The focus is on 10-13 year olds.

STATUS: Sponsored project

SOURCE OF GRANT: Johann Jacobs Foundation £65,439

DATE OF RESEARCH: 1996-1997

KEYWORDS: **child caregivers; clubs; holidays; parent attitudes; play; pupil attitudes; recreation; recreational activities**

1390

Institute of Education, Thomas Coram Research Unit, 27-28 Woburn Square, London WC1H 0AA
0171 612 6957

Moss, P. Mr

Provision for sponsored day care services for children in need

ABSTRACT: This study is exploring the use made by local authorities of voluntary and private day care services for children defined as 'in need', as encouraged by the Children Act 1989. It is looking at the extent and nature of local authority use of this resource, the process of placement, the recruitment and support of day care providers, parents' views about the service, the quality of the provision, and the effectiveness of placements in relation to social work objectives. Data will be collected using a variety of methods, including an analysis of local authority documents, secondary analysis of government day care statistics, a postal survey of local authorities, a study of sponsorship schemes in 12 local authorities (which will include a survey of day care providers) and case studies of the referral process and outcomes in 3 local authorities.

STATUS: Sponsored project

SOURCE OF GRANT: Department of Health £194,832

DATE OF RESEARCH: 1996-continuing

KEYWORDS: child caregivers; children act 1989; children at risk; day care; disadvantaged; social services

1391

Institute of Education, Thomas Coram Research Unit, 27-28 Woburn Square, London WC1H 0AA
0171 612 6957

Moss, P. Mr

Registration and inspection of day care provision: assessing quality

ABSTRACT: This study builds on earlier work at the Thomas Coram Research Unit which has developed self-assessment materials for use by day care providers in assessing, monitoring and enhancing the quality of the service they offer. The main aim of this follow-up work is to establish effective procedures for using these self-assessment materials so as to support day care providers who wish to enhance the quality of the care they provide, and to contribute to the process of local authority registration and inspection of day care providers. The study is a development project and involves: a preparatory stage, when procedures will be developed and the materials modified to make them more suitable for use by local authority regulatory staff; and a piloting stage, when the materials and accompanying procedures will be used in a small number of day nurseries and 4 local authorities.

STATUS: Sponsored project

SOURCE OF GRANT: Department of Health £258,345

DATE OF RESEARCH: 1996-continuing

KEYWORDS: caregivers; day care; inspection; quality control; social services

1392

Institute of Education, Thomas Coram Research Unit, 27-28 Woburn Square, London WC1H 0AA
0171 612 6957

Moss, P. Mr; Brannen, J. Dr

Secondary analysis of trends in parental employment of the Labour Force Survey

ABSTRACT: The project will build on past analysis of the Labour Force Survey (LFS) on parental employment carried out at the Thomas Coram Research Unit by providing: a) further analysis of economic activity trends of mothers, fathers, and at a household level; b) provide new analysis of working hours, non-standard employment, shiftwork in households with children.

STATUS: Sponsored project

SOURCE OF GRANT: Department for Education and Employment

DATE OF RESEARCH: 1996-1997

KEYWORDS: employed parents; employment; family life; labour market; working hours

1393

Institute of Education, Thomas Coram Research Unit, 27-28 Woburn Square, London WC1H 0AA
0171 612 6957

Candappa, M. Ms

Extraordinary childhoods

ABSTRACT: The aim of the research is to study the experiences of refugee children whose childhoods can be seen as 'extraordinary' in the upheaval and trauma many have experienced, and the way in which they have had to deal with life in a strange country in often taxing circumstances. The research will focus on a sample of 32 refugee children (including asylum seekers and those given exceptional leave to remain in Britain), exploring their social networks, their social responsibilities and experiences in relation to their parents, and as 'go-between' in relation to parents and the outside world. It will investigate refugee children's experience of services such as school, health care, and any specialist services provided for them in relation

to difficulties they face. For comparative purposes the experience of 2 smaller groups of indigenous white and minority ethnic immigrant (non-refugee) children, matched with the main group for age, gender, socio-economic status and religion, will be studied.

STATUS: Sponsored project

SOURCE OF GRANT: Economic and Social Research Council

DATE OF RESEARCH: 1996-1998

KEYWORDS: children; disadvantaged; immigrants; migrant children; refugees

1394

Institute of Education, Thomas Coram Research Unit, 27-28 Woburn Square, London WC1H 0AA
0171 612 6957

Smith, M. Dr

A study of stepchildren and stepparenting

ABSTRACT: The aims of this study are to describe how children in stepfamilies are parented and to investigate whether this differs markedly from parenting in original families. The study is investigating the process of formation and functioning in different types of stepfamily, to see which variables or models of stepfamily are associated with a good outcome for the child. Data will be collected from a representative community sample of approximately 200 stepfamilies, each with a child aged between 7 and 11 years of age, and where the stepfamily has been in existence for between 1 and 3 years.

STATUS: Sponsored project

SOURCE OF GRANT: Department of Health £398,744

DATE OF RESEARCH: 1996-continuing

KEYWORDS: family life; parent child relationship; parents; stepfamily

1395

Institute of Education, Thomas Coram Research Unit, 27-28 Woburn Square, London WC1H 0AA
0171 612 6957

Owen, C. Mr

Staffing of day care services with particular attention to gender issues

ABSTRACT: This study is concerned with the workforce in day care services for young children, both generally and with reference to issues raised by the gendered nature of the workforce and the implications of employing men in day care services. It will look at who works in these services, in what conditions and the relationship between staffing and quality. It will also examine: whether local authorities and institutions have policies on the recruitment of men to train and work in day care services; the experience of day care centres which have promoted a mixed gender workforce as a matter of policy; the views of parents and workers about men working in these services; and whether the gender of the staff group affects the behaviour of children, staff and parents. Data will be collected using a variety of methods, including postal surveys of local authorities and training institutions, case studies of nurseries which have implemented a mixed gender workforce policy and a wider study of a sample.

STATUS: Sponsored project

SOURCE OF GRANT: Department of Health £284,334

DATE OF RESEARCH: 1996-continuing

KEYWORDS: child care occupations; child caregivers; day care; men; sex differences; young children

1396

Institute of Education, Thomas Coram Research Unit, 27-28 Woburn Square, London WC1H 0AA
0171 612 6957

Smith, M. Dr

A normative study of children's injuries

ABSTRACT: The frequency and nature of minor injuries, so called 'normal trauma', as well as the context and circumstances in which these injuries occur, will be investigated in a community sample of children aged between birth and 8 years of age. Information on the nature of the injuries and details of the context in which they occurred will be collected from families. This will be followed by interviews with the caretaking parent during which standardised measures of child behaviour, parent affect and stress will also be completed. More detailed interviews will take place in a sub-sample of families to investigate the role of parental actions and expectations of child behaviour on injury causation or prevention, as well as parental views of appropriate supervision, safety measures and expectations of child behaviour.

STATUS: Sponsored project

SOURCE OF GRANT: Department of Health £404,005

DATE OF RESEARCH: 1997-continuing

KEYWORDS: **accidents; children; injuries; parents; safety; young children**

1397

Institute of Education, Thomas Coram Research Unit, 27-28 Woburn Square, London WC1H 0AA
0171 612 6957

Deven, F. Dr; Inglis, S. Dr; Petrie, P. Dr; Moss, P. Mr

State of the art overview of reconciliation of work and family

ABSTRACT: This project is a state of the art study on reconciliation of work and family life for men and women and the quality of care services, covering 4 objectives: 1) review of recent literature; 2) identification of gaps in knowledge; 3) identification of institutions that fund research; 4) identification of areas of study which the European Commission could support within the framework of the Community Action Programme on Equal Opportunities.

STATUS: Sponsored project

DATE OF RESEARCH: 1996-1997

KEYWORDS: **child caregivers; child minding; day care; employed parents; employment; europe; family life**

1398

Institute of Education, Thomas Coram Research Unit, 27-28 Woburn Square, London WC1H 0AA
0171 612 6957

Brannen, J. Dr

Children's concepts and experiences of care

ABSTRACT: This study is examining children's understandings of care and their experience both as carers and cared for. It focuses on children as subjects rather than objects of research and the ways in which children understand, experience and actively contribute to caring in a variety of family contexts. These contexts include birth families, single parent families, stepfamilies and children cared for by foster parents. The study has both quantitative and qualitative components. Data will be collected by means of self-completion questionnaires from children aged 10-12 in schools, and by means of indepth interviews conducted with children and their mothers living in different types of family context. The study will include children from a range of different ethnic and socio-economic backgrounds.

STATUS: Sponsored project

SOURCE OF GRANT: Department of Health £278,664

DATE OF RESEARCH: 1996-continuing

KEYWORDS: **child caregivers; childhood attitudes; children; family life; foster care; one parent family; parent child relationship; parents; stepfamily**

1399

Institute of Education, Thomas Coram Research Unit, 27-28 Woburn Square, London WC1H 0AA
0171 612 6957

Moss, P. Mr

Day care services for children under five

ABSTRACT: This is a stream of work encompassing 3 major projects: 1) staffing of day care services, with particular attention to gender issues, the provision of sponsored day care and quality in day care services. The objective is to provide a coordinated range of research that is directly relevant to public policy concerns, particularly following the implementation of the

Children Act, that builds on work already carried out by the Thomas Coram Research Unit.

STATUS: Sponsored project

SOURCE OF GRANT: Department of Health £281,964

DATE OF RESEARCH: 1996-continuing

KEYWORDS: **child caregivers; child development; day care; early experience; family life; parents; young children**

1400

Institute of Education, Thomas Coram Research Unit, 27-28 Woburn Square, London WC1H 0AL
0171 612 6957

Statham, J. Dr

Preliminary work towards an overview of the Children Act

ABSTRACT: Overview of projects funded by the Department of Health on the implementation of the Children Act 1989. Production of guidelines on presentation of research findings.

STATUS: Sponsored project

SOURCE OF GRANT: Department of Health

DATE OF RESEARCH: 1996-1998

KEYWORDS: **child welfare; children act 1989; day care; legislation**

1401

Institute of Education, Thomas Coram Research Unit, 27-28 Woburn Square, London WC1H 0AA
0171 612 6957

St James Roberts, I. Dr

Evaluation of the Islington CHANCE project

ABSTRACT: CHANCE involves the use of community 'mentors' who counsel, support and provide a role model for primary school children at risk for later criminal behaviour. By intervening early with such children and their families, the intention is to find a cost-effective preventative programme. The Institute is funded by the Home Office to evaluate: 1) whether CHANCE is being implemented successfully; 2) whether the planned improvements in the children's behaviour are being achieved.

STATUS: Sponsored project

SOURCE OF GRANT: Home Office £32,718

DATE OF RESEARCH: 1997-continuing

KEYWORDS: **behaviour modification; children at risk; crime prevention; intervention; primary school pupils**

1402

Institute of Education, Thomas Coram Research Unit, 27-28 Woburn Square, London WC1H 0AA
0171 612 6957

Aggleton, P. Prof.

Evaluation of Health Education Authority/Glaxo Wellcome drug education grant

ABSTRACT: The project involves an evaluation of the Health Education Authority/Glaxo Wellcome drugs education small grants scheme. In addition to a review of project purposes, training and evaluation will be offered to funded projects, and an overall evaluation of work undertaken will be prepared.

STATUS: Sponsored project

SOURCE OF GRANT: Health Education Authority

DATE OF RESEARCH: 1998-1998

KEYWORDS: **drug education; health education**

1403

Institute of Education, Thomas Coram Research Unit, 27-28 Woburn Square, London WC1H 0AA
0171 612 6957

Candappa, M. Ms

Living in the city: consultation exercise with young people

ABSTRACT: The objectives of the project are to: 1) obtain the views of children and young people on what it's like to live in the City of London; 2) identify the young people's wishes, needs and concerns regarding children's services to the City; 3) seek young people's ideas about whether and how the Corporation of London could improve the quality of their lives.

STATUS: Sponsored project

SOURCE OF GRANT: Thomas Coram Foundation £4,598

DATE OF RESEARCH: 1998-continuing

KEYWORDS: childhood attitudes; childrens services; urban environment; urban youth; youth attitudes

1404

Institute of Education, Thomas Coram Research Unit, 27-28 Woburn Square, London WC1H 0AA
0171 612 6957

Mooney, A. Ms

The long term effects of early non-parental day care on children's development

ABSTRACT: There is much interest in how maternal employment and early non-parental day care may affect children and their families. Yet much of the research in this area has focused on developmental outcomes of early childhood. The Thomas Coram Research Unit Day Care project, a major longitudinal study of couples who began parenting in the 1980s, presents a unique opportunity to examine the long-term effects of early day care experiences of these families. However, the success of a follow-up to the Day Care project will depend on the number of families who are available from the original sample. A 3-month pilot study has been funded to explore the feasibility of conducting a full-scale study which would focus on the relationship between early childcare experience, parental employment and cognitive and educational outcomes at 16-17 years of age. The pilot study will seek to contact the 215 families who were last contacted in 1993. To assess the feasibility of a full-scale study, the characteristics of the families agreeing to participate in a further round of data collection will be compared to those families who cannot be found or refuse to participate.

STATUS: Sponsored project

SOURCE OF GRANT: Joseph Rowntree Foundation £11,619

DATE OF RESEARCH: 1999-continuing

KEYWORDS: child development; child rearing; day care; early experience; employed parents; outcomes of education

1405

Institute of Education, Thomas Coram Research Unit, 27-28 Woburn Square, London WC1H 0AA
0171 612 6957

Owen, C. Mr; Mooney, A. Ms; Moss, P. Mr

Who cares? Childminding in the 1990s

ABSTRACT: The aim of the project is to study childminders as a distinctive group within the total child care workforce, and their place in the overall provision of childcare for children with employed parents. It aims to: 1) analyse the place of childminding in the provision of child care for children with employed parents and in relation to other forms of child care; 2) examine the education and employment histories of childminders; 3) examine the employment situation of childminders; 4) examine the views, motivation, commitment and satisfaction of childminders with respect to their work, including their views on different forms of organisation and status.

STATUS: Sponsored project

SOURCE OF GRANT: Joseph Rowntree Foundation £75,579

DATE OF RESEARCH: 1999-continuing

KEYWORDS: child caregivers; child minders; day care

1406

Institute of Education, Thomas Coram Research Unit, 27-28 Woburn Square, London WC1H 0AA
0171 612 6957

Petrie, P. Dr; Moss, P. Mr

Transforming children's services

ABSTRACT: The general aim of this project is to stimulate and support a fundamental re-thinking of the purposes, organisation and staffing of 'children's services', a term covering a wide range of services providing education, care, play, leisure and other opportunities for children amongst which schools play a major part. This will involve the preparation, publication and dissemination of a major report. The report will provide analysis of current inadequacies in children's services; a vision of what a transformed children's services might look like; and specific proposals for the steps needed to make that vision a reality over a specified period of time. The report will draw on examples of institutions and agencies which are already attempting to transform children's services, both in this country and abroad, as well as engaging a number of 'wise helpers' to assist in its preparation.

STATUS: Sponsored project

SOURCE OF GRANT: Paul Hamlyn Foundation £20,000

DATE OF RESEARCH: 1998-continuing

KEYWORDS: agency cooperation; childrens services

1407

Institute of Education, Thomas Coram Research Unit, 27-28 Woburn Square, London WC1H 0AA
0171 612 6957

Pugh, G. Ms; Moss, P. Mr

Coram community campus: a multi-agency child care network

ABSTRACT: The aim of the project is to contribute both to the development and evaluation of the Coram Children's Campus, an innovatory multi-agency and multi-functional model of service provision for young children and their families. The model offers a comprehensive, coherent and flexible approach to the needs of families through mainstream services, which are accessible and responsive to the varied needs of a diverse and economically disadvantaged community. The replicability of the model will be assessed. Work will also be undertaken to develop and apply methods that give children a voice both in the service and its evaluation. The project will involve 3 main components: a case study of the process of developing the service; interview based work with families; and an exploratory study of how to give meaning to the 'voice of the child'.

STATUS: Sponsored project

SOURCE OF GRANT: Joseph Rowntree Foundation £87,443

DATE OF RESEARCH: 1998-continuing

KEYWORDS: agency cooperation; childrens services; social services

1408

Institute of Education, Thomas Coram Research Unit, 27-28 Woburn Square, London WC1H 0AA
0171 6512 6957

Storey, P. Ms; Brannen, J. Dr

Young people and transport: access and opportunity

ABSTRACT: In rural areas, young people's access to personal mobility is particularly affected by their resources and consequently their access to education, training and employment. This project will raise the profile of the particular difficulties which face young people in rural areas as they enter further education, training and the job market. The main component is a case study conducted in rural areas of Somerset and Dorset. Data will be collected from 3 age groups (15, 17 and 23) of young people. These 3 age groups have been selected to represent key stages in rural young people's life cycles with regard to their transition to independent mobility. Data will be collected via focus groups, questionnaires and interviews. Forums in the case study area with young people and local public transport providers and managers to review the study and to develop local needs led service.

STATUS: Sponsored project

SOURCE OF GRANT: Joseph Rowntree Foundation £73,283

DATE OF RESEARCH: 1998-continuing

KEYWORDS: access to education; adolescents; mobility; rural environment; transport; youth

1409

Institute of Education, Thomas Coram Research Unit, 27-28 Woburn Square, London WC1H 0AA
0171 612 6957

Munton, A. Dr; Mooney, A. Ms

Promoting family support through childcare services

ABSTRACT: Historically, there has been little in the way of support services for families experiencing difficulties in Hungary. As a result, children have often been taken into state institutional care. Policy in this area has now changed. Under recent legislation, local authorities are required to establish a comprehensive and coordinated system of family support services. The project will specifically address the need for Hungarian local authorities to develop a new policy and practice, offering local authorities the benefit of learning from UK experience in this area. Through seminars and practice exchange, Hungarian and British colleagues will share information about modes of good practice. The project capitalises on the collaborative partnership between Bolcsodek Orszagos Modszertani Intezete (BOMI), Thomas Coram Research Unit and Save the Children Fund established during previous work funded by the British Council.

STATUS: Sponsored project

SOURCE OF GRANT: British Council £6,000

DATE OF RESEARCH: 1998-continuing

KEYWORDS: **child welfare; hungary**

1410

Institute of Education, Thomas Coram Research Unit, 27-28 Woburn Square, London WC1H 0AA
0171 612 6957

Tizard, B. Prof.

A study of academic retirement

ABSTRACT: The context of this proposal is the increasingly long and healthy proportion of the life span spent in retirement, with the consequent loss to society of potential productivity. Whilst many welcome retirement, academics are one group where some are reluctant to retire. As a basis for discussion about possible innovations to enable those who wish to do so to continue to be academically productive, it is proposed to obtain a detailed description from a large national sample of retired academics of their activities, academic or otherwise, the academic support they receive and would like, and their academic aspirations. The findings will be analysed in relation to such factors as age, gender, state of health, discipline, and level of pre-retirement academic productivity.

STATUS: Sponsored project

SOURCE OF GRANT: Nuffield Foundation £4,895

DATE OF RESEARCH: 1998-continuing

KEYWORDS: **academic staff; lecturers; retirement; teachers; teaching profession**

1411

Institute of Education, Thomas Coram Research Unit, 27-28 Woburn Square, London WC1H 0AA
0171 612 6957

Monck, E. Dr

Effects of concurrent planning in adoption of children under 9 years old

ABSTRACT: The progress of children from families showing high risk of neglect and/or abuse will be assessed over 2 years when they are referred to a specialist agency undertaking concurrent (compared to sequential) planning for rehabilitation with parent(s) or adoption. Two matched comparison groups (one with the same agency, but referred after extensive local authority social services input; the other receiving only social services input) will be followed for 2 years. The older children, birth parents and fostering/adopting parents will be separately interviewed, and aspects of successful placement will be assessed.

STATUS: Sponsored project

SOURCE OF GRANT: Nuffield Foundation £134,000

DATE OF RESEARCH: 1998-continuing

KEYWORDS: **adoption; child welfare; foster care**

1412

Institute of Education, Thomas Coram Research Unit, 27-28 Woburn Square, London WC1H 0AA
0171 612 6957

Aggleton, P. Prof.

Impact evaluation of Health Education Authority (HEA)/Standing Conference on Drug Abuse (SCODA) LOCATE Service

ABSTRACT: The principal aim of the work will be to provide evaluation support to the Health Education Authority (HEA)/Standing Conference on Drug Abuse (SCODA) LOCATE Drug Education and Prevention Service, and to offer an overview of the principal achievements of the service. It will do this by: 1) reviewing data collected through the monitoring forms used with enquiries to the service; 2) undertaking telephone interviews with a sample of enquirers to determine how useful they have found the information and advice they have received and in what ways their work has been affected by contact with the LOCATE service; 3) working with LOCATE staff to review the existing monitoring process, and provide training in monitoring and evaluation; 4) undertaking a collaborative review of the mapping process undertaken by SCODA and offer a set of recommendations on enhancing data collection; 5) preparing a review of the impact of the LOCATE Service as a whole.

STATUS: Sponsored project

SOURCE OF GRANT: Health Education Authority £19,648

DATE OF RESEARCH: 1998-continuing

KEYWORDS: **drug education; health education**

1413

Institute of Education, Thomas Coram Research Unit, 27-28 Woburn Square, London WC1H 0AA
0171 612 6957
London University, Institute of Education, 20 Bedford Way, London WC1H 0AL
0171 580 1122

Aggleton, P. Prof.; Whitty, G. Prof.

A review of effectiveness of training of health professionals in health promotion

ABSTRACT: As part of work to support the achievement of national targets set out in The Health of the Nation, and other local targets, the Health Education Authority (HEA) has prioritised work to enhance the capacity of health professionals, National Health Service managers and purchasers, and alliance partners to undertake and promote health promotion locally and nationally. This requires an improved knowledge base about the effectiveness of different kinds of training and professional development, as well as a better understanding of the above groups' training and support needs. In order to facilitate this, the HEA has commissioned a review of the research literature examining the effectiveness of the training currently received by professionals in health promotion.

STATUS: Sponsored project

SOURCE OF GRANT: Health Education Authority

DATE OF RESEARCH: 1996-1997

KEYWORDS: **health personnel; health promotion; health services; professional continuing education; professional development; training**

1414

Institute of Education, Thomas Coram Research Unit, 27-28 Woburn Square, London WC1H 0AA
0171 612 6957
London University, Institute of Education, 20 Bedford Way, London WC1H 0AL
0171 580 1122

Aggleton, P. Prof.; Whitty, G. Prof.

Young people's health network evaluation project

ABSTRACT: This project is intended to promote the effective evaluation of health promotion interventions with young people. It will identify evaluation styles appropriate for such interventions and gather evidence about the evaluation approaches used in a range of health-related projects in a variety of formal and informal settings. The findings of the study will be used to develop resource materials and training courses on evaluation for those working in health promotion with young people.

STATUS: Sponsored project

SOURCE OF GRANT: Health Education Authority £54,982

DATE OF RESEARCH: 1997-continuing

KEYWORDS: health education; health promotion; programme evaluation

1415

Institute of Education, Thomas Coram Research Unit, 27-28 Woburn Square, London WC1H 0AA
0171 612 6957
Oxford University, Department of Educational Studies, 15 Norham Gardens, Oxford OX2 6PY
01865 274024
London University, Institute of Education, Department of Primary Education, 20 Bedford Way, London WC1H 0AL
0171 580 1122

Hurry, J. Dr; Sylva, K. Prof.; Riley, J. Dr

Improving literacy teaching at National Curriculum key stage 1 through inservice

ABSTRACT: The study is an evaluation of a classroom programme for teaching literacy at National Curriculum key stage 1. The evaluation was carried out in reception classes in 12 inner London schools. Children were tested at the beginning and end of the year and classrooms were observed. The intervention group was compared with a comparison group and the innovative literacy programme was shown to be effective at raising children's reading scores.

STATUS: Sponsored project

SOURCE OF GRANT: Esmee Fairbairn Charitable Trust

DATE OF RESEARCH: 1996-1997

KEYWORDS: inservice teacher education; key stage 1; literacy education; primary education; reading teaching; reception classes; writing skills

1416

King's College, School of Education, Cornwall House, Waterloo Road, London SE1 8WA
0171 836 5454

Johnson, D. Prof.; Shayer, M. Dr; Adhami, M. Mr

Cognitive Acceleration in Mathematics Education (CAME)

ABSTRACT: It is well documented that many pupils 'mark time' in secondary school mathematics - and research has identified many misconceptions held, and errors made, by large number of pupils in the age range 11-16. Recent work in science education (the Cognitive Acceleration in Science Education (CASE) project) has demonstrated the potential for addressing the problems through changes in teaching which focus on developing pupils' ability to think. The main aim of the present project, Cognitive Acceleration in Mathematics Education (CAME) is to develop exemplary lessons in mathematics, embodying teaching and class-management skills which include a focus on intervention (learning activity aimed at increasing, or accelerating, intellectual development), as distinguished from instruction (utilising pupils' present competence to process mathematical concepts and procedures). The work seeks to embed the psychological principles of Concrete Preparation, Cognitive Conflict, Metacognition, Bridging and Zone of Proximal Development (ZPD) in planned/structured tasks which also facilitate pupil-pupil interaction, within the context of school mathematics in Years 7 and 8. Hence, this research represents a validation and implementation study of the feasibility of integrating in practice, recent developments in the fields of cognitive psychology, mathematics education research, and social psychology. Development work is being carried out with four teachers/classes in four schools in the London and Cambridge areas. Data collection is both quantitative, e.g. pre- and post-tests (of a larger cohort), and qualitative, e.g. detailed observation notes of CAME lessons.

STATUS: Sponsored project

SOURCE OF GRANT: Leverhulme Trust £108,890

DATE OF RESEARCH: 1993-1998

KEYWORDS: cognitive ability; intervention; learning strategies; mathematics education; secondary education; teaching methods

1417

King's College, School of Education, Cornwall House, Waterloo Road, London SE1 8WA
0171 836 5454

Ball, S. Prof.; Maguire, M. Dr; Macrae, S. Dr

Education markets in the post-16 sector of one urban locale

ABSTRACT: The research focuses on the post-16 transition in one local, urban, education and training market. It explores the market behaviours of producers (schools, colleges, employers etc), the choice making of consumers (students, parents) and the processes of transition and distribution of destinations. The project has 5 main aims: 1) to describe and begin to explain the dynamics of post-16 education and training markets in the urban context; 2) to explore and begin to explain choice-making (parents and young people) within post-16 provision and the role played by educational intermediaries in this process; 3) to explore and begin to explain the role played by differences in material, culture and social capital in the processes and possibilities of choice, particularly as these relate to 'race', class and gender; 4) to identify and begin to explore the nature of what we refer to as the 'informal learning society': that is, the experiences and prospects of those young people post-16, who fall outside education, training and paid employment; 5) to describe and analyse the market behaviour of the main providers in the post-16 education and training phase. A short questionnaire will be administered to a whole Year 11 cohort (110 students) in one local education authority (LEA) school and one local pupil referral unit (PRU). Interviews will take place with: 59 students, each interviewed 3 times; 10 parents, each interviewed once; 36 providers of education and training, each interviewed once; 15 intermediaries, each interviewed once. The overall intention is to create as full a picture as possible of the students' transition from school to their first year of post-16 experience, shaped by the dynamics of competition and perceived choice within our local market.

PUBLISHED MATERIAL: MACRAE, S., MAGUIRE, M. & BALL, S.J. (1996). 'Opportunity knocks: choice in the post-16 education and training market'. In: FOSKETT. N.H. (Ed). Markets and education: policy process and practice: Proceedings of an international symposium organised by the Centre for Research in Education Marketing, University of Southampton. Southampton: University of Southampton, School of Education, Centre for Research in Education Marketing. ; MACRAE, S., MAGUIRE, M. & BALL, S.J. (1997). 'Competition, choice and hierarchy in a post-16 education and training market'. In: TOMLINSON, S. (Ed). Education 14-19: critical perspectives. London: Athlone Press.

STATUS: Sponsored project

SOURCE OF GRANT: Economic and Social Research Council £101,850

DATE OF RESEARCH: 1995-1998

KEYWORDS: career choice; labour market; school leavers; school to work transition; sixteen to nineteen education; training

1418

King's College, School of Education, Cornwall House, Waterloo Road, London SE1 8WA
0171 836 5454

Maguire, M. Dr; Jones, C. Ms

An investigation into the school experience of ethnic minority student teachers

ABSTRACT: The investigation will provide an account of the in-school experiences of student teachers from black and other ethnic minority heritages during their Postgraduate Certificate in Education (PGCE) course. The project intends to explore the task of school-based mentoring as this constitutes a critical element in the successful passage through the training course. The study is ethnographic in design. A sample of students will be interviewed (6 white and 12 ethnic minority students will become key informants). Questionnaire data will be elicited from the whole cohort at 2 key points in the course. School teacher mentors will also be interviewed. The objectives of this research are: to accumulate data relating to the in-school experiences of ethnic minority student teachers in the new school focused courses; to contribute to knowledge and understanding in the areas of teacher 'race' relations and contemporary teacher education; as well as to consider the complexities involved in policy enactment (teacher education reforms and the drive to recruit ethnic minority teachers).

STATUS: Sponsored project

SOURCE OF GRANT: Economic and Social Research Council £29,197

DATE OF RESEARCH: 1995-1997

KEYWORDS: **black students; black teachers; ethnic groups; mentors; preservice teacher education; school based teacher education; student experience; student teachers**

1419

King's College, School of Education, Cornwall House, Waterloo Road, London SE1 8WA
0171 836 5454

Millett, A. Dr; Johnson, D. Prof.

OFSTED and primary mathematics: a critical analysis of policy and its interpretations

ABSTRACT: The overall aim of the research is to provide clarification of the range of interpretations regarding the improvement of primary mathematics through inspection. It cannot be assumed that there is any unambiguous interpretaton of government policy in regard to primary school mathematics, even by those involved in the inspection process itself. In the light of the ongoing public debate about standards in school mathematics, consistency in interpretation is of critical importance, particularly for the recipients of the process - schools, teachers and pupils. Qualitative methods of data collection and analysis will focus on 3 levels of interpretation of the Office for Standards in Education (OFSTED) policy towards primary mathematics: 1) Policy implementation, review and promotion - the analysis of policy through a critical study of selected government publications (OFSTED and School Curriculum and Assessment Authority (SCAA) and interviews with key personnel in the inspection process (4 interviews). 2) Those who carry out inspections in schools - interviews with primary inspectors (10 interviews) to identify any match or mismatch between interpretations of policy as elicited in the first level analyses and those of the inspectors who visit schools; the analysis of empirical evidence from inspections through a study of official inspection reports and the evidence on which they were based. 3) Schools which have been the subject of recent inspection - interviews with headteachers and mathematics coordinators in schools, which have recently been inspected (8 interviews), to investigate whether/how the priorities and views of the mathematics in the school as reported by the inspectors corresponded with their own.

STATUS: Sponsored project

SOURCE OF GRANT: Economic and Social Research Council £41,444

DATE OF RESEARCH: 1996-1997

KEYWORDS: **educational policy; educational quality; inspection; mathematics education; ofsted; primary education; school improvement**

1420

King's College, School of Education, Cornwall House, Waterloo Road, London SE1 8WA
0171 836 5454

Brown, M. Prof.; Johnson, D. Prof.; Street, B. Prof.; Wiliam, D. Dr; Askew, M. Mr

Leverhulme numeracy research programme

ABSTRACT: The research programme has a major focus on pupil attainment in numeracy, and effective ways of improving numeracy standards. The substantial experience and expertise in applied research in primary numeracy of the mathematics education staff in the School of Education places King's College in a unique position to mount this comprehensive programme of further research in this area which will take forward understanding of the nature and causes of low achievement in numeracy and provide insights into effective strategies for remedying the situation. It is expected that at the end of the 5 years the programme of research will have contributed towards: 1) understanding of the 'critical' points in progression in primary mathematics; 2) knowledge of how classroom practices influence standards of attainment; 3) identifying training and intervention strategies that demonstrably influence teachers' practices and pupil attainment; 4)

understanding the mechanisms of teacher change at both the individual and school level; and 5) understanding how schooling and 'social' factors interact in the development of numerate pupils. A review of a number of attempts to explain weaknesses in attainment suggested that the framework taken for the research programme includes the following factors: 1) classroom practice factors; 2) teacher factors; 3) school factors; 4) social context factors. The research consists of a core longitudinal project and 5 focus projects linked to it and to one another. The 5-year nature of the funding allows a unique opportunity for longitudinal study of progression in the development of numeracy in a significant sample of pupils, reflecting the long time-scales represented in school schemes of work and required for pupil learning.

STATUS: Sponsored project

SOURCE OF GRANT: Leverhulme Trust

DATE OF RESEARCH: 1997-continuing

KEYWORDS: **achievement; mathematics education; numeracy; teaching methods**

1421

King's College, School of Education, Cornwall House, Waterloo Road, London SE1 8WA
0171 836 5454

Collins, S. Ms; *Supervisor*: Osborne, J. Dr

Pupils, parents and teachers views of the school science curriculum and its contribution to the public understanding and appreciation of science

ABSTRACT: This research seeks to determine the views of pupils, parents and science teachers about the school science curriculum and, in particular, to ascertain those aspects of science education which these groups would value and perceive as relevant. It is a response to the need to inform the current debate on the school science curriculum in the UK and to represent the voice of parents and pupils in the debate so as to guide policy decisions on its possible reform in the year 2000 and beyond. The research will be undertaken using 40 focus groups of pupils or parents, separated by 3 dimensions - pupils v parents, male v female and scientific v non-scientific, drawn from mixed, full ability comprehensive schools in a range of areas. In the final phase, focus groups of science teachers will be used to determine their response to the main issues and themes emerging from the study with pupils and parents. This research seeks to understand and interpret the range of experiences and views, to document not only what these groups think about the content of science, but also why these views are held and how the curriculum could be improved to address their needs. A full report will be prepared and a summary report will be widely circulated. It is envisaged that the findings will be of major interest to the Qualifications and Curriculum Authority (QCA), professional scientific bodies and those engaged in promoting the public understanding of science.

STATUS: Sponsored project

SOURCE OF GRANT: Wellcome Foundation £89,000

DATE OF RESEARCH: 1997-continuing

KEYWORDS: **parent attitudes; public understanding of science; pupil attitudes; science curriculum; science education**

1422

King's College, School of Education, Cornwall House, Waterloo Road, London SE1 8WA
0171 836 5454

Lucey, H. Ms; Reay, D. Dr; *Supervisors*: Reay, D. Dr; Ball, S. Prof.

Secondary school transfer: children as consumers of education

ABSTRACT: This research project is an indepth study of the secondary school transfer process from the perspective of children. It will explore children's collective and individual understandings, experiences and negotiations of the process and will examine how they envisage the choices available to them. 125 children in 8 schools in 21 London Boroughs will be interviewed individually and in groups. These children will be in Year 6 of primary schooling. The group interviews will provide insights into how peer group norms operate while the individual interviews will allow for a concentration on particular children's experiences. The research will follow a target group of 40 children through into their destination secondary schools and will also draw on the perspectives of concerned adults by interviewing a sample of parents and primary and secondary school teachers. The dynamics of social factors will be examined, including social class, ethnicity, race, gender and religion in this transfer process.

STATUS: Sponsored project

SOURCE OF GRANT: Economic and Social Research Council £149,006

DATE OF RESEARCH: 1998-continuing

KEYWORDS: **parent choice; primary to secondary transition; secondary education; transfer pupils**

1423

London School of Economics and Political Science, Centre for Economic Performance, Houghton Street, London WC2A 2AE
0171 405 7686

Rogers, N. Mr

Graduate earnings 1974-1996

ABSTRACT: Using General Household Survey and Labour Force Survey data the study examines how far the graduate earnings premium has varied since the early 1970s and how far variations in the earnings premium can be explained within a supply and demand framework. Graduates' greater earnings provide a key indicator of the benefits of higher education to the individual and the economy as a whole. The study helps improve our understanding of the economic benefits of higher education and, in particular, inform our forecasts of the likely impact of the recent expansion of higher education and the new student support policies on the rates of return to higher education qualifications.

STATUS: Sponsored project

SOURCE OF GRANT: Department for Education and Employment £29,643

DATE OF RESEARCH: 1997-1998

KEYWORDS: **graduate employment; salaries**

1424

London School of Economics and Political Science, Centre for Educational Research, Houghton Street, London WC2A 2AE
0171 405 7686

Holdstock, C. Mrs; Noden, P. Dr; *Supervisor*: West, A. Dr

Evaluation and self-evaluation in the universities of Europe

ABSTRACT: This international project is examining evaluation in universities in 8 European countries. The research is looking at the various forms of evaluation that take place - internal and external evaluation, formal and informal evaluation, evaluation of teaching and non-teaching staff. In addition, the ways in which statistical indicators are used in evaluation are being explored. Other issues to be addressed include the link between higher education and employment. The countries involved in the research are: France, Italy, Norway, Germany, the UK, Portugal, Spain and Finland. The research methodology includes an analysis of the current state of play in the countries concerned and case studies of evaluation in 3 or 4 universities per country.

STATUS: Sponsored project

SOURCE OF GRANT: European Commission: DGXII

DATE OF RESEARCH: 1996-1998

KEYWORDS: **comparative education; educational quality; europe; evaluation; higher education; institutional evaluation; performance indicators; quality control; self evaluation - groups; universities**

1425

London School of Economics and Political Science, Centre for Educational Research, Houghton Street, London WC2A 2AE
0171 405 7686
London University, London School of Economics and Political Science, Greater London Group, Houghton Street, London WC2A 2AE
0181 672 9944
St George's Hospital Medical School, Department of Psychology, Cranmer Terrace, London SW17 0RE

Pennell, H. Ms; West, R. Prof.; Travers, T. Mr; *Supervisor*: West, A. Dr

The financing of school-based education

ABSTRACT: This research is focusing on the financing of school-based education in England. It looks at the allocation of resources by central governmnent to local government and by local government to schools. The aims are, first of all, to establish how the education budget is determined in a sample of local education authorities (LEAs) in authorities of different types; secondly, to establish factors involved in determining the education budget at the local authority level; thirdly, to establish how priorities within the education budget are determined, particularly in relation to under-fives education and the balance between primary and secondary funding; fourthly, to establish how money allocated for 'additional educational needs' - including for example, social disadvantage, non-statemented special educational needs, English as a second language - is used at school level; and finally, to propose alternative approaches to the funding of school-based education.

STATUS: Sponsored project

SOURCE OF GRANT: Economic and Social Research Council

DATE OF RESEARCH: 1996-continuing

KEYWORDS: **additional educational needs; early childhood education; economics education relationship; educational finance; local education authorities; primary education; secondary education**

1426

London School of Economics and Political Science, Centre for Educational Research, Houghton Street, London WC2A 2AE
0171 405 7686

Gosling, R. Mrs; Holdstock, C. Mrs; *Supervisor*: West, A. Dr

Quality in higher education: an international perspective

ABSTRACT: This research project is focusing on quality in higher education using an international perspective. It aims first of all to explore the various ways in which quality in higher education is perceived by two groups of 'consumers' of higher education - employers and students; secondly, to examine what sort of information is used to determine choices made - i.e. universities selected by students and graduates appointed by employers; thirdly, to explore the aims of higher education; and finally, to analyse the policy implications arising from the research findings in relation to both the providers of higher education - the government and universities - and the consumers of higher education. The research is being carried out by means of interviews with employers in multinational companies in the UK, France, Australia and the USA and by means of interviews with students. The methodology is primarily qualitative.

STATUS: Sponsored project

SOURCE OF GRANT: British Petroleum

DATE OF RESEARCH: 1995-1998

KEYWORDS: **educational quality; employer attitudes; employers; higher education; student attitudes; universities; university choice; work education relationship**

1427

London School of Economics and Political Science, Centre for Educational Research, Houghton Street, London WC2A 2AE
0171 405 7686

Pennell, H. Ms; Noden, P. Dr; Edge, A. Mrs; *Supervisor*: West, A. Dr

Educational reforms, choice and diversity

ABSTRACT: This research has been examining the ways in which the 'market reforms' in education in England and Wales are affecting choices for secondary schools made by parents, the ways in which schools are selecting pupils, and the ways in which schools are diversifying in response to the reforms. A range of themes have been explored including changing schools' admissions policies, the new types of schools that have been created, how the reforms have affected equity and the regulatory mechanisims that are needed to ensure equity. The research has been carried out by means of analysis of data from a variety of sources.

PUBLISHED MATERIAL: WEST, A. & PENNELL, H. (1996). 'Changing admissions policies and practices in Inner London: implications for policy'. In: GLATTER, R., WOODS, P.A. & BAGLEY, C. (Eds). Choice and diversity in schooling: perspectives and prospects. London: Routledge. ; WEST, A., PENNELL, H. & EDGE, A. 'Exploring the impact of school enrolment policies in England', Educational

Administration Quarterly. (in press). ; WEST, A. & PENNELL, H. 'Educational reform and school choice in England and Wales', Educational Economics. (in press).

STATUS: Team research

DATE OF RESEARCH: 1995-1998

***KEYWORDS*: admission criteria; educational change; parent choice; secondary education; selection**

1428

London School of Economics and Political Science, Centre for Educational Research, Houghton Street, London WC2A 2AE
0171 405 7686

Edge, A. Mrs; Stokes, E. Mrs; *Supervisor*: West, A. Dr

Quality and assessment in secondary education

ABSTRACT: This research focuses on quality as it relates to standards of outcomes in education. The overall aim is to establish the curriculum followed in the countries of the European Union/European Economic Area in specific subject areas and to explore the forms of assessment used (examinations and school-based assessment). The objectives are: 1) to describe and analyse the form and content of assessment at/around the end of lower secondary education and at the end of upper secondary general education with a particular focus on mathematics, science, the language of instruction and modern foreign languages; 2) to relate the assessment to the syllabus and curriculum followed; 3) to compare and contrast the curriculum coverage in these subjects and in the assessments carried out, and to highlight both common and unique features; and 4) to examine the outcomes at the end of lower secondary education and upper secondary general education.

STATUS: Sponsored project

SOURCE OF GRANT: European Commission: DGXXII, SOCRATES Programme Action III 3.1

DATE OF RESEARCH: 1996-1998

***KEYWORDS*: comparative education; curriculum; educational quality; europe; outcomes of education; secondary education**

1429

London School of Economics and Political Science, Centre for Educational Research, Houghton Street, London WC2A 2AE
0171 405 7686

Noden, P. Dr; *Supervisor*: West, A. Dr

Examining the impact of the specialist schools programme

ABSTRACT: This is a study financed by the Department for Education and Employment (DfEE). The overall aim of the project is to examine the impact of the specialist schools programme on participating schools and to identify 'good practice' for wider dissemination. An evaluation-type methodology is being used to examine the specialist schools programme in terms of inputs, processes, outputs and outcomes. In addition, a framework for measuring cost-effectiveness is being developed in conjunction with two consultants who are working on the project.

STATUS: Sponsored project

SOURCE OF GRANT: Department for Education and Employment

DATE OF RESEARCH: 1998-continuing

***KEYWORDS*: art colleges; language colleges; specialist schools; sports colleges; technology colleges**

1430

London School of Economics and Political Science, Centre for Educational Research, Houghton Street, London WC2A 2AE
0171 405 7686

West, A. Dr

Vocational education and training indicators: effectiveness of initial vocation education and training and training for the unemployed

ABSTRACT: This project is funded by the Centre for the Development of Vocational Training (CEDEFOP) and aims at developing a set of indicators to improve our understanding of the performance of initial vocation education and training for the unemployed. The project is designed to supplement the ongoing work within the Commission with the objective being to develop a new set of indicators that are concerned with the effectiveness of training.

STATUS: Sponsored project

SOURCE OF GRANT: Centre for the Development of Vocational Training (CEDEFOP)

DATE OF RESEARCH: 1998-continuing

***KEYWORDS*: educational quality; performance indicators; training; unemployment; vocational education**

1431

London School of Economics and Political Science, Centre for Educational Research, Houghton Street, London WC2A 2AE
0171 405 7686

Edge, A. Mrs; Stokes, E. Mrs; *Supervisor*: West, A. Dr

Examination and assessment of data on foreign language learning

ABSTRACT: This study, funded by the European Commission, has 4 main objectives: 1) It involves an assessment of the information required for initial and continuing vocational training purposes at community level on foreign language learning and competences. 2) It involves an evaluation following a common framework of the data already existing on foreign language learning and competences at regional, member state and community level. 3) New statistical indicators are to be developed. 4) Proposals for scenarios for possible data collection instruments at European Community level are to be proposed.

STATUS: Sponsored project

SOURCE OF GRANT: European Commission DG XXII

DATE OF RESEARCH: 1998-continuing

***KEYWORDS*: comparative education; europe; modern language studies; training; vocational education**

1432

London School of Economics and Political Science, Centre for Educational Research, Houghton Street, London WC2A 2AE
0171 405 7686

Dimitropoulos, A. Mr; *Supervisor*: West, A. Dr

Higher education admissions and student mobility within the European Union

ABSTRACT: This is a large research study funded by the European Commission and coordinated by the London School of Economics. It involves 5 countries the UK, France, Germany, Sweden and Greece. The overarching objective of the project is to shed light on higher education admissions policies and practices at national and university levels and to relate these to student mobility. In doing so it will examine the barriers to student mobility and the characteristics of students who choose to study in other European Union countries. It will also examine the forms of innovation needed to enhance student mobility.

STATUS: Sponsored project

SOURCE OF GRANT: European Commission DGXII

DATE OF RESEARCH: 1998-continuing

***KEYWORDS*: admission criteria; comparative education; europe; higher education; student mobility**

1433

London School of Economics and Political Science, Department of Social Policy and Administration, Houghton Street, London WC2A 2AE
0171 405 7686

Marques Cardoso, C. Ms; *Supervisor*: Glennerster, H. Prof.

Decentralised management of schools and school autonomy: education reforms in England and Portugal

ABSTRACT: The origins of the school reforms in England and Portugal - Local Management of Schools in England and school autonomy in Portugal, and an analysis of the implementation of barriers and politics of reform in the two countries.

STATUS: Individual research

DATE OF RESEARCH: 1992-1998

KEYWORDS: **comparative education; educational change; educational policy; local management of schools; portugal; school based management**

1434

London School of Economics and Political Science, Department of Social Policy and Administration, Houghton Street, London WC2A 2AE
0171 405 7686

Hendry, R. Mr; *Supervisors*: Glennerster, H. Prof.; Hills, J. Mr; Travers, T. Mr
Formula funding

ABSTRACT: The research investigates the means by which different social departments of government allocate resources to subordinate agencies using some method of formula funding. The particular departments of state and services involved are - education (schools), housing and health. The aim is to: 1) trace the evolution of formula funding; 2) trace the methods that are currently used both to justify and apply the formulae; 3) compare and contrast common approaches and differences; 4) bring the various factors together from different agencies, local and national; and 5) discuss how the nature of funding formulae affect the behaviour of local agencies. The methods used are documentary analysis and extensive interviewing.

STATUS: Sponsored project

SOURCE OF GRANT: Economic and Social Research Council

DATE OF RESEARCH: 1996-continuing

KEYWORDS: **educational finance; resource allocation; school support**

1435

Royal Holloway, Department of Psychology, Egham Hill, Egham TW20 0EX
01784 434455

Wilding, J. Dr; Tickle, S. Mrs
Learning styles and other factors associated with student performance

ABSTRACT: Measures of students' approaches to learning, and various personality factors, are being collected in a longitudinal study of the relation of such measures to academic performance, and the nature of changes over the undergraduate course in approaches and performances.

PUBLISHED MATERIAL: WILDING, J. & VALENTINE, E. (1992). 'Factors predicting success and failure in the first year examinations of medical and dental courses', Applied Cognitive Psychology, Vol 6, No 3, pp.247-261. ; WILDING, J. & HAYES, S. (1992). 'Relations between approaches to studying and note-taking behaviour in lectures'. Applied Cognitive Psychology, Vol 6, No 3, pp.233-246.

STATUS: Individual research

DATE OF RESEARCH: 1988-continuing

KEYWORDS: **learning strategies; study skills**

1436

Royal Holloway, Department of Psychology, Egham Hill, Egham TW20 0EX
01784 434455

Wilding, J. Dr; Valentine, E. Dr
Memory ability

ABSTRACT: A study of memory in teenage samples has supported the view that a general memory ability operating across a range of tasks can be identified which is distinct from general intelligence. This ability predicted 10 to 20% of the variance in a measure of performance in the GCSE public examination. Projected work includes a study of subjects with unusual ability for memorising number sequences and use of brain scanning techniques with subjects showing unusual memory ability.

PUBLISHED MATERIAL: WILDING, J. & VALENTINE, E. (1994). 'Memory champions', British Journal of Psychology, Vol 85, No 2, pp.231-244. ; WILDING, J. & VALENTINE, E. (1994). 'Mnemonic wizardry with the telephone directory - but stories are another story', British Journal of Psychology, Vol 85, No 4, pp.501-509. ; WILDING, J. & VALENTINE, E. (1997). Superior memory. Hove: Psychology Press.

STATUS: Sponsored project

SOURCE OF GRANT: Economic and Social Research Council

DATE OF RESEARCH: 1984-continuing

KEYWORDS: **cognitive ability; gifted; memory**

1437

Royal Holloway, Department of Psychology, Egham Hill, Egham TW20 0EX
01784 434455

Wilding, J. Dr
Attentional problems in children

ABSTRACT: The research aims to identify information-processing weaknesses in children rated by teachers as having poor attentional ability. A battery of computerised tests suitable for use with children has been developed. Results from one of these tasks, a test of ability to process visual information from several locations in parallel, correlate with teacher ratings of children's general attentional ability. It is hypothesised that children who show unstable attention in the classroom have a narrow attentional 'beam' and switch attention frequently from a main task in order to sample peripheral aspects of the environment. Further tests of this hypothesis are in progress.

PUBLISHED MATERIAL: GIANNOULIS, K. & WILDING, J. (1992). 'A deficit of iconic memory in children with attentional problems assigned to nurture groups', British Journal of Developmental Psychology, Vol 10, No 2, pp.199-201. ; WILDING, J. (1994). 'Attentional problems in the classroom and parallel processing ability', British Journal of Developmental Psychology, Vol 12, No 4, pp.539-553.

STATUS: Individual research

DATE OF RESEARCH: 1992-continuing

KEYWORDS: **attention; attention deficit disorders; concentration; hyperactivity**

1438

Royal Holloway, Department of Psychology, Egham Hill, Egham TW20 0EX
01784 434455

Wilding, J. Dr; Saeedi, N. Mrs; Pollicina, C. Mr
Use of computers with learning-disabled subjects

ABSTRACT: (A) Tasks are being developed on PC computers which are appropriate for different levels of handicap, using concept keyboards and touch screens for response. These enable measurement of ability, training in interaction with the computer and eventually use of the computer for other types of training and activity. (B) In cooperation with Anni Verdi in Rome, a program has been developed to measure and stimulate operational thinking. Performance by normal children aged 5-10 years has been assessed and baseline performance and improvement following training is being tested in a group of handicapped adults. Methods to assess memory ability and conceptual thought are also being developed.

STATUS: Individual research

DATE OF RESEARCH: 1990-continuing

KEYWORDS: **computer assisted learning; computer uses in education; concept keyboards; human computer interaction; information technology; learning disabilities; special educational needs; touch screens**

1439

Royal Holloway, Department of Psychology, Egham Hill, Egham TW20 0EX
01784 434455

Crowley, K. Mr; Wilding, J. Dr
Relations between musical ability and reading ability in children

ABSTRACT: A number of measures of musical ability and phonological competence are being collected from pre-readers in order to explore whether common underlying mechanisms exist. Follow-up measures of progress in reading will be collected and further tests are being devised to investigate communalities between the two areas of ability within a framework derived from the Working Memory Model of Baddeley and Hitch.

PUBLISHED MATERIAL: BARWICK, J., VALENTINE, E., WEST, J. & WILDING, J. (1989). 'Relations between reading and musical abilities', British Journal of Educational Psychology, Vol 59, pp.253-257.

STATUS: Individual research

DATE OF RESEARCH: 1992-continuing

KEYWORDS: **musical ability; phonology; reading ability**

1440

Royal Holloway, Department of Psychology, Egham Hill, Egham TW20 0EX
01784 434455

Williamon, R. Mr; *Supervisor*: Valentine, E. Dr

Memorization for music performance

ABSTRACT: The research focuses on expert memory to determine how less prepared musicians may implement the same learning techniques. Seven professional and seven intermediate pianists will perform three minuets from Bach's Notebook for Anna Magdalena Bach. The pieces are one page long, but their brisk tempos and demand for accuracy make them difficult to perform. Pianists will rate the complexity of each piece on eight dimensions: conceptual complexity, non-standard fingerings, technical difficulties, phrasing, dynamics, tempo, pedal use, and expressiveness. At each rehearsal, musicians will record themselves on a portable recorder. To ensure a relaxed consistent learning atmosphere, they will train in their own practice facilities; however, two consecutive final performances (recital setting) will be videotaped to evaluate the reliability of the learning procedures. A repeat performance, after a two-week repose, will test the musicians' retention.

STATUS: Individual research

DATE OF RESEARCH: 1996-continuing

KEYWORDS: **memory; music; music activities**

1441

Royal Holloway, Department of Psychology, Egham Hill, Egham TW20 0EX
01784 434455

Brewin, C. Prof.; Reynolds, M. Dr; Saxton, M. Dr

Promoting mental health in schoolchildren

ABSTRACT: Social stress lies behind many of the psychiatric disorders of childhood and adulthood. Psychiatric services are insufficient to treat more than a small proportion of vulnerable children, and this suggests that a preventive, community-based approach should be developed in parallel with more traditional specialist services. One obvious area to begin is to inculcate more effective ways of dealing with stress in schools. Research in the US has repeatedly demonstrated that programmed writing about stressful experiences over a comparatively brief period has beneficial effects on indices of stress such as immune function, absenteeism, and use of health services. This project will work with primary and secondary schools to adapt this research to a British context, including developing methods for reaching children with poor writing skills, and will evaluate the effectiveness of the methods in this new context.

STATUS: Sponsored project

SOURCE OF GRANT: Mental Health Foundation £29,056

DATE OF RESEARCH: 1997-1998

KEYWORDS: **coping; mental health; primary school pupils; secondary school pupils; stress - psychological; stress management**

1442

Royal Holloway, Department of Psychology, Egham Hill, Egham TW20 0EX
01784 434455

Funnell, E. Prof.; Pitchford, N. Dr

The effect of stroke on the development of reading in children

ABSTRACT: This study is designed to carry out the first systematic psycholinguistic investigation into the nature of reading disorders acquired at different ages by children who have suffered a stroke. 20 children with strokes affecting the language areas of the dominant hemisphere and 8 children with strokes to the non-dominant hemisphere will be studied. In phase 1 of the investigation, performance on standardised reading tests will be assessed according to the side of the brain affected and the age at which the stroke occurred. The results of this phase should show whether only strokes to the dominant hemisphere for language affect reading development and whether the severity varies according to the age at which the stroke occurs. In phase 2, performance on tests of particular reading processes will be reading age in order to know whether the pattern of the stroke

children's reading shows a normal, but delayed reading pattern, or whether the pattern deviates from the norm. In phases 3 and 4, children with specific reading deficits will be investigated more thoroughly and all children will be reassessed regularly to monitor reading progress. It is anticipated that the results of this project should enable early detection of children at risk of developing reading problems following stroke, and should also provide methods for evaluating individual children's difficulties and designing appropriate programmes for remediation.

PUBLISHED MATERIAL: PITCHFORD, N.J., FUNNELL, E., ELLIS, A.W., GREEN, S.H. & CHAPMAN, S. (1996). 'Recovery of spoken language in a 6 -year-old child following a left hemisphere stroke: a longitudinal study', Aphasiology, Vol 11, pp.83-102.

STATUS: Sponsored project

SOURCE OF GRANT: Medical Research Council £133,564

DATE OF RESEARCH: 1996-continuing

KEYWORDS: **language handicaps; medical conditions; reading ability; sick children; stroke**

1443

Royal Holloway, Department of Psychology, Egham Hill, Egham TW20 0EX
01784 434455
Lancaster University, Department of Psychology, Cartmel College, Bailrigg, Lancaster LA1 4YW
01524 65201

Hutton, U. M.; *Supervisors*: Towse, J. Dr; Hitch, G. Prof.

Strategic use of working memory resources in children and adults

ABSTRACT: The developmental increase in children's thinking (particularly during the primary school years) is self-evident. Not just in terms of the knowledge they possess, but in the style and capacity of their reasoning and thoughts. However, while the development itself is apparent, the psychological mechanisms - the cognitive strategies - underlying it are not fully understood. Previously, some researchers have argued that cognitive development can be characterised in terms of a working memory system with a relatively fixed processing capacity; the utilization of this capacity changes as mental operations become more efficient, so that tasks consume a smaller proportion of the total available resources which are freed for other purposes. However, there are alternative processing strategies which may be responsible for development; these theoretical positions deny that a single system is ubiquitously used, and place greater emphasis on the temporal dynamics of tasks in order to explain performance. By drawing upon and extending existing psychological measures of information processing, our work will attempt to discriminate between these competing theories, and provide experimental studies to compare them. Testing young children (and for comparison, adults) on different tasks will also help to reveal the similarities and differences in the processing of information related to skills such as reading and arithmetic.

STATUS: Sponsored project

SOURCE OF GRANT: Economic and Social Research Council £98,570

DATE OF RESEARCH: 1995-1998

KEYWORDS: **cognitive development; memory**

1444

University College London, Department of Psychology, Gower Street, London WC1E 6BT
0171 387 7050

Frederickson, N. Dr; *Supervisor*: Furnham, A. Prof.

The social acceptance of children with moderate learning difficulties in mainstream schools

ABSTRACT: The research aims to investigate and identify factors associated with the social acceptance of children with moderate learning difficulties who are integrated into mainstream middle schools. Methods of assessing social acceptance are first examined with a particular focus on the wide variety of methods which have been used for collecting and categorising sociometric information. A methodological study, carried out with a sample of 250 children, investigates the reliability and validity of a range of sociometric categorisation systems. The social acceptance of children with moderate learning difficulties (MLD) is then investigated through examining the distribution across sociometric categories of 114 MLD pupils aged 8-

12 years and their 1,227 mainstream classmates. Changes and continuities in social acceptance are explored through a 2-year follow-up of 40% of this sample. The third study of the series examines, separately for the mainstream (N=983) and MLD (N=108) populations, the relationship betweens social acceptance and a number of factors hypothesised or found in previous research to be associated with it. Aspects investigated in both the mainstream and MLD populations include behaviour, as reported by peers using the Guess Who Peer Assessment procedure; classroom social climate as assessed by the My Class Inventory (Fraser et al 1982). Aspects investigated in the MLD population include social adjustment as rated by class teachers using the Bristol Social Adjustment Guides (Stott 1974) and the class teacher's attitude to integration, assessed using the Classroom Integration Questionnaire (Kaufman et al 1985).

STATUS: Individual research

DATE OF RESEARCH: 1987-1993

***KEYWORDS*: classroom environment; learning disabilities; mainstreaming; pupil attitudes; pupil behaviour; social behaviour; special educational needs**

1445

University College London, Department of Psychology, Gower Street, London WC1E 6BT
0171 387 7050

Cameron, R. Dr; Frederickson, N. Dr

Market research survey for new part-time doctorate in educational psychology for practising educational psychologists

ABSTRACT: Professional training and practice in educational psychology have seen many changes during the past decade, however, these may eventually be regarded as relatively small when compared with predicted developments for the early years of the new millennium. In the case of Educational Psychology Services, the demands and expectations of customers - local education authorities, schools, parents, and allied services and disciplines - have generated ambitious new inservice training programmes for practising educational psychologists to enable them to keep abreast of a rapidly changing knowledge and skill base in psychology. From both inside the profession (GERSCH, I.S. (1997). 'Training matters', DECP Newsletter, No 77, pp.12-16) and outside (FREDERICKSON, N. & COLLINS, R. (1997). 'The future of professional training: views of aspiring applicants', Educational Psychology in Practice, Vol 12, No 3, pp.147-154) has come the recognition that current one-year Masters degree courses in Educational Psychology are unable to meet such a variety of demand. Very few people were surprised, therefore, when the recently recommended British Psychological Society accreditation criteria for professional training courses for chartered educational psychologists specified 3-year training from the year 2001 onwards (GERSCH, I.S. (1997). 'Radical changes in educational psychology training', The Psychologist, October 1997, pp.467-468). In the case of the University of London, approval has been given to a proposal from University College London and the Institute of Education to extend the current 1-year course to a 3-year Doctorate in Educational Psychology. At University College London, the objective is to establish a route by which experienced educational psychologists can update their skills and knowledge, and upgrade their qualifications. To achieve this, the need is to develop a Continuing Professional Development Doctorate in Educational Psychology course (part-time) to start in September 1998. The development proposal can be summarised as follows: 1) The use of focus-group methodology (MILLWARD, L. (1993). 'Focus groups'. In: BREAKWELL, G.M., HAMMOND, S. & FIFE-SHAW, C. (Eds). Research methods in psychology. London: Sage; VAUN, S., SCHUMM, J.S. & SINAGUB, J. (1996). Focus group interviews in education and psychology. London: Sage) to identify the major issues and themes for Educational Psychology Services in the London area relating to the proposal to extend the period of professional training for educational psychologists from 1 to 3 years. 2) A survey of the opinions of the major stakeholders in Educational Psychology - local education authority (LEA) officers, principal educational psychologists, mid-career educational psychologists, newly-qualified educational psychologists - across all the English local authority boroughs and counties. 3) Data from this survey would be used to refine and further develop the planned content and process of a 3-year, part-time Doctoral programme in Educational Psychology for practising educational psychologists. 4) The findings of this survey would also be written up for publication. As well as helping to shape the course of educational psychology

training in England and Wales, such a paper would also serendipitously highlight the benefits of the Doctorate in Educational Psychology course at University College London.

PUBLISHED MATERIAL: MILLWARD, L. (1993). 'Focus groups'. In: BREAKWELL, G.M., HAMMOND, S. & FIFE-SHAW, C. (Eds). Research methods in psychology. London: Sage. ; VAUHN, S., SCHUMM, J.S. & SINAGUB, J. (1996). Focus group interviews in education and psychology. London: Sage. ; MORRIS, S. (1997). 'Principal educational psychologists on extending professional training', DECP Newsletter, No 78, pp.26-31. ; FREDERICKSON, N. & COLLINS, R. (1997). 'The future of professional training: views of aspiring applicants', Educational Psychology in Practice, Vol 12, No 3, pp.147-154. ; GERSCH, I.S. (1997). 'Training matters', DECP Newsletter, No 77, pp.12-16.

STATUS: Sponsored project

SOURCE OF GRANT: Higher Education Funding Council £15,000

DATE OF RESEARCH: 1997-1998

***KEYWORDS*: educational psychologists; educational psychology; higher education; professional continuing education**

Loughborough University of Technology

1446

Department of Computer Studies, Loughborough LE11 3TU
01509 263171

Fish, J. Mr; *Supervisor*: Scrivener, S. Dr

Cognitive model for the design of sketching systems

ABSTRACT: A model is proposed for the mental representation of artist's sketches. Evidence is presented to support the theory that artists' sketches are hybrid images consisting of visible precept and a cognitive component of a superimposed mental image. It is further argued that sketches amplify the minds' ability to generate imagery from long term memory by facilitating translation between descriptive and depictive modes of representation. The model is used to suggest new improved computer software packages parts of which it is hoped to implement. The implication of the model for the way in which drawing is taught and the future use of sketching systems in education is analysed.

PUBLISHED MATERIAL: FISH, J.C.H. & SCRIVENER, S. (1990). 'Amplifying the mind's eye: sketching and visual cognition', Leonardo, Vol 23, No 1.

STATUS: Individual research

DATE OF RESEARCH: 1983-1993

***KEYWORDS*: computer assisted design; computer graphics; drawing**

1447

Department of Education, Loughborough LE11 3TU
01509 263171

Reid, I. Prof.

The development and application of socio-spatial indices

ABSTRACT: This project looks at the use of commercially based post code applications to school populations to allow for comparisons, and the construction and application of the derived scale of social advantage/social deprivation to school and pupil performance.

STATUS: Sponsored project

SOURCE OF GRANT: Bradford Metropolitan Council, Directorate of Education

DATE OF RESEARCH: 1990-1993

***KEYWORDS*: academic achievement; performance factors; scaling; school effectiveness; social environment; socioeconomic influences**

1448

Department of Education, Loughborough LE11 3TU
01509 263171

Demaine, J. Dr

Citizenship and education

ABSTRACT: A study of the concept of citizenship in the context of the National Curriculum requirement for teaching in schools.

STATUS: Individual research

DATE OF RESEARCH: 1991-1993

KEYWORDS: **citizenship education; national curriculum**

1449

Department of Education, Loughborough LE11 3TU
01509 263171

Demaine, J. Dr

Student evaluation of teaching in higher education in the UK

ABSTRACT: An investigation into student evaluation of teaching in higher education in the United Kingdom.

STATUS: Individual research

DATE OF RESEARCH: 1991-1993

KEYWORDS: **higher education; student evaluation of teacher performance; teacher effectiveness**

1450

Department of Education, Loughborough LE11 3TU
01509 263171

Demaine, J. Dr

Local Management of Schools

ABSTRACT: A study of the effects of Local Management of Schools (LMS) on a select group of schools in England.

STATUS: Individual research

DATE OF RESEARCH: 1991-1993

KEYWORDS: **educational administration; educational change; local management of schools; school based management**

1451

Department of Education, Loughborough LE11 3TU
01509 263171

Demaine, J. Dr

Socio-political attitudes of teacher trainers in the United Kingdom

ABSTRACT: An investigation into the socio-political attitudes of teacher trainers in the United Kingdom.

STATUS: Individual research

DATE OF RESEARCH: 1991-1993

KEYWORDS: **political attitudes; social attitudes; teacher attitudes; teacher education; teacher educators**

1452

Department of Education, Loughborough LE11 3TU
01509 263171

Thomas, J. Dr

History of educational psychology in Britain with special reference to university departments of education

ABSTRACT: This project includes the development of bibliographies on individual psychologists of education and case studies of individual university departments of education. It involves the use of primary and secondary historical services. The long term aim is a monograph on the history of educational psychology in Britain, including its clinical practice.

PUBLISHED MATERIAL: THOMAS, J.B. (1982). 'J.A. Green, educational psychology and the Journal of Experimental Pedagogy', History of Education Society Bulletin, No 29, pp.41-45. ; THOMAS, J.B. (1996). 'The beginnings of educational psychology in the Universities of England and Wales', Educational Psychology, Vol 16, No 3, pp.229-244.

STATUS: Individual research

DATE OF RESEARCH: 1982-continuing

KEYWORDS: **educational history; educational psychology; teacher education**

1453

Department of Education, Loughborough LE11 3TU
01509 263171

Thomas, J. Dr

Studies of teacher education in the Victorian day training college

ABSTRACT: The project aims to describe and analyse the work of education departments in universities from 1890 to 1918. It consists of case studies of individual institutions, biographical studies and investigations of related areas, for example, the development of the academic study of education and the greater opportunities for the professional education of women.

PUBLISHED MATERIAL: THOMAS, J.B. (1986). 'University College, London, and the training of teachers', History of Education Society Bulletin, Vol 37, pp.44-49. ; THOMAS, J.B. (1986). 'Students, staff and curriculum in a day training college (Cardiff)', Collected Original Resources in Education, Vol 10, No 3, Fiche 1 A04. ; THOMAS, J.B. (1988). 'University College, Bristol: pioneering teacher training for women', History of Education, Vol 17, No 1, pp.55-70. ; THOMAS, J.B. (1988). 'The beginnings of teacher training for men at University College, Bristol', History of Education Society Bulletin, Vol 41, pp.40-45. ; THOMAS, J.B. (1997). 'Our mistresses of method: women academics in the day training colleges 1890-1914', Journal of Educational Administration and History, Vol 29, No 2, pp.93-107.

STATUS: Individual research

DATE OF RESEARCH: 1978-continuing

KEYWORDS: **educational history; preservice teacher education**

1454

Department of Education, Loughborough LE11 3TU
01509 263171

Wild, G. Dr; *Supervisor*: Hinton, R. Dr

An investigation of communication problems for blind students in higher education

ABSTRACT: As a result of its experience in producing tactile diagrams, the department has in recent years been asked to help several blind students in higher education who are pursuing courses with a high content of visually orientated material. It has become apparent that not only are more blind students seeking to study courses which have an inherent visual content but also that courses which have in the past had a predominantly verbal structure are now making increasing use of visual resources. Resources which make it possible for a blind student to access visually orientated course work may exist but they are not always easily available or may require further development. Many existing students still struggle to obtain good quality resources and some students are refused entry to the courses of their choice partly because suitable resources are not available. The present study has been making detailed case studies of ten individual students pursuing a wide variety of courses with a significant visual content. Through maintaining contact with the students and their teaching and support staff it has: 1) established the degree and kind of support given to these students in enabling them to access the visually orientated elements of their course work; 2) advised staff on the provisions of suitable teaching materials and, where necessary, developed more effective resources; and 3) appraised the importance of such material in enabling the students to follow their courses successfully.

PUBLISHED MATERIAL: WILD, G. (1992). 'Requirements for tactile diagrams of visually impaired students in higher education: preliminary findings', Educare, No 42, pp.11-14. ; WILD, G. (1992). 'Tactile diagrams and visually impaired students', Intact, No 4. (Publication of Commission VII of the International Cartographic Association).

STATUS: Sponsored project

SOURCE OF GRANT: Leverhulme Trust £16,450

DATE OF RESEARCH: 1991-1993

KEYWORDS: **blindness; communication problems; higher education; nonverbal communication; special educational needs; visual impairments**

1455

Department of Education, Loughborough LE11 3TU
01509 263171

Shepherd, D. Ms; Ayres, D. Mr

Survey of Leicestershire LEA schools into their HIV/AIDS and health education provision (11-16 age range), compared with sample of Midland schools

ABSTRACT: The project aims were to explore the progress and curriculum provision for Human Immunodeficiency Virus/Acquired Immune Deficiency Syndrome (HIV-AIDS) education in a sample of 140 secondary schools in the East Midlands, particularly against local education authority (LEA) HIV-AIDS policy guidelines. Two questionnaires were sent to each school to extract different samples of information from headteachers and health education coordinators. Amongst the information sought was curriculum and teaching organisation and staffing, school policy and influence of governors, inservice teacher education (INSET) needs and provision, and constraints in teaching in the HIV-AIDS area.

STATUS: Sponsored project

SOURCE OF GRANT: Leicestershire Local Education Authority ; Leicestershire Health Authority

DATE OF RESEARCH: 1989-1993

KEYWORDS: **acquired immune deficiency syndrome; health education; sex education**

1456

Department of Education, Loughborough LE11 3TU
01509 263171

Simmons, C. Mr

A comparative study of adolescent values in England, the United States and Saudi Arabia

ABSTRACT: This research compares the results of three surveys. The subjects comprise 96 adolescents in an English comprehensive school, 125 adolescents in a private school in Virginia, USA, and 89 adolescents in two schools in Saudi Arabia. The subjects have a modal age of 14 years. The open-ended questionnaire comprised ten prompts designed to elicit responses concerning ideals and least ideals, most and least preferred companions, use of solitude, summum bonum, most and least desired outcomes to life and nascent philosophies. Two methods of analysis were used. First, references to dominant themes were totalled; secondly, responses were assigned to six categories according to the dominant values expressed from materialistic to altruistic. Similarities, but also significant differences, were found in the dominant themes and significant differences were also apparent in the values that were expressed. Most marked was the high value placed on parents and friendship by the English young people, the importance of being well adjusted and feeling good about themselves in the American group and the prominence given to Islam by the Saudi-Arabian adolescents.

PUBLISHED MATERIAL: SIMMONS, C. & SIMMONS, C. (1994). 'Personal and moral adolescent values in England and Saudi Arabia', Journal of Moral Education, Vol 23, No 1, pp.3-16. ; SIMMONS, C. & SIMMONS, C. (1994). 'A comparative study of English and Muslim adolescent values', Muslim Education Quarterly, Vol 12, No 1, pp.16-28. ; SIMMONS, C. 'A comparative study of educational and cultural determinants of adolescent values', Journal of Beliefs and Values: Studies in Religion and Education. (in press).

STATUS: Individual research

DATE OF RESEARCH: 1992-1998

KEYWORDS: **adolescents; aspiration; attitudes; cross cultural studies; pupil attitudes; saudi arabia; united states of america; values**

1457

Department of Education, Loughborough LE11 3TU
01509 263171

Hough, J. Prof.

Cost-benefit analysis in education

ABSTRACT: This project surveys techniques of cost-benefit analysis and their application to education and examines the practical problems and pitfalls that arise in such applications. Particular emphasis is made to cost-benefit studies in developing countries.

STATUS: Sponsored project

SOURCE OF GRANT: Overseas Development Administration (British Government) £11,000

DATE OF RESEARCH: 1991-1993

KEYWORDS: **cost effectiveness; developing countries; educational economics; educational finance; efficiency**

1458

Department of Education, Loughborough LE11 3TU
01509 263171

Hough, J. Prof.

The education system in England and Wales

ABSTRACT: This research is surveying developments in the education system in England and Wales with emphasis on changes since the Education Reform Act 1988. The research includes: The Department of Education and Science; local education authorities; the Education Reform Act 1988; the comprehensive school; the private sector of education; the education of the 16-19 age group and the further education sector; and higher education. In each case the project studys recent changes, especially those stemming directly from the Education Reform Act and considers the effects and consequences.

PUBLISHED MATERIAL: HOUGH, J.R. (1992). The education system in England and Wales: a synopsis. Papers in Education Series. Loughborough: Loughborough University of Technology, Department of Education.

STATUS: Sponsored project

SOURCE OF GRANT: Loughborough University of Technology: Department of Education

DATE OF RESEARCH: 1991-1993

KEYWORDS: **education reform act 1988; educational change; educational development; educational planning; educational policy; government role; local education authorities**

1459

Department of Education, Loughborough LE11 3TU
01509 263171

Thomas, J. Dr

The development of teacher education in British universities, including the development of education as an academic subject

ABSTRACT: This is research using archive and secondary sources which will examine case studies of university departments, produce biographical data, and provide specific studies of special topics, e.g. the history of educational psychology.

PUBLISHED MATERIAL: THOMAS, J.B. (Ed). (1990). British universities and teacher education: a century of change. London: Falmer Press. ; THOMAS, J.B. (1991). 'Educational research in the University of Wales: the half-century to 1940', Welsh Journal of Education, Vol 3, No 1, pp.10-20. ; THOMAS, J.B. (1992). 'Birmingham University and teacher training: day training college to department of education', History of Education, Vol 21, No 3, pp.307-321. ; THOMAS, J.B. (1996). 'The beginnings of educational psychology in the universities of England and Wales', Educational Psychology, Vol 16, No 3, pp.229-244.

STATUS: Individual research

DATE OF RESEARCH: 1978-continuing

KEYWORDS: **teacher education; universities**

1460

Department of Education, Loughborough LE11 3TU
01509 263171

Hinton, R. Dr

Development of effective tactile overlays, support material and user-training for an audio-tactile device for blind and disabled users

ABSTRACT: The Nomad audio-tactile device is a computer add-on which has a touch sensitive pad on which tactile diagrams and pictures can be placed for interactive use with a personal computer by blind students. It helps to overcome some of the problems of accurately linking information which would normally be in braille or tape to a clear tactile display, and of making use of the computing and data storing potential of the computer. Although this device has performed well in preliminary trials, it requires educational development to enable teachers to use it effectively with blind students following a normal curriculum. The research team will be collaborating with the mathematics, science and geography departments of Exhall Grange School, Coventry (initially to develop this device further and provide ancillary teaching resources).

PUBLISHED MATERIAL: HINTON, R.A.L. (1991). 'Working with Nomad: an audio-tactile device'. In: Proceedings of the World Congress of Technology, Arlington, Virginia, December 1991, Vol VI. ; HINTON, R.A.L. (1992). 'Children's reactions to Nomad', British Journal of Visual Impairment, Vol 10, No 1, pp.27-28. ; HINTON, R.A.L. (1992). 'Stimulating access to graphics for visually impaired students'. Special Update, June, pp.12-13. Coventry: National Council for Educational Technology. ; HINTON, R.A.L. (1992). 'Preparing for diagram use in higher education'. Paper delivered at Quinquenial Conference of International Council for the Education of the Visually Handicapped, Bangkok, 26-31 July 1992.

STATUS: Sponsored project

SOURCE OF GRANT: Nuffield Foundation £19,989

DATE OF RESEARCH: 1990-1993

KEYWORDS: **blindness; computer uses in education; diagrams; higher education; information technology; low vision aids; microcomputers; sensory aids; special educational needs; tactile adaptation; visual impairments**

1461

Department of Education, Loughborough LE11 3TU
01509 263171

Clowes, P. Mr; *Supervisor*: Busher, H. Dr

Managing professionals inside and outside education

ABSTRACT: This research project asks: 1) What are the questions and paradoxes of managing professionals in institutions? 2) What does the term 'professional' mean? 3) Who are the professional workers in education? 4) Are the terms 'professional' and 'management' compatible, and what are the key issues involved in this nexus? 5) Who are the people involved in management in education and what form does the management function take in schools?

STATUS: Individual research

DATE OF RESEARCH: 1992-1997

KEYWORDS: **management in education; professional personnel**

1462

Department of Education, Loughborough LE11 3TU
01509 263171

Busher, H. Dr; Hodgkinson, K. Mr

Managing interschool liaison under Local Management of Schools

ABSTRACT: The project will explore how schools are managing interschool liaison under Local Management of Schools (LMS). For example, how this is affecting the internal management of individual schools, and how this is affecting the staff development of teaching and ancillary staff. For the sake of brevity the term "ancillary" is used to cover all technical, clerical, cleaning and domestic staff. The project focuses upon a local cluster of schools - those in and around Loughborough and Shepshed. The aim is to interview primary, high and upper school headteachers, and deputy headteachers or vice-principals responsible for interschool liaison, in schools with a post which includes this as part of a job description. Each interview is likely to last an hour, and answers given will be treated confidentially. In addition the person interviewed will be asked to keep a diary for one week in each of the three school terms of the contacts he/she has with other schools.

STATUS: Sponsored project

SOURCE OF GRANT: Universities Funding Council £2,000

DATE OF RESEARCH: 1992-1993

KEYWORDS: **educational administration; institutional cooperation; local management of schools**

1463

Department of Education, Loughborough LE11 3TU
01509 263171

Harvey, J. Miss; *Supervisor*: Busher, H. Dr

Marketing an independent school

ABSTRACT: This research sets out to find out how headteachers and parents perceive a school, make choices, and give advice to potential pupils about whether or not to apply. One measure of the impact of this research on policy will be the changes in the number of pupils coming to the school. Another measure will be expressions by parents of increased satisfaction with the school. The research will include interviews with headteachers of precursor schools, and a survey of parents' views of schools.

STATUS: Individual research

DATE OF RESEARCH: 1991-1993

KEYWORDS: **independent schools; marketing; parent choice**

1464

Department of Education, Loughborough LE11 3TU
01509 263171

Hodgkinson, K. Mr; Wild, P. Dr

A flexible learning plan for information technology on primary school teaching practice

ABSTRACT: The development of a detailed profile of student use of information technology (IT) on teaching practice in primary schools. It will include a pilot study of 5 students, and a full design for 60 students. Students will record their work. The flexible learning plan (FLP) will then be formally assessed and student performance in IT will be matched against the Council for the Accreditation of Teacher Education (CATE) and Trotter Report recommendations.

STATUS: Sponsored project

SOURCE OF GRANT: Loughborough University of Technology £2,325

DATE OF RESEARCH: 1992-1993

KEYWORDS: **computer uses in education; information technology; preservice teacher education; student teachers; teaching practice**

1465

Department of Education, Loughborough LE11 3TU
01509 263171

Gatt, W. Mr; *Supervisor*: Wild, P. Dr

The development of information technology in Maltese schools

ABSTRACT: The development of information technology (IT) in Maltese schools is at an early stage. This project will investigate the position of Malta relative to the international IT scene, and within the political context of Malta in its recent past. An initial survey of secondary schools has already been carried out and a longitudinal study of developments will continue for the next three years.

STATUS: Individual research

DATE OF RESEARCH: 1994-continuing

KEYWORDS: **computer uses in education; information technology; malta**

1466

Department of Education, Loughborough LE11 3TU
01509 263171

Blease, D. Mr; Busher, H. Dr

Decision-making by teachers and technicians in secondary school science departments

ABSTRACT: The project is designed to explore how decisions are taken in secondary school science departments and in particular how the work of technicians affects and is organised by heads of departments. Confined in the first instance to schools in the East Midlands, data is being collected using semi-structured interviews with technicians, heads of science departments and headteachers, and includes working shadowing of technicians for up to 3 full days at a time. Much of the fieldwork is being undertaken by a part-time research assistant and the first results are expected to be reported sometime during the summer of 1996.

STATUS: Sponsored project

SOURCE OF GRANT: Loughborough University £10,000

DATE OF RESEARCH: 1995-1998

KEYWORDS: decision making; laboratory technicians; paraprofessional personnel; science education; science laboratories; science teachers; secondary education

1467

Department of Education, Loughborough LE11 3TU
01509 263171

Crisp, R. Mr; *Supervisor*: Hinton, R. Dr

The effect of visual impairment on the learning abilities of children who are classed as having learning difficulties and/or behavioural problems, but are not recognised as having a visual impairment

ABSTRACT: This research has surveyed 165 children of average age 9.5 years, selected as having learning difficulties or behavioural problems. Functional vision was tested and significant numbers were found with undetected visual impairments. In many cases behaviour and/or school progress improved when the visual impairment was: a) corrected by an optometrist's prescription; or b) compensated for by teacher strategy.

STATUS: Individual research

DATE OF RESEARCH: 1993-1998

KEYWORDS: emotional and behavioural difficulties; learning disabilities; special educational needs; vision tests; visual impairments

1468

Department of Education, Loughborough LE11 3TU
01509 263171

Wishart, J. Dr

Information technology and learning

ABSTRACT: The researcher is currently setting up research projects involving the use of multimedia CD-Roms and the Internet in schools. The goals are to identify successful strategies for use of information technology (IT) by teachers and learners and to understand individual differences in approach to IT.

STATUS: Individual research

DATE OF RESEARCH: 1996-1998

KEYWORDS: cd roms; computer networks; computer uses in education; information technology; internet; learning strategies; multimedia; primary education; secondary education; teaching methods

1469

Department of Education, Loughborough LE11 3TU
01509 263171

Blease, D. Dr; Wishart, J. Dr; Wild, P. Dr

Evaluation of the effects on teaching and learning of computer networks in schools

ABSTRACT: An investigation into the effectiveness of a newly installed computer network (100 personal computers) in a large comprehensive school. Unlike previous research on computer networks, this study concentrates on changes in teaching and learning styles brought about by the integration of the system into the secondary school curriculum. Methodology includes observation, questionnaire, interview and the monitoring of use of the network by electronic means.

STATUS: Sponsored project

SOURCE OF GRANT: Stanground College, Peterborough £1,000

DATE OF RESEARCH: 1996-1997

KEYWORDS: computer networks; computer uses in education; information technology; learning strategies; secondary education; teaching methods

1470

Department of Education, Loughborough LE11 3TU
01509 263171

Hinton, R. Dr; Hinton, D. Mrs

The use of tactile graphics in the teaching of chemistry at honours degree level

ABSTRACT: Chemistry is a subject where structural diagrams, graphs and various symbolic representations are an inevitable part of the language of the subject. This project is investigating all aspects of the use of tactile forms of these diagrams in the teaching of Chemistry of Honours Degree standard to blind students. The project will also provide necessary tactile teaching material for the students concerned.

STATUS: Sponsored project

SOURCE OF GRANT: Higher Education Funding Council for England

DATE OF RESEARCH: 1995-1998

KEYWORDS: blindness; chemistry; higher education; raised line drawings; science education; special educational needs; tactile adaptation; visual impairments

1471

Department of Education, Loughborough LE11 3TU
01509 263171

Wishart, J. Dr; *Supervisors*: Wild, P. Dr; Evans, M. Prof.

Internet in the community

ABSTRACT: This project is investigating the actual and planned use of the Internet in the local area, in particular by secondary schools and public library services. As experience in using the Internet remains quite limited outside tertiary education, information-gathering activities have been combined with training sessions for groups of teachers and librarians. Recommendations on whether, and in what ways, the university should support the introduction of networked resources into the local school and community information environments will be made to the university, in the light of the feedback received from participating institutions and individuals.

STATUS: Sponsored project

SOURCE OF GRANT: Loughborough University £30,000

DATE OF RESEARCH: 1996-1998

KEYWORDS: community information services; computer uses in education; information technology; internet; libraries; public libraries; secondary education

1472

Department of Education, Loughborough LE11 3TU
01509 263171

Hinton, R. Dr; Hinton, D. Mrs; Wild, G. Dr

The use of tactile graphics in the teaching of science at honours degree level

ABSTRACT: For blind students of the sciences, tactile diagrams of various kinds are an essential, though neglected, means of communication and learning. The focus is on effective understanding rather than on technology for its own sake and the diagrams per se. Approximately 2000 chemical diagrams have been produced, plus many in other subjects. Monitoring is by direct feedback from the blind students and their teachers.

PUBLISHED MATERIAL: WILD, G.E. & HINTON, R.A. (1992). 'Requirements for tactile diagrams of visually impaired students in higher education: preliminary findings', EDUCARE, No 42, pp.11-14. ; WILD, G.E. & HINTON, R.A. (1993). 'Visual information and the blind student: the problem of access', British Journal of Visual Impairment, Vol 11, No 3, pp.99-102. ; WILD, G.E. & HINTON, R.A. (1996). 'An evaluation study of the use of tactile diagrams on Open University science courses', British Journal of Visual Impairment, Vol 14, No 1, pp.5-9. ; HINTON, R.A. (1996). Tactile graphics in education. Edinburgh: Moray House Publications. ; A full list of publications is available from the researchers.

STATUS: Sponsored project

SOURCE OF GRANT: Higher Education Funding Council

DATE OF RESEARCH: 1995-continuing

KEYWORDS: **blindness; computer uses in education; diagrams; graphics; higher education; information technology; low vision aids; science education; sensory aids; special educational needs; tactile adaptation; visual impairments**

1473

Department of Education, Loughborough LE11 3TU
01509 263171

Hough, J. Prof.

Education and child labour

ABSTRACT: This study is working with the International Labour Office, Geneva, to further the links between the development of education systems and the elimination of child labour in developing countries.

STATUS: Sponsored project

DATE OF RESEARCH: 1997-continuing

KEYWORDS: **child labour; developing countries; development education**

1474

Department of Education, Loughborough LE11 3TU
01509 263171

Kasler, J. Mr; *Supervisor*: Hinton, R. Dr

Development of the strengths and weaknesses academic profile: a tool for career counselling of adults with specific learning disabilities

ABSTRACT: A strengths and weaknesses academic profile questionnaire has been prepared which is designed to grade career counselling for adults with learning disabilities. Pilot testing and validation of this questionnaire has been carried out and it will be administered to 100 adults in Israel.

STATUS: Individual research

DATE OF RESEARCH: 1996-continuing

KEYWORDS: **adults; career counselling; israel; learning disabilities; special educational needs; vocational guidance**

1475

Department of Education, Loughborough LE11 3TU
01509 263171

Wishart, J. Dr

Attitudes toward and use of information technology and individual locus of control

ABSTRACT: The researcher has previously established a small but significant correlation between having a positive attitude toward using information technology and having a more internal locus of control. A questionnaire survey is being carried out on 400 students in nurse and teacher training to follow up the presence of this correlation. With both teacher and nurse training courses currently being modified to include information and communications technology skills, it is important that lecturers are aware that those with a more external locus of control may need further support in this area.

STATUS: Individual research

DATE OF RESEARCH: 1997-continuing

KEYWORDS: **human computer interaction; information technology; locus of control**

1476

Department of Education, Loughborough LE11 3TU
01509 263171
Baptist University, Kowloon, Hong Kong
010 852 23397210
University of Twente, Department of Educational Administration, Netherlands
010 31 53893609

Wild, P. Dr; Fung, A. Dr; Visscher, A. Dr

Evaluation of information technology systems used to support administration in schools

ABSTRACT: A consequence of the Education Reform Act 1988 (ERA) is the need for information technology (IT) systems to support the Local Management of Schools (LMS). It is well known from research in the commercial and industrial sectors that the success rate for the implementation of such systems is as low as 20%. If the IT systems being installed in schools are to achieve their potential in helping to administer, or, more importantly, manage the working of the school then it is essential that some evaluation of the systems is carried out. A methodology developed at the Human Sciences and Advanced Technology (HUSAT) Research Institute at Loughborough University, called the User Acceptance Audit, is being modified for the school environment. A detailed task analysis is required of the management and administration within the schools so that the evaluation tool developed by HUSAT can be made context sensitive. This research is now being developed in the context of the Hong Kong School Administration and Management System (SAMS).

PUBLISHED MATERIAL: WILD, P., SCIVIER, J.E. & RICHARDSON, S.J. (1992). 'Evaluating information technology-supported Local Management of Schools: the User Acceptability Audit', Education Management and Administration, Vol 20, No1, pp.40-48. ; WILD, P. (1995). 'The use of task analysis and user acceptability audits in implementing information technology systems in schools'. In: BARTA, B-Z., TELEM, M. & GEV, Y. (Eds). Information technology in education management. London: Chapman and Hall. ; VISSCHER, A. & WILD, P. (1995). 'Future directions for research on information technology in educational management'. In: TINSLEY, J.D. & VAN WEERT, T.J. (Eds). World Conference on Computers in Education VI. London: Chapman and Hall.

STATUS: Sponsored project

SOURCE OF GRANT: Baptist University, Hong Kong ; Hong Kong Education Department

DATE OF RESEARCH: 1994-continuing

KEYWORDS: **computer uses in education; educational administration; information technology; local management of schools; management information systems; management systems; school based management**

1477

Department of Education, Loughborough LE11 3TU
01509 263171
Royal National Institute for the Blind Vocational College, Radmoor Road, Loughborough LE11 3BS
01509 611077

Todd, N. Mr; *Supervisor*: Hinton, R. Dr

The integration of visually impaired students in further education

ABSTRACT: This thesis is in three main parts. Part One reviews the general literature on the integration debate and looks at the debate in relation to the specific field of visual impairment. This examines the issues and gives a broad context to the particular area of the visually impaired student in mainstream further education. Part Two is a review of the field of integration support with particular reference to further education and individuals with visual impairment. There exist real concerns about the ability of the mainstream to provide an environment that will ensure that these individuals maximise their learning potential. These concerns seem principally related to making appropriate support services available so that the advantages of mainstreaming are not outweighed by the disadvantages of reduced levels of support. Part Three is a research project based on further education colleges in the Midlands. It attempts to identify and examine the support services that enable successful integration of visually impaired students. It also attempts to evaluate these factors to establish their relative value in this mainstreaming process. The evaluation is from the perspective of visually impaired students in further education rather than that of professionals in the visually impaired field. The survey was conducted by means of a structured questionnaire to Midlands further education (FE) colleges and a separate questionnaire to visually impaired students who were identified. Thirty-five FE colleges had visually impaired students in mainstream courses and from these eighty individual students completed the questionnaire. The statistical significance of the graded results were analysed by the Chi-square test.

STATUS: Individual research

DATE OF RESEARCH: 1988-1993

KEYWORDS: **further education; mainstreaming; special educational needs; visual impairments**

1478

Department of Education, Loughborough LE11 3TU
01509 263171
Warwick University, Department of Science Education, Coventry CV4 7AL
01203 523523

Melrose, J. Miss; *Supervisor*: Schwarzenberger, R. Prof.

An exploration into the notion of levels of attainment in mathematics

ABSTRACT: This research is a comparison of young children and older low-attainers in their thinking about mathematics topics including subtraction and three dimensional visualisation. The methods employed are principally individual interviews with the children together with reflections from their teachers.

STATUS: Individual research

DATE OF RESEARCH: 1989-1993

KEYWORDS: **low achievement; mathematics achievement; mathematics education**

1479

Department of Physical Education, Sports Science and Recreation, Management Loughborough LE11 3TU
01509 263171

Evans, J. Prof.

The impact of the National Curriculum and Local Management of Schools (LMS) on the provision of sport and physical education in schools

ABSTRACT: The research is monitoring the impact of the National Curriculum and Local Management of Schools (LMS) on the provision of sport and physical education (PE) in schools in England and Wales. The study is employing qualitative methodologies to monitor the effects of a National Curriculum for PE on processes of teaching and learning in PE and sport in schools.

STATUS: Sponsored project

SOURCE OF GRANT: Leverhulme Trust ; Economic and Social Research Council

DATE OF RESEARCH: 1990-1997

KEYWORDS: **educational change; local management of schools; national curriculum; physical education; sports**

1480

Department of Physical Education, Sports Science and Recreation, Management Loughborough LE11 3TU
01509 263171

Harris, J. Dr; *Supervisor*: Almond, L. Mr

Physical education: a picture of health? The implementation of health-related exercise in the National Curriculum in secondary schools in England

ABSTRACT: This thesis documents and explores factors influencing the way in which physical education's (PE) contribution to health in the form of health-related exercise (HRE) was viewed, approached and delivered by secondary school PE teachers following the introduction of a National Curriculum for physical education (NCPE). The methodology incorporated both quantitative and qualitative approaches. A national survey of 1000 secondary schools in England in 1993 elicited questionnaire responses from 72.8% of heads of PE departments from a proportionate sample of schools stratified by type, age range, gender, size and geographical location. Analysis employed the Statistical Package for Social Scientists (SPSS). Case studies were completed in 1995 in 3 randomly selected mixed sex state schools in the South, Midlands and North of England. Case study data analysis focused on the progressive identification of themes and concepts associated with the implementation of HRE in the National Curriuclum. The findings revealed that the NCPE's explicit attention to health issues was welcomed although views varied regarding interpretation, delivery and assessment of the requirements. Most schools had adopted a combination of approaches, involving discrete units and permeation through the activity areas within PE, and/or delivery through other curriculum areas. Consensus existed for some theoretical areas although a physiological bias was evident. There was limited evidence of a well-structured and coordinated approach to integrating health issues within the PE activity areas, and that delivered in discrete units often had a fitness-orientation, reflecting adaptation of the performance rationale underlying the 'traditional' games-dominated PE programme. Conceptual confusion prevailed regarding the multidimensional concept of HRE, and the varying relationships between PE, sport, health and fitness. The expression of health issues in the NCPE revealed limitations to the accommodation of HRE, mismatches between intentions and outcomes, and a tendency to reflect inequitable practices. Influences included school and individual characteristics, contextual constraints and prevailing ideologies. Creative interpretation of the NCPE remains possible in the form of innovative programmes which integrate health and PE, and which challenge physical fitness and sport performance orientations. A committed, comprehensive and coherent approach to health issues is rarely a central feature of school PE. Nevertheless, a shared vision of the expression of health in the NCPE clearly remains desirable and possible.

PUBLISHED MATERIAL: HARRIS, J. (1994). 'Physical education in the National Curriculum: is there enough time to be effective?', British Journal of Physical Education, Vol 25, No 4, pp.34-38. ; HARRIS, J. (1995). 'Physical education: a picture of health?', British Journal of Physical Education, Vol 26, No 4, pp.25-32. ; HARRIS, J. (1997). 'A health focus in physical education'. In: ALMOND, L. (Ed). Physical education in schools. London: Kogan Page. ; HARRIS, J. & CALE, L. (1997). 'How healthy is school PE? A review of the effectiveness of health-related PE programmes in schools', Health Education Jounral, Vol 56, No 1, pp.84-104. ; PENNEY, D. & HARRIS, J. (1997). 'Extra-curricular physical education: more of the same for the more able?', Sport, Education and Society, Vol 2, No 1, pp.41-54.

STATUS: Individual research

DATE OF RESEARCH: 1993-1997

KEYWORDS: **health; health promotion; national curriculum; physical activities; physical education; secondary education**

1481

Department of Physical Education, Sports Science and Recreation, Management Loughborough LE11 3TU
01509 263171

Luke, I. Mr; *Supervisor*: Hardy, C. Dr

The development of metacognitive ability and of learning strategies in physical education

ABSTRACT: It has been argued that the learner and the learning processes are as important as the teacher and the teaching processes in influencing the quantity, quality and type of learning that occurs (Weinstein & Mayer, 1986). Unfortunately, research into the learner and the learning processes is in its infancy in physical education (Mawer, 1995). However, through research into classroom learning, the concepts of learning styles, learning strategies and metacognition have emerged as being significant in improving and developing the learning processes (e.g. Dunn & Dunn, 1978, Weinstein & Mayer, 1986, Garofalo, 1987). The aim of the study is to utilise some of the research findings concerning learning styles, learning strategies and metacognition, and to examine the potential benefits of developing these areas with physical education classes.

STATUS: Sponsored project

SOURCE OF GRANT: British Gas PLC

DATE OF RESEARCH: 1994-1997

KEYWORDS: **learning strategies; metacognition; physical education**

1482

Department of Physical Education, Sports Science and Recreation, Management Loughborough LE11 3TU
01509 263171

Thorpe, R. Mr; *Supervisor*: Williams, C. Prof.

Helping children play games

ABSTRACT: The research objective is to establish a coherent and effective method of providing children with games playing opportunities commensurate with: 1) their ability and aspirations; 2) the circumstances within which the experience occurs and recognising the capabilities of the provider. The research takes the form of a number of separate but related papers which examine the factors contributing to children's playing of games. The development, testing and implementation of approaches to teaching games in the curriculum and providing games outside the curriculum are reported. Comparisons of children's interests and aspirations, and programmes designed to meet them, are examined in the United Kingdom and compared with those in Australia. The research has been carried out with various partners as appropriate.

STATUS: Individual research

DATE OF RESEARCH: 1994-1997

KEYWORDS: **australia; comparative education; games; physical education; sports**

1483

Department of Physical Education, Sports Science and Recreation, Management Loughborough LE11 3TU
01509 263171

Hagger, M. Mr; *Supervisors*: Cale, L. Dr; Evans, J. Prof.; Hardy, C. Dr

Children's attitudes, beliefs and perceptions of control and their relationship with self-reported intention and physical activity behaviour

ABSTRACT: The beneficial effects of physical activity to children's health have been recognised in recent years and this had led to a growing interest in the psychological correlates of children's physical activity behaviour. Understanding the determinants of children's physical activity is important to physical educators and health promoters in promoting physical activity and may have important implications in the development of PE curricula. This research project aims to examine the relationship between attitudes, beliefs and control and self-reported intention and physical activity behaviour in 12-14 year-old children. The primary focus of the project is to investigate the link between affective attitudes, a person's stated predisposition towards engaging in a certain behaviour, and stated intentions and self-reported behaviour. Further, the influence of past behaviour, self-efficacy and perceptions of control, which have also been recognised by health psychologists as influential variables on volitional behaviour (Terry & O'Leary, 1995), on children's attitudes, intention and physical activity behaviour will also be examined. Self-efficacy and control have been selected based on their pertinence to the theoretical approaches adopted as well as the important and relevant conceptual influence they may have on attitudes and behaviour. The constructs will be operationally defined and measured using standardised psychometric techniques within 3 social psychological theories: Ajzen's (1985) theory of planned behaviour; Kenyon's (1968) conceptual model for characterising physical activity; and Bandura's (1977) social cognitive theory. The influence of these constructs on intention and behaviour will be examined concurrently in a 'theoretical merger' as proposed by Brawley (1994) and structural equation techniques have facilitated this approach.

PUBLISHED MATERIAL: HAGGER, M.S., CALE, L. & ALMOND, L. (1995). 'The importance of children's attitudes towards physical activity'. In: LIDOR, R., ELDAR, E. & HARARI, I. (Eds). Proceedings of the AIESEP World Congress on Bridging the Gaps between Disciplines, Curriculum and Instruction. Netanya, Israel: Wingate Institute. ; HAGGER, M.S. & CALE, L. (1997). 'Validity and reliability of the CATPA, an instrument for assessing attitudes towards physical activity in British children', Exercise and Society, Vol 17 (Supplement), p.107. ; HAGGER, M.S., CALE, L. & ASHFORD, B. (1997). 'Children's physical activity levels and attitudes towards physical activity', European Physical Education Review, Vol 3, pp.144-164.

STATUS: Individual research

DATE OF RESEARCH: 1994-1998

KEYWORDS: **attitudes; children; exercise; physical activities; physical activity level; pupil attitudes**

1484

Department of Physical Education, Sports Science and Recreation, Management Loughborough LE11 3TU
01509 263171

Kay, W. Mr; *Supervisor*: Evans, J. Prof.

Physical education (PE) and the 'Political New Right': the development of a National Curriculum PE

ABSTRACT: This investigation centres on the making of the National Curriculum PE in England and Wales and on the way in which this has been influenced by the interests and aspirations of key figures, politicians and educationalists involved in the policy process. Methodologically, the study has drawn on the principles of qualitative research, to interrogate empirically the perspectives of influencial figures in the policy-making process. Conceptually, the study is grounded in social theory, in particular in insights drawn from neo-Marxism and discourse analysis. The research is intended to contribute to academic debate within sociology and cultural studies and to the professional development of physical education.

STATUS: Sponsored project

SOURCE OF GRANT: Loughborough University £27,000

DATE OF RESEARCH: 1995-1997

KEYWORDS: **educational policy; national curriculum; physical education; politics education relationship; sports**

1485

Department of Social Sciences, Loughborough LE11 3TU
01509 263171

Bagilhole, B. Dr

On the inside: equal opportunities in academic life. A research report on women, ethnic minority and disabled academics

ABSTRACT: Women academics in British universities make up a very small minority and are concentrated in the lower grades. Statistical evidence points to the fact that an important reason for this is that discrimination exists within the academic profession. However, there is very little empirical information on the nature of this discrimination and how it operates. This research study sought to identify and illuminate the processes that serve to maintain this discrimination through the experiences and perceptions of women academics themselves. A total of 43 women were interviewed at length using a semi-structured interview schedule. This explored issues such as recruitment and selection, probation, career development, appraisal, positions of power, the roles of women academics, the problem of being in small minorities functioning in a male environment, isolation, exclusion from male colleagues, and challenges to authority by male students. Women academics were found to have fewer support systems than their male colleagues, fewer role models or mentors, and little access to communication networks. They report problems with work relationships, and experience hostility from male colleagues and students. The majority had experienced discrimination within the university. This leads to the majority becoming convinced that the concept of a woman academic is problematic. They put pressure on themselves to perform better than their male colleages, and avoid being identified with other women. They become 'honorary men' and as such are in no position to support other women.

PUBLISHED MATERIAL: BAGIHOLE, B. (1992). On the inside: equal opportunities in academic life. A research report on women, ethnic minority and disabled academics. Loughborough: Loughborough University, Department of Social Sciences. ; BAGIHOLE, B. (1993). 'How to keep a good woman down: an investigation of the role of institutional factors in the process of discrimination against women academics', British Journal of Sociology of Education, Vol 14, No 3, pp.261-274. ; BAGIHOLE, B. (1993). 'Survivors in a male preserve: a study of British women academics' experiences and perceptions of discrimination in a UK university', Higher Education, Vol 26, No 4, pp.431-447.

STATUS: Sponsored project

SOURCE OF GRANT: Loughborough University of Technology £1,000

DATE OF RESEARCH: 1992-1993

KEYWORDS: **academic staff; employment opportunities; equal opportunities jobs; higher education; universities; women teachers; womens employment**

LSU College of Higher Education

1486

The Avenue, Southampton SO17 1BG
02380 216200
London University, Institute of Education, 20 Bedford Way, London WC1H 0AL
0171 580 1122

McDermid, J. Dr; *Supervisor*: Aldrich, R. Prof.

Nationality, class and gender in 19th century Scottish education: the schooling of working-class girls

ABSTRACT: The aim of this study is to place women in Scottish educational history, and in the process to question the gender-blindness of the Scottish educational tradition. Education was seen as integral to Scottish identity, but it also had to be adapted to English practices and legislation which stressed a female education in domesticity. The impact of the following factors on female education within Scotland are examined: 1) Class differences, and particularly working-class girls, and the class basis of the gender-specific curriculum. 2) Tensions between highland and lowland, urban and rural, east and west, Protestant and Catholic. Local studies are central to this study. There is also an examination of the female educators of working-class children. Key sources include Her Majesty's Inspectorate reports, minutes of the Committee of Council on Education, the first and second statistical accounts of Scotland, the Argyll Commission reports, school log books, local newspapers.

STATUS: Individual research

DATE OF RESEARCH: 1990-1997

KEYWORDS: **educational history; girls; womens education**

1487

The Avenue, Southampton SO17 1BG
02380 216200
Southampton University, Faculty of Educational Studies, Research and Graduate School of Education, Highfield, Southampton S09 5NH
02380 595000

Foskett, R. Ms; *Supervisor*: Simons, H. Prof.

Organisational change in primary schools in response to a client focused environment and increasing managerial autonomy

ABSTRACT: The main aim of the project focuses on the extent to which the management structures within primary schools have changed in response to a client-focused approach to the provision of education services. It considers how the legislative environment of competition, Local Management of Schools (LMS), corporate identity, customer charters etc have stimulated changes which have affected the structure, function and culture of the management of primary schools. The environment of operation of primary schools has undergone a series of major upheavals since the Education Reform Act 1988. The study is investigating the nature of these changes and how the 'business-culture' is influencing the collegiality of the schools. The nature of the research is exploratory and based on empirical evidence. It is a T-shaped study, with a broad survey being backed up by more detailed case study work. The study is taking a representative sample of primary schools in Hampshire and a contrasting area. The sample is approximately 100 schools, stratified on the following characteristics: All-through Primary schools/Junior Schools; Male Headteachers/Female Headteachers; Young Headteachers/Old Headteachers; Urban Catchment/Rural Catchment. The questionnaire study will identify specific issues to be further researched and clarified during the case study phase. Certainly questions involving the 'culture' of the school, perceptions versus reality, and inter-relationships will need to be supplemented by more qualitative research. A number of the schools sampled by questionnaire will be selected, from each of the categories in the stratified sample, for more detailed work.

STATUS: Individual research

DATE OF RESEARCH: 1995-continuing

KEYWORDS: **educational administration; head teachers; management in education; primary education**

Luton University

1488

Educational Services Unit, Park Square, Luton LU1 3JU
01582 734111

Fallows, S. Dr

Introduction of open learning into mainstream higher education

ABSTRACT: Open learning is seen as one possible solution to increased student numbers in higher education without increased resources. This research project seeks to increase understanding of the implementation of open learning in a mainstream higher education institution. The key points of interest are the implications of the use of open learning in different educational situations and with students from different backgrounds (such as younger/older; different ethnic backgrounds; first year/final year etc). The intention is to utilise the University of Luton as an initial 'test bed' with the aim of both informing the Luton situation and contributing to the wider debate.

PUBLISHED MATERIAL: FALLOWS, S.J. (1994). 'Integration of open learning into mainstream higher education'. In: KNIGHT, P. University-wide change, staff and curriculum development. Birmingham: SEDA Publications.

STATUS: Sponsored project

SOURCE OF GRANT: Luton University

DATE OF RESEARCH: 1993-1997

KEYWORDS: **higher education; open education**

1489

Educational Services Unit, Park Square, Luton LU1 3JU
01582 734111

Guest, K. Mr; *Supervisors*: Fallows, S. Dr; Van den Brink Budgen, R. Dr; Dillon, M. Mr

Evaluation of critical writing assessment tests as predictions of performance in higher education

ABSTRACT: This research stems from the development of aptitude profiling tests by the University of Cambridge Local Examination Syndicate (The MENO project), in particular those sections concerned with Critical Thinking, Communications and Literacy. The researcher has been involved in the development of these tests for 3 years; producing and evaluating materials, establishing marking criteria, and piloting the tests in institutions across the UK and abroad. This specific research project seeks to address the problems of: 1) how to assess the suitability of mature, non-standard entry students (i.e. those without conventional academic qualifications) able to benefit from a degree course; and 2) what makes a successful student (i.e. the required qualities and competences, generic skills, character traits, experiential or prior learning). It includes a critical review of approaches tried so far and what is currently available - practicality, strengths and limitations - and investigates the conceptual base of MENO, the design and testing of the experimental programme (with results and analysis), and discussion of future development of aptitude profiling as a diagnostic tool.

PUBLISHED MATERIAL: GUEST, K. (1992). Study skills booklet. Luton: University of Luton.

STATUS: Individual research

DATE OF RESEARCH: 1991-1997

KEYWORDS: **aptitude; assessment; critical thinking; higher education; mature students; prediction; selection; students**

1490

Educational Services Unit, Park Square, Luton LU1 3JU
01582 734111

Fallows, S. Dr

Support systems for supervisors of PhD research students

ABSTRACT: It is recognised that there is considerable 'wastage' between registration for a research degree and submission of thesis. Whilst some drop-out is inevitable, the current rates are deemed to be excessive. The role of the supervisor is likely to be a major factor. The study focuses on systems adopted by universities to maximise completion of research degrees. Of particular interest are systems designed to support supervisors.

STATUS: Individual research

DATE OF RESEARCH: 1993-continuing

KEYWORDS: **degrees - academic; higher education; research directors; student research; student wastage; theses**

1491

Educational Services Unit, Park Square, Luton LU1 3JU
01582 734111

Fallows, S. Dr; Steven, C. Ms

Implementing skills into the higher educational curriculum

ABSTRACT: A university degree is not an instant passport to employment. Many universities now recognise that providing the means to an indepth knowledge of an academic discipline is no longer enough; steps must also be taken to equip students with skills for their future employment. The University of Luton has subjected 'skills to make students employable' to extensive internal debate and now recognises four groups of skills and has established a set of key principles which underpin their delivery. The researchers' approach is just one method of addressing the 'skills to make students employable' issue and is seeking to bring together a collection of contributions which describe: 1) different models through which universities have recognised the issue and have taken strategic steps to implement schemes which ensure that students are assisted to develop their skills for employment; 2) approaches to the practical implementation of skills programmes at an operational level within specific subject areas. Two multi-author international publications are presently in preparation - one deals with strategic matters, the other with operational matters.

STATUS: Team research

DATE OF RESEARCH: 1997-continuing

KEYWORDS: communication skills; employment; higher education; information retrieval; literacy; numeracy; skill development; skills; students; work education relationship

1492

Educational Services Unit, Park Square, Luton LU1 3JU
01582 734111

Fallows, S. Dr; Ahmet, K. Dr

Students without an interest in given subjects

ABSTRACT: Many lecturers face the task of teaching their subject to students whose primary learning interest is elsewhere. This situation arises when it is deemed essential that students gain an insight into subjects that underpin their primary subjects. The research is drawing together an international set of case examples of how lecturers in different institutions and different disciplines tackle this important issue. An international multi-author publication is presently in preparation and will be published by Kogan Page early in 1999.

STATUS: Team research

DATE OF RESEARCH: 1997-continuing

KEYWORDS: comparative education; higher education; subject knowledge; teaching methods

1493

Educational Services Unit, Park Square, Luton LU1 3JU
01582 734111
Bedford Hospital, College of Nursing, Kempston Road, Bedford MK42 9DJ 01234 355122

Camiah, S. Mr; *Supervisors*: Fallows, S. Dr; Gabriel, F. Ms

Changing role of lecturers in nursing

ABSTRACT: Nurse education has, since the late 1980s, been moving from small generalist hospital-based provision within the National Health Service (NHS) to become part of mainstream higher education (HE). Different institutions are at different stages on the progression from NHS to HE. The study focuses on the role of the nursing lecturer as the provision becomes more HE-focused. The University of Luton is the primary (pilot) case example with additional studies involving a number of HE institutions.

STATUS: Individual research

DATE OF RESEARCH: 1997-continuing

KEYWORDS: nurse education; nurse teachers; nurses

1494

Faculty of Business, Park Square, Luton LU1 3JU
01582 734111
International Centre for Educational Leadership and Management, Lincoln University Campus, Brayford Pool, Lincoln LN6 7TS
01522 886071

Newcastle upon Tyne University, Department of Education, St Thomas Street, Newcastle upon Tyne NE1 7RU
0191 222 6000

Scott, M. Mr; *Supervisors*: Thody, A. Dr; Cole, T. Mr; Dennison, W. Dr

An investigation into the effectiveness of marketing techniques used by secondary schools

ABSTRACT: The aim of this research is to: 1) investigate the marketing techniques being used by a sample of secondary schools in Hertfordshire and Bedfordshire; 2) devise an appropriate model to test marketing effectiveness; 3) use the model to test the effectiveness of the marketing techniques used by the sample of schools; and 4) draw appropriate conclusions.

STATUS: Individual research

DATE OF RESEARCH: 1995-continuing

KEYWORDS: marketing; recruitment; secondary education

1495

Faculty of Health Care and Social Studies, Park Square, Luton LU1 3JU
01582 456843
York University, Department of Social Policy and Social Work, Heslington, York Y01 5DD
01904 430000

Brodie, I. Ms; *Supervisors*: Berridge, D. Prof.; Sinclair, I. Prof.

The exclusion from school of children looked after by local authorities

ABSTRACT: Exclusion from school has emerged as a prominent issue in recent years, with a dramatic increase in the numbers of exclusions being reported nationally. This has serious implications for children looked after by local authorities ('in care'). Looked after young people frequently encounter educational difficulties and have been identified as a group which experiences a high level of exclusion. This study focuses on young people looked after in residential accommodation. It aims to understand more about the way in which the exclusion process operates, by examining the interactions between, and the views of, the different individuals involved in this process - young people, teachers, social workers, carers, educational welfare officers and educational psychologists. The research investigates the factors which contribute to an exclusion taking place and influence the way in which it is experienced, including liaison between services. It also examines the way in which the exclusion process operates in the light of current legislation and guidance relating to the education of children looked after by the local authorities. The research is being carried out in two local authorities. Ten cases of permanent exclusion are being identified via children's homes in each authority. Cases include children of both primary and secondary school age. Interviews are then carried out with the range of individuals involved in each case. Case files are also examined.

PUBLISHED MATERIAL: BRODIE, I. Exclusion from school. Highlight Series No 136. London: National Children's Bureau. ; BERRIDGE, D. & BRODIE, I. 'Residential child care in England and Wales: the enquiries and after'. In: HILL, M. & ALDGATE, J. (Eds). Developments in child care: law, policy and practice. London: Jessica Kingsley.

STATUS: Individual research

DATE OF RESEARCH: 1994-continuing

KEYWORDS: child welfare; exclusion; problem children; residential care; social services; supervision

1496

Faculty of Management, Putteridge Bury Management Centre, Hitchin Road, Luton LU2 8LE
01582 482555

Churcher, J. Mr

Democratising Lithuanian schools

ABSTRACT: Social, political and economic changes are desired by the Lithuanian government and people alike. However, owing to the legacy of 50 years of Soviet control, it appears to be less likely that these changes will be as rapid as people anticipate. The focus of this study will be the effective way to bring about real and lasting fundamental change through the impact of: a) teachers and school leaders, introducing children to the reality and possibility of democracy; b) partnership programmes with educationalists from Western democratic countries. Much of the researcher's thinking around this subject results from partnership training visits to Lithuanian schools and political involvement within educational and party politics in the UK. First-hand observations and discussions in Lithuania (with school leaders, local authority officials and colleages in inservice provision) some three years after the ending of the Soviet period, show that many people still resist change, and for others, the benefits of democratisation and modernisation will still have to be worked upon and struggled over for many years. The following questions and comments, which may be included in the research are: a) To what extent are school leaders and teachers afraid of or reluctant to embark upon the democratisation of schools? b) To what extent are the expectations of some of the Lithuanian school leaders that the changes in educational direction and benefits of democratisation and modernisation will accrue to them almost overnight? c) Before there is a lasting national change, to what extent will there have to be a fundamental change in the nation's value system whereby hearts and minds are influenced, leading to a major change in the culture of society - and how can education contribute to the process? d) What are the similarities and differences between the concept of 'democracy' from both a liberal Western approach and from a Lithuanian post-Soviet standpoint? e) To what extent do Lithuanian school leaders and teachers see democracy being unbridled freedom for the individual or a right to be responsibly exercised within a social context, and how this may have an impact upon the curriculum and pedagogy of the schools?

STATUS: Individual research

DATE OF RESEARCH: 1994-continuing

KEYWORDS: **democracy; eastern europe; lithuania; politics education relationship; social change**

1497

Faculty of Management, Putteridge Bury Management Centre, Hitchin Road, Luton LU2 8LE
01582 482555

Foulkes, P. Mrs

Competences for specialist teacher assistants

ABSTRACT: The aim of the research is to devise a framework of competences appropriate to the role of the specialist teacher assistant. Using the group of specialist teacher assistants on the University of Luton's pilot, Department for Education and Employment (DfEE) funded programme, and in consultation with sponsoring schools, a framework of competences is currently being developed and will be applied during the course (academic year 1995-96) to provide a Specialist Teacher Assistant's Record of Achievement (STAR). Issues relating to the roles and responsibilities of non-teaching assistants form the focus of the research and the specification and assessment of competences are being explored.

STATUS: Individual research

DATE OF RESEARCH: 1995-continuing

KEYWORDS: **competency based education; staff development; support staff**

1498

Faculty of Management, Putteridge Bury Management Centre, Hitchin Road, Luton LU2 8LE
01582 482555
International Centre for Educational Leadership and Management, Lincoln University Campus, Brayford Pool, Lincoln LN6 7TS
01522 886071
Glasgow University, Department of Education, Glasgow G12 8QQ
0141 339 8855

Punter, A. Mrs; *Supervisors*: Thody, A. Dr; Macbeth, A. Dr; Macbeth, A. Dr

School governors from the business and industry community

ABSTRACT: No study has assessed the impact of legislation since 1986 requiring there to be representatives from the business and industry community on school governing bodies. This study aims to investigate the current business and industry sector role in school governance and the ways in which schools and business/industries interact in the context of school governance. The first phase of the work has featured a questionnaire survey to gather data from all the school governors employed by the sample of

twelve national companies which are members of the collaborating establishment, Industry in Education. Frequency and pattern analyses of governors from the sample companies have been carried out. Interviews of a representative sample of managers from the twelve companies were carried out to provide the management's perspective on the current and possible future role of governors from the business and industry community. The results and conclusions from this first phase of the study have been presented to the collaborating establishment and will form part of their report, to be published in Spring 1995. The results have also informed the next phase of the research, through a number of case studies, which will be an indepth study of the role of governors from the business community.

PUBLISHED MATERIAL: PUNTER, A. (1994). 'Collaborating with the business community'. Proceedings of the British Educational Management and Administration Society Conference, University of Manchester Institute of Science and Technology, September 1994. ; PUNTER, A. (1995). 'Issues in administration from the Commonwealth: school governance'. Proceedings of the American Educational Research Association Conference, San Francisco, April 1995. ; PUNTER, A. (1995). 'Leaders and leadership in schools and colleges'. Proceedings of the British Educational Management and Administration Society Conference, Balliol College, Oxford, September 1995. ; PUNTER, A. (1996). 'Partners in change'. To be presented at the British Educational Management and Administration Society Conference, Robinson College, Cambridge, March 1996.

STATUS: Collaborative

SOURCE OF GRANT: Industry in Education £20,000

DATE OF RESEARCH: 1993-1998

KEYWORDS: **educational administration; governing bodies; governing bodies; industry education relationship; school governors**

1499

Quality Assurance Division, Centre for Quality Assurance, Fairview House, Luton LU1 3JU
01582 734111

White, J. Mr; Atlay, M. Dr

Transferable skills in a university-wide modular credit scheme

ABSTRACT: The research looks at the extent to which the University of Luton has adopted a generic transferable skills template and embedded it throughout the entire curriculum of a large modular credit schedule which covers a significant number of subject disciplines. The research uses primary research data collected over the last 18 months and involves the analysis if over 25,000 questionnaires. The research considers differences in perceived levels of skills acquisition on an inter-disciplinary basis and identifies, where possible, generic differences in the way in which transferable skills are received by students in relation to particular disciplines. Future research will focus on how best to assess transferable skills and how to record from a student's transcript and profile.

STATUS: Team research

DATE OF RESEARCH: 1997-continuing

KEYWORDS: **higher education; modular courses; skills; transfer of learning**

1500

Teaching and Learning Directorate, CAA Centre, Park Square, Luton LU1 3JU
01582 734111

Zakrzewski, S. Dr; Bull, J. Dr

Computer-based assessment

ABSTRACT: The research focuses on the use of computer-based assessment techniques in higher education and involves 10,000 such assessments at the University of Luton in 1996/97. The focus of the study is: 1) staff perceptions; 2) student perceptions; 3) management strategies; 4) cost effectiveness.

STATUS: Team research

DATE OF RESEARCH: 1994-continuing

KEYWORDS: **assessment; computer assisted testing; computer uses in education; higher education; information technology**

1501

Teaching and Learning Directorate, CAA Centre, Park Square, Luton LU1 3JU
01582 734111

Bull, J. Dr; McKenna, C. Ms

Implementation and evaluation of computer-assisted assessment

ABSTRACT: The implementation and evaluation of computer-assisted assessment is part of Higher Education Funding Council's (HEFC's) Teaching and Learning Technology Programme (phase 3). The project is developing and piloting various models of implementation, which can be used by individuals, departments and institutions to introduce computer-assisted assessment (CAA). The project will evaluate the cost and learning effectiveness of CAA and provide a centre of expertise, advice and guidance for the implementation and evaluation of CAA in higher education.

STATUS: Sponsored project

SOURCE OF GRANT: Higher Education Funding Council for England

DATE OF RESEARCH: 1998-continuing

KEYWORDS: **assessment; computer assisted testing; computer uses in education; information technology**

1502

Teaching and Learning Directorate, Work Based Learning Unit, Park Square, Luton LU1 3JU
01582 734111

Weller, G. Mr; *Supervisors*: Fallows, S. Dr; Woods, R. Mr; Assiter, A. Prof.

A study of the criteria for designing schemes of work based learning as perceived by the stakeholders; with particular reference to work based learning at degree level, in specified degree fields

ABSTRACT: This investigation has been stimulated through issues which have arisen from Employment Department projects in the field of work based learning, for example, in projects based at the University of North London, University of Huddersfield, University of Portsmouth, and others as defined by Duckenfield & Stirner 1992. This study will consider the needs of the individual stakeholders by assessing the work based learning process using soft systems methodology, as developed by Checkland (1981). The criteria which may emerge from this investigation will be based on the main properties of a system for work based learning, which have been applied to the real world. This research will build on the current body of knowledge available in the field of work based learning for degree level study, much of which has been supported by the Employment Department, and the Council for National Academic Awards (CNAA) through the Association of Sandwich Education and Training (ASET). Central to this investigation is the hypothesis that there exists certain commonality of criteria for the design and assessment of schemes of work based learning, within specified degree fields. If these criteria were understood, then the future design and assessment of schemes of work based learning would become easier to develop, and better meet the needs of all stakeholders.

PUBLISHED MATERIAL: WELLER, G. (1993). 'Modes of employer participation in negotiated work based learning for academic and vocational credit'. Proceedings of the British Education Management and Administration Society Conference on 'Partnerships in Education: Successes and Stresses', 1993. ; WELLER, G. (1994). The work based learning project at the University of Luton. Luton: University of Luton Press. ; WELLER, G. (1995). 'Degree programmes by WBL study mode: issues on planning, delivery and partnership'. In: Proceedings of "Towards a Learning Workforce" Conference, Lancaster University, September 1995. ; WELLER, G. (1995). 'Work based learning in higher education: recognising new styles of partnership'. In: Proceedings of Middlesex University/CBI Conference on Work Based Learning Partnership, June 1995.

STATUS: Sponsored project

SOURCE OF GRANT: Department for Education and Employment ; Bedfordshire Training and Enterprise Council

DATE OF RESEARCH: 1994-continuing

KEYWORDS: **experiential learning; flexible learning; higher education; industry higher education relationship; on the job training; work education relationship**

Manchester Metropolitan University

1503

Crewe and Alsager Faculty, Department of Education, Crewe Campus, Crewe Green Road, Crewe CW1 1DU
0161 247 2000

Keating, I. Ms; *Supervisor*: Robertson, A. Dr

The impact of participation in a nursery on a group of socially and economically disadvantaged mothers

ABSTRACT: The research will consider the impact of participation in a nursery on a group of socially and economically disadvantaged mothers. From background reading, it is clear that early years at schooling play a particularly significant part in child development and attitudes towards schooling. It is accepted that fathers (and other members of the community) become involved in school but it is argued that the role of mothers is particularly significant. The researcher does not intend to reiterate the debate about the value and importance of parental involvement and its impact on children, but to focus on its impact on the mothers who have become involved. The research focus is two-fold: 1) The impact of parental involvement on mothers. 2) Which forms of parental involvement are most valued by different interest groups in a nursery. The research will take place in a nursery with the research subjects identified as mothers, staff and children. It is hoped to construct cost-benefit analyses from these three distinct perspectives. The research methods are essentially interpretative ethnographic. The researcher is anxious to disassociate herself from any possibility of exploiting the women she contacts for the purpose of her research. It is hoped that advantages should arise out of the research for the women (and in particular the mothers) involved in it.

STATUS: Individual research

DATE OF RESEARCH: 1991-1997

KEYWORDS: **early childhood education; mothers; nursery schools; parent participation**

1504

Crewe and Alsager Faculty, Department of Education, Crewe Campus, Crewe Green Road, Crewe CW1 1DU
0161 247 2000
Birmingham University, School of Education, Edgbaston, Birmingham B15 2TT
0121 414 3344

Burton, D. Ms; *Supervisor*: Riding, R. Dr

Cognitive style and personality

ABSTRACT: Research into cognitive style has yielded many different labels which, it is suggested, are different conceptions of the same dimensions. Dr Riding points to two principal cognitive styles: the Wholist-Analytic and Verbal-Imagery dimensions; and has developed a computer-presented Cognitive Styles Analysis (CSA) which measures one individual's position on these two dimensions. It has been found that cognitive style is related to aspects of personality with Verbalisers exhibiting extrovert behaviour and Imagers introvert behaviour. The aim of this study was to investigate the relationship between cognitive style, and outwardly manifested personality characteristics. One hundred and seventy-four 12 year old boys and girls were asked to rate the pupils in their tutor group on seven personality characteristics - humorous, shy, outgoing, patient, quiet, lively and serious. They were also given the CSA to determine each pupil's position on the two dimensions of Verbal-Imagery and Wholist-Analytic. A factor analysis indicates that the seven characteristics could be viewed as three groupings - lively, quiet and serious. A significant interaction was found between Verbal-Imagery style and characteristic grouping. The rating of Lively decreased from Verbaliser to Imager, Quiet was highest for the Intermediate Position of Bimodal, and Serious increased from Verbaliser to Imager. There was also a significant interaction of sex and characteristics grouping with the girls being higher on Quiet and Serious and the boys on Lively. A clear relationship between cognitive style and outwardly observable personality characteristics was shown. Further work is continuing using self-report measures.

STATUS: Individual research

DATE OF RESEARCH: 1991-1997

KEYWORDS: cognitive style; personality; secondary school pupils; sex differences

1505

Crewe and Alsager Faculty, Department of Education, Crewe Campus, Crewe Green Road, Crewe CW1 1DU
0161 247 2000
Manchester University, School of Education, Centre for Formative Assessment Studies, Oxford Road, Manchester M13 9PL
0161 275 2000

Ellis, S. Mr; *Supervisor*: Christie, T. Prof.

National Curriculum assessment in the 1990s: a critical review of the literature

ABSTRACT: The Education Reform Act 1988 has created an unprecedented climate of rapid curricular change in both primary and secondary schools. The management of change will be crucial if the reforms are to benefit all concerned; schools will need to increasingly involve themselves in review and evaluation at whole-school level. The role of research in this area has been largely ignored especially National Curriculum assessment monitoring and evaluation. There is a need to develop our understanding of assessment theory and to move towards a national system which is not just concerned with the 'products' of assessment, but also seeks to explore the underlying 'process' rationale. The central tension and 'dilemma' is the distinction between formative (classroom-based) and summative (external) national assessment. The way in which both primary and secondary schools are managing this conflict forms the broad rationale for this research. The main style of research is pluralistic evaluation as a multi-method approach (triangulation). The collection of data falls into two contexts: 1) Broad context: The focus is 2/3 tier educational institutions exploring the development, monitoring and evaluation of whole school approaches to curricular and assessment implementation. 2) Specific context: This context aims to narrow the field and includes the interlocking variables of continuity and progression, experience of the individual child and the foundation subject geography. The outcomes of the research will provide an examination of the 'state of the art' re-assessment in the National Curriculum. Furthermore, it will provide guidelines for 'good practice' re whole-school assessment issues. Issues of progression and continuity in assessment from the child's perspective are also addressed.

STATUS: Individual research

DATE OF RESEARCH: 1993-1997

KEYWORDS: assessment; national curriculum

1506

Crewe and Alsager Faculty, Department of Education, Crewe Campus, Crewe Green Road, Crewe CW1 1DU
0161 247 2000
Manchester University, School of Education, Oxford Road, Manchester M13 9PL 0161 275 2000

Barnes, E. Mrs; Supervisor: Pumfrey, P. Prof.

A longitudinal study of children's spelling development up to National Curriculum key stage 1

ABSTRACT: The research is set within the theoretical concept of the development of automaticity in children's spelling. It is a longitudinal study of children's progress from mark-making to conventional spelling under 3 somewhat distinctive pedagogic policies during infant school education. The aims are to: 1) collect on a termly basis samples of mark-making/ writing produced by key stage 1 pupils and describe developmental patterns in their spellings; 2) test hyptheses concerning the children's spelling development in relation to distinct agreed school policies theoretically governing the teaching and learning of spelling; 3) consider the theoretical and practical implications of the findings. From 71 infant and primary schools in a given division of a local education authority (LEA), information concerning agreed and written school policies governing the teaching and learning of writing and spelling were elicited. On the basis of this information, schools were categorised as 'developmental', 'eclectic' or 'traditional'. From schools of Group 2 size, 2 schools were selected at random from each of the 3 categories. Each school admitted 1 cohort each September and another each January. 184

children were involved. The research systematically sampled the children's naturalistic writing (and hence spelling) elicited in small groups on each of up to 9 occasions. Additionally, a standard spelling test was administered on 3 occasions. The Harvard Codes for Human Analysis of Transcripts (CHAT) and Computerised Language Analysis (CLAN) were used to analyse the naturalistic data. Both are included in the Child Lanaguage Data Exchange System (CHILDES).

STATUS: Individual research

DATE OF RESEARCH: 1990-1997

KEYWORDS: key stage 1; primary education; spelling; writing skills; writing teaching

1507

Crewe and Alsager Faculty, Department of Education, Crewe Campus, Crewe Green Road, Crewe CW1 1DU
0161 247 2000
University College Worcester, Henwick Grove, Worcester WR2 6AJ
01905 855000
Nottingham University, School of Education, University Park, Nottingham NG7 2RD
01159 515151

Fabian, H. Ms; *Supervisors*: Pascal, C. Prof.; Gammage, P. Prof.

Managing the admission and induction of children into school

ABSTRACT: The study aims to: 1) investigate the management of the admission and induction of children into school; 2) explore ways in which the transition from pre-school and home to school, and the first days in school, are managed; 3) identify how children are settled into school; 4) discuss how the nature of the transition may have influenced attitudes and learning behaviour. The study will ask: 1) What are the implications for practice or admission policies? 2) What strategies are employed which might make the transition, and first days in school, a stress-free experience? 3) How does the parents' attitudes and involvement affect the way in which children settle? 4) What are the children's perceptions of school? Approaches to the methodology will be located in sociological and ethnographical theory and will follow a naturalistic model of inquiry. In order to demonstrate the general features of induction in the locality a survey has been conducted, by means of a questionnaire, of 26 infant and primary schools in a town in the Midlands. Case studies are taking place in two schools in the area (one infant, one primary), with similar catchment areas but with different practice. A sample of 60 children who entered school during the academic year 1994/95 are being studied, together with their parents and teachers. Research methods include interviews, partipant and non-participant observation which will result in both qualitative and quantitative data.

STATUS: Individual research

DATE OF RESEARCH: 1993-1998

KEYWORDS: early childhood education; home school relationship; infant education; primary education; pupil school relationship; reception classes; school entrance age; young children

1508

Crewe and Alsager Faculty, Department of Educational Management, Hassall Road, Alsager, Stoke on Trent ST7 2HL
0161 247 2000

Turnock, J. Mr; *Supervisor*: Tolly, B. Dr

The role of the Church of England in the provision of education at Worfield Endowed Church of England (Aided) Primary School from 1546 to 1991, with particular reference to the governors' responsibility for curriculum, funding and building in the light of the Education Reform Act 1988.

ABSTRACT: The aim of this research is to clarify the purpose and application of educational endowments from the Brierley Charity of 1609, Lloyd and Parker Charity of 1613 and other trust deeds which were later amalgamated into the Worfield United Charities. It will also try to establish the changing role of the Church of England and the provision of free education. The project will look at the changes which took place in local thinking and to examine the influences of the major educational reform acts of the last 150 years. The researchers will establish whether the Foundation Governors' income from endowment is still regulated by the 1909 scheme, or whether subsequent variations have been legitimised by the Charity Commissioners. Links will be established between the elected Church Foundation Governors and their associated endowments with other members of the Governing Body in order to clarify responsibility for the curriculum and the ownership of the land and buildings of Worfield Primary School. It is also hoped to clarify the powers of the whole Governing Body in the light of new legislation under the Education Reform Act 1988.

STATUS: Sponsored project

SOURCE OF GRANT: Shropshire Local Education Authority £395

DATE OF RESEARCH: 1991-1993

KEYWORDS: church education relationship; educational history; educational legislation; financial support; free education; primary education; school governors

1509

Crewe and Alsager Faculty, Department of Educational Management, Hassall Road, Alsager, Stoke on Trent ST7 2HL
0161 247 2000

James, M. Mr; *Supervisor*: Seymour, R. Mr

Managing the implementation of the National Curriculum

ABSTRACT: This research examines the introduction of the National Curriculum as an exercise in the management of change. Literature reviews have been carried out on curriculum theory, a centrally controlled curriculum and various perspectives on the National Curriculum as well as educational change. The question of cross curricularity and subject overlap has emerged as extremely important. Five secondary schools will be studied. Interviews with the headteacher and deputy and the heads of science, geography and technology will take place. Data will then be collated and analysed to compare 'real world' perceptions and problems with the theoretical perspectives of the literature review. It is hoped that 'good practice' guidelines and additional knowledge on the management of change will emerge.

STATUS: Individual research

DATE OF RESEARCH: 1990-1993

KEYWORDS: core curriculum; curriculum development; educational administration; educational change; educational development; interdisciplinary approach; national curriculum

1510

Crewe and Alsager Faculty, Department of Educational Management, Hassall Road, Alsager, Stoke on Trent ST7 2HL
0161 247 2000

Hemmings, N. Mr; *Supervisor*: Seymour, R. Mr

Self managing schools - a practical way forward for secondary schools

ABSTRACT: The research aims to consider some of the practical effects of school management in the light of the Education Reform Act 1988 (ERA). In particular focusing upon the ways secondary schools have adapted to the new challenges that ERA has presented. A case study of representative schools has begun.

STATUS: Sponsored project

SOURCE OF GRANT: Stoke on Trent Local Education Authority £150

DATE OF RESEARCH: 1990-1993

KEYWORDS: education reform act 1988; educational administration; educational change; local management of schools; school based management; secondary education

1511

Department of Applied Community Studies, Didsbury Campus, 799 Wilmslow Road, Didsbury, Manchester M20 2RR
0161 247 2000

Stokes, I. Ms; *Supervisor*: Humphries, B. Dr

Black practice teachers in social work: a study of their number and contributions in four statutory agencies in Greater Manchester

ABSTRACT: This study is an investigation into black practice teachers in social work in three local authority social services departments and one probation service in an area of the north west of England. It attempts to

identify the numbers of black practitioners who were eligible to become practice teachers and whether such practitioners were interested in practice teaching. In addition, mechanisms in the agencies which determine how individuals are chosen to become practice teachers were examined and the effectiveness of such mechanisms were explored with the research subjects. The research is based on the notion of black perspectives in terms of taking into account the reality of black people's experiences. The data was gathered through questionnaire, interviews, group sessions, and analysis of relevant literature and policy and practice documents of the agencies. The report concludes that large numbers of black practitioners in the agencies were eligible to become practice teachers and a large percentage were interested in being practice teachers. The recommendations suggest ways in which all those involved in social work practice teaching could work to develop and realise these interests, at the same time as increasing the number of black practice teachers in the system.

STATUS: Sponsored project

SOURCE OF GRANT: Central Council for Education and Training in Social Work Practice Placement Initiative Grant £90,000

DATE OF RESEARCH: 1992-1993

KEYWORDS: blacks; ethnic groups; social work teachers

1512

Department of Hotel, Catering and Tourism Management, Hollings Faculty, Old Hall Lane, Manchester M14 6HR
0161 247 2000
Keele University, Department of Education, Keele ST5 5BG
01782 621111

Ineson, E. Dr; *Supervisor*: Kempa, R. Prof.

The predictive validity of criteria used in the selection of students for undergraduate courses and graduate training in hotel and catering management

ABSTRACT: This study investigated whether selection criteria, which were predictive of undergraduate Hotel and Catering Management (HCM) students' subsequent academic performance and their recruitment into employment, could be identified. The scant findings from previous HCM studies were supplemented by evidence from HCM prospectuses, application forms and interviews with selectors. Data were collected from 469 first year and 210 final year HCM undergraduates in England and Scotland and related to a series of performance measures. The predictive qualities of the data in relation to the performance measures were evaluated by appropriate statistical techniques including ANOVA and discriminant analysis. The findings confirmed that academic criteria were predominantly the most effective single predictors of HCM degree course success. However, slightly better predictions were obtained from a combination of academic and non-academic criteria. As far as recruitment to graduate management training was concerned, academic criteria did not have significant predictive value. Instead, these recruiters relied on a preconception that all graduates had acquired certain skills and competences, then sought evidence of managerial work experience, interpersonal skills and certain personal qualities. Ambition, measured at the commencement of the final undergraduate year, was the main criterion leading to Hotel and Catering employment. It was concluded that the selection criteria in operation were not very well matched with the performance outcomes, hence it was extremely difficult for undergraduate admission tutors to take a long term perspective. This PhD project was sponsored in part by the ASE division at NFER-Nelson.

PUBLISHED MATERIAL: INESON, E.M. (1987). 'The do's and don'ts of jobhunting', Hospitality, February. ; CHILDS, R. (1990). Graduate and managerial assessment data supplement. Windsor: ASE - a division of NFER-Nelson.

STATUS: Individual research

DATE OF RESEARCH: 1986-1993

KEYWORDS: hospitality industry; hotel and catering education; hotel management education; selection

1513

Didsbury School of Education, 799 Wilmslow Road, Didsbury, Manchester M20 2RR
0161 247 2000

Gutteridge, K. Dr; Hatch, G. Mrs; Lingard, D. Mr

A case study to compare the experience of teacher training students in primary and secondary schools

ABSTRACT: The research is a case study involving two secondary schools and four primary schools. The schools fall into two groups of one secondary and two primary schools in the same geographical area. The two geographical areas are contrasting in social type. All data on the student experience during a school practice forming part of year 3 of the B.Ed. course is being collected. A researcher will visit all six schools twice to observe classes and discuss the practice with the student. The latter will be taped. Student file entries will be collected together with school and tutor reports. The underlying purpose of the case study is to see whether it is possible to throw any light on the reasons that secondary students obtain lower gradings on school experience than primary students. This small-scale project may develop into a larger scale one if the current work shows any patterns which seem to merit a wider investigation.

STATUS: Sponsored project

SOURCE OF GRANT: Manchester Metropolitan University

DATE OF RESEARCH: 1992-1993

KEYWORDS: placement; preservice teacher education; primary education; secondary education; student teachers; teaching practice

1514

Didsbury School of Education, 799 Wilmslow Road, Didsbury, Manchester M20 2RR
0161 247 2000

Hustler, D. Prof.; Carter, K. Ms; Green, J. Ms; Halsall, R. Mr

An evaluation of 'The Recording Achievement and Higher Education Project'

ABSTRACT: The Recording Achievement and Higher Education project is a collaborative project across 15 higher education institutions and 11 local education authorities (LEAs) and associated schools and colleges. The project is designed to investigate how best to link and coordinate initiatives within and across both institutions and sectors, as regard to recording achievement. Work focuses on admissions processes into higher education and on the role of recording achievement processes within higher education. The evaluation team have: participated in project events and activities; undertaken an extensive interviewing programme; and sampled a range of project products. The evaluation work has been designed so as to have both formative and summative outcomes. An interim evaluation report has been produced and a project statement drawing on this work is available.

STATUS: Sponsored project

SOURCE OF GRANT: Department of Employment £10,000

DATE OF RESEARCH: 1992-1993

KEYWORDS: access to education; higher education; programme evaluation; records of achievement; student records

1515

Didsbury School of Education, 799 Wilmslow Road, Didsbury, Manchester M20 2RR
0161 247 2000

Johnson, P. Dr

The Book Art Project

ABSTRACT: The Book Art Project was inaugurated by a Crafts Council grant of 400 pounds in 1986, and further funding was provided by the Gulbenkian Foundation in 1990 (5,000 pounds). The main aims of the project are to: (1) further the literacy development of children through the book arts; (2) encourage the interrelationship of verbal and visual modes of communication in the curriculum; (3) enhance the role of the book arts as a cross-curricular model of processing information in education; (4) increase children's awareness of the cultural heritage of the book concept and their place in that tradition. This research programme is conducted entirely by the project director and involves medium to long term school-based skills through the book arts. Results and conclusions are published periodically. Project publications include Book Pack 1 (1990). Structures and authorship; Book Pack 2 (1992). Books across the curriculum; Book Pack 3 (1993). Introducing illustration to children; INSET

video (1992). Children making their own books. The Children's Press was established in 1992. The aim of the press is to encourage children to write and illustrate their own books by publishing a selection of titles each year.

PUBLISHED MATERIAL: JOHNSON, P. (1992). Pop-up paper engineering: cross-curricular activities in design engineering technology, English and art. London: Falmer Press. ; JOHNSON, P. (1993). 'Book art and the road to literacy', Primary English, No 3, pp.23-26. ; JOHNSON, P. (1993). Literacy through the book arts'. London: Hodder & Stoughton. ; JOHNSON, P. (1993). 'The Japanese connection', Language and Learning, Vol 15, No 2, pp.31-36. ; JOHNSON, P. (1995). Children making books. Reading: University of Reading, Reading and Language Information Centre. A full list of publications is available from the researcher.

STATUS: Sponsored project

SOURCE OF GRANT: Gulbenkian Foundation £5,000

DATE OF RESEARCH: 1990-continuing

KEYWORDS: art education; books; children as writers; childrens art; childrens literature; literacy; picture books

1516

Didsbury School of Education, 799 Wilmslow Road, Didsbury, Manchester M20 2RR
0161 247 2000

Archer, M. Mr; Hogbin, J. Mr; Pickard, A. Dr; Strahan, H. Ms; Palmerone, W. Ms

Supervision 'in action': a study of the process of supervision of initial teacher training students

ABSTRACT: The aim of the project is to investigate the process of school experience supervision, in order to identify and prioritise those elements necessary for an effective scheme for induction into supervisory skills. This is a small scale pilot project focused on the supervisory practices utilised by the five research collaborators in their supervision of a group of students in training. Thirty students are participating in the project chosen at random from two different year groups. The approach fits within the tradition of ethnographic research. All transactions associated with the supervision of students including tutorials, classroom observation, discussion with students and teachers are being documented. All tutorials and supervision are being tape recorded. The research concerns are to identify the nature of the activities associated with each style of 'event' and to identify the supervisory issues associated with each. The research is essentially self-analytical in its stance seeking to identify the concerns, intentions and reflections of the supervisors engaged in the project. The intention is to produce illuminative materials that can be used, in the first instance, within the School of Education, at Manchester Metropolitan University to help induct new supervisors to their role. It is likely that the materials will have direct relevance to experienced supervisors and to mentors.

STATUS: Sponsored project

SOURCE OF GRANT: Manchester Metropolitan University

DATE OF RESEARCH: 1992-1993

KEYWORDS: mentors; preservice teacher education; student teacher supervisors; supervision; supervisory methods; teaching practice

1517

Didsbury School of Education, 799 Wilmslow Road, Didsbury, Manchester M20 2RR
0161 247 2000

Harnor, M. Mr

Higher education students with epilepsy

ABSTRACT: It might be possible that public attitudes and expectations concerning people with epilepsy are less likely to be negative if individuals with the condition can increasingly establish themselves in occupations requiring graduate and post-graduate qualifcations. University level institutions generally maintain that they have equal opportunities policies. This study is concerned with students' perceptions of their own epilepsy and a range of personal, social and educational consequences whilst they are in higher education. A sample of 40 students so far has been reached through advertisement. Each received a suitably designed and trialled questionnaire concerned with 38 variables and a sub-sample interviewed. Many wrote substantial correspondence highlighting the need for this research. Those who answered received a brochure previously co-written for students and institutions. The personal and idiosyncratic nature of epilepsy and its treatment makes suitable multivariant analysis difficult although this is being attempted. Examples of some of the many findings are given by: 60% of those who had initial attacks under 19 years doing so at or near key school examination dates. Of those having attacks during an examination or within 24 hours either way, 37% had references made to the examiners; 43% had initial attacks post 18 years; 41% of those in college accommodation had been given priority; 86% felt people regarded them as different. Drugs worried many; 83% felt that these affected their academic performance. 77% felt the brochure would have been valuable to them.

STATUS: Sponsored project

SOURCE OF GRANT: Manchester Metropolitan University

DATE OF RESEARCH: 1990-continuing

KEYWORDS: **epilepsy; higher education; student attitudes; student health and welfare**

1518

Didsbury School of Education, 799 Wilmslow Road, Didsbury, Manchester M20 2RR
0161 247 2000

Hall, N. Mr; Robinson, A. Mrs

Using letter writing to develop young children's non-chronological writing

ABSTRACT: This project aims to provide experiences in relation to socio-dramatic play situations where children are required to write letters which contain non-chronological text. The children involved will be aged 5-7. Within each project setting opportunities will be created where the writing of a particular text form will become a reasonable and natural thing to do. In each setting the researchers will provide real responders to the children's letters. These replies will aim to draw out the children in a variety of textual forms. The textual forms the project will aim to introduce to the children will be: (1) persuasive/argumentative (subsuming apologies, complaints and application); (2) procedural (subsuming directions, rules and instructions); (3) explanatory; (4) descriptive. Two principal kinds of data will be recorded: (1) Transcriptions of teaching undertaken by the teacher or project workers in respect of the textual forms. Thus any discussions or explanations will be recorded and analysed. This will be done in order to identify the most useful teaching points; (2) The letters written by the children. Each group of children's letters will be analysed for appropriate use of the correct textual form. The analysis will be primarily linguistic, looking at genre form and the children's use of register.

PUBLISHED MATERIAL: HALL, N. & ROBINSON, A. (1995). Exploring writing and play in the early years. Manchester Metropolitan University Education Series. London: Fulton.

STATUS: Sponsored project

SOURCE OF GRANT: Royal Mail £7,000; Arjo Wiggins £7,000

DATE OF RESEARCH: 1993-continuing

KEYWORDS: **letters - correspondence; writing - composition; writing exercises; writing skills**

1519

Didsbury School of Education, 799 Wilmslow Road, Didsbury, Manchester M20 2RR
0161 247 2000

Arthur, C. Ms; *Supervisor*: Hall, N. Mr

An investigation into the concepts of punctuation held by children between the ages of 6 and 8

ABSTRACT: The intended research will focus on children's own observations of punctuation in the processes of reading, adding punctuation to existing text, and writing. It is hoped thereby to ascertain the children's concepts and understanding of punctuation, as much as possible, from the children's own statements. The difficulties with this are mainly to do with eliciting from children their knowledge about a subject which is of

little significance to them, which they would not naturally talk about at all, which is inevitably extremely complex, and which requires a metalanguage of which children are largely ignorant or confused. In an attempt to alleviate some of these problems the experimental procedure will involve children working in pairs on one task. It is hoped that this will 'force' children to be explicit about many of the things that are normally simply thought about. The pairs of children will undertake a variety of tasks. They will: (1) read and respond to passages with and without punctuation; (2) place punctuation in an unpunctuated passage; (3) engage in free writing during which the punctuation of texts will be observed and will be discussed immediately afterwards; (4) discuss or explain in interviews their use or understanding of punctuation. The children will be selected from Year 2 classes (pre-National Curriculum assessment) and Year 3 classes (post-National Curriculum assessment). For each pair of children a set of data will be collected, allowing comparison between the results of the various tasks set, and across age groups. Analysis of the data will be in terms of the underlying linguistic strategies revealed by the children's statements, reading responses, and writing.

PUBLISHED MATERIAL: HALL, N. & ROBINSON, A. (1996). Learning about punctuation. Language and Education Library No 9. Clevedon: Multilingual Matters.

STATUS: Sponsored project

SOURCE OF GRANT: Manchester Metropolitan University

DATE OF RESEARCH: 1992-continuing

KEYWORDS: **comprehension; punctuation; writing skills**

1520

Didsbury School of Education, 799 Wilmslow Road, Didsbury, Manchester M20 2RR
0161 247 2000

Rainer, J. Mr; Johnson, M. Mr; Black, M. Ms

Research into ways in which drama teaching in primary schools may have an impact on general classroom learning and interpersonal behaviour

ABSTRACT: The aims of the project are to: a) find whether drama teaching in primary schools has an effect on classroom behaviours and ethos; b) find whether such effects might be measured; c) find whether particular kinds of drama activity might have more effect than others; and d) devise an instrument which might measure (c). The project will use 8 teacher-researchers recruited from 5 primary schools across Greater Manchester/Cheshire to administer Professor B. Fraser's "My Class Inventory" - an instrument designed to quantify changes in classroom behaviour and ethos - before and after a programme of monitored drama activity. In addition, a research group will be set up with the task of designing an instrument which might quantify drama activity in order to assist more detailed classroom observation.

STATUS: Sponsored project

SOURCE OF GRANT: Manchester Metropolitan University; Higher Education Funding Council

DATE OF RESEARCH: 1993-continuing

KEYWORDS: **classroom environment; classroom management; drama; primary schools; pupil behaviour**

1521

Didsbury School of Education, 799 Wilmslow Road, Didsbury, Manchester M20 2RR
0161 247 2000

Wood, D. Mr; *Supervisors*: Goodwin, A. Mr; Langrish, J. Dr

Influences of increased school-based training in developing science teaching competences

ABSTRACT: A case study of the influence of increasing school-based teacher training on the development of science student teacher competences. The project will look at a range of influencing factors on student development in one university department of education in the United Kingdom. The influence of course input, school experience (including mentoring), previous experience and peer relationships will all be explored using observation, interview, questionnaire and document analysis. A longitudinal comparison spanning the implementation period of the British government's reforms to secondary teacher training (1992), will be made by collecting data from courses throughout this period of change (2-3 years). The sample size will be approximately 70 students per year in each year of the study, which will run for 2-3 years in all. The whole course will be sampled using questionnaires, but smaller samples will be selected for interview and observation.

STATUS: Individual research

DATE OF RESEARCH: 1993-1997

KEYWORDS: preservice teacher education; school based teacher education; science education; science teachers; student teachers

1522

Didsbury School of Education, 799 Wilmslow Road, Didsbury, Manchester M20 2RR
0161 247 2000

Naylor, S. Mr; Keogh, B. Ms

Cartoons as a teaching and learning approach in science

ABSTRACT: The research involves the use of simple pictorial representations of scientific ideas. These 'cartoons' present alternative viewpoints about everyday situations. The cartoons have been trialled by teachers in primary, secondary and higher education settings. The aim of the research is to explore the effectiveness of the cartoons in motivating learners, in eliciting their ideas, in re-structuring their ideas, and in drawing together the elicitation and re-structuring phases of the constructivist teaching sequence. Data from teachers indicates that the cartoons are effective in all of these respects.

PUBLISHED MATERIAL: KEOGH, B. & NAYLOR, S. (1993). 'Learning in science: another way', Primary Science Review, No 26, pp.22-23. ; KEOGH, B. & NAYLOR, S. (1996). Scientists and primary schools: a practical guide. Sandbach: Millgate House.

STATUS: Sponsored project

SOURCE OF GRANT: Higher Education Funding Council for England

DATE OF RESEARCH: 1993-continuing

KEYWORDS: cartoons; educational materials; science education

1523

Didsbury School of Education, 799 Wilmslow Road, Didsbury, Manchester M20 2RR
0161 247 2000

Procter, P. Mrs; Walker, K. Mr; Brake, J. Ms

Photography education

ABSTRACT: The investigation focuses on developmental work in photography education over a three year period. The key features of the work are: 1) To develop awareness of photography as an art form with broad applications and relevance across all phases of education. 2) To establish working relationships with teachers, students and children and develop school and community based photography projects and initiatives. 3) To use photography and digital media to produce educational resources and teaching materials relating to the National Curriculum Orders General Certificate of Education (GCSE) and inservice teacher education (INSET) needs. In collaboration with Viewpoint Photography Gallery, Salford, Oldham Art Gallery and targeted schools, a number of high profile projects will be coordinated and documented which will demonstrate the range of possibilities and the educational potential of photography in enhancing visual literacy. Central to the work will be issues of media representation, ways of broadening cultural enfranchisement, access and critical perspectives. The results of the work will be disseminated through contextualised exhibitions at a number of national venues and by CD ROM and/or video. Throughout the period of investigation a range of educational resources and publications will be produced to ensure national dissemination.

STATUS: Sponsored project

SOURCE OF GRANT: Manchester Metropolitan University; Higher Education Funding Council; Arts Council; North West Arts Board

DATE OF RESEARCH: 1994-1997

KEYWORDS: art education; photography; visual arts

1524

Didsbury School of Education, 799 Wilmslow Road, Didsbury, Manchester M20 2RR
0161 247 2000

Hatch, G. Mrs; Binns, B. Ms; Eade, F. Mr; Andrews, P. Mr; Luckley, P. Mr

Innovative teaching in mathematics

ABSTRACT: The project looks at various forms of innovative teaching in the classroom. The teaching may be innovative in two main ways: a) by approaches which use, for example, information technology, problem solving, investigative methods, games; b) the project studies the effect of a group of approximately 10 student teachers working in a school, accompanied by a lecturer, and using innovative approaches, and the subsequent development of these student teachers. Their work in school involves joint planning and delivery and allows secure experimentation. The research methods used involve personal diaries, direct observation, audio and video tape recording. For one year of the project the student group also involved Hungarian teacher trainees. Therefore some comparative work has been done between the systems in two countries.

PUBLISHED MATERIAL: ANDREWS, P. (1994). 'A snapshot of Hungarian teacher training', Mathematics Teaching, No 149, pp.20-22. ; TAHTA, D., POPE, S., WINTER, J., PINAL, A., KNIGHTS, G., GORMON, M., HATCH, G. & WELLS, B. (1994). 'Coming up to Russian expectations', Mathematics Teaching, No 146, pp.25-36. ; ANDREWS, P. (1994). 'Different approaches', MicroMath, Vol 10, No 1, pp.31-34. ; ANDREWS, P. (1995). 'Return to Budapest', Mathematics Teaching, No 151, pp.23-25.

STATUS: Sponsored project

SOURCE OF GRANT: Manchester Metropolitan University

DATE OF RESEARCH: 1993-continuing

KEYWORDS: innovation; learning activities; mathematical enrichment; mathematics education; preservice teacher education; student teachers; teaching methods; teaching practice

1525

Didsbury School of Education, 799 Wilmslow Road, Didsbury, Manchester M20 2RR
0161 247 2000

Campbell, A. Prof.; Kane, I. Mr; Moylett, H. Ms; Hustler, D. Prof.; Craig, B. Ms

Mentoring in schools

ABSTRACT: This is part of a national project working with the Universities of Oxford, Leicester, Swansea, Sussex and Keele. The Manchester research project 'mentoring in schools' is concerned with the systematic investigation of the role of the mentor focusing on: 1) the learning of mentoring skills to enhance initial teacher education; 2) continuous professional development for teacher mentors; 3) institutional changes in schools and higher education as a result of implementation of school-based teacher education; 4) the use of learning contracts as a possible framework for the development of professional competences; 5) common mentoring issues across primary and secondary schools; 6) mentoring in the whole school context with reference to primary schools. Data has been gathered via interview, questionnaire, diary, mentor's log and discussions and this has enabled the construction of case studies from which the following issues emerged as significant: 1) Primary school culture and mentoring: whole school approaches. 2) Challenges and conflicts posed by mentoring and the concepts of objectivity, confidentiality and trust. 3) Parents' and governors' views on school-based teacher education. 4) Differences and similarities between primary and secondary schools. 5) Varieties of mentoring depending on context. There are five interim reports which are available from Manchester Metropolitan University: 1) 'Similarities and differences' by I.S. Kane & B. Craig; 2) 'Tutors' views' by M. Whiteley; 3) 'Mentors and mentoring' by A. Campbell; 4) 'Parents and governors' by I.S. Kane; 5) 'Headteachers talking' by A. Campbell.

PUBLISHED MATERIAL: CAMPBELL, A. (1995). 'The mentoring school: some aspects of mentoring causing tensions and dilemmas for primary schools', Mentoring and Tutoring, Vol 2, No 3, pp.1-8. ; CAMPBELL, A. & KANE, I. 'Chapter mentoring in primary schools: tensions, dilemmas, problems and success'. In: MCINTYRE, D. &

HAGGER, H. (Eds). Mentoring in schools: developing the profession of teaching. London: David Fulton Publishers.

STATUS: Sponsored project

SOURCE OF GRANT: Esmee Fairbairn Charitable Trust £35,000

DATE OF RESEARCH: 1993-continuing

KEYWORDS: mentors; preservice teacher education; school based teacher education; student teacher supervisors

1526

Didsbury School of Education, 799 Wilmslow Road, Didsbury, Manchester M20 2RR
0161 247 2000

Harnor, M. Mr

Teachers with epilepsy

ABSTRACT: This study is concerned with teachers' perceptions of their own epilepsy and a range of possible personal, social and professional consequences. A sample of teachers (n=20) was reached, mainly through advertisement in the Epilepsy Press. Each was sent a questionnaire and all who responded (n=19) volunteered their telephone number, enabling further sample interviewing. Specific items concerned: seizure frequency and type; drug regimes; perceived effects of epilepsy and/or medication upon job performance; attack locations; headteacher, teacher and pupil awareness; restrictions upon teaching particular items; career impact; disclosure to employing authorities' medical services; disclosure to headteachers upon appointment or before; interviews; any suspension or discharge due to epilepsy; reinstatement and procedures; awareness of regulations or recommendations concerning teachers with epilepsy; awareness of any other teachers with epilepsy before this study.

STATUS: Individual research

DATE OF RESEARCH: 1993-continuing

KEYWORDS: epilepsy; health; teachers

1527

Didsbury School of Education, 799 Wilmslow Road, Didsbury, Manchester M20 2RR
0161 247 2000

Goodwin, A. Mr; Kelly, M. Mr; Cockett, M. Mr; Carter, K. Ms; Rodger, R. Ms; Green, J. Ms; *Supervisor*: Halsall, R. Mr

A study of the use of action research projects as a school improvement strategy

ABSTRACT: The North West Consortium for the Study of Effective Urban Schools has been recently established by the Didsbury School of Education at Manchester Metropolitan University, the Education Department at Manchester Victoria University, Manchester Local Education Authority and Salford Local Education Authority. Its aim is to encourage and support action research/development projects in schools, and consortium of schools, which are aimed at improving school effectiveness. A number of action research projects will, therefore, be undertaken. This particular study aims to oversee them with a view to 'evaluating' the impact of such projects on school improvement. In one sense, then, the focus is on action research as an improvement strategy. The exact number of action research projects is not yet finally determined but will probably be about 15-20 in total, each with a focus on a particular theme (e.g. parental involvement, baseline assessment, literacy, raising motivation). The 'overarching' evaluative study will involve participant observation, the use of pre- and post-project indicators regarding outcomes, and interviewing of school staff.

STATUS: Sponsored project

SOURCE OF GRANT: Manchester Metropolitan University

DATE OF RESEARCH: 1995-1997

KEYWORDS: action research; educational improvement; educational quality; school effectiveness

1528

Didsbury School of Education, 799 Wilmslow Road, Didsbury, Manchester M20 2RR
0161 247 2000

Hall, N. Mr

Learning to punctuate: an ecological and conceptual investigation

ABSTRACT: The overall aim of this project is to develop an account of children's developing beliefs about punctuation and to consider classroom influences on children's thinking about punctuation. It is an initial study and should raise a number of issues that could be the subject of later, more extended study. The objectives are: 1) To investigate the existence of a stage-developmental progression in young children's understanding of punctuation. 2) To investigate the relationship between developmental changes and classroom experiences. It is an essential criteria of the methodology that the above objectives are investigated within the normal classroom context. Such an investigation, with its need for comprehensive situational data, necessitates an intensive study of one group of children in their normal classroom environment through a qualitative approach. The project will locate itself in one classroom for a one year period. The children would be followed across a one year period while they are in Year 1 (approximately 6 years of age). Initial data will be collected about the knowledge of punctuation by the children in the class, their general ability with writing, and the teaching styles to which they have been exposed.

STATUS: Sponsored project

SOURCE OF GRANT: Economic and Social Research Council £29,000

DATE OF RESEARCH: 1994-continuing

KEYWORDS: classroom observation techniques; infant education; primary education; punctuation; writing skills; young children

1529

Didsbury School of Education, 799 Wilmslow Road, Didsbury, Manchester M20 2RR
0161 247 2000

Ackers, J. Ms; Griffin, B. Ms; Marsch, C. Ms; Grant-Mullins, N. Ms; *Supervisor*: Abbott, L. Ms

Shaping the future - educare for the under-threes

ABSTRACT: National research at the present time is tending to focus on the 3-5 year old stage and this project complements those on ongoing research projects which aim to evaluate and improve the learning of 3 and 4 year old children in a range of settings (Pascal 1994 and Belkin 1994). A critical question which the project is attempting to address is: given the diversity of provision for under-threes in what ways can continuity with the 3-5 stage be facilitated? The proposal is innovative and timely in the light of recent legislation regarding inspection and registration required by both the Children Act 1989 and the Education Reform Act 1988. The project aims to: 1) identify the training and support needs of adults working with under-threes including parents; 2) identify minimum standards with regard to the care and education of under-threes; 3) undertake a small scale comparison in two European countries with regard to the above; 4) involve early childhood students at initial and inservice training levels in ways which will contribute to their professional development and provide continuity with the later stages.

PUBLISHED MATERIAL: ABBOTT, L. & ROGER, R. (Eds). (1994). Quality education in the early years. Buckingham: Open University Press.; GRIFFIN, B. (1994). 'Look at me I'm only two'. In: ABBOTT, L. & ROGER, R. (Eds). Quality education in the early years. Buckingham: Open University Press. ; A full list of publications is available from the researchers.

STATUS: Sponsored project

SOURCE OF GRANT: Esmee Fairbairn Charitable Trust £25,100; Higher Education Funding Council for England £25,100

DATE OF RESEARCH: 1995-1997

KEYWORDS: child caregivers; early childhood education; early experience; educational quality; nursery education; preschool education; young children

1530

Didsbury School of Education, 799 Wilmslow Road, Didsbury, Manchester M20 2RR
0161 247 2000

Phillips, S. Mrs; Thomas, E. Ms; *Supervisor*: Johnson, M. Mr

Pupils with epilepsy and the Code of Practice for Identification and Assessment of Special Educational Needs

ABSTRACT: The Code of Practice on the Identification and Assessment of Special Educational Needs places a clear emphasis on the wishes of parents in determining and providing for the special educational needs of pupils. It underscores the importance of close collaboration between parents and all others involved with the child's health and educational needs. This is particularly true of epilepsy where many of the difficulties following diagnosis may be due to secondary effects, e.g. side effects of medication, parental anxiety and perceptions of the condition rather than the actual condition itself. It is therefore proposed to undertake qualitative research with a group of children and adolescents who have a history of epilepsy and their families. Inteviews will be conducted with them and the 'significant others' from their school, local education authority (LEA) and associated child health services who have been concerned in processes relating to the Code of Practice to establish what the diagnosis of an epileptic condition in a pupil means to that pupil and those significant others associated with him or her. The aims are: 1) to determine what this group of people anticipate will be the results for him or her; 2) to establish their expectations of each other in relation to the education of that pupil; and 3) from these understandings, to produce materials that will enhance the ability of those having a role in determining the future educational needs of the pupil to communicate effectively with each other in attaining the pupil's rights and fulfilling their responsibilities under the Code of Practice.

STATUS: Sponsored project

SOURCE OF GRANT: British Epilepsy Association £37,000

DATE OF RESEARCH: 1996-1997

KEYWORDS: code of practice; epilepsy; special educational needs

1531

Didsbury School of Education, 799 Wilmslow Road, Didsbury, Manchester M20 2RR
0161 247 2000

Moscovitch Steiner, M. Ms; Supervisor: Hustler, D. Prof.

Promoting global citizenship through mentor programmes in initial teacher education

ABSTRACT: The objectives of the research are: 1) to identify the best means of utilising the partnership teacher training programmes between schools and higher education institutions to promote the global dimension in initial teacher education; 2) to develop courses and modules which develop this understanding amongst student teachers; and 3) to facilitate action research activities amongst the participants - these will be teacher-mentors (both primary and secondary phases) and higher education tutors. Membership will be drawn from approximately 10 higher education institutions in England and Wales who will in turn identify local school-based partners. The work will entail pre- and post-course surveys of attitudes and opinions concerning both global issues (here defined as those to do with human rights, development, equal opportunities (gender, race), environment and citizenship) and appropriate teaching practices to explore these. It will identify teaching methodologies and interpersonal skills that are best suited to mentorship/partnership arrangements, insofar as they enable the teacher educators to equip student teachers to understand and be able to teach such matters appropriately.

STATUS: Sponsored project

SOURCE OF GRANT: Manchester Metropolitan University; Oxfam; Christian Aid; CAFOD; UNICEF; Action AID; Save the Children

DATE OF RESEARCH: 1996-1998

KEYWORDS: citizenship education; civil rights; environmental education; global approach; human rights; mentors; preservice teacher education; student teachers

1532

Didsbury School of Education, 799 Wilmslow Road, Didsbury, Manchester M20 2RR
0161 247 2000
British Dyslexia Association, 98 London Road, Reading RG1 5AU
01734 668271

Phillips, S. Mrs; Bryan, K. Ms; Supervisor: Johnson, M. Mr

An investigation into methods of identification and assessment of specific learning difficulties/dyslexia and effective intervention strategies which can be used by classroom and subject teachers in mainstream schools

ABSTRACT: The broad aims of this project are to: 1) establish practices for assessment and intervention which teachers find 'effective' for use in ordinary classrooms, with pupils with dyslexia; 2) identify other practices in the literature, in relation to the National Curriculum Attainment Targets; 3) trial methods to establish ease of incorporation within normal practice, and effectiveness in identifying specific learning difficulties and improving pupils' performance; 4) develop a training package to disseminate 'good practice'. During year 1, phase 1 will look at current practices: questionnaires will be sent to teachers with a qualification in specific learning difficulties from the Special Educational Needs Centre at Manchester Metropolitan University. The questionnaire will: list the specific strategies learned; rate these for effectiveness and ease of use; comment on methods not currently used; state metods used for identification and assessment of all pupils' difficulties in reading, writing and spelling; and list the intervention methods found effective. The research will determine whether National Curriculum English Assessment is effective in distinguishing children with specific learning difficulties, and establish whether other forms of assessment contribute 'valuable' information. Phase 2 will look at the results of using methods seen as effective and acceptable in normal classrooms. This will include: attainments in reading; writing and spelling and measures relating to general pupil performance; self-esteem; attitude to school; organisation of working and participation in the curriculum. A sample of pupils and parents will be interviewed to seek experiences of strategies used and degree of family involvement demanded. During year 2, phase 3, a short intensive course will be produced. Phase 3 will also include an investigation of the results of using selected methods in classrooms, by offering the project schools inservice training prior to trialling the methods in their classes; and evaluation of improvement in attainments in literacy as indicators of the effectiveness of the methods. In phase 4, following evaluation, the course will be converted into professional development activities made generally available to schools and local education authorities through an established publisher or produced within the University.

STATUS: Sponsored project

SOURCE OF GRANT: Department for Education and Employment

DATE OF RESEARCH: 1996-1998

KEYWORDS: assessment; diagnostic assessment; dyslexia; reading difficulties; special educational needs

1533

Didsbury School of Education, 799 Wilmslow Road, Didsbury, Manchester M20 2RR
0161 247 2000
Sheffield Hallam University, School of Leisure and Food Management, Totley Hall Lane, Sheffield S17 4AB
01142 720911

Hunt, P. Ms; Ludlow, M. Mrs; Supervisor: Woodcock, M. Miss; Rose, A. Miss

Home and health in the European Community

ABSTRACT: The project's aim is to investigate the extent to which the education systems (for ages 5-16) within the European Community (EC) address two of the World Health Organisation's (European Region) targets 'Health for all by the year 2000'. The selected targets are: Target 11 - Accidents, and Target 22 - Food Quality and Safety. The work involves: (a) an indepth review of literature relating to the structure of education systems of all Member States; (b) an indepth review of the teacher/delivery of health education within primary and secondary schools of all Member States; (c) a questionnaire (translated into the appropriate EC languages) distributed to four primary and four secondary schools in all Member States, to be completed by teachers; (d) study visits to two countries to work more closely with cooperating schools (case study). It is hoped that the work will be of value/interest to the World Health Organisation - Copenhagen (strong links have been established), to the various ministries of education and to other professionals/persons interested in school health education. The work will be recorded in a detailed 'report'/'document'.

STATUS: Sponsored project

SOURCE OF GRANT: All Saints Educational Trust £99,000

DATE OF RESEARCH: 1991-1993

KEYWORDS: **accidents; comparative education; european union; food standards; health education; nutrition education; safety education**

1534

Didsbury School of Education, 799 Wilmslow Road, Didsbury, Manchester M20 2RR
0161 247 2000

The David Lewis Centre for Epilepsy, Warford, Alderley Edge SK9 7UD
01565 872613

Harnor, M. Mr; Benham, K. Ms; Brown, S. Dr

Educational statements of special educational needs in children with complex epilepsy referred to a residential special school

ABSTRACT: The Education Act 1981, in England and Wales, with its equivalent in Scotland, requires that a child who appears to have a degree of difficulty which calls for special educational provision to be made for them, shall have an assessment of those needs made by the local education authority and, where appropriate, a 'statement' of those needs issued. The educational statements of 86 children referred to the David Lewis Centre as of December 1991 were researched. These emanated from 26 local education authorities throughout the UK. Complete statements were available for 54 (63%) children whilst the school had not actually been provided with the statements for 32 (37%). In 10 (19%) of the statements epilepsy was not mentioned at all. In another 20 (39%) descriptions were vague and inappropriate. A syndrome only was mentioned in 3 (6%). A sub-group of 16 children were chosen for comparison of statement contents with their teacher's personal perceptions of the children's needs. There was no significant difference. Multivariate statistical analysis of medical, educational and social data has initally failed to demonstrate any other consistent pattern. It was concluded that the medical portions of the statements, where present, were extremely unhelpful to clinicians. Educational aspects were variable but more adequate. (The project has now been extended to include admissions as of December 1994).

STATUS: Sponsored project

SOURCE OF GRANT: Manchester Metropolitan University

DATE OF RESEARCH: 1991-continuing

KEYWORDS: **epilepsy; special educational needs; special schools; statements special educational needs**

1535

Didsbury School of Education, 799 Wilmslow Road, Didsbury, Manchester M20 2RR
0161 247 2000

University of Manchester Institute of Science and Technology, PO Box 88, Sackville Street, Manchester M60 1QD
0161 236 3311

Taylor, P. Mr; *Supervisors*: Kelly, M. Mr; ApThomas, J. Mr; Cooper, C. Dr

The governance of primary schools: appropriate roles and relationships, perceived and actual, in the governing and managing of primary schools

ABSTRACT: The study aims to establish appropriate action, roles and relationships for effective governance of primary schools, deriving from an investigation of existing practice. Structured interviews are being used on a cross-section of headteachers, governors, parents, business people, support staff, teaching staff and support agencies (local education authority (LEA) members etc) for their views on the position as it now stands, and what they feel would be an effective way to conduct governor business. Secondly, a questionnaire will be designed and piloted on 'opportunity samples' of headteachers. The questionnaire will then be sent to a much larger sample of headteachers in at least 2 districts of Cheshire. At least 100 returns will be collected by this means. The study will use the data gathered from the interviews, questionnaires, wide ranging literature survey and industrial/commerical secondments to Marks and Spencer, Sainsbury's, Woolworth plc and the South East Cheshire Training and Enterprise Council (TEC), to develop proposals for good practice in the key areas of concern for the self-managing school (e.g. headteacher/ governing body relations, alternative spheres of influence and action, development of bases for effective learning organisations, and possible codes of practice).

STATUS: Individual research

DATE OF RESEARCH: 1993-continuing

KEYWORDS: **educational administration; governing bodies; primary education; school governors**

Manchester University

1536

School of Education, Oxford Road, Manchester M13 9PL
0161 275 2000

Cross, A. Mr

New technology in the National Curriculum

ABSTRACT: This enquiry seeks to explore the potential of the following for the delivery of the National Curriculum: a) word processors which use speech; b) datalogging; c) portable computers.

STATUS: Sponsored project

SOURCE OF GRANT: Manchester University

DATE OF RESEARCH: 1995-continuing

KEYWORDS: **computer uses in education; computers; data processing; information technology; national curriculum; word processing**

1537

School of Education, Oxford Road, Manchester M13 9PL
0161 275 2000

Naylor, J. Mrs

Individual goal-setting and the learning curve of PGCE modern languages students

ABSTRACT: The aim of this ten-year study has been to ascertain the learning curve of Postgraduate Certificate in Education (PGCE) students specialising in modern foreign languages. Data collected over the period of the study includes individual goals set by each year's intake of students (number varying from eight to thirty) for their teaching practice, goal monitoring, and evaluation of their own performance in the light of the goals set. Some patterns have emerged already and have been used as a basis for course design. The database is unique and is now to be investigated further.

STATUS: Individual research

DATE OF RESEARCH: 1982-continuing

KEYWORDS: **learning; postgraduate certificate in education; preservice teacher education; student teachers**

1538

School of Education, Oxford Road, Manchester M13 9PL
0161 275 2000

Cross, A. Mr; *Supervisor*: Robertson, A. Dr

An investigation of pedagogy related to the teaching of design and technology in the primary school

ABSTRACT: The hypothesis is that pedagogy significantly affects children's experience of design and technology; and that primary education lacks a clearly understood pedagogy for design and technology and that articulation of effective pedagogy whilst desirable is likely to remain problematic. The objectives of the research are: 1) How do teachers go about teaching design and technology? ((a) do teachers understand the subject; b) what teachers see as teaching design and technology; c) how their own knowledge of the subject affects their teaching - culture, class, age, gender; d) descriptors of teaching styles). 2) Examination of questions raised? ((a) justification of questions; b) range and scope of these questions; c) are the questions about pedagogy, related to it or extraneous; d) do such issues affect our view of design and technology as part of primary education). 3) An examination of how the main issues might be addressed? (a) further clarification/investigation; b) how teachers develop pedagogy and/or ideas about pedagogy). 4) What are the implications for the subject? (a) at school level; b) at national level).

PUBLISHED MATERIAL: CROSS, A. (1996). 'Comments related to the teaching of design and technology by school inspectors in primary school inspection reports', Journal of Design and Technology Education, Vol 1, No 2, pp.136-140.

STATUS: Individual research

DATE OF RESEARCH: 1995-continuing

KEYWORDS: design and technology; primary education; teaching methods; teaching process

1539

School of Education, Oxford Road, Manchester M13 9PL
0161 275 2000

Chung, L. Mr; *Supervisor*: Reid, D. Prof.

British and Chinese influences on the preservice training of secondary teachers in Hong Kong

ABSTRACT: Hong Kong is in the unique position of transition from a British Colony to Chinese sovereignty. Both, very disparate, cultures influence teacher training. This project sets out to look at the syllabus and attitudes to the professional studies component of initial teacher trainees in China (Beijing), UK (Manchester) and Hong Kong. An appropriate attitudes questionnaire will be developed and piloted in the three countries. An analysis of the data will lead to proposals for that element of the course for preservice teachers in Hong Kong.

STATUS: Individual research

DATE OF RESEARCH: 1995-continuing

KEYWORDS: china; cultural influences; hong kong; preservice teacher education

1540

School of Education, Oxford Road, Manchester M13 9PL
0161 275 2000

Moots, C. Ms; *Supervisor*: Reid, D. Prof.

Towards reducing the incidence of home-based accidents in the 0-5 age group

ABSTRACT: A data bank of accidents in the home of 2000+ children aged 0-5 years has been collated and analysed in terms of frequency and severity of accidents. This information is being used to develop an appropriate education programme focused at 'homeless' parents, and a number of intervention strategies are being developed, piloted and refined.

STATUS: Individual research

DATE OF RESEARCH: 1994-continuing

KEYWORDS: accidents; child welfare; home environment; injuries; safety; safety education; young children

1541

School of Education, Oxford Road, Manchester M13 9PL
0161 275 2000

Osman, K. Ms; *Supervisor*: Reid, D. Prof.

The teaching and learning of thinking skills by preservice science teachers in Malaysia

ABSTRACT: Included in the aims of the Malaysian science curriculum for secondary school children is a requirement for children to learn to think scientifically. The research design involves the writing of 3 topics (including the teaching of thinking skills to preservice postgraduate scientists being trained as science teachers in Malaysia) in contact and distance education format. The effects of the controlled teaching programmes are then considered by observing the student teachers' actions in their own science lessons and the extent to which they are using the techniques effectively. Appropriate feedback will be given and new observations made.

STATUS: Individual research

DATE OF RESEARCH: 1995-continuing

KEYWORDS: learning strategies; malaysia; preservice teacher education; science education; science teachers; thinking skills

1542

School of Education, Oxford Road, Manchester M13 9PL
0161 275 2000

Meekums, B. Ms; *Supervisor*: Sanderson, P. Dr

Women's perceptions of arts therapy groups for survivors of child sexual abuse

ABSTRACT: This research examines the perceptions of women clients of the mental health services at Tameside and Glossop Community and Priority Services NHS Trust who undertake a 20-week arts therapy programme for survivors of child sexual abuse. Specifically, the research addresses: the healing process, including clinical conditions supporting change; the effects of the research on both informants and researcher. The research is designed as 4 cycles, each building on the previous cycle. Each cycle concerns one 20-week programme for a different set of women. The methodology used is qualitative, theory-generating and reflective. Truth is viewed incrementally, informants being seen as potential co-researchers rather than subjects.

STATUS: Individual research

DATE OF RESEARCH: 1993-1998

KEYWORDS: art activities; art therapy; child abuse; child sexual abuse; sexual abuse; therapy; women

1543

School of Education, Oxford Road, Manchester M13 9PL
0161 275 2000

Pearson, D. Ms; *Supervisor*: Sanderson, P. Dr

Attitudes of secondary school teachers to the comic strip as an educational tool

ABSTRACT: It seems that the comic strip has not been given serious consideration for use in an educational context with mainstream pupils in England, across the whole range of curriculum subjects. This research is concerned with the potential value of different types and styles of comic strips with children of various age groups and academic ability. Factors influencing teacher attitudes, such as sex, age group, length and type of teaching experience, familiarity with medium, will form the independent variables. A survey design employing a questionnaire which incorporates comic strip material will be adopted. The latter will be developed in association with teachers and pupils, and subsequently form the basis of discussions with 6 groups of teachers drawn from schools throughout England. A content analysis of these discussions will produce statements, which will constitute the dependent variables. Data from a nationwide sample (n=1500) will be analysed using ANOVA and regression analysis.

STATUS: Individual research

DATE OF RESEARCH: 1995-continuing

KEYWORDS: cartoons; comics - publications; educational materials; secondary education; teacher attitudes; visual aids

1544

School of Education, Oxford Road, Manchester M13 9PL
0161 275 2000

Yiallourides, G. Mr; *Supervisor*: Sanderson, P. Dr

Factors influencing 9-14 Cypriot pupils' attitudes towards physical education

ABSTRACT: During the past 3 decades there has been a continuing interest in the attitudes of pupils to physical education (PE) particularly in the USA and the UK. Attitude measurement, however, has relied heavily on scales devised by Kenyon (1968) and, furthermore, there does not appear to be any PE attitude research relating to Cypriot pupils. This research will therefore focus on: the development of valid and reliable attitude scales; and the employment of those scales as measures of attitude to PE. Scales will be grounded in the opinions of pupils in Cyprus (n=32 boys and girls) and developed by means of a survey employing a questionnaire comprised of pupils' statements and a 5-point Likert scale (n=1000). Factor analysis statistical technique will be used. The emerging valid and reliable scales will form the dependent variables in a survey involving a sample of 2000 male and female pupils in Cyprus, between the ages of 9 and 13 years. Independent variables will include age, sex, social class, teacher and parental interests in PE. ANOVA and multiple regression analysis will be employed to ascertain the influence of the independent variables on attitudes to PE as measured by the scales.

STATUS: Individual research

DATE OF RESEARCH: 1994-1997

KEYWORDS: attitudes; cyprus; physical education; pupil attitudes

1545

School of Education, Oxford Road, Manchester M13 9PL
0161 275 2000

Savva, A. Ms; *Supervisor*: Sanderson, P. Dr

Evaluation of the artists in schools programme in Cyprus

ABSTRACT: For the past 8 years, professional musicians (n=120) and visual artists (n=20) have been employed in Cyprus primary schools on full-time or part-time bases, yet this arrangement has never been evaluated. This research aims at assessing the impact of the programme on the artists, teachers and children, by means of indepth case studies and questionnaire surveys. Case studies will be made of 4 representative primary schools, while the surveys will employ samples of 500 pupils, 100 teachers and 20 artists, drawn from 20 primary schools throughout Cyprus. Exploratory work involving interviews and/or observations with key administrators, headteachers, teachers, artists and children will clarify the research questions and hypotheses and also test research instruments; questionnaires will be 'grounded' in data gathered at this preliminary stage. Appropriate quantitative and qualitative methods of analysis will be employed.

STATUS: Individual research

DATE OF RESEARCH: 1995-continuing

KEYWORDS: **art activities; artists; artists in schools; cyprus; primary education**

1546

School of Education, Oxford Road, Manchester M13 9PL
0161 275 2000

Dyer, C. Dr; Choksi, A. Dr

District institutes of education and training: a comparative study in three Indian states

ABSTRACT: India's District Institutes of Education and Training (DIET) are relatively recent departures under new district planning initiatives. DIETs were set up as institutes both to provide pre- and inservice primary teacher education, and to act as an educational resource for the district. Each district may have 8,000-12,000 primary teachers. One of the project's main aims will be to facilitate and observe the process of developing critical practitioners who can make use of the nascent autonomy that district level planning offers, instead of the previously highly centralised system. The project will facilitate teacher educators visiting schools, reflecting on their findings, and adapting their training messages to fit in with their analyses of teachers' needs. A second project aim will be to draw on these participatory, action research cycles to bring policymakers into closer correspondence with processes in classrooms, so that subsequent policy inputs can be tuned to known realities within the district. The project will run for 2 years in the states of Gujarat, Madhya Pradesh and Rajasthan.

STATUS: Sponsored project

SOURCE OF GRANT: Department for International Development £209,500

DATE OF RESEARCH: 1998-continuing

KEYWORDS: **india; teacher education**

1547

School of Education, Oxford Road, Manchester M13 9PL
0161 275 2000

Martin, M. Ms

Research as a process of participatory learning, empowerment and social change in health development

ABSTRACT: The broad aim of the thesis is to explore the research process as a means of participatory learning, empowerment and social change in the struggle for health development. This applies to the experiences of researchers, subjects of research, and students of health research on professional courses in primary health care. The first two chapters set out the theoretical framework and context for the publications by examining relevant theories of health, development and research within an international context. Emphasis is given to participatory and feminist perspectives and broader issues of inequality as these have particular significance to health development. As participatory research is closely

linked to the educational ideas of the Brazilian educator, Paulo Freire, his educational philosophy forms part of the introductory theoretical discussion. The publications are introduced in the third chapter, first collectively and then individually. Where relevant, comment is provided concerning the contribution they make to knowledge in the particular area. The publications have been written over the past 4 years. They comprise a research report for the Overseas Development Administration, two articles published in international refereed journals, three book chapters and one refereed international conference paper. The final and concluding chapter raises questions for closer analysis and comment, with a view to future research and teaching. These include: problematising participation in research contexts; developing education for health and development professionals that strengthen the critical faculty through an awareness of alternative participatory and gendered perspectives in health development; reflecting on these issues within the global context of the market economy, and the drive towards individualism that has dominated public sector service throughout the past decade or more.

PUBLISHED MATERIAL: MARTIN, M. & HUMPHRIES, B. (1996). 'Representation and difference in cross-culture research: the impact of institutional structures', Feminism and Psychology, Vol 6, No 2, pp.210-215. ; MARTIN, M. 'Participatory research and the empowerment of women in health care', Social Change, Vol 30, No 2. (in press). ; A full list of publications is available from the researcher.

STATUS: Individual research

DATE OF RESEARCH: 1993-continuing

KEYWORDS: **health promotion; participatory research; research**

1548

School of Education, Oxford Road, Manchester M13 9PL
0161 275 2000

Reid, D. Prof.; Elm, A. Ms

Teachers' perceptions of the role of educational theory in preservice training

ABSTRACT: In England, government innovation has resulted in teachers being much involved in preservice teacher training, and in Sweden the role is being developed. There is a danger that increased levels of partnership between schools and universities will result in a divorcing of theory and practice in the education of teachers. Many practising teachers are disinclined to be trained as mentors and take part in teacher training. The supply of mentors crucially affects quality control procedures. This joint project sets out to determine the perceptions of these two groups of teachers in England and Sweden, that is, those already mentoring and those not wanting to become mentors. Kelly's repertory grid encourages individuals to inform their understanding of issues without compelling them to respond to an externally prescribed version of what they might or should be about. Such a phenomological approach encourages teachers to develop their own constructs of the value of different kinds of educational theory in teacher training. 60 interviewees (30 from England and 30 from Sweden) will be required to rank a number of statements about educational theory and to reflect on their actions. Ethnograph and Q-sort will be used to analyse the data, so that comparisons can be drawn between the perceptions of Swedish and English and participating and non-participating mentor teachers.

STATUS: Sponsored project

SOURCE OF GRANT: Swedish Government £7,600

DATE OF RESEARCH: 1997-continuing

KEYWORDS: **attitudes; comparative education; educational theories; mentors; preservice teacher education; student teachers; sweden**

1549

School of Education, Oxford Road, Manchester M13 9PL
0161 275 2000

Davies, J. Dr

The effects of the Literacy Hour on Year 2 children's reading attainment

ABSTRACT: The Literacy Hour has been introduced into primary schools as a major part of the National Literacy Strategy to raise standards in reading. This study (which is both cross-sectional and longitudinal) is nested within the larger ongoing study of the effects of the National

Curriculum in five primary schools over time. The sample consists of a random sample of equal numbers of boys and girls from Year 2 in these schools. All Year 2 children do the Primary Reading Test (France 1981). A random sample is taken (7 boys and 7 girls) from the scoring bands - 85; -95; -105; -115; 115+. These children will be tested on the word lists for Reception, Years 1 and 2 (National Literacy Strategy, Department for Education and Employment, 1998). The Stephen Jackson 'Get Reading Right' (Jackson, 1973) will be administered to them. The sample will be retested one year later and the next Year 2 sample also tested. Interviews with teachers will illumine the study. Analysis of the data will shed light on the effects of the Literacy Hour on children's reading attainment.

STATUS: Individual research

DATE OF RESEARCH: 1998-continuing

KEYWORDS: **literacy hours; national literacy strategy; primary education; reading; reading achievement; young children**

1550

School of Education, Oxford Road, Manchester M13 9PL
0161 275 2000

Marshall, J. Ms; Ralph, S. Dr

Attitudes of Postgraduate Certificate in Education (PGCE) students towards children with speech and language difficulties

ABSTRACT: Attitudes towards the inclusion/integration of children with speech and language difficulties do not appear to have been widely studied. The attitudes and beliefs of teachers towards children with various types of speech and language difficulty have also been studied by a number of authors. All found negative attitudes. There remains a need for further research. The aims of the project are: (1) to identify the main attitudes of trainee teachers towards children with speech and language difficulties; and (2) to determine if the attitudes of trainee teachers are affected by the use of workshops. The subjects are Manchester University PGCE students for the academic year 1998/9 (n=approx. 300). The project will be divided into three main phases: (a) Initial measurement of attitudes. (b) Workshops on challenging attitudes. (c) Repeat measurement of attitudes. Measurement of attitudes will be carried out using written questionnaires and focus groups. Workshops on challenging attitudes will be carried out using short videos and other visual materials involving children with speech and language difficulties. Participants will be asked to discuss their attitudes, thoughts and feelings towards children with speech and language difficulties. The data will be analysed statistically in order to describe the attitudes expressed and to determine if attitudes vary: (a) over time, (b) by participation in focus groups discussing attitudes, (c) by participating in workshops on attitudes. The project outcomes will be qualitative and quantitative data concerning the attitudes of trainee teachers towards children with speech and language difficulties and an indication of the factors which may affect those attitudes.

STATUS: Sponsored project

SOURCE OF GRANT: Royal College of Speech and Language Therapists £300; Manchester University £2,268

DATE OF RESEARCH: 1998-continuing

KEYWORDS: **attitudes; language handicaps; mainstreaming; special educational needs; speech handicaps; student teacher attitudes; teacher attitudes; teacher pupil relationship**

1551

School of Education, Oxford Road, Manchester M13 9PL
0161 275 2000

Boreham, N. Prof.; Lammont, N. Dr; Morgan, C. Mr

Curriculum models for information and communication technology (ICT) education in higher education

ABSTRACT: The research aims to document and interpret the diversity of provision for education in information and communication technology (ICT) in higher education, against the background of the call of the Dearing Report on higher education for relevance to graduate employment. The specific objectives of the project are to: (1) carry out 15 comparative case studies exploring the diversity of current ICT courses in higher education; (2) identify the curriculum models underlying the diversity of provision, with particular reference to their assumptions about (a) the

nature of ICT capability and (b) the way courses are linked to the graduate employment market; (3) develop criteria for evaluating curricula in this field; (4) conduct a dialogue with "users" representing employers, lecturers, students and policy making bodies to clarify the policy options for implementing Dearing's recommendation.

STATUS: Sponsored project

SOURCE OF GRANT: Economic and Social Research Council £36,000

DATE OF RESEARCH: 1998-continuing

KEYWORDS: **computer literacy; computer science education; computer uses in education; higher education; information technology**

1552

School of Education, Oxford Road, Manchester M13 9PL
0161 275 2000

Boreham, N. Prof.

Work process knowledge in technological and organizational development

ABSTRACT: This 10-country European research project is concerned with changes in the structure of employment that occur when organizations acquire greater flexibility and introduce new technologies in response to the pressures of competition. The project involves the University of Manchester, Universidade Nova de Lisboa, Portugal, Technical University of Denmark, University of Siena, Italy, Universitat Bremen, Germany, CNRS - University de Paris 8, France, Technical Research Centre of Finland, Linkoping Univeresity, Sweden, Fundacio CIREM, Spain and Katholieke Universitet Leuven, Belgium. It focuses on the knowledge needed by the workforce to adapt to these changes. The overall objective is to develop policies for facilitating the acquisition of this knowledge through human resource development, the design of new technologies and organizational development. The specific objectives are to: (1) identify critical changes in working practices associated with technological and organizational development, especially those likely to contribute to the European 'skills gap'; (2) integrate European traditions for conceptualising 'work process knowledge', including such topics as understanding work processes and constructing knowledge in the workplace; (3) describe and illustrate best practice for facilitating the acquisition of work process knowledge, including new approaches to learning in the workplace, the design of new technology itself and organizational development within enterprises; (4) generate and analyze policy options for facilitating acquisition of the knowledge needed for workers to participate fully in technological and organizational change in response to the pressures of competition; (5) make contributions to parallel European research projects, especially those dealing with (a) knowledge in work environments, (b) cognitive aspects of the design and application of new technologies in education and training, and (c) the determination of labour market requirements concerning vocational training. Details about the project and a literature review can be found on the web site - EU Thematic Network: http://www.man.ac.uk/education/euwhole/home.htm

STATUS: Collaborative

SOURCE OF GRANT: European Commission: DGXII £270,206

DATE OF RESEARCH: 1997-continuing

KEYWORDS: **employment; knowledge management; organisational development; technological advancement; work based learning; work environment**

1553

School of Education, Oxford Road, Manchester M13 9PL
0161 275 2000

Warburton, T. Dr; *Supervisor*: Ralph, S. Dr

The contribution of newspaper images to public dialogue about education

ABSTRACT: Narratives and debate about education are presented in the press. Some of these are represented by images like photographs and cartoons. Images such as these carry messages to readers. Some of these messages are explicit and some are implied. When readers take in this information its content becomes both a topic and a resource. This information helps individuals and groups to form their thinking about and their attitudes to education. The research intends to collect images and supporting texts from newspapers and to organise this material around topics, themes and key figures. This will allow firstly, to chart how the press treats such stories and images about education. Secondly, to identify key images. Thirdly, to analyse how narratives are represented in those images. Fourthly, to identify what images recur and are used as stereotypes and emblems over and over again. This will also allow the researchers to try to state a theory of public image-use in respect of educational images. The project will also allow them to construct some specific examples of narratives and debate, which can then be used with teacher groups to try to determine what effect the images have on how teachers construct dialogue about the themes and topics the case-studies represent.

PUBLISHED MATERIAL: WARBURTON, T. (1998). 'Cartoons and teachers mediated visual images as data'. In: PROSSER, J. (Ed). Image-based research: a sourcebook for qualitative researchers. London: Falmer Press. ; WARBURTON, T. & RALPH, S. (1999). 'Images of education generating teacher discourse'. In: RALPH, S. (Ed). Youth and the global media. Luton: John Libbey Media, University of Luton Press.

STATUS: Sponsored project

SOURCE OF GRANT: Economic and Social Research Council £39,950

DATE OF RESEARCH: 1999-continuing

KEYWORDS: **mass media; newspapers; press opinion; public opinion**

1554

School of Education, Centre for Adult and Higher Education, Oxford Road, Manchester M13 9PL
0161 275 2000

Stock, A. Prof.

Lifelong education as a significant cultural element in various European countries

ABSTRACT: Lifelong education is a concept adopted by UNESCO, the European Union and numerous national departments of government world-wide. It is not, however, frequently evident in practice although there are signs of development in certain countries, together with substantial prominence in a few. The research examines the manifestations of lifelong education as cultural phenomena in each country where concentrated 'social-anthropological' fieldwork is undertaken in similar communities. The information and data will, in the final analysis, be subjected to rigorous comparative examination and an end report prepared accordingly. To date, fieldwork in Denmark, the Netherlands and the UK has been the basis for two monographs and the work is continuing.

STATUS: Individual research

DATE OF RESEARCH: 1991-continuing

KEYWORDS: **adult education; comparative education; continuing education; cultural differences; europe; lifelong learning**

1555

School of Education, Centre for Adult and Higher Education, Oxford Road, Manchester M13 9PL
0161 275 2000
University of Georgia, Athens, Department of Adult Education, Tucker Hall, Athens GA 30602, USA
0101 706 542 2214

Davis, M. Mr; Holt, M. Dr

E-mail conferencing: creating and maintaining a virtual community

ABSTRACT: This project will explore the extent to which it has been possible to initiate, maintain and monitor the creation and development of an electronic community based in the departments of adult education in two universities. Face-to-face contact is being supported by an electronic list which will enable participants, numbering 25, to 'meet' to exchange ideas, research interests, problems and experiences. It will be semi-moderated in that common tasks will be agreed between faculties in both institutions. In addition, unmoderated one-to-one and one-to-subgroup communication will also be encouraged. The strategies, designed to develop a sense of community on the list, will involve writing activities derived from the use of auto/biography in adult education research. Participants will explore aspects of their experience of adult education - either as students or practitioners - and this data will be used as the basis for the identification of common research interests across the community.

STATUS: Sponsored project

SOURCE OF GRANT: University of Manchester Research Development Fund

DATE OF RESEARCH: 1996-continuing

KEYWORDS: **adult education; community; electronic mail; telecommunications; teleconferencing**

1556

School of Education, Centre for Audiology, Education of the Deaf and Speech Pathology, Oxford Road, Manchester M13 9PL
0161 275 2000

Lynas, W. Dr

The educational management of children with Usher Syndrome

ABSTRACT: The aim of the research is to develop sound principles for the educational management of children with Usher Syndrome. Diagnosed children and young people are observed in a variety of educational settings - special school for the deaf, unit, mainstream class, further education college and special provisions for deaf pupils/students with deteriorating vision are noted. The data collected include material from informal interviews with teaching staff and from the Usher pupils themselves. So far, 15 Usher children/young people have been observed.

PUBLISHED MATERIAL: LYNAS, W. (1991). 'Deaf children with Usher Syndrome', Journal of British Association of Teachers of the Deaf, Vol 15, No 2, pp.33-39. ; LYNAS, W. (1991). The educational management of children with Usher Syndrome. London: SENSE.

STATUS: Sponsored project

SOURCE OF GRANT: National Deaf-Blind and Rubella Association (SENSE)

DATE OF RESEARCH: 1989-1993

KEYWORDS: **deafness; hearing impairments; special educational needs**

1557

School of Education, Centre for Audiology, Education of the Deaf and Speech Pathology, Oxford Road, Manchester M13 9PL
0161 275 2000

Willis, S. Ms; *Supervisor*: Gallaway, C. Dr

Vocabulary acquisition in prelingually profoundly deaf children with cochlear implants

ABSTRACT: Acquiring vocabulary is a fundamental component of early language development and normally-developing children's vocabulary acquisition processes are now quite well understood. Much less is understood about this process in prelingually profoundly deaf children. With young cochlear implants (CI) users, gaining a better understanding of their early language development is of crucial importance. There are very few studies of the vocabulary development of such children. We have some idea of how their vocabulary develops over time in relation to their normally-hearing peers, but no quantitative or normative data. The aim of the study is, ultimately, to provide information which will inform practice with these children in clinical and educational settings. It will produce some indicators of expected vocabulary development in these young implant users, in order to assess the implications for clinical intervention and to provide information for clinicians, parents and teachers regarding likely patterns of development. The researcher is conducting a study to evaluate the acquisition of receptive and expressive spoken vocabulary in prelingually, profoundly deaf children who have received a multichannel CI. The study will be based on ongoing data collection undertaken through the researcher's post as specialist speech and language therapist with Manchester Paediatric Cochlear Implant Programme. The children on the programme receive regular oral/aural habilitation sessions over their first two years of CI use, and it is hoped that at least 20 children will be included in the study.

STATUS: Individual research

DATE OF RESEARCH: 1996-continuing

KEYWORDS: **deafness; hearing aids; hearing impairments; language acquisition; vocabulary development**

1558

School of Education, Centre for Audiology, Education of the Deaf and Speech Pathology, Oxford Road, Manchester M13 9PL
0161 275 2000
Birmingham University, School of Education, Edgbaston, Birmingham B15 2TT
0121 414 3344

Watson, L. Ms; *Supervisors*: Gallaway, C. Dr; Elphick, R. Mr

The early writing of hearing-impaired children: from scribble to sentences

ABSTRACT: The aim of the study is to investigate the development of early written language in hearing impaired pupils. A cohort of children will be followed for 2 years and samples of their writing and writing-related activities at home and at school will be collected.

STATUS: Individual research

DATE OF RESEARCH: 1994-continuing

KEYWORDS: **deafness; hearing impairments; partial hearing; special educational needs; writing - composition; writing skills**

1559

School of Education, Centre for Audiology, Education of the Deaf and Speech Pathology, Oxford Road, Manchester M13 9PL
0161 275 2000
London University, Royal Holloway, Department of Psychology, Egham Hill, Egham TW20 0EX
01784 434455

Gallaway, C. Dr; Saxton, M. Dr

Long-term effects of negative feedback in speech addressed to children

ABSTRACT: When young children are in the process of acquiring language, they make grammatical errors such as 'we goed to the park'. Since adult language is free from such errors, children's language-learning processes must include some procedure whereby they recover from grammatical mistakes. It is likely that parental corrections might stimulate this recovery process, but despite continued research effort since 1970 there is still little agreement as to how this procedure might work. Research effort to date has concentrated on the child's immediate responses to corrective input. Hence, very little is yet known about the longer-term impact of corrections on grammatical development. Accordingly, the present study intends to collect observational data on adult-child interactions in order to gauge the extent to which parental corrections are related to improvements in the child's grammar after a period of 12 weeks. A theory of corrective input advanced by the applicant will be used as a suitable framework for testing predictions about the likely effects of corrective input. The findings from this study will enhance the researchers' understanding of how normally developing children recover from grammatical errors. In addition, a better understanding of the role of corrections and modelling in grammatical acquisition will inform practice with children whose language is delayed for some reason, as in the case of deaf children acquiring spoken language.

STATUS: Sponsored project

SOURCE OF GRANT: Economic and Social Research Council £40,119

DATE OF RESEARCH: 1998-continuing

KEYWORDS: **child language; feedback; grammar; grammatical acceptability; language acquisition; speech**

1560

School of Education, Centre for Audiology, Education of the Deaf and Speech Pathology, Oxford Road, Manchester M13 9PL
0161 275 2000

Hopwood, V. Ms; *Supervisors*: Lynas, W. Dr; Gallaway, C. Dr

The teaching practices of teachers of the deaf and their implications for spoken language acquisition in deaf children

ABSTRACT: About 85% of deaf children are educated in mainstream settings, but there has been little research evaluating the linguistic experience of the deaf child in the mainstream class. The aim of this project is to examine language support and, in particular, the spoken language input received by deaf children in secondary schools. The nature of this linguistic experience is being evaluated in terms of its effects on fostering language acquisition.

STATUS: Individual research

DATE OF RESEARCH: 1996-continuing

KEYWORDS: **deafness; language acquisition; mainstreaming; special educational needs**

1561

School of Education, Centre for Audiology, Education of the Deaf and Speech Pathology, Oxford Road, Manchester M13 9PL
0161 275 2000

Maltby, M. Ms; *Supervisor*: Sugden, D. Prof.

Testing the speech perception skills of profoundly deaf children

ABSTRACT: The need for a single, simple test of speech perception for school-aged profoundly deaf children is discussed. Currently available tests are considered, but no one test fulfils all the requirements. This study therefore develops a speech perception test which is appropriate to profoundly deaf children over the full school age range. This test, called the Maltby Speech Test, uses meaningful words presented in pictorial form with a choice of response limited to the smallest possible closed set. It seeks to evaluate the ability to perceive, and to use in word recognition, a range of minimal speech cues, and it allows for practice items to ensure understanding of the requirements of the test. The sample of speech features selected for inclusion was based on an investigation of the available tests and literature. Validation makes statistical comparison between score on the test and degree of hearing loss. One hundred and forty-six children were given the test. These were children with all degrees of hearing level, from normal hearing to profound loss. All children were drawn from the Leeds education authority area. The sample included all profoundly deaf hearing aid users in Leeds. The results indicate a highly significant relationship between hearing loss and speech score on the Maltby test.

PUBLISHED MATERIAL: TATE, M. (1998). 'Winter deafness. A case study of a profoundly deaf child's additional hearing disability', Deafness and Education, Vol 22, No 1, pp.3-9.

STATUS: Individual research

DATE OF RESEARCH: 1995-continuing

KEYWORDS: **audiology; deafness; hearing impairments; special educational needs; speech communication; tests**

1562

School of Education, Centre for Audiology, Education of the Deaf and Speech Pathology, Oxford Road, Manchester M13 9PL
0161 275 2000

Hesketh, A. Mrs; Adams, C. Mrs; Nightingale, K. Ms

A comparison of therapy procedures for phonologically impaired children

ABSTRACT: Children with phonological output problems form a significant part of the paediatric speech and language therapist's caseload. It has been suggested that these children may have a deficit of phonological awareness which underlies their speech problem, and recently, clinical speech and language therapy for these children has increasingly come to include metaphonological (or phonological awareness) training. However, the research evidence for the existence of such a deficit is conflicting, and the efficacy of metaphonological training itself has received little attention. The objectives of the study are to clarify the status of phonological awareness skills in children with phonological problems, and to compare two approaches to therapy: a metaphonological approach which aims to raise the child's awareness of phonological features and contrasts not marked in his/her speech and a production based approach which gives the child many opportunities to attempt to produce the required sounds. Sixty children with phonological output problems were assessed, and their phonological awareness skills compared to a control group of 60 normally-speaking children. The speech-disordered children were divided into two groups (good and poor) on the basis of their metaphonological performance, and these two groups were further subdivided according to the therapy approach they received (metaphonological or articulatory). Ten sessions of therapy were provided, by one of two qualified speech and language therapists. Therapy approaches can therefore be compared, both directly and in relation to the underlying phonological awareness skills of the children. The study is ongoing, therefore results cannot be provided at this stage.

STATUS: Sponsored project

SOURCE OF GRANT: The Nuffield Foundation £70,452

DATE OF RESEARCH: 1997-continuing

KEYWORDS: phonology; special educational needs; speech handicaps; speech therapy

1563

School of Education, Centre for Educational Needs, Oxford Road, Manchester M13 9PL
0161 275 2000

Pumfrey, P. Prof.

The concerns of young people

ABSTRACT: This research concerns the psycho-social development of young persons aged from 11 to 18 years. The aim is to plot the changing concerns of males and females in relation to personal, educational and vocational issues. This is seen as a first step whereby young people can be helped to address their concerns in a variety of educational settings. Data are being collected from a variety of educational establishments using a specially devised checklist covering 15 major aspects of psycho-social development. In the present phase of the study, the current version of the Concerns Checklist is deliberately lengthy. To date, checklists from 5,000 pupils have been obtained. This database is being further extended.

STATUS: Individual research

DATE OF RESEARCH: 1992-continuing

KEYWORDS: adolescent attitudes; adolescents; attitudes; interests; personality; social development; vocational guidance

1564

School of Education, Centre for Educational Needs, Oxford Road, Manchester M13 9PL
0161 275 2000

Piotrowski, J. Ms; *Supervisor*: Pumfrey, P. Prof.

Attribution and responsibility for learning in mainstream primary schools

ABSTRACT: This research seeks to evaluate what effect, if any, the variables of gender, year, group, category of special need (where appropriate), term of birth and class size have upon self-esteem, attribution and responsibility for learning, and popularity in primary school children aged 7-11 years. The study is longitudinal over 2 years. The population comprises all such aged children in Stockport Local Education Authority (LEA), the sample being 24 classes on each occasion from 3 schools.

STATUS: Individual research

DATE OF RESEARCH: 1992-continuing

KEYWORDS: learning; locus of control; primary education; pupil behaviour; pupil responsibility; self esteem; social behaviour; special educational needs

1565

School of Education, Centre for Educational Needs, Oxford Road, Manchester M13 9PL
0161 275 2000

Davies, J. Dr

The National Curriculum and children's attainments in reading and mathematics in key stages 1 and 2 in six primary schools

ABSTRACT: The aim of this project is to observe the effects of the National Curriculum on children's attainments in reading and mathematics in Years 2 and 6 in 5 primary schools. The project uses a cross-sectional study which was devised to gather quantitative data on the cognitive and affective aspects of successive cohorts of Year 2 and 6 children's reading and mathematics. One cohort (1988/89) was tested prior to the introduction of the National Curriculum; the others were tested subsequently. A range of theoretically and practically important situational variables were also considered. The sample comprised all Year 2 and 6 children within six randomly selected primary schools from within one local education authority (n=approximately 2500). Each summer term the cohorts were tested using the following instruments: Primary Reading Test (France 1981); Mathematics 7 or 11 (NFER 1986); Self-Esteem

(Lawrence 1981); Attitudes towards School and School Activities ('Smiley' Scale, ILEA 1988); Adjustment to School (Child at School Schedule, ILEA 1988). One inter-correlational matrix will be drawn up for each of the cohorts. The hypothesis covering the mean scores of cohorts 1, 2, 3, 4, 5, 6, 7, 8, 9 and 10 on each of the dependent variables will be tested using: a) a series of 7 one-way anovas for each independent variable; b) a series of 6 two-way anovas each using cohort as one main effect: cohort x school; cohort x sex; cohort x length of infant experience; cohort x parental occupation; cohort x pre-school experience.

PUBLISHED MATERIAL: DAVIES, J. & BREMBER, I. (1995). 'The first and second mathematics standard assessment tasks at key stage 1: a comparison based on a five school study', Educational Review, Vol 47, No 1, pp.3-9. ; DAVIES, J., BREMBER, I. and PUMFREY, P.D. (1995). 'The first and second reading standard assessment tasks at key stage 1: a comparison based on a five school study', Journal of Research in Reading, Vol 18, No 1, pp.1-9. ; DAVIES, J. & BREMBER, I. (1997). 'Did the SATs lower Year 2 children' self-esteem? A 4 year cross-sectional study', Research in Education, Vol 57, pp.1-11. ; DAVIES, J. & BREMBER, I. (1997). 'The effects of pre-school experiences on reading attainment: a 4 year cross-sectional study', Educational Psychology, Vol 17, No 3, pp.255-266.; DAVIES, J. & BREMBER, I. (1997). 'The effects of pre-school experience on mathematical attainment in Year 2: a 4 year cross-sectional study', British Journal of Curriculum and Assessment, Vol 8, No 2, pp.33-36.

STATUS: Individual research

DATE OF RESEARCH: 1988-continuing

KEYWORDS: achievement; mathematics education; national curriculum; primary education; reading achievement

1566

School of Education, Centre for Educational Needs, Oxford Road, Manchester M13 9PL
0161 275 2000

Crutchley, A. Ms; Botting, N. Ms; Simkin, Z. Ms; Knox, E. Miss; *Supervisor*: Conti-Ramsden, G. Prof.

Educational transitions for specific language impaired children attending language units

ABSTRACT: The present project aims to investigate educational transitions experienced by 200 children with specific language impairment (SLI) attending their last year in infant language units. Specifically, the research will attempt to provide information on 2 interrelated but logically separate issues: 1) What factors influence decisions to integrate? 2) Which children do well if integrated into mainstream? Information on these issues will have important implications for: a) our understanding of specific language impairments; and b) the development of an integration policy for children with SLI attending language units.

STATUS: Sponsored project

SOURCE OF GRANT: Nuffield Foundation £108,000

DATE OF RESEARCH: 1995-continuing

KEYWORDS: language handicaps; language units; learning disabilities; mainstreaming; special educational needs; speech handicaps; transfer pupils

1567

School of Education, Centre for Educational Needs, Oxford Road, Manchester M13 9PL
0161 275 2000

Skipp, A. Ms; Windfuhr, K. Ms; *Supervisor*: Conti-Ramsden, G. Prof.

Verb learning and usage in children with a specific language impairment (SLI)

ABSTRACT: This project aims to assess how children with specific language impairment (SLI) learn and use verbs, in comparison to normal language development (NLD) children. Four novel verbs will be taught to each of the 64 children to act as "tracers" so that the researchers can see how easily children can comprehend verbs and their argument structure, spontaneously use verbs, and form generalisations and grammatical rules from them. The researchers will train the children with these verbs and then test their production and comprehension abilities of the verbs. The same procedure will be carried out with nouns as a control condition. This work will have an important contribution to theory and understanding of the nature of SLI, and to practice in terms of guidelines for intervention focusing on verb use.

STATUS: Sponsored project

SOURCE OF GRANT: Wellcome Trust

DATE OF RESEARCH: 1998-continuing

KEYWORDS: language acquisition; language handicaps; learning disabilities; specific language impairment; verbs

1568

School of Education, Centre for Educational Needs, Oxford Road, Manchester M13 9PL
0161 275 2000

Farrell, P. Dr; Balshaw, M. Dr; Polat, F. Dr

The management, role and training of learning support assistants

ABSTRACT: This research is in two parts. Part 1: This is a survey of training providers in England and Wales who run courses for Learning Support Assistants. All colleges of further and higher education, universities and location education authorities have been asked to complete a detailed questionnaire on the range of courses that they offer to Learning Support Assistants. Specifically the research team is interested in finding out about the length and content of training courses, whether they are award bearing, entry qualifications and collaboration arrangements with schools. Part 2: This phase of the research consists of site visits to 22 different "sites" where Learning Support Assistants work. The sites include mainstream and special schools, schools from the maintained and voluntary sector. The aim of the site visits is to seek the views of key stakeholders including Learning Support Assistants, teachers, LEA administrators, parents and if possible, pupils, on the work of Learning Support Assistants.

STATUS: Sponsored project

SOURCE OF GRANT: Department for Education and Employment £57,000

DATE OF RESEARCH: 1998-continuing

KEYWORDS: learning support; learning support assistants; mainstreaming; special educational needs; special schools; support services; support staff; training

1569

School of Education, Centre for English Language Studies in Education, Oxford Road, Manchester M13 9PL
0161 275 2000

Fay, R. Mr; *Supervisor*: O'Brien, T. Dr

Investigation of current trends concerning the use of cultural materials in English language teaching throughout Europe

ABSTRACT: The last 5 years (since 1990) have witnessed an increase in discussion within English language teaching circles about the role of culture and cultural awareness in language teaching. Initial investigations suggest that under the broad heading of culture and language teaching, a number of markedly different outlooks are being promoted and these differences of outlook seem to have some correspondence with the geo-political nature of the country where the language teaching is taking place. Using a questionnaire as the research instrument, the research aims to gather data from practising language teachers (primarily of English as a foreign/second language) about the role of culture in their teaching and their level of satisfaction with the materials currently available.

STATUS: Individual research

DATE OF RESEARCH: 1995-continuing

KEYWORDS: culture; english - second language; language teachers; second language teaching

1570

School of Education, Centre for English Language Studies in Education, Oxford Road, Manchester M13 9PL
0161 275 2000

Amiri, F. Mr; *Supervisor*: Motteram, G. Mr

The 'comeback' of grammar: the use of multimedia in 'grammar consciousness raising' about the English definite article

ABSTRACT: This research examines the reasons for the 'comeback' of grammar and investigates the concept of 'grammar consciousness raising' and the possible use of multimedia in 'grammar consciousness raising' about the English article system, especially the definite article. The research looks at some language acquisition theories, theories of 'teacher professionalism' and learners' views on grammar in order to find out why grammar is making a comeback. The learners' views on grammar are collected through a survey of about 400 language learners. The overwhelming majority of those who returned the questionnaire are in favour of grammar teaching and do not find it boring. Hawkins' theory of definiteness and indefiniteness is examined in detail and different models of teaching the English article system are analysed. A small multimedia program for teaching the English definite article, based on 'grammar consciousness raising', is being developed which will then be tested with a group of language learners in order to find out how such a system is used in practice by learners, whether the multimedia aspects of the program are regarded by learners as useful and motivating, and whether the program does in fact 'enhance the input' and result in an increase in the level of 'noticing' the definite article by learners in the future.

STATUS: Individual research

DATE OF RESEARCH: 1993-1997

KEYWORDS: english; grammar

1571

School of Education, Centre for Ethnic Studies in Education, Oxford Road, Manchester M13 9PL
0161 275 2000

Sharma, S. Mr; *Supervisors*: Verma, G. Prof.; Papastergiadis, N. Dr

A pedagogy of cultural difference

ABSTRACT: This study attempts to innovate a pedagogy of cultural difference beyond current theoretical approaches found in the discourse of multicultural and anti-racist education in Britain. It is contended that these educational approaches are flawed and predicated on politically inadequate conceptions of culture and identity. This has led to inadequate rationalist pedagogical practices being developed for contemporary social conditions that exhibit complex and changing patterns of social identity and subjectivity. By re-thinking an anti-essentialist notion of culture and drawing on recent post-structuralist theories of identity formation and representation, this study will theoretically map out an alternative basis for the possibility of developing liberatory pedagogical strategies, particularly in relation to understanding cultural difference.

STATUS: Individual research

DATE OF RESEARCH: 1994-continuing

KEYWORDS: antiracism education; cultural differences; multicultural education

1572

School of Education, Centre for Ethnic Studies in Education, Oxford Road, Manchester M13 9PL
0161 275 2000

Skinner, G. Mr; *Supervisor*: Verma, G. Prof.

Church schools and the education of Muslim children

ABSTRACT: Many Church of England primary schools recruit pupils from Muslim homes. Some such schools have all their pupils from Muslim backgrounds. This study looks at the response of church schools to the needs of Muslim pupils and sets this in the wider context of the debate on the role of church schools in plural Britain.

STATUS: Individual research

DATE OF RESEARCH: 1993-continuing

KEYWORDS: muslims; primary schools; religion and education; religious cultural groups; religious education; school worship; voluntary schools

1573

School of Education, Centre for Ethnic Studies in Education, Oxford Road, Manchester M13 9PL
0161 275 2000

Canterbury Christ Church College, North Holmes Road, Canterbury CT1 1QU
01227 767700

Verma, G. Prof.; Zec, P. Mr; Skinner, G. Mr; Gewirtz, D. Ms
Inter-ethnic relationships in secondary schools

ABSTRACT: Concern with race relations in the wider community as well as with related issues in the education system in the UK prompted this research. It aimed to provide a portrait of relationships in nine secondary schools in terms of their organisation, structures and interactive processes. It attempted to characterise prevalent attitudes and behaviour, centring on those of the pupils and those who taught them. The study further sought to discover how inter-ethnic relationships are influenced by the policies and practices of individual schools. The research was intended to yield positive models and examples of good practice which might be of help to schools with multi-ethnic populations. The methodology was mixed, entailing multi-site case-studies, largely ethnographic in emphasis; and an overall quantitative analysis of results from a questionnaire administered to all the 2,300 Year 8 and Year 10 pupils across the 9 schools. Indepth interviews were conducted with 281 Year 8 and Year 10 pupils, and with 190 teachers (including headteachers). The findings included: 1) Teachers confessing relative ignorance of ethnic minority pupils' cultural backgrounds. 2) Lack of inservice training in relevant fields. 3) The perceived effectiveness and value of school policies on inter-ethnic relationships and multicultural/anti-racist education turned on questions of ownership, practical implementation and monitoring. 4) Curriculum and other processes seemed to correlate more closely with the quality of inter-ethnic relationships than did curriculum content. 5) The more ethnically diverse the school, the more pupils from different ethnic backgrounds mixed socially. 6) The most commonly reported subject matter of verbal abuse across the 9 schools was race or colour. Ethnic minority pupils were more likely than others to mention race, language or religion as the focus of experienced abuse; muslims much more likely. 7) The more ethnically diverse the school, the better its inter-ethnic relationships were felt to be by pupils and teachers.
PUBLISHED MATERIAL: ZEC, P. (1993). 'Dealing with racial incidents in schools'. In: FYFE, A. & FIGUEROA, P. Education for cultural diversity. London: MacMillan. ; VERMA, G.K., ZEC, P.M. & SKINNER, G. (1994). The ethnic crucible: harmony and discord in secondary schools. London: Falmer.

STATUS: Sponsored project

SOURCE OF GRANT: Leverhulme Trust £65,000

DATE OF RESEARCH: 1990-1993

KEYWORDS: ethnic groups; ethnic relations; intergroup relations; multiculturalism; racial relations; school policy; secondary education

1574

School of Education, Centre for Formative Assessment, Oxford Road, Manchester M13 9PL
0161 275 2000

Boyle, B. Mr; Clarke, P. Dr; Christie, T. Prof.
Aims for the school curriculum

ABSTRACT: A questionnaire survey of 25,778 schools in England to gather and analyse data on schools' statements about their aims and priorities for their school curriculum. The consultation exercise was a starting point in the Qualifications and Curriculum Authority's (QCA) thinking for a potential National Curriculum review. 3,022 schools responded and their statements were analysed and reported by the University of Manchester's Centre for Formative Assessment Studies to QCA in 'Aims for the school curriculum: what does your school think?'. The reporting process from its conception was data driven in that the language used in the school responses informed the analytical framework. This meant that the data generated the categories used in the report to describe the aims and priorities of the schools, rather than the researchers impose a pre-defined structure on the project. The key themes included learning, social skills, school-parent partnership and school environment.
STATUS: Sponsored project

SOURCE OF GRANT: Qualifications and Curriculum Authority £80,000

DATE OF RESEARCH: 1997-continuing

KEYWORDS: curriculum development; national curriculum

1575

School of Education, Centre for Formative Assessment Studies, Oxford Road, Manchester M13 9PL
0161 275 2000

Harrison, I. Mr; *Supervisor*: Christie, T. Prof.
Evaluation of distance learning materials and workshops for the professional development of community pharmacists

ABSTRACT: National questionnaire surveys of the effectiveness of professional development courses offered to community pharmacists. The impact to be evaluated in terms of knowledge acquisition and skills development.
STATUS: Sponsored project

SOURCE OF GRANT: Manchester University

DATE OF RESEARCH: 1991-continuing

KEYWORDS: pharmaceutical education; pharmacists; professional development

1576

School of Education, Centre for Formative Assessment Studies, Oxford Road, Manchester M13 9PL
0161 275 2000

Davies, P. Mr; Digby, B. Mr; Boyle, B. Mr; Schiavone, T. Mr; *Supervisor*: Christie, T. Prof.
Development of National Curriculum key stage 3 geography standard assessment tasks

ABSTRACT: The aims of this project are: 1) The development of standard assessment tasks to national pilot stage (June 1993). 2) The development of national guidance for teacher assessment in geography (August-December 1993). 3) Change in focus of the development following amendments to the assessment arrangements for geography in March/June 1993.
STATUS: Sponsored project

SOURCE OF GRANT: Schools Examination and Assessment Council £560,000

DATE OF RESEARCH: 1992-1993

KEYWORDS: assessment; assessment by teachers; geography; national curriculum; standard assessment tasks; tasks and tests; tests

1577

School of Education, Centre for Formative Assessment Studies, Oxford Road, Manchester M13 9PL
0161 275 2000

Harrison, I. Mr; *Supervisor*: Christie, T. Prof.
Development of assessment system for work-based projects in electrical engineering

ABSTRACT: Research objectives are to establish the nature of the learning experience for students working in the group Enterprise Project Scheme organised by the Department of Electrical Engineering at Manchester University, and to develop appropriate assessment procedures and strategies for on-going teaching/learning.
STATUS: Sponsored project

SOURCE OF GRANT: Enterprise in Higher Education £11,500

DATE OF RESEARCH: 1991-continuing

KEYWORDS: assessment; electrical engineering

1578

School of Education, Centre for Formative Assessment Studies, Oxford Road, Manchester M13 9PL
0161 275 2000

Boyle, B. Mr; Christie, T. Prof.; Harrison, I. Mr
School sampling project

ABSTRACT: The school sampling project monitors the curriculum delivery and national assessment/public examination results from a sample of 1,000 schools across the range of types and sizes. The sample was originally drawn by the Qualifications and Curriculum Authority (QCA) but is now supplemented by the Centre for Formative Assessment Studies (CFAS) at the University of Manchester as phase numbers fall. Curriculum information is collected by questionnaire from primary headteachers, secondary curriculum deputy headteachers and discrete subject heads of department. Assessment and examination results are collected at pupil/subject level on a sample of 15 pupils per school. Reports are written for QCA on each data collection and analysis phase of the work. In 1997-98 the project informed QCA's advice to the Secretary of State on the school curriculum; the 1997-98 curriculum report 'Monitoring the school curriculum: reporting to schools'; the 1998 school standards reports issued by QCA to all schools; and advice on the use of value added information in schools. Schools are drawn from the sample to constitute QCA case studies, focus groups, or to form sub-samples for small-scale QCA research projects.

PUBLISHED MATERIAL: BOYLE, B. & CHRISTIE, T. (1997). Monitoring the school curriculum: reporting to schools. London: Qualifications and Curriculum Authority. ; BOYLE, B., CHRISTIE, T. & HARRISON, I. (1997). Standards at key stage 1: English and mathematics. Report on the 1997 National Curriculum assessments for 7 year olds. London: Qualifications and Curriculum Authority. ; BOYLE, B. & CHRISTIE, T. (1998). Monitoring the school curriculum: primary report. London: Qualifications and Curriculum Authority. ; BOYLE, B. & CHRISTIE, T. (1998). Monitoring the school curriculum: secondary report. London: Qualifications and Curriculum Authority.

STATUS: Sponsored project

SOURCE OF GRANT: Qualifications and Curriculum Authority £350,000

DATE OF RESEARCH: 1996-continuing

KEYWORDS: **academic achievement; assessment; monitoring; primary education; secondary education**

1579

School of Education, Centre for Formative Assessment Studies, Oxford Road, Manchester M13 9PL
0161 275 2000

Harrison, I. Mr; Bragg, J. Ms; *Supervisors*: Boyle, W. Mr; Boyle, T. Ms

Review of key stage 1 reading task assessment records

ABSTRACT: During the 1998 key stage 1 assessment data collection exercise by the School Sampling Project Centre for Formative Assessment Studies, Manchester University (CFAS/QCA), 96 schools provided 1121 reading assessment records. These records covered pupils assessed at level W to level 3. The miscues made by these children were categorised into the following groups: phonic, graphic, syntactic, contextual, self-correction, teacher told, told/incorrect attempt, omit. By level of attainment the most frequently used strategies were tabulated and percentagised and patterns of errors were recorded. A commentary on the issues was developed through analysis of the teachers' comments by level of pupil attainment. Analysis of reading strategies was conducted revealing a restricted menu, ie initial sounds, phonetically sounding, word building, simple words recognised (keywords), picture cues, context and incorrect self-correction.

STATUS: Sponsored project

SOURCE OF GRANT: Qualifications and Curriculum Authority (QCA) £2,500

DATE OF RESEARCH: 1998-1998

KEYWORDS: **assessment; assessment by teachers; key stage 1; primary education; reading; reading achievement**

1580

School of Education, Centre for Formative Assessment Studies, Oxford Road, Manchester M13 9PL
0161 275 2000
Examinations, Research and Testing Division, Ministry of Education, PO Box 189, Gabarone, Botswana

Beckles, D. Dr; Trutter, S. Ms; *Supervisor*: Christie, T. Prof.

Development of a Botswana national examinations processing system

ABSTRACT: Examinations Research and Testing Division (ERTD) of the Ministry of Education of the Government of Botswana is responsible for public examinations in Forms 4, 7 and 9. In 1999 they will also become responsible for Form 12 examinations currently run by Cambridge. All of these examinations are unashamedly norm referenced and the results are scaled to such an extent that there is no real information generated other than individual results slips of interest only to the candidate receiving them. For example, general standards in Form 7 English are high, with a grade A associated with an examination cut off around 83%, while standards in mathematics are low with a grade A associated with a cut off of 48%. Schools cannot act on this information because they do not know what is happening in the examination room or in ERTD. The project will explore new forms of reporting of examination results within criterion referenced formats which will call for reduced dependence on the currently dominant multiple choice format. The exploration will be public and form part of a wider debate on the reform of the Botswana educational system. A major outcome will be a software suite incorporating decisions made about curriculum structure and functions.

STATUS: Sponsored project

SOURCE OF GRANT: Government of Botswana £748,700

DATE OF RESEARCH: 1997-continuing

KEYWORDS: **assessment; botswana; criterion referenced tests; examinations**

1581

School of Education, Centre for Physical Education and Leisure Studies, Oxford Road, Manchester M13 9PL
0161 275 2000

Carroll, R. Dr

Assessment and examinations in physical education

ABSTRACT: Since the 1970s there has been a movement in schools into physical education examinations, first with Certificate of Secondary Education (CSE), later General Certificate of Secondary Education (GCSE) and A-levels. There has also been a similar movement by the further education sector into vocational qualifications such as City and Guilds and BTEC, and physical education has widened into the leisure industries. In addition there have been developments such as Records of Achievement (ROA) and the National Curriculum. The aim of the research has been to monitor such developments. The research has taken the form of a number of small projects and has been accumulative rather than one major project. This information has been collected from all the examination boards on statistics and structure, and from teachers and pupils on the functioning of examinations and assessment methods. Examples of Records of Achievement have also been collected, and questionnaires and interviews carried out. The findings show the dramatic take-up of examinations in physical education. These statistics are continually updated and published. Analysis of GCSE and National Curriculum has been made to show the changes which will have to be undertaken in these examinations.

PUBLISHED MATERIAL: CARROLL, R. (1990). 'Examinations and assessment in physical education'. In: ARMSTRONG, N. (Ed). New Directions in Physical Education. Human Kinetics, pp.137-160. ; CARROLL, R. (1990). 'The twain shall meet: GCSE and the National Curriculum', British Journal of Physical Education, Vol 21, No 3, pp.29-32. ; CARROLL, R. & JEPSON, J. (1991). 'ROA versus reports: what the pupils say', British Journal of Physical Education, Vol 22, No 2, pp.19-22.; CARROLL, R. (1991). 'Assessment in the national curriculum: what the teacher has to do', British Journal of Physical Education, Vol 22, No 2, pp.8-10. ; CARROLL, R. (1995). 'Professional and development issues in leisure, sport and education'. In: LAWRENCE, L., MURDOCH, E. & PARKER, S. (Eds). Examinations in physical education and sport: gender differences and influences on subject choice. Eastbourne: Leisure Studies Association, Chelsea School Research Centre, University of Brighton.

STATUS: Individual research

DATE OF RESEARCH: 1986-continuing

KEYWORDS: **assessment; examinations; physical education**

1582

School of Education, Centre for Physical Education and Leisure Studies, Oxford Road, Manchester M13 9PL
0161 275 2000

Karkou, V. Ms; *Supervisor*: Sanderson, P. Dr

An evaluation of the practice of creative arts therapists

ABSTRACT: There is a growing interest in the arts therapies as a means of diagnosing and especially treating those with a range of special needs, yet little information is available concerning the range and types of such therapies available in Britain. This research aims to answer a number of questions concerning: a) the backgrounds, training and client groups of arts therapists; and b) the theoretical basis and principles upon which they base their work, therapeutic methods and assessment of treatment outcomes. Any significant relationships between the independent variables (a) and the dependent variables (b) will be investigated. A survey design employing a questionnaire with a final total sample of approximately 600 art, music, dance and drama therapists will be adopted. The questionnaire will include statements gathered from a sample of arts therapists on the issues indicated in (b) by means of semi-structured interviews. Statistical analyses will include ANOVA and regressional analysis.

STATUS: Individual research

DATE OF RESEARCH: 1994-1997

KEYWORDS: art therapy; arts; dance; drama therapy; music therapy; special educational needs; therapists; therapy

1583

School of Education, Centre for Physical Education and Leisure Studies, Oxford Road, Manchester M13 9PL
0161 275 2000

Lavin, J. Mr; *Supervisor*: Carroll, R. Dr

The implementation of National Curriculum Physical Education in primary schools in Cumbria

ABSTRACT: This research investigates the implementation of National Curriculum Physical Education (PE) in primary schools in Cumbria. A questionnaire will be sent to all primary schools in Cumbria to collect data on facilities, time, teachers, curriculum, teachers' opinions, and how PE has changed since the introduction of the National Curriculum. This will be followed by a qualitative study of a selected number of schools, which includes observation and interviews with teachers.

STATUS: Individual research

DATE OF RESEARCH: 1994-continuing

KEYWORDS: national curriculum; physical education; primary education

1584

School of Education, Centre for Physical Education and Leisure Studies, Oxford Road, Manchester M13 9PL
0161 275 2000

Shropshire, J. Miss; *Supervisor*: Carroll, R. Dr

Children's physical activity levels and relationship to selected variables

ABSTRACT:This research investigates physical activity (PA) levels of a sample of children, aged 10-12 years (n=924), pre- and post-transfer to secondary school. The PA levels will be considered in terms of the most recent recommendations for criteria for health (Sallis and Patrick 1994). The PA levels will be related to selected variables: motivational orientations, perceived self-competence in sports, attitudes to school physical education, and social economic states as measured by free school meals. Changes over the year will also be examined in relation to school attenders and parental participation in sports/physical activity.

PUBLISHED MATERIAL: SHROPSHIRE, J. & CARROLL, R. (1997). 'Family variables and children's physical activity: influence of parental exercise and socio-economic status', Sport, Education and Society, Vol 2, No 1, pp.95-116.; SHROPSHIRE, J., CARROLL, R. & YIM, S. 'Primary school children's attitudes to physical education: gender differences', European Journal of Physical Education. (in press).

STATUS: Individual research

DATE OF RESEARCH: 1994-1997

KEYWORDS: physical activities; physical activity level; physical education; primary school pupils; pupil attitudes; secondary school pupils; sports

1585

School of Education, Centre for Physical Education and Leisure Studies, Oxford Road, Manchester M13 9PL
0161 275 2000

Murray, C. Dr

Secondary analysis of adolescent lifestyle data

ABSTRACT: This work involves the re-analysis of data collected over a number of years (1985-1988) with the intention of throwing some light on the transitional processes of our young people. The difficult to employ and the long-term unemployed provide a focus for the work. Reports focusing on one or more topics can be prepared for colleagues working in the field of adolescence and young adulthood, these include: social skills' longitudinal study; lifestyles and unemployment; ethnicity and its correlates; international comparison of young workers; and conceptual clarification.

PUBLISHED MATERIAL: MURRAY, C. & DAWSON, A. (1983). Five thousand adolescents. Manchester: Manchester University Press. ; CARASE, F., LAGREE, J.C. & MURRAY, C. (1985). Jeune chomeurs: modes de vie, occupation et sources de revenue de jeune chomeurs nontoucles per les programmes d'emploi ou de formation. Etude No 84196. Paris: EEC. ; MURRAY, C. & HARAN, D. (1986). The young manual worker in Britain and Sweden: social psychological study of occupational socialization. Manchester: University of Manchester, Centre for Adult and Higher Education. ; MAGUIRE, M., MURRAY, C. & ASHTON, D. (1988). 'Youth lifestyles, employment and the labour market: concepts in need of clarification', British Journal of Education and Work, Vol 2, No 2, pp.27-49.

STATUS: Individual research

DATE OF RESEARCH: 1996-continuing

KEYWORDS: adolescents; life style; school leavers; school to work transition; youth; youth employment; youth unemployment

1586

School of Education, Centre for Physical Education and Leisure Studies, Oxford Road, Manchester M13 9PL
0161 275 2000

Carroll, R. Dr; Jones, B. Mr; Hunter-Jones, J. Mr

Employers' and students' views of undergraduate work placements in the leisure industry

ABSTRACT: This research provides an overview of work placements in undergraduate courses in the leisure studies/management area, and provides detailed views of employers and students of their placements in one institution (University of Manchester). The research looks at the length and type of placements in over 100 courses. 70% of institutions had some form of vocational placement. The Manchester survey included 100 students and 88 employer organisations and analysed answers from questionnaires to both employers and students on the following topics: getting the placement; purposes of the placements; employers' involvement in placement; projects carried out by students; satisfaction with placement. A second phase using another 100 students will be completed in 1997.

PUBLISHED MATERIAL: JONES, B., CARROLL, R. & HUNTER-JONES, J. (1996). 'The role of industrial vocational experience in leisure management undergraduate degrees in the UK, with an evaluation of the experience in the leisure management degree at the University of Manchester'. Paper given at the LSA Annual Conference, The Netherlands, 1996.

STATUS: Team research

DATE OF RESEARCH: 1995-continuing

KEYWORDS: employer attitudes; higher education; job placement; leisure industry; student attitudes; student employment; work experience

1587

School of Education, Centre for Physical Education and Leisure Studies, Oxford Road, Manchester M13 9PL
0161 275 2000

Bannon, F. Ms; *Supervisor*: Sanderson, P. Dr

Aesthetic development and dance education

ABSTRACT: Dance experience as a means of aesthetic development has received little attention to date. This longitudinal research aims at monitoring and assessing the aesthetic development of students throughout a 3-year undergraduate specialist dance course. The methodology employed will combine aspects of the case study approach. The final samples will comprise a total of 24 students, 3 groups of 8 from each year group, beginning in September 1997. A pilot study will be undertaken in January 1997, involving 16 students divided evenly between 2 year groups. Interviews, observation, peer, self and tutor assessment monitoring methods will be employed to detail the progression of students in terms of individual aesthetic development during the course. Videotapes of a variety of dance performances will be essential research tools.

STATUS: Individual research

DATE OF RESEARCH: 1996-continuing

KEYWORDS: **aesthetic education; arts; dance; higher education**

1588

School of Education, Centre for Physical Education and Leisure Studies, Oxford Road, Manchester M13 9PL
0161 275 2000

Connell, J. Mr; *Supervisor*: Sanderson, P. Dr

The practice of dance teaching within the National Curriculum in Yorkshire secondary schools in the 1990s

ABSTRACT: Dance occupies an ambiguous position in the National Curriculum. Officially it is a constituent of physical education (although dance is not compulsory at secondary level) but in practice it is also often considered to be an arts activity. Interpretations of National Curriculum guidelines therefore vary considerably. This research aims at ascertaining more precisely current practice in one area of England, Yorkshire. Information will be gathered from 3 main sources: 1) questionnaires, involving 360 teachers of dance, including dance artists, working within various educational contexts, and with contrasting backgrounds and experience; 2) semi-structured interviews involving a sample of 16 drawn from those completing the questionnaire; 3) observations of 12 teachers. Appropriate qualitative and quantitative methods of analyses will be employed. A pilot study has been completed using the above methodology.

STATUS: Individual research

DATE OF RESEARCH: 1994-continuing

KEYWORDS: **arts; dance; national curriculum; secondary education**

1589

School of Education, Centre for Physical Education and Leisure Studies, Oxford Road, Manchester M13 9PL
0161 275 2000

Hunter-Jones, J. Mr; *Supervisors*: Kloss, D. Mrs; Carroll, R. Dr

Legal sanctions and their use in securing safely organised recreational activity

ABSTRACT: Physical recreation exposes participants to a higher risk of injury than most other leisure activities. Research by the Health and Safety Executive and the Department of Trade and Industry has established the particular vulnerability of such participants. Research has also demonstrated that many of these organised activities did not incorporate safe practice and injuries could have been avoided. The law in this area has been guided by the Rolans Committee Report of 1972 on Health and Safety at Work, which encouraged a partnership approach between employers, employees and the state, in order to develop safe practices, but subject to criminal sanctions where failures in safety procedure have been revealed. The alternative approach by the state is to force all risk activity providers to be subject to regular inspection and to have to conform to rigid prescribed conditions. The research considers these two approaches and seeks to identify which is likely to be the more effective in securing safety for the consumer.

STATUS: Individual research

DATE OF RESEARCH: 1997-continuing

KEYWORDS: **legal responsibility; recreational activities; safety**

1590

School of Education, Centre for Science and Technology Education, Oxford Road, Manchester M13 9PL
0161 275 2000
Universiti Sains Malaysia, Pusat Pongajian, Ilmu Pendidikan, 11800 Nimden, Penang, Malaysia

Ahmed, S. Prof.; *Supervisor*: Reid, D. Prof.

Teacher appraisal in Malaysia: towards a strategy

ABSTRACT: Current trends in Malaysian secondary education are towards a national system of teacher appraisal. What has Malaysia to learn from the British model, and what features of the Malaysian teacher population demand special attention? A survey of 1,200 teachers in Malaysia is being used to determine the attitudes and opinions of secondary school teachers to appraisal. A strategy for appraisal will be developed on the basis of the survey.

STATUS: Individual research

DATE OF RESEARCH: 1989-1993

KEYWORDS: **malaysians; secondary education; teacher evaluation**

1591

School of Education, Economics and Business Education Unit, Oxford Road, Manchester M13 9PL
0161 275 2000

Raffo, C. Mr

Cultural GNVQs and the transition from education to work - situational learning and the creative city

ABSTRACT: UK cities are going through a process of change and development. Manchester, in particular, is experiencing a movement away from a classic Fordist city to one where creative, diversity and carnivalesque consumption of the cultural and symbolic are pronounced. This is mediated and enhanced by a growth of micro and small businesses dedicated to cultural consumption. The strategies adopted by these businesses are often leading edge and the work generated through their activity, both formal and informal, is a major contributor to the regeneration of the city. General National Vocational Qualifications (GNVQs) have to date not accessed students effectively into the world of work. This research is geared to examining why GNVQs have not provided an appropriate bridge to work and in particular it will explore how students, through situational learning in the creative centre of the city, can enhance their understanding of work in this sector and develop their skills to be more effective contributors to this sector. The research will involve: a) a study of the GNVQ framework and its appropriateness as a qualification for guiding students into the world of work; b) an ethnographic study of cultural entrepeneurs and the business skills they demonstrate in their work; c) researching the effectiveness of situational learning as a means of enhancing GNVQ and the transition from education to work. The sample will be approximately 50 cultural entrepeneurs with 10 detailed ethnographic studies; and approximately 50 students studying GNVQs in Art and Design, Leisure and Tourism, and Media. Results to date show that many activities carried out by cultural entrepeneurs do not always fit education models provided by mainstream business theory, e.g. networking, the blurring of leisure and work, intuitive understanding of their market by being part of the market, the cultural value of products.

PUBLISHED MATERIAL: RAFFO, C., LOVATT, A. & O'CONNOR, J. (1996). 'Modernist 16-19 business education in a post-modern world: critical evidence of business practice and business education in the cultural industries', British Journal for Education and Work, Vol 9, No 3, pp.19-34.

STATUS: Individual research

DATE OF RESEARCH: 1996-continuing

KEYWORDS: **cultural industry; general national vocational qualifications; leisure industry; school to work transition; sixteen to nineteen education; vocational education; work education relationship**

1592

School of Education, Research and Graduate School, Oxford Road, Manchester M13 9PL
0161 275 2000

Al-Assaf, A. Dr; *Supervisors*: Verma, G. Prof.; Brember, I. Ms

Computer-based information systems and the role of the information technology managers in Saudi Arabia

ABSTRACT: Organisations are currently experiencing a revolution arising out of the rapid change from old to new technology. In compliance with this trend, the value of information technology (IT) managers to their organisation continues to increase. Because of their role as leaders at a critical juncture in the organisation's development, IT managers are able to model an organisational culture in unique ways. Thus IT manager behaviours may affect and influence the development and implementation of computer-based information systems (CBIS). However, the direction of IT, especially in developing countries, is mainly aimed at the technical processes and inadequate attention is being paid to the social implications of IT manager roles and behaviours. The primary objectives of the present study were to explore the social aspects affecting the development and implementation of CBIS in Saudi Arabia. The study sought to investigate: 1) the extent to which IT manager behaviours affect and influence CBIS development and implementation; 2) the leadership roles played by IT managers; 3) the relationship between IT manager leadership roles and user satisfaction, and whether any of those roles made a greater contribution to user satisfaction; 4) whether any differences existed between Saudi and non-Saudi IT managers in their leadership roles and behaviours in their approach to CBIS development and implementation in a Saudi setting. Building on existing work in the field of CBIS, explored through the relevant literature, 2 questionnaires were developed, validated and distributed to the IT manager (as system provider) and the financial manager (as system user) of 200 Saudi organisations. The findings reported in this study are built on the data from completed questionnaires returned by 81 IT managers and 72 system users. Analysis of the fieldwork data showed: 1) the strong influence of IT manager behaviours on the development and implementation of CBIS; 2) no significant relationship between IT manager behaviours and user satisfaction; 3) despite the vision setter role being the most important IT manager leadership role, both the analyser and motivator roles had more significant associations with IT manager behaviours than did the vision setter role; 4) no overall association between leadership roles and user satisfaction; 5) no significant correlation overall between Saudi and non-Saudi IT managers in CBIS development and implementation, although significant correlations were found between them on the motivator leadership role and the external control mechanism behaviour. Limitations of the study are also addressed, as are implications of the study and suggestions for further related research in the field of CBIS in Saudi Arabia are put forward.

STATUS: Individual research

DATE OF RESEARCH: 1994-1997

KEYWORDS: **information technology; saudi arabia**

1593

School of Education, Research and Graduate School, Oxford Road, Manchester M13 9PL
0161 275 2000

Ghmadi, M. Dr; *Supervisor*: Verma, G. Prof.

Implementation of humanities curriculum in Libyan secondary schools

ABSTRACT: The present study reports an investigation into the delivery of the humanities curriculum in secondary schools in Libya. Although that curriculum subsumes 7 separate subjects, the broad focus was adopted. The investigation concentrated on two central themes: 1) the teaching of the humanities; and 2) their resourcing. The former theme was sub-divided into three: classroom organisation and management; curriculum organisation; and the evaluation of teaching-learning activities. The latter theme addressed the availability and quality of resources, teacher provision, preparation, and use of resources. The investigation sought to identify problems and issues facing teachers in their implementation of the humanities curriculum. Data were gathered by the use of student and teacher questionnaires and of interviews. Questionnaires were completed by third year students and their humanities teachers in 10 secondary schools in Tripoli. Interviews were conducted with the headteachers of the 10 schools, 40 heads of humanities departments and all the specialist secondary school humanities advisers in Tripoli.

STATUS: Individual research

DATE OF RESEARCH: 1993-1997

KEYWORDS: **humanities; libya; secondary education**

1594

School of Education, Research and Graduate School, Oxford Road, Manchester M13 9PL
0161 275 2000

Jallad, M. Dr; *Supervisors*: Verma, G. Prof.; Skinner, G. Mr

The Islamic studies curriculum in Jordan

ABSTRACT: This thesis is based on an investigation of the teaching of the Islamic studies curriculum in Jordan. The main focus of the research was on elements of the tenth grade curriculum: objectives, content, teaching methods and assessment. The study was conducted in 22 schools located in Amman. The 3 research methods used in the study were survey, interview and observation, and both qualitative and quantitative data were generated. The questionnaire sample consisted of 1,164 students and 92 Islamic studies teachers. Interviews were conducted with 88 students, 22 Islamic studies teachers and 12 Islamic studies educational supervisors. Informal observation was also conducted in 22 Islamic studies classes. The thesis is divided into 2 sections: Chapters 1 to 4 set out the context of the study, including an introduction to Jordan and its education system, a discussion of Islamic studies in the light of curriculum theory and the methodological framework for the fieldwork; Chapters 5 and 6 consider the findings of the research and these findings are discussed in Chapter 7. Finally, Chapter 8 reflects on the study as a whole relating the fieldwork to the theory. In addition it offers some recommendations concerning the Islamic studies curriculum in Jordan and suggestions for further research. Islamic studies is one of the crucial and foundation subjects in Jordanian schools. Its importance is derived from its subject, the religion of Islam. However, it was found that the focus of the curriculum and the teaching-learning process of Islamic studies was mainly restricted to the subject matter or content. The main concern of the teachers was to deliver information to students which was achieved through lectures with little or no use made of other teaching styles. Few aids and activities were used in the process and assessment was confined to students' knowledge. The research also identified the importance of preparing Islamic studies teachers by ensuring that they had a good understanding of both Islam and educational matters. Several recommendations are put forward, including making better use of educational theory in developing and producing the curriculum, searching for a suitable model for the Islamic studies curriculum, minimising the role of textbooks in the teaching-learning process, and better and inservice training programmes for Islamic studies teachers.

STATUS: Individual research

DATE OF RESEARCH: 1994-1997

KEYWORDS: **islamic education; jordan**

1595

School of Education, Research and Graduate School, Oxford Road, Manchester M13 9PL
0161 275 2000

Ramadan, E. Dr; *Supervisor*: Verma, G. Prof.

Programmed learning and achievement in geography in Libyan secondary schools

ABSTRACT: A conference held in Libya at the end of the 1980s drew attention to the lack of quality of learning in Libyan schools and sought to address ways in which the situation might be remedied. One of the conference's recommendations was that a wider variety of teaching methods should be applied in Libyan classrooms. The present study sought to explore the effects of the use of programmed learning techniques as an aid to improve the quality of instruction. The project reports an experimental study into the effects of two modes of programmed learning, using immediate and delayed feedback on the learning of geography among seventh grade pupils in four single sex Libyan secondary schools, as compared to normal classroom teaching. The four schools, two serving urban and two, rural areas, were selected randomly to provide the research base. In each school, three seventh grade classes were randomly assigned to three different treatments, programmed learning with immediate or delayed feedback, and conventional teaching, the latter serving as a control group. The control group classes studied two units from the Libyan geography curriculum by conventional methods, while the experimental group classes worked from specially written programmed learning materials built on the same content. At the end of the experimental period, the pupils (n=358) in all twelve classes were tested on the knowledge they had acquired, to determine whether any significant learning gains had occurred through the use of programmed learning with either immediate or delayed feedback, as compared to conventional teaching. Further measures were obtained on pupils in the programmed learning groups in order to assess whether any other gains had been made. The programmed learning group pupils completed a self-esteem inventory, prior to and immediately after the experiment. They also completed a questionnaire on their experience of using programmed learning. The group leaders supervising the classes kept a detailed log of progress with the programmed learning materials, and the classes' normal geography teachers rated the pupils on their attitudes to geography, some three weeks after their return to normal teaching. The results of the experiment are fully reported and are sited in the theoretical context of operant conditioning and programmed learning. The programmed learning classes achieved higher mean scores on the achievement test than most of the control group classes, some differences reaching statistical significance. In addition, gains were found in mean self-esteem scores over the experimental period in the programmed learning classes, some of these also reaching statistical significance. Recommendations are made concerning the use of programmed learning in the Libyan education system to provide teachers with an additional method for promoting effective learning.

STATUS: Individual research

DATE OF RESEARCH: 1993-1997

KEYWORDS: **geography; libya; teaching methods**

Market and Opinion Research International (MORI)

1596

95 Southwark Street, London SE1 0HX
0171 928 5955

Everett, M. Mr

Information types and sources - their value to young people

ABSTRACT: The research assessed the effectiveness of careers information currently available to young people, both those planning to stay in education and those planning to enter the labour market. The research involved 462 semi-structured interviews with young people who had just completed Year 11. 8 different types of careers information documents were considered: post-16 options; destinations documents; post-16 school/college performance tables; college student achievement/ destinations (S50s); further education college prospectuses; 6th form prospectuses; training opportunities information; labour market information. Key findings for this study show that most young people find careers literature easy to understand, although many documents are not well known. Few documents have been extensively read or used by young people, although this varies by document type. Also young people who intended to continue in education were more aware of the different document types than those who intended to enter the labour market. Earlier and targeted distribution of materials may prove effective.

STATUS: Sponsored project

SOURCE OF GRANT: Department for Education and Employment £61,936

DATE OF RESEARCH: 1997-1998

KEYWORDS: **career awareness; career choice; information sources; secondary school pupils; vocational guidance**

1597

95 Southwark Street, London SE1 0HX
0171 928 5955

Everett, M. Mr

Effect of Jobseeker's Allowance on 16/17 year olds: survey of young people

ABSTRACT: Jobseeker's Allowance was introduced in October 1997 to replace Income Support and Unemployment Benefit. A small number of 16 and 17 year-olds are eligible to claim Jobseeker's Allowance under Severe Hardship provisions. This research interviews a sample of those 16 and 17 year-olds and looks at how their attitudes towards job search and training change over time. The research comprises indepth qualitative interviews with 70 16 and 17 year-olds and is a before and after design.

STATUS: Sponsored project

SOURCE OF GRANT: Department for Education and Employment £96,644

DATE OF RESEARCH: 1996-1997

KEYWORDS: **job search methods; training; unemployment; youth unemployment**

1598

95 Southwark Street, London SE1 0HX
0171 928 5955

Wardman, M. Mr; Stevens, J. Ms

Course switching: evaluating the impact of careers guidance on young people's early careers guidance

ABSTRACT: This study was commissioned in order to enhance the Department for Education and Employment's (DfEE) understanding about factors which are associated with young people making early changes to their initial post-16 education or training courses. A further aim of the study was to provide an insight into how Careers Education and Guidance (CEG) is related to young people making inappropriate decisions or changes. The study looked at young people who had switched from 4 different types of courses: A-level courses in school sixth forms and sixth form colleges; full-time National Vocational Qualification (NVQ) courses in further education colleges; intermediate level General National Vocational Qualification (GNVQ) courses in school sixth forms and Youth Training courses. The report presents findings from a qualitative study of young people aged 16 or 17 years old who had switched course within 9 months of starting their first post-16 education or training course. The fieldwork involved 2 stages. In the first stage 40 individual interviews were conducted with young people in May/June 1997. During the second stage of the fieldwork 208 semi-structured interviews took place in July/ August 1997. The findings show that although early post-16 course switching may be influenced by social, financial and personal factors, it results mainly from problems experienced by young people with their course. Schools, colleges and providers have a role to play in giving young people a more realistic picture of what their options might involve.

STATUS: Sponsored project

SOURCE OF GRANT: Department for Education and Employment £60,184

DATE OF RESEARCH: 1997-1997

KEYWORDS: **course selection - students; dropouts; further education; sixteen to nineteen education; training; vocational guidance**

1599

95 Southwark Street, London SE1 0HX
0171 928 5955

Everett, M. Mr

Evaluation of national traineeships

ABSTRACT: The first stage of the national evaluation of national traineeships has involved baseline interviews with a small number of Industry Training Organisations (ITOs)/National Training Organisations (NTOs), Training and Enterprise Councils (TECs) and Careers Services to obtain their views on the early implementation of the initiative. The objective is to identify strengths and weaknesses so that good practice can be disseminated to facilitate the development of the initiative and to help iron out any initial teething problems. Later stages of the evaluation will include surveys of both employers involved in the initiative and trainees, to examine the effectiveness of the initiative from their perspective.

Organisations interviewed in the first phase will be re-interviewed to gain their views once the initiative is more established. Overall, the evaluation will look at establishing and implementing the frameworks, employer involvement, quality of the young people's experience, marketing and funding.

STATUS: Sponsored project

SOURCE OF GRANT: Department for Education and Employment £106,356

DATE OF RESEARCH: 1997-continuing

KEYWORDS: national traineeship; training; work based learning; youth employment

1600

95 Southwark Street, London SE1 0HX
0171 928 5955

Wardman, M. Mr

Nursery education vouchers pilot areas: survey of the parents of 3 and 4 year olds

ABSTRACT: The aims of the survey were to: identify participation in different types of preschool provision in the Phase 1 areas of the nursery education voucher scheme; assess the impact of the introduction of the scheme on parental attitudes to and choice of different types of preschool provision for 4 year-olds; establish the range of reasons why not all eligible parents claimed vouchers, or, where they did, did not use them. Sample interview survey conducted with parents whose children were 3 or 4 either in Summer 1995 or Summer 1996. Interviews took place in Summer 1996.

STATUS: Sponsored project

SOURCE OF GRANT: Department for Education and Employment £93,261

DATE OF RESEARCH: 1996-1997

KEYWORDS: early childhood education; education vouchers; nursery education; parents; preschool education

MENCAP National Centre

1601

123 Golden Lane, London EC1Y ORT
0171 454 0454 / 0171 962 1280
Further Education Unit, Spring Gardens, Citadel Place, Tinworth Street, London SE11 5EH

Griffiths, M. Mr; Supervisor: Hood, P. Ms

Post-school learning opportunities for people with profound intellectual and multiple impairments

ABSTRACT: The aim of the project is to identify existing practice and the current perceptions of learning opportunities for adults with profound intellectual impairment who are likely to have multiple disabilities and to produce a curriculum framework for these learners. The project will use the following methods: (a) A nationwide survey by questionnaire (b) selection from the above and otherwise by a multi-disciplinary working group who will: (1) identify core learning experiences (2) generate a curriculum framework (3) produce and test learning material.

STATUS: Sponsored project

SOURCE OF GRANT: Department of Health £12,500; Further Education Unit £12,500

DATE OF RESEARCH: 1991-1993

KEYWORDS: access to education; adult basic education; adult learning; intelligence differences; learning disabilities; multiple disabilities; special educational needs

Middlesex University

1602

School of Lifelong Learning and Education, Trent Park, Bramley Road, London N14 4XS
0181 362 5000

Montgomery, D. Prof.

Distance learning: using cognitive process learning and assessment strategies to develop capability in higher education programmes

ABSTRACT: The research is based in critical thinking theory. Six teaching methods have been compiled and developed which can evoke critical thinking across curriculum subjects in schools and higher education: investigative learning and problem solving; cognitive study skills; experiential learning; collaborative learning; language experience methods; and games and simulations. The development research took place in teacher education, primary and secondary schools. The purpose was to train teachers on initial and inservice courses to enable pupils to develop higher order learning and cognitive skills which could be used across curriculum subjects. These had the express purpose of developing higher order cognitive skills and abilities in pupils and students as well as in their teachers. The success of the methods had been demonstrated with pupils with general and specific learning difficulties, children of average ability, able and highly able pupils, and those with emotional and behavioural difficulties in classroom settings. It showed the ways in which curriculum differentiation could effectively be achieved by a process termed 'developmental differentiation'. The project is now at the stage of addressing the issue of how similar results may be achieved in the distance learning mode and how practical competencies in teaching and learning, and collaborative team work capabilities may be achieved in what is in essence an individualised learning activity. The distance programme is delivered at Middlesex University as a 13 x 10 credit set of modules and a 50 credit dissertation module (180 credits) as an MA in Special Educational Needs and an MA in Specific Learning Difficulties. There is also a 10 credit new experimental module for the BA Qualified Teacher Status (QTS). There are 70 students on the MA programmes and 33 on the BA, from whom qualitative and quantitative data is being collected in the form of questionnaires, rating scales and feedback reports from pupils, students, assessors and researchers during the 1996-97 period. There will be a second phase project which will try to quantify the professional capabilities and cognitive skills developments involved.

PUBLISHED MATERIAL: MONTGOMERY, D. (1994). 'The promotion of high ability and intelligence through education and instruction'. Proceedings of the 3rd International Conference of the European Council of High Ability (ECHA), Munich University, Munich. Seattle: Hogresse & Huber. ; MONTGOMERY, D. (1995). 'Critical theory and practice in evaluation and assessment'. In: GIBBS, G. Improving student learning. Proceedings of the 2nd International Seminar, Oxford Brookes University, Oxford. ; MONTGOMERY, D. (1996). Educating the able. London: Cassell. A full list of publications is available from the researcher.

STATUS: Individual research

DATE OF RESEARCH: 1991-1997

KEYWORDS: cognitive processes; differentiated curriculum; distance education; learning strategies; metacognition; preservice teacher education; teaching methods

1603

School of Lifelong Learning and Education, Trent Park, Bramley Road, London N14 4XS
0181 362 5000

Montgomery, D. Prof.

The nature, origin and remediation of spelling difficulties

ABSTRACT: After 100 years of the visual processing paradigm being used to explain severe reading problems the switch to phonological explanations has been made in the experimental literature. The same changes have not yet taken place in the remedial teaching field, although there are the beginnings of change. For more than 100 years the whole emphasis in the area of poor literacy skills and dyslexia has been upon reading rather than spelling and writing difficulties. The purpose of this research is to promote the analysis and development of theory and practice in spelling teaching and remedial spelling through research. It is hypothesised that in severe literacy difficulties the core difficulties which need to be addressed are spelling rather than reading skills. Thus far it has been shown that articulation awareness is an area of difficulty in dyslexics but not in poor readers and control subjects (n=288) (replication study n=90). Techniques of teaching which address these difficulties and which promote phonological skills lacked by the dyslexics have been shown to be successful in promoting more than two years advancement in reading and spelling in one year, compared with five to eleven months of other schemes. A system of analysis of errors using a 4 Column Miscues Analysis is in development, together with a set of programmes and strategies for intervention. The plight of able 'dyslexics' is considered as a special subgroup within the larger population of dyslexics. High ability is defined as a WISC-R scale of 130 IQ on either verbal or performance quotients (n=30).

PUBLISHED MATERIAL: MONTGOMERY, D. (1994). 'Underachievement: the problems of gifted dyslexics and their remediation'. In: HELEK, K.A. & HANY, E.A. (Eds). Proceedings of the 3rd International Conference of the European Council for High Ability (ECHA), Munich University, Munich. Seattle: Hogresse & Huber. ; MONTGOMERY, D. (1995). 'Social abilities in able and highly disabled learners and the consequences for remediation'. Proceedings of the 4th International Conference of the European Council for High Ability (ECHA), Nijmegen University, The Netherlands. ; MONTGOMERY, D. Spelling remedial strategies. London: Cassell. (in press).

STATUS: Individual research

DATE OF RESEARCH: 1993-1997

KEYWORDS: **dyslexia; reading difficulties; remedial programmes; spelling; writing difficulties**

1604

School of Lifelong Learning and Education, Trent Park, Bramley Road, London N14 4XS
0181 362 5000

Taylor, P. Mr; *Supervisors*: Cave, J. Prof.; Tufnell, R. Prof.

An investigation into problem-solving in design and technology at National Curriculum key stage 3

ABSTRACT: The basis for the research is of particular interest in determining the effectiveness of problem stating and problem-solving and the relationships between teachers and pupils engaged in these processes. Part of this interest has been associated with the notion of progression and operational levels linked to pupils at key stage 3 working independently on open-ended design based problem-solving. The initial central aims of the investigation were to: 1) investigate the nature of problem-solving in design and technology at key stage 3 with special reference to the perceptions of teachers and pupils; and 2) study the interaction between teachers and pupils in the teaching of problem-solving in design and technology at key stage 3. The methodology for the initial stage was based on focus group interviews. Teachers and pupils in 12 sample schools were interviewed to gain an insight into their awareness, and use, of the factors of the problem-solving process. It is envisaged that the outcomes will contribute towards the ongoing debate about the role of problem-solving in design and technology linked to the development of National Curriculum technology. This might typically form the development of principles that will inform students training to be teachers of design and technology, as well as existing teachers of design and technology.

STATUS: Individual research

DATE OF RESEARCH: 1992-continuing

KEYWORDS: **design and technology; key stage 3; learning activities; problem solving; secondary education; secondary school pupils; teacher pupil relationship; teaching methods**

1605

School of Lifelong Learning and Education, Trent Park, Bramley Road, London N14 4XS
0181 362 5000

Blumenfrucht, J. Mrs; *Supervisors*: Freeman, J. Prof.; Jones, L. Mr; Halstead, V. Ms

Gifted children and the acquisition of language: the impact of expertise on stages of development and its practical implications for all students of language

ABSTRACT: The aims of the investigation are to: 1) ascertain how gifted children acquire language; 2) test whether the 'doors of learning' remain open longer in gifted children; 3) establish the strategies used by gifted children to acquire expertise in language; 4) discover whether these metacognitive and social strategies can be adapted to improve the language acquisition of all learners, and if so, how; and 5) define the place of bilingualism and multilingualism in 1-4 above. The early stage of the project would comprise indepth studies of the development of language using socio-historical and metacognitive sources, an extensive literature search for background information on gifted children and how they learn, i.e. expertise versus normal development as well as extensive analysis of systems for testing the above with a view to establishing a personal style of baseline assessment. (The means of assessment are to include conventional and computer assisted methods). Later a testing of hypotheses would be required where methodology would include all areas of research studied at Middlesex University for the Postgraduate Certificate in Research Methodology, ie. surveys, data preparation based on a variety of sources, qualitative and quantitative data analysis using statistical input, processing of data using SPSS, and depth interviewing. There would also be some observation of a variety of situations with tape recordings or video input. A control group will be established and closely monitored and an ongoing literature review would follow closely changes in thinking in all areas encompassed by the research topic.

STATUS: Individual research

DATE OF RESEARCH: 1998-continuing

KEYWORDS: **child language; gifted; language acquisition; language skills**

1606

School of Lifelong Learning and Education, Trent Park, Bramley Road, London N14 4XS
0181 362 5000

de Rijke, V. Ms; *Supervisors*: Campbell, P. Dr; Durant, A. Prof.; Segal, L. Dr

Metaphors of childhood: the garden and the school in 20th century literature and art

ABSTRACT: Background to this research was to study figures of childhood represented in 20th century literature and art, focusing on two metaphoric locations of the garden and the school. The field was limited to selected texts and images 1900-1996, such as Francis Hodgson-Burnett's 'The Secret Garden'; J.P. Hartley's 'The Go Between'; Henry James 'The Pupil' and Roald Dahl's 'Mathilda'. An historical introduction sets the context for the 20th century child sited in the garden and school, related to changes in psychological and pedagogic thinking. Metaphor is examined as both a literary and cultural trope, with a rich interdisciplinary literature for study. Broadly, the research's methodology has been psychoanalytic and literary criticism, attempting to relate theories of transference to metaphor, and thereon to reading the child. Part of the conclusion of the research is to blur the traditional categories of literature for children/ adults with texts about childhood. The researcher's final conclusions have not been reached about metaphor, though it is in relation to Freud's dreamwork where the primary processes of condensation, displacement and symbolism resist categories of time and space. It is possible that texts citing the child in the garden focus on the unconscious 'natural' childhood aspects of adult whereas the school links to cultural cultivations the adult aspect of the child. However, the end is still a secret.

PUBLISHED MATERIAL: DE RIJKE, V. & ZACHARKIW, A. (1995). 'Reading the child invention', Children's literature in Education Journal, Vol 26, No 3, pp.153-169. ; A full list of publications is available from the researcher.

STATUS: Individual research

DATE OF RESEARCH: 1994-continuing

KEYWORDS: **childhood; childrens literature; literature; metaphors; visual arts**

1607

School of Lifelong Learning and Education, Trent Park, Bramley Road, London N14 4XS
0181 362 5000

Holmes, K. Mrs; *Supervisors*: Costley, C. Dr; Grant, D. Mr

Sharing good practice: effective strategies used by the education welfare office working with the school non-attender

ABSTRACT: The principal function of the Education Welfare Service (EWS) is to help parents and local education authorities (LEAs) meet their statutory obligations on school attendance. The EWS is not a statutory service, but it is often a means by which LEAs respond to a range of statutory duties placed upon them. One of these duties is to prosecute parents, under Section 7 and Section 444 of the 1996 Education Act, who fail to ensure that their child is receiving an efficient full-time education. In order to prevent prosecution, the role of the Education Welfare Officer (EWO), through close cooperation with the school, is to assist and encourage the parent/s to fulfil their responsibility. From experience of working with a number of EWOs and with over 2 years working experience as an EWO, the researcher has identified 2 broad approaches of working practices - the traditional school board approach at one end of the continuum and the supportive approach at the other. It is the researcher's suggestion that for the EWO to maintain an effective working practice it is important to acquire skills and knowledge from both approaches. This study will investigate the wide range of professional skills involved in the working practice of the EWO along with how the professional develops effective strategies to engage the consumer of the service - the school non-attender. Data will be collected on the working practices of EWOs from 4 LEAs working with school non-attenders (predominantly serving multi-racial, working class, white middle-class and white working-class areas) - respondents representing inner London, outer London and the counties. The researcher will request 4 cases from each of the subject's current caseload with a school attendance rate of 50% or below, using a case study approach.

STATUS: Sponsored project

SOURCE OF GRANT: Middlesex University £19,500

DATE OF RESEARCH: 1997-continuing

KEYWORDS: attendance; educational welfare; truancy

1608

School of Lifelong Learning and Education, Trent Park, Bramley Road, London N14 4XS
0181 362 5000

Gutmann, D. Mr; *Supervisors*: Russell, T. Mr; Jack, D. Ms

An investigation into GNVQ in schools as preparation for employment

ABSTRACT: The thesis aims to show how effective General National Vocational Qualifications (GNVQs) can be a preparation for employment and whether it is more effective in some vocational areas than others. The background to this project is the researcher's teaching career in secondary education which has involved business and vocational education. GNVQs were introduced in 5 vocational areas to see the progression from GNVQ to employment, particularly for intermediate pupils. A pilot sample of 12 pupils in 1 school is proposed, followed by a sample of 18 in 3 case study schools. The sample will consist of all intermediate pupils who intend to enter employment and it is hoped to choose schools at different stages of GNVQ experience. It is proposed to identify pupils in case study schools to ascertain, on a longitudinal empirical basis, how their GNVQ courses have proved suitable to employers and employment. Qualitative and quantitative methods will be employed, based on questionnaires and interviews for the main empirical study, following-up an initial literature search. The research will be mostly classroom based.

STATUS: Individual research

DATE OF RESEARCH: 1997-continuing

KEYWORDS: employment; general national vocational qualifications; school leavers; secondary education; vocational education; work education relationship

1609

School of Lifelong Learning and Education, Trent Park, Bramley Road, London N14 4XS
0181 362 5000

Neale, J. Mr; *Supervisors*: Tufnell, R. Prof.; Cave, J. Prof.

Design and technology education in National Curriculum key stages 3 and 4

ABSTRACT: This investigation of secondary school pupils' attitudes to, and perceptions of, design and technology in the National Curriculum (1995 Order), aims to measure and compare attitudes and understanding of technology in general and design and technology at 3 points: 1) after 1

year of key stage 3 (Year 7); 2) after the National Curriculum assessment of design and technology at the end of key stage 3 (end of Year 9); 3) after completion of a GCSE design and technology course or half course (Year 11). The method used for stages (1) and (2) will be semi-structured questionnaires with possibility of an unstructured response. Qualitative data will be obtained from interviews in 3 Hertfordshire mixed secondary schools after GCSE in stage (3) and related to that obtained in stages (1) and (2).

PUBLISHED MATERIAL: NEALE, J.G. (1996). 'The new order for design and technology'. In: ANDREWS, R. Interpreting the new National Curriculum. Enfield: Middlesex University Press.

STATUS: Individual research

DATE OF RESEARCH: 1995-continuing

KEYWORDS: design and technology; key stage 3; national curriculum; pupil attitudes; secondary education; secondary school pupils

1610

School of Lifelong Learning and Education, Trent Park, Bramley Road, London N14 4XS
0181 362 5000

Howarth, M. Mr; *Supervisors*: Andrews, R. Prof.; Davies, S. Mr; Russell, T. Mr

Children and computers: the development of a graphic user interface to improve the quality of interaction

ABSTRACT: This project looks at computer interface design issues using education radio programmes as multimedia learning resources. The project was supported by the BBC during the time the researcher was a senior radio producer in the Education Directorate. The research tool is a popular key stage 1 music study series called Starcatcher, reformatted as a multimedia CD Rom. The Starcatcher CD Rom - the research tool - began with a study for the BBC of 12 schools in Hertfordshire as part of the CD Rom in primary schools initiative by the National Council for Educational Technology. The Starcatcher software development then took place at the Open University BBC Production Centre with the researcher as project manager. The budget was 20,000 pounds. The first school pilot resulted in some changes in software design assisted by input from a BBC Education Officer. The budget allowed for some reprogramming to subsequently take place. At this stage the project matured as a PhD proposal at Middlesex University. The subject was the design and functionality of the 8 different computer interfaces in the research tool. Following a literature search, a second pilot tested the methodology to be used. The descriptive method was chosen to use the researcher's 20 years of experience in the classroom professionally evaluating educational radio programmes. The main study design consisted of collection data using the triangulation process. The study involved observations of around 200 children in groups of 3; indepth interviews with 15 children; and interviews with 6 teachers. 4 schools were visited. Questions were grouped in 3 areas, screen instructions, screen design and movement of screen objects. The replies totalled 1,133 filecards.

PUBLISHED MATERIAL: HOWARTH, M. (1996). 'Visual elements and container metaphors for multi-media', British Journal of Educational Technology, Vol 28, No 2, pp.125-133.

STATUS: Individual research

DATE OF RESEARCH: 1994-continuing

KEYWORDS: cd roms; computer uses in education; information technology; multimedia

1611

School of Lifelong Learning and Education, Trent Park, Bramley Road, London N14 4XS
0181 362 5000

Newby, P. Prof.; Osborne, C. Mr; Jervis, P. Prof.; Wisdom, J. Mr

The development and accreditation of higher level skills

ABSTRACT: The project seeks to identify and elaborate a higher level skills curriculum to represent this curriculum in outcome terms and to establish a template that is a framework for student portfolio work. The project will reconceptualise skill within the higher education curriculum and will identify ways of moving academic practice and culture to achieve skills outcomes. A key feature of the project will be to map existing practice against the skills template.

STATUS: Sponsored project

SOURCE OF GRANT: Higher Education Regional Development Fund £44,000

DATE OF RESEARCH: 1998-continuing

KEYWORDS: **higher education; skills**

1612

School of Lifelong Learning and Education, Trent Park, Bramley Road, London N14 4XS
0181 362 5000

Newby, P. Prof.; Jervis, P. Prof.

Partnership structures and processes in local development programmes

ABSTRACT: The project is: 1) mapping the pattern and structure of partnerships; 2) exploring the part played by educational institutions; 3) researching the conditions that make for sound partnership and collaboration; and 4) identifying effective partnership management and reorganisation. The research will contribute to the literature on local management and economic development and the local economic role of the education system.

STATUS: Sponsored project

SOURCE OF GRANT: Middlesex University £10,000

DATE OF RESEARCH: 1998-continuing

KEYWORDS: **college community relationship; community development; partnerships; school community relationship**

1613

School of Lifelong Learning and Education, Trent Park, Bramley Road, London N14 4XS
0181 362 5000

Jones, L. Mr

The National Literacy Strategy and the able child at key stage 1

ABSTRACT: The research focuses on children at National Curriculum key stage 1 in Year 2 to gauge their comprehension and decoding skills evident from the selection of reading books required in a set period from February to March 1999. Standardised reading tests, tasks and tests, and teacher records will identify the sample of able children to be studied. The children's reading ability will be carefully monitored to examine compatibility between text and reader in terms of fluency, comprehension and interest. Other aspects related to word, sentence and text strands of the National Literacy Strategy will be explored to provide an informed understanding of each child's grasp of literacy.

STATUS: Individual research

DATE OF RESEARCH: 1999-continuing

KEYWORDS: **able pupils; key stage 1; national literacy strategy; primary education; reading; reading ability**

1614

School of Lifelong Learning and Education, Trent Park, Bramley Road, London N14 4XS
0181 362 5000

Cave, J. Prof.; Tufnell, R. Prof.

Technology Enhancement Programme (TEP) resource development

ABSTRACT: The Technology Enhancement Programme (TEP) was established in 1992 as an initiative of the Gatsby Charitable Foundation. Its overall mission is to enhance and enrich technology education in the United Kingdom, raise awareness of engineering and technology and encourage career take-up in areas of serious shortage. The programme is currently in the first year of its third 3-year phase, and is thus the longest running and most significant project of its kind ever undertaken. Each 3-year phase has had a different emphasis. The first phase laid foundations and provided selected schools with grant funding to develop premises and curriculum planning. The second phase widened the scheme to participation by any school in the UK and the third phase currently seeks to widen school participation from 1000 schools to double that

number by the year 2000. The third phase also seeks to build on the critical mass of new resources, publications and multimedia materials to provide a secure platform for a key part of the National Curriculum moving into the next millennium. The first two phases of TEP were managed by the Engineering Council and comprised a team of 5 full-time officers, and consultants with central infrastructural support. The officers provided advice and support for schools and encouraged the development of industrial links. They also organised industrial visits, conferences and regional meetings to keep all schools up-to-date with new developments in technology and engineering - and technology education. During the second phase, TEP offered a formal membership scheme in return for a commitment from schools to obtain matching industrial support. Over the period 1994-1997 membership grew from 80 schools to just under 1000 (approximately 25% of the UK total). During this period at least as many schools again purchased TEP publications and resources. The Middlesex University's Technology Education Centre (MUTEC) was brought into the programme in 1994 with a specific remit to develop new photocopiable and physical resources to support technology teaching. The centre also hosted TEP summer schools and developed a major multimedia resource with additional Gatsby funding. The current phase of TEP is now managed through the Gatsby Technical Education Project Office, a new umbrella organisation supporting other major curriculum development projects. TEP has a new and larger central support team offering basic support to schools but now providing inservice courses and other new membership benefits. Through direct contact with schools, public exhibitions, and expansion of its quarterly publication, 'News and Views', TEP has become a major national presence in technology education. Increasingly, it is also a significant international player representing the interests of the UK at conferences, supporting developing countries, and forging partnerships between European Union (EU) member states.

STATUS: Sponsored project

SOURCE OF GRANT: Gatsby Charitable Foundation

DATE OF RESEARCH: 1993-continuing

KEYWORDS: **educational materials; engineering; secondary education; technology; technology education**

1615

School of Lifelong Learning and Education, Trent Park, Bramley Road, London N14 4XS
0181 362 5000

Mitchell, S. Ms; Riddle, M. Mr

Improving the quality of argument in higher education

ABSTRACT: The background to this project was earlier work (see Mitchell 1994) which explored the place and nature of argument in Sixth Forms and higher education in various disciplines. That work suggested that argument was highly valued, but that there were difficulties with students' ability to argue, with disciplinary and institutional expectations and with the degree and quality of teaching that addressed that area. The current project aims to produce practical outcomes for the teaching and learning of argument in higher education. It has taken a collaborative approach, attempting to involve staff in the investigation of argument and in the development of strategies for improving understanding and application. The focus is particularly on the writing students do, but extends to consideration of their reasoning processes within disciplinary fields more generally.

PUBLISHED MATERIAL: MITCHELL, S. (1994). The teaching and learning of argument in sixth forms and higher education: final report. Hull, University of Hull, Institute of Education. ; MITCHELL, S. (1996). Improving the quality of argument in higher education: interim report. London: Middlesex University. ; RIDDLE, M. (Ed). (1997). The quality of argument: colloquium on issues of teaching and learning in higher education. London: Middlesex University, School of Education. ; MITCHELL, S. (1998). 'Teaching, learning and assessing argument', Encyclopedia of Language and Education, Vol 6. Dordrecht: Kluwer Academic Publishers.

STATUS: Sponsored project

SOURCE OF GRANT: Leverhulme Trust £63,270

DATE OF RESEARCH: 1995-continuing

KEYWORDS: **argument; higher education; learning strategies; secondary education; sixth forms**

1616

School of Lifelong Learning and Education, Trent Park, Bramley Road, London N14 4XS
0181 362 5000
Leeds University, School of Education, Leeds LS2 9JT
01132 431751

Stephenson, J. Prof.; Williams, R. Mr; Cairns, L. Dr

The social milieu of learning stimulated by National Vocational Qualifications

ABSTRACT: This research builds on the work of Williams, Cunningham and Stephenson (1998) on the Impact of National Vocational Qualifications (NVQs) on Corporate Capability which suggested that the social processes stimulated by participation in NVQs were more important to the development of corporate capability than the intended learning outcomes built into NVQ programmes. A review of the literature on social learning, including within organisations, suggested a number of features which, if present, might indicate that effective and useful learning was taking place. Holders of NVQs in 4 large organisations were interviewed about their NVQ learning experiences. Data from these and earlier interviews were reviewed in the context of the potential indicators of effective social learning which emerged from the literature review. A firmer list of indicators has been produced which are now being tested against the experiences of learners in 6 organisations not previously included in this or its earlier study. The final stage is to examine the extent to which the indicators survive scrutiny in the context of data from the final 6 cases, and to consider the extent to which it is possible to formulate advice for designers of NVQs and those responsible for their introduction to raise the effectiveness of NVQs as contributors to individual and corporate development.

STATUS: Sponsored project

SOURCE OF GRANT: RSA Examinations Board £20,000

DATE OF RESEARCH: 1998-continuing

KEYWORDS: **learning; national vocational qualifications; social development; vocational education**

1617

School of Lifelong Learning and Education, Trent Park, Bramley Road, London N14 4XS
0181 362 5000
Leeds University, School of Education, Leeds LS2 9JT
01132 431751

Stephenson, J. Prof.; Williams, R. Mr; Cunningham, L. Ms

The impact of National Vocational Qualifications (NVQs) on the development of corporate capability

ABSTRACT: The researchers were commissioned by the Royal Society of Arts Examinations Board, one of the main National Vocational Qualification (NVQ) awarding bodies, to report on the impact, if any, of NVQs on the development of corporate capability. Current literature on corporate development was reviewed and a list of possible indicators, as proposed by different authors, was produced. Three case studies of major organisations were prepared: a major city council; a privatised utility; and a national distribution company. Groups of NVQ holders were interviewed and were encouraged to describe their personal experiences of completing an NVQ qualification. Senior managers responsible for the introduction of NVQs were also interviewed. The data from these interviews were presented as case studies structured according to the 'indicators' of corporate capability identified from the literature. NVQs appeared to have little impact on corporate capability except in ways which were outside the intended outcomes. Learning through interaction with colleagues and through self and peer assessment were positive outcomes, leading the researchers to speculate that the process by which employees engaged with NVQs, and with each other, was more relevant to the development of corporate capability than the specified outcomes of the NVQs themselves.

PUBLISHED MATERIAL: WILLIAMS, R., CUNNINGHAM, L. & STEPHENSON, J. (1998). The use of NVQs as a means to develop corporate capability. Coventry: Royal Society of Arts Examination Board.

STATUS: Sponsored project

SOURCE OF GRANT: RSA Examinations Board £10,000

DATE OF RESEARCH: 1997-1997

KEYWORDS: **industry education relationship; national vocational qualifications; qualifications; training; vocational education; work education relationship**

1618

School of Lifelong Learning and Education, Trent Park, Bramley Road, London N14 4XS
0181 362 5000
London University, Institute of Education, 20 Bedford Way, London WC1H 0AL
0171 580 1122

Khwaja, C. Ms; *Supervisors*: Frost, J. Mrs; Barker, V. Dr

How does the level of engagement with the content of National Curriculum primary science vary with the level of confidence of the teacher, and does this level of engagement increase with teaching experience

ABSTRACT: There is a wealth of research showing that primary school teachers lack knowledge and understanding of the science that they are required to teach. An analysis of the current research into primary teachers' lack of knowledge and understanding in science, and a criticism of this work, has been carried out. The aim of the research is to: 1) describe what is happening in a primary science classroom; 2) identify the factors which contribute to the level of engagement with primary science by teachers; 3) find out if it is possible to quantify level of engagement with science; and 4) identify and describe those factors which contribute to teacher confidence with primary science. During their Postgraduate Certificate in Education (PGCE) year, the students' main concerns are managing pupil behaviour, organising the classroom, maintaining their teaching file and coping with being assessed. As the student gains in confidence in these areas, they are less of a concern, so the students' level of engagement with science should increase. 10 PGCE students were observed teaching and were then interviewed twice during their PGCE year, and twice during their first 2 years of teaching after qualification. The students' lessons have been scored using an observation tool which the researcher has developed over the last 3 years. The level of engagement with science for each lesson has been scored and the scores are based on both positive and negative engagement with science. The students have assessed their level of confidence to manage pupil behaviour; confidence to teach science; and confidence with science subject matter. The students have been interviewed to find out what sort of support they have received for science from their schools and local authority inspectorate.

PUBLISHED MATERIAL: KHWAJA, C. (1996). 'A look at primary science'. In: ANDREWS, R. (Ed). Interpreting the new National Curriculum. Enfield: Middlesex University Press.

STATUS: Individual research

DATE OF RESEARCH: 1994-continuing

KEYWORDS: **primary school teachers; science education; subject knowledge; teacher confidence**

1619

School of Lifelong Learning and Education, National Centre for Work-based Learning Partnerships, White Hart Lane, London N17 8HR
0181 362 5000

Naish, J. Ms; *Supervisors*: Taylor, K. Mr; Portwood, D. Prof.

Role theory and the work-based learning of creative artists: the case of William Shakespeare

ABSTRACT: The aims of the project are to: 1) identify and analyse learning from the work roles of artists, using role theory, in order to increase understanding of the dialectic between an artist's work and the production of 'works'; 2) identify, analyse and test this dialectic through the special case of Shakespeare's work role relationships with key stakeholders in his career, especially exploring the meaning and significance of the diverse role sets of which he was a member. The outcomes of the research are: 1) to contribute to the scholarly investigation of work-based learning as a field of study; to critically examine Shakespeare's performance of his work roles; to identify implications of this approach for study of other work roles - in the arts; 2) to develop and test a theoretical model, using role theory, that makes an original contribution to knowledge, about analysing work-based learning. The major outcome of the research will be increased understanding about the nature of the dialectic between work roles and the works of William Shakespeare.

STATUS: Individual research

DATE OF RESEARCH: 1996-continuing

KEYWORDS: **artists; work based learning**

National Deaf Children's Society

1620

15 Dufferin Street, London EC1Y 8PD
0171 250 0123

Wheatley, H. Ms

Children who are deaf: mainstream schools and bullying

ABSTRACT: The National Deaf Children's Society (NDCS) propose to produce and disseminate a leaflet to schools with units for deaf children across the United Kingdom. The leaflet will cover basic information such as identification and prevention strategies, together with sources of advice and information. It will be designed to heighten awareness in schools and services and lead people to ask for further support. NDCS will convene a small, focused Advisory Group which will pool suggestions for the material and identify current good practice. It is anticipated that this group will meet only 3 times - once at the beginning of the project, once to agree the materials, and at the end to review progress and decide upon any future action for the field. NDCS staff will coordinate the group, write and produce the leaflet, disseminate it to schools and services and pull together evaluation results. It is hoped that the Advisory Group will include representatives of: Delwyn Tattum, Kidscape, National Society for the Prevention of Cruelty to Children (NSPCC), Childline, Nuffield Centre for Speech and Hearing, and the British Association of Teachers of the Deaf. These are all organisations with whom the NDCS has a relationship and who are likely to have the relevant expertise upon which to draw. The funding available will not enable the Society to produce a booklet or resource pack, so the focus will be upon a high quality leaflet with 3 key purposes: 1) To raise awareness of issues surrounding bullying and deaf children particularly in a mainstream setting. 2) To guide staff working with deaf children to recognise signs and take action to prevent and reduce bullying in their school. 3) To offer information, advice and resources for staff by providing contact details and addresses of key organisations. The leaflet produced will be distributed to schools, and an evaluation of the usefulness of the leaflet will be undertaken.

STATUS: Sponsored project

SOURCE OF GRANT: Calouste Gulbenkian Foundation

DATE OF RESEARCH: 1997-1997

KEYWORDS: **bullying; deafness; hearing impairments; mainstreaming; special educational needs**

National Foundation for Educational Research

1621

The Mere, Upton Park, Slough SL1 2DQ
01753 574123

Harland, J. Dr; Kinder, K. Ms; *Supervisor*: Bradley, J. Dr

Patterns of local education authority inservice education and training of teachers (INSET) organisation

ABSTRACT: Recent changes in inservice education and training of teachers (INSET) funding arrangements have resulted in local education authorities (LEAs) adopting a wide range of strategies for the planning and delivery of professional development activities. The proposed research would mapped the major types and patterns of LEA INSET organisation with the intent of developing guidelines on good practice. A national survey of INSET coordinators was followed by case study work in five LEAs exhibiting different types of INSET policy and practice. The views of LEA and school staff was sought on the benefits, problems and

effectiveness of the varying approaches to INSET. A report on the project will be produced in 1993.

PUBLISHED MATERIAL: HARLAND, J., KINDER, K. & KEYS, W. (1993). Restructuring INSET: privatization and its alternatives. Slough: National Foundation for Educational Research.

STATUS: Sponsored project

SOURCE OF GRANT: National Foundation for Educational Research £64,000

DATE OF RESEARCH: 1991-1993

KEYWORDS: **educational administration; inservice teacher education; local education authorities**

1622

The Mere, Upton Park, Slough SL1 2DQ
01753 574123

Maychell, K. Ms; *Supervisor*: Bradley, J. Dr

Evaluation and monitoring at local education authority level

ABSTRACT: This eighteen-month research project had three main aims: 1) to gather detailed information on the operation of a range of local education authority (LEA) monitoring and evaluation strategies; 2) to carry out a national survey of LEA's and schools that would provide useful information when developing evaluation and monitoring strategies; and 3) to provide practical information and guidance to assist LEA's in the future development of good practice in this area of their work. The research was nearing completion as the Education (Schools) Act 1992 was going through parliament. The report takes these changes into account and describes LEA inspection and other strategies for monitoring schools in the crucial period prior to the introduction of the Government's 'privatisation' of school inspection, i.e. the Office for Standards in Education (OFSTED) inspections. It emerged that 60% of LEA's already carried out a programme of full inspections, though the numbers of schools inspected were generally much lower than the 25% of all schools which OFSTED must inspect each year. Of the 830 schools in the survey, half had never experienced full inspection. However, most headteachers and LEA chief inspectors/advisers were in favour of introducing four-yearly formal inspections, though they were overwhelmingly against private inspection teams. Only one in ten LEA respondents and one in five headteachers felt that separating advice and inspection would be in the best interest of schools.

PUBLISHED MATERIAL: MAYCHELL, K. (1993). Under inspection: LEA evaluation and monitoring. Slough: National Foundation for Educational Research.

STATUS: Sponsored project

SOURCE OF GRANT: NFER Membership Programme

DATE OF RESEARCH: 1991-1993

KEYWORDS: **evaluation; inspection; local education authorities; monitoring; ofsted**

1623

The Mere, Upton Park, Slough SL1 2DQ
01753 574123

Taylor, M. Dr; Bagley, C. Dr; *Supervisor*: Stoney, S. Dr

Multicultural education after ERA: concerns and challenges for the 1990s

ABSTRACT: The values underpinning the Education Reform Act 1988 (ERA) and the structures and targets set by the implementation of the National Curriculum and Local Management of Schools (LMS) raised new issues and challenges in the realisation of equal opportunities in the translation of multicultural antiracist policies into practice. This project sought to be diagnostic and responsive by establishing current concerns among local education authorities (LEAs) and identifying promising developmental strategies in relation to institutional, training and curricular issues. The research had three phases: a national questionnaire, interviews, and thematic case studies. Initially the project identified LEA concerns, constraints and challenges for multicultural antiracist education in post-ERA developments. As a result, four themes formed the focus of subsequent research: (1) the implementation of Section 11 changes; (2) Training and Enterprise Councils (TECs) and the Ethnic Minority Grant;

(3) equal opportunities in governor training; (4) the issues of cultural diversity in Religious Education and the Standing Advisory Councils on Religious Education (SACREs). Research dissemination has occurred during the project and included ongoing publications, seminars, conference presentations and talks to various audiences.

PUBLISHED MATERIAL: TAYLOR, M.J. (1992). Multicultural antiracist education after ERA: concerns, constraints and challenges. Slough: National Foundation for Educational Research. ; TAYLOR, M.J. (1992). Equality after ERA? Slough: National Foundation for Educational Research. ; TAYLOR, M.J. (1992). 'Empowering SACRE to support RE', Resource, Vol 15, No 1, pp.2-4. ; BAGLEY, C.A. (1992). Back to the future: Section 11 of the Local Government Act 1966: Local education authorities and multicultural/antiracist education. Slough: National Foundation for Educational Research. ; TAYLOR, M.J. & BAGLEY, C.A. (1995). 'Multicultural antiracist education - the LEA and TEC context. In: TOMLINSON, S. & CRAFT, M. (Eds). Ethnic relations and schooling: policy and practice in the 1990s. London: Athlone Press. A full list of publications is available from the researcher.

STATUS: Sponsored project

SOURCE OF GRANT: National Foundation for Educational Research £154,649

DATE OF RESEARCH: 1991-1993

KEYWORDS: antiracism education; education reform act 1988; educational planning; equal education; local education authorities; multicultural education

1624

The Mere, Upton Park, Slough SL1 2DQ
01753 574123

Sims, D. Mr; *Supervisor*: Stoney, S. Dr

Evaluation of the Construction Industry Training Board's curriculum centre initiative

ABSTRACT: The Construction Industry Training Board (CITB) has established 73 Curriculum Centres around the country with the aim of: (1) establishing 'construction' as a genuine context for cross-curricular learning; (2) providing practical facilities which will simulate real-work situations; and (3) providing a platform for a continuing dialogue between education and industry. The National Foundation for Educational Research was contracted to provide consultancy and devise materials for the self-evaluation of the initiative by the CITB and the Centres themselves. It also conducted periodic evaluative reviews of the self-evaluation outputs and of data collected independently by the Foundation. The evaluation proceeded in a series of phases. A preliminary phase (when a self-evaluation strategy and materials were devised) was completed in August 1991. The first phase of the main evaluation was completed in February 1992 and resulted in a report, published by the CITB, on the progress and outcomes of the initiative to date. During the remainder of 1992 further work (Phase 2) was conducted and resulted in an evaluation up-date report, a report on the employers' contribution to the initiative and an evaluation handbook. During Phase 3, in 1993, a series of evaluation workshops were organised in order to disseminate the evaluation findings and to support local self-evaluation.

PUBLISHED MATERIAL: SIMS, D. & STONEY, S. (1992). The CITB curriculum centre initiative: evaluation report. Norfolk: Construction Industry Training Board/National Foundation for Educational Research.; SIMS, D. & STONEY, S. (1992). The CITB curriculum centre initiative: evaluation update report. Norfolk: Construction Industry Training Board/National Foundation for Educational Research. ; SIMS, D. & STONEY, S. (1992). The CITB curriculum centre initiative: employer report. Norfolk: Construction Industry Training Board/National Foundation for Educational Research. ; SIMS, D. & STONEY, S. (1992). The CITB curriculum centre initiative: evaluation handbook. Norfolk: Construction Industry Training Board/National Foundation for Educational Research.

STATUS: Sponsored project

SOURCE OF GRANT: Construction Industry Training Board £10,680

DATE OF RESEARCH: 1991-1993

KEYWORDS: building trades education; construction - process; construction industry; cross curricular approach; technical education; vocational education

1625

The Mere, Upton Park, Slough SL1 2DQ
01753 574123

Earley, P. Mr; Kinder, K. Ms

The role of the local education authority in the professional development of new teachers

ABSTRACT: Awareness of the potentially powerful role of local education authorities (LEAs) and schools in programmes of professional development for new teachers has been heightened following the introduction of the new training routes to Qualified Teacher Status (QTS), the proposed changes in the nature and content of initial teacher training courses and the abolition of probation. A growing number of LEAs and schools are offering induction and training programmes designed to ensure the continuing development of the professional skills and competencies currently required of new teachers, not least in the delivery of the National Curriculum. This 18-month study is employing both survey and case study research methods to investigate the role of the LEAs in the extension of initial training. It intends to analyse the professional development programmes offered to new teachers and seek perceptions of the range of professionals involved on their effects and outcomes. The main aim of the research is to contribute to the improvement of the quality of support offered to new teachers. More specifically, the research has three aims: (i) to gather a broad base of information from all LEAs on their structures and procedures for training and supporting new teachers; (ii) to collect more detailed information from selected authorities and schools on professional development programmes in practice; and (iii) to ascertain the perceptions of a wide range of providers and practitioners on the benefits, problems and overall effectiveness of the various approaches to the induction and development of new teachers. The research will begin with a series of exploratory interviews in several LEAs to gather initial perspectives from key training personnel on the main issues relating to the induction and professional development of new teachers. The material collected from these interviews, complemented by the findings from recent research studies, will be used to develop a questionnaire which will be sent to each authority. An interim report based on the questionnaire findings will be available by autumn 1992. In the next phase of the research, interviews will be held with LEA personnel to clarify and expand upon the questionnaire data. About six LEAs will then be chosen for case study investigation. In each case study location, interviews will be held with relevant LEA personnel and all documentation relating to the professional development of new teachers will be collected. A sample of schools will be selected to represent the primary and secondary sectors as well as grant-maintained schools within each LEA. The work in the schools will involve interviews with headteachers, INSET coordinators, staff with responsibility for the guidance and support of new teachers, and the new teachers themselves. It will, of course, be important to ensure that teachers following different routes to QTS are included in the sample. The particular emphasis during the case study phase will be on collecting more detailed information on the content and delivery of training and support programmes in the selected LEAs and schools, whilst also focusing on emerging issues. A final report, drawing on both the survey and case study evidence will be produced at the end of the project.

PUBLISHED MATERIAL: EARLEY, P. (1992). Beyond initial teacher training: induction and the role of the LEA. Slough: National Foundation for Educational Research. ; EARLEY, P. & KINDER, K. (1994). Initiation rights: effective induction practices for new teachers. Slough: National Foundation for Educational Research. ; KINDER, K. & EARLEY, P. (1995). 'Key issues emerging from an NFER study of NQT's: models of induction support'. In: KERRY, T. & MAYES, A. Shelton. (Eds). Issues in mentoring. London: Routledge. ; EARLEY, P. (1995). 'Beginning teachers' professional development and the objectives of induction training'. In: KERRY, T. & MAYES, A. Shelton. (Eds). Issues in mentoring. London: Routledge.

STATUS: Sponsored project

SOURCE OF GRANT: National Foundation for Educational Research £135,000

DATE OF RESEARCH: 1992-1993

KEYWORDS: local education authorities; preservice teacher education; probationary teachers; teacher development; teacher education; teacher induction

1626

The Mere, Upton Park, Slough SL1 2DQ
01753 574123

Smith, P. Dr; *Supervisor*: Whetton, C. Mr

Standardisation of the LARR short-form test

ABSTRACT: The project has standardised a new version of the Canadian 'Linguistic Awareness in Reading Readiness (LARR) test' for use with British children at the start of formal schooling. The new version, 'The LARR short-form', will be published by NFER-Nelson. The standardisation involved administering the test to nearly 500 nursery children and over 2,300 children in reception classes in schools throughout England and Wales during October 1992. The test was found to be too demanding for the nursery children but appropriate for the reception sample. Norms were created for the age range from 4 years 0 months to 5 years 3 months. The results, together with administration instructions and guidance on interpreting the test scores, were written for the test manual. In parallel with the national standardisation, the test was also given to all reception age pupils in Wandsworth schools as part of the Local Education Authorities baseline assessment. The National Foundation for Educational Research (NFER) then carried out a local standardisation for Wandsworth.

PUBLISHED MATERIAL: 'LARR test of emergent literacy'. (1993). NFER-Nelson.

STATUS: Sponsored project

SOURCE OF GRANT: NFER-Nelson; Wandsworth Local Education Authority

DATE OF RESEARCH: 1992-1993

KEYWORDS: infant school pupils; nursery school pupils; reading; reading readiness; reception classes; tests

1627

The Mere, Upton Park, Slough SL1 2DQ
01753 574123

Hagues, N. Mr; Courtenay, D. Ms

Item bank testing

ABSTRACT: An item bank is a large collection of pre-trialled questions, a small proportion of which can be selected to construct a test to the user's specification and to a pre-determined level of difficulty. Because these tests are custom-made, the test is unique and hence a very high level of security can be guaranteed. The National Foundation for Educational Research maintains item banks in verbal reasoning, non-verbal reasoning, mathematics and English, and these have been used in recent years with pupils aged 8 to 14 for attainment testing, monitoring, screening and selection.

DATE OF RESEARCH: 1983-continuing

KEYWORDS: assessment; item banks; screening tests; test construction; test items; tests

1628

The Mere, Upton Park, Slough SL1 2DQ
01753 574123

Jamison, J. Mr; *Supervisor*: Stradling, R. Dr

Developing European awareness: the role of local education authorities and schools in the 1990s

ABSTRACT: As part of the preparation for the creation of a single European Market by the end of 1992, the Council of the European Community passed a resolution in May 1988 aimed at promoting and strengthening the European dimension at all levels of education. Although a growing number of local education authorities (LEAs) and schools are now taking steps to incorporate the European dimension, research evidence on established practice and new developments is still limited. The purpose of the evaluation therefore is to update and extend the database on LEA- and school-based initiatives on European Awareness, and to evaluate the impact of established LEA programmes on school practice. In addition, the project will determine how LEAs are supporting these activities. Finally, the project will identify successful practices and establish which initiatives are appropriate to different educational phases,

ability ranges and school contexts. Methods employed will include a survey of all LEAs in England and Wales by questionnaire, concerning their policy documents and initiatives on European Awareness, and a national survey of primary and secondary schools regarding the incorporation of European Awareness into the curriculum. These will be accompanied by case study research in schools in selected LEAs. The research team plans to produce a written report on activities at LEA level and a handbook for schools and advisory staff with supporting materials which could be used for staff development.

PUBLISHED MATERIAL: JAMISON, J. (1993). Developing European awareness: the role of local education authorities. Slough: National Foundation for Educational Research.

STATUS: Sponsored project

SOURCE OF GRANT: National Foundation for Educational Research £100,000

DATE OF RESEARCH: 1993-1993

KEYWORDS: curriculum development; european studies; european union; local education authorities

1629

The Mere, Upton Park, Slough SL1 2DQ
01753 574123

Sims, D. Mr; Harland, J. Dr; Tomlins, B. Dr; Twitchin, R. Mr; *Supervisor*: Stoney, S. Dr

Evaluation of the second year of the Training Credits pilot: three case studies

ABSTRACT: This evaluation sought to explore any changes in attitudes, culture and practice amongst young people, school staff, careers staff, employers and training providers which may have occurred as a result of the introduction of the Training Credits (TC) pilot and since the first round of evaluations. The project focused on the extent to which the original aims of the Training Credits pilots had been achieved, how much progress had been made in overcoming difficulties identified from the first-year evaluations and making practical recommendations to assist in the further development of the pilots. The three case studies employed the following research methods: postal questionnaires, telephone and face-to-face interviews, and group discussions. The number in each questionnaire sample were as follows: Year 11 students (760), Year 12/13 students (162), young people (731 TC-users; 47 non-TC users) and training providers (75). Interviews were conducted with up to 50 operational personnel such as Training and Enterprise Councils (TECs), local education authority (LEA) and Careers Service staff and 311 employers (160 TC-users; 151 non-TC users). Broadly, findings indicate that TECs were making strenuous efforts to promote the Training Credits pilot but were finding that outcomes and impact were being seriously constrained by the current recession. The main outcomes from the project were three case-study reports and one overall national report.

PUBLISHED MATERIAL: SIMS, D. & STONEY, S. (1993). Evaluation of the second year of training credits: final report. Slough: National Foundation for Educational Research.

STATUS: Sponsored project

SOURCE OF GRANT: Department of Employment £87,064

DATE OF RESEARCH: 1992-1993

KEYWORDS: credits; school to work transition; training; training and enterprise councils; vocational education; vocational guidance

1630

The Mere, Upton Park, Slough SL1 2DQ
01753 574123

Powell, R. Mr; Lewis, G. Mr; Jones, Ll. Ms; Lewis, T. Mr

Development of standard assessment tasks in Welsh for key stage 3 of the National Curriculum

ABSTRACT: This is an extension of the original contract for Welsh key stage 3 standard assessment tasks which ran from July 1989 to August 1991. The requirement is for the creation of standard assessment tasks to assess the range of attainment from Level 1 to Level 10 on both the Welsh and Welsh Second Language programmes contained in the Statutory Orders. Following pilots in 1991 and 1992 the first statutory assessment will be held in 1993. The standard assessment tasks comprise a long task for assessment of oracy and reading through oral response to be administrated in the classroom over three months, and written tests for assessment of writing and reading through written response.

STATUS: Sponsored project

SOURCE OF GRANT: School Examinations and Assessment Council £700,000

DATE OF RESEARCH: 1991-1993

KEYWORDS: assessment; attainment tests; national curriculum; standard assessment tasks; welsh

1631

The Mere, Upton Park, Slough SL1 2DQ
01753 574123

Taylor, M. Dr; *Supervisor*: Stoney, S. Dr

Values education in Europe

ABSTRACT: This project, the first collaborative exercise of the Consortium of Institutes of Development and Research in Education in Europe/Values Education in Europe Programme (CIDREE/VEEP), was commissioned by United Nations Educational Scientific and Cultural Organisation (UNESCO). It had three parts: (1) To provide guidelines for Values Education in Europe (this work was undertaken by Ian Barr, Chair of CIDREE/VEEP at the Scottish Consultative Council on the Curriculum, Dundee, Scotland); (2) To provide an annotated bibliography on Values Education in Europe from 1985-1992; (3) To provide an overview of the state of the art in Values Education in Europe. (2) and (3) were coordinated and undertaken by the National Foundation for Educational Research (NFER). The objectives of the project were to coordinate and facilitate the exchange of information and to build a foundation for undertaking further collaborative projects on a European scale. Almost 30 countries participated in the bibliography (up to 20 entries per country) and survey. Values Education has different emphases and scope in the education systems of Europe and the overview sought to establish common ground, and review historical and ideological backgrounds, aims and objectives, aspects of provision, theoretical influences, current concerns, teacher training, teaching methods, curriculum development research and evaluation and aspects of informal education relating to Values Education. There are three publications, corresponding to the three aspects of the project: guidelines, annotated bibliography and overview of state of the art. These were launched by UNESCO at an international conference in Norway in September 1993.

PUBLISHED MATERIAL: BARR, I. (Ed) (1994). A sense of belonging: guidelines for values for the humanistic and international dimension of education. CIDREE Vol 6. Dundee: Consortium of Institutions for Development and Research in Education in Europe/UNESCO. ; TAYLOR, M. (Ed) (1994). Values education in Europe: a select annotated bibliography for 27 countries (1985-1992). CIDREE Vol 7. Dundee: Consortium of Institutions for Development and Research in Education in Europe/UNESCO. ; TAYLOR, M. (Ed) (1994). Values education in Europe: a comparative overview of a survey of 26 countries in 1993. CIDREE Vol 8. Dundee: Consortium of Institutions for Development and Research in Education in Europe/UNESCO.

STATUS: Sponsored project

SOURCE OF GRANT: UNESCO £4,500; CIDREE £1,000; National Foundation for Educational Research £2,770

DATE OF RESEARCH: 1992-1993

KEYWORDS: europe; international educational exchange; values education

1632

The Mere, Upton Park, Slough SL1 2DQ
01753 574123

Jamison, J. Mr; Hamilton, K. Mrs; Stradling, R. Dr; Johnson, F. Ms; *Supervisor*: Saunders, L. Ms

Evaluation of the European Network of Health Promoting Schools

ABSTRACT: In 1993, the United Kingdom entered the European Network of Health Promoting Schools, a three-year developmental project in school health education. The Health Education Authority (HEA) has been

designated as the UK National Support Centre. Up to 30 schools will be selected throughout the UK to be pilot schools, 16 of these in England. Pilot schools will be offered support and advice in developing initiatives and disseminating their experiences. The 16 pilot schools in England will be matched with a further 32 schools which will act as controls. The aim of the project is to strengthen the capacity of primary, secondary and special schools, both local authority and grant-maintained, to be healthy environments for living, learning and working. This research project is the formal evaluation of the Health Education Authority's European Network of Health Promoting Schools project. It will evaluate the effectiveness of different approaches to the development of health promoting schools. It aims to assess the benefits to pupils of a whole school approach to health promotion in terms of their knowledge of health issues and their behaviour. Main methods employed will be as follows: Stage 1 - a screening survey of all schools which apply for membership of the project, followed by an audit of 150 of the applicants to identify 16 pilot and 32 control schools. Stage 2 - monitoring of the pilot and control schools over two school years. Stage 3 - a final complete audit of the pilot and control schools starting in May 1996. Reporting and dissemination activities will take place throughout the project, increasing in intensity from autumn 1995.

PUBLISHED MATERIAL: STRADLING, R. (1995). The health promoting school: a baseline survey. London: Health Education Authority.

STATUS: Sponsored project

SOURCE OF GRANT: Health Education Authority

DATE OF RESEARCH: 1993-1997

KEYWORDS: health education; health promoting schools; health promotion; programme evaluation

1633

The Mere, Upton Park, Slough SL1 2DQ
01753 574123

Lewis, G. Mr

Setting effective papers (differentation) in Welsh and Welsh second language at key stage 4

ABSTRACT: The project aimed to establish what questions and elements of papers, and which papers were most effective at differentiating pupils' performance at three ability range points - high, low and medium. Pupils' scores at these points were analysed, as were scripts, the respective mark schemes, and papers. Chief examiners were interviewed regarding best practice in setting papers.

STATUS: Sponsored project

SOURCE OF GRANT: School Curriculum and Assessment Authority £19,000

DATE OF RESEARCH: 1993-1993

KEYWORDS: assessment; attainment tests; differential performance; second language learning; welsh

1634

The Mere, Upton Park, Slough SL1 2DQ
01753 574123

Schagen, I. Dr; Gallacher, S. Dr; *Supervisor*: Saunders, L. Ms

Quantitative analysis for self evaluation (QUASE)

ABSTRACT: There is a perceived need for rigorous school self-evaluation, particularly in judging year-on-year performance on a range of outcome measures. For the purposes of self-evaluation, outcome measures need to be analysed in a way which takes into account the school context, the ability range of pupils and the 'value added' by the school over time; and are also flexible enough to measure the progress made by individual departments, year teams, etc. The National Foundation for Educational Research (NFER) has been developing a responsive package which will help schools to evaluate their own performance relative to the kind of students they have and to other key factors - in other words, a 'value added' approach' to judging achievements. The study has piloted an approach which: 1) utilises data already being collected for statutory purposes; 2) collects data felt by participating schools to be relevant in judging educational performance; 3) takes into account appropriate school/student input measures; 4) is sensitive enough to provide information at departmental/year group level. Secondary schools are participating in an ongoing study whose activities include: 1) developing appropriate ways of publicising the service to schools; 2) refining appropriate data collection instruments, including student intake measures; 3) generating a multi-level model for establishing appropriate norms against which schools and departments within schools can compare their own performance; and 4) identifying the most useful forms of feedback and follow-up for participants. All secondary schools in England and Wales may participate.

PUBLISHED MATERIAL: SCHAGEN, I. & SAUNDERS, L. (1994). 'Developing a system for school self-evaluation based on quantitative data'. Paper presented at the Annual Conference of the British Educational Research Association, Oxford, September 8-11. ; SAUNDERS, L. (1996). 'QUASE and the special education sector'. In: FLETCHER-CAMPBELL, F. (Ed). Value-added and special educational needs: proceedings of EMIE/NFER seminars 28 November 1995 (Slough) 14 March 1996 (Stockport). Slough: National Foundation for Educational Research. ; SCHAGEN, I. (1996). QUASE: quantitative analysis for self-evaluation. Technical Report 1996. Analysis of GCSE cohorts 1993 to 1995. Slough: National Foundation for Educational Research. ; SCHAGEN, I. (1996). QUASE: quantitative analysis for self-evaluation. Analysis of GCSE cohorts 1993 to 1995. NFER Research Summary. Slough: National Foundation for Educational Research; SCHAGEN, I. (1996). 'Male/female differences at the end of compulsory education in England and Wales'. Paper presented at the European Congress on Educational Research, Seville, September 25-28, 1996.

STATUS: Sponsored project

SOURCE OF GRANT: National Foundation for Educational Research £20,000; Participating schools and LEAs

DATE OF RESEARCH: 1994-continuing

KEYWORDS: **educational quality; institutional evaluation; performance indicators; school effectiveness; value added**

1635

The Mere, Upton Park, Slough SL1 2DQ
01753 574123

Sharp, C. Ms; *Supervisor*: Bradley, J. Dr

Evaluative reviews of alcohol research 1983-1992: alcohol education for young people

ABSTRACT: The review aimed to present the findings from English language studies of alcohol education published between 1983 and 1992, and to identify any gaps in the literature as a guide to future research. There have been three broad shifts in approaches to alcohol education in the past three decades. Informational programmes were common in the 1960's. In the 1970's 'affective' approaches enhanced self-esteem and developed students' social skills. The 'social influences' approach in use since the mid 1980's has focused on resisting external influences to drink. Results and conclusions of the review include: 1) Factors found to be related to alcohol use in adolescence concern: the family; the personality; the peer group; and the socio-cultural environment. 2) Evaluations of alcohol and drug education have found that it is easier to improve knowledge than to affect attitudes. Behavioural change is the most difficult to accomplish. 3) Social influences approaches to alcohol education have not generally proved effective in impacting on adolescent alcohol use. The fact that this approach has shown more promising results for tobacco and other drugs suggests that the relative social acceptability of alcohol may be a strong factor which cannot be easily overcome through education. 4) There is a need for more research in the UK. Large-scale, longitudinal studies of new approaches are needed, which consider the impact of programmes for different groups of participants. There is also a need for qualitative studies, particularly of peer group influence in alcohol and substance use.

PUBLISHED MATERIAL: SHARP, C. (1994). Alcohol education for young people: a review of the literature 1983-1992. Slough: National Foundation for Educational Research.

STATUS: Sponsored project

SOURCE OF GRANT: Alcohol Education and Research Council; Portman Group

DATE OF RESEARCH: 1993-1993

KEYWORDS: **alcohol education; drinking; health education**

1636

The Mere, Upton Park, Slough SL1 2DQ
01753 574123

Gorman, T. Dr; Hutchison, D. Dr; Trimble, J. Ms; *Supervisor*: Foxman, D. Mr

Avon collaborative reading study

ABSTRACT: All too often, pupils work in groups in school, but not as groups. Effective, collaborative groupwork is uncommon. This study shows one way it can be done, and how it can raise reading standards. In 1992-93, a project was carried out in a group of inner-city schools in Avon. It was designed to improve the reading performance of children aged 10 and 12. The children tackled questions about a poem or a passage of non-fiction, discussed their answers in groups, then had the chance to revise them. Over 100 groups of children were involved - a larger total than in any previous research of this type in Britain. The main results were: 1) All groups improved their answers to the questions. 2) Poorer readers improved their answers the most, and substantially more than better readers did. 3) The pupils' reports showed they had become more reflective about their reading. 4) Most pupils enjoyed collaborative reading. 5) Over two terms, the primary school pupils involved made a significant gain in scores on a standardised reading test. So groupwork can be effective, and can help to raise reading standards, when the task is focused and specific.

PUBLISHED MATERIAL: GORMAN, T., HUTCHISON, D. & TRIMBLE, J. (1993). Reading in reform: the Avon Collaborative Reading Project. Slough: National Foundation for Educational Research.

STATUS: Sponsored project

SOURCE OF GRANT: Avon Local Education Authority £5,000

DATE OF RESEARCH: 1992-1993

KEYWORDS: **group work; learning activities; reading improvement; reading strategies**

1637

The Mere, Upton Park, Slough SL1 2DQ
01753 574123

Clausen-May, T. Dr; Mason, K. Mr; Evans, S. Dr; Ravenscroft, L. Mrs; Claydon, H. Ms; Kentleton, N. Mr; *Supervisor*: Ruddock, G. Dr

The writing of National Curriculum key stage 3 mathematics tests for use in 1995-1999

ABSTRACT: The project is sponsored to produce mathematics tests for the higher level of the National Curriculum and classroom-based tasks for pupils working at levels 1 and 2. The tests and tasks are for use with pupils at the end of key stage 3 of the National Curriculum, Year 9. In 1995 they were based on the old version of the National Curriculum, while those for 1996 and 1997 reflect the revised version and from 1998 onwards include mental mathematics tests.

STATUS: Sponsored project

SOURCE OF GRANT: School Curriculum and Assessment Authority

DATE OF RESEARCH: 1994-1998

KEYWORDS: **assessment; key stage 3; mathematics achievement; mathematics education; national curriculum; secondary education; tasks and tests; tests**

1638

The Mere, Upton Park, Slough SL1 2DQ
01753 574123

Sharp, C. Ms; Maychell, K. Ms; Walton, I. Ms

Nursing and AIDS: material matters. Issues, information and teaching materials on HIV and AIDS for nurses

ABSTRACT: From April 1992 to March 1993 the National Foundation for Educational Research (NFER) carried out the second phase of a research study looking at information and educational materials on human immunodeficiency virus (HIV) and acquired immune deficiency syndrome (AIDS) for nurses and nurse educators. The research was funded by the Department of Health. The NFER's study built on work conducted by Akinsanya and Barnett, based at Anglia Polytechnic University. They conducted a questionnaire survey of colleges and university departments offering training on HIV/AIDS to students and qualified nurses, midwives and health visitors (collectively termed 'nurses' for the purposes of this document). The second phase of the research focused on nurse educators' decision-making processes in selecting and using materials on HIV/AIDS and looked at the information sources on HIV/AIDS currently used by nurses and nurse educators. The research also sought to identify key factors in the professional culture of nursing and nurse education which may help or hinder dissemination and knowledge utilisation in relation to HIV and AIDS.

PUBLISHED MATERIAL: SHARP, C., MAYCHELL, K. & WALTON, I. (1993). Nursing and AIDS: material matters. Issues, information and teaching materials on HIV and AIDS for nurses - a research study. Slough: National Foundation for Educational Research.

STATUS: Sponsored project

SOURCE OF GRANT: Department of Health

DATE OF RESEARCH: 1992-1993

KEYWORDS: **acquired immune deficiency syndrome; educational materials; nurses; sexually transmitted diseases**

1639

The Mere, Upton Park, Slough SL1 2DQ
01753 574123

Jowett, S. Dr; Payne, S. Ms; Walton, I. Ms; *Supervisor*: Bradley, J. Dr

National evaluation of demonstration schemes in pre-registration nurse education (Project 2000)

ABSTRACT: The launch of Project 2000 in 13 Demonstration Districts in England in late 1989/early 1990 was a substantial innovation in nurse education. While there was much enthusiasm and excitement about the introduction of Project 2000, it generated a considerable amount of hard work, stress and anxiety and it is crucial that lessons for the future are identified and dissected. The research was undertaken in 6 of the 13 first round Demonstration Districts in England. The main data collection was by interviews with college of nursing staff, senior nurse managers, senior service managers, practice-based nurses, staff in higher education and students. This was a longitudinal study in which interviews with the same key personnel took place at different points in time. The findings suggested good cause for optimism, particularly from the students vis-a-vis their role as qualified staff, and from staff whose professional development has been enhanced by the changes. A great many individuals have benefited from the opportunities Project 2000 offers, with implications for their enhanced performance as practitioners and educators. Although it was widely accepted that considerable problems had been encountered, there was also broad agreement about the viability and desirability of the changes Project 2000 promised.

PUBLISHED MATERIAL: JOWETT, S., WALTON, I. & PAYNE, S. (1992). The introduction of Project 2000: early perspectives from higher education. National Evaluation of Demonstration Schemes in Pre-registration Nurse Education (Project 2000). Interim Paper 4. Slough: National Foundation for Educational Research. ; JOWETT, S., WALTON, I. & PAYNE, S. (1992). The introduction of Project 2000: early perspectives from the students. National Evaluation of Demonstration Schemes in Pre-registration Nurse Education (Project 2000). Interim Paper 5. Slough: National Foundation for Educational Research. ; JOWETT, S. (1992). 'Project 2000: research on its implementation', Nursing Times, Vol 88, No 26, pp.40-43. ; JOWETT, S., WALTON, I. & PAYNE, S. (1992). Implementing Project 2000 in an interim report. Slough: National Foundation for Educational Research. ; JOWETT, S. (1995). 'Added value', Nursing Times, Vol 91, No 1, pp.55-57. A full list of publications is available from the researcher.

STATUS: Sponsored project

SOURCE OF GRANT: Department of Health £250,000

DATE OF RESEARCH: 1989-1993

KEYWORDS: **nurse education; professional education**

1640

The Mere, Upton Park, Slough SL1 2DQ
01753 574123

Kendall, L. Mrs; Hewitt, D. Dr

Contextualisation of school examination results

ABSTRACT: In 1994, the National Foundation for Educational Research (NFER) entered into contracts with a number of local education authorities (LEA's) to provide 'value added' analyses of the achievements of the pupils in their schools, as measured by GCSE results, including brief automated individual school reports. This work continued a programme initiated by the Association of Metropolitan Authorities in 1990. Each of the participating authorities was able to provide data on all its 16 year old pupils, including GCSE results and information relating to the background of the individual pupils such as sex and ethnicity, as well as the scores on tests taken when the pupils transferred to secondary school. In addition, variables relating to the school attended, such as size, denomination, and whether the school is coeducational or not, were collated. The combined data set provided comprehensive information on about 15,000 pupils. The outcomes of the project included an overall report, giving general findings for all LEA's and schools involved, with an appendix for each LEA giving results at school level for that LEA. Confidentiality was preserved, so that individual schools or LEA's could be identified only on a 'need to know' basis. The reports can form an integral part of an ongoing LEA process of school improvement, identifying aspects where further investigation by the LEA or the school could be targeted. Results for the 1998 GCSE examinations will be reported to these authorities in March 1999. 11 LEAs are participating in the 1997 analysis which will also include an investigation of the relationship between key stage 3 outcomes and GCSE results.

PUBLISHED MATERIAL: KENDALL, L. (1995). Examination results in context: report on the analysis of 1994 examination results. London: Association of Metropolitan Authorities. ; KENDALL, L. & AINSWORTH, L. (1997). Examination results in context: analysis of the 1996 examination results. London: Local Government Assocation Publications. ; KENDALL, L. (1997). Examination results in context: report on the analysis of 1995 examination results. London: Association of Metropolitan Authorities.

STATUS: Sponsored project

SOURCE OF GRANT: Consortium of local education authorities £13,835

DATE OF RESEARCH: 1994-continuing

KEYWORDS: **achievement; educational quality; examination results; outcomes of education; performance factors; performance indicators; school effectiveness; value added**

1641

The Mere, Upton Park, Slough SL1 2DQ
01753 574123

Dickson, P. Mr

Evaluation of LINGUA in the UK

ABSTRACT: The purpose of the evaluation was to assess progress in the UK on the implementation of the EC LINGUA programme. Interviews were carried out with those responsible for the management and administration of the programme, and a questionnaire survey sought views from those who had benefited from LINGUA grants. The information collected provided a detailed account of the work of the UK LINGUA Unit in promoting the programme, administering it and processing applications. The views of applicants threw light on the difficulties facing those seeking grants, who, nevertheless, provided evidence of the substantial benefits to be gained from the programme, not only in language learning, but also in personal and professional development.

PUBLISHED MATERIAL: DICKSON, P., with MOYS, A. & WIGHTWICK, C. (1994). LINGUA: the UK perspective. Slough: National Foundation for Educational Research.

STATUS: Sponsored project

SOURCE OF GRANT: Department for Education £35,000

DATE OF RESEARCH: 1993-1993

KEYWORDS: **international programmes; modern language studies; programme evaluation; second language learning; student exchange programmes**

1642

The Mere, Upton Park, Slough SL1 2DQ
01753 574123

Williams, M. Mrs; Francis, M. Mrs; *Supervisor*: Powell, R. Mr

National Curriculum key stage 1 Standard Task Development for Welsh

ABSTRACT: From the start of statutory National Curriculum key stage 1 assessment in 1989, Welsh was assessed as a component of the Core Standard Assessment Task. From 1992, Welsh has been assessed separately. This contract requires the development of a classroom task assessing speaking and listening, reading and writing. Materials are developed in consultation with teacher panels and trialled thoroughly before final copy is presented to the Assessment and Curriculum Authority for Wales (ACAC).

STATUS: Sponsored project

SOURCE OF GRANT: Assessment and Curriculum Authority for Wales

DATE OF RESEARCH: 1996-continuing

KEYWORDS: **assessment; national curriculum; standard assessment tasks; tasks and tests; tests; welsh**

1643

The Mere, Upton Park, Slough SL1 2DQ
01753 574123

Lewis, T. Mr; Breese, N. Mrs; Derbyshire, G. Mr; *Supervisor*: Powell, R. Mr

National Curriculum key stage 3 tasks and tests in Welsh and Welsh Second Language

ABSTRACT: This project is a continuation of the National Curriculum key stage 3 assessment development which began in July 1989. The present contract requires the development of Welsh and Welsh Second Language tests and classroom tasks for the end of key stage 3 in 1996, 1999 and 2000. Materials are developed in consultation with teacher panels and trialled thoroughly in schools before final copy is presented to the Assessment and Curriculum Authority for Wales (ACAC).

STATUS: Sponsored project

SOURCE OF GRANT: Assessment and Curriculum Authority for Wales

DATE OF RESEARCH: 1996-continuing

KEYWORDS: **assessment; key stage 3; national curriculum; secondary education; tasks and tests; tests; welsh**

1644

The Mere, Upton Park, Slough SL1 2DQ
01753 574123

Maychell, K. Ms; Pathak, S. Ms; *Supervisor*: Keys, W. Dr

The impact of inspection and action plans

ABSTRACT: Following an Office for Standards in Education (OFSTED) inspection, schools are required to prepare an action plan setting out specific action to be taken in response to the report and the timetable on which it will be carried out. The responsibility for producing the plan rests with the school's governing body. The final version of the plan must then be distributed to various parties involved with the school, such as parents, members of staff, the school's local education authority (LEA) and OFSTED. The primary purpose of action planning is to enhance the quality of pupils' learning experiences. The purpose of this research is to identify changes in policy and practice that result from schools' action plans, and to explore the ways in which schools approach the task of developing and implementing action planning. The research had two phases: a questionnaire survey of 200 primary and 225 secondary headteachers in schools inspected during Spring or Summer 1995; and case-study work in approximately 10 schools, where discussions were held with members of staff and governors focusing on their experiences of drawing up and implementing their action plans, the feedback they have received from registered inspectors and support from LEA personnel and others. Two reports of the study, covering phase I and phase II separately, will be published in 1997 and will be of interest to all those involved in the OFSTED inspection process.

STATUS: Sponsored project

SOURCE OF GRANT: NFER Membership Programme £80,000

DATE OF RESEARCH: 1995-1997

KEYWORDS: **development plans; educational planning; educational quality; inspection; ofsted; primary education; school effectiveness; secondary education**

1645

The Mere, Upton Park, Slough SL1 2DQ
01753 574123

Hagues, N. Mr; Courtenay, D. Ms; *Supervisor*: Whetton, C. Mr

Customised Testing Project

ABSTRACT: A new generation of item banks is being developed in the areas of verbal reasoning, non-verbal reasoning, mathematics and English, from which tests have been selected from 1995 onwards. All items are in multiple-choice format, which enables customers to machine-read their answer sheets for ease and speed of marking. The items and their associated psychometric data are stored in a computer database.

STATUS: Sponsored project

SOURCE OF GRANT: NFER-Nelson Publishing Company

DATE OF RESEARCH: 1994-continuing

KEYWORDS: **assessment; computer assisted testing; item banks; multiple choice tests; test construction; test items; tests**

1646

The Mere, Upton Park, Slough SL1 2DQ
01753 574123

Schagen, S. Dr; MacDonald, A. Ms; *Supervisor*: Stoney, S. Dr

Evaluation of Natwest Face 2 Face with Finance

ABSTRACT: NatWest Face 2 Face With Finance is a programme of educational acitivies designed to promote understanding of 'financial literacy' (personal money management). The National Foundation for Educational Research (NFER) has been commissioned by NatWest to assess the effectiveness of Face 2 Face in raising levels of financial literacy among young people of secondary school age. The project will use mainly quantitative analysis, although some qualitative work will be involved. The main research instrument will be a questionnaire given to young people before and after participation in Face 2 Face activities, in order to assess their level of financial literacy, and obtain a measure of improvement. Three cohorts of young people will take part in the evaluation. Groups will be chosen to reflect the range of Face 2 Face activities and the different curricular contexts in which they are used. Students in the first two cohorts will be sent a follow-up questionnaire, one and (where possible) two years later, in order to assess their retention of knowledge and the extent to which they are applying acquired skills to real-life situations. Teachers who complete placements at NatWest will be interviewed in order to discover what they achieved during their time at the Bank, and how they expect their teaching to develop as a result. Teacher interviews in 1995 and 1996 will be followed up in order to see whether their expectations had been fulfilled.

STATUS: Sponsored project

SOURCE OF GRANT: NatWest £106,548

DATE OF RESEARCH: 1995-1997

KEYWORDS: **budgeting; financial services; money management; secondary school pupils; secondments; teacher development**

1647

The Mere, Upton Park, Slough SL1 2DQ
01753 574123

Burley, J. Ms; McCulloch, K. Ms; *Supervisors*: Sainsbury, M. Dr; Ashby, J. Mr

Trialling of key stage 1 task and test materials for 1997

ABSTRACT: The School Curriculum and Assessment Authority (SCAA) are developing assessment tasks and tests for use at the end of National Curriculum key stage 1 in schools in 1997. The aim of this project is to administer a series of large scale trials of the tasks and tests in mathematics, reading and spelling in order to provide SCAA with the relevant information that they need to be able to refine the assessment instruments or to standardise them. Large scale, nationally representative, stratified samples of children in England and Wales are being drawn. In the case of developmental trials, 800 children are used and for standardisation trials, 2000 children are targeted. Analysis is carried out on the pupils' results arising out of each of the trials and further information is obtained from a questionnaire survey of the teachers who are taking part in the trials. A small number of school visits are made to observe teachers administering the tasks and tests and by means of brief and informal interviews to ascertain pupils' perceptions and teachers' opinions of the assessment materials.

STATUS: Sponsored project

SOURCE OF GRANT: School Curriculum and Assessment Authority £214,034

DATE OF RESEARCH: 1996-1997

KEYWORDS: assessment; key stage 1; national curriculum; primary education; tasks and tests; test construction; tests

1648

The Mere, Upton Park, Slough SL1 2DQ
01753 574123

Sizmur, S. Dr; Ashby, J. Mr

Introducing scientific concepts to children

ABSTRACT: The result of introducing children to scientific meanings is unpredictable, and a range of research literature attests to the difficulty pupils have in understanding fundamental principles underlying scientific knowledge. Teachers have a range of possibilities for introducing scientific topics, but there has been little attention given to the approaches actually employed by typical primary teachers. There is a need for an appraisal of such approaches, to identify where existing practice is effective and where it is in need of support. The aims of this project are to: 1) examine how scientific constructs are first introduced to children in primary classrooms; 2) develop a means of categorising these methods; 3) gather information on how children's understanding of the constructs might be related to the ways they are introduced. Two areas of science content, derived from the National Curriculum programmes of study for key stage 2, are addressed: the heart and circulation (from Life processes and living things); and periodic changes in the solar system (from Physical processes). Visits to participating schools will be arranged for the time the concept area was first introduced to the children. The means by which the concept area was introduced will be recorded, using appropriate methods such as audio or videotape and researcher notes. Supporting information will be gathered from teachers. Pupils will be interviewed in each school to determine their understanding of the concepts and any links to the activities in which they have participated.

STATUS: Sponsored project

SOURCE OF GRANT: NFER £51,383

DATE OF RESEARCH: 1995-1997

KEYWORDS: concept teaching; key stage 2; primary education; science education; scientific concepts

1649

The Mere, Upton Park, Slough SL1 2DQ
01753 574123

Harris, S. Mrs; *Supervisor*: Keys, W. Dr

Study into school admissions: problems affecting service children

ABSTRACT: Service families are subject to postings both within the UK and overseas. These postings can take place at any time of year and service parents may, as a result, have to obtain school places for their children at times which do not coincide with the start of the new school year. This study was commissioned by the Royal Air Force (RAF) to investigate the range of problems experienced by service parents with regard to obtaining places for their children, in both primary and secondary schools. The study involves: 1) a questionnaire survey of RAF parents randomly selected from 6 RAF bases in England (totalling approximately 1200 families); and 2) interviews with headteachers of a small number of schools which admit a large number of children from RAF service families. The study will produce a report presenting the findings of the questionnaire survey and the interviews with headteachers.

STATUS: Sponsored project

SOURCE OF GRANT: RAF Headquarters: Personnel and Training Command, Training Support and Education Branch £10,000

DATE OF RESEARCH: 1996-1997

KEYWORDS: access to education; admission criteria; parent choice; pupil mobility; servicemens children; transfer pupils

1650

The Mere, Upton Park, Slough SL1 2DQ
01753 574123

Sims, D. Mr; Christophers, U. Mrs; Lewis, G. Mr; Williams, S. Mr

An evaluation of training credits: West Wales Training and Enterprise Council (TEC) area

ABSTRACT: Subsequent to a baseline study evaluating the impact of training credits in the West Wales area, undertaken two years ago, follow-up work is being carried out in the same area. The research will look at any changes that have taken place in the attitudes of young people, their parents and employers in the area, towards the work-based route to qualifications. Large scale surveys will be undertaken with Year 11 students, young people in training using training credits and their parents. Additionally, careers coordinators, careers advisers and employers will be surveyed. Interviews will be carried out with a sub-set of each group.

STATUS: Sponsored project

SOURCE OF GRANT: West Wales Training and Enterprise Council

DATE OF RESEARCH: 1996-1997

KEYWORDS: attitudes; employer attitudes; parent attitudes; pupil attitudes; school to work transition; secondary school pupils; training; training credits; vocational education; work based learning; youth attitudes; youth employment

1651

The Mere, Upton Park, Slough SL1 2DQ
01753 574123

MacDonald, A. Ms; *Supervisor*: Weston, P. Mrs

Talking TVEI: young people's accounts of 14-18 progression

ABSTRACT: This paper presents the voices of young people who experienced the Technical and Vocational Education Initiative (TVEI) during their last two years of compulsory schooling, set within the context of national evidence on the lasting impact of TVEI in the education/ training field. The paper draws on young people's thoughts on the value of their experience in relation to key aspects of TVEI provision and their perceptions of the success of TVEI in achieving its goals. The comments formed part of the data gathered for the Cohort Study of TVEI Extension Students undertaken by the National Foundation for Educational Research (NFER) from 1991-1994 on behalf of the then Employment Department. This was a longitudinal study of two cohorts of young people, carried out as they progressed through the 14-18 age range. Postal questionnaires were administered annually over the four years, and young people were given the opportunity to air their views on a number of key issues related to TVEI aims. These open-ended comments provided a valuable insight into the views and experiences of the young people, in their own words. The comments showed that the young people were generally positive about what they had gained from their school-based TVEI experiences, although there were also some incisive criticisms. This paper thus provides an interesting addition to the more statistically signficant findings embraced by the reports on the cohort study published by the Employment Department.

PUBLISHED MATERIAL: MACDONALD, A. Talking TVEI: young people's accounts of 14-18 progression. Slough: National Foundation for Educational Research. (in press).

STATUS: Sponsored project

SOURCE OF GRANT: National Foundation for Educational Research £4,500

DATE OF RESEARCH: 1996-1997

KEYWORDS: pupil attitudes; school to work transition; secondary education; secondary school pupils; tvei; vocational education; youth attitudes

1652

The Mere, Upton Park, Slough SL1 2DQ
01753 574123

Lee, B. Ms; Evans, C. Ms; *Supervisor*: Keys, W. Dr

Factors affecting the take-up of 16-plus educational provision

ABSTRACT: Britain lags behind its major industrial competitors in the numbers of young people who stay in education beyond the compulsory school-leaving age. Although staying-on rates have started to improve, there is concern that many young people are not being educated to the full extent of their capabilities. The main aims of the research are to identify: the factors which induce young people to finish their education as soon as legally possible; the factors which encourage young people to remain in full-time education beyond the statutory leaving age; the factors which affect young people's decisions to select different types of post-16 educational provision; the specific factors which impact upon the aspirations of young males in inner city areas; examples of good practice in the provision of advice to young people on careers and post-16 provision. The study comprises 3 phases. The developmental phase consists of group and individual interviews with pupils in Years 8, 11 and 12. A self-completion questionnaire will be designed on the basis of these interviews. Surveys will be carried out of about 3,000 students in 50 secondary schools (and sixth form colleges, where appropriate). The questionnaire for Year 8 and Year 11 will seek information on students' career plans, post-16, sources of information and the reasons for their choices. The questionnaire for Year 12 will ask these questions retrospectively. A school/college questionnaire will also be used to obtain background information. The surveys will be complemented by case studies in order to develop and extend the data. The main outcome of the research will be a report outlining the main factors which affect students' post-16 intentions.

STATUS: Sponsored project

SOURCE OF GRANT: NFER Membership Programme

DATE OF RESEARCH: 1996-1997

KEYWORDS: **career choice; decision making; pupil attitudes; pupil destinations; school leavers; sixteen to nineteen education; vocational guidance**

1653

The Mere, Upton Park, Slough SL1 2DQ
01753 574123

Tabberer, R. Mr; Brooks, R. Ms; Hawker, J. Mrs

Survey of information technology in initial teacher training

ABSTRACT: The purpose of the research project is to map out the current state of information technology (IT) in initial teacher training (ITT). The Teacher Training Agency (TTA) hopes to use the findings to underpin the development of a national strategy for IT in ITT and to establish clear areas for further research and development. The survey will address the full range of ITT provision including higher education institution/school partnerships, school-centred initial teacher training, distance learning and employment-based schemes and also the full range of phase/subject provision including undergraduate, postgraduate, primary and secondary. In the first stage of the project, questionnaires were sent to 40 institutional providers of ITT and their partnership schools, where appropriate. In the spring term 1997 questionnaires will be sent to 168 ITT tutors, asking about their own use of IT in the ITT course. Finally, in the summer term, questionnaires will be distributed to 1500 trainees in the final term of their teacher training courses. They will be asked about their perceptions of their own IT capability as preparation for their role as teachers. The final report will be presented to the Teacher Training Agency in June 1997.

STATUS: Sponsored project

SOURCE OF GRANT: Teacher Training Agency £34,390

DATE OF RESEARCH: 1996-1997

KEYWORDS: **computer uses in education; information technology; preservice teacher education; school based teacher education**

1654

The Mere, Upton Park, Slough SL1 2DQ
01753 574123

Whetton, C. Mr; Sainsbury, M. Dr; McCulloch, K. Ms

Development of standardised test materials in English for Year 4

ABSTRACT: The School Curriculum and Assessment Authority (SCAA) intends to provide optional tests and assessment materials for use with pupils in Year 4 of the National Curriculum. This project will develop a series of tests in English. One test will cover reading, one writing and

one spelling. The tests will given rise to an indication of National Curriculum level and the reading and spelling tests will also yield standardised scores. The research project will involve an informal trialling stage with a group of teachers assisting in ensuring that the questions are suitable. There will then be three formal trials. The first two of these will be administered to samples of 400 pupils. The third is a standardisation trial and will involve 4,000 pupils.

STATUS: Sponsored project

SOURCE OF GRANT: School Curriculum and Assessment Authority

DATE OF RESEARCH: 1996-1997

KEYWORDS: **assessment; english; national curriculum; primary education; reading achievement; spelling; tasks and tests; tests; writing skills**

1655

The Mere, Upton Park, Slough SL1 2DQ
01753 574123

Gallacher, S. Dr; Brooks, R. Ms; *Supervisor*: Tabberer, R. Mr

Schools' use of information technology

ABSTRACT: The objectives are two-fold: 1) To map information technology (IT) equipment levels and use at a local education authority (LEA) level to complement the biennial Department for Education and Employment (DfEE) survey; and 2) To examine the conditions contributing to successful IT use with pupils having some degree of special educational needs. The first objective will be achieved by a questionnaire survey, developed jointly with the National Association for Advisers of Computing in Education (NAACE). The second will comprise case studies of at least 50 experienced IT-using pupils. The outcomes will be: a) reports to LEAs of IT provision and use in their area, against a national picture, along with summaries for participating schools; and b) an overview report of 'good practice' in IT use in the special needs area.

STATUS: Sponsored project

SOURCE OF GRANT: NFER Membership Programme

DATE OF RESEARCH: 1996-1997

KEYWORDS: **computer uses in education; information technology; local education authorities; special educational needs**

1656

The Mere, Upton Park, Slough SL1 2DQ
01753 574123

Sizmur, S. Dr; *Supervisor*: Whetton, C. Mr

Evaluation of integrated learning systems: phase III

ABSTRACT: The project is aiming to evaluate the impact of integrated learning systems (ILS) on pupil achievement levels. The National Foundation for Educational Research (NFER) is undertaking a largely quantitative study involving about 60 ILS-using schools and a smaller number of 'control' schools (not using ILS). Tests in 3 domains: mathematics, English and cognitive abilities, will be administered to Year 5, Year 6 and Year 8 pupils at the beginning and end of the 1996-97 academic year. Any changes in achievement levels will be assessed in relation to ILS exposure. Pupil attitudes will also be monitored. This work will be complemented by field studies (10) to deepen understanding of the process contributing to the observed outcomes. This study sits alongside work being undertaken by colleagues at Leicester and Durham universities.

STATUS: Sponsored project

SOURCE OF GRANT: National Council for Educational Technology

DATE OF RESEARCH: 1996-1997

KEYWORDS: **academic achievement; achievement; computer assisted learning; computer uses in education; educational software; information technology; integrated learning systems; multimedia; primary education; secondary education**

1657

The Mere, Upton Park, Slough SL1 2DQ
01753 574123

Gallacher, S. Dr; *Supervisor*: Tabberer, R. Mr

Improving schools' discussion forum

ABSTRACT: This ongoing work aims to draw upon the spread of the Internet as an educational and communication tool to stimulate discussion around the area of school improvement. The National Foundation for Educational Research (NFER) act as moderators - editing and stimulating the correspondence. So far, this has ranged from target-setting to baseline assessment. The discussion forum is part of the Department for Education and Employment's (DfEE) 'improving schools' strategy. One outcome, other than raised awareness and information levels, might be the compilation of discussions into a publication.

STATUS: Sponsored project

SOURCE OF GRANT: Department for Education and Employment

DATE OF RESEARCH: 1996-continuing

KEYWORDS: computer uses in education; educational improvement; information networks; information technology; internet; telecommunications

1658

The Mere, Upton Park, Slough SL1 2DQ
01753 574123

Gallacher, S. Dr; *Supervisor*: Tabberer, R. Mr

Evaluation of the Staffordshire targeted early education initiative

ABSTRACT: Class size really does matter. Whilst conflicting views appear to have resulted from research on the impact of class size on teaching and learning, in recent years a consistent theme has emerged. The weight of this evidence suggests that initiatives targeted on class size reductions in the early years of schooling have a significant and positive impact. In cooperation with several other local education authorities (LEAs) throughout England, Staffordshire is engaged in a series of activities aimed at examining the effect of reducing class sizes in Reception, Year 1 and Year 2. In total, 31 schools from some of the most disadvantaged areas of the county will be participating in the initiative. Within Staffordshire, the project is being overseen by a steering group which comprises 5 headteachers, LEA staff and members of the National Foundation for Educational Research (NFER) evaluation team. Staffordshire is allocating funding to schools with National Curriculum key stage 1 classes, based on the proportion of children in each school eligible for free school meals. The amounts allocated to each of the 31 schools range from 2,000 to 22,000 pounds. The main aim of the project is to fully utilise the potential of additional targeted funding, focused on the reduction of class sizes (and the implementation of other related strategies) to bring about improvements in children's levels of achievement. At an initial inservice teacher education (INSET) session, senior managers from each school were asked to formulate specific targets, detailing how the money would be spent, what they hoped to achieve, and how they were going to monitor progress toward these targets. From initial meetings, the participating schools suggested a common focus upon raising reading attainment. Whilst the main theme of the initiative deals with class size reduction, there may be limitations on schools' physical ability to achieve these ends. For instance, they may simply lack the space to be able to create more classes. Schools have therefore arrived at a variety of ways of lowering the adult:pupil ratio in their early years classes. This may involve greater use of trained National Nursery Examination Board (NNEB) staff or putting in more English as a Second Language (ESL) support. The initiative is planned to last for 3 years, with initial funding being allocated in September 1996. As with any development of this nature, there is the need to undertake an objective evaluation of the project during its lifetime and at its conclusion. The NFER has been asked to undertake this work in Staffordshire and has developed a framework of assessments and school visits in order to collect data about the participating schools, the children involved and the progress being made. In brief, this will involve assessing the reading ability of children in each of the 3 cohorts passing through Reception, Year 1 and Year 2 during the course of the project. This information will be collected annually, and at the very start of the project, along with background data relating to the pupils, the school and its environment. The collection of assessment data will be complemented by a series of visits to each of the schools. Through classroom observation and discussion with staff, the evaluation will be able to develop a more

rounded picture of the impact of the initiative, and to place the assessment data in context. In order to be more cost effective, the NFER is undertaking this work collaboratively, with LEA staff and teachers. It is intended that the research will inform: a) schools on 'best practice' in translating additional funding allocations into real pupil progress and on embedding the changes within the schools; b) the LEA about the success or failure of the programme, and better equip them to make strategic decisions in the future regarding funding; and c) other LEAs about the most and least successful elements of the programme. In addition, the experiences of other participating LEAs will be drawn upon at the conclusion of the project.

STATUS: Sponsored project

SOURCE OF GRANT: Staffordshire Local Education Authority

DATE OF RESEARCH: 1996-1997

KEYWORDS: achievement; class size; early childhood education; educational finance; educational improvement; key stage 1; primary education; reading achievement

1659

The Mere, Upton Park, Slough SL1 2DQ
01753 574123

Hagues, N. Mr; *Supervisor*: Whetton, C. Mr

Evaluation of the National Literacy Project

ABSTRACT: The National Foundation for Educational Research (NFER) has been approached by the Department of Education and Employment (DfEE) to undertake an evaluation of this new government initiative. Fifteen local education authorities (LEAs) have volunteered to take part and the project will use a variety of methods to raise the levels of achievement in literacy in its associated schools. Because it is important that the outcomes of such a large project are evaluated in a tangible way, a series of formal reading tests are to be given to pupils within the centres on several occasions during their primary school years. This will provide a series of interlinked longitudinal studies demonstrating the progress made by the pupils involved in the project.

STATUS: Sponsored project

SOURCE OF GRANT: Department of Education and Employment

DATE OF RESEARCH: 1996-1998

KEYWORDS: achievement; assessment; literacy; primary education; reading ability; reading achievement; reading tests

1660

The Mere, Upton Park, Slough SL1 2DQ
01753 574123

Sizmur, S. Dr; Ashby, J. Mr; Kirkup, C. Ms

Development and trialling of Year 4 assessments in science

ABSTRACT: Materials are to be developed to support teacher assessment in science during National Curriculum key stage 2. Up to 5 assessment units are to be produced, primarily for use at the end of Year 4. These will assess children's attainment against specific aspects of the programme of study for science, and will provide teachers with an indication of children's overall level of performance. The materials will be published by the School Curriculum and Assessment Authority (SCAA). The assessment activities comprise a combination of practical, written and oral tasks, and assess both experimental and investigative science and scientific knowledge and understanding. Each unit is first trialled informally by a group of teachers who are closely involved in the development. Following revisions, the materials are then subject to 2 rounds of formal trialling in a nationally representative sample of 50 schools.

STATUS: Sponsored project

SOURCE OF GRANT: School Curriculum and Assessment Authority

DATE OF RESEARCH: 1996-1997

KEYWORDS: assessment; assessment by teachers; key stage 2; national curriculum; primary education; science education; tasks and tests; tests

1661

The Mere, Upton Park, Slough SL1 2DQ
01753 574123

Sainsbury, M. Dr; Underhay, S. Mrs

Standard tests in English for pupils at the end of the second key stages of the National Curriculum in 1997, 1998, 1999

ABSTRACT: The purpose of this work is to provide assessments of individual pupils' attainments in National Curriculum English at the end of key stage 2 (Year 6, typical age of pupils, 11 years). The assessments will be made in relation to the statutory curriculum order for English. The tests will be predominantly written and timed. During the initial developmental stage of the work, the research team at the National Foundation for Educational Research (NFER) work intensively with teacher consultants, acting as material writers. Members of this panel reconvene in successive stages of the project to revise and adapt material. Draft materials are scrutinised by an internally appointed vetting panel, while the work as a whole is under regular supervision by the committees of the School Curriculum and Assessment Authority (SCAA). For each year's test, up to 3 times the required material is developed. Final selection is made on the basis of 2 pre-tests, each with a large nationally representative sample.

STATUS: Sponsored project

SOURCE OF GRANT: School Curriculum and Assessment Authority

DATE OF RESEARCH: 1996-1998

KEYWORDS: **assessment; english; key stage 2; national curriculum; primary education; reading achievement; tasks and tests; tests; writing skills**

1662

The Mere, Upton Park, Slough SL1 2DQ
01753 574123

Le Metais, J. Dr; O'Donnell, S. Miss; Boyd, S. Mrs

International review of curriculum and assessment frameworks

ABSTRACT: As part of its work in monitoring the curriculum in England, the School Curriculum and Assessment Authority (SCAA) commissioned the National Foundation for Educational Research (NFER) to undertake an international review of curriculum and assessment frameworks in Australia, Canada, England, France, Germany, Hungary, Italy, Japan, Korea, the Netherlands, New Zealand, Singapore, Spain, Sweden, Switzerland and the United States of America. The aims of the project are: 1) to build an accurately researched and ready-to-use resource, comprising a succinct description of the educational aims, structure and organisation, and of the curriculum and assessment framework in each country, collectively referred to as 'The Archive'; 2) to help SCAA analyse the outcomes of international comparisons; 3) to provide comparative tables and factual summaries in specific areas of interest; 4) to conduct thematic studies in specific areas to enable SCAA to evaluate the English National Curriculum and assessment frameworks; 5) to make the findings available to policymakers, researchers and practitioners. The project collects, summarises and analyses information from national sources, research and wider literature on a) national values and educational aims; b) the educational and organisational contexts, and c) whole curriculum and assessment structures. The descriptions for each country collectively constitute 'The Archive', which is subject to continual revision and updating. The guiding principles for data collection and presentation are: 1) each national summary provides a reliable account of key features of the curriculum and assessment framework in the country concerned, reflecting, as far as possible, the national structure, concepts and terminology; 2) where possible, statements are verified by national authorities; 3) legislation, regulations and other official statements are drawn upon to provide an indication of the intended arrangements in each country, supplemented by correspondence and interviews with official agencies in the countries concerned; 4) alternative sources (e.g. correspondence and interviews with educators in the countries concerned) may be used to provide insights into implementation; 5) the sources are indicated, so that users of 'the Archive' can evaluate the content and locate sources; 6) the thematic studies bring together the findings of 'The Archive' with additional research. In some cases, invitational seminars involving participants from most of the contributing countries are held, to provide a context for, and deeper insights into, the similarities and differences between countries. 'The Archive' is available as a pilot CD-Rom (known as INCA) or in published form as a series of individual national descriptions for each country. The pilot CD-Rom will be subject to formal evaluation between July and October 1997.

PUBLISHED MATERIAL: TABBERER, R. & LE METAIS, J. (1997). 'Looking behind international comparisons', Education Journal, Issue 9, pp.20-21. ; LE METAIS, J., O'DONNELL, S., BOYD, S. & TABBERER, R. (1997). INCA: the international review of curriculum and assessment frameworks archive (CD-Rom). London: School Curriculum and Assessment Authority. ; LE METAIS, J. & TABBERER, R. (1997). Comparative tables and factual summaries (International Review of Curriculum and Assessment Frameworks). London: School Curriculum and Assessment Authority. ; LE METAIS, J. (1997). Values and aims underlying curriculum and assessment. International Review of Curriculum and Assessment Frameworks Paper 1. London: School Curriculum and Assessment Authority. ; LE METAIS, J. & TABBERER, R. (1997). 'Why different countries do better: evidence from examining curriculum and assessment frameworks in 16 countries', International Electronic Journal for Leadership in Learning, The University of Calgary, Alberta, Canada. (Available on-line at: http://www.ucalgary.ca/-iejll/lemetais_v1n3.html).

STATUS: Sponsored project

SOURCE OF GRANT: School Curriculum and Assessment Authority

DATE OF RESEARCH: 1996-1998

KEYWORDS: **assessment; comparative education; curriculum; curriculum development**

1663

The Mere, Upton Park, Slough SL1 2DQ
01753 574123

Hutchison, D. Dr; Wilkin, A. Mrs; Kinder, K. Ms; Wood, H. Ms; Harman, J. Mr; Gorman, T. Dr; *Supervisor*: Brooks, G. Dr

Family literacy follow-up

ABSTRACT: In 1997 the Basic Skills Agency commissioned the National Foundation for Educational Research to follow up the parents and children who had participated in the FAmily Literacy Demonstration Programmes in 1994/95. The aim was to investigate the extent to which children had sustained the gains they had made during their courses, and the extent to which Family Literacy continued to have an impact on parents' employment and education. A total of 154 parents and 237 children were re-contacted between January and April 1997. Interviews were also carried out with the teachers of a subsample of the children, and with the Demonstration Programme coordinators. The main findings on the continuing benefits for children are as follows: (1) The 237 Family Literacy children re-contacted had maintained the gains made during the courses in vocabulary, reading and writing. (2) The parents and the Demonstration Programme coordinators were strongly of the opinion that the children were continuing to benefit. (3) The interviews with teachers showed that (a) Family Literacy children were superior to their peers in the support they received from their families, classroom behaviour, and probable success in school; and (b) Family Literacy children were equal to their peers in other academic and motivational respects. Thus overall the Family Literacy children were holding their own, and their educational prospects were better than they would have been without Family Literacy. The main findings on the continuing benefits for parents: (1) Of the 154 parents re-contacted, 66 (43 per cent) were in work in 1997, up from 29 (19 per cent) in 1994/95; and of these 66, 57 (86 per cent of those in work) attributed their gaining employment directly to Family Literacy. (2) Of the full group of 154, 92 (60 per cent) had taken at least one further course of study, whereas none were studying in 1994/95; and of these 92, 78 (51 per cent of the total) had achieved a further qualification; and 76 (49 per cent of the total) intended to continue studying. Thus the 'study rate' in this group had risen from zero to 60 per cent, and many had gained qualifications. (3) Of the 154 parents re-contacted, 133 (86 per cent) thought that their own reading and writing were continuing to benefit from Family Literacy; and 146 (95 per cent) thought that their ability to help their children with reading and writing was continuing to benefit. In the coordinators' opinion, these benefits arose mainly from increased literacy awareness and activity in the home. (4) Of the 154 parents re-contacted, 87 (56 per cent) said that they were involved with their children's schools; and of these 42 (48 per cent of those involved with schools) had become literacy helpers in the classroom. The rate of involvement of Family Literacy parents with their children's schools was double that of parents of children in a control group. (5) Of the 154 parents re-contacted, 141 (92 per cent) thought that they were continuing to benefit from Family Literacy in other ways, especially in confidence and in communication skills. Therefore the parents continued to benefit in employment, study, qualifications, literacy, ability to help their children, and involvement with their children's schools; and overall, Family Literacy parents continued to widen their participation in education and in society generally. The overall conclusion of this follow-up study is that it showed that the Family Literacy children had successfully maintained the gains they made during the courses, and that the parents had continued to widen their participation in education and society.

PUBLISHED MATERIAL: BROOKS, G., GORMAN, T.P., HARMAN, J., HUTCHISON, D., KINDER, K., MOOR, H. & WILKIN, A. (1997). Family Literacy Lasts: The NFER Follow-up Study of the Basic Skills Agency's Demonstration Programmes. London: Basic Skills Agency. ; BROOKS, G. (1998). 'The effectiveness for parents of family literacy programmes in England and Wales', Journal of Adolescent and Adult Literacy, Vol 42, No 2, pp.130-2.

STATUS: Sponsored project

SOURCE OF GRANT: Basic Skills Agency £70,000

DATE OF RESEARCH: 1996-1997

KEYWORDS: **family involvement; family literacy; family programmes; followup studies; literacy; parent participation; reading skills; writing skills**

1664

The Mere, Upton Park, Slough SL1 2DQ
01753 574123

Henkhuzens, Z. Ms; Flanagan, N. Ms; Hutchison, D. Dr; *Supervisor*: Brooks, G. Dr

Evaluation of early reading intervention schemes

ABSTRACT: Over the four years 1994-97 the proportion of children in England achieving below level 2 in reading in the Key Stage 1 National Curriculum tests averaged 21 per cent. What schemes are available to meet these children's needs, and how effective are they? This project was designed to provide some answers to these questions. The researcherse gathered information from local education authorities and from institutions of teacher education, and trawled the literature. The aim was to look for approaches which had been used with struggling but non-dyslexic children in at least one of Years 1 to 4 (or the equivalent) in the UK, and which had been the subject of a quantitative evaluation in the UK from which an impact measure could be calculated. The project concentrated on studies carried out in the UK to avoid the objection 'How do we know that it will work here?' Twenty studies were found which met this criteria. Because seven of the studies covered more than one approach the researchers were able to make quantitative comparisons of 30 approaches in all. The best-known of these is probably Reading Recovery, but they also analysed (among others): (1) the 1984 version of DISTAR; (2) an early (1994) version of THRASS; (3) the Basic Skills Agency's Family Literacy Demonstration Programmes; (4) the original Parental Involvement project in Haringey; (5) the Paired Reading approach in the version researched in Kirklees; (6) two Integrated Learning Systems initiatives; (7) the Cumbria Reding with Phonology project; (8) the Buckinghamshire Phonological Awareness Training scheme, plus several phonological approaches within larger projects; (9) work on self-esteem and reading carried out in Somerset between 1970 and 1984; (10) several other LEA initiatives; (11) an experimental study using Inference Training to improve comprehension; (12) the latest innovation for struggling readers in Year 3, Catch up; (13) just one study in which a school developed and researched its own approach; and (14) 'no treatment' (normal schooling) control groups in about half the studies, containing about 1000 children. Most of the studies measured children's reading just at the beginning and end of an initiative, but in seven studies there was a follow-up some time after the intervention had ended. The studies varied widely in scale. The Kirklees Paired Reading study was by far the largest, with 2372 children in experimental groups and 446 controls. Five studies had between 100

and 750 children, and the remaining 14 had fewer than 100. The smallest was a 'Pause, Prompt and Praise' experiment with just 20 children. The overall conclusions were that: (1) Generally, normal schooling ('no treatment') does not enable slow readers to catch up, thus reinforcing the case for early intervention. (2) Work on phonological skills should be embedded within a broad approach - most approaches which concentrated heavily on phonological aspects showed little impact. (3) Children's comprehension can be improved if directly targeted. (4) Working on children's self-esteem and reading in parallel has definite potential. (5) IT approaches only work if they are precisely targeted. (6) Large-scale schemes, such as Reading Recovery and Family Literacy, though expensive, can give good value for money. (7) Where reading partners are available and can be given appropriate training, partnership approaches can be very effective. (8) Most of the schemes which incorporated follow-up studies showed that children maintained the improvements they had made during the interventions.

PUBLISHED MATERIAL: BROOKS, G., FLANAGAN, N., HENKHUZENS, Z. & HUTCHISON, D. (1998). What Works for Slow Readers? The Effectiveness of Early Intervention Schemes. Slough: NFER.; BROOKS, G. (1999). 'What works for slow readers?', Support for Learning, Vol 14, No 1, pp.27-31.

STATUS: Sponsored project

SOURCE OF GRANT: National Foundation for Educational Research £40,000

DATE OF RESEARCH: 1995-1998

KEYWORDS: **intervention; literacy; reading; reading difficulties; reading teaching; remedial programmes; remedial reading**

1665

The Mere, Upton Park, Slough SL1 2DQ
01753 574123

Hutchison, D. Dr; Wilkin, A. Mrs; Harman, J. Mr; Kendall, S. Dr; *Supervisor*: Brooks, G. Dr

Evaluation of family literacy alternative models

ABSTRACT: The original model of family literacy established by the Basic Skills Agency in 1994 was for families where the parents had basic skills needs and the children were aged three to six. Very few families from linguistic minorities participated in the Demonstration Programmes evaluated by the NFER in 1994-95, and only families with a child in the relevant age range were targeted. In early 1997 the Agency implemented family literacy courses which followed three alternative models: (1) working with linguistic minority families where the parents had basic skills needs and the children were aged three to six; (2) working with parents with basic skills needs, and their children in Year 4; and (3) working with parents with basic skills needs, and their children in Year 7. In most cases, these models were delivered through courses of 10 to 12 weeks' duration during school terms, though adjustments to local circumstances were envisaged. Each course was designed for up to 10 parents and 12 children. The Basic Skills Agency commissioned the NFER to evaluate these alternative models in 1997-98. The aim of the evaluation was to establish whether the original model had been appropriately adapted for the new groups, and how effective courses following the new models had been. Background data were gathered on parents and children participating in 47 courses. Performance data were collected at the beginning and end of their courses on the attainment in literacy of 287 parents and 344 children. Observations were made of 43 teaching sessions, and 30 course staff were interviewed. The attempt to adapt the original Family Literacy model for families with a child in Year 7 was largely unsuccessful. This was partly because of problems of retaining parents on the coursese, and partly because of the very different circumstances of secondary schools. But the original model was successfully adapted both for linguistic minority families with a child aged three to six, and for families with a child in Year 4. The linguistic minorities model: A) The main linguistic minority recruited was speakers of Urdu and Punjabi. B) The parents significantly improved their literacy in English. C) The parents' ability to help their children had improved. D) The children made substantial progress in writing and in early literacy generally. E) Boys and girls made approximately equal gains. The Year 4 model: A) The parents significantly improved their literacy. B) The children made substantial progress in writing and in literacy generally. C) Boys and girls made approximately equal gains. Lessons: (1) The success of the linguistic minorities model showed that the original model can be successfully implemented with different linguistic/ethnic gorups. (2) The success of the Year 4 model shows that the original model can be successfully implemented at that point in the primary age range; but these courses need even more careful ground-laying and planning than those for the younger age range.

PUBLISHED MATERIAL: BROOKS, G., HARMAN, J., HUTCHISON, D., KENDALL, S. & WILKIN, A. (1999). Family literacy for new groups. London: Basic Skills Agency.

STATUS: Sponsored project

SOURCE OF GRANT: Basic Skills Agency £120,000

DATE OF RESEARCH: 1996-continuing

KEYWORDS: **english - second language; ethnic groups; family involvement; family literacy; family programmes; literacy; parent participation; reading skills; writing skills**

1666

The Mere, Upton Park, Slough SL1 2DQ
01753 574123

Gallacher, S. Dr; *Supervisor*: Weston, P. Mrs

Kent primary self-evaluation: survey of current assessment practice in primary schools

ABSTRACT: Building on a relationship which led to the 'Raising Attainment in Secondary Schools' Handbook, the National Foundation for Educational Research (NFER) is beginning a similar process to enhance Kent's approach to school self-evaluation, in the primary phase. The initial step involves auditing the range and uses of assessment materials across all 500-plus primary schools in the authority. This phase is being run jointly by Kent and the NFER, and is relying on a questionnaire to establish the current assessment picture.

PUBLISHED MATERIAL: SAUNDERS, L., STRADLING, B. & GALLACHER, S. (1996). Raising attainment in secondary schools. A handbook for self-evaluation. Slough: National Foundation for Educational Research.

STATUS: Sponsored project

SOURCE OF GRANT: Kent County Council Education Department

DATE OF RESEARCH: 1997-1997

KEYWORDS: **assessment; institutional evaluation; primary education**

1667

The Mere, Upton Park, Slough SL1 2DQ
01753 574123

Sims, D. Mr; Hewitt, D. Dr; *Supervisors*: Weston, P. Mrs; Schagen, I. Dr

Progress towards Foundation Targets 1 and 3 by English region

ABSTRACT: The overall purpose of the research is to use regional data to describe and account for differences in achievement related to Foundation Targets 1 and 3 between and within English regions. Within this remit, 3 aims have been identified, linked to description, explanation and improvement: 1) to clarify the spread of achievement across and within regions (for each Target, over time, in different types of institution and for different qualification routes); 2) to identify the factors that influence variations in achievement (including factors related to the individual, the institution, and the local economy); 3) to identify effective strategies for raising attainment, and suggest how these might be disseminated more widely. In order to address the issues raised and to achieve the research aims, 2 parallel strands are proposed for the research. The first and major strand would involve the collation, consolidation and analysis of data from all the relevant sources. The second strand would include interviews with national and regional personnel to identify and clarify issues which could contribute to the design of the analysis, and subsequently pursue the implications of the analysis in the 4 selected regions.

STATUS: Sponsored project

SOURCE OF GRANT: National Advisory Council for Education and Training Targets £29,837

DATE OF RESEARCH: 1996-1997

KEYWORDS: **academic achievement; foundation targets; national targets for education and training; regional variations; vocational education**

1668

The Mere, Upton Park, Slough SL1 2DQ
01753 574123

Sharp, C. Ms; Davis, C. Ms; *Supervisor*: Keys, W. Dr

Provision for under fives: a study of parental needs and expectations

ABSTRACT: Increased numbers of children are experiencing preschool provision and the Government's initiatives have made this an appropriate time to study parental needs and expectations of the provision for the under fives. The three main aims of the research are: 1) to identify parents' perceived needs and expectations for their children's preschool experience; 2) to highlight and describe provision which achieves a high level of parental satisfaction; 3) to examine to what extent parental views of what constitutes good provision equates with independent evaluation. The research is designed in three stages: a) A review of the literature and selection of six authorities for study; b) A questionnaire survey of parents in 36 nominated settings. c) Visits to each of the 12 settings which achieved the highest rating from parents. The findings will be published by the National Foundation for Educational Research.

STATUS: Sponsored project

SOURCE OF GRANT: National Foundation for Educational Research

DATE OF RESEARCH: 1996-1997

KEYWORDS: **early childhood education; nursery education; parent attitudes; parent choice; parents; preschool education**

1669

The Mere, Upton Park, Slough SL1 2DQ
01753 574123

Kendall, L. Mrs; *Supervisor*: Keys, W. Dr

Pupils with asthma

ABSTRACT: Estimates suggest that about 5% of school children have asthma requiring medical attention. This study aims to investigate how secondary school pupils obtain information on air quality, their response to such information and how to target this group more effectively. Phase 1 will establish the issues to be addressed and will include discussion with doctors, representatives of support and pressure groups and staff and pupils with asthma in about 5 schools. A brief review of the literature will also be undertaken. The information gained in this phase will be used to assist in the design of a questionnaire to be used in Phase 2. Pupils with asthma in about 200 secondary schools will be surveyed in order to ascertain their awareness and knowledge of air quality issues and the effect of this information on their lifestyle. The project will also seek to establish how communication of quality of air information can be improved for this age group. Information on school policy on asthma will also be obtained and a modified version of the school questionnaire will be sent to a small number of special schools. A report will be produced for the sponsors.

STATUS: Sponsored project

SOURCE OF GRANT: Department of Health

DATE OF RESEARCH: 1996-1997

KEYWORDS: **air quality; asthma; pupil health and welfare; school policy; secondary school pupils**

1670

The Mere, Upton Park, Slough SL1 2DQ
01753 574123

Birmingham, P. Mr; *Supervisor*: Keys, W. Dr

The NFER Annual Survey of Trends in Education: 1998

ABSTRACT: The Annual Survey of Trends in Education is a series of regular questionnaire surveys of primary schools focusing on key issues of educational practice. Its purpose is to obtain up-to-date views from headteachers and to ensure that these are given widespread coverage as part of the continuing debate on education. Each survey consists of a small number of 'barometer' questions designed to monitor trends in school perspectives over time. In addition, there is a special focus which changes each year. The survey began in 1994 with a pilot study and the special focus was on the resourcing of the curriculum at National Curriculum key stage 2. The 1995 survey included a focus on Science in the Primary School. The 1996 survey included a focus on Mathematics in the Primary School and the 1997 survey focused on English in the Primary School. The 1998 survey focuses on teacher appraisal. The 1998 survey consists of a questionnaire to a sample of 568 primary school headteachers. The sample consists of two sub-samples: 138 schools which had taken part in the 1997 survey; and a new sample of 430 schools. The results of the pilot survey were reported in Digests 1 and 2 (KEYS, W. (1995). Annual survey of trends in education Digest 1: results of the pilot study. Slough: NFER; and KEYS, W. (1995). Annual survey of trends in education. Digest 2: key issues in primary schools. Slough: NFER). The 1995 results were reported in Digest 3 (DAVIS, C. (1996). Annual survey of trends in education. Digest 3: current issues in education. Slough: NFER) and an additional report on Science in the Primary School (HARRIS, S. (1996) Science in primary schools. Slough: NFER). The 1996 results were reported in Digest 4 (HENKHUZENS, Z. (1997). Annual survey of trends in education. Digest 4: changes over time. Slough: NFER) and an additional report on Mathematics in the Primary School (HARRIS, S. & HENKHUZENS, Z. (1997). Mathematics in primary schools. Slough: NFER). The 1997 results were reported in Digests 5 and 6 (OSGOOD, J. & KEYS, W. (1998). Annual survey of trends in education. Digest 5: headteachers' main concerns. Slough: NFER; and BROOKS, G. & KEYS, W. (1998). Annual survey of trends in education. Digest 6: headteachers' views on English in the primary school. Slough: NFER).

STATUS: Sponsored project

SOURCE OF GRANT: NFER

DATE OF RESEARCH: 1998-continuing

KEYWORDS: **appraisal interviews; educational trends; english; head teachers; key stage 2; mathematics education; national curriculum; primary education; resource allocation; science education; surveys; teacher evaluation**

1671

The Mere, Upton Park, Slough SL1 2DQ
01753 574123

Henkhuzens, Z. Ms; *Supervisor*: Harris, S. Mrs

Primary school mathematics - implementing the post-Dearing National Curriculum

ABSTRACT: The NFER Annual Survey of Trends in Education consists of 2 parts: a special focus; and a section seeking headteachers' views on current issues in education. The main outcome of the 1996 survey will be a 4-page digest, published in Spring 1997, summarising the main findings. Mathematics in the Primary School is the special focus of the 1996 NFER Annual Survey. Issues covered include: planning and implementing the post-Dearing National Curriculum; the role and time allocation of the mathematics coordinator; approaches to mathematics teaching at key stages 1 and 2; and the successes and challenges faced by schools in the implementation of the post-Dearing National Curriculum. The questionnaire survey consisted of a sample of 400 maintained and grant-maintained primary schools containing key stage 1 and/or key stage 2 pupils. In addition to the questionnaire, schools were asked to include any curriculum plans or schemes of work and these will be analysed as part of the research. Follow-up work in schools will include face-to-face and telephone interviews with headteachers and mathematics coordinators and, if appropriate, classroom observation of mathematics work. The main outcome of the research will be a clear, user-friendly report designed for classroom practitioners, mathematics coordinators, headteachers and advisers. It will include the main findings of the study, highlight examples of good practice and include suggestions for the future. The report will be published in September 1997.

STATUS: Sponsored project

SOURCE OF GRANT: NFER Research Development Programme £22,000

DATE OF RESEARCH: 1997-1997

KEYWORDS: **key stage 1; key stage 2; mathematics education; national curriculum; primary education**

1672

The Mere, Upton Park, Slough SL1 2DQ
01753 574123

Coffey, M. Mr

A review of the feasibility of teachers' adaptability to organisational change

ABSTRACT: The aims of this research are primarily to investigate a basis for the future development of a test instrument. Such an instrument would determine how any teacher is predisposed to change in his/her workplace, how such a change would affect him/her, and how he/she could be helped to cope with such problems. This preliminary research entails a literature review of material on organisational change, both generally and as it applies to education. The end product would form the basis for the production of an instrument.

STATUS: Sponsored project

SOURCE OF GRANT: National Foundation for Educational Research £20,000

DATE OF RESEARCH: 1997-1997

KEYWORDS: **change; educational administration; educational change; institutional environment; organisational change; organisational climate; teacher attitudes; teachers**

1673

The Mere, Upton Park, Slough SL1 2DQ
01753 574123

Taylor, M. Dr; Lines, A. Mrs; *Supervisor*: Stoney, S. Dr

Values education in primary and secondary schools

ABSTRACT: Despite much public and educational debate about the state and status of values education in schools, little precise information exists about how schools approach values education, how their provision supports their stated values, why and how they choose certain curricular approaches and teaching strategies and what professional support is needed. This project will examine key factors in schools' formal and informal teaching in values education and provide evidence of coherent and interesting practice as a basis for policy-making and good practice guidelines. In particular, through an evaluation of the Citizenship Foundation's 'You, Me, Us!' materials for primary schools, it will provide evidence of the kind of materials schools take up, use and find effective, as well as their resource and support needs. Additionally, to inform the International Association for the Evaluation of Educational Achievement (IEA) Civic Education Project it will also consider to what extent secondary schools make provision for developing young people's awareness of democracy, their sense of national identity and their understanding of the disenfranchised and marginalised, by the age of 15 (see also IEA project). The research involves a nationally representative survey of 600 primary schools and 400 secondary schools; telephone interviews with up to 50 Personal and Social Education coodinators; mini case studies of 20-25 primary and secondary schools. The research will provide a much needed up-to-date picture of values education across primary and secondary schools in England and Wales. The outcomes will be: 1) a full project report; 2) a report to the Citizenship Foundation: an evaluation of the take-up and use of its 'You, Me, Us!' materials for primary schools; 3) inclusion of secondary school data on citizenship education in a report to IEA as part of the International Civic Education Project; and 4) a one-day seminar.

STATUS: Sponsored project

SOURCE OF GRANT: NFER Research and Development Programme £27,865; School Curriculum and Assessment Authority: International Association for the Evaluation of Educational Achievement £29,980; Citizenship Foundation £20,000

DATE OF RESEARCH: 1997-continuing

KEYWORDS: **citizenship education; moral education; primary education; secondary education; values; values education**

1674

The Mere, Upton Park, Slough SL1 2DQ
01753 574123

Harland, J. Dr; Bower, R. Mr; Wilkin, A. Mrs; Moor, H. Ms; *Supervisors*: Bradley, J. Dr; Kinder, K. Ms

Effective behaviour management in schools

ABSTRACT: As both Elton (1989) and Circular 8/94 'Pupil Behaviour and Discipline' (1994) suggest, teachers can and do make a significant difference to both pupil attainment and pupil behaviour. Beyond prevention and general behaviour management procedures, lie the issues of how schools deal with acknowledged difficult and deviant behaviour, and the kind of support available to them from outside agencies. Given recurring research and media focuses on pupil behaviour, this project will offer timely insight into the most effective strategies and practices in the management of behaviour at local educationa authority (LEA), school and classroom level. It will complement the NFER Membership Project 'The policy and practice of non-exclusion' in which one key research question will be how and which strategies for managing behaviour are capable of supporting any non-exclusion policy. The project's aims are: 1) to portray the range of support structures for behaviour management offered to schools by their LEA and other outside agencies; 2) to investigate the different behaviour management practices operating within schools and other institutions; 3) to garner multi-perspectives on effective policy and practice; and 4) to identify key factors linked to effective behaviour management at LEA, school and classroom level. The project will employ both quantitative and qualitative methods. An initial questionnaire will seek to identify the range of behaviour management support currently provided by LEAs. Case study work will be undertaken in a number of institutions, involving documentary analysis, interviews and classroom observation. A second survey will then be sent to a range of personnel in a representative sample of schools to elicit a multi-perspective overview of key issues, values and practices associated with effective behaviour management. It is envisaged that an interim report and short papers will be published during the research with a final report presenting the findings from all 3 of the project's phases.

STATUS: Sponsored project

SOURCE OF GRANT: NFER Membership Programme £200,000

DATE OF RESEARCH: 1996-1997

KEYWORDS: **behaviour management; behaviour problems; discipline; disruptive pupils; emotional and behavioural difficulties; local education authorities; pupil behaviour; support services**

1675

The Mere, Upton Park, Slough SL1 2DQ
01753 574123

Harland, J. Dr; Kinder, K. Ms; Vulliamy, G. Dr; Webb, R. Dr

Curriculum organisation and pedagogy at National Curriculum key stage 2: a literature review

ABSTRACT: This literature review aims to examine the claims made concerning effective classroom practice at National Curriculum key stage 2 (KS2) to identify those which can be substantiated by research evidence and to propose further research that could make a useful contribution to the debate. Currently claims are being made by policy-makers for increasing the effectiveness of teaching at key stage 2 by approaches such as separate subject teaching, subject specialism, ability grouping and whole class teaching. The justification for these claims, if given, generally appears to be derived from accounts of policy and practice in other countries or from Office for Standards in Education (OFSTED) inspection data. Consequently, there is uncertainty as to whether, and to what extent, such claims are influenced by personal predilections, political, ideological and/or economic motives or rooted in, and substantiated by past and ongoing research. There is clearly a need for such a literature review to explore and analyse the claims of policy-makers and in so doing identify the advantages and disadvantages of alternative forms of classroom practice at KS2 in differing schools and curriculum contexts. Such a review will investigate current claims and their origins and identify those which are substantiated by research. In order to identify aspects of effective practice it will examine research findings on both classroom processes and the outcomes of these processes. This will necessitate consideration of the diverse methodologies used in order to establish the relationship between research approaches, findings and implications for practice and to explore any apparent tensions or contradictions between findings which may arise from their location within different research traditions.

STATUS: Sponsored project

SOURCE OF GRANT: National Foundation for Educational Research; University of York, jointly £24,000

DATE OF RESEARCH: 1996-1997

KEYWORDS: **class organisation; classroom management; curriculum development; grouping - teaching purposes; key stage 2; primary education; teaching methods; teaching process**

1676

The Mere, Upton Park, Slough SL1 2DQ
01753 574123

Lewis, G. Mr; Williams, S. Mr

Evaluation of adult guidance for West Wales Training and Enterprise Council

ABSTRACT: This study examines the nature of adult guidance provided in the West Wales Training and Enterprise Council (TEC). It involves an ongoing client survey as well as examining the views of advisers and partnership organisations. An interim report was produced in November 1996.

STATUS: Sponsored project

SOURCE OF GRANT: West Wales Training and Enterprise Council

DATE OF RESEARCH: 1996-1997

KEYWORDS: **adult counselling; adults; career counselling; careers advisers; guidance; training; training and enterprise councils; vocational guidance**

1677

The Mere, Upton Park, Slough SL1 2DQ
01753 574123

Lewis, G. Mr; Williams, S. Mr

Evaluation of adult guidance for South Glamorgan Training and Enterprise Council

ABSTRACT: This study examines the nature of adult guidance provided in the South Glamorgan Training and Enterprise Council (TEC). It involves an ongoing client survey as well as examining the views of advisers and partnership organisations. A final report will be produced in March 1997.

STATUS: Sponsored project

SOURCE OF GRANT: West Wales Training and Enterprise Council

DATE OF RESEARCH: 1996-1997

KEYWORDS: **adult counselling; adults; career counselling; careers advisers; guidance; training; training and enterprise councils; vocational guidance**

1678

The Mere, Upton Park, Slough SL1 2DQ
01753 574123

Lewis, G. Mr; Williams, S. Mr

Evaluation of adult guidance for Gwent Training and Enterprise Council

ABSTRACT: This study examines the nature of adult guidance provided in the Gwent Training and Enterprise Council (TEC). It involves an ongoing client survey as well as examining the views of advisers and partnership organisations. A final report will be produced in March 1997.

STATUS: Sponsored project

SOURCE OF GRANT: Gwent Training and Enterprise Council

DATE OF RESEARCH: 1996-1997

KEYWORDS: **adult counselling; adults; career counselling; careers advisers; guidance; training; training and enterprise councils; vocational guidance**

1679

The Mere, Upton Park, Slough SL1 2DQ
01753 574123

Williams, S. Mr; Lewis, G. Mr

Use of English and Welsh as a medium of instruction

ABSTRACT: To examine how Welsh medium teachers deploy both languages in the classroom. Of particular interest, is how they manage language shift between topics of instruction.

STATUS: Sponsored project

SOURCE OF GRANT: National Foundation for Educational Research

DATE OF RESEARCH: 1996-1997

KEYWORDS: **classroom communication; english; language of instruction; primary education; secondary education; wales; welsh; welsh medium education**

1680

The Mere, Upton Park, Slough SL1 2DQ
01753 574123

Kerr, D. Mr; *Supervisor*: Weston, P. Mrs

Effective learning in grant-maintained schools and city technology colleges

ABSTRACT: One of the factors to be considered by schools in opting for grant-mainted (GM) status was the loss of direct association with the local authority, particularly in respect of curriculum support from the local education authority (LEA) advisory teams. City technology colleges (CTCs) had to plan from the start to establish, individually or jointly, their own curriculum support structure. The aim of this research is to provide a systematic review of the extent and effectiveness of curriculum delivery, monitoring and support sysems in schools outside the LEA system. Topics covered include curriculum policy, support and related inservice training in GM schools/technology colleges and CTCs. The research has two main strands: 1) A review of research (and other published material) on learning approaches, curriculum development and support and inservice provision in GM schools and CTCs since their inspection; 2) a questionnaire survey of all GM schools/colleges and CTCs to ascertain their current strategies for support of curriculum development and for related inservice training (INSET) support, and the factors affecting these strategies. The main outcome of the project will be a report which will provide an appraisal of current curriculum policy and practice within the GM and CTC sectors.

STATUS: Sponsored project

SOURCE OF GRANT: NFER Membership Programme £29,000

DATE OF RESEARCH: 1995-continuing

KEYWORDS: **advisory support; city technology colleges; curriculum development; grant maintained schools; inservice teacher education; secondary education**

1681

The Mere, Upton Park, Slough SL1 2DQ
01753 574123

Taylor, M. Dr; *Supervisor*: Stoney, S. Dr

Evaluation of the Association of Christian Teachers' Cross-Curricular Christianity (CHARIS) Project

ABSTRACT: Recent educational policy, guidance and inspection have given renewed prominence to spiritual, moral, social and cultural (SMSC) development. Recognition is also being accorded to these aspects of education in all curricular subjects. The CHARIS project, being undertaken by the Association of Christian Teachers, is producing classroom materials for English, Mathematics, French & German and Science at National Curriculum key stage 4 which aim to enhance SMSC development from a Christian perspective. In particular, the project aims to promote 14-16 year-old pupils' SMSC development, their understanding of Christian perspectives and world views. A concurrent evaluation of the project is being undertaken to: provide information on project development and management, consider issues in the development and dissemination of materials; and assess the extent to which the project achieves its own aims for pupils' SMSC development and the take-up of materials in secondary schools. The evaluation is being conducted by means of documentary analysis; observation of writing teams, interviews with team members and project directors; visits to schools trialling the materials including teacher interviews, class observation, pupil group interviews, telephone interviews with editors and designers; attendance at and contributions to project management meetings. The sponsor receives ongoing formative evaluation reports for its educational advisory group and trustees' meetings. A summative report will also be provided at the end of the project. It is hoped that a paper from the evaluation will be produced for an academic educational journal or book chapter. To

date, the CHARIS project has produced one set of materials for English, Mathematics and French & German available from the Stapleford House Education Centre, Freepost, Wesley Place, Stapleford, Nottingham NG9 7BR.

STATUS: Sponsored project

SOURCE OF GRANT: Jerusalem Trust £14,980

DATE OF RESEARCH: 1995-1997

KEYWORDS: **christianity; cross curricular approach; curriculum development; educational materials; key stage 4; moral development; moral education; religious education; secondary education; spiritual development**

1682

The Mere, Upton Park, Slough SL1 2DQ
01753 574123

Stoney, S. Dr; Sims, D. Mr; Lines, A. Mrs; Golden, S. Ms

An evaluation of the impact and added value of the Construction Industry Training Board's curriculum centres

ABSTRACT: The Construction Industry Training Board (CITB) commissioned the National Foundation for Educational Research (NFER) to conduct an evaluation of their Curriculum Centre Initiative. The aim of the Initiative is to promote construction and the built environment as a context for learning. Recently, partnerships between schools, colleges and employers have been developed which aim to facilitate progression into various vocational qualifications and to play a role in supporting Dearing's recommendation to offer a vocational aspect to the curriculum. The main aims of the evaluation were to assess the extent to which involvement in Curriculum Centre activities is associated with improved academic and vocational performance by students in Years 10 and 11, to gather perceptions of the value of the Initiative from those involved, and to identify the key elements which contribute to a successful Curriculum Centre. These aims were addressed firstly through a questionnaire survey of Year 10 and 11 students which gathered information on students' experience of Centre activities and their interest in vocational routes and qualifications. In addition, a value-added analysis of students' academic progress will be conducted using National Curriculum key stage 3 and GCSE results later in 1997. Secondly, the perceptions of schools, colleges and employers on the value and outcomes of the Initiative were investigated through face-to-face and telephone interviews. The research found that the Initiative is regarded as a worthwhile venture by those involved and raised awareness of the construction industry among teachers and students. There were signs that the Initiative was providing a foundation for progression to General National Vocational Qualifications (GNVQs)/General Scottish Vocational Qualifications (GSVQs) and National Vocational Qualifications (NVQs)/Scottish Vocational Qualifications (SVQs) and to the construction industry. Young people benefit from experiencing a broad curriculum which enables them to make informed choices for their future. Schools gain from accessing the expertise and resources of colleges. Employers improve their awareness of young people and education. A confidential report was produced for the sponsors.

STATUS: Sponsored project

SOURCE OF GRANT: Construction Industry Training Board

DATE OF RESEARCH: 1996-1997

KEYWORDS: **colleges of further education; construction industry; curriculum development; industry education relationship; key stage 3; national vocational qualifications; school college relationship; secondary education; value added; vocational education; work education relationship**

1683

The Mere, Upton Park, Slough SL1 2DQ
01753 574123

Golden, S. Ms; Sims, D. Mr

Review of industrial mentoring in schools

ABSTRACT: During the 1990s there has been a notable growth in schools' use of industrial mentors where they form part of the range of school-industry links which schools are developing. Mentors are valued for the contribution they can make to helping young people fulfil their potential and achieve. This research was funded by the National Foundation for Educational Research (NFER) and aimed to map out the range and main models of industrial mentoring schemes in schools and to identify the outcomes and benefits as perceived by those involved in mentoring, including teachers, mentees and mentors. This research was conducted through a postal questionnaire of 72 mentoring scheme coordinators, who were mostly based in Education Business Partnerships and Compact schemes, 20 of these coordinators also participated in telephone interviews. Further indepth information was gathered through face-to-face interviews with mentors, mentees and school teacher-coordinators in 4 schools. The research found that while mentoring schemes adapted to local needs, the majority provided one-to-one mentoring for under-achievers with potential in Years 10 and 11. Having recruited suitable mentors, which could be challenging, most schemes provided training and were beginning to develop ongoing support sessions, often as a result of identifying such a need through evaluation. It was found that the distinctive feature about mentoring - having an adult other than a family member or teacher, who is interested in an individual student had a positive impact on the young persons' self-esteem and their awareness of the world of work.

STATUS: Sponsored project

SOURCE OF GRANT: National Foundation for Educational Research

DATE OF RESEARCH: 1996-1997

KEYWORDS: compacts; education business partnerships; industry education relationship; key stage 4; link courses; mentors; pupil development; secondary education; underachievement; work education relationship

1684

The Mere, Upton Park, Slough SL1 2DQ
01753 574123

Kerr, D. Mr; *Supervisor*: Taylor, M. Miss

International Association for the Evaluation of Educational Achievement Civic Education Project: England case study

ABSTRACT: The International Association for the Evaluation of Educational Achievement (IEA) is currently organising a Civic Education Project in 24 countries worldwide focusing on citizenship in secondary education. Phase 1 of the project, to which this English case study contributes, addresses 3 core areas: young people's knowledge of democracy; sense of national identity; and their awareness of the disenfranchised and marginalised by the age of 14 or 15. The project involves a review of policy and research literature and interviews with a range of education professionals and 'opinion leaders', focusing on policy objectives, teaching strategies and materials and school-based activities in relation to the core questions as set out by the IEA. The work is being guided by a national expert panel. The report will also include an introduction to civic education and an annotated bibliography of 10-15 texts. The report will complement other current values education initiatives, provide a national case study of citizenship in secondary education in England and contribute to the comparative overview undertaken by IEA. A report to IEA on Citizenship (Civic) Education in England is due in May 1997. A separate publication by the NFER is to be considered.

PUBLISHED MATERIAL: KERR, D. (1998). Re-examining citizenship education: the case of England. National Case Study for IEA Civic Education Study Phase 1. Slough: NFER. ; KERR, D. (1999). 'Re-examining citizenship education in England'. In: TORNEY-PURTA, J., SCHWILLE, J. & AMADEO, J.A. Civic education across countries: 24 national case studies from the IEA Civic Education Project. Delft, Netherlands: International Association for the Evaluation of Educational Achievement/Eburon Publishers.

STATUS: Sponsored project

SOURCE OF GRANT: School Curriculum and Assessment Authority

DATE OF RESEARCH: 1997-1997

KEYWORDS: citizenship education; comparative education; democracy; global approach; international educational exchange; life skills; national identity; secondary education; social development; values education

1685

The Mere, Upton Park, Slough SL1 2DQ
01753 574123

Lewis, G. Mr; Powell, R Mr; Williams, S. Mr

Evaluation of Central Council for Education and Training in Social Work (CCETSW) language policy

ABSTRACT: All public bodies in Wales are now required to produce a statutory Language Plan to ensure equal treatment of Welsh with English. The present language policy of the Council for Education and Training in Social Work (CCETSW) was evaluated in terms of internal use of Welsh among staff and in CCETSW literature, the use of Welsh by training providers, and the views of students on the application of the policy. Advice was also supplied to CCETSW on amending its data collecting instruments and on revising its language policy to meet the criteria for a Language Plan. A report was sent to the sponsor.

STATUS: Sponsored project

SOURCE OF GRANT: Central Council for Education and Training in Social Work

DATE OF RESEARCH: 1996-1997

KEYWORDS: language policy; social work; wales; welsh

1686

The Mere, Upton Park, Slough SL1 2DQ
01753 574123

Kirkup, C. Ms; *Supervisors*: Whetton, C. Mr; Ashby, J. Mr

Trialling of standardised test materials for Year 4

ABSTRACT: The School Curriculum and Assessment Authority (SCAA) have commissioned the development of English tests in reading, writing and spelling for use with Year 4 pupils. The aim of this project is to administer a series of large scale trials of the tests in order to provide SCAA and the test development agency with the relevant information that they need to be able to refine the assessment instruments or to standardise them. Large scale, nationally representative, stratified samples of pupils in England and Wales are being drawn. In the case of the developmental trials, 400 pupils are used and for standardisation trials, 3500 children are targeted. Analysis is carried out on the pupils' results arising out of each of the trials and further information is obtained from a questionnaire survey of the teachers who are taking part in the trials.

STATUS: Sponsored project

SOURCE OF GRANT: School Curriculum and Assessment Authority

DATE OF RESEARCH: 1996-1997

KEYWORDS: assessment; english; key stage 2; primary education; reading skills; spelling; standardised tests; tasks and tests; test construction; tests; writing skills

1687

The Mere, Upton Park, Slough SL1 2DQ
01753 574123

Hargreaves, E. Ms; Burley, J. Ms; McCulloch, K. Ms; *Supervisor*: Sainsbury, M. Dr; Ashby, J. Mr

Trialling of National Curriculum key stage 1 task and test materials for 1998

ABSTRACT: The School Curriculum and Assessment Authority (SCAA) are developing assessment tasks and tests for use at the end of National Curriculum key stage 1 in schools in 1998. The aim of this project is to administer a series of large scale trials of the tasks and tests in mathematics, reading and spelling in order to provide SCAA with the relevant information that they need to be able to refine the assessment instruments or to standardise them. Large scale, nationally representative, stratified samples of children in England and Wales are being drawn. In the case of the developmental trials, 800 children are used and for standardisation trials, 2500 children are targeted. Analysis is carried out on the pupils' results arising out of each of the trials and further information is obtained from a questionnaire survey of the teachers who are taking part in the trials. A small number of school visits are made to observe teachers administering the tasks and tests and, by means of brief and informal interviews, to ascertain pupils' perceptions and teachers' opinions of the assessment materials.

STATUS: Sponsored project

SOURCE OF GRANT: School Curriculum and Assessment Authority

DATE OF RESEARCH: 1997-1997

KEYWORDS: assessment; key stage 1; national curriculum; primary education; standardised tests; tasks and tests; test construction; tests

1688

The Mere, Upton Park, Slough SL1 2DQ
01753 574123

Fletcher-Campbell, F. Dr; Cullen, M. Mrs; *Supervisor*: Bradley, J. Dr

The impact of delegation on local education authority support services for special educational needs

ABSTRACT: Since the introduction of Local Management of Schools, the organisation and management of support services for special educational needs have undergone considerable change. There are considerable variations in provision across England and Wales. Schools are affected by the nature of support services' work, by the mode and timing of their intervention and by the expertise available ; all this is particularly critical to addressing responsibilities laid down by the Code of Practice. The project aims to: 1) audit the resources within existing support services; 2) describe the services offered; 3) explore the patterns of delegation and the implications of each; 4) delineate the organisation and management of the services; 5) investigate the use of services made by schools and the effect of interventions on curricular provision and the addressing of needs; 6) evaluate the different models of support on schools' practice and meeting individuals' needs. Phase I involves a questionnaire survey of the support services in all local education authorities (LEAs) in England and Wales. In Phase II six authorities will be selected for indepth investigation of their services.

STATUS: Sponsored project

SOURCE OF GRANT: Council of Local Education Authorities £119,000

DATE OF RESEARCH: 1996-1998

KEYWORDS: code of practice; local education authorities; local management of schools; mainstreaming; special educational needs; support services

1689

The Mere, Upton Park, Slough SL1 2DQ
01753 574123

Morris, M. Miss; Jamison, J. Mr; *Supervisor*: Stoney, S. Dr

Evaluation of teaching and learning frameworks and use of employers

ABSTRACT: The quality and effectiveness of the British education system, and the way it could and does contribute to the country's economic effectiveness, has been of major interest to the government over the past 15 years. During the 1990s there has also been an interest in assessing outcomes, over and above academic qualifications, for insitutions and students, and identifying the relationship between these outcomes and specific school provision and processes. Identifying such relationships is not straightforward, due to the difficulties posed in identifying and measuring appropriate outcomes and because of the diversity of school structures, processes and local needs. Different initiatives have been implemented which have sought to raise young people's skills in work-related or cross-curricular areas, or to give coherence to young people's learning experiences in school. The National Curriculum (NC) is a key element of this strategy, but is not sufficient in itself, precisely because of the diversity between and within schools. Moreover, the cross-curricular themes and dimensions included within the NC pose their own problems in relation to implementation and coordination. It appears that there may be a significant loss of learning potential in schools because of this lack of coherence and integration across the curriculum: the question for policymakers and educational managers is how to optimise this potential. The two learning or outcomes frameworks (the LEntA Pathways project and the MELSO framework) that are the focus for the current research, are each premised on frameworks that purport to focus on student outcomes at NC key stages 3 and 4, although in rather different ways. One of the challenges is to impose a common frame of reference on these 2 initiatives, so that their relative merits can be explored and

assessed. The research will draw on the lessons learnt from the 'school effectiveness' research agenda, about the factors that need to be taken into account in comparing schools' performance, and also about the models that can be used to scrutinise student outcomes, including, but not restricted to, academic qualifications. It will also apply the understanding gained from studies on the management of change, which have assessed the effectiveness of in-school processes for managing initiatives in the light of schools' own priorities and circumstances. This will help form a model for input-output assessment for the secondary curriculum beyond the two particular initiatives of the research. The project aims to: 1) identify the specific objectives set by individual schools using the frameworks for pupil outcomes, including behaviour and attainment, and assess the progress achieved toward these objectives; 2) identify the changes in school management style, organisation (including information flows) and teaching and learning approaches which these schools have adopted as a result of implementing the frameworks, and assess the extent to which each of these have influenced changes in pupil outcomes, including behaviour and attainment; 3) provide an overall, indicative assessment of the potential of the frameworks to improve pupil outcomes and school effectiveness and the characteristics of the practice required to maximise such benefits. The research, to be conducted between July 1997 and September 1998, is primarily qualitative and focuses on 6 schools or clusters of schools. It will take an indepth approach to exploring each case study school's interpretation of the framework adopted, their individual experiences, and the impact that the framework had on the structures, processes and outcomes in the school. The research is in 3 stages: 1) Summer 1997 will centre on the development of an analytical schema that will provide the basis for the fieldwork. 2) Fieldwork activities, September 1997 to April 1998, will include: familiarisation visits and expert seminars in each school to introduce the evaluations; interviews with senior managers and key teachers and the establishment of a diary or critical incident strategy; data collection and document scrutiny; attendance at staff meetings, institutional planning meeting and INSET sessions; discussions with employers involved in framework-related activities; the collection of perception data through questionnaires to young people in Years 7 and 11 and discussion groups with young people in Years 6, 7 and 11 (12); 3) May 1998 to September 1998 will focus on the analysis of data and the preparation of reports.

STATUS: Sponsored project

SOURCE OF GRANT: Department for Education and Employment

DATE OF RESEARCH: 1997-1998

KEYWORDS: achievement; cross curricular approach; educational quality; employers; outcomes of education; pupil development; school effectiveness; secondary education; teaching process; work related curriculum

1690

The Mere, Upton Park, Slough SL1 2DQ
01753 574123

Lee, B. Ms

The identification of good practice in self-assessment for pupils with significant learning difficulties

ABSTRACT: Self-assessment skills are important for all young people and are now a formal requirement in many non-GCSE schemes, often used by pupils with learning difficulties at key stage 4. Self-assessment can contribute to the development of independence skills and to empowering young people with learning difficulties to plan their own development and identify the progress they are making. The research was funded by the National Lotteries Charities Board to investigate good practice. Case studies of 5 special schools were carried out between June 1997 and January 1998. A report was published in January 1999. It provides evidence of strategies used in schools to develop self-assessment skills and focuses, in particular, on pupils in key stage 4. It explores the many activities in place during this transitional period which provide opportunities for pupils to develop their self-critical skills. The report describes how teachers try to balance the promotion of pupils' confidence and self-esteem with the development of self-critical perspectives, so that pupils can take a realistic view of their strengths and weaknesses and make decisions about their plans for the future.

PUBLISHED MATERIAL: LEE, B. (1999). Self-assessment for pupils with learning difficulties. Slough: NFER.

STATUS: Sponsored project

SOURCE OF GRANT: National Lottery Charities Board

DATE OF RESEARCH: 1997-1998

KEYWORDS: **key stage 4; learning disabilities; pupil performance; secondary education; self evaluation - individuals; special educational needs**

1691

The Mere, Upton Park, Slough SL1 2DQ
01753 574123

Schagen, S. Dr

Financial literacy in the primary curriculum

ABSTRACT: In 1992, the National Foundation for Educational Research (NFER) prepared for NatWest a report which examined the concepts and competences of financial literacy and the opportunities for promoting and developing these within the school curriculum. A financial literacy programme for secondary schools was developed, piloted and evaluated and in September 1994 launched nationwide under the name Face 2 Face with Finance. Approximately 2,000 secondary schools have since registered their interest and involvement in the programme. NatWest now wishes to explore the opportunities for promoting work on financial literacy within the primary curriculum. The implementation of the National Curriculum and associated assessment procedures for key stages 1 and 2 means that only limited time is available for activities which might be regarded as 'optional extras'. Although the Dearing Review recommended that 20% of teaching time should be available for use at the individual school's discretion, primary schools responding to a recent survey said that they were intending to use this time for further work on basic literacy and numeracy, and/or the National Curriculum subjects. It would therefore be important to integrate learning about personal money management within the National Curriculum itself. The best opportunities are likely to be found in 3 areas: mathematics, information technology, and the cross-curricular themes, especially economic and industrial understanding. NatWest has asked the NFER to examine these opportunities in more detail, review existing practice and suggest possible future developments. The aims of the research will be to: 1) investigate the development of children's understanding of money matters during the primary years (ages 5 to 11) and the pedagogical questions relating to the delivery of financial literacy in the primary classroom; 2) explore methods and materials currently used to teach about money in primary schools, and find examples of good practice; 3) examine the availability of resources (such as information technology equipment) which might aid the effective delivery of financial literacy in primary schools; 4) identify the opportunities for incorporating financial literacy within the primary school curriculum; and 5) ascertain what kind of additional support or training would enable or encourage teachers to make full use of these opportunities. The project will involve the following: 1) The most recent National Curriculum Orders and curriculum guidance documents will be scanned, and the curriculum map provided in NFER's earlier report updated, with specific reference to key stages 1 and 2. 2) A literature review of research into children's understanding of money matters will be undertaken. Again, this will build on the earlier work, but relevant databases will be interrogated to ensure that more recent findings were included. 3) A telephone survey of relevant organisations will be undertaken, in order to obtain details of national and local initiatives relating to financial literacy in the primary school. Examples of good practice will be sought, together with information about the schools and teachers involved. 4) A postal survey of primary schools will be undertaken, in order to ascertain the extent of current work on financial literacy, and the likely take-up of support which might be offered as a result of this research. 5) Teachers identified during stages 3 and 4 will be interviewed by telephone in order to elicit further information about projects undertaken, and suggestions about the most effective methods of developing financial literacy in the primary school. At the end of the project, a report submitted to NatWest will: outline the findings of the literature review, and the implications for children's understanding of personal money management; map the concepts and competences of financial literacy against the National Curriculum requirements for core and foundation subjects at key stages 1 and 2; indicate the extent of existing financial literacy work in primary schools, and highlight examples

of good practice; and make recommendations for the most effective ways of developing financial literacy work in primary schools, and the support which teachers might welcome.

STATUS: Sponsored project

SOURCE OF GRANT: NatWest Group

DATE OF RESEARCH: 1996-1997

KEYWORDS: **cross curricular approach; key stage 1; key stage 2; mathematics education; money management; numeracy; primary education**

1692

The Mere, Upton Park, Slough SL1 2DQ
01753 574123

Lee, B. Ms; Brooks, R. Ms

Review of 16 plus educational provision

ABSTRACT: This literature review examined a large number of studies which have explored factors which influence the destinations of young people at 16. In particular, it explored the impact of: national education and economic systems; more localised factors such as schools and regional economics; and young people's individual characteristics such as their social class, gender and ethnicity.

STATUS: Sponsored project

SOURCE OF GRANT: National Foundation for Educational Research

DATE OF RESEARCH: 1997-1998

KEYWORDS: **access to education; ethnic groups; further education; pupil attitudes; school leavers; sex differences; sixteen to nineteen education; social class**

1693

The Mere, Upton Park, Slough SL1 2DQ
01753 574123

Sharp, C. Miss

Review of the research literature on the effects of arts teaching and learning: a mapping exercise

ABSTRACT: At an international conference on the arts in the curriculum, organised jointly by the Department of National Heritage and the School Curriculum and Assessment Authority (SCAA), participants had an opportunity to discuss research looking at the effects of additional teaching in art and music on the progress of children in reading and mathematics (FOX, A. & GARDINER, M.F. (1997). 'The arts and raising achievement'. Paper presented at the Arts in the Curriculum Conference, Lancaster House, London, 25 February 1997). It emerged that not only was this particular piece of research of interest, but that research studies of a similar nature have been carried out in the UK and elsewhere, but these are not widely known. It was felt that, if all the evidence were collected together, reviewed and widely disseminated, it would illuminate the relationships between arts teaching and pupil progress in the arts and in other areas. Such a review would be a useful document for arts practitioners, policymakers and researchers. As a first step, it is proposed that the NFER should conduct a mapping exercise to identify research studies carried out in the UK and worldwide. The mapping exercise would have the following aims: 1) To identify key pieces of research which have studied the impact of arts education on pupils' learning. 2) To map the range of research that has been conducted as a basis for a substantive review of the literature. At the mapping stage, the search would be broad, encompassing quantitative, qualitative and theoretical approaches, published work and ongoing studies of teaching and learning in the arts (defined as: music, art and design, media arts, drama, dance, and expressive writing). Two main methods would be adopted during the mapping phase: a library search; and a search through a network of contacts involved in educational research worldwide. The mapping exercise would yield a variety of information about research into the effects of arts education. A report will be submitted to SCAA, documenting the range of research that has been identified and outlining a strategy for compiling a full literature review, should further sponsorship be forthcoming. A full rigorous review of the research evidence would provide useful insights into the ways in which arts learning contributes to pupil learning, both in the arts and in other areas. It would help to raise

345

awareness of the value of the arts, and would identify areas for further study.

STATUS: Sponsored project

SOURCE OF GRANT: School Curriculum and Assessment Authority

DATE OF RESEARCH: 1997-1997

KEYWORDS: **art education; arts; creative writing; dance; drama; educational benefits; learning; literature; literature reviews; music**

1694

The Mere, Upton Park, Slough SL1 2DQ
01753 574123

Stoney, S. Dr; Saunders, L. Ms; Morris, M. Miss

Value-added measures of school effectiveness: a critical review

ABSTRACT: A critical review of value-added approaches to measuring school effectiveness is particularly important just now. Firstly there appears to be a growing recognition amongst the leading practitioners in this field that the major studies carried out in the mid-1980s may not be so relevant in the changing educational world of the 1990s: later research has thrown doubt on some of the earlier findings regarding factors which are demonstrably associated with effective schools or schools 'adding value' to their pupils' performance. Some of the changes introduced since the Education Reform Act 1988 are introducing new variables into the process of measuring so-called value-added. Secondly, there is still a lack of concensus about the procedures for measuring value-added, reflected in reports by the School Curriculum and Assessment Authority (SCAA) and the Office for Standards in Education (OFSTED). Part of the current debate focuses on the relative advantages of using National Curriculum assessments or nationally standardised cognitive ability tests as intake measures, and whether or not to adjust attainment scores by taking into account the socio-economic characteristics of the students and contextual information on each school as well as pupils' prior attainment. There is also a lively argument being conducted about whether or not multi-level modelling is the preferred statistical technique for analysing such data. Thirdly, the Dearing report on assessment and the National Curriculum and statements by the Department for Education and Employment (DfEE) indicate growing official support for the introduction of some kind of value-added approach for publicly reporting the annual performance of schools, in order to help drive up national standards of achievement. In effect, the academic debate on school effectiveness and how to measure it has now come to be incontrovertibly linked with the national political agenda for school improvement. This means that the range of interested parties now extends from politicians to school senior managers, and from academic researchers to lay governors. There is consequently a need not only to look at the technical and methodological evidence in relation to the measurement of value-added, but also to see how the different requirements of these key players can best be addressed through such measurements. The main aims of the review are to make a signficant contribution to the policy as well as to the methodological debates on value-added measures of school effectiveness, and to identify areas for further investigation by the NFER which will complement and inform its own innovative work in this field. To this end, a critical review of the value-added dimension of existing school effectiveness research - both national and international - is being undertaken which addresses issues of: 1) which outcome measures can or should be used (e.g. standard assessment task (SAT) results, GCSEs, A levels, National Vocational Qualifications (NVQs), General National Vocational Qualifications (GNVQs), post-16 destinations, other non-academic outcomes); 2) which intake measures can/should be used (e.g. cognitive ability tests, reading tests, National Curriculum assessments, baseline assessments on school entry); 3) which, if any, school context variables can/should be included; 4) which, if any, measures of social and educational disadvantage can/should be included; 5) which are the most rigorous and feasible statistical methods to be employed; 6) how to generate more differentiated analyses (e.g. by subject and/or groups of pupils); 7) what kind of conclusions can be robustly drawn from the results; and 8) what are the different uses to which the evidence can be put by schools and/or policymakers. The methods used include: a review of the research literature on the quantitative dimensions of school effectiveness, including work being done in other countries; a review of current thinking on the collection and use of data relating to school context and pupils' socio-economic backgrounds;

further analysis of value-added data which the NFER has collected for other purposes to test out hypotheses emerging from the review; strategic interviews with representatives of national bodies which have an interest in value-added measures; and a seminar of leading practitioners in the school effectiveness field to discuss the findings. The main outcomes will be a published report on all aspects of the critical review, academic journal articles and a briefing paper from the seminar of leading practitioners.

STATUS: Sponsored project

SOURCE OF GRANT: National Foundation for Educational Research

DATE OF RESEARCH: 1996-1998

KEYWORDS: **educational quality; outcomes of education; performance factors; performance indicators; school effectiveness; school improvement; value added**

1695

The Mere, Upton Park, Slough SL1 2DQ
01753 574123

Caspall, L. Ms; *Supervisor*: Whetton, C. Mr

Development and standardisation of the General Ability Test II

ABSTRACT: The General Ability Tests were first published in 1988 and comprise 4 tests namely verbal, numerical, non-verbal and spatial. The current General Ability Tests are based on normative samples in the following areas: 5th form secondary school pupils; A-level students and further education Business and Technician Education Council (BTEC) National Diploma students. The General Ability Tests are now undergoing development and standardisation in terms of normative data and the range of tests. The new version of materials will be for corporate users and guidance and further education users. The corporate users will use the materials as part of the selection process. Whereas the guidance and further education users will use the materials to identify areas of competence to assist individuals with career choices or as a tool to facilitate selection onto courses. The existing tests are to undergo revision all with a range of normative data. There will also be the development of a fifth test battery, which will be of mechanical reasoning content. There will be a combination of 8 test packages for the trials, and each package will be trialled on the following number of subjects: 100 Year 9 pupils; 100 Year 11 pupils; 100 Year 12 and 13 pupils, and 30 people in an occupational group. The trial tests would be administered by staff in the schools as a postal exercise. The standardisation sample will be a target of 1600 subjects, taking all 5 tests, as follows: 400 Year 9 pupils; 400 Year 11 pupils; 400 Year 13 pupils, taking A-levels; 200 office-based subjects from an occupational group and 200 technical-based subjects from an occupational group. The following analyses would be undertaken: classical item analysis including distractor analysis of each test for each sample; bias analyses using Mantel Haenszel procedures; mean scores and standard deviations for defined groups; correlations between each test for each sample; preparation of norms for each sample, along with percentile ranks and correlations with criterion-measures (GCSE).

STATUS: Sponsored project

SOURCE OF GRANT: NFER-NELSON

DATE OF RESEARCH: 1997-continuing

KEYWORDS: **ability tests; mechanical reasoning; nonverbal ability; numeracy; selection; spatial ability; tests; verbal ability**

1696

The Mere, Upton Park, Slough SL1 2DQ
01753 574123

Dickson, P. Mr

Development of a typology for language learning tasks

ABSTRACT: Recent work carried out by the National Foundation for Educational Research (DICKSON, P. (1996). Using the target language: a view from the classroom. Slough: NFER), and by the NFER in collaboration with Southampton University (e.g. MITCHELL, R. & MARTIN, C. (1997). 'Rote learning, creativity and "understanding" in classroom foreign language teaching', Language Teaching Research, Vol 1, No 1, pp.1-27) have included a focus on teachers' beliefs and accounts of classroom practice in modern foreign language (MFL) learning. The picture of classroom learning which emerged from these studies is one in which the following features dominated: 1) a major focus on meaning with relatively less emphasis than in the past on form; 2) an emphasis in the early stages on the learning of 'chunks' of language with no analysis of their linguistic content; 3) an emphasis in the early stages on 'rehearsal' type activities with little opportunity for the expression of personal meaning; 4) topics as the only organising principle of the syllabus; 5) no systematic approach to the learning of vocabulary and grammar; and 6) an acknowlegement of the role of motivation, reflected in the emphasis on interest and enjoyment. These observations on the current state of MFL learning in schools reflect the widely accepted aim of communication, embodied now in the National Curriculum Orders for MFLs, and, in response to the promptings of some second language acquisition (SLA) research, an increased dependence on acquisition as opposed to 'direct' learning. A central question arising from these observations is how the process of acquisition interacts with direct learning in the classroom context. There are two important issues associated with this question: 1) The learning of vocabulary and grammar in the context of the range of tasks and activities currently used by teachers. 2) The attitudes of pupils and their views on the experience of learning MFLs in the classroom - not in general terms, but in relation to the activities they undertake and the extent to which these are perceived to be effective for learning. These issues are the subject of separate proposals for research which would be based on a) an investigation of teachers' beliefs and practice in relation to relevant SLA theory and research, and b) a survey of pupils' attitudes to their language learning experience. These projects would focus on the selection and use of learning activities and the related questions of planning and management for effective classroom learning. The aim of this study is to develop a typology of classroom tasks/activities which would clarify the ways in which different tasks are oriented towards different learning objectives, and their impact on learners in terms of difficulty and effectiveness. The study will combine theoretical and practical knowledge and will be conducted in two parts: 1) a review of the literature on task-based language learning, as well as the use of tasks in SLA research; and 2) the collection of information from teachers to document the range of tasks/activities currently used and their views on the kinds of learning to which they contribute. The outcomes will be a review article produced on completion of the literature review, and an article summarising the discussions with teachers and featuring the task/activity typology.

PUBLISHED MATERIAL: DICKSON, P. (1996). Using the target language: a view from the classroom. Slough: National Foundation for Educational Research. ; MITCHELL, R. & MARTIN, C. (1997). 'Rote learning, creativity and "understanding" in classroom foreign language teaching', Language Teaching Research, Vol 1, No 1, pp.1-27.

STATUS: Sponsored project

SOURCE OF GRANT: National Foundation for Educational Research

DATE OF RESEARCH: 1997-1998

KEYWORDS: modern language studies; teaching methods

1697

The Mere, Upton Park, Slough SL1 2DQ
01753 574123

Sainsbury, M. Dr

Pupil performance in National Curriculum English key stages 1 and 2

ABSTRACT: This project will provide an indepth analysis of pupils' responses in the English national tests at National Curriculum key stages 1 and 2. Separate analyses will be made of reading, writing and spelling. Errors will be coded and quantified, and patterns of error discussed. The outcome will be a full report on each key stage, to be used in drafting the School Curriculum and Assessment Authority (SCAA) documents reporting on standards.

STATUS: Sponsored project

SOURCE OF GRANT: School Curriculum and Assessment Authority £30,000

DATE OF RESEARCH: 1997-1997

KEYWORDS: academic achievement; achievement; assessment; english; key stage 1; key stage 2; literacy; national curriculum; primary education; pupil performance; reading achievement; spelling; tasks and tests; tests; writing skills

1698

The Mere, Upton Park, Slough SL1 2DQ
01753 574123

Sainsbury, M. Dr

Baseline assessment scales for children with learning difficulties

ABSTRACT: In early 1997, the School Curriculum and Assessment Authority (SCAA) commissioned from the National Foundation for Educational Research (NFER) a set of Baseline Assessment Scales for use in assessing children in the first half term of primary school. This project will extend the scales so that they are suitable for children with learning difficulties. A group of teachers in special schools is involved in devising the new scales, and a field trial of 100 children in 15 schools will be conducted.

STATUS: Sponsored project

SOURCE OF GRANT: School Curriculum and Assessment Authority £10,000

DATE OF RESEARCH: 1997-1997

KEYWORDS: baseline assessment; learning disabilities; primary education; reception classes; school entrance age; special educational needs

1699

The Mere, Upton Park, Slough SL1 2DQ
01753 574123

Sainsbury, M. Dr

National Curriculum key stage 2 additional test administration (Summer Schools)

ABSTRACT: As a pilot project, the Government has set up 50 Summer Literacy Schools, each of which will provide 50 hours of literacy tuition for children falling below the expected level in reading at the age of 11 years. This project will evaluate the progress made by children attending the summer school, and compare it with that of a matched control group. A test similar to the National Curriculum key stage 2 reading test will be administered to both groups. A range of background information will be collected for each child, and there will also be questionnaires to ascertain the children's attitude to reading. The summer school sample consists of 1400 pupils and the control group of 2300 pupils.

STATUS: Sponsored project

SOURCE OF GRANT: School Curriculum and Assessment Authority £44,000

DATE OF RESEARCH: 1997-1997

KEYWORDS: achievement; assessment; attitudes; key stage 2; literacy; pupil attitudes; pupil improvement; reading achievement; reading attitudes; summer literacy schools; summer schools; tests

1700

The Mere, Upton Park, Slough SL1 2DQ
01753 574123

Brooks, R. Ms; Sukhandan, L. Dr; Flanagan, N. Ms; *Supervisor*: Sharp, C. Ms

Strategies to raise achievement at National Curriculum key stage 2

ABSTRACT: Recent Office for Standards in Education (OFSTED) reports have found standards among National Curriculum key stage 2 (KS2) pupils to be less satisfactory than at KS1, particularly in Years 3 and 4. The aim of this research is to identify the range and types of innovative strategies being deployed by teachers at KS2 to raise achievement, to observe and analyse the processes involved in these teaching strategies and the impact they have on pupils' classroom experiences. The research will culminate in a practical book for teachers. This will highlight examples of strategies which schools have found useful in raising achievement at KS2 through a number of case studies. Primary advisers in 157 local education authorities (LEAs) throughout England and Wales were asked to nominate 3 schools, which had specific strategies in place, to raise achievement at KS2. Positive replies were received from 100 (64%) of the LEAs. Altogether the LEAs nominated a total of 245 schools. The headteachers of the schools were then contacted by telephone and asked for brief details about their strategies. In total, information was received from 233 (95%) of the nominated schools. 12 of the 245 schools were then selected as case studies on the basis of the strategies they had implemented. Each of the case study schools was visited during the autumn or spring term of 1997/98. Information about the strategies was obtained through semi-structured interviews and observations. Relevant members of staff and pupils were interviewed in each school and parents, school governors and LEA officials were also interviewed, where appropriate. During the fieldwork visits efforts were made to obtain any relevant documentation relating to the strategy under review, such as lesson plans, school development plans and OFSTED reports. The book for teachers is to be published in the Summer 1999.

PUBLISHED MATERIAL: BROOKS, R., SUKHNANDAN, L. & SHARP, C. (1998). 'What are schools doing to raise achievement at KS2?', Education Journal, Vol 28-29, Issue 21.

STATUS: Sponsored project

SOURCE OF GRANT: National Foundation for Educational Research

DATE OF RESEARCH: 1997-1998

KEYWORDS: **achievement; classroom observation techniques; educational quality; key stage 2; primary education; pupil performance; school effectiveness; school improvement; teaching methods**

1701

The Mere, Upton Park, Slough SL1 2DQ
01753 574123

Johnson, F. Ms; *Supervisor*: Dickson, P. Mr

The role of health professionals in school-based health promotion

ABSTRACT: A growing emphasis on a 'partnership approach' to health promotion with young people has increasingly blurred what was, at one time, an absolute distinction between the teaching and medical professions. There is evidence to demonstrate that a variety of health professionals now play a greater part in the health promotion efforts of many schools, although the scope and nature of their contributions varies considerably. The main aims of the project are to: 1) present research evidence on the scope and nature of the role of health professionals in school-based health promotion; 2) explore emerging issues relating to schools' use of health professionals in school-based health promotion; 3) identify the significant features of cost-effective and educationally-effective use by schools of health professionals in school-based health promotion and provide initial evidence of good practice. This research will use a dual methodological approach. A literature search will be undertaken to provide a review of the literature written on this subject within the last decade. Key issues identified during the review will then form the basis of 5 exploratory visits and 50 telephone interviews with schools in the mainstream sectors in up to 5 local education authorities (LEAs) in order to investigate schools' perceptions of the role of health professionals, and the issues surrounding their deployment in schools. It will have a particular focus on clarifying what is meant by the term 'partnership approach'. The survey element of the project will be conducted with health education coordinators (or their equivalent) in the schools concerned.

STATUS: Sponsored project

SOURCE OF GRANT: National Foundation for Educational Research £16,000

DATE OF RESEARCH: 1997-continuing

KEYWORDS: **health personnel; health promotion; health services; nurses; primary education; pupil health and welfare; school health services; school nurses; secondary education**

1702

The Mere, Upton Park, Slough SL1 2DQ
01753 574123

Jamison, J. Mr; Johnson, F. Ms; Gray, J. Mrs; *Supervisor*: Dickson, P. Mr

The impact of class size

ABSTRACT: There is a widespread belief amongst parents, teachers and others that pupils learn more effectively in small classes. However, previous research into the relationship between class size and achievement at the secondary level has produced inconsistent results, possibly because of the difficulty of controlling for ability and the tendency for schools to group less able students together in small classes. Recent studies, notably the Tennessee Project STAR, have demonstrated the benefits of a marked reduction in class size in the early years of primary schooling. The Office for Standards in Education (OFSTED) review in 1995 also found evidence

of benefits in the early years of reduced class sizes, though pointing out that there is no simple link between class size and the quality of teaching and learning, and stressing the importance of teaching methods, class organisation and the way in which classroom assistants are used. In recent years, increasing numbers of schools have taken measures to reduce the size of early years classes. A survey by the National Union of Teachers (NUT) in 1991, for example, found more large (over 30) classes in Year 3 to Year 6 than in Year 1 and Year 2. The number of large reception classes was even smaller. Little is known, however, about the implications for schools and teachers of reducing class size at key stage 1, nor about how and why class size reductions may be translated into teaching and learning improvements. Key stage 1 class sizes are currently the renewed focus of lively educational and political debate. In identifying and investigating the key issues relating to the influence of class sizes on schools, teachers and pupils, it is intended that the NFER's research should both inform and help shape this debate. The aims of the study, which is being conducted between May 1997 and April 1998, are to: 1) investigate recent trends regarding the size of classes at key stage 1 in maintained schools in England and Wales; 2) investigate the nature of school policies on class size and the implications for schools of reducing class size at key stage 1; 3) generate information about the classroom experience of teachers of smaller classes; 4) elicit the views of teachers on how class size influences their classroom practice. The project is using both quantitative and qualitative research methods in its investigations. The methods employed encompass: 1) An initial survey of a sample of 1500 primary schools with pupils at key stage 1 using a short pro-forma to determine trends in class sizes, and to elicit information about staffing levels (teachers and assistants) and relevant policies; 2) A questionnaire survey of selected key stage 1 teachers, in up to 500 of the schools which respond to the initial survey, to investigate their views on class size and their perceptions of its influence(s) on their classroom practice; 3) Visits to 20 schools selected from the responses to the pro forma, 10 of which will be schools where class sizes at key stage 1 are large (more than 30) and 10 where they are very much smaller. Teachers will be interviewed at the beginning and end of the Autumn term of 1997 about their experiences in relation to class size and its effect on their classroom practice. The main outcome will be a final report which is to be produced in April 1998. In addition, a separate report on the findings from the pro forma survey will be produced in research summary format in the Autumn of 1997.

STATUS: Sponsored project

SOURCE OF GRANT: National Foundation for Educational Research

DATE OF RESEARCH: 1997-1998

KEYWORDS: **class size; educational quality; key stage 1; primary education; school policy; teacher attitudes**

1703

The Mere, Upton Park, Slough SL1 2DQ
01753 574123

Lewis, G. Mr

Implications of recent NFER research for the development of Welsh language policy and provision

ABSTRACT: The Welsh Unit of the National Foundation for Educational Research (NFER) has now conducted a wide range of research projects in such areas as careers guidance, adult guidance, health education and promotion, economic development and language planning. These are in addition to its major assessment and curricular projects dealing with Welsh as a first and second language. The NFER's portfolio of research and development studies have provided a variety of opportunities for considering Welsh language provision and the use of Welsh in a range of situations. For instance, during the course of one study it was found that there was a shortage of adult guidance through the medium of Welsh, and as a result, the relevant agencies decided to rectify this situation. However, a subsequent study found that there was little actual take-up of the Welsh-medium service. The availability of Welsh language provision and its relationship to take-up has been a feature of a number of other studies including a language audit for the Central Council for Education and Training in Social Work (CCETSW). It is timely, therefore, to review the evidence already gathered from NFER's unique body of work in Wales in order to analyse current language trends, and the ways in which providers determine their Welsh language policy and provision, and so help develop policy in this area. The chief aim of the project would be to draw out the implications of NFER's research for the development of Welsh language policy and provisions by education and training establishments in Wales. In particular, the review would examine: 1) How do organisations manage and resource their Welsh language provision? 2) How is the need for Welsh language provision established and how far does the type and level of provision meet expressed needs? 3) What indications are there about actual take-up of Welsh language provision? 4) What are the implications for the use of the Welsh language in different educational and training contexts? 5) What are the implications of the NFER's findings for future language planning and provision in Welsh? The review would adopt solely desk-based methods to review recent reports and data gathered by the NFER Welsh Unit. In addition to this review, reports and policy documents from other agencies would be analysed to place the NFER research into a wider context. The findings would be presented in the form a self-standing review paper, and the main conclusions would be presented in relevant journal articles. The intended audience for the report would be policymakers and managers within the education and training system who need to develop Welsh language plans and Welsh medium provision. The study would provide the stimulus for further research and would be a positive contribution to the education and training debate in Wales.

STATUS: Sponsored project

SOURCE OF GRANT: National Foundation for Educational Research

DATE OF RESEARCH: 1997-1997

KEYWORDS: bilingual education; language policy; wales; welsh; welsh medium education

1704

The Mere, Upton Park, Slough SL1 2DQ
01753 574123

Kinder, K. Ms; Haynes, J. Ms; *Supervisor*: Harland, J. Dr

The effects and effectiveness of arts education in schools

ABSTRACT: In order to substantiate the case for the arts in the curriculum there is a need for valid evidence on the outcomes of arts education in schools. This 3-year investigation will seek to identify the effects of arts education and examine the relationship between these effects and a wide range of factors associated with arts provision in schools. The study will aim to: 1) document and evidence the range of effects and outcomes attributable to school-based arts education including an examination of associations between students' participation in the arts and their general academic achievement; 2) examine the relationship between these effects and the key factors and processes associated with arts provision in schools; 3) illuminate good practice in schools' provision of high quality educational experiences in the arts; and 4) study the extent to which high levels of institutional involvement in the arts correlates with the qualities known to be associated with successful school improvement and school effectiveness. The study will use both qualitative and quantitative methods and 3 annual phases of research are planned. 5 secondary schools will be chosen as case studies based on a reputation for excellence in the arts. They will be involved throughout the phases, with interviews being undertaken with staff and students, observation of classroom practice, analysis of Quantitative Analysis for Self-Evaluation (QUASE) data, and interviews with members of the wider school community. Initial student cohorts of Year 7 and 9 students will be interviewed at all 3 phases. A survey of approximately 3,000 Year 11 students will also be undertaken prior to the sitting of GCSE examinations. An annual report on each phase will present interim findings with an overall report at the completion of the project. Dissemination events will be organised including an international seminar.

PUBLISHED MATERIAL: HARLAND, J., KINDER, K., HAYNES, J. & SCHAGEN, I. (1998). The effects and effectiveness of arts education in schools. Commissioned by the Royal Society for the Encouragement of Arts, Manufacturers and Commerce. Interim Report 1. Slough: NFER.

STATUS: Sponsored project

SOURCE OF GRANT: Royal Society of Arts; Arts Council of England; Wigan LEA; Powys LEA ; NFER

DATE OF RESEARCH: 1997-continuing

KEYWORDS: art education; arts; dance; drama; educational quality; music; outcomes of education; secondary education

1705

The Mere, Upton Park, Slough SL1 2DQ
01753 574123

Harland, J. Dr; Kinder, K. Ms; Ashworth, M. Mrs; Haynes, J. Ms

Creative arts partnerships in education: stage one evaluation

ABSTRACT: CAPE UK (Creative Arts Partnerships in Education) is an initiative which aims to provide a secure base for partnerships between schools and arts organisations to influence the perception and status of creativity as a key element in the education process across the curriculum. The NFER has been commissioned to conduct an evaluation of Stage 1 of this initiative which will take place within the Leeds and Manchester local education authorities. This Stage 1 evaluation will pursue 4 main aims: 1) To identify the staff's and management's peception of the current status, extent and level of creativity in teaching and learning. 2) To identify the expectations, intentions and anxieties of participating schools about becoming involved in the project. 3) To enable the project's management to make decisions about what organisational and managerial strategies and structures, and what teaching strategies involving external agencies, can promote creativity in schools. 4) To establish the baselines from which future change and development can be charted as the project progresses. The research will commence with a pilot survey to 23 participating schools. Following the pilot survey, case study methodology will be employed. The equivalent of 5 full fieldwork days will be spent in each of 6 school sites with interviews being undertaken with the headteacher, other senior managers, all arts-related teachers, teachers of other subjects, governors, relevant local education authority personnel and external agents (e.g. artists). Observations will also be conducted and accompanied by informal conversations with students. The 6 case studies will be selected in consulation with the CAPE UK Steering Group to represent a range of different types, settings and organisational structures. Outcomes will consists of a written report presenting an analysis of the survey and case-study data, a piloted and refined questionnaire for use in gauging school baseline details, and baseline data on the participating schools. Interactive feedback sessions will be undertaken individually with the case-study schools and collectively with the remaining surveyed schools.

STATUS: Sponsored project

SOURCE OF GRANT: CAPE UK £39,951

DATE OF RESEARCH: 1997-1998

KEYWORDS: art activities; art education; artists; arts; arts centres; cooperation; cooperative programmes; creative art; partnerships

1706

The Mere, Upton Park, Slough SL1 2DQ
01753 574123

Harland, J. Dr; Tambling, P. Ms; Kinder, K. Ms; Haynes, J. Ms; Henkhuzens, Z. Ms

Orchestral educational programmes

ABSTRACT: Since the mid-1980s, there has been a growing expectation that publicly funded arts organisations should develop education programmes. Consequently, along with other performing arts organisations in the UK, orchestras have experienced expansion in their education work over the last 10 years. This research will pursue 4 main aims: 1) To analyse the aims and purposes of educational work in orchestras, in terms of participants' perceptions of the needs of orchestras, the funding system, and the wider community. 2) To examine how these aims are translated into practice by studying the design and range of recent orchestral educational programmes. 3) To investigate the relationship between the educational work and the overall artistic mission of the orchestras and how the identity of each orchestra relates to their education policy. 4) To use the results of the research to inform developments in the policy and practice of orchestral education policy. The research will adopt a multi-site case study methodology in 6 orchestras. The equivalent of 4 full fieldwork days will be spent with each orchestra with interviews being conducted with orchestral players, workshop leaders, conductors, composers, educational personnel and key management and board members. The 6 case studies will be selected by purposive random sampling. From a random sample of UK orchestras, 6 will be chosen to provide examples to illustrate a range of different types and approaches, for example, size of the organisation, type of clients worked with, type of staffing, and geographical spread. The main outcome will be a final report.

STATUS: Sponsored project

SOURCE OF GRANT: Arts Council of England £23,830

DATE OF RESEARCH: 1997-1998

KEYWORDS: arts; music; orchestras

1707

The Mere, Upton Park, Slough SL1 2DQ
01753 574123

Harris, S. Mrs; *Supervisor*: Keys, W. Dr

Pilot study to develop test materials for an international study of 10 year olds mathematics achievement

ABSTRACT: This is a pilot study to develop test materials designed to provide information about the levels of mathematics achievement by 10 year-old pupils in England, Germany, Denmark and the Netherlands. The tests and questionnaires are being developed collaboratively by experts from each participating country. The study involves samples of about 100 pupils in up to 5 schools in each country. The intention is for the materials developed in the pilot study to be used in a large-scale comparative study using fully representative samples of schools and pupils in each country.

STATUS: Sponsored project

SOURCE OF GRANT: Nuffield Foundation £10,000

DATE OF RESEARCH: 1997-1998

KEYWORDS: achievement; assessment; comparative education; international educational exchange; mathematics achievement; mathematics education; primary education; primary school pupils; tests

1708

The Mere, Upton Park, Slough SL1 2DQ
01753 574123

Evans, J. Mrs; *Supervisors*: Bradley, J. Dr; Fletcher-Campbell, F. Dr

The operation of the Special Educational Needs Tribunal

ABSTRACT: The Special Educational Needs Tribunal (SENT) was established under the terms of the Education Act 1993 (and consolidated in the Education Act 1996) as the independent body to which parents can appeal against decisions taken by local education authorities (LEAs) with regard to the assessment of, and subsequent provision for, pupils with special educational needs. The number of appeals brought to the SENT is higher than was originally expected and there are indications that further increases are likely. The distribution of appeals across LEAs however is uneven. A survey by the Association of Metropolitan Authorities and the Association of County Councils (LGA 1997) identified a number of concerns relating to the wider impact of the SENT on local policy, strategic planning and provision and the distribution of finite resources. This research aimed to explore the impact of the SENT at LEA level. It analysed and compared events leading up to and resulting from SENT decisions in a sample of appeals, investigated the wider, long-term effects of upheld appeals and explored factors which seemed to result in a low incidence of appeals. Proformas were sent to all LEAs in England and Wales. Telephone interviews were used to follow-up approximately 30-40 responses and of these, a sample of 25 LEAs were chosen as case studies.

PUBLISHED MATERIAL: EVANS, J. (1998). Getting it right: LEAs and the Special Educational Needs Tribunal. Slough: NFER. ; EVANS, J. 'The impact of the Special Educational Needs Tribunal on LEAs' policy and planning for special educational needs', Support for Learning. (in press).

STATUS: Sponsored project

SOURCE OF GRANT: National Foundation for Educational Research

DATE OF RESEARCH: 1997-1998

KEYWORDS: appeals procedure; parent grievances; special educational needs; special educational needs tribunal

1709

The Mere, Upton Park, Slough SL1 2DQ
01753 574123

Jamison, J. Mr; Hamilton, K. Mrs; Johnson, F. Ms; Lewis, G. Mr; Saunders, L. Ms; Ashby, P. Mrs; *Supervisor*: Dickson, P. Mr

European Network of Health Promoting Schools: Evaluation of the project in England - dissemination phase

ABSTRACT: Having completed the research phase of the evaluation of the European Network of Health Promoting Schools (ENHPS) in March 1997, the National Foundation for Educational Research (NFER) has now proceeded to the dissemination phase of the project. This work continues to be sponsored by the Health Education Authority (HEA). A range of publications is planned for the Summer and Autumn of 1997. These include: 1) A summary of key findings from the ENHPS Survey of Parents (published by the HEA in July 1997). 2) The Health Promoting School: a summary of the ENHPS Evaluation Project in England - to be published by the HEA during the Autumn term of 1997. 3) The main report of the Evaluation of the ENHPS Project in England - to be published by the HEA in the Autumn term of 1997. A series of 7 regional events is planned for October and November 1997 to be managed by the HEA in partnership with local health and education professionals. Members of the NFER evaluation team will present findings from the evaluation at each of these events. The HEA has produced a resource to support the development of health promoting schools. NFER project staff have been co-authors of this document and are conducting an evaluation of its potential effectiveness, by surveying teachers in 18 schools in England. The HEA plans to publish the resource in the Summer of 1998.

STATUS: Sponsored project

SOURCE OF GRANT: Health Education Authority

DATE OF RESEARCH: 1997-1997

KEYWORDS: health education; health promoting schools; health promotion; programme evaluation

1710

The Mere, Upton Park, Slough SL1 2DQ
01753 574123

Jamison, J. Mr; Blenkinsop, S. Miss

A review of the literature on drugs education, 1992-1998

ABSTRACT: This ongoing research focuses on the sensitive issue of drug education. It aims to provide a review of the literature written on this subject between 1992 and 1998, in order to reflect the changes in legislation that have taken place during this time and the considerable work undertaken within schools and in other settings in developing drugs education for young people. It will also aim to provide conceptual clarification in an area made more problematic by difficulties in defining drugs education, and to draw together the messages from various disparate pieces of research to provide a document of interest to anyone working in the broad area of health education or research.

SOURCE OF GRANT: NFER

DATE OF RESEARCH: 1997-continuing

KEYWORDS: drug education; health education; literature reviews

1711

The Mere, Upton Park, Slough SL1 2DQ
01753 574123

Hamilton, K. Mrs

A study of non-affiliates schools' awareness of the Technology Enhancement Programme (TEP)

ABSTRACT: The technology enhancement programme (TEP) is supported by the Gatsby Charitable Foundation, and aims to 'enhance and enrich technology education and training'. It now has a paid-up membership in excess of 900 schools and further education colleges. TEP commissioned research has revealed a large scale endorsement of its work amongst teachers in its affiliated schools. The large majority of secondary schools, however, remain outside the scheme, and little was known about levels of awareness about TEP amongst technology staff in these schools. The NFER was therefore commissioned to conduct a telephone survey of secondary schools not appearing amongst the TEP member schools. 110 interviews with heads of technology or equivalent were conducted during the summer term 1997 across the 4 countries in the United Kingdom. The interviews showed that: 1) the large majority of respondents (90%) had heard of TEP; awareness was particularly high in England and Wales; 2) 85% confirmed that they received a copy of 'News and Views', the regular TEP newsletter; 3) interviewees were largely positive about TEP but were often vague about what exactly it did.

STATUS: Sponsored project

SOURCE OF GRANT: Gatsby Charitable Foundation: Technology Enhancement Programme

DATE OF RESEARCH: 1997-1997

KEYWORDS: secondary education; technology education

1712

The Mere, Upton Park, Slough SL1 2DQ
01753 5764123

Evans, G. Mrs; Williams, M. Mrs; Williams, S. Mr; Jones, E. Ms; Lewis, T. Mr; John, P. Ms; *Supervisor*: Powell, R. Mr

Baseline assessment in Wales

ABSTRACT: The 1997 Education Bill provides for the implementation of a statutory system of baseline assessment for all maintained primary, infant and nursery schools in England and Wales. By September 1998, these schools will be required to have a baseline assessment scheme in place. In December 1996, the Curriculum and Assessment Authority for Wales (ACAC) began a process of consultation to ascertain the form which baseline assessment should take in Wales. The National Foundation for Educational Research (NFER) was commissioned to conduct a survey of current practice, and then carried out a first-phase consultation in the form of a questionnaire survey of local education authority (LEA) opinion of the main findings of that survey of current practice. Both reports were submitted to ACAC in April 1997. The NFER was also commissioned by ACAC to carry out the second phase of the work. This involved a national consultation on a preferred model for baseline assessment, and the trialling of that model in a sample of schools. Final recommendations were reported to ACAC in December 1997. During the survey of current practice, a wide range of assessment schemes at present in use in various Welsh LEAs was collected. The first stage of the project required the analysis of these schemes in order to draw up several possible differing models for a national baseline assessment. Three of these models were selected through discussions with the project's monitoring group and used as the subject of the national consultation. A draft national framework for baseline assessment, used as the criterion for accrediting future assessment schemes, was drawn up and included as a consultation document. The national consultation on the assessment models and the national framework contained 3 elements: 1) a questionnaire survey of all schools in Wales with classes of under-5s; 2) 3 regional seminars for teachers and LEA personnel; 3) a national conference for LEAs and other interested bodies. The response to the consultation was analysed and one assessment model selected on the basis of that response. This model was refined and trialled with a sample of some 40-50 English and Welsh medium schools during the Autumn of 1997. The results of these trials were analysed and the findings submitted to ACAC, together with final recommendations for future baseline assessment in Wales.

STATUS: Sponsored project

SOURCE OF GRANT: Curriculum and Assessment Authority for Wales (ACAC)

DATE OF RESEARCH: 1997-1997

KEYWORDS: assessment; baseline assessment; early childhood education; infant school education; nursery school education; primary education; reception classes; school entrance age; wales; young children

1713

The Mere, Upton Park, Slough SL1 2DQ
01753 574123

Jones, G. Mrs; Evans, S. Mrs; Lewis, T. Mr; *Supervisor*: Powell, R. Mr

The development of statutory tasks and tests in Welsh for key stage 3

ABSTRACT: The Education Reform Act 1988 required statutory assessment of pupils in the core subjects in all maintained schools at the ages of 7, 11 and 14. Welsh (First Language) is a core subject in those schools in Wales which teach it as such, and the development of statutory assessment materials in Welsh at key stage 3 began in 1989. The development was sponsored by the School Examinations and Assessment Council (SEAC), and then the School Curriculum and Assesment Authority (SCAA) until 1995, when the Curriculum and Assessment Authority for Wales (ACAC) assumed responsibility for the assessment of Welsh. The present contract requires the development of materials for use in schools in 1998, 1999 and 2000. The materials produced for 1998 include tasks and tests. Oracy and oral response to reading material is assessed through the classroom task. This includes a magazine for pupils containing the stimulus material, a question book, mark schemes and teachers' guidelines. The task assesses the full range of National Curriuculum levels from 1 to 'Exceptional Performance'(EP). The materials are arranged in 3 thematic units, and individual activities are targeted at tiers of levels 1-2, 3-4. 5-6 and 7-EP. Each activity includes reading material and stimulus material for oral discussion. Pupils attempt these activities in groups of 3 and are awarded levels for oracy and reading (oral response) by their subject teacher after the group activity. The materials also include written tests for levels 3-EP. Test Paper 1 assesses reading (written response) on 2 tiers, 3-6 and 5-EP. Paper 2 assesses writing on a single tier from 3-EP. The tests are marked by external markers. Pupil levels on the reading assessments in the task and test are aggregated to provide a combined level for reading. Levels in the 3 attainment targets are then aggregated to provide a subject level. The development of materials follows a structured cycle. Discussions between the development team and its teacher panel yield ideas and themes which are worked up into early draft materials. These are trialled informally in schools during the Autumn term before a draft of the whole assessment package is submitted to ACAC in December. Following comments and amendments, the tasks and tests are evaluated through a national pre-test during the Winter and a second pre-test after Easter. The final materials are then agreed with ACAC and submitted for publication in July/August. The reading material assessed through the task was originally restricted to imaginative and literacy texts, while response to more factual material was assessed through the tests. However, in 1998 tasks and tests contain texts of both a literary and a factual or persuasive nature. Writing is assessed in the test through 2 questions, the first requiring transactional writing and the second a creative response.

STATUS: Sponsored project

SOURCE OF GRANT: Curriculum and Assessment Authority for Wales (ACAC)

DATE OF RESEARCH: 1996-continuing

KEYWORDS: assessment; key stage 3; national curriculum; secondary education; tests; welsh

1714

The Mere, Upton Park, Slough SL1 2DQ
01753 574123

Lewis, T. Mr; Davies, M. Mr; *Supervisor*: Powell, R. Mr

The development of key stage 3 non-statutory tasks and tests in Welsh Second Language

ABSTRACT: Following the Education Reform Act 1988, Welsh as a second language was made a foundation subject and compulsory for pupils up to Year 11 in all schools where it was not taught as pupils' first language and as a core subject. The compulsory obligation in key stage 4 was postponed to allow schools in some areas more time to ensure staff and resources were in place, but this dispensation ends in 2000. The development of second language assessment materials for key stage 3 began in 1989, simultaneously with statutory assessments for Welsh first language. The second language assessments were subsequently made non-statutory, but their development has continued to be sponsored, first by the School Examinations and Assessment Council (SEAC) and the School Curriculum and Assessment Authority (SCAA), and now by the Curriculum and Assessment Authority for Wales (ACAC). The assessment materials have been distributed to all schools in Wales which order them. The present 1-year contract requires the development of materials for use in schools in 1998. The 1998 materials are designed to assess all 3 attainment targets, and include a classroom task and written tests. The task includes a pupil magazine, Ifanc, a Question Book and a Teacher Guide with mark schemes. Assessment of oracy, reading and writing can all be carried out through the task which assesses the full range of attainment from National Curriculum level 1 to Exceptional Performance (EP). The materials are arranged in 3 thematic units, with activities targeted at tiers of levels 1-2, 3-4, 5-6 and 7-EP. Each activity, except those at levels 1-2, contains reading and stimulus material for oral discussion. Pupils attempt the activities in groups of 3 and are then awarded levels for oracy and reading (oral response) by their subject teacher. The magazine also contains stimulus material for classroom assessments of reading (written response) and writing on the above tiers of levels. The assessment package also includes written tests on 2 tiers - at levels 3-6 and 5-EP. Each test contains 2 questions to assess reading and one to assess writing. The reading assessment material on levels 5-6 is common to both tiers. An important innovation in the 1998 second language package is the bridging material. The 2 assessment packages for Welsh, first and second language, contain common material whereby attainment of the 2 groups of pupils can be bridged and a continuum of attainment established. The task material to assess oracy and reading (oral response) is the same for second language levels 7-EP and first language levels 3-4, and either first or second language levels can be awarded for pupil attainment on this material. These non-statutory materials can be used by teachers to support their (statutory) teacher assessment for the subject, or as internal school examination materials. The development of materials has followed a similar yearly cycle. Discussions between the development team and its teacher panel help to identify areas and themes which are worked up into early draft materials. These are trialled informally in schools before the whole assessment package is submitted to ACAC in December. Following amendments, the tasks and tests are evaluated through a national pre-test during the Winter and a second pre-test after Easter. The final materials are then agreed with ACAC and prepared for publication during June/July.

STATUS: Sponsored project

SOURCE OF GRANT: Curriculum and Assessment Authority for Wales (ACAC)

DATE OF RESEARCH: 1996-1997

KEYWORDS: assessment; key stage 3; national curriculum; secondary education; tests; welsh

1715

The Mere, Upton Park, Slough SL1 2DQ
01753 574123

Hutchison, D. Dr

Developments in bias and differential item functioning

ABSTRACT: The project is a combination of literature review and secondary analysis. It aims to: a) review the recent developments in testing based on Item Response Theory and raw data methods for differential item functioning (DIF), especially those dealing with non-dichotomous items; b) review what is required in software for these, and make recommendations for software as appropriate; c) compare the results of different types of DIF analysis.

STATUS: Sponsored project

SOURCE OF GRANT: NFER Reseaach Development Fund

DATE OF RESEARCH: 1997-1997

KEYWORDS: bias; differential item functioning; item analysis; statistical analysis; test bias; test theory; testing

1716

The Mere, Upton Park, Slough SL1 2DQ
01753 574123

Bower, R. Mr; Moore, H. Ms; Wilkin, A. Mrs; *Supervisor*: Harland, J. Dr; Kinder, K. Ms

Schools' use of non-contact days

ABSTRACT: The origins of non-contact days (NCDs) lie with the Teachers' Pay and Conditions Act of 1987 which legislated that 5 non-teaching days would be available per academic year. Recently, however, concerns about the efficacy of NCDs organisation and delivery have emerged,

including schools' planning; organisation and management of NCDs; their focus; scope and content; and their implications for staff and pupils. The project aims are to: 1) document and evaluate how schools use their NCDs; 2) examine teachers' perceptions of the merit of NCD activities; and 3) illustrate their successful practices. The study will contribute significantly to how schools design and manage NCDs, assist the development of effective LEA support and generate a framework for the analysis of wider issues, including: 1) consideration of current practice against the latest 'standard fund' guidance and other regulations; 2) NCDs, design, implementation, structure and content, as well as links with school development plans; 3) inspection and appraisal; 4) appropriateness of timing; 5) levels of resources deployed; 6) the amount of LEA involvement; 7) evaluating NCDs. Data collection techniques will be: detailed case studies in 6 schools (3 primary and 3 secondary) selected to illustrate successful or interesting practises in NCDs organisation and use, over one academic year; and condensed fieldwork visits to interview staff, at the end of the academic year, in a representative sample of 60 schools. A report of the study's findings will be produced by the end of November 1998, along with an executive summary.

STATUS: Sponsored project

SOURCE OF GRANT: NFER Membership Programme

DATE OF RESEARCH: 1997-1998

KEYWORDS: inservice teacher education; non contact days; professional development; teacher development; teaching profession

1717

The Mere, Upton Park, Slough SL1 2DQ
01753 574123

Sainsbury, M. Dr

Error analysis of Year 4 English tests

ABSTRACT: English tests for Year 4 were supplied to schools, for optional use, by the School Curriculum and Assessment Authority (SCAA) in the Summer term of 1997. In order to give teachers additional useful information about children's responses, this project conducted further analyses of scripts from pre-tests. In reading, children's correct and incorrect responses to each question were coded, quantified and analysed. In writing, various characteristics of children's compositional and presentational skills were identified and described. In spelling, incorrect attempts were quantified. The results of the study contributed towards a report supplied to all schools in the Autumn term of 1997.

STATUS: Sponsored project

SOURCE OF GRANT: School Curriculum and Assessment Authority

DATE OF RESEARCH: 1997-1997

KEYWORDS: english; primary education; reading achievement; spelling; tests; writing skills

1718

The Mere, Upton Park, Slough SL1 2DQ
01753 574123

Harris, S. Mrs; *Supervisor*: Keys, W. Dr

Review of literature relating to INSET for information technology (IT)

ABSTRACT: Within the last 10 years, information technology (IT) has been established as part of the National Curriculum and there has been a relative fall in the cost of hardware. However, are teachers adequately prepared to utilise these resources to maximise the educational benefit for their pupils? Furthermore, apart from issues of competence and confidence in the use of IT, are there other factors which influence the level of integration of IT within classroom teaching at both primary and secondary school level? This study will review the available literature so as to clarify the current position. The main aim of the literature review will be to prepare a short report presenting the findings relating to inservice training for teachers in the use of information technology to support the curriculum (i.e. as opposed to the use of IT for administrative purposes) and the implementation of IT in primary and secondary schools in the UK. It is anticipated that the review will identify gaps in the research evidence which would benefit from further investigation. The review of literature will encompass empirical work, theoretical work and guidance documents as appropriate. Main areas to be covered are likely to include: a) inservice education for teachers (INSET) in IT; b) the impact of utilising computers in the classroom on teachers' existing pedagogy; c) factors which impact on the level of computer integration; d) the IT coordinator. The main source for references will be the British Education Index on International ERIC.

PUBLISHED MATERIAL: HARRIS, S. (1999). INSET for IT: a review of the literature relating to preparation for and use of IT in schools. Slough: NFER.

STATUS: Sponsored project

SOURCE OF GRANT: NFER Research and Development Fund

DATE OF RESEARCH: 1997-1998

KEYWORDS: **computer uses in education; information technology; inservice teacher education; literature reviews; primary education; secondary education**

1719

The Mere, Upton Park, Slough SL1 2DQ
01753 574123

Evans, G. Mrs; *Supervisor*: Powell, R. Mr

Pretesting key stage 2 Welsh tasks and tests

ABSTRACT: Statutory tasks and tests to assess Welsh at key stage 2 were developed since their inception in 1993 by the PASG agency at Bangor. However, the Curriculum and Assessment Authority for Wales (ACAC) have now awarded separate contracts for development and pretesting. The pretesting project involves receiving the draft assessment materials from the development agency and pretesting them in a national sample of Welsh-medium schools. The task materials assess oracy, oral response to reading material, and writing, and a reading test assesses written response to text. Teachers trial some three-quarters of the materials themselves and the National Foundation for Educational Research (NFER) officers visit schools to pretest the remainder. A first national pretest with some 70 schools is held in January/February each year, and a smaller second national pretest in March/April. The results of pupil performance in the task and test, together with a teacher questionnaire on the appropriateness of the materials and assessment arrangements, are analysed by the NFER. A report on each pretest is then submitted to ACAC with recommendations for amendments to the materials.

STATUS: Sponsored project

SOURCE OF GRANT: Curriculum and Assessment Authority for Wales

DATE OF RESEARCH: 1997-continuing

KEYWORDS: **assessment; key stage 2; primary education; tests; welsh**

1720

The Mere, Upton Park, Slough SL1 2DQ
01753 574123

Sims, D. Mr

College service-level agreements: follow-up evaluation

ABSTRACT: This study is a follow-up evaluation of the service level agreement (SLA) between Learning Partnership West (previously Careers Service West) and local colleges. The evaluation aims to establish whether there has been any change in the understanding of the SLA's purpose, to ascertain how it is used and to find out what impact it has had on learning and student support. The main research method is a programme of group discussions with college staff. The data will be analysed and a report will be widely disseminated.

STATUS: Sponsored project

SOURCE OF GRANT: Learning Partnership West £7,000

DATE OF RESEARCH: 1997-1998

KEYWORDS: **career education; careers service; programme evaluation; vocational guidance**

1721

The Mere, Upton Park, Slough SL1 2DQ
01753 574123

Sainsbury, M. Dr

Development of English tests and tasks at National Curriculum key stage 1 for the years 2000-2002

ABSTRACT: Children at the end of key stage 1 of the National Curriculum, at about the age of 7, are assessed in a range of ways, according to their level of attainment. In reading, pupils at levels 1 and 2 take an individual assessment task in which they read aloud to their teacher and discuss what they have read. Children at levels 2 and 3 take a written comprehension test. Children at all 3 levels produce a piece of writing according to direction from their teachers in the course of an informal assessment task. There is also a spelling test, which is compulsory for levels 2 and 3 and optional for level 1. This project will develop all these materials for use in the 3 years from 2000-2002. The work will involve: selection of texts and devising of questions for the comprehension tests; selection of books for the task booklist; review and revision of the instructions for the writing task; development of spelling tests. All materials will be subject to 2 rounds of large-scale field trials. Materials under development will be subject to review by practising teachers and by specialists in a range of relevant fields, as well as by the Qualifications and Curriculum Authority (QCA) consultants and officers.

SOURCE OF GRANT: Qualifications and Curriculum Authority

DATE OF RESEARCH: 1998-continuing

KEYWORDS: **assessment; english; key stage 1; national curriculum; primary education; reading achievement; tasks and tests; tests; writing skills**

1722

The Mere, Upton Park, Slough SL1 2DQ
01753 574123

Sainsbury, M. Dr; Twist, L. Ms

Development of English tests and tasks at National Curriculum key stage 2 for the years 2000-2002

ABSTRACT: Children at the end of key stage 2, at about the age of 11, are assessed by means of 3 English tests addressing levels 3-5 of the National Curriculum: reading; writing; and spelling and handwriting. Pupils of particularly high attainment, who may achieve level 6, take an additional extension paper. This project will develop all these materials for use in the 3 years from 2000-2002. The work will involve: selection of texts and devising of questions for the reading tests; production of suitable prompts for the writing tests; development of spelling tests. For each of these, 2 alternative test packs will be produced each year. All materials will be subject to 2 rounds of large-scale field trials. Materials under development will be subject to review by practising teachers and by specialists in a range of relevant fields, as well as by the Qualifications and Curriculum Authority (QCA) consultants and officers.

STATUS: Sponsored project

SOURCE OF GRANT: Qualifications and Curriculum Authority

DATE OF RESEARCH: 1998-continuing

KEYWORDS: **assessment; english; handwriting; key stage 2; national curriculum; primary education; reading achievement; spelling; tasks and tests; tests; writing skills**

1723

The Mere, Upton Park, Slough SL1 2DQ
01753 574123

Sainsbury, M. Dr

Development of English tests for Years 3, 4 and 5

ABSTRACT: It is the policy of the Qualifications and Curriculum Authority (QCA) to provide test and assessment materials which allow teachers to monitor the progress of their pupils in the course of National Curriculum key stage 2. Currently, a range of materials is available, addressed at Year 4, and QCA wishes to supplement these. Sets of English tests will be produced for Years 3 and 5 in the course of the 1997-8 school year. A further set for Year 4 will be produced during 1998-9. This project will develop these sets of materials. For reading, a variety of texts will be sought and questions developed to address a range of the key skills set out in the key stage 2 programmes of study. There will be a writing test where children are required to produce 2 pieces of writing of different types. Spelling will be assessed separately by means of a 20-word test, with the words set in context in a passage. The tests will be subject to 2 rounds of field trials and a large-scale standardisation, but this work is contracted separately.

STATUS: Sponsored project

SOURCE OF GRANT: Qualifications and Curriculum Authority

DATE OF RESEARCH: 1997-1998

KEYWORDS: **ability tests; assessment; english; primary education; reading achievement; spelling; tests; writing skills**

1724

The Mere, Upton Park, Slough SL1 2DQ
01753 574123

Sainsbury, M. Dr

Survey of literacy hours

ABSTRACT: From September 1998, all primary schools will be required to have a literacy hour. The details of this requirement are not entirely clear, although it is likely that the structure of these hours will be based on that of the existing National Literacy Project. This project aims to estabish the prevalence and structure of literacy hours in schools in early 1998, before the introduction of the formal requirement. By means of a survey of local education authorities and, where necessary, of individual schools, it will investigate how many schools currently operate a literacy hour. Further, it will include a documentary analysis to establish the structure, content and methods of existing models of literacy hour, including that of the National Literacy Project. This should provide a framework for the analysis of the new requirements, and could also underpin a wider evaluation of the success of the literacy hour initiative.

PUBLISHED MATERIAL: SAINSBURY, M. (1998). Literacy hours: a survey of the national picture in the Spring term of 1998. Slough: NFER.

STATUS: Sponsored project

SOURCE OF GRANT: NFER Research and Development Fund

DATE OF RESEARCH: 1998-1998

KEYWORDS: **literacy; literacy hours; national literacy project; primary education; reading**

1725

The Mere, Upton Park, Slough SL1 2DQ
01753 574123

Lee, B. Ms; Sukhnandan, L. Dr

Streaming, setting and grouping pupils by ability

ABSTRACT: The research will carry out a thorough review of the literature on streaming, setting and grouping of pupils and identify questions for a further investigation to be carried out in schools. The study will examine the literature on the effects of different grouping arrangements in the following areas: primary and secondary schools; different curriculum areas; classes of different sizes. Research on teacher attitudes to grouping and their teaching and learning approaches will also be explored. A written review of the literature will be produced and the findings analysed in the context of the current situation in Britain in the 1990s, where pressure for more streaming and setting appears to be growing.

PUBLISHED MATERIAL: SUKHNANDAN, L. & LEE, B. (1998). Streaming, setting and grouping by ability: a review of the literature. Slough: NFER.

STATUS: Sponsored project

SOURCE OF GRANT: NFER Research and Development Programme

DATE OF RESEARCH: 1998-1998

KEYWORDS: **grouping - teaching purposes; literature reviews; primary education; secondary education; setting; streaming; teacher attitudes**

1726

The Mere, Upton Park, Slough SL1 2DQ
01753 574123

Milne, A. Mrs; Minnis, M. Ms

Evaluation and testing programme for the National Literacy Project

ABSTRACT: The National Foundation for Educational Research (NFER) has been asked by the Qualifications and Curriculum Authority (QCA) to undertake a testing programme as part of the evaluation of the National Literacy Project. The aim of the programme is to monitor progress within the project by collecting and analysing pupil test results and background data. Analysis and reporting, including the calculation of progress measures, is taking place at pupil level, school level, local education authority (LEA) level and nationally. The project began in Autumn 1996 and will finish in Summer 1998. Two cohorts of pupils in 15 LEAs are taking part for a period of two academic years. The pupils are tested on entry to the project and again on exit. The first cohort (30,000 pupils) completed exit tests in Summer 1998. Analysis of these test results showed that, generally, scores had improved beyond what would have been expected. The second cohort (30,000 pupils) will undertake exit tests in Summer 1999. Progress made by these pupils will be compared to a matched control group (9,000 pupils) undertaking the same testing regime but with no input from the National Literacy Project.

PUBLISHED MATERIAL: SAINSBURY, M. (1998). Evaluation of the National Literacy Project. Summary Report. London: Department for Education and Employment.

STATUS: Sponsored project

SOURCE OF GRANT: Qualifications and Curriculum Authority £125,693

DATE OF RESEARCH: 1996-continuing

KEYWORDS: **assessment; literacy; longitudinal studies; national literacy project; primary education; tests**

1727

The Mere, Upton Park, Slough SL1 2DQ
01753 574123

Milne, A. Mrs; Minnis, M. Ms

Evaluation and testing programme for the National Numeracy Project

ABSTRACT: The National Foundation for Educational Research (NFER) has been asked by the Qualifications and Curriculum Authority (QCA) to undertake the testing programme associated with the evaluation of the National Numeracy Project. The aim of the programme is to monitor progress within the project by collecting and analysing pupil test results and background data. Analysis and reporting is taking place at pupil level, school level, local education authority (LEA) level and nationally. The National Numeracy Project involves 3 cohorts of pupils in 13 LEAs. Each cohort of pupils (approximately 30,000) takes part in the project for 2 academic years and undertakes a specially designed test on entry, midway and on exit from the project. The first cohort of pupils entered the project in January 1997 and completed exit tests in Summer 1998. Analysis of these test results showed a significant improvement in numeracy skills as measured by the tests, particularly in mental calculations. The second cohort will be undertaking exit tests in Summer 1999. Progress made by these pupils will be compared to a matched control group (9,000 pupils) undertaking the same testing regime but with no input from the National Numeracy Project.

PUBLISHED MATERIAL: MINNIS, M., FELGATE, R. & SCHAGEN, I. (1999). National Numeracy Project: Technical report. Slough: NFER.

STATUS: Sponsored project

SOURCE OF GRANT: Qualifications and Curriculum Authority £168,459

DATE OF RESEARCH: 1997-continuing

KEYWORDS: **assessment; longitudinal studies; mathematics education; national numeracy project; numeracy; primary education; tests**

1728

The Mere, Upton Park, Slough SL1 2DQ
01753 574123

Taylor, M. Dr

Research and development support for remotivating young people through social mentoring and values education

ABSTRACT: This consultancy is offering research and development support to Values Education for Life (VEFL), a charity based in East

Birmingham, working with disadvantaged and disaffected young people, whom it aims to remotivate through a programme of social mentoring and values education. With support from the European Social Fund, VEFL has also developed a training programme for adult social mentors, which focuses on values education and is accredited by the University of Central England. VEFL is now extending its work through a pilot partnership project being undertaken with the social mentors and young people in Years 8 and 9 in a Birmingham secondary school. In weekly PSE lessons, social mentors are working as volunteers with form tutors, sharing their skills, experience and specific awareness of socio-cognitive development from their training with staff and students. The consultancy (financed by the Department for Education and Employment through VEFL) is acting as a 'critical friend' to the project in its development over two years. It is undertaking a programme of qualitative research inquiry with both VEFL and the school, involving: individual interviews with project and school managers, mentors and teachers; class observations; and focus groups with mentors, teachers and pupils. The evaluation is focusing on the training for social mentoring and its transfer to another institutional context; school processes and activities and the effects on and implications for the school of participating in such a project; pupil participation and development; and implications for VEFL and its future development. The case study will offer an overview of issues for schools and partnership projects attempting to develop new ways of remotivating young people through socio-moral development within the school.

STATUS: Sponsored project

SOURCE OF GRANT: Department for Education and Employment via Values Education for Life

DATE OF RESEARCH: 1997-continuing

KEYWORDS: adolescents; consultancy; disadvantaged; disaffection; mentor training; mentors; moral development; social development; social mentoring; values education; youth

1729

The Mere, Upton Park, Slough SL1 2DQ
01753 574123

Fletcher-Campbell, F. Dr; Brooks, R. Miss; Harland, J. Dr; Kinder, K. Ms; Lewis, G. Mr; *Supervisor*: Bradley, J. Dr

Evaluation of the National Professional Qualification for Headship (NPQH)

ABSTRACT: Headteachers are faced with an unparalleled array of challenges in the present educational climate and the spotlight is firmly focused on them to prove effective leadership in support of the Government's thrust to improve standards. They have to fulfil responsibilities in areas as diverse as curriculum and assessment, staff development and finance, each of which require strategic and operational management, as well as maintaining a presence in the community and considering aspects of marketing. The task of ensuring overall coherence for all these operations is formidable and there is widespread agreement that headteachers cannot be adequately prepared for headship merely by 'on-the-job' training or by holding a deputy's post. In view of this situation, and as part of its programme of professional development throughout a teacher's career, the Teacher Training Agency (TTA) has initiated a professional qualification for headteachers - the National Professional Qualification for Headship (NPQH). It has commissioned the NFER to undertake an evaluation of the training and assessment arrangements for this qualification in its first year of operation. The evaluation aims to assess the quality of the procedures and processes adopted by the Regional Training Centres and Assessment Centres appointed to deliver the NPQH, and to provide the TTA with formative evidence as a basis for future planning. Visits will be made to each of the 10 Training Centres and the 10 Assessment Centres and to the provider of the Supported Open Learning route to gaining the qualification. In each area, a variety of research strategies will be used in order to collect a range of perspectives and allow for the triangulation of data. Strategies will include: 1) indepth semi-structured interviews with all the Centre Managers focusing on the organisation and management of the Centres with respect to the TTA's criteria for quality, and the policies, procedures, and practices which have been established in order to fulfil these criteria; 2) an examination and analysis of any data collected by the Centres in the course of their internal monitoring, review and evaluation procedures; 3) a survey of a sample of candidates, exploring their perceptions of their

experiences of the process to date, followed by focus groups involving a small sample of candidates to explore in greater detail some of the issues raised in the responses to the candidate survey; 4) obervation of the process of assessment and training; 5) interviews with a sample of assessors and trainers; 6) an examination and analysis of course materials produced for the NPQH; and 7) a questionnaire survey of all LEAs in England and Wales to ascertain their involvement with the regional centres. The project will report to the TTA at various stages during and at the end of the project, to indicate any difficulties arising as training and assessment for the qualifcation are implemented, and also suggested solutions that are grounded in emerging good practice in order to facilitate the TTA's own development work.

STATUS: Sponsored project

SOURCE OF GRANT: Teacher Training Agency

DATE OF RESEARCH: 1998-1998

KEYWORDS: head teachers; national professional qualification for headship; professional development; teacher development; teaching profession

1730

The Mere, Upton Park, Slough SL1 2DQ
01753 574123

Cullen, M-A. Mrs; Osgood, J. Ms; Kelleher, S. Ms; *Supervisor*: Fletcher-Campbell, F. Dr

Alternative educational provision at National Curriculum key stage 4

ABSTRACT: A number of local authorities, public sector and voluntary organisations work with schools and units to provide alternative, or adapted, education for pupils perceived as unlikely to benefit from the GCSE/General National Vocational Qualification (GNVQ) mainstream curricula. This project aims to identify, describe and analyse effective practice - that is, practice which meets needs, supports young people at a difficult time of their lives, and equips them to plan positively for their future in employment, education or training. The criteria for effective practice will develop in the course of the project as understanding of aims, objectives and working practices of alternative educational initiatives is gained. Questionnaires will be sent to schools and providers in 14 local education authorities across England and Wales. Case study work will be carried out in a number of schools using different sorts of provision. In each case study school, a small number of pupils involved in such initiatives will be asked to become the focus of a detailed study of how alternative educational provision works in practice. This will involve interviewing the pupils themselves but also relevant staff in the pupils' schools and in other organisations involved in the initiatives - both those working directly with the initiatives and those responsible for referring the pupils to them. The views of the pupils' parents/carers will also be sought. The main outcome of the project will be a Good Practice Guide for schools and providers.

STATUS: Sponsored project

DATE OF RESEARCH: 1998-continuing

KEYWORDS: alternative education; disaffection; disruptive pupils; key stage 4; local education authorities; secondary school pupils; special educational needs; suspension; truancy; voluntary agencies

1731

The Mere, Upton Park, Slough SL1 2DQ
01753 574123

Ashby, J. Mr; Harris, S. Mrs; Sturman, L. Ms

Test development and pre-testing 2000-2002 National Curriculum key stage 2 science

ABSTRACT: The Education Reform Act 1988 required national testing of children in all maintained schools at the age of 7, 11, 14 and 16. For children nearing the end of key stage 2 (age 11), science tests at levels 3-6 are currently administered in May each year. The aim of the project is to develop materials for use in the national assessment of science in England at key stage 2 in the years 2000 to 2002. The specification requires written tests covering attainment targets 2-4 at levels 3-5, together with an extension test for level 6. Questions are written by a team of teacher-writers and submitted to the National Foundation for

Educational Research (NFER) for review. The review process incorporates the views of external specialists in science and in primary teaching. Following review, questions are developed further and trialled informally. This results in a pool of questions from which tests can be constructed. Later reviews focus on the accessibility of the tests to children with special educational needs or who are learning English as an additional language. Two national pre-tests are carried out, with the final pre-test making use of tests in as close to the final form as possible. From this exercise, accurate statistical data on the performance of the tests are obtained. The tests are accompanied by mark schemes, which are refined in conjunction with external marking agencies.

STATUS: Sponsored project

SOURCE OF GRANT: Qualifications and Curriculum Authority

DATE OF RESEARCH: 1998-continuing

KEYWORDS: **assessment; key stage 2; national curriculum; primary education; science education; tests**

1732

The Mere, Upton Park, Slough SL1 2DQ
01753 574123

Lewis, G. Mr; Williams, S. Mr

Evaluation of adult guidance for Mid-Glamorgan Training and Enterprise Council

ABSTRACT: This study examined the model adopted for delivering adult guidance in the Mid-Glamorgan Training and Enterprise Council (TEC) area. It also appraised the network groupings that underpinned the provision of adult guidance. The study also demonstrated a number of client gains accrued from this provision. A report has been sent to Mid-Glamorgan TEC.

STATUS: Sponsored project

SOURCE OF GRANT: Mid-Glamorgan Training and Enterprise Council £5,000

DATE OF RESEARCH: 1997-1998

KEYWORDS: **training and enterprise councils**

1733

The Mere, Upton Park, Slough SL1 2DQ
01753 574123

Lewis, G. Mr; Williams, S. Mr; Lewis, T. Mr

Evaluation of Competitiveness Fund in Wales

ABSTRACT: This study examined the impact of the funding provided by the Competitiveness Fund to enhance the links between employers and further education (FE) colleges. It gathered views from all Training and Enterprise Councils (TECs) and FE colleges in Wales, as well as a sample of 150 employers. It found that the Fund met its objectives and enhanced liaison between employers and colleges. This was mainly achieved by enabling colleges to deliver training linked to modern apprenticeships by providing industrial grade equipment. A report has been sent to the council of Welsh Training and Enterprise Councils.

STATUS: Sponsored project

SOURCE OF GRANT: Council of Welsh Training and Enterprise Councils £22,000

DATE OF RESEARCH: 1997-1998

KEYWORDS: **educational finance; employers; further education; training and enterprise councils**

1734

The Mere, Upton Park, Slough SL1 2DQ
01753 574123

Lewis, G. Mr; Williams, S. Mr

Take-up of Welsh language provision in Care training

ABSTRACT: This study examined the extent of the take-up of Welsh medium training leading to the Diploma in Social Work and National Vocational Qualification (NVQ) in Care. It found that students were reluctant to avail themselves of the whole range of Welsh medium provision. The study recommendations argue for enhancing the link

between the vocational value of the use of Welsh and actual training. A report was presented to the Central Council for Education and Training in Social Work (CCETSW).

STATUS: Sponsored project

SOURCE OF GRANT: Central Council for Education and Training in Social Work £12,000

DATE OF RESEARCH: 1997-1998

KEYWORDS: **social work; social work studies; welsh; welsh medium education**

1735

The Mere, Upton Park, Slough SL1 2DQ
01753 574123

Barraclough, S. Miss; *Supervisor*: Evans, J. Mrs

Educational interventions for pupils with autistic spectrum disorders

ABSTRACT: Increasing numbers of pupils are being identified as affected by disorders on the autistic spectrum. This may be due to a number of factors including: more effective assessment; greater awareness of these disorders; or, an increase in incidence. Such pupils have a range of difficulties across a triad of impairments: social impairment (difficulties in interacting with both adults and peers); communication impairment (difficulties in all aspects of communication); and flexibility impairment (characterised by repetitive stereotyped behaviour). These difficulties, taken together, constitute autistic spectrum disorders. As more is learnt about educational interventions for pupils with these difficulties, a greater variety of teaching methods has emerged to deal with them, and currently there is no consensus about the effectiveness of these different approaches. The National Foundation for Educational Research (NFER) research is focusing on interventions for younger children (preschool and key stage 1) and will explore the ways in which autistic spectrum disorders are identified, the ways in which parents are supported, issues of inter-agency collaboration and the range of educational interventions being used in local education authorities.

STATUS: Sponsored project

SOURCE OF GRANT: NFER

DATE OF RESEARCH: 1998-continuing

KEYWORDS: **autism; intervention; special educational needs**

1736

The Mere, Upton Park, Slough SL1 2DQ
01753 574123

Lee, B. Ms; Brooks, R. Ms

Review of professional development in further education

ABSTRACT: The further education (FE) sector has witnessed considerable change over the past decade. The introduction of incorporation, franchising arrangements, new courses and curricula have placed increasing demands on FE managers, lecturers and learning support staff to develop new competences in a wide range of areas. This project will review research, conducted over the past 10 years, which has explored issues connected to professional development in FE. The report will discuss the findings in relation to recent changes in the sector and will identify areas for future research.

STATUS: Sponsored project

SOURCE OF GRANT: NFER

DATE OF RESEARCH: 1998-continuing

KEYWORDS: **colleges of further education; further education; professional development; staff development; teacher development**

1737

The Mere, Upton Park, Slough SL1 2DQ
01753 574123

Rudd, P. Dr; *Supervisor*: Saunders, L. Ms

Overview of school effectiveness and school improvement literature

ABSTRACT: In the last 5 years or so there has been a huge expansion in the literature on school effectiveness and school improvement. The literature is currently so vast that those concerned with school improvement barely have time to consider new publications and their implications. This is especially true for practitioners who often have very little time to assimilate research findings and even less time to implement recommendations and governmental requirements. The need for assistance with the literature on school improvement at a practitioner level is likely to increase as official frameworks for target-setting and school self-evaluation are put into place. One aspect of the school improvement literature, that relating to 'Value added measures of school effectiveness', has been subjected to critical review in another NFER project, but this has been of a rather specialist nature and a more generalised overview of the literature is now required. The overview will relate to both primary and secondary schools. The aim will be to cut a path through the 'jungle' of school improvement research so that practitioners, policymakers, local education authority advisers, academics and others with concerns in this area can make sense of this ever-expanding literature. This will enable those with specialised interests to access the relevant literature quickly and efficiently. An important part of the project will be to provide an overview by devising and organising appropriate thematic areas. Appropriate themes and classifications of the literature will be developed as the review progresses. Three articles/publications will be produced from this project: 1) The full review, combining both theoretical and practical themes related to school improvement. 2) A shorter report emphasising the latest developments in school improvement in practice. This could be aimed at practitioners and policymakers. 3) A journal article. This will present the latest theoretical developments in a coherent form for those with an academic interest in the school improvement literature.

STATUS: Sponsored project

SOURCE OF GRANT: NFER

DATE OF RESEARCH: 1998-continuing

KEYWORDS: **educational quality; literature reviews; school effectiveness; school improvement**

1738

The Mere, Upton Park, Slough SL1 2DQ
01753 574123

Sainsbury, M. Dr

Evaluation of the National Literacy Project

ABSTRACT: The first cohort of the National Literacy Project involved approximately 250 schools in 17 local education authorities (LEAs) and ran from Autumn 1996 to Summer 1998. Participating schools implemented a new literacy policy including a daily literacy hour. Training and consultancy advice was available to these schools. This research aimed to evaluate the success of the project in terms of pupils' progress in reading and their attitudes to reading. Tests and attitude questionnaires were administered at the beginning and end of the period, and results analysed in the light of a range of background factors.

PUBLISHED MATERIAL: SAINSBURY, M. (1998). Evaluation of the National Literacy Project. Summary Report. London: Department for Education and Employment.

STATUS: Sponsored project

SOURCE OF GRANT: Department for Education and Employment

DATE OF RESEARCH: 1998-1998

KEYWORDS: **literacy; national literacy project; primary education; programme evaluation; pupil improvement; reading; reading achievement; reading skills**

1739

The Mere, Upton Park, Slough SL1 2DQ
01753 574123

Sainsbury, M. Dr

Key stage 1 English test development and pretesting 2000-2002

ABSTRACT: All 7 year-olds at the end of key stage 1 are required to take national tests in English covering reading and writing at Levels 1-3 of the National Curriculum. This research project will develop the tests to be used in the years 2000 to 2002. The development process each year consists of initial work with teachers and consultants, and then 2 large-scale pre-tests. Each year, 2 complete sets of tests are produced, and one of these chosen for final use.

STATUS: Sponsored project

SOURCE OF GRANT: Qualifications and Curriculum Authority

DATE OF RESEARCH: 1998-continuing

KEYWORDS: **assessment; english; key stage 1; national curriculum; primary education; tasks and tests; test construction; tests**

1740

The Mere, Upton Park, Slough SL1 2DQ
01753 574123

Sainsbury, M. Dr

Evaluation of Summer School programme

ABSTRACT: The incoming government in 1997 instituted a programme of summer schools for 11 year-old pupils who had not reached the standard expected of their age, Level 4 of the National Curriculum. In 1998, this summer school programme was expanded considerably to include: over 500 Summer Literacy Schools; a pilot programme of 15 Summer Literacy Schools for pupils with special educational needs; and a pilot programme of 50 Summer Numeracy Schools. This research project aims to evaluate all three of these types of summer school, using all the schools in the 2 pilot programmes and a 10% sample of the Summer Literacy Schools. The evaluation has 3 strands. Participating children are tested at the beginning and end of the summer school period to ascertain their progress in literacy or numeracy. At the same time, pupils complete a questionnaire to judge their attitudes to literacy or numeracy. The third element of the study is a qualitative investigation into target-setting processes within summer schools.

PUBLISHED MATERIAL: SAINSBURY, M., CASPALL, L., MCDONALD, A., RAVENSCROFT, L. & SCHAGEN, I. (1999). Evaluation of the 1998 summer schools programme: full report. Slough: NFER.

STATUS: Sponsored project

SOURCE OF GRANT: Department for Education and Employment

DATE OF RESEARCH: 1998-1998

KEYWORDS: **literacy; mathematics education; numeracy; programme evaluation; pupil attitudes; pupil improvement; reading; special educational needs; summer literacy schools; summer numeracy schools; summer schools**

1741

The Mere, Upton Park, Slough SL1 2DQ
01753 574123

Sainsbury, M. Dr

Follow-up of pupils in 1997 summer schools

ABSTRACT: The incoming government in 1997 instituted a programme of summer schools for 11 year-old pupils who had not reached the standard expected of their age, Level 4 of the National Curriculum. During the summer holidays of 1997, 50 Summer Literacy Schools were set up, each to provide 50 hours of focused literacy tuition for about 30 pupils. The evaluation of this initiative showed that, although there were gains in confidence and enthusiasm amongst the pupils, their reading attainments, as measured by end of key stage tests, fell over the summer period, as did those of pupils not attending summer schools. In July 1998, the same pupils, now at the end of Year 7, were tested again, and completed the same attitude questionnaire, to ascertain how their reading attainments and attitudes had progressed in the intervening year.

STATUS: Sponsored project

SOURCE OF GRANT: Department for Education and Employment

DATE OF RESEARCH: 1998-1998

KEYWORDS: **followup studies; pupil improvement; reading; reading achievement; summer literacy schools; summer schools**

1742

The Mere, Upton Park, Slough SL1 2DQ
01753 574123

Ruddock, G. Dr

International comparisons of pupil performance: TIMSS - R (Repeat)

ABSTRACT: The TIMSS - Repeat study is a smaller scale repeat of the TIMSS instrument carried out in 1995, to obtain international comparisons of pupil attainment in mathematics and science. The TIMSS - R study will collect data on pupil attainment at age 13, in about 12 countries. Trials will take place in 1998, with testing and data collection in 1999, and results reported in 2000.

STATUS: Sponsored project

SOURCE OF GRANT: Department for Education and Employment

DATE OF RESEARCH: 1998-continuing

KEYWORDS: **academic achievement; comparative education; cross national studies; mathematics education; pupil performance; science education**

1743

The Mere, Upton Park, Slough SL1 2DQ
01753 574123

Keys, W. Dr

OFSTED/DfEE joint research on homework policy and guidance

ABSTRACT: The aim of the project was to provide a sound basis for the development of national guidelines on homework, promised in the 1997 White Paper 'Excellence in Schools'. It involved a systematic review of research literature; analysis of the OFSTED database; a structured telephone questionnaire survey of 368 schools identified through the database as having good homework practice; visits to 29 of the schools; and a questionnaire survey of about 1000 National Curriculum key stage 2 and 3 pupils at those schools. It found that homework was most effective when: 1) schools had clear policies and all parties - teachers, pupils and parents - knew what was expected of them; 2) homework was planned alongside school schemes of work; 3) pupils received prompt, clear feedback on their work; 4) there was firm leadership and a team approach, to ensure consistent practice.

STATUS: Sponsored project

SOURCE OF GRANT: Department for Education and Employment £18,800

DATE OF RESEARCH: 1997-1998

KEYWORDS: **homework; literature reviews; primary education; secondary education**

1744

The Mere, Upton Park, Slough SL1 2DQ
01753 574123

Morris, M. Miss; Lines, A. Mrs; Golden, S. Ms

Follow-up evaluation on the impact of enhanced Careers Education and Guidance on young people in Years 9 and 10 and transition at 16

ABSTRACT: The Department for Education and Employment (DfEE) conducted a baseline study in 1995 to look at Careers Education and Guidance (CEG) provision and its impact on young people in Years 9 and 10. The new project follows on from this original study. It aims to examine CEG in Years 9 and 10 and identify changes in provision since 1995. It will also examine the extent to which changes in implementation and provision of CEG have influenced pupil outcomes in Years 9 and 10. The project's second aim is to examine transition at 16 and early post-16 outcomes. The influence of CEG provision received in Year 9 and subsequently will be looked at. The research will consist of indepth interviews with careers and schools' staff and quantitative surveys of young people in Years 10, 11 and first year post-16. Research findings are pending.

STATUS: Sponsored project

SOURCE OF GRANT: Department for Education and Employment

DATE OF RESEARCH: 1997-1998

KEYWORDS: **career education; secondary education; vocational guidance**

1745

The Mere, Upton Park, Slough SL1 2DQ
01753 574123

Ashby, J. Mr

Use of assessment information in schools

ABSTRACT: The use that schools make of National Curriculum assessment information with individuals or bodies outside of the school is in part specified by statute but it is the use of such information within schools that will have an impact upon standards. There has been rapidly growing interest in the use of assessment results by schools for value-added and for self-evaluation. The aim of the project is to ascertain the range of uses that schools at key stages 1 and 2 have for their assessment results and the procedures that they use to utilise their results. The study is looking at all 3 subjects in the core curriculum but with an emphasis on primary science. Data have been obtained from a questionnaire survey of a nationally representative sample of schools in England and Wales and this will be complemented by a series of case studies. The specific issues that are the focus of the project are how assessment information such as scores from statutory tests, National Curriculum level outcomes and item-level information are used in the curriculum management and planning for whole year, year group, class groups and individual children.

STATUS: Sponsored project

SOURCE OF GRANT: NFER

DATE OF RESEARCH: 1998-continuing

KEYWORDS: **assessment; curriculum mapping; information utilisation; key stage 1; key stage 2; national curriculum; primary education**

1746

The Mere, Upton Park, Slough SL1 2DQ
01753 574123

Ashby, J. Mr; Griffin, H. Ms; Kirkup, C. Ms

Welsh test development key stage 2 science 2000-02

ABSTRACT: The aim of the project is to develop test instruments that will be used in schools in Wales for the statutory assessment of science at the end of key stage 2 for years 2000 to 2002. The project is structured in 3 development cycles each lasting a year. The current development cycle is focused upon the development of instruments for the year 2000, the second cycle will focus upon the development of instruments for the year 2001 and the last cycle will develop instruments for the year 2002. Each of the development cycles has 3 phases. Test questions are written and informally trialled by groups of teacher-writers during the first phase. The test questions are pre-tested in the second phase with a representative sample of 800 pupils in Wales. Prior to pre-testing, all test questions are vetted by panels of judges, including members who are expert in physics, chemistry, biology, primary science, children with special educational needs and pupils learning English as an additional language. The information that is obtained from the first pre-test is used to inform the item selection for the final versions of the instruments. These undergo a second pre-test during the last phase of the development cycle, using the same sample specifications as for the first pre-test. All test material is developed concurrently in both English and Welsh and first and second pre-testing takes place in both languages.

STATUS: Sponsored project

SOURCE OF GRANT: ACCAC

DATE OF RESEARCH: 1998-continuing

KEYWORDS: **assessment; key stage 2; national curriculum; primary education; science education; tasks and tests; test construction; tests; wales**

1747

The Mere, Upton Park, Slough SL1 2DQ
01753 574123

Ashby, J. Mr; Evans, S. Dr; Claydon, H. Ms; Phillips, J. Ms

Welsh test development key stage 1 mathematics 2000-02

ABSTRACT: The aim of the project is to develop task and test instruments that will be used in schools in Wales for the statutory assessment of mathematics at the end of National Curriculum key stage 1 for years 2000 to 2002. The project is structured in 3 development cycles each lasting a year. The current development cycle is focused upon the development of instruments for the year 2000, the second cycle will focus upon the development of instruments for the year 2001 and the last cycle will develop instruments for the year 2002. Each of the development cycles has 3 phases. Test questions and task parts are written and informally trialled by groups of teacher-writers during the first phase. The test questions are pre-tested in the second phase with a representative sample of 800 pupils in Wales. The tasks are pre-tested with 400 pupils in Wales. Prior to pre-testing, all task parts and test questions are vetted by panels of judges, including members who are expert in primary mathematics, children with special educational needs and pupils learning English as an additional language. The information that is obtained from the first pre-test is used to inform the item selection for the final versions of the tasks and tests. These undergo a second pre-test during the last phase of the development cycle, using the same sample specifications as for the first pre-test. All test material is developed concurrently in both English and Welsh and first and second pre-testing takes place in both languages.

STATUS: Sponsored project

SOURCE OF GRANT: ACCAC

DATE OF RESEARCH: 1998-continuing

KEYWORDS: **assessment; key stage 1; mathematics; national curriculum; primary education; tasks and tests; test construction; tests; wales**

1748

The Mere, Upton Park, Slough SL1 2DQ
01753 574123

Fletcher-Campbell, F. Dr

Target setting in special schools

ABSTRACT: From September 1998 all schools will have to set and publish targets to demonstrate relevant and measurable year-on-year improvements. Schools, local education authorities (LEAs) and government agencies are therefore focusing on how data can be used to achieve this. This is particularly difficult for special schools whose pupils' achievement may not be able to be measured according to progress through National Curriculum levels or GCSE scores. There is, subsequently, a need for a set of finer-tuned assessment criteria for use with these pupils. The National Foundation for Educational Research (NFER) is working on behalf of the Qualifications and Curriculum Authority (QCA) to develop a set of assessment criteria for target setting in special schools.

PUBLISHED MATERIAL: GREAT BRITAIN. DEPARTMENT FOR EDUCATION AND EMPLOYMENT, STANDARDS AND EFFECTIVENESS UNIT. (1999). Supporting the Target Setting process: guidance for effective target setting for pupils with special educational needs. London: DfEE.

STATUS: Sponsored project

SOURCE OF GRANT: Qualification and Curriculum Authority

DATE OF RESEARCH: 1998-1998

KEYWORDS: **educational quality; special educational needs; special schools; target setting**

1749

The Mere, Upton Park, Slough SL1 2DQ
01753 574123

Sukhnandan, L. Dr

Gender differences in achievement

ABSTRACT: The aim of this study is to explore the range of strategies currently operating in schools to address gender differences in achievement. From the range of strategies which the research hopes to identify, 20 will be selected as examples of 'good practice'. The project will investigate the rationale behind schools' adoption of certain strategies, the way in which they have been implemented and why some are successful. A set of guidance materials will be produced for schools wishing to adopt similar strategies.

STATUS: Sponsored project

SOURCE OF GRANT: NFER

DATE OF RESEARCH: 1998-continuing

KEYWORDS: **academic achievement; achievement; pupil performance; secondary education; sex differences**

1750

The Mere, Upton Park, Slough SL1 2DQ
01753 574123

Brooks, R. Ms

Evaluation of university summer schools

ABSTRACT: In 1997, the Sutton Trust funded a summer school, for pupils in the first year of their A-level studies at Oxford University. The aim of the summer school was to encourage high-achieving pupils from non-privileged backgrounds to apply to leader universities and to enrich their A-level studies. In 1998, the Trust funded 4 summer schools for pupils (at Oxford, Cambridge, Bristol and Nottingham universities). The project will use a series of questionnaires and interviews to evaluate how far the summer schools met the Sutton Trust's aims of encouraging young people from non-privileged backgrounds to apply to leading universities and enriching their A-level studies.

STATUS: Sponsored project

SOURCE OF GRANT: The Sutton Trust

DATE OF RESEARCH: 1998-continuing

KEYWORDS: **a level examinations; access to education; higher education; programme evaluation; summer schools; universities; widening participation**

1751

The Mere, Upton Park, Slough SL1 2DQ
01753 574123

Sharp, C. Ms

Study support: a review of opinion and research

ABSTRACT: The Government's target is for half of secondary schools and a quarter of primary schools to be providing regular out-of-lesson-time learning activities by 2001. The National Foundation for Educational Research (NFER) is carrying out a review of expert opinion and research literature on the benefits and effects of this type of support.

STATUS: Sponsored project

SOURCE OF GRANT: Department for Education and Employment

DATE OF RESEARCH: 1997-1998

KEYWORDS: **learning activities; literature reviews; out of school hours; primary education; secondary education; study support centres**

1752

The Mere, Upton Park, Slough SL1 2DQ
01753 574123

Sharp, C. Ms

An evaluation of playing for success

ABSTRACT: 'Playing for success' is a new initiative which involves Premier Division football clubs in the provision of out-of-school learning activities for pupils in inner city areas. Its aim is to target those young people who underachieve at school by using their interest in football as a trigger to encourage them to study. The evaluation will provide an initial indication of the effectiveness of the scheme and identify those features which lead to success in terms of participation, gains in motivation, positive attitudes towards learning and enhanced learning outcomes. Seven of the centres are being evaluated. The first group will include Newcastle United, Sheffield Wednesday and Leeds United (the three centres already running).

STATUS: Sponsored project

SOURCE OF GRANT: Department for Education and Employment

DATE OF RESEARCH: 1998-continuing

KEYWORDS: **extracurricular activities; football; sports; underachievement**

1753

The Mere, Upton Park, Slough SL1 2DQ
01753 574123

Spear, M. Dr; *Supervisor*: Lee, B. Ms

Review of the research literature on teacher motivation

ABSTRACT: This review is investigating the factors which contribute to teacher motivation and job satisfaction. In addition, the effect of teacher motivation and morale upon teachers' career moves is being explored.

STATUS: Sponsored project

SOURCE OF GRANT: NFER

DATE OF RESEARCH: 1998-1998

KEYWORDS: career development; literature reviews; teacher morale; teacher motivation; teachers; teaching profession

1754

The Mere, Upton Park, Slough SL1 2DQ
01753 574123

Schagen, S. Dr; Dickson, P. Mr

Evaluation of Phase 3 of the Technology Enhancement Programme

ABSTRACT: The Technology Enhancement Programme (TEP) is part of the Gatsby Foundation's Technical Education Project. Launched nationally in 1991, it produces publications, materials and equipment aimed at enhancing the technology curriculum in schools and colleges. The National Foundation for Educational Research (NFER) has been commissioned to evaluate Phase 3 of TEP. The project will run from September 1998 to March 2001. A screening survey of 200 TEP-affiliated schools will be undertaken in the Autumn term of 1998. This will provide some background information and enable us to assess the degree of each school's participation in TEP. 15 of the responding schools will be invited to cooperate in further research. This will involve administering questionnaires to all Year 10 students in Spring 1999, and a follow-up questionnaire to the same students in Autumn 2000, when they are in the sixth Form. Each school will be visited during the school year 1999/2000 by a researcher who will interview key members of staff and (in certain schools) hold discussion groups with participating students. Proformas will be sent to parents and governors. The impact of TEP in the case study schools will also be investigated through a comparative analysis of GCSE results. Interim reports will be produced in Summer 1999 and Summer 2000. A final report will be submitted to TEP in March 2001.

STATUS: Sponsored project

SOURCE OF GRANT: Gatsby Charitable Foundation

DATE OF RESEARCH: 1998-continuing

KEYWORDS: engineering; secondary education; technology education

1755

The Mere, Upton Park, Slough SL1 2DQ
01753 574123

Davies, M. Ms; *Supervisor*: Stoney, S. Dr

Recent policy and strategy development in the Careers Service: a review

ABSTRACT: Since the implementation of the National Curriculum in 1989, careers education and guidance has been formally recognised as a cross-curricular theme within schools. Following the publication of the 1997 Education Act, it has been given statutory status, with Clause 43 ensuring that, for the first time, Careers Service staff are guaranteed access to schools and further education colleges. Such curriculum changes are but one element of a whole series of policy and strategy initiatives that have had implications for the work of the Careers Service. In addition to supporting core contract work in schools, Government strategies are also redirecting Careers Services towards more work with the disaffected. The recent publication of the Government's strategy document 'Investing in Young People' emphasised its commitment to a range of measures aimed at raising participation in learning beyond the age of 16 and decreasing disaffection and 'drop out' through the development of a wider range of vocational and work-related options in the curriculum. Central to the strategy is the part to be played by the Careers Service in targeting

guidance and support to those who are seen as needing it most. Initiatives such as the New Start projects rely heavily on Careers Service inputs, while services are the designated local nodes for issuing the new Learning Card. Work with adults is also high on the agenda with Careers Service activities focused on the various Welfare to Work programmes, including the 'New Deal' for clients in the 18-24 and over-24 age brackets. However, alongside this commitment to professional support for careers education and guidance is a growing concern with the quality and effectiveness of that provision, especially given the diverse roles the Careers Service are being encouraged to adopt. Careers Services have been subject to scrutiny by a variety of bodies, including the Audit Commission, Government offices and other local and regional partnerships. The Department for Education and Employment's (DfEE) Choice and Careers Division has conducted a number of Performance Review surveys, while national and local evaluations of a range of Careers Service initiatives have been commissioned from the NFER, National Institute for Careers Education and Guidance and other research bodies. Each of these surveys has served different policy customers and has been given a different emphasis. This review would have 2 key aims: 1) to identify the implications of current policy and strategy developments within the Careers Service for careers education and guidance practice within schools and post-school education and training; 2) to undertake a critical review of the policy and strategy developments in order to conceptualise and inform future research in this area. The review would be undertaken in 2 stages. An initial trawl of strategy and policy documents, particularly those emerging since the 1997 Education Act, would be conducted in order to identify the underlying trends and directions in the various careers education and guidance-led policies. Secondly, a critical review of these documents and also of recent careers-related research, would also be conducted and the key research and policy messages identified and highlighted. The key outcomes of this review would be an article for publication in an academic and/or user journal, highlighting the main implications of current strategy developments for the education and training system as well as the Careers Service itself. It is anticipated that the review would inform future careers-related research by NFER colleagues.

STATUS: Sponsored project

SOURCE OF GRANT: NFER

DATE OF RESEARCH: 1998-1998

KEYWORDS: career counselling; career education; careers service; vocational guidance

1756

The Mere, Upton Park, Slough SL1 2DQ
01753 574123

Taylor, M. Dr

Circle Time: its aims, use and effectiveness in primary schools

ABSTRACT: Circle Time is a technique which is in widespread use in primary schools and has been widely addressed in staff development. It is an increasingly popular method for promoting self-esteem and the development of pupils' values, attitudes and personal qualities. It is associated with many of the key aspects of Values Education, particularly moral, spiritual and emotional development, Personal and Social Education, character education, developing an ethos of caring, teaching by example, fostering democratic values and pro-social behaviour, and involving pupils in the formation of classroom rules. However, as a strategy with potential to enhance learning, Circle Time is under-researched. Specific aims of Circle Time may include, for example, the development of self-awareness and the ability to talk about feelings, trust, responsibility and cooperation. Furthermore, it is claimed that Circle Time can enhance pupils' self-esteem and help develop empathy, caring behaviour and a sense of belonging to a group or community. Circle Time can also be used to create shared rules and encourage their acceptance, as well as promoting problem-solving and conflict resolution. Circle Time should be a carefully structured activity. Typically, everyone, including the teacher, sits in a circle. An object is passed around the circle, and each individual has the opportunity to contribute when holding it. Each speaker has the right to express personal views and opinions and to be listened to with interest and respect, but negative comments about other members of the group are not permitted. The teacher may offer a starter phrase or may invite the children to suggest ways of resolving specific problems which have arisen in the class. This basic structure for Circle Time may be varied in a number of ways as indicated by one of its main proponents (MOSELEY, J. (1993). Turn your school around. Wisbech: LDA; and MOSELEY, J. (1996). Quality Circle Time in the primary classroom. Wisbech: LDA) and in training. The research would investigate the aims, uses and perceptions of effectiveness of Circle Time in a sample of primary schools in England. Circle Time may have a range of aims. The project would investigate teachers' aims for Circle Time and whether these were in line with the schools' aims for pupils' spiritual, moral, social and cultural development; teachers' understanding of what is meant by the values, attitudes, personal qualities, skills, dispositions or behaviour identified as the goals of Circle Time; and how teachers know if Circle Time has met the goals they have identified for it. It would seek to view and describe ways in which Circle Time is used by primary teachers in order to provide examples of positive practice and to raise issues associated with successful and less successful experiences of Circle Time from the perspectives of pupils and teachers. How do pupils learn to discuss and develop arguments, change their attitudes and gain interpersonal skills? What kind of techniques does the teacher adopt in participating in and commenting on the discussion? What kinds of topics or techniques make for good Circle Time? Another aim would be to explore teachers' and pupils' perceptions of learning across a number of skill areas basic to personal and social interaction and how these are addressed in Circle Time. What distinctive contribution does Circle Time make? Do pupils feel Circle Time has been of benefit to them? The effect of Circle Time on the school, and on teaching and non-teaching colleagues, would also be explored and the implications for teacher training considered. The project would involve several research activities: 1) Familiarisation with the research literature and the curriculum materials available to teachers for Circle Time, and contact with proponents of Circle Time, to gain a sense of history and development of the technique and some perceptions regarding aims, use, effectiveness and training; 2) Drawing on an existing database to compile a list of primary schools using Circle Time, and contacting a representative sample of 100 schools by phone for a short exploratory interview. 3) Selecting 20 primary schools for day visits to view Circle Time with at least two teachers and debriefing about the lessons and their perceptions of Circle Time; interviewing a member of the senior management; holding focus groups with pupils; and collecting relevant documentation. 4) From these schools, selecting 5 for further visits, to evaluate outcomes for teachers and pupils and identify aspects of personal and social development. What kinds of learning occur? Is it transferable to other curriculum areas? Does the strategy influence whole-school approaches?

STATUS: Sponsored project

SOURCE OF GRANT: NFER

DATE OF RESEARCH: 1998-continuing

KEYWORDS: circle time; moral development; primary education; pupil development; self esteem; teaching methods; values education

1757

The Mere, Upton Park, Slough SL1 2DQ
01753 574123

Schagen, I. Dr

Methods for tracking and displaying individual pupil progress

ABSTRACT: This project is investigating the feasibility and validity of combining pupil assessments from different sources at different times to enable pupils' progress to be tracked over time. In particular, ways of combining National Curriculum assessment results and commercial test standardised scores on a single display are being investigated. After developing a conceptual framework for the work, a draft paper containing this and some examples of possible displays will be sent to interested schools and local education authorities (LEAs). It is hoped that these will provide both feedback on these proposed methods and data for testing them. A report will be produced which evaluates the proposed methods and the feasibility of applying them in current or projected work for schools and LEAs.

STATUS: Sponsored project

SOURCE OF GRANT: NFER

DATE OF RESEARCH: 1998-continuing

KEYWORDS: academic achievement; assessment; primary education; pupil improvement; secondary education

1758

The Mere, Upton Park, Slough SL1 2DQ
01753 574123

Schagen, I. Dr; Kendall, L. Mrs; Morrison, J. Ms; Hewitt, D. Dr

Secondary research and analysis of value-added data

ABSTRACT: Since 1993, the National Foundation for Educational Research (NFER) value-added projects for secondary schools have collected and analysed a large quantity of data. The major focus of these projects each year has been the feedback of results to schools and local education authorities (LEAs), but at regular intervals reports have been produced of overall analyses of data collected in particular years. This project would make full use of all the data collected over these years to address important research questions about school effectiveness, trends in performance and relationships between performance and background variables. It would maintain and enhance the Foundation's academic reputation in this field, and would give important leads into important potential areas of research. The outcome of the research will be a published report, plus possibly academic papers.

STATUS: Sponsored project

SOURCE OF GRANT: NFER

DATE OF RESEARCH: 1998-continuing

KEYWORDS: educational quality; performance indicators; school effectiveness; secondary education; value added

1759

The Mere, Upton Park, Slough SL1 2DQ
01753 574123

Jamison, J. Mr; Johnson, F. Miss; Blenkinsop, S. Miss; Lewis, G. Mr

Evaluation of drug education resources for young people

ABSTRACT: 'Drugs - the facts' and 'The Score - facts about drugs' are two drug education resources for young people aged 11-14 and 14-16 published by the Health Education Authority. These are mainly intended as free standing resources to inform young people about the risks involved in misusing drugs and solvents, and are designed for use in a variety of settings, including the home, schools, youth clubs and GP surgeries. This project aims to investigate how the resources have been made available to young people, and how they have been used, and to assess the impact which the resources have had by exploring the views of young people, their parents and health and education professionals. A report will be produced for the Health Education Authority in Spring 1999, along with an executive summary.

STATUS: Sponsored project

SOURCE OF GRANT: Health Education Authority

DATE OF RESEARCH: 1998-continuing

KEYWORDS: drug education; health education

1760

The Mere, Upton Park, Slough SL1 2DQ
01753 574123

Kerr, D. Mr

International review of curriculum and assessment frameworks (INCA): Thematic Study Citizenship Education

ABSTRACT: The Citizenship Education study is part of a wider review which provides reliable, detailed information to enable the Qualifications and Curriculum Authority (QCA) to evaluate the curriculum and assessment frameworks in England and to contextualise the outcomes of international comparisons. Specifically, it aims to support QCA's current work in Citizenship Education by: 1) establishing national practice (England, France, Hungary, Italy, Japan, Korea, the Netherlands, New Zealand, Singapore, Spain and Sweden and selected states in Australia, Canada, Germany, Switzerland and the USA) in the case of systems, or aspects, which are centrally controlled (through documentary research); and 2) obtaining as much information on systematic regional variation, or the degree to which non-enforceable guidelines are followed, as is feasible within the resources available (through an invitational seminar involving participants from most of the contributing countries). It is expected that where opinion is involved, or where regional or institutional diversity is permitted within the system, the information obtained will not be definitive as to practice in schools. Areas of study include: current provision (from INCA and other sources) for the 5-18 age range, curriculum aims, organisation and structure, implementation (teaching and learning approaches), support (teacher training and learning materials), assessing and evaluating the impact of Citizenship Education and current and future developments in different countries.

PUBLISHED MATERIAL: KERR, D. (1999). 'Citizenship education: an international perspective'. Keynote paper presented at the QCA International Seminar on Citizenship Education: an International Perspective, 27-29 January, 1999. ; KERR, D. (1999). Citizenship education: an international perspective. International Review of Curriculum and Assessment Frameworks Paper 4. London: Qualifications and Curriculum Authority.

STATUS: Sponsored project

SOURCE OF GRANT: Qualifications and Curriculum Authority

DATE OF RESEARCH: 1998-continuing

KEYWORDS: citizenship education; comparative education

1761

The Mere, Upton Park, Slough SL1 2DQ
01753 574123

Saunders, L. Ms; Rudd, P. Dr; Davies, D. Ms

Schools' use of value added data

ABSTRACT: The National Foundation for Educational Research (NFER) has a well-established programme of work in the field of school effectiveness and particularly in undertaking so-called 'value-added' analyses of school performance. But even though 'value-added' is now well developed in methodological and analytical terms, the issue of support for schools in managing and using such data needs much closer examination. Such support is more than ever necessary, as increasingly sophisticated statistical data is generated by the Department for Education and Employment (DfEE), the Qualifications and Curriculum Authority (QCA), local education authorities (LEAs) and schools themselves. The debate about 'value-added' - to which the NFER has made a major contribution - has shown how challenging the technical, conceptual and ethical issues are. Early in 1998, leading experts in value-added and school effectiveness/improvement research met at the NFER and agreed that better guidance and protocols are needed, based on empirical evidence of what is happening in schools. This project is providing that evidence. The aims of the project are to investigate how far and under what circumstances value-added analyses have a role to play in school improvement and the raising of pupils' attainment in different institutional contexts; and to draft some guidelines for good practice. The project draws directly on, and contributes to, the NFER's Quantitative Analysis for Self-Evaluation (QUASE) service for secondary schools, which provides a range of analyses of performance at GCSE. More generally, it will help to supply the important 'missing link' between school effectiveness (the statistical evidence) and school improvement (the in-school processes).

STATUS: Sponsored project

SOURCE OF GRANT: NFER

DATE OF RESEARCH: 1998-continuing

KEYWORDS: educational quality; school effectiveness; school improvement; secondary education; value added

1762

The Mere, Upton Park, Slough SL1 2DQ
01753 574123

Saunders, L. Ms; Rudd, P. Dr; Davies, D. Ms

The effectiveness of school self-evaluation strategies

ABSTRACT: Much of the recent work of the Department for Education and Employment (DfEE) has focused on developing a systematic approach to self-evaluation by schools in raising the level of all young people's achievements. The main issue is whether - beneath the rhetoric - there

really is a culture of self-evaluation in schools in which target-setting and related processes can take root and flourish. This project capitalises on the interest generated by a recently-completed National Foundation for Educational Research (NFER) project for the DfEE on 'raising standards through systematic school self-review'. It will explore questions such as: 1) What are the aims, for individual schools, of undertaking self-evaluation? For what purposes is 'self-evaluation' being used? To what extent are these different uses mutually compatible/consistent? 2) Where does the 'ownership' of school self-evaluation lie? What, if any, changes in the culture of schools need to be encouraged if 'self-evaluation' is to become a reality? 3) Do schools at different stages of development ('improving', 'stagnating', 'deteriorating', 'failing') tend to have different approaches to self-evaluation? 4) What role(s) can the local education authority (LEA) play in helping schools to become better at self-evaluation? The outcome will be a report on models of school self-evaluation.

STATUS: Sponsored project

SOURCE OF GRANT: NFER

DATE OF RESEARCH: 1998-continuing

KEYWORDS: educational quality; institutional evaluation; school effectiveness; school improvement; self evaluation - groups; target setting

1763

The Mere, Upton Park, Slough SL1 2DQ
01753 574123

Saunders, L. Ms; Dickson, P. Mr; Jamison, J. Mr

Evaluation of curriculum reform in Slovenia

ABSTRACT: Slovenia, a relatively new and small country, became independent in 1991 upon the disintegration of Yugoslavia. Like other Eastern European countries, Slovenia has been going through a period of intense professional, public and political concern about the role education should play in a democratic polity based on a market economy; about the role the state should play in national education provision; and about the extent to which the curriculum should embody new values. An ambitious programme of curriculum reform has been set in train; there is a consequent need to develop methods to enable an expert evaluation to be carried out of the quality and effects of these reforms over the next 5 or 6 years. The Pedagoski Institut (the Slovenian Institute of Educational Research) in Ljubljana wishes to commission the National Foundation for Educational Research (NFER), as an independent institution based in another European country with a mature democratic system, to assist, in the first instance, with developing an appropriate evaluative framework for use by the National Evaluation Commission and its sub-committees. The commission is fully supported by the Ministry of Education and Sports. The outcome will be a draft evaluation framework.

STATUS: Sponsored project

SOURCE OF GRANT: Slovenian Institute of Educational Research

DATE OF RESEARCH: 1999-continuing

KEYWORDS: curriculum development; educational change; slovenia

1764

The Mere, Upton Park, Slough SL1 2DQ
01753 574123

Powell, R. Mr; Lewis, G. Mr; Saunders, L. Ms

Raising attainment in Merthyr Tydfil

ABSTRACT: The Department of Education, Merthyr Tydfil County Borough Council, commissioned the National Foundation for Educational Research (NFER) to assist with strategies for raising the achievement of pupils in all its schools. The initial programme of work was to conduct and report on a questionnaire survey of primary and secondary schools, to determine the use made of standardised tests across the Borough. The survey covered the kinds of tests used, the pattern of their use in different key stages, the purposes for which schools administer tests and the ways in which they report results to governors and parents. Follow-up work is planned to raise awareness in schools of the issues relating to testing and target-setting; and to share good practice. The outcome will be a confidential report for the Department of Education, Merthyr Tydfil County Borough Council.

STATUS: Sponsored project

SOURCE OF GRANT: Merthyr Tydfil County Borough Council

DATE OF RESEARCH: 1998-1998

KEYWORDS: academic achievement; achievement; assessment; pupil improvement

1765

The Mere, Upton Park, Slough SL1 2DQ
01753 574123

Saunders, L. Ms; Schagen, I. Dr; Caspall, L. Miss

Slough school improvement and value-added project

ABSTRACT: The Education Department of Slough Borough Council has commissioned the National Foundation for Educational Research (NFER), along with another organisation, Schools Information Management Systems (SIMS), to assist in establishing and developing a borough-wide project in school improvement and value-added measures of performance. The elected members and officers are seeking to build a rigorous approach to the development, analysis and use of an informative evidence-base on young people's achievements and performance in the primary, secondary and special sectors. The NFER's contributions during the first year of the project (April 1998-March 1999) are to: 1) write an evaluative commentary, and make recommendations, on baseline assessment schemes for use in primary schools; 2) undertake comparative analyses of performance, initially for key stages 2 and 4, which will show the performance of Slough schools, collectively and individually, against national norms; 3) provide inservice teacher education (INSET) and professional support to local education authority (LEA) and school staff, as needed, on the interpretation and use of 'value-added' measures of performance; 4) provide general input and support through attendance at key meetings.

STATUS: Sponsored project

SOURCE OF GRANT: Slough Borough Council

DATE OF RESEARCH: 1997-continuing

KEYWORDS: educational quality; performance indicators; primary education; school effectiveness; school improvement; secondary education; value added

1766

The Mere, Upton Park, Slough SL1 2DQ
01753 574123

Stoney, S. Dr; Sims, D. Mr; Lines, A. Mrs

Supporting adult learners to achieve success (ATLASS)

ABSTRACT: Supporting adult learners to achieve success (ATLASS) is an adult education action project, funded through the European Commission's Socrates Programme. It is a close collaboration between the National Foundation for Educational Research (NFER), the Institut National de Recherce Pedagogique (INRP), France and the Landesinstitut fur Schule and Weiterbuildung, Germany. The project began in September 1997 and will end in August 1999. Its main aim is to 'identify and disseminate across Europe, the best ways of enabling adult learners, particularly those with few or no qualifications and poor educational backgrounds, to make progress in, remain motivated throughout, and successfully complete, their learning programmes'. The first year has been spent in collecting the detailed testimony of adult learners and practitioners involved with different educational programmes in the 3 countries. During this time, a paper that compares the concepts and terms used in the learner support area within the 3 language areas has been produced and is being published by the NFER in December 1998. The second year is focusing on the production of a main report, a briefing paper for policymakers, guidance and training materials for practitioners and a booklet of handy hints for adult learners. The outcome will be a comparative text of concepts and terms (1998) and main report, briefing paper for policymakers, guidance and training materials for practitioners and booklet of handy hints for adult learners (1999).

STATUS: Sponsored project

SOURCE OF GRANT: European Commission

DATE OF RESEARCH: 1997-1998

KEYWORDS: adult education; adult learning; comparative education; international educational exchange; support services

1767

The Mere, Upton Park, Slough SL1 2DQ
01753 574123

Schagen, S. Dr; Kerr, D. Mr; *Supervisor*: Dickson, P. Mr

Effective progression from primary to secondary schooling

ABSTRACT: The project examines curriculum continuity and individual progression in the light of the introduction of the National Curriculum and associated assessment procedures. It also explores local structures and activities designed to facilitate continuity and progression. After an initial telephone survey of 104 secondary schools, the project focused on indepth case study work in 10 different areas. A secondary school in each area was visited 3 times, and interviews undertaken with a range of teachers; group discussions with Year 7 pupils were also held. Some of the feeder primary schools (in most cases, 2 for each secondary school) were also visited. A full report of the research findings will be published by the National Foundation for Educational Research (NFER), probably in March 1999.

STATUS: Sponsored project

SOURCE OF GRANT: NFER

DATE OF RESEARCH: 1996-continuing

KEYWORDS: developmental continuity; national curriculum; primary education; primary to secondary transition; secondary education

1768

The Mere, Upton Park, Slough SL1 2DQ
01753 574123

Schagen, S. Dr; Taylor, M. Dr; *Supervisor*:#@ Stoney, S. Dr

Cross-curricular learning: a review

ABSTRACT: To help schools provide a 'broad and balanced curriculum' for their pupils, the National Curriculum Council (NCC) recommended that certain cross-curricular dimensions, skills and themes should be included. Five themes were defined, but the priority accorded them in schools has varied. There is, however, widespread recognition of the need to adequately prepare students for life as 21st century adults. The Government has established advisory groups on citizenship, Personal, Social and Health Education (PSHE), creative and cultural education and sustainable development education. In the light of these developments, a comprehensive review of cross-curricular learning will be undertaken. A wide range of published research and policy documents will be examined. Interviews with key members of government committees will be undertaken where possible. Among other things, the project will explore: 1) links and overlaps between the themes; 2) the concepts, knowledge, attitudes and skills involved; and 3) the aims and desired outcomes of cross-curricular study. The main outcome will be a paper which will address the whole area of cross-curricular learning. It will seek to: 1) distinguish the main issues and questions to be addressed; 2) summarise the findings from relevant research; 3) provide an analysis of current thought and policy; 4) map the learning and skills which relate to cross-curricular themes; and 5) indicate specific areas where further research might prove valuable.

STATUS: Sponsored project

SOURCE OF GRANT: NFER

DATE OF RESEARCH: 1998-continuing

KEYWORDS: citizenship education; creative and cultural education; cross curricular approach; cultural education; personal social and health education; primary education; secondary education; sustainable development

1769

The Mere, Upton Park, Slough SL1 2DQ
01753 574123

Kinder, K. Ms; Atkinson, M. Ms; Halsey, K. Ms; Kendall, S. Dr; Moor, H. Ms; Wilkin, A. Mrs; *Supervisor*: Harland, J. Dr

Exclusion: effective practice

ABSTRACT: In the light of evidence that the numbers of pupils excluded from school are increasing, this study will examine a range of activity and intervention which deals with pupils following a permanent exclusion, including those excluded for more extreme examples of anti-social behaviour. It will adjudge the effectiveness and cost-effectiveness of this work. It will research examples of innovative practice, as well as existing approaches that are perceived to be successful. It will focus on the provision and support currently available within the education service, as well as from health and social services, youth justice and the police. Particular attention will be given to examples of multi agency approaches and liaison. The aims of the project are to: 1) identify a range of activity, support and intervention available to permanently excluded pupils, including those exhibiting serious offending behaviours within mainstream school; 2) study the processes and components of these strategies (including re-integration) to ascertain key factors in successful post-exclusion support; 3) analyse the effects of these interventions and determine the effectiveness and cost-effectiveness of various approaches. The project will involve an intensive case study approach. Following on the views of young people themselves and observations of practice and indepth interviews with a range of persons involved with excluded pupils, including staff in special units and off-site provision, school staff, parents, social and health workers, police, youth officers and voluntary agencies.

STATUS: Sponsored project

SOURCE OF GRANT: NFER

DATE OF RESEARCH: 1998-continuing

KEYWORDS: **antisocial behaviour; behaviour problems; disruptive pupils; exclusion; intervention**

1770

The Mere, Upton Park, Slough SL1 2DQ
01753 574123

Atkinson, M. Ms; Halsey, K. Ms; Kendall, S. Dr; Wilkin, A. Mrs; *Supervisor*: Kinder, K. Ms

Pupil disaffection in Merseyside: causes and experiences

ABSTRACT: The Merseyside Learning Partnership, through the Inter Agency Development Programme, commissioned this study looking into the perceived factors of pupil disaffection within the partnership authorities and how that disaffection is experienced by youngsters and their families. The study investigated the 'pupil careers' of a sample of young people from the partnership authorities (including home and community influences) who had demonstrated some degree of disengagement and dislocation from their mainstream schooling opportunities. It identified key factors and commonalities among the sample which were associated with disaffection. It explored the range of experiences, attitudes and feelings that accompanied the disaffected behaviours of the sample. It also explored the perceived efficacy of alternative provision and support programmes experienced by the sample and identified key features which had achieved some reduction in disaffected attitudes and/or behaviour. The study involved an indepth interview programme with 50 young people from Years 7 to 10 who had a range of disaffected behaviour; from those with attendance problems to school refusers; and from those in danger of fixed term exclusion; to those who were permanently excluded. A series of contextualising interviews were carried out with youngsters' parents/carers and the educational professionals (teachers and support staff) who work with them. Other data such as school performance measures and records of attendance and behaviour were also collected.

PUBLISHED MATERIAL: KINDER, K., KENDALL, S., HALSEY, K. & ATKINSON, M. Disaffection talks. Slough: NFER. (in press).

STATUS: Sponsored project

SOURCE OF GRANT: Merseyside Inter Agency Development Group

DATE OF RESEARCH: 1998-1998

KEYWORDS: **alternative education; behaviour problems; disaffection; disruptive pupils; exclusion; truancy**

1771

The Mere, Upton Park, Slough SL1 2DQ
01753 574123

Jamison, J. Mr; Sims, D. Mr

Evaluation of Work Based Training for Adults Strands: Two's Company and into Business Scheme

ABSTRACT: This research focuses on strategies which are aimed at enabling the long-term unemployed to return to ongoing employment, both as employees and as self-employed people. It will provide an evaluation of two strands of the Work Based Training for Adults programme of Calderdale and Kirklees Training and Enterprise Council (TEC) - Into Business Scheme and Two's Company. Employers, employees and self-employed people involved in the two schemes will be interviewed, both face-to-face and by telephone. The project will also provide guidance for future strategies which the TEC might consider to help sustain a skilled, motivated and flexible workforce in its area.

STATUS: Sponsored project

SOURCE OF GRANT: Calderdale and Kirklees Training and Enterprise Council

DATE OF RESEARCH: 1998-continuing

KEYWORDS: **adult vocational education; adults; employment; training; unemployment; work based learning**

1772

The Mere, Upton Park, Slough SL1 2DQ
01753 574123

Brooks, G. Dr

The effectiveness of literacy tuition in basic skills programmes

ABSTRACT: The Basic Skills Agency has commissioned the National Foundation for Educational Research (NFER) to study the effectiveness of literacy tuition in adult basic skills programmes, that is, the amount of progress which adults make on such programmes. The aims of the project are to investigate: 1) the progress made by students in mainstream adult literacy programmes provided by local education authorities (LEAs) and further education (FE) colleges; and 2) factors associated with improvement in literacy. Assessment instruments were devised in 1998; these cover students' reading and writing attainment. Testing is being carried out in the academic year 1998/99, pre-testing in the Autumn term, and post-testing in the Summer term. Background data on all sampled students are also being collected, plus information from the adult literacy tutors of the tested students. Gain scores will be analysed against the background variables and the information from tutors. A second post-test is planned for the Autumn term of 1999, in order to see whether students have maintained their gains. The principal outcome of the project will be a final report to the Basic Skills Agency which would be submitted in December 1999.

STATUS: Sponsored project

SOURCE OF GRANT: Basic Skills Agency

DATE OF RESEARCH: 1997-continuing

KEYWORDS: **adult learning; adult literacy; literacy**

1773

The Mere, Upton Park, Slough SL1 2DQ
01753 574123

Fletcher-Campbell, F. Dr

Links between special and ordinary schools (second re-run)

ABSTRACT: This research will follow up one of the strands of a research project undertaken at the National Foundation for Educational Research (NFER) from 1983-1985, namely the strand that explored links between ordinary and special schools. In 1994 a questionnaire was sent to all special schools in England and Wales with the aim of identifying any sharing of pupils, staff or material resources between establishments; the sharing could be reciprocal or one way. This survey will be repeated in 1999.

STATUS: Sponsored project

SOURCE OF GRANT: NFER

DATE OF RESEARCH: 1999-continuing

KEYWORDS: **institutional cooperation; mainstreaming; partnerships; special educational needs; special schools**

1774

The Mere, Upton Park, Slough SL1 2DQ
01753 574123

Wilkinson, D. Mr; *Supervisor*: Keys, W. Dr

Out of school learning activities: LEA survey

ABSTRACT: A survey of local education authorities' (LEAs) involvement in out-of-school hours learning activities began in November 1998. The intention of the survey was to build on existing knowledge of LEA schemes and help to develop a national picture of the role LEAs have in supporting, initiating and monitoring out of school hours learning. A questionnaire was designed following consultation with the Department for Education and Employment (DfEE), LEA representatives and colleagues involved with similar projects at the National Foundation for Educational Research (NFER). Essentially, the questionnaire sought information regarding study support activities LEAs supported or initiated. Questions focused on LEA policies, types of activities/provision supported, and the organisation/staffing of activities or schemes. A report will be made to the DfEE during the first half of 1999 detailing the findings of the survey.

STATUS: Sponsored project

SOURCE OF GRANT: Department for Education and Employment

DATE OF RESEARCH: 1998-continuing

KEYWORDS: **learning activities; local education authorities; out of school hours; study support centres**

1775

The Mere, Upton Park, Slough SL1 2DQ
01753 574123

Kendall, L. Mrs

Benchmarking for London LEAs

ABSTRACT: School-level aggregate information, including local education authority (LEA), school and pupil characteristics and end-of-key-stage outcomes, has been collated by LEAs for each of their schools. Statistical techniques are being used to identify 'families' of schools. LEAs will be provided with tables enabling comparisons to be made between schools in the same 'family', for each of the key stages 1, 2, 3 and 4.

STATUS: Sponsored project

SOURCE OF GRANT: Consortium of London LEAs

DATE OF RESEARCH: 1998-continuing

KEYWORDS: **benchmarking; educational quality; local education authorities; outcomes of education; primary education; secondary education**

1776

The Mere, Upton Park, Slough SL1 2DQ
01753 574123

Sims, D. Mr; Golden, S. Ms; Lewis, G. Mr; Williams, S. Mr

Longitudinal study of the impact of the Curriculum Centre Initiative

ABSTRACT: Early in the 1990s the Construction Industry Training Board (CITB) recognised the poor image which the industry had in the eyes of young people who where potential recruits. In order to respond to this, the CITB established its Curriculum Centre Initiative which aimed to help schools, colleges and employers to work in partnership to use construction as a context and resource for learning and consequently 'to open the eyes of youngsters to the importance of the world of construction'. Since the inception of the Initiative, evaluations have been conducted by the National Foundation for Educational Research (NFER) which have shown that it has a positive impact on the young people's awareness of the industry and that nearly half of those involved anticipated entering construction either immediately after leaving school or some time in the future. Local evidence from individual Curriculum Centres suggests that Initiative 'graduates' do return to college to undertake training in construction, but the influence of their involvement in the Initiative on this decision has not been explored in depth. The CITB has commissioned the NFER to conduct a longitudinal qualitative study of 50 young people who left school in the Summer of 1998 to investigate the longer term impact of the Initiative on their transition from school to their post-16 destinations and their progression routes into the world of work. The research, which will consist of a series of interviews with young construction trainees over 2 years, will investigate their Curriculum Centre experiences and the extent to which these influenced their subsequent decisions. In addition, interviews will be conducted with relevant professionals including college tutors, CITB staff and employers. The first phase of the research will report in January 2000. A final report will be written for the CITB. An executive summary will be disseminated to participants.

STATUS: Sponsored project

SOURCE OF GRANT: Construction Industry Training Board

DATE OF RESEARCH: 1999-continuing

KEYWORDS: **building trades education; construction industry; followup studies; industrial training; industry; industry education relationship; school to work transition; sixteen to nineteen education; training; vocational education; work education relationship**

1777

The Mere, Upton Park, Slough SL1 2DQ
01753 574123

Mason, K. Mr

NFER study of out-of-lesson time learning activities pilot schemes

ABSTRACT: There are 50 pilot schemes throughout England that have received Department for Education and Employment (DfEE) funding to set up or extend out-of-lesson time learning activities for pupils. These schemes include single schools, consortia of schools and other institutions. The research involves initial and follow-up visits to each of the 50 schemes in the period May 1998 to February 1999. Interviews are being held with the coordinator of each scheme. Across the schemes, some of the staff involved at all levels are also being interviewed, as well as some of the targeted pupils, parents and adult mentors involved, whether from the business sector or other volunteers. Up to 10 schemes are being chosen for indepth case study work to highlight aspects of good practice. These schemes will involve a series of interviews with the staff and pupils involved, as well as observation of the scheme in action. A main outcome of the research is to be a report to the DfEE in May 1999, which will describe the main factors in setting up and running out-of-lesson time learning activities. The intention is that the report will serve as a guide for schools and others wishing to initiate or extend their operations in this direction.

STATUS: Sponsored project

SOURCE OF GRANT: Department for Education and Employment

DATE OF RESEARCH: 1998-continuing

KEYWORDS: **learning activities; out of school hours; study support centres**

1778

The Mere, Upton Park, Slough SL1 2DQ
01753 574123

Clausen-May, T. Dr; McDonald, A. Mr

An annotated review of spatial ability and mathematics education

ABSTRACT: Following the publication of Spatial Ability: a Handbook for Teachers, it is now the right time to build on the interest this has aroused and to take the research further. The Handbook has aroused interest in the field of mathematics education, and the relationship between spatial ability and mathematics performance and teaching needs to be explored further. The main objective would be to produce an annotated literature review in the area of spatial ability and mathematics education. The annotated bibliography will be of considerable interest, particularly to people involved in mathematics education in schools and colleges. The review will focus closely on those aspects of the research into spatial ability and styles of thinking and learning which have a bearing on mathematics education, and those aspects of mathematics education which have a bearing on spatial ability. Each entry will include a brief summary of the main points of the book or article. Significant themes which appear across several publications will be identified, and brought together in a separate note or appendix. This will lead to the publication of an article relating the two strands of research. The work could also lead to further research, identified in the course of the literature review. This would involve spatial ability and mathematics education, and could, for example, lead to the development of resource materials designed to make aspects of mathematics which are usually presented 'symbolically' more accessible to spatially able pupils.

PUBLISHED MATERIAL: CLAUSEN-MAY, T. & SMITH, P. (Eds). (1998). Spatial ability: a handbook for teachers. Slough: NFER.

STATUS: Sponsored project

SOURCE OF GRANT: NFER

DATE OF RESEARCH: 1999-continuing

KEYWORDS: literature reviews; mathematics education; spatial ability

1779

The Mere, Upton Park, Slough SL1 2DQ
01753 574123

Milne, A. Mrs; Minnis, M. Ms

Evaluation of National Literacy and Numeracy Strategies

ABSTRACT: The National Foundation for Educational Research (NFER) has been asked by the Qualifications and Curriculum Authority (QCA) to undertake the administration and analysis of standardised tests to support the evaluation of the effectiveness of the National Literacy and Numeracy Strategies. Two samples of schools have been identified by the Office for Standards in Education (OFSTED) covering approximately 70 local education authorities (LEAs). In total 700 schools are involved in the testing. One sample of schools will administer mathematics tests to Years 3, 4 and 5 and the other will administer English tests to these year groups. Tests will be administered in June 1999 and again in 2000 and 2001. Analysis and reporting will be taking place at pupil level, school level and nationally. Multilevel modelling will be used as part of the statistical analysis in order to investigate the relationship between background factors and attainment. Each participating school will receive a report on their pupils' achievements and national findings will be reported to QCA.

STATUS: Sponsored project

SOURCE OF GRANT: Qualifications and Curriculum Authority

DATE OF RESEARCH: 1999-continuing

KEYWORDS: achievement; assessment; literacy; mathematics education; national literacy strategy; national numeracy strategy; reading; tests

1780

The Mere, Upton Park, Slough SL1 2DQ
01753 574123

Lee, B. Ms

Survey of statistics and research units for Education Management Information Exchange (EMIE)

ABSTRACT: Local education authorities (LEAs) have always relied on their research and/or statistics officers to supply valid data to inform their policy and practice but recently the Government's drive to raise standards in education has led to a rapid expansion of their role and given them a crucial part to play in collecting, analysing and disseminating information to support school improvement. The National Foundation for Educational Research (NFER) is currently investigating the services which LEAs might wish to commission the Foundation to carry out, and as part of that process, it was thought useful to ascertain how LEAs organise their own research and information gathering functions. A questionnaire survey will be carried out of all LEAs asking them whether they have a dedicated unit or team and investigating the functions of such a team. Information will also be collected on who has responsibility for such functions when a specific team is not in place. The questionnaire will be designed by EMIE and staff from Policy and Curriculum Studies (PCS) working in collaboration.

STATUS: Sponsored project

SOURCE OF GRANT: NFER

DATE OF RESEARCH: 1998-continuing

KEYWORDS: educational research; local education authorities; statistics

1781

The Mere, Upton Park, Slough SL1 2DQ
01753 574123

Morris, M. Miss; Rudd, P. Dr; Nelson, J. Ms; Davies, D. Ms

The contribution of careers education and guidance to school effectiveness in 'partnership' schools

ABSTRACT: Careers education and guidance has long been a central aspect of the vocational and training initiatives implemented by successive governments in order to meet the skill needs of global competition. However, it was not until the introduction of the White Paper 'Excellence in Schools' in 1998 that the Government highlighted aspects of careers education and guidance as significant elements of its strategy for promoting higher educational standards and more effective schools. In 1995 the Department for Education and Employment (DfEE) sponsored the National Foundation for Educational Research (NFER) to conduct a research report into the role of the careers service in careers education and guidance in schools, which identified a number of schools that adopted a 'guidance community' or 'partnership school' approach to careers education and guidance. This model indicated a significant degree of interaction between schools and careers services, the wider school curriculum, employers and the business community. There is evidence to suggest that appropriate careers education and guidance provision delivered through such a model can contribute to the effective development of young people's careers-related skills and learning outcomes. However, it is less clear whether such provision has any wider educational implications. This research, which has been commissioned by the DfEE, seeks to explore the extent to which schools that deliver careers education and guidance within a partnership framework can be identified as effective, and the extent to which they promote high educational standards. The outcomes will be: 1) a main report addressing the aims and research questions that have framed the project, written for an essentially policy and managerial audience; and 2) a short feasibility study report, with a specification for a future quantitative study of the impact of careers education and guidance on school effectiveness.

STATUS: Sponsored project

SOURCE OF GRANT: Department for Education and Employment

DATE OF RESEARCH: 1998-continuing

KEYWORDS: career choice; career education; careers service; employers; partnerships; school leavers; school to work transition; secondary education; vocational guidance; work education relationship

1782

The Mere, Upton Park, Slough SL1 2DQ
01753 574123

Lee, B. Ms; Spear, M. Dr

NFER Centre for local education authority research and development

ABSTRACT: The Centre was set up to carry out research and consultancy for individual local education authorities (LEAs) and their schools, tailored to their particular needs. It draws upon the specialist expertise and experience of staff across the Foundation. Since its inception, in September 1997, it has carried out projects in a wide range of areas, including: learning community schemes (home-school agreements, parental involvement, Saturday schools, summer school); secondary and primary admission arrangements; secondary transfer arrangements; training and qualifications of early years staff; classroom assistants. LEAs and other bodies are invited to contact the Centre Coordinator if they wish to discuss the possibility of the Centre carrying out some work for them.

STATUS: Sponsored project

SOURCE OF GRANT: NFER

DATE OF RESEARCH: 1997-continuing

KEYWORDS: consultancy; educational research; local education authorities

1783

The Mere, Upton Park, Slough SL1 2DQ
01753 574123

Morris, M. Miss; Nelson, J. Ms

Measuring the impact on learners and teachers of the Learning Partnership West Skills Certificate for students in key stage 4

ABSTRACT: The development of 'key skills' amongst young people forms a significant and growing element of the local and national training agenda. These key skills are currently identified as: communication, information technology, application of number, working with others, improvement of self-learning and performance and problem-solving. It is likely that, from the year 2000, all post-16 school leavers may have to work towards a Qualifications and Curriculum Authority (QCA) recognised key skills certificate. Learning Partnership West (LPW) has worked with local education authorities (LEAs), schools, businesses and training providers, to develop a Key Skills Certificate. This Certificate aims to facilitate the progression of young people from key stage 3 to key stage 4, to contribute to an enhancement of their understanding of key skills and their relevance to adult and working life, and to prepare them for the advent of the planned QCA post-16 key skills assessment. Since September 1998, 12 schools and one college in the LPW area have been piloting the Key Skills Certificate with Year 10 students, and LPW has now commissioned the National Foundation for Educational Research (NFER) to assess the extent to which the implementation of this Certificate has improved student motivation and achievement, and has developed a greater understanding amongst students and teachers of how to work towards key skills and demonstrate their achievement. There will be 2 main outcomes from this research: 1) A brief interim report in March 1999, which will summarise initial findings from fieldwork visits, telephone interviews and a baseline questionnaire; and 2) A final report in September 2000, which will provide a qualitative and quantitative evaluation of the impact of the Key Skills Certificate.

STATUS: Sponsored project

SOURCE OF GRANT: Learning Partnership West

DATE OF RESEARCH: 1998-continuing

KEYWORDS: core skills; key skills; key stage 4; qualifications; secondary education; sixteen to nineteen education

1784

The Mere, Upton Park, Slough SL1 2DQ
01753 574123

Jamison, J. Mr; Lewis, G. Mr; Blenkinsop, S. Miss

Focus groups with secondary school pupils on food hygiene materials

ABSTRACT: Education about food and healthy eating is a key element in the UK Government's healthy schools programme. Many of those concerned with improving the nation's health and well-being agree that young people need to learn about all aspects of food: 'nutrition education is not only about the nutritional value of food, but also about budgeting for food, and choosing, preparing and cooking it' (Independent Enquiry into Inequalities in Health, Acheson, 1998). A Eurobarometer survey in 1997 revealed that for 68% of consumers, food safety was a major concern. In response to this concern, the EC has launched a European Food Safety Campaign. As part of this, in the UK, the Health Education Authority (HEA) intends to focus a food safety and hygiene campaign on young people. The objective is to ensure that young people become aware of the importance of basic rules of food hygiene and develop an appropriate level of understanding of the underlying principles. A schools' resource of teaching materials will be developed by HEA and sent to all UK secondary schools. The National Foundation for Educational Research (NFER) has been commissioned by the HEA to identify which are the most popular food hygiene materials currently in use with secondary school pupils, to determine what messages about food safety and hygiene are remembered by pupils, to identify the most suitable materials for conveying the key messages to pupils and to gather pupils' reactions to draft materials prepared as part of the HEA school resource. This will be undertaken through a series of focus group interviews with secondary school pupils in England, Wales, Scotland and Northern Ireland during February 1999. A report will be submitted to the HEA in March 1999.

STATUS: Sponsored project

SOURCE OF GRANT: Health Education Authority

DATE OF RESEARCH: 1999-continuing

KEYWORDS: cookery; design and technology; food; food service; hygiene; safety; secondary education

1785

The Mere, Upton Park, Slough SL1 2DQ
01753 574123

Johnson, F. Miss; Stoney, S. Dr; Williams, S. Mr; Davies, M. Ms

The Duke of Edinburgh's Award qualitative study

ABSTRACT: The Duke of Edinburgh's Award offers all young people between the ages of 14 and 25 a flexible programme of individual and non-competitive, self-selected activities which become more challenging as participants progress through the Award's three levels. The aims of the project are to conduct an exploratory study, in 5 areas across the country, of views about the Award amongst Award participants and non-participants, unit leaders and staff in operating authorities. The research will focus on how the awareness, image and take-up of the Award can be improved for young people, especially for young people from less economically-favoured backgrounds, those with special needs and those in the 18-25 age range. It will also examine possibilities for simplifying the management and delivery of the Award at local level.

STATUS: Sponsored project

SOURCE OF GRANT: Duke of Edinburgh's Award Scheme

DATE OF RESEARCH: 1998-1998

KEYWORDS: extracurricular activities; youth opportunities; youth organisations

1786

The Mere, Upton Park, Slough SL1 2DQ
01753 574123

Le Metais, J. Dr; Greenaway, E. Mrs

Compilation of European glossary on education terminology (Volume 2: education establishments)

ABSTRACT: This is the second volume in a series of glossaries intended to facilitate the understanding of educational terminology used in Europe. The first volume, on qualifications, covered the 15 Member States of the European Union and the 3 European Economic Area countries. The present volume will cover these countries and, in addition, the 10 countries of Central and Eastern Europe and Cyprus. The project involves the compilation of a glossary of terms relating to education institutions at primary, secondary and higher education level. It is being carried out in collaboration with the Eurydice European Unit in Brussels.

STATUS: Sponsored project

SOURCE OF GRANT: NFER

DATE OF RESEARCH: 1998-continuing

KEYWORDS: educational terminology; europe; vocabulary

1787

The Mere, Upton Park, Slough SL1 2DQ
01753 574123

Kinder, K. Ms; Kendall, S. Dr; Atkinson, M. Ms; *Supervisor*: Harland, J. Dr

The policy and practice of non-exclusion

ABSTRACT: For some time, the rising number of pupils experiencing permanent exclusion from school has been a focus for academic research as well as a topic of media interest. The over-representation of Year 10 and 11 pupils, boys, Afro-Caribbean pupils and young people with special needs among those excludees has also been well documented. Perhaps less often noted, however, has been the positive and preventative to support at-risk pupils which is currently underway in a number of schools and local education authorities (LEAs). For instance, there have been examples of LEA behavioural support teams contracting with schools to provide temporary, pre-exclusion places in off-site units. Equally, GEST

20 funding has facilitated the introduction of a range of innovative school-based strategies offering behavioural/pastoral or curriculum-related support to pupils displaying disaffected tendencies. Yet, how far these approaches are directly linked to an intention and commitment not to permanently exclude is not always apparent. It is therefore timely to look at schools who do operate a policy of non-exclusion and investigate the strategies and practice which accompany this. The project's aims are to: 1) identify and illuminate the practice of schools which operate a non-exclusion policy; 2) provide an evaluative overview of the efficacy and impact of this approach; and 3) identify key factors in its success. The project will adopt a case study approach, thus allowing for a sustained and indepth focus on the characteristics and culture of the selected schools. Equally, the relationship between school policy statements on exclusions and subsequent practice (as experienced by staff, pupils, parents and the community, associated personnel from LEA services) is a key issue of this research. The project is linked to the NFER's Effective Behaviour Management project. One key research question will be how and which strategies for managing behaviour are capable of supporting any non-exclusion policy. The study will utilise the survey of a representative sample of 120 secondary schools which is also part of the Effective Behaviour Management project. It will obtain data on the characteristics of non-excluding schools as well as the perceived efficacy and existence of a non-exclusion policy.

STATUS: Sponsored project

SOURCE OF GRANT: NFER

DATE OF RESEARCH: 1997-1998

KEYWORDS: exclusion; school policy

1788

The Mere, Upton Park, Slough SL1 2DQ
01753 574123

Lee, B. Ms; Derrington, C. Ms

The LEA role in school improvement

ABSTRACT: A number of major initiatives, introduced by central Government since 1997, mark a significant shift in the duties that local education authorities (LEAs) are required to perform. With the emphasis on raising standards in schools, ministers have made it clear that LEAs are expected to play a vital, supporting role although former levels of direct influence over schools have been reduced over the past decade. These new responsibilities are outlined in the White Paper 'Excellence in Schools' (DfEE, 1997). The Education Act 1997 gave the Chief Inspector of Schools the power to inspect the performance of LEAs and the School Standards and Framework Act 1998 gives the Secretary of State new powers of intervention where an LEA is judged to be failing. The new Act also requires LEAs to publish Education Development Plans. In addition, LEAs must have regard to a new Code of Practice on effective relations within schools. From April 1999, a revised system of funding will reduce centrally-held budgets and increase delegation to schools. This project aims to investigate the impact of the changing role and the LEA's contribution to raising standards in schools. It will seek to identify the strengths and opportunities afforded by the revised role as well as the major challenges and areas of conflict. The research will be carried out by means of case studies in a number of LEAs. Interviews will be held with LEA personnel, school staff and governors.

STATUS: Sponsored project

SOURCE OF GRANT: NFER

DATE OF RESEARCH: 1998-continuing

KEYWORDS: educational quality; local education authorities; performance indicators; primary education; school effectiveness; school improvement; secondary education; value added

1789

The Mere, Upton Park, Slough SL1 2DQ
01753 574123

Sims, D. Mr; Kinder, K. Ms; Fletcher-Campbell, F. Dr

Expert support for New Start projects

ABSTRACT: In 1998 the Department for Education and Employment (DfEE) launched the New Start strategy to tackle disaffection among 14

to 17 year-olds. It is funding local partnerships of statutory and voluntary organisations to assess the scope of disaffection and to coordinate and disseminate action to address this problem. The partnerships may include local education authorities, training and enterprise councils (TECs), the careers service, the probation service, social services, the youth service, schools, colleges, employers and training organisations, and voluntary and community groups. The National Foundation for Educational Research (NFER) provides expertise and advice at the national level to DfEE staff, at regional level to North East and North West Government Office staff, and at local level to individual partnerships. This work includes advising Government Offices on strategic developments in this field, supporting partnerships in devising frameworks for development, helping them to build research findings into their action plans, and assisting with dissemination activities. The outcomes will include contributions to the development of New Start partnerships and strategies and presentations at New Start conferences and workshops.

STATUS: Sponsored project

SOURCE OF GRANT: Department for Education and Employment

DATE OF RESEARCH: 1997-continuing

KEYWORDS: agency cooperation; disaffection; new start; partnerships; pupil alienation

1790

The Mere, Upton Park, Slough SL1 2DQ
01753 574123

Sims, D. Mr

Partnerships against social exclusion

ABSTRACT: A network of representatives of 6 European countries was established in September 1998 to work on a project called Partnerships Against Social Exclusion. Coordinated by the National Council of Education in Portugal, and including members from Belgium, France, Germany, Spain and the UK, the purpose of the network is to: 1) examine the meanings and definitions of social exclusion; 2) compare and share different types of partnership strategy and models of formation, development, operation, maintenance and evaluation; 3) write country-specific reports on the work of educational partnerships in dealing with social exclusion; and 4) produce an overall summary of the key findings and main observations contained in the individual reports. Network members meet twice to exchange information and to draw together critical messages on effective partnerships against social exclusion. The project will provide 6 national reports and a summary report which will be sent to the European Commission.

STATUS: Sponsored project

SOURCE OF GRANT: European Commission

DATE OF RESEARCH: 1999-continuing

KEYWORDS: disadvantaged; europe; partnerships; social exclusion

1791

The Mere, Upton Park, Slough SL1 2DQ
01753 574123

Sims, D. Mr; Golden, S. Ms; Davies, D. Ms

Construction Industry Training Board (CITB) trainee characteristics survey

ABSTRACT: The Construction Industry Training Board (CITB) commissioned the National Foundation for Educational Research (NFER) to carry out a project, between September 1998 and March 1999, to collect and analyse key data on its trainees which could be used for monitoring, management and quality assurance purposes. A postal survey was undertaken of CITB and non-CITB apprentices to find out why they chose to go into construction, the main influences on their career choice, their views on the Construction Skills Learning Exercise and recruitment interviews, and what they think about their training programme. The results may be used as baseline data for follow-up surveys in 1999-2000 and 2000-2001. The outcome will include an overall report to the CITB, reports for Area Offices and an oral presentation of the findings and their implications.

STATUS: Sponsored project

SOURCE OF GRANT: Construction Industry Training Board

DATE OF RESEARCH: 1998-continuing

KEYWORDS: **apprenticeships; building trades education; construction industry; trainees; training; vocational education**

1792

The Mere, Upton Park, Slough SL1 2DQ
01753 574123

Kerr, D. Mr; *Supervisor*: Dickson, P. Mr

Teacher training and the new 16-19 agenda

ABSTRACT: The aim of this project is to investigate the range of approaches to post-16 on Postgraduate Certificate of Education (PGCE) initial teacher training courses and to consider their effectiveness in training teachers for the post-16 phase. The project will document the range of initial teacher training (ITT) programmes, identify patterns of approach to post-16 and examine the experiences of those involved in training to teach the post-16 phase. This will be achieved through a postal enquiry to all initial teacher training providers, followed by a survey of student teachers and tutors in 3 subject areas which cover the range of post-16 pathways and qualifications: science, modern foreign languages (MFL) and history. A final phase of the study may be included to provide indepth case study research in 5 training programmes, each with different approaches and strategies for the post-16 phase. The outcomes will inform the growing national debate on post-16, initial teacher training and teacher quality.

STATUS: Sponsored project

SOURCE OF GRANT: NFER

DATE OF RESEARCH: 1998-continuing

KEYWORDS: **preservice teacher education; sixteen to nineteen education**

1793

The Mere, Upton Park, Slough SL1 2DQ
01753 574123

Golden, S. Ms; *Supervisor*: Sims, D. Mr

Evaluation of the mentoring bursary programme

ABSTRACT: Mentoring has become a widely used support and enabling strategy in a broad range of contexts including education, management and business. The mentoring bursary programme was established in Autumn 1998 to promote the adoption of mentoring for young people with different needs in a variety of settings. A total of 20 projects are being supported by the programme which is managed by the National Mentoring Network on behalf of the Department for Education and Employment (DfEE). The Network has commissioned the National Foundation for Educational Research (NFER) to provide professional advice to individual projects and to assess the overall impact of the bursary programme. The research team is collecting a wide range of data from the projects which they will be visiting twice during the course of the evaluation which started in October 1998. This data will include written materials, qualitative interviews, and project-level monitoring data and evaluation results. The evaluation report will be presented in October 1999 and will include key findings and their implications for future policy development in this important area. The findings will be presented in a final report to the DfEE in October 1999 which will be disseminated through the National Mentoring Network.

STATUS: Sponsored project

SOURCE OF GRANT: National Mentoring Project

DATE OF RESEARCH: 1998-continuing

KEYWORDS: **adolescents; mentoring; mentors; national mentoring network; programme evaluation; secondary school pupils**

1794

The Mere, Upton Park, Slough SL1 2DQ
01753 574123

Kerr, D. Mr; Lines, A. Mrs; Taylor, M. Dr; *Supervisor*: Dickson, P. Mr

IEA Civic Education: Phase 2

ABSTRACT: This is a major project, funded by the Department for Education and Employment (DfEE), investigating national development in civic or citizenship education for 14 year-olds within an international context. It is a two-phase study, carried out under the aegis of the International Association for the Evaluation of Educational Achievement (IEA). In the first phase, each of the 24 participating countries gathered information in their own country on approaches to civic education and completed a comprehensive National Case Study Report for inclusion in the international database. England's report (Kerr, 1999) traces the background to citizenship education and relates it to current debates about political awareness and social cohesion. It describes the diversity of practice in schools and sets out the challenges involved in incorporating citizenship education into the school curriculum. The second phase started in 1998 and will consist of a major international survey in 29 countries of young people's attitudes, experiences and understanding of citizenship education. The goal of Phase 2 is to identify and examine in a comparative framework the ways in which young people are prepared to undertake their role as citizens in democracies and societies aspiring to democracy, as well as the aspects of political identity that are important to them. A primary purpose will be to obtain a picture of how young people are initiated into the various levels and types of political community of which they are members; this will include an investigation of influences in and out of school. The Phase 2 work in England will be conducted between November 1998 and June 2001. About 150 schools will take part in a survey which will include tests to be completed by students and questionnaires for students, teachers and schools. A sample of about 2,500 14 year-olds in the 150 schools will be required to complete a test lasting 90 minutes assessing 5 types of student capacities: knowledge, skills, concepts, attitudes and actions. A second population, which includes students in their last year of upper secondary education, is optional and will not feature in the survey in England. Questionnaires will be administered to teachers (3 in each of the survey schools) on 'civics related' subjects, and to headteachers on issues relating to policy, provision and organisation. The outcomes will include: 1) A volume containing the National Case Study reports from Phase 1 will be published by IEA in early 1999. 2) A national report on Phase 2 results in England and the international report on key international and national findings will be ready for publication in 2001. 3) Other dissemination of the results will be carried out through supplementary reports, press releases, the use of the Internet, meetings, research articles and conferences

PUBLISHED MATERIAL: KERR, D. (1999). 'Re-examining citizenship education in England'. In: TORNEY-PURTA, J., SCHWILLE, J. & AMADEO, J-A. (Eds). Civic education across countries: twenty-four national case studies from the IEA Civic Education project. Amsterdam: Eburon Publishers for the International Association for the Evaluation of Educational Achievement (IEA).

STATUS: Sponsored project

SOURCE OF GRANT: Department for Education and Employment

DATE OF RESEARCH: 1998-continuing

KEYWORDS: **citizenship education; pupil attitudes**

1795

The Mere, Upton Park, Slough SL1 2DQ
01753 574123

Saunders, L. Ms; Schagen, S. Dr

Teacher education in study support

ABSTRACT: Study support - learning activity outside normal lessons which young people participate in voluntarily - is an important element of the Government's proposals to raise levels of achievement in young people. Extending Opportunity, a national framework for study support published by the Department for Education and Employment (DfEE) earlier this year, sets out the context for the national development of study support activities and initiatives. The impact of this kind of initiative is dependent not only on what is done but on how it is done. For study support to be as effective as possible, training opportunities need to be available for teachers to develop their skills in this area of work. The University of Keele and Christchurch College, Canterbury, are jointly developing inservice teacher education (INSET) in study support for secondary teachers through a DfEE funded project. Two sites (one in the Midlands and one in the South) have been selected for the following activities: surveying and analysing existing provision; carrying out a training needs analysis; designing a pilot training course; and fostering professional networks. A second DfEE project, undertaken by Education Extra, is aimed at primary teachers, and has sites in the London Borough of Newham, the London Borough of Croydon, East Sussex and Rochdale. The National Foundation for Educational Research (NFER) has been asked to act as external evaluator to the initial phase of both projects during the period October 1998 - March 1999. The initial evaluation will be essentially formative, both for the implementation of the training provision and for the refining of policy for the second stage. The outcome will be the production of an evaluation report, plus input into proposals for post-pilot phase.

STATUS: Sponsored project

SOURCE OF GRANT: Department for Education and Employment

DATE OF RESEARCH: 1998-continuing

KEYWORDS: **inservice teacher education; out of school hours learning; study support; teacher development**

1796

The Mere, Upton Park, Slough SL1 2DQ
01753 574123

Sims, D. Mr; Golden, S. Ms; Nelson, J. Dr

National Vocational Qualifications (NVQs) case studies

ABSTRACT: The Department for Education and Employment (DfEE), which now has overall responsibility for the promotion of National Vocational Qualifications (NVQs), commissioned the National Foundation for Educational Research (NFER) (November 1998-March 1999) to produce an accessible resource of case study material on the use and outcomes of NVQs and an outline strategy for disseminating it. A postal survey was used to collect information from organisations and individuals on key themes such as reasons for taking up NVQs, the experience and challenges of using them, the impact and benefits, and lessons learned. Drawn from a range of industrial sectors, the information is being developed into a computerised database of case studies. The database, which will contain a minimum of 60 case studies, has been designed so that it may be used interactively to deal with enquiries.

STATUS: Sponsored project

SOURCE OF GRANT: Department for Education and Employment

DATE OF RESEARCH: 1998-continuing

KEYWORDS: **databases; national vocational qualifications; outcomes of education; vocational education; vocational qualifications**

1797

The Mere, Upton Park, Slough SL1 2DQ
01753 574123

Ashworth, M. Mrs; Atkinson, M. Ms; Halsey, K. Ms; Haynes, J. Ms; *Supervisors*: Kinder, K. Ms; Harland, J. Dr

An evaluation of North East Lincolnshire: promoting positive behaviour strategy - a multi-agency approach to teachers' continuing professional development

ABSTRACT: This evaluation focused on 2 examples of multi-agency activity in North East Lincolnshire. Firstly, the work of the multi-agency support team (MAST) in 6 case study primary schools, and secondly, the development of multi-agency courses to encourage collaboration between individuals working with young people in a number of related areas. The aims were to examine the impact of both the MAST team and the courses on teachers, schools and other professionals to explore the relationship between continuing professional development (CPD) outcomes and the forms of CPD provided and to identify any additional benefits to schools of multi-agency activity, such as improving attendance, reducing the incidence of disruptive behaviour or the incidence of exclusions. The main approach was qualitative indepth interviews. For the courses, both the perceptions of course attenders and course providers were sought concerning the impact on practice and school policy; the challenges and advantages of multi-agency and cluster attendance; and areas for further development. For the MAST activities in case study schools, both teachers and MAST personnel were interviewed twice: first for perceptions of

the activities while they were in operation, and again, once the project was completed, for perceptions of the impact of the MAST activity as a whole. Baseline data was also collected from the case study schools, wherever possible, on exclusions, attendance and behaviour. The final results from the evaluation were to be presented in a report at the end of June 1999.

STATUS: Sponsored project

SOURCE OF GRANT: North East Lincolnshire LEA; NFER

DATE OF RESEARCH: 1998-continuing

KEYWORDS: **agency cooperation; local education authorities; professional continuing education; teacher development**

1798

The Mere, Upton Park, Slough SL1 2DQ
01753 574123

Greenaway, E. Mrs

International review of curriculum and assessment frameworks: thematic study lower secondary education

ABSTRACT: The lower secondary education study is the fifth thematic study based on INCA, the Archive of the International Review of Curriculum and Assessment Frameworks (IRCAF) project. INCA comprises descriptions (by individual country) of curriculum and assessment frameworks in 16 countries (England, France, Hungary, Italy, Japan, Korea, the Netherlands, New Zealand, Singapore, Spain and Sweden and selected states in Australia, Canada, Germany, Switzerland and the USA). The thematic studies provide reliable, detailed information on the specific area under review. This is used by the Qualifications and Curriculum Authority (QCA) to evaluate the curriculum and assessment framework in England and to contextualise the outcome of international comparisons. The Lower Secondary Education thematic study brings together findings from INCA with additional research. An invitational seminar will be held in June 1999, involving IRCAF project staff, QCA staff and invited participants from most of the 16 countries, to assist this process. Specifically, this thematic study aims to: 1) provide richer descriptions of practice in this area in the 16 countries concerned; 2) clarify the role and nature of lower secondary education; 3) offer an analysis of the fundamental issues in this area as they relate to the curriculum and assessment framework in England. Areas of study focus on aspects of the current provision (from INCA and other sources) for the 11-14 age range including: 1) structures and organisation of lower secondary provision; 2) curriculum aims, organisation and structure; 3) implementation, looking at teachers, teaching and learning approaches and learning materials; 4) values and attitudes and how these are reflected or reinforced in the curriculum; 5) assessment arrangements; 6) current and future developments in different countries.

STATUS: Sponsored project

SOURCE OF GRANT: Qualifications and Curriculum Authority

DATE OF RESEARCH: 1998-continuing

KEYWORDS: **assessment; comparative education; curriculum development; secondary education**

1799

The Mere, Upton Park, Slough SL1 2DQ
01753 574123

Harland, J. Dr; Kinder, K. Ms; Pitts, S. Dr; Ashworth, M. Ms; Halsey, K. Ms

Extending young people's access to cultural organisations

ABSTRACT: Against a backcloth of concerns about the relatively low level of young people's cultural inclusion, especially in the years immediately following the end of compulsory schooling, the study sets out to: (a) review the available evidence and key literature on young people's attendance at artistic events and cultural venues; (b) conduct an audit of the most recent and significant initiatives aimed at broadening such access; (c) examine qualitative evidence on a sample of young people's attitudes towards engagement with the arts; (d) identify strategies that may be effective in mediating the arts and, in particular, explore the potential efficacy of cultural intermediaries, mediators and peer mentors.

STATUS: Sponsored project

SOURCE OF GRANT: Calouste Gulbenkian Foundation £8,000; Arts Council of England £8,000; NFER £5,915

DATE OF RESEARCH: 1999-continuing

KEYWORDS: arts; attitudes; cultural activities; cultural opportunities; culture; young adults; youth; youth attitudes

1800

The Mere, Upton Park, Slough SL1 2DQ
01753 574123

Hutchison, D. Dr; Kendall, S. Dr; Wilkin, A. Mrs; *Supervisor*: Brooks, G. Dr

Evaluation of intensive Basic Skills courses

ABSTRACT: In February 1999 the Basic Skills Agency received funding to establish intensive basic skills courses to be mounted by nine local education authorities/colleges of further education in England. The courses were to be completed by Easter 1999. The Agency commissioned research into these courses on a pre-test/post-test basis. The instruments used were the same as in the 1998/99 NFER evaluation of adult literacy provision, also conducted for the Basic Skills Agency.

STATUS: Team research

SOURCE OF GRANT: Basic Skills Agency

DATE OF RESEARCH: 1999-continuing

KEYWORDS: accelerated learning; achievement; adult basic education; adult literacy; course evaluation; intensive basic skills; literacy

1801

The Mere, Upton Park, Slough SL1 2DQ
01753 574123

Brooks, R. Ms; Fletcher-Campbell, F. Dr; Foxman, D. Dr; Sharp, C. Ms

Consultancy to Basic Skills Agency on its evaluation of Innovative Development Projects

ABSTRACT: The Basic Skills Agency is supporting 32 innovatory development projects in 1998/99. The projects fall into five areas (numbers of projects in brackets): (a) 'Catch up' programmes for 14- to 16-year-olds in secondary schools (7); (b) increasing the involvement of parents in helping their children to improve their basic skills in secondary schools (8); (c) developing new approaches to basic skills provision for adults (6); (d) developing new approaches to English for Speakers of Other Languages (ESOL) provision (2); (e) children and young people in care (9). NFER is providing consultancy in each of these specialist areas, and on evaluation of educational innovations in general.

STATUS: Sponsored project

SOURCE OF GRANT: Basic Skills Agency £13,000

DATE OF RESEARCH: 1998-continuing

KEYWORDS: adult basic education; adult literacy; basic skills; consultancy; educational innovation; english - second language; intervention; literacy; looked after children; numeracy; parent participation

1802

The Mere, Upton Park, Slough SL1 2DQ
01753 574123

Brooks, G. Dr; Shay, J. Mrs; Cross, J. Mrs

Evaluation of PEEP (Peers Early Education Partnership)

ABSTRACT: The Peers Early Education Partnership (PEEP) is a birth-to-school-entry programme based on the Littlemore/Blackbird Leys Estate in Oxford, England. PEEP is managed by a board of Trustees, and those Trustees have commissioned an independent evaluation of the programme from the National Foundation for Educational Research (NFER). This evaluation began on 1 February 1998, and (if all the necessary funding is secured) will run until 31 January 2005. The aim of the evaluation is to study all children born between 1 April 1998 and 31 March 1999 in the PEEP area and in a comparison area in Banbury, where no provision such as PEEP exists. The Littlemore/Blackbird Leys area of Oxford was chosen by the developers of PEEP because of the low literacy levels of pupils entering the Peers School at age 13. The area is one of severe material deprivation. The town of Banbury (excluding its middle-class area) is the comparison area. By Easter 1999, the samples had been recruited (300 families in each area) and were very similar.

PUBLISHED MATERIAL: BROOKS, G., SHAY, J., CROSS, J. & SMITH, G. (1998). The NFER Evaluation of the Peers Early Education Partnership (PEEP): Interim Report to the PEEP Trustees. Slough: NFER.

STATUS: Team research

SOURCE OF GRANT: PEEP Trustees, Esmee Fairbairn Charitable Trust

DATE OF RESEARCH: 1998-continuing

KEYWORDS: disadvantaged environment; early childhood education; intervention; literacy; longitudinal studies; programme evaluation

1803

The Mere, Upton Park, Slough SL1 2DQ
01753 574123

Taylor, M. Dr

Evaluation of the curriculum resources of the Stapleford Centre

ABSTRACT: Recent educational policy, guidance and inspection have given renewed prominence to spiritual, moral, social and cultural (SMSC) development in all curricular subjects. This evaluation constitutes a second consultancy being undertaken for the Jerusalem Trust. The first consultancy (1994-7) was an evaluation of the Charis project (undertaken by the Association of Christian Teachers) which produced two sets of classroom materials for English, Mathematics, French & German and (one set for) Science at key stage 4, with the aim of enhancing SMSC development from a Christian perspective. The evaluation (see publication below) provided information on project development and management, considered issues in the development and dissemination of materials, and assessed the extent to which the project achieved its own aims for pupils' SMSC development and the take-up of materials in secondary schools. The present consultancy (December 1997-2000) is both a continuation and an extension of the first. Initially, the evaluation is continuing to investigate the take-up and use of the key stage 4 Charis materials in schools. This is being undertaken through telephone interviews with a representative sample of over 50 schools from those which have purchased the materials. Following this, up to 10 school visits are being undertaken to observe materials in use in classrooms, interview teachers, and undertake focus groups with pupils. The evaluation is focusing on the influence of the materials on teachers' awareness of how to develop moral and spiritual dimensions of the curriculum, teaching strategies and on pupils' learning. This phase of the evaluation is likely to be completed by August 1999. In addition, the evaluation has a broader remit to review the management, development, take-up, use and influence of a range of other curriculum resources - for religious education, collective worship, personal and social education and spiritual, moral social and cultural education - being developed by the Stapleford Centre with sponsorship from the Jerusalem Trust. These resources include the development of Charis materials for key stage 3, as well as the ongoing production of established magazines such as Cracking RE. This aspect of the evaluation is being conducted by means of: documentary analysis; attendance at management meetings; observation of writing teams, interviews with team members and project directors; and is likely to include further contact with schools. Issues to be considered will include cost effectiveness and impact of the Centre's resources on schools' development of provision for SMSC.

PUBLISHED MATERIAL: TAYLOR, M.J. (1997). 'Evaluation of the Association of Christian Teachers' Cross-Curricular Christianity Charis Project'. Final Report. A Report to the Jerusalem Trust.

STATUS: Sponsored project

SOURCE OF GRANT: Jerusalem Trust

DATE OF RESEARCH: 1997-continuing

KEYWORDS: curriculum development; educational materials; moral education; personal and social education; religious education; spiritual development

1804

The Mere, Upton Park, Slough SL1 2DQ
01753 574123

Taylor, M. Dr

Preparing teachers as educators in values, attitudes, beliefs and behaviour

ABSTRACT: Current reviews of the aims and purposes of the National Curriculum, prior to its revision in 2000, are focusing on the broad area of personal and social education of young people. School-based research indicates that teachers accept responsibility for this as part of their role, but lack preparation and confidence. Indeed, current debate about values education in schools tends to overlook the need for teacher preparation to deliver a consistent and coherent curricular experience for pupils. To do this teachers require both initial training and continuing professional development. On the other hand, teacher training institutions have recently been required to pay renewed attention to the affective dimension - education in values, attitudes, beliefs and behaviour. How then are school needs and training requirements being addressed? This collaborative research, undertaken by University College of St Martin, Lancaster and NFER, aims to build an up-to-date national picture of teacher training institutions offering courses related to values education and the nature of these courses. Provision for teacher training in a wide range of values-related issues, such as personal and social education, religious education, collective worship and citizenship will be addressed. A survey questionnaire is being sent to all teacher training institutions in England and Wales. It will be followed up by telephone interviews with course leaders and analysis of documentation. A report will be produced, setting the research data in the context of current national policy, and reviewing the wider implications for teacher preparation to deliver personal and social education.

SOURCE OF GRANT: NFER

DATE OF RESEARCH: 1998-continuing

KEYWORDS: **citizenship education; inservice teacher education; personal and social education; preservice teacher education; religious education; school worship; teacher development; values education**

1805

The Mere, Upton Park, Slough SL1 2DQ
01753 574123

Hutchison, D. Dr; Kendall, S. Dr; Wilkin, A. Mrs; *Supervisor*: Brooks, G. Dr

Evaluation of adult literacy provision

ABSTRACT: The aims of the project are to investigate: (1) the progress made in literacy by adults in mainstream basic skills programmes provided by local education authorities and colleges of further education in England and Wales; and (2) factors associated with improvement in literacy by adults in such provision. Pre-tests were carried out between October 1998 and April 1999, and post-tests between March and June 1999. On both occasions, students were asked to complete a simple writing task, and a reading test. Items for the reading tests were drawn from several sources, including the 1995 International Adult Literacy Study (conducted in Britain by the Office for National Statistics). Tutors' views were investigated by questionnaire.

STATUS: Team research

SOURCE OF GRANT: Basic Skills Agency £205,000

DATE OF RESEARCH: 1998-continuing

KEYWORDS: **adult basic education; adult literacy; adults achievement; literacy; reading achievement; reading tests**

1806

The Mere, Upton Park, Slough SL1 2DQ
01753 574123

Brooks, G. Dr; Keys, W. Dr

Pamphlet on international comparisons in the core subjects

ABSTRACT: The independent thinktank Politeia commissioned NFER to provide the first draft and factual basis for a pamphlet comparing the performance in reading, mathematics and science of students aged 9 and 13 in a small number of countries (England, Scotland, USA, New Zealand, France, Germany, Japan, Switzerland, Netherlands). The information was drawn from the 1991 Reading Literacy study conducted by the International Association for the Evaluation of Educational Achievement (IEA) - together with the 1996 replication of that study in England and Wales, and the Third International mathematics and Science Study (TIMSS), also conducted by the IEA.

STATUS: Sponsored project

SOURCE OF GRANT: Politeia

DATE OF RESEARCH: 1999-continuing

KEYWORDS: **academic achievement; achievement; comparative education; international educational exchange; literacy; mathematics achievement; mathematics education; performance; primary education; reading; reading achievement; science education; scientific ability; secondary education**

1807

The Mere, Upton Park, Slough SL1 2DQ
01753 574123

Brooks, G. Dr; Harman, J. Mr; Hutchison, D. Dr; *Supervisor*: Brooks, G. Dr

Evaluation of the reading intervention strategy of the first steps initial literacy programme

ABSTRACT: In 1998, the Western Australia-based authors of the First Steps initial literacy teaching continuum devised the Reading Intervention Strategy, a remedial intervention for children who, although in First Steps classrooms, were not making satisfactory progress in reading. The Strategy was implemented in a small number of schools in the town of Reading, Berkshire, all of which were already using First Steps. The Education Department of Western Australia commissioned an evaluation of the Strategy, and the pre-test was carried out. However, less than one term in, the implementation of the Strategy itself was abandoned, and the evaluation was therefore cut short.

STATUS: Team research

SOURCE OF GRANT: Education Department, Western Australia

DATE OF RESEARCH: 1998-continuing

KEYWORDS: **intervention; literacy; programme evaluation; reading; reading strategies; remedial reading**

1808

The Mere, Upton Park, Slough SL1 2DQ
01753 574123

Kinder, K. Ms; Atkinson, M. Ms; Wilkin, A. Mrs; Kendall, S. Dr; Halsey, K. Ms

The role of the LEA in reducing truancy

ABSTRACT: In the light of recent developments, such as the establishment of a link between truancy and crime and the publication of the social exclusion report, in which the government commits to a reduction in truancy and details plans for this to be translated into targets at both school and local education authority level, this study aims to: (1) Identify the activity undertaken by the Education Welfare Service in reducing truancy; (2) Audit multi-agency approaches that are used to address non-attendance and examine how these affect truancy rates; (3) Examine key staffing issues that have implications for reducing truancy; (4) Report and evaluate examples of effective practice in reducing truancy; (5) Examine the overall contribution of local education authorities to reducing truancy. The study will involve an initial audit of education welfare service activity followed by qualitative in-depth interviews with personnel from 20 local education authorities at strategic level. More intensive case study work in five local authorities, where interventions have made a positive impact on attendance, will include interviews with pupils, parents and community members. An interim report, providing an overview of the contribution of local authority services, to the reduction of truancy and the issues identified at strategic level, will be followed by a final report presenting and evaluating examples of innovative and effective practice.

STATUS: Sponsored project

SOURCE OF GRANT: Council for Local Education Authorities

DATE OF RESEARCH: 1999-continuing

KEYWORDS: **attendance; educational welfare; local education authorities; truancy**

1809

The Mere, Upton Park, Slough SL1 2DQ
01753 574123

McDonald, A. Mr

The prevalence and effects of test anxiety in school children

ABSTRACT: This project reviews the literature on the prevalence and effects of test anxiety on children in compulsory education. Tests are identified as a major source of concern to many children, and the overall prevalence of test anxiety appears to be increasing, possibly due to increased testing in schools and pressures associated with this. Studies of children are generally in accordance with the wider literature, namely that test anxiety impairs test performance, although this is moderated by individual differences and the testing environment. Methodological problems in the literature are discussed, and suggestions for further research made.

STATUS: Sponsored project

SOURCE OF GRANT: NFER

DATE OF RESEARCH: 1999-continuing

KEYWORDS: **anxiety; pupils; stress - psychological; test anxiety; tests**

1810

The Mere, Upton Park, Slough SL1 2DQ
01753 574123

Rudd, P. Dr; Jamison, J. Mr; Johnson, F. Miss; Davies, D. Ms; Ashby, P. Mrs; Dobby, J. Mr; Felgate, R.Miss; *Supervisor*: Saunders, L. Ms

Evaluation of pilot beacon schools

ABSTRACT: The NFER has been commissioned by the Department for Education and Employment (DfEE) to evaluate the pilot Beacon Schools initiative during the period March 1999 to September 1999. The 75 schools selected for DfEE funding during the pilot phase (identified through the Office for Standards in Education (OFSTED) inspection evidence) began operating as Beacon Schools in September 1998. The initiative will be extended to include a further 125 schools from September 1999. Beacon Schools are one dimension of the DfEE drive to base strategies for school improvement in school. This 'site based' model is complemented by a partnership principle, and, as such, Beacon Schools are intended to play a formative role for other schools in identifying, disseminating and promoting good practice in key areas such as leadership, teaching and monitoring of pupils' progress. The project aims to evaluate the range and quality of Beacon Schools activities to support and promote good practice, the use made by Beacon Schools of resources, the perceived value of Beacon School activities to their 'target audience' (of non-Beacon schools, local education authorites and providers of teacher training), and the likelihood of Beacon School activities leading to school improvement, especially raised standards. The outcome will be a report on the Beacon School questionnaire responses, supported by a technical appendix and a detailed final report which will evaluate the achievements, effectiveness and value of Beacon Schools.

STATUS: Sponsored project

SOURCE OF GRANT: Department for Education and Employment

DATE OF RESEARCH: 1999-continuing

KEYWORDS: **beacon schools; dissemination of good practice; educational quality; good practice; high performing schools; nursery education; primary education; school effectiveness; school improvement; secondary education; special schools**

1811

The Mere, Upton Park, Slough SL1 2DQ
01753 574123

O'Donnell, S. Mrs; *Supervisor*: Le Metais, J. Dr

International review of curriculum and assessment frameworks

ABSTRACT:1714-17181710-1714 The International Review of Curriculum and Assessment Frameworks draws mainly on primary sources from national authorities in 16 countries (Australia, Canada, England, France, Germany, Hungary, Italy, Japan, Korea, the Netherlands, New Zealand, Singapore, Spain, Sweden, Switzerland, USA). It is intended to inform Qualifications and Curriculum Authority's (QCA) review of the curriculum and assessment in England and to provide a context for interpreting the findings of international surveys. The comparative country descriptions

constitute an excellent reference tool for policymakers, practitioners and researchers interested in: (1) stated values and educational aims; (2) educational structures; (3) institutional organisation; (4) curriculum content and organisation; (5) assessment frameworks. The thematic studies bring together the findings of INCA, additional research and an invitational seminar. The first three studies are: values and aims in curriculum and assessment frameworks; primary education: expectations and provision; and mathematics in the school curriculum: an international perspective.

PUBLISHED MATERIAL: LE METAIS, J. (1997). Values and aims in curriculum and assessment frameworks. International Review of Curriculum and Assessment Frameworks Paper 1. London: School Curriculum and Assessment Authority. ; LE METAIS, J. & TABBERER, R. (1997). 'Why different countries do better: evidence from examining curriculum and assessment frameworks in 16 countries', International Electronic Journal for Leadership in Learning. Calgary, Alberta, Canada: The University of Calgary. ; TABBERER, R. (1997). Primary education: expectations and provision. International Review of Curriculum and Assessment Frameworks Paper 2. London: School Curriculum and Assessment Authority. ; LE METAIS, J. (1998). 'Values and aims in curriculum and assessment systems: a 16 nation review'. In: MOON, R. & MURPHY, P. Curriculum in context (E836 Course Reader One). London: Sage. ; RUDDOCK, G. (1998). 'Mathematics in the school curriculum: an International perspective. International Review of Curriculum and Assessment Frameworks Paper 3. London: Qualifications and Curriculum Authority. A full list of publications is available from the researchers.

STATUS: Sponsored project

SOURCE OF GRANT: Qualifications and Assessment Authority

DATE OF RESEARCH: 1998-continuing

KEYWORDS: **assessment; comparative education; curriculum development**

1812

The Mere, Upton Park, Slough SL1 2DQ
01753 574123

Brooks, G. Dr

Evaluation of family numeracy pilot projects

ABSTRACT: NFER has been evaluating the Basic Skills Agency's family numeracy project by advising on methods of evaluation, and analysing and interpreting statistics. The main finding was that children in Family Numeracy courses made greater progress than children in control groups (nurseries with no Family Numeracy teaching).

STATUS: Sponsored project

SOURCE OF GRANT: Basic Skills Agency

DATE OF RESEARCH: 1997-1997

KEYWORDS: **early childhood education; family numeracy; mathematics education; numeracy; nursery education; parent participation; parent pupil relationship; young children**

1813

The Mere, Upton Park, Slough SL1 2DQ
01753 574123

Osgood, J. Miss

The coordination of childcare and education services for under fives

ABSTRACT: The aim of this project is to evaluate the strategies devised for the integration of services for children under five. It involves the investigation of Early Years Development Plans of local authorities from across England in order to identify: the range of strategies which have been adopted; how the plans are implemented; examples of effective practice; and the advantages and disadvantages of different models in relation to particular local contexts. The project will consist of two phases. Phase one will involve familiarisation of the main strategies adopted by local authorities for the coordination of the services for under fives, as detailed in Early Years Development Plans. The second phase will involve the selection of eight local authorities for detailed case study investigation. An interview programme would be carried out, focusing upon the evolution, aims and objectives, implementation, monitoring and evaluation, successes and challenges and any modifications made to the plans. The final report would provide examples of different approaches to providing services for young children, highlighting the particular advantages and disadvantages of each.

STATUS: Sponsored project

SOURCE OF GRANT: NFER

DATE OF RESEARCH: 1999-continuing

KEYWORDS: **coordination; day care; early childhood education; local education authorities; nursery education; preschool education; young children**

1814

The Mere, Upton Park, Slough SL1 2DQ
01753 574123

Mason, K. Mr

Homework in mathematics and science at key stage 3

ABSTRACT: This research is focusing on the findings on the effectiveness of homework in raising achievement, drawing on the data from the Third International Mathematics and Science Study (TIMSS).

STATUS: Sponsored project

SOURCE OF GRANT: NFER Research Development Fund

DATE OF RESEARCH: 1998-1998

KEYWORDS: **academic achievement; achievement; comparative education; homework; key stage 3; mathematics education; science education; secondary education**

1815

The Mere, Upton Park, Slough SL1 2DQ
01753 574123

Mason, K. Mr

Use of mathematics textbooks at key stage 2

ABSTRACT: Secondary analyses of the Third International Mathematics and Science Study (TIMSS) dataset were carried out in order to identify and compare the extent and nature of textbook use in teaching mathematics to nine-year-olds TIMSS Population 2) in England and other countries.

STATUS: Sponsored project

SOURCE OF GRANT: NFER

DATE OF RESEARCH: 1998-1998

KEYWORDS: **comparative education; key stage 2; mathematics education; primary education; textbooks**

1816

The Mere, Upton Park, Slough SL1 2DQ
01753 574123

Keys, W. Dr

Third International Mathematics and Science Study (TIMSS) multi-level modelling

ABSTRACT: This project consists of secondary analyses of the Third International Mathematics and Science Study (TIMSS) datasets designed to identify the factors associated with mathematics and science achievement for nine-year-olds (TIMSS Population 1) and 13-year-olds (TIMSS Population 2) in England and a small number of other countries.

STATUS: Sponsored project

SOURCE OF GRANT: NFER Research Development Fund

DATE OF RESEARCH: 1998-1998

KEYWORDS: **academic achievement; achievement; comparative education; mathematics education; multilevel modelling; primary education; science education; secondary education; statistical analysis**

1817

The Mere, Upton Park, Slough SL1 2DQ
01753 574123

Maychell, K. Ms

Survey to identify the incidence of able 16-18-year-olds

ABSTRACT: This study surveyed maintained and independent schools, sixth-form and tertiary colleges. Institutions were asked to: estimate the number of 16- to 19-year-olds who met the Qualifications and Curriculum Authority's (QCA) working definition of very able; and provide information on the enrichment courses, activities and experiences they provided for such students.

STATUS: Sponsored project

SOURCE OF GRANT: Qualifications and Assessment Authority

DATE OF RESEARCH: 1997-1998

KEYWORDS: **able pupils; enrichment activities; sixteen to nineteen education**

1818

The Mere, Upton Park, Slough SL1 2DQ
01753 574123
Brunel University, School of Education, Twickenham Campus, 300 St Margaret's Road, Twickenham TW1 1PT
0181 891 0121

Ruddock, G. Dr; Harris, D. Prof.; Tomlins, B. Dr; Brooks, G. Dr; Salt, S. Mr; *Supervisors*: Whetton, C. Mr; Foxman, D. Mr

Evaluation of National Curriculum assessment at key stage 3 in mathematics, science, English and technology

ABSTRACT: The project evaluated the first nationwide National Curriculum assessment of fourteen year olds in science and mathematics in 1992, and in English and technology in 1993. The results of these were surveyed and the procedures used evaluated. One focus of evaluation was the validity and reliability of the results. Three elements made up the study: a statistical survey of results; case studies of schools' management of the assessment process; and review of the assessment materials used. Reports on the 1992 mathematics and science pilot have been published, while that on the 1993 English and technology is due to be available in 1995.

PUBLISHED MATERIAL: RUDDOCK, G. et al. (1992). Teacher assessment in mathematics and science at key stage 3: a report. London: School Examinations and Assessment Council. ; RUDDOCK, G. et al. (1993). Evaluation of National Curriculum Assessment in mathematics and science at key stage 3: the 1992 National Pilot. Final Report. London: School Examinations and Assessment Council.

STATUS: Sponsored project

SOURCE OF GRANT: School Examinations and Assessment Council £569,000

DATE OF RESEARCH: 1991-1993

KEYWORDS: **assessment; english; evaluation; mathematics education; national curriculum; science education; secondary education; technology education**

1819

The Mere, Upton Park, Slough SL1 2DQ
01753 574123
Further Education Development Agency, Citadel Place, Tinworth Street, London SE11 5EH
0171 840 5400

Lee, B. Ms; Davies, P. Mr; *Supervisor*: Keys, W. Dr

Factors affecting the take-up of 16-plus educational provision: college study

ABSTRACT: This study forms part of a larger National Foundation for Educational Research (NFER) project in which school students in Years 8, 11 and 12 are being surveyed and interviewed. The same issues will be investigated in schools and colleges, with an appropriate focus. The main outcome of the research will be a report outlining the main factors which affect students' post-16 intentions. The study comprises 3 phases. The developmental phase consists of group interviews with first year students in further education (FE) colleges. A self-completion questionnaire will be designed on the basis of these interviews. A survey will be carried out of about 1,000 students in 25 FE colleges. The questionnaire will seek information on what students knew about the range of post-16 provision available to them and their career plans before they left school, as well as the reasons for their choice. A college questionnaire will also be used to obtain background information. The surveys will be completed by case studies in order to develop and extend the data.

STATUS: Sponsored project

SOURCE OF GRANT: Further Education Development Agency

DATE OF RESEARCH: 1996-1997

KEYWORDS: career choice; decision making; further education; pupil destinations; school leavers; secondary education; secondary school pupils; sixteen to nineteen education; student attitudes; vocational guidance

1820

The Mere, Upton Park, Slough SL1 2DQ
01753 574123
London Research Centre, 81 Black Prince Road, London SE1 7SZ
0171 787 5666

Kendall, L. Mrs; McCallum, I. Mr; Euteneuer, R. Mr

Research into factors influencing GCSE performance in London boroughs

ABSTRACT: The National Foundation for Educational Research (NFER) has been involved in research which puts the General Certificate of Secondary Education (GCSE) examination results of pupils in inner London into context, taking into account factors related to individual pupils' ethnicity, gender, fluency in English, entitlement to free school meals and prior achievement. The London Research Centre (LRC) has been investigating the links between pupils' home characteristics, using small area census data, and their achievements. These two strands will be combined to develop a more sophisticated understanding of the influences relating most strongly to performance at GCSE level. This pilot study will use existing data for a small number of inner London boroughs to investigate the relative contributions of different measures of pupils' socio-economic circumstances in describing pupil achievement. By using multilevel modelling techniques, this pilot study would also explore the extent to which it is possible to identify those secondary schools which are particularly effective with various sub-groups of pupils, such as those from particular ethnic groups, or from particular socio-economic groups. A report will be produced outlining the findings of the analysis. In addition, the work will provide an understanding of the extent to which the procedures and analysis used in the pilot could be transferred to a full-scale survey of London secondary schools.

STATUS: Sponsored project

SOURCE OF GRANT: Peabody Trust £9,000; NFER £1,100; London Research Centre £1,350

DATE OF RESEARCH: 1998-continuing

KEYWORDS: academic achievement; examination results; general certificate of secondary education; school effectiveness; secondary education; urban schools

1821

The Mere, Upton Park, Slough SL1 2DQ
01753 574123
London University, Institute of Education, 20 Bedford Way, London WC1H 0AL
0171 580 1122

Harris, S. Mrs; Preston, C. Mrs; *Supervisor*: Foxman, D. Mr

Survey of the provision, acquisition and use of computer software in primary and secondary schools

ABSTRACT: Information technology (IT) is one of the attainment targets of Technology in the National Curriculum. The main aim of the project was to investigate the current use of educational software in schools, in terms of what is being used, how it is is being used and which aspects of the curriculum are being supported. The research was carried out by means of: 1) questionnaire surveys of a random sample of 400 primary and 600 secondary schools; 2) telephone interviews with IT coordinators in a sub-sample of primary and secondary schools selected from respondents to the survey; 3) visits to local education authority (LEA) computer centres; 4) interviews with IT coordinators in a number of 'focus' schools outside the random sample, which explored issues covered

in the questionnaire in more depth; and 5) a questionnaire survey of 50 educational software publishers. The report on the project provides: information on schools' software purchases; the software in use in schools; and the systems and strategies available to support school use of software. The contributions of LEAs and educational software publishers are also explored. Finally, some perspectives on the future (in terms of needs and possible developments) are collated from schools, LEAs and educational software publishers.

PUBLISHED MATERIAL: HARRIS, S. & PRESTON, C. (1993). Software in schools: the provision, acquisition and use of computer software in primary and secondary schools. Slough: National Foundation for Educational Research.

STATUS: Sponsored project

SOURCE OF GRANT: National Council for Educational Technology £38,000

DATE OF RESEARCH: 1993-1993

KEYWORDS: computer software; computer uses in education; educational software; information technology; technology education

1822

The Mere, Upton Park, Slough SL1 2DQ
01753 574123
Plymouth University, Faculty of Arts and Education, Rolle School of Education, Douglas Avenue, Exmouth EX8 2AT
01395 255309

Taylor, M. Dr; Halstead, J. Dr; *Supervisor*: Stoney, S. Dr

A review of research on the development of values, attitudes and personal qualities

ABSTRACT: Pupils' values and the role of schools in developing young people's attitudes and personal qualities have come under greater scrutiny, both because of various horrific social acts perpetrated by children and because of renewed attention given to the provision for spiritual, moral, social and cultural development in the Office for Standards in Education (OFSTED) inspections. This review of published research, undertaken in the UK and USA over the last 10 years or so, aims, in relation to 5-16 year-olds, to: 1) clarify concepts and terminology; 2) consider the social context, non-school influences on young people's values, controversial issues and a values framework for schools; and 3) examine values, attitudes and personal qualities developed through school life, specific strategies and programmes, aspects of the curriculum, and as indicated in individual assessment and school evaluation. The review, which will in effect constitute an overview of the state of the art in values education, will include a full bibliography and indicate further areas for research, curriculum development and school practice. A publication of around 20,000 words, arranged under key topics and accessible to the informed educational reader, is envisaged.

STATUS: Sponsored project

SOURCE OF GRANT: Office for Standards in Education £16,000

DATE OF RESEARCH: 1996-1997

KEYWORDS: attitudes; individual development; moral development; moral values; ofsted; personal qualities; primary education; pupil attitudes; secondary education; values; values education

1823

The Mere, Upton Park, Slough SL1 2DQ
01753 574123
Sheffield College, PO Box 345, Sheffield S2 2YY
01142 602600

Sims, D. Mr; Golden, S. Ms; Strath, I. Mr; *Supervisor*: Le Metais, J. Dr

Strategic market research - a study of overseas services

ABSTRACT: British Training International (BTI) was established in November 1997 to establish and position the UK as the recognised world leader in providing vocational education, training and related services. The aims of the project are: 1) Support BTI and its partners in their long-term strategic planning and development by providing independent evidence and customer views on the main reasons for take-up and use of UK vocational standards, qualifications and training perceptions of the effectiveness of the UK's products and services characteristics of quality service provision. 2) Disseminate key messages to UK providers, including the potential for competence-based vocational training, accreditation and related services in overseas markets. The project will include four case studies, consultation of documentation and semi-structured face-to-face interviews in the UK (to refine the interview schedule) and overseas, with staff in a range of agencies and individuals including government bodies, training organisations, employers and some employees. The outcome is a confidential report to BTI: Strategic Market Research - a Study of Overseas Services.

PUBLISHED MATERIAL: LE METAIS, J. (1998). 'Walking on quicksand'. Paper presented at the British Training International Conference on Building International Excellence, Queen Elizabeth II Conference Centre, London, 28 October, 1998. ; SIMS, D. (1998). 'Lessons from abroad'. Paper presented to the British Training International Conference on Building International Excellence, Queen Elizabeth II Conference Centre, London, 28 October, 1998.

STATUS: Sponsored project

SOURCE OF GRANT: British Training International

DATE OF RESEARCH: 1998-1998

KEYWORDS: **international educational exchange; training; vocational education**

1824

The Mere, Upton Park, Slough SL1 2DQ
01753 574123
Surrey University, School of Educational Studies, Guildford GU2 5XH
01483 300800

Rudd, P. Dr; Evans, K. Prof.; Behrens, M. Ms; Kaluza, J. Dr; Woolley, C. Ms

Taking control: personal agency and social structures in young adult transitions in England and the new Germany

ABSTRACT: The question of whether there now exists a period of 'extended dependency' in young people's transitions is central to the Economic and Social Research Council's Youth, Citizenship and Social Change Programme. This research addresses this question through investigation of control and personal agency among young adults (18 to 25 years old) as they pass through extended periods of transition in education and training, work and unemployment, in selected localities experiencing economic transformation in England and new Germany. The study will investigate how, in different ways, choice and uncertainty can be important dimensions in young people's biographies in contemporary societies. Their experiences and their futures are not exclusively determined by socialising and structural influences, but also involve elements of subjectivity, choice and agency. The research will contribute to understanding of the processes involved in becoming 'independent' and 'personally effective' in different national and institutional settings. The research involves collaboration between the National Foundation for Educational Research (NFER) Department of Evaluation and Policy Studies and the University of Surrey Department of Educational Studies. Researchers in these institutions will take responsibility for organising fieldwork and analysis in relation to 3 cities: the 3 proposed geographical settings are Leipzig and Hanover (Germany) and Derby (England). The aims of the project are to: 1) contribute to theoretical development of the area, through dissemination of findings in the academic peer-reviewed media as well as through a book; and 2) involve researchers and users (young people, practitioners and policymakers) in debate about the most effective ways to support transitional processes in the 18-25 age range. This will take place through meetings, seminars and conference inputs.

STATUS: Sponsored project

SOURCE OF GRANT: Economic and Social Research Council

DATE OF RESEARCH: 1998-continuing

KEYWORDS: **citizenship; employment; higher education to work transition; school to work transition; social change; training; unemployment; young adults; youth**

1825

The Mere, Upton Park, Slough SL1 2DQ
01753 574123
Ulster University, Magee College, School of Education, Northland Road, County Londonderry BT48 7JL
01504 265621

Ashworth, M. Mrs; Moor, H. Ms; Wilkin, A. Mrs; Montgomery, A. Ms; Kendall, L. Mrs; *Supervisors*: Harland, J. Dr; Kinder, K. Ms

The Northern Ireland Curriculum Cohort Study

ABSTRACT: Building on a 16-month pilot study conducted in 5 post-primary schools, the cohort inquiry represents an important and innovative development in the methods used to monitor the implementation of the Northern Ireland Curriculum. The cohort study aims to provide evidence of the impact of the curriculum as a total package from the perspective of the learner in terms of: 1) relevance and appropriateness; 2) breadth, balance and coherence; and 3) enjoyment and manageability. This evidence should be generalisable to the whole key stage 3 population in Northern Ireland. The research will also examine evidence of the extent to which the aims of the Northern Ireland curriculum are evident in its implementation; the extent to which the objectives of cross-curricular themes are being addressed through the curriculum; and the appropriateness of methods of assessment and evaluation. Additionally, in collaboration with researchers from the University of Ulster, the cohort study will include an analysis of the extent to which values are being imparted and assimilated. The study will employ both quantitative and qualitative methods and consist of 3 main strands: 1) An annual pupil questionnaire. 2) An annual school questionnaire. 3) 5 case-study schools. The main outcomes of the cohort study will comprise: a) an annual report analysing data from the 3 research methods (i.e. Year 8, 9 and 10 reports); b) a final report analysing all the data from Years 7 to 10; c) conferences with focus groups to disseminate the results and discuss their implications for practice.

STATUS: Sponsored project

SOURCE OF GRANT: Northern Ireland Council for Curriculum and Examinations Authority

DATE OF RESEARCH: 1996-continuing

KEYWORDS: **cross curricular approach; curriculum development; learning experience; national curriculum - northern ireland; northern ireland; pupil attitudes; secondary education; teaching methods**

1826

The Mere, Upton Park, Slough SL1 2DQ
01753 574123

Bhabra, S. Ms; *Supervisor*: Sharp, C. Ms

An evaluation of Step by Step: Improving the Quality of Life for All

ABSTRACT: The aim of this project is to evaluate a resource pack produced by Buckinghamshire County Council. The objective of the pack, known as Step by Step: Improving the Quality of Life for All, is to promote children's health, environmental awareness and road safety. Step by Step was developed to address three main issues arising from the growing trend for children to be transported to and from school by car. Firstly, being driven to school has contributed to children's poor physical fitness. Secondly, frequent car transportation inhibits children from developing sufficient 'pedestrian skills'. (A lack of pedestrian skills is one explanation for the high number of road injuries amongst 11- and 12-year-olds.) Thirdly, the high use of private cars has implications for the environment: it contributes to road congestion and poor air quality. Evaluation of the resource pack will be carried out through a questionnaire survey, sent to all middle and combined schools in Buckinghamshire. Questionnaires will be distributed to key stage 2 teachers who have received copies of the resource pack.

STATUS: Sponsored project

SOURCE OF GRANT: Buckinghamshire County Council

DATE OF RESEARCH: 1999-continuing

KEYWORDS: **environment; health; physical fitness; pupil journeys; pupils; traffic safety; transport; travel; walking**

National Institute for Careers Education and Counselling

1827

Sheraton House, Castle Park, Cambridge CB3 OAX
01223 460277

Watts, A. Mr

European careers guidance survey

ABSTRACT: The survey is studying the educational and vocational guidance services available to young people and adults in the twelve Member States. Its aim is to illuminate the different structures and strategies adopted in these countries in a way which will enable Member States to: (a) learn from each other's experience; (b) develop stronger networks across national boundaries in support of the Single European Market. Particular attention is being paid to: (i) Changes which have taken place since the survey of guidance services for young people carried out by Watts et al. in 1985/1987; (ii) The structure of guidance services for adults, which were not examined in any detail in the earlier survey. Country-studies are being commissioned from experts in each Member State; they will be revised during a one-week study visit to the country in question by a member of the project's central team (Tony Watts, UK; Peter Plant, Denmark; Dr Jean Guichard, France; Professor Luisa Rodriguez, Spain).

PUBLISHED MATERIAL: WATTS, A.G., GUICHARD, J., PLANT, P. & RODRIGUEZ, M.L. (1994). Education and vocational guidance in the European Community. Luxembourg: Office for Official Publications of the European Communities.

STATUS: Sponsored project

SOURCE OF GRANT: European Commission - ECUs £136,500

DATE OF RESEARCH: 1992-1993

KEYWORDS: **adult counselling; career counselling; europe; european union; vocational guidance**

1828

Sheraton House, Castle Park, Cambridge CB3 0AX
01223 460277

Hawthorn, R. Ms

Impact of the media on career choice

ABSTRACT: The project will look at the extent to which broadcast media were believed to have influenced the career decisions of a sample of 50 individuals, to include young people who have recently entered their first full-time employment, and older adults who have made career changes. The semi-structured interviews will cover influence on beliefs about broader issues, such as economic climate, as well as more detailed beliefs about specific occupations. Questions will be included which explore in particular whether images of occupations in science and technology are adversely affected by the media. The analysis will explore the extent to which theories of career choice allow for informal influence of this kind, and the implications for careers education and guidance for young people and for adults.

STATUS: Sponsored project

SOURCE OF GRANT: Times Educational Supplement £12,000

DATE OF RESEARCH: 1995-continuing

KEYWORDS: **career choice; career education; mass media; mass media effects; vocational guidance**

1829

Sheraton House, Castle Park, Cambridge CB3 0AX
01223 460277
Free University of Brussels, 50 Ave Franklin Roosevelt, 1050 Brussels, Belgium
010322 6502111

Watts, A. Prof.; Van Esbroeck, R. Prof.

New skills for vocational counsellors in higher education

ABSTRACT: The aim of the project is to provide an up-to-date overview of the current structure of guidance and counselling services in higher education, the roles and tasks of those who work in such services, and the training for such roles. The project is concerned to identify the extent to which training provision exists within the European Union to equip those in these roles with the new skills they require to meet the changing needs of an increasingly diverse student body, within a European labour market. It is designed to provide a basepoint for exploring the extent to which postgraduate and post-experience training modules might be made available across Europe, possibly leading to a European Master's degree in guidance and counselling in higher education.

PUBLISHED MATERIAL: **WATTS, A.G. & VAN ESBROECK, R. (1998). New skills for new futures. Brussels: VUB University Press.**

STATUS: Sponsored project

SOURCE OF GRANT: European Union Leonardo Programme £114,896

DATE OF RESEARCH: 1997-1998

KEYWORDS: **career counselling; higher education; vocational guidance**

1830

Sheraton House, Castle Park, Cambridge CB3 0AX
01223 460277

Munro, M. Mrs; Elsom, D. Dr

The influence of careers advisers and science teachers on students' decisions about science subjects and subsequent careers

ABSTRACT: The background to this project is concern about how careers' departments and science departments in schools interact over guidance to pupils about post-16 subject choices. The project will seek perceptions and experiences from careers advisers working in 6 sample careers companies in the UK and through questionnaires. Analysis of these will be followed up by detailed case studies in 5/6 schools selected on the basis of evidence of good collaborative practice. The outcomes of the research will be a report analysing key findings, with case studies and examples of good practice, together with recommendations for further staff development, both for careers advisers and science teachers.

STATUS: Sponsored project

SOURCE OF GRANT: Department for Education and Employment; Employers Federation; Engineering and Marine Training Authority; The Salters' Institute; The Royal Academy of Engineering

DATE OF RESEARCH: 1998-continuing

KEYWORDS: **career choice; careers advisers; choice of subjects; science education; vocational guidance**

National Institute of Adult Continuing Education

1831

21 De Montfort Street, Leicester LE1 7GE
01162 551451

McGivney, V. Dr

Part-time and temporary workers and the National Targets for Education and Training

ABSTRACT: The aim of the enquiry was to investigate the nature and extent of the training offered to part-time and temporary workers to see whether the National Targets for Education and Training can be achieved. The study was in two parts: a context analysis using existing research; and empirical research in employing organisations, involving interviews with personnel and training managers and with part-time and temporary staff. The results showed that although large 'leading edge' companies have improved the training they offer 'peripheral' or 'atypical' workers, and reduced differentials between part-time and full-time employees, part-time workers as a whole still receive far less training than full-time workers. Their opportunities for promotion and progression also remain limited. Unless this state of affairs can be improved, the National Lifelong Education and Training Targets stand little chance of being achieved.

PUBLISHED MATERIAL: McGIVNEY, V.K. (1994). Wasted potential: training and career progression for part-time and temporary workers. Leicester: National Institute of Adult Continuing Education. ; McGIVNEY,

V.K. (1994). 'Part-time workers and the achievement of the National Targets for Education and Training', Adults Learning, Vol 6, No 1, pp.38-40.

STATUS: Sponsored project

SOURCE OF GRANT: Department of Employment £21,500

DATE OF RESEARCH: 1993-1993

KEYWORDS: **job training; part time employment; temporary employment; training**

1832

21 De Montfort Street, Leicester LE1 7GE
01162 551451

Wertheimer, A. Ms; *Supervisor*: Sutcliffe, J. Ms

Adult learners and mental health

ABSTRACT: This project was a joint venture between the National Institute of Adult Continuing Education (NIACE) and the Further Education Development Agency (FEDA). The project aimed to explore good practice in relation to continuing education for adults with mental health difficulties. As the Further Education Funding Council report 'Inclusive Learning' (1996) showed, this group of learners is currently under-represented in continuing education. A detailed postal survey was sent to all colleges and local education authorities (LEAs) in England and Wales. Over 20 case study visits were made to colleges, LEAs and other organisations. Students with mental health difficulties were asked for their perspectives. The survey material and case study information has been written up under themes and set against national developments and policy issues. The findings show that although provision is very patchy nationally, there are examples of good practice which can be developed and built on.

PUBLISHED MATERIAL: WERTHEIMER, A. (1997). Images of possibility: creating learning opportunities for adults with mental health difficulties. Leicester: National Institute of Adult Continuing Education.

STATUS: Sponsored project

SOURCE OF GRANT: Local Government Association

DATE OF RESEARCH: 1996-1997

KEYWORDS: **adult education; learning disabilities; special educational needs**

1833

21 De Montfort Street, Leicester LE1 7GE
01162 551451

Jacobsen, Y. Ms; *Supervisor*: Sutcliffe, J. Ms

All things being equal

ABSTRACT: The project aims to document issues and interesting practice in providing continuing education for adults with learning difficulties from marginalised groups. This includes, for example, people with profound and multiple learning difficulties, older learners, people from ethnic minority groups and those who have the dual label of learning difficulties and mental health problems. Earlier research by the National Institute of Continuing Education (NIACE) and the Norah Fry Research Centre called 'Still a chance to learn?' (1996) had shown that certain groups were starting to miss out. For this research, colleges and local education authorities (LEAs) in England and Wales were invited to share details of their practice in this area of work. A wide-ranging programme of site visits has been undertaken, to include colleges, LEAs and voluntary organisations. Early indications are that there is little imaginative practice for these groups of learners, and that even where things have been developed, the work is often very fragile and under threat of cuts.

PUBLISHED MATERIAL: SUTCLIFFE, J. & JACOBSEN, Y. (1998). All things being equal? Leicester: NIACE. ; SUTCLIFFE, J. & JACOBSEN, Y. (1998). Continuing education and equal opportunities for adults with learning difficulties. York: Joseph Rowntree Foundation. ; SUTCLIFFE, J. & JACOBSEN, Y. (1998). 'All things being equal?', Adults Learning, Vol 10, No 3, pp.6-7.

STATUS: Sponsored project

SOURCE OF GRANT: Joseph Rowntree Foundation £58,000

DATE OF RESEARCH: 1997-1998

KEYWORDS: **adult education; learning disabilities; special educational needs**

1834

21 De Montfort Street, Leicester LE1 7GE
01162 551451
Hillcroft College, South Bank, Surbiton KT6 6DF
0181 399 2688

McGivney, V. Dr; *Supervisor*: Aird, E. Mrs

Women in education and training: barriers to access; informal starting points and progression issues

ABSTRACT: The study involved a literature search and interviews with staff and women students in a range of education and training courses. It showed that the principal barriers that deter women from participating in education and training - lack of finance, lack of childcare, lack of confidence in their abilities - stem from cultural attitudes and expectations underpinned by social and economic structures and policies. Help with education/training costs and childcare most facilitates women's access to education/training and their progression within it. The project revealed that informal re-entry learning schemes have enabled a great number of women without qualifications to take the first step back into education, training and employment. However, the reliance on 'special' funding for women's re-entry courses, coupled with the changes brough about by the Further and Higher Education Act, have resulted in a sharp reduction in the informal learning opportunities available for women. Women are still expected to fit into a system established mainly for the benefit of men. The project showed that formal education and training providers need to adapt not only the courses they offer, but also delivery methods, teaching approaches, support structured and institutional 'ethos' in order to give women equal access to training, qualifications and employment opportunities.

PUBLISHED MATERIAL: MCGIVNEY, V. (1993). Women, education and training: barriers to access, informal starting points and progression issues. Leicester: National Institute of Adult Continuing Education. ; MCGIVNEY, V. (1994). 'Women, education and training: a research report', Adult Learning, Vol 5, No 5, pp.118-120.

STATUS: Sponsored project

SOURCE OF GRANT: Training, Enterprise and Education Directorate

DATE OF RESEARCH: 1992-1993

KEYWORDS: **access to education; adult education; retraining; womens education**

National Institute of Economic and Social Research

1835

2 Dean Trench Street, Smith Square, London SW1P 3HE
0171 222 7665

Kirkland, J. Mr

Supply and demand issues for engineering, science and mathematics graduates

ABSTRACT: Information is being gathered on the supply of, and demand for, graduates in engineering, science and mathematics. There is concern that the best undergraduates do not enter degree courses in these subjects, that such courses do not attract sufficient female entrants and that even those people who do graduate and enter the professions tend not to remain there. At the same time, despite employers' complaints concerning the quality of graduate skills available to them, little hard information is available on what their needs are at different levels (e.g. technician, graduate,'high flier').

STATUS: Sponsored project

SOURCE OF GRANT: Department for Education and Employment £58,824

DATE OF RESEARCH: 1997-1998

KEYWORDS: **engineering; graduate employment; mathematics education; science education**

Nene College of Higher Education

1836

Park Campus, Boughton Green Road, Northampton NN2 7AL
01604 735500

Silcock, P. Dr

A new model of reflective professional practice and professional development

ABSTRACT: The aim of the project is to develop a new model of reflective professional practice and professional development. This research proposes a new theory of reflective professional practice and professional development, integrating Donald Schon's radical model with more traditional, academic conceptions. It is based on a close analysis of the evolving relationship between human thought and action. Implications for learning transfer and course development are included.

PUBLISHED MATERIAL: SILCOCK, P.J. (1994). 'The process of reflective teaching', British Journal of Educational Studies, Vol 42, No 3, pp.273-285.

STATUS: Individual research

DATE OF RESEARCH: 1993-continuing

KEYWORDS: **educational theories; professional development; reflective teaching; teaching profession**

1837

Park Campus, Boughton Green Road, Northampton NN2 7AL
01604 735500

Martin, J. Dr

Women and the politics of educational reform, 1870-1950

ABSTRACT: This project builds on earlier work for a PhD thesis examining the role of women in the formation of a national education system in late-Victorian and Edwardian England. Focusing on the female members of the London School Board, the thesis explores the links between private life, social and political networks, and the entry of women to the public domain. It examines the stance adopted by individual women board members on the formal curriculum, the administration of reformatory institutions, and attitudes towards working-class children in school, considered in terms of the interacting dynamics of gender and class. The researcher is now taking this work forward to examine the work of women members of Education Committees and is especially interested in the work of Shena D. Simon on the Manchester Education Committee. The research will look at the work of a number of women involved in the politics of educational reform during the specified time period. It will describe and assess women's contribution to education as well as any difficulties they may have experienced working in the world of English local government.

PUBLISHED MATERIAL: MARTIN, J. (1991). 'Hard-headed and large-hearted': women and the industrial schools', History of Education, Vol 20, No 3, pp.187-201. ; MARTIN, J. (1994). 'The only place for women was home?, Gender and policy in elementary education, 1870-1904', History of Education, December 1994. ; MARTIN, J. Women and schooling in Victorian and Edwardian England. London: Cassell. (in press).

STATUS: Sponsored project

SOURCE OF GRANT: Nene College of Higher Education £500

DATE OF RESEARCH: 1994-continuing

KEYWORDS: **educational history; politics education relationship; women**

1838

Park Campus, Boughton Green Road, Northampton NN2 7AL
01604 735500
London University, Institute of Education, 20 Bedford Way, London
WC1H 0AL
0171 580 1122

Rogers, J. Ms; *Supervisor*: Cowan, R. Dr

Language and symbolism in the learning of mathematics

ABSTRACT: Previous research has identified mathematical symbolism as a source of misunderstanding and anxiety. This study aims to investigate the relationship between language, the use of symbols, and success in dealing with written algorithms and number operations. Methodology will be by empirical research. Quantitative data and statistical analyses will be combined with individual case design and the analysis of qualitative data. Initially, subjects will be selected from a representative sample in the British primary school sector, aged 5-11 years.

STATUS: Individual research

DATE OF RESEARCH: 1994-1997

KEYWORDS: **mathematical linguistics; mathematics education; primary education; primary school pupils; symbols - mathematics**

1839

Park Campus, Boughton Green Road, Northampton NN2 7AL
01604 735500
Northamptonshire Inspection and Advisory Service, John Dryden
House, The Lakes, Bedford Road, Northampton NN4 7DD
01604 236242

Fisher, E. Dr; Barry, B. Ms

Children using CD-ROMs for information searches

ABSTRACT: The increasing availability of large amounts of information on computers and the requirements of the National Curriculum have led to a need for children in schools to develop skilled strategies for computer information searches. Schools are responding to this need by obtaining and using CD-Roms in the classrooms. However, little is known about how effectively these resources are used, what user skills are needed, and how these can best be developed. One feature of computer-provided information is that the available range is normally extensive, and certainly much greater than was available to most individuals when their sources were confined to books. Whilst this increased availablity provides exciting opportunities, it also introduces new difficulties which need new skills for coping. Inexperienced individuals faced with a wealth of new information may find difficulty in selecting what is appropriate. It is well established (Eysenck & Keene, 1990) that 'experts' on particular tasks use very different task strategies from 'novices', who are often so overwhelmed with the details of the new situation that they fail to develop effective overall task plans. It has also been found that children, when offered a wide choice of information on computers, for example with simple statistical packages, make selections based on inappropriate and poorly-thought-through criteria (SLANT project, Economic and Social Research Council 1990-92). The aim of this study is to establish precisely what chidren in primary schools do when faced with computer information search facilities, and how best to help them improve their strategies. It will be carried out in 3 stages: Stage 1 - to establish how chidren use books and CD-Roms to carry out information search strategies; Stage 2 - a workshop to be run by the researchers for teachers, in which findings will be shared and ideas for improved task/strategies will be developed; Stage 3 - the improved tasks to be implemented and evaluated.

STATUS: Sponsored project

SOURCE OF GRANT: Nene College of Higher Education

DATE OF RESEARCH: 1996-1997

KEYWORDS: **cd roms; computer uses in education; information seeking; information technology; primary education**

1840

Park Campus, Boughton Green Road, Northampton NN2 7AL
01604 735500
University of Oporto, Faculdade de Psigologia E de Ciencias, Da
Educa Cao, R Do Campo Alegre 1055, 4150 Porto, Portugal
010 3512 6079739

Stanley, J. Dr; Wyness, M. Dr; Stoer, S. Dr; Cortesao, L. Dr

Schooling - England and Portugal

ABSTRACT: The project is examining the involvement of parents in their children's schooling by taking a broad socio-cultural sample of parents drawn from urban, rural and multi-ethnic areas in Portugal and England. The project,using qualitative data, is uncovering a diversity of parental experiences and needs which seem to challenge ideal-typical descriptions found in prevailing policy and discourse.

STATUS: Sponsored project

DATE OF RESEARCH: 1995-continuing

KEYWORDS: **disadvantaged; parent participation; parent school relationship**

New College Durham
1841

Division of Health, Care and Education, Neville's Cross Centre, Darlington Road, Durham DH1 4SY
0191 375 4000

Walker, S. Mr; Reece, I. Mr; Hunt, J. Mr; Rosethorn, C. Mrs; Harvey, R. Mr; Thompson, G. Ms

Post-compulsory education and training: a survey of practice

ABSTRACT: The aim of the research is to observe, record and analyse what is happening in post-compulsory education and training. Approximately 100 lessons will be observed this year. The observers are teacher trainers and the observed are existing lecturers and trainers who are undertaking some teacher training courses. The current focus is examining what takes place in the introductions to, and conclusions of, lessons. Planned learning outcomes will be compared with actual learning outcomes.

PUBLISHED MATERIAL: REECE, I. & WALKER, S. A practical guide to teaching, training and learning. Sunderland: Business Education Publishers. (in press).

STATUS: Sponsored project

SOURCE OF GRANT: New College Durham £5,000

DATE OF RESEARCH: 1997-continuing

KEYWORDS: **classroom observation techniques; further education; sixteen to nineteen education; teaching methods; training**

Newcastle upon Tyne University
1842

Department of Education, St Thomas Street, Newcastle upon Tyne NE1 7RU
0191 222 6000

Lewis, T. Ms; *Supervisor*: Skelton, C. Ms

Gender differentiated career paths to senior posts in secondary education

ABSTRACT: A qualitative study of the careers of women teachers in positions of middle management. Three case study schools have been used together with interviews of a women teachers management group from one local education authority (LEA). The data suggests that women teachers in middle management experience constraints to their career development because of the subjects they teach, the timetabling of their school days, personal commitments and lack of appropriate staff development.

STATUS: Individual research

DATE OF RESEARCH: 1990-1997

KEYWORDS: **career development; middle management; secondary school teachers; teaching profession; women teachers**

1843

Department of Education, St Thomas Street, Newcastle upon Tyne NE1 7RU
0191 222 6000

Wells, M. Dr; *Supervisor*: Westgate, D. Mr

Contrasting grammar-teaching strategies in modern foreign languages

ABSTRACT: The background to the project blends the teacher-researcher's complementary desires to gain perspective on a significant aspect of her own practice and to investigate grammar-teaching within the context and recommended practices of National Curriculum (NC) modern foreign language teaching, with its emphasis on teaching in/through the target language and covert approaches to structure. The research begins from related literature, with a historical review of issues surrounding language development and, in particular, of change in modern foreign languages teaching. It follows an action research format, set in a 13-18 comprehensive school, monitoring the performances of a single year-group occupying comparable classes over their 3-year course in French to General Certificate in Secondary Education (GCSE) (1991-94). A longitudinal study, it takes as its focal point, the question of the advantages or disadvantages attaching to either explicit or implicit grammar teaching at various stages. The study sets out to observe effects of the broadly distinct teaching strategies - made contrastive by the presence or absence of explicit grammar-summaries delivered in English (as a concession agreed in the NC Non-Statutory Guidance to the policy outlined above). Data have been gathered on both classroom processes and learning outcomes at various points, including final GCSE scores. The study also explores issues relating to the conduct of such research, including attitudes and responses of teachers and pupils to their participation in the study. In disclosing the pattern of results which systematically took shape during the 3 years, the report will discuss findings in the context of current practice. It is thus intended to set local insights in a wider perspective and to identify aspects which may have more general significance.

PUBLISHED MATERIAL: WELLS, M.C. (1994). 'Reflecting on grammar teaching'. In: PECK, A. & WESTGATE, D. (Eds). Language teaching in the mirror. London: Centre for Information on Language Teaching and Research.

STATUS: Individual research

DATE OF RESEARCH: 1991-1997

KEYWORDS: **grammar; modern language studies**

1844

Department of Education, St Thomas Street, Newcastle upon Tyne NE1 7RU
0191 222 6000

Todd, C. Ms; *Supervisor*: Carrington, L. Mr

Equal opportunities (gender) and teacher unions: a comparative study of the United Kingdom and the United States of America

ABSTRACT: This research focuses on the professional lives and careers of women teachers in the United Kingdom and United States of America. It includes a substantial case study of the Californian Teachers' Association and an empirical investigation undertaken in the Auburn area of that state. An investigation of the National Union of Teachers and a case study of women teachers in Hexham, Northumberland, is also being undertaken.

STATUS: Individual research

DATE OF RESEARCH: 1991-continuing

KEYWORDS: **equal opportunities - jobs; professional associations; teacher associations; teacher employment; teaching profession; unions; united states of america**

1845

Department of Education, St Thomas Street, Newcastle upon Tyne NE1 7RU
0191 222 6000

Brand, J. Ms; *Supervisor*: Carrington, L. Mr

A comparative study between physical education teaching in post-independent Zimbabwe and physical education in England and Wales during the same period (1980-91)

ABSTRACT: This research examines recent developments in physical education in Zimbabwe and England and Wales. It focuses upon policy makers', headteachers' and pupils' perceptions of provision in the country concerned.

STATUS: Individual research

DATE OF RESEARCH: 1991-continuing

KEYWORDS: **comparative education; physical education; zimbabwe**

1846

Department of Education, St Thomas Street, Newcastle upon Tyne NE1 7RU
0191 222 6000

Jones, K. Mr; *Supervisor*: Atkins, M. Dr

School inspection, school effectiveness and school improvement: the impact of OFSTED inspections on theoretical and practical perspectives

ABSTRACT: The main aims of the Office for Standards in Education (OFSTED) school inspection arrangements were emphasised in the 1993 OFSTED Corporate Plan. The new system would at the same time "inform parents", "make schools more directly accountable for standards", and "provide an agenda for school improvement". This study attempts to engage with the third aim noted above. By means of a longitudinal study of developments in two North-East secondary schools throughout the full cycle of their first and second OFSTED inspections, the study will seek to examine a number of inter-related questions: 1) What is it that schools - and in particular individuals and functioning groups - do when preparing for an OFSTED inspection? 2) How much confidence do staff have in the inspection process, and how valid a view do they feel the report(s) present? Do they feel any sense of commitment to putting right weaknesses identified by an inspection team? 3) Where staff have accepted an OFSTED report, how do they then implement (i.e. formulate and energise) the governors' action plan? How do staff and governors perceive the process? What do individuals do? Who takes responsibility for what? 4) What do individuals of different status and with various responsibilities and roles actually do over time to "improve the school" as a direct consequence of an OFSTED inspection? What help do they receive (internally and externally)? 5) How do schools measure the "school improvements" that have come from an OFSTED inspection?

STATUS: Individual research

DATE OF RESEARCH: 1994-1997

KEYWORDS: **educational improvement; educational quality; inspection; inspectors - of schools; ofsted; school effectiveness**

1847

Department of Education, St Thomas Street, Newcastle upon Tyne
NE1 7RU
0191 222 6000

Todd, E. Ms; *Supervisor*: Easen, P. Dr

An investigation of the meaning of partnership in the assessment of special educational needs

ABSTRACT: This research aims to look in more detail at the meaning of partnership in the formal process of assessing children's special educational needs. This research widens the current interest in parent partnership and the growing interest in the child's perspective to investigate the perspectives of all those involved in an assessment to find out how the assessment is perceived and to find out different perspectives of the nature of partnership involved. The first phase of the research is a case study of a parent partnership scheme run by educational psychologists and operating in a northern urban education authority. The operation of the scheme during its first year is described and discussed with reference to field notes and minutes of meetings taken during the researcher's involvement with the scheme. Semi-structured interviews are also carried out with those involved in the scheme. An investigation of this scheme raises questions about the possibilities for parent partnership within existing legislative and professional frameworks. It also raises questions about other kinds of partnerships within the process, such as between the teacher and the psychologist, the child and the parent. The second phase of the research is a number of case studies of assessments which have recently been completed under the Education Act 1993. Semi-structured interviews and documents from the assessment will be used to look at the persepectives of all the people involved in the assessment in order to investigate the different possibilities and problems for partnership between all those involved.

STATUS: Individual research

DATE OF RESEARCH: 1994-1997

KEYWORDS: **assessment; cooperation; diagnostic assessment; educational psychologists; parent participation; partnerships; pupil attitudes; special educational needs; statements - special educational needs**

1848

Department of Education, St Thomas Street, Newcastle upon Tyne
NE1 7RU
0191 222 6000

Reimann, N. Ms; *Supervisor*: Westgate, D. Mr

German 'Languages for All' provision in higher education: an evaluation study with particular reference to student dropout

ABSTRACT: This study intends to increase our knowledge about the processes involved in learning German within the specific setting of 'Languages for All' schemes. It is based in the tradition of language classroom research and focuses on individual reasons for student dropout. Institutional factors (integration of language element into courses, institutional policies), personal factors (students' motivation, attitudes, expectations, perceptions, previous language learning experience) and classroom factors (content of the course, classroom processes and interaction) are addressed mainly by means of qualitative methods, without totally excluding quantitative forms of enquiry. Student perceptions of and reactions to the language learning experience form the core of the study; the main body of the data consists of intro-/retrospection and classroom observation. It has been planned to investigate a number of schemes, however the indepth approach taken might severely limit the amount of cases studied.

PUBLISHED MATERIAL: REIMANN, N. (1996). 'Ab initio and beyond: staying in and dropping out'. Paper given at Ab initio German: Trends and Perspectives, University of York, 22-23 March 1996. ; REIMANN, N. (1997). 'Languages for all in HE: researching the student perspective'. Paper given at the Case for a National Languages Policy - the Contribution of Further, Higher and Adult Education, CILT, London, 29 November 1997. ; REIMANN, N. 'Ab initio German and beyond: a case study of staying in and dropping out', Interface (Bradford Studies in Language Culture and Society), Vol 3. (in press).

STATUS: Individual research

DATE OF RESEARCH: 1995-1998

KEYWORDS: **dropouts; german; higher education; modern language studies; student wastage**

1849

Department of Education, St Thomas Street, Newcastle upon Tyne
NE1 7RU
0191 222 6000

Baumfield, V. Dr; Leat, D. Dr; Higgins, S. Mr; Taverner, S. Ms; Meagher, N. Mr

Keys to effective thinking skills teaching

ABSTRACT: The research investigates the extent to which a variety of thinking skills programmes shares features which are crucial to their success. It then seeks to understand how the necessary and sufficient processes, which lie at the heart of successful thinking skills teaching, operate in the classroom. The following questions are addressed: 1) What theories of children's cognitive development and learning are the programmes based on? 2) What processes of teaching are recommended? 3) What is the balance of emphasis between method and content? 4) To what extent are the methods and content proposed congruent with those operational in the classroom? 5) How do teachers implement the programmes and justify deviations from recommended practice and content? 6) What recommendations can be made on the basis of 1-5 to teachers wanting to teach thinking skills? A sample of teachers, drawn from the Newcastle upon Tyne University database of teachers, involved in thinking skills programmes will be observed teaching lessons and will then participate in semi-structured interviews. The results of the observations, and the perceptions of the teachers in the interviews, will be compared with the analysis of the programme documentation. Programme documentation and teacher interviews will be analysed using NUD.IST. Observation will involve customised observer software developed by the project.

STATUS: Sponsored project

SOURCE OF GRANT: YAPP Foundation £1,300

DATE OF RESEARCH: 1996-1997

KEYWORDS: **classroom observation techniques; learning strategies; primary education; secondary education; teacher attitudes; teaching methods; thinking skills**

1850

Department of Education, St Thomas Street, Newcastle upon Tyne
NE1 7RU
0191 222 6000

Warren, S. Mr; *Supervisors*: Skelton, C. Ms; Carrington, L. Mr

Boys and classroom groups: their behaviours and strategies for improving them

ABSTRACT: This study focuses on masculinities and primary schooling. It is a qualitative study of primary age boys which explores the behaviours and strategies they adopt in daily classroom life. The research explores the view that boys' behaviours are more problematic than girls which results in discipline problems for teachers. It is intended that the research will illuminate ways in which teachers can address boys' negative classroom behaviours.

STATUS: Individual research

DATE OF RESEARCH: 1993-1998

KEYWORDS: **behaviour; boys; discipline; masculinity; primary education; primary school pupils; sex differences**

1851

Department of Education, St Thomas Street, Newcastle upon Tyne
NE1 7RU
0191 222 6000

Lloyd, J. Mr; *Supervisor*: Dennison, W. Dr; Bavidge, M. Dr

Headteacher leadership: an investigation in leadership in primary schools

ABSTRACT: The aims of this PhD research project are: 1) to extend leadership research in headteacher education; 2) to identify Office for Standards in Education (OFSTED) concept of leadership; and 3) to offer an explication of headteacher leadership for primary schools. The research will be qualitative and will include interpretations of leadership through: 1) conceptual analysis; 2) paradigm model analysis of authors in educational leadership; 3) content analysis of OFSTED reports and case studies of a few primary schools; 4) interviews of headteachers (primary) and OFSTED inspectors. The research will also be quantitative, this will involve a critical analysis of a) leadership questionnaires, e,g. Hersey and Blanchard (1973); b) models of leadership; c) the OFSTED database. The size of the project will be: 1) 25 pre-April 1996 primary school reports (North East England); 2) 25 post-April 1996 primary school reports (North East England); 3) 1 longitudinal study (1 year) and 3 short interviews in 3 schools of headteacher, deputy and 1 other member of staff to ascertain evidence of situational leadership; 4) interviews with 4 inspectors to explicate their concept(s) of leadership.

STATUS: Individual research

DATE OF RESEARCH: 1994-1997

KEYWORDS: **head teachers; leadership; primary education**

1852

Department of Education, St Thomas Street, Newcastle upon Tyne
NE1 7RU
0191 222 6000

Taverner, S. Mr; Baumfield, V. Dr; Leat, D. Dr

Whole school planning at key stage 3

ABSTRACT: This project is contracted by the School Curriculum and Assessment Authority (SCAA) to carry out a focused study of whole school planning at key stage 3 in order to inform the review of the National Curriculum. The five main foci are: 1) how schools are seeking to establish a balance between the basics and the broader curriculum and the significance attached to non-core subjects; 2) how far intended flexibility is used to devise a curriculum which reflects local needs; 3) how the requirements for information technology (IT) capability and use of language are being addressed through a whole school approach; 4) how schools are seeking to address the broad aims of the Education Reform Act 1988; 5) which aspects of curriculum organisation and teaching do schools identify with raising pupils' attainment in the National Curriculum. Questionnaires were sent to a representative sample of schools across the North East of England. Selection was partly informed by local education authorities (LEAs) and Office for Standards in Education (OFSTED) reports as the sample including a range of practice. Interviews were carried out in order to obtain some detailed case study material and the main findings were that: 1) pressure of National Curriculum tests meant some subjects were given more emphasis; 2) there is a lack of expertise and staff confidence in using IT rather than a shortage of equipment; 3) social, moral, spiritual and cultural aspects permeated the

curriculum, especially Personal and Social Education, but spiritual was the most challenging to deliver; 4) raising attainment was a real focus for schools, but in reality this leads to too much data with schools who are uncertain how to use it effectively.

STATUS: Sponsored project

SOURCE OF GRANT: Schools Curriculum and Assessment Authority £15,000

DATE OF RESEARCH: 1997-1997

KEYWORDS: **curriculum development; key stage 3; national curriculum; secondary education; whole school approach**

1853

Department of Education, St Thomas Street, Newcastle upon Tyne
NE1 7RU
0191 222 6000

Hall, I. Mr; Smith, F. Dr; *Supervisors*: Taverner, S. Ms; Hardman, F. Dr

The relevance of GCSE mathematics and English and key skills units as preparation for employment

ABSTRACT: This project looks at the relevance of GCSE mathematics and English and key skills units as preparation for employment. A report will feed into the forthcoming review of GCSE syllabuses and the National Curriculum at key stage 4. The sample size will be a maximum of 50 young people who left school at the age of 16 in either 1996 or 1997. The project will focus on small (20 employees) and medium (20-200 employees) companies. Employers will be identified with the help of Tyneside and Northumberland Training and Enterprise Councils (TECs) in order to obtain a representative sample of types and location of employer. Employers and their young employees will be interviewed using a semi-structured schedule which will focus on: 1) the specific communication and numeracy skills needed to satisfactorily carry out their job; 2) how well GCSE mathematics and English and key skills units prepared them for their work; 3) strategies used by employers to 'plug any gaps' in the knowledge, skills and understanding identified by them, and whether such gaps should/could have been addressed through schooling. Where possible, semi-structured interviews, on a similar theme, will also take place with the relevant teachers at the schools attended by the sample of young people. Teachers will be questioned as to how the programmes of learning are structured and taught within their subject area. Results and conclusions will follow.

STATUS: Sponsored project

SOURCE OF GRANT: Qualifications and Curriculum Authority £20,000

DATE OF RESEARCH: 1998-1998

KEYWORDS: **core skills; employment; english; general certificate of secondary education; job skills; key skills; key stage 4; mathematics education; school leavers; school to work transition; school to work transition; secondary education; skills; work education relationship**

1854

Department of Education, St Thomas Street, Newcastle upon Tyne
NE1 7RU
0191 222 6000

Thompson, I. Mr; Clark, J. Ms

An investigation of the mental calculation strategies used by children in Years 4 and 5 for the addition and subtraction of two-digit numbers

ABSTRACT: The main aim of the project is to attempt to answer the question 'What are the strategies that young children use to perform two-digit additions and subtractions mentally?' The following related questions have been derived from this general question: 1) Is it possible to classify mental calculation strategies in terms of their level of sophistication? 2) What are the common errors made by children when adding or subtracting mentally? 3) To what extent do the strategies used by less able pupils differ from those employed by the more able? 4) Do girls perform significantly differently from boys in the area of mental calculation? 5) Do the strategies used by children in Year 4 differ from those used in Year 5? Twelve schools from several different local education authorities (LEAs) will be selected to represent a variety of social backgrounds, and twelve children from each of Year 4 and Year 5 will be interviewed in each school. Class teachers will be asked to select two boys and two girls from each of three different attainment groups within each school year. These groups will comprise four children whose attainment in number could be considered to be below average; four children whose attainment is deemed to be of average standard; and four who are currently performing at an above-average level. The interview protocols will be transcribed and analysed in a variety of ways commensurate with the research questions outlined above.

STATUS: Sponsored project

SOURCE OF GRANT: Nuffield Foundation £8,415

DATE OF RESEARCH: 1998-continuing

KEYWORDS: **addition; arithmetic; learning strategies; mathematics achievement; mathematics education; mental arithmetic; primary education; sex differences; subtraction**

1855

Department of Education, St Thomas Street, Newcastle upon Tyne NE1 7RU
0191 222 6000

Baumfield, V. Dr; Leat, D. Dr; Taverner, S. Ms

North East school based research consortium

ABSTRACT: This is a collaborative project between: University of Newcastle; Heaton Manor School; Longbenton Community College; Prudhoe Community High School; St Mary's Roman Catholic Comprehensive School; Walker School; Newcastle Local Education Authority; North Tyneside Local Education Authority and Northumberland Local Education Authority. The consortium is concerned with the impact that involvement in interventions, designed to improve pupils' critical thinking, has on teachers' professional development and aims to support teachers as they engage with research in the pursuit of monitoring any improvements in pupils' learning. The objectives are to: 1) provide opportunities for teachers to develop craft knowledge through the implementation of a thinking skills programme including strategies for evaluating pupils' learning strategies and markers for effective classroom practice; 2) establish a cohort of highly skilled teacher coaches who are confident in their engagement with research and able to support the development of less experienced colleagues effectively; 3) extend the higher education institution (HEI)/school partnership to incorporate a research dimension; and 4) develop the links across the consortium and the region to ensure wide dissemination of the findings and draw contacts into active involvement in an evidence-based research culture by generating their own projects. Partners in the consortium will use a range of methods of data collection and analysis in accordance with the focus of their project. Data collected will relate to three variables: teacher input; classroom processes; and pupil outcomes. There will be a wealth of quantitative and qualitative data therefore which allows: 1) longitudinal studies of teachers, pupils and classroom environments; 2) statistical analysis; 3) comparative analysis (including between school and between subject analysis). The data generated by individual school level projects will form the basis for medium and long term research projects analysing the patterns of classroom interaction and the emergent role of the teacher coach.

STATUS: Sponsored project

SOURCE OF GRANT: Teacher Training Agency £105,000; Consortium of schools; Local Education Authorities; University of Newcastle

DATE OF RESEARCH: 1998-continuing

KEYWORDS: **pupil improvement; teacher development; teacher researchers; thinking skills**

1856

Department of Education, St Thomas Street, Newcastle upon Tyne NE1 7RU
0191 222 6000

Straker, A. Miss; *Supervisor*: Carrington, L. Mr

Children's contructions of nationhood: a cross cultural study

ABSTRACT: The aim of this study is to determine the underlying constructs from which children build their understanding of the concept of nationhood. The focus is on the structures which dictate their interpretations of nationhood, rather than on any individual's sense of their own national affiliation. Integral to this study of primary school children is its comparative nature. This will illustrate the degree to which any particular constructs may be seen as fundamental and universal or situation dependent.

STATUS: Individual research

DATE OF RESEARCH: 1997-continuing

KEYWORDS: **cross cultural studies; national identity; primary school pupils**

1857

Department of Education, St Thomas Street, Newcastle upon Tyne NE1 7RU
0191 222 6000

Elliott, J. Mr; Baez, M. Mrs; Crowther, D. Miss; *Supervisors*: Dyson, A. Prof.; Millward, A. Mr

Examination of practice in mainstream schools for children with special educational needs

ABSTRACT: The aims of this project were: 1) The establishment of baseline data relating to current practice in mainstream schools as they prepared for the implementation of the Code of Practice. This baseline will make it possible to monitor the impact of the Code of Practice and to carry out subsequent evaluations of the extent to which it has enhanced special needs provision in schools. 2) The construction of a survey instrument which can be used not only in the investigation of current practice, but also in any future investigations to monitor changes that have been brought about by the Code of Practice. 3) The identification of key issues which face Northern Ireland schools in respect of the Code of Practice so that appropriate guidance and support can be offered both by the Department of Education for Northern Ireland (DENI) and by the Education and Library Boards. 4) The identification of examples of effective current practice in mainstream schools. The investigation comprised two major elements: a) a questionnaire survey of all mainstream schools in Northern Ireland aimed at identifying the major features of current practice and provision in respect of special educational needs; b) case study work in a representative sample of a minimum of 30 schools drawn from all Board areas. These case studies illuminated the complexity of practice and provision; explored underlying factors which shaped that practice; identified the problems likely to be faced by schools in implementing the Code of Practice; and identified examples of effective practice which other schools might consider. The final report was published by the Department of Education for North Ireland in 1998.

STATUS: Sponsored project

SOURCE OF GRANT: Department for Education for Northern Ireland

DATE OF RESEARCH: 1996-1998

KEYWORDS: **mainstreaming; northern ireland; special educational needs**

1858

Department of Education, St Thomas Street, Newcastle upon Tyne NE1 7RU
0191 222 6000

Dyson, A. Prof.; Lin, M. Dr; Millward, A. Mr

Effective communication between school, local education authorities, health and social services in the field of special educational needs

ABSTRACT: This research was commissioned by the Department for Education and Employment and the Department of Health and was undertaken by the Special Needs Research Centre in the Department of Education, Newcastle upon Tyne University, over the academic year of 1996-97. The research aimed to identify obstacles to effective inter-agency cooperation. The investigation was conducted in 10 local education authorities (LEAs) in England. It took the forms of interviews with headteachers, special educational needs coordinators (SENCOs) and parents at a sample of schools, and with officers and senior management from LEAs, health and social services. Case studies were conducted into examples of significant and effective practice which were identified from nominations by national professional bodies and from the literature. The findings revealed a number of models of inter-agency cooperation for pupils with special educational needs. A series of recommendations were made relating to effective cooperation between schools and other agencies. An analytic model was developed which can be used by individual agencies as a means of reviewing their current practice and also charting a course for future development.

STATUS: Sponsored project

SOURCE OF GRANT: Department for Education and Employment; Department of Health

DATE OF RESEARCH: 1996-1997

KEYWORDS: **agency cooperation; health services; local education authorities; mainstreaming; social services; special educational needs**

1859

Department of Education, St Thomas Street, Newcastle upon Tyne
NE1 7RU
0191 222 6000

Harrison, T. Mr; *Supervisor*: Moseley, D. Mr

Effective pedagogical use of information and communication technology in the teaching and learning of literacy and numeracy in primary schools

ABSTRACT: With reference to the rapid expansion of the use of information and communication technology (ICT) in the last decade, educators have strong interests in the innovative potentials of computers in teaching and learning. There are many barriers against the successful innovation. Apart from the question about the availability of hardware and software, teachers have a significant role in promoting its use. The attitude towards its use and the pedagogical challenge of integrating ICT with traditional teaching practice are common factors for the effectiveness of use. Various aspects of support, which include effort put in by the school and/or outside agents, need to be established on the basis of the contextual variables in teaching and learning. The present research adopts the approach of identifying and promoting examples of effective practice of using ICT to support the teaching and learning of literacy and numeracy. Particular attention is placed on the frequency and intensity of using ICT and the pedagogical decision-making processes in relation to the teaching strategy and level of ICT provision. Data collection methods include classroom observation, semi-structured interview, survey questionnaire, concept mapping and repertory grid exercise.

STATUS: Individual research

DATE OF RESEARCH: 1997-continuing

KEYWORDS: **computer uses in education; information technology; literacy; numeracy; primary education; teaching methods**

1860

Department of Education, St Thomas Street, Newcastle upon Tyne
NE1 7RU
0191 222 6000

Baumfield, V. Dr; Taverner, S. Ms

Withdrawals from Postgraduate Certificate in Education courses in secondary mathematics and science

ABSTRACT: As part of a project funded by the Teacher Training Agency (TTA) the researchers looked at the pattern of withdrawal from one year Postgraduate Certificate of Education (PGCE) courses secondary mathematics and science. A representative sample of institutions were contacted and questionnaires distributed to students who had withdrawn, either before taking up their place, or once the course had commenced. The reasons given by the students for their withdrawal were analysed as were other factors, such as their class of degree. Institutions with a range of withdrawal rates were interviewed by telephone to establish what procedures, if any, they took to maintain contact with students between the date of their acceptance onto the course and their registration day. Main findings were that students withdrew for one of five main reasons: 1) financial reasons - another year of grant and increased expenses while on teaching placement; 2) negative image of teaching - discouraged those from taking up a place; 3) need for scientists to be proficient in more than one subject; 4) perceived lack of support from host school and training institution during teaching placements.

STATUS: Sponsored project

SOURCE OF GRANT: Teacher Training Agency £5,000

DATE OF RESEARCH: 1996-1997

KEYWORDS: **dropouts; postgraduate certificate in education; preservice teacher education; student recruitment; student wastage**

1861

Department of Education, St Thomas Street, Newcastle upon Tyne
NE1 7RU
0191 222 6000

Moseley, D. Dr; Higgins, S. Mr

Effective teaching methods using information and communications technology

ABSTRACT: The Teacher Training Agency (TTA) is committed to improving the standards of pupils' achievements and quality of their learning through improving the quality of teaching, raising the standards of teacher education and training, and promoting teaching as a profession. As part of this work the TTA has commissioned the University of Newcastle to undertake research into effective classroom pedagogy using information and communications technology (ICT) in primary schools. It is intended that this research will help teachers raise pupils' achievements by extending and enhancing their pedagogy through increasing their capacity to make informed choices about when and where to use ICT and to understand the implications of using this technology. The project aims to: 1) test and develop a generic framework highlighting the potential benefits and pitfalls in ICT use in classrooms, particularly in the areas of literacy and numeracy; 2) help teachers raise pupil achievements in these areas through supporting informed choice about the use of ICT in the classroom; 3) refine and illustrate specific aspects of the framework through detailed classroom case studies of effective teacher practice and development. The research is being carried out in 3 main stages: Stage 1: a range of schools will be identified (some using data from the Performance Indicators in Primary Schools Project (PIPS) based at Durham University) and the extent of ICT provision determined. Stage 2: approximately 30 classrooms from these schools and other 'ICT-rich' schools will be investigated to identify pedagogical factors which may correlate with increased pupil attainment. Stage 3: this evidence will be used with a group of about 20 teachers to plan specific development projects for their own classrooms. Evidence for the effectiveness of this development will focus on impact upon pupil attainment and will include support for pupils with special educational needs (SEN) in mainstream classes. The proposed outcomes include: 1) a report to the TTA on the research findings and case studies of school based development; 2) a framework for effective pedagogy using ICT with examples of research-based practice; 3) a database of research on ICT in primary schools; 4) a website containing a research summary for teachers and researchers.

STATUS: Sponsored project

SOURCE OF GRANT: Teacher Training Agency £180,000

DATE OF RESEARCH: 1997-continuing

KEYWORDS: **computer uses in education; information technology; primary education; teacher effectiveness; teaching methods**

1862

Department of Education, St Thomas Street, Newcastle upon Tyne
NE1 7RU
0191 222 6000

Jimenez, M. Ms; *Supervisor*: Westgate, D. Mr

Inservice teacher training in the UK: implications for policy in Colombia

ABSTRACT: The study aims first to provide an account of the currently varied forms of inservice support and training (INSET) available to UK teachers, as well as of current and projected trends. The analysis is in part evaluative, drawing upon views of both providers and clients. Data have been gathered across several regions of the UK, through interviews and questionnaires, subjected to both quantitative and qualitative analysis. Essentially a case study, its conclusions will nevertheless be further scrutinised for lessons (e.g. from an increasingly market-driven model of INSET) which have relevance to policy development in Colombia.

STATUS: Individual research

DATE OF RESEARCH: 1995-continuing

KEYWORDS: **colombia; inservice teacher education**

1863

Department of Education, St Thomas Street, Newcastle upon Tyne
NE1 7RU
0191 222 6000

Dyson, A. Prof.; Millward, A. Mr; Lin, M. Dr; Crowther, D. Miss

The role of the special educational needs coordinator in schools

ABSTRACT: This project investigated the management of the role of the special educational needs coordinator (SENCO) in the light of the Code of Practice (Department for Education and Employment (DfEE), 1994). The research was commissioned by the DfEE. The fieldwork was undertaken by the Special Needs Research Centre in the University of Newcastle during the 1995-96 academic year. The research aimed to identify the problems that SENCOs felt themselves to be facing in managing their role as delineated by the Code and the strategies that they were developing in order to manage that role effectively. The investigation took the form of a questionnaire survey of all mainstream schools in 7 local education authorities (LEAs) and follow-up case study visits of a sample of schools. The findings revealed that the Code presented SENCOs with both opportunities and challenges. Many SENCOs developed strategies in order to implement the Code effectively. The end of the project report makes a series of recommendations relating to the management of the SENCO role.

PUBLISHED MATERIAL: CROWTHER, D., DYSON, A., LIN, M. & MILLWARD, A. (1997). The role of SEN coordinator in schools: analytic report. Newcastle upon Tyne: University of Newcastle, Department of Education.

STATUS: Sponsored project

SOURCE OF GRANT: Department for Education and Employment

DATE OF RESEARCH: 1995-1997

KEYWORDS: **mainstreaming; special educational needs; special educational needs coordinators**

1864

Department of Education, St Thomas Street, Newcastle upon Tyne
NE1 7RU
0191 222 6000

Robson, E. Ms; Clark, J. Ms

Evaluation of the training strategy of Reviving the Heart of the West End Single Regeneration Budget (SRB) programme

ABSTRACT: The training strategy is a central part of the Reviving the Heart of the West End programme and aims to address the need for local provision which overcomes the barriers which continue to prevent/inhibit many people from accessing and participating in training. The evaluation will aim to examine whether the strategy has achieved its own overall aims and objectives and has: 1) improved the 'employability' and employment prospects of local people; 2) met the needs of all sections of the community; and 3) achieved an appropriate balance between pre-vocational support and vocational support. More specifically, the evaluation study aims to examine the effectiveness and impact of 5 local projects which work at the core of the strategy. The research will be broken down into 3 phases. Phase 1: participant observation of the 5 projects in action; semi-structured interviews with key staff; collection and collation of 'hard' data; focus group discussions with users; identification of the samples of users to 'track'; interviews with representatives of outside partners/ collaborators. Phase 2: interviews with key individuals; interviews with 'users'; focus group discussion with key staff; focus group discussions with other groups. Phase 3: interviews with 'users'; semi-structured interview with the coordinator; focus group discussion with key staff of the 5 projects; focus group discussions with other groups; data analysis, writing up and report preparation.

STATUS: Sponsored project

SOURCE OF GRANT: Reviving the Heart of the West End £12.000

DATE OF RESEARCH: 1999-continuing

KEYWORDS: **programme evaluation; social exclusion; training; unemployment; vocational education**

1865

Department of Education, St Thomas Street, Newcastle upon Tyne
NE1 7RU
0191 222 6000

Bonnett, A. Dr; Pearce, D. Dr; Tomlin, R. Mr; Skelton, C. Dr; Nayak, A. Mr; Smith, F. Dr; *Supervisor*: Carrington, B.

Recruitment of ethnic minorities into teaching

ABSTRACT: This research aims to examine the motivations and attitudes of ethnic minority students towards teaching. Focusing on the 1998/99 entry to the Postgraduate Certificate in Education (PGCE), the study will address the following questions: 1) What do students perceive as the main constraints upon ethnic minority participation in teacher education? 2) What are their experiences during training? 3) How might teacher training institutions encourage ethnic minority students to take up places on their courses? The study is being carried out over a period of 28 months. During the first year, a questionnaire will be administered to a national sample of minority students from a range of ethnic backgrounds. The survey will provide information on: the students' motives for entering teaching; the factors influencing their choice of course and institution; their images of teaching as a profession; and their perceptions of the barriers to ethnic minority recruitment. Interviews will be conducted with PGCE staff involved in student selection, mentor training and quality assurance. Towards the end of the PGCE year, individual and group interviews with a sub-sample of students will be undertaken. Course information, policy statements relating to admissions and other documentary material will also be examined. In the second year of the study, follow-up interviews will be conducted with a cross-section of newly-qualified ethnic minority teachers in their first teaching posts.

STATUS: Sponsored project

SOURCE OF GRANT: Teacher Training Agency £100,000

DATE OF RESEARCH: 1998-continuing

KEYWORDS: **ethnic groups; postgraduate certificate in education; preservice teacher education; student recruitment; student teachers**

1866

Department of Education, St Thomas Street, Newcastle upon Tyne
NE1 7RU
0191 222 6000

Dyson, A. Prof.; Millward, A. Mr; Clark, J. Ms; Lin, M. Dr; Hall, E. Ms

Examining the link between housing policy and education

ABSTRACT: The investigation was prompted by a number of recent developments at the interface of housing and education policy, and is mainly focused on a primary school which is geographically at the centre of a social housing estate where the principal landlord is a single Housing Association (HA). The school believes that it is the Trust's lettings policy, which has for some time been based on a notion of housing 'need', that has resulted in a concentration within the area of families experiencing special educational needs. The researchers set out to explore the alleged causal link, and were asked to: 1) analyse the problems reported by the school in terms of perceptions of staff and of any hard evidence of changes in attainment and behaviour; 2) explore possible relationships between the problems reported by the school and changes within the local community which might be attributable to the HA's policies; 3) investigate the school's responses to the reported changes and their relationship with any responses being made by other agencies within the community; 4) compare the responses in the area with those made by schools and other agencies in two (broadly) similar communities; 5) make recommendations about how the school's responses might be further developed and how it might be coordinated with other community responses. What appears to have emerged through this research is that there has been a series of changes which were unavoidable from the landlord's point of view. These changes seem to have been gradual and have had a cumulative effect. While they may not exactly be dramatic, they are nonetheless, significant. Schools are relatively stable institutions, and if there are changes made externally, for example, in the population of the surrounding community, than the school has to cope with these changes. If the school is not prepared for such changes, then it can take a long time to turn it in a different direction. Because the changes have not been particularly dramatic, it was not only the school which was not prepared. None of the other agencies were fully aware of what was happening and there has been, therefore, no overall community strategy. The problems highlighted by the research are problems generated by change rather than absolute levels of social need. Because the area does not constitute one of the country's 'worst estates', it has been by-passed by the area initiatives characteristics of government policy. Moreover, given the pressures and resource constraints under which social agencies operate, it is inevitable that they will focus on areas of significant need, particularly where 'crises' force the area to public and political attention. This may paradoxically result in areas such as this becoming more marginalised, and to the failure to develop and resource an overall strategy to manage change until it is too late. A full research report has been presented to the Joseph Rowntree Foundation.

STATUS: Sponsored project

SOURCE OF GRANT: Joseph Rowntree Foundation £50,000

DATE OF RESEARCH: 1997-continuing

KEYWORDS: **disadvantaged; housing; primary education; social problems; special educational needs**

1867

Department of Education, St Thomas Street, Newcastle upon Tyne NE1 7RU
0191 222 6000

Ecclestone, K. Ms; Hall, I. Mr

Quality assurance and quality control in internal assessment across qualifications

ABSTRACT: There is a fine balance between national standards based on the reliability and consistency of teachers' assessment decisions and the ability of teachers to respond to the interests of their students and trainees via coursework (internal assessment). A move in recent years to use internal assessment in qualifications reflects policy concerns to motivate more students to take formal accreditation, to make assessment more valid and authentic by covering more skills and qualities than is possible through traditional external assessment and to respond more flexibly to local conditions. At the same time, a radical aim of outcome-based assessment is to make students more active and equal partners in being able to judge the quality of their own work. Yet, as qualifications must increasingly provide progression between and across different pathways, sectors and institutions, concerns for externally monitored rigour and consistency have grown. These tensions mean that the Qualifications and Curriculum Authority (QCA) and awarding bodies face difficult decisions about implementing terms of quality assurance and control which relate authentically to teachers' and students' own approaches to assessment. The broad aims of the research project are: 1) To inform QCA about the range and effectiveness of quality assurance and quality control features across a range of different qualifications which use internal assessment. 2) To inform and contribute to the QCA's aim of securing a rigorous system of regulation for national tests and qualifications. The research involves a literature review; documentary analysis of quality assurance/quality control procedures for awarding bodies; structured interviews with groups of teachers and students in the post-14 qualifications (General Certificate of Secondary Education (GCSE), A-level, General National Vocational Qualification (GNVQ) Advanced, Business and Technician Education Council (BTEC) National Diploma, National Vocational Qualification (NVQ)) in two colleges, two schools and a workplace offering NVQs, awarding body officers, Further Education Funding Council (FEFC) inspectors. A report will be produced for QCA.

STATUS: Sponsored project

SOURCE OF GRANT: Qualifications and Curriculum Authority £23,503

DATE OF RESEARCH: 1999-continuing

KEYWORDS: **assessment; assessment by teachers; coursework; qualifications; quality control**

1868

Department of Education, St Thomas Street, Newcastle upon Tyne NE1 7RU
0191 222 6000

Brunel University, School of Education, Twickenham Campus, 300 St Margaret's Road, Twickenham TW1 1PT
0181 891 0121

Baez-Olmeno, M. Dr; *Supervisors*: Sandow, S. Dr; Garner, P. Dr

Reproduction of cultural dependence in the special education systems of Latin America with special reference to Chile

ABSTRACT: In 1990, when democracy was reinstalled in Chile, education was made a priority and significant innovations were introduced in the system. The view that innovations might engender contradictory outcomes was not fully addressed and change was expected to take place through these programmes and supported by new educational policy. This study introduces the concept of a culturally dependent educational system which relies on foreign models, as hindering the process of producing positive educational outcomes. This study examines the reproduction of cultural dependence in Chilean special education. It looks in detail at the historical basis of the creation of this state and the implications derived from the economic dependence on foreign capital, and culturally dependent on foreign educational tenets and models of practice. The conceptual framework of the study is drawn from the critical examination of the radical-functionalist discourse and in particular, from dependence theory. This adoption is based on the assumption that these can also be extended to explain wider issues associated with economic dependence, especially those related to the education system. This is because Latin American countries and Chile in particular have geared educational reforms to support and to favour economic development. The methodological underpinning is derived from the combination of historiography and an ethogenic approach. It draws attention to the relevance of historical processes and detailed qualitative fieldwork of collecting accounts of participants in context. The study therefore documents selected participants' accounts at different levels of the Chilean education system. Data were collected through extended accounts by participants in interviews and through the collection and analysis of relevant official documents. The findings of the study reveal that while teachers in mainstream schools lack awareness of the state of cultural dependence in which they are immersed, teachers in special schools have a minimal understanding of the effect of this cultural dependence on the implementation of integration policies. Individuals at different levels of the Ministry of Education take the view that policies are somewhat subject to interpretation by actors located within specific contexts, and what they have done to support teachers appears to be little in comparison with the scope of expected outcomes. Emerging from this study is the notion of a special education system which needs redefinition of the discourse of appropriation by protagonists of policy, models and practice. The study is established upon the abiding conviction that cultural dependence can be reversed. For this to occur, actions should be taken by the Chilean Ministry of Education to define the features of producing a culturally independent system of special education. This study opens a way to such a direction.

STATUS: Individual research

DATE OF RESEARCH: 1994-1998

KEYWORDS: **chile; latin america; special educational needs**

1869

Department of Education, St Thomas Street, Newcastle upon Tyne NE1 7RU
0191 222 6000
Coopers and Lybrand, 1 Embankment Place, London WC2N 6NN
0171 583 5000

Elliott, J. Mr; Crowther, D. Miss; *Supervisors*: Dyson, A. Prof.; Millward, A. Mr

Costs and outcomes for pupils with moderate learning difficulties in special and mainstream schools

ABSTRACT: The aims of this project are: 1) The analysis of the full costs associated with making provision for pupils with moderate learning difficulties (MLD) in a range of settings. 2) A review of the literature on outcome measures for the education of children with MLD with a view to recommending a set or bank of appropriate measures. 3) The identification of the ways in which further research in this field might be carried out - particularly in terms of full cost-effectiveness studies of MLD provision. 4) The development of a set of 'profiles' of children with MLD which can, in the absence of any operationalised definition of

MLD, be used as the basis for further research in this field. 5) The development of methodology for costing different forms of MLD provision at both local education authority (LEA) and school level. The investigation will comprise: a) constructing a sample of 8 LEAs to reflect the range of LEA types; b) identifying a panel of experienced special educational needs (SEN) staff to write brief profiles of actual MLD students; c) categorising these profiles in order to carefully construct a set of 'synthetic' profiles which represent the range of MLD students; d) face-to-face interviewing in the 8 LEAs and a nominated sample of 32 schools in order to identify the structure of the SEN provision; explore what provision, if any, would be made for pupils matching each of the profiles; collect financial data in order to assess the costs of the MLD provision; and e) literature review on outcome measures.

STATUS: Sponsored project

SOURCE OF GRANT: Department for Education and Employment

DATE OF RESEARCH: 1997-1998

KEYWORDS: cost effectiveness; educational finance; learning disabilities; mainstreaming; outcomes of education; special educational needs; special schools

1870

Department of Education, St Thomas Street, Newcastle upon Tyne NE1 7RU
0191 222 6000
Nanyang Technological University, National Institute of Education, Bukit Timam Road, Singapore 259756
01065 7911744

Baumfield, V. Dr; Han, C. Dr; Higgins, S. Mr; Tan, C. Dr

Pedagogy for thinking: a cross-cultural analysis

ABSTRACT: Recent developments in education policy have seen the emergence of two parallel movements in curriculum design; the implementation of thinking skills programmes and the promotion of citizenship education. In both Singapore and the UK, the coincidence of these developments has been marked with initiatives swiftly following one another. In the UK, the government's White Paper 'Excellence in Schools' (1997) advocated the teaching of thinking skills as a contributor to excellence in schools. There are now increased opportunities to introduce critical thinking into the curriculum in all the key stages of the National Curriculum. In Singapore the slogan 'Thinking schools, learning nation' was used by Prime Minister Goh Chok Tong to encapsulate the aspirations for the role of education in the 21st century. A thinking programme, which has been piloted, is in the process of being gradually implemented in all secondary schools in Singapore. A study of the thinking programme using discourse and/ or conversation analysis would provide depth of understanding with regard to the forms of interaction, and the learning and teaching processes, in the classroom. This would increase knowledge of how thinking programmes work, and the effect that the pedagogy used in such programmes would have on citizenship education. It could also contribute to the development and greater effectiveness in the implementation of the thinking programme. The study is conceived as a joint research project, lasting approximately 3 years, between the National Institute of Education (Nanyang Technological University) and Newcastle University. It is the second of 3 projects planned between the 2 institutions and the project builds on the work that has been carried out by Dr Vivienne Baumfield of Newcastle University in the evaluation and analysis of thinking programmes. The project will focus on the pedagogy in lessons where thinking skills are used. A study of pupil-teacher and pupil-pupil interactions will enable researchers to analyse the extent to which the classroom discourse matches the model of learning envisaged by programme designers (that of the designers of the thinking programme in the case of Singapore), as well as the wider theoretical context. The aim is ultimately to identify and provide a cross-cultural perspective on the pedagogy encouraging thinking and/or the developing of a community of enquiry. It is also to provide feedback to curriculum developers and practitioners, and so contribute to the ongoing research and development on thinking programmes in Singapore. Implications for citizenship education will also be explicated.

STATUS: Sponsored project

SOURCE OF GRANT: British Council £4,200; National Institute of Education £58,035; University of Newcastle £10,000

DATE OF RESEARCH: 1998-continuing

KEYWORDS: citizenship education; comparative education; singapore; thinking skills

1871

Department of Education, St Thomas Street, Newcastle upon Tyne NE1 7RU
0191 222 6000
Newcastle upon Tyne University, Department of Speech, King George VI Building, Newcastle upon Tyne NE1 7RU

Sadler-Meazzini, J. Mrs; *Supervisor*: Westgate, D. Mr

A longitudinal study of the educational performance and speech and language development of language impaired children during the first three years of school

ABSTRACT: This longitudinal study examines: a) the educational performance and b) the speech and language development of 44 children diagnosed as having a speech and/or language impairment at the onset of their schooling within one local education authority (LEA) in the North East of England. The aim is to examine the influence of certain variables, such as type and pervasiveness of the language disorder, behaviour and social development, non-verbal ability of the children, and the attitudes and knowledge of teachers. These have intuitively been felt by the professionals working in this field to influence the educational performance and language development of children who at the beginning of their school career present a severe speech and/or language impairment. Such information will be invaluable to parents, speech and language services, and local education authorities alike, when making decisions regarding the individual needs of these children, their educational provision, and the allocation of increasingly scarce human and financial resources.

STATUS: Individual research

DATE OF RESEARCH: 1993-1998

KEYWORDS: academic achievement; language handicaps; performance; special educational needs; speech handicaps; young children

1872

Department of Education, St Thomas Street, Newcastle upon Tyne NE1 7RU
0191 222 6000
Newcastle upon Tyne University, Department of Geography, Daysh Building, Newcastle upon Tyne NE1 7RU
Newcastle upon Tyne University, Department of Town and Country Planning, Claremont Tower, Newcastle upon Tyne NE1 7RU

Carrington, L. Mr; Bonnett, A. Dr; Gilroy, R. Ms

British and Canadian anti-racist initiatives in public sector education and training

ABSTRACT: This is a comparative study of the development and implementation of anti-racist initiatives in public sector education and training in the UK and Canada. As well as examining policies and debates at a national level, particular consideration is given to developments in four metropolitan areas: Toronto and Vancouver in Canada; and London and Newcastle upon Tyne in the UK. Semi-structured interviews are employed to examine the perceptions of grass-roots activists, pressure groups, practitioners, administrators, politicians and scholars in an attempt to identify some of the key dilemmas faced by those dealing with this issue. It is hoped that an international study of this kind will indicate the future direction for anti-racist education and training in each of the countries concerned.

STATUS: Sponsored project

SOURCE OF GRANT: Canadian Government: Institutional Research Award Program £9,700

DATE OF RESEARCH: 1994-1997

KEYWORDS: antiracism education; canada; comparative education; training

Newman College

1873

Genners Lane, Bartley Green, Birmingham B32 3NT
0121 476 1181

Darnton, A. Ms; *Supervisor*: Hoey, M. Prof.

This way through the woods: new directions in the analysis of narrative

ABSTRACT: This thesis takes as its basic premise the proposition that the grammar of narrative discourse posited by Longacre (1976, 1983) and based upon the tagmemic system of analysis provides a most efficient model of narrative organisation; a model against which examples of narrative texts can be usefully measured and by means of which their effectiveness may, to a greater or lesser extent, be accounted for. However, it also recognises that there are problems with the model, problems that occur in the main because of a tendency on Longacre's part both to gloss over certain details of the tagmemic system and to overlook, in respect of a description of narrative, the relative importance of others. Specifically, these problems consist of: the lack of any notional structure equivalent of the surface structure features, title, aperture and finis; the difficulty in the demarcation of episode boundaries; the non-grammatical nature of certain peak markers; the number of surface elements marked by turbulence and the positioning of those elements in respect of the organisation of the notional structure. The thesis discusses solutions to each of these problems, stressing particularly the need to take account of what is happening at levels of the tagmemic system above that of the discourse, wave perspective and the role played by the referential hierarchy, it is the last problem that is given greatest attention. Evidence is offered for the existence of an area of surface structure turbulence, regularly occurring and consistently sited, additional to the two originally described by Longacre and the proposition put forward that this turbulence is indicative of the existence of an element within the notional structure not previously identified. This new notional structure element, here given the label of Igniting Moment, is then described in respect of its grammatical and referential characteristics including its role in the overall narrative pattern which is summarised as that of focusing the predictions of the audience as to the eventual outcome of the plot or more colloquially as 'This way through the woods'. Finally, the validity of the suggested amendments to the Longacre model is tested when those amendments are brought into use to facilitate the satisfactory analysis of a hitherto problematic text and a revised version of the model is then proposed.

STATUS: Individual research

DATE OF RESEARCH: 1993-1998

KEYWORDS: **discourse analysis; narration**

1874

Genners Lane, Bartley Green, Birmingham B32 3NT
0121 476 1181

Lavelle, A. Mr; *Supervisor*: Swan, M. Mr

Using software in mathematics to develop independent learning, in data handling

ABSTRACT: This research investigates the use of software in mathematics, typically spreadsheets, by undergraduates, in developing understanding of graphs in an indendent mode. Interviewing students whilst explaining their thinking as they explore graphs with spreadsheets is the main source of data collection. Interesting results relating to perceptions of lines and curves are emerging.

STATUS: Individual research

DATE OF RESEARCH: 1996-continuing

KEYWORDS: **computer uses in education; educational software; graphs; higher education; information technology; mathematics education; spreadsheets**

1875

Genners Lane, Bartley Green, Birmingham B32 3NT
0121 476 1181

Al-Nakeeb, Y. Dr; Woodfield, L. Ms; Carry, A. Mr

Time management and levels of physical activity during physical education lessons

ABSTRACT: Physical activity has generally been recognised as having a positive effect on a number of chronic diseases, such as cardiovascular diseases (Bouchard et al, 1994). Presently, it is commonly accepted that children should engage in a minimum of 3 sessions per week of activities that last 20 minutes or more at a time and that require moderate to vigorous levels of exertion. Physical education (PE) in school is recognised commonly by professionals as possibly the most appropriate environment for the promotion of health related physical activity (HRPA). The purpose of this study was twofold: 1) to examine the management of PE time in schools; and 2) to assess levels of children's physical activity in PE lessons and to investigate the disparity between the areas of gymnastics, dance, games and swimming. 62 PE lessons in primary schools were observed. The children were aged between 5 and 11 years. The data was collected using an adaptation of the continuous observation procedure validated by O'Hara et al, 1989. 4 categories of intensity of physical activity were identified and recorded, points were then converted into a predicted heart rate in order to compare the results with other studies that used heart rate monitoring. According to this procedure, moderate to vigorous physical activity (MVPA) was identified as that which resulted in heart rate above 139 bpm. The analysis of the results indicated that: 1) only 53% of the total PE lessons time was spent in activity; the rest was lost in changing, transferring and getting ready; 2) the highest percentage of MVPA was in swimming lessons, whilst the lowest was in dance, with approximately one-third of the total time observed, in activity, being spent with heart rate above 139 bpm; 3) there were only few occasions where MVPA was maintained for a period in excess of 10 minutes. The results of this study highlighted the need to take the following measures: a) appropriately structured lessons to increase child involvement with the focus of the lessons being engaging children in physical activity; b) better use of space and support materials; c) more efficient use of time allocated to PE lessons; d) improving quality of teaching styles and delivery to emphasise continuous MVPA.

PUBLISHED MATERIAL: A full list of publications are available from the researchers.

STATUS: Team research

DATE OF RESEARCH: 1997-continuing

KEYWORDS: **health activities; physical activity level; physical education; physical fitness; time management**

1876

Genners Lane, Bartley Green, Birmingham B32 3NT
0121 476 1181
Birmingham University, School of Education, Edgbaston, Birmingham B15 2TT
0121 414 3344

Moore, M. Dr; *Supervisor*: Wade, B. Prof.

An evaluation of a local Bookstart project

ABSTRACT: The research examines the effectiveness of early book gifting (i.e. to babies). It is longitudinal (from 4 months of age to 5 years) and examines differences between two cohorts of 70 children; one cohort receiving a book pack at 4 months, 8 months, 18 months and 40 months from health visitors and nursery. Comparisons between groups are made at several stages: 1) in the home: evidence of books and book sharing; 2) nursery school: language and nursery skills, speech and language skills, interaction and social skills, behaviour; 3) reception class: baseline assessment. Methods include observation of behaviour, standardised tests of speech and language and a standardised preschool behaviour checklist. Interviews with teaches and parents, and baseline assessments (school).

STATUS: Individual research

DATE OF RESEARCH: 1996-continuing

KEYWORDS: **babies; books; childrens literature; early childhood education; early experience; language acquisition; literacy; preschool children; young children**

1877

Genners Lane, Bartley Green, Birmingham B32 3NT
0121 476 1181
Exeter University, School of Education, St Luke's, Heavitree Road, Exeter EX1 2LU
01392 263263

Davenport, A. Mr; *Supervisors*: Peacock, A. Dr; Desforges, C. Prof.

The social and cognitive anatomies of degree construction and partnership

ABSTRACT: Ethnographic account of degree construction in process. Emphasis is placed upon insider accounts and phenomenological understandings of the research process itself. The study maps the construction of a new undergraduate and a new postgraduate programme over a period of 3 years. It seeks to show how the structural, organisational and individual levels of explanation articulate an interact. The main aim of the case study is to illustrate the way in which insider research has become a neglected element in research in education as a whole and how it is a very powerful tool for exploring issues of generalisability and relatability within a qualitative paradigm.

STATUS: Individual research

DATE OF RESEARCH: 1998-continuing

KEYWORDS: **degrees - academic; higher education; research**

1878

Genners Lane, Bartley Green, Birmingham B32 3NT
0121 476 1181
University of Wales, Swansea, Department of Education, Hendrefoilan, Swansea SA2 7NB
01792 201231

Myers, K. Mr; *Supervisors*: Lowe, R. Prof.; Grosvenor, I. Dr

The education of refugee children in Britain 1937-1945

ABSTRACT: This research provides an historical perspective on contemporary debates relating to refugees and asylum. Using a case study approach and reconstructing the life experiences of Jewish and Spanish refugee children in Britain, this project analyses a number of key issues in the field. First, particular attention is paid to issues relating to education as this can be seen as critical in aiding refugee settlement. Second, an assessment of the affect of migration on both an individual's sense of identity and on the collective understanding of national identity is offered. Third, the idea of educational agency is explored with regard to the formation of identity, in both individuals and as part of wider cultural groups. In addition to the use of both public and private documentation collections, the collection, interpretation and analysis of refugee testimonies forms an integral part of this study. This research project will provide an important addition to the literature available to policymakers and scholars and will significantly enhance the researchers' undestanding of the issues surrounding the nature of the refugee question as we approach the next millenium.

STATUS: Individual research

DATE OF RESEARCH: 1995-continuing

KEYWORDS: **educational history; identity; immigrants; national identity; refugees**

NICER Research Unit

1879

Queen's University of Belfast, School of Education, 69 University Street, Belfast BT7 1HL
01232 245133

D'Arcy, J. Mr; Thompson, K. Miss; Leitch, C. Miss; McMahon, J. Ms; Rainey, N. Mrs; McGillion, P. Ms; *Supervisor*: Sutherland, A. Ms

Annual follow-up of newly-trained teachers

ABSTRACT: In collaboration with the teacher training institutions in Northern Ireland, the Northern Ireland Council for Educational Research (NICER) carries out an annual survey of newly-qualified teachers. The investigation seeks to describe the newly-qualified teachers in terms of their subject specialism, sector emphasis and type of training; to identify employment status by the same characteristics; to take note of teachers' experiences in seeking teaching posts and to examine trends in teacher employment. Data are collected by means of an annual questionnaire survey to all teachers who qualified the previous summer. Over the years considerable changes have been observed in the numbers of teachers qualifying, in the percentage who fail to find employment and in the ratio of permanent to non-permanent teaching posts obtained by newly-qualified teachers.

PUBLISHED MATERIAL: D'ARCY, J.M. (1990). Teachers newly-qualified in 1989. Belfast: Northern Ireland Council for Educational Research. ; THOMPSON, K. (1991). Teachers newly-qualified in 1990. Belfast: Northern Ireland Council for Educational Research. ; LEITCH, C.M. & SUTHERLAND, A.E. (1992). Teachers newly-qualified in 1991. Belfast: NICER Research Unit, School of Education, The Queen's University of Belfast. ; SUTHERLAND, A.E., MCMAHON, J.M. & RAINEY, N.A. (1993). Teachers newly-qualified in 1992. Belfast: NICER Research Unit, School of Education, The Queen's University of Belfast.; A full list of publications is available from the NICER Research Unit.

STATUS: Sponsored project

SOURCE OF GRANT: Department of Education for Northern Ireland

DATE OF RESEARCH: 1978-continuing

KEYWORDS: **labour market; newly qualified teachers; northern ireland; teacher employment; teacher recruitment; teaching profession**

1880

Queen's University of Belfast, School of Education, 69 University Street, Belfast BT7 1HL
01232 245133

Sutherland, A. Ms

Northern Ireland teachers who train in Great Britain

ABSTRACT: The aims of the research are to explore the reasons why a considerable number of Northern Ireland students go to Great Britain for initial teacher training (ITT) courses, especially Postgraduate Certificate in Education (PGCE) courses, whether they wish to return to teach in Northern Ireland and, if they do, how successful they are in finding teaching posts. One hypothesis is that the shortage of teacher training places in Northern Ireland drives many students 'across the water'. Two simultaneous surveys are in progress. Firstly, all Northern Ireland teachers identified as having qualified in Great Britain in 1995 or 1996 and as having taken up a teaching post in Northern Ireland the following academic year have been asked about their qualifications, the nature of their ITT course, the type of appointment held, the number of job applications made and their reasons for training in Great Britain and then returning to Northern Ireland. Secondly, students completing the first or final year of a teaching course have been asked about their qualifications, for their reasons for going to train in Great Britain and whether they hope to return to teach in Northern Ireland. Those qualifying this year have also been asked if they have found a teaching post for 1997-98.

STATUS: Sponsored project

SOURCE OF GRANT: Department of Education for Northern Ireland £12,000

DATE OF RESEARCH: 1997-1997

KEYWORDS: **course selection - students; employment opportunities; followup studies; graduate employment; graduate surveys; newly qualified teachers; northern ireland; preservice teacher education; student recruitment; student teachers; teacher employment; teaching profession**

North Cheshire College

1881

Padgate Campus, Fearnhead Lane, Warrington WA2 0DB
01925 814343
Lancaster University, Department of Management Learning, Gillow House, Bailrigg, Lancaster LA1 4YX
01524 65201

Lloyd, P. Mr; *Supervisor*: Davies, J. Mrs

Assessment of work experience in relation to management learning

ABSTRACT: The aim of this research is to investigate and evaluate the validity of supervised work experience as a degree course component that: (1) Enables students to acquire knowledge and skills. (2) Enables students to complement the college based learning prior to the placement period. (3) Enables students to develop appropriate and meaningful learning strategies following work experience periods. (4) Facilitates course development through 'wash back' on existing learning programmes. (5) Promotes staff development in terms of updating current practices within the industrial/commercial environment. (6) Enhances host awareness and sympathy towards participation in supervised work experience programmes. (7) Accurately assesses student development and performance in terms of: (a) personal/social skills; and (b) academic/cognitive skills. A further aim is to test the above through a process of primary and secondary research into short- and long-term supervised work experience programmes in several institutions offering a range of vocational related courses. It also aims to establish the theoretical concepts via primary and secondary sources of the notions underpinning: (1) experiential learning; (2) education and training; (3) teaching and learning methods; (4) assessment and profiling; and (5) competence and competition.

STATUS: Individual research

DATE OF RESEARCH: 1991-1993

KEYWORDS: industry higher education relationship; management studies; placement; work experience

North East Wales Institute of Higher Education

1882

School of Education, Postal Point 36, Plas Coch, Mold Road, Wrexham LL11 2AW
01978 290666

Harris, D. Mrs; *Supervisors*: Costello, P. Dr; Norris, R. Mr; Edwards, G. Miss

The role of argument in higher education for the professions: three case studies in education, management and nursing

ABSTRACT: The fundamental questions the research will address are: 1) How is argument defined or described in education, management and nursing studies? 2) What functions does argument serve in these areas? (i.e. Who is arguing? Who is the audience? What is the subject matter? In what contexts? To what ends?). 3) What constitutes a good argument in education, management and nursing? 4) How is argument taught and learned? 5) What role does argument play in the assessment of student performance? These questions will be explored by the analysis of discourse, both spoken and written, produced in a range of interactions between students and tutors, students and students, and students and tutors and the researcher. This would include texts such as: 1) Guidance and advice produced by institutions, departments or individuals on the subjects of study skills, assignments, assessment and written work; 2) examination questions and answers; 3) examiners' reports; 4) coursework assignments and projects; 5) dissertations; 6) tutors' comments and assessments; 7) lectures, seminars, tutorials, discussion groups; and 8) accounts given in interviews with tutors and students. The research will study the processes of argumentation to determine their functions in higher education: at undergraduate level, in developing the skills of emergent teachers, nurses and managers; and at postgraduate level, in refining professional practice and furthering personal development.

STATUS: Individual research

DATE OF RESEARCH: 1994-1997

KEYWORDS: argument; critical thinking; higher education; management studies; nurse education; persuasive discourse; preservice teacher education; professional education

1883

School of Education, Postal Point 36, Plas Coch, Mold Road, Wrexham LL11 2AW
01978 290666

Humphreys, B. Mrs; *Supervisor*: Costello, P. Dr

Economic and industrial understanding and work-related school activities in the secondary school curriculum

ABSTRACT: The purpose of this piece of research is to evaluate current practice in the delivery of Economic and Industrial Understanding (EIU)

and other work-related activities at National Curriculum key stages 3 and 4 in sceondary schools in North East Wales. Elements of the work-related curriculum such as EIU, industry/business days/weeks, work experience, mock interviews, teacher placements in industry and careers education and guidance will be investigated in relation to the value attached to these activities by the various parties involved. The study will collect and analyse the views of pupils, teachers and members of the business community in relation to their experience of various work-related activities organised by schools. It is intended to ascertain whether the time, effort and resources being devoted to such activities is seen to be worthwhile by each of the participating groups. The investigation will examine whether the pupils find the experiences to be a worthwhile and effective part of their preparation for the future; whether teachers (both those who are and are not involved in the organisation and implementation of such activities) consider such events to be an effective and valued use of time and resources; and whether the industrialists who participate find such events beneficial to themselves, their company and the pupils. Having studied the views of the parties involved and compared their evaluation of shared experiences, recommendations for good practice will be proposed.

STATUS: Individual research

DATE OF RESEARCH: 1996-continuing

KEYWORDS: economic and industrial understanding; industry education relationship; secondary education; secondments; vocational education; vocational guidance; work education relationship; work experience programmes

1884

School of Education and Humanities, Postal Point 36, Plas Coch, Mold Road, Wrexham LL11 2AW
01978 290666

Bowen, M. Ms; *Supervisor*: Costello, P. Dr

Special education and teacher training: an effective model of partnership between schools and a higher education institution

ABSTRACT: The research has been undertaken in order to ensure that, as newly qualified teachers, trainee teachers following a BA Qualified Teacher Status (QTS) course at a higher education institution (HEI) will have the necessary knowledge and skills to meet the special educational needs (SEN) of pupils in their care. The aim of the research is to do this by developing an effective model of partnership between primary schools and the HEI. Following the research, recommendations will be made as to how the quality of SEN training in initial teacher training can be improved in line with Department for Education and Employment (DfEE) proposals. The study will identify and evaluate existing practice in other HEIs using questionnaires and interviews with a sample group. It will also identify and evaluate the practice of the HEI in which the study takes place using questionnaires and interviews with trainee teachers, mentors and liaison tutors. This research data will be used to design and implement a mentor and liaison tutor training programme and a school-based SEN training programme for all BA (QTS) year one students. These programmes will be evaluated and based upon the findings, a core group of mentors will be involved in devising a suitable training programme in SEN for years two and three of the BA (QTS).

STATUS: Individual research

DATE OF RESEARCH: 1997-continuing

KEYWORDS: higher education; mentor training; partnerships; preservice teacher education; special educational needs

1885

School of Education and Humanities, Postal Point 36, Plas Coch, Mold Road, Wrexham LL11 2AW
01978 290666

Bleakley, c. Ms; *Supervisor*: Costello, P. Dr; Fairbairn, G. Dr

Promoting initial and continuing professional development: 3 case studies

ABSTRACT: The purpose of this research is to develop a coherent framework that places both initial and continuous professional development alongside accreditation of teaching, quality assurance, appraisal and staff development in higher education (HE). The research is grounded in the belief that professional development portfolios can provide the focus for staff to appreciate the inter-connectedness of all the different elements cited above and their relationship with individual and organisational development. This research investigates and compares models for initial and continuing professional development for academic staff currently employed in 3 higher education institutes and how portfolios are being used to support accreditation of professional academic practice. This will be conducted through the use of interviews and questionnaires. A critical review of the literature on initial and continuing professional development and the use of portfolios will be undertaken alongside an examination of the concept of lifelong learning. The resulting data will be used to inform the design and implementation of a flexible, integrated framework for initial and continuing professional development using portfolios as the main instrument for providing evidence of reflective evaluation of one's professional practice. Programmes in this framework will include accreditation of professional practice designed for new or inexperienced staff and an accredited prior experiential learning route (APEL), designed to accommodate the needs of experienced staff in higher education (HE). The portfolio and the resulting professional profile will be designed to meet the requirements of the new Institute of Learning and Teaching in Higher Education (ILTHE). The research will include an analysis of evaluative data from individuals participating on the initial and continuing professional development programmes; subject mentors; course tutors and representatives from the North East Wales Institute of Higher Education senior management team. Further developments will be advocated in the light of the research findings, the national context and demands of the ILTHE.

STATUS: Individual research

DATE OF RESEARCH: 1998-continuing

KEYWORDS: academic staff; accreditation of prior learning; higher education; lifelong learning; professional development; teacher development

North Westminster Community School

1886

Marylebone Lower House, Penfold Street, London NW1 6RX
0171 262 8000

Desai, P. Mr; Miah, M. Mr; Alinajeeb, A. Mr

Conflict between Bangladesh young men in Camden and Westminster

ABSTRACT: This study explores the reasons for the series of conflicts which occurred between Bangladeshi young men from Camden and Westminster. The study uses qualitative methods, including indepth interviews and group discussions. The sample comprises Bangladeshi men aged 15-18 in both areas, as well as interviews with youth workers. The conclusions suggest the causes lie in 2 areas: 1) the context of deprivation within which these young men live; and 2) the loyalty which some young men feel towards their peer group and area, and the consequent rivalry with other groups.

STATUS: Sponsored project

SOURCE OF GRANT: Gulbenkian Foundation

DATE OF RESEARCH: 1996-1997

KEYWORDS: bangladeshis; conflict; ethnic groups; peer relationship; youth

Northbrook College of Design and Technology

1887

Broadwater Road, Worthing BN14 8HJ
01903 231445
Sussex University, Institute of Education, Falmer, Brighton BN1 9RG
01273 606755

Thrower, M. Mr; *Supervisor*: Pateman, T. Dr

The Hegelian objective mind in education

ABSTRACT: Hegel included no systematic exposition and theory of education or system of pedagogy in his published philosophical work, yet in his

professional life he was heavily involved in teaching and preparing his philosophical text for assimilation by his students. Additionally, his philosophical system depended heavily on education as a vehicle for delivering the state of true knowledge. The research attempts to collate his various writings on education. His theory of education is then tested against the general philosophy to ensure consistency of approach. Additionally, philosophical, historical, sociological and political perspectives are brought to bear on the material. Contextual analysis includes a review of his personal relationships with family, friends and patrons as well as a study of the organisation of German schools in the 19th century. The relevance of Hegel's theories to modern practice are discussed where appropriate.

STATUS: Individual research

DATE OF RESEARCH: 1991-1998

KEYWORDS: educational history; educational philosophy; philosophy

Northern College

1888

Aberdeen Campus, Hilton Place, Aberdeen AB24 4FA
01224 283500

Payne, F. Mrs; *Supervisor*: Wood, S. Mr

The knowledge of and attitudes towards Scottish history of S4 pupils in Scottish schools

ABSTRACT: This research is based on a questionnaire that was completed by 3,200 S4 pupils in schools selected to provide coverage of different parts of Scotland, and different sizes and types of school. Pupils completed the questionnaire regardless of whether they had dropped history at the end of S2. The project aimed to explore a key issue in curriculum design in terms not only of pupils' knowledge of major events, people, and dates, but also in terms of their attitudes to the importance of Scottish history and their actual beliefs about a number of key issues concerned with the relationship of Scotland and England. The research has contributed to the work of the Scottish History Review Group - a national working party set up by the Scottish Consultative Council on the Curriculum. The data gathered has been processed and indicates negligible knowledge of Scottish history, a fairly positive view that it matters, and misconceptions about Anglo-Scottish relationships in the past that may well play a part in shaping current attitudes. The project also explored pupils' views on what they regarded as the most hepful way of working and the extent to which they saw their knowledge and attitudes being the result of school study or of influences outside school.

PUBLISHED MATERIAL: WOOD, S. & PAYNE, F. (1997). The knowledge of and attitudes towards Scottish history of S4 pupils in Scottish schools. Aberdeen: Northern College. ; WOOD, S. & PAYNE, F. (1997). 'In search of a Scottish identity? S4 pupils' knowledge of and attitudes towards Scottish history', Education in the North, New Series, No 5, pp.11-15.

STATUS: Sponsored project

SOURCE OF GRANT: Scottish Consultative Council on the Curriculum £2,000; Scottish Higher Education Funding Council £2,500

DATE OF RESEARCH: 1995-1997

KEYWORDS: curriculum development; history; national identity; pupil attitudes; scotland; secondary education

1889

Aberdeen Campus, Hilton Place, Aberdeen AB24 4FA
01224 283500

Coutts, N. Mr; Denoon, D. Mr; Bain, Y. Mrs

Project REM

ABSTRACT: The project seeks to investigate the colloborative development and use of multimedia learning and teaching resources for teacher education made available via specially written multimedia database software available via the Internet. Materials and shared learning and teaching will pilot a 'virtual Erasmus of university' experience for students of the 11 collaborating institutions led by the University of Wales, Bangor.

STATUS: Sponsored project

SOURCE OF GRANT: EU Telematics 4th Framework £126,200

DATE OF RESEARCH: 1996-1998

KEYWORDS: computer assisted learning; computer networks; computer uses in education; information technology; international educational exchange; internet; multimedia; telecommunications

1890

Aberdeen Campus, Hilton Place, Aberdeen AB24 4FA
01224 283500

Coutts, N. Mr; *Supervisor*: Tuson, J. Dr; Northcroft, D. Dr; McAleese, R. Prof.

Technology-mediated learning dialogues

ABSTRACT: It is proposed to investigate the extent to which two different technology-mediated learning environments, asynchronous text-based computer conferencing and synchronous video-based conferencing, can sustain the forms of learning dialogues and exchanges associated with the the effective use of discussion as a medium for learning in face-to-face settings.

STATUS: Individual research

DATE OF RESEARCH: 1996-continuing

KEYWORDS: computer uses in education; dialogues - language; discussion; information technology; preservice teacher education; telecommunications; teleconferencing

1891

Aberdeen Campus, Hilton Place, Aberdeen AB24 4FA
01224 283500

Fyfe, R. Dr; Mitchell, E. Ms

Transition to literacy

ABSTRACT: This project develops from earlier research which suggested that young children have knowledge, experience and thinking strategies which could be exploited to ease their transition into literacy, but which tend not to be activated by teachers using currently favoured approaches. The project attempts to devise development activities which would exploit these abilities.

PUBLISHED MATERIAL: FYFE, R., LEWIS, G. & MITCHELL, E. (1996). Investigating the transition to literacy: a report to the Scottish Office Education Department. Aberdeen: Northern College, Language Research and Development Unit.

STATUS: Sponsored project

SOURCE OF GRANT: Scottish Office Education and Industry Department £12,000

DATE OF RESEARCH: 1996-1997

KEYWORDS: beginning reading; literacy; primary education; reading; young children

1892

Aberdeen Campus, Hilton Place, Aberdeen AB24 4FA
01224 283500

Simpson, M. Prof.; Goulder, J. Mrs

Continued evaluation of the 5-14 programme in secondary schools

ABSTRACT: The study is an extension of the Evaluation of the 5-14 Programme with a particular focus on the classroom. The main areas of enquiry are: 1) the impact of the implementation on classroom practices, the characteristics of good practice and the factors which promote it; 2) the influence on the organisation of learning and teaching and the provision of a coherent learning experience; 3) the role of assessment in the provision of reliable information on pupils; progress and attainment; 4) teachers' responses to 5-14 and what types of support are proving helpful to them. The study focuses on the 2 transition points P7-S1 and S2-S3 in 3 mathematics and 3 English departments. Progress in other curricular areas are monitored. Methods include a large scale survey to provide a wider range of information.

PUBLISHED MATERIAL: SIMPSON, M. & GOULDER, J. (1997). Implementing 5-14 in secondary schools: continuity and progression.

Aberdeen: Northern College. ; GOULDER, J. & SIMPSON, M. (1998). 'Promoting continuity and progression: implementing the 5-14 development programme in secondary school mathematics and English language departments', Scottish Educational Review, Vol 30, No 1, pp.15-28.

STATUS: Sponsored project

SOURCE OF GRANT: Scottish Office Education and Industry Department £60,000

DATE OF RESEARCH: 1995-1997

KEYWORDS: assessment; curriculum development; five to fourteen curriculum; primary education; scotland; secondary education

1893

Aberdeen Campus, Hilton Place, Aberdeen AB24 4FA
01224 283500

Drinkwater, R. Ms; *Supervisor*: Simpson, M. Prof.

Information and communications technology in teaching and learning

ABSTRACT: The project examines teaching and learning opportunities gained from the use of information and communications technology (ICT). This is in the context of schooling and virtual learning in the home or other institutions. The research has involved an extensive review of current literature, projects and initiatives throughout the world. Most of this information was gained from the Internet. Observations and interviews took place in 6 Scottish schools. This was to determine the level of ICT use, the attitudes that teachers hold towards ICT and any effects upon pupil learning. The research has found that some schools in America are further forward in their innovative use of ICT than in the UK. The use of ICT by individual teachers regardless of location is determined by many factors, including competence, confidence and the level and type of ICT training. Quantifiable effects of ICT upon pupil learning are difficult to measure. Pupils appear to be enthusiastic, motivated, and enjoy collaborating with others. The literature has reported improvements in writing and presentation skills. Much of this research is speculative; looking at the types of schooling models that are currently being used with a view to looking at 'the school of the future'. The final part of the project examines learning theory and the practical use of ICT. This will form the part of a teaching module for student teachers.

STATUS: Sponsored project

SOURCE OF GRANT: Northern College; Grampian Enterprise Limited, jointly £24,800

DATE OF RESEARCH: 1998-continuing

KEYWORDS: computer uses in education; information technology; learning; pupil attitudes; teacher attitudes; teaching methods

1894

Dundee Campus, Gardyne Road, Dundee DD5 1NY
01382 464000
Open University, Institute of Educational Technology, Walton Hall, Milton Keynes MK7 6AA
01908 274066

Fyfe, W. Mr; *Supervisors*: Cowan, J. Dr; Morgan, A. Dr

Development of approaches to learning

ABSTRACT: The purpose behind this research is to examine the development of student approaches to learning in formal education. It is based largely on research carried out by the phenomenological school into deep and surface approaches to learning, but also attempts to take account of work in other areas of human development, e.g. in child development and in adult learning. Of particular interest is the well documented decrease in the level of learner sophistication noted in higher education. A variety of explanations have been given for this occurrence, including the suggestion that it is related to the learner's experiences in school education. Another view might be that the current nature of all formal education is responsible for this deterioration and possibly higher education may even be most to blame. The research will also focus on aspects of course design, such as the amount of responsibility given to learners, as a possible source of the different approaches to learning. Two lines of investigation are proposed: 1) A complete year group of students in a B.Ed course (about 80 students) will be followed from first to fourth year, through interviews and questionnaires/inventories. Part of this investigation will ask them to reflect on their learning experiences before higher education. 2) A small sample of school pupils will be interviewed in their final year of secondary schooling and at various points in higher education. The underlying hypothesis is that deep approaches to learning are natural and that surface approaches are caused by formal education.

PUBLISHED MATERIAL: FYFE, W. & LOGAN, J.L. (1994). 'Flexible learning units in B.Ed year 2 mathematics'. In: PARSONS, C. & GIBBS, G. Course design for resource based learning - education. Oxford: Oxford Brookes University, The Oxford Centre for Staff Development. ; FYFE, W. (1995). 'Learning environments and students' perceptions of learning'. In: GIBBS, G. (Ed). Improving student learning through assessment and evaluation. Oxford: Oxford Brookes University, The Oxford Centre for Staff Development.

STATUS: Individual research

DATE OF RESEARCH: 1993-1998

KEYWORDS: **cognitive style; higher education; learning strategies; learning theories; secondary education**

1895

Aberdeen Campus, Hilton Place, Aberdeen AB24 4FA
01224 283500
Strathclyde University, Department of Business and Computer Education, Jordanhill Campus, Southbrae Drive, Glasgow G13 1PP
0141 950 3000

Simpson, M. Prof.; Lynch, E. Miss; Payne, F. Mrs; Hughes, S. Mrs; Munro, R. Mr

Information and communications technology in initial teacher education in Scotland

ABSTRACT: There were 3 separate and semi-independent strands in the research project which the investigation focused on: 1) The confidence and information and communications technology (ICT) competence of preservice students on course entry and exit. 2) The range of ICT-related skills and strategies deployed by staff in teacher education institutes (TEIs). 3) The perceptions and requirements of the students' future employers. The research was conducted using the following methods: a) nationally distributed questionnaires to staff and students of all TEIs in Scotland, and to a small sample of schools; b) semi-structured interviews with course directors, students and local authority staff; c) diaries kept by students of their ICT experiences in courses and school experience. The findings indicate that the incoming students present a picture of a cohort of students who vary enormously in their skills, but a substantial proportion of whom have mastered the basic skills. While the needs of many of the existing students had clearly been met, dissatisfaction was expressed by students in all courses about the context and quality of the teaching experiences offered. The majority of staff expressed strongly positive attitudes towards the use of ICT and its potential contribution to education. However, the data suggest that the frequency of the use of software and other strategies for the integration of ICT into the delivery of courses is at a fairly low level. Staff encouraged students to use certain ICT facilities or to think about their use, but the incidence of direct teaching of the use, or of coverage, of key pedagogical aspects appeared low.

PUBLISHED MATERIAL: SIMPSON, M., HUGHES, S., LYNCH, E., MUNRO, R. & PAYNE, F. (1997). Information and communications technology in teacher education in Scotland. Aberdeen: Northern College.

STATUS: Sponsored project

SOURCE OF GRANT: Scottish Office Education and Industry Department £53,866

DATE OF RESEARCH: 1996-1997

KEYWORDS: **computer literacy; information technology; preservice teacher education; student teachers**

Northern Ireland Council for the Curriculum, Examinations and Assessment

1896

Clarendon Dock, 29 Clarendon Road, Belfast BT1 3BG
01232 261200

Abbott, L. Mrs; Maguire, R. Dr; D'Arcy, J. Mr; McCune, R. Mr

The transition from GCSE science to GCE A-level science

ABSTRACT: The introduction of the Northern Ireland Curriculum has ensured that all pupils follow courses in science at key stages 3 and 4. Thus, at key stage 4, pupils take either a balanced science course (usually Double Award) or the separate sciences. This 2-year project (1995-97) examined the experiences of pupils proceeding to the study of A-level science from a range of General Certificate of Secondary Education (GCSE) science backgrounds, following them through to their final grades. The project also sought to identify and evaluate the strategies being used by science teachers delivering A-level science courses to pupils who had undertaken different routes at key stage 4. Questionnaires were administered to a stratified sample of science pupils in both their Lower and Upper VI years, and were also sent to Heads of Science in post-primary schools in Northern Ireland offering A-level science subjects. Case studies were carried out with a further stratified sample of A-level science pupils and with their science teachers. Interim findings would suggest that the majority of schools had adopted appropriate measures to bridge the gap between balanced science courses (such as Double Award) and General Certificate of Education (GCE) A-level, and most had set criteria with regard to pupils' entry to A-level sciences. The majority of pupils in the latter part of their Lower VI year, who had taken the separate sciences at GCSE felt that they had been well prepared for A-level science, whereas most Double Award pupils felt that they had been less well prepared.

STATUS: Team research

DATE OF RESEARCH: 1995-1997

KEYWORDS: **a level examinations; general certificate of secondary education; key stage 4; national curriculum - northern ireland; science education; secondary education**

1897

Assessment Clarendon Dock, 29 Clarendon Road, Belfast BT1 3BG
01232 261200

McCullough, J. Mrs; *Supervisor*: Gallagher, C. Ms

Teaching and learning graphical skills in the context of the Northern Ireland Curriculum

ABSTRACT: Graphical communication is one of the first means of personal expression for children and a strong natural link exists between the early development of mapping and drawing skills and the development of reading and writing skills. Graphical communication is also recognised as being an important tool in the development of pupils' understanding of difficult concepts and an important form of communication in adult life. As such graphical skills deserve their place in the school curriculum. The issues associated with the treatment of graphical skills in the context of the Northern Ireland Curriculum have been identified from reviews of the current literature and the Programmes of Study of the Northern Ireland Curriculum, and from a qualitative analysis of questionnaires and indepth interviews with teachers, Education and Library Board Officers and initial teacher trainers. The research highlights the fact that, although teachers generally recognise the importance of graphical communication for both teaching and learning, graphical skills are not necessarily being taught in a coherent way across the curriculum. This may contribute to pupils' poor ability to transfer their graphical skills from one context to others. Also highlighted are a number of general and subject specific difficulties which pupils encounter when learning graphical skills and the advantages and disadvantages of using information technology (IT) as a means of developing pupils' graphical skills. Drawing on the research findings, a number of recommendations are made as to how curriculum planners, initial teacher trainers, inservice providers, school departments and teachers themselves can raise awareness and ultimately improve pupils' understanding and use of graphical skills. These recommendations suggest that teachers would benefit from guided support material showing graphical skills progression, identifying common difficulties encountered by pupils and showing how the teaching of these skills could be coordinated across the curriculum.

STATUS: Sponsored project

SOURCE OF GRANT: Northern Ireland Council for the Curriculum, Examinations and Assessment

DATE OF RESEARCH: 1995-1997

KEYWORDS: curriculum development; drawing; graphical skills; national curriculum - northern ireland; northern ireland

Nottingham Trent University

1898

Faculty of Education, Clifton Hall, Clifton, Nottingham NG11 8NS
01159 418418

Rist, R. Mrs; Supervisors: Bloomfield, A. Dr; Williams, C. Dr

An investigation into the suitability of traditional training for classical ballet students

ABSTRACT: The aims of the project are to: 1) determine if traditional methods of training remain appropriate for the ballet dancer; 2) to examine these traditional methods from a scientific point of view; and 3) seek the effectiveness of alternative teaching approaches and training methodology (including perception, attitudes and responses of the developing dancer). Many professional classical dancers have significant muscular imbalances and many classical dance students have long-term over-use injuries. As the standard of the classical technique continues to change and evolve into a technically demanding athletic style, the traditional classical training developed over the last 300 years may be inappropriate to train the 1990s dancer. Reasons for this may be the increased technical demands now placed on the dancer. The research will aim to show that the principles of dance science could be applied to the dancer to provide a different technique to train classical dancers. The traditional approach to class may be questioned, if found wanting a new approach may be developed. The project will involve investigation of the traditional methods of classical ballet training from a scientific viewpoint in order to examine the training of a young ballet student. The premise is that the traditional approach, while leaving the young dancer deficient in particular aspects of injury, may also result in overtraining with respect to other components of fitness.

STATUS: Individual research

DATE OF RESEARCH: 1994-1998

KEYWORDS: dance

1899

Faculty of Education, Clifton Hall, Clifton, Nottingham NG11 8NS
01159 418418

Wilson, K. Mr; Supervisor: Hayes, M. Ms

The art of asking questions and its application to the development of computer aided learning packages

ABSTRACT: It is rare for a subject to be taught in exactly the same order and style, as it is written down in a textbook. This is, however, what a lot of computer aided learning packages attempt to do. The aims of this project are to: 1) discover what sort of answers are offered by existing teaching packages to the questions of the learners; 2) discover what types of questions are used during the teaching/learning process and what patterns there are to the way that they are asked; 3) construct a teaching package for a specific subject area which will reflect these patterns of questioning and test its performance; and 4) develop some general principles for the design of teaching packages which might be applicable to other fields of knowledge. In order for a teaching package to be effective, it must present information in a way that will answer the learner's questions at the right time and in the right way, even if those questions are implicit and not fully formulated. The researcher intends to conduct a survey of the way that students use questions to acquire knowledge in a specific subject area. If it is possible to determine some pattern in the way that students require answers to questions, it should be possible to construct a teaching package which can reflect this. The package will then be tested experimentally to see if it leads to improved student performance.

STATUS: Individual research

DATE OF RESEARCH: 1995-1998

KEYWORDS: computer assisted learning; computer uses in education; educational software; information technology; questioning techniques

1900

Faculty of Education, Clifton Hall, Clifton, Nottingham NG11 8NS
01159 418418

Youngman, A. Mrs; Supervisors: O'Neil, M. Mr; Rothera, M. Mr

The dynamics of learning, teaching and assessment: a study of innovatory practice in promoting deep-active student learning

ABSTRACT: The aims of the project are: a) To conduct a programme of research into initiatives designed to encourage the development of deep-active learning by means of innovatory approaches to learning, teaching and assessment. This is based on strategies identified by Gibbs (1992) and O'Neil (1995) which help to foster a deep-active approach to learning - independent learning personal development, problem-based learning, reflection, independent group work, learning by doing, developing learning skills, project work. Gibbs stressed these should be complemented by a well-developed knowledge base, congruent assessment methods and adequate access to learning resources, including information technology. b) To explore the strengths and weaknesses of innovatory curriculum design, delivery and assessment approaches focused on the correspondence of theory with practice. c) To evaluate the effectiveness of such methods and to make recommendations for future applications of the approaches used, based on research findings.

STATUS: Individual research

DATE OF RESEARCH: 1994-1997

KEYWORDS: assessment; learning strategies; learning theories; teaching methods

1901

Faculty of Education, Clifton Hall, Clifton, Nottingham NG11 8NS
01159 418418

Gray, A. Ms; Supervisors: Johnston, J. Ms; Bastiani, J. Dr

The development of attitudes to science in the parents of primary age children

ABSTRACT: Scientific knowledge and understanding has been shown to be related to attitudes to science (RAPER, G, & STRINGER, J. (1987). Encouraging primary science. London: Cassell; HARLEN, W. (1992). The teaching of science: studies in primary education. London: David Fulton; JOHNSTON, J. (1996). Early explorations in science. Milton Keynes: Open University Press). As formation of these attitudes begins before the start of formal schooling (SMAIL, B. (1984). Girl friendly science: avoiding sex bias in the curriculum. York: Longman), examination of parental attitudes to science would inform practice on two levels: it would inform primary practice in the development of attitude to science; and provide an account of parental views of science. This research concentrates on developing an extensive typology for attitudes to science, examining issues of self-concept and choice. This will provide a theory for the development of attitude to science. The methods used in this research have been tailored to provide rich qualitative data from a variety of perspectives. Context analysis (KRIPPENDORFF, C. (1991). Content analysis. Beverly Hills: Sage Publications) is used to decode narrative interview text into categories and so give a framework for the interpretation of additional data. Discussion groups and observation of participants in the science intervention programme are used as another source of data to supplement the more detailed perspective with a broader view, more easily generalised across situations.

PUBLISHED MATERIAL: SMAIL, B. (1994). Girl friendly science: avoiding sex bias in the curriculum. York: Longman. ; RAPER, C. & STRINGER, J. (1987). Encouraging primary science. London: Cassell. ; KRIPPENDORFF, C. (1991). Content analysis. Beverly Hills: Sage Publications. ; HARLEN, W. (1992). The teaching of science: studies in primary education. London: David Fulton.

STATUS: Individual research

DATE OF RESEARCH: 1995-1998

KEYWORDS: attitudes; parent attitudes; primary education; science education

1902

Faculty of Education, Clifton Hall, Clifton, Nottingham NG11 8NS
01159 418418
London University, Goldsmiths College, Department of Design Studies, New Cross, London SE14 6NW
0171 919 7171

Bowen, R. Mr; *Supervisors*: Ovens, P. Dr; Kimbell, R. Prof.

Improving aspects of performance in design and technology education for pupils, teachers and university students

ABSTRACT: The aims of the project are to investigate how classroom practices influence the progression of children's learning in design and technology in primary school classrooms, and to apply this understanding to the work of practising and trainee teachers. The major aspect of the researcher's work is teaching undergraduate and inservice teacher education (INSET) courses in Design and Technology. The purpose of the research is to improve student and teacher classroom practice. It is expected that the research will improve: a) the researcher's teaching performance - because it will be based on better knowledge; b) the quality of the work of the Primary Design and Technology Curriculum Group because of the transmission of knowledge to the group via course planning and other meetings; c) the quality of Design and Technology teaching in the family of schools the researcher will be working with. There is concern, evidenced by personal contact with teachers and from Her Majesty's Inspectorate (HMI) Reports (1991, 1992) that, whilst there is good quality Design and Technology being undertaken in schools, the majority of the activity is 'one-off' in nature and lacks a coherent structure over the medium and long terms. This research intends to examine how teacher and pupil performance can be improved. It is intended to analyse the influence of differing classroom practices on the progression of children's learning, examine frameworks for improving performance and express considered opinions about the nature and intentions of the subject from a range of perspectives, the teacher, the child and the researcher.

PUBLISHED MATERIAL: BOWEN, R. & WADE, W. (1993). 'Joining with industry: innovative curriculum materials for technology and science in primary schools'. In: SMITH, J.S. (Ed). IDATER 1993: International Conference on Design and Technology Research and Curriculum Development, Loughborough University of Technology, Department of Design and Technology, 1st-4th September, 1993.

STATUS: Individual research

DATE OF RESEARCH: 1993-1997

KEYWORDS: design and technology; learning activities; teaching methods

Nottingham University

1903

Department of Continuing Education, Education Building, University Park, Nottingham NG7 2RD
01159 515151

Wood, A. Mr; *Supervisor*: Jotham, R. Dr

The role of information technology in the education of socially handicapped children

ABSTRACT: Particular topics in numeracy and literacy areas are taught to groups of children in a special school for maladjusted children in formats which (a) do not use information technology (IT); and (b) use IT extensively. Observers, who are normally present in classes, record characteristics such as attention span systematically for individual children in order to establish primary data for comparison.

STATUS: Individual research

DATE OF RESEARCH: 1989-1993

KEYWORDS: behaviour disorders; computer uses in education; information technology; special educational needs; special schools

1904

Department of Continuing Education, Education Building, University Park, Nottingham NG7 2RD
01159 515151

Jones, D. Dr; Stephens, M. Prof.

Adult education in the United Kingdom and China

ABSTRACT: Working with colleagues at Shandung Teachers University, it is intended to carry out a comparative study of adult education in the United Kingdom and China which will examine: (a) theories and philosophies of adult education; (b) organisation and structure of adult education; (c) aims and purposes of adult education; (d) target groups; (e) institutions for adult education; (f) teaching methods; (g) developments and trends in adult education.

STATUS: Individual research

DATE OF RESEARCH: 1992-1993.

KEYWORDS: adult education; china; comparative education

1905

Department of Continuing Education, Education Building, University Park, Nottingham NG7 2RD
01159 515151

Sherman, I. Mr; Barnes, K. Mr; *Supervisor*: Jotham, R. Dr

The potential of computer-mediated-communication for developing social and educational opportunities for adults with physical and sensory difficulties

ABSTRACT: The aim is to establish a communication network for training and related activities between disabled centres and individual users in the East Midlands with links through the Joint Academic Network and the Packet Switch system to researchers, practitioners and other disabled people in the United Kingdom and worldwide. The efficient use of the network will be evaluated by monitoring traffic and by consultation with disabled users and professionals working with them.

PUBLISHED MATERIAL: A list of publications is available from the researchers.

STATUS: Sponsored project

SOURCE OF GRANT: Leverhulme Trust £55,000; Universities Funding Council £10,400

DATE OF RESEARCH: 1989-1993

KEYWORDS: communications; computer networks; disabilities; training; wide area networks

1906

Department of Continuing Education, Education Building, University Park, Nottingham NG7 2RD
01159 515151

Jotham, R. Dr; Ellis, M. Mrs

Aspects of educational practice in the physical sciences and information technology

ABSTRACT: The aim of this project is to evaluate, comment upon and improve educational practice in science and information technology. The methodology involves direct experimentation work with student groups, followed by discussion with students and tutors. The research also includes extensive studies of statistical information on the extent, diversity and logistics of provision of adult education in this general area.

PUBLISHED MATERIAL: A list of publications is available from the researchers.

STATUS: Individual research

DATE OF RESEARCH: 1970-continuing

KEYWORDS: adult education; computer uses in education; educational practices; higher education; information technology; physical sciences; science education

1907

Department of Continuing Education, Education Building, University Park, Nottingham NG7 2RD
01159 515151

Henson, C. Rev.; *Supervisors*: Mackie, K. Prof.; Parsons, W. Dr

The space within an interdisciplinary study of voluntary groups engaging with AIDS and HIV

ABSTRACT: The aim of the research is to discover a model for adult education based on voluntary groups engaging with Acquired Immune Deficiency Syndrome (AIDS) and Human-Immunodeficiency Syndrome (HIV); and to understand the ethical and theological implications of this model. The research will include interviews with selected voluntary groups and a comparative study of educational philosophies.

STATUS: Individual research

DATE OF RESEARCH: 1989-1993

KEYWORDS: acquired immune deficiency syndrome; adult education; ethics; sexually transmitted diseases; voluntary agencies

1908

Department of Continuing Education, Education Building, University Park, Nottingham NG7 2RD
01159 515151

Morgan, W. Prof.

Political education, voluntary associations and civil society in state socialist countries

ABSTRACT: The research seeks to identify and analyse the relationship of adult political education and voluntary associations to the emergence of civil society in state socialist countries. The key concepts will be defined theoretically and examined empirically through a series of related historical and sociological studies.

PUBLISHED MATERIAL: MORGAN, W.R. (1989). 'Homo-Sovieticus - political education and civil society in the Soviet Union'. In: MORGAN, W.P. (Ed). Proceedings of the Standing Conference of University Teachings and Research into the Education of Adults. Nottingham. ; MORGAN, W.P. (1989). 'Workers adult education in the Soviet Union', Bulletin of the International Congress of University Adult Education, Vol 2, No 1, Spring 1989.

STATUS: Sponsored project

SOURCE OF GRANT: British Council; Beatrice Webb Trust

DATE OF RESEARCH: 1989-1993

KEYWORDS: adult education; citizenship education; political influences; social change; socialist countries; voluntary agencies

1909

Department of Continuing Education, Education Building, University Park, Nottingham NG7 2RD
01159 515151

Thompson, E. Mrs; *Supervisors*: Morgan, W. Prof.; Stock, A. Prof.

An international information and resources collection in adult education and training

ABSTRACT: The aim of the research project is to establish an international information and bibliographical resources collection on adult education and training which will be of value to researchers engaged in international and comparative studies. The project involves the establishment of a database and production of a bibliography on comparative adult education and training.

STATUS: Sponsored project

SOURCE OF GRANT: Universities Funding Council £15,000

DATE OF RESEARCH: 1990-1993

KEYWORDS: adult education; adults; comparative education; continuing education; databases; vocational education

1910

Department of Continuing Education, Education Building, University Park, Nottingham NG7 2RD
01159 515151

Wong, K. Mr; *Supervisors*: Morgan, W. Prof.; Shipstone, D. Dr

Evaluation of the process of curriculum design of technical and vocational education in Hong Kong

ABSTRACT: An evaluation of the process of curriculum design in technical and vocational education in Hong Kong will be undertaken. Special reference will be made to the interaction between education, training, employment and economic outcomes. It is also intended to identify present and likely difficulties, and to suggest ways of linking technical and vocational education with the general education system in order to ensure an adequate supply of competent technical personnel for the 1990s and beyond 1997.

STATUS: Individual research

DATE OF RESEARCH: 1989-1993

KEYWORDS: curriculum evaluation; economics education relationship; hong kong; training; tvei; work education relationship

1911

Department of Continuing Education, Education Building, University Park, Nottingham NG7 2RD
01159 515151

Hannah, J. Dr

Adult refugee access to education and the labour market in the UK and Australia

ABSTRACT: For humanitarian, economic and social reasons, it is important that adult refugees have access to education, training and employment, thus maximising their own potential to either settle in the host country or, when circumstances allow, return to the home country and contribute towards redevelopment. Focusing upon the following broad areas, this study will analyse and compare experience in the UK and Australia: 1) On-arrival education, occupation and skill; recognition and transferability. 2) Sources of advice, guidance and support in accessing education, training and employment. 3) Preand post-arrival labour market experience (participation rates, unemployment, pre- and post-arrival occupation). 4) Access to, and experience of, education and training.

PUBLISHED MATERIAL: HANNAH, J. (1997). 'Borders crossed - boundaries to break: refugee participation in further and higher education in Sydney'. In: ARMSTRONG, P., MILLER, N. & SUKAS, M. Crossing borders, breaking boundaries research in the education of adults. Proceedings of the 27th Annual SCUTREA Conference, 1997.

STATUS: Sponsored project

SOURCE OF GRANT: Commonwealth Relations Trust

DATE OF RESEARCH: 1996-continuing

KEYWORDS: access to education; adults; australia; labour market; refugees

1912

Department of Continuing Education, Education Building, University Park, Nottingham NG7 2RD
01159 515151

Lee, M. Ms; *Supervisors*: Murphy, R. Prof.; Jones, D. Dr

A study of collaborative learning in 3 adult education schemes

ABSTRACT: This research explores the world of collaborative learning through a qualitative case study of 3 British adult education schemes. The research spans 2 questions: 1) What are the values of collaborative learning for adult learners? 2) How does collaborative learning affect the roles of the learning community, both participants and facilitators? Collaborative learning is used in this thesis to refer to a generic term for educational approaches involving joint intellectual effort by adult participants, or adult participants and facilitators together marked by symmetry of power relations. In most collaborative learning situations the participants are working in groups of 2 or more, mutually searching for understanding, solutions or meaning, or creating a product. There is wide variability in collaborative learning activities but most centre on the participants' exploration or application of the material at hand, not simply on the facilitator's presentation or explication of it. Facilitators who use collaborative learning approaches tend to perceive themselves less as expert transmitters of knowledge and more as midwives of a more emergent learning process. The research analysis vivifies the principles and processes of collaborative learning. It illuminates 3 core values: cultivating critical openness; drawing upon life experiences; and engaging the whole person in learning. 4 barriers emerge as counterpoints to collaborative learning: gravitation towards the cognitive dimension; culture of individualism; dysfunctional group dynamics; and hierarchical structures fostering dependency syndrome. The roles of collaborative learning communities flow dialogically between the overlapping and distinctive roles of participants and facilitators. The interplay of roles spans 2 overarching spheres: creating a conducive climate; and working with shared resources.

STATUS: Individual research

DATE OF RESEARCH: 1995-1998

KEYWORDS: adult education; cooperative learning

1913

Department of Continuing Education, Education Building, University Park, Nottingham NG7 2RD
01159 515151

Barker, J. Ms; *Supervisor*: Parker, S. Prof.

The nature of mental health nurses' knowledge

ABSTRACT: The roots of mental health nurse (MHN) practice are said to lay in interpersonal interventions/relationships and it is this belief which guides curriculum planning in nurse education. However, research has consistently shown that whilst education programmes prescribe and promote an interpersonal approach, the described practice of MHNs is somewhat different. Developing a clear understanding of the knowledge used in day-to-day interactions with clients/patients would allow the development of effective education programmes facilitating the development of those skills viewed essential to the effective practice of mental health nursing. Adopting Michael Foucault's framework which suggests that power forms knowledge and products discourse, it is posited here that the MHN does not produce a regime of knowledge, rather power relations inscribe on the nurse forms and domains of knowledge. Utilising Foucault's genealogy, 3 areas will be addressed: 1) The identification and formation of domains of MHN's knowledge. 2) The organisation of normative systems within mental health nursing. 3) The relation of mental health nursing to other groups. This will encompass the accessing of the general 'archive' relating to MHNs and identifying the power relations which direct the behaviour/perceptions of, towards MHNs.

STATUS: Individual research

DATE OF RESEARCH: 1996-continuing

KEYWORDS: mental health; nurse education; nurses

1914

Department of Continuing Education, Education Building, University Park, Nottingham NG7 2RD
01159 515151

Tsay, L-J. Ms; *Supervisor*: Jones, D. Dr

The role of the study tour in cultural studies in adult education in Taiwan

ABSTRACT: This research project was conducted in the UK with Taiwanese students who came to Europe to either study languages or to do cultural travel (or both). The aims of the study are to: 1) categorise the study tours in the researcher's samples of research and to identify their characteristic features; 2) find out students' possible changes in learning and how they are affected by the study tour; and 3) identify the role and purposes of the study tour. The research focuses on the learning impact the study tour can make upon adult students who go abroad (Europe, especially the UK) to study a particular interest for a period of time from a few days to months. Although the research area and samples are for Taiwanese consideration, however some ideas from the research can be applied to most study tours. The sample consisted of 219 students and the research methods included interview, questionnaire and participant observation. At this stage, it is found that the influence of the overseas study tour is vital on adult learners, in terms of cultural studies and adult education.

STATUS: Individual research

DATE OF RESEARCH: 1995-1998

KEYWORDS: adult education; culture; study abroad; taiwan

1915

Department of Continuing Education, Education Building, University Park, Nottingham NG7 2RD
01159 515151

Alshehri, A. Mr; *Supervisor*: Jones, D. Dr

An evaluation of art teacher preparatory programmes in Saudi Arabia for teachers at school level

ABSTRACT: The research will evaluate art teacher preparatory programmes in Saudi Arabia and the aims of the project are to: 1) analyse contemporary directions in art training in Britain; 2) establish criteria to evaluate art teacher preparatory programmes in Saudi Arabia; 3) identify the strengths and weaknesses of the programmes; 4) provide suggestions and recommendations to develop the programmes further. It is hoped to answer the following questions: 1) What are the most important aspects of teacher training programmes as indicated by staff responses? 2) What are the most important aspects of teacher training programmes as indicated by student teachers' responses? 3) What are the strengths and weaknesses of the programme? 4) What recommendations can be made to develop the programme? Programmes will be evaluated under the following headings: 1) Programme organisations: timetable - length of programme; student selection; assessment. 2) Programme goals. 3) Programme content consisting of: general knowledge development; professional development; subject specialism. 4) Equipment and teaching methods. Data will be collected from 3 sources: department documents; interviews with the course directors; and questionnaires for use with staff and student teachers

STATUS: Individual research

DATE OF RESEARCH: 1995-1998

KEYWORDS: art teachers; preservice teacher education; saudi arabia

1916

Department of Continuing Education, Education Building, University Park, Nottingham NG7 2RD
01159 515151

Fuse, M. Ms; *Supervisor*: Jones, D. Dr

Critical evaluation of Mezirow's transformation theory

ABSTRACT: Jack Mezirow's transformation theory of adult learning is generally considered to have made a critical turn in American adult education theory, particularly by introducing Habermas's critical social theory in the field. However, it has also invited a number of criticisms and diverse interpretation. This study is an attempt to critically evaluate this theory, by clarifying Mezirow's ontological assumptions and examining the epistemological foundation of this theory. For this purpose, a thorough review of the relevant literature by Mezirow and his critics are conducted, including Mezirow's single empirical study on this subject, which has been almost completely neglected in the critiques examined. In addition, an interview with Mezirow has been done by the author to complement the study of the literature. This paper will argue that transformation theory has several weaknesses at the level of theorisation, including the conceptual ambiguity of terms and the eclectic ways of incorporating other theories. This would imply that transformation theory largely lacks epistemological coherence, which is a necessary condition of a proper theory. It will also be argued that transformation theory is characterised by humanistic assumptions of adults and liberal ideals of social formation. It will be concluded that transformation theory does not break out of conventional liberal/humanistic settlement and is not, as it is sometimes assumed to be, likely to give a foundation for radical adult education.

STATUS: Individual research

DATE OF RESEARCH: 1996-1998

KEYWORDS: adult education; educational theories

1917

Department of Continuing Education, Education Building, University Park, Nottingham NG7 2RD
01159 515151

Rofli, N. Mrs; *Supervisor*: Jones, D. Dr

The attitudes and perceptions of Malaysians towards the arts and arts education

ABSTRACT: The research focuses on the study of attitudes and perceptions of Malaysians towards arts and arts education. Three decades have gone by since the formulation of the National Culture Policy, a political statement formulated in 1971 to address the problems of a multi-racial population. Since then, new challenges in the form of modernisation, the influx of foreign workers, changing values and consumerism have brought about a marked social change among Malaysians. As an integral and visible component of culture, the arts reflect Malaysia's political and social manifestation of the country towards the various upheavals that have been experienced and are being experienced. The issue of values and the arts is central to contemporary debates about the relationship of modernity and identity, both collective (cultural) identity and the individual or self-identity. The importance of understanding how Malaysians relate to the arts and arts education is looked at in the context of: 1) the arts as a medium of unity; 2) the arts as a visible portrayal of national identity; 3) arts for arts sake and the preservation and propagation of the (traditional) art forms; 4) modernisation, globalisation, international influences and its impact on local values. The research will use indepth interviews for data generation and will concentrate on two research population categories: 1) Malaysians who have a connection with the arts; and 2) Malaysians who have no connection with the arts; and with a selected panel of respondents who will fit one of several main categories. The categories are level of education, sex, location (rural/urban) and ethnic group. 16 respondents will be selected. The research objectives are to: 1) determine the perception and attitude of Malaysians towards the arts and arts education; 2) ascertain whether different ethnic groups have different perceptions of the arts and arts education; 3) identify the major influences which determine the understanding and participation of the population in the arts. The results of the research on the attitude and perception of Malaysians towards arts and arts education will: a) provide vital information to policymakers when drawing up or revising policies on the arts and arts education, particularly the national culture policy and the national education policy; b) become an important resource in the planning of activities by public and non-governmental arts administrators, arts organisations and social workers; c) contribute in strengthening the arts curriculum in schools and the institutions of higher learning; d) become an essential indicator to arts funding policies to both the public and private sectors.

STATUS: Individual research

DATE OF RESEARCH: 1997-continuing

KEYWORDS: **art education; arts; malaysia**

1918

Department of Continuing Education, Education Building, University Park, Nottingham NG7 2RD
01159 515151

Green, P. Ms

Educational opportunities for socially excluded adults

ABSTRACT: This action research project developed from an earlier project working with adults with a disability. The aim is to develop educational opportunities for socially excluded adults. Courses are being run in a variety of locations: Social Services Day Centres; Community Groups' premises; and Adult Education Centres. During the 4 years of the project, 400 students (80% at least with a physical/sensory disability) will be targeted. It is hoped that the project will produce data on the best ways to meet the educational needs of adults with a disability; implications for methods of delivery; and the curriculum. It should also produce data on the training needs of tutors working with adults with a disability and how such needs could be addressed.

STATUS: Sponsored project

SOURCE OF GRANT: Higher Education Funding Council for England £234,284

DATE OF RESEARCH: 1995-continuing

KEYWORDS: **access to education; adult education; adults; disabilities; educational needs; special educational needs**

1919

Department of Continuing Education, Education Building, University Park, Nottingham NG7 2RD
01159 515151

Canto, N. Ms; *Supervisors*: Hannah, J. Dr; Morgan, W. Prof.

International collaboration agreements and their consequences for the development of postgraduate education in Brazil

ABSTRACT: The research addresses the question of how international cooperation is affecting Brazilian higher education, particularly at postgraduate level. It seeks to critically evaluate the impact of international agreements operating between Brazil and the United Kingdom, France and Germany, assessing their contribution to the national programme of Brazilian postgraduate education. In common with most developing countries which have experienced colonisation, the current Brazilian university system has its roots in a western European model. Throughout the last decade a persistent criticism of international cooperation is that it has become very expensive, and the current provision is no longer appropriate. In particular, it is argued that it is no longer necessary to send such large numbers of student abroad, since the national postgraduate programmes are now mature and of high quality. Consequently, the country should give priority to overseas scholarships where students are engaged in joint research projects which consolidate inter-institutional

relationships. From the researcher's point of view, there is a danger that this position is gaining prevalence in Brazil, despite the fact that it is largely unresearched and unsubstantiated. Whilst studies of students abroad and the CAPES evaluation system have been undertaken, there is not a single paper evaluating joint research projects. It therefore seems important and timely to critically evaluate the contribution of international cooperation agreements to Brazilian postgraduate education.

STATUS: Individual research

DATE OF RESEARCH: 1995-continuing

KEYWORDS: **brazil; graduate study; higher education; international cooperation; international educational exchange**

1920

Department of Continuing Education, Education Building, University Park, Nottingham NG7 2RD
01159 515151

Dale, M. Dr

Institutional implementation of accreditation of prior experiential learning

ABSTRACT: A study based on interviews with officials and published and unpublished documentary sources in 3 departments of the University of Nottingham. The study is part of a wider investigation into the theory and practice of accreditation of prior learning in the UK and USA to inform new developments in South Africa. The Nottingham study found that academics are primarily concerned with issues of control over learning, and accrediting prior learning is problematic because they only have control over the assessment of learning. The study found that this issue of control is rooted in a misconception that learning is finite and accrediting prior learning deals only with past learning. Assessment processes can be defined which concentrate on the contemporary state of the learning assessed and its future potential. It is therefore unhelpful to use the term 'prior learning'.

PUBLISHED MATERIAL: DALE, M. (1997). 'Accreditation of prior (experiential) learning: paradigms, policies and practices at the University of Nottingham, United Kingdom and University of Cape Town, Department of Adult Education and Extra Mural Studies, Republic of South Africa. Nottingham: University of Nottingham, Department of Continuing Education.

STATUS: Sponsored project

SOURCE OF GRANT: University of Cape Town, South Africa

DATE OF RESEARCH: 1997-1998

KEYWORDS: **accreditation of prior learning; comparative education; experiential learning; higher education; south africa; united states of america**

1921

Department of Continuing Education, Education Building, University Park, Nottingham NG7 2RD
01159 515151

Herrington, M. Ms; Sanderson, A. Dr; Woolfson, H. Ms; Henry, H. Ms; East, C. Mrs; *Supervisor*: Dale, M. Dr

Mental health hidden disabilities and learning support

ABSTRACT: A development project aimed at institutional change in relation to students with disabilities. An inclusive action research stance is taken on a number of issues: 1) Mental health of students - numbers reporting, conditions, effect on academic performance. 2) Staff development - exploring the implications of a social model of disability with all levels of staff. 3) Voice recognition systems - as a potential barrier to learning for some dyslexic students. The project will report on the effectiveness of strategies for institutional change in relation to disability issues and identify good practice.

STATUS: Sponsored project

SOURCE OF GRANT: Higher Education Funding Council for England £180,000; Nottingham University

DATE OF RESEARCH: 1997-continuing

KEYWORDS: **dyslexia; learning support; mental health; special educational needs; support services**

1922

Department of Continuing Education, Education Building, University Park, Nottingham NG7 2RD
01159 515151

Naylor, M. Ms; Hofton, D. Ms; *Supervisors*: Dale, M. Dr; Sherman, I. Mr

Periphera

ABSTRACT: The Periphera project as a whole sets out to investigate and to demonstrate the utility and practical viability of telematics applications for marginalised groups. Seven partners throughout Europe are looking at key groups who may benefit from the flexibility of access to information and to work opportunities offered by the power of the new telematics technologies. The University of Nottingham research is looking at the benefit and possible use of telematics for people with disabilities. People with disabilities are a group of citizens who are not directly addressed by the main developments in the new European society. Yet, in contrast, it is widely felt that they are key groups who may benefit from the flexibility of access to information and to work opportunities offered by the power of the new telematics technologies. The work involves members of The NewLink Project Limited, a self-help charity which trains disabled people in information technology. The objectives include the delivery of specialised training to individuals in a number of locations through the use of telematics links, to support remote access to further training and work.

STATUS: Sponsored project

SOURCE OF GRANT: Telematics Application Programme (TWRA)

DATE OF RESEARCH: 1996-1998

KEYWORDS: **disabilities; information technology; special educational needs; telecommunications**

1923

Department of Continuing Education, Education Building, University Park, Nottingham NG7 2RD
01149 515151

Morgan, W. Prof.; Xi-Suo, L. Prof.; Bo, J. Dr

Chinese students in Britain in the 1930s and 1940s

ABSTRACT: This investigation is an historical account of the presence of Chinese students in Britain in the 1930s and 1940s; the reasons for their sojourn in Britain; their places and subjects of study; their cultural experience; and their subsequent careers in China and elsewhere. A number of case studies will also be undertaken, such as Fei Xido Tung, social anthropologist, and Chun Chun-Yel, author and literary critic.

STATUS: Sponsored project

SOURCE OF GRANT: British Academy Award £5,000

DATE OF RESEARCH: 1996-1998

KEYWORDS: **chinese; educational history; higher education; overseas students**

1924

Department of Continuing Education, Education Building, University Park, Nottingham NG7 2RD
01159 515151

Morgan, W. Prof.; San, P. Prof.

Educational policy and development in the Socialist Republic of Vietnam

ABSTRACT: To investigate the educational policy and planning in the Socialist Republic of Vietnam, in the context of economic and social transition to the market economy, and to examine specifically the role of adult and continuing education and of higher education in this process. There will also be a focus on the position of migrants, minorities and refugees, especially those who have returned to Vietnam from abroad. A sociological and anthropological approach will be adopted.

STATUS: Sponsored project

SOURCE OF GRANT: British Council Higher Education Link Programme

DATE OF RESEARCH: 1998-continuing

KEYWORDS: **educational development; educational policy; vietnam**

1925

Department of Continuing Education, Education Building, University Park, Nottingham NG7 2RD
01159 515151

Tong Yiu-Woon, J. Mr; *Supervisors*: Day, C. Prof.; Morgan, W. Prof.

Quality and effectiveness issues in distance education - with reference to the Open Learning Institute of Hong Kong

ABSTRACT: Distance education in Hong Kong has gained an increasingly important role in the tertiary education arena. This is particularly evident by the formal establishment of the Open Learning Institute in Hong Kong. The research in the quality and effectiveness issues, with particular reference to the Hong Kong model, will provide solid evidence of the state of distance education in Hong Kong. Perceptions from the students, tutors and employers were obtained and analysed and the research findings will contribute to new or additional knowledge to the quality and effectiveness in distance education.

STATUS: Individual research

DATE OF RESEARCH: 1992-1998

KEYWORDS: **distance education; hong kong**

1926

Department of Continuing Education, Education Building, University Park, Nottingham NG7 2RD
01159 515151

Atkin, C. Mr; *Supervisor*: Morgan, W. Prof.

The effect of learner and institutional culture on learner choices at ages 16 and 18

ABSTRACT: The research aims to: 1) identify the factors that influence the decision-making processes of young people considering post-16 education; and 2) evaluate institutional characteristics that attract learners. The research will be based in rural Lincolnshire and the urban outskirts.

STATUS: Individual research

DATE OF RESEARCH: 1997-continuing

KEYWORDS: **further education; higher education; school leavers; school to further education transition; school to higher education transition; sixteen to nineteen education**

1927

Department of Continuing Education, Education Building, University Park, Nottingham NG7 2RD
01159 515151

Hue Doan, D. Miss; *Supervisor*: Morgan, W. Prof.

International cooperation and its impacts on the development of higher education in Vietnam since 1987

ABSTRACT: Vietnam's diplomatic relations with the outside world have been gradually improved since 1987. The adoption of a free market economy helped attract an influx of foreign investment entirely from capitalist countries. In the midst of change, Vietnam's higher education found itself at a crossroads. Vietnamese education has to do a dual job: preserving good features from its national heritage and learning from the outside world knowledge and experience necessary for its development. The objectives of the study are to investigate: 1) the factors that affect international cooperation in the context of Vietnam; 2) the forms of international cooperation affecting the development of Vietnam's higher education; 3) the impacts of international cooperation on Vietnam higher education. The investigation will be based on: indepth interviews with foreign investors/funders, top Vietnamese educational officials, university administrators and faculty; and an examination of relevant government documents.

STATUS: Individual research

DATE OF RESEARCH: 1997-continuing

KEYWORDS: **higher education; international cooperation; vietnam**

1928

Department of Continuing Education, Education Building, University Park, Nottingham NG7 2RD
01159 515151

Prichard, C. Mr; *Supervisor*: Wallis, J. Dr

Making managers in UK further and higher education

ABSTRACT: This PhD thesis is a critical investigation of the formation of managers in the UK further and higher education (FHE) sector. It explores the character and problematics that surround the development of senior FHE post-holders as managers in the first half of the 1990s. The work draws on interviews with more than 70 senior post-holders in 4 universities and 4 further education colleges and observation in 1 university and 1 college. It analyses the narratives and practices that make up the changing working lives of the respondents. These are discussed in relation to recent social theory, particularly around approaches to 'discourse', 'the body', and 'identity/subjectivity'. This in turn is set against the backdrop of broad political-economic circumstances and conditions. 2 key issues are addressed in the thesis: 1) the problematics that surround the development of managers; and 2) the gendered dimensions of this formation. The thesis is in 3 sections: 1) Epistemological commitments and ontological priorities (this divides into 3 chapters: a) managing discourse and discouraging managers; living bodies and inscribing bodies; and the relative thickness of human material, approaching 'identity' and 'subjectivity'). 2) Speaking historically, politically and of literatures (this divides into 3 chapters: a) making sense of making managers, a review of the critical further and higher education management literature; b) from methodology to research methods; and c) further and higher education's turbulent years). 3) Making managers in further and higher education (this divides into 3 chapters: a) doing the business, constructing the supervisors of production in further and higher education; b) just how managed is the new further and higher education?; and c) university and college management: is it men's work?). The concluding chapter draws out the keypoints from the thesis, discusses these in the context of possible futures for further and higher education, and suggests directions for further research work.

PUBLISHED MATERIAL: PRICHARD, C. (1996). 'Making managers accountable , or making managers? The case of a code for management in a higher education institution', Educational Management and Administration, Vol 24, No 1, pp.79-91. ; PRICHARD, C. (1996). 'University management: is it men's work?'. In: COLLINSON, D.L. & HEARN, J. (Eds). Men as managers, managers as men: critical perspectives on men, masculinity and managements. London: Sage Publications. ; PRICHARD, C. & WILLMOTT, H. (1997). 'Just how managed is the UK University', Organization Studies, Vol 18, No 2, pp.287-316.

STATUS: Individual research

DATE OF RESEARCH: 1995-1997

KEYWORDS: **administrators; colleges of further education; educational administration; further education; higher education; management in education; universities**

1929

Department of Continuing Education, Education Building, University Park, Nottingham NG7 2RD
01159 515151

Watson, V. Ms; *Supervisor*: Hall, E. Dr

An examination of the training and education of black counsellors in higher education and private institutions

ABSTRACT: Counselling education is a major growth area in the education of adults, women in particular. Counselling approaches are used in the medical profession, public services, teaching, and in the voluntary sector in order to assist individuals with relationship issues, mental health problems and career related concerns. Increasingly, black students are entering higher education via Access routes, often provided through courses offered by continuing/adult education departments in universities in the UK. For those black students seeking counselling training and qualification, there appears to be little acknowledgement of the existing broad range of therapeutic interventions which have proved to be effective with clients who are not white. At present, the main counsellor accreditation bodies in the UK only recognise counselling training which is in line with common eurocentric approaches. The hypothesis of this research is that current training and education programmes in the UK which predominantly focus on eurocentric counselling approaches, are an inadequate preparation for counsellors in general, but particularly so far for black trainees. The focus of the research will be on investigating the experience of black counsellors and their training in the light of the debate on transcultural issues in counselling as it is pursued in higher education institutions.

STATUS: Individual research

DATE OF RESEARCH: 1996-continuing

KEYWORDS: **black counsellors; counsellor training; higher education**

1930

Department of Continuing Education, Education Building, University Park, Nottingham NG7 2RD
01159 515151

Othman, A. Mr; *Supervisor*: Morgan, W. Prof.

The role of the National Vocational Training Council in the management of vocational training in Malaysia

ABSTRACT: In Malaysia the responsibility to produce skilled manpower has rested heavily on the government. This can be seen by the increasing number of public training institutions in almost every 5-year development plan. Malaysia has achieved much in producing skilled manpower through this effort. However, despite the significant increase in terms of training capacities and output over the years, Malaysia is still critically short of skilled manpower. In searching for the answer, this study tries to focus on the role of the National Vocational Training Council (NVTC). Its central premise is that the internal efficacy of NVTC and its relationship with other organisations within the Malaysian vocational training system, address distinct but equally important needs towards organisational effectiveness. The study seeks to answer the following main question: How effective has the NVTC been in playing its role as an intermediary agency in the vocational training system of Malaysia? In carrying out this research, a number of different methods of data collection are employed, such as questionnaire, interview, documents review, and participant observation. Subjects of this study include the NVTC staff (67), representatives of the public and private organisations who sit in the Council Committee (23). The results show that communication, coordination and cooperation between and within divisions or sections of NVTC, as well as leadership capabilities are crucial in ensuring the effectiveness of NVTC in playing its role as the intermediary agency.

STATUS: Individual research

DATE OF RESEARCH: 1994-1998

KEYWORDS: **malaysia; training; vocational education**

1931

Department of Continuing Education, Education Building, University Park, Nottingham NG7 2RD
01159 515151
Associacao Portuguesa de Paralisia Cerebral, Rua Delfim Maia, 4300 Porto, Portugal

Jotham, R. Dr; Da Cunha, A. Sr

Comparative study of information technology training for disabled people in Britain and Portugal

ABSTRACT: A Portugese researcher will spend two months in the United Kingdom gathering information on the training of disabled people in information technology. This will be followed by gathering comparative data in Portugal and the results will be collated to generate a report which will be published in both English and Portugese.

STATUS: Sponsored project

SOURCE OF GRANT: Gulbenkian Foundation £5,000

DATE OF RESEARCH: 1991-1993

KEYWORDS: **adult vocational education; comparative education; computer uses in education; disabilities; information technology; portugal; special educational needs; training; united kingdom**

1932

Department of Continuing Education, Education Building, University Park, Nottingham NG7 2RD
01159 515151
Nottingham Trent University, Trent Surveys, Burton Street, Nottingham NG1 4BU
01159 418418

Hadfield, M. Dr; Haw, K. Dr; Watling, R. Dr; Kane, S. Mr; *Supervisors*: Dale, M. Dr; Morgan, W. Prof.; Priest, B. Ms

Evaluation of single regeneration bid round 2 and 3 - City of Nottingham

ABSTRACT: An evaluation study combining questionnaire survey and focus group video evidence. The impact of urban programme initiatives under a single regeneration bid is analysed by a household survey sampled before the main initiative and towards the end of the initiative. Qualitative evidence of impact is collected via community and neighbourhood groups with video exchange with professionals, such as local government officials. A particular focus is on training and educational needs among disadvantaged/unemployed and on strategies for community capacity building. The sample is up to 10,000 households in inner city Nottingham. The first publication will be in 1998, then in late 1999.

STATUS: Sponsored project

SOURCE OF GRANT: Nottingham City Council

DATE OF RESEARCH: 1997-continuing

KEYWORDS: urban areas; urban improvement

1933

Department of Continuing Education, Education Building, University Park, Nottingham NG7 2RD
0115 9 515151
Stamford College, Faculty Office, Drift Road, Stamford PE9 1XA
01780 764141

Baldwin, J. Mr; *Supervisors*: Parker, S. Prof.; Dale, M. Dr

The management styles of further education managers during rapid and extensive change: a case study

ABSTRACT: The research is concerned with ascertaining whether managers in a further education (FE) college are equipped to cope with and are using the appropriate management style(s) in light of the changes that have occurred since FE incorporation. The researcher is a manager in a small/medium sized FE college and, as a participative observer, is researching the styles of management that colleagues are using and ascertaining whether they are being successful. The researcher believes that college managers are being forced to behave differently by changes brought about since incorporation and questions whether: a) are they equipped to cope with managerialism and rapid change? 2) should they attempt to resist managerialism? A qualitative approach will be used recording critical incidents, interviewing colleagues in depth, and underpinning this with quantitative techniques such as questionnaires to provide basic broad details of the college staff's view of their manager's behaviour. It is hoped that the research will provide insights into how managers under stress behave, which management strategies are most successful, and whether managerialism is appropriate in educational institutions.

STATUS: Individual research

DATE OF RESEARCH: 1995-continuing

KEYWORDS: administrators; colleges of further education; educational administration; educational change; further education; leadership styles; management in education

1934

Department of Continuing Education, Education Building, University Park, Nottingham NG7 2RD
0115 9 515151
University of Arkansas, Fayetteville AR 72701, USA
001 501 575 5781

Dale, M. Dr; Claflin, V. Dr

Academic individuation among older learners in universities: US/UK academic study

ABSTRACT: A small scale study using grounded theory approach, working with older learners in at least two universities in the USA and UK, to explore how older learners adapt and survive in a university setting. The study will use focus group research with individual questionnaires to cover factual background and the sample size will be 20 individuals.

STATUS: Sponsored project

SOURCE OF GRANT: US State sources

DATE OF RESEARCH: 1997-continuing

KEYWORDS: comparative education; higher education; mature students; united states of america; universities

1935

Department of Continuing Education, Education Building, University Park, Nottingham NG7 2RD
0115 9 515151
University of Manitoba, Faculty of Education, Winnipeg, Manitoba R3T 2NZ
001204 2696629

Day, M. Ms; *Supervisors*: Hannah, J. Dr; Pangman, C. Dr

Empowerment through training? A critical evaluation for the taking charge initiative for lone mothers

ABSTRACT: Canadian and Manitoban governments have identified lone mothers as a drain on the economy of both the nation and the provence, and have designated adult education programmes as the means of empowering women and facilitating social change. While many of these courses are designed to enable these women to take more control of the social and economic components of their lives, and to make significant social changes for women is commendable, there is little research which supports this approach. The aims of the study are to: 1) study the ways in which women become empowered through various kinds of training; 2) learn how training equips, or fails to equip, women to take control of their lives; 3) know and understand more about the process of women becoming empowered. Three semi-structured interviews were completed with 24 women who volunteered to be part of the research project and who were participants in 5 different training programmes designed especially for women. 3 facilitators were interviewed at the end of the programmes and the data collection took place over 1 calendar year. The majority of the women were receiving social assistance payments. The analysis showed that, in order for training programmes to assist women to become empowered, programmes require combinations of specific components and special programme delivery modes. These combinations may vary considerably from one woman to another. In some instances anger appears to be the triggering factor, while knowledge seems to support and strengthen other women's desire for personal empowerment. Women's desire for empowerment directly affects their determination and 'will-to-empower'. The mode of programme delivery is important because many women had negative experiences previously in educational environments and were afraid. Connected instructors and classroom environments where the teacher/student power relationship were equal helped women to feel safe and affirmed. In these settings women learned better, faster and were able to find their voices to name barriers, share opinions and ask questions. Hope seems to be the spark that ignites women's energy to become empowered.

STATUS: Individual research

DATE OF RESEARCH: 1995-1998

KEYWORDS: canada; training; unmarried mothers; women

1936

Department of Psychology, Blind Mobility Research Unit, University Park, Nottingham NG7 2RD
01602 515151

Flannigan, H. Ms; Craig, D. Mr; *Supervisor*: Dodds, A. Dr

The development of a scale to measure psychological adjustment to sight loss

ABSTRACT: A scale to measure psychological adjustment to sight loss has been developed in the form of a 50-item questionnaire. Sub-scales to measure anxiety, depression, self esteem, self-efficacy, locus of control, attitudes to sight loss, acceptance of blindness, and attributional style enable the assessment of psychological factors underlying emotional states. Psychometric analysis of a database comprising 469 clients presenting for rehabilitation has resulted in factorial validation of the questionnaire items. The instrument is able to identify clients experiencing psychological difficulties, and it is also sensitive to changes resulting from interventions. Lisrel structural modelling analysis has resulted in a model whereby the cognitive factors underlying emotional states can be related to those emotional states.

PUBLISHED MATERIAL: DODDS, A.G., BAILEY, P., PEARSON, A. & YATES, L. (1991). 'Psychological factors in acquired impairment: the development of a scale of adjustment', Journal of Visual Impairment &

Blindness, Vol 85, No 7, pp.306-310. ; DODDS, A.G., NG, L. & YATES, L. (1992). 'Residential rehabilitation: 2 - psychological outcome of rehabilitation, New Beacon, LXXVI (902), pp.373-377. ; DODDS, A.G., FLANNIGAN, H. & NG. L. (1993). 'The Nottingham Adjustment Scale: a validation study', International Journal of Rehabilitation Research, Vol 16, No 2, pp.177-184. ; DODDS, A.G. (1993). Rehabilitating blind and visually impaired people: a psychological approach. London: Chapman & Hall.

STATUS: Sponsored project

SOURCE OF GRANT: Department of Health: Health and Personal Social Services Research Programme

DATE OF RESEARCH: 1990-1993

KEYWORDS: **adaptive behaviour - of disabled; attitude measures; blindness; emotional adjustment; measurement techniques; rehabilitation; visual impairments**

1937

Department of Psychology, Centre for Organisational Health and Development, University Park, Nottingham NG7 2RD
01159 515151

Smewing, C. Mr; *Supervisors*: Cox, T. Prof.; Griffiths, A. Dr; Leyden, G. Mr

Health of schools as organisations: development and application of a theory of organisational health

ABSTRACT: The project concerns the nature, and measurement of the health of schools as organisations, and the identification of its antecedents and correlates. Essentially, the research seeks to understand how school performance and teacher well-being might be optimised through organisational development. The theory of organisational health, and its practical application, draw on general systems thinking, and on aspects of complexity theory. In practice, the project is progressing through an ongoing series of theoretical studies, field research and evaluated intervention studies. The latter have been conducted in schools in the UK, and also in Singapore and Taiwan. The field studies have largely involved interview and questionnaire-based surveys, often longitudinal in nature, analysed using multivariate statistical techniques including LISREL. The intervention studies have been carried out at the school level, and employed quasi-experimental designs.

PUBLISHED MATERIAL: BROCKLEY, T. & COX, T. (1984). 'The experience and effects of stress in teachers', British Educational Research Journal, Vol 10, No 1, pp.83-87. ; COX, T., COX, S. & BOOT, N. (1989). 'Stress in schools: a problem solving approach'. In: COLE, M. & WALKER, S. (Eds). Teaching and stress. Milton Keynes: Open University Press. ; COX, T., KUK, G. & LEITER, M. (1993). 'Burnout, health, work stress and organizational healthiness'. In: SCHAUFELI, W., MASLACH, C. & MAREK, T. (Eds). Professional burnout: recent developments in research and theory. Washington, D.C.; London: Taylor & Francis. A full list of publications is available from the researcher.

STATUS: Sponsored project

SOURCE OF GRANT: Various sponsors

DATE OF RESEARCH: 1986-continuing

KEYWORDS: **educational environment; institutional environment; organisational climate; organisational development; stress - psychological; teaching conditions**

1938

School of Education, University Park, Nottingham NG7 2RD
01159 515151

Hall, E. Dr; Hall, C. Dr

Outcomes of experiential learning

ABSTRACT: This is an ongoing project which examines the outcomes of experiential interpersonal skills training programmes which have been developed over the years at the Centre for the Study of Human Relations at the University of Nottingham. A series of studies have been conducted, partly associated with four Ph.D students. All of the evaluations have involved experienced teachers who attended six-day residential courses or extended award bearing courses to gain an M.Ed. or an Advanced Diploma. Data has been collected before, during and up to three years after the courses. Data was collected using standardised questionnaires, interviews, diaries of critical incidents, outcomes of goal setting, learning

journals and data collected during experiential exercises during the courses. A consistent pattern has emerged over several studies. The participants reported significant changes in both their personal and professional lives. These changes involved reports of reductions in stress, a greater sense of control over one's life and a shift to a more humanistic approach to discipline issues. These changes involved relationships with both students and colleagues. There was also a strong 'Sleeper effect' in several of the studies in which a significant improvement was obtained at the end of the course, followed by a much more substantial increase one year later. Further studies have involved the evaluation of the development of the same forms of training with students in schools. The project has now been extended to evaluate the effects of 5 days experiential training for teachers on the behaviour and attendance of students in primary schools. This was funded by Nottingham County Council and the new local education authority (LEA) invited a further extension.

PUBLISHED MATERIAL: HALL, E., HALL, C. & LEECH, A. (1990). A scripted fantasy in the classroom. London: Routledge. ; HALL, C. & DELANEY, J. (1992). 'How a personal and social education programme can promote friendship in the infant class', Research in Education, No 47, pp.29-39. ; DAY, C., HALL, C.A., GAMMAGE, P. & COLES, M. (1993). Leadership and curriculum in the primary school: the roles of senior and middle management. London: Paul Chapman Publishing. ; HALL, E. (1994). 'The social relational approach'. In: KUTNICK, P. & ROGERS, C. (Eds). Groups in schools. London: Cassell. ; HALL, E., HALL, C. & SIRIN, A. (1996). 'Professional and personal development for teachers: the applications of learning following a counselling module', British Journal of Educational Psychology, Vol 66, No 3, pp.383-398. A full list of publications is available from the researchers.

STATUS: Sponsored project

SOURCE OF GRANT: Nottingham University: School of Education £4,000 Universities Funding Council £4,000; Enterprise in Higher Education £7,500

DATE OF RESEARCH: 1974-continuing

KEYWORDS: **experiential learning; interpersonal competence; locus of control; outcomes of education; stress - psychological; student experience; teacher education**

1939

School of Education, University Park, Nottingham NG7 2RD
01159 515151

Phillips, R. Dr; Gillespie, J. Mr

Multimedia in the mathematics classroom

ABSTRACT: This research follows up a major curriculum development project for the English National Curriculum Council (NCC) which produced interactive video materials to support mathematics teaching at key stages 3 and 4 (the 11 to 16 age group). Three double-sided laservision discs with supporting print material and software were completed by the Shell Centre and New Media during 1992. The package entitled 'The world of number' offers a rich and varied resource for teachers and their students to use, together with explicit suggestions for lesson activities. The present project is collecting data from seven schools which trialled the original development and agreed to continue as frequent users of the materials. The research focuses on the mathematics departments in these schools and in particular on two teachers: one experienced and one inexperienced in using the materials. Through a mixture of classroom observation and interviews, the range of classroom activities supported by the materials is studied, including those that take place away from the equipment. A wide range of issues are under consideration including the merits of whole class and small group activities, the roles adopted by teachers and students, and the potential of the technology to support activities which are difficult or impossible to carry out in other ways. The research will collect teachers' views on the efficacy of the materials and any practical problems that arise in using them.

PUBLISHED MATERIAL: NATIONAL CURRICULUM COUNCIL (1992). The world of number: an interactive video resource for teaching secondary mathematics. York: National Curriculum Council. ; GILLESPIE, J. & PHILLIPS, R.J. (1992). 'The use of multimedia materials for modelling in the secondary mathematic classroom', Proceedings of Working Group 14, ICME -7, Quebec. ; PHILLIPS,

R.J. (1992). 'Gazing in the bright lights', Times Educational Supplement, 21 February, pp.40.

STATUS: Individual research

DATE OF RESEARCH: 1992-1993

KEYWORDS: **classroom research; computer uses in education; educational materials; information technology; interactive video; mathematics education; multimedia**

1940

School of Education, University Park, Nottingham NG7 2RD
01159 515151

Murphy, R. Prof.; Fraser, D. Mrs; Worth-Butler, M. Mrs

An outcome evaluation of the effectiveness of pre-registration midwifery programmes of education

ABSTRACT: Midwifery education has recently seen the introduction of a new 'direct entry' (pre-registration) programme, alongside the traditional programme of midwifery education which required students to be previously registered as general nurses. Whilst many practitioners have welcomed the possibility of a more cost-effective programme which emphasises the 'normal' nature of midwifery, many have reservations about the competence of midwives trained through the programme, to care for a woman who has a medical, surgical or psychiatric problem. This project sets out to evaluate the effectiveness of the pre-registration programme in producing midwives who are competent to practise at the point of registration. Assessment tools currently being used in the programmes will be examined and used to develop a new assessment tool which will then be used to evaluate the outcomes of the pre-registration programme. A second phase of the study will involve looking at midwives who have trained through the pre-registration programme, one year on. Career intentions and patterns and intention rates will be examined alongside a comparative assessment of their knowledge, attitudes and competencies as midwives. Evidence regarding the effectiveness of the programme will be gathered through interviews, observations and document analysis.

STATUS: Sponsored project

SOURCE OF GRANT: English National Board for Nursing, Midwifery and Health Visiting £150,000

DATE OF RESEARCH: 1993-1997

KEYWORDS: **medical education; nurses; obstetrics**

1941

School of Education, University Park, Nottingham NG7 2RD
01159 515151

Cotton, A. Mr; *Supervisor*: Bennett, S. Mr

A mathematics curriculum for social justice

ABSTRACT: Mathematics educators with an interest in issues of social justice concentrate their efforts in two key areas: 1) countering the underachievement of students from minority groups; and 2) meeting the growing demand for mathematicians and scientists in the increasingly technological workplace. The issue of student empowerment is a key one in this debate. These arguments have been developed to include the notion of equity. This is the idea that mathematics can and indeed should prepare students to restructure the social systems in order to remove the barriers that women, minorities and other experience in their jobs and in the social institutions with which they interact. Much energy has been spent alleviating what are seen by many as the detrimental effects of the mass of government legislation over the last ten years; energy which may have been better spent proposing and building an alternative agenda around notions of education for social justice. The research aim is to build a model for a mathematics curriculum on ideas of social justice and to propose an action plan for the implementation of this curriculum. The research plan is: 1) A philosophical overview of the ideas underpinning social justice. 2) Interviews with groups of a focus group of pupils to examine and refine their notions of social justice in the mathematics classroom. 3) The development of curriculum material for use within mathematics classrooms to evaluate pupils' notions of social justice. 4) The building of a model for a mathematics curriculum and an action plan for its development. The model to recognise the power of mathematics

as a tool for social change and to take as a starting point the ideas of social justice developed throughout the study.

STATUS: Individual research

DATE OF RESEARCH: 1994-1998

KEYWORDS: **curriculum development; justice; mathematics education; social change; social values**

1942

School of Education, University Park, Nottingham NG7 2RD
01159 515151

Nye, R. Ms; *Supervisor*: Hay, J. Dr

Understanding children's spirituality: clearing away the confusion in religious education

ABSTRACT: The Education Reform Act 1988 and subsequent government publications require that schools give serious attention to spirituality in the curriculum. Unfortunately, as a recent survey by the Culham Institute has shown, there is widespread confusion about the meaning of the term spirituality within the teaching profession and very little research information about the content of children's spirituality. The task of this project is to investigate how spirituality manifests itself in contemporary British children aged 5/6 and 10/11. The theoretical basis of the project is the hypothesis of Alister Hardy that spiritual awareness is a natural function of the human species which has evolved because it has survival value to the individual. On this supposition, spirituality in some form is a potential in all children. The problem is to identify what will count as falling within the category and to develop an understanding of how this expresses itself in the contemporary context. Using the methodology of grounded theory, recorded conversations were conducted with groups of children (selected for differences of gender, culture, religious belief etc) at National Curriculum key stages 1 and 2 and an analysis made of the transcribed texts. The intention was to develop a coherent battery of information and to create a detailed theory of children's spirituality.

PUBLISHED MATERIAL: HAY, D. & NYE, R. (1998). The spirit of the child. London: Harper Collins.

STATUS: Sponsored project

SOURCE OF GRANT: 3 Trust Funds £70,000

DATE OF RESEARCH: 1994-1997

KEYWORDS: **key stage 1; key stage 2; primary education; religion; religious education**

1943

School of Education, University Park, Nottingham NG7 2RD
01159 515151

Yuk-Hang, S. Ms; *Supervisor*: Shipstone, D. Dr

Science and Technology in Society education for primary pupils in Hong Kong

ABSTRACT: Since the 1970s, there has been growing awareness of the need to incorporate social or societal aspects of science into the science curriculum and a number of science curriculum reforms have incorporated a Science and Technology in Society (STS) approach. STS has been variously implemented in these reforms, however. At one end of the scale science content is used as the basic organiser of the curriculum, with due emphasis given to applications in daily life, technological aspects and social relevance. At the other is the use of STS issues as the central organiser, with science content being developed from these. This research seeks to suggest what type of STS approach to science teaching would be most suitable at primary level in Hong Kong and to evaluate the consequences of adopting this approach through the implementation of a school-based curriculum project. A literature review will examine the variety of meanings attached to STS worldwide, the historical development of the STS movement and the various curricular approaches employed with STS. Teachers' views on the desirable nature of an STS approach and its value will be determined through individual interviews and a questionnaire survey. The school-based project will be developed through revision of one section of the Hong Kong General Studies curriculum in response to the teachers' views together with evidence currently available on the children's cognitive development, moral development and societal thinking. The evaluation of this project will inform proposals for further development of STS within the primary school curriculum in Hong Kong.

STATUS: Individual research

DATE OF RESEARCH: 1994-1998

KEYWORDS: **hong kong; science education; science technology and society; technology education**

1944

School of Education, University Park, Nottingham NG7 2RD
0115 9 515151

Swan, M. Mr

Diagnostic teaching in GCSE mathematics in further education

ABSTRACT: Further education colleges contain thousands of students aged 16-19, currently attempting to gain GCSE mathematics qualifications in one year. There is no evidence to suggest that the teaching methods adopted in such courses are any different from the methods that have been used and, for these students, have failed at secondary level. The proposed work involves research and development. It aims to develop classroom activities that encourage students to confront and overcome common difficulties in supportive social contexts. It seeks to measure the impact of such activities in typical classrooms. The approach involves situations which foster reflective thinking. The research has its roots in diagnostic teaching and metacognition. Previous work at the Shell Centre has included funded projects in both of these areas. During months 1-15, tests and observation instruments will be devised, and baseline data concerning the learning effects of college lecturers' own methods will be obtained. Data concerning the most common conceptual errors will be gathered. The handbook of diagnostic classroom activities will be developed, piloted and revised. 8 lecturers will be invited to take part, from 4 different colleges. In months 16-24, 4 lecturers will be invited to introduce the diagnostic activities with fresh, comparable, cohorts of students. Comparisons will be drawn between the conceptual understanding developed by the 2 cohorts for each lecturer.

STATUS: Sponsored project

SOURCE OF GRANT: Esmee Fairbairn Charitable Trust £51,072

DATE OF RESEARCH: 1995-1997

KEYWORDS: **diagnostic teaching; further education; general certificate of secondary education; mathematics education; reflective teaching; sixteen to nineteen education; teaching methods**

1945

School of Education, University Park, Nottingham NG7 2RD
0115 9 515151

Hadfield, M. Dr; Tolley, H. Dr; Harris, A. Dr; Berresford, J. Mr; *Supervisor*: Day, C. Prof.

Professional leadership in schools

ABSTRACT: The research aims to contribute to knowledge of leadership in schools. It focuses upon reputationally good headteachers, what influences them, and their influence upon the development of the communities whom they serve. The research uses a synthesis of existing literature and small scale qualitative research with case studies of 12 National Association of Headteachers (NAHT) members. It will result in a report which will revisit purposes, contexts and practices of headship and through this contribute to the enhancement of the work of all those in school leadership roles.

STATUS: Sponsored project

SOURCE OF GRANT: National Association of Headteachers £10,000

DATE OF RESEARCH: 1997-continuing

KEYWORDS: **educational administration; head teachers; leadership; management in education**

1946

School of Education, University Park, Nottingham NG7 2RD
0115 9 515151

Coyle, D. Mrs

Bilingual integration of languages and disciplines: interplay between learners' linguistic and strategic competence in secondary classes

ABSTRACT: The research is set within the context of a pilot study since such essential data sites, i.e. secondary school classrooms where the curriculum is delivered in a foreign language, are not widely available in the state sector in the UK, unlike some other European countries especially France and Germany. The research aims to investigate the relationship between strategic and linguistic competence of secondary pupils learning geography through the medium of a foreign language (French and Spanish respectively). Two classes of Year 9 pupils (14 year olds) were targeted in different schools. Within the qualitative paradigm, a case study approach applying socio-cultural learning theory in a Vygotskian sense was used, monitoring almost 60 pupils in general and 16 pupils in detail - 8 in each class representing the range of ability in the respective classes. The study indicates that significantly high levels of linguistic competence are also mirrored by high levels of strategic competence - facilitated by a learning environment which encouraged spontaneous use of language, cognitively challenging material and motivating content. Pupil questionnaires were analysed for background information and attitudes, transcripts of lessons were made to monitor learner talk, specific language activities were recorded to test linguistic competence (e.g. solving a logic puzzle, discussing environmental issues) and specific strategies were monitored through a learning log. Intensive interviews were also carried out to provide triangulation. The conclusions reached emphasise key social elements of the learning context which are crucial to maintaining high levels of concentration, motivation and linguistic strategic competence, i.e. they are dependent on the balance of meaningful social interaction.

STATUS: Individual research

DATE OF RESEARCH: 1995-1998

KEYWORDS: **bilingual education; immersion programmes; language of instruction; modern language studies; secondary education**

1947

School of Education, University Park, Nottingham NG7 2RD
0115 9 515151

Wilmut, J. Mr; Burke, P. Mr; Rainbow, R. Mr; Macintosh, H. Mr; Gillespie, J. Mr; *Supervisors*: Murphy, R. Prof.; Goodman, L. Dr

Independent evaluation of the key skills qualification pilot phase

ABSTRACT: The Nottingham team involved in this research had a close involvement in work leading to the key skills qualifications which are now being piloted. The evaluation is concerned with all aspects of the appropriateness and quality of the qualification and the processes that lead up to the award. The evaluation model reflects the complexity of the interconnections within the pilot which involve schools, further education (FE) colleges, awarding bodies, employers, professional bodies and government agencies. The methodology includes surveys conducted in all centres on 3 occasions during the year and followed up by telephone contacts. Case studies conducted in about 30 centres with 2 visits in each year; close contact with the awarding bodies; expert panels drawn from the employment and education sectors and meeting twice. Liaison with other evaluators and the Qualifications and Curriculum Authority and ongoing reports. As this evaluation is not yet concluded, final results are not available.

STATUS: Sponsored project

SOURCE OF GRANT: Qualifications and Curriculum Authority

DATE OF RESEARCH: 1997-continuing

KEYWORDS: **core skills; key skills; qualifications**

1948

School of Education, University Park, Nottingham NG7 2RD
0115 9 515151

Hopkins, D. Prof.; Harris, A. Dr; Day, C. Prof.

Improving quality of education for all (IQEA)

ABSTRACT: Improving the quality of education for all (IQEA) arose from discussions at the Cambridge Institute of Education, arising from the work of Mel Ainscow, David Hopkins, Mel West and Geoff Southworth, with schools and their development after about 1991. The project envisaged developing schools, both through specific improvement projects related to reaching and learning in the classroom, and the development of specific management conditions within the school - leadership, staff development, involvement coordination, reflection and enquiry, and collaborative planning. It is intended that these two development processes take place contemporaneously. Schools have the services of a research officer and a consultant. A series of meetings, primarily for the IQEA coordinating group within the school, are organised to discuss strategies for coordinating research activities and for feeding research findings into the school system. IQEA network now consists of about 150 English schools and there are two flourishing branches based at the Schools of Education at Nottingham and Cambridge Universities. Branches also exist in Iceland and Puerto Rico.

PUBLISHED MATERIAL: AINSCOW, M., HOPKINS, D., SOUTHWORTH, G. & WEST, M. (1994). Creating conditions for school improvement: a handbook for staff development activities. London: David Fulton. ; HOPKINS, D., AINSCOW, M. & WEST, M. (1994). School improvement in an era of change. London: Cassell. ; HOPKINS, D., WEST, M. & AINSCOW, M. (1996). Improving the quality of education for all: progress and challenge. London: David Fulton. ; HOPKINS, D., WEST, M., AINSCOW, M., HARRIS, A. & BERESFORD, J. (1997). Creating the classroom conditions for school improvement: a handbook for staff development activities. London: David Fulton.

STATUS: Collaborative

DATE OF RESEARCH: 1991-continuing

KEYWORDS: **educational quality; school effectiveness; school improvement**

1949

School of Education, University Park, Nottingham NG7 2RD
01159 515151

Haw, K. Dr; Coyle, D. Ms; Gillespie, J. Mr; *Supervisor*: Murphy, R. Prof.

Research and monitoring of bilingual education project at Hasland Hale Community School

ABSTRACT: For 1998-99, 3 of the 7 classes at this Derbyshire comprehensive school are, for about half the total lesson time, being taught history, geography, mathematics, Personal and Social Education (PSE) and other studies. The school's aims are: 1) improving students' foreign language abilities; 2) making the ability to understand and communicate effectively in a foreign language an entitlement for all - not just for an able minority of 'linguists'; 3) developing confidence and independent learning skills; and 4) develop language for an immediate purpose. The research team is already monitoring this remarkable initiative within the limits imposed by current funding, based around the comparisons between the bilingual and normal classes currently in Year 7 and with the results of previous year's results from the current Year 8. The aims of the monitoring programme are to discern any significant learning gains and losses and to draw appropriate conclusions. The monitoring programme for 1998-99 will include the following: 1) Devise and carry out survey of students attitudes in bilingual and 'normal' classes; complete analysis of initial staff questionnaire. 2) Identify, track and interview representative students, interview parents, analyse results of interviews. 3) Conduct end of year surveys and interviews with staff and students, collect and analyse end of year data from school assessments. 4) Compare end of year results and for both bilingual and normal classes; compare results with measures of students' attainment and ability before entering the school; produce a report on year's programme for school and for wider audiences. The team is anxious to continue the monitoring and research into 1999-2001.

STATUS: Sponsored project

SOURCE OF GRANT: Nottingham University £4,000

DATE OF RESEARCH: 1998-continuing

KEYWORDS: **bilingualism; french; immersion programmes; language of instruction; modern language studies; secondary education**

1950

School of Education, University Park, Nottingham NG7 2RD
01159 515151

Cox, A. Ms; *Supervisors*: Hopkins, D. Prof.; Youngman, M. Dr; Harrison, C. Prof.

The adaptation, implementation and dissemination of Success for All in England 1998-2001

ABSTRACT: Success for All (SFA) is a comprehensive programme for restructuring primary schools when pupils are 'at risk' of not developing functional literacy by the end of key stage 1. The programme was developed at John Hopkins University, Baltimore, and uses research-based approaches to curriculum, instruction, assessment and classroom management with one-to-one tutoring being provided for those pupils falling behind in their reading. A report on the initial implementation (September 1997-March 1998) has been completed. The purpose of this research was to provide empirical evidence on the process of implementation of SFA in England, and to assess how such an innovation programme could contribute to the Government's National Literacy Strategy (NLS). The results of the initial research study show an excellent match between the NLS and SFA, and that the progress made in the 6 primary schools involved in the pilot programme matched the progress of schools with a similar social context in the United States of America. The qualitative outcomes showed behaviour in schools had improved as a result of the cooperative learning strategies built into the programme, and teachers were positive about the impact of the programme on the children. The newly acquired research grant will fund a further 6 pilot schools as well as continuing the existing pilot programme. It will allow research in more detail of the relationship between intelligence quotients and reading progress within the programme and in control schools. A steering committee is to be established comprising of experts in the field of reading from within the University of Nottingham and an external university. The committee will design the next stage of the research and monitor its progress.

PUBLISHED MATERIAL: HOPKINS, D. et al. (1998). Evaluation of the initial effects and implementation of success for all. Nottingham: University of Nottingham. ; HOPKINS, D., HARRIS, A., YOUNGMAN, M. & WORDSWORTH, J. 'Evaluation of the initial effects and implementation of success for all in England', United Kingdom Reading Association Journal. (in press).

STATUS: Sponsored project

SOURCE OF GRANT: The Fischer Foundation Research Machines £664,000

DATE OF RESEARCH: 1998-continuing

KEYWORDS: **intervention; literacy education; primary education; reading; reading difficulties; reading improvement; school improvement; success**

1951

School of Education, University Park, Nottingham NG7 2RD
01159 515151

Convery, A Ms; *Supervisor*: Hopkins, D. Prof.

Changing attitudes to Europe: initial teacher education and the European Dimension

ABSTRACT: Student teachers on a one-year Postgraduate Certificate in Education (PGCE) course reacted in a negative way to an input on the European Dimension. This study was designed to investigate the reasons. The aims of the study were formulated as research questions: 1) What are the attitudes of student teachers to Europe? 2) Do student teachers' attitudes to Europe change during the course of the training year? 3) Does the inclusion of a European Dimension in the teacher education curriculum help to change attitudes to Europe? 4) What is meant by the term 'European Dimension'? Data for the study was gathered through the use of a pre- and post-course questionnaire, over 5 consecutive years. Each year group was composed of 250-300 student teachers, from the disciplines of English, geography, history, mathematics, modern languages and science. A series of indepth interviews was also carried out with a small group of student teachers. Finally, a combined questionnaire was used with groups of student teachers from Austria, France, Germany, the Netherlands and Portugal, to enable cross-cultural comparisons to be carried out. The research is underpinned by Bronfenbrenner's Ecology of Human Development which describes a process of mutual accommodation between the human organism and its surroundings. For the purpose of this study, Bronfenbrenner's microsystem is the immediate setting in which the student teacher operates, and his macrosystem is the European Union. The data is currently being analysed and the results will shortly be available.

PUBLISHED MATERIAL: CONVERY, A. et al. (1997). Pupils' perceptions of Europe: identity and education. London: Cassell. ; CONVERY, A. (1997). 'The case for the European Dimension', Primary Geographer, Vol 29, pp.4-6. ; CONVERY, A. et al. (1997). 'An investigative study into pupils' perceptions of Europe', Journal of Multilingual and Multicultural Development, Vol 18, No 1, pp.1-16.

STATUS: Individual research

DATE OF RESEARCH: 1992-continuing

KEYWORDS: **attitudes; europe; european dimension; preservice teacher education; student teacher attitudes; student teachers**

1952

School of Education, University Park, Nottingham NG7 2RD
01159 515151

Burke, P. Mr; Greatbach, D. Dr; Rainbow, R. Mr; Tolley, H. Dr; Wilmut, J. Mr; *Supervisor*: Murphy, R. Prof.

A study of the validity and transferability of National Vocational Qualifications (NVQs)/ Scottish Vocational Qualifications (SVQs) in the workplace

ABSTRACT: The distinctive features of Scottish Vocational Qualifications (SVQs)/National Vocational Qualifications (NVQs) is their competence-based form, which states assessment requirements. The focus is on outcomes appropriate to a specified occupation and specified to the point of transparency for both candidates and assessors. The validity of assessment is determined by: a) its relation to the standard; and b) the standards relation to the competencies demanded in the workplace. Further, judgements about the validity of the assessments must take account of the contexts within which competencies are to be demonstrated. The first part of the project was a feasibility study which aimed to provide a summary of past evidence on the validity and transferability of SVQs/NVQs in the workplace; and a series of methodological options for the subsequent stage. The aims of this second stage are to develop a number of research designs for future investigations into the topic and a variety of methodologies for the collection and analysis of data. These will include: a) tracking candidates and employees; and b) cross-sectional studies of sample groups at different stages of training. Samples will be drawn from a large tertiary college and a large tertiary college and a large company which employs workers across a range of occupational sectors. The research outcomes include practical guidelines for the design and management of future investigation.

STATUS: Sponsored project

DATE OF RESEARCH: 1998-continuing

KEYWORDS: **competency based education; national vocational qualifications; scottish vocational qualifications; skills; transfer of learning; vocational education; vocational qualifications; work education relationship**

1953

School of Education, University Park, Nottingham NG7 2RD
01159 515151
Nottingham Trent University, Faculty of Education, Clifton Hall, Clifton, Nottingham NG11 8NS
01159 418418

Biddulph, M. Mr; *Supervisors*: Griffiths, M. Prof.; Woods, G. Prof.

The Turing project: researching self-identity and self-esteem as dimensions in the personal/professional lives of gay/bisexual men who are educators

ABSTRACT: The Turing project is a piece of qualitative research investigating self-identity and self-esteem as key variables in the experiences of a cohort of gay/bisexual men who are educators. The project is named after Alan Turing who was a university academic, genius and gay man. In 1954, the police who investigated a burglary at his home also investigated his lifestyle and charged him with gross indecency. Turing reluctantly pleaded guilty and he was put on probation on the condition that he was treated with hormones. Shortly afterwards he killed himself by eating an apple impregnated with cyanide. He was 42. Alan Turing's story has an element of tragedy - his academic brilliance was seen as both useful and acceptable - his sexual orientation was seen at the time as being unacceptable. This tension provides the backdrop to the aims and objectives of the research which are as follows. The aim is to acquire a greater understanding of the lives and experiences of gay/bisexual men who are educators. The objectives are to: 1) use theoretical perspectives and the voices of research participants to gain a sense of what gay identity means to individuals; how this evolves over time; how it is related to other aspects of self-identity; 2) gain an understanding of what self-esteem means for gay/bisexual men who are educators in terms of their 'journey' to the point that they are at now, reviewing critical incidents, difficult times and sources of support; considering how self-esteem is related to teacher identity; 3) to acquire an understanding of the professional context and environment in which gay/bisexual men who are educators work considering specifically the discourses of educational institutions; the historical relationship between homosexuality and education; the system of power relations that exists between identity, homophobia and heterosexism in educational institutions; 4) gain an understanding of how gay/bisexual men who are educators 'interface' with their environments in terms of the process of constructing and negotiating a gay-teacher identity; the mechanisms and ways in which these are presented in education contexts and gay contexts; reviewing the role of past personal/professional experience in constructing these complex identities. The data consists of transcripts from semi-structured interviews that were conducted with the research participants. In analysing the text, grounded theory is being utilised to identify themes and phenomena. The initial results of the analysis are contained in unpublished conference papers which analyse the role of critical incidents as key dimensions of professional experience. Sexual orientation is still noticeably absent from the equal opportunities policies of many educational establishments, particularly in schools. Alan Turing's experience may have been an extreme example of how self-esteem and self-identity clashed with the accepted professional norms of the day. A key question is: so what has changed?

STATUS: Individual research

DATE OF RESEARCH: 1995-continuing

KEYWORDS: **homosexuality; self esteem; teachers**

1954

School of Education, University Park, Nottingham NG7 2RD
01159 515151
Open University, Vocational Qualifications Centre, Walton Hall, Milton Keynes MK7 6AA
01908 274066

Wilmut, J. Mr; Rainbow, R. Mr; Burke, P. Mr; Macintosh, H. Mr; Gillespie, J. Mr; *Supervisor*: Murphy, R. Prof.

Implementing a dissemination strategy for key skills in higher education

ABSTRACT: During 1996/97 the University of Nottingham and the Open University were commissioned by the Department for Education and Employment (DfEE) to undertake 3 research and development projects in 'key skills in higher education'. The aims of this project are: 1) to provide an effective dissemination strategy for the earlier work; and 2) to create a forum for continuing debate. There are several strands of the strategy: a) a series of regional workshops for academics and employers looking at employability (Nottingham University); and a series of workshops by the Open University to disseminate their materials; b) the development and piloting of a range of guidance, support and consultancy services; c) the management and promotion of Nottingham University's website (keyskillsnet.org.uk) and the Open University's resource database website (accessible through above URL); d) the establishment of a number of demonstration sites based in higher education institutions where good practice has been established; e) a longitudinal study of the nature and extent of the usage made of the key skills packages, which will be conducted across a range of disciplines; f) a forum of exchange which will allow institutions to access the different initiatives and approaches to key skills.

PUBLISHED MATERIAL: MURPHY, R. et al. (1997). The key skills of students entering higher education. Nottingham: University of Nottingham, School of Education. ; MURPHY, R. et al. (1997). Supporting key skills in high education: a staff development pack. Nottingham: University of Nottingham, School of Education.

STATUS: Sponsored project

SOURCE OF GRANT: Department for Education and Employment

DATE OF RESEARCH: 1998-continuing

KEYWORDS: **core skills; higher education; key skills**

1955

School of Education, University Park, Nottingham NG7 2RD
0115 9 515151
Queen's University of Belfast, School of Education, 69 University Street, Belfast BT7 1HL
01232 245133
Leeds University, School of Education, Leeds LS1 9JT
01132 431751
Warwick University, Institute of Education, Coventry CV4 7AL

Harrison, C. Prof.; Alexander, J. Ms; Clarke, S. Mr; Medwell, J. Ms

KAL-CAL (knowledge about language - computer assisted learning): the evaluation of a suite of computer programs aimed at improving student teachers' knowledge about language, and their own knowledge of grammar and punctuation rules

ABSTRACT: The project aims to disseminate and evaluate the KAL-CAL (knowledge about language - computer assisted learning) program over a minimum of 12 university education departments in the UK. The program modules are interactive, and are in 2 groups: the first 5 modules give information about how children use language and how they learn to write and spell. The final 3 modules give the user information about his or her own abilities in spelling, punctuation and grammar, and offer the opportunity to improve. The program runs over a network within Windows 95 and stores data on a number of aspects of the user's performance and interaction. During the Teaching and Learning Technology Programme (TLTP) Phase 1 project (1994-95), the modules were developed and evaluated on a field-trial basis at the universities of Nottingham and Warwick. Initial evaluations of the modules were positive (Harrison and McCartney, 1994) and a clear relationship was found between the nature of the course being studied (B.Ed or Postgraduate Certificate in Education (PGCE) and which modules were most valued by the student teachers. 3 types of problems were encountered in running the program over a network, during this evaluation phase. These were: a) a small number of bugs in some modules; b) problems with soundcard management; c) bugs in the record-keeping section of the software. A great deal was accomplished for the 5,000 pounds which had been the sum awarded to the KAL-CAL project, but its implementation and wider use were hampered by a lack of funds for development. This project therefore has the specific subgoals of: 1) fixing known bugs and making the program stable over a network; 2) implementing use of the program with a much greater number of students; 3) evaluating in greater detail than was possible in the development phase the gains made; and 4) running and evaluating a dissemination seminar for colleagues in other universities. The evaluation design will draw upon Stake's (1979) responsive evaluation model, which makes use of a variety of methodologies, as negotiated with key participants and end users. There will be 3 main components of the evaluation: 1) An evaluation of students' use of the program across institutions, and their learning gains in spelling, grammar, punctuation and knowledge about language (KAL) (collected automatically by the program). 2) An evaluation of lecturers' and students' attitudes to using and learning from this program (collected by questionnaire). 3) An evaluation of the costs and benefits involved (based on algorithms developed and refined during the life of the project, and making use of expertise already available within TLTP Support Network Centres).

PUBLISHED MATERIAL: HARRISON, C., MCCARTNEY, V., BRYDGES, S. & WRIGHT, S. (1993). The KAL-CAL project. Authorware professional for windows: suite of five computer programs for self-study of knowledge about language. Nottingham: Nottingham University, Teaching and Learning Technology Project. ; HARRISON, C. & MCCARTNEY, V. (1994). 'The KAL-CAL project: a computer-aided approach to knowledge about language for student teachers', Education Today, Vol 44, No 3, pp.33-36.

STATUS: Collaborative

DATE OF RESEARCH: 1998-continuing

KEYWORDS: computer uses in education; grammar; information technology; preservice teacher education; punctuation; spelling; student teachers

Office for Standards in Education

1956

Alexandra House, 33 Kingsway, London WC2B 6SE
0171 421 6800

Yeomans, A. Ms

Specialist Teacher Assistant Pilot Scheme - evaluation

ABSTRACT: The Specialist Teacher Assistant (STA) Pilot Scheme was launched in September 1994. It is designed to train serving classroom assistants in primary schools in the knowledge and skills necessary for assisting qualified teachers and supporting learning in reading, writing, numeracy and related skills at key stage 1 level of the National Curriculum. The Department for Education and Employment (DfEE) will be funding 51 local education authorities (LEAs) in England in 1997/98 and 1998/99, through the Standards Fund (formerly GEST), to enable them to purchase training from existing training providers, or to set up new provision locally. OFSTED is monitoring and evaluating the scheme and will produce a good practice guide and an evaluation of the first year of the scheme in 1997.

PUBLISHED MATERIAL: DAVIES, R. et al. (1996). The specialist teacher assistant pilot scheme: the first year. London: OFSTED.

STATUS: Sponsored project

SOURCE OF GRANT: Department for Education and Employment £40,000

DATE OF RESEARCH: 1997-1997

KEYWORDS: classroom assistants; primary education; specialist teacher assistants

Open University

1957

Centre for Higher Education Research and Information (QSC), 344-354 Grays Inn Road, London WC1X 8BP
0171 447 2506

Brennan, J. Mr; Williams, R. Ms

Quality assurance in higher education in Central and Eastern Europe

ABSTRACT: The aim of the project is to support the development of quality assurance in the higher education systems of 11 countries in Central and Eastern Europe; Albania; Bulgaria; Czech Republic; Estonia; Hungary; Latvia; Lithuania; Poland; Romania; Slovenia; Slovakia. The project comprises the following elements: 1) a review of recent higher education legislation in the 11 countries; 2) over 20 evaluations of educational programmes and institutions; 3) sharing of experience through multi-national seminars; 4) publication of a 'quality manual' and associated guidelines.

PUBLISHED MATERIAL: BRENNAN, J. et al. (1998). Quality assurance in higher education: a legislative review and needs analysis of developments in Central and Eastern Europe. London: Open University, Quality Support Centre. ; BRENNAN, J. et al. (1998). Quality assurance in higher education. London: Open University, Quality Support Centre. ; KRISTOFFERSEN, D., SURSOCK, A. & WESTERHEIJDEN, D. (1998). Manual of quality assurance: procedures and practices. London: Open University, Quality Support Centre.

STATUS: Sponsored project

SOURCE OF GRANT: EC PHARE £750,000

DATE OF RESEARCH: 1997-1998

KEYWORDS: comparative education; eastern europe; educational quality; higher education; international educational exchange; quality assurance

1958

Centre for Higher Education Research and Information (QSC), 344-354 Grays Inn Road, London WC1X 8BP
0171 447 2506

Brennan, J. Mr; Shah, T. Ms; Johnstone, B. Dr

Higher education and graduate employment in Europe

ABSTRACT: This is a comparative study of the employment experiences of graduates from 9 countries of the European Union. It aims to investigate the early employment experiences of graduates and to examine differences between countries, between institutional and course types, and according to socio-biographic factors such as gender, age, ethnicity, and social class. Samples of around 4,000 graduates per country will be contacted by postal questionnaire 3 years after their graduation. The survey data will be complemented by interviews with graduates and employers. The project commenced in January 1998 and will be completed by December 1999. It is being conducted jointly by research groups from 10 European countries under the overall direction of Professor Ulrich Teichler of the German University of Kassel.

STATUS: Sponsored project

SOURCE OF GRANT: EC Targeted Socio-Economic Research Programme (TSER) £90,000

DATE OF RESEARCH: 1997-continuing

KEYWORDS: **comparative education; employment; europe; followup studies; graduate employment; graduate surveys; student destinations**

1959

Centre for Higher Education Research and Information (QSC), 344-354 Grays Inn Road, London WC1X 8BP
0171 447 2506

Brennan, J. Mr; Williams, R. Ms
Accreditation of higher education institutions in Bulgaria

ABSTRACT: The aim of this project was to support the development of a system of evaluation and accreditation for Bulgarian higher education. This has involved the drafting of guidelines, policy analysis, training and seminars for academic and administrative staff in Bulgarian universities and institutes. The project was undertaken during 1996 and 1997 and was completed at the end of 1997. Several project publications in Bulgarian have been produced.

STATUS: Sponsored project

SOURCE OF GRANT: EC PHARE £250,000

DATE OF RESEARCH: 1996-1997

KEYWORDS: **accreditation - institutions; bulgaria; higher education**

1960

Centre for Higher Education Research and Information (QSC), 344-354 Grays Inn Road, London WC1X 8BP
0171 447 2506

Brennan, J. Mr; Frederiks, M. Dr; Shah, T. Ms
Analysis of the extent to which recommendations for quality improvement made by subject peer assessors have been acted upon

ABSTRACT: Teaching quality was introduced into British higher education in 1993. This project, funded by the Higher Education Funding Council for England (HEFCE), evaluated the extent to which recommendations made by assessors had been acted upon by institutions. This was achieved through 12 institutional case studies and covered all the first 15 subjects assessed by the HEFCE during 1993-1995 and a balance of excellent, satisfactory and unsatisfactory grading.

PUBLISHED MATERIAL: BRENNAN, J., FREDERIKS, M. & SHAH, T. (1997). Improving the quality of education: the impact of quality assessment on institutions. London: Open University, Quality Support Centre.

STATUS: Sponsored project

SOURCE OF GRANT: Higher Education Funding Council for England £47,000

DATE OF RESEARCH: 1996-1997

KEYWORDS: **educational quality; higher education; quality control**

1961

Centre for Higher Education Research and Information (QSC), 344-354 Grays Inn Road, London WC1X 8BP
0171 447 2506

Little, B. Ms
Key skills assessment

ABSTRACT: The Council for Industry in Higher Education's (CIHE) broad aim is to consider how employers and academics might together develop an agreed and mutually recognised system for assessing and accrediting key skills in graduates. The CIHE has commissioned the Open University's Quality Support Centre to undertake a limited project looking at the assessment of undergraduate key skills on work placements and/or work experience. The aims of the project are to: 1) identify current practices in the assessment of key skills in undergraduate work placements; and 2) identify those aspects which could usefully be adopted/adapted to help current undergraduates demonstrate to future employers key skills developed in a workplace environment. The project is drawing case study examples from a range of employment sectors and is covering a range of disciplines.

STATUS: Sponsored project

SOURCE OF GRANT: Council for Industry in Higher Education

DATE OF RESEARCH: 1997-1998

KEYWORDS: **assessment; core skills; employers; higher education; job placement; key skills; skill development; skills; students; work based learning; work experience**

1962

Centre for Higher Education Research and Information (QSC), 344-354 Grays Inn Road, London WC1X 8BP
0171 447 2506

Brennan, J. Mr; Devries, P. Dr; Williams, R. Ms
An evaluation of the flexibility in teaching and learning scheme

ABSTRACT: The Scottish Higher Education Funding Council (SHEFC) administered 3 flexibility in teaching and learning schemes (FITLS) between 1993 and 1996 under which bids were invited from Scottish higher education institutions for projects, and the successful bids funded by SHEFC. The remit of the schemes was to encourage wider access to, and more flexible forms of learning provision within, Scottish higher education. In 1996 SHEFC invited bids for an evaluation of FITLS which was awarded to the Quality Support Centre. The evaluation was to consider the extent to which the schemes' objectives were achieved, the extent of the embedding of projects, the impact of the schemes on higher education in general, the value for money, the administration of the scheme, and the lessons learnt. In undertaking the evaluation, interviews, surveys and documentary analysis were undertaken to gain information about the operation of the scheme from fund holders and project teams, student managers and administrators in Scottish higher education institutions, SHEFC officials, and members of SHEFC's Teaching and Learning Advisory Group. 6 of the funded projects were examined in detail. The outcome of the evaluation was a report to SHEFC covering the main issues which the evaluation was asked to address.

STATUS: Sponsored project

SOURCE OF GRANT: Scottish Higher Education Funding Council £27,000

DATE OF RESEARCH: 1996-1997

KEYWORDS: **access to education; flexible learning; higher education; scotland**

1963

Centre for Higher Education Research and Information (QSC), 344-354 Grays Inn Road, London WC1X 8BP
0171 447 2506

Brennan, J. Mr; Shah, T. Ms
Quality management, quality assessment and the decision-making process

ABSTRACT: This project is funded by the Organisation for Economic Cooperation and Development (OECD) with support from the Higher Education Funding Council for England (HEFCE) and the European Union. It is investigating the purposes, methods and intended outcomes of different national systems of quality assurance and their impact on institutional management and decision-making. Over 30 universities from different parts of the world are undertaking case studies of the impact of external quality assurance on their own institutions. Various national quality assurance bodies are also contributing to the project.

PUBLISHED MATERIAL: BRENNAN, J. & SHAH, T. (1997). 'Quality assessment, decision-making and institutional change', Tertiary Education and Management, Vol 9, No 1. ; SHAH, T. (1997). 'Quality management, quality assessment and the decision-making process: the project on institutional impact'. In: BRENNAN, J., DE VINE, P. & WILLIAMS, R. Standards and quality in higher education. London: Jessica Kingsley.

STATUS: Sponsored project

SOURCE OF GRANT: Organisation for Economic Cooperation and Development £28,000

DATE OF RESEARCH: 1994-1998

KEYWORDS: **comparative education; educational quality; europe; higher education; quality assurance; quality control**

1964

Centre for Higher Education Research and Information (QSC), 344-354 Grays Inn Road, London WC1X 8BP
0171 447 2506

Brennan, J. Mr; Shah, T. Ms; Mills, J. Mr

Feasibility study of obtaining employment data on part-time students/graduates

ABSTRACT: The project aims to examine the feasibility of collecting employment data on part-time students and graduates. In collaboration with 6 partner universities, the project also aims to examine the ways in which this kind of information can best be used to improve the relevance of higher education provision to part-time students and to employers. A subsidiary aim is to describe the employment experiences of a sample of part-time students and graduates. The research consists of 3 main strands: consultation and interviews with partner institutions and employers; the development and piloting of a data collection instrument; and examination of the uses of the data produced.

STATUS: Sponsored project

SOURCE OF GRANT: Department for Education and Employment

DATE OF RESEARCH: 1998-1998

KEYWORDS: **graduate employment; higher education; part time students; student employment**

1965

Centre for Higher Education Research and Information (QSC), 344-354 Grays Inn Road, London WC1X 8BP
0171 447 2506
Brunel University, Department of Government, Centre for the Evaluation of Public Policy and Practice, Uxbridge UB8 3PH
01895 274000

Little, B. Ms; Brennan, J. Mr; Henkel, M. Ms; Kogan, M. Prof.

Changing relationships between higher education and the State

ABSTRACT: A series of seminars on the theme of changing relationships between higher education and the State were organised by the Open University's Quality Support Centre and Brunel University's Centre for the Evaluation of Public Policy and Practice. The aims of the seminar were to conceptualise and exemplify the changing relationship; conceptualise and exemplify the impact of recent government reforms upon higher education institutions. Specific topics addressed included: the impact of evaluation mechanisms; the funding of higher education; higher education and work; studies in higher education institutions; managing a diverse system of higher education. Presentations at seminars covered both international perspectives, conceptual analyses and case study examples, drawn from the UK, mainland Europe and Scandinavia. Participants comprised a mix of researchers, together with policymakers, executive members of intermediate bodies and institutional leaders.

PUBLISHED MATERIAL: HENKEL, M. & LITTLE, B. (1998). Changing relationships between higher education and the State. London: Jessica Kingsley.

STATUS: Sponsored project

SOURCE OF GRANT: Economic and Social Research Council £9,960

DATE OF RESEARCH: 1996-1998

KEYWORDS: **comparative education; educational finance; educational policy; government intervention; higher education; politics education relationship**

1966

Centre for Research in Teacher Education, 4 Portwall Lane, Bristol BS1 6ND
01179 299641
Reading University, School of Education, Bulmershe Court, Woodlands Avenue, Earley, Reading RG6 1HY
01189 875123
Exeter University, School of Education, St Luke's, Heavitree Road, Exeter EX1 2LU
01392 263263

Deane, M. Mrs; Macaro, E. Dr; Poulet, G. Mr

Mendeval: mentor development and evaluation

ABSTRACT: This project involves the Open University; Reading University; Exeter University; Pedagogische Akademie des Bundes Osterreich, Austria; Provinciale Hogeschool Limburg, Belgium; Hogeschool West-Vlaanderen, Belgium; Hogeschool Rotterdam and Omstreken, Netherlands; and Universidad de Almeria, Spain. The aims are to harmonise understanding of the role of mentors (teachers who train student teachers in schools) in the training of modern languages student teachers); 2) find out the commonality of mentors' practices towards the creation of a European model; and 3) create mentor training materials to respond to modern languages mentors' needs at European level. The sample will be modern languages teacher educators (teacher trainers in institutions and mentors) in 5 European countries. It will involve questionnaires and interviews. The expected outcomes and products will be: 1) a better understanding of the role of mentor throughout Europe; 2) a European perceptive on the role of mentor; 3) a glossary of terms in 6 European languages; 4) a European bibliography of publication on mentoring; and 5) a multimedia bank of materials for mentor training.

STATUS: Sponsored project

SOURCE OF GRANT: European Commission

DATE OF RESEARCH: 1999-continuing

KEYWORDS: **comparative education; language teachers; mentor training; mentors; modern language studies; preservice teacher education**

1967

Institute of Educational Technology, Walton Hall, Milton Keynes MK7 6AA
01908 274066

Chambers, E. Ms

Humanities higher education (especially distance education)

ABSTRACT: The named researcher and other members of the Humanities Higher Education Research Group (HERG) at the Open University are committed to investigating all aspects of the teaching and study of the humanities at tertiary and 'access' to tertiary levels: theory; policy; curriculum; principles of course design and development; pedagogy (including applications of new technology and multimedia teaching; course evaluation; student characteristics; study skills and assessment. The following projects are current: 1) Reading, discourse and learning - access to humanities higher education. 2) Uses of computer mediated communication in humanities distance education (EU Socrates with colleagues in Europe). 3) Evaluation of multimedia teaching in the humanities. 4) An innovative approach to teaching classical texts in translation: Home and Greek tragedy. Research methods include: questionnaire studies; telephone interview; face-to-face interview (individuals and student groups); analysis of student demographic and institutional data (e.g. dropout, assignment and examination grades/pass rates etc); scrutiny of assignment scripts, computer conferencing transcripts, text and multimedia teaching materials; participant-observation; focus groups. Surveys are normally conducted with samples of between 200-600; interviews, observation studies, etc usually involve between 8-25 subjects. The HERG runs the national Humanities and Arts Higher Education Network (HAN) with members drawn from over 90 institutions of higher education and professional bodies. Members of the network exchange information and papers, undertake collaborative research projects, meet annually at a conference, and are negotiating to establish an academic journal of humanities higher education.

PUBLISHED MATERIAL: CHAMBERS, E.A. (1995). 'Course evaluation and academic quality'. In: LOCKWOOD, F. (Ed.). Open and distance learning today. London: Routledge. ; CHAMBERS, E.A. (1996). 'Course-based research in humanities distance education', Media and Technology for Human Resource Development, Vol 17, No 3, pp.79-89.; CHAMBERS, E.A. & WINCK, M. (1996). Same difference? experience of a European distance education course in two cultures. Tubingen: Deutsches Institut fur Fernstudienforschung. ; CHAMBERS, E.A. & NORTHEDGE, A. (1997). The arts good study guide. Milton Keynes: Open University. ; CHAMBERS, E.A. (1997). 'The domain network: a model for collaborative research in distance education'. In: EVANS, T., JAKUPEC, V. & THOMPSON, D. (Eds). Research in distance education, Vol 4. Geelong: Deakin University Press.

STATUS: Sponsored project

SOURCE OF GRANT: Open University

DATE OF RESEARCH: 1975-continuing

KEYWORDS: **adult students; distance education; humanities; mature students; open universities; student attitudes**

1968

Institute of Educational Technology, Walton Hall, Milton Keynes MK7 6AA
01908 274066

Kirkup, G. Ms; Kirkwood, A. Mr; Jones, A. Dr

Home use of domestic information and communication technologies to support distance learning

ABSTRACT: The Institute of Educational Technology Home Computing Group was originally set up in 1988 to evaluate the impact of the Home Computing Policy, but has since broadened its work as recent technical developments and a convergence of communications and information technology (IT) mean that it is no longer appropriate (or perhaps even possible) to focus only on computers. In the next few years, forms of household leisure technology, which will have IT capacities as well as support a variety of media, will be widely available in the UK and most of Europe. Some of these, but it is not yet clear which, will have great potential as educational devices. Therefore, in addition to monitoring of student access to, and use of personal computers, research needs to be done on the educational potential of, and student access to, other kinds of new IT media. One of the group's aims is to develop generalisable knowledge about the educational potential of, and access to, new IT media. Particular ongoing work includes: 1) analysing and presenting baseline information on ownership of and access to IT equipment in domestic and work environments which can support Open University study; 2) bringing this information together with other national data on household ownership of equipment; 3) investigating tutors' access to IT and attitudes towards it, evaluating innovative course components related to IT, e.g. the use of CD-Roms for resource based learning, and computer mediated communication. Research methods include survey questionnaires at points in the year, interviews and self-completion diaries.

PUBLISHED MATERIAL: JONES, A., KIRKUP, G. & KIRKWOOD, A. (1992). Personal computers for distance education: the study of an innovation. London: Paul Chapman. ; KIRKUP, G. & JONES, A. with JELFS, A., KIRKWOOD, A. & TAYLOR, J. (1995). 'Diversity, openness and domestic information and communication technologies'. In: SEWART, D. (Ed). One world, many voices: quality in open and distance learning. Milton Keynes, Open University and International Council for Distance Education. ; KIRKWOOD, A. (1995). 'Over the threshold: media technologies for home learning'. In: LOCKWOOD, F. (Ed). Open and distance learning today. London: Routledge. ; KIRKWOOD, A., JONES, A. & JELFS, A. (1996). 'Changing the role of tutors in distance education with information and communication technologies', Association for Learning Technology Journal, Vol 4, No 1, pp.35-39.

STATUS: Sponsored project

SOURCE OF GRANT: Open University

DATE OF RESEARCH: 1988-continuing

KEYWORDS: **computer uses in education; distance education; information technology; microcomputers; open universities**

1969

Institute of Educational Technology, Walton Hall, Milton Keynes MK7 6AA
01908 274066

Burt, G. Mr

The curriculum as culture and ideology

ABSTRACT: According to the common-sense view, education is about indiviudal people 'learning' ideas and skills. It is an apolitical activity, which meets the needs of individuals and of society as a whole. The aim of the curriculum as culture and ideology project is to challenge this view. Education is not about people learning ideas and skills; it is about cultural ideas and practices taking possession of people. Education then is simply one of a number of arenas in which different culutres and ideologies with differential powers seek to promote themselves, and hence come into conflict. Cultures seek to promote themselves in every sphere of society. Hence cultures demand education about every social sphere. The aim of the research project is to study educational provision with a view to identifying the cultural and ideological promotions involved. Currently under study are the arenas of educational technology, educational computing, mathematics and technology education, management education and community education. Teaching materials in these areas involve cultural and ideological promotion relating to issues of gender, class, ethnicity, individualism, technicism and militarism. Proposals for how education might be redesigned to take account of this critique are also being developed.

PUBLISHED MATERIAL: BURT, G.J. (1989). 'Social forces and school computing', British Journal of Educational Technology, Vol 20, No 2, pp.140-141. ; BURT, G.J. (1989). 'Computers in schools as culture and ideology', International Council for Distance Education Bulletin, Vol 20, pp.19-24. ; BURT, G.J. (1989). 'Beyond educational technology: the new discipline of cultural and ideological technology', Research in Distance Education, Vol 1, No 3, pp.9-11. ; BURT, G.J. (1989). 'The message behind the medium', Information Technology and Learning, December, pp.55-56. ; BURT, G.J. (1991). 'Culture and ideology in the training literature', Educational Technology and Training International, Vol 28, No 3, pp.229-237. A full list of publications is available from the researcher.

STATUS: Individual research

DATE OF RESEARCH: 1988-1993

KEYWORDS: **cultural influences; curriculum; educational philosophy; ideology**

1970

Institute of Educational Technology, Walton Hall, Milton Keynes MK7 6AA
01908 274066

Whalley, P. Dr; Williams, D. Dr

A 'virtual' microscope

ABSTRACT: This project is concerned with developing a 'virtual' microscope which allows the student to choose, manipulate and examine rock samples on the computer screen. Embedding the 'virtual' microscope within a general multi-media database will provide the student with a powerful tool for enquiry and learning. The primary problems that the researchers intend to tackle are pedagogic not technical - what does or does not aid student learning in the summer school environment, and how may computer-based materials be integrated with the other media being used. An important part of the project will be the developmental testing of the materials at Open University summer schools with the general aim of finding the right balance between questioning and support for the student. An immediate use of the materials will be to enrich the experience of the less mobile students attending these summer schools. Whilst other students go out collecting samples 'in the field', these students will be able to make detailed analyses of equivalent rock samples and consequently be able to make greater contributions to group discussions. A simple extension of the project on the lines of the well known 'Eco-Disc' project would allow the student to 'move' around computer based images and video clips of the hill or quarry and choose from where they would like a 'sample' to be taken. This would obviously empower disabled students to undertake courses and projects from which they would otherwise be blocked.

STATUS: Sponsored project

SOURCE OF GRANT: Open University: Institute of Educational Technology £60,300

DATE OF RESEARCH: 1993-continuing

KEYWORDS: computer assisted learning; earth science; educational equipment; microscopes; simulation; special educational needs

1971

Institute of Educational Technology, Walton Hall, Milton Keynes MK7 6AA
01908 274066

Taylor, M. Mrs; Valentine, C. Mr; *Supervisor*: Vincent, A. Prof.

Access to teaching materials for visually impaired learners

ABSTRACT: Compact disc versions (electronic and audio) of print course material from a number of Open University (OU) courses are being produced for students who are unable to use conventional print. This approach is part of a long term strategy to provide disabled students with the choice of the most appropriate medium for course texts. The first courses were made available to selected students in 1994. Sixteen courses have subsequently been transformed. Desktop or portable computers, with CD-ROM drives and appropriate enabling technologies, are being used by students to access modified versions of electronically published print materials. This modification involves the replacement of mark-up commands used for publishing through print and adding new mark-up commands that provide an appropriate layout of text for the CD-ROM delivery medium as well as taking into account that the text will be used with screenreaders (synthetic speech) or other enabling technologies. A retrieval program (ReadOut) has been developed that is compatible with enabling technologies, and allows for a more structured presentation of the course material and a higher level of interactivity. The project continues with funding from the Guide Dogs for the Blind Association, the Higher Education Funding Council for England and the Open University Development Fund.

PUBLISHED MATERIAL: HAWKRIDGE, D. & VINCENT, T. (1992). Learning difficulties and computers: access to the curriculum. London: Jessica Kingsley. ; VINCENT, T. (1994). 'Distance teaching and visually impaired students: an electronic environment'. In: All our learning futures: the role of technology in education. Glasgow: Scottish Council for Educational Technology.

STATUS: Sponsored project

SOURCE OF GRANT: Higher Education Funding Council for England ; Guide Dogs for the Blind Association

DATE OF RESEARCH: 1993-continuing

KEYWORDS: blindness; cd roms; computer uses in education; information technology; special educational needs; speech synthesisers; visual impairments

1972

Institute of Educational Technology, Walton Hall, Milton Keynes MK7 6AA
01908 274066

Hatzipanagos, S. Mr; *Supervisors*: Hodgson, B. Dr; Scanlon, E. Dr

Physics education and information technology. Simulations for physics learners: reality versus abstraction

ABSTRACT: Computer-based simulations in physics can result in what Champagne (1980) calls 'the student's private Newtonian revolution' by helping students to differentiate between their individual 'Aristotelian' frameworks and the formalisms of Newtonian physics. Implications arise about the degree to which pupils expect and perceive simulations to be real and how those perceptions affect their interaction with the simulation. The focus of this research is combining real experiments with computer-simulated laboratories in order to compare the two and enhance the simulations' credibility. The outcome should be to convince students that the same rules apply in simulations and in the real world.

STATUS: Individual research

DATE OF RESEARCH: 1993-1998

KEYWORDS: computer simulation; computer uses in education; information technology; physics; simulation

1973

Institute of Educational Technology, Walton Hall, Milton Keynes MK7 6AA
01908 274066

Scanlon, E. Dr; Taylor, J. Dr; Whitelock, D. Dr

Mediating science learning at a distance with new technology

ABSTRACT: The aims of the study are to: 1) measure the effects of different mediating technologies on collaboration between pairs of participants in science problem solving; 2) develop methodologies within a social constructivist perspective for analysing and studying effective collaboration on a range of features including task performance; 3) investigate a number of analytical tools to demonstrate modes and measures of pair interactions; and 4) report both methodological issues and research findings to the distance learning community and to the research community at large. The researchers propose to evaluate the 'state of the art' technologies which will support distance learners in science problem solving tasks. Their interest is in measuring the effects of computer supported learning environments. Science based computer assisted learning software has been evaluated in its use with both children in schools and adults at the Open University. The two main types of studies proposed are: a) naturalistic and b) laboratory-based. The laboratory-based studies will provide refinement for the techniques used to conduct the studies, the data capture and analysis. A more naturalistic setting will then be used in which to replicate and validate the findings. The focus is to explore the potential of collaborating technologies for distance learning and to match task performance with a number of collaborative conditions.

PUBLISHED MATERIAL: SMITH, R., O'SHEA, T., O'MALLEY, C., SCANLON, E & TAYLOR, J. (1991). 'Preliminary experiments with a distributed, multi-media problem solving environment'. In: BOWERS, J.M. & BENFORD, S.D. (Eds) Studies in computer supported cooperative work: theory, practice and design. Kidlington: Elsevier Science Ltd. ; SCANLON, E., O'SHEA, T., SMITH, R., O'MALLEY, C. & TAYLOR, J. (1993). 'Running in the rain: using a shared simulation to solve open-ended physics problems', Physics Education, Vol 28, No 2, pp.107-113. ; WHITELOCK, D., TAYLOR, J., O'SHEA, T., SCANLON, E., CLARK, P. & O'MALLEY, C. (1993). 'Challenging models of elastic collisions with a computer simulation', Computers and Education, Vol 20, No 1, pp.1-9.

STATUS: Sponsored project

SOURCE OF GRANT: Open University

DATE OF RESEARCH: 1994-1998

KEYWORDS: computer assisted learning; computer uses in education; cooperation; distance education; group work; information technology; science education

1974

Institute of Educational Technology, Walton Hall, Milton Keynes MK7 6AA
01908 274066

Oram, I. Mr; *Supervisors*: Kaye, A. Mr; Thomson, A. Prof.

Use of computer supported collaborative learning in management education

ABSTRACT: The case study is a common method of tuition in management education. It is particularly used in graduate management courses such as the Master of Business Administration (MBA). Typically a small group of students work together on a case. The case, possibly one of many in a term's case pack, can be anywhere from 1 to 50 pages of paper and often poses a specific question. The group analyses the case, develops a proposed course of action and presents the proposal to the rest of the class (and tutor) for comment. Prima facie, this is fertile ground for Computer Supported Collaborative Learning (CSCL). The group must collaborate to develop a solution. For part-time or distance students, computer mediated communication offers a proven means of collaboration. Computer searching and manipulation of data offers a means of comprehensively analysing a large case. Many management education institutions are adopting CSCL; whether for educational or commercial reasons is a matter of debate. What they do not know is whether or not CSCL has any impact on the learning outcomes. The research programme addresses this issue.

STATUS: Individual research

DATE OF RESEARCH: 1994-1997

KEYWORDS: case studies; computer uses in education; cooperative learning; distance education; group work; information technology; management studies

1975

Institute of Educational Technology, Walton Hall, Milton Keynes MK7 6AA
01908 274066

Edirisingha, E. Mr; *Supervisor*: Hawkridge, D. Prof.

Interactive media in agricultural education

ABSTRACT: This study will test the feasibility of using interactive media for farmers learning at a distance. It is of potential importance in the UK, because of the growing necessity to change existing farming practices. Changing European agricultural policies, changing relationships between the agricultural sector and countryside affairs, and environmental and safety aspects force farmers to change their agricultural practices. Traditional media such as broadcasting and audio and videocassettes have been used with some success in agricultural education, but little has been done to test the feasibility of using interactive media such as computer-based and conferencing technologies. Since farmers are physically isolated, widely dispersed and heterogeneous, as far as possible the learning opportunities should be available on their farms. Interactive media could provide effective learning experiences for farmers whose attitudes towards learning are very much shaped by their life style. This research will attempt to investigate: how farmers learn in their social and occupational context; how farmers learn from interactive media; and how interactive media contribute to effectiveness of learning. The study will be in five stages: 1) literature review for developmental and evaluative evidence from earlier studies in the UK and elsewhere; 2) ethnographic study of farmers' approach to their continuing education, their updating needs, and their attitudes to interactive media; 3) modelling of the characteristics of farmers, their updating needs, and interactive media; 4) field test and evaluation of selected examples of relevant software/media; 5) revision of the model in the light of the field test and evaluation.

STATUS: Individual research

DATE OF RESEARCH: 1994-1997

KEYWORDS: **agricultural education; computer uses in education; distance education; farmers; information technology; interactive video; telecommunications; teleconferencing**

1976

Institute of Educational Technology, Walton Hall, Milton Keynes MK7 6AA
01908 274066

Lewin, C. Dr; *Supervisors*: Fung, P. Dr; Jones, A. Dr

The development and evaluation of software for teaching reading at primary level

ABSTRACT: Before developing an intelligent computer assisted reading system for children with reading levels substantially below their chronological age, the types of software currently being employed in the primary classroom need to be evaluated. Incorporating the major strengths and addressing the weaknesses of such software, together with the wealth of research literature on the theory of learning to read, is a necessary step in forming sound foundations for the design of an innovative learning platform. Two types of software will be evaluated. One is a case study of an implementation of talking word processors (The Somerset Talking Computer Project). The second is an evaluation of the educational significance of the use of talking book software, which brings children's books to the computer screen in an interactive and visually exciting form, using digitised speech. From these reviews two main points emerge. Firstly, in any educational capacity, the interaction with computers and software is strongly motivating for children. Secondly, the addition of speech synthesis or digitised speech enables constant reinforcement of the sound of a word with its written form, and contributes significantly to the possible improvements in reading ability. This could be significant in providing specialised support and phonological coaching to poor readers. The findings will form the basis for an intelligent system. This is based on a model of a child reading to and interacting with an intelligent and supportive tutor in a multisensory forum, utilising sound and vision to its best educational effect.

STATUS: Individual research

DATE OF RESEARCH: 1994-continuing

KEYWORDS: **computer assisted reading; computer uses in education; information technology; primary education; reading difficulties; reading teaching; talking computers**

1977

Institute of Educational Technology, Walton Hall, Milton Keynes MK7 6AA
01908 274066

Oliver, M. Mr; *Supervisors*: Fung, P. Dr; O'Shea, T. Prof.

Supporting learning modal logics through visualisation and manipulation tools

ABSTRACT: It has already been established that computers can aid the learning of classical first order logics in two ways: 1) by graphical representations of the language, which make it more approachable, and 2) by providing automated proof checkers, which remove some of the tedium traditionally associated with the topic. The researcher intends to consider ways in which these results can be extended to the area of modal logics, and to find appropriate graphical interfaces and examples with which to manage and explain the concepts. Furthermore, it is not clear whether graphical interfaces are still useful once familiarity with symbolic systems has been established for example, once first order logic has been learnt using a tool such as Tarski's World (Barwise and Etchemendy, 1990), will there be any significant benefit from introducing the new concepts of modality using graphics? In order to assess and answer these problems, it is planned to use two test groups of 15-20 students, and supplement these results with case studies. The outcome of this work should help to ascertain whether or not modal logistics benefit from a graphical treatment and, if so, to provide criteria for the development of an appropriate software tool.

STATUS: Individual research

DATE OF RESEARCH: 1994-continuing

KEYWORDS: **computer graphics; computer uses in education; educational software; information technology; logic**

1978

Institute of Educational Technology, Walton Hall, Milton Keynes MK7 6AA
01908 274066

Scanlon, E. Dr; Fung, P. Dr; Hennessy, S. Dr

Portable information technologies for supporting graphical mathematics investigations (PIGMI)

ABSTRACT: The primary purpose of this project is to investigate the potential uses of portable information technologies (particularly graphing calculators and palmtop computers) in supporting foundation and secondary school level mathematics teaching. The researchers are examining the impact of a recent shift towards calculating and computing tools as increasingly accessible, everyday technologies on the nature of learning in a traditional area of the mathematics curriculum. The focus is on the roles of portable tools in facilitating students' graphing skills and understandings of graphical representations, using investigations of real world problems. Studies are being conducted with school students and students of an Open University foundation mathematics course.

PUBLISHED MATERIAL: HENNESSY, S., FUNG, P., SCANLON, E. & NORTHERN, L. (1998). 'Graphing with palmtops', Micromath, Vol 14, No 2, pp.30-33. ; HENNESSY, S. 'The potential of portable technologies for supporting graphing investigations', British Journal of Educational Technology, Vol 30, No 1, pp.57-60. (in press). ; HENNESSY, S., FUNG, P. & SCANLON, E. 'The potential of portable technologies for supporting graphing investigations: overview of the PIGMI project', Journal of Computer-Assisted Learning. (in press).

STATUS: Sponsored project

SOURCE OF GRANT: Open University £58,217

DATE OF RESEARCH: 1996-continuing

KEYWORDS: **computer graphics; computer uses in education; information technology; mathematics education; sex differences**

1979

Institute of Educational Technology, Walton Hall, Milton Keynes MK7 6AA
01908 274066
De Montfort University, Department of Media and IT, The Gateway, Leicester LE1 9BH
01162 551551
Humberside University, School of Policy Studies, Inglemire Avenue, Hull HU6 7LU
01482 440550

Lefrere, P. Dr; Brown, S. Prof.; Karran, T. Dr

PILOT (Project information, linking, orientation and training)

ABSTRACT: The researchers are developing a telematic support system for work-based projects and placements, and student projects in general. The system is designed for use by all higher education (HE) institutions. It will link people who want placements and training, with people who can provide placements and training. It uses a rapid-response electronic system, with multimedia databases, accessed via the Internet/JANET. This should ensure better matching of project placements to students' competencies; and enhance inter-personal, presentational and self-appraisal skills and career prospects, particularly for disadvantaged or minority groups. Another outcome will be dissemination of best practice about organisation of placements and projects. The first users of the system are employers (seeking trained personnel for projects) and universities (seeking appropriate work placements and projects for students). In due course, the system will be extended beyond placements and projects, to provide on-the-job training for people already in work. Research is needed into many aspects of the system, particularly its educational aspects. These include studies of learners who use the system to create multimedia CVs, design their own study programs, access materials appropriate to their learning styles, conduct self-assessment and receive feedback at a distance from educational institutions, which become facilitators rather than direct providers of this learning process. Some of these aspects will be studied, but other complementary studies are welcomed. Interested researchers can discuss their plans with any of the partner institutions (the Open University, De Montfort and Humberside).

STATUS: Sponsored project

SOURCE OF GRANT: British Telecom £100,000

DATE OF RESEARCH: 1995-continuing

KEYWORDS: **computer networks; computer uses in education; industry higher education relationship; information technology; placement; student projects**

1980

Institute of Educational Technology, Walton Hall, Milton Keynes MK7 6AA
01908 274066
Hertfordshire University, Sensory Disability Research Unit, Department of Psychology, College Lane, Hatfield AL10 9AB
01707 284000

Pearson, M. Dr; *Supervisors*: Cooper, M. Mr; Petrie, H. Dr

Investigation into the applications of 3-dimensional synthesised soundfields, based on Ambisonics, for sensory impaired learners

ABSTRACT: Much promise has been held up, and some demonstrated, for the application of virtual worlds in education. The ability to learn through exploring worlds that would be otherwise inaccessible because of their size, location, timescale or dangerous nature is attractive and offers potential benefit at all levels of education. This has applications in a wide range of subject areas; a few examples could include the explorations of: 1) atomic structures, the solar system, observation of otherwise invisible forces (e.g. magnetic field patterns); 2) exploration within the human body, intracellular processes, bio-tech procedures; 3) complex data analysis, representation of multidimensional functions; 4) long timescale time variant processes e.g. human population distributions. Now if this benefit is to be extended to blind and partially sighted students then the creation of rich audio virtual worlds that faithfully convey what is conventionally offered in the visual medium is needed. There is still much basic research required into the perceptual and technical issues pertaining to the practical implementation of such audio worlds. This is particularly the case as the target is that these implementations will be readily achieved in the classroom or student's home with minimal specialised and only relatively low cost computing and audio facilities. This is the context of an ongoing collaborative work between the Multimedia and Enabling Technology Group at the Open University and the Sensory Disabilities Research Unit at the University of Hertfordshire.

PUBLISHED MATERIAL: COOPER, M. & TAYLOR, M.E. (1998). 'Ambisonic sound in virtual environments and applications for blind people'. Proceedings of the 2nd European Conference on Disability, Virtual and Associated Technologies, Skovde, Sweden, September 1998.

STATUS: Collaborative

DATE OF RESEARCH: 1998-continuing

KEYWORDS: **blindness; computer simulation; information technology; multimedia; partial vision; spatial audio; special educational needs; virtual reality; visual impairments**

1981

Institute of Educational Technology, Walton Hall, Milton Keynes MK7 6AA
01908 274066
Scottish Council for Research in Education, 15 St John Street, Edinburgh EH8 8JR
0131 557 2944

Laurillard, D. Prof.; Plowman, L. Dr

Narrative construction and the comprehension of interactive multimedia (MENO: Multimedia, Education and Narrative Organisation)

ABSTRACT: The research investigates the relationship between the design of educational interactive multimedia programmes and the cognitive processes engendered by their use by both groups and individuals. The research will study the interrelationship between the learning tasks, the narrative (or macro-structure), the classroom context and the users (interpreting users as teachers and children). The researchers will adopt methods which combine a naturalistic approach, which takes account of the situatedness of use and the larger learning context (observation and informal interviews), with the systematic manipulation of specific design features. This will enable them to establish how these materials can be designed in such a way that they reflect and support the ways in which students think and operate in learning situations and to increase usability, enjoyment and understanding. The researchers have already established the limitations of existing designs and the need for this enquiry. This has been acknowledged by the readiness of commercial producers of such materials to be involved in and support this research. Working in collaboration with them allows the research team to address their concerns at every stage from design and evaluation of prototypes to the most appropriate formats for dissemination of findings. As a result of this research, a better understanding of learners' cognitive processes when using interactive media will have been gained. The researchers will then be able to contribute guidelines and exemplars of improved instructional design practices which will benefit both learners and producers of these materials.

PUBLISHED MATERIAL: PLOWMAN, L. (1996). 'Narrative, linearity and interactivity: making sense of interactive multimedia', British Journal of Educational Technology, Vol 27, No 2, pp.92-105. ; LAURILLARD, D.M. 'Learning formal representations through multimedia'. In: HOUNSELL, D., MARTON, F. & ENTWHISTLE, N. The experience of learning. Edinburgh: Scottish Academic Press. (in press).

STATUS: Sponsored project

SOURCE OF GRANT: Economic and Social Research Council £232,420

DATE OF RESEARCH: 1995-1998

KEYWORDS: **cognitive processes; computer uses in education; educational software; human computer interaction; information technology; multimedia**

1982

Mathematics Faculty, Centre for Mathematics Education, Walton Hall, Milton Keynes MK7 6AA
01908 274066

Galpin, B. Mr; Graham, A. Mr

Establishing the spreadsheet as a mathematical tool

ABSTRACT: Starting from a personal interest in and use of the spreadsheet, the researchers are now working at the problem of promoting this software as a useful tool for doing mathematics at all levels. In particular the intent is to research effective ways of bringing the software to the attention of teachers of mathematics, helping them reach the point where they can use the tool with confidence themselves, not only in their administrative work but also to enhance their own mathematical understanding. To this end a range of examples of spreadsheet applications which are appropriate for use by teachers at all levels will be collected and published.

PUBLISHED MATERIAL: GRAHAM, A. & GALPIN, B. et al (1993). Supporting primary number work. Milton Keynes: Open University.

STATUS: Individual research

DATE OF RESEARCH: 1992-1993

KEYWORDS: computer uses in education; educational software; information technology; mathematics education; spreadsheets

1983

North West Region, Chorlton House, 70 Manchester Road, Chorlton-cum-Hardy, Manchester M21 1PQ
0161 861 9823
Underley Hall School, Kirkby Lonsdale, Carnforth LA6 2HE
01524 271206

Litt, L. Dr; Pain, J. Dr

Asessment of handwriting and its relationship to spelling and reading in six and a half to seven and a half year old children

ABSTRACT: The research arises from the development of a dictation test for use with top infant (six and a half to seven and a half year old) children. Data (total scores) is available for several thousand children. From these, a sub-sample of some 500 scripts is being analysed in detail so that comparisons may be made between handwriting characteristics and attainments in spelling and reading. Anomalies identified in these comparisons will be investigated on an individual basis to identify causal factors.

STATUS: Individual research

DATE OF RESEARCH: 1991-1993

KEYWORDS: handwriting; infant school pupils; reading; spelling; writing skills

1984

School of Education, Walton Hall, Milton Keynes MK7 6AA
01908 274066

Tyler, S. Ms; *Supervisor*: Light, P. Prof.

Spatial cognition: childrens' pictorial representations

ABSTRACT: Modern accounts of childrens' drawings still take intellectual/visual realism (or elaborations) as their focal point. The current research treats drawing as problem-solving, with solutions determined/constrained by factors such as lack of particular spatial concepts. However, Piaget's accounts of the child's construction of representational space, and his premise of perception in 2D are not accepted. Thus in the first experiments, which focused on inconsistencies in response when children are requested to draw an array in which one object is partly hidden by another, the dimensions of the objects were systematically varied (2D/3D). Results showed that children aged 4-7 years are sensitive to object dimensions. When 2D equivalents of 3D objects are used children are less likely to segregate either outlines or 2D cutouts when drawing or arranging materials on paper, than when the objects are 3D. They are able to arrange 2D materials so that one is partially hidden, provided the arrangement is made 'in space' so that many gaps can be left to represent object depth. They can also match arrays, using identical materials. The findings show that childrens' difficulties are confined to the 2D drawing surface, and that they have no problems with understanding simple spatial relationships, with allowing objects to be partially hidden, or with viewpoint. Other findings showed that children will treat 3D objects as 2D provided object depth is not an essential feature (as it is in spheres, cones etc.). A current experiment is investigating whether partial occlusion can be facilitated by triggering what may be schemas for drawing familiar objects - schemas that may be 2D in concept.

STATUS: Sponsored project

SOURCE OF GRANT: Economic and Social Research Council £21,000

DATE OF RESEARCH: 1990-1993

KEYWORDS: cognitive ability; depth perception; drawing; problem solving; spatial ability; visual perception

1985

School of Education, Walton Hall, Milton Keynes MK7 6AA
01908 274066

Bancroft, D. Dr

Temporal inference research project

ABSTRACT: It is arguably the case that much human reasoning and problem solving rests on an understanding of the temporal inter-relations between events. Early and effective development of temporal understanding may then make a considerable contribution to wider cognitive skills. There has been a considerable amount of European laboratory based research investigation of the development of children's understanding of time. One outcome is the suggestion that the co-ordination of temporal concepts is problematic for children until late in childhood since it depends on considerable cognitive sophistication. Another possibility is that young children are capable of dealing with temporal concepts when not obstructed by 'interfering' factors. There is also evidence from the psycholinguistic tradition which suggests that children use the language of 'time' effectively from a very early age. The aim of the project is to investigate children's ability to reason about, and manipulate the concepts of Order and Duration in order to resolve some of the theoretical issues and to identify means of encouraging the development of temporal reasoning. Children aged between 4 and 7 years are presented with temporal problems on a microcomputer. Children have either mouse or concept keyboard control of the computer, thus allowing a behavioural indication of comprehension. Results to date indicate that, although not all temporal problems are of equal complexity, children of this age are capable of producing sophisticated solutions and that this ability can be developed and promoted.

STATUS: Sponsored project

SOURCE OF GRANT: Open University

DATE OF RESEARCH: 1987-continuing

KEYWORDS: cognitive development; reasoning; temporal integration; time perspective

1986

School of Education, Walton Hall, Milton Keynes MK7 6AA
01908 274066

Edwards, R. Dr

Educational responses to adult employment

ABSTRACT: The aim of this research is to critically examine the policies and practices which produce and respond to adult unemployment in contemporary society and the role of education and training discourse and programmes in overcoming and/or reproducing adult unemployment. This is pursued through desk research and interviews with policy makers, practitioners and participants in the field. Conclusions are always provisional, dependent on the changing constellation of policy and practice.

PUBLISHED MATERIAL: EDWARDS, R. (1991). 'The Canadian jobs strategy', Unemployment Bulletin, Autumn, pp.8-13. ; EDWARDS, R. (1991). 'The inevitable future? post-Fordism and open learning', Open Learning, Vol 6, No 2, pp.36-43. ; EDWARDS, R. (1991). 'Guidance and unemployment in Canada', Adults Learning, Vol 2, No 10, pp.279-282. ; EDWARDS, R. 'Winners and losers: the education and training of adults'. In: RAGGATT, P. & UNWIN, L. (Eds). Change and intervention: vocational education and training. London: Falmer Press.

STATUS: Sponsored project

SOURCE OF GRANT: Canadian High Commission £1,800

DATE OF RESEARCH: 1990-1993

KEYWORDS: adult vocational education; employment patterns; training; unemployment

1987

School of Education, Walton Hall, Milton Keynes MK7 6AA
01908 274066

Faulkner, D. Dr; Miell, D. Dr

The effects of friendships and social isolation on young children's adjustment to school life

ABSTRACT: This ongoing project began with an exploratory longitudinal study of 37, 4-5 year old children throughout their first term of formal schooling. A number of methods for examining the impact of early friendships on the children's success in settling into school were tested:

pairs of friends and isolated children were observed over 11 weeks. Interaction in the clasroom was recorded on video-tape; teacher interviews were conducted; children were interviewed about their friendships and took part in a communication game. This research has shown, as predicted, that children who enter school in the company of a previously established friend adjust better to the demands of school than children who find it difficult to establish friendships. The research also showed that the former are more socially competent than the latter in a range of formal and informal school settings. Subsequent research with Reception/Year 1 children in a number of schools has confirmed these initial results and has shown that pairs of friends out-perform randomly paired children on a range of classroom-based tasks such as joint story construction, model building, and story sequencing tasks. This research has also shown that 'isolated' children (i.e. those who are not selected as play-partners by their classmates), work better on these tasks when they are paired with a child from an estabished friendship pair, than when partnered with a 'popular' child from the same class. The current investigations have been designed to compare in detail the non-verbal and verbal communication skills of 'popular' and less popular children. The researchers are also carrying out studies which interrogate social understanding and children's concepts of friendship. Initial findings suggest that the less popular ('isolated') children have less well developed concepts of friendship than their peers. Intervention studies which attempt to develop these children's social understanding, social competence and communication skills are being planned. This research forms part of a programme of research being carried out by the Social Dynamics in Development and Learning research group at the Open University.

STATUS: Sponsored project

SOURCE OF GRANT: Nuffield Foundation; Open University

DATE OF RESEARCH: 1992-continuing

KEYWORDS: **communication skills; early childhood education; friendship; infant school pupils; primary education; reception classes; social development; social isolation; young children**

1988

School of Education, Walton Hall, Milton Keynes MK7 6AA
01908 274066

Bennett, N. Dr

The impact of single-sex teaching in a mixed school on patterns of school choice

ABSTRACT: This is a case study of the impact of a decision by one school to alter its teaching and pupil organisation in response to intense local competition and over-supply of secondary school places, and in a climate of turbulence and local structural change. Interviews with local headteachers and with school staff, and a questionnaire to parents choosing the local schools for September 1995 intake, will be combined with documentary analysis to investigate perceptions of the change, expectations of the teachers on student recruitment, and compare these with patterns of recruitment and parents' expressed reasons for their choice of school. A follow-up survey of the 1997 intake parents is being negotiated.

STATUS: Individual research

DATE OF RESEARCH: 1993-1997

KEYWORDS: **marketing; parent choice; school organisation; single sex classes**

1989

School of Education, Walton Hall, Milton Keynes MK7 6AA
01908 274066

Evens, H. Ms; Spence, M. Ms; *Supervisors*: McCormick, R. Prof.; Murphy, P. Ms

Mathematics by design

ABSTRACT: The aim is to investigate the use of mathematics within design and technology (D&T). Activities in schools in England, at National Curriculum key stage 2 (KS2) and key stage 3 (KS3) will reveal the way mathematics is used in D&T and how this relates to pupil mathematical experience in mathematics lessons. From this the researchers can advise teachers on improving the opportunities for this use. Case studies of a D&T project are carried out (3 at KS3 and

2 at KS2), involving video-recording of pupil project activity, pupil interviews to ascertain their mathematical understanding, and interviewing D&T and mathematics teachers for their perceptions of the mathematics involved in the project, what they expect of pupils, and actions that can be taken within a school to improve the use of mathematical opportunities (e.g. coordination between D&T and mathematics departments). Interim results indicate that the language the teachers use in the 2 types of classrooms (D&T and mathematics) is different and is related to the tools and context of each along with the aims of the teaching. Thus a D&T teacher will talk of 'projecting information' when the mathematics teacher will talk about the geometrical concepts of 'reflection', 'rotation' and 'translation'. These differences relate to the drawing instruments used by D&T teachers and the fact they focus on procedures, whereas the mathematics teacher focuses upon concepts. Pupils need both approaches and it is evident that they currently cannot use in D&T the concepts they have encountered in mathematics lessons.

PUBLISHED MATERIAL: DESIGN COUNCIL. (1996). Maths by design. London: Design Council. ; EVENS, H. & MCCORMICK, R. (1996). 'The use of mathematics in design and technology'. Paper presented to the European Conference on Educational Research, Seville, Spain, 24-27 September 1996.

STATUS: Sponsored project

SOURCE OF GRANT: Design Council; Open University

DATE OF RESEARCH: 1995-1997

KEYWORDS: **design and technology; key stage 2; key stage 3; mathematical applications; mathematics education; primary education; secondary education**

1990

School of Education, Walton Hall, Milton Keynes MK7 6AA
01908 274066

Paechter, C. Dr

Educating the Other: a feminist perspective on gender and education

ABSTRACT: The concept of woman as Other, in de Beauvoir's sense, is a useful lens through which to view the education of girls and young women. While the Othering of subordinated groups has been a pervasive feature of both Western and non-Western thought, such treatment, especially in the context of the Western dualistic tradition, has most constantly been applied to women. This scholarly research looks at the ways in which the dualistic tradition of Western philosophical thought has positioned men as Subject, women as Other, through the association of reason both with essential humanness and with the male gender. In it the researcher is investigating how women, girls and those inhabiting subordinated masculinities and femininities, are positioned as Other within the school setting. This work is useful not only in the field of gender but because it provides a lens through which to look at a number of issues of equity in education. By examining the female Other we are also able to see how other groups become disadvantaged in a system developed according to the asusmption of a white male subject. The work thus has implications for action, within schools as well as in society at large, to overcome systemic inequity.

PUBLISHED MATERIAL: PAECHTER, C.F. Educating the other. London: Falmer Press (in press).

STATUS: Individual research

DATE OF RESEARCH: 1996-1998

KEYWORDS: **equal education; feminism; girls; sex differences; womens education**

1991

School of Education, Walton Hall, Milton Keynes MK7 6AA
01908 274066

Twining, P. Mr; *Supervisors*: McCormick, R. Prof.; Underwood, J. Dr

Computer innovation and the management of change in primary education

ABSTRACT: New technology is having a significant impact on most aspects of life in the industrialised world. These changes create a situation in which those involved with primary education need to rethink many aspects of what they do and how they do it. It is argued that information technology (IT) has the potential to alter the curriculum (what children need to learn), progression (the order in which you learn things), mathetics (how you learn) and hence pedagogy (how you teach). It is not clear what these changes would look like; there are many possible views. However all of them would require the use of IT as a tool for learning and this will require changes in primary practice. This research aims: 1) to investigate the factors which affect the extent to which IT is used as a tool for learning in primary education; and 2) to identify the most effective strategies for enhancing the extent to which teachers use IT in ways which result in their rethinking their practice? Explicit models of the factors affecting IT use in primary education will be used as metacognitive tools to enhance the researcher's understanding. These models will be tested against data collected in primary schools. A case study methodolgy, which incorporates both qualitative and quantitative techniques will be used. A triangulation procedure will be implemented which will involve comparing the evidence from each mode of data collection in order to corroborate it.

PUBLISHED MATERIAL: TWINING, P. (1995). 'Making barriers explicit: some problems with the computer innovation literature'. In: WILLIS, D.A. et al (Eds). Technology and teacher education annual: Proceedings of the 6th International Conference of the Society for Information Technology and Teacher Education (SITE), San Antonio, Texas, 22-25 March, 1995. Greenville, NC: Society for Technology and Teacher Education.

STATUS: Individual research

DATE OF RESEARCH: 1995-continuing

KEYWORDS: computer uses in education; information technology; primary education; teaching methods

1992

School of Education, Walton Hall, Milton Keynes MK7 6AA
01908 274066

Williams, S. Dr; *Supervisor*: Raggatt, P. Mr

The politics of competence: a study of policy

ABSTRACT: The introduction of competence-based vocational qualifications the National Vocational Qualifications (NVQ) system - has been central to recent vocational education and training reforms and has itself become an important and contentious area of public policy. This research investigates the process through which this particular concept came to dominate vocational education and training policy and assesses the significance of economic, institutional and political factors in its development and implementation. The study focuses on: 1) the extent to which structural factors, including institutional and political short-termism and ideological considerations, combined during implementation to reconstruct the broad notion of competence, which underpinned the initial policy, as a much narrower concept; and 2) the factors which contributed to the resilience of the NVQ system and its extension to new areas - General National Vocational Qualifications (GNVQs) and professional activities - despite widespread criticism and low take-up by employers. It considers the extent to which the use of national standards was attractive both as a means of fostering a training market and of exerting greater central control over vocational education and training provision. Key areas of public policy analysis examined include: the interaction between ministers, with their often short-term goals, and officials; coherence and continuity between policy formation and implementation and between government departments; the role and accountability of quangos. Two principal research methods are used: 1) documentary analysis; and 2) 70+ indepth, semi-structured interviews with ministers, senior civil servants and other senior officials and representatives of organisations with major responsibilities for, or interests in, competence-based vocational qualifications

PUBLISHED MATERIAL: WILLIAMS, S. & RAGGAT, P. 'Contextualising public policy in vocational education and training: the origins of competence-based vocational qualifications', Journal of Education and Work. (in press).

STATUS: Sponsored project

SOURCE OF GRANT: Economic and Social Research Council £55,000

DATE OF RESEARCH: 1997-1998

KEYWORDS: competency based education; educational policy; national vocational qualifications; politics education relationship; training; vocational education

1993

School of Education, Walton Hall, Milton Keynes MK7 6AA
01908 274066

Levacic, R. Ms; Woods, P. Prof.; Hardman, J. Mr

The impact of competition on secondary schools

ABSTRACT: The impact of competition on secondary schools (ICOSS) project is investigating the implications for schools, in terms of resourcing and examination performance, of the more competitive climate created by structural and procedural changes to the education system introduced at the end of the 1980s. Using administrative data on over 300 secondary schools from 6 local education authorities (LEAs), it addresses questions such as: 1) 'What has been the impact over time on school rolls and budgets? 2) Have certain trends emerged? 3) To what extent are these the result of parental choice? 4) How does success in the market relate to schools' examination performance and the socio-economic status (SES) of pupils? Other questions relate to the dynamics of the market and schools' responses: 1) How do more open enrolment, local school management and pupil-led formula-funding interact in practice? 2) Under what conditions do these structural elements provide incentives for schools to respond? 3) What significance is given to these incentives by schools? 4) How do they relate to schools' educational activity? 5) What role does the LEA play in all of this? Other datasets, including a survey of headteachers' perceptions of competition, combine with and complement the school-level administrative data to help answer these questions. Interviews with headteachers of 16 schools, in varying competitive situations, begin to examine the local dimension to competition and cooperation between schools. A process which is to be continued through more intensive case study work in 4 of all these schools, as well as interviews with LEA personnel. To date, the study has generated several papers describing the trends and associations in and between 'market success' (both in relation to pupil recruitment and financial reward) and factors such as examination performance, pupil SES, and grant maintained status.

PUBLISHED MATERIAL: HARDMAN, J. & LEVACIC, R. (1997). 'Impact of competition on secondary schools'. In GLATTER, R., WOODS, P.A. & BAGLEY, C. (Eds). Choice and diversity in schooling: perspectives and prospects. London: Routledge. ; LEVACIC, R. 'Local management of schools in England: results after 6 years', Journal of Education Policy. (in press). ; LEVACIC, R. & HARDMAN, J. 'Competing for resources: the impact of social disadvantage and other factors on English secondary schools' financial performance', Oxford Review of Education. (in press).

STATUS: Sponsored project

SOURCE OF GRANT: Economic and Social Reserach Council £126,530

DATE OF RESEARCH: 1995-1998

KEYWORDS: competition; educational markets; parent choice; secondary education

1994

School of Education, Walton Hall, Milton Keynes MK7 6AA
01908 274066

Bennett, N. Dr; Smith, R. Dr

The impact on practice of programmes of educational leadership and management development

ABSTRACT: The impact on practice of programmes of educational leadership and management development (IMPPEL) project derives from the demands of the Teacher Training Agency (TTA), that programmes of continuing professional development (CPD) should include an assessment of their impact upon practice. It sets out to: 1) problematise the concept of practice; and 2) examine ways of investigating the impact of a training or development programme on that practice. The project will rest on a substantial literature review and an extensive survey of CPD provision in the field of educational leadership and management. From this, a number of distinctive case studies will be explored and exploratory discussions are taking place to compare programmes in other countries, with those examined in the UK. The IMPPEL project is conceived as a pilot study from which a more vigorous and extensive examination of CPD and its impact on professional practice can be developed.

STATUS: Team research

DATE OF RESEARCH: 1998-continuing

KEYWORDS: **educational administration; leadership; management development; management in education; professional development**

1995

School of Education, Walton Hall, Milton Keynes MK7 6AA
01908 274066

Spence, M. Dr; *Supervisor*: Murphy, P. Ms

Primary science and mathematics project

ABSTRACT: The project explores the mathematical demands typically required in science tasks and teachers' and children's understanding of these and their approaches to them. The aim is to consider opportunities for developing and consolidating mathematical competence through science activities in ways that support and enhance children's learning of science. The first completed case study was of Year 6 children exploring forces. Children were video and audio-taped in science and mathematics classes. Observations in both classes revealed a gap between the way measurement was used in science and mathematics. Children's approaches to accuracy differed and their perceptions of the mathematics in the process of measurement in science revealed that they saw 'measure' as something separate from mathematics and number. The actual process of measurement was science not mathematics in the view of these children.

PUBLISHED MATERIAL: SPENCE, M. (1998). 'Measurement in primary science and maths', Primary Science Review, Vol 53, pp.6-9.

STATUS: Team research

DATE OF RESEARCH: 1996-continuing

KEYWORDS: **mathematics education; primary education; science education**

1996

School of Education, Walton Hall, Milton Keynes MK7 6AA
01908 274066

Jeffrey, B. Mr ; Woods, P. Prof.

The effects of OFSTED inspections on primary teachers and their work

ABSTRACT: A new system of schools inspection, under the Office for Standards in Education (OFSTED), was set up in 1992. Nominally, independent, it was appointed within the frame of the general restructuring of public institutions and of the Government's marketization and managerialization of the education system in the late 1980s and early 1990s. As the operations of OFSTED bear directly on inspectors and teachers, it provides good opportunities to study the effects on them of restructuring and how they cope with the powers of the State. The values behind the new reforms contrast sharply with the prevailing child-centred discourse preferred by primary school teachers. Inspectors, in the actual execution of inspections, represented themselves as moderating the approach in a kind of humanistic managerialism which apparently goes some way to meeting the teachers' position. However, this is not how the inspections were experienced by the teachers. They were conscious of a deep and damaging value clash in the areas of knowledge, pedagogy, assessment and culture. Their lives, selves and work became colonized by the OFSTED process. At the more traumatic moments, they felt deprofessionalized. Like the inspectors, however, they devised their own coping strategies, involving both distancing and engagement, staging performances and various other strategical measures. Both inspectors and teachers avail themselves of a range of discourses in negotiating personal ways through structural constraints. However, their solutions are boundaried in their own life worlds rather than meeting across them in common purpose. They are personal, rather than structural, solutions.

PUBLISHED MATERIAL: JEFFREY, B. & WOODS, P. (1996). 'Feeling de-professionalized: the social construction of teacher emotions during an OFSTED inspection', Cambridge Journal of Education, Vol 26, No 3,

pp.325-344. ; WOODS, P., JEFFREY, B., TROMAN, G. & BOYLE, M. (1997). Restructuring schools, reconstructing teachers: responding to changes in the primary school. Buckingham: Open University Press. ; JEFFREY, B. & WOODS, P. (1998). Testing teachers: the effect of school inspections on primary teachers. London: Falmer Press. ; WOODS, P., JEFFREY, B., TROMAN, G., BOYLE, M. & COCKLIN, B. (1998). 'Team and technology in writing up research', British Educational Research Journal, Vol 24, No 5, pp.573-592. ; WOODS, P., BOYLE, M., JEFFREY, B. & TROMAN, G. 'A research team in ethnography', International Journal of Qualitative Studies in Education. (in press).

STATUS: Sponsored project

SOURCE OF GRANT: Economic and Social Research Council £27,887

DATE OF RESEARCH: 1996-1998

KEYWORDS: **inspection; inspectors - of schools; ofsted; primary school teachers; teacher morale; teacher role**

1997

School of Education, Walton Hall, Milton Keynes MK7 6AA
01908 274066

Woods, P. Prof.; Boyle, M. Ms

Child-meaningful learning in bilingual school

ABSTRACT: How do multicultural children and their parents experience the very beginning of their school careers? How do teachers mediate the demands of the educational system, and how do the children adapt? What kind of access to the National Curriculum is offered to multicultural children? In answering these questions the researchers did 2 years' intensive research in 3 multi-ethnic institutions. They explored teachers' values and beliefs and how they attempted to put them into practice. At times, teachers were constrained to get things done because of pressures operating on them; but at other times, taught creatively in a way particularly relevant to the children's concerns and cultures. The researchers studied the children's experiences on their transition to school, and argue that they were inducted into not only a general pupil role, but also one based on an Anglicised model of pupil. Opportunities for learning which children found most meaningful came notably from free play, but these became gradually more limited as they approached and then engaged with the National Curriculum. These young children were forming complex identities as they sought to respond to the varying influences operating them. Their parents saw a cultural divide opening up between home and school. The researchers suggest that one way to tackle the problems revealed in the research is through the institution of a 'learning community'.

PUBLISHED MATERIAL: BOYLE, M. & WOODS, P. (1996). 'The composite head: coping with changes in the primary headteacher's role', British Educational Research Journal, Vol 22, No 5, pp.549-568. ; WOODS, P., JEFFREY, B., TROMAN, G. & BOYLE, M. (1997). Restructuring schools, reconstructing teachers: responding to change in the primary school. Buckingham: Open University Press.; BOYLE, M. (1998). 'Storytelling, relevance and the bilingual child', English in Education, Vol 32, No 2, pp.15-23. ; WOODS, P., BOYLE, M. & HUBBARD, N. (1999). Multicultural children in the early years: creative teaching, meaningful learning. Clevedon: Multilingual Matters.

STATUS: Sponsored project

SOURCE OF GRANT: Economic and Social Research Council £82,930

DATE OF RESEARCH: 1994-1997

KEYWORDS: **bilingualism; early childhood education; english - second language; ethnic groups; multilingualism; primary education**

1998

School of Education, Walton Hall, Milton Keynes MK7 6AA
01908 274066

Troman, G. Dr; Woods, P. Prof.

The social construction of teacher stress

ABSTRACT: The incidence of teacher stress is increasing, and having a serious impact on the quality of teaching and the efficient running of the educational system. This research is exploring the sources of teacher stress at various levels, particularly with a view to the impact of the changed nature of work on teachers' roles and identities; and to the different experiences of males and females. The researchers are charting the career of stress through its various phases, with particular interest in the social construction of emotions, and in the phenomenon of self-renewal following a period of stress and burnout. To complement existing work on teacher stress, qualitative research methods are being used on a limited, but controlled, sample to explore cases in depth. The main research focuses on primary teachers, but is combined with similar research by a linked full-time research student working at the secondary level. This affords a powerful basis for the generation of theory, which will be employed in informing policy and practice relating to teacher stress, and to stress in other professions. Working with occupational health professions, the researchers are seeking to aid their inservice training activities with school personnel and other professional groups.

STATUS: Sponsored project

SOURCE OF GRANT: Economics and Social Research Council £45,831

DATE OF RESEARCH: 1997-continuing

KEYWORDS: **primary school teachers; stress - psychological; teacher role; teacher workload; teachers**

1999

School of Education, Centre for Language and Communication, Walton Hall, Milton Keynes MK7 6AA
01908 274066

Bourne, J. Prof.

Teaching and learning strategies in multi-ethnic schools

ABSTRACT: The study examines practice in a number of successful multi-ethnic primary and secondary schools. It identifies the key features of good practice in school organisation and teaching strategies which are transferable between schools with ethnically diverse populations and intakes. The study involved 'indepth' work in primary and secondary schools which apparently were successful for all pupils and which had over 10% of pupils from at least one of the following ethnic group backgrounds: Bangladeshi, Black Caribbean and Pakistani. Involved interviews with staff, pupils and parents and also classroom observation.

STATUS: Sponsored project

SOURCE OF GRANT: Department for Education and Employment £74,480

DATE OF RESEARCH: 1996-1997

KEYWORDS: **ethnic groups; learning strategies; primary education; secondary education; teaching methods**

2000

School of Education, Centre for Language and Communication, Walton Hall, Milton Keynes MK7 6AA
01908 274066

Mercer, N. Prof.; Wegerif, R. Dr; Littleton, K. Dr

The talk, reasoning and computers project (TRAC)

ABSTRACT: The talk, reasoning and computers (TRAC) project investigated 2 issues of current concern. Firstly, research on the role of talk in the process of classroom education has led to claims that education is a process of linguistic socialisation. In relation to this, the study produced 3 main findings: 1) that exploratory talk helps groups to reason together; 2) children's use of exploratory talk can be increased through coaching; and 3) individual scores on a standard non-verbal reasoning test significantly increased in those children coached in exploratory talk. Surveys show that computers are being under-used in primary schools because, in many cases, teachers are not sure how to integrate work with computers into the curriculum. In response to this need, a specific strategy for the integration of computers into the primary classroom was explored. The project consisted of the development, implementation and evaluation of an educational intervention programme in 3 separate schools. This programme began with the coaching of reasoning through talk and then used specially designed items of software to support this kind of talk in 2 curriculum areas: citizenship and science. A combination of 2 main methods were used in evaluating the effects of the intervention programme: an experimental design, including measures of both group and individual reasoning ability; and the qualitative discourse analysis of changes in children's talk supported by the use of new computer-based methods.

PUBLISHED MATERIAL: WEGERIF, R. & MERCER, N. (1997). 'Using computer-based analysis to integrate quantitative and qualitative methods in the investigation of collaborative learning', Language and Education, Vol 11, No 4, p.271-286.; WEGERIF, R., MERCER, N., LITTLETON, K. & DAWES, L. (1997). 'Research note: the talk reasoning and computers (TRAC) project', Journal of Computer Assisted Learning, Vol 13, No 1, pp.68-72. ; WEGERIF, R., MERCER, N. & DAWES, L. (1998). 'Software design to support discussion in the primary classroom', Journal of Computer Assisted Learning, Vol 14, pp.199-211. ; MERCER, N. & WEGERIF, R. (1998). 'Is "exploratory talk" "productive talk"?. In: LITTLETON, K. & LIGHT, P. (Eds). Learning with computers: analysing productive interactions. London: Routledge. ; MERCER, N. (1998). 'Development through dialogue: a socio-cultural perspective on the process of being educated'. In: QUELHAS, A. & PEREIRA, F. (Eds). Cognition and context. Analise Psicologica Special Edition. Lisbon: IPSA.

STATUS: Sponsored project

SOURCE OF GRANT: Economic and Social Research Council £29,000

DATE OF RESEARCH: 1996-1998

KEYWORDS: **child language; computer uses in education; information technology; primary education; reasoning; speech; verbal communication**

2001

School of Education, Centre for Language and Communication, Walton Hall, Milton Keynes MK7 6AA
01908 274066

Stierer, B. Dr

An examination of academic literacy practices and the construction of professional knowledge within Masters level courses in education

ABSTRACT: This research conceptualises university masters programmes in education as a site where 2 orders of discourse compete: the discourses associated with training and professional development, and the discourses of the academy - principally those of the social sciences. School teachers studying within these programmes, typically part-time and inservice, struggle to reconcile their identifiers, and their personal/professional purposes for studying, with the authority and control of higher education institutions. These 2 orders of discourse are especially evident in the literacy practices of such programmes. The project has therefore examined: privileged genres of academic writing; the experience of school teachers as literacy learners in a specialised context; and the ways in which school teachers' negotiation of writing requirements articulates with their professional knowledge, experience, expertise and aspirations. This has led to wider questions of epistemology, agency and identity: 1) What 'counts' as knowledge within these programmes? 2) How are teachers expected to use written language to construct that knowledge? 3) Where do they locate themselves in relation to that knowledge? 4) Do the discursive practices within these programmes position students as expert teachers or as novice academics? Data comprises tape-recorded interviews with students and teaching faculty in universities in the UK and USA, course materials, students' written assignments, and written feedback from faculty. The project has drawn widely for the theoretical frame used in the analysis, including work in literacy studies, critical discourse analysis, literary criticism, the politics of expert knowledge, the culture and discourses of professional groups, and neo-Vygotskian perspectives on language and the construction of knowledge.

PUBLISHED MATERIAL: LEA, M. & STIERER, B. 'Student writing in higher education: new contexts. Buckingham: Open University Press and Society for Research into Higher Education. (in press). ; STIERER, B. 'School teachers as students: academic literacy practices and the construction of professional knowledge in Masters level courses in education'. In: LEA, M. & STIERER, B. (Eds). Student writing in higher education: new contexts. Buckingham: Open University Press and Society for Research into Higher Education. (in press).

STATUS: Individual research

DATE OF RESEARCH: 1996-continuing

KEYWORDS: **masters courses; teacher development; teacher education; writing composition**

2002

School of Education, Centre for Language and Communication, Walton Hall, Milton Keynes MK7 6AA
01908 274066

Coffin, C. Ms; Wegerif, R. Dr; Lea, M. Ms

Academic writing online

ABSTRACT: The academic writing online (AWO) project pursues research aims through realising a practical objective. The practical objective is to develop a short course to help academics and research students publish articles in relevant international English language journals. The research aims of the project are to develop and pilot new technologies and new pedagogies for teaching and learning using computer mediated communication (CMC) and to explore and assess the potential of CMC as a medium to support accelerated linguistic socialisation within a discourse community. The course design was based upon a socio-cultural model of teaching and learning using computer mediated (CMC) and to explore and assess the potential of CMC as a medium to support accelerated linguistic socialisation within a discourse community. The course design was based upon a socio-cultural model of teaching and learning as a process of guided induction into a community of practice. A pilot course was run internationally followed by a continuing series of internal courses to Open University researchers. Participants in the pilot course consisted of 10 European Association for Research on Learning and Instruction (EARLIE) members from 9 different countries, 7 of whom completed the course. Evaluation indicated that the most successful aspects of the course which related to a more innovative 'learning community' approach proved less successful than hoped. Collaborative learning through peer-review and discussion was nonetheless a valued and significant part of the course. The theoretical findings of the pilot AWO project, on the relation between the World Wide Web (WWW) and socially situated models of teaching and learning, proved more ambiguous. Further research continues to explore this issue.

STATUS: Team research

DATE OF RESEARCH: 1996-continuing

KEYWORDS: distance education; information technology; internet; online systems; telecommunications; writing - composition; writing for publication

2003

School of Education, Centre for Language and Communication, Walton Hall, Milton Keynes MK7 6AA
01908 274066

Hulme, R. Mr; *Supervisors*: Wegerif, R. Dr; Mercer, N. Prof.

Literacy education and computer mediated communication in the primary classroom

ABSTRACT: Literacy and the turn to electronic networks are perhaps the two issues in education which currently have the highest profile in the news and in political debates. These are normally treated as two quite separate issues yet many commentators have argued that the shift from a print medium to an interactive electronic medium has the potential to transform the nature of literacy and of education for literacy. This project will investigate the relationship between electronic computer mediated communication (CMC) and the teaching and learning of literacy in primary schools. The project will have three aims: 1) to investigate theoretical frameworks for understanding both electronic literacy and the role of new media in teaching literacy; 2) to research findings on the application of CMC to the teaching of literacy; and 3) to contribute to the further development of computer-based methods for investigating the teaching and learning of literacy using CMC. While the details of this study will be influenced by the findings of the first phase of the research, it is proposed investigating how the potential of CMC to combine several modes of communication, video, audio, graphics and text can be best used to facilitate the teaching and learning of literacy.

STATUS: Individual research

DATE OF RESEARCH: 1998-continuing

KEYWORDS: computer uses in education; information technology; literacy; primary education; reading; writing - composition

2004

School of Education, Centre for Language and Communication, Walton Hall, Milton Keynes MK7 6AA
01908 274066

Goodman, S. Dr; Swann, J. Dr; Lea, M. Ms

Academic literacies in a distance-taught English language course

ABSTRACT: This project explores academic literacy on the Open University undergraduate course, 'The English Language: past, present and future', a course explicitly designed with a diverse student body in mind (for students from the UK, Europe and Singapore with a range of academic backgrounds). The research, which is influenced by recent research on academic literacy, and on literacy practices more generally (e.g. Lea and Street, 1998) focuses particularly on literacy requirements in the course texts, how these are mediated by tutors and how they are received and negotiated by students. It will thus attempt to answer the question: What kinds of literacy practices are students engaged in during their study of 'The English Language' and how do these practices differ between students, or groups of students? Participants include 11 associate lecturers teaching for the Open University in England, Singapore and Greece, as well as students in their teaching groups. Much of the project will focus on the analysis of data on studying the course, with data including tuition and study diaries completed by participants, as well as samples of student assignments and associate lecturers' comments.

STATUS: Team research

DATE OF RESEARCH: 1998-continuing

KEYWORDS: cultural differences; distance education; english; literacy; writing - composition

2005

School of Education, Centre for Language and Communication, Walton Hall, Milton Keynes MK7 6AA
01908 274066

Scrimshaw, P. Mr; Lewin, C. Dr; Mercer, N. Prof.; Wegerif, R. Dr

National Curriculum key stage 1 with low cost word processors project

ABSTRACT: The aim of the project is to evaluate the impact of information and communications technology (ICT) on literacy standards at key stage 1 using low cost word processors. A secondary consideration is to evaluate the management of a significant amount of ICT equipment in schools. It is linked to the National Literacy Strategy and the implementation of the literacy hour in primary schools. In addition, the project will investigate the impact of computers on: teachers' professional development, home school links and the literacy of pupils for whom English is an additional language. 16 schools from 6 local education authorities are participating in the project and they have identified up to 4 classes from Years 1 and 2. Each school has been provided with 30 low cost word processors. A mixed methodology has been adopted, including a case by case analysis of the schools. A second phase is planned for April 1999-July 2000.

STATUS: Sponsored project

SOURCE OF GRANT: British Educational Communications and Technology Agency £21,000

DATE OF RESEARCH: 1998-continuing

KEYWORDS: computer uses in education; home school relationship; information technology; literacy; primary education; word processing

2006

School of Education, Centre for Language and Communication, Walton Hall, Milton Keynes MK7 6AA
01908 274066
De Montfort University, Polhill Avenue, Bedford MK41 9EA
01234 351671

Mercer, N. Prof.; Wegerif, R. Dr; Lewin, C. Dr; Littleton, K. Dr; Dawes, L. Ms

The schools-based project: raising achievement through thinking and language skills (RATTLS) - phase 1

ABSTRACT: The raising achievement through thinking and language skills (RATTLS) project continues from an earlier project at the Centre for Language and Communications developing an approach to teaching the use of language as a tool for thinking in primary schools. The project has an added focus on literacy and involved 6 schools (one as control group) and 11 Year 4 and 5 classes. A specially designed set of lessons, which introduced 'ground rules for talk' were developed in order to help students to develop skills in 'exploratory talk'. A literacy pre-test and post-test, as well as a reasoning test, were used to test post-intervention reading and reasoning skills. Classes were also videoed to record children's development throughout the intervention. Video-recordings and other observations indicate that the introduction of the 'ground rules for talk' and associated activities had the effect hoped for in that, given opportunities to put them into practice, most children seemed to appreciate their value and use them well. Results of the sample group who completed the reasoning test showed distinct improvement in group reasoning abilities which tends to confirm the link between the use of 'exploratory talk' and the development of improved reasoning. Analysis of results of the literacy tests did not show any obvious improvement, but for the unexpected reason that the test seems to have been too simple for most of the children. A second phase of the project is currently being planned including Year 3. The literacy assessment will be re-designed for phase 2 to overcome this problem.

STATUS: Sponsored project

SOURCE OF GRANT: Milton Keynes Local Education Authority £2,000

DATE OF RESEARCH: 1997-1998

KEYWORDS: **child language; group work; language skills; literacy; primary education; reasoning; thinking skills; verbal communication**

2007

School of Education, Centre for Research and Development in Teacher Education, Walton Hall, Milton Keynes MK7 6AA
01908 274066

Swarbrick, A. Ms

The Iliad project (International Languages Inservice at a Distance)

ABSTRACT: The Iliad project involves the Open University with the University of Karlstad, Sweden; Universidad Publica de Navarra, Spain; British Broadcasting Corporation, London; Centre for Information on Language Teacher and Research, London; Institut Universitaire de Formation de Maitres de Paris, France; IUFM des Pays de Loire, France; and Padagogisches Institut des Bundes in Wien, Austria. The project is creating a web-based, interactive communications network and resource bank for language teachers across Europe. The resource includes: 1) multimedia and multilingual resources targeting key aspects of the curriculum in the late primary and early secondary phase in each participating country; 2) expert commentary and analyses of classroom scenes; and 3) electronic conferencing for languages teachers. The project objectives are to: 1) raise awareness of what is culturally specific in languages classrooms in different countries; 2) compare and link primary and secondary school practice in the teaching and learning of modern foreign languages (MFL) using practical exemplars; 3) complement existing training materials (pre-service and inservice) used in partner countries; 4) increase positive attitudes amongst learners and teachers towards ideas from other phases and countries; and 5) raise awareness of how MFL methodology is affected by cultural factors. The project's main activities will focus on creating the Iliad interactive resource bank using educational and technological expertise in each of the partner countries (Spain, France, Austria, Sweden and the UK). Five issues common to all partner countries will form the initial focus: classroom management; planning sequences of lessons; pupil motivation; topics/issues preferred by students; and learning resources. The expected outcomes and products of the project include: 1) establishing a core of high quality resources; 2) access to contemporary ideas and practices within the multilingual 'site' through subscription; 3) facilitation of discussion through face-to-face inservice provision or through the virtual community of languages teachers established through the Iliad electronic network; 4) production of print and video based pack of materials arising from the development of the 'site'.

STATUS: Sponsored project

SOURCE OF GRANT: European Union Socrates (Lingua A) £108,557

DATE OF RESEARCH: 1998-continuing

KEYWORDS: **computer uses in education; information technology; international educational exchange; internet; modern language studies; multilingual materials; multimedia**

2008

School of Education, Walton Hall, Milton Keynes MK7 6AA
01908 274066
Universidade Aberta, Palacio Ceia, Rua da Escola, Politeenica 141-147, 1200 Lisbon, Portugal
Utrecht University, IVLOS Institute of Education, PO Box 80127, 3508 TC, Utrecht, Netherlands
University of Tampere, Department of Teacher Education, Box 346, 13131 Hameenlinna, Finland

Moon, R. Prof.; Banks, F. Mr; Hobbs, S. Ms; Ferreira, M. Dr; Veen, W. Dr; Niemi, H. Prof.

Open and distance learning in initial teacher education in Europe (ODLITE)

ABSTRACT: Open and distance learning methodologies are being exploited in a range of professional and vocational contexts. In cooperation with colleagues in Finland, The Netherlands and Portugal, this project will seek to survey the extent to which such teaching and learning strategies are being used in the field of initial teacher education across Europe. The project will combine quantitative methods with a small number of selected case studies to give an indication of the range of activity in elementary, secondary and vocational teacher preparation courses, and point to good practice in this new and growing area.

STATUS: Sponsored project

SOURCE OF GRANT: European Union: SOCRATES £94,650

DATE OF RESEARCH: 1996-1997

KEYWORDS: **comparative education; distance education; open education; preservice teacher education**

2009

School of Education, Walton Hall, Milton Keynes MK7 6AA
01908 274066
Warwick University, Department of Psychology, Coventry CV4 7AL
01203 523523

Norgate, S. Dr; *Supervisors*: Lewis, V. Prof.; Collis, G. Dr

Physical and social influences on pretend play in blind children

ABSTRACT: The project involves a detailed study of the development of pretend play in blind children. It includes charting the development of different types of pretend play; identifying ways in which the physical setting and social setting influence pretend play in relation to: a) the beliefs that each child's parents and teacher have about the value of pretence for psychological development; b) the view of the parents and teacher of each child on how much and what the child can see; and c) the child's level of visual impairment determined opthalmologically. 18 blind/severely visually impaired children, with no additional impairments, aged between 18 months and 6 years, are being studied both at home and nursery/school. The study will provide the first detailed account concerning the nature of pretence and the factors influencing its occurrence in blind children. The findings will be of considerable theoretical importance, both to theories of development in blind children and theories concerning the processes underlying development in sighted children. The findings will also have immediate practical implications for how parents and teachers can optimise the development of pretence in blind children by suggesting ways of organising play space, types of toys and the roles of adults and other children.

PUBLISHED MATERIAL: COLLIS, G. & LEWIS, V. (1997). 'Implications for theory and practice'. In: LEWIS, V. & COLLIS, G. (Eds). Blindness and psychological development 0-10 years. Leicester: BPS Books. ; LEWIS, V. & COLLIS, G. (1997). 'Theoretical and practical issues in studying children with severe visual impairments'. In: LEWIS, V. & COLLIS, G. (Eds). Blindness and psychological development 0-10 years. Leicester: BPS Books. ; LEWIS, V. & COLLIS, G. (1997). (Eds). Blindness and psychological development 0-10 years. Leicester: BPS Books. ; LEWIS, V. & BOUCHER, J. Test of pretend play (ToPP). San Antonio: Psychological Corporation. (in press).

STATUS: Sponsored project

SOURCE OF GRANT: Leverhulme Foundation Trust £49,330

DATE OF RESEARCH: 1996-1998

KEYWORDS: **blindness; imagination; play; pretend play; special educational needs; visual impairments**

2010

Science Faculty, Centre for Science Education, Walton Hall, Milton Keynes MK7 6AA
01908 274066

Sharp, G. Ms; *Supervisors*: Whitelegg, E. Ms; Murphy, P. Ms

Cognitive Acceleration in Science Education (CASE) related to age intervention and gender differentiation

ABSTRACT: The project is to investigate a variety of science teaching intervention procedures with particular reference to age of intervention and gender differentiation, with the aim of discovering what types of intervention can be used to improve the science education of individual pupils within the 10 to 12 year old age range. The project is looking in detail at one recent intervention programme, the Cognitive Acceleration in Science Education (CASE) project, and comparing the effects of this to other intervention strategies, including inservice teacher education (INSET) on equal opportunities, primary science collaborative learning methods, single sex teaching, etc. Much of the initial research will be to collate information on intervention strategies that have been used on a city, national and international basis. Whilst carrying out this research the project will use the 30 activity lessons as designed by Shayer et al with Year 7 pupils and will introduce the use of these materials at one of the feeder schools. The evaluation packs as provided by the CASE project will be used. New sets of evaluation and analysis documents will also be developed. Self-assessment, as well as group and individual interviews, will be used with pupils and teachers. The standard assessment tasks for the National Curriculum will be used with all the pupils and although these will be testing knowledge rather than cognitive understanding, they may be of some use.

STATUS: Individual research

DATE OF RESEARCH: 1993-continuing

KEYWORDS: intervention; science education; sex differences

2011

Science Faculty, Centre for Science Education, Walton Hall, Milton Keynes MK7 6AA
01908 274066

Scanlon, E. Dr; Spence, M. Dr; Hodgson, B. Dr; Whitelegg, E. Ms; Issroff, K. Dr; Hall, S. Ms; *Supervisor*: Murphy, P. Ms

Collaborative learning and primary science (CLAPS)

ABSTRACT: The project examined teachers' approaches to investigative science in primary classrooms. The goal was to provide detailed pictures of how individuals within a group interacted and how these interactions developed over time and impacted on learning; and to investigate the links between activities and outcomes. Teachers typically approach science by planning a series of activities within a topic. Both the teachers' intentions and the learning outcomes for students can be better understood if the links between activities and outcomes are examined. Ongoing classwork is video and audio-recorded. Target groups of students were selected to focus on indepth. Interviews were carried out with teachers and target students. A delayed probe was administered to target students, and questionnaires were administered to the whole class. The researchers show how teachers' interactions can foster or create barriers to social interactions and describe some of the ways students' understanding of tasks and roles in groups can lead to breakdowns in collaboration. Opportunities for collaboration depend significantly on the task context and structure provided by the teachers. Two crucial features are that students perceive a common goal and that the task is structured to be a true group task.

PUBLISHED MATERIAL: WHITELEGG, E., MURPHY, P., SCANLON, E. & HODGSON, B. (1992). 'Investigating collaboration in primary science classrooms: a gender perspective'. Vol 1. Proceedings of East and West European GASAT Conference, Eindhoven, Netherlands, October 1992. ; WHITELEGG, E., MURPHY, P., SCANLON, E. & HODGSON, B. (1993). Group work on science investigations - do girls and boys differ? In: BENTLEY, D. & WATTS, M. (Eds). Primary science and technology: practical alternatives. Buckingham: Open University Press. ; SCANLON, E., MURPHY, P., HODGSON, B. & WHITELEGG, E. (1994). 'A case study approach to studying collaboration in primary science classrooms'. In: FOOT, H.C. (Ed). Group and interactive learning: proceedings of the international conference on group and interactive learning, Strathclyde, 1994. Southampton: Computational Mechanics Publications. ; MURPHY,

P., SCANLON, E., HODGSON, B. & WHITELEGG, E. (1994). 'Developing investigative learning in science - the role of collaboration'. Proceedings of the ECUNET European Conference on Curriculum, University of Twent, Enshed, The Netherlands, August 31-September 2, 1994. ; SCANLON, E., ISSROFF, K. & MURPHY, P. (1998). 'Collaboration in a primary science classroom: mediating science activities through new technology'. In: LITTLETON, K. & LIGHT, P. (Eds). Learning with computers: analysing productive interactions. London: Routledge.

STATUS: Team research

DATE OF RESEARCH: 1993-continuing

KEYWORDS: classroom observation techniques; group work; learning activities; primary education; science activities; science education

2012

Science Faculty, Centre for Science Education, Walton Hall, Milton Keynes MK7 6AA
01908 274066

Erlick, S. Mr; *Supervisor*: Thomas, J. Dr

The effect of science education on the attitudes of adult science learners

ABSTRACT: The aim of the research is to determine the effect of science education on the attitudes of adult learners towards science and contemporary issues such as genetic engineering and nuclear power. It attempts to ascertain the degree of any change in attitudes towards these issues and which factors have caused it. Survey research is being undertaken of all adult students (1000+) on the Open University Science Matters Course. Five postal surveys (pre, post and at 3 critical mid-points in course) have been administered to students taking the 1996 presentation of the course. Results from a pilot study indicate that the most consistent effect of science education on attitudes is confirmation. There is evidence for attitude change but this is differentiated between the issues concerned. The research has relevance specifically to the learning of science by adults and generally for the public understanding of science.

PUBLISHED MATERIAL: ERLICK, S. (1996). 'Attitudes and attitude change amongst adult science learners'. Proceedings of ESERA 3rd European Summer School on Theory and Methodology of Research in Science Education, 1996. ; THOMAS, J. & ERLICK, S. 'The effect of adult science education on attitudes to controversial issues in science and the implications for the public understanding of science', Studies in the Education of Adults. (in press).

STATUS: Individual research

DATE OF RESEARCH: 1995-1998

KEYWORDS: adult education; adult learning; attitudes; controversial issues course content; genetic engineering; mature students; nuclear energy; science education; student attitudes

2013

Science Faculty, Centre for Science Education, Walton Hall, Milton Keynes MK7 6AA
01908 274066

Tresman, S. Dr; Stevens, V. Dr

Approaches to adult learning in primary science during courses of professional development

ABSTRACT: This project aims to investigate the ways in which primary teachers are able to access science during programmes of professional development. Studies are underway to examine concept acquisition by teachers in relation to entry qualifications in science, and the elements found to be effective in tutorial provision and assessment in establishing explicit bridges between content and teaching practice. The use of mixed-media resources, reflective diaries, and the relationship between the Open University and course leaders and tutors is also analysed. The potential to transfer elements of such programmes of continuing professional development to international settings is explored.

PUBLISHED MATERIAL: TRESMAN, S. & FOX, D. (1996). Meeting in-service needs in primary science, using reflective diaries: Occasional Paper No 10. Milton Keynes: Open University, Centre for Science Education. ; TRESMAN, S., with TWISS, S., PATTINSON, R., HAGAN, C. & GLOVER, J. (1996). 'A novel approach to developing INSET', Primary Science Review, Vol 45, pp.26-27. ; TRESMAN, S. (1996). 'Empowering primary teachers to work with confidence and expertise in science'. A workshop presented to the Malta Forum for Science Education, September 1996.

STATUS: Sponsored project

SOURCE OF GRANT: Open University; British Council

DATE OF RESEARCH: 1996-continuing

KEYWORDS: inservice teacher education; primary education; primary school teachers; science education; teacher attitudes; teacher development

2014

Science Faculty, Centre for Science Education, Walton Hall, Milton Keynes MK7 6AA
01908 274066

Sharp, G. Ms; *Supervisors*: Whitelegg, E. Ms; Murphy, P. Ms

A longitudinal study investigating pupil attitudes to science in school

ABSTRACT: The research questions are as follows: 1) What is the current position of girls in science (1978-1996)? 2) To what extent does this position reflect a change in pupils'/girls' attitude to science as a subject/profession? 3) Does the Cognitive Acceleration in Science Education (CASE) intervention project have a positive influence on both achievement and attitudes? 4) What other factors influence achievement in science, attitudes to school science and the uptake of science post-16? The research has involved 3 secondary schools in Coventry and a county secondary school. One third of each schools' first year intake were randomly selected and surveyed. 20 pupils from each city school plus 4 pupils from the county school were interviewed. The city pupils were interviewed over 3 years and the county pupils over 2 years. 20 pupils were interviewed at one city school in Year 10. Teachers were interviewed and Year 9 classes observed at one school. The results are presently being analysed. Differences between boys' and girls' attitudes have been noted with respect to confidence, topic area preference, willingness to continue science studies, interest in science and importance of school science.

PUBLISHED MATERIAL: WHITELEGG, E. (1996). 'Gender effects in science classrooms'. In: WELFORD, G., OSBORNE, J. & SCOTT, P. (Eds). Research in science education in Europe: current issues and themes. London: Falmer Press.; SHARP, G. (1996). 'Achieving the four E's: education, employment, equality, empowerment'. Paper presented at the GASAT Conference, Ahmedabad, India, 5-10 January 1996.

STATUS: Individual research

DATE OF RESEARCH: 1994-continuing

KEYWORDS: pupil attitudes; science education; secondary education; secondary school pupils; sex differences

2015

Science Faculty, Centre for Science Education, Walton Hall, Milton Keynes MK7 6AA
01908 274066

Sumner, A. Miss; *Supervisors*: Solomon, J. Prof.; Thomas, J. Dr

Environmental education in secondary school

ABSTRACT: Environmental education is currently under much debate. The government wishes to see educators providing pupils with a sound basis of knowledge and understanding of the world around them in order that they develop into responsible citizens who can make informed decisions and have the ability to become actively involved in the sustainable use of their environment. The guidance given by the government provides advice on setting out a policy and planning implementation of environmental education into schools (National Curriculum Council, 1990). The research is concerned with the practicalities of implementing such a cross-curricular theme in a secondary school, that, as a grant maintained girls' grammar school, is quite well resourced for this undertaking. It is intended to determine how successful the current practice has proven to be in achieving the above, and whether the pupils are able to transfer their environmental knowledge from one discipline to another easily. The researcher will study a group of 27 Year 8 pupils, using questionnaires and direct observations, as well as an investigation of the policy views held by the headteacher and environmental education coordinator.

STATUS: Individual research

DATE OF RESEARCH: 1997-continuing

KEYWORDS: cross curricular approach; environmental education; secondary education; transfer of learning

2016

Science Faculty, Centre for Science Education, Walton Hall, Milton Keynes MK7 6AA
01908 274066

Whitelegg, E. Ms; Edwards, C. Mr

Investigation of the transfer of learning physics concepts amongst post-16 students across a variety of learning contexts

ABSTRACT: This research arises out of a new curriculum development initative - the Supported Learning in Physics Project (SLIPP). The curriculum project consists of 8 units of text-based student learning material which provides a self-study programme in physics for post-16 students to use with the support of their teachers. By using specific learning strategies, in particular developing concept acquisition through discussion of real life contexts, the project aims to motivate students to learn by increasing their interest in physics. This strategy accepts that knowledge is acquired in a context, so the context for learning matters. Transfer of knowledge across contexts is problematic and the debates about transfer contentious. The research will investigate the transfer phenomenon using the contexts in the SLIPP materials and in non-contextual situations normally found in the traditional school laboratory. A pilot study will be used to develop the research instrument that will allow for cross-context testing of students and this instrument will be used in a further indepth study across a wider school/college population with a greater variation of learning contexts.

STATUS: Sponsored project

SOURCE OF GRANT: Open University £16,000

DATE OF RESEARCH: 1998-continuing

KEYWORDS: physics; sixteen to nineteen education; transfer of learning

2017

Science Faculty, Centre for Science Education, Walton Hall, Milton Keynes MK7 6AA
01908 274066

Lunn, S. Mr; *Supervisor*: Solomon, J. Prof.

The promotion of school science and the future of scientific culture in Europe

ABSTRACT: This project will link science teachers in 8 or 9 European countries and involve them in collaborative curriculum innovation in areas which will affect the scientific culture of ordinary citizens. From these Internet discussions, the researchers will attempt to understand and model how teachers from diverse cultures react to similar initial stimuli.

STATUS: Sponsored project

SOURCE OF GRANT: European Union £56,000

DATE OF RESEARCH: 1997-continuing

KEYWORDS: comparative education; curriculum development; europe; international educational exchange; internet; science education; science teachers; telecommunications

2018

Science Faculty, Centre for Science Education, Walton Hall, Milton Keynes MK7 6AA
01908 274066

Lunn, S. Mr; *Supervisors*: Solomon, J. Prof.; Thomas, J. Dr

Primary teachers' understandings of the nature of science and the purposes of science education

ABSTRACT: Much research on primary science teaching is based on testing teachers' subject knowledge and finding holes in it, leading to a 'deficit model' of teachers' understanding and to inservice training aimed at plugging gaps in knowledge. It can also be observed, however, that primary science is prospering: children like it; do well in standardised assessments; and look good in international comparisons, so teachers must be doing something right. This project is looking more closely at how they do this: 1) at how teachers' understandings of science content and of teaching, learning, and children in general are transformed and articulated in 'pedagogical content knowledge' - in particular at how this might develop following reflection on the nature of the subject matter, and at how such development might be manifest in teachers' planning and teaching. 8 teachers of 5 to 11 year-old pupils are taking part, looking at the planning and delivery of a science topic and discussing the nature of science and the purposes of teaching it. This will be a longitudinal study spread over 5 terms, using think-aloud protocols, semi-structured interviews and classroom observation. Domain mapping and data analysis will use a range of graphical techniques including systematic networks. A 1996 pilot project showed that teachers' perceptions of science are diverse and pluralistic, and that they may develop or evolve over time, and that at least some primary teachers have now taken 'ownership' of science as a subject, and have extended or are trying to extend their autonomy in terms of content and presentation.

PUBLISHED MATERIAL: LUNN, S. & SOLOMON, J. 'Primary teachers views of National Curriculum science', British Educational Research Journal. (in press). ; LUNN, S. (1998). Analysis of interview data using systemic networks: primary teachers' views of science. Milton Keynes: Open University, Centre for Science Education.

STATUS: Individual research

DATE OF RESEARCH: 1997-continuing

KEYWORDS: **primary education; primary school teachers; science education; subject knowledge; teacher attitudes**

2019

Science Faculty, Centre for Science Education, Walton Hall, Milton Keynes MK7 6AA
01908 274066
Open University, Institute of Educational Technology, Walton Hall, Milton Keynes MK7 6AA

Whitelegg, E. Ms; Hodgson, B. Dr; Scanlon, E. Dr; Spensley, F. Dr

Women in physics - conceptions of career progress

ABSTRACT: The science education community has been greatly concerned over the past 30 years about girls' low participation and under-achievement in education in the physical sciences. There has been much research and development in curriculum design, teaching strategies, learning interventions, classroom practice and career counselling to ensure that girls are not precluded from jobs that require some knowledge of, or training in, physics and chemistry. But what of those girls who were attracted into - or perhaps were determined to get into - higher education, into postgraduate studies and then careers in physics and chemistry. How have they fared? Has their education, both formal and informal, been appropriate and supportive of their aspirations? Have practices of outcomes at this level changed over time? The research is looking at a broad picture of women's higher education experience in physics from curriculum design through teaching and learning strategies to mentoring and peer support - and its relationship to career progression. The research began by conducting an interview study of women physicists from different areas of physics, from different educational backgrounds, within broad categories of career patterns and of varying ages. The experiences of these interviewees have been located within a broad mapping of women PhD physicists in Britain over the last 50 years and comparisons have been drawn with a similar study of women physicists and chemists in Sweden and with mathematicians in the USA.

STATUS: Sponsored project

SOURCE OF GRANT: Open University

DATE OF RESEARCH: 1997-continuing

KEYWORDS: **career development; girls; graduate employment; higher education; physics; science education; womens education; womens employment**

Oxford Brookes University

2020

School of Education, Wheatley Campus, Wheatley, Oxford OX33 1HX
01865 485930

Wellens, S. Dr; *Supervisors*: Silver, H. Prof.; Gaunt, D. Ms

Education/industry partnerships in England and Wales, and in the United States: a comparative analysis

ABSTRACT: This study focuses on education/industry partnerships to analyse why differences in the political and governmental structures of England and Wales, and the United States, and differences in the policy process - rational in Britain and incremental in the United States - led to different systemic responses to similar economic, ideological and sociological pressures of the late 1970s and 1980s. It explains why industry in Britain sought to improve conditions through changing teaching and learning methods, while American business sought to reform the organisational and management structure of schools. Policial structures and methods of policy and decision making are compared to explain the differences in industry's approach to educational change in each country. The partnership focus then leads into a consideration of historical, governmental, political and other aspects, as well as educational policies, practices and contexts which affect the policy and decision making process. An examination is made of the role of the historical perspective in each country with particular attention to the differing concepts of vocationalism. The study concluded with a focus on the changes and trends in partnerships as well as related issues that emerged in both countries from 1990 to 1993 and suggests that the different responses demonstrated by the comparison of education/industry partnerships may be extended to other issues in education and beyond. The process of policy making in Britain and the United States is directly related to the way the governmental, political and other structures operate in each country.

STATUS: Individual research

DATE OF RESEARCH: 1990-1993

KEYWORDS: **comparative education; educational policy; industry education relationship; partnerships; politics education relationship; united states of america**

2021

School of Education, Wheatley Campus, Wheatley, Oxford OX33 1HX
01865 485930

Harkin, J. Dr

Core skills in National Vocational Qualifications

ABSTRACT: The project implemented the proposals of a national working party on core skills (National Curriculum Council (NCC), British Technician and Education Council (BTEC), National Council for Vocational Qualifications (NCVQ) etc). Four teams of tutors/trainers were selected from the following occupational areas, Engineering, Business Administration, Hairdressing, Health Care, to trial the core skills specifications with groups of learners. The outcomes of the project were fed back to the National Council for Vocational Qualifications in order to refine the core skills specifications, and to provide data to help form guidance to Examining Bodies.

STATUS: Sponsored project

SOURCE OF GRANT: National Council for Vocational Qualifications £70,000

DATE OF RESEARCH: 1991-1993

KEYWORDS: **basic skills; national vocational qualifications; vocational education**

2022

School of Education, Wheatley Campus, Wheatley, Oxford OX33 1HX
01865 485930

Jones, C. Mrs; *Supervisors*: Wilson, M. Ms; Silver, H. Prof.; Measor, L. Dr

A longitudinal study of some factors influencing children's attitudes to science between the primary and secondary stages of education

ABSTRACT: The proposed investigation will aim to evaluate children's attitudes to science, and the changes (if any), over a period of 4 years, between the primary and secondary stages of education. It will follow on from the numerous research findings which have shown concern about science uptake in the later years of schooling and, particularly, the low uptake by girls in physical sciences. The investigation, to discover children's attitudes to science, will use structured mini-essays (at primary level); questionnaires; and interviews of children as they leave their primary school in July 1994, in the secondary school (after 1 term), and annually until age

14. It will take account of in-school and out-of-school factors and allow for an analysis of gender differences. Ideally, the survey will be extended so as to assess outcome (as measured by uptake of science components after age 16) at the end of National Curriculum key stage 4. The project proposes to use 3 primary schools in the area, each of which 'feed' about 60 children per annum into one large, coeducational comprehensive school at age 11. Expected sample size should be of the order of 150 children per annum.

STATUS: Individual research

DATE OF RESEARCH: 1994-continuing

KEYWORDS: **primary secondary education; primary to secondary transition; pupil attitudes; science experiments; sex differences**

Oxford University

2023

Department for Continuing Education, 1 Wellington Square, Oxford OX1 2JA
01865 270360

Thomas, G. Dr

Scientific literacy

ABSTRACT: The project builds on the national survey of public understanding of science carried out by the researcher and other collaborators in 1988. Its aim is to establish a framework for the public understanding of science which meets the (conflicting) aspirations of the scientific profession, the proponents of participatory democracy, economic utility, and cultural literacy. @#Published Material:#@ DURANT, J.R., EVANS, G.A. & THOMAS, G.P. (1989). 'The public understanding of science', Nature, Vol 340, pp.11-14. ; DURANT, J., EVANS, G. & THOMAS, G. (1992). 'Public understanding of science in Britain: the role of medicine in the popular representation of science', Public Understanding of Science, Vol 1, pp.161-182. ; THOMAS, G. (1993). 'Science in the public mind: a cause for concern?'. Schering Lecture No 15. Berlin: Schering Research Foundation.

STATUS: Individual research

DATE OF RESEARCH: 1988-continuing

KEYWORDS: **attitudes; public opinion; scientific literacy**

2024

Department for Continuing Education, 1 Wellington Square, Oxford OX1 2JA
01865 270360

Gray, M. Dr

Knowledge management

ABSTRACT: This study involves an analysis of and development in the institutional economics of knowledge management. The aim has been to address 3 key policy related questions: 1) Do quasi-private organisations need to manage knowledge? 2) What is the economic incentive for knowledge management? 3) What institutional forms of economic activity are associated with knowledge-based competition? Results are to be disseminated in articles and conference papers.

STATUS: Individual research

DATE OF RESEARCH: 1997-continuing

KEYWORDS: **information systems; knowledge management**

2025

Department of Educational Studies, 15 Norham Gardens, Oxford OX2 6PY
01865 274024

Judge, H. Dr

Teacher education in context

ABSTRACT: This research will involve a cross-national study of the relationship of teacher education to higher education in France, the United States and Britain.

PUBLISHED MATERIAL: JUDGE, H.G. (1988). 'Cross national perceptions of teachers', Comparative Education Review, Vol 32, No 2, pp.143-158. ; JUDGE, H.G. (1990). 'The education of teachers in England and Wales'.

In: GUMBERT, E. (Ed). Fit to teach: teacher education in international perspective. Georgia: Georgia State University.

STATUS: Sponsored project

SOURCE OF GRANT: Spencer Foundation - Chicago £300,000

DATE OF RESEARCH: 1988-1993

KEYWORDS: **comparative education; france; higher education; teacher education; united states of america**

2026

Department of Educational Studies, 15 Norham Gardens, Oxford OX2 6PY
01865 274024

Jaworski, B. Dr; Lee, C. Ms

Mathematics teacher enquiry (MTE) project

ABSTRACT: This project involved the study of the processes and practices of mathematics teachers' research into self-chosen aspects of their own teaching, with a scrutiny of the associated developments in mathematics teaching. Methodology in the project was seen at two levels: the local level, in terms of each teacher's research; and the global level in terms of the study of the teachers' research as a whole. The methodology of the teacher researchers, a central study of the project, was closely related to the substance of their research and both substance and methodology evolved. At the global level, research was qualitative and interpretive. Data was collected through participant observations in classrooms, conversations between researchers at both levels, and project meetings. It consists of reflective writing, field notes, and (transcribed) audio-recordings. Triangulation was built into data collection. Analysis followed, loosely, the concept of data-grounded theory involving close scrutiny of the data with triangulation from a variety of sources. Emergent theory of teachers' research activity fitted strongly with a view of action research relating to critical reflective practice. The teachers were seen as reflective practitioners, developing knowledge and awareness through enhanced metacognitive activity. Their research was characterised as evolutionary, in contrast with established patterns of action research. Despite differences in the substance of each teacher's research there were commonalities which provide insights into the conducting of research by teachers and its potential for the development of mathematics teaching. The special nature of mathematics in this research, and the role of external researchers in the project, were important considerations.

PUBLISHED MATERIAL: JAWORSKI, B. & LEE, C. (1994). 'Studying the process of teacher research in the development of mathematics teaching'. Proceedings of the British Society for Research into Learning Mathematics Conference, London, December, 1994. ; JAWORSKI, B. & LEE, C. (1997). 'Teachers can do research', Mathematics Teaching, Vol 158, pp.8-11. ; JAWORSKI, B. & LEE, C. (1997). 'Some investigations about mathematical talk', Mathematics Teaching, Vol 159, pp.33-37. ; JAWORSKI, B. & EDWARDS, J. (1997). 'Research into raising self-esteem in low attainers', Mathematics Teaching, Vol 162, pp.23-25. ; JAWORSKI, B. (1998). 'Mathematics teacher research: process practice and the development of teaching', Journal of Mathematics Teacher Education, Vol 1, No 1, pp.1-29.

STATUS: Sponsored project

SOURCE OF GRANT: Oxford University £8,000

DATE OF RESEARCH: 1994-1997

KEYWORDS: **classroom research; mathematics teachers; researchers; teacher development; teachers**

2027

Department of Educational Studies, 15 Norham Gardens, Oxford OX2 6PY
01865 274024

Davies, C. Dr; Preston, J. Dr

Teaching and learning writing across the curriculum

ABSTRACT: This research concerns the literacy demands, especially the writing demands, that pupils must cope with daily across the school curriculum in order to succeed in their learning. The kinds of literacy skills indicated here include: the ability to read a wide range of texts from different subject areas, purposefully and systematically; the ability to record, develop and organise knowledge and ideas through note-making; the ability to write according to the discourse demands of different subject areas. During the initial exploratory phase of the research, the two central questions are: 1) To what extent are different pupils capable of meeting the actual writing and reading demands that they encounter in the course of their learning? 2) What do teachers do to enable pupils of varying abilities to meet those demands? The present exploratory stage of the research focuses on a number of Year 6 classes in 3 different primary and middle schools, and combines the testing of pupils' literacy skills, observation of lessons across the curriculum, interviews with pupils and with teachers. The central focus is upon the extent to which teachers and pupils share explicit understandings about the nature and specific requirements of different writing tasks.

STATUS: Sponsored project

SOURCE OF GRANT: Oxford University £9,000

DATE OF RESEARCH: 1995-1998

KEYWORDS: **content area reading; content area writing; cross curricular approach; literacy; middle school education; primary education; reading skills; study skills; writing across the curriculum; writing skills**

2028

Department of Educational Studies, 15 Norham Gardens, Oxford OX2 6PY
01865 274024

Kruger, C. Mr; Mant, J. Mrs; *Supervisor*: Summers, M. Mr

Developing primary school teachers' and children's understanding of energy efficiency and energy waste

ABSTRACT: The project focused on primary teachers' and children's understanding of energy efficiency and energy waste, and how this understanding developed following, respectively, teacher training and classroom teaching. In the first phase of this project an opportunity sample of 6 primary teachers took part in a 3-day inservice training course on all aspects of energy. Their ideas about energy were probed, by means of indepth structured interviews, before and after training. In the second phase, 5 of these teachers then went on to teach energy to the children in their classes. The understanding of a sample of children from each class was probed, again by means of structured indepth interviews, before and after teaching. This research into teachers' and children's ideas highlighted 2 key areas: awareness of both is crucial for a comprehensive understanding of energy issues. The first area is energy conservation as a human action (turning off the lights, walking instead of driving). Here, teachers and children already had many ideas which could be readily developed into scientific understanding. The second area is energy efficiency in terms of minimising unintended outcomes. For both teachers and children understanding of this was initially, on the whole, absent. However, understanding developed significantly following training and teaching. The research showed that basic ideas about energy waste which underpin energy conservation (using less energy) and the critically important scientific concept of efficiency can be made accessible non-specialist primary teachers to an 'average' group of primary school children.

PUBLISHED MATERIAL: KRUGER, C., SUMMERS, M., MCNICHOLL, J., MANT, J. & CHILDS, A. (1998). Teaching energy and energy efficiency effectively: teacher education materials for primary and non-specialist secondary teacher education. Hatfield: Association for Science Education.; SUMMERS, M., KRUGER, C., MANT, J. & CHILDS, A. (1998). 'Developing primary teachers' understanding of energy efficiency', Educational Research, Vol 40, No 3, pp.311-328.

STATUS: Sponsored project

SOURCE OF GRANT: Institute of Electrical Engineers £18,000; Esso UK PLC £6,000; Oxford University £5,500

DATE OF RESEARCH: 1997-1998

KEYWORDS: **electricity; energy education; primary education; science education; teaching methods**

2029

Department of Educational Studies, 15 Norham Gardens, Oxford OX2 6PY
01865 274024

Walford, G. Dr

The implementation of policy on faith-based grant maintained schools

ABSTRACT: This research continues earlier research on the activities of pressure groups within education that lead to important changes to the Education Act 1993. This Act allows existing private schools to 'opt into' the state sector and become sponsored grant maintained schools. The current research is concerned to investigate the policy implementation process and will follow the paths of various faith-based private schools into the grant maintained sector.

PUBLISHED MATERIAL: WALFORD, G. (1995). 'The Christian Schools Campaign - a successful eudcational pressure group?', British Educational Research Journal, Vol 21, No 4, pp.451-464. ; WALFORD, G. (1995). 'The Northbourne amendments: Is the House of Lords a garbage can?', Journal of Education Policy, Vol 10, No 5, pp.413-425. ; WALFORD, G. (1996). 'Diversity and choice in school education: an alternative view', Oxford Review of Education, Vol 22, No 2, pp.143-154. ; WALFORD, G. (1996). 'School choice and equity in England and Wales', Oxford Studies in Comparative Education, Vol 6, No 1, pp.49-62. ; WALFORD, G. (1997). 'Diversity, choice and selection in England and Wales', Educational Administration Quarterly, Vol 33, No 2, pp.158-169.

STATUS: Sponsored project

SOURCE OF GRANT: Oxford University £3,500

DATE OF RESEARCH: 1995-1998

KEYWORDS: **church and education; educational legislation; educational policy; grant maintained schools; independent schools; primary education; religion and education; secondary education**

2030

Department of Educational Studies, 15 Norham Gardens, Oxford OX2 6PY
01865 274024

Van Rooy, W. Ms; *Supervisors*: Hayward, G. Dr; Hagger, H. Dr

A-level biology teachers' thinking about controversial issues

ABSTRACT: This research focuses on the manner by which a small group of experienced A-level biology teachers think about the teaching of biological controversial issues. The study examines the thinking of biology teachers as they go about their normal day to day teaching of biology. Of major interest are the possibilities and problems which teachers see for the incorporation of state of the art biological research into current teaching practice as a means of teaching biological concepts. Seven experienced A-level teachers participated in the initial set of interviews, of whom 4 later became case studies. These 4 teachers were interviewed and observed teaching a group of A-level students over a period of between 6-8 weeks. Each teacher chose a controversial issue which would fit into the time frame - the issues investigated were organ transplantation, infertility, diabetes and animal experimentation. The data collected so far shows a richness and complexity of thinking underlying the pedagogic decision-making of teachers when deciding to use controversial issues as part of their biology teaching. The data also seems to indicate that curriculum developers and innovators in biology education would do well to take into account teacher thinking, classroom contexts and syllabuses with respect to the development, implementation and use of innovative teaching approaches and resource materials.

STATUS: Individual research

DATE OF RESEARCH: 1993-1997

KEYWORDS: **biology; biology teachers; controversial issues - course content; science education; secondary education; teacher attitudes**

2031

Department of Educational Studies, 15 Norham Gardens, Oxford OX2 6PY
01865 274024

Alexiadou, N. Ms; *Supervisors*: Hayward, G. Dr; Brock, C. Dr

Markets and further education

ABSTRACT: The Further and Higher Education Act 1992, granted further education (FE) colleges independent status within the public sector. The government's intention behind this shift of status was to to achieve a combination of the benefits of the private sector in terms of operational effectiveness and efficiency, with a sense of public accountability and responsiveness to national policies. The main structural changes within FE include the creation of a new central funding agency, the Further Education Funding Council (FEFC), and the introduction of new inspection arrangements. Overall, the introduction of the market is intended to increase consumer choice and power, increase participation in education and training, and at the same time, serve the changing needs of the local and national economy. Based on these reforms, this study is based on the idea that the market orientation introduced in the FE sector, has driven colleges to: a) be sensitive and responsive to the market forces and work within the framework of a quasi-market; b) perceive and treat their students as 'customers'. Initiatives such as the Student's Charter, training credits, growing emphasis on student's choice at all levels of education, in combination with an increasingly diverse and competing providers' environment, aim at the formation of students as 'sovereign customers'. The aim of the thesis will be to describe, analyse and conceptualise the effects of the changes brought by the market driven legislation in two FE colleges. A set of issues emerge from such a context which provide the focus of the research: 1) In what ways and to what extent do key informants (i.e. senior managers, governors, lecturers and students) in two FE colleges, perceive their institutions as having responded to the 1992 reforms? It will be central to the research to investigate the ways in which, and the extent to which, the market ideology has been 'domesticated' by colleges. 2) How and why do these perceptions vary across the two case study colleges? 3) How do they relate to the beliefs, values and attitudes of the key informants? 4) In what ways and to what extent do FE colleges perceive and treat their students as customers to whom they sell their services; and in what ways and to what extent do further education students perceive colleges as the providers of service? These questions aim at researching: a) the perceptions of the changes as seen by key informants; b) the colleges' organisational responses to the quasi-market arrangement; c) the impact of the market ideology on the college culture, including students and staff at all levels; d) the process of implementation of policy within FE colleges. The research will involve case studies of the two colleges. This will include interviewing, study of sources such as college documents, informal conversations and observation of events.

PUBLISHED MATERIAL: ALEXIADOU, N. (1996). 'Further education: a quasi-market'. Paper presented at the British Comparative and International Education Society (BCIES) Conference on Education as a Commodity: After the Market?, St Aidan's College, University of Durham, 27-29 September 1996.

STATUS: Individual research

DATE OF RESEARCH: 1995-1998

KEYWORDS: educational markets; further education

2032

Department of Educational Studies, 15 Norham Gardens, Oxford OX2 6PY
01865 274024

Rickinson, M. Mr; *Supervisors*: Corney, G. Dr; Hayward, G. Dr

The teaching and learning of environmental issues in geography: a classroom-based study

ABSTRACT: That a geographical education encompasses personal values as well as intellectual facts is now fairly widely acknowledged. In spite of this, there is an acute lack of empirical work into the ways in which values-rich people-environment issues are being dealt with in geographical education. The research therefore constitutes an investigation into the teaching and learning of environment-development issues in National Curriculum key stage 3 geography classrooms. It seeks to address the following questions: 1) How are geography teachers teaching environment-development modules to key stage 3 classes? 2) Why are they teaching in these ways? 3) How are pupils making sense of the content, tasks and processes of these lessons? 4) How are the teachers' and pupils' views of the content, tasks and processes of such lessons similar and/or different? The adopted methodology is qualitative, being small in scale (focusing on the teacher and 4 pupils from one Year 8/9 class in 3 successive schools), and grounded in approach (following an emergent methodology and a progressive focusing of substantive concerns). Features of particular importance include: 1) a focus on actual classroom practice, and pupils' and teachers' experiences of this; 2) a concern to generate authentic perspectives from both pupils and teachers; and 3) a recognition of the importance of researcher-participant relationships. The data generation

methods include: classroom observation and audio recording of lessons, teacher and pupil lesson impression sheets, and semi-structured teacher and pupil interviewing after lessons.

STATUS: Individual research

DATE OF RESEARCH: 1995-1998

KEYWORDS: classroom observation techniques; environmental education; geography; teaching methods; values

2033

Department of Educational Studies, 15 Norham Gardens, Oxford OX2 6PY
01865 274024

N'Tchougan-Sonou, C. Mrs; *Supervisor*: Brook, C. Dr

Values learned through formal education: a comparative study of Anglophone and Francophone Ewes in Ghana and Togo

ABSTRACT: This comparative study seeks to illustrate the impact of anglophone and francophone influences, derived from British and French colonialism, as well as the forces of globalization, on a single ethnic group which is divided by a national border in West Africa. The two educational systems and how they function within the case study communities are the foci of the research. These communities represent a natural experiment: Hohoe and Kpalime are neighbouring towns (approximately 25 kilometers apart) in Ghana and Togo respectively. They share the dominant ethnic population - the Ewe - and were divided by a national border only in the year 1919. In order to highlight the effect of formal schooling on native values, observations and interviews focus on classrooms, teachers and pupils in selected schools in the two towns, with care given to ground the research within its local community by interviewing market women, unschooled youth, community leaders and civil servants as well. The overall context of this research is that of West Africa, where the societies are characterised by a lack of economic and social opportunity and the schools by a lack of sufficient materials, resourcing and funding. This situation has a strong bearing on and inter-relationship with the social and educational variables under consideration. Since Kpalime and Hohoe do not face the debilitating handicaps of extreme poverty, cultural disaffection with schooling, linguistic delivery, etc which plague many areas of both countries, the educational systems themselves, and not the external problems blocking them, are highlighted.

STATUS: Individual research

DATE OF RESEARCH: 1996-continuing

KEYWORDS: africa; developing countries; togo; values

2034

Department of Educational Studies, 15 Norham Gardens, Oxford OX2 6PY
01865 274024

Birbili, M. Ms; *Supervisor*: Walford, G. Dr

The experience of working in Greek higher education

ABSTRACT: The purpose of this study is to obtain a profile of the workplace experiences of a number of academics from two types of Greek higher education institutions - a university and a non-university - and to ascertain how the two groups view each other. The study was designed to draw its data from semi-structured, indepth interviews with academics from two different types of higher education institutions. In agreement with the idea that it is not possible to understand academics in isolation from their immediate occupational context by interviewing them as independent entities, and that the contextual nature of academic life requires a 'case by case' investigation, a case study approach was thought to be the most appropriate for the purposes of this research. A total of 50 academics, selected from 4 departments - 2 from each type of institution - were interviewed. Since there is strong support in the professional literature for distinguishing between subject areas when examining academics' perceptions of their workplace, in order to be able to 'compare' the situation in the 2 institutions, 'similar' departments from each type of institution were chosen.

STATUS: Individual research

DATE OF RESEARCH: 1995-1998

KEYWORDS: greece; higher education

2035

Department of Educational Studies, 15 Norham Gardens, Oxford
OX2 6PY
01865 274024

Economou, A. Ms; *Supervisor*: Phillips, D. Dr

The formulation, acceptance and implementation of the European dimension in British compulsory schooling: a comparative study between England, Wales and Scotland

ABSTRACT: The present research investigates the way that policy on the European dimension in compulsory schooling is formulated at central government level in Great Britain; the role of non-departmental organisations such as the Central Bureau for International Visits and Exchanges, the Qualifications and Curriculum Authority, the Office for Standards in Education, Curriculum and Assessment Authority for Wales, the Scottish Curriculum Council etc; the role of the European Parliament Office in London, the European Commission Offices in Great Britain, the National Union of Teachers, Society of Education Officers, Association of Directors of Education in Scotland, etc. In addition, the study looks at the way that the local education authorities (LEAs) in Great Britain approach the European dimension in compulsory schooling. Finally, 3 primary and 3 secondary schools which encourage the European dimension have been chosen in order to see how the implementation of the European dimension in compulsory education can be achieved. The data draws from documents and interviews with officials from the central government, non-departmental organisations and associations; questionnaires have also been used in order to elicit information about the work of the LEAs (all over Great Britain) on the European dimension; the headmasters, the Year 6 and Year 11 pupils and their teachers have been interviewed; the pupils were also given a questionnaire. The study will develop empirical and theoretical conceptualisations for alternative models in relation to the implementation of the European dimension within compulsory education in Great Britain. The data is yet to be analysed.

STATUS: Individual research

DATE OF RESEARCH: 1995-continuing

KEYWORDS: comparative education; european dimension; european studies; primary education; secondary education

2036

Department of Educational Studies, 15 Norham Gardens, Oxford
OX2 6PY
01865 274024

Jaworski, B. Dr; Potari, D. Dr

The teaching triad project

ABSTRACT: This is ongoing research which attempts to make sense of the complexity of mathematics teaching at secondary school level. The fieldwork has been conducted in partnership between two teachers and two researchers over one school term in two UK secondary schools. A theoretical construct, the Teaching Triad, is used both as an analytical device (by the researchers) and as a reflective agent for teaching development (by the teachers). The Teaching Triad consists of three domains: management of learning; sensitivity to students; and mathematical challenge. It was derived from analysis of one teacher's teaching over a substantial period of observations, followed by its theoretical testing against the work of other teachers (JAWORSKI, B. (1994). Investigating mathematics teaching: a constructivist enquiry. London: Falmer Press.) The current work is designed both to test the triad further as an analytical and descriptive device, and to consider its use by teachers to stimulate reflective activity. Data has been collected through classroom observations, interviews between researchers and teachers, and collaborative meetings of all participants. A micro-analysis of classroom transcript data has 'mapped' instances from classroom interactions onto the Teaching Triad, and led to a macro-analysis validated through other data sources. The research is leading to characterisation of the observed teaching with insights into issues central to the construction of teaching. Issues emerging relate to the cognitive and affective domains of mathematics teaching; to a distinguishing of subtly differing styles of teaching and their relations to pupils' learning; and to teachers' developing awareness of issues in their teaching and their relation to future classroom activity and lesson design.

PUBLISHED MATERIAL: JAWORSKI, B. (1992). 'Mathematics teaching. What is it?', For the Learning of Mathematics, Vol 12, No 1, pp.8-14. ;

JAWORSKI, B. (1994). Investigating mathematics teaching: a constructivist enquiry. London: Falmer Press.

STATUS: Sponsored project

SOURCE OF GRANT: Oxford University £825

DATE OF RESEARCH: 1997-1998

KEYWORDS: classroom observation techniques; mathematics education; secondary education; teaching methods

2037

Department of Educational Studies, 15 Norham Gardens, Oxford
OX2 6PY
01865 274024

Okada, A. Mr; *Supervisors*: Phillips, D. Dr; Goodman, R. Dr

Equality of opportunity in post-war England and Japan: a comparative study of educational policy, 1944-1970

ABSTRACT: This thesis is designed as a comparative study of England and Japan in educational policy. It aims to throw light on the evolution and historical transformation of the concept of 'equality of opportunity' as applied to educational policies in these countries, and on the multiplicity and complexity of factors which bring about changes in the meaning of equality of educational opportunity. In addition, the universality and the uniqueness of the process of changing the concept will be analysed and clarified through the comparisons between England and Japan. It attempts to analyse the pattern of the shift of the concept of equality of educational opportunity through a cross-national comparison of England and Japan and to examine the question of what are the similarities and differences in the process of transformation. Cross-national comparison is essential in evaluating claims of similarities and differences. Isolated study of equality of opportunity in a particular society cannot by itself address the question of whether a process of historical transformation of the concept is typical or anomalous. To formulate such an explanation it has been necessary to analyse the factors which effected changes in the concept. Such analysis is mainly a descriptive synthesis of the dialectical interplay between egalitarianism and meritocracy. The continual presence of, on the one hand, the progressives' idea that all children are on more or less the same developmental road and have a natural right to secondary education and on the other, the conservatives' idea that children differ greatly in basic academic ability and expected social function, is central to the researchers' understanding of the key terms of this study. The placing of emphasis upon either one or the other of the two premises of egalitarianism and meritocracy roughly corresponded with the historical shifts in the major concepts of equality of opportunity in education. This thesis attempts to throw light on this dialectic, and to examine the relationship between such factors and the historical transformation of the concept of equality of educational opportunity through comparison between the cases of England and Japan. The researcher will then examine whether there is a universal dynamic behind the historical shift of the concepts or not, and if not, what factors have led to uniqueness.

STATUS: Individual research

DATE OF RESEARCH: 1994-1998

KEYWORDS: comparative education; educational history; educational policy; equal education; japan

2038

Department of Educational Studies, 15 Norham Gardens, Oxford
OX2 6PY
01865 274024

Colman, P. Mr; Griffin, R. Ms; Barclay, A. Mr; *Supervisor*: Woolnough, B. Mr

Evaluation of engineering education schemes in Scotland

ABSTRACT: An evaluation based on 'expert witness' approach of the effectiveness of different types of engineering education schemes in Scotland. It involves survey, interview of experts, questionnaire surveys of students and teachers, and case studies of schools.

STATUS: Sponsored project

SOURCE OF GRANT: Scottish Enterprise £20,500

DATE OF RESEARCH: 1997-1998

KEYWORDS: engineering education; scotland

2039

Department of Educational Studies, 15 Norham Gardens, Oxford OX2 6PY
01865 274024

McIntyre, B. Mr; Supervisor: Woolnough, B. Mr

Evaluation of CREST and GETSET

ABSTRACT: An evaluation was made of the Creativity in Science and Technology (CREST) award scheme and its associated Girls Entering Tomorrow Science Education and Technology (GETSET). The research consisted of student and teacher questionnaires and case studies of participating schools. Girls who had done GETSET in 1994 (Year 9) were traced through to their Year 12 studies.

PUBLISHED MATERIAL: MCINTYRE, B. & WOOLNOUGH, B. (1996). Enriching the curriculum: part 1. Oxford: Oxford University, Department of Educational Studies. ; WOOLNOUGH, B. (1997). Enriching the curriculum: part 2. Oxford: Oxford University, Department of Educational Studies.

STATUS: Sponsored project

SOURCE OF GRANT: OST; Unilever; National Council of Vocational Qualifications; Zeneca; Esso; Association for Science Education, jointly £15,000

DATE OF RESEARCH: 1996-1997

KEYWORDS: **girls; science education; secondary education; technology education; womens education**

2040

Department of Educational Studies, 15 Norham Gardens, Oxford OX2 6PY
01865 274024

Woolnough, B. Mr

Factors affecting school success in producing engineers and scientists: international project

ABSTRACT: This is a collaborative project involving the University of Oxford; Normal University, Beijing; Coimbra University, Portugal; Sophia University, Tokyo; University of British Colombia, Vancouver; and Curtin University, Perth. The original research (Woolnough 1991, 1994 and 1995) which looked at the factors affecting schools success in producing engineers and scientists in England was paralleled in China, Japan, Australia, Canada and Portugal. Students aged 18 years were surveyed, by questionnaire and case study, to see what factors affected their choice of career towards or away from engineering and science.

PUBLISHED MATERIAL: WOOLNOUGH, B., GUO, Y., LEITE, M.S., DE ALMEIDA, M.J., RYU, T., WANG, Z. & YOUNG, D. (1997). 'Factors affecting student choice of career in science and engineering: parallel studies in Australia, Canada, China, England, Japan and Portugal', Research in Science and Technological Education, Vol 15, No 1, pp.105-121.

STATUS: Collaborative

DATE OF RESEARCH: 1993-1997

KEYWORDS: **career choice; comparative education; engineering education; engineers; science education**

2041

Department of Educational Studies, 15 Norham Gardens, Oxford OX2 6PY
01865 274024

Forbes, S. Mr; *Supervisors*: Wilson, J. Mr; Pring, R. Prof.

Personal, emotional and social development in holistic education

ABSTRACT: Over the last several decades the number of education initiatives describing themselves as holistic has dramatically increased as parents, educators and students feel that an alternative to mainstream schools is needed. At least 7,500 schools calling themselves alternative or holistic have been created worldwide, as well as an uncounted number of special programs designed to be used in and out of state schools for limited periods. Unfortunately, there is little or no consensus as to what holistic education means, what it purports to do, or how it intends to do it, although they usually involve non-traditional views of the learning process and learning goals. Most of these innovations have remained unknown and unscrutinised, and there has been little effort to make coherent sense of the field as a whole. This investigation seeks to make coherent sense of the major threads in theories of holistic education within the larger field of pedagogy. Whilst it may be useful for educators to have the materials from this research available and to draw their own conclusions from it, it is likely that an analysis of these holistic education theories and practices, combined with philosophical, sociological and psychological insights from elsewhere that lend greater substance to these theories and practices, may yield certain general principals and procedures that schools interested in alternative approaches to education could find useful.

STATUS: Individual research

DATE OF RESEARCH: 1996-1998

KEYWORDS: **alternative education; holistic approach**

2042

Department of Educational Studies, 15 Norham Gardens, Oxford OX2 6PY
01865 274024

Aczel, J. Mr; *Supervisors*: Solomon, J. Prof.; Pring, R. Prof.

Learning equations using a computerised balance model: a Popperian approach to learning symbolic algebra

ABSTRACT: This study investigates, using a perspective based on the work of Karl Popper, how students aged 10-15 can learn about simple linear equations, with particular reference to the use of a computerised balance model of an equation. Popperian epistemology implies a conjectural view of knowledge, in which rigour depends on the potential for intersubjective criticism; while a Popperian approach to psychology sees learning and understanding occurring through trial and improvement of strategic theories in response to concerns, rather than through the development of context-free modes of thought. From this perspective, explanatory constructs from research into learning algebra such as letter interpretations and equation metaphors are seen as recontextualised meta-algebraic theories rather than as slowly maturing underlying algebraic cognitive structures. A research instrument is developed to detect learning in a range of principal algebraic concerns - representation, interpretation, transformation and utilisation. A computer program called Equation is also constructed, which acts as a research tool to explore the educational limitations of the balance model of an equation. Fieldwork is carried out to test relevant conjectures, involving around 100 students. It is argued that a concern for symbolic algebra can be initiated firstly by using the balance model to promote formal operations on equations and secondly by encouraging the formulation of equations to find an unknown number in a word problem. In addition, by providing progressive challenge and feedback on the effects of operations, it is possible for students to create, test and improve strategic theories for a number of transformation and representation problems.

PUBLISHED MATERIAL: ACZEL, J.C. (1998). 'Learning algebraic strategies using a computerised balance model'. Proceedings of the 22nd International Conference for the Psychology of Mathematics Education, Stellenbosch, South Africa.

STATUS: Individual research

DATE OF RESEARCH: 1995-1998

KEYWORDS: **algebra; computer uses in education; equations - mathematics; information technology; mathematics education; models**

2043

Department of Educational Studies, 15 Norham Gardens, Oxford OX2 6PY
01865 274024

Nardi, E. Dr; Hegedus, S. Dr; *Supervisor*: Jaworski, B. Dr

Characterisations and issues of mathematics teaching in undergraduate tutorials

ABSTRACT: This project is a study of mathematics teaching at undergraduate level. It is a one-year collaborative project between researchers in mathematics education and university mathematics teachers. It draws on the findings from 2 previous studies: 1) a detailed study of first-year undergraduates' learning difficulties in their encounter with the abstractions of advanced mathematics within a tutorial-based pedagogy; and 2) a study of the tutors' responses to and interpretations of these difficulties. The study moves beyond a focus on mathematical learning to a study of the pedagogical processes involved in first-year undergraduate teaching and their relationship to epistemological and cognitive processes previously conceptualised. Its aim is, firstly, to characterise current conceptualisations of mathematics teaching as reflected in practice and interpreted by tutors and researchers; and secondly to identify issues arising from these practices and their implications for mathematical learning. Tutorials, taught by participant tutors, are observed by the researchers who make field notes but take no part in the teaching. Through semi-structured (audio-recorded) interviews, tutors are drawn into an identification and exploration of teaching approaches and their relationship to epistemological issues in the mathematical content of the tutorial and to the cognitive and affective dimensions of the students' learning. Subsequently significant episodes are identified and categorised. The analysis results in documentation and grouping of practices, processes and the thinking of participants. Researcher interpretations are fed back to participants for respondent validation and to initiate discussion on the implications of the research findings for future practices. Periodic meetings of tutors and researchers encourage the collaborative nature of the research and support validatory procedures. They provide a forum through which the implications of the project for developments in mathematics teaching at this level can be addressed.

STATUS: Sponsored project

SOURCE OF GRANT: Economic and Social Research Council £36,138

DATE OF RESEARCH: 1998-continuing

KEYWORDS: **higher education; mathematics education; teaching methods**

2044

Department of Educational Studies, 15 Norham Gardens, Oxford OX2 6PY
01865 274024

Summers, M. Mr; Kruger, C. Mr; Childs, A. Dr; Mant, J. Mrs

Developing primary school teachers' understanding of the science for environmental issues

ABSTRACT: The over-riding aim is to contribute to the development of effective environmental education in primary schools. The specific objectives are to: 1) explore primary school teachers' understanding of key environmental concepts; 2) identify: a) misconceptions; b) areas of partial understanding, and c) missing concepts; 3) produce a practical guide for preservice and inservice teacher education which will: a) provide accounts of the science of environmental issues at a level appropriate for primary school teachers; b) identify typical misconceptions and compare these with a scientific perspective; c) suggest how the scientific concepts underpinning an understanding of environmental issues can be incorporated into teacher education courses (especially the new Initial Teacher Training National Curriculum for Primary Science); and National Curriculum work in schools. Indepth interviews with an opportunity sample of 24 primary teachers are being used to elicit existing understanding of the targeted issues (energy use, pollution, the carbon cycle, sustainability, biodiversity, ozone, global warming, life-cycle analysis). The findings will be used to construct survey questionnaires designed to uncover the prevalence of different conceptions in these areas in a much larger sample of teachers.

STATUS: Sponsored project

SOURCE OF GRANT: Esso UK PLC £10,000; ICI £8,000

DATE OF RESEARCH: 1998-continuing

KEYWORDS: **environment; environmental education; primary education; primary school teachers; science education**

2045

Department of Educational Studies, 15 Norham Gardens, Oxford OX2 6PY
01865 274024

Walford, G. Dr

Faith-based schools: a comparative study of England and the Netherlands

ABSTRACT: This research will examine and compare current state policy and practice on faith-based schools in Britain and the Netherlands. To develop a genuine comparative approach, the first stage of the research

will investigate the historical development of each educational system within its social and historical context. While all religious schools will be considered, the research will have a particular focus on state-funded schools for religious minorities - in particular, Muslim and fundamentalist Christian schools. Information will be gained about current Government policy and practice through published documentation and a series of interviews with politicians, officials and religious leaders in each country. Such indepth interviews with those with power in education have been shown in previous research to be highly informative. In addition to broad issues of policy, these interviews will focus on the potential and real equity effects of state-funded faith-based schools. The third stage of the research will consist of a series of case studies of schools and their local environment in each country. Four case studies will be conducted in each country - two being of Muslim schools and two of fundamentalist Christian schools. The case studies selected for more intensive study will be chosen for their theoretical rather than statistical significance. A form of 'compressed ethnography' will be used to build an account of the nature of each school, focusing on the equity effects of such state-funded schools for children within the school, and those in the neighbourhood.

PUBLISHED MATERIAL: WALFORD, G. (1994). 'The new religious grant-maintained schools', Educational Management and Administration, Vol 22, No 2, pp.123-130. ; WALFORD, G. (1995). 'Faith-based grant-maintained schools: selective international policy borrowing from The Netherlands', Journal of Education Policy, Vol 10, No 3, pp.245-257. ; WALFORD, G. (1995). 'The Christian schools campaign - a successful educational pressure group?', British Educational Research Journal, Vol 21, No 4, pp.451-464. ; WALFORD, G. (1997). 'Sponsored grant-maintained schools: extending the franchise?', Oxford Review of Education, Vol 23, No 1, pp.31-44. ; WALFORD, G. (1998). 'Durkheim, democracy and diversity: some thoughts on recent changes in England'. In: WALFORD, G. & PICKERING, W.S.F. (Eds). Durkheim and modern education. Routledge International Studies in the Philosophy of Education, Vol 6. London and New York: Routledge.

STATUS: Sponsored project

SOURCE OF GRANT: Spencer Foundation £70,000

DATE OF RESEARCH: 1998-continuing

KEYWORDS: **christianity; comparative education; islamic education; netherlands; religion and education; voluntary schools**

2046

Department of Educational Studies, 15 Norham Gardens, Oxford OX2 6PY
01865 274024

Scrivener, C. Mr; *Supervisor*: Corney, G. Mr

Teaching of local environmental issues in geography

ABSTRACT: Issues-based studies are characteristic of a people-environment approach to geography. The teaching of local environmental issues within the geography curriculum provides teachers with the opportunity to connect classroom learning to pupils' direct experiences. Such issues are complex and value-laden, often controversial, likely to be ephemeral and time-bound, and represent a contrast to the common subject matter of geography. This has implications for the pedagogical practices associated with teaching and learning. Local environmental issues also provide the opportunity for teachers and pupils, working collaboratively, to create 'new knowledge' which may have considerable value to the local community within which it is generated. A local environmental issue may provide a context for pupils to move beyond awareness raising and to engage in sustainable environmental practices through practical action. The purpose of the research is to investigate the thinking and practice of geography teachers who use local environmental issues in their teaching, and to discover how and why they plan and organise teaching and learning activities. This is a qualitative study which adopts a case study approach involving an indepth study of the thinking and practice of a small number of teachers. Data is collected through semi-structured interviews, classroom observation and related interviews. Analysis is being undertaken through 'constant comparative' categorisation.

STATUS: Individual research

DATE OF RESEARCH: 1997-continuing

KEYWORDS: **controversial issues - course content; environmental education; geography; local issues; teaching methods**

2047

Department of Educational Studies, 15 Norham Gardens, Oxford
OX2 6PY
01865 274024
Cardiff University, School of Education, Senghennydd Road, Cardiff
CF2 4YG
01222 874000
London University, Institute of Education, 20 Bedford Way, London
WC1H 0AL
0171 580 1122

Sylva, K. Prof.; Melhuish, E. Prof.; Sammons, P. Dr; Siraj-Blatchford, I. Dr

Effective provision of preschool education

ABSTRACT: This project compares and contrasts the developmental progress, including performance at key stage 1, of 3,000 children from a wide range of social and cultural backgrounds, some of whom are second language learners of English, who have differing preschool experiences as well as early entry to reception from homes. The project will establish whether some preschool centres are more effective than others in promoting children's cognitive and social/emotional development during the preschool years (3 to 5) and during the beginning of primary educatiion (4 plus to 7 years). The individual characteristics ('quality' indicators) of preschool education in centres found to be most and least effective will be identified. The study adopts a 'school effectiveness' design and incorporates qualitative methods as well.

STATUS: Sponsored project

SOURCE OF GRANT: Department for Education and Employment
£1,428,295

DATE OF RESEARCH: 1997-continuing

KEYWORDS: **early childhood education; key stage 1; nursery education; outcomes of education; preschool education; preschool effectiveness; primary education; school effectiveness**

2048

Department of Educational Studies, 15 Norham Gardens, Oxford
OX2 6PY
01865 274024
Institute of Psychiatry, De Crespigny Park, London SE5 8AF
0171 919 3467

Nikapota, A. Dr; Cox, A. Prof.; Sylva, K. Prof.

Cross cultural study of emotional and behavioural problems in children: families' perceptions and ways of using resources

ABSTRACT: This project will explore cross-cultural differences in parent perceptions of child behavioural and emotional problems, with specific behaviours shown by their child. Enquiry will be made into criteria used by them in rating behaviours which could indicate the existence of emotional or behavioural problems in their children and ways of dealing with such problems. Information will also be obtained on the constructions placed by parents on specific behaviours and, finally, on the perceived relevance and availability of child mental health resources. Cultural differences will be looked at in relation to between group comparison of three ethnic groups and within group comparison.

STATUS: Sponsored project

DATE OF RESEARCH: 1995-1997

KEYWORDS: **child psychiatry; cross cultural studies; emotional and behavioural difficulties; ethnic groups; family problems; parent attitudes; special educational needs**

2049

Department of Educational Studies, 15 Norham Gardens, Oxford
OX2 6PY
01865 274024
Institute of Psychiatry, Department of Child and Adolescent Psychiatry,
De Crespigny Park, London SE5 8AF
0171 919 3467

Scott, S. Dr; Sylva, K. Prof.

Enabling parents: supporting specific parenting skills with a community programme

ABSTRACT: This study investigates the effects of an innovative intervention programme to support parents' management of child behaviour and learning. From a community sample of 600 parents of 5 year-old children, 120 parents of the most vulnerable children will be selected to participate in the project. Half the parents will receive intensive intervention, the remaining 60 receive less intensive, advice-only telephone support. The intervention programme aims to help parents to develop the positive social skills of their children and to enhance their literacy - the aim of this project is to assess the effectiveness on both sets of outcomes.

STATUS: Sponsored project

DATE OF RESEARCH: 1998-continuing

KEYWORDS: **intervention; literacy; parent education; parent participation; parent pupil relationship; pupil behaviour**

2050

Department of Educational Studies, 15 Norham Gardens, Oxford
OX2 6PY
01865 274024
London University, Institute of Education, 20 Bedford Way, London
WC1H 0AL
0171 580 1122

Corney, G. Mr; *Supervisor*: Slater, F. Dr

Student geography teachers' thinking and teaching about environmental issues

ABSTRACT: Teaching about environmental issues is an important part of the secondary school geography curriculum. It presents teachers with choices about the nature of subject matter and approaches to teaching and learning. Student teachers begin their Postgraduate Certificate in Education (PGCE) course with experiences, beliefs and pre-conceptions about the nature of subject matter and approaches to teaching and learning; during their course they have experiences which may influence their beliefs, and they have opportunity to put their beliefs into practice. The purpose of the research is to investigate their beliefs and practice in this area during their PGCE course, and to try to discover how these are influenced by various factors. This is a qualitative study consisting of several types of data. Data was collected for a complete cohort of 30 geography student teachers through a structured writing exercise on 3 occasions during the year; 5 students were followed as case studies, and additional data was collected through semi-structured interviews, classroom observation and related interviews. Analysis is being undertaken through 'constant comparative' categorisation. Further analysis is needed before results and conclusions are identified.

PUBLISHED MATERIAL: CORNEY, G.J. (1994). 'Teaching environmental topics by beginning geography teachers'. Proceedings of the Environmental Education in the 21st Century International Conference on Environmental Education, Guanzhou, China, 1994. ; CORNEY, G.J. (1995). 'An eclectic approach to qualitative research design'. In: WILLIAMS, M. (Ed). Understanding geographical and environmental education: the role of research. London: Cassell. ; CORNEY, G.J. (1997). 'Conceptions of environmental education'. In: SLATER, F., LAMBERT, D. & LINES, D. (Eds). Education, environment and economy. London: University of London, Institute of Education. ; CORNEY, G.J. (1998). 'Learning to teach environmental issues', International Research in Geographical and Environmental Education, Vol 7, No 2, pp.90-105.

STATUS: Individual research

DATE OF RESEARCH: 1992-continuing

KEYWORDS: **environmental education; geography; preservice teacher education; student teacher attitudes; student teachers; values**

2051

Department of Educational Studies, 15 Norham Gardens, Oxford
OX2 6PY
01865 274024
London University, Institute of Education, Thomas Coram Research
Unit, 27-28 Woburn Square, London WC1H 0AA
0171 612 6957

Sylva, K. Prof.; Hurry, J. Dr

Early reading intervention: long term effects and costs

ABSTRACT: This study is the third follow-up assessment of children's reading and spelling progress after intervention at the age of 6 years. The original research evaluated the effectiveness of Reading Recovery and specifically phonological training up to 15 months after post intervention. In the present study the researchers seek to establish the long-term affects of both Reading Recovery and phonological training, 3 and a half years after intervention. In the summer term of 1994, 366 children of the original 390 were traced and tested. In the autumn term 339 of these children were traced and tested again. In addition to testing the original cohort of children some of their classmates have also been tested. Once the data are prepared the researchers will compare both children who received Reading Recovery and those who received the phonological intervention with the original control group. These comparisons will allow the researchers to determine the extent to which either intervention has a significant effect after 3 and a half years.

STATUS: Sponsored project

SOURCE OF GRANT: School Curriculum and Assessment Authority

DATE OF RESEARCH: 1996-1997

KEYWORDS: intervention; primary education; pupil improvement; reading ability; reading difficulties; reading teaching; remedial programmes; remedial reading

2052

Department of Educational Studies, 15 Norham Gardens, Oxford OX2 6PY
01865 274024
Oxford University, Institute of Economics and Statistics, St Cross Building, Manor Road, Oxford OX3 3UL
01865 276434
Warwick University, Industrial Relations Research Unit, Warwick Business School, Coventry CV4 7AL
01203 524275

Pring, R. Prof.; Mayhew, K. Mr; Keep, E. Dr

Economic and Social Research Council Centre for knowledge, skills and organisational performance

ABSTRACT: While the supply of knowledge and skills is important to economic success, it is increasingly recognised that demand for them, and their usage within the productive process, are equally critical. Conventional wisdom maintains that skills now form the sole source of sustainable competitive advantage within developed economies. Evidence, however, is mounting that many UK firms are not pursuing competitive advantage through skills, and that linkages between knowledge, skills and economic performance are more complex and conditional than had been assumed. Much is known about mechanisms of skill supply, much less about the demand for and deployment of skills in employment and their place within firms' competitive strategies. The Centre will examine these issues by focusing on a causal cycle that reintegrates demand and supply; acquisition, deployment and management of skill; and factors internal and external to the organisation that influence the role skills play in determining performance. Such research will address concerns central to major policy and theoretical debates. The research will be organised around four interlocking, multidisciplinary themes: 1) the nature, origin and relative force of different models of competitive advantage and the role skills play within them; 2) the operationalisation of competitive and skill usage strategies; 3) the relationship between the supply of, demand for, and deployment of knowledge and skills; 4) the evaluation of policy interventions and institutional mechanisms that could encourage adoption of high skills strategies.

STATUS: Sponsored project

SOURCE OF GRANT: Economic and Social Research Council £1,920,000

DATE OF RESEARCH: 1998-continuing

KEYWORDS: employment; knowledge; skill development; skills; training

2053

Department of Educational Studies, 15 Norham Gardens, Oxford OX2 6PY
01865 274024
South Bank University, School of Computing, Information Systems and Mathematics, 103 Borough Road, London SE1 0AA
0171 928 8989

Watson, A. Ms; *Supervisors*: Lerman, S. Dr; Davies, C. Dr

An investigation into how teachers make judgements about what pupils know and can do in mathematics

ABSTRACT: The aim of the project is to describe the variety of ways teachers informally assess pupils' mathematics, what kinds of evidence they recognise and how they use these to form judgements of their pupils. The study is within the UK context which expects continuous assessment of mathematics to be planned and recorded by teachers, incorporated into future planning and included as part of formal assessment at the end of each National Curriculum key stage. Informal interviews were carried out with 30 teachers from primary, middle and secondary phases, concentrating on Years 6 and 7. A further study was undertaken to observe 10 pupils in 2 mathematics classrooms and compare the researcher's observations to the teachers' development of views about their mathematical achievement and potential during one term's work. The results suggest that informal assessment is complex, intimately bound up with every aspect of teaching and owing much to a range of non-mathematical factors and influences. It is argued that all informal judgements contribute to high-stakes decisions in mathematics teaching, such as grouping, setting and levels of entry as well as final grading. Teachers' professional judgements need to be recognised as potential sources of unfairness being, to a large extent, based on non-mathematical, incomplete evidence and unexamined inferences.

PUBLISHED MATERIAL: WATSON, A. (1995). 'Evidence for pupils' mathematics achievements', For the Learning of Mathematics, Vol 15, No 1, pp.16-20. ; WATSON, A. (1996). 'Teachers' notions of ability', Mathematics Education Review, Vol 8, pp.27-35. ; WATSON, A. (1997). 'Coming to know pupils: a study of informal teacher assessment of mathematics'. Proceedings of the 21st Conference of International Group for Psychology of Maths Education.

STATUS: Individual research

DATE OF RESEARCH: 1994-1998

KEYWORDS: assessment; assessment by teachers; mathematics education; primary education; secondary education

2054

Department of Educational Studies, 15 Norham Gardens, Oxford OX2 6PY
01865 274024
University of London, Royal Free Hospital, School of Medicine, Leopold Muller Department of Child and Family Mental Health, Rowland Hill Street, London NW3 4PF
0171 830 2860

Sylva, K. Prof.; Stein, A. Prof.; Leach, P. Dr

Families, children and childcare

ABSTRACT: This project studies different ways young children are cared for and how this influences the development of children and their families. The sample will be broadly representative of babies born in the UK and 600 families in London and 600 families in Oxfordshire will take part. The project starts while families are planning and making their earliest child care choices and stays in touch while parents, care providers and children are experiencing different child care arrangements. This is a unique opportunity to increase the researchers' understanding of the influence of different types of child care, personal or purchased, on children's developments.

STATUS: Sponsored project

DATE OF RESEARCH: 1997-continuing

KEYWORDS: child caregivers; child development; child minding; day care; family life; young children

2055

Department of Educational Studies, 15 Norham Gardens, Oxford OX2 6PY
01865 274024
Warwick University, Centre for Education and Industry, Coventry CV4 7AL
01203 523523

Pring, R. Prof. ; Hayward, G. Dr ; Huddleston, P. Mrs

Skills, knowledge and organisational performance (Theme 3: vocational education and training)

ABSTRACT: Theme 3 addresses questions concerned with the vocational benefits of certain intervention in full-time and part-time education and training. By 'vocational benefits' is meant the economic and employment advantages it gives both to individuals and to society at large. Such an enquiry will look at the effects of curriculum developments, changing qualifications, recruitment and retention post-16, access to higher education and lifelong learning. The different enquiries will include literature review of the evidence in terms of policy related questions; case studies of young people and of institutions over a period of time, etc. The research is at an early stage and, through networking and conference, more exact questions are being formulated.

STATUS: Sponsored project

SOURCE OF GRANT: Economic and Social Research Council £2,000,000; Oxford University; Warwick University

DATE OF RESEARCH: 1998-continuing

KEYWORDS: **skill development; skills; training; vocational education; work education relationship**

Paisley University

2056

Craigie Campus in Ayr, Faculty of Education, Beech Grove, Ayr KA8 0SR
01292 886000

Gibson, G. Mr

Student teachers' views on gender issues in education

ABSTRACT: A small group of female students in the third year of a four year B.Ed (Primary) course at a Scottish university took part in paired discussion of a number of questions concerning the effects of gender differences in education. Analysis of transcripts suggested that students held contradictory views about particular issues, while advocating gender equality as a broad aim. Views about gender in education seemed to derive from a liberal feminist 'equal opportunities' perspective, with no evidence being found of any more radical frameworks being used to conceptualise the influences of gender differences in schools. These findings are in keeping with earlier researchers' findings about attitudes of teachers and student teachers towards gender issues. The findings led to some changes in course design in the faculty where it was carried out. Further work is planned in relation to students who have taken the amended courses.

STATUS: Individual research

DATE OF RESEARCH: 1992-continuing

KEYWORDS: **gender equality; preservice teacher education; sex differences; student teacher attitudes; student teachers**

2057

Craigie Campus in Ayr, Faculty of Education, Beech Grove, Ayr KA8 0SR
01292 886000

Livingston, K. Ms; *Supervisor*: Humes, W. Dr

The European dimension in teacher education: a comparative study

ABSTRACT: This research project is carrying out an investigation into the European dimension in education. It focuses particularly on teacher education. It hopes to identify the influences that shape changes in teacher education in relation to the European dimension at an institutional and individual lecturer level. The project includes 5 countries, namely, the Netherlands, Denmark, Slovakia, Portugal and Scotland. The aims of the project are to: 1) analyse the influence of European policy documents which seek to encourage the implementation of a European dimension in education; 2) find out if there are national policy documents which provide direction on incorporating a European dimension in education; 3) analyse course documentation in order to identify the inclusion of a European dimension in teacher education in different European countries; 4) investigate teacher educators' understanding of the definition of the European dimension in education and the rationale for its inclusion in teacher education courses; 5) compare the implementation of the European dimension in different European countries; 6) provide examples of good practice in the implementation of the European dimension in teacher education. The methodology for the project includes: 1) content analysis of European and national documents related to the promotion of the European dimension in education; 2) analysis of specific teacher education course documentation which includes the European dimension; 3) textual analysis of the responses of indepth semi-structured interviews carried out with teacher educators in different institutions, ministries of education officials and staff from intermediary non-governmental agencies; 4) cross-analysis of the interview responses from different European countries.

STATUS: Individual research

DATE OF RESEARCH: 1995-continuing

KEYWORDS: **comparative education; denmark; european dimension; european studies; netherlands; portugal; preservice teacher education; scotland; slovakia**

Peter Clyne Associates

2058

Education and Training Consultancy, 33 Altenburg Gardens, London SW11 1JH
0171 228 5946

Clyne, P. Mr

Review of the use by the Preschool Playgroups Association of its grant from the Department for Education

ABSTRACT: The objective of this study is to carry out an independent evaluation of the effectiveness of the work of the regional training and development officers and branch tutor organisers employed by the Preschool Playgroups Association and of the value of the Diploma in Playgroup Practice. The methods used include: (1) structured interviews with the staff concerned; (2) collection of job descriptions and training statistics; (3) visits to a range of training courses in different parts of the country; (4) visits to playgroups led by trained and untrained staff; and (5) reading and noting published curriculum and training materials.

STATUS: Sponsored project

SOURCE OF GRANT: Department for Education £16,925

DATE OF RESEARCH: 1993-1993

KEYWORDS: **child caregivers; play groups; preschool education; qualifications; training**

Plymouth University

2059

Enterprise Unit, 92 Cobourg Street, Plymouth PL4 8AA
01752 232376

Davies, J. Mr

Mentors in education and training

ABSTRACT: Mentors were introduced into Plymouth University's inservice Certificate in Education course in 1985 as a means of providing a link between the students' course of study and their place of work. As mentors have come to take an increasingly important role in education and training, so a need for mentor training has been identified. In order to design coherent training programmes, it is essential to have a clear view of the roles of both mentors and proteges. Through the literature, this research aims to clarify and identify established roles, to create a typology, and to suggest training programmes appropriate to the different roles.

STATUS: Sponsored project

SOURCE OF GRANT: Plymouth University: Rolle Faculty of Education £750; Plymouth University: Enterprise in Higher Education £750

DATE OF RESEARCH: 1991-1993

KEYWORDS: **inservice teacher education; mentors; training**

2060

Department of Mathematics and Statistics, Centre for Teaching Mathematics, Drake Circus, Plymouth PL4 8AA
01752 600600

Maull, W. Dr; *Supervisors*: Berry, J. Prof.; Stockel, C. Dr

Teaching differential equations using multimedia methods

ABSTRACT: Various bodies have expressed concerns over the falling mathematical ability of engineering undergraduates. In an experiment at Plymouth the researcher observed engineering and mathematics students carrying out the same mathematical modelling exercise, and noted significant different differences. It is proposed that the way in which engineers and engineering students 'do mathematics' is different and that the mathematics teaching of engineering students should take this into account. A questionnaire has been devised which asks respondents to rank various options in order of how well they represent a particular idea or situation, or how closely they resemble a target idea. From the preferences expressed, some picture of the mathematical ideas of the respondents can be built up. After a pilot study, about 40 each engineering and mathematics undergraduates have been questioned at the start of their first year, and again at the end of their first year. Final year students are also being questioned at the end of their studies. Groups of L6 and U6 A-level mathematics pupils and engineering graduates working in local manufacturing companies are also being sampled as a comparison. The pilot study showed an apparent maturing of mathematical ideas between final year engineering students and practising engineers. The main study appears to show slight differences between the students of mathematics and engineering at intake: these are expected to increase as they progress through their courses. In the light of these results, a multimedia package is being developed to teach differential equations concepts to engineering students in a modelling context.

PUBLISHED MATERIAL: MAULL, W., BERRY, J. & STOCKEL, C. (1995). 'Teaching engineering mathematics through computer technology'. In: Proceedings of the 13th International Conference on Production Research, Jerusalem, 1995.

STATUS: Individual research

DATE OF RESEARCH: 1994-1997

KEYWORDS: **concept formation; engineering education; higher education; mathematical concepts; mathematics education; students**

2061

Department of Mathematics and Statistics, Centre for Teaching Mathematics, Drake Circus, Plymouth PL4 8AA
01752 600600

McMichael, P. Mr; Marcer, M. Ms; Green, K. Ms; *Supervisors*: Rowlands, S. Dr; Graham, E. Dr; Berry, J. Prof.

Student conceptual understanding in mechanics

ABSTRACT: The majority of students hold intuitive ideas about concepts in mechanics. These intuitive ideas are often in conflict with reality. For example, many students maintain that the force acting on a ball thrown upward is the force given by the thrower and is stored in the object. This leads to an upward force on an object during its upward motion. The Socratic method of strategic questioning is a teaching strategy to try to challenge and undo student misconceptions. The aim of this research project is to develop and carry out the Socratic method with school children.

PUBLISHED MATERIAL: ROWLANDS, S., GRAHAM, E. & BERRY, J. (1998). 'Identifying stumbling blocks in the development of student understanding of moments of forces', International Journal of Mathematics in Science and Technology, Vol 29, No 4, pp.511-531.

STATUS: Individual research

DATE OF RESEARCH: 1997-continuing

KEYWORDS: **concept formation; mathematics education; mechanics - physics; questioning techniques**

2062

Department of Mathematics and Statistics, Centre for Teaching Mathematics, Drake Circus, Plymouth PL4 8AA
01752 600600

Walker, B. Mr; Graham, E. Dr; *Supervisors*: Graham, E. Dr; Berry, J. Prof.; Patrick, M. Dr

Research in the use of telematics for tutorial support in mathematics

ABSTRACT: The project is beginning to look at whether video conferencing can be used to provide mathematics support for students. The project will focus on the experiences of students working in a workshop environment, but that need mathematics support. The experiences of students having face-to-face tutorials will be compared with those who have them via video conferencing. At the current stage of the work, a programme of research is being formulated.

STATUS: Individual research

DATE OF RESEARCH: 1998-continuing

KEYWORDS: **higher education; mathematics education; telecommunications; teleconferencing; tutorials**

2063

Department of Mathematics and Statistics, Centre for Teaching Mathematics, Drake Circus, Plymouth PL4 8AA
01752 600600
Leeds University, School of Education, Leeds LS2 9JT
01132 431751

Berry, J. Prof.; Johnson P. Mr; Maull, W. Dr; Monaghan, J. Dr

Assessment using computer algebra systems

ABSTRACT: The introduction of advanced hand held technology into the teaching and learning of mathematics will have a considerable effect on the syllabus and assessment of mathematics at all levels. For mathematics at upper secondary level it is believed that weak students gain their marks from routine questions of a type that advanced calculators would trivialise. This research project will examine A-level mathematics scripts of students on questions which have routine and non-routine parts. The question to be examined is, do lower attaining students gain a significant number of their marks on the routine parts of such questions.

STATUS: Collaborative

DATE OF RESEARCH: 1998-continuing

KEYWORDS: **algebra; assessment; calculators; computer uses in education; mathematics education; secondary education**

2064

Department of Mathematics and Statistics, Centre for Teaching Mathematics, Drake Circus, Plymouth PL4 8AA
01752 600600
Office of the Superintendent of Manhattan High Schools, 122 Amsterdam Avenue, New York, NY 10023

Picker, S. Ms; *Supervisors*: Berry, J. Prof.; Maull, W. Dr

Student beliefs and perceptions of mathematics

ABSTRACT: The aim of this project is to research secondary students' beliefs about mathematics and investigate students' perceptions of mathematicians and what mathematicians do. One aspect of the research will be to determine if different applications of mathematics can serve as an intervention in students who have been identified as having misconceptions about mathematics and to see if their beliefs have changed over time of the course.

PUBLISHED MATERIAL: PICKER, S. (1997). 'Using discrete mathematics to give remedial students a second chance'. In: ROSENSTEIN, J.G., FRANZBLAU, D.S. & ROBERTS, F.S. (Eds). Discrete mathematics in the schools. Series in Discrete Mathematics and Theoretical Science No 36. Corby: American Mathematical Society.

STATUS: Individual research

DATE OF RESEARCH: 1997-continuing

KEYWORDS: **mathematics education; pupil attitudes; secondary education; secondary school pupils**

2065

Department of Mathematics and Statistics, Drake Circus, Plymouth PL4 8AA
01752 600600
Plymouth University, Department of Psychology, Drake Circus, Plymouth PL4 8AA

Fortescue-Hubbard, W. Ms; *Supervisors*: Dyke, P. Prof.; Shaw, S. Dr; Edworthy, J. Dr

A study into the development of a game for learning multiplication tables

ABSTRACT: There is a statutory requirement for pupils to have 'mental recall' of multiplication and division facts by level 4 of the National Curriculum as stated in the orders of September 1995. Traditionally multiplication tables have been associated with drudgery, boredom and frustration, for some it is an overwhelming experience. The experience may leave a lasting impression, and may exclude any other, leading children to have a harmful attitude to mathematics. Practice is the medium suggested to strengthen association between factors and product in a basic fact leading to automatic activation. Research has established that when errors are made, immediate corrective feedback prevents students from practising incorrect responses. Random practice develops the ability to access efficiently the component skills in a problem-solving situation, leading to superior retention of skills. Material that is generated rather than simply read has a distinct retention advantage. Taking the cognitive aspects discussed into account the main aim of the study was to design a learning apparatus/game to assist pupils and adults to gain mastery of multiplication and division tables, and provide a theoretical analysis of its effectiveness. The game Perfect Times has now been developed and granted a patent and published. The associated properties are now receiving further investigation. An investigation has also been carried out into the current teaching methods employed to teach mastery of multiplication tables and assess mental recall. An experimental comparison of methods for teaching mastery of multiplication and division tables is to be carried out in Years 5 and 6. The sample is to be 1,200 pupils from 20 different schools. The methods will be Perfect Times, Cover, Copy and Compare, traditional chanting, and controls. This is to be a 3-way factorial design with 2 fixed factors: the treatment conditions and Year group, and a random factor: a school with one covariate ability, as defined by Mathematics National Curriculum Level. The analysis will be the analysis of covariance. The different teaching methods employed will be summarised in an annotated bibliography.

PUBLISHED MATERIAL: FORTESCUE-HUBBARD, W. (1995). '"Perfect times" providing a possible answer for adults to learn mastery of multiplication tables and provide a positive learning experience'. A workshop session presented at the ALM2 Conference, University of London, Goldsmiths College, London, 1995. ; FORTESCUE-HUBBARD, W. & BEERE, H.G. (1996). Perfect times: the perfect game to master multiplication tables. Teachers' Booklet. Exmouth: Southgate Publishers. ; FORTESCUE-HUBBARD, W. (1996). Perfect times: a game for teaching multiplication tables. Exmouth: Southgate Publishers. ; FORTESCUE-HUBBARD, W. (1996). 'Perfect times for multiplication', Strategies, Vol 6, No 4, pp.31-34. ; FORTESCUE-HUBBARD, W. & REID, F. (1997). 'Mastery of multiplication tables: the associated issues'. Paper presented at the British Psychological Society Conference, Edinburgh, April 1997.

STATUS: Individual research

DATE OF RESEARCH: 1994-continuing

KEYWORDS: arithmetic; games; learning activities; mathematics education; memory; mental arithmetic; multiplication tables; primary education; teaching methods

2066

Faculty of Arts and Education, Rolle School of Education, Douglas Avenue, Exmouth EX8 2AT
01395 255309

Silver, H. Prof.

Good schools, effective schools: judgements and their history

ABSTRACT: A study of the development of research interests in effective schools and school differences in the 1970s-1980s, in the United States and Britain, in a historical context. The investigation covers perceptions of what has constituted a good school, who has had the power to define what is good, and the criteria that have been used for different kinds of schooling. It considers the difference between 19th and earlier 20th century judgements about the quality of schooling and the research-based interest in effective schools after the decline in confidence in the outcomes of schooling in the late 1960s and early 1970s. It looks at the implementation of effective schools criteria in individual American states and in Congressional legislation in 1988. The study also examines alternatives to school reform based on the effective schools research - in the US essential and accelerated schools and forms of restructuring, and in the UK government-sponsored approaches to curricula and assessment. The study is mainly document-based, except for visits to Connecticut, Rhode Island and Washington DC to visit administrators and schools.

PUBLISHED MATERIAL: SILVER, H. (1991). 'Poverty and effective schools', Journal of Education Policy, Vol 6, No 3, pp.271-285. ; SILVER, H. (1991). Educational research and the policy environment: the case of 'effective schools', liber amoricum for H. Remak, Indiana University. ; SILVER, H. (1994). Good schools, effective schools: judgments and their history. London: Cassell.

STATUS: Individual research

DATE OF RESEARCH: 1989-1993

KEYWORDS: comparative education; educational history; educational quality; school effectiveness; united states of america

2067

Faculty of Arts and Education, Rolle School of Education, Douglas Avenue, Exmouth EX8 2AT
01395 255309

Dyer, A. Mr

Re-storying the landscape

ABSTRACT: An environmental education project aimed at using all of the arts in the interpretation and discovery of the natural world. Children are encouraged to rediscover some of the stories about particular or nearby landscapes, or invent new ones. The experimental phase of the project took place at Killerton Park near Exeter in Devon, with a group of children taking part in a 'Dragon Quest'. A day visit programme has been developed and trialled for two years with over 100 schools. Workshops, conference and consultation presentations have been given throughout Britain and Europe. The results will be published in a handbook for teachers, leaders and parents.

STATUS: Sponsored project

SOURCE OF GRANT: National Trust ; Plymouth University, jointly £1,039

DATE OF RESEARCH: 1990-continuing

KEYWORDS: environmental education; field studies; geographic location; local studies; story telling

2068

Faculty of Arts and Education, Rolle School of Education, Douglas Avenue, Exmouth EX8 2AT
01395 255309

Gill, J. Mrs; *Supervisors*: Halstead, J. Dr; Hannan, A. Dr

The nature and justifiability of the Act of Collective Worship in schools

ABSTRACT: The act of collective worship continues to be a compulsory element in the daily organisation of all maintained schools, and this legal requirement, together with the current debate on the spiritual, moral and cultural development of children and young people, constitutes the background within which this research is sited. Its aims are to: 1) examine the purpose, provision and implementation of the act of worship; 2) identify, explore and analyse its explicit and implicit features, together with the responses and perceptions of its participants; and 3) examine the issues raised, with particular reference to the development of spiritual, moral and cultural values, and the justification of its compulsory place in the curriculum of contemporary, secular and pluralist society. Data collection involves the use of observation, interview and questionnaire; this includes material from both primary and secondary schools in rural and inner-city areas, and from the public and private sectors. The study will examine the overt content and context of the act of worship and the underlying values and attitudes which are transmitted, seeking to identify the intentional and unintentional features of the hidden curriculum which are also present. Questions concerning the nature and purpose of the act of worship in a society which is both pluralist and secular, and which requires schools to provide pupils with a framework of religious and moral values, will be addressed.

STATUS: Individual research

DATE OF RESEARCH: 1993-continuing

KEYWORDS: moral development; religion and education; religious attitudes; school worship; values education

2069

Faculty of Arts and Education, Rolle School of Education, Douglas Avenue, Exmouth EX8 2AT
01395 255309

Lee, C. Mr; *Supervisors*: Hannan, A. Dr; Hayes, D. Dr; Nias, J. Prof.

Bullying in the primary school: a case study

ABSTRACT: This research is an examination of the perceptions of staff, pupils and parents of bullying in a primary school. It seeks to gain insights through a case study of a single school which is involved in developing policy and practice into incidence, definition, management and impact of a phenomenon that has received considerable recent publicity. There is a need for a body of qualitative longitudinal research which places the problem in the context of one school's perceptions and the perspectives of the children, their teachers, other staff and parents on bullying which have yet to be investigated, although some research has been undertaken into teacher perception in the secondary sector. The school is one which has been considering the issue of bullying and has been made aware of the issues and implications of the research through an ethics protocol and has been willing to permit the forms of access and research cited in the document. The case study into issues highlighted above will be conducted by semi-structured interviews with school staff, parents and pupils, and by non-participant observation. This analysis of the various perspectives on bullying is intended to facilitate greater understanding of the issue in the school context and may provide valuable information for schools as they seek to comply with the requirements of inspection criteria.

STATUS: Individual research

DATE OF RESEARCH: 1994-continuing

KEYWORDS: **bullying; discipline problems; primary education**

2070

Faculty of Arts and Education, Rolle School of Education, Douglas Avenue, Exmouth EX8 2AT
01395 255309

Tyrer, R. Mr; *Supervisors*: Rodd, J. Dr; Hannan, A. Dr; Lee, C. Mr

Analysis of the relationship between Individual Education Plans and classroom activities

ABSTRACT: The Education Act 1993 establishes the principle that pupils with special educational need who are giving 'cause for concern' should be subject to a 5-stage model of assessment. From stage 2 each pupil should have an Individual Education Plan (IEP) giving clear details of specific provision, programmes, targets and time limits. There is a general consensus that IEPs should be functional and age appropriate, but there is evidence to strongly suggest that there is little relationship between the content of the IEP and instructional activities. The aim of this research is to provide information on the overall value of the process centred on IEPs by examining the quality of practice. Following a literature search and construction of an ethics protocol, it is proposed, at this stage, to examine the IEPs of pupils in Year 6, along with other qualitative data, and follow them through Year 7 and the transition to secondary school. The method will involve the analysis of IEPs, the categorisation of goals into exclusive domains which will allow for the pupils to be rated and compared. This will be accompanied by teacher, pupil and parent interview, and classroom observation.

STATUS: Individual research

DATE OF RESEARCH: 1995-continuing

KEYWORDS: **individual education plans; individual needs; learning activities; primary education; secondary education; special educational needs**

2071

Faculty of Arts and Education, Rolle School of Education, Douglas Avenue, Exmouth EX8 2AT
01395 255309

Gulliver, J. Mr; *Supervisors*: Taylor, G. Dr; Nias, J. Prof.; Mackenzie, R. Mr

Educative encounters relating to pupils' writing in the humanities

ABSTRACT: Prompted by a concern for an empirical exploration of the past, if any, that assessment plays in supporting children's learning. this research focuses on teacher-pupil interaction in a primary classroom in relation to writing in the humanities. It is concerned with how a teacher interprets and responds to pupils' learning in continuing classroom life. It seeks answers to 2 questions: 1) How does the teacher, within the course of interaction, form ideas about pupils' learning on which they build for teaching purposes? 2) How, in interaction, does the teacher attempt to turn these ideas to educative advantage? Addressing these questions, it is believed, promises to contribute to the development of understanding of how assessment functions within a (needed) reasoned theory of how the negotiation of meaning as socially arrived at could be intrepreted as a pedagogical axiom (Bruner, 1986, Actual minds, possible worlds). The approach is interpretive. It centres on the work of a single teacher with a whole class in a primary school. It is primarily based on stimulated recall techniques to elicit the teacher's thinking in action. In its current phase, now nearing completion, it involves the analysis of the teacher's thinking about the children's actions at observational interpretive and evaluative levels.

STATUS: Individual research

DATE OF RESEARCH: 1993-1997

KEYWORDS: **assessment; assessment by teachers; classroom research; primary education; primary school teachers; teacher pupil relationship**

2072

Faculty of Arts and Education, Rolle School of Education, Douglas Avenue, Exmouth EX8 2AT
01395 255309

Lewis, M. Mrs

Using parody to enhance children's understanding of written generic structures

ABSTRACT: A small scale pilot study to investigate whether using fiction picture books that parody non-fiction genre (e.g. 'How dogs really work' by Alan Snow, which parodies a workshop manual), can help develop children's understanding of the generic structure of the type of text that is being parodied. Picture book parody texts are growing in number and are common place in the book collections of primary classrooms. We do not know what children understand of such texts and whether they confuse or illuminate their subsequent understanding of the non-fiction genre thus parodied. As picture books are often aimed at the younger, and therefore less experienced, readers it is unclear whether they even recognise that a parody is being offered them. If they do 'get the joke' this implies an understanding of the structures and language features characteristic of the textual genre being parodied. Case study data was collected from working with a mixed ability group of Year 3 and Year 5 children. Their initial reactions to various types of text were recorded, work was undertaken using parody texts and their subsequent responses on returning to the original text type was noted. The data is in the process of being examined and written up and it is not yet possible to give conclusions.

STATUS: Sponsored project

SOURCE OF GRANT: Plymouth University £1,400

DATE OF RESEARCH: 1996-1997

KEYWORDS: **books; childrens literature; literary genres; nonfiction; parody; primary education; reading**

2073

Faculty of Arts and Education, Rolle School of Education, Douglas Avenue, Exmouth EX8 2AT
01395 255309

Sharp, J. Mr

Children's astronomy

ABSTRACT: Astronomy is an established subdomain within the primary science component of a centrally organised National Curriculum of subjects currently operating in maintained schools throughout England and Wales. Witnessed also by its presence in the primary science curricula of other countries throughout the world, astronomy education provision is clearly thought to carry considerable educational value. Despite this, relatively little is known about the nature and development of children's ideas in the field of learning astronomy itself, particularly with regard to learning outcomes in classroom situations. Research currently under way is directed towards the following questions: 1) To what extent does lerning and scientific conceptualization take place over time? (developmental study of 7, 9 and 11 year-olds). 2) To what extent does learning and scientific conceptualization take place after 'formal instruction'? (quasi-experimental study of 10-11 year-olds). 3) What are the learning routes and pathways involved in the learning process?

PUBLISHED MATERIAL: SHARP, J.G. (1993). 'Earth and space science: missing link or lost cause?', Teaching Earth Sciences, Vol 18, No 1, pp.29-30. ; SHARP, J.G. (1995). 'Children's astronomy: implications for curriculum developments at key stage 1 and the future of infant science in England and Wales', International Journal of Early Years Education, Vol 3, No 3, pp.17-49.; SHARP, J.G. (1996). 'Children's astronomical beliefs: a preliminary study of Year 6 children in South-West England', International Journal of Science Education, Vol 18, No 6, pp.685-712. ; SHARP, J.G. & HITCHIN, R. (1996). 'Up, up and away: activities for introducing your class to the earth and beyond', Primary Science Review, Vol 44, pp.3-5.

STATUS: Individual research

DATE OF RESEARCH: 1993-continuing

KEYWORDS: **astronomy; science education**

2074

Faculty of Arts and Education, Rolle School of Education, Douglas Avenue, Exmouth EX8 2AT
01395 255309

Hannan, A. Dr; Enright, H. Dr; Ballard, P. Dr

Using research: comparing teachers, doctors (GPs) and surgeons

ABSTRACT: Professor David Hargreaves, in his 1996 lecture to the Teacher Training Agency, argued that educational research should and could have much more relevance for, and impact on, the professional practice of teachers than it now has. He compared teachers and doctors in terms of the use they made of research and advocated that teaching should shift towards evidence-based practice on the medical model. This project attempts to provide some preliminary evidence about the comparisons made by reporting the results of a pilot survey of teachers in 4 schools (1 secondary, 1 primary, 1 junior and 1 infant), GPs in 5 group practices and surgeons in one district general hospital. The findings show how teachers, GPs and surgeons differ in their understanding of the nature of research, their use of research and their own activities as researchers.

PUBLISHED MATERIAL: HANNAN, A. & ENRIGHT, H. (1998). Using research: the results of a pilot study comparing teachers, general practitioners and surgeons, EducatiON-LINE at http://www.leeds.ac.uk/educol

STATUS: Sponsored project

SOURCE OF GRANT: Plymouth University

DATE OF RESEARCH: 1996-1998

KEYWORDS: **educational research; medical research; medicine; physicians; research; research utilisation; teachers**

2075

Faculty of Arts and Education, Rolle School of Education, Douglas Avenue, Exmouth EX8 2AT
01395 255309

Hannan, A. Dr

The Catholic church and grant-maintained status for schools

ABSTRACT: A survey has been undertaken of every Catholic grant-maintained (GM) school in England to ascertain the views of headteachers, on the process of 'opting out' of local education authority (LEA) control and the moral considerations involved with particular reference to the position of the Catholic church. Further information has been gathered on such issues by means of a two-hour interview with a Roman Catholic bishop involved in the establishment of a GM school.

STATUS: Individual research

DATE OF RESEARCH: 1996-1997

KEYWORDS: **catholic schools; church and education; educational administration; educational finance; grant maintained schools; head teachers; roman catholic church; school based management**

2076

Faculty of Arts and Education, Rolle School of Education, Douglas Avenue, Exmouth EX8 2AT
01395 255309

Silver, H. Prof.; Hannan, A. Dr; English, S. Ms

Innovations in teaching and learning in higher education: Phase 1

ABSTRACT: The past decade has seen increased attention to methods of teaching and learning, and the 1997 Dearing report, Higher Education in the Learning Society, has further emphasised the need for innovative responses to the challenges facing higher education. Universities are having to react to pressures which have arisen from increased student numbers and diversity, the need to promote lifelong learning and a learning society, and satisfying the requirements of employment and citizenship, at a time of reduced public funding. Traditional teaching has struggled to cope with these demands leading to the adoption of innovative approaches involving such methods as problem-based learning, open learning, independent learning, distance learning and computer-based or supported learning. These methods are intended to be both more efficient in terms of reducing costs per student and more effective in terms of enhancing student learning. The project, part of the Economic and Social Research Council's Learning Society Programme, will focus on innovations such as these that seek to shape the learning interface of students with teachers, one another, the technologies and materials. A sample of some 20 UK higher education institutions will be visited, selected on the basis of innovations identifed through data collected in the 1990s by such bodies as the Open Learning Foundation, the Partnership Trust, Higher Education for Capability, and the Staff and Educational Development Association and its predecessors. An interim report will be produced in the first year, and will form the basis of widespread dissemination and consultation.

PUBLISHED MATERIAL: SILVER, H., HANNAN, A. & ENGLISH, J. (1998). Innovation: questions of boundary, EducatiON-LINE at http://www.leeds.ac.uk/educol ; SILVER, H. (1998). Innovations in teaching and learning in higher education: an annotated bibliography (mainly since 1980), EducatiON-LINE at http://www.leeds.ac.uk/educol ; SILVER, H. (1998). 'The languages of innovation: listening to the higher education literature, EducatiON-LINE at http://www.leeds.ac.uk/educol ; SILVER, H. (1998). 'Why innovate? Some preliminary findings from 'Innovations in teaching and learning in higher education'. Paper presented at the Conference on Managing Learning Innovation: The Challenges of the Changing Curriculum, Lincoln University Campus, University of Lincolnshire and Humberside, 1-2 September 1998. ; A full list of publications is available from the researchers or by visiting the web site at http://www.fae.plym.ac.uk/itlhe.html

STATUS: Sponsored project

SOURCE OF GRANT: Economic and Social Research Council; Higher Education Quality Council, jointly £66,000

DATE OF RESEARCH: 1997-1998

KEYWORDS: **computer assisted learning; computer uses in education; distance education; educational innovation; higher education; independent study; information technology; learning strategies; open education; teaching methods**

2077

Faculty of Arts and Education, Rolle School of Education, Douglas Avenue, Exmouth EX8 2AT
01395 255309

Fisher, R. Dr; Lewis, M. Mrs

Different readings? Children's and teachers' perceptions and readings of non-fiction texts

ABSTRACT: The aims of the project are: a) to find out whether children come to school already understanding the difference between narrative fiction and non-narrative information books and to identify any observable difference in response by children to the two genres including any expression of preference; b) to analyse the ways in which class teachers mediate the two genres and whether this has any identifiable impact on children's response; c) to identify any changes evidenced by children in their approach or attitude to reading non-narrative information books after a year in school. A pilot study is being undertaken in one school in 1996/97. This will extend to more schools in 1997/98, depending on funding. During their first week in school and at the end of their first year, reception children will be asked to share a story book and a non-fiction book on the same topic. The class teachers will be audiotaped reading books of their choice at two weekly intervals during the year. The research will attempt to indicate what knowledge of, and preference for, different types of books children bring with them on starting school and how these may develop.

STATUS: Individual research

DATE OF RESEARCH: 1996-1998

KEYWORDS: **books; childrens literature; fiction; literary genres; nonfiction; primary education; reading interests; reception classes; young children**

2078

Faculty of Arts and Education, Rolle School of Education, Douglas Avenue, Exmouth EX8 2AT
01395 255309

Lee, C. Mr; *Supervisors*: Hannan, A. Dr; Nias, J. Prof.

Teacher perceptions of bullying and its management

ABSTRACT: The research of bullying has usually involved questionnaires set by the researcher. However, this piece of work will seek to use a variety of scenarios, followed by structured interviews, to gain access to teachers' views on the extent and management of the behaviour in their schools. The primary school, which has received less attention than the secondary sector, will be the principal focus of the work. Research will centre on: the behaviours that teachers consider to be bullying; the extent to which they see it as a problem in their schools; and the impact of the teacher's gender, age, experience and status within the school to determine any variations in the definition. There is a need to determine whether teachers build stereotypes of bullies and victims, and to examine their reactions to incidents reported to them. Management issues to be addressed include: perceived location and timing of bullying; efficacy of policies adopted; the subject; and the degree to which this is seen as reflecting the extent of the problem. Teachers' attitudes towards their role and responsibility in the management of the matter will be considered. Teachers' views on a number of specific initiatives in the management of bullying, such as 'the no-blame approach', 'bully courts' and 'shared concern method', and their potential value to the primary school will be sought.

STATUS: Individual research

DATE OF RESEARCH: 1994-1997

KEYWORDS: **antisocial behaviour; behaviour problems; bullying; discipline policy; discipline problems; teacher attitudes**

2079

Faculty of Arts and Education, Rolle School of Education, Douglas Avenue, Exmouth EX8 2AT
01395 255309

Hannan, A. Dr; Silver, H. Prof.; English, S. Ms

Innovations in teaching and learning in higher education: Phase 2

ABSTRACT: The first phase of the project focused on the experiences of innovators. The second phase is intended to relate the findings to institutional cultures and structures, looking at relevant university machineries and procedures at individual, departmental, faculty and institutional levels. This will involve investigating relevant policymaking; responsiveness to external policies and programmes; directions in which teaching and learning are driven; the control of funding and support processes; the machinery of implementation. In addition to the study of committees and the roles of responsible units and individuals, the research will explore where and how significant planned changes are introduced, and how proposals for innovations are handled by the system. Having studied 15 institutions in the first phase, the project intends to revisit and examine in these ways 4 of those previously included and also the Open University. The study was based on interviews, focus groups and documentation. The result will be an analysis of how institutions manage the promotion (or otherwise) of innovation; how (and how well) processes for promoting and embedding innovation operate; perceptions of the value of such innovation and of the importance of internal and external sources of encouragement and support.

STATUS: Sponsored project

SOURCE OF GRANT: Economic and Social Research Council; Department

for Education and Employment; Higher Education and Funding Council for England, jointly £53,293

DATE OF RESEARCH: 1998-continuing

KEYWORDS: **educational innovation; higher education; learning strategies; teaching methods; universities**

2080

Faculty of Arts and Education, Rolle School of Education, Douglas Avenue, Exmouth EX8 2AT
01395 255309

Fisher, R. Dr; Lewis, M. Mrs; Davis, B. Ms

The implementation of the literacy hour in small rural schools

ABSTRACT: This project aims to investigate how teachers of mixed age classes in small rural schools implement the literacy hour and to identify effective ways of working. 10 schools will be selected and teachers from a Reception/key stage 1 class and a key stage 2 class in each of the schools will be interviewed about their literacy teaching. At the beginning of the Autumn term a standardised reading/writing test will be used with children in these classes. For the remainder of the year, 10 visits will be made to the target schools to observe the literacy hour, collect work samples and undertake an informal interview with the target teachers. In July 1999 the children will be re-tested and a follow-up interview will be conducted with each teacher involved. The research will indicate how effective the implementation of the literacy hour has been in these small schools. It will examine the gains in literacy achievement made by the children and identify problems and issues encountered by teachers in the implementation of the literacy hour. It will analyse the ways in which teachers have attempted to overcome these difficulties and will identify successful strategies they have used.

PUBLISHED MATERIAL: FISHER, R. & LEWIS, M. 'Anticipation or trepidation: teachers' views on the literacy hour', Reading. (in press).

STATUS: Sponsored project

SOURCE OF GRANT: Economic and Social Research Council £41,000

DATE OF RESEARCH: 1998-continuing

KEYWORDS: **key stage 1; key stage 2; literacy hours; national literacy strategy; primary education; reading; reception classes; rural schools; small schools**

2081

Faculty of Arts and Education, Rolle School of Education, Douglas Avenue, Exmouth EX8 2AT
01395 255309

Rodd, J. Dr

International leadership project: a collaborative study of leadership in early childhood in Australia, England, Finland, Russia and USA

ABSTRACT: This study, in collaboration with the University of Oulu, Finland; University of Melbourne, Australia; John Carroll University, Ohio, USA; and Karelian State University, Russia, investigated aspects of leadership in early childhood professionals in these countries. Selected samples of early childhood professionals working in child care and education were asked to complete a survey of daily tasks which examined the type of activity undertaken and with whom during a typical data. These data were supplemented by observational data collected from the range of early childhood services which are representative of service provision in each country. The quantitative and qualitative data analyses provide a picture of the similarities and differences in the work undertaken by early childhood professionals and illustrate the context in which leadership can be assumed in the various countries. Comparative analyses of phase 1 of this study will be followed by phase 2 in which leadership will be studied as a situational phenomenon using case study as the primary methodology. Phase 3 of the study aims to examine the development of leadership and its relationship to quality in early childhood services using action research as the primary methodology. The results of phase 1 suggest that leadership is a complex and subtle phenomenon requiring sophisticated tools for meaningful examination.

PUBLISHED MATERIAL: RODD, J. (1998). 'Action research in early childhood settings throughout the world'. In: HUJALA, E. (Ed). The international leadership project: Australia, England, Finland, Russia and the United States. Oulu, Finland: University of Oulu. ; RODD, J. (1998). 'Leadership in early childhood in England: a national review'. In: HUJALA, E. (Ed). The international leadership project: Australia, England, Finland, Russia and the United States. Oulu, Finland: University of Oulu.

SOURCE OF GRANT: Plymouth University; Finnish Academy

DATE OF RESEARCH: 1996-continuing

KEYWORDS: child caregivers; comparative education; early childhood education; international studies; leadership

2082

Faculty of Arts and Education, Rolle School of Education, Douglas Avenue, Exmouth EX8 2AT
01395 255309

Hayes, D. Dr

Competence for teaching project

ABSTRACT: In recent years there has been a strong move towards school-based teacher training, partnership schemes, mentoring and the emergence of large numbers of teachers who have responsibility for students. Some teachers have specialised in dealing with trainee teachers and have been involved in liaising with colleagues, attending meetings at the local higher education establishment, observing students at work and reviewing student progress through structured meetings and informal discussions. The role of classroom teachers has also been important as they have helped students to refine their plans, deliver lessons successfully and gain a fuller understanding of professional responsibilities. Their task has become a demanding and significant one. Although a lot of effort has rightly been expended in helping teachers with the task of mentoring students in school, surprisingly little has been written from the student perspective. Important issues such as what student teachers find easy and less easy to deal with during different phases of their course, the teaching skills that they find most demanding and their awareness of the social and cultural factors which impinge upon their ability to survive and prosper in their placement schools, have received small attention. Along with other training providers, the Faculty of Arts and Education has developed close working relationships with mentors over a period of years, supported by documentation, regular training and refresher courses, and the occasional conference. This research forms part of a more extensive piece of research, the Competence for Teaching Project, made possible through internal funding through the University of Plymouth. The research was initiated to contrast the perceptions of school-based mentors and the student primary teachers about the difficulties that student teachers experienced in coping with different aspects of classroom teaching skills. The purpose of discovering their contrasting views was twofold: a) to determine where students were having most difficulty in order to make necessary modifications to their preparation for teaching at college; b) to gain greater awareness of the gap between the perceived and actual difficulties of inexperienced student teachers as a means of enhancing mentors' insights into the developmental process.

PUBLISHED MATERIAL: HAYES, D. (1997). 'Teaching competences for qualified primary teacher status in England', Teacher Development, Vol 1, No 2, pp.165-174. ; HAYES, D. (1998). 'Teaching skills, perceptions and invisible boundaries: an insight into the thoughts of trainee teachers on school placement', Primary Practice, No 15, pp.35-38. ; HAYES, D. (1998). 'Walking on egg shells: the significance of socio-cultural factors in the mentoring of primary school students', Mentoring and Tutoring, Vol 6, Nos 1/2, pp.67-76. ; HAYES, D. (1999). Planning, teaching and class management in primary schools: meeting the standards. London: David Fulton. (in press).

STATUS: Individual research

DATE OF RESEARCH: 1997-continuing

KEYWORDS: competency based teacher education; mentors; preservice teacher education; school based teacher education; student teacher attitudes; student teachers

2083

Faculty of Arts and Education, Rolle School of Education, Douglas Avenue, Exmouth EX8 2AT
01395 255309
Nottingham University, School of Education, University Park, Nottingham NG7 2RD
01159 515151

Lewis, M. Mrs; Fisher, R. Dr; Harrison, C. Prof.; Grainger, T. Dr

Curiosity kits: using non-fiction book bags with reluctant boy readers (The Nuffield Exel Project: Phase 2)

ABSTRACT: As part of the National Year of Reading a new scheme to encourage reluctant boy readers to take books home is being trialled. Non-fiction book bags containing books, artefacts and related magazines (which are aimed at encouraging the male in the household to share reading with the child) have been prepared. Sets of 30 bags have been placed in Year 4 classes in 4 target schools from January 1999. 4 control schools in the same towns have also been identified. Details of books the pupils take home and details of who they share the book with at home are being collected in all 8 classes. This will continue throughout the year. Group interviews on attitudes to reading are being conducted with reluctant and failing boy reader in all schools prior to the introduction of the bags in the target schools. These interviews will be repeated after 2 terms, the teachers interviewed and, if possible, some parents. The data will be analysed to see if the introduction of the bags leads to any variation in the pattern of taking books home/ sharing within the home and to any changing attitude amongst the targeted group of reluctant/failing boy readers. Target schools will be compared to the control (no bag) schools. This research is being undertaken on behalf of the United Kingdom Reading Association.

STATUS: Sponsored project

SOURCE OF GRANT: Department for Education and Employment

DATE OF RESEARCH: 1997-continuing

KEYWORDS: books; boys; childrens literature; literacy; nonfiction; primary education; reading; reading difficulties; reading habits; underachievement

2084

Faculty of Arts and Education, Rolle School of Education, Douglas Avenue, Exmouth EX8 2AT
01395 255309
Plymouth University, Department of Mathematics and Statistics, Centre for Teaching Mathematics, Drake Circus, Plymouth PL4 8AA
01752 600600

Pratt, N. Mr; *Supervisors*: Berry, J. Prof.; Maull, W. Dr; Woods, P. Prof.

Perceptions of the nature of mathematics in relation to National Numeracy Strategy

ABSTRACT: This research, which is still in its very early stages, aims to examine the way in which students in initial teacher training (ITT) perceive the nature of mathematics and the effects of these perceptions on their teaching of the National Numeracy Strategy (NNS). In particular it starts from the assertion that the NNS proposes a set of practices stemming from a framework of beliefs about the nature of mathematics and its teaching, which may or may not be shared by the student teachers in question. It is likely therefore that there will be student teachers who are carrying out these practices despite the fact that they do not share the set of beliefs from which they came. The study aims to examine the result of this possible tension. A phenomenographic approach is intended, based on the conjecture that many previous studies of students' 'beliefs' have, in practice, elicited higher level, reflected thinking which is unlikely to match classroom practice where decisions tend to be made on the intuitive level rather than the reasoned level. The use of phenomenography is aimed at trying to examine students' perceptions of mathematics via their 'human experience' rather than via 'reflected upon' thought. The study is a small scale one involving around 10 students. The practice of these students should provide an insight into the way in which internalised understanding of mathematics interacts with practice in the classroom, and the practice of the NNS in particular.

STATUS: Individual research

DATE OF RESEARCH: 1998-continuing

KEYWORDS: mathematics education; national numeracy strategy; preservice teacher education; student teachers

2085

Faculty of Arts and Education, Rolle School of Education, Douglas Avenue, Exmouth EX8 2AT
01395 255309
Warwick University, Institute of Education, Coventry CV4 7AL
01203 523523

Lewis, M. Mrs; Wray, D. Prof.

Using literacy to access the curriculum (The Nuffield Exel Project, Phase 2)

ABSTRACT: Following on from the work undertaken in primary schools by the Extending Literacy (EXEL) project from 1992-95, it became evident that there was a need to explore with secondary teachers the specific literacy demands of different curriculum areas and to help develop strategies that would support students in the literacy demands of the secondary curriculum. A combined research and curriculum development project was therefore proposed. The initial stage of the project involved collecting evidence (via questionnaire of 342 secondary teachers in 8 randomly selected secondary schools in 3 local education authorities) of teachers' existing knowledge about literacy and their existing use of supportive literacy strategies within their subject teaching. This data is currently being analysed using the Statistical Package for Social Scientists (SPSS). 12 secondary schools in 4 authorities were then involved in developing units of work which incorporated supportive literacy strategies within specific units of work, in a variety of subject departments. Case study evidence is being gathered including interviews with teachers, interviews with pupils and samples of students' work. Work is ongoing on these case studies. It is too early in the project to give results and conclusions but the first research report on teachers' use of literacy strategies is due for publication shortly and indicates that secondary teachers are still more likely to help their students avoid the literacy demands of texts than offer them support in engaging with texts.

STATUS: Sponsored project

SOURCE OF GRANT: Nuffield Foundation £80,000

DATE OF RESEARCH: 1997-continuing

KEYWORDS: literacy; reading; secondary education

2086

Faculty of Arts and Education, School of Humanities and Cultural Interpretation, Douglas Avenue, Exmouth EX8 2AT
01395 255309

Bainbridge, K. Ms; *Supervisor*: Halstead, J. Dr

Adolescence, values, and sex education

ABSTRACT: The research is examining values in an educational context, and specifically the values systems of adolescents, to gain an understanding of the varied and sometimes conflicting values networks that shape, influence and advise their perceptions. A controversial area of the school curriculum, sex education is examined - including the influences of moral, political, cultural, religious and economic agendas. Ethnographic research is being conducted in a Devon secondary school, through a longitudinal tracking study of a Year 9 tutor group. Health education is being specifically monitored, including a county-based sex education programme from the local health authority. Through informal observation techniques, a background examination of cultural, social and religious values is being carried out, including parental values and the core values of the school. Also examined are sources of the adolescents' values, including the media and the peer group. Specific research aims are: 1) To study values in education, and to examine specifically sex education in this context. 2) To assess the values underpinning school-based sex education using a longitudinal secondary school study, in the context of the wider values networks that have a contributing influence on adolescents. 3) To re-examine sex education in schools in light of this study.

STATUS: Sponsored project

SOURCE OF GRANT: Higher Education Funding Council

DATE OF RESEARCH: 1994-1997

KEYWORDS: adolescent attitudes; adolescents; secondary education; sex education; values

2087

Faculty of Arts and Education, School of Humanities and Cultural Interpretation, Douglas Avenue, Exmouth EX8 2AT
01395 255309
James Cook University, School of Education, Queensland, Australia 4811 University of Texas at Arlington, 700 College Street, Arlington, Texas TX 76092, USA

Peel, R. Dr; Patterson, A. Dr; Gerlach, J. Dr

Beliefs about 'English': an international comparison

ABSTRACT: The project has been designed to investigate the beliefs held by specialists in English about the scope and purpose of the area in which they work. That area itself is undergoing constant redefinition and enlargement as developments such as media education, information technology and networking, debates about literacy and linguistics, genre and reading methods, and discussions about post-structural theory and its relationship to classroom practice all impact on the pedagogy and methodology of 'English'. At a time of great ferment and turbulence, when 'English' itself becomes the site for anxieties about the future of civilisation and the moralising effect of education, it is important to establish how teachers are responding to these changes, and to see if it is possible to draw some conclusions about the set of practices known as subject of 'English'. This is the aim of the research, and by comparing the results of separate investigations currently underway in England, Australia and the United States, the researchers intend to assemble a report that could be of considerable importance for the development of 'English' teaching as we enter the 21st century.

PUBLISHED MATERIAL: PEEL, R. & HARGREAVES, S. (1995). 'Beliefs about English: trends in Australia, England and the United States', English in Education, Vol 29, No 3, pp.38-49. ; PEEL, R. & CURTIS, F. (1996). 'Becoming and being a specialist: anticipating and experiencing higher education English', Teaching in Higher Education, Vol 1, No 2, pp.227-243.

STATUS: Collaborative

DATE OF RESEARCH: 1992-1997

KEYWORDS: australia; comparative education; english; english studies teachers; united states of america

2088

Institute of Marine Studies, Drake Circus, Plymouth PL4 8AA
01752 600600

Kennerley, A. Dr

The education and training of merchant seafarers, 1890-1990

ABSTRACT: The aim is to make a critical study of the need, policy and provision of education and training for mercantile marine personnel of all capacities and levels, in relation to changing industrial requirements; state policy and legislation, and the involvement of charities, shipping employers, professional bodies, trade unions, local authorities, and various government departments, in making provision. By 1890 the dominant influence in the education and training of merchant marine officers (masters, mates and engineers) had long been the system of licensing, through examinations for certificates of competency, operated by the Marine Department of the Board of Trade, for which preparation was offered by endowed nautical schools, schools supported by the Science and Art Department, and private teachers. There was no structured education and training for ratings, though a number of static training ships had come into existence in the second half of the century, orphanages, industrial schools, reformatory schools, which trained in seamanship alongside an elementary education, and supplied boys to the shipping industry. Many of these operated under the Home Office. Shore-based education and training provision was already split between pre-sea courses for boys, and post experience courses mainly directed at cramming for the licenses. The State was reluctant to fund training and look askance at cramming. The employers wanted trained manpower, but were reluctant to fund structured training. The debate on the balance continued through the 20th century. Throughout the 20th century, the interaction of the developing State approach to post-school education and training with the education and training needs of merchant shipping has been a critical dimension. To what extent would the maritime world be able to participate and benefit from State provision? In the 40 years of the Science and Art Department (from 1853) the relationship had not been easy. The technical education of initiatives of the 1890s provided new opportunities, taken up with respect to nautical education, for example, in Liverpool. Certainly progressively, maritime educational and training establishments were absorbed into the State system. But each new initiative by the State created problems for the maritime world, as for example the proposal for day continuation in the 1918 Education Act. Nevertheless, particularly at the pre-sea level, ways were found of taking advantage, though often through the devising of special regulations. The more advanced education connected with officer licensing began to be matched with arrangements in other technical subject areas in the 1960s with the introduction of ONC, OND,

HNC, HND courses in maritime subjects and the devising of nautical degrees. With the development of NVQs in the 1980s, maritime education and training found that State approaches had come round to what it had effectively been doing to some extent throughout the century. While there have been several investigations impinging on the current state and future direction of education and training for merchant shipping manpower during this century, no study has been attempted which examines the subject over the whole period since the start of modern technical education. The study used archival analysis of institutional, local and national records, and shipping industry records to establish the scale of demand and provision at various levels and to derive the interaction of national tertiary education policy with the industry's requirement for educated and trained personnel.

STATUS: Individual research

DATE OF RESEARCH: 1997-continuing

KEYWORDS: **educational history; nautical education**

2089

Institute of Marine Studies, Drake Circus, Plymouth PL4 8AA
01752 600600

Kennerley, A. Dr

The making of the University of Plymouth

ABSTRACT: The aim is to research, write up and publish an analytical study of the history of the provision and delivery of higher education which culminated in the designation of the University of Plymouth, taking into account the local, regional and national contexts while doing justice to the elements that make up the current establishment. It will involve archival analysis of institutional, local and national records, to draw out the changing nature of local and national policy and funding, and the changing scale and nature of the student body, facilities and methods of operation; supplemented by oral methods for the more recent period and an examination of relevant published literature. The University of Plymouth is a multi-site establishment which has grown from mid-19th century roots partly through the incorporation of independent establishments. Thus this study examines the histories of the current education, agriculture, art and design faculties on the university branch campuses at Exmouth, Newton Abbot and Exeter, and of course developments on the Plymouth campus, which includes a school of navigation as well as the range of technological, scientific, commercial and social science subjects which are characteristic of tertiary education in Plymouth.

STATUS: Sponsored project

SOURCE OF GRANT: Plymouth University £30,000

DATE OF RESEARCH: 1997-continuing

KEYWORDS: **higher education; universities**

Policy Studies Institute

2090

100 Park Village East, London NW1 3SR
0171 468 0468

White, M. Dr; Bryson, A. Mr; Payne, J. Ms; Callender, C. Ms

Student loans: who borrows and why?

ABSTRACT: Data from the 1995/6 Student Income and Expenditure Survey are used to investigate the factors which influence a student's decision to take out a student loan. Potential explanatory variables which are of particular interest include: the students' knowledge of the loans system, the age, gender, social group and ethnicity of the student and his or her financial circumstances. Logistic regression techniques are used to develop a series of statistical models which investigate these links.

PUBLISHED MATERIAL: PAYNE, J. & CALLENDER, C. (1997). Student loans: who borrows, and why? PSI Report No 848. London: Policy Studies Institute.

STATUS: Sponsored project

SOURCE OF GRANT: Department for Education and Employment £19,276

DATE OF RESEARCH: 1996-1997

KEYWORDS: **educational finance; higher education; student financial aid; student loans; students**

Portsmouth University

2091

Academic Development Centre, University House, Winston Churchill Avenue, Portsmouth PO1 2UP
01705 876543
Sheffield University, Division of Education, 388 Glossop Road, Sheffield S10 2JA
01142 768555

Selway, I. Mrs; *Supervisor*: Rowland, S. Mr

Organisational change and professional practice in a restructured higher education institution

ABSTRACT: Exploration of the dimensions of structural change within the higher education sector as a whole, using a post-modern paradigm and critical theory framework. Locating University of Portsmouth within this context, changes in professional practice will be explored to identify the effects of the transformation of higher education on the professional identity of academics. The methodology is enthnographic, using a 'stories at work' approach, as well as collaborative enquiry. An initial review of policy documents, both national and 'local' to the institution, will employ content analysis and the concept of neo-narrative to identify metaphors of meaning, language use and ideological 'shifts' concerning the purpose of higher education.

STATUS: Individual research

DATE OF RESEARCH: 1994-continuing

KEYWORDS: **higher education; organisational change; organisational climate; professional recognition; teaching profession**

2092

Centre for Disabilities, Department of Psychology, King Henry Building, King Henry 1st Street, Portsmouth PO1 2DY
01705 876543

Byrne, A. Ms; *Supervisors*: MacDonald, J. Dr; Buckley, S. Prof.; Fellows, B. Dr

Investigating the literacy, language and memory skills of children with Down's Syndrome and their mainstream peers

ABSTRACT: This longitudinal study is charting the literacy and other cognitive skills of 24 children with Down's Syndrome and 2 comparison groups of children selected from their mainstream classes. One group were average readers (n=42) and the other group were matched to the children with Down's Syndrome on reading ability (n=31). The baseline data revealed that the children with Down's Syndrome had uneven performance profiles with relatively advanced reading skills, compared to their other cognitive skills. The group of reading matched children attained significantly higher scores than the children with Down's Syndrome on all measures other than reading. This reading matched group, who were generally of below average reading ability for their age, were also signficantly delayed relative to the average readers on measures of language, number and memory. As a group the average readers were average on all measures. All 3 groups are being followed longitudinally to explore the progress of the children and to look at the developmental interrelationships between reading, language and memory skills. The children have also completed a series of experimentally controlled reading tasks. The tasks were designed to look more closely at the strategies the children are using to read. The results are currently being analysed to establish the age and stage of reading development at which the children move from using a logographic strategy to an alphabetic strategy and to compare strategy use in the 3 groups of children. The children are currently being studied for another year.

PUBLISHED MATERIAL: BUCKLEY, S. & BYRNE, A. (1994). 'The links between language, literacy and memory skills in children with Down's Syndrome', Portsmouth Down's Syndrome Trust Newsletter, Vol 4, No 2, pp.9-11. ; BYRNE, A., BUCKLEY, S., MACDONALD, J. & BIRD, G. (1995). 'Investigating the literacy, language and memory skills of children with Down's Syndrome', Down's Syndrome: Research and Practice, Vol 3, No 2, pp.53-58. ; BUCKLEY, S., BIRD, G. & BYRNE, A. (1996). 'Reading acquisition by young children with Down's Syndrome'. In: GUNN, P. & STRATFORD, B. (Eds). New approaches to Down's Syndrome. Second Edition. London: Cassell.

STATUS: Individual research

DATE OF RESEARCH: 1993-1998

KEYWORDS: **cognitive ability; downs syndrome; literacy education; mainstreaming; memory; reading ability; reading skills; special educational needs**

2093

Centre for Disability Studies, Department of Psychology, King Henry Building, King Henry 1st Street, Portsmouth PO1 2DY
01705 876543

Nye, J. Ms; *Supervisors*: Fluck, M. Dr; Buckley, S. Prof.

Development of numerical skills in children with Down's Syndrome

ABSTRACT: In 1994/95 as part of a BSc (Hons) Psychology Degree, the researcher carried out a study which documented the numerical and receptive language abilities of children with Down's Syndrome. A group of 16 children with Down's Syndrome in Hampshire and West Sussex were studied. A battery of tests were implemented, including 4 tests of numerical skills. Each of the numerical tests was thought to have advantages for assessing skills in this population, depending on the situation and purpose of assessment. In addition, a positive correlation was found between receptive grammar and numerical skills. The relationship between numeracy and receptive vocabulary was not significant. This study highlighted how little is known about the development of numerical knowledge and skills in this population, nor about effective intervention strategies. This is supported by reports from teachers involved in the research at the Sarah Duffen Centre concerning mainstream schooling. The current research aims to improve this situation. It is investigating the social aspects of numerical skills development, connecting with previous projects at Portsmouth University that have been conducted with typically developing children. The focus of the research is parent-child interaction, including parental scaffolding of counting procedures and strategies, cardinal reference by parent and number vocabulary used during interactions.

PUBLISHED MATERIAL: NYE, J., CLIBBENS, J. & BIRD, G. (1995). 'Numerical ability, general ability and language in children with Down's Syndrome', Down's Syndrome: Research and Practice, Vol 3, No 3, pp.92-102. ; NYE, J. & BIRD, G. (1996). 'Developing number and maths skills', Portsmouth Down's Syndrome Trust Newsletter, Vol 6, No 2, pp.1-7.

STATUS: Individual research

DATE OF RESEARCH: 1995-1998

KEYWORDS: **downs syndrome; mother child relationship; numeracy; parent participation; scaffolding; special educational needs**

2094

Centre for Disability Studies, Department of Psychology, King Henry Building, King Henry 1st Street, Portsmouth PO1 2DY
01705 876543

Appleton, M. Miss; *Supervisors*: Buckley, S. Prof.; Bull, R. Prof.; Fellows, B. Dr

Reading and language development: a comparison of preschool children with Down's Syndrome, hearing impairment or typical development

ABSTRACT: This PhD work involves conducting a 2-year longitudinal study examining reading and language development in preschool children with either Down's Syndrome, hearing impairment or typical development. The aims of the research are to assess reading development in these children and to consider whether reading actually aids language development in children with Down's Syndrome or hearing impairment. The research follows the progress of 20 children with typical development, 20 children with Down's Syndrome and 14 children with hearing impairment. Data is collected on each child's language ability and developmental ability. Language ability was measured on the Reynell Language Development Scales (which measures verbal comprehension and verbal expression). Developmental ability was measured on either the British Ability Scales (which measures visual recognition, verbal comprehension, naming vocabulary and digit recall) for children over the age of 3.5 years, or the Bayley Scales of Infant Development for the younger children. Statistical analysis on the initial data suggests that the typical developers obtained higher scores on both language and developmental ability than did children with Down's Syndrome or hearing impairment. Children with hearing impairment scored significantly higher on digit recall than children with Down's Syndrome. Apart from this score there was no significant difference

found between children with Down's Syndrome and children with hearing impairment. The progress of these children's language developmental and reading ability will be followed over 2 years.

STATUS: Individual research

DATE OF RESEARCH: 1994-continuing

KEYWORDS: **downs syndrome; early childhood education; hearing impairments; language acquisition; reading ability; reading skills; special educational needs; young children**

2095

Centre for Disability Studies, Department of Psychology, King Henry Building, King Henry 1st Street, Portsmouth PO1 2DY
01705 876543

Bird, G. Mrs; Byrne, A. Ms; *Supervisor*: Buckley, S. Prof.

Mainstream education of children with Down's Syndrome

ABSTRACT: This study aims to develop models of good practice for mainstreaming children with Down's Syndrome. Many aspects of the placement are being investigated, including factors relating to the school, the management of the placement, the child and their family, access to the curriculum and adaptation of teaching materials, particularly with regard to the specific learning profile associated with Down's Syndrome and the children's invid025l needs. The children's social development is also a focus of research and this links with placement management, educational progress/attainment and individual differences. This research is collaborative with schools, educational psychologists, local education authorities (LEAs), parents and others involved to obtain information about mainstreaming and meeting the educational needs of children with Down's Syndrome in order to inform and promote good practice nationally.

PUBLISHED MATERIAL: BIRD, G. & BUCKLEY, S.J. (1994). The educational needs of children with Down's Syndrome: a resource pack for teachers. Portsmouth: University of Portsmouth.

STATUS: Sponsored project

SOURCE OF GRANT: Portsmouth Down's Syndrome Trust; Down's Syndrome Association; David Solomon Trust

DATE OF RESEARCH: 1990-continuing

KEYWORDS: **downs syndrome; mainstreaming; special educational needs**

2096

Centre for Disability Studies, Department of Psychology, King Henry Building, King Henry 1st Street, Portsmouth PO1 2DY
01705 876543

Buckley, S. Prof.; MacDonald, J. Dr

Memory and language development in children with Down's Syndrome

ABSTRACT: This project is a continuation of research which piloted a programme to teach memory strategies to children with Down's Syndrome in 1993. This demonstrated that the children could be trained to use rehearsal and organisation strategies as a way to increase memory span. Fourteen of the children involved in this earlier training have been revisited to assess the long term effects of the training. After 3 years, the effects of the training have not been maintained. However, the researchers found interesting and significant advances in short term memory, vocabulary and grammar for children with Down's Syndrome who have learned to read since the study began. A revised teaching programme has been developed along with new materials for use in the research, and also for sale to parents and teachers. Currently, about 30 children from 3 special schools in Surrey are taking part in research to evaluate the programme. An important aim of the new programme is to persuade the schools and/or parents to continue with some level of training after the initial intensive course. It is only by maintaining the memory skill over time that there will be the chance to investigate: a) whether memory development will continue; and b) whether increased memory capacity will result in the improved language development that would be theoretically predicted.

PUBLISHED MATERIAL: LAWS, G., BUCKLEY, S., MACDONALD, J., BIRD, G. & BROADLEY, I. (1995). 'The influence of reading instruction on language and memory development in children with Down's Syndrome', Down's Syndrome: Research and Practice, Vol 3, No 2, pp.59-64. ; LAWS, G., MACDONALD, J., BUCKLEY, S. & BROADLEY, I. (1995). 'Long term maintenance of trained memory strategies in children with Down's Syndrome', Down's Syndrome: Research and Practice, Vol 3, No 3, pp.

STATUS: Sponsored project

SOURCE OF GRANT: Higher Education Funding Council for England

DATE OF RESEARCH: 1994-continuing

KEYWORDS: cognitive development; downs syndrome; language acquisition; literacy education; memory; special educational needs

2097

Centre for Disability Studies, Department of Psychology, King Henry Building, King Henry 1st Street, Portsmouth PO1 2DY
01705 876543

Le Prevost, P. Ms; *Supervisors*: Bull, R. Prof.; Buckley, S. Prof.

The value of early intervention programmes for children with Down's syndrome in relation to the development of all dimensions of their communication skills

ABSTRACT: The value of intervening with a specific programme, to assist the development of communication skills, has been the subject for discussion for many years, as has the contents of that intervention. Children with Down's syndrome have been recognised as having difficulty with communication skills, and it is now established that these skills are affected over and above their other intellectual abilities. It has also been recognised that there is an underlying short-term memory deficit. Combine this with poor auditory skills, immature muscle patterns and weak muscle power which can also be present. However, there is a wide variation in the final outcome in children who have appeared to have the same environmental experiences, and a disparity in the achieved ability levels of the various aspects of communication. The object of this study is to look at a group of children who have had a structured early intervention programme, and to compare them with a matched group, who have had a range of less structured early intervention programmes that occur more frequently in the UK.

STATUS: Individual research

DATE OF RESEARCH: 1995-continuing

KEYWORDS: communication skills; downs syndrome; intervention; special educational needs

2098

Centre for Disability Studies, Department of Psychology, King Henry Building, King Henry 1st Street, Portsmouth PO1 2DY
01705 876543

Ramruttun, M. Ms; *Supervisors*: Fluck, M. Dr; Buckley, S. Prof.

The friendships and peer relationships of children who have Down's syndrome a longitudinal study

ABSTRACT: What little research has been done indicates that young children with Down's syndrome become isolated in settings designed for typically developing children because they fail to conform to the rules of mutual gaze and lack the behaviours needed for peer-related social competence. This study examines the development of peer relationship skills in 5 and 7 year-olds with Down's syndrome in mainstream schools studied over 2 years and compared with typically developing peers of similar sociometric status.

STATUS: Individual research

DATE OF RESEARCH: 1996-continuing

KEYWORDS: communication skills; downs syndrome; friendship; mainstreaming; nonverbal communication; peer acceptance; peer relationship; primary education; social skills; special educational needs

2099

Centre for Disability Studies, Department of Psychology, King Henry Building, King Henry 1st Building, Portsmouth PO1 2DY
01705 876543
Open University, School of Education, Walton Hall, Milton Keynes MK7 6AA
01908 274066

Ramruttun, B. Mr; *Supervisors*: Fluck, M. Dr; Buckley, S. Prof ; Oates, J. Mr

A longitudinal study of early attentional, social, and pre-linguistic communication capacities of young infants with Down's syndrome and non-delayed children

ABSTRACT: Infants with Down's syndrome have been found to be delayed in pre-linguistic communicative behaviours such as gazing when compared with control subjects matched on mental age. It has been argued recently, however, that mental age may not reflect the infant's true cognitive capacity, and that visual attention and novelty preference are more appropriate measures. This research tests the hypothesis that: 1) early pre-linguistic communication will be significantly related to these two variables; 2) when matched on these variables, children with Down's syndrome will show similar levels of communication skills as typically developing children.

STATUS: Individual research

DATE OF RESEARCH: 1996-continuing

KEYWORDS: communication skills; downs syndrome; infants; nonverbal communication

2100

School of Education and Continuing Studies, Cambridge Building, Cambridge Road, Portsmouth PO1 2LF
01705 876543

White, J. Mrs; *Supervisors*: Jones, K. Dr; Selway, I. Mrs; Birch, R. Dr

Access to higher education

ABSTRACT: Thames Valley Enterprise, a Training and Enterprise Council (TEC), has commissioned Portsmouth University to undertake a 3 year research project to help underpin its commitment to the attainment of the National Targets for Education and Training. Its rationale is that with the increased expectation of school/further education (FE) students achievement at National Vocational Qualification (NVQ) level 3 equivalent, and the use of these achievements to access higher education (HE), it is necessary to evaluate the effectiveness of advice and support offered to those students at identified key stages. The research will monitor students through two key stages of progression, these being identified as: the beginning of Year 10 to end of Year 11 (or equivalent); and the beginning of Year 12 (or equivalent) to end equivalent 1st year higher education. Schools will be selected from the Thames Valley area using student achievement levels at Level 3 as criteria. The key research method will be tracking of small groups of students. Due reference will be made to the inherent variables and to the characteristics of longitudinal research. It is expected that quantitative data will come mainly from secondary sources with primary sources providing most qualitative data. Research methods will include: ongoing literature search; gathering and analysis of secondary data; structured interviews at planned, spaced intervals; group discussions; case study; some direct observation; and account (student and other). The research project is being monitored by a steering group consisting of senior staff from Thames Valley Area Education and Careers Service, Portsmouth University and Thames Valley Enterprise.

STATUS: Sponsored project

SOURCE OF GRANT: Thames Valley Enterprise

DATE OF RESEARCH: 1994-1997

KEYWORDS: access to education; further education; higher education; national vocational qualifications

2101

School of Education and Continuing Studies, Cambridge Building, Cambridge Road, Portsmouth PO1 2LF
01705 876543

Stepien, D. Mrs; *Supervisors*: Lawrence, B. Dr; Murray, L. Dr; Lupton, C. Dr

Children living in temporary accommodation: educational disadvantage in the early years of schooling

ABSTRACT: Previous research suggests that 'deprivation does damage' and points to the importance of the family environment as factors influencing the educational attainment of children. There has been a general growth nationally in the number of families bringing up young children in temporary accommodation. However, little research has been carried out with regard to educational development. In collaboration with statutory and voluntary agencies in the Portsmouth area, this 3 year research project is investigating the impact of residence in temporary accommodation on the intellectual and social functioning of children. The notion of deprivation has been extended to include the concept of 'disruption'. Four empirical indicators 'disruption', 'housing', 'family status' and 'neighbourhood area' will be related to school-based measures of attainment in an attempt to provide an assessment of whether social, emotional or functional aspects of schooling are affected, in particular, by disruption. The research involves a cohort of over 220 children taken from 7 primary schools which are being tracked through the first 2 years of their formal schooling. In addition, case studies of a number of families from this original cohort will be undertaken. The mid-term results suggest that children who have been disrupted in their housing and/or their schooling are doing less well than those who have not been disrupted. Children who have lived or are living in temporary accommodation are doing less well in terms of their vocabulary development but (paradoxically) are well adjusted in the school situation. The research has also pointed to the inherent difficulties in this field and the necessity for collaboration between a range of statutory and voluntary agencies. Four reports have been produced in 1995: Report to the Bill Sargent Fund/ Portsmouth Housing Association Group; The Robert Centre Report; an interim report to the contributing agencies/Portsmouth City Council; and the Schools Profile Data.

STATUS: Sponsored project

SOURCE OF GRANT: Portsmouth City Council £5,000; Portsmouth Social Services £5,000; Portsmouth Housing Trust £2,000

DATE OF RESEARCH: 1994-1997

KEYWORDS: academic achievement; child development; disadvantaged; family problems; home environment; home school relationship; homeless people; housing; primary education

2102

School of Education and Continuing Studies, Cambridge Building, Cambridge Road, Portsmouth PO1 2LF
01705 875543

Murray, L. Dr

Research-led programme evaluation: Postgraduate Certificate in Education (post compulsory education)

ABSTRACT: This research project represents a cooperative research-led programme evaluation of the 'industry standard' Certificate in Education (CIE) and Postgraduate Certificate in Education (PGCE) for trainers, tutors, lecturers and adult education personnel, courses conducted by Portsmouth University. The research is cooperative in that franchised stakeholders in the courses - the further education (FE) colleges of Chichester, Eastleigh, Chippenham, Basingstoke and South Downs participate in data gathering activities. The evaluation is 'research-led' in that a process of orderly gathering of evidence based on interviews, standardised occupational interest inventories, course evaluation proformas and documentary content-analysis is used to underpin claims to knowledge and assertions of worth. The evaluation focuses on 4 components: 1) Organisational arrangements for the courses; 2) Curriculum and pedagogy; 3) Student responses to course delivery; 4) Academic and support staff responses. The viability and worth of CIE/PGCE courses nationwide will be illuminated in a post-Dearing 16-19 and beyond Education Reform Act; and Further Education Development Agency (FEDA)/Further Education National Training Organisation (FENTO) proposals for 'standards' in such courses.

PUBLISHED MATERIAL: MURRAY, L. (1998). 'Research into the social purposes of schooling', Pastoral Care in Education, Vol 16, No 3, pp.28-35. ; MURRAY, L. & LAWRENCE, B. Practitioner based enquiry - principles for postgraduate research. London: Falmer Press. (in press).

STATUS: Collaborative

DATE OF RESEARCH: 1997-continuing

KEYWORDS: course evaluation; further education; postgraduate certificate in education

2103

School of Education and Continuing Studies, Cambridge Building, Cambridge Road, Portsmouth PO1 2LF
01705 876543
Hampshire County Council, Education Department, The Castle, Winchester SO23
8UG
01962 841841

Murray, L. Dr; Stepien, D. Mrs

Family literacy in Hampshire: a regional application of the Basic Skills Agency Family Literacy Programme

ABSTRACT: The research was a replication in a regional context (Hampshire) of the National Foundation for Educational Research (NFER) evaluations of the Basic Skills Agency Family Literacy Demonstration Programmes. A characteristic of the Basic Skills Agency Family Literacy Programme is the joint delivery by adult and early years educators. The programme aims to raise standards and prevent failure by offering combined programmes for parents with limited basic skills and their children. This evaluation was commissioned by Hampshire County Council to monitor the effectiveness of courses provided in five infant schools across the county. Results from the course evaluations included: improvements in parents' reading and writing scores; a substantial increase in the average frequency of literacy related activities in the home during the courses; and at a 12-week subsequent measurement point, a dramatic improvement in children's average reading and writing scores during the courses and sustained in post-course testing. As a summary finding, parents and teachers stressed children's improved attitudes and motivation to learn as well as improved literacy skills.

PUBLISHED MATERIAL: STEPIEN, D. & MURRAY, L. (1997). Family literacy in Hampshire: a regional application of the Basic Skills Agency Family Literacy Programme. Winchester: Hampshire County Council. ; RALLS, C. & MURRAY, L. (1997). 'Twelve children's perceptions of reading', New Era in Education, Vol 78, No 3, pp.70-79.

STATUS: Sponsored project

SOURCE OF GRANT: Hampshire County Council £5,000; Portsmouth University £1,600

DATE OF RESEARCH: 1997-continuing

KEYWORDS: adult literacy; family literacy; literacy; parent participation; reading; reading difficulties; reading skills; writing skills

2104

Social Services Research & Information Unit (SSRIU), Halpern House, 1-2 Hampshire Terrace, Portsmouth PO1 2QF
01705 876543

Sheppard, C. Dr; Lupton, C. Dr

Evaluation of an innovatory home-school support project

ABSTRACT: Recent case-studies of primary school exclusions conducted by the SSRIU (Hayden 1994, Hayden et al, 1996) have encountered families under stress appealing for support in coping with their children's behaviour. Teachers are reporting an increase in the incidence and severity of problem behaviour in very young children. Exclusion of children from hard-pressed schools is exacerbating problems for families already in difficulty (Cohen 1994; Parsons, 1995; Hayden, 1996). Research is thus revealing an urgent need for preventative programmes to be developed. Effective preventative work, it is argued, will need to take place at pre-school and/or primary level and to encompass the home and school environments (Farrington, 1996). The project being evaluated aims to develop an integrated home-school support programme across a whole community and has incorporated into its design quantitative outcome measurements. Our evaluation of this project will provide the qualitative dimension regarding process and outcome from the perspectives of key workers, parents, teachers and children. This one year evaluation of the project will run from September 1996 until August 1997. The research, which has been funded by The Nuffield Foundation, will employ a case study approach, using the technique of pluralistic evaluation. This will facilitate an in-depth examination of a fluid social process and enable an assessment of the impact of the project over time from the perspectives of all key participants. A multi-method approach will be used to collect documentary, observational, institutional and interview data. It is hoped that the findings from this evaluation will contribute to the compelling and growing body of evidence which advocates intervention at an early age in order to prevent more serious problems developing within families.

PUBLISHED MATERIAL: PARSONS, C. et al (1994). The experience of excluded primary school children and their families. FPSC/Joseph Rowntree Foundation.; COHEN, R. et al. (1994). Schools out. London: Barnardos and Family Services Units. ; HAYDEN, C. (1994). 'Primary age children excluded from school: a multiagency focus for concern', Children and Society, Vol 8, No 3, pp.257-273. ; FARRINGDON, D. (1996).

Understanding and preventing youth crime. York: York Publishing Services/ Joseph Rowntree Foundation.

STATUS: Sponsored project

SOURCE OF GRANT: The Nuffield Foundation

DATE OF RESEARCH: 1996-1997

KEYWORDS: **behaviour problems; disruptive pupils; exclusions; family problems; home school relationship; primary education; primary school pupils; pupil behaviour**

Queen's University of Belfast
2105

School of Education, 69 University Street, Belfast BT7 1HL
01232 245133

McAleese, L. Mr; McConnell, B. Miss; *Supervisor*: Jarman, R. Miss

A survey of science at Northern Ireland Curriculum key stage 4 in a sample of Northern Ireland schools

ABSTRACT: This study investigated a range of issues associated with science provision at Northern Ireland Curriculum key stage 4 . The research included surveys of: 1) the organisation, timetabling and teaching arrangements for the science curriculum within schools; 2) the uptake of single science, double science and triple science courses and the factors influencing pupils' choice of option; 3) pupils' performance in single science, double science and triple science courses and their subsequent course/career choices. A sample of 30 post-primary schools, stratified by school type and management type, was drawn. Over a period of 3 years, a series of semi-structured interviews was conducted in the project schools with the major stakeholders: the head of science, the head of careers and the pupils. In addition, questionnaires were adminstered to the pupils, pre-course and post-course, to investigate their attitudes to science and to survey their reasons for choosing particular science programmes.

PUBLISHED MATERIAL: JARMAN, R. & MCALEESE, L. (1996). 'A survey of children's reported use of school science in their everyday lives', Research in Education, No 55, pp.1-15. ; JARMAN, R. & MCALEESE, L. (1996). 'Recent developments in the science education of 14-16 year-olds in Northern Ireland or "A tale of two policies"', The Curriculum Journal, Vol 7, No 3, pp.345-360. ; JARMAN, R. & MCALEESE, L. (1996). 'Physics for the star-gazer: pupils' attitudes to astronomy in the Northern Ireland Science Curriculum', Physics Education, Vol 321, No 4, pp.223-226. ; JARMAN, R., MCALEESE, L. & MCCONNELL, B. (1997). A survey of science at key stage 4: special studies. Belfast: Queen's University of Belfast, School of Education. ; JARMAN, R., MCALEESE,L. & MCCONNELL, B. (1997). A survey of science at key stage 4: executive study. Belfast: Queen's University of Belfast, School of Education. A full list of publications is available from the researchers.

STATUS: Sponsored project

SOURCE OF GRANT: Department of Education for Northern Ireland £92,891

DATE OF RESEARCH: 1993-1997

KEYWORDS: **choice of subjects; key stage 4; national curriculum - northern ireland; pupil attitudes; science education; secondary education**

2106

School of Education, 69 University Street, Belfast BT7 1HL
01232 245133

Jarman, R. Miss; *Supervisor*: Curragh, E. Dr

Secondary teachers' planning for primary science/secondary science curricular continuity: the impact of the Northern Ireland Curriculum

ABSTRACT: The study aims to compare secondary science teachers' planning for primary science/secondary science curricular continuity just prior to, and at, a number of critical stages subsequent to the introduction of the Northern Ireland Curriculum. During 1989/90, semi-structured interviews were conducted with heads of science in secondary schools to explore their perceptions on primary science and primary science/secondary science continuity, and their practice in respect of primary science/secondary science links and continuity. This provided baseline information for phase

2 of the study. A sample of 50 schools were revisited on a number of occasions after the first cohort of children to experience the full curriculum at key stage 2 had progressed to key stage 3. These schools' perceptions and practices in respect of primary/secondary continuity in science were again explored.

PUBLISHED MATERIAL: JARMAN, R. (1995). 'Science is a green field site: a study of primary science/secondary science continuity in Northern Ireland', Educational Research, Vol 37, No 2, pp.141-157.

STATUS: Individual research

DATE OF RESEARCH: 1989-1997

KEYWORDS: **developmental continuity; national curriculum - northern ireland; primary secondary education; primary to secondary transition; science education**

2107

School of Education, 69 University Street, Belfast BT7 1HL
01232 245133

McMahon, J. Ms; *Supervisor*: Gardner, J. Prof.

Teaching and learning technology project evaluation

ABSTRACT: The evaluation is looking at the impact of computers in teaching and learning within the Queen's University of Belfast, with implications for higher education in general. The overall objective is to identify the attitudinal, environmental policy and teaching/learning factors which inhibit or facilitate student usage of computers. The project is longitudinal in nature and involves observation of the various computing facilities at the University, as well as interview and questionnaire surveys with samples of students and members of staff. This target group will be monitored over the following 2 years to assess changes in attitudes and student computer usage patterns and competence.

STATUS: Sponsored project

SOURCE OF GRANT: Department of Education for Northern Ireland ; Higher Education Funding Council for England

DATE OF RESEARCH: 1993-1997

KEYWORDS: **computer assisted learning; computer uses in education; higher education; information technology**

2108

School of Education, 69 University Street, Belfast BT7 1HL
01232 245133

Barr, A. Ms; *Supervisor*: Kilpatrick, R. Dr

Suspensions and expulsions from schools in Northern Ireland

ABSTRACT: Phase 1 of the research identified levels and patterns of suspensions and expulsion from schools in Northern Ireland while Phase 2 examined the preventative and reintegration strategies used in primary and secondary schools. Phase 3 which will commence in September 1997 will consist of a series of case studies examining the processes operated in schools where good or innovative practice was identified in Phase 2 of the study. Additionally, young people who are frequently suspended or have been expelled will be followed-up in order to identify educational, family or social factors which may contribute to exclusion from school for behavioural reasons.

STATUS: Sponsored project

SOURCE OF GRANT: Department of Education for Northern Ireland

DATE OF RESEARCH: 1996-1997

KEYWORDS: **discipline; exclusion; northern ireland; primary education; secondary education**

2109

School of Education, 69 University Street, Belfast BT7 1HL
01232 245133

Shuttleworth, I. Dr; *Supervisors*: Kilpatrick, R. Dr; Thompson, W. Mr

Scoping study on children/youth living in Making Belfast Work areas

ABSTRACT: The study aims to: 1) assess the needs of children and young people in the 0-25 year-old age group living in socially deprived areas of Belfast; 2) establish a baseline in terms of services provided by the statutory and voluntary sectors to meet those needs, and 3) identify any gaps in the current provision. Secondary analysis of existing data will be conducted to describe the target population under 5 headings namely: demographic, economic, education, social and health factors. Service provision will be profiled by means of a questionnaire to all providers, and young people (or their parents) will also be asked to complete a questionnaire indicating what services they use and their location. To identify needs, focus groups will be run with young people and a range of professionals and this information will be backed-up by a questionnaire administered to larger groups of children and professionals. The information on provision and uptake of facilities will be mapped to identify where and how far young people are travelling to services and any gaps in provision. The analysis of the focus group information will identify perceived needs and this information will be related to the demographic data and again mapped to identify gaps in services. A literature review will identify accounts of best practice in addressing the needs of young people and consider the methodological issues in evaluating how needs and the relative social deprivation of young people can best be assessed.

STATUS: Sponsored project

SOURCE OF GRANT: Making Belfast Work

DATE OF RESEARCH: 1997-1997

KEYWORDS: **children; community services; disadvantaged; needs; northern ireland; social services; youth**

2110

School of Education, 69 University Street, Belfast BT7 1HL
01232 245133

Knipe, D. Mr; *Supervisors*: McEwen Dr; McGuiness, C. Dr

CRAGS: A cognitive framework for A-levels and GNVQs

ABSTRACT: One of the chief obstacles to reforming the curriculum for 16-19 year-olds is the entrenched division in our national intellectual culture between academic knowledge and the traditionally lower esteemed vocational training. A-levels, for example, are widely perceived as the 'gold standard' of academic values at this stage of education. Proponents of General National Vocational Qualifications (GNVQs), by contrast, argue that A-levels are too narrowly focused and unrelated to students' future needs at work. By concentrating on a number of core vocational skills and specific knowledge, GNVQ students are better prepared for their work than their A-level counterparts. The project will seek to investigate these claims by: 1) developing a learning framework that captures continuities between how subject knowledge and styles of thinking in A-level, and core thinking and vocational skills in GNVQs, are realised in the ways in which the 2 curricula are taught and learnt; 2) investigating the variations in student knowledge and skills acquired during A-level and GNVQ courses; 3) enabling teachers and lecturers, through action research, to observe and reflect on the design and delivery of knowledge and skills in A-level and GNVQ classrooms; 4) analysing, through a series of case studies, teachers' and students' construction and use of knowledge and skill in the 2 curricula over an extended period of time; and 5) creating a curricular framework such that A-levels and GNVQs might be more easily combined and their common features would become more transparent.

STATUS: Sponsored project

SOURCE OF GRANT: Economic and Social Research Council £60,000

DATE OF RESEARCH: 1996-1998

KEYWORDS: **a level examinations; academic education; academic vocational divide; cognitive development; curriculum development; general national vocational qualifications; thinking skills; vocational education**

2111

School of Education, 69 University Street, Belfast BT7 1HL
01232 245133

McKeown, E. Mr; *Supervisors*: McEwen, A. Dr; Johnston, J. Dr

Factors influencing A-level students' attitudes to primary teaching as a career

ABSTRACT: The central aim of this study is to investigate the reasons for the widening gap between the numbers of men and women choosing to enter primary teaching. In Northern Ireland, the 1992 primary teacher population was 21% male and 79% female. The specific objectives of the project are to generate data from a wide range of perspectives which will permit a clearer understanding of the phenomenon. The study will examine the perceptions of 6th Form students, careers teachers, training college admissions officers, preservice teachers and probationary teachers as to factors which influence decision-making regarding primary teaching as a career.

STATUS: Sponsored project

SOURCE OF GRANT: Equal Opportunities Commission £12,000

DATE OF RESEARCH: 1997-1997

KEYWORDS: **career choice; men teachers; northern ireland; preservice teacher education; primary school teachers; teachers; teaching profession; women teachers**

2112

School of Education, 69 University Street, Belfast BT7 1HL
01232 245133

Neil, S. Dr

Diversification in modern languages in schools in Northern Ireland

ABSTRACT: French has traditionally been the main foreign language offered as first foreign in the post-primary sector in Northern Ireland. In recent years several schools have introduced other languages as alternatives to French in Year 8 and in some schools elaborate models of language provision are in operation. This project sets out to investigate patterns of language provision and to investigate aspects of good practice. Interviews will be conducted with school principals, heads of language departments and with pupils.

STATUS: Sponsored project

SOURCE OF GRANT: Department for Education Northern Ireland £15,000

DATE OF RESEARCH: 1997-1998

KEYWORDS: **modern language studies; northern ireland; secondary education**

2113

School of Psychology, David Keir Building, Stranmillis Road, Belfast BT9 5AG
01232 245133
Queen's University of Belfast, School of Education, 69 University Street, Belfast BT7 1HL

McGuinness, C. Dr; Greer, B. Dr; Daly, P. Dr; Salters, M. Mr; McGillion, P. Ms; Curry, C. Dr

ACTS: Activating Children's Thinking Skills

ABSTRACT: The Activating Children's Thinking Skills (ACTS) project is an initiative aimed at developing thinking skills within the context of the Northern Ireland Curriculum. In the first phase of the project (January 1995-March 1996) the researchers identified core concepts with regard to thinking skills; analysed the Programmes of Study and Levels of Attainment within the curriculum in order to identify 'opportunities' for developing higher order thinking; liaised with teachers in Northern Ireland who are already involved in structured programmes to develop thinking skills; interviewed good practice teachers, both primary and secondary, about their views on the obstacles and opportunities for developing thinking skills within the Northern Ireland Curriculum. The second phase of the project (June 1996-September 1997) is proceeding with development work at key stage 2 using an infusion approach across the curriculum. The infusion method seeks to identify contexts within the curriculum where particular thinking skills can be developed (e.g. problem solving, causal reasoning, classification) and to develop lesson plans where these thinking skills and topic understanding can be explicit and simultaneously pursued. Working closely with 17 primary teachers, the purpose is to produce an ACTS Handbook for key stage 2 teachers which will include contributions from the participating teachers.

STATUS: Sponsored project

SOURCE OF GRANT: Northern Ireland Council for the Curriculum Examinations and Assessment

DATE OF RESEARCH: 1995-1997

KEYWORDS: **cognitive development; learning processes; learning strategies; primary education; teaching methods; thinking skills**

Reading University

2114

Department of Linguistic Science, Whiteknights, Reading RG6 2AL
01189 875123

Yamada-Yamamoto, A. Dr; Richards, B. Dr

Japanese children in the UK: cultural, educational and language issues

ABSTRACT: This research aimed to obtain an overview of the linguistic, educational and cultural experience of Japanese children who are temporarily resident in the UK. Data collection included the following: 1) a questionnaire survey of 320 Japanese families, including 591 children. Information was collected about length of stay, schools attended, parental background and the linguistic environment of the children; 2) interviews with a subsample of Japanese parents about linguistic and educational concerns; 3) longitudinal case studies of 5 Japanese children's acquisition of English; children were recorded at 3-4 weekly intervals in conversation with a trained interlocuter; 4) a case study of one Japanese child's early school experiences: video-recorded data of the child at school; interviews with his parents and teacher. Findings show that Japanese parents experience many difficulties resulting from differing cultural expectations of the educational process. However, while they are naturally concerned about their children's maintenance and development of Japanese, they value equally the acquisition of English and Japanese in their children. During the preschool years, in particular, children are exposed to considerably more Japanese than English.

PUBLISHED MATERIAL: YAMADA-YAMAMOTO, A. & RICHARDS, B.J. (Eds). (1998). Japanese children abroad: cultural, educational and language issues. Clevedon: Multilingual Matters. ; RICHARDS, B.J. & YAMADA-YAMAMOTO, A. 'The linguistic experience of Japanese pre-school children and their families in the UK', Journal of Multilingual and Multicultural Development. (in press).

STATUS: Sponsored project

SOURCE OF GRANT: Toyota Foundation £22,500; Matsushita International Foundation £8,250; Great Britain Sasakawa Foundation £2,650; Japan Foundation Endowment Committee £4,000

DATE OF RESEARCH: 1994-continuing

KEYWORDS: **bilingualism; cultural differences; english - second language; ethnic groups; japanese; japanese people; migrant children**

2115

Department of Linguistic Science, Whiteknights, Reading RG6 2AL
01189 875123
London University, Birkbeck College, Department of Applied Linguistics, Malet Street, London WC1E 7HX
0171 580 6622

Williams, A. Dr; *Supervisor*: Cheshire, J. Prof.

The influence of a non-standard dialect on children's school writing

ABSTRACT: The close relationship that is claimed between speech and early writing would suggest that children who speak a non-standard dialect would include some non-standard forms in their school writing, although standard English is the variety required in schools. The study investigated the occurrence in school writing of syntactic and morphological features of the dialect spoken in Reading, Berkshire. Sixty children (30 boys/30 girls) from 3 age groups, 9/10, 11/12, 13/14, who spoke non-standard, Reading English were selected from schools in Reading and their school writing in the form of all the extended written texts produced in their English books over a period of 2 terms, was compared with that of 60 children, matched for age, sex and ability who spoke standard English. Analysis of the written data indicated that children who spoke non-standard English also included non-standard forms in their written texts. Boys consistently used non-standard forms more frequently than girls and there was a significant age-related decrease in the use of non-standard forms across all groups. Spellings influenced by the Reading accent showed an age-related decrease, suggesting that older writers rely less on phonological strategies. Increased use of subordination in the texts of the older children evidenced a growing awareness of the requirements of written style, although discourse features, in adults usually confined to speech, occurred in the texts of all groups. The considerable variation in teachers' corrections and comments suggested that policies for dealing with non-standard dialect forms in children's writing have yet to be implemented.

PUBLISHED MATERIAL: WILLIAMS, A. (1989). 'Dialect in school written work'. In: CHESHIRE, J., EDWARDS, V., MUNSTERMANN, H. & WELTENS, B. (Eds). Dialect and education: some European perspectives. Clevedon: Multilingual Matters. ; WILLIAMS, A. (1993). 'Talk written down? The sociolinguistics of school writing'. In: DANES, F., CMERKOVA, S. & HARLOVA, D. (Eds). Writing versus· speaking: language, text, discourse, communication. Tubingen: Gunther Narr Verlag.; WILLIAMS, A. (1994). 'Writing in Reading: syntactic variation in children's school writing in Reading, Berkshire'. In: MELCHERS, G., JOHANNESSON, N.L. (Eds). Non-standard varieties of language. Stockholm: Almqvist and Wiksell.

STATUS: Individual research

DATE OF RESEARCH: 1985-1986

KEYWORDS: **children as writers; dialect studies; english; language variation; primary school pupils; secondary school pupils; sociolinguistics; verbal communication; writing - composition; written language**

2116

Department of Linguistic Science, Whiteknights, Reading RG6 2AL
01189 875123
London University, Queen Mary and Westfield College, Department of Linguistics, Mile End Road, London E1 4NS
0171 975 5555

Kerswill, P. Dr; Williams, A. Dr; Cheshire, J. Prof.

The role of adolescents in dialect levelling

ABSTRACT: The aim of the project is to investigate a phenomenon increasingly recognised by both linguists and lay people in recent years, the apparent decrease in phonological and syntactic differences between dialects. Three towns with differing demographic characteristics have been selected as research sites: Milton Keynes, Reading and Hull. The researchers aim firstly to describe and analyse the speech of young people from contrasting social backgrounds in each area, and compare their speech patterns with those of elderly residents, and secondly to attempt to identify the regional and social characteristics of dialect levelling processes. The main subjects of the research will be adolescents, since this age group seems to be particularly innovative in its use of language. Thirty-two 14/15 year old pupils from comprehensive schools will be recruited in each town and samples of formal and informal speech recorded. Interviews with sixteen elderly residents of each town will also be recorded for purposes of comparison. The data for each subject will comprise a reading list, an interview with a fieldworker and, in the case of the adolescents, responses to tasks designed to elicit phonological and grammatical variables. Approximately twelve phonological and twelve grammatical and discourse features currently involved in social and geographical diffusion will be transcribed, coded and analysed using a combination of quantitative and qualitative methods.

STATUS: Sponsored project

SOURCE OF GRANT: Economic and Social Research Council £137,000

DATE OF RESEARCH: 1995-1998

KEYWORDS: **adolescents; dialect studies; english; language variation; sociolinguistics; speech communication**

2117

Department of Linguistic Science, Whiteknights, Reading RG6 2AL
01189 875123
Reading University, Department of Psychology, Whiteknights, Reading RG6 2AL

Shockey, L. Dr; Watkins, A. Dr

Perception of conversational English by native and non-native speakers

ABSTRACT: The research shows there are two primary strategies for the unravelling of ambiguity which occurs in relaxed, unselfconscious speech: short-term strategy, which relies on the perceiver's knowledge of phonetics, phonology and lexicon; and long-term strategy, which relies on the perceiver's knowledge of semantics and pragmatics. Native speakers use both of these with skill, but non-native speakers rely very heavily on the second. This makes speech perception slower for them, because it involves processing of large spans of speech after reception, rather than 'real time' processing. The current research attempts to quantify the seriousness of this effect and to suggest language teaching techniques which will lessen the effect.

STATUS: Team research

DATE OF RESEARCH: 1993-continuing

KEYWORDS: english - second language; second language teaching; speech communication

2118

Department of Psychology, Whiteknights, Reading RG6 2AL
01189 875123

Leather, C. Dr; Turner, J. Dr; *Supervisor*: Henry, L. Dr

The development of the rehearsal strategy

ABSTRACT: This project investigated the development of the verbal rehearsal strategy in children and related this to current theories of memory development. Memory was tested using a touch screen which allowed recall to be examined without the interference of spoken output and, thus, allowed the effects of output interference and verbal rehearsal to be distinguished. Accuracy data and reaction times were collected. The first series of experiments investigated the effect of the modality of presentation upon rehearsal strategy development in children aged 4 to 10 years. Evidence for rehearsal was taken from word length effects, self-reported memory strategies and video-recordings. With probed, non-verbal, recall, rehearsal was found to emerge at about 7 years in both modalities. When full, nonverbal, recall was used rehearsal was found at 4 years. This result is inconsistent with the prediction by Gathercole and Hitch (1993), based on the working memory model, that rehearsal should develop earlier with auditory presentation. Rehearsal training was conducted which demonstrated that 5 year-olds can be taught rehearsal techniques successfully and that work length effects will then occur for auditory presentation. A second series of experiments explored the influence of familiarity with the memory items upon the development of rehearsal. No effect of familiarity was found for 5 year-olds while significant effects were found for older children and for adults. The development of rehearsal and the familiarity effect occur concurrently. Disassociations between word length effects and familiarity effects, however, suggest that the familiarity effect is not a consequence of rehearsal. The results are consistent with the familiarity effect being produced by a strategic reintegration or reconstruction process.

PUBLISHED MATERIAL: HENRY, L.A., LEATHER, C., TURNER, J.E. & SMITH, P.T. 'Exploring the development of the rehearsal strategy'. In: HOFFMAN, J. & SEBALD. A. (Eds). Cognitive psychology in Europe. ; TURNER, J.E., HENRY, L,A. & SMITH, P.T. (1998). 'The influence of familiarity upon short-term memory in children'. Proceedings of the British Psychological Society Conference, 1998.; HENRY, L., TURNER, J.E. & SMITH, P.T. 'Modality effects and the development of rehearsal strategies in children', Journal of Experimental Child Psychology. (in press).

STATUS: Sponsored project

SOURCE OF GRANT: Medical Research Council £100,000

DATE OF RESEARCH: 1994-1997

KEYWORDS: child development; child psychology; memory; rehearsal

2119

Faculty of Education and Community Studies, Department of Arts and Humanities in Education, Bulmershe Court, Earley, Reading RG6 1HY
01189 875123

Pegg, L. Mrs; *Supervisor*: Kemp, A. Prof.

National programme of training for primary school music consultants

ABSTRACT: The purpose of the project is to provide a programme of inservice training for primary school music teachers who wish to develop consultancy skills. This training is offered on a national basis, organised in various locations throughout the country, and consists of four-week phased courses of the kind held at the University of Reading Music Education Centre since 1982. These courses offer teachers an updated view of recent developments in the primary music curriculum and training in the processes of consultancy work amongst colleagues. They also offer conferences for primary headteachers within their structure. A second important facet of the project will be the development of regional groups of music consultants to encourage on-going professional interchange and aftercare.

PUBLISHED MATERIAL: SMITH, J. (1987). Music consultancy in Berkshire primary schools. Reading: Royal County of Berkshire Music Department. ; KEMP, A.E. (1988). 'Towards national adoption of music consultancy in primary schools'. In: BARTON, M. & STEWART, A. (Eds). British Music Education Year Book 1988/89. London: Rhinehold. ; KEMP, A.E. & WOOTTON-FREEMAN, S. (1988). 'New tasks for music in primary schools and teacher training', International Journal of Music Education, No 11, pp.21-24. ; PEGG, L.J. (1992). 'If music is for all pupils then it must be for all teachers', Early Education, No 7, pp.8. ; KEMP, A.E. (1993). 'School within communities; are music opportunities being missed?'. In: KEMP, A.E. & PEGG, L.J. Consultancy Matters. Reading: Reading University.

STATUS: Sponsored project

SOURCE OF GRANT: Music Industries Association £75,000; Caloustie Gulbenkian Foundation £15,000

DATE OF RESEARCH: 1988-1993

KEYWORDS: consultants; inservice teacher education; music; music teachers; primary school teachers

2120

Faculty of Education and Community Studies, Department of Arts and Humanities in Education, Bulmershe Court, Earley, Reading RG6 1HY
01189 875123

Drever, M. Mrs; *Supervisor*: Richards, B. Dr

Teaching English in a multilingual classroom

ABSTRACT: The research has two aims: (1) to carry out a survey of strategies used by class teachers in the teaching of the English language in a multilingual context, i.e. in a class composed of pupils from more than one linguistic home background, including English mother tongue, and (2) to suggest strategies which might benefit all pupils in attaining a competent level of English performance in order to cope with more sophisticated and subject specific language, semantically and structurally, as they move up the curriculum. The research will use classroom observation, interviews and questionnaires.

STATUS: Individual research

DATE OF RESEARCH: 1990-1993

KEYWORDS: english; minority groups; multilingualism; teaching methods

2121

Faculty of Education and Community Studies, Department of Arts and Humanities in Education, Bulmershe Court, Earley, Reading RG6 1HY
01189 875123
Theale Green School, Bath Road, Reading RG7 5DA
01189 875123

Kempe, A. Mr; Holroyd, R. Mr

Imaging

ABSTRACT: The end product of the research will be four books for use in top primary/lower secondary classrooms. Three pupil books will contain a range of resources on three separate topics. Literature, visual material, realia and research or creative tasks will be bound together by a linking narrative for each of the three topics. An accompanying teacher's book will outline how each individual resource may be used as part of an enactive learning programme and suggest various strategies by which the resources may be combined into dramatic structures. Within the whole project, there will be opportunities to meet the stated attainment targets of English in the National Curriculum document and some reference will also be made to the history, science, and craft, design and technology (CDT) documents. Most of the material is being trialled at a comprehensive school in Reading. Other elements are being used on inservice teacher education (INSET) courses and a programme of primary school sessions. The final publications will hopefully provide the basis for a more extensive and refined publishing programme aimed at meeting the needs of the National Curriculum without destroying current good practice.

PUBLISHED MATERIAL: KEMPE, A. & HOLROYD, R. (1986). 'Team teaching: cheap relief for a taxing problem', 2D Vol 6, No 1, pp.60-71. ; KEMPE, A. (1992). 'Enthusiastic beginners'. Drama, Vol 1, No 1, pp.13-16.

STATUS: Individual research

DATE OF RESEARCH: 1988-1993

KEYWORDS: drama education; educational materials; english; english studies curriculum; national curriculum

2122

Faculty of Education and Community Studies, Department of Arts and Humanities in Education, Bulmershe Court, Earley, Reading RG6 1HY
01189 875123

Fletcher-Campbell, F. Dr; *Supervisor*: Straughan, R. Dr

The caring school

ABSTRACT: Most schools claim to be caring institutions but it is not clear as to how this claim should be interpreted. The research analyses accounts in the literature and as given by a small sample of secondary headteachers. A philosophical analysis of the concept of the caring school is then undertaken before practical recommendations for schools' policy and practice are made.

STATUS: Individual research

DATE OF RESEARCH: 1988-1993

KEYWORDS: educational environment; educational philosophy; pastoral care education; pupil school relationship; pupil welfare

2123

Faculty of Education and Community Studies, Department of Arts and Humanities in Education, Bulmershe Court, Earley, Reading RG6 1HY
01189 875123

Richards, B. Dr; Chambers, F. Dr; Richards, M. Mrs

Oral assessment in modern languages

ABSTRACT: The project is a study of oral testing in French. The aim is to compare the reliability and validity of different assessment criteria currently used by GCSE examining groups and to investigate whether characteristics of teacher-examiners influence their ratings of candidates' performance. The main focus is on the assessment of 'free conversation'. The project involves: (1) a literature review; (2) a review of the syllabuses, administrative practices and marking schemes of the GCSE examining groups; (3) a survey of current practices in selected schools; (4) development of three sets of criteria for assessing free conversation which reflects different approaches used by examining groups; (5) obtaining tape recordings of 75 children who were examined in the 1990 GCSE examination. This sample represents the full range of oral marks awarded at GCSE; (6) selection of a sub-sample of 30 children from the above to represent the middle ability range; (7) preparation of two versions (two different random orders) of a set of pre-recorded tapes of the 30 children completing a free conversation task; (8) piloting the three sets of assessment criteria and accompanying instructions and mark sheets; (9) assessment by four groups of six teachers representing native and non-native speakers in comprehensive and selective schools, of the 30 conversations on two separate occasions, one month apart; (10) assessment by 22 PGCE Modern Languages students of the 30 conversations; and (11) validation of the GCSE speaking task by using 15-year old children attending two schools in France.

PUBLISHED MATERIAL: CHAMBERS, F. & RICHARDS, B.J. (1992). 'Criteria for oral assessment', Language Learning Journal, No 6, pp.5-9. ; CHAMBERS, F. & RICHARDS, B.J. (1992). A deux (videotape and accompanying notes). Reading: University of Reading, Department of Arts and Humanities in Education. ; CHAMBERS, F. & RICHARDS, B.J. (1993). 'Oral assessment: the views of language teachers', Language Learning Journal, No 7, pp.22-26. ; CHAMBERS, F. & RICHARDS, B.J. (1993). Native and non-native responses in oral interviews: implications for foreign language teachers and the assessment of oral performance. Departmental Working Paper. Reading: University of Reading, Department of Arts and Humanities in Education. ; RICHARDS, B.J. & CHAMBERS, F. (1993). Oral assessment in modern languages: summary of findings. Working Paper No 1. Reading: University of Reading, Department of Arts and Humanities in Education.

STATUS: Sponsored project

SOURCE OF GRANT: Reading University Research Endowment Fund £30,000

DATE OF RESEARCH: 1990-1993

KEYWORDS: assessment; french; general certificate of secondary education; modern language studies; oral tests

2124

Faculty of Education and Community Studies, Department of Community Studies, Bulmershe Court, Earley, Reading RG6 1HY
01189 875123

Denicolo, P. Dr

Part-time research students: the integration of this role with others in their professional lives

ABSTRACT: This research is derived from concerns about providing relevant and appropriate support for part-time research students in particular, although it may also produce results of significance to full-time research students. It is commonly accepted that research towards a higher degree is, inter alia, demanding, time-consuming, and requiring a high degree of motivation. Yet, a large number of part-time research students are mature and hence have many roles in life, personal and professional, which compete with their research student role. This research seeks to understand some of the effects that this role has on students' lives, in particular how it contributes to and constrains other roles. A personal construct theory approach (Kelly 1955) will be used to indicate commonalities of perspectives as well as to provide case studies which illuminate possible benefits, opportunities and difficulties derived from such an undertaking. Thus, it is speculated, the results will contribute to the provision of appropriate advice and support for prospective and current students.

PUBLISHED MATERIAL: DENICOLO, P. & POPE, M.L. (1994). 'A postgraduate's journey - an interplay of roles'. In: ZUBER-SKERRIT, O. & RYAN, Y. (Eds). Quality in postgraduate education. London: Kogan Page.

STATUS: Individual research

DATE OF RESEARCH: 1993-continuing

KEYWORDS: graduate study; mature students; part time students; student research

2125

Faculty of Education and Community Studies, Department of Education Studies and Management, Bulmershe Court, Earley, Reading RG6 1HY
01189 875123

Dawkins, J. Mr; *Supervisor*: Fidler, B. Prof.

Local management of secondary schools in Berkshire - an evaluation

ABSTRACT: The aim of this research is to monitor and evaluate the implementation of Local Management of Schools (LMS) in secondary schools in Berkshire to assess over the initial period if the quality of education in those schools has been enhanced by the provision of LMS. The researcher will aim to: (i) keep abreast of, and include current research in terms of a developing national perspective of the implementation of LMS; (ii) to detail within Berkshire the changes planned within the Local Education Authority as direct result of delegated budgets in secondary schools; (iii) evaluate (by means of a detailed case study of 3 secondary schools) the LMS pilot scheme; (iv) evaluate 3 further (non-pilot) schools as case studies; and (v) conclude whether the quality of education has been enhanced by the provision of LMS. Research will be carried out through questionnaires and follow up interviews of LEA officers and governors, teachers and administrators from at least six secondary schools.

STATUS: Sponsored project

SOURCE OF GRANT: Berkshire Local Education Authority £450

DATE OF RESEARCH: 1989-1993

KEYWORDS: educational change; evaluation; local management of schools; school based management; secondary education

2126

Faculty of Education and Community Studies, Department of Education Studies and Management, Bulmershe Court, Earley, Reading RG6 1HY
01189 875123
De Montfort University, 37 Lansdowne Road, Bedford MK40 2BZ
01234 351966

Keiner, J. Ms; Grugeon, E. Mrs

Evaluation of the National Oracy Project

ABSTRACT: The National Oracy Project was established to promote good practice in oral work across the curriculum and to develop appropriate modes of assessment for pupils aged 3 to 18 years. This evaluation of the National Oracy Project aims to explore the extent to which the Project's work fulfils its stated aims. A case study approach has been adopted, drawing on a selection of seven local authority consortia of teacher-based groups involved in the Project, in conjunction with studies of the National Project Team; its relationship with National Curriculum Council and other national educational policy bodies; and publications an other data emerging from the project. Methods used include analysis of published material and other documents; field visits and interviews; and participant observation. Results and conclusions will be published in a final report.

STATUS: Sponsored project

SOURCE OF GRANT: National Curriculum Council £22,000

DATE OF RESEARCH: 1990-1993

***KEYWORDS*: oracy; oral language; programme evaluation; speech communication**

2127

Faculty of Education and Community Studies, Department of Education Studies and Management, Bulmershe Court, Earley, Reading RG6 1HY
01189 875123

Singh, A. Dr; Spear, M. Dr

A local authority based demonstration trial of 'good practice' in road safety education

ABSTRACT: The primary aim of the project is to develop, implement and evaluate policies of 'good practice' in road safety education for children aged 5-16. The initial phase of the project is being spent developing guidelines for the management and co-ordination of road safety education both at local authority and at school level in collaboration with educational advisers, teachers, road safety officers, health education officers and the police; and in conducting a pilot trial in one local authority. During the second phase of the research, the revised policy document will be implemented through inservice training in all the primary and secondary schools (about 130 schools) within the selected areas of the two trial authorities. The third phase of the research will be concerned with monitoring the implemented programmes closely in 20 primary and 10 secondary schools in order to assess the impact on educational outcomes over a given period of time, for example in pupils' knowledge, skills, attitudes, behaviour and future intentions regarding road safety. The research design will be quasi-experimental. The input, process and evaluation data will be obtained through visits, interviews, questionnaires, telephone calls, observation of lessons and unobtrusive observation of actual behaviour on the roads. The cost effectiveness of programmes including measures of changes in casualty rate will also be assessed. The final phase of the research will comprise feedback to the participants, dissemination of the findings and the production of a report designed to assist local authorities and schools in implementing such policy(ies) effectively and economically.

STATUS: Sponsored project

SOURCE OF GRANT: Department of Transport: Transport and Road Research Laboratory £407,303

DATE OF RESEARCH: 1988-1993

***KEYWORDS*: safety education; traffic safety**

2128

Faculty of Education and Community Studies, Department of Education Studies and Management, Bulmershe Court, Earley, Reading RG6 1HY
01189 875123
Newcastle upon Tyne University, Department of Psychology, Ridley Buildings, Newcastle upon Tyne NE1 7RU
0191 222 6000

Stainthorp, R. Dr; *Supervisor*: Snowling, M. Prof.

A longitudinal study of the development of reading strategies in 7-11 year old children

ABSTRACT: This research is a longitudinal study of a group of sixteen children from a mainstream primary school. The children's reading strategies were studied by means of a series of experiments during their time in National Curriculum key stage 2 (age 7-11 years). The experimental programme included a series of repeated measures tasks investigating word and non-word reading accuracy; the effects of context on word and non-word reading; lexical and phonological decision tasks using ordinary non-words and pseudo-homophones. Finally, the children were interviewed about their reading habits and asked to fill in a UK version of an Author Recognition Test. The results indicated that good readers were able to use a decoding strategy when reading from age 7, but that poor readers had difficulty in so doing. This lack of a decoding strategy appeared to hinder progress, particularly in the development of an extensive sight vocabulary.

STATUS: Individual research

DATE OF RESEARCH: 1988-1993

***KEYWORDS*: reading processes; reading skills; reading tests**

2129

Faculty of Education and Community Studies, Department of Education Studies and Management, Bulmershe Court, Earley, Reading RG6 1HY
01189 875123

Fox-Lee, L. Ms; *Supervisor*: Brehony, K. Dr

The Montessori movement and English elementary education 1909-1939

ABSTRACT: The project aims to account for the career of the Montessori system in England between 1909-1939. Documentary analysis is used to cover a spectrum from published books, journal articles and other printed media, to school logbooks and Her Majesty's Inspector (HMI) reports. The concepts of ideology and discourse are foregrounded and the investigation seeks to demonstrate the role of tropes, rhetoric and poetics in the Montessori system's impact upon educational discourse.

STATUS: Individual research

DATE OF RESEARCH: 1993-1997

***KEYWORDS*: educational history; educational theories; elementary schools; montessori method**

2130

School of Education, Bulmershe Court, Woodlands Avenue, Earley, Reading RG6 1HY
01189 875123

Denicolo, P. Dr

Teaching for salient learning: actioning espoused theories in the face of perceived constraints

ABSTRACT: Rapid developments in knowledge, technology and policy in educational institutions enforce reflection on practice, both by teachers and learners. Building on data and results from previous staff development work, this research will investigate firstly the relationship between espoused theories of teaching and learning, theories-in-use and perceived imposed theories held by teachers. Informal research suggests that, although such teachers recognise the value of developing transferable, learning-to-learn skills in their students, they nevertheless feel constrained in their teaching strategies by overloaded syllabi and the expectations (perceived) of the culture and systems in which they work. A literature review and an indepth investigation of this, using a Personal Construct Theory approach across a range of provision, will ground the consequent research in both theory and practice. The second phase will consist of pilot trials, implementing a series of specific teaching strategies which are congruent with espoused theories but which take account of practical constraints. The results will be evaluated by triangulation of all participant views with comparisons of successful achievement between these and former students. The third phase will incorporate a similar study, using revised strategies from the second phase with a new group of students, to confirm and extend results and will also involve a follow-up study of the original student group to investigate the persistence of any new learning skills and their transfer to new learning situations. This will involve a variety of investigatory techniques with the original students and their new teachers as participants.

PUBLISHED MATERIAL: DENICOLO, P.M. (1993). 'Personal and professional development across the public and private sector'. Paper given at Management in the Public Sector Conference, Kingston University, July 1993. ; MAUND, L. & DENICOLO, P.M. (1994). 'Conflict stimulation and learning'. Paper given at Second European Personal Psychology Conference, EPCA, St. Andreasberg, Germany, April 1994.

STATUS: Individual research

DATE OF RESEARCH: 1992-1997

KEYWORDS: **learning strategies; learning theories; teaching methods**

2131

School of Education, Bulmershe Court, Woodlands Avenue, Earley, Reading RG6 1HY
01189 875123

Harwood, A. Dr; *Supervisor*: Denicolo, P. Dr

The effects of institutional and curricula course changes in further and higher education with regard to implications for staff development

ABSTRACT: The introduction of National Vocational Qualifications and the requirements of business and technology education for competence-based learning have resulted in changes in the role of teaching staff as 'lecturers' to 'facilitators' of learning with a greater degree of work placement involvement and more flexible modes of operation. Institutional changes have also resulted in changes in role for staff in colleges of further education, requiring their involvement in costing, marketing, quality assurance; while at the same time experiencing reduced security of tenure. Both aspects of change require skills and abilities which were not necessarily part of 'traditional' teaching roles and, therefore, call for appropriate staff development.

PUBLISHED MATERIAL: HARWOOD, A. & DENICOLO, P. (1994). 'Views on personal and professional development: listening to people's voices'. Proceedings of Second European Personal Psychology Conference, EPCA, St. Andreasberg, Germany, April 1994. ; HARWOOD. A. (1996). Skills for employment and education: towards a synergy of teachers', learners' and employers' perspectives. PhD Thesis. Reading: University of Reading.

STATUS: Individual research

DATE OF RESEARCH: 1991-continuing

KEYWORDS: **academic staff; educational change; further education; teacher development**

2132

School of Education, Bulmershe Court, Woodlands Avenue, Earley, Reading RG6 1HY
01189 875123

Stainthorp, R. Dr; Hughes, D. Mrs

Young early readers: a longitudinal study of the development of reading of a group of children able to read fluently prior to National Curriculum key stage 1

ABSTRACT: The young early readers project is a longitudinal study of the development of reading performance, cognitive characteristics and educational experiences of a group of 16 children who were identified as being fluent readers before they had begun their formal schooling. The background to the research is the original study by Margaret Clark (1976) but it is being carried out in the light of contemporary models of reading development. A further group of 14 children have been included in the study as a control group. These have been matched on age, sex, vocabulary development, socio-economic status, pre-school experiences and expected first school class. Over a period of 3 years all the children will be tested on a number of standardised and non-standardised measures. In addition, their parents and classroom teachers will be interviewed periodically. Preliminary results suggest that there are significant differences between the young early readers and their matched controls on all aspects of phonological awareness.

STATUS: Sponsored project

SOURCE OF GRANT: Reading University £45,000

DATE OF RESEARCH: 1993-1997

KEYWORDS: **child development; early reading; reading ability; young children**

2133

School of Education, Bulmershe Court, Woodlands Avenue, Earley, Reading RG6 1HY
01189 875123

Sellers, M. Mrs; *Supervisor*: Croll, P. Prof.

Home-based early intervention with hearing impaired children and their families

ABSTRACT: Although there is a body of work on various aspects of the development of young hearing impaired children in relation to, for example, audiology and child language acquisition, there does not appear to be any significant literature on the 'whole' development of the hearing impaired child within the context of the family, particularly in relation to the provision of home-based early intervention. The present study therefore focuses on home-based early intervention. It locks into the broad theoretical area of child development, and is expected to contribute: 1) a comprehensive analysis of perceived needs and of current provision; 2) an understanding of professional and non-professional decision making in this area; 3) identification of 'best practice' and proposals for enhancement of provision; and 4) suggestions for further research.

STATUS: Individual research

DATE OF RESEARCH: 1992-1998

KEYWORDS: **early childhood education; early experience; hearing impairments; intervention; parent participation; special educational needs**

2134

School of Education, Bulmershe Court, Woodlands Avenue, Earley, Reading RG6 1HY
01189 875123

Taylor, B. Mrs; *Supervisor*: Fidler, B. Prof.

Curriculum continuity from infants to junior schools

ABSTRACT: The aim of the research is to investigate the extent to which the National Curriculum and its associated testing has impacted on curriculum continuity in the transititon from infants to junior schools and how such continuity might be improved. The research has involved surveys of all-through primary schools and separate infants and junior schools to investigate curriculum continuity, before and after the start of testing at key stage 1. From these results, a need to improve curriculum continuity from key stage 1 to key stage 2 was established. The difficulties of improving continuity were investigated in a linked case study of infant and junior schools using action research.

STATUS: Individual research

DATE OF RESEARCH: 1990-1998

KEYWORDS: **developmental continuity; infant school education; junior schools; key stage 1; key stage 2; primary education; transfer pupils**

2135

School of Education, Bulmershe Court, Woodlands Avenue, Earley, Reading RG6 1HY
01189 875123

Fox-Lee, L. Ms; *Supervisor*: Brehony, K. Dr

The Dalton Laboratory Plan in England

ABSTRACT: This research includes: 1) broad survey of 'progressive' educators in England after World War 1; 2) examination of educational networks and the influence of the New Education Fellowship on progressive teaching; 3) specific examination of the work of Helen Parkhurst, her collaboration with Montessori and the development of the Laboratory Plan; 4) examination of the schools adopting the Plan in England, and the documents relating to practice, inspection and theory; 5) a consideration of gender in the implementation of the Plan; 6) consideration of subsequent educational methods drawing on the theories underpinning Parkhurst's work.

STATUS: Individual research

DATE OF RESEARCH: 1993-1998

KEYWORDS: **early childhood education; individualised methods; intervention; teaching methods**

2136

School of Education, Bulmershe Court, Woodlands Avene, Earley, Reading RG6 1HY
01189 875123

Gilbert, J. Prof.; Boulter, C. Dr; Buckley, B. Dr; Oversby, J. Dr; Pawel, S. Mr; Davies, T. Mr; Taylor, B.Mr

Models in science and technology: research in education (MISTRE)

ABSTRACT: The MISTRE Group is an international collaborative venture concerned with all aspects of models and modelling in science and technology, and in science education and technology education. The group includes colleagues from the National Portrait Gallery in London, the Science Museum in London, and from universities in Australia, New Zealand, South Africa and the USA. MISTRE seeks to explore the ways in which individuals construct and use mental models; the ways in which these models are presented as public domain models; the processes by which public models gain social acceptance, to become conceptual models; the use made of mental models, public models, and conceptual models, in the conduct and the teaching and learning of science and technology; models of the science community and of the science education community. The intention is also, subsequently, to present the outcomes of this exploration, within academic literature, in forms which can directly influence the conduct of science and technology education. In order to do so MISTRE conducts research and development projects on an international collaborative basis; holds seminars wherever members can assemble together; presents work at conferences; publishes, both individually and collectively.

PUBLISHED MATERIAL: GILBERT, J. (Ed). (1993). Models and modelling in science education. Hatfield: Association for Science Education. ; LOWE, R. & BELL, C. (1993). Successful instructional diagrams. Key Topics in Educational and Training Technology Series. London: Kogan Page. ; PRIEST, M. & GILBERT, J. (1994). 'Learning in museums: situated cognition in practice', Journal of Education in Museums, Vol 15, pp.16-18.; GILBERT, J. & BOULTER, C. (1994). 'Modelling across the curriculum: the demands and actualities of a unifying theme from science in the primary school'. In: VAN TROMMEL, J. (Ed) Science and technology education in a demanding society. Proceedings of the 7th International Symposium, Enschede, Netherlands, 1994.

STATUS: Team research

SOURCE OF GRANT: Reading University; National Portrait Gallery; Science Museum; Australian Research Council; CAPES, Brazil; Ministry of Education, New Zealand

DATE OF RESEARCH: 1993-continuing

KEYWORDS: **international educational exchange; models; science education; science technology and society; technology education**

2137

School of Education, Bulmershe Court, Woodlands Avenue, Earley, Reading RG6 1HY
01189 875123

Levesque, D. Mr; *Supervisor*: Watson, K. Prof.

Whose money? Whose education system? Perception gaps in aid management in Pakistan

ABSTRACT: Against a background of the ongoing desire of aid organisations to provide effective programmes, and the British Government's insistence on value for tax payers money, the research examines the policies and perceptions of aid donors recipients in education projects in Pakistan. It traces the development of aid priorities, primarily of the British Government and the World Bank and how these have interacted with the needs of the Pakistan Government and Ministries of Education. Two case studies are presented. The first, in the North West Frontier Province, describes the formation of a five year multi-donor funded primary education development programme from the perspective of a donor programme designer. This is contrasted with comments expressed by Pakistan officials during the two years of preparation. The second looks at the implementation of a similar primary programme in Sindh Province with specific reference to the training of senior managers. A series of questionnaires and interviews establishes the perspective of 99% of the serving senior education officials. The conclusions are compared to the original project documents and the objectives set by the donors. The results show that, historically, education development projects have only been moderately successful and despite donor efforts to improve participation in design and implementation, significant perception gaps continue to limit the cost effectiveness of aid programmes. Improvements can be expected through improving participation at all levels, the establishment of process rather than blueprint projects, and a realistic timetable for change.

STATUS: Individual research

DATE OF RESEARCH: 1991-continuing

KEYWORDS: **developing countries; development aid; economics education relationship; educational development; educational policy; pakistan**

2138

School of Education, Bulmershe Court, Woodlands Avenue, Earley, Reading RG6 1HY
01189 875123

Quist, D. Mrs; *Supervisor*: Cowan, B. Dr

Improving the quality of primary school teaching in Ghana: an examination of the potential role of school centred staff development programmes

ABSTRACT: Historically most teacher improvement efforts have focused on the individual, a perspective still reflected in the traditional inservice programmes of many developing countries. Recently, the value of, and need for school centred inservice programmes, has been fairly well documented by a range of educationists, from the international agencies to teachers at the 'grass roots'. What is less clear, is the way in which these programmes may be implemented and sustained in areas with few resources and an inadequate support system. This research, which focuses on Ghana, seeks to establish how far school centred staff development programmes are a viable and sustainable option for teacher improvement in primary schools. Two rather different purposes for staff development have been outlined in the available literature. One definition suggests that it should be aimed at training teachers in skills. The other, 'developmental' view, suggests that it should be designed to provide the continuing personal and professional growth of teachers within a supportive school climate. The research field work will explore which view is more appropriate in the present context of Ghanaian primary schools. The study will use a more qualitative approach involving policy analysis, questionnaires, interviews and observation. The study will look at a random sample of four primary schools in different contexts (rural urban - private/government), analyse the personal and professional 'needs' of both staff and management and identify the particular constraints which may affect the implementation of staff development in those schools.

STATUS: Individual research

DATE OF RESEARCH: 1994-1998

KEYWORDS: **developing countries; ghana; inservice teacher education; teacher development**

2139

School of Education, Bulmershe Court, Woodlands Avenue, Earley, Reading RG6 1HY
01189 875123

Welsh, M. Rev.; *Supervisor*: Watson, K. Prof.

The development and impact of Seventh-Day Adventists tertiary education in Jamaica

ABSTRACT: The study seeks to examine the development of Seventh-Day Adventists tertiary education in Jamaica through an analysis of relevant policy documents; local reactions to the spread of Seventh-Day Adventists education; the underline philosophy of Seventh-Day Adventists (SDA) and the development of the SDA educational position within the country with special reference to the tertiary level. The research will be divided into three broad areas: 1) An historical analysis of the development of SDA education. 2) An evaluation of the impact of SDA education. 3) Suggestions for future developments and relationships with the state sector. Data used will include documentary analysis of Ministry of Education files; and Institute of Jamaica (library) minutes and records of West Indies Union Conference of SDA. Qualitative and quantitative methodologies will be used. It is hoped that this study will throw light on one important aspect of educational development in the Caribbean region.

STATUS: Individual research

DATE OF RESEARCH: 1994-continuing

KEYWORDS: **church and education; jamaica; religion and education; religious cultural groups**

2140

School of Education, Bulmershe Court, Woodlands Avenue, Earley, Reading RG6 1HY
01189 875123

Hughes, D. Mrs; *Supervisor*: Stainthorp, R. Dr

The writing development of a group of young early readers

ABSTRACT: This research project is a longitudinal cohort study of the development of writing of a criterion group of 15 children who were able to read fluently on entry to full-time education at National Curriculum key stage 1 and a matched group of 14 children who were not able to read fluently on entry to school. The aims of the research are to document and analyse the writing development of the children during key stage 1, in terms of spelling, punctuation, handwriting and compositional aspects. The development of those cognitive processes underlying writing will also be studied. This information will then be related to the development of reading and to the children's experiences at home and school, with a view to being able to show how teaching strategies may be informed by such knowledge. A repeated measures design is being used. In order to make comparisons concerning progress and to relate this to home and school experiences, data is being collected at three points - 1994, 1995 and 1996 - and from three main sources - the children, their parents (or main caretaker) and their schools and teachers. A battery of standardised and non-standardised assessments is being used to collect information from the children. Information concerning their progress and their experiences at home and school is being obtained by conducting semi-structured interviews with parents and teachers.

PUBLISHED MATERIAL: HUGHES, D. (1995). 'The handwriting skills of young early readers', Handwriting Review, Vol 9, pp.50-67. ; HUGHES, D. (1995). 'The writing development of a group of young fluent readers: work in progress', The British Psychological Society Education Section Review, Vol 19, No 2, pp.76-78. ; STAINTHORP, R. & HUGHES, D. (1995). 'Young early readers: a preliminary report'. In: RABAN-BISBY, B., WOLFENDALE, S. & BROOKS, G. (Eds). Developing language and literacy in the English National Curriculum. Stoke-on-Trent: Trentham Books. ; STAINTHORP, R. & HUGHES, D. (1998). 'Phonological sensitivity and reading: evidence from precocious readers', Journal of Research in Reading, Vol 21, No 1, pp.53-68.

STATUS: Individual research

DATE OF RESEARCH: 1993-1998

KEYWORDS: cognitive processes; early reading; handwriting; infant education; key stage 1; literacy education; primary education; punctuation; spelling; writing skills; young children

2141

School of Education, Bulmershe Court, Woodlands Avenue, Earley, Reading RG6 1HY
01189 875123

White, D. Mr; *Supervisors*: Pope, M. Prof.; Badger, D. Mr

Inter-professional working with people learning disabilities

ABSTRACT: The research aims to investigate the problem of knowledge learning disability and the processes by which this knowledge is acquired, with particular reference to education and training. Inter-professional working within this area provides the focus for a number of discourses. The proposal is that conflict between discourses is managed through an 'everyday/practical' interpretation of particular policies and philosophies such as 'normalisation' and 'empowerment'. These discourses move between control and autonomy and involve a number of professions and interests, and actors may use more than one discourse about learning disability at one time. This is an under-theorised area in sociology, though some writers have applied what they see as a socioligical perspective. In particular the use of 'social models' of disability presents problems when used to explain the lives of people with learning disabilities. A postgraduate course for people working in the field is being observed and a range of professionals will be interviewed to investigate their knowlege base. Workers in group homes are also being interviewed; their relative training and education needs will be examined.

STATUS: Individual research

DATE OF RESEARCH: 1995-continuing

KEYWORDS: interprofessional relationship; learning disabilities; professional development; residential care

2142

School of Education, Bulmershe Court, Woodlands Avenue, Earley, Reading RG6 1HY
01189 875123

Vigneswaren, P. Ms; *Supervisor*: Pope, M. Prof.

The role of education in the treatment of sexually abused/abusing adolescents

ABSTRACT: The aims of the research are: 1) To explore the role of education in the treatment of adolescent males who have a history of sexually traumatic and traumatised patterns of behaviour, in a therapeutic setting. 2) To investigate the perceptions of sexually abused/abusing adolescents regarding educational provision and its impact on their therapeutic exposure. 3) To develop a model for a centre of educational excellence within a therapeutic environment for the positive development of sexually abusing young men. Within this, to evaluate the project at the researcher's place of work. The research will address inter alia the following research questions: 1) Identification and definition of criteria for excellence in education. 2) Abused/abusing young men - what is unique to this client group? 3) What is the current educational provision for young people in this category in the UK, America and Europe? 4) What are the constraints posed by difficulties in inter-agency liaison and the lack of inter-professional education and training? 5) What are the educational needs of this client group and how could these best be met? 6) How does this proposed provision reconcile with ongoing therapeutic approaches to provide consistency of care? 7) How can successful reintegration into the mainstream of education and society be facilitated? The methodology will be to conduct a literature survey including American and European literature in this field, and to carry out a documentary analysis of mission statements, educational material etc. It will also include action research case studies of 12 young people and comparison with a control group matched in terms of age, family background and nature of offence. This will include depth interviews with the young people concerned - including the use of repertory grid techniques (Kelly 1955). Significant others, including family, staff and educational providers, will also be interviewed.

STATUS: Individual research

DATE OF RESEARCH: 1993-1998

KEYWORDS: access to education; adolescents; behaviour modification; rehabilitation; sex offenders; sexual abuse; therapy

2143

School of Education, Bulmershe Court, Woodlands Avenue, Earley, Reading RG6 1HY
01189 875123

Denicolo, P. Dr

Higher degree research supervision: constructs and perspectives

ABSTRACT: Considerable experience of supervising PhD students, experience of the research process and of supporting colleagues as novice supervisors, led to a recognition of the need to research the process itself. Complaints about the quality of supervision appear regularly in the education press, yet little is provided by way of institutional guidance, in the main, other than information on regulations, nor is there a substantial literature available for reference. What there is of the literature tends mainly to consist of advice to students on how to survive the process or to be of the generalised description of the difficulty of the process. A notable exception is the documentation of the experience of one tutor and her supervisors by Salmon (1993). This research aims to elaborate this work, documenting the experience of a large number of students and supervisors in order to distinguish frequently recurring problems and solutions and idiosyncratic ones, so that both supervisors and students might learn from the experience of others. The research is conducted within a personal constructivist framework, using a range of instruments to encourage participants to articulate their perspectives and constructs. This is a longitudinal study as well as an indepth one. To date, more than 50 students have contributed, along with 10 staff.

PUBLISHED MATERIAL: DENICOLO, P.M. & POPE, M. (1994). 'A postgraduate's journey - an interplay of roles'. In: ZUBER-SKERRITT, O.

& RYAN, Y. (Eds). Quality in postgraduate education. London: Kogan Page.

STATUS: Individual research

DATE OF RESEARCH: 1994-continuing

KEYWORDS: doctoral degrees; graduate study; higher education; research; student research; supervision; supervisors

2144

School of Education, Bulmershe Court, Woodlands Avenue, Earley, Reading RG6 1HY
01189 875123

Courtenay, M. Mrs; *Supervisors*: Gilbert, J. Prof.; Pope, M. Prof.

The teaching, learning and use of infection control practices in nursing

ABSTRACT: The research was designed to answer the following questions: 1) The theoretical principles underpinning infection control are derived from microbiology. Which of these principles, and infection control procedures building on these principles, are taught to student nurses, qualified nurses and health care assistants? 2) What knowledge should be taught? 3) What of this knowledge is learnt? 4) What of this knowledge is used by student nurses, qualified nurses and health care assistants to support their clinical practice regarding infection control? 5) To what extent have the recent reforms in the National Health Service (NHS) and nurse education affected nursing practice? 6) What links exist between the answers to the first four questions? 7) To what extent do present nurse education and health care assistant training programmes produce staff with the appropriate knowledge and skills to deliver effective nursing care in the area of infection control? An ethnographic approach was adopted within a naturalistic framework. Data was collected from three programmes of nurse education - traditional registered nursing training; a BSc in nursing studies programme; and Project 2000 training - and a health care assistants training programme. The data was also collected from two twenty-six bed mixed male and female medical wards. Observations, interviews and documentary evidence was used to gather this data, which is now being analysed.

STATUS: Individual research

DATE OF RESEARCH: 1991-1997

KEYWORDS: nurse education; nurses; practical nursing

2145

School of Education, Bulmershe Court, Woodlands Avenue, Earley, Reading RG6 1HY
01189 875123

Ewens, E. Dr; *Supervisors*: Pope, M. Prof.; Howkins, E. Mrs

Changing role perceptions of students on integrated courses in community nursing: a case study approach

ABSTRACT: The National Health Service (NHS) and Community Care Act 1990 has placed inter-professional collaboration high on the agenda. The Post-Registration Education and Practice Document produced by the United Kingdom Central Council for Nursing, Midwifery and Health Visiting (UKCC) in 1994, has identified 8 community nurse specialists who can share a common core programme with specialist study and practice integrated into the course. A body of knowledge is building around the processes involved in preparing professionals who can collaborate in practice. The development of trust, mutual respect and understanding of one's own and others' professional roles is considered as some of the pre-requisites for collaborative practice. (HORNBY, S. (1993). Collaborative care: interprofessional, interagency and interpersonal. Oxford: Blackwell Scientific Publications). This study aims to explore the changing role perceptions of students on these integrated courses in community nursing. This study uses a longitudinal case study approach involving the indepth investigation of two integrated courses in community nursing. A personal construct psychology framework is used to explore the personal thinking of the key participants involved in these courses in relation to roles of different health and social care professionals. A triangulation of methods are being used including observation, interviews, and the repertory grid technique. Repertory grid elicitation took place with students from both courses on commencement of the course (63 out of a total of 80 students completed a grid), and a follow-up case study sample of students (n=26) were interviewed at the end of their course. A further interview is planned with them for early 1996. Single interviews have been carried out with

community practice teachers (n=25) and tutors (n-14). All the interviews are structured through the use of the repertory grid technique.

PUBLISHED MATERIAL: EWENS, E.A. (1995). 'Shared learning: integrated courses in community nursing'. Paper given at the 6th Annual International Nurse Education Tomorrow Conference, Durham University, Durham, September 5-7, 1995.

STATUS: Individual research

DATE OF RESEARCH: 1993-1998

KEYWORDS: community services; interprofessional relationship; nurse education; nurses

2146

School of Education, Bulmershe Court, Woodlands Avenue, Earley, Reading RG6 1HY
01189 875123

Mignot, P. Mr; *Supervisor*: Denicolo, P. Dr

Metaphor: a paradigm for interpreting 'self' and 'career'

ABSTRACT: This research project provides an account of an investigation into the nature of 'career' identities of young men. The account initially describes the development and implementation of a methodology that places joint emphasis on the personal and social domains of the research exercise, in order to realise an emancipatory praxis through collaboration between participants. The methodology addresses not only how individuals construct meaning in their lives, but also how power relations are constructed , maintained and implemented. The account then describes the programme of empirical research which was undertaken in an urban youth centre with participants drawn from members of the centre's community. The participants were invited to construct a photographic record of aspects of their life that were significant to them in 'career' terms. These photographs provided the basis for a hermeneutic interpretation of individual and collective constructions of reality; this interpretation was undertaken through identifying the metaphorical constructs embedded within the discourse of the participants as they described their photographic 'texts'. The account concludes by considering both the liberating and constraining effects of the generative metaphors contained in the discourse of the participants as they construct and maintain their 'career' identities.

PUBLISHED MATERIAL: GOTHARD, W.P. & MIGNOT, P. 'Career counselling for the 21st century: integrating theory and practice', International Journal for the Advancement of Counselling. (in press).

STATUS: Individual research

DATE OF RESEARCH: 1995-continuing

KEYWORDS: career choice; career counselling; discourse analysis; metaphors; vocational guidance

2147

School of Education, Bulmershe Court, Woodlands Avenue, Earley, Reading RG6 1HY
01189 875123

Denicolo, P. Dr

Dilemmas experienced by teachers, teacher educators and educational researchers

ABSTRACT: This research derives from the experience of self and colleagues from a review of the literature which frequently notes the dilemmic nature of decisions required in the field of education. A PhD was supervised in the field (Miller 1994) and the current research builds on the literature base of this work, as well as on papers produced on the dilemmic nature of educational research. Explorations are continuing, using a personal construct psychology approach, with teachers, teacher educators and education researchers about how they experience and deal with the dilemmic situations they encounter, so that a review of personal strategies of coping can be documented. It is also intended that common dilemmas will be identified, described and followed-up in terms of the kind of strategies found to be effective. The techniques used in the research include interviews structured by personal construct techniques, such as repertory grids, time lines and concept-maps. Some results have already been, or are about to be, published.

PUBLISHED MATERIAL: MILLER, P. (1994). 'Perspectives on the recognitiion and resolution of dilemma within an educational framework'.

Unpublished PhD Thesis, Surrey University. ; DENICOLO, P.M. (1996). 'Productively confronting dilemmas in educational practice and research'. In: KOMPF, M., BOND, R., DVORET, D. & BOAK, T. (Eds). Changing research and practice: teachers' professionalism, identities and knowledge. London: Falmer Press.

STATUS: Individual research

DATE OF RESEARCH: 1995-continuing

KEYWORDS: **educational researchers; problems; teacher educators; teachers**

2148

School of Education, Bulmershe Court, Woodlands Avenue, Earley, Reading RG6 1HY
01189 875123

Albanese, M. Ms; *Supervisor*: Denicolo, P. Dr

Analyzing the use of the right and left brain in the writing process

ABSTRACT: The aim of the research is to understand when and how we use the left hemisphere (analytical) and the right hemisphere (creative) during the writing process, specifically academic writing.

STATUS: Individual research

DATE OF RESEARCH: 1995-continuing

KEYWORDS: **brain hemisphere functions; writing processes**

2149

School of Education, Bulmershe Court, Woodlands Avenue, Earley, Reading RG6 1HY
01189 875123

Denicolo, P. Dr; Harwood, A. Dr

Teaching approaches which promote learning skills required by current and future European employers

ABSTRACT: Two institutions of higher education, one in the UK and a comparable one in Portugal, are participating in a project to identify: 1) staff perspectives on the kinds of skills required of their graduate students by the social and economic forces of the European market; 2) staff perspectives on the teaching methods which develop those skills; 3) students' perspectives on their development of such skills during the course of their studies. In each institution, comparable departments have been selected and participants' views collected using questionnaires and interviews. Both of these have been designed to be culturally relevant in each context. The first part of the study will indicate common and different perspectives within and between institutions, the strengths and weaknesses of each, and lessons to be learned by each other. The second part will aim to test the consistency of perspectives across each local geographic region, using an extended number of institutions.

PUBLISHED MATERIAL: HARWOOD, A. (1996). Skills for employment and education: towards a synergy of teachers', learners' and employers' perspectives. PhD Thesis. Reading: University of Reading.

STATUS: Sponsored project

SOURCE OF GRANT: British Council Treaty of Windsor Project £4,000

DATE OF RESEARCH: 1994-continuing

KEYWORDS: **employment potential; european union; graduate employment; higher education; skill development; students; transfer of learning; work education relationship**

2150

School of Education, Bulmershe Court, Woodlands Avenue, Earley, Reading RG6 1HY
01189 875123

Apraiz, E. Ms; *Supervisors*: Denicolo, P. Dr; Thornton, C. Mrs

Communication in learning disabilities

ABSTRACT: The main aim of this research will be to gain a better insight into some of the ways of feeling and thinking, in people with learning disabilities, by enabling them to express their feelings and thoughts whilst experiencing guided mental walks via pictures of works of art. This study will take as a model a controlled intervention study of the effect on psychomedical health in elderly women, recently undertaken in Sweden by Dr. Britt-Maj Wikstrom, for the National Institute for Psychological Factors and Health, Karolinska Institute, Stockholm, Sweden. A great deal of research is required into communications and learning disabilities to ensure this group of people use their capabilities to the full, and benefit from therapies such as counselling. This research will begin with a pilot study concerning the effects of a visual stimulation programme provided in the form of pictures of works of art in a group of 6-8 adults with moderate learning disabilities. The question investigated here will be: 'What are the feelings and thoughts of the people involved with regard to abstract topics such as God, Heaven and Hell'. The answer to some of these questions should shed some light into the ways this group of people feel and think. Possible changes of mood and behaviour will be observed. A second study will be carried out after exploration and refinement of the method used in the pilot study, using 2-3 groups of a similar sample of people. In collaboration with other professionals, qualitative and quantitative analysis will be taken against changes in behaviour to investigate both emotional and intellectual skills.

STATUS: Individual research

DATE OF RESEARCH: 1996-continuing

KEYWORDS: **adults; art therapy; learning disabilities; pictorial stimuli; pictures; special educational needs; verbal communication**

2151

School of Education, Bulmershe Court, Woodlands Avenue, Earley, Reading RG6 1HY
01189 875123

Stainthorp, R. Dr

Learning spelling: handwriting versus the computer

ABSTRACT: Cunningham and Stanovich (1991) have reported that when children are in the early stages of learning to spell, handwriting is a more powerful medium for learning than using a computer. In their research, the computer was one which gave only visual feedback and no aural feedback. The Somerset Talking Pendown project suggests that when aural feedback is incorporated into a teaching programme, it can be an effective instructional aid. This project is designed as a replication of Cunningham and Stanovich's work with the added variable that aural feedback will be available when children are using the computer. National Curriculum key stage 1 children in a mainstream primary school will act as subjects for a controlled learning experiment with handwriting and computer keyboarding as the two variables.

PUBLISHED MATERIAL: STAINTHORP, R. (1997). 'Learning to spell: handwriting does not always beat the computer', Dyslexia, Vol 3, pp.229-234.

STATUS: Sponsored project

SOURCE OF GRANT: Reading University

DATE OF RESEARCH: 1996-1997

KEYWORDS: **computer uses in education; handwriting; information technology; key stage 1; literacy education; primary education; spelling; talking computers; writing skills; writing teaching**

2152

School of Education, Bulmershe Court, Woodlands Avenue, Earley, Reading RG6 1HY
01189 875123

Stainthorp, R. Dr

Settling children into school: home-school transition policies

ABSTRACT: Research shows that children's reading performance at the end of their first year in school is related, among other things, to the ease with which they settle into school. This research project is designed to investigate the procedures that schools adopt for making home-school links around the time that children are about to start school. A group of 14 teachers wrote accounts of their own schools' procedures and from these a questionnaire was developed. The questionnaire is being sent to a wide range of National Curriculum key stage 1 schools. As a cross-cultural comparison, the questionnaire will also be answered by teachers in Sydney, Australia. Preliminary data suggest that the UK schools have a wide variety of approaches but that all are ensuring that home-school links are developed.

STATUS: Individual research

DATE OF RESEARCH: 1995-1997

KEYWORDS: **home school relationship; home to school transition; infant school pupils; key stage 1; parent participation; primary education; pupil school relationship; reception classes; school entrance age; young children**

2153

School of Education, Bulmershe Court, Woodlands Avenue, Earley, Reading RG6 1HY
01189 875123

Croll, P. Prof.; Moses, D. Ms

One in Five: special educational needs from the 1970s to the 1990s

ABSTRACT: The study is concerned with the extent and nature of special educational needs (SEN) in primary schools and, through a replication of the One in Five (Croll and Moses, 1985) study, will provide a unique comparison with the situation in the early 1980s. Change over the period will be analysed in the context of major legislation and other developments. The research has relevance to appropriate provision for SEN and for understanding of the process of educational change.

PUBLISHED MATERIAL: CROLL, P. & MOSES, D. Special educational needs in the primary school. London: Cassell.

STATUS: Sponsored project

SOURCE OF GRANT: Economic and Social Research Council £120,000

DATE OF RESEARCH: 1997-continuing

KEYWORDS: **educational history; educational policy; primary education; special educational needs**

2154

School of Education, Bulmershe Court, Woodlands Avenue, Earley, Reading RG6 1HY
01189 875123

Croll, P. Prof.; Moses, D. Ms

Trajectories of special educational needs

ABSTRACT: The study will provide a dynamic account of developments in special education over the last 15 years by: a) using government statistical data to construct typologies of the development of provision at local education authority (LEA) level; and b) by interviewing LEA officers and headteachers to construct an explanatory framework for the emergence of different trajectories. Differing patterns of special educational provision will be analysed and located within models of centre-local relations in education, influences and constraints on education policy and on elements of conflict and consensus in thinking about special educational needs.

PUBLISHED MATERIAL: CROLL, P. & MOSES, D. (1998). 'Pragmatism, ideology and educational change: the case of special educational needs', British Journal of Educational Studies, Vol 46, No 1, pp.11-25.

STATUS: Sponsored project

SOURCE OF GRANT: Economic and Social Research Council £27,000

DATE OF RESEARCH: 1996-1998

KEYWORDS: **educational policy; special educational needs**

2155

School of Education, Bulmershe Court, Woodlands Avenue, Earley, Reading RG6 1HY
01189 875123

Copeland, I. Dr

The school prospectus: special, primary, secondary and independent schools

ABSTRACT: Since 1982, the school prospectus or brochure has become an instrument for central control of schools, such that it compels schools annually to publish information in precise categories. This is for the intended benefit of parents who may thus locate schools in an education quasi-market. The sample consists of some 600 brochures for the academic year 1997-98 from schools in 7 local authorities in Central, Southern England. A comparison with a similar sample for 1992-93 for primary and secondary schools is made. Analysis reveals that the fulfilment of stipulated requirements proves more challenging for secondary than primary schools.

Some requirements are met by less than half the brochures while others are variable. The new requirements highlighted by Department for Education and Employment documents sent to all schools were poorly addressed. This was particularly so in the requirement to furnish comparative national data for National Curriculum tasks and tests and for the General Certificate of Secondary Education. The recording of rates of absence, authorised and unauthorised, also fluctuated. Statements for sporting aims were also frequently omitted.

STATUS: Sponsored project

SOURCE OF GRANT: Standing Conference on Studies in Education £450

DATE OF RESEARCH: 1998-1998

KEYWORDS: **educational markets; marketing; parent choice; school brochures**

2156

School of Education, Bulmershe Court, Woodlands Avenue, Earley, Reading RG6 1HY
01189 875123

Fidler, B. Prof.; Morris, R. Dr

The local authority contribution to school improvement - benchmarking

ABSTRACT: The aim of the research is to investigate the contribution to school improvement by 5 local education authorities (LEAs). The initial stage of the research was to collect data about LEA activities which contributed to improvements in their schools. Data was collected by interview with designated officers. The provision of comparative data to schools emerged as a key LEA contribution to school improvement. The next stage of the research will access schools' views of the value of benchmarking data and investigate how such data is used by schools for improvement purposes.

STATUS: Team research

DATE OF RESEARCH: 1996-1998

KEYWORDS: **benchmarking; educational quality; local education authorities; school effectiveness; school improvement**

2157

School of Education, Bulmershe Court, Woodlands Avenue, Earley, Reading RG6 1HY
01189 875123

Rahman, M. Mr; *Supervisors*: Fidler, B. Prof.; Ogden, J. Dr

The impact of management information systems for education in the Malaysian context

ABSTRACT: The aim of the research is to investigate the extent to which the newly implemented education management information system (EMIS) in Malaysia is providing timely, complete, accurate, relevant and reliable data and to investigate possible ways of improving these aspects of data collection. The study will monitor the early stages of the implementation of EMIS and particularly its impact on schools. The extent to which schools use the data collected for EMIS will be investigated. This may be compared with the use English schools make of the schools information and management system (SIMS) developed in the UK.

STATUS: Individual research

DATE OF RESEARCH: 1997-continuing

KEYWORDS: **computer uses in education; information technology; malaysia; management information systems**

2158

School of Education, Bulmershe Court, Woodlands Avenue, Earley, Reading RG6 1HY
01189 875123

Butt, F. Ms; *Supervisor*: Fidler, B. Prof.

The effects of policy changes in the funding of liberal adult education in universities with particular reference to the 1992 Policy Review

ABSTRACT: The research aims to study the implementation of policy changes in the funding of liberal adult education in the universities following the 1992 policy review. Implementation will be studied for its effects on institutions, departments, courses and individual students. Survey data has been collected from 7 universities. Focus groups of students have also been used as a source of data. A model of policy implementation in higher education is to be developed.

STATUS: Individual research

DATE OF RESEARCH: 1997-continuing

KEYWORDS: **adult education; continuing education; educational finance; universities**

2159

School of Education, Bulmershe Court, Woodlands Avenue, Earley, Reading RG6 1HY
01189 875123

Davies, T. Mr; Jones, P. Mr; Howe, T. Mr; *Supervisor*: Dillon, P. Dr

Educational research in innovation, design and society

ABSTRACT: The research of the group is concerned with the relationship between technology, in its various manifestations, and technological education, in its various contexts. The processes of innovation and design are seen as central to technological developments and the group believe that technological change is best understood through its socio-economic and cultural contexts. The goal of the group, at the approach of the millennium, is to produce definitive publications on aspects of educating for a technological future.

PUBLISHED MATERIAL: JONES, P. (1997). 'Cultural constructs of technology: a different paradigm for technological literacy'. Proceedings of the 7th International Conference on Design and Technology Educational Research and Curriculum, Loughborough University, 1997. ; DILLON, P., WRIGHT, B. STILL, M. & THORNTON, P. (1997). 'Conducting research over the internet. An interactive, image-based instrument for investigations in environmental education', Journal of Information Technology for Teacher Education, Vol 6, No 2, pp.147-156. ; DAVIES, T. (1997). 'Models in technology and technology education'. In: GILBERT, J.K. (Ed). Models and modelling in science and technology. New Bulmershe Papers. Reading: University of Reading, Department of Science and Technology Education.; DILLON, P.J. (1998). 'Information technology and higher education'. Special Issue of the Journal of Information Technology for Teacher Education, Vol 7, No 1.

STATUS: Sponsored project

SOURCE OF GRANT: Reading University; Endowment Trust Fund

DATE OF RESEARCH: 1992-continuing

KEYWORDS: **design; technological advancement; technology education**

2160

School of Education, Bulmershe Court, Woodlands Avenue, Earley, Reading RG6 1HY
01189 875123

Osborne, M. Mr; *Supervisors*: Pope, M. Prof.; Bailey, R. Dr

An investigation into the characteristics of individual performers/players as compared to team players

ABSTRACT: The 'hypothesis' will examine the assumption that different categories of sports attract or tolerate people with different personality characteristics. The personal constructs that successful sports performers utilise, and their self image, may be shown to vary in relation to the 'demands' of their particular activity. In particular, individual participants (e.g. athletes, golfers, tennis players and perhaps solo musicians for example) may need to exhibit different 'acceptance' and 'responsibility' characteristics from those associated with team sportsmen/women. Golfers and skiers for example have no team mates, referees or 'direct' opponents to 'blame', and it may be that attitudes and behaviours of this type of performer differ significantly from others - particularly in successful participants. The work of Kelly and Rogers may be helpful in identifying parameters of suitability of personality 'models' of successful participants, similar to the way that exercise physiology has identified physical constraints for explosive versus endurance events and informed training, selection and resource allocation on this basis. The implications for training and selecting sportsmen and women on the basis of 'mental' suitability may be informed through this investigation. Having tried to help sports participants - from club and recreational level, through to professional and international level - with

sports related psychological issues, it seems apparent that there is often a need to adopt an eclectic, negotiated programme of diagnostic and 'corrective' processes to help reach or regain a state of mind which enables the performer to operate at optimum levels of awareness and arousal for successful participation in their sport at appropriate level. In addition to sport psychology inventories, counselling techniques are necessarily involved in such situations. Developing a diagnostic model and concommitant 'treatment' process is an underlying 'raison d'etre' of the study. The target groups are amateur, professional, club and international players from both categories. The distinctive nature of golf will be emphasised. The methodology will include: 1) literature review of behavioural and construct material; 2) interview - players, coaches and administrators; 3) possible development of appropriate inventories - with quantitative and qualitative analysis, in addition to the utilisation of existing research tools from sports and mainstream psychology; and 4) observation and guided introspection. Whilst there is currently a very strong emphasis on a large psychometric approach to the study of sports related psychological phenomena, it is proposed that an eclectic 'Rogerian/Construction Theory' view of the issues highlighted in the investigation will help provide information on a 'fit-for-purpose' mental profile for sportsmen in different fields of competitive and cooperative endeavour.

STATUS: Individual research

DATE OF RESEARCH: 1998-continuing

KEYWORDS: **individual activities; individual characteristics; sports; sports psychology; team sports**

2161

School of Education, Bulmershe Court, Woodlands Avenue, Earley, Reading RG6 1HY
01189 875123

Macfadyen, T. Mr; *Supervisors*: Bailey, R. Dr; Croll, P. Prof.

Identifying and addressing exceptional ability as a special need in physical education

ABSTRACT: The development of the most gifted children raises crucial questions concerning the organisation of education and the curriculum. The aim of this research is to provide a clearer picture of the nature of gifted pupils in physical education and to suggest the most appropriate ways of educating exceptionally able pupils. Basing itself within the special needs perspective the research will consider how current rhetoric is being translated into practice. Through critical analysis of recent guidance, schools' practice in this area will be investigated. More specifically the study will centre upon how giftedness in physical education is being treated. The focus will be upon how the needs of exceptionally able children can be 'ordinarily met' in physical education. Resource and curricular implications for pupils statemented as having a special need in physical education will be explored. The National Curriculum for Physical Education (1995) states that all children should be provided with a broad and balanced curriculum that should be taught 'in ways appropriate to their abilities'. Assuming this premise, the second major strand of the project will investigate the current provision of physical education for the most gifted pupils in mainstream schools. The research will be based on a triangulation method utilising both qualitative and quantitative perspectives to include: 1) interviews with teachers of physical education; 2) a large scale survey of physical education departments in England; 3) an indepth look at the relevant documentation of Government, local education authorities and schools. Analysis of the data will attempt to formulate a model of good practice in the delivery of physical education to those pupils of exceptional ability.

STATUS: Individual research

DATE OF RESEARCH: 1999-continuing

KEYWORDS: **exceptional persons; gifted; gifted disabled; physical education; special educational needs**

2162

School of Education, Bulmershe Court, Woodlands Avenue, Earley, Reading RG6 1HY
01189 875123

Macaro, E. Dr; *Supervisor*: Croll, P. Prof.

Analysis of foreign language classroom interaction with particular reference to teacher recourse to first language (L1)

ABSTRACT: This thesis explores the oral interaction between student teachers and their pupils in foreign language classrooms in England. It focuses particularly on the ways in which 6 student teachers use English, the first language (L1) of the majority of the pupils in those classrooms, as opposed to French, the foreign language which is being taught. According to the National Curriculum for Modern Foreign Languages for England and Wales, the foreign language is the medium in which virtually all of the lesson should be conducted. This fact, in addition to theories and methods of language teaching, forms the backdrop to the analysis of the interaction. The student teachers' use of English is analysed both quantitatively and qualitatively. However, much greater emphasis is placed on the qualitative analysis of the interaction, using (among others) discourse analysis techniques, such that research questions about what are the causes of the use of English and what are the effects of that use can attempt to be answered. Additionally, using an ethnographic framework, issues related to student teacher thinking are explored. The findings suggest high levels of variance of interaction patterns amongst subjects. Nevertheless, overall, low levels of L1 use were detected and the evidence suggests that student teacher L1 does not, necessarily, lead to pupil L1 use. The findings of this thesis underline and contribute to the current educational debate about the exclusion of the first language and its possible demotivating effect. The findings are applicable not only to the foreign language classroom in England, but also to other second language classrooms in a variety of learning contexts.

PUBLISHED MATERIAL: MACARO, E. (1998). The analysis of foreign language classroom interaction with particular reference to teacher recourse to L1. Unpublished PhD Thesis. Reading: University of Reading.

STATUS: Individual research

DATE OF RESEARCH: 1995-1998

KEYWORDS: **language usage; modern language studies; native speakers**

2163

School of Education, Bulmershe Court, Woodlands Avenue, Earley, Reading RG6 1HY
01189 875123

Kanellopoulos, P. Mr; *Supervisor*: Kemp, A. Prof.

An ethnographic study of primary schoolchildren's culture of musical improvisation

ABSTRACT: The research focuses on the examination of the social nature of children's practices of musical improvisation, and on the children's conceptions of these practices. An ethnographic approach was adopted. Fieldwork was carried out in a classroom of ten 8 year-olds who had not received any kind of musical training, in Piraeus, Greece, between February and June 1996. The findings suggest that the children's improvisation did not emerge as a response to sounds per se, but as a socially significant practice of music-making. Getting down to making music in the presence of others became a signifying force, in the sense that the children's conduct as music-makers and listeners was subjected to subtle and dynamic negotiation, both verbal and non-verbal. In other words, the attitude developed towards spontaneous music-making mediated their actual music-making and their conception of it. Moreover, it is argued that through their engagement with improvisation, the children learned that music-making is an open-ended process which is both deeply fulfilling and a mode of inquiry. Their improvisations constituted instances of positing questions and developing answers through self-determined action. These questions had nothing to do with skills: they had to do with concepts, which are immanent to the nature of music and its making. The consistency of the developed practices leads to the suggestion that these children created, not two hundred or so improvisations, but one single, collectively shaped Oevre. Also, during the discussion of their work (which emerged as a mode of objectivation), the children developed remarkable meta-musical thinking, which stemmed from and at the same time informed their practices.

STATUS: Individual research

DATE OF RESEARCH: 1995-continuing

KEYWORDS: **greece; music; music activities**

2164

School of Education, Bulmershe Court, Woodlands Avenue, Earley, Reading RG6 1HY
01189 875123

Macaro, E. Dr

Learner strategies in modern foreign languages: awareness and training

ABSTRACT: There has, in recent years, been an increasing interest in the strategies that 'good' language learners use, much of this centred on adult learners. Very little work has been carried out in the secondary sector, particularly in the UK. A pilot project into strategy use was carried out at the University of Reading and initial findings suggested that, for example, girls use many more strategies than boys and more often. The main project involving schools in the Reading area and the area around Rome (Italy) has provided further evidence of gender as a variable in strategy use. When comparing strategy use across the two countries it becomes clear that different teaching styles and educational context do make a difference. It also raises the issue of whether questionnaire scales using descriptions of frequency use can be compared across national learning contexts. A strategy training programme was initiated in both countries. One of the most interesting results from the training is that experimental groups made significant gains when compared to control groups in the area of training for memorisation of vocabulary and formulaic phrases. Other interesting insights were offered by the 'think-aloud' techniques which were applied to learners in both countries.

PUBLISHED MATERIAL: MACARO, E. (1998). 'Learner strategies: piloting awareness and training', Tuttitalia, No 18, pp.10-16.

STATUS: Sponsored project

SOURCE OF GRANT: European Union (Socrates) £11,000

DATE OF RESEARCH: 1997-continuing

KEYWORDS: **comparative education; italy; learning strategies; modern language studies; secondary education**

2165

School of Education, Bulmershe Court, Woodlands Avenue, Earley, Reading RG6 1HY
01189 875123

Bhatti, G. Dr

Aspirations and achievements: teenagers into young adulthood. A longitudinal study of Asian young people

ABSTRACT: This is a follow up research which grew out of a doctoral study of 50 Asian (Pakistani, Bangladeshi and Indian) boys and girls. Initial findings of doctoral work are going to be published by Routledge in April 1999. The book is entitled 'Asian children at home and at school: an ethnographic study. The researcher is going to re-visit the same families - or as many as possible after nearly 8 years from the initial research. The aim is to find out how many of the 25 boys and 25 girls achieved their aspirations. The target sample is 50. These are predominantly Muslim families with some Sikh and Hindu families as well. The main focus will be the young people and what they made of their lives since leaving school. The main method will be ethnography.

STATUS: Individual research

DATE OF RESEARCH: 1999-continuing

KEYWORDS: **achievement; asians; aspiration; ethnic groups; followup studies**

2166

School of Education, Bulmershe Court, Woodlands Avenue, Earley, Reading RG6 1HY
01189 875123

Ewens, E. Dr; *Supervisors*: Howkins, E. Mrs; Pope, M. Prof.

The changing role perceptions of students on integrated courses in community health care nursing

ABSTRACT: This study explores the changing role perceptions of students on integrated courses in Community Health Care nursing. The integrated course, based on the principles of interprofessional education, was introduced to address the low levels of collaboration created by isolated training. Concern however was expressed that this type of learning would lead to a loss of specialist role identity and result in the creation of the generic community nurse. The impact of the integrated course on promoting interprofessional collaboration, whilst maintaining a specialist role identity, is unknown. The research is a comparative case study of two integrated courses involving the research methods of observations, interviews and the repertory grid technique. At the start of the courses, repertory grids were elicited from 67 students (out of a possible 80), 26 students were selected and followed up in 2 interviews, including further repertory grid elicitation at the end of the courses and after 6 months in practice. An interview with grid elicitation also took place with 24 community practice teachers and 14 tutors. The findings show that: 1) all the students gain a secure professional role identity and successfully take up roles within the healthcare system; 2) understanding of each other's roles does not develop and this points to the failure of the course in promoting interprofessional collaboration. The integrated course is a successful curriculum in preparing graduate practitioners for their specialist role but the impact of interprofessional education in this process is left in doubt.

STATUS: Individual research

DATE OF RESEARCH: 1993-1998

KEYWORDS: **community health services; nurse education; nurses**

2167

School of Education, Bulmershe Court, Woodlands Avenue, Earley, Reading RG6 1HY
01189 875123

Ashwell, N. Mr; *Supervisors*: Denicolo, P. Dr; Lynch, P. Dr

A critical study of collaborative responses by community-based projects and organisations to the sexual health education needs of young people

ABSTRACT: Organisations and agencies in the primary health care fields are being encouraged to work together, yet a number of factors significantly inhibit such cooperation. The research explores the nature of the difficulties that organisations and agencies, associated with sexual health education, encounter as they attempt to collaborate. Data is being collected through questionnaires, semi-structured interviews, and from observations of group meetings documentation. Personal Construct Psychology (PCP) is being used to explore people's attitudes to collaboration utilising repertory grids and for the narrative interview. The research explores the extent to which PCP is an appropriate approach for such research. Preliminary results indicate the important contribution that the diversity of organisational cultures and the differing perceptions of such diversity make to the process of collaboration. Results should be universally applicable to any group of agencies or organisations wishing to develop a collaborative working relationship.

STATUS: Individual research

DATE OF RESEARCH: 1995-continuing

KEYWORDS: **agency cooperation; health education; sex education**

2168

School of Education, Bulmershe Court, Woodlands Avenue, Earley, Reading RG6 1HY
01189 875123

Walkington, H. Miss; *Supervisor*: Gayford, C. Dr

Reflections of places, reflecting on practice

ABSTRACT: The research aims to elicit teachers' images of, aims and practice regarding developing localities about which they are teaching at key stage 2. A suite of complementary methods, questionnaires, interviews, a focus group and text analysis of teaching packs all contribute to a qualitative research design. Two contrasting groups of teachers are being studied: VSO returned volunteers, and teachers with no direct experience of the developing world, to ascertain the impact of such long-term experience upon images, aims and practice. Results so far point towards more dynamic and multi-faceted place images, aims more oriented to global citizenship education and practice oriented to development education methodologies than teachers with only vicarious attachment to the locality about which they are teaching. The teaching resources display underlying ideologies which appear to be unnoticed by teachers using them. The suggestion is that a more critical pedagogy should form the basis of teacher education/training and inservice work to ensure that ideologies and bias can be effectively reflected upon in images, aims, practice and resources.

STATUS: Individual research

DATE OF RESEARCH: 1996-continuing

KEYWORDS: **developing countries; geography; geography teachers; world studies**

2169

School of Education, Bulmershe Court, Woodlands Avenue, Earley, Reading RG6 1HY
01189 875123

Denicolo, P. Dr; Fuller, M. Prof.; Boulter, C. Dr

The assessment of M.Phil/PhD degrees

ABSTRACT: The general aim of this project is to inform and improve the practice of examination of doctoral degrees. Novice and experienced examiners and doctoral research supervisors alike would welcome clarification of criteria and procedures so that they might better ensure comparability of standards and fair operation of assessment. This is a 3 part project. Part 1 uses documentary analysis of university documents (UK) which provide information, rules and procedures about doctoral assessment. These will be reviewed for similarities and differences. Part 2 will use indepth interviews and personal construct psychology techniques to explore how the regulations and criteria are interpreted and implemented by key informants (registrars, researcher directors, supervisors and examiners). Part 3 will use similar methods and questionnaires to explore the views of participants, including students, in a range of selected case vivas.

STATUS: Team research

DATE OF RESEARCH: 1997-continuing

KEYWORDS: **assessment; degrees - academic; doctoral degrees; higher education**

2170

School of Education, Bulmershe Court, Woodlands Avenue, Earley, Reading RG6 1HY
01189 875123

Denicolo, P. Dr; Pope, M. Prof.

An evaluation of the benefits and limitations of formal programmes of research training for doctoral students

ABSTRACT: Formal training for research students is demanded by research councils but there exists no empirical evidence that this produces better support or completion rates than individual or group supervision. This research seeks to explore whether there is evidence that attendance on research training courses benefits the students and the supervisors. The study will use quantitative data on successful completions; rates of completion and the provision of research training will be collected from a range of institutions for a range of disciplines and analysed for correlations. A qualitative phase will follow in which a sample of students, supervisors and managers of courses/research will be interviewed using personal construct psychology techniques to explore perceived significant benefits and limitations of different forms or research training.

STATUS: Team research

DATE OF RESEARCH: 1999-continuing

KEYWORDS: **degrees - academic; doctoral degrees; higher education; student research**

2171

School of Education, Bulmershe Court, Woodlands Avenue, Earley, Reading RG6 1HY
01189 875123

Denicolo, P. Dr; Pope, M. Prof.

A review of the definitive differences between forms of higher degree (MA, MSc, M.Res, ED.D, M.Phil, PhD)

ABSTRACT: The Harris Report recommends the improvement of practice and greater consistency between institutions in relation to higher degrees. Criteria to differentiate these forms of degrees are vague in documents and mainly implicit in practice. This research aims to make these more transparent and explicit. Literature on the topic is being compiled, collated and documents are being analysed to identify definitions currently used. Salient differences and similarities in criteria are being identified between and within different degree forms. A qualitative phase will follow in which academics from different disciplines and institutions will be interviewed using personal construct psychology techniques to identify how different forms and levels of higher degrees are identified in practice.

STATUS: Team research

DATE OF RESEARCH: 1999-continuing

KEYWORDS: **degrees - academic; doctoral degrees; higher education; masters degrees**

2172

School of Education, Bulmershe Court, Woodlands Avenue, Earley, Reading RG6 1HY
01189 875123
Buckinghamshire College, Newlands Park Campus, Goreland Lane, Chalfont St Giles HP8 4AD
01494 874441

Parsons, C. Ms; *Supervisor*: Fidler, B. Prof.

The internationalisation of higher education institutions

ABSTRACT: The internationalisation of higher education can be defined as 'the incorporation of an international dimension in teaching, learning and research'. Published research has traditionally concentrated on the educational aspects of this dimension, with limited attention paid to the roles of institutional strategy and policy. There have been few attempts to understand whether the approach to internationalisation might change over time, as institutional experience increases. The concept of 'partner' institutions is similarly under-researched. The research therefore aims to develop and test an analytical framework for studying institutions at an advanced stage of internationalisation. The influences of macro environmental, institutional and individual factors will be considered. Finally, recommendations for institutional policy will be derived from the analytical framework. Participant observation, interviews and documentary evidence will be used in the collection of qualitative data from four higher education institutions, two in the UK and two in Germany. Findings will be presented in case study form.

STATUS: Individual research

DATE OF RESEARCH: 1994-continuing

KEYWORDS: **higher education; institutional cooperation; international educational exchange**

2173

School of Education, International Centre for Research in Music Education, Bulmershe Court, Woodlands Avenue, Earley, Reading RG6 1HY
01189 875123

Pegg, L. Mrs; *Supervisors*: Kemp, A. Prof.; Richards, B. Dr

Kinaesthetic, linguistic, auditory and visual modes of mental imagery in children's music learning processes

ABSTRACT: The research builds on an initial investigation 'Kinaesthetic, auditory, visual and linguistic imagery in children's music learning processes (Pegg, 1991). The use of four modalities in musical memory were investigated: kinaesthetic, visual, auditory and linguistic. The study employed a quantitative methodology with randomised samples for each modality. The subjects were children aged 8 to 9 years, subjects were asked to respond to music in different groups (randomised) utilising one given modality. Later they were involved in a musical memory test. The findings suggested that each of the four modalities could be utilised by individuals. The use of the kinaesthetic modality did not lead to any observable difference in musical memory trace. The present study aims to attempt further clarification of the area where little specific research exists and where existing studies lack comparability because of differences in focus and methodology. It also aims to assemble data concerning the modes of imagery utilised in children's musical memory processes, amongst individuals and at different ages and stages of development. The study commences with a summary of the earlier literature review, discusses the research methodology employed and re-examines the critical analysis of the findings. Subjects will be children aged 6 to 7, 8 to 9 and 10 to 11 years. Relevant and ethnically acceptable methodologies are discussed and a multi-faceted approach identified using qualitative, quantitative and more naturalistic approaches. Data from each methodology will be assembled and analysed section by section. Finally the results will be compared, contrasted and synthesised, conclusions reached and future research identified. Implications for practice will be discussed.

PUBLISHED MATERIAL: PEGG, L.J. (1991). Kinaesthetic, auditory, visual and linguistic modalities in children's music learning processes. Unpublished MA Dissertation. Reading: University of Reading. ; PEGG, L.J. (1994). The principles of influential music educators. Reading: University of Reading, International Centre for Research in Music Education. ; PEGG,

L. (1998). Music. Leamington Spa: Scholastic.

STATUS: Individual research

DATE OF RESEARCH: 1997-continuing

KEYWORDS: **kinaesthetic perception; music**

2174

School of Education, Bulmershe Court, Woodlands Avenue, Earley, Reading RG6 1HY
01189 875123
London University, Institute of Education, 20 Bedford Way, London WC1H 0AL
0171 580 1122

Earley, P. Mr; Ferguson, N. Mr; Fidler, B. Prof.; Ouston, J. Dr

The inspection of primary schools: factors associated with school development and becoming a self-evaluating institution

ABSTRACT: The research aims to discover why some primary schools are more effective than others in using inspections organised by the Office for Standards in Education (OFSTED) as a catalyst for development. The investigation will involve surveys of two groups of schools - those that were inspected in the spring term 1997 and those to be inspected in the summer term 1998. The periods of preparation for inspection and action planning following inspection will both be investigated. From these surveys a small number of representative case studies will be undertaken.

STATUS: Sponsored project

SOURCE OF GRANT: Nuffield Foundation £52,893

DATE OF RESEARCH: 1998-continuing

KEYWORDS: **inspection; institutional evaluation; ofsted; primary education; school development planning; school effectiveness; school improvement**

2175

School of Education, Bulmershe Court, Woodlands Avenue, Earley, Reading RG6 1HY
01189 875123
London University, King's College, Department of Nursing Studies, Cornwall House Annexe, Waterloo Road, London SE1 8WA
0171 836 5454

Goding, L. Mrs; *Supervisor*: Pope, M. Prof.

An investigation into the intuitive nature of health visiting practice

ABSTRACT: The research will focus on the intuitive nature of health visiting practice. The issues raised will be analysed in relation to theory/practice integration within the education of community nurses at degree level. The assumption is that insights and intuition are essential components of performance and these abilities are neglected in the education and assessment of community nurse practice. The research will seek to: 1) investigate the relationship between theory and practice with reference to the education and the intuitive aspects of health visiting practice; 2) examine the perceptions of community practice teachers regarding intuitive practice; 3) incorporate a comparative element, looking at assessment of the intuitive aspects of performance in two other professions, to broaden the research perspective, serving to enlighten the assessment of community nurse practice. It is hoped that the data collected will enable the creation of a strategy for the education and assessment of community nurse practice in conjunction with appropriate education for community practice teachers. It is anticipated that qualitative data will be obtained by the use of semi-structured, taped interviews followed by written examples of intuitive practice. Observation with videotaping followed by individual interviews will also be undertaken with community practice teachers and their clients which, in combination with the other methods of data collection, will enhance the researcher's understanding of intuitive performance.

PUBLISHED MATERIAL: GODING, L. (1997). 'Can degree level practice be assessed?', Nurse Education Today. (in press).

STATUS: Individual research

DATE OF RESEARCH: 1994-1998

KEYWORDS: **community health services; health personnel; health visitor education; health visitors; intuition; nurse education; nurses**

2176

School of Education, Reading and Language Information Centre, Bulmershe Court, Woodlands Avenue, Earley, Reading RG6 1HY
01189 875123

Abbas, S. Mrs

Access to Information on Multi-cultural Education Resources (AIMER)

ABSTRACT: AIMER is a database project which offers students, teachers, advisers and others information on multicultural antiracist teaching materials. In recent years there has been a proliferation of booklets, packs and other resources produced within local education authorities (LEAs) and other organisations. AIMER acts as a clearing house for materials of this kind. In addition to a postal inquiry service, it publishes resource lists on a wide range of topics which are updated on an annual basis. It is possible either to buy individual resource lists or the whole set at a substantial discount in the form of a single volume, 'Photocopiable resources to support the multicultural dimension of the National Curriculum'. A publications list is available on request.

DATE OF RESEARCH: 1987-continuing

KEYWORDS: **databases; multicultural education; resource materials**

2177

School of Education, Reading and Language Information Centre, Bulmershe Court, Woodlands Avenue, Earley, Reading RG6 1HY
01189 875123

An, R. Ms; *Supervisor*: Edwards, V. Prof.

Learning in two languages and cultures: the experience of mainland Chinese families in Britain

ABSTRACT: The project will explore perceptions of British education of parents from the People's Republic of China temporarily resident in the UK. The study will be based upon the Reading Chinese community which is typical of other university towns all over the UK. It consists of some 50 research staff and students, including 18 married couples and children. As a member of the community in question, the researcher will have access to all the families in question. Interview data will be collected from 3 groups: Chinese parents, Chinese children and British teachers and will be supplemented by observational data in schools. This research is taking place within an ethnographic framework and as such, aims to generate rather than test hypotheses. It uses a wide range of methodologies including participant observation, indepth interviews with parents, teachers and videotaped recordings of teaching situations. The researcher will analyse this data using NUD*IST, a package designed for handling qualitative data. Study of the Chinese community is likely to make a contribution to the theorising on the nature of different ethnic minority communities. It also contributes to the study of comparative education.

STATUS: Individual research

DATE OF RESEARCH: 1996-continuing

KEYWORDS: **chinese; comparative education; cultural differences; english second language; ethnic groups; migrant children; parent attitudes**

2178

School of Education, Reading and Language Information Centre, Bulmershe Court, Woodlands Avenue, Earley, Reading RG6 1HY
01189 875123

Edwards, V. Prof.

Fabula: bilingual multimedia stories for children

ABSTRACT: This is a collaborative project with: Reading University; Brighton University; DTP Workshop, Dublin; The Linguistics Institute of Ireland; Universitat Popeu Flavia, Barcelona; Kankobo Ikastola, France; and GCO, The Netherlands. Fabula is a project involving teachers and children, software designers, information designers, translators, and researchers in various fields including language and literacy learning, human computer interface, and typography and graphic communication. The aim is to develop an authoring tool, to enable teachers to create illustrated bilingual multimedia storybooks to help primary school children learn a second language (and gain a deeper understanding of their first) through the written word, supported by pictures and sound. As children read the 'pages' of these storybooks, using the specially developed Fabula viewer software, they will be able to exploit the unique opportunities provided by a multimedia environment to interact with the texts and pictures, in particular exploring the equivalencies and differences between their two languages. The Fabula team will also assist with the design and production of support materials, both on and off-line.

STATUS: Collaborative

DATE OF RESEARCH: 1998-continuing

KEYWORDS: **bilingualism; computer software; computer uses in education; english - second language; information technology; multimedia; second language learning**

2179

School of Education, Reading and Language Information Centre, Bulmershe Court, Woodlands Avenue, Earley, Reading RG6 1HY
01189 875123
Reading University, Department of Typography and Graphic Communication, 2 Earley Gate, Whiteknights, Reading RG6 2AL

Walker, S. Dr; Edwards, V. Prof.

Interactive multimedia in primary schools: perspectives on design and classroom use (IMPS)

ABSTRACT: The project is looking at children's responses to conventions for access, navigation, typography and picture/text interaction. It is also concerned with issues of classroom management: how do teachers introduce interactive materials to their class and how can they use them in their schemes of work. A key part of the project is the development of a descriptive framework: 1) to allow teachers to gain some kind of generic overview of the ways that information is organised on interactive multimedia; 2) to compare points of contact/conflict with paper-based materials; and 3) to highlight issues of interface design and information structuring that children find helpful or difficult to understand. The development of the framework will be based on descriptive work in relation to characteristics of print material as well as approaches to multimedia design. It will focus on access, navigation, typography, picture/text interaction. It is hoped that the outcome of the project will provide teachers and designers with a way of talking about the graphic and linguistic conventions used in multimedia, as well as contributing to ways of describing graphic language.

STATUS: Sponsored project

SOURCE OF GRANT: British Library

DATE OF RESEARCH: 1996-continuing

KEYWORDS: **computer uses in education; information technology; multimedia; primary education**

2180

School of Education, Bulmershe Court, Woodlands Avenue, Earley, Reading RG6 1HY
01189 875123
Reading University, Department of Agricultural Extension and Rural Development, 3 Earley Gate, Whiteknights Road, Reading RG6 2AL

Taylor, P. Mr; *Supervisors*: Garforth, C. Dr; Cowan, B. Dr

Policy formation, implementation and evaluation of inservice training of trainers: the development of an institutional policy for inservice training of teachers (INSET) at Botswana College of Agriculture

ABSTRACT: In Botswana, many changes are taking place which affect the agricultural industry and the distribution of population between rural and urban areas. A vital element of the development process, education and training must meet and supply evolving needs of all members of the population. As an institution unique in Botswana, Botswana College of Agriculture (BCA) must ensure that its staff is in a position to respond professionally to the new demands placed upon them. One means by which this may be achieved is through inservice training of staff. This research aims to examine the role and strategies of inservice training of teachers (INSET) at Botswana College of Agriculture in the context of the situation in Botswana, in order to determine the effectiveness of policies and methods relating to INSET. Teaching and administrative staff, students and written sources at Botswana College of Agriculture, personnel of the Ministries of Agriculture and Education and other external agencies in Botswana will comprise the sources of data. A triangulatory approach will be adopted for this project in an attempt to gather data which will allow a systematic analysis of the situation pertaining at BCA. This will involve a case study, including a review of relevant literature, interviews and use of diary keeping. The research will also employ a quantitative element via the use of questionnaires, where appropriate, in order to gather data which may illuminate the findings of the case study.

STATUS: Individual research

DATE OF RESEARCH: 1994-1997

KEYWORDS: agricultural colleges; agricultural education; botswana; developing countries; inservice teacher education; staff development

2181

School of Education, Bulmershe Court, Woodlands Avenue, Earley, Reading RG6 1HY
01189 875123
Reading University, Faculty of Education and Community Studies, Department of Arts and Humanities in Education, Bulmershe Court, Earley, Reading RG6 1HY

McKee, G. Dr; Knott, R. Dr; *Supervisors*: Richards, B. Dr; Malvern, D. Mr

A new research tool: mathematical modelling in the measurement of lexical diversity

ABSTRACT: Most measures of lexical diversity or repetitiveness have the disadvantage of being dependent on the size of the language sample used for measurement. For the Type-Token-Ratio (TTR), for example, the more tokens that are included from a transcript or text the lower the ratio will be. This phenomenon has distorted research findings in a number of areas of educational and linguistic research. A solution to the problem is to model the curvilinear relationship between TTR values and the number of tokens. Mathematically modelling the probability of new vocabulary being introduced into longer and longer texts offers a method for measuring lexical diversity that is not dependent on the size of the sample of words in the way that TTR and other measures are. An equation and a set of procedures for curve fitting are used to produce a single parameter, D, which provides the best fit for the TTR versus Token curve for any language sample. The advantages of this approach are that the measure is not a function of sample size, all the data available in a transcript are made use of, and the values for D represent the TTR versus Token curve rather than a single point on it. The project has developed softward ("vocd") which will act on any transcript in the CHAT format of the CHILDES project. In fact, the text-handling part of the program has been modelled on FREQ in Brian MacWhinney's CLAN software, and unless other options are chosen will divide up any transcript into types and tokens in the same way as FREQ. The difference from FREQ is that it outputs a sequential list of words from the target speaker from which random samples of words are extracted and on which the mathematical algorithms then operate. The software calculates and averages TTRs for given token sizes and produces a series of such averages for subsamples of increasing token size. Curve fitting procedures then output the value for D that represents the best fit between the actual and theoretical TTR versus Token curve. At the moment, the software exists in a UNIX version. After further testing and validation work, and the implementation of additional options, the researchers hope to offer a final version to Brian MacWhinney for inclusion in CLAN. Validation of D as a measure has produced encouraging results on 32 month-old children acquiring English, adult learners of English as a second language, teenage learners of French as a foreign language, samples of academic writing and children's narratives in Inuktitut. An annotated bibliography relating to Type-Token, Type-Type and other measures of lexical richness, and lexical style can be viewed on the World Wide Web at: http://www.rdg.ac.uk/ehsrichb.

PUBLISHED MATERIAL: MALVERN, D.D. & RICHARDS, B.J. (1996). 'A new measure of lexical diversity'. In: WRAY, A. & RYAN, A. (Eds). Evolving models of language. Papers from the Annual Meeting of the British Association of Applied Linguistics, University of Wales, Swansea, September 1996. ; RICHARDS, B.J. & MALVERN, D.D. (1996). 'Swedish verb morphology in language impaired children: interpreting the type/token ratios', Logopedics Phoniatrics Vocology, No 21, pp.109-111. ; RICHARDS, B.J. & MALVERN, D.D. (1997). Quantifying lexical diversity in the study of language development. New Bulmershe Papers. Reading: University of Reading. ; RICHARDS, B.J. & MALVERN, D.D. (1997). Type-token and type-type measures of vocabulary diversity and lexical style: an annotated bibliography. Reading: University of Reading, Faculty of Education and Community Studies. ; MCKEE, G., MALVERN, D.D.,

RICHARDS, B.J. & KNOTT, R. (1998). VocD: software for measuring vocabulary diversity through mathematical modelling. Reading: University of Reading.

STATUS: Sponsored project

SOURCE OF GRANT: Economic and Social Research Council £30,614

DATE OF RESEARCH: 1995-1998

KEYWORDS: child language; information technology; language research; lexicology; vocabulary

2182

School of Education, Bulmershe Court, Woodlands Avenue, Earley, Reading RG6 1HY
01189 875123
Surrey University, School of Educational Studies, Guildford GU2 5XH
01483 300800

Dearmun, A. Dr; *Supervisors*: Denicolo, P. Dr; Lathlean, J. Prof.

The experiences of recently qualified BA (Hons) child branch graduates

ABSTRACT: The aims are to: 1) explore the experiences of newly qualified graduate children's nurses; and 2) elicit information about the children's nurses' perception of their role, their responsibilities, their philosophy of care, satisfactions, dissatisfactions, stressors, support needs and career aspirations. The first graduates from the BA (Hons) Paediatric Nursing in the United Kingdom qualified in 1993 and 1994. The cohorts comprised of three and seven graduates respectively. To date there have been very few published indepth studies exploring the transition from student to staff nurse and examining the experiences of recently qualified graduates. There have been notable exceptions, however none of these focused upon nurses in the paediatric field. It is suggested that a study in this area is particularly timely in view of the generalist - specialist debate and discussions about the future of children's nursing. This study used a qualitative approach to data collection in which indepth tape recorded interviews were conducted at three monthly intervals. Each graduate was also encouraged to keep a critical incident diary and provide a pictorial profile of their first year as a qualified nurse. Data collection commenced in August 1993 and was completed in October 1995.

STATUS: Individual research

DATE OF RESEARCH: 1992-1997

KEYWORDS: childrens nurses; followup studies; graduate surveys; nurse education; nurses

2183

School of Education, Bulmershe Court, Woodlands Avenue, Earley, Reading RG6 1HY
01189 875123
UNISA University of South Africa, Department of Comparative Education and Management, 0001 Pretoria, South Africa

Cowan, B. Dr; Botha, N. Dr

The provision, monitoring and evaluation of management training and development in primary and secondary schools in the PWV area of South Africa

ABSTRACT: The principal purpose of this joint project is to combine training with research. It is intended to run a series of courses related to educational management, both in schools and with principals and teachers from different institutions. The main aim of these courses is to provide opportunities for schools in the PWV area of South Africa to evaluate their management needs, and to satisfy them in order to provide a more satisfactory education for their pupils, to create better oppportunities for multi-racial integration, to improve partnerships with communities and parents, and to ensure a more efficient use of resources. The running of courses will be strongly linked with research into the impact of the above courses and other training programmes with which headteachers are involved. Because the impact of training programmes is often lost due to lack of follow-up, evaluation and monitoring of training will be assessed over both a short and longer (three year) period of time. Headteachers will be encouraged to keep diaries, related to training, throughout the period of research. It is intended that the outcomes of the research will be presented in several ways: a report given to the two universities, the British Council and UNESCO's International Institute for Educational Planning (IIEP); publications in appropriate international journals; a book, which deals not only with material covered in the report, but considers broader and more personal perspectives about training in relation to the changing nature of education in South Africa.

STATUS: Sponsored project

SOURCE OF GRANT: British Council

DATE OF RESEARCH: 1995-1998

KEYWORDS: educational administration; head teachers; management development; management in education; secondary education; south africa

2184

School of Education, Bulmershe Court, Woodlands Avenue, Earley, Reading RG6 1HY
01189 875123
University of Erfurt, Erfurt, Thuringen, Germany
Sozialwissenschaftliches Institut Munchen, Munich, Germany

Braband, G. Mr; Frohlich, W. Mr; *Supervisor*: Gellert, C. Prof.

The acquisition of academic competency in Europe

ABSTRACT: The aim of the project is analysis and description of conditions and processes of student learning in 8 European university systems. The countries involved are: France, Britain, Italy, Germany, Austria, Netherlands, Sweden, Spain. A questionnaire survey among students, more than 5000 questionnaires sent out, with about 25% return. The subject areas involved are: sociology/political science, history, physics, engineering. Interviews were also held with students and expert talks with government and labour market representatives. The hypotheses investigated were: 1) intensity and conditions of student learning can be taken as an adequate efficiency and quality measure in international comparison; 2) in that respect it is more important how than what students learn; and 3) the employment systems and labour markets in Continental Europe have recently moved into the direction of the Anglo-American models by increasingly looking for generic skills and other personality-related attributes in graduates. The project is to be completed in early 1999 with book publication (in German) in late 1999. Articles are also to be expected in English.

PUBLISHED MATERIAL: GELLERT, C. (1998). 'The changing conditions of teaching and learning in European higher education'. In: GELLERT, C. (Ed). Innovation and adaptation in higher education: the changing conditions of advanced teaching in Europe. London: Jessica Kingsley.

STATUS: Sponsored project

SOURCE OF GRANT: Ministry of Science and Education, Thuringen

DATE OF RESEARCH: 1997-continuing

KEYWORDS: comparative education; europe; higher education; learning strategies; universities

2185

School of Education, Bulmershe Court, Woodlands Avenue, Earley, Reading RG6 1HY
01189 875123
University of the West of England, Faculty of Education, Redland Campus, Redland Hill, Bristol BS6 6UZ
01179 741251

Haggarty, L. Dr; Postlethwaite, K. Prof.

The development of effective learning in a secondary school

ABSTRACT: This is an action research project involving collaboration between two university lecturers and a group of teachers in a secondary comprehensive school. Issues for investigation are defined by teachers. The group explores these relying on the lecturers to provide access to current theoretical ideas and research findings. The group devises solutions and trials them in school. The lecturers take particular responsibility for evaluating actions. Various members of the group are involved in preparing papers for publication. Topics investigated to date include differentiation through the strategy of mastery learning, transfer of learning, pupil motivation and teacher-pupil communication. A secondary research question involves the role of lecturers in such school-based research.

PUBLISHED MATERIAL: HAGGARTY, L. & POSTLETHWAITE, K. (1995). 'Working as consultants on school-based teacher-identified problems', Education Action Research, Vol 3, No 2, pp.169-181. ;

HAGGARTY, L., POSTLETHWAITE, K. & BURGESS, J. (1995). 'Reading scales', Mathematics in School, Vol 24, No 5, pp.10-12. ; HAGGARTY, L., HINES, J. & POSTLETHWAITE, K. (1997). The identification of actions teachers can take to improve learning through an examination of student academic performance in relation to prior attainment as measured by NFER Cognitive Abilities Tests scores. A report for the Teacher Training Agency. London: TTA. ; HAGGARTY, L., HINES, J. & POSTLETHWAITE, K. (1998). Communication between students and their teachers about learning. A report for the Teacher Training Agency. London: TTA.

STATUS: Sponsored project

SOURCE OF GRANT: Teacher Training Agency £50,500

DATE OF RESEARCH: 1991-continuing

KEYWORDS: action research; differentiated curriculum; learning theories; mastery learning; pupil motivation; school effectiveness; secondary education; transfer of learning

2186

School of Education, Bulmershe Court, Woodlands Avenue, Earley, Reading RG6 1HY
01189 875123
University of the West of England, Faculty of Education, Redland Campus, Redland Hill, Bristol BS6 6UZ
01179 741251

Orme, J. Mrs; *Supervisors*: Haggarty, L. Dr; Postlethwaite, K. Dr; Croll, P. Prof.

Aspects of partnership model for teacher education: an enquiry into ways in which mathematics students learn

ABSTRACT: The Reading University Secondary Postgraduate Certificate in Education (PGCE) course has developed a partnership model with local schools over the last 3 years. The resulting model has been informed by the notion of the 'reflective practitioner' and other literature on student teacher learning, in particular publications by Calderhead and by McIntyre. A major aspect of the model therefore is that of the student as an active learner, analysing their practice in terms of theory, research and the local context. A further element in this reflective learning is the student's own perspective of what makes a good mathematics teacher. This perspective is arrived at through a wide variety of experiences many of which are rooted in the student's past. These biographical or historical experiences also give rise to a personal agenda only part of which the student may acknowledge. The purpose of this study is to investigate student learning, and in particular to explore the role personal agenda plays in this learning. The methodology is to be that of a naturalistic enquiry: an indepth study of a small group of PGCE students who are planning to teach mathematics, with particular case studies of a subset of those students. The aim, using this methodology, is to develop a possible model of student teacher learning. The study will use a rich variety of data collection techniques including: analysis of student's initial position statements, questionnaires, analysis of other written statements including student assignments, taped interviews, observation and the systematic collection of comments made in less structured settings.

STATUS: Individual research

DATE OF RESEARCH: 1993-continuing

KEYWORDS: institutional cooperation; partnerships; postgraduate certificate in education; preservice teacher education

Research International
2187

6-7 Grosvenor Place, London SW1X 7SH
0171 656 5000

Emery, B. Ms

Employers' contributions to youth training initiatives

ABSTRACT: The aim of the study was to estimate employers' total financial contributions to Modern Apprenticeships (MA) and Youth Training (YT) institutions in England in 1995-96. The study did not cover other contributions made by employers such as on-the-job supervision and premises overheads, nor benefits to the employer in the form of trainees' productive contribution to the organisation's output. A random sample of

4,000 establishments was contacted by telephone to screen for whether they had Youth Trainees or Modern Apprenticeships in 1995-96. Those which did were categorised into those who: 1) made no financial contributions; 2) made contributions which were fully offset by payments received from Training and Enterprise Councils (TECs) or training providers contracted to TECs; and 3) made contributions which were not fully offset by payments received from TECs or training providers. The screening survey found that 13% of establishments had apprentices or trainees, while of those with trainees/apprentices, 74% made payments that were not fully offset by payments from the TEC or elsewhere. Virtually every employer paid their trainees/apprentices a wage/allowance. The average wage/allowance was 80 pounds per week. Smaller numbers of employers made payments in respect of training fees, fees for assessment and certification, tools grants, travel allowances and payments to the TEC or training providers. Employers made an estimated net financial contribution to YT and MA of 630 million pounds in 1995-96. The great majority of this sum (nearly 85%) was in the form of wages/allowances.

STATUS: Sponsored project

SOURCE OF GRANT: Department for Education and Employment £77,956

DATE OF RESEARCH: 1996-1997

KEYWORDS: **employers; financial support; modern apprenticeships; training; youth; youth training**

Research Surveys of Great Britain Limited

2188

Taylor Nelson AGB House, Westgate, London W5 1UA
0181 967 4259

Russell, N. Mr

Youth Cohort Study: Cohort 8, Sweep 2 (18 year olds)

ABSTRACT: The survey provides data for England and Wales, which are representative of the 18/19 age cohort, following up respondents to a similar survey 2 years earlier. It will provide information about the education, training and labour market routes they have followed since leaving compulsory schooling and the qualifications they have gained. The survey will make an important contribution to more accurate cost comparisons across education and training routes. It will capture information on modern apprentices and their outcomes, switching between routes, and participation and attainment by ethnic origin and socio-economic group. It will provide a baseline for new initiatives including Investors in Young People. Cohort 8 Sweep 2 is a postal survey of the nearly 16,000 young people in England and Wales who responded to COhort 8 Sweep 1. Fieldwork takes place between February and May 1998, consisting of a postal questionnaire, followed by a postcard reminder and 2 written reminders. There will be, for the first time, the offer of a telephone interview for those that fail to respond. This will boost overall response, but in particular will broaden the range of young people on which we have good information, as many of this age group are less likely to respond to written questionnaires.

STATUS: Sponsored project

SOURCE OF GRANT: Department for Education and Employment £188,000

DATE OF RESEARCH: 1997-1998

KEYWORDS: **cohort analysis; modern apprenticeships; school leavers; school to work transition; sixteen to nineteen education; training; vocational education; youth; youth cohort study; youth employment**

Robert Gordon University

2189

School of Information and Media, 352 King Street, Aberdeen AB9 2TQ
01224 262000

Robertson, J. Miss; *Supervisor*: Williams, D. Dr

The application of computer aided learning to the development of information skills in further education

ABSTRACT: The project seeks to examine the way in which further education

(FE) students explore and utilise sources of information. The intial test group are National Diploma in Business Studies students at Telford College, Edinburgh and subsequently the students of similar courses in other Scottish FE colleges. A Hypertext system has been developed to guide students through information searches, and to log individual student's use of the system. These logs will be analysed to evaluate learning patterns.

STATUS: Individual research

DATE OF RESEARCH: 1990-1993

KEYWORDS: **computer assisted learning; further education students; hypertext; information seeking; information sources**

2190

School of Information and Media, 352 King Street, Aberdeen AB9 2TQ
01224 262000
Beaufort-Delta Divisional Board of Education, Bag Service 12, Inuvik, NWT XOE OTO, Canada

Branch, J. Ms; *Supervisors*: Williams, D. Dr; Robertson, E. Dr; Haycock, K. Dr

Adolescents and CD ROM encyclopaedias: the development of a model based on a critical analysis of the information-seeking process of Canadian and Scottish 12-15 year old students, across a range of abilities, when accessing CD ROM encyclopeadias

ABSTRACT: Students come to the school library with a wide range of abilities, interests and levels of maturity and it is essential that all their information needs be addressed. A popular new information source, the CD ROM encyclopaedia, is now available in many school libraries. The aim of this research is to identify the information-seeking process that 12-15 year old Canadian and Scottish students, across a range of abilities, use to gather information using CD ROM encyclopaedias. Relevant literature from education, library and information science, and other related fields will be reviewed to gather learning theories and models which may be applied to this specific, real-life situation. By gathering qualitative and quantitative data, the information-seeking process of 12-15 year old students will be related to these existing theories and models. A new model will be developed, tested and refined that will describe this specific information-seeking process. Future benefits of the model will be discussed and suggestions made to theorists, researchers and practitioners in the fields of education and design.

STATUS: Individual research

DATE OF RESEARCH: 1995-continuing

KEYWORDS: **cd roms; computer uses in education; encyclopaedias; information seeking; information technology; library skills; multimedia; school libraries; secondary education**

2191

School of Information and Media, 352 King Street, Aberdeen AB9 2TQ
01224 262000
Napier University, Department of Print Media, Publishing and Communication, 219 Colinton Road, Edinburgh EH14 1DJ
0131 444 2266
Sheffield University, Department of Journalism, Sheffield S10 2TN
01142 768555

Barford, J. Ms; *Supervisors*: Williams, D. Dr; Beveridge, R. Mr; Gunter, B. Prof.

The effectiveness of information provision in relation to teachers' selection and use of broadcast resources in schools

ABSTRACT: The project examines the extent to which information about educational broadcasts influences their selection and use by secondary school teachers. Effective selection may be influenced by the material and intellectual form in which information is presented, and a key issue is the relationship between information supplier and user. The proposed plan of work will investigate teachers' perceptions and needs, and interpretation of information provided. It will also examine the rationale behind information suppliers' understanding of these perceptions and needs. Methodology will take the form of semi-structured interviews with information producers and suppliers, educational advisers, and secondary school teachers. The evaluation may also be extended to consider the effectiveness of programme information in a user environment.

STATUS: Individual research

DATE OF RESEARCH: 1994-1998

KEYWORDS: educational broadcasting; educational materials; educational radio; educational television; information dissemination; information needs; teachers; teaching guides

2192

School of Information and Media, 352 King Street, Aberdeen AB9 2TQ
01224 262000
Northern College, Aberdeen Campus, Department of Language Studies, Hilton Place, Aberdeen AB24 4FA
01224 283500

Sutton, A. Mrs; *Supervisors*: Williams, D. Dr; Anderson, C. Ms; Lewis, G. Dr

The development of critical attitudes to reading for information 5-14

ABSTRACT: This project proposes to examine the expected progression of pupils from Level D to Level E within the 5-14 strand of English language, entitled 'Reading for Information'. This involves the development of pupils from being able 'to collect and collate information', to being able to evaluate the usefulness of information for a particular purpose and being able to use it for a piece of personal research. Literature searches have shown that there has been little work done on the question of this skill developing across the primary/ secondary transition period and in the context of 5-14 targets. This study will cover this period. The study will also specify and trace the progression of the key skills at this stage and focus on the continuity, or lack of continuity, of the application of these skills, between primary and secondary school. At PhD stage, once the necessary skills have been defined, the study will examine whether or not this development is an educational progression, or a result of other factors such as maturity, social factors or family background. This stage will concentrate on the educational experience of a group of students, in order to assess what effect the teaching of information skills has had. The study will involve linking the progression of skills with the existing 5-14 documentation, necessitating discussions and interviews with staff, and resulting in the creation of a checklist of skills and an accompanying set of attainment targets. Classroom observation will be used to define indicators and observational strategies, and again to implement these strategies in the course of the research. Further observation and indepth interviews with students and staff will be used in the final stages of the research to examine individual educational experiences.

STATUS: Individual research

DATE OF RESEARCH: 1996-continuing

KEYWORDS: information seeking; primary education; primary to secondary transition; projects - learning activities; reading; secondary education

2193

School of Public Administration and Law, 352 King Street, Aberdeen AB9 2TQ
01224 262000

Fairley, J. Prof.

The integration of sectoral and local approaches to vocational education and training in Scotland

ABSTRACT: The project set out to examine the effectiveness of the interface between the 120 Industry Training Organisations (ITOs) and the 22 Local Enterprise Companies (LECs) in Scotland. Questionnaires were sent to 120 ITOs and 22 LECs and very good response rates were achieved. The results suggest that LECs and ITOs work well together in a few sectors. However, there are clear problems of lack of awareness and understanding on both sides of the interface.

PUBLISHED MATERIAL: FAIRLEY, J. (1995). 'Training strategy in Scotland merging the sectoral and the local perspectives', Regional Studies, Vol 29, No 6. ; FAIRLEY, J. (1996). 'Vocational education and training in Scotland towards a strategic approach?', Scottish Educational Review, Vol 28, No 1, pp.50-60.

STATUS: Sponsored project

SOURCE OF GRANT: Robert Gordon University

DATE OF RESEARCH: 1994-1997

KEYWORDS: industry training organisations; local enterprise companies; scotland; training

2194

School of Public Administration and Law, 352 King Street, Aberdeen AB9 2TQ
01224 262000
Edinburgh University, Department of Politics, Old College, South Bridge, Edinburgh EH8 9YL
0131 650 1000

Fairley, J. Prof.; Brown, A. Dr

The current education reform process in Eire

ABSTRACT: Examination of the developing process of educational reform in Eire. Research is conducted by means of regular interviews with key interest groups and participant observation in key forums of policy debate.

PUBLISHED MATERIAL: BROWN, A. & FAIRLEY, J. (1993). 'Pressures for reform in contemporary Irish education', Scottish Educational Review, Vol 25, No 1, pp.34-45.

STATUS: Sponsored project

SOURCE OF GRANT: Nuffield Foundation

DATE OF RESEARCH: 1992-1997

KEYWORDS: educational administration; educational change; ireland

Roehampton Institute London

2195

Roehampton Lane, London SW15 5PU
0181 392 3000

Sangster, M. Ms; *Supervisor*: Rogers, L. Mr

Exploring mathematical thinking in the early years

ABSTRACT: The aim is to closely examine young children's style of learning mathematics. By carefully examining their approach and developing understanding of pattern, it is hoped to identify some of the ways children build concepts, and particularly whether they are able to transfer this information to other areas of mathematics. Information will be collected by observation and interview.

STATUS: Individual research

DATE OF RESEARCH: 1993-1997

KEYWORDS: mathematical concepts; mathematics education; young children

2196

Roehampton Lane, London SW15 5PU
0181 392 3000

Nakase, A. Prof.; Nade, T. Mr; *Supervisors*: Mason, R. Dr; Bruntlett, S. Mr

Teaching craft inheritance in Britain and Japan

ABSTRACT: The four year project is a joint venture between research teams in Joetsu and De Montfort Universities to investigate the use of computers to develop a resource base for crafts, and as a teaching/learning strategy for delivering crafts input into the National Curriculum (Art) in schools. The proposed outcomes of the research are two prototype bilingual multimedia applications for teaching crafts heritage in schools, which are part of a larger crafts resource. Access to collections of domestic and rural crafts has been secured in Tokyo and Leicestershire Museums, and the project has been set up as a collaborative venture involving museum educators and teachers and pupils in schools. The programme of research is built on previous investigations by team members into computer applications in art and design, teaching crafts heritage and education for international understanding.

PUBLISHED MATERIAL: IWANO, M. (1991). 'Museum education in school', Museum Education Studies, Vol 2, No 1, pp.10-11. ; BRUNTLETT, S. (1992). 'Uses of CD ROM in the art and design classroom as a teaching learning resource', Micro User, Vol 10, No 4, p.26. ; SUSUMAGO, K. (1993). 'The present state of crafts teaching in Japanese schools'. Paper presented at De Montfort University Research Colloquoia, March 1993.

STATUS: Sponsored project

SOURCE OF GRANT: De Montfort University £1,000; DAIWA Foundation £2,000

DATE OF RESEARCH: 1993-1998

KEYWORDS: **art education; arts; computer uses in education; cultural education; handicrafts; international educational exchange; japan; museums**

2197

Roehampton Lane, London SW15 5PU
0181 392 3000

Taber, K. Dr; *Supervisors*: Watts, M. Dr; Barber, V. Dr

Understanding chemical bonding

ABSTRACT: This research is an exploration of pre-university students' understanding of bonding in chemistry. Data collection is by one-to-one focused interviews set out as a series of detailed case studies. Learners' understandings are fragmentary and lack coherence for what is a fundamental concept in chemistry.

PUBLISHED MATERIAL: TABER, K. & WATTS, D.M. (1996). 'The secret life of the chemical bond: students' anthropomorphic and animistic references to bonding', International Journal of Science Education, Vol 18, No 5, pp.557-568. ; WATTS, D.M. & TABER, K. (1996). 'An explanatory gestalt of essence: students' conceptions of 'natural' in physical phenomena', International Journal of Science Education, Vol 18, No 8, pp.939-954.

STATUS: Team research

DATE OF RESEARCH: 1992-1997

KEYWORDS: **chemical bonding; chemistry; science education; scientific concepts**

2198

Roehampton Lane, London SW15 5PU
0181 392 3000

Lee, S. Ms; Wilkes, J. Ms

The developing role of the school experience tutor

ABSTRACT: The project, ongoing since 1993, is researching the changing role of tutors supervising students on primary initial teacher education programmes when they are in school. The process of change which has resulted in the new roles of higher education link tutor and school-based mentor has been documented in published articles and conference papers. The recent phase focused on the perceptions of all those affected by the changes - headteachers, tutors, mentors, students, class teachers - and on the professional development required to support the new roles. The project is based on Roehampton Institute's Faculty of Education's partnership schools and uses semi-structured interviews and questionnaires to allow for a full exploration of the issues. During 1996-97 the research moves into consideration of: a) the implications for the career pathways of those teachers closely involved in primary partnership; and b) the possible effects of those partnerships on the quality of the children's learning environment.

PUBLISHED MATERIAL: LEE, S. & WILKES, J. (1995). 'The training triangle', Managing Schools Today, Vol 5, No 3, pp.16-18. ; LEE, S. & WILKES, J. (1995). 'Mentoring and the professional development of teachers', Mentoring and Tutoring, Vol 3, No 2, pp.33-38. ; LEE, S. & WILKES, J. (1996). 'The changing role of the school experience tutor', British Journal of In-service Education', Vol 22, No 1, pp.99-112.

STATUS: Sponsored project

SOURCE OF GRANT: Roehampton Institute £5,000

DATE OF RESEARCH: 1993-1997

KEYWORDS: **preservice teacher education; school based teacher education; student teacher supervisors; supervisors; teaching practice**

2199

Roehampton Lane, London SW15 5PU
0181 392 3000

Shaughnessy, J. Ms; *Supervisors*: Jackson, P. Dr; Evans, R. Dr

An evaluation of PGCE students' training and implications for developing reflective practice in initial teacher education

ABSTRACT: The study will examine the progress of the cohort of students on a one-year Postgraduate Certificate in Education (PGCE) Primary course. The aim of the study is to chart the perceptions of the students and investigate the training issues related to developing reflective practice in initial teacher education. Absent from the current debate about primary teacher education is a contemporary research project of the complexity and richness of the Nias studies at the Cambridge Institute of Education. These studies were completed before the Education Reform Act 1988 when circumstances were radically different from today. Portrayal of the widespread PGCE training model, within a context of educational reform in teacher education programmes, will illuminate the training process at Roehampton Institute.

STATUS: Individual research

DATE OF RESEARCH: 1994-1997

KEYWORDS: **postgraduate certificate in education; preservice teacher education; reflection; reflective teaching; student teachers; teacher development**

2200

Roehampton Lane, London SW15 5PU
0181 392 3000

Lee, S. Mrs

Self-assessment in primary mathematics

ABSTRACT: The intention was to begin to develop strategies for involving primary children in assessing their own performance and understanding of mathematics. Guidelines were distributed to participants suggesting possible starting points for work with children. Activities carried out with the children were monitored through feedback forms, interviews with students/teachers and visits to the schools. There was involvement in the project by students in Year 3 and Year 4 of a BA Qualified Teacher Status (QTS) Degree Programme, Postgraduate Certificate in Education (PGCE) students and experienced teachers. Main points from feedback received include: 1) self-assessment is worth pursuing; 2) it should be part of the overall assessment process; 3) its usefulness and success depends on developing a good rapport with the children and a common understanding of what is required. More specifically it was found that: 1) simply recording errors and considering their cause was insufficient; 2) discussion and completion of written records was more helpful; 3) discussion without self-assessment could lead to the teacher making the interpretation of what the child meant, losing the important self-analysis; 4) self-analysis came from developing clear targets and expectations with the children; and 5) successful involvement in self-assessment by the children has implications for the teacher's own professional development, in particular the level to which he/she is successfully 'matching' the tasks to the children's ability and providing a degree of challenge. The importance of agreeing targets is one of the strategies found to be valuable. This requires an understanding of what knowledge skills and learning are to be assessed and what would constitute evidence that this had taken place or that the agreed targets had been met. Further work is required to develop this.

STATUS: Sponsored project

SOURCE OF GRANT: Roehampton Institute £300

DATE OF RESEARCH: 1993-1993

KEYWORDS: **assessment; mathematics achievement; mathematics education; primary school pupils; self evaluation - individuals**

2201

Roehampton Lane, London SW15 5PU
0181 392 3000

Geddes, H. Ms; *Supervisors*: Best, R. Prof.; Kutnick, P. Dr

Attachment and learning: an investigation into links between maternal attachment experience, reported life events, behaviour causing concern at referral and difficulties in the learning situation

ABSTRACT: This research is concerned with children with emotional and behavioural problems and associated learning difficulties who have been referred to Child Guidance Units and sought to investigate possible links between aspects of children's life experiences, with particular reference to patterns of maternal attachment and their difficulties in the learning situation. The investigation is framed by the theoretical model of Attachment Theory and informed by previous findings concerning factors affecting school based learning. The data were derived from 66 case histories of children experiencing difficulties in learning where the difficulty had been attributed to social and emotional factors. The source of the case histories was archive files in Child Guidance Units. The resulting data were subsequently analysed in a predominantly qualitative and interpretive paradigm, principally by content analysis informed by empirical findings from Attachment Theory research. Analysis of data concerning maternal attachment experience resulted in the identification of two distinct samples of insecure attachment, avoident and resisent/ambivalent, forming sub-samples which were the basis of further investigation and analysis. A number of differences between the two groups with regard to life experiences were evident. The avoident attacment sub-sample reported a higher rate of father absence and was significantly associated with the events 'death', 'loss' and 'separation'. The resistent/ambivalent attachment sub-sample was significantly associated with the event, 'mental and/or physical illness in the family including drug and/or alcohol abuse'. No particular association was identified between attachment experience and reported behaviour at referral. An unexpected outcome concerning ethnicity indicated significantly high rates of non-white referral in the avoident group and low rates of non-white referral in the resistent/ambivalent group. A strong association between maternal attachment experience and distinct patterns of response in the learning situation was indicated. Possible characteristics of learning skills were also indicated linked to attachment experience. The nature of the different patterns of response in the learning situation are identified and implications for learning and teaching are discussed in relation to the findings.

STATUS: Individual research

DATE OF RESEARCH: 1993-1998

KEYWORDS: attachment behaviour; emotional and behavioural difficulties; family problems; learning; mother child relationship; social experience; special educational needs

2202

Roehampton Lane, London SW15 5PU
0181 392 3000

White, P. Ms; *Supervisors*: Welch, G. Prof.; Sundberg, J. Prof.; Chiltern, E. Dr

The application of digital signal processing techniques to improved methods for the analysis and assessment of children's voices

ABSTRACT: Speech technology has evolved mostly through experiments with the voices of adult males. Unfortunately, far fewer studies have been reported on the speech of adult females or of children, that is, speech with a high fundamental frequency (F0). The mean F0 of adult male speech is more than an octave lower than the F0 of children's speech. Also, adult females have F0 values which are closer to the frequency of children's voices than to that of adult males. Children's voices, therefore, are in some ways incomparable to those of adults, and it is not surprising that standard procedures for the formant analysis of adult speech can prove less than reliable for use with children. In particular, a high fundamental frequency leads to widely-spaced harmonics which makes the estimation of formant locations difficult. Formant analysis is an extremely useful tool in the measurement and assessment of speech and singing. As researchers inevitably find themselves working with a broader range of subjects, including adult females, children, and trained and untrained singers, it is becoming increasingly necessary to attempt to improve, or find an alternative to, the standard analysis methods. The aims of the research, therefore, are: a) to identify fully the problems involved in using standard analysis techniques with children's voices; b) to assess and compare any analysis methods suggested in the research literature; and c) to offer some suggestions for future development.

PUBLISHED MATERIAL: WHITE, P.J. (1995). 'Some acoustic measurements of children's voiced and whispered vowels', Voice, Vol 4, No 1, pp.1-14.

STATUS: Individual research

DATE OF RESEARCH: 1993-1997

KEYWORDS: acoustics; speech communication; voice

2203

Roehampton Lane, London SW15 5PU
0181 392 3000

Masters, B. Mr; *Supervisor*: Jackson, P. Dr

Steiner Education from founding principles to contemporary praxis: an evaluation of Steiner philosophy of education from its origins to the present day

ABSTRACT: The thesis examines and evaluates the educational philosophy of the Rudolf Steiner Waldorf schools movement. The research falls essentially into 3 parts: philosophical and textual research into the Steiner Archive Documents (the 'Konferenzen'); critique of current Steiner-Waldorf theory; implications of the critique for the movement.

PUBLISHED MATERIAL: MASTERS, B. (1993). 'Report on the political campaign conducted by Waldorf schools in the UK and Northern Ireland', Child & Man: Journal for Waldorf Education, Vol 27, No 3, pp.23-29. ; MASTERS, B. (1994). 'Talk, talk, talk ..', Child & Man: Journal for Waldorf Education, Vol 28, No 1, pp.10-12. ; MASTERS, B. (1994). 'Retrospective: 75 years of Waldorf education', Child & Man: Journal for Waldorf Education, Vol 28, No 2, pp.2-6.; MASTERS, B. (1994). 'Brien Masters interviews Linda Nunhofer', Child & Man: Journal for Waldorf Education, Vol 28, No 2, pp.8-12. ; MASTERS, B. (1997). 'Imagination', Steiner Education: Journal for Waldorf Education, Vol 31, No 2, pp.2-5. A full list of publications is available from the researcher.

STATUS: Individual research

DATE OF RESEARCH: 1993-1997

KEYWORDS: steiner waldorf schools

2204

Roehampton Lane, London SW15 5PU
0181 392 3000

McCreery, E. Ms; *Supervisors*: Welch, G. Prof.; Best, R. Ms; Slee, N. Ms

Spiritual development and the education of young children

ABSTRACT: The research is grounded in the legal requirements for schools to promote the spiritual development of the children in their care. The study aims to investigate how the spiritual is addressed in schools for pupils at National Curriculum key stage 1. Of particular interest is how teachers see their role in developing the spiritual. The study focuses on a small number of first schools and includes interviews with headteachers, classroom teachers and children. The intention is to identify common attitudes and practices. Of particular value are instances of creative and positive ways in which schools are addressing this area. From the study it is anticipated that some ways forward might be identified to help schools develop their provision for promoting children's spiritual development.

PUBLISHED MATERIAL: MCCREERY, E. (1994). 'Towards an understanding of the notion of the spiritual in education', Early Child Development and Care, Vol 100, pp.93-99. ; MCCREERY, E. (1996). 'Talking to young children about things spiritual'. In: BEST, R. (Ed) Education, spirituality and the whole child. London: Cassell.

STATUS: Individual research

DATE OF RESEARCH: 1993-1998

KEYWORDS: religious education; spiritual development; young children

2205

Roehampton Lane, London SW15 5PU
0181 392 3000

Lathey, G. Dr; *Supervisors*: Reynolds, K. Dr; Evans, R. Dr

Modern English and German language autobiographical children's literature set in the Third Reich and the Second World War

ABSTRACT: The focus of the research is fictionalised autobiography, and the experiences of children in Britain and Germany as recollected in middle age. Differences and similarities between experiences and the writers' reconstruction of the past from a contemporary perspective, will be explored. The role of writing as therapy and cross-cultural links are to be examined from a range of theoretical perspectives. An analysis of the timing, audience and purpose of recent children's literature on the war years in both Britain and Germany will form an important concluding chapter to the study.

STATUS: Individual research

DATE OF RESEARCH: 1991-1997

KEYWORDS: autobiographies; childrens literature; war

2206

Roehampton Lane, London SW15 5PU
0181 392 3000

Lee, S-W. Mr; *Supervisor*: Evans, R. Dr

A study of the relevance of Friedrich Froebel to the Christian education of young children

ABSTRACT: In the educational thought of Froebel, we are confronted with a panoramic view of the universe of knowledge and experience. Motivated by a profound grasp of the Creator-creature relationship in Christian theology, Froebel was able to provide a radical, holistic view of the task of Christian education. For Froebel, one's relationship to nature was nothing less than a religious communion, a drawing close to the Creator. Froebel's conception of God is big, comprehensive and cosmic. All truth, all knowledge, all reality is from God. Thus, in Froebel's educational theory, knowledge and truth have an inherently religious aspect. Humanity is made in the image of God, not to pursue its own ends, but to pursue a course of development according to the rules and laws of God. Education is not confined to just one compartment of human life; it must be free to address every part of the pupil's being, body, will, mind and spirit. Thus, education must span many subjects and embrace religion, science and art. The method of education must not be removed from real life but must engage the pupil at many levels of life and activity. Because education is such a holistic activity it cannot be dealt with in a compartment labelled 'school'. Parents are guardians of a sacred trust, responsible to God, to the child, and to all humanity. This is why Froebel placed such importance upon women. Upon women depends the welfare of the child, and thus the future welfare of the human race. Education is the process of coming to a knowledge of and love for this Triune Creator through His creation, via His holy institution of the family. Froebel has laid a most valuable foundation for Christian education theory; now, his shortcomings must be corrected and the insights of the intervening century must be added to his seminal work.

STATUS: Individual research

DATE OF RESEARCH: 1990-1993

KEYWORDS: **christianity; religious education; young children**

2207

Roehampton Lane, London SW15 5PU
0181 392 3000

Rose, D. Mr; *Supervisors*: Best, R. Prof.; Whitty, G. Prof.

A consideration of the inherent conflict between local faith representation on Standing Advisory Council for Religious Education (SACRE) and the Agreed Syllabus requirements for the RE curriculum in schools

ABSTRACT: The aims of the research are to: 1) explore the impact of plurality of faiths within England and Wales, and to consider how this is reflected in policy-making committees in relation to religious education (RE); 2) explore the mechanisms and rationale exercised for a 'faith' to be included in, or rejected from, religious education in the classroom as prescribed by the local Agreed Syllabus. The first part of the research was by questionnaire sent to every local education authority (LEA) in England and Wales. The data gleaned revealed specific anomalies which required further discussion. The next parts of the research will consider: 1) the nature of current legislation in relation to local representation; 2) the nature of the 'faiths' themselves - rationale for inclusion/rejection; and 3) the way forward, i.e. dealing with the anomalies.

STATUS: Individual research

DATE OF RESEARCH: 1993-1997

KEYWORDS: **religious cultural groups; religious education**

2208

Roehampton Lane, London SW15 5PU
0181 392 3000

Welch, G. Prof.; Sergeant, D. Dr; White, P. Ms

Singing development in early childhood

ABSTRACT: The project has aimed to chart and compare the singing development of children aged 3 to 8 years, and to identify aspects of teaching that might promote or hinder the development of singing abilities. Previous research has indicated that preschool children focus first on the words of songs, before focusing on the rhythm and pitch contour. As there has been little research concerning the significance of such elements in school singing, it was decided to include assessment components such as glissandi (pitch glides), pitch patterns and single pitches, as well as the performance of two songs, in the research protocol. The intention was to gain insight into the effects of musical context on a child's vocal pitch accuracy, using subjective and objective assessment methods. To date, information has been gathered on over 800 subjects. One hundred and eighty-four subjects form the longitudinal part of the study. The longitudinal data analysis has revealed significant differences within and between years in children's singing competences on the various components of the testing protocol. There is a clear hierarchy of singing ability, biased towards single pitches, melodic fragments and simple glides. In contrast, vocal pitch-making in the context of a song was consistently found to be the most difficult singing task across all 3 years. Analysis also revealed that differences exist between schools in the distribution of mean response ratings. It appears that differences in educational environment and teaching strategies are significant in singing development.

PUBLISHED MATERIAL: WELCH, G.F. & WHITE, P.J. (1993/4). 'The developing voice: education and vocal efficiency - a physical perspective', Bulletin of the Council for Research in Music Education, Vol 119, pp.146-156. ; WELCH, G.F. (1994). 'The assessment of singing', Psychology of Music, Vol 22, No 1, pp.3-19. ; WELCH, G.F., SERGEANT, D.C. & WHITE, P.J. (1995/6). 'The singing competences of five year old developing singers', Bulletin of the Council for Research in Music Education, Vol 127, pp.155-162. ; WELCH, G.F., SERGEANT, D.C. & WHITE, P.J. (1996). 'Age, sex and vocal tasks as factors in singing 'in-tune' during the first years of schooling'. Proceedings of the Sixteenth ISME International Research Seminar, Frascati, July 1996.

STATUS: Sponsored project

SOURCE OF GRANT: Leverhulme Trust £102,000; Roehampton Institute £36,342

DATE OF RESEARCH: 1990-1997

KEYWORDS: **music; music activities; singing; young children**

2209

Roehampton Lane, London SW15 5PU
0181 392 3000

Jackson, P. Dr

Distinctive approaches to early childhood education: Froebel, Steiner and Montessori

ABSTRACT: An investigation into the philosophies, policies, practices and effects of Froebel, Montessori and Steiner-Waldorf education, with special reference to early childhood education. It included, in addition to empirical, conceptual and historical methods, the successful supervision of PhDs on Froebel and Steiner. A follow-up project will, it is hoped, investigate how the culturally distinct forms of the 3 approaches - Froebel, Montessori and Steiner - have developed worldwide, and their relationships to the original theory and practice. Over and above the intrinsic scholarly worth of the project, the intention is to establish best practice for the upbringing of young children, especially now that multiprofessional community-based kindergartens combining education with child welfare are attracting Governmental attention in the UK.

PUBLISHED MATERIAL: JACKSON, P.W. (1996). 'Pre-school'. In: DOCKING, J.W. (Ed). National school policy: major issues in education policy for schools. London: David Fulton. ; JACKSON, P.W. (1996). 'Diversity'. In: DOCKING, J.W. (Ed). National school policy: major issues in education policy for schools. London: David Fulton. ; JACKSON, P.W. (1997). 'Froebel and the Hitler jugend', Early Child Development and Care, Vol 117, pp.45-65. ; JACKSON, P.W. (1997). 'Child-centred education for Pacific-rim cultures?', International Journal of Early Childhood Education, Vol 2, pp.5-19. ; JACKSON, P.W. & LEE, S.W. 'Froebelian developments in the Republic of Korea', Early Child Development and Care. (in press).

STATUS: Sponsored project

SOURCE OF GRANT: Roehampton Institute

DATE OF RESEARCH: 1994-1997

KEYWORDS: **early childhood education; educational theories; montessori method; steiner waldorf schools; teaching methods**

2210

Roehampton Lane, London SW15 5PU
0181 392 3000

Alsop, S. Dr; *Supervisors*: Evans, R. Dr; Watts, M. Dr

Public understanding of radiation and radioactivity

ABSTRACT: This research explores public understandings of radiation and radioactivity. Data is gathered from 4 main samples by means of questionnaires and focused one-to-one interviews. Particular samples have been drawn from geographical regions of the UK where there is high incidence of background radiation from emissions of naturally occurring radon gas. The study uses a model of informal learning in science to analyse the changing conceptions of adults as they interpret official information of the risks to their health.

STATUS: Individual research

DATE OF RESEARCH: 1991-1997

KEYWORDS: **attitudes; public opinion; public understanding of science; radiation; risk; scientific literacy**

2211

Roehampton Lane, London SW15 2PU
0181 392 3000

Lathey, G. Dr

European children's literature in translation

ABSTRACT: In an attempt to inspire interest in translated children's fiction, the project aims to offer teachers, parents, librarians and children an annotated booklist of translated children's literature currently in print. The booklist is to be published by the Thimble Press. The introduction of the list points to the importance of reading literature set in other cultures, and of introducing readers to some of the best European writers for children. Pieces on national developments in children's literature, written by experts in various European countries, will provide a context for the annotations.

STATUS: Individual research

DATE OF RESEARCH: 1993-1997

KEYWORDS: **annotated bibliographies; bibliographies; books; childrens literature; european literature; fiction; literature**

2212

Roehampton Lane, London SW15 5PU
0181 392 3000

Collins, F. Ms; *Supervisors*: Riordan, J. Prof.; Laycock, E. Ms

Telling tales: what do children and stories tell us about themselves and about each other?

ABSTRACT: This project arises from a professional interest, as a storyteller, and a research interest, as an educationist, in the contribution made by hearing and retelling traditional tales to the primary school child's developing knowledge and understanding of the world. Many projects have focused on language skills in oracy work. This research looks at memory, creativity, visualisation amongst other skills promoted and developed through the oral tradition, and asks the question: are we, as teachers, undervaluing the valuable oral skills which children bring to school, and missing the opportunity to work within an oral tradition to empower and enable children as language users and learners? A survey of the working methods and techniques of 38 storytellers working in the revival tradition contributes a unique picture of the ways in which storytelling is used now. This is complemented by fieldwork with children in primary classrooms. The conclusions and results are still pending.

PUBLISHED MATERIAL: COLLINS, F. (1996). 'Storytelling as a cerative art', Language Matters, No 2. ; COLLINS, F. (1996). 'Forgotten skills, living memory: using storytelling in the classroom', Early Childhood Development and Care, Vol 116.

STATUS: Sponsored project

SOURCE OF GRANT: Roehampton Institute £15,000

DATE OF RESEARCH: 1994-1997

KEYWORDS: **classroom communication; language skills; narration; oracy; primary school pupils; story telling**

2213

Roehampton Lane, London SW15 5PU
0181 392 3000

Riley, K. Prof.; Docking, J. Dr; Johnson, H. Ms; Mahony, P. Prof.; Rowles, D. Mr

An examination of the changing role and effectiveness of local education authorities

ABSTRACT: There has been little work in the UK about what constitutes an effective local education authority (LEA). Despite major changes in recent years, education authorities continue to play a significant part in the organisation management and delivery of education services. The opting out provision has existed for several years and yet the vast majority of schools in England and Wales remain with the local authority. Typically this fact has been described in negative terms - the schools have chosen not to opt out. However, if one describes it as a positive decision - the schools have opted for LEA membership - some questions about this decision spring to mind. 1) What benefits accrue to the schools, and to whom within schools? 2) Are these benefits stronger for some schools in some LEAs than for other, and if so why? 3) How should the schools and the LEAs act to strengthen the positive aspects of the relationship, and minimise any negative aspects? 4) In particular, how can the capacity of schools for development be supported? These questions provide a starting point for this exploratory study of the changing role and effectiveness of LEAs; and their contribution to quality and school improvement. The study will take into account relevant external exterior criteria but will emphasise the judgements of those who are the primary users of education authority services. It will examine the educational leadership of education authorities, seeking to characterise what this means and how vision is translated into policy, priority and concrete action.

PUBLISHED MATERIAL: RILEY, K.A. (1993). Managing for quality in an uncertain climate. Luton: Local Government Management Board. ; JOHNSON, H. & RILEY, K.A. (1995). 'The impact of quangos and new government agencies on education'. In: RIDLEY, F.F. & WILSON, D. (Eds). The quango debate. Oxford: Oxford University Press. ; RILEY, K.A., JOHNSON, H. & ROWLES, D. (1995). Managing for quality in an uncertain climate. Report II. Luton: Local Government Management Board. ; RILEY, K.A. & ROWLES, D. 'Inspection and school improvement in England and Wales: national contexts and local realities'. In: TOWNSEND, T. (Ed). Restructuring, quality and effectiveness: problems and possibilities for tomorrow's schools. London: Routledge. (in press).

STATUS: Sponsored project

SOURCE OF GRANT: Local authorities; Higher Education Funding Council

DATE OF RESEARCH: 1995-1997

KEYWORDS: **educational administration; local education authorities**

2214

Roehampton Lane, London SW15 5PU
0181 392 3000

Whitby, V. Mrs; *Supervisors*: Kutnick, P. Dr; Mahony, P. Prof.

The quality of science in the primary school

ABSTRACT: The aim of the project is to explore the issues that relate to the quality of science in the primary school: 1) The history of the primary science curriculum. 2) Teachers' own scientific knowledge and teachers' confidence. 3) How do schools organise their primary science curriculum? 4) What constraints do schools experience? 5) How can these issues be resolved? Six schools will be used to explore these issues in depth.

STATUS: Individual research

DATE OF RESEARCH: 1994-1998

KEYWORDS: **primary education; science education**

2215

Roehampton Lane, London SW15 5PU
0181 392 3000

Bedford, D. Mrs; Iwano, M. Dr; *Supervisors*: Mason, R. Prof.; Kutnick, P. Dr

National survey of craft in Art and Design and Technology curricula and courses at National Curriculum key stages 3 and 4 in England and Wales: Part 2 - teachers' views

ABSTRACT: A national survey of craft education in Art and Design Technology at National Curriculum key stages 3 and 4 was carried out in October 1994. It set out to obtain factual data about the provision for and the practice of craft education since the introduction of the National

Curriculum and to ascertain teachers' views of its educational status and value. The survey was both statistical and quantitative, it was recognised that qualitative data would also be required to enable policy making, issues were therefore identified in part one (Mason and Iwano 1995). The qualitative research for part two cross-checked and clarified the data and findings of part one. It commenced in April 1996 and was completed by July 1997 when it was presented in the form of a report with conclusions for recommendations based on the following concerns: 1) making activities which effectively promote conceptual and practical learning in ceramics, metal, textiles and wood; 2) impact of decreased consumable budgets, increased student numbers and other resource issues on effective delivery; 3) teachers' professional development needs with regard to the knowledge and understanding of the historical, technological and cultural contexts of craft; and 4) purposes and value of craft education and strategies for promoting it in schools. 126 teachers from 18 schools took part in the second stage. Research instruments included an inventory of quality indicators, a semi-structured interview schedule for use with Art and Design and Technology teachers, observation of specialist resources and accommodation, recording craft processes and outcomes and reviewing school and course documents.

PUBLISHED MATERIAL: MASON, R. & IWANO, M. (1995). National survey of craft in Art and Design and Technology curricula and courses at key stages 3 and 4 in England and Wales. Final Report of the first stage of the survey. London: Roehampton Institute.

STATUS: Sponsored project

SOURCE OF GRANT: Roehampton Institute; Crafts Council

DATE OF RESEARCH: 1996-1997

KEYWORDS: **art education; craft work education; design and technology; handicrafts; key stage 3; key stage 4; secondary education; teacher attitudes**

2216

Roehampton Lane, London SW15 5PU
0181 392 3000

Houghton, N. Mr; Bedford, D. Ms; *Supervisors*: Mason, R. Prof.; Steers, J. Dr; Allison, B. Prof.

An investigation into pupils' views of the role of craft in Art and Design and Technology secondary education in England and Wales

ABSTRACT: Craft in British secondary schools is considered by many people to be inferior to academic subjects and its purpose in the curriculum is unclear. It is taught as an element of two National Curriculum subjects: art, and design and technology and its role appears to be different (and confused). Since 1988, secondary education has experienced changes brought about by the Education Reform Act and the introduction of the National Curriculum which may have had an impact on the teaching of craft. A national survey is being carried out to discover from teachers the nature, extent and quality of craft education, in the light of these changes, part one of which is complete and published. This research builds on the findings of part one of the national survey and is attempting to find out: 1) what secondary pupils think of craft and how they learn about it, both inside and outside school; 2) what does, or does not motivate them to engage in craft activity; and 3) what influences their views about craft.

STATUS: Sponsored project

SOURCE OF GRANT: Roehampton Institute; Crafts Council, jointly £25,000

DATE OF RESEARCH: 1996-1998

KEYWORDS: **art education; craft work education; design and technology; handicrafts; key stage 3; key stage 4; pupil attitudes; secondary education**

2217

Roehampton Lane, London SW15 5PU
0181 392 3000

Park, J. Ms; *Supervisors*: Mason, R. Prof.; Bailey, G. Dr; Ahn, H. Prof.

An investigation into the role and contribution of art history to multicultural reform in Korea

ABSTRACT: The main problem addressed in this research is that Korean art education is based on outdated Western theory mediated through Japan.

Despite Korean Government policy on internationalisation and the fact that the National Curriculum has been reformed 7 times in the last 50 years in response to changing social needs, there remains an orthodoxy of so-called 'creative self-expression' related to Western theory dating from the period 1920-1950. This analytical and descriptive study is using ethnographic and action research methods to develop curriculum content for Korean art education derived from indepth analyses of contemporary Korean art and culture. The intention is to establish a basis for multicultural curriculum reform in secondary art education in Korea, identifying key principles which might underpin the Korean concepts of cultural pluralism and cultural identity.

STATUS: Individual research

DATE OF RESEARCH: 1994-1997

KEYWORDS: **art education; curriculum development; korea; multicultural education**

2218

Roehampton Lane, London SW15 5PU
0181 392 3000

Blatherwick, M. Ms; *Supervisors*: Mason, R. Prof.; Bailey, G. Dr; Taylor, C. Dr

An investigation of the potential of art criticism for the teaching of intercultural understanding

ABSTRACT: The object of this study is to investigate the potential for art criticism, as it relates to visual literacy, to be used as a means of promoting intercultural understanding in the upper elementary schools of New Brunswick. A key motivation for this research is based on the need for children to become more aware of the culturally relevant experiences of other children from different cultural backgrounds. This concept is a major goal in school policy in Canada. It has been suggested that works of art can be especially effective means of developing cognition of others' experience; visual art is considered a form of communication. Therefore it is assumed that visual images may serve well as a means of increasing students' knowledge and understanding of various cultural perspectives. Within the province of New Brunswick teachers at the upper elementary level do not include a critical approach to learning about the content of visual images. Since intercultural understanding is being promoted as a goal of the educational system, and visual images/art have the ability to convey meaning, images created by a culturally diverse student population might provide teachers with a resource or instrument for teaching about this concept. Methods have been tested out previously which have used the images of children as learning resources. What remains undetermined is: 1) the way in which the visual art curriculum should be altered to include this approach; and 2) the effectiveness of this approach in increasing intercultural understanding. The investigation will involve: 1) Researching methods of art criticism, the meaning and role of intercultural understanding. 2) Collecting personal images created by elementary students from different cultural backgrounds. 3) Training teachers in methods/approaches of art criticism. 4) Observing and documenting the teachers' ability to implement the method in a classroom setting. 5) Assessing the effectiveness of: a) the teacher's ability to implement the method; and b) the method's ability to increase the intercultural understanding of the students. 6) Providing possible recommendations for curriculum change.

STATUS: Individual research

DATE OF RESEARCH: 1994-1998

KEYWORDS: **arts; canada; criticism; cultural education; intercultural communication; multicultural education**

2219

Roehampton Lane, London SW15 5PU
0181 392 3000

Moura Correia, A. Miss; *Supervisors*: Mason, R. Prof.; Lima Cruz, M. Prof.

Prejudice reduction in teaching and learning Portuguese cultural heritage

ABSTRACT: The proposed study will expand on previous MA research into Portuguese teachers' concepts of art and education, in that it sets out to assess and develop their understanding of Portuguese art heritage with reference to cross-cultural interaction and exchange. The proposed programme of curriculum development and research will seek to investigate, develop and test out curriculum strategies and content for teaching Portuguese art heritage that address the above issues. The aim of this study overall is to design, implement and evaluate an experimental social reconstructionist curriculum focusing on an aspect of Portuguese colonial heritage, namely Indo-Portuguese religious art. The content will be issues-based in the sense that it will deal with questions of equality of opportunity and discrimination in present day Portugese society that affect middle school students in their daily life.

STATUS: Individual research

DATE OF RESEARCH: 1995-continuing

KEYWORDS: **arts; cultural education; portugal**

2220

Roehampton Lane, London SW15 5PU
0181 392 3000

Jackson, A. Dr; Kutnick, P. Dr

Group interaction at the microcomputer

ABSTRACT: In the majority of British primary schools, children use the computer in groups of 2 or 3. This is partly due to the lack of resources, ie. most classrooms still only have 1 or 2 computers to share between around 30 children. Group work on computers is also justified for pedagogic reasons. Previous research comparing children working in groups or alone has revealed an advantage for children working in groups although tasks undertaken have generally been problem solving programs. This study examined the performance of pairs and individual children (6 year olds) on a drill and practice program to investigate whether the group superiority effect for problem solving programs can be applied to other tasks. The research was based in a local infant school, and involved around 90 Year 1 boys and girls. Children worked at a mathematical drill and practice program either in single sex, similar ability pairs, or alone; a control group was also used. In addition to recording performance on the computer task, interactions were videotaped for later analysis. In comparison to the evidence from problem-solving activities, individuals were found to have a significant advantage over pairs during the drill and practice task. Analysis is currently underway to ascertain whether this was due to differences in on task and off task behaviour between groups and individuals.

PUBLISHED MATERIAL: JACKSON, A. & KUTNICK, P. (1996). 'Groupwork and computers: task type and children's performance', Journal of Computer Assisted Learning', Vol 12, No 3, pp.162-171.

STATUS: Sponsored project

SOURCE OF GRANT: Roehampton Institute London £3,362; Froebel Educational Institute £865

DATE OF RESEARCH: 1994-1997

KEYWORDS: **computer uses in education; group work; information technology; primary education; problem solving; pupil performance**

2221

Roehampton Lane, London SW15 5PU
0181 392 3000

Evans, R. Dr; Jackson, A. Dr; Stein, G. Ms

Using information technology in action and transition planning

ABSTRACT: At present only a handful of local careers services have started using the Internet which is and will be ideally placed to transmit up-to-date information to schools online. This project has developed one of the first such Internet sites in the UK. This project involved the development and evaluation of an Internet site with a number of key features. Options include access to leaflets on a wide variety of careers, links to other careers' sites, advice on how to get a job, links to higher education institutions and local further education colleges, and work experience reports. Further developments are underway to give teachers and pupils the opportunity to make appointments direct with the local careers service by e-mail, receive daily updates on what jobs are available locally, and access to a conferencing facility. In addition to the development of the website, a further aspect of the project was to trial the use of an action planning program within selected schools. The program was used with Year 10 pupils to assess their responses and its ease of use. The outcomes of this process are then transmitted to the local careers service using the Internet site and used to inform career interviews. These features are being evaluated by staff and pupils in 5 local secondary schools by means of questionnaires and follow-up interviews. Final results are not available at present but interim evaluations have been

very favourable and have helped facilitate the development of the Internet site.

STATUS: Sponsored project

SOURCE OF GRANT: AZTEC (Technology Enterprise Council for South West London £30,000

DATE OF RESEARCH: 1996-1997

KEYWORDS: **career awareness; career education; careers service; computer uses in education; electronic mail; employment opportunities; information technology; internet; labour market; school to work transition; secondary education; vocational guidance**

2222

Roehampton Lane, London SW15 5PU
0181 392 3000

Jackson, P. Dr

Continuation of distinctive approaches to early childhood education: Froebel, Steiner, Montessori

ABSTRACT: To the original investigation of the philosophy, policies, practices and effects of 2 distinctive approaches to early childhood educationMontessori and Steiner - has been added a third: Froebel. The investigation has already produced published papers and will eventually take book form. The key idea is that current conceptions of these approaches are distorted generalisations which require considerable revision. Through historical and philosophical research, different versions of these approaches will be identified. The identification will enable analysis to be more accurately focused so that evaluation of the appropriateness of these approaches to the education of young children can be made.

PUBLISHED MATERIAL: LEE, S-W., EVANS, R. & JACKSON, P. (1994). 'Froebel and Christianity', Early Child Development and Care', Vol 100, pp.1-42. ; JACKSON, P. (1996). 'Pre-school'. In: DOCKING, J.W. (Ed). National school policy: major issues in education policy for schools. Roehampton Text Series. London: David Fulton. ; JACKSON, P. (1996). 'Diversity'. In: DOCKING, J.W. (Ed). National school policy: major issues in education policy for schools. Roehampton Text Series. London: David Fulton. ; JACKSON, P. & LEE, S-W. (1996). 'Froebel and the Hitler Jugend: the Britishing of Froebel', Early Child Development and Care, Vol 117, pp.45-65.

STATUS: Sponsored project

SOURCE OF GRANT: Roehampton Institute £1,000; Froebel Company £500

DATE OF RESEARCH: 1994-1997

KEYWORDS: **early childhood education; educational theories; froebel schools; montessori method; steiner waldorf schools; teaching methods**

2223

Roehampton Lane, London SW15 5PU
0181 392 3000

Pinsent, P. Ms

Children's literature and equality issues

ABSTRACT: The aim of the research is to analyse some of the many children's books in the area of gender, 'race', disability and other 'equality' issues, in order to determine: a) the effectiveness of the means with which they deal with such subjects; b) the extent to which the author's ideology, overt and covert, affects such treatments; c) the qualify of the books as literature or, in the case of non-fiction, as sources of information; and d) the way in which they may be useful to teachers in attempting to fulfill the demands of the National Curriculum, both in terms of literature and of equality. The interim conclusion is that, since it is impossible for any writer to be without certain ideological presuppositions, the important thing is for authors, teachers, librarians, and, as far as is possible, children, to be aware of the way in which these affect their writing. This has implications for initial and inservice teacher education, and for the way books are handled in schools. There are in any case far too many books already in existence, within and outside schools, for consciousness only to be directed towards provision of resources, important though this is; education is essential so that children may be able to detect and handle bias in materials of all kinds. Books which may themselves reveal prejudices in their writers may be amongst the most effective instruments to assist pupils in gaining this kind of ability. This project has resulted in a book, published in 1997, and several articles, but is continuing.

PUBLISHED MATERIAL: PINSENT, P. (1995). '"We speak English in this school": the depiction of immigrant children'. In: BROADBENT, N. (Ed). Researching children's literature: a coming of age. Southampton: LSU College of Higher Education. ; PINSENT, P. (1996). 'Race and feminism in some recent children's books', Feminist Theology, No 13, pp.96-107. ; PINSENT, P. (1997). Children's literature and the politics of equality. Roehampton Teaching Studies. London: David Fulton. ; PINSENT, P. (1997). 'Reference books for children: a brief historical survey'. In: HANCOCK, S. (Ed). Guide to children's reference books and multimedia material. Aldershot: Scolar.

STATUS: Individual research

DATE OF RESEARCH: 1989-continuing

KEYWORDS: **antiracism education; books; childrens literature; disabilities; gender equality; race; racial attitudes; sex differences**

2224

Roehampton Lane, London SW15 5PU
0181 392 3000

Addo, A. Dr

Melody countours and language in Ghanaian children's singing

ABSTRACT: The purpose of this study is to examine the relationship between tone production and language among children of varying cultural backgrounds. The questions are: 1) Is there a relationship between language patterns and the expected melody of a Ghanaian children's play song? and b) Is there a relationship between the melody contour the children sung and the language? An analysis and a comparison of a selected singing game, Obiara, performed by a group of Ghanaian children and a group of English children was conducted. A pitch measurement device (Kay Elemetrics Computerised Speech Laboratory 5.1 (CSL) programme was used to construct a computer-assisted transcription of what the children sung. An expected transcription was also constructed from relative pitch judgements made in reference to the pitches in Obiara by the researcher and 3 other individuals. Two transcriptions of Obiara provided a description of the relationship between a) the expected transcription and the tones of the language; and b) what the children sung and the tones of the language. Fits between movement of expected tones, sung tones, and language tones were calculated and compared as percentages of the total number of movements in the song. The results so far show that in the adults' estimation 77.8% of the time the children followed the macro contour of the Akan language. The computer assisted transcription also revealed the same results. The findings indicate that language and music enculturation influence children's singing development.

PUBLISHED MATERIAL: ADDO, A.O. (1996). 'A multimedia analysis of selected Ghanaian children's play songs', Bulletin of the Council for Research in Music Education, Vol 129, pp.1-23.

STATUS: Sponsored project

SOURCE OF GRANT: Roehampton Institute London £3,000

DATE OF RESEARCH: 1996-continuing

KEYWORDS: **ghana; music; music activities; singing**

2225

Roehampton Lane, London SW15 5PU
0181 392 3000

Shaughnessy, J. Ms; *Supervisor*: Jackson, P. Dr

Becoming a teacher: analysis of a Postgraduate Certificate of Education (PGCE) course

ABSTRACT: Analysis and evaluation of a Postgraduate Certificate of Education (PGCE) course taking account of the students' personal experiences. The project includes a pilot study of 1993-94 PGCE cohort; review of literature; collection of data (application forms, interview notes, diaries, feedback sheets, researcher's observations, etc); preliminary practice; final practice (interviews, reports, diaries); implications of the findings of the investigations in the context of the review of literature; and recommendations.

STATUS: Individual research

DATE OF RESEARCH: 1993-1997

KEYWORDS: **postgraduate certificate in education; preservice teacher education; reflective teaching; student experience; student teacher attitudes; student teachers**

2226

Roehampton Lane, London SW15 5PU
0181 392 3000

McGrath, C. Ms; *Supervisors*: Watts, D. Dr; Kutnick, P. Dr

Promoting relevance in school science

ABSTRACT: This research is exploring the fostering of personal and social relevance within school science. In particular, the study is exploring the use and effectiveness of materials specifically designed to promote relevance: the Association for Science Education's 'Science and technology in society' books. Data is being gathered through survey questionnaires and focused interviews.

STATUS: Individual research

DATE OF RESEARCH: 1994-1997

KEYWORDS: **relevance - education; science education; science interests**

2227

Roehampton Lane, London SW15 5PU
0181 392 3000

Mallick, J. Ms; *Supervisors*: Kutnick, P. Dr; Watts, M. Dr; O'Connor, L. Ms

An investigation into parent-child communication about drugs

ABSTRACT: There is an acknowledged need to bring parents and children effectively into drug prevention initiatives and effective communication is identified as an important part of this process. Research indicates there is a generation gap between the parent and youth cultures surrounding drugs and this gap impedes effective communication between them. Therefore, it is important to identify and explore the key factors within the parent and youth cultures surrounding drugs and identify more clearly the gap as well as the issues surrounding parent-child communication about drugs. The aims of the study are to: 1) investigate the nature of parent-child communication around drug issues from the perspectives of young people and parents of young people; 2) facilitate and measure the development of effective communication about drug issues between parents and young people. This study will be set within the framework of personal construct theory (PCT) (Kelly, 1955). The initial phase of research will use focus groups of young people and parents to explore the emergent themes. An intervention will then be developed using PCT techniques to facilitate and measure the development of effective communication between parents and children about drugs. From the findings future recommendations can be made for prevention initiatives to effectively address drug education for both parents and young people.

PUBLISHED MATERIAL: MALLICK, J., EVANS, R. & STEIN, G. 'Parents and drug education: parents' concerns, attitudes and needs', Drugs: Education, Prevention and Policy, Vol 5, No 2. (in press).

STATUS: Individual research

DATE OF RESEARCH: 1996-continuing

KEYWORDS: **drug education; drug education; parent child relationship**

2228

Roehampton Lane, London SW15 5PU
0181 392 3000

Rinne, P. Mr; *Supervisors*: Mason, R. Prof.; Bailey, G. Dr

A study of the use of drawing in the National Curriculum key stage 3: with special reference to developing strategies for raising teachers' understanding of its general educational significance

ABSTRACT: The research grew out of a desire to investigate both the use of art across the secondary school curriculum and the ill-defined concept of graphicacy. Observation in local secondary schools revealed large numbers of drawings on display in all subject areas but reasons why teachers included them were not clear. A decision was taken to research their use and a review of literature revealed that no research of any significance had been conducted on the topic. Key research questions formulated as follows: 1) What are the existing requirements within the National Curriculum for the use of drawing? 2) How much drawing do pupils actually do, what types of drawing and in what subjects? 3) Why do non-specialist teachers include drawing and how do they teach it? (Do they have the necessary knowledge and skills?). 4) How can their understanding of its educational value (both general and subject-specific) be increased? The research method included profiles of children's drawings over one school year, an action study and an attitude survey. Tentative conclusions so far are that, as a teaching-learning strategy, drawing is used a great deal, but that its educational value is poorly understood.

STATUS: Individual research

DATE OF RESEARCH: 1992-1998

KEYWORDS: **art education; key stage 3; secondary education**

2229

Roehampton Lane, London SW15 5PU
0181 392 3000

Gould, G. Ms; Walsh, A. Ms; *Supervisors*: Watts, M. Dr; Alsop, S. Dr

The Questcup project

ABSTRACT: This project explores the production and use of learners' questions in classroom situations. Questions have given rise to a taxonomy of learners' questions, and a study has been made, using classroom observations and diary methods, of questions as critical incidents in teachers' professional activities.

PUBLISHED MATERIAL: WATTS, D.M., GOULD, G.F. & ALSOP, S.J. (1997). 'Questions of understanding: categorising pupils' questions in science', School Science Review, Vol 78, No 285, pp.101-107. ; WATTS, D.M., ALSOP, S.J., GOULD, G.F. & WALSH, A. (1997). 'Prompting teachers' constructive reflection. Pupils' questions as critical incidents', International Journal of Science Education, Vol 19, No 9, pp.1025-1037.

STATUS: Team research

DATE OF RESEARCH: 1995-continuing

KEYWORDS: **classroom observation techniques; pupils questions; science education**

2230

Roehampton Lane, London SW15 5PU
0181 392 3000

Alsop, S. Dr; *Supervisor*: Watts, M. Dr

The transition from formal to informal learning in science

ABSTRACT: This project explores a model to describe informal learning of science in the domain of public understanding of science. The model is drawn from formal school 'conceptual change learning' and is modified to encompass affective and cognitive components. The data is drawn from surveys and interviews with 5 sample learners.

PUBLISHED MATERIAL: ALSOP, S.J. & WATTS, D.M. (1997). 'Sources from a Somerset village: a model for informal learning about radiation and radioactivity', Science Education, Vol 81, No 6, pp.633-650. ; WATTS, D.M. & ALSOP, S.J. (1997). 'A feeling for learning: modelling affective learning in school science', Curriculum Journal, Vol 8, No 3, pp.351-365.

STATUS: Team research

DATE OF RESEARCH: 1994-continuing

KEYWORDS: **public understanding of science; science education**

2231

Roehampton Lane, London SW15 5PU
0181 392 3000

Forland, H. Dr; Dock, G. Mr; *Supervisor*: Watts, D. Dr

Self-esteem in science education

ABSTRACT: This project explores self-esteem in the learning of science by non-science undergraduates. It uses questionnaire and interview data to gauge levels of self-awareness and self-esteem as these influence subject choice, positive attitudes and grade performance in science studies.

STATUS: Individual research

DATE OF RESEARCH: 1997-1998

KEYWORDS: **higher education; science education; self esteem; students**

2232

Roehampton Lane, London SW15 5PU
0181 392 3000

Alsop, S. Dr; Dock, G. Mr; *Supervisor*: Watts, D. Dr

Communicare Nelle Science

ABSTRACT: This project is researching the inter-relationships between the teaching of science, home language and modern foreign languages. In collaboration with Italy, France, Greece and Portugal, classroom intervention materials have been designed and evaluated which explore teachers' collaboration across these subject disciplines. The materials use print, video, and information technology (IT) formats, suitable for use with 14-18 year-old students.

STATUS: Sponsored project

SOURCE OF GRANT: Socrates Lingua Project £30,000

DATE OF RESEARCH: 1995-1998

KEYWORDS: **cross curricular approach; modern language studies; science education; secondary education**

2233

Roehampton Lane, London SW15 5PU
0181 392 3000

Kutnick, P. Dr

Gender and school achievement in the Caribbean

ABSTRACT: Generally higher levels of school achievement have been informally reported in various countries of the English speaking Caribbean. This study drew upon quantitative and qualitative research methods to substantiate the relative performance of boys and girls at the classroom level and with regard to a representative sample, paternal and maternal occupation, type of school attended, preschool attendance, help for learning in and around the home. Three parts were included in the study: a representative sample of pupils aged 8-18 in Barbados; a representative sample of pupils aged 8-18 in St Vincent and classroom observations in Trinidad. The study found that: 1) girls perform better than boys in core subjects (English, mathematics, science) when using average scores; 2) in elite schools, boys and girls (and children from a range of parental occupations) perform similarly; 3) top performing pupils live with both parents and these parents come from higher occupational levels; 4) classrooms are run in a traditional manner and this is most likely to include high attaining pupils and exclude low attainers; 5) girls are more likely to form support groups among themselves which can enhance classroom performance.

PUBLISHED MATERIAL: KUTNICK, P., LAYNE, A. & JULES, V. (1997). Gender and school achievement in the Caribbean. London: Department for International Development.

STATUS: Sponsored project

SOURCE OF GRANT: Department for International Development £35,000

DATE OF RESEARCH: 1996-1997

KEYWORDS: **academic achievement; achievement; caribbean; sex differences**

2234

Roehampton Lane, London SW15 5PU
0181 392 3000

Best, R. Prof.

The professional and developmental needs of the deputy headteacher

ABSTRACT: In a context in which the Teacher Training Agency (TTA) is introducing a programme of staged training leading to qualifications for headteachers, subject leaders and advanced-skills teachers and newly qualified teachers (NQTs), the developmental needs of deputy headteachers seem to be neglected. This project uses a questionnaire (to be distributed and collected with the assistance of the Secondary Heads Association (SHA) and semi-structured interviews to establish secondary deputy heads' perspectives on their training needs. Respondents will be asked to evaluate the training they received before and since becoming deputy headteachers, to report and prioritise their perceived training needs at present and to indicate their agreement or otherwise with statements concerning the relevance, quality and utility of a range of forms of training and support. Attention will be paid to the importance of personal support and pastoral care for incumbents in this demanding role. It is anticipated that a number of distinctive deputy 'types' will be identified and appropriate programmes of training and support proposed.

STATUS: Sponsored project

SOURCE OF GRANT: National Association for Pastoral Care in Education £1,050; Incorporated Froebelk Educational Institute £277; Secondary Heads Association

DATE OF RESEARCH: 1997-continuing

KEYWORDS: deputy head teachers; teacher development; teaching profession

2235

Roehampton Lane, London SW15 5PU
0181 392 3000

Mahony, P. Prof.; Hextall, I. Mr

The impact on teaching of the National Professional Qualifications

ABSTRACT: Since its establishment in September 1994, the Teacher Training Agency (TTA) has undertaken a raft of activities which constitute a fundamental restructuring of a National Professional Qualification (NPQ) framework which consists of national standards and qualifications for various stages within the teaching career. There is currently much debate about the reconstruction of professionalism in teaching. These debates reflect three main themes: tensions involved in concepts of professionalism; transformations in the social and economic contexts within which public sector professionals are located and specific changes in the nature, control and definition of teaching as an occupational category. Issues of representation, accountability and governance are also being widely debated within a burgeoning international literature. All these elements are pertinent to the NPQ developments. Using a combination of documentary analysis, questionnaire survey and interviews, the project aims to investigate the assumptions, procedures and mechanisms through which the NPQ policy has been established, including analysis of the processes of consultation and response, the manner in which policy is being translated into practice and its impact on teaching.

PUBLISHED MATERIAL: MAHONY, P. (1997). 'Talking heads: feminist perspectives on public sector reform in teacher education', Discourse, Vol 18, No 1, pp.87-102. ; MAHONY, P. & HEXTALL, I. (1997). The policy context and impact of the TTA: a summary. London: Roehampton Institute London. ; MAHONY, P. & HEXTALL, I. (1997). 'Problems of accountability in reinvented government: a case study of the Teacher Training Agency', Journal of Education Policy, Vol 12, No 4, pp.267-278.; MAHONY, P. & HEXTALL, I. (1997). 'Sounds of silence: the social justice agenda of the Teacher Training Agency', International Studies in Sociology of Education, Vol 7, No 2, pp.137-156. ; MAHONY, P. & HEXTALL, I. (1998). 'Effective teachers for effective schools'. In: SLEE, R., TOMLINSON, S. & WEINER, G. (Eds). School effectiveness for whom? London: Falmer Press.

STATUS: Sponsored project

SOURCE OF GRANT: Economic and Social Research Council £71,588

DATE OF RESEARCH: 1997-continuing

KEYWORDS: head teachers; national professional qualification for headship; teacher development; teaching profession

2236

Roehampton Lane, London SW15 5PU
0181 392 3000

Evans, R. Dr; Coggans, N. Dr; Spencer, I. Ms; *Supervisor*: O'Connor, L. Mrs

Drugs education in schools: identifying the added value of the police service within a model of best practice

ABSTRACT: This is a collaborative project between the Drugs Education and Prevention Research Unit at Roehampton Institute London and the Association of Chief Police Officers Drugs Sub-Committee. The project

arose out of previous research carried out at Roehampton Institute London (1995-1997) which used an extensive literature review, first hand research with approximately 4500 5-18 year-olds in 3 London boroughs, and representative teachers, police officers, health promotion educators and school governors, to inform a model of 'best practice' in drugs education. This research has been published as O'CONNOR, L., O'CONNOR, D. & BEST, R. (1998). Drugs: partnerships for policy, prevention and education. London: Cassell. The significance of the above research for the current project lies in the finding that police officers are major contributors to school drugs education, and to school drugs policies to address incidents of misuse. Given the current constraints on police budgets and competing priorities on 'core' policing objectives, the present project aims to identify the most effective, focused contribution the police service can make to school drugs education, which is capable of demonstrating added value to this area. Three key questions are being addressed through the research aims and design: 1) What is currently being done? (What is the extent and nature of the police contribution to school drugs education/policies?) 2) What should be done? (What is the best contribution that the police can make, in the light of research evidence effectiveness, national and local policy recommendations, and the needs of schools as organisations?) 3) What can be done? (What is realistic and achievable given competing priorities and current constraints on police resources?) The research methods are: 1) An international literature review of drugs education effectiveness and police involvement in school drugs education. 2) Questionnaires to all police forces in England and Wales and one representative Scottish force, to ascertain the aims, content, methods and intended outcomes of police efforts, the number of police officers involved and how these are prepared for their role. 3) Six case studies of forces chosen on information contained in returned questionnaires and enclosed background materials. Criteria for inclusion includes variations in the involvement of officers in the classroom and school drugs policies, programme rationale, content and delivery, the contribution of other agencies, location, mix and size of rural and urban forces. 4) A series of focus groups (11-18 year-olds) across a selection of London boroughs (8-10) to ascertain young people's perceptions, experiences and expectations of police involvement in school drugs education, to compare and contrast with police perceptions of their own contribution in this area. The report is to be published at the end of March 1999.

PUBLISHED MATERIAL: O'CONNOR, L. (1998). 'Drugs education in schools: identifying the added value of the police service with a model of best practice', Police Research and Management, Summer 1998, pp.37-46.

STATUS: Collaborative

DATE OF RESEARCH: 1997-continuing

KEYWORDS: drug education; health education; police; police school relationship

2237

Roehampton Lane, London SW15 5PU
0181 392 3000

Lathey, G. Dr

The reception history of Erich Kastner's children's books in the UK

ABSTRACT: It is the aim of this research project to trace the reception history of Erich Kastner's children's books, particularly 'Emil and the Detectives', in the UK. This involves the collection and analysis of press reviews and critical attention since the first English version of 'Emil' was published in 1931, and a comparative analysis of different translations. Interviews have also been conducted to establish children's responses to 'Emil' across several decades.

STATUS: Sponsored project

SOURCE OF GRANT: Thyssen Steel

DATE OF RESEARCH: 1998-continuing

KEYWORDS: books; childrens literature

2238

Roehampton Lane, London SW15 5PU
0181 392 3000

Watts, M. Dr; Hollins, M. Dr

Family science

ABSTRACT: The project involved 3 primary schools in the South West

London area where pupils and parents were invited to participate in 2 'family science nights' at each school. The first night introduced a series of astronomy topics, entertainment and practical tasks, and set project tasks to each family group. The second night was convened 6 weeks later when, after further 'info-tainment' the family groups reported on their projects. At each school were audiences of 20, 40 and 120 respectively, with excellent responses on the '2nd night tasks'. Support and evaluation of the overall project was undertaken by a team of 8 undergraduates from the Institute. The research shows very positive support for 'family learning'. A report on the family science project has been prepared for the Particle Physics and Astronomy Research Council.

STATUS: Sponsored project

SOURCE OF GRANT: Particle Physics and Astronomy Research Council £3,000

DATE OF RESEARCH: 1997-continuing

KEYWORDS: **astronomy; family involvement; science activities; science education**

2239

Roehampton Lane, London SW15 5PU
0181 392 3000
De Montfort University, Lens Media Centre, The Gateway, Leicester LE1 9BH 011625 51551
Universidade Federal de Santa Maria, Centro de Artes e Letras, Cidade Universitaria, Camobi, 97-119 Santa Maria RS, Brazil
Universidade Estadual de Campinas, Departmento de Metodologia do Ensino, Faculdade de Educacao, R. Bertrand Russel, Campinas SP, Brazil

Mason, R. Prof.; Richter, I. Prof.; Almeida, C. Prof.; Cruickshank, I. Ms; Casey, L. Ms

Aesthetic value in the home and its contribution to family life

ABSTRACT: This project sets out to determine the contribution of women's crafts in the home to family life and the social/economic order. The target group are working class housewives from 3 distinctive cultural groups in the Santa Maria region of Brazil who practice handcrafts in the home. A cross-cultural team of researchers are adopting a life-history approach to reconstructing these women's domestic art worlds using semi-structured interviews and photographic documentation of their aesthetic and other interests and concerns. The project will have research and curriculum development outcomes in the form of: a) illustrated case studies of the women and their aesthetic interests together with analysis of their social and occupational determinants and contribution to family life; and b) a portable educational resource for use in art teacher training in Britain and Brazil.

STATUS: Sponsored project

SOURCE OF GRANT: British Council; CAPES £24,000

DATE OF RESEARCH: 1996-continuing

KEYWORDS: **arts; brazil; handicrafts; preservice teacher education; women**

2240

Roehampton Lane, London SW15 5PU
0181 392 3000
De Montfort University, School of Arts and Humanities, Centre for Postgraduate Teacher Education, The Gateway, Leicester LE1 9BH 01162 551551

Smith, J. Mrs; *Supervisors*: Mason, R. Prof.; Allison, B. Prof.

An investigation into the training, early professional career and publications of the Sheffield artist and art educator Elizabeth Styring Nutt (1870-1946)

ABSTRACT: Elizabeth Styring Nutt (1870-1946) emigrated to Canada in 1919 to take up a post as Principal of Nova Scotia College of Art. Her prominence as an art educator there has been fairly well researched, but little is known of her formative years in Britain, she is not referred to in standard British art education histories. Lack of reference to Nutt appears to parallel that of many British women artists, educators and writers whose careers developed despite the challenges and problems created by a male dominated society. This interdisciplinary research, which falls within the area of the history of art and design education, draws together insights from 3 fields, those of biographical history, the theory and development of art education and feminist theory. Within the framework of feminist theory, and with particular reference to gender issues, the research investigates 19th century British art teacher training and examines Nutt's religious background, art philosophy, educational values, curriculum content and the professional expertise gained by her in Britain and taken to Canada. The research is based on analysis of primary archival source material, e.g. reports identified in the Sheffield Local Studies Library, Sheffield School of Art and Nova Scotia College of Art and Design, newspaper and magazine articles in the British and Canadian press and paintings, art work and texts by Nutt. This material will be evaluated with reference to secondary sources, e.g. articles in the Victorian periodical press, contemporary feminist literature and interviews with Nutt's relatives.

STATUS: Individual research

DATE OF RESEARCH: 1993-1998

KEYWORDS: **art education; art teachers; artists; educational history**

2241

Roehampton Lane, London SW15 5PU
0181 392 3000
London University, Goldsmiths College, Department of Design Studies, Technology Education Research Unit, New Cross, London SE14 6NW
0171 919 7171

Mahony, P. Prof.; Johnson, H. Ms; Kimbell, R. Prof.; Miller, S. Ms; Saxton, J. Mr

Decisions by design

ABSTRACT: The project explores the extent to which - and the ways in which - design activity can be used to enhance the decision making of school managers. The researchers are concerned with the ways in which decisions get made, rather than the structures that exist in schools or the substance of the decisions that result. Specifically, interest is in the extent to which these decision making processes reflect design behaviour; and in the consequences for decision making when those responsible for the decisions are made aware of the procedures of design thinking. The project aims to: 1) examine and document in 6 case study schools (3 primary and 3 secondary) - the decision making procedures that operate in the senior management teams (SMTs) in those schools; 2) expose the SMTs to a variety of design experiences - both direct and indirect - requiring them at the same time to reflect upon them; 3) present and debate school management challenges and opportunities in ways that enable the SMTs to recognise designerly responses to them; 4) monitor the extent to which - and the ways in which - these experiences modify the decision making procedures of SMTs.

STATUS: Sponsored project

SOURCE OF GRANT: Design Council £88,000

DATE OF RESEARCH: 1995-1997

KEYWORDS: **administrators; decision making; design; educational administration; management in education; management teams; primary education; secondary education**

2242

Roehampton Lane, London SW15 5PU
0181 392 3000
London University, Institute of Education, 20 Bedford Way, London WC1H 0AL
0171 580 1122

Smedley, S. Ms; *Supervisors*: Miller, J. Prof.; Turvey, A. Ms

Male students in primary initial teacher education

ABSTRACT: The researcher has worked as a primary teacher and now works as a tutor in primary initial teacher education (ITE). This study has grown out of her personal and professional interests in gender and difference. The study is an exploration of male student teachers' moves into the feminised culture of primary teaching. Male students have been interviewed at different stages of their ITE course. Issues relating to the researcher's position as a woman studying men are considered. The aim is to investigate how the experiences and understanding of male students can be theorised. Analysis of the data suggests that male students' position as teachers of young children is complex and often ambivalent. Close reading of selected extracts from the data shows that gender and social class shape the ways the students are able to understand their experiences and their expectations. The research also has an historical dimension, tracking the significance of gender and class in primary teaching and primary ITE from the late 19th century. Data from college archives is used as illustrative material. Conclusions will consider pedagogical implications for primary ITE.

PUBLISHED MATERIAL: SMEDLEY, S. (1997). 'Men on the margins': male student primary teachers', Changing English, Vol 4, No 2, pp.217-227. ; SMEDLEY, S. (1998). 'Perspectives on male student primary teachers', Changing English, Vol 5, No 2, pp.147-159.

STATUS: Individual research

DATE OF RESEARCH: 1995-continuing

KEYWORDS: **men; men teachers; preservice teacher education; primary school teachers; sex differences; student teachers**

2243

Roehampton Lane, London SW15 5PU
0181 392 3000
London University, King's College, School of Education, Cornwall House, Waterloo Road, London SE1 8WA
0171 836 5454

Rose, D. Mr; *Supervisor*: Ball, S. Prof.

An exploration of cultural restorationism and its impact since the 1988 Education Reform Act, with particular reference to religious education

ABSTRACT: This study will analyse the tensions and key influences brought to bear in determining religious education (RE) policy. It will consider this within the context of post-war developments for RE providers with attention being given to selected Education Acts and government directives. Consideration will be given to pressures exerted by key bodies such as the National Curriculum Council (NCC) and School Curriculum and Assessment Authority (SCAA) when judgements are made concerning the content of RE. The study will include the following significant areas: 1) The politics of RE, considering both statute, terminology used and post-war tensions within policy-making for the subject. This includes analysis of post-war literature in seeking to identify the tensions and various interpretations of terms used in relation to RE especially at a local level. 2) A consideration of the disparity in thinking between the Standing Advisory Council for Religious Education (SACRE) at local education authority (LEA) level and that of the key influencers including the Department for Education (DFE) Department for Education and Science (DES), SCAA, OFSTED and key figures, whether politicians or religiously orientated. LEA perceptions will be gained through questionnaire and analysis of responses (initially undertaken in 1992 but with the possibility of follow-up). 3) The main focus of the study to highlight the effects of decision making will be that of the cultural restorationists. Analysis will include a literature survey from the 1960s to date, together with an exploration of the perceptions of those closely involved. The underlying tension from the secular perspective and what may be deemed an opposite extreme, the conservative Christian perspective, will be considered. 4) Current ambiguities in RE policy making will be highlighted and an 'expose' given.

PUBLISHED MATERIAL: ROSE, D.W. (1996). 'Religious education, spirituality and the acceptable face of indoctrination'. In: BEST, R. (Ed). Education, Spirituality and the Whole Child. London: Cassell. ; ROSE, D.W. (1998). 'A survey of representative groups on SACRE', Journal of Contemporary Religion, Vol 13, No 3, pp.383-393.

STATUS: Individual research

DATE OF RESEARCH: 1995-continuing

KEYWORDS: **curriculum development; educational policy; humanism; ofsted; religious education**

2244

Roehampton Lane, London SW15 5PU
0181 392 3000
London University, King's College, School of Education, Cornwall House, Waterloo Road, London SE1 8WA
0171 836 5454

Gifford, S. Ms; *Supervisors*: Brown, M. Prof.; Askew, M. Mr

Under fives learning about number in the nursery school

ABSTRACT: Recent research and mathematics educationalists (Young

Loveridge, 1987, Tahta, 1991) have questioned the validity of the influence of Piaget on views of how children learn about number. There are two aspects to this, in terms of what it is about number that children are learning and how they are learning. The aims of this study are to chart how a few individual children with different degrees of competence and experience in number develop their competence as shown in the school situation between the ages of 3 and 5. The questions to be answered are: 1) How do various aspects of number competence develop in relation to each other and in a variety of contexts, with different individuals? 2) How do individuals respond to various experiences on offer? 3) What factors might influence children's learning, both in and out of school? Data will be collected mainly by observation, with audio and videotaping, on weekly visits over 2 years. These observations will be supplemented by observations from staff and interviews with parents.

STATUS: Individual research

DATE OF RESEARCH: 1995-continuing

KEYWORDS: **early childhood education; mathematics education; numbers; nursery education; preschool education; young children**

2245

Roehampton Lane, London SW15 5PU
0181 392 3000
Merton, Sutton and Wandsworth Health Authority, Specialist Health Promotion Service, 61 Glenburnie Road, Tooting, London SW17 7DU

Best, R. Prof.; Best, D. Dr; *Supervisor*: O'Connor, L. Ms

Identifying young people's knowledge and awareness of drug use and misuse and the critical success factors for the development of effective drugs education policies and programmes which meet the needs of young people

ABSTRACT: A comprehensive assessment of drug education needs, issues and policy was carried out in the South London boroughs of Merton, Sutton and Wandsworth in 1996. This involved direct assessment of 4,415 children attending school (1,941 primary school children and 34 children attending a special needs school completed a 'draw and write' task, while 2,440 secondary school children filled in a questionnaire). This was supplemented by a questionnaire to teachers at each of the participating schools, a series of group discussions with secondary children who had participated in the questionnaire phase, interviews with key informants working in the drug education area and a series of seminar workshops carried out at the initial dissemination of the questionnaire results. The 'draw and write' task revealed increasing levels of drug knowledge in primary school children with age. While many of the 4-5 year olds had little understanding of even the term 'drugs', this increased significantly by the age of 7-8 years, and by 10-11 years a substantial proportion of primary children have a relatively sophisticated concept of a range of drug issues. The questionnaire results showed that while 26% of the sample drank alcohol at least once a week, only 5% smoked cigarettes with the same frequency, while 17% had tried an illicit drug, most commonly cannabis. Both regular drinking and regular smoking were predictors of illicit drug use, with regular drinkers around 9 times more likely to have tried an illicit drug than irregular drinkers, while regular smokers were around 6 times more likely to have tried an illicit drug than irregular smokers. 126 respondents described themselves as dependent smokers (19% of the smokers in the survey) and those who did so were around 22 times more likely to have tried an illicit drug than were irregular smokers or non-smokers. The implications derived from the research are that education on smoking, drinking and illicit drug use should be integrated to a considerably greater extent. The research also concludes that schools should adopt a 'whole-school' approach in which drug education is an open and participative activity that goes beyond the school gates to involve the community and in which young people themselves are permitted a more active and reflexive role. A report will be published in-house.

PUBLISHED MATERIAL: O'CONNOR, L., O'CONNOR, D. & LANG, P. (Eds). (1998). Drugs policy, prevention and education. London: Cassell.

STATUS: Sponsored project

SOURCE OF GRANT: Home Office £8,000; Linbury Trust £8,000; First Continental £2,000; Price Waterhouse £3,000

DATE OF RESEARCH: 1995-1997

KEYWORDS: **drinking; drug abuse; drug education; health education; primary education; secondary education; smoking**

2246

Roehampton Lane, London SW15 5PU
0181 392 3000
The Hong Kong Institute of Education, Grantham Campus, 42 Gascoigne Road, Kowloon, Hong Kong
010852 23885061

Au, K. Ms; *Supervisors*: Mason, R. Prof.; Watts, M. Dr

Educational evaluation: its role in improving subject knowledge and competences of secondary art teachers in Hong Kong

ABSTRACT: For decades there has been no formal evaluation or assessment to ensure the quality of art teaching in Hong Kong. The aim of the proposed research is to establish levels of subject knowledge and competencies as currently perceived by secondary art teachers in Hong Kong. It is also proposed to study how evaluation of art teaching can be applied in inservice teacher education for professional development purposes. Data will be collected through a questionnaire survey to a random sample of secondary art specialist teachers. Findings evolved from the questionnaire data will form the basis of a professional development programme. Inservice art teachers will devise small scale action research projects in collaboration with the researcher. In the projects they will apply clusters of subject knowledge and competencies to classroom practice with the aim of improving the quality of their teaching.

STATUS: Individual research

DATE OF RESEARCH: 1995-1998

KEYWORDS: **art education; art teachers; hong kong; inservice teacher education**

Royal College of Nursing Institute

2247

20 Cavendish Square, London W1M OAB
0171 409 3333

Savage, J. Dr

Emotions in practice: a study of Balint seminar training as experiential learning for qualified nurses

ABSTRACT: This pilot study takes an ethnographic approach, focusing on the work of one established group of nurses (9) who, through prolonged seminar training, are skilled in using their emotional reactions to patients as a tool for responding to distress. 9 seminars will be attended and recorded, and all participants will be interviewed regarding their experience of seminar training. Data will be subjected to thematic and narrative analysis. The study aims to describe the experiential process that is associated with Balint seminar training, with a view to evaluating this as a model for clinical supervision. As a parallel concern, the study is interested in developing theoretical understanding of the role of emotions in nurses' knowledge and practice.

STATUS: Sponsored project

SOURCE OF GRANT: Royal College of Nursing Institute

DATE OF RESEARCH: 1998-continuing

KEYWORDS: **emotions; experiential learning; nurse education; nurses**

2248

20 Cavendish Square, London W1M OAB
0171 409 3333

Price, B. Mr; *Supervisors*: Lucock, R. Dr; Clark, L. Dr

A grounded theory of student support amongst distance learning nurse undergraduates

ABSTRACT: This research consists of a grounded theory inquiry (Glaser and Strauss 1967, Glaser 1992) into the ways in which students experience and negotiate support on a post registration, distance learning nursing studies degree. The study follows the precepts of classical grounded theory with a commitment to theoretical sampling, constant comparison of data, memo writing and the evolution of a substantive theory centred upon the basic social process involved in this mode of study support. The researcher is using a variety of data gathering techniques including the interview of students and their lay supporters, the interview of tutor-counsellors, participant observation of tutorials and analysis of correspondence between the Institute and its students. Students, lay supporters, tutors and Institute are afforded a brief on the research before being invited to sign an informed consent form. Thereafter respondents are invited to ask for research updates. A central concern of this study has been to illuminate the hidden, non institutional support that students draw upon, whilst they continue with employment and family commitments. This research is seen as complementary to the more traditional focus upon academic helping roles and services.

STATUS: Individual research

DATE OF RESEARCH: 1996-continuing

KEYWORDS: **distance education; nurse education; nurses**

2249

20 Cavendish Square, London W1M 0AB
0171 409 3333
Bath University, Claverton Down, Bath BA2 7AY
01225 826826

Manley, K. Mrs; *Supervisors*: Luccock, R. Dr; James, C. Dr

The clinical nurse specialist's role in facilitating the development of nurses and nursing in order to provide a quality nursing service: an action research project

ABSTRACT: The Hamric and Spross (1989) Model of Clinical Nurse Specialist a Unique Role in the United Kingdom is the focus of this study. The Role has: four specific sub-roles (expert practice, educator, researcher and consultant); and explicit criteria and competencies are expected, e.g. a Masters Degree/PhD and Postgraduate Teaching Certificate; expert skills and competencies in change management, collaboration, leadership, facilitation etc. The post resulted from a values clarification exercise involving all staff working on a nursing development unit, who also agreed to evaluate it. Action research was selected as it was congruent with the values of staff, in that it is both collaborative and emancipatory; it also focuses on action, and the messy and real world of practice. The post itself is inextricably linked with the unit's purpose. The purpose of the project was therefore threefold: ultimately it was about improving the service to patients and their families; secondly, it was about trying to understand and make sense of the processes involving the researcher and her colleagues as collaborative researchers in achieving this end; and thirdly, to try and understand the clinical nurse specialist's role in facilitating this process. Action research cycles therefore have centred around three main issues: 1) the macro-overriding theme on how to improve the service to patients and their families; 2) A middle theme with action cycles relating to each of the unit's eight objectives; and 3) action research cycles, focusing on the clinical nurse specialist's own actions in facilitating the process. Several methods of data collection have been used throughout as evidence at various stages of the action research cycles, these have included unstructured interviews, focused group discussions, reflective practice notes and document analysis. Deep analysis is currently being undertaken. The post has been successfully refunded by the hospital trust.

PUBLISHED MATERIAL: MANLEY, K., CRUSE, S. & KEOGH, S. (1996). 'Job satisfaction of intensive care nurses practising primary nursing and a comparison with those practising total patient care', Nursing in Critical Care, Vol 1, No 1. ; MANLEY, K., HAMILL, J.M. & HANLON, M. 'Nursing staff's perceptions and experiences of primary nursing on intensive care four years on', Journal of Clinical Nursing. (in press).

STATUS: Individual research

DATE OF RESEARCH: 1993-1997

KEYWORDS: **nurse education; nurses**

Royal National Institute for the Blind

2250

224 Great Portland Street, London W1N 6AA
0171 388 1266

Clunies-Ross, L. Ms; Keil, S. Mrs

Blind and partially sighted children in Britain: their incidence and special needs at a time of change

ABSTRACT: This research concerns children up to the age of 16 who are visually impaired, i.e. children whose lack of functional vision means that they require braille, modified large print or tape resources in order to access the curriculum. As demographic details of visually impaired children are not available from any central source there is no means of assessing the national level of need for specialist visual impairment provision, teacher training, teaching resources and/or examination requirements. A structured questionnaire sent to key personnel in local authority visual impairment services in England, Scotland and Wales and to all schools for sensory impaired children in 1997 seeks to establish numbers of visually impaired and multi-disabled visually impaired children in age bands of under 5, 5 to 10, 11 to 16; numbers with a Statement or Record of Need and the numbers using braille or moon for reading or writing. The survey also seeks information on pupils' educational placement, information on definitions used by local authority visual impairment services to identify children as visually impaired and multi-disabled visually impaired, and on local education and unitary authority service structures and staffing levels. Changes to visual impairment services since local government reorganisation in 1994 are documented, and future development plans noted. Three selected areas will provide 'case study' examples to illuminate the numerical data. It is intended that the information collected and disseminated will assist education authorities and other service providers to plan and deliver appropriate specialist provision to meet the needs of visually impaired children.

STATUS: Sponsored project

SOURCE OF GRANT: The Nuffield Foundation £34,200

DATE OF RESEARCH: 1996-1998

KEYWORDS: **blindness; braille; partial vision; special educational needs; visual impairments**

2251

224 Great Portland Street, London W1N 6AA
0171 388 1266

Franklin, A. Ms; Masters, K. Ms; Smith, L. Mr; *Supervisors*: Clunies-Ross, L. Ms; Cole-Hamilton, I. Ms

Shaping the future: RNIB children and young people's need and aspirations survey

ABSTRACT: The survey is exploring the views and experiences of 600, randomly selected, visually impaired and multi-disabled visually impaired children and young people with a view to informing and influencing the nature and delivery of provision in education, health, social and other public services. The subjects and participants are as follows: 1) Multi-disabled children of 5-16 years old: the needs and views of these children are being ascertained primarily through their parents and primary professional carers. A small number of case studies will be undertaken to give some more indepth information and to allow a few children the opportunity to take part themselves. 2) Multi-disabled young people of 16-25 years old: parents are being invited to take part on behalf of these young people and some limited work will be undertaken with a small number of young people themselves. 3) Blind and partially sighted children of average learning ability of primary school age. The main participants are the child's parent(s). Some small group work and one to one interviews will take place with a small sample of the children. 4) Blind and partially sighted children of average learning ability of secondary school age: the students will take part themselves in the study and their parents will take a much smaller part. 5) Blind and partially sighted students in 6th forms, further and higher education will participate themselves. The research is in 3 stages. Focus groups have been held to establish priorities for and issues for a questionnaire survey. A questionnaire survey will provide quantitative data and further focus groups will allow more indepth discussion of issues of particular importance. Final reports will be available in July 1999.

STATUS: Sponsored project

SOURCE OF GRANT: Royal National Institute for the Blind £227,000

DATE OF RESEARCH: 1998-continuing

KEYWORDS: **aspiration; blindness; needs; special educational needs; visual impairments**

Scarman Centre for the Study of Public Order

2252

University of Leicester, 6 Salisbury Road, Leicester LE1 7QR
01162 522458

Gill, M. Dr; Hearnshaw, S. Mr

Personal safety for those who work in education

ABSTRACT: The aims of this study were to identify: the number and type of violent incidents confronting pupils and staff; the strategies put in place for ensuring or enhancing the personal safety of pupils and staff; examples where schools have responded effectively to crime problems. The research provided recommendations for good practice. A postal survey of staff in over 2,000 schools as well as face-to-face interviews, plus a review of literature.

PUBLISHED MATERIAL: GILL, M. & HEARNSHAW, S. (1997). Personal safety and violence in schools. DFEE Research Report RR21. London: HMSO.

STATUS: Sponsored project

SOURCE OF GRANT: Department for Education and Employment £19,204; Suzy Lamplugh Trust

DATE OF RESEARCH: 1996-1997

KEYWORDS: **safety; school safety; violence**

Scottish Council for Research in Education

2253

15 St John Street, Edinburgh EH8 8JR
0131 557 2944

Black, H. Mr; Devine, M. Mrs; Fenwick, N. Ms; Gray, D. Mr; Mingard, S. Dr

Schools Assessment Research and Support Unit (SARSU)

ABSTRACT: The Schools Assessment Research and Support Unit (SARSU) carries out a rolling programme of action research and exploratory studies in assessment. It also encourages the dissemination of research findings and provides a support service for local authorities' inservice staff development programmes in assessment.

PUBLISHED MATERIAL: BLACK, H.D., DEVINE, M., TURNER, E. & HARRISON, C. (1988). Standard Grade Assessment: a support package for schools. Edinburgh: SCRE/SARSU; in collaboration with the Scottish Education Department. ; BLACK, H.D. & DEVINE, M. (1988). Mathematics checkpoint 7: assessment materials for primary 7 pupils. Edinburgh: SCRE/SARSU. ; TURNER, E., BLACK, H.D., HALL, J. & DEVINE, M. (1989). Technology in Home Economics. Edinbugh: SCRE/SARSU. ; BLACK, H.D., DEVINE, M. & TURNER, E. (1989). Aspects of assessment: a primary perspective. Edinburgh SCRE/SARSU. ; TURNER, E., BLACK, H.D. & DEVINE, M. (1990). Technology: an annotated bibliography. Edinburgh: SCRE/SARSU. A full list of publications is available from the researcher.

STATUS: Sponsored project

SOURCE OF GRANT: Local authorities; Scottish Council for Research in Education; Scottish Office Education Department

DATE OF RESEARCH: 1983-1993

KEYWORDS: **action research; assessment; educational research; school based assessment**

2254

15 St John Street, Edinburgh EH8 8JR
0131 557 2944

Thorpe, G. Mr; Docherty, G. Ms; Whitcombe, D. Mr; Bichard, A. Dr

Central Support Unit: the Assessment of Achievement Programme

ABSTRACT: The Central Support Unit (CSU) has been funded by the Scottish Office Education Department to provide the technical support and infra-structure for its Assessment of Achievement Programme (AAP). The

AAP is a systematic programme, designed to monitor pupil attainment. Individual teams with knowledge and expertise in the particular subject under study are established to have responsibility for the content-specific part of the projects. The CSU provides technical support to all projects across the subject spectrum. This support includes: advice on experimental design; sampling; liaison with schools; collation, distribution and collection of test materials; computing the desired analyses and advising on the statistics of these. Part of the general support of the AAP will incorporate the development and continuous updating of a set of guidelines for AAP projects. These guidelines will assist the project teams in the efficient design of their assessment programmes, will offer a repertoire of analytic approaches designed to enable the teams to extract different kinds of information from their data, and will make practical suggestions which will help to overcome anticipated difficulties.

PUBLISHED MATERIAL: 'Noticeboard' - a newsletter for schools and Feedback booklets covering the 1989 science and 1990 mathematics surveys are available from the Scottish Council for Research in Education.

STATUS: Sponsored project

SOURCE OF GRANT: Scottish Office Education Department

DATE OF RESEARCH: 1987-1997

KEYWORDS: academic achievement; achievement rating; assessment; educational research

2255

15 St John Street, Edinburgh EH8 8JR
0131 557 2944

Munn, P. Mrs; Blair, A. Ms; Lowden, K. Mr; Powney, J. Dr; McPake, J. Ms; Arney, N. Mr

Adult education: provision, guidance and progression

ABSTRACT: The research will be carried out in four studies. It will provide a broad based national picture of opportunities for progression and of guidance while enabling more detailed information on adults' experiences and on the operation of particular systems to be collected. The four studies are: (1) case studies of adults' experiences of guidance, provision and progression, Scottish Council for Research in Education (SCRE) and Scottish Community Education Council (SCEC); (2) a survey of opportunities for progression, focusing particularly on inter-sector links and on links between formal and informal services, together with indepth analysis of opportunities for progression within one region; (3) a survey of guidance provision together with indepth analysis of a small number of new initiatives and an assessment of user experience (SCRE); and (4) a special study of adults in schools, investigating the opinions of adults and of the schools about the advantages of this form of provision (SCRE).

STATUS: Sponsored project

SOURCE OF GRANT: Scottish Office Education Department £149,671

DATE OF RESEARCH: 1991-1993

KEYWORDS: access to education; adult education; adult students; community education; educational guidance; mature students; student attitudes

2256

15 St John Street, Edinburgh EH8 8JR
0171 557 2944

Powney, J. Dr

Teacher appraisal and equality

ABSTRACT: The aim of the research study is to elucidate the main issues and concerns about appraisal and equal opportunities as identified by the Association of Teachers and Lecturers (ATL) membership. Broad research questions include: How does the actual process of appraisal being used in different education authorities and schools enhance or inhibit the implementation of equal opportunities policies? What does an analysis of those who are appraised and those who are the appraisers contribute to equal opportunities practices? What are participants' expectations of appraisal schemes? Are targets emerging from different appraisals yielding useful information about trends in equal opportunities for school staff?

STATUS: Sponsored project

SOURCE OF GRANT: Association of Teachers and Lecturers

DATE OF RESEARCH: 1993-1993

KEYWORDS: equal opportunities - jobs; teacher development; teacher evaluation; teaching profession

2257

15 St John Street, Edinburgh EH8 8JR
0131 557 2944

Devine, M. Ms; Harlen, W. Prof.; Thorpe, G. Mr

Third International Mathematics and Science Study (TIMSS) survey

ABSTRACT: Over 40 countries participated in the Evaluation of Educational Achievement (IEA) Third International Mathematics and Science Study. The study had 3 main areas of investigation: 1) the intended curriculum based on an analysis of curriculum guidelines and textbooks; 2) the implemented curriculum using questionnaires for teachers and pupils; 3) the attained curriculum using tests of pupils' attainment. Information ws obtained from questionnaires for schools, teachers and pupils and from assessment tasks completed by Primary 3/Primary 5 and Secondary 1/ Secondary 2.

PUBLISHED MATERIAL: GREAT BRITAIN. SCOTTISH OFFICE EDUCATION AND INDUSTRY DEPARTMENT. (1996). Achievements of Secondary 1 and Secondary 2 pupils in mathematics and science. Third International Mathematics and Science Study (TIMSS). Edinburgh: Scottish Office Education and Industry Department. ; GREAT BRITAIN. SCOTTISH OFFICE EDUCATION AND INDUSTRY DEPARTMENT. (1997). Achievements of Primary 4 and Primary 5 pupils in mathematics and science. Third International Mathematics and Science Study (TIMSS). Edinburgh: Scottish Office Education and Industry Department.

STATUS: Sponsored project

SOURCE OF GRANT: Scottish Office Education and Industry Department £143,856

DATE OF RESEARCH: 1992-1997

KEYWORDS: comparative education; curriculum development; international educational exchange; mathematics education; science education

2258

15 St John Street, Edinburgh EH8 8JR
0131 557 2944

Black, H. Mr

Evaluation of the Glasgow University Enterprise in Higher Education Initiative

ABSTRACT: Glasgow University was one of the first round of Enterprise in Higher Education (EHE) projects. Glasgow EHE began in March 1989 and finished in February 1994. This project seeks to evaluate the impact of the activities which have taken place under the auspices of the initiative. In particular it will explore the extent to which: 1) the EHE initiative has secured effective links between the University and employers; 2) it has developed appropriate skills in students; 3) it has resulted in a more responsive curriculum. The results of the evaluation will be used to inform considerations of the University's future strategy in relation to the EHE initiative.

STATUS: Sponsored project

SOURCE OF GRANT: Glasgow University ; Scottish Enterprise, jointly £19,791

DATE OF RESEARCH: 1993-1993

KEYWORDS: enterprise in higher education; industry higher education relationship

2259

15 St John Street, Edinburgh EH8 8JR
0131 557 2944

Powney, J. Dr

Evaluation of headteacher review in Tayside Region

ABSTRACT: The aim of this study is to elucidate the main issues, concerns and suggested improvements emerging from the first phase of the headteacher review in Tayside in order to improve the current headteacher guidelines.

PUBLISHED MATERIAL: LOWDEN, K. & POWNEY, J. (1993). Evaluation of headteacher review in Tayside Region: a report of findings and recommendations. SCRE Research Report No 51. Edinburgh: Scottish Council for Research in Education. ; LOWDEN, K. (1994). Developing headteacher management skills through performance review. SCRE Spotlight No 46. Edinburgh: Scottish Council for Research in Education.

STATUS: Sponsored project

SOURCE OF GRANT: Tayside Region

DATE OF RESEARCH: 1993-1993

KEYWORDS: **head teachers; teacher development; teaching profession**

2260

15 St John Street, Edinburgh EH8 8JR
0131 557 2944

Powney, J. Dr

Adult education: provision, guidance and progression. Study 3: educational guidance for adults in Scotland

ABSTRACT: The Scottish Office Education Department is funding a large scale research project concerned with adult education in Scotland. The project is made up of four individual, yet related studies. This third study aims to: map existing guidance provision for adults; compare and contrast different approaches to provision and also to assess the effectiveness of different approaches in terms of adults who use guidance services.

PUBLISHED MATERIAL: LOWDEN, K. & POWNEY, J. (1993). Where do we go from here: adult educational guidance in Scotland. SCRE Research Report No 48. Edinburgh: Scottish Council for Research in Education.

STATUS: Sponsored project

SOURCE OF GRANT: Scottish Office Education Department

DATE OF RESEARCH: 1992-1993

KEYWORDS: **access to education; adult education; adult students; educational guidance; mature students; scotland**

2261

15 St John Street, Edinburgh EH8 8JR
0131 557 2944

Powney, J. Dr

School development planning

ABSTRACT: This project will monitor school development planning in action and so provide empirical evidence of strategies and solutions adopted. It will disseminate examples of effective practice and assist schools in their planning and evaluation.

STATUS: Sponsored project

SOURCE OF GRANT: Scottish Office Education Department £19,405

DATE OF RESEARCH: 1992-1993

KEYWORDS: **educational planning; school based management**

2262

15 St John Street, Edinburgh EH8 8JR
0131 557 2944

Munn, P. Mrs

Discipline support pack

ABSTRACT: The aim of the project is to review the existing evidence concerning the establishment and maintenance of good discipline in schools and to use this as a basis for the production of a resource pack for use in primary and secondary schools in Scotland. This includes the trialling of the pack in a limited number of schools.

PUBLISHED MATERIAL: MUNN, P., JOHNSTONE, M., WATSON, G. & EDWARDS, L. (1993). Action on discipline in the primary school: a support pack. Edinburgh: Scottish Council for Research in Education. ^MUNN, P., JOHNSTONE, M., WATSON, G. & EDWARDS, L. (1993). Action on discipline in the secondary school: a support pack. Edinburgh: Scottish Council for Research in Education.

STATUS: Sponsored project

SOURCE OF GRANT: Scottish Office Education Department £20,631

DATE OF RESEARCH: 1992-1993

KEYWORDS: **classroom discipline; discipline; discipline policy; educational materials**

2263

15 St John Street, Edinburgh EH8 8JR
0131 557 2944

Munn, P. Mrs

Adult education in the UK: policy, provision and practice

ABSTRACT: Part of the process of developing a synthesis paper on adult education in European Community member states.

PUBLISHED MATERIAL: BLAIR, A., MCPAKE, J. & MUNN, P. (1993). Facing Goliath: adults' experiences of participation, guidance and progression in education. SCRE Research Report No 46. Edinburgh: Scottish Council for Research in Education. ; MUNN, P., TETT, L. & ARNEY, N. (1993). Negotiating the labyrinth: progression opportunities for adult learners. SCRE Research Report No 47. Edinburgh: Scottish Council for Research in Education. ; LOWDEN, K. & POWNEY, J. (1993). Where do we go from here? Adult educational guidance in Scotland. SCRE Research Report No 48. Edinburgh: Scottish Council for Research in Education. ; BLAIR, A., MCPAKE, J. & MUNN, P. (1994). Adults in schools. SCRE Research Report No 58. Edinburgh: Sottish Council for Research in Education.

STATUS: Sponsored project

SOURCE OF GRANT: European Community

DATE OF RESEARCH: 1991-1993

KEYWORDS: **adult education**

2264

15 St John Street, Edinburgh EH8 8JR
0131 557 2944

Thorpe, G. Mr

Factors influencing entry to higher education

ABSTRACT: The two main aims of this research are: 1) To assess the changes since 1991 in the social class and parental occupation of school leavers, determining the relationships between social class and measures of parental education with staying on at school, school qualifications, application to enter higher education, and entry to higher education. 2) To determine the best means of projecting entry to higher education.

STATUS: Sponsored project

SOURCE OF GRANT: Scottish Office Education Department £15,470

DATE OF RESEARCH: 1992-1993

KEYWORDS: **access to education; higher education; socioeconomic background; student recruitment**

2265

15 St John Street, Edinburgh EH8 8JR
0131 557 2944

Munn, P. Mrs

Entry requirements for higher education

ABSTRACT: This project aims to identify the formal published higher education entry (HE) requirements for a sample of faculties/courses covering both general entry requirements for each HE institution and the faculty requirements. It also aims to clarify the application of these rules and describe any arrangements for exemption from parts of courses for candidates with certain qualifications, e.g. HND or GCE 'A' levels. Finally, it will provide an indication of the incidence of special classes in HE to bring candidates up to an adequate level of attainment to cope on the mainstream course.

STATUS: Sponsored project

SOURCE OF GRANT: Scottish Office Education Department

DATE OF RESEARCH: 1992-1993

KEYWORDS: **access to education; admission criteria; higher education; student recruitment**

2266

15 St John Street, Edinburgh EH8 8JR
0131 557 2944

Powney, J. Dr

Monitoring the Moray House pilot PGCE (Secondary) course

ABSTRACT: The main aims of the study are to describe some of the advantages and disadvantages of increasing school experience time and to identify the implications of this change for the different partners involved in pre-service teacher training.

PUBLISHED MATERIAL: POWNEY, J., EDWARD, S., HOLROYD, C. & MARTIN, S. (1993). Monitoring the pilot: the Moray House Institute PGCE (Secondary). SCRE Research Report No 52. Edinburgh: Scottish Council for Research in Education. ; POWNEY, J., EDWARD, S., HOLROYD, C. & MARTIN, S. (1993). Towards more school based training? Interchange No 20. Edinburgh: Scottish Council for Research in Education/Scottish Office Education Department.

STATUS: Sponsored project

SOURCE OF GRANT: Scottish Office Education Department

DATE OF RESEARCH: 1992-1993

KEYWORDS: **postgraduate certificate in education; preservice teacher education; teaching practice**

2267

15 St John Street, Edinburgh EH8 8JR
0131 557 2944

Johnstone, M. Mrs

Teachers' workload and associated stress

ABSTRACT: This project aims to provide: a snap-shot of teacher workload in different schools (i.e. nursery, primary, secondary) and at different levels of responsibility together with some breakdown of the workload in terms of context, time spent in various tasks, and potential stress.

PUBLISHED MATERIAL: JOHNSTONE, M. (1993). Teachers workload and associated stress. SCRE Research Report No 53. Edinburgh: Scottish Council for Research in Education. ; JOHNSTONE, M. (1993). Time and tasks: teacher workload and stress. SCRE Spotlight No 44. Edinburgh: Scottish Council for Research in Education. ; JOHNSTONE, M. (1993). Teachers' workload and associated stress. Edinburgh: Educational Institute of Scotland.

STATUS: Sponsored project

SOURCE OF GRANT: Educational Institute of Scotland

DATE OF RESEARCH: 1992-1993

KEYWORDS: **stress - psychological; teacher role; teacher workload; time management**

2268

15 St John Street, Edinburgh EH8 8JR
0131 557 2944

Black, H. Mr

The teaching of foreign languages for vocational purposes in further education

ABSTRACT: The overall aim is to identify evidence and analyse the effectiveness of different teaching approaches in order to provide practical advice for further education colleagues and others wishing to improve their provision. It will examine: 1) teaching approaches used in particular vocational contexts, eg catering, computing or engineering; 2) how foreign language skills for vocational purposes are assessed; 3) the evidence as to the effectiveness of different teaching approaches and those approaches considered most effective by lecturers and students.

PUBLISHED MATERIAL: HALL, J. & BANKOWSKA, A. (1994). Vocational languages: foreign languages for vocational purposes in further and higher education. SCRE Research Report No 56. Edinburgh: Scottish Council for Research in Education. ; HALL, J. & BANKOWSKA, A. (1994). Foreign languages for vocational purposes in further and higher education. Interchange No 25. Edinburgh: Scottish Office Education Department.

STATUS: Sponsored project

SOURCE OF GRANT: Scottish Office Education Department £20,966

DATE OF RESEARCH: 1992-1993

KEYWORDS: **further education; languages for specific purposes; modern language studies; second language teaching; vocational education**

2269

15 St John Street, Edinburgh EH8 8JR
0131 557 2944

Black, H. Mr

5-14 diagnostic procedures

ABSTRACT: As part of the 5-14 development programme, national guidelines on assessment have been issued (1991), and national tests in English language and mathematics were introduced in 1990. These were aimed primarily at improving teachers' assessments of children's progress for reporting to parents and to improve learning and teaching. This study will produce materials to help teachers identify what underlies pupils' performances so that they can build on strengths and overcome weaknesses. The project will review existing diagnostic materials and 'by building on existing research and teaching practice' will develop diagnostic units on selected aspects of learning in language, mathematics and science. Later stages of the project may cover other areas of the curriculum.

PUBLISHED MATERIAL: BLACK, H.D. (1993). Taking a closer look at mathematics - around town: a resource pack for teachers. Edinburgh: Scottish Council for Research in Education. ; BLACK, H.D., DEVINE, M.S. & PEARSON, M. (1993). Taking a closer look at mathematics - space: fact and fiction: a resource pack for teachers. Edinburgh: Scottish Council for Research in Education.

STATUS: Sponsored project

SOURCE OF GRANT: SCRE; Scottish Office Education Department, jointly £19,500

DATE OF RESEARCH: 1991-1993

KEYWORDS: **achievement tests; assessment; primary secondary education; school based assessment**

2270

15 St John Street, Edinburgh EH8 8JR
0131 557 2944

Black, H. Mr

Health education in schools

ABSTRACT: This project will review the nature and extent of provision for health education and health promotion in primary and secondary schools. It will also review the support available to schools from education authorities, health boards and other bodies.

PUBLISHED MATERIAL: DEVINE, M. (1993). Encouraging healthy living: health education in Scottish schools. SCRE Spotlight No 41. Edinburgh: Scottish Council for Research in Education. ; DEVINE, M., BLACK, H. & GRAY, D. (1993). Health education in Scottish schools: a survey of primary and secondary schools. SCRE Research Report No 44. Edinburgh: Scottish Council for Research in Education.

STATUS: Sponsored project

SOURCE OF GRANT: Scottish Office Education Department SCRE Contract

DATE OF RESEARCH: 1992-1993

KEYWORDS: **health education; health promotion; pupil needs; scotland**

2271

15 St John Street, Edinburgh EH8 8JR
0131 557 2944

Glissov, P. Dr; *Supervisor*: Powney, J. Dr

Effectiveness of Access courses: longitudinal study

ABSTRACT: The aim of this project is to assess the effectiveness of science and social science Access courses in preparing adults for degree level study. The research will provide a greater understanding of the strengths and weaknesses of Access courses, as well as recommendations for good practice both in Access courses themselves and in higher education responsiveness to Access students. This project will track the progress of students from the earlier project Access courses in Science and Social Science funded by the Leverhulme Trust.

PUBLISHED MATERIAL: MUNN, P., JOHNSTONE, M. & LOWDEN, K. (1993). Students' perceptions of Access Courses: a survey. SCRE Research Report No 43. Edinburgh: Scottish Council for Research in Education.

STATUS: Sponsored project

SOURCE OF GRANT: Scottish Office Education Department £14,193

DATE OF RESEARCH: 1994-1997

KEYWORDS: access programmes; course evaluation; educational quality; higher education; mature students; programme effectiveness; science education; social sciences

2272

15 St John Street, Edinburgh EH8 8JR
0131 557 2944

Devine, M. Mrs

Impact of managed effective learning (MEL) in schools upon key student outcomes

ABSTRACT: This research was commissioned in 1994 to provide an evaluation of a development project entitled managed effective learning in schools to key student outcomes (MELSO). The project involved 12 schools adopting a management framework which explicitly linked a range of learning and teaching styles to specific skill outcomes which students could be expected to learn. These include: qualifications (including but wider than GCSEs), knowledge of work and business, literacy and numeracy, ability to manage progression, and personal effectiveness e.g. time management, teamwork, self reliance and communication. Schools could add their own outcomes to this common list. The research project was planned to help inform both the Department for Education and Employment's (DfEE) refinement of the framework for schools, and schools' own planning of provision. MELSO students showed increased confidence in using personal effectiveness skills and were more positive about target setting and planning learning activities. A wider range of teaching styles were used in MELSO schools and pupil centred learning was emphasised. Teachers in MELSO schools felt increased responsibility to help students understand the world of work. Commensurate with this, the range and quality of activities undertaken between MELSO schools and businesses increased. MELSO schools were more systematic in auditing current teaching practice and were, therefore, increasingly able to identify gaps in their development programmes. In addition, most MELSO schools have decided to continue with the programme beyond its official life. MELSO has provided an impetus for change and enabled schools to carry through improvements more quickly than they would otherwise have done. There were no significant improvements regarding literacy and numeracy, or GCSE attainment. However, these kind of improvements are unlikely to show in the short term and would not be visible within the timescale of the project.

PUBLISHED MATERIAL: DEVINE, M., REID, M. & THORPE, G. (1998). The impact of managed effective learning on key student outcomes. DfEE Research Report No RR 42. London: The Stationery Office. ; DEVINE, M., REID, M. & THORPE, G. (1998). The impact of managed effective learning in key student outcomes. Research Brief. London: Department for Education and Employment.

STATUS: Sponsored project

SOURCE OF GRANT: Department for Education and Employment

DATE OF RESEARCH: 1994-1997

KEYWORDS: improvement programmes; learning activities; life skills; literacy; managed effective learning; numeracy; school to work transition; secondary education

2273

15 St John Street, Edinburgh EH8 8JR
0131 557 2944

Thorpe, G. Mr; Whitcombe, D. Mr; Russell, S. Ms

Central Support Unit: the Assessment of Achievement Programme - second contract

ABSTRACT: The Assessment of Achievement Programme (AAP) identifies general strengths and development needs in English language, mathematics

and science for the P4, P7 and S2 populations; compares performance over time of nationally representative samples of pupils in P4, P7 and S2 on assessment tasks in these curricular areas. Surveys in each of the three curricular areas are carried out at three-yearly intervals. The findings contribute to the identification of policy issues for the Scottish Office Education and Industry Department (SOEID) and education authorities and are published as summary reports and dissemination materials for teachers with information and teaching issues (the Feedback series and AAP Noticeboard newsletter). The role of the Central Support Unit is to provide the AAP with support services and advice in areas common to all main projects. The services include sampling, liaison with schools, distribution and collection of written materials, data preparation, analysis and structuring for the AAP data archive.

STATUS: Sponsored project

SOURCE OF GRANT: Scottish Office Education and Industry Department £176,451

DATE OF RESEARCH: 1994-1997

KEYWORDS: academic achievement; achievement rating; assessment; educational research; primary education; secondary education

2274

15 St John Street, Edinburgh EH8 8JR
0131 557 2944

Harlen, W. Prof.; Malcolm, H. Ms

Continued extension to the evaluation of the 5-14 programme in primary schools

ABSTRACT: The study was an extension of the evaluation of the 5-14 programme with a particular focus on the classroom. The main areas of enquiry were: a) the impact of the implementation on classroom practices, the characteristics of good practice and the factors which promote it; b) the influence on the organisation of learning and teaching and the provision of a coherent learning experience; c) the role of assessment in the provision of reliable information on pupils' progress and attainment; d) teachers' responses to 5-14 and what types of support are proving helpful to them. The study focused on five case study schools and was supplemented by a large scale survey of schools to provide a wider range of information.

PUBLISHED MATERIAL: MALCOLM, H. & SIMPSON, M. (1997). Implementing 5-14 in primary and secondary schools: steady development? Interchange No 49. Edinburgh: Scottish Office Education and Industry Department/Research and Intelligence Unit. ; MALCOLM, H. & SCHLAPP, U. (1997). 5-14 in the primary school: a continuing challenge. SCRE Research Report No 82. Edinburgh: Scottish Council for Research in Education.

STATUS: Sponsored project

SOURCE OF GRANT: Scottish Office Education and Industry Department £60,695

DATE OF RESEARCH: 1995-1997

KEYWORDS: assessment; curriculum development; five to fourteen curriculum; primary education; scotland; teaching methods

2275

15 St John Street, Edinburgh EH8 8JR
0131 557 2944

Thorpe, G. Mr

Impact of managed effective learning (MEL): associated schools

ABSTRACT: This is one of the strands of the Managed Effective Learning (MEL) project. It will provide participating schools with aggregate year group results for Years 9, 10 and 11, and changes in these over the next 3 years. The instruments are pupil questionnaires related to links between school work and two basic competency tests in numeracy and literacy.

STATUS: Sponsored project

SOURCE OF GRANT: Department for Education and Employment

DATE OF RESEARCH: 1995-1998

KEYWORDS: attainment tests; improvement programmes; learning activities; life skills; literacy; managed effective learning; managed effective learning; numeracy; secondary education/2276*@

2276

15 St John Street, Edinburgh EH8 8JR
0131 557 2944

Powney, J. Dr; Glissov, P. Dr

Effectiveness of Access courses: longitudinal study (follow-up of students)

ABSTRACT: This project will track the progress of students from the earlier Scottish Council for Research in Education (SCRE) project which assessed the effectiveness of science and social science Access courses in preparing adults or degree level study.

STATUS: Sponsored project

SOURCE OF GRANT: Scottish Office Education Department £14,193

DATE OF RESEARCH: 1993-1997

KEYWORDS: **access programmes; access to education; adult students; followup studies; higher education; mature students; science education; social sciences**

2277

15 St John Street, Edinburgh EH8 8JR
0131 557 2944

Hall, J. Dr; Edwards, L. Ms; Brown, C. Ms; Maclean, P. Ms

Effective use of computer technology in careers guidance

ABSTRACT: This is a joint project with JIIG-CAL Limited. The project aims to evaluate the influence of computer technology on the careers education and guidance of students in schools, its impact on schools as organisations, and its effect on the relationship between schools and careers services.

PUBLISHED MATERIAL: HALL, J., BROWN, C., EDWARDS, L. & MACLEAN, P. (1998). Effective use of computers in careers guidance. London: Department for Education and Employment.

STATUS: Sponsored project

SOURCE OF GRANT: Department for Education and Employment Careers Service Branch

DATE OF RESEARCH: 1996-1997

KEYWORDS: **career awareness; careers service; computer uses in education; information technology; school to work transition; secondary education; vocational guidance**

2278

15 St John Street, Edinburgh EH8 8JR
0131 557 2944

Powney, J. Dr; Lowden, K. Mr

Evaluation of drug education in Scottish schools

ABSTRACT: Major developments have been taking place in drug education in schools and the study documents current practices and assesses their success. The aims are to provide a national picture of drug education in Scotland, to describe drug education programmes in operation and how they were selected and to measure their impact on pupils' knowledge, attitudes and behaviour. The study includes censuses of secondary schools and major surveys of primary schools, surveys of school staff and pupils and illuminative qualitative work.

STATUS: Sponsored project

SOURCE OF GRANT: Scottish Office Education and Industry Department £163,047

DATE OF RESEARCH: 1996-continuing

KEYWORDS: **drug education; health education; primary education; secondary education**

2279

15 St John Street, Edinburgh EH8 8JR
0131 557 2944

Harlen, W. Prof.; McPake, J. Ms; Malcolm, H. Mrs; Powney, J. Dr; Tinklin, T. Ms

Teachers' and pupils' days in the primary classroom: an observation study

ABSTRACT: This study aims to understand and describe learning and teaching in primary classrooms. Observation, interviews with teachers and pupils and review of pupils' work provide information on teachers' and pupils' experiences in the primary classroom. It is exploring how these can be related to the Scottish Office Education and Industry Department (SOEID) indicators of the quality of learning and teaching and what teachers and pupils see as influencing their work.

STATUS: Sponsored project

SOURCE OF GRANT: Scottish Office Education and Industry Department

DATE OF RESEARCH: 1996-1998

KEYWORDS: **classroom observation techniques; educational experience; educational quality; learning activities; primary education; primary school pupils; primary school teachers; teaching methods**

2280

15 St John Street, Edinburgh EH8 8JR
0131 557 2944

Hall, J. Dr; Tinklin, T. Ms

Policy and provision for disabled students in higher education institutions

ABSTRACT: The project investigated the experience of disabled students in a number of higher education institutions in Scotland. Information was gathered through shadowing and interviewing 12 such students. The project also investigated institutional policy and provision for disabled students and the way in which they are defined. The project collaborated with the current Scottish Higher Education Funding Council (SHEFC) study 'Council Initiative in Support of Students with Disabilities - Evaluation' conducted by Sheila Riddell, Jill Duffield, Rena Phillips and Sally Brown at Stirling University.

PUBLISHED MATERIAL: HALL, J. & TINKLIN, T. (1998). Disabled students in higher education. SCRE Spotlight No 66. Edinburgh: Scottish Council for Research in Education. ; HALL, J. & TINKLIN, T. (1998). 'Policy and provision for disabled students in higher education', Research in Education, SCRE Newsletter No 62, p.2. ; HALL, J. & TINKLIN, T. (1998). Students first: the experiences of disabled students in higher education. SCRE Research Report No 85. Edinburgh: Scottish Council for Research in Education.

STATUS: Sponsored project

SOURCE OF GRANT: Scottish Office Education and Industry Department £46,694

DATE OF RESEARCH: 1996-1997

KEYWORDS: **access to education; accessibility - for disabled; disabilities; higher education; special educational needs; students**

2281

15 St John Street, Edinburgh EH8 8JR
0131 557 2944

Wilson, V. Ms; Malcolm, H. Ms; McFall, L. Ms; Finnigan, J. Ms; McPake, J. Ms

The management of change including Devolved School Management, in small primary schools

ABSTRACT: This project investigates the management of change in small primary schools in Scotland. It is aiming to identify management strategies and activities adopted by headteachers. It evaluates the effectiveness of these strategies and activities and assesses their impact.

PUBLISHED MATERIAL: WILSON, V. & MCPAKE, J. (1998). Managing change in small Scottish primary schools. SCRE Research Report No 86. Edinburgh: Scottish Council for Research in Education.

STATUS: Sponsored project

SOURCE OF GRANT: Scottish Office Education and Industry Department £89,971

DATE OF RESEARCH: 1996-1998

KEYWORDS: **change strategies; educational administration; educational change; head teachers; local management of schools; primary education; school based management; scotland; small schools**

2282

15 St John Street, Edinburgh EH8 8JR
0131 557 2944

Powney, J. Dr; Hall, S. Mr

Longitudinal study of Scottish Wider Access Programme (SWAP) students

ABSTRACT: This project tracked a cohort of 80 students, whose transition into higher education was investigated in an earlier Leverhulme funded study. This study tracked these students through the rest of their higher education studies and into eventual employment, using telephone interviews.

PUBLISHED MATERIAL: HALL, S. & POWNEY, J. (1998). Scottish Access students in higher education. SCRE Research Report No 84. Edinburgh: Scottish Council for Research in Education. ; HALL, S. (1998). It was a worthwhile slog! Scottish Access students in higher education. SCRE Spotlight No 68. Edinburgh: Scottish Council for Research in Education.

STATUS: Sponsored project

SOURCE OF GRANT: Scottish Office Education and Industry Department £14,193

DATE OF RESEARCH: 1993-1997

KEYWORDS: **access programmes; followup studies; higher education; student destinations**

2283

15 St John Street, Edinburgh EH8 8JR
0131 557 2944

Hall, J. Dr; Devine, M. Mrs; Thorpe, G. Mr; Edwards, L. Ms

Research to develop a new Police Standard Entrance Test

ABSTRACT: The research aims to produce a revised standard entrance test for police forces which will: 1) be related to the essential elements of a police officer's job and reflect the qualities required to make a competent and effective officer; 2) take full account of the 2-year initial training programme for recruits and assist in identifying applicants who can satisfy the demands of that programme; 3) provide similar opportunities of success to different groups of candidates; 4) contain safeguards (allowing multiple versions of the test for security and re-testing purposes); 5) be capable of being administered by forces in an efficient and effective manner, especially with regard to marking; 6) complement any additional processes undertaken by forces in their recruitment process and form an integral part of that process. The programme of work for the project includes: familiarisation with existing tests; drafting initial test ideas; consulting interested parties; preparing pilot tests; trialling pilot tests; analysing pilot results; and preparing final versions of the proposed tests.

STATUS: Sponsored project

SOURCE OF GRANT: Scottish Office £39,381

DATE OF RESEARCH: 1997-1998

KEYWORDS: **entrance test; personnel selection; police; recruitment; selective admission**

2284

15 St John Sreet, Edinburgh EH8 8JR
0131 557 2944

Russell, S. Ms; Thorpe, G. Mr; Whitcombe, D. Mr

Assessment of Achievement Programme: Central Support Unit - third contract

ABSTRACT: The role of the Central Support Unit is to provide the Assessment of Achievement Programme (AAP) with support services and statistical advice. The services include sampling, data preparation and analysis.

STATUS: Sponsored project

SOURCE OF GRANT: Scottish Office Education and Industry Department £165,000

DATE OF RESEARCH: 1997-continuing

KEYWORDS: **academic achievement; achievement rating; assessment; educational research; primary education; secondary education**

2285

15 St John Street, Edinburgh EH8 8JR
0131 557 2944

Hall, J. Dr; Brown, C. Ms

Evaluation of the Superhighway Project to Research the Impact of Networking Technologies (SPRINT)

ABSTRACT: The use of information and communications technology (ICT) in schools is growing at a considerable pace. Many schools now make use of e-mail and the World Wide Web for both obtaining and originating information materials. However, conventional (narrow band) access to ICT has a number of drawbacks for schools, not least of which is the data transmission speed which greatly limits the amount and types of information which can reasonably be transmitted or downloaded. The Superhighway Project to Research the Impact of Networking Technologies (SPRINT) aims to link 6 schools in Edinburgh and West Lothian to a broad band communications infrastructure and to equip the schools with a wide range of technology which will enable them to benefit from this. The Scottish Council for Research in Education (SCRE) evaluation will gather data on the progress of the schools implementing the SPRINT project, and to identify those innovations which are successful and which are less successful, together with the factors which are responsible for that success or lack of success. This evaluation is commissioned by Lothian and Edinburgh Enterprise Limited.

STATUS: Sponsored project

SOURCE OF GRANT: Lothian and Edinburgh Enterprise Limited

DATE OF RESEARCH: 1997-1998

KEYWORDS: **computer uses in education; electronic mail; information technology**

2286

15 St John Street, Edinburgh EH8 8JR
0131 557 2944

Powney, J. Dr; Hall, S. Mr; Silver, H. Prof.

Closing the loop: an exploratory study of the impact of student feedback on learning and teaching in higher education

ABSTRACT: The focus of this study was the impact of student feedback on measures taken by 2 or 3 higher education institutions to foster and improve student learning. 3 themes were addressed: 1) How do higher education institutions collect feedback from students about their learning and teaching experiences? 2) What action to improve teaching and educational provision is taken on the basis of student feedback? 3) What evidence is there that students' learning is enhanced when changes are made as a result of student feedback?

STATUS: Sponsored project

SOURCE OF GRANT: Quality Assurance Agency

DATE OF RESEARCH: 1997-1998

KEYWORDS: **feedback; higher education; learning; students**

2287

15 St John Street, Edinburgh EH8 8JR
0131 557 2944

Wilson, V. Ms; Devine, M. Mrs; Hall, J. Dr; Hamilton, S. Ms; Pirrie, A. Dr

Effectiveness of multi-disciplinary education in health care: evaluation

ABSTRACT: This project aims to provide working definitions of multi-disciplinary learning and teaching, to map its extent and perceived effectiveness, and provide guidelines and examples of good practice.

PUBLISHED MATERIAL: PIRRIE, A., WILSON, V., ELSEGOOD, J., HALL, J., HAMILTON, S., HARDEN, L., LEE, D. & STEAD, J. (1998). Evaluating multidisciplinary education in health care. SCRE Research Report No 89. Edinburgh: Scottish Council for Research in Education.

STATUS: Sponsored project

SOURCE OF GRANT: Department of Health

DATE OF RESEARCH: 1996-1998

KEYWORDS: **allied health occupations; cross curricular approach; education; health services; medical education**

2288

15 St John Street, Edinburgh EH8 8JR
0131 557 2944

McPake, J. Ms; Davidson, J. Ms; Harlen, W. Prof.; Powney, J. Dr
Teachers' and pupils' days in the primary classroom: extension

ABSTRACT: This project extends the classroom observation to include a sample of Primary 4 and Primary 7 classes which are 'set' for some subjects, e.g. languages or mathematics, to ascertain the effects on pupils' and teachers' experiences.

STATUS: Sponsored project

SOURCE OF GRANT: Scottish Office Education and Industry Department

DATE OF RESEARCH: 1998-continuing

KEYWORDS: **classroom observation techniques; educational experience; educational quality; learning activities; primary education; primary school pupils; primary school teachers; teaching methods**

2289

15 St John Street, Edinburgh EH8 8JR
0131 557 2944

McPake, J. Ms; Harlen, W. Prof.
Higher Still evaluation - cohort studies

ABSTRACT: The study is one of a series of studies which will evaluate the Higher Still development programme. The study has two components each of which will track S5 pupils through their S5 and S6 years - the first cohort in 1998-99 before Higher Still is implemented, and the second in 2000-01 after the implementation of Higher Still is well in progress. Over 100 pupils in 18 schools will be tracked on each occasion. Information about the schools will be collected by questionnaire and from other sources.

STATUS: Sponsored project

SOURCE OF GRANT: Scottish Office Education and Industry Department
£59,900

DATE OF RESEARCH: 1998-continuing

KEYWORDS: **higher still; qualifications; scotland; secondary education; sixteen to nineteen education**

2290

15 St John Street, Edinburgh EH8 8JR
0131 557 2944

Powney, J. Dr; McPake, J. Ms; Hall, S. Mr; Hamilton, S. Ms; Lyall, L. Ms
Review of education of people from minority ethnic groups in Scotland

ABSTRACT: The review investigates the availability of statistical information on ethnic minorities in Scotland covering all aspects of education and training. The research literature from Scotland and other countries is examined to identify particular issues. A major focus of the review is teaching and learning.

PUBLISHED MATERIAL: POWNEY, J., MCPAKE, J., HALL, S. & LYALL, L. (1998). Education of minority ethnic groups in Scotland: a review of research. SCRE Research Report No 88. Edinburgh: Scottish Council for Research in Education.

STATUS: Sponsored project

SOURCE OF GRANT: Scottish Office Education and Industry Department
£5,000

DATE OF RESEARCH: 1998-1998

KEYWORDS: **access to education; equal education; ethnic groups; guides; learning strategies; literature reviews; scotland; teaching methods; training**

2291

15 St John Street, Edinburgh EH8 8JR
0131 557 2944

Powney, J. Dr; Hall, S. Mr; Lowden, K. Mr
Evaluation of the Scotland Against Drugs Primary School Initiative

ABSTRACT: Scotland Against Drugs (SAD) is funding a major initiative

of inservice training in drug education for primary teachers in Scotland. The Scottish Council for Research in Education (SCRE) is evaluating the pilot programme and subsequent phases. The evaluators will attend and evaluate, in collaboration with the trainers and participants, the pilot staff development events. Methods include observation, self-completion questionnaires and discussion groups. The findings from this preliminary work will inform the production of the modules to be available for local authorities to use if they wish in their own approaches to drug education. Early next academic session the evaluators will identify the nature of drug education plans in all local authorities and, selecting a sample representing the range of models, work with these more closely over the subsequent year. Trainers and participants will be observed, interviewed and/or asked to keep records of the initiative activities. Once the booklet/reference guide is introduced, the evaluators will survey a representative sample of Scottish schools about the usefulness of the materials, either as complementary to staff development, or as a free standing resource. Finally, seminars will provide authorities with opportunities to review their own initiatives alongside others and consider their desirability, 'sustainability' and cost effectiveness.

STATUS: Sponsored project

SOURCE OF GRANT: Scotland Against Drugs

DATE OF RESEARCH: 1998-continuing

KEYWORDS: **drug education; health education; inservice teacher education; primary education; primary school teachers; scotland; teacher development**

2292

15 St John Street, Edinburgh EH8 8JR
0131 557 2944

Hall, S. Mr; Powney, J. Dr; Hamilton, S. Ms; Pirrie, A. Dr; Pitcairn, J. Mr
Institutional support for overseas students

ABSTRACT: Full fee non-European Union overseas students are present in considerable numbers in Scottish higher education. They are a heterogeneous category of students from a range of backgrounds and with a variety of needs. This research sets out to identify those needs and the extent to which they are being met by Scottish educational institutions. Documents on policy and provision from all higher education institutions (HEIs) and a selection of other establishments are analysed, and interviews conducted with students, students' representatives and staff about the needs of overseas students and the provision made by institutions. The resulting guidelines can be used to inform future practice.

STATUS: Sponsored project

SOURCE OF GRANT: Scottish Office Education and Industry Department
£29,522

DATE OF RESEARCH: 1998-1998

KEYWORDS: **higher education; overseas students; pastoral care - education; scotland; student needs**

2293

15 St John Street, Edinburgh EH8 8JR
0131 557 2944

Harlen, W. Prof.; Schilling, M. Mr
Science on-line support network for schools (SOLSN) evaluation

ABSTRACT: Science on-line support network for schools (SOLSN) project is a feasibility study on using the Internet for interactive professional development in science for primary teachers. The evaluation is to inform decisions about the further development of this project. Teachers at 11 schools involved in the feasibility study were interviewed about using the technology.

PUBLISHED MATERIAL: HARLEN, W. & SCHILLING, M. (1998). Evaluation of the science on-line support network (SOLSN) feasibility study. SOEID Research Report. Edinburgh: Scottish Office Education and Industry Department.

STATUS: Sponsored project

SOURCE OF GRANT: Scottish Office Education and Industry Department
£5,000

DATE OF RESEARCH: 1998-1998

KEYWORDS: **computer uses in education; information technology; inservice teacher education; internet; primary education; science education; teacher development**

2294

15 St John Street, Edinburgh EH8 8JR
0131 557 2944

Harlen, W. Prof.

Review of the teaching of science

ABSTRACT: The review examines the UK and international literature on research carried out in primary and secondary schools into teaching approaches and techniques which have proved effective in the teaching of science. It also considers teacher education, both pre-service and continuing professional development.

STATUS: Sponsored project

SOURCE OF GRANT: Scottish Office Education and Industry Department
£5,000

DATE OF RESEARCH: 1998-1998

KEYWORDS: **inservice teacher education; literature reviews; preservice teacher education; primary education; science education; science teachers; secondary education; teacher development; teaching methods**

2295

15 St John Street, Edinburgh EH8 8JR
0131 557 2944

Devine, M. Mrs; Plowman, L. Ms; Reid, M. Ms

Evaluation of pilot professional development schemes for dentists and GPs

ABSTRACT: This project will evaluate pilot professional development schemes for dentists in the North East of Scotland and GPs in Scotland. The evaluation of general professional training for dentists involves questionnaires to all dentists in training in Scotland and interviews with trainers and trainees in the General Professional Training (GPT) scheme. The evaluation of the Higher Professional Training (HPT) Programme for GPs in a qualitative study comprises indepth group and individual interviews with the HPT fellows and interviews with key participants from the universities and host practice GPs.

STATUS: Sponsored project

SOURCE OF GRANT: Scottish Council for Postgraduate Medical and Dental Education £60,000

DATE OF RESEARCH: 1996-1998

KEYWORDS: **dentists; physicians; professional development**

2296

15 St John Street, Edinburgh EH8 8JR
0131 557 2944

Devine, M. Mrs; Plowman, L. Ms; Musselbrook, K. Ms

Evaluation of West Midlands general professional training programmes for dentists

ABSTRACT: This project aims to evaluate the General Professional Training (GPT) programmes for dentists in the West Midlands; explores the experience and perceptions of trainees and trainers in the GPT scheme and compares these experiences and perceptions with dentists who have followed different career pathways.

STATUS: Sponsored project

SOURCE OF GRANT: West Midlands General Professional Training Programme Scheme £40,543

DATE OF RESEARCH: 1997-1998

KEYWORDS: **dental education; dentists; professional education**

2297

15 St John Street, Edinburgh EH8 8JR
0131 557 2944

Powney, J. Dr; Hall, S. Mr

Impact study of Higher Education and Equality Guide

ABSTRACT: A survey is being conducted of all higher education institutions to evaluate the impact of the Higher Education Equality Guide on progress in equality and to identify areas which need further support.

STATUS: Sponsored project

SOURCE OF GRANT: Commission for Racial Equality; Committee of Vice-Chancellors and Principals; Equal Opportunities Commission

DATE OF RESEARCH: 1998-1998

KEYWORDS: **access to education; equal education; ethnic groups; guides; higher education**

2298

15 St John Street, Edinburgh EH8 8JR
0131 557 2944

Powney, J. Dr

Review of school administration systems in European countries

ABSTRACT: The primary aim of the study is to review school administrative structures and procedures in a sample of European countries (including England, France, and possibly Norway) and other countries, for example, USA and New Zealand. The review will focus on identifying who does what in schools which may be defined as 'administrative'.

STATUS: Sponsored project

SOURCE OF GRANT: Scottish Office Education and Industry Department

DATE OF RESEARCH: 1998-1998

KEYWORDS: **comparative education; educational administration; management in education; school based management; school organisation**

2299

15 St John Street, Edinburgh EH8 8JR
0131 557 2944

Thorpe, G. Mr; Whitcombe, D. Mr; Russell, S. Ms

OECD survey of student attainment in reading, mathematics and science at age 15

ABSTRACT: This study is one of a series of 3 surveys which will be carried out on behalf of the OECD as part of its educational indicators programme. It will assess the attainment of 15 year-old students in reading, mathematics and science. The survey will use written assessment materials to measure the performance of 4500 students from 150 schools. The first survey, for which this is the fieldwork contract, will assess reading as its major domain with subsidiary assessments in mathematics and science. About 30 countries will be involved in the survey.

STATUS: Sponsored project

SOURCE OF GRANT: Scottish Office Education and Industry Department £77,397

DATE OF RESEARCH: 1999-continuing

KEYWORDS: **achievement; assessment; comparative education; literacy; mathematics achievement; mathematics education; numeracy; pupil performance; reading; reading achievement; science education; secondary education**

2300

15 St John Street, Edinburgh EH8 8JR
0131 557 2944

Hall, J. Dr

Review of music instruction in Scotland

ABSTRACT: This project reviews the arrangements for instrument tuition in Scottish education authorities since local government reorganisation, and provides a picture of overall current provision for music instruction across Scotland. It also draws on available literature to describe provision in other countries of the UK.

STATUS: Sponsored project

SOURCE OF GRANT: Scottish Office Education and Industry Education Department

DATE OF RESEARCH: 1998-1998

KEYWORDS: **music; music activities; musical instruments; scotland**

2301

15 St John Street, Edinburgh EH8 8JR
0131 557 2944

Harlen, W. Prof.

Wales curriculum review: additional survey

ABSTRACT: Parallel with the main review of the Wales curriculum which was to inform changes to be introduced in 2000, this additional survey considers the opinions of all schools and related bodies in Wales on the form that any immediate modifications in 1998 might take.

STATUS: Sponsored project

SOURCE OF GRANT: Curriculum and Assessment Authority for Wales

DATE OF RESEARCH: 1998-1998

KEYWORDS: **curriculum development; national curriculum; wales**

2302

15 St John Street, Edinburgh EH8 8JR
0131 557 2944
Glasgow University, Youth Education and Employment Research Unit, Glasgow G12 8QQ
0141 339 8855

Powney, J. Dr; Hall, S. Mr; Furlong, S. Dr; Biggart, A. Mr

The effectiveness of youth work with vulnerable young people

ABSTRACT: Drawing on the views of providers of community education services and of young people this project identified the effectiveness and costs of different programmes of community education. Programmes intended for young people at risk, including those where there is inter-professional and inter-sectoral collaboration were of particular interest. This was a collaborative project with Glasgow University, Youth Education and Employment Research Unit.

PUBLISHED MATERIAL: FURLONG, A., CARTMEL, F., POWNEY, J. & HALL, S. (1997). Evaluating youth work with vulnerable young people. SCRE Research Report No 83. Edinburgh: Scottish Council for Research in Education. ; POWNEY, J., FURLONG, A., CARTMEL, F. & HALL, S. (1997). Youth work with vulnerable young peopole. Interchange No 51. Edinburgh: Scottish Office Education and Industry Department/Research and Intelligence Unit. ; FURLONG, A. & CARTMEL, F. (1998). 'Youth work in a changing world', Research in Education, SCRE Newsletter No 62, pp.6-7.

STATUS: Sponsored project

SOURCE OF GRANT: Scottish Office Education and Industry Department £74,957

DATE OF RESEARCH: 1996-1997

KEYWORDS: **community education; programme effectiveness; youth; youth problems; youth work**

2303

15 St John Street, Edinburgh EH8 8JR
0131 557 2944
Nottingham University, School of Education, University Park, Nottingham NG7 2RD
01159 515151

Harlen, W. Prof.; Thorpe, G. Mr; Murphy, R. Prof.

The impact of Higher Still on attainment in core skills

ABSTRACT: Higher Still includes the specification of core skills to be taught in courses and advice on the assessment of these skills will be issued to schools, The expectation is that this identification of and focus on core skills will feed through into improved pupil attainment. The study investigates standards of attainment at S5 and S6 before and after the implementation of Higher Still using comparable and representative samples of pupils. The assessment instruments will as far as possible be derived for the unit assessments being developed as part of the Higher Still programme.

STATUS: Sponsored project

SOURCE OF GRANT: Scottish Office Education and Industry Department £119,390

DATE OF RESEARCH: 1998-continuing

KEYWORDS: **core skills; higher still; key skills; scotland; secondary education**

2304

15 St John Street, Edinburgh EH8 8JR
0131 557 2944
South Bank University, School of Education, Politics and Social Sciences, 103 Borough Road, London SE1 0AA
0171 928 8989

Powney, J. Dr; McPake, J. Ms; Weiner, G. Prof.

Higher education and equality - a manager's manual

ABSTRACT: The aim of the work is to produce a publication that will enable managers and senior academic and specialist staff in universities to formulate and pursue equality objectives and outcomes as part of their management and quality assurance work. The publication will encompass equal opportunities issues relevant to all staff in higher education institutions, including non-academic staff, students and curriculum issues and will need to be current for use in the academic year 1997/8.

PUBLISHED MATERIAL: POWNEY, J., WEINER, G. & HAMILTON, S. (1997). Higher education and equality: a guide. Manchester: Equal Opportunities Commission.

STATUS: Sponsored project

SOURCE OF GRANT: Equal Opportunities Commission; Commission for Racial Equality

DATE OF RESEARCH: 1996-1997

KEYWORDS: **academic staff; educational administration; equal education; equal opportunities - jobs; higher education; management in education; students; support staff; universities**

2305

15 St John Street, Edinburgh EH8 9JR
0131 557 2944
Stirling University, Institute of Education, Stirling FK9 4LA
01786 467600

Harlen, W. Prof.; Thorpe, G. Mr; *Supervisor*: Johnstone, R. Prof.

Attainment of pupils in Gaelic Medium Units

ABSTRACT: This project, under the overall directorship of Professor Johnstone of Stirling University, is addressing questions concerned with the comparative performance of pupils (Primary 3-7) educated in Gaelic Medium Units and those not. The research work involves jointly the Research Centre for Gaelic Affairs at Leirsinn, Skye and the Scottish Council for Research in Education (SCRE), with Lersinn concentrating on national assessment and contextual factors, and SCRE on the Assessment of Achievement components of the study.

STATUS: Sponsored project

SOURCE OF GRANT: Scottish Office Education and Industry Department £103,000

DATE OF RESEARCH: 1996-1998

KEYWORDS: **academic achievement; gaelic; gaelic medium education; language of instruction; primary education; pupil performance; scotland**

2306

15 St John Street, Edinburgh EH8 8JR
0131 557 2944
Stirling University, Institute of Education, Stirling FK9 4LA
01786 467600

Harlen, W. Prof.; Malcolm, H. Ms; Pake, J. Ms; Johnstone, R. Prof.; Low, L. Ms

Foreign languages in the upper secondary school in Scotland

ABSTRACT: The study aims to understand why students opt against studying modern foreign languages at Higher level, and is focusing on 6 major areas: Standard Grade and its relationship to Highers; school policies, options and timetable structures; pupil attitudes; teacher views; parent attitudes and perceptions of modern foreign languages (MFL) in the working world. Interrogation of existing databases at the Scottish Qualifications Authority (SQA) will be followed by work in 12 case study schools where detailed information will be gathered from staff and pupils. A national survey of S4 and S5 pupils and principal teachers of modern foreign languages will follow. Information is also being gathered from parents, careers officers and business representatives. Data gathering procedures will include: 1) interrogation of Scottish Examination Board (SEB) and Scottish Vocational Education Council (SCOTVEC) databases; 2) group interviews with pupils in S2, S3, S4 and S5; 3) interviews with school staff, careers officers, business representatives; 4) telephone interviews with parents; 5) questionnaires to pupils in S4 and S5 (case study schools) and 6) national survey of principal teachers and S4 and S5 pupils.

STATUS: Sponsored project

SOURCE OF GRANT: Scottish Office Education and Industry Department £93,456

DATE OF RESEARCH: 1996-1998

KEYWORDS: **choice of subjects; higher grade examinations; modern language studies; pupil attitudes; scotland; scottish certificate of education; secondary education; teacher attitudes**

2307

15 St John Street, Edinburgh EH8 8JR
0131 557 2944
Strathclyde University, Faculty of Education, Department of Business and Computer Education, Jordanhill Campus, Southbrae Drive, Glasgow G13 1PP
0141 950 3000

Somekh, B. Dr; Hall, J. Dr; McPake, J. Ms; Munro, R. Mr

Scottish 'superhighways' evaluation

ABSTRACT: As part of a UK initiative, the Scottish Council for Research in Education (SCRE) was evaluating two Scottish projects. The evaluators were asked to establish the extent to which 'superhighways' can enrich the delivery and experience of education, help young people meet the challenges they face on entering employment and provide skills for lifelong learning.

PUBLISHED MATERIAL: SCOTTISH OFFICE EDUCATION AND INDUSTRY DEPARTMENT. (1997). Superhighways to learning. Issue No 1. Edinburgh: Scottish Office Education and Industry Department. ; WELSH OFFICE, DEPARTMENT OF EDUCATION NORTHERN IRELAND, DEPARTMENT FOR EDUCATION AND EMPLOYMENT, SCOTTISH OFFICE. (1997). Preparing for the information age: synoptic report of the Education Departments' Superhighways Initiative. London: Department for Education and Emloyment. Also available on-line at: http://vtc.ngfl.gov.uk/reference/edsi/

STATUS: Sponsored project

SOURCE OF GRANT: Scottish Office Education and Industry Department; Department for Education and Employment; Department of Education for Northern Ireland; Welsh Office, Department of Education

DATE OF RESEARCH: 1996-1997

KEYWORDS: **computer uses in education; electronic mail; information technology; internet; secondary education**

2308

15 St John Street, Edinburgh EH8 8JR
0131 557 2944
University of Northumbria at Newcastle, Ellison Building, Ellison Place, Newcastle upon Tyne NE1 8ST
0191 232 6002

Powney, J. Dr; Edward, S. Ms

Career entry profiles for newly qualified teachers

ABSTRACT: This evaluation, conducted with the University of Northumbria at Newcastle, covered the first cycle of preparation and use of career entry profiles developed by the Teacher Training Agency (TTA). It aided the development of materials and guidance for the introduction of profiles for all new teachers qualifying in England from July 1997.

STATUS: Sponsored project

SOURCE OF GRANT: Teacher Training Agency

DATE OF RESEARCH: 1996-1997

KEYWORDS: **career entry profiles; newly qualified teachers; profiles; teaching profession**

Secondary Heads Association

2309

130 Regent Road, Leicester LE1 7PG
01162 471797

Miller, P. Mr; Horn, J. Mr; Bray, R. Mr; Gemmell, M. Mrs; Griffin, M. Mrs; Taylor, P. Mr

Investigation into drama provision in secondary schools in England and Wales with special reference to National Curriculum key stage 4

ABSTRACT: The aims of the project were to: 1) obtain an up-to-date national picture of drama provisions focused upon key stage 4 (KS4) and the use of drama techniques in other subjects across the secondary school curriculum; 2) build up a portfolio of evidence on the social effects of pupils' involvement in drama; 3) identify examples of good practice from across the nation; 4) publish to a wide audience the results of the work, particularly disseminating good practice and advocating the benefits of sound drama work at least up to the end of compulsory education. The working group devised and administered a questionnaire sent to a sample cross-section of Secondary Heads Association (SHA) 8,000 members who are Headteachers and Deputies from the majority of the country's secondary schools, maintained and independent. These members have direct access to the reality of the curriculum as it currently operates in the nation's secondary schools. The questionnaire was designed to elicit 4 pieces of information: 1) The present provision of drama in KS4 for boys/girls and in different types of school. 2) Changes which have taken place recently since the preparation of 'Whither the Arts' and under the influence of the Dearing revisions to the National Curriculum. 3) The extent to which and how drama techniques are deployed across the curriculum, including use of external facilitators. 4) School leaders' perceptions of the social effects of drama, particularly in terms of resolution of adolescent conflict; education for family life ('parenting'); and mediation, tolerance and conflict resolution. 5) Cultural diversity and cross-cultural understanding. Good practice is identified in case-studies to provide examples which schools can use to build or improve their present provision.

PUBLISHED MATERIAL: MILLER, P., HORN, J., BRAY, R., GEMMELL, M., GRIFFIN, M. & TAYLOR, P. (1998). Drama sets you free. Leicester: Secondary Heads Association.

STATUS: Sponsored project

SOURCE OF GRANT: Calouste Gulbenkian Foundation £5,000; Esmee Fairbairn Charitable Trust £5,000

DATE OF RESEARCH: 1997-1998

KEYWORDS: **drama; key stage 4; secondary education**

2310

130 Regent Road, Leicester LE1 7PG
01162 471797

Bray, R. Mr; Gardner, C. Mr; Parsons, N. Mr; *Supervisor*: Downes, P. Mr

Can boys do better?

ABSTRACT: This project will result in a booklet concerned with under-achievement in boys and strategies for improvement. Schools find predominantly poor results from boys. The causes are complex and the authors argue that schools must face up to the problem and develop appropriate strategies.

STATUS: Team research

DATE OF RESEARCH: 1996-1997

KEYWORDS: **academic achievement; achievement; boys; pupil performance; secondary education; sex differences; underachievement**

Sheffield Hallam University

2311

Computer and Management Sciences, City Campus, Sheffield S1 1WB
01142 720911

Drew, D Dr; Demack, S. Mr

The methodology of research in race and education

ABSTRACT: Research on 'race' and education has always generated controversy. Some papers produced by Sheffield Hallam University have excited interest about the way research can illustrate the extent of unequal treatment, racial discrimination and racism. Two papers (Gillborn and Drew, 1992 and 1993) have been subject to critical scrutiny in books on the politics of social research. The researchers have also worked on a critique of statistical research on race and education over the last decade for a book published by the Open University Press in 1998, entitled 'Researching Racism in Education' by Paul Connolly and Barry Troyna.

PUBLISHED MATERIAL: GILLBORN, D. & DREW, D.J. (1992). 'Race, class and school effects', New Community, Vol 18, No 4, pp.551-565. ; GILLBORN, D. & DREW, D.J. (1993). 'The politics of research: some observations on methodological purity', New Community, Vol 19, No 2, pp.354-360. ; DREW, D. & DEMACK, S. (1998). A league apart: statistics in the study of 'race' and education'. In: CONNOLLY, P. & TROYNA, B. (Eds) Researching racism in education: politics, theory and practice. Buckingham: Open University Press.

STATUS: Sponsored project

SOURCE OF GRANT: Sheffield Hallam University

DATE OF RESEARCH: 1995-continuing

KEYWORDS: educational research; ethnic groups; race; racial discrimination; research methodology

2312

Learning and Teaching Research Institute, ADSETS Centre, Sheffield S1 1WB
01142 720911

Johnson, R. Ms

Generating and interpreting evaluative data about teaching and learning

ABSTRACT: The research method employed will provide elucidatory information about teacher perceptions of purpose, process and content of student feedback through examination of: relationship to the concept of "student feedback"; their perceptions of the value and validity of student comment; attitudes towards methodologies and processes and the significance of this, and reactions to the results as per their content and indicatory nature. The study will examine the means by which a feedback process functions in relation to the individual constructions of identity as a teacher in higher education who: operates within conceptions of the parameters of subject discipline and the institutional culture; works according to individual and social value systems; has a social and functional position in relation to students; may have an individual level of concern for and expertise in educational ideas and techniques, and may have an individual readiness to extract meaning from the results. The study will investigate how the content of feedback from students demonstrates student awareness of variables which have been argued to have an affect on student learning and their ability to articulate them; how the particular method employed can have a consciousness raising effect on students which could be considered of educational merit. The study would like to reveal how pertinent issues of the cultural context for and freedom to criticise are perceived to be for the students interviewed, and whether this is described by the students as having an effect on the nature of the feedback information relayed. Close analysis of dialogue produced by the researcher and the teacher participants through collaborative and reflexive examination of the dynamics and issues operating within a system of feedback will aim to assist a shift in understanding of its nature from that held to be a reliably mechanical means of quality measurement, towards that of a dynamic and political process, showing variation in outcome appropriate to its character as a subjective, inter-personal and socially constructed task.

STATUS: Sponsored project

SOURCE OF GRANT: Sheffield Hallam University

DATE OF RESEARCH: 1996-continuing

KEYWORDS: feedback; higher education; students

2313

Mathematics Education Centre, 25 Broomgrove Road, Sheffield S10 2NA
01142 720911

Gardiner, J. Mr; *Supervisors*: Hudson, B. Dr; Wilson, D. Mr; Povey, H. Dr

Hand-held dynamic geometry in the classroom - a socio-cultural analysis

ABSTRACT: The project investigates the use of dynamic geometry in the lower years of secondary school using Cabri on the Texas TI 92. Data have been collected at two secondary schools in Years 7 and 8 classrooms. Evidence is presented on the influence of a dynamic geometry environment on pupils' ideas of conviction and proof, in particular of how spontaneous and scientific concepts (Vygotsky 1962) interweave and interact. The importance of mediation by teacher and technology in this dialectic is examined, as is the influence of the technology on pupils' ideas of construction and proof and on the idea of necessary and sufficient conditions. A further socio-cultural aspect is that of the implications of the use of handheld technology. The availability of the dynamic geometry environment on a small machine can be used to stimulate interaction between pupils and between pupil and workbook and the classroom material has been written with this in mind. Directions for further work, in the socio-cultural implications of handheld technology and the importance of dynamic images in promoting learning, are proposed. More general ideas on the possible impact of handheld technology on teaching and learning are being developed.

STATUS: Individual research

DATE OF RESEARCH: 1996-continuing

KEYWORDS: geometry; technology

2314

School of Education, City Campus, Sheffield S1 1WB
01142 720911

Stirton, J. Mr; *Supervisor*: Cashdan, A. Prof.

An investigation into the issues associated with the investigation of children with a history of epilepsy in mainstream secondary students

ABSTRACT: The project initially identified 3 comprehensive schools in different authorities which had, over the previous 3 years, moved towards whole school approaches for children with special educational needs. In each of the schools children on the special educational needs register with a history of epilepsy were identified. Each of the children noted was studied through structured observation, interview and by scanning both educational and medical records. Staff views were sought through a questionnaire, structured interviews and an attitudinal inventory. Extensive field notes were maintained. The evidence adduced suggested that prevailing views as to the nature of discrimination towards children with a history of epilepsy were over simplistic and that teacher responses were more sympathetic than had been previously assumed.

STATUS: Individual research

DATE OF RESEARCH: 1991-continuing

KEYWORDS: epilepsy; mainstreaming; secondary education; special educational needs; teacher attitudes

2315

School of Education, City Campus, Sheffield S1 1WB
01142 720911

Dawson, E. Ms; *Supervisors*: Boulton, P. Ms; Weatherald, C. Ms; Trickey, S. Dr

Learning choices: a grounded theory study of adult returners

ABSTRACT: This research seeks to determine the nature, extent and effect of psychological and sociological influences on the learning choices of adult returners, that is, adults who left school with few qualifications, who, after a period of time away from education identify a desire or a need to re-enter the system. It intends to consider the influence on choice of third parties and the affect of available provision, determining how perceptions and choices change as adults re-enter and progress through their chosen route. By adopting a grounded theory methodology, the research intends to develop valid, reliable and testable theory grounded in the data which provides an original contribution to knowledge.

STATUS: Individual research

DATE OF RESEARCH: 1995-1998

KEYWORDS: adult students; higher education; mature students

2316

School of Education, City Campus, Sheffield S1 1WB
01142 720911

Smith, R. Dr

Primary student teachers' use of subject knowledge

ABSTRACT: This was a longitudinal study of the development and use of subject knowledge by primary student teachers during their 4-year course of training. One cohort of students specialising in science (n=17) was traced from entry in 1992 to qualification in 1996. Data was collected by: 1) documents (entry qualifications, background experience from applications; teaching practice plans, evaluations and assessments); 2) questionnaires and exercises exploring students' learning priorities, orientation and views of learning; 3) tests and task eliciting their subject knowledge in science and their pedagogical content knowledge. Interviews with 5 students were conducted in year 1, year 3, and at the end of their course. Analysis revealed a shift of concerns from personal goals toward management and learning professional skills and subsequently toward assessment and promotion of individual pupils' learning. Subject knowledge and pedagogic knowledge grew in relation to its use in teaching, but gaps in scientific knowledge to underpin teaching remained. Case studies and papers will examine the growth of an integrated repertoire of professional knowledge against the background of a shifting perception of primary teaching.

PUBLISHED MATERIAL: SMITH, R.G. (1993). 'The development by student teachers of a repertoire of subject knowledge in primary science'. Paper given at the International Conference on Teacher Education, Tel Aviv, June 1993. ; SMITH, R.G. & LLOYD, J. (1995). '"I'd need to do a lot of reading myself before teaching this". How do primary teachers know what science to teach?'. Paper given at the CONASTA 95 Annual Conference of Australian Science Teachers Association, Brisbane, September 1995. ; SMITH, R.G. (1996). 'Learning what you need to know. Continuity and change in the professional development of primary teachers in training'. Paper given at European Conference on Educational Research, Seville, September 1996. ; SMITH, R.G. & LLOYD, J. (1997). '"Before teaching this I'd do a lot of reading": preparing primary student teachers to teach science', Research in Science Education, Vol 27, No 1, pp.141-154.

STATUS: Sponsored project

SOURCE OF GRANT: Learning and Teaching Institute £6,000

DATE OF RESEARCH: 1992-1997

KEYWORDS: **preservice teacher education; science education; science teachers; student teachers; subject knowledge; teacher development**

2317

School of Education, Collegiate Crescent, Sheffield S10 2BP
01142 720911

Brand, J. Mr; *Supervisor*: Holland, M. Dr

Using professional development portfolios to enhance students' learning in secondary initial teacher training

ABSTRACT: A new 3-year BSc Hons. secondary programme was started in 1994 by 125 students (subjects: physical education, mathematics, science, design and tchnology). This programme incorporated an assessed portfolio of professional development for all students which was designed to enhance learning opportunities throughout the degree and make a bridge between university-based work and school experience. The research seeks to identify key issues in the implementation of this scheme. In particular, the value placed on students aiming at schools with portfolios by mentors who are responsible for developing and assessing competences in practical teaching. It is intended to research the usefulness of the portfolios to final year students when seeking jobs, and eventually to follow-up the use made by heads of department/mentors of the portfolio during the first year of employment. The researchers are also examining developments in the use of portfolios in teacher training at other UK institutions and in the US.

STATUS: Sponsored project

SOURCE OF GRANT: Enterprise Funding £6,000

DATE OF RESEARCH: 1996-1997

KEYWORDS: **portfolios - background material; preservice teacher education; profiles; student teachers; teacher development**

2318

School of Education, City Campus, Sheffield S1 1WB
01142 720911

Smith, R. Dr; Lloyd, J. Dr; Young, P. Ms

Primary student teachers' attitudes and knowledge in science

ABSTRACT: The project aims to: 1) analyse student teachers' attitudes to science and their understanding of the subject as they progress through the undergraduate route of primary initial teacher training (ITT); 2) relate findings to National Curriculum Orders at key stages 1 and 2 to competences to be required of newly qualified teachers. Methods used include questionnaires, tests and interviewing students.

STATUS: Sponsored project

SOURCE OF GRANT: Learning and Teaching Research Institute £7,500

DATE OF RESEARCH: 1996-continuing

KEYWORDS: **newly qualified teachers; primary school teachers; science education; student teacher attitudes; student teachers**

2319

School of Education, City Campus, Sheffield S1 1WB
01142 720911

Peacock, G. Mr; Nott, M. Mr; Smith, R. Dr

Continuity and progression in specific areas of science

ABSTRACT: There is concern over progression in pupils' science learning and particularly over continuity between key stages. Monitoring of the National Curriculum has shown that, in some areas of science, pupils may be repeating work carried out at an earlier key stage. This project used questionnaires and focused interviews to explore the extent of the problem in 3 specific areas of science at key stages 1, 2 and 3: investigations, plants and changes of state. Primary and secondary schools in 3 local education authorities (LEAs) were surveyed. 121 responses from teachers were received. In each LEA interviews were conducted with advisory staff and with teachers in all 3 key stages. Analysis will be completed in February 1998.

STATUS: Sponsored project

SOURCE OF GRANT: Qualifications and Curriculum Authority £8,000

DATE OF RESEARCH: 1997-1998

KEYWORDS: **developmental continuity; key stage 1; key stage 2; key stage 3; national curriculum; primary education; science education; secondary education**

2320

School of Education, City Campus, Sheffield S1 1WB
01142 720911

Lowe, G. Mr; *Supervisors*: Holland, M. Dr; Hudson, B. Dr; Simkins, T. Dr

School improvement through inspection?

ABSTRACT: The study will analyse the impact of school development in 6 comprehensive schools. The research seeks to: 1) identify factors in schools and the inspection process which influence schools' response to inspection; 2) analyse how factors interact in the implementation of inspection recommendations; 3) analyse data on the impact of inspection on school development; 4) test Office for Standards in Education's (OFSTED) assumptions about the impact on school development; 5) identify teachers' perceptions of the link between inspection and school improvement; 6) determine the basis for judgements about school improvement in 6 comprehensive schools; and 7) develop valid, reliable and testable theory grounded in the data which provides an original contribution to knowledge of the process of inspection-induced change.

PUBLISHED MATERIAL: LOWE, G. Inspection in the classroom: rhetoric and reality'. In: Life after inspection: school and LEA responses. London: PCP. (in press).

STATUS: Individual research

DATE OF RESEARCH: 1996-continuing

KEYWORDS: **inspection; ofsted; school improvement; teacher attitudes**

2321

School of Education, City Campus, Sheffield S1 1WB
01142 720911

Holland, M. Dr; Fowler, T. Mr; Drew, D. Dr

Barnsley 'highway to success'

ABSTRACT: Sheffield Hallam University is conducting a 5-year longitudinal study to measure the effect of the Highway to Success Programme on the educational provision in Barnsley. Data will be collected by surveys (sample size 1000) to parents, pupils and teachers, together with interviews and focus groups. The main themes of the research are: preschool and family learning; transition from infant to primary, primary to secondary; and improving curriculum skills.

STATUS: Sponsored project

SOURCE OF GRANT: Barnsley Council £150,000

DATE OF RESEARCH: 1998-continuing

KEYWORDS: achievement; developmental continuity; family involvement; preschool education; pupil improvement

2322

School of Education, City Campus, Sheffield S1 1WB
01142 720911

Holland, M. Dr

Student teachers' conceptions of professionalism

ABSTRACT: The research seeks to discover student teachers' views on teaching as a professional occupation at the start and finish of a 3-year undergraduate course for secondary students. The sample size is 100 students. Methods used are individual surveys and interviews. It is intended to extend the sample to teacher mentors and also to students following primary routes.

STATUS: Individual research

DATE OF RESEARCH: 1997-continuing

KEYWORDS: preservice teacher education; student teachers; teaching profession

2323

School of Education, City Campus, Sheffield S1 1WB
01142 720911

Povey, H. Dr; Coldron, J. Mr

Women's careers in teaching

ABSTRACT: The project aimed to look at the causes of women's under-representation in senior posts in schools in Denmark, England and the Netherlands. A total of 80 women (in-service and pre-service) and 20 managers/headteachers (male or female). This work was reported in a stage 1 report in 1992. In stage 2, colleagues from each institution developed curricula and materials to use with pre-service and in-service teachers and managers to help women gain senior posts. In stage 3, these were published in 1997 in a resource and practical guide that combined research and action to help those in schools. A parallel activity was a case study of a school in England which looks at the causes of lack of promotion for a female member of staff and evaluates a radical management initiative to include women staff in the all-male executive team.

PUBLISHED MATERIAL: COLDRON, J.H., HITCHINGS-DAVIS, V. and POVEY, H. (1993). Report of the first phase of the women's careers in teaching project. An action project of the European Union in collobaration with Dutch and Danish universities. Sheffield: Sheffield Hallam University, School of Education. ; COLDRON, J.H. & POVEY, H. (1995). 'Women's careers in teaching: how can we redress the balance?'. Proceedings of the 20th Conference of the Association for Teacher Education in Europe (ATEE), Oslo, 1995. ; POVEY, H. & COLDRON, J. (Eds). (1997). Women's careers in teaching: a practical guide. Sheffield: Sheffield Hallam University Press.; POVEY, H. & COLDRON, J.H. (1998). 'Still a tough job to reach the top', Times Educational Supplement, No 4256, 23 January, TES FRIDAY, pp.22-23.

STATUS: Sponsored project

SOURCE OF GRANT: European Union £44,374

DATE OF RESEARCH: 1991-1997

KEYWORDS: career development; careers; head teachers; promotion occupational; teaching profession; women teachers; womens employment

2324

School of Education, City Campus, Sheffield S1 1WB
01142 720911

Johnson, S. Mr; Elliott, S. Mr; Hudson, B. Dr

Re-learning algebra

ABSTRACT: This is an ongoing project into the learning of algebra by students at university level, all of whom have studied algebra previously. It addresses the conceptions of algebra held by students and the differences/similarities between students whose main subject is mathematics, and those who need mathematics to support their study. The function of language and discussion in helping students both to articulate and re-formulate their conceptions is investigated and also the significance of the students' role as teachers in helping them to accommodate a more useful conception of algebra. The work draws on that of a range of authors and researchers, including Arcavi, Sierpinska, Kaput and Cobb.

STATUS: Sponsored project

SOURCE OF GRANT: Sheffield Hallam University £6,000

DATE OF RESEARCH: 1994-continuing

KEYWORDS: algebra; higher education; mathematics education

2325

School of Education, City Campus, Sheffield S1 1WB
01142 720911

Williams, J. Mr

An international comparative study of school governance and parental involvement

ABSTRACT: A comparative study of approaches to the governance of schools in different parts of the world. Field data from North America, Europe and Africa will be used to explore the rationale for and experience of different models of community involvement in schools. The study is based on visits to schools in the aforementioned continents and the analysis of policy documentation. This is supplemented by Ministry of Education papers from several other countries. The aim of the research is to identify the key questions that need to be answered when proposing a model for school governance, community and parental involvement in schools.

STATUS: Individual research

DATE OF RESEARCH: 1997-1998

KEYWORDS: comparative education; educational administration; governing bodies; parent participation; school governors

2326

School of Education, City Campus, Sheffield S1 1WB
01142 720911

Smith, J. Ms

General National Vocational Qualifications and progression to higher education: the student experience

ABSTRACT: In 1995/6 this project focused on the experience of Advanced General National Vocational Qualification (GNVQ) students in further and higher education. The aim of this year's work was to produce a 'baseline' survey of student experience to inform future research, development and quality assurance work at Sheffield Hallam University and further education colleges. Qualitative and quantitative data were gathered from students in five further education colleges in the region and from former GNVQ students studying in their first year at Sheffield Hallam University. The college sample represented 10 per cent of the Year 2 Advanced GNVQ student group and the university sample 17 per cent of first year students with GNVQ qualifications. Data were collected by questionnaire and semi-structured audio-taped group discussion. Areas explored included course choice, expectations and impressions, teaching and learning methods, core skills, comparison with A-level courses and the value of GNVQs for progression. The findings showed that while students have a positive orientation towards their studies, their perceptions need to be interpreted against objective measures of achievement. Issues relating to retention, student interaction with teachers and higher level group and other process skills were among the issues recommended for further investigation. Follow-up research is planned linking tracking data on student performance and withdrawal to further study of some of the key findings. A summary report of work carried out in 1995/6 is available.

PUBLISHED MATERIAL: SMITH, J. (1996). Bridge or barrier?: Student experience of Advanced GNVQ as a progression route. Sheffield: Sheffield Hallam University. ; SMITH, J. (1998). 'Beyond the rhetoric: are General

National Vocational Qualifications doing students any good', Journal of Vocational Education and Training, Vol 50, No 4, pp.537-548.

STATUS: Sponsored project

SOURCE OF GRANT: Sheffield Hallam University

DATE OF RESEARCH: 1998-continuing

KEYWORDS: academic vocational divide; further education; general national vocational qualifications; sixteen to nineteen education; vocational education; vocational qualifications

2327

School of Education, City Campus, Sheffield S1 1WB
01142 720911

Boulton, P. Ms; Coldron, J. Mr

Parents' reflections on schools

ABSTRACT: The project took the form of wide-ranging interviews with the parents/carers of children who had reached the end of compulsory schooling. It built on a previous project conducted five years before, examining parents' choice of schools. The interviews addressed issues around parental satisfaction with schools and with choices made.

PUBLISHED MATERIAL: COLDRON, J. & BOULTON, P. (1996). 'What do parents mean when they talk about "discipline" in relation to their children's schools?', British Journal of Sociology of Education, Vol 17, No 1, pp.53-64. ; BOULTON, P. & COLDRON, J. (1996). 'Does the rhetoric work? Parental responses to new right policy assumptions', British Journal of Educational Studies, Vol 44, No 3, pp.296-306.

STATUS: Sponsored project

SOURCE OF GRANT: Sheffield Hallam University

DATE OF RESEARCH: 1997-1998

KEYWORDS: discipline; parent attitudes; parent choice; parent school relationship; secondary education

2328

School of Education, City Campus, Sheffield S1 1WB
01142 720911

Boulton, P. Ms; Coldron, J. Mr

Positive action for women's careers in teaching - a case study of one secondary school

ABSTRACT: The project investigates the events leading to the establishment of an all-male management team in a secondary school, and examines the measures taken by the school to mitigate the effects of an all-male team. An evaluation is being made of the effectiveness of measures taken which primarily took the form of an enlargement of the management team to include women elected by a women's group. A case study of a woman faculty head who was expected to apply for the vacant management position and did not, revealed some subtle ways in which gender affected the actions of individuals.

PUBLISHED MATERIAL: BOULTON, P. & COLDRON, J. (1998). 'Why women teachers say "stuff it" to promotion: a failure of equal opportunities?', Gender and Education, Vol 10, No 2, pp.149-161. ; COLDRON, J. & BOULTON, P. (1998). 'The success and failure of positive action to mitigate the effects of an all male management team in a secondary school', British Educational Research Journal, Vol 24, No 3, pp.317-331.

STATUS: Sponsored project

SOURCE OF GRANT: Sheffield Hallam University

DATE OF RESEARCH: 1996-1998

KEYWORDS: careers; equal opportunities - jobs; management in education; school organisation; sex differences; teaching profession; women teachers; womens employment

2329

School of Education, City Campus, Sheffield S1 1WB
01142 720911

Monteith, M. Mrs

Information technology competences for intending teachers

ABSTRACT: To develop agreed lists of information technology (IT) competences as benchmarks for students, university staff, and staff in placement schools. Representatives from 34 schools attended one of four seminars at Sheffield Hallam University and drew up lists of preferred IT competences. Subsequently, all participants commented on lists so that quite specific lists were finally agreed.

PUBLISHED MATERIAL: MONTEITH, M. (1994). 'IT competences for intending teachers'. Paper presented at National Council for Educational Technology Conference, Birmingham, 1994. ; MONTEITH, M. (1995). 'IT competences for intending teachers'. Paper presented at Computer Aided Learning Conference, University of Cambridge, 1995.

STATUS: Sponsored project

SOURCE OF GRANT: Sheffield Hallam University

DATE OF RESEARCH: 1997-1998

KEYWORDS: competence; computer literacy; information technology; preservice teacher education; student teachers

2330

School of Education, City Campus, Sheffield S1 1WB
01142 720911

Monteith, M. Mrs

The use of individual time for word-processing with young children

ABSTRACT: The research aim is to observe the stages in children's word-processing in the early years, and relate these stages to previous research on children's writing development. Twenty-two children of Year 1 and Year 2 over two years spent 10-15 minutes per week word-processing; observations and tests were made of their reading and writing development.

PUBLISHED MATERIAL: MONTEITH, M. (1996). 'Combining literacies: the use of "individual time" for word-processing with young children'. In: NEATE, B. (Ed). Literacy saves lives. Shepreth: United Kingdom Reading Association. ; MONTEITH, M. (1996). 'The use of word-processors with children who are learning to read'. In: Teacher Training and Values Education, selected papers from the 18th Annual Conference of the Association for Teacher Education in Europe (ATEE).

STATUS: Sponsored project

SOURCE OF GRANT: Sheffield Hallam University

DATE OF RESEARCH: 1997-1997

KEYWORDS: computer uses in education; information technology; literacy; primary education; reading; word processing; writing - composition; young children

2331

School of Education, City Campus, Sheffield S1 1WB
01142 720911

Garrett, V. Mrs

Educational leadership

ABSTRACT: Ten educational leaders were interviewed investigating various themes.

PUBLISHED MATERIAL: GARRETT, V. (1997). 'Principals and headteachers as leading professionals'. In: RIBBINS, P. (Ed). Leaders and leadership in the school, college and university. London: Cassell. ; GARRETT, V. (1997). 'Conversation: Rosemary Whinn-Sladden with Viv Garrett'. In: RIBBINS, P. (Ed). Leaders and leadership in the school, college and university. London: Cassell. ; GARRETT, V. (1997). 'Managing change'. In: DAVIES, B. & ELLISON, L. (1997). School leadership for the 21st century: a competency and knowledge approach. London: Routledge. ; GARRETT, V. with BOWLES, C. (1997). 'Teaching as a profession: the role of professional development'. In: TOMLINSON, H. (Ed). Managing continuing professional development in schools. London: Paul Chapman.

STATUS: Sponsored project

SOURCE OF GRANT: Sheffield Hallam University

DATE OF RESEARCH: 1995-1997

KEYWORDS: head teachers; leadership; principals

2332

School of Education, City Campus, Sheffield S1 1WB
01142 720911

Coldron, J. Mr; Boulton, P. Ms; Povey, H. Dr

Teacher education in Europe: equal opportunities (TENET Project)

ABSTRACT: The aims are: (1) an evaluation of pre-service teacher education courses at Sheffield Hallam University's School of Education; and (2) to develop an action plan for the enhancement of the education of students concerning gender issues in the classroom.

PUBLISHED MATERIAL: BOULTON, P., COHEN, L. & COLDRON, J.H. (1992). Ways and meanings: gender, process and teacher education. Sheffield: PAVIC. ; BOULTON, P. & COULDRON, J.H. (1993). 'Equal opportunities, teacher education and Europe'. In: SIRAJ-BLATCHFORD, I. (Ed). Race, gender and the education of teachers. Buckingham: Open University Press.

STATUS: Sponsored project

SOURCE OF GRANT: Sheffield Hallam University

DATE OF RESEARCH: 1992-continuing

KEYWORDS: course evaluation; equal education; preservice teacher education; sex differences

2333

School of Education, City Campus, Sheffield S1 1WB
01142 720911
Roehampton Institute London, Roehampton Lane, London SW15 5PU
0181 392 3000
Reading University, School of Education, Bulmershe Court, Woodlands Avenue, Earley, Reading RG6 1HY
01189 875123

Bentley, D. Prof ; *Supervisors*: Mahony, P. Prof.; Gilbert, J. Prof.

Feminist science education? Views of teachers on the feasibility of the issue

ABSTRACT: The research is in 2 parts: Part 1 - the views of young women, is completed from 3 sources: questionnaire to 1,000 Year 8/9 pupils; interviews with young women at Sixth Form stage; and post-18 in first year of university. (12 in each cohort). These views of science, science education and teaching form part of the evidence for Part 2. Part 2 - life history, involves interviews of 6 science teachers, 2 in primary, 2 in secondary and 2 in higher education. Data from Part 1, as well as research critiques of science by feminists, forms the major source, along with life history as scientists for the interviews of teachers.

STATUS: Team research

DATE OF RESEARCH: 1995-1997

KEYWORDS: feminism; girls; higher education; pupil attitudes; science education; science teachers; secondary education; sex differences; student attitudes; teacher attitudes; women

2334

School of Education, City Campus, Sheffield S1 1WB
01142 720911
Sheffield University, Division of Education, 388 Glossop Road, Sheffield S10 2JA
01142 768555

Nott, M. Mr; Wellington, J. Dr

Teachers' understanding of the nature of science

ABSTRACT: Through paper and pencil tests, interviews using critical incidents, questionnaires and semi-structured interviews the researchers have, over the last 6 years, probed teachers' understanding of the nature of science, particularly in relation to practical work. It was found that: the teachers' responses to practicals that go wrong raised questions about teachers' norms, morals and ethics when dealing with practical work and controversial issues by developing a set of critical incidents; the teachers would either 'talk their way through it' or 'rig' or 'conjure'. 'Talking your way through it' is where the teacher encourages the pupils to critically evaluate the experiment and the way that it has been conducted to determine why the results do not agree with predictions or accepted theory. 'Rigging' is where the teacher learns to adjust variables in a practical so that it does

always work. 'Conjuring' occurs when the results are fraudulently produced. The researchers also investigated further with students undertaking doctoral research who had a similar science education and training to the sample of trainee teachers. It was found that a majority of the science graduates on a teacher training programme conducted some practical work in schools in a fraudulent manner, i.e. they 'conjured' to get the right empirical results. The results indicate that trainee teachers can initiate counter-normative behaviour themselves or be initiated by mentors or laboratory technicians. It was found that the teachers conjure to ensure the production of matters of fact; to ensure the smooth running of classroom life; in consideration of the ability of the pupils. It is a custom that is endemic in schools and it may be institutionalised and written into schemes of work. It was claimed that this counter-normative behaviour is a normal part of practical work on undergraduate programmes. This raised the question as to whether it was only the deviants who entered teaching after graduating. An equivalent sample of science graduates on a doctoral programme was interviewed to determine if they had conjured as undergraduates. It was found that the majority of both groups had conjured results for practical exercises as undergraduates. All the doctoral research students could understand why their fellow graduates would need to conjure with and in front of children. None of the doctoral students said that they conjured as researchers although some were convinced that other researchers may do. The conclusion is that normative scientific behaviour is inculcated through investigations and open-ended activities where the audience to be persuaded is one's own peers; counter-normative scientific behaviour is encouraged by the current systems of university laboratory work where the audience to be persuaded is one's assessor.

PUBLISHED MATERIAL: NOTT, M. & WELLINGTON, J. (1993). 'Your nature of science: an activity for science teachers', School Science Review, Vol 75, No 270, pp.109-112. ; NOTT, M. & WELLINGTON, J. (1995). 'Critical incidents in the science classroom and the nature of science', School Science Review, Vol 76, No 276, pp.41-46. ; NOTT, M. & WELLINGTON, J. (1996). 'Probing teachers' views of the nature of science: how should we do it and where should we be looking?'. In: WELFORD, G., OSBORNE, J. & SCOTT, P. (Eds). Research in science education in Europe. London: Falmer Press. ; NOTT, M. & WELLINGTON, J. (1996) 'When the black box springs open: practical work in school science and the nature of science', International Journal of Science Education, Vol 18, No 7, pp.807-818. ; NOTT, M. & WELLINGTON, J. 'Producing the evidence: science teachers' initiation into practical work', Research in Science Education. (in press).

STATUS: Collaborative

DATE OF RESEARCH: 1992-continuing

KEYWORDS: science education; science teachers; scientific literacy

2335

School of Education, City Campus, Sheffield S1 1WB
01142 720911
Sheffield University, Division of Education, 388 Glossop Road, Sheffield S10 2JA
01142 768555

Elliott, S. Mrs; *Supervisors*: Hudson, B. Dr; O'Reilly, D. Dr

Visualisation and using technology in mathematics education

ABSTRACT: Visualisation is being recognised increasingly as an important aspect of mathematical reasoning. Studies have revealed that activities which encourage the construction of images can greatly enhance mathematics learning. Indeed, potentially, technology could assume a very powerful and influential role in stimulating and shaping students' powers of visualisation, and as such may prove to contribute significantly to the depth of students' understanding. This project seeks to identify and evaluate ways in which existing technology can be utilised to help improve and develop students' powers of visualisation and to encourage their usage of these skills. Previous research into visualisation has suggested that in order to achieve a deeper and more meaningful understanding of mathematics, visual representations of ideas need to be linked to other modes of mathematical thinking and other forms of representation. This research is based on this premise. Initially, the research will involve designing classroom materials with the aim of promoting the development of students' powers of visualisation using technology in the A-level mathematics classroom. Following the development of these materials and a small pilot study, data will be collected in two cycles involving more indepth analysis of the influence of the technology on students' abilities to visualise mathematically and will include post-trial written tests. The main focus of this research will be on the graphing of functions. A qualitative interpretivist methodology will be adopted, based on a case study approach.

STATUS: Individual research

DATE OF RESEARCH: 1997-continuing

KEYWORDS: **computer uses in education; information technology; mathematics education; technology; visualisation**

2336

School of Health and Community Studies, Collegiate Crescent, Sheffield S10 2BP
01142 720911

Rosie, A. Dr

Value conflicts in educational settings

ABSTRACT: The concept of professionalism may be seen as contested. Different views of professionalism have held greater influence at some times than others. Shifts in definition and approaches to professionalism frequently involve competing values, whether understood in terms of a value base or more generally. This research explores the way in which competing values lead to debate over professionalism through case study research. It aims to chart value conflicts and offer various interpretations based on theoretical work. An action research project was conducted with a group of part-time adult youth workers on a 3 year training programme. The case study involved observation and dialogue between the researcher. The sample consisted of 14 workers from different authorities on a single three-year part-time course. Each student worker had a fieldwork supervisor who was also included in the research. Methodology involved: observation including participation as tutor, interviews, diaries, log records and document analysis. The study showed that two competing discourses of professionalism structured student experience. These discourses could be understood in terms of concepts derived from postmodernism. Further work will be undertaken on professional understanding and student teachers to examine comparison and contrast.

PUBLISHED MATERIAL: ROSIE, A. (1994). 'Contested discourse: exploration of two discourses in youth work training', Journal of Contemporary Ethnography, Vol 23, No 3, pp.330-354.

STATUS: Individual research

DATE OF RESEARCH: 1990-continuing

KEYWORDS: **values; youth leaders**

2337

School of Health and Community Studies, Collegiate Crescent, Sheffield S10 2BP
01142 720911

Morley, C. Ms; Hartley, P. Mr; *Supervisors*: Rosie, A. Dr; Bufton, S. Ms

How do social science undergraduate students experience the teaching of social theory?

ABSTRACT: The research began from the observation that social science undergraduate students find their social theory studies particularly demanding, but they often achieve their best marks in this field. Initial questions include: 1) Why do they do better in social theory than other subjects? 2) Is it simply because they work harder when they find it difficult? 3) Is it to do with the way it is taught? The final year (Year 3) course consists of a lecture, seminar and tutorial programme. A sample of students (n=8) were interviewed using semi-structured interviews and this data is being coded and analysed through grounded theory. A literature review is being prepared. The initial findings suggest that a key factor is the quality of tutorial provision including group tutorial work. The analysis is also likely to provide a way of developing and extending Jean Lane's analysis of social practice (Lane 1988, 1991, 1993) to provide a model with generalisability to higher education.

STATUS: Sponsored project

SOURCE OF GRANT: Sheffield Hallam University £3,000

DATE OF RESEARCH: 1997-1998

KEYWORDS: **higher education; social sciences; social theories**

2338

School of Health and Community Studies, Collegiate Crescent, Sheffield S10 2BP
01142 720911

Bufton, S. Ms; *Supervisors*: Ashworth, P. Prof.; Rosie, A. Dr; Sykes, R. Mr

Access students: the accessibility of higher education for the working class

ABSTRACT: This is a longitudinal, qualitative study of the experiences of former Access students in 3 institutions of higher education: an old and a new university, and a college of higher education. The central argument is that Access entrants to higher education form a distinct sub-group of mature students and that research is required to identify the nature of this distinctiveness. The experiences of Access students in higher education are being explored with particular emphasis on issues of identity and changes in identity. The central explanatory concept employed is that of disjunction and it is argued that Access students, who are more likely to be drawn from the working class than mature students generally, may experience serious problems of disjunction in higher education. The research seeks to explore the nature of any disjunction encountered and the experiences and feelings of the students as they progress through different types of higher education institution.

STATUS: Individual research

DATE OF RESEARCH: 1992-continuing

KEYWORDS: **access programmes; access to education; higher education; working class**

2339

School of Health and Community Studies, Collegiate Crescent, Sheffield S10 2BP
01142 720911

Monteith, M. Ms; Borre, S. Ms; Hojsholt-Poulsen, L. Mr

SISTER - Spatial Interface for Stimulation Education and Recreation

ABSTRACT: The Spatial Interface for Stimulation Education and Recreation (SISTER) project will investigate the potential of new technologies in early stage learning. The concept of a computer interface will be extended to include spatial interaction with position tracking and extensive use of sound. Children's activity will be away from the computer screen and into the classroom. The computer and network will act as sources for ideas and activities. This project is an early stage exploration of the potential in virtual reality (VR) based systems for pedagogical purposes. It will not focus on VR applications with helmets or gloves nor follow a cave design. It will apply simpler technology in the form of low cost, low precision tracking devices based on the instrumentation of a room and artefacts. Both laboratory testing and use with children in kindergartens/nursery schools will feed back to the development of the technology. There will be 3 pilot groups in Norway, Denmark and England where young children use this technology. All observations and measurements of activity and development of skills will be published as research papers on the Internet.

STATUS: Sponsored project

SOURCE OF GRANT: Esprit

DATE OF RESEARCH: 1998-continuing

KEYWORDS: **computer uses in education; early childhood education; virtual reality; young children**

2340

School of Health and Community Studies, Collegiate Crescent, Sheffield S10 2BP
01142 720911

Povey, H. Dr

Mathematics, social justice and teacher education

ABSTRACT: This is a follow-up to an earlier research project involving some of the original participants as case students. An action research account of an intervention with respect to gender on a mathematics Postgraduate Certificate in Education (PGCE) course in 1989-90. Two years after the intervention, 3 of the students (non teachers) who had been involved were interviewed, with a view to finding out what impact, if any, this had had on their beliefs, understandings, commitment and practice. A model of the ways of knowing of (non) teachers of mathematics was constructed and one epistemology, that based on the authority of self and reason, was linked to an emancipatory curriculum and to critical mathematics education. The implications for initial teacher education were considered briefly. The research was conducted as a praxis-oriented inquiry and both have been influenced by feminism, critical theory and post-modern tendencies. The project is continuing to analyse mathematics teaching and learning with a view to construing these activities in such a way as to make available their potential for emancipatory education. A particular emphasis on epistemology and the concept of authority. Also including a focus on information technology.

PUBLISHED MATERIAL: POVEY, H. (1995). Ways of knowing of student and beginning mathemamatics teachers and their relevance to becoming a teacher working for change. PhD Thesis. Birmingham: Birmingham University. ; POVEY, H. & BURTON, L. (1995). 'Working for change in teacher education: some steps for Monday morning'. In: BURTON, L. & JAWORSKI, (Eds). Technology in mathematics teaching: a bridge between teaching and learning. Bromley: Chartwell-Bratt. ; POVEY, H. & BURTON, L. (1996). 'Competency in the mathematics classroom - the example of equal opportunities'. In: HUSTLER, D. & MACINTYRE, D. (Eds). Developing competent teachers. London: David Fulton. ; POVEY, H. (1996). 'Constructing a liberatory discourse for mathematics classrooms', Mathematics Education Review, No 8.

STATUS: Individual research

DATE OF RESEARCH: 1990-continuing

KEYWORDS: **mathematics; preservice teacher education**

2341

School of Urban and Regional Studies, Pond Street, Sheffield S1 1WB
01142 720911
York University, Department of Educational Studies, Heslington, York
YO1 5DD
01904 430000

Grainger, N. Mr; *Supervisor*: Davies, I. Dr

The Europeanisation of higher education

ABSTRACT: A literature review has been undertaken of citizenship rights in Europe and educational issues. Preliminary questions included 'What are the rights and responsibilities of people working and/or studying at higher educational institutions in Europe?' This question leads to the issue - Are they the best? People have views on what their rights should be. The European Union view (or policies) is being sought from its documentation. The views of experts are being sought on European higher education exchanges, and also the views of some students and exchange coordinators, in the light of their experiences on exchanges, overseas placements etc. Following the above interviews or discussions, there would be an examination of implications for higher/vocational education and student goals and other matters relating to rights issues and the concepts of European citizenship.

STATUS: Individual research

DATE OF RESEARCH: 1993-continuing

KEYWORDS: **citizenship; europe; higher education; overseas employment; overseas students; student exchange programmes; study abroad**

2342

Survey and Statistical Research Centre, Collegiate Crescent, Sheffield
S10 2BP
01142 720911

Wallace, W. Mr

Survey of small awarding bodies

ABSTRACT: This is the fourth Survey of Small Awarding Bodies, the first being conducted in 1993. The main aim of the survey is to provide data to allow the coverage provided by the National Information System for Vocational Qualifications (NISVQ) database to be estimated. The survey was conducted by means of a postal questionnaire, with telephone follow-ups. Questionnaires were sent to a total of 349 organisations, identified from a database of awarding bodies maintained by the contractor. The survey asked for details of other vocational qualifications awarded (i.e. not National Vocational Qualification (NVQ) or General National Vocational

Qualification (GNVQ) during the period 1 October 1995 to 30 September 1996. A total of 168 questionnaires were returned and used in the analysis. The analysis indicated a total of 255,000 other vocational qualification (VQ) awards made by awarding bodies outside the NISVQ database. The conclusion of the survey was that there appeared to be approximately 250 awarding bodies who did not contribute to NISVQ, and the coverage of other VQs on NISVQ was approximately 55%.

STATUS: Sponsored project

SOURCE OF GRANT: Department for Education and Employment £6,340

DATE OF RESEARCH: 1996-1997

KEYWORDS: **awarding bodies; national information system for vocational qualifications; vocational qualifications**

Sheffield University
2343

Department of Psychology, Sheffield S10 2TN
01142 768555

Boulton, M. Dr; Laver, R. Ms; Cowie, H. Dr; *Supervisor*: Smith, P. Prof.

Prejudice, isolation and bullying: intervention in ethnically mixed classes

ABSTRACT: Research has shown that racial prejudice, social isolation and bullying are far from uncommon during the middle school period. In a previous one year Economic and Social Research Council (ESRC) funded project, the research team found that prejudice could be ameliorated to some extent, and liking of peers increased, in classes where teachers were trained in and used cooperative group work (CGW). The central feature of this approach is the opportunity to learn through the expression and exploration of diverse ideas and the cooperative solution of problems, in groups formed across ethnic and gender barriers. In the present project, the CGW curriculum was refined and more focused in some respects, based on previous experience. An attempt was made to replicate the positive results of the previous study, using both quantitative and qualitative methods. In general, while some positive results were obtained, the research demonstrated the difficulty of cooperative group work with rejected or bullying pupils.

PUBLISHED MATERIAL: BOULTON, M.J. & SMITH, P.K. (1991). 'Bullying and withdrawn children'. In: VARMA, V.P. (Ed). Truants from life: theory and therapy. London: David Fulton. ; COWIE, H., BOULTON, M.J. & SMITH, P.K. (1992). 'Bullying: pupil relationships'. In: JONES, N. & JONES, E.B. (Eds). Learning to behave: curriculum and whole school management approaches to discipline. London: Kogan Page. ; COWIE, H., SMITH, P.K., BOULTON, M. & LAVER, R. (1994). Cooperation in the multi-ethnic classroom. London: David Fulton. ; SMITH, P.K., COWIE, H. & BERDONDINI, L. (1995). 'Cooperation and bullying'. In: KUTNICK, P. & ROGERS, C. (Eds). Groups in schools. Poole: Cassell.

STATUS: Sponsored project

SOURCE OF GRANT: Economic and Social Research Council £82,496

DATE OF RESEARCH: 1990-1993

KEYWORDS: **bullying; cooperation; ethnic relations; intergroup relations; intervention; middle school education; pupil behaviour; social isolation**

2344

Department of Psychology, Sheffield S10 2TN
01142 768555

Smith, P. Prof.; Sharp, S. Ms; Ahmad, Y. Ms; Boulton, M. Dr; Cowie, H. Dr; Thompson, D. Dr

The DFE Sheffield Bullying Project: a follow up survey on bully/victim problems in one local education authority with monitoring and evaluation of the actions and interventions taken as a result of the survey

ABSTRACT: The Department for Education (DFE) Sheffield Bullying Project aims to identify through evaluation, ways in which schools can effectively tackle the problem of bullying. The project follows on from a survey which took place in November 1990 which monitored the nature and extent of bullying in 24 Sheffield schools (number of pupils = 6,758). Twenty three of these schools, (16 primary, 7 secondary) wished to continue with the intervention project. All of the schools have at a minimum developed a whole school anti-bullying policy which clarifies for staff, pupils and parents what bullying is and what can be done about it. Other interventions have also been explored. These include strategies for tackling bullying through the curriculum; strategies for working directly with bullies and victims; and strategies for enhancing the playground environment. Data gathered through regular monitoring, pupil and staff interviews and observation were combined with information gathered from a follow-up survey in November 1992 to indicate how successful schools have been in reducing levels of bullying, and which interventions work best. Results were encouraging with a substantial reduction in bullying in most schools. A Pack resulting from the project findings has been disseminated widely by the Department for Education.

PUBLISHED MATERIAL: SHARP, S. & SMITH, P.K. (1991). 'Bullying in UK schools: the DES Sheffield Bullying Project', Early Child Development Care, No 77, pp.47-55. ; COWIE, H. & SHARP, S. (1992). 'Students themselves tackle the problem of bullying', Pastoral Care in Education, Vol 10, No 4, pp.31-37. ; COWIE, H., SHARP, S. & SMITH, P.K. (1992). 'Tackling bullying in schools: the method of common concern', Education Section Review, Vol 16, No 2, pp.55-57. ; SHARP, S. & SMITH, P.K. (1993). 'Tackling bullying in the Sheffield Project'. In: TATTUM, D. (Ed). Understanding and managing bullying. London: Heinemann. ; SHARP, S. & SMITH, P.K. (Eds). (1994). Tackling bullying in your school: a practical handbook for teachers. London: Routledge.

STATUS: Sponsored project

SOURCE OF GRANT: Department for Education £173,972

DATE OF RESEARCH: 1991-1993

KEYWORDS: **antisocial behaviour; behaviour problems; bullying; discipline; discipline policy; pupil behaviour**

2345

Department of Psychology, Sheffield S10 2TN
01142 768555

Fawcett, A. Dr; *Supervisor*: Nicolson, R. Prof.

Interactive teaching assistant in reading for dyslexic children and adults

ABSTRACT: The difficulty confronting designers of reading remediation schemes for dyslexics is that of devising a scheme that is both effective and cost-effective. It would appear from attempts to date that simple approaches are not effective (and hence not cost-effective). There are effective approaches, but these require extended support from a highly trained professional. Consequently, though such schemes are justifiable in terms of the 'stitch in time' principle, they are inevitably very costly and hence not viable for the large-scale support needed. The solution proposed is to use computer-based methods to streamline and automate the various training processes, and to develop an 'Interactive Teaching Assistant' (ITA) to provide an integrated package. Standard approaches have shown the success of computer-based teaching methods for dyslexic children; with an 'intelligent tutoring system' a computer program is able to orchestrate the various aspects of computer-based training; however we suggest that it is usually both better and cheaper to develop an ITA which supports, rather than replaces, the teacher. We name the proposed ITA for reading RITA - Readers' Interactive Teaching Assistant. The overall project design involves the construction of a prototype integrated reading skills environment for 10-50 year olds. The system will be tested with 2 very different groups of users; dyslexic students identified via our adult screening test and 10-15 year old dyslexic children who have already participated in the theoretical research programme.

PUBLISHED MATERIAL: NICOLSON, R.I. & FAWCETT, A.J. (1997). 'Development of objective procedures for screening and assessment of dyslexic students in higher education', Journal of Research in Reading, Vol 20, No 1, pp.77-83. ; NICOLSON, R.I. & FAWCETT, A.J. (1997). Towards the construction of RITA, a Readers' Interactive Teaching Assistant. Abstracts of the British Dyslexia Association, 25th Anniversary Conference, York, 1997. ; FAWCETT, A.J. & NICOLSON, R.I. 'Learning disabilities in adults: screening and diagnosis in the UK'. In: VOGEL, S. & REDER, S. (Eds). Bridging the gap, learning disabilities, literacy and adult education. (in press).

STATUS: Sponsored project

SOURCE OF GRANT: Leverhulme Trust £97,000

DATE OF RESEARCH: 1995-1997

KEYWORDS: **computer assisted learning; computer assisted reading; computer uses in education; dyslexia; information technology; reading; reading difficulties**

2346

Department of Psychology, Sheffield S10 2TN
01142 768555
Manchester University, School of Education, Oxford Road, Manchester M13 9PL
0161 275 2000

Moss, H. Ms; Nicolson, M. Mrs; *Supervisors*: Fawcett, A. Dr; Reason, R. Dr

Systematic identification and remediation for reading difficulty

ABSTRACT: Literacy underpins education. There is now widespread concern over the standards of literacy in UK schools, particularly for children with special educational needs. Research evidence suggests that the earlier children with special needs can be identified, the more effective (and cost-effective) intervention will be, provided that the intervention is tailored to the child's abilities and skills. The authors have between them developed systematic procedures for identifying children at risk for reading difficulty, together with systematic teaching strategies to overcome reading difficulty. The Readers Interactive Teaching Assistant (RITA) system (developed by the Sheffield group) uses a computer to augment and support traditional teaching methods, and has as its teaching methodology the Interactive Assessment and Teaching (IA&T) system developed by the Manchester group. This research adapts the approach to young children, and will evaluate the effectiveness of 2 interventions (RITA and IA&T alone) compared with standard classroom approaches to literacy development. In a study to investigate the effectivness of IA&T, 62 at-risk children were supported in groups of 4 twice-weekly over 10 weeks, with the emphasis on word building and phonics skills. The intervention proved effective, with a mean improvement in reading standard score for the trained group, compared with a deterioration for the controls. 88% of the 'problem readers' (children whose reading after training was still at least 6 months behind) had 'at risk' or 'borderline risk' scores on the Dyslexia Early Sreening Test (DEST) compared with only 28% of the 'recovered readers', indicating that the DEST provides a valuable predictive index not only of reading failure, but also of those children likely to need specialist support.

PUBLISHED MATERIAL: NICOLSON, R.I. & FAWCETT, A.J. (1997). 'Development of objective procedures for screening and assessment of dyslexic students in higher education', Journal of Research in Reading, Vol 20, No 1, pp.77-83. ; NICOLSON, R.I. & FAWCETT, A.J. (1997). Towards the construction of RITA, a Readers' Interactive Teaching Assistant. Abstracts of the British Dyslexia Assocation, 25th Anniversary Conference, York, 1997. ; FAWCETT, A.J. & NICOLSON, R.I. 'Learning disabilities in adults: screening and diagnosis in the UK'. In: VOGEL, S. & REDER, S. (Eds). Bridging the gap, learning disabilities, literacy and adult education. (in press).

STATUS: Sponsored project

SOURCE OF GRANT: Nuffield Foundation £70,000

DATE OF RESEARCH: 1998-continuing

KEYWORDS: **computer assisted learning; computer assisted reading; computer uses in education; diagnostic assessment; information technology; intervention; literacy; reading; reading difficulties**

2347

Department of Psychology, Sheffield S10 2TN
01142 768555
Tapton Mount School for the Blind, 20 Manchester Road, Sheffield S10 5DG
01142 667151

Spencer, C. Dr; Blades, M. Dr; Ungar, S. Mr

Evaluation of mobility education for young blind children

ABSTRACT: The researchers' previous work on the education for mobility of the visually handicapped has included: (1) development of spatial concepts; (2) the hierarchy of skills underlying successful mobility; (3) the evaluation of experimental programmes to improve aspects of training; and (4) the evaluation of tactile maps in learning a novel area. One such project - on the parental approach to independence and mobility skills for children prior to school - has led the researchers to embark upon the present project, which will study children through the years prior to entry to blind school, and their first few years of formal mobility training within the school. Research will be conducted in conjunction with Tapton Mount, the special school for the visually handicapped in Yorkshire and surrounding counties. The aim is to plan and test mobility training programmes designed to develop the child's techniques for (1) acquiring and storing knowledge of spatial layout; (2) updating one's position within a locale; and (3) applying systems of spatial concepts to plan routes. In 1994 and Economic an Social Research Council (ESRC) grant will extend this work into the training of blind adults.

PUBLISHED MATERIAL: BLADES, M. & SPENCER, C.P. (1990). 'The development of 3-6 year olds' map using ability: the relative importance of landmarks and map alignment', Journal of Genetic Psychology, No 151, pp.181-194. ; MORSLEY, K., SPENCER, C.P. & BAYBUTT, K. (1991). ' Is there any relationship between a child's body image and spatial skills? British Journal of Visual Impairment, No 9, pp.41-43. ; MORSLEY, K., SPENCER, C.P. & BAYBUTT, K. (1991). 'Two techniques for encouraging movement and exploration in the visually impaired child', British Journal of Visual Impairment, No 9, pp.75-78. ; SPEMCER, C., MORSLEY, K., UNGAR, S., PIKE, E. & BLADES, M. (1992). 'Developing the blind child's cognition of the environment: the role of direct experience and map given experience', Geoforum, No 23, pp.191-197.

STATUS: Sponsored project

SOURCE OF GRANT: Economic and Social Research Council

DATE OF RESEARCH: 1990-1993

KEYWORDS: **blindness; mobility aids; visual impairments; visually handicapped mobility**

2348

Division of Adult Continuing Education, 196-198 West Street, Sheffield S1 4ET
01142 768555

Hunt, C. Mrs

The philosophy and practice of community education, using Derbyshire as a case study

ABSTRACT: Various models have been devised to make sense of the variety of ideologies, interests and outcomes encompassed by the notion of community education (CE). This research draws together and examines some of these models as they are reflected in the practice of one local authority: Derbyshire. In 1987, the County Council introduced a unique and comprehensive CE policy which attempted to develop CE through both schools and local communities. Not only were more than 100 new professional appointments made, but 37 local community education councils (CECs) were set up. Each of these comprised over 30 'lay' members to whom collective responsibility for administering a substantial budget was devolved. Within 6 years however, as a result of legislative and linked financial changes, the majority of the professional posts had been disestablished, the delivery of CE had been reorganised twice and the CECs were in disarray. This research attempts to document and analyse the 'Derbyshire CE experience' by drawing on the words of practitioners and participants wherever possible. It takes a 'grounded theory' approach and seeks to find 'the consequential in the inconsequential', while operating within an ethical framework which emphasises research 'with' rather than 'on' people.

STATUS: Sponsored project

SOURCE OF GRANT: Nuffield Foundation £3,000

DATE OF RESEARCH: 1990-1997

KEYWORDS: **adult education; community education**

2349

Division of Adult Continuing Education, 196-198 West Street, Sheffield S1 4ET
01142 768555

Fang, X. Ms; *Supervisor*: Hampton, W. Prof.

Going into the sea: the relationship of socio-economic developments and changes to the developments and changes in the education and training of adults in China and the UK, with comparative aspects in Hong Kong (1978-1996)

ABSTRACT: By using qualitative methodology, mainly through documentary analysis supported by a large number of semi-structured interviews, this study explores the relationship of socio-economic developments and changes to the developments and changes in the education and training of adults in China, the UK and Hong Kong. The study argues that, as with other aspects of education, the education and training of adults can never be developed in isolation but always reflects, and is influenced by, socio-economic development and changes. On the one hand, socio-economic development and changes are driving forces for the development in the education and training of adults. On the other hand, in response to changes in the socio-economic context, management models for the education and training of adults will change. The study suggests that such management models can be illustrated as a triangle with orientations towards the 3 corners, that is, academic, planning and market orientations. The main finding of the study is that, despite their differences, the management models for the education and training of adults in the 2 countries and the region of Hong Kong, in various degrees, are moving together towards the market orientation because of the movement of international privatisation since the late 1970s. However, they will not move to the top position of the market orientation, but will continue to be a mixture of the 3 orientations.

PUBLISHED MATERIAL: PAN, M. & FANG, X. (1993). 'The prsent status of continuing education in China'. Paper presented at the International Conference on Developments in Continuing Education: an East-West Perspective, Hong Kong, November 1993. ; FANG, X. (1995). 'Adult education in China'. Paper given at the International Conference in Adult Continuing Education, Hungary, September 1995. ; FANG, X. (1996). 'British NVQ (National Vocational Qualifications)', Higher Education Abroad, No 1. ; FANG, X. (1996). 'Changes in British university adult education'. In: ZUKAS, M. (Ed). Diversity and development: futures in the education of adults: Proceedings of the 26th Annual SCUTREA Conference, University of Leeds 1996. Leeds: University of Leeds, Department of Adult Education.

STATUS: Individual research

DATE OF RESEARCH: 1993-1997

KEYWORDS: **adult education; china; comparative education; hong kong; training**

2350

Division of Education, 388 Glossop Road, Sheffield S10 2JA
01142 768555

Wiltsher, C. Mr; *Supervisor*: Carr, W. Prof.

The concept of education in higher education in England 1960-1996 with particular reference to adult continuing education

ABSTRACT: During the period 1960-1996, higher education in England has undergone many changes. In the same period, extra-mural provision by universities, now called adult continuing education, has also changed. Most of the changes have occurred in response to external pressures. This study seeks to discover whether the concept(s) of education used in universities and adult continuing education departments, implicitly or explicitly, has (have) changed too and, if so, in what ways. One part of the study will aim to analyse the concept(s) of education found in public documents such as government papers, The Robbins Report, papers from the Committee of Vice Chancellors and Principals (CVCP) and similar bodies, and policy documents produced by universities and appropriate departments. Any general view emerging will then be tested in a case study of the University of Sheffield and its adult provision.

STATUS: Individual research

DATE OF RESEARCH: 1995-1998

KEYWORDS: **adult education; continuing education; educational history; extension education; higher education; universities**

2351

Division of Education, 388 Glossop Road, Sheffield S10 2JA
01142 768555

Calvert, M. Mr; *Supervisor*: Quicke, J. Prof.

Personal and Social Education teaching and staff development: a suitable case for treatment?

ABSTRACT: Pastoral care is a particularly problematic area. Within it the teaching of Personal and Social Education (PSE) is extremely difficult to manage, deliver and evaluate. There is a common picture of ill-prepared, poorly resourced and reluctant teachers who are required to teach the subject. The research focuses on the impact that staff development can make to what many would argue is an important aspect of the curriculum. It will need to embrace a number of bibliographies: staff development, pastoral care, school effectiveness, school improvement, personal bibliographies and management of change. It will involve investigating such areas as: models of PSE provision, models of staff development, management models and evaluating change. The researcher will use qualitative data from interviews and work closely with schools that are undertaking staff development work in this area. The research will identify strategies for staff development in the context of whole school effectiveness.

PUBLISHED MATERIAL: CALVERT, M. & HENDERSON, J. (1994). 'Newly qualified teachers: do we prepare them for their pastoral role?', Pastoral Care in Education, Vol 12, No 2, pp.7-12. ; CALVERT, M. & HENDERSON, J. (1995). 'Leading the team: managing pastoral care in the secondary setting'. In: BELL, J. & HARRISON, B.T. (Eds). Visions and values in managing education: successful leadership principles and practice. London: David Fulton.

STATUS: Individual research

DATE OF RESEARCH: 1994-continuing

KEYWORDS: pastoral care - education; personal and social education; secondary education; teacher development

2352

Division of Education, 388 Glossop Road, Sheffield S10 2JA
01142 768555
Leeds University, School of Education, Leeds LS2 9JT
01132 431751

Rudduck, J. Prof.; Taggart, L. Ms

Gender and equal opportunities in secondary schools

ABSTRACT: The aim of the research was to identify secondary schools in urban areas which were seen to be making progress with gender at a whole-school level. Interviews were conducted with teachers (and, in some settings, with pupils) in five 'case study' schools, and with a range of teachers and advisors outside those schools whose experience was relevant to the concerns of the research. The report presents the stories told by different 'gender leaders' who took the initiative in developing a whole-school gender policy; yet also offers four profiles of different ways into the task of building a gender policy. The various threads are drawn together in one full study of the progress made - and the problems encountered - in one comprehensive school over a three year period. Major themes of the report are the tension between the individual in the institution and between accommodation and resistance.

PUBLISHED MATERIAL: HARRIS, S. & RUDDUCK, J. (1991). Keeping gender on the agenda: a portfolio of material for students. Sheffield: University of Sheffield, Division of Education, QQSE Research Group. ; RUDDUCK, J. (1993). Developing a gender policy in secondary schools. Milton Keynes: Open University Press.

STATUS: Sponsored project

SOURCE OF GRANT: British Petroleum £38,000

DATE OF RESEARCH: 1990-1993

KEYWORDS: equal education; gender equality; school policy; secondary education; whole school approach

Social and Community Planning Research

2353

35 Northampton Square, London EC1V OAX
0171 250 1866

Courtenay, G. Ms; Hedges, B. Mr

England and Wales youth cohort study (YCS)

ABSTRACT: The youth cohort study (YCS) now spans a decade. The first YCS survey was designed in 1984, and developed out of earlier work, in particular the Scottish School Leavers Survey (then carried out by the Centre for Educational Sociology at Edinburgh University), and the Sheffield and Bradford Pilot Study (carried out by the Division of Education at Sheffield University). The research is primarily about transitions and change. It focuses on young people's activities after compulsory education. It is about the transition from school to further (then higher) education, or to the labour market. It seeks to identify and explain the factors that influence the transitions (for example, educational attainment, training opportunities, experiences at school). The YCS is funded by the Department for Education and Employment (DfEE). It is designed and administered by the Social and Community Planning Research (SCPR), who are also responsible for the preliminary reports on each cohort, and for much of the methodological work arising from (and contributing to) the surveys. In addition to the YCS reporting undertaken by SCPR, there is a parallel 'academic work programme' in which the funding departments specify substantive topics of interest for reports. From 1984-1993 this reporting was done by the Division of Education at Sheffield University. Since then, the academic work programme has been carried out by the Policy Studies Institute (PSI). Other universities and institutions have also contributed to this work programme (for example, the Institute of Employment Research at Warwick University). The first YCS cohort was surveyed in 1985, and the most recent in 1994. The research covers seven cohorts and over twenty surveys, with a considerably larger number of reports on a wide range of topics. The questionnaires have been designed, over the ten years of the YCS, to be broadly comparable, but external changes and shifts in areas of policy interest have brought about changes - some minor, others fundamental. There are various reports on separate surveys within each cohort published by the Department of Employment in their Research Series.

STATUS: Sponsored project

SOURCE OF GRANT: Department for Education and Employment

DATE OF RESEARCH: 1984-continuing

KEYWORDS: cohort analysis; further education; school leavers; school to work transition; sixteen to nineteen education; vocational education; youth; youth cohort study; youth employment

2354

35 Northampton Square, London EC1V OAX
0171 250 1866

Lynn, P. Mr; Taylor, S. Mr

Scottish school-leavers survey (SSLS)

ABSTRACT: The Scottish Office Education Department has sponsored surveys of school leavers since the early 1970's. Throughout the 1980's these were known as the Scottish Young Persons Survey (SYPS), but following a review of the use made of the findings, the survey was redesigned in 1991 and became the Scottish School Leavers Survey (SSLS). The survey obtains information on the educational and employment activities of young people after they leave school, as well as background characteristics, such as parents' level of education and social class, family circumstances, and housing tenure. Since 1994, the survey has also included questions about experiences at school. The survey data is then linked with information on school qualifications obtained from the Scottish Examination Board (SEB) and Scottish Vocational Educational Council (SCOTVEC). The resultant data set is used by the survey contractor (Social and Community Planning Research) to write reports, by SOED for policy purposes, and is available to the wider research community via the Economic and Social Research Council (ESRC) data archive. The SSLS has two components - an annual survey of leavers, and a follow-up survey of an age cohort. The survey of leavers, carried out each spring (1993, 1994, 1995, 1996, 1997 etc) involves a 10% sample of those who had left school in the previous academic session, who may have left from S4 aged 16, from S5 aged 16 or 17, or from S6 aged 17 or 18. Only pupils with special educational needs are excluded. The first follow-up survey was carried out in 1995, based on a sample of people who entered S4 in autumn 1991, many of whom had already been included in the 1993 or 1994 leavers' surveys. The surveys are carried out by post, using self-completion booklets, with response rates of around 75% (though qualifications, along with sex, school type, region and stage of leaving are known for 100% of the sample). Sample size is around 4,000 per survey.

PUBLISHED MATERIAL: LYNN, P. (1994). The Scottish school-leavers survey: the 1992 leavers. Edinburgh: Scottish Office Education Department.;

LYNN, P. & FARRANT, G. (1994). The Scottish School-leavers Survey Series: 1993 Leavers Survey, Technical Report. London: Social and Community Planning Research. ; LYNN, P. & PURDON, S. (1994). 'An analysis of factors affecting response to a postal survey of young people. Paper presented to the International Conference of the Royal Statistical Society, Newcastle upon Tyne, September 1994. ; LYNN, P. (1995). The Scottish school-leavers survey: the 1993 leavers. Edinburgh: Scottish Office Education Department. ; LYNN, P. The Scottish school-leavers survey: the 1994 leavers. Edinburgh: Scottish Office Education Department. (in press).

STATUS: Sponsored project

SOURCE OF GRANT: Scottish Office Education Department; Department of Employment, jointly £75,000 per annum

DATE OF RESEARCH: 1992-continuing

KEYWORDS: **cohort analysis; further education; school leavers; school to work transition; sixteen to nineteen education; surveys; youth employment**

2355

35 Northampton Square, London EC1V 0AX
0171 250 1866

Field, J. Ms; Sproston, K. Ms

Study of the career paths of postgraduate students funded by the research councils

ABSTRACT: The Research Councils have commissioned the Social and Community Planning Research (SCPR) to carry out a study of the career paths of former postgraduate students whose funding terminated in one of two years: 1987-88, and 1988-89. The Research Councils comprise: Engineering and Physical Science Research Council (ESPRC), Biotechnology and Biological Sciences Research Council (BBSRC), Natural Environment Research Council (NERC), Natural Environment Research Council (NERC), Particle Physics and Astronomy Research Council (PPARC) and the Medical Research Council (MRC) from the Research Councils' records of awards, a representative sample of research and advanced course students has been randomly selected. The selected sample consists of 3,800 former postgraduates from about 120 different higher education institutions throughout the UK. Initially, institutions will be approached to provide the most recent known addresses of sample members, then a 20-page questionnaire will be sent to the former students, asking about their views and attitudes towards their postgraduate study, and collecting details of jobs since Research Council funding ended.

STATUS: Sponsored project

SOURCE OF GRANT: The Research Councils and the Office of Science and Technology

DATE OF RESEARCH: 1996-1997

KEYWORDS: **careers; followup studies; graduate surveys; higher education; students**

2356

35 Northampton Square, London EC1V 0AX
0171 250 1866

Beinart, S. Ms; Smith, P. Dr

Continuous adult learning survey

ABSTRACT: This is the first of a series of Department for Education and Employment (DfEE) sponsored surveys designed to monitor levels and types of learning undertaken by the adult population of Britain. Six thousand 1-hour interviews are being conducted with a random sample of adults aged between 16 and 69. Computer assisted personal interviewing (CAPI) methods are being used throughout. Results will be analysed and reported on during the summer of 1997.

STATUS: Sponsored project

SOURCE OF GRANT: Department for Education and Employment

DATE OF RESEARCH: 1996-1997

KEYWORDS: **adult education; adult learning; adults; continuing education; lifelong learning; training**

2357

35 Northampton Square, London EC1V 0AX
0171 250 1866

Finch, S. Mr

Youth Cohort Study A-level data matching

ABSTRACT: The aim of the project was to match the GCE A/AS examination results obtained from the Youth Cohort Study (YCS), Cohort 7 Sweep 2 (England only) with the corresponding information held in the University of Bath qualifications database. The Social and Community Planning Research (SCPR) took the matched file from the University of Bath and then incorporated this back into the YCS database. The Bath database includes both Winter 1995 and Summer 1996 A/AS results. These were matched to the YCS survey of 18/19 year-olds in Spring 1996. The specific objectives of the project were to: 1) add the A/AS matched data to all existing Cohort 7 Sweep 2 databases; 2) update analyses previously carried out using A/AS results; 3) investigate the extent and pattern of under and over reporting of A/AS results in the YCS; 4) investigate attrition between Sweeps 1 and 2 by the number of A/AS levels.

STATUS: Sponsored project

SOURCE OF GRANT: Department for Education and Employment £2,300

DATE OF RESEARCH: 1998-1998

KEYWORDS: **a level examinations; cohort analysis; examination results; school leavers; school to work transition; sixteen to nineteen education; training; vocational education; youth; youth cohort study; youth employment**

2358

35 Northampton Square, London EC1V 0AX
0171 250 1866

Finch, S. Mr

Youth Cohort Study database manipulation and enhancement

ABSTRACT: The aim is to improve the Youth Cohort Study data held by the Department for Education and Employment (DfEE). It will increase the flexibility of the Department's Quanvert database by adding more variables. This will improve particularly the information on qualifications. The Quanvert database has the variables needed to do the more common data requests. However the demands on it are becoming increasingly varied and require a more flexible approach to looking at the data. In particular, much of the qualifications data are available in summary form only. There is a continuing need to supply data to tight deadlines and the Quanvert database allows this. The work will consist primarily of programming new variables for Cohorts 5-8 and providing documentation for these. There will be only a small number of variables for the earlier Cohorts (1-4).

STATUS: Sponsored project

SOURCE OF GRANT: Department for Education and Employment £1,900

DATE OF RESEARCH: 1998-1998

KEYWORDS: **cohort analysis; databases; qualifications; youth cohort study**

2359

35 Northampton Square, London EC1V 0AX
0171 250 1866

Finch, S. Mr

Youth Cohort Study estimates of independent further education (FE)

ABSTRACT: The aim was to improve the quality of information on the type of educational establishment attended by young people in Cohort 8 Sweep 1 of the Youth Cohort Study (YCS). Coverage is for England only. Within the YCS respondents were asked to tick a box for the type of educational establishment which they attended at the time of the survey. They were also asked to write in the name and address of the establishment. The project matched these names and addresses with the Department for Education and Employment's (DfEE) register of educational establishments to create: 1) an alternative list of educational establishments; 2) a 'best estimate' of establishment type using data from both the tick boxes and the match; 3) an embryo list of presumed independent colleges. This will inform estimates of the proportion of young people in independent colleges. It will also allow an assessment of the quality of the data regularly collected in the YCS on educational establishment and allow us to plan improvements to the next Cohort's questionnaires. The matching exercise was successful, with 94% of valid responses being matched.

STATUS: Sponsored project

SOURCE OF GRANT: Department for Education and Employment £5,940

DATE OF RESEARCH: 1997-1998

KEYWORDS: cohort analysis; colleges of further education; further education; independent colleges; sixteen to nineteen education; training; vocational education; youth; youth cohort study

2360

35 Northampton Square, London EC1V 0AX
0171 250 1866

Finch, S. Mr

Youth Cohort Study data access service

ABSTRACT: The Youth Cohort Study (YCS) is a Department for Education and Employment (DfEE) funded programme of longitudinal surveys of young people in England and Wales to look at their education, training and labour market experience in the first two and a half years following the completion of compulsory education. The Data Access Service was a contract with the Social and Community Planning Research (SCPR), who were also responsible for the design and administration of the surveys. Requests for YCS information were received from various sources, and those which were too complex to be dealt with by the DfEE were then passed on to SCPR, who hold the data from the YCS surveys in a large database. The analysis was carried out by their programmers, which were sent back to the Youth and Further Education division at DfEE. Previous data access requests have included attainment of those in full-time education by the number of A/AS levels studied and educational institution attended.

STATUS: Sponsored project

SOURCE OF GRANT: Department for Education and Employment £20,000

DATE OF RESEARCH: 1996-1997

KEYWORDS: a level examinations; cohort analysis; examination results; school leavers; school to work transition; sixteen to nineteen education; training; youth; youth cohort study; youth employment

2361

35 Northampton Square, London EC1V 0AX
0171 250 1866

Hales, J. Mr; Smith, P. Mr

Youth Cohort Study Cohort 7 Sweep 2

ABSTRACT: This survey collected data from a sample of 18 year-olds who were first contacted 2 years earlier when they were 16. The survey provides information about their education, training and labour market experiences since they were last surveyed, and the qualifications that they have gained. Data about socio-demographic characteristics such as ethnic origin, socio-economic groups, living arrangements and parental background are also collected. The survey covered about 13,000 young people in England and Wales. As well as information about the current activities of 18 year-olds, the data from this survey, when combined with that collected 2 years earlier, provides a comprehensive picture of the experiences of young people in the first two and a half years since leaving compulsory education and links this to GCSE attainment at school.

STATUS: Sponsored project

SOURCE OF GRANT: Department for Education and Employment £137,983

DATE OF RESEARCH: 1995-1998

KEYWORDS: cohort analysis; examination results; general certificate of secondary education; school leavers; school to work transition; sixteen to nineteen education; training; vocational education; youth; youth cohort study; youth employment

2362

35 Northampton Square, London EC1V 0AX
0171 250 1866

Finch, S. Mr

Youth Cohort Study - Cohort 9 Sweep 1 (16 year olds)

ABSTRACT: The survey provides data for England and Wales which are representative of the 16/17 age cohort to inform policy in relation to young people's education, training and the transition to the labour market. The main objective is to map the current whereabouts of young people in a way that captures the full range of education, training and labour market activities they are engaged in. It will record the activities young people have been engaged in since leaving compulsory education and monitor the extent and usefulness of careers provision received. Data is also collected on qualifications studied and gained, occupation, working hours and earnings of jobs. New questions for Cohort 9 include disability, attitudes and exclusions from school. Cohort 9 Sweep 1 will be a postal survey of 22,500 young people covering England and Wales, with a telephone interview supplement to boost response. It will cover young people in the first year after they are eligible to have left school, who will therefore be aged 16/17. It will involve postal questionnaires and reminders. Those not responding to reminders will, where possible, be contacted by telephone with the offer of a telephone interview. Fieldwork will take place between February and June 1998.

STATUS: Sponsored project

SOURCE OF GRANT: Department for Education and Employment £203,221

DATE OF RESEARCH: 1997-1998

KEYWORDS: attitudes; cohort analysis; qualifications; school leavers; school to work transition; sixteen to nineteen education; training; vocational education; youth; youth cohort study; youth employment

2363

35 Northampton Square, London EC1V 0AX
0171 250 1866

Hales, J. Mr; Smith, P. Mr

Youth Cohort Study Cohort 8 Inter-Sweep contact letter

ABSTRACT: The Youth Cohort Study (YCS) is a longitudinal programme of surveys. Under its current design, young people are first surveyed some 8 months after leaving compulsory education, when they are 16, and followed up again 2 years later when they are 18. Cohort 8 was started in 1996 with a survey of 16 year-olds. This project aimed to re-contact the Cohort 8 sample, to retain their interest and collect details of any change of address, in order to maximise the likely response rate to the second sweep. Young people were sent a newsletter of interesting YCS findings and a change of address return postcard. Only young people who responded to the first sweep were contacted.

STATUS: Sponsored project

SOURCE OF GRANT: Department for Education and Employment £7,900

DATE OF RESEARCH: 1997-1997

KEYWORDS: cohort analysis; school leavers; school to work transition; sixteen to nineteen education; training; vocational education; youth; youth cohort study; youth employment

2364

35 Northampton Square, London EC1V 0AX
0171 250 1866

Prior, G. Ms

Survey of parents of 3 and 4 year olds

ABSTRACT: A national survey of parents of 3 and 4 year-old children is being undertaken in Spring 1998 to measure participation in preschool education and childcare. This survey will be compared with a baseline survey conducted in Spring 1997. Face-to-face interviews with 4,284 parents of children who were 3 and 4 in the Summer and Autumn terms 1997 and Spring term 1998.

STATUS: Sponsored project

SOURCE OF GRANT: Department for Education and Employment £188,161

DATE OF RESEARCH: 1997-1998

KEYWORDS: day care; early childhood education; nursery education; parents; preschool education

2365

35 Northampton Square, London EC1V 0AX
0171 250 1866

Finch, S. Mr; Stratford, N. Ms; Pethick, J. Ms

Survey of parents of 3 and 4 year olds: national baseline study for early years provision

ABSTRACT: A national baseline survey has been conducted amongst parents of 3 and 4 year-olds, prior to the national introduction of early years services. Results of this survey will be compared with future surveys, in later years, to identify any changes in levels and patterns of participation in early years provision amongst these age groups. A Face-to-face interview survey with 8,800 parents of 3 and 4 year-old children was conducted in March 1997. Key finding was that participation in nursery education amongst 4 year-olds was 91% and amongst 3 year-olds 88%.

PUBLISHED MATERIAL: STRATFORD, N., FINCH, S. & PETHICK, J. (1997). Survey of parents of three and four year old children and their use of early years services. DFEE Research Report RR 31. London: Department for Education and Employment.

STATUS: Sponsored project

SOURCE OF GRANT: Department for Education and Employment £257,651

DATE OF RESEARCH: 1996-1997

KEYWORDS: day care; early childhood education; nursery education; parents; preschool education

2366

35 Northampton Square, London EC1V 0AX
0171 250 1866

Nove, A. Ms; Snape, D. Ms; Chetwynd, M. Mr

Advancing by degrees: a study of graduate recruitment and skills utilisation

ABSTRACT: This study focuses on the extent to which the skills of new, and reasonably new, graduates are being fully used in different sectors of the economy. It investigates the extent to which it causes - or results from - a change in the nature of work. The report includes some information on early graduate career development.

PUBLISHED MATERIAL: NOVE, A., SNAPE, A. & CHETWYND, M. (1998). 'Advancing by Degrees', Labour Market Trends, Vol 106, No 4, pp.167-170.

STATUS: Sponsored project

SOURCE OF GRANT: Department for Education and Employment £ 92,741

DATE OF RESEARCH: 1996-1997

KEYWORDS: graduate employment; graduates; job skills; labour market

Somerset County Council

2367

Education Development Service, Keats Road, Taunton TA1 2JB
01823 330574
University College of St Mark and St John, Derriford Road, Plymouth PL6 8BH
01752 777188
Exeter University, School of Education, St Luke's, Heavitree Road, Exeter EX1 2LU
01392 263263

Whiteley, A. Mr; Jordan, R. Mr; *Supervisor*: Hughes, M. Prof.; Rolph, P. Dr

Class size/small schools

ABSTRACT: Somerset Local Education Authority (LEA) is working with the University College of St Mark and St John, Plymouth, and the University of Exeter on a collaborative research project aimed, ultimately, at supporting and improving small primary schools. The aims are: 1) To identify key factors conducive to a partnership between the LEA and groups of small primary schools. 2) To develop and evaluate policy initiatives aimed at improving small schools. 3) To consider appropriate ways of measuring effectiveness. 4) To identify processes through which improvement may be initiated and sustained. 5) To identify key factors influencing the effectiveness of small schools (such as funding and deployment of resources).

DATE OF RESEARCH: 1995-continuing

KEYWORDS: class size; local education authorities; primary education; school effectiveness; school size; small schools

South Bank University

2368

School of Computing, Information Systems and Mathematics, 103 Borough Road, London SE1 OAA
0171 928 8989

Walker, K. Mr; *Supervisor*: Lerman, S. Dr

A socio-historical study of the development of individualized learning schemes in mathematics education, with particular reference to the Secondary Mathematics Individualized Learning Experiment (SMILE)

ABSTRACT: The aims of the curriculum study are to document the historical development of individualized learning schemes in mathematics education, with particular reference to the Secondary Mathematics Individualized Learning Experiment (SMILE) in its social setting. The major objective of the project is the publication of a book, and associated papers, discussing the results of the research. This book will include: 1) What is SMILE? - an examination of the resources, methods and activities associated with the SMILE scheme. 2) The context of SMILE - a re-examination of developments in British mathematics education 1900-1972 from the perspective of individualized learning. 3) The Kent mathematics project. 4) The start of SMILE (the first 5 years). 5) The growth of SMILE (issues and perspectives over the next 10 years) with curriculum analysis. 6) SMILE and the establishment (CSE, GCE, GCSE examinations and the National Curriculum). 7) SMILE in the classroom - issues and perspectives. 8) Individualized learning in the 1990's.

PUBLISHED MATERIAL: WALKER, K.R. (1991). 'SMILE update'. Paper presented at the Pedagogic Text Analysis and Content Analysis Conference, Harnosand, Sweden, Nov 4-6, 1991.

STATUS: Individual research

DATE OF RESEARCH: 1991-1993

KEYWORDS: individualised methods; mathematics education; teaching methods

2369

School of Computing, Information Systems and Mathematics, 103 Borough Road, London SE1 OAA
0171 928 8989
London University, King's College, School of Education, Cornwall House, Waterloo Road, London SE1 8WA
0171 836 5454

Winbourne, P. Mr; *Supervisors*: Lerman, S. Dr; Johnson, D. Prof.

Paradigm shifts in algebra: its nature, its learning, its teaching and its application

ABSTRACT: Modern technology makes available new forms of representation and communication of mathematics which will influence the language and perception of mathematics and the nature of mathematical thinking. This research will first survey and discuss existing curricular paradigms. In particular, it will be concerned to survey current beliefs about the nature of algebra and of mathematical modelling. The research will build on previous work about the increasing accessibility, mediated by technology, of modelling activity and the important role that modelling should have in mathematics learning and seek to determine the level of algebraic understanding that is necessary for students to become effective modellers. Through modelling - particularly computer modelling - children can become metacognitively aware of learning processes and relate the modelling process in maths to the way we 'model' the world. The research will examine how technology can facilitate this metacognition drawing on Vygotsky's insights of the functioning of the zone of proximal development. The study and elucidation of changing curricular paradigms will parallel discussion of the development of mathematical thinking, from a historical, psychological and social perspective. An additional question to be addressed is the neutrality or otherwise of technological development. This research will examine the implications of the existence of powerful tools such as symbol manipulators and graphical calculators for beliefs about learning and the nature of mathematics.

STATUS: Individual research

DATE OF RESEARCH: 1993-1998

KEYWORDS: algebra; mathematical models; mathematics education

2370

School of Education, Politics and Social Sciences, 103 Borough Road, London SE1 OAA
0171 928 8989

Weiner, G. Prof.; Adams, E. Ms

External evaluation of the Lambeth Technical and Vocational Education Initiative (TVEI)

ABSTRACT: This five year evaluation has already involved case studies of Technical and Vocational Education Initiative (TVEI) implementation in selected schools. An interim report was completed in July 1995. An evaluation of the Lambeth European Awareness Festival was completed in July 1996. A further report is anticipated at the end of the project.

STATUS: Sponsored project

SOURCE OF GRANT: Lambeth TVEI £33,000

DATE OF RESEARCH: 1993-1998

KEYWORDS: programme evaluation; tvei

2371

School of Education, Politics and Social Sciences, 103 Borough Road, London SE1 0AA
0171 928 8989

Hutchinson, G. Ms; *Supervisors*: Weiner, G. Prof.; David, M. Prof.

Decline of a subject: the case of home economics

ABSTRACT: The thesis presents an historical and sociological study of home economics to explain how a curriculum subject has developed and changed over the last 100 years. The subject which was at first concerned entirely with an educational context has now widened to include an industrial context. The case study focuses on the perspectives of a group of home economists working in industry, who graduated in 1990. A feminist research methodology was used to explore the views and experiences of this group of home economists on their education, higher education courses, job and career prospects. This involved the choice of a multi-method research approach incorporating qualitative and quantitative methods to allow those involved in the study to express their views about the first two years of employment. Progressive focusing enabled exploration of the factors influencing decisions to study home economics; methods such as telephone interviews, work-diary accounts and group interviews enhanced the reflexive and interpretative aspects of the study. The study identified tensions which exist within home economics deriving from its gendered status and affiliation to private spheres of knowledge, and specifically how home economists resolve these tensions. The positioning of home economics education, with reference to recent changes in the subject content and its shift in application to industrial rather than domestic contexts is analysed in relation to feminist theories. The 'collective voice' of women home economists reveals that they experience a tension between their own values and reasons for choosing home economics and those of the public world which define and attribute status to their employment roles. Home economics has been and continues to be a site for contestation and debate around cultural, social and political issues determining the status of women and the value attributed to what they know and do.

PUBLISHED MATERIAL: HUTCHINSON, G. (1993). 'The title debate', The Home Economist, Vol 12, No 6, pp.2-4. ; HUTCHINSON, G. (1994). 'Empowering home economists: career development in focus', The Home Economist, Vol 13, No 5, pp.8-9. ; HUTCHINSON, G. (1994). 'Meeting the challenge: the 1990s food technology teacher', Modus, Vol 12, No 7, pp.196-198. ; HUTCHINSON, G. (1995). 'Planning schemes of work for KS3 design and technology', Modus, Vol 13, No 1, pp.14-16.

STATUS: Individual research

DATE OF RESEARCH: 1989-1997

KEYWORDS: career choice; home economics; professional education; womens employment

2372

School of Education, Politics and Social Sciences, 103 Borough Road, London SE1 0AA
0171 928 8989

Adams, E. Ms

Interface between the practice, process and reception of public art

ABSTRACT: The project is derived from findings of the Public Art Policy Review carried out by Eileen Adams for the London Arts Board in 1994. The Review identified the need to create evaluative methods for Public Art. The aim was to consider how they might be used to develop the practice of Public Art, to promote critical debate and to inform education initiatives. The research sought to develop an evaluative framework that can be tested through a single case study. The study will investigate: 1) how a Public Art project is developed; 2) the processes, interactions, roles and relationships involved; 3) what perceptions are developed through this experience; 4) what meanings, values and judgements are developed through the experience of Public Art by the public. This was documented through participant observation, illustrated journals, a photographic record, interviews, focus groups and expert seminars. The work was carried out in 30 days between September 1995 and March 1997. Thus study is a pilot aimed at a fuller research programme to explore the issues in greater depth and in the context of a wider range of practice. The second stage, lasting 3 years, is planned for 1997-2000. The results will be directed at artists, commissioners, funders, arts organisations, local authority officers, elected members, the public and critics.

STATUS: Sponsored project

SOURCE OF GRANT: London Arts Board £9,400

DATE OF RESEARCH: 1995-1997

KEYWORDS: arts; community arts; public facilities

2373

Social Sciences Research Centre, 103 Borough Road, London SE1 0AA
0171 928 8989
London University, Institute of Education, 55-59 Gordon Square, London WC1H 0NT
0171 580 1122

David, M. Prof.; Edwards, R. Dr; Alldred, P. Ms

Children's understandings of parental involvement in education

ABSTRACT: There is a wide-ranging consensus that parents' involvement in their children's education is both necessary and beneficial. Education policy stresses parental choice and responsibilities, and strategies have been developed to encourage parental participation at home and at school, and to link home and school more effectively. However, there is little knowledge about the part that children play in the processes of parental involvement in education. This indepth research uses individual, pair and group interviews with primary and secondary school children from a range of backgrounds, to foreground children's experiences and perspectives on mothers' and fathers' involvement in their education. A range of daily and intermittent school curricula and other educational activities will be addressed, as will the setting (home or school) in which these take place. The study will also take account of the broader meaning of 'family' and 'education', and how these relate, in the lives of girls and boys. The findings will be of relevance to policy discussions of parental involvement in children's education, including home-school contracts, at national government, local education authority and individual school levels. More generally, it will contribute to a recognition of children's activity in society.

PUBLISHED MATERIAL: EDWARDS, R. & DAVID, M. (1997) 'Where are the children in home-school relations? Notes towards a research agenda', Children and Society, Vol 11, No 3, pp.194-200. ; EDWARDS, R. & ALLDRED, P. (1999) 'Children and young people's views of social research: the case of research on home-school relations', Childhood, Vol 6, No 2, May 1999.

STATUS: Sponsored project

SOURCE OF GRANT: Economic and Social Research Council £87,880

DATE OF RESEARCH: 1997-continuing

KEYWORDS: home school relationship; parent participation; parent pupil relationship; primary education; pupil attitudes; secondary education

Southampton University

2374

Department of Sociology and Social Policy, Highfield, Southampton SO9 5NH
02380 595000

Shilling, C. Dr

Educational differentiation and social space

ABSTRACT: Research consists firstly, of a review of the literature on the role of social space in educational differentiation with particular reference to the place of space in structuration theory. Secondly, an ethnographic study has been conducted into the use of space in two school libraries. Particular attention is given to teacher and pupil attempts to colonise and regulate this educational space.

PUBLISHED MATERIAL: SHILLING, C. & COUSINS, F. (1990). 'Social use of the school library: the colonisation and regulation of educational space', British Journal of Sociology of Education, Vol 11, No 4, pp.411-430. ; SHILLING, C. (1991). 'Social space, educational differentiation and gender inequalities', British Journal of Sociology of Education, Vol 12, No 1, pp.23-45.

STATUS: Individual research

DATE OF RESEARCH: 1990-1993

KEYWORDS: equal education; personal space; school space

2375

Department of Sociology and Social Policy, Highfield, Southampton SO9 5NH
02380 595000
London University, King's College, School of Education, Cornwall House, Waterloo Road, London SE1 8WA
0171 836 5454

Shilling, C. Dr; Ball, S. Prof.

New directions in education policy sociology

ABSTRACT: 'New Directions in Education Policy Sociology' is a Nuffield Foundation funded conference taking place in March 1993. It is also intended that the Conference proceedings will (in part) contribute to a book, with the same title, addressing theoretical and methodological issues in the field of education policy sociology.

STATUS: Sponsored project

SOURCE OF GRANT: Nuffield Foundation

DATE OF RESEARCH: 1993-1993

KEYWORDS: educational policy; sociology of education

2376

Faculty of Educational Studies, Centre for Language in Education, Highfield, Southampton SO9 5NH
02380 595000

Brumfit, C. Prof.; Mitchell, R. Dr

'Knowledge about language', language learning and the National Curriculum

ABSTRACT: This project aims to investigate the nature of children's understanding of the nature of language and how it works, and how this is developed through experience of English/Modern Languages work in school. Teachers of English and Modern Languages have been encouraged by the Kingman Report, (Department of Education and Science Committee of Inquiry into the Teaching of English Language (1988). Report of the Committee of Inquiry into the Teaching of English Language. London HMSO), the Language in the National Curriculum (LINC) programme, and National Curriculum programmes for their subjects, to pay more attention to developing children's knowledge about language. Traditionally however, teachers in the different language subjects have dealt with 'Knowledge about Language' (KAL) in rather different ways. Moreover, in spite of much debate, little is known about school age children's resulting knowledge and beliefs about the nature of language, and the relationship between such knowledge and the development of children's practical language skills. Fieldwork consists of case studies carried out during the school year 1991-92 in the English and Modern Languages departments of three Hampshire schools. A period of approximately 8 weeks is being spent in each school, spread over three terms. The focus is on pupils in Year 9; teachers of both subjects are being interviewed, and English/Modern Language classes are being observed and recorded, to learn how and when language matters are discussed, and in what terms. Children will also be interviewed, to explore their developing knowledge about language, and its relationship with classroom discussions and activities. The development of their language skills will also be monitored, through analysis of their day to day work, and possible links with their developing knowledge about language will be explored.

STATUS: Sponsored project

SOURCE OF GRANT: Economic and Social Research Council £52,000

DATE OF RESEARCH: 1991-1993

KEYWORDS: english; language skills; modern language studies

2377

Faculty of Educational Studies, Centre for Language in Education, Highfield, Southampton SO9 5NH
02380 595000

Williams, S. Mr; *Supervisor*: Brumfit, C. Prof.

A longitudinal study of interpersonal affect in native speaker/non-native speaker interaction

ABSTRACT: The reflexive relationship between affect and communication is implied by Berger, (BERGER, C.F. (1979). 'Beyond initial interaction: uncertainty, understanding and the development of interpersonal relationships'. In: HOWARD, G. & StCLAIR, R.N. (Eds). Language and Social Psychology. Oxford: Basil Blackwell), who suggests that communication over time is central to the development and disintegration of interpersonal relationships. This research concerns the association of interpersonal affect and various factors in native speaker (NS) non-native speaker (NNS) interaction in an academic setting. Both external and internal factos are examined, including (a) motivation; (b) discourse structure; (c) discourse quality; and (d) NNS fluency. It asks the following questions: (1) what sorts of speech events do formal conversation meetings comprise (e.g. how much is conversation and how much pedagogic discourse?); (2) are there (i) qualitative or (ii) NNS fluency differences between the conversation of dyads representing four kinds of scheme histories, namely those who, relative to other dyads, (a) get on and stop meeting; (b) get on and continue meeting; (c) do not get on and continue meeting and (d) do not get on and stop meeting. Recordings were made of a series of meetings from the English language conversation scheme organised by Southampton University Students Union. Participants were requested to complete self-reflection sheets after each meeting and at regular intervals. The research also involved using Personal Construct Theory (PCT) repertory grids and a pragmatic oral test. The grids were used to track affective influences on the discourse, and the oral test to measure NNS language learning progress. Participants' own notions of a satisfactory conversation were also considered. Participants were also interviewed to discover language learning histories, the range of convenience of elicited PCT constructs and, at the end of the scheme, were asked for their retrospective impressions of the meetings. Transcriptions from the recordings are being analysed, and the findings will have implications for language learning and language teaching methodology.

PUBLISHED MATERIAL: WILLIAMS, S. (1992). 'Playful - aloof': using personal construct theory as a measure of interpersonal affect in native speaker/non-native speaker conversation', Centre for Language in Education Occasional Paper. Southampton: University of Southampton. ; WILLIAMS, S. (1992). 'The disqualified half': gender representation in a children's reading scheme'. In: BLUE, G. (Ed). Perspectives on reading, CLE Working Papers 2. Southampton: University of Southampton.

STATUS: Individual research

DATE OF RESEARCH: 1990-1993

KEYWORDS: communication research; conversation; native speakers; second language learning; verbal communication

2378

Faculty of Educational Studies, Centre for Language in Education, Highfield, Southampton SO9 5NH
02380 595000

Edwards, J. Mr; *Supervisor*: Benton, M. Prof.

Curriculum change and its effects on school departmental culture, with particular reference to secondary school English

ABSTRACT: This research aims to illuminate how curriculum change operates in English teaching in secondary schools, particularly during a period of great and controversial shifts of emphasis accompanying the development of the National Curriculum. Historical discussion and analysis provide the context for the study. An interview-based enquiry with 80 departmental heads of English is set against this background. Syllabus content, teaching style, the effects of external control, vis-a-vis personal and professional autonomy, are the main issues to be pursued.

STATUS: Individual research

DATE OF RESEARCH: 1991-1997

KEYWORDS: **curriculum development; educational change; english; english studies curriculum; national curriculum; secondary education**

2379

Faculty of Educational Studies, Centre for Science Communication, Highfield, Southampton SO9 5NH
02380 595000

Ratcliffe, M. Dr; Fullick, P. Mr; *Supervisor*: Kelly, P. Prof.

Issues in science and decision making

ABSTRACT: With the implementation of the National Curriculum all pupils up to the age of 16 will be expected 'to study scientific controversies' and 'begin to understand the power and limitations of science in solving problems'. There is also a growing need to address the public understanding of science. The objectives of this research are: (1) To identify some of the features of the role of the individual in collective decision making, and to identify the particular thinking skills and capacities which individuals need in order to take decisions about science based issues. This objective to be met through (a) literature search from fields of education, sociology, psychology and management; and (b) examination of case studies relating to decision making about science based issues in the public domain. (2) To examine, through action research in classrooms - (a) the ways in which pupils make decisions about aspects of science which affect them personally, and scientific issues which, at the time, may have only a marginal impact on their daily lives; and (b) the ways in which teachers manage this decision making process. Methodology will be observation in classes in the age range 14-18 in order to achieve objective 2. Techniques will include: observation schedules, video analysis, interviews and questionnaires involving both pupils and teachers. It is hoped to develop curriculum materials from this research.

STATUS: Sponsored project

SOURCE OF GRANT: Southampton University: School of Education £3,000

DATE OF RESEARCH: 1992-1993

KEYWORDS: **decision making; national curriculum; science education; scientific literacy**

2380

Faculty of Educational Studies, Department of Health Education, Highfield, Southampton SO9 5NH
02380 595000

Box, V. Ms

United Kingdom primary health care cancer education/training audit

ABSTRACT: The objectives of this research are: (i) Audit of multi-disciplinary cancer education training, topic and process, in statutory and voluntary agencies. (ii) Audit of existing resources for cancer education and prevention. (iii) Consultation with professionals about 'needs' in relation to cancer education. The methodology will involve: (a) interviewing of/by individuals at national, regional and district levels; (b) a questionnaire given to primary health care facilitators; and (c) focus group interviews with mixed groups of health professionals.

STATUS: Sponsored project

SOURCE OF GRANT: Department of Health; Europe Against Cancer, jointly £20,000

DATE OF RESEARCH: 1992-1993

KEYWORDS: **cancer education; health education; preventive medicine; primary health care**

2381

Faculty of Educational Studies, Department of Health Education, Highfield, Southampton SO9 5NH
02380 595000

McWhirter, J. Dr; Wetton, N. Mrs; Williams, T. Mr; *Supervisor*: Weare, K. Ms

A whole life, a healthy life

ABSTRACT: The aim is to research and write a health education programme for 10-14 year-old pupils in elementary schools in Hungary. The materials are being trialled in 10 schools and data is being collected in these and 10 reference schools. The implementation is supported by twice-yearly professional development for teachers using the materials. Open-ended illuminative research tools have been designed specifically for this project beginning with a draw and write about what health means to pupils; what changes they envisage in their lives; what disturbs the balance of their lives; and an open-ended questionnaire on how they envisage their future health. The materials are based on active learning approaches, are pupil-centred, and constructed to follow a spiral curriculum with horizontal cohesion and emphasise the importance of a whole school approach to health education.

PUBLISHED MATERIAL: MCWHIRTER, J., WETTON, N. & WILLIAMS, T. (1996). 'Health education for Hungary', Health Education, Vol 1, pp.8-15.

STATUS: Sponsored project

SOURCE OF GRANT: Ministry of Welfare (Hungray) via World Bank loan £500,000

DATE OF RESEARCH: 1995-continuing

KEYWORDS: **health education; hungary**

2382

Faculty of Educational Studies, Department of Health Education, Highfield, Southampton SO9 5NH
02380 595000

McWhirter, J. Dr; King, A. Ms; *Supervisor*: Weare, K. Ms

Children's changing perceptions of risk - an evaluation of the Getting it Right project

ABSTRACT: The aim of the project was to evaluate a police-school liaison for primary schools. 24 schools in Hampshire and 10 schools in Dorset volunteered to take part in the study. Hampshire schools were pilot schools for the Getting it Right project, while Dorset were non-intervention comparison schools. Pupils in Year 4 were asked to draw and write about 'risk' and their responses were coded, and compared with a post-intervention response after 18 months. Significant differences were found between boys and girls, between control and intervention groups, and between pre- and post- intervention responses. The data were compared with a similar study of adult perceptions of risk and the results suggest that pupils in intervention schools had a more mature perception of risk after the intervention than before. A report will be submitted to Hampshire Constabulary.

PUBLISHED MATERIAL: MCWHIRTER, J. & WETTON, N. (1998). 'Getting it right: the case for risk education'. In O'CONNOR, D. et al. (Eds). Drugs: policy, prevention and education. Cassell Studies in Pastoral Care and Personal Social Education. London: Cassell.

STATUS: Sponsored project

SOURCE OF GRANT: Hampshire Constabulary £11,000

DATE OF RESEARCH: 1994-1997

KEYWORDS: **police school relationship; primary education; risk; safety education; sex differences**

2383

Faculty of Educational Studies, Department of Health Education, Highfield, Southampton SO9 5NH
02380 595000

McWhirter, J. Dr; Coleman, H. Dr; McCann, D. Dr; *Supervisors*: Warner, J. Prof.; Weare, K. Ms

Evaluation by case study of a school-based intervention to improve the management and decrease the morbidity of children with asthma

ABSTRACT: The aim of the project is to evaluate a model for the effective communication about asthma within the school setting. The objectives are to: 1)) offer intervention and support to help staff to develop a whole school approach to asthma management; b) monitor changes in school policy with respect to asthma management; c) monitor changes in staff attitudes, knowledge, awareness of asthma in childhood; d) monitor changes of all pupils with respect to their awareness, knowledge, and understanding and perceptions of asthma, its causes and its management; e) monitor changes in morbidity, perceptions of asthma, self esteem, knowledge and understanding of asthma in asthmatic children and the self esteem of asthmatic pupils. Asthma is the most common chronic disease of childhood. It is a leading cause of absenteeism and can lead to poor academic performance and low self esteem. Schools are key settings in the government strategy to improve the health of young people and the National Asthma Campaign has identified the need for each school to have a policy outlinining its approach to asthma. A recent report has highlighted the important partnership of health professionals and school staff in minimising the effects of chronic childhood diseases in education. Studies have shown that school staff have limited knowledge and are concerned about asthma. The Southampton based Group for Asthma Education in Schools (GAMES) has carried out a pilot study in local schools using trained school nurses to educate school staff. As with other studies this initiative led to an increase in knowledge and awareness amongst teachers, but no measures of morbidity were attempted. In other studies where attempts have been made to measure morbidity changes, no improvements have been detected. This project would develop and evaluate a modified GAMES initiative using a controlled case study approach. The study proposed will use a wide range of techniques, including previously validated questionnaires and semi-structured interviews which will yield quantitative and qualitative data. The study will also employ a draw and write technique to determine pupils' perceptions of asthma. This will enable the team to determine the awareness, knowledge and understanding of the pupils in the study while providing a starting point for the development of classroom activities. The study design will be quasi-experimental. 10 primary schools (350+ pupils per school) will be subject to detailed examination before, during and after an intervention modelled on the GAMES project and compared with 10 control schools which will not receive the support of the GAMES project. The wide range of quantitative and qualitative data to be collected will enable the team to build up a case study of each school, and these case studies will illuminate the processes by which a school modifies policies and practice with respect to asthma management. It is expected that at least 100 children in each of the experimental and control groups will be asthmatic. A range of data, including teachers' records, GP records and prescription details will reveal the exent to which the intervention has affected morbidity in these children.

STATUS: Sponsored project

SOURCE OF GRANT: NHS Research and Development Fund £209,000

DATE OF RESEARCH: 1998-continuing

KEYWORDS: asthma; medical conditions; medical needs; whole school approach

2384

Faculty of Educational Studies, Research and Graduate School of Education, Highfield, Southampton SO9 5NH
02380 595000

Benton, M. Prof.

Readings in literature and painting, 1700-1900, and their relevance to pedadogy

ABSTRACT: This cross-curricular research aims to illuminate the historical and theoretical connections between painting and literature focusing especially on the 18th and 19th centuries in Britain. Theoretical enquiries into the spectator role in respect of both art forms will be followed by a study of 8 major themes: painting; theatre and fiction in the 18th century; landscape painting and literary pictorialism; the idea and image of childhood; narrative in visual and verbal forms; the idea of the poetic in both arts; painting, poetry and the canon. These historical themes will then be related to current cross-curricular work in secondary schools.

PUBLISHED MATERIAL: BENTON, M.G. (1995). 'The self-conscious spectator', The British Journal of Aesthetics, Vol 35, No 4, pp.361-373. ; BENTON, M.G. (1995). 'From a Rake's Progress to Rosie's Walk: lessons in aesthetic reading', The Journal of Aesthetic Education, Vol 29, No 1, pp.33-46. ; BENTON, M.G. (1997). 'Anyone for Ekphrasis?', British Journal of Aesthetics, Vol 37, No 4, pp.367-376. ; BENTON, M.G. & BUTCHER, S. (1998). 'Painting Shakespeare', Journal of Aesthetic Education, Vol 32, No 3, pp.53-66.

STATUS: Individual research

DATE OF RESEARCH: 1994-1997

KEYWORDS: art education; art history; arts; cross curricular approach; literary history; literature; secondary education

2385

Faculty of Educational Studies, Research and Graduate School of Education, Highfield, Southampton SO9 5NH
02380 595000

Hemsley-Brown, J. Dr; *Supervisor*: Foskett, N. Dr

Higher education awareness amongst school pupils

ABSTRACT: This study is an examination of the perceptions and understanding that school pupils have of the nature, purpose, operation and value of higher education. Using a sample of pupils in schools in Hampshire, it is examining these issues through questionnaires and individual and focus group interviews with pupils, and interviews with teachers and careers advisers. The work is being undertaken with a sample of pupils in each of Years 6, 8 and 10.

STATUS: Sponsored project

SOURCE OF GRANT: Hampshire Training and Enterprise Council £30,000; Universities and Colleges Admissions Service £2,000

DATE OF RESEARCH: 1995-1998

KEYWORDS: career awareness; higher education; pupil attitudes; vocational guidance

2386

Faculty of Educational Studies, Research and Graduate School of Education, Highfield, Southampton SO9 5NH
02380 595000

Fullick, P. Mr; *Supervisor*: Davis, G. Prof.

Discussion of science practical work and secondary science students' understanding of the nature of science

ABSTRACT: Founded in 1995, the on-line journal, ScI-Journal, publishes young people's accounts of school science investigations. One of the aims of the journal is to enhance young people's understanding of the nature of science by encouraging them to engage in debates with one another about practical science work that they have done. In order to acquire evidence about whether peer-group discussion of science practical work can lead to a better understanding of the nature of science, a year-long study has been conducted in a city secondary school. The school is an 11-16 girls comprehensive, and the class studied is a high-ability group of 15 year-old girls taking GCSE science. Working with the class chemistry and physics teachers, activities were devised which encouraged the development of a classroom in which knowledge claims and practical ideas were subject to critical scrutiny by peers. The development of ideas about the nature of science were probed through a series of small-group interviews (n=5) conducted at points during the year. These interviews used historically-situated materials linked to the curriculum to act as a stimulus for discussion. Analysis of the data from the study suggests that this approach may help to link the practical work done by students to the work of 'real' scientists.

PUBLISHED MATERIAL: FULLICK, P.L. (1995). 'Teaching science using ScI-Journal - an electronic journal for science pupils', Education in Science, Vol 165, pp.26-27. ; FULLICK, P.L. (1997). 'Using an online journal to teach students about science'. In: BURGE, Z.L. & COLLINS, M.P. (Eds). Wired together: computer-mediated communication in K-12. Volume 4: Writing, reading and language acquisition. Cresskill, New Jersey: Hampton Press.

STATUS: Individual research

DATE OF RESEARCH: 1995-1998

KEYWORDS: computer uses in education; discussion; electronic publishing; internet; online journal; practical science; science education; scientific literacy; secondary education

2387

Faculty of Educational Studies, Research and Graduate School of Education, Highfield, Southampton SO9 5NH
02380 595000

Andrews, S. Mr; *Supervisor*: Brumfit, C. Prof.

The metalinguistic awareness of Hong Kong secondary school teachers of English

ABSTRACT: The research investigates the metalinguistic awareness (TMA), with particular reference to grammar, of non-native speaker teachers of English in Hong Kong secondary schools. It explores potential influences upon the development of an individual teacher's metalinguistic awareness, observes the ways in which TMA can affect a teacher's professional activity, and examines how it interacts with other aspects of pedagogical content knowledge. At the same time, the study attempts to provide insights into the TMA of the specific group of teachers under investigation, graduates without professional training. The research took place in 2 stages. The first was a baseline study, intended to provide an overview of the TMA of untrained graduate teachers of English in Hong Kong secondary schools. A random sample of 188 subjects was involved in the baseline study, which consisted of a battery of testing tasks: a group interview, a multiple-choice test of grammar/vocabulary, a composition, and a test of language awareness. In addition, subjects completed a questionnaire about their beliefs and attitudes towards language, language learning and language teaching. The second stage of the research, the main study, focused in depth upon the TMA of a sample of 17 teachers selected from the main study group. For this part of the study a range of qualitative techniques were employed: principally semi-structured interview, classroom observation, questionnaire, together with 3 pedagogically-related tasks involving explaining a grammar point, planning a grammar-focused lesson, and correcting grammatical errors. The study will be completed in summer 1999.

PUBLISHED MATERIAL: ANDREWS, S.J. (1996). 'Metalinguistic awareness and lesson planning'. In: STOREY, P., BUNTON, D. & HORE, P. (Eds). Issues in language in education. Hong Kong: Hong Kong Institute of Education. ; ANDREWS, S.J. (1997). 'Metalinguistic awareness and teacher explanation', Language Awareness. Special Issue: Papers from the 3rd International Conference of the Association for Language Awareness, Vol 6, Nos 2 & 3, pp.147-161.

STATUS: Individual research

DATE OF RESEARCH: 1994-continuing

KEYWORDS: english - second language; grammar; hong kong; language teachers

2388

Faculty of Educational Studies, Research and Graduate School of Education, Highfield, Southampton SO9 5NH
02380 595000

Kamanda, M. Mr; *Supervisor*: Brumfit, C. Prof.

The bases of language and literacy policy for contemporary Sierra Leone

ABSTRACT: Sierra Leone, like most of Sub-Saharan Africa, has demonstrated the desire to innovate and indigenise its education system, by instituting the 6.3.3.4 Basic Education curriculum and new language and education policies. A striking feature of these policies is that they provide for and emphasise literacy in the child's mother-tongue and in at least one other community language. As a language teacher trainer, the researcher is concerned about and interested in ways in which the influence of past policies, which had promoted, enhanced and entrenched the use of English language are likely to impact on successful implementation of the current package. The main aim of this study therefore is to review and clarify language and literacy policies in Sierra Leone during the period 1961-1995, so as to be able to propose a principled base for such a policy as we approach the 21st century. The scope of the study will encapsulate policy and planning of literacy and language in Sierra Leone and Britain. It will also examine English mother-tongue and second language teaching in the respective countries, and the teaching of African languages in Sierra Leone. This comparative outlook will enrich the findings and comprehensively inform whatever conclusions that will be drawn from the search. The study will consist mainly of documentary analysis of primary, secondary and tertiary sources of information. A quasi-fieldwork component will focus mainly on a representative sample of teachers, students and parents of minority languages in Britain. The objective will be to test for their attitudes, aspirations and problems of teaching and acquiring tongues other than the language of mainstream culture. Although the method of analysis will mainly be qualitative, tables and other forms of graphic presentation of information will be used for illustrations. The findings of the study will enable the researcher to construct a principled basis for language and literacy policy for Sierra Leone, a former colony of Britain, caught in a new wave of change. Such principles will be useful to language policymakers and planners on the one hand, and others who are involved in implementation and evaluation of policy packages.

PUBLISHED MATERIAL: KAMANDA, M.C. (1997). 'Literacy as social practice: contemporary international debate', Centre for Language in Education Briefing Document, No 9.

STATUS: Individual research

DATE OF RESEARCH: 1996-continuing

KEYWORDS: language policy; sierra leone

2389

Faculty of Educational Studies, Research and Graduate School of Education, Highfield, Southampton SO9 5NH
02380 595000

Hyatt, J. Ms; Zamorski, B. Ms; Potulicka, E. Prof.; Melosik, Z. Prof.; Mizerek, H. Dr; Korporowicz, L. Dr; *Supervisor*: Simons, H. Prof.

Training for education reform management (TERM) evaluation

ABSTRACT: This project set out to train senior Polish academics and their assistants in the art of case study evaluation concurrent with the conduct by each of them of a component of educational reform in the training for education reform management (TERM) programme. The programme TERM and the external evaluation were funded under the PHARE programme, sponsored by the European Union and administered by the Foundation for the Development of the Education System, Ministry of national Education (MoNE), Poland. The project which took place from 1995-97 consisted of intensive periods of evaluation training in England and a series of week long evaluation seminars in Poland at different stages throughout the two years. In between the seminars and study visits, the team of evaluators conducted a case study of the impact of one of the major components of the TERM programme. In addition the external evaluators from England conducted a technical evaluation of the management and organisation of the programme. The final report comprises the five case studies and the technical evaluation, plus a self-evaluation from the Polish evaluators of what they had learned about evaluation through the process and how they intended to utilise their educational evaluation expertise in the future.

STATUS: Sponsored project

SOURCE OF GRANT: European Union £209,968

DATE OF RESEARCH: 1995-1997

KEYWORDS: educational change; evaluation; poland

2390

Faculty of Educational Studies, Research and Graduate School of Education, Highfield, Southampton SO9 5NH
02380 595000

Ratcliffe, M. Dr

Evaluation of learning about socio-scientific issues

ABSTRACT: This research, in collaboration with the University of California, follows from a PhD study 'Adolescent decision-making about socio-scientific issues' (M. Ratcliffe, 1996) and seeks to evaluate the nature and quality of learning about the use of scientific and other evidence through the study of socio-scientific issues within the secondary science curriculum. The first phase examines the suitability of the structure of learning outcomes (SOLO) taxonomy and a decision-making framework as tools for assessment of 13-15 year-olds' written responses to socio-scientific issues in which information has to be evaluated (200 14-15 year-olds in mixed comprehensive schools in Southern England). The second phase of the research evaluates the use of different learning activities in assisting pupils in: 1) understanding the nature and limitations of scientific evidence; 2) understanding the nature of ethics; 3) clarification of values. The range of learning activities are drawn from FULLICK P. & RATCLIFFE, M. (1996). Teaching ethical aspects of science. Totton: Bassett Press. Outcomes from the first phase provide evaluation tools for the second phase. The sample of schools for the second phase includes two mixed comprehensives in Southern England and two high schools in California.

STATUS: Collaborative

DATE OF RESEARCH: 1997-continuing

KEYWORDS: **ethics; science curriculum; science education; secondary education**

2391

Faculty of Educational Studies, Research and Graduate School of Education, Highfield, Southampton SO9 5NH
02380 595000

Moss, G. Dr; Attar, D. Ms

Fact and fiction: the gendering of reading in the 7-9 age group

ABSTRACT: The fact and fiction research project is designed to look at boys' development as readers at home and in school, at the point when they first begin to read independently. Key issues to be explored are: 1) whether boys' preferences for factual genres rather than fiction impacts on their progress in reading; 2) how the difference in genre preferences between boy and girl readers emerges and is sustained both at home and in school; 3) how to describe the kinds of competencies boys develop in relation to the texts they prefer, and the extent to which these differ from the kinds of competencies acquired from the reading of narrative fiction; 4) the potential for expanding both the range of texts on the primary school curriculum, and the ways in which they are used. The research will be undertaken in the form of 4 case studies. These will identify how the reading of fact and fiction texts is currently undertaken at home and at school; the main differences children perceive between the range of texts they read; the extent to which children are developing different repertoires of reading skills in relation to different texts; the relationship between reading competencies developed in informal settings and those which form the basis of classroom activity.

STATUS: Sponsored project

SOURCE OF GRANT: Economic and Social Research Council £86,400

DATE OF RESEARCH: 1996-1998

KEYWORDS: **books; boys; childrens literature; fiction; nonfiction; primary education; primary school pupils; reading; reading habits; sex differences**

2392

Faculty of Educational Studies, Research and Graduate School of Education, Highfield, Southampton SO9 5NH
02380 595000

Beale, D. Mrs; *Supervisor*: Mitchell, R. Dr

Interactions around books: early years' children becoming literate

ABSTRACT: After working for many years as an early years class teacher, in mainstream and special schools, the researcher aimed to find out how interaction between children in these settings might enhance their development towards becoming literate. Of particular interest was what they said to each other when they shared stories or looked at books in a library. However, the researcher needed a variety of tasks and activities involving literacy skills, assessment of ability and interests, teacher's views, and visit to homes to talk to parents, to gain a full view of each child. Having access to both a mainstream infant school, and to a special school for children with moderate learning difficulties, it was possible to select 5 children - 4 boys and a girl, of similar ages, from each setting. The children were observed, in snapshot periods, for 2 academic years, from the time they started school. They were recorded on cassette, occasionally videotaped, as they interacted over tasks, and browsed in their school libraries. The final session was in a public library, where 4 children from each school were recorded talking to each other, and to staff, about the books they found as they looked around. Some read quite competently for themselves, other relied on other children or adults to provide them with information. Early analysis reveals strategies and game playing being used to learn, or to tell, required information, highlighting contrasts between how they reacted when sharing books with adults, or when with other children.

STATUS: Individual research

DATE OF RESEARCH: 1993-continuing

KEYWORDS: **books; childrens literature; early childhood education; interaction; libraries; literacy; reading; young children**

2393

Faculty of Educational Studies, Research and Graduate School of Education, Highfield, Southampton SO9 5NH
02380 595000

Johnston, B. Ms; *Supervisor*: Mitchell, R. Dr

A proposed framework for teaching analytical writing: a principled, holistic pedagogic approach

ABSTRACT: Writing analytically at university is a major problem for many students, especially those for whom English is their second language, who wrestle with knowing how to express their own opinion; having to construct and sustain a convincing argument; knowing how to interact with external sources of information, often containing large amounts of highly technical and complex information; and throughout this process maintaining intellectual and personal confidence. This research project proposes some principles for a teaching programme to guide students at various levels through the analytical writing process to produce acceptable written products. These principles are intended to be practical in application, although grounded in theories of learning, writing and critical thinking. The project involved an action research study of a class of 15 second language students in an English-medium university in the Middle East. In the project, the researcher implemented an early version of a teaching programme based on the principles that she was in the process of developing. The researcher wrote indepth case studies of 5 of the students in the class and discussed how their writing developed in response to the teaching programme and other contextual influences. The writing development of the students was extremely complex, displaying overall development according to the strategies taught, but including many developmental features such a uneven development across strategy areas; apparent retrogressions as students employed new writing strategies on more complex writing assignments and had difficulty in controlling their writing processes and products; and continuing searching around by students to find appropriate ways of writing/analysing in the complex world of academic writing.

STATUS: Individual research

DATE OF RESEARCH: 1994-1998

KEYWORDS: **analysis; higher education; writing - composition**

2394

Faculty of Educational Studies, Research and Graduate School of Education, Highfield, Southampton SO9 5NH
02380 595000

Edwards, J. Ms; *Supervisors*: Davis, G. Prof.; Jones, K. Mr

Pupil discourse, exploratory talk and mathematical learning in secondary classrooms

ABSTRACT: The aim of the study is to analyse pupil-pupil talk in the normal setting of small group activity in a secondary mathematics classroom. Pupil-pupil talk will be analysed to identify exploratory mathematical talk which involves pupils engaging critically and constructively with each others' ideas so that statements and suggestions are challenged and justified. The study will determine whether the incidence of exploratory mathematical talk is affected by the degree to which teacher and pupils share common beliefs about the role of small group talk as a means to mathematical learning.

PUBLISHED MATERIAL: A list of publications is available from the researcher.

STATUS: Sponsored project

SOURCE OF GRANT: Economic and Social Research Council

DATE OF RESEARCH: 1997-continuing

KEYWORDS: **classroom communication; discussion; mathematics education; secondary education; small group teaching; verbal communication**

2395

Faculty of Educational Studies, Research and Graduate School of Education, Highfield, Southampton SO9 5NH
02380 595000

Jones, K. Mr

The mediation of learning within a dynamic geometry environment

ABSTRACT: The focus of this study is the mediation of mathematics learning. The study addresses the question of how the learning of aspects of plane geometry by children in the secondary mathematics classroom is mediated by the use of the dynamic geometry environment Cabri-Geometre. The central objective of the study is to trace the development of mastery of relevant elements of both the dynamic geometry package and the specialist language associated with plane geometry. Fieldwork consists of longitudinal case studies of pairs of pupils using the computer package within their regular mathematics class.

PUBLISHED MATERIAL: JONES, K. (1996). 'Coming to know about "dependence" within a dynamic geometry environment'. In: PUIG, L. & GUITIERREZ, A. (Eds). Proceedings of the 20th Conference of the International Group for the Psychology of Mathematics Education, University of Valencia, Spain, 1996. ; JONES, K. (1997). 'Children learning to specify geometrical relationships using a dynamic geometry package'. In: PEHKONEN, E. (Ed). Proceedings of the 21st Conference of the International Group for the Psychology of Mathematics Education, University of Helsinki, Helsinki, 1997.

STATUS: Sponsored project

SOURCE OF GRANT: Southampton University £2,352

DATE OF RESEARCH: 1994-1998

KEYWORDS: **geometry; learning; mathematics education; secondary education**

2396

Faculty of Educational Studies, Research and Graduate School of Education, Highfield, Southampton SO9 5NH
02380 595000

Hegedus, S. Mr; *Supervisors*: Hirst, K. Dr; Jones, K. Mr

Analysing the metacognitive behaviour of undergraduates solving certain calculus problems

ABSTRACT: This project aims to analyse the metacognitive behaviour of undergraduates to understand more about their knowledge in solving single and multi-variable integration. The study was designed on Schoenfield's (1985) method of using think-aloud verbal transcripts (SCHOENFELD, A. (1985). Mathematical problem-solving. Hove: Lawrence Erlbaum Associates), and using protocol analysis to investigate the mathematical thinking of first year undergraduates. Three groups of students were used. The model was adopted through a 3-stage empirical process by allowing interventions and analysing their impact with reference to the students' thought processes. The study concentrated on self-regulatory metacognitive behaviour including reflection, organisation, monitoring and extraction (ROME) which developed the ROME model of analysis. The results of the study offered more mathematical interpretations of students' self-regulatory behaviour solving single, double and triple integration problems. It also developed the ROME model of analysis which can be used to analyse metacognitive behaviour of problem-solvers in other fields of mathematics.

PUBLISHED MATERIAL: HEGEDUS, S.J. (1996). 'Analysing the metacognitive behaviour of students solving an integral'. Proceedings of the British Society for Research in Learning Mathematics, Loughborough, 1996. ; A full list of publications is available from the researcher.

STATUS: Sponsored project

SOURCE OF GRANT: Economic and Social Research Council

DATE OF RESEARCH: 1994-1998

KEYWORDS: **calculus; cognitive processes; higher education; mathematics education; metacognition; students**

2397

Faculty of Educational Studies, Research and Graduate School of Education, Highfield, Southampton SO9 5NH
02380 595000

Hague, E. Ms; *Supervisor*: Grenfell, M. Dr

Gesture in the English as a Foreign Language (EFL) classroom

ABSTRACT: This research examines how cross-cultural differences in the use of gesture can present a problem to English as a Foreign Language (EF) students. While some gestures made by British EFL teachers in the course of their teaching may be interpreted correctly by some students, many gestures are confusing to students who have different linguistic and cultural backgrounds. Moreover, because many gestural messages are both transmitted and received subconsciously, the source of the problem may go unrecognised. The research aims to catalogue these recognitions and misrecognitions as a way of enhancing non-verbal communication in cross-cultural teaching situations.

STATUS: Individual research

DATE OF RESEARCH: 1995-continuing

KEYWORDS: **body language; cultural differences; english - second language; nonverbal communication; second language learning**

2398

Faculty of Educational Studies, Research and Graduate School of Education, Highfield, Southampton SO9 5NH
02380 595000

Grenfell, M. Dr; Harris, V. Ms

Language learning strategies

ABSTRACT: This research deals with the strategies pupils develop in learning modern foreign languages. It is based on a developmental project in London which sought to enhance pupils' autonomy in the language classroom. Some 120 pupils were involved. Questionnaire and observation techniques were used. Further research has examined individuals' linguistic profiles in detail. Here, introspection and retrospection, as well as discourse analysis techniques have been used. The aim of the research is to build up a taxonomy of strategies used by learners at distinct developmental levels. Further research examines the feasibility of strategy instruction, its effectiveness and the applicability of findings from 'good language learner' research to classroom methodologies.

PUBLISHED MATERIAL: GRENFELL, M. & HARRIS, V. (1994). 'How do pupils learn (I)?', Language Learning Journal, Vol 9, pp.7-11. ; GRENFELL, M. & HARRIS, V. (1994). 'How do pupils learn (II)?', Language Learning Journal, Vol 10, pp.22-25. ; GRENFELL, M. (1994). 'Flexible learning: the teacher's friend?', Modern English Teacher, Vol 3 & 4, pp.7-13. ; GRENFELL, M. & HARRIS, V. Learning to learn - strategies and the language learner. London: Routledge. (in press).

STATUS: Collaborative

DATE OF RESEARCH: 1992-continuing

KEYWORDS: **learning strategies; modern language studies**

2399

Faculty of Educational Studies, Research and Graduate School of Education, Highfield, Southampton SO9 5NH
02380 595000

Grenfell, M. Dr

Bourdieu and education

ABSTRACT: This research is based on the work of the French social theorist, Pierre Bourdieu. It involves an epistemological critique of educational research methods and the development of approaches and techniques to conduct research within a Bourdieuian framework. The work is coordinated at Southampton University but involves a national and international network of scholars working in this field. An inaugural conference of some 60 delegates was held in Southampton in 1997. Topics and research covered on language and education include: teacher education; adolescents' career decision making; classroom discourse; bilingual education; higher education experience for mature students; comparative studies of 6th form teachers; the relationship between home and school; primary education; curriculum and policy reform.

PUBLISHED MATERIAL: GRENFELL, M. (1992). 'What it is to speak', Modern and Contemporary France Review, Vol 4, pp.82-84. ; GRENFELL, M. (1996). 'Bourdieu and initial teacher education - a post structuralist approach', British Educational Research Journal, Vol 22, No 3, pp.287-303. ; GRENFELL, M. & JAMES, D. Bourdieu and education: acts of practical theory. London: Falmer Press. (in press).

STATUS: Individual research

DATE OF RESEARCH: 1991-1998

KEYWORDS: **educational theories; research methodology; social theories**

2400

Faculty of Educational Studies, Research and Graduate School of Education, Highfield, Southampton SO9 5NH
02380 595000

Grenfell, M. Dr

Modern language teacher education

ABSTRACT: This research is a longitudinal study of modern language trainee teachers. It is based on a cohort of 24 students undertaking a 1-year training course. 8 students are presented in detail as individual case studies. Interview, questionnaire and classroom observation data gathering techniques are used to present the professional development of their pedagogic competence. Data is analysed in terms of the interaction between personal experience and attributes, and aspects of situational contexts. Training is presented as a problematic process in which tensions build on developing teaching skills. Various other approaches to teacher education - both theoretical and practical - are critically analysed along with trends in national policy.

PUBLISHED MATERIAL: GRENFELL, M. (1996). Bourdieu and initial teacher education - a post-structuralist approach', British Educational Research Journal, Vol 22, No 3, pp.287-303. ; GRENFELL, M. (1996). 'La formation comme champ', Revue du Centre de Recherche sur La Formation, Vol 4, pp.587-594. ; GRENFELL, M. (1997). 'Theory and practice in modern language teacher training', Language Learning Journal, Vol 16, pp.12-15. ; GRENFELL, M. Training teachers in practice. Clevedon: Multilingual Matters. (in press).

STATUS: Individual research

DATE OF RESEARCH: 1992-1998

KEYWORDS: language teachers; modern language studies; preservice teacher education

2401

Faculty of Educational Studies, Research and Graduate School of Education, Highfield, Southampton SO9 5NH
02380 595000

Foskett, N. Dr; Hemsley-Brown, J. Dr

Career perceptions and decision-making amongst young people in schools and colleges

ABSTRACT: This project is examining the perceptions that young people aged 10, 14 and 17 have of specific careers. In particular, it is focusing on the perceptions they have of nursing, engineering, and their chosen career, to identify: 1) the factors influencing the perceptions they hold; 2) the processes by which these perceptions develop; 3) the influence of these perceptions on the educational and training choices young people make; 4) the implications for careers education and guidance of insights into young people's perceptions. The research involved a sample of 400 young people in South East England and the West Midlands, using both focus groups and questionnaires.

STATUS: Sponsored project

SOURCE OF GRANT: Higher Education Information Services Trust £30,000; Department of Health £5,000

DATE OF RESEARCH: 1997-1998

KEYWORDS: career choice; careers; engineering; nursing; pupil attitudes

2402

Faculty of Educational Studies, Research and Graduate School of Education, Highfield, Southampton SO9 5NH
02380 595000

Anderson, Y. Miss; *Supervisor*: Erben, M. Mr

The collaborative process (a European project)

ABSTRACT: This project, sponsored by the European Commission, is to produce educational materials for nurses across Europe in career promotion. The researcher has led a group of people drawn from different countries to develop these materials by writing collaboratively. The process by which this has been achieved has been recorded in action and the resultant data will be used to develop grounded theory. Key questions include: 1) Why collaborate? 2) What is collaboration and how does it work? 3) What processes are operating when a group comes together in this way? The group consists of 1 nurse educator each from: France; Germany; Portugal; Luxembourg; Belgium; Holland; Ireland; Norway and Scotland; and 2 health educators (including the researcher) from the University of Southampton.

STATUS: Sponsored project

SOURCE OF GRANT: European Union

DATE OF RESEARCH: 1996-continuing

KEYWORDS: career choice; comparative education; nurse education; nurses

2403

Faculty of Educational Studies, Research and Graduate School of Education, Highfield, Southampton SO9 5NH
02380 595000

D'Authreau, J. Mr; *Supervisors*: Figueroa, P. Dr; Sharland, E. Dr

Why do children in local authority care achieve so little in the education system?

ABSTRACT: There have been a number of studies which have demonstrated that children who have come into the local authority care system do not fare well in the educational system, often leaving school with few if any educational qualifications. Many of the studies have focused on children who are in residential care, with education on or off the premises. More recent studies have indicated that children who have been fostered, even if this is in long term 'stable' placements, also often achieve little. The aim of the study is to explore for a particular population of one local authority the nature and circumstances of children they are looking after and their experience of the educational system. The intention is to gain a better understanding of why these children appear to be failing to achieve. The study is in 2 parts: 1) The first is a survey of 50 children through their social workers establishing background information about their social and educational circumstances to develop a profile of this population. 2) The second part involves a small number of individual case studies by semi-structured interview, and semi-structured interviews with education and social work professionals. At this point the first stage has been completed, and a profile of the population has been developed. The results confirm many of the findings of previous studies.

STATUS: Individual research

DATE OF RESEARCH: 1995-continuing

KEYWORDS: achievement; child welfare; educationally disadvantaged; foster care; social services; underachievement

2404

Faculty of Educational Studies, Research and Graduate School of Education, Highfield, Southampton SO9 4NH
02380 595000

McKeever, M. Ms; *Supervisor*: Figueroa, P. Dr

Case study of a school for black workers at a white university in South Africa, 1988-1995

ABSTRACT: This is a qualitative, interpretative study of a school set up by black workers and staffed by black students and intellectuals at a white university in South Africa during the transition from apartheid to democracy. The school, although located at a university, was not of the university, and was largely built on the vernacular knowledge and organisational systems of those excluded from the formal power-knowledge systems that underpinned apartheid. The school will be situated within the culture of the anti-apartheid movement with its unique symbols, rituals, theatre, art and literature. The history of the school will be reconstructed from all existing documentary sources. Three different interviewers will be used: a researcher; a black intellectual; and a black worker, to allow for triangulation of the interview data allowing for any bias that may occur because of the race, class or educational background of the interviewer. Analysis will involve triangulation of the themes that emerge from the interviews, the documentary sources and the cultural, artistic and literary texts of the anti apartheid movement. At all times the Western epistemological traditions underpinning formal education will be foregrounded and contrasted with the ontological and epistemological systems that workers brought with them to the school. The development of the school from a marginal oppositional grouping to the role it played in the formulation and implementation of national adult educational policy in many ways mirrors the macro change from apartheid to democracy.

PUBLISHED MATERIAL: MCKEEVER, M. (1996). 'The literature of the "illiterate"', Rapal Bulletin, No 31, pp.14-19.

STATUS: Individual research

DATE OF RESEARCH: 1995-continuing

KEYWORDS: **adult education; blacks; south africa; works schools**

2405

Faculty of Educational Studies, Research and Graduate School of Education, Highfield, Southampton SO9 5NH
02380 595000

Warsh, M. Dr; *Supervisor*: Figueroa, P. Dr

Teacher preparedness for multicultural/anti-racist education: a case study of the professional development programme at Simon Fraser University

ABSTRACT: This study examined multicultural/anti-racist (MCAR) teacher education in the Professional Development Programme (PDP) at Simon Fraser University (SFU) in Burnaby, British Columbia, Canada. It was concerned with the institutional milieu in which MCAR teacher education operates and its limitations, and with the national, regional and theoretical context for MCAR teacher education in Canada and British Columbia. It sought to ascertain: 1) how the institutional and organisational characteristics of the PDP influence MCAR teacher education at the formal and less than formal levels; 2) the philosophical perspectives on MCAR teacher education held in the Faculty; and 3) the degree to which these perspectives are apparent in individual teaching practices. It also sought to identify any barriers to further development of MCAR teacher education. The study employed research methods from the alternative tradition to evaluation research. Interviews, participant observation, document analysis and questionnaires were used. MCAR teacher education at SFU was found to function within Lynch's (1986) ad hoc multicultural level and Baptiste and Baptiste's (1980) process-oriented level. MCAR teacher education in the PDP has been given a marginal status and is not infused throughout programme offerings. Several barriers were found to the growth of MCAR teacher education: resistance to, and lack of knowledge about and understanding of, MCAR teacher education by teacher educators themselves, plus several institutional policies and practices which also act as barriers. Nevertheless, some growth and development of MCAR teacher education has been evident and further growth seems possible.

STATUS: Individual research

DATE OF RESEARCH: 1990-1997

KEYWORDS: **antiracism education; canada; multicultural education; preservice teacher education**

2406

Faculty of Educational Studies, Research and Graduate School of Education, Highfield, Southampton SO9 5NH
02380 595000

Figueroa, P. Dr; Nehaul, K. Ms

Parenting, academic success and Caribbean heritage pupils

ABSTRACT: How can Caribbean-heritage parents contribute to their children's progress in school? The present exploratory project focuses on this question which, despite much research on Caribbean-heritage pupils, has been almost entirely neglected. This project thus aims to gain insight into ways in which Caribbean-heritage parents do or can promote their children's education. It also aims to help build up a broader picture of influences on these children's educational performance. A third aim is to develop parent-teacher communication to improve learning. Specific goals will include: identifying educationally supportive home-based activities; understanding better how being black and in some ways culturally different impinge on the educational process; and promoting parent-teacher partnerships. The project will employ case studies of a small number of pupils starting secondary school in September 1997 (about 18 pupils in 3 urban comprehensive schools). Pupils and parents will be interviewed so as to identify parental strengths and relevant home-based activities, and other relevant influences and experiences, that impinge on the pupils' performance in school. Teachers are also to be interviewed and classroom activities observed. Finally, work is to be done with parents, pupils and teachers together, so as to try to develop and work towards specific targets and strategies for improving pupil performance. These case studies will help to advance the researchers' understanding of how Caribbean-heritage parents can work alongside schools, and should contribute to the development of models of relevant parent-pupil-teacher partnerships. Insights may also be gained which have wider relevance to home-school partnerships.

STATUS: Sponsored project

SOURCE OF GRANT: Economic and Social Research Council £41,608

DATE OF RESEARCH: 1997-1998

KEYWORDS: **afro caribbean youth; ethnic groups; home school relationship; parent participation; parent school relationship; youth**

2407

Faculty of Educational Studies, Research and Graduate School of Education, Highfield, Southampton SO9 5NH
02380 595000

Wong, L. Ms; *Supervisor*: Figueroa, P. Dr

The assimilation of youth immigrants from mainland China into the educational system in Hong Kong

ABSTRACT: The changeover of the rule of Hong Kong from Britain to China on 1 July 1997 has resulted in immense and sudden influx of immigrants from mainland China to Hong Kong, including youths aged between 10 to 18. It is vital to analyse the progress and assimilation of the youth immigrants from mainland China into the current educational system in Hong Kong. This research will focus on the experiences of these young immigrants on the policies developed, and on their implementation. The methodology will include a survey of relevant Hong Kong schools, interviews with headteachers, teachers, social workers and young immigrants from mainland China.

STATUS: Individual research

DATE OF RESEARCH: 1997-continuing

KEYWORDS: **china; hong kong; immigrants**

2408

Faculty of Educational Studies, Research and Graduate School of Education, Highfield, Southampton SO9 5NH
02380 595000

Bourne, J. Prof.; Smith, K. Mr; Kenner, C. Ms; Barton-Hide, D. Ms

Career ladder for classroom assistants

ABSTRACT: There is a perceived need for appropriate career ladders into teaching for those working as classroom assistants who have the potential to meet the standards required for Qualified Teacher Status (QTS). The aim of this Teacher Training Agency (TTA) funded project is to outline a possible national framework for progression to QTS and to identify the implications for implementation. The project is focusing on 3 main areas of research: identifying the current professional development training opportunities that exist for classroom assistants, analysing the appropriateness and effectiveness of this training and outlining a national and accessible framework for progression to QTS. Information will be collected from teachers, classroom assistants and training providers through interviews and focus groups across a number of regions. These regions will be selected according to the level and quality of work currently being carried out and on the potential and interest for further development. The study will attempt to encompass a comprehensive range of course provision and to include a full range of current pathways working towards QTS. National information gathered from questionnaires targeted at classroom assistants, teachers and training providers will provide a method for verifying the regional research within a national context. The overall aim will be to provide classroom assistants with clear and accessible training routes for working towards QTS. Importantly, the project will also aim to make these training opportunities useful and beneficial to classroom assistants who want training but do not want to obtain QTS.

STATUS: Sponsored project

SOURCE OF GRANT: Teacher Training Agency £25,000

DATE OF RESEARCH: 1998-continuing

KEYWORDS: **classroom assistants; qualified teacher status; teacher education**

2409

Faculty of Educational Studies, Research and Graduate School of Education, Highfield, Southampton SO9 5NH
02380 595000

Tsouroufli, M. Ms; *Supervisor*: Figueroa, P. Dr

Teachers' sex role ideology and the education of female students in Greece: an ethnographic study in a secondary school

ABSTRACT: The study aims to describe and analyse teachers' ideas about the roles of the sexes and to discover any gender stereotypes or prejudices of Greek teachers towards women, and particularly, towards female and male students. It also aims to discover any possible connections between teachers' sex role ideology and their behaviour in the classroom. The study was carried out in one secondary school in Greece. The approach followed was qualitative ethnographic and includes the use of the following research methods: oral life history interviews, classroom observation, semi-structured interviews. The study was conducted over a period of 3 months. The school was located in a working class area but the teachers who participated in the study live in different areas. 5 teachers participated in the study, 1 male and 4 females (1 teacher each of mathematics, modern Greek, physics, religious education and English). One class (B3) which all the selected teachers taught was chosen where 52 hours of observation in total took place.

STATUS: Individual research

DATE OF RESEARCH: 1996-continuing

KEYWORDS: **greece; sex differences; teacher attitudes**

2410

Faculty of Educational Studies, Research and Graduate School of Education, Highfield, Southampton SO9 5NH
02380 595000

Pointet, A. Mr; *Supervisor*: Figueroa, P. Dr

Underachieving boys

ABSTRACT: This research project arises from a concern about the underachievement of boys vis-a-vis girls at all ages and in just about every subject. The particular focus will be on the 11-16 age range and will use qualitative research methods involving semi-structured interviews and participant observation. Initially, the researcher will interview a sample of 10 boys from Years 7, 9 and 11 but the intention is to interview a sample of girls as well. Classroom observation and informal interviews with teaching colleagues will hopefully give balance to the research. In terms of methodology, background reading has veered the researcher towards an action research/ethnography approach. Whilst the qualitative research will be centred on one 11-16 inner city mixed comprehensive, the national situation regarding boys and underachievement will be at the forefront of this research. As a result of the investigation, the aim is to explain the cause of boys' underachievement and suggest some possible solutions to the problem.

STATUS: Individual research

DATE OF RESEARCH: 1998-continuing

KEYWORDS: **academic achievement; achievement; boys; secondary education; sex differences; underachievement**

2411

Faculty of Educational Studies, Research and Graduate School of Education, Highfield, Southampton SO9 5NH
02380 595000

Pike, M. Mr; *Supervisor*: Benton, M. Prof.

Keen readers (fostering keen adolescent readers of pre-20th century poetry at GCSE)

ABSTRACT: The research is designed to discover how teaching and learning strategies can be developed to foster keen adolescent readers of pre-20th century poetry. The term 'keen' includes both senses of the word: intellectually acute and also enthusiastic (Benton, M. (1998). Secondary worlds, p.ix). Investigating these twin elements of keenness involves a study of the aesthetic, cognitive and motivational aspects of response. This research is an attempt to acquire knowledge of the dynamic system that governs 'the relation of cognitive and emotional development to the growth of aesthetic capabilities' (Rosenblatt. (1985). Researching response to literature and the teaching of literature, p. 43). The relationship between discourse and thinking is explored in order to create readers who are intellectually perceptive and capable of making effective literacy judgements. Vygotsky is the dominant theorist (psychology) drawn upon but recent work by Edwards and Mercer (Common knowledge, 1987) is also developed. Theories of communication and cognition are applied to pedagogy and discourse in the classroom. The role of teacher and pupils as language users is explored in the context of classroom practice. Models of the reading process will be evaluated in the light of findings. A 3-year longitudinal ethnographic case study of 6 selected readers (4 male, 2 female) from Year 9 to Year 11. A broadly qualitative approach is used as the research is concerned with exploring processes. Extensive audio recording and transcription of situated classroom discourse as well as analysis of written work at GCSE has been carried out. The findings are intended to have a wide application to both literary and learning theory as well as to pedagogy in English teaching.

STATUS: Individual research

DATE OF RESEARCH: 1996-continuing

KEYWORDS: **english; literature; poetry; reading interests; secondary education**

2412

Faculty of Educational Studies, Research and Graduate School of Education, Highfield, Southampton SO9 5NH
02380 595000

Okuni, A. Mr; *Supervisor*: Benton, M. Prof.

Initial teacher training for the teaching of literature in English to second language (L2) students in Uganda

ABSTRACT: The study is prompted by the need to understand teaching and learning of literature in English in a second language context and, in particular, the need to develop an indepth understanding of low interest and academic achievement in literature in secondary schools in Uganda. For the purpose of this study attention will be focused on the nature and possible effect(s) of initial teacher preparation for literature teaching within secondary school Postgraduate Diploma in Education (PGDE) courses. This inquiry will concentrate on exploring the effectiveness of the training in knowledge of instructional objectives and methods and ability to use the methods appropriate for teaching literature. A qualitative (ethnographic and case study) research design will be adopted for this study. A sample of the relevant member(s) of staff and student teachers at a teacher training institution will be selected 'purposively'. A triangulation of data collection methods will include using: observation, interviews, questionnaires, profiles and documentary analysis. Data analysis will utilise 'grounded theory' procedures and will entail both ongoing review during data collection and more detailed systematic conceptual analysis after leaving the field.

STATUS: Individual research

DATE OF RESEARCH: 1997-continuing

KEYWORDS: **english - second language; second language teaching; uganda**

2413

Faculty of Educational Studies, Research and Graduate School of Education, Highfield, Southampton SO9 5NH
02380 595000
Leeds Metropolitan University, Department of Leisure and Sports Studies, Calverley Street, Leeds LS1 3HE
01132 832600
Loughborough University, Department of Physical Education, Sports Science and Recreation, Management Loughborough LE11 3TU
01509 263171

Clarke, G. Ms; *Supervisors*: Scraton, S. Prof.; Flintoff, A. Dr; Evans, J. Prof.

The lives and lifestyles of lesbian physical education teachers

ABSTRACT: This research focuses upon the lives of 14 white able-bodied lesbian physical education teachers working in secondary schools in England. In so doing it examines how they make sense of their lives and sexual identities within the specific context of physical education. To gain such insights a theoretical framework that centred on lesbian feminism and incorporated elements of postmodern and poststructural thinking was adopted. A biographical methodology was utilised as an approach particularly well suited to gaining a closely textured account of lesbian lives within the educational system and for interpreting data generated by the life story interviews. As well as offering a detailed examination of selves in specific settings the research was additionally concerned to make visible the structural and interactional injustices confronting lesbian teachers. The findings of the research reveal the complexities and contradictions of the lives of these lesbian teachers and how, at times, they may appear to collude with hegemonic heterosexual discourses, whilst resisting and challenging them. It is argued that hererosexual regulation has proved unable to assert complete dominance in the area under investigation and that, in fact, resistance to a would-be hegemony has been (dependent upon situation) both volubly opposed and silently challenged. The narratives from the life stories demonstrate that hereosexuality can be imitated and mirrored in acts of necessary subterfuge. By engaging in such heterosexual performance it is contended that power and resistance may be exercised and mobilised. However for the lesbian teachers in this research such undercover activity is more often than not prompted by fear of exposure and the consequent likelihood of dismissal. Running through this thesis is a claim that not only should these voices from the margins be heard, but also that what they are saying has direct relevance to the legal framing and defining of civil rights.

PUBLISHED MATERIAL: CLARKE, G. (1995). 'Outlaws in sport and education? Exploring the sporting and education experiences of lesbian physical education teachers'. In: LAWRENCE, L., MURDOCH, E. & PARKER, S. (Eds). Professional and development issues in leisure, sport and education. Eastbourne: Leisure Studies Association. ; CLARKE, G. (1996). 'Conforming and contesting with (a)difference: how lesbian students and teachers manage their identities', International Journal of Studies in Sociology of Education, Vol 6, No 2, pp.191-210. ; CLARKE, G. (1997). 'Playing a part: the lives of lesbian physical education teachers'. In: CLARKE, G. & HUMBERSTONE, B. (Eds). Researching women and sport. London: Macmillan. ; CLARKE, G. (1998). 'Working out: lesbian teachers and the politics of (dis)location', Journal of Lesbian Studies, Vol 2, No 4, pp.85-99. ; CLARKE, G. (1998). 'Voices from the margins: resistance and regulation in the lives of lesbian teachers'. In: ERBEN, M. Biography and education: an edited collection. London: Falmer Press.

STATUS: Individual research

DATE OF RESEARCH: 1993-1998

KEYWORDS: **homosexuality; lesbianism; physical education teachers; sexual identity**

2414

Faculty of Educational Studies, Research and Graduate School of Education, Highfield, Southampton SO9 5NH
02380 595000
Southampton University, School of Nursing and Midwifery, Southampton General Hospital, Tremona Road, Southampton SO16 6YD
01703 796554

Simons, H. Prof.; Long, G. Mr; Clark, J. Ms; Gobbi, M. Ms

Nurse education and training evaluation in Ireland

ABSTRACT: Commissioned by the Department of Health, Dublin, in collaboration with An Board Altranais, this independent external evaluation is evaluating the introduction of the General Nurse Registration/Diploma Programme in Ireland over 2 years from May 1996-May 1998. The evaluation takes the form of a major case study over 2 years of the first site of operation of the 'new' Registration/Diploma programme in Galway. This is supplemented by shorter field visits to other sites for comparative purposes (both urban and those initially maintaining traditional programme) and interviews with major stakeholders. In the second year, the database is extended further to include questionnaires on outcomes and focus group discussions with representatives of key groups in implementation from the additional sites which came on stream with the Registration/Diploma Programme in 1995 and 1997.

STATUS: Sponsored project

SOURCE OF GRANT: Department of Health, Dublin in collaboration with An Board Altranais

DATE OF RESEARCH: 1996-1998

KEYWORDS: **ireland; nurse education; nurses**

2415

Research and Graduate School of Education, Highfield, Southampton SO9 5NH
02380 595000

Butcher, S. Mrs; *Supervisor*: Benton, M. Prof.

An examination of the benefits of cross-curricular study of English and the visual arts at post-16 level

ABSTRACT: The research takes as its field of reference the classically established relationship between the sister arts of painting and poetry, a relationship which has prospered within English literature since the Renaissance, reaching its height in the 18th century. The last 20 years have seen a renewed interest in comparative studies in this area with important implications for education. Literary studies in particular have moved beyond their primary discipline and sought to identify structures of meaning which are shared by both painting and literature. Such a cross-disciplinary approach to the Arts has begun to be reflected through the availability of A-level courses which offer theatre studies, media studies, film studies, communication studies and expressive arts in addition to the traditional English literature course. These subjects now often make use of a common critical grammar when evaluating communicative texts (whether expressed visually or linguistically). The research has explored the historical, theoretical and practical case for a new A-level in English with the visual arts. The last four of the A-level subjects quoted above are rooted firmly in the 20th century and therefore fail to develop the comparative opportunities a wider historical range offers. The proposed new course is underpinned by an examination of the relationship which is established separately with painting and poetry, of the potentialities of each medium and of the benefits offered by combined study. The initial research questions focus on the relationship which the viewer/reader develops with visual and verbal texts and explores the cognitive and affective processes involved. The specifically educational questions are as follows: 1) In what ways can an awareness of these processes, and of their similarities and differences across the two disciplines, foster a mutually enriched understanding in students of the art forms? 2) What insights into cultural and historical conditions are available to students who become fluent in interpreting these complementary arts? At the initial stage, the researcher aimed to gather a wide understanding of the perception of the role of the reader and viewer. At the second stage, fieldwork was carried out in four post-16 settings documenting and evaluating the quality and range of responses to selected visual and verbal texts. The methodology was qualitative and involved detailed scrutiny of the responses of A-level English students, with the aim of analysing their responses in depth. Oral, written and graphic means were used to monitor students' work and semi-structured interviews were conducted with students. Analysis and evaluation of the data so gathered will be used to help identify the most appropriate emphases, in both content and method, in the future development of the proposed A-level syllabus.

PUBLISHED MATERIAL: BENTON, M.G. & BUTCHER, S.M. 'Painting Shakespeare', Journal of Aesthetic Education. (in press).

STATUS: Individual research

DATE OF RESEARCH: 1995-continuing

KEYWORDS: **art education; arts; literature; painting - visual arts**

2416

Teaching Support and Media Services, Highfield, Southampton SO9 5NH
02380 595000

Smith, I. Mr; *Supervisor*: Allen, W. Mr

Optimising international links and exchange programmes between departments of photography

ABSTRACT: This project is concerned with the study of links and exchanges as mechanisms for promoting a greater mutual understanding of the nature and structure of college and university courses in photography in Europe. The investigation involves case studies of selected interchange programmes, the establishment of a data base of European courses in photography and an analysis of the characteristics of photographic courses with a view to identifying the potential for a European Scheme for credit accumulation and transfer. The project has reached the stage of having produced a published data base of European courses in photography through the 'Photolink International' scheme which is supported by Kodak Limited and ERASMUS.

PUBLISHED MATERIAL: SMITH, I.R. (1990). 'Directory of photographic education: A European survey', Photolink International.

STATUS: Sponsored project

SOURCE OF GRANT: Kodak Limited; ERASMUS

DATE OF RESEARCH: 1988-1993

KEYWORDS: **international educational exchange; photography**

St Andrew's College of Education
2417

Duntocher Road, Bearsden, Glasgow G61 4QA
0141 943 1424

McGilp, J. Dr; Michael, M. Ms

The development of language through partnership and quality experiences

ABSTRACT: The purpose of the study is threefold: (1) to provide different learning experience in language for pupils; (2) to involve parents and teacher in partnership; (3) to gain parent and pupil responses to the learning opportunities provided and to partnership. The study builds on extensive work carried out in the Australian Catholic University (Aquinas' Campus) by Dr McGilp. The research will be conducted in Clydebank. The researcher and headteacher have an established working relationship and with the senior stages teacher (P6) will collaboratively work with parents to establish partnership through which to carry out the investigation. Qualitative and quantitative data will be obtained by questionnaire and interview. Improvements in pupil linguistic competence and the factors contributing to this will be recorded. The final published study will compare results with those in a paralelled Australian study.

STATUS: Sponsored project

SOURCE OF GRANT: St Andrew's College of Education

DATE OF RESEARCH: 1993-1993

KEYWORDS: **language acquisition; language skills; learning experience; parent participation; parent teacher cooperation; partnerships**

2418

Duntocher Road, Bearsden, Glasgow G61 4QA
0141 943 1424

Bourne, V. Mr; Blee, H. Mr; Barr, M. Ms; Webster, D. Mr; Dixon, J. Mr

Probationer teachers' views of college courses

ABSTRACT: The investigation will determine how successfully the B.Ed course has been in preparing teachers for their first and second years of teaching. Strengths of the course will be identified together with suggestions for changes/additions as seen from probationer teachers' points of view. Areas for investigation will include: (1) the teacher's perception of competence and its origin; (2) the nature of the school induction programme; (3) the effectiveness of partnership between the school and St Andrew's College during B.Ed degree; (4) major gaps in course, e.g. language, positive behaviour, planning, classroom administration; (5) any difference between East/West/Tayside regions. A questionnaire will be issued to all students qualifying with a B.Ed degree from this college in the last two years. The response will be evaluated and summarised. Some interviews may be carried out to illuminate the questionnaire responses.

STATUS: Sponsored project

SOURCE OF GRANT: St Andrew's College of Education £220

DATE OF RESEARCH: 1993-1993

KEYWORDS: **course evaluation; preservice teacher education; probationary teachers**

2419

Duntocher Road, Bearsden, Glasgow G61 4QA
0141 943 1424

Ker, M. Ms; Whyte, A. Mr

Using the school grounds

ABSTRACT: The aims of this project are: (1) To evaluate the use of school grounds in Dunbarton Division; to compare this with recent research carried out elsewhere; and to help teachers in a selected group of schools to recognise the unique potential of each site, build on that, and challenge these teachers to fully exploit the grounds as a resource. (2) To devise strategies to assist these schools; improve the effective use of these environments involving the whole community; and to investigate the impact of these developments on pupil creativity. (3) To encourage interest in such development more widely. The project will involve students on the B.Ed 2 course 'Improving the College Grounds'. A questionnaire will be devised for students to use with pupils and teachers about their use of school grounds. The project will also involve working with the Educational Development Service, to promote the work in schools. Questionnaires and semi-structured interviews will be used in pilot schools. The outcomes of the project will include: instruments for evaluating and assessing impact of improved landscapes; a report with agenda for change; and training in the process of education authority art teachers.

STATUS: Sponsored project

SOURCE OF GRANT: Dunbarton Division, Strathclyde £9,000; St Andrew's College of Education £120

DATE OF RESEARCH: 1992-1993

KEYWORDS: **campuses; educational facilities improvement; school space**

2420

Duntocher Road, Bearsden, Glasgow G61 4QA
0141 943 1424

Conroy, J. Mr; McClure, M. Sist.

Attitudes to religious education among college students

ABSTRACT: The background to the research is that there has been a dearth of information as to the opinion of young adults about their school Religious Education (RE); and that there has been a national syllabus for RE extent for a number of years. The aims of the research are: (1) to discover (a) the effects of the National Syllabus on young college students; (b) the attitudes of young people in general; and (c) the educational background against which attitudes develop; (2) To carry out comparative analysis with research completed in Europe and other parts of Britain. (3) To use the data as a springboard for a wider research project which goes beyond undergraduates. (4) To discover the efficacy of current pedagogies. The research methods will include a research questionnaire for all students; the development of a database; integration of the database using keyword/concept software; and statistical regression analysis.

STATUS: Sponsored project

SOURCE OF GRANT: St Andrew's College of Education

DATE OF RESEARCH: 1992-1993

KEYWORDS: **religious education; student attitudes**

2421

Duntocher Road, Bearsden, Glasgow G61 4QA
0141 943 1424

Cooper, W. Mr

Control technology

ABSTRACT: The aim of the project is to determine the extent to which upper primary school pupils are able to undertake control activities in the classroom. An action research approach will be used where pupils will be observed working on directed practical activity. Interviews of colleagues involved in the activities will also be undertaken together with evaluation of worksheets and achievement objectives.

STATUS: Sponsored project

SOURCE OF GRANT: St Andrew's College of Education

DATE OF RESEARCH: 1992-1993

KEYWORDS: **control technology; primary education**

2422

Duntocher Road, Bearsden, Glasgow G61 4QA
0141 943 1424

Hutchison, M. Mrs

Science and technology in the primary school: implications of the Review and Development Group's Publication 3 (RDGP3) for curricular integration

ABSTRACT: The aims of this research are to: (1) research existing practices in primary schools for the development of science and technology; (2) explore the problems which exist in integrating science within environmental studies in relation to the recommendations of 5-14 Review and Development Group 3; and (3) develop and pilot materials for a primary school programme in Science and Technology which will take account of existing practices and the recommendations of RDG3. The research will include: personal investigation of a sample of schools; evidence from Science and Technology Regional Organisation (SATRO); evidence from Strathclyde Regional Inspectorate; extended survey working with students as researchers in schools; design of materials; and piloting and evaluating materials. A report will be published with recommendations for policy and practice in relation to science and technology education in Scottish primary schools including specific targets and attainment levels with identified resources for achieving these.

STATUS: Sponsored project

SOURCE OF GRANT: St Andrew's College of Education £440

DATE OF RESEARCH: 1992-1993

KEYWORDS: **primary education; science education; technology education**

2423

Duntocher Road, Bearsden, Glasgow G61 4QA
0141 943 1424

O'Brien, J. Mr; McGettrick, B. Prof.; McPhee, A. Mr; McDonald, S. Mrs; Boyle, J. Mr; Blee, H. Mr; Luti, P.Mr

Valued forms of support for secondary school teachers in times of curriculum change and development

ABSTRACT: The investigation examines the nature and type of support offered to teachers to facilitate curriculum change and educational development. The project will aim to identify those forms of support which have been regarded as essential, helpful and effective. It examines such initiatives as Standard Grade, Revised Higher and National Certificate. The main focus is on what can best be done centrally to: (1) provide materials and different forms of support; and (2) stimulate types of support which teachers find helpful. A triangulation approach to the illumination of the issues across a number of subjects will be used. The views and experiences of teachers in the subjects chosen will be considered in relation to three aspects of support for development: a focus on materials or subjects; a focus on school support; a focus on agencies. This will be achieved in workshop discussions, subsequent devising of a questionnaire; five case studies; fifty schools sampled by questionnaire and structured interviews; interviews with a limited number of personnel from support agencies such as the Scottish Examination Board (SEB), Scottish Consultative Committee on the Curriculum (SCCC), Scottish Council for Educational Technology (SCET); and analysis of collected data. A report to the Scottish Office Education Department (SOED) will identify types of support viewed as valuable experiences for teachers; it may also indicate possible further investigations which could inform decision making on the support for curriculum development and change.

STATUS: Sponsored project

SOURCE OF GRANT: Scottish Office Education Department £16,700

DATE OF RESEARCH: 1993-1993

KEYWORDS: **curriculum development; secondary school teachers; teacher development**

2424

Duntocher Road, Bearsden, Glasgow G61 4QA
0141 943 1424

Mumford, J. Ms

Development of 5-14 Mathematics Programme

ABSTRACT: The project aimed to find ways of illustrating how mathematics can be taught with particular reference to a current school text and in relation to 5-14 mathematics guidelines. The work included document analysis, participant observation and discussion of effective practice. A chapter for a book on 5-14 mathematics which contextualises the philosophy of the subject within current approaches resulted from the work.

PUBLISHED MATERIAL: MUMFORD, J. (1993). 'Assessing with HBJ mathematics'. In: MENZIES, Y., MUMFORD, J. & SKINNER, G. Mathematics in context. London: Harcourt, Brace, Jovanovich.

STATUS: Sponsored project

SOURCE OF GRANT: Collins Publishing

DATE OF RESEARCH: 1992-1993

KEYWORDS: **mathematics education**

2425

Duntocher Road, Bearsden, Glasgow G61 4QA
0141 943 1424

Gibson, D. Mr; Thomson, A. Mr

Paediatric surgery and medicine course

ABSTRACT: The project aims to develop open and flexible learning materials incorporating video, computer and text resources for undergraduate and postgraduate students in paediatric medicine and surgery. These materials will extend and vitalise a newly developed textbook written specifically for an existing course, freeing course staff from lectures and enabling them to increase the quality time they spend with students, while at the same time increasing student throughput. The materials will also act as a key resource in supported self-study activities associated with full-time and part-time courses.

STATUS: Sponsored project

SOURCE OF GRANT: Glasgow University; Yorkhill Hospital Trust; Various pharmaceutical companies, jointly

DATE OF RESEARCH: 1993-1998

KEYWORDS: educational materials; flexible learning; material development; medical education

2426

Duntocher Road, Bearsden, Glasgow G61 4QA
0141 943 1424

McDonald, S. Mrs

A model for staff development in information technology within initial teacher training

ABSTRACT: The Structure and Process in Teacher Education (SPRITE) initiative has given the College an opportunity to try out a new form of staff development in information technology (IT), targetting a group of staff working as a team towards a specific goal. The project involves one full-time equivalent post on IT staff development. A seconded teacher and a College staff member will focus on: 1) learning to make overlays for touch keyboard and creating overlays for a particular context; and 2) the location and piloting of resurces on a theme for a class of 7 year olds.

STATUS: Sponsored project

SOURCE OF GRANT: St Andrew's College of Education; Scottish Office Education Department

DATE OF RESEARCH: 1991-1993

KEYWORDS: **computer uses in education; information technology; staff development; teacher education**

2427

Duntocher Road, Bearsden, Glasgow G61 4QA
0141 943 1424

Wilson, R. Mr; Cullen, L. Mrs

Influencing the lunchtime experience through curricular development: development of a research tool

ABSTRACT: The first outcome of this project is the development of an appropriate research instrument to be used within the pilot programme 'Influencing the lunchtime experience through curricular development'. The aims of this project are placed in a context which takes account of individual pupils and their lifestyles, how they relate to groups within the school and how they are influenced by the curriculum in its various forms - formal, informal and hidden. Previous research on pupil choices of food at lunchtime, Turner et al (1995) and Ross (1995) indicated that influences such as pupil perceptions of 'healthy food' and school organisation were seen as the factors affecting what children think and actually do at school lunchtimes. This project is part of the larger development programme and is intended to produce an appropriate research tool to meet the first aim of the programme: to develop an understanding of the priorities placed on different lunchtime behaviours by pupils. Methods include interview of key school staff, survey of pupils' views by questionnaire (n=47 P7 pupils) and follow-up interviews of selected pupils. The next step is to use instrument to assess impact of a curricular programme on healthy eating on P7 pupils' attitudes and behaviours at lunchtime. A final report will be produced during 1997 for the Health Promotion Department, Greater Glasgow Health Board.

STATUS: Sponsored project

SOURCE OF GRANT: Health Promotion Department, Greater Glasgow Health Board £2,000

DATE OF RESEARCH: 1996-1997

KEYWORDS: **eating habits; food; nutrition; primary education; primary school pupils; pupil attitudes; school meals**

2428

Duntocher Road, Bearsden, Glasgow G61 4QA
0141 943 1424

Gibson, D. Mr; Thomson, A. Mr

A flexible approach to postgraduate teacher education

ABSTRACT: The purpose of this project is to examine ways of developing a flexible approach to postgraduate teacher education through the development of a range of learning materials in open access, technology-based format to replace 251 of the taught components within the Postgraduate Certificate of Education (PGCE) secondary Professional Studies programme.

STATUS: Sponsored project

SOURCE OF GRANT: Scottish Higher Education Funding Council £57,000

DATE OF RESEARCH: 1997-continuing

KEYWORDS: **flexible learning; postgraduate certificate in education; preservice teacher education; teaching methods**

2429

Duntocher Road, Bearsden, Glasgow G61 4QA
0141 943 1424
Strathclyde University, Faculty of Education, Department of Educational Studies, Jordanhill Campus, Southbrae Drive, Glasgow G13 1PP
0141 950 3000

Forde, C. Ms; Casteel, V. Mrs; Reeves, J. Ms

A framework for management development in Scottish schools

ABSTRACT: With the increasing emphasis in Scotland on the role of school managers in the provision of effective learning, there has been a growing concern about meeting the development needs of school managers and aspirants. The aims of this project were to survey current provision and develop a strategic approach to management development for Scottish schools. The project includes a number of investigations: 1) a survey of regional authority provision of school management training through semi-structured interviews of staff in each region which indicated that a common developmental framework was desirable; 2) a survey of opinion regarding the accuracy of a functional analysis of school management for Scottish schools using focus groups and questionnaires which led to the development of a framework for management development to include functions, abilities and qualities; 3) a survey of attitudes using focus groups concerning the resultant framework to be conducted February-March 1997.

PUBLISHED MATERIAL: REEVES, J. & WIGHT, J. (1995). Towards a framework for management in Scottish schools. A report on current provision by regional authorities. Report to the Scottish Office Education Department. ; CASTEEL, V., REEVES, J., FORDE, C. & LYNAS, R. (1997). A framework for leadership and management development in Scottish Schools. Glasgow: Scottish Qualification for Headship Development Unit. ; A full list of publications is available from the Scottish Qualification for Headship Development Unit.

STATUS: Sponsored project

SOURCE OF GRANT: Scottish Office Education and Industry Department

DATE OF RESEARCH: 1994-1997

KEYWORDS: **educational administration; educational administrators; management development; management in education; school based management; scotland**

St Andrews University
2430

Department of Psychology, St Andrews, Fife KY16 9AJ 01334 76161
Craigie College of Education, Beech Grove, Ayr KA8 OSR
01292 260321

Holligan, C. Dr; *Supervisor*: Johnston, R. Dr

Segmentation ability and patterns of reading failure: the nature of the relationship

ABSTRACT: The aim of this research is to examine: (a) how poor readers recognise words; (b) in what way this is qualitatively distinct from that of normal readers; and (c) why this leads to impaired nonword reading. A study is also being made of poor readers' memory difficulties, and the importance of visual skills to the early stages of reading development.

STATUS: Sponsored project

SOURCE OF GRANT: Wellcome Trust £61,000

DATE OF RESEARCH: 1992-1993

KEYWORDS: **dyslexia; reading difficulties; reading failure; reading skills; word recognition**

St Mary's College
2431

191 Falls Road, Belfast BT12 6FE
01232 327678

Keane, M. Dr; Randall, A. Dr; Vandijk, H. Dr; Wierdsma, M. Dr; Dillon, M. Dr; Artigues, A. Dr

Cultural diversity in Europe: a handbook for teacher education students

ABSTRACT: This is a joint project between: St Mary's College; De Montfort University; St Patrick's College, Dublin; Windeshein Christelijke Hogeschool, Zwolle, Netherlands; University of the Balaerics, Palma de Mallorca, Spain; and the Institut de la Providence, Champion, Belgium. In spite of the inexorable move towards 'an ever-closer union' cultural differences within many European countries are becoming increasingly apparent. Reactions to such differences of race, language, religion and/or culture may be tolerant and respectful. On the other hand, reactions may be racist and violent. The nature of cultural diversity, as well as the social, economic, political and educational implications, needs to be understood as part of the education of student teachers all over Europe, many of whom will teach in multi ethnic and multi cultural environments. This project aims, therefore, to provide insights into salient aspects of the cultural diversity which exists in a range of countries within Europe, compiled by teacher educators who live and work in these countries. A compendium of case studies on the nature and varied effects of linguistic, religious and ethnic differences forms the core of a handbook which also provides methods for using the materials. It is envisaged that the handbook may be used with students in either transnational groupings or within their own institutions.

STATUS: Collaborative

DATE OF RESEARCH: 1993-continuing

KEYWORDS: **cultural differences; educational materials; europe; guides; multiculturalism; preservice teacher education**

2432

191 Falls Road, Belfast BT12 6FE
01232 327678

McKendry, E. Dr

'Seanchai - Storyteller': storytelling in Ireland

ABSTRACT: The British Broadcasting Corporation (BBC), Northern Ireland series 'Seanchai - Storyteller' has been produced in Irish language and then in English versions. The project will provide background and classroom notes to support the series, firstly in English and then in Irish. The target audience is key stages 3 and 4 (secondary, supporting the English and Irish-medium programmes of study and the cultural heritage cross-curricular theme in the Northern Ireland Curriculum. The original project material will be supplemented in the future. A booklet to accompany the BBC Northern Ireland television series 'Seanchai - Storyteller' will be produced in Spring 1997.

STATUS: Sponsored project

SOURCE OF GRANT: British Broadcasting Corporation

DATE OF RESEARCH: 1995-1998

KEYWORDS: **childrens television; cultural education; educational television; folk culture; irish; literature; northern ireland; story telling**

2433

191 Falls Road, Belfast BT12 6FE
01232 327678

McKendry, E. Dr

Phonetic influence and the learning of Irish

ABSTRACT: The phonetic system of Irish is fundamentally different from that of English, particularly in regard to the phenomenon of 'Caol agus Leathan', broad and slender consonants. Teachers and learners of Irish alike are often unaware of the importance of this distinction, sometimes with bizarre results. Emphasis upon the affricatives in Ulster Irish has also dulled aural discrimination across the consonantal range. The research will centre upon the needs of learners and teachers, and consider the approach required in teacher training.

PUBLISHED MATERIAL: McKENDRY, E. (1997). 'Phonetic influence and the learning of Irish'. In: HENRY, A. (Ed). Language in Ireland. Belfast Working Papers in Language and Linguistics, Vol 12. Newtownabbey: University of Ulster, Department of Communication Studies.

DATE OF RESEARCH: 1994-1997

KEYWORDS: **irish; language teachers; languages; phonemics; phonetics**

2434

191 Falls Road, Belfast BT12 6FE
01232 327678

McKendry, E. Dr

Languages in Ireland

ABSTRACT: Despite its geographical position at the periphery of Europe, Ireland has a remarkably rich variety in its linguistic experience. This project aims to give an overview of languages in Ireland, from prehistoric, through Indo-European, Old Irish, Latin, Scandinavian, French, to Modern Irish and English, including Ulster Scots. The material produced will be flexible, for use in lecture presentation (academic, local history groups, community etc), or for classroom application (Northern Ireland Curriculum key stages 2-4 and A-level), with suitable exercises and activities. The project is specifically targeted in schools to the Cross-curricular Themes of Cultural Heritage and Education for Mutual Understanding in the Northern Ireland Curriculum. It is hoped that development for the Internet and an interactive CD-Rom will also result. The material was first collated as a contribution to the language element in 'Timescapes' - an interactive CD-Rom programme sponsored by the Department of Education for Northern Ireland (DENI) in collaboration with its Museums Branch and produced by the Northern Ireland Centre for Learning Resources (NICLR).

DATE OF RESEARCH: 1995-continuing

KEYWORDS: **cd roms; cultural education; ireland; languages; literature; northern ireland; primary education; secondary education**

2435

191 Falls Road, Belfast BT12 6FE
01232 327678

McKendry, E. Dr

The cultural element in language learning after education reform in Northern Ireland

ABSTRACT: The Northern Ireland version of the National Curriculum in Britain broadly reflects the approach towards language learning contained in the National Curriculum - no compulsory second language at key stages 1 and 2 (primary), but a compulsory language at key stages 3 and 4 (secondary). (Provision for Welsh in Wales and Irish-medium education in Northern Ireland may be considered as regional variations). Possible reasons for this rejection of the compulsory early learning of languages in the UK will be examined. The paper will concentrate, however, on the debate surrounding the link between language, culture and the curriculum, which contributed to the emergence of cultural heritage as a compulsory cross-curricular theme in the Northern Ireland Curriculum. In the search for a means of provision for Irish within the general Northern Ireland Curriculum, cultural arguments and political pragmatism, as well as those of language learning, dominated in the compromise which emerged. Through 'cultural heritage' and its companion theme 'education for mutual understanding', the concept of 'culture and language learning' was given an added dimension within the context of language learning in Northern Ireland. In Northern Ireland's English-medium primary schools, language learning provision can, unusually, be interpreted as being subservient to the cultural dimension. Implications for classroom practice, at primary and secondary levels, will be discussed.

PUBLISHED MATERIAL: MCKENDRY, E. (1989). 'The way forward and the Irish language in Northern Ireland's education system', Eire/Ireland, Vol XXIV, No 2, pp.128-139. ; MCKENDRY, E. (1994). 'Irish in Northern Ireland'. In: NI DHEA, E. et al (Eds). The lesser used languages and teacher education: towards the promotion of the European dimension. Limerick: Mary Immaculate College. ; MCKENDRY, E. (1997). 'The cultural element in language learning after education reform in Northern Ireland'. Proceedings of the Royal Irish Academy/IRAAL Symposium on Culture and Language Learning, University of Limerick, November 1996.

STATUS: Individual research

DATE OF RESEARCH: 1996-1997

KEYWORDS: **cross curricular approach; cultural education; irish; national curriculum - northern ireland; northern ireland; second language learning**

St Mary's University College

2436

Waldegrave Road, Strawberry Hill, Twickenham TW1 4SX
0181 240 4000

Howard, J. Mrs

The secondary school as a place of adult learning, with special reference to school based initial teacher training

ABSTRACT: The study is focused on the school as a place of adult learning. The experience of a cohort of students on initial teacher training in schools is monitored throughout their undergrduate course, together with the experience of the teachers in school who are acting as mentors. The aim is to consider how both teachers and students function as adult learners. The culture of the school in supporting their learning is a particular area of attention.

STATUS: Individual research

DATE OF RESEARCH: 1995-continuing

KEYWORDS: **adult learning; mentors; preservice teacher education; school based teacher education; student teacher supervisors; student teachers; teaching practice**

2437

Waldegrave Road, Strawberry Hill, Twickenham TW1 4SX
0181 240 4000

Daley, A. Dr; Buchanan, J. Mrs

Aerobic dance and physical self-perceptions in female adolescents: some implications for physical education

ABSTRACT: Whilst there is widespread empirical evidence indicating a positive relationship between physical activity and mental health, literature examining this relationship with reference to feminine typed physical activity has been limited. The present study was conducted to determine the effects of physical exercise upon physical self-perceptions in female adolescents with specific regards to participation in aerobics. 113 adolescent females were recruited to either an aerobics plus physical education group (n=43) or a physical education only condition (n=70). All participants completed the PSPP before and after the 5 week aerobics class intervention. The aerobics classes took place after school hours. Results revealed that the aerobics group demonstrated significantly improved physical self-perceptions over time but the physical education only group did not. These findings indicate that female adolescents' feelings about their physical selves may be enhanced through the use of gender appropriate physical exercise within secondary schools.

PUBLISHED MATERIAL: DALEY, A.J. & BUCHANAN, J. 'Aerobic dance and physical self-perceptions in female adolescents: some implications for physical education', Research Quarterly for Exercise and Sport. (in press).

STATUS: Individual research

DATE OF RESEARCH: 1997-1998

KEYWORDS: **adolescents; aerobics; girls; physical education; self concept; self esteem**

2438

Waldegrave Road, Strawberry Hill, Twickenham TW1 4SX
0181 240 4000

Sullivan, J. Dr; *Supervisors*: Walsh, P. Dr; Lawton, D. Prof.

Catholic education: distinctive and inclusive

ABSTRACT: The thesis examines the coherence of the claim that Catholic education is both distinctive and inclusive. Central questions explored are: 1) What is the nature of, foundation for and implications of the claim that Catholic schools offer a distinctive approach to education? 2) To what extent does the claim to distinctiveness entail exclusiveness or allow for inclusiveness? How far can distinctiveness and inclusiveness (in the context of Catholic education) be reconciled? An extended commentary on key Roman Catholic documents about Catholic education is provided. This is related to the particular context of Catholic schools in England and Wales, where an ambivalence in the purposes of Catholic schools is indicated and a way for them to avoid the ambivalence by being both distinctive and inclusive is suggested. The study works at the interface between Christian (and more specifically Catholic) theology, philosophical analysis and educational theory and practice with regard to the raison d'etre of Catholic schools. Through a retrieval and application of the notion of 'living tradition' it is shown that within Catholicism there are intellectual resources which enable Catholic schools to combine distinctiveness with inclusiveness, although there will be limits on the degree of inclusiveness possible. In the face of criticisms of their potentially inward-looking role in a pluralist society, it is argued that Catholic schools contribute to the common good. The argument should enhance clarity about purpose for Catholic educators and it has implications for other forms of faith-based education.

PUBLISHED MATERIAL: SULLIVAN, J. (1997). 'Blondel and a living tradition for Catholic education', Catholic Education: A Journal of Inquiry and Practice, Vol 1, No 1, pp.67-76. ; SULLIVAN, J. (1997). 'Leading values and casting shadows', Pastoral Care, Vol 15, No 3, pp.8-12. ; SULLIVAN, J. (1998). 'Compliance or complaint', Irish Educational Studies, Vol 17, pp.183-193. ; SULLIVAN, J. 'From promulgation to reception', Doctrine and Life. (in press). ; SULLIVAN, J. 'Leading values and casting shadows in Church schools', Education and Ethos, Vol 1, No 1. (in press). A full list of publications is available from the researcher.

STATUS: Individual research

DATE OF RESEARCH: 1994-1998

KEYWORDS: **catholic educators; catholic schools; church and education**

2439

Waldegrave Road, Strawberry Hill, Twickenham TW1 4SX
0181 240 4000

Scholefield, L. Ms; *Supervisor*: Walsh, P. Dr

The tale of two cultures: a case study of the symbols, stories, rituals and values of a Roman Catholic and a Jewish secondary school

ABSTRACT: The research explores the culture of a Catholic and Jewish voluntary aided, co-educational, 11-18, secondary school through two case studies. The relationship between what happens in the schools and the theology of education in Christianity and Judaism is discussed. Culture is understood as the symbols, stories, rituals and values of the school. This is an inter-faith study and uses the concept of dialogue in several ways. The case studies included student questionnaires, participant observation, interviews of staff and students, and document analysis. It is not a full blown ethnographic study but has many of the characteristics of ethnography. The researcher defines the theoretical paradigm as open inclusivism within a wider hermeneutical or interpretive tradition of research. The education which the Catholic students have experienced stresses the importance of the uniqueness of the individual, combined with the building of community within the school but not particularly related to the wider church. The Jewish school is trying to teach the language of Jewish tradition so that students can lead Jewish lives. There is a family atmosphere built up in this school. In neither school are the students strongly committed to institutional religion and the explicit religious elements are only partially integrated into the school. The culture comes most sharply into focus in dealing with death and dying as well as on special occasions and in connection with places such as Lourdes and Israel.

STATUS: Individual research

DATE OF RESEARCH: 1994-continuing

KEYWORDS: **catholic schools; church and education; cultural education; jewish education; religion and education; religious education; secondary education**

2440

Waldegrave Road, Strawberry Hill, Twickenham TW1 4SX
0181 240 4000

Leahy, J. Ms; *Supervisor*: Daley, A. Dr

A comparison of self-perceptions in participants and non-participants of extra curricular physical activities

ABSTRACT: The positive relationship between physical activity and self-esteem has been consistently documented, although evidence regarding the psychological effects of participation in extra-curricual physical activities (ECPA) has been limited. The aim of the present study was to consider the relationship between participation in ECPA in male and female secondary school adolescents. Adolescents (Year 8 and Year 9) who participated in ECPA were identified and 63 children were randomly selected to complete Harter's (1982) Self-perception Profile for Adolescents. Additionally, 42 children who did not participate the ECPA were randomly selected from the Year 8 and Year 9 class registers and asked to complete the Self-perception Profile for Adolescents. Results revealed a significant group main effect. ECPA participants reported significantly higher global self-worth, romantic appeal and athletic, social, physical appearance and job competence scores compared to non-ECPA participants. These findings suggest that participation in extra-curricular physical activities may influence adolescents self-perceptions in a beneficial manner.

PUBLISHED MATERIAL: DALEY, A.J. & LEAHY, J. (1998). 'A comparison of self-perceptions in participants and non-participants of extra-curricular physical activities', European Journal of Physical Education, Vol 3, No 1, p.107.

STATUS: Individual research

DATE OF RESEARCH: 1998-1998

2441

Waldegrave Road, Strawberry Hill, Twickenham TW1 4SX
0181 240 4000

O'Gara, A. Ms; *Supervisor*: Daley, A. Dr

Age, gender and motivation for participation in extra-curricular physical activities in secondary school adolescents

ABSTRACT: The aim of the present study was to consider the relationship between age and children's motives for participation in extra-curricular physical activities. Secondly, this relationship was considered in relation to gender. A motivation inventory was completed by 145 children who were students at a mixed comprehensive school and results revealed that age and gender were the main effects. It appeared that Year 7 and Year 10 children are motivated to take part in extra-curricular activities for different reasons. Boys and girls also reported differing reasons for participation in extra-curricular physical activities.

PUBLISHED MATERIAL: DALEY, A.J. & O'GARA, A. (1998). 'Age, gender and motivation for participation in extra-curricular physical activities in secondary school adolescents', European Physical Education Review, Vol 4, No 1, pp.47-53.

STATUS: Individual research

DATE OF RESEARCH: 1998-1998

2442

Waldegrave Road, Strawberry Hill, Twickenham TW1 4SX
0181 240 4000
Catholic Education Service, 39 Eccleston Square, London SW1V 1BX

Martin, M. Sist.; *Supervisors*: Walsh, P. Dr; Faley, A. Rev.

Catholic education and change - with particular reference to the teaching of religious education and the introduction of the new curriculum directory for Catholic schools

ABSTRACT: The Catholic Bishops of England and Wales have requested the preparation of classroom materials for the first 3 years of secondary school in religious education (RE). The materials are to be based upon the Curriculum Directory for Catholic Schools, a document presenting the heart of the content for RE classroom teaching. This work is part of a whole national project in RE and involves consultation, piloting and preparation for materials for all Catholic secondary schools in England and Wales. The structure of the consultation and piloting is organised with Harper Collins publishers through the National Project for RE, which is composed of RE advisers from 22 dioceses in England and Wales. The result will be 3 textbooks for classroom RE for National Curriculum key stage 3 pupils.

STATUS: Sponsored project

SOURCE OF GRANT: Harper Collins

DATE OF RESEARCH: 1997-continuing

KEYWORDS: **catholic schools; church and education; curriculum development; educational materials; material development; religious education; textbook preparation**

2443

Waldegrave Road, Strawberry Hill, Twickenham TW1 4SX
0181 240 4000
Mexican Embassy, 42 Hertford Street, London W1Y 7TF
0171 499 8586

Cook, K. Dr; Phillips, A. Mr; Dalton, R. Mr; Brooks, L. Mr

Meet Mexico

ABSTRACT: The aim of this project is to produce a CD-Rom on Mexico for use in National Curriculum key stage 2 geography lessons in UK schools. The product will provide material for the study of a distant locality. It is centred on a family in the village of Tocuaro in Michoacan State in Central Mexico. The project has been designed around the Horta family and, following 3 weeks work in Mexico during which video, slide and other resources were obtained, a series of issues will be examined. These will work outwards from the family and its home, the village and the local environment. Links will be made with environmental issues such as the survival of the monarch butterfly which spends its winters in forests near Tocuaro. The future of Lake Patzcuaro will also be considered in terms of its rapid shrinkage in recent years. Links will also be made with Paricutin volcano which is nearby and with wider Mexican issues. Despite recent changes to key stage 2 requirements, it is felt that teachers will continue to require good resources. The 'Meet Mexico' pack and the CD-Rom will hopefully meet these needs, encouraging pupils to study a country and its people often neglected in UK schools. The process being carried out, regarding the production of the CD-Rom and the special needs of working with an international organisation such as an Embassy and its staff, will form the basis of a report for the Geographical Association.

STATUS: Sponsored project

SOURCE OF GRANT: ICI £1,000; Geographical Association £300; St Mary's University College £8,000; Mexican Embassy £1,000

DATE OF RESEARCH: 1997-continuing

KEYWORDS: **educational materials; geography; key stage 2; material development; mexico; primary education**

Staffordshire University

2444

Business School, Department of Economics, Leek Road, Stoke-on-Tent ST4 2DE
01782 294000

Davies, P. Mr

The relationship between staff and curriculum development in economics and business studies

ABSTRACT: The background to the project is the diversity and change in the curriculum profile and substance of economics and business studies in the 11-18 curriculum. It relates to the development of this subject area as a planning unit within the curriculum and provides a basis for reflection on ideas about stages in the development of a subject area. The objective is to establish the teaching commitments of staff with expertise in economics and business studies, how that expertise is being developed, and how that expertise bears upon planning decisions for school curricula. The first stage in the research was to review national (England and Wales) data available since 1980 on the teaching of economics and business studies. The second stage was a questionnaire survey of 600 schools in the north-west of England (which received a response rate of above 40%). The third stage will be interviews with economics and business studies teachers and deputy headteachers, reviewing the history of developments in that institution, their career histories, and their attribution of the causes of these developments.

STATUS: Individual research

DATE OF RESEARCH: 1993-continuing

KEYWORDS: **business education; curriculum development; economics education; teacher attitudes; teacher development**

2445

Business School, Department of Economics, Leek Road, Stoke-on-Trent ST4 2DE
01782 294000

Davies, P. Mr

Teacher assessment in geographical education

ABSTRACT: The introduction of national curricula in England, Wales and Northern Ireland has thrust the assessment of 11-14 year olds into the limelight. Teachers have faced the job of interpreting statements of attainment which purport to describe strands of progression. The validity of describing geographical achievement in this way, the sense of the particular statements of attainment which have now been set in statute, and the reliability of teachers' assessments of pupils' work have each been called into question. The aim of this project is to identify how geography teachers differentiate between levels of achievement, this includes: (a) identifying procedures used; (b) isolating criteria adopted; (c) exemplifying criteria with evidence; (d) isolating changes in criteria used by teachers and relating such changes to possible influences; and (e) comparing the consistency of teachers' judgments when using the same criterion. Initial investigation will focus on the written tests for National Curriculum key stage 3 geography in England, Wales and Northern Ireland prepared by the Centre for Formative Assessment (CFAS) at the University of Manchester. The work of CFAS in developing statutory instruments for assessment at key stage 3 for England, Wales and Northern Ireland provides a valuable database of pupil responses and teachers' interpretation of mark schemes. The work of three groups of teachers will be studied over the period September 1993 to September 1995. There will be approximately one dozen teachers in each group drawn from Greater Manchester, North Wales and Northern Ireland.

STATUS: Individual research

DATE OF RESEARCH: 1993-1997

KEYWORDS: **assessment; assessment by teachers; geography; national curriculum**

Stirling University

2446

Department of Education, Stirling FK9 4LA
01786 467600

Low, L. Mrs; Duffield, J. Mrs; Bankowska, A. Dr; *Supervisors*: Brown, S. Prof.; Johnstone, R. Prof.

Evaluation of national pilot projects: foreign languages in primary schools (Scotland)

ABSTRACT: As part of a major government initiative, pilot projects have been set up to test the feasibility of introducing foreign language teaching into the primary schools associated with twelve secondary schools. The commonest model involves collaboration between class teachers from P6 to P7 and visiting modern language teachers from the secondary school. The main aims of the evaluation are: (1) assessment of the linguistic attainments of children involved in the pilot projects including comparisons with those children not involved; (2) evaluation of the project courses including commentary on factors such as the nature of the course and pedagogical methods which influence the linguistic performance of the children involved. The first aim has involved speaking and listening assessments carried out with pairs of pupils in the foreign language. In 1991 these compared 'project' and 'non-project' pupils in S1 and S2. In 1992 attention was on progression from Primary 7 onwards with 'project' pupils only. Within class assessments carried out by teachers have also been analysed. The second aim has been addressed through an interview study with class teachers and others involved at every level in the management of the projects, and a lesson observation study of primary and secondary classes. The result of the evaluation remains confidential until April 1993. An extension, to September 1994, will investigate the gains in linguistic attainments of pupils commencing their foreign language at different stages in the primary school, effective teaching approaches and various wider implications for the organisation of primary and secondary schools.

STATUS: Sponsored project

SOURCE OF GRANT: Scottish Office Education Department £172,901

DATE OF RESEARCH: 1991-1993

KEYWORDS: **language proficiency; modern language studies; primary education**

2447

Department of Education, Stirling FK9 4LA
01786 467600

Morris, B. Mr; Stronach, I. Prof.

Evaluation of the management of change: TVEI Tayside

ABSTRACT: The research was commissioned by Tayside Region to assess the effectiveness of the approach to management of change adopted by Tayside Technical and Vocational Education Initiative (TVEI). The research was based on interviews (102) in seven case study schools and with TVEI and Regional personnel. The interim evaluation findings were incorporated into a report/questionnaire distributed to a stratified sample (72) of staff in an additional 9 schools for comment (86% return rate). Research findings include: 1) Tayside TVEI has sponsored a comprehensive work experience programme; contributed to the development of procedures for forward planning and allocation of resources in schools; and introduced information technology to a wide range of teachers and pupils. It has been less successful in influencing teaching sytles and introducing profiling. 2) The creation of internal TVEI related school management posts has encouraged women into school management teams (albeit temporarily). 3) The departmental 'bidding' mechanism for allocating resources has tended to emphasise equipment purchase and to contain developments within subject boundaries. 4) Project 'responsiveness' has assisted acceptance in schools but created problems in establishing project identity and direction. 5) Where elements of TVEI were incorporated into policy, at school and Regional level ('led'), there was considerable impact. Where TVEI was 'licensed' to operate, development was 'patchy' and idiosyncratic. Decisions as to whether to 'license' or 'lead' were made throughout the system. 6) There is some evidence to suggest that change was being 'over reported' by school management and 'under reported' by some principal and classroom teachers.

STATUS: Sponsored project

SOURCE OF GRANT: Tayside Regional Council £14,000

DATE OF RESEARCH: 1992-1993

KEYWORDS: **change strategies; educational innovation; programme evaluation; tvei**

2448

Department of Education, Stirling FK9 4LA
01786 467600

Stronach, I. Prof.; Turner, E. Mrs; Waterhouse, S. Dr Lloyd, J. Dr

Schools - industry links

ABSTRACT: A national survey of schools-industry provision, based on interview, documentation and questionnaire. In addition, selected case studies of 'exemplary' and 'typical' practice. The project will attempt to generate largely qualitative accounts of costs and benefits of different types of initiative, and will, where possible, make recommendations for future policy.

STATUS: Sponsored project

SOURCE OF GRANT: Scottish Office Education Department £46,000

DATE OF RESEARCH: 1992-1993

KEYWORDS: **industry education relationship; school to work transition; vocational education**

2449

Department of Education, Stirling FK9 4LA
01786 467600
Stirling University, Division of Educational Policy and Development, Stirling FK9 LA
01786 473171

Mannion, G. Mr; *Supervisors*: Waterhouse, S. Dr; Sankey, K. Ms

A cooperative inquiry/action research project using narrative to investigate a community's 'sense of place'

ABSTRACT: This research adopts a poststructuralist position to acknowledge the widely expressed 'narrative' of what is seen by many as a global human/ environmental problematic or 'crisis'. The interdependent and complex nature of the problem as reported by environmentalists, the media, and the public at large appears simultaneously personal, interpersonal, ecological and political. The problems of development and the environment seem intimately interdependent. Concurrently, there is sustained concern about the nexus of environmental issues and issues of global inequality. As a result postmodern educational responses to this complex web of personal, interpersonal, ecological and political issues also generates a debate about a need for a deconstruction of the underlying technological and scientific 'paradigm' towards a more speculative, non-repesentationalist view of reality that is experienced 'intertextually'. It is common for writers dealing with 'education for sustainability' (and formerly environmental education) to advocate an holistic approach to adequately address the issues that are, by their nature multidisciplinary. This approach is also seen as useful in that it challenges the reductionist paradigm so often cited as influential in creating the problems we face. Holism of a poststructuralist form, by philosphically and methodoligically underpinning critique, would encourage teachers to challenge existing models for environmental education and development education. Within this model, educative processes that would focus our 'storied residence' are advocated as worthy of investigation in this research proposal. The questions that arise in this particular research are: 1) Is there a viable process of shared story-telling (narrative research) that would enable a group of teachers (or 'community of learners' in a school) to respond in an active way to environmental issues and issues of 'sustainability'. 2) Would teachers, or other members of a local community, that participate in the proposed action research project using narrative, gain a clear(er) ability to express their 'sense of place' in relation to local or global environmental/developmental issues? 3) Would these teachers (or other locals) go on to engage in particular kinds of 'action for the environment or for justice' in their own lives, locality, or in their teaching profession? It is envisaged that a full teaching staff in a primary school would self-select to engage in an action research, cooperative inquiry/process using narrative to enquire into the community's 'sense of place'. This research seeks to employ specific holistic story-telling methodologies within a model of cooperative inquiry that seek to encourage empowerment, personal transformation, and increased self-reliance in addressing isuses that impinge on the question of a 'sustainable future'. The double role of researcher as 'cooperative inquirer' and 'catalytic intervener' will undoubtedly require careful handling.

STATUS: Individual research

DATE OF RESEARCH: 1996-continuing

KEYWORDS: environmental education; narration; story telling; sustainable development

2450

Division of Academic Innovation and Continuing Education, Stirling FK9 4LA
01786 473171

Mannion, G. Mr; *Supervisor*: Sankey, K. Ms

Children's sense of place: children's participation in the planning and design of outdoor spaces

ABSTRACT: The research focuses on the question of how children's participation in the planning and design of outdoor spaces get narrated in the process of planning, design and maintenance of outdoor (school) environments.

STATUS: Individual research

DATE OF RESEARCH: 1996-continuing

KEYWORDS: campus planning; environmental education; school grounds

2451

Division of Academic Innovation and Continuing Education, Stirling FK9 4LA
01786 473171

Ireland, L. Ms; *Supervisor*: Sankey, K. Ms

Education for an ecologically sustainable society

ABSTRACT: An action research project to investigate aspects of the implementation of an holistic curriculum founded in the ideologies of deep ecology and sustainability. It begins from the premise put forward by a number of environmental education researchers (including David Orr) that a discipline-centric curriculum is no longer appropriate for the 21st century and that the kind of changes required will involve changes in: a) the content of the curriculum; b) how institutions function; c) the organisation and physical environment of institutions; and d) the purposes of learning. The research is set within the context of an independent small school and the Scottish Office Curriculum Guidelines 5-14.

STATUS: Individual research

DATE OF RESEARCH: 1997-continuing

KEYWORDS: curriculum development; environmental education; sustainable development

2452

Division of Academic Innovation and Continuing Education, Stirling FK9 4LA
01786 473171

Nixon, J. Prof.; Furay, V. Mr; *Supervisor*: Sankey, K. Ms

Education for sustainability in Scottish secondary schools

ABSTRACT: The report provides an overview of education for sustainability in Scottish secondary schools. The evidence suggests that overall provision is sporadic and that, even where education for sustainability is being developed, whole-school change is likely to be conceived in the main as modest modifications to existing structures. The report outlines the very different starting points that schools have adopted in seeking to develop education for sustainability and goes on to show how 3 particular schools have sought to develop and extend their work in this area. Finally, the report offers some specific recommendations regarding the way in which Scottish Natural Heritage and other agencies might support secondary schools in developing programmes of work in the area of education for sustainability. The central message is that any support programme that is developed by Scottish Natural Heritage and other agencies should work with schools that are already committed to education for sustainability. By celebrating their small steps, the network of participating schools may gradually be extended. The aim, then, would be twofold: to help schools develop and extend their work in education for sustainability and to disseminate instances of good practice more widely. The approach would be realistic, taking account of the existing pressures on schools and teachers and recognising the scarcity of provision nationwide. It would encourage incremental change and acknowledge that in complex hierarchical structures (which is what schools invariably are) change takes time. The report's findings were that while whole-school change is an important aspiration, schools require a strategy in order to begin to realise that aspiration. Indeed, too strong an emphasis on the 'whole-school' dimension may serve to mask the reality of a secondary school curriculum that is defined and, in the main taught, in terms of tightly framed subject areas and of a teaching force that is differentiated and, in Scotland, professionally registered according to subject specialism. It requires time together with a realistic current climate (of low teacher morale, high public accountability and centrally imposed change) schools that are trying to take education for sustainability seriously need help in making it workable. A report has been submitted to the Scottish Natural Heritage.

STATUS: Sponsored project

SOURCE OF GRANT: Scottish Natural Heritage

DATE OF RESEARCH: 1997-1998

KEYWORDS: curriculum development; environmental education; scotland; sustainable development; whole school approach

2453

Institute of Education, Stirling FK9 4LA
01786 467600

Ferrie, A. Mr; *Supervisors*: Osborne, M. Prof.; Morgan-Klein, B. Ms

Routes into higher education - a comparison of progression and peformance

ABSTRACT: An investigation of the Access route as a preparation for higher education, including a comparison of performance of Access, A-level and higher grade students in 4 Scottish universities and an analysis of the relevance of variables such as class and gender.

PUBLISHED MATERIAL: LEOPOLD, J. & OSBORNE, M.J. (1996). 'The performance of former in-house Access students at a Scottish university', Journal of Access Studies, Vol 11, pp.120-131. ; OSBORNE, M., DOCKRELL, R. & REEVE, F. (1996). 'Access to higher education through the accreditation of work based learning', Journal of Further and Higher Education, Vol 20, No 2, pp.81-96. ; OSBORNE, M.J., LEOPOLD, J. & FERRIE, A. (1997). 'The performance of mature students at a Scottish university', Higher Education, Vol 33, pp.1-22.

STATUS: Sponsored project

SOURCE OF GRANT: Scottish Wider Access Programme - West of Scotland Consortium

DATE OF RESEARCH: 1995-continuing

KEYWORDS: academic achievement; access programmes; access to education; higher education; mature students; nontraditional students; performance

2454

Institute of Education, Stirling FK9 4LA
01786 467600

Lawson, K. Ms; *Supervisors*: Drever, E. Dr; Cope, P. Dr

Microteaching as microcosm: how students learn to be teachers

ABSTRACT: This qualitative research will look at microteaching as a potential microcosm of teacher education, and seek to describe the factors that shape and constrain students in learning to be teachers. Initital teacher education (ITE) at Stirling University incorporates a new approach towards microteaching which has evolved from the traditional skills/behaviourist models into an interpretive framework, emphasising problem-solving and self-evaluation. Teacher fellows from local schools participate as student supervisors. This departure emulates changes in the wider sphere of teacher education, in particular current emphasis on reflective practice, apprenticeship models, mentoring, and partnership with schools. The research aims to look at: how students develop teacher expertise; implicit and explicit concepts of learning; environmental influences on teacher development; how students think about their lessons and evaluate their practice; changing behaviour and pedagogical thinking; transfer of ideas and values and craft knowledge through interaction; supervisory approaches; attitudes to learning, support structures and student motivation. A longitudinal study will follow a cohort of students through the ITE programme at Stirling University. Ethnographic methodology will be used in compiling 'case histories'. Data will be collected from interviews with students at key stages in the ITE programme (during microteaching, videotapes of microlessons will form a basis for discussion); participant observation of student supervisory sessions; non-participant observation of microlessons and school placement lessons. Interview data will also be gathered from graduate teachers who have completed the programme.

STATUS: Sponsored project

SOURCE OF GRANT: Economic and Social Research Council

DATE OF RESEARCH: 1995-1998

KEYWORDS: microteaching; preservice teacher education; student teachers; teaching experience; teaching methods

2455

Institute of Education, Stirling FK9 4LA
01786 467600

Brown, S. Prof.; Riddell, S. Prof.; Allan, J. Ms

Special schools and multiple policy innovations

ABSTRACT: In recent years special schools have undergone changes in the nature and size of their populations and in the roles they are expected to fulfil. They have also been influenced by a variety of policy innovations, for example parental choice and the delegation of budgets to schools. This research will investigate the culture and practices within special schools in Scotland and changing patterns among pupil populations and regional policies. It will examine the impact of multiple policy innovations, particularly parental choice, School Boards, devolved school management, local government reform and the 5-14 programme, on special schools. In the context of these innovations, the research will explore how disability, equality, progress, empowerment and support for pupils with special educational needs are construed and evaluated by professionals and parents. Data will be collected from policy-makers within national and local governments during the period of transition to single tier authorities. Case studies will be conducted in two local authorities, affected differently by local government reform, and in eight special schools.

STATUS: Sponsored project

SOURCE OF GRANT: Economic and Social Research Council

DATE OF RESEARCH: 1995-1997

KEYWORDS: educational policy; scotland; special educational needs; special schools

2456

Institute of Education, Stirling FK9 4LA
01786 467600

Morris, B. Mr; Stephen, C. Dr

An evaluation of the drug awareness resource for primary schools "I don't want to be like that" project

ABSTRACT: This is an evaluation of a primary school drug education initiative sponsored by Glasgow Council Education Department and the Greater Glasgow Health Board. The programme is centred on a production by the Fablevision Theatre Company. The research will be conducted as 4 case studies. In 2 of the schools, the programme will take the form of a video of the theatre production with supporting written materials, in contrast to the true production experienced in the other 2 schools. The research will consist of: interviews with theatre personnel and project sponsors; interviews with teachers before and after performance or video; 'draw and write' exercises with pupils before and after the performance or video. The final report will be produced in June 1997.

STATUS: Sponsored project

SOURCE OF GRANT: Health Promotion Department, Greater Glasgow Health Board £4,999

DATE OF RESEARCH: 1997-1997

KEYWORDS: drug education; health education; primary education; programme evaluation; theatre arts

2457

Institute of Education, Stirling FK9 4LA
01786 467600

Low, L. Mrs; Stephen, C. Dr; Cope, P. Dr; Morris, B. Mr; *Supervisors*: Brown, S. Prof.; Waterhouse, S. Dr; Bell, D. Prof.

Pre-school education voucher initiative (Scotland): national evaluation of the pilot year

ABSTRACT: The research will look at the way in which the voucher policy affects provision in preschool education and at the effectiveness of the operation of the schemes. This will involve monitoring the way in which the scheme is administered and the experience of parents and providers during the pilot year. The researchers are interested in how the existence of the new system affects the supply of preschool places and whether there are any unexpected 'side effects', especially in availability and access. Data from 2 main sources will be looked at. The first source will be the documentary and statistical data made available by the Scottish Office and by Capita (the company which is contracted to administer the voucher scheme nationally). The second source will be the people who are directly involved in the 4 pilot areas. Data from this second source will be gathered by interviewing samples of parents, of providers and of local authority representatives. The main research questions focus upon emerging patterns of provision, the early experience of parents, providers (and potential providers), particularly in relation to expansion of provision and opportunities for exercising choice. Of special interest will be the economic issues of supply and demand, the effects in remote rural areas, the impact on children with special needs. Data collection involves semi-structured interviews (face-to-face and telephone) and case studies in 4 pilot areas. Telephone interviews with a sample of 80 providers, and 1,000 parents.

STATUS: Sponsored project

SOURCE OF GRANT: Scottish Office Education and Industry Department £81,817

DATE OF RESEARCH: 1996-1997

KEYWORDS: access to education; early childhood education; education vouchers; educational finance; educational markets; nursery education; parent choice; preschool education; programme evaluation; scotland

2458

Institute of Education, Stirling FK9 4LA
01786 467600

Cloonan, M. Dr; *Supervisor*: Osborne, M. Prof.

Cost benefit analysis in continuing education

ABSTRACT: This is a European Universities Continuing Education (EUCEN) sponsored project examining the use of cost-benefit analysis in 4 countries: France, Ireland, Italy and Scotland. The work is being carried out by Working Group 5 of EUCEN's Thematic Network Project (THENCUE). The research is based on formal interviews with continuing education providers in 8 institutions (2 from each country). The result will be a qualitative survey on the use of cost-benefit analysis in the provision of continuing education.

STATUS: Sponsored project

SOURCE OF GRANT: European Universities Continuing Education

DATE OF RESEARCH: 1998-1998

KEYWORDS: comparative education; continuing education; cost effectiveness

2459

Institute of Education, Stirling FK9 4LA
01786 467600

Oberski, I. Dr; Cloonan, M. Dr; *Supervisors*: Osborne, M. Prof.; Seagraves, L. Mrs

European learning in smaller companies

ABSTRACT: The project has been established to introduce a postgraduate certificate in small and medium-sized enterprise management into small and medium enterprises (SMEs) in Scotland, Spain, Finland and Italy making use of web-based technology for distance learning and electronic networking. The research will investigate the impact of this approach to management training in these companies which have entered the programme in comparison with non-participating businesses. The stakeholders to be considered are the owner/manager, the learner and the providers.

STATUS: Sponsored project

SOURCE OF GRANT: European Union Directorate General XXII Leonardo da Vinci

DATE OF RESEARCH: 1997-continuing

KEYWORDS: computer uses in education; distance education; europe; graduate study; industry higher education relationship; information technology; internet; management development; small businesses

2460

Institute of Education, Stirling FK9 4LA
01786 467600

Canning, R. Mr

New technology and work-based learning

ABSTRACT: This research is aimed at developing a number of case studies in the use of new technology and work-based learning. The organisations involved are all small and medium-sized enterprises who are supporting their staff on flexible learning programmes leading to professional and vocational qualifications. The new technologies are: the Internet, video-conferencing, and computer conferencing. The research will evaluate aspects of cost-effectiveness, quality of learning and the workplace as a learning community.

STATUS: Sponsored project

DATE OF RESEARCH: 1997-continuing

KEYWORDS: information technology; internet; small businesses; teleconferencing; vocational qualifications; work based learning

2461

Institute of Education, Stirling FK9 4LA
01786 467600

Gray, P. Mr; *Supervisors*: Morgan-Klein, B. Ms; Nixon, J. Prof.

Spatiality and adult learning

ABSTRACT: The research will investigate various constructions of space as experienced by adult learners in order to address issues such as the theory/practice gap in environmental education, and the transfer of skills between different learning environments.

STATUS: Individual research

DATE OF RESEARCH: 1998-continuing

KEYWORDS: adult education; adult students; environmental education; space utilisation; spatial ability

2462

Institute of Education, Stirling FK9 4LA
01786 467600

Cloonan, M. Dr; Canning, R. Mr

Scottish Vocational Qualifications: an analysis of enrolment and completion rates

ABSTRACT: An analysis of enrolment and completion rates for Scottish Vocational Qualifications (SVQs). SVQs are now an important and established part of work-based learning in Scotland. However, they have been plagued by high levels of non-completion. The project aims to establish a "natural" completion rate for SVQs. It further seeks to examine the reasons for non-completion and to suggest key reforms to providers which will improve completion rates.

STATUS: Sponsored project

SOURCE OF GRANT: Scottish Qualifications Authority £10,000

DATE OF RESEARCH: 1998-continuing

KEYWORDS: course completion rate; dropouts; scotland; scottish vocational qualifications; vocational education; vocational qualifications; work based learning

2463

Institute of Education, Stirling FK9 4LA
01786 467600

Canning, R. Mr; *Supervisor*: Cloonan, M. Dr

Scottish and National Vocational Qualifications: a comparison of take-up and usage between Scotland and England

ABSTRACT: A comparison of take-up rates for Scottish Vocational Qualifications (SVQs) in comparison with National Vocational Qualifications (NVQs). The research will aim to establish whether the existence of "competitors" for SVQs - including NVQs, and National Certificate Modules - is affecting take-up rates for SVQs. The aim is also to establish whether meaningful comparisons between England and Scotland in terms of vocational education can be made.

STATUS: Sponsored project

SOURCE OF GRANT: Scottish Qualifications Authority (SQA) £10,000

DATE OF RESEARCH: 1998-continuing

KEYWORDS: national vocational qualifications; scotland; scottish vocational qualifications; vocational education; vocational qualifications; work based learning

2464

Institute of Education, Stirling FK9 4LA
01786 467600

Cloonan, M. Dr; Osborne, M. Prof.

Performance indicators in Slovakia's higher education institutions

ABSTRACT: An analysis of the introduction of performance indicators into the Slovakian higher education system. Comparisons are made with the UK's system of Teaching Quality Assessment and the UK's Research Assessment Exercise.

STATUS: Sponsored project

SOURCE OF GRANT: European Union Tempus Project £1,584

DATE OF RESEARCH: 1998-continuing

KEYWORDS: educational quality; higher education; performance indicators; slovakia

2465

Institute of Education, Stirling FK9 4LA
01786 467600
Napier University, Faculty of Arts and Social Science, Merchiston Campus, 10 Colinton Road, Edinburgh EH10 5DT
0131 455 2270

Riddell, S. Prof.; Phillips, R. Mrs; Duffield, J. Mrs; Sutherland, E. Ms; Cox, A. Mrs; Amery, P. Mr; *Supervisor*: Brown, S. Prof.

Support for students with disabilities: evaluation of Scottish Higher Education Funding Council initiatives

ABSTRACT: A team based at the Universities of Stirling and Napier has been commissioned by the Scottish Higher Education Funding Council (SHEFC) to evaluate the impact of 3 SHEFC initiatives (1993-96) relating to support for students with disabilities in all 21 Scottish higher education institutions (HEIs). The evaluation is based on interviews, documentary analysis, a questionnaire to managements of higher education institutions, and 6 case studies of Scottish HEIs in varied circumstances. The SHEFC initiatives were: 1) The Disabled Students Initiative (DSI): audit of provision in 1993-94 which produced interim and final reports and the student guide 'Access to success'. 2) The Staff Initiative (SSD-S) which created a National Coordinator post and provided funds for each HEI to employ a half-time adviser/coordinator for students with disabilities; (two phases, 1994-95 and 1995-96). 3) The Equipment Initiative (SSD-E) which provided funds to HEIs acting in consortia for appropriate equipment and buildings adaptation (two phases, 1994-95 and 1995-96). The purpose of the evaluation is to investigate the conception, management, conduct, value for money and impact upon institutions of the initiatives. Preliminary results indicate a majority view that the initiatives had a decisive impact on the development of support for students with disabilities. The Staff Initiative was seen as the key component and the best value for money. External factors including campaigns by people with disabilities had contributed to such progress as had taken place. The goal of full inclusion of students with disabilities was still distant.

STATUS: Sponsored project

SOURCE OF GRANT: Scottish Higher Education Funding Council £28,500

DATE OF RESEARCH: 1996-1997

KEYWORDS: access to education; disabilities; higher education; programme evaluation; scotland; special educational needs; students; support services

2466

Institute of Education, Stirling FK9 4LA
01786 467600
Scottish Arts Council, 12 Manor Place, Edinburgh EH3 7DD
0131 226 6051

Turner, E. Mrs; *Supervisor*: Dow, S. Ms

The arts-education interface in transition: evaluating quality

ABSTRACT: The project is being supported by the Scottish Arts Council, the Calouste Gulbenkian Foundation and the Esmee Fairbairn Charitable Trust. Work is being carried out in cooperation with major arts organisations in Scotland, e.g. the Scottish Chamber Orchestra. The project has been developed in collaboration with arts organisations following on from the project undertaken for the Scottish Arts Council in 1992 (SCOTTISH ARTS COUNCIL. (1993). Perceptions of policy, provision and practice. Edinburgh: Scottish Arts Council). The project is studying a number of arts-education projects (case studies) and seeks to answer the following questions: 1) Do examples of excellent activities exist at the arts-education interface? 2) What general lessons can be drawn from those examples, in terms of quality criteria, to enhance relationships and future partnerships between formal education and the arts during a time of organisational transition? Ideally each case study will involve: observation of planning meetings, rehearsals and arts education events; interviews with key arts workers; follow-up in selected primary and secondary schools using group interviews with pupils and interviews and/or focus groups with teachers; and further observation of selected events and follow-up interviews in schools. It is the intention that arts events and schools will be 'revisited' in the second year of the project to identify possible modifications in arts organisations' practice and longer term effects in schools. The number of case studies depends on the funding available and the extent of the projects chosen for study.

STATUS: Sponsored project

SOURCE OF GRANT: Scottish Arts Council; Calouste Gulbenkian Foundation; Esmee Fairbairn Charitable Trust

DATE OF RESEARCH: 1996-1997

KEYWORDS: art education; arts; cultural education

Stranmillis College

2467

Department of English, Belfast BT9 5DY
01232 381271

Patterson, G. Dr

The teaching of poetry writing in primary and secondary schools

ABSTRACT: This project examines the relationship between teachers' knowledge and understanding of the practices of experienced writers from the poetry and critical writing of poets from a variety of backgrounds and their ability to provide classroom experiences which enable pupils to behave like real writers.

PUBLISHED MATERIAL: PATTERSON, G. (1996). '"Unless soul clap its hands and sing": literature, cultural heritage and a divided society', Irish Studies Review, No 14, pp.26-32.

STATUS: Individual research

DATE OF RESEARCH: 1986-1997

KEYWORDS: poetry; primary education; secondary education; writing composition

Strathclyde University

2468

Careers Service, 26 Richmond Street, Glasgow G1 1XH
0141 552 4400

Graham, B. Miss

Professional development for support staff in higher education careers services

ABSTRACT: This study investigated the extent and nature of staff development and training for support staff in higher education careers services (i.e. staff other than careers advisers). The survey investigated issues such as training providers and sources of funding for staff development. It also examined outcomes in relation to career development for support staff and enhancement of customer service. The findings demonstrated a high level of training and staff development in the target population. Involvement in such activities was found in both small and large careers services, the most essential factors in provision being the attitudes of careers service managers and institutional policy on staff development at all levels. There were definite correlations between adequate staff development and good customer service.

STATUS: Sponsored project

SOURCE OF GRANT: Association of Graduate Careers Advisory Services £1,000

DATE OF RESEARCH: 1997-1997

KEYWORDS: careers service; higher education; staff development

2469

Careers Service, 26 Richmond Street, Glasgow G1 1XH
0141 552 4400

MacKenzie, K. Mr

Destinations of contract research staff in some Scottish universities

ABSTRACT: This research investigated the destinations of contract research staff in 6 Scottish universities over a period of 6 months, with a sample of just over 100 respondents. A larger survey was also conducted of over 500 contract research staff employed in these institutions to determine their career aspirations, knowledge of career options open to them, and methods of seeking their next post. They were also asked where they would look for careers guidance. The findings show that a large majority continue in academic research, which is the preferred option of over 70%. The majority take further short-term appointments with only a small outflow to other occupations. Most contract research staff would like to use higher education careers services for guidance and help with job seeking, but the remit of most careers services is to work with students, not staff.

STATUS: Sponsored project

SOURCE OF GRANT: Scottish Higher Education Funding Council

DATE OF RESEARCH: 1997-1997

KEYWORDS: careers; employment opportunities; followup studies; researchers

2470

Careers Service, 26 Richmond Street, Glasgow G1 1XH
0141 552 4400
Higher Education Careers Service Unit, Prospects House, Booth Street East, Manchester M13 9EP
0161 277 5291
Newcastle upon Tyne University, Careers Service, Armstrong Building, Newcastle upon Tyne NE1 7RU
0191 222 7748

Lamb, L. Mrs; Taylor, J. Ms; *Supervisor*: Raderecht, P. Ms

Understanding the graduate labour market

ABSTRACT: Much labour market information is collected, but it is under-utilised because potential beneficiaries are unaware of its existence or find it inaccessible and do not understand its relevance to them. This project aims to investigate how better use can be made of existing labour market information (regional and national) in order to: 1) inform the academic planning process; 2) introduce the use of labour market intelligence (i.e. the interpretation of labour market information) into careers education so that students and graduates can be better informed in the process of career choice and job search). Methodology involves setting up regional fora of labour market intelligence providers in the Northumbria and West of Scotland areas. Outputs will include proposed models for the use of labour market intelligence in academic planning and careers education. The outcome will be a report to the Department for Education and Employment (DfEE).

STATUS: Sponsored project

SOURCE OF GRANT: Department for Education and Employment £80,000

DATE OF RESEARCH: 1998-continuing

KEYWORDS: careers service; employment; graduate employment; labour market; vocational guidance

2471

Centre for Research in Quality in Education, Jordanhill Campus, Southbrae Drive, Glasgow G13 1PP
0141 950 3000
Keele University, Department of Education, Keele ST5 5BG
01782 621111

MacBeath, J. Prof.; Myers, K. Prof.; Smith, I. Prof.; McCabe, J. Prof.

Study support: evaluation and development project

ABSTRACT: The Prince's Trust is financing a three year evaluation and development project supported by the Department for Education and Employment (DfEE). The study support evaluation and development project is attempting to discover whether study support makes a difference to the achievement of those students who attend out-of-hours study sessions and if so how it does so. Fifty-four schools in England, Scotland and Wales, all of which are offering study support, are participating in the study. Their partnership authorities have contributed to the financing of the project which will run from 1997 to 2000. The education authorities and Partnership areas are Tower Hamlets, Newham, Camden, Bedfordshire, Sandwell, Birmingham, Sheffield, Merseyside, Durham and Newcastle. The project is tracking for three years 8,000 Year 9 students and 1,000 Year 7s. At the outset of the project (autumn 1997) baseline data were gathered, so that predictions of performance measurement at GCSE (national public examinations at 16+) could be used as a benchmark for measures of value-added, to compare students who attend study support with their peers who do not, and to compare regular attendees with those who attend on an occasional or spasmodic basis. Differentiation by type of study support used will also be an important variable. Baseline measures include: NFER-Nelson standardised non-verbal reasoning test; NFER student attitude questionnaire; student attitude to study support software (self-administered by those students who attend study support); teacher questionnaire (to all teachers in the school).

PUBLISHED MATERIAL: MYERS, K., MACBEATH, J. & ROBERTSON, I. (1998). 'Changing your life through study support: how will we know if it makes a difference?' Paper presented at the AERA Conference, San Diego, 1998. ; MYERS, K., MACBEATH, J. & ROBERTSON, I. (1998). 'Study support: will it make a difference? How will we know?' Paper presented at the BERA Conference, Belfast, August, 1998. ; MACBEATH, J. & MYERS, K. (1999). 'Evaluating out of school learning'. Paper presented at the International Congress for School Effectiveness and School Improvement, San Antonio, Texas, January 3-6, 1999.

STATUS: Sponsored project

SOURCE OF GRANT: Prince's Trust Participating schools Department for Education and Employment

DATE OF RESEARCH: 1997-continuing

KEYWORDS: academic achievement; achievement; learning activities; out of school hours learning; pupil attitudes; secondary education; study support

2472

Department of Psychology, Graham Hills Building, 40 George Street, Glasgow G1 1QE
0141 552 4400

McLaren, B. Mr; Whelan, K. Ms; Supervisors: Thomson, J. Dr; Tolmie, A. Dr; Foot, H. Prof.

Visual search and selective attention in the context of pedestrian behaviour: a developmental and training study

ABSTRACT: A significant number of child pedestrian accidents involve victims who fail to detect an approaching vehicle, despite having looked for traffic as enjoined by road safety education. Such accidents may be attributable to immature search strategies. This research therefore has two priorities: firstly, to determine what features of the traffic environment children of different ages perceive as salient, and how they pick these up, and secondly, to explore whether intervention can promote better search strategies. The project has two phases: In the first, 48 children in each of 4 age groups (5, 7, 9 and 11 year olds), plus 48 adults, will report on their observations of both real and simulated traffic environments in which a range of visual and auditory features have been controlled. The aim is to determine: 1) how children's performance stands relative to adults', and how it improves with age; 2) the effect on performance of increasing both relevant and irrelevant features, and of making explicit the task's connection with road crossing; 3) the extent to which performance in simulated and real environments is related; and 4) whether individual differences are associated with other identifiable factors. The second phase will examine whether children's search skills at the roadside can be improved through training in simulated environments. Two intervention techniques, peer-based collaborative problem solving and adult-led training, will be assessed using 36 children in each of two age groups (5 and 7 year olds), with children being pre- and post-tested on both search and road crossing skills.

PUBLISHED MATERIAL: FOOT, H.C., THOMSON, J., TOLMIE, A. & MCLAREN, B. (1994). 'Interactive learning approaches to road safety education: a review'. In: FOOT, H.C., HOWE, C.J., ANDERSON, A., TOLMIE, A. & WARDEN, D. (Eds). Group and interactive learning: Proceedings of the International Conference on group and interactive learning. Southampton: Computational Mechanics Publications. ; THOMSON, J.A., TOLMIE, A., FOOT, H.C. & MCLAREN, B. (1996). Child development and the aims of road safety education: a review and analysis. Report to the Department of Transport. London: Her Majesty's Stationery Office.

STATUS: Sponsored project

SOURCE OF GRANT: Department of Transport £100,134

DATE OF RESEARCH: 1995-1997

KEYWORDS: accidents; child development; traffic safety; visual perception

2473

Department of Psychology, Graham Hills Building, 40 George Street, Glasgow G1 1QE
0141 552 4400

Jeager, P. Mr; Supervisor: Howe, C. Prof.

The role of externalised symbolic and non-symbolic mediating structures in developing pupils' technological problem-solving capabilities

ABSTRACT: The aim of the proposed research is to discover new methods and conditions to facilitate more efficient development of technological problem-solving capability. The major three phases of the research would be prepared for by two minor investigations: a questionnaire would help to create four stratified samples of 15 pupils in terms of problem-solving styles; and some individual interviews with pupils of the most extreme problem-solving styles would help to choose appropriate tasks for the major phases. Phases A and B would examine pupils' technological problem-solving behaviour and the extent of transfer between tasks under different conditions. The conditions examined would be certain manifestations of symbolic, non-symbolic and mixed externalisations of pupils' thoughts as aids for the problem-solving process. This would involve a 45-minute long observation of technological problem-solving, immediately followed by a retrospective interview, both on a one-to-one basis, with each of the 45 pupils chosen in the experimental groups, in both Phases A and B. These sessions would be videotaped. There would be one experimental lesson subsequent to the interviews for each class in both phases, during which pupils would solve technological problems in some way analogous to the ones pupils of the experimental groups solved during the interviews, aiming to find out differences between performances of pupils from different experimental groups. Based on the findings of Phases A and B, an alternative methodology would be devised which would be implemented in one group of first year secondary pupils (Phase C) for one school term. In this longitudinal study pupils of both this experimental group and a control group would be continually observed, tested and compared in their development.

STATUS: Individual research

DATE OF RESEARCH: 1998-continuing

KEYWORDS: design and technology; problem solving

2474

Department of Psychology, Graham Hills Building, 40 George Street, Glasgow G1 1QE
0141 552 4400

McWilliam, D. Miss; *Supervisor*: Howe, C. Prof.

A study into the discussion skills of nursery school children

ABSTRACT: Educational guidelines, such as the Scottish Office Education Department (SOED) S-14 English Language Document (1991), tend to suggest that young children are incapable of complex discussion, including understanding others' viewpoints or justifying their own perspective. Previous findings have thrown some doubt on this, and the present set of 3 studies aims to clarify and elaborate on earlier work by systematically observing, recording and categorising preschoolers' exchanges in the natural set-up of their nursery schools. The first study comprised of 125 children and focused upon conflictual exchanges whilst the second study consisted of 82 children engaged in cooperative dialogue. For comparison, a State-run nursery plus private preschool were involved in the 2 studies, with more boys than girls in each. From the recordings, different types of linguistic strategies were identified and categorised to give a general indication of language complexity. Complexity was then examined in relation to gender, social class, and type of play activity. Results indicate that young children are linguistically more adept than SOED guidelines suggest, and this is especially true when they are engaged in either symbolic or construction play. No significant gender differences were found in either study but the private school children appear verbally more skilful, in conflict situations, than their State school peers. The third and final part of this research builds on the given findings by introducing an intervention programme to increase these complex speech acts via modelling and practice. An overall improvement in the use of these verbal strategies is predicted, which may be helpful for future educational policy and practice.

STATUS: Individual research

DATE OF RESEARCH: 1997-continuing

KEYWORDS: child language; discussion; nursery school pupils; preschool children; young children

2475

Department of Psychology, Centre for Research into Interactive Learning, Graham Hills Building, 40 George Street, Glasgow G1 1QE
0141 552 4400

Duchak, V. Dr; Rattray, C. Ms; *Supervisor*: Howe, C. Prof.; Tolmie, A. Dr

Bridging the Piaget-Vygotsky gap: conceptual and procedural knowledge in science group work

ABSTRACT: Previous research in science education has identified activities that improve pupils' understanding of physical phenomena and activities that improve their grasp of investigative procedures. Successfully integrating these activities into single tasks, so that conceptual grasp is improved via appropriate investigation, would be highly desirable and would meet a main objective of both the National Curriculum and the Scottish 5-14 Programme. Achieving the aim is not, however, straightforward and in many circumstances the relevant activities appear to be mutually antagonistic. However, while the problems must be recognised, past research by the investigators suggests that integration is possible, given group tasks which involve the negotiation of joint conceptualisations, and the assisted testing of consensual viewpoints. The present research will examine this possibility in the contexts of shadow formation and heat transfer. Children aged 9 to 12 will be pre-tested on both their conceptual grasp of the salient variables, and their understanding of how to conduct systematic tests of whether these variables are important. Once the pre-tests are complete, children will be assigned to threesomes and set to work on the relevant group tasks or appropriate control tasks. A few weeks after the group sessions, all participating children will be post-tested using the same method as for the pre-tests. Individual pre- to post-test change in both conceptual and procedural understanding will be calculated, and analysed with respect to the group task engaged in, and on-task activity. A further issue is the manner in which external guidance is provided; and more specifically, whether it is better to risk the potentially intrusive effect of having an adult present to help with testing, or to avoid this by having a computer provide directions and feedback, albeit with less sophisticated tailoring to circumstances than a human would exhibit. Thus the work on shadow formation will contrast the use of a computer and an adult researcher to provide help with the testing.

STATUS: Sponsored project

SOURCE OF GRANT: Economic and Social Research Council £80,059

DATE OF RESEARCH: 1996-1998

KEYWORDS: concept teaching; group work; practical science; primary education; science education; science experiments; scientific concepts; teaching methods

2476

Department of Psychology, Centre for Research into Interactive Learning, Graham Hills Building, 40 George Street, Glasgow G1 1QE
0141 552 4400

Noble, A. Mr; *Supervisors*: Smith, P. Dr; Howe, C. Prof.

Conceptual gain and successful problem-solving in primary school mathematics

ABSTRACT: There is evidence that collaborative problem-solving can facilitate conceptual understanding in mathematics, and this had led to group work being promoted in curricular guidelines, e.g. the Scottish 5-14 Programme. However, it is not clear that children of all ability levels can benefit nor that conceptual gain is invariably translated into problem-solving success. In addition, there are indications that gender may be relevant to collaborative interactions and possibly also to learning outcome. The project is an attempt to shed further light on these issues through a teaching intervention which involves group and pair-based problem solving in 4 Primary 6 classes. Four control classes work on the same problems in the traditional, individual fashion over the same time period. Pre- and post-teaching measures are being taken to compare conceptual and problem-solving gain in the intervention and control classes. The effects of ability and gender on gains are also being considered, as are ability and gender effects on collaborative interactions within the intervention classes.

STATUS: Sponsored project

SOURCE OF GRANT: Economic and Social Research Council £25,883

DATE OF RESEARCH: 1996-1997

KEYWORDS: concept teaching; group work; mathematical concepts; mathematics education; primary education; problem solving; sex differences; teaching methods

2477

Department of Psychology, Centre for Research into Interactive Learning, Graham Hills Building, 40 George Street, Glasgow G1 1QE
0141 552 4400

Terras, M. Dr; Rattray, C. Ms; *Supervisors*: Howe, C. Prof.; Foot, H. Prof.; Cheyne, W. Dr

Quality in preschool provision: the role of the parents

ABSTRACT: The research is concerned with the roles, views and perceptions of parents with respect to the quality of preschool provision. It is being conducted in 2 parts: the first part involving a questionnaire-based survey of a large sample of Scottish parents; and the second, an indepth interview-cum-observational follow-up with a more selected group. The survey asks parents of Primary 1 children about their earlier usage of preschool provision, their satisfaction with the provision, the desired and actual extent of their involvement (as helpers, fundraisers, etc) and their knowledge of the differences between the various forms of provision (playgroups, day nurseries, nursery schools, etc). The results will be analysed with reference to a range of demographic variables, including region of Scotland and urban vs. rural residence. The interview/observational follow-up focuses on the parents of preschool children. More detailed information is being sought on the consequences of parental involvement in preschool establishments, bearing in mind the possible implications for staff, children and the parents themselves. Also of interest are changes in aspirations, satisfactions and knowledge at different points in the child's development.

STATUS: Sponsored project

SOURCE OF GRANT: Scottish Office Education and Industry Department £47,307

DATE OF RESEARCH: 1997-1998

KEYWORDS: early childhood education; educational quality; parent participation; preschool education

2478

Department of Psychology, Centre for Research into Interactive Learning, Graham Hills Building, 40 George Street, Glasgow G1 1QE
0141 552 4400

Warden, D. Dr; Christie, D. Mr; Cheyne, W. Dr; Fitzpatrick, H. Dr; Reid, K. Ms

Promoting children's interpersonal awareness and behaviour by peer interaction

ABSTRACT: This project examines the relationship between children's prosocial and antisocial behaviour, their interpersonal awareness and their gender, and it evaluates the effects on children's social understanding and behaviour of regular and structured classroom peer group activities which involve discussions of interpersonal behaviours and motivations. Groups of 9/10 year-old children from 12 primary schools in Strathclyde will be identified by established methods as being typically prosocial or antisocial, and as being likely or not to be involved in bullying interactions. Control and experimental samples of these children will be assessed on several measures of interpersonal understanding. Experimental samples will then participate for 2 months in a structured sequence of group activities involving discussions and role plays of prosocial and antisocial interactions. The same measures of interpersonal understanding will be applied to all children after the intervention. It is intended that this research will contribute to our understanding of the characteristics of male and female prosocial children, bullies and victims, and of the relationship between children's interpersonal awareness and social behaviour, and provide an effective and enjoyable set of classroom activities which will help to foster children's prosocial behaviour.

PUBLISHED MATERIAL: WARDEN, D., CHRISTIE, D., KERR, C. & LOW, J. (1996). 'Children's prosocial and antisocial behaviour as perceived by children, parents and teachers', Educational Psychology, Vol 16, No 3, pp.365-378. ; WARDEN, D. & CHRISTIE, D. (1997). Teaching social behaviour: classroom activities to foster children's interpersonal awareness. London: David Fulton.

STATUS: Sponsored project

SOURCE OF GRANT: Economic and Social Research Council £136,295

DATE OF RESEARCH: 1998-continuing

KEYWORDS: **antisocial behaviour; bullying; interpersonal competence; primary education; social behaviour**

2479

Department of Psychology, Centre for Research into Interactive Learning, Graham Hills Building, 40 George Street, Glasgow G1 1QE
0141 552 4400
Strathclyde University, Scottish School of Further Education, Jordanhill Campus, Southbrae Drive, Glasgow G13 1PP
0141 950 3000

Soden, R. Dr; Low, J. Ms; *Supervisors*: Anderson, A. Dr; Halliday, J. Dr; Howe, C. Prof.

Bridging the academic/vocational divide by integrating critical thinking

ABSTRACT: In recent years, considerable concern has been expressed concerning the inflexibility of separate academic and vocational tracks with little opportunity for transfer between these. The project is based on the view that a necessary step towards addressing this problem is the teaching of critical thinking skills alongside vocational subject matter. Thus, the project's first stage is an observational study in 3 colleges of further education, ascertaining the extent to which critical thinking is supported in the context of studying health and social care. The second stage is an attempt to boost the support in the 3 colleges via a 10-week teaching programme which involves: a) the modelling of critical thinking in dialogues between researchers, e.g. the use of evidence to support one's own views and to rebut the views of others; b) the use of critical thinking in discussions of project work between students; c) the deployment of skills learned through discussion in written project reports. The programme is being evaluated via videorecordings of the students' discussions and comparisons with project work from both previous years within the colleges and additional control colleges.

STATUS: Sponsored project

SOURCE OF GRANT: Economic and Social Research Council £26,312

DATE OF RESEARCH: 1996-1997

KEYWORDS: **academic vocational divide; critical thinking; further education; vocational education**

2480

Faculty of Education, Department of Applied Arts, Jordanhill Campus, Southbrae Drive, Glasgow G13 1PP
0141 950 3000

Dawes, M. Mr; Hart, D. Mr; Borland, D. Mr; Lochrin, B. Mr; Welsh, R. Mr; *Supervisor*: Coutts, G. Mr

Digital Education Group at Strathclyde University (DEG@S)

ABSTRACT: The group aims to: identify and disseminate good practice in art and technology education; develop high quality research and teaching materials embracing art and technology; provide a forum to discuss and promote art and technology at all levels in education; develop and promote links within and external to the university; to develop research activity in the field of art, design and technology.

PUBLISHED MATERIAL: Web site: http://www.strath.ac.uk/Departments/ Applied Arts/DEGAS/DEG@Shomepagev.2.html

STATUS: Sponsored project

SOURCE OF GRANT: 1st Glasgow 1999 £21,000

DATE OF RESEARCH: 1998-continuing

KEYWORDS: **art education; computer uses in education; design and technology; educational materials; information technology; technology education**

2481

Faculty of Education, Department of Applied Arts, Jordanhill Campus, Southbrae Drive, Glasgow G13 1PP
0141 950 3000
Strathclyde University, Scottish School of Further Education, Jordanhill Campus, Southbrae Drive, Glasgow G1 1PP

Byrne, C. Mr; Sheridan, M. Mr; Soden, R. Dr; Halliday, J. Dr; Hunter, S. Mr

Teaching core skills in Higher Still Music courses: developing conceptions and practice

ABSTRACT: The research will focus on two particular 'core skills' which are included in the new Higher Still units on musical composition. These core skills are 'planning and organising' and 'critical thinking'. Composition is not only part of all proposed Higher Still music courses from Access level to Advanced Higher, but also influences pupils' learning of other musical competencies in these courses such as listening and performing. The overall purpose of the research is to improve the teaching of core skills by helping teachers to develop a conception which makes sense to them of 'planning and organising' and of 'critical thinking' and to implement this conception in their teaching. The findings are expected to be applicable in other Higher Still subjects. The purpose of Stage 1 is to build up a picture of music teachers' existing classroom practices and their conceptions of learning musical composition; this will provide baseline data for Stage 2 of the research. The researchers will analyse videotaped observations of lessons and interview data relating to the teachers' conceptions. In Stage 2 the researchers will engage in developmental activities with the secondary 3 teachers who participated in Stage 1 as they move through secondary 4 work in the same subject with the same pupils. These activities will include discussing video and interview data with teachers and encouraging change in conceptions and practices by introducing ideas from psychologically informed literature on 'teaching thinking'.

STATUS: Sponsored project

SOURCE OF GRANT: Strathclyde University

DATE OF RESEARCH: 1998-continuing

KEYWORDS: **core skills; higher still; key skills; music; musical composition; scotland; secondary education**

2482

Faculty of Education, Department of Business and Computer Education, Jordanhill Campus, Southbrae Drive, Glasgow G13 1PP
0141 950 3000

Baker, J. Ms; Coutts, G. Mr; Hughes, S. Mrs

Tempus Estonia Republic: information technology in teacher education

ABSTRACT: To develop a system of inservice postgraduate awards for teachers in Estonia in information technology (IT) which will be based upon a common framework adapted from that of the Universities of Strathclyde and Barcelona. Also a course in IT for initial teacher education.

STATUS: Sponsored project

DATE OF RESEARCH: 1994-1997

KEYWORDS: **computer uses in education; estonia; information technology; international educational exchange; teacher education**

2483

Faculty of Education, Department of Community Education, Jordanhill Campus, Southbrae Drive, Glasgow G13 1PP
0141 950 3000

Hayward, B. Dr; *Supervisor*: Hough, M. Mr

Homesickness: causes and effects

ABSTRACT: To assess the process of transition experienced by six young people from Skye as they move to higher education.

STATUS: Sponsored project

SOURCE OF GRANT: Faculty Research Committee £900

DATE OF RESEARCH: 1997-continuing

KEYWORDS: **higher education; homesickness; students**

2484

Faculty of Education, Department of Community Education, Jordanhill Campus, Southbrae Drive, Glasgow G13 1PP
0141 950 3000

Rowlands, C. Mr; ter Horst, J. Ms; *Supervisor*: Seddon, J. Mr

Young people and alcohol

ABSTRACT: An investigation of the attitudes of young people to alcohol in the late 1990s in the Netherlands and Scotland.

STATUS: Sponsored project

SOURCE OF GRANT: Faculty Research Committee £800

DATE OF RESEARCH: 1997-continuing

KEYWORDS: **adolescent attitudes; alcohol education; netherlands; scotland**

2485

Faculty of Education, Department of Community Education, Jordanhill Campus, Southbrae Drive, Glasgow G13 1PP
0141 950 3000

Ferguson, R. Mr; *Supervisor*: Milburn, T. Mr

Youth streetwork in South Lanarkshire

ABSTRACT: The aims of the project are: (a) mapping current work and assessing value; (b) action research with two pilots; (c) set pilots within strategy of South Lanarkshire Council; and (d) identify and record good practice.

STATUS: Sponsored project

SOURCE OF GRANT: South Lanarkshire Council £18,000

DATE OF RESEARCH: 1998-continuing

KEYWORDS: **youth work**

2486

Faculty of Education, Department of Community Education, Jordanhill Campus, Southbrae Drive, Glasgow G13 1PP
0141 950 3000

Hampson, I. Ms; *Supervisor*: Fagan, G. Mr

Young people say...

ABSTRACT: The aim of the project is to identify the attitudes and values of young people in Scotland towards the Third World and investigate how they may be confronted within good youthwork practice.

STATUS: Sponsored project

SOURCE OF GRANT: IDEAS £6,000; CADISPA £6,000

DATE OF RESEARCH: 1997-1998

KEYWORDS: **adolescent attitudes; developing countries; youth attitudes; youthwork**

2487

Faculty of Education, Department of Mathematics, Science and Technological Education, Jordanhill Campus, Southbrae Drive, Glasgow G13 1PP
0141 950 3000

Murdoch, G. Mr

Young engineers clubs

ABSTRACT: The aim of the project is to review the effectiveness of being a young engineer on career prospects.

DATE OF RESEARCH: 1995-continuing

KEYWORDS: **career development; careers; engineering; engineers**

2488

Faculty of Education, Department of Mathematics, Science and Technological Education, Jordanhill Campus, Southbrae Drive, Glasgow G13 1PP
0141 950 3000

Simpson, M. Prof.; Kirkwood, M. Mr; Gray, D. Mr; Munro, B. Mr; *Supervisor*: Stark, R. Mrs

The impact of information and communication technology (ICT) initiatives on pupil attainment

ABSTRACT: The aims of the project are: (1) to provide measures of pupil attainment in information and communication technology (ICT) skills and knowledge; and (2) before and after the major government initiatives are implemented, to provide an estimate of the gains made as a result.

STATUS: Sponsored project

SOURCE OF GRANT: Scottish Office Education and Industry Department £195,275

DATE OF RESEARCH: 1998-continuing

KEYWORDS: **achievement; computer uses in education; information technology**

2489

Faculty of Education, Department of Primary Education, Jordanhill Campus, Southbrae Drive, Glasgow G13 1PP
0141 950 3000

Kleinberg, S. Mrs

Inquiry learning and teaching

ABSTRACT: Development of a model of the process of inquiry learning and identification of what the teacher needs to plan if children are to be helped to learn to inquire and learn through inquiry. Application of the model has led to a range of projects on inquiry learning in language, science, drama and mathematics.

DATE OF RESEARCH: 1995-1998

KEYWORDS: **inquiry; learning strategies; teaching methods**

2490

Faculty of Education, Department of Primary Education, Jordanhill Campus, Southbrae Drive, Glasgow G13 1PP
0141 950 3000

Ellis, S. Mrs

Writing in the 5-14 curriculum

ABSTRACT: The influence of context, content and process approaches on curriculum and teacher frameworks; the development and understanding of characterisation in the stories children write.

DATE OF RESEARCH: 1997-continuing

KEYWORDS: **children as writers; writing - composition**

2491

Faculty of Education, Department of Primary Education, Jordanhill Campus, Southbrae Drive, Glasgow G13 1PP
0141 950 3000

Dunlop, A-W. Mrs

Early intervention: project evaluations

ABSTRACT: The evaluation of the Reading Discovery Project, funded by Scottish Office Education and Industry Department (SOEID), and the evaluation of the Knightsbridge Project for under fives and their families, funded by that project.

STATUS: Individual research

DATE OF RESEARCH: 1997-1998

KEYWORDS: **beginning reading; early childhood education; intervention; reading; reading teaching; young children**

2492

Faculty of Education, Department of Primary Education, Jordanhill Campus, Southbrae Drive, Glasgow G13 1PP
0141 950 3000

Dunlop, A-W. Mrs

Continuity and progression - pre-school to primary education

ABSTRACT: Current practice in curricular and pastoral continuity from pre-school into primary education including the part that parents play in continuity; how far it provides primary school entrants with continuity of educational and pastoral experiences and whether the improvement of continuity practice enhances educational opportunities and achievements. A further project will look at how the quality of the relationships and interaction within learning and teaching contributes to curricular continuity.

DATE OF RESEARCH: 1997-1998

KEYWORDS: **developmental continuity; preschool to primary transition**

2493

Faculty of Education, Department of Primary Education, Jordanhill Campus, Southbrae Drive, Glasgow G13 1PP
0141 950 3000

Grogan, D. Mrs

Effective use of playrooms

ABSTRACT: The status of play within the early years curriculum and teachers' involvement during play.

DATE OF RESEARCH: 1996-1997

KEYWORDS: **early childhood education; play**

2494

Faculty of Education, Department of Primary Education, Jordanhill Campus, Southbrae Drive, Glasgow G13 1PP
0141 950 3000

Gavienas, E. Mrs

Group teaching in primary schools

ABSTRACT: The research will look at: teacher frameworks underpinning decisions about the seating arrangements for group teaching in primary classrooms; and the effect on learning of "extracting" attainment groups to a common seating area to teach and "visiting" them to teach.

DATE OF RESEARCH: 1997-1998

KEYWORDS: **class organisation; grouping - teaching purposes; primary education**

2495

Faculty of Education, Department of Primary Education, Jordanhill Campus, Southbrae Drive, Glasgow G13 1PP
0141 950 3000

Hughes, A. Mrs

Professionalism in early childhood education; support for learning in part-time degrees

ABSTRACT: The research involves studies of a group of predominately women workers in an emerging profession in which degree level study has only just become available. The research considers: (i) the nature of support required for part-time students from a non-academic background but who are experienced in practice; (ii) the constructs of professionalism in early childhood work and the implications for course design and for practice.

STATUS: Individual research

DATE OF RESEARCH: 1997-1998

KEYWORDS: **child care givers; early childhood education; higher education; part time degrees; preschool education; preschool teachers**

2496

Faculty of Education, Department of Primary Education, Jordanhill Campus, Southbrae Drive, Glasgow G13 1PP
0141 950 3000

Mackay, R. Mr

Structure and nature of school experience in Teacher Education Institutions

ABSTRACT: Comparative studies in Scottish and Dutch Teacher Education Institutions (TEI) investigating the roles of TEI supervisors and school supervisors and the concerns of first and fourth year students regarding their teaching.

DATE OF RESEARCH: 1997-1998

KEYWORDS: **comparative education; preservice teacher education; school based teacher education; student teacher supervisors; student teachers**

2497

Faculty of Education, Department of Primary Education, Jordanhill Campus, Southbrae Drive, Glasgow G13 1PP
0141 950 3000

Logue, J. Mrs

Talking activities in the primary school

ABSTRACT: Study of the role, use and organisation of oral activities across the curriculum and stages. Recommendations to develop the talking outcome of the 5-14 English Language curriculum.

DATE OF RESEARCH: 1996-1998

KEYWORDS: **oral language; primary education; verbal communication**

2498

Faculty of Education, Department of Primary Education, Jordanhill Campus, Southbrae Drive, Glasgow G13 1PP
0141 950 3000

Laing, M. Miss

Attitudes in environmental studies and environmental education

ABSTRACT: Case studies of effective implementation of environmental education; ethos, values and children's ability to act on sustainability issues.

DATE OF RESEARCH: 1997-1998

KEYWORDS: **attitudes; environment; environmental education; pupil attitudes; sustainable development**

2499

Faculty of Education, Department of Primary Education, Jordanhill Campus, Southbrae Drive, Glasgow G13 1PP
0141 950 3000

Kleinberg, S. Mrs

Early intervention

ABSTRACT: Comparative studies of early intervention projects and issues that arise from them.

DATE OF RESEARCH: 1997-1998

KEYWORDS: **early childhood education; intervention**

2500

Faculty of Education, Department of Primary Education, Jordanhill Campus, Southbrae Drive, Glasgow G13 1PP
0141 950 3000

Pearson, M. Mrs

Diagnostic assessment in mathematical problem solving

ABSTRACT: Skills and strategies used by children in problem-solving and how and why teachers intervene.

DATE OF RESEARCH: 1997-1998

KEYWORDS: **mathematics education; problem solving**

2501

Faculty of Education, Department of Primary Education, Jordanhill Campus, Southbrae Drive, Glasgow G13 1PP
0141 950 3000

Pearson, M. Mrs

Reflections on learning

ABSTRACT: The aim of the project is to study how individuals learn in an organisational context and the impact on organisational change.

STATUS: Individual research

DATE OF RESEARCH: 1997-1998

KEYWORDS: **learning processes; learning strategies; organisational change**

2502

Faculty of Education, Department of Primary Education, Jordanhill Campus, Southbrae Drive, Glasgow G13 1PP
0141 950 3000

Twiddle, B. Mr

National Centre: Education for Work and Enterprise

ABSTRACT: The aim of the project is to develop strategies to promote education for work (enterprise education; support for learning and teaching; transition from school to work). This is a joint project with Education Business Partnership Network, Scottish Councils Education Industry Network and the Centre for Careers Education and Guidance.

STATUS: Individual research

DATE OF RESEARCH: 1998-continuing

KEYWORDS: **enterprise education; industry education relationship; school to work transition; vocational education; work education relationship**

2503

Faculty of Education, Department of Primary Education, Jordanhill Campus, Southbrae Drive, Glasgow G13 1PP
0141 950 3000

Smyth, G. Ms

Teaching and assessing bilingual learners

ABSTRACT: The aim of the project is to study how teachers meet the demands of the multilingual primary classroom. Issues arising from teaching methodologies, assessment issues and the teacher's underpinning knowledge will be looked at.

STATUS: Individual research

DATE OF RESEARCH: 1997-continuing

KEYWORDS: **bilingualism; english - second language; ethnic groups; multilingualism; primary education**

2504

Faculty of Education, Department of Primary Education, Jordanhill Campus, Southbrae Drive, Glasgow G13 1PP
0141 950 3000

Allan, J. Mr

Reading for information

ABSTRACT: Case studies of different approaches taken by schools to the teaching of information skills; involves developing and trialling new materials and approaches.

DATE OF RESEARCH: 1997-1998

KEYWORDS: **information seeking; teaching methods**

2505

Faculty of Education, Department of Social Studies Education, Jordanhill Campus, Southbrae Drive, Glasgow G13 1PP
0141 950 3000

Hillis, P. Dr

History education in Scotland

ABSTRACT: The aim of the project is to enhance the reputation of history teaching. The outcome will be an edited book.

DATE OF RESEARCH: 1998-continuing

KEYWORDS: **history**

2506

Faculty of Education, Department of Social Studies Education, Jordanhill Campus, Southbrae Drive, Glasgow G13 1PP
0141 950 3000

Hillis, P. Dr

External assessment in Higher Still Higher History

ABSTRACT: To develop a fair style of external assessment in history.

DATE OF RESEARCH: 1998-continuing

KEYWORDS: **assessment; higher still; history; scotland; sixteen to nineteen education**

2507

Faculty of Education, Department of Social Studies Education, Jordanhill Campus, Southbrae Drive, Glasgow G13 1PP
0141 950 3000

Foxon, C. Mr; *Supervisor*: Gray, I. Mr

Developing a database for religious and moral education in Scottish schools

ABSTRACT: This database is intended to provide students and others with a quick and easy way to identify a wide range of resources to support the teaching of topics which address attainment targets within the 5-14 programme of religious and moral education.

PUBLISHED MATERIAL: Web site: http://www.strath.ac.uk/Departments/ Social Studies/RE/Database.

DATE OF RESEARCH: 1996-1998

KEYWORDS: **computer uses in education; databases; educational materials; information storage; information technology; moral education; religious education; scotland**

2508

Faculty of Education, Department of Social Studies Education, Jordanhill Campus, Southbrae Drive, Glasgow G13 1PP
0141 950 3000

Calderhead, D. Mr; *Supervisor*: Hillis, P. Dr

Auld Reekie and the Dear Green Place of Living and Working

ABSTRACT: The aim of the project is to enhance use of information and communication technology in history teachers. The output will be CD ROM.

DATE OF RESEARCH: 1997-1998

KEYWORDS: **cd roms; computer uses in education; history; information technology**

2509

Faculty of Education, Department of Social Work, Jordanhill Campus, Southbrae Drive, Glasgow G13 1PP
0141 950 3000

Thorne, J. Ms; *Supervisor*: Chakrabarti, M. Prof.

Having regard to racial, religious, cultural and linguistic needs of Scotland's Children (Scotland) Act 1995

ABSTRACT: The aim of the project is to produce guidance materials to show how social work services for children should take account of matters of race, religion, language and culture.

STATUS: Sponsored project

SOURCE OF GRANT: Social Work Services; Inspectorate of the Scottish Office, jointly £18,000

DATE OF RESEARCH: 1998-continuing

KEYWORDS: **childrens services; cultural differences; english - second language; ethnic groups; racial differences; religious differences; scotland; social services**

2510

Faculty of Education, Department of Special Educational Needs, Jordanhill Campus, Southbrae Drive, Glasgow G13 1PP
0141 950 3000
Strathclyde University, Faculty of Education, Department of Speech and Language Therapy, Jordanhill Campus, Southbrae Drive, Glasgow G13 1PP

MacKay, G. Dr; Anderson, C. Mrs; Baldry, H. Mrs; Clark, K. Mrs

Provision for pupils with disorders of language and communication

ABSTRACT: The research reviewed the varieties and extent of provision in 11 new West of Scotland education authorities created by local government reorganisation in 1996. Widespread provision for pupils with disorders of language and communication is relatively recent in Scottish education, and it seemed important to take stock of the field, and to identify trends and priorities in its development. Recommendations on terminology, the development of provision for pupils, and the training needs of staff were identified.

PUBLISHED MATERIAL: MACKAY, G., ANDERSON, C., BALDRY, H. & CLARK, K. 'Educational provision for pupils with disorders of language and communication in West Central Scotland', Scottish Educational Review, Vol 29, No 2, pp.154-162.

STATUS: Sponsored project

SOURCE OF GRANT: Strathclyde University

DATE OF RESEARCH: 1996-1997

KEYWORDS: **communication disorders; scotland; services; special educational needs; speech handicaps**

2511

Faculty of Education, Division of Business & Computer Education, Jordanhill Campus, Southbrae Drive, Glasgow G13 1PP
0141 950 3000
Northern College, Computer Education Department, Dundee Campus, Gardyne Road, Dundee DD5 1NY
01382 464000

Munro, R. Mr; Lamont, M. Mrs

SPRITE (Supporting and Promoting Information Technology in Education)

ABSTRACT: The aim of this project is to improve, enhance and encourage the use of information technology (IT) by college staff (throughout Scotland) and assist the permeation of IT use in college courses.

STATUS: Sponsored project

SOURCE OF GRANT: Strathclyde University; Northern College; Scottish Office Education Department

DATE OF RESEARCH: 1991-1993

KEYWORDS: **colleges; computer uses in education; information technology**

2512

Faculty of Education, Division of Inservice Training, Jordanhill Campus, Southbrae Drive, Glasgow G13 1PP
0141 950 3000

McCall, C. Dr; Ellis, S. Mrs; Grant, M. Mrs; Hughes, A. Mrs

Philosophical inquiry in values education

ABSTRACT: This project aims to disseminate the method of philosophical inquiry in values education and to use this in staff development in values education.

STATUS: Sponsored project

SOURCE OF GRANT: Gordon Cook Foundation £40,000

DATE OF RESEARCH: 1991-1993

KEYWORDS: **moral education; philosophy; values education**

2513

Faculty of Education, Division of Language and Literature, Jordanhill Campus, Southbrae Drive, Glasgow G13 1PP
0141 950 3000

Williams, W. Mr

Scottish Standard Grade Beginners Latin Course: design of a course book

ABSTRACT: The aim of this project is to design a beginners Latin course book based on the elements of the Scottish Standard Grade.

STATUS: Sponsored project

SOURCE OF GRANT: Strathclyde University £500

DATE OF RESEARCH: 1988-1993

KEYWORDS: **educational materials; latin; textbook preparation**

2514

Faculty of Education, Division of Special Educational Needs, Jordanhill Campus, Southbrae Drive, Glasgow G13 1PP
0141 950 3000

Hewitt, C. Mrs; Hamill, P. Mr; Robertson, P. Mrs

Below average attainment project

ABSTRACT: This project aims to describe and evaluate the variety of services designed to support the progress of pupils with learning difficulties and social disadvantage.

STATUS: Sponsored project

SOURCE OF GRANT: Scottish Office Education Department £69,638

DATE OF RESEARCH: 1991-1993

KEYWORDS: **disadvantaged; learning disabilities; low achievement; special educational needs; support services**

2515

Faculty of Education, Jordanhill Campus, Southbrae Drive, Glasgow G13 1PP 0141 950 3000
Edinburgh University, Centre for Educational Sociology, 7 Buccleuch Place, Edinburgh EH8 9LW
0131 650 4186

Semple, S. Ms; Howieson, C. Ms

A longitudinal study of young people and careers

ABSTRACT: This is a longitudinal study of a small number of young people in Ayrshire over a three year period. The intention is to identify the changes that occur in young people's thinking and consider the influences on them as they move out of compulsory education and into subsequent education, training and work opportunities. It will chart how their attitudes to training, the labour market, continuing education and lifelong learning develop and change as their experiences grow. The young people will be contacted at four points over the study. The second strand of the research focuses on those individuals identified by the young people as significant to their thinking and decisions; the aim is to gain an understanding of the nature and extent of their influence and impact. Delay in obtaining agreement to proceed means that the first contact of the young people will now be in late 1998; meanwhile the research team is developing research instruments and identifying potential participants. The project is led by Sheila Semple of the University of Strathclyde.

STATUS: Sponsored project

SOURCE OF GRANT: Scottish Office Enterprise Ayrshire; Ayrshire Careers Partnership; Ayrshire Education Business Partnership

DATE OF RESEARCH: 1997-continuing

KEYWORDS: **careers; school leavers; school to work transition; sixteen to nineteen education; training; vocational guidance; youth attitudes; youth employment**

2516

Faculty of Education, Scottish School of Further Education, Jordanhill Campus, Southbrae Drive, Glasgow G13 1PP
0141 950 3000

Niven, S. Mr; McFarlan, E. Miss; Foong, A. Dr; *Supervisors*: Stillie, D. Mr; McQueeney, E. Mrs

Accreditation of experienced derived learning for second-level nurses: 3 phases

ABSTRACT: The aim of the projects is to devise and test an assessment instrument which will accredit the experience derived learning of second-level nurses, to enable them to gain access, with credit, to courses leading to first level qualification.

PUBLISHED MATERIAL: FOONG, A.L. & MACKAY, G. (1996). 'An examination of the psycho-social perspective of educational/developmental opportunities for enrolled nurses: the forgotten species', Nurse Education Today, Vol 16, No 1, pp.94-97.

STATUS: Sponsored project

DATE OF RESEARCH: 1990-1993

KEYWORDS: **accreditation of prior learning; assessment; clinical experience; experiential learning; nurse education; nurses**

2517

Faculty of Education, Scottish School of Sports Studies, Jordanhill Campus, Southbrae Drive, Glasgow G13 1PP
0141 950 3000

Boyd, B. Dr; Allison, P. Mr; *Supervisor*: Green, B. Mr

Sport and drug education action research project

ABSTRACT: To establish the effectiveness of the combined drug education and sporting experience and the extent to which this intervention could be used as an example of good practice for future work.

PUBLISHED MATERIAL: FORREST, J., GREEN, B., ALLISON, P., BOYD, B. & TWADDLE, G. (1998). Sport and Drug Education Action Research Project: Evaluation Report. University of Strathclyde, Faculty of Education, Glasgow. ; FORREST, J. & GREEN, B. (1998). 'Drug Education and Sports: an unholy alliance?: a report on an innovative drugs intervention in Scottish primary schools'. In: Proceedings of Working Together for Better Health - International Conference, Cardiff, 1998.

STATUS: Sponsored project

SOURCE OF GRANT: Glasgow Drugs Prevention Team £10,000

DATE OF RESEARCH: 1997-1998

KEYWORDS: **drug education; physical education; sports**

Sunderland University

2518

School of Computing and Information Systems, St Peter's Campus, St Peter's Way, North Sands, Sunderland SR6 0DD
0191 515 2000

Lejk, M. Mr; *Supervisors*: Wyvill, M. Mr; Farrow, S. Dr

Group assessment on undergraduate computing courses in higher education in the UK

ABSTRACT: The research question is: 'What are the reasons behind assessment of students in groups on undergraduate computing courses in the UK, what are the perceived problems and benefits of the methods used, and how can these problems be overcome?'. The methods used are: 1) Interview with recognised experts who have a clear view of the purposes of computing courses and the ways in which group assessment can contribute to the achievement of these purposes. 2) Surveys and interviews with computing tutors. 3) Surveys and interviews with students. 4) Design and implementation of a number of interventions to test the veracity of some of the assumptions arising from 1, 2 and 3 above and to compare the effectiveness of different approaches to group assessment. It is anticipated that this will involve investigation of: a) methods of group formation; and b) methods of peer assessment.

PUBLISHED MATERIAL: LEJK, M. (1994). 'Team assessment, win or lose', The New Academic, Vol 3, No 3, pp.10-11. ; DEEKS, D. & LEJK, M. (1995). 'Real-world computing', The New Academic, Vol 4, No 3, pp.15-16. ; LEJK, M. (1996). 'Learning together', The New Academic, Vol 5, No 3, pp.6-7. ; LEJK, M., WYVILL, M. & FARROW, S. (1996). 'A survey of methods of deriving individual grades from group assessment', Assessment and Evaluation in Higher Education, Vol 21, No 3, pp.267-280.

STATUS: Individual research

DATE OF RESEARCH: 1994-1998

KEYWORDS: **assessment; computer science; group work; higher education**

2519

School of Education, Hammerton Hall, Gray Road, Sunderland SR2 8JB
0191 515 2000

Constable, H. Prof.; Meyer, W. Mr

The European dimension in inservice teacher education

ABSTRACT: On 24 May 1988, the European Community Council adopted a resolution aimed at promoting and reinforcing the European Dimension in Education. The aim was to strengthen young people's sense of European identity, to improve their knowledge of the Community and to prepare them to take part in the future economic and social development of the Community. Certain sections of the resolution relate to inservice teacher education (INSET) and suggest that in this area the European Dimension might be fostered by providing courses and activities of an awareness-raising type and by opening up certain INSET activities to teachers from other European Community member states. As part of an investigation carried out by the Association for Teacher Education in Europe the University of Sunderland conducted a survey of UK and Irish INSET providers in order to establish the level and type of relevant INSET provision. It was found that in the UK provision of European Dimension INSET was strongest in the following regions: Scotland; Northern Ireland; Northern England; Yorkshire and Humberside; South-Western England. In Southern Ireland, work was generally limited both in extent and scope. In the UK, it was found that some of the most effective work was being done by groups of local education authorities working together in collaboration with higher education institutions and the Central Bureau for Educational Visits and Exchanges. Much depended on local and individual enthusiasm. There was a feeling in the field that the UK central government was failing to give a lead.

PUBLISHED MATERIAL: CONSTABLE, H. & MEYER, W. (1994). The European dimension in inservice teacher education in the United Kingdom and Ireland. Sunderland: University of Sunderland, School of Education.

STATUS: Sponsored project

SOURCE OF GRANT: European Commission Association

DATE OF RESEARCH: 1993-1993

KEYWORDS: **european studies; european union; inservice teacher education; intercultural programmes**

2520

School of Education, Hammerton Hall, Gray Road, Sunderland SR2 8JB
0191 515 2000

Constable, H. Prof.; Meyer, W. Mr

Evaluation of teacher and headteacher appraisal in Sunderland

ABSTRACT: The 1986 Education Act contained enabling legislation for teacher appraisal and in December 1990 the Secretary of State for Education announced a national, compulsory scheme under which all teachers in service were to be appraised by the end of the 1994-95 school year. The School of Education of the University of Sunderland was commissioned by the Sunderland Local Education Authority (LEA) to evaluate the introduction and early stages of its appraisal scheme. The main research techniques were observations of appraisal inservice teacher education (INSET) sessions; interviews with teachers, headteachers, and LEA personnel; and the administering of a questionnaire to 500 teachers and headteachers. It was found that appraisal was generally favoured as a means of professional development and it was felt that the LEA had succeeded in introducing its scheme in a sensitive and efficient way. Fears were expressed that central government would act to bring in a strict accountability model of appraisal and would link appraisal to remuneration. Appraisal was found to be more popular with headteachers than with other teachers; and more popular in primary than in secondary schools. Appraisal was found useful in regard to clarifying roles and setting priorites but it was not thought that it would improve morale or equal opportunities. Fears were expressed about the confidentiality aspect and there was concern about the future availability of funding for cover and INSET requirements. A frequently expressed worry was that appraisal was a glutton for time.

PUBLISHED MATERIAL: CONSTABLE, H. & MEYER, W. (1993). An evaluation of teacher and headteacher appraisal in Sunderland. Sunderland: University of Sunderland, School of Education.

STATUS: Sponsored project

SOURCE OF GRANT: Sunderland Local Education Authority £4,800

DATE OF RESEARCH: 1992-1993

KEYWORDS: **academic staff development; head teachers; teacher evaluation; teaching profession**

2521

School of Education, Hammerton Hall, Gray Road, Sunderland SR2 8JB
0191 515 2000

Atkinson, E. Ms; *Supervisor*: Newton, D. Dr

Identification of some causes of demotivation amongst National Curriculum key stage 4 pupils in studying technology, with special reference to design and technology

ABSTRACT: The importance of technology education and the failure to interest a larger proportion of young people, including the more able and girls, at a time of considerable technological change in society, has been the concern of educationalists and others in the United Kingdom throughout the second half of this century. Given its importance, it is vital that the technology curriculum offered to pupils motivates them to participate fully. Technology in schools requires pupils to apply skills and knowledge to develop solutions to practical problems. As the subject area has developed so has the use of the design process as a method of delivering and examining subject content and capability. It would appear from the initial research that long-term pieces of coursework, fundamental to the delivery of technology, may well prove to be tangible indicators in the identification of the causes of pupil demotivation. An initial survey was carried out in 50 schools teaching technology in 7 local education authorities in the North East of England. Eight schools were then selected and during Phase 1 a specific sample of 179 Year 11 pupils completed a questionnaire. From the analysis of that data, 40 pupils were selected for further indepth study. Phase 2 involved 126 Year 10 pupils from the same 8 case study schools. Through a questionnaire and a cognitive style test a sample of 50 pupils was identified. Phase 3 is concerned with those pupils who are now being observed and interviewed at regular intervals throughout the production of their major projects for their General Certificate in Secondary Education (GCSE) technology examination. It is intended that analysis of the collected data will highlight the key factors involved in causing demotivation and that this will lead to the development of teaching/learning strategies which could improve the situation.

PUBLISHED MATERIAL: ATKINSON, E.S. (1993). 'Identification of some causes of demotivation amongst key stage 4 pupils in studying technology with special reference to design and technology'. In: SMITH, J.S. (Ed) IDATER 93: International Conference on Design and Technology, Loughborough University, Department of Design and Technology, September 1993.

STATUS: Individual research

DATE OF RESEARCH: 1992-1997

KEYWORDS: **demotivation; design and technology; girls; key stage 4; motivation; secondary education; sex differences; technology education**

2522

School of Education, Hammerton Hall, Gray Road, Sunderland SR2 8JB
0191 515 2000

Lauchlan, F. Mr; *Supervisors*: Elliott, J. Dr; Swann, J. Dr

An investigation of the efficacy of dynamic assessment in educational settings

ABSTRACT: Dynamic assessment aims to address the learning difficulties of children in a more effective manner than the present means of assessment, such as standardised tests. The most definitive aspect of dynamic assessment is the provision of examiner assistance during the assessment. While the roles of examiner and child are clearly defined during traditional assessment methods, dynamic assessment encourages an environment where the examiner and child are perceived as working together. It is argued that a child's learning potential can be measured by analysing the ability of the child to improve his/her performance as a result of assistance (Vygotsky, 1978). The research is investigating the dynamic assessment technique on 3 main themes as follows: 1) Is dynamic assessment an accurate means of measuring the learning potential of children? 2) Does dynamic assessment provide more information about a child's intellectual and affective functioning than what is already known from teacher observations and standardised assessments? 3) Does cognitive intervention enhance children's independent problem-solving skills; ability to profit from assistance; ability to transfer or generalise these skills to 'academic areas' such as reading and arithmetic? There are 69 children and 6 teachers involved in the research. All 69 children were assessed in January-March 1996 using both the dynamic assessment method and a standardised test. Half of the sample then received a cognitive intervention programme (instrumental enrichment, Feuerstein, Rand, Hoffman and Miller, 1980). Post-intervention assessments are presently ongoing. The 6 teachers were interviewed on their perceptions of dynamic assessment.

PUBLISHED MATERIAL: LAUCHLAN, F. (1996). 'The contribution of Vygotsky to the development of dynamic assessment: an accurate representation?'. Paper presented at the Piaget-Vygotsky Centenary Conference, Annual Conference of the British Psychological Society, Brighton, April 1996. ; ELLIOTT, J., LAUCHLAN, F. & STRINGER, P. (1996). 'Dynamic assessment and its potential for educational psychologists. Part 1 - theory and practice', Educational Psychology in Practice, Vol 12, No 3, pp.152-160. ; LAUCHLAN, F. (1997). 'Dynamic assessment: an alternative means of assessing children with learning difficulties'. Proceedings of the Annual Conference of the Scottish Educational Research Association, 1996. ; STRINGER, P., ELLIOTT, J. & LAUCHLAN, F. (1997). 'Dynamic assessment and its potential for educational psychologists. Part 2 the zone of next development?', Educational Psychology in Practice, Vol 12, No 4, pp.234-39.

STATUS: Individual research

DATE OF RESEARCH: 1995-1998

KEYWORDS: **assessment; intervention; learning disabilities; special educational needs**

2523

School of Education, Hammerton Hall, Gray Road, Sunderland SR2 8JB
0191 515 2000

Addison, S. Mr; *Supervisors*: Reay, G. Mrs; Whitley, S. Mr

Styles of learning and teaching in higher education

ABSTRACT: Students differ in the way they prefer to learn, for example each has his or her own learning style. Lecturers tend to choose teaching methods which reflect their own preferences in learning. These teaching methods can be disadvantageous to students with different learning styles to the lecturers. This research aims to investigate the extent to which teaching and learning in higher education can be improved through an understanding and application of the variety of learning styles among students. A total of 6 individual case studies within 3 different schools of the University of Sunderland will be conducted. Each case study will involve the design and implementation of a teaching approach which will take into account different student learning styles, and the specific subject being taught, and the lecturer's learning style. Learning styles will be diagnosed by using the Cognitive Style Analysis (CSA) developed by Dr Richard Riding. The number of students in each case study varies from 10 to 180. This research will test the suitability and evaluate the effect on the quality of the learning when identifying and catering to student learning styles across 3 disciplines in higher education.

STATUS: Individual research

DATE OF RESEARCH: 1995-1998

KEYWORDS: **academic staff; cognitive style; higher education; learning strategies; lecturers; teaching methods**

2524

School of Education, Hammerton Hall, Gray Road, Sunderland SR2 8JB
0191 515 2000

Watkinson, B. Mr; *Supervisors*: Constable, H. Prof.; Hutton, N. Dr

The profession of science teachers in higher education

ABSTRACT: Although there have been studies on the nature of teaching expertise, they have almost always involved school teachers and there has been little, if any, research into differences between expert and novice lecturers in higher education. The project will be a longitudinal study examining the processes by which new teachers progress to become expert teachers. It will critically analyse the processes and find suitable terms for the stages in the progression from novice to expert. The progression from naive teacher will be followed mainly by autobiographical interviews but, where appropriate, questionnaires and observation will be used to detect changes and advancement through the stages of skill development. As the development of expertise may progress at different rates depending on the method of instruction used by the lecturer, the progression of the teacher will be followed whilst using a variety of teaching and learning methods.

STATUS: Individual research

DATE OF RESEARCH: 1995-continuing

KEYWORDS: **academic staff; higher education; lecturers; professional development; science teachers; teacher development; teaching profession**

2525

School of Education, Hammerton Hall, Gray Road, Sunderland SR2 8JB
0191 515 2000

Spedding, P. Mrs; *Supervisors*: Constable, H. Prof.; Dockerty, A. Dr

Matching demands: teachers' strategies for differentiation in science

ABSTRACT: The aim of this project is to investigate and identify the ways in which teachers match demands and expectations to pupils' learning needs. Making the appropriate demand on pupils has been a long-standing matter of interest to teachers and researchers. Match is a dynamic process, setting tasks appropriate to pupils' existing skills and ideas and at the same time raising achievements and expectations. Developing and using strategies for differentiation is both an integral part of teachers' work and a key point of their expertise. Concerns continue to be expressed about levels of match, attainment and differentiation and may point only to the fact that this key aspect of teachers' expertise is exceptionally difficult to describe. Developing strategies for differentiation and match remains difficult until such strategies can be described clearly and meaningfully. This project sets out to describe and map the strategies teachers use. Arising from this will be implications for the development of practice, initial training and inservice training. The theoretical background to the enquiry will be investigated by a review of the literature and attention to the common sense theory of practitioners. It aims to develop a typology of ways in which teachers match the demands they make to the pupils they teach extending the investigation to explanation of how these strategies work. Methods for collecting, recording and analysing findings will be by a combination of interviews, observations and consultation with teachers, school management, teacher trainers, professional bodies, inservice trainers and inspectors.

STATUS: Individual research

DATE OF RESEARCH: 1995-1998

KEYWORDS: **differentiated curriculum; individualised methods; learning strategies; pupil needs; science education; teaching methods**

2526

School of Education, Hammerton Hall, Gray Road, Sunderland SR2 8JB
0191 515 2000

Ding, L. Ms; *Supervisors*: Ecclestone, K. Ms; Swann, J. Dr

An investigation of university students' and tutors' attitudes towards and uses of assessment feedback: case studies in the UK and China

ABSTRACT: Assessment has a significant impact on learning. How student learning is influenced by the nature of assessment tasks has been the subject of considerable debate. However, the influence of assessment feedback has not received comparable attention. There has been limited systematic empirical exploration in this area. This research investigates university students' and tutors' attitudes towards, and uses of, assessment feedback. The aim is to: a) develop existing theory about the impact of assessment feedback in higher education; and b) formulate recommendations as to how university tutors can use assessment feedback more strategically. The research project consists of 4 comparative case studies, 2 undertaken in a UK university and 2 in a university in China. Each case study involves an analysis of documented assessment policy, tutors' written feedback to students and semi-structured interviews with 4 tutors and 15 students. Case

study findings will be analysed and cross-cultural comparison made. Implications will be drawn for assessment policy and practice in both countries.

STATUS: Individual research

DATE OF RESEARCH: 1996-continuing

KEYWORDS: **assessment; china; comparative education; feedback; higher education; learning**

2527

School of Education, Hammerton Hall, Gray Road, Sunderland SR2 8JB
0191 515 2000

Sellami, A. Mr; *Supervisors*: Reay, G. Mrs; Breet, F. Dr

Cultural awareness and intercultural competence in higher education

ABSTRACT: The research will focus on the way in which culture is transmitted and learnt in foreign language higher education. The investigation will consider the case of English as a foreign language (EFL) in Morocco with a context provided by French as a foreign language (FFL) in England. The aim of the study is to identify the role of intercultural competence in foreign language (FL) teaching and learning. Emphasis will be laid on intercultural competence which is implicit in the teaching and learning of foreign languages, as dictated by the demands placed on the teaching and learning activity and as translated into good, flexible and proficient communication both inside and outside the classroom. By intercultural competence is meant the ability of a FL learner to behave adequately and in a flexible manner when confronted with actions, attitudes and expectations of representatives of the foreign culture. Such a capability implies awareness and understanding of cultural differences between one's own and the foreign culture and the ability to handle cross-cultural difficulties which may result from these discrepancies. The 4 traditional skills of speaking, listening, writing and reading have largely ignored the basic element of the interaction between forms and the meanings associated with them, between usage and use. The need arises for more than just the teaching and learning about the foreign language and culture; due importance should also be attached to the teaching and learning of the two. This will contribute to the enhancement in learners of cultural awareness and cultural understanding. The proposed methodology of the study combines quantitative and qualitative data. Methods will include interviews, questionnaires and textbook and document analysis. A pilot study will be undertaken based in the University of Sunderland, School of Social and International Studies (England) and Ibn Zohr University, Department of English Language and Literature (Morocco). The sample will include lecturers of French/English respectively, and first year and final year students of French/English language. An evaluation of the pilot study will inform the final methodology of the study. Outcomes will be measured using statistics, attitudinal measurement and analysing qualitative data for interviews.

STATUS: Individual research

DATE OF RESEARCH: 1996-continuing

KEYWORDS: **cultural awareness; higher education; intercultural communication; modern language studies**

2528

School of Education, Hammerton Hall, Gray Road, Sunderland SR2 8JB
0191 515 2000
Durham University, School of Education, Leazes Road, Durham DH1 1TA
0191 374 2000

Elliott, J. Dr; *Supervisor*: Coffield, F. Prof.

Locus of control beliefs in children with emotional and behavioural difficulties: an exploratory study

ABSTRACT: The study examines control related beliefs of 240 children aged between nine and sixteen, and considers the implications of these beliefs for therapeutic intervention. All subjects have been referred to the educational psychology service because of perceived behavioural difficulties, and each child's behaviour is scored on nine behavioural dimensions. The data used for analysis are drawn from self-report scales, semi-structured interviews and case files. Both quantitative (using multivariate techniques) and qualitative modes of data analysis are employed and the stengths and weaknesses of each approach are noted. The research challenges many assumptions contained within the locus of control literature and highlights the difficulty of adopting findings from nomothetic research for the purpose of clinical intervention.

STATUS: Individual research

DATE OF RESEARCH: 1988-1993

KEYWORDS: child psychiatry; emotional and behavioural difficulties; locus of control; special educational needs

Surrey University

2529

Department of Educational Studies, Guildford GU2 5XH
01483 300800

Blamire-Prosser, J. Mrs; *Supervisor*: Jarvis, P. Prof.

Vocational education and training and the labour market: an economic curriculum model

ABSTRACT: The research examines Government policies for Vocational Education and Training (VET) between 1981 and 1991 against changes in the labour market supply and demand and curriculum theories, notably vocationalism, core skills and competence-based curricula. Data sources include government reports, official papers and commentaries, and a case study into the effects of planning work-related further education in London in 1990. The research identifies characteristics derived from monetarism and the ideology of market forces as: economy, efficiency and effectiveness. The main premise of the model is that a money-led curriculum serves and is subservient to, the requirements of the labour market and economic individualism. This justifies the value in Government policy placed on vocationalism, control by employers and changes to the organisation of the education and training system to reflect competitive commercialism. This gives rise to restructuring to create an internal market and the substitution of price mechanisms, consumerism and centralism for educational issues in planning the curriculum. The key issues are the tensions between public and private cost; scarcity and choice expressed by consumer preferences; price mechanisms operating on funding for institutions and courses; and the utility value of VET. The research redefines the curriculum model based on economy, efficiency, effectiveness and equity, reciprocal transfer of values between VET and the post-industrial labour market, and suggests alternative structures for both.

STATUS: Individual research

DATE OF RESEARCH: 1989-1993

KEYWORDS: curriculum development; economics education relationship; educational policy; labour market; politics education relationship; vocational education

2530

Department of Educational Studies, Guildford GU2 5XH
01483 300800

Dean, J. Dr; *Supervisor*: Hobrough, J. Dr

A study of effective advisory work in local education authorities

ABSTRACT: This study of 4 widely differing local education authority (LEA) advisory teams, initially involved the working out of criteria by which judgements of effectiveness might be made. These were then incorporated into questionnaires which were sent to 100 headteachers and 200 teachers in each of the authorities. The questionnaires were complemented by interviews with groups of advisers, advisory teachers, primary and secondary headteachers and teachers whose schools had been inspected. Headteachers and teachers were also asked for their priorities for advisory work. In addition, there was a national survey of what was currently happening to advisory teams. Important findings included the fact that the team which separated inspection and advice did less well; the best team was very well managed but also had the highest staffing ratio; and that small teams were important in supporting people doing this work. There was a strong correlation between relationships with headteachers and teachers and successful inspection, advice and inservice work, and between knowledge, skill and experience and these three areas. The criteria offer a means by which other teams might evaluate their work.

PUBLISHED MATERIAL: DEAN, J. (1991). The organisation of LEA inspectorate/advisory teams. Slough: National Foundation for Educational Research. ; DEAN, J. (1992). Effectiveness in the advisory services. Slough: National Foundation for Educational Research. ; DEAN, J. (1993). Headteachers' and teachers' priorities for advisory work and inspection. Slough: National Foundation for Educational Research. ; DEAN, J. (1993). A survey of the organisation of LEA inspection and advisory services. Slough: National Foundation for Educational Research. ; DEAN, J. (1994). What headteachers and teachers think about inspection. Slough: National Foundation for Educational Research. A full list is available from the researcher.

STATUS: Individual research

DATE OF RESEARCH: 1991-1993

KEYWORDS: advisers; inservice teacher education; inspection; local education authorities; organisational effectiveness

2531

Department of Educational Studies, Guildford GU2 5XH
01483 300800

Brown, A. Dr; Blackman, S. Dr

Evaluation of Young Engineers

ABSTRACT: The project investigated key curricular issues concerning the operation of Young Engineers clubs. The evaluation was illuminative, with the issues investigated including the reasons for schools and teachers becoming involved in the initiative; the different patterns of commitment, achievement and progression of pupils; and any change or reinforcement of attitudes towards engineering.

PUBLISHED MATERIAL: BLACKMAN, S. & BROWN, E. (1994). Evaluation of young engineers. Guildford: University of Surrey.

STATUS: Sponsored project

SOURCE OF GRANT: Standing Conference on Schools Science and Technology £12,000

DATE OF RESEARCH: 1992-1993

KEYWORDS: clubs; curriculum enrichment; engineering; engineers; industry education relationship

2532

Department of Educational Studies, Guildford GU2 5XH
01483 300800

Germon, S. Ms; *Supervisor*: Walters, N. Rev.

Needs analysis of staff development for volunteers in continuing education

ABSTRACT: The project aims to use the experience of engaging with volunteers on a collaborative project, with the Community Education Department of the Open University, and Surrey Community Action Learning Programme, in order to research social policy implications, recruitment policy and process, initial training needs analysis for organisations and individual volunteers, progressional paths, and the interface between the volunteer and the professional. The objective is to identify staff development programmes that meet the 'real' rather than perceived needs of the volunteer in adult continuing education. Methods include a case study of the collaborative project, questionnaire survey with managers of volunteers and volunteers themselves, (approximate sample size 200) followed by selective interviews.

STATUS: Sponsored project

SOURCE OF GRANT: Universities Funding Council £21,486

DATE OF RESEARCH: 1992-1993

KEYWORDS: community education; continuing education; staff development; training; voluntary service; volunteers

2533

Department of Educational Studies, Guildford GU2 5XH
01483 300800

Evans, K. Prof.; Brown, A. Dr

Technical and training mastery in the workplace

ABSTRACT: This research aims to explore the issues involved in the implementation of attempts to develop people who combine both technical and training mastery in the workplace and to make recommendations on the development of a strategy which addresses delivery as well as policy issues. It is intended that the research findings should be of interest to both practitioners and policy makers. The researchers will investigate attempts to promote the development of 'key workers' - people who combine both technical and training mastery in the workplace. (This will cover both individual company initiatives and the attempt by City and Guilds of London Institute (CGLI) to develop a national system for accreditation of skilled 'masters'). It is also intended to identify factors significant in the success or failure of such initiatives with reference to selected international comparisons.

PUBLISHED MATERIAL: BROWN, A., EVANS, K., BLACKMAN, S. & GERMON, S. (1994). Key workers: technical and training mastery in the workplace. Bournemouth: Hyde Publications.

STATUS: Sponsored project

SOURCE OF GRANT: Leverhulme Trust £37,650

DATE OF RESEARCH: 1991-1993

KEYWORDS: **industrial training; on the job training; trainers**

2534

School of Educational Studies, Guildford GU2 5XH
01483 300800

Evans, K. Prof.

Citizenship and competence for times of social change

ABSTRACT: The time taken to reach adult status has lengthened in all the industrialised countries of the world. At the same time the risks for young people trying to 'make their way' and achieve their personal goals have increased. In this context, the provision of resources and support to assist young people in making the transition has become increasingly important. Yet little is known about the way that young people are adjusting to the new circumstances, still less what kinds of personal, social and financial support they need to become full citizens, and what roles education, training, work and the community should have in providing it. This is divided into 2 parts. Part 1 considers the experiences of young adults in the status passage to adulthood, focusing on the 4 domains of work, education, family and community. In Part 2, this exploration of patterns of experience and transition behaviour leads into analysis and discussion of the structures and policies which are needed to support successful transition. Drawing on recent comparative studies with Germany and Canada carried out by the researcher, various models are considered, and criteria are proposed which may be applied in different cultural contexts. Emphasis is placed on the significance of learning throughout, developing the argument that the central objective of public policy must be to foster active maximal approaches to citizenship in a perspective of lifelong learning.

PUBLISHED MATERIAL: EVANS, K. (1995). 'Competence and citizenship: towards a complementary model for times of critical social change', British Journal of Education and Work, Vol 8, No 2, pp.14-27. ; EVANS, K. & TAYLOR, M. (1997). 'The interplay between education and work among young adults in Canada and Britain'. Paper presented at the Canadian Association for the Study of Adult Education (CASAE) Conference, Newfoundland, St Johns, June 1997. ; EVANS, K. & FURLONG, A. (1997). 'Niches, pathways, trajectories or navigations?'. In: BYNNER, J., CHISHOLM, L. & FURLONG, A. (Eds). Youth citizenship and social change. Aldershot: Ashgate. ; EVANS, K. (1998). Shaping futures: learning for competence and citizenship. Aldershot: Ashgate.

STATUS: Individual research

DATE OF RESEARCH: 1994-1998

KEYWORDS: **citizenship; life skills; lifelong learning; young adults**

2535

School of Educational Studies, Guildford GU2 5XH
01483 300800

Evans, K. Prof.

The learning society: colleges for the community in Canada and Britain

ABSTRACT: A comparative analysis of the roles of Canadian community colleges, and those of colleges in the newly independent further education sector in Britain, which are evolving towards a new future under 'incorporation'. It reviews factors and events significant in change, and their outcomes, in community colleges in Canada comparing these with colleges of further education in Britain, in order to identify the lessons that can be learned from the experiences of each. The objectives of the research

are to: 1) uncover how the institutions' missions have evolved and are evolving, with reference to social and cultural trends and norms in the two countries; 2) examine ways in which the institutions' programmes are reflecting and responding to socio-economic, demographic and educational changes, in practice; 3) identify factors promoting and impeding institutional change; 4) draw out lessons for future development in both countries. Four community colleges in contrasting economic areas in Ontario and British Columbia have been studied by means of field visits carried out over a period of one month by the proposer who already has a working knowledge of the systems and policies of education in these provinces through previous studies. Further contextual data will be gathered through official reports and documents, interviews with government officials and a range of independent experts. In each of the colleges, a 'vertical' cross-section has been taken of the organisation. Interviews have been conducted at the levels of principal, senior management, programme management (selected programmes at a variety of levels), and samples of teachers in these selected programmes. In Britain, meta-analyses of the experiences of colleges' post-incorporation have been carried out, around these questions, supplemented by interview/data provided by relevant policy bodies.

PUBLISHED MATERIAL: EVANS, K. (1997). 'Reshaping colleges for the community in Canada and Britain', Journal of Research in Post-Compulsory Education, Vol 1, No 2, pp.205-229.

STATUS: Sponsored project

SOURCE OF GRANT: Canadian Government

DATE OF RESEARCH: 1994-1997

KEYWORDS: **canada; colleges of further education; community colleges; comparative education; further education**

2536

School of Educational Studies, Guildford GU2 5XH
01483 300800

Okorocha, E. Mrs; *Supervisors*: Loewenthal, D. Dr; Griffin, C. Dr

Overseas students' uptake and non-uptake of counselling for problems: implications for adjustment strategies and cross-cultural counselling

ABSTRACT: The objective of this thesis is to investigate the academic, personal and social experiences of overseas students as they study in the United Kingdom. This includes an investigation of their sources of assistance and the extent to which they avail themselves of counselling about problems of adjustment to life and study in the UK. A further purpose is to explore the issues that create barriers for counsellors and staff (academic and non-academic) working with them. These perspectives are explored, by a combination of qualitative and quantitative approaches and are related through the extensive use of triangulation. The findings show that all three groups of respondents consider that the experiences of overseas students can and should be made more satisfactory by: a) increased awareness of overseas students' problems of adjustment and the issues which create barriers in working with them; b) provision of structured assistance to help overseas students to adjust to the British system of education and social life without losing their cultural heritage; c) assistance to counsellors and staff in acquiring or improving their cross-cultural skills to work more effectively with overseas students; d) employemnt of at least one overseas person with whom students can identify in each support services team; e) demonstration that institutions offer value for money in the educational services they provide, together with sound support services enabling students to make effective use of facilities provided. Recommendations based on these findings will be made to staff, counsellors and institutions; students' unions; and current and future overseas students.

PUBLISHED MATERIAL: OKOROCHA, E. (1994). 'Barriers to effective counselling of overseas students: implications for cross-cultural counselling'. Paper presented at the Society for Research into Higher Education Annual Conference, University of York, 19-21 December 1994.; OKOROCHA, E. (1995). 'Strategies for effective pastoral care and counselling of people from other faiths and cultures'. Paper presented at the East Anglican Ministerial Training Course, Wesley House, Cambridge, 16 January 1995. ; OKOROCHA, E. (1996). 'Cultural clues to student guidance', Times Higher Education Supplement, 7 June 1996, p.13. ; OKOROCHA, E. (1996). 'The international student experience: expectations and realities', Journal of Graduate Education, Vol 2, No 3, pp.80-84. ; OKOROCHA, E. (1997). 'High fees, no reward', Times Higher Education Supplement, Research Opportunities Section, 16 May 1997, p.vi.

STATUS: Individual research

DATE OF RESEARCH: 1993-1997

KEYWORDS: counselling services; cultural differences; higher education; overseas students; pastoral care - education; student counselling; student health and welfare; students

2537

School of Educational Studies, Guildford GU2 5XH
01483 300800

Rudd, P. Dr; *Supervisor*: Evans, K. Prof.

Structure and agency in youth transitions: young people's perspectives on vocational further education

ABSTRACT: The research examines the school to work transitions of 2 samples of 16-19 year-old college students in terms of their vocational preparation, skill development and expectations of labour market entry. The study links with a programme of research developed in the University of Surrey from the Economic and Social Research Council's 16-19 Initiative. The study aims to describe, analyse and evaluate current processes of vocational preparation primarily from the persepectives of the young people themselves. A multi-method approach involving a structured questionnaire and a series of ethnographic group interviews is used to try to discover something of the 'lived realities' of these young people. A central aim of the study is to explore structure and agency in young people's lives in the light of their perceptions of the 'new vocationalism' and to assess how much control they feel they have over the further education phase of the school to work transition. Part I considers some of the aims and contexts of the research and outlines the methodology used. A number of substantive issues arising from the literature on the school to work transition are discussed. Parts II-IV consider school to work transitions in national, local, college, group and individual settings. Use is made of Evans and Heinz's distinction between policy as espoused, policy as enacted and policy as experienced to structure the main body of the thesis. Part II outlines policy as espoused, that is national policy on vocational aspects of further education as expressed mainly in official documents. Part III looks at how these national policies are enacted, i.e. what actually happens in practice in the 2 contrasting local labour markets and colleges featured in the study. Parts II and III taken together summarise the structural influences that may be impacting upon these young people's school to work transitions. Part IV, policy as experienced, presents the day-to-day experiences of vocational education as expressed by the 'matched' samples of young people. Both quantitative data (from a structured questionnaire survey) and qualitative data (from the group interviews) are reported with special reference to possible manifestations of structure and agency in these experiences. Finally in Part V practical and theoretical implications are considered and the findings of the study are used to assist in clarifying and developing the 'individualisation thesis' and a variety of concepts relating to youth transitions.

PUBLISHED MATERIAL: RUDD, P. & EVANS, K. (1996). 'Structure and agency in youth transitions: from trajectory to biography'. Paper presented at the ESRC Conference on British Youth Research: the New Agenda, Universityo f Glasgow, January 1996. ; RUDD, P. (1997). Structure and agency: students' perspectives on vocational further education. PhD Thesis. Guildford: University of Surrey. ; RUDD, P. & EVANS, K. (1998). 'Structure and agency in youth transition', Journal of Youth and Policy, Vol 1, No 1, pp.39-62.

STATUS: Individual research

DATE OF RESEARCH: 1993-1997

KEYWORDS: adolescent attitudes; attitudes; further education; labour market; national vocational qualifications; school leavers; school to work transition; sixteen to nineteen education; skill development; training; vocational education; youth; youth employment

2538

School of Educational Studies, Guildford GU2 5XH
01483 300800

Swan, R. Mr; *Supervisor*: Jarvis, P. Prof.

Christian ministers' perceptions of maturity and their effect on parish education

ABSTRACT: Christian ministers are usually the key educators for religious education within parishes. It is their perceptions of maturity which inform the educational aims of any adult religious education (ARE) that occurs. As the ministers are largely untrained in educational theory it is vitally important to examine the relevance of the aims which their constructs of maturity produce. Such a study can investigate the maturity of the ministers' perceptions and it can ascertain whether adult learners' needs are being addressed. The research utilises psychological studies of maturity and development, and compares them to religious theories - especially James Fowler's 'Stages of faith'. It also discusses the nature of liberal education and its suitability in parish education. The overall approach is phenomenological.

STATUS: Individual research

DATE OF RESEARCH: 1992-1997

KEYWORDS: adult education; christianity; church and education; clergy; maturity - individuals; religious education

2539

School of Educational Studies, Guildford GU2 5XH
01483 300800

Wilson, B. Mr; *Supervisor*: Evans, K. Prof.

Entry to, or progress through, the coach education programme of the national governing body of athletics by adult volunteers affiliated to athletics clubs in Surrey: is this affected by reading ability

ABSTRACT: The research concerns the formal training of volunteers in sport. It compares the literacy, personal resource perceptions and motivations of 5 groups of volunteers in athletics to see how these may affect their decisions to become qualified coaches and to progress through the coach education programme. Literacy is being measured by comparing the Flesch scores of their leisure reading (newspapers, magazines and books) with the coach education manuals and reference books required. This is being triangulated against their perceptions of the difficulty of the education programme and their educational qualifications. Their personal resource perceptions are being measured in relation to time, cost and family/work commitments. Their motivation is being measured on a scale corresponding to Reiss's 15 Desire Profile. The methodology involves interviewing about 100 individuals. Use is being made of various statistical measures, including multivariate analysis. The samples are being triangulated against data in the Basic Skills Agency 1997 UK Literacy and Numeracy Survey; the Sports Council 1995 Survey for "Valuing Volunteers in UK Sport"; and the Scottish Sports Council 1996 Survey for "Factors influencing the Motivations of Sports Coaches".

STATUS: Individual research

DATE OF RESEARCH: 1995-continuing

KEYWORDS: adult literacy; sports coaching

2540

School of Educational Studies, Guildford GU2 5XH
01483 300800

Kinchin, I. Mr; *Supervisors*: Evans, K. Prof.; Hay, D. Dr

Concept mapping biological education

ABSTRACT: This research is attempting to address a perceived need to develop a mechanism to make the benefits of concept mapping more accessible to the classroom teacher. A qualitative approach to concept map analysis is presented which will encourage classroom use. The method is also seen as a way to promote cognitive conflict and facilitate meaningful learning. This work is linked to a contructivist view of teaching and learning and builds on the literature related to student misconceptions in the sciences.

PUBLISHED MATERIAL: KINCHIN, I.M. (1998). 'Constructivism in the classroom: mapping your way through'. Paper presented at the British Educational Research Association Annual Student Conference, The Queen's University of Belfast, 26-27 August, 1998.

STATUS: Individual research

DATE OF RESEARCH: 1997-continuing

KEYWORDS: biology; concept mapping; concept teaching; science education

2541

School of Educational Studies, Centre for Research in Nursing and Midwifery Education, Guildford GU2 5XH
01483 300800

Woodward, V. Miss

An ethnographic study into the meanings and manifestations of professional caring in nursing and midwifery hospital settings and implications for education

ABSTRACT: Based on an interest in the impact of policies affecting contemporary nursing and midwifery practice and education, the research examines the phenomenon of professional caring. Caring is explored at length in the nursing literature, but rarely against the context of day-to-day practice. The research addresses this deficit and explores the interpretations and values practitioners attach to the concept of caring and how these are manifest clinically. The research was undertaken with the intention to extrapolate findings to the educational context in order to investigate potential educational strategy. The study adopts an ethnographic approach, which involves two hospital-based case studies and convenience samples of six palliative care nurses and seven midwives within a postnatal/antenatal ward. Qualitative data were generated through non-participant observation and semi-structured interviews. Contextual data, such as patient to staff ratios and admission and discharge numbers were also collected, in addition to patient/client comments regarding care when the opportunity arose. Data were transcribed, followed by abductive thematic analysis and interpretation. Comparison of observational and interview data across settings identify qualitative differences in how caring is conceptualised, articulated and manifest. While the maternity setting experiences greater pressure of work, this does not totally explain the practice differences. In particular, the use of a theoretical model to guide care, strong team identity and clinical leadership within the palliative care setting appear to produce visionary rather than routinised, task-oriented practice. In addition to educational strategy, this implicates socialisation processes as the means to establish and perpetuate caring values. Recommendations for a strategy to place caring at the centre of practice highlight the need for organisational and educational collaboration. There is emphasis placed on the importance of clinical leadership and a clinically based educator to facilitate team solidarity through reflection on clinical practice against a theoretical framework which encompasses caring value.

PUBLISHED MATERIAL: WOODWARD, V. (1997). 'Professional caring: a contradiction in terms?', Journal of Advanced Nursing, Vol 26, pp.999-1004. ; WOODWARD, V. (1998). 'Caring, patient autonomy and the stigma of paternalism', Journal of Advanced Nursing, Vol 28, No 5.

STATUS: Individual research

DATE OF RESEARCH: 1995-1998

KEYWORDS: nursing; obstetrics

2542

School of Educational Studies, Guildford GU2 5XH
01483 300800
Lancaster University, Department of Educational Research, Cartmel College, Bailrigg, Lancaster LA1 4YW
01524 65201

Preece, J. Dr

Talking differently - discourse positions and margins in university continuing education

ABSTRACT: This research explores the notion of different, and mismatching, discourse practices between those that characterise the academic institution, and those which are understood by people who are most on the margins of participation in continuing education. It explores how discourse is manifested in different ways and the excluding effect the discourse of continuing education has on accessibility for some adults. The research asks: 1) Are there different discourse, perspectives and values amongst cultural groups who are under-represented in the university continuing education system and, if so, how are they sustained? 2) What influences the discourse under discussion (for example, policy, people, agencies, academic experiences)? 3) How do university criteria exclude an invalidate certain discourses from academic acceptability, and why? 4) How does the institution have to change to accommodate the different discourses and perspectives of people outside the system - and what justification is there for demanding such change? The researcher's main sources of data are from:

interviews with adults who are new learners in Lancaster University's outreach programme; interviews with role model tutors and coordinators for these new learners; and interviews with academic continuing education staff. In addition, records of departmental planning meetings and taped samples of classroom discourses will be referred to.

PUBLISHED MATERIAL: PREECE, J. (1998). 'Focault's institutional power males: an analysis of the interdependent relations between power and language in continuing education department documents', South African Journal of Higher Education, vol 12, No 2. ; PREECE, J. (1998). 'Researching difference'. In: BEN, R. et al. (Eds). Educating Rita and her sisters. Leicester: National Institute of Adult Continuing Education.

STATUS: Individual research

DATE OF RESEARCH: 1993-1998

KEYWORDS: access to education; adult education; communication; continuing education; dialogues - language; discourse; nontraditional students**

2543

School of Educational Studies, Guildford GU2 5XH
01483 300800
Lancaster University, Department of Educational Research, Cartmel College, Bailrigg, Lancaster LA1 4YW
01524 65201

Preece, J. Dr; Houghton, A-M. Ms

Community education, guidance and higher education access

ABSTRACT: This is a 2-year part-time action research project which is exploring the range of guidance and support strategies required to support lifelong learning in communities of socio-economic groups 4 and 5. The project explores tutor and student identification of guidance issues and needs across a range of community locations in Lancashire and South Cumbria. Quantitative data on pre- and post course guidance needs is collected from approximately 100 students per annum, followed up by interviews with 20 tutors. Preliminary findings so far suggest that there is a learning support gap which needs to be bridged between the informal learning support provided in community locations and the more formal guidance provision of colleges and universities. Students in communities tend to have their needs anticipated by community providers. Students are often not ready for the level of self direction required by institutions for them to access formal guidance provision.

PUBLISHED MATERIAL: OGLESBY, L. & HOUGHTON, A. (1997). 'Exploring threshold standards for guidance and learner support', Managing Guidance in Higher Education, Vol ; HOUGHTON, A. & BOKHARI, R. (1998). 'Guiding differently: the importance of supporting community learners', Adults Learning, Vol 9, No 7, pp.15-17.

STATUS: Sponsored project

SOURCE OF GRANT: Higher Education Funding Council £150,000

DATE OF RESEARCH: 1996-continuing

KEYWORDS: access to education; community education; guidance; higher education; lifelong learning**

2544

School of Educational Studies, Guildford GU2 5XH
01483 300800
Lancaster University, Department of Educational Research, Cartmel College, Bailrigg, Lancaster LA1 4YW
01524 65201

Preece, J. Dr; Houghton, A-M. Ms

Families into higher education project (FIHEP)

ABSTRACT: The families into higher education project (FIHEP) is a 3-year, part-time project which started in the latter half of 1996. The aim of the project is to introduce the idea of university education to parents from minority ethnic communities who may not normally consider such an option for their children and to research specific cultural issues around accessing Western higher education provision. The research explores issues of cultural and religious identity and the influence of community values for Muslim and Hindu families in East Lancashire, perceptions of higher education for girls. The project works with parents and their children to encourage discussion at home, as well as enable the university to learn more about family expectations or concerns and engender mutual understanding of possibilities for the future. The project aims to work with a total of 5 primary schools and a minimum of 50 parents. It operates in 4 phases: a short course for parents entitled 'Your child's future' documented by tutor diary notes; school curriculum activities for a class of primary children around the theme of 'university'; a day visit by parents and children to Lancaster University; follow-up interviews with parents to explore their views on cultural and religious values regarding western universities and to explore the effect of Lancaster University's intervention on their thinking. It is intended to expand this project, if additional funds can be found, to include a 3-year longitudinal study of study options made at secondary school. A progress report has been provided for the Esmee Fairbairn Trust and Lancaster University.

PUBLISHED MATERIAL: PREECE, J. & BOKHARI, R. (1996). 'Making the curriculum culturally relevant', Journal of Further and Higher Education, Vol 20, No 3, pp.70-80. ; PREECE, J. 'Families into higher education project: a higher education awareness raising action research project with schools and parents', Higher Education Quarterly, Vol 53. (in press).

STATUS: Sponsored project

SOURCE OF GRANT: Esmee Fairbairn Trust £22,500; Lancashire County Council £15,000

DATE OF RESEARCH: 1996-continuing

KEYWORDS: **access to education; cultural background; ethnic groups; higher education**

2545

School of Educational Studies, Guildford GU2 5XH
01483 300800
Lancaster University, Department of Educational Research, Cartmel College, Bailrigg, Lancaster LA1 4YW
01524 65201

Preece, J. Dr; Houghton, A-M. Ms

Flexible accreditation, communities and higher education

ABSTRACT: This is a 3-year part-time action research project which is exploring the impact of university intervention into the development programmes of different educational attitudes and influences amongst people whose backgrounds include disability, working class, special school or minority culture experiences. In particular the project is exploring how a flexible accreditation (foundation credit) scheme, with a negotiated curriculum, can motivate learners. The project collects statistical information on approximately 150 learners per annum. Indepth interviews are taking place with 40 learners and approximately 8 tutors or key community contacts. Preliminary findings indicate that a wide range of socio-economic and under-represented groups will take part in higher education experiences if they have ownership over curriculum content and style of provision.

PUBLISHED MATERIAL: PREECE, J. (1997). 'Academic practise for disaffected youth? Reinterpreting university and community boundaries'. In: ARMSTRONG, P., MILLER, N. & ZUKAS, M. (Eds). Crossing borders, breaking boundaries. London: SCUTREA. ; PREECE, J. (1997). 'Gender, race and religion: community education and the struggle for cultural capital'. Paper presented at the UACE Annual Conference, Dublin. ; PREECE, J. (1998). 'Has it made any difference that we are a university?'. In: PREECE, J. (Ed). Beyond the boundaries: exploring the potential of widening participation in higher education. Leicester: National Institute of Adult Continuing Education. ; PREECE, J. 'Making the curriuclum culturally relevant through a higher education core skills framework', South African Journal of Higher Education, Vol 13, No 1 (in press).

STATUS: Sponsored project

SOURCE OF GRANT: Higher Education Funding Council £50,000

DATE OF RESEARCH: 1996-continuing

KEYWORDS: **access to education; community education; higher education; nontraditional students; widening participation**

2546

School of Educational Studies, Guildford GU2 5XH
01483 300800
Monash University, Clayton 3168, Australia
University of Port Elizabeth, Centre for Organisational and Academic Development, PO Box 1600, 6000 Port Elizabeth, South Africa

University of Sofia, Faculty of Primary Education, 69-A Blvd, Shipchenski Prohod, 1574 Sofia, Bulgaria

Preece, J. Dr; Heagney, M. Ms; Blunt, R. Prof.; Popov, N. Prof.

'More means different' - a comparative study: how inclusive are university missions and practices?

ABSTRACT: This is a collaborative research project between: Surrey University; Monash University, Australia; University of Port Elizabeth, South Africa; and the University of Sofia, Bulgaria. The focus of the research is to explore how higher education (HE) missions, perceptions and practices for broadening access differ cross nationally. The goal is to find out what lessons can be learnt about future participation strategies from an international study of different institutional behaviours. For example, how has globalisation affected each country in its policymaking and how has that materialised for individual institutions in practice? The project is in 2 stages: 1) A pilot phase will require each researcher to provide a case study of their institution's contribution to broadening access. Case studies will look at how the institutional infrastructure caters for 'disadvantaged' students. 2) The case studies will conclude with an analysis of how national and global contexts are influencing each institution's decision-making regarding the widening of access. It will make recommendations for the research focus of the second phase.

STATUS: Collaborative

DATE OF RESEARCH: 1998-continuing

KEYWORDS: **access to education; comparative education; higher education; widening participation**

2547

School of Educational Studies, Guildford GU2 5XH
01483 300800
ZAROF (Zentrum fur Arbeits-und Organisationsforschung), Leipzig 04347, Germany

Behrens, M. Ms; Kaluza, J. Dr; Fobe, K. Dr; *Supervisor*: Evans, K. Prof.

Skill formation, socio-economic attitudes and transition behaviours of young adults in Eastern Germany; comparison with Western Germany and England

ABSTRACT: In 1994, the Anglo-German foundation published the book 'Becoming adults in England and Germany' (Evans and Heinz 1994), the product of the comparative study of transitions to adulthood in the 4 contrasting labour markets of Swindon, Liverpool, Bremen and Paderborn. The timing of the research was such that it was not possible to include a labour market/city from the former East Germany. Since that time, further research has been conducted by the University of Surrey team into the processes of entering and maintaining a place in skilled employment in English and German cities, comparing matched samples with their counterparts in the Netherlands. The present collaborative study fills a significant gap in this work. The work to be carried out by ZAROF will focus on the specific labour market in the new federal states in Germany. It will address important policy issues identified by ZAROF through previous work, but making substantive proposals for the development of social concepts for vocational training, material assistance of young adults and on the possibility of exerting influence upon the development of personal and social values. The work to be carried out by the University of Surrey will centre on the further comparative analysis of data from previous and current Anglo-German studies, leading to the construction of a typology of strategies for support of transitions into skilled employment which will highlight strategic choices and policy options available to policymakers in both countries. The study will track processes by which individuals progress to experienced worker status in the labour markets of new federal states. It will compare these with failed transitions into the labour market and skilled careers. It will be able to investigate attitudes towards work and education and the ways these reflected in transition behaviours in the chosen labour market. It will thus extend theoretical constructions of transitions behaviour and career outcomes by exploring the part played by socio-economic attitudes, values and beliefs in the federal states: see model from earlier work (Evans and Heinz 1995).

PUBLISHED MATERIAL: EVANS, K. & HEINZ, W.R. (1994). Becoming adults in England and Germany. London: Anglo-German Foundation for the Study of Industrial Society. ; EVANS, K. & HEINZ, W.R. (1995). 'Flexibility, learning and risk: work, training and early careers in England and Germany', Education and Training, Vol 37, No 5, pp.3-11. ; EVANS, K., BEHRENS, M. & KALUZA, J. (1998). "We had everything before us

....". Skill formation, socio-economic attitudes and transition behaviours of young adults in Eastern Germany: comparison with Western Germany and England. London and Bonn: Anglo-German Foundation.

STATUS: Sponsored project

SOURCE OF GRANT: Anglo-German Foundation £33,450

DATE OF RESEARCH: 1997-1998

KEYWORDS: attitudes; comparative education; east germany; employment; germany; labour market; skill development; skilled workers; training; vocational education; young adults; youth

Sussex University

2548

Institute of Education, Education Development Building, Falmer, Brighton BN1 9RG
01273 606755

Thomson, A. Dr; *Supervisor*: Gray, F. Dr

The role of non-traditional partners in continuing education provision

ABSTRACT: The general research aim was to examine the nature of liberal adult education provision by 'non-traditional' agencies (including voluntary bodies, charities, museums, arts centres, local societies and commercial tour operators). Specific aims were to examine the objectives, motives and target groups of non-traditional continuing education (CE) providers, the type and quality of provision; and the diversity of changing relationships between traditional (and specifically university CE departments) and non-traditional providers. The objectives were to clarify the array of provision and to assess the opportunities for, and limitations to, collaboration between mainstream and non-traditional providers. The project was pursued by way of three inter-connected case studies: 1) An historical investigation, based on documentary sources and secondary material, of the creation and development of the boundaries of adult continuing education in Britain throughout the 20th century, examining how certain providers have attained 'traditional' status while non-traditional agencies have sometimes challenged accepted boundaries. 2) An examination, via a postal questionnaire of English and Welsh university CE departments and indepth interviews with key individuals within selected departments, of the relationships of university CE centres with non-traditional partners, highlighting the value, potential and problems of collaboration. 3) A study of the evolution, from 1969 to 1992, of relationships between both traditional and non-traditional agencies in Sussex and the University of Sussex, Centre for Continuing Education. Research methods included questionnaires and face to face interviews.

PUBLISHED MATERIAL: THOMSON, A. (1992). 'Sustaining the cutting edge: non-traditional partners in adult education provision'. Adults learning, Vol 3, No 6, pp.154-156. ; THOMSON, A. (1992). 'New cultural contexts for university adult education: the potential of partnerships with non-traditional agencies'. In: MILLER, N. & WEST, L. Changing culture and adult learning. Canterbury: University of Kent at Canterbury, SCUTREA.

STATUS: Sponsored project

SOURCE OF GRANT: Universities Funding Council £30,000

DATE OF RESEARCH: 1991-1993

KEYWORDS: adult education; continuing education; liberal education; nontraditional education; partnerships

2549

Institute of Education, Education Development Building, Falmer, Brighton BN1 9RG
01273 606755

Stephens, D. Dr

Culture as a frame of reference in education and development

ABSTRACT: This research aims to provide a critique of current dominant, i.e. economic, frames of reference in education and development. A comprehensive review of secondary source literature in both Britain and North America will be followed by the development of a model of analysis which utilizes the concepts of culture and cultural identity. This model will then be applied to existing development projects in cultural contexts of which the author/researcher is familiar, e.g. Kenya, Sierra Leone, Nigeria.

The research draws upon the researcher's masters and doctoral theses: Cultural Identity and Secondary Education in Sierra Leone, 1976 and Attitudes to Education Across Two Generations in Northern Nigeria, 1982 and recent research in Ghana which examined the question of girls' access to schooling from a cultural perspective. The research will also address questions of research methodology and the development of aid policy in relation to cultural issues. A book is currently being prepared for publication.

STATUS: Sponsored project

SOURCE OF GRANT: UNICEF

DATE OF RESEARCH: 1992-continuing

KEYWORDS: africa; cultural influences; developing countries; educational policy; nigeria

2550

Institute of Education, Education Development Building, Falmer, Brighton BN1 9RG
01273 606755

Ryle, M. Mr

Cultural studies and curriculum development in adult education

ABSTRACT: This project involves: 1) discussion of the relation between 'cultural studies' and longer-established subjects/disciplines within the humanities, with especial reference to questions of teaching and learning; 2) dissemination/discussion articles on current and future course and curriculum development within the Centre for Continuing Education at Sussex University; and 3) theoretical articles and historical/genre-based research in literature and cultural studies.

PUBLISHED MATERIAL: RYLE, M. (1994). 'Long live literature? Eng lit, radical criticism and cultural studies', Radical Philosophy, Vol 67, pp.21-27. ; RYLE, M. (1995). 'Cultural studies and adult learners: literature and theory'. In PRESTON, P. Literature in the adult class: tradition and challenge. Nottingham: University of Nottingham. ; RYLE, M. (1996). 'Histories of cultural populism', Radical Philosophy, Vol 78, pp.27-33. ; RYLE, M. (1998). 'Adult learning and new social movements: teaching/learning environmental politics'. In: ALHEIT, P. & KAMNLER, E. (Eds). Lifelong learning and its impact on social and regional development. Bremen: Douat Verlag.

STATUS: Individual research

DATE OF RESEARCH: 1992-1998

KEYWORDS: adult education; cultural education; curriculum development; humanities

2551

Institute of Education, Education Development Building, Falmer, Brighton BN1 9RG
01273 606755

Colclough, C. Dr; Lewin, K. Prof.

Modelling the financing of Education for All

ABSTRACT: This research is designed to explore the challenge created by the Jomtien Conference which committed many developing countries to pursue strategies for Education For All. In this work which follows on from a round table paper presented at the conference by the authors, the implications of resourcing Education for All are pursued in depth. The research explores the parameters, which are related to different levels of participation in developing countries, in the first cycle of the school system. It develops a computer simulation model to project forward enrolments and costs under different scenarios. A series of cost saving, cost shifting and quality enhancing reforms are introduced in order to explore the impact they have on the financial viability of Education for All strategies. The last part of the research explores the implications of these for the domestic financing of Education for All and needs for external assistance.

PUBLISHED MATERIAL: COLCLOUGH, C. & LEWIN, K.M. (1993). Educating all the children: strategies for education in the south. Oxford: Oxford University Press

STATUS: Sponsored project

SOURCE OF GRANT: UNICEF

DATE OF RESEARCH: 1990-1993

KEYWORDS: **developing countries; development aid; development education; financial support**

2552

Institute of Education, Education Development Building, Falmer, Brighton BN1 9RG
01273 606755

Cooper, B. Dr; Torrance, H. Dr; *Supervisor*: Lacey, C. Prof.

Andhra Pradesh primary education project

ABSTRACT: Sussex University is providing staff as evaluation consultants for the largest basic education project funded by the Overseas Development Administration. This project focuses on human resource development through the physical upgrading of educational facilities and a quality improvement programme for over 50,000 schools. It involves reciprocal visits between Sussex and Andhra Pradesh for evaluation team members and the joint analysis of quantitative and qualitative data.

PUBLISHED MATERIAL: LACEY, C., COOPER, B. & TORRANCE, H. (1993). 'Evaluating the Andhra Pradesh primary education project: problems of design and analysis', British Educational Research Journal, Vol 19, No 5, pp.535-554. ; COOPER, B., LACEY, C. & TORRANCE, H. (1995). 'Evaluating the Andhra Pradesh primary education project: problems of design and analysis'. In: ROBERTS, B., WOODS, C. & CUSHING, B. (Eds). The sociology of development. International Library of Critical Writings in Sociology No 2. Cheltenham: Edward Elgar. ; COOPER, B., LACEY, C. & TORRANCE, H. (1996). 'The role of evaluation in large scale educational interventions: lessons from the Andhra Pradesh primary education project'. In: LYNCH, J., MODGIL, C. & MODGIL, S. (Eds). Education and development: tradition and innovation. Volume 1: concepts, approaches and assumptions. International Debates Series. London: Cassell.; COOPER, B., LACEY, C. & TORRANCE, H. (1996). 'Making sense of large scale evaluation data: the case of the Andhra Pradesh primary education project', International Journal of Educational Development, Vol 16, No 2, pp.125-140.

STATUS: Sponsored project

SOURCE OF GRANT: Overseas Development Administration; British Council

DATE OF RESEARCH: 1989-1997

KEYWORDS: **developing countries; development education; india; learning activities; primary education; teaching methods**

2553

Institute of Education, Education Development Building, Falmer, Brighton BN1 9RG
01273 606755

Cole, G. Mr; *Supervisor*: Eraut, M. Prof.

Assessing competence in the professions

ABSTRACT: This project studied existing and developing ways of assessing competence to practise in a variety of professions. An initial survey of 30 groups was followed by case studies of 11 professions: architecture; chartered surveying; civil engineering; electrical engineering; nursing; optometry; social work; teaching in Scotland; management accountancy; industrial management; and personnel management. The report presents comparative data and discusses the principal issues arising. Two kinds of assessment evidence are distinguished: 1) evidence derived by observation and questioning directly from performance on-the-job, products arising from work or reports about that work; and 2) evidence of capabilities which enable performance such as the use of underpinning knowledge, personal skills and qualities, and professional thinking. Separate chapters of the report are devoted to standards and criteria, sources of evidence and assessment, and verification procedures. Issues discussed in the final chapter include the purposes of an assessment system, the role and character of standards, choosing appropriate sources of evidence, and the implementation of assessment policy.

PUBLISHED MATERIAL: ERAUT, M. & COLE, G. (1993). 'Assessing competence in the professions'. Report No 11. Research and Development Series. Department of Employment, Strategy Unit. ; ERAUT, M & COLE, G. (1993). 'Assessment of competence in higher level occupations', Competence and Assessment Issue 21. ; ERAUT, M. (1993). 'Implications for standards development', Competence and Assessment Issue 21.

STATUS: Sponsored project

SOURCE OF GRANT: Department of Employment £47,000

DATE OF RESEARCH: 1992-1993

KEYWORDS: **assessment; competence; job performance; professional occupations**

2554

Institute of Education, Education Development Building, Falmer, Brighton BN1 9RG
01273 606755

Lewis, M. Ms

Mentor development

ABSTRACT: A group of 12 teachers were followed through a year of mentoring primary (PGCE) students. The project involved mentors working in pairs, visiting each other at work with students, engaging in discussion and regular meetings to identify issues and needs of newly appointed mentors. The aim of the project ws to explore ways new mentors learned the skills of mentoring. An experienced mentor was paired with an inexperienced mentor. Mentors kept diaries and records, the project researcher observed the process in action, interviewed mentors, analysed records and diaries. Outcomes demonstrated: a) the need for support and training; b) the viability of the method used. Additionally, a range of issues and content considered relevant to mentoring and training needs were identified. Project findings are being analysed.

STATUS: Sponsored project

SOURCE OF GRANT: Paul Hamlyn Foundation

DATE OF RESEARCH: 1991-1993

KEYWORDS: **mentors; preservice teacher education; supervisory training; teaching practice**

2555

Institute of Education, Education Development Building, Falmer, Brighton BN1 9RG
01273 606755

Chivers, T. Dr; *Supervisors*: Abbs, P. Dr; Pateman, T. Dr

Autobiography and insight: life review in group contexts

ABSTRACT: Developing academic and popular interest in autobiography forms the background to this research. The principal aims are to: 1) clarify the nature of insight and meaning in life review; 2) suggest ways of promoting this insight and meaning; 3) develop the role of the small group in this process; 4) develop the convenor's role thereby. Every fortnight, the researcher convenes a small group, drawn from members of a local University of the Third Age, who meet to read out sections of their autobiographies for discussion. There is a series of such groups, varying somewhat in size. The methodology is action research as the aims seek to move participants towards the creation of new selves by the review process, deepen group understanding and improve convenor performance. The principal method is participant observation, following the interpretive paradigm. In addition, there are evaluative discussions, questionnaires and interviews. To simplify, it could be said that insight is sought via an enhanced understanding of the social self. A programme of topics with related sensitising questions is issued to each group for optional use by participants. The forthcoming thesis will contain chapters on: the debate about the self and identity; action research modelled on self-discovery; the development of andragogy; the role of the emerging self-image; group transformation; and convenor development.

STATUS: Individual research

DATE OF RESEARCH: 1994-1998

KEYWORDS: **autobiographies; group behaviour; self evaluation - individuals**

2556

Institute of Education, Education Development Building, Falmer, Brighton BN1 9RG
01273 606755

Mandy, P. Mr; *Supervisor*: Becher, T. Prof.

The professionalisation of podiatry/chiropody

ABSTRACT: This study aims to investigate the professional development of chiropody with particular reference to its status and the effect this may have had on development. The study will be conducted against the background of another profession, dentistry. The following research questions will be addressed: 1) How has the chiropody profession developed? 2) What is the status of the profession of chiropody? 3) What effect has the status had on professional development? 4) Has the development of the profession been in the best interest of the clientele? Data collection will be from historical records, official documents, interviews and questionnaire. Results are currently being analysed.

STATUS: Individual research

DATE OF RESEARCH: 1993-continuing

KEYWORDS: chiropody; dentistry; health services; professional development; professional recognition

2557

Institute of Education, Education Development Building, Falmer, Brighton BN1 9RG
01273 606755

Robinson-Pant, A. Mrs; *Supervisors*: Street, B. Dr; Torrance, H. Dr

The link between women's literacy and development in Nepal

ABSTRACT: The aim of this research is to look at 2 contrasting literacy programmes in Nepal to analyse how women's lives have been affected by becoming literate. In many developing countries, literacy has been seen as the key to 'women's development' resulting in a proliferation of women's literacy programmes run by both Governments and Non Governmental organisations. Nepal is one such example of a country where literacy programmes have been used extensively as an entry point for involving women in development activities. The researcher's own experience of working in this field in Nepal has made her question what impact these literacy programmes have on women's lives: in particular, to question whether there is a strong link between gaining literacy skills and change (whether simply economic or social and cultural too) and whether the kind of literacy programmes currently provided meet women's perceived needs. It is hoped that this research will provide new insights into why and how women's literacy programmes work - from the participants' point of view - thereby exploring future directions for such programmes. The fieldwork will adopt an ethnographic approach to studying women participants in a traditional and a more radical literacy programme in Nepal. Methods from participatory rural appraisal (PRA), a participatory action research approach within rural development, will be combined with the more usual anthropological methods, such as participant observation, to explore their value in an educational context.

PUBLISHED MATERIAL: ROBINSON-PANT, A. (1997). The link between women's literacy and development. D.Phil Thesis. Brighton: University of Sussex.

STATUS: Individual research

DATE OF RESEARCH: 1994-1997

KEYWORDS: developing countries; development education; literacy education; nepal; women; womens education

2558

Institute of Education, Education Development Building, Falmer, Brighton BN1 9RG
01273 606755

Russell, S. Ms; *Supervisor*: Griffiths, V. Dr

Adolescent girls' diary writing and personal writing: the educational importance

ABSTRACT: The aim is to show the educational values of adolescent girls' personal writing by using samples of their writing, diaries, letters etc, published and unpublished material, past and present diaries - including research into the Mass-Observation diarists contained in the archive at the University of Sussex.

STATUS: Individual research

DATE OF RESEARCH: 1991-continuing

KEYWORDS: adolescents; children as writers; diaries; girls; letters correspondence; personal narratives; writing - composition

2559

Institute of Education, Education Development Building, Falmer, Brighton BN1 9RG
01273 606755

Adamczyk, P. Mr; Williams, D. Mr; Willson, M. Mr

Concept mapping and its wider applications

ABSTRACT: This research is looking at the acquisition and consolidation of concepts via the technique of concept mapping in primary and secondary school pupils as well as undergraduate and postgraduate students, both home and overseas. It also includes activities with teachers following inservice training courses. The work is concerned to investigate and evaluate the following applications of concept mapping: 1) monitoring and evaluation of the effectiveness of a teaching programme through comparative assessment of the learner's concept acquisition; 2) facilitation of the creation of an individual's own learning programme through self investigation of knowledge and understanding; 3) diagnostic tool for misconceptions; 4) its use as an aid for differentiation; 5) its application with individuals having special educational needs; 6) its use for peer tutoring and in a group learning environment. Future developments will look at applications of the technique in computerised learning, distance learning and management applications.

PUBLISHED MATERIAL: ADAMCZYK, P., WILLIAMS, D. & WILLSON, M. (1994). 'Evaluating science INSET through concept mapping', British Journal of Inservice Education, Vol 20, No 1, pp.121-30. ; WILLSON, M., WILLIAMS, D. & ADAMCZYK, P. (1994). 'Concept mapping: a multi-level and multi-purpose tool', School Science Review, Vol 76, No 275, pp.116-124. ; WILLSON, M. & WILLSON, S. (1994). 'Concept mapping as an assessment tool', Primary Science Review, No 34, pp.14-16. ; ADAMCYZK, P. & WILLSON, M. (1996). 'Physics education: using concept maps with trainee physics teachers', Physics Education, Vol 31, No 6, pp.374-381.

STATUS: Team research

DATE OF RESEARCH: 1992-1997

KEYWORDS: cognitive development; concept teaching; higher education; learning; primary education; primary school pupils; secondary education; secondary school pupils; students

2560

Institute of Education, Education Development Building, Falmer, Brighton BN1 9RG
01273 606755

Becher, T. Prof.

Professional strategies for coping with change

ABSTRACT: This is an ethnographic study of how practitioners in 6 professional fields (medicine, pharmacy, law, accountancy, architecture and structural engineering) adapt to a variety of changes in the demands on their competence. It is hoped that the analysis of their coping strategies will throw light on professional practice and help to influence initial preparation for the relevant careers as well as policies for continuing professional development. The research is now completed and the resulting book 'Professional Practices' is to be published in 1999.

STATUS: Sponsored project

SOURCE OF GRANT: Economic and Social Research Council

DATE OF RESEARCH: 1993-1997

KEYWORDS: change; professional continuing education; professional development

2561

Institute of Education, Education Development Building, Falmer, Brighton BN1 9RG
01273 606755

Bowker, J. Mr; *Supervisor*: Torrance, H. Dr

Media education and curriculum innovation

ABSTRACT: Within the United Kingdom, in recent years (1988-1998), formal courses in media studies have been introduced into the National Curriculum and from October 1995 media education is included in the Order for English (which will not change for 5 years) for 5-16 year olds. In the domestic domain, new media technologies are rapidly changing the informal environment for learning, thus placing greater expectations on schools. The aim of the research is to characterise the types of learning experiences children have, contrasting formal media studies/education with informal learning about media. This will be achieved by means of a 3-year tracking study of 100 children selected from age intervals: 7, 11, 14 and 16. Are there differences perceived by children and teachers (and parents) between formalised learning and informal experiences with media consumption and production? Theoretical frameworks include: cultural production; cultural aesthetics; audience studies; psychological development; children's talk analysis; concepts of modality; whole school improvement and innovation; and the politics of education. The methodology consists of small group interviews, individual teacher, parental interviews, and the use of audio-visual activities to record observation and data. The results of the survey are intended to benefit researchers into media education, archivists and teachers.

PUBLISHED MATERIAL: BOWKER, J. (Ed.) (1992). Classroom materials for teachers and pupils at key stage 3. London: British Film Institute.

STATUS: Individual research

DATE OF RESEARCH: 1995-continuing

KEYWORDS: **curriculum development; learning experience; media studies; primary education; secondary education**

2562

Institute of Education, Education Development Building, Falmer, Brighton BN1 9RG
01273 606755

Lewin, K. Prof.

Financing secondary schools in developing countries

ABSTRACT: This research is concerned to explore problems that are arising in the financing of secondary schools in a range of developing countries. The project is mounted in collaboration with the Institute of Educational Planning, Paris. During the first phase, computer modelling is being undertaken and a number of case studies are planned, mostly in sub-Saharan African countries. The second phase involves case studies in Zimbabwe, Malawi, Mauritius, Sri Lanka and China.

PUBLISHED MATERIAL: LEWIN, K.M. (1994). 'Cost recovery and the role of the state'. Paper for the 12th Commonwealth Ministers of Education Conference, Pakistan, November 1994, London, Commonwealth Secretariat.; LEWIN, K.M. (1995). 'The costs of secondary schooling in developing countries: patterns and prospects'. Proceedings of the Oxford Conference, New College, Oxford, 21-26 September 1995. ; LEWIN, K.M. (1996). 'The costs of secondary schooling in developing countries: patterns and prospects', International Journal of Educational Development, Vol 16, No 4. ; LEWIN, K.M. (1996). 'Financing secondary schools: an education and development dilemma'. Proceedings of World Congress of Comparative Education, Sydney, July 1996.

STATUS: Sponsored project

SOURCE OF GRANT: Overseas Development Administration

DATE OF RESEARCH: 1994-continuing

KEYWORDS: **africa; developing countries; educational development; educational finance; secondary education**

2563

Institute of Education, Education Development Building, Falmer, Brighton BN1 9RG
01273 606755

Lewin, K. Prof.

The financing of education in Mauritius

ABSTRACT: This research is being conducted in the context of the Education Master Plan for Mauritius. It has involved a comprehensive view of the financing of the Mauritian education system with a view to providing improved services and access at comparable levels of cost. The Education Master Plan provides for a number of policy initiatives which carry financial obligations which have to be met in a sustainable way. A series of reports have been produced indicating how this might be achieved and what strategies appear to be most promising.

PUBLISHED MATERIAL: A full list of publications is available from the researcher.

STATUS: Sponsored project

SOURCE OF GRANT: Government of Mauritius

DATE OF RESEARCH: 1994-1997

KEYWORDS: **educational development; educational finance; educational planning; mauritius**

2564

Institute of Education, Education Development Building, Falmer, Brighton BN1 9RG
01273 606755

Lewin, K. Prof.

The development of science and technology education policy in South Africa

ABSTRACT: This research is concerned with developing a framework within which policy on science and technology education may be developed for South Africa. It is being undertaken with the University of Durban-Westville and other colleagues in South Africa.

PUBLISHED MATERIAL: LEWIN, K.M. (1995). Building research capacity: initiatives in science technology education policy at the University of Durban-Westville and elsewhere in South Africa. London: Overseas Development Administration. ; LEWIN, K.M. (1995). 'Development policy and science education in South Africa: reflections on post-Fordism and praxis', Comparative Education, Vol 31, No 2, pp.201-221. ; NAIDOO, P. & LEWIN, K.M. 'Policy and planning of physical science education in South Africa: myths and realities. Durban: University of Durban Westville, Macro Education Policy Unit. ; A full list of publications is available from the researcher.

STATUS: Sponsored project

SOURCE OF GRANT: Overseas Development Administration

DATE OF RESEARCH: 1994-1998

KEYWORDS: **educational policy; science education; south africa; technology education**

2565

Institute of Education, Education Development Building, Falmer, Brighton BN1 9RG
01273 606755

Bauress, W. Mr; *Supervisors*: Abbs, P. Dr; Pateman, T. Dr

Max Beckmann and the self portrait in 20th century German painting: a continuing tradition

ABSTRACT: The research is a direct outcome of work as a teacher in trying to develop pupils' critical thinking skills in response to Art. Our ideas of self, the 'conversations that we are', are in need of clarification amongst art educators. Part of the difficulty of trying to develop 'Knowledge and Understanding in Art' (National Curriculum attainment target 2) arises because, although much of our artistic tradition has been a reflection of the sense of ourselves as beings with inner depths and of the connected notion that we are 'selves', our interpretation of the history of art does not seem to recognise and relate to this fact in a clear way. Although there is a strong continuing tradition of self-portraiture within painting and although it is closely related to the genre of autobiography, there has in fact been very little written about it, and consequently there does not exist a useful framework in which its place and value can be considered. The study should help to redress this weakness and demonstrate within the tradition of European painting the power and importance of the self-portrait as a means to self-recognitition and self-knowledge. The research is divided into 3 parts: 1) Part 1 will examine the tradition of German self-portraiture from the time of Durer until 1920. 2) The main part of the research will focus on the self-portraits of Max Beckmann. Although his self-portraits will be described chronologically this aspect of the research will focus on how his self-portraits reflect important themes or concerns relating to his other paintings. 3) The self-portraits of German artists since the return to figuration in the early 1960s.

STATUS: Individual research

DATE OF RESEARCH: 1993-1997

KEYWORDS: art education; arts; self expression

2566

Institute of Education, Education Development Building, Falmer, Brighton BN1 9RG
01273 606755

Gordon, M. Mrs; *Supervisors*: Stephens, D. Dr; Stuart, J. Dr

An investigation into occupational health nursing: the influence of an educational programme on attitudes to health and safety

ABSTRACT: The research intention is to investigate the influence of an occupational health nursing education programme on attitudes to workplace health and safety in two contexts, an industrialised society (UK) and a developing country (Zambia). Occupational health (OH) is concerned with the promotion of health and safety in the working environment, and traditionally trained nurses require additional specialist education to gain skills and knowledge, moving from a hospital, treatment oriented reactive practice to a preventive, proactive attitude. Short courses, organised from the UK, in Zambia provide the only available source of specialised programme. The research questions are: 1) Is there a need for short courses in Zambia/UK? 2) Are concepts transferable from one culture to another? 3) What is the health and safety status before and after the course? 5) Is there a change from reactive to proactive nursing? 5) What are the views of those involved? The methodology takes an illuminative/idiographic approach and includes: participative action, oriented to enter the cultural context, with role of facilitator rather than outside researcher; life history/ oral testimony interviews and group focused interviews; comparative case studies; non-participant observation. Framework within STOKES, R. (1967). Countenance model for evaluation. The two case studies - one in Zambia, one in the UK, include the following methods: 1) Antecedents: document collection/questionnaire (students); 2) Transactions: student group focused interview/individual life history interviews (students and teachers)/ non-participant observation, evaluation questionnaire. 3) Outcomes: reflective diary, committee, interviews of employer, worker, unions, statistics on health and safety in individual workplaces (co-researchers), and questionnaire at six months, fieldwork visits at 12 months, interviews and observation at workplace (researcher). Thematic data analysis: data from Case Study 1 (Zambia - sample size 11) will be used in the design of Case Study 2 (UK - sample size 20).

STATUS: Individual research

DATE OF RESEARCH: 1993-1997

KEYWORDS: attitudes; nurse education; occupational safety and health; safety; zambia

2567

Institute of Education, Education Development Building, Falmer, Brighton BN1 9RG
01273 606755

Cooper, B. Dr; Dunne, M. Dr

Assessment of mathematics at National Curriculum key stages 2 and 3: pupils' interpretations and performance

ABSTRACT: There is good reason to believe that there is an increasing mismatch between officially recommended 'good practice' in school mathematics and the current forms of assessment of mathematics in the National Curriculum. This mismatch is likely to compromise existing 'good practice' and hinder further improvement of teaching methods. It is also possible that the increased emphasis on pencil and paper tests will disadvantage some pupils systematically. The research will investigate the ways in which pupils at key stages 2 and 3 of the National Curriculum, with varying pedagogic experiences, and with varying background characteristics, interpret and respond to National Curriculum assessment demands in mathematics. A key focus will be the validity of pencil and paper tests.

PUBLISHED MATERIAL: COOPER, B. (1994). 'Authentic testing in mathematics? The boundary between everyday and mathematical knowledge in National Curriculum testing in English schools', Assessment in Education: Principles, Policy and Practice, Vol 1, No 2, pp.143-166. ; COOPER, B. (1995). 'Authentic testing in mathematics? The boundary between everyday and mathematical knowledge in National Curriculum testing in English Schools'. In: CRAFT, A. (Ed). Primary education: assessing and planning learning. London: Routledge. (reprint of above). ; COOPER, B. (1996). 'Using data from clinical interviews to explore students' understanding of mathematics test items: relating Bernstein and Bourdieu on culture to questions of fairness in testing'. Paper presented at the Symposium on Investigating Relationships between Student Learning and Assessment in Primary Schools, American Educational Research Conference, New York, April 1996. ; COOPER, B. 'Assessing National Curriculum mathematics in England: exploring children's interpretation of key stage 2 tests in clinical interviews', Educational Studies in Mathematics. (in press).

STATUS: Sponsored project

SOURCE OF GRANT: Economic and Social Research Council £118,000

DATE OF RESEARCH: 1995-1997

KEYWORDS: assessment; key stage 2; key stage 3; mathematics achievement; mathematics education; mathematics tests; national curriculum; primary education; secondary education

2568

Institute of Education, Education Development Building, Falmer, Brighton BN1 9RG
01273 606755

Chapman, P. Mr; *Supervisor*: Eraut, M. Prof.

The implementation of the National Vocational Qualifications (NVQs) in care in the health service

ABSTRACT: The researcher has been heavily involved in the Care Sector Consortium, the lead body in care for developing National and Scottish Vocational Qualifications (NVQs). Well over 20 qualifications have been available since 1992. Registration for them has been considerable, but assessment and qualification acquisition has been slow. The aim of the research is thus to investigate the implementation, in particular, of Levels 2 and 3 NVQs in Care for a new grade of staff called health care assistants. The research will follow a case study approach in which the 4-6 'cases' will consists of approved assessment centres. It will be qualitative, and based on face-to-face interviews with training managers, service managers, assessors and candidates. Interviews will be semi-structured and it is anticipated that the following themes will emerge: access problems; confusion of training agenda with industrial relations; shortage of time for candidate and assessor to get together; over-assessment; concern about documentation jargon; ladders to higher level qualifications and links to other disciplines; professional role-boundary blurring.

STATUS: Individual research

DATE OF RESEARCH: 1993-1997

KEYWORDS: caregivers; health personnel; health services; national vocational qualifications; vocational education

2569

Institute of Education, Education Development Building, Falmer, Brighton BN1 9RG
01273 606755

Eraut, M. Prof.; Gray, A. Dr

Effectiveness of labour market oriented training for the long-term unemployed

ABSTRACT: The core aim of this project is to get a better understanding of what works and what does not work in training for the long-term unemployed through the comparative analysis and evaluation of such programmes. More specifically, the objectives of the project are: 1) To develop a set of hypotheses with regard to effectiveness-enhancing conditions in labour market oriented training for the long-term unemployed. 2) To test these hypotheses in a comparative research project in order to: a) identify the organisational, curricular and instructional characteristics of labour market oriented training programmes for the long-term unemployed that influence the effectiveness of these training programmes; b) identify the contextual conditions under which these characteristics render labour market oriented training programmes more or less effective. 3) To develop an integral multilevel model of effectiveness of training for the long-term unemployed. 4) To test the generalizability of this model across European countries. 5) To investigate and interpret possible differences between countries by examining contextual background information about the socio-economic situation and the situation on the labour market. 6) To provide both policymakers and managers and trainers working in training institutes/ programmes for the long-term unemployed with information and suggestions on the way labour market training for this target group can be improved. 7) To develop on the bases of the outcomes of the proposed study a monitoring instrument that can be used in practice by managers/training staff for assessing the effectiveness and quality of their own training programme.

STATUS: Sponsored project

SOURCE OF GRANT: European Commission £80,000

DATE OF RESEARCH: 1996-continuing

KEYWORDS: **europe; labour market; training; unemployment; vocational education**

2570

Institute of Education, Education Development Building, Falmer, Brighton BN1 9RG
01273 606755

Eraut, M. Prof.

Evaluation of vocational training for science graduates in the National Health Service (EVETSIN)

ABSTRACT: Project EVETSIN is a 2-year evaluation of the Vocational Training of Scientists in the National Health Service (NHS). The main foci of the evaluation were: 1) clinical scientists in the pathology based disciplines of biochemistry, cytogenetics, molecular genetics and microbiology; 2) biomedical scientists (MLSOs); 3) medical physicists, clinical engineers and audiological scientists; and 4) medical technical officers (MTOs) in cardiology and rehabilitation engineering. Both initial vocational qualifications and higher training after qualifications were included in the brief as well as the continuing problem of matching training to the rapidly changing needs and varying expectations of different types of hospital. The findings were that most MLSOs and clinical scientists regard their initial training as relevant and of good quality, but there is also a minority of less satisfied trainees whose numbers vary with the professional group and the regions in which they are trained. The areas of greatest weakness from a trainee's viewpoint are too little feedback and aspects of the work where they would like more training. Very few trainers were trained for their training role, and a minority were judged to be not very good at it. Many trainers expressed the view that they were given neither the time nor the training to perform their role properly. Assessment procedures vary across the professions but are generally not as robust as those in higher education. External assessors are used by clinical scientists and MLSOs to conduct searching oral examinations, but some professions provide these assessors with more direct evidence of competence than others. Thus the initial training of clinical scientists and MLSOs is generally satisfactory but weak in a few aspects. It is also very vulnerable to service demands because, apart from the designated Grade A trainee scheme for clinicial scientists (not all of whom get this opportunity), there is no separate formal allocation of time for training. The training of MTOs is far less satisfactory. There is no terminal certificate of competence backed by rigorous assessment, most training manuals are very dated and academic courses do not closely match the learning needs of trainees. The report recommends that urgent attention be given to this problem and that an R&D initiative be pursued to develop realistic policy options for MTO training commensurate with their current, and anticipated future, responsibilities.

STATUS: Sponsored project

SOURCE OF GRANT: National Health Service Research and Development Unit £245,000

DATE OF RESEARCH: 1996-1998

KEYWORDS: **graduate employment; health personnel; health services; medical laboratory technicians; professional development; scientists; training**

2571

Institute of Education, Education Development Building, Falmer, Brighton BN1 9RG
01273 606755

Eraut, M. Prof.; Adamczyk, P. Mr; Morley, L. Ms; Owen, P. Ms; Sexton, T. Mr

Evaluation of the role of vocational components in 14-19 curriculum models

ABSTRACT: The context for this study is the piloting of Part One General National Vocational Qualification (GNVQ), which has itself been enabled by the reduction in volume of the mandatory parts of the National Curriculum at key stage 4. The evaluations of Part One GNVQ pilots by the Office for Standards in Education (OFSTED) and the National Council for Vocational Qualifications (NCVQ) will focus mainly on intrinsic criteria. Do Part One GNVQ courses motivate students and enable them to acquire the knowledge, skills and attitudes envisaged by the course designers? Are they accessible to students within their target population and do they attract such students (and their parents)? What factors facilitate quality learning on Part One GNVQ courses? The formative aspects of these evaluations will inform: 1) modifications to the curriculum specifications and assessment regime; and 2) quality improvement programmes for schools based on the experience of the pilot. The research is primarily concerned with evaluating the Part One GNVQ criteria and within the wider context of 14-19 curriculum models. The issues addressed are: 1) For which key stage 4 students are Part One GNVQ and GNVQ units best suited? 2) To where and with what ease will GNVQ students progress at 16+? 3) How do Part One GNVQ and GNVQ unit qualifications compare with other types of vocational courses at key stage 4? These issues concern the kind of qualification niche which Part One GNVQ should occupy and the nature and extent of its competitive advantage within that niche. However, the external evaluation also has scope for 2 formative elements. Guidance has to be offered to students considering Part One GNVQ from 1996 and 1997, and all 3 evaluations will contribute to the advice NCVQ can offer to schools. Ease of progression is affected by post-16 guidance and induction and the range and quality of provision; and this evaluation should also contribute to NCVQ advice to post-16 institutions.

STATUS: Sponsored project

SOURCE OF GRANT: National Council for Vocational Qualifications £37,600

DATE OF RESEARCH: 1995-1997

KEYWORDS: **key stage 4; national vocational qualifications; secondary education; sixteen to nineteen education; vocational education**

2572

Institute of Education, Education Development Building, Falmer, Brighton BN1 9RG
01273 606755

Hunt, C. Ms

The use of fictionalised autobiography in personal development

ABSTRACT: This topic arises out of the teaching of creative writing over 5 years at the University of Sussex, in which students have been encouraged to draw on personal memory and experience as a way into fiction writing. In the course of the teaching the researcher has become aware of the extent to which important issues of the self emerge in the fiction writing process, especially when one is fictionalising from personal experience, and the potential for self-exploration which this approach offers. The main aims of the research are: a) to examine the link between writing fictional autobiography and personal development; b) to develop a theoretical (essentially psychoanalytic) basis for the use of fictional autobiography in personal development, and c) to suggest ways in which the writing of fictional autobiography may be used in a therapeutic setting. For the first part of the research, questionnaire research was carried out with current and former students, and interviews conducted. The material indicates that a consciously fictionalised life narrative may have, in certain respects, definite advantages over a straightforward autobiographical narrative, from the point of view of self-understanding.

PUBLISHED MATERIAL: HUNT, C. (1995). 'Autobiography and the imagination', Writing in Education, No 7, pp.25-26. ; HUNT, C. (1998). 'Finding a voice-exploring the self: autobiography and the imagination in a writing apprenticeship'. Auto/Biography, Vol 6, Nos 1-2, pp.93-98. ; HUNT, C. & SAMPSON, F. (Eds). (1998). The self on the page: theory and practice of creative writing in personal development. London: Jessica Kingsley.

STATUS: Individual research

DATE OF RESEARCH: 1994-1998

KEYWORDS: **autobiographies; creative writing; fiction; self concept; self evaluation - individuals; writing - composition**

2573

Institute of Education, Education Development Building, Falmer, Brighton BN1 9RG
01273 606755

Lewin, K. Prof. ; Stuart, J. Prof.

The Mpumalanga primary school initiative

ABSTRACT: This research and development programme is concerned with the first major bilateral basic education project in South Africa. The Link Institute arrangement provides for contributions to curriculum development in the college of education system, interventions in the areas of management and staff development, the redevelopment of approaches to the professional aspects of teacher training, support for the development of teacher centres, and contributions to the accreditation and assessment system. Approximately 8 staff will be involved in different elements of the programme and will work closely and collaboratively with colleagues in Mpumalanga over a period of 3 years. Research and development activity will develop from analytic exercises profiling existing provision and identifying effective practices. It is intended to collect baseline data to provide the basis for evaluation and monitoring of interventions and establish effectiveness. An important element within the project is to contribute to research capacity building and to develop analysis skills through joint activities which generate reliable data on different aspects of the project. It is anticipated that a wide variety of publications will flow from the project as it develops.

STATUS: Sponsored project

SOURCE OF GRANT: Overseas Development Administration £350,000

DATE OF RESEARCH: 1996-continuing

KEYWORDS: **colleges of education; preservice teacher education; south africa**

2574

Institute of Education, Education Development Building, Falmer, Brighton BN1 9RG
01273 606755

Lewin, K. Prof.

Educational development in China

ABSTRACT: This research is concerned with a wide-ranging view of recent developments in the education sector in China. Areas of interest cover the school system, teacher education, assessment and higher education. Critical reviews of each of these areas are being developed collaboratively with colleagues in the universities of Beijing Normal, Hangzhou, and East China Normal University in Shanghai and with the London University Institute of Education. Current output consists of a book, two papers and five monographs as follows: China Research Monograph 6 'Access, equity and efficiency: perspectives on the Chinese school system'; China Research Monograph 7 'Quality and quantity in technical and vocational schooling in China'; China Research Monograph 8 'Policy and practice in higher education in China'; China Research Monograph 9 'Examinations and assessment, practice, procedure and problems in China'; China Research Monograph 10 'The education and training of teachers in China: methods and issues'. These are published by the Cultural and Education Section of the British Embassy, Beijing, 1996 and each provides a critical and analytic commentary of major developments and recent policy shifts.

PUBLISHED MATERIAL: LEWIN, K.M. et al. (1994). Educational innovation in China: tracing the impact of the 1985 reforms. Harlow: Longman. ; LEWIN, K.M. (1995). 'Basic education amongst national minorities: the case of the Yi in Sichuan Province, China', Prospects, Vol 25, No 4, pp.623-637. ; LEWIN, K.M. (1997). 'The sea of items returns to China: backwash, selection and the diploma disease revisited', Assessment in Education, Vol 4, No 1, pp.137-159.

SOURCE OF GRANT: British Council ; Spencer Foundation, jointly £15,000

DATE OF RESEARCH: 1991-1998

KEYWORDS: **china; educational change; educational development; educational policy**

2575

Institute of Education, Education Development Building, Falmer, Brighton BN1 9RG
01273 606755

Lewin, K. Prof.

Educational futures in emerging Asia

ABSTRACT: This research is concerned with charting recent trends in development in education throughout the Asian region. It is part of a global study coordinated by the Harvard Institute for International Development. Its purpose is to identify current policy issues at a sub-regional level which are likely to be prominent in the development agenda for the next 15 years. Rapid growth in some parts of Asia is changing educational needs at an unprecedented rate; at the same time, in parts of South Asia and elsewhere, there remain problems of high illiteracy, and basic education is yet to be universalised. Standards of achievement also vary dramatically across the region and create different policy problems in different groups of countries. Economic, demographic and environmental changes will have an impact on educational development in the region as will globalisation and the spread of new information-based technologies. These will create challenges which planning and policy systems will need to respond to.

PUBLISHED MATERIAL: LEWIN, K.M. 'Education in emerging Asia: patterns, policies and futures into the 21st century', International Journal of Educational Development. (in press).

STATUS: Sponsored project

SOURCE OF GRANT: Asian Development Bank

DATE OF RESEARCH: 1996-1998

KEYWORDS: **asia; comparative education; developing countries; educational development**

2576

Institute of Education, Education Development Building, Falmer, Brighton BN1 9RG
01273 606755

Lewin, K. Prof.; Bude, U. Dr

Improving primary school leaving examinations in science and agriculture

ABSTRACT: This research has collated and analysed primary school leaving examinations across the African continent from 14 countries. A series of research and development seminars have been organised which have provided insights into the quality, reliability and validity of instruments currently in use. A further international seminar is planned for 1997 on the basis of this work, and 2 volumes collecting together the analysis so far will be published.

PUBLISHED MATERIAL: BUDE, U. & LEWIN, K.M. (Eds). Improving test design: constructing tests, analysing results and improving assessment quality in primary schools in Africa: volume 1. Bonn: Deutsche Stiftung fur Internationale Entwicklung. ; BUDE, U. & LEWIN, K.M. (Eds). Improving test design: assessment of science and agriculture in primary schools in Africa: 12 country cases reviewed. Volume 2. Bonn: Deutsche Stiftung fur Inernationale Entwicklung.

STATUS: Sponsored project

SOURCE OF GRANT: Deutsche Stiftung fur Internationale Entwicklung

DATE OF RESEARCH: 1996-1998

KEYWORDS: **africa; agricultural education; developing countries; examinations; primary education; science education**

2577

Institute of Education, Education Development Building, Falmer, Brighton BN1 9RG
01273 606755

Lewin, K. Prof.; Caillods, F. Dr; Gottelmann-Duret, G Dr

Planning secondary science education in developing countries

ABSTRACT: This research is based on a 5-year programme at the International Institute of Educational Planning (IIEP), funded by a variety of donors. It examines planning issues that relate to science education. Output includes a wide range of publications produced by the IIEP as a result of multi-country studies, detailed indepth case studies of particular countries (especially Malaysia and Morocco), commentaries from regional workshops held to disseminate various research findings arising in the course of the research programme, and a series of state of the art reviews. The final synthesis of the project will be published by Pergamon and contains details of the many products from this programme.

PUBLISHED MATERIAL: LEWIN, K.M. (1993). 'Planning policy on science education in developing countries', International Journal of Science Education, Vol 15, No 1, pp.1-15. ; LEWIN, K.M. (1995). 'Resources for science and technology education in Africa'. Paper given at the Conference of the Association of Science and Technology Educators for Africa, University of Durban-Westville, South Africa, December 5-10, 1995. ; LEWIN, K.M. (1995). Practical work and the need for equipment'. Paper given at The Forum on Planning Science Education at Secondary Level, African Regional Conference, Magaliesburg, South Africa, August 28-September 1, 1995. Paris: International Institute for Educational Planning.; LEWIN, K.M. (Ed). (1996). Planning secondary science education: progress and prospects in the African region. Paris: International Institute of Educational Planning. ; A full list of publications is available from the researcher.

STATUS: Sponsored project

SOURCE OF GRANT: International Institute of Educational Planning, Paris £75,000

DATE OF RESEARCH: 1992-1997

KEYWORDS: **comparative education; developing countries; educational planning; malaysia; morocco; science education; secondary education**

2578

Institute of Education, Education Development Building, Falmer, Brighton BN1 9RG
01273 606755

Norris, M. Miss; *Supervisor*: Miller, C. Dr

The use of knowledge by registered nurses

ABSTRACT: The past decade has seen a number of changes which have had a direct impact on nursing practice. These can be seen as being professionally driven (i.e. statements from the United Kingdom Central Council for Nursing, Midwifery and Health Visiting (UKCC) in 1986, 1994 and 1995) or as being politically driven, i.e. following the National Health Service and Community Care Act (1990). The impact of these changes offer many exciting opportunities for registered nurses but the need to define the role of the nurse and nursing's contribution to health care is becoming more and more apparent. Changing patterns of health care delivery into the 21st century demand that nurses develop appropriate patterns of care delivery in an ever changing political and professional climate. How do registered nurses use their knowledge in practice? They are, after all, the role models and the clinical teachers for nursing students. What is it like to nurse in the UK in the current climate of the internal market economy with the rapidly changing provision of health care? How does their education prepare them for their practice? One way to explore these questions is to go and find out. The research sample was students undertaking a 4-year part-time degree programme for registered nurses. The diversity of clinical settings together with a wide range of roles and grades gives a richness of nursing experience within the group which allowed the researcher to see the world of nursing from a number of different perspectives. Initial purposeful interviews were conducted with a randomly selected group of students (8) which established 4 core categories each with emerging themes. Following this a series of non-participant observations was carried out within five National Health Service (NHS) Trusts and in a variety of clinical settings. In total 27 registered nurses were observed in clinical settings as disparate as Intensive Care to Care of the Elderly; in the NHS and in the private sector. Half the observation sample (16) were followed-up with an indepth interview. The question posed was 'tell me about your perceptions of nursing'. The observations produced some startling findings and the researcher, an experienced nurse, found many of the sessions unsettling and concerning. The indepth interviews elicited feelings such as 'scary', 'frightening', 'stressful', 'unsupported', 'a battle field'. Participants talked about low morale, inappropriate staffing levels, organisational and resource constraints, in relation to maintaining and developing their practice. Some registered nurses were able to use their knowledge effectively and were able to reflect on their practice and 'make sense' of the situations they found themselves in (the survivors); others seemed to have either given up the struggle or never engaged (the battle hardened) and the final group felt completely overcome by the constraints placed upon them (the battle weary). Avoiding cues from the patients was a recurring theme and this appeared to be associated with operating a survival strategy which reduced their nursing care from patient centred care to task orientation. They felt dissonance between their espoused values and beliefs about nursing practice and their ability to enact these values. In some cases there were those nurses who had tried to change nursing practice only to be ostracised and isolated by

their colleagues, one was referred to as a 'bad apple' at a team meeting. Some 20 years ago earlier studies (Bendall, 1975; Orton, 1981; Ogier, 1983; Melia, 1987) revealed similar problems of organisational issues, education process issues and professional issues in relation to the practice of nursing. What happens to registered nurses when they enter the world of nursing? Does post registration education enable them to develop survival strategies that enhance their nursing practice rather than reduce patient centred care?

STATUS: Individual research

DATE OF RESEARCH: 1996-continuing

KEYWORDS: **nurse education; nurses; nursing; practical nursing**

2579

Institute of Education, Education Development Building, Falmer, Brighton BN1 9RG
01273 606755

Scotland, M. Mrs; *Supervisor*: Becher, T. Prof.

The implications of power and gender on nurse education

ABSTRACT: Project 2000 is an innovative nurse education programme which introduces the concept of the preceptor. This qualitative study of Project 2000 student nurses revealed that the preceptors played an important part in facilitating the students' learning in the community workplace. Before the programme started the preceptors were resistant to and resentful of Project 2000 and displayed a significant lack of commitment. By the end of the first 3-year programme the preceptors' attitude towards Project 2000 remained unchanged. The impact of power and gender was substantial throughout the study. In particular they were influential factors in determining the preceptors' attitude and behaviour towards the student nurses. The traditional hierarchy of nursing appeared to persist; that is, the patriarchy of the medical profession and the ideology of nursing remained as they were a hundred years ago. This resulted in the preceptors' ambiguous relationship with the student nurses. At times they were supportive and caring, whilst at others they were manipulative and controlling. The student nurses developed different strategies to minimise the effects of this ambiguity and maximise the benefits of their community experience. The characteristics of nursing practice are complex and varied, and much of the learning is gained through tacit knowledge. This leads to the question whether the student nurses will remain subservient or model their preceptors' dominant and controlling behaviour once they have qualified. The study identifies such problematic issues and offers a possible solution in the form of a community network model. In the model, emphasis is placed upon a student-centred, experiential approach, enabling students to have more control of their own learning and to become more politically aware of the underlying issues within the National Health Service (NHS). This enhanced awareness and consciousness should enable nurses in the future to make informed choices in relation to their own practice as well as being part of the decision-making process in a wider context.

STATUS: Individual research

DATE OF RESEARCH: 1993-1998

KEYWORDS: **nurse education; nursery nurses**

2580

Institute of Education, Education Development Building, Falmer, Brighton BN1 9RG
01273 606755

Drake, P. Ms; *Supervisor*: Bliss, J. Prof.

Mathematics across the undergraduate curriculum

ABSTRACT: The study aims to begin to compile a portfolio of circumstances when mathematics is taught and learned successfully across the undergraduate curriculum. Of particular interest are the perspectives brought by enthusiastic non-specialist teachers of mathematics. Research questions to be explored include: (1) characteristics of successful teaching experience; teachers' choice of problems; context of problems; teachers' empathy with students; difficulties in teaching maths. (2) What draws 'non-specialists' into teaching mathematics; noteworthy experiences of learning; enthusiasm; attitude to mathematics; career changes. The study is set in one university (currently) and takes a qualitative approach. Critical incidents are elicited which signal significant good/bad learning/reflective experiences on the part of teachers.

STATUS: Individual research

DATE OF RESEARCH: 1997-continuing

KEYWORDS: **higher education; mathematics education; mathematics teachers**

2581

Institute of Education, Centre for International Education, Education Development Building, Falmer, Brighton BN1 9RG
01273 606755

Stuart, J. Dr; Lewin, K. Prof.; Stephens, D. Dr

Multisite teacher education research

ABSTRACT: This collaborative project arose out of the Higher Education Links Programme of the British Council. Based on already existing partnerships, Sussex University is coordinating teams in Ghana (University of Cape Coast); Lesotho (National University of Lesotho); Malawi (CERT Chancellor College); South Africa (University of Durban-Westville); and Trinidad and Tobago (University of the West Indies). This will investigate teacher education from the following 3 perspectives: a) the patterns of initial qualification, costs and benefits; how they developed in recent years, and what options are available to policymakers; b) the identity and role of the teacher in different cultures; c) the process - curricular and otherwise - by which new teachers acquire and learn to apply the understanding, skills and attitudes needed to become effective professional practitioners in their local schools. The research design will include core components where comparable data will be collected in each country, together with context-specific components aimed at generating particular insights into certain aspects of teacher education. Some data will be collected from documents and statistics and through interviewing of key informants and of small samples of stakeholding groups, such as Ministry officials, trainees, college tutors, qualified teachers, and community representatives. Local case studies will employ ethnographic techniques to gain deeper understanding of the processes involved. The results are planned to include: a comparative analysis of teacher education curricula; an analysis of the costs and benefits associated with different training pathways; insights into how cultural and ideological contexts affect teachers and their training; recommendations for college lecturers.

STATUS: Collaborative

DATE OF RESEARCH: 1998-continuing

KEYWORDS: **comparative education; developing countries; preservice teacher education**

2582

Institute of Education, Graduate Research Centre in Education, Falmer, Brighton BN1 9RG
01273 606755

Torrance, H. Dr; Pryor, J. Dr

Investigating and developing formative assessment in primary schools

ABSTRACT: Many claims are being made about the efficacy and effectiveness of formative approaches to assessment. Little is known about how teachers come to understand and practice formative assessment in the classroom. This project is taking an action research approach to investigating and developing formative assessment. A small group of teachers is working as a research team with the principal investigators to explore the problems and possibilities of formative assessment and document the process of developing formative assessment in the classroom. An edited collection of teacher accounts will be produced.

PUBLISHED MATERIAL: TORRANCE, H. & PRYOR, J. (1998). Investigating formative assessment. Buckingham: Open University Press.

STATUS: Sponsored project

SOURCE OF GRANT: Economic and Social Research Council £68,000

DATE OF RESEARCH: 1997-1998

KEYWORDS: **assessment; formative evaluation; primary education**

2583

Institute of Education, Education Development Building, Falmer, Brighton BN1 9RG
01273 606755
Institute of Nursing and Midwifery, Sussex University, Ashdown House, Falmer, Brighton BN1 9RT
01273 570038

Eraut, M. Prof.; Cole, G. Mr; Senker, P. Mr; Alderton, J. Ms

Learning society: development of knowledge and skills in employment

ABSTRACT: What is being learned at work? How is it being learned? And what are the factors which affect the amount and direction of learning in the workplace? These 3 key questions lie at the heart of this research project forming part of the Economic and Social Research Council's (ESRC's) Learning Society Programme. The research team started with 2 basic assumptions that learning occurs in employment throughout a person's working life, and that people learn at work without necessarily being recipients of training. Evidence was collected by double interviews, 6 and 12 months apart, with 120 managers, professionals and technicians in the engineering, business and healthcare sectors. It was found that formal education and training provided only a small part of what is learned at work - indeed most of the learning described in the interviews was non-formal, neither clearly specified nor planned. Instead it arose naturally out of the demands and challenges of work - solving problems, improving quality and/or productivity, or coping with change - and out of social interactions in the workplace with colleagues, customers or clients. In retrospect, it may be described as learning from experience. Learning from other people is sometimes facilitated by organised learning support, which may be formally organised by the Centre or informally organised at local level. The former includes apprenticeships and trainee schemes; while monitoring, shadowing or coaching is more likely to be locally arranged, and generally more effective when it is. The researchers found that working for qualifications and short training courses were important for some people at particular stages in their career. Generally, initial training was judged better when it was both broad in scope and involved periods in the workplace as well as in the classroom, laboratory, or workshop. Mid-career management and professional qualifications were judged highly effective because they were able to use and build on prior experience of work. Management courses involved small groups and projects played an important role in helping people shift their thinking from an operational to a strategic level. What is less recognised, however, is the importance of less visible, work-based learning in developing the capability to use what has been learned off-the-job in work situations. This is especially true for short courses which have very little impact unless they are appropriately timed and properly followed up at work. The analysis is that at the individual level, learning depends on confidence, motivation and capability - especially when capability is viewed as something acquired rather than something innate. This, in turn, depends on people's work having the appropriate degree of challenge, on how they are managed and on the micro culture of the immediate work environment. The key person is the local manager whose management of people and role in establishing a climate favourable to learning, in which people seek advice and help each other to learn quite naturally, is critical for those who are managed. It follows that all the mechanisms at organisational level used to promote learning, the most significant is likely to be the appointment and development of its managers. However, while approaches to management development normally emphasise motivation, productivity and appraisal, comparatively little attention is given to supporting the learning of subordinates, allocating and organising work, and creating a climate which faciitates informal learning. Such an imbalance may result from ignorance about how much learning does (and how much more learning might) take place on-the-job.

PUBLISHED MATERIAL: ERAUT, M., ALDERTON, J., COLE, G. & SENKER, P. (1998). 'The learning society: the highest stage of human capitalism?'. In: COFFIELD, F. (Ed). Learning at work. Bristol: Policy Press. ; ERAUT, M. et al. (1998). Development of knowledge and skills in employment. University of Sussex Institute of Education Research Report No 5. Brighton: University of Sussex, Institute.

STATUS: Sponsored project

SOURCE OF GRANT: Economic and Social Research Council £120,000

DATE OF RESEARCH: 1995-1997

KEYWORDS: **learning organisation; management development; on the job training; professional continuing education; skill development; work based learning**

2584

Institute of Education, Education Development Building, Falmer, Brighton BN1 9RG
01273 606755

Merton Sixth Form College, Department of Mathematics, Central Road, Morden SM4 5SE
0181 640 9564

Rutter, D. Mr; *Supervisor*: Cooper, B. Dr

Using and applying mathematics post-16

ABSTRACT: The National Curriculum aims to develop and assess students in the use and application of mathematics, and this is a significant aspect of General Certificate of Secondary Education (GCSE) syllabi. In the tertiary sector a wide range of academic, General National Vocational Qualification (GNVQ) and vocational courses assess the use and application of mathematics either as a core skill or embedded in a vocational assignment. This research aims to explore the relationship between the work going on in secondary and tertiary institutions in this area of the curriculum, and to identify practices which are correlated with a successful change of sector for the student. The research will be a case study of 4 secondary and 2 tertiary institutions, and there will be close monitoring of a sample of students from each. Two cohorts will be tracked through their final year of secondary and first year of tertiary education. A variety of methods will be used to facilitate triangulation: interview, questionnaire, and objective testing. In addition, the researcher's action research in a tertiary institution will form a significant part of the work.

STATUS: Individual research

DATE OF RESEARCH: 1994-1998

KEYWORDS: **mathematical applications; mathematics education; sixteen to nineteen education**

2585

Institute of Education, Education Development Building, Falmer, Brighton BN1 9RG
01273 606755
Seychelles Polytechnic, PO Box 77, Mahe, Republic of Seychelles

Pennycuick, D. Dr; Stuart, J. Dr; Lacey, C. Prof.; Towner, E. Ms

Monitoring inservice and research programme: Seychelles B.Ed. project

ABSTRACT: The Government of the Seychelles, in collaboration with the University of Sussex, established a split Batchelor of Education degree course (B.Ed) for Seychelles trainee teachers to equip them to teach in the Seychelles National Youth Service (NYS) and secondary schools. This course has been supported by a programme of monitoring, inservice and research, which included exchange visits by staff from Sussex and the Seychelles School of Education. A main objective of the research was to evaluate the effect of the training programme on the quality of education in NYS. It comprised four separate components, each undertaken collaboratively by Sussex staff and Seychellois educationists. While using a variety of research styles and methods, all contained an element of action research, in that most of the researchers were also involved in teaching on the B.Ed. course, and used the findings to improve the training programme both at Sussex and in Seychelles. Mathematics education was studied in October-December 1989 using multi-site case-study at NYS and primary levels. The first implementation of the Final Teaching Project (in which returning students must carry out and report on a reflective enquiry into their own teaching, before they can gain their degree) was evaluated in October-November 1990, using a responsive model. Teaching styles, teacher support, and school organisation at the NYS were studied before and after the Sussex graduates returned (February-March 1990, 1992), using classroom observation schedules and interviews. A small but significant shift in classroom practice was found. In October-December 1991 environmental education was surveyed at all educational levels and some inservice work carried out with teachers.

PUBLISHED MATERIAL: A list of publications is available from the researcher.

STATUS: Sponsored project

SOURCE OF GRANT: Overseas Development Agency £101,000

DATE OF RESEARCH: 1988-1993

KEYWORDS: **preservice teacher education; seychelles**

2586

School of Cognitive and Computing Sciences, Sussex House, Falmer, Brighton BN1 9RH
01273 606755

Yuill, N. Dr

Adults' conceptions of the origin, development and modifiability of personality traits: the influence of studying psychology

ABSTRACT: The project investigates the content of undergraduates' concepts of personality, and how the structure of these concepts may change as a result of studying psychology. Students of psychology will be questioned about their conceptions of personality traits when starting and after one year of their course, and their responses compared with non-psychology students, using a coding scheme adapted from research with children.

STATUS: Sponsored project

SOURCE OF GRANT: Nuffield Foundation £2,290

DATE OF RESEARCH: 1992-1993

KEYWORDS: **personality traits; psychology**

2587

School of Cognitive and Computing Sciences, Sussex House, Falmer, Brighton BN1 9RH
01273 606755

Yuill, N. Dr; Oakhill, J. Dr; Garnham, A. Dr

Development of working memory in children

ABSTRACT: This project aims to investigate the role of working memory in children's text comprehension. Recent research has shown that reading skills are highly reliant on working memory: the ability not just to store information, but also to perform manipulations on that information at the same time, as in mental arithmetic. Various tests of working memory have been developed for adults so as to identify its different components (linguistic, numerical and spatial) and to show how demands of storage are traded off against processing requirements. However, little is known about how working memory develops, and what influence this development has on the acquisition of reading skills. We will examine the development of the different components of working memory between the ages of 7 and 11, and the relation of working memory to reading skills. It is not known whether working memory becomes differentiated with age or whether distinct systems exist from an early age. The data will also show whether working memory is related more closely to inferential skills than to memory for verbatim information, an assumption often made in work on children's text comprehension. A working memory test that seems not to be related to comprehension skills in adults is spatial working memory (i.e. memory for location). However, this aspect of memory may be related to developing text comprehension in children, because fluent readers develop 'place-keeping' skills that allow the selective reinspection of text, and children who are good readers are better at this reinspection than are poor ones. This conjecture will be tested by correlating spatial working memory skills with reading comprehension ability.

STATUS: Sponsored project

SOURCE OF GRANT: University of Sussex £10,000

DATE OF RESEARCH: 1994-1998

KEYWORDS: **memory; reading skills**

2588

School of Cognitive and Computing Sciences, Sussex House, Falmer, Brighton BN1 9RH
01273 606755

Yuill, N. Dr

The role of word-play in improving children's text comprehension

ABSTRACT: This project aims to investigate whether making children aware of linguistic inferences by using word-play and riddles will improve text comprehension. Previous research has identified a group of 7-8 year old children who, although fluent readers, have noticeable difficulty with text comprehension. Although much is known about the specific deficits of such children, little research has been done on the most effective remedial techniques for them, and no-one has investigated the use of word-play as proposed here. Explicit instruction in inference skills, used for older children, is not suitable for young children, but it is important to address reading deficiencies as early in children's development as possible. A source of practice in making linguistic inferences not requiring explicit instruction are the word games that children engage in naturally at around this age. For example, some authors have shown how the everyday activity of rhyming games can help 5-6 year olds in learning to decode the written word because it increases their awarenes of sounds and corresponding letter patterns. In a similar way, it is possible that practice with 'plays on words' such as riddles and puns, is a way of fostering awareness of alternative meanings, and hence comprehension skills. The research involves assessing riddle comprehension of various types and developing a treatment programme to address comprehension skills in children who have either poor or good comprehension. Post-tests will be used to assess whether the training improves both specific and general comprehension skills. Computer software is also being developed aimed at improving text comprehension.

PUBLISHED MATERIAL: YUILL, N. (1996). 'A funny thing happened on the way to the classroom: jokes, riddles and metalinguistic awareness in understanding and improving poor comprehension in children'. In: CORNOLDI, C. & OAKHILL, J. (Eds). Reading Comprehension disabilities: processes and intervention. Hove: Erlbaum. ; A full list of publications is available from the researcher.

STATUS: Sponsored project

SOURCE OF GRANT: University of Sussex £4,120

DATE OF RESEARCH: 1992-continuing

KEYWORDS: reading comprehension; reading games; word recognition

2589

School of Cognitive and Computing Sciences, Sussex House, Falmer, Brighton BN1 9RH
01273 606755

Direne, A. Mr; *Supervisor*: Sharples, M. Dr

Methodology and tools for designing concept tutoring systems

ABSTRACT: The research describes how high-level knowledge about visual images should be represented and further interpreted through system-active and system-passive tutorial interactions. The ideas lend themselves to the design and implementation of intelligent tutoring systems aimed at the teaching of abnormalities in highly visual domains like medical radiology, magnetic resonance imaging and ultrasonography. Most past work in visual concept tutoring has concentrated on the theoretical principles of how humans acquire expertise in visual recognition. The few implementations there have been are domain-specific. A methodology has been developed for managing the complexity of tutoring systems design and a model of dialogue interpretation has been developed for implementing tutorial interactions. The method and the model are supported by computer-based tools that integrate the multi-layer environment, Representations for Understanding Images (RUI).

STATUS: Individual research

DATE OF RESEARCH: 1989-1993

KEYWORDS: computer science; computer uses in education; information technology; visual perception

2590

School of Cognitive and Computing Sciences, Sussex House, Falmer, Brighton BN1 9RH
01273 606755

Luckin, R. Ms; *Supervisors*: du Boulay, B. Prof.; Sharples, M. Dr

ECOLAB: explorations in the zone of proximal development

ABSTRACT: This thesis presents an interpretation of Vygotsky's Zone of Proximal Development (ZPD) which builds upon the increasing acceptance of computers into the culture of the school classroom and respects the need for educational software to be integrated with the broader teaching strategy of the school. The computer is cast in the role of a more able partner for the learner. The notion of the ZPD is extended and clarified to encompass two further concepts. The Zone of Available Assistance (ZAA) and the Zone of Proximal Adjustment (ZPA). The first of these concepts describes the various forms of assistance that are at the disposal of the more able partner. The second concept: the ZPA, defines the quantity and quality of assistance that is selected for use in particular collaborative activities of the learner and partner. The interpretation of the ZPD is used in the formulation of a software design framework. This framework is implemented in the 'Ecolab' software which offers instruction about food webs to primary school children. There

are 3 system variations within the 'Ecolab', each of which has a different instructional profile: VIS is based upon the Vygostskian instructional model used in the construction of the design framework. WIS is inspired by a contingent approach to instruction and NIS is a system which makes no instructional decisions for the child. The development of WIS and NIS has allowed the effective evaluation of VIS. An empirical evaluation study, undertaken with a class of 10-11 year-old children, confirmed the viability of the partnership role allocated to the computer system. It also supported the hypothesis that interactions which are consistent with the creation of a ZPD between system and child generate increased learning gains. The interactions which occurred when the system attempted to adjust the demands of the learning encounter to a particular user, were also more sensitive to variations in learner ability and learning style. The implementation of the 'Ecolab' shows that a concept like the ZPD can be interpreted in a manner which is informative to the software design process.

PUBLISHED MATERIAL: LUCKIN, R. (1995). Creating a computerised ZPD: The Eighth White House papers. In: HOWELL, J. & WOOD, J. (Eds). Cognitive Science Research Paper No. 390. Brighton: University of Sussex, School of Cognitive and Computing Sciences. ; LUCKIN, R. (1996). 'EuroAIED TRIVAR: Exploring the "zone of proximal development"'. Proceedings of the European Conference of Artificial in Education, Lisbon, Portugal, October 1996. ; LUCKIN, R. (1996). 'You'll never walk alone in Vygotsky's zone'. In: NOBLE, J. & PARSOWITH, S.R. The Ninth White House Papers. Graduate research in the cognitive and computing sciences at Sussex. Research Paper No 440. Brighton: University of Sussex. ; LUCKIN, R. 'VIS: assisting child-computer collaboration in the zone of proximal development' In: BLISS, J., LIGHT, P. & SALJO, R. (Eds). Learning sites. Oxford: Pergamon. (in press).

STATUS: Individual research

DATE OF RESEARCH: 1994-1997

KEYWORDS: computer assisted learning; computer uses in education; educational theories; information technology

2591

School of Cognitive and Computing Sciences, Sussex House, Falmer, Brighton BN1 9RH
01273 606755

Banerjee, R. Mr; *Supervisor*: Yuill, N. Dr

The development of self-presentation in children

ABSTRACT: Despite the ubiquity of research on self-presentation in the social psychological literature, very little research has been directed towards self-presentation in children. This research project is concerned with clarifying the development of children's use and understanding of self-presentational tactics. Furthermore, the probable link between the development of self-presentation and the understanding of mind will be explored. This exploratory work will involve experimentally examining 4-10 year old children's responses to fictitious narratives or hypothetical scenarios, as well as direct observation of their self-presentational skills in simulated situations. The research will cover a wide range of self-presentational tactics - e.g. self-promotion, ingratiation, modesty - manifested in verbal, non-verbal and expressive behaviour. Examples of current research concerns are children's ability to manipulate verbal self-descriptions for various goals, and their understanding of face-saving emotional displays. It is hoped that this research will shed new light on children's social-cognitive skills. Previous research suggests that self-presentation is likely to be an important aspect of behaviour in middle childhood. In particular, because of its significant role in both peer interactions and child-adult interactions, the research is likely to be of interest to educators wishing to gain a fuller understanding of social processes evident in the educational context.

STATUS: Individual research

DATE OF RESEARCH: 1995-1998

KEYWORDS: child development; self expression; social behaviour; social cognition

2592

School of Cognitive and Computing Sciences, Sussex House, Falmer, Brighton BN1 9RH
01273 606755

Teather, B. Dr; du Boulay, G. Prof.; Cuthbert, L. Dr; De Andres Garcia, F. Mr; *Supervisors*: du Boulay, B. Prof.; Sharples, M. Dr; Teather, D. Prof.

Computer support in neuroradiology via interactive overviews of disease spaces

ABSTRACT: This is a team project with Sussex University, De Montfort University, the National Hospital for Neurology and Neurosurgery, and Birmingham University to improve the training of radiologists by applying an analysis of working practices, learning methods, professional development, tutoring techniques, and medical image description to the design of a tutoring system for Magnetic Resonance Imaging (MRI). Fundamental research will be undertaken which involves psychological investigation into diagnosis in a complex and uncertain domain, namely diagnosis of brain lesions using MR. In support of the research aims the researchers will further develop an existing prototype decision support aid, building on the results of a recent Economic and Social Research Council (ESRC) Cognitive and Engineering grant. Methods of reducing uncertainty and imprecision will be focused upon: a) by using visualisation techniques to help a radiologist to assess the areas of uncertainty and imprecision (e.g. displaying regions of uncertainty for each case in the overview space; giving visual displays of the relative certainty of competing diagnoses); b) by improving the precision of the image discription language by using statistical methods to assess the diagnostic power of the language; and c) by operationalising some of the terms of the image description language (such as margin graded or sharp and comparison of signal intensities) so that it can be used as a check or diagnostic support.

PUBLISHED MATERIAL: DU BOULAY, G.H., TEATHER, B., TEATHER, D., JEFFERY, N.P., SHARPLES, M. & DU BOULAY, B. (1996). 'MEDIATE: Medical image description and training environment'. Paper presented at the 22nd Congress European Society of Neuro Radiology, Milan, 17-21 September 1996. ; SHARPLES, M., DU BOULAY, B., JEFFERY, N. TEATHER, D., TEATHER, B. & DU BOULAY, G.H. (1996). 'Interactive display of typicality and similarity using multiple correspondence analysis'. In: BLANDFORD, A. & THIMBELBY, H. (Eds). Proceedings of HCI 96, London, 20-23 August 1996. ; TEATHER, B., JEFFERY, D., TEATHER, D., DU BOULAY, G.H., SHARPLES, M. & DU BOULAY, B. (1996). 'MEDIATE' - for learning, teaching and diagnostic help with MRI of the brain', British Journal of Radiology, Vol 69, p.273 (Radiology UK, Supplement). ; JEFFERY, N., DU BOULAY, G.H. TEATHER, B. & TEATHER, D. (1997). 'Expert-novice differences in the interpretation of MR-Imaging of the brain'. Paper presented at the BIR Conference, Radiology UK, 21 May 1997. ; A full list of publications is available from the researchers.

STATUS: Sponsored project

SOURCE OF GRANT: Economic and Social Research Council £90,000

DATE OF RESEARCH: 1998-continuing

KEYWORDS: **computer assisted learning; health personnel; professional development; radiology**

2593

School of Cognitive and Computing Sciences, Sussex House, Falmer, Brighton BN1 9RH
01273 606755

Aldrich, F. Dr; Davies, M. Mr; *Supervisors*: Scaife, M. Dr; Rogers, Y. Dr

Explaining external cognition for designing and engineering interactivity

ABSTRACT: The aim of this project (eco-i) is to develop and apply a theory of external cognition to the design and evaluation of interactive information for innovative technologies. The area focused on is educational software/ webware and, in particular, representing complex concepts in ecology and biology. These are subjects that children and teachers have a difficult time learning and teaching using traditional materials (e.g. books, video). Central to this approach is finding ways of exploiting the dynamic and interactive properties provided by multimedia. For example, a range of 'dynalinks'; dynamic links between multiple representations, that vary in abstraction, and change their behaviour with respect to each other, have been developed. Empirical studies have shown this to be an effective approach to enabling children to understand better abstract concepts, and importantly to be able to make inferences from them. To design the interactive educational software, the researchers have developed their own 'informant design' framework. This advocates efficiency of input from different people at different stages of the design process (e.g. teachers, children, educational

technologists). Using this methodology a suite of software prototypes has been developed and evaluated.

PUBLISHED MATERIAL: SCAIFE, M. & ROGERS, Y. (1996). 'External cognition: how do graphical representations work?', International Journal of Human-Computer Studies, Vol 45, pp.185-213. ; ROGERS, Y. & ALDRICH, F. (1996). 'In search of clickable dons: learning about HCI through interacting with Norman's CD-Rom', SIGCHI Bulletin, Vol 28, No 3, pp.335-360. ; A full list of publications is available from the researchers.

STATUS: Sponsored project

SOURCE OF GRANT: Economic and Social Research Council Cognitive Engineering Initiative Grant £128,000

DATE OF RESEARCH: 1995-1997

KEYWORDS: **biology; computer assisted learning; computer system design; computer uses in education; ecology; educational software; human computer interaction; information technology; multimedia; science education**

2594

School of Cognitive and Computing Sciences, Sussex House, Falmer, Brighton BN1 9RH
01273 606755

Cooper, P. Ms; *Supervisor*: Yuill, N. Dr

Social interaction and social cognition in deaf children

ABSTRACT: This study compares social interaction and social cognition in different groups of children with hearing impairment: those in exclusively oral classrooms, those in sign-only schooling, and those integrated in mainstream classrooms. The focus is on both successes and failures in entering a group of peers, and on children's social cognitive abilities: theory of mind and social role-taking. It is expected that the results will be relevant not only to academics in social-cognitive development, but also to the families and educators of the deaf.

STATUS: Individual research

DATE OF RESEARCH: 1996-continuing

KEYWORDS: **deafness; hearing impairments; interpersonal competence; mainstreaming; social cognition; social integration; special educational needs; special schools**

2595

School of Cognitive and Computing Sciences, Sussex House, Falmer, Brighton BN1 9RH
01273 606755

Ramirez-Uresti, J. Mr; *Supervisor*: du Boulay, B. Prof.

Teaching a learning companion

ABSTRACT: The present research is in the field of Learning Companion Systems (LCS). LCS are a new kind of Intelligent Tutoring Systems (ITS). In an LCS, besides the traditional agents of an ITS - a computerized tutor and a human student - there is a third agent, a companion, which plays the role of a computerised student. The aim of this reearch is to explore the hypothesis that a learning companion with less knowledge than a human student will help the student to learn by encouraging her to teach the companion. At present an LCS is being developed in the domain of Binary Boolean Algebra. This system will be used in experiments with learning companions of various knowledge levels to test the hypothesis described before.

STATUS: Individual research

DATE OF RESEARCH: 1995-continuing

KEYWORDS: **computer assisted learning; computer system design; computer uses in education; human computer interaction; information technology**

SWA Consulting

2596

The Old Booking Hall, 2A Station Road, Clowne, Chesterfield S43 4RW
01246 570333

Watson, A. Mr

The evaluation of the impact of 'new' organisations on the delivery of the Careers Service

ABSTRACT: The report looks at the implementation and implications of change on 6 careers service companies which were awarded 5-year contracts by the Department of Education and Employment in April 1996. The research comprised case studies of 6 career service companies. 26 interviews were conducted with individuals in each area. Interviews were held with members of the company and major stakeholders, such as headteachers and training providers. Information was gathered at 2 stages in order to chart change. The first stage consisted of baseline interviews which were conducted prior to contracts being awarded. The second stage occurred 18 months later. Findings looked at changes in culture, organisational structure, operations and support systems. The findings show that new careers companies placed a high priority on shifting towards a business-like culture, the work of boards has become more effective and longer term strategies are more evident. However, many operational staff have experienced the last 5 years as a difficult period.

STATUS: Sponsored project

SOURCE OF GRANT: Department for Education and Employment £97,719

DATE OF RESEARCH: 1996-1998

KEYWORDS: **careers advisers; careers service; vocational guidance**

2597

The Old Booking Hall, 2A Station Road, Clowne, Chesterfield S43 4RW
01246 570333

Watson, A. Mr

Evaluation of key stage 4 vocational and work-related demonstration project

ABSTRACT: In the 14-19 White Paper, 'Learning to Compete: Education and Training for 14-19 Year Olds', the Department for Education and Employment (DfEE) has stated that it will support innovative approaches to delivering vocational provision for 14-16 year olds. In order to test further the feasibility and efficacy of different approaches to realising this commitment, the Education Business Links Division will be supporting up to 20 demonstration projects. These projects will be developed by Training and Enterprise Councils (TECs) and local education authorities (LEAs) in partnership with schools. Further education (FE) colleges/training providers and local agencies, build upon and/or adding to existing partnership arrangements. The projects will seek to improve young people's motivation and attainment and better prepare them for working life by promoting key skills and providing further opportunities for work-related learning, through better school, college and employer links. The research is intended to evaluate this initiative by assessing, for a typical selection of projects, the impact on young people, positive externalities and the factors which promote or inhibit the success of projects. This will require collation of data on student performance and management information and detailed case studies amongst participating TECs, LEAs, schools, employers, colleges and other agencies. Results will be utilised to inform further policy development, identify and disseminate key aspects of effective approaches.

STATUS: Sponsored project

SOURCE OF GRANT: Department for Education and Employment £88,157

DATE OF RESEARCH: 1997-continuing

KEYWORDS: **fourteen to nineteen education; secondary education; training; vocational education; work education relationship**

2598

The Old Booking Hall, 2A Station Road, Clowne, Chesterfield S43 4RW
01246 570333

Watson, A. Mr

Analysis of outcomes from the careers guidance process

ABSTRACT: The report attempts to assess the impact of Careers Education and Guidance (CEG) on Year 11 pupils in the East Midlands. The study sought to gather data on, and analyse, the relationships between, on the one hand, the quantity and quality of CEG received by Year 11 pupils (inputs) and the skills and knowledge of the pupils (the outcomes). The data in the report is based on complete data sets for 603 pupils from 20 schools across the East Midlands. CEG inputs are comprised of those provided from both the school and careers service. Information was also gathered on background factors. Learning outcomes were assessed from 2 pupil questionnaires

(baseline and follow-on) and independent assessment by face-to-face interview. The findings suggest that Careers Service provided inputs which tend to be of a generally high quality. Pupils appear to have reached a high level of learning outcome by the end of Year 11, although they had already reached a generally high level of learning outcome by the start of Year 11. On the whole progress achieved tends to be more commonly associated with background factors than CEG inputs.

STATUS: Sponsored project

SOURCE OF GRANT: Department for Education and Employment £118,301

DATE OF RESEARCH: 1996-continuing

KEYWORDS: **career counselling; careers service; secondary education; secondary school pupils; vocational guidance**

Teesside University

2599

School of Computing and Mathematics, Borough Road, Middlesbrough TS1 3BA
01642 218121

Richards, S. Mr; *Supervisors*: Barker, P. Prof.; Manji, K. Dr

End-user interfaces to electronic books

ABSTRACT: The term 'electronic book' is a metaphor which is used to describe an application which aims to deliver information in an electronic form. The rapid advances in storage technologies, for example Compact Disc Read Only Memory (CD ROM) and Magneto Optical Rewritable Optical Disk (MOROD), have allowed such books to deliver huge quantities of information in a wide variety of presentation media forms. Such developments, along with the advances in digital information presentation; video and audio compression and decompression in real-time; high resolution colour display devices; and hypermedia information networks, can facilitate the creation of extremely rich and stimulating information delivery environments. The very newness of these technologies has meant that the full capabilities and potentials as applied to electronic books, has as yet not been fully investigated. The current research aims to develop extremely rich electronic book environments which are capable of tailoring the information which they deliver to individual user requirements. Information will be presented in the form of digital video, sound, animation, hypertext and hyperimages in order to assess the pedagogic impact of such information delivery strategies. This is to be effected by investigating the effectiveness of different page structures based upon the following models: simple page model; composite page model; overlay page model; and the viewport page model. Through the adoption of such a strategy it will then be possible to assess the efficacy of various page structures, presentation media and access techniques within learning and training environments.

PUBLISHED MATERIAL: RICHARDS, S.M. & BARKER, P.G. (1991). 'Page structures for electronic books', Educational and Training Technology International, Vol 28, No 4, pp.291-301.

STATUS: Sponsored project

SOURCE OF GRANT: Science and Engineering Research Council; Dean Associates

DATE OF RESEARCH: 1990-1993

KEYWORDS: **cd roms; computer assisted learning; electronic books; human computer interaction; hypermedia; information technology; multimedia**

2600

School of Computing and Mathematics, Borough Road, Middlesbrough TS1 3BA
01642 218121

Lamont, C. Mr; *Supervisors*: Barker, P. Prof.; Manji, K. Dr

Human-computer interfaces to reactive graphical images

ABSTRACT: A reactive graphical image is one that changes its form when pointed at by a computer user using a mouse or a touch screen. Such reactive graphical images can be combined with multimedia presentations (the blending of moving video, sound, and graphics in one display environment) to form the basis of effective interactive multimedia courseware for use in the computer based training (CBT) industries. Work has initially been undertaken to provide custom editors within the PC/PILOT and PROPI authoring environments. A custom editor is designed to enhance the authoring capability of a CBT production environment by allowing parameters to be embedded within a lesson to access external material and devices. Such methods can enhance the usability and training value of a CBT lesson. Initially, custom editors have been built to incorporate videodisc still images or moving video sequences into a lesson, and for displaying graphics images on a remote terminal. However, because videodisc technology is based on analog data, it cannot effectively provide variable speed motion with continued sound synchronisation and effective graphics overlays. Thus the thrust of multimedia technology development is to provide all these features in one digital environment. Future custom editors will be built to take full advantage of this digital video interactive (DVI) technology. Once the full range of graphical custom editors has been designed and built, evaluations will be conducted to assess the quality of design and the usability of the products that are generated. Extensive end-user evaluations will also be conducted in order that a set of models and guidelines which reflect good design practice can be derived from the research.

STATUS: Sponsored project

SOURCE OF GRANT: Science and Engineering Research Council; A.P. Chesters and Associates

DATE OF RESEARCH: 1990-1993

KEYWORDS: computer assisted learning; computer uses in education; educational software; information technology; interactive video

2601

School of Computing and Mathematics, Borough Road, Middlesborough TS1 3BA
01642 218121

Pearson, E. Dr; *Supervisors*: Green, S. Dr; Oswald, A Dr

Computer presentation of a language and reading scheme for the assessment of language in children with special educational needs

ABSTRACT: This thesis is concerned with multimedia presentation of a Language Through Reading (LTR) scheme. It explores the benefits of such an application for the learning experience of children with language difficulties. In particular, the program's effectiveness as a means of collecting evidence of errors in the linguistic productions of such children is investigated. The potential for the development of a program of natural language analysis designed to provide an assessment of the child's typed inputs to the LTR application is also explored. The aim is to provide information on the lexical, syntactic and semantic aspects of the child's productions. The first part of the thesis (Chapters 2 and 3) describes theories of learning and language development and the causes of language disorder and examines the benefits of the computer in the education of children with special needs. A series of experiments and observations were carried out to establish the effectiveness of the LTR application as a means of collecting evidence of grammatical errors. The aim was to discover any significant differences in the children's attitude to the two modes of delivery, or in the quality of the assessment. These experiments and their findings are described in Chapter 4. Chapter 5 details the results of two surveys designed to determine those features of computer-based learning and assessment which teachers regard as most important. The second survey was aimed more specifically at enabling a comparison between the assessment features included in the developed prototype using the data from the classroom experiments and those features of assessment regarded by teachers as most important. The program of natural language analysis, its capabilities and limitations are described in Chapter 6. The program, written in Prolog, is designed to assess the child's typed inputs as a result of his interactions with the LTR interface. Chapter 7 provides an analysis of the possibilities for further research as a result of the findings of this body of work. Suggestions include the extension of the assessment process to provide a developmental profile of the child's current capabilities. The addition of a program of remediation tailored to the needs of the individual to increase the potential of the LTR package as a complete learning and assessment tool is also discussed. The thesis concludes (Chapter 8) that the LTR learning and assessment package is successful in providing a useful overall picture of the child's specific problem areas. It also provides a stimulating and independent learning environment for the child and a solid base from which further work in this very important field can be developed.

PUBLISHED MATERIAL: GREEN, S. (1995). 'Multimedia and electronic books in the development of language teaching materials for special needs children. Leadership for creating education: integrating the power of techology'. Proceedings of the 12th International Conference on Technology and Education, Orlando, Florida, USA, March 1995. ; GREEN, S. & SINCLAIR, F. (1995). 'From special needs to neural nets'. Proceedings of the 12th International Conference on Technology and Education, Orlando, Florida, USA, March 1995.

STATUS: Individual research

DATE OF RESEARCH: 1993-1997

KEYWORDS: assessment; computer assisted learning; computer uses in education; information technology; language skills; multimedia; reading schemes; special educational needs

2602

School of Computing and Mathematics, Borough Road, Middlesborough TS1 3BA
01642 218121

Birtle, M. Dr

Effective project work in computer science (EPCOS)

ABSTRACT: This is a collaborative project between the following universities: Teesside, Kent, Leeds, Manchester, Open, Exeter, London (Imperial College), York and Southampton. The part of the project handled by the University of Teesside is the Negotiated Learning Contracts. Negotiated cooperative learning is the notion that individuals and teams can negotiate their own learning objectives in projects. Negotiation takes place between student and student (within teams), between teams and tutors, and between individual students and tutors. This is a desirable objective because it can be argued that a negotiation process can improve learning autonomy in students. Learning autonomy is the ability to identify learning needs (or objectives), marshall the resources required to address the needs, learn effectively, and self-assess outcomes, or to have the outcomes assessed by someone else. These are key transferable skills for lifelong learning. The purpose of this work will be to devise a transferable management framework within which negotiation regarding learning can be carried out through the use of learning contracts.

STATUS: Sponsored project

SOURCE OF GRANT: Higher Education Funding Council for England (weighted equally between partners): £250,000

DATE OF RESEARCH: 1996-continuing

KEYWORDS: computer science; computer uses in education; contracts; higher education; information technology; learning objectives; projects - learning activities

Thames Valley University

2603

Centre for Information Management, St Mary's Road, Ealing, London W5 5RF
0181 579 5000
The Open University of Tanzania, PO Box 23409, Dar Es Salaam, Tanzania
01025 51 68992

Mcharazo, A. Mr; *Supervisors*: Olden, A. Dr; McGarry, K. Dr; Roberts, S. Dr

Distance learning in the African context: a case study of Tanzania's new Open University and the learning resource needs of its students

ABSTRACT: In 1993 the Open University of Tanzania was launched, one of the first such institutions in Africa, south of the Sahara. This move is a new initiative in terms of providing an alternative educational system for the many whom the small number of traditional full-time institutions cannot accommodate. Hopefully this educational innovation will prove to be useful both to individuals and the nation at large. However, the information profession sees this move as a challenge to the present practices of information provision which are characterised or influenced by the needs of traditional full-time institutions. Distance learning is a very complex operation which requires, among other things, proper planning and sufficient resources. In the developed countries, for example, the success of open universities is attributed to provision of adequate resources to meet the diverse needs of their communities. It is felt that, despite the effort, consideration, and thought that have gone into the establishment of the Open University of Tanzania, the provision of learning resources may not have been adequately addressed, and that there is a need to study the needs of the students. This research intends to study the situation and come up with specific recommendations of value to the Open University and more general recommendations of value to other developing countries which face similar conditions. The research strategy used is the case study and fieldwork is conducted in Tanzania. The specific methods for collecting research data are: 1) investigation of the wider context; 2) consultation of records and other documents; 3) survey (students, lecturers and administrators, librarians, students and staff of other open universities); and 4) experiment.

STATUS: Individual research

DATE OF RESEARCH: 1996-continuing

KEYWORDS: africa; developing countries; distance education; educational resources; information needs; open universities; tanzania

2604

Department of English Language Teaching, Walpole House, 18-20 Bond Street, Ealing, London W5 5AA
0181 579 5000

Harrison, A. Mr; *Supervisor*: Skehan, P. Prof.

Language assessment in the classroom

ABSTRACT: The overall aim is to work out a practical system for continual assessment to be carried out by learners and teachers in English as a Foreign Language (EFL) classrooms. As a starting point, an analysis of course books was devised which used Apple Macintosh's HyperCard to provide the analyser with a necessarily large mass of guidance in digestible form. The analysis was used on a variety of course books, in particular three commonly used at intermediate level. The system has now been applied in several schools to the course book in use with particular classes, and has resulted in specifications for assessment materials which have been tried out experimentally with the relevant students. The materials take the form of 'scenarios' providing realistic, locally relevant purposes for which the students need to use the language they have learnt. The intention is to provide two kinds of information: diagnostic, which requires detailed notes on language points for the student's future reference; and achievement/proficiency, which is concerned more generally with the student's success in coping with the 'real life' demands of the scenario. Ideally, both kinds of information should be available shortly after the scenario has been completed.

STATUS: Individual research

DATE OF RESEARCH: 1989-1997

KEYWORDS: assessment; computer uses in education; english - second language; information technology; second language learning; textbooks

2605

Department of English Language Teaching, Walpole House, 18-20 Bond Street, Ealing, London W5 5AA
0181 579 5000

Mehnert, U. Ms; *Supervisor*: Skehan, P. Prof.

The effects of planning on the speech production of second language learners in the context of task-based instruction

ABSTRACT: This research is aimed at investigating the effect that pre-task speech planning has on the oral performance of second language (L2) learners. It is argued that advance speech planning involves the activation and retrieval of knowledge about linguistic forms and their meaning from long-term to working memory and thus represents an effective way for L2 learners to handle communicative strains and pressures in a task-based learning environment, focus more on form and as a result improve their performance. A series of related experimental studies are designed to investigate issues such as the effect of different amounts of planning time and methods of improving the effectiveness of pre-task planning. Subjects are adult learners of German at intermediate and advanced levels performing monologic speaking tasks. The data collected is analysed with respect to various measures of speech fluency, accuracy and complexity as well as lexical density. In the first study, evidence was found that brief planning time tends to influence accuracy levels while longer periods for planning produce more complex language rather than progressively greater accuracy. Results for fluency and lexical density show a steady increase with more planning time. The next study will focus on the manner in which planning time is used and how pre-task planning activities by L2 learners can be supported so as to lead to even greater improvements in performance as compared to unguided planning.

STATUS: Individual research

DATE OF RESEARCH: 1995-1998

KEYWORDS: german; modern language studies

2606

Department of English Language Teaching, Walpole House, 18-20 Bond Street, Ealing, London W5 5AA
0181 579 5000

Barduhn, S. Ms; *Supervisors*: Skehan, P. Prof.; Borrill, J. Dr

Factors influencing success on the Certificate in English Language Teaching to Adults (CELTA)

ABSTRACT: This is an investigation of why some people learn how to teach more quickly than others on the Certificate in English Language Teaching to Adults (CELTA). The data was taken from 3 courses, with a total of 44 participants. There were 5 research instruments: 1) The Honey-Mumford questionnaire; 2) 9 focus group recorded interviews; 3) reflection books (dialogue journals); 4) an assignment on learner styles; 5) a repertory grid. Two computer programmes are used to help analyse the data: SPSS and NUD*IST (non-numerical instructured data, indexing, searching and theorising). Results and conclusions cannot be declared at the present time, although learner styles, experience and outlook will probably be significant.

PUBLISHED MATERIAL: BARDUHN, S. (1996). 'Teacher thinking'. Paper presented at the British Council Conference on Teacher Training, Milan, 1996.

STATUS: Individual research

DATE OF RESEARCH: 1994-1998

KEYWORDS: adult education teachers; certificate in english language teaching to adults; language teachers; learner characteristics; teacher education

2607

Faculty of Humanities and Languages, 1 The Grove, London W5 5DX
0181 579 5000
Durham University, School of Education, Leazes Road, Durham DH1 1TA
0191 374 2000

Roberts, C. Ms; Byram, M. Prof.

Cultural studies in advanced language learning: the year abroad in undergraduate courses

ABSTRACT: The aim of this research is to develop a more integrated approach to language and culture on four year language degree courses. At the Thames Valley University this will be done by introducing principles of ethnography in the second year of the degree course. Students will write ethnographies of the target culture while abroad, which will then be evaluated. Two language staff will learn ethnographic approaches and their learning will be documented. They will then develop a new course for the language students.

STATUS: Sponsored project

SOURCE OF GRANT: Economic and Social Research Council £44,000

DATE OF RESEARCH: 1990-1993

KEYWORDS: cultural education; degree requirements; ethnography; higher education; second language learning; study abroad

The Federal Trust

2608

Dean Bradley House, 52 Horseferry Road, London SW1P 2AF
0171 799 2818

Morrell, F. Mrs

European Citizenship 1999

ABSTRACT: European Citizenship 1999 is a collaborative institutional project whose aim is to produce a set of curriculum materials in the official languages of the European Union. The materials will be made available to all schools in the secondary education sector throughout the Union, prior to the European parliamentary elections of 1999.

STATUS: Sponsored project

SOURCE OF GRANT: European Commission; British Telecom

DATE OF RESEARCH: 1995-continuing

KEYWORDS: citizenship education; curriculum development; educational materials; european studies; european union; material development

The Host Consultancy

2609

PO Box 144, Horsham RH12 1YS
01403 211440

Berry-Iound, D. Ms

Group work process, role and impact

ABSTRACT: The research aimed to map out current organisation and objectives for group work in Careers Education and Guidance (CEG). It focused on the role of the careers services in planning, developing and delivering group work, although information is also presented about the contribution of schools. This study was commissioned in order to provide the Department for Education and Employment (DfEE) with an overview of current practice regarding group work in Years 9, 10 and 11. It focuses on the role of the Careers Service in the planning, development and delivery of group work, although information is also presented about the contribution of schools. Previous research evidence about its quality and level of usage has been limited. In order to map group work provision, 350 schools were selected and postal questionnaires were sent to careers advisers and coordinators working in these schools. Subsequently an examination of 15 case study schools occurred. This involved interviews with careers coordinators and advisers, plus a survey of 385 pupils. The main findings show that group work is considered to be effective by practitioners, when well delivered, but that more could be achieved by careers companies providing written guidelines, by enhanced objective setting and by integration of group work within CEG in schools.

STATUS: Sponsored project

SOURCE OF GRANT: Department for Education and Employment £44,645

DATE OF RESEARCH: 1996-1997

KEYWORDS: careers service; group work; secondary education; vocational guidance

The Tavistock Institute

2610

39 Tabernacle Street, London EC2A 4DE
0171 417 8310

Sommerlad, E. Dr; Moerkamp, T. Dr; Erlicher, L. Ms

Linking learning and work in youth training: a European partnership research project

ABSTRACT: Funded by the European Commission under the PETRA initiative, this collaborative research project has been undertaken by researchers in three countries: the UK, the Netherlands and Italy. Its focus is on the workplace as a setting for learning, in particular the strategies for structured learning (on and off the job) which are intended to foster the development of transferable skills as part of broad occupational competence. Case studies of company-based training were undertaken in the three countries. The UK case study examines work-based learning in the water industry, drawing on qualitative data from a series of interviews in five different companies and more detailed investigation of youth training within two company settings.

PUBLISHED MATERIAL: ERLICHER, L., MOERKAMP, T., & SOMMERLAD, E. (1993). Quality aspects of alternance in vocational education and training. London: The Tavistock Institute.

STATUS: Sponsored project

SOURCE OF GRANT: European Commission: PETRA Initiative

DATE OF RESEARCH: 1991-1993

KEYWORDS: off the job training; on the job training; partnerships; skill development; training; transfer of training; work experience programmes; youth training

2611

39 Tabernacle Street, London EC2A 4DE
0171 417 8310

Holly, L. Dr; Searle, C. Mr

Access and aspiration: oral history project to encourage young people of the inner city to gain entry to, and succeed in, higher education

ABSTRACT: This research is based at Earl Marshal Comprehensive School which serves an area in the North East of Sheffield. This is a neighbourhood suffering from many of the features of a disadvantaged inner city area. However, this is also an area vibrant with a mix of communities. The School is multi-racial and multi-lingual, with a strong commitment to anti-racism and internationalism. Students include many Asian girls who are often discouraged from aspiring to higher education by the low expectations which are ingrained in this society in relation to class, gender and race. Some young women come from families where expectations for daughters continue to be related to domesticity and marriage. The aims of this action research study are three fold: 1) To encourage young women in the fourth year of study at Earl Marshal School to reflect on the influences from the wider society and from their families, which mould their lives. 2) To consider ways out of stereotypes and limitations whilst respecting those aspects of society and culture which sustain and support these young women. 3) To help the young women to develop the confidence to build on their achievements and lay the foundation for progress towards higher education if that is in their plans.

STATUS: Sponsored project

SOURCE OF GRANT: Calouste Gulbenkian Foundation (UK branch) £4,000; Sheffield TVEI: £5,000

DATE OF RESEARCH: 1992-1993

KEYWORDS: access to education; cultural background; equal education; ethnic groups; higher education; inner city; womens education

2612

30 Tabernacle Street, London EC2A 4DE
0171 417 0407

Stern, E. Mr; Turbin, J. Ms

Continuing vocational training: the evaluation of the FORCE programme

ABSTRACT: Continuing training for those in employment is becoming increasingly important across Europe. There is also widespread consensus among both employers and trade unions that continuing vocational training (CVT) can make a contribution to competitiveness as well as to enhancing the introduction of new technologies. The FORCE programme is a major CVT initiative of the Task Force Human Resources of the European Commission. The programme supports innovative projects in all 12 member states of the European Union. These projects include pilot training schemes, exchanges between firms, and vocational qualification schemes. Among the interesting features of this European programme is the extent to which delivery within each country is a collaborative effort between national authorities and social partners. At a European level the programme involves close cooperation between the Commission and other European and nationally based agencies. The Tavistock Institute's Evaluation Development and Review Unit has been responsible for the external evaluation of the FORCE programme beginning in 1993. This external evaluation is the first of 2 evaluation rounds required as part of the FORCE decision of the European Council of Ministers. It is an interim evaluation focusing on implementation issues and early evidence of programme effectiveness. The terms of reference for the evaluation include a review of both the organisational structures through which FORCE is implemented, and the results insofar as these are available. The evaluation has involved a consortium of research institutes in all European countries. The Institute worked closely with 2 groups in particular: Groupe Quaternaire (Paris) and the Danish Technological Institute (Aarhus), which had management responsibility for this evaluation alongside the Tavistock Institute.

STATUS: Sponsored project

DATE OF RESEARCH: 1993-continuing

KEYWORDS: **europe; on the job training; programme evaluation; staff development; vocational education**

2613

30 Tabernacle Street, London EC2A 4DE
0171 417 0407

Hills, D. Ms; Abraham, F. Ms; Child, C. Ms; Holly, L. Dr; King, A. Ms; Radcliffe, P. Ms

The role of training materials in the preparation of social services staff for major change (Children Act, Community Care)

ABSTRACT: A team from the Tavistock Institute's Evaluation Development and Review Unit has been involved in two evaluative studies of training resources and materials designed to assist Social Services Departments (SSDs) in the training of staff. These studies, funded by the Department of Health, have evaluated training materials designed to help training sections prepare staff for implementation of the Children Act 1989 and the National Health Service and Community Care Act 1990. The pace of change within SSDs has placed considerable pressure on the capacity of training sections and, on the whole, availability of training materials and other resources has been welcome. However, the utilisation and take-up of new resources also depends on the strategies being adopted by SSDs. These studies have highlighted that close collaboration between training sections and those involved in implementing change at a policy and service development level is essential if departments are to be able to make effective use of these resources.

STATUS: Sponsored project

DATE OF RESEARCH: 1993-continuing

KEYWORDS: **educational materials; on the job training; social services; staff development**

2614

39 Tabernacle Street, London EC2A 4DE
0171 417 8310

Cullen, J. Dr; Frade, C. Mr; Stern, E. Mr

Concerted action on learning and pedagogic research

ABSTRACT: The concerted action on learning and pedagogic research project forms part of The Tavistock Institute's Evaluation Development Review Unit's (EDRU) portfolio of European projects focusing on education and training. It provides expertise and know-how in learning and pedagogic research for participants involved in developing and piloting learning technology applications. EDRU organises and manages a forum of experts involved in concerted action which, through meetings also attended by representatives of the DELTA projects, informs the projects on the pedagogic aspects of their innovations, and develops instruments to enable the projects to assess the pedagogic effectiveness of learning technology applications. Key outputs of the concerted action will include a major workshop on pedagogic research, and a book on pedagogic issues in relation to flexible and distance learning.

STATUS: Sponsored project

DATE OF RESEARCH: 1993-continuing

KEYWORDS: **computer uses in education; europe; information technology; teaching methods; training; vocational education**

The Who Cares? Trust

2615

Kemp House, 156-160 City Road, London EC1V 2NP
0171 251 3117

Fletcher, B. Ms

Equal chances: improving the education of children in care

ABSTRACT: There are 52,000 children and young people in care in England and Wales. Approximately 65% live in foster placements and the rest are looked after in a variety of residential placements. As a discrete group these children dramatically underachieve at school. As a consequence of being separated from their families and placed in public care they are denied the same educational opportunities as other children. Education is, if anything, more vital to this group of young people than others in the general population. From the age of 16 they are required to 'leave care' and live independently often with no consistent adult support. Without the confidence, qualifications and lifeskills which effective schooling can provide, they go on to be over-represented among the young unemployed, homeless and prison population. Looked after children are not different from other children in terms of their potential to benefit from education. They differ from other children having undergone distressing and damaging experiences which result in them being separated from their families. The education of these children is accorded a low priority and at school they are treated differently. The stigma of public care means that they are more frequently bullied by other pupils and suffer the intrusive interest of both pupils and teachers. Carers and teachers have low expectations of them, and it takes a considerable time for them to be found a school place. These children often experience frequent moves from one home to another and this means frequent moves of school, long periods out of school and falling behind with school work. It also means lack of continuity of carers, teachers and friendships. The most significant disadvantage faced by these young people is the lack of a consistent interested adult who can monitor their progress, offer praise and encouragement and act as an advocate when necessary. For children in care, the local authority, as 'corporate parent', is supposed to look after their educational interests. Despite legal requirements and recommended action contained in government guidance, local authorities appear to be doing little to remedy the educational disadvantage experienced by children in care. In collaboration with The Who Cares? Trust, a national charity committed to addressing the needs of young people in public care, the Gulbenkian Foundation now wishes to initiate a major project that will provide a national lead in assisting local authorities to meet the educational needs of young people in the care system. One metropolitan authority (Bradford) and one unitary authority (Brighton and Hove) agreed to participate. The initiative involves several projects: 1) Mapping and meeting need - one of the main reasons why local authorities continue to neglect the needs of looked after pupils is because they do not monitor their progress or ensure that the right people have relevant information to take action quickly, e.g. schools may not know that some of their pupils are in care, while carers and social workers may not know that a child in their care is at risk of exclusion. 2) A buddying scheme - most of the school-based problems looked after pupils identify are concerned with being treated differently. This project focuses upon inclusion by developing a scheme which welcomes and supports all pupils new to a school, whatever their family circumstances. It provides new pupils with peer support a befriender who is trained. Children in care will be provided with a befriender and will be given support in deciding what information they wish to share with other pupils and staff. Buddying is a way of allowing the whole school community to think through and work through what it is like to be different. 3) Exclusion and school attendance (Bradford); Post-16 opportunities (Brighton and Hove) - these projects are aimed at tackling some of the issues which concern local authorities but which may not be addressed by Projects 1 and 2 which concentrate on the needs of all looked after pupils. The outcomes of the initiative should be: a better educational experience for looked after children; more robust and effective policies; raised awareness of the needs of looked after pupils; higher expectations of these pupils; improved school attendance; fewer unnecessary moves of school (and placement); integration of looked after children's educational needs into Children's Services Planning and other local authority policies; structural changes which facilitate communication between education and social services; better professional practice.

PUBLISHED MATERIAL: Reports will include a quarterly newsletter, seminars, consultancy and promotional material.

STATUS: Sponsored project

SOURCE OF GRANT: Calouste Gulbenkian Foundation and various other organisations

DATE OF RESEARCH: 1997-1998

KEYWORDS: **attendance; child welfare; educational improvement; educationally disadvantaged; exclusion; foster children; friendship; local education authorities; looked after children; peer support system; pupil needs; residential care; sixteen to nineteen education; social services; underachievement**

Trinity College

2616

Carmarthen, Dyfed SA31 3EP
01267 237971

Francis, L. Prof.; Lewis, C. Mr

Secondary school pupils' attitudes towards science and religion (Northern Ireland)

ABSTRACT: This project is re-analysing data collected from 2,000 secondary school pupils attending Catholic and Protestant schools in Northern Ireland in order to explore the relationship between attitudes to science, religion, creationism and scientism. Attitudes are measured by Likert type scales.

PUBLISHED MATERIAL: A full list of publications is available from the researchers.

STATUS: Sponsored project

SOURCE OF GRANT: Trinity College

DATE OF RESEARCH: 1992-continuing

KEYWORDS: **northern ireland; pupil attitudes; religious education; scientific attitudes; secondary school pupils**

2617

Carmarthen, Dyfed SA31 3EP
01267 237971

Francis, L. Prof.

Religiosity and wellbeing

ABSTRACT: This study explores the relationship between religion and psychological wellbeing among a sample of 5,000 11-16 year old secondary school pupils. Wellbeing is measured as a Likert type inventory. Religiosity is measured by self-reported practice of personal prayer and church attendance, and by a twenty-four item Likert type attitude scale.

PUBLISHED MATERIAL: FRANCIS, L.J. & BURTON, L. (1994). 'The influence of personal prayer on purpose in life among Catholic adolescents', Journal of Beliefs and Values, Vol 15, No 2, pp.6-9. ; FRANCIS, L.J. & EVANS, T.E. (1996). 'The relationship between personal prayer and purpose in life among churchgoing and non-churchgoing 12-15 year olds in the UK', Religious Education, Vol 91, pp.9-21.

STATUS: Sponsored project

SOURCE OF GRANT: Trinity College

DATE OF RESEARCH: 1994-continuing

KEYWORDS: **religion; secondary school pupils; well being**

2618

Carmarthen, Dyfed SA31 3EP
01267 237971

Francis, L. Prof.

The measurement of personality among primary school pupils

ABSTRACT: The measurement of personality among primary school pupils has been sharpened by the development of the Revised Junior Eysenck Personality Questionnaire (JEPQ-R). As yet, however, no comparability study has reported on the empirical performance of these new scales alongside the earlier established measures. This project aims to explore the reliability and validity of the JEPQ-R among a sample of 800 primary school pupils.

STATUS: Sponsored project

SOURCE OF GRANT: Trinity College

DATE OF RESEARCH: 1992-continuing

KEYWORDS: **personality; personality measures; primary school pupils**

2619

Carmarthen, Dyfed SA31 3EP
01267 237971

Francis, L. Prof.; Evans, T. Rev.

The development of a Welsh language edition of the Junior Eysenck Personality Questionnaire

ABSTRACT: Since its development in 1975 the Junior Eysenck Personality Questionnaire (JEPQ) has been translated into a number of other languages. The aim of the present project is to develop and test empirically a Welsh language edition of the JEPQ for use among a secondary school population.

STATUS: Sponsored project

SOURCE OF GRANT: Trinity College

DATE OF RESEARCH: 1992-continuing

KEYWORDS: **personality measures; welsh**

2620

Carmarthen, Dyfed SA31 3EP
01267 237971

Francis, L. Prof.

Influence of religion and personality on secondary school pupils' attitudes towards substance use

ABSTRACT: This project aims to compare the attitudes of churchgoing 13-15 year olds to smoking, alcohol, and drugs, according to the denomination attended. In order to build up a significant sample of churchgoing adolescents, the attitude inventory has been completed by 20,000 secondary school pupils.

PUBLISHED MATERIAL: FRANCIS, L.J. (1993). 'Religiosity and attitude towards drug use among 13-15 year olds in England', Addiction, Vol 88, No 5, pp.665-672. ; FRANCIS, L.J. (1996). 'The relationship between Eysenck's personality factors and attitude towards substance use among 13 to 15 year olds', Personality and Individual Differences, Vol 21, pp.633-640. ; FRANCIS, L.J. (1997). 'The impact of personality and religion on attitude towards substance use among 13-15 year olds', Drug and Alcohol Dependence, Vol 44, pp.95-103.

STATUS: Sponsored project

SOURCE OF GRANT: Trinity College

DATE OF RESEARCH: 1992-continuing

KEYWORDS: **drinking; drug abuse; personality; pupil attitudes; religious attitudes; secondary school pupils; smoking; substance abuse**

2621

Carmarthen, Dyfed SA31 3EP
01267 237971

Francis, L. Prof.; Jones, S. Rev.

School today: bullying, personality and values

ABSTRACT: This study explores the relationship between personality, bullying, religious victimisation, self-concept and values among secondary school pupils in Wales. Personality is measured by the short form Revised Junior Eysenck Personality Questionnaire. Self-concept is measured by the Coopersmith Inventory. Two new Likert type scales have been developed to assess the tendency to be either bully or victim. Values are measured by a Likert instrument. So far over 20,000 13-15 year-olds have participated in the project.

PUBLISHED MATERIAL: FRANCIS, L.J. & JONES, S.M. (1994). 'The relationship between Eysenck's personality factors and fear of bullying among 13-15 year-olds in England and Wales', Evaluation and Research in Education, Vol 8, No 3, pp.111-118.

STATUS: Sponsored project

SOURCE OF GRANT: Trinity College

DATE OF RESEARCH: 1993-continuing

KEYWORDS: **antisocial behaviour; behaviour problems; bullying; personality; secondary school pupils; values**

2622

Carmarthen, Dyfed SA31 3EP
01267 237971

Francis, L. Prof.; Gibson, H. Prof.

The influence of Catholic schools on pupil attitudes towards Christianity

ABSTRACT: This project aims to examine the attitudes of Catholic pupils towards Christianity and to compare the attitudes of those pupils educated in Catholic schools with those educated in non-denominational schools in Scotland. This project re-analyses data collected from over 6,000 pupils in Dundee.

STATUS: Sponsored project

SOURCE OF GRANT: Trinity College

DATE OF RESEARCH: 1992-continuing

KEYWORDS: **christianity; pupil attitudes; religion; religious attitudes; roman catholic church**

2623

Carmarthen, Dyfed SA31 3EP
01267 237971

Francis, L. Prof.; Wilcox, C. Mrs

Religion, sex and sex role identity

ABSTRACT: While sex is consistently found to be a significant predictor of the dimensions of religiosity among children and adolescents as well as among adults, theoretical explanations for this finding remain confused. The aim of the present project is to explore the extent to which sex differences in religiosity can be accounted for in terms of the personality dimensions of masculinity and femininity proposed by Bem's Sex Role Inventory, rather than by the simple categorisation of gender, among a sample of 1,300 13-16 year olds. These data are being compared with data provided by undergraduate students.

PUBLISHED MATERIAL: FRANCIS, L.J. & WILCOX, C. (1996). 'Religion and gender orientation', Personality and Individual Differences, Vol 20, No 1, pp.119-121. ; WILCOX, C. & FRANCIS, L.J. (1997). 'Beyond gender stereotyping: examining the validity of the Bem Sex Role Inventory among 16-19 year old females in England', Personality and Individual Differences, Vol 23, pp.9-13. ; FRANCIS, L.J. & WILCOX, C. (1998). 'Religiosity and femininity: do women really hold a more positive attitude toward Christianity?', Journal for the Scientific Study of Religion, Vol 37, pp.462-469.

STATUS: Sponsored project

SOURCE OF GRANT: Trinity College

DATE OF RESEARCH: 1992-continuing

KEYWORDS: **pupil attitudes; religion; religious attitudes; secondary school pupils; sex differences**

2624

Carmarthen, Dyfed SA31 3EP
01267 237971

Francis, L. Prof.

Religion, personality and self-concept

ABSTRACT: This project aims to compare the empirical properties of three measures of self-concept and to explore the relationship between self-concept and religiosity among fifth year secondary school pupils on a database of 700 respondents. These findings are being compared with those from a sample of 500 primary school pupils using one measure of self concept.

PUBLISHED MATERIAL: FRANCIS, L.J., CARTER, M. & JONES, S.H. (1995). 'The properties of the Lipsitt Self Concept Scale in relationship to sex, social desirability, reactionism and extroversion', Personality and Individual Differences, Vol 19, pp.619-624. ; FRANCIS, L.J. & WILCOX, C. (1995). 'Self-esteem: Coopersmith and Rosenberg compared', Psychological Reports, Vol 76, p.1050. ; JONES, S.H. & FRANCIS, L.J. (1996). 'Religiosity and self-esteem during childhood and adolescence'. In: FRANCIS, L.J. Research in religious education. Leominster: Gracewing.; FRANCIS, L.J. & GIBBS, D. (1996). 'Prayer and self-esteem among 8-11 year olds in the UK', Journal of Social Psychology, Vol 136,

pp.791-793.

STATUS: Sponsored project

SOURCE OF GRANT: Trinity College

DATE OF RESEARCH: 1992-continuing

KEYWORDS: **personality; pupil attitudes; religion; religious attitudes; secondary school pupils; self concept**

2625

Carmarthen, Dyfed SA31 3EP
01267 237971

Francis, L. Prof.; Kay, W. RevDr

Teenage religion and values today

ABSTRACT: A modified form of the CENTYMCA Attitude Inventory developed by Leslie Francis in Teenagers and the Church (Collins, 1984) and Youth in Transit (Gower, 1982) is being completed by 30,000 13-15 year old pupils through state maintained and independent secondary schools in England and Wales. The inventory employs Likert type scales to measure religiosity, social, personal and moral values. The aim of the project is to explore the role of religion in shaping teenage values.

PUBLISHED MATERIAL: FRANCIS, L.J. & MULLEN, K. (1993). 'Religiosity and attitudes towards drug use among 13-15 year olds in England', Addiction, Vol 88, pp.665-672. ; FRANCIS, L.J. & JONES, S.H. (1994). 'The relationship between Eysenck's personality factors and fear of bullying among 13-15 year olds in England and Wales', Evaluation and Research in Education, Vol 8, No 3, pp.111-118. ; JONES, S.H. & FRANCIS, L.J. (1995). 'The relationship between Eysenck's personality factors and attitude toward truancy among 13-15 year olds in England and Wales', Personality and Individual Differences, Vol 19, No 2, pp.225-233.; FRANCIS, L.J. & KAY, W.K. (1995). Teenage religion and values. Leominster: Gracewing.

STATUS: Sponsored project

SOURCE OF GRANT: Trinity College

DATE OF RESEARCH: 1990-continuing

KEYWORDS: **attitude measures; pupil attitudes; religion; religious attitudes; secondary school pupils; values**

2626

Carmarthen, Dyfed SA31 3EP
01267 237971

Francis, L. Prof.

The measurement of personality among secondary school pupils

ABSTRACT: The measurement of personality among secondary school pupils has been sharpened by the development of the Revised Junior Eysenck Personality Questionnaire (JEPQ-R). As yet, however, no comparability study has reported on the empirical performance of these new scales alongside the earlier established measures. This project aims to explore the reliability and validity of the JEPQ-R among a sample of 2,000 secondary school pupils.

PUBLISHED MATERIAL: FRANCIS, L.J. (1996). 'The development of an abbreviated form of the Revised Eysenck Personality Questionnaire (JEPQR-A) among 13-15 year olds', Personality and Individual Differences, Vol 21, pp.835-844.

STATUS: Sponsored project

SOURCE OF GRANT: Trinity College

DATE OF RESEARCH: 1994-continuing

KEYWORDS: **personality; personality measures; secondary school pupils**

2627

Carmarthen, Dyfed SA31 3EP
01267 237971

Francis, L. Prof.; Evans, T. Rev.

The development of a Welsh language edition of the Francis Scale of Attitude Toward Christianity

ABSTRACT: Since its development and publication in 1978 the Francis Scale of Attitude Toward Christianity has been employed in over a hundred independent studies. Translations have been developed in Chinese, German, Norwegian, Dutch and French. The aim of the present project is to provide a Welsh edition of the instrument and to trial this among primary school pupils, secondary school pupils, undergraduate students and adults.

PUBLISHED MATERIAL: EVANS, T.E. & FRANCIS, L.J. (1996). 'Measuring attitude toward Christianity through the medium of Welsh'. In: FRANCIS, L.J. Research in religious education. Leominster: Gracewing.

STATUS: Sponsored project

DATE OF RESEARCH: 1995-continuing

KEYWORDS: attitude measures; attitudes; christianity; religious attitudes; welsh

2628

Carmarthen, Dyfed SA31 3EP
01267 237971

Kay, W. RevDr

Piaget revisited: neo-Piagetian aspects of religious development

ABSTRACT: Piaget's influence on curriculum development in the 1960s and 1970s led to the acceptance of various assumptions in relation to religious development. Piaget's own thought, and the emergence of neo-Piagetian perspectives, make it worthwhile re-examining these assumptions.

PUBLISHED MATERIAL: KAY, W.K., FRANCIS, L.J. & GIBSON, H.M. (1996). 'Attitude to Christianity and the transition to formal operational thinking', British Journal of Religious Education, Vol 19, pp.45-55.

STATUS: Sponsored project

DATE OF RESEARCH: 1995-continuing

KEYWORDS: attitudes; child development; religious attitudes

2629

Carmarthen, Dyfed SA31 3EP
01267 237971
Cardiff University, Department of Welsh, PO Box 920, Cardiff CF1 3XP
01222 874000

Jones, D. Miss; *Supervisor*: Jones, G. Prof.

Assessment of linguistic attainments of pupils in Welsh immersion programmes

ABSTRACT: This thesis assesses the linguistic attainments of children in Welsh immersion programmes, i.e. children from English-speaking backgrounds who attend Welsh-medium schools. Forty-five 8 year-old subjects are asked to retell a story previously shown on video and to partake in a group discussion task. In addition, they are required to write the story in their own words. Ten control pupils, with Welsh as a first language, are used for comparison. The data are analysed within the Interlanguage and Communicative Competence frameworks. Detailed quantitative and qualitative analyses of some aspects of their linguistic competence are carried out. Preliminary results indicate that the grammatical and sociolinguistic aspects of their communicative competence are weaker than their discourse and strategic competences. These results are consistent with the findings of other studies on second language acquisition in immersion programmes. Furthermore, processes of simplification, overgeneralisations and transfer are seen to be at work.

STATUS: Individual research

DATE OF RESEARCH: 1993-continuing

KEYWORDS: achievement; bilingualism; immersion programmes; linguistic competence; second language learning; welsh; welsh medium education

2630

Carmarthen, Dyfed SA31 3EP
01267 237971
Welsh Education Centre, Old College, Aberystwyth SY23 3BX
01970 622121

Grififths, B. Dr; Williams, M. Miss; Phillips, S. Ms; Rousson, L. Mrs; Lowri, M. Mrs; *Supervisors*: Greller, W. Dr; Davies, M. Mr

Welsh-French/French-Welsh dictionary; Welsh-German/German-Welsh dictionary

ABSTRACT: The French-Welsh dictionary contains over 50,000 entries, over 140,000 references and over 176,000 translations, and the German-Welsh dictionary similarly. Both dictionaries have full pronunciation for French and German words (Welsh, itself a phonetic language, not necessarily this), examples illustraing meaning and correct usage as well as colloquial words, idioms and 'sayings. They include coverage of general words from the field of politics, science, technology, literature, economics, business and media communication. There is full coverage of verb conjugations, as well as of acronyms and proper nouns in French and German and Welsh. There are also tables indicating numbers, times and dates in both dictionaries. Both will be an invaluable asset for the study of the 3 languages - by Welsh-medium students studying French and German as well as for French and German students wishing to study Welsh. The new corpus of Welsh entries are up-to-date and based on the most recent lexical research in Welsh.

PUBLISHED MATERIAL: GRELLER, W. (1999). German-Welsh concise dictionary. Aberystwyth: Canolfan Astudiaethau Addysg.

STATUS: Sponsored project

SOURCE OF GRANT: Curriculum and Assessment Authority for Wales (ACCAC) £455,000

DATE OF RESEARCH: 1996-continuing

KEYWORDS: dictionaries; french; german; modern language studies; welsh

Ulster University

2631

Coleraine Campus, School of Education, Cromore Road, Coleraine, County Londonderry BT52 1SA
01265 44141

McGarvey, B. Prof.; Harper, D. Mr; Day, J. Mrs

Differentiated learning in science project

ABSTRACT: The development and trials of schemes of work for the Northern Ireland Science Curriculum at key stages 1, 2 and 3. These schemes incorporate the principles of continuity, progression and differentiation.

STATUS: Sponsored project

SOURCE OF GRANT: Northern Ireland Curriculum Council £213,378

DATE OF RESEARCH: 1992-1993

KEYWORDS: curriculum development; differentiated curriculum; individualised methods; northern ireland; science education

2632

Coleraine Campus, School of Education, Cromore Road, Coleraine, County Londonderry BT52 1SA
01265 44141

Harvey, P. Mr; *Supervisor*: Austin, R. Dr

Junior Certificate History in the Republic of Ireland: purpose, problems and potential

ABSTRACT: The aim of this study is to explore the ways in which a national curriculum change in the teaching of history in the Republic of Ireland is being implemented in the classroom. A sample of teachers are completing questionnaires, and resource materials are being designed, used and evaluated to measure student reaction to the proposed changes. The research is set in the wider context of the history of curriculum change in the Republic of Ireland and the perceived value and interest of history to young people.

STATUS: Individual research

DATE OF RESEARCH: 1991-1997

KEYWORDS: curriculum development; history; ireland

2633

Coleraine Campus, School of Education, Cromore Road, Coleraine, County Londonderry BT52 1SA
01265 44141

Austin, R. Dr

The role of electronic mail in modern language learning

ABSTRACT: The project tested the language skills and level of cultural awareness of two groups of linked school pupils before and after an electronic mail (e-mail) project. The pupils in Northern Ireland were aged 14, while those in Germany were 14-16. Significant gains in language competence, cultural awareness and information technology skills were registered.

PUBLISHED MATERIAL: AUSTIN, R. & MENDLICK, F. (1993). 'The role of electronic mail in cultural awareness and language development', ReCALL, Issue No 9, pp.19-23. ; AUSTIN, R. & MENDLICK, F. 'Electronic mail in modern language development', Neusprachliche Mitteilungen aus Wissenschaft und Praxis. (in press).

STATUS: Sponsored project

SOURCE OF GRANT: British Telecom

DATE OF RESEARCH: 1993-1993

KEYWORDS: **cultural awareness; electronic mail; intercultural communication; language proficiency; modern language studies; telecommunications**

2634

Coleraine Campus, School of Education, Cromore Road, Coleraine, County Londonderry BT52 1SA
01265 44141

Austin, R. Dr

The impact of computer conferencing on teaching and learning in history

ABSTRACT: This project is studying the ways that computer conferencing in history can improve learning. In particular, it is examining how this form of interaction affects student motivation, appreciation of other perspectives, awareness of new research and the development of writing skills. The project is ongoing and has been broadened to include the role of the Internet in learning history.

PUBLISHED MATERIAL: AUSTIN, R. (1994). 'Computer conferencing in history: a pilot study at 16-18', Teaching History, No 75, April, pp.33-35. ; AUSTIN, R. (1995). Computer Conferencing in history: studying the past with the technology of the future. London: The Historical Association.; AUSTIN, R. (1995). 'Quality learning through computer conferencing'. In: TINSLEY, J.D. & VAN WEERT, T.J. (Eds). Liberating the learner. Proceedings of the World Conference on Computers in Education VI. London: Chapman and Hall. (published on behalf of the International Federation for Information Processing)

STATUS: Sponsored project

SOURCE OF GRANT: British Telecom

DATE OF RESEARCH: 1993-1997

KEYWORDS: **computer uses in education; history; information technology; internet; learning strategies; teaching methods; teleconferencing**

2635

Coleraine Campus, School of Education, Cromore Road, Coleraine, County Londonderry BT52 1SA
01265 441411

Montgomery, A. Ms; *Supervisor*: Smith, A. Dr

Values in education in Northern Ireland

ABSTRACT: The aims of the project are to: 1) research existing approaches to values in education through the Consortium of Institutions for Development and Research in Education in Europe (CIDREE); 2) generate specific 'profiles' of different initiatives; 3) evaluate the current provision for values in education in the context of the Northern Ireland Curriculum. The initial research for this project has now been completed and published. The report recommends further development work in 3 areas: 1) Better definition of the values dimension within the Northern Ireland Curriculum. 2) Pilot programmes at different key stages. 3) More influence in the provision of teacher training and professional development programmes. The project is proceeding in a developmental way in anticipation of the Northern Ireland Curriculum Review in 2001. The project is also participating in the NFER project 'The Northern Ireland Curriculum Cohort Study' in association with John Harland.

PUBLISHED MATERIAL: MONTGOMERY, A. & SMITH, A. (1997).

Values in education in Northern Ireland. Coleraine: University of Ulster.

STATUS: Sponsored project

SOURCE OF GRANT: Northern Ireland Council for the Curriculum, Examinations and Assessment

DATE OF RESEARCH: 1995-1998

KEYWORDS: **moral education; national curriculum - northern ireland; values; values education**

2636

Coleraine Campus, School of Education, Cromore Road, Coleraine, County Londonderry BT52 1SA
01265 44141

Pritchard, R. Dr

Educational reform in East Germany after unification

ABSTRACT: The project includes: 1) A critical description of the former system in the German Democratic Republic (DDR): its political values; strengths and weaknesses; curriculum and textbooks; teacher education; equipment and staff. 2) The planning of the school reform by the West German authorities: discussions about various options; official goals; legal basis and guidelines; organisation of cooperation between East and West Germans, e.g. in ministries; cooperation between old and new Bundeslanden. 3) Implementation of the reform process: material conditions (time, finance, staff, buildings etc); psychological conditions (differing attitudes, leadership styles, expectations, fear versus hope); political conditions; new forms of school organisation (e.g. Gymnasien instead of Einheitsschule, introduction of the Dual System instead of Polytechnischer Unterricht); curriculum renewal (abolition of certain school subjects, introduction of new subjects, new textbooks); new directions in pedagogy; staff and personnel (loss of jobs, school leadership, the position of women under altered political conditions); and teacher education and retraining. 4) Assessment and evaluation of the reform process from different points of view.

STATUS: Sponsored project

SOURCE OF GRANT: Economic and Social Research Council £11,920

DATE OF RESEARCH: 1995-1997

KEYWORDS: **east germany; educational change; germany**

2637

Coleraine Campus, School of Education, Cromore Road, Coleraine, County Londonderry BT52 1SA
01504 265621

McCully, A. Mr; O'Doherty, M. Ms; Smyth, P. Mr; *Supervisor*: Smith, A. Dr

Exploring controversial issues: a media approach

ABSTRACT: A three-year research and development project funded by the European Union in collaboration with Channel 4 Schools and Ulster Television. The project involves the production of a high quality television series ('Off the Walls') of five programmes which address some of the more controversial aspects of life in Northern Ireland. A research and development team based in the School of Education at the University of Ulster is working closely with teachers and youth workers to explore how it can best be used with young people; to develop a strategy for widespread dissemination of the series and its associated methodologies; and to evaluate the impact of the series on young people. A video produced by Channel 4 'Off the Walls' of five Channel 4 schools programmes concerning identity, culture, religion and politics in Northern Ireland is available, together with 'Speak your Piece: Exploring Controversial Issues' - a guide for teachers, youth and community workers to accompany the Channel 4 television series.

PUBLISHED MATERIAL: SMITH, A. & ROBINSON, A. EMU: The initial statutory years. Coleraine: University of Ulster, School of Education.

STATUS: Sponsored project

SOURCE OF GRANT: European Union; Channel 4; Ulster Television Company

DATE OF RESEARCH: 1995-1998

KEYWORDS: **controversial issues - course content; culture; education for mutual understanding; educational broadcasting; educational television; northern ireland; politics; values education**

2638

Coleraine Campus, School of Education, Cromore Road, Coleraine, County Londonderry BT52 1SA
01265 44141

Austin, R. Dr

The role of computer conferencing in handling controversial issues

ABSTRACT: This research project explores the ways that controversial issues can be explored using computer conferencing. Data has been collected from student teachers by questionnaire, and the transcript of conference discourse has been analysed.

STATUS: Individual research

DATE OF RESEARCH: 1995-continuing

KEYWORDS: controversial issues - course content; telecommunications; teleconferencing

2639

Coleraine Campus, School of Education, Cromore Road, Coleraine, County Londonderry BT52 1SA
01265 44141
London University, Institute of Education, 20 Bedford Way, London WC1H 0AL
0171 580 1122

Smith, A. Dr; Bourne, R. Mr

Young people's understanding of human rights

ABSTRACT: This 4-country study of young people's understanding of human rights is being coordinated at the University of London Institute of Education and is being carried out in Northern Ireland, India, Botswana and Zimbabwe. In Northern Ireland a questionnaire survey was administered to 20 14-year-olds and 20 16-year-olds in each of 5 schools, giving a total sample of 200 pupils. The questionnaire items related to 7 broad areas as follows: 1) law and the administration of justice; 2) equality of opportunity; 3) the teaching of history; 4) civic and social rights and responsibilities; 5) violence; 6) issues concerning identity (gender, language, culture, religion and politics); 7) pupil perspectives on future provision for human rights education. In addition, semi-structured interviews on human rights education obtained the perspectives of 5 headteachers, 10 teachers, 3 education advisers and 20 pupils (4 from each school).

PUBLISHED MATERIAL: SMITH, A. & BIRTHISTLE, U. (1997). Young people's understanding of human rights in Northern Ireland. Coleraine: University of Ulster.

STATUS: Sponsored project

SOURCE OF GRANT: Commonwealth Secretariat

DATE OF RESEARCH: 1996-1997

KEYWORDS: civil rights; human rights; northern ireland; secondary education; secondary school pupils

2640

Jordanstown Campus, School of Education, Shore Road, Newtownabbey, County Antrim BT37 0QB
01232 365131

Hutchinson, B. Dr

Appraising appraisal: quality assurance and control in the University of Ulster

ABSTRACT: A small scale qualitative research evaluation project investigating: the extent to which the recently established University staff appraisal scheme realised its intentions; the adequacy of the purposes and conceptions embedded in the appraisal scheme; the relationship between staff appraisal and other University-wide procedures. Documentary analysis and semi-structured, tape-recorded interviews were the main methods of investigation to supplement a critical review of literature. Findings: staff very much appreciated the appraisal interview; not many appraisals had been conducted along the devised themes suggested by management; this had more 'bad' effects than 'good' ones; no evidence to suggest that appraisal actually changed anything for the better - yet.

PUBLISHED MATERIAL: HUTCHINSON, B. (1993). Appraising appraisal: quality assurance and control in the University of Ulster. Coleraine: University of Ulster.

STATUS: Sponsored project

SOURCE OF GRANT: Ulster University: Faculty of Education £2,600

DATE OF RESEARCH: 1991-1993

KEYWORDS: academic staff evaluation; quality assurance; quality control; teacher evaluation; universities

2641

Jordanstown Campus, School of Education, Shore Road, Newtownabbey, County Antrim BT37 0QB
01232 365131

Crouch, C. Mr

Children and television

ABSTRACT: The research aims to provide a broad picture of children's use and understanding of television. To date, the preferences of children of primary school age (i.e. 7 to 11/12) have been explored (sample of 3,700+ from Northern Ireland, England, Australia surveyed) and results have indicated early gender differences; females tending to prefer soap opera programmes increasingly by age. A second wave of research (sample of 1,000 Australian, circa 1,000 Northern Ireland 12-12/16 year olds) involves survey by questionnaire on a wide range of issues but with special emphasis on television and learning. Children aged 12-16 in non-English speaking countries (i.e. Spain and Hungary) have also been surveyed using the same (translated) questionnaire.

PUBLISHED MATERIAL: CROUCH, C. (1989). 'Television and primary schoolchildren in Northern Ireland: 1: television programme preferences', Journal of Educational Television, Vol 15, No 13, pp.163-170. ; CROUCH, C. (1989). 'Soap in the eyes: primary schoolgirl TV preferences', Metro: Media and Education Magazine, (Australia), No 81, pp.18-22. ; CROUCH, C. (1991). 'The emergence of soap: primary schoolchildren's TV preferences in Northern Ireland, England and Australia', Research in Education, No 46, pp.73-83.

STATUS: Individual research

DATE OF RESEARCH: 1988-continuing

KEYWORDS: adolescents; children; television

2642

Jordanstown Campus, School of Education, Shore Road, Newtownabbey, County Antrim BT37 0QB
01232 365131

Donnelly, C. Miss; *Supervisors*: Dallat, J. Dr; McKeown, P. Mrs

A comparative investigation of the effects of aspects of education reform on primary schools of different management types in Northern Ireland

ABSTRACT: The fundamental reorganisation of the Northern Ireland education system since the Education Reform (N.I.) Order 1989 has been designed with the intention of improving a public service and increasing the position of the individual. The implications of these reforms for all schools in Northern Ireland are substantial, in terms of the new patterns of governance, delegated management, consumer choice and the regulation of the curriculum. The Northern Ireland experience of educational reform is, however, significantly different from the reforms introduced in the rest of the UK as a result of the different character of the Northern Ireland school system, which is one where the ethos, atmosphere, pupil intake and the government of each type of school reflects a lucid religious and cultural loyalty. It appears likely that such loyalties will shape the responses of the schools to the main dimensions of reform. It is, therefore, an opportune moment to examine the current ways primary schools are coping with particular strands of the reforms according to their managerial designation (controlled, integrated or maintained). This research aims to be an empirical investigation which examines the development and experiences of the different types of primary school as a result of the Education Reform (N.I.) Order 1989. It is intended that the study will be comparative, so as to accommodate the disparate nature of the school system in Northern Ireland. It is intended to conduct an examination of the distinct types of school (i.e. controlled, maintained and integrated) and their various perceptions, experiences and approaches to implementing a key aspect of educational reform.

STATUS: Individual research

DATE OF RESEARCH: 1994-1997

KEYWORDS: educational administration; educational change; educational legislation; national curriculum - northern ireland; northern ireland; primary education

2643

Jordanstown Campus, School of Education, Shore Road, Newtownabbey, County Antrim BT37 0QB
01232 365131

Morgan, T. Mr; *Supervisors*: Lovett, T. Prof.; Field, J. Prof.

Community education and music

ABSTRACT: The central theme of this research concerns developmental education as it relates to community based music. The music context will be assessed by using the qualitative method of 'self-directed learning' processes within local Northern Ireland communities. This will include both traditions, i.e. Catholic and Protestant. A comparison will then be made of musical forms in 'working class' communities, including the relationship with and between local organisations and the professional music services, administered by education and library boards.

STATUS: Individual research

DATE OF RESEARCH: 1995-continuing

KEYWORDS: community education; music; music activities

2644

Jordanstown Campus, School of Education, Shore Road, Newtownabbey, County Antrim BT37 0QB
01232 365131

Hutchinson, B. Dr; McKeown, P. Ms; Wilkinson, C. Dr; Whitehouse, P. Dr

The Impact project

ABSTRACT: The project will examine the experience of learning, and the value and use made of action research by participants and graduates of the MSc Education Management course. Action research encourages and supports critical reflective attitude to one's practice and professional and social context so that improvements in understanding can be translated into improved practice, and vice-versa. Major contemporary reforms in education apparently undermine such an effort. The project will seek to appreciate the changing conditions education managers now work in, so that the MSc, currently under revision, can be appropriately modified in terms of content, pedagogy and assessment modes. Initially approximately 20 headteacher graduates, selected from a range of schools and colleges, will be interviewed (semi-structured) to ascertain their use of action research, their current concerns, and their views of the NPQH proposals; additionally they will be asked to judge the impact learning action research has had on them and in turn what impact they consequently have had on their schools and colleges. Following analysis of the interview transcripts, a questionnaire will be constructed and issued to all graduates. Concurrently, existing participants will be followed-up with an intensive investigation of a small number of organisations (probably 4-6) to gauge the impact of recent reforms and the headteachers' participation on the programme.

STATUS: Sponsored project

SOURCE OF GRANT: Ulster University £2,000

DATE OF RESEARCH: 1997-1997

KEYWORDS: action research; head teachers; management in education; management studies; school improvement

2645

Magee College, School of Education, Northland Road, County Londonderry BT48 7JL
01504 265621

Carlin, J. Ms; *Supervisor*: Smith, A. Dr

An investigation of selection at age 11 in Northern Ireland

ABSTRACT: This research forms the basis for doctoral studies over a 5-year period to investigate the origins, impact and reasons for the continued existence of a selection procedure from primary schools at age 11 in Northern Ireland.

STATUS: Individual research

DATE OF RESEARCH: 1995-continuing

KEYWORDS: northern ireland; secondary education; selective admission

University College Bretton Hall

2646

West Bretton, Wakefield WF4 4LG
01924 830261

Bell, G. Prof.; Chisholm, T. Mr

The European dimension of inservice teacher education in the arts: research based teaching in the arts

ABSTRACT: A Symposium (March 1997) and Conference (August 1997) were held at Woolley Hall and University College Bretton Hall. 35 participants and contributors from 9 European countries engaged in debate, practical workshops and evaluation and planning sessions, exploring the relationship between research in the arts and practice in European schools and teacher training institutions. Colleagues from a variety of institutions and educational backgrounds in different member states were invited to work together in a residential setting to explore these concerns. The European Dimension of Inservice Teacher Education in the Arts formed a unique element in the European Union/Socrates programme in 1997. Its key features were partnership, mutual learning, communication, transferability, dissemination, research-based teaching and the identification of training imperatives. Consideration was also given to educational aims and objectives, curriculum provision, education and training issues in the arts, teaching methods, policy formation, assessment and evaluation, the synthesising of theory and practice, socio-political factors and influences and the impact of research on classroom practice. Initial thoughts and papers from the Symposium were brought together in a publication (BELL, G.H. & CHISHOLM. T. (Eds). (1997). Research based teaching in the arts: towards a European dimension. Wakefield: University College Bretton Hall). Papers and other data from the Conference are in the final editorial stage for publication in 1998.

PUBLISHED MATERIAL: BELL, G.H. & CHISHOLM, T. (Eds). (1997). Research based teaching in the arts: towards a European dimension. Wakefield: University College Bretton Hall.

STATUS: Sponsored project

SOURCE OF GRANT: European Union Socrates £20,000

DATE OF RESEARCH: 1997-1998

KEYWORDS: art education; arts; european dimension; inservice teacher education

2647

West Bretton, Wakefield WF4 4LG
01924 830261

Crick, M. Dr; Daniels, S. Ms

Evaluation of the University of First Age (Kirklees LEA) Summer School

ABSTRACT: The Kirklees University of the First Age (UFA) Summer School took place over 2 weeks in July 1998, involving Year 7 pupils from 10 schools. The model is the Birmingham scheme, which has been in operation for 2 years, offering an enrichment experience via approaches to teaching and learning based on Howard Gardner's theory of Multiple Intelligences, exploring connections between curriculum areas. The UFA aims to provide quality learning opportunities for all pupils of all abilities including the disaffected and those who underachieve, outside the traditional school hours, thus leading to a raising of achievement, attainment and motivation. The selected curriculum areas were: music/mathematics, citizenship, information and communication technology. The data was generated through: 1) participation and non-participation observations; 2) interviews during July and again in September with students, peer mentors, staff tutors and headteachers; 3) informal discussion; 4) analysis of documentation, learning logs and evaluations completed by students, peer mentors and staff tutors; 5) sound and video recording. The 5 elements most valued by students were: 1) working with other people and making new friends; 2) developing self-confidence; 3) a different approach to learning; 4) the specific content of the sessions; 5) enjoyment. All felt they would learn better in 'normal' school if they had more support and more concentrated and linked teaching. A quality experience was definitely provided and motivation was clearly raised. A conclusion regarding achievement and attainment will only be feasible when the Summer School is thoroughly integrated into the UFA-centred year round activities of participating schools.

STATUS: Sponsored project

SOURCE OF GRANT: University of First Age budget

DATE OF RESEARCH: 1998-1998

KEYWORDS: pupil improvement; pupil motivation; secondary education; summer schools

2648

West Bretton, Wakefield WF4 4LG
01924 830261

Barker, B. Ms; *Supervisors*: Long, R. Dr; Sewell, A. Dr

An approach to the effective teaching of adolescent pupils with learning difficulties with specific reference to Gardner's Theory of Multiple Intelligences

ABSTRACT: The purpose of this research is to identify, apply and evaluate changes to the researcher's own teaching practice following critical reflection upon the theories of 3 American psychologists, Howard Gardner, Daniel Goleman and Mihalyi Cziksczentmihalyi, whose respective theories on 'multiple intelligences', 'emotional intelligence', and the concept of 'flow' are creating a significant impact on educational practice worldwide. A specific focus is to look at the assessment and recording procedure currently in use and compare it with a format designed to record wherever possible the 7 intelligences specified by Gardner and to demonstrate the 'seamless' approach of learning which is not restricted to school curriculum and content. It is the intent to develop and reflect pupil profiles, parental involvement, project work and portfolios of work within a reporting system. The context for this research is a special school for students with learning difficulties on the urban fringe of a town in the North East of England. The school educates pupils with a wide range of learning difficulties within the age range 11-19.

STATUS: Individual research

DATE OF RESEARCH: 1998-continuing

KEYWORDS: educational psychology; intelligence; learning disabilities; special educational needs; teaching methods

2649

West Bretton, Wakefield WF4 4LG
01924 830261

Long, R. Dr; Holloway, K. Mr

The development of shared practice groups to improve the teaching of mental arithmetic in primary schools - the 'it figures' project

ABSTRACT: Previous experience with inservice education for primary teachers suggested that teachers often learned a great deal from informal discussions with one another. To test this notion, a 'shared practice group' was set up with teachers from 5 primary schools in Kirklees Local Education Authority (LEA) to explore the teaching of mental arithmetic at key stage 2. The 'shared practice group' met on a regular basis (every 6 to 7 weeks), teachers bringing in examples of children's work to share with colleagues. The group was supported by a facilitator (Kevin Holloway) who is a mathematics tutor at Bretton Hall. Features of 'shared practice groups' were critically examined, and 3 key issues were discussed: 1) collaborative approaches to professional learning; 2) reflection and reflexivity in teacher development; 3) the role of the 'shared practice group' facilitator. Teachers and children were enthusiastic about the impact of the 'shared practice group' on their classroom work and there were strong indications that this could be a powerful tool for teacher development and school improvement.

PUBLISHED MATERIAL: HOLLOWAY, K. (1997). 'Exploring mental arithmetic', Mathematics Teaching, No 160, pp.26-28. ; HOLLOWAY, K. & LONG, R. (1998). 'The development of shared practice groups to improve teaching in primary schools'. In: Proceedings of the International Congress of School Effectiveness and Improvement (ICSEI), University of Manchester, Manchester, 1998. (CD Rom). ; HOLLOWAY, K. & LONG, R. 'The development of shared practice groups to improve teaching in primary schools', Journal of In-Service Education. (in press).

STATUS: Sponsored project

SOURCE OF GRANT: University College Bretton Hall £3,500; Kirklees LEA £3,500

DATE OF RESEARCH: 1996-1998

KEYWORDS: arithmetic; mathematics; mental arithmetic; primary education; school improvement; teacher development

2650

West Bretton, Wakefield WF4 4LG
01924 830261

Long, R. Dr; Stogdon, C. Mrs

Building effective staff teams to improve pupil achievement

ABSTRACT: The primary school improvement (PSI) pilot study in 1994 indicated clearly that interpersonal factors were implicated in the success or otherwise of improvement strategies in the primary school. There appeared to be a clear need to build the capacity of the school to deal with conflict and stress. Today, the stress levels within school are certainly no less, and the pressure on teachers has not diminished, so there is still a pressing need to help teachers deal with stress and conflict, and help schools to build effective staff teams to improve pupil achievement. The present study aims to work with infant and junior schools which have recently amalgamated, to explore methods of working with school staff to help them deal with conflict and foster and develop effective teamwork.

STATUS: Sponsored project

SOURCE OF GRANT: Kirklees LEA

DATE OF RESEARCH: 1998-continuing

KEYWORDS: primary education; school improvement; stress - psychological; teamwork

2651

West Bretton, Wakefield WF4 4LG
01924 830261

Long, R. Dr

Shaping the future: building a vision of primary education for the next century

ABSTRACT: Drawing from a range of literature reviews, key issues and concerns facing primary education are identified and examined. Areas explored include: 1) learning needs for the knowledge society; 2) systems and structures of schooling; 3) the primary curriculum of the future; 4) family and community involvement; 5) the potential impact of information and communication technology (ICT) and new technologies. From this analysis, a summary of the main issues and dilemmas will be brought to a variety of stakeholders in primary education - children, parents, teachers - and their views and opinions will be synthesised to begin to build a vision of primary education for the next century.

PUBLISHED MATERIAL: LONG, R. 'Shaping the future: building a vision of primary (elementary) education for the next century'. Paper for the International Congress for School Effective and Improvement 1999. (in press).

STATUS: Individual research

DATE OF RESEARCH: 1998-continuing

KEYWORDS: educational development; primary education; school community relationship; school improvement

2652

West Bretton, Wakefield WF4 4LG
01924 830261

Taylor, M. Ms; *Supervisor*: Crick, M. Dr

A critical study of students with physical and sensory disabilities in the visual arts in higher education

ABSTRACT: Historically, people with physical and sensory disabilities had little or no presence in the visual arts. In the last decade, a small number of disabled artists have emerged but professional, mainstream artists, designers, teachers and policymakers with a disability are rare. Their absence, professionally, is reflected by the disproportionately low numbers of students with disabilities that apply to, and are accepted onto, visual arts courses leading to graduate qualifications (universities central admissions service data). The research is to determine the factors that differentiate those students with disabilities studying in higher education from the large numbers of their disabled peers who do not access this level of learning. The main research method will be case study interviews. Students with physical disabilities will be sampled across 3 years of study. Where numbers are higher (sensory impairment) a questionnaire survey will be carried out. The main method of research will be complemented by an analysis of relevant literature or policy, with a focus on the social, political and cultural attitudes which have informed the concept of equal opportunities for disabled people. An exploration of how disabled children can be precluded from acquiring a visual language - and whether such preclusion is consolidated by the educational experience, will be made. Included within this research study will be those students currently studying on the Bretton Hall/Hereward College degree programme. This initiative is designed to enhance access for students with disabilities to higher education courses in the arts and is unique in its provision.

PUBLISHED MATERIAL: TAYLOR, M. (1998). 'Art students with a future', Target (Muscular Dystrophy), Summer 1998, pp.3-4.

STATUS: Individual research

DATE OF RESEARCH: 1998-continuing

KEYWORDS: **art education; arts; disabilities; higher education; special educational needs; visual arts**

2653

West Bretton, Wakefield WF4 4LG
01924 830261

Braund, M. Mr; Crebbin, C. Mr; Lloyd, J. Dr; Phipps, R. Mr

Bretton Hall - Zeneca primary science project

ABSTRACT: The School of Primary Education at University College Bretton Hall developed an inservice course for continuing professional development in primary science involving two teachers from each of 15 schools in Barnsley local education authority (LEA). One teacher was the science coordinator and the other a non-specialist 'partner teacher'. It was envisaged that both teachers from each school would support each other throughout the course. The first phase, Autumn 1997, provided 3 days of training for coordinators and partner teachers in scientific investigations; aspects of subject knowledge; industrial liaison; process of partnership teaching; monitoring/assessment; role of the coordinator; and curriculum planning. Each school was given a 1,000 pounds grant for science equipment. The curriculum enabled informed decisions to be made on how to spend the grant. How the grant was spent has been carefully analysed and a paper submitted to a journal for consideration for publication in October 1998. The second phase of the project concentrated on partnership teaching. This process involved each pair planning lessons with subject knowledge and process skills foci, participative observation in respective classrooms. Each session was followed by professionally challenging but supportive critical reflection about the teaching process. 5 days of funding were allocated to this aspect of the course. A paper on the Zeneca primary science project will be presented at the University of Durham at the 'Fourth Conference for Teacher Education in Primary Science: the Challenge of Change' from 6-9 July 1999.

PUBLISHED MATERIAL: LLOYD, J. (1998). 'Improving primary science teaching in partnership with industry', Science Teacher Education, 23 September, p.8.

STATUS: Sponsored project

SOURCE OF GRANT: Zeneca £160,000

DATE OF RESEARCH: 1998-continuing

KEYWORDS: **inservice teacher education; primary education; science education; teacher development**

2654

West Bretton, Wakefield WF4 4LG
01924 830261

Stephenson, T. Dr

Performing arts education: an examination of the interface between BTEC National Diploma and higher education course provision

ABSTRACT: The 1990s have witnessed a period of rapid change and development for everyone participating in the further and higher education sectors. Traditional demarcations have been eroded and the number of students entering courses has rapidly increased. This study examines some of the principal debates that have been raised during this period through an

analysis of the work of two further education colleges in the North East of England. The focus of the research is on Business and Technology Education Council (BTEC) National Diploma courses in performing arts, and the way in which they interface with courses in higher education. The two colleges provide case studies through which the primary debate of access is examined. Subsidiary issues regarding course content, vocational training, academic standards, resource issues and the expectations of staff and students are also examined. The entire study is located within a contextual framework which examines the broader effects of policy changes with regard to the arts and education, the development of vocational courses and statistical evidence pertaining to the interface of BTEC courses and degree programmes. Opinions have been gathered from a number of staff engaged in education and training in both sectors. These have been supplemented by the views of students on BTEC National Diploma courses and illuminated through exploration of the regional context in which the courses operate. The scope of this research project has required the adoption of an appropriately flexible research technique. A number of differing, yet complementary, research techniques will be used within a framework of multi-method analysis. This was deemed to be the most effective manner in which meaningful conclusions could be reached due to the subjective nature of much of the information to be examined.

PUBLISHED MATERIAL: STEPHENSON, T.J. (1999). 'Access to HE performing arts courses'. In: BUTTERWORTH, P. (Ed). National arts education archive occasional papers. Vol 13. Wakefield, Bretton Hall: National Arts Education Archive.

STATUS: Individual research

DATE OF RESEARCH: 1994-1997

KEYWORDS: **business and technology education council; further education; higher education; theatre arts**

2655

West Bretton, Wakefield WF4 4LG
01924 830261

Long, R. Dr

Arts education and the National Curriculum: a case study of a first school

ABSTRACT: Historically, post-war primary education in England was seen as an active, practical endeavour, where young children explored and came to make sense of the world through a curriculum which contained a good deal of art, craft, poetry and nature study. The primary classroom of the nineties must look at first glance a very different place, with its emphasis on a subject-oriented National Curriculum and the acquisition of basic skills. This case study examines how one school attempts to 'deliver' the National Curriculum through a humanistic, arts-based curriculum.

STATUS: Individual research

DATE OF RESEARCH: 1996-continuing

KEYWORDS: **art education; arts; national curriculum; primary education**

2656

West Bretton, Wakefield WF4 4LG
01924 830261

Long, R. Dr; Clark, A. Mrs

Using 'shared practice groups' to support the implementation of the National Literacy Hour at key stage 1

ABSTRACT: 'Shared practice groups', where teachers from a small number of schools meet on a regular basis to discuss and develop their practice in a particular area, have been shown to be a useful means of developing practice in teaching mental arithmetic at key stage 2. The present study aims to further explore 'shared practice groups' as a means of teacher development, focusing on the teaching of literacy at key stage 1 through the implementation of the National Literacy Hour. The National Literacy Hour has been implemented in all primary schools in England with a view to raising standards. The 'shared practice group' in this study is comprised of key stage 1 teachers from 4 schools in Royston, Barnsley, who met every 3 to 4 weeks to share and compare their approaches to implementing the National Literacy Hour.

STATUS: Team research

DATE OF RESEARCH: 1998-continuing

KEYWORDS: **key stage 1; literacy; literacy hours; primary education; teacher development**

2657

West Bretton, Wakefield WF4 4LG
01924 830261

Braund, M. Mr

Using drama to improve student teachers' understanding in the physical sciences

ABSTRACT: Students find ideas in physical sciences abstract and they may have persistent misconceptions. One way of improving understanding is to use active, creative approaches in teaching. Drama is one example. The research evaluated the dramas/improvisations used by 37 student teachers as part of their second year undergraduate course in initial teacher training (ITT). Students were asked to use drama, mime etc to explain to their peers concepts in the domain of generation and transmission of electrical energy. Students' presentations have been analysed using a behavioural framework and students questioned and interviewed on video. The findings show that students' drama helps them to explain abstract ideas and that they value this approach to learning science. A case is made for use of drama generally in teaching science in schools and colleges and a list of requirements for this to happen more widely is provided.

PUBLISHED MATERIAL: BRAUND, M.R. (1998). 'Using drama to improve student teachers' scientific understanding', Science Teacher Education, Vol 23, pp.6-7.

STATUS: Individual research

DATE OF RESEARCH: 1997-continuing

KEYWORDS: **drama; preservice teacher education; science education; student teachers**

2658

West Bretton, Wakefield WF4 4LG
01924 830261

Braund, M. Mr

An evaluation of the use of school ponds

ABSTRACT: Over the last 10 years a significant investment has been made in constructing new ponds in schools across the UK. This has been a central part of a move to develop and enhance the often barren landscapes of schools and to provide for learning that takes place in the outdoor classroom. Little was previously known about the educational effectiveness of school ponds, the potential for further development or problems that schools might have with them. The research surveyed 50 schools with and without ponds in 10 local authorities by way of a questionnaire to elicit information on design, use and maintenance. The findings show that there is great potential for further development of ponds but that cost, fears of vandalism and problems with plant overgrowth pose significant barriers. Educational work carried out at ponds was found to be very short-term and limited to studies in one season. Parents, children and the community rarely have lasting connections with pond maintenance or extended study and this is particularly so for ponds in secondary schools.

PUBLISHED MATERIAL: BRAUND, M.R. (1997). 'School ponds: their current status and likely contribution to education, conservation and local environmental enhancement'. In: BOOTHBY, J. (Ed) 'British pond landscapes. Action for protection and enhancement'. Proceedings of the UK Conference of the Pond Life Project, University College, Chester, 1997.; BRAUND, M.R. & KERSEY, R. (1998). 'Getting the best from your school pond', Primary Science Review, No 54, pp.8-11. ; BRAUND, M.R. 'Ponds and education in the UK: problems and possibilities'. In: BOOTHBY, J. (Ed) 'Pond use and conservation'. Proceedings of the International Conference of the Pond Life Project, Vaerstedhalt Castle, Maastricht, Netherlands. (in press).

STATUS: Individual research

DATE OF RESEARCH: 1996-1998

KEYWORDS: **educational facilities; environmental education; school grounds; school ponds; water resources**

2659

West Bretton, Wakefield WF4 4LG
01924 830261

Adams, E. Ms; Chisholm, T. Mr

Site specific: art, design, built environment education in initial teacher education

ABSTRACT: Site specific is a research project in initial teacher education, a collaboration between 6 institutions in England, Scotland and Wales (University College Bretton Hall; St Andrews College; University of Central England; Middlesex University; Strathclyde University and University of Wales Institute of Education) to investigate work in schools that links art, design, built environment and education. The project will investigate the influences on such work and the theories that underpin it. It will explore how new ideas and practices are able to impact on the school curriculum. It will identify opportunities and constraints for students to extend and enrich work in schools. Elements of course work in some Postgraduate Certificate in Education (PGCE), B.Ed and BA Community Arts courses, together with examples of work in schools generated by students and teachers, will be documented and evaluated and the results disseminated. Publications will describe and explain ideas for study, learning methods and teaching strategies. A report will analyse and evaluate the opportunities, constraints and strategies evident in the work of student teachers using the built environment as a resource for art and design education. In addition, an illustrated book containing examples of programmes of work, learning and teaching methods and examples of pupils' work will be produced. The materials will be of use to student teachers and practising teachers as well as artists, designers, architects, planners and landscape architects who work in schools and other educational contexts.

PUBLISHED MATERIAL: ADAMS, E. (1997). 'Connections between public art and art and design education in schools', Journal of Art and Design Education, Vol 16, No 3. ; COUTTS, G. & DAWES, M. (1998). 'Drawing on the artist outside: towards 1999', Journal of Art and Design Education, Vol 17, No 2. ; ADAMS, E. & CHISHOLM, T. Art, design and the built environment. A programme for teacher education', Journal of Art and Design Education. (in press).

STATUS: Collaborative

DATE OF RESEARCH: 1998-continuing

KEYWORDS: **arts education; built environment; design; preservice teacher education**

2660

West Bretton, Wakefield WF4 4LG
01924 830261

Burtonwood, N. Dr

Cultural identity and liberal democracy: curriculum implications

ABSTRACT: A critical response to recent communitarian attempts to construct curriculum models which seek to combine a concern for group-based identity with an individual autonomy consistent with liberal democracy.

PUBLISHED MATERIAL: BURTONWOOD, N. (1995). 'Beyond local cultures: towards a cosmopolitan art education', Journal of Art and Design Education, Vol 14, No 2, pp.205-212. ; BURTONWOOD, N. (1996). 'Beyond culture: a reply to Mark Halstead', Journal of Philosophy of Education, Vol 30, No 2, pp.295-299. ; BURTONWOOD, N. (1996). 'Culture, identity and the curriculum', Educational Review, Vol 48, No 3, pp.227-236. ; BURTONWOOD, N. (1998). 'Liberalism and communitarianism: a response to two recent attempts to reconcile individual autonomy with group identity', Educational Studies, Vol 24, No 3, pp.295-304.

STATUS: Individual research

DATE OF RESEARCH: 1995-1998

KEYWORDS: **cultural differences; curriculum development; identity**

2661

West Bretton, Wakefield WF4 4LG
01924 830261

Liversidge, J. Ms; *Supervisor*: Braund, M. Mr

Children's perceptions of animals from literature and the relationships to science learning in the primary school

ABSTRACT: This research will explore the images of animals transmitted via children's books and the effects that these have on children's perceptions of animal relationships in the wild. Children aged 10 and 11 will be read stories portraying animal interrelationships. These children will then be asked a number of questions that test their understanding of similar interrelationships in the natural environment. The results will be analysed and discussed so that issues relating to the teaching of biological concepts at this age can be explored.

STATUS: Individual research

DATE OF RESEARCH: 1998-continuing

KEYWORDS: **animals; books; childrens literature; primary education; science education**

2662

West Bretton, Wakefield WF4 4LG
01924 830261
Leeds University, School of Education, Leeds LS2 9JT
01132 431751

Bruce, R. Mr; *Supervisors*: Threlfall, J. Dr; Orton, A. Dr

Factors within preschool educational settings that affect the number attainment of young children

ABSTRACT: A nationally supported initiative of an early intervention type was undertaken in a range of preschool settings located in the district of Dewsbury, West Yorkshire, during the mid-1990s. A core aim of the initiative was the promotion of learning in the field of number. This study provides a quantitative and qualitative analysis of the effect of participation in the project on the number attainments of the children involved. The study also provides new insights into the number abilities of young children, together with the conditions and factors within preschool settings that appear to impact upon such abilities. Three settings involved in the initiative were matched with three similar settings using a quasi-experimental post-test non-equivalent groups design. Data regarding the number abilities of the children were obtained using a series of specially developed assessment instruments. The total sample consisted of 93 children of which 50 were girls, with an average age of 4 years and 4 months. The main findings indicate that the impact of the initiative was limited in 2 out of the 3 settings studied. The initiative had most impact when the socio-economic status of the families involved was relatively low. The impact of this type of early intervention programme on increasing number attainment is questioned. Findings also suggest that previous studies might have overestimated the number abilities of children of this age. Implications regarding specific areas of number including ordinality, subitising and strategies used for solving problems involving number operations are also considered.

STATUS: Individual research

DATE OF RESEARCH: 1993-continuing

KEYWORDS: **early childhood education; mathematics education; numbers; numeracy; preschool education; young children**

2663

West Bretton, Wakefield WF4 4LG
01924 830261
Leeds University, School of Education, Leeds LS2 9JT
01132 431751

Gedman, J. Ms; *Supervisors*: Smith, P. Mr; Clarke, S. Mr

The underachievement of boys in English

ABSTRACT: Boys' underachievement in English enjoys immense topicality. There is both quantitative and qualitative evidence at national, regional and local level to suggest that boys are performing less well in English from girls. The aim of this research is to examine particular strategies, within the confines of the English classroom. Although it is assumed that English teachers pay close attention to advanced reading skills, it has been suggested that systematic deployment of a number of techniques is unusual. These techniques, which could be used with pupils of all levels, are to be used as tools with which English teachers could effectively raise achievement in the English classroom. Lunzer and Gardner' Directed Activities Related to Texts (DARTs) is the model on which it is intended to base this research at classroom level. The culture of the catchment area will also be examined to understand the pressure placed upon pupils from home. How influential is the school in raising the ambitions of the pupils? How important is it for the boys to adopt the 'uncool to learn' attitude? Investigating the aspirations of pupils and their parents may go some way to understanding why so many

boys are now underachieving. The combination of close classroom 'boy-friendly' strategies and the investigation into the 'laddish' culture of the catchment area will raise many issues: social, cultural, political and educational.

STATUS: Individual research

DATE OF RESEARCH: 1998-continuing

KEYWORDS: **achievement; boys; english; reading; sex differences; underachievement**

2664

West Bretton, Wakefield WF4 4LG
01924 830261
Sheffield University, Division of Adult Continuing Education, 196-198 West Street, Sheffield S1 4ET
01142 768555

Burke, C. Dr; *Supervisor*: McConnell, D. Prof.

Computer supported collaborative learning: the use of an interactive web site and integral e-mail discussion in enhancing the learning process in higher education

ABSTRACT: This is an action research project which seeks to investigate the potential use of the Internet and e-mail discussion in enhancing or changing the learning and teaching process. The research is based at University College Bretton Hall and is part of a module offered at level 2 as a core module within the Child and Family Studies Degree Programme. The web site which has been designed for the research is entitled 'A journey through the history of state education in Britain' and provides a means by which students are encouraged to access Internet based resources. The web site uses the notion of 'role play' in an attempt to engage the students with past themes, personalities and experiences. Central to the learning process is an e-mail discussion organised to enable flexible but consistent discussion of issues raised through the web site. The sample of students number 28. Research is underway and results and conclusions will be available January 1999. The web site reference is: http://panizzi.shef.ac.uk/med/cathy/intro.html

STATUS: Individual research

DATE OF RESEARCH: 1997-continuing

KEYWORDS: **computer uses in education; higher education; history; internet; teaching methods**

University College Chester

2665

Cheyney Road, Chester CH1 4BJ
01224 375444
Newcastle upon Tyne University, Department of Speech, King George VI Building, Newcastle upon Tyne NE1 7RU
0191 222 6000

Williams, F. Mr; *Supervisor*: Mogford-Bevan, K. Dr

The speech of adult strangers to a child from ages 10 months to 3 years 10 months

ABSTRACT: The research was conducted over a period of three years. The aim was to gather a corpus of linguistic data for transcription and analysis. Adult strangers were chosen for a) availability; b) age (55+); c) gender (female), and asked to speak to the child for 2-3 minutes. The linguistic changes the adults made in their talk to the child were compared with the changes made by the child's mother. These comparative changes reflect a number of factors in adult-child discourse such as: a) the significance of familiarity in the fine-tuning hypothesis; b) the ability of adults to adjust to the level of the child's language. Measures of well-formedness, grammatical complexity and semantic range were used for purposes of comparison in the data.

STATUS: Individual research

DATE OF RESEARCH: 1994-continuing

KEYWORDS: **child language; discourse analysis; speech communication; verbal communication**

University College of Ripon and York St John

2666

Centre for Sports Science, Leisure and Tourism, Lord Mayor's Walk, York YO3 7EX
01904 656771

Thombs, S. Dr

Categorisation and analysis of discrete manual movements in Down syndrome children aged 6 to 16 years

ABSTRACT: 40 Down syndrome children, aged 6 to 16 years, were grouped into 5 age categories (6 years through 7 years 11 months; 8 years through 9 years 11 months; 10 years through 11 years 11 months; 12 years through 13 years 11 months; and 14 years through 15 years 11 months) and examined on a number of manual tasks. These involved a variety of hand actions during peg displacement, transportation, manipulation and relocation. Discrete movement times were noted and a system devised to categorise groups of comparable discrete movements and define areas of manual operation. Pairwise comparisons of age groups for each movement category, based on estimated marginal means for discrete movement time, indicated that 69.64% of the observed significant differences between age groups represented differences between age group 1 and older age groups. These significant differences are noted, to a greater or lesser extent in 56.25% of the recorded movement categories and 44.64% of the observed significant differences. Further evidence from age group profiles, examining discrete movement time within comparable movement categories, confirmed that some children have a preference for operational area and an affinity with certain manual movements. The child's inability to quickly complete a given task may, therefore, be partly a reflection of task orientation.

STATUS: Individual research

DATE OF RESEARCH: 1997-1998

KEYWORDS: **downs syndrome; motor development; special educational needs**

2667

Faculty of Professional, Management and Teaching Studies, Lord Mayor's Walk, York YO3 7EX
01904 656771

Sellick, M. Dr; *Supervisor*: Tomkinson, P. Dr

Effects of recent change in secondary teacher education : a longitudinal comparison

ABSTRACT: The central focus is on 2 cohorts of trainees taking a one-year Postgraduate Certificate in Education (PGCE) for secondary school teaching in 1993-94 and 1994-95 and each group's first year of full-time work in school. It traces changes in secondary teacher training in England since 1944. The particular changes made by one higher education institution to comply with the Department for Education and Circular 9/92 are outlined. The research methodology employed was questionnaires, hierarchically focused interviews and case study compilations on 2 samples of 6 students generating data in depth rather than breadth. These methods yielded data concerning 2 cohorts of 20 trainee teachers as they progressed from students to newly qualified teachers (NQTs) and some of the changes that took place in 35 associated schools with regard to attitudes to teacher education and the role of the school based trainer, mentor or more experienced colleague. It was concluded that some of the changes were for the better, some for the worse while much remained the same. For the better the second group of students seemed more able to undertake the immediate role of classroom teacher but were less able than those in the first group to articulate a rationale for their teaching. Both students and teachers were concerned about the lack of time in a one-year course, whatever the pattern of division between university and school, but the final interviews with teachers indicated a growing awareness of the necessity for a coherent pattern of teacher education from initial, through induction to continuing inservice education.

PUBLISHED MATERIAL: SELLICK, D. (1994). 'When is a mentor a preceptor?', Education Today, Vol 44, No 3, pp.49-53. ; SELLICK, D. (1996). 'Learning to use the mirror: reflection and teacher education', Education Today, Vol 46, No 4, pp.11-16.

STATUS: Individual research

DATE OF RESEARCH: 1993-1998

KEYWORDS: **postgraduate certificate in education; preservice teacher education; secondary school teachers**

University College of St Mark and St John

2668

Derriford Road, Plymouth PL6 6BH
01752 777188

Thatcher, A. Prof.

Engaging the curriculum - a theological programme

ABSTRACT: The Programme commissions internationally renowned authors to produce materials which engage Christan theology with most of the subjects on the curricula of the 24 church colleges of higher education in England and Wales. Use of the materials will be optional. They will be launched at national conferences. Work is in progress in the first four areas: sociology; science education; English; spiritual and moral development. The first essay, by Professor David Martin, 'Christian foundations, sociological fundamentals', is complete. The phased publication of a series of essays, together with additional papers about the implementation of curricular proposals, is planned throughout the present decade.

STATUS: Sponsored project

SOURCE OF GRANT: Council of Church and Associated Colleges; St Gabriel's Trust £10,000

DATE OF RESEARCH: 1993-continuing

KEYWORDS: **church and education; curriculum development; material development; religious education; theological education; voluntary colleges**

2669

Derriford Road, Plymouth PL6 6BH
01752 777188

Laker, A. Dr

An investigation into the connection between school physical education experiences and lifetime activity

ABSTRACT: The purpose of the study is to establish whether there is a connection between school physical education (PE) and level of activity in adult life. Active lifestyles are a main factor in adult health and the study's findings may have implications for the way PE is taught in schools. A pilot study will be carried out in the local area. Samples of inactive, moderately active, and very active adults will be surveyed to ascertain their memories and perceptions of their school physical education as a determinant of their current activity level. It is hoped to collaborate with other institutions in conducting a national survey along the lines of the pilot. At this stage, the treatment of the data is uncertain, but it is likely to use one of the regression techniques.

STATUS: Sponsored project

SOURCE OF GRANT: College of St Mark and St John

DATE OF RESEARCH: 1995-1997

KEYWORDS: **lifetime sports; physical activities; physical activity level; physical education; recreational activities**

2670

Derriford Road, Plymouth PL6 6BH
01752 777188

Laker, A. Dr

The teaching of non-physical aims in physical education

ABSTRACT: The project is looking at ways to teach physical education (PE) for the achievement of all National Curriculum aims, not only the physical ones. The first phase places the non-physical outcomes of physical education in context with curriculum documents and especially the National Curriculum document. It explains the problem and highlights the contradiction that currently exists. The next stage was to develop and implement a training programme for student teachers that will equip them to teach in a way that places increased emphasis on the affective domain, but not at the expense of the physical domain. The construction, content and delivery of this training programme constituted the second phase. The third phase covered the teaching by the sample students in schools. The results of the project were obtained from a variety of sources: taped and transcribed interviews with pupils and student teachers, analysis of videotaped lessons, and reflective journals kept by the student teachers. This research is now progressing on two themes. Firstly, the development of a theoretical framework which legitimises the inclusion of affective outcomes and charts their promotion in physical education. This includes a socio-cultural and political critique of the perceived importance of the affective within the education system. The second theme is the interpretation of the theoretical into the practical. Application in school settings, teacher strategies, and the assessment of outcomes, form part of this theme. It is anticipated that each of the two themes will result in a project report.

PUBLISHED MATERIAL: LAKER, A. (1995). 'Physical education lessons in England: content and perceptions'. In: Proceedings of ICHPER.SD 38th World Congress, Gainesville, USA, July 1995. ; LAKER, A. (1996). 'The aims of physical education within the revised National Curriculum: lip service to the affective', Pedagogy in Practice, Vol 2, No 1, pp.23-30. ; LAKER, A. (1996). 'Learning to teach through the physical, as well as of the physical', British Journal of Physical Education, Vol 27, No 4, pp.18-22.

STATUS: Individual research

DATE OF RESEARCH: 1993-continuing

KEYWORDS: affective objectives; physical education; preservice teacher education

2671

Derriford Road, Plymouth PL6 8BH
01752 777188
Plymouth University, Department of Psychology, Drake Circus, Plymouth PL4 8AA
01752 600600

Laker, A. Dr; Jones, K. Mr; Lea, S. Dr

A longitudinal study of evolving student teacher concerns and socialisation

ABSTRACT: Research into the concerns of student teachers in secondary physical education has increased recently. However, there is still little research that traces the changes that occur over a series of teaching practices. The purpose of this study is to chart those changes in concerns and also to investigate how this affects the students' socialisation into the profession. A cohort of B.Ed (Hons) secondary physical education students were tracked in their last 3 years of the 4-year degree course. Quantitative and qualitative instruments were used to gather data from the students about their concerns and perceptions of teaching practice. The baseline report indicates that 3 areas were prominent for them: firstly, subject knowledge; secondly, management and organisation; and thirdly, relationship with staff and pupils. Initial indications from later data show that students begin to regard themselves as 'teachers' during their last practice, when they take 'ownership' of their practice and professional development and socialisation. Future publications will deal with formal and informal support systems, occupational socialisation, quantitative and qualitative changes that take place during the 3 years.

PUBLISHED MATERIAL: LAKER, A. & JONES, K. 'A longitudinal study of evolving student teacher concerns: baseline report', European Journal of Physical Education. (in press).

STATUS: Collaborative

DATE OF RESEARCH: 1996-continuing

KEYWORDS: physical education; preservice teacher education; student teachers; teaching practice

University College of St Martin

2672

Bowerham Road, Lancaster LA1 3JD
01524 384384

Horsfall, B. Mr; *Supervisor*: Rogers, C. Dr

Do schools make a difference: school effectiveness and special educational needs

ABSTRACT: This research project is about school effectiveness in the primary school and focuses specifically on the nature of school effectiveness in terms of provision for pupils with special educational needs (SEN). It inevitably concerns itself with both cognitive and socio-psychological outcomes, and on school and individual teacher effect. It considers the relationships between the current research into school effectiveness and the substantive goals for pupils promoted by theoretical perspectives on mainstream provision in special educational needs. The research focuses on a number of agents, policymakers, deliverers and in particular the recipients of that delivery, the pupils themselves. It also addresses some of the complexities brought to light by the interfaces between them. The following questions are considered: 1) What are the substantive criteria by which schools might be considered effective? 2) What might be considered as 'effective' provision for children with SEN? 3) In what ways are these two matched? 4) What do primary schools and the various agents within them perceive as effectiveness in terms of provision for SEN? 5) What degree of convergence occurs in these perceptions? 6) Do schools which are 'effectiveness minded' make a difference for pupils with SEN? 7) At which point in the continuum of system policy to teaching practice might effectiveness best be ensured? 8) How does this align with the varied 'effectiveness' criteria which can be drawn from SEN and school effectiveness research? Data are currently being collected by a three stage progressive focusing methodology using an initial sample of 50 primary schools. Results are expected early in 1998.

STATUS: Individual research

DATE OF RESEARCH: 1993-continuing

KEYWORDS: educational quality; mainstreaming; primary education; school effectiveness; special educational needs

2673

Rydal Road, Ambleside LA22 9BB
01539 433066

Cooper, H. Dr

Young children's thinking in history

ABSTRACT: This research began as a PhD thesis (awarded in 1991, London University, Institute of Education), and has led to further case studies which have been published. It was undertaken originally while the researcher was a full-time primary school teacher, and is an empirical investigation of her practice. Subsequent studies have been undertaken in collaboration with teachers and university initial teacher training students. Theories of cognitive development relevant to children's thinking in history are examined. An experiment is set up to investigate the ability of 3 groups, each consisting of 20 8-year-old children, to make deductions and inferences about a range of historical sources. Teaching strategies based on discussion of key sources using learned concepts are evaluated. Assessment scales, based on cognitive psychology and previous research, were devised. Findings suggested that children of 8-years-old are able to make valid deductions and inferences about pictures, artefacts, diagrams, maps and writing. Discussions were more wide-ranging than written answers, whether an adult was present or not. Teaching strategies influenced the quality of children's responses.

PUBLISHED MATERIAL: COOPER, H.J. (1992). Young children's thinking in history', Teaching History, No 69, pp.8-13. ; COOPER, H.J. (1995). 'The teaching of history in primary schools: implementing the revised National Curriculum. 2nd Edition. London: David Fulton. ; COOPER, H.J. (1994). 'Exploring links between whole-class teaching and small group discussion', TOPIC, Issue 15, Item 2, pp.1-8. ; COOPER, H.J. (1995). History in the early years. Teaching and learning in the first 3 years of school Series. London: Routledge. ; COOPER, H. & COUNSELL, C. (1999). 'History and literacy'. In: ARTHUR, J. & PHILLIPS, R. Issues in the teaching of history. London: Routledge. (in press). A full list of publications is available from the researcher.

STATUS: Individual research

DATE OF RESEARCH: 1988-continuing

KEYWORDS: cognitive development; discussion - teaching technique; educational materials; history; primary education; primary sources; resource materials; scaffolding; teaching methods; thinking skills

2674

Bowerham Road, Lancaster LA1 3JD
01524 384384

Collison, J. Dr

Mentoring relationships and effective mentoring

ABSTRACT: One of the findings of a recent 3-year project (Edwards and Collison, 1996) to study the impact of school-based teacher education within the accelerated degree programme was the fact that the effectiveness of mentoring could be affected by the stance adopted by either or both the mentor and the student teacher. Using the idea of 'addressivity' (from the work of Bakhtin, see for example MORRIS, P. (Ed), (1994). The Bakhtin Reader. London: Edward Arnold) to describe how student teachers and their mentors interacted, the researchers found that they frequently selected a style of interaction that could be described as 'pilot guest/host'. This preoccupation with politeness was a serious handicap preventing the student teachers from viewing themselves, and from being viewed by their mentors, as learners. Clearly there is a need to seek ways of overcoming what we ironically call politeness. The findings of this research have informed subseqent mentor training and have led to the introduction of a programme of student preparation for mentoring; both of which have focused on the position of student teachers as learners in the classroom and appropriate expert/novice relationships. The aim of the current research is to assess the effectiveness of this new style mentor training.

STATUS: Sponsored project

SOURCE OF GRANT: University College of St Martin £1,000

DATE OF RESEARCH: 1996-1997

KEYWORDS: **mentors; preservice teacher education; school based teacher education; student teachers**

2675

Bowerham Road, Lancaster LA1 3JD
01524 384384

Lindley, J. Ms; *Supervisor*: Sikes, P. Dr

Women's careers in special education

ABSTRACT: The research is concerned with women's careers in special education, drawing upon personal life histories to inform outcomes. Using semi-formal interviews in a one-to-one situation, women from different phases of education who are currently working in special education in the North West of England have given taped interviews of their experiences, interweaving professional development with personal narrative. The research is currently at a stage of data collection and it is envisaged that analysis and presentation of findings will be presented in Summer 1999 onwards.

STATUS: Individual research

DATE OF RESEARCH: 1996-continuing

KEYWORDS: **careers; special education teachers; special educational needs; womens employment**

2676

Bowerham Road, Lancaster LA1 3JD
01524 384384

Carroll, S. Ms; *Supervisor*: Lindley, J. Ms

'Use IT': increasing the use of Open and Distance Learning materials by primary level fairground and traveller children

ABSTRACT: The 'Keep IT going' and 'Use IT' project seeks to address the problem of insufficient use of Open and Distance Learning (ODL) materials developed for primary level traveller and fairground traveller children. The project is planned to run for 3 years and initial research has already started. The process will involve collaboration between the Traveller Education Service (TES), in Lancashire; partner schools; and the University College of St Martin. There will be further links with European partners - to be initiated in September 1998. The research will be directed towards the work of TES based in local primary schools and focusing on families and parents of traveller children. The main question in the initial stages of the project is how to motivate traveller children and their parents to participate and use ODL materials. This will be undertaken by teachers working closely in school drop-in centres.

STATUS: Sponsored project

SOURCE OF GRANT: Cormenius II

DATE OF RESEARCH: 1997-continuing

KEYWORDS: **computer uses in education; distance education; information technology; transient children; travellers - itinerants**

2677

Rydal Road, Ambleside LA22 9BB
01539 433066
Lancaster University, Department of Educational Research, Cartmel College, Bailrigg, Lancaster LA1 4YW
01524 65201

Simco, N. Dr; *Supervisor*: Smith, L. Dr

Initial teacher training and professional development within dimensions of classroom activity ambiguity

ABSTRACT: The research seeks to illuminate aspects of the professional development of students undergoing initial teacher training. In particular it aims to richly describe classrooms where students are operating, and to draw from this description common strands of professional progress made by beginning teachers. The study has, as a central focus, the development made along two dimensions of 'ambiguity', namely the degree of activity openness enabled and the degree of teacher clarity in delivering activity. In this respect activity will be described in four 'cells': 1) activity which is open and clear; 2) activity which is closed and clear; 3) activity which is open and vague; 4) activity which is closed and vague. The empirical work has two elements. The first element focuses on the professional progress of ten students during final teaching practice on a B.A. Qualified Teacher Status (QTS) course, and uses semi-structured observation and pre- and post-activity interviews with students, teachers and children. The second strand explores, through a questionnaire, a whole year group's beliefs about the openness and clarity of their teaching prior to and after teaching practice.

PUBLISHED MATERIAL: SIXSMITH, S.C. & SIMCO, N.P. (1994). 'Developing a mentoring scheme in primary initial teacher education', Mentoring and Tutoring, Vol 2, No 1, pp.27-31. ; SIMCO, N.P. (1995). 'Using activity analysis to investigate primary classroom environments', British Educational Research Journal, Vol 21, No 1, pp.49-60. ; SIMCO., N.P. (1995). 'Changes in student teachers' beliefs about classroom activity'. Paper presented to the European Conference on Educational Research, University of Bath, 14-17 September, 1995. ; SIMCO, N.P. & WARIN, J. (1997). 'Validity in image-based research, an elaborated illustration of the issues', British Educational Research Journal, Vol 23, No 5, pp.661-672.

STATUS: Individual research

DATE OF RESEARCH: 1990-1998

KEYWORDS: **classroom environment; preservice teacher education; student teachers; teacher development; teaching practice**

2678

Bowerham Road, Lancaster LA1 3JD
01524 384384
Leeds University, School of Education, Leeds LS2 9JT
01132 431751

Twiselton, S. Mrs; *Supervisors*: Edwards, A. Prof.; Beard, R. Dr

The teaching of literacy in initial teacher training

ABSTRACT: Initial research into the classroom experience of primary student teachers showed that a number of factors (not least the grounds on which they were being assessed by mentors) combined to lead to a focus on management rather than learning. In particular the skill of 'contingent teaching' was being neglected by both students and mentors. The aims of the research are as follows: 1) Identify the range of literacy teaching skills and knowledge demonstrated by students at different stages of their course, and by experienced teachers. 2) Identify the main criteria used by those involved with the assessment of the students. 3) Identify factors related to the development of contingency literacy teaching skills. Twenty to thirty case study students are being tracked through their teacher education course, via observations, interviews and copies of plans etc. The research will also include observations of and interviews with experienced teachers. The research is at an early stage but initial findings show a great difference, according to experience, between the range of strategies and knowledge drawn on at any given moment. The experienced teachers operate within a synchronic framework whereas the trainees are only able to focus on one thing at a time.

PUBLISHED MATERIAL: TWISELTON, S. (1996). 'The assessment of classroom competence: what is actually being assessed and how does it relate to student learning?', Education Section Review, Vol 20, No 1, pp.30-32. ; TWISELTON, S. (1997). 'Contingent literacy teaching: a comparison between novices and expert teachers'. Proceedings of the British Educational Research Association Conference, York University, 1997. ; EDWARDS, A. & TWISELTON, S. (1997). 'Pedagogy: the missing ingredient in primary ITT'. Proceedings of the European Association of Research into Learning and Instruction Conference, Athens, 1997. ; RICHARDS, C., SIMCO, N.,& TWISELTON, S. (Eds). New directions in ITT. London: Falmer Press. (in press). ; EDWARDS, A. & TWISELTON, S. 'Specialist teacher assistants', Junior Education. (in press).

STATUS: Individual research

DATE OF RESEARCH: 1996-continuing

KEYWORDS: **literacy education; preservice teacher education; student teachers; teaching practice; teaching skills**

2679

Bowerham Road, Lancaster LA1 3JD
01524 384384
National Foundation for Educational Research, The Mere, Upton Park, Slough SL1 2DQ
01753 574123

Gates, B. Dr; Taylor, M. Dr

Moral education in teacher training

ABSTRACT: Current debate about values education in schools tends to overlook the need for teacher preparation to deliver a consistent and coherent curricular experience for pupils. To do this teachers require both initial training and continuing professional development. The last survey on religious education in teacher training, which also included moral education, was undertaken in the mid-1980s. This research is an attempt to build an up-to-date picture of teacher training institutions offering moral education courses and the nature of these courses. A survey questionnaire will be sent to all teacher training institutions in England and Wales. It will be followed-up by telephone interviews and analysis of documentation. The information obtained will complement other current inquiries into values education. A report, setting the research data in the context of current national policy, will be produced.

STATUS: Collaborative

DATE OF RESEARCH: 1997-1997

KEYWORDS: **moral education; moral values; preservice teacher education; teacher development; values education**

2680

Bowerham Road, Lancaster LA1 3JD
01524 384384
University College of St Martin, Rydal Road, Ambleside LA22 9BB
01539 433066
Manchester Metropolitan University, Didsbury School of Education, 799 Wilmslow Road, Didsbury, Manchester M20 2RR
0161 247 2000

Jacques, K. Ms; Collison, J. Dr; Richards, C. Prof.; Simco, N. Dr; Richards, C. Prof.; Simco, N. Mr; *Supervisor*: Campbell, A. Prof.

Developing the teaching profession through partnership

ABSTRACT: There are 3 main aims to the project: 1) To determine how trainee teachers learn their craft from mentors in school. 1) To investigate the role of pedagogy and its relationship with effective pupil learning. 3) To develop a typology of successful mentoring. The project draws upon the school-based experiences of students, mentors, college tutors, headteachers and Office for Standards in Education (OFSTED) inspectors. Increased partnership between schools and higher education and other agencies concerned with initial teacher education is having an effect on professionalism, especially the way in which trainees learn to become teachers. The project will provide evidence on the nature of the affects and the quality of newly qualified teachers.

STATUS: Team research

DATE OF RESEARCH: 1997-continuing

KEYWORDS: **institutional cooperation; mentors; newly qualified teachers; partnerships; preservice teacher education; school based teacher education; student teachers; teacher development; teaching profession**

2681

Rydal Road, Ambleside LA22 9BB
01539 433066
University of Lapland, Faculty of Education, PO Box 122, Fin 96101, Rovaniemi, Finland

Cooper, H. Dr; David, R. Mr; Thorley, J. Dr; Huggins, M. Mr; Pekkala, L. Mr

An investigation of what children of primary school age in a range of European countries know and understand about the past and how they acquired that knowledge

ABSTRACT: This research was a pilot study, it is hoped to secure findings for more extensive research. Research related to the teaching and learning of history throughout Europe was discussed at a meeting of experts organised by the Council of Europe, in Strasbourg, in 1995 (DECS/Rech (95) 30). In response to the question 'How and where do young people of school age acquire their notion of history?' it was agreed that history teaching in school has to take account of pupils' out-of-school notions, prejudices and stereotypical ideas. Children in primary school are rarely taught history. Therefore the ideas about the past which they acquire before formal history education begins are significant. A small pilot study was undertaken collaboratively by researchers in Britain, Romania, Lapland, Greece and Holland. The sample of children in each country consists of groups of children in the 7-8 year-old age range and in the 10-11 year-old age range. Each group of children using their mother tongue made a concept map showing what they knew about the past and how they knew it. Data for each country was translated into English and analysed using common categories. Data from the 5 countries was collated and evaluated, and questions for further research were identified.

PUBLISHED MATERIAL: COOPER, H.J. (1997). 'Yabba-dabba-doo! It's time for the history lesson', Times Educational Supplement, Research Focus, 10 October 1997, p.18. ; COOPER, H. 'The European dimension: what do children know about the past in countries where there is no primary curriculum?'. In: ARTHUR, J. & PHILLIPS, R. (Eds). Issues in the teaching of history. London: Routledge. (in press). ; A full list of publications is available from the researchers.

STATUS: Collaborative

DATE OF RESEARCH: 1995-continuing

KEYWORDS: **europe; history; knowledge level; primary education; primary school pupils**

University College Scarborough

2682

Filey Road, Scarborough YO11 3AZ
01723 370815

Coman, P. Mr; *Supervisor*: Williams, R. Mr

Primary school pupils' perceptions of German people: the effects of studying the National Curriculum unit 'Britain since 1930'

ABSTRACT: The research examines the impact of an aspect of the National Curriculum key stage 2 in History. Specifically it examines the effect of the topic 'Britain since 1930' upon pupil perceptions of German people. It involves 3 focus schools and a wider sample of 20 schools for corroborative data. It involves both qualitative and quantitative methods, including questionnaire, content analysis, observation of teaching, field notes and an adaptation of Kelly's Repertory Grid. Results indicate that the topic makes pupils more favourably disposed to contemporary German people because it sets the war within a limited historical context. Girls are more strongly influenced in a favourable direction by the topic, regarding contemporary German people as less aggressive, more socially acceptable and more like British people than they did previously. However, both girls and boys retain a suspicion of an apparently innate German pre-disposition to war that lies beneath the surface as a hidden character flaw.

PUBLISHED MATERIAL: COMAN, P. (1996). 'Reading about the enemy: school textbook representation of Germany's role in the war with Britain during the period from April 1940 to May 1941', British Journal of Sociology of Education, Vol 17, No 3, pp.327-340.

STATUS: Individual research

DATE OF RESEARCH: 1993-1998

KEYWORDS: german people; history; national curriculum; primary education; pupil attitudes; war

University College Suffolk

2683

Suffolk College, Ipswich IP4 1LT
01473 255885

Greig, A. Dr; *Supervisor*: Hinde, R. Prof.

Communication and relationships at playgroup

ABSTRACT: The original PhD research was carried out at Cambridge University between 1988 and 1992. The study aim was to investigate the role of interpersonal relationships in communication of preschool children. Twenty-four males and 24 females were selected to take part according to strict friendship criteria. The age range was 3.5 to 4.5 years. Same-sex pairs of friends and non-friends (1 child on 2 occasions; once with a friend and once with a non-friend) were observed playing in a naturalistic Wendy house situation (standardised) on 3 successive 15 minute sessions. In addition, 4 pairs of cross-sex pairs were examined. Parents of the subjects were interviewed, and the researchers conducted temperament Q-sorts on the child, and parenting attitude questionnaires. Temperament Q-sorts remain unanalysed. The results indicate that communication of ideas, action and emotion are unaffected by parenting beliefs. Cognitive aspects are largely unaffected by friendship status between children. It is in the area of emotion that friendship appears to make a difference to communication and the effect is different across males and females. The research may now continue on social dominance and communication. There are also possibilities for publications.

STATUS: Individual research

DATE OF RESEARCH: 1988-continuing

KEYWORDS: communication research; friendship; peer relationship; play groups; preschool children

2684

Suffolk College, Ipswich IP4 1LT
01473 255885

Robinson, J. Ms; Leamon, J. Ms

Documentary analysis of nursing degree curricula in England (DANCE project)

ABSTRACT: The recent proliferation of undergraduate programmes in nursing has created a situation where it is difficult to know the extent to which degrees in nursing are comparable in terms of scope and academic level. This research aims to: 1) compare and contrast the way in which degree programmes are organised, structures which support them and their relationship with other programmes, as described in curriculum documents; 2) examine the way programme content is described and extent to which they are integrated to relate to nursing; 3) compare learning outcomes in relation to teaching and learning methods, assessment strategies, notions of academic progression and achievement of degree level work; 4) describe range and nature of variation which exists nationally between nursing degree courses. Curricula documents from 40 nursing degree courses will be subjected to documentary analysis, sampled to include the majority of pre-registration degrees and a cross section of post-registration degrees.

STATUS: Sponsored project

SOURCE OF GRANT: English National Board for Nurses, Midwives and Health Visitors £30,000

DATE OF RESEARCH: 1997-1998

KEYWORDS: curriculum development; nurse education; nurses

University College Worcester

2685

Henwick Grove, Worcester WR2 6AJ
01905 855000

Emery, H. Mrs; Picard, P. Ms; *Supervisor*: Phillipson, S. Mr

Pattern of teaching and learning at National Curriculum key stage 2

ABSTRACT: The objectives are to be achieved by working with local education authority (LEA) inspection teams and eight individual case study schools in Hereford and Worcester, and Sandwell. They are to: 1) Develop a picture of the nature of teaching and learning in National Curriculum key stage 2 in the two LEAs, focusing particularly upon patterns of curriculum and classroom organisation in the case study schools. 2) Work in partnership with eight case study schools on key concerns they are developing in implementing the National Curriculum at key stage 2 and how the College can support them. Particularly focusing on developing mentoring for teaching experience placements, and developing initial teacher training (ITT) courses and inservice teacher education (INSET) provision. 3) Provide specific feedback on examples of teaching and learning in reading. 4) Provide staff development for members of the College's Later Primary Years Team by participating in the survey. The case study schools reflect a range of sizes, locations and patterns of organisation. At the end of the research a conference will be held for schools to share their development work with others.

STATUS: Sponsored project

SOURCE OF GRANT: Worcester College of Higher Education £5,000

DATE OF RESEARCH: 1993-1993

KEYWORDS: classroom research; learning strategies; national curriculum; primary education; reading teaching; teaching methods

2686

Henwick Grove, Worcester WR2 6AJ
01905 855000

Wakefield, P. Mr; Ghaye, A. Dr

Successful schools

ABSTRACT: This was a collaborative, action research project between Worcester College of Higher Education, the National Primary Centre, and Sandwell, Solihull, Walsall and Wolverhampton local education authorities (LEAs), which enabled all those in a school's community to get a better understanding of the factors and influences upon school success. Thirty-six schools in the four local education authorities in the West Midlands participated in the project. The three main features of the resulting report are: 1) That the 'voices' of children, teachers, LEA officers and other adults are reported and analysed. 2) The school findings are related to contemporary research on school improvement. 3) The presentation of eight features which our research tells us are characteristics of developing all successful schools.

PUBLISHED MATERIAL: NATIONAL PRIMARY CENTRE. (1993). Disadvantaged but successful: successful schools. Oxford: National Primary Centre.

STATUS: Sponsored project

SOURCE OF GRANT: Sandwell Local Education Authority; Solihull Local Education Authority; Walsall Local Education Authority; Wolverhampton Local Education Authority, jointly: £10,000

DATE OF RESEARCH: 1991-1993

KEYWORDS: educational quality; school effectiveness; success

2687

Henwick Grove, Worcester WR2 6AJ
01905 855000

Mould, C. Mrs; *Supervisor*: Pascal, C. Prof.

The influence of teachers' learning stance on the effectiveness of the early learning of four year olds in schools in England

ABSTRACT: The aim of this research is to critically analyse and evaluate the relationship between four year old children and teachers in effective early learning throughout a diverse range of schools in England. The research study stems from the belief that interactions between the adult and the child are critically significant in determining the effective nature of the learning experience. A methodological triangulation approach has been adopted, producing both qualitative and quantitative data. To further refine validity a democratic approach to quality evaluation is respected throughout. The research framework divides into two separate yet interdependent studies. 1) Empirical research: investigating, documenting and assessing attitudinal qualities teachers demonstrate and the significance these have on teaching effectiveness. The study focused on ten Birmingham local education authority (LEA) schools with four year olds in their reception classes. (Fieldwork period February - April 1995). 2) Collaborative action research: data obtained from four of the experimental groups that participated in the original fieldwork. The researcher is working collaboratively with the class teacher. (Fieldwork period October 1995-May 1996). Assessment focused on two significant factors in the quality of learning facilitation: a) child's level of involvement during the process; b) form of attitudinal qualities demonstrated by the teacher to support and facilitate learning. The rigorous analysis of this original research provided the foundation of the collaborative action research study. The empirical observations proved to be a critical stage in establishing a firm grounding for collaborative extension. A growing awareness of the role of the pedagogue flavoured the approach. This initiated the concept of extending the research focus with known participants. During eighteen months the researcher and the teacher will be developing in unison, the outcome being one of professional development for both. This consequently leads to an enhanced effectiveness of the early learning for young children. It is proposed that the role of the researcher in the classroom could be extended as a form of inservice training. It is intended that this research will be used as a form of development that maximises the unique potential of the person behind the professional. Practitioners could utilise this approach as part of their professional development and inservice training.

PUBLISHED MATERIAL: MOULD, C. (1995). 'The influence of teachers' learning stance on the effectiveness of the early learning of four year olds in schools in England'. Paper presented at the Annual European Conference on the Quality of Early Childhood Education, Paris, 7-9 September 1995.

STATUS: Individual research

DATE OF RESEARCH: 1994-1997

KEYWORDS: early childhood education; educational quality; primary education; teacher effectiveness; young children

2688

Henwick Grove, Worcester WR2 6AJ
01905 855000

Pascal, C. Prof.; Bertram, A. Mr

Four year olds in reception classes in Birmingham

ABSTRACT: The project is an 18 month study of the quality of educational provision for four year old children in Birmingham primary schools. This authority has had a policy of annual admission to primary schools for over 10 years. The aim of this project is to document systematically the quality of provision and practice offered to the four year olds in all Birmingham primary schools, as a basis for a programme of quality improvement across the Authority. Evidence will be gathered in the first phase (January 1996-June 1996) on a cohort of 200+ primary schools using qualitative and quantitative methods, including structured observations, interviews and questionnaires. In the second phase a sample of these schools (20%) will be followed up in more depth to provde detailed material to guide the development of policy and practice in the Authority.

PUBLISHED MATERIAL: PASCAL, C. (1990). Under-fives in the infant classroom. Stoke-on-Trent: Trentham Books.

STATUS: Sponsored project

SOURCE OF GRANT: Birmingham Local Education Authority £60,000

DATE OF RESEARCH: 1996-1997

KEYWORDS: early admission; early childhood education; primary education; reception classes; school entrance age; young children

2689

Henwick Grove, Worcester WR2 6AJ
01905 855000

Elliott, G. Dr

Preparation for higher education: the context of effective student learning

ABSTRACT: This is a case study of the context of effective student learning, which focuses upon courses and programmes designed to prepare students for higher education (HE). Many argue that incorporation has encouraged a flourishing 'market' in post-compulsory education, which has driven both competitive and collaborative relationships within and between the further education and higher education sectors. Critical analysis of the present further/higher education context, including the extent to which modular and credit-based structures are manifestations of consumerism in education, informs the work. Access and Foundation courses are increasingly characterised by modules and credits with the majority now assimilated within the Open College Network. This research questions whether such schemes presage an increase in scheme-driven bureaucracy, and asks whether segmentation of qualification structures serves the needs of learners. The role of learner support is a particular focus of this study, which is based upon the expectations and experiences of a group of 12 Access and Foundation full-time students as they proceed through their one year programme. The data is drawn from direct observations, reflective accounts, and semi-structured open-ended interviews. A qualitative data computer software package is employed in data analysis. A theoretical framework is being developed, based upon the model of critical student-centred pedagogy developed by Paulo Freire. This approach is particularly appropriate to an analysis of educational structures and processes which takes adequate account of the characteristics and needs of adult learners, as well as a pervasive and interrelated range of social and political factors.

PUBLISHED MATERIAL: ELLIOTT, G. (1995). 'Managing Access: preparing mature students for higher education', Innovation and Learning in Education, Vol 1, No 2, pp.10-16. ; ELLIOTT, G. (1996). Crisis and change in vocational education and training. Higher Education Policy Series Vol 36. London: Jessica Kingsley.

STATUS: Individual research

DATE OF RESEARCH: 1995-1997

KEYWORDS: access programmes; access to education; further education; higher education; introductory courses; mature students; nontraditional students; students

2690

Henwick Grove, Worcester WR2 6AJ
01905 855000
Brighton University, Faculty of Education, Sport and Leisure, Falmer, Brighton BN1 9PH
01273 600900
Sheffield Hallam University, Mathematics Education Centre, 25 Broomgrove Road, Sheffield S10 2NA
01142 720911

Perkins, M. Mrs; Supervisors: Ghaye, A. Dr; Dombey, H. Prof.; Cashdan, A. Prof.

The preparation of student teachers to be teachers of reading

ABSTRACT: The overall aim is to explore the nature of the knowledge required to be an effective teacher of reading. Within the above aim it is expected that the following objectives will also be addressed: 1) To analyse the primary professional English initial teacher education (ITE) courses at Worcester College of Higher Education; 2) To explore the extent to which the courses satisfy the perceived needs of college, students, schools and other external demands; 3) To identify effective teaching and learning strategies, to improve the quality of primary professional work in reading at the College. One of the main concerns in primary initial teacher education is the preparation of students to be teachers of reading and this concern is emphasised in the Department for Education Circular 14/93: The Initial Training of Primary School Teachers - New Criteria for Courses. Her Majesty's Inspectorate (HMI) reports in 1989 and 1993 on the teaching of reading in primary schools indicate that the quality of teaching is the key factor in pupils' success or otherwise, and that 'practice was not underpinned by sufficiently clear, coherent and comprehensive reading policies'. This has implications for the training of teachers as is identified in Circular 14/93 which specifies time to be spent on reading by student but not the specific content of that time. This study aims to explore that area by looking in depth at work in one institution. This case study will generate a knowledge base of the pre-requisites for a teacher of reading. Principally the study will use an action research approach, supported by a phenomenographic perspective in which teaching will be reflected on and analysed in order to improve practice. The model to be used is called 'emancipatory action research', which critically examines values underpinning behaviours. The starting point for the research is: 'What do I need to know in order to be an effective teacher of reading?' and 'How can I best communicate this knowledge to others?'. The focus of the research, therefore, is the knowledge, beliefs and experiences necessary for the teacher of reading and how these are transmitted to intending teachers. It is expected that the knowledge thus gained will impinge on both ITE and inservice teacher education (INSET) courses and that the research will be a key feature in both staff and course development. Data will be collected and triangulated through: a) reflective journals kept by the researcher and another member of the course team; b) video recordings of selected teaching sessions; c) interviews with approximately 36 students on the primary BA Qualified Teacher Status (QTS) course, 12 teachers, a local education authority (LEA) adviser and 3 College tutors; d) formal and public documentation - course outlines, student handouts, assignments, government documentation and documentation from at least one other institution. Analysis of the perceptions of the participants, including the researcher, will be within the phenomenographic paradigm, creating 'categories of description' about the teaching of reading. From these a knowledge base will be formed which will be used in planning future student experiences to prepare them as teachers of reading.

STATUS: Individual research

DATE OF RESEARCH: 1994-1998

KEYWORDS: **preservice teacher education; primary school teachers; reading teachers; reading teaching; student teachers**

University of Central England in Birmingham

2691

Centre for Research into Quality, 90 Aldridge Road, Perry Barr, Birmingham B42 2TP
0121 331 5000

Harvey, L. Prof.; Moon, S. Ms; Geall, V. Ms; Bower, R. Mr; Bowes, L. Ms; Montague, G. Ms

Graduates' work: organisational change and students' attributes

ABSTRACT: Graduates' Work systematically explores the views of a wide range of employers and recent graduates to identify the knowledge, abilities and skills that future graduates will need to be successful at work. Over 250 indepth semi-structured interviews were conducted in over 90 organisations: large and small, public and private, manufacturing and service, and not for profit. Respondents were specifically invited to comment on the changing nature and subsequent needs of employing organisations and what skills and abilities graduates would need to be successful within them. Respondents were probed for clear definitions of the types and abilities they sought in new recruits and their reasons for seeking them. Interviewees were also asked whether they felt that degree courses equipped students with these skills and, if not, what was the best method of obtaining them. Teamworking, communication and inter-personal skills along with intellect, flexibility, adaptability and a willingness to learn were identified as some of the essential skills for success at work. Employers and graduates felt that degree programmes enabled students to develop some of these skills, but identified work experience as the most effective way to become 'work-ready'.

STATUS: Sponsored project

SOURCE OF GRANT: Council for Industry and Higher Education; Department for Education and Employment; Association of Graduate Recruiters

DATE OF RESEARCH: 1996-1997

KEYWORDS: **employer attitudes; employers; graduate employment; graduate surveys; higher education; work education relationship; work experience**

2692

Centre for Research into Quality, 90 Aldridge Road, Perry Barr, Birmingham B42 2TP
0121 331 5000

Bowes, L. Ms; Blackwell, A. Ms; Williams, A. Ms; Williamson, E. Ms

A report of staff and student perceptions of the impact of the reforms to the student funding arrangements

ABSTRACT: There has been much speculation about the impact of Government's reforms to the student funding arrangements on students and the higher education (HE) sector as a whole. The University of Central England is monitoring the perceived and actual impact of these reforms in a longitudinal study. All staff and a quarter of the student population were, and will continue to be, surveyed on an annual basis to gauge their perceptions of the impact of the changes. In 1998, a questionnaire was used to survey staff and students. Students were asked to rate the extent to which they agreed with the Government's decision to introduce fees and abolish maintenance in the finance section of the annual student satisfaction survey. Three-quarters of full-time students stated that they strongly disagreed with the decision to introduce fees and over 80% strongly disagreed with the abolition of maintenance. Staff were asked in a more extensive survey to rate the extent to which they believed that the reforms would impact on aspects of the HE sector, the student profile, welfare and support services, staff and the institution and whether this impact would be positive or negative. Qualitative comments on each of the areas were also invited. Preliminary findings demonstrate that staff overwhelmingly disagree with the reforms and believe that they will have a strong negative impact on most of the above. Staff are particularly concerned that students will become more instrumental in their approach to higher education and choose courses with both a vocational bent and high earning potential.

STATUS: Sponsored project

SOURCE OF GRANT: University of Central England in Birmingham

DATE OF RESEARCH: 1998-continuing

KEYWORDS: **educational finance; grants; higher education; student financial aid; student loans**

2693

Centre for Research into Quality, 90 Aldridge Road, Perry Barr, Birmingham B42 2TP
0121 331 5000

Harvey, L. Prof.; Blackwell, A. Ms; Bowes, L. Ms; Aston, J. Ms; Geall, V. Ms; Moon, S. Ms

A report of staff satisfaction at the University of Central England in Birmingham

ABSTRACT: The Staff Satisfaction Survey is a large-scale quantitative survey conducted at the University of Central England (UCE). It is designed to elicit academic and non-academic staffs' views of their experience as a UCE employee. The results of the survey identify clear areas for action and feed directly into the strategic planning processes at the institution. A questionnaire is used to survey all staff, with the exception of visiting lecturers and other hourly paid staff and weekly paid manual workers for whom the majority of the questionnaire is irrelevant. Staff generate the issues that are included in the questionnaire through focused-group discussions. Respondents are asked to indicate their satisfaction with, and the importance of, all aspects of their experience as a UCE employee. The satisfaction and importance scores are aggregated, combined and converted into a letter, A-E. The results are reported in tabular form, where an upper case 'A' denotes an important area of satisfaction and an upper case 'D' or 'E' denotes an important area of dissatisfaction. The tables are used basis for consultation between the Vice-Chancellor and Deans and Heads of Services where strategies for improvement are agreed. Staff expressed dissatisfaction with a number of aspects of their employment. Action since the survey has focused on staff development opportunities, communication and the academic environment.

STATUS: Sponsored project

SOURCE OF GRANT: University of Central England in Birmingham

DATE OF RESEARCH: 1996-1997

KEYWORDS: **academic staff; higher education; job satisfaction; support staff; universities; work attitudes**

2694

Centre for Research into Quality, 90 Aldridge Road, Perry Barr, Birmingham B42 2TP
0121 331 5000

Aston, J. Ms; Blackwell, A. Ms; Williamson, E. Ms; Williams, A. Ms; Harvey, L. Prof.; Bowes, L. Ms

The 1998 report on the student experience at University of Central England in Birmingham

ABSTRACT: The student satisfaction survey is conducted on an annual basis at the University of Central England (UCE). It is a large quantitative survey designed to elicit students' views of their total student experience. The results of the survey identify clear areas for action and feed directly into the strategic planning processes at the institution. A questionnaire is used to survey a quarter of the students at UCE. The questions are generated from issues raised by students in Group Feedback Strategy. Respondents are asked to indicate their satisfaction with, and the importance of, all aspects of their experience as a student at UCE. The satisfaction and importance scores are aggregated, combined and converted into a letter, A-E. The results are reported in tabular form, where an upper case 'A' denotes an important area of satisfaction and an upper case 'D' or 'E' denotes an important area of dissatisfaction. The tables are used as a basis for consultation between the Vice-Chancellor and Deans and Heads of Services where strategies for improvement are agreed.

STATUS: Sponsored project

SOURCE OF GRANT: University of Central England in Birmingham

DATE OF RESEARCH: 1997-1998

KEYWORDS: **educational experience; higher education; student attitudes; students; universities**

2695

Faculty of Education, Westbourne Road, Edgbaston, Birmingham B15 3TN
0121 331 6100

Cavendish, M. Mr; *Supervisors*: Hellawell, D. Prof.; Hall, E. Miss; Hatcher, R. Mr

Going grant-maintained: a case study of change from a management perspective

ABSTRACT: The Education Reform Act (1988) provided for a new category of school known as 'grant maintained'. These schools, owned and managed by their governing bodies, have evoked considerable controversy since the first few were introduced in 1989. One of these early self-governing schools is the setting for a case-study undertaken by its headteacher who explores how change was managed, particularly by governors, associate staff and members of the school's senior management team. Data is gathered from extensive one-to-one dialogues and group sessions which explore individual perceptions of the change process. The researcher also draws on evidence from personal field notes and from relevant documents. It is argued that some theories about management processes in schools need to take more account of the person-centred approach. Case-studies can reveal a greater complexity than is sometimes admitted. The writer asserts that data gathering and analysis from within a school, in this case by the headteacher, demonstrates most strikingly the need for more detailed studies of the roles of the principal actors when evaluating the management of change. In particular, attention is drawn to the importance for researchers in educational management of exploring the unpredictability of change processes. The writer concludes that the successful management of change is often unplanned and that implementation failure often has its roots in interpersonal relationships. Where change is successfully managed there tends to have been a climate of trust, openness and positive regard within the institutions.

STATUS: Individual research

DATE OF RESEARCH: 1991-continuing

KEYWORDS: **educational administration; educational change; grant maintained schools; management in education; school based management**

2696

Faculty of Education, Westbourne Road, Edgbaston, Birmingham B15 3TN
0121 331 6100

Brooks, R. Ms; Duckworth, R. Ms; *Supervisor*: Hellawell, D. Prof.

Social skills training in the classroom: effects on sociometric status

ABSTRACT: The aims of this research are: (1) To present a review of current sociometric research and materials in the area of children's friendship choices and social adjustment in the classroom. (2) Use sociographic techniques to assess the patterns of specific friendship choices which exist in classes (e.g. popular children, reciprocated pairs, isolates, etc.). (3) Assess the personality and behavioural characteristics of specific 'types' of children (as identified in (2) using the Junior Eysenck and behavioural observations. (4) Intervene to coach the identified 'isolated' children in specific social skills, e.g. asking questions, offering directions to peers. (5) Ascertain what effect/s the social skill training (as in (4)) has on overall peer acceptance and popularity within the class. (6) Provide an indepth examination of individual isolates, including the perceptions of friendship, and reasons for sociometric choices made. (7) For individual isolates (as in (6)) examine the family structure, number of siblings, contact with other social networks (e.g. clubs, church) which affect their social experience and competence.

STATUS: Individual research

DATE OF RESEARCH: 1992-1997

KEYWORDS: **friendship; intergroup relations; interpersonal competence; peer relationship; pupil behaviour; social isolation; social skills**

2697

Faculty of Education, Westbourne Road, Edgbaston, Birmingham B15 3TN
0121 331 6100

Harrison, D. Mrs; *Supervisor*: Brown, K. Mr

Development and progress of special educational needs provision in mainstream: using an interdisciplinary approach to enhance provision for special educational needs in a mainstream school

ABSTRACT: This research will involve: a) Investigation of mainstream provision for special educational needs in Birmingham: attitudes of headteachers, teachers and critical friends to pupil support; constraints under which providers and purchasers consider themselves to be working, i.e. government funding, political will, availability of relevant professional support and resources in Central England. b) Investigation of the strategies in use by teachers at stages 1 and 2 of the Code of Practice and a comparative study of provision for a sample of 3 pupils with special needs comprising case studies which will investigate their progress over a 3 year period. c) Investigation of a networking system involving an interdisciplinary approach between departments of education, housing, health and social services which can be compared to existing provision as in (b). Strategies to support pupils at stages 1 and 2 of the Code of Practice, as well as the class teacher and special needs coordinator prior to statutory assessment and statementing which will be drawn up, trialled and evaluated for their effect upon the quality of learning in the classroom as a whole, since 'what is good practice for special educational needs is good practice for all'. Results will be analysed and effective strategies shared throughout the disciplines involved.

STATUS: Individual research

DATE OF RESEARCH: 1995-1997

KEYWORDS: **agency cooperation; code of practice; mainstreaming; special educational needs**

2698

Faculty of Education, Westbourne Road, Edgbaston, Birmingham B15 3TN
0121 331 6100

Eyles, J. Mrs; *Supervisors*: Eggleston, J. Prof.; Hoskyns, J. Dr

Initial teacher training and the development of partnership with schools

ABSTRACT: Framed in the context of the present political climate it is hypothesised that the involvement of primary schools in the professional training and education of initial teacher training students will be that of 'partnership'. Partnership schemes with initial training establishments will lead to different patterns of education and training for students and some of these may be delivered more effectively than in conventional schemes. The key aspects of this research will be to: 1) explore primary headteachers' views of their schools' involvement in teacher training and education; 2) carry out an indepth analysis and evaluation of the involvement of schools in the West Midlands with the University of Central England in the professional training and education of initial teacher training students; 3) consider the quality of training provision; and 4) place all of this in the current political context.

STATUS: Individual research

DATE OF RESEARCH: 1994-1998

KEYWORDS: head teachers; institutional cooperation; partnerships; preservice teacher education; school based teacher education

2699

Faculty of Education, Westbourne Road, Edgbaston, Birmingham B15 3TN
0121 331 6100

McGrath, J. Mr; *Supervisor*: Franklin, L. Dr

Lifelong learning - barriers and opportunities: a case study

ABSTRACT: A case study of how mature non-traditional students who have decided to undertake university level education for the first time. The aim of the research will be to identify the factors which prompted the students to participate in higher education for the first time and to detail the decision-making process that they went through.

STATUS: Individual research

DATE OF RESEARCH: 1997-continuing

KEYWORDS: higher education; mature students; nontraditional students

2700

Faculty of Education, Westbourne Road, Edgbaston, Birmingham B15 3TN
0121 331 6100
Newman College, Genners Lane, Bartley Green, Birmingham B32 3NT
0121 476 1181

Miller, S. Mr; Taylor, P. Prof.; *Supervisor*: Hellawell, D. Prof.

The teacher education curriculum in the member states of the European Community

ABSTRACT: The basis of the research was an initial survey of the existing literature and its reflective analysis. This was followed by two stages of empirical enquiry: the first was based on a structured questionnaire, the rationale for which was provided by the analysis of the research literature; the second was based on sample interviews in six member states of the European Community. Data for a final section of the research was based on the work undertaken by the European Community to foster between-country activities in the field of teacher education.

PUBLISHED MATERIAL: HELLAWELL, D., MILLER, S. & TAYLOR, P. (1993). The teacher education curriculum in the member states of the European Community. Brussels: Association for Teacher Education in Europe.

STATUS: Sponsored project

SOURCE OF GRANT: Commission of the European Communities, Brussels £20,000

DATE OF RESEARCH: 1991-1993

KEYWORDS: european union; preservice teacher education; teacher education curriculum

2701

Faculty of Education, Westbourne Road, Edgbaston, Birmingham B15 3TN
0121 331 6100
Worcester College of Technology, Deansway, Worcester WR1 2JF
01905 725555

Allard, W. Mrs; *Supervisors*: Hellawell, D. Prof.; Franklin, L. Dr

Management in further education - a case study

ABSTRACT: The role of further education (FE) in the provision of management development and training for managers operating in the health care sector has experienced potent changes over the last 6 years. The context for this research into the implications of policy changes at a macro and micro level is based on 3 discrete but interrelating dimensions. Firstly, the implementation of the National Health Service (NHS) and Community Care Act 1990 which has introduced major cultural changes within the NHS and has had a significant influence on the roles and responsibilities of care sector managers. Secondly, the revolution that has taken place in terms of the approach to the design and delivery of management programmes in response to the evolution of management and the corresponding shift in qualifications. Thirdly, the effect of incorporation and the impact of applying private sector management techniques in FE and the subsequent effect on the way the first two points are addressed. This thesis is essentially a case study of cultural change researched and managed through a detailed study of Worcester Management Centre which is an autonomous arm of Worcester College of Technology. Initially, the investigation aimed to systematically review, analyse and interpret in order to address the following primary and secondary aims. Primary aims: 1) to assess the effect of applying private sector management techniques in FE on the choice of management development programmes which should be delivered; 2) to analyse the impact of incorporation on the future provision of management qualifications. Secondary aims: 1) to focus on the shift in emphasis from traditional to competence-based management programmes relevant to the development of managers; 2) to provide evidence which may be interpreted and applied by education and training providers. The researcher's contribution to the body of academic knowledge on educational management arises from an investigation and interpretation of the implications for managers in the future. This is an attempt to present more than a philosophical dialogue which dissects the emergent themes underlying management philosophy. Instead, this thesis offers an informed and worthwhile contribution which sets the parameters for a critique through the eyes of a participant researcher facilitator. By seeking to establish parameters, the researcher was able to develop a real understanding and recognition of the significance of social relationships and sensitivities at a variety of organisational levels. The contribution emerges through a simultaneous analysis of the constituent parts of the organisation at operational and strategic levels which was reinforced by the imperative to remain connected to the whole picture. This led to a set of interpretations and perceptions that suggested successful educational management in the future will be characterised by the following features: 1) a research dominated and facilitative style of management which encourages a re-definition of the role of the manager as a researcher facilitator; 2) a management style focused on positive realism; 3) management by association; and 4) emergent virtual organisations as natural environments and vehicles for the fostering of learning cultures and continuing professional development.

PUBLISHED MATERIAL: A full list of publications is available from the researcher.

STATUS: Individual research

DATE OF RESEARCH: 1997-1998

KEYWORDS: educational administration; further education; management in education

University of Central Lancashire

2702

Department of Chemistry, Preston PR1 2HE
01772 201201

Dodd, J. Dr; *Supervisor*: Hart, A. Mrs

A competence framework in chemistry

ABSTRACT: Recent changes in Business and Technology Education Council (BTEC) policy towards 'competences and transferable skills' call for an urgent response from course teams. The Faculty of Science at the University of Lancashire has granted the research a six-month secondment (February-August 1992) to make progress in this area. The aim of the project was to develop a competence framework, primarily (but not exclusively) for HND/HNC courses in chemistry - along with supporting materials and delivery systems. The activities involved liaison with other course teams in Faculty/University, and with the Faculty Support Group; visits to other institutions (to discover examples of good practice); consultation in industry to provide resource material, and to discuss joint assessment procedures in student placements and works based projects; and the development of related student centred learning materials. The outcomes of the research provided a coherent strategy for a competence framework in BTEC chemistry/science courses; the development of quality materials for use in teaching/learning situations; and the facilitating (and assessment) of transferable skills within the curriculum.

STATUS: Sponsored project

SOURCE OF GRANT: Enterprise and Higher Education £2,500

DATE OF RESEARCH: 1992-1993

KEYWORDS: business and technology education council; chemistry; competency based education; science education; skills; transfer of learning

2703

Department of Computing, Preston PR1 2HE
01772 201201
Sheffield University, Division of Education, 388 Glossop Road, Sheffield S10 2JA
01142 768555

Mallatratt, J. Dr; *Supervisor*: Opie, C. Dr

Inservice education and training (INSET) to support information technology (IT) use across the secondary curriculum

ABSTRACT: The research focused upon the effectiveness of Government policies aimed at supporting teachers to use information technology (IT) within the delivery of other subjects in the curriculum. The approach to the research was to follow the processes of formulation and implementation of national policies intended to affect inservice education and training (INSET) related to information technology. The main programmes included were the Local Education Authority Training Grants Scheme (LEATGS), the Education Support Grants (ESG) scheme and the Technical and Vocational Education Initiative (TVEI). The sample was comprised of five local education authorities (LEAs) within England and Wales, chosen to give variation in size and in nature (e.g. rural and urban). Within these authorities, twenty-nine schools were selected for detailed investigation. Approximately seventy key personnel, involved in the development and implementation of national, local and school policies, were identified and given extended interviews. Data was further triangulated by the use of a questionnaire with a simple random sample of 30% of the teachers in the selected schools. The research established that, although a significant amount of training had been delivered which was aimed at improving the capability of teachers to use IT within their own subject domains, much of the training had not been as effective as it might have been. The findings from previous studies into the correlates of effective INSET, appeared to have been ignored by some of the key personnel involved either in the design or delivery of IT-related INSET provision.

PUBLISHED MATERIAL: MALLATRATT, J. (1990). 'A review of the effectiveness of national policies in the UK aimed at providing inservice training support to teachers to enable them to use computers in non-computing subjects'. Paper presented at EURIT 90, Herning, Denmark, April 1990. ; MALLATRATT, J. (1990). 'Needs and provision: a consideration of the inservice education and training of teachers to use computers across the secondary school curriculum', Computer Education, No 64, pp.25-27. ; MALLATRATT, J. (1992). 'Staff development (INSET) policies to support the use of IT across the curriculum: the good news'. Paper presented at IDATER 92, Loughborough University of Technology, September 1992. ; MALLATRATT, J. (1993). 'The preparation of teachers to use information technology across the curriculum: a critique of the approaches in England and Wales'. Paper presented at IFIP WG 3.1/3.5 Open Conference: Information and Changes in Learning, Gmunden, Austria, June 1993.

STATUS: Individual research

DATE OF RESEARCH: 1987-1993

KEYWORDS: **computer uses in education; information technology; inservice teacher education**

2704

Department of Education Studies, Preston PR1 2HE
01772 201201
University of Amsterdam, Network Educational Science, Grose Bickerstraat, Amsterdam, Netherlands
Aristotle University, Thessaloniki, Greece

Heywood-Everett, G. Dr; Billingham, S. Dr; Alkan, M. Dr; Papanoum, Z. Dr

Parents and schools (PAS) project

ABSTRACT: The aim of this research was to ascertain the degree of consensus or dissonance between teachers' and parents' views over a critical range of issues. Its design looked to a group problem-solving approach whereby parents and teachers (separately and then together) engaged in an activity which produced quantitative and qualitative data concerning their mutual priorities. 5 schools (UK) and 4 schools (Greece) took part in the first stage of the project. A further 2 schools (The Netherlands) will be reporting from their own approach. In all cases, the schools were at the primary level. Parent groups were self-selecting whereas in each of the

schools, all school staff participated. Preliminary results indicate a marked difference in priorities between parents and teachers over issues to be discussed. In the main (across the Greek and UK schools) teachers were interested in policy-oriented discussions with parents whereas parents tended to be interested in classroom-based discussions with teachers. This has real implications for how parents are perceived, not only as a cohesive group, but also as 'partners' with teachers as promoted by ideologists of inclusiveness across Europe.

PUBLISHED MATERIAL: HEYWOOD-EVERETT, G. 'Problem-solving as home:school strategy and research methodology', Educational Research and Evaluation. (in press).

STATUS: Sponsored project

SOURCE OF GRANT: European Union: Task Force for Social Sciences £17,000

DATE OF RESEARCH: 1994-1998

KEYWORDS: **comparative education; ethnic groups; greece; netherlands; parent participation; parent school relationship**

2705

Department of Psychology, Preston
01772 201201
Wolverhampton University, Department of Psychology, Molineux Street, Wolverhampton WV1 1SB
01902 321000

McDonald, M. Ms

Gender roles in adolescent girls

ABSTRACT: A sample of 43 girls aged 10-15 years from the northwest of the United Kingdom were interviewed about their own, and other girls' preferences and choices regarding sports, school subjects, occupations and leisure interests. Their gender-role attitudes were also examined by means of two other methods: (1) responses to vignettes involving gender-role dilemmas; (2) repertory grids involving supplied and elicited elements. Grids were represented a year later to provide a limited longitudinal design. The interview data has been analysed separately in relation to the four topics. Quantitative analysis showed that the answers for both sports and school subjects departed from established stereotypes. There was little support for the hypothesis that gender-role activities become accentuated at adolescence. Qualitative analysis revealed a number of gender related themes in these answers. The remaining data from the project is being analysed. Supplementary studies have been provided by rating-scale investigations of the gender-stereotyping of school subjects (Archer & Freedman, 1989; Archer & Macrae, 1991), and the research has been integrated into more general theoretical work on gender-role development (Archer, 1984, 1989).

PUBLISHED MATERIAL: ARCHER, J. & FREEDMAN, S. (1989). 'Gender-stereotypic perceptions of academic disciplines', British Journal of Educational Psychology, No 59, pp.306-313. ; ARCHER, J. & MACDONALD, M. (1991). 'Gender roles and school subjects in adolescent girls', Educational Research, Vol 33, No 1. ; ARCHER, J. (1989). 'Childhood gender roles: structure and development', The Psychologist, No 9, pp.367-370. ; ARCHER, J. & MACDONALD, M. (1990). 'Gender roles and sports in adolescent girls', Leisure Studies, No 9, pp.225-240.

STATUS: Sponsored project

SOURCE OF GRANT: University of Central Lancashire

DATE OF RESEARCH: 1984-1993

KEYWORDS: **girls; sex differences; sex stereotypes**

2706

Department of Public Policy, Preston PR1 2HE
01772 201201

Hurst, A. Prof.

Policies and provision for disabled students - international approaches and experiences

ABSTRACT: Based on published information, personal visits and commissioned papers, the project aims to identify different approaches to policies and provision for students with disabilities in higher education, with a view to disseminating good practices and highlighting common concerns. Following a brief overview of the context and higher education system in each country, there is a focus on aspects of provision: publicity, admissions and entry, academic support, accommodation, and student finances. In addition, there are case studies of invididual institutions. Reference is also made to national policy initiatives and to the role of umbrella organisations, such as in England the work of SKILL (the National Bureau for Students with Disabilities).

STATUS: Individual research

DATE OF RESEARCH: 1993-continuing

KEYWORDS: access to education; comparative education; disabilities; higher education; special educational needs; students; universities

University of East Anglia

2707

School of Education and Professional Development, Norwich NR4 7TJ
01603 456161

Cockburn, A. Dr

Teaching under pressure

ABSTRACT: Stress in the teaching profession is reaching critical proportions, yet there is very little comprehensible and comprehensive help and advice for teachers. The aim of this study is to produce a practical and insightful guide for trainee, beginning and experienced teachers, on the sources, responses and possible solutions to the negative aspects of stress in their lives. Using a sample of local primary teachers and structured and clinical interview techniques, this investigation will examine teachers' experiences of stress, their awareness of its effects and how, if at all, they manage it.

STATUS: Sponsored project

SOURCE OF GRANT: Nuffield Foundation £1,332

DATE OF RESEARCH: 1993-1993

KEYWORDS: stress - psychological; stress management; student teachers; teachers; teaching profession

2708

School of Education and Professional Development, Norwich NR4 7TJ
01603 456161

Fox, J. Ms; Walker, B. Ms; *Supervisor*: Kushner, S. Dr

Young mothers' education project

ABSTRACT: This was an evaluation of a small peer education project whereby young mothers were trained to run workshops in schools and youth clubs. The aims of the programme were to inform young people of the realities of young parenthood, and to provide information on contraception. Unstructured interviews were conducted with the organisers of the project, participants in 2 schools and 2 youth clubs, the young mothers themselves (5 of which were indepth interviews), and their youth/community workers. The evaluation considered the effectiveness of the training the young mothers received, the conduct of the workshops and their reception by the participants, and the effect of the programme on the young mothers. The evaluation concluded that the scheme was so small that it could only be viewed as a feasibility study and, as such, in spite of the inevitable tensions and uncertainties inherent in pioneering work of this kind, it would justify further support. The role of the youth/community workers was seen as important; the young mothers made personal gains as a result of involvement with the programme; and the programme, though small, was felt by the participants to be an improvement on current sex education provision - where it existed. However, the project relied heavily on the commitment of the youth/community workers involved and the enthusiasm of the volunteer young mothers whose idea it was.

PUBLISHED MATERIAL: FOX, J., WALKER, B. & KUSHNER, S. (1993). It's not a bed of roses. Young mothers' education project evaluation report. Norwich: University of East Anglia, Centre for Applied Research in Education.

STATUS: Sponsored project

SOURCE OF GRANT: Norwich Health Authority

DATE OF RESEARCH: 1993-1993

KEYWORDS: community education; contraception; early parenthood; family planning; mothers; parenthood education; peer teaching; sex education

2709

School of Education and Professional Development, Norwich NR4 7TJ
01603 456161

MacDonald, B. Prof.; Stronach, I. Prof.; Kushner, S. Dr; Norris, N. Dr; MacLure, M. Dr

The information technology and educational research policy evaluation

ABSTRACT: This was a policy evaluation of the Economic and Social Research Council (ESRC) funding and the management and organisation of research initiatives. The evaluation was based on naturalistic, case-study methodology. It followed the principle that the evaluation of research policy has to be founded upon accounts of the experience of the research projects; i.e. that research evaluation and policy evaluation were inseparable. The themes illuminated and analysed in depth by the evaluation included: interdisciplinarity; research careers in the social sciences; the coordination of research initiatives and the process of refereeing; and selection and commissioning of research programmes.

PUBLISHED MATERIAL: MACDONALD, B. & STRONACH, I. (1988). The InTER programme: the independent policy evaluation. InTER occasional publications 6/88. Lancaster: University of Lancaster, Department of Psychology. ; STRONACH, I. & MACDONALD, B. (1989). Making a start: the origins of a research programme. A first report from the independent evaluators of the ESRC Research Programme Information Technology in Education (InTER). Norwich: University of East Anglia, Centre for Applied Research in Education. ; STRONACH, I. & MACDONALD, B. (1991). Faces and future: an inquiry into the jobs, lives and careers of educational researchers in an ESRC initiative. A report from the independent evaluators of the ESRC Research Programme Information Technology in Education (InTER). Norwich: University of East Anglia, Centre for Applied Research in Education. ; KUSHNER, S. (1991). ESRC initiatives and their coordinators: organising for innovation in the social sciences. A report from the independent evaluators of the ESRC Research Programme Information Technology in Education (InTER). Norwich: University of East Anglia, Centre for Applied Research in Education. ; NORRIS, N., DAVIES, R., PETTIGREW, M. & KUSHNER, S. (1992). Research careers in the social sciences - a policy review paper for the ESRC. Commissioned by the ESRC's Research Resources Board. Mimeo. Norwich: University of East Anglia, Centre for Applied Research in Education. A full list of publications is available from the researcher.

STATUS: Sponsored project

SOURCE OF GRANT: Economic and Social Research Council £150,000

DATE OF RESEARCH: 1988-1993

KEYWORDS: educational research; information technology; policy; research; research opportunities; social science research

2710

School of Education and Professional Development, Norwich NR4 7TJ
01603 456161

McBride, R. Dr

Egyptian teachers: jobs and lives

ABSTRACT: The aim of the research is to raise the voice of Egyptian teachers and to reveal what is hidden or repressed. The researcher will track Egyptian teachers' views during a period of major change; this will include a study of gender and feminism in the Egyptian system. In addition the research is intended to act as a form of inservice teacher education (INSET) which will deconstruct existing role expectations, and provide INSET which will empower and support self-reconstruction. Methods are qualitative; there will be considerable use of teachers' narratives. Between 200 and 300 Egyptian teachers will participate during each year of the project.

STATUS: Sponsored project

SOURCE OF GRANT: Egyptian Government

DATE OF RESEARCH: 1993-1997

KEYWORDS: egypt; teachers

2711

School of Education and Professional Development, Norwich NR4 7TJ
01603 456161

Brown, C. Mrs

Parent-helpers, children and the understanding of science: investigating interactions on school visits to hands-on science galleries

ABSTRACT: Parent-helpers accompany many school groups on visits to hands-on science galleries in museums and science centres. Their role as participants in such events is relatively unknown. A pilot study of parents and children on informal holiday visits to hands-on science galleries described the different types of interactions which can be observed and the effect of gender. The current study will investigate these interactions in the more formal context of school visits.

PUBLISHED MATERIAL: BROWN, C.A. (1995). 'Making the most of family visits: some observations of parents with children in a Museum Science Centre', International Journal of Museum Management and Curatorship, Vol 14, No 1.

STATUS: Sponsored project

DATE OF RESEARCH: 1996-1998

KEYWORDS: **parent participation; parent pupil relationship; school visits; science education; science teaching centres**

2712

School of Education and Professional Development, Norwich NR4 7TJ
01603 456161

Browne, A. Ms

The impact of the vouchers on the education of children under 5 in Norfolk

ABSTRACT: Norfolk is one of the 4 local education authorities (LEAs) taking part in the pilot for the voucher scheme. Norfolk had a low level of existing state provision for 3 and 4 year-olds prior to April 1996. The aims are to examine the impact of the voucher scheme using the Government's rationale for the scheme which was: 1) to increase provision; 2) to enhance quality; 3) to ensure parental choice. The methods include: interviews with parents; headteachers; early years' inspectors and advisory teachers; staff and providers working in the private and voluntary sectors; and examination of nursery inspection reports. The preliminary findings are that state provision for 4 year-olds has increased; provision in the private and voluntary sectors has become less stable; and some provision for 3 year-olds has been lost. The quality of provision is emerging as a major issue. The indication is that quality education is not being provided. Parents in the first phase experienced no increase in choice of provision. Further data is being collected and analysed.

PUBLISHED MATERIAL: BROWNE, A. (1998). 'The effect of the voucher initiative on early years provision', Early Years, Vol 18, No 2.

STATUS: Individual research

DATE OF RESEARCH: 1996-1997

KEYWORDS: **early childhood education; education vouchers; nursery education; parent choice; preschool education; young children**

2713

School of Education and Professional Development, Norwich NR4 7TJ
01603 456161

Sinkinson, A. Ms; *Supervisor*: Brown, G. Prof.

Investigating the link between concrete materials and formalisation in secondary school mathematics

ABSTRACT: The research, in progress, follows on from previous research which shows that children find it very difficult to bridge the gap between concrete mathematical activities and the more formalised, symbolic mathematics which they are expected to adopt. It is a study to investigate the effect of introducing a middle stage into the teaching and learning process. This stage is designed to be different from both the concrete materials and formalisation phases of teaching, but to effectively link the 2 with the aim of making the formalisation more accessible to children. The research covers 2 mathematical topics currently taught at National Curriculum key stages 3 and 4: Pythagoras' theorem and the formula for calculating the area of parallelogram. 4 teachers form the sample for each topic. Each teacher teaches the topic to 2 'matched' classes: one is taught using the teacher's existing scheme of concrete materials leading to a formalisation, the other 'matched' class is taught a similar scheme with the addition of a middle, 'bridging' phase, written by the researcher. All classes are pre-tested, post-tested and a sample of each class is interviewed by the researcher immediately after the teaching and again 3 months later. Analysis
of results will show the effect of the 'bridging' phase of teaching.

STATUS: Individual research

DATE OF RESEARCH: 1994-1998

KEYWORDS: **mathematical concepts; mathematics education; secondary education; teaching methods**

2714

School of Education and Professional Development, Norwich NR4 7TJ
01603 456161

Tomakin, E. Mr; *Supervisors*: MacLure, M. Dr; McBride, R. Dr

A tutor's use of inservice training for teacher development and action research in foreign language teaching in Turkey

ABSTRACT: Educational action research studies were made use of in the United States in the 1950s and in the UK in the 1960s, and a great deal of actin research studies were undertaken in various fields such as nursing, insurance, hospitals, as well as educational studies. The main motivation of these studies has become either to solve the problem or to improve practice. Teachers are generally regarded as the 'researchers' of action research studies. In the same token, this study, which will be employed at a new environment firstly, aims to 'improve foreign language teaching' on the basis of teachers as researchers movement. It becomes clear that to enable teachers as researchers they should be equipped with the specific knowledge and the process of action research as well as its objectives, criteria and evaluation. Firstly, this study employs an inservice course in which participants study the minimal requirement and the core of action research (literature review). The methodology of the study is a qualitative case study and the methods of data collection are diary study, dialogue journals, interview, classroom observations and analytic memos. The study has already started and 7 volunteer teachers included for the time being. By the end of this study, it is expected that teachers will have insight into qualitative research; have critical eyes to their teaching sessions; produce potential actions to be used during their teaching session; and make inferences (hypotheses and statements) from their investigations.

STATUS: Sponsored project

SOURCE OF GRANT: Turkish Government

DATE OF RESEARCH: 1997-1997

KEYWORDS: **action research; language teachers; teacher researchers; turkey**

2715

School of Education and Professional Development, Norwich NR4 7TJ
01603 456161

Maruthavanar, P. Mr; *Supervisors*: McBride, R. Dr; Mayhew, P. Dr

Information technology in educational management - in educational systems: a Malaysian perspective

ABSTRACT: In Malaysia, with the introduction of the Multimedia Super Corridor and Smart Schools, the development and use of information technology in school administration is both an exciting opportunity and a demanding challenge. Though schools are relatively small organisations with typically flat and uncomplicated hierarchy, they are bureaucratically, professionally and politically complex organisations. All the basic processes that occur in large organisations can be found in the school, with the addition of its characteristic school-specific teaching and teaching-related systems. The researcher plans to use a prototyping approach to develop an operational system that would hold management level information for a Malaysian secondary school. Microsoft Access and Microsoft Visual Basic would be used to develop most of the modules. These modules would include matters related to curriculum, examinations, finance, extra-curricular activities, scholarships, timetabling, discipline, personnel, resources and special needs.

STATUS: Individual research

DATE OF RESEARCH: 1996-continuing

KEYWORDS: **computer uses in education; educational administration; information technology; malaysia; management information systems**

2716

School of Education and Professional Development, Norwich NR4 7TJ
01603 456161

Battersby, J. Mr; *Supervisor*: Elliott, J. Prof.

Reducing pupil disaffection through environmental education

ABSTRACT: Pupils express their disaffection with the school curriculum through their disruptive behaviour, disengagement from the learning process and through under-achievement in their work. This study considers the potentially positive effect that environmental education can have on: pupils' attitudes to learning; their ability to demonstrate positive achievement; their involvement and cooperation in lessons; their behaviour and their attitude to school, as well as their general educational progress. The study also considers some of the reasons for the differences in pupils' attitudes, behaviour and perceptions of their learning through environmental education. This is one of a number of research studies into pupil disaffection, centred at the University of East Anglia, and involves local teachers and local schools in school centred action research initiatives. The study is based on evidence collected from questionnaires, observations and interviews of pupils and teachers from 3 schools in East Anglia. Early indications from an initial pilot study suggest that learning about the environment has had a positive effect on pupils' attitude to school and to their curriculum, and that such a curriculum has the potential to reduce disaffection with it and with school as well as contributing to reducing pupil under-achievement.

STATUS: Individual research

DATE OF RESEARCH: 1997-continuing

KEYWORDS: **curriculum; disaffection; environmental education; pupil attitudes**

2717

School of Education and Professional Development, Norwich NR4 7TJ
01603 456161

Ebbutt, D. Mr; Howard, L. Ms; *Supervisor*: Elliott, J. Prof.

Distance learning materials for basic education teaching diploma (inservice) for Namibia: a research project

ABSTRACT: This project will produce distance learning materials to be delivered by November 1998 in 'Lower Primary' and 'Educational Theory and Practice' targeted at inservice teachers in Namibia. The materials are premised on practice-based inquiry (action research) wherein the inservice teachers carry out research on their own practice. The project team will make 3 visits to Namibia to field test the acceptability/viability of the materials as they are developing. Both named researchers have wide experience of education in Africa. The team will produce a succession of research papers that reflect the issues: a) to do with action research in a developing country; b) to do with distance learning in a developing country. It is through the (in press) paper, and those scheduled, that this project is categorised as a 'research' rather than a development project.

PUBLISHED MATERIAL: ELLIOTT, D. & ELLIOTT, J. (1997). 'Supporting practitioner inquiry in a developing country through distance learning materials: some key issues - paper presented at the European Conference for Educational Research at Frankfurt 24-27 September 1997'. In: Reform Forum: Journal for Educational Reform in Namibia, No 6. (in press).

STATUS: Sponsored project

SOURCE OF GRANT: Swedish International Development Agency

DATE OF RESEARCH: 1998-1998

KEYWORDS: **developing countries; distance education; educational materials; inservice teacher education; material development; namibia**

2718

School of Education and Professional Development, Norwich NR4 7TJ
01603 456171

Bridges, D. Prof.

Philosophy and educational research

ABSTRACT: This is a continuing programme of personal enquiry and writing (but including collaborative endeavours) designed to explore the interface between philosophy and educational research and, more particularly, to close what is observed to have been an artificial and unproductive divide. The researcher has produced a series of linked papers which have included discussion of: philosophy as a form of research; the epistemological boundaries between the empirical and the philosophical; and the issues raised

by 'contract' research; and will continue to write on the ethics of researching across cultural boundaries and the dispensability of 'truth' in the discourse of research.

STATUS: Individual research

DATE OF RESEARCH: 1995-continuing

KEYWORDS: **educational research; philosophy**

2719

School of Education and Professional Development, Norwich NR4 7TJ
001603 456161
Addis Ababa University, PO Box 1176, Addis Ababa, Ethiopia
00251 550844

Bridges, D. Prof.; Masheshe, A. Dr

Teacher education in a developing country: Ethiopia - a portrayal

ABSTRACT: This project sets out to generate a portrayal of teacher education in Ethiopia built up of a series of mini case studies. These will be the product of fieldwork conducted by staff from the University of East Anglia in cooperation with staff and students from Addis Ababa University. A first stage of the research will focus on the different sources which have contributed to both the theoretical and organisational construction of teacher education as it is today. This will include a study of some of the indigenous educational traditions in Ethiopia and consider to what extent they have found expression in either contemporary educational practice in schools or in teacher education. A second phase will focus on the interface between the university and schools in the process of teacher education.

STATUS: Sponsored project

DATE OF RESEARCH: 1998-continuing

KEYWORDS: **developing countries; ethiopia; teacher education**

2720

School of Education and Professional Development, Centre for Applied Research in Education, Norwich NR4 7TJ
01603 456161

Juat Ngoh, T. Miss; *Supervisor*: Cockburn, A. Dr

A study of primary science teachers' teaching behaviour

ABSTRACT: Teachers have a vast array of ideas, views, ways of thinking and feelings which influence their classroom behaviour. When the teacher's views, aims or thinking are in agreement with his/her classroom behaviour, teaching is more likely to be effective. However, this is not necessarily the case; much will depend upon the teacher's awareness of their teaching behaviour. The aims of this research are to: 1) explore primary science teachers' views of the nature of science and what it means to teach science from their perspective; 2) examine what goes on in science classrooms to see teachers' teaching behaviour; 3) investigate major factors facilitating and constraining the teaching of science in a classroom; 4) examine the nature of the relationship between teachers' views of the nature of science, their teaching behaviour and the quality of learning in pupils; and 5) examine the impact of primary science teachers' teaching behaviour and quality of pupils' learning on the primary school science curriculum. The sample consists of 8 to 10 primary science teachers and pupils in Malaysia. Data will be collected through: interviews with participants (teachers and pupils); direct observations of ongoing science lessons and teachers' teaching behaviour in a naturalistic setting; and analysis of documents such as the primary school science curriculum, other educational documents, science textbooks, teachers' lesson plans, pupils' worksheets and pupils' monthly test worksheets. A total of 56 to 70 lessons will be observed through this research.

STATUS: Individual research

DATE OF RESEARCH: 1997-continuing

KEYWORDS: **malaysia; primary school teachers; science education; science teachers; teacher behaviour**

2721

School of Education and Professional Development, Centre for Applied Research in Education, Norwich NR4 7TJ
01603 456161

Mohamed, A. Mr; *Supervisors*: Norris, N. Dr; Schostak, J. Prof.

A case study of the BA (teaching English as a second language) programme in British universities: the experience of Malaysian inservice teachers

ABSTRACT: This is a study to understand the main issues involved in the training of inservice Malaysian English as second language (ESL) teachers, sponsored by the Teacher Training Division of the Malaysian Ministry of Education and trained by the Consortium of British Universities in Britain (a consortium of 9 universities - 6 in England, 2 in Scotland and 1 in Wales), by conducting a case study based on qualitative as well as quantitative methodology. There are 4 main objectives in the research and they are to conduct: a preliminary study; an exploratory study; a survey; and a supplementary inquiry. The objective of the preliminary study is to obtain introductory information regarding the programme. During the preliminary study a number of universities under the 'Consortium of British Universities' were contacted and relevant documents pertaining to the programme were obtained. The second objective of the study is to further explore the issues involved through document analysis and interviewing. The exploratory study was completed in January 1997 and the researcher is now preparing for the next stage of the study - the survey. This involved the preparation and administration of a questionnaire. The questionnaire will be analysed and further qualitative work will be undertaken. The objective of this work is to obtain more descriptive data in order to understand the main issues involved in the case. It is hoped that by the end of this stage sufficient data will have been collected and analysed to understand the case and the main issues involved.

STATUS: Individual research

DATE OF RESEARCH: 1995-1998

KEYWORDS: **english - second language; language teachers; teacher education**

2722

School of Education and Professional Development, Centre for Applied Research in Education, Norwich NR4 7TJ
01603 456161

Magyar, A. Ms; *Supervisor*: MacLure, M. Dr

Deconstructing the boundaries of culture studies in a French and English rural primary school

ABSTRACT: The thesis is constructed around ethnographic fieldwork carried out in two small rural schools, one in France and one in England. The central notion is that language does not merely 'describe' realities, but rather 'constructs' realities. It follows that it is what the participants make of the rural schools and what working in a rural school might feel like that is of interest here. However, the researcher is not an 'objective' outsider but is herself implicated in this constructive process. Thus the thesis adopts a reflexive and sceptical stance towards the status of the interpretations (including the textual ones of the thesis itself) and the manner in which they are presented. The research addresses both substantive and methodological issues. Substantively, the thesis explores the ways in which the rural and the educational might inter-relate in the two investigative sites. It argues that the debate about small rural schools has been obliged to abide by the conventions of particular political frameworks in order to be heard and asks how might these schools be 'read' outside of these frameworks. The methodology adopted, that of cross-cultural comparison, raises important issues about the researcher's 'visualising practices', arguing for a more reflexive account of the process of 'crossing cultures'. The methodological question has been: how and whether comparison across cultures can enrich and enhance meaning in an ethnographic inquiry, while at the same time avoiding 'easy ethnocentricity'. The introductory Chapters 1 to 3, review relevant literature and map out key methodological issues. The pivotal textual results of the comparative process are the portrayals of the 2 schools in Chapter 4. Chapters 5 and 6 take issue with these portrayals as 'textual constructions', arguing that they inevitably exclude other 'stories'. Both chapters suggest alternative 'readings' of the 2 schools in their rural context. Finally, Chapter 7 turns to the teachers and explores issues of identity, asking what it might mean, what it might feel like, to be a teacher in a small rural school.

STATUS: Individual research

DATE OF RESEARCH: 1992-1997

KEYWORDS: **comparative education; france; rural schools; small schools**

2723

School of Education and Professional Development, Centre for Applied Research in Education, Norwich NR4 7TJ
01603 456161

Brown, K. Ms; *Supervisor*: MacLure, M. Dr

The first five years

ABSTRACT: This research project focuses on the first 5 years' experience of language teachers gaining Qualified Teacher Status in Modern Foreign Languages at the University of East Anglia. There is a national shortage of language teachers and recruitment to initial teacher training is low. This project aims to track those who do train, to find out how many stay in the profession and what the factors are which cause others to leave. An important element of the project is the opportunity it affords for reflection by teachers on the quality of their initial training programme after a few years of service. It will also help to identify further professional development needs. Teachers will be interviewed at 2 points in their first year of teaching, and once a year in subsequent years. They will also complete questionnaires over the five year period. Between 20 and 30 student teachers qualify each year from this Postgraduate Certificate of Education course - many go on to teaching posts in the area.

STATUS: Individual research

DATE OF RESEARCH: 1996-continuing

KEYWORDS: **followup studies; graduate surveys; language teachers; modern language studies; newly qualified teachers; teacher development; teaching profession**

2724

School of Education and Professional Development, Centre for Applied Research in Education, Norwich NR4 7TJ
01603 456161

Doherty, P. Mr; *Supervisor*: Elliott, J. Prof.

The curriculum dimensions of pupil disaffection

ABSTRACT: The research project 'The curriculum dimensions of pupil disaffection' is a collaborative project. It will involve up to 8 Norwich area secondary schools; Postgraduate Certificate of Education (PGCE) subject tutors from the University of East Anglia (UEA); subject teachers in participating schools; pupils; and parents. It will be coordinated by senior researchers at the Centre for Applied Research in Education (CARE) at UEA. An element of this project will involve investigating the pupils' perceptions of curriculum disaffection. The aim of the project is to shift the focus of any search for solutions to pupil disaffection away from individual psychology models and toward those that contain a socio-historic perspective. This requires a re-conceptualisation of disaffection from deficit behaviour (which structurally confines solutions within the fields of 'remedial'; 'compensatory'; and 'special' education), towards a model of disaffection as rationale choice. The focus will not therefore be on the pathologies of pupil disruption or absence, but on the pathology of presence. This shifts the subsequent enquiries from solely exhibiting the behavioural manifestations associated with disaffection, to include the majority school population, whom, whilst exhibiting few external 'indicators' of disaffection, may experience a lack of engagement with the formal school curriculum that manifests itself in high levels of under-achievement. The methodological techniques will be both quantitative and qualitative, incorporating survey and case study strategies. The initial stages involve the pupils in developing a questionnaire in each school. This process aims to generate a conceptualisation of disaffection as it affects pupils, and not impose an external frame of reference upon those perceptions. After this developmental process, a representative sample of the school population will complete the questionnaire and the results will be enumerated. Across school comparative analysis will occur in conjunction with the other strands of the project (PGCE tutors; parents; teachers; UEA researchers etc). The second (and somewhat longer) stage of the project involves 'shadowing' a number of pupils through a full academic year of their school career (these will not necessarily be pupils who exhibit the behavioural signs commonly associated with disaffection). A case study of disaffection at the individual, school and area levels will be developed through indepth interviews with these pupils at differing stages of their school careers. The project will conclude by drawing together the different strands of the research (cross-school analysis etc) and a report will be published in the form of a PhD thesis in 1999.

STATUS: Sponsored project

SOURCE OF GRANT: University of East Anglia

DATE OF RESEARCH: 1996-continuing

KEYWORDS: curriculum; disaffection; pupil attitudes; secondary education; secondary school pupils

2725

School of Education and Professional Development, Centre for Applied Research in Education, Norwich NR4 7TJ

01603 446161

Puteh, M. Mrs; *Supervisors*: Haylock, N. Dr; Norris, N. Dr

A case study: factors attributed to mathematics anxiety and its impact on teacher trainees in Malaysia

ABSTRACT: The focus of this study is to investigate the factors that contributed to the teacher trainees' mathematics anxiety and further on, to investigate the impact, if any, of this phenomena on the teacher trainees generally, such as their decision-making: lifestyle, sense of self, behaviour with regard to mathematics and also in their further understanding of mathematics taught to them. Other research projects have been undertaken in order to determine the factors that are responsible for this anxiety, and many explanations have been suggested, or discovered to have had an impact on the students' mathematics anxiety. Nevertheless very few studies have only focused on mathematics anxiety in particular, and tried to explain why it had occurred in the first place. The first phase of this study tries to unwrap the factors that surround this phenomena, and especially tries to look into the effect it has on the teacher trainees, such as: their attitudes towards mathematics, confidence in mathematics, their perceptions of mathematics, their teachers' method of teaching and learning strategies, their perceived usefulness of the subject, their parental attitudes towards mathematics, peer group expectations and effects, gender differences, and other factors. The theoretical background only acts as a guideline for further pursuance into the factors as this is a qualitative research and hence the focus is to understand the current phenomena and to obtain a rich and indepth knowledge of the issue. This study also explores whether the teacher trainees' mathematics anxiety will affect their teaching strategies and beliefs. Questionnaires, interviews and observations will be used to give indepth insight into the issue. Questionnaires were first used in order to select the teacher trainees that perceive themselves as having mathematics anxiety. These teacher trainees will then be further interviewed to give an insight into the cause and effect of this mathematics anxiety. Observations of actual classes of mathematics are videotaped. The focus of the observations are on the teacher trainees and the lecturers teaching them in order to understand the complex interactions that are involved. Further interviews with the teacher trainees and also with the lecturers are carried out after each observation session in order to help the researcher uncover any unidentified cause of action by the lecturer or the teacher trainees. The second phase of the study aims to uncover the effect, if any, of this mathematics anxiety on the teacher trainees' teaching practices. Their strategies in teaching mathematics, and how their own mathematics anxiety affects them in all aspects of their sense of self as a mathematics teacher. The research hopes to give some insight on how these teachers cope with their pupils' mathematics anxiety while coping with their own anxiety at the same time.

STATUS: Individual research

DATE OF RESEARCH: 1995-1998

KEYWORDS: anxiety; mathematics anxiety; mathematics education; preservice teacher education; student teachers

2726

School of Education and Professional Development, Centre for Applied Research in Education, Norwich NR4 7TJ

01603 456161

Perez del Aguila, V. Mrs; *Supervisor*: MacLure, M. Dr

An evaluation study of the Wawa Wasi home child care programme in Peru

ABSTRACT: Wawa Wasi is the National Home Care System in Peru coordinated by the government and UNICEF in order to provide an integrated care system for children under the age of 6. The system includes and supports all types of day care experiences (public, private, communal, cooperative, local authority funded, etc) and promotes other alternatives, particularly for poor women who work more than 10 hours outside the house and need a secure and cheap place to leave their children under the age of 3. Thus, 'Community Educational Homes' have been created over the last 3 years in urban shanty towns. They have been set up in houses of local women who are selected and trained as the community's caregivers. Since this is a new experience, the aim of this study is to carry out evaluative research to find an early indication of the government action and its impact. Strengths and weaknesses are likely to increase the understanding of the problem and contribute to the improvement of the programme. To accomplish this goal, the research will include an analysis of the public policy on early childhood education in Peru with focus on an indepth qualitative case study of 4 community educational homes in which beneficiaries' perceptions will have an overriding role. Documentary analysis, interviews, focus groups and participant and non-participant observation will be the main techniques used in data collection. The findings of this research intend to support the view that investment in early childhood education programmes is important for the economic development of a society and is a strategy for poverty reduction in developing countries.

STATUS: Individual research

DATE OF RESEARCH: 1996-continuing

KEYWORDS: child caregivers; day care; developing countries; early childhood education; peru; programme evaluation

2727

School of Education and Professional Development, Centre for Applied Research in Education, Norwich NR4 7TJ

01603 456161

University of East Anglia, School of Education and Professional Development, Keswick Hall Centre for Research and Development in Religious Education, Norwich NR4 7TJ

Bell, J. Miss; *Supervisors*: Elliott, J. Prof.; Rudge, L. Mrs

Curriculum and professional development in religious education: syllabus implementation studies between 1996 and 1999

ABSTRACT: Religious education is the only subject in the school curriculum that demonstrates formal curriculum development at a local level. This project will research the implementation and impact of new agreed syllabuses in local education authorities (LEAs) in the Eastern Region. The LEAs that have agreed to be involved are different in cultural and geographical composition and are at different stages in the implementation of their own syllabuses. Attention will also be given to church-aided and grant maintained schools that can choose whether or not to use their local agreed syllabus. The aim of the project is to contribute to the understanding of local curriculum design and the impact of the agreed syllabuses in religious education on teachers, pupils and local communities. A longitudinal approach will be taken. Standing Advisory Councils in Religious Education (SACREs) agreed syllabus conferences, LEA departments and schools will be visited at various stages of the implementation. Each LEA will be treated as an individual case study. Whilst the project has an evaluative dimension, it is not an evaluation commissioned by an outside body and has no underlying thesis to prove. The perspectives of SACREs, LEAs, schools and faith communities will be sought. To gather such data, qualititative research methods will be used, such as: interviews, observation, written surveys and literature reviews of LEA material and related studies.

STATUS: Individual research

DATE OF RESEARCH: 1996-continuing

KEYWORDS: curriculum development; primary education; religious education; secondary education

2728

School of Education and Professional Development, Centre for Applied Research in Education, Norwich NR4 7TJ

01603 456161

Musonda, L. Mr; *Supervisor*: Elliott, J. Prof.

Institutional perceptions and management of educational change/reform

ABSTRACT: Teacher training institutions (TTI) often find themselves having to translate and manage educational changes/reforms determined exclusively by a political agenda. It is argued that the current social/educational changes are altering the theory, pedagogy and management of teacher education so fundamentally that TTIs are finding themselves in a dilemma to efficiently plan and manage teacher education. The need arises to develop institutional capacities to respond imaginatively to these challenges. It is doubtful if TTIs have developed their own problem-solving structures and processes to adapt these internal and external changes. The research therefore aims at investigating how TTIs perceive, adapt and manage change initiated at higher system levels. This will be a case study of 3 teacher training institutions (1 in the UK and 2 in Zambia). The study will attempt a comparative analysis of the above 2 educational contexts - Zambia and the UK. It will mainly involve interviews, observations and documentary analysis.

STATUS: Individual research

DATE OF RESEARCH: 1997-continuing

KEYWORDS: change strategies; educational change; higher education; organisational change; preservice teacher education; zambia

2729

School of Education and Professional Development, Centre for Applied Research in Education, Norwich NR4 7TJ
01603 456161

Cockburn, A. Dr

Mathematics which is challenging to teach in the early years of schooling

ABSTRACT: Serious mathematics books in primary teacher education tend to be of 2 types: those which focus almost exclusively on the research literature and those which explain mathematical concepts for the intending teacher. The majority of students, who find time to read, tend to opt for the latter variety. Typically, even the most successful of these are fairly single-minded in their endeavour to explain mathematical concepts and procedures. Rarely, if ever, do such books make any distinction between topics which are straightforward to teach and those which appear to cause considerable difficulty for teachers and pupils alike. This project will illustrate and examine the research findings based on a study of 12 elementary school teachers, their pupils and the research literature. The focus will be on mathematical topics which the teachers have found particularly difficult to teach (e.g. place value and time). It will describe how the group endeavoured to develop their teaching skills through the sharing of: 1) an underlying understanding of the complexities involved in the learning of some mathematical concepts; 2) teaching techniques used in other countries (e.g. there are wide variations in the way place value is taught; 3) group member's own practical successes when working with concepts which others find difficult to teach. A book and several papers on effective ways to teach surprisingly challenging concepts will be produced.

STATUS: Individual research

DATE OF RESEARCH: 1997-1997

KEYWORDS: concept teaching; mathematical concepts; mathematics education; primary education

2730

School of Education and Professional Development, Centre for Applied Research in Education, Norwich NR4 7TJ
01603 456161

Kite, K. Ms; *Supervisor*: MacDonald, B. Prof.

A study to describe and analyse some of the contextual factors which may affect the learning of trained nurses in an intensive therapy unit (ITU)

ABSTRACT: One of the objectives of this study is to produce an account of nursing practice and a detailed case study analysis of the contextual influences upon registered nurses' learning in the British intensive care unit under study. Another is the opportunity the study will provide for nurses to reflect upon their practice and so to identify their personal learning needs. It is intended that through this mechanism, the personal and professional development of those participating in the study will be facilitated. Finally, a broad aim of the study is that it should inform both the design and requirement for the continuing education of nurses. Methodologically, this research is interesting for it is important to realise that it is not just research for development, but developmental research. Although detailed case study analysis is by nature non-generalisable, the main themes and principles derived from the study will be generalisable. The research methodology has been naturalistic in nature, using some of the features of ethnographic enquiry. As such, the techniques of participant observation and interview have been the main research methods. Selection of participants was made from staff working on an 8-bedded intensive therapy unit (ITU) in a district general hospital. To date, participant observation has been carried out on 25 occasions ranging from 4 to 11 hours, and over 75 interviews on other occasions. Preliminary analysis of the data suggests that the high-risk nature of the work due to the enormous consequence of error, plays an important role in the learning of these nurses 'on the job'. The range and depth of 'knowledges' required by these nurses is considerable bearing in mind their undisputed function in judgement making. Interestingly, the geographical layout of the unit combined with the nature of the work, may influence patterns of feedback on performance for all nurses along with policy influences at this time of unprecedented change in the National Health Service.

PUBLISHED MATERIAL: KITE, K. (1996). 'Participant observation? Some methodological considerations about a study in progress entitled: Developmental research in the workplace. A study to describe and analyse some of the contextual factors which may influence the learning of registered nurses in an intensive care unit (ITU)'. Paper presented at the American Educational Research Association Conference, New York City, 8-12 April 1996.

STATUS: Individual research

DATE OF RESEARCH: 1994-1997

KEYWORDS: learning; nurses; practical nursing; professional development

2731

School of Education and Professional Development, Centre for Applied Research in Education, Norwich NR4 7TJ
01603 456161

Meng, C. Mr; *Supervisor*: Kushner, S. Dr

The experience of schooling: how do the pupils view it? A case study of a Malaysian primary school

ABSTRACT: Despite the pupils' centrality to the education system, it is rather surprising that those involved in education do not seek their feelings, ideas, and insights. This research hopes to balance the lopsided situation by exploring the pupils' experience. There is a need to know what pupils think about life in schools and how such views can help to make school life more relevant to them. The objectives of this research are: to explore the pupils' view of schooling and examine the meanings they have accorded to their experience in context, and to explore the pupils' expectation of schooling. This research will use a case study approach to understand the phenomenon of its particular context - the case of the pupils' experience of schooling. The research sample consists of a group of primary school pupils from 2 classes. The desirable size of the interview sample is 20 pupils. The methods of investigation will be interviews, observations, and collection of documents. Quasi participant observation will be undertaken. Interviews will be conducted with individual and small groups of pupils after trust is gained by the researcher. The headteacher and teachers will be interviewed. These interviews are of the semi-structured and unstructured type. Relevant documents, including examples of pupils' work, will also be collected from the school and the relevant education departments.

STATUS: Individual research

DATE OF RESEARCH: 1997-continuing

KEYWORDS: educational experience; malaysia; primary school pupils; pupil attitudes

2732

School of Education and Professional Development, Centre for Applied Research in Education, Norwich NR4 7TJ
01603 456161

Therese, A. Sr.; *Supervisors*: MacLure, M. Dr; Kushner, S. Dr

Creating communities of full regard: relationships, race and religious education

ABSTRACT: This piece of qualitative research was conducted in a small Roman Catholic primary school and considers the overlapping cultures of children and adults by focusing upon multicultural/antiracist teaching and learning as a part of a Roman Catholic/religious education ethos. This was done in the first instance by looking at classrooms and their places by extension. Teachers, the headteacher and staff in the school, presented as 'snapshots' in the study, provide a backdrop of the world of adults. The world of the child is also presented through various interviews and interactions with children. However, as a part of the 26-month study, 2 children worked with the researcher as co-researchers and this forms the basis of the documentation 'from a child's world'. This also gives one dimension of context of 'relationships'. These adults and children are also overlapped by the Office for Standards in Education (OFSTED) inspection which occurred during this time. Some of the implications of this are discussed. This study focuses on the shifting boundaries of ethnicities/ 'cultures' of various sorts, and movement towards a deeper understanding of both conflict and harmony between children and adults. Several methods were used at different times during the study. These included observation and interview, one instance of action research, one instance of boundary/ edge research. The study 'connects things' which are not always connected.

STATUS: Individual research

DATE OF RESEARCH: 1994-1997

KEYWORDS: antiracism education; multicultural education; primary education; religious education

2733

School of Education and Professional Development, Centre for Applied Research in Education, Norwich NR4 7TJ
01603 456161

Doherty, J. Ms; *Supervisor*: MacLure, M. Dr

Women and higher education: participation and experience

ABSTRACT: This research will explore the implications of increased participation in higher education (HE) by female students. Taking numerical representations as a starting point, it will explore the complex relationships between access to HE, student experience and educational outcomes. Women now constitute 51% of undergraduates in the UK. Nevertheless, despite such apparent levelling of gender inequalities, specific disparities continue to exert an influence on the experiences of female undergraduates. Not only are women disproportionately distributed across subject areas, they are under-represented in more 'prestigious' institutions and remain marginalised in academic employment. The aim of the project is to systematically examine the relationships between undergraduates' presence in HE and their experiences. The project will contain an assessment of participation and experience in 2 different types of higher education institutions (HEI): one established and one 'new' university. Focusing upon 2 departments in each HEI, it will compare the experiences of female and male students in 2 subject areas (where female students are either under- or over-represented). A combination of both quantitative and qualitative methods will be employed during the project. The initial stages of the research will involve assessing the participation of female and male undergraduates in each department, followed by unstructured observation of students in their lectures/seminars. A small number of students will act as 'key informants', raising issues that have resonance to their own experience. These issues will go on to form the basis of the next stage of the research: a survey of students' experiences. The survey will be completed by a random sample of students. Its findings, and other issues raised by the participants will be discussed in greater depth during follow-up interviews. These will be less structured and involve a smaller opportunistic sample.

STATUS: Individual research

DATE OF RESEARCH: 1997-continuing

KEYWORDS: higher education; sex differences; student experience; womens education

2734

School of Education and Professional Development, Centre for Applied Research in Education, Norwich NR4 7TJ
01603 456161

Walker, B. Ms; *Supervisor*: MacLure, M. Dr

Secondary school parents evenings: a qualitative study

ABSTRACT: Parents' evenings provide one of the main opportunities in secondary schools for dialogue between parents and teachers. In a policy climate which has promoted parental choice, accountability, and shared responsibility between school and home for children's educational and social development, the annual parents' evening is thus a key event, symbolically

at least. Yet there have been few studies of secondary parents' evenings. Those which exist suggest that they can be unsatisfactory events for those involved. This research examines the organisation and conduct of parents' evenings in 6 secondary schools, and explores the implications for parental involvement, home-school relations and professional training. The research uses qualitative methods, aiming for indepth understanding of parents' evenings in a relatively small number of schools. The study seeks to understand the meanings and significance which the participants bring to, and take from, parents' evenings, as revealed in interviews and observation. Additionally, the research is distinctive in paying special attention to the parent-teacher interviews which form the main business of the annual parents' evening. Existing research into parents' evenings consists mainly of after-the-event reports by the participants (parents, teachers, and, occasionally, students). The research uses methods drawn from discourse analysis to document the negotiations of meaning, power and identity which take place in parent-teacher interviews.

STATUS: Sponsored project

SOURCE OF GRANT: Economic and Social Research Council £23,885

DATE OF RESEARCH: 1997-1998

KEYWORDS: parent participation; parent school relationship; parents evenings; secondary education

2735

School of Education and Professional Development, Centre for Applied Research in Education, Norwich NR4 7TJ
01603 456161

Wallis, L. Mr; *Supervisor*: MacLure, M. Dr

Teaching English as a foreign language: some sociological aspects

ABSTRACT: Teaching English as a foreign language (TEFL) appears as one of the most uncritical and unthinking forms of education. In places where English was once the language of ruler and administrator, it has been seen as having a much diminished presence. By this token, English is merely a technical language with wholly isolated characteristics and features, or at best a foreign language with various implicit connections to the larger English-speaking world. There is a conveniently politically-neutral view whereby the whole historical trajectory of the incidence of teaching foreign languages to non-native speaking students is seen as closely tied up with international trade. In this view, which seems to underpin much of the current thinking, purchasers need the language key either to unlock the Western knowledge or to obtain access to academic lifestyle privileges. This perspective of English as an International Language (the EIL view) holds sway in much of the current writing. The research will challenge this one-dimensional 'end of empire' view and instead look at a whole range of likely explanations for the perceived behaviour-patterns of the participants' perceptions of what constitutes 'good' TEFL practice and a 'good' TEFL institution. Field data will come from e-mail responses and also interviews at the English Language Centre at King Fahd University in Dhahran as a case study; interviewing native-speaking English lecturers during the 1998 autumn semester. The analysis will explore various perspectives as they arise from the investigations in the first part of the research and from the field data.

STATUS: Individual research

DATE OF RESEARCH: 1997-continuing

KEYWORDS: english - second language; second language teaching

2736

School of Education and Professional Development, Norwich NR4 7TJ
01603 456161
Georgetown College, Kentucky, KY 40324, USA
502 863 8011

Brown, G. Prof.; Shaw, G. Dr

Studies of Attention Disordered Hyperactive (ADHD) children

ABSTRACT: A series of experiments is in progress to explore the cognitive skills of children with attention disorders and hyperactivity. In particular the research is investigating unusual facets of memory and high levels of non-verbal creativity in Attention Disordered Hyperactive (ADHD) children. There is also strong evidence of high levels of mixed laterality, left handedness and allergic conditions.

PUBLISHED MATERIAL: SHAW, G.A. & BROWN, G. (1990). 'Laterality and creativity concomitants of attentional problems', Developmental Neuropsychology, Vol 6, No 1, pp.39-59. ; SHAW, G.A. & BROWN, G. (1991). 'Laterality, implicit memory and attention disorders', Educational Studies, Vol 17, No 1, pp.15-23. ; BROWN, G. (1991). 'Some more equal than others', The Vernon-Wall Lecture to the Education Section of the British Psychological Society, Blackpool, 1991.

STATUS: Sponsored project

SOURCE OF GRANT: University of East Anglia ; Georgetown College

DATE OF RESEARCH: 1989-1993

KEYWORDS: **attention deficit disorders; cognitive ability; hyperactivity; learning disabilities; memory**

2737

School of Education and Professional Development, Norwich NR4 7TJ
01603 456161
University College Suffolk, Suffolk College, Ipswich IP4 1LT
01473 255885
Suffolk and Great Yarmouth College of Nursing and Midwifery, Department of Nursing Studies, Education Centre, Ipswich Hospital, Heath Road, Ipswich IP4 5PD

Bedford, H. Ms; Robinson, J. Ms; *Supervisors*: Phillips, T. Mr; Schostak, J. Prof.

Assessment of competencies in nursing and midwifery education (ACE Project)

ABSTRACT: The research investigated the assessment of competencies in nursing and midwifery education, focusing on the experiences of staff and students in classrooms and clinical areas. Through observation, interviewing and the collection of documentary evidence, case studies of the structures and processes of assessment were constructed. In seeking ways of understanding the complex nature of professional competence, the research asked whether current assessment practices were adequate for identifying and evaluating integrated theory and practice. It looked in particular at processes for collecting and analysing evidence of competence, and at structures for critical dialogue about that evidence. Fieldwork was carried out in nine colleges of nursing, midwifery, health studies and their associated placement institutions in East Anglia, London and the North East. During the first phase, data was collected from all nine colleges, and issues relating to planning, design, use, monitoring, and development of assessment documents and procedures were identified. A grounded theory was developed from which themes and issues emerged for study at a smaller number of fieldsites in the second phase.

PUBLISHED MATERIAL: PHILLIPS, T., SCHOSTAK, J., BEDFORD, H. & ROBINSON, J. (1992). The assessment of competencies in nursing and midwifery education and training (the ACE project): interim report. Norwich: University of East Anglia, School of Education. ; PHILLIPS, T., BEDFORD, H., SCHOSTAK, J. & ROBINSON, J. (1993). The assessment of competencies in nursing and midwifery education and training (the ACE project). Research highlights 4. London: The English Board for Nursing, Midwifery and Health Visiting. ; BEDFORD, H., PHILLIPS, T., ROBINSON, J. & SCHOSTAK, J. (1994). The assessment of competencies in nursing and midwifery education and training (the ACE project): final report. London: The English National Board for Nursing, Midwifery and Health Visiting. ; BEDFORD, H., PHILLIPS, T., ROBINSON, J. & SCHOSTAK, J. (1994). The assessment of competencies in nursing and midwifery education and training (the ACE project): executive summary. London: The English National Board for Nursing, Midwifery and Health Visiting.

STATUS: Sponsored project

SOURCE OF GRANT: The English National Board for Nursing, Midwifery and Health Visiting £95,000

DATE OF RESEARCH: 1991-1993

KEYWORDS: **assessment; competence; nurse education; obstetrics**

2738

School of Education and Professional Development, Norwich NR4 7TJ
01603 456161
University of East Anglia, School of Education and Professional Development, Keswick Hall Centre for Research and Development in Religious Education, Norwich NR4 7TJ

Rudge, L. Mrs; *Supervisor*: Elliott, J. Prof.

Perceptions of policy on religious education and related areas 1993-98

ABSTRACT: Religious education (RE) in state schools is part of the basic legislated curriculum. It is organised through local education authorities (LEAs) not through the School Curriculum and Assessment Authority (SCAA). However, central control of RE exists through legislation and guidance contained in summarised form in DFE Circuluar 1/94. This PhD research project examines the tensions between local and national initiatives and developments in RE, and in related areas such as school collective worship. It aims to monitor the impact of the legislation on schools, individuals, LEAs, their Standing Advisory Councils on RE (SACREs) and local communities - including faith communities. The methods used are essentially action research and oral history (interviews, data analysis, classroom observations, analysis of public meetings, surveys), based mainly in case study sites in the East of England, set against a detailed overview of the national/international position of religion in the school curriculum. Interim results are available from the researcher.

PUBLISHED MATERIAL: RUDGE, L. (1995). 'RE in England: choice, diversity and freedom?', Religion og Livssyn (Norwegian teachers' publication), Vol 2, pp.22-28. ; RUDGE, L. (1996). 'Future trends in RE', Resource Journal of the Professional Council for RE, Vol 18, no 3, pp.4-8.

STATUS: Individual research

DATE OF RESEARCH: 1993-continuing

KEYWORDS: **educational legislation; educational policy; religious education; school worship**

University of East London

2739

Centre for Institutional Studies, Maryland House, Manbey Park Road, London E15 1EY
0181 590 7722

Howlett, S. Mr; *Supervisor*: Locke, M. Mr

Governance in public and community services

ABSTRACT: A series of studies have been undertaken to monitor the impact of policy developments on the governance of further and higher education and on voluntary organisations.

PUBLISHED MATERIAL: LOCKE, M. (1989). 'Sweet charity', Management in Education, Vol 3, No 2, pp.7-8. ; LOCKE, M. (1989). 'Can collegiality and entrepreneurialism exist together', Management in Education, Vol 3, No 4, pp.6-7. ; LOCKE, M. (1992). 'The application of "trust" in the management of institutions'. Paper presented to the Annual Conference of the British Educational Management and Administrative Society, September 1992. ; LOCKE, M. (1996). '"Trust" in the governance and management of voluntary organisations'. Paper presented to the International Research Symposium on Public Services Management, Aston University, March 1996. ; LOCKE, M. & HOWLETT, S. (1997). 'Stakeholders in the governance of voluntary organisations'. Paper presented to the International Research Symposium on Public Services Management, Aston University, September 1997.

STATUS: Sponsored project

SOURCE OF GRANT: University of East London

DATE OF RESEARCH: 1970-continuing

KEYWORDS: **community services; educational administration; educational change; educational policy; further education; higher education; management in education; voluntary agencies**

2740

Centre for Institutional Studies, Maryland House, Manbey Park Road, London E15 1EY
0181 590 7722

Hillier, Y. Dr; *Supervisor*: Locke, M. Mr

Informal practitioner theory in adult basic education

ABSTRACT: Adult basic education relies heavily on notions of 'good practice'. This study seeks to identify the elements of good practice used by practitioners in adult basic education and to relate these to adult education theory. This is in response to claims that practitioners do not take account of formal theory per se, but use informal theory to develop their practice. Thirty adult basic education practitioners, drawn from a sub-regional training group, will be interviewed using Kelly's Repertory Grid. This technique elicits constructs which will be used to identify underlying assumptions about 'good practice'. This will be used to create a formal statement of the informal theory.

STATUS: Individual research

DATE OF RESEARCH: 1990-1993

KEYWORDS: **adult basic education; adult educators; educational practices; teaching methods; theory practice relationship**

2741

Centre for Institutional Studies, Maryland House, Manbey Park Road, London E15 1EY
0181 590 7722

Lewis, A. Mr; *Supervisors*: Pratt, J. Prof.; Graham, J. Mr

The construction and use of mechanisms for obtaining student feedback in UK universities

ABSTRACT: The increasing use of mechanisms, for obtaining feedback on quality from students in higher education, raises questions about which of the various parties involved in the process is influencing the construction of the mechanisms and benefiting from the resulting feedback. In order to discover how student feedback mechanisms are being used in higher education, the research will examine the approach to the construction and use of mechanisms of the stakeholders involved: the institution, the various subject departments and the students. The research is concerned to discover whether or not their requirements of the mechanisms are compatible and, if there are differences, to what extent these dictate different preferences in the design of the mechanism. The research will be concerned to identify the political and ideological context of the development of student consultation. The research will investigate the selection and use of feedback methodologies for different types of courses in a sample of UK universities and will include indepth field surveys. The research will investigate the selection of feedback methodologies and their uses by academic staff and students on a sample of courses in order to determine which variables have an influence. To support this objective a taxonomy of feedback mechanisms will be developed on the basis of the epistemological and ideological considerations which inform them. It is hoped that comment will be forthcoming, from this point of view, on the appropriateness and shortcomings of the choices made.

STATUS: Individual research

DATE OF RESEARCH: 1993-1998

KEYWORDS: **educational quality; feedback; higher education; quality control; student attitudes; students**

2742

Centre for Institutional Studies, Maryland House, Manbey Park Road, London E15 1EY
0181 590 7722

Tuffin, R. Ms; *Supervisor*: Sampson, A. Ms

Young children's views of their environment: a pilot project

ABSTRACT: The aim of the project is to find out children's opinions of their area, their experiences of crime, and obtain their views on how the area may be made safer by focusing on their coping strategies in situations when they are afraid of being victimised. The work includes: walkabouts with children in a local primary school; consultation meetings with the staff; questionnaire for group discussions on experiences of crime; 30 indepth face-to-face interviews with 15 children aged 7/8 years and 15 children aged 10/11 years. This is a pilot project and it is hoped to obtain further funding to undertake a larger project and to make a video to assist young children to develop effective safety strategies.

STATUS: Sponsored project

SOURCE OF GRANT: University of East London £500; SDP Limited £2,200

DATE OF RESEARCH: 1995-1997

KEYWORDS: **community; crime; environment; primary school pupils; pupil attitudes; safety**

2743

Centre for Institutional Studies, Maryland House, Manbey Park Road, London E15 1EY
0181 590 7722

Jackson, S. Ms; *Supervisors*: Humm, M. Prof.; Locke, M. Mr

Spinsters and mistresses: returning the academic to women

ABSTRACT: This research considers the position of women in higher education asking whether, in order to succeed at university, women have to learn to be part of a male defined academic structure. In a male dominated and patriarchal system with a masculine determined curriculum, will women have to deny themselves and learn to 'play the game'. The empirical research will follow a group of women students through their degrees at the University of East London. It will compare the experiences of these 'combined studies' students on both women's studies and their other chosen subjects. It will consider their experiences in the classroom and lecture theatre, their written and assessed work, and the curriculum they are following. The theoretical research will focus on locating oppression, the creation of meaning and ownership of knowledge, and educational theories.

STATUS: Individual research

DATE OF RESEARCH: 1995-continuing

KEYWORDS: **higher education; sex differences; women; womens education**

2744

Centre for Institutional Studies, Maryland House, Manbey Park Road, London E15 1EY
0181 590 7722

Pratt, J. Prof.; Richards, N. Mr

Metropolitan higher: the establishment of higher education in London

ABSTRACT: Staff from several London universities and other educational institutions are collaborating on a project investigating the establishment of higher education in London throughout the 19th and early 20th centuries.

PUBLISHED MATERIAL: PRATT, J. & RICHARDS, N. (1998). 'Higher education and the London economy'. In: GLYNN, S. (Ed). London higher. London: Athlone Press.

STATUS: Collaborative

DATE OF RESEARCH: 1996-1998

KEYWORDS: **colleges of higher education; educational history; higher education; institutes of higher education; polytechnics; universities**

2745

Centre for Institutional Studies, Maryland House, Manbey Park Road, London E15 1EY
0181 590 7722

Eley, V. Ms; *Supervisor*: Pratt, J. Prof.

The history of the polytechnics

ABSTRACT: This study collates and analyses data on the policy and development of the polytechnics from the mid 1960s until their achievement of university status in 1992.

PUBLISHED MATERIAL: PRATT, J. (1997). The polytechnic experiment: 1965 to 1992. Buckingham: Open University Press.

STATUS: Sponsored project

SOURCE OF GRANT: Leverhulme Foundation £11,000; Committee of Directors of the Polytechnics £5,000

DATE OF RESEARCH: 1993-1997

KEYWORDS: **higher education; polytechnics**

2746

Centre for Institutional Studies, Maryland House, Manbey Park Road, London E15 1EY
0181 590 7722

Fernandes, M. Ms; *Supervisor*: Locke, M. Mr

Training needs analysis for voluntary organisations

ABSTRACT: The project is attempting to develop a simple kit for analysing training and development needs of people in voluntary organisations. It takes a person-centred, problem-solving approach, intending to help identify a range of measures available for individuals. It has been piloted in local organisations.

STATUS: Team research

SOURCE OF GRANT: London Docklands Development Corporation £3,925; University of East London

DATE OF RESEARCH: 1995-1998

KEYWORDS: **staff development; training; voluntary agencies; volunteers**

2747

Centre for Institutional Studies, Maryland House, Manbey Park Road, London E15 1EY
0181 590 7722

Pratt, J. Prof.

The development of Fachhochschulen in Austria

ABSTRACT: John Pratt was Rapporteur for a team of Organisation for Economic Cooperation and Development (OECD) examiners which reviewed the development of higher education policy in Austria, and he is a consultant to the Austrian Ministry of Science and Research for a project to monitor and evaluate the development of the policy to establish Fachhochschulen and its impact.

PUBLISHED MATERIAL: ORGANISATION FOR ECONOMIC COOPERATION AND DEVELOPMENT. (1993). Review of higher education policy in Austria: examiners' report and questions. Paris: OECD.; PRATT, J. (1993). 'Creating a binary policy in Austria', Higher Education Quarterly, Vol 47, No 2, pp.142-162. ; PRATT, J. (1994). 'Lehren aus der Gesichte: Die Osterreichische Eutwicklung aus Britischen sicht'. In: HOLLINGER, S., HACKL, E. & BRUMER, C. (Eds). Fachhochschulen - unburokratischm brauchbar und kure. Vienna: Passagen Verlag.

STATUS: Sponsored project

SOURCE OF GRANT: Austrian Ministry of Science and Research

DATE OF RESEARCH: 1993-1997

KEYWORDS: **austria; binary system; higher education; polytechnics**

2748

Centre for Institutional Studies, Maryland House, Manbey Park Road, London E15 1EY
0181 590 7722

Pratt, J. Prof.

Unification of higher education 1992-1997

ABSTRACT: A 'unified' system of higher education was created by the Further and Higher Education Act 1992. The Act enabled the polytechnics and major colleges to acquire university titles and established new funding and quality assurance agencies. It marked recognition that Britain had a system of 'mass' higher education. The years immediately following the Act offer a unique opportunity to examine its development as a single whole. The study will identify the 1992 policy intentions, examine whether they have been reflected in the strategic responses of institutions, and assess the impact of the new mechanisms of funding and control. The study will focus on strategic policy issues. It will attempt to identify the overall aims of the main parties involved in the decision to unify the system, in particular, the government and the institutions in the previous sectors, and the extent to which they were congruent or disparate. The study will examine the extent to which the aims of the parties were achieved in the years up to the Dearing Report, through analysis of the overall development of the system and the institutional sub-groups, and of the strategic responses of a sample of institutions from the previous sectors. It will examine the impact of the new forms of funding and control on a sample of institutions, and whether these are conducive to the policy aims or have differential effects.

STATUS: Individual research

DATE OF RESEARCH: 1997-continuing

KEYWORDS: **educational change; higher education; polytechnics**

2749

Centre for Institutional Studies, Maryland House, Manbey Park Road, London E15 1EY
0181 590 7722

Roberts, F. Ms; *Supervisor*: Sampson, A. Ms.

Evaluation of the Stratford City Challenge Stratford's standard primary schools project

ABSTRACT: The research will evaluate the Stratford City Challenge Stratford Standard Primary Project. The project aims to raise the level of pupil achievement in 7 primary and 2 nursery schools in the city challenge area by funding the purchase of information technology (IT) equipment. The computers will then be used to develop pupils' literacy and IT skills and enhance the delivery of other curriculum areas. Parents and Newham College of Further Education students are being trained to provide support in the classrooms to those children who are taking part in the computer assisted reading scheme. The link teacher in each school will be interviewed and some parents, students and pupils will also be interviewed to establish their opinions of the impact of the project. Test results, where they are available, will also be analysed in order to establish the impact of the programme on the pupils' literacy and IT skills.

STATUS: Sponsored project

SOURCE OF GRANT: Stratford Development Partnership Ltd

DATE OF RESEARCH: 1998-1998

KEYWORDS: **achievement; computer assisted reading; computer uses in education; information technology; literacy; pupil performance; reading**

2750

Centre for Institutional Studies, Maryland House, Manbey Park Road, London E15 1EY
0181 590 7722

Roberts, F. Ms; *Supervisor*: Sampson, A. Ms

Evaluation of the Stratford City Challenge Youth Pinnacle Programme

ABSTRACT: The research evaluates the Stratford City Challenge Youth Pinnacle Programme. Youth Pinnacle aimed to improve young people's job search skills. It provided 563 Year 10 and 11 pupils in 3 secondary schools with experience in writing a curriculum vitae and attending a mock interview. In the course of the evaluation, 244 pupils completed structured questionnaires. 30 interviewers from businesses and professional interviewers completed telephone questionnaires, and 3 teachers, one from each school, were interviewed in person. The data was analysed using SPSS. Pupils were asked to rate their skills before and after their participation in the programme. The interviewers were asked to rate the skills of pupils from each school. The results show that the programme does appear to have achieved its aims. The vast majority of pupils and all the interviewers and teachers who took part in the research thought that the programme was useful, and both the pupils and interviewers perceived an increase in the pupils' job seeking skills following their participation in the programme.

PUBLISHED MATERIAL: ROBERTS, F. (1997). Evaluation of the Stratford City Challenge Youth Pinnacle Programme. CIS Commentary No 64. London: University of East London, Centre for Institutional Studies.

STATUS: Sponsored project

SOURCE OF GRANT: Stratford Development Partnership Ltd

DATE OF RESEARCH: 1997-1997

KEYWORDS: **job search methods; school leavers; school to work transition; secondary school pupils; vocational guidance**

2751

Centre for Institutional Studies, Maryland House, Manbey Park Road, London E15 1EY
0181 590 7722

Grady, A. Dr; *Supervisor*: Locke, M. Mr

International postgraduate education

ABSTRACT: The study includes: 1) reviews of postgraduate education as a channel for technology transfer; 2) a survey of experiences of international postgraduate students at a UK university. It builds on a PhD study of 45

postgraduate students in UK universities by questionnaire, together with extensive review of literature.

PUBLISHED MATERIAL: GRADY, A. & LOCKE, M. (1997). 'The progress of technology transfer and the channel of international education', Industry and Higher Education, October, pp.278-286. ; GRADY, A. & LOCKE, M. (1997). 'Research and advisory centre for international education', Mediterranean Journal for Educational Studies, Vol 2, No 1.

STATUS: Individual research

DATE OF RESEARCH: 1997-1998

KEYWORDS: **graduate study; higher education; overseas students; universities**

2752

Group for Research into Access and Student Programmes, Barking Campus, Longbridge Road, Dagenham RM8 2AS
0181 590 7722
University of East London, Department of Combined Social Sciences, Barking Campus, Longbridge Road, Dagenham RM8 2AS

Ainley, P. Dr; Robbins, D. Dr

A comparison of student and staff experiences at two contrasted higher education institutions

ABSTRACT: A cross section of 51 final year undergraduates at Kent University has been interviewed for comparison with a geographical selection of 50 final year undergraduates at the University of East London. This is intended to bring out the differences and similarities in the experience of higher education by 'stereotypical' - 18-21 year old middle class students moving from school to work and home to living away via residential higher education; and the 'new' - mature female, ethnic minority and working class students living at home whilst studying. The student interviews are supplemented by staff interviews at the two higher education institutions.

PUBLISHED MATERIAL: AINLEY, P. (1994). Degrees of difference: higher education in the 1990s. London: Lawrence and Whishart.

STATUS: Sponsored project

SOURCE OF GRANT: Department of Employment: Enterprise in Higher Education Initiative

DATE OF RESEARCH: 1991-1993

KEYWORDS: **academic staff; ethnic groups; higher education; mature students; middle class students; student attitudes; student experience; working class**

University of Kent at Canterbury
2753

Department of Sociology and Social Anthropology, Canterbury CT2 7NZ
0181 316 8000

Davey, B. Mr; *Supervisor*: Ainley, P. Dr

The student charter project

ABSTRACT: The report starts with working definitions for a charter and other related terms, compact and contract. It then traces some early developments in charters and examines why there has been renewed interest in the concept in recent years. The link between charters and quality is examined, followed by the results of a survey of all higher education institutions in the UK with case studies of charter implementation in three of them. The different types of charters are set against the Institute of Public Policy Research's definitions of quality.

PUBLISHED MATERIAL: DAVEY, B. (1992). 'The student charter project report'. Canterbury: Enterprise Kent, University of Kent.

STATUS: Sponsored project

SOURCE OF GRANT: Department of Employment: Enterprise in Higher Education Initiative £12,000

DATE OF RESEARCH: 1992-1993

KEYWORDS: **educational quality; higher education; institutional role; performance contracts**

University of North London
2754

School of Teaching Studies, Marlborough Building, 383 Holloway Road, London N7 ORN
0171 607 2789

O'Keefe, D. Dr; Stoll, P. Mrs; Cole, H. Mrs

Truancy research project

ABSTRACT: The present research covers 20 randomly selected local education authorities (LEAs) in England. In each of these, every fourth school is to be visited, to a total of 150 schools. In each school visited all year 10 and 11 pupils are surveyed through confidential and anonymous questionnaires. The aim is to uncover the incidence of truancy, especially Post Registration Truancy, and the incidence of alienation from the school curriculum. The analysis of the findings will be aided by those of a staff questionnaire aimed at uncovering the school ethos and socio-economic status. The most innovative factor in the research is the guiding expectation that truancy is essentially a sociological rather than a psychological phenomenon, and intimately related to the school curriculum.

PUBLISHED MATERIAL: O'KEEFE, D. (1981). 'Truancy, industry and the school curriculum'. In: FLEW, et al (Eds). The Pied Pipers of Education. London: Social Affairs Unit. ; O'KEEFE, D. & STOLL, P. (1989). Officially present. London: IEA Education Unit.

STATUS: Sponsored project

SOURCE OF GRANT: Department of Education and Science £185,000

DATE OF RESEARCH: 1991-1993

KEYWORDS: **pupil behaviour; truancy**

2755

School of Teaching Studies, Marlborough Building, 383 Holloway Road, London N7 ORN
0171 607 2789
Bath Spa University College, Newton Park, Newton St Loe, Bath BA2 9BN
01225 875875

Hutchings, M. Ms; *Supervisors*: Ross, A. Prof.; Coulby, D. Dr

Children's perceptions of work and the sources of their understanding

ABSTRACT: An investigation into primary aged children's thinking about work, examining (through semi-structured interviews) the way in which children draw on their experiences (in the home, school, community and through the media) and from them construct their understanding of work (including paid and unpaid work, and work at school).

PUBLISHED MATERIAL: HUTCHINGS, M. (1989). Children's ideas about the world of work. London: Polytechnic of North London Press. ; HUTCHINGS, M. (1990). 'Children's thinking about work'. In: ROSS, A. (Ed). Economic and industrial awareness in the primary school. London: Polytechnic of North London Press.

STATUS: Individual research

DATE OF RESEARCH: 1986-1993

KEYWORDS: **employment; primary school pupils; social cognition; work attitudes**

University of the West of England
2756

Faculty of Computer Studies and Management, Frenchay Campus, Coldharbour Lane, Bristol BS16 1QY
01179 656261

Cartwright, D. Mr; *Supervisors*: Thomas, P. Prof.; Jones, S. Dr

Technology to support reflective thinking through speech capture in collaborative learning environments

ABSTRACT: This study investigates the use of technology in collaborative learning. The focus is on 'advanced learning' which refers to aspects of higher education and professional development. A review of learning theory suggests that a constructivist perspective is most appropriate for individual knowledge construction. Learning in a community of practice is explained by the principle of legitimate peripheral participation where learners participate in systems of knowing. Knowledge is a cultural construction, mediated through language and results from social practice. The role of conversation as a mode of communication is prominent. A study of the characteristics of advanced learning in this kind of setting reveals that it is individualistic, skill-oriented and exploratory. The activity revolves around the solution of complex problems. Complex problems do not have a straightforward solution, they are 'fuzzy' and difficult to define. Learning to solve complex problems, demands development of certain skills. Creativity, critical thinking, argumentation and reflection are all necessary. Of these, reflective thinking is the least understood and has little technological support. This study investigates how reflective thinking may be supported by capturing collaborative learning conversations and allowing the individual learners to reflect on the emergent knowledge contained. A conceptual model is developed for reflection in learning and a study made of reflective conversations to identify categories of reflective thought. These results are then used to inform the design of a speech capture tool which supports reflective learning.

PUBLISHED MATERIAL: THOMAS, P.J., LEES, D.Y. & CARTWRIGHT, D. (1995). 'The Centre for Personal Information Management: organisational overview'. Proceedings of HCI '95 Conference, Huddersfield, 1995. ; CARTWRIGHT, D. (1997). 'Supporting emergent knowledge capture in collaborative learning environments'. Proceedings of the HCI '97 Conference, 1997. ; CARTWRIGHT, D., THOMAS, P.J. & JONES, S. (1998). 'Collaborative learning using a speech capture tool'. Proceedings of CiP '98 Conference, York, April 1998.

STATUS: Individual research

DATE OF RESEARCH: 1995-1998

KEYWORDS: computer uses in education; cooperative learning; higher education; information technology; reflection

2757

Faculty of Computer Studies and Mathematics, Frenchay Campus, Coldharbour Lane, Bristol BS16 1QY
01179 656261

Jukes, K. Prof.

A framework for enabling higher level information technology updating and continuous professional development of the existing regional workforce

ABSTRACT: With demographic decline, rapid technological change, the use of information technology (IT) in all sectors of the market, and the impact of the downturn in the defence industry, the peace dividend and the recession, organisations have increasingly recognised the need to place effort into the continuing professional development (CPD) of the retained workforce. In IT and end-user support, historical skill shortages were historically plugged by personnel without formal training. Rapid changes in technology, tools and methodologies, and their strategic impact on competitiveness and the quality of information have led to a need to ensure staff have a firmer grounding in the subject. The University of the West of England has addressed this over recent years through the development of tailored training programmes, part-time MSc's, part-time HNC/D programmes and top-ups to Degree level from HNC/D. Each of these areas has moved forward by modular provision and the development of credit rating structures. The project includes the following objectives: 1) the development of a formal network of employers and universities in the region to collaborate in providing modules for CPD with a range of levels, locations, and modes of delivery; 2) the setting up of access mechanisms to the network by other parties including small and medium sized enterprises (SMEs) and very small organisations; 3) fieldwork to research and establish requirements for and approaches to CPD; and 4) the establishment of a database of modules and providers, the database being in a variety of forms for effective access and use.

STATUS: Sponsored project

SOURCE OF GRANT: Avon Training and Enterprise Council; Training, Enterprise and Education Directorate; Department of Employment, jointly £69,000

DATE OF RESEARCH: 1991-1993

KEYWORDS: computer uses in education; higher education; information technology; professional development

2758

Faculty of Computer Studies and Mathematics, Frenchay Campus, Coldharbour Lane, Bristol BS16 1QY
01179 656261

Wallace, C. Mr

Conceptual models and their cognition

ABSTRACT: The use of graphical notations to depict conceptual models is widespread in software engineering. Despite this, there has been little work done on the perception of such notations by students learning software design methods, nor is there much evidence of the application of graphic design principles in the 'engineering' of such notations. This study is aimed at a particular conceptual modelling notation, namely class-models in object-oriented design. Numerous variations in notation exist and the study will investigate the comparative ease of comprehension and construction of two polar extremes amongst these notations. The test instruments being developed are largely comprehension tests which will be administered to stratified groups of students. By comparison, it is expected that the tests will also be used with experienced systems designers.

STATUS: Individual research

DATE OF RESEARCH: 1996-1998

KEYWORDS: computer software; computer system design; information technology

2759

Faculty of Computer Studies and Mathematics, Frenchay Campus, Coldharbour Lane, Bristol BS16 1QY
01179 656261

Tuckett, J. Mrs; *Supervisors*: Thomas, P. Prof.; Jones, S. Dr

Human factors of the mobile multimedia university

ABSTRACT: The 1990s have seen radical changes within the educational system which have resulted in greater participation in post-school education. This, coupled with funding cutbacks, puts a severe strain on the present educational system. The researchers believe that one way of relieving this pressure is through the use of technology. This research recognises the combination of education and technology as a powerful force. The mobile multimedia university (MMU) project investigates the opportunities afforded by the developments taking place in mobile computing and communications technologies. The convergence of technologies which allow packetisation and integration of different categories of information - data, image, voice - now allow the development of new technologies which support the learning process, e.g. distance learning, video-conferencing, and particularly for the MMU, the use of medical imaging over different network configurations. In the future, such information is expected to be delivered across wired and wireless networks in a seamless fashion. The focus of the research is on user need and, as such, a Delphi survey has taken place which attempts to establish the current state of education and technology and where developments are likely to take place within the next 5-10 years.

PUBLISHED MATERIAL: TUCKETT, J. & THOMAS, P. (1996). 'Accessing the digital campus and the digital library'. Paper presented at the Conference on 3D and Multimedia on the Internet, WWW and Networks, Bradford, 16-18 April, 1996. ; TUCKETT, J., JONES, S.R. & THOMAS, P.J. (1997). 'The future of technology in higher education - a Delphi survey'. Proceedings of the RUFIS Conference, Prague, 1997. ; TUCKETT, J., THOMAS, P.J., JONES, S.R. & MEECH, J. (1997). 'Poster: the mobile multimedia university'. Proceedings of the ALT-C97 Conference, September 1997.

STATUS: Sponsored project

SOURCE OF GRANT: Hewlett-Packard; University of the West of England

DATE OF RESEARCH: 1995-1998

KEYWORDS: computer assisted learning; computer networks; computer uses in education; higher education; information technology; multimedia; telecommunications

2760

Faculty of Computer Studies and Mathematics, Frenchay Campus, Coldharbour Lane, Bristol BS16 1QY
01179 656261

Cartwright, D. Mr; *Supervisors*: Thomas, P. Prof.; Jones, S. Dr

Computer-supported collaborative learning: an audio tool for critical thinking

ABSTRACT: Work for this thesis has focused on investigating technological support for learning; in particular the learning of research skills. Developing research skills focuses around the qualities of learning how to learn and developing critical thinking skills, which are concordant with constructivist theories of learning. Design of technology with constructivist principles is currently manifest in the field of Computer-Supported Collaborative Learning (CSCL). Within this field there is much scope for the development of systems and tools to support new ways of learning. Theories of how learning occurs suggest that at the research level there is a knowledge-based process occurring for the learner which involves the synthesis of acquired knowledge and the construction of new knowledge. In the practice of argument and discussion between learning peers (a form of collaborative learning) a construction of shared meaning occurs, through which new knowledge emerges. Usually this emergent knowledge is not captured and so cannot be explicity reflected on or further explored. This project will investigate how learning can be enhanced if supported by technology which will effectively captive audio, and allow reflection on and manipulation of emergent knowledge of this kind. It is expected that an audio captive tool will be prototyped and user tested.

STATUS: Sponsored project

SOURCE OF GRANT: Hewlett Packard Laboratories £20,000

DATE OF RESEARCH: 1995-1998

KEYWORDS: **audiovisual education; computer assisted learning; computer uses in education; group work; information technology; learning theories; talking computers**

2761

Faculty of Computer Studies and Mathematics, Frenchay Campus, Coldharbour Lane, Bristol BS16 1QY
01179 656261

Sanderson, F. Ms; *Supervisors*: Lacohee, H. Dr; Thomas, P. Prof.

Understanding personal communication: significant factors influencing children's use of electronic communication

ABSTRACT: This project is an enquiry into children's use of communications technologies, located within the contexts of the family and home. It considers children's use of electronic communications, particularly online services, in order to identify the significant factors which affect the extent and quality of use. It considers: 1) some of the factors which underlie children's use of communications technologies, particularly electronic communications; 2) contextual factors, such as family practices with communications technologies, and family 'styles'; 3) constraints on young children's use of new technologies, including physical access constraints, as well as those inherent in the technologies themselves; 4) emergent patterns and purposes of communications' technology use, which might form an element of a 'universal communications behaviour' schema. Dependent upon first analysis of existing datasets, the project may focus on children of particular ages, perhaps the transition from home to school, or from primary to secondary school age.

STATUS: Sponsored project

SOURCE OF GRANT: British Telecom

DATE OF RESEARCH: 1997-continuing

KEYWORDS: **children; computer uses at home; computer uses in education; computers; home computers; human computer interaction; information technology; telecommunications**

2762

Faculty of Education, Redland Campus, Redland Hill, Bristol BS6 6UZ
01179 741251

Attwood, G. Ms; *Supervisors*: Blunden, G. Dr; Bone, J. Mrs; Croll, P. Prof.

Competence in context: an investigation into the appropriateness of competence-based assessment schemes in contrasting educational settings

ABSTRACT: This research is for a PhD. Its aim is to investigate whether competence is a sufficient and/or appropriate assessment measure of achievement in a range of educational contexts. A review of the policy background, and implementation of the National Vocational Qualification (NVQ) provides a backdrop by which to explore the various theoretical models and approaches to assessment. The empirical data involved 2 case studies. The first is a practical assessment scheme offered by the Royal Society of Art Examination Board to assess basic information technology skills. The second case study focused on the effects of the introduction of exit competences as a requirement for the assessment of students of initial teacher training. The 2 studies look into tutor's perceptions of what has happened. This is followed by a comparison of the 2 very different models in terms of similiarity and difference. The conclusions suggest that there is a role for competence-based assessment as it offers transparency of what is required but that the model that is selected within a range of possible competence-based models needs to be very carefully thought out. At the skills level highly prescriptive and behaviourist model can be used successfully but in professional areas the model needs to address criteria that cannot be easily defined.

PUBLISHED MATERIAL: ATTWOOD, G. (1995). 'Teacher perceptions of a skills-based competence assessment scheme', British Journal of Curriculum and Assessment, Vol 6, No 1, pp.26-31.

STATUS: Individual research

DATE OF RESEARCH: 1992-continuing

KEYWORDS: **assessment; competency based education**

2763

Faculty of Education, Redland Campus, Redland Hill, Bristol BS6 6UZ
01179 741251

Raphael Reed, L. Ms

Working with boys

ABSTRACT: A critical investigation of the reported crisis around boys and schooling, integrating the insights from recent academic writing on gender and education, with practitioner orientated theorisation of the issues. The project, using an ethnographic methodology, explores closely the relationship between teachers and boys in one class in a secondary school context from Year 9 through to Year 11. Specifically it investigates: 1) the ways in which gender and sexualities construct and are constructed by the interactions between teachers and pupils focusing on masculinities; 2) how issues around masculinity impinge upon the learning process for boys in the classroom context; and 3) how working with boys impacts upon both the identity formation and educational practices of teachers. The aim is to develop further our understanding of attempts to engage with and intervene in the dynamics of masculinities in the learning process and thereby to further re-evaluate existing equal opportunities perspectives.

PUBLISHED MATERIAL: RAPHAEL REED, L. (1995). 'Reconceptualising equal opportunities: a study of radical teacher culture in transition'. In GRIFFITHS, M. & TROYNA, B. (Eds). Antiracism, culture and social justice. Stoke on Trent: Trentham Books. ; RAPHAEL REED, L. (1995). Working with boys: a new research agenda. The Redland Papers. Bristol: University of the West of England, Faculty of Education. ; RAPHAEL REED, L. (1998). 'Power, pedagogy and persuasion: schooling masculinities in the secondary school classroom', Journal of Education Policy, Vol 13, No 4, pp.501-517. ; RAPHAEL REED, L. (1998). 'Zero tolerance: gender performance and school failure'. In EPSTEIN, D., ELWOOD, J., HEY, V. & MAW, J. (Eds). Failing boys? Issues in gender and achievement. Buckingham: Open University Press. ; RAPHAEL REED, L. 'Boys and underachievement. Reality or backlash?', Education Today and Tomorrow. (in press).

STATUS: Individual research

DATE OF RESEARCH: 1995-continuing

KEYWORDS: **boys; equal education; masculinity; secondary education; sex differences**

2764

Faculty of Education, Redland Campus, Redland Hill, Bristol BS6 6UZ
01179 741251

Thomas, G. Prof.; Webb, J. Dr

Evaluation of Barnardos Somerset inclusive project

ABSTRACT: Evaluation was made of the closure of a special school and its conversion to a service. The project was found to be highly successful.
PUBLISHED MATERIAL: THOMAS, G., WALKER, D. & WEBB, J. (1997). The making of the inclusive school. London: Routledge.

STATUS: Sponsored project

SOURCE OF GRANT: Barnardos £30,000

DATE OF RESEARCH: 1996-1997

KEYWORDS: closures; mainstreaming; special educational needs; special schools

2765

Faculty of Education, Redland Campus, Redland Hill, Bristol BS6 6UZ
01179 741251

Thomas, G. Prof.

Best practice among special schools on special measures: the role of action planning in improvement

ABSTRACT: Research is being undertaken into the effects of action planning in helping special schools to come off special measures. Work is in progress.

STATUS: Sponsored project

SOURCE OF GRANT: Department for Education and Employment £20,000

DATE OF RESEARCH: 1997-1998

KEYWORDS: inspection; special educational needs; special schools

2766

Faculty of Education, Redland Campus, Redland Hill, Bristol BS6 6UZ
01179 741251

Eke, R. Dr; *Supervisor*: Croll, P. Prof.

Children's media learning in primary schools

ABSTRACT: This thesis describes a study which investigates children's experience of media education in a small selection of primary classrooms with a view to informing pedagogic practice and conceptions of children's understanding of media, especially television. The investigation springs from a consideration of curriculum proposals for primary media education and reports of curriculum implementation. The approaches to teaching and learning about the media embedded in these proposals are pursued through a focus on children's learning about and from television. Developmental evidence of children's television learning, although problematic, can inform the provision of media education in primary schools. Social constructivist approaches to children's viewing provide a perspective on social viewing, and on children making sense of their viewing. They have the potential to address pupils' practical activity as meaning makers. The social constructivist emphasis on context, and on issues of 'scaffolding' and 'handover' inform the approach to data analysis employed. The approach brings together issues of curriculum provision and pupil learning through a structured analysis of classroom utterances. The categories that inform this analysis allow an exploration of the nature of scaffolded media learning in a variety of teaching contexts. The analysis of the transcripts demonstrates the value of a systematic analysis of utterances, and its sensitivity to teaching context and content. A significant rise in the number and level of areas of media attainment visited by 10 and 11 year-olds, compared to younger pupils, is reported. Distinctions are found between whole-class teaching and small group activity, and between image study and image making. The principal outcomes of the study are reviewed and suggestions offered for further research. The thesis makes a small, original contribution to the study of children's media learning from a social constructivist perspective.

PUBLISHED MATERIAL: EKE, R. (1995). 'Context and utterance', Study of Children's Media Learning and Journal of Educational Television', Vol 21, No 2, pp.101-111.

STATUS: Individual research

DATE OF RESEARCH: 1994-1997

KEYWORDS: mass media; primary education; scaffolding; television

2767

Faculty of Education, Redland Campus, Redland Hill, Bristol BS6 6UZ
01179 741251

Forrest, M. Dr; Ching Yee, W. Ms

Primary Latin project: evaluation

ABSTRACT: The Primary Latin project was established during the academic year 1996-97. Funding in the region of 20,000 pounds was raised by private subscription to enable Barbara Bell, Head of Classics, Clifton High School, to work full-time on the design and writing of a short Latin Language Programme aimed at pupils in key stage 2 of the National Curriculum. The materials are being used on a trial basis during 1997-98 and are due to be published in 1999 by Cambridge University Press. Funding from project sources has enabled a small-scale evaluation to be carried out during the second semester of 1997-98. Questionnaires were distributed to the 20 teachers who are trialling the materials in both the maintained and independent sectors. Visits will be undertaken to schools with a view to collecting data from teachers and pupils and parents. Interest will focus on the evidence of transferable learning between the language programme and other areas of the curriculum, notably English and history.

STATUS: Sponsored project

SOURCE OF GRANT: Private Benefactions £4,000

DATE OF RESEARCH: 1998-continuing

KEYWORDS: latin; primary education

2768

Faculty of Education, Redland Campus, Redland Hill, Bristol BS6 6UZ
01179 741251

James, D. Dr

Assessment practices and mature student experiences in higher education

ABSTRACT: This resource fellowship project arose from work undertaken as part of a PhD study, completed in 1996. Its main aim is to conduct detailed investigation into the nature and significance of common assessment practices in higher education through the use of comparative case studies. Within this, the research explores the impact of institutional histories and cultures on assessment practices and examines the utility of different theoretical frameworks which are brought to bear on assessment (e.g. technical, humanistic, sociological).

PUBLISHED MATERIAL: JAMES, D. (1995). 'Mature studentship in higher education beyond a 'species' approach', British Journal of Sociology of Education, Vol 16, No 4, pp.451-466. ; JAMES, D. (1996). Mature studentship in higher education. PhD thesis. Bristol: University of the West of England. ; JAMES, D. & GRENFELL, M. (1998). Bourdieu and educational research. London: Falmer Press.

STATUS: Individual research

DATE OF RESEARCH: 1996-1998

KEYWORDS: assessment; higher education; mature students; student experience

2769

Faculty of Education, Redland Campus, Redland Hill, Bristol BS6 6UZ
01179 741251

Postlethwaite, K. Prof.; Gilbert, P. Mr

The sex-files

ABSTRACT: The project further developed a CD-Rom sex education resource called seX Files which had previously been produced by one of the research team. It delivered training sessions to classroom assistants, youth workers, school governors and health education workers in the use of this interactive multimedia resource (IMM) and developed insights into the use of IMM generally. It evaluated this training. The training sessions were designed following consultation with the Health Promotion Service, Avon (formerly Bristol Area Specialist Health Promotion Services), youth services in several local authorities in the Bristol area, lecturers in the Faculty of Health and Social Care and the University of the West of England and, because of the focus on classroom assistants, with special educational needs coordinators in primary and secondary schools. These consultations indicated that the seX Files resource was a valuable tool for sex education, that the content was appropriate and accurate, and the presentation engaging; that schools welcomed the idea of using IMM in personal, health and social education (PHSE) and related areas; that special educational needs coordinators (SENCOs) welcomed the notion of classroom assistants using IMM for PHSE with individuals and small groups out of the mainstream classroom. Initial market research indicated a strong interest in training workshops from all the target groups. In practice, 37 of the 45 who attended were classroom assistants, with some representation from the other groups. This appeared to be for practical reasons concerned with the timing of the workshops and timing and targeting of the advertising. Workshops involved discussion of what makes a good IMM resource, instruction on setting up an IMM computer, and familiarisation with the seX Files CD-Rom. This was followed by group work such as the design of activities for use with young people to support and complement one section of the CD-Rom in the context of a session in school or elsewhere. The workshop was evaluated by pre- and post-questionnaires. The project demonstrated a high level of interest in training in the use of new technologies, recognition of their value in education and anxiety about how best to use them. The researchers identified a need for basic information and communications technology (ICT) training for classroom assistants and governors. It was useful to have different professional groups together in the workshops to exchange ideas about a range of approaches to topics such as sex education which have controversial elements. It was clear that each professional group also had specific needs which might better be addressed in specific sessions (e.g. the classroom assistants needed further help on managing the resource with pupils with special educational needs). Participants demonstrated that they found IMM less confusing and less difficult after the workshop. They also made clear that the workshop was thought provoking in relation to the place of IMM in education. A common view was that IMM resources should be distributed with teachers' guides and photocopiable activity handouts for pupils.

PUBLISHED MATERIAL: GILBERT, P. (1998). The seX FILES: final report. Bristol: University of the West of England.

STATUS: Sponsored project

SOURCE OF GRANT: Higher Education Funding Council for England £11,498

DATE OF RESEARCH: 1998-1998

KEYWORDS: **cd roms; computer uses in education; information technology; multimedia; sex education**

2770

Faculty of Education, Redland Campus, Redland Hill, Bristol BS6 6UZ
01179 741251

Shabajee, P. Mr; *Supervisors*: Altwood, G. Ms; Postlethwaite, K. Prof.

ARKive education research project

ABSTRACT: ARKive will be a multimedia database which will contain film, photographs, sound and text-based information on all recognised endangered species worldwide and all UK species for which film and photographs are available. The ARKive Education Research project started in March 1996 to identify how ARKive can be designed and constructed to be of maximum use in UK schools. This research is focused on 3 main areas: 1) What are the key factors which would make ARKive an effective educational multimedia resource for pupils? 2) What are the key factors which would make ARKive an effective educational multimedia resource to support the teachers? 3) What are the most effective design and production processes for ARKive to enable it to meet the needs of pupils and teachers? The project is due to end and report in March 1999.

PUBLISHED MATERIAL: SHABAJEE, P. 'Making values and beliefs explicit as a tool for the effective development of educational multimedia software - a prototype', British Journal of Educational Technology. (in press). ; SHABAJEE, P., COSTELLO, K., HARNETT, P. & EGAN, R. 'Discovering Cabot's Bristol: exploring the potential of multimedia approaches for effective learning'. Proceedings of the HAN 1988 (HumanITies, Information Technology in the Arts and Humanities) Conference, 1998. (in press).

STATUS: Sponsored project

SOURCE OF GRANT: Single Regeneration Grant £18,000; Higher Education Funding Council for England £24,500

DATE OF RESEARCH: 1996-continuing

KEYWORDS: **computer uses in education; conservation - environment; environmental education; information technology; multimedia; wildlife**

2771

Faculty of Education, Redland Campus, Redland Hill, Bristol BS6 6UZ
01179 741251

Whitehead, J. Ms; Taylor, A. Ms

Teaching supply in modern foreign language: recruitment and supply of foreign native speakers

ABSTRACT: The research looks at the shortfall in recruitment to initial teacher training courses in modern foreign languages (MFL) and how the recruitment of foreign native speakers is helping meet the shortfall. The aim of the research was to document the numbers of foreign native speakers undertaking courses leading to the award of qualified teacher status (QTS), to discover their reasons for training in England, as well as their experiences during training and success in obtaining teaching posts. The aim was also to document steps providers of teacher training had taken to recruit foreign native speakers and how the providers believed these students had coped with the training. All institutions (68) offering initial teacher training in MFL were circulated with questionnaires and, where course leaders indicated a willingness to participate in the research (43), questionnaires were sent to the foreign native speakers from whom a sample was chosen for semi-structured interviews. The findings revealed that foreign native speakers constituted a third of those admitted to initial teacher training in 1997-98. Without these students the shortfall in recruitment would have been 47%. Training institutions believed that students' prior experience as foreign language assistants had helped their adjustment to training, whilst the students believed their personalities and determination had been key factors. 87% of the students planned to seek teaching posts in the UK on completion of their training.

STATUS: Sponsored project

SOURCE OF GRANT: Teacher Training Agency £11,033

DATE OF RESEARCH: 1998-1998

KEYWORDS: **language teachers; modern language studies; overseas students; preservice teacher education; student teachers; teacher supply and demand**

2772

Faculty of Education, Redland Campus, Redland Hill, Bristol BS6 6UZ
01179 741251

Harnett, P. Mrs; *Supervisors*: Lee, J. Mr; Forrest, M. Dr

Development in the history curriculum in state primary schools in the 20th century

ABSTRACT: The study is tracing the development of the history curriculum in primary schools during this century. It identifies particular traditions in the history curriculum and illustrates how they are represented within the current history National Curriculum. The study explores the justification for including history within the primary school curriculum and investigates how its subject status has developed since the Education Reform Act 1988. Future research will examine the changing nature of history's status in relationship with other subject areas prior to the curriculum review in 2000. Data is drawn from official documents including government handbooks, reports and discussion papers, together with books on teaching history and selected children's textbooks. The current history curriculum as experienced in schools is also investigated through interview data with primary school teachers and through a questionnaire sent to 280 primary schools.

PUBLISHED MATERIAL: HARNETT, P. (1996). The development of the history curriculum in state primary schools in twentieth century England. Redland Papers. Issue No 3. Bristol: University of the West of England. ; HARNETT, P. (1997). 'Developments in the primary history curriculum during the twentieth century'. In: PENDRY, A. & O'NEILL, C. Principles and practice: analytical perspectives on curriculum reform and changing pedagogy from history teacher educators. Lancaster: Standing Conference of History Teacher Educators. ; HARNETT, P. (1998). 'Heroes and heroines: exploring a nation's past. The history curriculum in state primary schools in the twentieth century', Bulletin of the History of Education Society, Vol 62, pp.83-95.

STATUS: Individual research

DATE OF RESEARCH: 1996-continuing

KEYWORDS: **educational history; history; national curriculum; primary education**

2773

Faculty of Education, Redland Campus, Redland Hill, Bristol BS6 6UZ
01179 741251

Tarr, J. Ms; *Supervisors*: Thomas, G. Prof.; Postlethwaite, K. Prof.; Vincent, C. Dr

Professionals' and parents' concepts of special educational needs

ABSTRACT: The main focus of this study is the educational experiences of the child who for some reason is identified as having difficulty in learning. A social model is used for beginning understanding this construction of 'special needs' which will explore the role, function and perceptions of parents and professionals engaged in the life of the child. The social model implies that the context surrounding the child plays a crucial part in the experiences of the child. Issues being explored will cover notions of parents' culture and the community; professionalism, identity and culture; social justice and the recognition of difference. The methodology takes a naturalistic approach and will be conducted through interviews with 6 sets of parents/carers and at least 6 professionals working with children. It is intended that findings will enhance understanding of provision for children with special educational needs at stage 3 and above of the Code of Practice (1994) and move towards a framework for multi-agency working that provides respect and recognition for the child and parents/carers.

STATUS: Individual research

DATE OF RESEARCH: 1996-continuing

KEYWORDS: **learning disabilities; parent attitudes; special educational needs**

2774

Faculty of Education, Redland Campus, Redland Hill, Bristol BS6 6UZ
01179 741251

Ashley, M. Mr; *Supervisors*: Menter, I. Mr; Croll, P. Prof.; Clough, N. Mr

Value as a reason for action in environmental education

ABSTRACT: The research explores the relationship between pro-environmental behaviour and the way in which children make value judgements about the environment. 300 pupils aged 11 and 14 were selected from urban and rural schools. A questionnaire was administered to the whole sample which established that high levels of knowledge of how one 'ought' to behave towards the environment existed. Much less scientific understanding of reasons that might justify the behaviour was found. Intention to act was found not to correlate with either naive moral or scientific knowledge. Questions about willingness to pay established that services such as health and education were valued by a majority of subjects, whilst environmental protection was an economic marginal. Detailed structured interviews with 45 of the middle school pupils took place during the following year. These sought to establish the relative amounts of value placed on aspects of outdoor environments by groups identified as users and non-users of national parks and outdoor education. The user group valued the outdoors significantly more than the non-user groups. However, the main reasons for the higher valuations were for hedonistic reasons such as adventure games or viewing popular species of mammals. Environmental awareness had minimal effect on the results. The study concluded that children are socialised into an anthropocentric culture which treats the natural world as though it is a commodity to be consumed. Children's hedonistic orientations may be insufficient to generate moral commitment to pro-environmental behaviours. The study proposed further work to identify the development in children of non-material values.

PUBLISHED MATERIAL: ASHLEY, M. (1995). 'Why the moralistic approach to environmental education will never work', Environmental Education, Autumn, p.16. ; ASHLEY, M. (1998). 'Economics, environment and the loss of innocence'. In: HOLDEN, C. & CLOUGH, N. (Eds). Children as citizens: education for participation. London: Jessica Kingsley.; ASHLEY, M. 'Sustainability and the humanities: towards uncertain futures'. In: ASHLEY, M. (Ed). Improving teaching and learning in the humanities. London: Falmer Press. (in press).

STATUS: Individual research

DATE OF RESEARCH: 1993-1998

KEYWORDS: **environment; environmental education; moral development; secondary education; values**

2775

Faculty of Education, Redland Campus, Redland Hill, Bristol BS6 6UZ
01179 741251
Cardiff University, School of Education, Senghennydd Road, Cardiff CF2 4YG
01222 874000

Lee, J. Mr; Fitz, J. Dr

Quality control in schools: the role of Her Majesty's Inspectorate (HMI) as policy makers in a climate of change

ABSTRACT: In the context of change the main aim of the research is to explore the role of national inspection in England and Wales in the making of education policy. The specific objectives of the research are: 1) To investigate the practice of Her Majesty's Inspectors (HMIs) in maintaining quality and pursuing curriculum innovation. 2) To compare the practice of the Office for Standards in Education (OFSTED) with that of HMI in order to: a) explore the extent that theory and practice of instruction is proposed to schools; b) clarify the role of both in the creation and revision of the National Curriculum; and c) explore the role of both in the accreditation of an initial teacher training (ITT) curriculum. 3) To investigate the impact of OFSTED on teachers' perception of their professionalism. The empirical focus of the research will include: published and unpublished documents; interview data from retired members of HMI and members of OFSTED teams; and interview data from schools and teachers who have been inspected under the auspices of OFSTED.

PUBLISHED MATERIAL: LEE, J. & FITZ, J. 'Constituting good practice: HMI and its influence on policy and pedagogy: some provisional findings'. In: DAVID, S. (Ed). Control and accountability in educational settings. London: Cassell (in press).

STATUS: Sponsored project

SOURCE OF GRANT: University of the West of England

DATE OF RESEARCH: 1993-1997

KEYWORDS: **educational policy; inspection; inspectors - of schools; ofsted; quality control**

2776

Faculty of Education, Redland Campus, Redland Hill, Bristol BS6 6UZ
01179 741251
Cardiff University, School of Education, Senghennydd Road, Cardiff CF2 4YG
01222 874000

Lee, J. Dr; Eke, R. Dr; Fitz, J. Dr

Inspection, quality and improvement: the role of registered inspectors, school reports and school responses to reports ensuring improvement

ABSTRACT: There have been some concerns about whether inspection reports on schools are of a consistent enough quality to provide clear feedback and guidance on a school's strengths and weaknesses and thus lead to improvement. The aims are to: 1) investigate the quality of inspection information, criticism and guidance provided for primary and secondary schools; 2) consider the relationship between the experience of registered inspectors and the frequency with which they conduct inspections on the quality of inspection outcomes. The principal objectives are to: 1) investigate the acceptance of external evaluation and its use; 2) investigate the quality of inspection reports in relation to the experience of registered inspectors and the number of inspections they lead; and 3) investigate the source of registered inspectors in the future and their training needs. Research will be conducted in 3 sequential but overlapping stages. It is envisaged that the project will last the equivalent of one academic year. Data analysis will be ongoing. Stage 1: Analysis of a sample of Office for Standards in Education (OFSTED) schools reports and of OFSTED documents related to schools inspection. Analysis of LEA documents relating to inspection and offering advice and guidance to schools and of documentation provided by contractors. A questionnaire survey, and a sample of registered inspectors. Stage 2: A questionnaire survey of 360 school headteachers and a sample of registered inspectors who have inspected and reported on those schools. Stage 3: Collection of interview data from 20 headteachers and chairs of governors, 20 registered inspectors, 5 contractors, 6 local education authority (LEA) and relevant staff at OFSTED.

STATUS: Sponsored project

SOURCE OF GRANT: CfBT £15,550

DATE OF RESEARCH: 1998-continuing

KEYWORDS: **inspection; inspectors - of schools; ofsted; school improvement; school reports**

2777

Faculty of the Built Environment, Frenchay Campus, Coldharbour Lane, Bristol BS16 1QY
01179 656261
Bath University, School of Education, Claverton Down, Bath BA2 7AY
01225 826826

Avgerinou, M. Ms; *Supervisor*: Ericson, J. Mr

Visual Literacy: anatomy and diagnosis

ABSTRACT: This research project was initially launched to explore the theoretical framework of the construct of Visual Literacy (VL). The focus of the research evolved around attempts to delineate VL skills and to measure them. Test construction theory principles and standards were employed so as to support the validity and reliability of the experimental testing instrument. The initial research questions were consequent upon the hypothesis that VL is measurable. As the research progressed, three separate but inter-related aims emerged. First to make a distinctive contribution towards our perception of the VL construct and the inherent skills; secondly, to create a VL ability index, and lastly to provide a defensible body of evidence to sustain future attempts towards standardisation of VL tests. As the chance to have had a large number of subjects to administer the test on appeared rather slender considering the nature and time constraints of the present project, it seemed more reasonable at the time to arrange for individual, recurrent trials of the test, and consider them as "item pilotings" which would indicate potential refinements of the testing instrument. Accordingly, one pre-pilot and five pilot test administrations took place. In total, 50 subjects (adults) participated. Data were collected in the UK, and the US. To ensure the validity of the instrument, an attitude towards visual communication questionnaire was devised and distributed to all participants. In addition, a VL expert group was formed in order to assess the theoretical framework, as well as the ways it had been expressed through the individual test items. Eleven VL abilities were identified as most pertinent to a VL index, which however had focused solely on the VL reading/interpreting skills. High internal consistency was evidenced indicating that (a) all items are somehow related; and, (b) all measured abilities are part of the suggested VL index. Furthermore, the test seems to have tested for abilities related to VL, and not for something else. The research findings are by no means fully explanatory and conclusive: they are merely descriptive and indicative of the complex nature, and the location of the research methodology problems. Yet, constructing a Visual Literacy index should not be seen as an impossible mission anymore. It is hoped that this project has signposted the way forward and thus facilitated any subsequent research in this area.

PUBLISHED MATERIAL: AVGERINOU, M. & ERICSON, J. (1997). 'A review of the concept of visual literacy', British Journal of Educational Technology, Vol 28, No 4, pp.280-291.

STATUS: Individual research

DATE OF RESEARCH: 1993-continuing

KEYWORDS: visual literacy; visual perception

University of Wales, Aberystwyth

2778

Department of Education, PO Box 2, Aberystwyth SY23 2AX
01970 623111

Watkins, W. Mr; *Supervisor*: Daugherty, R. Prof.

A study of the role of internal verification procedures in programmes leading to the award of Part 1 General National Vocational Qualifications (GNVQs)

ABSTRACT: Evidence has been gathered, through questionnaires and interviews, from a sample of secondary schools in South Wales. The data obtained relates to practice in a range of circumstances and across several GNVQ programme areas. The study explores the interpretation and implementation, by practitioners and managers in schools, of the national requirements which seek to maximise consistency of judgements through internal verification procedures.

STATUS: Individual research

DATE OF RESEARCH: 1995-continuing

KEYWORDS: assessment; general national vocational qualifications; moderation - marking; secondary education; vocational education

2779

Department of Education, PO Box 2, Aberystwyth SY23 2AX
01970 623111

Chandler, D. Dr; Roberts-Young, D. Mr

The construction of identity in personal home pages on the World Wide Web (WWW)

ABSTRACT: This is an ongoing study of personal home pages on the World Wide Web (WWW) which have been created by children and young people. It is being conducted in part through on-line interviews and content analysis and in part through face-to-face interviews with children and young people in Wales. The empirical focus is on Wales, though broader surveys have already been undertaken. The researchers are initially gathering contacts both through the Web itself and through personal contacts with schools, local education authorities, information technology specialists etc. Consideration will be given to both home pages constructed in a school setting and those which are constructed outside school. A particular concern is with the way in which young people are using personal home pages in the shaping of their public identities. The theoretical focus is primarily phenomenological, and priority will be given to establish the various functions which personal home pages may have for the individuals involved by focusing on their own ways of framing their use of the Web. In the textual analysis of the pages themselves, content analysis will be combined with semiotic approaches in order to establish the basic syntagmatic forms and paradigmatic variations in this new genre.

PUBLISHED MATERIAL: CHANDLER, D. (1997). 'Writing oneself in cyberspace (World Wide Web document)'. Paper presented at the Writing Development in Higher Education Conference, Aberystwyth, April 1997.

STATUS: Team research

DATE OF RESEARCH: 1997-continuing

KEYWORDS: computer uses at home; computer uses in education; home computers; identity; information technology; internet

2780

Department of Education, PO Box 2, Aberystwyth SY23 2AX
01970 623111

Ghuman, P. Dr

*Asian adolescents in Sydney and California; and Britain and Canada

ABSTRACT: Young people of Indian and Pakistani origin can be caught between the conflicting demands of two well-intentioned institutions (those of school and home) and suffer from heightened anxiety and guilt, which can subsequently affect their scholastic performance and social adjustment. The ensuing educational and social issues have been investigated by several researchers in Britain and elsewhere. The researcher has conducted many investigations into the concerns of Asian parents and their young people since 1974, and has widely published the findings in books and journal articles. The picture which has emerged is a lot more sanguine than was, and is, being imagined by the popular press, TV, and some teachers, social workers and politicians. The young people of South Asian origins are using a variety of strategies to acculturate into the fabric and structures of the society in which they are living. Theses include: cultural synthesis; clear differentiation of role behaviours (especially by girls) at home and school; development of novel cultural idioms; and development of bicultural identities. The researcher's last major project was a comparative one which studied the acculturation of British Asian and Indo-Canadian adolescents. Marked differences between the two groups emerged which are closely related to the socio-political climate of the day and the history and pattern of settlement of Asian communities. The research will now be extended to cover Australia and the USA. The aims of the research are to: 1) compare the acculturation patterns of South Asian young people in Australia with those of their counterparts in Britain, USA and Canada; 2) provide richer and indepth theoretical underpinnings to the research findings on ethnic identity and biculturalism. An account of the research will be published in a book published by Multilingual Matters which should be of value to teachers and others concerned with the education of ethnic minority young people.

PUBLISHED MATERIAL: GHUMAN, P.A.S. (1994). Coping with two cultures: British Asian and Indo-Canadian adolescents. Clevedon: Multilingual Matters.; GHUMAN, P.A.S. (1997). 'Integration or assimilation: a study of Asian adolescents', Educational Research, Vol 39, No 1, pp.23-25.

STATUS: Sponsored project

SOURCE OF GRANT: Nuffield Foundation £2,950

DATE OF RESEARCH: 1995-continuing

KEYWORDS: adolescents; asians; biculturalism; cultural background; ethnic groups

2781

Department of Education, PO Box 2, Aberystwyth SY23 2AX
01970 623111

Llewellyn, M. Mr; *Supervisor*: Chandler, D. Dr

Popular music in the Welsh language and the development of youth identity

ABSTRACT: The researcher hopes to develop critical approaches towards popular music in the Welsh language that will enable conclusions to be drawn about the roles played by musical participation in the wider culture of society. In particular, it is hoped to gain an understanding of music's part in developing and sustaining identity and a sense of belonging, especially but not exclusively among young people. The methodology will be primarily ethnographic: qualitative and reflexive.

STATUS: Individual research

DATE OF RESEARCH: 1997-continuing

KEYWORDS: music; popular music; welsh; youth culture

2782

Department of Education, PO Box 2, Aberystwyth SY23 2AX
01970 623111

Griffiths, M. Ms; *Supervisor*: Chandler, D. Dr

Children, gender and advertising

ABSTRACT: Since the majority of past research on sex-stereotyping in advertising has concentrated on adults, particularly women, the research considers the degree to which children are presented as either 'boys' or 'girls'. The researcher considers the possibility that advertisements present children with models of 'appropriate gender behaviour' and the influence that such advertisements actually have. Samples of 117 British toy advertisements, televised prior to Christmas 1996 have been collected. These advertisements were classified by the researcher and a group of 10 independent coders, as appealing to one of three audience groups: male, female or mixed. An extensive content analysis of the sample has been completed and levels of statistical significance regrading the differences between the audience groups have been calculated. A number of ethnographic interviews with both adults and children have been conducted, and they have been encouraged to discuss their immediate impressions of advertisement presentation and the impressions these advertisements have made on them personally. The scope of the research will now expand to include more ethnographic interviews, especially with children, and interviews with the advertisers themselves, to establish exactly how they target their audiences. More emphasis will be placed on children's perceptions of their own and the opposite gender, as a result of the mass media as a whole.

STATUS: Individual research

DATE OF RESEARCH: 1995-continuing

KEYWORDS: advertising; children; marketing; mass media; sex differences; sex stereotypes; stereotypes; television

2783

Department of Education, PO Box 2, Aberystwyth SY23 2AX
01970 623111

Williams, I. Ms; Thorpe, R. Mr

Primary education in rural Wales

ABSTRACT: This research focuses on schools and their communities and, in particular, the small primary school in Wales, and strategies relating to primary education in rural areas including inservice teacher education (INSET). The study has examined the ways in which small rural school in Wales are collaborating and how this has been supported by the local education authorities (LEAs) before and since local government reorganisation. The research has been conducted through questionnaire survey, semi-structured interview and review of literature and documentary

evidence. An early finding was that collaborative practice between small schools was widespread and deemed essential by both providers and receivers of INSET. Recommendations made were that future INSET should focus on small school issues and provision should be made to support collaborative practice between schools. Factors relating to effective collaboration were examined and mode of leadership was found to be important. More recently, the relative effectiveness of support frameworks in providing for teachers' training needs was examined and the general conclusion that flexibility and teacher ownership within a defined overall structure was most effective. Whilst literature evidence suggests that small schools appear to be doing marginally better than their larger counterparts there seems to be a case for combining the advantages of a smaller unit with those of a larger one through some form of collaboration. The options that are open to LEAs for primary education in rural areas are the subject of current research.

PUBLISHED MATERIAL: WILLIAMS, I., THORPE, R., & JAMES, Ll. (1995). INSET in small primary schools in Wales. A report to the Welsh Office. Aberystwyth: University of Wales, Aberystwyth/Welsh Office. ; WILLIAMS, I. & THORPE, R. (1997). 'In-service education of teachers in small primary schools in Wales', Journal of In-Service Education, Vol 23, No 2, pp.179-191. ; WILLIAMS, I. & THORPE, R. (1997). 'The professional development of teachers (INSET) in small primary schools in Wales - a study of collaborative practice', Welsh Journal of Education, Vol 6, No 1, pp.33-55. ; WILLIAMS, I. & THORPE, R. 'Small primary schools in rural Wales: frameworks of collaboration', Journal of Research into Rural Education. (in press).

STATUS: Sponsored project

SOURCE OF GRANT: Welsh Office, Cardiff £90,000

DATE OF RESEARCH: 1993-continuing

KEYWORDS: inservice teacher education; institutional cooperation; local education authorities; primary education; rural schools; small schools; wales

2784

Department of Education, PO Box 2, Aberystwyth SY23 2AX
01970 623111

Chandler, D. Dr

Learning television realities

ABSTRACT: The primary aim of this research is to investigate children's understanding of what is 'real' on television. Children's television viewing deserves the attention of educationalists for two reasons. Firstly, with children's annual viewing in the UK taking up on average more time than they spend in school, it has been aptly dubbed 'the alternative curriculum'. Secondly, because we may have something to learn from a medium whose codes and conventions (the complexity of which we tend to forget) children learn to interpret without any formal instruction. The realism of television programmes and the ability of child viewers to distinguish real from fantasy programmes are often seen as important factors to be considered in assessing such issues as children's comprehension of TV and any influence which watching TV may have on children. This project aims to map out and illustrate some key features in the development of children's 'modality judgements' of TV realities, focusing on their use of 'internal' criteria, such as knowledge of TV production (e.g. acting, make-up, stage sets, scale models) and of formal features of the medium (e.g. animation, 'camera tricks'), and also on their use of 'external' criteria (both lived experience and indirect knowledge of the world). Such modality judgements become more complex and flexible as children mature. So far the research has involved a major review of the existing research literature (published in the Journal of Educational Media). It has also involved fieldwork in schools. The fieldwork, which involved 48 individual interviews and 12 small-group discussions with children in 3 Welsh primary schools (in the age ranges 4-5, 7-8 and 10-11), sought to chart key differences in emphasis. Data analysis is in progress.

PUBLISHED MATERIAL: CHANDLER, D. (1997). 'Children's understanding of what is "real" on television: a review of the literature', Journal of Educational Media, Vol 23, No 1, pp.65-80.

STATUS: Sponsored project

SOURCE OF GRANT: University of Wales, Aberystwyth £1,500

DATE OF RESEARCH: 1996-continuing

KEYWORDS: childrens television; mass media; television; television research; television viewing

2785

Department of Education, PO Box 2, Aberystwyth SY23 2AX
01970 623111

Thomas, G. Mr

Quality schools: the effects of the new inspection arrangements

ABSTRACT: A new, and revolutionary, system of schools inspection was introduced in England and Wales by the Education (Schools) Act 1992. The effects of inspections on schools in Wales were investigated by visiting 6 schools shortly after inspection. 36 semi-structured interviews were carried out with staff at all levels. 4 schools were revisited 12-18 months after their inspections; again, a cross-section of staff was interviewed in each school. Specific areas covered by the interviews were analysed, and the results compared with other published and unpublished material (for example, documents from the Association of Metropolitan Authorities relating to inspections). Papers were prepared which focus on the following areas: 1) A description of how schools prepare for inspection. 2) The stress caused to teachers by inspection. 3) The problems which can arise when schools are inspected by teams based on inspectors from their own local education authority (LEA). Major conclusions include the following: a) improvements do take place in schools prior to inspection, but these are mainly to do with teamwork, organisation and documentation, rather than teaching and learning; b) the inspection handbook and training days are useful during preparation; c) many teachers are stressed by the long delay between the announcement of an inspection and the event itself, and some become very distressed if inspectors refuse to provide feedback on their performance; d) inspection of schools by inspectors from the same LEA can damage relationships between schools and the LEA.

PUBLISHED MATERIAL: THOMAS, G. (1995). 'Preparing for inspection: the process and its effects', Welsh Journal of Education, Vol 5, No 1, pp.16-26. ; THOMAS, G. (1996). 'It's good to talk', Management in Education, Vol 10, No 3, p.25. ; THOMAS, G. (1996). 'The new schools' inspection system: some problems and possible solutions', Educational Management and Administration, Vol 24, No 4, pp.355-369. ; THOMAS, G. (1997). 'Some moral grey areas in the new school inspection system', Welsh Journal of Education, Vol 6, No 2, pp.17-28.

STATUS: Individual research

DATE OF RESEARCH: 1994-1997

KEYWORDS: educational quality; inspection; inspectors - of schools; ofsted; school effectiveness; wales

2786

Department of Education, PO Box 2, Aberystwyth SY23 2AX
01970 623111

Thomas, G. Mr

The development of a policy: a case study

ABSTRACT: The 1992 Education (Schools) Act 1992 brought about major changes in the system of schools' inspection in England and Wales, and created new agencies (Office for Standards in Education (OFSTED)) in England and the Office of Her Majesty's Chief Inspector (OHMCI) (Wales) to oversee the new process. The final version of the Act incorporated a number of significant changes when compared to the original proposals, as a result of government compromises and defeats in the House of Lords. The Act was controversial at the time of its introduction, and the manner in which it has been implemented has remained a matter of debate ever since. The broad aim of this project is to look at the way in which the policy was developed, including the political context which led to its introduction. The methods employed will include interviews with some of the individuals involved with developing the policy, and the investigation of contemporary records (including newspaper reports and Hansard). A preliminary report was presented at a seminar on education policy in Wales on 21 November 1997. Provisional conclusions include the following: government policy was influenced by ideas published by the Centre for Policy Studies (a right-wing think-tank); the final Act differed significantly from the government's intentions because it was forced to accept changes as a result of opposition in the House of Lords.

PUBLISHED MATERIAL: THOMAS, G. (1995). 'Preparing for inspection: the process and its effects', Welsh Journal of Education, Vol 5, No 1, pp.16-26. ; THOMAS, G. (1996). 'It's good to talk', Management in Education, Vol 10, No 3, p.25. ; THOMAS, G. (1996). 'The new schools' inspection system: some problems and possible solutions', Educational Management and Administration, Vol 24, No 4, pp.355-369. ; THOMAS, G. (1997). 'Some moral grey areas in the new school inspection system', Welsh Journal of Education, Vol 6, No 2, pp.17-28.

STATUS: Individual research

DATE OF RESEARCH: 1997-continuing

KEYWORDS: educational change; educational quality; inspection; inspectors of schools; legislation; ofsted; ohmci - wales; school effectiveness

2787

Department of Education, PO Box 2, Aberystwyth SY23 2AX
01970 623111

Jobe, A. Mr; Lai Seng, L. Dr; Davids, L. Mr; Coly, G. Mr; Hakalima, S. Dr; *Supervisor*: Woodhall, M. Ms

Cost-effectiveness of publishing educational materials in national and local languages in Africa

ABSTRACT: The research consisted of two workshops (held in Dakar, Senegal) on the cost-effectiveness of publishing educational materials in national and local languages in Africa, and a series of case studies on the development and use of educational materials in national and local languages in 5 countries: The Gambia, Madagascar, Namibia, Senegal and Zambia. The first workshop, held in March 1996, discussed and agreed a common framework and methodology for the case studies. Participants included Maureen Woodhall (University of Wales, Aberystwyth), as facilitator of the workshops, and national experts from each of the 5 countries. (Abdoulie Jobe, The Gambia; Louis Lai Seng, Madagascar; Laurentius Davids, Namibia; Gaston Pierre Coly, Senegal; Shadrek Hakalima, Zambia). The case studies were conducted between April and June 1996, and a second workshop was held in July 1996, to discuss preliminary findings. The 5 case studies covered the following topics: 1) the social, economic and educational context; 2) language policy; 3) policy on publishing in national/ local languages; 4) strategies for minimising costs; 5) costs of publishing materials in national/local languages; 6) benefits and effectiveness; 7) conclusion: the cost-effectiveness of educational materials in national/local languages. The final stage of the research was the preparation and publication of a report on the results of the case studies, which included a summary of the conclusions of the workshops and case studies and presented the 5 case studies. The research demonstrated the value of a cost-benefit or cost-effectiveness framework for analysing the problems and advantages of publishing educational materials in national and local languages in Africa. The case studies faced many problems, including difficulties of obtaining accurate data on either costs or benefits, but it was agreed that it is important to collect and disseminate such data, and to examine policies on language and publication of educational materials in Africa in terms of costs and effectiveness.

PUBLISHED MATERIAL: WOODHALL, M. (1997). Cost-effectiveness of publishing educational materials in African languages. London: Association for the Development of Education in Africa. ; WOODHALL, M. (1997). 'Cost-effectiveness of educational materials in local and national languages: evidence from African case studies', Welsh Journal of Education, Vol 6, No 2, pp.69-83.

STATUS: Team research

DATE OF RESEARCH: 1996-1997

KEYWORDS: africa; african languages; cost effectiveness; educational materials; mother tongue

2788

Department of Education, PO Box 2, Aberystwyth SY23 2AX
01970 623111

Chandler, D. Dr

Webcams and the presentation of self by males

ABSTRACT: This research follows on from the study of personal home pages on the Web. It is a study of the use of live web cameras (webcams) in association with personal home pages. Such cameras serve to shift personal space to public space even more than personal home pages do. The primary focus of the study is on the self-presentation strategies of male webcam users. The study excludes 'spycams' and focuses on online cameras set up by those who appear on them. It seeks to describe primarily the camera-users' framing of the experience, but also, where the cameras are linked to online chat systems, describes the reactions of 'visitors'. Online interviews and e-mail dialogues are the primary means of gathering data and some of the sites are being studied in detail over time. The implications of this use of new technologies for the development of adolescent identities will be explored.

PUBLISHED MATERIAL: CHANDLER, D. & ROBERTS-YOUNG, D. (1998). 'The construction of identity in the personal homepages of adolescents'. Available on-line at: http://www.aber.ac.uk ; CHANDLER, D. & ROBERTS-YOUNG, D. (1999). 'The construction of identity in the personal homepages of adolescents'. In: MARQUET, P., MATHEY, S. & JAILLET, A. (Eds). Proceedings of the IN-TELE 98 European Conference on Educational Uses of the Internet and European Identity Construction. Berne: Peter Lang Publishers.

STATUS: Individual research

DATE OF RESEARCH: 1998-continuing

KEYWORDS: **adolescents; identity; internet; self expression; teleconferencing**

2789

Department of Education, PO Box 2, Aberystwyth SY23 2AX
01970 623111

Evans, W. Dr

The quality of learning in Welsh secondary schools: the evidence of examiners, 1890s to 1990s

ABSTRACT: A hitherto unused archive - the annual report of examiners - is being analysed on a subject-by-subject basis (viz. English, Welsh, Latin, History etc) to ascertain the qualities demanded by examiners over the last 100 years. Each subject is examined with reference to overall subject and curriculum changes. It is hoped that a contribution will be made to the ongoing debate about standards in secondary schools.

STATUS: Individual research

DATE OF RESEARCH: 1998-continuing

KEYWORDS: **assessment; educational history; educational quality; examinations; examiners; secondary education; wales**

2790

Department of Education, Aberystwyth SY23 2AX
01970 623111
Scottish Council for Research in Education, 15 St John Street, Edinburgh EH8 8JR
0131 557 2944

Daugherty, R. Prof.; Williams, I. Mm; Thomas, G. Mr; Harlen, W. Prof.; Lowden, K. Mr

Wales curriculum review: National Curriculum key stages 1, 2 and 3

ABSTRACT: The aim of the project was to gather evidence concerning implementation of the National Curriculum in Wales in preparation for decisions to be made by the Welsh Office, on advice from the Qualifications, Curriculum and Assessment Authority for Wales (ACCAC), concerning a revision of the National Curriculum scheduled for the year 2000. In the first phase, evidence was collected from documentary sources, from case study schools, from local education authorities and from Departments for Her Majesty's Chief Inspector of Schools (OHMCI) (Wales). During the second phase a questionnaire building on the project's initial analysis was circulated to a sample of primary and secondary schools. A wide range of organisations with an interest in education was also consulted. In the final phase, submission of a final report to the Authority in July 1998, all the available evidence was analysed and the project's main findings and recommendations were presented.

STATUS: Sponsored project

SOURCE OF GRANT: Curriculum and Assessment Authority for Wales £110,685

DATE OF RESEARCH: 1997-1998

KEYWORDS: **curriculum development; key stage 1; key stage 2; key stage 3; national curriculum; primary education; secondary education; wales**

2791

Department of Education, PO Box 2, Aberystwyth SY23 2AX
01970 623111
The Forum for African Women Educationalists (FAWE), 12th Floor, International House, Mama Ngina Street, PO Box 53168, Nairbobi, Kenya

Woodhall, M. Ms; Ng'ethe, N. Prof.

An evaluation of the forum for African women educationalists (FAWE)

ABSTRACT: The Forum for African Women Educationalists (FAWE) is an international non-governmental organisation (NGO) based and registered in Nairobi, Kenya. It was established in 1992 to provide an opportunity for a small but influential group of women Ministers of Education to work together to campaign for policy reform and innovation to improve the participation and performance of girls and women in all levels of education in Sub-Saharan Africa. It now has 58 members, from 30 African countries, 28 associate members and national chapters have been established in 25 countries, with a further 6 in the process of formation. In 1998 FAWE commissioned an external evaluation of the achievements, impact, strengths and weaknesses of the organisation after its first 6 years. The evaluation team consisted of 2 independent researchers, one from Africa and one from the UK, who carried out the evaluation on the basis of extensive interviews in 6 African countries (Ethiopia, Ghana, Guinea, Kenya, Mali and Tanzania), and interviews with FAWE's donor partners (including Association for the Development of Education in Africa (ADEA), Association of African Universities (AAU), Rockefeller Foundation, UNESCO and UNICEF). The report, presented to the Executive Committee of FAWE in December 1998, gives an historical account of the development of FAWE, examines its goals and objectives, work programme, governance and management structures, and assesses the impact of the organisation, its current challenges and possible future development, and presents a number of recommendations.

PUBLISHED MATERIAL: WOODHALL, M. & NG'ETHE, N. (1998). Forum for African women educationalists (FAWE): external evaluation report. Nairobi, Kenya: Forum for African Women Educationalists.

STATUS: Collaborative

DATE OF RESEARCH: 1998-1998

KEYWORDS: **africa; developing countries; girls; womens education**

2792

Department of Education, PO Box 2, Aberystwyth SY23 2AX
01248 351151
University of Wales, Bangor, School of English and Linguistics, College Road, Bangor LL57 2DG

Borsley, R. Dr; Aldridge, M. Dr; Jones, B. Mr; Roberts, I. Prof.

The acquisition of Welsh syntax

ABSTRACT: The aim of the project is to investigate the development of syntax in children who acquire Welsh as their first language. The model of Principles and Parameters is used to analyse early syntax, and a particular aim is to investigate the emergence of functional categories. A naturalistic corpus of adult-child conversations is used as the data base. There are 6 children between the ages of approximately 18 and a half months to 31 months. They were recorded in their homes. This Welsh data is investigated not only as a contribution to Welsh studies and, in particular, the early acquisition of Welsh syntax, but also to evaluate ideas about parameter-setting and functional categories that have emerged in recent work on the development of syntax. The corpus is made available to other researchers through the Childes database.

PUBLISHED MATERIAL: ALDRIDGE, M., BORSLEY, R.D., CLACK, S., CREUNANT, G. & JONES, B.M. (1997). 'The acquisition of NPs in Welsh'. Proceedings of the GALA 97 Conference on Language Acquisition: Knowledge, Representation and Processing Conference, University of Edinburgh, 1997.

STATUS: Sponsored project

SOURCE OF GRANT: Economic and Social Research Council £45,590

DATE OF RESEARCH: 1996-1997

KEYWORDS: **child language; grammar; language acquisition; syntax; welsh**

2793

Department of Information and Library Studies, Llanbadarn Fawr, Aberystwyth, Dyfed SY23 2AX
01970 623111

Preston, G. Mrs; Barber, J. Mrs; *Supervisor*: Baggs, C. Mr

To initiate a distance learning undergraduate degree course in information and library studies

ABSTRACT: In the light of current moves towards providing greater opportunities for mature adults with non-traditional educational qualifications to gain access to higher education, and the Universities Funding Council's (UFC) programme to encourage flexibility in course provision, it was proposed to set up a research and development programme to initiate a distance learning undergraduate degree course in information and library studies. The aim of the project is to investigate the scope and management of current distance learning provision; to evaluate the relative merits of different methods of course provision, including developments in educational technology; to look at methods of assessment for student-centred learning; and to develop quality control mechanisms appropriate for academic and professional validation. High attrition rates experienced in some models of distance learning provision make it important to assess how inherent problems such as student support and adequate resourcing may be overcome. This will lead to the design of a course aimed at mature non-traditional entrants currently or recently employed in a library or information environment, who wish to gain a professional qualification. The production of student-centred learning packages will involve research into developing Computer Assisted Learning (CAL) and video-conferencing to supplement traditional print-based materials.

STATUS: Sponsored project

SOURCE OF GRANT: Universities Funding Council £63,100

DATE OF RESEARCH: 1992-1993

KEYWORDS: **distance education; flexible learning; information science; librarianship education; mature students**

2794

Department of Information and Library Studies, PO Box 2, Aberystwyth SY23 2AX
01970 623111

Nkosi, L. Ms; *Supervisor*: Lonsdale, R. Mr

Information services to black South African youth

ABSTRACT: South Africa has embarked on a programme of reconstruction and development to redress inequities created by apartheid policy. Information is the life-blood of a developing society, and every person has a fundamental right to participate in free and equal exchange of information. However, while South Africa has excellent libraries and sophisticated infrastructure for information provision, the majority of the population do not have access to the simplest of library and information services. There are few libraries that provide specialised services to young people, but these do not address black needs. Little has been written on the special needs of young blacks, who are the country's future. The aim of this study is to correct this deficiency by assessing the information needs of young blacks and developing a model for an information service that can be used to cater for these needs. The study will focus on the Eastern Cape Province. Within this selected region, a study will be made in 3 areas - a rural, peri-urban and an urban area. Appropriate literature will be examined and contact will be made with funders of alternative services, and library and information associations to identify services to young blacks. Questionnaires and interviews will be conducted with black youths, service providers, librarians, and leaders in the communities to assess the needs of these youth.

STATUS: Individual research

DATE OF RESEARCH: 1995-continuing

KEYWORDS: **black youth; information dissemination; information needs; libraries; south africa**

University of Wales, Bangor

2795

School of Education, Deiniol Road, Bangor LL57 2UW
01248 351151

Rees, W. Dr

Counselling in different settings

ABSTRACT: The aim of this research is to discover whether there is a common core of counselling skills and approaches in different settings. Interviews have been taped and transcribed with hospital chaplains, hospital social workers, probation officers, drugs workers, and student counsellors

STATUS: Individual research

DATE OF RESEARCH: 1992-1993

KEYWORDS: **counselling; counsellor characteristics; counsellor performance; counsellors**

2796

School of Education, Deiniol Road, Bangor LL57 2UW
01248 351151

Baker, C. Prof.; Prys Jones, S. Dr

Encyclopedia of bilingualism and bilingual education

ABSTRACT: The encyclopedia will contain over 150 topics arranged in 4 sections: individual and family bilingualism; bilingual communities and societies; cultural and political aspects of bilingualism; bilingual education. The encyclopedia will contain foundational text on each topic, plus illustrations of recent research, plus plentiful graphics, illustrations and short text boxes. Publication has been targeted for mid-1997.

STATUS: Sponsored project

SOURCE OF GRANT: University of Wales, Bangor £20,000

DATE OF RESEARCH: 1994-1997

KEYWORDS: **bilingual education; bilingualism; encyclopaedias; material development; reference materials; second language learning**

2797

School of Education, Deiniol Road, Bangor LL57 2UW
01248 351151

Owen, M. Mr; Liber, O. Mr; Britain, A. Dr; *Supervisors*: Owen, M. Mr; Liber, O. Mr

Reseau d'Enseignement Multimedia: REM

ABSTRACT: The research is sponsored by the Telematics Applications Programme of Directorate General DGXIII-C of the European Commission (EC). It involves the University of Wales and 10 other European higher education institutions. The project's aim is to develop a collaborative, multimedia learning environment which works across telematic networks. It provides an integration of communication tools, and multimedia resources organised in knowledge models. The user needs analysis in devising the system has been based on constructivist principles and practices, offering a structured workflow and strong human-human interaction supported by technology for communication and access to resources. A major theme of the research is the use of the technology in learning about Europe across Europe in supporting the Erasmus and Comenius programmes of DGXXII of the EC. The project integrates a range of technologies for synchronous and asynchronous communication for a range of learning models, e.g. project work, debates, simulations.

STATUS: Sponsored project

SOURCE OF GRANT: European Commission DGXIII-C £1.2 million; Apple Computers £100,000

DATE OF RESEARCH: 1996-1998

KEYWORDS: **computer system design; computer uses in education; europe; information technology; international educational exchange; multimedia; networks; telecommunications**

2798

School of Education, Deiniol Road, Bangor LL57 2UW
01248 351151

McLeay, H. Ms; *Supervisors*: Williams, I. Prof.; Baker, C. Prof.

Imagery and the mental manipulation of deformable objects

ABSTRACT: The first phase of the research involved 21 subjects in performing a series of spatial tests requiring the comparison of diagrams of interlaced ropes, or knots, at varying orientations. Knots were chosen not only because they are deformable and the manipulative tasks form a contrast to previous work on rigid objects, but also because there is a mathematical structure to the study of their properties. The results were compared with previous work on the mental manipulation of rigid and semi-rigid objects. The results revealed that certain knot shapes are easier to process than others and that, as with rigid objects, rotation of one of the deformable objects increases the processing time. It was expected that tasks with higher numbers of crossings, which were predicted to be of higher complexity, would have longer processing times. However, this was found not to be the case. Skills and strategies involved in doing the tests are now being investigated and a further study using a refined set of test items is underway. A different methodology is being used to carry out a further investigation requiring subjects to verbalise their strategies as they attempt the tasks. Five basic strategies can be identified at this stage.

PUBLISHED MATERIAL: MCLEAY, H. & PIGGINS, D. (1996). 'The mental manipulation of 2-D representations of knots as deformable structures', Educational Studies in Mathematics, Vol 30, pp.399-414.

STATUS: Individual research

DATE OF RESEARCH: 1995-continuing

KEYWORDS: **imagery; knots; mathematics education; mental manipulation; visualisation**

2799

School of Education, Deiniol Road, Bangor LL57 2UW
01248 351151

Baker, C. Prof.

Continuity in Welsh language education

ABSTRACT: This research paper has 10 main points: 1) Families are not reprproducing the Welsh langugae in their children to a sufficient extent to maintain the language. If both parents are Welsh speaking, there is a 92% chance of their child becoming Welsh speaking. If one parent is Welsh speaking and the other not, there is between a 49% and 54% chance of the child becoming Welsh speaking, varying with the gender of the child and the gender of the Welsh speaking parent. Therefore the production of Welsh through schooling becomes a vital part of Welsh language maintenance. 2) Mudiad Ysgolion Meithrin plays an important role in Welsh language maintenance by increasing the supply of Welsh speakers after the shortfall in the home reproduction of Welsh as well as strengthening the language in those children who speak Welsh at home. 3) A map of the geographical distribution of Mudiad Ysgolion Meithrin shows a considerable spread of units with variations in density mostly consonant with population spread and Welsh language population spread. 4) Welsh medium education has expanded remarkably since the late 1950s. Graphs are provided to show the Welsh language education revolution that has occurred in four decades. 5) Primary schools are shown to play a major role in increasing the supply of Welsh speakers. Welsh Office statistics show that 20.9% of pupils are in primary schools where Welsh is the sole, main or part medium of teaching in the class. By the age of 11, around one in five children in Wales are fluent in Welsh. According to the 1991 Census, 36.1% of all children who are Welsh speaking come from homes where neither parent speaks Welsh. Primary schools thus play a major role in Welsh language production. 6) Through second language Welsh lessons, a large population of second language Welsh speakers, albeit with different levels of fluency (approximately 70% of the school population) have been produced in primary schools. 7) In the first year of secondary schooling, only 12.9% of pupils are taught Welsh as a first language. That is, between primary and secondary schooling, around 87% to 8% of children in Wales move from being first language to second language Welsh. At GCSE, only 5.7% of all examination entries are through the medium of Welsh, and at Advanced level, only 5.2% of all examination entries are through the medium of Welsh. The report explores the discontinuity in Welsh language education from primary to secondary school with a district by district analysis. 8) The paper continues by examining the amount of Welsh medium education in further education and higher education establishments in Wales. The percentage of students formally assessed in Welsh in further education colleges in Wales in 1996/97 is 2.31%. Coleg Meirion-Dwyfor (70%), Coleg Llysfasi

(41.56%), Coleg Harlech (22.56%) and Coleg Menai (10.88%) are the four colleges with over 10% of students assessed in Welsh. The overall percentage had dropped from 2.92% in 1996/97 to 2.31% in 1997/98. This represents a drop in Welsh medium assessments of 21%. 9) The percentage of higher education students in Wales following Welsh medium courses in 1996/97 (in part or in full) was 1.6%, with Trinity College, Carmarthen (18.4%), the University of Wales, Bangor(6.2%) and the University of Wales, Aberystwyth (2.4%) having the highest percentages of students following Welsh medium courses. In 1995/96, 42.3% of students from Wales attended universities in England.

STATUS: Individual research

DATE OF RESEARCH: 1998-continuing

KEYWORDS: **bilingualism; wales; welsh; welsh medium education**

University of Wales, Swansea
2800

Department of Education, Hendrefoilan, Swansea SA2 7NB
01792 201231

Maynard, T. Dr; Lowe, K. Ms

Boys, girls and writing in the primary schools

ABSTRACT: Over the past year, lecturers from the Department of Education, University of Wales, Swansea, have been working collaboratively with the staff of St Thomas Primary School, and with the English Advisor for the City and County of Swansea, in order to explore boys' and girls' attitudes towards and attainment in literacy. Initially, staff at the school were interviewed to ascertain their initial perceptions of boys' difficulties - particularly with writing. In general boys' attitudes towards writing were seen by teachers as a greater problem than their actual ability. Orally many boys displayed imaginative and sensitive use of language but this was not always apparent in their written work. Subsequently it was decided to undertake a more systematic and detailed examination of children's writing throughout the school: having explored children's perceived difficulties, there was a need to ascertain their actual difficulties. Teachers identified a sample of 6 children in their classes - boys and girls - who were recognised as having differing abilities in writing. These children were interviewed in order to ascertain their opinions about literacy and all writing undertaken by the sample group was collected over a period of 6 weeks. This data is currently being analysed.

STATUS: Team research

DATE OF RESEARCH: 1997-continuing

KEYWORDS: **boys; girls; primary education; sex differences; writing composition**

2801

Centre for Applied Language Studies, Singleton Park, Swansea SA2 8PP
01792 205678

Meara, P. Dr

Word recognition problems among Arabic-speaking learners of English

ABSTRACT: The background of the research lies in the problems Arabic learners of English seem to have in distinguishing English words with similar consonant structure, e.g. broad/bread; curl/cereal. After several initial attempts to design test procedures which would replicate this type of error, a computer-based word-recognition test was developed in which firstly vowels and then secondly consonants were systematically deleted from word stimuli presented to the subjects. The test records response-times and error rates for each subject. Two initial experiments of this type indicated that there was a significant difference between the responses of, on the one hand, Arabic speaking subjects and on the other, native speakers and speakers of European languages written in Roman script. This difference was maintained in the final experiment where Arabic speaking subjects were compared with Japanese, Thai and European language speakers as well as native speakers of English, a total of 131 subjects. In spite of the overall significance of the results of the Arabic speaking group, there were considerable individual differences between subjects; this has prompted the final phase of the study in which it is hoped to design a simple diagnostic test to predict those subjects who are most likely to have word-handling difficulties of the type analysed here. Such a test would have considerable classroom value.

PUBLISHED MATERIAL: RYAN, A. & MEARA, P. (1991). 'The case of the invisible vowels: Arabic speakers reading English words', Reading in a Foreign Language, Vol 7, No 2, pp.531-540.

STATUS: Individual research

DATE OF RESEARCH: 1987-1993

KEYWORDS: **arabs; english - second language; vowels; word recognition**

2802

Centre for Applied Language Studies, Singleton Park, Swansea SA2 8PP
01792 205678

Meara, P. Dr

Lexical behaviour in a second language

ABSTRACT: This project comprises a group of linked studies aimed at improving our understanding of vocabulary acquisition in foreign languages. The project includes: (1) a large scale bibliographical survey; (2) development of lexical tests; and (3) a set of linked PhD projects on lexical difficulties of second language speakers.

PUBLISHED MATERIAL: A list of publications is available from the researcher.

STATUS: Sponsored project

SOURCE OF GRANT: Eurocentres; Longmans; TVEI; University of Oxford Local Examinations Delegacy; BBC English

DATE OF RESEARCH: 1981-continuing

KEYWORDS: **second language learning; vocabulary development**

2803

Centre for Applied Language Studies, Singleton Park, Swansea SA2 8PP
01792 205678

Rodriguez-Sanchez, I. Mr; *Supervisor*: Meara, P. Dr

Matrix models in long-term vocabulary retention

ABSTRACT: Based on Meara (1990), this research tries to assess the usefulness and scope of Matrix models in predictory long-term vocabulary retention. Using versions of yes-no tests, word frequency samples, and subjects of different proficiency levels of Spanish, the model has provided promising results so far. The matrices used were 2x2 and 4x4, and the correlation between the vocabulary size predicted by those matrices a) several months before; and b) the actual vocabulary size have been found to be highly significant. The validity of this tool would be of major utility when comparing teaching methods, subject aptitudes etc.

PUBLISHED MATERIAL: MEARA, P. (1990). 'Matrix models of vocabulary acquisition', Aila Review, Vol 6, pp.66-74. ; MEARA, P. & RODRIGUEZ-SANCHEZ, I. (1993). 'Matrix models on vocabulary acquisition: an empirical assessment'. Proceedings of the Symposium on Vocabulary Research, Creal, Ottawa, 1993.

STATUS: Individual research

DATE OF RESEARCH: 1993-continuing

KEYWORDS: **matrices; second language learning; vocabulary development**

2804

Centre for Applied Language Studies, Singleton Park, Swansea SA2 8PP
01792 205678

Fitzpatrick, T. Ms; *Supervisor*: Meara, P. Dr

Measuring productive vocabulary in second language

ABSTRACT: The research project focuses on the design and application of a new test of language learners' productive vocabulary. The test uses word association techniques to explore the second language (L2) learner's active vocabulary, requiring subjects to produce a set of single word responses to a series of prompt words. The set of words produced by each subject is then processed and an association profile is produced for each subject, based on the number of infrequent words they produce. Findings seem to indicate a strong correlation between the results of this test and general L2 language

competence. The research project uses data from test subjects to explore the validity and reliability of the test, and goes on to suggest possible test applications. L2 learners are tested at regular intervals and the patterns of their association profiles are analysed. Test results are also compared with the subject's performance in more conventional tests of L2. Native speakers are also tested in order to provide a context for learners' results. Finally, the new test is examined in relation to current theories of vocabulary acquisition, retention and recall in the L2.

STATUS: Individual research

DATE OF RESEARCH: 1997-continuing

KEYWORDS: **second language learning; tests; vocabulary**

2805

Department of Education, Hendrefoilan, Swansea SA2 7NB
01792 201231

Rowe, M. Mr; Tanner, H. Mr; Davies, L. Ms; Morgan-Jones, P. Mr; Prichard, J. Ms

Teacher competencies and professional development

ABSTRACT: Action research is being conducted in Swansea, Aberystwyth and Bangor to develop a framework of competencies for use in initial teacher education. Techniques and documentation are being developed to establish records of achievement for student teachers. The success of the competencies and records of achievement will then be evaluated.

STATUS: Sponsored project

SOURCE OF GRANT: University of Wales

DATE OF RESEARCH: 1991-1993

KEYWORDS: **competence; competency based teacher education; preservice teacher education; records of achievement; student teachers**

2806

Department of Education, Hendrefoilan, Swansea SA2 7NB
01792 201231

Furlong, J. Prof.

The role of the mentor in initial teacher education

ABSTRACT: This is an indepth study of the work of eight 'mentors' in different programmes of initial teacher education.

STATUS: Sponsored project

SOURCE OF GRANT: Paul Hamlyn Foundation £14,000

DATE OF RESEARCH: 1992-1993

KEYWORDS: **mentors; preservice teacher education**

2807

Department of Education, Hendrefoilan, Swansea SA2 7NB
01792 201231

Jephcote, M. Mr; *Supervisor*: Williams, M. Prof.

Economic awareness as a curriculum entitlement for Welsh pupils

ABSTRACT: The study is to facilitate the development of economic awareness in primary and secondary schools in Wales. The project has curriculum development and curriculum research aspects. On the research side the focus is on the preparation of case studies of individual schools and upon pupils' cognitive growth.

STATUS: Sponsored project

SOURCE OF GRANT: Welsh Office; Esme Fairbairn Trust

DATE OF RESEARCH: 1990-1993

KEYWORDS: **cross curricular approach; curriculum development; economics education; enterprise education; primary education; secondary education; wales**

2808

Department of Education, Hendrefoilan, Swansea SA2 7NB
01792 201231

Maynard, T. Dr; *Supervisor*: Furlong, J. Prof.

The role of the university tutor in the development of trainees' teaching skills and knowledge while on block teaching practice

ABSTRACT: Through a series of studies which explore the nature and content of primary school teachers' practical professional knowledge, student teachers' development of this knowledge, and the contribution made to this process by both the school mentor and university tutor, this research seeks to identify and define a distinctive role for the university tutor in student teachers' school-based learning.

PUBLISHED MATERIAL: MAYNARD, T. & FURLONG, J. (1993). 'Learning to teach and models of mentoring'. In: MCINTYRE, D., HAGGER, H. & WILKIN, M. (Eds). Mentoring: perspectives on school-based teacher education. London: Kogan Page. ; FURLONG, J. & MAYNARD, T. (1995). Mentoring student teachers: the growth of professional knowledge. London: Routledge. ; MAYNARD, T. (1996). 'Mentoring subject-knowledge in the primary school'. In: MCINTYRE, D. & HAGGER, H. (Eds). Mentors in school: developing the profession of teaching. London: David Fulton. ; MAYNARD, T. (1996). 'The missing element? Early years teachers' attitudes to subject knowledge'. In: COX, T. (Ed). The National Curriculum and the early years: challenges and opportunities. London: Falmer Press. ; MAYNARD, T. (Ed). (1997). An introduction to primary mentoring: principles, processes and subject knowledge. London: Cassell.

STATUS: Individual research

DATE OF RESEARCH: 1994-1997

KEYWORDS: **academic staff; mentors; school based teacher education; student teacher supervisors; student teachers; teaching practice**

2809

Department of Education, Hendrefoilan, Swansea SA2 7NB
01792 201231

Jones, S. Mrs; *Supervisor*: Tanner, H. Mr

An investigation into the effect of calculator use on basic arithmetic skills

ABSTRACT: It is important that policy decisions on the use of calculators in schools are taken on the basis of research evidence rather than supposition and political expediency. This ongoing project aims to: 1) survey secondary schools in Wales to determine the predominant mode of calculator use in mathematics; 2) determine common methods and misconceptions in key areas of basic arithmetic and compare these with the results of studies by the Assessment of Performance Unit (APU) and the Concepts in Secondary Mathematics and Science (CSMS) project; 3) determine the extent to which basic arithmetic skills have changed since the large scale introduction of calculators; 4) compare the basic skills of pupils in schools with differing calculator policies. Questionnaires sent to every secondary school in Wales will explore the attitude of the head of mathematics to the use of calculators, whether or not schools have a policy on calculator use, and the modes of use encouraged. Open-ended interviews conducted with 20 Year 8 pupils will trial items for the written assessment papers, determine common errors and misconceptions, and identify pupils' approaches to key problems. All Year 8 pupils in a stratified sample of 10% of secondary schools in Wales (drawn from league table performance at GCSE) will be assessed by written papers. Overall results will be compared with those reported by APU and CSMS before calculator use became common, and comparisons made between schools with differing policies for calculator use. A series of research papers are planned: a) describing children's common misconceptions in number; b) comparing basic skills in number between the early 1980's and the present day; c) comparing basic skills and mode of calculator use.

STATUS: Sponsored project

SOURCE OF GRANT: University of Wales Swansea £2,500

DATE OF RESEARCH: 1994-1998

KEYWORDS: **arithmetic; calculators; mathematics education**

2810

Department of Education, Hendrefoilan, Swansea SA2 7NB
01792 201231

Lowe, R. Prof.

Schooling and social change, 1964-1970

ABSTRACT: This study provides an overview of the ways in which the sweeping social and economic changes of the modern period have impacted upon the education system. The research evaluates the ways in which schools and universities were moulded by external events and the part they played in promoting the modernisation of society. The study has explored: 1) the nature of the economic transformation of the period; 2) the growing awareness of gender issues; 3) new patterns of suburbanisation; 4) the changing ethnic composition of modern Britain; 5) the bureaucratisation of society and the rise of new politics.

PUBLISHED MATERIAL: LOWE, R. (1994). 'Suburbs and schools: the generation of at-risk children in post-war Britain', Aspects of Education, No 50, pp.142-155. ; LOWE, R. (1996). 'Postmodernity and historians of education: a view from Britain', Paedagogica Historica, Vol 32, No 2, pp.307-323. ; LOWE, R. (1997). Schooling and social change, 1964-1990. London: Routledge.

STATUS: Individual research

DATE OF RESEARCH: 1990-1997

KEYWORDS: **economic change; educational history; ethnic groups; politics education relationship; sex differences; social change**

2811

Department of Education, Hendrefoilan, Swansea SA2 7NB
01792 201231

Tanner, H. Mr; Jones, S. Mrs; *Supervisors*: Dobbins, D. Dr; Burton, L. Prof.

Developing mathematical thinking through practical problem solving and modelling

ABSTRACT: Phase 1: Eight Welsh secondary schools participated in an action research project which developed approaches to teaching and assessing mathematical thinking skills involved in practical modelling situations. The metacognitive skills of planning, monitoring and evaluating were found to be integral to successful modelling. Learning to model involves socialization into the consensual realities of a wider mathematical culture and the teacher plays a pivotal role in the generation of this consensus through the legitimization of linguistically expressed subjectivities. Participation in peer and self-assessment involves the student in a recursive, self-referential learning process which supports the explicit development of metacognitive skills. Phase 2: The aim was to develop and evaluate a thinking skills course to accelerate students' cognitive development in mathematics. The project aimed to accelerate the development of formal modes of thought by enhancing metacognitive skills. A quasi-experiment was set up in which 314 students aged between 11 and 13 followed a thinking skills course and were compared with matched control groups using pre-tests, post-tests, delayed tests and structured interviews. Assessment instruments were devised to assess students' levels of cognitive development, and their ability to use strategic and metacognitive skills. Statistical data were supported by participant observations. Intervention students performed significantly better than control students in both cognitive and metacognitive post-tests. Cognitive skills had not been taught directly by the course and transfer is claimed. Accelerated performance exhibited by intervention groups was maintained in delayed testing. Teaching metacognitive processes resulted in accelerated and sustained cognitive development.

PUBLISHED MATERIAL: TANNER, H.F.R. & JONES, S.A. (1993). Hands on maths: a project funded by the Welsh Office. Swansea: University of Wales, Swansea. ; JONES, S.A. & TANNER, H.F.R. (1994). 'Using peer and self assessment to develop modelling skills with students aged 11 to 16: a socio-constructive view', Educational Studies in Mathematics, Vol 27, No 4, pp.413-431. ; TANNER, H.F.R. & JONES, S.A. (1995). 'Teaching mathematical skills to accelerate cognitive development'. Proceedings of the Psychology of Mathematics Education Conference No 19, Recife, Brazil, 1995. ; TANNER, H.F.R. & JONES, S.A. (1995). Better thinking, better mathematics: thinking skills course to accelerate mathematical development. Swansea: University of Wales, Swansea.

STATUS: Sponsored project

SOURCE OF GRANT: Welsh Office

DATE OF RESEARCH: 1990-1998

KEYWORDS: **mathematical models; mathematics education; problem solving; secondary education; thinking skills**

2812

Department of Education, Hendrefoilan, Swansea SA2 7NB
01792 201231

Kennewell, S. Mr; *Supervisor*: Tanner, H. Mr

The role of computer modelling in the teaching and learning of algebra during ages 11-14

ABSTRACT: This project is a PhD study framed by the questions: 1) What influence does the learning and application of computer modelling have on the development of pupils' understanding of algebra? 2) In what ways do various conditions concerning software tools, teachers' knowledge, pupil activities, etc contribute to these effects? 3) How might we optimise the contribution of computer modelling activities to the teaching and learning of elementary algebra? Following a number of preliminary studies which identified the need to study characteristics of the pupils' mathematics teaching environment, the main fieldwork involves collaboration between the researcher and two teachers in each of two schools. This work is exploring relationships between variables concerning teachers' subject and pedagogical knowledge, computer modelling activities, related non-computer activities, computer software and pupils' conceptual development concerning mathematical variables and the interpretation, construction and equivalence of algebraic expressions. A mixed quantitative and qualitative methodology has been adopted, involving the use of pre- and post-testing, teacher and pupil interviewing, and participant observation. Early evidence indicates that there are significant variations of ways in which mathematical knowledge is represented amongst teachers as well as variations in the levels of development of pupils' concepts and skills. It is hypothesised that the use of information technology (IT) changes the ways in which we know mathematics towards a more dynamic representation, but that teachers who have not developed dynamic ways of representing mathematical concepts themselves will have difficulty in integrating IT into their teaching.

STATUS: Individual research

DATE OF RESEARCH: 1993-1998

KEYWORDS: algebra; computer uses in education; educational software; information technology; mathematical models; mathematics education

2813

Department of Education, Hendrefoilan, Swansea SA2 7NB
01792 201231

Parkinson, J. Dr

A study of investigative work in A-level chemistry

ABSTRACT: The purpose of this research is to investigate the extent to which A-level chemistry students are carrying out practical work that requires them to select variables and plan their own experiments. A questionnaire has been sent to all chemistry teachers who enter candidates for one examination board. The responses will show the frequency of use of investigative work at A-level and the nature of the tasks set. The final report will contain examples of investigations that can be used to assess students' practical skills at A-level.

STATUS: Sponsored project

SOURCE OF GRANT: Royal Society of Chemistry £1,200

DATE OF RESEARCH: 1998-1998

KEYWORDS: a level examinations; chemistry; practical science; science education; science experiments; sixteen to nineteen education

2814

Department of Education, Hendrefoilan, Swansea SA2 7NB
01792 201231

Kennewell, S. Mr; Parkinson, J. Dr; Tanner, H. Mr

Whole school approaches to the development of information technology capability

ABSTRACT: In view of the relatively low numbers of pupils meeting expected levels of attainment in information technology (IT), there is a need to understand the factors affecting the quality of teaching and learning of IT. The project aims to identify indicators of successful performance in developing pupils' IT capability on a whole school basis, and relate such successes to characteristics of pupils and their learning experiences; to characteristics of teachers and their pedagogical practices, and to characteristics of schools, their policies, and their models of curriculum and assessment in IT. The main study will involve the use of questionnaires in 30 primary and secondary schools across Wales and case studies of 6 schools which exemplify high achievement in developing pupils' IT capability. The questionnaires will probe pupils' IT access, experience, attitudes and self-assessment of capability; teachers' access, experience, attitudes and curricular use of IT; and schools' policies, curriculum models, resources and training. The case studies will involve interviews, document analysis, curriculum audit and classroom observation to focus in depth on matters which may influence schools' success in developing pupils' IT capability.

STATUS: Sponsored project

SOURCE OF GRANT: ACCAC £34,216

DATE OF RESEARCH: 1997-1998

KEYWORDS: achievement; computer uses in education; information technology; wales; whole school approach

2815

Department of Education, Hendrefoilan, Swansea SA2 7NB
01792 201231

Lowe, R. Prof.

Writing the history of education: a survey of the last 25 years

ABSTRACT: This involves the preparation of a four volume set of 'Readings in the History of Education' which will survey the development of this field of study over the most recent 25 years and identify key contemporary trends and issues. This is to be published by Routledge in 2000 or as soon as possible after that date.

STATUS: Individual research

DATE OF RESEARCH: 1996-continuing

KEYWORDS: educational history

2816

Department of Education, Hendrefoilan, Swansea SA2 7NB
01792 201231

Morris, B. Ms; *Supervisor*: Maynard, P. Dr

Raising standards of literacy in 3 South Wales secondary schools

ABSTRACT: Using as its basis 3 contrasting but typical South Wales schools, the research will investigate: 1) interpretations of literacy, including contemporary ones by teachers, pupils, parents, policymakers and educationists; 2) attitudes towards literacy, including why literacy is important and who is responsible for teaching/developing it; 3) specific contexts: 3 comprehensive schools' strategies for raising standards of literacy will be studied and these strategies will be matched against the perceptions and attitudes examined in (1) and (2) above. The methods of research used will be predominantly interview and questionnaire.

STATUS: Individual research

DATE OF RESEARCH: 1998-continuing

KEYWORDS: literacy education; reading; secondary education; writing composition

2817

Department of Education, Hendrefoilan, Swansea SA2 7NB
01792 201231

Patterson, E. Dr

Developing literacy through science

ABSTRACT: Much of the literacy teaching and learning in the primary school is dependent on the reading and writing of fiction, which many children particularly boys - do not find appealing. Science has the potential to provide a rich and varied context for the development of literacy skills. To enable pupils to effectively develop reading and writing skills, the use of 'scaffolds' to help them order their thinking are being developed. The aims and intended outcomes are: 1) develop structures which will serve as 'scaffolds' to support pupils in the acquisition of literacy skills; 2) facilitate and support the development of class teachers' practice in literacy teaching by providing opportunities to carry out trials of a range of strategies for improving literacy; 3) use scientific knowledge, understanding and processes as a context for the development of literacy skills. The research is being carried out in 3 schools, from September 1998 to July 1999. The class teachers are closely involved in directing the research. The structures which are being used to support pupils' writing are: 1) Concept maps used for the development of sentence structure (Novak, J.D., Gowin, B.D. & Johansen, G.T. (1983). 'The use of concept mapping and knowledge vee mapping with junior high school science students', Science Education, Vol 67, No 5, pp.625-645). 2) Context maps to structure writing (Bloom, J.W. (1995). 'Assessing and extending the scope of children's contexts of meaning: context maps as a methodological perspective', International Journal of Science Education, Vol 17,No 2, pp.167-187. 3) Writing grids and writing frames to develop writing in different genres (description, exposition, explanation, report) (Franklin, S. (1998). 'Writing, the novel and genres - an English perspective', English in Education, Vol 32, No 2, pp.25-34; Lewis, M. & Wray, D. (1996). Writing frames. Reading: University of Reading).

PUBLISHED MATERIAL: NOVAK, J.D., GOWIN, B.D. & JOHANSEN, G.T. (1983). 'The use of concept mapping and knowledge vee mapping with junior high school science students', Science Education, Vol 67, No 5, pp.625-645. ; BLOOM, J.W. (1995). 'Assessing and extending the scope of children's contexts of meaning: context maps as a methodological perspective', International Journal of Science Education, Vol 17, No 2, pp.167-187. ; LEWIS, M. & WRAY, D. (1996). Writing frames. Reading: University of Reading. ; FRANKLIN, S. (1998). 'Writing, the novel and genres - an English perspective', English in Education, Vol 32, No 2, pp.25-34.

STATUS: Individual research

DATE OF RESEARCH: 1998-continuing

KEYWORDS: **literacy; primary education; reading; scaffolding; science education**

2818

Department of Education, Hendrefoilan, Swansea SA2 7NB
01792 201231

Gough, J. Dr; *Supervisor*: Sanders, S. Dr

The implementation of key stage 4 Welsh second language in schools in the English speaking areas of South Wales

ABSTRACT: The research is into the effect of the introduction of Welsh second language as a compulsory element of the key stage 4 curriculum from September 1999. It will involve 12 secondary schools in predominantly English speaking areas of South Wales. The researcher is interested to see if there will be an increase in the numbers of students with A*-C grades at GCSE in Welsh who complete their compulsory schooling in 2001. It may be that most will follow a short course which will be significantly inferior to the full GCSE course. Changes in the curriculum will affect other subjects, and the researcher will want to monitor the numbers studying a modern foreign language before and after the introduction of Welsh second language.

STATUS: Individual research

DATE OF RESEARCH: 1998-continuing

KEYWORDS: **key stage 4; secondary education; welsh**

2819

Department of Education, Hendrefoilan, Swansea SA2 7NB
01792 3201231
University of Jyvaskyla, Department of Teacher Education, PO Box 35 C132, SF-40351 Jyvaskyla, Finland

Parkinson, J. Dr; Asunta, T. Dr

Pupils' attitudes towards information technology

ABSTRACT: The research planned is a collaborative research project between the Education Departments of the University of Wales, Swansea and the University of Jyvaskyla looking at pupils' attitudes towards information technology with particular reference to its use in science. Research so far completed includes a study of pupils' attitudes towards science, mathemtics, English and design and technology at National Curriculum key stage 3. A sample of 1038 pupils completed an attitude questionnaire in each of the above areas and a smaller group from each cohort was interviewed. The results have been published. A further study was carried out comparing the attitudes of British and Qatari pupils towards computers. A sample of 400 pupils (200 from each country) completed an attitude questionnaire. The results showed that the mode of use has a signficant influence on pupils' attitudes. Boys had more positive attitude than girls and British pupils more positive than Qatari pupils.

PUBLISHED MATERIAL: STABLES, A., DAVIES, S., HENDLEY, D., PARKINSON, J., STABLES, S. & TANNER, H. (1995). 'Attitudes to English in key stage 3', English in Education, Vol 29, No 3, pp.29-36. ; HENDLEY, D., PARKINSON, J., STABLES, A. & TANNER, H. (1996). 'Pupils' attitudes to technology in key stage 3 of the National Curriculum: a study of pupils in South Wales', International Journal of Technology and Design Education, Vol 6, pp.15-29. ; PARKINSON, J., HENDLEY, D., STABLES, A. & TANNER, H. Pupils' attitudes to science in key stage 3 of the National Curriculum: a study of pupils in South Wales', Research in Science and Technological Education. (in press).

STATUS: Collaborative

DATE OF RESEARCH: 1992-continuing

KEYWORDS: **attitudes; computer uses in education; computers; information technology; pupil attitudes; science education**

2820

Department of Political Theory and Government, Singleton Park, Swansea SA2 8PP
01792 205678
University of Wales Swansea, Department of Education, Hendrefoilan, Swansea SA2 7NB
01792 201231

Moran, A. Mr; *Supervisors*: Phillips, R. Ms; Haddock, B. Mr

Implications of the thought of G.B. Vico for a pragmatic philosophy of education

ABSTRACT: This work describes the educational theories which derive from the epistemological and psychological models implicit in the New Science of G.B. Vico. The possible influence of Vico's thought is related historically and structurally to that of the 19th century Italian pragmatists and thence to American pragmatism. It is argued that important aspects of the implied-educational thought of pragmatists, particularly Peirce, James and Dewey, derive from the work of Vico, either by importation or by analytical affinity in the derivation of the pragmatists 'original' thought. It is suggested that to make a direct connection between Vico's work, and those aspects of pragmatism which inform modern educational practice, will provide an improved model for present educational theory.

STATUS: Individual research

DATE OF RESEARCH: 1992-1998

KEYWORDS: **educational theories; epistemology**

University of Wales Institute, Cardiff

2821

Central Management, Llandaff Centre, Western Avenue, Cardiff CF5 2SG
01222 551111

Adams, S. Ms; *Supervisors*: Birchenough, A. Prof.; Thomas, M. Dr; Brannigan, C. Prof.

An investigation into student satisfaction and dissatisfaction in an institution of higher education

ABSTRACT: Student satisfaction in the higher education (HE) sector forms an area of research which has recently received increasing attention in the UK. (This research is already well established in the USA). Its assessment may be important for reasons of public accountability, as this has attained increasing prominence, primarily through recent quality initiatives within H, in conjunction with cross-referenced information. Information on student satisfaction can help institutional management to both understand the 'student experience' and to prioritise course and facilities improvements. The aims of this study are therefore to further institutional management's knowledge of the student perspective and experience. The research seeks to identify specific areas of student satisfaction and dissatisfaction for continuing students at a medium-sized British higher education establishment, over the period January 1994 to December 1996. It will also extend the current satisfaction and dissatisfaction work to cover all those students who have withdrawn from courses (voluntary or involuntary). It will be valuable to determine if there are differences between these groups and to explore whether dissatisfaction may lead to withdrawal; an action which has far reaching individual and institutional consequences. The sample to be used is: approximately 2000 (randomly selected) continuing students per year; and approximately 600 (total sample) withdrawn students per year. Methods include: annual postal questionnaires to continuing students (designed following student discussions and sent to 25% random sample); and withdrawn students (designed following semi-structured discussions with key members of staff and sent to total number of withdrawn students). The researcher may also carry out follow-up interviews with some students. The outcome will be the provision of relevant recommendations for institutional action based on findings from two sets of survey data. To survive and prosper, institutions must meet the needs of their client group - that is, the students themselves.

PUBLISHED MATERIAL: ADAMS, S. (1994). 'Student satisfaction: development of a comprehensive model', Concord, Vol 4, No 2, pp.35-36. (In-house journal of Cardiff Institute of Higher Education).

STATUS: Individual research

DATE OF RESEARCH: 1994-1997

KEYWORDS: **higher education; student attitudes; student experience**

2822

Department of Education, Cyncoed Centre, Cyncoed Road, Cardiff CF2 6XD
01222 551111

Laugharne, J. Ms; *Supervisor*: Bellin, W. Dr

An examination of Welsh/English bilingual children's storytelling, with particular reference to the oral story as a genre and the language domains of home and school

ABSTRACT: The study examines the oral stories in Welsh by 9 and 10 year-old children in 3 Welsh medium Cardiff schools at a time of considerable expansion in Welsh medium education and an upturn in numbers of young Welsh speakers. The children told stories about the contrasting language domains of home and school. The study investigated cultural and metalinguistic issues and the genre of the bilingual oral story. Labov's (1972) model was applied and a set of criteria devised to judge more and less successful stories in the data. Background language information, based on the children's own responses, gave indications of those children who spoke most and least Welsh in the home domain. It was found that neither the language background of the children nor the originating domain of the story had a great impact on its outcome. However, the immediate context was important and the telling of the stories in Welsh in the school domain did have a strong effect. It appeared to inhibit use of English and code-switching and to encourage translation. There has been little research carried out on the oral story in a bilingual context, in Wales or in other countries. This study contributes to the area by focusing closely on young English/Welsh bilingual children telling stories about home and school.

STATUS: Individual research

DATE OF RESEARCH: 1991-1997

KEYWORDS: **bilingualism; narration; story telling; welsh; welsh medium education; welsh speaking schools**

2823

Department of Education, Cyncoed Centre, Cyncoed Road, Cardiff CF2 6XD
01222 551111
Kristiansand University, Agder College, Department of Humanities, Postuttak 4604, Kristiansand, Norway
01047 381 41445

Laugharne, J. Ms; Baird, A. Dr; Maagero, E. Ms; Seip Tonnossen, E. Ms

Children's meeting with narrative texts: a joint research project between University of Wales Institute, Cardiff and Ayder College, Norway

ABSTRACT: This is a comparative study of the reading process and how understanding is influenced by cultural, linguistic and textual frames. This study is based on reception theory which emphasises the role of the reader as an important and necessary part of creating meaning from texts (ECO UMBERTO (1993). Six walks in the fictional woods. Cambridge, M.A.: Harvard University Press). Connections are made between reception theory and the child reader. The study seeks to explore cultural dimensions in terms of a reader who approaches texts as either a first or second language

learner. Different inferences from a text may be made as a result of the above factors. A cohort of 20 children from Norway and Wales were presented with four texts and their responses as readers will be analysed (all texts were available in both English and Norwegian). The results were presented in four linked conference papers at the 20th International Congress for Modern Languages and Literature, Regensburg, Germany, August 1996. Links were explored between analysis of the children's responses and analysis of the 'model reader'.

PUBLISHED MATERIAL: LAUGHARNE, J., BAIRD, A., MAAGERO, E. & TONNESSON SEIP, E. (1997). Children's meeting with narrative texts. Kristiansand, Norway: Kristiansand University.

STATUS: Collaborative

DATE OF RESEARCH: 1995-continuing

KEYWORDS: **bilingualism; cross cultural studies; literature; narration; reader response**

2824

Department of Education, Cyncoed Centre, Cyncoed Road, Cardiff CF2 6XD
01222 551111
South Wales Police Authority, Police Headquarters, Cowbridge Road, Bridgend CF31 3SU

Ball, G. Dr; Barry, S. Insp.; Warton, K. Ms; Tattum, D. Mr

School Watch

ABSTRACT: Schools Liaison Officers have encouraged schools throughout the South Wales Police area to establish School Watch Committees. There are currently in excess of 100 such committees already established in primary schools within the South Wales area. Committees have been established consisting usually of Year 6 children, who meet every 2 weeks with a police officer and a teacher to discuss ways of improving the school environment. The groups of children are called School Watch Committees and they elect a chairperson and other officers so that they function like any other committee. The teacher and police officer act purely as advisors and have no vote. The committees' primary aim is to target the following areas: vandalism to school property; litter; vandalism to personal property; truancy; bullying. The purpose of this research is to assess the effectiveness of the School Watch programme by evaluating the extent to which the 5 areas noted above are perceived to occur. The research objectives are: 1) to assess the effectiveness of the School Watch programme in primary schools in the South Wales area in eradicating anti-social behaviour traits; 2) to determine the reasons for any variation in the level of success of the School Watch programme; 3) to establish a database of information to enable further evaluation to be undertaken by 2003.

PUBLISHED MATERIAL: BALL, G. et al. (1997). 'School watch: working with pupils to make schools safer places'. In: TATTUM, D.P. & HERBERT, G. (Eds). Bullying: home, school and community. London: David Fulton.

STATUS: Sponsored project

SOURCE OF GRANT: Police Research Group

DATE OF RESEARCH: 1996-continuing

KEYWORDS: **antisocial behaviour; bullying; committees; police school relationship; primary education; pupil participation; school safety; truancy; vandalism; wales**

2825

Department of Education, Cyncoed Centre, Cyncoed Road, Cardiff CF2 6XD
01222 551111
University of Wales, Aberystwyth, Department of Education, PO Box 2, Aberystwyth SY23 2AX
01970 623111

Ball, G. Dr; Davies, L. Mrs

Using and applying mathematics at key stage 3 of the National Curriculum

ABSTRACT: The purpose of the study is to determine the extent to which process-based mathematics teaching occurs at National Curriculum key stage 3 in secondary schools in Wales. Central to the study are the interpretations and perceptions teachers hold in relation to Attainment Target 1 (AT1) - Using and Applying Mathematics. A representative sample of twenty secondary schools (10%) was chosen to reflect the diversity of secondary provision in Wales. Semi-structured interviews were held with heads of mathematics departments and mathematics teachers. All but one of these interviews were tape-recorded and later transcribed. Initial analysis of data indicates that there is no single interpretation of AT1 held by teachers, and that a wide variety of opinion exists as to the value of process-based work in mathematics teaching and learning.

PUBLISHED MATERIAL: BALL, G. & DAVIES, L. (1995) 'The incidence and nature of investigative activities in the teaching of mathematics at key stage 3 in Welsh secondary schools', Welsh Journal of Education, Vol 5, No 1, pp.55-68. ; BALL, G. & DAVIES, L. (1995). 'Gwaith Ymchwiliol yng Nghymru - Arolwg Cenedlaethol', Mathlwg, Vol 8, pp.8-11. ; DAVIES, L. (1995). Integration of mathematical process and content at key stage 3. Aberystwyth Education Papers. Aberystwyth: University of Wales, Aberystwyth. ; BALL, G. & DAVIES, L. (1996). 'The use of investigative activities on the teaching of mathematics at key stage 3 in Welsh secondary schools', Education Today, Vol 46, No 2, pp.24-30.

STATUS: Sponsored project

SOURCE OF GRANT: University of Wales £3,000

DATE OF RESEARCH: 1995-1998

KEYWORDS: **mathematical applications; mathematics education**

Warwick University

2826

> Centre for Education and Industry, Coventry CV4 7AL
> 01203 523523

Huddleston, P. Mrs; *Supervisors*: Woolhouse, J. Prof.; Tomlinson, J. Prof.

The secondment of professional staff between education and industry

ABSTRACT: The research is concerned with the professional development of outcomes of teacher secondments/placements into business and industry at both individual and institutional level. In particular, the impact of placement experiences on curriculum development is being investigated. The methodology includes questionnaire and personal interviews of teachers who have undertaken placements; longitudinal studies; core studies; and evaluation of placement studies.

STATUS: Sponsored project

SOURCE OF GRANT: Goldsmiths' Company of London £165,000

DATE OF RESEARCH: 1988-1993

KEYWORDS: **industrial secondments; industry education relationship; teacher development**

2827

> Centre for Education and Industry, Coventry CV4 7AL
> 01203 523523

Richardson, W. Dr; Finegold, D. Dr

The education policies of large companies

ABSTRACT: The project is an analysis of the education policies of large companies in the United Kingdom. Research methods include literature reviews (general and that of specific companies') and interviews with companies' managers. The research characterises the development of companies' education policies, how they are formulated and who is responsible for their operation. Analyses of results is presented in two ways: (a) stages of evolution in a company's relationship with education; (b) variables which shape company behaviour.

PUBLISHED MATERIAL: RICHARDSON, W. & FINEGOLD, D. (1991). Making education our business (interim report). Warwick: Warwick University.

STATUS: Sponsored project

SOURCE OF GRANT: British Petroleum £100,000; Department for Education £12,500; Department of Employment £12,500

DATE OF RESEARCH: 1989-continuing

KEYWORDS: **corporate education; industry education relationship; staff development**

2828

> Centre for Education and Industry, Coventry CV4 7AL
> 01203 523523

Miller, A. Mr; *Supervisor*: Woolhouse, J. Prof.

Building effective school-business links

ABSTRACT: In 1992 the Department for Education carried out a quantitative survey of school-business links during the 1991-92 academic year. The survey questionnaire was sent to a random sample of 865 primary and 554 secondary schools in England. At the same time a qualitative survey was commissioned from the Centre for Education and Industry, University of Warwick. A 'qualitative' questionnaire was sent to a 10% random sample of schools included in the main survey. The report based on the survey is unpublished and confidential to the Department. The second stage of the research involved joint visits by Her Majesty's Inspectorate (HMI) and researchers of the School Curriculum Industry Partnership Central Team to twenty schools. Six primary and six secondary schools were selected from the schools in the qualitative survey. They were supplemented with other schools identified by HMI as containing practice which would complement that found in the survey schools. Twenty case studies were written, based on the use of HMI criteria and methods of collecting evidence interviews with staff and pupils; examination of samples of pupils' work and other documents; lesson observation; and interviews with business partners. The published report includes 'good practice' points that schools wishing to improve quality should consider, as well as numerous examples of good practice in school-business links.

PUBLISHED MATERIAL: MILLER, A. (1993). Building effective school-business links: a practical guide to improving quality. London: Department for Education.

STATUS: Sponsored project

SOURCE OF GRANT: Department for Education; Department of Employment; Esso PLC, jointly £75,000

DATE OF RESEARCH: 1991-1993

KEYWORDS: **cooperative programmes; industry education relationship**

2829

> Centre for Education and Industry, Coventry CV4 7AL
> 01203 523523

Huddleston, P. Mrs; Anderson, J. Mrs

An evaluation of the pilot year of the School Associate Programme

ABSTRACT: The evaluation commenced in January 1993 and covered two pilot School Associate Programmes in Essex and Durham. The focus of the evaluation: highlights potential strengths and weaknesses of the schemes; identifies good practice; and provides case study exemplars for dissemination. The evaluation involved a series of face-to-face interviews using semi-structured schedules with School Associates (business people working in schools), teacher mentors, headteachers, company training officers and project managers. Results highlight a wide range of practice and of opportunities for business people to work in schools. However, conclusions identify the need for appropriate recruitment, selection, induction and training of Associates. Management and ownership of the Programme by all parties is stressed and a need for better understanding of the culture of education and of business is important to maximise the potential of such exchanges.

STATUS: Sponsored project

SOURCE OF GRANT: Paul Hamlyn Foundation £12,450

DATE OF RESEARCH: 1993-1993

KEYWORDS: **cooperative programmes; industry education relationship; programme evaluation; secondments**

2830

> Centre for Education and Industry, Coventry CV4 7AL
> 01203 523523
> London University, Institute of Education, 20 Bedford Way, London WC1H 0AL
> 0171 580 1122

Woolhouse, J. Prof.; Richardson, W. Dr; Spours, K. Dr; Young, M. Dr

Learning for the future

ABSTRACT: The project will examine all aspects of post-compulsory vocational education and training in order to assess the options for development of the national system in a direction compatible with expected developments in labour markets and work-based skills. In addition to an introductory issues paper ('Changes and challenges' - see below) the research will be organised around four main themes: 1) modularisation and credit; 2) full-time vocational learning; 3) work-based learning; 4) funding, incentives and institutional arrangements. The researchers will undertake desk research as well as interviewing all the national agencies and public bodies responsible for and associated with current policy and practice. The final report will outline clear conclusions and recommendations for the development of vocational education and training in England and Wales.

PUBLISHED MATERIAL: WOOLHOUSE, J.G., YOUNG, M., RICHARDSON, W. & SPOURS, K. (1994). Changes and challenges: 14-19 education and training. Warwick: University of Warwick.

STATUS: Sponsored project

SOURCE OF GRANT: Government departments; Charitable foundations; Industrial firms, jointly £180,000

DATE OF RESEARCH: 1993-1997

KEYWORDS: **qualifications; sixteen to nineteen education; training; vocational education**

2831

Centre for Educational Development, Appraisal and Research (CEDAR), Coventry CV4 7AL
01203 523523

Pole, C. Dr

Life histories of black teachers: giving voice

ABSTRACT: This is a study of the lives and careers of 20 black/Asian teachers which focuses on the lived experience of teaching in the UK. Teachers have been selected to reflect different ethnic origin, age, sex and length of service in the UK. Issues explored include educational background of the teacher and his/her family, reasons for joining the teaching occupation, career paths and experiences, experience of racism/sexism, religious and other forms of discrimination, career aspirations and expectations. The life history method places prime importance on the individual agency of the social sector. The method seeks to unravel the subjective experience of the individual black teacher and locate this within its wider social, political and educational context.

STATUS: Sponsored project

SOURCE OF GRANT: Economic and Social Research Council £30,000

DATE OF RESEARCH: 1996-1998

2832

Centre for Educational Development, Appraisal and Research (CEDAR), Coventry CV4 7AL
01203 523523

Galloway, S. Ms; Winfield, G. Ms; Costley, D. Dr; Pike, G. Mr; *Supervisor*: Burgess, R. Prof.

Higher level vocational qualifications

ABSTRACT: Since October 1995 Coventry and Warwickshire Training and Enterprise Council (TEC) and the University of Warwick have jointly funded research and development activities in the area of higher level qualifications and continuing vocational education. A joint steering committee has allowed representatives from both sponsors to have access to findings from each phase and has strengthened links between these two bodies and the local business community. Initially, the project investigated the views of employers and employees about work-based learning and higher level vocational qualifications. Outcomes included a review of policy in this area, a questionnaire on the take-up of vocational qualifications in local companies, and 8 case studies of firms and university departments involved in vocational education. A development phase encouraged local employers to invest in vocational education and training, and they nominated employees to take part in personal development training. Recent elements of this programme have been case studies of the role of professional bodies in promoting continuing professional development in first the legal profession and secondly the engineering profession. A review of the use of professional development profiles is in progress and an analysis of the impact of the Kennedy and Dearing Reports for vocational developments in higher education has been completed. During 1997-98 work funded by the University focuses on vocational elements in existing postgraduate post-experience education and on facilitating access to higher level continuing professional development (CPD). Various papers have been produced by the researchers in connection with this project.

STATUS: Sponsored project

SOURCE OF GRANT: Coventry and Warwickshire Training and Enterprise Council; Warwick University, jointly

DATE OF RESEARCH: 1995-1998

KEYWORDS: **professional continuing education; vocational education; vocational qualifications**

2833

Centre for Educational Development, Appraisal and Research (CEDAR), Coventry CV4 7AL
01203 523523

Band, S. Ms; Kaivanto, K. Mr; *Supervisors*: Burgess, R. Prof.; Ferlie, E. Prof.

Pilot audits of research exploitation in the social sciences

ABSTRACT: Focused on 4 departments in the Faculty of Social Studies at the University of Warwick, the study will survey current practice, provide a critical analysis of strengths and weaknesses in the exploitation and dissemination process, seek to highlight recent successful exploitations and the processes behind them, identify options for improving exploitation processes, both in university systems and the supporting role of the Economic and Social Research Council (ESRC). The study will explore different modes of dissemination and examine their appropriateness for different audiences, having regard to both formal systems and informal working practices, 2 research groups at each of the 4 departments will be selected as case studies for detailed analysis.

STATUS: Sponsored project

SOURCE OF GRANT: Economic and Social Research Council

DATE OF RESEARCH: 1997-1998

KEYWORDS: **social science research**

2834

Centre for Educational Development, Appraisal and Research (CEDAR), Coventry CV4 7AL
01203 523523

Baldauf, B. Ms; Sprokkereef, A. Ms; Verhoeven, J. Prof.; *Supervisor*: Burgess, R. Prof.

Postgraduate education and training in Europe

ABSTRACT: Within an ever closer European Community detailed information on higher education and postgraduate training becomes more and more important for higher education institutions as well as for policymakers. This cross-national project (Warwick University with 6 research institutions in Europe) focused on a particular area within higher education: postgraduate education and training, especially doctoral study; ongoing political and academic debates and the organisation of doctoral study, both at national and at institutional level. Among the topics covered in particular are: recruiting and selecting doctoral students; financing doctoral studies; training programmes; supervision; evaluation and career prospects of doctoral students. The project covered Austria, Belgium, Germany, Greece, England, France, Italy, Portugal, Spain and the Netherlands. The first part of the project was devoted to a description and an analysis of postgraduate education and training at national level based on literature review and statistical data. The second part seeks to gather and analyse data at an international level. A case study in engineering as well as in business studies was conducted in each country. Each case study was based on documentary evidence and 12 to 25 semi-structured one-hour interviews, mainly with doctoral students and supervisors.

STATUS: Sponsored project

SOURCE OF GRANT: Human Capital and Mobility Programme of the EU

DATE OF RESEARCH: 1994-1997

KEYWORDS: **comparative education; doctoral degrees; europe; graduate study; higher education**

2835

Centre for Educational Development, Appraisal and Research (CEDAR), Coventry CV4 7AL
01203 523523
Warwick University, Centre for the Study of Social History, Coventry CV4 7AL

Dowling, M. Dr; *Supervisors*: Burgess, R. Prof.; Steedman, C. Prof.

Teacher training as the social history of ideas

ABSTRACT: This project is being run by the Centre for Educational Development, Appraisal and Research and the Centre for Social History at the University of Warwick. It is concerned with looking at the training of teachers from the period immediately after the Education Act 1944 to the James Report of 1972 (GREAT BRITAIN. DEPARTMENT OF EDUCATION AND SCIENCE. COMMITTEE OF INQUIRY INTO TEACHER TRAINING. (1972). Teacher education and training. London:HMSO). The following former training colleges have been chosen for the project: the City of Coventry Training College, Whitelands, Southlands, the College of St Bede, Durham and St Mary's, Strawberry Hill. The project will include investigating the archives of these colleges: student records, prospectuses, course outlines, and booklists (where available). It will also include interviews with former staff and students of the colleges. The researchers are anxious to know what they remember about their experiences especially with regard to the content of their courses, the total experience of college life, the relevance of their training when they came into teaching situations. In addition to interviews there will be a postal questionnaire which will cover many of the same topics as the indepth interviews. The information which is gleaned from the specific colleges will be put into a more general context of continuity and change in English education over the period under review. This will include societal changes, the structure of education, new methods of teaching, issues concerning the teaching unions, the continued development of the teaching profession and the role of the teacher.

STATUS: Sponsored project

SOURCE OF GRANT: Leverhulme Trust £89,829

DATE OF RESEARCH: 1996-continuing

KEYWORDS: **educational history; preservice teacher education**

2836

Centre for English Language Teacher Education, Coventry CV4 7AL
01203 523523

Nesi, H. Dr; Tsai, C. Ms

The development and evaluation of online computer-assisted language learning materials for English for academic purposes

ABSTRACT: The proposed project is to build up a coherent package of English language learning materials which can be accessed by non-native speaker students via the Warwick University network. The programs intended for use are commercially produced, but will be 'authored' by the Centre for English Language Teaching (CELT) staff, with due regard for the students' subject specialisms and levels of expertise. It is anticipated that students will be introduced to the first phase of materials at the beginning of the 1992-1993 academic session, and the use made of the materials will then be monitored by means of Warwick University's Novell 1.12 Netware package, supplemented by questionnaires and interviews with selected subjects. The aim is to discover which types of Computer Assisted Language Learning (CALL) activity are (a) used most frequently; and (b) judged to be most effective by university-level learners of English for academic purposes. In further phases of the project the intention is to expand and modify the materials in accordance with these findings.

STATUS: Individual research

DATE OF RESEARCH: 1992-1993

KEYWORDS: **computer assisted language learning; english - second language; english for academic purposes; overseas students; second language learning**

2837

Centre for English Language Teacher Education, Coventry CV4 7AL
01203 523523

Karavas, E. Ms; *Supervisor*: Khan, J. Ms

English language teaching curriculum renewal in Greek secondary schools: the teachers' response

ABSTRACT: The research focuses on the Greek English language teachers' response to a new English language course that was recently implemented in Greek secondary schools. The course is based on a weak version of the communicative learner-centred approach. The aims of the research are: a) to investigate the impact of the course on teachers' classroom behaviour; and b) to assess teachers' educational attitudes. Classroom observation and interviews are being used in order to fulfil the first aim. Questionnaires are being used in relation to the second aim.

STATUS: Individual research

DATE OF RESEARCH: 1990-1993

KEYWORDS: **english - second language; greece**

2838

Centre for English Language Teacher Education, Coventry CV4 7AL
01203 523523

Hara, Y. Mrs; *Supervisor*: Hedge, P. Ms

The composing strategies of Japanese learners in the process of writing English

ABSTRACT: The research is intended to explore strategies used by Japanese learners of English in the process of writing. The design of the study involves qualitative analysis of think aloud protocols to be taken from the subjects. Other research instruments will include interviews and questionnaires. The intended subjects are Japanese college students taking a preparatory course of English for Academic Purposes at the University of Warwick. Observation of the students, some 12-15 in number, will be undertaken over 3 or 4 months during their course. It is expected that the results of the analysis will give some pedagogical implications about how foreign language learners of English at the tertiary level could be encouraged to write English more fluently and appropriately with fewer constraints caused by language switching.

STATUS: Individual research

DATE OF RESEARCH: 1994-1997

KEYWORDS: **english - second language; english for academic purposes; overseas students; second language learning; writing processes**

2839

Centre for English Language Teacher Education, Coventry CV4 7AL
01203 523523

Rea-Dickins, P. Dr; Gardner, S. Dr; Shearsby, C. Mr; Howard, S. Ms; Clayton, E. Ms

Investigating English as an additional language (EAL) language assessment in an early years bilingual intervention project

ABSTRACT: The research aims to investigate the range and validity of the assessment procedures used in the Early Years Intervention Project (EYIP) - an ongoing project which is being implemented to address problems of low levels of achievement in English. The research initially centred on assessment procedures and processes from the perspective of different stakeholders: class teachers, language support teachers and bilingual education assistants. The methodology has included a survey to all stakeholders of main assessment issues; a questionnaire to all EYIP language support teachers to gather quantitative data; a structured interview in each of the 9 schools; and classroom observations. The results suggest that there is a variety of well coordinated assessment procedures in place that are working very effectively to feed into teaching and administration in the EYIP. Assessment has been found to be a significant part of the working curriculum, and has raised issues in relation to the reliability and validity of classroom-based assessment.

PUBLISHED MATERIAL: REA-DICKINS, P., GARDNER, S. with CLAYTON, E. (1998). Investigating the language assessment of learners with EAL. Report for Minority Group Support Services. Warwick: University of Warwick, Centre for English Language Teacher Education, Language Testing and Evaluation Unit. ; GARDNER, S. (1998). 'Representations of literacy'. Paper presented at the NALDIC Conference, University of Birmingham, November 1998. ; GARDNER, S. & REA-DICKINS, P. (1998). 'Literacy and oracy assessment in a bilingual intervention project: the roles of English language stages'. Paper presented at the BAAL Conference, University of Manchester, September 1998.

STATUS: Sponsored project

SOURCE OF GRANT: Single Regeneration Budget Coventry City Council

DATE OF RESEARCH: 1998-continuing

KEYWORDS: assessment; bilingualism; english - second language; intervention; key stage 1; primary education

2840

Centre for English Language Teacher Education, Coventry CV4 7AL
01203 523523

Pringle, J. Mrs; *Supervisor*: Rixon, S. Ms

That the teaching of mathematics is an effective means of teaching English as an additional language at key stage 2

ABSTRACT: Children who are learning English as an additional language rarely receive language support in mathematics. This study attempts to show that this is a wasted opportunity, not only because it may be a useful deployment of the language support teacher's time, but also because of the much more fundamental link between the development of the concepts of mathematics and those of language. By the time they have reached the age of 7, the children already have a well-developed understanding of their world through their mother-tongue and they do not lack the ability to form concepts. The mathematical concepts contained in the curriculum at key stage 2 become increasingly more cognitively demanding and these closely match the concepts contained within the language of instruction, i.e. English. The children who took part in this study were all born in the UK, except one who was born in Bangladesh and who arrived here with his family at the age of one year. Their situation of finding themselves unable to keep pace with the demands of the primary curriculum, particularly at key stage 2, is not unusual. This is a longitudinal study of children learning an additional language through mathematics. The course book (Ginn Level 3) was analysed for the frequency of the structures of language as they arose in the text. Situations were then set up to investigate indications of language transfer to other areas of the curriculum. All sessions were recorded.

STATUS: Individual research

DATE OF RESEARCH: 1994-continuing

KEYWORDS: bilingualism; english - second language; key stage 2; mathematics education; primary education

2841

Centre for English Language Teacher Education, Coventry CV4 7AL
01203 523523

Ok Lee, H. Ms; *Supervisor*: Rixon, S. Ms

A longitudinal study of learner training for group independence in a Korean state primary school

ABSTRACT: In South Korea English language teaching in state primary schools started with children in Year 3 (age 8 to 9) in March 1997. They have been learning English twice a week (2x40 minutes). This research is composed of a baseline study and action research. The baseline study (November to December 1997) was to get the general picture of the extent and type of classroom interaction in Year 3 English lessons. Responses to questionnaires, classroom observations, and teacher interviews, through small samples, showed that peer interaction was very little and mechanical. Action research (May 1998 to February 1999) was an attempt to improve the quality of teaching and learning as a foreign language in mixed ability large classes by promoting peer interaction. The researcher is training two classes of children in Year 4 to do group work by themselves. Each class was divided into 8 heterogeneous groups (6 children per group). Activities for group work, in accordance with the topics of the textbook, have been increased by 4 times per unit. Research instruments include questionnaire, self-assessment sheet, tape-recording and observation (2 groups), learner diary (2 groups), interview (2 groups), and the researcher's own reflection. The results have not yet been identified, but they will include whether and how learner training has changed children's attitudes towards group work, whether and how much it has contributed to develop children's speaking skills. While most research into group work, so far, has been conducted not only at university level but in laboratory conditions, this longitudinal study will be conducted both at the primary level and in natural classrooms.

STATUS: Individual research

DATE OF RESEARCH: 1996-continuing

KEYWORDS: english - second language; primary education; south korea

2842

Centre for English Language Teacher Education, Coventry CV4 7AL
01203 523523

Daoud, S. Ms; *Supervisors*: Hedge, P. Ms; Rea-Dickins, P. Dr

English as a foreign language (EFL)/English for specific purposes (ESP) teachers development and innovation: a case study

ABSTRACT: Little research has been done in the area of English as a foreign language (EFL)/English for specific purposes (ESP) teacher development and its influence on pedagogical innovation. This case study contributes to filling in this gap. It was carried out at the ESP Centre, Damascus University, in 1996-97. The overall aim of the research was to explore the potential of teacher-initiated action research for teacher and curriculum development in that and similar contexts. The researcher, a teacher in the context, assumed a participatory and facilitating role. The project had 2 main phases: baseline and main. The main aims of the baseline investigation was to a) substantiate the relevance and viability of a project proposal based on the findings of an earlier study by the same researcher in the context; and b) to collect baseline data. Several instruments were used, the main being indepth interviews with 23 out of 30 members of staff. The main aim of the interviews was to articulate an accurate picture of staff needs and potential for change working as a group to tackle a specific problem. The problem, considered the most challenging by all, was the how of teaching and learning research paper writing under considerable constraints. In the light of the findings, the project proposal was refined, and a programme of activities was agreed with participants. The overall aim of the main/intervention phase was to provide participants with learning opportunities and support to self-direct their professional development and meet their needs working individually and collaboratively. Because of staff loss and other constraints, the programme had to be redefined in the process of implementation. The main phase had 2 main stages: orientation and research and dissemination. The former had the main aims of supporting participants to orientate themselves in: a) current approaches to teaching academic writing; and b) action research. The latter stage was for carrying out classroom action research and sharing the findings. 20 out of 23 teachers participated in different ways, rates and intensities: 5 marginally, 7 moderately and 8 actively. Active participants carried out action research, and 5 of them presented papers at a regional conference. In this project, tools of research were used for development. Among them, feedback to and from participants was one main research and development strategy. Others were diaries, conference papers, recordings of project activities and meetings etc. Analysis of the data identified several strands of staff and pedagogical developments and different responses to the programme. These are presented in comparable ways cross-sectionally on the group level and longitudinally on the individual level (case studies). Findings of the cross-sectional analysis show relationships between level of involvement and teacher response or reaction. Generally, the higher the level of involvement, the more positive the response. Overall, reflection level is higher in experienced teachers. On the other hand, novices tend to be more reflexive and tolerant of peer critical evaluation. Risk taking ability tends to be higher in novices; they admit errors and tolerate sacrifices in self-esteem more than experienced teachers. But striking individual differences were also found. Findings are discussed for their implications for teacher development and innovation.

PUBLISHED MATERIAL: DAOUD, S. (1996). 'Action research: a need and a challenge for EFL/ESP practitioners'. In: CARTAZZI, M., RAFIK GALEA, S. & HALL, B. (Eds). Aspects of language teaching, learning and research methodology in the context of education. Leicester: University of Leicester, School of Education and School of Modern Languages.

STATUS: Individual research

DATE OF RESEARCH: 1995-continuing

KEYWORDS: english - second language; language teachers; second language teaching; syria

2843

Centre for English Language Teacher Education, Coventry CV4 7AL
01203 523523

Chichester Institute of Higher Education, Centre for International Education and Management, Bognor Regis Campus, Upper Bognor Road, Bognor Regis PO21 1HR
01243 816000

Kiely, R. Mr; *Supervisor*: Rea-Dickins, P. Dr

Programme evaluation by teachers in their own classrooms: an observational study

ABSTRACT: This study examines the evaluation of English language programmes by teachers for development and quality assurance purposes. The research involves a survey of the literature in educational evaluation and English language applied linguistics to determine the role of evaluation in teaching and programme management routines. The empirical work uses an ethnographic approach - observation and interviews - to investigate how teachers use evaluation in their work. Case studies describe evaluation practices in the professional life of teachers, and in the teaching of an English for academic purposes (EAP) programme. The case studies relate practice in evaluation to professional value on the one hand, and institutional policies on the other.

PUBLISHED MATERIAL: KIELY, R. (1998). 'Programme evaluation by teachers: issues of policy and practice'. In: REA-DICKINS, P. & GERMAINE, K. (Eds). Managing evaluation and innovation in language teaching. Harlow: Addison Wesley Longman.

STATUS: Individual research

DATE OF RESEARCH: 1995-continuing

KEYWORDS: **english - second language; programme evaluation; second language teaching**

2844

Centre for Research in Elementary and Primary Education, Coventry CV4 7AL
01203 523523

Phillips, E. Ms; *Supervisor*: Alexander, R. Prof.

Curriculum coordination in primary schools

ABSTRACT: The project is a collaboration of researchers from Warwick University and 4 local education authorities (LEAs) - Birmingham, Buckinghamshire, Oxfordshire and Warwickshire. The project aims: 1) To survey and study in detail strategies for curriculum coordination in primary schools in 4 LEAs. 2) To examine the role of the curriculum coordinator in relation to the changing demands and contexts of primary education. 3) To identify conditions for effective coordination in practice. 4) To identify and analyse problems and obstacles to success. 5) To analyse implications for policy and practice. The methods include: 1) questionnaire survey of 240 schools in 4 LEAs; 2) interviews with headteachers, coodinators and class teachers in 48 schools; and 3) school and classroom observation. The project is interesting as an example of collaborative research between a university and 4 LEAs, and for its use of seconded teachers as research staff, as well as for its substantive engagement with curriculum management.

STATUS: Sponsored project

SOURCE OF GRANT: Birmingham, Buckinghamshire, Oxfordshire and Warwickshire Local Education Authorities £25,000

DATE OF RESEARCH: 1997-1998

KEYWORDS: **coordination; curriculum; educational administration; primary education; school organisation; subject coordinators**

2845

Centre for Research in Elementary and Primary Education, Coventry CV4 7AL
01203 523523

Mills, K. Ms; Schweisfurth, M. Ms; *Supervisor*: Alexander, R. Prof.

Primary education in five cultures

ABSTRACT: The aims of the project are to: 1) undertake a comparative analysis of aspects of primary education in the UK, USA, Russia, France and India; 2) focus on the interplay of educational policies and school/classroom practices; 3) give particular attention to pupils aged 6 and 9, and to classroom discourse; 4) venture into the relatively under-researched field of comparative classroom analysis and to contribute to the development of

theory and methodology. The methods include: 1) A 2-level study in each country: level 1 (policy/system) accessed by interviews with policymakers/administrators; and level 2 (practice) accessed by interviews with teachers and headteachers, and through classroom observation. 2) Data (currently being analysed) including interview transcripts/notes; videotapes; photographs; observation notes; documentation; and lesson transcripts (Russian, French and Hini - medium lessons translated into English).

PUBLISHED MATERIAL: ALEXANDER, R.J. (1995). 'Task, time, talk and text: signposts to effective teaching'. In: KUMAR, K. (Ed). School effectiveness and learning achievement at the primary stage: international perspectives. Delhi: National Council for Educational Research and Training. ; ALEDANDER, R.J. (1996). Unfinished journey: pedagogy and discourse in school effectiveness research. Delhi: National Council for Educational Research and Training. ; ALEXANDER, R.J. (1996). Other primary schools and ours: hazards of international comparison. CREPE Occasional Paper No 1. Warwick: University of Warwick, Centre for Research in Elementary and Primary Education.

STATUS: Sponsored project

SOURCE OF GRANT: Leverhulme Trust £13,000; British Council £1,250; University of Warwick Research Innovations Fund £9,000

DATE OF RESEARCH: 1994-continuing

KEYWORDS: **classroom communication; classroom observation techniques; comparative education; discourse; france; india; primary education; russia; teaching methods; united states of america**

2846

Centre for Research in Elementary and Primary Education, Coventry CV4 7AL
01203 523523

Costley, D. Dr; Band, S. Ms; Wardle, K. Ms; *Supervisors*: Burgess, R. Prof.; Morrison, M. Dr

The role of libraries in a learning society

ABSTRACT: The aim of the study is to investigate the role of the Library and Information Service in promoting lifelong learning. Its strategic objectives are to demonstrate good practice and to provide evidence of the added value that libraries can provide in supporting lifelong learning. The specific objectives are to apply case study approaches to demonstrate effective practice set in the context of age, diverse communities, and the specific purposes of learning. This is being achieved through examining issues relating to: 1) learners and a range of learner experiences; 2) the public library service and a range of other library providers; 3) library provision and use in educational settings; 4) partnership arrangements between public libraries, educational institutions and issues concerned with education, training and employment issues. The research report is to be submitted to the Library and Information Commission by 31 December 1997.

STATUS: Sponsored project

SOURCE OF GRANT: Library and Information Commission

DATE OF RESEARCH: 1997-1997

KEYWORDS: **libraries; lifelong learning; public libraries**

2847

Centre for Research in Elementary and Primary Education, Coventry CV4 7AL
01203 523523

Packwood, A. Dr; Sinclair Taylor, A. Ms

An evaluation of the first steps approach to literacy

ABSTRACT: The First Steps approach to literacy was developed in Western Australia by a project team led by Alison Dewsbury. Extensive data from English speaking countries was collated and used to develop a series of developmental continua for reading, writing, spelling and oracy. Alongside the continua, descriptors for each stage and major teaching emphases were identified. There is also an integrated system of assessment and recording. The approach has had notable success in Australia and has been the subject of a series of evaluation projects. Now First Steps has been brought to the UK, the Australian project team are keen to have its impact on classroom effectiveness evaluated. This small scale study will focus particularly on the First Steps approach to writing. A small number of self-selected schools in a large metropolitan borough will be the focus of a series of indepth case studies. A range of methods of data collection will be used including: classroom observation; documentary analysis; questionnaire; interview; and the collection of children's work.

STATUS: Sponsored project

SOURCE OF GRANT: Heinemann Educational Publishers £11,144

DATE OF RESEARCH: 1997-1998

KEYWORDS: literacy; reading; writing exercises; writing teaching

2848

Centre for Research in Elementary and Primary Education, Coventry CV4 7AL
01203 523523
Bristol University, Graduate School of Education, Centre for Curriculum and Assessment Studies, 22 Berkeley Square, Bristol BS8 1JA
01179 289000
Oxford University, Department of Educational Studies, Centre for Comparative Studies in Education, 15 Norham Gardens, Oxford OX2 6PY
01865 274024

Alexander, R. Prof.; Broadfoot, P. Prof.; Phillips, D. Dr

Theories, methods and applications of comparative educational research: a reassessment

ABSTRACT: A series of 6 seminars, followed by an international conference, designed to re-assess the character and purposes of comparative educational research. Membership will be by invitation and will include researchers and research users from the UK and overseas. The themes for the seminars are: 1) the state of the discipline (Oxford, Summer 1997); 2) researching classrooms and schools (Warwick, Autumn 1997); 3) researching pupil achievement (Bristol, Spring 1998); 4) researching education and development (Warwick, Summer 1998); 5) researching education policy (Oxford, Autumn 1998); 6) researching teachers and teaching (Bristol, Spring 1999). The theme of the final conference (Warwick, Summer 1998) has yet to be announced. Proceedings from the seminars are to be published by Triangle Books.

STATUS: Sponsored project

SOURCE OF GRANT: Economic and Social Research Council £14,800

DATE OF RESEARCH: 1997-continuing

KEYWORDS: educational research; seminars

2849

Centre for Research in Ethnic Relations, Coventry CV4 7AL
01203 523523

Taylor, P. Mr

Ethnic minorities in higher education

ABSTRACT: The main aims of the project are to: (1) obtain greater knowledge of ethnic minority participation in higher education; (2) study the perceptions formed by these students and (3) consider the role of higher education institutions in the continuation of discrimination. In order to pursue these aims several different institutions are being studied. Data obtained from various sources (including the Universities Central Council for Admissions (UCCA)) were used to study participation. Consideration of students' experiences and perceptions of higher education will be facilitated by interview and survey material. These studies are to be placed in the context of the institutional policies and practices which affect students, in particular ethnic minorities

PUBLISHED MATERIAL: TAYLOR, P. (1992). 'Ethnic group data and application to higher education', Higher Education Quarterly, Autumn. ; TAYLOR, P. (1992). 'Ethnic group data for university entry', Project report for the Committee of Vice-Chancellors and Principals, Coventry: Centre for Research in Ethnic Relations.

STATUS: Sponsored project

SOURCE OF GRANT: Economic and Social Research Council

DATE OF RESEARCH: 1991-1993

KEYWORDS: educational discrimination; ethnic groups; higher education; student recruitment

2850

Centre for Research in Ethnic Relations, Coventry CV4 7AL
01203 523523

Hyder, K. Mrs

The effects of the Education Reform Act 1988 on black communities

ABSTRACT: Pupils of Caribbean background have a long history of educational disadvantage in Britain. The main aim of the study is to examine developments in local authorities and their schools which arise from the Education Reform Act 1988 and which may further disadvantage black pupils. Advantages, disadvantages and the overall effect of the Act will be investigated using a questionnaire to be circulated to all local education authorities in 1993. A second aim of the study is to look in detail at the process of assessment. This is one of the few aspects of the Act with potential benefits for black pupils. The project will examine the hypothesis that the structures and networks developed for assessment will be used by authorities and schools to monitor and respond to inequalities. The third aim is to observe classroom teaching and assessment in order to clarify the more controversial causes of 'underachievement/achievement'. Particular attention will be paid to the role of teacher knowledge and awareness of black children's backgrounds and the mechanisms through which these inform teaching processes and influence academic success. For the second and third aims, the research will focus on a sample of Year Two learners in schools in two authorities. Research methods will include classroom observations and interviews of teachers, pupils and parents.

STATUS: Sponsored project

SOURCE OF GRANT: Economic and Social Research Council

DATE OF RESEARCH: 1992-1993

KEYWORDS: achievement; afro caribbean youth; assessment; black pupils; education reform act 1988; equal education; ethnic groups; low achievement

2851

Centre for Research in Ethnic Relations, Coventry CV4 7AL
01203 523523

Abbas, T. Mr; *Supervisor*: Anwar, M. Prof.

South Asian ethnicity and educational class: a relational analysis

ABSTRACT: This PhD research attempts to describe, analyse and theorise the principal determinants engendering the processes behind the educational achievements of South Asians in schools and colleges in Birmingham. Indepth interviewing has occurred in 6 schools (all of which are very different to each other) and 1 college of further education, and 87 pupils and students have been interviewed. 114 postal questionnaires have been returned from 3 colleges from a total sample of 383. SPSS is to be used to analyse the questionnaire data. Presently, approximately 222 parents are to be sampled, half of which were the parents of the original total pupil sample, for indepth interviewing within their homes. Before the end of the 1996-97 school year, a range of teachers from the schools and other relevant professionals are also be interviewed. Examination results of GCSE and A-levels , being gender and ethnic specific, will help to determine a further quantitative picture. The fieldwork will finish by July 1997. The thesis seeks to examine the way in which differing South Asians, in vastly differing schools, achieve in various educational spheres. There is an analysis of what education means for South Asians in general and then by triangulating between parents, pupils and teachers on the one level and by analysing the examination results and the postal questionnaire data to reveal quantitative tendencies on the other, a more complete analysis is expected - all of which ought to aid the development of a research thesis that is distinctively different from earlier studies. In summary, this research: 1) is a greater focus on each of the main 3 South Asian groups; 2) has involved a much deeper qualitative and quantitative analysis in general as it is wholly being undertaken by a sole South Asian male researcher; 3) suggests the more involved relevance of various colonial and imperial histories to migrant South Asian communities in Britain; 4) suggests the effects of Islamophobia on Muslim groups in particular.

STATUS: Individual research

DATE OF RESEARCH: 1995-1998

KEYWORDS: academic achievement; achievement; asians; ethnic groups; secondary education; secondary school pupils

2852

Centre for Research in Ethnic Relations, Coventry CV4 7AL
01203 523523

Verhoeven, M. Dr; *Supervisor*: Joly, D. Dr

School experience in two different multicultural societies: Belgium and Britain

ABSTRACT: It is well known that Belgium and Britain have got different immigration histories and policies. The British tradition is often described as 'multiculturalist', while the Belgian model (at least in the French speaking part) tends to be more associated with the assimilationist French model. The two educational systems have then developed different kinds of policies to deal with the presence of ethnic pupils. The aim of the present project is to analyse and compare these different educational strategies, and then to focus on the school experience and socialisation process of adolescents from different ethnic groups in Brussels and Birmingham. Our theoretical framework will be constructed using three axes of reflexion: 1) the recent theories of ethnicity; 2) the sociology of school; 3) new theories of socialisation and school experience. The main questions of the research are: 1) How can the strategies developed by both educational systems to deal with multiculturalism be characterised? 2) How do these educational strategies affect the adolescents' school experience and socialisation (i.e. their integration, their strategies, their projects)? 3) How do the nature and characteristics of the different ethnic groups chosen (modes of integration, status, school mobilisation, for example) influence their school experience? The research methods will be qualitative. After a general review of the educational strategies developed in both countries to deal with multicultural situations, 'case studies' in 3 state secondary schools will be realised to analyse each school's own strategy (through observation and interview with key people). Finally the researchers will use indepth qualitative interviews to analyse adolescents' school experience, focusing on the last year of compulsory education.

STATUS: Individual research

DATE OF RESEARCH: 1998-continuing

KEYWORDS: **belgium; comparative education; educational experience; ethnic groups; multiculturalism; social integration**

2853

Centre for Research in Ethnic Relations, Coventry CV4 7AL
01203 523523

Kockuzu, A. Mr; *Supervisor*: Anwar, M. Prof.

Education of Muslim children in a multicultural society

ABSTRACT: Britain is a multicultural, multi-racial, multi-religious, multi-faith society. Muslims have been living intensively in this country for almost 40 years. Naturally they would like to establish their own schools in multicultural settings. They would also like to benefit from the State's grant for their schools. There are some obstacles to be removed. Islamophobia is another threat for Muslims who are in Europe. In this project the researcher would like to point out the current situation of Muslim pupils in state schools. Their problems and expectations will be under research.

STATUS: Individual research

DATE OF RESEARCH: 1996-continuing

KEYWORDS: **islamic education; multiculturalism; muslims; religious cultural groups; religious education**

2854

Centre for Research in Ethnic Relations, Coventry CV4 7AL
01203 523523
Warwick University, Centre for Educational Development, Appraisal and Research (CEDAR), Coventry CV4 7AL

Roach, P. Mr; Morrison, M. Dr; *Supervisors*: Layton Henry, Z. Prof.; Burgess, R. Prof.

Public libraries, ethnic diversity and citizenship

ABSTRACT: The research, which was undertaken between April 1996 and September 1997, has focused on the relationship between public library services and communities characterised by ethnic diversity. Moreover, the research has sought to consider a number of critical questions as these related to the nature of public library services and the extent to which those services are made accountable to, and regarded as legitimate by, ethnically diverse communities. This research has sought to examine: 1) the values and role of the public library service in an increasingly diverse society; 2) the measures taken by public library services to assess and address the needs of ethnic minority groups; 3) the extent to which ethnic minorities are involved in the process of public library services; 4) the factors which affect ethnic minority use of and satisfaction with public library services; 5) the role of ethnic minority community sector agencies in supporting the development of and access to public library services. There have been 3 main aspects to the research: a) a literature review; b) a focused postal audit of 12 library authorities; and c) detailed case studies of 4 library authorities. A critical examination of these issues has enabled the researchers to identify key opportunities for and constraints to the provision of an ethnically diverse public library service through a consideration of: the relationship between the library service and its multi-ethnic population; the extent to which the library service reflects and is responsive to needs within an ethnically diverse setting; the arrangements in place for minority consultation and involvement; the requirements for the development of an ethnically diverse public library service. This report of the research provides evidence of the findings obtained together with guidance for developing practice improvements and recommendations for policy and strategic action at the local and national levels within the public library area.

PUBLISHED MATERIAL: ROACH, P. & MORRISON, M. (1997). 'Libraries - the place on the hill?', Library Record, August 1997.

STATUS: Sponsored project

SOURCE OF GRANT: British Library; 4 Local Education Authorities

DATE OF RESEARCH: 1996-1997

KEYWORDS: **citizenship; ethnic groups; libraries; public libraries**

2855

Department of Continuing Education, Coventry CV4 7AL
01203 523523

McKie, J. Ms; *Supervisor*: Leicester, M. Dr

Representations of technology: IT and adult learning

ABSTRACT: The refiguration of adult and child is explored in the context of discourse about lifelong learning and media representations of technological products (technology is both dominant in the media and dispersed by information technology (IT). The researcher discusses the ways in which advertising for 'educational' technologies juxtaposes and manipulates the concepts of adult and child. Discourse about lifelong learning is prevailing recognition of the new viability of the adult in educational terms (and this recognition is itself driven by demographic and market factors). How does the new viability of the adult student square with marketing for technology that uses the obsolescence of the adult as a strategy to sell products? To reinstate the adult as a legitimate subject of technological discourse, the researcher looks to lifelong learning with its attendant emphasis on flexible access and skills and on holistic and cross-disciplinary epistemologies.

PUBLISHED MATERIAL: MCKIE, J. (1996). 'Is democracy at the heart of IT? Commercial perceptions of technology', Sociological Research Online, Vol 1, No 4.

STATUS: Individual research

DATE OF RESEARCH: 1995-1998

KEYWORDS: **adult education; advertising; computers; educational software; information technology; lifelong learning; marketing**

2856

Department of Continuing Education, Coventry CV4 7AL
01203 523523

Field, J. Prof.

Globalization and lifelong learning

ABSTRACT: In recent years, the introduction of major policy changes has been justified by reference to the influence of globalization. Much of the resulting literature has tended to define globalization in largely economic terms; to judge it largely as a negative phenomenon, which has damaged social cohesion; and to see its impact upon education and training as primarily a narrowing of both the purpose of learning and its content. This study seeks to compare the impact of globalization upon education and training in the Republic of Ireland, Germany and the UK. It draws upon existing discussions over the extent to which the economy is indeed undergoing a globalizing process; it considers the cultural and social dimensions of globalization; and it takes education and training systems to be the active agents of globalization, and not simply their passive victims. It is based largely upon a review of the secondary literature in the fields of international economic activity and social policy; and upon documentary analysis and interview data in the field of educational and training policy and practice.

PUBLISHED MATERIAL: FIELD, J. (1997). 'Globalization and lifelong learning: a critical perspective on the policies of the European Union', International Journal of Studies in Education, Vol 1, No 2, pp.81-93. ; FIELD, J. 'Globalization and the Republic of Ireland: lifelong learning and the Celtic tiger'. In: MULENGA, D. (Ed). Globalization and adult education. New Haven: Yale University Press. (in press).

STATUS: Individual research

DATE OF RESEARCH: 1998-continuing

KEYWORDS: **adult education; comparative education; economic development; germany; globalization; ireland; lifelong learning**

2857

Department of Continuing Education, Continuing Education Research Centre, Coventry CV4 7AL
01203 523523

Duke, C. Prof.

Continuing education and organisation change in universities

ABSTRACT: This is a study of change in university continuing education in Britain as a window into change in higher education generally. The traditional, often marginalised, extramural departments are giving way to new structures and arrangements. Continuing education is gaining a much wider meaning and being 'mainstreamed' in policy and organisation. The research studys these trends and processes, and considers implications for higher education generally.

PUBLISHED MATERIAL: DUKE, C. (1991). 'Restructuring for better service in continuing university education', New Education, Vol 13, No 1, pp.57-68. ; DUKE, C. (1991). 'University continuing education: identities, prospects and perspectives'. In: FIELDHOUSE, R. (Ed). The organisation of Continuing Education in Universities. UDACE. ; DUKE, C. (1991). 'Lifelong education and the universities of the United Kingdom', Higher Education in Europe, Vol XVI, No 1, pp.46-55.

STATUS: Sponsored project

SOURCE OF GRANT: Universities Funding Council £30,000; Training, Enterprise & Education Directorate

DATE OF RESEARCH: 1990-1993

KEYWORDS: **adult education; continuing education; higher education; organisational change; universities**

2858

Department of Continuing Education, Continuing Education Research Centre, Coventry CV4 7AL
01203 523523

Duke, C. Prof.; Merrill, B. Dr

Comparative European study on the access of adults to universities: policies and practice

ABSTRACT: The aim of the project is to compare the adult access policies implemented in British universities with those in Belgian and Swedish universities. The project will include: 1) A description of the universities' policies and practices regarding: a) admissions conditions and procedures; b) course schedule; c) course location; d) curriculum; e) pedagogy; and f) student services. 2) An evaluation of the observed policies and practices in these 6 areas and their effects on adult access. 3) An analysis of the organisational dynamics underlying the development of the observed access policies and practices. This is a European comparative study involving at present the Universite Catholique de Louvain, Belgium, and the University of Stockholm, Sweden and future partners to join from Eire, Spain and Germany. A case study approach is used. Stage 1 is completed and is a general description and analysis of the national contexts in a comparative perspective on adult access and education systems. Stage 2, also completed, is a description of the universities' policies and practices (6 points outlined

above) using quantitative approaches and a case study method of Louvain University and Warwick University. Stage 3, in progress, comprises case studies of the institutions involved in the project, and a study of the experiences of adult students, and lecturers, in relation to the access of adults to universities. Qualitative methods were used such as indepth semi-structured interviews. Stage 4, in progress, will look at adult access and organisational dynamics. Future partners will employ the same methodology.

PUBLISHED MATERIAL: BOURGEOIS, E., DUKE, C., GUYOT, J.L., MERRILL, B. & DE ST GEORGE, P. (1994). Comparing access internationally: the context of the Belgian and English higher education systems. Warwick: University of Warwick, Department of Continuing Education, Continuing Education Research Centre.

STATUS: Sponsored project

SOURCE OF GRANT: Higher Education Funding Council

DATE OF RESEARCH: 1992-continuing

KEYWORDS: **access to education; comparative education; educational policy; higher education; mature students; universities**

2859

Department of Continuing Education, Continuing Education Research Centre, Coventry CV4 7AL
01203 523523

Blaxter, L. Dr; Hughes, C. Dr; Tight, M. Dr

Career paths: adult education and adult lives

ABSTRACT: A field study of 6 organisations in the West Midlands and interviews with 120+ adults about the place of education in their lives. The focus of the analysis will use key concepts - careers, organisation, human resources, development and lifelong learning. The analysis is ongoing.

PUBLISHED MATERIAL: BLAXTER, L. & HUGHES, C. (1995). 'Women, class and education: ravelling the threads'. Paper presented at the Towards a Learning Workforce Conference, University of Lancaster, 1995. ; TIGHT, M. (1995). 'Education, work and adult life: a literature review', Research Papers in Education, Vol 10, No 3, pp.383-400. ; HUGHES, C., TIGHT, M. & BLAXTER, L. (1996). 'Living lifelong education: the experience of some working class women', Adults Learning, Vol 7, No 7, pp.109-171. ; BLAXTER, L., HUGHES, C. & TIGHT, M. (1997). 'Education, work and adult life: how adults relate their learning to their work, family and social lives'. In: SUTHERLAND, P. (Ed). Adult learning: a reader. London: Kogan Page.

STATUS: Team research

DATE OF RESEARCH: 1993-continuing

KEYWORDS: **adult education; careers; continuing education; lifelong learning; staff development; vocational education**

2860

Department of Continuing Education, Continuing Education Research Centre, Coventry CV4 7AL
01203 523523

Alzaroo, S. Mr; *Supervisors*: Bown, L. Prof.; Blaxter, L. Dr

Educational inequalities in Palestinian schools: how can nonformal education help?

ABSTRACT: This study tries to conceptualise nonformal education in the Palestinian West Bank and Gaza Strip, and explore its role in overcoming educational inequalities in Palestinian formal schooling, particularly in bridging the gap bteween the sexes, rural-urban areas, vocational-general education, and between the West Bank and Gaza Strip. The research depends on indepth interviews. The methodology utilised a plethora of approaches including: comparative approach, statistical approach, historical approach.

STATUS: Individual research

DATE OF RESEARCH: 1995-1998

KEYWORDS: **equal education; nonformal education; palestine**

2861

Department of Continuing Education, Continuing Education Research Centre, Coventry CV4 7AL
91203 523523

Spencer, D. Mr; *Supervisor*: Leicester, M. Ms

The Primary Schools Programme (an adult education programme for women): a site of struggle and a catalyst for change

ABSTRACT: The Primary Schools Programme (PSP) in Coventry is an adult education programme which attracts working class women. Classes take place part-time, during the day, in local primary schools and are generally certificated, e.g. GCSEs and A-levels. Since its inception in 1981, approximately 15,000 women have enrolled. The study uses documentary evidence to show the PSP as a site of struggle. Two questionnaires, one from 1986 (263 replies), the second from 1992 (305 replies) are analysed to give an indication of who the students are and why they attend PSP classes. 21 past and present students were interviewed and asked about changes in their lives as a result of attending classes. The women spoke of a growth in self-confidence and social awareness. An interaction takes place between life experience and academic knowledge leading to critical thinking. This produces changes in relationships and sometimes a sense of isolation at university and in new careers because the women feel neither working class nor middle class. The researcher is the founder of the PSP and a tutor on the PSP and a man, some self-reflectivity is therefore included.

STATUS: Individual research

DATE OF RESEARCH: 1991-1997

KEYWORDS: **adult education; adult students; followup studies; outcomes of education; student development; womens education; working class**

2862

Department of Continuing Education, Continuing Education Research Centre, Coventry CV4 7AL
01203 523523
Northern College, Wentworth Castle, Stainborough, Barnsley S75 3ET
01226 206232
Further Education Development Agency, Citadel Place, Tinworth Street, London SE11 5EH
0171 840 5400

Merrill, B. Dr; Byrd, P. Dr; Fryer, R. Prof.; Smith, G. Mr; Morris, A. Mr

The further education college and its communities

ABSTRACT: The aims are: 1) To investigate the changing nature of relationships between colleges, the communities they serve, and the local organisations with which they interact, seeking to identify the value further education is adding to an area. 2) To examine ways in which strategic research partnerships can be developed in the further education sector and identify a model for partnership research. This is a collaborative project in which further education staff have been trained to undertake the research in their institutions. It is also a comparative study looking at further education colleges and their communities in the West Midlands and South Yorkshire. Further education colleges, in recent years, have experienced policy and structural changes which have affected their relationships with the local community. The project looks at local people's perceptions of the role of further education colleges in order to develop a conceptual understanding of community within the context of further education colleges. However, another important outcome will be to identify the processes for developing a model of good practice for partnership research.

STATUS: Sponsored project

SOURCE OF GRANT: Further Education Development Agency £120,000

DATE OF RESEARCH: 1996-1998

KEYWORDS: **college community relationship; colleges of further education; community; community education; further education**

2863

Department of Continuing Education, Coventry CV4 7AL
01203 523523
Edinburgh University, Faculty of Education, Centre for Continuing Education, Moray House, Holyrood Campus, Holyrood Road, Edinburgh EH8 8AQ
0131 651 6296
Ulster University, Jordanstown Campus, School of Education, Shore Road, Newtownabbey, County Antrim BT37 OQB
01232 365131

Spence, L. Ms; Burns, A. Dr; *Supervisors*: Field, J. Prof.; Schuller, T. Prof.

Divergence between initial and continuing education performance in Scotland and Northern Ireland

ABSTRACT: Conventionally, it is widely assumed that high achievement rates in initial schooling will generate high participation levels in lifelong learning. Empirically, this is not the case in the two UK regions with the highest levels of achievement among school-leavers: in Scotland and Northern Ireland, which consistently perform well in terms of school leavers' qualifications, participation in most forms of adult education and training is well below the averages for the UK. The study focuses upon the nature and causes of this apparent divergence. Methodologically, it involves: 1) detailed analysis of the statistical basis for comparison within the UK; 2) a collection of stakeholders' views, using 10 sectoral focus groups in each of the 2 societies concerned; 3) an indepth exploration of perceptions of the relationship between initial and continuing learning, based on 60 interviews; and 4) collection of data from a small number of comparator societies (including Malta, Sweden, Bremen, Hokkaido, and Canada). Conceptually, the study has made significant use of the notion of social capital developed by James Coleman and Robert Putnam. In Coleman's and Putnam's hands, this notion refers to the strength or weakness of social networks, norms and trust in any given social space. Coleman argues that strong social capital can be decisive in contributing to high initial educational performance; Putnam that high social capital can foster both civic engagement and economic prosperity. This study is the first to explore the role of social capital in lifelong learning, and to consider the role of lifelong learning in building social capital.

PUBLISHED MATERIAL: FIELD, J. & SCHULLER, T. (1995). 'Is there less adult learning in Scotland and Northern Ireland? A preliminary analysis', Scottish Journal of Adult and Continuing Education, Vol 2, No 2, pp.71-82.; SARGANT, J., FIELD, T. & SCHULLER, T. et al. (1997). The learning divide. Leicester: National Institute of Adult Continuing Education. ; SCHULLER, T. & FIELD, J. 'Social capital, human capital and the learning society', International Journal of Lifelong Education. (in press).

STATUS: Sponsored project

SOURCE OF GRANT: Economic and Social Research Council £98,000

DATE OF RESEARCH: 1996-1998

KEYWORDS: **comparative education; continuing education; further education; higher education; lifelong learning; northern ireland; participation rate; scotland**

2864

Department of Continuing Education, International Centre for Education Development, Coventry CV4 7AL
01203 523523
Birmingham University, Centre for West African Studies, Edgbaston, Birmingham B15 2TT
0121 414 3344

Bown, L. Prof.; *Supervisor*: Rimmer, D. Mr

The British contribution to higher education in Africa. Part of a larger project on the British intellectual engagement with Africa

ABSTRACT: The study is a contribution to a publication celebrating the centenary of the Royal African Society in 1999, on the theme of British Intellectual Engagement with Africa. It will cover approximately 45 university institutions in the English-speaking countries of tropical Africa, mainly looking at their history in the last half-century, although there will be a preliminary survey of earlier developments. The three main modes of establishment will be studied and major issues elicited, such as curriculum, international equivalences and recognition, pay differentials between British and national staff. The role of the African universities in national life will be compared with the British experience and current engagement through staff and student interchange and 'link' schemes will be examined. Additionally, a sample of universities in three African countries will be taken and the places of qualification of academic staff will be analysed, to ascertain what proportion have been trained in the UK.

STATUS: Sponsored project

SOURCE OF GRANT: Royal African Society

DATE OF RESEARCH: 1996-1998

KEYWORDS: **africa; developing countries; educational development; higher education; international cooperation; international educational exchange; universities**

2865

Department of Continuing Education, International Centre for Education Development, Coventry CV4 7AL
01203 523523

Arthur, L. Ms; *Supervisor*: Preston, R. Dr

Achieving effective consultancy

ABSTRACT: Recent research, based on cross-national case studies set out to identify the parameters of good practice and effectiveness of international consultancy in education and social development. The present study is being developed to identify how the ways in which consultancy is undertaken affects its outcomes and to analyse the ways in which improvement in stratgegy increases effectiveness. The study uses cross-national comparisons between rich and poor countries. Research council funding is being sought.

PUBLISHED MATERIAL: ARTHUR, L., PRESTON, R. et al (1995). Quality and overseas consultancy: understanding the issues. Manchester: British Council. ; PRESTON, R. (1996). 'Consultancy research and human development'. In: BUCHERT, L. & KING, K. (Eds). Consultancy and research in international education: the new dynamics. Bonn: NORRAG/ DSE.

STATUS: Team research

DATE OF RESEARCH: 1997-continuing

KEYWORDS: **consultancy; educational development; international educational exchange; social development**

2866

Department of Continuing Education, International Centre for Education Development, Coventry CV4 7AL
01203 523523
State University of New York at Buffalo, New York NY 14260
001 716 6452000

Preston, R. Dr; Ilon, L. Dr

Chaos and stability: education in the global age

ABSTRACT: The study is of a series of case studies from different countries by 20 authors concerned to analyse the ways in which social stability and change interacts with education at a time of adjustment to a world global economy. They range from macro level analyses of multilateral organisations' influence on national educational agendas, to community studies of the implications of education for pastorals in India. The project is the preparation of an edited volume to be published, hopefully, during the course of 1998.

STATUS: Team research

DATE OF RESEARCH: 1997-1998

KEYWORDS: **comparative education; economic development; educational change; educational development; globalization**

2867

Department of Continuing Education, International Centre for Education in Development, Coventry CV4 7AL
01203 523523

Karifis, G. Mr; *Supervisor*: Preston, R. Dr

The transition from higher education to working life: the experience of European Union postgraduate students of human and social sciences in a British university

ABSTRACT: The research is comparative and traces issues that relate to the way higher education students of human and social sciences develop their attitudes and form their values towards education, employment and themselves in their transition from higher education to working life. The aim of this study is to describe the way postgraduate students of human and social science develop these attitudes, conceptualise transition, and furthermore to analyse the way/s in which they evaluate their educational experience in relation to their work expectations. The hypothesis is that the way students in the European Union (EU) conceptualise transition from higher education to work, explicity relates to their evaluation of life experience and the development or change of self in relation to the other. The study further suggests that the way these students conceptualise transition from higher education to work consists of an autonomous form of learning, which may involve levels of sociological and psychological stress derived from the value attached to an awareness of the motives of self and others. The sample consists of 12 European Union nationals who are postgraduate students of human and social sciences in a British university. Data collection utilises non-directive interviews, feedback reports from the informants on the interviews, and a research diary. Analysis of the data involves the use of case-oriented comparison that employs a dialectical paradigm of conversational analysis. Each case is seen as a whole. The analysis is performed in relation to certain contextual categories that relate to the emotional state of the informant during the transition from higher education to work, the values of the informant, the attitudes and sentiments of the informant, the informant's opinions on a subject, and the cognitive formulation of ideas on a subject. These broad categories embrace a number of dialectical paradigms, such as work-unemployment, me-others, money-creativity, movement stability etc. The outcomes of this categorisation are then put in a broader context that relates to concepts of work, education, learning, knowledge, etc. At an educational level, the study adopts a socio-anthropological perspective towards the issue of transition and the way higher education students conceptualise it. At the same time however, it acknowledges the psychological extensions that describe transition and suggests that transition may be conceptualised as a period of autonomous learning that has emotional and cognitive effects in students' lives. At a theoretical level the study promotes an alternative method of approaching the issue of transition to work by providing new research categories. At EU level, the study describes a different aspect of lifelong learning that relates to the evaluation of students' life in an EU university and the way these lives affects their further occupational choices.

STATUS: Individual research

DATE OF RESEARCH: 1996-1998

KEYWORDS: **employment; higher education to work transition; student attitudes; students; work attitudes**

2868

Department of Continuing Education, Coventry CV4 7AL
01203 523523
University of Louvain, Department des Sciences de l'Education, Place du Cardinal Mercierio, B-1348, Louvain-la-Neuve, Belgium
University of Barcelona, CREA, Edificio Llevant, Planta Vall d'Hebron, 08035 Barcelona, Spain

Merrill, B. Dr; Hill, S. Dr

Accreditation of prior experiential learning in Europe

ABSTRACT: This is a development project to promote the policies and practice of accreditation of prior experiential learning (APEL) across Europe through the development, establishment and dissemination of a European database. Year 1 of the project focused on 3 European countries: Belgium, Spain and the UK. Year 2 of the project has extended to include the following countries: Germany and Sweden. A quantitative and qualitative survey of APEL good practices has been undertaken in several European countries in 3 educational fields: further and higher education; adult and continuing education; and professional and vocational training. This data has led to the development of a database. The ultimate aim is to extend the provision of APEL within Europe and hence widen access and lifelong learning opportunities for adults through the: provision of examples of good practice at different educational levels and fields; exchange of knowledge relating to APEL; and development of cooperation between universities and adult education institutions to develop APEL strategies within a European context.

STATUS: Sponsored project

SOURCE OF GRANT: European Union: Socrates

DATE OF RESEARCH: 1996-1998

KEYWORDS: **access to education; accreditation of prior learning; adult education; comparative education; europe; experiential learning; further education; higher education**

2869

Department of Science Education, Coventry CV4 7AL
01203 523523

Harwood, D. Mr

The debriefing process in active learning

ABSTRACT: Previous research has shown that the teacher becomes the focus of interaction in active learning whenever he or she is present with the teaching group. This research aims to study the nature of the teacher's statements and questions during the debriefing porcess and identify the effects they have upon pupil participation. Teachers who are experienced in active learning, have volunteered to participate. The 'debriefing' phase of the lesson will be videotaped and transcribed. As a result of collaboration beteween teacher and researcher, a commentary will be written to accompany the transcript. Guidelines for debriefing 'active learning' will be identified.

PUBLISHED MATERIAL: HARWOOD, D.L. (1989). 'The nature of teacher-pupil interaction in the "Active Tutorial Work" approach: using interaction analysis to evaluate student-centred approaches', British Educational Research Journal, Vol 15, No 2, pp.177-194. ; HARWOOD, D.L. (1991). 'Guidelines for debriefing active learning: an interim report'. Coventry: University of Warwick/Warwickshire Local Education Authority. (Available from the author).

STATUS: Sponsored project

SOURCE OF GRANT: Warwickshire Local Education Authority £350

DATE OF RESEARCH: 1990-1993

KEYWORDS: **classroom communication; learning activities; teacher pupil relationship; teacher role; teaching methods**

2870

Institute of Education, Coventry CV4 7AL
01203 523523

Abbott, I. Mr

The City Technology College initiative with particular reference to the establishment of a City Technology College on Teesside

ABSTRACT: The study aims to assess the effectiveness and impact of a city technology college on the educational system of a deprived urban area, particularly the effect the college will have on the local education authority schools within the locality. The means of collecting data will include indepth interviews, observation and the use of questionnaires and surveys. Specifically extensive contacts have been made with the institutions and individuals involved in this process. It is expected that a wide range of issues will be identified including the role of the industrial sponsors, the position of the local authority, the effect on schools and colleges, the response of teachers and the impact on parents, pupils and staff involved in the college. The study will be looking at a rapidly developing area and it is expected that it will provide data which will be of use in determining future policy decisions.

PUBLISHED MATERIAL: ABBOTT, I.D. (1991). 'British and American approaches to science and technology', Education and Training, Vol 33, No 1, pp.5-7. ; ABBOTT, I.D. (1991). 'School industry links: an American perspective', Head Teachers Review, pp.10-12, Winter.

STATUS: Individual research

DATE OF RESEARCH: 1989-1993

KEYWORDS: **city technology colleges; disadvantaged environment; industry education relationship; school community relationship**

2871

Institute of Education, Coventry CV4 7AL
01203 523523

Lewis, A. Dr

Communication between non-handicapped children and pupils with severe learning difficulties

ABSTRACT: This research is investigating the nature of communication between non-handicapped (NH) children and pupils with severe learning difficulties (SLD). The children interact in dyads or triads and each group comprises at least one NH and one SLD child. NH-SLD interaction has been video-recorded for approximately 60 minutes each week throughout a year of weekly integration sessions. Thirty-six NH children (ages ten years, one month to eleven years, one month at the start of the year) and nine pupils with SLD (ages twelve years, four months to fifteen years, eight months at the start of the year) have been involved. Analyses of data is being carried out utilising frameworks developed in an earlier study (Lewis and Carpenter, 1990; Lewis, 1990) involving younger children in NH-SLD dyads.

PUBLISHED MATERIAL: LEWIS, A. (1990). 'Six and seven year old 'normal' children's talk to peers with severe learning difficulties', European Journal of Special Needs Education, Vol 5, No 1, pp.13-23. ; LEWIS, A. & CARPENTER, B. (1990). 'Discourse, in an integrated school setting, between six and seven year old non-handicapped children and peers with severe learning difficulties'. In: FRASER, W.I. (Ed). Key issues in mental retardation. London: Routledge. ; LEWIS, A. (1991). 'Entitled to learn together?'. In: ASHDOWN, R., CARPENTER, B. & BOVAIR, K. (Eds). Meeting the curriculum challenge. Lewes: Falmer Press. ; LEWIS, A. (1994). Children's understanding of disability. London: Routledge.

STATUS: Sponsored project

SOURCE OF GRANT: Warwick University: Research and Innovations Fund £1,300

DATE OF RESEARCH: 1990-1993

KEYWORDS: **communication research; integration studies; learning disabilities; special educational needs; verbal communication**

2872

Institute of Education, Coventry CV4 7AL
01203 523523

Lewis, A. Dr

Primary school children's understanding of severe learning difficulties

ABSTRACT: This research investigated non-handicapped (NH) children's understanding of the nature of severe learning difficulties (SLD). The literature on social cognition was reviewed in order to identify developmental changes during middle childhood in understanding about others. As a result of this review two questions about children's understanding of SLD were identified. These two questions were: which cues of SLD are salient for NH children, and do NH children recognise the irrevocability of SLD? Two age groups, 7 and 11 year olds, were selected for interview because research on social cognition (Aboud, 1988; Schneider, 1991) suggests that there will be marked differences between these two age groups in terms of their understanding of SLD. Nineteen 7 year olds (mean age seven years, two months) were interviewed individually. Thirty-two 11 year olds (mean age eleven years, one month) were interviewed in small friendship groups of four children. All children interviewed had participated in integration projects involving children with SLD. Findings indicated that the 7 year olds were confused about the nature of SLD and tended to believe that children with SLD had transitory sensory, but not cognitive, impairments. The 11 year olds also misunderstood the nature of SLD although they were clearer than the younger children about the irrevocability of SLD. For the 11 year olds, intra-SLD group, as well as inter group (SLD-NH), differences were recognised. These findings are consistent with research into the development of other aspects of social cognition, for example, children's understanding of gender and race.

PUBLISHED MATERIAL: LEWIS, A. (1992). 'Group child interviews as a research tool', British Educational Research Journal, Vol 18, No 4, pp.413-421. ; LEWIS, A. (1993). 'Integration, education and rights', British Educational Research Journal, Vol 19, No 3, pp.291-302. ; LEWIS, A. (1993). 'Primary school children's understanding of severe learning difficulties', Educational Psychology, Vol 13, No 2, pp.133-145. ; LEWIS, A. (1995). Children's understanding of disability. London: Routledge.

STATUS: Individual research

DATE OF RESEARCH: 1990-1993

KEYWORDS: **children; comprehension; integration studies; learning disabilities; primary school pupils; pupil attitudes; special educational needs**

2873

Institute of Education, Coventry CV4 7AL
01203 523523

Raban, B. Prof.

Evaluation of the National Curriculum core subjects (English) at key stages 1, 2 and 3

ABSTRACT: The aim of this National Curriculum Council (NCC) monitoring programme is to ensure that problems which teachers are facing in implementing National Curriculum English are fully understood to discover: whether the difficulty lies in the Order; whether it is a question of teacher knowledge and understanding; or whether statement(s) of attainment are pitched inappropriately for pupils within a particular key stage. An analysis of the English Orders will provide a conceptual and practical framework for fieldwork in schools. Between 70-80 schools will be visited in 10 local education authorities (LEAs) throughout England. Teachers, parents and governors will be interviewed. Classrooms will be observed and school documents inspected. Access to key stage 1 standard assessment task data, examples of pupils' work and interviews with LEA personnel will form the body of evidence required to address the issues specified by the NCC.

STATUS: Sponsored project

SOURCE OF GRANT: National Curriculum Council £377,000

DATE OF RESEARCH: 1991-1993

KEYWORDS: **english; english studies curriculum; evaluation; monitoring; national curriculum**

2874

Institute of Education, Coventry CV4 7AL
01203 523523

Richardson, W. Dr

Participation in education and training: age group 16-19

ABSTRACT: A research seminar will convene on six occasions over two years. Six designated themes are identified: (1) determinants of individuals decisions; (2) qualifications as a predictor of post education destination; (3) funding structures; (4) the status of qualifications; (5) access; (6) quality in teaching and learning

STATUS: Sponsored project

SOURCE OF GRANT: Economic and Social Research Council £7,500

DATE OF RESEARCH: 1992-1993

KEYWORDS: **access to education; further education; sixteen to nineteen education; student participation; tertiary education; vocational education**

2875

Institute of Education, Coventry CV4 7AL
01203 523523

Troyna, B. Prof.

Local Management of Schools and racial equality

ABSTRACT: The research explores how the recent educational reforms have affected the status of (and commitment to) racial equality issues in a local education authority and a sample of its secondary schools.

PUBLISHED MATERIAL: TROYNA, B. (1995). 'The local management of schools and racial equality'. In: CRAFT, M. & TOMLINSON, S. (Eds). Ethnic relations in schools in the 1990's. London: Athlone Press.

STATUS: Sponsored project

SOURCE OF GRANT: Commission for Racial Equality £33,000

DATE OF RESEARCH: 1992-1993

KEYWORDS: **equal education; local management of schools; racial discrimination; racial integration; school based management; secondary education**

2876

Institute of Education, Coventry CV4 7AL
01203 523523

Gardner, P. Mr; Pickering, J. Dr

Mature students and higher education

ABSTRACT: Research into how mature students at university perceive younger undergraduates; how they get on in halls of residence; and how course selectors view mature students.

PUBLISHED MATERIAL: GARDNER, P. & PICKERING, J. (1991). 'Learning with yuppies: or, on counselling mature students', Pastoral Care in Education, Vol 9, No 1, pp.13-19. ; GARDNER, P. & PICKERING, J. (1992). 'Learning to live with Madonna: or mature students on campus', Pastoral Care in Education, Vol 10, No 4, pp.3-8. ; PICKERING, J. & GARDNER, P. (1992). 'Access: a selector's perspective', Journal of Access Studies, Vol 7, No 2, pp.220-233.

STATUS: Individual research

DATE OF RESEARCH: 1992-1997

KEYWORDS: **access to education; higher education; mature students; student attitudes; student housing; student recruitment**

2877

Institute of Education, Coventry CV4 7AL
01203 523523

Phillips, G. Mr; *Supervisor*: Gardner, P. Mr

Moral principles and moral education

ABSTRACT: An enquiry into the nature of objectivity in morality and moral education which includes a critical consideration of ethical subjectivism, relativism and proceduralism. The inquiry concentrates in the main on moral realism and considers the extent to which moral realism can withstand the objections of its critics and can provide an account of the provibility and nature of moral knowledge and a secure foundation for moral education.

PUBLISHED MATERIAL: PHILLIPS, G. (1991). 'Personal, social and moral education'. In: ENTWISTLE, N. (Ed). A Handbook of Educational Ideas. London: Croom Helm.

STATUS: Individual research

DATE OF RESEARCH: 1987-1993

KEYWORDS: **educational philosophy; ethics; moral education; moral values; realism; reasoning**

2878

Institute of Education, Coventry CV4 7AL
01203 523523

Morris, A. Mr; *Supervisor*: Halpin, D. Dr

Pupil performance in Catholic schools

ABSTRACT: Using data on examination performance in secondary schools in one West Midlands local education authority, as well as detailed case study work in two secondary Catholic schools in the same area, this investigation explores the extent to which the philosophy and practice of contrasting kinds of Catholic school contributes either way to academic output.

STATUS: Individual research

DATE OF RESEARCH: 1993-1997

KEYWORDS: **academic achievement; catholic schools; school effectiveness**

2879

Institute of Education, Coventry CV4 7AL
01203 523523

Pritchard, A. Mr

The extent to which children's learning may be enhanced by the use of information technology

ABSTRACT: The study: 1) examines literature; 2) identifies present information technology curriculum content in two sample schools; and 3) assesses consequences for learning enhancement.

STATUS: Individual research

DATE OF RESEARCH: 1993-continuing

KEYWORDS: **computer uses in education; information technology**

2880

Institute of Education, Coventry CV4 7AL
01203 523523

Vincent, C. Dr; Warren, S. Mr

Community and collectivism: the role of parents' organisations in the education system

ABSTRACT: The principal aim of this project is to further theoretical and empirical understanding of parents' roles in relation to the education system through an analysis of the relationship between parents' organisations and their client groups. This will shed light on the nature of dominant discourses concerning acceptable forms of lay participation in the education system, and how those discourses are perceived, and subsequently reinforced or subverted by such organisations and their client groups. In broad terms, therefore, the research focuses on the role of parent-centred organisations. Parent-centred organisations (PCOs) are local, community-based organisations. They may include groups run by parents, or groups for parents established by professionals working in local education authorities (LEAs) or the voluntary sector. Such organisations are usually independent of any individual school and offer a range of facilities and services, including advice, information and sometimes advocacy services. More specifically, three particular aspects of their operation are being examined: 1) the interactions between parent-centred organisations and their clients; 2) the relationships between the PCOs and other agencies; and 3) the PCOs' conceptions of an 'appropriate' parental role in relation to state education. The work of Antonio Gramsci is used as a starting point with which to examine and conceptualise the formation of relationships between PCO staff and their clients. Much of Gramsci's writing focused on the interaction of different social groups and the manner in which power relationships are formed and maintained. The case studies include: a general parent-centred organisation answering a range of educational enquiries; specialist PCOs focusing on special education, and the experiences of black parents; and a small, self-help parents' group. Data is being collected through a range of qualitative research methods, primarily semi-structured interviewing, but also observation and document analysis. The researchers have provided each parents' organisation with written feedback based on the views gathered, and concerning a range of organisational and managerial issues.

PUBLISHED MATERIAL: VINCENT, C. (1997). 'Community and collectivism: the role of parents' organisations in the education system', British Journal of Sociology of Education, Vol 18, No 2, pp.271-283. ; VINCENT, C. & WARREN, S. (1997). 'A "different kind" of professional? Case studies of the work of parent-centred organisations', International Journal of Inclusive Education, Vol 1, No 2, pp.143-161. ; VINCENT, C. & WARREN, S. 'Motherhood, education and transition', British Journal of Sociology of Education. (in press).

STATUS: Sponsored project

SOURCE OF GRANT: Economic and Social Research Council £30,000

DATE OF RESEARCH: 1996-continuing

KEYWORDS: **community organisations; organisations - groups; parent organisations; parent participation**

2881

Institute of Education, Coventry CV4 7AL
01203 523523

Solity, J. Mr

Psychological assessment and children's reading

ABSTRACT: The aim of the research is to evaluate the impact of a framework for teaching and assessing reading in reception classrooms. Five experimental and five control schools will be identified and the intervention will last for two academic years until children reach the end of Year 1. The framework will teach children a range of skills and strategies that draw on recent research, that are generalisable and that can be related to any teaching approaches or philosophies about teaching reading. The framework will address the following areas: 1) an analysis of what children are expected to read; 2) the research on phonological awareness and the strategies which are hypothesised to have the greatest impact on children's progress; 3) non phonological generalisable skills and strategies; 4) teaching methods; 5) the frequency and duration of teaching; 6) strategies for listening to children read; 7) approaches to the regular assessment of children's learning. The evaluation will examine: 1) the impact of the reading framework on the reading of 5-6 year old children; 2) how successfully are the issues raised when teachers implement the framework; and 3) the extent to which 'reading difficulties' are prevented.

STATUS: Sponsored project

SOURCE OF GRANT: Essex Local Education Authority £53,164

DATE OF RESEARCH: 1995-continuing

KEYWORDS: **assessment; beginning reading; primary education; reading achievement; reading difficulties; reading teaching; young children**

2882

Institute of Education, Coventry CV4 7AL
01203 523523

Harris, B. Mr; *Supervisors*: Tomlinson, J. Prof.; Husbands, C. Dr

GCSE: institutional and individual perspectives

ABSTRACT: The project was developed from the researcher's interest in the pastoral curriculum, partly as a result of previous work on BA and MA degrees and partly because of what seemed a curious lack of research into how individuals and institutions deal with the pressures of examinations. Consequently, the aim of the project is to look at institutional and individual perspectives in the specific context of the General Certificate in Secondary Education (GCSE) examinations, and to attempt to define, using the GCSEs as the example, whether or not institutional and individual interests harmonise or conflict in terms of academic and pastoral strategies for achieving examination success. The sample includes six secondary schools, including three large comprehensives, two grant-maintained single-sex schools and a small independent coeducational grammar school. The basic method is to track Year 11 pupils through the whole academic year 1995-96, including their eventual results and destinations, using questionnaires for all Year 11 pupils, interviews with senior staff and Year 11 tutors, and discussions and diaries with small 'sample' groups of four to twelve pupils in each school. The research is still in progress and therefore conclusions cannot yet be reached, but a great deal of data is being collected which sheds light on the pressures on pupils, and suggests that there are pastoral and individual elements to examination pressure and 'non-academic' strategies which can be used by institutions to combat the pressures.

STATUS: Individual research

DATE OF RESEARCH: 1994-1997

KEYWORDS: **anxiety; examinations; general certificate of secondary education; pastoral care - education; pupil needs; secondary education; stress psychological; test anxiety**

2883

Institute of Education, Coventry CV4 7AL
01203 523523

Phillips, E. Mrs; *Supervisors*: Lloyd-Smith, M. Mr; Harwood, D. Mr

Meeting the needs of gifted children

ABSTRACT: A study to investigate: a) ways in which the needs of 'gifted' children are defined; b) strategies and programmes for meeting those needs; and c) methods adopted to monitor and evaluate these strategies. The study will concentrate on pupils in National Curriculum key stages 3 and 4. A comparison will be made, using the existing research evidence, between official policies and guidelines and current practice in schools. Against this background an empirical study is being conducted in which perceptions of pupils' needs and their special provision will be investigated, using samples of pupils identified as 'gifted', parents of these pupils and teachers in the schools they attend. Issues to be explored will include: definitions of and assumptions about 'giftedness', the adequacy of match between needs and provision, variations in policy and practice according to gender, age and curriculum subject.

STATUS: Individual research

DATE OF RESEARCH: 1994-1997

KEYWORDS: **gifted; key stage 3; key stage 4; pupil needs; secondary education; special provision - gifted**

2884

Institute of Education, Coventry CV4 7AL
01203 523523

Begley, A. Ms; *Supervisor*: Lewis, A. Dr

The aspirations and perceptions of children and adolescents with Down's syndrome towards schooling

ABSTRACT: This research project is concerned with the self-concept of children and adolescents with Down's syndrome. The aim is to investigate how children with Down's syndrome between the ages of 7 and 13 years see themselves (their self-image), and how they evaluate themselves (their self-esteem). The self-image and self-esteem of children with Down's syndrome will be compared to the self-image and self-esteem of children with typical development, and children with mental retardation. In addition to the differences between different groups of children, the effects of age and school type (mainstream or special school) on the self-image and self-esteem of children with Down's syndrome will also be examined.

STATUS: Sponsored project

SOURCE OF GRANT: Down's Syndrome Research Association

DATE OF RESEARCH: 1995-continuing

KEYWORDS: **downs syndrome; mainstreaming; pupil attitudes; self concept; self esteem; special educational needs; special schools**

2885

Institute of Education, Coventry CV4 7AL
01203 523523

Eggleston, S. Prof.

Pupil decision-making at the end of compulsory schooling

ABSTRACT: Questionnaires and structured interviews with 120 15-16 year old pupils in a sample of 12 schools, and interviews with teachers and parents, will be used to identify causal factors in decision on the nature and direction of continuing education after compulsory schooling ends.

STATUS: Sponsored project

SOURCE OF GRANT: Leverhulme Foundation £12,000

DATE OF RESEARCH: 1995-1997

KEYWORDS: **decision making; pupil attitudes; pupil destinations; school leavers; sixteen to nineteen education**

2886

Institute of Education, Coventry CV4 7AL
01203 523523

Evans, L. Ms; *Supervisor*: Sikes, P. Dr

Early years teachers' perceptions of their role

ABSTRACT: This research project aims to examine the ways in which early years teachers perceive their role, how they came to these perceptions, and how these perceptions relate to institutional and national contexts. A life history approach is being used to trace earlier influences upon current understandings of what it is to be a teacher of young children. A series of indepth interviews are being used to collect personal and professional biographies of nursery and reception teachers.

STATUS: Individual research

DATE OF RESEARCH: 1995-1998

KEYWORDS: **early childhood education; infant school teachers; nursery school teachers; primary education; primary school teachers; reception classes; teacher attitudes; teacher role; teaching profession; young children**

2887

Institute of Education, Coventry CV4 7AL
01203 523523

Rakhit, A. Ms; *Supervisor*: Sikes, P. Dr

The career experiences of Asian female teachers: a case study approach

ABSTRACT: The research examines and appraises the career experiences of Asian female teachers in one local education authority (LEA) in the context of national background. By focusing on the interaction between Asian female teachers and other teachers and white pupils and parents, the research has attempted to answer the question: what is it like to be a black teacher in a British school? The work is based upon indepth life history interviews. The sample size was 20 female teachers of South Asian origin working in primary or secondary sectors of education. The research provides an account of Asian female teachers' perceptions of their treatment in the British education system. The research suggests that racism at all levels influences the career prospects of Asian female teachers.

STATUS: Individual research

DATE OF RESEARCH: 1992-1998

KEYWORDS: **asians; black teachers; careers; ethnic groups; teaching profession; women teachers**

2888

Institute of Education, Coventry CV4 7AL
01203 523523

Baldacchino, J. Dr

Education and the arts as agents of contingency: discursive analyses in aesthetics, culture and learning

ABSTRACT: This is an ongoing project which embarks on the relationship between aesthetics and education. The major premise is that for such an analysis to achieve credibility, there must be a radical distancing from the customary definitions of education (viz. schooling, curricular engineering, standardised teacher-training, etc). This distancing aims to challenge the long-held views of art and education as unequivocal necessities that have long held human knowledge captive to their standardised cultural practices. In this project there are long moments of pause and abstention from any discussion of education per se. Here, the researcher's main interest goes back to the ways of motives, interpretations and praxis, and their effects on the reading of human expression and its pragmatic grammars. This pause is intended to provide a consolidated basis for the aesthetic and cultural argument of the arts in order to modify the theoretical platform of educational studies. This research began by addressing aesthetic theory with a special focus on German Idealism and its Marxist and Post-Marxist derivatives - now published as BALDACCHINO, J. (1996). Post-Marxist Marxism: Questioning the Answer. Aldershot: Avebury. It proceeded with an analysis of art's contingency, as manifested in the development of modernity and its derivatives - now published as BALDACCHINO, J. (1998). Easels of Utopia: Art's Fact Returned. Aldershot: Ashgate. The researcher is currently engaged in further investigations of culture as a reading of its genealogical discourse, particularly evident in the works of theorists like Norberto Bobbio and Benedetto Croce. It is hoped that this will be followed by an analysis of the dialects of learning providing a locus for new forms of address and definition.

PUBLISHED MATERIAL: BALDACCHINO, J. (1994). 'Art's gaming lost: within the make-belief of curricular certainty', Curriculum Studies, Vol 2,No 3, pp.333-344. ; BALDACCHINO, J. (1996). Post-Marxist Marxism: questioning the answer: different and realism after Luckacs and Adomo. Aldershot: Avebury. ; BALDACCHINO, J. (1997). 'Imposing freedom: the cultural game of "adult education"'. In: MAYO, P. & BALDACCHINO, G. (Eds). Beyond schooling. Malta: Mireva Publications. ; BALDACCHINO, J. (1998). Easels of Utopia: art's fact returned. Aldershot: Ashgate.

STATUS: Individual research

DATE OF RESEARCH: 1994-continuing

KEYWORDS: **aesthetic values; art history; arts; culture**

2889

Institute of Education, Coventry CV4 7AL
01203 523523

Vincent, C. Dr; Warren, S. Mr

Supporting refugee children in school: a focus on home-school links

ABSTRACT: This research is based on the hypothesis that positive home-school relationships can be beneficial to parents, children and teachers. Thus it studies relationships between refugee parents and educational professionals in order to identify factors that encourage or hinder the strengthening of home-school contact and communication. Building on data gathered in a pilot study and other research, the project consists of case studies of 4 primary schools in 2 inner urban local education authorities (LEAs). It deals with data gathered through indepth interviews with parents, teachers and others, and observation of parent-professional interactions. This research draws together 2 particular issues which feature widely in current education debates. One is the nature of links between race, ethnicity and educational progress and achievement. The second issue is the role of parents in relation to the education system. The research is underpinned by 2 central concerns: the heterogeneous nature of the refugee population; and the need to contextualise education policy research. The project looks specifically at 3 questions: 1) What are the views of teachers concerning the school's relationship with refugee families and communities? 2) What are the views of parents from different refugee communities concerning their relationships with their children's school? 3) What are the wider issues with which refugee families have to contend and, to what degree, can/should schools provide help and support? The aim of the research is to identify and publicise examples of successful developments and initiatives.

STATUS: Sponsored project

SOURCE OF GRANT: Nuffield Foundation £34,007

DATE OF RESEARCH: 1997-1998

KEYWORDS: home school relationship; refugees

2890

Institute of Education, Coventry CV4 7AL
01203 523523

Sikes, P. Dr; Everington, J. Ms

Personal commitment and professional religious education: becoming an RE teacher

ABSTRACT: Relatively little is known about how teachers of religious education (RE) in secondary schools perceive and experience their work. Within contemporary society, the social identities attached to religious commitment or association of whatever kind, tend not to be positive - that this is the case may have implications for those teaching the subject, both in terms of their own personal and professional sense of self, and with regard to their relationships with their pupils. This research is using life history and narrative approaches to follow a cohort of 16 Postgraduate Certificate in Education (PGCE) students through their training and into their first year in the profession. The aim is to begin to understand: 1) who becomes an RE teacher at the turn of the century; 2) why they opt for this career choice; 3) what it is like to be an RE teacher; 4) why they teach in the ways that they do; 5) what challenges they face, which strategies they adopt, and how their personal and professional knowledge develops.

STATUS: Sponsored project

SOURCE OF GRANT: Warwick University £1,990

DATE OF RESEARCH: 1997-continuing

KEYWORDS: preservice teacher education; religious education; religious education teachers; student teachers; teaching profession

2891

Institute of Education, Coventry CV4 7AL
01203 523523

Schweisfurth, M. Ms; *Supervisor*: Alexander, R. Prof.

Teachers and process of change in Russia and South Africa

ABSTRACT: Educational reform is often examined from an exclusively 'macro' perspective, while the processes at the 'micro' level, so essential to its success or failure, are overlooked. This study aims to explore primary school teachers' experiences of large-scale political, social and educational change in the new democracies of Russia and South Africa. The research focuses on the key personal, professional and social influences on teachers' attitudes and practice which affect their willingness and ability to effect reform. The first, exploratory phase of the research involved familiarisation with the context and main issues through a range of interviews, observations and documentary analysis. In the second phase, key themes which emerged from analysis of first-stage data will form the framework for case studies of 6 teachers in each country. Within the group of subjects, a range of different educational contexts and experiences (such as urban/rural settings and newly-qualified/experienced teachers) will be included. Data for the case studies will be gained from a series of hierarchically-focused semi-structured interviews, and classroom observation. Early analysis of first-phase data has pointed to the roles of reflective practice and practical and economic constraints.

STATUS: Individual research

DATE OF RESEARCH: 1995-continuing

KEYWORDS: educational change; political influences; primary school teachers; russia; social change; south africa

2892

Institute of Education, Coventry CV4 7AL
01203 523523

Ipgrave, J. Ms; *Supervisors*: Jackson, R. Prof.; Nesbitt, E. Dr

Interfaith encounter in the primary classroom: challenges to identity and belief

ABSTRACT: The influence of interaction with peers of different religious backgrounds on young people's religious development has received little attention. Studies of Muslim children in school have not examined their contribution to their peers' religious development. The aim is to examine the effect of non-Muslim pupils' interaction with Muslim peers on their perceptions of their religious identity and of their understanding of their own and other religious traditions. The methodology is ethnographic - observation with minimal and total participation (as teacher/researcher) and interviews (structured and unstructured). Children will be considered as class members, group members and as individuals. The study focuses on 16 non-Muslim children from 4 classes in 2 primary schools in Highfields, Leicester.

STATUS: Individual research

DATE OF RESEARCH: 1997-continuing

KEYWORDS: ethnic groups; muslims; primary school pupils; religious cultural groups

2893

Institute of Education, Coventry CV4 7AL
01203 523523

Doherty, N. Ms; *Supervisors*: Packwood, A. Dr; Francis, E. Dr

The emerging feminine sentence in education theory and practice and in educational research

ABSTRACT: This research is based on the thesis that there presently exists an emerging orientation to education that can be called 'a feminine sentence'. The researcher gives definition to the feminine aesthetic form through literature and literary criticism - specifically the writings of Virginia Woolf. Predominant educational theorists are cited as reflecting various elements of the feminine sentence in their projects. Concepts such as frailty, vulnerability, fragmented self, womb-like images, and interrelated themes such as openness, fluidity and transference and transformation are explored and given value in education and educational research. As part of the dissertation the concept of 'a feminine sentence', as defined, forms the basis for two empirical research projects in the field of education: one at an international level and the other at a local level.

STATUS: Individual research

DATE OF RESEARCH: 1996-continuing

KEYWORDS: aesthetic values; educational theories

2894

Institute of Education, Coventry CV4 7AL
01203 523523

Northcote, V. Ms; *Supervisor*: Yeomans, R. Dr

The role of the National Society of the Church of England in the development of the use of illustrated teaching material for religious education c.1870-1914

ABSTRACT: This research is designed to illuminate the way Christian images came to be used by the Church of England in the schools supported by the National Society. The period covered is c.1870-1914 because this was a crucial one in both the history of art and the development of educational ideas. It ends in 1914 because the deep changes in society during and following the First World War inevitably caused changes in teaching methods from that time. However, the grandchildren of the children educated during that period still hand on perceptions of religious truth gained from these late Victorian and early Edwardian images. The research is contextualised by ethnography, philosophy, semiotics and educational theory. On the basis of analysis to date of National Society archives, it suggests the Society played a significant role in the educational theory of the period.

STATUS: Individual research

DATE OF RESEARCH: 1997-continuing

KEYWORDS: church and education; educational history; religious education

2895

Institute of Education, Coventry CV4 7AL
01203 523523

Miller, J. Ms; *Supervisor*: Jackson, R. Prof.

Developing a hermenuetical approach to religious education through the visual arts

ABSTRACT: The argument of this thesis is that contemporary religious education (RE) frequently fails to interest or challenge many pupils in schools today. The reason suggested for this is that it often consists of a narrow phenomenological approach to the six principal religions represented in Great Britain, whether studied systematically or thematically. This thesis argues that a different approach to religious education should be adopted in which: a) religious education would be seen as different from religious studies; b) there will be a study of 'religion' as well as religions; c) religious education will engage with questions of 'ultimate concern'; and d) necessitate the use of other disciplines, including philosophy and theology. Given the links that exist between religion and art, the spiritual and art, the use of symbolism in religion and art, and the expression of meaning through art, an effective way of developing this approach to religious education could be through the use of the visual arts. A critique of the ways in which art has been used in RE in the past will be given. A hermeneutical approach, which is being advocated here, will be developed and trialled in schools to evaluate its effectiveness. The data produced will enable conclusions to be drawn on the use of visual art as part of a hermeneutical approach to religious education.

STATUS: Individual research

DATE OF RESEARCH: 1997-continuing

KEYWORDS: arts; religious education

2896

Institute of Education, Coventry CV4 7AL
01203 523523

Nesbitt, E. Dr; *Supervisor*: Jackson, R. Prof.

A longitudinal study of young British Hindus' perceptions of their religious tradition

ABSTRACT: This research provides a longitudinal dimension to the Warwick University team's earlier studies of the religious nurture of Hindu children (JACKSON, R. & NESBITT, E. (1993). Hindu children in Britain. Stoke-on-Trent: Trentham Books). The aims included ascertaining, through ethnographic methods (mainly semi-structured interviews): 1) how 22 young British Hindus perceived their relationship to the Hindu tradition; 2) continuities and changes in this relationship since their interviews 8 years before; 3) whether they regarded their tradition as a total worldview or as affecting only limited areas of their lives; 4) the influence of factors including gender, 'ethnic' background, education, media, peer group. Of particular interest were their experiences of caste and family (obligations and relationships), dietary imperatives, Indian languages, characteristic belief and ritual practice. Continuities were more evident than change, while individuals' actual practice (dietary, linguistic, etc.) shows variation (e.g. because university is less conducive than home). Attitudes have remained constant in significant respects. For example, all strongly affirm their Hindu identity and belief in God. They tend to avoid beef and want their mother tongue to continue in the next generation. While they share the intention to marry, their views on the balance between family guidance and individual initiative in selecting spouses vary. The visiting preacher, Morari Bapu, and (in some cases) the teaching of Sampradayas (religious groupings) had influenced young people. The acknowledgement of Hinduism in school varied. This had implications for young Hindus' perceptions of their tradition.

PUBLISHED MATERIAL: NESBITT, E. (1998). 'Bridging the gap between young people's experience of their religious tradition at home and at school: the contribution of ethnographic research', British Journal of Religious Education, Vol 20, No 2, pp.98-110. ; NESBITT, E. (1998). 'The contribution of nurture in a sampradaya to young British Hindus' understanding of their tradition'. In: MENSKI, W. (Ed). From generation to generation: religious reconstruction in the South Asian diasapora. Basingstoke: Macmillan. ; NESBITT, E. The impact of Morari Bapu's Kathas on Britain's young Hindus'. In: LIPNER, J. (Ed). Youth and youthfulness in the Hindu tradition. Calgary: Bayeux Arts Inc. (in press).

STATUS: Sponsored project

SOURCE OF GRANT: Leverhulme Trust

DATE OF RESEARCH: 1995-1998

KEYWORDS: asians; ethnic groups; hindu culture; hinduism; longitudinal studies; religious cultural groups; youth

2897

Institute of Education, Coventry CV4 7AL
01203 523523

Ellis, P. Dr

Sound therapy: a new approach for children with severe and profound and multiple learning difficulties

ABSTRACT: Sound therapy is a non-invasive approach which combines aspects of music, sound, technology and aesthetics. Since 1994 the researcher has been developing this approach in conjunction with a local special school. A number of children with profound and multiple learning difficulties have been involved in a programme of research and development to ascertain whether progression and development can result from this approach. To this end, a longitudinal qualitative research tool, 'layered analysis', has been developed to enable a clear and unambiguous record of changing behaviour to be made. The results of this work indicate that even the most severely handicapped child can be reached. Communication can be established and developed and self esteem, self confidence, a range of physical skills and the general quality of life and experience can be improved and enhanced.

PUBLISHED MATERIAL: ELLIS, P. (1995). 'Developing abilities in children with special needs: a new approach', Children and Society, Vol 9, No 4, pp.64-79. ; ELLIS, P. (1996). 'Layered analysis: a video-based qualitative research tool to support the development of a new approach for children with special needs', Bulletin for the Council for Research in Music Education, Vol 130, pp.65-74. ; ELLIS, P. (1997). 'The music of sound: a new approach for children with severe and profound and multiple learning difficulties', British Journal of Music Education, Vol 14, No 2, pp.173-186.

STATUS: Sponsored project

SOURCE OF GRANT: ESPRIT (EU) Programme £158,479

DATE OF RESEARCH: 1994-continuing

KEYWORDS: learning disabilities; music therapy; sound therapy; special educational needs

2898

Institute of Education, Coventry CV4 7AL
01203 523523

Daskalogianni, A. Mr; *Supervisors*: Bills, L. Dr; Tall, D. Prof.

Attitudes and expectations towards mathematics: the transition from school to university

ABSTRACT: The project aims to address the question 'Does the change of nature between elementary and advanced mathematical thinking result in a change of students' attitude towards mathematics?'. The researcher will seek to find answers to this question in the cognitive and social environments, through the use of interviews and questionnaires addressed to a sample of school students moving on to degree courses in mathematics.

STATUS: Individual research

DATE OF RESEARCH: 1998-continuing

KEYWORDS: attitudes; higher education; mathematics education; pupil attitudes; secondary education; student attitudes

2899

Institute of Education, Language Centre, Coventry CV4 7AL
01203 523523

Barnes, A. Mrs; *Supervisors*: Husbands, C. Dr; Powell, B. Dr

The development of modern foreign languages (MFL) teachers - from Postgraduate Certicate in Education (PGCE) student to Newly Qualified Teacher (NQT)

ABSTRACT: The research focus is the development of Postgraduate Certificate in Education (PGCE) modern foreign language (MFL) students - from applicant to working Newly Qualified Teacher (NQT). It will look at their attitudes, confidence and competence and is an investigation into change, stages and effects on whole cohorts and separate sub-groups. The background is the growth of professional knowledge and the relationship between subject knowledge and pedagogical competence is a major issue at present in teacher education. The research questions are: 1) How, when and why do MFL PGCE students' attitudes to a range of teaching and learning issues change from application to working as an NQT? 2) How, when and why does MFL PGCE students' confidence in a range of teaching and personal competences change from application to working as an NQT? How is this development in confidence linked to competence? In relation to the above issues, what effect do gender, native speaker and age factors have? A particular focus is the development of linguistic competence throughout this period. The research strategy/method(s) are a combination of survey ("snapshot" questionnaire(s) on a longitudinal basis); case study (video discussions and other data); and other evidence - mentors' reports, students' assignments, mentor questionnaires. The sample of two years' cohorts of modern foreign languages students (41 Warwick students 1996-97, 47 Warwick students 1997-98, 10 Oxford students 1997-98 will be tracked).

PUBLISHED MATERIAL: BARNES, A. (1996). 'Maintaining language skills in the initial training of foreign language teachers', Language Learning Journal, No 14, pp.58-64.

STATUS: Individual research

DATE OF RESEARCH: 1997-continuing

KEYWORDS: **modern language studies; newly qualified teachers; preservice teacher education; student teachers; teacher development; teaching profession**

2900

Institute of Education, Language Centre, Coventry CV4 7AL
01203 523523

Barton, A. Ms; *Supervisors*: Powell, R. Dr; Sealey, A. Ms

Boys' underachievement in GCSE modern languages: assessing the effectiveness of single-sex initiatives

ABSTRACT: The research investigates the effects of single-sex teaching on boys' attitudes to and academic performance in modern languages in secondary school. The study is a response to the long-standing and marked disparity between boys' and girls' achievements in the subject. It tests the hypothesis that a modification of teaching strategies within these groups to accommodate sex-specific strengths and weaknesses may increase pupil motivation and counteract boys' underachievement. The project adopts a case-study approach to observe the practices of a small number of mixed comprehensive schools in the UK who are teaching languages to one or more segregated cohort. Data is predominantly attitudinal and collected by means of group and individual interviews with teachers and pupils, short and long questionnaires, classroom observation and informal discussion with staff. The research reviews the possible reasons for boys' underachievement; contextualises the single-sex modern languages classroom by describing similar small-scale projects in other disciplines; describes and analyses the effectiveness of teaching strategies observed in use with all boys' groups in the case study schools; considers boys' learning preferences and styles; and represents teachers' and pupils' opinions on the success of single-sex initiatives.

PUBLISHED MATERIAL: BARTON, A. (1997).'Boys' under-achievement in GCSE modern languages: reviewing the reasons', Language Learning Journal, No 16, pp.11-16.

STATUS: Individual research

DATE OF RESEARCH: 1995-continuing

KEYWORDS: **achievement; boys; modern language studies; pupil attitudes; sex differences; underachievement**

2901

Institute of Education, Coventry CV4 7AL
01203 523523
London University, Institute of Education, 20 Bedford Way, London
WC1H 0AL
0171 580 1122

Lindsay, G. Prof.; Hall, C. Ms; Jordan, R. Ms; Dockrell, J. Prof.

Services for children with specific speech and language difficulties

ABSTRACT: This study aims to examine the services provided for children with specific speech and language difficulties (SSLD); the views of key practitioners and parents; and to describe the children's profiles of difficulties and needs. Children in 2 local education authorities (LEAs) and their relevant health trusts were identified by schools, speech and language therapists

and educational psychologists as being SSLD. These samples were supplemented by children in 2 special schools designed for children with SSLD. A total of 67 children have been assessed. Teachers, educational psychologists, speech and language therapists and parents have been interviewed. A wide variety of language attainment and non-verbal ability tests were used to assess the children, together with teacher and parent completed rating scales. Self-esteem was also examined. The initial study showed variation in the professionals' views of which children had SSLD, and also that these frequently had associated difficulties. The present study has found that children with SSLD have significant literacy difficulties in addition. The interview data are currently being analysed.

STATUS: Sponsored project

SOURCE OF GRANT: Gatsby Charitable Foundation

DATE OF RESEARCH: 1996-1998

KEYWORDS: **health services; language handicaps; special educational needs; speech handicaps; speech therapy**

2902

Institute of Education, Coventry CV4 7AL
01203 523523
Sheffield University, Division of Education, 388 Glossop Road,
Sheffield S10 2JA
01142 768555

Lindsay, G. Prof.; Desforges, M. Dr

Baseline assessment: development of the Infant Index (now Baseline-plus)

ABSTRACT: The Infant Index was produced to aid teachers of 5 year-old children to identify special educational needs (SEN). Stage 1 comprised the development of the Infant Index and analyses of reliability and construct validity. The present phase is a longitudinal study over 3 years to evaluate the predictive validity of the scale (cohort = 6000 children). A new, computer-read version of the Infant Index has also been produced - Baseline plus. This has been made available to schools as part of the government's accreditation of the baseline assessment schemes - published by Ed-Excel.

PUBLISHED MATERIAL: DESFORGES, M. & LINDSAY, G. (1995). The infant index. London: Hodder and Stoughton. ; DESFORGES, M & LINDSAY, G. (1995). 'Baseline assessment', Educational and Child Psychology, Vol 12, No 3, pp.42-51. ; DESFORGES, M. & LINDSAY, G. with EDEXCEL. (1998). Baseline plus. London: EdExcel. ; LINDSAY, G. (1998). 'Baseline assessment: a positive or malign initiative?'. In: NORWICH, B. & LINDSAY, G. (Eds). Baseline assessment. Tamworth: NASEN.

STATUS: Sponsored project

SOURCE OF GRANT: Sheffield Local Education Authority

DATE OF RESEARCH: 1994-continuing

KEYWORDS: **baseline assessment; primary education; reception classes; special educational needs; young children**

2903

Institute of Education, Coventry CV4 7AL
01203 523523
South Bank University, School of Education, Politics and Social
Sciences, 103 Borough Road, London SE1 0AA
0171 928 8989

Packwood, A. Dr; Scanlon, M. Ms; Weiner, G. Prof.

Getting published: a study of writing, refereeing and editing practices

ABSTRACT: This study is a response to a growing interest in the criteria and means by which writing is judged to be worthy of publication. It seeks to answer such questions as 'who gets published?', 'on what basis?', 'for what purposes?' and 'for what readership?'. It proposes to explore the roles,amechanisms and purposes of writing for publication with an aim both to elucidate theory and question practice. It has investigated the ways in which the relationship between theory, research, methodologies and practice are reflected in selected education, sociology and psychology journals. It has also looked at discourse practices and conventions in terms of how they construct experience, by whom and for whom. The research comprises two distinct but interrelated phases involving textual analysis, and an investigation of writing, refereeing and editorial practices. This includes a survey of a maximum of 30 journals taken from education, sociology and psychology. The survey covers the official journals of each of the learned societies; plus 19 other journals from education; 4 from sociology and 4 from psychology. The survey reviews 2 issues per annum for each journal over a 10 year period (1986-1996) - a total of 600 issues. Three questionnaires have been developed and administered: to current editors of the journals surveyed; to a 10% sample of the membership of the 3 learned societies; and to a sample (approximately 300) of authors of papers in the journals surveyed. This research is a significant means by which the world of publishing can be rendered accessible to the expanded academic community. The research offers a critical appraisal of publishing and its relation to other areas such as research and the development of theory and methodological practices. It offers important insights into the intersection between text and practice.

STATUS: Sponsored project

SOURCE OF GRANT: Economic and Social Research Council £50,180

DATE OF RESEARCH: 1996-1998

KEYWORDS: **publications; publishing industry; writing for publication**

Westminster College

2904

North Hinksey, Oxford OX2 9AT
01865 247644

Bigger, S. Dr

Heart of England Training and Enterprise Council's education initiatives: a sponsored research evaluation

ABSTRACT: Heart of England Training and Enterprise Council (TEC) have funded a number of educational initiatives in local schools and further education (FE) colleges, and in community education. These seek to further vocational programmes or to encourage links between educational establishments and employers. This research evaluated 3 particular projects: 1) General National Vocational Qualification (GNVQ) developments in Oxfordshire. 2) Compact initiatives and mentoring in schools. 3) Women returner provision. The research has been carried out using questionnaires, interviews and participant observation covering all providers in these sectors. The reports are scheduled to be completed by April and will contain a detailed critique and recommendations.

PUBLISHED MATERIAL: BIGGER, S.F. (1996). GNVQ in Oxfordshire. Abingdon: Heart of England TEC.

STATUS: Sponsored project

SOURCE OF GRANT: Heart of England Training and Enterprise Council £10,000

DATE OF RESEARCH: 1996-1997

KEYWORDS: **adult education; community education; compacts; education business partnerships; further education; general national vocational qualifications; industry education relationship; mentors; secondary education; training; training and enterprise councils; vocational education; women returners; work education relationship**

2905

North Hinksey, Oxford OX2 9AT
01865 247644
Oxford University, Department of Educational Studies, 15 Norham Gardens, Oxford OX2 6PY
01865 274024

Atkinson, S. Ms; *Supervisors*: McIntyre, D. Mr; Lewis, I. Mr

An action research study into the role of a mathematics coordinator in a primary school

ABSTRACT: The role of the mathematics coordinator is explored in the context of school-based inservice education of teachers (INSET). The research looks at changes that took place in a primary school over three years; the ways that teachers coped with change; what the facilitating role of the coordinator involved; and when the facilitating was most successful. The nature of action research is discussed in relation to the feasibility of the concept of teacher-researcher and to the nature of the teacher's 'self' in a demanding situation.

STATUS: Individual research

DATE OF RESEARCH: 1985-1993

KEYWORDS: **inservice teacher education; mathematics education; primary education**

Westminster University

2906

309 Regent Street, London W1R 8AL
0171 911 5000

Openshaw, S. Mr; *Supervisors*: Billing, D. Dr; Roweth, B. Mrs

The transferability of core skills

ABSTRACT: The background to this project is partly the Enterprise in Higher Education Initiative (EHEI) which promotes curriculum and staff development, and aims to develop general skills by integrating them into discipline based degree courses. Also, surveys show that employers claim to prize general abilities of graduates more highly than subject specific knowledge and skills. This research is, therefore, exploring the extent to which core abilities are transferable. The assumption of transferable skills is not established, and this project aims, through the design and application of tests, to generate more reliable data. The study hopes to look at undergraduates from this and other universities. It is also hoped that by revealing the differences and similarities in subject methodologies as applied, for example, to analysis and problem-solving, there will be implications for a firmer basis of interdisciplinary courses and enterprises.

STATUS: Individual research

DATE OF RESEARCH: 1994-1997

KEYWORDS: **higher education; skill development; skills; students; transfer of learning; universities**

2907

Educational Initiative Centre, 35 Marylebone Road, London NW1 5LS
0171 911 5000

Alpin, C. Ms; Walsh, S. Ms; *Supervisor*: Shackleton, J. Prof.

Over and under-education in the UK graduate labour market

ABSTRACT: This research examines the apparent under-utilisation of the skills of employed graduates in the UK using Labour Force Survey data. It develops two measures of 'overeducation' and indicates the characteristics of the 'overeducated'. It also sheds light on the 'undereducated' - those performing graduate jobs without a degree. These people are disproportionately white males.

PUBLISHED MATERIAL: ALPIN, C., SHACKLETON, J.R. & WALSH, S. (1998). 'Overand undereducation in the UK graduate labour market', Studies in Higher Education, Vol 23, No 1, pp.17-34.

STATUS: Team research

DATE OF RESEARCH: 1996-1997

KEYWORDS: **employment opportunities; graduate employment; higher education; labour market; overeducated; undereducated; work education relationship**

2908

Harrow Business School, Northwick Park, Harrow HA1 3TP
0171 911 5000

Huscroft, M. Ms; Gleeson, E. Mr

Studio based practice and large student groups

ABSTRACT: This research is based on a case study of two modules currently running at the University of Westminster. The modules are 'design as communication' and 'design processes'. The study analyses the first 3 years of the modules from September 1995 to November 1997 with the student groups ranging from 55 in the first year to 70 in the third. The 2 researchers designed the curriculum and the teaching strategies, and were responsible for the delivery and evaluation of the students' performance on the modules as well as the management of the staff team and staff induction to the pedagogy. The priorities were to provide the students with supportive systems and course management, to make the modes of assessment compatible with the student centred approach, to create individual 'learning spaces' and personal choices within the context of a large group and to develop student autonomy and learning support groups. The aim of the case study is to evaluate firstly, the effectiveness of modules in achieving their aims and secondly, whether their aims were appropriate to the students' needs. The methods are case study and action research. The research is not yet finalised, but at present it points towards the recognition that the most effective learning takes place in small groups where the students can engage in practical activities followed by periods of individual reflection and evaluation which can be contextualised through discussion.

STATUS: Team research

DATE OF RESEARCH: 1997-1998

KEYWORDS: **design; group work; higher education; learning activities; peer teaching**

2909

Harrow Business School, Northwick Park, Harrow HA1 3TP
0171 911 5000
London University, Institute of Education, 20 Bedford Way, London WC1H 0AL
0171 580 1122

Evans, L. Mr; *Supervisor*: Wolf, A. Prof.

Accreditation in prior experiential learning in action

ABSTRACT: This project will research the use of prior learning as a means of entry into undergraduate management education and a review of students' experience, accreditation of prior experiential learning systems, subsequent course experiences and eventual degree classification. This will concentrate on the accreditation of prior experiential learning module and the extent of credit provided.

STATUS: Individual research

DATE OF RESEARCH: 1997-continuing

KEYWORDS: **access to education; accreditation of prior learning; higher education; management studies; nontraditional students**

Wolverhampton University

2910

School of Education, Walsall Campus, Gorway Road, Walsall WS1 3BD
01902 321000

Birley, G. Dr

University examinations in science 1870-1900

ABSTRACT: This research will look at the content of science syllabuses and examination papers set by universities during the period 1870-1900, and relate this to examiners' interests and current scientific developments. The aim is to establish the role of the examinations and the extent to which the examination movement helped to codify scientific disciplines.

STATUS: Sponsored project

SOURCE OF GRANT: Royal Society ; Wolverhampton University

DATE OF RESEARCH: 1990-1993

KEYWORDS: **educational history; examination syllabuses; science education; university examinations**

2911

School of Education, Walsall Campus, Gorway Road, Walsall WS1 3BD
01902 321000

Tam, C. Mrs; *Supervisors*: Birley, G. Dr; Moreland, N. Dr; Pearl, L. Dr

An investigation of factors associated with high achievement in degree performance in higher education science students

ABSTRACT: Using biographical information and basic information of socio-economic group, age, gender, etc., a study is being conducted of the outcomes of student learning against the inputs in order to determine what factors and study skills are associated with high achievement in science and technology undergraduates.

STATUS: Individual research

DATE OF RESEARCH: 1993-1997

KEYWORDS: **academic achievement; achievement; background; science education; students**

2912

School of Education, Walsall Campus, Gorway Road, Walsall WS1 3BD
01902 321000

Farley, K. Mr; *Supervisors*: Birley, G. Dr; Gomez, G. Dr

Implementing the National Curriculum History in primary schools

ABSTRACT: This is an ethnographic study of three primary schools, in one local education authority, which will examine the effects upon the teaching of history following the introduction of the National Curriculum in history. Recent years have seen the development of process-based methods of teaching history in the primary school, and the study aims to discover the extent to which the introduction of new curricula has enabled this process to continue.

STATUS: Individual research

DATE OF RESEARCH: 1993-1997

KEYWORDS: **history; national curriculum; primary education**

2913

School of Education, Walsall Campus, Gorway Road, Walsall WS1 3BD
01902 321000

Evans, D. Mrs; *Supervisors*: Birley, G. Dr; Hyde, B. Miss

Professional practice and emotional development in the student nurse

ABSTRACT: This research is studying the relationship between professional practice and the emotional development of the student nurse. It aims to test the assumption that psychological congruence will facilitate the integration of psychiatric theory and practice. On the basis of this study, a programme will be developed which, it is intended, will improve theory/practice integration. This programme will be evaluated.

STATUS: Individual research

DATE OF RESEARCH: 1993-1997

KEYWORDS: **emotional development; nurse education; nurses; professional development; student development**

2914

School of Education, Walsall Campus, Gorway Road, Walsall WS1 3BD
01902 321000

Harrison, S. Mr; *Supervisors*: Birley, G. Dr; Mathias, J. Dr

Open and flexible learning systems in the National Health Service

ABSTRACT: Flexible and open learning systems currently being introduced into the public service and National Health Service systems of Britain are being evaluated, against more traditional levels of delivery, in one hospital training school.

STATUS: Individual research

DATE OF RESEARCH: 1992-1997

KEYWORDS: **flexible learning; medical education; open education; teaching methods**

2915

School of Education, Walsall Campus, Gorway Road, Walsall WS1 3BD
01902 321000

Han, M. Miss; *Supervisors*: Birley, G. Dr; Elliott, D. Mr

A longitudinal study of gifted children in Singapore

ABSTRACT: This is an examination of a series of programmes for gifted children in Singapore. It involves the development and validation of selection tests and an evaluation of the effectiveness of the programmes.

STATUS: Individual research

DATE OF RESEARCH: 1993-1997

KEYWORDS: **gifted; programme evaluation; singapore**

2916

School of Education, Walsall Campus, Gorway Road, Walsall WS1 3BD
01902 321000

Aston, S. Ms; *Supervisors*: Moreland, N. Dr; Brown, C. Dr; Birley, G. Dr

Student pathways: a longitudinal study of a cohort of students following a variety of full-time awards within one university

ABSTRACT: This study is concerned with the experiences which students moving through a variety of university courses receive. This will involve the experiences both inside and outside university and how these affect their ability to cope with the exigencies of university life. The aims of the study therefore are: 1) To conduct a longitudinal study of students within the School of Education at Wolverhampton University by collecting quantitative and qualitative data of their experiences. 2) To identify, document and research the students' understandings of the variety of coping strategies and colonisation activities used by the students to navigate their way through academic and non-academic aspects of university life. 3) To extend the theoretical understanding of the context and experiences of the university for student behaviour and learning experiences.

STATUS: Sponsored project

SOURCE OF GRANT: University of Wolverhampton

DATE OF RESEARCH: 1995-continuing

KEYWORDS: **higher education; student experience; students; universities**

2917

School of Education, Walsall Campus, Gorway Road, Walsall WS1 3BD
01902 321000

Allan, J. Ms; *Supervisors*: Birley, G. Dr; McKay, J. Miss

An action research study of learning outcomes in higher education

ABSTRACT: This research investigates the implications for curriculum design in higher education of a 'learning outcomes' model of curriculum development. It looks at both the students' and the lecturers' perceptions of learning outcomes and the implications for modularity of this development.

STATUS: Sponsored project

SOURCE OF GRANT: University of Wolverhampton

DATE OF RESEARCH: 1993-1997

KEYWORDS: **curriculum development; higher education; learner educational objectives; learning modules; modular courses; outcomes of education**

2918

School of Education, Walsall Campus, Gorway Road, Walsall WS1 3BD
01902 321000

Abell, B. Mr; *Supervisors*: Pomeroy, R. Mr; Birley, G. Dr; McKay, J. Miss

Managing reflection: a study of the development of mentoring in the implementation of Department for Education Circular 9/92 - Initial Teacher Training (Secondary Phase)

ABSTRACT: The research is conducted in two parts. First of all, the range and type of mentoring arrangements currently used in schools will be examined. There will then be an identification and analysis of the reflection practices of individual students.

STATUS: Sponsored project

SOURCE OF GRANT: University of Wolverhampton

DATE OF RESEARCH: 1993-1997

KEYWORDS: **mentors; preservice teacher education; reflection; school based teacher education; student teachers**

2919

School of Education, Walsall Campus, Gorway Road, Walsall WS1 3BD
01902 32100

Birley, G. Dr

A case study of the setting up and operation of a City Technology College

ABSTRACT: This project examines the setting up and operation of a City technology college. It therefore examines the total curriculum and financial context in which the institution originated and currently operates. Data has been collected from project directors, industrial sponsors and architects. It is intended to collect further data from school staff, governors, managers and curriculum advisers.

STATUS: Sponsored project

SOURCE OF GRANT: Nuffield Foundation £4,500

DATE OF RESEARCH: 1996-1998

KEYWORDS: **city technology colleges; secondary education**

2920

Wolverhampton Business School, Compton Park, Wolverhampton WV3 9DX
01902 321000

Williams, S. Ms; *Supervisors*: Birley, G. Dr; Davies, G. Dr

Assessment of action learning type sets as a management strategy

ABSTRACT: This research examines the varied learning experiences of Master of Business Administration (MBA) students in relation to self-directed learning. It relates their learning experience to their progress and dilemmas on a personal development module which makes use of action learning type sets as a learning strategy.

STATUS: Individual research

DATE OF RESEARCH: 1993-1997

KEYWORDS: **business administration education; learning activities; learning strategies; management studies**

York University

2921

Department of Educational Studies, Heslington, York YO1 5DD
01904 430000

Davies, I. Dr; *Supervisor*: Lister, I. Prof.

Guidelines for political education

ABSTRACT: There were three main sections to this research. Firstly, a combination of narrative and analysis which shows the early call for guidelines for political education, the West German example, Department of Education and Science (DES) and Local Education Authority (LEA) guidelines. The researcher sought to illuminate the nature of different guidelines, considering to what extent they addressed aims, content, methods, evaluation and suggesting how they related to the recommendations made by key political educators. Secondly, the research examined the perceptions of guidelines by the producers, the political educators, teachers and gatekeepers who may include headteachers, governors, and local education authority (LEA) officers and a sample of politicians. Finally, the research sought to enquire how the guidelines help practice and focus on the relation between reality and theory in a number of Local Education Authorities.

PUBLISHED MATERIAL: DAVIES, I. (1988). 'Guidelines for political education', Social Science Teacher, Vol 18, No 2, pp.37-39. ; DAVIES, I. (1993). 'The reform of education: how and why are documents produced for teachers and are they perceived to be of any value?', Curriculum, Vol 14, No 2, pp.114-123. ; DAVIES, I. 'Whatever happened to political education?', Educational Review. (in press).

STATUS: Individual research

DATE OF RESEARCH: 1987-1993

KEYWORDS: **curriculum development; guidelines; political science studies**

2922

Department of Educational Studies, Heslington, York YO1 5DD
01904 430000

Stone, C. Mrs; *Supervisor*: Horbury, A. Dr

The implementation of the National Curriculum through topic work

ABSTRACT: The thesis considers the implementation of the National Curriculum predominantly through topic work. The aim was to consider the impact of the National Curriculum on primary school teachers. The overall research strategy adopted was that of case study. The research took place in two schools in the North of England; a twenty-one class combined infant and junior school and a nine class infant school. Two days a week were spent at both these schools as a participant for a period of four terms.

Data was collected through classroom observation, two rounds of lengthy semi-structured interviews in July 1990 and 1991 and from documentary materials. The data analysis revealed that topic work usage varied considerably from class to class and an emergent typology of topic work in the context of the National Curriculum is presented. It can be argued that through their attempts to implement the National Curriculum in this way the difficulties of acquiring 'clarity' are revealed. 'Clarity' in terms of this reform appears to be important at different levels: 1) in respect of the overall intentions of the Education Reform Act 1988; 2) in relation to the National Curriculum itself; 3) in respect of their own practice and the changes required of them. At each of these levels there seems to be considerable barriers to the necessary process of clarification which, when taken together, create a formidable obstacle to reform. It therefore appears likely that although the National Curriculum may bring about change it may not produce reform.

PUBLISHED MATERIAL: STONE, C.E. 'An emergent typology of topic work in the context of the National Curriculum', Journal of Teacher Development. (in press).

STATUS: Individual research

DATE OF RESEARCH: 1990-1993

KEYWORDS: **educational change; national curriculum; projects - learning activities; pupil projects; teaching methods**

2923

Department of Educational Studies, Heslington, York YO1 5DD
01904 430000

Arnold, M. Mr; *Supervisor*: Millar, R. Dr

Teaching a scientific mental model: a case study using analogy to construct a model of thermal processes

ABSTRACT: The research involves teaching a scientific mental model of thermal processes to early secondary school students, using a water flow analogy to introduce the idea of thermal equilibrium. The three ideas of heat, temperature and thermal equilibrium were progressively differentiated. A pilot study shows that students and adults use a basic 'on = hot, off = cold' model of thermal phenomena. A teaching approach to address this issue was developed with 180 year 8 and year 10 students, and subsequently taught to 90 year 8 students in normal science lessons. Written and observational data on the students' developing conceptions was obtained, and a sample of students interviewed, tape recorded and the transcipts analysed. Sixteen weeks later a written post-test was administered to determine the extent to which previously learned material had been retained. The water analogy enabled most students to understand thermal equilibrium more clearly, and this idea assists many students to differentiate heat and temperature within a model of thermal processes. Some students were able to extend the model to other systems in dynamic equilibrium. Teaching a coherent mental model in which the relevant concepts are inter-related appears to be a valuable technique for science education, and the use of analogy facilitates the understanding of the difficult concept of thermal equilibrium.

PUBLISHED MATERIAL: MILLAR, R. & ARNOLD, M. (1987). 'Being constructive: an alternative approach to the teaching of introductory ideas in electricity', International Journal of Science Education, Vol 9, No 5, pp.553-563.

STATUS: Individual research

DATE OF RESEARCH: 1988-1993

KEYWORDS: **physics education; science education; scientific concepts; thermodynamics**

2924

Department of Educational Studies, Heslington, York YO1 5DD
01904 430000

Key, M. Ms; *Supervisors*: Waddington, D. Prof.; Lazonby, J. Mr

How do A-level chemistry students perceive the chemical industry and how might their perceptions and views be influenced by their A-level chemistry course and its teaching?

ABSTRACT: The perceptions and views of a sample of A-level chemistry students have been monitored during their A-level course. Teachers and students have completed questionnaires at 3 different points during the 2 years. Schools and colleges using Northern Examining Board syllabuses,

Nuffield syllabus and Salters' syllabus were included in the sample of about 100 institutions.

STATUS: Individual research

DATE OF RESEARCH: 1992-1998

KEYWORDS: **a level examinations; chemical industry; chemistry; industry education relationship; pupil attitudes; science education; secondary education**

2925

Department of Educational Studies, Heslington, York YO1 5DD
01904 430000

Vulliamy, G. Dr; Webb, R. Dr; Horbury, A. Dr

A comparative study of curriculum change in primary education in England and Finland

ABSTRACT: The research incorporates the English component of a comparative study of curriculum change in primary education in England and Finland. While England revised its detailed and prescriptive National Curriculum, in September 1994 Finland discontinued its long-standing statutory national curriculum in order to encourage schools to be more responsive to community and pupils' needs. An examination of the ways in which change is brought about by a combination of national legislation and reactions and responses at local authority and school level will contribute to the understanding of the nature of educational change in the current market-orientated climate. The research involves qualitative case studies of 6 schools in England, conducted by 3 English researchers, and 6 schools in Finland, conducted by 4 Finnish researchers (funded by Finnish organisations).

STATUS: Sponsored project

SOURCE OF GRANT: University of York £3,827

DATE OF RESEARCH: 1994-1997

KEYWORDS: **comparative education; curriculum development; educational change; finland; national curriculum; primary education**

2926

Department of Educational Studies, Heslington, York YO1 5DD
01904 430000

Sudworth, S. Ms; *Supervisor*: Webb, R. Dr

Teachers' personal and professional change at National Curriculum key stage 1

ABSTRACT: This research is a longitudinal study of the introduction of the National Curriculum and its associated assessment at key stage 1. It aims to explore the relationship between imposed change at national and local level and teachers' responses to change influenced by their values and past experience. The research involves qualitative data collection in 6 case-study schools including the shadowing of a primary classteacher and a headteacher.

STATUS: Individual research

DATE OF RESEARCH: 1988-1997

KEYWORDS: **educational change; key stage 1; national curriculum; primary education; primary school teachers; teacher attitudes; teaching profession**

2927

Department of Educational Studies, Heslington, York YO1 5DD
01904 430000

Webb, R. Dr; Vulliamy, G. Dr; Sudworth, S. Ms

Challenging youth crime: an evaluation of a Home Office social workers in schools project

ABSTRACT: The research is an evaluation of a Home Office project which involves the appointment of 5 specialist staff to work with troublesome pupils in schools in 5 areas of 2 education authorities which have been targeted because of their rising exclusion rates. These 'home-school support workers' are intended to help youngsters stay in school when their behaviour might normally lead to exclusion. They intend this to be achieved by: counselling of individual pupils; assisting parents to find answers to their children's problems; promoting good links between schools and external agencies, such as social services, police and probation; and helping to develop school policies on behaviour and discipline. The evaluation has 3 overall aims. Firstly, it will evaluate the project's processes and outcomes, charting its successes and failures. Secondly, the evaluation will fulfill a formative role, with regular oral reports and interim annual written reports being fed back to project workers to facilitate the development of the scheme. Thirdly, it will play a wider research role by informing policymakers both of the context and nature of pupil disruption and of the manner in which schools and teachers are already addressing such problems. It will also provide detailed protrayals of the pupils with behavioural difficulties and their family situations. A range of approaches to data collection is being used including interviews and observation in 7 case-study schools, shadowing the home-school support workers, questionnaires to teachers and pupils, and the collection of relevant statistical data from schools and the support agencies.

STATUS: Sponsored project

SOURCE OF GRANT: Home Office £63,532

DATE OF RESEARCH: 1996-continuing

KEYWORDS: **adolescents; behaviour problems; discipline; discipline problems; disruptive pupils; educational welfare; exclusion; home school relationship; juvenile crime; pupil behaviour; secondary education; secondary school pupils; social workers**

2928

Department of Educational Studies, Heslington, York YO1 5DD
01904 430000

Ellis, J. Mr; Killip Mosedale, A. Ms; Price, R. Ms; *Supervisor*: Bennett, J. Dr

Pupils' attitudes to school science

ABSTRACT: The research study has 3 main aims: 1) to provide a base line of information about attitudes to science currently held by young people; 2) to enable comparisons about attitudes to be made amongst groups of pupils following different science courses; 3) to inform future curriculum development by helping with the identification of particular areas to target for action. The study is currently in the second year of a 3-year programme. An open response questionnaire has been developed and trialled to gather the views of pupils on key stages 2-4 in 11 strands which yield information on attitudes to science. Each strand comprises 15 statements, and 50-70 open responses are being gathered for each statement. These will then be used to develop categories in a fixed response instrument to measure attitudes to science. In the first instance, this instrument will be used to gather data from approximately 100 pupils in each of 6 schools, though it is hoped that time and resources would permit the sample size to be expanded.

STATUS: Sponsored project

SOURCE OF GRANT: The Salters' Institute of Chemistry £5,000

DATE OF RESEARCH: 1997-continuing

KEYWORDS: **primary education; pupil attitudes; science education; secondary education**

2929

Department of Educational Studies, Heslington, York YO1 5DD
01904 430000
University of Cape Town, Department of Physics, Rondebosch 7700, Cape Town, South Africa
01027 21650 9111

Campbell, R. Dr; Lubben, F. Mr; Buffler, A. Dr; Allie, S. Dr; Kaunda, L. Dr

Procedural understanding of disadvantged first year science students

ABSTRACT: This project stems from the PACKS project in the UK (funded by the Economic and Social Research Council and aims to document the procedural understanding of students entering a physics department from educationally disadvantaged backgrounds. The longer term aim is to inform the development of a curriculum appropriate to such students.

PUBLISHED MATERIAL: ALLIE, S., BUFFLER, A., KAUNDA, L., CAMPBELL, B. & LUBBEN, F. (1997). 'Procedural understanding of first year university science students'. Proceedings of SAARMSE Fifth Annual Meeting, 22-26 January, University of Witwatersrand, Johannesbury, South Africa, 1997. ; ALLIE, S., BUFFLER, A., KAUNDA, L., CAMPBELL, B. & LUBBEN, F. (1997). 'Analysing how students communicate science investigations'. Proceedings of SAARMSE Fifth Annual Meeting, 22-26 January, University of Witwatersrand, Johannesburg, South Africa, 1997.

STATUS: Sponsored project

SOURCE OF GRANT: York University; University of Cape Town; British Council Foundation for Research and Development

DATE OF RESEARCH: 1996-1997

KEYWORDS: **educationally disadvantaged; higher education; nontraditional students; physics; science education**

2930

Department of Educational Studies, Heslington, York YO1 5DD
01904 430000
University of Toronto, Faculty of Education, 371 Bloor Street West, Toronto, Ontario, Canada M55 2R7

Pike, G. Dr; *Supervisor*: Vulliamy, G. Dr

Global education: international dimensions

ABSTRACT: The research seeks to identify the theoretical frameworks and ideologies underlying approaches to global education in different continents with special reference to Britain, Canada, and the USA. Global education policies in these continents are being researched with a combination of document analysis, questionnaires and telephone interviews from leading exponents in the field. The research also seeks to explore the variety of meanings attached to global education by practising teachers who use such approaches. Data collection for this involves qualitative interviews with teachers in England and case studies of schools in Canada and the USA.

STATUS: Individual research

DATE OF RESEARCH: 1991-1997

KEYWORDS: **canada; comparative education; global approach; teaching methods; united states of america**

2931

Department of Educational Studies, Heslington, York YO1 5DD
01904 430000
York University, Department of Chemistry, Heslington, York YO1 5DD

Bennetta J. Dr; Lazonby, J. Mr; Parvin, J. Ms; Waddington, D. Prof.; Stevenson, M. Ms

Primary pupils' views of the chemical industry

ABSTRACT: The project aims to document primary age pupils' views of the chemical industry, before and after intervention strategies in the form of curriculum enrichment materials have taken place. Data have been gathered via interviews with pupils and staff. The main phase of the study employed a pencil and paper inventory with pupils and questionnaires and interviews with staff. A detailed report of the project is currently in preparation and funding is being sought for a further development of the work.

STATUS: Sponsored project

SOURCE OF GRANT: Thomas Swan Company

DATE OF RESEARCH: 1995-1998

KEYWORDS: **chemical industry; chemistry; primary education; primary school pupils; pupil attitudes; science education**

2932

Department of Language and Linguistic Science, Heslington, York YO1 5DD
01904 430000
Universite Louis Pasteur, LADISIS, URA 668 - CNRS, Section Psycholinguistique, 12 rue Goethe, 67000 Strasbourg, France
00 33 88 35 82 04

Russell, J. Dr; Verma, M. Mr; *Supervisors*: Warner, A. Dr; Le Page, R. Prof.; Tabouret-Keller, A. Prof.

International group for the study of language standardisation and the vernacularisation of literacy

ABSTRACT: Biennial workshops in 1986, 1988, 1990 and 1992 have brought together a group of people each actively concerned with vernacular education, especially in the former colonies of Britain and France, but also in Europe and the Americas. The results of this work have been put into a book, Vernacular Literacy Revisited, to be published in 1997.

PUBLISHED MATERIAL: TABOURET-KELLER, A., et al. (1997).

Vernacular literacy: an examination of the practicalities. Oxford: Clarendon.; TABOURET-KELLER, A. et al. (1997). Vernacular literacy: a re-evaluation of the International Group for the Study of Language Standardization and Vernacularization of Literacy (IGLSVL). Oxford: Clarendon.

STATUS: Sponsored project

SOURCE OF GRANT: ESRC £3,000; Nuffield Foundation £2,000; York University £600; CNRS - Paris £2,000; British Academy £2,000; British Council £1,500

DATE OF RESEARCH: 1986-1997

KEYWORDS: developing countries; language policy; language standardisation; literacy; mother tongue

2933

Department of Psychology, Heslington, York YO1 5DD
01904 430000

McDougall, S. Ms; *Supervisors*: Ellis, A. Prof.; Hulme, C. Prof.; Monk, A. Dr

Extent and correalates of variability among different groups of readers

ABSTRACT: The study has two principal aims. The first aim is to investigate whether different groups of readers matched on reading age show the same or different patterns of reading performance when latency as well as accuracy, and variability, as well as central tendency are taken into consideration. This should resolve current controversy over the extent to which dyslexic reading performance follows simply from their reading age or includes a differential deficit in, for example, phonological processing. The groups concerned will be: (1) dyslexic children (high IQ) with specific and unexpected reading retardation; (2) poor readers (low IQ) with nonspecific learning difficulties; (3) precocious readers (high IQ) whose reading age is ahead of their chronological age; and (4) normal readers. If reading age is the sole determinant of group reading patterns, then these four groups should not differ from one another. The second aim is to discover whether different reading patterns related to different patterns of strength and weakness in performance on tasks which do not involve reading per se, but tap aspects of cognition which may be relevant to the acquisition of reading. Different patterns of strength and weakness in reading skill will be related to different patterns of strength and weakness in basic visual and phonological processes. A broader subsidiary aim of this project is to evaluate the extent to which information-processing accounts of a skill such as reading can also provide the dimensions for characterising individual differences in cognitive ability.

STATUS: Sponsored project

SOURCE OF GRANT: Economic and Social Research Council £56,966

DATE OF RESEARCH: 1990-1993

KEYWORDS: cognitive ability; dyslexia; reading difficulties; reading skills

2934

Department of Psychology, Heslington, York YO1 5DD
01904 430000

Eames, C. Dr; *Supervisor*: Cox, M. Dr

Drawing ability in gifted and non-gifted autistic children

ABSTRACT: The development of depth representation in the drawings of normal children is now beginning to be understood. This research project was carried out to see whether the development of depth portrayal in the drawings of autistic children follows a 'normal' path. Comparing autistic children with Down's Syndrome children and normal children, matched on non-verbal mental age, it was found that autistic children are developmentally delayed in their depth representation rather than showing anomalous strategies of depth portrayal.

PUBLISHED MATERIAL: EAMES, K. & COX, M.V. (1994). 'Visual realism in the drawings of autistic, Down's syndrome and normal children', British Journal of Developmental Psychology, Vol 12.

STATUS: Sponsored project

SOURCE OF GRANT: Medical Research Council £13,680

DATE OF RESEARCH: 1989-1993

KEYWORDS: autism; downs syndrome; drawing; gifted; special educational needs; visual arts

2935

Department of Psychology, Heslington, York YO1 5DD
01904 430000

Catte, M. Miss; *Supervisor*: Cox, M. Dr

Emotional indicators in children's human figure drawings

ABSTRACT: Human figure drawings (HFDs) have long been used as a projective technique to assess the mental health or personality of the artist. Various methods have been proposed and used by clinicians for analysing a drawing and many studies assessed the reliability and validity of the scoring systems. However, faults in the designs of these studies and a lack of replication of results meant that the conclusions which could be drawn from the research were limited. This research project investigated the emotional indicators (Koppitz, 1968) in the HFDs of children with emotional/behavioural difficulties, compared to normally adjusted children matched for chronological age (CA) and mental age (MA). No significant differences were found between the indicator scores of 18 clinical sample children still in mainstream school and either the CA or MA matched control samples' HFDs. Statistically significant differences were found, however, between the indicator scores of 44 clinical sample children from special schools and both the CA and MA matched control samples' HFDs. Following a normative data collection of 1600 drawings a revised list of indicators was formulated due to changes in the children's drawings between 1968 and 1996. The drawings previously collected were scored for these new revised indicators but the results remained the same. Thus the differences in indicator scores between the clinical and the normally adjusted children, which only occurred with a more severely disturbed clinical sample, could not be explained by differences in mental age, or the fact that the indicator list was out of out date.

STATUS: Individual research

DATE OF RESEARCH: 1995-1998

KEYWORDS: child psychology; drawing; emotional and behavioural difficulties; human figure drawing; identification - psychology; personality assessment; projective measures; special educational needs

2936

Department of Psychology, Heslington, York YO1 5DD
01904 430000

Carroll, J. Ms; *Supervisor*: Snowling, M. Prof.

Precursors of phonological awareness

ABSTRACT: This project aims to identify the precursors of phonological awareness in preschool children. A series of studies on children aged 2.06 to 4 years will first identify sensitive tests of phonological processing and phonological learning. These tests will then be used, together with assessments of vocabulary and non-verbal ability, to follow a cohort of 3 year-olds longitudinally for 12 months, being the phase of development in which it is anticipated that metalinguistic skills begin to emerge. Outcome measures will include phonological awareness tasks and pre-literacy measures.

STATUS: Individual research

DATE OF RESEARCH: 1998-continuing

KEYWORDS: child language; language acquisition; phonology; young children

2937

Department of Psychology, Heslington, York YO1 5DD
01904 4300000

Nation, K. Dr; *Supervisor*: Snowling, M. Prof.

The relationship between children's language and reading skills

ABSTRACT: The aim of this study is to identify the cognitive and linguistic characteristics of children who have specific reading comprehension difficulties, in the absence of deficits in basic (decoding) skills. It is estimated that 10% of the primary school population have such difficulties. Results to date confirm earlier findings that these children have normal phonological skills. However, the researchers have found that they have impairments of vocabulary knowledge, semantic and syntactic processing, seen most clearly in their poor listening comprehension. The current research focuses on the mechanisms that account for the impact of poor comprehension on learning to read. Experiments investigating priming from sentence and word contexts are being used to explore differences between 20 poor comprehenders and controls. A small-scale longitudinal study is following these children over 2 years.

PUBLISHED MATERIAL: SNOWLING, M.J. & NATION, K. (1997). 'Phonology, language and learning to read'. In: HULME, C. & SNOWLING, M.J. (Eds). Dyslexia: biology, cognition and intervention. London: Whurr Publishers. ; HULME, C. & SNOWLING, M. (Eds). (1997). 'Dyslexia: biological bases, identification and intervention'. Proceedings of the Fourth International Conference of the British Dyslexia Association, University of York, 1997. ; NATION, K. & SNOWLING, M.J. (1997). 'Assessing reading difficulties: the validity and utility of current measures of reading skill', British Journal of Educational Psychology, Vol 67, pp.359-370. ; NATION, K. & SNOWLING, M.J. (1998). 'Individual differences in contextual facilitation: evidence from dyslexia and poor reading comprehension', Child Development, Vol 69, No 4, pp.996-1011.

STATUS: Sponsored project

SOURCE OF GRANT: Wellcome Trust £91,000

DATE OF RESEARCH: 1996-continuing

KEYWORDS: **language skills; reading comprehension; reading difficulties**

2938

Department of Psychology, Heslington, York YO1 5DD
01904 430000
Chinese Academy of Sciences, Institute of Psychology, Beijing, China

Perara, J. Dr; Fan, X. Prof.; *Supervisor*: Cox, M. Dr

Teaching methods and children's drawing skills in the UK and China

ABSTRACT: The purpose of the present investigation was to compare children's development of drawing in 2 cultures - the UK and China - and to examine and compare the teaching methods employed in schools in these 2 cultures. The teaching of formal techniques of drawing is discouraged in UK schools, mainly on the grounds that it stifles children's creativity. The consequence is that the standard of drawing is allegedly low and, in fact, rather few children display much creativity. In contrast, the standard of drawing and painting in China is remarkably high; Chinese children routinely collect international awards and an exhibition of their work is currently on tour in the UK. We assume that the Chinese children are no more innately gifted than are UK children, but that their talent has been fostered in their culture, in particular through the relatively formal approach of teaching right from the kindergarten. However, in the West little is known about these teaching methods, so one of the aims of this research project was to video-record a sample of art lessons for 6-13 year olds in China and to compare them with art lessons for children in the UK. A second aim was to collect data from both Chinese and UK children (480 Chinese and 480 UK children in normal classes, and 240 Chinese children in special art classes) in order to compare the standard of drawing in the 2 cultures. There were 3 topics drawn from imagination and 5 from models; these were compared on overall artistic merit (i.e. ratings by art educators) and on a number of technical measures. In fact the drawings produced by children in the UK and in Chinese normal schools were evaluated at a similar level; however, the drawings of the art school schildren received higher scores. Classroom practices in China are formal and class-based, those in the UK are informal and group/individual based.

STATUS: Sponsored project

SOURCE OF GRANT: Royal Society £6,140; Economic and Social Research Council £60,790

DATE OF RESEARCH: 1995-1997

KEYWORDS: **art education; china; comparative education; drawing; teaching methods**

2939

Department of Psychology, Heslington, York YO1 5DD
01904 430000
Cumbria Education Service, 5 Portland Square, Carlisle CA1 1PU
01228 606060

Hatcher, P. Dr; *Supervisors*: Hulme, C. Prof.; Snowling, M. Prof.

Phonological skills and the prevention of children's reading difficulties

ABSTRACT: This research grows out of an earlier study by Hatcher, Hulme and Ellis, 1994, which tested the idea that children make most progress in learning to read when training to improve phonological skills is combined with the process of learning to relate the sounds of words to their spelling patterns. In line with our 'phonological linkage hypothesis' the researchers found that reading delayed 7 year-olds made reading gains at twice the average rate when previously they had been falling behind. The present study is applying the ideas from the previous study to class teaching in the first 2 years of school. The relative effectiveness of different levels (rhyme and phoneme awareness) of phonological training was also assessed. 20 classes of children have been split into 4 matched groups of 5. The taught control group is receiving a systematic phonic approach to reading. In addition to this programme, the 3 other groups are receiving either phonological training based upon rhyme, phoneme or rhyme and phoneme units. A fifth group of 5 schools is acting as an unseen control group. Measures of literacy, phonological awareness, IQ, speech rate, memory and language skills were taken at the beginning of the study, when the children had been in school for about 6 weeks, and again after a year in school. The same measures will be taken after a second year of training has ceased. The results of the study will be analysed using multivariate techniques (taking account of class and individual scores) and structural equation modelling.

STATUS: Sponsored project

SOURCE OF GRANT: Economic and Social Research Council £230,000

DATE OF RESEARCH: 1996-continuing

KEYWORDS: **beginning reading; key stage 1; phonology; primary education; reading ability; reading skills**

2940

Department of Psychology, Heslington, York Yo1 5DD
01904 430000
Dyslexia Institute, 133 Gresham Road, Staines TW1 2AJ
01784 463935

Griffiths, Y. Ms; *Supervisors*: Snowling, M. Prof.; Rack, J. Dr

Individual differences in developmental dyslexia

ABSTRACT: The study is concerned with investigating how individual differences in a dyslexic child's cognitive skills (e.g. their language strengths and weaknesses) can predict the development of their reading and spelling skills, both quantitatively and qualitatively. 59 developmental dyslexic children, reading between the 7 and 9 year-old level, with at least a 2-year delay, were tested on a large battery of tasks. The battery was designed to measure abilities on a large range of speech and language processing tasks (e.g. phonological awareness, nonword repetition, nonword and exception word reading, and usual and auditory span measures). Individual differences in reading profiles at the behavioural level were investigated by comparing the individual performance on the test battery with a group of younger children, reading at the same level as the dyslexic group (pair-wise matched in reading age with each dyslexic child). Developmental differences in the stability of these individual reading profiles were investigated by following the progress over time on these cognitive measures.

STATUS: Sponsored project

SOURCE OF GRANT: Dyslexia Institute

DATE OF RESEARCH: 1996-1998

KEYWORDS: **dyslexia; special educational needs**

2941

Department of Psychology, Heslington, York YO1 5DD
01904 4300000
Kyoto University, Faculty of Education, Kyoto 606-01, Japan

Cox, M. Dr; Koyasu, M. Prof.

Children's pictorial representation of figures in action - UK/Japan comparisons

ABSTRACT: This cross-cultural research project will compare children's drawings of the human figure in the UK and Japan. In recent years manga comic books have become popular in Japan and distinctive manga graphic styles have been observed in children's drawings. Thus, children have borrowed a graphic style from popular media and have broadened their repertoire of graphic skills. One particular feature of the manga comics is the variety of poses of figures in action. The hypothesis is that Japanese children will be more skilled at drawing action figures than will UK children. Boys in Japan will be more skilled than girls since action comics are read more by boys. Data will be collected from 6-7 year-olds and 10-11 year-olds, equal numbers of boys and girls in each sample, in both UK and Japan. Each child will draw 3 figures man standing and looking at viewer, man running towards right, man running towards the viewer. All drawings are from imagination. The drawings will be rated by both UK and Japanese rates on a number of scales and technical measures.

STATUS: Collaborative

DATE OF RESEARCH: 1998-continuing

KEYWORDS: **cartoons; childrens art; comics - publications; comparative education; cross cultural studies; drawing; japan**

2942

Language Teaching Centre, Heslington, York YO1 5DD
01904 43000
Universitat Munchen, Lehrstuhl fur die Didaktik der Englischen Sprache und Literatur, Schellingstrasse 3, D-8000 Munchen 40, Germany
02180 2995

Green, P. Mr; Hecht, Kh. Prof.

Learner language

ABSTRACT: This was a project to investigate learner language and compare it at all stages with the language of native peers. The project involved German (and, for certain tasks, French, Hungarian, Italian and Swedish) school learners of English and English school pupils in performing communicative tasks in English (letter writing, oral and written narrative, and oral transaction) and completing tasks of grammatical and lexical competence. There were over 6000 pupil productions. The productions were analysed from the following standpoints: (1) linguistic form; (2) content; (3) communicative effectiveness; (4) strategies; (5) self correction/monitoring; (6) grammatical and lexical competence and performance; (7) development of communicative competence; (8) assessment/reactions by natives and non-natives. Conclusions were very varied. @#Published Material:#@ GREEN, P.S. & HECHT, Kh. (1985). 'Native and non-native evaluation of learners' errors in written discourse', System, Vol 13, No 2, pp.77-79. ; GREEN, P.S. & HECHT, Kh. (1987). 'The influence of accuracy on communicative effectiveness', British Journal of Language Teaching, Vol 25, No 2, pp.79-84. ; GREEN, P.S. & HECHT, Kh. (1988). 'The sympathetic native speaker - a GCSE role-play for the teacher', Modern Languages, Vol 69, No 1, pp.3-10. ; GREEN, P.S. & HECHT, Kh. (1990). 'Investigating learners' language'. In: BRUMFIT, C.J. & MITCHELL, R. (Eds). Research in the language classroom. Basingstoke: MacMillan. ; GREEN, P.S. & HECHT, Kh. (1993). 'Language awareness of German pupils', Language Awareness, Vol 2, No 3, pp.125-142. A full list of publication is available from the researcher.

STATUS: Sponsored project

SOURCE OF GRANT: British Council Academic Linking Scheme £600; European Community £1,400; EC Erasmus £1,400; York University £1,000; Leverhulme Trust £2,500

DATE OF RESEARCH: 1980-1993

KEYWORDS: **comparative education; english; german; language tests; modern language studies; native speakers; second language teaching**

James E. Clyde
CONSTRUCTION INSPECTION: A FIELD GUIDE TO PRACTICE

Harold J. Rosen and Philip M. Bennett
CONSTRUCTION MATERIALS EVALUATION AND SELECTION:
A SYSTEMATIC APPROACH

C. R. Tumblin
CONSTRUCTION COST ESTIMATES

Harvey V. Debo and Leo Diamant
CONSTRUCTION SUPERINTENDENTS JOB GUIDE

Oktay Ural, Editor
CONSTRUCTION OF LOWER-COST HOUSING

Robert M. Koerner and Joseph P. Welsh
CONSTRUCTION AND GEOTECHNICAL ENGINEERING USING
SYNTHETIC FABRICS

J. Patrick Powers
CONSTRUCTION DEWATERING: A GUIDE TO THEORY AND
PRACTICE

Walter Podolny, Jr., and Jean M. Muller
CONSTRUCTION AND DESIGN OF PRESTRESSED CONCRETE
SEGMENTAL BRIDGES

*Construction and Design
of Prestressed Concrete
Segmental Bridges*

Construction and Design
of Prestressed Concrete Segmental Bridges

Walter Podolny, Jr., Ph.D., P.E.

Bridge Division
Office of Engineering
Federal Highway Administration
U.S. Department of Transportation

Jean M. Muller

Chairman of the Board
Figg and Muller Engineers, Inc.

1807 1982

A Wiley-Interscience Publication

John Wiley & Sons
New York   Chichester   Brisbane   Toronto   Singapore

Library of Congress Cataloging in Publication Data:

Podolny, Walter.
    Construction and design of prestressed concrete
    segmental bridges.

    (Wiley series of practical construction guides
    ISSN 0271-6011)
    "A Wiley-Interscience publication."
    Includes index.
    1. Bridges, Concrete—Design and construction.
    2. Prestressed concrete construction.   I. Muller, Jean M.
    II. Title.   III. Series.

TG355.P63   624.2   81-13025
ISBN 0-471-05658-8   AACR2

Printed in the United States of America

10 9 8 7 6 5 4 3 2 1

Series Preface

The Wiley Series of Practical Construction Guides provides the working constructor with up-to-date information that can help to increase the job profit margin. These guidebooks, which are scaled mainly for practice, but include the necessary theory and design, should aid a construction contractor in approaching work problems with more knowledgeable confidence. The guides should be useful also to engineers, architects, planners, specification writers, project managers, superintendents, materials and equipment manufacturers and, the source of all these callings, instructors and their students.

Construction in the United States alone will reach $250 billion a year in the early 1980s. In all nations, the business of building will continue to grow at a phenomenal rate, because the population proliferation demands new living, working, and recreational facilities. This construction will have to be more substantial, thus demanding a more professional performance from the contractor. Before science and technology had seriously affected the ideas, job plans, financing, and erection of structures, most contractors developed their know-how by field trial-and-error. Wheels, small and large, were constantly being reinvented in all sectors, because there was no interchange of knowledge. The current complexity of construction, even in more rural areas, has revealed a clear need for more proficient, professional methods and tools in both practice and learning.

Because construction is highly competitive, some practical technology is necessarily proprietary. But most practical day-to-day problems are common to the whole construction industry. These are the subjects for the Wiley Practical Construction Guides.

M. D. Morris, P.E.

v

Preface

Prestressed concrete segmental bridge construction has evolved, in the natural course of events, from the combining of the concepts of prestressing, box girder design, and the cantilever method of bridge construction. It arose from a need to overcome construction difficulties in spanning deep valleys and river crossings without the use of conventional falsework, which in some instances may be impractical, economically prohibitive, or detrimental to environment and ecology.

Contemporary prestressed, box girder, segmental bridges began in Western Europe in the 1950s. Ulrich Finsterwalder in 1950, for a crossing of the Lahn River in Balduinstein, Germany, was the first to apply cast-in-place segmental construction to a bridge. In 1962 in France the first application of precast, segmental, box girder construction was made by Jean Muller to the Choisy-Le-Roi Bridge crossing the Seine River. Since then the concept of segmental bridge construction has been improved and refined and has spread from Europe throughout most of the world.

The first application of segmental bridge construction in North America was a cast-in-place segmental bridge on the Laurentian Autoroute near Ste. Adele, Quebec, in 1964. This was followed in 1967 by a precast segmental bridge crossing the Lievre River near Notre Dame du Laus, Quebec. In 1973 the first U.S. precast segmental bridge was opened to traffic in Corpus Christi, Texas, followed a year later by the cast-in-place segmental Pine Valley Bridge near San Diego, California. As of this date (1981) in the United States more than eighty segmental bridges are completed, in construction, in design, or under consideration.

Prestressed concrete segmental bridges may be identified as precast or cast in place and categorized by method of construction as balanced cantilever, span-by-span, progressive placement, or incremental launching. This type of bridge has extended the practical and competitive economic span range of concrete bridges. It is adaptable to almost any conceivable site condition.

The objective of this book is to summarize in one volume the current state of the art of design and construction methods for all types of segmental bridges as a ready reference source for engineering faculties, practicing engineers, contractors, and local, state, and federal bridge engineers.

Chapter 1 is a quick review of the historical evolution to the current state of the art. It offers the student an appreciation of the way in which segmental construction of bridges developed, the factors that influenced its development, and the various techniques used in constructing segmental bridges.

Chapters 2 and 3 present case studies of the predominant methodology of constructing segmental bridges by balanced cantilever in both cast-in-place and precast concrete. Conception and design of the superstructure and piers, respectively, are discussed in Chapters 4 and 5. The other three basic methods of constructing segmental bridges—progressive placement, span-by-span, and incremental launching—are presented in Chapters 6 and 7.

Chapters 2 through 7 deal essentially with girder type bridges. However, segmental construction may also be applied to bridges of other types. Chapter 8 discusses application of the segmental concept to arch, rigid frame, and truss bridges. Chapter 9 deals with the cable-stayed type of bridge and Chapter 10 with railroad bridges. The practical aspects of fabrication, handling, and erection of segments are discussed in Chapter 11.

In selected a bridge type for a particular site, one of the more important parameters is economics. Economics, competitive bidding, and contractual aspects of segmental construction are discussed in Chapter 12.

Most of the material presented in this book is not

original. Although acknowledgment of all the many sources is not possible, full credit is given wherever the specific source can be identified.

Every effort has been made to eliminate errors; the authors will appreciate notification from the reader of any that remain.

The authors are indebted to numerous publications, organizations, and individuals for their assistance and permission to reproduce photo-graphs, tables, and other data. Wherever possible, credit is given in the text.

WALTER PODOLNY, JR.
JEAN M. MULLER

Burke, Virginia
Paris, France

January 1982

Contents

*Construction and Design
of Prestressed Concrete
Segmental Bridges*

1

Prestressed Concrete Bridges and Segmental Construction

1.1 Introduction

The conception, development, and worldwide acceptance of segmental construction in the field of prestressed concrete bridges represents one of the most interesting and important achievements in civil engineering during the past thirty years. Recognized today in all countries and particularly in the United States as a safe, practical, and economic construction method, the segmental concept probably owes its rapid growth and acceptance to its founding, from the beginning, on sound construction principles such as cantilever construction.

Using this method, a bridge structure is made up of concrete elements usually called segments (either precast or cast in place in their final position in the structure) assembled by post-tensioning. If the bridge is cast in place, Figure 1.1, travelers are used to allow the various segments to be constructed in successive increments and progressively

prestressed together. If the bridge is precast, segments are manufactured in a special casting yard or factory, transported to their final position, and placed in the structure by various types of launch-

FIGURE 1.1 Cast-in place form traveler.

1

FIGURE 1.2. Oleron Viaduct, segmental construction in progress. One typical precast segment placed in the Oleron Viaduct.

ing equipment, Figure 1.2, while prestressing achieves the assembly and provides the structural strength.

Most early segmental bridges were built as cantilevers, where construction proceeds in a symmetrical fashion from the bridge piers in successive increments to complete each span and finally the entire superstructure, Figure 1.3. Later, other construction methods appeared in conjunction with

the segmental concept to further its field of application.

1.2   Development of Cantilever Construction

The idea of cantilever construction is ancient in the Orient. Shogun's Bridge located in the city of Nikko, Japan, is the earliest recorded cantilever bridge and dates back to the fourth century. The Wandipore Bridge, Figure 1.4, was built in the seventeenth century in Bhutan, between India and Tibet. It is constructed from great timbers that are corbeled out toward each other from massive abutments and the narrowed interval finally capped with a light beam.[1]

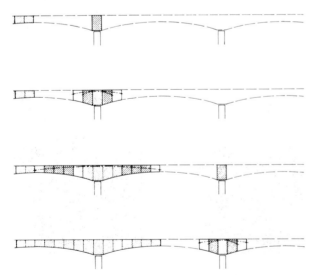

FIGURE 1.3. Cantilever construction applied to prestressed concrete bridges.

FIGURE 1.4. Wandipore Bridge.

Thomas Pope, a New York carpenter, was so inspired by these structures that he used the concept in his "Flying Lever Bridge." In 1810 he built a 50 ft (15 m) model on a scale of $\frac{3}{8}$ in. to 1 ft (1 to 32 m) representing half of a proposed 1800 ft (549 m) span. It was to be a single wooden structure crossing the Hudson River near New York City, Figure 1.5. According to witnesses the 50 ft (15 m) unsupported arm withstood a 10 ton (9 mt) weight. Pope published the design of his daring and interesting concept the following year. Although arched in form, the optimistic span was a cantilever beam in principle, with the "flying levers" projected from great masonry abutments, fitted out on the New York side as apartments. Pope's presentation of this design was accompanied by the following couplet[2]:

Let the broad arc the spacious Hudson stride
And span Columbia's rivers far more wide
Convince the world America begins
To foster Arts, the ancient work of kings.
Stupendous plan! which none before e'er
    found,

That half an arc should stand upon the
    ground
Without support while building, or a rest;
This caus'd the theorist's rage and sceptic's
    jest.

Prefabrication techniques were successfully combined with cantilever construction in many bridges near the end of the nineteenth century, as exemplified by such notable structures as the Firth of Forth Bridge, Figure 1.6, and later the Quebec Bridge, Figure 1.7, over the Saint Lawrence River. These structures bear witness to the engineering genius of an earlier generation. Built more recently, the Greater New Orleans Bridge over the Mississippi River, Figure 1.8, represents modern contemporary long-span steel cantilever construction.

Because the properties and behavior of prestressed concrete are related more closely to those of structural steel than those of conventional reinforced concrete, the application of this material to cantilever construction was a logical step in the continuing development of bridge engineering.

FIGURE 1.5. Pope's Flying Lever Bridge.

FIGURE 1.7. Quebec Bridge.

FIGURE 1.6. Firth of Forth Bridge.

FIGURE 1.8. Greater New Orleans Bridge.

This application has evolved over many years by the successive development of many concepts and innovations. In order to see how the present state of the art has been reached, let us briefly trace the development of prestressed concrete and in particular its application to bridge construction.

1.3　Evolution of Prestressed Concrete

The invention of reinforced concrete stirred the imagination of engineers in many countries. They envisioned that a tremendous advantage could be achieved, if the steel could be tensioned to put the structure in a permanent state of compression greater than any tensile stresses generated by the applied loads. The present state of the art of prestressed concrete has evolved from the effort and experience of many engineers and scientists over the past ninety years. However, the concept of prestressing is centuries old. Swiss investigators have shown that as early as 2700 B.C. the ancient Egyptians prestressed their seagoing vessels longitudinally. This has been determined from pictorial representations found in Fifth Dynasty tombs.

The basic principle of prestressing was used in the craft of cooperage when the cooper wound ropes or metal bands around wooden staves to form barrels.[3] When the bands were tightened, they were under tensile prestress, which created compression between the staves and enabled them to resist hoop tension produced by internal liquid pressure. In other words, the bands and staves were both prestressed before they were subjected to any service loads. The wooden cartwheel with its shrunk-on iron rim is another example of prestressed construction.

The first attempt to introduce internal stresses in reinforced concrete members by tensioning the steel reinforcement was made about 1886 when P. H. Jackson, an engineer in San Francisco, obtained a United States patent for tightening steel rods in concrete members serving as floor slabs. In 1888, C. E. W. Döhring of Berlin secured a patent for the manufacture of slabs, battens, and small beams for structural engineering purposes by embedding tensioned wire in concrete in order to reduce cracking. This was the first attempt to provide precast concrete units with a tensioned reinforcement.

Several structures were constructed using these concepts; however, only mild steel reinforcement was available at the time. These structures at first behaved according to predictions, but because so little prestress force could be induced in the mild

steel, they lost their properties because of the creep and shrinkage of the concrete. In order to recover some of the losses, the possibility of retightening the reinforcing rods after some shrinkage and creep of the concrete had taken place was suggested in 1908 by C. R. Steiner of the United States. Steiner proposed that the bond of embedded steel bars be destroyed by lightly tensioning the bars while the concrete was still young and then tensioning them to a higher stress when the concrete had hardened. Steiner was also the first to suggest the use of curved tendons.

In 1925, R. E. Dill of Nebraska took a further step toward freeing concrete beams of any tensile stresses by tensioning high-tensile steel wires after the concrete had hardened. Bonding was to be prevented by suitably coating the wires. He explicitly mentioned the advantage of using steel with a high elastic limit and high strength as compared to ordinary reinforcing bars.

In 1928, E. Freyssinet of France, who is credited with the modern development of prestressed concrete, started using high-strength steel wires for prestressing. Although Freyssinet also tried the method of pretensioning, where the steel was bonded to the concrete without end anchorages, the first practical application of this method was made by E. Hoyer about 1938. Wide application of the prestressing technique was not possible until reliable and economical methods of tensioning and end anchorage were devised. From approximately 1939 on, E. Freyssinet, Magnel, and others developed different methods and procedures. Prestress began to gain some importance about 1945, while alternative prestressing methods were being devised by engineers in various countries.

During the past thirty years, prestressed concrete in the United States has grown from a brand-new idea into an accepted method of concrete construction. This growth, a result of a new application of existing materials and theories, is in itself phenomenal. In Europe the shortage of materials and the enforced economies in construction gave prestressed concrete a substantial start. Development in the United States, however, was slower to get underway. Designers and contractors hesitated mainly because of their lack of experience and a reluctance to abandon more familiar methods of construction. Contractors, therefore, bid the first prestressed concrete work conservatively. Moreover, the equipment available for prestressing and related techniques was essentially new and makeshift. However, experience was gained rapidly, the quality of the work improved,

FIGURE 1.9. Freyssinet's Esbly Bridge on the Marne River.

FIGURE 1.10 Walnut Lane Bridge, Philadelphia (courtesy of the Portland Cement Association).

and prestressed concrete became more and more competitive with other materials.

1.4 Evolution of Prestressed Concrete Bridges

Although France took the lead in the development of prestressed concrete, many European countries such as Belgium, England, Germany, Switzerland, and Holland quickly showed interest. As early as 1948, Freyssinet used prestressed concrete for the construction of five bridges over the Marne River near Paris, with 240 ft (74 m) spans of an exceptionally light appearance, Figure 1.9. A survey made in Germany showed that between 1949 and 1953, out of 500 bridges built, 350 were prestressed.

Prestressing in the United States followed a different course. Instead of linear prestressing, circular prestressing as applied to storage tanks took the lead. Linear prestressing as applied to beams did not start until 1949. The first structure of this type was a bridge in Madison County, Tennessee, followed in 1950 by the well-known 160 ft (48.80 m) span Walnut Lane Bridge in Philadelphia, Figure 1.10. By the middle of 1951 it was estimated that 175 bridges and 50 buildings had been constructed in Europe and no more than 10 structures in the United States. In 1952 the Portland Cement Association conducted a survey in this country showing 100 or more structures completed or

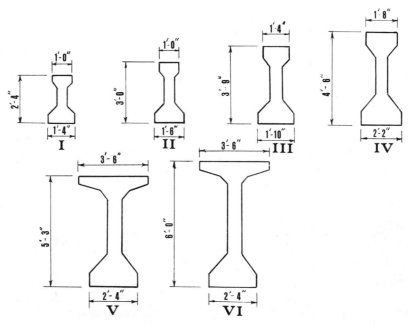

FIGURE 1.11. AASHTO-PCI I-girder cross sections.

under construction. In 1953 it was estimated that there were 75 bridges in Pennsylvania alone.

After the Walnut Lane Bridge, which was cast in place and post-tensioned, precast pretensioned bridge girders evolved, taking advantage of the inherent economies and quality control achievable with shop-fabricated members. With few exceptions, during the 1950s and early 1960s, most multispan precast prestressed bridges built in the United States were designed as a series of simple spans. They were designed with standard AASHTO-PCI* girders of various cross sections, Figure 1.11, for spans of approximately 100 ft (30.5 m), but more commonly for spans of 40 to 80 ft (12 to 24 m). The advantages of a continuous cast-in-place structure were abandoned in favor of the simpler construction offered by plant-produced standardized units.

At this time, precast pretensioned members found an outstanding application in the Lake Pontchartrain crossing north of New Orleans, Louisiana. The crossing consisted of more than 2200 identical 56 ft (17 m) spans, Figures 1.12 through 1.14. Each span was made of a single 200 ton monolith with pretensioned longitudinal gird-

*American Association of State Highway and Transportation Officials (previously known as AASHO, American Association of State Highway Officials) and Prestressed Concrete Institute.

FIGURE 1.12. Lake Pontchartrain Bridge, U.S.A.

ers and a reinforced concrete deck cast integrally, resting in turn on a precast cap and two prestressed spun piles. The speed of erection was incredible, often more than eight complete spans placed in a single day.

In the middle 1960s a growing concern was shown about the safety of highways. The AASHTO Traffic Safety Committee called in a 1967 report[4] for the ". . . adoption and use of two-span bridges for overpasses crossing divided highways . . . to eliminate the bridge piers normally placed adjacent to the shoulders," Figure 1.15. Interstate highways today require overpasses with two, three, and four spans of up to 180 ft (54.9 m) or longer. In the case of river or stream crossings,

FIGURE 1.13. Lake Pontchartrain Bridge, U.S.A.

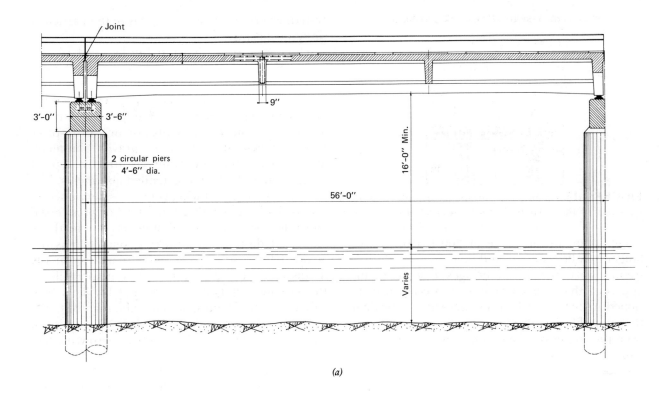

(a)

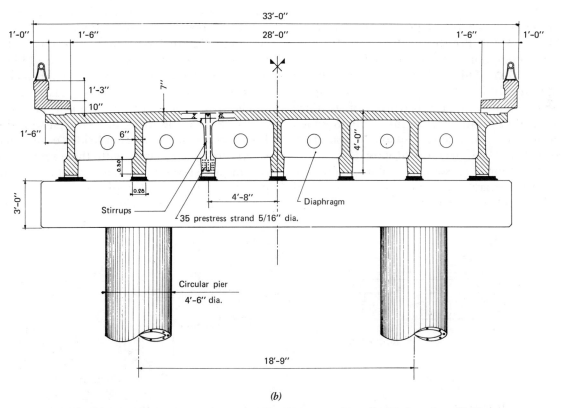

(b)

FIGURE 1.14. Lake Pontchartrain Bridge, U.S.A. (a) Longitudinal section. (b) Transverse section.

7

STANDARD 4-SPAN INTERSTATE CROSSING

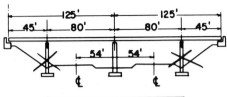

Span for Skewed Bridges	
Skew	Span
30°	144'
45°	177'
60°	250'

FIGURE 1.15. Standard four-span interstate crossing (courtesy of the Portland Cement Association).

longer spans in the range of 300 ft (91.5 m) or longer may be required, and there is a very distinct trend toward longer-span bridges. It soon became apparent that the conventional precast pretensioned AASHTO-PCI girders were limited by their transportable length and weight. Transportation over the highways limits the precast girder to a length of 100 to 120 ft (30.5 to 36.6), depending upon local regulations.

1.5   Long-Span Bridges with Conventional Precast Girders

As a result of longer span requirements a study was conducted by the Prestressed Concrete Institute (PCI) in cooperation with the Portland Cement Association (PCA).[5] This study proposed that simple spans up to 140 ft (42.7 m) and continuous spans up to 160 ft (48.8 m) be constructed of standard precast girders up to 80 ft (24 m) in length joined by splicing. To obtain longer spans the use of inclined or haunched piers was proposed.

The following discussion and illustrations are based on the grade-separation studies conducted by PCI and PCA. Actual structures will be illus-

trated, where possible, to emphasize the particular design concepts.

The design study illustrated in Figure 1.16 uses cast-in-place or precast end-span sections and a two-span unit with AASHTO I girders.[6] Narrow median piers are maintained in this design, but the abutments are extended into the spans by as much as 40 ft (12 m) using a precast or cast-in-place frame in lieu of a closed or gravity abutment. When site conditions warrant, an attractive type of bridge can be built with extended abutments.

A similar span-reducing concept is developed in Figure 1.17, using either reinforced or prestressed concrete for cantilever abutments. An aesthetic abutment design in reinforced concrete was developed for a grade-separation structure on the Trans-Canada Highway near Drummondville in the Province of Quebec, Figure 1.18. This provided a $32\frac{1}{2}$ ft (9.9 m) span reduction that led to the use of type IV Standard AASHTO I girders to span $97\frac{1}{2}$ ft (29.7 m) to a simple, narrow median pier.

A cast-in-place reinforced concrete frame with outward-sloping legs provides a stable, center supporting structure that reduces span length by 29 ft (8.8 m), Figure 1.19. This enables either standard box sections or I sections 84 ft (25.6 m) long to be used in the two main spans. This layout was used for the Hobbema Bridge in Alberta, B.C., Canada, shown in Figure 1.20. This bridge was built with precast channel girder sections, but could be built with AASHTO I girders or box sections. The median frame with inclined legs was cast in place.

The schematic and photograph in Figures 1.21 and 1.22 show the Ardrossan Overpass in Alberta. It is similar to the Hobbema Bridge except that the spans are longer and, with the exception of a cast-in-place footing, the median frame is made up of precast units post-tensioned together, Figure 1.21. The finished bridge, Figure 1.23, has a

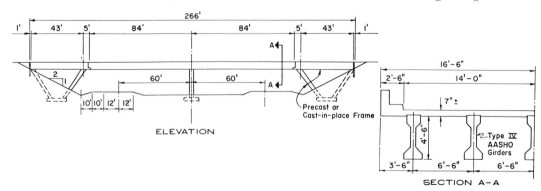

ELEVATION

SECTION A-A

FIGURE 1.16. Extended abutments (courtesy of the Prestressed Concrete Institute, from ref. 6).

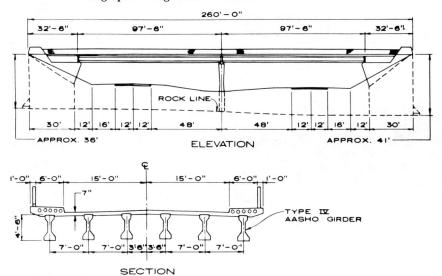

FIGURE 1.17. Cantilevered abutments (courtesy of the Prestressed Concrete Institute, from ref. 6).

FIGURE 1.18. Drummondville Bridge (courtesy of the Portland Cement Association).

pleasing appearance. The standard units were channel-shaped stringers 64 in. wide and 41 in. deep (1.6 m by 1.04 m). The use of precast units allowed erection of the entire superstructure, including the median frame, in only three weeks. The bridge was opened to traffic just eleven weeks after construction began in the early summer of 1966.

By use of temporary bents, Figure 1.24, standard units 60 ft (18.3 m) long can be placed over the median pier and connected to main span units with cast-in-place reinforced concrete splices located near the point of dead-load contraflexure.

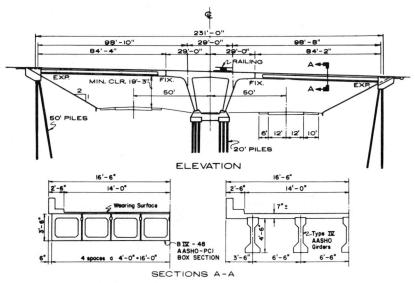

FIGURE 1.19. Median frame cast in place (courtesy of the Prestressed Concrete Institute, from ref. 6).

FIGURE 1.20. Hobbema Bridge, completed structure (courtesy of the Portland Cement Association).

This design is slightly more expensive than previous ones but it provides the most open type two-span structure.

The structural arrangement of the Sebastian Inlet Bridge in Florida consists of a three-span unit over the main channel, Figure 1.25. The end span of this three-span unit is 100 ft (30.5 m) long and cantilevers 30 ft (9 m) beyond the piers to support a 120 ft (36.6 m) precast prestressed drop-in span, Figure 1.26. The end-span section was built in two segments with a cast-in-place splice with the help of a falsework bent. The Napa River Bridge at Vallejo, California (not to be confused with the Napa River Bridge described in Section 2.11), used a precast concrete cantilever-suspended span concept similar to the Sebastian Inlet Bridge, at about the same time. The only difference was that the cantilever girder was a single girder extending

from the side pier over the main pier to the hinge-support for the suspended span.

The type of construction that uses long, standard, precast, prestressed units never quite achieved the recognition it deserved. As spans increased, designers turned toward post-tensioned cast-in-place box girder construction. The California Division of Highways, for example, has been quite successful with cast-in-place, multicell, post-tensioned box girder construction for multispan structures with spans of 300 ft (91.5 m) and even longer. However, this type of construction has its own limitations. The extensive formwork used during casting often has undesirable effects on the environment or the ecology.

1.6   Segmental Construction

Segmental construction has been defined[7] as a method of construction in which primary load-supporting members are composed of individual members called segments post-tensioned together. The concepts developed in the PCI-PCA studies and described in the preceding section come under this definition, and we might call them "longitudinal" segmental construction because the individual elements are long with respect to their width.

In Europe, meanwhile, segmental construction proceeded in a slightly different manner in conjunction with box girder design. Segments were cast in place in relatively short lengths but in full-roadway width and depth. Today segmental construction is usually understood to be the type developed in Europe. However, as will be shown later, the segments need not be of full-roadway

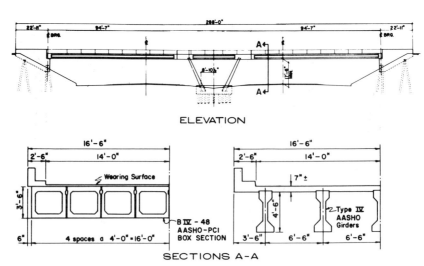

ELEVATION

SECTIONS A-A

FIGURE 1.21. Median frame precast (courtesy of the Prestressed Concrete Institute, from ref. 6).

FIGURE 1.22. Ardrossan Overpass precast median frame (courtesy of the Portland Cement Association).

FIGURE 1.23. Completed Ardrossan Overpass (courtesy of the Portland Cement Association).

width and can become rather long in the longitudinal direction of the bridge, depending on the construction system utilized.

Eugene Freyssinet, in 1945 to 1948, was the first to use precast segmental construction for prestressed concrete bridges. A bridge at Luzancy over the Marne River about 30 miles east of Paris, Figure 1.27, was followed by a group of five precast bridges over that river. Shortly thereafter, Ulrich Finsterwalder applied cast-in-place segmental prestressed construction in a balanced cantilever fashion to a bridge crossing the Lahn River at Balduinstein, Germany. This system of cantilever segmental construction rapidly gained wide acceptance in Germany, after construction of a bridge crossing the Rhine at Worms in 1952, as shown in Figure 1.28,[8] with three spans of 330, 371, and 340 ft (100, 113, and 104 m). More than 300 such structures, with spans in excess of 250 ft (76 m), were constructed between 1950 and 1965

in Europe.[9] Since then the concept has spread throughout the world.

Precast segmental construction also was evolving during this period. In 1952 a single-span county bridge near Sheldon, New York, was designed by the Freyssinet Company. Although this bridge was constructed of longitudinal rather than the European transverse segments, it represents the first practical application of match casting. The bridge girders were divided into three longitudinal segments that were cast end-to-end. The center segment was cast first and then the end segments were cast directly against it. Keys were cast at the joints so that the three precast elements could be joined at the site in the same position they had in the precasting yard. Upon shipment to the job site the three elements of a girder were post-tensioned together with cold joints.[10,11]

The first major application of match-cast, precast segmental construction was not consummated

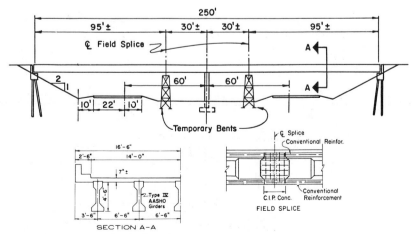

FIGURE 1.24. Field splice for continuity (courtesy of the Prestressed Concrete Institute, from ref. 6).

FIGURE 1.25. Sebastian Inlet Bridge (courtesy of the Portland Cement Association).

until 1962. This structure, designed by Jean Muller and built by Entreprises Campenon Bernard, was the Choisy-le-Roi Bridge over the Seine River south of Paris, Figure 1.29. This concept has been refined and has spread from France to all parts of the world.

The technology of cast-in-place or precast segmental bridges has advanced rapidly in the last decade. During its initial phase the balanced cantilever method of construction was used. Currently, other techniques such as span-by-span, incremental launching, or progressive placement also are available. Any of these construction methods may call on either cast-in-place or precast segments or a combination of both. Consequently, a variety of design concepts and construction methods are now available to economically produce segmental bridges for almost any site condition.

Segmental bridges may be classified broadly by four criteria:

1. The ultimate use of the bridge—that is, highway or railway structure or combination thereof. Although many problems are common to these two categories, the considerable increase of live loading in a railway bridge poses special problems that call for specific solutions.

2. The type of structure in terms of statical scheme and shape of the main bending members. Many segmental bridges are box girder bridges, but other types such as arches or cable-stayed bridges show a wide variety in shape of the supporting members.

3. The use of cast-in-place or precast segments or a combination thereof.

4. The method of construction.

The sections that follow will deal briefly with the last three classifications.

1.7 Various Types of Structures

From the point of view of their statical scheme, there are essentially five categories of structures: (1) girders, (2) trusses, (3) rigid frames, (4) arch frames, and (5) cable-stayed bridges.

1.7.1 GIRDER BRIDGES

Box girders in the majority of cases are the most efficient and economical design for a bridge. When constructed in balanced cantilever, box girder decks were initially made integral with the piers while a special expansion joint was provided at the center of each span (or every other span) to allow

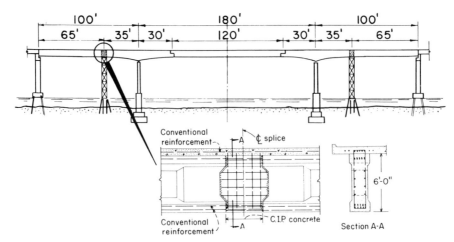

FIGURE 1.26. Sebastian Inlet Bridge (courtesy of the Prestressed Concrete Institute, from ref. 6).

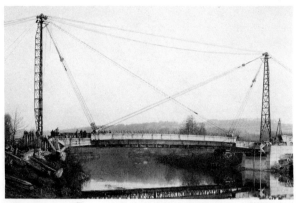

FIGURE 1.27. Luzancy Bridge over the Marne River.

FIGURE 1.28. Worms Bridge (courtesy of Dyckerhoff & Widmann).

FIGURE 1.29. Choisy-le-Roi Bridge.

for volume changes and to control differential deflections between individual cantilever arms. It is now recognized that continuity of the deck is desirable, and most structures are now continuous over several spans, bearings being provided between deck and piers for expansion.

Today, the longest box girder bridge structure that has been built in place in cantilever is the Koror Babelthuap crossing in the Pacific Trust territories with a center span of 790 ft (241 m), Figure 1.30.[12] A box girder bridge has been proposed for

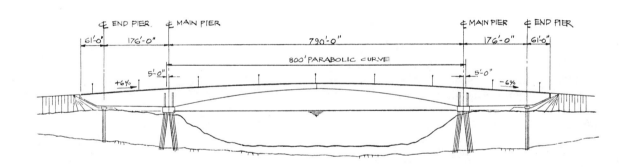

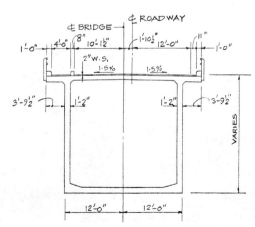

FIGURE 1.30. Koror-Babelthuap Bridge, elevation and cross section (ref. 12).

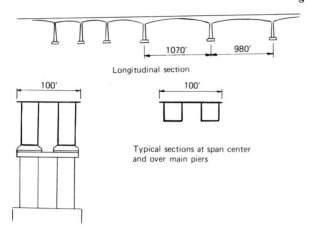

1070'   980'

Longitudinal section

100'   100'

Typical sections at span center
and over main piers

FIGURE 1.31.   The Great Belt Project.

the Great Belt Project in Denmark with a 1070 ft
(326 m) clear main span, Figure 1.31. The box
girder design has been applied with equal success to the construction of difficult and spectacular
structures such as the Saint Cloud Bridge over
the Seine River near Paris, Figure 1.32, or to the
construction of elevated structures in very congested urban areas such as the B-3 Viaducts near
Paris, Figure 1.33.

1.7.2   TRUSSES

When span length increases, the typical box girder
becomes heavy and difficult to build. For the purpose of reducing dead weight while simplifying
casting of very deep web sections, a truss with open
webs is a very satisfactory type that can be conveniently built in cantilever, Figure 1.34. The technological limitations lie in the complication of connections between prestressed diagonals and
chords. An outstanding example is the Rip Bridge
in Brisbane, Australia, Figure 1.35.

FIGURE 1.32.   Saint Cloud Bridge, France.

FIGURE 1.33.   B-3 Viaducts, France.

The cantilever method has potential applications
between the optimum span lengths of typical box
girders for the low ranges and of stayed bridges for
the high ranges.

1.7.3   FRAMES WITH SLANT LEGS

When the configuration of the site allows, the use
of inclined legs reduces the effective span length.

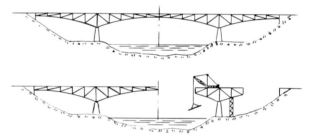

FIGURE 1.34.   Long-span concrete trusses.

FIGURE 1.35.   Rip Bridge, Brisbane, Australia.

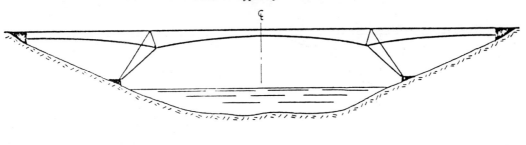

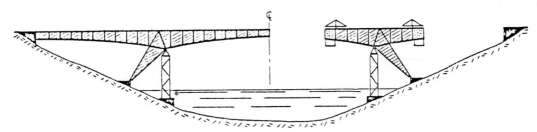

FIGURE 1.36. Long-span frame.

Provisional back stays or a temporary pier are needed to permit construction in cantilever, Figure 1.36. This requirement may sometimes present difficulty. An interesting example of such a scheme is the Bonhomme Bridge over the Blavet River in France, Figure 1.37.

The scheme is a transition between the box girder with vertical piers and the true arch, where the load is carried by the arch ribs along the pressure line with minimum bending while the deck is supported by spandrel columns.

1.7.4 CONCRETE ARCH BRIDGES

Concrete arches are an economical way to transfer loads to the ground where foundation conditions are adequate to resist horizontal loads. Eugene Freyssinet prepared a design for a 1000 meter (3280 ft) clear span 40 years ago. Because of construction difficulties, however, the maximum span built to date (1979) has been no more than 1000 ft (300 m). Construction on falsework is made difficult and risky by the effect of strong winds during construction.

The first outstanding concrete arch was built at Plougastel by Freyssinet in 1928 with three 600 ft (183 m) spans, Figure 1.38. Real progress was achieved only when free cantilever and provisional stay methods were applied to arch construction, Figure 1.39. The world record is presently the Kirk Bridge in Yugoslavia, built in cantilever and com-

FIGURE 1.37. Bonhomme Bridge.

FIGURE 1.38. Plougastel Bridge, France.

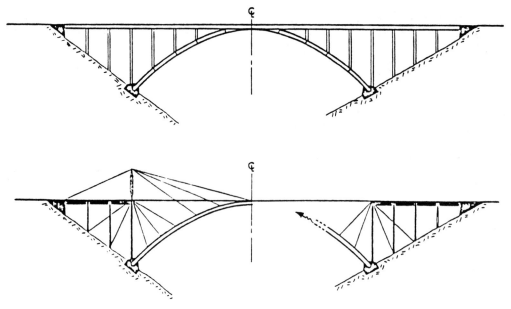

FIGURE 1.39. Concrete arches.

FIGURE 1.40. Kirk Bridges, Yugoslavia.

pleted in 1979 with a clear span of 1280 ft (390 m), Figure 1.40.

1.7.5 *CONCRETE CABLE-STAYED BRIDGES*[18]

When a span is beyond the reach of a conventional girder bridge, a logical step is to suspend the deck by a system of pylons and stays. Applied to steel structures for the last twenty years, this approach gained immediate acceptance in the field of concrete bridges when construction became possible

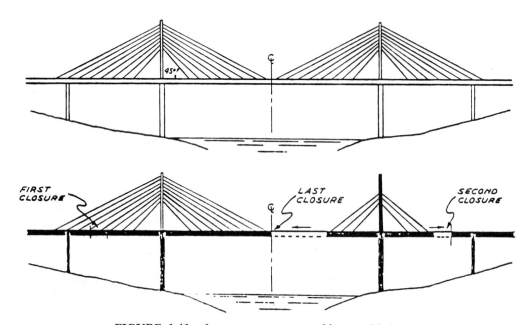

FIGURE 1.41. Long-span concrete cable-stayed bridges.

FIGURE 1.42. Brotonne Bridge, France.

and economical in balanced cantilever with a large number of stays uniformly distributed along the deck, Figure 1.41. The longest span of this type is the Brotonne Bridge in France with a 1050 ft (320 m) clear main span over the Seine River, Figure 1.42. Single pylons and one line of stays are located along the centerline of the bridge.

1.8   Cast-in-Place and Precast Segmental Construction

1.8.1   CHARACTERISTICS OF CAST-IN-PLACE SEGMENTS

In cast-in-place construction, segments are cast one after another in their final location in the structure. Special equipment is used for this purpose, such as travelers (for cantilever construction) or formwork units moved along a supporting gantry (for span-by-span construction). Each segment is reinforced with conventional untensioned steel and sometimes by transverse or vertical prestressing or both, while the assembly of segments is achieved by longitudinal post-tensioning.

Because the segments are cast end-to-end, it is not difficult to place longitudinal reinforcing steel across the joints between segments if the design calls for continuous reinforcement. Joints may be treated as required for safe transfer of all bending and shear stresses and for water tightness in aggressive climates. Connection between individual lengths of longitudinal post-tensioning ducts may be made easily at each joint and for each tendon.

The method's essential limitation is that the strength of the concrete is always on the critical path of construction and it also influences greatly the structure's deformability, particularly during construction. Deflections of a typical cast-in-place cantilever are often two or three times those of the same cantilever made of precast segments.

The local effects of concentrated forces behind the anchors of prestress tendons in a young concrete (two or four days old) are always a potential source of concern and difficulties.

1.8.2   CHARACTERISTICS OF PRECAST SEGMENTS

In precast segmental construction, segments are manufactured in a plant or near the job site, then transported to their final position for assembly. Initially, joints between segments were of conventional type: either concrete poured wet joints or dry mortar packed joints. Modern segmental construction calls for the match-casting technique, as used for the Choisy-le-Roi Bridge and further developed and refined, whereby the segments are precast against each other, preferably in the same relative order they will have in the final structure. No adjustment is therefore necessary between segments before assembly. The joints are either left dry (in areas where climate permits) or made of a very thin film of epoxy resin or mineral complex, which does not alter the match-casting properties. There is no need for any waiting period for joint cure, and final assembly of segments by prestressing may proceed as fast as practicable.

Because the joints are of negligible thickness, there is usually no mechanical connection between the individual lengths of tendon ducts at the joint.

Usually no attempt is made to obtain continuity of the longitudinal conventional steel through the joints, although several methods are available and have been applied successfully (as in the Pasco Kennewick cable-stayed bridge, for example). Segments may be precast long enough in advance of their assembly in the structure to reach sufficient strength and maturity and to minimize both the deflections during construction and the effects of concrete shrinkage and creep in the final structure.

If erection of precast segments is to proceed smoothly, a high degree of geometry control is required during match casting to ensure accuracy.

1.8.3   CHOICE BETWEEN CAST-IN-PLACE AND PRECAST CONSTRUCTION

Both cast-in-place methods and precast methods have been successfully used and produce substantially the same final structure. The choice depends on local conditions, including size of the project, time allowed for construction, restrictions on access and environment, and the equipment available to the successful contractor. Some items of interest are listed below:

1. *Speed of Construction*   Basically, cast-in-place cantilever construction proceeds at the rate of one pair of segments 10 to 20 ft (3 to 6 m) long every four to seven days. On the average, one pair of travelers permits the completion of 150 ft (46 m) of bridge deck per month, excluding the transfer from pier to pier and fabrication of the pier table. On the other hand, precast segmental construction allows a considerably faster erection schedule.

a.   For the Oleron Viaduct, the average speed of completion of the deck was 750 ft (228 m) per month for more than a year.

b.   For both the B-3 Viaducts in Paris and the Long Key Bridge in Florida, a typical 100 to 150 ft (30 to 45 m) span was erected in two working days, representing a construction of 1300 ft (400 m) of finished bridge per month,

c.   Saint Cloud Bridge near Paris, despite the exceptional difficulty of its geometry and design scheme, was constructed in exactly one year, its total area amounting to 250,000 sq ft (23,600 sq m).

It is evident, then, that cast-in-place cantilever construction is basically a slow process, while precast segmental with matching joints is among the fastest.

2. *Investment in Special Equipment*   Here the situation is usually reversed. Cast-in-place requires usually a lower investment, which makes it competitive on short structures with long spans [for example, a typical three-span structure with a center span in excess of approximately 350 ft (100 m)].

In long, repetitive structures precast segmental may be more economical than cast-in-place. For the Chillon Viaducts with twin structures 7000 ft (2134 m) long in a difficult environment, a detailed comparative estimate showed the cast-in-place method to be 10% more expensive than the precast.

3. *Size and Weight of Segments*   Precast segmental is limited by the capacity of transportation and placing equipment. Segments exceeding 250 tons are seldom economical. Cast-in-place construction does not have the same limitation, al-

though the weight and cost of the travelers are directly proportional to the weight of the heaviest segment.

4. *Environment Restrictions*   Both precast and cast-in-place segmental permit all work to be performed from the top. Precast, however, adjusts more easily to restrictions such as allowing work to proceed over traffic or allowing access of workmen and materials to the various piers.

1.9   *Various Methods of Construction*

Probably the most significant classification of segmental bridges is by method of construction. Although construction methods may be as varied as the ingenuity of the designers and contractors, they fall into four basic categories: (1) balanced cantilever, (2) span-by-span construction, (3) progressive placement construction, and (4) incremental launching or push-out construction.

1.9.1   *CAST-IN-PLACE BALANCED CANTILEVER*

The balanced or free cantilever construction concept was originally developed to eliminate falsework. Temporary shoring not only is expensive but can be a hazard in the case of sudden floods, as confirmed by many failures. Over navigable waterways or traveled highways or railways, falsework is either not allowed or severely restricted. Cantilever construction, whether cast in place or precast, eliminates such difficulties: construction may proceed from the permanent piers, and the structure is self-supporting at all stages. The basic principle of the method was outlined in Section 1.1 (Figure 1.3).

In cast-in-place construction the formwork is supported from a movable form carrier, Figure 1.1. Details of the form travelers are shown in Figure 1.43. The form traveler moves forward on rails attached to the deck of the completed structure and is anchored to the deck at the rear. With the form traveler in place, a new segment is formed, cast, and stressed to the previously constructed segment. In some instances a covering may be provided on the form carrier so that work may proceed during inclement weather, Figure 1.44.

The operation sequence in cast-in-place balanced cantilever construction is as follows:

1.   Setting up and adjusting carrier.
2.   Setting up and aligning forms.

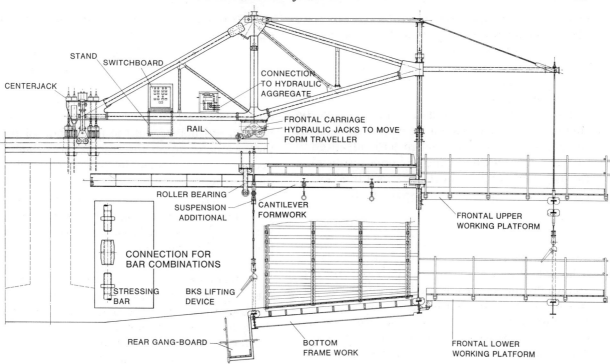

FIGURE 1.43.   Form traveler (courtesy of Dyckerhoff & Widmann).

3. Placing reinforcement and tendon ducts.

4. Concreting.

5. Inserting prestress tendons in the segment and stressing.

6. Removing the formwork.

7. Moving the form carrier to the next position and starting a new cycle.

Initially, the normal construction time for a segment was one week per formwork unit. Advances in precast segmental construction have been applied recently to the cast-in-place method in order to reduce the cycle of operations and increase the efficiency of the travelers. With today's technology it does not seem possible to reduce the construction time for a full cycle below two working days, and this only for a very simple structure with constant cross section and a moderate amount of reinforcing and prestress. For a structure with variable depth and longer spans, say above 250 ft (75 m), the typical cycle is more realistically three to four working days.

Where a long viaduct type structure is to be constructed of cast-in-place segments, an auxiliary steel girder may be used to support the formwork, Figure 1.45, as on the Siegtal Bridge. This equip-

FIGURE 1.44.   Bendorf Bridge form traveler (courtesy of Dyckerhoff & Widmann).

FIGURE 1.45.   Siegtal Bridge, use of an auxiliary truss in cast-in-place construction.

ment may also be used to stabilize the free-standing pier by the anchoring of the auxiliary steel girder to the completed portion of the structure. Normally, in construction using the form traveler previously described, a portion of the end spans (near the abutments) must be cast on falsework. If the auxiliary steel girder is used, this operation may be eliminated. As soon as a double typical cantilever is completed, the auxiliary steel girder is advanced to the next pier. Obviously, the economic justification for use of an auxiliary steel girder is a function of the number of spans and the span length.

1.9.2. PRECAST BALANCED CANTILEVER

For the first precast segmental bridges in Paris (Choisy-le-Roi, Courbevoie, and so on, 1961 to 1965) a floating crane was used to transfer the precast segments from the casting yard to the barges that transported them to the project site and was used again to place the segments in the structure. The concept of self-operating launching gantries was developed shortly thereafter for the construction of the Oleron Viaduct (1964 to 1966). Further refined and extended in its potential, this concept has been used in many large structures.

The erection options available can be adapted to almost all construction sites.

1. *Crane Placing* Truck or crawler cranes are used on land where feasible; floating cranes may be used for a bridge over navigable water, Figure 1.46. Where site conditions allow, a portal crane may be used on the full length of the deck, preferably with a casting yard aligned with the deck near

FIGURE 1.46. Segment erection by barge-mounted crane, Capt. Cook Bridge, Australia (courtesy of G. Beloff, Main Roads Department, Brisbane, Australia).

one abutment to minimize the number of handling operations, Figure 1.47.

2. *Beam and Winch Method* If access by land or water is available under the bridge deck, or at least around all permanent piers, segments may be lifted into place by hoists secured atop the previously placed segments, Figure 1.48. At first this method did not permit the installation of precast pier segments upon the bridge piers, but it has been improved to solve this problem, as will be explained later.

3. *Launching Gantries* There are essentially two families of launching gantries, the details of which will be discussed in a later chapter. Here we briefly outline their use.

In the first family developed for the Oleron Viaduct, Figures 1.49 and 1.50, the launching gantry is slightly more than the typical span length, and the gantry's rear support reaction is applied near the far end of the last completed cantilever. All segments are brought onto the finished deck and placed by the launching gantry in balanced cantilever; after completion of a cantilever, after placing the precast segment over the new pier, the launching gantry launches itself to the next span to start a new cycle of operations.

In the second family, developed for the Deventer Bridge in Holland and for the Rio Niteroi Bridge in Brazil, the launching gantry has a length approximately twice the typical span, and the reaction of the legs is always applied above the permanent concrete piers, Figures 1.51 and 1.52.

Placing segments with a launching gantry is now in most cases the most elegant and efficient method, allowing the least disturbance to the environment.

1.9.3 SPAN-BY-SPAN CONSTRUCTION

The balanced cantilever construction method was developed primarily for long spans, so that construction activity for the superstructure could be accomplished at deck level without the use of extensive falsework. A similar need in the case of long viaduct structures with relatively shorter spans has been filled by the development of a span-by-span methodology using a form traveler. The following discussion explains this methodology.[13,14,15,16]

In long viaduct structures a segmental span-by-span construction may be particularly advantageous. The superstructure is executed in one direc-

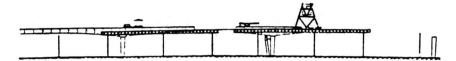

COUPE TRANSVERSALE

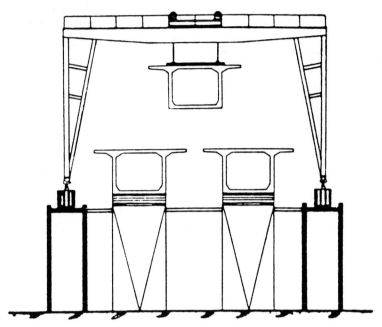

FIGURE 1.47. Mirabeau Bridge at Tours, France.

tion, span by span, by means of a form traveler, Figure 1.53, with construction joints or hinges located at the point of contraflexure. The form carrier in effect provides a type of factory operation transplanted to the job site. It has many of the advantages of mass production commonly associated with precast plant operations as well as the added advantage of permitting versatile adjustments in

FIGURE 1.48. Hoist placing at Pierre Benite Bridges, France.

the field. The form traveler may be supported on the piers, or from the edge of the previously completed construction, at the joint location, and at the forward pier. In some instances, as in the approaches of Rheinbrücke, Düsseldorf-Flehe, the movable formwork may be supported from the ground, Figure 1.54. The form traveler consists of a steel superstructure, which is moved from the completed portion of the structure to the next span to be cast. For an above-deck carrier, large formwork elements are suspended from steel rods during concreting. After concreting and post-tensioning, the forms are released and rolled forward by means of the structural steel outriggers on both sides of the form traveler's superstructure. For a below-deck carrier, a similar procedure is followed.

Many long bridges of this type have been built in Germany, France, and other countries. Typical construction time for a 100 ft (30 m) span superstructure is five to eight working days, depending upon the complexity of the structure. Deck configuration for this type of construction is usually a monolithic slab and girder (T beam or double T), box girder, or a mushroom cross sec-

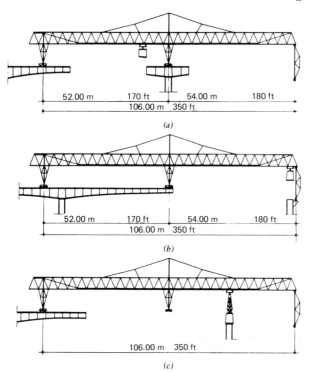

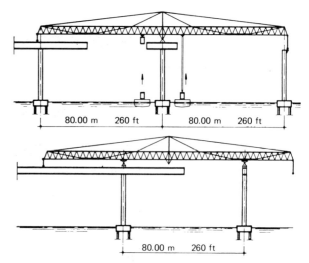

FIGURE 1.51. Second family of launching gantries, Rio Niteroi Bridge.

FIGURE 1.49. First family of launching gantries (Oleron Viaduct).

span. Prestressing tendons then assure the assembly of the various segments in one span while achieving full continuity with the preceding span, Figures 1.55 and 1.56. The floating crane used to place the segments over the truss also moves the truss from span to span. The contractor for the Seven Mile Bridge modified the erection scheme from that used for Long Key Bridge by suspending a span of segments from an overhead falsework truss. This is the first application of a method that seems to have a great potential for trestle structures in terms of speed of construction and economy.

tion. This method has been used recently in the United States on the Denny Creek project in the state of Washington.

In its initial form, as described above, the span-by-span method is a cast-in-place technique. The same principle has been applied in conjunction with precast segmental construction for two very large structures in the Florida Keys: Long Key Bridge and Seven Mile Bridge, with spans of 118 ft (36 m) and 135 ft (40 m), respectively. Segments are assembled on a steel truss to make a complete

1.9.4 PROGRESSIVE PLACEMENT CONSTRUCTION

Progressive placement is similar to the span-by-span method in that construction starts at one end of the structure and proceeds continuously to the

FIGURE 1.50. Placing precast segments on the Oleron Viaduct.

FIGURE 1.52. Rio Niteroi launching girder.

FIGURE 1.53. Span-by-span construction using a form traveler (courtesy of Ulrich Finsterwalder).

FIGURE 1.54. Form traveler supported from the ground, Düsseldorf-Flehe Bridge.

_ PRINCIPE DE POSE _

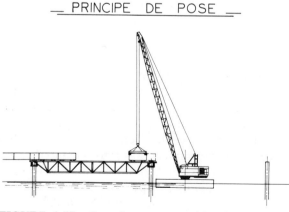

FIGURE 1.55. Span-by-span assembly of precast segments.

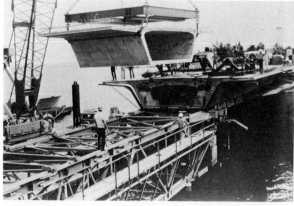

FIGURE 1.56. Placing segments on assembly truss for Long Key Bridge.

other end. It derives its origin, however, from the cantilever concept. In progressive placement the precast segments are placed from one end of the structure to the other in successive cantilevers on the same side of the various piers rather than by balanced cantilevers on each side of a pier. At present, this method appears practicable and economical in spans ranging from 100 to 300 ft (30 to 90 m).

Because of the length of cantilever (one span) in relation to construction depth, a movable temporary stay arrangement must be used to limit the cantilever stresses during construction to a reasonable level. The erection procedure is illustrated in Figure 1.57. Segments are transported over the completed portion of the deck to the tip of the cantilever span under construction, where they are positioned by a swivel crane that proceeds from one segment to the next. Approximately one-third of the span from the pier may be erected by the free cantilever method, the segments being held in position by exterior temporary ties and final prestressing tendons. For the remaining two-thirds of the span, each segment is held in position by temporary external ties and by two stays passing through a tower located over the preceding piers. All stays are continuous through the tower and anchored in the previously completed deck structure. The stays are anchored to the top flange of the box girder segments so that the tension in the stays can be adjusted by light jacks.

Used for the first time in France on several structures, Figure 1.58, progressive placement is being applied in the United States for the construction of the Linn Cove Viaduct in North Carolina. In this bridge the precast pier construction proceeds also from the deck to solve a difficult problem of environmental restrictions.

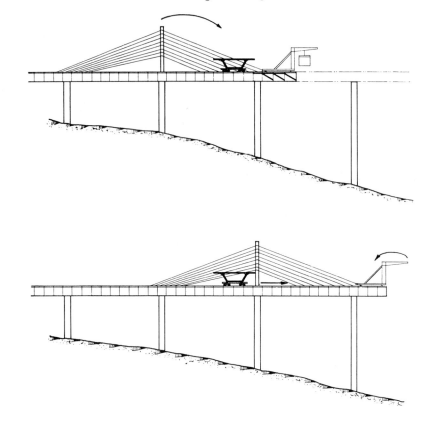

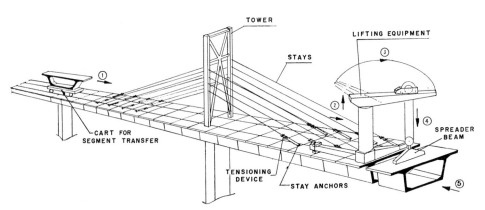

FIGURE 1.57. Progressive placement erection procedure.

The progressive placement method may also be applied to cast-in-place construction.

1.9.5. INCREMENTAL LAUNCHING OR PUSH-OUT CONSTRUCTION

This concept was first implemented on the Rio Caroni Bridge in Venezuela, built in 1962 and 1963 by its originators, Willi Baur and Dr. Fritz Leonhardt of the consulting firm of Leonhardt and Andra (Stuttgart, Germany).[17]

Segments of the bridge superstructure are cast in place in lengths of 30 to 100 ft (10 to 30 m) in stationary forms located behind the abutment(s), Figure 1.59. Each unit is cast directly against the previous unit. After sufficient concrete strength is reached, the new unit is post-tensioned to the previous one. The assembly of units is pushed forward in a stepwise manner to permit casting of the succeeding segments, Figure 1.60. Normally a work cycle of one week is required to cast and launch a segment, regardless of its length. Operations are

FIGURE 1.58. Fontenoy Bridge, progressive placing construction.

scheduled so that the concrete can attain sufficient strength over a weekend to allow launching at the beginning of the next week. Generally, fabrication in the on-site factory can be done in the open, although in inclement weather a protective covering may be provided.

Bridge alignment in this type of construction may be either straight or curved; however, the curve must have a constant radius. This requirement of constant rate of curvature applies to both horizontal and vertical curvature. The Val Ristel Bridge in Italy, which was incrementally launched on a radius of 492 ft (150 m), is illustrated in Figure 1.61. Roadway geometry thus is dictated by construction, as opposed to the present practice in the United States, in which construction is dictated by geometry.

To allow the superstructure to move forward, special low-friction sliding bearings are provided at the various piers with proper lateral guides. The main problem is to insure the resistance of the

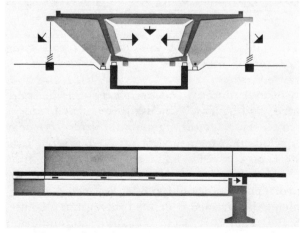

FIGURE 1.59. Casting bed and launching arrangement (courtesy of Prof. Fritz Leonhardt).

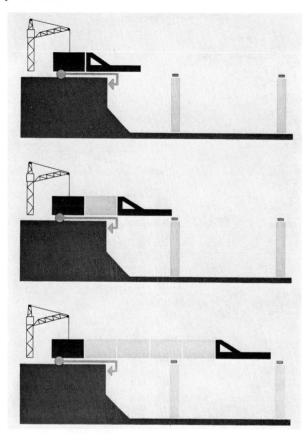

FIGURE 1.60. Incremental launching sequence (courtesy of Prof. Fritz Leonhardt).

superstructure under its own weight at all stages of launching and in all sections. Four methods for this purpose are used in conjunction with one another.

1. A first-stage prestress is applied concentrically to the entire cross section and in successive increments over the entire length of the superstructure.

2. To reduce the large negative bending moments in the front (particularly just before the superstructure reaches a new pier) a fabricated structural steel launching nose is attached to the lead segment, Figure 1.62.

3. Long spans may be subdivided by means of temporary piers to keep bending moments to a reasonable magnitude. This construction technique has been applied to spans up to 200 ft (60 m) without the use of temporary falsework bents. Spans up to 330 ft (100 m) have been built using temporary supporting bents. The girders must have a constant depth, which is usually one-twelfth to one-sixteenth of the longest span.

4. Another method has been used successfully in France to control bending moments in the

FIGURE 1.61. Incremental launching on a curve (courtesy of Prof. Fritz Leonhardt).

FIGURE 1.62. Steel launching nose (courtesy of Prof. Fritz Leonhardt).

deck in the forward part of the superstructure. A system using a tower and provisional stays is attached to the front part of the superstructure. The tension of the stays and the corresponding reaction of the tower on the deck are automatically and continuously controlled during all launching operations to optimize the stress distribution in the deck, Figure 1.63.

After launching is complete, and the opposite abutment has been reached, additional prestressing is added to accommodate moments in the final structure, while the original uniform prestress must resist the varying moments that occur as the superstructure is pushed over the piers to its final position.

Today, the longest incrementally launched clear span is over the River Danube near Worth, Germany, with a maximum span length of 550 ft (168 m). Two temporary piers were used in the river for launching. The longest bridge of this type is the Olifant's River railway viaduct in South Africa with 23 spans of 147 ft (45 m) and a total length of 3400

ft (1035 m). The incremental launching technique was used successfully for the first time in the United States for the construction of the Wabash River Bridge at Covington, Indiana.

1.10 Applications of Segmental Construction in the United States

The state of the art of designing and constructing prestressed concrete segmental bridges has advanced greatly in recent years. A wide variety of structural concepts and prestressing methods are used, and at least a thousand segmental bridges have been built throughout the world. We may conclude that segmental prestressed concrete construction is a viable method for building highway bridges. There are currently no known major problems that should inhibit utilization of segmental prestressed concrete bridges in the United States. They have been successfully consummated in other countries and are increasingly being employed in the United States.

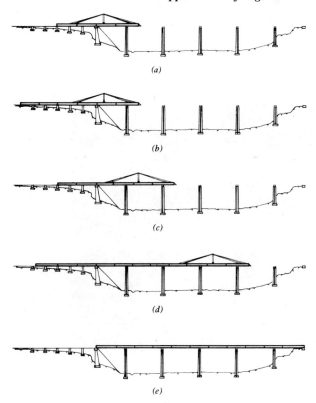

(a)

(b)

(c)

(d)

(e)

FIGURE 1.63. Incremental launching with provisional tower and stays.

FIGURE 1.64. Three Sisters Bridge.

One of the earliest projects for which segmental construction was considered was the proposed Interstate I-266 Potomac River Crossing in Washington, D.C., Figure 1.64, otherwise known as the Three Sisters Bridge. This structure contemplated a 750 ft (229 m) center span with side spans of 440 ft (134 m) on reverse five-degree curves, built with cast-in-place segmental construction. Because of environmental objections, this project never reached fruition.

The JFK Memorial Causeway (Intracoastal Waterway), Corpus Christi, Texas, Figure 1.65, represents the first precast, prestressed, segmental, balanced cantilever construction completed in the United States. It was opened to traffic in 1973. Designed by the Bridge Division of the Texas Highway Department, it has a center span of 200 ft (61 m) with end spans of 100 ft (30.5 m).

The first cast-in-place, segmental, balanced cantilever, prestressed concrete bridge constructed in the United States is the Pine Valley Bridge in California, on Interstate I-8 about 40 miles (64 km) east of San Diego. Designed by the California Department of Transportation, the dual structure, Figure 1.66, has a total length of 1716 ft (53.6 m)

FIGURE 1.65. JFK Memorial Causeway, Corpus Christi, Texas.

FIGURE 1.66. Pine Valley Bridge (courtesy of CALTRANS).

FIGURE 1.67.   Rendering of Houston Ship Channel Bridge.

with spans of 270, 340, 450, 380, and 276 ft (82.3, 103.6, 137.2, 115.8, and 84.1 m).

As indicated previously, numerous segmental bridge projects have been constructed or are contemplated in the United States. Many of them will be discussed in detail in the following chapters. Among the most significant are the Houston Ship Channel Bridge with a clear span of 750 ft (228 m), which will be the longest concrete span in the Americas, Figure 1.67, and the Seven Mile Bridge, which will be the longest segmental bridge in North America, Figure 1.68.

FIGURE 1.68.   Rendering of Seven Mile Bridge.

1.11   Applicability and Advantages of Segmental Construction

Segmental construction has extended the practical range of span lengths for concrete bridges. Practical considerations of handling and shipping limit the prestressed I-girder type of bridge construction to spans of about 120 to 150 ft (37 to 46 m). Beyond this range, post-tensioned cast-in-place box girders on falsework are the only viable concrete alternative. At many sites, however, falsework is not practical or even feasible, as when crossing deep ravines or large navigable waterways. Falsework construction also has a serious impact upon environment and ecology.

Prestressed concrete segmental construction has been developed to solve these problems while extending the practical span of concrete bridges to about 800 ft (250 m) or even 1000 ft (300 m). With cable-stayed structures the span range can be extended to 1300 ft (400 m) and perhaps longer with the materials available today.[13] Table 1.1 summarizes the range of application of various forms of construction by span lengths.

Although the design and construction of very-long-span concrete segmental structures pose an important challenge, segmental techniques may

TABLE 1.1   Range of Application of Bridge Type by Span Lengths[a]

Span	Bridge Types
0– 150 ft	I-type pretensioned girder
100– 300 ft	Cast-in-place post-tensioned box girder
100– 300 ft	Precast balanced cantilever segmental, constant depth
250– 600 ft	Precast balanced cantilever segmental, variable depth
200–1000 ft	Cast-in-place cantilever segmental
800–1500 ft	Cable-stay with balanced cantilever segmental

[a] 1 ft = 0.3048 m.

find even more important applications in moderate span lengths and less spectacular structures. Especially in difficult urban areas or ecology-sensitive sites, segmental structures have proven to be a valuable asset.

Today most sites for new bridges can be adapted for segmental concrete construction. The principal advantages of segmental construction may be summarized as follows:

1. Segmental construction is an efficient and economical method for a large range of span lengths and types of structure. Structures with sharp curves and variable superelevation may be easily accommodated.

2. Concrete segmental construction often provides for the lowest investment cost. Savings of 10 to 20% over conventional methods have been realized by competitive bidding on alternate designs or by realistic cost comparisons.

3. Segmental construction permits a reduction of construction time. This is particularly true for precast methods, where segments may be manufactured while substructure work proceeds and be assembled rapidly thereafter. Further cost savings ensue from the lessening of the influence of inflation on total construction costs.

4. Segmental construction protects the environment. Segmental viaduct-type bridges can minimize the impact of highway construction through environmentally sensitive areas. Whereas conventional cut-and-fill type highway construction can scar the environment and impede wildlife migration, an elevated viaduct-type structure requires only a relatively narrow path along the alignment to provide access for pier construction. Once the piers have been constructed, all construction activity proceeds from above. Thus, the impact on the environment is minimized.

5. Interference with existing traffic during construction is significantly reduced, and expensive detours can be eliminated. Figure 1.69 indicates how precast segments may be handled while traffic is maintained with a minimum disturbance.

6. Segmental construction contributes toward aesthetically pleasing structures in many different sites. A long approach viaduct (Brotonne, Figure 1.70), a curved bridge over a river (Saint Cloud, Figure 1.71), or an impressive viaduct over a deep valley (Pine Valley, Figure 1.66) are some examples where nature accepts human endeavor in spite of its imperfections.

7. Materials and labor are usually available locally for segmental construction. The overall labor requirement is less than for conventional construction methods. For the precast option a major part of the work force on site is replaced by plant labor.

8. As a consequence, quality control is easier to perform and high-quality work may be expected.

9. Segmental bridges when properly designed and when constructed by competent contractors under proper supervision will prove to be practically free of maintenance for many years. Only bearings and expansion joints (usually very few for continuous decks) need to be controlled at regular intervals.

FIGURE 1.69. Saint Cloud Bridge, segments placed over traffic.

FIGURE 1.70. Brotonne Bridge approach.

10. During construction, the technique shows an exceptionally high record of safety.

Precast segmental construction today is competitive in a wide range of applications with other materials and construction methods, while it adds a further refinement to the recognized advantages of prestressed concrete.

FIGURE 1.71. Saint Cloud Bridge, France, curved bridge over a river.

References

1. H. G. Tyrrell, *History of Bridge Engineering*, Henry G. Tyrrell, Chicago, 1911.

2. Elizabeth B. Mock, *The Architecture of Bridges*, The Museum of Modern Art, New York, 1949.

3. T. Y. Lin, *Design of Prestressed Concrete Structures*, John Wiley & Sons, Inc., New York, 1958.

4. Anon., "Highway Design and Operational Practices Related to Highway Safety," Report of the Special AASHO Traffic Safety Committee, February 1967.

5. Anon., *Prestressed Concrete for Long Span Bridges*, Prestressed Concrete Institute, Chicago, 1968.

6. Anon., "Long Spans with Standard Bridge Girders," *PCI Bridge Bulletin*, March–April 1967, Prestressed Concrete Institute, Chicago.

7. "Recommended Practice for Segmental Construction in Prestressed Concrete," Report by PCI Committee on Segmental Construction, *Journal of the Prestressed Concrete Institute*, Vol. 20, No. 2, March–April 1975.

8. Ulrich Finsterwalder, "Prestressed Concrete Bridge Construction," *Journal of the American Concrete Institute*, Vol. 62, No. 9, September 1965.

9. F. Leonhardt, "Long Span Prestressed Concrete Bridges in Europe," *Journal of the Prestressed Concrete Institute*, Vol. 10, No. 1, February 1965.

10. Jean Muller, "Long-Span Precast Prestressed Concrete Bridges Built in Cantilever," *First International Symposium, Concrete Bridge Design*, ACI Publication SP-23, Paper 23–40, American Concrete Institute, Detroit, 1969.

11. Jean Muller, "Ten Years of Experience in Precast Segmental Construction," *Journal of the Prestressed Concrete Institute*, Vol. 20, No. 1, January–February 1975.

12. Man-Chung Tang, "Koror-Babelthuap Bridge—A World Record Span," Preprint Paper 3441, ASCE Convention, Chicago, October 16–20, 1978.

13. C. A. Ballinger, W. Podolny, Jr., and M. J. Abrahams, "A Report on the Design and Construction of Segmental Prestressed Concrete Bridges in Western Europe—1977," International Road Federation, Washington, D.C., June 1978. (Also available from Federal Highway Administration, Offices of Research and Development, Washington, D.C., Report No. FHWA-RD-78-44.)

14. Ulrich Finsterwalder, "New Developments in Prestressing Methods and Concrete Bridge Construction," *Dywidag-Berichte*, 4-1967, September 1967, Dyckerhoff & Widmann KG, Munich, Germany.

15. Ulrich Finsterwalder, "Free-Cantilever Construction of Prestressed Concrete Bridges and Mushroom-Shaped Bridges," *First International Symposium, Concrete Bridge Design*, ACI Publication SP-23, Paper SP 23-26, American Concrete Institute, Detroit, 1969.

16. C. A. Ballinger and W. Podolny, Jr., "Segmental Construction in Western Europe—Impressions of an IRF Study Team," *Proceedings*, Conference conducted by Transportation Research Board, National Academy of Sciences, Washington, D.C., TRR 665, Vol. 2, September 1978.

17. Willi Baur, "Bridge Erection by Launching is Fast, Safe, and Efficient," *Civil Engineering—ASCE*, Vol. 47, No. 3, March 1977.

18. Walter Podolny, Jr., and J. B. Scalzi, "Construction and Design of Cable-Stayed Bridges," John Wiley & Sons, Inc., New York, 1976.

2

Cast-in-Place Balanced Cantilever Girder Bridges

2.1 Introduction

Developed initially for steel structures, cantilever construction was used for reinforced concrete bridges as early as fifty years ago. In 1928, Freyssinet used the cantilever concept to construct the springings of the arch rib in the Plougastel Bridge, Figure 2.1. The reactions and overturning moments applied by the falsework to the lower part of the arch ribs were balanced by steel ties connecting the two short cantilevers. A provisional prestress was thus applied by the ties to the arch ribs with the aid of jacks and deviation saddles.

The first application of balanced cantilever construction in a form closely resembling its present one is due to a Brazilian engineer, E. Baumgart, who designed and built the Herval Bridge over the Rio Peixe in Brazil in 1930. The 220 ft (68 m) center span was constructed by the cantilever method in reinforced concrete with steel rods extended at the various stages of construction by threaded couplers. Several other structures fol-

lowed in various countries, particularly in France. Albert Caquot, a leading engineer of his time, built several reinforced concrete bridges in cantilever. Shown in Figures 2.2 through 2.4 is Bezons Bridge over the River Seine near Paris, with a clear center span of 310 ft (95 m), being constructed in successive cantilever segments with auxiliary trusses. This bridge design was prepared in 1942. The method was not widely used at that time, because the excessive amount of reinforcing steel

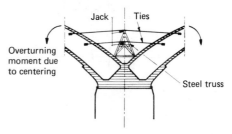

FIGURE 2.1. Cantilever construction of arch springings for Plougastel Bridge, France.

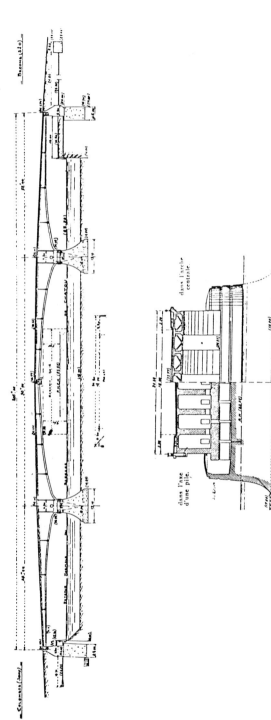

FIGURE 2.2. Bezons Bridge over the Seine River, France, typical longitudinal and transverse sections.

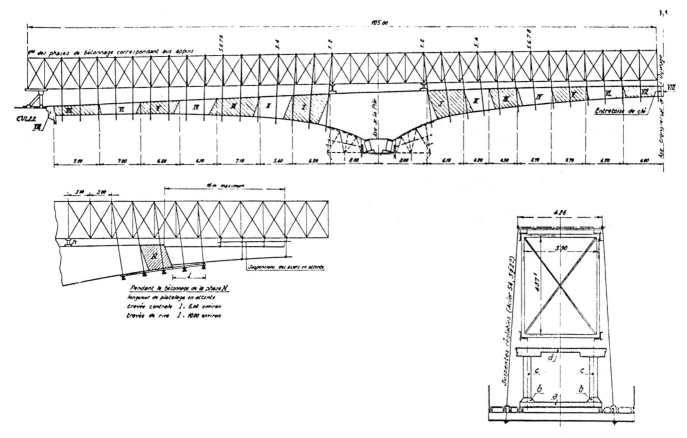

FIGURE 2.3. Bezons Bridge, construction procedure.

required to balance the cantilever moments produced the tendency toward cracking inherent in an overreinforced slab subject to permanent tensile stresses.

The introduction of prestressing in concrete structures dramatically changed the situation.

Used successfully in 1950 and 1951 by Finsterwalder with the German firm of Dyckerhoff & Widmann for the construction of the two bridges of Balduinstein and Neckarrews, balanced cantilever construction of prestressed concrete bridges experienced a continuous popularity in Germany

FIGURE 2.4. Bezons Bridges under construction.

FIGURE 2.5. La Voulte Bridge, France.

and surrounding countries. Nicolas Esquillan designed and built a large bridge by the cantilever method over the Rhine River in France, La Voulte Bridge (1952), where an overhead truss was used during construction, Figure 2.5.

Between 1950 and 1965 more than 300 such bridges were constructed in Europe alone. Initially all structures were prestressed by high-strength bars, and hinges were provided at the center of the various spans. Later other prestressing methods with parallel wire or strand tendons were also used. More important, a significant improvement in structural behavior and long-term performance was made possible by the achievement of deck continuity between the various cantilever arms. The first cantilever bridges with continuous decks were designed and built in France in 1962: the Lacroix Falgarde Bridge and Bouguen Bridge, Figures 2.6 and 2.22. Subsequently, the advantages of continuity were recognized and accepted in many countries.

From 1968 to 1970 cantilever construction was considered for the Three Sisters Bridge in Washington, D.C., Figure 1.64. This project never reached the construction stage. The first cast-in-place balanced cantilever segmental bridge built in the United States is the Pine Valley Creek Bridge in California (1972 to 1974), Figure 2.7. To date, all segmental bridges constructed in the United States have been either precast or cast-in-place cantilever construction, with the following exceptions:

Wabash River Bridge, incrementally launched (Chapter 7)

Denny Creek and Florida Keys Bridges, span-by-span construction (Chapter 6)

FIGURE 2.6. Bouguen Bridge in Brest, France. First continuous rigid-frame structure built in balanced cantilever.

FIGURE 2.7. Pine Valley Creek Bridge.

Linn Cove Viaduct, progressive placement construction (Chapter 6)

The balanced cantilever method of construction has already been briefly described. In this chapter we shall see how this method has been implemented on various structures before we go on to consider specific design and technological aspects.

2.2 *Bendorf Bridge, Germany*

An early and outstanding example of the cast-in-place balanced cantilever bridge is the Bendorf autobahn bridge over the Rhine River about 5 miles (8 km) north of Koblenz, West Germany. Built in 1964, this structure, Figure 2.8, has a total length of 3378 ft (1029.7 m) with a navigation span of 682 ft (208 m). The design competition allowed the competing firms to choose the material, configuration, and design of the structure. Navigation requirements on the Rhine River dictated a 328 ft (100 m) wide channel during construction and a final channel width of 672 ft (205 m). The winning design was a dual structure of cast-in-place concrete segmental box girder construction, consummated in two distinct portions. In part one

FIGURE 2.8. Bendorf Bridge (courtesy of Dyckerhoff & Widmann).

(west) are the river spans consisting of a symmetrical seven-span continuous girder with an overall length of 1721 ft (524.7 m). In part two (east) are the nine-span continuous approach girders with the spans ranging from 134.5 ft (41 m) to 308 ft (94 m) and having an overall length of 1657 ft (505 m), Figures 2.9 and 2.10.

The continuous, seven-span, main river structure consists of twin, independent, single-cell box girders. Total width of the bridge cross section is 101 ft (30.86 m). Each single-cell box has a top flange width of 43.3 ft (13.2 m), a bottom flange width of 23.6 ft (7.2 m), and webs with a constant thickness of 1.2 ft (0.37 m). Girder depth is 34.28 ft (10.45 m) at the pier and 14.44 ft (4.4 m) at midspan representing, with respect to the main span, a depth-to-span ratio of 1/20 and 1/47, respectively. Girder depth of the end of this seven-span unit reduced to 10.8 ft (3.3 m). The main navigation span has a hinge at midspan that is de-

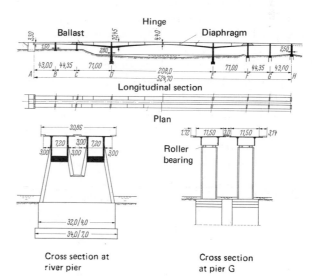

FIGURE 2.9. Bendorf Bridge, Part One (West), longitudinal section, plan, and cross sections at the river pier and pier G, from ref. 1 (courtesy of Beton- und Stahlbetonbau).

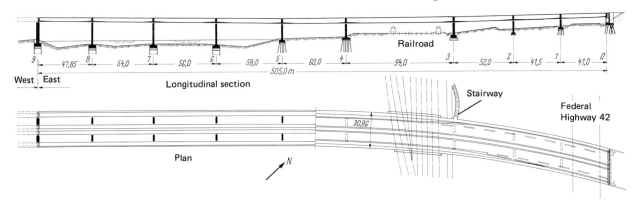

FIGURE 2.10. Bendorf Bridge, Part Two (East), longitudinal section and plan, from ref. 1 (courtesy of Beton- und Stahlbetonbau).

signed to transmit shear and torsion forces only, thus allowing the superstructure to be cast monolithically with the main piers.[1,2] After construction of the piers, the superstructure over the navigable portion of the Rhine was completed within one year. The repetition of the procedure in 240 segments executed one after the other offered numerous occasions to mechanize and improve the erection method.[3,4]

The deck slab has a longitudinally varying thickness from 11 in. (279.4 mm) at midspan to 16.5 in. (419 mm) at the piers. The bottom flange varies in thickness from 6 in. (152 mm) at midspan to 7.87 ft (2.4 m) at the piers. To reduce dead-weight bending-moment stresses in the bottom flange concrete, compression reinforcement was used extensively in regions away from the piers. Thicknesses of the various elements of the cross section are controlled partly by stress requirements and partly by clearance requirements of the tendons and anchorages.

The structure is three-dimensionally prestressed: longitudinal prestressing uniformly distributed across the cross section; transverse prestressing in the top flange; and inclined prestressing in the webs. A total of 560 Dywidag bars $1\frac{1}{4}$ in. (32 mm) in diameter resists the negative bending moment produced by a half-span, Figure 2.11.

The maximum concrete compressive stress in the bottom flange at the pier is 1800 psi (12.4 MPa). As a result of the three-dimensional prestress the tensile stresses in the concrete were negligible. The longitudinal prestressing is incrementally decreased from the pier to the hinge at midspan and to the adjacent piers; thus, shear stresses in the webs on both sides of the main piers are almost constant. Therefore, the web thickness remains constant and the diagonal prestressing remains very nearly constant.

Construction began on March 1, 1962. After completion of the foundations and piers, balanced cantilever operations began from the west river pier in July 1963 and were completed at the end of that year. Segments were 12 ft (3.65 m) in length in the river span and 11.4 ft (3.48 m) in the remaining spans. Segments were cast on a weekly cycle. As the segments became shallower, the construction cycle was advanced to two segments per week. During winter months, to protect operations from inclement weather, the form traveler was provided with an enclosure, Figure 2.12.

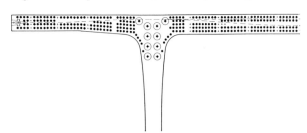

FIGURE 2.11. Bendorf Bridge, cross section showing tendons in the deck, ref. 2, (courtesy of the American Concrete Institute).

FIGURE 2.12. Bendorf Bridge, protective covering for form traveler (courtesy of Ulrich Finsterwalder).

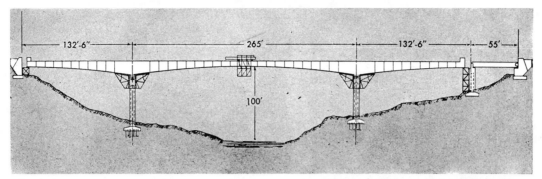

FIGURE 2.13.   Ste. Adele Bridge, elevation, from ref. 5 (courtesy of *Engineering News-Record*).

In the construction of the approach spans, the five spans from the east abutment were built in a routine manner with the assistance of falsework bents. The four spans over water were constructed by a progressive placement cantilever method (see Chapter 6), which employed a temporary cable-stay arrangement to reduce the cantilever stresses.

2.3   Saint Adele Bridge, Canada

This structure, built in 1964 (the same year as the Bendorf Bridge), represents the first segmental bridge, in the contemporary sense, constructed in North America. It crosses the River of the Mules near Ste. Adele, Quebec, and is part of the Laurentian Autoroute. It is a single-cell box girder continuous three-span dual structure with a center span of 265 ft (80.8 m) and end spans of 132 ft 6 in. (40.4 m), Figure 2.13. At one end is a prestressed concrete 55 ft (16.8 m) simple span. The bridge has a 100 ft (30.5 m) vertical clearance over the river in the canyon below.

The variable-depth girder is 16 ft 3 ⅜ in. (4.96 m) deep at the piers and 6 ft (1.83 m) deep at midspan and its extremities, Figure 2.14. Each dual structure consists of a single-cell rectangular box 23 ft (7 m) wide with the top flange cantilevering on each side 9 ft (2.75 m) for a total width of 41 ft (12.5 m), Figure 2.15, providing three traffic lanes in each direction. Thickness of bottom flange, webs, and top flange are respectively 1 ft 1¾ in. (0.35 m), 1 ft 6 in. (0.46 m), and 1 ft (0.3 m).[5]

A total of 70 prestressing tendons were required in each girder. Each tendon of the SEEE system consists of seven strands of seven 0.142 in. (3.6 mm) wires. The seven strands are splayed out through a steel ring in the anchorage and held in a circular pattern by steel wedges between each of the strands. The number of tendons anchored off at each segment end varies with the distance from the pier, increasing from an initial six tendons to eight tendons at the eighth segment, then decreasing to two tendons at the eleventh segment at midspan. There are an additional 44 positive-moment tendons in the center span located in the bottom flange.[5]

FIGURE 2.14.   Ste. Adele Bridge, view of variable-depth box girder (courtesy of the Portland Cement Association).

FIGURE 2.15.   Ste. Adele Bridge, view of end of box girder segment (courtesy of the Portland Cement Association).

FIGURE 2.16. Ste. Adele Bridge, dual structure under construction by the balanced cantilever method, from ref. 5 (courtesy of *Engineering News-Record*).

Forty-seven segments are required for each structure, eleven cantilevered each side of each pier, a closure segment at midspan of the center span, and a segment cast in place on each abutment. Segments cast by the form traveler were 10 ft 7⅜ in. (3.24 m) in length.[5] Four traveling forms were used on the project: one pair on each side of the pier for each of the dual structures, Figures 2.16 and 2.17.

The forms were supported by a pair of 42 ft (12.8 m) long, 36 in. (914.4 mm) deep structural steel beams spaced 15 ft (5.57 m) on centers, that cantilevered beyond the completed portion of the structure. Initially the cantilevered beams were

FIGURE 2.17. Ste. Adele Bridge, view of form travelers cantilevering from completed portion of the structure, from ref. 5 (courtesy of *Engineering News-Record*).

counterweighted with 70 tons (63.5 mt) of concrete block, which was gradually diminished as construction proceeded and the depth of the segments decreased. The first pair of segments (at the pier), each with a length of 21 ft 2¾ in. (6.47 m), were cast on a temporary scaffolding braced to the pier, Figure 2.18, which remained fixed in position throughout the erection process.[5]

Construction of four segments per week, one at each end of a cantilever from two adjacent piers, was attained by the following five-day construction cycle[5]:

First day: Traveling forms moved, bottom flange formed, reinforced, and cast. In the parallel span there was a one-day lag such that crews could shift back and forth between adjacent structures.

Second day: Reinforcement placed for webs and top flange.

Third day: Concrete placed for webs and top flange, cure begun.

Fourth day: Tendons placed and prestressing jacks positioned while concrete was curing.

Fifth day: Prestressing accomplished. Forms stripped; preparations made to repeat cycle.

The cycle began on Monday. Since there was a lag of one day on the parallel structure, a six-day work week was required. Upon completion of the eleventh segment in each cantilever the contractor installed temporary falsework to support the abutment end and then cast the closure segment at midspan. Counterweights were installed at the abutment end to balance the weight of the closure forms and segment weight. After installation and stressing of the continuity tendons, abutment segments were cast and expansion joints installed.[5]

2.4   Bouguen Bridge in Brest and Lacroix Falgarde Bridge, France

The Bouguen Bridge in Brittany, West Province in France, is the first rigid-frame continuous structure built in balanced cantilever (1962 to 1963). The finished bridge is shown in Figure 2.6, while dimensions are given in Figure 2.19. It carries a three-lane highway over a valley 145 ft (44 m) deep—Le Vallon du Moulin à Poudre—and provides a link between the heart of Brest city and Le Bouguen, a new urban development.

The total length of bridge is 684 ft (208 m). The main structure is a three-span rigid frame with

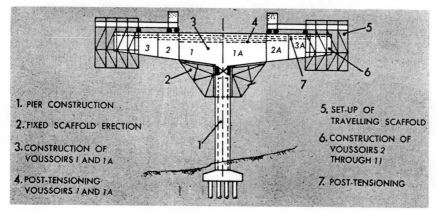

FIGURE 2.18. Ste. Adele Bridge, schematic of construction sequence, from ref. 5 (courtesy of *Engineering News-Record*).

piers elastically built-in on rock foundations with span lengths of 147, 268, and 147 ft (45, 82, and 45 m). At one end the deck rests on an existing masonry wall properly strengthened; at the other end a shorter rigid frame with a clear deck span of 87 ft (26.5 m) provides the approach to the main bridge.

The deck consists of two box girders with vertical webs of variable height, varying from 15 ft 1 in. (4.6 m) at the support to 6.5 ft (2 m) at midspan and the far ends of the side spans. Width of each

box girder is 10 ft (3 m); web thickness also is constant throughout the deck and is equal to $9\frac{1}{2}$ in. (0.24 m).

Piers consist of two square box columns 10 ft by 10 ft (3 × 3 m) with wall thickness of $9\frac{1}{2}$ in. (0.24 m) located under each deck girder. Two walls $8\frac{1}{2}$ in. (0.22 m) thick with a slight recess used for architectural purposes connect the two columns. Both piers are of conventional reinforced concrete construction, slip-formed at a speed reaching 14 ft (4.25 m) per day in one continuous operation.

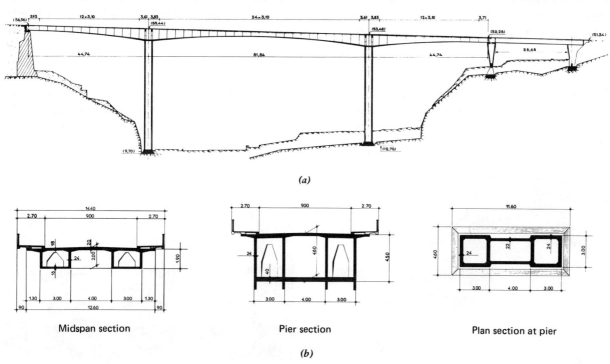

(a)

Midspan section   Pier section   Plan section at pier

(b)

FIGURE 2.19. Bouguen Bridge, France, general dimensions. (*a*) Longitudinal section. (*b*) Cross sections.

FIGURE 2.20. Bouguen Bridge, construction of east cantilever.

The superstructure box girders are connected to the pier shaft by transverse diaphragms made integral with both elements to insure a rigid connection between deck and main piers. Construction of the deck proceeded in balanced cantilever with 10 ft (3 m) long segments cast in place in form travelers with a one-week cycle, Figures 2.20 and 2.21. High-early-strength concrete was used and no steam curing was required. Concrete was allowed to harden for 60 hours before application of prestress. The following cube strengths were obtained throughout the project:

60 hours (time of prestress)	3700 psi (25.5 MPa)
7 days	5500 psi (37.9 MPa)
28 days	7000 psi (48.3 MPa)
90 days	8200 psi (56.5 MPa)

Only one pair of form travelers was used for the entire project, but each traveler could accommodate the construction of both girders at the same time.

During construction of the deck, much attention was given to the control of vertical deflections. Adequate camber was given to the travelers to fully compensate for short- and long-term concrete deflections. The cumulative deflection at midspan of the first cantilever arm was $1\frac{1}{2}$ in. (40 mm) at time of completion. Concrete creep caused this deflection to reach 3 in. (75 mm) at the time the second cantilever arm reached the midspan section. Proper adjustment of the travelers allowed both cantilever arms to meet within $\frac{1}{8}$ in. (3 mm) at the time continuity was achieved. Flat jacks were provided over the outer supports to allow for any further desired adjustment.

The structure is prestressed longitudinally by tendons of eight 12 mm strands:

76 tendons over the top of the pier segment,

32 tendons at the bottom of the crown section,

20 tendons in the side spans,

and transversely by tendons of seven 12 mm strands.

The Lacroix Falgarde Bridge over Ariege River in France, built in 1961 and 1962, is similar to the Bouguen Bridge and represents the first continuous deck built in balanced cantilever (see the photograph of the finished bridge, Figure 2.22). It consists of three continuous spans 100, 200, and 100 ft (30.5, 61, and 30.5 m). The single box girder has a depth varying between 4 ft 5 in. and 10 ft 6 in. (1.35 to 3.2 m). Dimensions are given in Figure 2.23. The superstructure rests on both piers and abutments through laminated bearing pads.

The deck was cantilevered and the construction started simultaneously from the two piers with four travelers working symmetrically. During con-

FIGURE 2.21. Bouguen Bridge, view of the traveler.

FIGURE 2.22. Lacroix-Falgarde Bridge, view of the structure during construction.

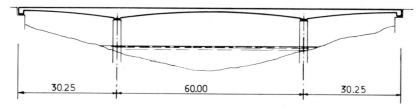

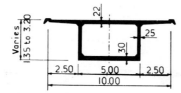

FIGURE 2.23. Lacroix-Falgarde Bridge, elevation and cross section.

struction, the deck was temporarily fixed to the piers by vertical prestress. The structure is prestressed longitudinally by tendons of twelve 8 mm strands and transversely by tendons of twelve 7 mm strands.

2.5 Saint Jean Bridge over the Garonne River at Bordeaux, France

Completed in April 1965, the Saint Jean Bridge in Bordeaux is a remarkable application of the new concepts developed at that time in cast-in-place cantilever construction. The main structure has an overall length of 1560 ft (475 m) and is continuous with expansion joints only over the abutments. The deck is free to expand on neoprene bearings located on all river piers, Figure 2.24. A very efficient method of pier and foundation construction was also developed, which will be described in more detail in Chapter 5.

The bridge was built in the heart of the city of Bordeaux over the Garonne River between a 175-year-old multiple-arch stone structure and a 120-year-old railway bridge designed by Eiffel, the engineer who designed the Eiffel Tower.

The main structure includes six continuous spans. The central spans are 253 ft (77 m) long and allow a navigation clearance of 38 ft (11.60 m) above the lowest water level, while the end spans are only 222 ft (67.80 m) long. Short spans at both ends, 50 ft (15.40 m) long, provide end restraint of the side spans over the abutments. The overall width of the bridge is 88 ft (26.80 m), consisting of six traffic lanes, two walkways, and two cycle lanes. Superstructure dimensions are shown in Figure 2.25.

The deck consists of three box girders. The constant depth of 10.8 ft (3.30 m) has been increased to 13 ft (3.90 m) over a length of 50 ft (15 m) on each side of the piers to improve the bending capacity of the pier section and reduce the amount of cantilever prestress. No diaphragms were used except over the supports. The results of a detailed analysis performed to determine the transverse behavior of the deck confirmed this choice (see detailed description in Chapter 4).

Longitudinal prestressing consists of tendons with twelve 8 mm and twelve $\frac{1}{2}$ in. strands. Transverse prestressing consists of tendons with twelve 8 mm strands at 2.5 ft (0.75 m) intervals. Vertical prestressing is also provided in the webs near the supports.

As indicated in Figure 2.26, three separate pier columns support the three deck girders. They are capped with large prestressed transverse diaphragms. The piers are founded in a gravel bed located at a depth of 45 ft (14 m) below the river level by means of a reinforced concrete circular caisson

FIGURE 2.24. Saint Jean at Bordeaux, view of the completed structure.

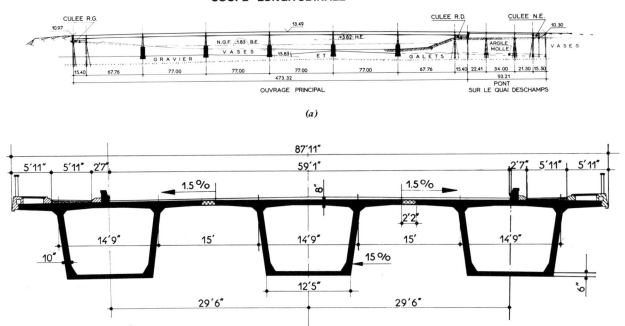

FIGURE 2.25. Saint Jean at Bordeaux. (*a*) Longitudinal and (*b*) cross sections.

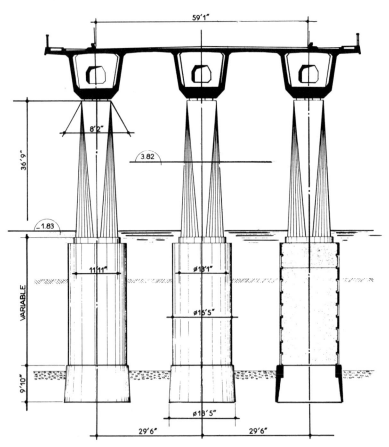

FIGURE 2.26. Saint Jean Bridge at Bordeaux, typical section at river piers.

FIGURE 2.27. Saint Jean Bridge at Bordeaux, work progress on piers and deck.

18.5 ft (5.60 m) in diameter and 10 ft (3 m) high, floated and sunk to the river bed and then open-dredged to the gravel bed. Precast circular match-cast segments prestressed vertically make up the permanent walls of caissons, while additional segments are used temporarily as cofferdams and support for the deck during cantilever construction. A lower tremie seal allows dewatering and placing of plain concrete fill inside the caisson. The reinforced concrete footing and pier shaft are finally cast in one day.

The superstructure box girders were cast in place in 10 ft (3.05 m) long segments using twelve form travelers, allowing simultaneous work on the three parallel cantilevers at two different piers. The 20 ft (6.1 m) long pier segment was cast on the temporary supports provided by the pier caissons, allowing the form travelers to be installed and cantilever construction to proceed. Six working days were necessary for a complete cycle of operations on each traveler. Work progress is shown in Figures 2.27 and 2.28. Total construction time for the entire 130,000 sq ft (12,000 m²) was approximately

FIGURE 2.28. Saint Jean Bridge at Bordeaux, cantilever construction on typical pier.

one year, as shown on the actual program of work summarized in graphic form in Figure 2.29. To meet the very strict construction deadline of the contract, it was necessary to bring to the project site another set of three travelers to cast the last cantilever on the left bank and achieve continuity with the southern river pier cantilever. Altogether, meeting the two-year construction schedule was recognized as an engineering achievement.

Exactly one hundred years earlier, Gustave Eiffel had built the neighboring railway bridge in exactly two years—food for thought and a somewhat humbling reflection for the present generation.

2.6 Siegtal and Kochertal Bridges, Germany

The Siegtal Bridge near the town of Sieger, north of Frankfort, Germany, represents the first industrial application of cast-in-place cantilever construction with an auxiliary overhead truss. This method was initially developed by Hans Wittfoht and the firm of Polensky-und-Zollner and subsequently used for several large structures in Germany and other countries. One of the most recent and remarkable examples of this technique is the Kochertal Bridge between Nüremberg and Heilbron, Germany. Both structures will be briefly described in this section, while a similar application in Denmark is covered in another section of this chapter.

Siegtal Bridge is a twelve-span structure 3450 ft (1050 m) long resting on piers up to 330 ft (100 m) high, with maximum span lengths of 344 ft (105 m), Figure 2.30. Two separate box girders carry the three traffic lanes in each direction for a total width of 100 ft (30.5 m), Figure 2.31. Structural height of the constant-depth box girder is 19 ft (5.8 m), corresponding to a span-to-depth ratio of 18. The deck is continuous throughout its entire length, with fixed bearings provided at the three highest center piers and roller bearings of high-grade steel for all other piers and end abutments. Piers have slip-formed reinforced concrete hollow box shafts with a constant transverse width of 68 ft (20.7 m) and a variable width in elevation with a slope of 40 to 1 on both faces.

The superstructure was cast in place in balanced cantilever from all piers in 33 ft (10 m) long segments with an auxiliary overhead truss supporting the two symmetrical travelers, and a cycle of one week was obtained without difficulty for the construction of two symmetrical 33 ft (10 m) long seg-

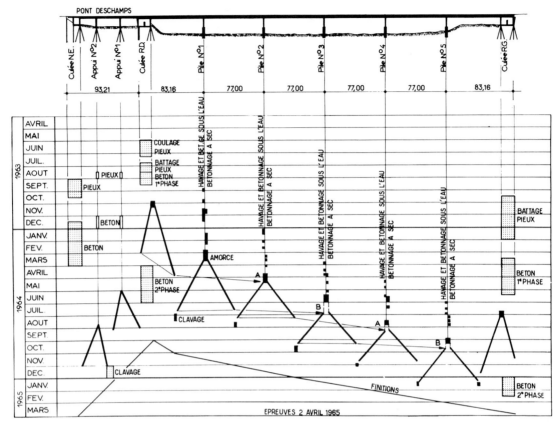

FIGURE 2.29. Saint Jean Bridge at Bordeaux, actual program of work.

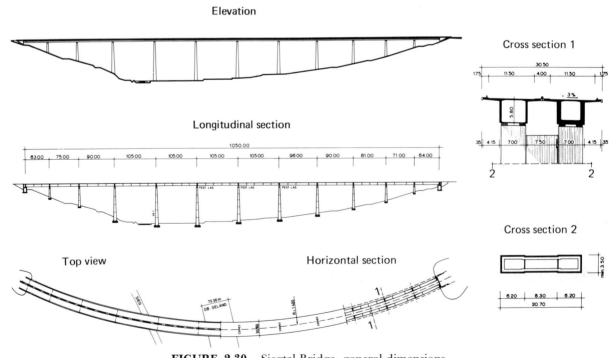

FIGURE 2.30. Siegtal Bridge, general dimensions.

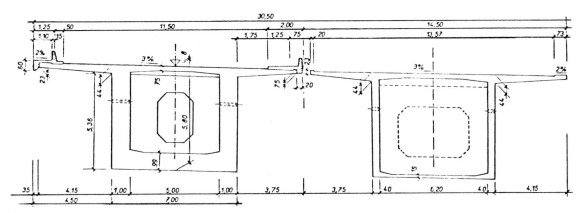

FIGURE 2.31. Siegtal Bridge, typical cross section.

ments. The auxiliary truss was also first used to cast the pier segment above each pier, Figure 2.32, before cantilever construction could proceed, Figure 2.33. Because the pier shafts are flexible and have limited bending capacity, it was inadvisable to subject them to unsymmetrical loading conditions during deck construction. Thus, the overhead truss also served the purpose of stabilizing the cantilever arms before continuity was achieved with the previous cantilever.

The auxiliary steel truss is made of high-strength steel (50 ksi yield strength). Prestressing is applied to the upper chord, which is subjected to high tensile stresses in order to reduce the weight of the equipment. The overall length of the truss is 440 ft (135 m) long to accommodate the maximum span length of 344 ft (105 m). The total weight of the truss and of the two suspended travelers, allowing casting of two 33 ft (10 m) long segments, was 660 t (600 mt). Deck concrete was pumped to the various segments through pipes carried from the finished deck by the auxiliary truss, Figures 2.34 and 2.35.

Work commenced on the superstructure in March 1966. The first box girder was completed in April 1968. The truss and travelers were immediately transferred to the second box girder, which was completed in September 1969. Thus, the average rate of casting was as follows:

First bridge: 3450 ft (1050 m) in 25 months, or 140 ft (42 m) per month

Second bridge: 3450 ft (1050 m) in 17 months, or 200 ft (62 m) per month

Both bridges: 6900 ft (2100 m) in 42 months, or 160 ft (50 m) per month

An outstanding contemporary example of the same technique is the Kochertal Bridge in Germany, shown in final progress in Figure 2.36. General dimensions of the project are given in Figure 2.37. Total length is 3700 ft (1128 m) with typical spans of 453 ft (138 m) supported on piers up to 600 ft (183 m) in height. The single box girder superstructure with precast outriggers carries six traffic lanes for a total width of 101 ft (30.76 m). Box piers were cast in climbing forms with 14.2 ft (4.33 m) high lifts. The top section is constant for all piers with outside dimensions of 16.4 by 28.2 ft

FIGURE 2.32. Siegtal Bridge, pier segment casting.

FIGURE 2.33. Siegtal Bridge, cantilever construction.

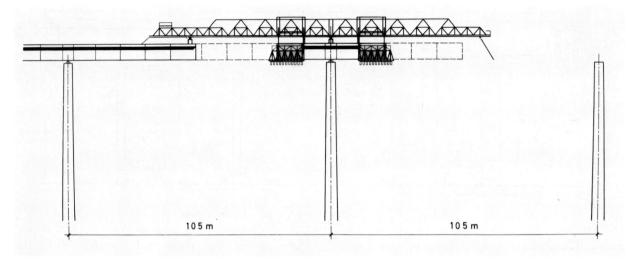

FIGURE 2.34. Siegtal Bridge, elevation of overhead truss and travelers.

(5 by 8.6 m). The four faces are sloped to increase the dimensions at foundation level to a maximum of 31.2 by 49.2 ft (9.5 by 15 m) for the highest piers. Wall thickness varies progressively from top to bottom, to follow the load stresses, from 20 in. (0.5 m) to 36 in. (0.9 m).

The constant-depth superstructure is cast in two stages, Figure 2.38: (1) the single center box with a width of 43 ft (13.1 m) and a depth of 23 ft (7 m), and (2) the two outside cantilevers resting on a series of precast struts. To meet the very tight construction schedule of 22 months it was necessary to use two sets of casting equipment, working simultaneously from both abutments toward the center. Each apparatus was made of an overhead truss

equipped with a launching nose to move from pier to pier and two suspended travelers working in balanced cantilevers, casting segments on a one-week cycle, Figure 2.39.

2.7 Pine Valley Creek Bridge, U.S.A.

The first prestressed concrete cast-in-place segmental bridge built in the United States was the Pine Valley Creek Bridge on Interstate I-8 between San Diego and El Centro, California, Figures 1.66 and 2.7, opened to traffic late in 1974. This structure is located approximately 40 miles (64 km) east of San Diego and 3 miles (4.8 km) west of the

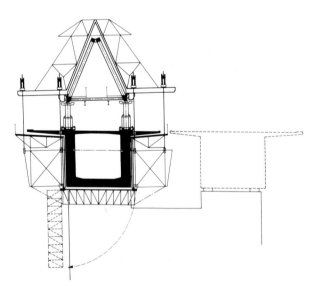

FIGURE 2.35. Siegtal Bridge, typical section of truss and travelers.

FIGURE 2.36. Kochertal Bridge, general view of project.

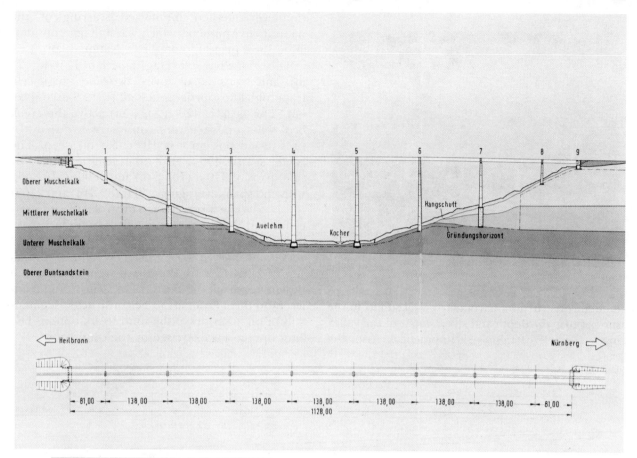

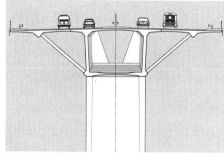

FIGURE 2.37. Kochertal Bridge, elevation, plan and cross section.

(*a*)

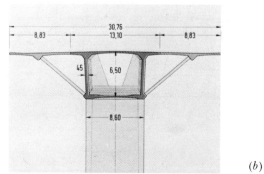

(*b*)

FIGURE 2.38. Kochertal Bridge, typical cross sections. (*a*) First stage casting. (*b*) Final stage.

community of Pine Valley and within the Cleveland National Forest. Interstate I-8 crosses over a semiarid region that is highly erodible when the ground cover is disturbed; consequently stringent controls were imposed on access roads and ground-cover disturbances. Structure type was influenced by the following factors: site restrictions, economics, ecological considerations, and Forest Service limitations. After comparing various possible schemes such as steel arch, deck truss, or steel box girder, the California Department of Transportation selected a concrete box girder bridge predicated on the use of cantilever seg-

FIGURE 2.39. Kochertal Bridge, cantilever construction.

mental construction, particularly well suited to the site because the depth and steep slopes of the valley made the use of falsework impractical. Also, the cantilever method minimized scarring of the natural environment, which was a major consideration for a project located in a National Forest.

The bridge has an average length of 1716 ft (523 m) and consists of twin two-lane single-cell, trapezoidal box girders each 42 ft (12.8 m) out-to-out. The deck is 450 ft (137 m) above the creek bed. The superstructure consists of five spans of prestressed box girders 19 ft (5.8 m) deep. The center span is 450 ft (137 m) in length, flanked by side spans of 340 ft (103.6 m) and 380 ft (115.8 m), with end spans averaging 270 ft (82.3 m) and 276 ft (84.1 m). The bridge was constructed with four cantilevers. Pier 2 has cantilevers 115 ft (35.1 m) in length, piers 3 and 4 have 225 ft (69.6 m) cantilevers, and pier 5 has 155 ft (47.2 m) cantilevers,[6,7,8] Figure 2.40. Provisions were made in the design to permit the portions of spans 1 and 5 adjacent to the abutments to be constructed segmentally or on falsework at the contractors' option. The later option was exercised by the contractor.[9,10]

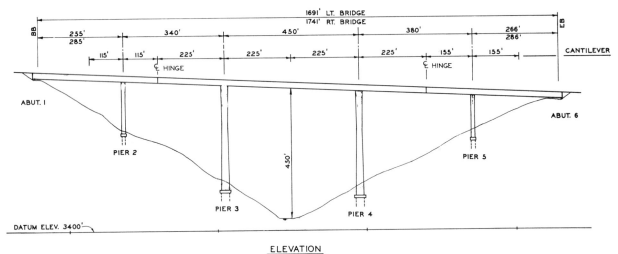

ELEVATION

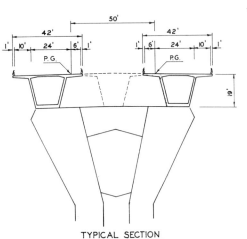

TYPICAL SECTION

FIGURE 2.40. Pine Valley Creek Bridge, elevation and typical section, from ref. 8.

Hinges were provided in spans 2 and 4 at the end of the main cantilevers. In the preliminary design, consideration was given to the concept of a continuous structure for abutment to abutment without any intermediate joints. Continuity has many advantages insofar as this particular structure is concerned. However, it has the significant disadvantage of large displacements under seismic loading conditions. Because of the extreme difference in height and stiffness between piers, it was determined that all the horizontal load was being transmitted to the shorter piers, which were not capable of accepting it.[9]

The pier foundations posed some interesting construction problems. The top 20 ft (6 m) of the rock material at the structure site was badly fissured, with some fissuring as deep as 40 ft (12 m). Narrow footings only 1 ft (0.3 m) wider than the pier shafts, tied down with rock anchors, were preferred to the conventional spread footings to minimize the amount of excavation.

Although the piers are spectacular because of their size, they are not unique in concept. The two main piers, 3 and 4, are approximately 370 ft (113 m) in height and are made up of two vertical cellular sections interconnected with horizontal ties. In a transverse direction the piers have a constant width to facilitate slip-form construction, while in the longitudinal direction the section varies parabolically, with a minimum width of 16 ft (4.9 m) approximately one-third down from the top. At this point they flare out to 23 ft by 24 ft (7 by 7.3 m) at the soffit. The pier wall thickness is a constant 2 ft (0.6 m).[6,9]

Earthquake considerations produce the critical design load for the piers. The 1940 El Centro earthquake was used as the forcing function in the design analysis. Design criteria required that the completed structural frame withstand this force level without exceeding stress levels of 75% of yield. The pier struts are an important element in the seismic design of the piers. They provide ductility to the piers by providing energy-absorbing joints and an increased stability against buckling for the principal shaft elements. Because of the size of the struts in relation to the pier legs, the majority of the rotation in the strut-leg joint occurs in the strut. Thus, a very high percentage of transverse confining reinforcement was required in the strut to insure the ductility at this location.[6,9]

Although preliminary design anticipated the slip-forming technique for construction of the piers, the contractor finally elected to use a self-climbing form system. Steel forms permitted 22 ft

(6.7 m) high lifts, and they were given a teflon coating to facilitate stripping while producing a high-quality finished concrete surface.

Construction of the pier caps was especially challenging. The pier caps, Figure 2.41, consist of two arms 60 ft (18.3 m) in height, which project outward at an approximate angle of 60° from each stem of the pier shafts. These arms are constructed in four lifts in such a manner that the forms for each lift are tied into the previous lift. Upon completion of the pier cap arms they are tied together and the top strut is formed, reinforcement placed, and cast. The pier cap is prestressed transversely in order to overcome side thrust from the superstructure.

The superstructure consists of two parallel trapezoidal box girders 42 ft (12.8 m) wide and 19 ft (5.8 m) deep with a 38 ft (11.6 m) space between the boxes, such that an additional box girder may be constructed for future widening, Figures 2.40 and 2.42. The boxes, in addition to being post-tensioned longitudinally, have transverse prestressing in the deck slab, together with sufficient mild steel reinforcement to resist nominal construction loads, allowing the transverse prestressing operations to be removed from the critical path. The

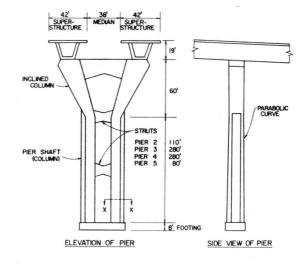

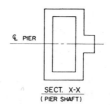

FIGURE 2.41. Pine Valley Creek Bridge, elevation, side view, and cross section of pier, from ref. 7 (courtesy of the Portland Cement Association).

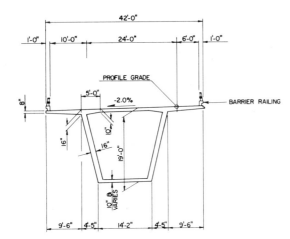

FIGURE 2.42. Pine Valley Creek Bridge, typical box girder cross section, from ref. 7 (courtesy of the Portland Cement Association).

sloping webs and large deck overhangs were used to minimize the slab spans and the number of girder webs and to accentuate a longitudinal shadow line, thus reducing the apparent depth. The web thickness of 16 in. (406 mm) was selected to permit side-by-side placement of the largest tendon then being used in bridge construction and to keep the shear reinforcement to a reasonable size and spacing, Figure 2.42. The bottom slab at midspan is 10 in. (254 mm) thick and flares out to 6.5 ft (1.98 m) at the pier.[6,7,9] Construction of the superstructure proceeded in a balanced cantilever fashion, Figures 2.7 and 2.43.

As shown in Figure 2.44, the erection scheme proposed by the contractor allowed all superstructure work to be performed in a continuous sequence, essentially from the top. Four form travelers were used for the cantilever construction of this project, one at each end of each cantilever arm. Basically, one traveler consisted of an overhead steel truss used to support the formwork for the typical 16.5 ft (5 m) long segments. The truss is anchored, at the rear, to the previously cast segment, while the front end is equipped with hydraulic jacks used for grade adjustment. High-density plywood was used for all formed surfaces. A total of 172 cast-in-place segments were required for the entire structure. Falsework was required close to abutments 1 and 6 to complete the side spans beyond the balanced cantilever arms. Formwork used in that portion of the structure could be reused above each intermediate pier cap to construct the 35 ft (10.7 m) long pier segment before the actual cantilever construction proceeded.

The cross section of the superstructure allowed

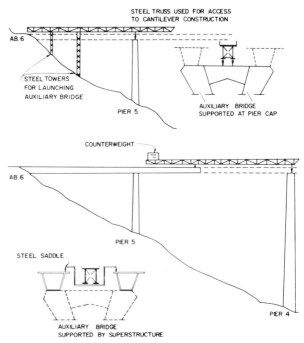

FIGURE 2.43. Pine Valley Creek Bridge, auxiliary bridge, from ref. 7 (courtesy of the Portland Cement Association).

an auxiliary truss to be located between the two concrete box girders, Figure 2.43. This auxiliary bridge consisted of a structural steel truss 10 ft (3.05 m) square in cross section and 320 ft (97.5 m) in length. In a stationary position it was supported at the leading end on the pier cap strut and at the rear end of a steel saddle between the two concrete boxes. It was designed such that the front end could be cantilevered out 225 ft (68.6 m), which is one-half the main span. Electric winches allowed longitudinal launching between the concrete box girders. When pier 5 was completed, the auxiliary bridge was erected in span 5–6, utilizing temporary support towers near abutment 6. Subsequent 30 ft (9.1 m) lengths of auxiliary truss were attached at the abutment and incrementally launched toward pier 5, until its front end was supported on the pier cap. The pier table was then constructed and cantilever construction commenced until the structural hinge in span 4–5 was reached. Upon completion of the closure joint in span 5–6 the auxiliary truss was launched forward until the front end reached pier 4. The form travelers were dismantled from the tip of the cantilever and reerected on the pier table at pier 4, and cantilever

FIGURE 2.44. (Opposite) Pine Valley Creek Bridge, erection scheme proposed by the contractor, from ref. 10.

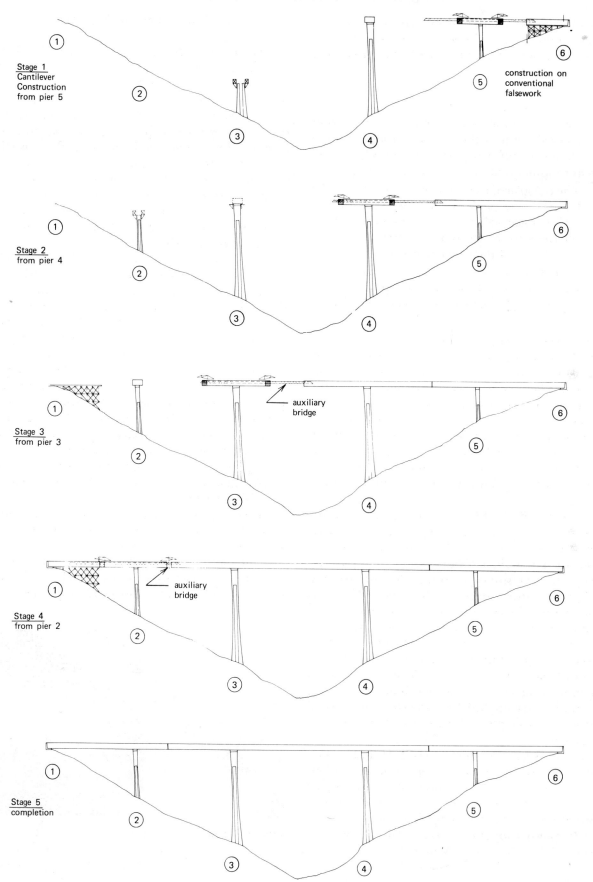

Stage 1
Cantilever
Construction
from pier 5

construction on
conventional
falsework

Stage 2
from pier 4

Stage 3
from pier 3

auxiliary
bridge

Stage 4
from pier 2

auxiliary
bridge

Stage 5
completion

51

construction was started again. This cycle was repeated until closure was achieved in span 1–2.

The use of the auxiliary truss had the following advantages[10]:

1. Men and materials for the superstructure could reach the location of construction from abutment 6 over the auxiliary bridge and the already completed portion of the superstructure without interfering with the valley below.

2. The construction equipment (tower cranes and hoists) at the piers was required only for the actual construction of the piers and could be relocated from pier to pier without waiting for completion of the superstructure.

3. Except for construction of abutment 1 and pier 2, site installation for the entire project was located at one location, near abutment 6.

Concrete was supplied from a batching plant located approximately 2 miles (3.2 km) from the site. Ready-mix trucks delivered the concrete at abutment 6. The concrete was then pumped through 6 in. (152 mm) pipes down the slope to the foot of piers 5 and 4. The concrete for the superstructure was pumped through a pipeline installed in the auxiliary truss right into the forms. A second pump with a similar installation was located at abutment 1 to supply concrete for abutment 1 and pier 2.[10]

A 5000 psi (35 MPa) concrete was specified for the superstructure, presenting no unusual problems. However, to maintain a short cycle for the construction of the individual segments it was necessary to have sufficient strength for prestressing 30 hours after concrete placement. This was difficult to achieve, since the specifications did not allow type III cement and certain additives. A solution was to prestress the individual tendons necessary to support the following segment to 50 percent of their final force. The form carrier could then be advanced and the remainder of the prestressing force applied after the concrete reached sufficient strength and before casting the next segment.[10]

Prestressing was achieved using 1¼ in. (32 mm) diameter Dywidag bars. Longitudinal tendons were provided in 33 ft (10 m) lengths and coupled as the work progressed. Temporary corrosion protection of the bars was obtained by blowing "VPI" powder into the ducts and coating each bar with vinyl wash or "Rust-Van 310."[8]

2.8 Gennevilliers Bridge, France

The Gennevilliers Bridge, Figures 2.45 and 2.46, is a five-span structure with a total length of 2090 ft (636 m). At its southern end it is supported on a common pier with the approach viaduct from the port of Gennevilliers. It crosses successively an entrance channel to the port, a peninsula situated between the channel, and the Seine River itself, Figure 2.47. It is part of the A15 Motorway, which traverses from the Paris Beltway through Gennevilliers, Argenteuil, the valley d'Oise, and on to the city of Cergy-Pontoise. The present structure provides a four-lane divided highway with provision for a future twin structure.

The superstructure is a variable-depth two-cell box girder with spans of 345, 564, 243, 564 and 371 ft (105, 172, 74, 172 and 113 m). Depth varies from 29.5 ft (9 m) at intermediate piers to 11.5 ft (3.5 m) at midspan of the 564 ft (172 m) spans and its extremities, with a depth of 23 ft (7 m) at midspan of the short center span, Figure 2.46. Depth-to-span ratios of the 564 ft (172 m) spans at midspan and at the piers are respectively 1/49 and 1/19. The curved portion of the structure has a radius, in plan, of 2130 ft (650 m). The longitudinal grade is a constant 1.5 percent within the zone of curvature. Because the short center span is subjected to negative bending moment over its entire length, the structure behaves much as a continuous three-span beam.

In cross section, Figure 2.48, the two-cell box girder has a bottom flange varying in width from 42.2 ft (12.86 m) at midspan to 30.5 ft (9.3 m) at the pier, for the 564 ft (172 m) span. Thickness of the bottom flange varies from 47 in. (1.2 m) at the pier to 8 in. (20 cm) at midspan. The top flange has

FIGURE 2.45. Gennevilliers Bridge, view of curved five-span structure.

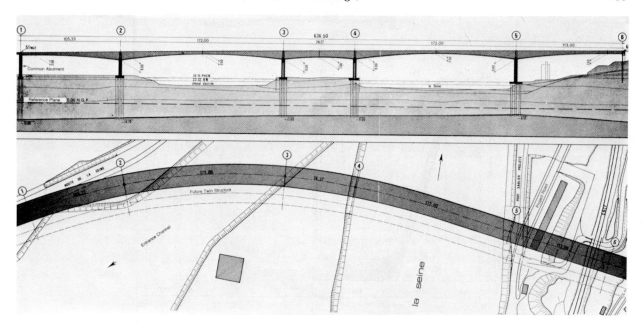

FIGURE 2.46. Gennevilliers Bridge, plan and elevation, from ref. 11.

an overall width of 60.6 ft (18.48 m) with a 6 ft (1.83 m) overhang on one side and 6.2 ft (1.88 m) on the other. Thickness of the top flange is a constant 8 in. (20 cm). The center web has a constant thickness of 16 in. (400 mm). Exterior webs, which are inclined 18° to the vertical, vary in thickness from 16 in. (400 mm) at the pier to 12 in. (300 mm) at midspan. Diaphragms, Figure 2.49, are located at the supports. The superstructure is prestressed in three directions, with strand tendons being utilized longitudinally and transversely and bar tendons utilized for the webs. Interior anchorage

FIGURE 2.47. Gennevilliers Bridge, aerial view of the completed bridge.

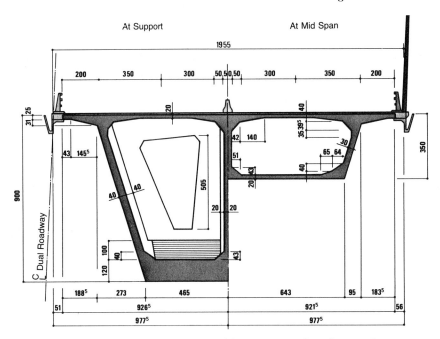

FIGURE 2.48. Gennevilliers Bridge, cross section, from ref. 11.

FIGURE 2.49. Gennevilliers Bridge, interior view showing diaphragm.

blocks for the longitudinal prestressing are located at top slab level.

The superstructure is fully continuous over its total length of 2090 ft (636 m) between the northern abutment and the southern transition pier with the approach viaduct. The deck rests upon the four main piers supported by large elastomeric pads. The superstructure was cast in place using the balanced cantilever method according to the step-by-step scheme shown in Figure 2.50. Segments over the piers (pier segments) were constructed first on formwork, in a traditional manner, except for their unusual length [26 ft (7.9m)] and weight [850 t (770 mt)].

Four travelers were used for casting the typical 11 ft (3.35 m) long segments varying in weight from 242 t (220 mt) near the piers to 110 t (100 mt) at midspan.[11] The travelers were specially designed to achieve maximum rigidity and prevent the usual tendency to crack a newly cast segment under the deflections of the supporting trusses of conventional travelers. The framework used for this purpose was made of self-supporting forming panels assembled into a monolith weighing 120 t (110 mt) and prestressed to the preceding part of the superstructure to make the unit substantially deflection free, Figure 2.51. Stability, especially under wind loads or in the event of an accidental failure of the travelers during the construction period, was maintained by a pair of cables on each

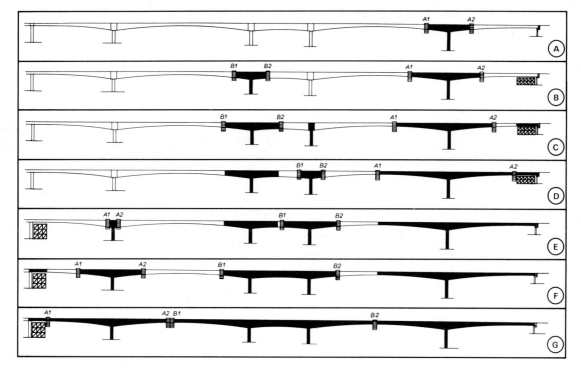

FIGURE 2.50. Gennevilliers Bridge, erection sequence, from ref. 11.

side of the pier connecting the superstructure to pier base.

2.9 Grand'Mere Bridge, Canada

This three-lane cast-in-place segmental bridge is located on Quebec Autoroute 55 and crosses the St. Maurice River approximately 3 miles (4.8 km) north of Grand'Mere, Quebec, Figure 2.52. Water depth at the bridge site is over 110 ft (35.5 m), with an additional 150 ft (45.75 m) depth of sand, silt,

and debris above bedrock. The river flow at the bridge site is 3.6 ft/sec (1.1 m/sec).

During the preliminary design stage in 1973 and 1974, several structural solutions were considered. The use of short spans of precast concrete AASHTO sections or structural steel girders requiring a number of piers was immediately abandoned because of river depth and current velocity at the site. Site conditions required the development of an economical long clear span with as few piers as possible in the river. Options available

FIGURE 2.51. Gennevilliers Bridge, superstructure under construction.

FIGURE 2.52. Grand'Mere Bridge, general view showing parabolic soffit of center span, (courtesy of the Portland Cement Association).

were structural steel, post-tensioned precast segmental, and several options of cast-in-place prestressed concrete, varying in span, cross section,
and pier requirements. The design finally selected
for preparing the bid documents was a concrete
cantilever single-cell box with a center span of 540
ft (165 m), a 245 ft (75 m) western land span, and a
150 ft (46 m) eastern land span for a total length of
935 ft (285 m). The design actually used for construction, Figure 2.53, for the same total length,
has a main span increased to 595 ft (181 m) and
two equal 170 ft (52 m) long side spans. The corresponding slight increase in cost of the superstructure was far more than offset by eliminating the
need to build a caisson in 48 ft (15 m) of water 98 ft
(30 m) above bedrock for the west pier. This redesign, developed in cooperation with the contractor,
allowed an overall saving of approximately 20% of
the project cost.

The two identical 170 ft (51.9 m) long land spans
cantilever from the main piers and act as counterweights for the main span. From a depth of 32 ft
(9.8 m) at the main piers they taper to a depth of 28
ft (8.5 m) at a point 130 ft (39.6 m) from the main

FIGURE 2.53. Grand'Mere Bridge, center span
parabolic arch soffit (courtesy of the Portland Cement
Association).

piers, where they are supported by a secondary
pair of 4 ft by 4 ft (1.2 by 1.2 m) bearing capped
piers. The 40 ft (12.2 m) wedge-shaped shore ends
of the land spans taper from the secondary piers to
grade at the top of the abutment. The abutments,
which are just 16 in. (406 mm) thick, are designed
to support the approach slab only, Figure 2.54.

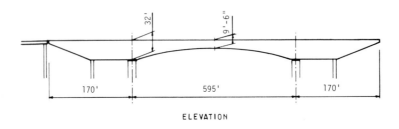

ELEVATION

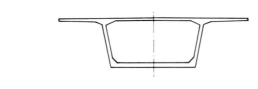

TYPICAL SECTION

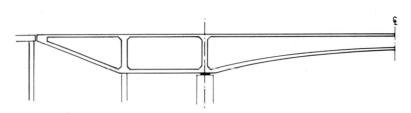

DETAIL OF ABUTMENT

FIGURE 2.54. Grand'Mere Bridge, general arrangement. (*a*) Elevation.
(*b*) Typical section. (*c*) Detail of abutment.

Modular, confined rubber expansion joints are provided in the roadway above the abutments. The wedge portions of the land spans are solid concrete, helping counterbalance the weight of the main span under service conditions as well as during the construction stage. The land spans have a web thickness of 2 ft (0.6 m), a 3 ft (0.9 m) thick bottom slab, and a 15 in. (381 mm) thick top flange. A 2 ft (0.6 m) thick diaphragm is located 78 ft (23.8

m) outboard of the secondary piers to form a chamber between the solid wedge end and the diaphragms. This chamber was incrementally filled with gravel in three stages to counterbalance the main span as it was progressively constructed. The bottom soffit of the west land span was supported on temporary steel scaffolding. However, because of the terrain slope, the east land-span bottom soffit was plywood-formed on a bed of sand spread

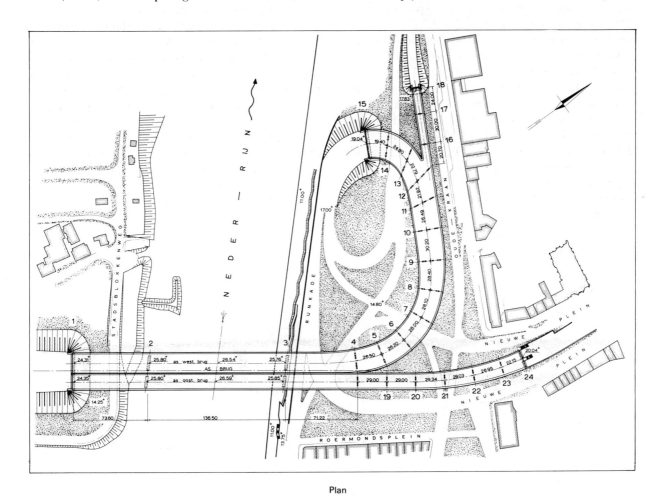

Plan

(a)

Elevation

(b)

FIGURE 2.55. Arnhem Bridge. (a) Plan. (b) Elevation.

over the rock. Upon completion of concreting and curing, the sand was hosed out from under the formwork, allowing it to be stripped.[12]

2.10   *Arnhem Bridge, Holland*

The Arnhem Bridge, Figure 2.55, is a cast-in-place, lightweight concrete, segmental bridge crossing the Rhine River with a center span of 448 ft (136 m), a south end span of 234 ft (71 m), and a north end span of 238 ft (72 m) connecting to approach ramps. It is a dual structure composed of two-cell box girders, Figure 2.56a. The western structure has two 30 ft (9.1 m) roadways for automobile traffic. The eastern structure has a 23 ft (7 m) roadway reserved for bus traffic, a 17 ft (5.3 m) roadway for bicycles and motorcycles, and a 7 ft (2.1 m) pedestrian walkway. Ramp structures are of prestressed flat slab construction, Figure 2.56b.

The main three-span river crossing with an overall width of 122.7 ft (37.4 m) consists of two double-cell box girders that vary in depth from 6.5 ft (2.0 m) at midspan to 17 ft (5.3 m) at the piers. The western rectangular box girder has a width of 49 ft (14.8 m) with 10 ft (3 m) top flange cantilevers for an overall width of 68.4 ft (20.84 m). The eastern rectangular box girder has a width of 35.4 ft (10.8 m) with top flange cantilevers of 8.6 ft (2.62 m) for a total width of 52.6 ft (16.04 m), Figure 2.56a.

Construction of the main spans is by the conventional cast-in-place segmental balanced cantilever method with form travelers. The form travelers are owned by the Dutch Government and leased to the contractors. Strand tendons were used for post-tensioning, and the lightweight concrete had a weight of about 110 lb/ft³ (1780 kg/m³), Figure 2.57.

Temporary supports at the pier were used for unbalanced loading during construction, Figure 2.58. Precast exposed aggregate facia units were used for the entire length of the structure and its approaches, Figures 2.59 and 2.60.

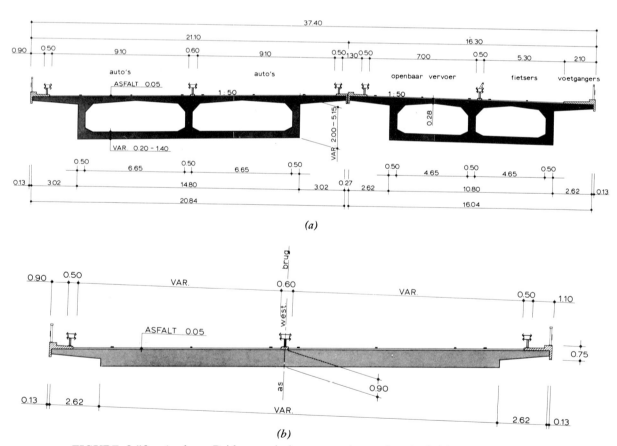

FIGURE 2.56. Arnhem Bridge, typical cross sections of main bridge and flat-slab ramp. (*a*) Main structure. (*b*) Prestressed flat-slab ramp.

FIGURE 2.57. Arnhem Bridge, center-span cantilevers.

FIGURE 2.59. Arnhem Bridge, view of prestressed flat-slab ramp structure.

FIGURE 2.58. Arnhem Bridge, temporary pier supports for unbalanced moments.

FIGURE 2.60. Arnhem Bridge, precast exposed aggregate facia units.

2.11 *Napa River Bridge, U.S.A.*

The Napa River Bridge, Figure 2.61, is located on Highway 29 just south of the city of Napa, California, and provides a four-lane, 66 ft (20 m) wide roadway over the Napa River to bypass an existing two-lane lift span and several miles of city streets. The 68 ft (20.7 m) wide, 2230 ft (679.7 m) long bridge consists of 13 spans varying in length from 120 to 250 ft (36.58 to 76.2 m) and a two-cell trapezoidal box girder varying from 7 ft 9 in. (2.36 m) to 12 ft (3.66 m) in depth, Figure 2.62. Three hinged joints were provided at midspan in spans 2, 6, and 10. These joints involved elaborate connections incorporating elastomeric bearing pads and hard-rubber bumper pads to withstand severe movement and shock during an earthquake, Figure 2.63. All other joints between the cantilevers were normal cast-in-place closure joints.[13] The superstructure is fixed to the piers, primarily for seismic resistance.

The Structures Division of the California Department of Transportation (CALTRANS) developed plans and specifications for three alterna-

FIGURE 2.61. Napa River Bridge, aerial view.

tive types of construction, Figure 2.62, as follows:

A. A conventional continuous cast-in-place prestressed box girder bridge of lightweight concrete.

B. A continuous structural-steel trapezoidal box girder composite with a lightweight concrete deck.

C. A cantilever prestressed segmental concrete box girder bridge allowing either cast-in-place

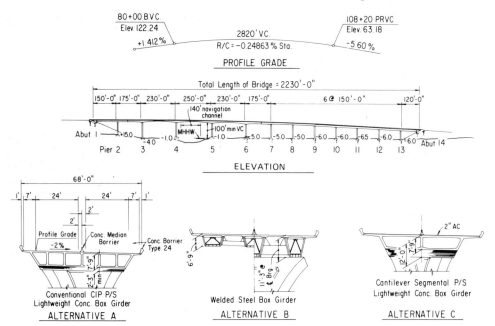

FIGURE 2.62. Napa River Bridge, profile grade, elevation, and alternate sections.

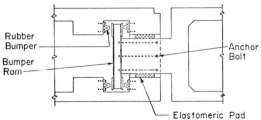

FIGURE 2.63. Napa River Bridge, mid-span hinge joint with seismic bumbers.

or precast segments. Erection was allowed on falsework or by the free cantilever method.

Because of poor foundations and a readily available aggregate supply, all alternatives utilized lightweight concrete in the superstructure. Alternative C utilized transverse prestressing in the deck to reduce the number of webs to three, as compared to seven webs required in alternative A. Of seven bids received and opened on November 6, 1974, six were for alternative C and the seventh and highest was for alternative B. No bids were submitted for alternative A.

Design of the superstructure required lightweight concrete with a compressive strength of 4500 psi (316 kg/cm²) at 28 days and 3500 psi (246 kg/cm²) prior to prestressing. The three-web winning alternative required a minimum of formed surfaces and forced the majority of longitudinal prestressing into the flanges, resulting in maximum prestress eccentricity, and therefore an economical solution.

Contract plans showed the minimum prestress force required at each section and permitted the use of either 270 ksi (1862 MPa) strand or 150 ksi (1034 MPa) bar tendons. Prestressing force diagrams were provided for both materials. The contractor had the option of balancing segment length against prestress force to achieve the most economical structure. In addition, the plans provided the contractor with the option of a combination of diagonal prestressing and conventional reinforcement in the webs for shear reinforcement or the utilization of conventional stirrup reinforcement only. The design was based upon a 40,000 psi (276 MPa) prestress loss for the 270 ksi (1862 MPa) strand and 28,000 psi (193 MPa) loss for the 150 ksi (1034 MPa) bars. Because the loss of prestress is a function of the type of lightweight aggregate used, the contractor was required to submit test values for approval concerning the materials to be used and relevant calculations.[14]

The contractor elected to use the cantilever cast-in-place alternative supported on falsework until each segment was stressed, Figure 2.64. Falsework bents with ten 70 ft (21.3 m) long, 36 in. (914 mm) deep, wide-flange girders support each balanced cantilever. The falsework was then moved to the next pier, leaving the cantilever free-standing, Figure 2.65. The entire formwork, steel girders, and timber forms were lowered by winches from the cantilever girder after all negative post-tensioning was completed. Positive post-tensioning followed midspan closure pours.[13]

The 250 ft (76.2 m) long navigation span was constructed with a complicated segment sequence because of a U.S. Coast Guard requirement that a 70 ft (21.3 m) wide by 70 ft (21.3 m) high navigation channel be maintained. Approximately 60 ft (18.3 m) of span 4, over the navigable channel, was constructed in three segments on suspended falsework by the conventional cast-in-place segmental method.[13]

All transverse and longitudinal post-tensioning tendons consist of $\frac{1}{2}$ in. (12.7 mm) diameter strands. Longitudinal tendons are twelve $\frac{1}{2}$ in. (12.7 mm) diameter strand, with anchorages located in the top and bottom flanges such that all stressing was done from inside the box girder. Loops are used for economy and efficiency, as shown in Figure 2.66. The longest span over the navigation channel is prestressed by 50 (twelve $\frac{1}{2}$ in. strand) tendons. Transverse prestress in the top flange allowed a 10 ft (3 m) cantilever on each side of the two-cell box girder. Transverse tendons consist of four $\frac{1}{2}$ in. diameter strands encased in flat ducts 2.25 by 0.75 in. (57 by 19 mm) with proper splay at both ends to accommodate a flat bearing at the edge of the deck slab.

2.12 Koror-Babelthuap, U.S. Pacific Trust Territory

This structure currently represents (1979) the longest concrete cantilever girder span in the world. It connects the islands of Koror and Babelthuap, which are part of the Palau Island chain of the Caroline Islands located in the United States Trust Territory some 1500 miles (2414 km) east of the Philippines, Figure 2.67.

FIGURE 2.64. Napa River Bridge, free-standing cantilever and supporting bents for falsework

FIGURE 2.65. Napa River Bridge, falsework bents (courtesy of Phil Hale, CALTRANS).

FIGURE 2.66. Napa River Bridge, longitudinal loop tendons.

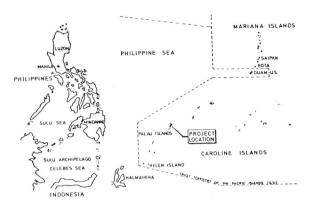

FIGURE 2.67. Koror-Babelthuap Bridge, location map, from ref. 15.

In elevation this structure has a center span of 790 ft (241 m) with side spans of 176 ft (53.6 m) that cantilever another 61 ft (18.6 m) to the abutments, Figure 1.30. Depth of this single-cell box girder superstructure varies parabolically from 46 ft (14 m) at the pier to 12 ft (3.66 m) at midspan of the main span, Figure 2.68. The side span decreases linearly from the main pier to 33 ft 8 in. (10.26 m) at the end piers and then to 9 ft (2.74 m) at the abutments. The structure has a symmetrical vertical curve of 800 ft (243.8 m) radius from abutment to abutment with the approach roadways at a 6% grade.[15]

Superstructure cross section, Figure 1.30, is a single-cell box 24 ft (7.3 m) in width with the top flange cantilevering 3 ft 9½ in. (1.16 m) for a total top flange width of 31 ft 7 in. (9.63 m), providing two traffic lanes and a pedestrian path. The webs have a constant thickness of 14 in. (0.36 m). Bottom flange thickness varies from 7 in. (0.18 m) at midspan of the center span to 46 in. (1.17 m) at the

main pier and then to 21 in. (0.53 m) at an intermediate diaphragm located in the end span. This diaphragm and the one at the end pier form a ballast compartment. Another ballast compartment is located between the end-pier diaphragm and the abutment. The bottom flange under the ballast compartments is 3 ft (0.9 m) thick in order to support the additional load of ballast material. Top flange thickness varies from 11 in. (0.28 m) at midspan of the main span to 17 in. (0.43 m) at the main pier and has a constant thickness of 17 in. (0.43 m) in the end spans.[15]

The superstructure is monolithic with the main piers, with a permanent hinge at midspan to accommodate concrete shrinkage, creep, and thermal movements. The hinge can only transfer vertical and lateral shear forces between the two cantilevers and has no moment-transfer capacity.[15] The superstructure was constructed in segments with the end spans on falsework and the main span in the conventional segmental cantilever manner, using form travelers. After foundations were completed, a 46 ft (14 m) deep by 37 ft (11.3 m) pier segment was constructed, Figure 2.69, in three operations: first the bottom flange, then the webs and diaphragm, and finally the top flange. Upon completion of the pier segment, form travelers were installed and segmental construction begun. Two form travelers were used to simultaneously ad-

FIGURE 2.68. Koror-Babelthuap Bridge, parabolic soffit of main span (courtesy of Dr. Man-Chung Tang, DRC Consultants, Inc.).

FIGURE 2.69. Koror-Babelthuap Bridge, pier segment (courtesy of Dyckerhoff & Widmann).

FIGURE 2.70. Koror-Babelthuap Bridge, main-span cantilevers advancing (courtesy of Dyckerhoff & Widmann).

vance the main-span cantilevers, Figure 2.70. Segments for this project were 15 ft (4.57 m) in length.[15]

On this project, each segment took slightly more than one week to construct. A typical cycle was as follows:[15]

1. When the concrete strength in the last segment cast reached 2500 psi (17.2 MPa), a specified number of tendons, ranging from six to 12, were stressed to 50 percent of their final force, thus enabling the form traveler to advance in preparation for the following segment.

2. Advancing the form traveler also brought forward the outside forms of the box. The forms were cleaned while rough adjustments of elevation were made.

3. Reinforcement and prestressing tendons were placed in the bottom flange and webs. The inside forms were advanced and top flange reinforcement and tendons placed.

4. After the previous segment concrete had reached a strength of 3500 psi (24.1 MPa), the remaining tendons were stressed. The previous segment had to be fully prestressed before concrete for the subsequent segment could be placed.

5. Fine adjustment of the forms for camber and any required correction was made.

6. New segment concrete was placed and cured.

7. When the new segment reached a concrete strength of 2500 psi (17.2 MPa), the cycle was repeated.

The structure was prestressed longitudinally, transversely, and vertically. Three hundred and

two longitudinal tendons were required at the pier segment. As the cantilever progressed, 12 to 16 tendons were anchored off at each segment, with eight longitudinal tendons remaining for the last segment in a cantilever at midspan. As the structure has a hinge at midspan, there were no continuity tendons in the bottom flange. Transverse tendons in the top flange were spaced at 22 in. (0.56 m) centers. Vertical tendons were used in the webs to accommodate shear. Spacing for the vertical web tendons was 30 in. (0.76 m) in the center span and 15 in. (0.38 m) in the end spans. All tendons were $1\frac{1}{4}$ in. (32 mm) diameter bars.[15]

Side spans were constructed on falsework resting on compacted fill. The sequence of segmental construction in the side spans was coordinated with that in the main span, so that the unbalanced moment at the main pier was maintained within prescribed limits.

2.13   Vejle Fjord Bridge, Denmark

This structure crosses the Vejle Fjord about 0.6 mile (1 km) east of the Vejle Harbor. It is part of the East Jutland Motorway, which will provide a bypass around the city of Vejle, Denmark. A total length of 5611 ft (1710 m) makes it the second longest bridge in Denmark.

Bid documents indicated two alternative designs, one in steel and one in concrete. The steel alternative called for a superstructure composed of a central box girder with cantilevered outriggers supporting an orthotropic deck and fjord spans of 413 ft (126 m). The second alternative required a prestressed concrete superstructure with a central box girder to be constructed by the balanced cantilever method utilizing either precast or cast-in-place segments, with fjord spans of 361 ft (110 m). The successful alternative was the cast-in-place segmental prestressed concrete box girder.

The bridge, in plan, is straight without any horizontal curvature. It does have a constant grade of 0.5% falling toward the north. Navigation requirements were a minimum 131 ft (40 m) vertical and 246 ft (75 m) horizontal clearance. Water depth in the fjord is generally 8 to 11.5 ft (2.5 to 3.5 m) except at the navigation channel, where the depth increases to 23 ft (7 m). Under the fjord bed are layers of very soft foundation materials, varying in depth from 26 to 39 ft (8 to 12 m). Therefore, the piers in the fjord are founded on 8 in. (0.2 m) square driven reinforced concrete piles varying in length from 100 to 130 ft (30 to 40 m), Figure 2.71. Piers on the south bank are founded on

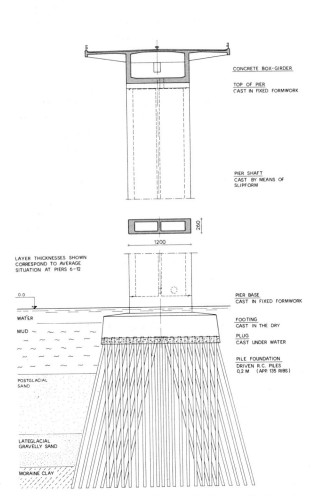

FIGURE 2.71. Vejle Fjord Bridge, fjord piers founded on driven reinforced concrete piles.

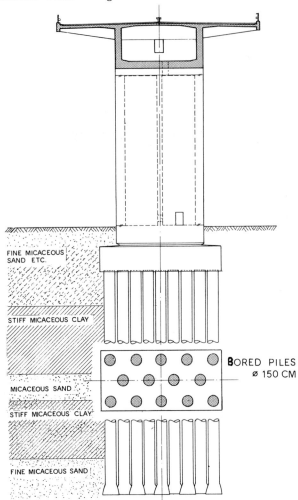

FIGURE 2.72. Vejle Fjord Bridge, land piers founded on bored piles.

bored reinforced concrete piles, 59 in. (1500 mm) in diameter, Figure 2.72. On the north bank one pier is founded on driven reinforced concrete piles and one is supported directly on a spread footing.

The cross section of the bridge, Figure 2.73, which carries four traffic lanes with a median barrier, is a variable-depth single box with a vertical web and prestressed transverse ribs. Total width between edge guard rails is 87 ft (26.6 m). Box girder width is 39.4 ft (12 m), with a depth varying from 19.7 ft (6 m) at the pier to 9.8 ft (3 m) at midspan. Each segment is cast with a length of 11.3 ft (3.44 m). Transverse top flange ribs are spaced at 22.6 ft (6.88 m) centers—that is, every other segment joint.

The total bridge length is divided into four separate sections by three expansion joints located at the center of spans 4–5, 8–9, and 12–13. Longitudinal prestress is achieved by Dywidag (twelve

0.6 in. diameter strand) tendons, as are the transverse prestress in the top slab and the continuity prestress in the bottom slab.

A 492 ft (150 m) long steel launching girder and two special form travelers were used for casting in place the full width of the 11.3 ft (3.4 m) long segments in balanced cantilever. Insulating forms followed the form travelers in order to prevent the formation of fissures due to adverse temperature gradients. In addition, the steel girder stabilized the concrete structure during construction and was used for the transportation of materials, equipment, and working crew. The total weight of the girder including the two travelers was approximately 660 t (600 mt). A typical longitudinal section of a cantilever is shown in Figure 2.74, along with the structure erection procedure.

Work on the bridge started in the summer of 1975 and was scheduled for completion in 1980.

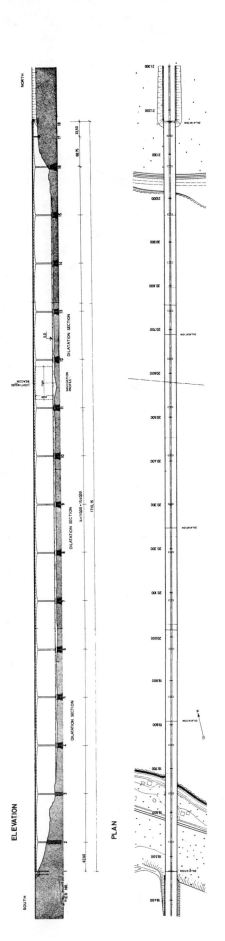

CROSS SECTION 1:200

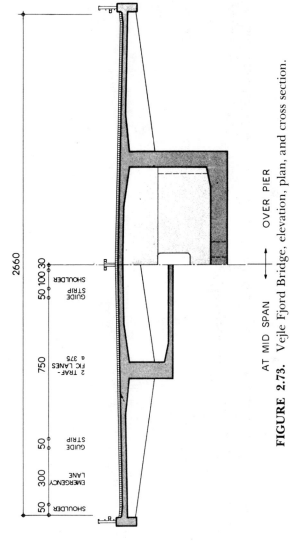

AT MID SPAN   OVER PIER

FIGURE 2.73. Vejle Fjord Bridge, elevation, plan, and cross section.

65

BOX-TYPE GIRDER

LONGITUDINAL SECTION

POSITION OF PRESTRESSING TENDONS

₵-CENTRE LINE OF SPAN

₵-CENTRE LINE OF SPAN

CONSTRUCTION PRINCIPLES

① CONCRETING OF SYMMETRICAL SECTIONS FROM PIER TOWARDS MID-SPAN. SECTIONS OF 3.44 M LENGTH CAST IN ORDER AS SHOWN. THE LAUNCHING GIRDER Ⓐ IS IN A FIXED WORKING POSITION. THE CONCRETE SUPER-STRUCTURE INCLUDING CARRIAGES Ⓑ IS CANTILEVER-ED AND UNSUPPORTED. DISBALANCE OF THE SYSTEM DUE TO ALTERNATE CASTING OF SECTIONS IS COUNTERACTED BY THE LAUNCHING GIRDER Ⓐ
WORKING CYCLUS PER SECTION: PLACING OF MILD STEEL AND PRESTRESSING TENDONS. CONCRETING, PRESTRESSING OF TENDONS. REMOVAL OF CARRIAGE Ⓑ TO THE FOLLOW-ING SECTION.

② CONNECTION TO PREVIOUSLY ESTABLISHED BRIDGE SECTION BY CONCRETING OF CENTRE SECTION IN MID-SPAN AND PRE-STRESSING ADDITIONAL TENDONS IN GIRDER BOTTOM-SLAB AND BRIDGE DECK (CONTINUITY-TENDONS)

③ LAUNCHING OF GIRDER Ⓐ TO NEW WORKING POSITION OVER ADJOINING PIER. SUPERSTRUCTURE SECTION ON TOP OF PIER HAS BEEN CONCRETED PREVIOUSLY ON CANTILEVER-ED SCAFFOLDING Ⓒ

④ TRANSPORT OF CARRIAGES Ⓑ ALONG THE LAUNCHING GIRDER Ⓐ TO THE FOLLOWING CANTILEVER SECTION.

⑤ CANTILEVERING OF CONCRETE STRUCTURE AS DESCRIBED UNDER ①. THE SUPERSTRUCTURE IS BUILD SIMULTA-NEOUSLY FROM THE NORTHERN AND THE SOUTHERN END OF THE BRIDGE BY MEANS OF IDENTICAL EQUIPMENT AND THE SAME CONSTRUCTION PRINCIPLES.

⑥ THE EDGE BEAMS OF THE BRIDGE DECK ARE FINALLY CON-CRETED IN A SEPARATE WORKING OPERATION.

AUXILIARY EQUIPMENT ETC.

Ⓐ LAUNCHING GIRDER, LENGTH 105 M, WEIGHT APP. 300 Mp
THE GIRDER HAS THE FOLLOWING FUNCTIONS:
- STABILIZING THE CONCRETE STRUCTURE DURING CON-STRUCTION
- TRANSPORTING OF MATERIALS AND EQUIPMENT
- ACCESS FOR WORKING CREW
THE GIRDER IS LAUNCHED SUCCESSIVELY ACCORDING TO PROGRESS FROM PIER TO PIER.

Ⓑ CARRIAGES FOR CONCRETING, WEIGHT 150 Mp PER CARRIAGE
EQUIPPED WITH FORM FOR CASTING OF SUPERSTRUC-TURE SECTIONS OF 3.44 M IN THE FULL WIDTH OF THE BRIDGE

Ⓒ CANTILEVERED SCAFFOLDING
FOR CASTING OF SUPERSTRUCTURE SECTION ON TOP OF PIERS.

Ⓓ SLIP FORM
FOR CONCRETING OF PIER SHAFTS.

SUPERSTRUCTURE, PRINCIPLE OF EXECUTION

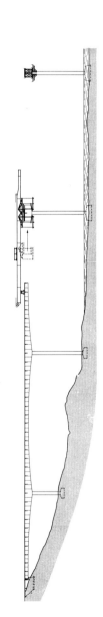

END SECTION CAST ON SCAFFOLDING

FIGURE 2.74. Vejle Fjord Bridge, longitudinal section and erection sequence.

FIGURE 2.75. Vejle Fjord Bridge, launching girder.

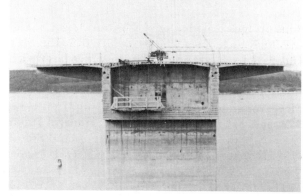

FIGURE 2.77. Vejle Fjord Bridge, pier segment with diaphragm.

FIGURE 2.76. Vejle Fjord Bridge, transverse ribs.

FIGURE 2.78. Vejle Fjord Bridge, construction view, spring 1978 (courtesy of H. A. Lindberg).

Construction progress in the spring of 1978 is illustrated in Figures 2.75 through 2.78. Figure 2.79 is an aerial view showing the structure nearing completion. To keep within the construction schedule, it was finally necessary to use two complete sets of launching girders and twin travelers working simultaneously from both ends of the bridge.

FIGURE 2.79. Vejle Fjord Bridge, aerial view from the northwest.

2.14 Houston Ship Channel Bridge, U.S.A.

This bridge, a rendering of which is shown in Figure 1.67, includes a main structure over the Ship Channel in Houston, Texas, and two approach viaducts. The main structure is a three-span continuous box girder, cast in place in balanced cantilever. Span lengths are 375, 750, and 375 ft (114, 229, and 114 m). The navigation channel is 700 ft (213 m) wide at elevation 95 ft (29 m) and 500 ft (752 m) wide at elevation 175 ft (53.4 m), Figure 2.80.

The three-web box girder carries four traffic lanes separated by a 2 ft 3 in. (0.7 m) central barrier and has two 3 ft 9 in. (1.14 m) parapets. The box girder is fixed to the top of the main piers to make the structure a three-span rigid frame. Support for the box girder is provided by elastomeric bearings on top of the transition piers, where it is separated from the approach viaducts by expansion joints.

Foundations The two center piers and two transition piers rest on 24 in. (610 mm) diameter driven steel pipe piles. The center piers each rest upon 255 piles with a unit pile capacity of 140 t (127 mt). Footings are 81 ft (24.7 m) wide, 85 ft (26 m) long, and 15 ft (4.6 m) deep. These footings are surrounded by a sheet pile cofferdam and are poured on a 4 ft (1.2 m) thick subfooting seal concrete. The transition pier footings are 50 ft (15.2 m) wide, 35 ft (10.7 m) long, and 5.5 ft (1.7 m) thick and rest on 70 piles each of 100 t (90 mt) bearing capacity.

Piers The main piers provide for the stability of the cantilevers during construction (unbalanced construction loads and wind loads) and participate in the capacity and behavior of the structure under service loads (long-term loads due to creep and shrinkage, superimposed dead loads, and live loads). They are, therefore, heavily reinforced; their dimensions are:

Total height (from top of footing to bottom of pier segments): 160 ft 10 in. (49 m)

Length (parallel to centerline of highway): 20 ft constant (6.1 m)

Width: variable from 38 ft at the bottom to 27 ft 7 in. at the top (11.6 to 8.4 m)

Pier cross section: rectangular box, with 2 ft (0.6 m) constant wall thickness

The transition piers support the last segment of the main structure side span and the last span of the approaches. The pier shaft is a rectangular box with 1 ft 4 in. (0.4 m) thick walls. Their heights are 152 ft (46 m) at one end and 164 ft (50 m) at the other end of the bridge. The length, parallel to the centerline of the highway, varies from 18 to 8 ft (5.5 to 2.4 m); the width is 38 ft (11.6 m) constant. Atop the pier, a 6 ft 8 in. (2 m) cap carries the permanent elastomeric bearings and all the temporary jacks and concrete blocks that will be used at the time of the side-span closure pour. All four piers are slip-formed.

Box Girder Superstructure Dimensions of the variable-depth box girder were dictated by very stringent geometry requirements. Vertical alignment of the roadway was determined by the maximum allowable grade of the approach viaducts and the connection thereof with the roadway system on both banks. The clearance required for the ship channel left, therefore, only a structural depth of 21.8 ft (6.6 m) at the two points located 250 ft (76 m) on either side of the midspan section. The soffit is given a third-degree parabolic shape to increase the structural depth near the piers in order to compensate for the very limited height of

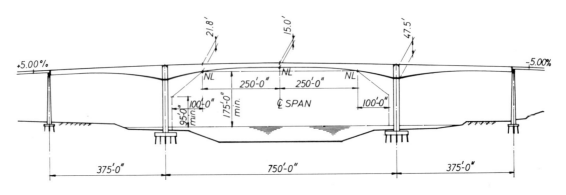

FIGURE 2.80. Houston Ship Channel Bridge, longitudinal section.

the center portion of the main span. Maximum depth at the pier is 47.8 ft (14.6 m), with a span-to-depth ratio of 15.3. Minimum depth at midspan is 15 ft (4.6 m), with a span-to-depth ratio of 49. Over the 500 ft (152 m) center portion of the main span the span-to-depth ratio is 23, compared to a usual value between 17 and 20. Typical dimensions of the box section are shown in Figure 2.81. Post-tensioning is applied to the box section in three dimensions:

Longitudinal prestress is provided by straight-strand tendons (twelve 0.6 in. diameter or nineteen 0.6 in. diameter strands), as shown schematically in Figure 2.82.

Transversely, the top slab is post-tensioned by tendons (four 0.6 in. diameter strands) in flat ducts placed at 2 ft (0.6 m) centers.

Vertically, the three webs are also post-tensioned as prescribed in the specifications to a minimum

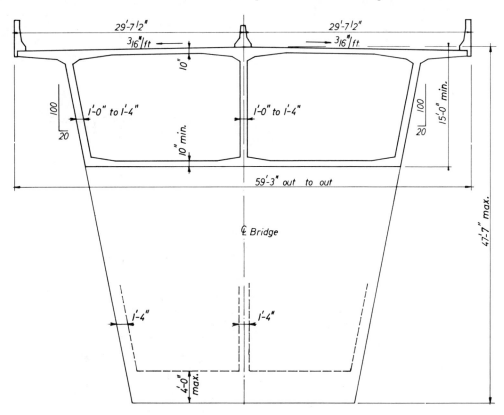

FIGURE 2.81. Houston Ship Channel Bridge, box section.

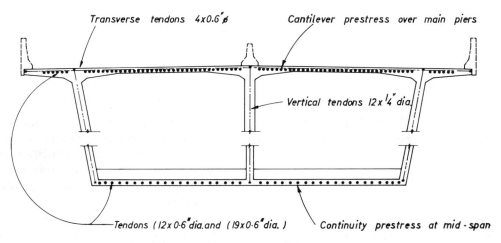

FIGURE 2.82. Houston Ship Channel Bridge, longitudinal prestress.

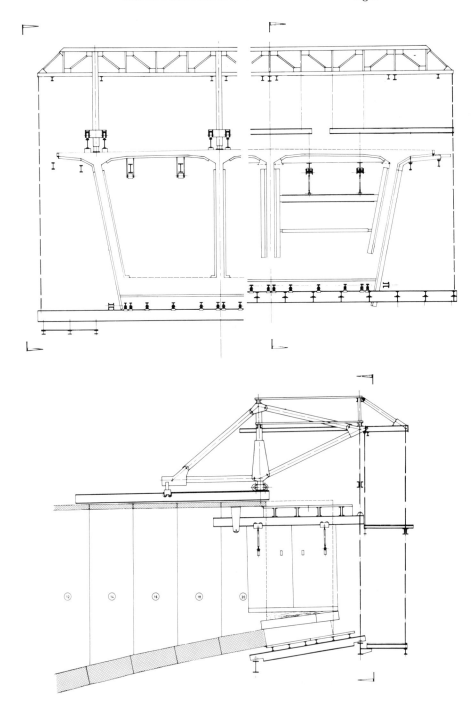

FIGURE 2.83.   Houston Ship Channel Bridge, details of travelers.

compressive stress equal to $3f'_c$; that is, 230 psi (1.6 MPa) for a concrete strength f'_c = 6000 psi (41.4 MPa).

Details of the form traveler are shown in Figure 2.83.

Pier segments over the main piers are of unusual size and posed a very interesting design problem, arising from the transfer of the superstructure un-

balanced moments into the pier shafts. Additional vertical post-tensioning tendons are provided in the two 2 ft (0.6 m) thick pier diaphragms for this purpose. End segments over the transition piers were designed to allow either the approaches or the main structure to be completed first, as these are two separate contracts.

It is possible to make an adjustment at the end piers to compensate either for differential settle-

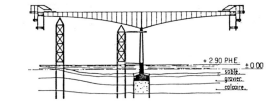

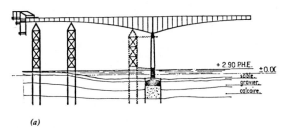

(a)

FIGURE 2.84. Medway Bridge, U.K. (*a*) Typical construction sequence. (*b*) View of finished bridge.

ments or for any deviation of the deflections from the assumed camber diagram used for construction.

Provisions have been made for unexpected additional concrete shrinkage and creep problems; empty ducts have been placed in the pier segment diaphragms and at midspan to allow for future possible installation of additional tendons located inside the box girder but outside the concrete section, should the need for such tendons arise.

2.15 Other Notable Structures

There are so many outstanding and interesting cast-in-place cantilever bridges in the world today that it is impossible to discuss the subject adequately in the space available here. Mention should be made, however, of several notable structures not yet covered by a detailed description.

2.15.1 MEDWAY BRIDGE, U.K.

One of the first very long-span cantilever bridges was the Medway Bridge. This structure used a series of temporary falsework bents to provide stability during construction, Figure 2.84.

2.15.2 RIO TOCANTINS BRIDGE, BRAZIL

This structure has a center span of 460 ft (140 m) and two side spans of only 174 ft (53 m), Figures 2.85 and 2.86.

2.15.3 PUENTE DEL AZUFRE, SPAIN

This bridge is located very high over a deep canyon of the Rio Sil. Cantilever cast-in-place was the ideal answer to allow construction with a minimal contact with the environment, Figures 2.87 and 2.88.

2.15.4 SCHUBENACADIE BRIDGE, CANADA

This three-span bridge with a center span of 700 ft (213 m) crosses the Schubenacadie River, near Truro, Nova Scotia. High tidal range, swift currents, ice, and adverse climatic conditions made the construction of this structure very challenging, Figures 2.89 and 2.90.

2.15.5 INCIENSO BRIDGE, GUATEMALA

The main three-span rigid frame structure with a center span of 400 ft (122 m) is of cast-in-place balanced cantilever construction, and the approach spans are of precast girders, Figures 2.91 and 2.92. The very severe 1977 earthquake left the center structure completely undamaged, while the usual damage took place in the approach spans.

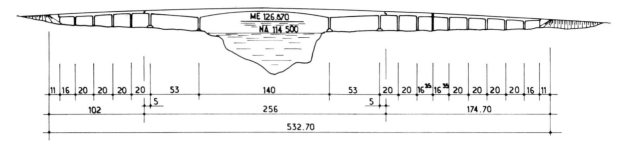

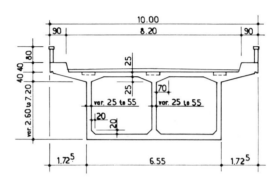

FIGURE 2.85. Rio Tocantins Bridge, Brazil, typical elevation and cross section.

2.15.6 *SETUBAL BRIDGE, ARGENTINA*

This three-span structure with a main span of 460 ft (140 m) rests on two main river piers with twin vertical walls and piles, with a transition footing at water elevation, Figures 2.93 and 2.94.

2.15.7 *KIPAPA STREAM BRIDGE, U.S.A.*

This bridge is located in the Island of Oahu in the State of Hawaii. The dual structure has an overall width of 118 ft (36 m) to accommodate six traffic lanes, three in each direction, and consists of two double-cell box girders of constant depth with interior spans of 250 ft (76.2 m), Figures 2.95 and 2.96. Construction was by cast-in-place cantilever with segments 15 ft 3 in. (4.65 m) long. The bridge has pleasant lines, which blend aesthetically with the rugged deep-valley site.

2.15.8 *PARROTS FERRY BRIDGE, U.S.A.*

This structure, built in California for the Corps of Engineers, represents a major application of lightweight concrete for cast-in-place cantilever construction, Figure 2.97.

2.15.9 *MAGNAN VIADUCT, FRANCE*

Located just off the French Riviera in Southern France, this four-span continuous structure rests on 300 ft (92 m) high twin piers of an I-shaped section. Superstructure was cast in place in two stages (first the bottom slab and webs and then the top slab) to reduce the weight and cost of travelers. Figures 2.98 and 2.99 show the principal dimensions and views of one cantilever and the finished structure, Figure 2.100.

FIGURE 2.86. Rio Tocantins Bridge, Brazil, view of the finished bridge.

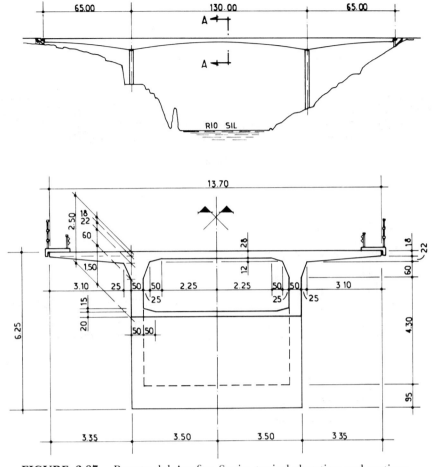

FIGURE 2.87. Puente del Azufre, Spain, typical elevation and sections.

2.15.10 PUTEAUX BRIDGE, FRANCE

These are twin bridges crossing the Seine River near Paris. Because of very stringent clearance and geometry requirements, the available structural depth was only 5.9 ft (1.8 m) for the clear 275 ft (83.8 m) span and 4.8 ft (1.47 m) for the clear 214 ft (65.3 m) span, making both structures very slender, Figures 2.101 and 2.102. Stiff "V" piers in both structures help reduce the flexibility of the deck.

2.15.11 TRICASTIN BRIDGE, FRANCE

This structure spans the Rhone River with no piers in the river, which necessitates a long center span and two very short side spans anchored at both ends against uplift. The center portion of the main span is of lightweight concrete, while the two zones over the piers where stresses are high are of conventional concrete, Figures 2.103 and 2.104.

2.15.12 ESCHACHTAL BRIDGE, GERMANY

This bridge is located near Stuttgart, Germany. The superstructure consists of a large single-cell box girder with large top flange cantilevers supported by precast struts. Because of the weight involved, the central box was cast in one operation; struts were installed and flanges cast subsequently, Figures 2.105 and 2.106.

FIGURE 2.88. Puente del Azufre, Spain.

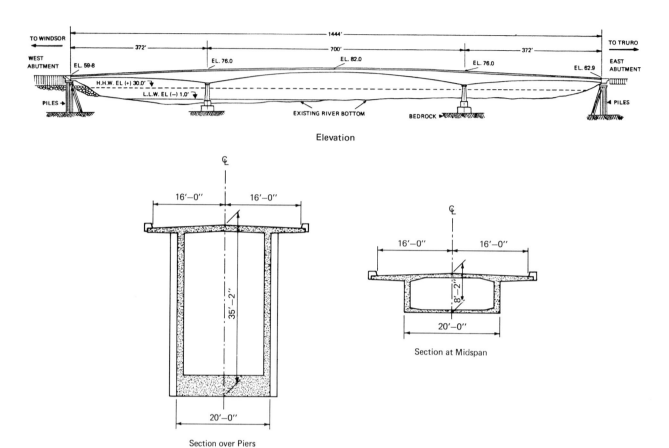

FIGURE 2.89. Shubenacadie Bridge, elevation and sections, from ref. 16.

FIGURE 2.90. Shubenacadie Bridge, support system for unbalanced cantilever moment at pier (courtesy of the Portland Cement Association).

FIGURE 2.91. Incienso Bridge, Guatemala, view of the structure.

74

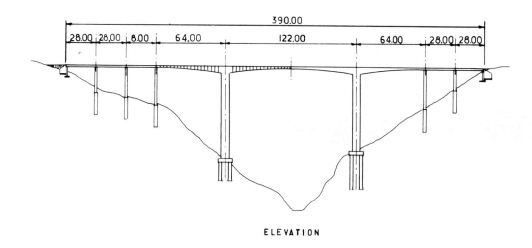

ELEVATION

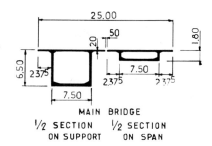

MAIN BRIDGE
½ SECTION   ½ SECTION
ON SUPPORT   ON SPAN

FIGURE 2.92.   Incienso Bridge, Guatemala, dimensions.

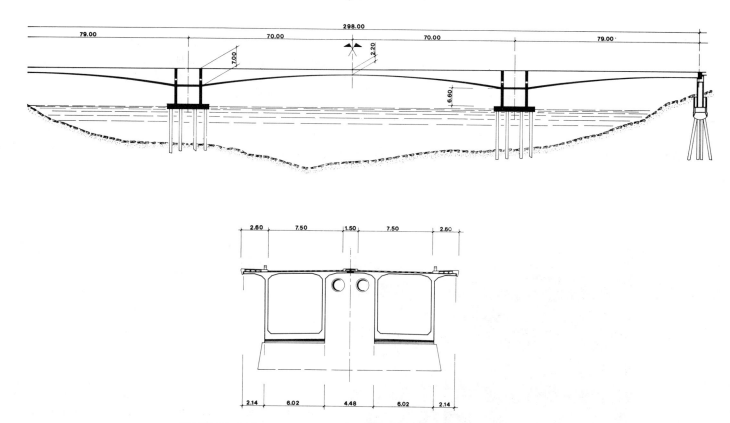

FIGURE 2.93.   Setubal Bridge, Argentina, dimensions.

FIGURE 2.94. Setubal Bridge, Argentina, view of the bridge.

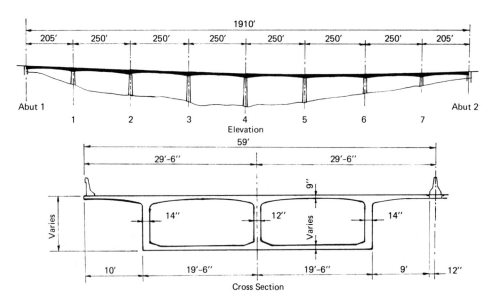

FIGURE 2.95. Kipapa Stream Bridge, elevation and cross section.

FIGURE 2.96. Kipapa Stream Bridge, construction view (courtesy of Dyckerhoff & Widmann).

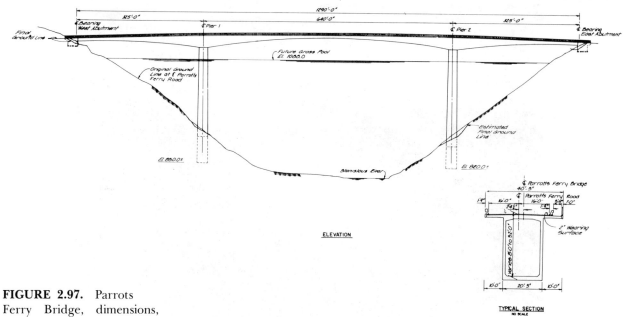

ELEVATION

TYPICAL SECTION
NO SCALE

FIGURE 2.97. Parrots Ferry Bridge, dimensions, ref. 17.

COUPE LONGITUDINALE

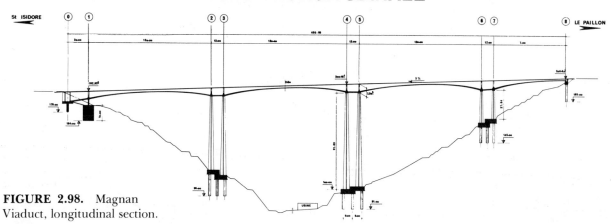

FIGURE 2.98. Magnan Viaduct, longitudinal section.

FIGURE 2.99. Magnan Viaduct, view of a cantilever.

FIGURE 2.100. Magnan Viaduct, aerial view of the completed bridge.

FIGURE 2.101. Puteaux Bridge, aerial view of the completed bridge.

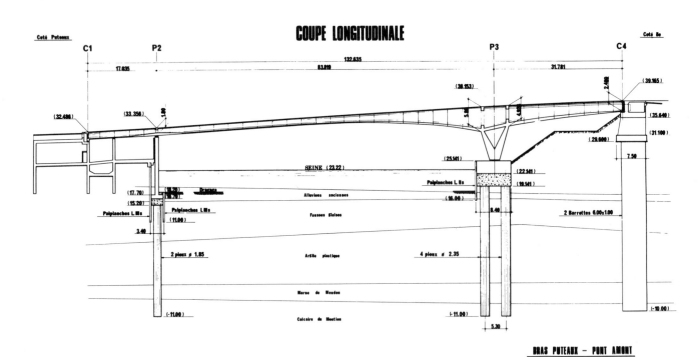

FIGURE 2.102. Puteaux Bridge, longitudinal section.

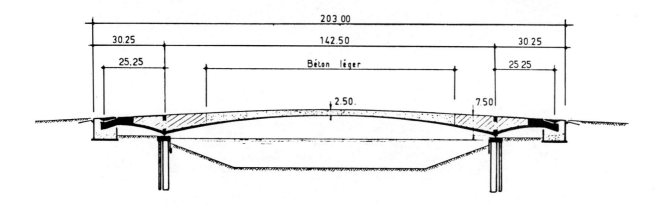

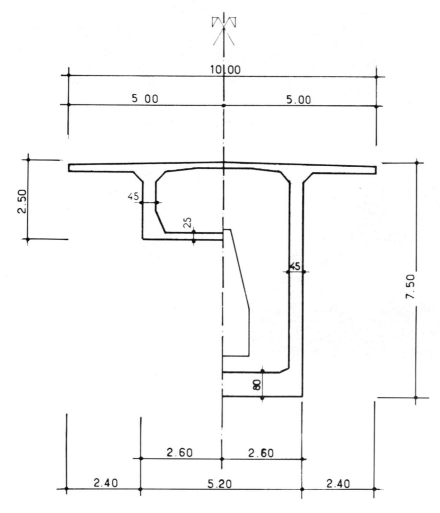

FIGURE 2.103. Tricastin Bridge, dimensions.

FIGURE 2.104. Tricastin Bridge, view of finished bridge.

FIGURE 2.105. Eschachtal Bridge, casting flange cantilevers.

FIGURE 2.106. Eschachtal Bridge, view of outrigger struts.

2.16 Conclusion

The many structures described above show the versatility of cast-in-place balanced cantilever construction, particularly in the field of very-long-span bridges with few repetitive spans. The design aspect of these structures will be discussed in Chapter 4 and construction problems in Chapter 11.

References

1. H. Thul, "Brückenbau," *Beton- und Stahlbetonbau*, 61 Jahrgang, Heft 5, Mai 1966.

2. Ulrich Finsterwalder, "Prestressed Concrete Bridge Construction," *Journal of the American Concrete Institute*, Vol. 62, No. 9, September 1965.

3. Ulrich Finsterwalder, "New Developments in Prestressing Methods and Concrete Bridge Construction," *Dywidag-Berichte*, 4-1967, September 1967, Dyckerhoff & Widmann KG, Munich, Germany.

4. Ulrich Finsterwalder, "Free Cantilever Construction of Prestressed Concrete Bridges and Mushroom-Shaped Bridges," *First International Symposium, Concrete Bridge Design*, ACI Publication SP-23, Paper SP23-26, American Concrete Institute, Detroit, 1969.

5. "Bridge Built Atop the Scenery With Cantilevered Travelers," *Engineering News-Record*, June 18, 1964.

6. Dale F. Downing, "Cantilever Segmental Prestressed Cast-in-Place Construction of the Pine Valley Creek Bridge," presented to the AASHO Annual Meeting, Los Angeles, California, November 11–15, 1973.

7. "Pine Valley Creek Bridge, California," Bridge Report SR 161.01 E, Portland Cement Association, Skokie, Ill., 1974.

8. Richard A. Dokken, "CALTRANS Experience in Segmental Bridge Design," *Bridge Notes*, Division of Structures, Department of Transportation, State of California, Vol. XVII, No. 1, March 1975.

9. A. P. Bezzone, "Pine Valley Creek Bridge—Designing for Segmental Construction," Meeting Preprint 1944, ASCE National Structural Engineering Meeting, April 9–13, 1973, San Francisco.

10. Richard Heinen, "Pine Valley Creek Bridge: Use of Cantilever Construction," Meeting Preprint 1981, ASCE National Structural Engineering Meeting, April 9–13, 1973, San Francisco.

11. "A.15 et A.86 raccordement autoroutier dans le nord du departement des hauts-de-seine," Ministere de L'Equipement Direction Departemental de L'Equipement des Hauts-de-Seine, Paris, September 1976.

12. "Bridge Has 595 ft Post-tensioned Span," *Heavy Construction News*, August 2, 1976.

13. "Napa River Bridge, Napa, California," Portland Cement Association, Bridge Report, SR 194.01 E, 1977.

14. "Alternate Bidding for California's Napa River Bridge Won by Cast-in-Place Prestressed Concrete Segmental Construction," Prestressed Concrete Institute, Post-Tensioning Division, Special Bridge Report.

15. Man-Chung Tang, "Koror-Babelthuap Bridge—A World Record Span," Preprint Paper 3441, ASCE Convention, Chicago, October 16–20, 1978.

16. D. W. MacIntosh and R. A. Whitman, "The Shubenacadie Bridge, Maitland, Nova Scotia," Annual Conference Preprints, Roads and Transportation Association of Canada, Ottawa, 1978.

17. "Concrete Alternate Wins Competitive Bidding Contest for Long Span California Bridge," Bridge Report, Post-Tensioning Institute, April 1977.

3

Precast Balanced Cantilever Girder Bridges

3.1   Introduction

As indicated in Chapter 1, precast segmental construction had its origins (in the contemporary sense) in France in 1962 as a logical alternative to the cast-in-place method of construction. To the advantage of segmental cantilever construction, primarily the elimination of conventional falsework, the technique adds the refinements implicit in the use of precasting.

The characteristics of precast segmental construction are:

1. Fabrication of the segments can be accomplished while the substructure is under construction, thus enhancing erection speed of the superstructure.

2. By virtue of precasting and therefore maturity of the concrete at the time of erection, the time required for strength gain of the concrete is removed from the construction critical path.

3. As a result of the maturity of the concrete at the time of erection, the effects of concrete shrinkage and creep are minimized.

4. Superior quality control can be achieved for factory-produced precast concrete.

However, geometric control during fabrication of segments is essential, and corrections during erection are more difficult than for cast-in-place segmental construction. In addition, the connection of longitudinal ducts for post-tensioning tendons and the continuity of reinforcing steel, if they are required in the design, are less easily achieved in precast than in cast-in-place methods.

Although precast segmental had been used as early as 1944 for the Luzancy Bridge over the Marne River, Figure 1.27, wide acceptance began when match-casting techniques were developed. Basically, the principle of fabrication of precast segments is to cast them in a series one against the other in the order in which they are to be assembled in the structure. The front face of a segment, thus, serves as a bulkhead for casting the rear face of the subsequent segment. Methods of fabrication of precast segments will be discussed in Chapter 11.

Segments are erected in balanced cantilever starting from a segment over the pier, which is the first to be placed. Modifications to the initial principle have further increased the flexibility of erection procedures. Two major modifications are (1) temporary prestress ties to secure two or more successive segments and thus free the erection equipment, and (2) cantilever prestressing tendons anchored inside the box sections instead of at the segment face as on early structures. These refinements mean that the placing of segments and the threading and stressing of tendons become independent operations.

Efficient application of this method has resulted in the use of cantilever construction in moderate-to small-span structures where it had previously been considered uneconomical. Examples are the B-3 South Viaduct (Section 3.14) composed of spans ranging from 98 ft (30 m) to 164 ft (50 m) and the Alpine Motorway Bridges (Section 3.15) where the spans range between 60 ft (18 m) to 100 ft (30 m).

It is interesting to note a constant evolution toward increased transverse dimensions and weight of precast segments. Problems in precasting, transporting, and placing segments that are constantly becoming heavier and wider are being progressively resolved. Chapter 4 will deal with this progressive evolution as applied to some French precast segmental bridges and will discuss typical cross sections of some precast segmental bridges constructed or in the design stage in the United States.[1,2]

In continuous structures expansion joints may be spaced very far apart. Continuous bridges up to 3300 ft (1000 m) in length have been constructed without intermediate joints; however, this may not be an upper limit, provided that the design of bearings and piers is correctly integrated into the total design of the structure. Free longitudinal movement of the bridge due to creep and temperature change is allowed for by placing the structure on elastomeric or sliding (teflon) bearings. We can also use pier flexibility to accommodate these movements by fixing the superstructure to the piers. In this case, flexibility can be obtained either by pier height or by the use of single or double thin-slab walls, thus reducing the piers flexural resistance.

The first precast segmental bridge to be built on the North American Continent was the Lievre River Bridge on Highway 35, 8 miles (13 km) north of Notre Dame du Laus, Quebec, with a center span of 260 ft (79 m) and end spans of 130 ft (40 m), built in 1967. It was followed in 1972 by the Bear River Bridge, Digby, Nova Scotia (Section 3.9), with six interior spans of 265 ft (81 m) and end spans of 204 ft (62 m). The JFK Memorial Causeway, Corpus Christi, Texas (Section 3.10), opened to traffic in 1973, was the first precast segmental bridge to be constructed in the United States. In the United States, as of this writing, the authors are aware of more than 30 precast segmental bridge projects that are either completed, under construction, or in the design stage. Some are listed in Table 3.1.[3]

3.2   Choisy-le-Roi Bridge and Other Structures in Greater Paris, France

The first bridge to use the precast segmental cantilever technique with epoxied match-cast joints was built at Choisy-le-Roi near Paris between 1962 and 1964. It carries National Highway 186, a part of the Paris Great Belt system, over the Seine River just east of Orly Airport, Figure 3.1. This structure is a three-span continuous bridge of constant depth with end spans of 123 ft (37.5 m) and a center span of 180 ft (55 m), Figures 3.2 and 3.3.

This bridge replaced one constructed in 1870, which had a superstructure of six steel girders with five spans of approximately 75 ft (23 m). This structure, determined to be no longer adequate as early as 1939, was severely damaged during World War II. It in turn had replaced an ancient bridge of five 66 ft (20 m) oak arch spans designed by the famous mathematician Claude-Louis-Marie Navier.[4]

In 1961, a study by the Administration of Bridges and Roads allowed two options, one in prestressed concrete and the other in steel, each having three continuous spans of 123 ft (37.5 m), 180.4 ft (55 m), and 123 ft (37.5 m). Four prestressed concrete solutions were considered. The successful solution is illustrated in Figure 3.2.

The overall width of the superstructure for this dual bridge is 93.2 ft (28.4 m), Figure 3.3. Each bridge consists of two single-cell rectangular box girders. The superstructure accommodates dual two-lane roadways of 23 ft (7 m), two 13 ft (4 m) sidewalks, and a 10 ft (3 m) median.[4,5] Individual box girders have a constant depth of 8.2 ft (2.5 m),

TABLE 3.1. Precast Segmental Concrete Bridges in North America

Name and Location	Date of Construction	Method of Construction[a]	Span Lengths, ft (m)
Lievre River, Notre Dame du Laus, Quebec	1967	B.C.	130 – 260 – 130 (39.6 – 79.2– 39.6)
Bear River, Digby, Nova Scotia	1972	B.C.	203.75 – 6 @ 265 – 203.75 (62.1 – 6 @ 80.77 – 62.1)
JFK Memorial Causeway, Corpus Christi, Texas	1973	B.C.	100 – 200 – 100 (30.5 – 61 – 30.5)
Muscatuck River, U.S. 50, North Vernon, Indiana	1975	B.C.	95 – 190 – 95 (29 – 58 – 29)
Sugar Creek, State Route 1620, Parke County, Indiana	1976	B.C.	90.5 – 180.5 – 90.5 (27.6 – 55 – 27.6)
Vail Pass, I-70 West of Denver, Colorado (4 bridges)	1977	B.C.	134 – 200 – 200 – 134 (40.8 – 61 – 61 – 40.8) 134 – 200 – 200 – 145 (40.8 – 61 – 61 – 44) 151 – 155 – 210 – 210 – 154 (46 – 47.2 – 64 – 64 – 47) 153 – 210 – 210 – 154 (46.6 – 64 – 64 – 47)
Penn DOT Test Track Bridge, Penn Sate University, State College, Pa.	1977	O.F.	124 (37.8)
Turkey Run State Park Parke County, Indiana	1977	B.C.	180 – 180 (54.9 – 54.9)
Pasco-Kennewick, Columbia River between Pasco and Kennewick, Washington (cable-stay spans)	1978	B.C.	406.5 – 981 – 406.5 (124 – 299 – 124)
Wabash River, U.S. 136, Covington, Ind.	1978	I.L.	93.5 – 4 @ 187 – 93.5 (28.5 – 4 @ 57 – 28.5)
Kishwaukee River, Winnebago Co. near Rockford, Ill. (dual structure)	1979	B.C.	170 – 3 @ 250 – 170 (51.8 – 3 @ 76.2 – 51.8)
Islington Ave. Ext., Toronto, Ontario	1979	B.C.	2 @ 161 – 200 – 5 @ 272 (2 @ 49 – 61 – 5 @ 83)
Kentucky River, Frankfort, Ky. (dual structure)	1979	B.C.	228.5 – 320 – 228.5 (69.6 – 97.5 – 69.6)
Long Key, Florida (contract let late 1978)		S.S.	113 – 101 @ 118 – 113 (34.4 – 101 @ 36 – 34.4)
Linn Cove, Blue Ridge Parkway, N.C. (contract let late 1978)		P.P.	98.5 – 163 – 4 @ 180 – 163 – 98.5 (30 – 49.7 – 4 @ 54.9 – 49.7 – 30)
Zilwaukee, Michigan (dual structure) (bids opened late 1978)		B.C.	26 N.B. spans total length 8,087.5 (2,465) 25 S.B. spans total length 8,057.5 (2,456) maximum span 392 (119.5)

[a]Method-of-construction notation: B.C.—balanced cantilever, I.L.—incremental launching, O.F.—on falsework, P.P.—progressive placement, S.S.—span-by-span.

top flange width of 21.65 ft (6.6 m), and a bottom flange width of 12 ft (3.66 m). Webs have a constant thickness of $10\frac{1}{4}$ in. (0.26 m), and the top flange is of constant section throughout its length with a minimum thickness of 7 in. (0.18 m) at its crown, Figure 3.3. The bottom flange thickness is 6 in. (0.15 m), except near the river piers where the thickness increases to 15.75 in. (0.4 m) to accommodate cantilever bending stresses. The downstream half of the bridge (consisting of two

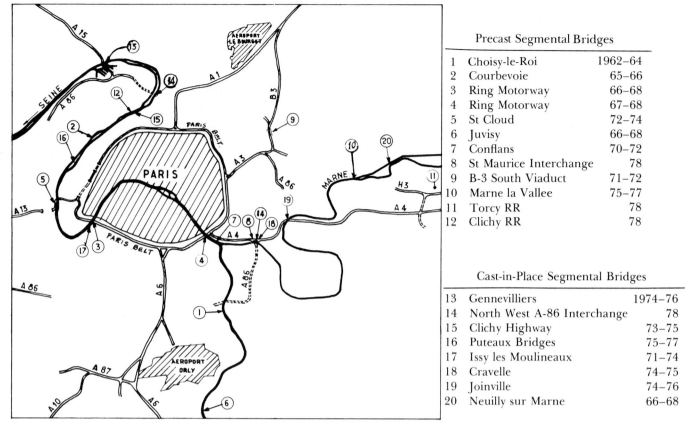

Precast Segmental Bridges		
1	Choisy-le-Roi	1962–64
2	Courbevoie	65–66
3	Ring Motorway	66–68
4	Ring Motorway	67–68
5	St Cloud	72–74
6	Juvisy	66–68
7	Conflans	70–72
8	St Maurice Interchange	78
9	B-3 South Viaduct	71–72
10	Marne la Vallee	75–77
11	Torcy RR	78
12	Clichy RR	78

Cast-in-Place Segmental Bridges		
13	Gennevilliers	1974–76
14	North West A-86 Interchange	78
15	Clichy Highway	73–75
16	Puteaux Bridges	75–77
17	Issy les Moulineaux	71–74
18	Cravelle	74–75
19	Joinville	74–76
20	Neuilly sur Marne	66–68

FIGURE 3.1.   Location map of segmental bridges in greater Paris, France.

box girders) was constructed first, alongside the existing bridge. After removal of the existing bridge, the second or upstream half was constructed. Each dual structure was constructed by the balanced cantilever method utilizing Freyssinet tendons for the longitudinal prestressing. Box girder segments were 8.2 ft (2.5 m) in length and weighed 22 tons (20 mt), except the pier segments

which were 16.4 ft (5 m) in length and weighed 60.6 tons (55 mt). The pier segments also contained two diaphragms which provided continuity with the inclined wall piers, Figure 3.3.

The segments were fabricated in a precasting yard on the left bank of the Seine approximately a mile (1.6 km) upstream of the project site, Figure 3.4. Although this bridge might be considered of moderate importance with respect to span lengths, its importance lies in the method of fabrication. It was the first to use segments precast by the match-casting technique. Segments were cast in the precasting yard as a series of 8.2 ft (2.5 m) long units, one against the other, on a continuous soffit form which had been carefully adjusted to the intrados profile of the bridge with allowance for camber. This came to be known as the "long-line" method (see Chapter 11). Two sets of steel forms riding the soffit form and overnight steam curing allowed the production of two segments per working day. To prevent bonding of the segments to each other in the casting form, a special peel-off bond breaker was sprayed over the end of the segment before the adjacent segment was cast. The segments were

FIGURE 3.2.   Choisy-le-Roi Bridge.

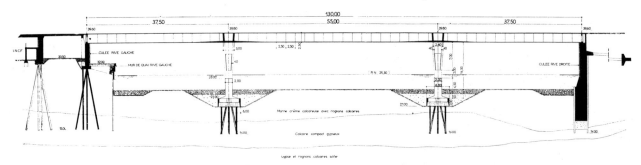

Elevation

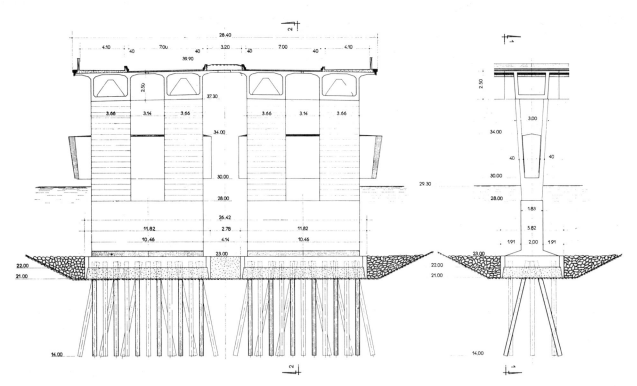

Elevation and cross section of river piers

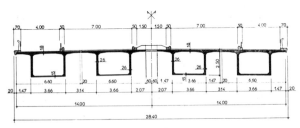

Cross section of superstructure

FIGURE 3.3. Choisy-le-Roi Bridge, dimensions: elevation, elevation and cross section of River piers, cross section of superstructure.

subsequently stripped from the soffit form at their match-cast joints and reassembled at the bridge site in balanced cantilever on each side of the river piers.[4]

A floating crane handled the segments at the casting yard. After the units were loaded on barges and transported to the project site, the same crane placed the segments over a retractable jig rolling inside the box girder in the completed portion of the bridge and was thus freed for another segment placing operation. A platform mounted on jacks on the jig, Figure 3.5, allowed for adjustment of the segment at the desired position.[4] A 1 ft (0.3 m) wide gap was temporarily maintained between the faces of the segments to allow workmen to apply

FIGURE 3.4.   Choisy-le-Roi Bridge, view of the precasting yard.

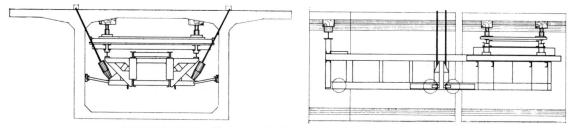

FIGURE 3.5.   Choisy-le-Roi Bridge, retractable erection jig.

the epoxy joint material. The jig was then retracted and prestressing tendons were placed and stressed to connect the two symmetrical segments on each side of the previously completed portion of the cantilevers on either side of the pier.[5]

Placing of the precast segments in a cantilever fashion on each side of the pier progressed step by step, as indicated in Figure 3.6. Tendon layout is illustrated in Figure 3.7. Upon completion of the two twin cantilevers from the river piers, a cast-in-place closure pour was consummated at midspan and a second series of prestressing tendons were placed in the bottom flange to achieve continuity between the two center-span cantilevers. These tendons were given a draped profile to allow the location of tendon anchorages in the top flange of the box girder. Both series of tendons, cantilever and continuity, overlap each other and contribute

FIGURE 3.6.   Choisy-le-Roi Bridge, segment placing with floating crane.

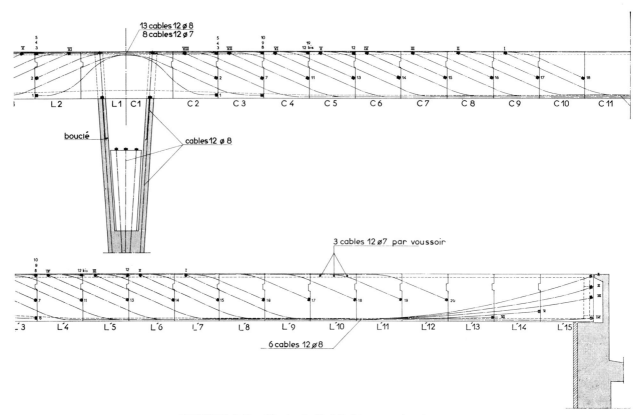

FIGURE 3.7. Choisy-le-Roi Bridge, tendon layout.

to a substantial reduction in the shear forces in the webs as a result of the vertical component of the prestress. The side spans were constructed in a similar manner. The three precast segments adjacent to the abutments were assembled on falsework. After a closure pour between these segments and the cantilever from the river pier, positive-moment tendons were placed and stressed in the end span to achieve continuity. Because the midspan area of the center span had little capacity to withstand moment reversal under ultimate load,

additional short tendons were located in the top flange to achieve full reinforcement continuity with the longest cantilever tendons.[5]

The same construction technique used for the Choisy-le-Roi Bridge was used for the Courbevoie Bridge, built between 1965 and 1967, which also crosses the Seine in the northwest suburb of Paris, Figure 3.1. The bridge has three symmetrical spans of 130, 200, and 130 ft (40, 60, and 40 m) for a total length of 460 ft (140 m), Figure 3.8. Four box girders of constant depth carry the 115 ft (35

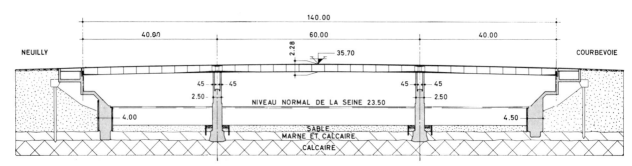

FIGURE 3.8. Courbevoie Bridge, elevation.

m) wide deck, Figure 3.9. The available depth of only 7.5 ft (2.28 m) made necessary a very slender structure; depth-to-span ratio for the main span is 1/26.[5,6]

Each river pier is an assembly of two half-piers, Figures 3.9 and 3.10, which are fixed at the level of the foundation. Each half-pier consists of a rectangular shaft 9 by 26 ft (2.8 by 8 m), which supports two pairs of prestressed concrete walls, above the normal water level, in the form of a parallelogram of 18 in. (0.45 m) thickness and 10.5 ft (3.2 m) width. The walls are arranged in a "V" in the transverse direction of the bridge and have a dimension of 6.7 ft (2.05 m) out-to-out of walls in the longitudinal direction.[6] The girders are fixed at the piers and supported on elastomeric bearings at the abutments. A total of 148 precast segments of 12.5 ft (3.8 m) length were required for the superstructure. They were fabricated in four months at the rate of two segments per day, in two sets of steel forms, electrically heated and insulated with polyurethane lining.[5]

Erection at the site was accomplished by a floating crane. After careful adjustment of the pier segments, they were erected at the rate of four per day. The temporary jig used at Choisy-le-Roi for adjustment of the segments was replaced in this project by two temporary steel beams bolted to the top of each segment and connected to the completed section of the cantilever by prestressing bars.[5]

The girder was prestressed longitudinally and transversely, through three longitudinal cast-in-place strips between the top flange cantilevers of the box girders. The completed structure is shown in Figure 3.10.

3.3 Pierre Benite Bridges Near Lyon, France

These two large bridges carry the motorway from Paris to the Riviera south of Lyon near the Pierre Benite hydroelectric plant, Figure 3.11. There are two separate bridges, one over the draft channel of the power plant and the other over the Rhone River. Both structures are twin bridges, each bridge consisting of two single-cell box girders. Typical dimensions in longitudinal and cross sections are shown in Figures 3.12 and 3.13. The same constant depth of 11.8 ft (3.6 m) is used for all spans of the two bridges. However, a haunch under the intrados of the box girders increases the

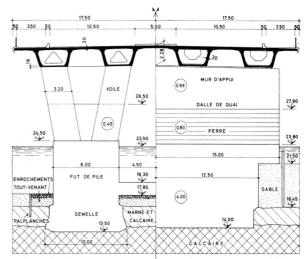

FIGURE 3.9. Courbevoie Bridge, cross section at river pier and abutment.

FIGURE 3.10. Courbevoie Bridge, view of completed bridge.

FIGURE 3.11. Pierre Benite Bridge, view of the finished bridge.

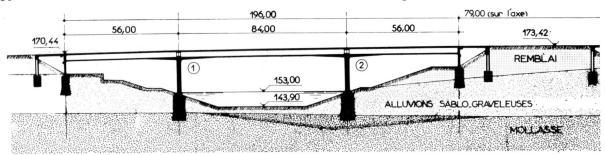

Bridge over draft channel

(a)

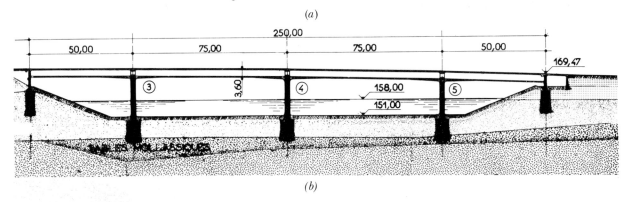

(b)

FIGURE 3.12. Pierre Benite Bridge, longitudinal sections. (a) Bridge over draft channel. (b) Bridge over Rhone River.

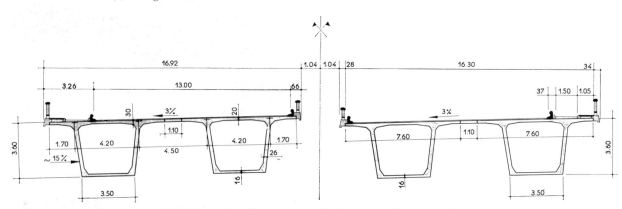

FIGURE 3.13. Pierre Benite Bridge, typical cross section.

structural depth over the piers to a maximum of 14 ft (4.28 m) for the 276 ft (84 m) span. All piers rest on compressed-air caissons and are made of solid cylindrical columns 6.5 ft (2 m) in diameter which support the cast-in-place pier segment, including skew diaphragms between the two individual box girders of each bridge. This pier segment served as the starting base for precast segment placing in balanced cantilever for the superstructure.

The 528 segments were precast near the southern bank of the draft channel. This application of precast segmental construction was the occasion to conceive and develop for the first time the short-

line precasting method, whereby the segments are cast in a formwork located in a stationary position. Each segment is cast between a fixed bulkhead and the preceding segment, in order to obtain a perfect match. After a learning curve of a few weeks, each of the two short-line-method casting machines was used to cast one segment every day. Details and specific problems of the short-line method will be described in Chapter 11. Figure 3.14 shows the precast segments as they were fabricated, temporarily stored, loaded on barges by a very simple portal structure equipped with winches, and finally transported to the construction site.

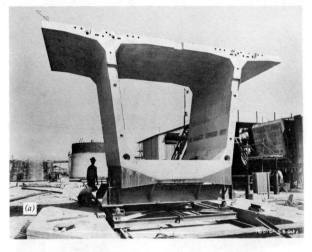

FIGURE 3.14. Pierre Benite Bridge, precasting yard and loading portal. (*a*) Precasting yard. (*b*) Loading portal.

Placing of all segments in the two twin structures was achieved in balanced cantilever, using the cast-in-place pier segments as a starting base. This project used the newly developed "beam-and-winch" erection system, illustrated in Figure 3.15 together with a close-up view of a typical segment-placing operation. Electric winches are supported in a cantilever position from the completed part of the deck to allow each segment to be lifted off the barge and placed in its final position.

Because of high-velocity river currents on one structure, it was considered advisable to transfer the segments from the barge to the winch system close to the piers to allow temporary anchorage of the barge. Therefore, segments had to be moved longitudinally from the barge position to their final location. A special trolley carried the winches and the suspended segment while riding along rails fixed to the finished deck. A general view of the

construction site with segment placing in progress is shown in Figure 3.16.

Both precasting and placing operations were carried out successfully. All the segments were placed in the structures in 13 months. The only regret was that this erection system did not provide for precast pier segments. The geometry of the cast-in-place pier segments was further complicated by the skew of the bridges, such that the contractor expended as much labor on this aspect of construction as in precasting and positioning all the precast segments.

3.4 Other Precast Segmental Bridges in Paris

The first two match-cast bridges, Choisy-le-Roi and Courbevoie, were followed by a series of other crossings over the Seine River. All contracts for design and construction were obtained on a competitive basis with other types of materials or construction methods.

The next two structures were for the construction of the Paris Belt Motorway which crosses the Seine at two locations, one downstream of the city and one upstream; see the location map, Figure 3.1. They were followed by several others, which are briefly described in this section.

3.4.1 PARIS BELT (DOWNSTREAM)

These twin bridges, Figure 3.17, carry four traffic lanes. Dimensions are shown in Figures 3.18 and 3.19. Maximum span length is 302 ft (92 m) and the structural depth of the four box girders is 11 ft (3.4 m), increased toward the piers to a maximum of 21.3 ft (5.5 m) by straight haunches. Because of the skew between the axis of the bridge and the flow of the Seine, the pier shafts were given a special lozenge shape, which proved very efficient for the hydraulic flow and is of pleasant appearance. The limited bending capacity of the shafts called for temporary supports during cantilever construction operations.

Precast segments were manufactured on the bank of the Seine with two casting machines (short-line method). For the part of the bridge superstructure located over the river, segments were placed with a floating crane, Figure 3.20. In fact, almost half the bridge length was placed over land out of reach of the floating crane. The beam-and-winch equipment used at Pierre Benite Bridge was substituted for the crane to place these segments. There was also need of additional falsework on one bank to compensate for the unusually long

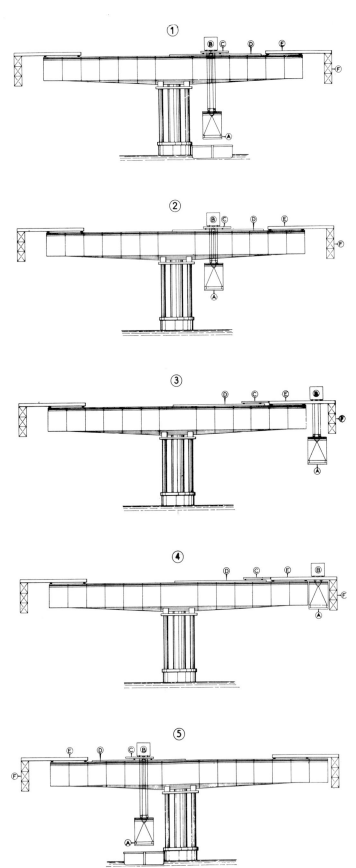

FIGURE 3.15. Pierre Benite Bridge, segment placing scheme (*left* and *top right*).

FIGURE 3.16. Pierre Benite Bridge, under construction.

FIGURE 3.17. Paris Belt (Downstream), view of finished bridge.

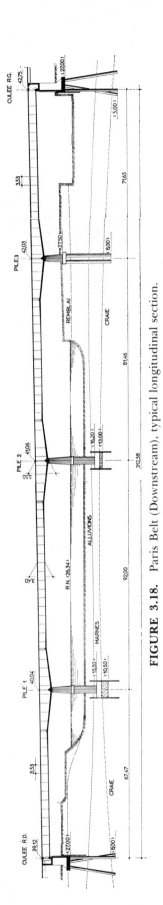

FIGURE 3.18. Paris Belt (Downstream), typical longitudinal section.

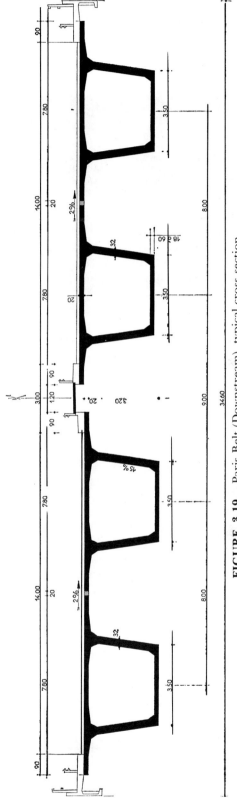

FIGURE 3.19. Paris Belt (Downstream), typical cross section.

93

FIGURE 3.20. Paris Belt (Downstream), segment placing.

FIGURE 3.21. Paris Belt (Upstream), view of the finished bridge.

end span, which could not be changed because of stringent pier location requirements.

3.4.2   *PARIS BELT (UPSTREAM)*

On the other side of Paris another segmental structure, also carrying the Belt Motorway over the Seine, was designed for five traffic lanes in either direction, Figure 3.21. The twin bridges have dimensions similar to those of the downstream bridge, and each structure has two parallel box girders connected by transverse prestress. Dimensions are shown in Figures 3.22 and 3.23. A circular intrados profile was used in lieu of the straight haunches. All segments were precast on the river bank in the immediate vicinity of the bridge, using

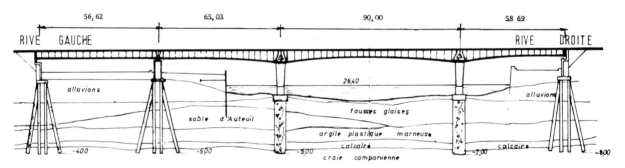

FIGURE 3.22.   Paris Belt (Upstream), longitudinal section.

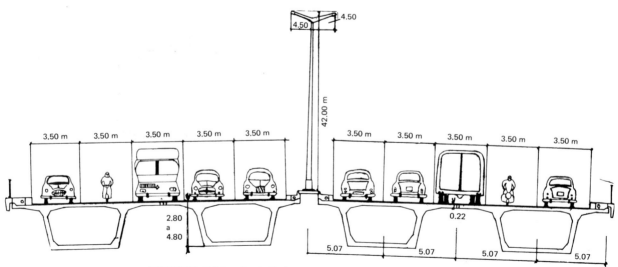

FIGURE 3.23.   Paris Belt (Upstream), typical cross section.

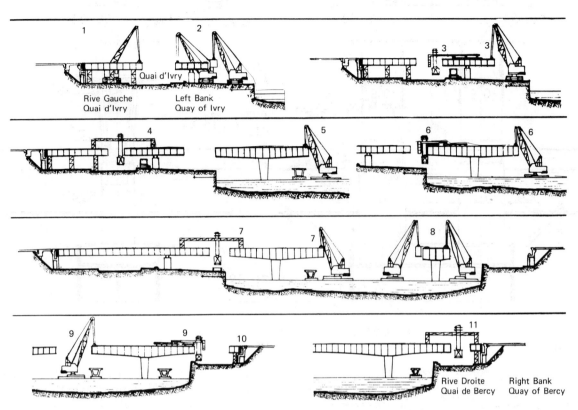

PHASES D'EXECUTION DU TABLIER   SEQUENCES OF THE DECK CONSTRUCTION

FIGURE 3.24. Paris Belt (Upstream), typical segment placing scheme.

the same two casting machines used previously for the downstream bridge.

Placing segments in the structure posed some interesting problems, as shown in the sequence diagrams of Figure 3.24. Pier segments were too heavy to be handled as one unit and were subdivided into two segments, assembled upon the pier shaft before cantilever placing could start. A

FIGURE 3.25. Juvisy Bridge, completed structure.

crane, either on crawlers or on a barge, together with the beam-and-winch equipment handled all segment placing.

3.4.3 JUVISY BRIDGE

This bridge, Figure 3.25, is also on the Seine just south of Choisy-le-Roi; see the location map, Figure 3.1. Dimensions are shown in Figure 3.26. Segments were cast by the short-line method near the site and placed with a floating crane. An auxiliary falsework on both banks allowed segment placing and assembly beyond the reach of the floating crane.

3.4.4 TWIN BRIDGES AT CONFLANS

These twin bridges, Figure 3.27, placed about 320 ft (100 m) apart to allow for interchange ramps on both banks, are upstream of Paris where the Seine and Marne Rivers merge; see the location map, Figure 3.1. Dimensions and construction methods were similar to those of the Courbevoie Bridge already described.

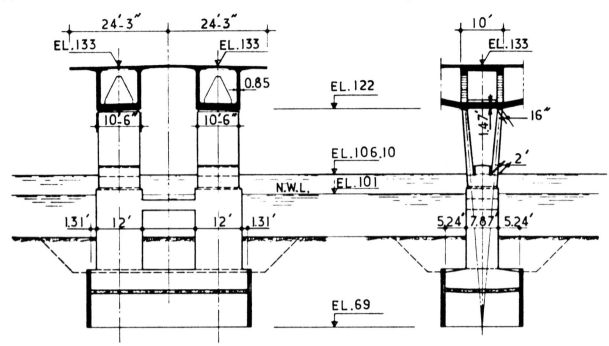

FIGURE 3.26.   Juvisy Bridge, cross section.

FIGURE 3.27.   Twin Bridges at Conflans, finished bridge.

3.5   *Oleron Viaduct, France*

The Oleron Viaduct provides a link between the mainland of France and the resort island of Oleron off the Atlantic West Coast 80 miles (128 km) north of Bordeaux. This structure has a total length between abutments of 9390 ft (2862 m). In the navigable central part of the structure are 26 spans of 260 ft (79 m), Figure 3.28. Approach spans consist of two at 194 ft (59 m), sixteen at 130 ft (39.5 m), and two at 94 ft (29 m). The superstructure is supported by 45 piers and was assembled by prestressing match-cast segments, using epoxy joints.

Balanced cantilever construction was accomplished utilizing a launching gantry for erection.

In the approach spans the superstructure has a constant depth of 8.2 ft (2.5 m). Depth of the center spans varies from 14.9 ft (4.5 m) at the piers to 8.2 ft (2.5 m) at midspan, Figure 3.29. The rectangular box segment has a bottom flange width of 18 ft (5.5 m) and a top flange width of 34.8 ft (10.6 m). Webs have a constant thickness of 12 in. (0.3 m), while the top and bottom flanges are 8 in. (0.2 m) and 7 in. (0.18 m) thick, respectively, Figure 3.30. Typical segment length is 10.8 ft (3.3 m).

Expansion of the deck is provided in every fourth span by a special stepped (ship-lap) joint with horizontal elastomeric bearing pads, Figure

FIGURE 3.28.   Oleron Viaduct, completed structure.

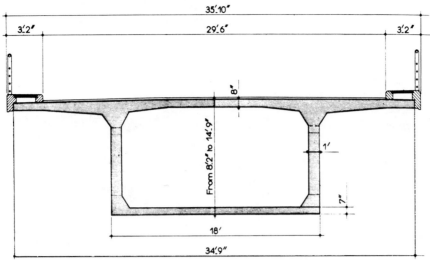

FIGURE 3.29. Oleron Viaduct, typical cross section, from ref. 5 (courtesy of the American Concrete Institute).

3.30. Throughout the total length of structure there are ten expansion joints: one at each abutment and eight intermediate ones. The latter are located at points of contraflexure in a typical interior span subjected to a continuous uniform load.[5] The segments with the expansion joint have the same length as typical segments and are in fact two half-segments that are temporarily preassembled with bolts, with a special layout of temporary and permanent prestressing tendons. It is then possible to maintain the balanced cantilever erection procedure beyond the expansion joint to midspan. Later on, when continuity has been achieved in the adjacent spans, the expansion-joint segment is "unlocked" to perform in the intended manner.

The precasting plant was located in the vicinity of the mainland abutment. Production in this plant was scheduled so that the 24 segments required for a typical 260 ft (79 m) central span could be fabricated in nine working days. Segments were produced by the long-line method, described in Chapter 11. Four sets of steel forms rode a bench that was carefully aligned to the longitudinal profile of the roadway and the variable-depth soffit with due provision for camber. Segments were match-cast in the same relative order in which they were subsequently assembled at the site.[5] An aerial view of the casting yard is shown in Figure 3.31.

Handling of segments in the casting and storage yard was accomplished by a special railway-mounted gantry capable of handling loads varying

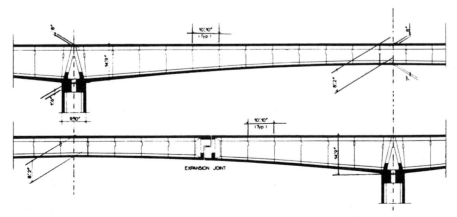

FIGURE 3.30. Oleron Viaduct, typical center span elevation, from ref. 5 (courtesy of the American Concrete Institute).

FIGURE 3.31. Oleron Viaduct, aerial view of casting yard.

FIGURE 3.32. Oleron Viaduct, construction view showing cantilever span, from ref. 5 (courtesy of the American Concrete Institute).

from 45 tons (42 mt) for the center-span segment to 80 tons (73 mt) for the pier segment. A lowboy dolly riding on rails of the finished bridge and pushed by a farm tractor transported the segments from storage to their location for assembly.

Cantilever erection at the site was accomplished by a launching gantry, Figure 3.32. This gantry was the key to the successful operation of this project. Although the structure is erected over water, the use of floating equipment would have been difficult, expensive, and subject to uncertainty because of the great tidal range and the shallowness of water in most of the area traversed by the structure. Floating equipment would have been able to reach the approach piers only at high tide. During low tide the marsh area, which is the location of France's famed Marennes oyster beds, could not accept any tire-mounted or crawler-mounted equipment. Consequently, it was decided to work entirely from above with a launching gantry. This new technique was developed for the first time for this structure and was later refined for other structures. For the typical central spans the erection cycle required between eight and ten working days.[5]

Construction began in May 1964, three months after design work had started. The first segment was cast in July and placed in August 1964. Side spans laid on a curve were completed in December and the launching gantry was then modified for construction of the center spans. The last of the 870 precast segments was in place in March 1966, and the bridge opened to traffic in May, after an overall construction time of two years[5]; see the summary of the work program in Figure 3.33. A

view of the final structure is shown in Figures 3.28 and 3.34.

The Oleron Viaduct was the first application of the launching-gantry concept for placing segments in cantilever. Several structures were later designed and built with the same construction method. Mention should be made here of three special bridges:

1. *Blois Bridge over the Loire River* The principal dimensions are given in Figure 3.35. The superstructure box girders rest on the pier shafts through twin elastomeric bearings, which allow thermal expansion while providing partial restraint for bending-moment transfer between deck and piers. Consequently, savings are obtained both in the deck and in the foundations. All segments were placed in the bridge with an improved version of the launching gantry first designed for the Oleron Viaduct. High-strength steel and stays were used to provide minimum weight with a satisfactory stiffness during operations, Figure 3.36. High-strength bolt connections were used throughout to make the gantry completely capable of dismantling and easily transportable to other construction sites.

2. *Aramon Bridge over the Rhone River* This was the next structure where the same gantry could be used, Figure 3.37.

3. *Seudre Viaduct* Located just a few miles south of Oleron over the Seudre River, this 3300 ft (1000 m) long viaduct was also of precast segmental construction and used the same launching gan-

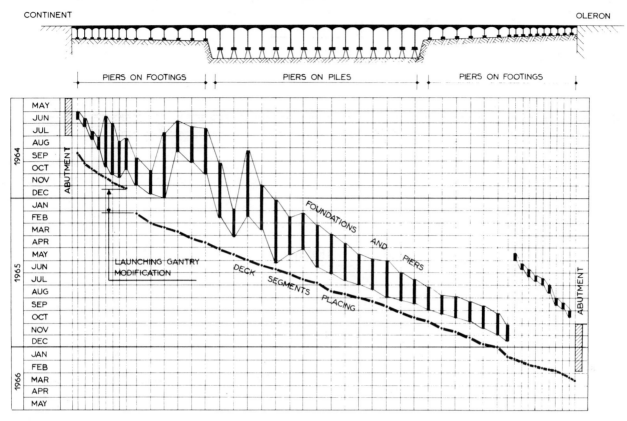

FIGURE 3.33. Oleron Viaduct, program of work.

try. The finished structure is shown in Figure 3.38. Foundations for the center spans were built inside sheet pile cofferdams in spite of very swift tidal currents.

3.6 Chillon Viaduct, Switzerland

The 7251 ft (2210 m) long dual structures of the Chillon Viaduct are part of European Highway E-2 and are located at the eastern end of Lake Geneva passing through an environmentally sensitive area and very close to the famed Castle of Chillon, Figure 3.39. In addition, the structures have very difficult geometrical constraints consisting of 3% grades, 6% superelevation, and tight-radius curves as low as 2500 ft (760 m). Each structure has 23 spans of 302 ft (92 m), 322 ft (98 m), or 341 ft (104 m). The variable spans allowed the viaduct to be fitted to the geology and topography, providing minimum impact on the scenic forest. The viaducts are divided by expansion joints into five sections of an approximate length of 1500 ft (457 m).

Twin rectangular slip-formed shafts were used for the piers, varying in height from 10 to 150 ft (3 to 45 m). Stability during construction was excellent and required little temporary bracing except between the slender walls to prevent elastic instability.[1] With the exception of three piers in each

FIGURE 3.34. Oleron Viaduct, aerial view of finished bridge.

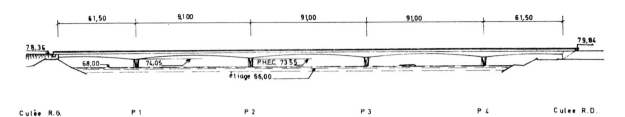

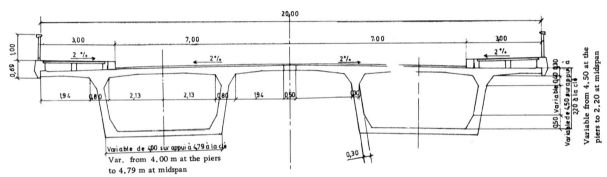

FIGURE 3.35. Blois Bridge, elevation and typical cross section.

viaduct, all piers are hinged at the top. The piers that are less than 72 ft (22 m) high are hinged at the base; taller piers are fixed at their base, being sufficiently flexible to absorb longitudinal move-

ment of the superstructure.

The superstructure consists of a single-cell rectangular box with a cellular cantilever top flange, Figure 3.40, and with a depth varying from 18.5 ft

FIGURE 3.36. Blois Bridge, launching gantry operating on the superstructure.

FIGURE 3.37. Aramon Bridge, launching gantry.

FIGURE 3.38. Seudre Bridge, finished structure.

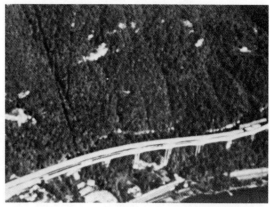

FIGURE 3.39. Chillon Viaduct, aerial view.

(5.64 m) at the longer-span piers to 7.2 ft (2.2 m) at midspan. Widths of top and bottom flange are respectively 42.7 ft (13 m) and 16.4 ft (5 m). Dimensions of the two typical cantilevers are noted in Figure 3.41. Maximum segment weight was 88 tons (80 mt). A cellular cantilever top flange was used because the overall width of the top flange ex-

ceeded 40 ft (approx. 12 m) and the cantilever length was 13.15 ft (4 m). An alternative would have been to provide stiffening ribs as used in the Saint Andre de Cubzac Viaducts (Section 3.11) and the Sallingsund Bridge (Section 3.13).

Segments were precast in a yard at one end of the structure with five casting machines, allowing

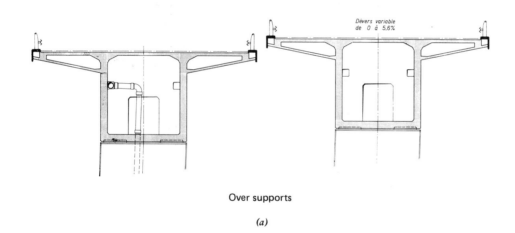

Over supports

(a)

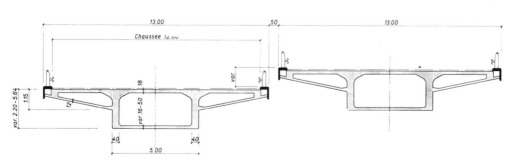

At mid-span

(b)

FIGURE 3.40. Chillon Viaduct, cross sections. (a) Over supports. (b) At midspan.

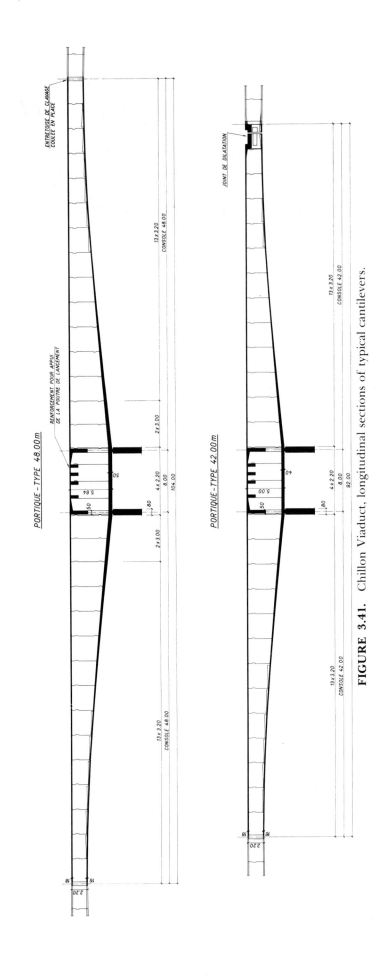

FIGURE 3.41. Chillon Viaduct, longitudinal sections of typical cantilevers.

FIGURE 3.42. Chillon Viaduct, precasting yard.

an average production of 22 to 24 segments per week (see aerial view, Figure 3.42).

Erection was by the conventional balanced cantilever method with a launching gantry designed to accommodate the bridge-deck geometry in terms of curve and variable superelevation. The overall length of the gantry was 400 ft (122 m) and the total weight 250 tons (230 mt). Special features of this gantry will be discussed in Chapter 11. Cantilever placing of precast segments is shown in Figure 3.43.

This structure is truly an achievement of modern technology with emphasis upon the aesthetic and ecological aspects of design.

3.7 Hartel Bridge, Holland

The 1917 ft (584.5 m) long Hartel Bridge crosses a canal in Rotterdam, Figure 3.44, and consists of the following elements:

FIGURE 3.43. Chillon Viaduct, cantilever construction with launching gantry.

Sections I, II, and V, conventional cast-in-place prestressed concrete box girders

Sections III and IV, precast prestressed concrete segmental box girders

Two steel bascule bridges.

The original design contemplated that the total structure would be constructed as conventional cast-in-place box girders on falsework. Substitution at the contractor's request of cast-in-place segmental construction by precast segmental construction for sections III and IV saved the extensive temporary pile foundation system necessary to avoid uneven settlement of falsework because of initial soil conditions. The redesign proposed two single-cell rectangular box girders as opposed to one three-cell box girder, Figure 3.44, omitting the center portion of the bottom flange and providing thinner webs and a thicker bottom flange.

In the segmental box girder design the dimensions of the deck slab are constant over the entire length, girder depth varies from 4.92 ft (1.5 m) to 17 ft (5.18 m), the webs have a constant thickness of 13.8 in. (0.35 m), and the bottom flange thickness varies from 10 in. (0.26 m) to 33 in. (0.85 m). Up to a depth of 9.35 ft (2.85 m) the segments have a length of 15.8 ft (4.8 m); over 9.3 ft (2.85 m) the length decreases to 12.3 ft (3.75 m).

The vertical curvature of the bridge was made constant for the full length of sections III and IV by increasing the radius from 9842.5 ft (3000 m) to 19,029 ft (5800 m), which resulted in a repetition of eight times half the center span. This repetition justified precast segments.

A long-line casting bed (see Chapter 11) was constructed on the centerline of the bridge box girders at ground level, Figure 3.45. Thus, a portal crane was able to transport the cast segments to the storage area and also erect them in the superstructure, Figure 3.46. The end spans have three more segments than half the center span; these were supported on temporary falsework until all the prestressing tendons were placed and stressed, Figure 3.46.

The first segment cast was the pier segment; each of the remaining segments was then match-cast against the preceding segment. The pier segment was positioned on bearings on top of the pier, Figure 3.47, and the two adjoining segments were positioned (one after the other) and the joints glued with epoxy resin. Temporary high-tensile bars located on the top of the deck slab and in the bottom flange were stressed to prestress the three

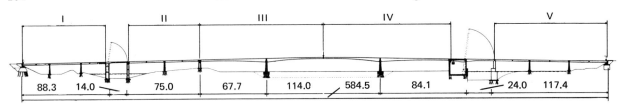

Elevation

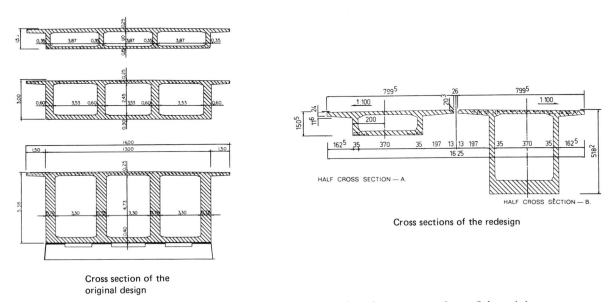

Cross section of the
original design

Cross sections of the redesign

HALF CROSS SECTION — A.

HALF CROSS SECTION — B.

FIGURE 3.44. Hartel Bridge, typical dimensions: elevation, cross sections of the original design, cross sections of the redesign (courtesy of Brice Bender, BVN/STS).

segments together. After the epoxy had hardened, the permanent tendons were placed and stressed. The two segments adjoining the pier segment were supported during erection on flat jacks on the top of the outside struts of a steel scaffolding bearing on the pier foundation. Thus, the flat jacks were used for adjustment of the segments to achieve proper geometry control. The remaining segments were

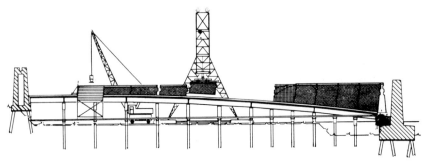

FIGURE 3.45. Hartel Bridge, method of casting segments (courtesy of Brice Bender, BVN/STS.

FIGURE 3.46. Hartel Bridge, portal crane for handling segments.

FIGURE 3.48. Hartel Bridge, completed structure.

FIGURE 3.49. Deventer Bridge, placing segments with the launching gantry.

erected in the conventional balanced cantilever method. The completed structure is shown in Figure 3.48.

Other structures using precast segmental construction were subsequently designed and built in the Netherlands. Shown in Figure 3.49 is the bridge over the Ijssel at Deventer, where segments in the 247 ft (74 m) spans were placed with a launching gantry. The overall length of the gantry was 520 ft (156 m), allowing the legs to bear on the permanent concrete piers and impose no loading on the deck during construction, Figure 3.50.

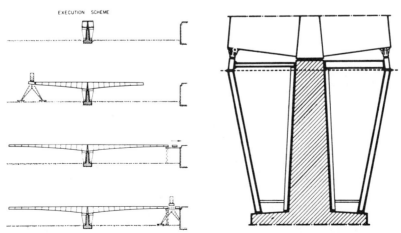

FIGURE 3.47. Hartel Bridge, erection sequence and detail of temporary pier bracing (courtesy of Brice Bender, BVN/STS).

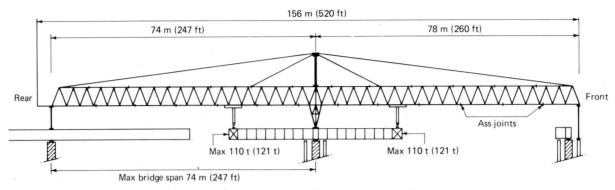

FIGURE 3.50. Deventer Bridge, elevation of gantry.

3.8   Rio-Niteroi Bridge, Brazil

The Rio-Niteroi Bridge crosses the Guanabara Bay connecting the cities of Rio de Janeiro and Niteroi, thereby avoiding a detour of 37 miles (60 km). This structure also closes the gap in the new 2485 mile (4000 km) highway that interconnects north and south Brazil and links the towns and cities on the eastern seaboard, Figure 3.51. Although the route taken by the bridge across the Bay seems somewhat indirect, it was selected because it avoids very deep water and is clear of the flight path from Santos Dumont Airport.

Total project length is approximately 10.5 miles (17 km), of which about 5.65 miles (9.1 km) is over water. The alignment begins at the Rio side with a 3940 ft (1200 m) radius curve, then a straight section, within which are located steel box girder navigation spans totaling 2872 ft (848 m) in length. This is followed by an island, where the viaduct is interrupted by a road section of 604 ft (184 m), and finally another 3940 ft (1200 m) radius curve arriving at Niteroi.

The precast segmental concrete viaduct sections have a total length of 27,034 ft (8240 m) representing a total deck area of 2,260,000 sq ft (210,000

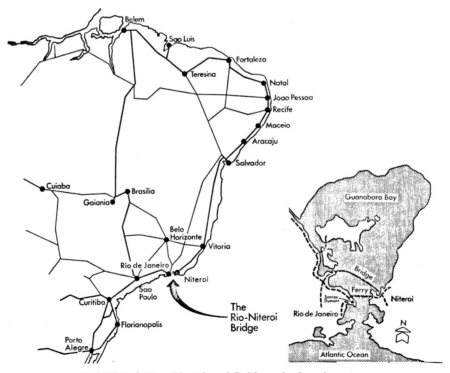

FIGURE 3.51. Rio Niteroi Bridge, site location map.

m²), making this bridge the largest structure of its type. An aerial view of the crossing under traffic is shown in Figure 3.52. The superstructure has 262 ft (80 m) continuous spans with an expansion joint at every sixth span, Figure 3.53. It consists of two rectangular box girders for a total width of 86.6 ft (26.4 m) and a constant depth of 15.4 ft (4.7 m). A 2 ft (0.6 m) cast-in-place longitudinal closure joint

between the top flange cantilevers provides continuity between the two box girder segments. Typical segments have a length of 15.75 ft (4.8 m) and weigh up to 120 tons (110 mt). The pier segments are 9.2 ft (2.8 m) in length. Special segments are used for expansion joints.

Longitudinal prestressing tendons consist of twelve $\frac{1}{2}$ in. (13 mm) diameter strands in the top and bottom flanges with a straight profile, while the resistance to shear stresses is obtained by vertical web prestress, Figure 3.54.

All segments were manufactured in a large precasting yard on a nearby island. Ten casting machines (eight for the typical segments and two for the pier and hinge segments) were laid in two independent parallel lines, each equipped with a portal crane for carrying the segments to the storage area and the loading dock. More than 3000 segments were subsequently barged to their location in the structure and erected by four launching gantries working simultaneously on each of the two parallel box girders and on either side of the bay, Figures 3.55 and 3.56. The rate of segment placing was remarkable. A typical span was assembled and completed in five working days. Between the months of February and July 1973, an average of

FIGURE 3.52. Rio-Niteroi Bridge, view of the completed structure.

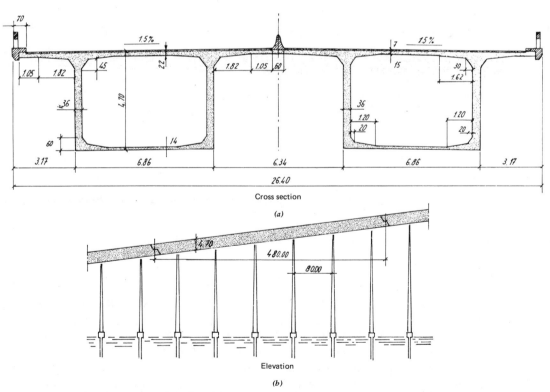

Cross section

(a)

Elevation

(b)

FIGURE 3.53. Rio-Niteroi Bridge, cross section and elevation. (a) Cross section. (b) Elevation.

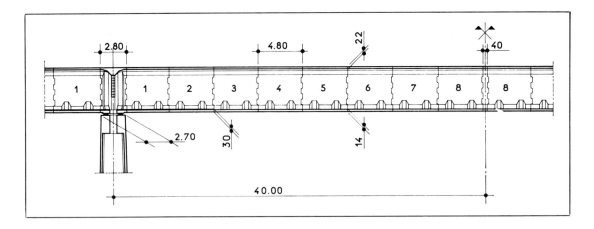

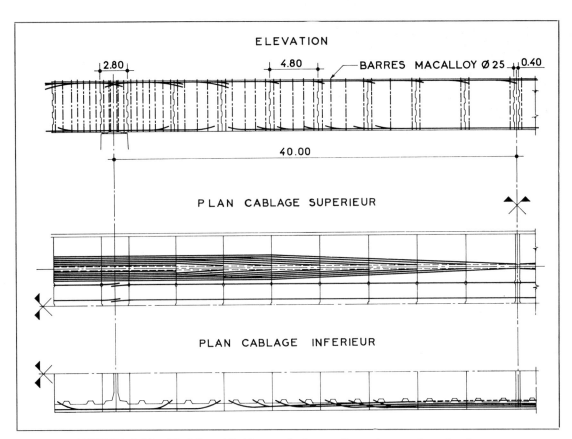

FIGURE 3.54. Rio-Niteroi Bridge, typical span dimensions and tendon layout.

278 precast segments per month were installed in the structure by the four launching gantries, representing an area of 180,000 sq ft (17,000 m²) of finished bridge per month. At the same speed, Oleron Viaduct could have been built in two months. Such is the measure of the determination and enthusiasm of engineers and constructors of the New World.

3.9 Bear River Bridge, Canada

The Bear River Bridge is about 6 miles (9.7 km) east of Digby, Nova Scotia, on trunk route 101 between Halifax and Yarmouth, near the Annapolis Basin; it replaces an 85-year-old structure. Preliminary studies showed, and construction bid prices verified, that precast segmental was more economical than steel construction by nearly 7%.[7,8]

FIGURE 3.55. Rio-Niteroi Bridge, cantilever construction.

Total structure length is 1998 ft (609 m) with six interior spans of 265 ft (80.8 m) and end spans of 204 ft (62.1 m), Figure 3.57. The layout has very severe geometry constraints. In plan, the east end of the bridge has two sharp horizontal curves connected to each other and to the west end tangent by two spiral curves; minimum radius is 1150 ft (350 m). In elevation, the bridge has a 2044 ft (623 m) vertical curve with tangents of 5.5 and 6.0 percent. Two sets of short-line forms employed by the contractor to cast the segments met the variable geometry requirements admirably. The accuracy of casting was such that only nominal elevation adjustments were required at the abutments and the center-span closure pours.[8]

The single-cell box girder superstructure is continuous for the total length of the bridge. Typical cross-section dimensions are indicated in Figure 3.58. Prestressing tendon layout is illustrated in Figure 3.59 for a typical interior span. Fifty-five tendons were required for negative moments and 22 for positive-moments. The majority of nega-

tive-moment tendons were inclined in the web and anchored at the face of the segments. Anchorage of six tendons at the face of the first segment adjacent to the pier segment (three in each web) produced a large upward shear force at the face of the pier segment, which was not overcome until the erection of several additional segments. The midspan positive-moment tendons are continuous through the cast-in-place closure joint at midspan. These tendons, indicated by capital letters in Figure 3.59, were placed in preformed ducts upon completion of erection of the segments in a span and the closure pour consummated. All positive-moment tendons were anchored in the top flange. The precast segments are typically 14 ft 2 in. (4.3 m) in length and the closure pour at midspan is 4 ft 4 in. (1.3 m) long.[7,8]

The precast segments are reinforced with prefabricated mild steel reinforcement cages, in addition to the primary longitudinal prestressing tendons, Figure 3.60, and transverse prestressing in the top flange. Web shear reinforcement varies depending on the location of the segment. The 145 precast segments were cast in a plant located near the bridge. This plant was equipped with two casting molds, each producing one segment per day. A 12-hour steam curing period was used and a concrete strength at 28 days of 5000 psi (34.5 MPa) was achieved.[7]

Because of the curved layout of the bridge and its relative shortness, the use of a launching gantry would have been uneconomical. Segments were placed by a 200 ton (180 mt) mobile crane on land, or on a barge over water, Figure 3.61. Construction of this bridge started in May of 1971, and it was opened to traffic on December 18, 1972.

3.10 *JFK Memorial Causeway, U.S.A.*

A portion of the JFK Memorial Causeway represents the first precast, prestressed, segmental box girder completed in the United States. Opened to traffic in 1973, this 3280 ft (1000 m) long structure spans the Gulf Intercoastal Waterway in Texas to connect Corpus Christi and Padre Island. It was designed by the Bridge Division of the Texas Highway Department under the supervision of Wayne Henneberger. The Center for Highway Research, University of Texas at Austin, under the supervision of Prof. John E. Breen, assisted in the design and also built and tested a one-sixth scale model of the bridge to check design requirements and construction techniques.[9]

FIGURE 3.56. Rio-Niteroi Bridge, launching gantries.

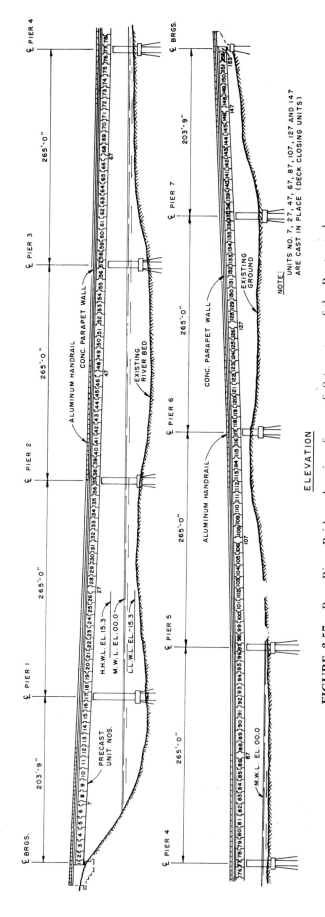

FIGURE 3.57. Bear River Bridge, elevation, from ref. 8 (courtesy of the Prestressed Concrete Institute).

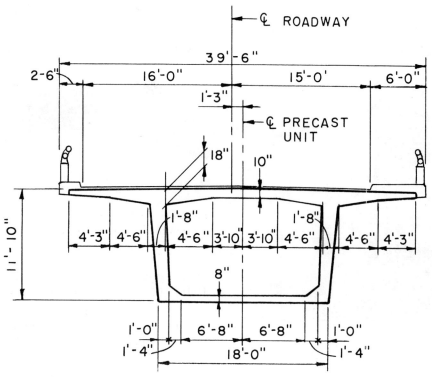

FIGURE 3.58. Bear River Bridge, typical cross section, from ref. 8 (courtesy of the Prestressed Concrete Institute).

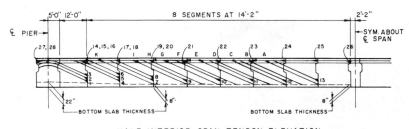

HALF INTERIOR SPAN TENDON ELEVATION

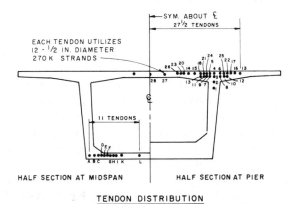

TENDON DISTRIBUTION

FIGURE 3.59. Bear River Bridge, typical center-span tendon elevation and distribution, from ref. 8 (courtesy of the Prestressed Concrete Institute).

111

FIGURE 3.60. Bear River Bridge, longitudinal pre-stress ducts in forms (courtesy of the Prestressed Concrete Institute).

FIGURE 3.61. Bear River Bridge, erection by barge-mounted crane (courtesy of the Prestressed Concrete Institute).

The structure consists of thirty-six 80 ft (24.4 m) long approach spans of precast, prestressed bridge beams and the 400 ft (122 m) total length segmental bridge spanning the Intercoastal Waterway. The segmental portion of this structure has a center span of 200 ft (61 m) with end spans of 100 ft (30.5 m). The segments were precast, transported to the site, and erected by the balanced cantilever method of construction using epoxy joints, Figure 3.62. The precast, segmental superstructure consists of constant-depth twin box girders with a 2 ft (0.61 m) cast-in-place longitu-

FIGURE 3.62. JFK Memorial Causeway, balanced cantilever construction (courtesy of J. E. Breen).

dinal closure strip, Figure 3.63. Segments are 10 ft (3.05 m) in length and in cross section, are 8 ft (2.44 m) in depth, and have a nominal top flange width of 28 ft (8.53 m). The top flange or deck is of constant dimension longitudinally but of variable thickness in a transverse direction. The bottom flange is of constant dimension transversely but varies longitudinally from 10 in. (254 mm) at the pier to 6 in. (152 mm) at 25 ft (7.62 m) from the pier center.

Segments were cast with male and female alignment keys in both the top and bottom flanges as well as large shear keys in the webs, Figure 3.64. Integral diaphragms were cast with the pier segments, Figure 3.65. Both matching faces of the segments were coated with epoxy, and temporary erection stressing at both top and bottom of the segments precompressed the joint before installation of the permanent post-tensioning tendons. The segments were erected by a barge-mounted crane. As each segment was erected, it was tilted 21 degrees from the in-place segment, so that a pair of hooks in the top of the segment being erected engaged pins in the segment previously erected. The new segment was then pivoted down by the sling until its shear key slipped into the mating shear key of the previously erected segment.[9] Figure 3.66 shows a permanent tendon being tensioned and the temporary working platform.

The design concept on this project utilized prestressing tendons in the top flange for dead-load cantilever stresses; after closure at midspan, continuity tendons were installed for the positive moment, Figure 3.67. Research on the model testing of the bridge is documented in references 10 through 15 with particular emphasis in reference 14 on lessons learned during construction that might facilitate or improve similar projects.

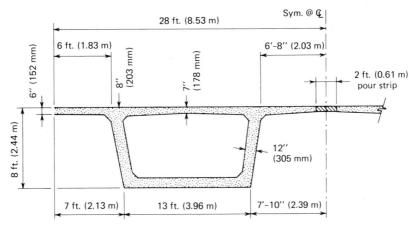

FIGURE 3.63. JFK Memorial Causeway, typical cross section. Bottom slab thickness varies from 10 in. (254 mm) at pier to 6 in. (152 mm) at 25 ft (7.62 m) from pier center.

FIGURE 3.64. JFK Memorial Causeway, precast segment in casting yard (courtesy of J. E. Breen).

FIGURE 3.65. JFK Memorial Causeway, construction view showing pier segments with diaphragms (courtesy of J. E. Breen).

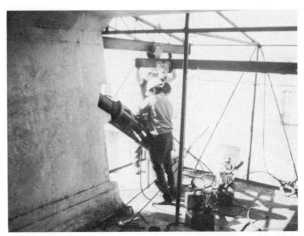

FIGURE 3.66. JFK Memorial Causeway, prestressing permanent tendon (courtesy of J. E. Breen).

3.11 Saint André de Cubzac Bridges, France

Opened to traffic in December 1974 after a construction period of 29 months, this important structure crosses the Dordogne River north of Bordeaux on the South Atlantic Coast. A view of the finished bridge is shown in Figure 3.68. The main river crossing has a total length of 3800 ft (1162 m) with approach land spans of 190 ft (59 m) and main river spans of 312 ft (95.3 m), Figure 3.69. Two intermediate expansion joints located at the point of contraflexure in the transition spans separate the deck into three sections for concrete volume changes. The center section has a length of 1920 ft (585 m). The main piers have rectangular hollow box shafts supported by circular open-dredged caissons 30 ft (9 m) in diameter. Approach piers have an I section.

Another structure, constructed under the same contract, consisted of twin bridges 1000 ft (307 m) in length with typical 162 ft (49.5 m) spans in an

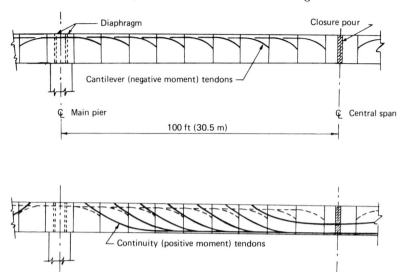

FIGURE 3.67. JFK Memorial Causeway, system of prestressing tendons.

FIGURE 3.68. Saint André de Cubzac Bridge, view of the finished bridge over the Dordogne River.

area north of the main crossing where poor soil conditions did not permit stability of an embankment. Altogether the deck area is 97,000 sq ft (29,500 m²), entirely of precast segmental construction. The typical cross section is a single box 54.4 ft (16.6 m) wide with transverse ribs both in the side cantilevers and between webs, Figure 3.69, to provide structural capacity to the deck slab under traffic loads. A casting yard located along the bank of the Dordogne River produced the 456 segments for both bridges (main crossing and north viaducts) in three casting machines (two for the typical segments and one for the special segments such as pier, hinge, or end segments). Moderate steam curing at 86°F (30°C) for 12 hours in a movable kiln enclosing the newly cast segment and its match-cast counterpart allowed a one-day cycle and proved very efficient in avoiding any geometric corrections.

Segments were placed in the structure by the beam-and-winch method either on land (for the northern viaducts or the approach spans of the main river crossing) as shown in Figure 3.70 or over water for the main spans as shown in Figure 3.71. This project was the occasion for a further improvement in the placing scheme by beam and winch, whereby the pier segments could be precast and placed with the same type of equipment as shown in principle in Figure 3.72. A provisional tower prestressed against the pier side face allowed the pier segment to be installed upon the pier cap, with the beam and winch later used for cantilever placing. To keep the segment weight to a maximum of 110 t (100 mt) the pier segment, representing the starting base of each cantilever, had been divided into two halves placed successively, Figure 3.73. Figure 3.74 shows the lifting of the last closure segment.

3.12   Saint Cloud Bridge, France

A connection between the peripheral Paris Ring Road and the Western Motorway (A-13) required the construction of a bridge over the Seine extended by a viaduct along the left bank leading to the Saint Cloud Tunnel, Figures 3.75 and 3.76. This structure has two traffic lanes in each direction. It will be duplicated later by a similar adjoining structure when the congested Saint Cloud Tunnel is duplicated. Original design of this bridge contemplated a steel structure. However, an alternative design utilizing precast segments and

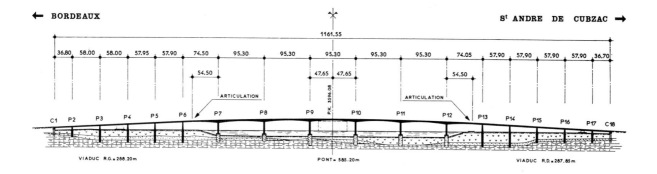

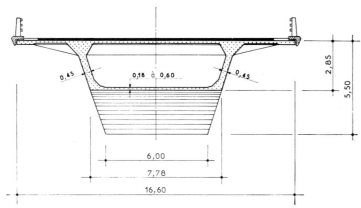

FIGURE 3.69. Saint André de Cubzac Bridge, elevation and cross section.

FIGURE 3.71. Saint André de Cubzac Bridge, beam-and-winch segment placing over water.

FIGURE 3.70. Saint André de Cubzac Bridge, beam-and-winch segment placing over land.

115

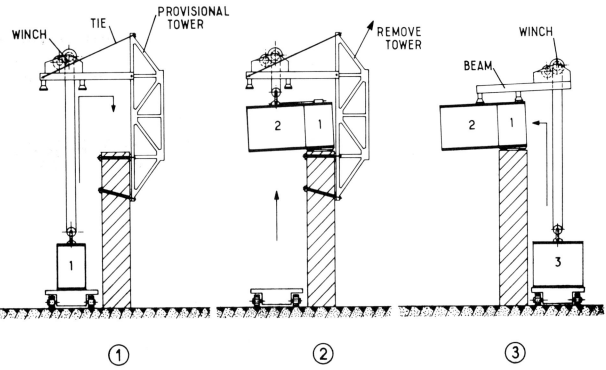

FIGURE 3.72. Saint André de Cubzac Bridge, placing precast pier segments.

FIGURE 3.73. Saint André Cubzac Bridge, lifting second half pier segment.

FIGURE 3.74. Saint André de Cubzac Bridge, placing closure segment in last span.

FIGURE 3.75. Saint Cloud Bridge, overall view.

the balanced cantilever method of construction, submitted by the contractor, permitted substantial savings and was accepted by the authorities.

The bridge has a total length of 3618 ft (1103 m) with a constant-depth superstructure. It includes two sections: the bridge over the Seine, which is a 1736 ft (529 m) long curved structure; and a 1883 ft (574 m) long viaduct, which follows a straight layout along the bank of the Seine and then crosses the Place Clemenceau, on a 2260 ft (690 m) radius curve, by an access ramp to the Saint Cloud Tunnel. It includes 16 spans divided as follows (refer to Figure 3.76):

Seine Bridge: 160.8, 288.7, 333.8, 296.0, 150.9, and two 219.5 ft spans (49, 88, 101.75, 90.25, 46, and two 66.9m)

Common area: 66.4 ft (20.24 m) up to the expansion joint, and then 153.1 ft (44.66 m), total 219.5 ft (66.9 m)

Viaduct: five 219.5; 285.4, 210.0, and 137.8 ft spans (five 66.9; 87, 64, and 42 m)

Architectural considerations led to the choice of a 11.8 ft (3.6 m) constant-depth three-cell box girder with sloping external webs with no overhangs, Figure 3.77. Segments are 7.4 ft (2.25 m) in length with a record width of 67 ft (20.4 m), their average weight varying from 84 to 143 tons (76 to 130 mt). Since the superstructure has a constant depth, the bending capacity is adjusted to the moment dis-

tribution by varying the bottom flange thickness, which decreases from 31.5 in. (800 mm) at the river piers to 7 in. (180 mm) at midspan. To accommodate the curvature of the bridge the segments in this area are cast, in plan, in a trapezoidal shape. A 4.5% superelevation is obtained by placing the units over the piers in an inclined position.

Three-dimensional prestressing was used in the superstructure: the main longitudinal prestress, transverse prestress in the deck, and a vertical prestress in the webs to accommodate shear. After the closure joint at midspan was cast, additional longitudinal prestress tendons were installed to provide continuity.

Superstructure segments were precast in a plant on the right bank of the Seine. Two casting molds were used for fabrication of the segments. Each mold had an external formwork and an internal retractable formwork. The adjacent, previously cast segment was used as a bulkhead to achieve a match-cast joint.

For erection, segments were transported on a trolley to a cable-stayed launching gantry of unusual size and capacity. It was of high-yield steel construction, 402 ft (122.5 m) in length and weighing 250 tons (235 mt), with a maximum load capacity of 143 tons (130 mt). The constant-depth gantry truss was supported on central and rear legs, which were tunnel shaped to allow passage of the precast segments endwise. At the central support, a 52.5 ft (16 m) high tubular tower topped

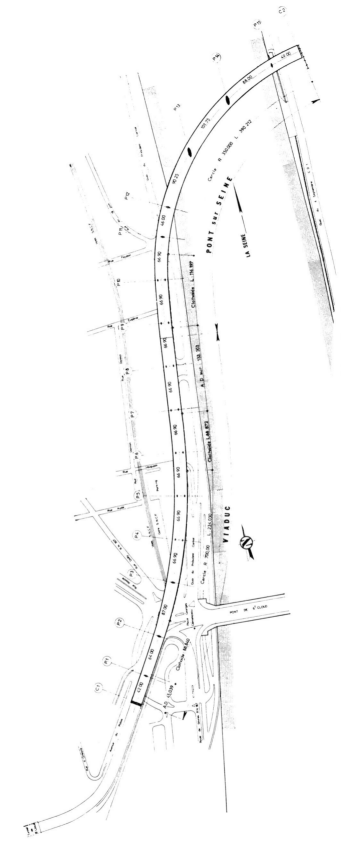

FIGURE 3.76. Saint Cloud Bridge, plan view.

118

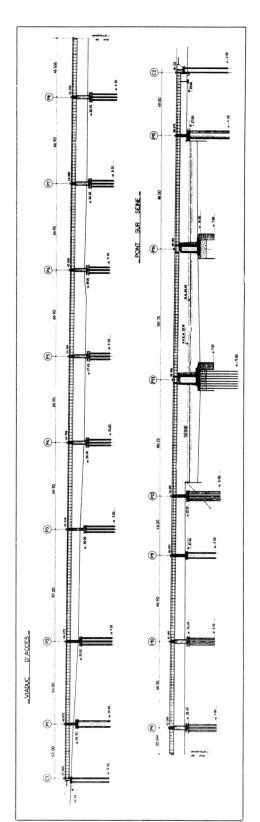

VIADUC D'ACCÈS

PONT SUR SEINE

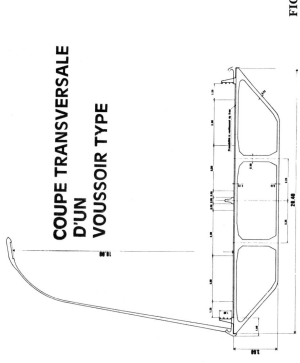

COUPE TRANSVERSALE
D'UN
VOUSSOIR TYPE

FIGURE 3.77. Saint Cloud Bridge, longitudinal and typical cross section.

with a saddle provided a large eccentricity to the three pairs of cable stays, which improved the negative-moment capacity at this support location. At the forward end of the gantry an additional leg was used as a third support point during launching and pier segment placing, Figure 3.78. The launching girder was moved forward on rails mounted on the completed superstructure, by sliding on pads placed at the central and rear legs. The launching girder, in cross section, was triangular in shape. The base of this triangle included two structural steel I sections, which served as tracks for the segment transportation trolley. The diagonal bracing of the launching girder consisted of tubular steel members. The girder was fabricated in ten sections, approximately 39 ft (12 m)

FIGURE 3.78. Saint Cloud Bridge, segment placing.

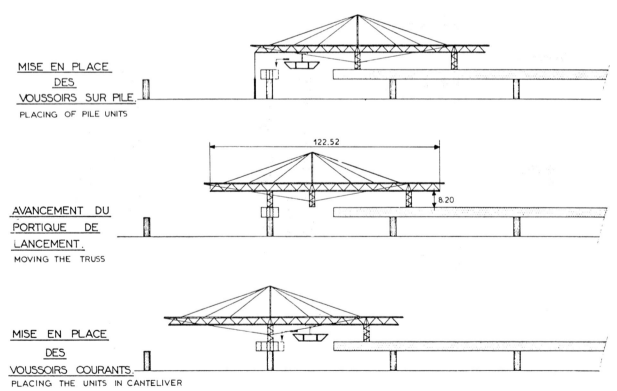

FIGURE 3.79. Saint Cloud Bridge, sequence of operations in moving launching girder.

in length, so as to be transportable over the highways. These units were assembled at the job site by prestressing bars.

The sequence of operations in moving the launching girder forward is illustrated in Figure 3.79 and included the following operations:

Placing pier segment: The gantry was supported on three points: the rear leg, the central leg placed near the end of the completed cantilever, and the temporary front leg supported just in front of the pier.

Launching of the gantry: The gantry slid on rails at the rear leg and rolled over an auxiliary support placed atop the pier segment. The central leg, during this travel, crossed the gap between the cantilever end and the pier unit.

Placing typical segments in cantilever: In this phase the gantry was supported at two points: the central leg placed over the pier and the rear leg anchored

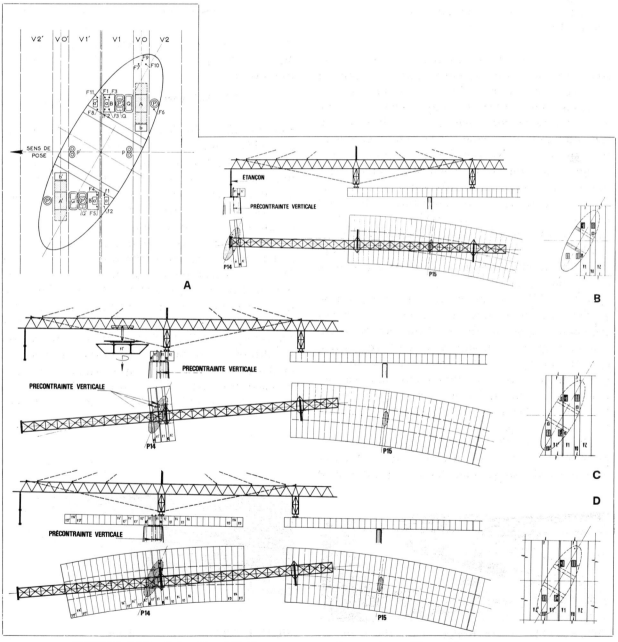

FIGURE 3.80.   Saint Cloud Bridge, sequence of operations of launching gantry over the river.

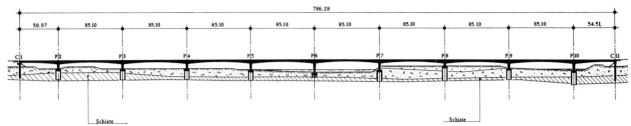

FIGURE 3.81. Angers Bridge, longitudinal section.

at the end of the last completed cantilever. The segments were lifted by the trolley at the rear end of the girder, moved forward, after a rotation of a quarter turn, and then placed alternatively at each end of the cantilevers under construction.

As a result of the horizontal curvature of the structure, the transverse positioning of a segment was accomplished both by moving the segment transportation trolley sideways relative to the girder [possible side travel of 3 ft (0.9 m) on either side] and by moving the launching gantry itself sideways relative to its bearing support on the bridge. Thus, the construction of a cantilever required one, two, or three different positions of the gantry, according to the curvature radius and length of span, as shown in Figure 3.80. Work started in October 1971 and was completed in December 1973. Placing the 527 precast segments in the 3600 ft (1097 m) long superstructure took exactly one year.

In terms of erection speed, a more interesting project was successfully carried out on a precast segmental bridge awarded to Campenon Bernard. A unique set of circumstances arose where a bridge over the Loire River at Angers could be fitted to use simultaneously the dimensions and casting machines of Saint Andre de Cubzac Bridge, which had recently been completed, and the gantry of Saint Cloud Bridge.

The 2577 ft (786 m) long structure rests on 10 piers and has 280 ft (85.1 m) typical spans, Figures 3.81 and 3.82, using a single box girder with ribbed

deck slab units identical to the sections used at Saint Andre de Cubzac. The construction contract was signed in August 1974 and the superstructure was completed in May 1975. All segments were placed between January and May 1975, in a little less than five months, corresponding to an average erection speed of 26 ft (8 m) per day of finished deck.

3.13 Sallingsund Bridge, Denmark

Sallingsund in Northern Jutland between Arrhus and Thisted is a site of great natural beauty. Construction of a bridge in such an environment was the object of careful study, which concluded, after an international competition, in the selection of a precast segmental structure, Figure 3.83, resting on piers of a unique design.

This structure has two end spans of 167 ft (51 m) and 17 interior spans of 305 ft (93 m). There are 18 piers between the two abutments. The level of the roadway reaches 100 ft (30.5 m) above the water at the center span and 82 ft (25 m) at the abutments. The two center spans are navigation spans requiring 85 ft (26 m) vertical clearance over a width of 197 ft (60 m). The bridge deck accommodates two traffic lanes, approximately 13 ft (4 m) each, two cycle paths, and two sidewalks for a total width of 52.5 ft (16 m), Figure 3.84. The

FIGURE 3.82. Angers Bridge, view of the completed structure.

FIGURE 3.83. Sallingsund Bridge, view of the completed structure.

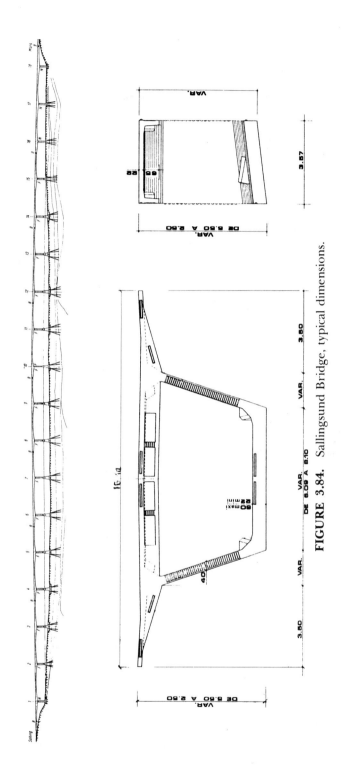

FIGURE 3.84. Sallingsund Bridge, typical dimensions.

superstructure consists of precast concrete box girder segments 11.7 ft (3.57 m) in length, with epoxy match-cast joints, which are prestressed together. Segment depth varies from 8.2 ft (2.5 m) at midspan to 18 ft (5.5 m) at the pier.

The precast superstructure segments were match-cast by the short-line method (see Chapter 11). There are altogether 453 segments varying in weight from 86 t (78 mt) to 118 t (107 mt). The typical segment shown in Figure 3.85 has web corrugated shear keys together with top and bottom flange keys. Hinge segments equipped with a roadway expansion joint for thermal movement of the superstructure are placed every other span near the point of contraflexure. A hinge segment with its diaphragm is shown in Figure 3.86. Segments are placed in the structure in cantilever with a cable-stayed launching gantry. Transfer from the casting area and the storage yard to the construction site and the launching gantry is achieved by a low-bed dolly pushed by a tractor, Figure 3.87. The gantry shown in Figure 3.88 should look

familiar to the reader, as it was previously used at the Saint Cloud and Angers Bridges.

Each pier in the water consists of the following, as shown in Figure 3.89:

Twenty-four pipe piles filled with reinforced concrete after driving

A guiding template and a tremie concrete seal

A precast substructure block and precast ice breaker

A cast-in-place hollow box shaft with cap for receiving the superstructure

Chapter 5 gives a detailed description of the foundation principles in design and construction.

3.14   B-3 South Viaducts, France

The South Viaducts of the B-3 Motorway, Figure 3.90, east of Paris, are 1.25 miles (2 km) in length

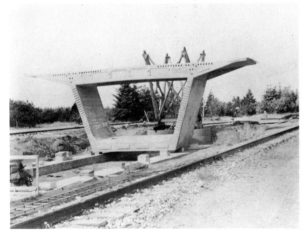

FIGURE 3.85. Sallingsund Bridge, view of a typical segment.

FIGURE 3.87. Sallingsund Bridge, segment transport.

FIGURE 3.86. Sallingsund Bridge, hinge segment with diaphragm.

FIGURE 3.88. Sallingsund Bridge, launching gantry.

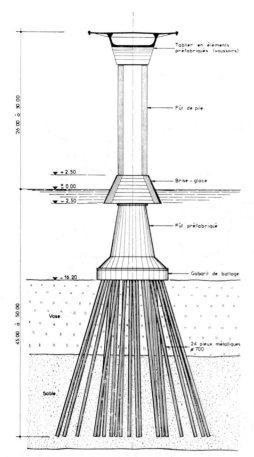

FIGURE 3.89. Sallingsund Bridge, elevation of main piers in water.

and have 860,000 sq ft (80,000 m²) of bridge deck. The project is in a congested area that required the crossing of railway tracks, canals, and more than 20 roads; its diverse structural geometry contains curves, superelevation ranging from 2.5 to 6% and grades up to 5%.

FIGURE 3.90. B-3 South Viaduct, overall view.

Figure 3.91 presents a plan of this project and shows a subdivision in accordance with the type of cross sections used. It includes the following main subdivisions:

1. The main viaduct VP 1-A through VP 1-J.
2. The main viaduct VP 2-A and VP 2-B.
3. The viaducts V1 and V2, which are access ramps to the main viaduct VP 2.
4. The viaducts V3 and V4, which are access ramps to the National Road RN3.

The original design for this project, prepared by the French authorities, was based on conventional cast-in-place construction of the superstructure in complete spans using movable formwork. The contractor proposed a more economical design based on the use of precast segments. The alternative design had advantages in erection, wherein parts were erected by a launching truss and parts by a mobile crane in conjunction with an auxiliary truss and winch. The use of precast units allowed a deeper and thus a more economical superstructure, because the space required for formwork did not have to be deducted in the clearance requirements over existing roads and other facilities.

The superstructure has a constant depth of 6.5 ft (2 m), consisting of three different cross sections, Figure 3.91. Different width and transitions were accommodated by varying the width of the cast-in-place median slab connecting the top flanges of the precast segments. Only the V3 and V4 access ramps were of conventional cast-in-place construction.

The webs of the precast segments have a constant thickness of 12 in. (310 mm), increased in some cases to 20 in. (500 mm) near a pier. Webs are stiffened by an interior rib, which also serves to anchor the longitudinal prestressing inside the box rather than in the web at the end of a segment. Where the webs are not thickened near a support, they are prestressed vertically by bars to accommodate shear forces. The top flanges of the segments are cantilevered 10 ft (3 m). In the case of segment types 2 and 3, Figure 3.91, the top flange cantilever between box sections is 9 ft (2.75 m). The top flange follows the superelevation of the roadway. The thickness of the cast-in-place longitudinal slab between box girders varies from 7.9 to 13.8 in. (200 to 350 mm), depending upon its width.

The total superstructure is supported on neoprene or sliding bearings. Expansion joints are spaced at distances up to 1970 ft (600 m) and are

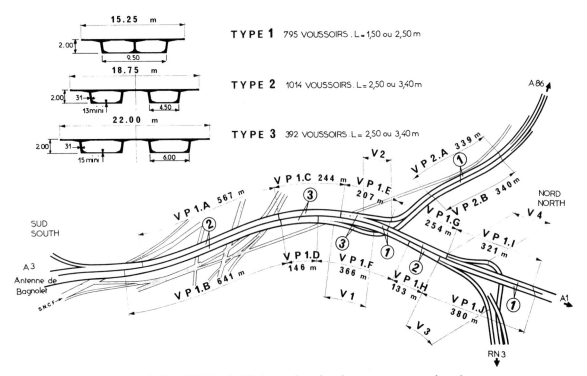

FIGURE 3.91. B-3 South Viaduct, plan showing segment type location.

located in special hinge joints near a pier. Superstructure spans vary from 89.6 to 174 ft (27 to 53 m), with 90% of them being in the range of 111 to 125 ft (34 to 38 m).

This project required 2225 precast segments, all manufactured by the short-line method (see Chapter 11), which involved the following operations:

1. Subassembly of mild steel reinforcing on a template.
2. Storage of subassembly units.
3. Assembly of complete reinforcement cages including tendon ducts.
4. Placing of the cages in the forms.
5. Concreting and curing of the segments.
6. After concreting and curing, transportation of the segment by a dolly to a position where one end would act as a bulkhead for the casting of the next segment. At the same time its position was adjusted to conform to the proper geometric configuration of the superstructure.
7. Transfer of the segment that had previously acted as the bulkhead to temporary storage for further curing.

8. Transfer of the segment, eight hours after curing, to a more permanent storage until required for erection.
9. Return of the mold bottom, after temporary storage, to the casting area for reuse.

Curing of the segments was accomplished with low-pressure steam in the following $4\frac{1}{2}$-hour cycle:

1. An initial $1\frac{1}{2}$-hour curing period at 35°C.
2. A two-hour temperature rise reaching 65°C.
3. A one-hour curing period at a level of 65°C.

The short curing cycle can be accomplished if the following conditions are satisfied: use of a proper cement, preheating of the materials to 35°C, rigid forms, and proper supervision. Casting of a segment required nine hours, allowing two segments per day per form; the four forms used produced a total of eight segments per day.

Erection of precast segments by the launching gantry shown in Figure 3.92 is schematically illustrated in Figure 3.93. After being rotated 90°, segments V2 and V'2 were placed at the same time by means of two trolleys suspended from the bottom chord of the launching girder, Figure 3.94.

FIGURE 3.92. B-3 South Viaduct, launching gantry in operation.

The matching faces of the segments being erected and the previously erected segments, V1 and V′1, were coated with epoxy joint material. Segments V2 and V′2 were then attached to the previously erected segments by temporary prestressing. During the erection operation of V2 and V′2 a transport dolly delivered segment V′3, then V3, and so on. In this manner the erection of segments could be carried out without being delayed by transportation of the segments from the storage area. In addition, the threading and stressing of the permanent prestressing tendons were independent of the erection cycle, since the tendons were anchored in the internal ribs and could be prestressed inside the box girder.

Where the span length was less than 125 ft (38 m), the pier segments were placed by the gantry in its normal working position. The pier segment position was adjusted from a platform fixed to the top of the pier to avoid delaying the placement of cantilever segments at the preceding pier. For the few

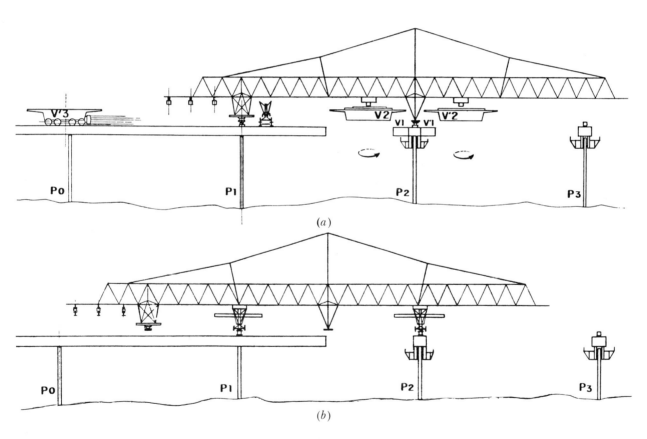

FIGURE 3.93. B-3 South Viaduct, erection sequence. (*a*) Placing the units: The two trolleys bring the units V2 and V′2 which will be placed, after rotation at 90°, against the units V1 and V′1. During this time, the lorry carries the units V′3, then V3, and so on. (*b*) Launching the truss: The rear and the central legs are lifted above the piers P0 and P1. The truss is supported by trestles and trolleys in P1 and P2 and moves forward by the action of the trolley motors until the legs reach P1 and P2. Thus the truss has advanced along one span length and can place the pile-unit in P3 and the cantilevers from P2.

FIGURE 3.94. B-3 South Viaduct, placing two segments in balanced cantilever.

larger spans, the pier segment was placed after closure of the preceding completed spans and advancement of the launching gantry. The center leg was advanced out onto the last completed half-span cantilever, but it remained in the proximity of the pier. Launching of the gantry to the next span was achieved by using the two segment transportation dollies temporarily fixed on the completed superstructure by two auxiliary steel trusses. The high degree of mechanization of the gantry together with the repetitive nature of the project allowed speedy erection. A typical 130 ft (39 m) span was erected and completed in two working days.

To maintain the construction schedule and minimize required erection equipment, the super-structure segments were placed simultaneously by two different methods. The launching gantry previously described placed 57% of the segments and a mobile crane in conjunction with a movable winch frame erected the remaining ones. The latter method was used where access was available for a truck-mounted crane and the segment transportation dolly. The truck-mounted crane could easily be used along the centerline of the structure to place segments at outboard cantilever ends. However, its use became complicated in the midspan area, particularly when it was used to place the closure segments. To solve this problem, an auxiliary truss equipped with a winch was used in conjunction with the mobile crane. This truss was supported at one end over the pier where cantilever construction proceeded and at the other end over the last completed cantilever arm, which might or might not require a temporary support pier, Figure 3.95. The segments were lifted by a trolley-mounted winch traveling along the truss. This truss was also used to stabilize the cantilevers during erection, since it was fixed to the pier and the completed portion of the superstructure. After the pier segment was positioned by the mobile crane, the frame was launched with the trolley in a counterweight position at the rear of the frame. When the span exceeded 65 ft (20 m), the front of the frame was held by the crane.

This structure exemplifies an innovative application of precast balanced cantilever segmental construction to a difficult urban site and shows its adaptability to almost any site conditions.

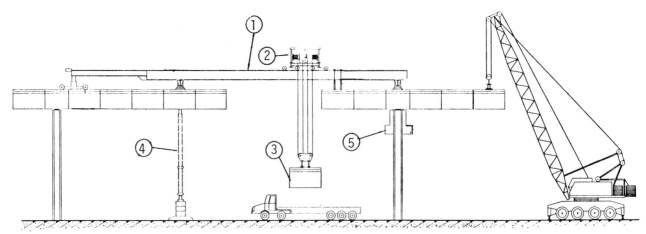

FIGURE 3.95. B-3 South Viaduct, auxiliary truss for segment assembly (crane placing). (1) Auxiliary truss, (2) winch for segment lifting, (3) precast segment, (4) possible temporary support (as required), and (5) concrete cantilever stability device.

3.15 Alpine Motorway Structures, France

The new Rhone-Alps Motorway system in South East France includes 220 miles (350 km) of tollways, of which 60 miles (100 km) are an optional section, between the cities of Lyons, Grenoble, Geneva, and Valence in order to improve communications between Germany and Switzerland on one hand and South France and Spain on the other. The motorway is situated among the beautiful western slopes of the Alpine mountain range (see the location map, Figure 3.96). The first 160 miles (250 km) include the following structures:

Ten viaducts varying in length between 500 and 1300 ft (150 to 400 m)

Two hundred overpass bridges

Fifty underpasses

Such a project afforded an exceptional occasion to optimize the structures in terms of initial investment and low maintenance costs.

The underpasses had to accommodate a variable and often considerable depth of fill to reduce the constraints of the longitudinal profile in this mountainous region. The ideal answer was found in the use of reinforced concrete arch structures, which proved extremely well adapted and had a cost approximately half that of conventional girder bridges.

Apart from the first section of the motorway (East of Lyons), which had to be built immediately and therefore called for conventional solutions (cast-in-place prestressed concrete slab), and except for certain special situations (excessive skew, railroad crossing, and so on), a careful study showed that the remaining 150 overpass bridges should be of precast concrete segmental construction, which were 20% more economical than other methods and practically maintenance free. The study further showed that segmental construction

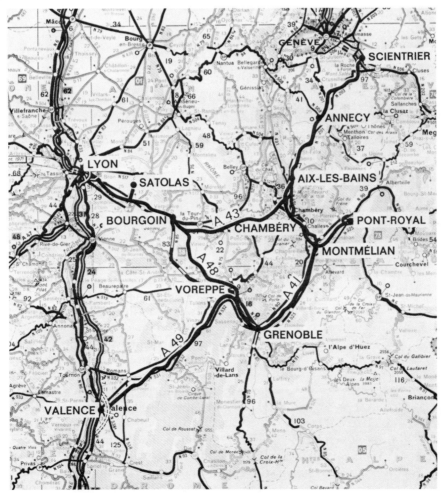

FIGURE 3.96. Alpine Motorway, location map.

should be extended to viaduct structures and that all segments for both overpasses and viaducts could be economically built in a single factory located near the center of gravity of the motorway network. The maximum carrying distance was no more than 75 miles (120 km) and the average was 40 miles (60 km). Figures 3.97 and 3.98 are views of a typical viaduct and a typical overpass in the motorway network.

The two-span and three-span overpass bridges have spans ranging from 59 to 98 ft (18 to 30 m). A variety of standardized precast cross sections were developed for this project, depending upon span and width requirements. The first structures used single and double-cell trapezoidal box sections, although later on voided slab sections were preferred, as illustrated in Figure 3.99*a*. This solution proved aesthetically pleasing and very simple to manufacture and assemble. The viaducts had to satisfy a wide range of environmental requirements. It was found that span lengths could be limited at all sites to a maximum of 200 ft (60 m),

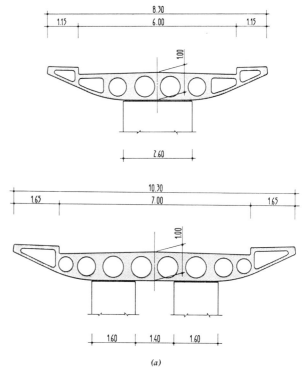

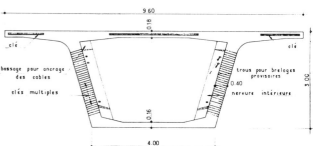

(*a*)

FIGURE 3.99. Alpine Motorway, typical sections of overpass and viaducts. (*a*) Overpass segments. (*b*) Viaduct segments.

FIGURE 3.97. Alpine Motorway, view of a viaduct.

FIGURE 3.98. Alpine Motorway, view of an overpass.

which allowed a constant-depth superstructure with precast segments, Figure 3.99*b*.

Segment manufacture was carried out in a factory close to the new motorway with easy access to the existing highway system, which was used to haul all segments to their respective sites. The factory had two parallel bays, Figures 3.100 and 3.101, one for the overpass segments and one for the viaduct segments. Segments for the overpasses, Figure 3.100, were match-cast by the short-line method with their longitudinal axis in a vertical position. The bottom segment was a previously cast unit. The segment at the top was then match-cast against the segment on the bottom. After the unit being cast had reached the required strength, the bottom unit was removed for storage, and the en-

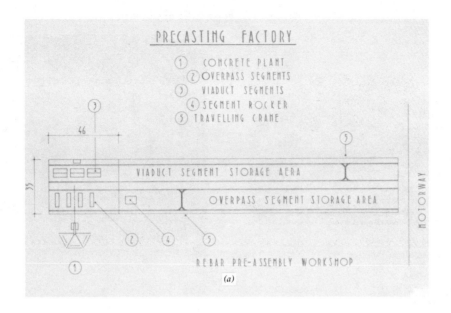

(a)

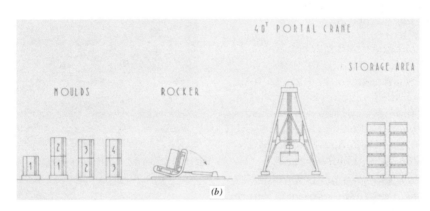

(b)

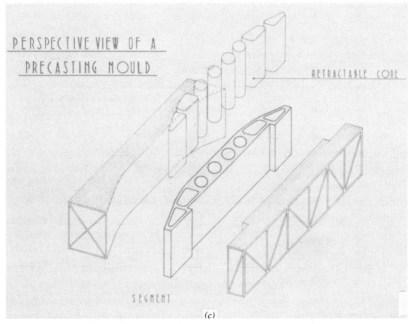

(c)

FIGURE 3.100. Alpine Motorway, precasting factory.

FIGURE 3.101. Alpine Motorway, general view of precast factory and segment storage.

tire process repeated. Figure 3.102 is a view of a segment in a vertical match-casting position.

Erection procedure for a typical three-span overpass structure was as follows:

1. After the foundations and pier columns had been constructed, precast concrete slabs were placed on sand beds adjacent to the piers to form foundations for the steel falsework towers. The precast slabs and towers were reusable for subsequent bridges. The erection commenced with placement of the first segment on top of four partially extended 25-ton jacks, Figure 3.103a.

2. The second and third segments were placed and prestressed to the first segment, Figure 3.103b. The joints between the segments were epoxy coated as the segments were erected. The prestressing of the second and third segments to the first segment consisted of temporary bars above the top surface of the segments, and other temporary tendons within the segments near the bottom of the segments. The four 25-ton hydraulic jacks under the first segment were then replaced by four partially extended 100-ton hydraulic jacks positioned under segments two and three. The jacks were supported on teflon sliding bearings.

3. The remaining segments were then erected, forming cantilevers on each side of the falsework towers, Figure 3.103c. The prestressing of the segments consisted of temporary tendons positioned above the segments, as indicated in Figure 3.103.

4. The erection of the segments could take place simultaneously at both piers, or one could precede the other, Figure 3.103d. Observe that at this stage of erection each assembly of segments was independently supported on four large hydraulic jacks and hence could be raised, lowered,

FIGURE 3.102. Alpine Motorway, vertical match casting of segments.

or rotated if required to adjust its position with respect to its pier or to its counterpart at the opposite pier. This method eliminated the need for a cast-in-place closure joint at midspan of the central span. Through the adjustment of the hydraulic jacks, perfect mating of the two centermost match-cast segments could be achieved when the assemblies of segments were slid together as indicated. The time required to erect the superstructure was significantly reduced by avoiding the use of a cast-in-place closure joint.

5. At this point in the erection, the first group of permanent prestressing tendons were inserted in preformed holes through the segments, after which they were stressed and grouted, Figure 3.103e.

6. The process proceeded with the erection of the remaining segments, Figure 3.103f.

7. After installation of precast match-cast abutments, a second group of permanent tendons was installed, and finally the temporary falsework and temporary prestressing was removed, Figure 3.103g.

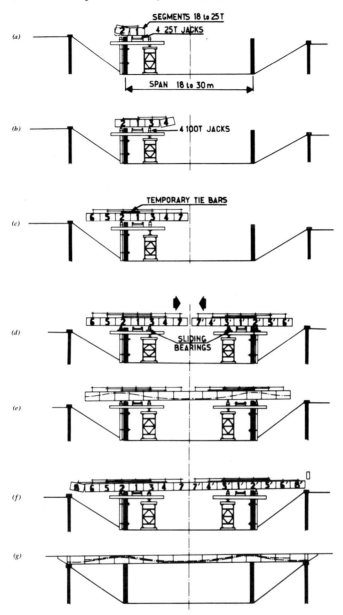

FIGURE 3.103. Alpine Motorway Bridges, erection scheme for typical three-span overpasses. (*a*) Placing the first and second segments. (*b*) Transfer to 100-ton jacks. (*c*) First half completed. (*d*) Joining precast assemblies by sliding. (*e*) Threading and stressing cables. (*f*) Placing the end segments. (*g*) Threading and stressing last cables.

Overpass structures of two spans could be erected using the technique illustrated above for three-span structures, Figure 3.104. As would be expected, the longer spans required the use of additional falsework towers. An overpass bridge, foundations plus piers and superstructure, could be constructed in less than two weeks. Figure 3.105 shows a typical segment being placed in the over-pass bridge with a mobile crane. Temporary pre-stress over the deck slab is shown in Figure 3.106.

The viaducts required the manufacture of larger segments in the same precasting factory used for the overpass segments, but with casting proceeding in the usual short-line horizontal fashion. Three casting machines were used simultaneously to pro-duce all viaduct segments.

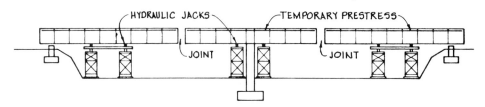

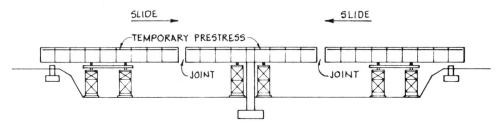

FIGURE 3.104. Alpine Motorway Bridges, erection scheme for two-span overpass bridges.

Erecting segments in the various structures required the use of a launching gantry of an exceptionally light and elaborate design, allowing easy transportation and erection from site to site, Figure 3.107. A typical 200 ft (60 m) long cantilever including 25 segments, one pier segment weighing 48 t (44 mt), and 24 typical segments weighing 36 t (33 mt) could be accomplished in six to eight working days, including launching the gantry to the following pier and achieving continuity with the preceding cantilever. The maximum rate of segment placing was 12 units in a single day.

This project is another interesting application of mass-production techniques and the standardization of segmental construction.

3.16 Bridge over the Eastern Scheldt, Holland

The bridge over the Eastern Scheldt, otherwise known as the Oosterschelde Bridge, Figure 3.108,

FIGURE 3.105. Alpine Motorway, segment placing in overpass with crane.

FIGURE 3.106. Alpine Motorway, provisional prestress over deck slab.

FIGURE 3.107. Alpine Motorway, segment placing in viaducts with launching gantry.

FIGURE 3.108. Bridge over the Eastern Scheldt, overall view of the structure.

is part of a project known as the Delta Works, which closed the mouths of many rivers and streams southwest of Rotterdam to protect the coastline from flooding. The bridge consists of fifty-five 300 ft (91.4 m) spans, a roadway width of 35 ft (10.7 m), and a vertical navigation clearance of 50 ft (15.2 m). Parameters considered in the choice of structural type and span were economics, foundation restraints, and ice loads.

Substructure consists of three cylinder piles with a caisson cap and an inverted V pier, Figure 3.109. The superstructure was assembled from seven precast elements, one pier segment, and two each of three progressively smaller segments to produce one double cantilever span of 300 ft (91.4 m). The bridge design, therefore, consists of very large prestressed cylinder piles, precast pier elements post-tensioned together, and precast superstructure elements erected and post-tensioned together to form a double cantilever system with a joint at each midspan location. Because of open-sea conditions,

time restraints for construction, and scarcity of labor, prefabrication was required to a very high degree. Since the precast pile elements would be large and heavy, it was decided that the pier and superstructure segments should be equally large and heavy, in the range of 400 to 600 tons.[16]

A casting yard, Figure 3.110, capable of producing all the various precast elements for the structure was constructed near one end of the bridge. This facility provided all the advantages of yard production techniques and the potential for high quality control.

The 14 ft (4.27 m) diameter cylinder piles have 14 in. (0.35 m) thick walls and were cast vertically in 20 ft (6 m) lengths. They were then rotated into a horizontal position where they were aligned, joints concreted, and the pile post-tensioned. In this manner piles were produced in required lengths up to 165 ft (50 m). The assembled pile was then transported by barge to the site, where a derrick picked it up at one end and rotated it into its verti-

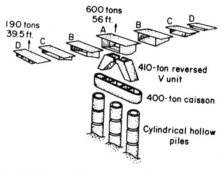

FIGURE 3.109. Bridge over the Eastern Scheldt, schematic of precast elements in the structure (courtesy of the Portland Cement Association).

FIGURE 3.110. Bridge over the Eastern Scheldt, view of precasting plant (courtesy of the Portland Cement Association).

cal position. Cylinder piles weighted from 300 to 550 tons (270 to 500 mt). The pier cap was also precast at the same yard, where it was post-tensioned circumferentially and vertically. The inverted V portion of the pier was also precast with provision for on-site post-tensioning to achieve final assembly.[16]

Figure 3.111 shows the bridge under construction. The temporary enclosures between each section are to protect the cast-in-place joint concrete against cold weather. Cast-in-place joints 16 in. (0.4 m) wide were used, with faces of the precast elements serrated to act as shear keys.

The superstructure segments were all set from a traveling steel gantry, Figure 3.111, that extended over two and one-half spans at a time. Segments were barged to their final location, then hoisted in symmetrical order about each pier. The joints were concreted and the primary stressing completed be-

fore the next series of segments were hoisted into position. Erection sequence is depicted in Figure 3.112. An aerial view of various stages of construction is shown in Figure 3.113. A typical cycle for two spans of superstructure, not including the pier segment, involving the raising, concreting, and stressing of 12 segments, was three weeks.

3.17   Captain Cook Bridge, Australia

This structure carries a six-lane highway over the Brisbane River in Brisbane, Australia, as part of the Riverside Expressway and South-West Freeway designed to relieve the city's overloaded traffic system.

The navigation requirements were for a 300 ft (91.4 m) wide horizontal clearance with a vertical clearance of 45 ft (13.7 m) across 200 ft (61 m) and 40 ft (12 m) at either extremity. However, a 600 ft (183 m) span became necessary because of the skew crossing. Adequate bearing rock, at a reasonable depth, was found at the south bank such that the pier could be founded on a spread footing. At the north end, because of the steeply rising bank, the anchor span was limited to a span of 140 ft (42.7 m) and the abutment was designed as a counterweight connected to the superstructure by a prestressed tie-down wall, Figure 3.114.[17]

Once the navigation span requirements had been met, the remaining span lengths were selected to meet design requirements, while the superstructure depth boundaries had to fall within a maximum allowable grade requirement of 3% and the flood level. The superstructure is a dual

FIGURE 3.111.   Bridge over the Eastern Scheldt, view of launching truss and enclosure for cast-in-place joints (courtesy of the Portland Cement Association).

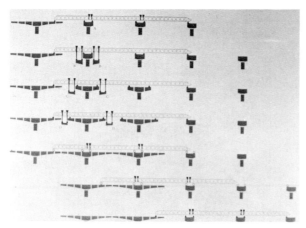

FIGURE 3.112.   Bridge over the Eastern Scheldt, schematic of erection sequence (courtesy of the Portland Cement Association).

FIGURE 3.113.   Bridge over the Eastern Scheldt, aerial view of construction showing various phases (courtesy of the Portland Cement Association).

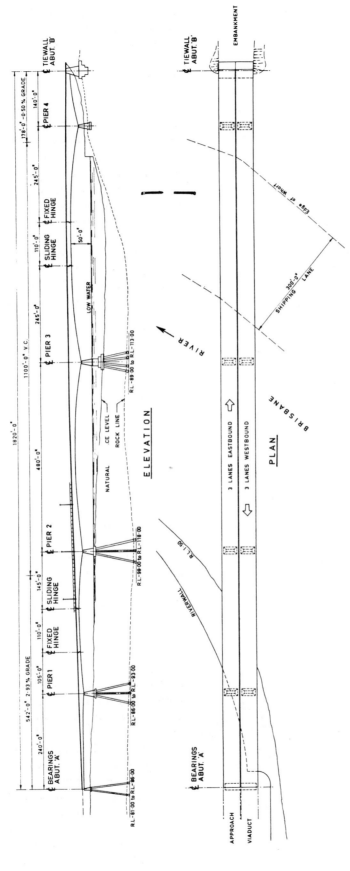

FIGURE 3.114. Capt. Cook Bridge, plan and elevation, from ref. 17.

structure of prestressed concrete segmental two-cell boxes, Figures 3.115 and 3.116.[17]

Steel rocker bearings were used to support the superstructure at piers 1, 3, and 4, and large-diameter single steel roller bearings were used at pier 2. Lubricated bronze bearings sliding on stainless steel were used at the north abutment and for the movable bearings at the suspended spans. Steel finger joints, allowing a 10 in. (250 mm) maximum movement, were provided at each slid-

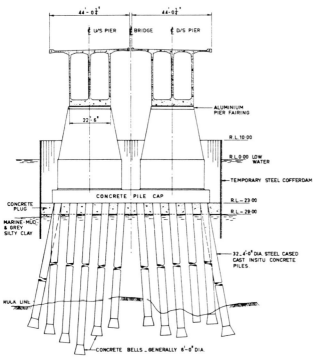

FIGURE 3.115. Capt. Cook Bridge, cross section at pier 3, from ref. 17.

FIGURE 3.116. Capt. Cook Bridge, two-cell box girder segment being erected (courtesy of G. Beloff, Main Roads Department).

ing bearing location and rubber and steel finger joints at the remaining locations.[17]

The box girder segments have a maximum depth of 32 ft (9.75 m) and a minimum depth of 6 ft (1.83 m). Segment length is 8 ft 8 in. (2.64 m). A 16 in. (0.4 m) cast-in-place, fully reinforced joint was used between segments. Maximum segment weight is 126 tons (114 mt). A total of 364 precast segments were required in the superstructure with the two segments over the tie-wall in the south abutment being cast in place.[17]

The contractor chose to locate the precasting operation on the river bank near the south abutment. This casting yard consisted of a concrete mixing plant, steam-curing plant, three adjustable steel forms, segment tilting frame, and a gantry crane to transport the segments to a storage area along the river bank. Segments were designed so that the top flange and upper portion of the webs had a constant thickness. The depth and lower portion accommodated all variations, allowing the contractor to cast in two sets of adjustable forms. Segments were cast with their longitudinal axis in a vertical position for ease of concrete placement around the prestressing ducts. Separate interior forms were constructed for each box to permit variations in the bottom flange and web thickness and size of fillets. After casting and curing, segments were lifted into a tilting frame to realign the segment into its normal position ready for handling and storage.[17]

A floating crane, designed and built by the contractor, was used for erection of the segments. It was essentially a rectangular pontoon with mounted A-frame lifting legs rising to 120 ft (36.6 m) with adequate clearance to service the finished deck level, while the stability was sufficient to transport the segments to the erection position, Figure 3.117. An extended reach was required to position segments on the first two spans in the shallow water near the bank.[17]

Segments on each side of the pier were supported on falsework anchored to the pier shafts, Figure 3.118. From this point additional segments, as they were erected, were supported on a cantilever falsework from the completed portion of the structure. This falsework was fixed under the completed girder and supported from deck level, Figure 3.119. When the capacity of the pier to carry the segment unbalanced load was reached, a temporary prop support on driven piles was constructed before cantilever erection could continue. Segment erection then proceeded on each side until either the joint position of the suspended

FIGURE 3.117. Cap. Cook Bridge, segment being transported by barge derrick to final position (courtesy of G. Beloff, Main Roads Department).

span was attained or the closure gap in span 3 was reached. The completed structure was opened to traffic in 1971, Figure 3.120.

3.18 Other Notable Structures

In Sections 3.2 through 3.15 the historical development of precast segmental bridges with match-cast joints has been illustrated by examples,

FIGURE 3.118. Capt. Cook Bridge, support for segments on each side of pier (courtesy of G. Beloff, Main Roads Department).

FIGURE 3.119. Capt. Cook Bridge, cradle support trusses and temporary support tower (courtesy of G. Beloff, Main Roads Department).

ranging from the first structure at Choisy-le-Roi to the largest applications such as the Rio Niteroi and Saint Cloud bridges. Emphasis has been placed on North American experience as well as on the advantages of precast segmental construction for urban structures (B-3 Viaducts) or repetitive applications (Alpine Motorways). Two particularly outstanding structures, deserving special mention because of their size and characteristics where precast segmental was used with conventional joints (not match-cast) were the Oosterschelde and Captain Cook Bridges (Sections 3.16 and 3.17). Before closing this important chapter, let us briefly give due credit to several other contemporary match-cast segmental bridges.

3.18.1 CALIX BRIDGE, FRANCE

This 14-span superstructure has a maximum span length of 512 ft (156 m) over the maritime

FIGURE 3.120. Capt. Cook Bridge, completed structure (courtesy of G. Beloff, Main Roads Department).

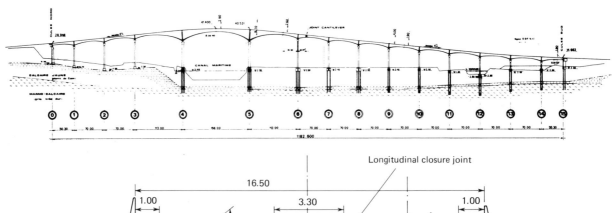

Longitudinal closure joint

FIGURE 3.121.   Calix Viaduct, near Caen, France general dimensions.

FIGURE 3.122.   Calix Viaduct, placing precast segments in superstructure.

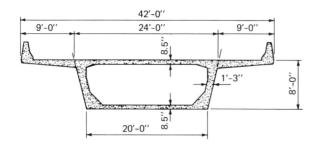

Section near midspan

FIGURE 3.123.   Vail Pass Bridge, cross-section general dimensions.

waterway and typical 230 ft (70 m) spans in the approaches on both banks. Dimensions are shown in Figure 3.121. The deck consists of two parallel box girders connected by a precast prestressed slab strip. All segments, with a maximum weight of 49 t (43 mt), were cast in a long bench and placed with a tower crane traveling between the box girders in the approaches. Segments were barged in for the main span, and a beam and winch system was used for hoisting them into place, Figure 3.122.

3.18.2   *VAIL PASS BRIDGES, U.S.A.*

These bridges are located on Interstate I-70 over Vail Pass near Vail, Colorado, in a beautiful setting at an altitude between 9000 and 10,000 ft (2700 and 3000 m) above sea level where winter conditions are critical and the construction period is very short. Dimensions are shown in Figure 3.123, and a view of one finished bridge appears in Figure 3.124.

3.18.3   *TRENT VIADUCT, U.K.*

This structure carries the M-180 South Humberside motorway over the River Trent and consists of dual roadways of three lanes each, with a central median. Precast segmental construction was selected against a steel plate girder design with a reinforced concrete deck slab. The bridge is sym-

FIGURE 3.124. Vail Pass Bridge, a completed precast segmental structure (courtesy of International Engineering Company, Inc.).

FIGURE 3.126. Trent Bridge, launching gantry finishing the deck.

metrical with four spans of 159, 279, 279, and 159 ft (48.5, 85, 85, and 48.5 m).

Each roadway is supported by an independent superstructure of twin concrete box girders varying in depth from 16 ft (4.9 m) at the piers to 7 ft (2.1 m) at midspan of the center spans. Principal dimensions are shown in Figure 3.125. Each box girder is made up of 91 precast segments 10 ft (3 m) long, varying in weight between 38 t (35 mt) to 82 t (75 mt). All segments were placed in balanced cantilever with a launching gantry shown in operation in Figure 3.126, with precast units being delivered on the finished deck.

3.18.4 L-32 TAUERNAUTOBAHN BRIDGE, AUSTRIA

This structure is located between Salzburg and Villach, Austria, as part of a new motorway connecting Germany and Yugoslavia. The 22-span twin bridge has a total length of 3820 ft (1167 m) distributed as follows: 110, twenty at 180, and 110

ft (33.5, twenty at 55, and 33.5 m). Box piers have a maximum height of 330 ft (100 m). The constant-depth superstructure of 12.5 ft (3.8 m) is made up of 722 segments match-cast in a job-site factory equipped with four casting machines, Figure 3.127. A launching gantry was used to place all segments in the two bridges in balanced cantilever, Figure 3.128.

3.18.5 KISHWAUKEE RIVER BRIDGE, U.S.A.

This dual structure carries U.S. Route 51 over the Kishwaukee River near the city of Rockford, Illinois. Dimensions are shown in Figure 3.129. Prestressing is achieved in the transverse and longitudinal directions by bar tendons. All segments were placed in the structure by a launching gantry, shown in Figure 3.130, which represents the first application of this method in the United States.

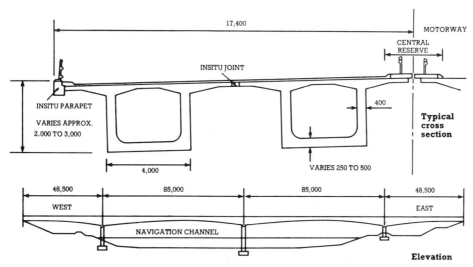

FIGURE 3.125. Trent Bridge, typical dimensions.

FIGURE 3.127. L-32 Tauernautobahn Bridge, casting machine.

FIGURE 3.128. L-32 Tauernautobahn Bridge, launching gantry.

3.18.6 *KENTUCKY RIVER BRIDGE, U.S.A.*

This structure crossing the Kentucky River is located in Franklin County just south of Frankfort, Kentucky. It is a three-span structure with a 323 ft (98.5 m) center span and 228.5 ft (70 m) side spans. In cross section the superstructure consists of two rectangular boxes. It is the first precast segmental bridge to be constructed in the United States using the long-bed casting method, Figure 3.131. A view during construction is shown in Figure 3.132.

3.18.7 *I-205 COLUMBIA RIVER BRIDGE, U.S.A.*

This large project represents one of the major applications of precast segmental construction in the United States. The 5770 ft (1759 m) long structure carries Interstate I-205 from Vancouver, Washington, across the North Channel of the Columbia River to Government Island near Portland, Oregon. Twin structures carry two 68 ft (20.7 m) wide roadways with span lengths varying between 600 ft (183 m) and 242 ft (74 m). Typical dimensions of

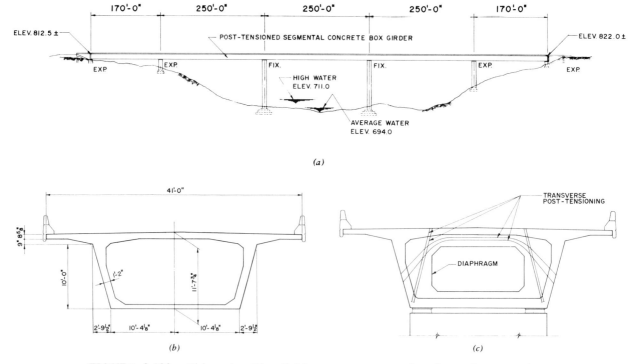

FIGURE 3.129. Kishwaukee River Bridge, superstructure elevation and cross sections. (*a*) Elevation. (*b*) Section at midspan. (*c*) Section at pier. (From ref. 18.)

FIGURE 3.130. Kishwaukee River Bridge, view during construction showing launching truss.

FIGURE 3.131. Kentucky River Bridge, long-line casting bed.

FIGURE 3.132. Kentucky River Bridge, during construction.

the main spans over the river are shown in Figure 3.133. Dimensions of the cross section, as designed, are shown in Figure 3.134. However, the contractor, under a value engineering option in the contract documents (see Chapter 12), elected to redesign the cross section to a two-cell box section, Figure 3.135. The contractor exercised the option allowed in the bidding documents to select his own construction method and proceeded with casting in place in conventional travelers the two cantilevers adjacent to the main navigation channel (piers 12 and 13), while all other spans are of precast segmental construction. Figure 3.136 shows a rendering of the structure.

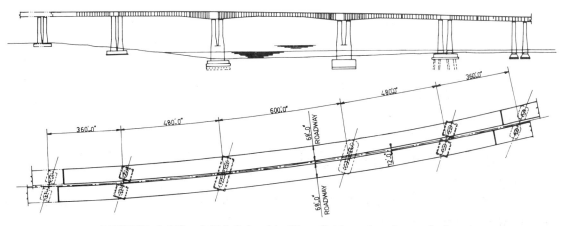

FIGURE 3.133. I-205 Columbia River Bridge, elevation and plan.

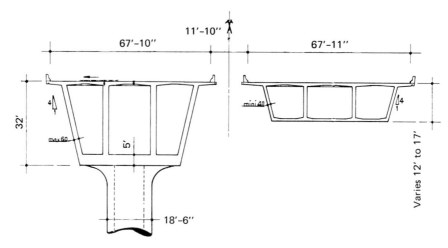

FIGURE 3.134.   I-205 Columbia River Bridge, cross sections.

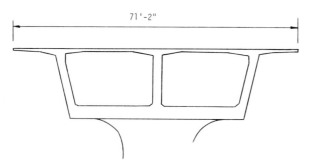

FIGURE 3.135.   I-205 Columbia River Bridge, revised cross section.

3.18.8   *ZILWAUKEE BRIDGE, U.S.A.*

This bridge is another important example of precast segmental construction in the United States. Located in central Michigan, this 8080 ft (2463 m) long structure carries dual four-lane roadways over the Saginaw River near Zilwaukee, Michigan. Principal dimensions are shown in Figure 3.137.

FIGURE 3.136.   I-205 Columbia River Bridge, rendering of the structure.

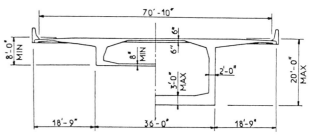

CROSS SECTION OF PRECAST SEGMENTS

FIGURE 3.137.   Zilwaukee Bridge, typical dimensions.

The 51 spans vary in length from 155 ft to 392 ft (47 to 119 m). An additional three-span ramp carries some traffic onto the southbound high-level bridge. Navigation clearance is 125 ft (38 m) above the Saginaw River.

For a total deck area of 1,180,000 sq ft (110,000

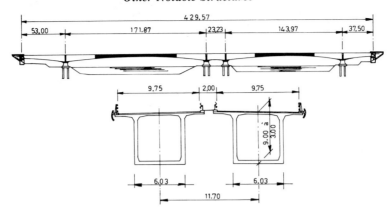

FIGURE 3.138. Ottmarsheim Bridge, general dimensions.

m²) there are 1590 large segments varying in length from 8 to 12 ft (2.4 to 3.65 m) with a maximum weight of 160 t (144 mt). Segments were produced in a production-line operation with short-line casting and placed in the structure in balanced cantilever with a large launching gantry accommodating two successive spans.

3.18.9 OTTMARSHEIM BRIDGE, FRANCE

This bridge in East France close to Germany and the Rhine River at the Ottmarsheim hydroelectric plant is today the longest clear span of precast segmental construction and the first major application of lightweight concrete to this type of structure. Principal dimensions are shown in Figure 3.138. As shown in the longitudinal section, lightweight concrete was used only in the center portion of the two main spans over the navigable waterway and over the outlet channel of the power plant. Figure 3.139 is a view of the completed structure.

3.18.10 OVERSTREET BRIDGE, FLORIDA, U.S.A.

This structure crosses the Intracoastal Waterway near Panama City in Western Florida. Dimensions are shown in Figures 3.140 and 3.141. The main navigation span is 290 ft (88 mm) long between piers to avoid any construction in the water fender system during operation. Approach spans are 125 ft (38 m) long and rest on I-shaped piers bearing on precast piles. The main piers consist of twin I piers of the same design. The total length of structure is 2650 ft (808 m) divided as follows: 95, seven at 125, 207.5, 290, 207.5, seven at 125, and 95 ft (29, seven at 38, 63, 88, 63, seven at 38, and 29 m). Precast segments 10 ft (3 m) long and

weighing a maximum of 50 t (45 mt) are designed to be placed in balanced cantilever with an auxiliary overhead truss (and winch system) in the approach spans to stabilize the deck over the flexible piers during construction.

3.18.11 F-9 FREEWAY, MELBOURNE, AUSTRALIA

This very important project is a recent application of precast segmental construction to urban elevated structures. The constraints relating to location of piers and construction over highway and railway traffic are comparable to the conditions encountered at the B-3 South Viaducts in Paris, France.

The principal project dimensions are shown in Figure 3.142. All segments will be placed in the twin bridge using two launching gantries, which incorporate the latest technological developments in safety and efficiency.

FIGURE 3.139. Ottmarsheim Bridge, view of the completed structure.

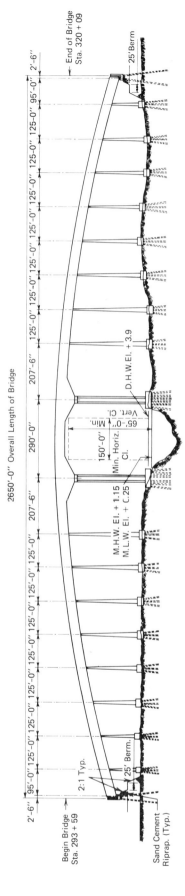

FIGURE 3.140. Overstreet Bridge, Florida, elevation.

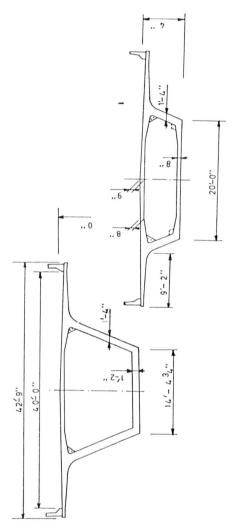

FIGURE 3.141. Overstreet Bridge, Florida, cross sections.

146

References

1. Jean Muller, "Ten Years of Experience in Precast Segmental Construction," *Journal of the Prestressed Concrete Institute,* Vol. 20, No. 1, January–February 1975.

2. C. A. Ballinger, W. Podolny, Jr., and M. J. Abrahams, "A Report on the Design and Construction of Segmental Prestressed Concrete Bridges in Western Europe—1977," International Road Federation, Washington, D.C., June 1978. (Also available from Federal Highway Administration, Office of Research and Development, Washington, D.C., Report No. FHWA-RD-78-44.)

3. Walter Podolny, Jr., "An Overview of Precast Prestressed Segmental Bridges," *Journal of the Prestressed Concrete Institue,* Vol. 24, No. 1, January–February 1979.

4. J. Mathivat, "Reconstruction du Pont de Choisy-le-Roi," *Travaux,* Janvier 1966, No. 372.

5. Jean Muller, "Long-Span Precast Prestressed Concrete Bridges Built in Cantilever," *First International Symposium, Concrete Bridge Design,* Paper SP 23-40, ACI Publication SP-23, American Concrete Institute, Detroit, 1969.

6. Andre Bouchet, "Les Ponts en Beton Precontraint de Courbevoie et de la Grande-Jatte (Hauts-de-Seine)," *La Technique des Travaux,* Juillet-Aout 1968.

7. "Bear River Bridge," STUP Bulletin of Information, November–December 1972.

8. "Nova Scotia's Bear River Bridge—Precast Segmental Construction Costs Less and the Money Stays at Home," *Bridge Bulletin,* Third Quarter 1972, Prestressed Concrete Institute, Chicago.

9. "John F. Kennedy Memorial Causeway, Corpus Christi, Texas," Bridge Report SR 162.01 E, Portland Cement Association, Skokie, Ill., 1974.

10. G. C. Lacey, and J. E. Breen, "Long Span Prestressed Concrete Bridges of Segmental Construction State of the Art," Research Report 121-1, Center for Highway Research, The University of Texas at Austin, May 1969.

11. S. Kashima and J. E. Breen, "Epoxy Resins for Jointing Segmentally Constructed Prestressed Concrete Bridges," Research Report 121-2, Center for Highway Research, The University of Texas at Austin, August 1974.

12. G. C. Lacey and J. E. Breen, "The Design and Optimization of Segmentally Precast Prestressed Box Girder Bridges," Research Report 121-3, Center for Highway Research, The University of Texas at Austin, August 1975.

13. R. C. Brown, Jr., N. H. Burns, and J. E. Breen, "Computer Analysis of Segmentally Erected Precast Prestressed Box Girder Bridges," Research Report 121-4, Center for Highway Research, The University of Texas at Austin, November 1974.

14. S. Kashima and J. E. Breen, "Construction and Load Tests of a Segmental Precast Box Girder Bridge Model," Research Report 121-5, Center for Highway Research, The University of Texas at Austin, February 1975.

15. J. E. Breen, R. L. Cooper, and T. M. Gallaway, "Minimizing Construction Problems in Segmentally Precast Box Girder Bridges," Research Report 121-6F, Center for Highway Research, The University of Texas at Austin, August 1975.

16. Ben C. Gerwick, Jr., "Bridge over the Eastern Scheldt," *Journal of the Prestressed Concrete Institute,* Vol. 11, No. 1, February 1966.

17. "A Proud Achievement—The Captain Cook Bridge," Issued by the Commissioner of Main Roads—1972, Main Roads Department, Brisbane, Queensland, Australia.

18. "Prestressed Concrete Segmental Bridges on FA 412 over the Kishwaukee River," *Bridge Bulletin,* No. 1, 1976, Prestressed Concrete Institute, Chicago.

4

Design of Segmental Bridges

4.1 Introduction

Design of concrete highway bridges in the United States conforms to the provisions of The American Association for State Highway and Transportation Officials (AASHTO) "Standard Specifications for Highway Bridges." For railway structures, specifications of the American Railway Engineers Association (AREA) should be consulted. For the most part, the provisions in these specifications were written before segmental construction was considered feasible or practical in the United States.

Before discussing design considerations, the authors wish to emphasize that no preference for either cast-in-place or precast methods of construction is implied here. The intent is simply to present conditions that the designer should be aware of to produce a satisfactory design. Both concepts are viable ones, and both have been used to produce successful structures.

In general, the segmental technique is closely related to the method of construction and the structural system employed. This is why segmental construction, either cast in place or precast, has been often identified with the cantilever construction used in so many applications. It is logical to take bridge structures built in cantilever as a basis for the design considerations developed in this chapter. Where other methods, such as incremental launching or progressive placement, require special design considerations, such problems are discussed in the appropriate chapters.

4.2 Live-Load Requirements

In comparing practices in other countries to those in the United States, an important parameter to keep in mind is that of live-load requirements. Figure 4.1 illustrates the considerable differences among code requirements in various countries.[1] For a simple span of 164 ft (50 m) and width of 24.6 ft (7.5 m), the German specification requires a live-load design moment 186% greater and the French requires one 290% greater than that of AASHTO. Some Canadian provinces use the AASHTO specifications but arbitrarily increase the live load by 25%.

The depth-to-span and width-to-depth ratios for segmental construction presently advocated in the United States have been adopted from European practice. The lighter live loads used in the United States should permit further refinements in our design approach.

4.3 Span Arrangement and Related Principles of Construction

In the balanced cantilever type of construction, segments are placed in a symmetrical fashion about a pier. The designer must always remember that construction proceeds with symmetrical cantilever deck sections centered about the piers and *not* with completed spans between successive piers.[2]

For a typical three-span structure, the side spans should preferably be 65 percent of the main center span instead of 80 percent in conventional cast-in-place structures. This is done to reduce to a minimum the length of the deck portion next to the abutment, which cannot be conveniently built in balanced cantilever, Figure 4.2a.

Where span lengths must vary, as between a main span and an approach span, it is best to introduce an intermediate span whose length will average the two flanking spans, Figure 4.2b. In this manner the cantilever concept is optimized.

Individual cantilever sections are generally made continuous by insertion of positive-moment ten-

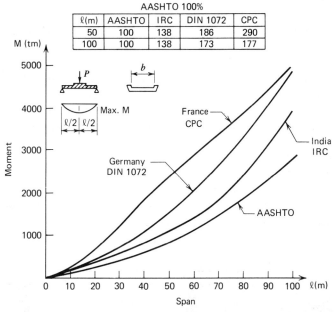

ℓ(m)	AASHTO	IRC	DIN 1072	CPC
50	100	138	186	290
100	100	138	173	177

FIGURE 4.1. Maximum live-load moment (simple span) (F. Leonhardt, *New Practice in Concrete Structures*, IABSE, New York, 1968).

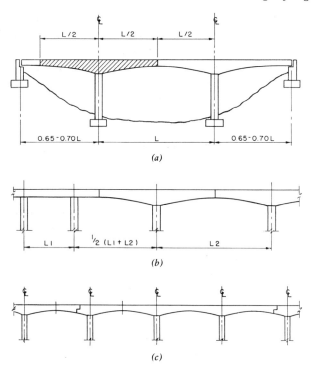

FIGURE 4.2. Cantilever construction showing choice of span lengths and location of expansion joints.

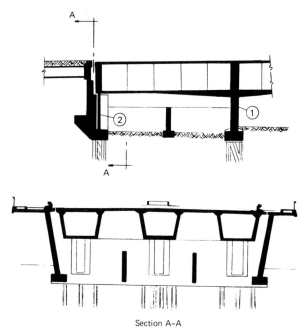

FIGURE 4.4. End restraint at abutment.

dons upon closure. It is preferred not to have any permanent hinges at midspan. Continuous decks without joints have been repeatedly constructed to lengths in excess of 2000 ft (600 m) and have proved satisfactory from the standpoint of maintenance and riding quality.

For very long viaduct-type structures, intermediate expansion joints are inevitable to accommodate volume changes. These joints should be located near points of contraflexure, Figure 4.2c, to avoid objectionable slope changes that occur if the joint is located at midspan. This consideration will be discussed in more detail in Section 4.4.

In many cases it may not be possible to provide the desirable optimum span arrangement. Thus, the end span may be greater or less than the optimum span length desired.[2] In the case of a long end span, the superstructure might be extended over the abutment wall to provide a short additional span. As shown in Figure 4.3, a conventional

bearing (1) is provided over the front abutment wall. A rear prestressed tie (2) opposes uplift and permits cantilever construction to proceed outward from the abutment to the joint (J1), where a connection can be effected with the cantilever from the first intermediate pier. Figure 4.4 shows an alternative scheme with a constant-depth section, as opposed to a haunched section, where the deck has been encased within the abutment wing walls for architectural purposes. For the normal end span, a special segment is temporarily cantilevered out so as to reach the first balanced cantilever constructed from the next pier, Figure 4.5. Alternatively this portion could be cast in place on falsework, if site conditions permit.

In a short-end-span situation, cantilever construction starts from the first pier and reaches the abutment on one side well before the midspan section of the adjacent span, Figure 4.6. An uplift reaction must be transferred to the abutment during construction and in the completed structure. Consequently, the webs of the main box girder deck are cantilevered over the expansion

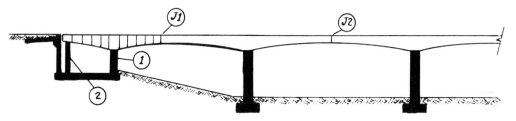

FIGURE 4.3. End restraint in abutment.

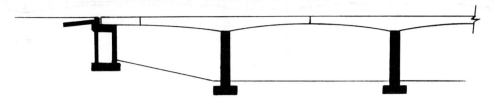

FIGURE 4.5. Conventional bearing on abutment.

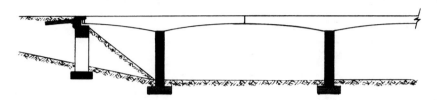

FIGURE 4.6. Anchorage for uplift in abutment.

joint into slots provided in the main abutment wall, Figure 4.7. The neoprene bearings are placed above the web cantilever rather than below to transfer the uplift force while allowing the deck to expand freely.

Interesting examples of such concepts are given in the three following bridges:

Givors Bridge over the Rhone River, France, shown in Figure 4.8. The main dimensions are given with the typical construction stages of the superstructure.

Tricastin Bridge over the Rhone River, France (Section 2.15.11). No river piers were desired for the structure, which dictated a main span of 467 ft (142.50 m), and there was no room on the banks to increase the side spans so as to avoid the end uplift. Two very short side spans of only 83 ft (25.20 m) provide the end restraint of the river span. The uplift is transferred to the abutments, which are earth filled to provide a counterweight, Figure 4.9. The magnitude of the uplift force has been re-duced by the use of lightweight concrete in the center of the main span.

Puteaux Bridges over the Seine River, near Paris (Section 2.15.10).

A few bridges have even been built in cantilever entirely from the abutments. The Reallon Bridge in France is one such structure, Figure 4.10, where very special site conditions with regard to bridge profile and shape of the valley were best met with this concept.

Another set of circumstances may be encountered when it is not possible to select the desired span lengths to optimize the use of cantilever construction. Such was the situation of the bridge over the Seine River for the Paris Ring Road, where a side span on the left bank could not be less than 88 percent of the main river span over the river, while very stringent traffic requirements governed the placement pattern of precast segments on the right bank, Figure 4.11.

4.4 Deck Expansion, Hinges and Continuity

4.4.1 HINGES AT MIDSPAN

Historically, the first prestressed concrete bridges built in cantilever were provided with a hinge at the center of the various spans. Such hinges were designed to transfer vertical shear between the tips of two adjacent cantilever arms (which could develop under the live loading applied over one arm only in half the span length) while enduring a free expansion of the concrete deck under volume changes (concrete creep and seasonal variations of temperature). Continuity of the deflection curve

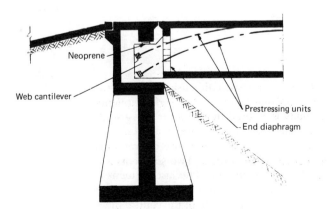

FIGURE 4.7. Longitudinal section.

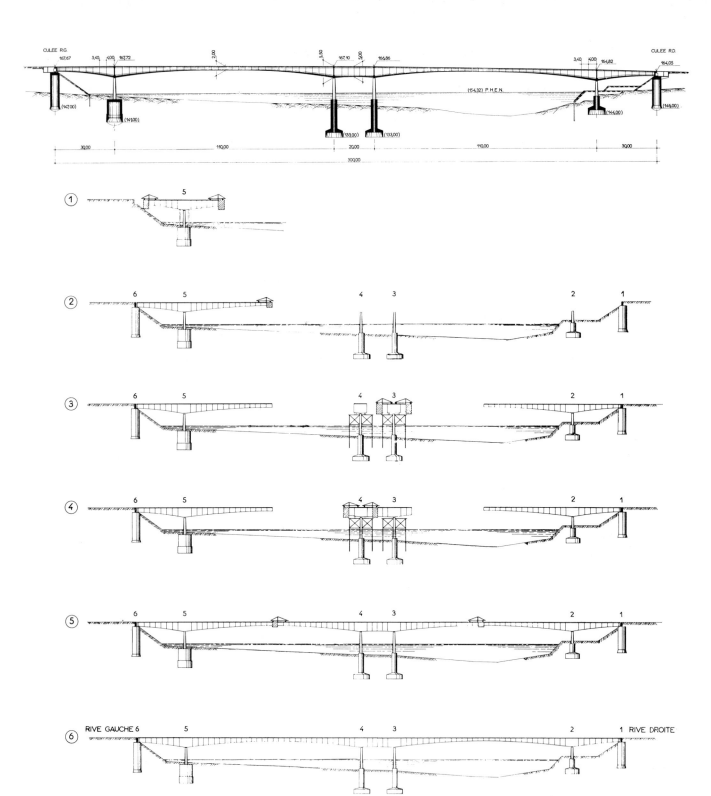

FIGURE 4.8. Givors Bridge over the Rhone River, France, span dimensions and typical construction stages. (1) Construction of left bank river pier segment. The eight segments either side of the pier are erected, and pier stability is assured by temporary props. (2) The connection between deck and abutments is made. Temporary props are removed and the seven remaining segments are placed in cantilever. (3) The above operation is repeated on the right bank. The central pier segments are poured. Two segments are erected on either side of each pier, supported by scaffolding. (4) The last segment is placed in the central span, continuity is achieved between the two cantilevers, and the scaffolding is removed. (5) The remaining 16 segments on either side of the central piers are placed. (6) The 110 m spans are completed by pouring the closure segments and tensioning the continuity prestress. The superstructure is now complete.

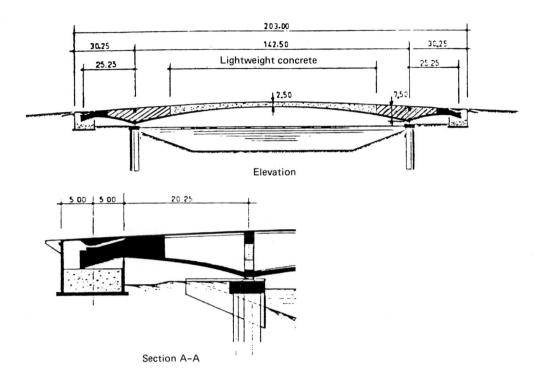

Elevation

Section A-A

Plan

FIGURE 4.9. Tricastin Bridge over the Rhone River, France.

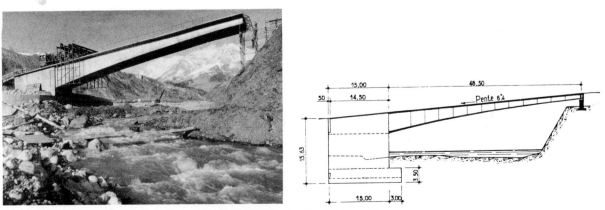

FIGURE 4.10. Reallon Bridge, France.

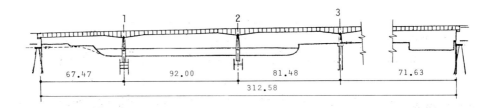

PHASE 1   construction of central cantilever

PHASE 2   construction of right bank cantilever

PHASE 3   closure of central and right bank cantilever

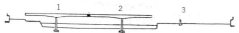

PHASE 4   joining of right bank cantilever with abutment

PHASE 5   construction of left bank cantilever

PHASE 6   closure of left bank and central cantilever

PHASE 7   joining of left bank cantilever with abutment

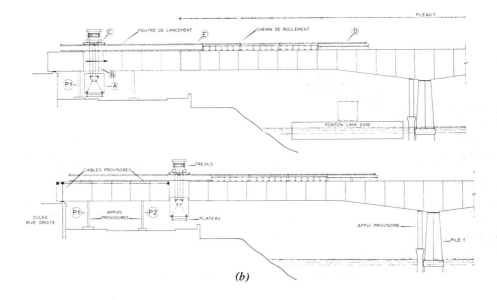

(b)

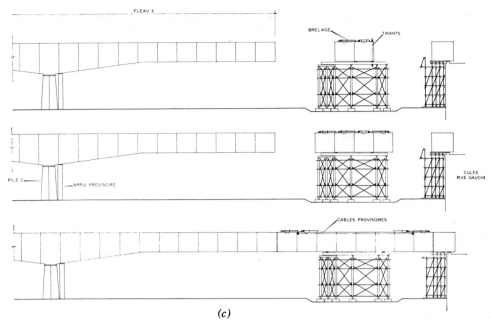

(c)

FIGURE 4.11. Paris Belt (Downstream). (*a*) Typical construction stages. (*b*) Segment assembly—right bank. (*c*) Segment assembly—left bank.

was thus obtained in terms of vertical displacement but not insofar as rotation at the hinge point was concerned.

Remember that in this type of structure the deck is necessarily fixed at the various piers, which must be designed to carry the unbalanced moments due to unsymmetrical live-load patterns over the deck. On the other hand, these structures are simple to design because they are statically determinate for all dead loads and prestressing, and the effect of live load is simple to compute. Because there are no moment reversals in the deck, the prestressing tendon layout is simple.

Some disadvantages were accepted as the price of simplicity of design:

The deck has a lower ultimate capacity as compared with a continuous structure, because there is no possible redistribution of moments.

Hinges are difficult to design, install, and operate satisfactorily.

There are many expansion joints, and regardless of precautions taken in design, construction, and operation they are always a source of difficulty and high maintenance cost.

The major disadvantage, revealed only by experience, related to the exceeding sensitivity of such structures to steel relaxation and concrete creep.

Because of the various hinges at midpoints of the spans, there is no restraint to the vertical and angular displacements of the cantilever due to the effect of creep. Steel relaxation and the corresponding prestress losses tend to make matters worse, while concrete creep is responsible for a progressive lowering of the center of each span. With time, there is an increasing angle break in the deck profile at the hinge. The magnitude of the deflection has been reported to be in excess of one foot (0.03 m).

The difficulties experienced with this type of construction are such that most government officials in Western Europe will no longer permit its use.[3]

4.4.2 CONTINUOUS SUPERSTRUCTURES

Further research concerning the exact properties and behavior of materials for such structures having a midspan hinge would enable more accurate prediction of the expected deflection and thus better control. A far more positive approach is to eliminate the fundamental cause of the phenomenon by avoiding all permanent hinges and achieving full continuity whenever possible.

To show the relative behavior of a continuous structure and one with hinges at midspan, a numerical application was made for the center span of the Choisy-le-Roi Bridge in two extreme cases:

TABLE 4.1. Comparison of Crown Deflections (Hinged versus Continuous Structure)

		Cast-in-Place Hinged Structure			Precast Continuous Structure		
No.	Load Stage	E (10⁶ psi)	y (in.)	ω (in. × 10³/in.)	E (10⁶ psi)	y (in.)	ω (in. × 10³/in.)
1	Girder weight	4.3	1.80	2.4	5.1	1.50	2.0
2	Initial prestress	4.3	−1.50	−2.0	5.1	−0.90	−1.2
3	Cumulative	4.3	0.30	0.4	5.1	0.60	0.8
4	5% Deviation of prestress	—	23%		—	7%	
5	Continuity prestress	—	—	—	6.4	−0.30	0
6	Superimposed load	6.4	0.30	0.4	6.4	0.10	0
7	Finished structure (initial)	—	0.60	0.8	—	0.40	0.8
8	Concrete creep and losses	2.1	1.10	1.4	2.1	−0.10	0
9	Finished structure (final)	—	1.70	2.2	—	0.30	0.8
10	Live loads	6.4	0.90	1.1	6.4	0.30	0

Explication of symbols:
E = modulus of elasticity for each particular loading stage
y = vertical deflection at crown
ω = total angular break at crown (expressed in thousandths of inch per inch)

Derivation of results:
(3) = (1) + (2)   girder weight and initial prestress
(7) = (3) + (5) + (6) finished structure (initial stage)
(9) = (7) + (8)   finished structure (final stage)

Cast-in-place cantilever with a hinge at midspan, and

Precast segmental continuous construction.

Results comparing the two structures are shown in Table 4.1 and in Figures 4.12 through 4.14.

The study shows no significant difference between the two types of structures with respect to the theoretical behavior of the cantilever method under combined dead load and initial prestress, Figure 4.12. In fact, the angle change at midspan is even slightly less for the hinged structure, because the prestress offsets a greater percentage of dead-load moments, 83 percent instead of 58 percent.

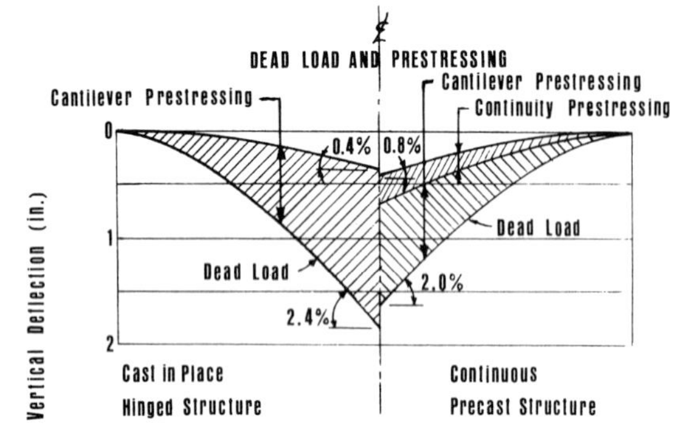

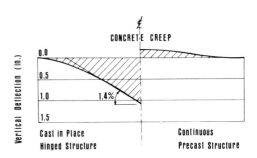

FIGURE 4.13. Comparison of deflection caused by creep (hinged versus continuous structure).

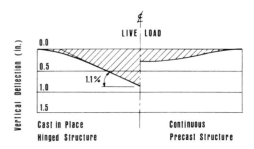

FIGURE 4.14. Comparison of deflections caused by live load (hinged versus continuous structure).

FIGURE 4.12. Comparison of deflection under dead load and prestressing (hinged versus continuous structure).

When the effect of concrete creep is considered, however, there is a significant difference between the two types of structures, Figure 4.13. The hinged structure has a vertical deflection of 1.1 in. (28 mm) and a corresponding total angle break of 0.0028 in./inch. This value is twice that shown in Table 4.1 and Figure 4.13 for the angle change of *one* cantilever, the value of 2.8 being the total angle break of the two abutting cantilevers. The continuous structure indicates a camber of 0.1 in. (3 mm), and no angle break will ever appear because of full continuity.

Further, the effect of deviation of actual prestress load from the design prestress load points out an important difference in the sensitivity of the two systems. Assuming the actual prestress in the structure to differ from the design assumption by 5%, the corresponding maximum deflection is increased by 23% in the hinged structure but only

7% in the continuous structure. Therefore, the continuous structure is three times less sensitive to possible deviations from the assumed material properties.

Live-load deflections of the continuous structure are three times more rigid than the hinged structure, Figure 4.14. The deflection of a typical span of the Oleron Viaduct in France is compared with a continuous span and with a crown hinged span in Figure 4.15.

From these data it is obvious that the fullest use of continuity and the elimination of hinges at midspan whenever possible is beneficial to the structural behavior of the bridge, to safety and comfort of traffic, and to the structure's aesthetic appearance.

In practice, the continuity of the individual cantilever arms at midspan is obtained by another set of prestressing tendons, usually called continuity

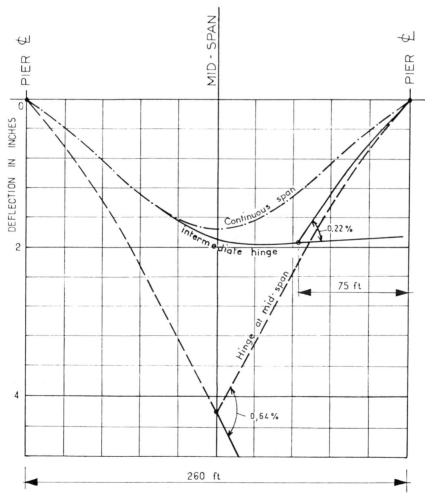

FIGURE 4.15. Comparisons between live-load deflections for continuous or hinged structures.

prestressing, which is installed along the span in a continuous structure. Details of the design aspects of this prestress will be discussed in Section 4.8.

4.4.3 *EXPANSION OF LONG BRIDGES*

When the continuity of the superstructure is selected as optimum for the behavior of the structure, one must keep in mind that proper measures should be concurrently taken to allow for expansion due either to short-term and cyclic volume changes or to long-term concrete creep.

The piers may be made flexible enough to allow for such expansion or may be provided with elastomeric bearings to reduce the magnitude of horizontal loads to acceptable levels when applied to the substructure. This important aspect of the overall bridge design concept is considered in Chapter 5.

Several structures are currently made continuous in lengths of 1000 to 2000 ft (300 to 600 m) and in exceptional cases even 3000 ft (900 m). For longer structures, full continuity between end abutments is not possible because of the excessive magnitude of the horizontal movements between superstructure and piers and related problems. Therefore, intermediate expansion joints must be provided. For long spans they should not be placed at the center of the span, as in the early cantilever bridges, but closer to the contraflexure point to minimize the effect of a long-term deflection. Such a concept was developed initially for the Oleron Viaduct and is currently used on large structures such as the Saint Cloud Bridge in Paris, Sallingsund Bridge in Denmark, and the Columbia River and Zilwaukee Bridges in the United States.

Detailed computations were made in the case of the Oleron Viaduct to optimize the location of the expansion joint in a typical 260 ft (80 m) span, Figure 4.15 shows the shape of the deflection curve for a uniform live loading with the three following assumptions:

Fully continuous span

Span with a center hinge

Span with an intermediate hinge located at 29 percent of the span length from the adjacent pier (actual case)

The advantages of having moved the hinge away from the center toward the quarter-span point are obvious:

Maximum deflection under live load is reduced in the ratio of 2.2 to 1.

Maximum angle break under live load is reduced in the ratio of 3.0 to 1.

For dead-load deflections the difference is even more significant, such that there is no substantial difference between the actual structure and a fully continuous one.

The variation of the angle break at the hinge point versus the hinge location along the span length is shown in Figure 4.16. There seems to be little doubt that the structure is improved by selection of a proper location for the hinge and the expansion joint.

Theoretically, the ideal hinge position is between points *A* and *B*, which are the contraflexure points for dead and live loads. From a construction standpoint, such a location for the hinge complicates the erection process, for the hinge must be temporarily blocked and subsequently released when the span is complete and continuity is achieved. We will consider this subject in detail after examining the layout of longitudinal prestress in cantilever bridges (Section 4.8.6).

It was recently discovered, in the designing of the Sallingsund Bridge, that the optimum location

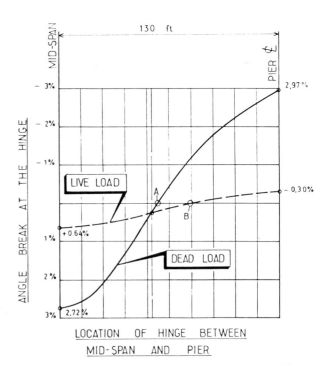

FIGURE 4.16. Variation of angle break at the hinge with hinge location along the span.

of the hinge to control the deflections under service-load conditions does not simultaneously permit achievement of the overall maximum capacity under ultimate conditions. This question will be discussed later in this chapter.

The preceding discussion of hinge location applies particularly for very long spans or for slender structures. For moderate spans with sufficient girder depth it has been found that careful detailing of the prestress in the hinged span can allow the hinge to be maintained at the centerpoint for simplicity (spans less than 200 ft with a depth to span ratio of approximately 20). Such was the case for the cantilever alternatives of the Long Key and Seven Mile Bridges in Florida.

4.5 Type, Shape, and Dimensions of the Superstructure

4.5.1 BOX SECTIONS

The typical section best suited for cantilever construction is the box section, for the following reasons:

1. Because of the construction method, dead-load moments produce compression stresses at the bottom fiber along the entire span length, and maximum moments occur near the piers. The typical section therefore must be provided with a large bottom flange, particularly near the piers, and this is achieved best with a box section.

The efficiency of the box section is very good, and for a given amount of concrete provides the least amount of prestressing steel. The efficiency of a section is usually measured by the following dimensionless coefficient:

$$\rho = \frac{r^2}{c_1 c_2}$$

with the notations as given in Figures 4.17 and 4.18, where some basic formulas are presented.

The efficiency would be $\rho = 1$ if the concrete were concentrated in thin flanges with webs of negligible thickness. On the other hand, a rectangular section has an efficiency of only 1/3. The usual box section efficiency is $\rho = 0.60$, which is significantly better than that of an I girder.

2. Another advantage of the large bottom flange is that the concrete area is sufficiently large at ultimate load to balance the full capacity of the prestressing tendons without loss in the magnitude of the lever arm.

3. The elastic stability of the structure is excellent both during construction and under service conditions, because the closed box section has a large torsional rigidity.

4. In wide bridge decks where several girders must be used side by side, the large torsional stiffness of the individual box girders allows a very satisfactory transverse distribution of live loads without intermediate diaphragms between piers.

5. Because of their torsional rigidity, box girders lend themselves to the construction of curved bridge superstructures and provide maximum flexibility for complicated tendon trajectories.

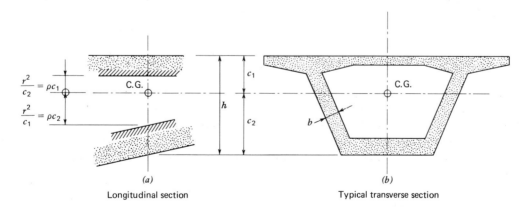

(a) Longitudinal section   (b) Typical transverse section

FIGURE 4.17. Typical characteristics of a box section: Total section height: h; cross-section area: A; moment of inertia: I; position of centroid; c_1, c_2; radius of gyration: r given by $r^2 = I/A$; efficiency ratio: $\rho = r^2/c_1 c_2$; limits of central core: $r^2/c_2 = \rho c_1$; $r^2/c_1 = \rho c_2$; for the usual box girder: $\rho = 0.60$.

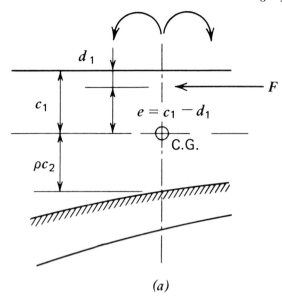

(a)

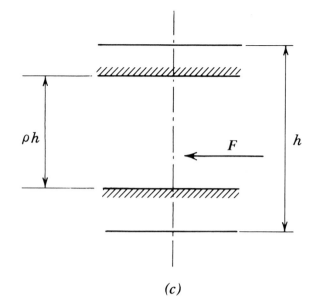

(c)

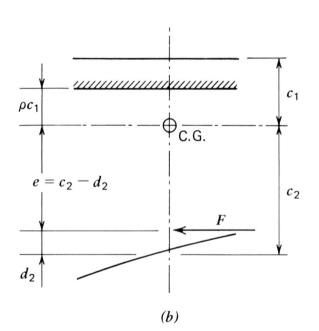

(b)

FIGURE 4.18. Typical prestress requirements of a box girder. (*a*) For maximum negative moment over the pier ($DL + LL$): total moment = M; required prestress = $F = M/z$ with $z = c_1 - d_1 + c_2$; usually over the pier $z \simeq 0.75\ h$. (*b*) For maximum positive moment at midspan ($DL + LL$): total moment = M; required prestress = $F = M/z$ with $z = c_2 - d_2 + c_1$; usually at midspan $z \simeq 0.70h$. (*c*) For variable moments (LL): total moment variation = ΔM (sum of positive and negative LL moments); required prestress = $F = \Delta M/\rho h$ ($\rho \simeq 0.60$).

The optimum selection of the proportions of the box section is generally a matter of experience. A careful review of existing bridges provides an excellent basis for preliminary design. The various parameters that should be considered at the start of a design are:

Constant versus variable depth

Span-to-depth ratio

Number of parallel box girders

Shape and dimensions of each box girder, including number of webs, vertical or inclined webs, thickness of webs, top and bottom flanges

All these factors are closely related to each other, and they also depend largely upon the construction requirements—for example, the size of the project that will require a large investment in sophisticated casting equipment.

4.5.2   *SHAPE OF SUPERSTRUCTURE IN ELEVATION*

Constant depth is the easiest choice and affords the best solution for short and moderate spans, up to 200 ft (60 m). However, constant depths have been used for aesthetic reasons for spans to 450 ft (140 m), such as the Saint Cloud Bridge in Paris and the

Pine Valley and Columbia River Bridges in the United States, Figure 4.19a.

When the span increases, the magnitude of dead-load moments near the piers normally requires a variation of structural height and a curved intrados. When clearance requirements allow, a circular intrados is the easier and more aesthetically pleasing choice, although in some cases (such as the Houston Ship Channel Bridge) a more complex profile must adjust to the critical corners of the clearance diagram. Between the constant-depth and the curved-intrados solutions, Figure 4.19, intermediate options may be used, such as:

The semiconstant depth, where the concrete required in the bottom flange near the piers is placed outside the typical section rather than inside the box (constant dimension for the interior cell). This solution has been used on two bridges in France and is aesthetically satisfactory, Figure 4.19b.

Straight haunches (bridge for the Ring Road in Paris). In this case caution must be exercised to insure compatibility of the local stresses induced by the abrupt angle change of the bottom soffit at the start of the haunch, where a full diaphragm is usually needed inside the box, Figure 4.19c.

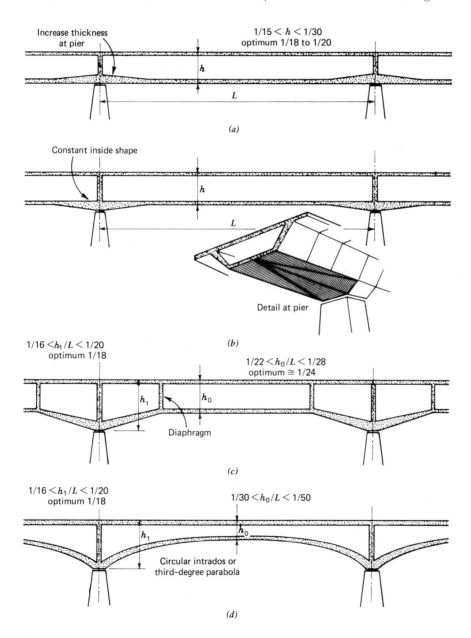

FIGURE 4.19 Longitudinal profile for segmental bridges. (*a*) Constant depth. (*b*) Semiconstant depth. (*c*) Straight haunches. (*d*) Variable depth.

4.5.3 *CHOICE OF TYPICAL CROSS SECTION*

Web spacing is usually selected between 15 and 25 ft (4.5 and 7.5 m) to reduce the number of webs to a minimum, simplifying construction problems while keeping transverse bending moment in the top and bottom flanges within reasonable limits.

A superstructure up to 40 ft (12 m) in width is thus normally made up of a single cell box girder with two lateral cantilevers, the span of which is slightly less than one-fourth the total width (7 to 8 ft for a 40 ft width).

For wide bridges, multicell box girders may be used:

Three webs, two cells: as in the B-3 South Viaduct and the Deventer Bridge
Four webs, three cells: as in the Saint Cloud Bridge and the Columbia River Bridge

Alternatively, large lateral cantilevers and a large span length between webs are accepted with special provisions to carry the deck live loads transversely:

Transverse flange stiffeners as in the Saint Andre de Cubzac, Vejle Fjord, and Zilwaukee Bridges
Side boxes as in the Chillon Viaduct

Alternatively several boxes may be used side by side to make up the superstructure. Figures 4.20 through 4.24 give the dimensions of a few structures selected at random from various countries throughout the world.

4.5.4 *DIMENSIONS OF THE TYPICAL CROSS SECTION*

Three conditions must be considered in determining the web thickness:

Shear stresses due to shear load and torsional moments must be kept within allowable limits
Concrete must be properly placed, particularly where draped tendons occur in the web
Tendon anchors, when located in the web, must distribute properly the high prestress load concentrated at the anchorages

Following are some guidelines for minimum web thicknesses:

8 in. (200 mm) when no prestress ducts are located in the web

10 in. (250 mm) when small ducts for either vertical or longitudinal post-tensioning tendons occur in the web
12 in. (300 mm) when ducts for tendons (twelve $\frac{1}{2}$ in. diameter strands) occur in the web
14 in. (350 mm) when an anchor for a tendon (twelve $\frac{1}{2}$ in. diameter strands) is anchored in the web proper

Most codes underestimate the capacity of two-way slabs, such as the roadway slab or top flange of a box girder bridge, whether prestressed transversely or mild-steel reinforced. There is a great reserve of strength due to the frame action between slabs and webs in the transverse direction.

The minimum slab thickness to prevent punching shear under a concentrated wheel load is approximately 6 in. (150 mm). However, it is recommended that a slab thickness of not less than 7 in. (175 mm) be used to allow enough flexibility in the layout of the reinforcing steel and prestressing ducts and obtain an adequate concrete cover over the steel and ducts.

Recommended minimum top flange thickness versus the actual span length between webs should be:

Span less than 10 ft (3 m)   7 in. (175 mm)
Span between 10 and 15 ft   8 in. (200 mm)
(3 to 4.5 m)
Span between 15 and 25 ft   10 in. (250 mm)
(4.5 to 7.5 m)

Over 25 ft (7.5 m), it is usually more economical to substitute a system of ribs or a voided slab for a solid slab.

Early bridges used very thin bottom flanges in order to reduce critical weight and dead-load moments. A 5 in. (125 mm) thickness was used in bridges, such as the Koblenz Bridge in Germany. It is very difficult to prevent cracking of such thin slabs due to the combined effect of dead load carried between webs and longitudinal shear between web and bottom flange. For this reason, it is now recommended that a minimum thickness of 7 in.

FIGURE 4.20. Typical dimensions of some cast-in-place segmental cantilever bridges in France. Year of construction and maximum span length (ft): (*a*) Moulin a Poudre (1963), 269. (*b*) Morlaix (1973), 269. (*c*) Bordeaux St. Jean (1965), 253. (*d*) Givors (1967), 360. (*e*) Oissel (1970), 328

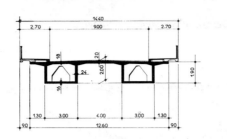

(a)

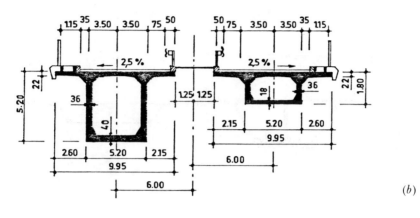

(b)

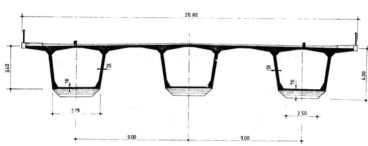

(c)

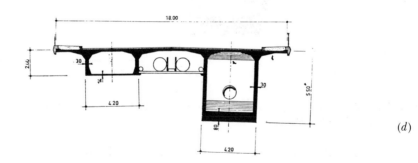

(d)

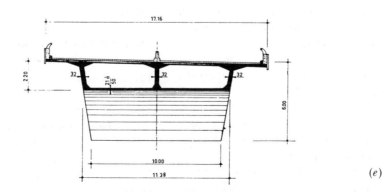

(e)

163

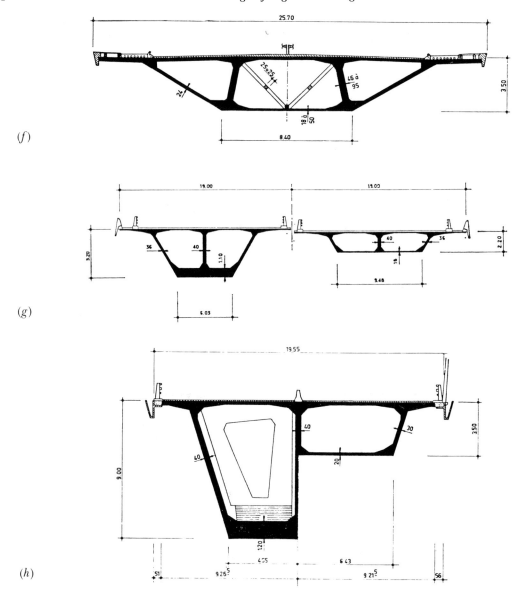

(f)

(g)

(h)

FIGURE 4.20 (*Continued*) (*f*) Viosne (1972), 197. (*g*) Joinville (twin deck) (1976), 354. (*h*) Gennevilliers (1976), 564.

(175 mm) be used, regardless of the stress requirements. Where longitudinal ducts for prestress are distributed in the bottom flange, a minimum thickness of 8 to 10 in. (200 to 250 mm) is usually necessary, depending on the duct size.

Near the piers, the bottom slab thickness is progressively increased to resist the compressive stresses due to longitudinal bending. In the Bendorf Bridge, 680 ft (207 m) span, the bottom flange thickness is 8 ft (2.4 m) at the main piers and is heavily reinforced to keep the compressive stresses within allowable limits.

After this brief review of the various conceptual choices for dimensioning the deck members, con-

sideration should be given to the design of such members with particular emphasis on the following points:

Distribution of load between box girders in multibox girder bridges

Effect of temperature gradients in the structure

4.6 Transverse Distribution of Loads Between Box Girders in Multibox Girders

We noted earlier that wide decks can conveniently consist of two or even three separate boxes trans-

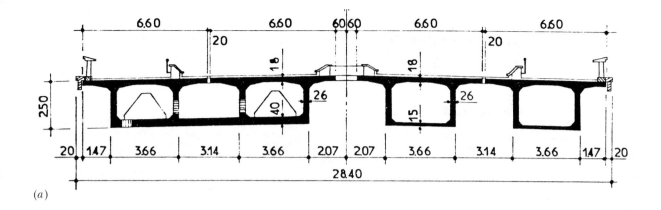

(a)

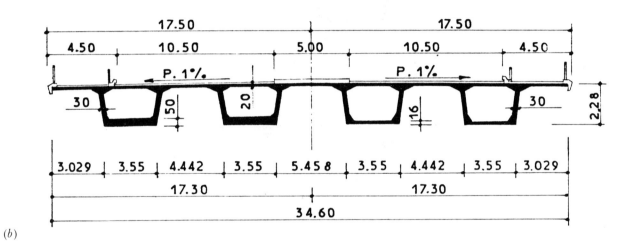

(b)

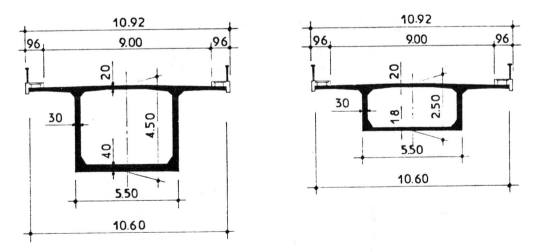

(c)

FIGURE 4.21. Typical dimensions of some precast segmental cantilever bridges in France. Year of construction and maximum span length (ft): (*a*) Choisy-le-Roi (1965), 180; (*b*) Courbevoie (1967), 197; (*c*) Oleron Viaduct (1966), 260; (*d*) Seudre (1971), 260; (*e*) B-3 South Viaduct (1973), 157; (*f*) St. Andre de Cubzac (1974), 312; (*g*) St. Cloud (1974), 334; (*h*) Ottmarsheim (1976), 564.

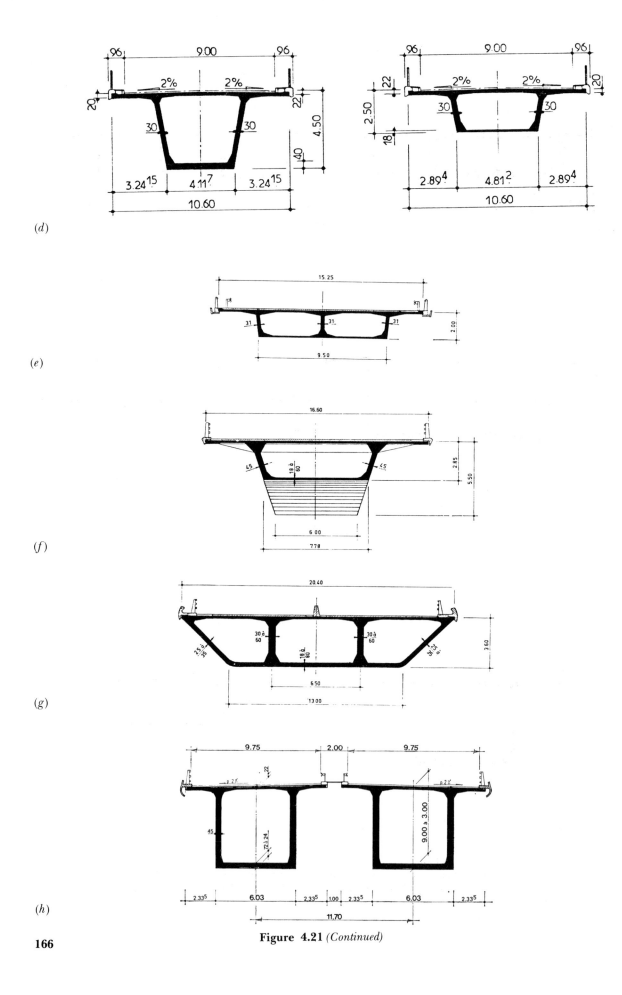

(d)

(e)

(f)

(g)

(h)

Figure 4.21 (*Continued*)

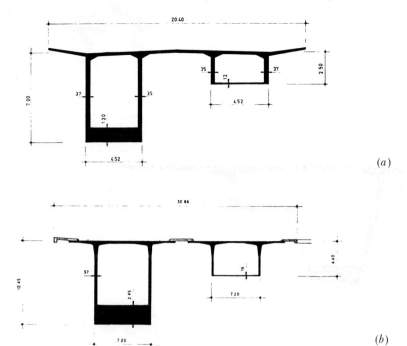

(a)

(b)

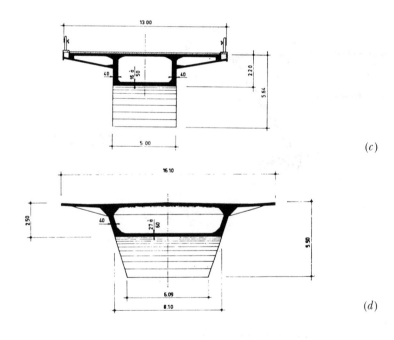

(c)

(d)

(e)

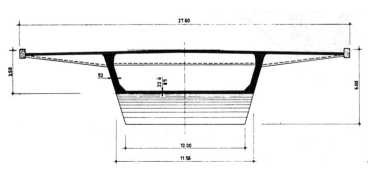

FIGURE 4.22. Typical dimensions of some segmental cantilever bridges in Europe. Year of construction and maximum span length (ft): (a) Koblenz, Germany (1954), cast in place, 374; (b) Bendorf, Germany (1964), cast in place, 682; (c) Chillon, Switzerland (1970), precast, 341; (d) Sallingsund, Denmark (1978), precast, 305; (e) Vejle Fjord, Denmark (1979), cast in place, 361.

167

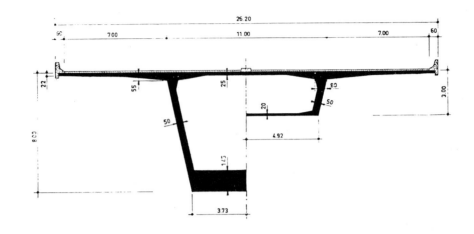

(a)

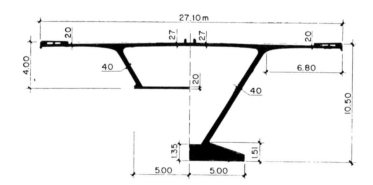

(b)

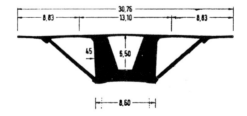

(c)

FIGURE 4.23. Typical dimensions of some segmental cantilever bridges in Europe. Year of construction and maximum span length (ft): (*a*) Felsenau, Switzerland (1978), cast in place, 512; (*b*) Tarento, Italy (1977), cast in place, 500; (*c*) Kochertal, Germany (1979), cast in place, 453.

Typical Cross Section

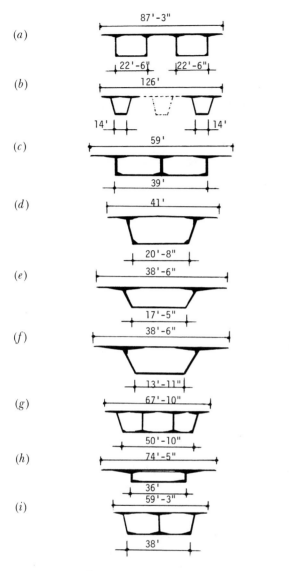

FIGURE 4.24. Typical dimensions of some segmental cantilever bridges in the Americas. Year of construction and maximum span length (ft): (*a*) Rio Niteroi, Brazil (1971), precast, 262; (*b*) Pine Valley, U.S.A. (1974), cast in place, 450; (*c*) Kipapa, U.S.A. (1977), cast in place, 250; (*d*) Kishwaukee, U.S.A., precast, 250; (*e*) Long Key, U.S.A., precast, 118; (*f*) Seven Mile, U.S.A., precast, 135; (*g*) Columbia River, U.S.A., cast in place and precast, 600; (*h*) Zilwaukee, U.S.A., precast, 375; (*i*) Houston Ship Channel, U.S.A., cast in place, 750.

girders, on one hand, and the torsional rigidity of such box girders on the other hand, would result in a very satisfactory transverse distribution of live loads between box girders. There is no need for diaphragms between girders as normally provided for I-girder bridgers.

Comprehensive programs of load testing of several bridges, including accurate measurements of deflections for eccentric loading, fully confirmed the results of theoretical analysis. This analysis has been reported in various technical documents, and only selected results will be presented in this section.

The first bridge analyzed in this respect was the Choisy-le-Roi Bridge. A knife-edge load *P* is considered with a uniform longitudinal distribution along the span, Figure 4.25. When this load travels crosswise from curb to curb, each position may be analyzed with respect to the proportion of vertical load carried by each box girder, together with the corresponding torsional moment and transverse moment in the deck slab. These analyses have made it possible to draw transverse influence lines for each effect considered, such as longitudinal bending moments (over the support or at midspan), torsional moments, or transverse moments.

For longitudinal moments it is convenient to use a dimensionless coefficient, Figure 4.25*c*, which represents the increase or decrease of the load carried by one box girder in comparison with the average load, assuming an even distribution between both girders. Numerical results show that the transverse distribution of a knife-edge load placed on one side (next to the curb) of a twin box girder produces bending moments in each box that are 1.4 and 0.6 times the average bending moment. For the same configuration, a typical deck with I girders would have an eccentricity coefficient of approximately 4 compared with 1.4 for the box girders. There are, however, two side effects to such an encouraging behavior, which relate to torsion stresses and transverse bending of the deck slab.

Torsional Moments in the Box Girder An unsymmetrical distribution of live loads in the transverse direction tends to warp the box girders and cause shear stresses. It is their high torsional rigidity which produces a favorable distribution of loads between girders. However, the maximum torsional moments usually occur when only one-half the structure (in cross section) is loaded, and the resulting stresses do not cumulate with the shear stresses produced by the full live-load shear force.

versely connected by the top flange. A detailed analysis was made of such decks with regard to the distribution of live load between the various boxes. It was found that in normal structures of this type, the combined effect of the flexural rigidity of the roadway slab acting transversely as a rigid frame with the webs and bottom slab of the various box

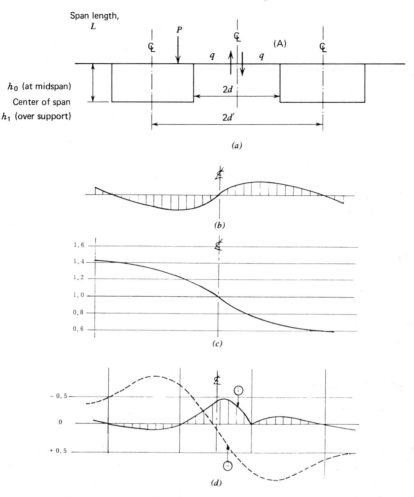

FIGURE 4.25. Principle of transverse distribution of loads between box girders. (*a*) Dimensions. (*b*) Influence line of the shear in the connecting slab. (*c*) Transverse influence line of longitudinal moment. (*d*) Transverse bending influence line at section A.

Transver Moments in the Deck Slab The deck slab cannot be considered as a continuous beam on fixed supports because of the relative displacements on the two boxes due to unsymmetrical loading. Figure 4.25*d* shows the consequence. If the slab were resting on fixed supports, the influence line for the moment in a section such as (A) would be the typical line (1). Because the box girders undergo certain deflections and rotations, the effect is to superimpose the ordinates of another line such as (2).

Numerically, the difference is not as great as may be expected at first sight, because line (1) pertains to the effect of local concentrated truck loads while line (2), being the result of differential movements between box girders, pertains to the effect of uniformly distributed loads. In summary, deck moments are increased by only 20 to 30% over their normal values if flexibility of the box

girders is ignored. As a matter of practical interest, actual numerical values for several bridges in France with either two or three box girders that have all shown excellent performance for more than 10 years are presented in Figures 4.26 and 4.27.

4.7   Effect of Temperature Gradients in Bridge Superstructures

Experience has shown the sensitivity of long-span cantilever bridges to concrete creep. This resulted in the preference for continuous rather than hinged cantilevers. However, two more problems arose from this significant change in design approach, both being the immediate result of continuity. These problems are (1) effect of temperature gradient in bridge decks and (2) redistribution

	Bridge	Spans	2d (ft)	2d' (ft)	h_0/h_1	Eccen. Coeff.
①	Givors	360' (110m)	15.7	29.5	6.6/18.0	1.14
②	D/S Paris Ring Parkway	300' (92m)	13.1	26.2	11.1/18.0	1.10
③	U/S Paris Ring Parkway	(90m) 295'	15.4	33.9	9.2/15.7	1.21
④	Corde	(79m) 260'	14.1	23.3	5.9/14.7	1.22
⑤	Juvisy	220' (66m)	14.6	24.9	5.2/10.7	1.23
⑥	Choisy-le-Roi	180' (55m)	11.1	22.3	8.2 constant	1.28

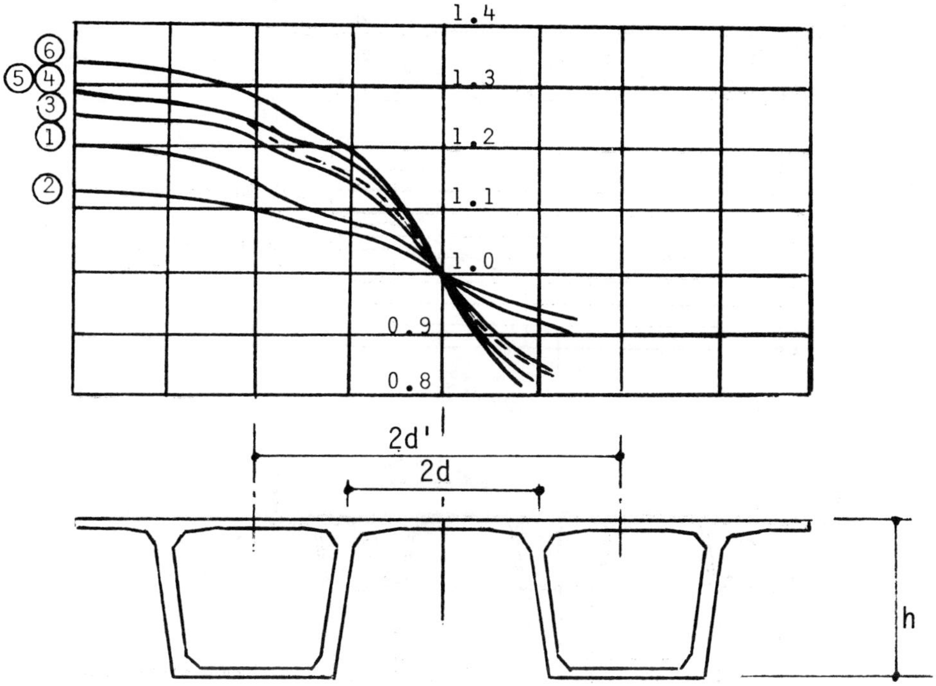

FIGURE 4.26.   Transverse distribution of loads between box girders, numerical values for several two-box girders.

of internal stresses due to long-term effects (steel relaxation and concrete creep). The importance of these two new problems was discovered experimentally. All structures are designed, according to the provisions of the various codes, for changes of temperature that are assumed to apply to the entire section. Significant bending moments in the superstructure occur only as a result of the frame action with the piers where a rigid connection is achieved between sub- and superstructure. Actual

measurements on existing structures confirm this assumption. The average concrete section undergoes a progressive shortening due to shrinkage and concrete creep superimposed naturally with the usual seasonal temperature variations, Figure 4.28*b*. The total concrete strain of 120×10^{-6} in./in. was very moderate for a period of four years.

Daily readings, on the same bridge, of strains and magnitude of reactions over the abutment

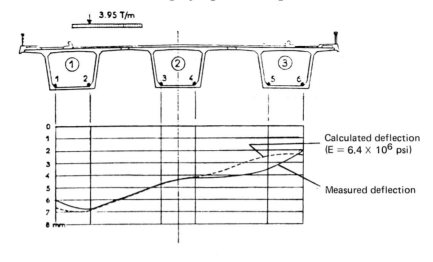

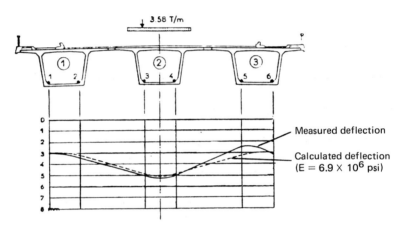

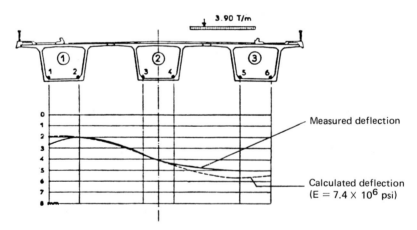

FIGURE 4.27.   Transverse distribution of loads between box girders.

brought to light a factor that had previously been ignored. This was the differential exposure of the bridge deck to the sun on warm summer days. This situation is aggravated for bridges crossing a river, where the bottom flange is kept cool by the water and the usual black pavement placed over the top flange concentrates the sun's radiation. Within a 24-hour period the reaction over the abutment could vary as much as 26%, Figure 4.28c. The equivalent temperature difference between top and bottom flanges reached 18°F (10°C). The maximum stress at the bottom flange level, due

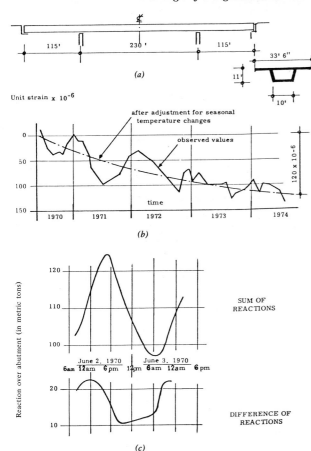

(a)

(b)

(c)

FIGURE 4.28. Champigny Bridge, observed values of concrete strains and deck reactions. (*a*) Typical dimensions. (*b*) Long-term shortening of bridge deck due to concrete creep superimposed with temperature variations. (*c*) Daily temperature variations as exemplified by change in reactions over abutments.

only to this temperature gradient, reached 560 psi (3.9 MPa), a value completely ignored in the design assumptions.

Various countries of Western Europe have now incorporated special provisions on temperature gradients as a result of this knowledge. In France, the following assumptions are required:

1. Add the effect of a 18°F (10°C) temperature gradient to the effect of dead loads and normal volume changes (such as shrinkage, creep, and maximal temperature differences). The effect of gradient is computed with an instantaneous modulus of elasticity (usually 5 million psi).

2. Add the effect of a 9°F (5°C) temperature gradient to the combined effect of all loads (including live load and impact) and volume changes, again using an instantaneous modulus of elasticity.

The effect is usually computed by assuming the gradient to be constant throughout the bridge superstructure length, which is not necessarily the case.

Figure 4.29 shows the result for the case of a typical span built-in at both ends (this is the case of a long structure with many identical spans). The stress at the bottom fiber depends only upon the following two factors:

Variation of height between span center and support (ratio h_1/h_0)

Position of the center of gravity within the section (ratio c_2/h_0)

The lowest stress is obtained for a symmetrical section and a constant-depth girder.

The stress increases rapidly when the variation in depth is more pronounced. For normal proportions the effect of gradient is increased by 50% in variable-depth girders compared to constant-depth girders (240 psi versus 160 psi for a 9°F gradient and a modulus of 5×10^6 psi).

4.8 Design of Longitudinal Members for Flexure and Tendon Profile

4.8.1 PRINCIPLE OF PRESTRESS LAYOUT

The longitudinal prestress of a cantilever bridge, whether cast in place or precast, consists of two families of tendons:

1. As construction in cantilever proceeds, the increasing dead-load moments are resisted at each step of construction by tendons located in the top flange of the girder and symmetrically placed on either side of the pier, Figures 4.30 and 4.31*a*. These are known as cantilever tendons.

2. Upon completion of individual cantilevers, continuity is achieved by a second family of tendons essentially placed at the center of the various spans, Figure 4.31*b*. Because girder load moments are small, except through long-term redistribution, because of the construction procedure, the continuity prestress is designed to resist essentially the effect of:
   a. Superimposed loads (pavement, curbs, and the like).
   b. Live loads.
   c. Temperature gradient.

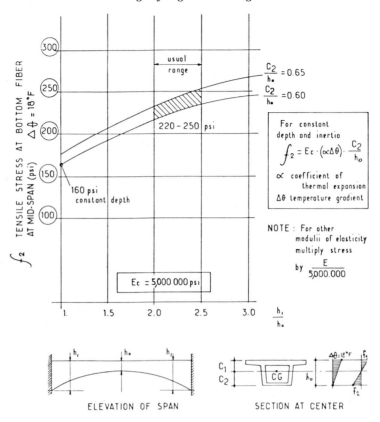

FIGURE 4.29.   Effect of thermal gradient on box girder decks.

d. Subsequent redistribution of girder load and cantilever prestress.

Tensile stresses are large at the bottom flange level, but seldom will continuity prestress gain the full advantage of the available eccentricity because of the stress conditions at the top flange level. Usually this prestress is divided into tendons, B1 or B2, located in the bottom flange, and a few tendons such as B3 which overlap the longer cantilever tendons, Figure 4.31b.

For the best selection of prestressing methods, it is essential to use prestressing units of a capacity large enough to reduce the number of tendons in the concrete section, particularly in very long spans. On the other hand, there must be a sufficient number of tendons to match with the number of segments in the cantilever arms. Also, units with an excessive unit capacity will pose serious problems for the transfer of concentrated high loads, particularly for cast-in-place structures, where concrete strength at the time of prestress is always a critical factor within the construction cycle.

In practical terms, prestress bars are as well adapted to short and medium spans as strand ten-

dons (such as twelve $\frac{1}{2}$ in. diameter strands). For very long spans (above 500 ft) large-capacity tendons (such as nineteen 0.6 in. diameter strands) with a final prestress force of about 700 kips afford a very practical solution for cantilever prestress. For continuity prestress the size of tendons is governed by the possibility of locating the tendon anchors in such areas and with such provisions as to allow a proper distribution of the concentrated load to the surrounding concrete section. Units such as twelve $\frac{1}{2}$ in. diameter or twelve 0.6 in. diameter are usually well adapted with careful detailing for this purpose.

4.8.2   *DRAPED TENDONS*

In early applications, both families of prestress were given a draped profile in the web of the box section to take advantage of the vertical component of prestress to reduce the shear stresses. In such a configuration there is a considerable overlapping of tendons in the web, because the cantilever prestress is anchored in the lower part of the web and the continuity prestress is anchored at the top flange level; see the layout in Figure 4.31c. For a constant-depth section and for segments of equal

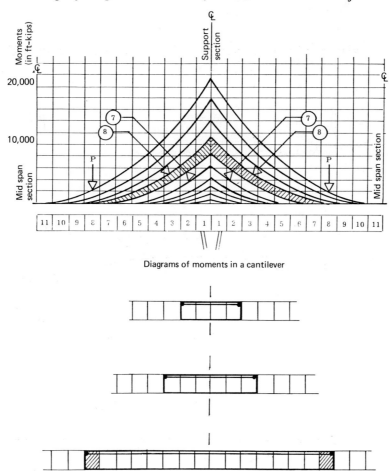

Diagrams of moments in a cantilever

FIGURE 4.30. Typical cantilever moments and prestress. When placing unit 8, the increase of bending moment is represented by the hatched area and the resultant curve is transferred from position 7 to position 8. Additional sets of cantilever prestressing tendons are placed each time a pair of segments is erected. This procedure allows the magnitude of prestress to follow very closely the various steps of construction.

length, it is easy to completely standardize the layout of prestress in various segments.

Mechanization of the casting operations is a very desirable feature, all prefabricated reinforcing cages being identical, with ducts always at the same locations. A substantial amount of repetition may still be obtained in variable-depth members as seen in Figure 4.32, which represents a typical span of the Oleron Viaduct. The two disadvantages of such a prestress layout are:

Cantilever tendon anchors are located in the web and it is difficult to prevent web cracking, particularly in cast-in-place structures, except through the use of thicker webs and smaller tendons.

Continuity tendons extend above deck level at both ends. The installation of the anchor with the block-out for stressing is difficult in the casting

form, and good protection against water seepage to the tendons in the finished structure is a critical factor.

4.8.3 STRAIGHT TENDONS

Tendons are in this configuration located in the upper and lower flange of the box girder and anchored near the web in their respective flanges. There is no draped profile for the tendons within the web and consequently no reduction of shear stresses due to a vertical component of prestress. This is a disadvantage of this scheme, which may often require vertical prestress to maintain shear stresses within allowable limits. On the other hand, the two advantages are:

Simplicity in both design and construction

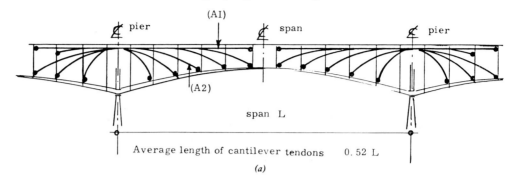

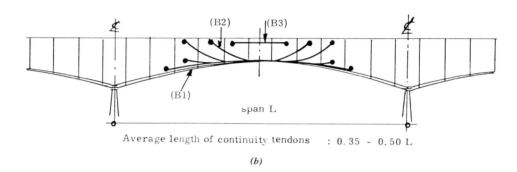

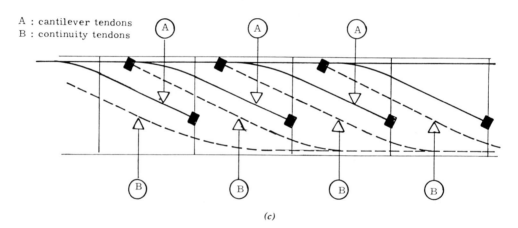

FIGURE 4.31. Typical layout of longitudinal prestress. (*a*) Cantilever tendons. (*b*) Continuity tendons. (*c*) Standardized layout of tendons for constant-depth segments.

Significant reduction in friction losses of the prestress tendons for both curvature and wobble effects, and consequent savings on the weight and cost of the longitudinal prestress of at least 10%, all else being equal

The Rio Niteroi Bridge (described in Section 3.8) used straight tendons, Figure 4.33. Typical characteristics of the deck are as follows:

Span length	262 ft
Width of a box	42 ft
Two webs at	14.2 in. each
Longitudinal cantilever prestress	42 (12 $\frac{1}{2}$ in. diam. strands)
Longitudinal continuity prestress	14 (12 $\frac{1}{2}$ in. diam. strands)
Vertical prestress	1 in. diameter bars

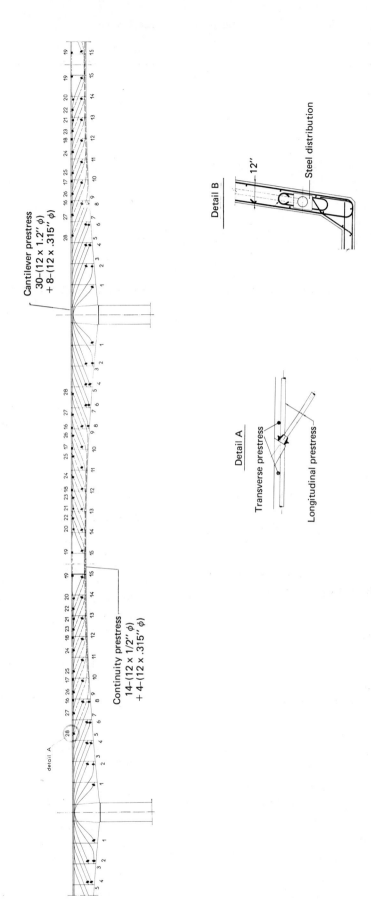

FIGURE 4.32. Oleron Viaduct, longitudinal prestress.

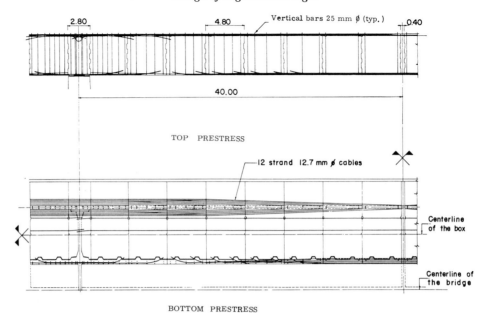

FIGURE 4.33. Rio-Niteroi Bridge, typical prestress layout.

Critical stresses near the pier are:

Longitudinal compression	850 psi
Vertical compression	400 psi
Maximum shear stress	580 psi
Diagonal stresses	−110 psi (tensile), and 1360 psi (compressive)

Typical details of tendon profiles and anchorages are portrayed for Linn Cove Viaduct in North Carolina, U.S.A., in Figures 4.34, 4.35, and 4.36.

4.8.4 SUMMARY OF TENDON PROFILES AND ANCHOR LOCATIONS

In the two preceding configurations, tendons were anchored in the following manner:

1. For cantilever prestress:
   a. On the face of the segment in the fillet between top flange and web.
   b. On the face of the segment along the web.
   c. In a block-out near the fillet between top flange and web, but inside the box.
2. For the continuity prestress:
   a. At the top flange level.
   b. In a block-out near the fillet between web and bottom flange.

c. In a block-out in the bottom flange proper away from the webs.

Configurations 1c, 2b, and 2c all permit prestressing operations to be performed safely and efficiently inside the box, Figure 4.37, permitting such operations to be removed from the critical path of actual placement or construction of the segments. Only those tendons required for balancing the self-weight of the segments need to be installed at each step of construction. The balance of the required prestressing may thus be installed later, even after continuity is achieved between several cantilever arms. Tendons for the additional prestress may then be given a profile comparable to that used in cast-in-place bridges with a length extending over several spans. The practical limit to this procedure is excessive sophistication and related high friction losses in the tendons.

4.8.5 SPECIAL PROBLEMS OF CONTINUITY PRESTRESS AND ANCHORAGE THEREOF

Tendons for continuity prestress may not, or even should not, always be located in the fillet between web and bottom flange. They may be located in the bottom flange proper. When a variable-depth member is used, the bottom flange has a curvature in the vertical plane, which must be followed by the prestress tendons. Unless careful consideration is

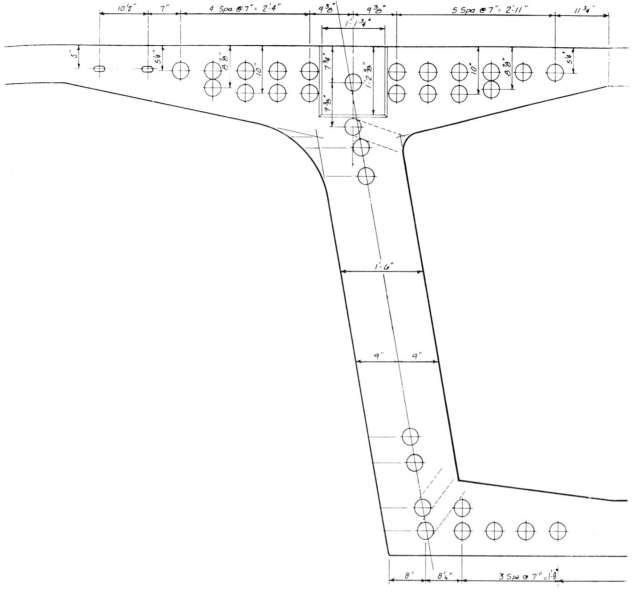

FIGURE 4.34. Linn Cove Viaduct, typical cross section showing prestress ducts.

given to that fact at the concept and detailed design stages, difficulties are likely to develop; we may see this by looking at Figures 4.38 and 4.39, which show the free-body diagrams of stresses in the bottom flange due to the curvature, together with a numerical example. Curvature of a tendon induces a downward radial load, which must be resisted by transverse bending of the bottom flange between the webs.

Longitudinal compressive stresses in the bottom flange similarly induce an upward radial reaction in the flange, counteracting at least in part the effect of the tendons. Unfortunately, when the full live load and variable effects, such as thermal gradients, are applied to the superstructure, the lon-

gitudinal stresses vanish and consequently the partial negation of the effect of tendon curvature is lost. Therefore, the effect of tendon curvature adds fully to the dead-load stresses of the concrete flange. The corresponding flexural stresses are four to five times greater than the effect due to dead load only, and if sufficient reinforcement is not provided for this effect, heavy cracking is to be expected and possibly failure. Practically, the situation may be aggravated by deviations in the location of the tendon ducts in the segments compared to the theoretical profile indicated on the drawings. At the point between segments, ducts are usually placed at their proper position; but if flexible tubing is used with an insufficient number of sup-

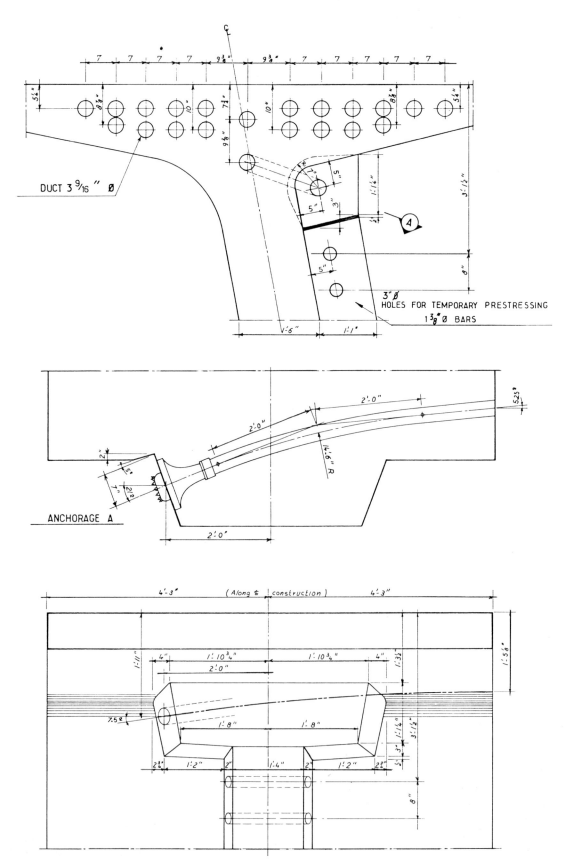

FIGURE 4.35. Linn Cove Viaduct, top flange prestress details.

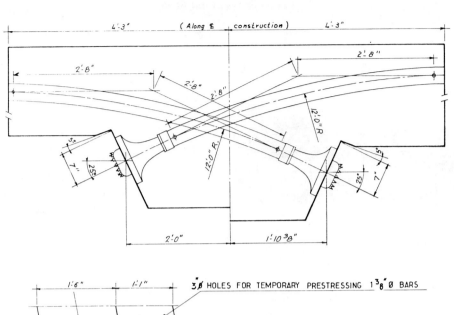

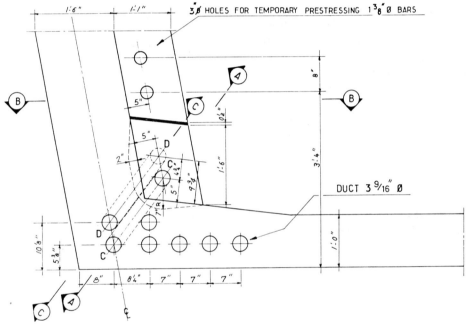

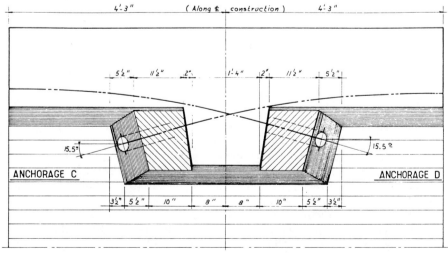

FIGURE 4.36. Linn Cove Viaduct, bottom flange prestress details.

FIGURE 4.37. B-3 South Viaduct, prestressing operations in box girder.

porting chairs or ties, the duct profile will have an angle break at each joint. In addition to the increased friction losses, there is a potential danger of local spalling and bursting of the intrados of the bottom flange, Figure 4.40. Rigid ducts properly secured to the reinforcement cage and placed at the proper level over the soffit of the casting machine or traveler will avoid this danger.

Another item concerning potential difficulties in continuity prestress relate to the projection of the anchor block-out in the bottom flange and where anchor blocks are not close to the fillet between web and bottom flange. When this method is used in conjunction with a very thin bottom flange (a

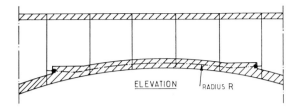

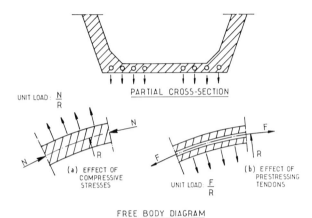

FIGURE 4.38. Secondary stresses due to curved tendons in the bottom flange.

flange as thin as 5 or 6 in. has been used in early bridges), it is almost impossible to distribute the concentrated load of the anchor block in the slab without subsequent cracking. For a 7 or 8 in. flange it is recommended that no more than two anchor

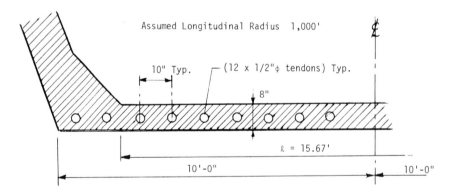

FIGURE 4.39. Secondary stresses due to curved prestressing tendons, numerical example. Assumed longitudinal radius = 1000 ft. Weight of bottom slab = 100 psf. Effect of compressive stresses: unloaded bridge, f_c = 2000 psi, compressive radial load: $f_c t/R$ = (2000 × 8 × 12)/1000 = 200psf; loaded bridge, 0 psi. Effect of prestressing tendons: stranded tendons (twelve $\frac{1}{2}$ in. dia strands) at 10 in. interval with a 280 kip capacity, corresponding radial load: F/R = 280,000/[(10/12)1000] = 336, say 340 psf. Total loads on bottom slab: (1) during construction, load = 100 psf; (2) unloaded bridge, load = 100 − 200 + 340 = 240 psf; (3) loaded bridge, load = 100 + 340 = 440 psf, moment = $w\ell^2/12$ = 9 kips ft/ft, stress in bottom slab: $f = M/S$ = (9000 × 12)/[(12 × 64)/6] = 840 psi.

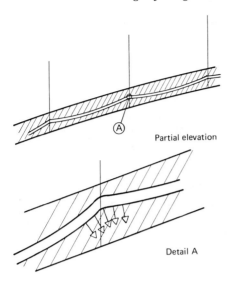

FIGURE 4.40. Effect of misalignment of continuity prestress.

blocks for (12 $\frac{1}{2}$ in. diameter strands) tendons be placed in the same transverse section in conjunction with additional reinforcing to resist bursting stresses. Wherever possible, the anchor blocks for continuity tendons should be placed in the fillet between the web and flange where the transverse section has the largest rigidity.

4.8.6 LAYOUT OF PRESTRESS IN STRUCTURES WITH HINGES AND EXPANSION JOINTS

Section 4.4.3 explained how the expansion joints in the superstructure should be located preferably near the contraflexure point of a span rather than at midspan as in previous structures. However, there is a resultant complication in the construction process, because cantilever erection must proceed through the special hinge segment. A typical construction procedure and the related prestress layout are presented in Figure 4.41. For the geometry of the structure in this figure, the construction proceeds as follows:

a. Place the first five segments in balanced cantilever and install cantilever prestress for resistance against dead load.

b. Place the lower half of the special segment and the corresponding tendons.

c. Install the upper half of the special hinge segment with permanent, or provisional bearings, and provisional blocking to permit transfer of longitudinal compressive stresses. Cantilever

tendons may be made continuous through the expansion joint or equipped with couplers.

d. Resume normal cantilever segment placing and prestressing to the center of the span, with tendons crossing the joint.

e. Achieve continuity with previous cantilever by pouring closure joint and stressing continuity tendons. Layout of these tendons includes anchors in the special hinge segment to transfer the shear forces in the completed structure.

f. Remove temporary blocking at hinge. Release tension in cantilever tendons holding segments 7, 8, and 9 or cut tendons across the hinge after grouting.

4.8.7 REDISTRIBUTION OF MOMENTS AND STRESSES THROUGH CONCRETE CREEP

In a statically indeterminate structure the internal stresses induced by the external loads depend upon the deformation of the structure. In prestressed concrete structures such deformations must include not only short-term but also long-term deformation due to relaxation of prestressing steel and concrete creep. In conventional structures such as cast-in-place continuous superstructures, the effect is not significant if all loads and prestress forces are applied to the statical design of the completed structure, which is the common case of construction on scaffolding. The behavior of cantilever bridges, particularly cast-in-place structures, is quite different, because the major part of the load (the girder load often represents 80% of the total load in long spans) is applied to a statical concept that is different from the completed design. As soon as continuity is achieved, the structure tends to resist the new situation in which it has been placed; this is one aspect of a very general law in mechanics whereby consequences always oppose their cause.

A very simple example is presented in Figure 4.42, which will provide the basis for a better appreciation of the problem. Assume two identical adjacent cantilever arms built-in at both ends and free to deflect at the center. The self-weight produces a moment:

$$M_0 = \frac{wa^2}{2} = \frac{wL^2}{8}$$

at both ends with a corresponding deflection and rotation at the center of y and ω.

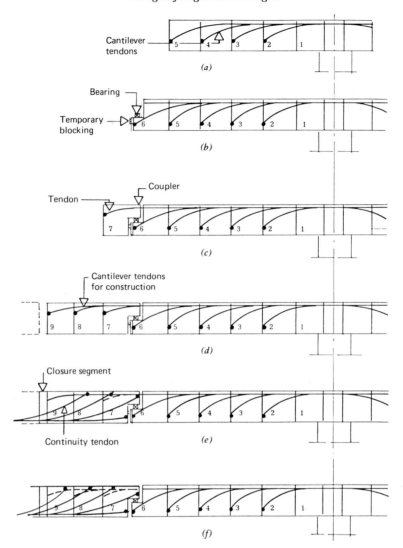

FIGURE 4.41. Construction procedure and prestress in a span with an expansion joint.

If the load is applied for a short time, the value of E to take into account is E_i (instantaneous modulus). Assuming that continuity is achieved between the cantilevers as shown in Figure 4.42c, there cannot be an angle break at the center, but only a progressive deformation of the completed span. After a long time the concrete modulus has changed from its initial value E_i to a final value E_f, which may be approximately 2.5 times less than E_i.

Because the external loads are unchanged and the structure is symmetrical, the only change in the state of the structure is an additional constant moment M_1 developing along the entire span and increasing progressively with time until the concrete creep has stabilized. At all times the magnitude of this moment adjusts in the structure to maintain the assumed continuity at the center.

The additional deflection at midspan, y_2, takes place in a beam with fixed ends under the effect of its own weight and only because of the progressive change of the concrete modulus from the value E_i to the value E_f.

Considering the concrete strain at any point of the structure, the total strain ϵ_f is the sum of two terms:

$$\epsilon_f = \epsilon_1 + \epsilon_2$$

where ϵ_1 = strain before continuity is achieved,
       ϵ_2 = strain after continuity is achieved.

Hooke's law relating stress and strain at a particular point in time states:

$$\epsilon_1 = \frac{f_1}{E_i}$$

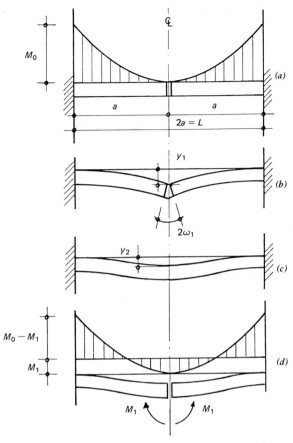

FIGURE 4.42. Redistribution of stresses through concrete creep.

Similarly there is a relationship between the additional strain ϵ_2 and the corresponding stress f_2 produced at the same location by the same loads applied in the continuous structure. One may write:

$$\epsilon_2 = \frac{f_2}{E_c}$$

where E_c, the creep modulus, is given by:

$$\frac{1}{E_c} = \frac{1}{E_f} - \frac{1}{E_i}$$

or

$$\epsilon_2 = f_2 \left(\frac{1}{E_f} - \frac{1}{E_i} \right)$$

Thus:

$$\epsilon_f = \frac{f_1}{E_i} + f_2 \left(\frac{1}{E_f} - \frac{1}{E_i} \right)$$

The corresponding total *stress* in the structure then becomes:

$$f = f_1 \frac{E_f}{E_i} + f_2 \left(1 - \frac{E_f}{E_i} \right)$$

In other words, the effect of concrete creep is to place the final stresses in the structure in an internal state (either of moments, shear forces, deflections, or stresses) intermediate between:

The initial statical design with free cantilevers, and
The completed design with continuity.

Assume, for example, $E_f/E_i = 0.40$. Thus:

$$f = 0.40f_1 + 0.60f_2$$

The relationship is equally true for moments, shear forces, or deflections.

Moments over the support are:

In the free cantilevers, $M = M_0$
In the continuous structure, $M = \frac{2}{3}M_0$

The final moment is therefore:

$$M_0 - M_1 = 0.40M_0 + 0.60(\tfrac{2}{3}M_0) = 0.80M_0$$

and

$$M_1 = \underline{0.20\ M_0}.$$

At midspan, moments are:

In the free cantilevers, $M = 0$
In the continuous structure, $M = M_0/3$

and the actual final moment:

$$M_1 = 0.60\ \frac{M_0}{3} = \underline{0.20M_0}$$

The above derivation applies not only to external loads but also to the effect of prestressing. Continuity prestress applied to a continuous structure gives little internal redistribution of moments except in multispan structures, where the spans react with one another according to the actual construction procedure. Cantilever prestress, which acts to offset an appreciable part of the dead-load moments, tends to reduce the distribution of moments due to external loads, Figure 4.43.

Up to now the concrete modulus has been assumed to take only the two values E_i and E_f (short-term and long-term values). In fact, because construction of a cantilever takes several weeks (or even several months in the case of cast-in-place structures), account must be taken of the concrete strains versus the age and the duration of loading.

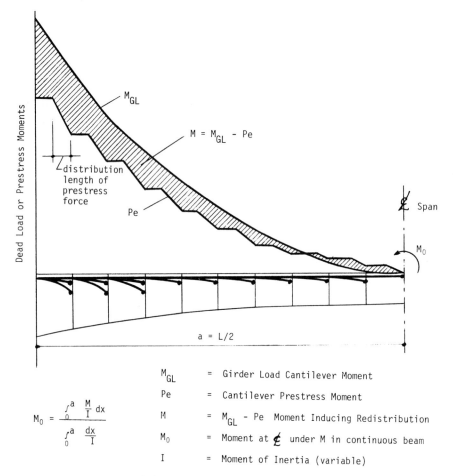

$$M_0 = \dfrac{\int_0^a \dfrac{M}{I}\,dx}{\int_0^a \dfrac{dx}{I}}$$

M_{GL} = Girder Load Cantilever Moment

Pe = Cantilever Prestress Moment

M = $M_{GL} - Pe$ Moment Inducing Redistribution

M_0 = Moment at ℄ under M in continuous beam

I = Moment of Inertia (variable)

FIGURE 4.43. Computation of moment redistribution due to dead load and cantilever prestress.

Such relationships are presented for normal-weight prestressed concrete and average climate in Figure 4.44.

Concrete strains are presented for convenience as a dimensionless ratio between the actual strain and the reference strain of a 28-day-old concrete subjected to a short-term load.

We see that short-term strains vary little with the age of the concrete at the time of loading except at a very early age. However, long-term strains are significantly affected by the age of the concrete. For example, a three-day-old concrete will show a final strain 2.5 times greater than a three-month-old concrete. This is particularly important for cast-in-place structures with short cycles of construction (two pairs of segments cast and prestressed every week, which has now become common practice).

Two other factors play an important role in the redistribution of stresses in continuous cantilever bridges:

1. Relaxation of prestressing steel and prestress losses. Because the stress in the prestressing steel varies with time (a part of that variation being due precisely to the concrete creep), the internal moments that produce the deformation of the structure and therefore originate the redistribution of stresses vary continually. This factor is important because the resultant moments in the cantilever arms (dead load and prestress) are given by the difference of two large numbers, and a variation on one usually has an important effect upon the result, Figure 4.43.

2. Change of the mechanical properties of the concrete section. For the sake of simplicity the gross concrete section is usually adopted for computation of bending stresses. In fact, the section to be used should be:

   a. The net section (ducts for longitudinal prestress deducted from the concrete sec-

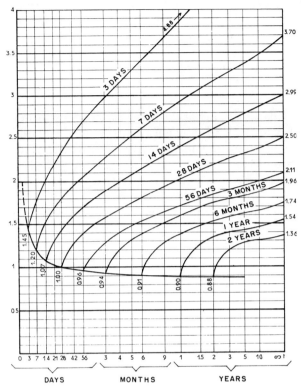

DAYS   MONTHS   YEARS

FIGURE 4.44. Concrete strains versus age and duration of loading. Note that strain is given as a dimensionless ratio between the actual strain and the reference strain of a 28-day-old concrete subjected to short-term load.

tion) for effect of girder load and prestress up to the time of tendon grouting.

b. The transformed section (with incorporation of the prestress steel area with a suitable coefficient of transformation) after grouting, where the coefficient of equivalence $n = E_s/E_c$, ratio of the modulus of steel and concrete, should be taken as a variable with time, from 5 to 12 or even 15.

The above discussion indicates the complexity of the problem with respect to the material properties and indicates the unreliable results of the early designs.

The only acceptable solution is the global approach, whereby a comprehensive electronic computer program analyzes step by step the state of stresses in the structure at different time intervals and whenever any significant change occurs, thus following the complete history of construction.

Such programs are now available and have proven invaluable in helping us understand the behavior of segmental bridges. They provide efficient tools for the final design of the structure.

Because it is difficult for some engineers to depend fully upon computer solutions in approaching a design problem, it is desirable to have orders of magnitude of the moment redistribution for preliminary proportioning and dimensioning of the structure. The following guidelines are based on experience and judgment.

1. Consider the case of a symmetrical span made up of two equal cantilevers fixed at the ends and built symmetrically. Compute girder load moments of the typical cantilever and prestress moments using the *final* prestress forces and the *transformed concrete* sections with $n = 10$ (average).

2. Compute the moment at midspan due to the difference of the above two loading cases (Figure 4.43). More generally, compute in the final structure the moments in the various spans due to the difference between cantilever girder load and moments and final prestress moments, including the restraint due to piers if applicable.

3. Reference is made now to the formula given previously and repeated here for convenience:

$$f = f_1 \frac{E_f}{E_i} + f_2 \left(1 - \frac{E_f}{E_i}\right)$$

where f = final stress (or moment or shear load in the structure at any point),

f_1 = stress at the same point obtained by adding all partial stresses for each construction step using the corresponding statical scheme of the structure,

f_2 = stress at the same point assuming all loads and prestress forces to be applied on the final structure with the final statical scheme,

E_i = initial or intermediate modulus of elasticity (short-term or for the duration of loading before continuity),

E_f = final modulus (long-term).

Using different assumptions on the construction sequence of bridge decks and the corresponding strains as given by Figure 4.44, we find that the average value of E_f/E_i would vary from 0.50 to 0.67. It is recommended that the conservative value of 0.67 be used in this approximate method. Thus the actual moment due to redistribution should be 0.67, the value computed under paragraph 2. This moment must be added to the effect of live load and thermal gradient at midspan.

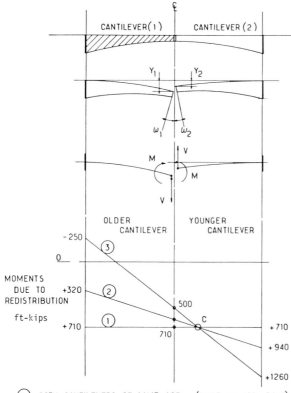

FIGURE 4.45. Variation of redistribution moment in cantilever construction with the construction procedure.

4. Correspondingly, the support moment (over the piers) is decreased by the same amount. In fact, the construction of cantilevers in successive stages is such that continuity is achieved in each span be-

tween cantilevers of different ages, and the redistribution of support moment may thus vary in wide proportions, Figure 4.45. To keep on the safe side, it is not recommended that the reduction in support moment be taken into account in designing the prestress forces.

It is interesting at this stage to give some orders of magnitude of moment redistribution by considering some fundamental formulas given as reference in Figure 4.46.

It has been assumed:

That the secondary moment due to the stressing of continuity tendons is 6% of the total moment over the support,

That the distance, d, between the center of gravity of the cantilever tendons and the top slab is equal to $0.05h$.

That the center of gravity, depending upon the section dimensions, may vary between ($c_1/h = 0.4$ and $c_2/h = 0.6$) and ($c_1/h = 0.6$ and $c_2/h = 0.4$),

That the efficiency factor is $\rho = 0.60$.

From the data indicated above and in Figure 4.46, the percentage of prestressing steel, p, may be determined as follows:

assuming a final stress in the tendons of 160 ksi

assuming a maximum compressive stress in the bottom flange of 2000 psi:

$$P = A_c f_{c(\text{avg})} = 2000 \frac{c_1 A_c}{h}$$

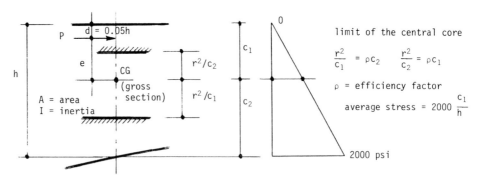

FIGURE 4.46. Approximate moment redistribution (moments over support). Total moment: $M_T = M_{GL} + M_{SL} + M_{LL}$, where M_{GL} = girder load moment, M_{SL} = superimposed load moment, M_{LL} = live-load moment (including impact). Assumed secondary moment due to continuity prestress: $0.06\,M_T$. Final prestress force: $P = 0.94M_T/[e + (r^2/c_1)] = 0.94M_T/(e + \rho c_2)$. Prestress moment (1): $Pe = 0.94M_T/[1 + (\rho c_2/e)]$. Moment-inducing redistribution: $M_{GL} - Pe$, given by (2): $(M_{GL} - Pe)/M_T = M_{GL}/M_T - 0.94/[1 + (\rho c_2/e)]$.

$$A_s = \frac{p}{f_s} = \frac{c_1 A_c}{80h}$$

$$p = \frac{A_s}{A_c} = \frac{c_1}{80h}$$

For a symmetrical section, $c_1 = 0.5h$, and p would, thus, be equal to 0.63%, a reasonable and common value. The transformed percentage area of the steel with $n = 10$ is equal to:

$$np = 0.125 \frac{c_1}{h}$$

All mechanical properties of the section change to make the denominator of equation (2) in Figure 4.46 increase and, consequently, the moment-inducing redistribution increase also. This fact, which was completely overlooked for many years, is clearly seen in Figure 4.47, where the percentage of moment-inducing redistribution in the various

sections is plotted versus the position of the centroid with or without transformed area.

It is interesting to study the effect of an accidental variation in the prestress load due to excessive friction in the ducts. Assume, for example, a reduction of 5% in the prestress load for the case $c_1/h = 0.5$ (symmetrical section over the support) and $M_{GL}/M_T = 0.80$.

The intial values of $(M_{GL} - Pe)/M_T$ are changed as follows:

	100% Prestress	95% Prestress	Percent Variation
Gross area	0.236	0.264	1.12
Transformed area	0.265	0.292	1.10

The combined effect of tendon grouting and of added friction losses increases the redistribution of moments by 25%.

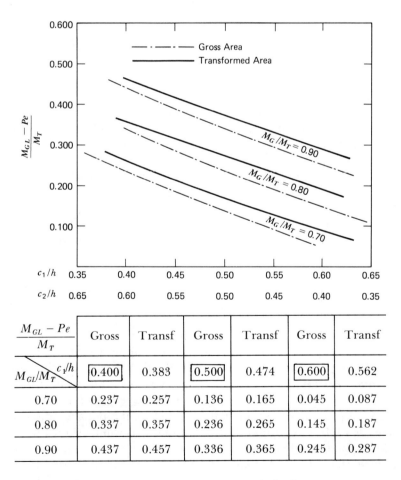

| c_1/h | 0.35 | 0.40 | 0.45 | 0.50 | 0.55 | 0.60 | 0.65 |
| c_2/h | 0.65 | 0.60 | 0.55 | 0.50 | 0.45 | 0.40 | 0.35 |

$\dfrac{M_{GL} - Pe}{M_T}$	Gross	Transf	Gross	Transf	Gross	Transf
M_{GL}/M_T ⟍ c_1/h	0.400	0.383	0.500	0.474	0.600	0.562
0.70	0.237	0.257	0.136	0.165	0.045	0.087
0.80	0.337	0.357	0.236	0.265	0.145	0.187
0.90	0.437	0.457	0.336	0.365	0.245	0.287

Figure 4.47. Moment redistribution, numerical values over support.

4.8.8 PREDICTION OF PRESTRESS LOSSES

The prediction of losses in prestressed concrete has always been subject to uncertainty. This is due to the high stress levels used for the prestressing steel, the variable nature of concrete, and its propensity to creep and shrink. As recently as 1975, AASHTO made a major revision to its code to provide improved methods for predicting prestress losses. The Structural Engineers Association of California has an excellent report on creep and shrinkage control for concrete in general. The report concludes that special attention should be given to material selection and proportioning. For creep and shrinkage calculations many European engineers recommend the guidelines of the Fédération Internationale de la Precontrainte, Comité Européen du Béton (FIP-CEB).

The design computations for segmental prestressed concrete bridges are very involved for the construction phase. Every time a segment is added or a tendon is tensioned, the structure changes, and it must be reanalyzed. As the segment ages, the concrete and prestressing steel creep, shrink, and relax. Thus, each segment has its own life history and an elastic modulus that depends upon the age and composition. To accurately compute all of these effects by hand, throughout the life of the structure, would be very difficult, particularly during the construction phase. Comprehensive computer programs such as "BC" (Bridge Construction) and others have been recently developed and are now available to aid the design engineer.

In addition to construction analysis, these programs will check the completed bridge in accordance with AASHTO specifications. It is possible to revise them to satisfy other codes or loadings, such as AREA.

Not only are all prestress losses properly evaluated and taken into account, but redistributions of moments due to concrete creep and steel relaxation are automatically incorporated in the design analysis.

4.9 Ultimate Bending Capacity of Longitudinal Members

Basically, the design approach of segmental bridges is one of service load. It is important, however, not to lose sight of the ultimate behavior of the structure to ensure that safety is obtained throughout.

In simply supported structures, the ultimate capacity is very simply analyzed by comparing in the section of maximum moment:

The total design load moment including girder load and superimposed load (*DL*) and live load (*LL*)

The ultimate bending moment of the prestressed section M_u

Depending on the governing codes and the usual practice in various countries, this comparison may be done in various ways:

Apply a load factor on *DL* and *LL* and a reduction factor for materials on M_u

Apply a single factor K on ($DL + LL$) and compare with M_u

Apply a single factor K on LL only and compare $DL + KLL$ with M_u

In all cases, the designer must first compute the ultimate capacity of the section considering the concrete dimensions and characteristics of prestressing tendons (and possible conventional reinforcement). From previous studies it may be shown that the ultimate moment of a prestressed section is computed very simply by considering a dimensionless factor called the weight percentage of prestressing steel, q (see Figure 4.48).

To account for the fact that the concrete characteristics are less reliable than those of the prestressing steel, which are well known and very constant, f_s' is usually taken equal to the guaranteed minimum tensile strength, whereas f_c' is assumed to be only 80% of the 28-day cylinder strength.

Considering now the case of segmental superstructures, which are most generally continuous structures, one may take the conventional approach of considering the various sections of the member (for example, support section and midspan sections in the various spans) as independent from one another in much the same way as for simple members. Such simplification overlooks the capacity of the redundant structure to redistribute, internally, the applied loads, which seems to be a conservative assumption.

In fact, it is not always as conservative and safe as it looks, as will be shown by an example computed numerically for a typical span of the Rio Niteroi Bridge. For such a span the design moments are as follows (in foot-kips × 1000):

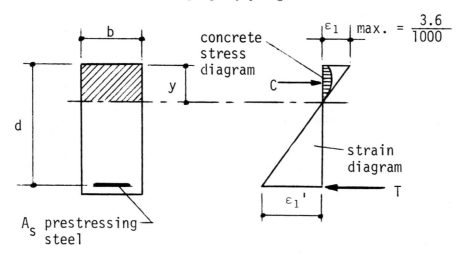

FIGURE 4.48. Ultimate moment of a prestressed section. (1) Dimensionless coefficient, $q' = (A_s/bd)(f'_s/f'_c)$, where A_s = area of prestressing steel, b = width of section, d = effective depth of section (distance between centroid of prestress and extreme compression fiber), f'_s = ultimate tensile strength of prestressing steel, f'_c = ultimate compressive strength of concrete. (2) Value of ultimate moment: for $q' < 0.07$, $M_u = 0.96A_s f'_s d$; for $0.07 < q' < 0.50$, $M_u = (1 - 0.6q')A_s f'_s d$.

	Support	Midspan
Girder load	116	0
Superimposed load	10	5
Total dead load (*DL*)	126	5
Total live load (*LL*)	29	22
Total (*DL* + *LL*)	155	27

Live-load moment in simple span: 37

The ultimate moments have been computed for all sections for both positive and negative bending. The envelopes of ultimate moments are shown in Figure 4.49.

Neglecting any moment redistribution, the situation would be the following over the support and at midspan:

	Section	
Moment	Support	Midspan
M_u	256	79
DL	126	5
LL	29	22
M_u =	1.65(*DL* + *LL*)	2.93(*DL* + *LL*)
or M_u =	*DL* + 4.5 *LL*	*DL* + 3.4*LL*

The picture is substantially different when looking at redistribution due to plastic hinges. Assuming an overall increase of both dead and live load simultaneously (loading arrangement A), we ob-

tain the overall safety factor by comparing the sum of ultimate moments over the support and at midspan:

$$256 + 79 = 335$$

and the sum of simple span moment due to *DL* and *LL*:

DL: 126 + 5 =	131
LL	37
Total	168

The overall safety factor is thus:

$$K = \frac{335}{168} = \underline{2.0}$$

approximately 20% higher than for the support section considered alone. In fact, it is more important and more realistic to consider only an increase of the live load, which is the only variable factor in the structure. Proceeding as before, the safety factor on *LL* only would be:

$$K = \frac{335 - 131}{37} = 5.5$$

However, this is not the actual safety factor of the structure, because there exists a more aggressive loading arrangement than that where all spans are live loaded. In the case where the live load is applied to only every second span [arrangement

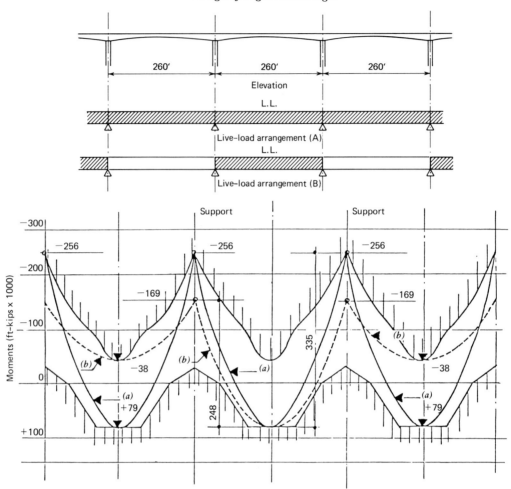

FIGURE 4.49. Ultimate bending capacity of a continuous deck.

(b) in Figure 4.49], the first plastic hinge will appear at the center of the unloaded spans with a negative moment (tension at the top fiber) and the support moment reaches the following limiting value:

Ultimate negative moment at midspan: 38

Actual dead-load moment in simple span:

$$126 + 5 = \underline{131}$$
$$169$$

This value of 169 is substantially lower than the ultimate moment at that support section considered by itself ($M_u = 256$).

The failure appears when the second plastic hinge appears at the center of the loaded span under positive moment (tension at the bottom fiber). The limiting value of the safety factor K is such that:

$$169 + 79 = 131 + K \cdot 37 \quad \text{and} \quad K = 3.2$$

In such structures a very important characteristic must be emphasized. At the time of ultimate load failure, due either to negative moment in the unloaded spans or positive moments in the loaded spans, the maximum moment over the support has only slightly increased above the value at design load (169 against 155) and is far below the ultimate moment of the section (256). Three interesting consequences may be derived from this fact:

1. Because the overall safety of the structure is not dependent upon the ultimate moment near the supports, it is not necessary to dimension the bottom flange of the concrete section in this area to balance the ultimate capacity of the prestressing tendons.

2. The global safety factor of the structure depends directly on the capacity of the sections near midspan for both positive and negative moments. The capacity for positive moments is given by the continuity tendons placed in the

bottom flange for service-load conditions. The capacity for negative moments depends upon the tendons placed at the top flange level to overlap the cantilever tendons of the two individual cantilever arms. The magnitude of this overlap prestress does not appear as a critical factor when designing the structure for service loads, yet it plays an important role in the ultimate behavior of the structure.

3. At ultimate load, it was shown that the areas of the members close to the supports are subjected to moments only slightly in excess of design load moments and in most cases below cracking moments. No early failure due to combined shear and bending is anticipated.

In long structures where hinges and expansion joints are provided in certain spans, the same design principles may be applied to analyze the ultimate capacity. Hinges represent singular points through which the moment diagrams must go regardless of the loading arrangement under consideration. It was found that the optimum location of the hinge with regard to ultimate safety is somewhat different from the location allowing the best control of long-term deflections. It may be of interest therefore to move the hinge slightly toward the center of the span, which has a further advantage of simplifying construction.

4.10 Shear and Design of Cross Section

4.10.1 INTRODUCTION

Designing prestressed concrete members for shear represents a challenging task for the engineer, because there are many differences of opinion and large variations in the requirements of the various codes. In particular the ACI code and the AASHTO specifications differ in several ways from the FIP-CEB and other European codes.

It is common practice in many countries to design reinforced concrete and prestressed concrete members for shear by allowing the concrete to carry a proportion of the shear loads while stirrups (formerly in conjunction with inclined bars) carry the rest. A complete agreement has not yet been reached on this aspect of design for shear:

The French codes (CCBA, for example) allow nothing to be taken by the concrete and the total shear to be carried by the transverse steel, which is certainly an overconservative approach. Obviously,

the beneficial effect of longitudinal compression (either in columns subject to axial load or in prestressed members) is taken into account.

The recent FIP-CEB code allows some proportion of the shear to be carried by the concrete.

ACI code allows a larger proportion of shear to be carried by the concrete with a consequent savings in stirrup requirements.

4.10.2 SHEAR TESTS OF REINFORCED CONCRETE BEAMS

Tests were recently carried out in France in order to increase the knowledge of this phenomenon, both on simply reinforced concrete and on prestressed members.[4] Static tests on reinforced concrete I beams showed that the steel stress in stirrups increases linearly with the load and is three times smaller than it would be if the concrete carried no shear, Figure 4.50. In this respect, all codes are fully justified in taking the concrete into account as a shear-carrying component.

However, dynamic testing on the same beams showed a very different behavior. A cyclic load was applied between one-third and two-thirds of the ultimate static load for one million cycles, whereupon the beam was statically tested to failure, Figure 4.51. Before cracking, the elastic behavior of the homogeneous member kept the steel stress in the stirrups very low. However, before 10,000 cycles, a crack pattern had appeared that remained to the end of the test and became more and more pronounced with a continuous increase of the inclined crack width. Crack opening reached $\frac{1}{16}$ in. (1.5 mm) at the end of the dynamic test. Most probably stirrup rupture took place about 600,000 cycles, although the ultimate static capacity of the

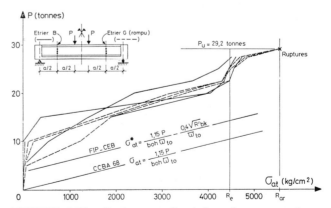

FIGURE 4.50. Static test of reinforced concrete I-beam steel stress in stirrups.

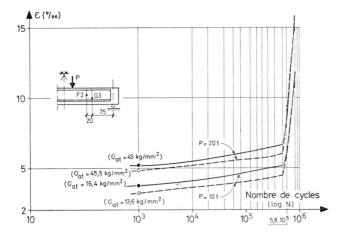

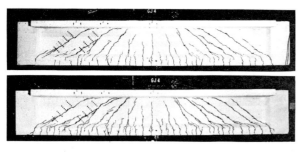

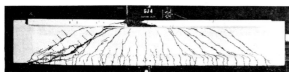

FIGURE 4.51. Dynamic test of reinforced concrete I-beam web cracking and variation of steel stress in stirrups.

beam after dynamic testing was substantially the same as for the other beams, which were tested only under static loads. Such tests show that the conventional approach of designing web reinforcement for static loading with a large part of the shear carried by the concrete may not provide adequate safety in the actual structures as soon as web cracking is allowed to develop.

4.10.3 DIFFICULTIES IN ACTUAL STRUCTURES

Another source of information is afforded by the behavior of existing structures. Fortunately, examples of difficulties imputable to shear in cantilever box girder bridges are scarce. The authors are aware of only two such contemporary examples, which are summarized here for the benefit of the design engineer.

The first example relates to a box girder bridge deck constructed by incremental launching and shown in Figure 4.52. Permanent prestress was achieved by straight tendons placed in the top and bottom flanges, as required by the distribution of moments. During launching an additional uniform prestress was applied to the constant-depth single box section, which produced an average compressive stress of 520 psi (3.60 MPa). Near each pier there was a vertical prestress designed to reduce web diagonal stresses to allowable values.

During launching a diagonal crack appeared through both webs between the blisters provided in the box for anchorage of top and bottom prestress. The corresponding shear stress was 380 psi (2.67 MPa), and there was no vertical prestress in that zone. The principal tensile stress at the centroid of the section was 200 psi (1.40 MPa), which is far below the cracking strength of plain concrete. In fact, the webs of the box section were subjected to additional tensile stresses due to the distribution of the large concentrated forces of the top and bottom prestress. The truss analogy shown in Figure 4.52 indicates clearly that such tensile stresses are superimposed on the normal shear and diagonal stresses due to the applied dead load and may therefore produce cracking. This could have been prevented by extending the vertical prestress in the webs further out toward midspan.

The second example concerns a cast-in-place variable-depth double box girder bridge with maximum span lengths of 400 ft. Because the bridge was subsequently intended to carry monorail pylons, two intermediate diaphragms were provided at the one-third and two-thirds points of each span, as shown in Figure 4.53. Prestress was applied by straight tendons in the top and bottom flanges and vertical prestress in the webs to control shear stresses. Diagonal cracking was observed in the center web only near the intermediate diaphragms with a maximum crack opening of 0.02 in. (0.6 mm). Repair was easily accomplished by adding vertical prestress after grouting the cracks.

A complete investigation of the problems encountered revealed that cracking was the result of the superposition of several adverse effects, any one of which was almost harmless if considered separately: (1) The computation of shear stresses failed to take into account the adverse effect (usually neglected) of the vertical component of continuity prestress in the bottom flange of a girder with variable height. (2) The distribution of shear stresses between the center and side webs was made under the assumption that shear stresses were equal in all three webs. In fact the center web

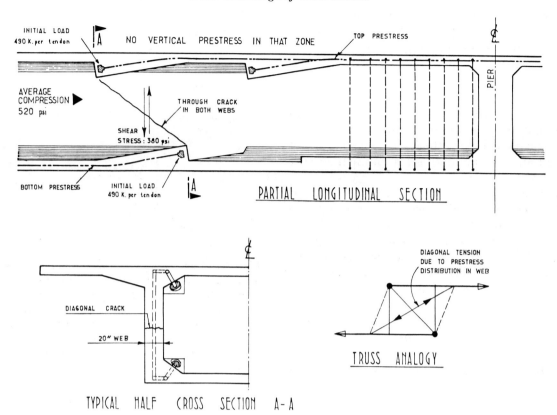

FIGURE 4.52. Example of web cracking under application of high prestress forces.

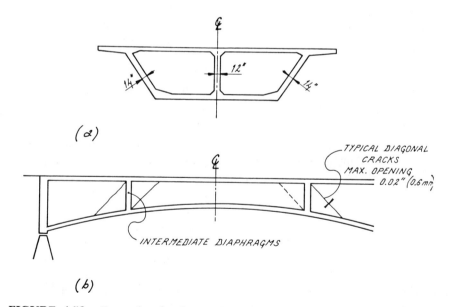

FIGURE 4.53. Example of web cracking in a 400 ft span. (*a*) Typical cross section. (*b*) Partial longitudinal section.

carries a larger proportion of the load, and shear stresses were underestimated for this web. (3) The vertical web prestress was partially lost into the intermediate diaphragms, and the actual vertical compressive stress was lower than assumed. (4)

Present design codes do not provide a consistent margin of safety against web cracking when vertical prestress is used. This margin decreases significantly when the amount of vertical prestress increases. In the present French code, the safety factor against web cracking is 2 when no vertical prestress is used and only 1.3 for a vertical prestress of 400 psi. (5) At present, vertical prestress is usually applied with short threaded bars, and even when equipped with a fine thread they are not completely reliable unless special precautions are taken under close supervision. Even a small anchor set significantly reduces the prestress load, and it is not likely that the actual prestress load is only three-fourths or even two-thirds of the theoretical prestress.

It should, however, be emphasized that the difficulties mentioned above have led to progress in this field, and the increase in knowledge has ensured that these examples remain rare exceptions. Practically all existing box girder bridges have performed exceptionally well under the effects of shear loads and torsional moments.

4.10.4 DESIGN OF LONGITUDINAL MEMBERS FOR SHEAR

The essential aspects of this important problem are:

Dimensioning of the concrete section particularly in terms of web thickness

Design of transverse and/or vertical prestress and of conventional reinforcement

The two major considerations are:

At the design stage (or, in modern code language, serviceability limit state) prevent or control cracking so as to avoid corrosion and fatigue of reinforcement.

At the ultimate stage (or load factor design concept state or ultimate limit state) provide adequate safety.

For the box sections used in cantilever bridges the behavior under shear must be investigated:

In the webs.

At the connections between web and top flange (including the outside cantilevers) and web and bottom flange. Figures 4.54 and 4.55 show a suggested method to compute shear loads and shear stresses.

Modern computer programs analyze the box girder cross sections perpendicular to the neutral axis and take into account all loads projected on the neutral axis and the section. Equivalent results

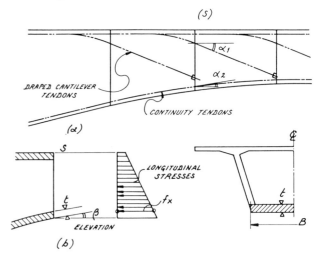

FIGURE 4.54. Computation of net applied shear load. (*a*) Vertical component of prestress. (*b*) Effect of inclined bottom flange (Resal effect). (*c*) Net shear force. Shear force due to applied loads = V; deduct vertical component of draped tendons = $-\Sigma P \sin \alpha_1$; add vertical component of continuity tendons = $+\Sigma P \sin \alpha_2$; deduct Resal effect = $-f_x \cdot t \cdot B \tan \beta$; total is net applied shear force = V_o.

are obtained by considering stresses on sections perpendicular to the top flange (which is usually the orientation of joints between segments) and projecting the loads on the section for determining shear stresses. The total net shear force is the sum of the following terms:

Shear force due to applied loads.

Reduction due to vertical component of draped tendons where used.

Increase due to inclination of continuity tendons in the bottom flange for variable-depth girders.

Reduction due to the inclined principal compressive stresses in the bottom flange (usually called the Resal effect after the engineer who first studied members of variable depth). Because the direction of the principal stresses in the web is not fully determined, it is usual to neglect the added reduction of shear force derived from web stresses.

Shear stresses may further be computed from shear force and torsion moment using the conventional elastic methods.

Tests have shown that the presence of draped tendon ducts in the webs, even if grouted after tensioning, changes the distribution of shear stresses. To take this effect into account, it is suggested to compute all shear stresses using a net web thickness that is the actual thickness minus one-half the duct

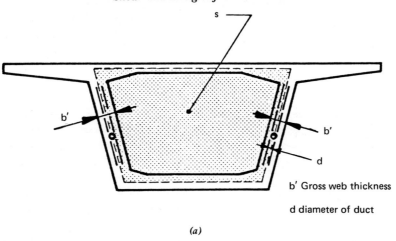

b' Gross web thickness

d diameter of duct

(a)

FIGURE 4.55. Computation of shear stress. Typical box section: net web thickness = $b = b' - \frac{1}{2}d$; shear stress due to shear force V_o net applied shear load = $v = V_o \cdot Q/[(\Sigma b) \cdot I]$, where Q = statical moment at centroid, b = net web thickness, I = gross moment of inertia, V_o = net applied shear load; shear stress due to the torsion moment = $v = C/(2 \cdot b \cdot S)$, where C = torsion moment, b = net web thickness, S = area of the middle closed box. *Note:* check the shear stress at centroid level.

diameter. Ducts for vertical prestress need not be taken into account because they are smaller and parallel to the vertical stirrups, which compensates for the possible small effect of the prestress ducts.

Web-thickness dimensioning depends upon the magnitude of shear stress in relation to the state of compressive stress. In the case of monoaxial compression (only longitudinal prestress and no vertical prestress) the diagonal principal tensile stress must be below a certain limit to insure a proper and homogeneous margin of safety against web cracking with its resulting long-term damaging effects. Figure 4.56 suggests numerical values based on the latest state of the art that are believed to be realistic and safe. Numerical values for allowable shear stresses under design loads are given in Figures 4.57 and 4.58 for 5000 and 6000 psi concrete.

Web thickness must therefore be selected in the various sections along the span to keep shear stresses within such allowable values. It may be that construction requirements or other factors make it desirable to accept higher shear stresses. It is necessary in this case to use vertical prestress to create a state of biaxial compression. Figure 4.56*b* indicates the corresponding procedure. The vertical compressive stress must be at least 2.5 times the excess of shear stress above the value for monoaxial compression.

When vertical prestress is used, the beneficial effect of increasing the length of the horizontal component of the potential crack in the web created by

the horizontal compression due to prestress is partially lost. In fact, if both horizontal and vertical compressive stresses are equal, $f_x = f_y$, the direction of the principal stress is given by $\beta = 45°$ as in

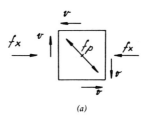

(a)

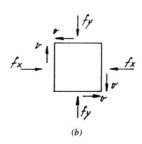

(b)

FIGURE 4.56. Allowable shear stress for mono- and biaxial compression in box girders. (*a*) Monoaxial compression: allowable shear stress = $v = 0.05f'_c + 0.20f_x$; corresponding diagonal tension = f_p given by $v^2 = f_p(f_x + f_p)$. (*b*) Biaxial compression: allowable shear stress = $v = 0.05f'_c + 0.20f_x + 0.40f_y$; corresponding diagonal tension = f_p given by $v^2 = (f_x + f_p)(f_y + f_p)$.

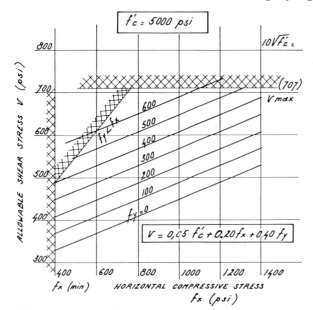

FIGURE 4.57. Allowable shear stresses for $f'_c = 5000$ psi.

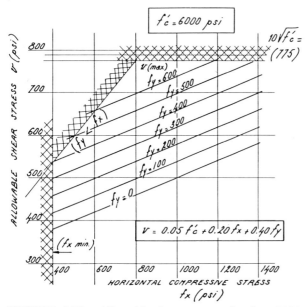

FIGURE 4.58. Allowable shear stresses for $f'_c = 6000$ psi.

ordinary reinforced concrete. If a higher vertical stress is used, a crack with $\beta > 45°$ could develop, with a consequent reduction of the horizontal length over which concrete and reinforcement must carry the total shear. To prevent such a situation, it is deemed preferable to use a vertical compressive stress not greater than the longitudinal compressive stress, $f_y < f_x$.

Finally, considering present knowledge on the behavior of prestressed concrete beams under high shear stresses, it is not recommended that shear

stresses higher than a limiting value of $10\sqrt{f'_c}$ be accepted prior to careful investigation based on specific experimental research.

In this respect, a very interesting case arose for the construction of the Brotonne Viaduct in France (described in Chapter 9), where an exceptionally long span called for minimum weight and consequently high concrete stresses. The most critical condition for shear stresses developed in the 8 in. (0.20 m) webs near the piers of the approach spans, where a maximum shear stress of 640 psi (4.5 MPa) was accepted together with an unusually low longitudinal compression stress of 500 psi (3.45 MPa). Vertical prestress was used in this case. The chart for a 6000 psi concrete, Figure 4.58, would give:

In monoaxial state with $f_x = 500$ psi, $V = 400$ psi.

In biaxial state with $f_y = 550$ psi, $V = 620$ psi, which is substantially equal to the actual shear stress of 640 psi.

A test was conducted to study the behavior of the precast prestressed web panels in the normal design load stage and up to failure, Figure 4.59. Results are shown in Figure 4.60. The ultimate capacity of the web was very large and probably far in excess of the needs. It is believed that web

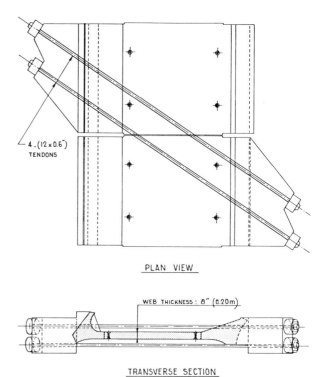

FIGURE 4.59. Brotonne Viaduct, test set-up for precast web panels.

Stresses at design stage (approach viaduct):

Horizontal compressive stress	500 psi
Vertical compressive stress	550 psi
Shear stress	640 psi

Results of test at rupture:

$$\frac{840}{630} = 1.3$$

Normal Load	630 t	
Ultimate shear	840 t	
Horizontal compressive stress		1650 psi
Vertical compressive stress		580 psi
Shear stress (elastic theory)		3300 psi
uniform		2200 psi

Joint destroyed and multiple keys sheared off. Panels intact.

FIGURE 4.60. Brotonne Viaduct, results of precast web panel tests.

cracking control can be obtained only by proper stress limits at the design load level.

When designing longitudinal bridge members for shear, another important factor remains to be considered, which has sometimes been overlooked by inexperienced designers. It concerns longitudinal shear stresses developing between the webs and the top and bottom flanges as shown in Figure 4.61. When web stresses have been verified at the level of the centroid, it is not necessary to make a detailed study at other points of the web [such as levels (d) and (e)], although the principal tensile stress near the pier may be slightly higher at point (d) than at the center of gravity. On the other hand, to keep the integrity of the box girder, it is very important to verify that shear and diagonal stresses in sections (a), (b), and (c) are within the

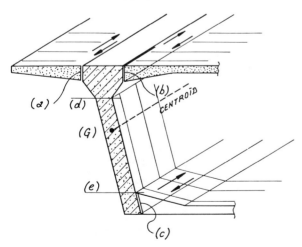

FIGURE 4.61. Longitudinal shear between web and flanges.

same allowable values as set forth previously for the webs and that a proper amount of reinforcing steel crosses each section.

This leads to the design of transverse reinforcement in the cross section to resist shear stresses. According to the provisions of the ACI Code and the AASHTO specifications, the web shear steel requirements are controlled by the ultimate stage. The net ultimate shear force is given by the following formula, based on the current partial load factors:

$$V_u = 1.30V_{DL} + 2.17V_{LL} + V_P$$

where V_u = net shear force at ultimate stage,
V_{DL} = actual shear force due to the effect of all dead loads, including the reduction due to variable depth where applicable,
V_{LL} = shear force due to live loads including impact,
V_P = unfactored vertical component of prestress where applicable.

Effects of temperature gradients and volume changes are usually small in terms of shear load and may be neglected except in rigid frames. On the contrary, shear due to moment redistribution and secondary effects of continuity prestress must be included. A partial safety factor on material properties is applied to the ultimate load state.

4.11 *Joints Between Match-Cast Segments*

Joints between match-cast segments are usually filled with a thin layer of epoxy to carry normal and shear stresses across the joint. In the early structures, a single key was provided in each web of the box girder to obtain the same relative position between segments in the casting yard and in the structure after transportation and placing. This key was also used to transfer the shear stresses across the joint before polymerization of the epoxy, which has substantially no shear strength before hardening. Figure 4.62 summarizes the force system in relation to a typical segment both during erection and in the completed structure.

Provisional assembly of a new segment to the previously completed part of the structure is usually achieved by stressing top (and sometimes bottom) longitudinal tendons, which induce forces F_1 (and F_2). The resultant F of $F_1 + F_2$ resolves with the segment weight W into a resultant R. The vertical component of R can be balanced only by a reac-

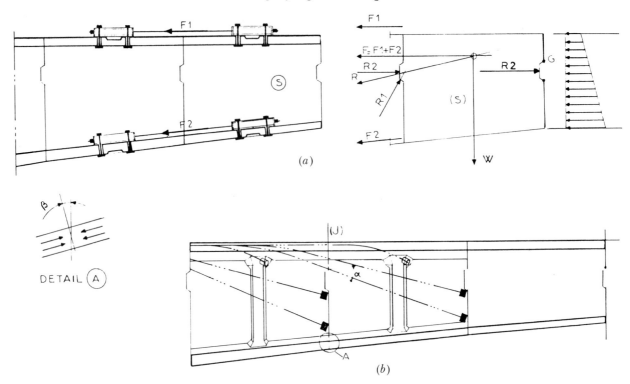

FIGURE 4.62. Typical segment in relation to the force system. (*a*) Provisional assembly of segment(s). (*b*) Segment(s) in the finished structure.

tion such as R_1 given by the inclined face of the key, while the balance of the normal force is R_2 which produces a distribution of longitudinal compressive stresses. In the finished structure, all normal and shear stresses are naturally carried through the joints by the epoxy material, which has compressive and shear strengths in excess of the segment concrete.

A series of interesting tests were performed for the construction of the Rio-Niteroi Bridge in Brazil to verify the structural behavior of epoxy joints between match-cast segments. A 1-to-6 scale model was built and tested to represent a typical deck span near the support and the corresponding seven segments as shown in Figure 4.63.

A crack pattern developed in the web when the test load was increased above design load, as shown in Figure 4.64. The epoxy joints had no influence on the continuity of the web cracks, and the behavior of the segmental structure up to ultimate was exactly the same as that of a monolithic structure. Failure occurred for concrete web crushing when the steel stress in the stirrups reached the yield point. The corresponding shear stress was 970 psi (6.8 MPa) for a mean concrete cylinder strength of 4200 psi (29.5 MPa).

The first bending crack had previously occurred for a load equal to 93 percent of the computed cracking load, assuming a tensile bending strength of 550 psi (3.9 MPa). Other tests were performed

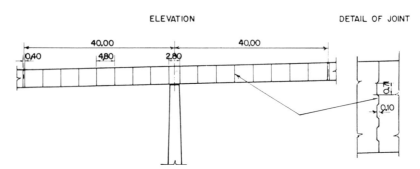

FIGURE 4.63. Rio-Niteroi Bridge, partial elevation and joint detail.

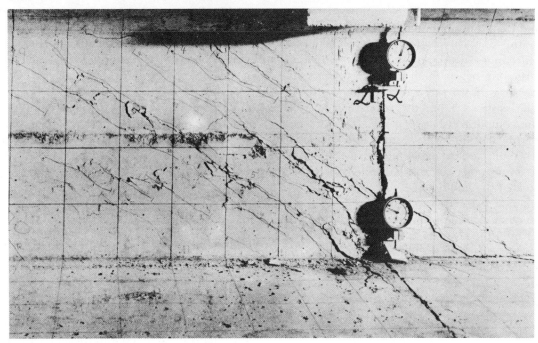

FIGURE 4.64. Rio-Niteroi Bridge, web crack pattern at ultimate in model test.

in order to study the transfer of diagonal principal compressive stresses across the segment joints as shown in Figure 4.65. Prismatic test specimens

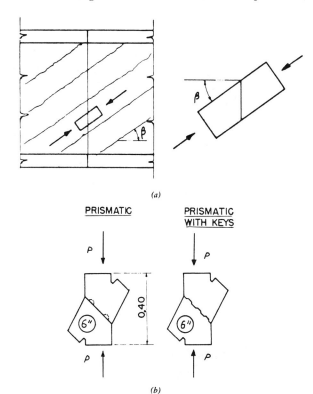

FIGURE 4.65. Rio-Niteroi Bridge, test specimens for web. (*a*) Crack pattern in web and related test specimen. (*b*) Actual test specimens.

were prepared, some with and some without shear keys across the joint, and tested for various values of β, the angle between the principal stress and the neutral axis of the girder. In the case of the Rio Niteroi Bridge the value of β is between 30 and 35°. For a reinforced concrete structure $\beta = 45°$.

A preliminary test showed that the epoxy joint had an efficiency of 0.92 as compared to a monolithic specimen with no joint (ratio between the ultimate load P on the prismatic specimen with an epoxy joint and with a monolith specimen). For various directions of the joint the results are as follows:

β	0°	15°	30°	45°	60°
Efficiency	0.94	0.92	0.98	0.95	0.70

It can be seen that for values of β smaller than 45° (which covers the entire field of prestressed concrete members) the compressive strength is hardly affected by the presence of the inclined joint. All these tests confirmed earlier experimental studies to show that epoxy joints are safe provided that proper material quality together with proper mixing and application procedures are constantly obtained.

Several early incidents in France, and some more recently in the United States, have shown that these conditions are not always achieved. The logical step in the development and improvement of epoxy joints was therefore to relieve the epoxy of any structural function. The multiple-key (or castellated-joint) design embodies this concept and provides for simplicity, safety, and cost savings. Webs and flanges of the box section are provided with a large number of small interlocking keys designed to carry all stresses across the joint with no structural assistance from the resin. Figure 4.66 shows the comparison between the structural behavior of an early joint with a single web key and a joint with multiple keys, assuming that the epoxy resin has improperly set and hardened. It is now recommended that multiple keys be used in all precast segmental projects, as shown in Figure 4.67. With the current dimensions used for depth and height of multiple keys, the overall capacity of the joint is far in excess of the required minimum to transfer diagonal stresses safely up to the ultimate load state.

4.12   Design of Superstructure Cross Section

The typical cross section of a box girder deck is a closed frame subjected to the following loads, Figure 4.68:

Girder weight of the various components (top and bottom flanges, webs)

Superimposed loads essentially applied to the top flange (barrier, curbs and pavement) and sometimes to the bottom flange, as when utilities are installed in the box girder

Live loads applied on the deck slab

A typical box girder element limited by two parallel cross sections, Figure 4.68*b*, is in equilibrium because the applied loads are balanced by the difference between shear stresses at the two limiting sections. To design the typical cross section the assumption is usually made that the shape of the section remains unchanged and that the closed frame may be designed as resting on immovable supports such as A and B. Bending moments are created in the various sections of the frame due to the applied loads. Maximum moments occur in the deck slab due to live loads in sections such as (a), (b), and (f).

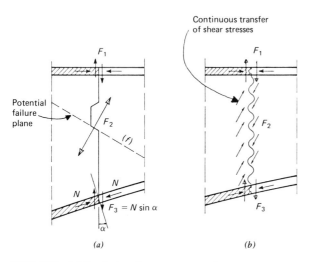

FIGURE 4.66. Joint between match-cast segments, comparison between single- and multiple-key concepts.

FIGURE 4.67. Precast segment with multiple keys.

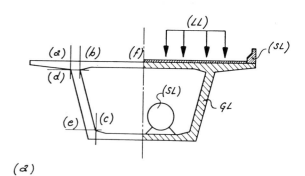

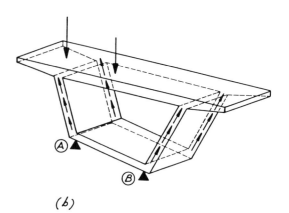

FIGURE 4.68. Design of deck cross section. (*a*) Typical loading on cross section. (*b*) Free-body diagram.

Because the webs are usually much stiffer than the flanges and the side-deck slab cantilevers and the center-deck slab between webs are built into the webs, most of the deck-slab moments are transferred to the web, with a maximum value in section (d) at the connection between web and top flange. In bridges where transverse or vertical prestress or both are used, the design of the deck cross section is not greatly affected by the fact that moments and normal forces computed in the frame superimpose their effects on the shear stresses due to longitudinal bending mentioned in Section 4.10.

The case is more critical when only conventional transverse reinforcing steel is used in both flanges and webs. A common method, based on experience, is to compute the steel area required on either face at critical sections such as (a) through (e), shown in Figure 4.68, for the following:

1.   Shear stresses in the longitudinal members.
2.   Transverse bending of the frame.

The minimum amount of steel should not be less than the larger of the following:

item 1 plus one-half of item 2,

item 2 plus one-half of item 1, or

0.7 times the sum of item 1 and item 2.

4.13   Special Problems in Superstructure Design

All design aspects covered in the preceding sections pertain to the design of deck members for bending and shear regardless of the local problems encountered over the piers or abutments and at intermediate expansion joints when required. This section will now deal with such local problems, which are of great practical importance.

4.13.1   DIAPHRAGMS

It was mentioned in Section 4.6 that the combined capacities of the deck slab in bending and the box girder in torsion allow a very satisfactory transverse distribution of live loads between girders in the case of multiple box girder decks. It has therefore been common practice to eliminate all transverse diaphragms between box girders except over the abutments. Diaphragms inside the box section are still required over the intermediate piers in most projects.

4.13.2   SUPERSTRUCTURE OVER PIERS

The simplest case is exemplified in Figure 4.69, where a deck of constant depth rests upon the pier cap with bearings located under the web of the box girder. The reaction is transferred directly from the web to the bearings, and there is need only for a simple inside diaphragm designed to transfer the shear stresses, due to possible torsion moments, to the substructure. A more complicated situation arises when the bearings are offset with regard to the webs, Figure 4.70. Reinforcing and possibly prestressing must be provided in the cross section immediately above the pier to fullfill the following functions:

Suspend all shear stresses carried by the web under point A, where a 45° line starting at the bearing edge intersects the web centerline (hatched area in the shear diagram).

Balance the moment $(R \cdot d)$ induced by the bearing offset.

Looking at other schemes, we find that decks of variable depth pose several challenging problems. Figure 4.71 shows an elevation of a box girder resting on twin bearings designed to improve the rigidity of the pier-to-deck connection and consequently reduce the bending moments in the deck, which will be described in greater detail in Chapter 5.

When the loading arrangement is symmetrical in the two adjacent spans, the transfer of the deck reaction into the piers through the four bearings is just as simple as for the case shown in Figure 4.69. Matters look very difficult for an unsymmetrical loading condition either in the completed structure, Figure 4.71, or during construction, Figure 4.72. Let us assume that the total deck reaction is transferred to the pier through one line of bearings only (for example, R_1 in Figure 4.71, for an excess of load in the left span). The compression C_2 carried by the bottom flange at the right is no longer balanced by the corresponding reaction R_2, and an abrupt change in the system of internal forces results in a large vertical tensile force T_2, which has to be suspended on the total width of the box section by special reinforcement or prestress. In long-span structures, these local effects are of no small magnitude. Taking the example of a 40 ft (12 m) wide box with a 20 ft (6 m) wide bottom flange and a span of 300 ft (90 m), the load carried by the bottom flange will probably be around 3000 t (2720 mt) and the angle change above the right bearing

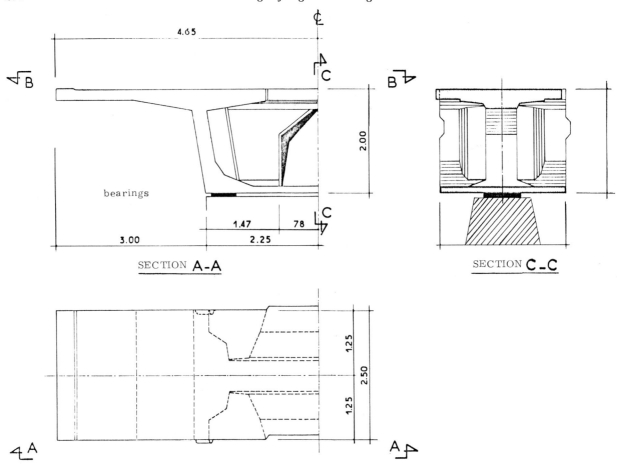

FIGURE 4.69. Pier segment for deck of constant depth and simple support.

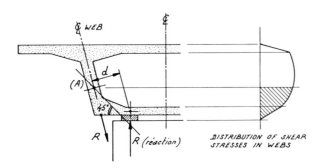

FIGURE 4.70. Deck over piers with offset bearings.

about 10 percent. The corresponding unbalanced load is therefore 300 t (272 mt), and this is more than enough to split the pier segment along the section between the web and the bottom flange if proper consideration has not been given to the problem with respect to design and detailing.

The situation may be even more critical during construction, Figure 4.72, if the unbalanced mo-ment induces uplift in one of the two bearings. The load of the anchor rods (2) has to be added to the unbalanced load resulting from the angle change of the bottom flange.

The diaphragm systems shown in Figures 4.71 and 4.72 are of the Δ type where both inclined diaphragm walls intersect at the top flange level. Any unsymmetrical moment that produces a ten-sion force in the top flange T and a compression force in the bottom flange may thus be balanced by normal loads such as F_1 and C_1, Figure 4.71, with no secondary bending. In this respect, then, it is a satisfactory scheme. Detailing may, however, be difficult because of the concentration of rein-forcement or prestress tendon anchors in the top flange area, which usually is already overcrowded with longitudinal tendon ducts. A simple and more practical design, although less satisfactory from a theoretical point of view, is to provide vertical diaphragms above the bearings. This is the logical choice when the deck is rigidly connected with a

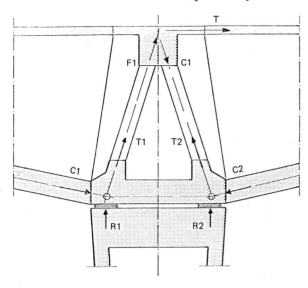

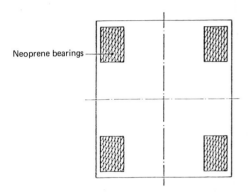

Neoprene bearings

FIGURE 4.71. Deck of variable depth, permanent deck-to-pier bearing arrangement.

box pier and where the pier walls are continued in the deck, as shown in Figure 4.73. Here again the transfer of all symmetrical loads between deck and pier is simple, and design difficulties arise for unsymmetrical loading. At the connecting points *A* and *B*, Figure 4.73, between the top flange and the vertical diaphragms, the part of the top flange tension load T such as T_1 induces into the diaphragm another tension load T_2, and both loads result in an unbalanced diagonal component T_3, which must be resisted both by the webs and by special provisions such as stiffening beams.

4.13.3   END ABUTMENTS

A special segment will be provided at both ends of the bridge deck with a solid diaphragm to transfer torsional stresses to the bearings, as shown in Figure 4.74. The expansion joint is, therefore, adequately supported by the end diaphragm on one side and the abutment wall on the other side.

4.13.4   EXPANSION JOINT AND HINGE SEGMENT

The expansion joints required at intermediate points in very long structures need a special segment to transfer the reaction between the two sides of the deck. When the expansion joint is located close to the point of contraflexure there is no provision for any uplift force, even with a load factor on the live loading.

The hinge segment is therefore made up of two half-segments, as shown in Figure 4.75:

The bearing half (reference *A*), which is connected by prestress to the shorter part of the span

The carried half (reference *B*), connected by prestress to the longer part of the span

Measures are taken to continue cantilever construction through the hinge segment until closure is achieved at midspan; see Section 4.8.6.

Inclined diaphragms provide an efficient way to suspend or transfer the reaction through the bearings into the flanges and webs on both sides of the box section, Figure 4.75.

One of the largest structures incorporating a hinge segment of this type is the Saint Cloud Bridge, described in Section 3.12. A typical detail of this segment is shown in Figure 4.76.

4.14   Deflections of Cantilever Bridges and Camber Design

Each cantilever arm consists of several segments, fabricated, installed, and loaded at different points in time. It is important therefore to predict accurately the deflection curves of the various cantilevers so as to provide adequate camber either in the fabrication plant for precast segmental construction or for adequate adjustment of the form travelers for cast-in-place construction.

When the structure is statically determinate, the cantilever arm deflections are due to:

The concrete girder weight

The weight of the travelers or the segment placing equipment

The cantilever prestress

After continuity between individual cantilevers is achieved, the structure becomes statically indeterminate and continues to undergo additional deflections for the following reasons:

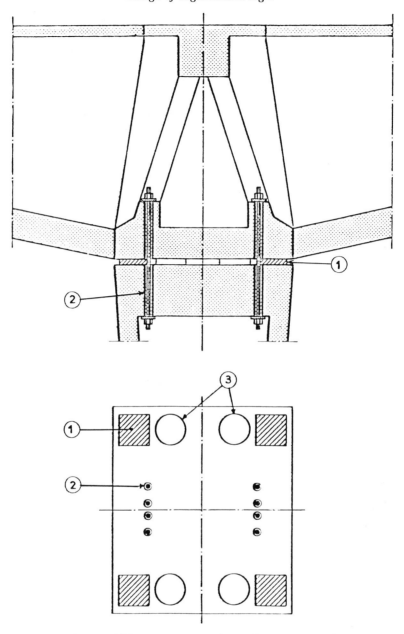

FIGURE 4.72.   Temporary pier and deck connection.

Continuity prestress

Removal of travelers or segment placing equipment

Removal of provisional supports and release of deck to pier connections

Placing of superimposed loads

Subsequent long-term deflections due to concrete creep and prestress losses will also take place. Compensation for the following three types of deflections must be provided for by adequate camber or adjustment:

1. Cantilever arms.

2. Short-term continuous deck.

3. Long-term continuous deck.

It has already been mentioned that the concrete modulus of elasticity varies both with the age at the time of first loading and with the duration of the load (see Section 4.8.7). Deflections of types 2 and 3 above are easily accommodated by changing the theoretical longitudinal profile by the corresponding amount in each section to offset exactly all future deflections. A more delicate problem is to

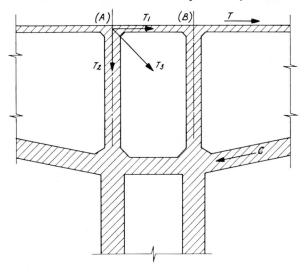

FIGURE 4.73. Pier segment with vertical diaphragms.

accurately predict and adequately follow the deflections of the individual cantilever arms during construction. It is necessary to analyze each construction stage and to determine the deflection curve of the successive cantilever arms as construction proceeds, step by step. A simple case with a five-segment cantilever is shown in Figure 4.77. The broken line represents the envelope of the various deflection curves or the space trajectory followed by the cantilever tip at each construction stage.

By changing the relative angular positions of the various segments by small angles, such as $-\alpha_1$, $-\alpha_2$, and so on, the cantilever should be assembled to its final length with a satisfactory longitudinal profile as shown in Figure 4.78, for the simple case considered. The practicalities of this important problem are covered in Sections 11.4 and 11.6.

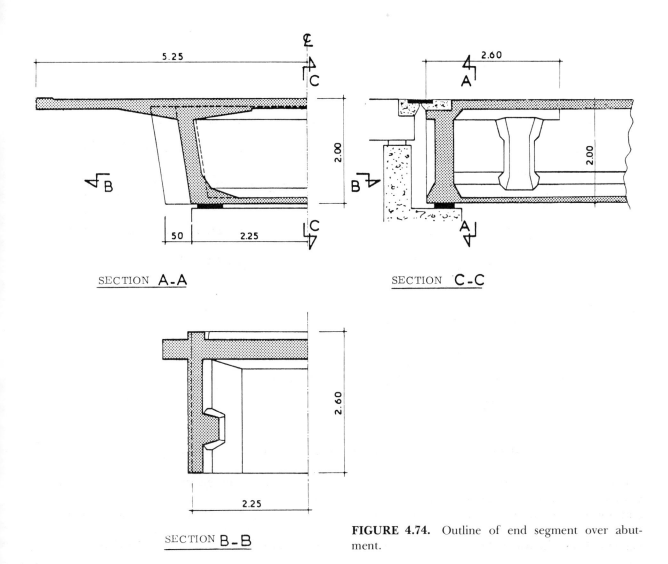

SECTION **A-A**

SECTION **C-C**

SECTION **B-B**

FIGURE 4.74. Outline of end segment over abutment.

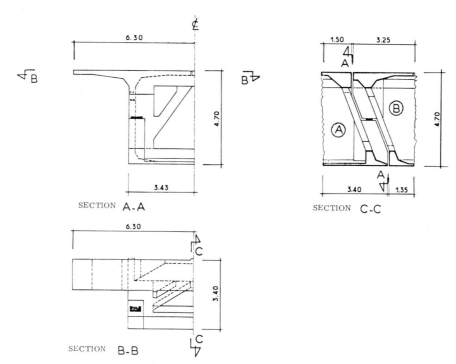

FIGURE 4.75. Hinge segment with expansion joint.

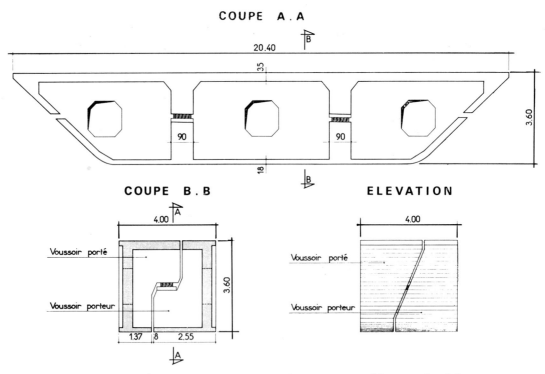

FIGURE 4.76. Saint Cloud Bridge, hinge segment with expansion joint.

It is interesting to compare the relative importance of deflections and camber for cast-in-place and precast construction. Figure 4.79 shows values for an actual structure, where computations have been made for the two different methods. The cal-culational assumptions given in Figure 4.79 indi-cate that in most cases the difference would be even more significant if a cast-in-place cycle of less than one week were employed and if precast seg-ments were stored for more than two weeks. How-

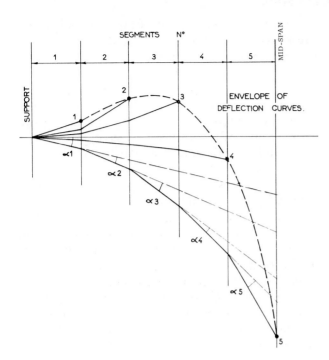

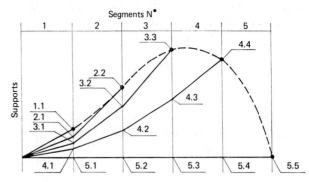

FIGURE 4.78. Choice and control of camber.

FIGURE 4.77. Deflections of a typical cantilever.

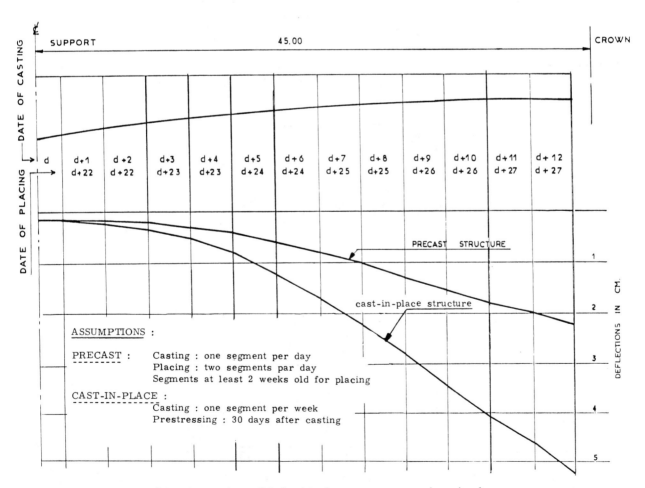

FIGURE 4.79. Comparison of deflections between precast and cast in place structures.

ever, one would normally expect a cast-in-place cantilever arm to resist deflections two or three times greater than the precast equivalent.

4.15   Fatigue in Segmental Bridges

Basically, prestressed concrete resists dynamic and cyclic loadings very well. Eugene Freyssinet demonstrated this fact fifty years ago. He tested two identical telegraph poles under dynamic loading. One was of reinforced concrete and the other of prestressed concrete; both were designed for the same loading conditions. The reinforced concrete member failed after a few thousand cycles, while the prestressed concrete member sustained the dynamic load indefinitely (several million cycles).

Fatigue in concrete itself has never been a problem in any known structure, because a variation of compressive stress in concrete may be supported indefinitely. When reference is made to fatigue in prestressed concrete, it is always inferred that fatigue problems arise in the prestressing steel or conventional reinforcing steel as a result of cracking due either to bending or to shear. If cracking could be avoided in prestressed concrete structures, the fatigue problem would be completely eliminated.

Figure 4.80 shows the resistance to fatigue of prestressing strands currently used in prestressed concrete structures. The diagram shows the limit of stress variation causing fatigue failure versus the mean stress in the prestressing steel. For convenience, both values are expressed as a ratio with respect to the ultimate tensile strength. For a steel stress of 60% of the ultimate the acceptable range of variation is ±8% of the ultimate for a number of cycles between 10^6 and 10^7. Using, for example, 270 ksi quality strand, this variation is therefore ±22,000 psi or a total range of 44,000 psi.

Because dynamic loading on a bridge is of a short-term nature, the concrete modulus is high and the ratio between steel and concrete moduli is of the order of 5. Consequently, the maximum concrete stress in an uncracked section that would cause a fatigue failure would be 44,000/5 = 8800 psi, a value which is probably ten times the stress variation under design live loads in highway box girder bridges. An uncracked prestressed concrete structure is therefore completely safe with respect to fatigue, regardless of the magnitude of live loads. A limited amount of cracking, although considered unadvisable from a corrosion point of view, is not critical if kept under control.

Tests and experience show that a grouted prestressing tendon can transfer bond stresses up to

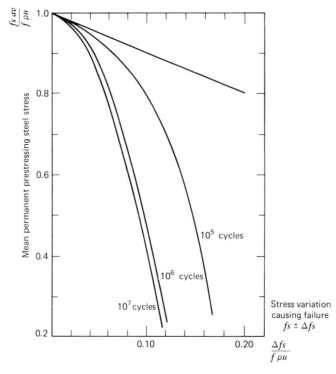

FIGURE 4.80.   Resistance to fatigue of prestressing strands.

500 psi to the surrounding concrete. Taking the example of a typical (twelve $\frac{1}{2}$ in. diameter strand) tendon with an outside diameter of 2.5 in. (64 mm), a stress variation of 40,000 psi in the steel produces a tendon force variation of 73,000 lb (33 mt), and the bond development length across a crack is then $73,000/(500 \times 2.5 \times \pi) = 18$ in. (0.46 m), see Figure 4.81. The corresponding crack width ϵ is equal to the elongation of the prestressing steel between points A and B with the triangular stress diagram—that is, 40 ksi over an average length of 18 in., or

$$\epsilon = \frac{40}{E'_s = 26,000} \times 18 = \underline{0.028 \text{ in. } (0.7 \text{ mm})}$$

A safe crack width limit of <u>0.015 in.</u> (0.4 mm) can be accepted to eliminate the danger of fatigue in the prestressing steel. In fact, instances of fatigue in segmental structures are extremely few and far between.

An isolated case has been reported of a bridge in Düsseldorf, Germany, where failure occurred as a result of fatigue of prestressing bars. The cast-in-place structure was prestressed with high-strength bars coupled at every construction joint. After ten years of service, a joint opened up to $\frac{3}{8}$ in. (10 mm) and caused bar failures at the couplers. An investigation revealed that a bearing had frozen and prevented the structure from following the longitudinal movements due to thermal variations. This accidental restraint induced high tensile stresses in the concrete and caused cracking, which first appeared in the construction joints precisely where bar couplers were located. The live-load stress level in the prestressing steel increased from 850 psi (6 MPa) for the previously uncracked section to 14,000 psi (96 MPa) for the cracked section and induced failure in the bars. A recommendation was made as a result of this fatigue problem that couplers should be moved at least 16 in. (0.40 m) away from the construction joints and that reinforcing steel should be provided through the joints if practical. Another sensitive factor relating to fatigue in web reinforcing steel was mentioned in Section 4.10.2 for reinforced concrete test beams. No such danger would exist in prestressed concrete if shear and diagonal stresses were kept within the limits that control web cracking.

In conclusion, fatigue in prestressed concrete is not a potential danger if design and practical construction take into account a few simple rules:

1. Avoid bending cracks in girders by allowing no tension or only a limited amount at either top or bottom fibers for normal maximum loads, such as the combination of dead loads, prestressing, and design live loads including moment redistribution and half the temperature gradient.

2. Avoid web cracking by keeping diagonal tensile stresses within allowable limits by proper web thickness and possibly vertical prestress.

3. Design and maintain bearings and expansion joints that allow free volume changes in decks. Temperature stresses that cannot be controlled can give rise to enormous forces that may either tear the deck apart or destroy the piers and abutments. In this respect, elastomeric bearings, which work by distortion and cannot freeze, are safer than friction bearings, which are more easily affected by dust and weathering of the contact surfaces.

Insofar as crack control in segmental structures is concerned, it is usually felt in Europe that excessive concrete cover over the reinforcing steel and prestress tendons does not prevent corrosion but merely increases the crack width.[3] For example, the typical 2 in. (50 mm) cover commonly used in bridge decks in the United States is considered extreme in Europe. The 4 in. (100 mm) cover for concrete exposed to sea water would be a complete surprise to European engineers.

Several examples of common practice in segmental bridges are given as a simple comparative reference in Table 4.2.

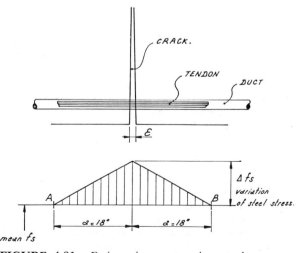

FIGURE 4.81. Fatigue in prestressing steel across a cracked section.

TABLE 4.2. Concrete Cover to Reinforcing Steel and Prestress Tendons in Europe

Concrete cover (in.)	Description
Germany	
$1\frac{1}{8}$ to 2	Reinforcing steel
$1\frac{1}{2}$	Outside exposure, tendons
$1\frac{1}{4}$	Inside exposure, tendons
France	
1	Transverse reinforcing steel
$1\frac{1}{2}$	Longitudinal reinforcing steel or tendons (normal atmosphere)
2	Corrosive atmosphere (salt water)
Netherlands	
$1\frac{1}{8}$	Reinforcing steel and tendons (normal exposure)
$1\frac{3}{8}$	Lightweight concrete
2 to $2\frac{3}{8}$	Salt water exposure

4.16 Provisions for Future Prestressing

For larger segmental bridges, it may be necessary to modify the prestress forces after construction. An example would be a bridge built using cantilever construction where positive-moment (continuity) tendons are added after erection. Or, as discussed in Section 4.8.6, some tendons may be released to articulate a joint. In addition to these adjustments immediately after construction, additional prestressing may be required at a later date to correct for unanticipated creep deflection or for additional loads such as for a new wearing surface. In Europe on some bridges spare tendon ducts are provided for this reason. A reasonable assumption would be to provide for 5 to 10% of the total prestress force for possible future addition.

Since the tendon anchorages for the spare ducts are inside the box girder and generally located at the web-flange fillet, they are readily accessible. If future prestressing is needed, it is only necessary to insert the required tendon in the duct, jack it to its designed load, anchor and grout it. Since all this work can be done inside a box girder, it is not necessary to interrupt traffic, and the workmen are fully protected.[3]

4.17 Design Example

The Houston Ship Channel Bridge now under construction in Texas, U.S.A., is an outstanding example of segmental construction and represents the longest box girder bridge in the Americas as of this writing. Typical dimensions were given in Section 2.14. This section will deal with some design aspects of this prestressed concrete segmental bridge.

4.17.1 LONGITUDINAL BENDING

Each of the four identical cantilever arms is made up of:

Ten segments 8 ft long (maximum weight 415 kips)

Six segments 12 ft long (maximum weight 464 kips)

Thirteen segments 15 ft long (maximum weight 457 kips)

Longitudinal tendons are as follows:

Cantilever tendons: 42 (nineteen 0.6 in. dia strands) + 50 (twelve 0.6 in. dia). Twelve additional bars used during construction are incorporated in the permanent prestress system.

Continuity tendons in side spans: 20 (twelve 0.6 in. dia).

Continuity tendons in center span: 40 (twelve 0.6 in. dia).

A typical layout of the cross section was given in Figure 2.82.

The main loading combinations considered in the design are summarized in Table 4.3. The lon-

TABLE 4.3. Houston Ship Channel Bridge, Main Design Load Combinations

Loading Case	Description	Allowable Tension on Extreme Fiber, Top or Bottom (ksf)
(1)	$(G) + (P) + (E)$	0
(2)	$(D) + (P) + (L + I)$	0
(3)	$(D) + (P) + (L + I) + \frac{1}{2}(\Delta T) + (T)$	25
(4)	$(D) + (P) + \frac{1}{2}(L + I) + (\Delta T) + (T)$	25
(5)	$(D) + (P) + (W)$	25

Notations: (G) girder load, (D) total dead load including superimposed dead load, $(L + I)$ live load plus impact, (P) prestress, (E) construction equipment, (ΔT) temperature gradient of 18°F between top and bottom fiber, (T) temperature and volume changes, (W) wind load on structure.
Concrete strength and stresses: f'_c = 6000 psi = 864 ksf (42.1 MPa).
Basic allowable compressive stress: $0.4 f'_c$ = 346 ksf (16.8 MPa).

gitudinal bending of the box girder has been analyzed using the BC program, which considers the effects of the creep, shrinkage, and relaxation at each construction phase. Figure 4.82 shows the diagram of prestress forces due to cantilever and continuity tendons at two different dates:

After completion of the structure and opening to traffic (780 days after start of deck casting)

After relaxation and creep have taken place (4000 days)

Significant values of the prestress forces are given in Table 4.4. The variation of stresses in the center and side spans is shown in the following diagrams for the corresponding loading cases:

Figures 4.83 and 4.84, all dead loads and prestress at top and bottom fibers

Figures 4.85 and 4.86, live load and temperature gradient at top and bottom fibers

It is easily shown from these diagrams that all stresses in the various sections are kept within the allowable values mentioned in Table 4.3. The

TABLE 4.4. Houston Ship Channel Bridge, Significant Values of Prestress Forces

Prestress Force (kips)	Day 780	Day 4000	Percent Loss
Maximum cantilever prestress in side span	54,710	51,310	6.2
Maximum cantilever prestress in center span	54,390	49,280	9.4
Maximum continuity prestress in side span	9,540	8,760	8.2
Maximum continuity prestress in center span	18,130	16,780	7.5

maximum compressive stress at the bottom fiber level appears in the section located 124 ft from the pier and is equal to 335 ksf under the combined effect of all dead and live loads and prestress.

4.17.2 REDISTRIBUTION OF MOMENTS

The exceptional size of the structure gives rise to a moment redistribution of particular importance. The BC program allows a complete analysis of the behavior of the structure under the separate and combined effects of loads and prestress; also the effect of concrete creep and steel relaxation can be considered separately.

Figure 4.87 shows the variation of stresses at top and bottom fibers along the center span between days 780 and 4000, which correspond to bridge opening date and the time when materials will have stabilized (concrete creep and shrinkage having taken place and prestress having reached its final value). The magnitude of the variation is remarkable, particularly at bottom flange level where it exceeds *100 ksf* (700 psi or 4.90 MPa).

To isolate the effect of concrete creep on moment and stress redistribution, a section near midspan may be analyzed where cantilever prestress is neglibile. Results for the section located at a distance of 352 ft from the pier are summarized in Figure 4.88. The redistribution moment is equal to 52,000 ft-kips.

It is interesting to compare this result, obtained through the elaborate analysis of the BC program, with the result of the approximate method outlined in Section 4.8.7. Figure 4.89 shows the moments in a typical cantilever under girder load and final prestress. The prestress moment has been computed using a reduced eccentricity obtained by

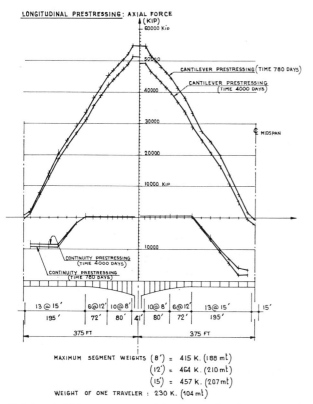

FIGURE 4.82. Houston Ship Channel Bridge, typical segment layout and longitudinal prestress.

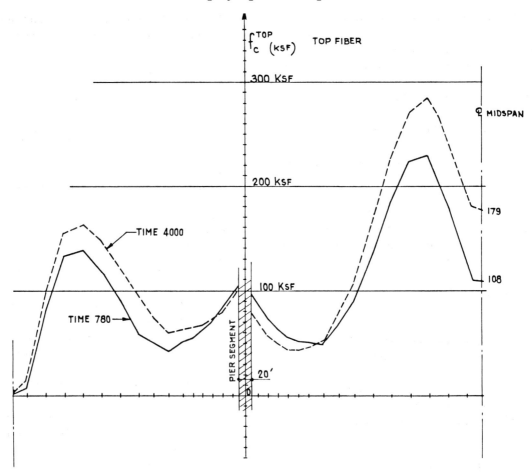

FIGURE 4.83. Houston Ship Channel Bridge, top fiber prestress for *(DL)* + *(P)* at time 780 days and 4000 days. Stresses at top fiber of the deck. Dead load at time 780 days when the bridge is just opened to traffic and at time 4000 days.

transforming the steel area in the concrete section. Therefore, the prestress moment is equal to:

$$Pe(1 - np)$$

where e = geometric eccentricity,
       n = 10, transformed coefficient,
       p = percentage of prestress steel in the section (varying between 0.5 and 0.7%).

The total midspan moment produced in the continuous span with fixed ends under the combined effect of girder load and final prestress is equal to 84,000 ft-kips. Therefore, the actual redistribution moment obtained by the BC program is equal to:

$$\frac{52,000}{84,000} = \underline{62\%} \text{ of the total moment}$$

The recommendation given in Section 4.8.7 to take a ratio of 2/3 gives a satisfactory approximation.

4.17.3 STRESSES AT MIDSPAN

Because of the moment redistribution the bottom fiber near midspan is subjected to increasing tensile stresses while the top fiber is always under compression. It is therefore sufficient to consider the state of stresses at the bottom fiber after creep and relaxation.

The results are shown in Table 4.5. It is instructive to compare the relative magnitude of the various factors influencing the stresses at midspan (stresses in ksf at bottom fiber):

1.	Live load	44
2.	Moment redistribution (difference between 250 for GL and 159 for prestress)	91
3.	Temperature gradient	48
4.	Temperature fall	18

TABLE 4.5. Houston Ship Channel Bridge, Stresses at Midspan

Stresses (ksf)	Bottom Fiber	
	Partial	Cumulative
Moment redistribution due to GL	+250	
Moment redistribution due to prestress	−159	
Moment redistribution due to $(GL) + (P)$	+ 91	
All dead loads and all final prestress (from BC program including moment redistribution)		−66
Live load + impact	44	
Temperature gradient, $\Delta T = 18°F$	48	
Temperature fall, $T = -40°F$	18	
Loading combination (2),[a] $(D) + (P) + (L + I)$		−22 Max
Loading combination (4),[b] $(D) + (P) + \frac{1}{2}(L + I) + \Delta T + T$		+22 (25)

[a]See loading combinations in Figure 4.85.
[b]Combination of Maximum $\Delta T + T$ (maximum temperature differential is improbable in winter).

The influence of the temperature fall (effect 4) is imputable to the frame action between deck and piers and would not appear in a conventional deck resting on its piers with flexible bearings. Considering only the other three factors combined, as in loading combination (4) of Table 4.3, the maximum tensile stress at the bottom fiber of the midspan section is:

$$91 + 44 + \frac{48}{2} = \underline{159 \text{ ksf}}$$

The live-load stress is only 44 ksf or 44/159 = 28 percent of the total.

In all good faith, a design engineer would have completely overlooked effects 2 and 3 only a few years ago and consequently underdesigned considerably the continuity prestress. The situation has now completely changed, and the knowledge of materials together with the powerful tool of the computer allows segmental structures to be designed safely and realistically.

It is as well to remember that the Houston Ship Channel Bridge is of exceptional size (which tends to increase the importance of dead load and moment redistribution) and that American live loads are light in comparison with those used in other countries, particularly in France and Great Britain. These two factors tend to increase the importance of moment redistribution in relation to the effect of loads computed in the conventional manner.

4.17.4   SHEAR

The variation of shear stresses along the center span under design loads is given in Figure 4.90 together with the corresponding longitudinal compressive stress at the centroid.

The most critical section is located 187 ft from the pier centerline. The numerical values in this section are as follows:

1. Vertical dead-load shear force: 4350 kips.
    Resal effect: the compressive stress at the centerline of the bottom slab is 192 ksf and the angle with the horizontal is 0.055 radians.
    Bottom slab area: 53.5 sq ft.
    Resal effect: 192 × 53.5 × 0.055 = 570 kips.
    Net dead-load shear: 3780 kips.
2. Live-load shear force: 430 kips.
3. Corresponding shear stresses in this section:

    $I/Q = 14$ ft web thickness

    $b = 4$ ft

    Total shear stress under design load (no load factor):

    $$V = 3780 + 430 = 4210 \text{ kips}$$

    Shear stress:

    $$v = \frac{4210}{14 \times 4} = 75.2 \text{ ksf}$$

4. Longitudinal compressive stress: $f_x = 160$ ksf
5. Vertical prestress. The contract specifications called for a vertical prestress for the entire deck giving a minimum compressive stress of:

    $$3\sqrt{f_c'} = 232 \text{ psi} = 33.5 \text{ ksf}$$

6. Verification of allowable shear stress.
    Using the formula proposed in Section 4.10.4:

    $$v = 0.05f_c' + 0.20f_x + 0.40f_y$$

    the allowable shear stress is:

    $$v_{\max} = 0.05 \times 864 + 0.20 \times 160 + 0.40 \times 33.5 = 88.6 \text{ ksf}$$

    while the actual shear stress is only 75.2 ksf

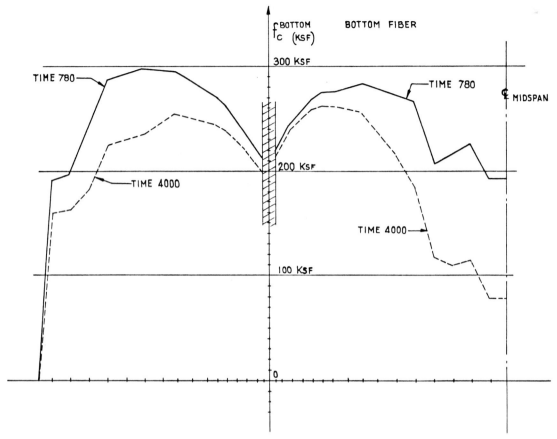

FIGURE 4.84. Houston Ship Channel Bridge, bottom fiber stresses for $(DL) + (P)$ at time 780 days and 4000 days. Stresses at bottom fiber of the deck. Dead load at time 780 days when the bridge is opened to traffic and at time 4000 days.

7. Principal stresses at design loads for the state of stress:

$$v = 75.2, \quad f_x = 160, \quad \text{and} \quad f_y = 33.5 \text{ ksf}$$

The two principal stresses are $\underline{-1}$ (tension) and $\underline{195}$ (compression).
The angle of the principal stress with the horizontal is given by:

$$\tan \beta = 0.466$$

If vertical prestresses were not used, the principal stresses would become:

$$-30 \text{ (tension) and } \underline{190} \text{ (compression)}$$

8. Principal stresses at ultimate stage.
For the load factors $1.3D + 2.17L$, including the effect of prestress, the ultimate shear force is:

$$V_u = 5710 \text{ kips}$$

Corresponding shear stress:

$$v_u = 102 \text{ ksf}$$

Principal stress: -23 (tension) and 217 (compression).

Direction of the principal stress given by:

$$\tan \beta = 0.56$$

Web shear cracking at this level of stress would be unlikely. Assuming that the concrete carried none of the ultimate shear across the potential crack shown in Figure 4.91, the total shear load should be resisted by the vertical tendons and the conventional stirrups acting on a length equal to:

$$\frac{I}{Q} \times \frac{1}{\tan \beta} = \frac{14}{0.56} = 25 \text{ ft}$$

The unit force per foot of girder is therefore:

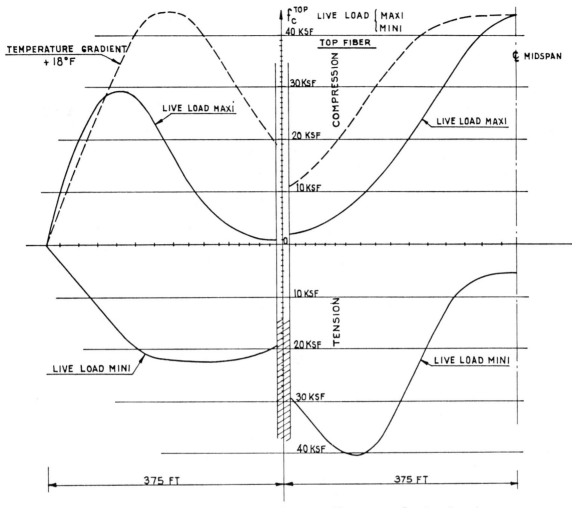

FIGURE 4.85. Houston Ship Channel Bridge, top fiber stresses for $(L + I)$ and $(\Delta T = 18°F)$.

$$\frac{5710}{25} = 228 \text{ kips/lineal ft}$$

The ultimate capacity of tendons and stirrups is:

Tendons in three webs	220 kips/lineal ft
Stirrups—0.88 in.²/lineal ft per web at 60 ksi	158 kips/lineal ft
	278 kips/lineal ft

The condition $V_u/\phi < V_s$ becomes:

$$\frac{228}{0.85} = 268 < 378 \text{ kips/lineal ft}$$

and is easily met.

If no vertical prestress had been used, the slope of the shear crack would be:

$$\tan \beta = 0.487$$

Using the limiting value $\tan \beta = 0.5$ instead of the actual value (as explained in Section 4.10.4), the

shear force per unit length of girder to be carried across the crack is:

$$\frac{1}{0.85} \times \frac{5710}{0.14} \times 0.5 = 240 \text{ kips/lineal ft}$$

The corresponding amount of steel (grade 60) would be for each web:

$$\frac{1}{3} \times \frac{240}{60} = 1.33 \text{ in.}^2/\text{lineal ft}$$

This amount of steel would still be reasonable (0.7%).

4.17.5 DESIGN OF THE CROSS-SECTION FRAME

Owing to the magnitude of the project, particular attention was given to this problem. Five finite element analyses were performed to analyze:

The local effects in the transverse frame,

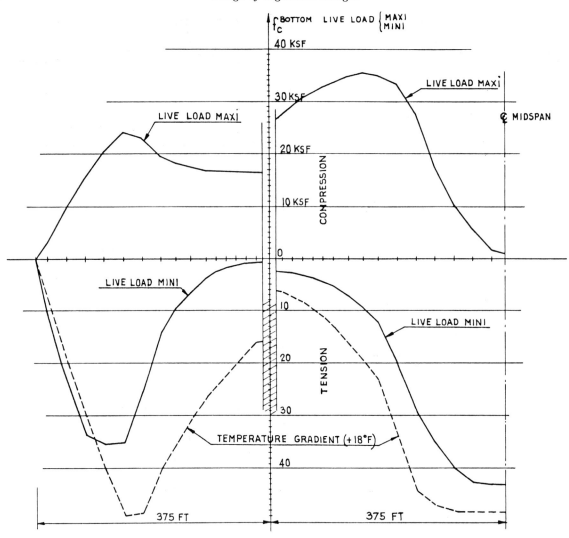

FIGURE 4.86. Houston Ship Channel Bridge, bottom fiber stresses for ($L + I$) and (ΔT = 18°F).

The possible differential deflections between the three webs of the box section,

The relative behavior of sections close to the piers or at midspan,

The effect of diaphragm restraint near the pier.

The dimensions of the cross section at midspan are given in Figure 4.92 with the nine critical sections where moments and axial loads were computed for as many as fourteen loading combinations.

A typical set of results is shown in Figure 4.93 for the midspan section. For the section located 187 ft from the pier centerline (already considered for maximum shear stresses), the moments and axial loads are substantially the same as for the midspan section. Excluding the vertical prestress, the most critical loading arrangement gives the following

values at the upper section of the outside web (section e of Figure 4.92).

Moment 11.9 kip-ft/ft

Axial load 5.4 kip/ft

The steel section required at design stage for grade 60 steel stirrups is 0.34 in.²/lineal ft. Applying the recommendations of Section 4.10.4 for the simple case of a section without web prestress, the requirements for steel on both faces of the web would be:

For shear of the longitudinal member:

$$\tfrac{1}{2} \times 1.33 = 0.67 \text{ in.}^2/\text{lineal ft}$$

For bending of the transverse member:

$$0.34 \text{ in.}^2/\text{lineal ft}$$

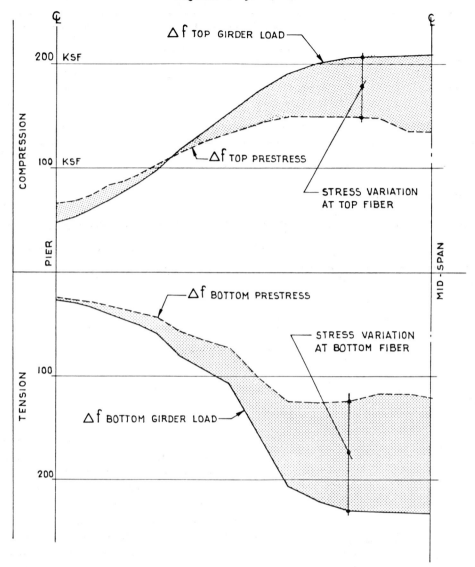

FIGURE 4.87. Houston Ship Channel Bridge, variation of stresses due to creep and relaxation.

The minimum area should thus be the higher of the following values:

$0.67 + \frac{1}{2} \times 0.34$	$= 0.84$ in.²/lineal ft
$\frac{1}{2} \times 0.67 + 0.34$	$= 0.67$ in.²/lineal ft
$0.7(0.67 + 0.34)$	$= 0.71$ in.²/lineal ft

In the actual structure, the stirrups in this section are #6 bars at 12 in. centers, giving on each face a steel area of 0.44 in.² together with the minimum vertical prestress of 44.2 kips/lineal ft (average compressive stress of 230 psi).

The ultimate capacity of the section reinforcement is therefore:

With vertical prestress: 378/3 = 126 kips/lineal ft

Without vertical prestress: 2 × 0.84 × 60 = 101 kips/lineal ft

4.18 Quantities of Materials

Before closing this chapter, it is interesting to give some statistical results concerning the quantities of materials required in segmental box girder bridges. Unit quantities have been computed by dividing the total quantities for the bridge superstructure by the deck area, using the total width of the prestressed concrete structure. The

Loading Case	Stresses, Top Fiber (ksf)		Stresses, Bottom Fiber (ksf)	
	780 Days	*4000 Days*	*780 Days*	*4000 Days*
Cantilever Prestress	− 6.36	130.32	−20.20	−161.08
Girder + superimposed dead load	−56.93	−266.50	61.89	293.50
Total	−63.29	− 136.18	41.69	132.42
Variation from 780 days to 4000 days		−72.89		+90.73

Note 1: Tensile stresses are positive.

Note 2: This moment is the difference between girder load, 142,000 ft-kips, and cantilever prestress, 90,000 ft-kips.

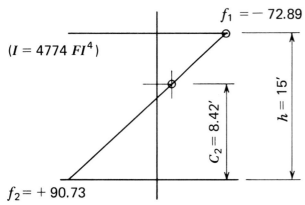

$$f_1 = -72.89$$

$$(I = 4774 \ FI^4)$$

$$C_2 = 8.42'$$

$$h = 15'$$

$$f_2 = +90.73$$

FIGURE 4.88. Houston Ship Channel Bridge, analysis of section at 352 ft from pier.

Corresponding moment variation:

$$\Delta M = (f_1 + f_2) \frac{I}{h}$$

$$= (72.89 + 90.73) \frac{4774}{15}$$

$$\Delta M = 52,000 \text{ ft-kips}$$

average concrete quantity per span foot varies with the span length. For each structure considered, the span length used is the average span of the various two-arm cantilevers. The longitudinal prestressing steel is given in pounds per cubic yard of deck concrete versus the same span length. It is assumed that prestressing tendons are made up of strands with 270 ksi guaranteed ultimate strength. From the charts given in Figures 4.94 and 4.95, it may be seen that the average quantities of materials may be represented by the following approximate formulae:

Concrete (ft³/ft²) ≃ 1.0 + (L/250)

Longitudinal prestress (lb/ft²) ≃ 1.0 + (L/60) (for spans up to 750 ft)

4.19 Potential Problem Areas

As with any type of construction with any material, problems arise that require the attention of not only the designers, but contractors and subcontractors as well. No matter how good the design, if

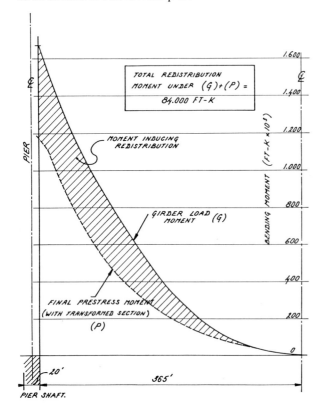

TOTAL REDISTRIBUTION MOMENT UNDER (G)+(P) = 84,000 FT-K

MOMENT INDUCING REDISTRIBUTION

GIRDER LOAD MOMENT (G)

FINAL PRESTRESS MOMENT (WITH TRANSFORMED SECTION) (P)

BENDING MOMENT (FT-K ×10³)

PIER

PIER SHAFT.

20'

565'

FIGURE 4.89. Houston Ship Channel Bridge, rapid computation of moment redistribution.

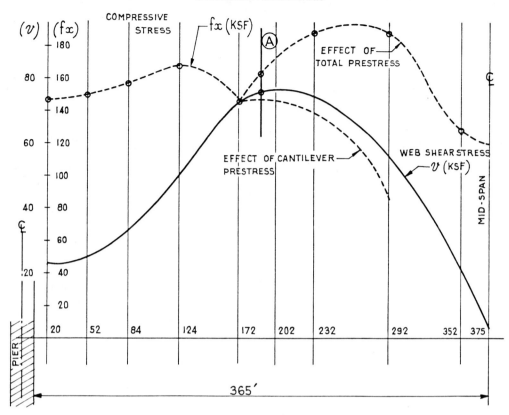

FIGURE 4.90. Houston Ship Channel Bridge, variation of web shear stress and average compressive stress in center span under design load.

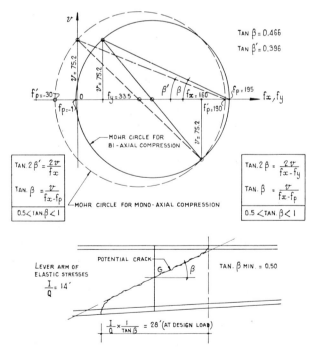

the structure is not properly constructed, there will be problems. Conversely, no matter how diligent the contractor, if the design details are poor, problems will result. Obviously, if the design and the construction are poor, problems are compounded.

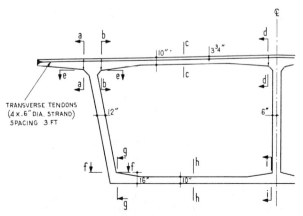

FIGURE 4.91. Houston Ship Channel Bridge, shear and principal web stresses in section 187 ft from Pier (under design loads).

FIGURE 4.92. Houston Ship Channel Bridge, design of transverse frame at midspan.

Section	a	b	c	d	e	f	g	h	i
M, dead load	−5.67	−6.29	2.37	−6.05	1.22	−3.15	−2.96	2.14	−5.29
M, Prestressing	16.59	13.22	−0.92	8.01	3.01	0.22	0.08	0	0.06
M, DL + P/T	10.92	6.93	1.45	1.96	4.23	−2.93	−2.88	2.14	−5.23
M, live load with |M| maxi	−5.24	−6.68	5.03	−8.82	5.88	−1.25	−1.25	0.35	−0.78
M, DL + P/T + LL + I	4.11	−1.75	7.98	−9.51	11.87	−4.55	−4.50	2.59	−6.25
N, dead load	0.06	−0.53	−0.65	−0.59	4.24	6.08	0.55	0.66	0.53
N, transverse prestressing	50.75	51.06	51.26	51.35	−0.31	−0.31	−0.29	−0.29	−0.29
N, DL + P/T	50.81	50.53	50.61	50.76	3.93	5.77	0.26	0.37	0.24
N, live load	—	—	—	—	1.10	—	—	—	—
N, DL + P/T + LL + I	50.81	50.53	50.61	50.76	5.36	5.77	0.26	0.37	0.24

Note: Web vertical prestress is not included.

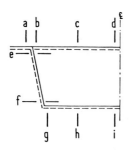

Compressive axial forces are positive. Positive bending moments cause tension at the broken line face.

SIGN CONVENTION

FIGURE 4.93. Houston Ship Channel Bridge, moments and axial forces in transverse frame at midspan.

Problems are generally associated with quality control, poor design details, or a lack of understanding as to how the structure will behave, either through ignorance or because a particular phenomenon is unknown to the current state of the art, or a combination of all these factors. The following list of problem areas, as they are known to the authors, is presented so that those involved in designing and building segmental bridges may take adequate measures and precautions to avoid these problems.

1. Improper performance of epoxy due to mishandling of mixing and application procedure, particularly in rain and cold weather. The consequences are largely reduced by the use of adequate shear keys in webs and in both top and bottom flanges of the box section.

2. Grout leakage between adjoining ducts at joints between segments, particularly in precast segmental construction. Conformity of the ducts at the joints is a desirable feature if practical. The use of tendons outside the concrete eliminates this problem.

3. Tensile cracks behind tendon anchorages, particularly for high-capacity continuity tendons in the bottom flange of box sections.

4. Transverse cracking or opening of joints, or adjacent thereto, due to the combination of several factors such as:

    a. Underestimation of moment redistribution due to concrete creep.

    b. Thermal gradients in the box section.

    c. Warping of segments due to improper curing procedures.

    Several such points have been already addressed in this chapter; others are discussed in Chapter 11. Should the recommendations given be followed both in design and construction methods and in supervision, no more difficulties of this nature are to be expected.

5. Laminar cracking in deck slab or in bottom flange due to wobble and improper alignment of ducts at the joints between adjacent segments. Such incidents have been experienced more often in cast-in-place construction than in precast construction. However, care should always be taken insofar as deck alignment is concerned in all segmental projects.

6. Freezing of water in ducts during construction, especially those anchored in the deck slab (vertical prestressing tendons or draped continuity tendons).

7. Excessive friction in ducts due to wobble. Proper alignment will reduce friction factors in segmental construction to those currently observed in conventional cast-in-place post-tensioned construction.

8. Improper survey control in segment manufacture for precast segments as well as in the field for cast-in-place segments.

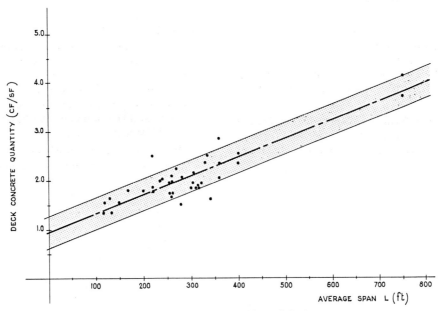

FIGURE 4.94. Average quantities of deck concrete.

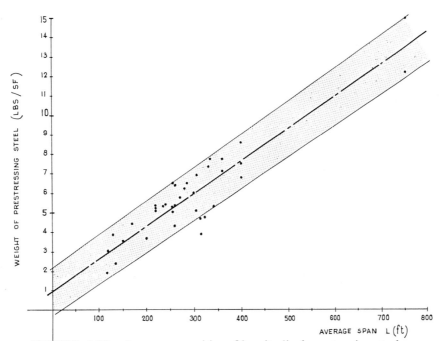

FIGURE 4.95. Average quantities of longitudinal prestressing steel.

References

1. F. Leonhardt, "New Trends in Design and Construction of Long Span Bridges and Viaducts (Skew, Flat Slabs, Torsion Box)," International Association for Bridge and Structural Engineering, Eighth Congress, New York, September 9–14, 1968.

2. Jean Muller, "Ten Years of Experience in Precast Segmental Construction," *Journal of the Prestressed Concrete Institute*, Vol. 20, No. 1, January–February 1975.

3. C. A. Ballinger, W. Podolny, Jr., and M. J. Abrahams, "A Report on the Design and Construction of Segmental Prestressed Concrete Bridges in Western Europe—1977," International Road Federation, Washington, D.C., June 1978. (Also available from Federal Highway Administration, Offices of Research and Development, Washington, D.C., Report No. FHWA-RD-78-44.)

4. "Effets de l'effort tranchant," Federation Internationale de la Precontrainte, London, 1978.

5

Foundations, Piers, and Abutments

5.1 Introduction

Probably the area most challenging to the civil engineer is that of foundation design and construction, presenting the largest potential dangers but also yielding the most significant savings to proper design concepts or refined construction methods. The first industrial application of prestressed concrete was related to solving an insurmountable problem of foundation underpinning.

225

The transatlantic terminal built in Le Havre Harbor in France on the English Channel was opened for operation in 1934 to receive the new generation of fast passenger ships between Europe and America. Improper foundation of the rear bays of the new building caused immediate constant settlements at the rate of $\frac{1}{2}$ in. (12.7 mm) per month with no foreseeable limit, except the total ruin of the facility, Figure 5.1. Eugene Freyssinet proposed a unique system of underpinning, which was immediately accepted and implemented, whereby prestressed concrete piles were manufactured in the basement of the existing building in successive increments and progressively driven by hydraulic jacks to reach the stable lower soil strata, found at a depth of more than 100 ft (30.5 m), Figure 5.2. This example should certainly make one cautious against excessive optimism in foundation design; at the same time it exemplifies the remarkable potential of prestressed concrete in solving unusual problems.

In concrete bridges, often greater savings may be expected from optimization of foundation and pier design than from the superstructure itself. This chapter will deal with certain specific aspects of piers, abutments, and foundations for bridges built in balanced cantilever. Similar concepts may be extended to cover other construction methods (span-by-span, incremental launching, and so on).

Piers with many different shapes have been used in conjunction with cantilever construction. For example, single piers, double piers, and moment-resistant piers have all been used. The cantilever segmental construction method has an important influence and bearing on the design concept of the structure. Resistance and elastic stability of piers during construction require careful investigation. Temporary piers or temporary strengthening of permanent piers or a combination of both have been used. However, the choice of piers that have adequate stability without temporary aids is highly desirable. Piers of a box section, or twin flexible legs, either vertical or inclined, are equally satisfactory.

The use of full continuity in the superstructure implies that proper steps have been taken to allow for volume changes (shrinkage, creep and thermal expansion) at the supports. Bridges such as the Choisy-le-Roi (Section 3.2), Courbevoie (Section 3.2), and the Chillon Viaduct (Section 3.6) show how the use of piers with flexible legs makes it possible to achieve full deck continuity and to build frame action between deck and piers without impairing the free expansion of the structure. The converging pier legs used at Choisy-le-Roi reduce and even cancel the amount of bending transferred to the pier foundations. Vertical parallel legs such as those in the Courbevoie and Chillon

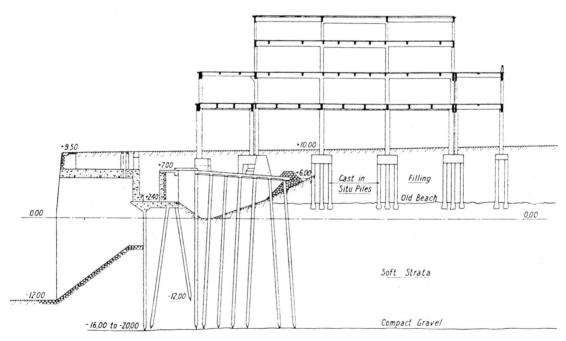

FIGURE 5.1. Le Havre transatlantic terminal, typical section.

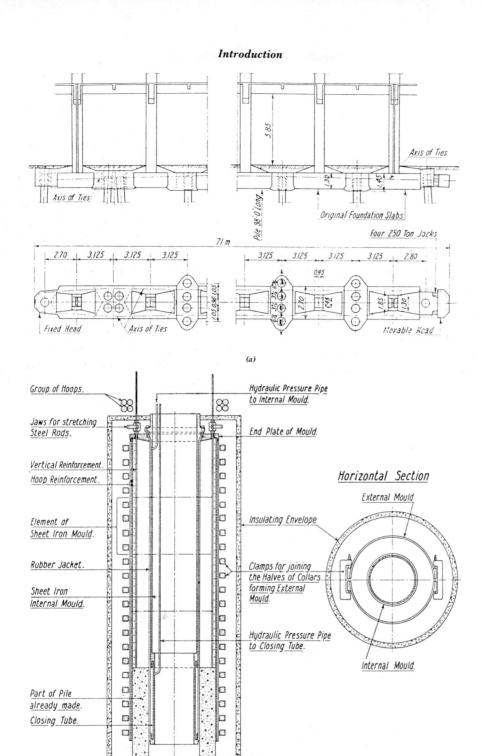

FIGURE 5.2. Le Havre transatlantic terminal. (*a*) Vertical section and plan of composite foundation girder. (*b*) Details of pile mold.

structures may be used on multispan structures because their additional flexibility accommodates larger horizontal displacements. For longer structures, bearings with a variable number of laminated elastomeric pads may be used to provide the desired horizontal flexibility.

If in the finished structure single slender piers are designed solely to transfer the deck loads to the foundations (including horizontal loads), the piers may be unable to resist the unsymmetrical moments due to the cantilever construction (i.e., with an unbalance of one segment and the equipment load). Thus, temporary shoring is required, often at considerable cost. In some cases, the stability of the cantilever under construction has been provided by the launching gantry used for placing the segments.

With double piers, two flexible legs (either inclined or vertical) make up the pier structure, which usually is supported on a single foundation. Stability during construction is excellent and requires little temporary equipment, except for some bracing between the slender walls to prevent elastic instability.

Moment-resistant piers are designed to withstand the unbalanced moments during construction by providing a temporary vertical prestress between the deck and the pier cap, thus producing a rigid connection. Flat jacks are usually placed between the pier top and the pier segment soffit to permit the substitution of temporary bearings for the permanent neoprene pads. When the ratio between span lengths and pier height allows it, the rigid connection and corresponding frame action may be maintained permanently between the superstructure and piers.

Piers do not necessarily have to be a massive solid cross section; a box section, Figure 5.3, may be more effective and more economical. In the United States it was generally felt that a solid pier was more economical. However, for tall piers the economics of pier casting should be evaluated against the cost of the additional dead load supported by the pier shaft and transferred to the foundations. It may be desirable to precast the pier as tubular segments that are prestressed vertically to each other as well as to the foundation; this concept was used for the Linn Cove Viaduct in North Carolina and the Vail Pass structures in Colorado.

In certain cases the tubular section may be replaced by an I section, Figure 5.4. However, the low resistance to torsion of this section imposes certain precautions to limit the deformation of the cantilevering superstructure during construction, in particular with respect to the effect of wind forces.

For the case of a continuous structure on short stiff piers, the volumetric changes of the concrete (shrinkage, creep, and thermal expansion) compound the redundant effect of longitudinal prestressing to produce, by virtue of the rigidity of the

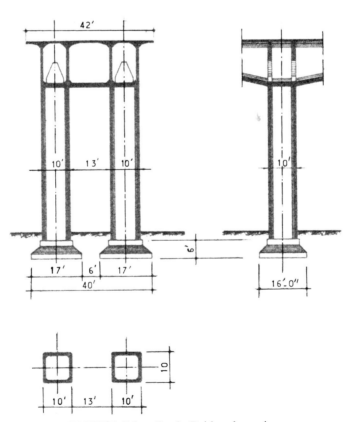

FIGURE 5.3.   Corde Bridge, box pier.

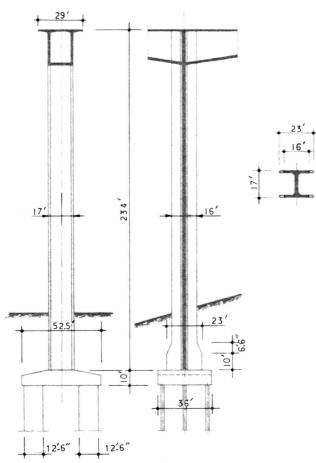

FIGURE 5.4. Pyle Bridge, I-section pier.

piers, bending forces that must be transmitted to the foundations, thus condemning the use of a rigid connection between the superstructure and its support. This disadvantage then requires the introduction of a continuous superstructure resting on a number of supports that permit the longitudinal movement of the superstructure (neoprene pads, teflon, and the like). However, it is necessary to insure the stability of the superstructure during cantilever construction. This may be accomplished as stated earlier by the use of temporary shoring in the proximity of the pier or by providing a temporary fixity at the pier.

Another solution is the use of piers with twin slender flexible legs. The transmission of horizontal loads in the direction of the longitudinal axis of the bridge is accommodated by the legs' flexibility. This type of pier offers three advantages:

1. Efficient fixity of the superstructure to the piers with regard to the vertical loads by the action of the separate supports,

2. Large flexibility in the horizontal plane (relative to the displacements parallel to the longitudinal axis of the superstructure), permitting the resolution of the problem of expansion posed by the continuous structure,

3. Stability of the superstructure during construction by a simple temporary bracing.

In the final structure, the leg flexibility is sufficient to accommodate the longitudinal braking forces.

When the geometry of the structure permits, it is more economical to incline the walls in order to reduce the bending moment transmitted to the foundation. If the legs are hinged at the superstructure and if the axes of the two legs converge near the level of the foundation, the bending moment is either canceled or minimized and the distribution into the supporting soil is essentially uniform, as for a vertical reaction, Figure 5.5. This type of structure is similar to a frame or an arch. The thrust produced by the effect of a horizontal load parallel to the longitudinal axis of the bridge is translated into a tension force on one leg, which then acts as a tie beam, and a compressive force in the other leg, which then acts as a strut. For this reason it is often necessary to prestress the legs to accommodate the tension force.

When the legs are vertical, they do not profit appreciably from the frame or arch action, and the stability is essentially contained in their bending resistance. For the case where the legs are hinged at both ends, no resistance is offered and it is neces-

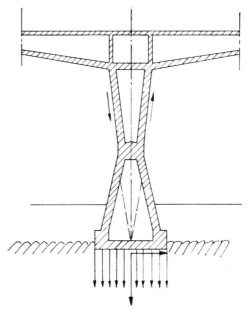

FIGURE 5.5. Piers with flexible walls.

sary to stiffen a pier to provide a fixed point in the structure.

Because of pier flexibility a careful analysis is required to assure the elastic stability of the structure. The legs supporting the superstructure are in effect very slender, and their resistance to buckling must be carefully examined. This type of pier structure will be examined in greater detail in the sections that follow.

Another family of piers that lends itself to cantilever construction is that of moment-resisting piers with a double row of neoprene bearings between the pier top and the superstructure, such as to benefit from pier rigidity during construction or in the finished structure while allowing free expansion of the continuous deck, Figure 5.6. The proper choice of dimensions for the neoprene bearings will allow control of the amount of bending transferred to the foundation; in fact, rigid piers with double neoprene bearings behave in much the same way as piers with twin flexible legs.

We see, then, that piers and foundations for cantilever concrete bridges will fall into one of the four following categories:

1. Moment-resisting piers either fixed or hinged to the superstructure.
2. Moment-resisting piers with double neoprene bearings.
3. Piers with twin flexible legs.
4. Conventional flexible piers properly strengthened during construction to resist unbalanced loading conditions.

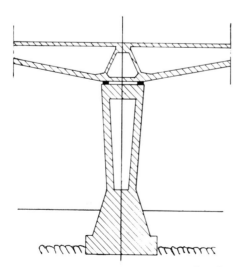

FIGURE 5.6. Piers with twin neoprene bearings.

After reviewing the loads applied to the piers and considering some suggestions pertaining to the aesthetics of piers and abutments for concrete segmental bridges, we shall deal separately with each of the four pier types. The chapter will conclude with a review of several types of abutments and the effect of unequal pier settlements on the stress in the superstructure.

5.2 Loads Applied to the Piers

All loads must be carefully considered in the design of the piers and their foundations, both in the finished structure and during its construction.

5.2.1 LOADS APPLIED TO THE FINISHED STRUCTURE

In addition to the various loading arrangements taken into account for conventional structures and used in combination as set forth in the AASHTO specifications, for example, it is necessary to include some design aspects particular to segmental cantilever construction as follows:

1. When a frame action is realized between superstructure and piers, proper transfer of moments to piers must be considered, particularly under unsymmetrical live loading. The piers are thus an integral part of the structural system and their flexibility must be first evaluated and then incorporated in the overall structural system. Figure 5.7 shows the usual parameters used to define the flexibility of a pier as the relationship between the applied loads (M, Q, and N) and the corresponding components of the deformation at the same point (θ, u, and v). The four flexibility coefficients A, B, C, and K must include all components of the pier and its foundation: soil, piles (if used), footing, pier shaft (or walls), neoprene bearings (if used). Loads and deformations are taken at the level of the deck girder neutral axis.

The deck construction scheme usually imposes special loads to the substructure. Piers adjacent to an expansion joint located at the point of contraflexure (see discussion of this aspect in Chapter 4) are subjected to appreciable bending moments due both to the relaxation of the hinge after cantilever construction and to live loading placed on either side of the hinge. Loads applied to the structure by the construction equipment result also in moment transfer in piers connected to the superstructure. Two typical cases often encountered are:

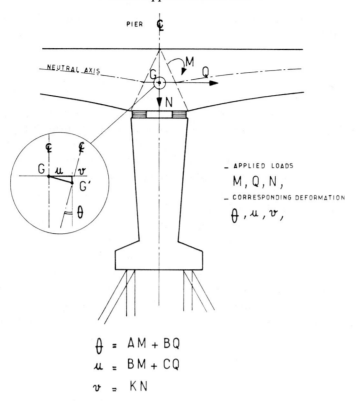

$$\theta = AM + BQ$$
$$u = BM + CQ$$
$$v = KN$$

FIGURE 5.7. Basic components of pier flexibility.

a. In precast segmental construction with segments placed with a launching gantry, the gantry leg reactions are applied to a temporary static scheme and released in another static scheme (after continuity between two adjacent cantilever arms is realized).

b. In case-in-place cantilever construction, the weight of travelers is applied to the free cantilever arms during construction but it is removed from the structure after continuity is achieved. On long spans the effect on the deck is usually beneficial, but important moments may simultaneously be induced.

2. Volume changes (shrinkage and thermal variations) and long-term shortening of materials (concrete creep and steel relaxation) both induce moments and horizontal loads in the piers, which must be included in the design.

5.2.2 *LOADS APPLIED DURING CONSTRUCTION*

Balanced cantilever construction imposes on the piers a loading configuration that is globally symmetrical. Unbalanced conditions appear, however, as a result of intermediate construction stages (normal loads due to a traveler or a segment out of balance), the application of random loads (difference between actual and computed dead loads or wind gusts), or accidental conditions (such as the fall of a traveler).

Normal Loads The most critical condition appears for one segment out of balance at the outboard end of the cantilever arm. Even in the case of cast-in-place construction with symmetrical travelers allowing simultaneous casting of both corresponding segments, the assumption of the total segment weight out of balance is a safe one, because no total guarantee can be given that concrete pouring will proceed simultaneously at either end of the cantilever. If construction equipment is designed to be installed on the deck, Figure 5.8, it

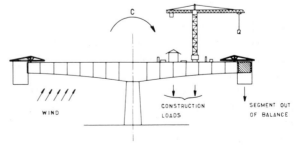

FIGURE 5.8. Loading conditions during construction.

must be accounted for in the design of the pier. For example, a tower crane is often used on one side of a cantilever.

Random Loads   Random loads essentially are such as to produce systematic geometric difference, although within acceptable tolerances. With proper workmanship and supervision, it is reasonable to assume such difference in weight at ±2%. It corresponds to a variation of top slab thickness of $\frac{3}{8}$ in. (9.5 mm) for a 40 ft (12 m) wide box with a cross-sectional area of 60 ft² (5.6 m²). However, it is very unlikely that the maximum weight decrease in one cantilever arm would appear simultaneously with the maximum weight increase in the other. It is therefore reasonable to limit the moment transferred to the pier to 2% of the maximum deck cantilever moment due to the girder weight. Other random loads related to the construction are produced by the small equipment, trucks, storage on the deck of materials such as post-tensioning tendons, and so on. An equivalent uniform load of 5 psf (24.4 kg/m²), together with a moving concentrated load of 20 k (9 mt), should be a safe allowance to cover these random loads.

Taking as an example the Houston Ship Channel Bridge, which was considered in Section 4.17, the effect of these three random loads would be:

difference in dead weight,
    1,600,000 ft-kips × 2%   32,000 ft-kips
random uniform load,
    (5 × 60)/1000 × 365²/2   20,000 ft-kips
random concentrated load,
    20 kips × 365 ft   7,000 ft-kips
                                    ─────────────
                                    59,000 ft-kips

This moment should be compared to the effect of one segment out of balance at the far end of a cantilever:

$$300 \text{ kips} \times 367 \text{ ft} = 110,000 \text{ ft-kips}$$

One last source of random loading is provided by gusts of wind that apply an uplift pressure or suction to the box girder intrados during construction. For long spans and construction sites exposed to hurricanes, it is desirable to make special aerodynamic tests. For an incident angle of 10° above the horizon, the upward pressure would be 5 psf (0.2394 MPa) during construction. This value may be substantially increased in exposed sites. For construction of the Gennevilliers Bridge, a maximum pressure of 9 psf (0.4309 MPa) was recorded in the wind-tunnel tests.

Accidental Loads   These are the result of a construction incident or of human failure, causing either the fall of a traveler in cast-in-place construction or of the lifting equipment in the case of precast construction. Such loads should be multiplied by a factor of 2, representing the impact coefficient for the case of immediate loading. It is never envisaged to consider the fall of a cast-in-place segment and traveler after casting, nor the fall of a precast segment immediately after its placement in the structure. A very long record of safety in such construction methods justifies that approach. However, in the case where the consequences of such major accident would be exceptionally disastrous (where, for example, the work takes place over a highway or a railway under operation), special provisions should be incorporated in the design and in construction procedures to double all safety features at each step of erection.

5.3   Suggestions on Aesthetics of Piers and Abutments

The problem of aesthetics is subjective and controversial. There is, however, a consensus among engineers, owners, and users that certain bridge structures are more pleasing than others. At a time when so much emphasis is being placed on protection of our environment and of nature from aggressive man-made structures, it may be helpful to review some ground rules based on experience that contribute to aesthetics of concrete bridges with very little added cost.

5.3.1   STRUCTURE LAYOUT

Generally speaking, an attempt should be made to match the structure to the environment and to preserve the existing landscape. Avoid long, high embankments at the ends of the bridge as well as long, high retaining walls that accentuate the intrusion of the new structure. Allow the number and shape of the piers to maintain a maximum of transparence. Cost optimization of superstructure span lengths will normally help to avoid serious aesthetical mistakes. It is equally disgraceful to see a heavy, long-span superstructure rampant over the ground as a multitude of closely spaced, high piers supporting a slender deck floating up in the air. The true appearance of a structure is usually not conveyed by the drawings, where often a distorted scale is used for convenience.

Finally, it is very important to keep the unity of appearance of a structure crossing different obstacles, in spite of the practical difficulties that may be entailed when project coordination involves different owners or agencies. When an overpass crosses, for example, a freeway and a parallel railroad track, nothing may be worse than to build two separate structures (probably of different height) connected by a short embankment contained at both ends by wing walls of variable height, Figure 5.9.

5.3.2 AESTHETICS OF PIERS

A significant advantage of segmental construction is to allow deck continuity, rather than simply supported structures. There is no longer a need for heavy bents protruding underneath the superstructure soffit. Piers can have simple graceful lines and be designed to receive directly the box girders of the superstructure.

Box piers of prismatic section but with curvilinear shapes improve the appearance over the conventional rectangular section. The approach piers of the Brotonne Viaduct, Figure 5.10, utilized that concept and also the piers for the Linn Cove Viaduct in North Carolina. More refined shapes may be used, such as for the river piers of the Blois Bridge, Figure 5.11, where the sculpture of the faces was designed to recall the appearance of a pier with twin inclined walls similar to that of the Juvisy Bridge, Figure 3.25. Architectural studies may be pursued further and reach beyond the immediate structural needs of the designer. An interesting example is afforded by the river piers

FIGURE 5.10. Piers for the Brotonne approach viaduct.

of the railroad bridge at Clichy near Paris, Figure 5.12.

A difficulty arises often for skewed bridges when bents include multiple pier shafts. A satisfactory solution was developed for the Paris Downstream Belt Bridge, Figure 5.13. The four columns of a river pier are given the shape of a lozenge, with one axis of symmetry matching the alignment of the superstructure while two of the four faces exactly align the four columns in the direction of the river flow.

FIGURE 5.11. Piers with architectural shapes for Blois Bridge.

FIGURE 5.9. An unacceptable example of an overpass built as two separate structures.

FIGURE 5.12. Piers for Clichy Railroad Bridge.

FIGURE 5.13. Piers for a skew bridge (Paris Ring Road).

When the piers will be seen only from a great distance, it is usually not worthwhile to call for a special treatment of the concrete faces. The eye will judge only the general shape of the structure and its overall proportions. For urban bridges the situation is very different and often justifies some architectural treatment of the piers. The river piers of the Saint Cloud Bridge were cast with a system of closely spaced vertical grooves, which greatly enhance their appearance at very little added cost, Figure 5.14.

5.3.3   *AESTHETICS OF ABUTMENTS*

At both ends, the structure has to blend with the existing landscape with a minimum of disturbance. Between the two systems of wing walls shown in Figure 5.15, the preference should strongly be with type (a), which allows a much more gradual transition between the lines of the superstructure and those of the approach embankment.

When tapered webs are used in the superstructure box girders, it has been found that the lateral wing walls in the abutments can be given the same

FIGURE 5.14. Saint Cloud Bridge. (*a*) River piers. (*b*) General view.

inclination to improve the transition between deck and abutments. Figure 5.16.

5.4   *Moment-Resisting Piers and Their Foundations*

We shall cover this topic by describing salient features of several characteristic structures.

5.4.1   *MAIN PIERS FOR THE BROTONNE VIADUCT, FRANCE*

The two main pylon piers for the Brotonne Viaduct rest on 41 ft (12.46 m) diameter cylindrical

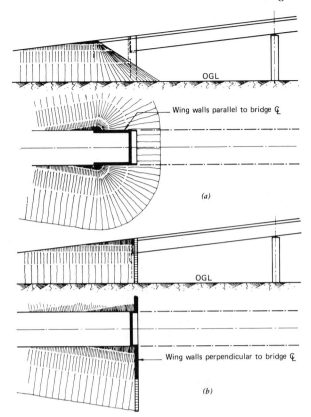

FIGURE 5.15. Wing walls and abutments.

FIGURE 5.16. Inclined wing walls in end abutment (Bordeaux St. Jean Bridge).

columns with a maximum wall thickness of 9.3 ft (2.83 m) and are 115 ft (35 m) below ground level in a limestone stratum overlain by alluvium, silt, and gravel beds. The maximum reaction at footing level is 19,000 tons. Typical dimensions of a main foundation system are shown in Figure 5.17.

It was decided to select the theoretical foundation level at 115 ft (35 m) below the original ground level, where the limestone bed had the following minimum characteristics determined from laboratory soil tests and in situ tests: angle of internal friction 20°, cohesion 5 tons/ft², and a pressure limit (on triaxial tests) of 45 tons/ft². The foundation system had to resist very large loads (both vertical and horizontal) together with important overturning moments.

The main foundation column embedded in the soil and resting on the lower limestone stratum was analyzed as a rigid body subjected to the applied loads (M, V, and H) shown in Figure 5.18 and receiving from the soil lateral reactions along the shaft and vertical reactions under the base. Values of lateral and vertical reactions were ascertained for the various soil strata and the equilibrium was determined by considering the total body to be subjected to an angle of rotation α around the in-

stantaneous center of rotation C. The coordinates of point C are the following:

Vertically, it represents the level where lateral reactions from the soil change sign (change from direct passive pressure on the front face to counterreaction at the back face).

Horizontally, it is the position of the neutral axis for the stress under the base.

The maximum loading configuration is represented numerically in Figure 5.18 along with the diagrams for:

Lateral reactions on the column

Bending moments along the column

Bearing stress under the base

If there were no lateral support, the bending moment at the base would have been 370,000 ft-kips. In fact, the actual moment is only 130,000 ft-kips,

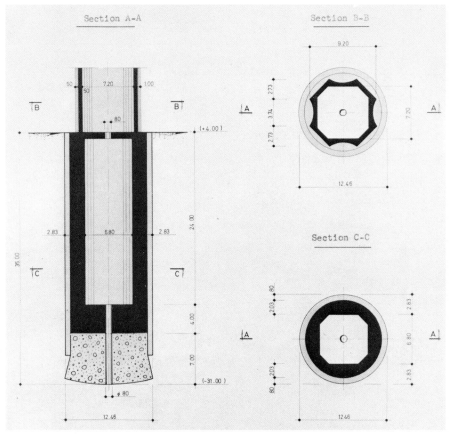

FIGURE 5.17.   Brotonne Viaduct, pylon foundations.

which explains why the extreme fiber stress is no more than 24 tons/ft² while the average bearing pressure is 14.25 tons/ft².

The actual safety factor for the foundation against soil failure is between 3 and 4, depending on the assumptions of soil characteristics.

Insofar as the construction method is concerned, each main foundation column was built in the dry inside a cofferdam made up of a continuous slurry trenched concrete wall excavated down to the limestone stratum, Figure 5.19. Grouting of the base allowed dewatering of the site after excavation to inspect the foundation material and confirmation of the actual soil characteristics by in situ soil tests. Following this inspection, the cofferdam was flooded and a tremie seal was placed at the base to prevent any risk of washing out of the footing concrete due to water seepage; the water head was above 100 ft (30 m). The reinforced concrete footing was cast in the dry above the seal and the foundation shaft was then slip-formed inside the cofferdam. The pier shaft was given the shape of an octagon with curvilinear sides for aesthetic reasons. The general dimensions of the foundation shaft and of the pier shaft allowed a very natural and direct transfer of loads at ground level with no need for a heavily reinforced footing. The construction of both foundations went very satisfactorily. The only incident was created by the fact that one panel of the cofferdam in the south pier was excavated out of plumb at its lower end. Consequently, the continuity of the horizontal ring to resist the hydrostatic pressure was not realized at the lower part of the cofferdam. Grouting of the surrounding soil was achieved in this area and an additional reinforced concrete ring was cast inside before the completion of excavation and final dewatering.

Regular survey measurements at the site have shown that settlements of both pier foundations have been very minimal and are now stabilized.

5.4.2   PIERS AND FOUNDATIONS FOR THE SALLINGSUND BRIDGE, DENMARK

The substructure and piers of this structure present an interesting construction methodology and use of materials, Figures 3.89 and 5.20. The piles are steel tubes, which are concreted after driving. Their length is about 98 ft (30 m), the diameter is

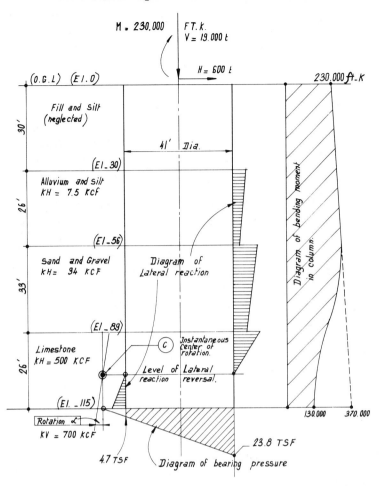

FIGURE 5.18. Brotonne Viaduct, loads and soil reactions on column of main foundations.

$27\frac{1}{2}$ in. (700 mm) and the wall thickness is about 0.4 in. (10 mm). Each pier has 24 piles. The first piles driven are tested in compression and tension be-

FIGURE 5.19. Brotonne Viaduct, view of pier excavation.

fore the remaining piles are driven. When the driving is accomplished, the template trough is filled with tremie concrete around the pile tops up to the upper edge of the template.

The template is precast at a plant located in the harbor. It is shaped like a circular slab surrounded by an annular trough, in which there are holes for the piles. The template is transported to the pier locations by the floating crane and lowered down to rest on three temporary vertical piles. The bottom is about 52.5 ft (16 m) below the water level. For an exact positioning in its submerged position, it is provided with an alignment tower, the top of which is always above water, Figure 5.21.

The pier box, shaped like a truncated cone approximately 39.3 ft (12 m) high, is precast in three lifts at the precasting plant in the harbor. First its lower part is cast on staging above water. During the following lifts it is progressively sunk. Since after the third stage it is too heavy to be lifted by the floating crane, it is provided with a lid, and com-

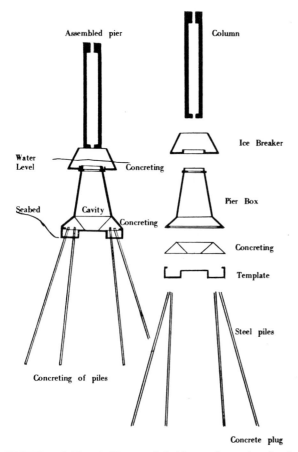

FIGURE 5.20. Sallingsund Bridge, schematic of substructure.

pressed air is pumped into the cavity. The floating crane then transports the pier box to the pier location and lowers it down to rest on the template. A reinforced concrete ring structure is made by connecting the pile tops to the pier box by reinforcing and concreting the space between them, Figure 5.21.

The icebreaker's shell is a reinforced concrete box, precast at the harbor site, Figure 5.22, transported to the pier location by means of the floating crane and placed on top of the pier box. Its top is then 8.2 ft (2.5 m) above and its bottom 8.2 ft (2.5 m) below the water level. When the box is in place, the water in the cavity of the pier box and the icebreaker box is pumped out. Next, the piles are filled with concrete and the pile tops and the lower part of the pier box are cast together. Finally the cavity of the icebreaker is filled with concrete. A schematic sequence of operations in constructing the substructure is shown in Figure 5.21.

Piers are cast in place in lifts 10 ft (3 m) high by means of climbing forms and are hexagonal, Fig-

ure 5.23. The finished bridge is shown in Figure 5.24.

5.4.3 CONCEPT OF PRECAST BELL PIER FOUNDATION FOR THE I-205 COLUMBIA RIVER BRIDGE, U.S.A.

A somewhat comparable system to that used for the Sallingsund Bridge was contemplated for approach spans 15 through 26 of the I-205 Columbia River Bridge in the State of Oregon, as shown schematically in Figures 5.25 and 5.26. Steel H piles of 200 ton capacity were to be driven through a template box, allowing tremie concrete to be placed inside the trough. The precast segments were designed to be stacked upon one another above the template to make up the pier shaft and transfer the superstructure load to the piles.

This scheme was not actually used, as the contractor decided on a more conventional method of construction. However, the scheme of precast bell pier foundations was used on the Richmond-San Rafael Bridge and the San Mateo-Hayward Bridge, both in San Francisco Bay, and the Columbia River Bridge at Astoria, Oregon. A comprehensive discussion of these structures is presented by Gerwick in reference 3.

5.4.4 MAIN PIERS FOR THE HOUSTON SHIP CHANNEL BRIDGE, U.S.A.

Each main channel pier, Figure 5.27, is made up of the following:

A rectangular shaft 161 ft (49 m) high with a cross section varying in dimensions from 20 × 38 ft (6.10 × 11.60 m) at the base to 20 × 28 ft (6.10 × 8.50 m) at the top. The section is a single-cell box with wall thicknesses of 2 ft (0.61 m).

A reinforced concrete footing 75 × 81 × 15 ft (22.90 × 24.70 × 4.60 m).

A group of two hundred and twenty-five 24 in. (0.61 m) diameter steel pipe piles having a wall thickness of $\frac{1}{2}$ in. (12.7 mm).

The superstructure is completely integral with the two main channel piers to form a rigid frame, both during construction and in the finished structure, Figures 1.67 and 2.80.

Stresses in the concrete and reinforcing steel were analyzed in both stages with the service-load design approach, and ultimate strength was verified by the load-factor method. The analysis is

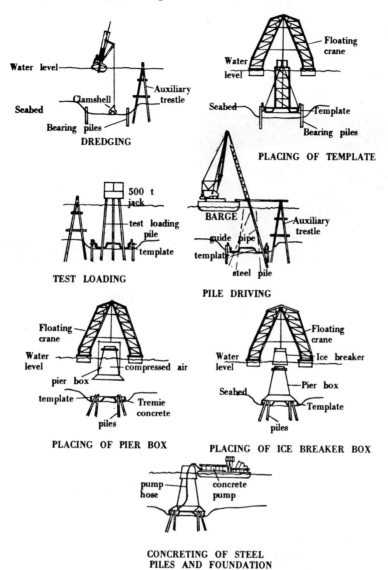

FIGURE 5.21. Sallingsund Bridge, schematic of substructure operations.

rather strenuous, because in the completed structure only there were 19 unit loads combined into 37 load combinations for service-load design and into 42 loading combinations for load-factor design.

The concrete cross-sectional area together with the corresponding reinforcing steel area is as follows:

top: $A_c = 176$ ft^2,
       $A_s = 200$ no. 11 bars $= 297$ in.^{2},
       $p = 1.17\%$

bottom: $A_c = 216$ ft^2,
        $A_s = 264$ no. 11 bars $= 392$ in.^{2},
        $p = 1.26\%$

Under service load the average concrete stress of the cross section is as follows:

top: 31,700 kips $\div$ 176 ft^2 = 180 kips/ft^2
bottom: 36,600 kips $\div$ 216 ft^2 = 170 kips/ft^2

In large structures, such as the Houston Ship Channel Bridge, the average concrete stress in the pier shafts usually varies between 160 and 200 kips/ft^2. The use of a varying-width pier in the transverse direction allows the maximum stress and the required amount of reinforcing steel to increase at a slow rate with the pier height, while a prismatic pier shaft will be subjected to a very critical stress at the base.

FIGURE 5.22.   Sallingsund Bridge, aerial view of pre-cast yard and harbor for substructure construction.

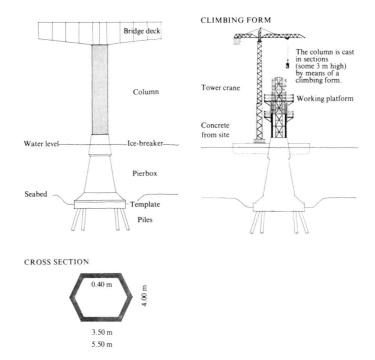

CROSS SECTION

0.40 m
4.00 m
3.50 m
5.50 m

FIGURE 5.23.   Sallingsund Bridge, schematic of pier construction.

FIGURE 5.24.   Sallingsund Bridge, view of finished bridge.

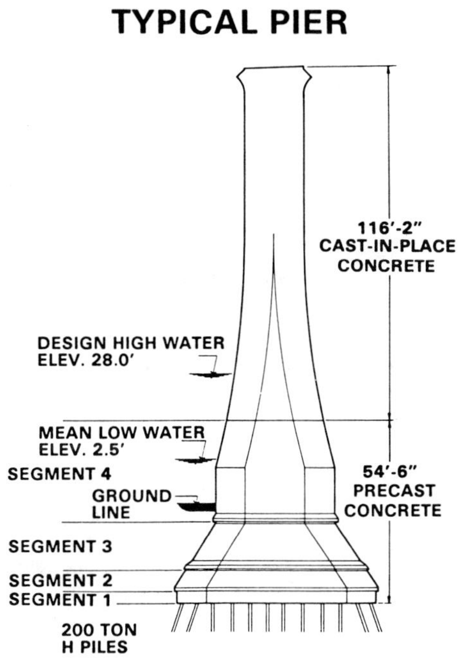

TYPICAL PIER
116'-2"
CAST-IN-PLACE
CONCRETE
DESIGN HIGH WATER
ELEV. 28.0'
MEAN LOW WATER
ELEV. 2.5'
SEGMENT 4
GROUND
LINE
54'-6"
PRECAST
CONCRETE
SEGMENT 3
SEGMENT 2
SEGMENT 1
200 TON
H PILES

FIGURE 5.25. I-205 Columbia River Bridge, main piers and foundations.

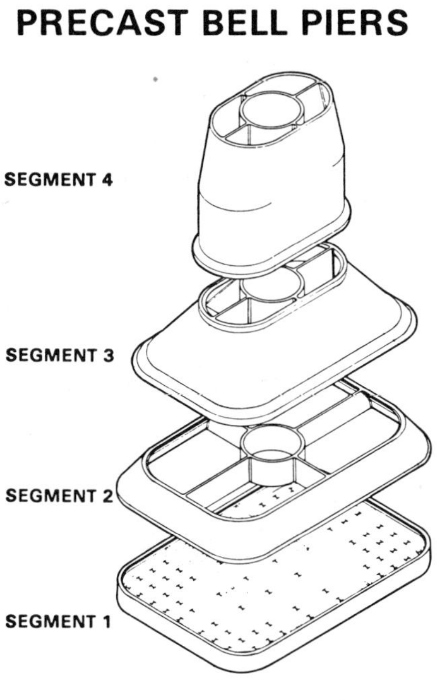

PRECAST BELL PIERS
SEGMENT 4
SEGMENT 3
SEGMENT 2
SEGMENT 1

FIGURE 5.26. I-205 Columbia River Bridge, schematic of construction of precast bell piers.

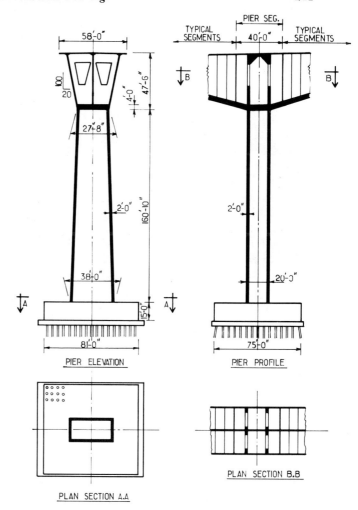

58'-0"
47'-6"
4'-0"
27'-8"
2'-0"
160'-10"
38'-0"
15'-0"
81'-0"
PIER ELEVATION
PIER SEG.
TYPICAL
SEGMENTS
40'-0"
TYPICAL
SEGMENTS
2'-0"
20'-0"
75'-0"
PIER PROFILE
PLAN SECTION A.A
PLAN SECTION B.B

FIGURE 5.27. Houston Ship Channel Bridge, main river piers.

5.5 Piers with Double Elastomeric Bearings

5.5.1 SCOPE AND GENERAL CONSIDERATIONS

Recognizing the inherent advantages of a rigid connection between piers and superstructure (stability during construction and increased superstructure stiffness reducing the effect of live load), the designer is rapidly limited in its use in long bridges because of unacceptable effects of volume changes. This situation allowed the birth of a new type of structure developed to maintain the two desirable features that were previously contradictory: flexural rigidity on one hand and horizontal flexibility on the other. The concept of the double row of elastomeric bearings was first developed for the Oleron Viaduct and used thereafter on a great many bridges.

With piers of this type, two observations are required concerning the transfer of forces between the superstructure and pier. The first observation concerns the transfer of service loads, Figure 5.28a. Under the effect of unsymmetrical loads, the upper and lower flanges of the superstructure are respectively subjected to unequal tension forces T_L and T_R and compressive forces C_L and C_R. If a vertical diaphragm is positioned over each of the two rows of bearings, the center portion of the top flange of the pier segment, to be in equilibrium, must accept the tension force $T_L - T_R$. This is not a satisfactory disposition, as the thickness of the flange and amount of reinforcing have to be increased between the two rows of bearings, and there is the risk of cracking.

However, if the two diaphragms are inclined and converge at the level of the top flange, the differential in tension, $T_L - T_R$, is divided into two components of force, C (compression) and T (tension), directed into the plane of the diaphragm, while the tension force may be accommodated by prestressing the diagonal bracings.

Another important aspect of the pier segment design relates to the imbalanced loading condition resulting at the bottom flange from the unequal reactions R_1 and R_2 of the bearings, which calls for careful analysis of the stress developing in the diagonal bracings in all loading stages of the structure.

The second observation concerns the superstructure-pier connection during the temporary phase of constructing the superstructure in cantilever, Figure 5.28b. To accommodate a moment unbalance resulting from the construction procedure, the pier segment is supported on four temporary bearings of steel or concrete, ①, and temporarily fixed by prestressing to the top of the pier, ②. After closure at midspan occurs, producing a continuous span, the joint is "unlocked" by releasing the prestressing. Flat jacks, ③, are then activated so as to substitute permanent bearings for the temporary bearings.

5.5.2 DESCRIPTION OF STRUCTURES

Many structures have been designed and built utilizing the system of piers incorporating a double row of neoprene bearings. This section will describe the salient features of three particular bridges as exemplifying the advantages of this system as used in connection with a variety of foundation schemes.

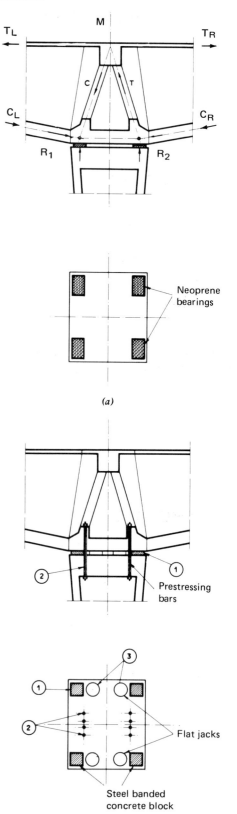

FIGURE 5.28. Connection of superstructure and pier. (a) In service. (b) In temporary construction phase.

Oleron Viaduct, France

Of the 45 piers, only the 27 piers supporting the center portion of the viaduct with span lengths of 260 ft (79 m) are designed with a double row of bearings. In this portion of the viaduct there is an expansion joint every fourth span, and the elastomeric bearings had to accommodate the volume changes of the deck in a maximum distance of three spans (i.e., 780 ft or 237 m). Out of these 27 piers equipped with a double row of bearings, 12 are founded on spread footings constructed directly on limestone rock inside a temporary sheet pile cofferdam, Figure 5.29. The other 15 piers are supported by a system of pipe piles driven to the limestone, which in this area is at a depth of 75 ft (23 m) below mean water level, Figure 5.30.

The 12 piles in each pier consist of four vertical piles, one at each corner, and eight battered piles, so inclined as to resist the horizontal loads (longitudinal and transverse) applied to the structure. For the most critical loading combination (comparable to the AASHTO requirements) the maximum load in a pile is 330 t (300 mt), which should be reduced to compare to American practice by a factor of 1.33. The comparable design load would then be 250 t (230 mt) for a pipe pile 20 in. (500 mm) in diameter with a thickness of $\frac{1}{2}$ in. (12.7 mm) driven to refusal in the rock and filled with concrete after driving. The corresponding steel stress of the pipe alone would be 16 ksi (110 MPa), a somewhat higher value than normally used in similar circumstances. When considering the global section of concrete and steel, the stress in the concrete is only 800 psi (5.5 MPa)—a very reasonable value, confirmed by the fact that none of the 15 piers showed any sign of settlement during the fifteen years of operation of this viaduct. The pipe piles were driven open-ended and excavated inside by a homemade airlift system conceived by the driving subcontractor. It took only a few minutes to perform this operation on each pile.

For the piers on piles, a tremie seal was used inside the cofferdam to allow dewatering and construction of the reinforced concrete footing poured in the dry.

All box pier shafts were slip-formed to a maximum height of 82 ft (25 m) at the rate of 15 to 20 ft (4.5 to 6 m) a day, and the construction of a shaft took approximately one week, Figure 5.31.

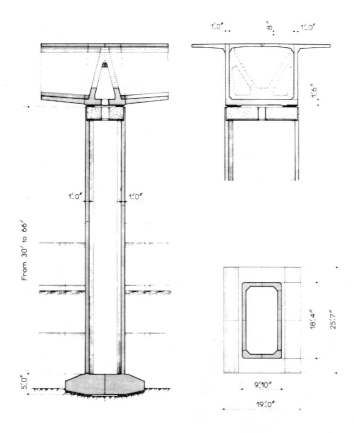

FIGURE 5.29. Oleron Viaduct, piers on spread footings.

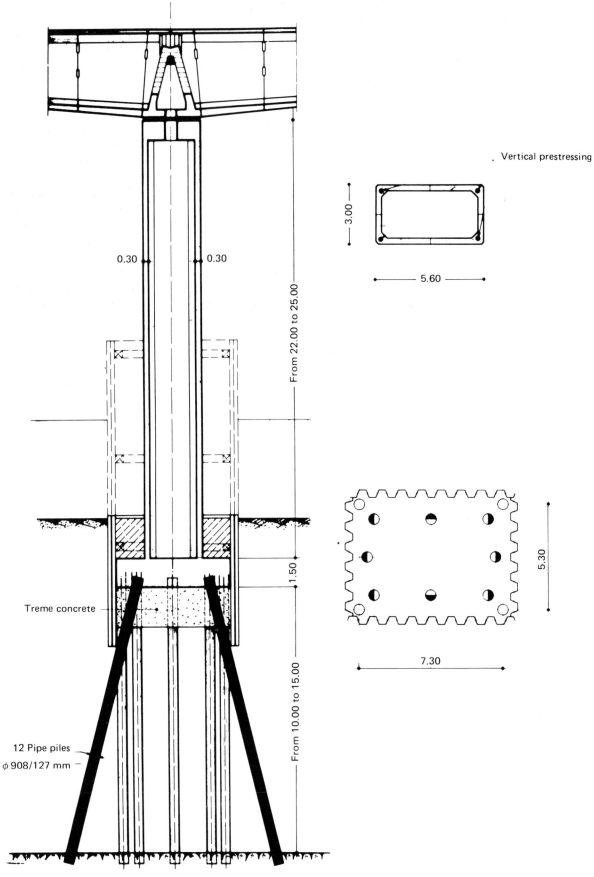

Vertical prestressing

0.30   0.30

3.00

5.60

From 22.00 to 25.00

1.50

Treme concrete

From 10.00 to 15.00

12 Pipe piles
ϕ 908/127 mm

5.30

7.30

FIGURE 5.30. Oleron Viaduct, piers on piles.

FIGURE 5.31. Oleron Viaduct, aerial view of foundations.

Blois Bridge, France

The Blois Bridge crossing the Loire River is a five-span, prestressed, precast concrete segmental superstructure consisting of twin box girders with the following span dimensions: 202, three at 300, 202 ft (61, three at 91, 61 m). It is supported by four river piers elastically restrained at the superstructure with a double row of bearings. Dimensions of a typical pier are given in Figure 5.32 and a view of a finished pier in Figure 5.11.

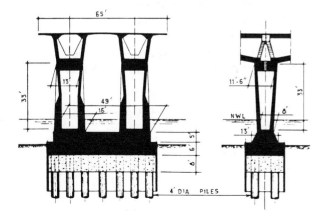

FIGURE 5.32. Blois Bridge, dimensions of river piers.

The special feature of this project is that a very comprehensive optimization study of the substructure system with a double row of bearings allowed the use of only half as many piles as the basic scheme with single bearings, without increasing the unit bearing capacity of the piles.

Upstream Paris Belt Bridge, France

This important bridge was built over the Seine River to carry Europe's most heavily traveled urban freeway, the Paris Beltway. As shown in a longitudinal section, Figure 3.22, it has two major river piers resting on a unique foundation system, while land piers and abutments are conventionally founded on piles.

A typical transverse section of the bridge shows the orientation of the piers, Figure 5.33, and various cross sections through the piers is shown in Figure 5.34. Each of the twin bridges carries four lanes of traffic on two box girders, which are supported on two separate pier shafts connected below water by a single footing. Two lower foundation shafts extend under this footing to a maximum depth of 70 ft (21 m) to carry the bridge loads to the supporting soil strata through a series of heterogeneous seams of silt, fine sand, and clay.

Each of these lower shafts (there are eight such shafts for the two river piers) was built inside a rectangular steel sheet pile cofferdam, driven as low as possible before excavation. The shafts were extended below the tip of the sheet piles to reach the load-bearing soil by incremental stages of excavation and continuous concrete lining, Figure 5.35. Cement grouting and temporary lowering of the aquifer by pumping allowed this work to be performed in the dry. Except for the minor blowout in one of the eight shafts, which called for special grouting work, the foundation project was performed safely and successfully. Figure 5.36 shows one of the river piers completed and receiving the precast pier segment of the superstructure.

5.5.3 PROPERTIES OF NEOPRENE BEARINGS

Notation

A neoprene bearing may be designated by the following physical parameters, Figure 5.37a:

a and b = plan dimensions of bearing ($a < b$)
n = number of elastomer sheets
t = thickness of one elastomer sheet
$2e$ = thickness of the internal steel sheet (twice the external sheet)
$A_b = a \cdot b$ = area of bearing

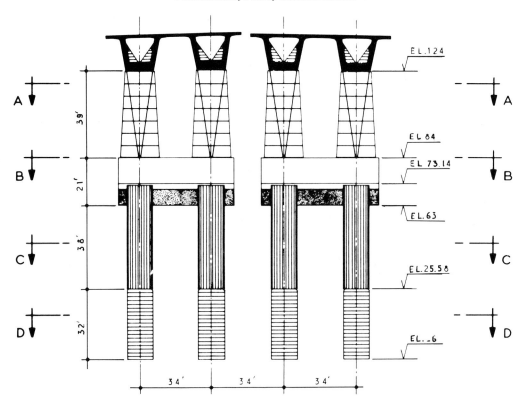

FIGURE 5.33. Upstream Paris Belt Bridge, typical elevation of river piers.

An example, with dimensions in millimeters, is as follows:

$$a \times b \times n(t + 2e)$$
$$300 \times 400 \times 2(10 + 2)$$

Where differing thickness of steel plates are used, the successive thicknesses of steel and elastomer are given:

$$a \times b \times n(\qquad)$$
$$300 \times 400 \times 2(5 + 8 + 2 + 8 + 1)$$

Deformation of Neoprene Bearings

The relationship between Young's modulus (E) and the shear modulus (G) is presented in Table 5.1. The shear modulus, G, of neoprene varies not

TABLE 5.1. Elastic Constants

Hardness (IRHD ± 4)	Young's Modulus E (N/mm^2)	Shear Modulus G (N/mm^2)
45	1.80	0.54
50	2.20	0.64
55	3.25	0.81
60	4.45	1.06
65	5.85	1.37

only with the material hardness, as indicated in Table 5.1, but also with the rate of loading. Tabulated values are for the case of slow loading; for an instantaneous loading the value of G is doubled.

Vertical Deformation (Compression) Under a normal force V every lamination is subjected to a vertical shortening, v, Figure 5.37b, such that:

$$v = C \frac{t^3}{GA_b a^2} V$$

C is a coefficient that depends on the plan dimensions of the bearing and that expresses the restraint effect on the lamination by the steel plate; refer to Table 5.2.

For a bearing consisting of n stacks or laminations, the value of the shortening is equal to:

$$v = C \frac{nt^3}{GA_b a^2} V \qquad (5\text{-}1)$$

Rotational Deformation Under a bending moment M the upper face of each lamination undergoes a rotation θ relative to the lower face:

$$\theta = C' \frac{t^3}{GA_b a^2} M$$

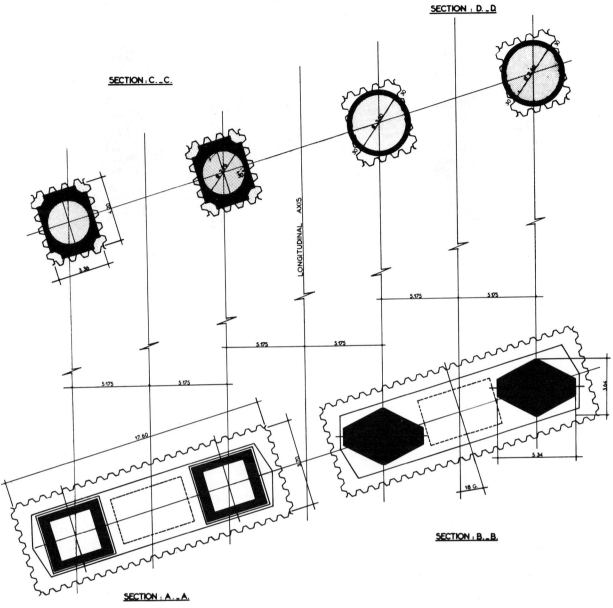

FIGURE 5.34. Upstream Paris Belt Bridge, typical horizontal sections of river piers.

C' is a coefficient that depends on the plan dimensions of the bearing and that expresses the restraint effect on the laminations by the steel plate; refer to Table 5.3. The value a is the dimension in plan of the bearing measured perpendicular to the axis of rotation, Figure 5.37b.

TABLE 5.2. Values of the Coefficient C

b/a	0.5	0.6	0.7	0.75	0.8	0.9	1.0	1.2	1.4	1.5	2	3	4	5	10	∞
C	5.83	4.44	3.59	3.28	3.03	2.65	2.37	2.01	1.78	1.70	1.46	1.27	1.18	1.15	1.07	1

TABLE 5.3. Values of the Coefficient C'

b/a	0.5	0.6	0.7	0.75	0.8	0.9	1.0	1.2	1.4	1.5	2	3	4	5	10	∞
C'	136.7	116.7	104.4	100.0	96.2	90.4	86.2	80.4	76.7	75.3	70.8	66.8	64.9	63.9	61.9	60

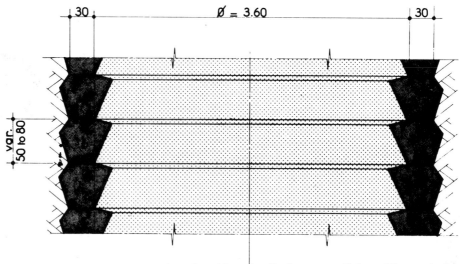

FIGURE 5.35.   Upstream Paris Belt Bridge, detail of concrete lining of lower shafts.

FIGURE 5.36.   Upstream Paris Belt Bridge, view of a finished pier.

For a bearing consisting of n stacks or laminations, the value of the rotation is equal to:

$$\theta = C' \frac{nt^3}{GA_b a^4} M \qquad (5\text{-}2)$$

Horizontal Deformation (Distortion)   Under a horizontal force, Q, the upper face of each lamination, relative to the lower face, undergoes a horizontal displacement u:

$$u = \frac{t}{GA_b} Q$$

with a corresponding distortion u/t.

For a bearing consisting of n stacks or laminations, the value of the horizontal displacement is equal to:

$$U = \frac{nt}{GA_b} Q \qquad (5\text{-}3)$$

5.5.4   DEFORMATION OF PIERS WITH A DOUBLE ROW OF NEOPRENE BEARINGS

In structures where deck and piers are rigidly fixed, it is necessary to analyze accurately the deformation of the various piers to incorporate their proper stiffness into the model of the total structure. This is particularly important for unsymmetrical live loading applied to one pier and for the effect of volume changes. There is a relationship between the loads applied at the top of one pier (usually at the level of the neutral axis of the deck over the pier) and the corresponding displacements at the same point that depends solely upon the mechanical properties of the pier and its foun-

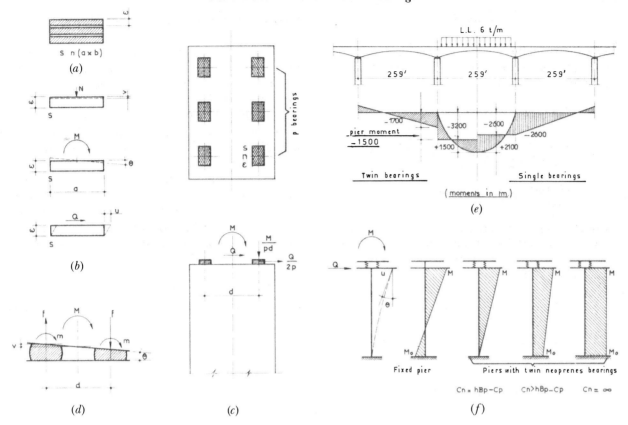

FIGURE 5.37. Piers with double row neoprene bearings (Oleron Viaduct). The most widely used polychloroprene is Neoprene (trademark of Du Pont de Nemours).

dation, Figure 5.7. The elasticity coefficients A, B, C, and K may be computed from the material properties and dimensions of the pier.

For example, a pier with constant section and the following properties:

Height h, area of cross section A_p

Moment of inertia I

Modulus of elasticity E

assumed to be fixed at the base onto a totally rigid foundation, has the following elasticity coefficients:

$$A = \frac{h}{EI}, \qquad B = \frac{h^2}{2EI}, \qquad C = \frac{h^3}{3EI},$$

$$K = A - \frac{B^2}{C} = \frac{h}{4EI}$$

In structures where neoprene bearings are placed between piers and deck, the corresponding change in elasticity of the system must be taken into account. In fact, the presence of two rows of neoprene bearings, spaced at a distance d, pro-

duces a partial fixity of the superstructure on the piers. The neoprene bearings intervene in the deformation of the pier by their normal force ($\pm M/pd$) produced by the moment M, Figure 5.37c. The rotational stiffness of the neoprene bearings may be neglected.

The moment M applied at the top of the pier may be divided into components f and m in the bearings, Figure 5.37d, such that:

$$M = fd + 2m, \qquad \theta = 2v/d$$

with:

$$m = \frac{GA_b pa^4}{C'nt^3}\,\theta$$

$$f = \frac{GA_b pa^2}{Cnt^3}\,v$$

from which:

$$M = \frac{pGA_b a^2}{nt^3}\left(\frac{d^2}{2C} + \frac{2a^2}{C'}\right)\theta$$

In the majority of cases the quantity $2a^2/C'$ is small relative to $d^2/2C$.

Example

Dimensions of the neoprene bearing: 600×600 mm. Spacing between the axes of the neoprene bearings: $d = 2.4$ m.

$$\frac{b}{a} = 1, \qquad C = 2.37, \qquad C' = 86.2$$

$$M = \frac{pGA_b a^2}{nt^3} \left(\frac{\overline{2.4^2}}{2 \times 2.37} + \frac{2 \times \overline{0.6^2}}{86.2} \right) \theta$$

$$= \frac{pGA_b a^2}{nt^3} (1.215 + 0.008)\theta$$

In neglecting the second term in the parenthesis, in other words the rotational stiffness of the neoprene, it can be seen that the error is slight, of the order of 1%. Therefore:

$$\theta = \frac{2nCt^3}{pGA_b a^2 d^2} M$$

Accordingly, the flexibility coefficients of the neoprene bearings may be written as:

$$A_n = C \frac{2n}{pd^2} \frac{t^3}{GA_b a^2}$$

$$B_n = 0 \qquad\qquad (5\text{-}4)$$

$$C_n = \frac{n}{2p} \frac{t}{GA_b}$$

$$K_n = \frac{n}{2p} \frac{t}{EA_b}$$

where p represents the number of neoprene bearings per row. Therefore, if the flexibility coefficients of the pier shaft are denoted by A_p, B_p, C_p, and K_p, the total flexibility coefficient may be defined as:

$$A = A_p + A_n$$

$$B = B_p$$

$$C = C_p + C_n$$

$$K = K_p + K_n$$

5.5.5 PROPERTIES OF PIERS WITH A DOUBLE ROW OF NEOPRENE BEARINGS

Piers with a double row of neoprene bearings have properties similar to those of piers with flexible legs, by insuring an effective fixity for loads while allowing the free expansion of the superstructure.

This fixity presents the advantage of reducing the bending moments in the spans without much increase of the moment in the bearings, Figure 5.37e.

During construction of the superstructure by cantilevering, stability in the temporary construction phase may be provided by the substitution of concrete pads for the neoprene bearings and the use of a temporary vertical prestressing.

By a judicious choice of neoprene thickness, it is possible to reduce the bending moments applied to the foundation. Consider a pier with a double row of neoprene bearings supporting a continuous superstructure. For a bending moment M at the top of the pier, under the effect of a loading in the superstructure with no horizontal displacement, the bending moment transmitted to the base of the pier is (Figure 5.37f):

$$M' = M + Qh$$

where h represents the height of the pier. Because $u = 0$, one may write:

$$BM + CQ = 0$$

from which:

$$Q = -\frac{BM}{C}$$

and

$$M' = \left(1 - \frac{Bh}{C} \right) M = \left(1 - \frac{B_p h}{C_p + C_n} \right) M = \phi M$$

The value of the coefficient ϕ varies with the thickness of neoprene pads. If it is desired to transfer no moment to the foundation at the level of the pier base, $M' = 0$, the transfer coefficient ϕ must be equal to 0, from which:

$$C_n = hB_p - C_p \qquad\qquad (5\text{-}5)$$

On the other hand if the neoprene thickness becomes very large, the value of ϕ tends to the limiting value of 1 and the bending moment remains constant in the pier; that is, $M' = M$, Figure 5.37f.

As an example, consider a pier with a constant moment of inertia, fixed at its base, with a double row of neoprene bearings and supporting a maximum reaction of 1000 tons.

Pier characteristics: Assume a box section with external dimensions of 5.0×3.0 m and a wall thickness of 0.30 m, $h = 33$ m, $I = 7$ m^4:

$$EA_p = \frac{h}{I} = 4.71$$

$$EB_p = \frac{h^2}{2I} = 77.7$$

$$EC_p = \frac{h^3}{3I} = 1715$$

Four neoprene bearings are arranged in two rows at a spacing of 2.4 m in the longitudinal direction of the bridge. Dimensions of each bearing are 600 × 400 × 3(12 + 2) (see Section 5.5.3).

Flexibility of the neoprene bearing: $a = 0.40$ m, $b/a = 1.5$, $C = 1.7$, $A_b = 0.24$ m^2, $n = 3$, $p = 2$, $t = 1.2 \times 10^{-2}$ m, $G = 160$ t/m^2, $E_c = 3.9 \times 10^6$ t/m^2:

$$EA_n = EC \frac{2n}{pd^2} \frac{t^3}{GA_b a^2} = 0.97$$

$$EB_n = 0$$

$$EC_n = E \frac{nt}{2pGA_b} = 915$$

Total flexibility of the pier:

$$EA = 4.71 + 0.97 = 5.68$$

$$EB = 77.7$$

$$EC = 1717 + 915 = 2630$$

Elasticity of the pier in the structure:

$$EK = E\left(A - \frac{B^2}{C}\right) = 5.68 - \frac{(77.7)^2}{2630} = 3.38$$

Elasticity of the pier without neoprene:

$$EK = E\left(A - \frac{B^2}{C}\right) = 0.25 \frac{h}{I} = 1.18$$

Coefficient of moment transmission in the pier:

$$\phi = 1 - \frac{Bh}{C} = 1 - \frac{77.7 \times 33}{2630} = +0.03$$

The bending moment M' transmitted to the base of the pier is very small (3% of M). For the moment M' to be theoretically equal to zero:

$$EC_n = \frac{EC_p}{2} = 860$$

and the corresponding thickness of neoprene is then:

$$EC_n = \frac{n}{2p} \frac{t}{GA_b} E$$

or

$$nt = \frac{2(EC_n)pGA_b}{E}$$

$$= \frac{2 \times 860 \times 2 \times 160 \times 0.24}{3.9 \times 10^6} = 0.034 \text{ m}$$

$$nt = 34 \text{ mm}$$

A comparison of the constants A, B, C, and K with the number of neoprene laminations (for this example) is presented in Table 5.4. If the height of pier were changed from 33 m to 20 m, the total neoprene thickness would correspondingly change from 34 mm to 8 mm.

5.5.6 INFLUENCE OF THICKNESS AND ARRANGEMENT OF NEOPRENE BEARINGS ON THE VARIATION OF FORCE IN A THREE-SPAN STRUCTURE

In order to better understand the influence of the thickness of neoprene pads, studies have been conducted to determine the variation of the bending moment in a three-span continuous structure when only the number of neoprene laminations at the top of the intermediate piers is modified.

The structure considered is a symmetric superstructure of three continuous spans supported on two identical piers; it consists of a box girder with a variable moment of inertia, whose spans are 44 m, 70 m, and 44 m.

Bending moments in the superstructure and piers are calculated under the following assumptions:

Superstructure fixed at the pier

Superstructure partially fixed elastically at the piers with neoprene bearings with the varying lamina of 1, 2, 3, 6, or 9 (thickness 12 mm)

Superstructure supported on the piers by simple supports

Assumptions used in the conduct of the study are:

Superimposed dead load represented by a uniform load, $q = 1.9$ t/m

Expansion of the deck at a rate of 2×10^{-4}, corresponding to an increase in temperature of 20°C.

Shrinkage of the deck at a rate of 4×10^{-4}, corresponding to a decrease of temperature of 20°C combined with the effect of shortening and time-dependent deformations (creep) resulting from prestressing (2×10^{-4}).

TABLE 5.4.

Coefficient	Number of Neoprene Lamina					
	0	1	2	3	4	5
EA	4.71	5.03	5.36	5.68	6.00	6.33
EB	77.7	77.7	77.7	77.7	77.7	77.7
EC	1715	2020	2325	2630	2935	3240
$EK = E\left(A - \dfrac{B^2}{C}\right)$	1.18	2.03	2.76	3.38	3.93	4.46
$\phi = \dfrac{M_0}{M}$	-0.50	-0.27	-0.10	$+0.03$	$+0.13$	$+0.21$
Diagram of bending moment in the pier ($h = 33$ m) (top)	$+1.00$	$+1.00$	$+1.00$	$+1.00$	$+1.00$	$+1.00$
(bottom)	-0.50	-0.27	-0.10	$+0.03$	$+0.13$	$+0.21$
Diagram of bending moment in the pier ($h = 20$ m) (top)	$EK = 0.71$			$EK = 3.19$		
(bottom)	-0.50	$+0.17$	$+0.42$	$+0.56$	$+0.64$	$+0.70$

Applied load $S_2 = 4.5$ t/m in the center span

Applied load $S_1 = 6.8$ t/m in the end spans

Braking force $F = 15$ t on the superstructure, corresponding to approximately one-twentieth of the structure dead load

The bending moments in the superstructure as a result of the above loads are tabulated in Tables 5.5a through 5.5c:

Table 5.5a: bending moment at the top of the pier

Table 5.5b: bending moment at the base of the pier

Table 5.5c: maximum bending moments in the superstructure

This study leads us to the following observations:

1. Regarding the superstructure, the maximum moments vary little with the number of neoprene laminations. When the number of laminations increases from one to six, the maximum bending moment at the support decreases by 4% and the maximum positive moment in the center span increases by 10%. The extreme case of nine lamina is to be avoided because of risk of instability presented by the tall stack of neoprene ($a/nt < 5$). Compared with a simple bearing support, the double row of bearings provides an important decrease in moment in the spans for a relatively smaller increase of moment at the pier support.

2. Regarding the pier, there exists an optimum thickness of neoprene allowing a minimal transfer of moment to the level of the foundations. In the example considered this thickness is equal to three lamina of 12 mm, which corresponds closely to the value determined in Section 5.5.4 for the case of a structure restrained horizontally.

TABLE 5.5a. **Bending Moment at the Top of the Pier as Function of the Bearing Thickness**[a]

Loading	0 (Fixed Pier)	1	2	3	6	9
		Number of Neoprene Lamina				
Superstructure D.L., $q = 1.9$ t/m	+ 124	+ 106	+ 93	+ 84	+ 68	+ 58
Deck expansion, $+2 \times 10^{-4}$	+ 92	+ 68	+ 53	+ 43	+ 27	+ 19
Deck shrinkage, -4×10^{-4}	− 184	− 36	− 106	− 86	− 54	− 38
Σ moments (no L.L.) +M	+ 216	+ 174	+ 146	+ 127	+ 95	+ 77
−M	− 60	− 30	− 13	− 2	+ 6	+ 20
L.L in center span, $S_2 = 4.5$ t/m	+1700	+1440	+1270	+1150	+ 930	+790
L.L. in end spans, $S_1 = 6.8$ t/m	−1420	−1240	−1120	−1030	− 850	−740
Braking force, $F = 15$ t	± 101	± 97	± 93	± 90	± 80	± 74
Maximum moments +M	+2017	+1711	+1059	+1367	+1105	+941
−M	−1581	−1367	−1226	−1122	− 924	−795

[a] Values have been calculated at the intersection of the axis of the pier with the center of gravity of the superstructure.

TABLE 5.5b. **Bending Moment at the Base of the Pier as Function of the Bearing Thickness**

Loading	0 (Fixed Pier)	1	2	3	6	9	Simple Support, $t = 24$ mm
		Number of Neoprene Lamina					
Superstructure D.L., $q = 1.9$ t/m	− 62	− 31	− 15	− 4	+ 13	+ 20	0
Deck expansion $+2 \times 10^{-4}$	− 202	−157	−129	−111	− 77	− 60	−130
Deck shrinkage -4×10^{-4}	+ 404	+314	+258	+222	+154	+120	+260
Σ moments (no L.L.) +M	+ 342	+283	+243	+218	+167	+140	+260
−M	− 264	−188	−144	−115	− 64	− 40	−130
L.L. in center span, $S_2 = 4.5$ t/m	− 820	−435	−198	− 47	+176	+265	0
L.L. in end spans $S_1 = 6.8$ t/m	+ 197	− 74	−207	−265	−380	−400	0
Braking force, $F = 15$ t	± 159	±163	±167	±170	±180	±186	(±520)
Maximum moments +M	+ 698	+609	+577	+558	+527	+591	+780
−M	−1243	−786	−518	−550	−624	−626	−650

5.6 Piers with Twin Flexible Legs

5.6.1 INTRODUCTION

The concept of piers with twin flexible legs was first used with the first match-cast segmental bridge of Choisy-le-Roi. It was further used on several other precast segmental bridges either in France or Europe and more recently in the United States. Several examples of such structures will be described below with particular emphasis on the design and construction methods of the foundation system.

TABLE 5.5c. Maximum Bending Moments in the Superstructure as Function of the Bearing Thickness

Loading		Number of Neoprene Lamina: 0 (Fixed Pier)	1	2	3	6	9	Simple Support
Moments at support	Center span	−3125	−3060	−3020	−2985	−2925	−2895	−2660
	Side span	−3105	−2960	−2845	−2770	−2635	−2545	−2055
Moments in span	Center span, ($0.5\ l_2$)	+ 910	+ 960	+ 990	+1015	+1060	+1090	+1270
	Side span, ($0.4\ l_1$)	+ 890	+ 935	+ 965	+ 980	+1020	+1040	+1200

5.6.2 RIVER PIERS AND FOUNDATIONS FOR CHOISY-LE-ROI, COURBEVOIE, AND JUVISY BRIDGES, FRANCE

These structures were described in Chapter 3.

Choisy-le-Roi Bridge over the Seine

This structure is composed of two parallel twin bridges, Figure 3.3 and 5.38. Each structure has a continuous three-span superstructure in prestressed concrete with spans of 123 ft (37.50 m), 180.4 (55 m), and 123 ft (37.50 m), fixed at the center piers and forming a symmetric frame.

Piers are supported on a system of steel pipe piles driven to refusal in rock. The superstructure is supported on two slender inclined legs having a thickness of 16 in. (0.40 m) and inclined to the vertical axis at 0.065. Dimensions of the substructure are shown in Figure 3.3. The precast legs with an approximate weight of 27.5 ft (25 mt) have their centerlines converging to a point approximately at the level of the foundations so as to reduce the bending moments to the foundation. The legs are joined to the body of the pier at one end and to the superstructure at the other end by prestressing tendons. Before construction of the superstructure by the balanced cantilever method, the legs are temporarily stiffened by a triangular steel framework in the space between them. The construction stages are described graphically in Figure 5.38.

Courbevoie and Juvisy Bridges over the Seine

The Courbevoie Bridge is very similar in concept to the Choisy-le-Roi Bridge. It consists of a continuous three-span superstructure with symmetrical spans of 131 ft (40 m), 197 ft (60 m), and 131 ft (40 m).

Each river pier consists of two half-structures whose foundations are fixed in dense rock, Figure 3.9. The top portion of each half-pier consists of two vertical slender legs, oriented, in plan, perpendicular to the longitudinal axis of the bridge, and in a transverse section of the bridge, disposed in the shape of a V. These legs, which have a parallelogram form, are spaced in a longitudinal direction at 6 ft 9 in. (2.05 m) on center with a constant wall thickness of 18 in. (0.45 m). The legs were precast and joined to the superstructure and the lower portion of the pier by prestressing tendons.

The Juvisy Bridge consists of six prestressed concrete continuous spans with a total length of 700 ft (213.5 m). Spans are successively from the left bank 62 ft (18.8 m), 62 ft (18.8 m), 137 ft (41.8 m), 218 ft (66.6 m), 137 ft (41.8 m), and 84 ft (25.7 m).

The two piers located in the Seine are split piers resting on a common foundation, Figure 3.26. The foundations were constructed inside a sheet pile cofferdam, which permitted the flexible legs to be fixed at the bottom and hinged at the top. The thickness of the legs varied from 24 in. (0.60 m) at their base to 16 in. (0.40 m) at the top. They were symmetrically inclined at 0.0805 to the vertical and were cast in place and prestressed.

5.6.3 PIERS AND FOUNDATIONS OF CHILLON VIADUCTS, SWITZERLAND

This structure, 1.24 miles (2 km) in length, is a twin parallel viaduct overlooking Lake Leman and following a sinuous route corresponding to the contour of the hillside on which it is located, Figure 5.39. It

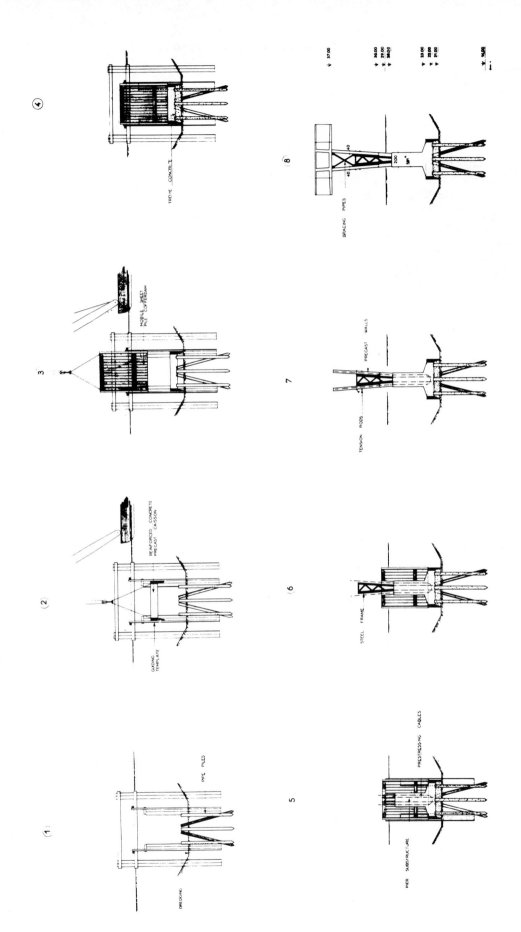

FIGURE 5.38. Choisy-le-Roi Bridge, construction stages of foundations and piers.

255

FIGURE 5.39. Chillon Viaduct, general view.

consists of 23 continuous spans of prestressed concrete, span lengths being 301.8 (92 m), 321.5 (98 m), or 341.2 ft (104 m). Four expansion joints divide each viaduct into sections with a maximum length of 1890 ft (576 m). The longitudinal stability of each section is provided either through a fixed bearing over the end abutment or by special fixed piers designed to withstand the horizontal reactions of the superstructure.

The piers, Figure 5.40, consist of two slender vertical legs with a constant thickness of 2 ft 8 in. (0.80 m). Height of pier varies in increments of 26 ft (8 m) with a maximum height of 118 ft (36 m). Legs less than 72 ft (22 m) in height are hinged at the top and bottom. Legs over 72 ft (22 m) in height are fixed at the base and hinged to the superstructure.

Because of the leg spacing there is no tension generated in the legs, so no vertical prestressing is required. During construction of the superstructure the stability of the pier is increased by temporary steel bracing anchored into the legs.

5.6.4   *MAIN PIERS AND FOUNDATIONS OF THE MAGNAN VIADUCT, FRANCE*

The Magnan Viaduct consists of four continuous spans; span lengths are 413 ft (126 m), two at 433 ft (132 m), and 249 ft (76 m), Figure 2.98. The piers are constructed of twin H-shaped shafts 40 ft (12 m) on center and with a maximum height of 318 ft (95 m) above the valley floor, Figures 5.41*a* and 5.41*b*. These piers are similar to slender vertical legs of variable cross section fixed at the base. Because this structure is located in an area of seismic activity, the superstructure is fixed at the west abutment and restrained transversly at the piers and the other abutment.

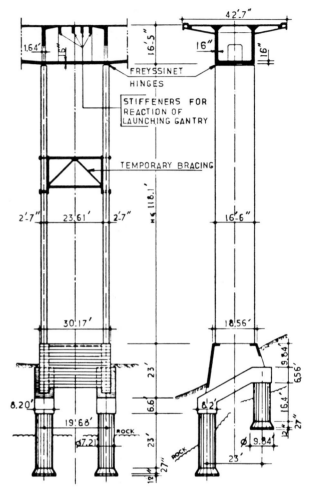

FIGURE 5.40.   Chillon Viaduct, pier section.

5.6.5   *MAIN PIERS AND FOUNDATIONS FOR THE DAUPHIN ISLAND BRIDGE, U.S.A.*

The Dauphin Island Bridge is an 18,000 ft (5.5 km) long structure over Mobile Bay connecting Dauphin Island to the mainland of Alabama. In order to permit ship traffic, the central portion of the structure was designed with a three-span continuous unit of 211, 400, and 211 ft (64, 122, and 64 m). This provided a clear shipping channel of 350 ft (107 m) horizontally and 85 ft (26 m) vertically. This project is currently (1980) under construction and is anticipated to be completed by late 1981.

Each main pier of this three-span structure consists of twin, I-shaped walls spaced longitudinally at 21.5 ft (6.6 m) on center, Figure 5.42. An individual wall is 24 ft 7 in. (7.5 m) wide and is moment-connected to the single cell box girder superstructure as well as to the footing.

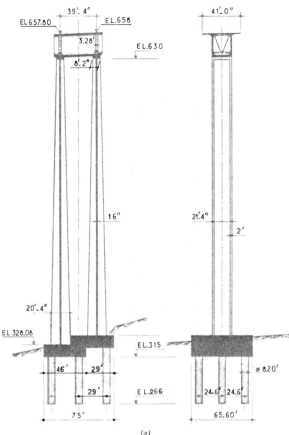

FIGURE 5.41. Magnan Viaduct. (*a*) Pier section. (*b*) Completed pier.

The foundation is to be made with circular, standard sheet pile construction. Alternate pilings were detailed on the plans to be either 30 in. (0.76 m) square precast, pretensioned concrete or 54 in. (1.37 m) hollow, cylindrical, precast, posttensioned concrete. Piling will be driven to a capacity of 450 kips (204 mt) for the 30 in. (0.76 m) square pile or 550 kips (249 mt) for the 54 in. (1.37 m) cylindrical pile. A dewatering seal will be poured under water after the piles have been driven. This seal will be located 25 ft (7.6 m) below the water surface and have a thickness of 5 ft (1.5 m). After dewatering, a circular footing with a diameter of 44 ft (13.4 m) and a thickness of 10 ft (3.05 m) will be poured. The twin wall piers will be constructed from a point 10 ft (3.05 m) below the water level and reach a total height of approximately 93 ft (28 m).

The design included checking of AASHTO loads and combinations, including a stream flow of 3.5 fps (1 mps). Additionally, the structure was checked at an ultimate condition for a storm wind of 200 mph (322 km/h). The load factor for this condition was taken as 1.0.

5.6.6 DEFORMATION AND PROPERTIES OF PIERS WITH FLEXIBLE LEGS

The following notation is used (Figure 5.43):

M, Q, N = components of external load acting at point O,

m, t, n = components of load acting at the top of the leg of the pier, oriented to the axis of the leg,

θ, u, v = displacements corresponding to M, Q, N at point O,

ω, α, β = displacements corresponding to m, t, n at the top of the leg,

E = modulus of elasticity of the concrete leg,

l = length of the leg between points A and B,

$2d$ = spacing of the legs at the top between points A and A′,

a = cross sectional area of leg,

i = moment of inertia of a leg,

$\rho_0 = ad^2/2i$ dimensionless coefficient,

ϕ = angle of inclination of the legs with the vertical.

Identical and symmetrical legs, of length l, are inclined to the vertical by the angle ϕ. The cross-sectional area and moment of inertia of each leg at a distance x from the top, A or $A′$, are respectively $a(x)$ and $i(x)$.

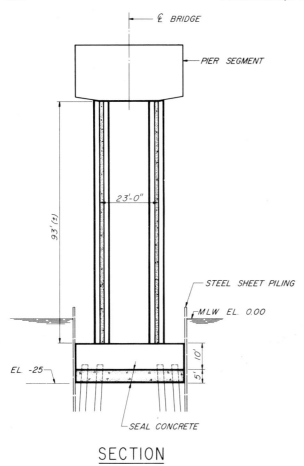

SECTION

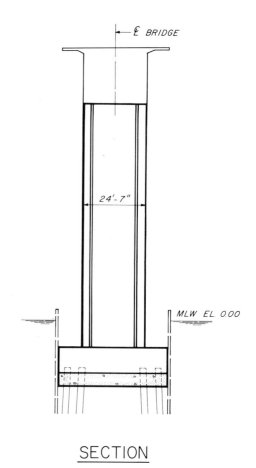

SECTION

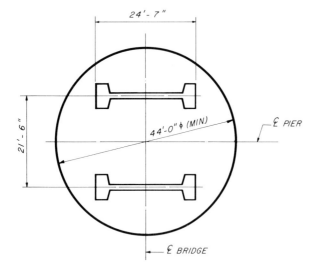

PLAN VIEW

FIGURE 5.42. Dauphin Island Bridge, dimensions of main piers and foundations.

The symbol σ is designated as an equivalent area of the leg such that:

$$\frac{1}{\sigma} = \frac{1}{l} \int_0^l \frac{dx}{a(x)}$$

and U, V, and W the characteristic integrals as:

$$U = \int_0^l \frac{dx}{i(x)}, \qquad V = \int_0^l \frac{x\,dx}{i(x)},$$

$$W = \int_0^l \frac{x^2\,dx}{i(x)}.$$

At the level of the superstructure, AA', the combined area and moment of inertia of the two legs, designated by A and I respectively, is represented by:

$$A = 2a \quad \text{and} \quad I = 2i + 2ad^2$$

with $2d$ being the distance between the two legs at the top.

Setting $\rho_0 = ad^2/2i$, the combined moment of inertia of the two legs becomes $I = 2i(1 + 2\rho_0)$.

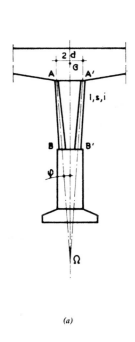
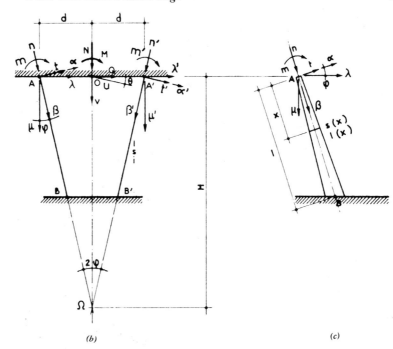

FIGURE 5.43. Piers with flexible legs, notations.

The positive directions of forces and displacements are indicated by the arrows in Figure 5.43.

The deformations of the pier are given by linear equations that relate the displacements of the top of the pier (θ, u, v) to the applied forces (M, Q, N). Legs AB and $A'B'$ are assumed to be connected at their ends by two rigid and indeformable sections AA' and BB'. Section BB' is assumed fixed (no translation), and the deformation equations are given by:

$$\theta = AM + BQ$$
$$u = BM + CQ$$
$$v = KN$$

where A, B, C, and K represent deformation coefficients of the legs.

Force components M, Q, N acting at point O (center of AA') are the resultant of the external forces applied to the pier, and θ, u, v are the corresponding components of displacement of the section AA' at point O (Figure 5.43b). To determine the forces m, t, n and m', t', n' in the legs at A and A' requires the formulation of the equations of equilibrium, deformation, and compatibility.

1. *Equilibrium equations:* The equilibrium of the system about point O is given by

$$M = m + m' + d \sin \phi (t + t')$$
$$\quad - d \cos \phi (n - n')$$

(5-6)

$$Q = (t + t') \cos \phi + (n + n') \sin \phi$$
$$N = - (t - t') \sin \phi + (n + n') \cos \phi$$

2. *Deformation equations:* Displacement ω, α, β and ω', α', β' at points A and A' (with respect to the axis of the legs) are given by:

$$\omega = \omega_0 + \int_0^l \frac{m + tx}{Ei} \, dx = \omega_0 + \frac{mU}{E} + \frac{tV}{E}$$

$$\alpha = \omega_0 l + \int_0^l \frac{m + tx}{Ei} x \, dx = \omega_0 l + \frac{mV}{E} + \frac{tW}{E}$$

$$\beta = \frac{n}{E} \int_0^l \frac{dx}{a} = \frac{nl}{E \sigma} \tag{5-7}$$

where ω_0 is the rotation of the leg AB at B, and E is the modulus of elasticity of the concrete. Corresponding equations give the displacements ω', α', β' at point A'.

Displacements of points A and A' with respect to the axis of the pier, θ, λ, μ and θ', λ', μ' are determined as

$$\theta = \omega$$
$$\lambda = \alpha \cos \phi + \beta \sin \phi$$
$$\mu = \alpha \sin \phi + \beta \cos \phi$$

$$\theta' = \omega'$$

$$\lambda' = \alpha' \cos \phi - \beta' \sin \phi$$

$$\mu' = \alpha' \sin \phi + \beta' \cos \phi$$

3. *Compatibility equations:* The conditions of compatibility between the displacements of point A, A', and O require that

$$\theta = \omega = \omega' \quad \text{(if there are no hinges at } A \text{ and } A')$$

$$u = \lambda = \lambda' \tag{5-9}$$

$$\mu = v - d\theta$$

$$\mu' = v + d\theta$$

The foregoing equations are sufficient to calculate θ, u, and v as functions of the applied loads represented by M, Q, and N.

Four practical cases need to be considered:

Legs fixed at both ends

Legs fixed at the superstructure and hinged at the base

Legs hinged at the superstructure and fixed at the base

Legs hinged at both ends

For any of these four cases the legs may be of constant or variable cross section, either inclined or vertical. A comprehensive study was made of this problem by J. Mathivat and reported in references 1 and 2, with several complete derivations of formulas applying to each particular case.

An important practical application is that of twin vertical walls with constant cross section, for which equations become very simple. Table 5.6 summarizes the value of the global equivalent coefficients of elasticity of the pier. In this case $\rho_0 = ad^2/2i$, which becomes $\rho_0 = 6(d/h)^2$ with $2d$ the distance on centers of both legs and h the wall thickness. Usually ρ_0 varies between 30 and 80.

It is evident, in fact, that a pier made up of twin legs behaves much in the same way as a conventional pier with a cross-sectional area A and a moment of inertia I insofar as the effect of vertical loads and moments on vertical displacements and rotation is concerned.

The behavior is completely different when considering the horizontal displacement due to the application of a horizontal load (braking force or thermal expansion). The conventional value of the

TABLE 5.6 Flexibility Coefficients of a Pier with Twin Vertical Walls of Constant Cross Section[a]

Flexibility Coefficient	Multiplier Coefficient	End Conditions for Legs			
		Fixed Top and Bottom	Fixed Top Hinged Bottom	Hinged Top Fixed Bottom	Hinged Top and Bottom
Exact Formulas					
A	$\dfrac{l}{EI}$	1	$1 + \dfrac{1}{2\rho_0}$	$1 + \dfrac{1}{2\rho_0}$	$1 + \dfrac{1}{2\rho_0}$
B	$\dfrac{l^2}{2EI}$	1	$2\left(1 + \dfrac{1}{2\rho_0}\right)$	0	0
C	$\dfrac{l^3}{3EI}$	$1 + \dfrac{\rho_0}{2}$	$\left(1 + \dfrac{1}{2\rho_0}\right)(3 + 2\rho_0)$	$1 + 2\rho_0$	∞
Approximate Formulas[b]					
A	$\dfrac{l}{EI}$	1	1	1	1
B	$\dfrac{l^2}{2EI}$	1	2	0	0
C	$\rho_0 \dfrac{l^3}{3EI}$	0.5	2	2	∞

[a]Notation: $I = 2i(1 + 2\rho_0)$, equivalent global inertia of twin walls. $\rho_0 = ad^2/2i = 6(d/h)^2$, with $2d$ distance between walls, h wall thickness.
[b]When $1/\rho_0$ is negligible with regard to 1.

elasticity coefficient $C = \dfrac{l^3}{3EI}$ is multiplied by the dimensionless factor $1 + \rho_0/2$ in the case of vertical walls fixed top and bottom or by $(1 + 2\rho_0)$ for walls hinged at one end.

The elasticity coefficient becomes infinitely large for double-hinged vertical walls, which proves simply that stability toward horizontal loads must be obtained through some other restraint in the structure such as fixed connections or elastomeric bearings over the abutments.

A detailed study of several typical cases was conducted for the Choisy-le-Roi Bridge, considering in particular:

Legs fixed at both ends

Legs hinged at both ends

Legs fixed on top and hinged at the base

Table 5.7 presents the essential results of this study, which also includes consideration of the flexibility of the body of the pier to the base of the foundation, where:

M_0 = bending moment in the superstructure at the pier section (side of the center span),

M_1 = bending moment in pier (top section),

Q = horizontal reaction in the pier.

The following conclusions may be drawn from the study:

The superstructure is very efficiently fixed over the river piers by the twin inclined wall system. The end moment for the center span totally fixed at both ends would be 255. The actual end moment varies between 230 and 232 (i.e., 90% of the fixed end moment).

The elasticity of the pier depends very little upon the conditions of fixity of the walls at the top and bottom (0.92 to 1.03).

The position of the point of contraflexure in the pier varies very little when the pier is subjected to a moment only; it is considerably more sensitive to the effect of a horizontal load.

The horizontal rigidity of the pier varies appreciably with the degree of fixity of the legs.

5.6.7 ELASTIC STABILITY OF PIERS WITH FLEXIBLE LEGS

It has been shown that the use of twin flexible legs (whether vertical or inclined) provides an economic solution to the dilemma between rigidity for bending versus rotation and flexibility for horizontal load versus displacement. In this respect the elastic stability of the system is the limiting factor, because there must always be an ample margin against buckling.

Assume the bridge superstructure to be displaced horizontally by u under a random horizontal load. The resistance against such displacement is offered by the pier rigidity, including the bending resistance of the legs if they are at least partially fixed at the top or bottom and possibly including the horizontal rigidity of the bearings over the abutments.

The minimum value of the vertical reaction in the pier (or the normal force in the legs), for which the imposed displacement does not have a tendency to spontaneously diminish until the cause provoking the displacement vanishes, represents the critical buckling load of the pier. This critical load is generally smaller than that where the legs are considered isolated and subjected to the same load conditions.

TABLE 5.7. Choisy-le-Roi Bridge: behavior of River Piers under Horizontal and Vertical Loads[a,b]

Type of Legs	Flexibility Coefficients			Elasticity E_k	Unit Vertical Load in Center Span		Unit Horizontal Load Applied to Deck		Unit Volume Change		
	A	B	C		M_0	M_1	M_0	M_1	M_0	M_1	Q
Fixed	4.06	54.6	973	0.92	−232	−157	+3.4	+5.7	+7.4	+24.7	2.4
Fixed/hinged	12.7	234	4670	0.98	−231	−154	+5.1	+8.7	+6.4	+21.5	1.3
Hinged	—	—	—	1.03	−230	−150	+6.3	+10.7	+5.9	+19.7	0.9

[a]Notation: A, B, C = flexibility coefficients of pier. E_k = global elasticity of pier. M_0 = end moment of center span (in tm). M_1 = bending moment at pier top (in tm). Q = horizontal reaction in pier.

[b]Units: All coefficients in metric system. A uniform vertical load of 1 t/m is applied over the center span. A unit horizontal load of 1 t is applied at deck level. A unit shortening of the deck is applied such that $E\Delta = 10^3$.

The deformations (θ, u) produce internal forces $(m, t, n$ and $m', t', n')$ in the top of the legs, which require the following conditions:

$$m_1 = m'_1, \qquad t_1 = t'_1, \qquad n_1 = -n'_1$$

If R_θ represents the rigidity of the superstructure against rotation and R_u toward longitudinal displacements, and if M and Q represent the moment and horizontal force that the superstructure transmits to the pier, we have:

$$M = -R_\theta \theta \, f \, (m_1, t_1, n_1) \qquad (5\text{-}10)$$
$$Q = -R_u u \, g(t_1, n_1)$$

These equations may be transformed to substitute the deformations of the superstructure (θ, u) for those of the legs:

$$R_\theta \omega \, f'(m_1, t_1, n_1) \qquad (5\text{-}11)$$
$$R_u(\alpha \cos \phi - \beta \sin \phi) \, g'(n_1, t_1)$$

with $a\omega = \alpha \sin \phi + \beta \cos \phi$ and $\beta = (l/E\sigma)n_1$.

The condition of initial load of the leg (expressed by n_0) is modified from the case of the displacement imposed to the structure and becomes:

Normal force: $\qquad n_0 + n_1$

Bending moment: $\qquad m_1$

Transverse force: $\qquad t_1$

The additional forces m_1 and t_1 may be expressed as a function of the displacement of the legs (ω, α) and of the initial force n_0. By substituting these forces, as functions of α and ω, into equations 5-11, we obtain a system of linear equations in three unknowns, n, α, ω.

When we assume that the displacements (α, ω) are different from zero when the cause inducing the displacement vanishes, the determinate form of the three equations is nil, which allows us to obtain the value of critical load n_{1c}.

The critical buckling force of one pier leg may be expressed as:

$$n_{cr} = r^2 \frac{Ei}{l^2}$$

where r is a dimensionless coefficient which may be related to the usual Euler formula for buckling:

$$n_{cr} = \pi^2 \frac{Ei}{\lambda^2}$$

with λ equal to the effective buckling length. Thus the equivalent buckling length of one leg as part of the total pier system will be:

$$\lambda = \frac{\pi l}{r}$$

The example of the Choisy-le-Roi Bridge will again be considered. Seven typical cases were investigated with either vertical or inclined legs and different leg end restraints. Also the horizontal restraint of the bridge over the abutment was varied. Table 5.8 summarizes the results for the following numerical values:

Wall length $l = 8.50$ m, on center spacing $2d = 2.00$ m

Area $a = 6.40$ m², moment of inertia $i = 0.085$ m⁴

Neoprene pads over the abutments: area $A_b = 1.28$ m², $E/G = 20,000$

The first six cases are hypothetical assumptions used for comparison. Case 7 is the actual case of the Choisy-le-Roi Bridge with the legs hinged at the base and fixed to the superstructure.

TABLE 5.8. Choisy-le-Roi Bridge: Elastic Stability of Twin-Flexible-Legged Pier for Various Support Conditions

Case Number	Conditions of Legs at River Piers	Support Condition at Abutments	$\dfrac{\lambda}{l}$	Factor of Safety
1	Hinged vertical legs	Rigidity neglected	∞	0
2	Vertical legs hinged at the base and fixed at the top	Rigidity neglected	2.00	1.1
3		Five neoprene pads	1.20	2.8
4		Three neoprene pads	1.00	4.0
5	Vertical legs fixed top and bottom	Rigidity neglected	1.00	4.0
6	Legs inclined 6.5%, hinged at base, fixed at top	Rigidity neglected	0.88	5.2
7	Legs inclined 6.5%, hinged at base, fixed at top (actual case of Choisy-le-Roi)	Three neoprene pads	0.97	4.8

The designer should be aware that the following three factors play an essential role in the elastic stability of the structure:

Inclination of the legs to the vertical

Horizontal rigidity of the neoprene bearings at the abutments

Fixity conditions of the ends of the legs in the piers

The fundamental difference between cases 2 and 6 (Table 5.8) indicated by the considerable increase in the factor of safety (1.1 to 5.2) is due to the introduction in case 6 of the arch effect of the inclined legs. Horizontal displacements of the superstructure cannot occur without mobilizing the bending stiffness of the pier assembly. For case 2 the elastic stability relies solely on the bending stiffness of the legs, and the critical buckling force is the same as for a beam fixed at one end and free at the other.

5.7 Flexible Piers and Their Stability During Construction

5.7.1 SCOPE

In the preceding paragraphs we considered piers having a bending capacity allowing the deck cantilever construction to proceed with no further strengthening. Such moment-resisting piers are usually joined to the superstructure to benefit from the frame action, both to reduce the cost of foundations and minimize the effect of live loading in the superstructure.

Another type of substructure remains to be considered here, one more conventional in design and where the piers receive the vertical reaction of the superstructure through a single row of bearings. Such piers are usually flexible, and the stability during cantilever construction requires that temporary supports be added to the self-bending strength of the pier shaft.

5.7.2 DESCRIPTION OF REPRESENTATIVE STRUCTURES WITH TEMPORARY SUPPORTS

Downstream Paris Belt Bridge, France

The four river pier shafts previously described and illustrated in Section 5.3.2 rest on a reinforced concrete substructure built inside a cofferdam sealed with tremie concrete. Dimensions are shown in Figure 5.44.

Because of the limited dimensions of the pier shafts and their consequent marginal bending capacity, a temporary support was used during construction for stability of the superstructure before deck continuity was achieved. Only one support was used for each pier, Figure 5.45, on one side of the concrete shaft within the space available inside the temporary cofferdam. Consequently the lever arm between the pier and support centerlines was only 8.5 ft (2.40 m), so that a heavy reaction was imposed on the temporary support.

The maximum reaction computed for the case of one precast segment out of balance, including the lifting equipment, was 1170 tons (1060 mt). Including provisions for random loads and the added reaction of the temporary prestressing tendons, the maximum design reaction in the support was 2030 tons (1840 mt). Each temporary support consisted of:

A 40 in. (1 m) steel pipe filled with concrete, Figure 5.46, resting on the spread footing of the permanent pier

A V-shaped concrete frame placed upon the pipe and allowing the deck reaction to be transferred directly from the box section webs to the pipe

Vertical prestressing tendons were also anchored in the pier footing and stressed from deck level to prevent accidental overturning of the cantilever, although limitations were imposed during construction to always start segment placement on the side of the temporary support.

Temporary connection between the pier segment and the concrete pier shaft included one looped tendon and four high-strength bars. An immediate consequence of the high vertical reaction imposed upon the deck by the temporary support in case of unbalanced loading was a reversal of shear stresses between the temporary and the permanent supports. This situation was even more critical because of the permanent draped tendons, shown in the detail of Figure 5.47, located in that zone together with the Resal effect produced by the inclined bottom flange. The corresponding shear stress in the webs reached a maximum of 680 psi. Two special tendons (twelve $\frac{1}{2}$ in. diameter strands) were placed on either side of each web of the box girder to reduce the shear stresses to allowable values. In fact, these four tendons worked as a tension tie between the top and bottom flanges of the box girder across the distance between the permanent and temporary support.

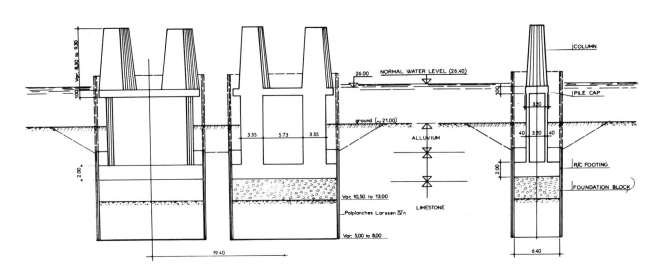

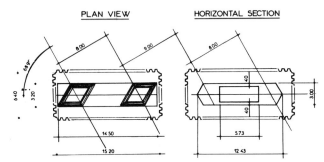

FIGURE 5.44. Downstream Paris Belt Bridge, dimensions of river piers.

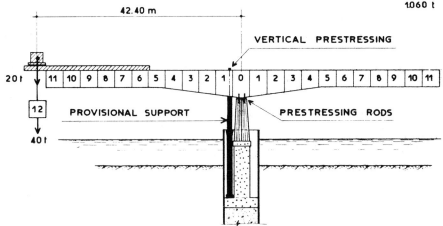

FIGURE 5.45. Downstream Paris Belt Bridge, schematic of temporary support and stability of river pier during construction.

264

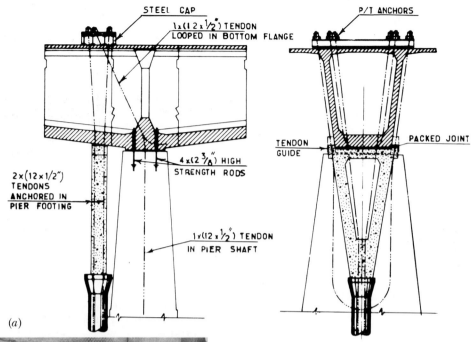

STEEL CAP

1x(12 x 1/2") TENDON
LOOPED IN BOTTOM FLANGE

P/T ANCHORS

2x(12 x 1/2")
TENDONS
ANCHORED IN
PIER FOOTING

4 x (2 3/8") HIGH
STRENGTH RODS

1x(12 x 1/2") TENDON
IN PIER SHAFT

TENDON
GUIDE

PACKED JOINT

(a)

(b)

FIGURE 5.46. Downstream Paris Belt Bridge, details of temporary support. (*a*) Dimensions of support. (*b*) View of support.

This problem has been described at some length to show that a single temporary support subjected to high loads may call for a rather complex arrangement to satisfy all requirements of stability and resistance of all parts of the structure at each construction stage.

Saint Jean Bridge In Bordeaux, France

For aesthetic reasons the river piers were designed as rather slender shafts, which had to accommodate an important variation of the waterline due to tidal effects in the mouth of the Garonne River. The bridge was relatively low above the water, particularly at high tide.

Each pier shaft was founded on an open-dredged concrete caisson anchored in a bed of sand and gravel of good quality, overlying a deep formation of marl and clay.

Dimensions of the piers and foundations are shown in Figure 5.48. The caisson had a cutting-edge diameter of 18 ft 4 in. (5.60 m) and the maximum average bearing pressure on the sand and gravel bed was 8.1 t/ft² at the time of first loading; the foundation settlement was a maximum of 1.1 in. (28 mm) and the long-term additional settlement was negligible, 0.16 in. (4 mm).

Construction of the piers called for the use of an auxiliary floating platform that could be raised on eight temporary pipe piles, comparable in principle to the legged jacking platforms used on offshore work, Figures 5.49 and 5.50. The reinforced concrete caisson was floated into place, suspended from the platform resting on its legs, and incorporated into the permanent structure. As excavation proceeded inside the caisson to lower it to its final elevation, precast segments were added to increase the height of the caisson wall as required.

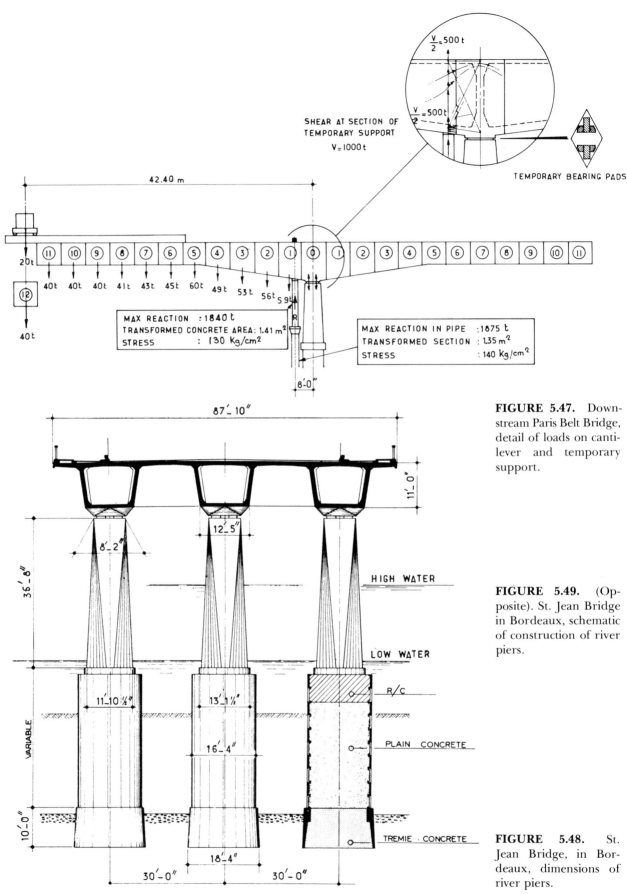

SHEAR AT SECTION OF
TEMPORARY SUPPORT
V = 1000 t

TEMPORARY BEARING PADS

42.40 m

20t

⑪ ⑩ ⑨ ⑧ ⑦ ⑥ ⑤ ④ ③ ② ① ⓪ ① ② ③ ④ ⑤ ⑥ ⑦ ⑧ ⑨ ⑩ ⑪

40t 40t 40t 41t 43t 45t 60t 49t 53t 56t 59t

⑫

40t

MAX REACTION : 1840 t
TRANSFORMED CONCRETE AREA: 1.41 m²
STRESS : 130 Kg/cm²

MAX REACTION IN PIPE : 1875 t
TRANSFORMED SECTION : 1.35 m²
STRESS : 140 kg/cm²

8'-0"

FIGURE 5.47. Downstream Paris Belt Bridge, detail of loads on cantilever and temporary support.

87'-10"

11'-0"

12'-5"

8'-2"

36'-8"

HIGH WATER

LOW WATER

11'-10½"

13'-1½"

R/C

16'-4"

PLAIN CONCRETE

VARIABLE

10'-0"

TREMIE · CONCRETE

18'-4"

30'-0" 30'-0"

FIGURE 5.49. (Opposite). St. Jean Bridge in Bordeaux, schematic of construction of river piers.

FIGURE 5.48. St. Jean Bridge, in Bordeaux, dimensions of river piers.

266

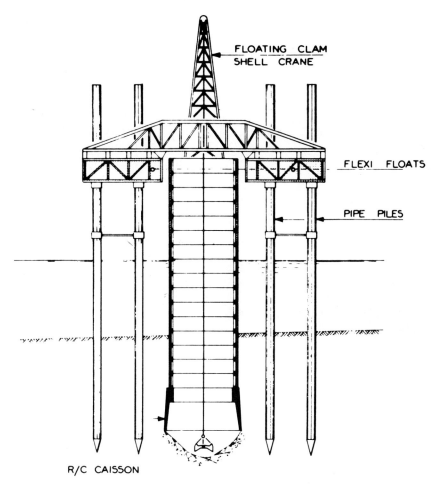

FLOATING CLAM
SHELL CRANE

FLEXI FLOATS

PIPE PILES

R/C CAISSON

BORDEAUX — PLACING RIVER CAISSONS — ELEVATION
1.018 _ 72 _

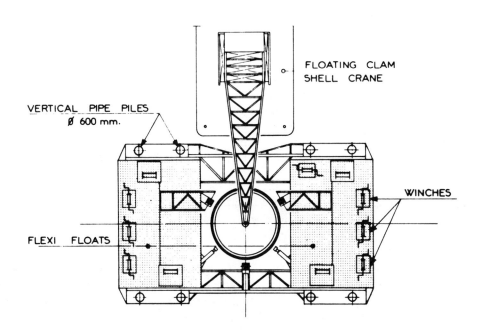

FLOATING CLAM
SHELL CRANE

VERTICAL PIPE PILES
Ø 600 mm.

WINCHES

FLEXI FLOATS

FIGURE 5.50. St. Jean Bridge at Bordeaux, platform on legs used for river pier caissons. (*a*) Platform in floating stage. (*b*) Platform on legs and caisson during excavation.

Match casting was used for making the various segments, and it proved very efficient and very simple.

The cofferdam required to build the pier shaft in the dry was made up of temporary additional caisson ring segments stacked upon the permanent caisson and bolted together. This cofferdam was used during construction of the deck to make a moment-resisting pier shaft as a substitute to the flexible permanent pier. The deck was therefore resting only upon the cofferdam and the lower caisson through two temporary caps, offering a stable base for unbalanced loading, Figure 5.51*a*.

After cantilever construction was finished and continuity achieved in the deck, flat jacks were used to transfer the total reaction of the box girder from the temporary caps and cofferdam onto the permanent concrete piers. All the temporary ring segments above low water were further removed. This example shows how the foundations and even part of the substructure can be used to minimize the cost of temporary supports required for cantilever construction.

5.7.3 REVIEW OF THE VARIOUS METHODS OF PROVIDING STABILITY DURING CANTILEVER CONSTRUCTION

A situation is considered here where the permanent pier cannot provide adequate stability during cantilever construction. Several methods may be used, either separately or in combination, to provide the required stability under the loading combinations briefly reviewed in Section 5.2.

Temporary Eccentric Prestress   In the general case where the construction procedure allows the unbalanced segment in a typical cantilever to be placed always on the same side of the pier, the unbalanced moment varies between 0 and Wd (segment weight W at a distance d from the pier centerline as shown in Figure 5.52).

Assume a temporary vertical tendon, anchored in the pier foundation or in a separate dead-man, to be stressed for this unbalanced loading configuration to a load P such that

$$P\delta = \frac{Wd}{2}$$

and the unbalanced moment in the pier now becomes

$$\pm \frac{Wd}{2}$$

and the actual bending capacity of the pier is theoretically doubled. The true gain is somewhat lower, because it is not practical to change the tendon load at each stage of segment placing. A proper temporary connection with high-strength rods between pier and deck must always be provided.

Unsymmetrical Distribution of Segments with Regard to the Pier   If the pier segment is eccentrically placed with regard to the pier shaft centerline, Figure 5.53, a permanent moment is applied to the pier when an even number of segments is incorporated in the deck. Dimensions may be such that the maximum unbalanced moment due to one segment's being placed on the proper side of the pier will result in applying only half to the pier. This approach results in significant complications in the layout of the prestress tendons in the deck. Both methods described thus far have one disadvantage, in that the deck cantilever is never in balance over the pier and so it is more complicated to following up the geometry of the deck during construction.

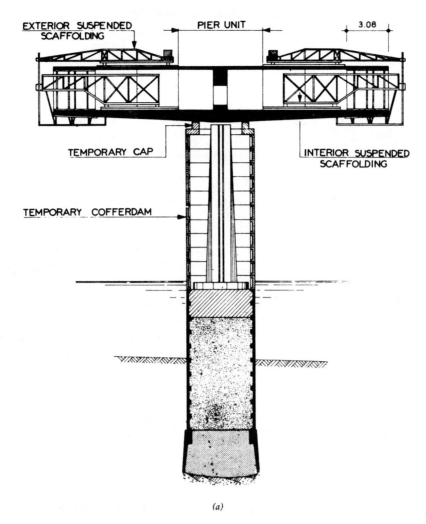

EXTERIOR SUSPENDED SCAFFOLDING

PIER UNIT

3.08

TEMPORARY CAP

INTERIOR SUSPENDED SCAFFOLDING

TEMPORARY COFFERDAM

(a)

(b)

FIGURE 5.51. St. Jean Bridge at Bordeaux, temporary arrangement of piers for deck cantilever construction. (a) Schematic of temporary cofferdam and deck support. (b) View of the pier segment and travelers.

269

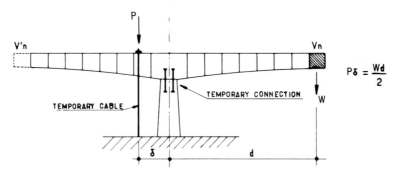

FIGURE 5.52. Temporary stability of deck and pier during construction by prestressing tendon.

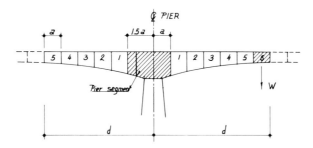

FIGURE 5.53. Unsymmetrical pier segment.

Stability of the Concrete Cantilever Provided by the Deck Construction Equipment   Figure 5.54 outlines a few typical schemes developed for either cast-in-place or precast construction where the stability during cantilever placing is achieved by the construction equipment itself, such as an overhead truss or launching gantry. Several such examples were previously described in Chapters 2 and 3:

Overhead truss in cast-in-place construction, Siegtal Bridge or Pine Valley Creek Bridge

Launching gantry in precast construction, Rio Niteroi Bridge and the B-3 South Viaducts

Overhead beam in precast construction, B-3 South Viaducts; a similar scheme is being contemplated for several contemporary projects in the United States.

Temporary Supports (Figure 5.55)   If a single temporary support is used on one side of the pier at a distance a, the reactions are as follows:

$$\text{pier:} \qquad V - \frac{M}{a}$$

$$\text{temporary support:} \qquad + \frac{M}{a}$$

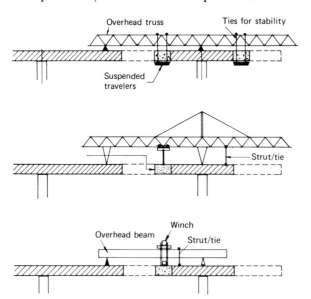

FIGURE 5.54. Cantilever stability by deck construction equipment.

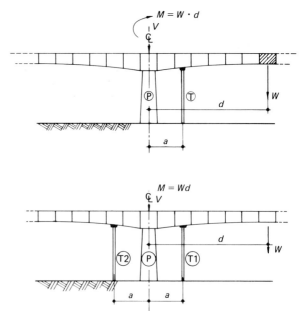

FIGURE 5.55. Cantilever stability by temporary support(s).

If two symmetrical temporary supports are used, the system is statically indeterminate and the actual distribution of reactions depends upon the respective flexibilities of the pier and of the supports. The load distribution is as follows:

	Temporary Support, T_1	Pier, P	Temporary Support, T_2
Effect of vertical load V	ρV	$(1 - 2\rho)V$	ρV
Effect of moment M	$-\dfrac{M}{2a}$	0	$+\dfrac{M}{2a}$
Total	$\rho V - \dfrac{M}{2a}$	$(1 - 2\rho)V$	$\rho V + \dfrac{M}{2a}$

If it is desired that the temporary supports never be subject to an uplift force, to resist which requires anchors and adequate foundations, the stiffness of the support must be such that a sufficient proportion of the vertical load compensates the effect of the moment. The minimum value of ρ must be such that:

$$\rho V - \frac{M}{2a} \geq 0 \quad \text{or} \quad \rho \geq \frac{M}{2a}$$

Consequently the maximum reaction at support T_2 becomes at least equal to M/a, which is precisely the value of the reaction for a single support with the same loading configuration. The double support system is therefore exactly twice as expensive as the single support system. The only advantage is to allow the construction of the deck to proceed indifferently from either side of the pier or to maintain an equal safety of the system should a mistake be made in the required sequence of operations for the case of a single support.

Temporary Stays In a limited number of structures, stability during construction was provided by temporary vertical or inclined stays anchored in special foundation blocks or in the permanent footing of the pier, Figure 5.56.

When feasible, this last system is particularly simple, because the temporary stays are usually made of simple prestressing tendons and are far less expensive than rigid temporary supports. Such a system must be used in conjunction with a strong temporary connection between pier and deck to reach an adequate level of safety.

5.8 Abutments

5.8.1 SCOPE

Although the abutments provided at both ends of the bridge are not necessarily of special design when associated with cantilever and segmental construction, it may be of interest to review briefly several types of structures actually used in completed projects.

The abutments serve a twofold purpose:

They provide the first and last support to the bridge superstructure, allowing a smooth transition of the roadway surface from the deck to the

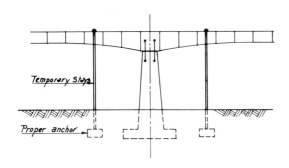

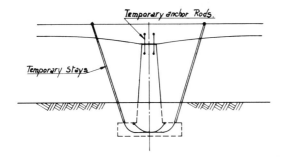

FIGURE 5.56. Cantilever stability by temporary stays.

approaches while allowing free expansion with an adequate roadway and sidewalk joint,

They make the retaining wall contain the fill of the approach embankment where geometric conditions require it. Design and construction methods of the abutments depend greatly upon the soil conditions and the level of the water table when present.

Basically, the two functions outlined above may either be integrated into a single structure or filled by two separate structures. On the other hand, the function of a retaining wall may be greatly minimized by allowing the approach fill to take a slope of repose under the structure.

By variously combining these characteristics, twelve different sketches were prepared in Figures 5.57 through 5.68 as an outline of typical structures encountered in practice. For convenience, these designs have been grouped into six different categories as described in the following paragraphs.

5.8.2 *COMBINED ABUTMENT/RETAINING WALL*

Type IA (Figure 5.57) A simple retaining wall perpendicular to the bridge centerline and anchored to a conventional spread footing both contains the approach fill and provides the deck end bearing. The back wall receives a transition slab to avoid the roadway profile discontinuity so frequent in earlier bridges between the rigid deck and the flexible pavement over the approach embankment. Two side walls of triangular shape contain the fill inside the abutment.

Type IB (Figure 5.58) The retaining wall is made of a vertical wall and a lower slab properly strengthened by longitudinal buttresses. The entire system is founded on piles.

Type IC (Figure 5.59) Where the poor quality of the soil makes it difficult to resist the horizontal loads due to earth pressure combined with braking and thermal reactions, the previous system may be founded on a system of vertical piles, while the

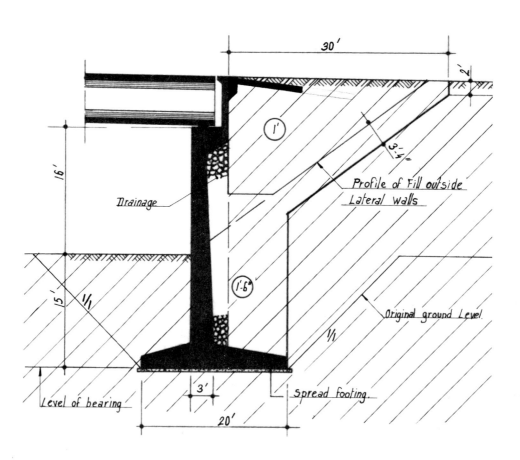

FIGURE 5.57. Abutment type IA.

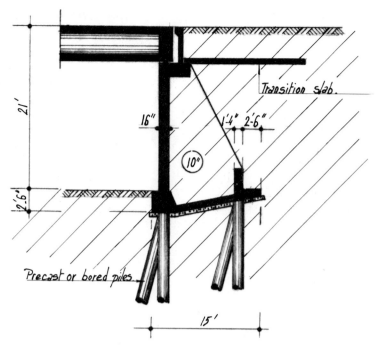

FIGURE 5.58. Abutment Type IB.

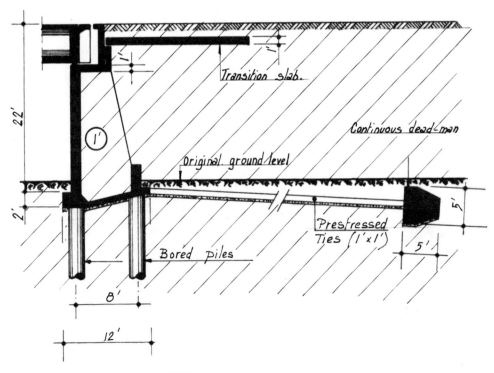

FIGURE 5.59. Abutment type IC.

horizontal loads are resisted by embedded pre-stressed concrete ties anchored in the back into a continuous dead-man.

5.8.3 SEPARATE END SUPPORT AND RETAINING WALL

Type II (Figure 5.60) The two functions of deck support and retaining wall are entrusted to two separate structures. Shown in this figure is a front vertical column, resting on spread footings or piles, which provides the deck end bearing. Behind this column and separate thereto, a reinforced earth retaining wall contains the approach fill.

5.8.4 THROUGH FILL ABUTMENT

The fill extends under the bridge deck with a stable slope (3:2 to 2:1) to reduce as much as possible the amount of earth pressure applied to the abutment.

Type IIIA (Figure 5.61) Vertical longitudinal walls connect the lower spread footing to the abutment superstructure. It is important to avoid horizontal cross bracings at intermediate levels embedded in the fill, because settlements may cause significant overloads in such members such as to cause failure.

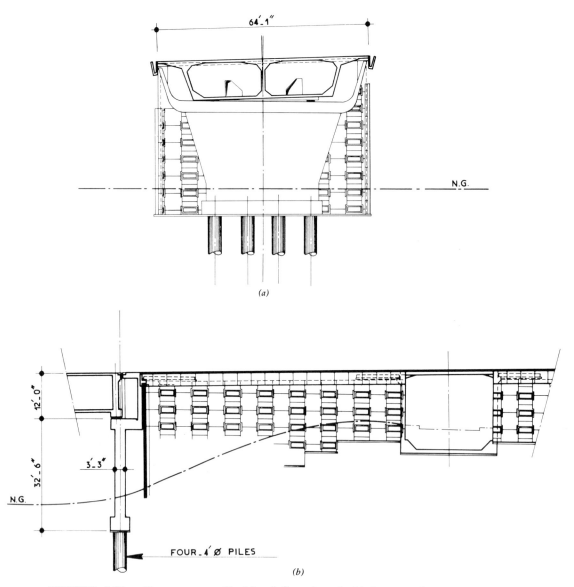

FIGURE 5.60. Abutment type II with reinforced earth. (*a*) Cross section. (*b*) Elevation and longitudinal section.

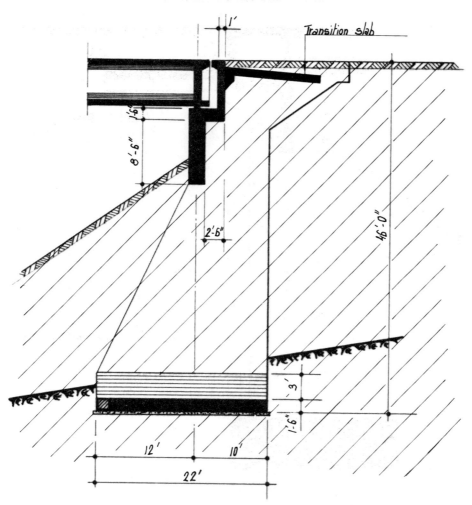

Transition slab

FIGURE 5.61. Abutment type IIIA.

Type IIIB (Figure 5.62) The same system may be adapted to the case where a high water table and poor soil conditions call for pile foundation built in a cofferdam.

5.8.5 HOLLOW BOX ABUTMENT

Type IVA (Figure 5.63) Another way to avoid high earth-pressure loads on the abutment, where it is not possible or desired to extend the approach fill under the deck, is to build the abutment as a box with a front wall providing the deck end support and the cover slab carrying the roadway between the bridge deck and the approach fill. Such a structure may be founded on spread footing or on piles (as shown in the sketch).

Type IVB (Figure 5.64) The same structure may rest both at the front and at the rear on open-dredged caissons excavated under water to the load-bearing soil.

5.8.6 ABUTMENTS DESIGNED FOR UPLIFT

The principle has been described previously in Chapter 4 (design) and for actual structures in Chapters 2 and 3 (cast-in-place or precast cantilever bridges).

Type VA (Figure 5.65) A large caisson is open-dredged and filled after completion of the excavation to the required foundation level with tremie concrete so as to obtain a sufficient weight to resist the uplift reaction from the deck.

Type VB (Figure 5.66) Another variation of the same concept was developed for the Saint Jean Bridge at Bordeaux to combine into a single abutment a front downward bearing and a rear uplifting bearing to fix the last span of the bridge while retaining its free expansion.

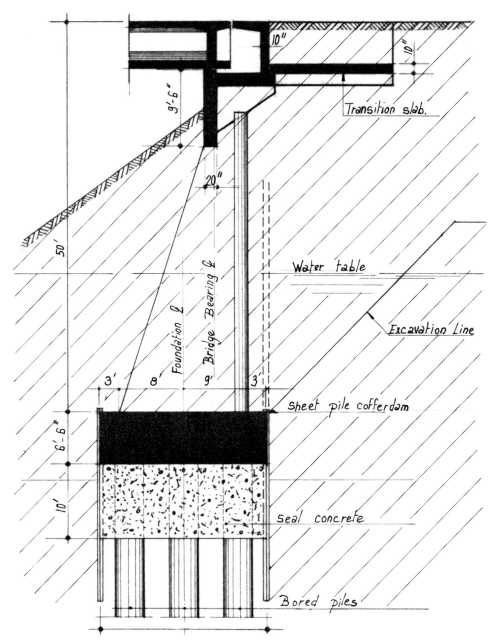

FIGURE 5.62. Abutment type IIIB.

5.8.7 *MINI-ABUTMENT*

For decks of small height, when prevailing conditions allow the fill to be placed around the deck, the abutment reduces to a very simple inexpensive structure shown as types VIA and VIB in Figures 5.67 and 5.68.

5.9 *Effects of Differential Settlements on Continuous Decks*

The question has often been raised as to the adequacy of allowing continuous decks to rest on piers subjected to possible differential settlements. The authors are aware of a few cases where differential

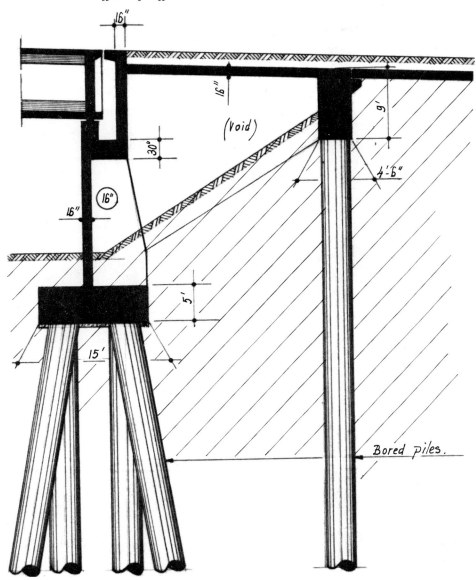

FIGURE 5.63. Abutment type IVA.

settlements were responsible for problems pertaining to the integrity of the superstructure (such as opening of joints between successive segments). Differential settlements, however, are very seldom critical in most soil conditions. In the isolated cases where they may be critical, precautions can be taken to counteract their eventual effects upon the structure.

5.9.1 EFFECTS OF AN ASSUMED PIER SETTLEMENT ON THE STRESSES IN THE SUPERSTRUCTURE

Starting with the simple case shown in Figure 5.69, where a continuous beam of constant depth with a large number of identical spans is subjected to the settlement of one pier by a given amount, one may easily derive the effect in terms of moments and stresses in the superstructure. Taking the fixed end moment $\mu = 6\,EIu/l^2$, the moments over the piers and at midspan are:

Over the pier subjected to settlement	$+0.732\mu$
Over the adjacent piers	-0.464μ
Midspan moment	$+0.134\mu$
Quarter-span moment	$+0.433\mu$

The stress produced in the superstructure is $f = Mc/I$, where c is the distance between the centroid

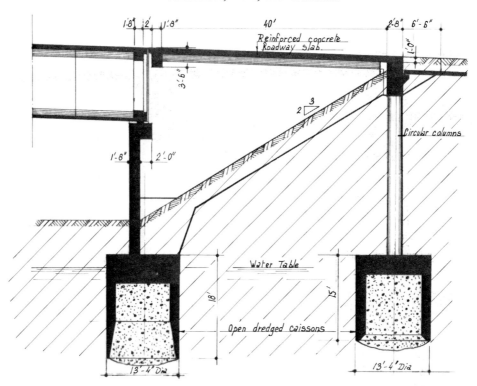

FIGURE 5.64. Abutment type IVB.

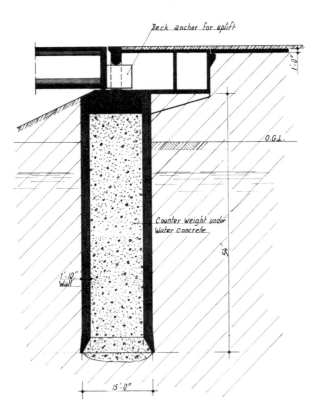

FIGURE 5.65. Abutment type VA.

and upper or lower flange. If the moment is expressed as $M = k\mu$, the stress becomes:

$$f = k \frac{6Ecu}{l^2}$$

which can be rewritten as follows:

$$f = 6kE \frac{c}{h} \frac{h}{l} \frac{u}{l}$$

The value of c/h varies between 0.4 and 0.6 and that of h/l between $\frac{1}{18}$ and $\frac{1}{22}$.

Considering the quarter-span point close to the pier where settlement occurred, the stress in the superstructure will be, with $k = 0.433$ and $E = 300,000$ kips/ft² (for long-term loading):

$$f = 23,400 \frac{u}{l}$$

For a settlement $u = \frac{1}{1000}$ the stress is equal to 23 kips/ft² at the bottom fiber, a very nominal value. For a 100 ft span, the corresponding settlement is $u = 0.1$ ft $= 1.2$ inches.

The amount of settlement to be considered is only that part taking place after continuity is achieved in the deck and so after most of the load has been applied to the structure.

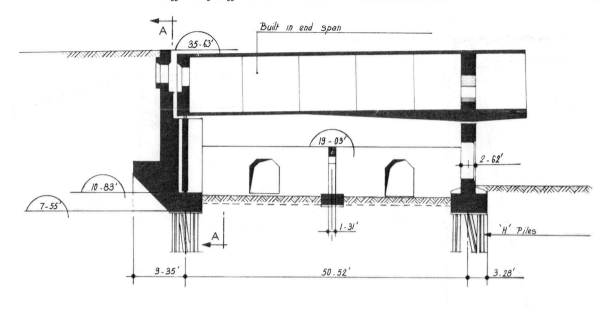

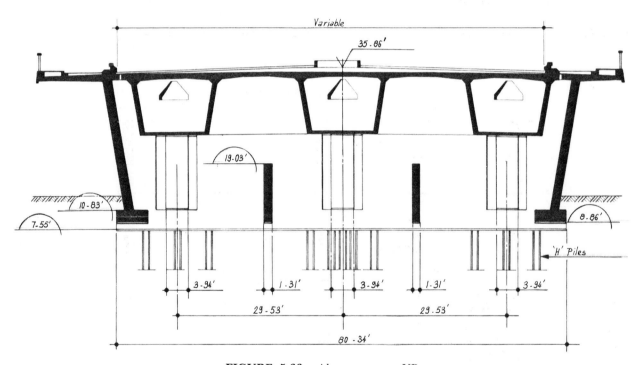

FIGURE 5.66. Abutment type VB.

5.9.2 PRACTICAL MEASURES FOR COUNTERACTING DIFFERENTIAL SETTLEMENTS

In most cases, the foreseeable differential settlements may be absorbed by the structure without any corrective measures and no special provisions need be taken in that respect.

For some structures the situation may call for special consideration. Such was the case, for example, with the Houston Ship Channel Bridge, where large long-term settlements could be anticipated at the time of design. In such instances, provisions for eventual realignment of the deck profile must be incorporated into the design.

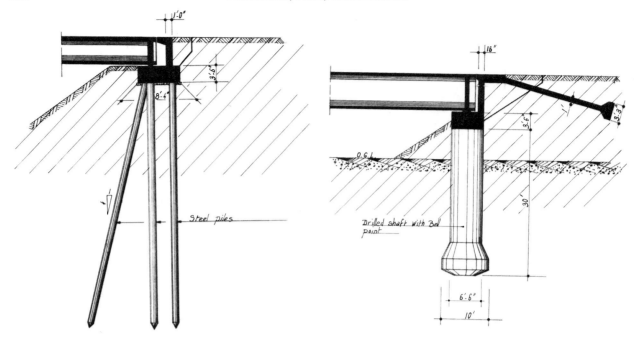

FIGURE 5.67. Abutment type VIA.   **FIGURE 5.68.** Abutment type VIB.

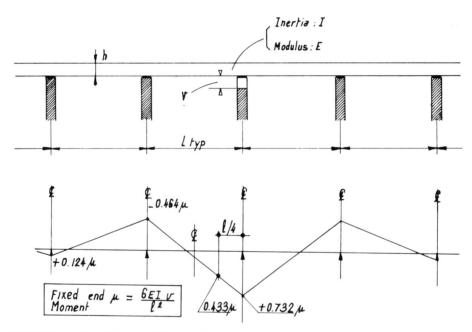

FIGURE 5.69. Effect of differential settlement on a continuous beam with equal spans and constant depth.

References

1. J. Mathivat, "Reconstruction du pont de Choisy-le-Roi," *Travaux*, Janvier 1966, No. 372.

2. J. Mathivat, "Structures de piles adaptees a la construction par encorbellement," Problems speciaux d'etude et d'execution des overages, *Journees A.F.P.C.*, Avril 22–23, 1974.

3. Gerwick, Ben C. Jr., "Bell-Pier Construction, Recent Developments and Trends," *Journal of the American Concrete Institute*, Proc. V. 62, No. 10, October 1965.

6

Progressive and Span-by-Span Construction of Segmental Bridges

6.1 Introduction

The concepts of the progressive placement and span-by-span methods of segmental construction were introduced in Sections 1.9.4 and 1.9.3, respectively. This chapter will explore these concepts in greater detail. These two methods have not made the conventional cast-in-place on falsework method obsolete; the conventional method is still applicable and economical where site, environmental, ecological, and economic considerations permit. What these two methods do is to open up a field where prestressed concrete structures were hitherto not practical and where they now can economically compete with structural steel.

The progressive placement and span-by-span methods are similar in that construction of the superstructure starts at one end and proceeds continuously to the other, as opposed to the balanced cantilever method where superstructure is constructed as counterbalancing half-span cantilevers

on each side of the various piers. Also, both methods are adaptable to either cast-in-place or precast construction.

6.1.1 PROGRESSIVE PLACEMENT METHOD

This method was developed to obviate the construction interruption manifested in the balanced cantilever method, where construction must proceed symmetrically on each side of the various piers. In progressive placement, the construction proceeds from one end of the project in continuous increments to the other end; segments are placed in successive cantilevers from the same side of the various piers. When the superstructure reaches a pier, permanent bearings are placed and the superstructure is continued in the direction of construction.

The first implementation of this method, which used cast-in-place segments, was on the Ounasjoki Bridge near the Arctic Circle in Finland. It was

281

later extended to the first use of precast segments in the Rombas Viaduct in eastern France.

The essential advantages of this method are as follows:

1. The operations are continuous and are carried out from that part of the structure already constructed. Access for personnel and materials is conveniently accomplished over the surface of the structure already completed (free of the existing terrain). This may be of importance with regard to urban viaducts cantilevering over numerous obstacles.
2. Reactions to the piers are vertical and not subject to any unsymmetrical bending moments, thus avoiding the need for temporary bracing during construction.
3. The method is adaptable to curved structure geometry.

The following are the disadvantages:

1. It is difficult, if not impossible, to utilize this method in the construction of the first span. Usually the first span must be erected on falsework. In some rare instances it may be possible to cantilever the first span from the abutment.
2. Forces imposed upon the superstructure, depending on the method of construction, are completely different (in sign and order of magnitude) from those present in the structure under service load. Consequently, a temporary external support system is required during construction in order to maintain the stresses within reasonable limits and minimize the cost of unproductive temporary prestressing. Falsework bents may be used (as in the Linn Cove Viaduct), but the more usual solution is that of a mobile temporary mast and cable-stay system (Figure 1.57). For the progressive placement method the mast and cable-stay system is relocated progressively over the piers as construction advances.
3. In this system the piers are subjected to a reaction from the self-weight of the superstructure approximately twice that in the final static arrangement of the structure. However, this is generally not critical to the design of the piers and foundations, as the effect of the dead load is rarely larger than half the total load including horizontal forces.

When cast-in-place segments are used in conjunction with the progressive placement method, the rate of construction is less than that for the balanced cantilever method, in that there is only one location of construction activity. That is, only one segment can be cast (at the end of the completed portion of the structure) rather than two (one at each end of the balanced cantilevers). This slowness may be minimized by the use of longer segments, but this solution is limited by the low resistance of the young concrete. On the other hand, the use of epoxy-joined precast segments may permit an average rapidity of construction comparable to that of balanced cantilever with a launching girder.

6.1.2   SPAN-BY-SPAN METHOD

As indicated in Chapter 1, the span-by-span method was developed to meet the need for constructing long viaducts with relatively short spans such as to incorporate the advantages of balanced cantilever construction.

From a competitive point of view, the capital investment in the equipment for this type of construction is considerable. It has been suggested[1] that one-third of the cost of the equipment be depreciated for a given site and that at least four uses would be required to achieve full depreciation, including interest on the capital investment. However, costly modifications that may be required because of changes in bridge widths or span limitations are not considered in the above write-off policy. It would, therefore, be advisable for a contractor investing in this type of equipment to consider some type of modular planning so that modification for future projects might be kept to a minimum. It might be possible to have a basic piece of equipment with interchangeable elements. There is, of course, the potential of leasing this equipment to others as a means of retiring the capital investment.

Wittfoht[1,2] has categorized stepping segmental construction into four subgroups:

1. With-on-the ground nontraveling formwork.
2. With traveling formwork or on-the-ground stepping formwork.
3. With off-the-ground stepping formwork.
4. In opposite directions starting from a pier.

The first category is generally used where there are a large number of approximately equal spans of a low height above existing terrain. It is generally limited to structure lengths of approximately 1000 ft (300 m) and to nonuniform span lengths that prohibit a forming system of uniform size.

Normally in span-by-span construction the superstructure is of constant cross section (at least insofar as external dimensions are concerned), and the work proceeds from one abutment to the other. If a large center span exists, it will be formed first, possibly to an inflection point in the adjacent spans. The formwork is allocated such that it is used to cast the spans in the approaches proceeding from the center, in both directions, toward the abutments. Forms and scaffolding are disassembled and reerected in an alternating sequence and in elements that can be conveniently handled by a crane.

In the second category of span-by-span construction, for economical justification of equipment, the total length of structure must be at least 1000 ft (300 m), the overall cross section constant, the structure of low height, and the terrain along the longitudinal axis approximately level. Maximum span for this category is approximately 165 ft (50 m), and a large number of equal spans are required to achieve repetitiveness and thus economy.[3]

The falsework and forms are generally a span length (either the dimension from pier to pier or from inflection point to inflection point), Figure 6.1.[3] The formwork is fixed to the scaffolding and travels with it. The bottom of the formwork is designed with a hinge or continuous trap-door device such that the scaffolding and forms can travel past and clear the piers. The scaffolding is moved forward on rails. If a foundation for the scaffolding, forms, and weight of superstructure is found to be too costly or unsafe, a scheme may be used where the rails carry only the load of the scaffolding and formwork. Once in position, the scaffolding is supported at the piers, or at the forward pier, and the completed structure at the rear by auxiliary brackets; thus construction loads are transmitted to the pier foundations.

Where conditions exist as in the previous category, but the structure is high with reference to the terrain or crosses over difficult terrain or water, the third category may be used, whereby during the stepping and casting operations the equipment is supported by the piers or by a pier and the previously completed portion of the structure.

Where consecutive spans in the range of 160 to 500 ft (50 to 150 m) are contemplated and the factors mentioned above prevail, the type of con-

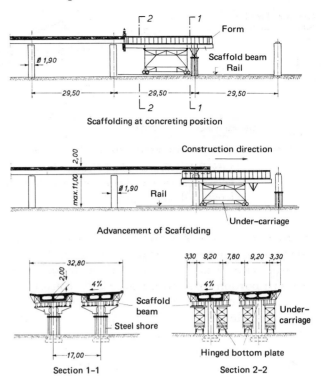

FIGURE 6.1. Schematic of procedure for movable scaffolding, from reference 3 (courtesy of Zement und Beton).

struction indicated by the fourth category may be considered. This system uses a gantry rig that has a length one and one-half times that of the span. In this method segments are cast in each direction from a pier, as in the balanced cantilever method, except that the form traveler and segment being cast are supported by the gantry. This method is actually a balanced cantilever method and not a span-by-span method of construction as defined here.

The advantages of the span-by-span method of construction, besides those associated with segmental construction in general, pertain to the prestressing steel requirements. Since the segments are supported by the form travelers, there are no cantilever stresses during construction, and prestress requirements are akin to those of conventional construction on falsework or those for the final condition of the structure.

6.2 Progressive Cast-in-Place Bridges

6.2.1 APPROACH SPANS TO THE BENDORF BRIDGE, GERMANY

As discussed in Section 2.2, the Bendorf Bridge was constructed in two parts. The western portion

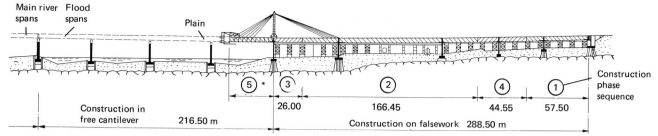

FIGURE 6.2.   Bendorf Bridge, Part Two (East), construction procedure, from reference 1 (courtesy of Beton- and Stahlbetonbau). Phase 5 by progressive placing, segment length 4.00 m.

(part one), Figure 2.9, consists of a symmetrical seven-span continuous girder constructed by the cast-in-place balanced cantilever method. The eastern portion (part two), Figure 2.10, consists of a nine-span continuous approach structure having an overall length of 1657 ft (505 m) with spans ranging from 134.5 ft (41 m) to 308 ft (94 m).

In the construction of the approach spans, Figure 6.2, the five spans from the east abutment were built in a routine manner with the assistance of falsework bents. The four spans over water were constructed by the progressive placement method, using cast-in-place segments and a temporary cable-stay arrangement to reduce the cantilever stresses. The temporary stay system consisted of a structural steel pylon approximately 65 ft (20 m) high and stays composed of Dywidag bars.

6.2.2 *OUNASJOKI BRIDGE, FINLAND*

This structure is near the city of Rovaniemi, Finland, and crosses the Ounas River just above its junction with the River Kemi near the Arctic Circle. The structural arrangement consists of two 230 ft (70 m) interior spans and end spans of 164 ft (50 m), prestressed longitudinally and transversely.

The first end span and 75 ft (22.75 m) of the second span were cast-in-place in a conventional manner on falsework inside a temporary wind-shielded protective cover, Figure 6.3. Outside temperature during this operation ranged from -20 to $-30°C$. Subsequent progressive cantilever construction was performed with the aid of a temporary pylon and stays, Figure 6.4. The same stages were repeated in the remaining spans. The superstructure was cast-in-place with the assistance of one form traveler, Figure 6.5. During these stages of construction, for protection against low temperatures, form traveler and form were fully enclosed, Figure 6.5. This enclosure was insulated with 4 in. (100 mm) of fiberglass.

Hardening of the concrete took an average of 76 hours. Temperature of the concrete was maintained between 35 and 45°C at mixing and between 20 and 25°C during casting. Curing inside the form traveler enclosure was assisted by warm-air blowers. Concrete strength was 5000 psi (34.5 MPa). Segment length was 11.5 ft (3.5 m), and it was possible to reach a casting rate of two segments a week.

Construction started in 1966 and was completed in 1967. Table 6.1 lists the temperatures recorded during seven months of the construction period. The progressive placement method proved effective and work progressed throughout the year even during arctic conditions.

FIGURE 6.3.   Ounasjoki Bridge, temporary protective structure (courtesy of Dyckerhoff & Widmann).

TABLE 6.1. Ounasjoki Bridge, Temperature Variations

Temperature	Month						
	March	April	May	June	July	August	September
Average °C	−2.5	−0.4	+5.6	+11.7	+14.3	+14.8	+8.7
Maximum °C	+5.8	+9.9	+24.6	+24.9	+25.7	+28.5	+19.3
Minimum °C	−26.4	−16.8	−12.2	+0.1	+3.0	+5.8	−4.7

FIGURE 6.4. Ounasjoki Bridge, winterproof traveling form (courtesy of Dyckerhoff & Widmann).

6.2.3 VAIL PASS BRIDGES, U.S.A.

The Vail Pass structures are part of Interstate I-70 near Vail, Colorado, in an environmentally sensitive area. Of the 21 bridge structures in this project, seventeen were designed and bid on the basis of alternate designs (Chapter 12). In the segmental alternative the contractor was allowed the option to construct as cast-in-place segmental. A group of four bridges approximately 7 miles (11.3 km) southeast of Vail were successfully bid as cast-in-place segmental and used the concept of progressive placement.

Two of these structures are contained in a four-span dual structure over Black Gore Creek, Figure 6.6. The other two structures are a three-span

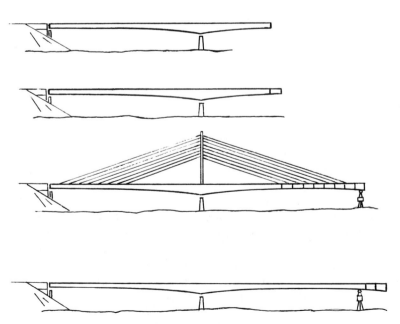

FIGURE 6.5. Ounasjoki Bridge, progressive placing scheme.

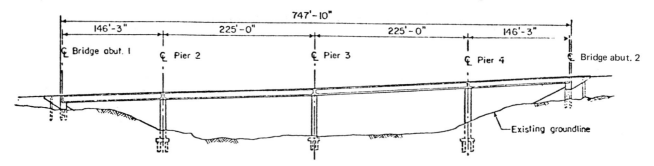

TYPICAL ELEVATION

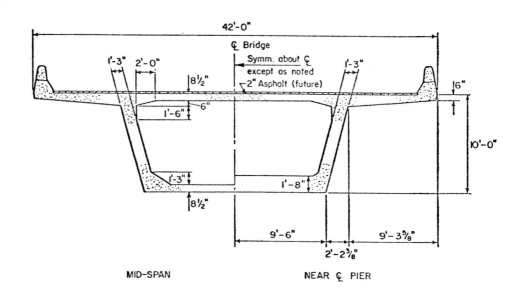

TYPICAL SECTION

FIGURE 6.6. Vail Pass Bridges, Black Gore Creek Bridge, typical elevation and section.

eastbound bridge and a four-span westbound bridge, both crossing Miller Creek, Figure 6.7.

Because the structures are relatively short and the spans small, they were constructed by the progressive placement method with temporary falsework bents. The work and time required to transport and reassemble the form travelers (as in the balanced cantilever method) was thereby minimized. Construction started from both abutments and proceeded progressively toward the center of each bridge.[4]

For each of the two structures in the Miller Creek Bridge, form travelers were assembled atop 30 ft (9.1 m) long segments at the abutments. As segment casting began, the side spans were supported at every second segment by a temporary bent. After reaching the first pier, segment con-

struction proceeded in normal fashion to midspan of the eastbound structure. In the westbound structure, when midspan of both interior spans was reached, temporary bents were again used to complete the remaining half-spans to the center pier. After reaching the center of the bridge, one form traveler of each bridge was dismantled, and the remaining form traveler was used to cast the closure pour. In this manner the form travelers for each bridge were assembled and dismantled only once, as opposed to the method of assembling two forms at each pier and dismantling upon completion of two half-span cantilevers about each pier.

For the Black Gore creek structures, to save critical construction time, both end spans of one structure and one end span of the other structure were built on falsework, while the form travelers

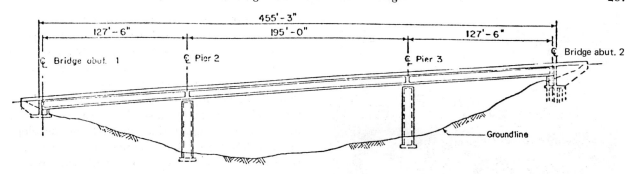

E. B. ELEVATION

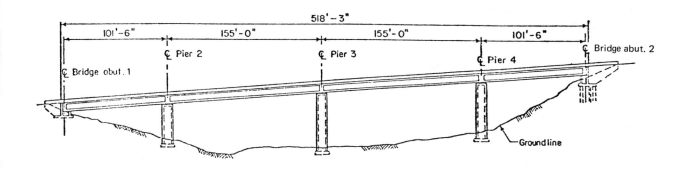

W. B. ELEVATION

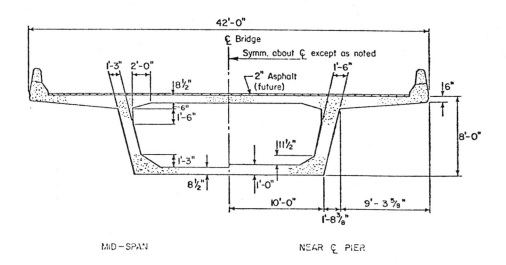

MID–SPAN   NEAR ℄ PIER

TYPICAL SECTION

FIGURE 6.7. Vail Pass Bridges, Miller Creek Bridge, typical elevation and section.

were occupied at the Miller Creek Bridges. Upon completion of their work at Miller Creek, the form travelers were transported over the completed end spans of the Black Gore Creek Bridges and construction continued in the progressive placement manner, Figure 6.8.

Because of the limited construction time a three-day cycle was required for segment casting.

FIGURE 6.8. Vail Pass Bridges, Black Gore Creek Bridge, under construction (courtesy of Dr. Man-Chung Tang, DRC Consultants, Inc.).

Construction specifications required a concrete strength of 3500 psi (24 MPa) at the time of post-tensioning and 5500 psi (38 MPa) at 28 days. Since the time required for forming and placing of rebar and tendons is somewhat fixed, the only operation that could be adjusted was the concrete curing time. This was accomplished by using a special water-reducing agent that allowed the development of 3500 psi (24 MPa) concrete in 18 hours. Because of lack of experience with the specific water reducer, honeycombing was experienced in the early stages of construction. Eventually a 2½ day cycle was achieved.

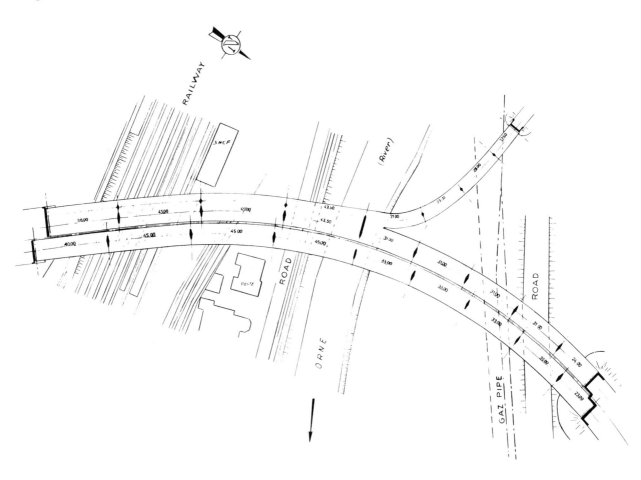

ROMBAS
-PLAN VIEW-

(a)

FIGURE 6.9. Rombas Viaduct, plan and sections. (a) Plan. (b) Typical bridge sections. (c) Typical segment section.

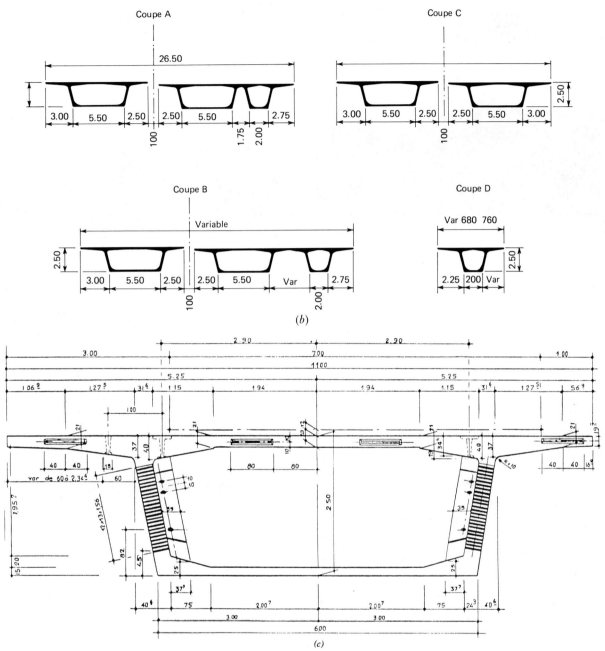

Figure 6.9. *(Continued)*

6.3 Progressive Precast Bridges

6.3.1 ROMBAS VIADUCT, FRANCE

The Rombas Viaduct is a constant-depth superstructure, supported on neoprene bearings, with nine continuous spans ranging from 75 ft (23 m) to 148 ft (45 m). This structure is curved in plan with a minimum radius of 900 ft (275 m) and of a variable width, owing to the presence of an exit ramp, Figure 6.9. Total length is 1073 ft (327 m),

and the viaduct has two parallel single-cell boxes. In cross section each single-cell box is 8.2 ft (2.5 m) deep and has a width of 36 ft (11.0 m). A construction view of the end of a segment is presented in Figure 6.10.

Construction of this structure employed the progressive placing of the precast segments. Temporary stability was provided by a cable-stay system, Figures 1.57 and 6.11, which advanced from pier to pier as the construction progressed. Segments were progressively placed, starting from one

FIGURE 6.10.   Rombas Viaduct, end view of segment.

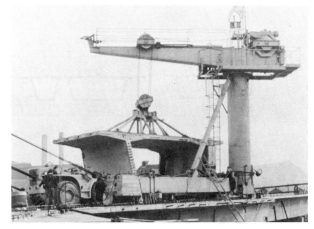

FIGURE 6.12.   Rombas Viaduct, view of swivel crane.

FIGURE 6.11.   Rombas Viaduct, view of cable stays and mast.

abutment, by means of a swiveling hoist, Figure 6.12, advancing along the deck.

6.3.2   *LINN COVE VIADUCT, U.S.A.*

A progressive placement scheme is being used for the Linn Cove Viaduct on the Blue Ridge Parkway in North Carolina, Figures 6.13 and 6.14. It is a

FIGURE 6.13.   Linn Cove Viaduct, photomontage.

FIGURE 6.14.   Linn Cove Viaduct, artist's rendering.

1243 ft (378.84 m) eight-span continuous structure with spans of 98.5, 163, 4 at 180, 163, and 98.5 ft (30.02, 49.68, four at 54.86, 49.68, and 30.02 m) and sharp-radius curves, Figure 6.15. In cross section it is a single-cell box girder with the dimensions indicated in Figure 6.16.

Because of the environmental sensitivity of the area, access to some of the piers is not available. Therefore, the piers will be constructed from the tip of a cantilever span, with men and equipment

being lowered down to construct the foundation and piers. The piers are precast segments stacked vertically and post-tensioned to the foundation, Figure 6.17.

The extreme curvature of the alignment makes the use of temporary cable stays impractical. Temporary bents at midspan will be used to reduce cantilever and torsional stresses during construction to acceptable levels. The temporary bents are erected in the same manner as the permanent

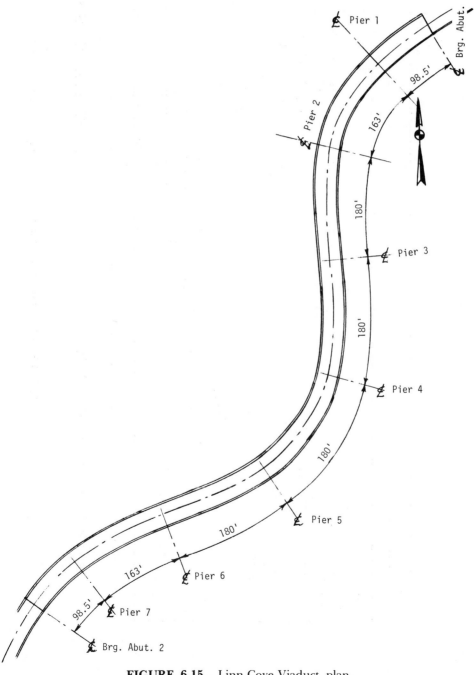

FIGURE 6.15. Linn Cove Viaduct, plan.

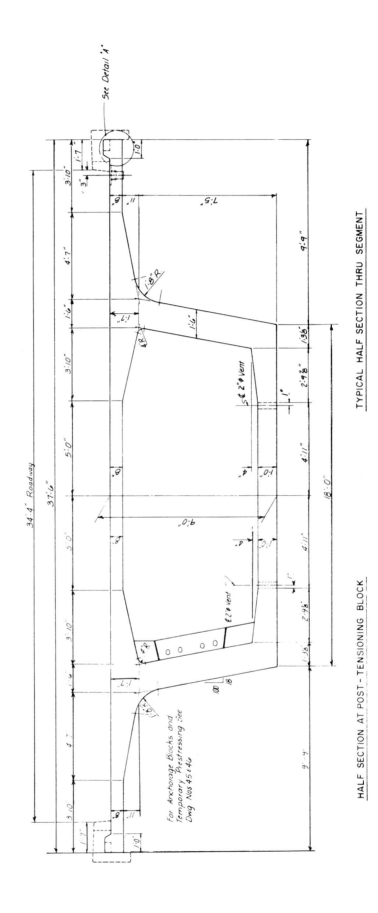

HALF SECTION AT POST-TENSIONING BLOCK

TYPICAL HALF SECTION THRU SEGMENT

FIGURE 6.16. Linn Cove Viaduct, typical segment cross section.

292

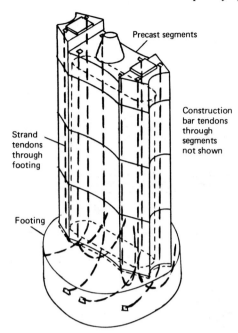

FIGURE 6.17. Linn Cove Viaduct, segmental pier.

piers, using a stiff-leg derrick at the end of the completed cantilevered portions of the structure, Figure 6.18. When the temporary bents are no longer required, they are dismantled and removed by equipment located on the completed portion of the bridge deck.

6.4 Span-by-Span Cast-in-Place Bridges

6.4.1 KETTIGER HANG, GERMANY

The first application of the off-ground methodology (category 3), Section 6.1.2, was in 1955 on the Kettiger Hang structure near Andernach (Federal Highway 9), Figure 6.19.[3] This system consists of four scaffolding trusses of slightly more than a span length and two cantilever girders of about a two-span length. The scaffolding trusses support the entire concrete weight during casting. The cantilever girders serve to transfer or advance the scaffolding trusses to the next span to be cast. The concrete form or mold rides with the scaffolding trusses and is thus repeatedly reused.

6.4.2 KRAHNENBERG BRIDGE, GERMANY

A variation of the off-the-ground system was used on the Krahnenbergbrücke near Andernach constructed from 1961 to 1964, Figure 6.20.[1,3] This structure has a length of 3609 ft (1100 m), a constant depth of 6.56 ft (2.0 m), a width of 60.7 ft (18.5), and spans of 105 ft (32 m). The site is on a slide-susceptible hillside, requiring difficult foundations, and its curved alignment follows the topography, all of which economically favored the span-by-span technique.

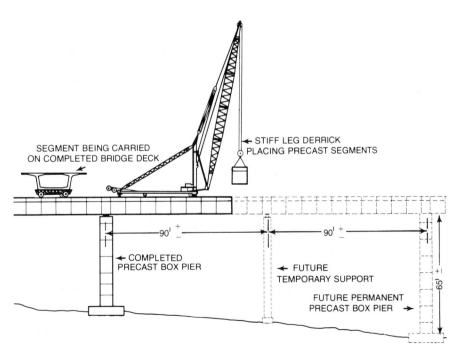

FIGURE 6.18. Linn Cove Viaduct, erection scheme for progressive placement.

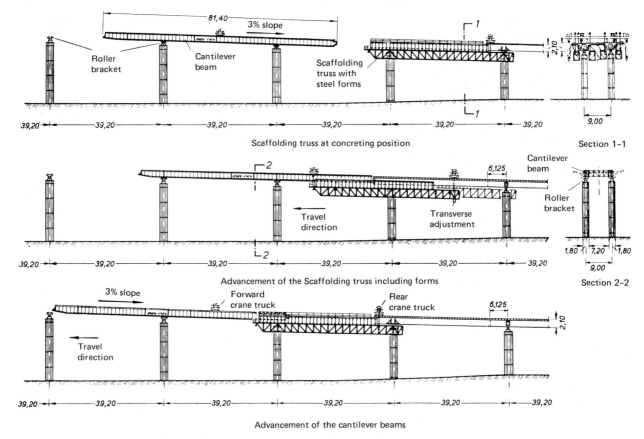

FIGURE 6.19. Kettiger Hang, schematic of the construction procedure, from reference 3 (courtesy of Zement und Beton).

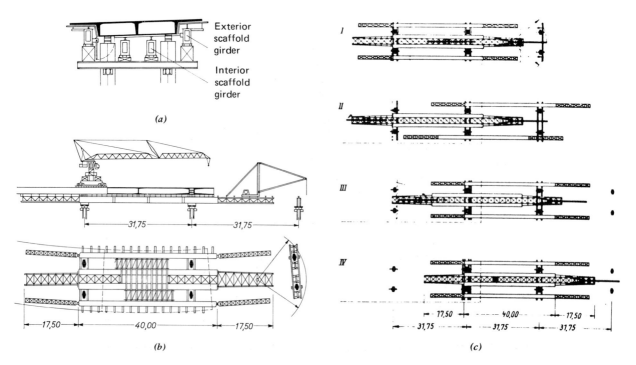

294

In this project four formwork supporting girders were used. Two interior girders were rigidly connected together by transverse horizontal bracing. The formwork was arranged so that the forms hinged at the bottom and folded down to allow passage, during advancement, past the piers, Figure 6.20a. The four girders were supported on the hexagonal piers by transverse support beams attached to the pier. In this manner the four longitudinal formwork support girders were supported on two piers, while an additional set of transverse support beams were attached to the forward pier. Figure 6.20b.

Latticework cantilever extensions at both ends of the longitudinal formwork support girders extended their length to twice the span length, so that a stable support was provided by the transverse support girders during advancement. The outside girders had joints or links at the connection with the cantilever latticework so that the curvature of the structure could be accommodated during their advancement. The elevation of the outside girders was adjusted by hydraulic jacks to accommodate superelevation. During the advancement operation the outside girders were advanced first and then the center two girders, Figure 6.20c. When the forward end of the interior girders reached the transverse supporting beams, the rear transverse beams of the previously cast span were no longer required. They were dismantled from the pier. These transverse beams were erected on the next forward pier by a crane, Figure 6.20b.

The exterior formwork of the two-cell box girder was attached to the longitudinal support girders and only required adjustment for curvature. The interior forms of the cells were dismantled and reassembled on the next span after reinforcement was placed in the bottom flange and webs.

FIGURE 6.20. (*Opposite*). Krahnenberg Bridge, schematic of construction, from reference 1 (courtesy of the American Concrete Institute). (*a*) Cross section. (*b*) Formwork equipment in working position. (*c*) I: Working position: reinforcing, and concreting on formwork equipment; installing the supporting construction on the next following pier by means of derrick and straight-line trolley. II: After concreting and prestressing: lowering of equipment; opening of formwork flaps; shifting forward of outer girders; dismantling of the first rear supporting girder by straight-line trolley; intermediate storage at center pier. III: Partial pony-roughing of center girder; dismantling and placing in intermediate for storage of second rear girder. IV: Final shifting forward of center girders; jacking up of equipment; closing of formwork flaps; new working position.

Average casting rate was 706 ft³ per hr (20 m³). Fourteen days was required for construction of a span.

6.4.3 *PLEICHACH VIADUCT, GERMANY*

In 1963 construction started on the 1148 ft (350 m) long Pleichach Viaduct[1,3] carrying a federal highway between Wurzburg and Fulda; it was the first use of the span-by-span technique for a dual structure, Figure 6.21. Span length is 119 ft (36.25

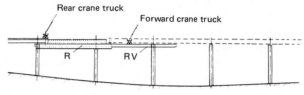

Scaffolding girder at concreting position

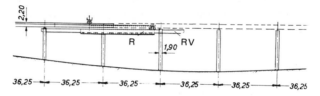

Advancement of the scaffolding girder including forms

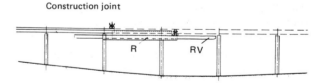

Advancement of the scaffolding and cantilever girders

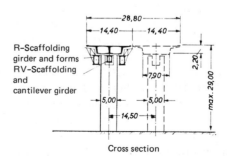

FIGURE 6.21. Pleichach Viaduct, schematic of the construction procedure, from reference 3 (courtesy of Zement und Beton).

m), with each two-cell box girder having a width of 47.2 ft (14.4 m) and a depth of 7.2 ft (2.2 m). The superstructure construction equipment was erected behind an abutment in a position to construct one superstructure. Upon reaching the opposite abutment, the equipment was shifted laterally for the return trip to construct the other superstructure. Because of the narrowness, only one longitudinal support girder was required, as opposed to the two girders required for the Krahnenberg Bridge. This girder is slightly longer than twice the span length. The two outside girders are approximately one span length.

The outside girders were advanced simultaneously by a carrier traveling at the front of the central girder and at the rear by carriers running on the deck of the previously completed section. During concreting, the two outside girders are supported on brackets at the forward pier and suspended from the completed portion of the superstructure. The center girder, relieved of the load of the two outside girders, is then advanced one span and again connected to the outside girders by the hinged bottom formwork, thus functioning as an auxiliary support girder. This sequence of operations is commonly referred to as the "slide-rule principle."

The piers have a width of 16.4 ft (5 m) and have an opening at the top to allow passage of the central support girder, Figure 6.21. The width of the pier is determined by the need for sufficient bearing area for the bearings and clearance for the central support girder. Whether the central opening at the top of the pier should be concreted in is one of aesthetics.

6.4.4 ELZTALBRÜCKE, GERMANY

The Elztalbrücke,[5,6] Figure 6.22, was constructed in 1965 at Eifel, West Germany, approximately 18.6 miles (30 km) west of Koblenz. It crosses the deep valley of the Elz River with a total structure length of 1244 ft (379.3 m), Figure 6.23. The superstructure has a width of 98.4 ft (30 m) and is supported on a single row of octagonal piers up to 328 ft (100 m) in height, Figure 6.24. Owing to the height of the valley, conventional construction on falsework would have been economically prohibitive. Therefore, a span-by-span system of self-supporting traveling scaffolding was used, Figure 1.53.

The Autobahn between Montabauer and Trier, which had been in planning before World War II,

FIGURE 6.22. Elztalbrücke, view of completed structure (courtesy of Dipl. Ing. Manfred Bockel).

had to cross two large natural obstacles, the Rhine River north of Koblenz (see the Bendorf Bridge, Section 2.2) and the Elz Valley. In 1962 tenders were called for on the Elz Valley structure. Bidders were provided with the grade requirements, dimensions for a single or a dual structure, the location of the abutments, and the foundation conditions.

A consortium of Dyckerhoff & Widmann AG, Wayss & Freytag KG, and Siemens-Bauunion GmbH investigated four possible prestressed concrete construction possibilities[5]:

1. A three-span variable depth structure similar to the Bendorf Bridge
2. A six-span constant-depth structure
3. A frame bridge
4. A nine-span "mushroom" construction with a center row of piers

These four schemes were proposed, as were a large number of different ones in both steel and concrete by other firms. The successful low bid was for scheme 4 above. The nine-span "mushroom" construction was approximately 4% less costly than an orthotropic-deck, three-span continuous steel girder and 7% less costly than a prestressed concrete girder bridge of six spans.[6]

The Elztalbrücke, extending the methodology used earlier for primarily low-level urban viaducts, was the first application of the "mushroom" cross section for a high-level structure crossing a deep valley. Previously, this type of construction, because of its short, stiff piers, required a number of expansion joints in the deck to accommodate thermal forces, elastic shortening, creep, and shrinkage. In this structure, owing to the flexibility of the tall piers, only one expansion joint was used,

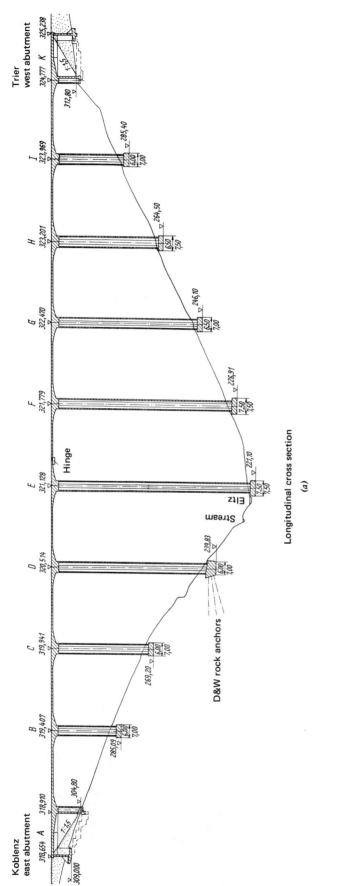

Longitudinal cross section

(a)

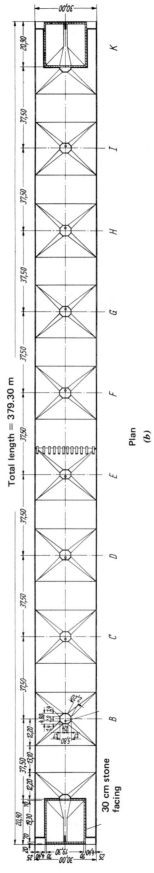

Total length = 379.30 m

Plan

(b)

FIGURE 6.23. Elztalbrücke, longitudinal cross section and plan, from reference 5 (courtesy of Der Bauingenieur). (a) Longitudinal cross section. (b) Plan.

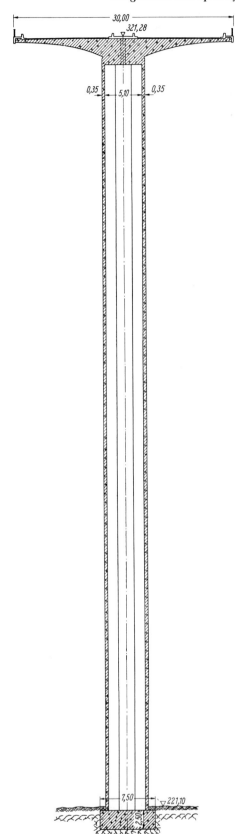

FIGURE 6.24. Elztalbrücke, cross section at pier E, from reference 5 (courtesy of Der Bauingenieur).

in the center span. This joint is located 38 ft (11.6 m) from pier E. The superstructure is monolithically connected at all piers and the abutments.

At the center of each span is a 43 ft (13.1 m) long, massive flat plate, which in cross section has a thickness varying from the centerline (crown of roadway) of $25\frac{1}{2}$ in. (650 mm) to $17\frac{3}{4}$ in. (450 mm) at the outside edges. The "mushroom" portion of the span varies in thickness, transversely and longitudinally, to 8 ft (2.45 m) at the pier. The superstructure is prestressed longitudinally and transversely.

The octagonal piers have, in cross section, external dimensions of 15.75 by 19 ft (4.8 by 5.8 m) with a wall thickness of $11\frac{3}{4}$ to $12\frac{3}{4}$ in. (300 to 350 mm). Any given pier has a constant cross section for its entire height. The percentage of vertical reinforcement, with a concrete cover on the outer and interior faces of 1.5 in. (40 mm), varies from 0.8 to 1.2% of the gross concrete area. Piers were constructed by slip-forming. The eight pier shafts were constructed in seven months. The tallest pier, 311.6 ft (95 m) in height, was slip-formed and cast at a rate of about 26 ft (8 m) per day and thus required 12 days to construct. The top 4 ft (1.2 m) portion of the pier was cast with the superstructure by the traveling scaffolding. On the top of the slip-formed pier four 7.2 ft (2.2 m) high pedestals were cast to provide the support for the cantilever girder from the traveling scaffolding, Figure 6.25.[5]

The traveling scaffolding was assembled at abutment A after completion of the abutment and the half-mushroom projecting therefrom. This form traveler, Figure 6.26, accommodates a full-width span-length segment of 123 ft (37.5 m). After the first span, two weeks were required to complete a superstructure span. The first opera-

FIGURE 6.25. Elztalbrücke, construction view (courtesy of Dipl. Ing. Manfred Bockel).

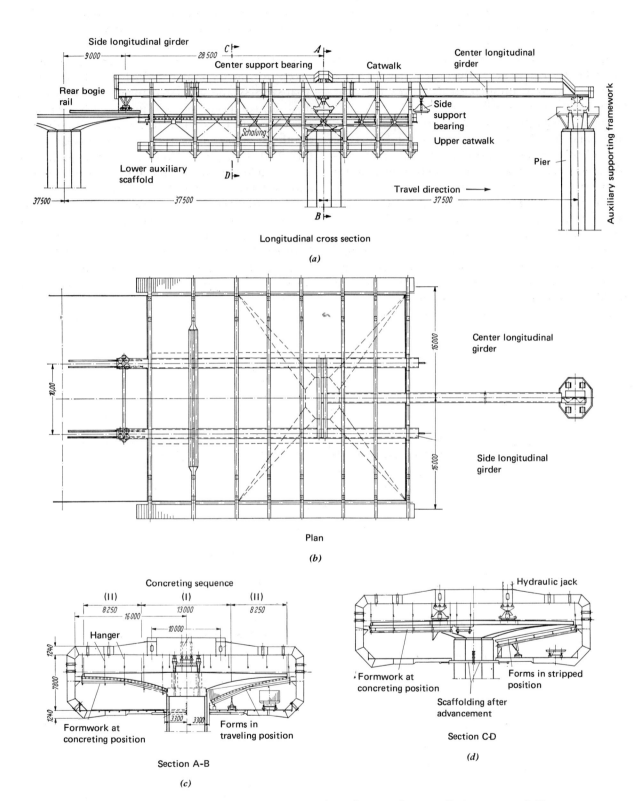

FIGURE 6.26. Elztalbrücke, form traveler, from reference 5 (courtesy of Der Bauingenieur). (*a*) Longitudinal cross section. (*b*) Plan. (*c*) Section *A-B*. (*d*) Section *C-D*.

299

tion was to cast a 42.65 ft (13 m) wide center portion of the bridge. After hardening and initial stressing, the two outside edges, each 27 ft (8.25 m) wide, were cast. Subsequently the form traveler was advanced to cast the next span.[5]

As mentioned previously, an expansion joint is located in the center span. During construction this joint was "locked" until construction reached pier G; then the joint was released.[5]

During concreting the forms are suspended by steel bars, and during advancement the forms are carried by the bottom arm of the transverse cantilevered steel members. The form traveler, Figure 6.26, essentially consists of two approximately 141 ft (43 m) long longitudinal girders and eight transverse frames in a "C" configuration which surrounds the deck construction. The transverse frames may be provided with a covering to protect the workmen and the construction from the weather. At the forward end an approximately 72 ft (22 m) long cantilever beam, located on the centerline, is projected to the next pier for support.

6.4.5   *GUADIANA VIADUCT, PORTUGAL*

This structure is located on national route 260 crossing the Guadiana River between Beja and Serpa, Portugal. The viaduct has a total length of 1115 ft (340 m) and consists of 197 ft (60 m) spans except for the river spans, which are 164 ft (50 m). Transversely, the superstructure is 53.8 ft (16.4 m) in width composed of two single-cell box girders. Each box girder is 19.35 ft (5.9 m) wide, with the depth varying from 6.5 ft (2.0 m) at midspan to 9.8 ft (3.0 m) at the piers. After construction of the box girders, a longitudinal centerline closure is poured and cantilevered sidewalks are constructed.

The superstructure is constructed by the span-by-span method, from inflection point to inflection point, by an overhead self-launching form carrier, Figure 6.27. The form carrier consists of 279 ft (85 m) long trusses of a depth varying from 9.8 ft (3.0 m) to 16.4 ft (5.0 m). Forms for concreting the superstructure are supported by two series of suspenders. One set pierces the concrete flanges and

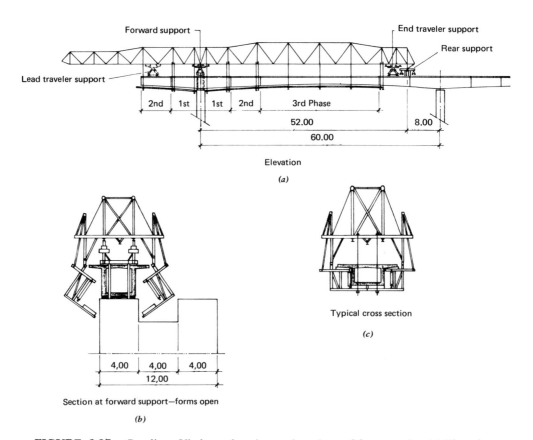

FIGURE 6.27.   Guadiana Viaduct, elevation and sections of form carrier. (*a*) Elevation. (*b*) Section at forward support—forms open. (*c*) Typical cross section.

is located inside the box cell. The other set is arranged outside the box and supports the forms when stripped and traveling past the piers in an open position, Figure 6.27.

During concreting of the superstructure the form carrier is supported on the forward pier by an arrangement of a telescoping tubular cross frame, at the rear; it is supported on the superstructure at a location 26 ft (8.0 m) forward of the rear pier. When the form carrier is being launched forward, it moves over a support at the tip of the completed superstructure cantilever (near the inflection point), and its rear support rides on the surface of the completed superstructure. The form carrier (including all equipment) weighs 209 tons (190 mt).

6.4.6   LOISACH BRIDGE, GERMANY

The federal autobahn between Munich and Lindau has an alignment that transverses the Murnauer swamp area near Ohlstadt and thus crosses the Loisach River and the old federal highway B-2 (Olympiastrasse), Figure 6.28. Because of flooding and poor soil conditions an embankment was not possible, and a decision was made requiring a dual viaduct bridge structure with a total length of 4314 ft (1315 m).[7]

The 232.8 ft (70.96 m) main span crossing the Loisach River is a variable-depth single-cell box girder constructed by the free cantilever method. Depth of the box girder varies from 9.84 ft (3.0 m) to 5.58 ft (1.7 m), Figure 6.29. The approach spans are of a T-beam cross section, Figure 6.29, constructed by the span-by-span method with the form carriers running below the superstructure. Figure 6.30 is a longitudinal section of the bridge within the area of the approach spans, showing the form carrier running below the level of the top slab. Figure 6.31 shows the form traveler in action.

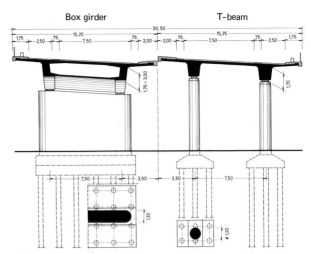

FIGURE 6.29. Loisachbrücke, cross sections, from reference 8 (courtesy of Dyckerhoff & Widmann).

The dual structure has a total width of 100 ft (30.5 m), Figure 6.29, and each half is supported on two circular piers, excepting the Loisach span which is supported on wall piers. In the total length, the dual structures are subdivided into three sections by two transverse joints, Figure 6.28. In plan the structure has a radius of 4265 ft (1300 m) at the Munich end, and the curvature reverses at the Loisach with a radius of 6562 ft (2000 m).[8] The completed structure is shown in Figure 6.32.

The circular piers are 4 ft (1.2 m) in diameter and are supported on 20 in. (500 mm) driven piles with an allowable load capacity of 176 tons (160 mt). Pile depths vary from 42 to 72 ft (13 to 22 m). A total of 1182 piles were driven for a total length of piling of 63,650 ft (19,400 m), with an average length of pile of 53.8 ft (16.4 m). Load capacity of the piles was determined from eleven load tests taken to 265 tons (240 mt).

Because of the poor soil conditions and ground-water pressure, the substructure was con-

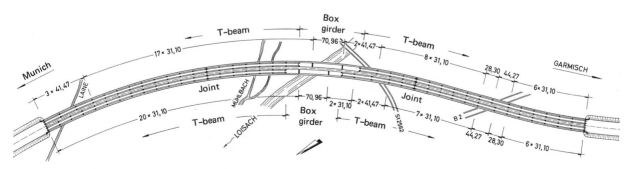

FIGURE 6.28. Loisachbrücke, layout and underside view of bridge, from reference 8 (courtesy of Dyckerhoff & Widmann).

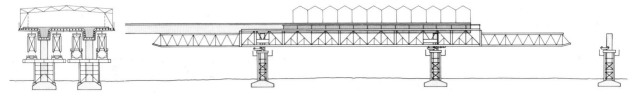

FIGURE 6.30. Loisachbrücke, longitudinal and cross section showing form traveler (courtesy of Dipl. Ing. Manfred Bockel).

FIGURE 6.31. Loisachbrücke, view of form traveler in action (courtesy of Dipl. Ing. Manfred Bockel).

FIGURE 6.32. Loisachbrücke, view of completed structure (courtesy of Dipl. Ing. Manfred Bockel).

structed in pits enclosed by sheet piling. The round piers vary in height from 9.8 to 23 ft (3 to 7 m). Because of the delay in pile driving, resulting from the soil conditions, the foundation completion was delayed from October 1970 to April 1971.

The 73 T-beam spans were constructed with two span-by-span form travelers whose operations were synchronized. On the Munich side of the Loisach four 223 ft (68 m) long and 4.26 ft (1.30 m) high principal form support girders are supported in the 100 ft (31 m) spans on cross beams at each pier, which in turn are supported off the pile caps. For the longer spans an auxiliary support was re-

quired at midspan. The radius and superelevation in a support length were held constant. Superelevation varies from +5.5 to −4%. For a normal span 8830 ft³ (250 m³) of concrete were placed in nine hours.[8]

Because of the tight time schedule, work was continued through the winter months in defiance of the extreme harsh weather conditions in the Loisach Valley. A weather enclosure was mounted on the form traveler and heated by warm-air blowers. In this enclosure the reinforcement and preheated concrete was placed. In addition, the fresh concrete was protected by heat mats. In this manner the work could proceed up to an outside temperature of 5°F (−15°C). Construction cycle per span was gradually reduced, after familiarization, from an original 14 days to seven days. Following completion of the western roadway up to the Loisach the form traveler was transferred to the eastern roadway for the return trip to the Munich abutment. All 38 spans on the Munich side were completed by the end of February 1972, saving nine weeks in the construction schedule.

On the Garmisch side of the Loisach the movable scaffold system consisted of four principal girders 292 ft (89 m) in length and 9.8 ft (3.0 m) deep, Figure 6.33. Superelevation varies from +4 to −5.5%.

Because of the delay in the pile driving, the first span was started in December 1970 with a 12-week delay. The last approach span on the left of the Garmisch side was completed in August of 1971. The traveler was then transferred to the other roadway for the return trip and all 35 bridge spans were completed by March 1972. By a gradual reduction of the work cycle from 14 days to seven days, nine weeks were saved in the construction schedule. Not only was the loss of time resulting from the foundation work made up, but a time advantage was attained.

The four box girder spans (two in each dual structure) on either side of the principal span over the Loisach were cast on stationary falsework. Auxiliary cross beams to support the falsework girder were supported on driven piles. The two main

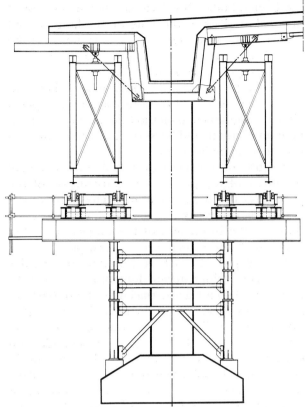

FIGURE 6.33. Loisachbrücke, cross section of movable scaffold system, from reference 8 (courtesy of Dyckerhoff & Widmann).

spans of 232.8 ft (70.96 m) were constructed by the free cantilever method. Thirteen segments of 16.4 ft (5 m) were required; six segments were cast from one pier and then the cantilever form travel-

ers were transferred to the opposite pier for the remaining seven segments.[8]

After a construction time of approximately 30 months the bridge was completed in 1972, shortly before beginning of the Olympic Games.

6.4.7 RHEINBRÜCKE DUSSELDORF-FLEHE, GERMANY

This is an asymmetric cable-stayed bridge with an inverted concrete Y-pylon, Figures 6.34 through 6.37. The overall length from abutment to abutment is 3764 ft (1147.25 m). The Rhine River span is 1205 ft (367.25 m) long and is a rectangular three-cell steel box girder with outriggers to support a 135 ft (41 m) wide orthotropic deck, Figures 6.36 and 6.37. At the pylon there is a transition from the steel box girder to prestressed concrete box girders, which are used for the thirteen 197 ft (60 m) spans in the approach viaduct. The structure is continuous throughout its entire length, having expansion joints only at the abutments.

The approach viaduct has from pier 9 up to pier 13, Figure 6.37, a five-cell box girder cross section with a width of 96.8 ft (29.5 m) and a depth of 12.5 ft (3.8 m). This heavy cross section, Figure 6.36, resists the anchorage forces from the cable stays. For the balance of the viaduct length from abutment to pier 9 the cross section consists of two single-cell boxes, a continuation of the exterior cells of the five-cell box girder cross section. However, the interior webs of each box are of less

FIGURE 6.34. Rheinbrücke Dusseldorf-Flehe, artist's rendering (courtesy of Dyckerhoff & Widmann).

FIGURE 6.35. Rheinbrücke Dusseldorf-Flehe, view from construction end of approach viaduct looking toward the pylon under construction.

thickness than that of the five-cell cross section. The width of each box then becomes a constant 23 ft (7.0 m) outside-to-outside of webs. A diaphragm occurs at each pier.

The approach spans were constructed segmentally by the span-by-span method with construction joints at approximately the one-fifth point of the span. As described in Section 6.1.2, the method used here employed movable falsework, Figures 1.54 and 6.38, supported from the ground. The 197 ft (60 m) spans were poured in place in one unit from construction joint to construction joint. This required continuous placement of as much as 3200 cubic yards (2500 m³) of concrete. After each section was cast in place and reached sufficient strength, the prestress tendons were stressed and the falsework was moved forward to repeat the cycle.

6.4.8 DENNY CREEK BRIDGE, U.S.A.

The Denny Creek Bridge is the first implementation of the span-by-span method of construction in the United States. It is located a few miles west of Snoqualmie Pass in the state of Washington and will carry the I-90 westbound traffic down off the pass. It is a three-lane, 20-span, prestressed concrete box girder design with a total length of 3620 ft (1103 m) on a 6% grade, Figure 6.39. The contractor, Hensel Phelps Construction Company, elected a construction method similar to those used in many German and Swiss designs where the area is environmentally sensitive.

Because of the ecological and environmental sensitivity of the project site, construction of the piers was carried out under extreme space restrictions. The contractor was allowed a narrow access road for the full length of the project and additional work and storage area at each pier.[9]

The 19 pier shafts have a hollow rectangular cross section with exterior dimensions of 16 by 10 ft (4.88 by 3.05 m), a wall thickness of 2 ft (0.61 m), and heights ranging from 35 to 160 ft (10.7 to 48.8 m), Figure 6.40. Twelve piers are supported on rectangular footings. The other seven piers are supported on pier shafts sunk through talus and till and keyed into solid bed rock, Figure 6.41. Pier-shaft diameter is 12 ft (3.66 m) with a maximum depth of shaft below the terrain of 80 ft (24.38 m).

The superstructure was constructed in three stages, Figure 6.42. In the first stage, bottom flange and webs were constructed from a 330 ft (100 m) long movable launching truss, Figure 6.43. The two trusses used for constructing the "U" portion of the box section rested on landing wings at the piers, Figures 6.44 and 6.45, as the launching truss moved up the valley, sliding from pier top to pier top. The construction schedule called for one span every two weeks. The entire scaffold system was supported on six jacks to adjust for proper alignment, two jacks at the rear of the span or initial pier and four jacks at the advance section or next pier.

The launching truss was designed to support the outside steel forms of the box section, Figure 6.46, and to facilitate removal of the inside forms,[9] Figure 6.42. Track-mounted cranes installed at the top of the truss frame lifted and moved the inside forms from the web, hanging them on the truss so that they were moved forward with the advancement of the launching truss. Figure 6.47 is an interior view of the working area between trusses. Visible are the overhead track for the 15 ton (13.6 mt) cranes located near each web. Also visible are the cable hangars from the roof frame for the bottom slab support during casting.

The steel trapezoidal box form used for con-

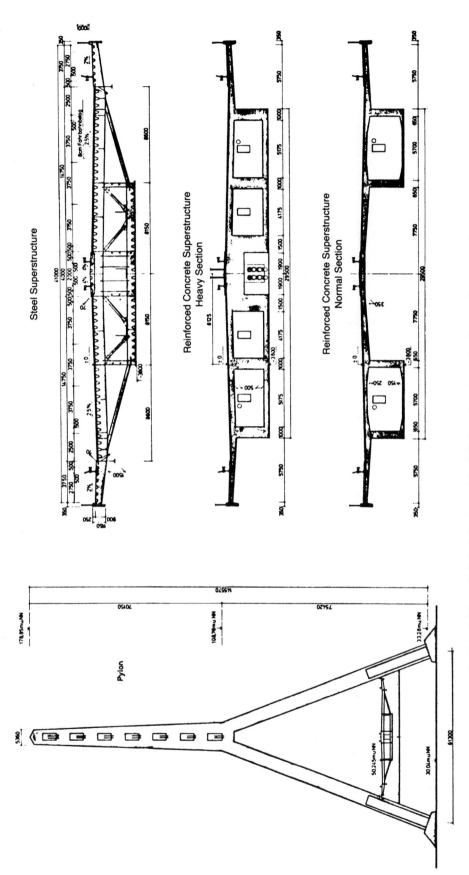

FIGURE 6.36. Rheinbrücke Dusseldorf-Flehe, elevation of pylon and cross sections.

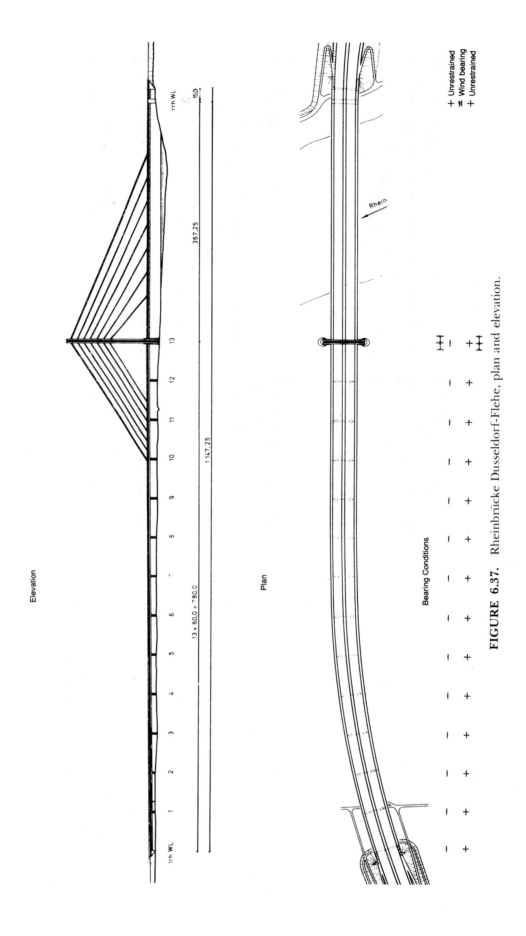

FIGURE 6.37. Rheinbrücke Dusseldorf-Flehe, plan and elevation.

FIGURE 6.38. Rheinbrücke Dusseldorf-Flehe, end view of girder.

struction was insulated with styrofoam, Figure 6.48, and had heat cables installed (actuated if need be) to help maintain the temperature and rate of cure. Also, heat blankets were available to go over the section to reduce heat loss and maintain a constant temperature in cold weather.

Concrete was batched from a plant erected near the west abutment using the highway right-of-way. The contractor used three 8 cu yd (6.1 m³) ready-mix trucks for mixing the concrete, which was then pumped to the proper location. Superstructure pours were about 300 cu yd (229.4 m³) and took about nine hours, using two concrete pumps and the track-mounted cranes installed in the truss frame. Concrete strength required was 5000 psi (34.47 MPa). The contractor obtained 3500 psi (24.13 MPa) in three days using $\frac{3}{4}$ in. (19 mm) aggregate. The 28-day strength ranged from 6100 to 6600 psi (42.06 to 45.51 MPa).

In stage two the top flange between the webs was placed. Metal forms, Figure 6.49, were supported from the bottom flange and webs, Figure 6.42.[9]

In stage three the two top flange cantilevers were placed, Figure 6.42, by a movable carriage that rode on top of the box cast in stage two, Figure 6.42. Upon completion of stage three, the transverse prestressing of the top flange was accomplished. The completed section is 52 ft (15.08 m) wide, providing three traffic lanes.

The Washington DOT sponsored the design. Three alternatives were prepared for bidding purposes. One was an in-house state design; the other two were prepared by outside consultants. The Dyckerhoff & Widmann design proved to be

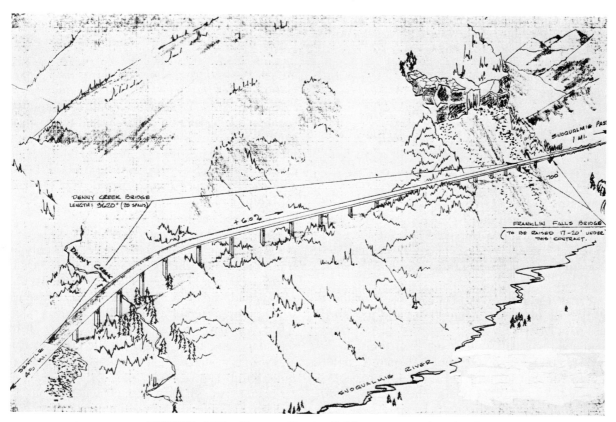

FIGURE 6.39. Denny Creek Bridge, perspective sketch.

FIGURE 6.40. Denny Creek Bridge, view of piers under construction (courtesy of J. L. Vatshell, Washington DOT).

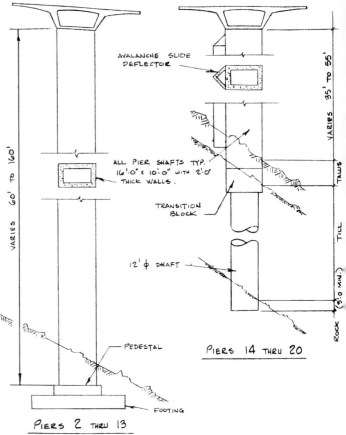

FIGURE 6.41. Denny Creek Bridge, substructure types.

the most economical. VSL Corporation was the subcontractor providing the prestressing expertise.

6.5 Span-by-Span Precast Bridges

6.5.1 LONG KEY BRIDGE, U.S.A.

Long Key Bridge in the Florida Keys carries U.S. Highway 1 across Long Key south to Conch Key. The existing bridge consists of 215 reinforced concrete arch spans, ranging in length from 43 to 59 ft (13.1 to 18 m) for a total bridge length of 11,960 ft (3645 m).

The new bridge, presently under construction, is 50 ft (15.2 m) between centerlines and just north and parallel to the existing structure. It is a precast segmental box girder constructed by the span-by-span method and consisting of 101 spans of 118 ft (36 m) and end spans of 113 ft (34.4 m) for a total length of 12,144 ft (3701 m). The roadway width between barrier curbs is 36 ft (11 m), Figure 6.50, to accommodate a 12 ft (3.66 m) roadway and a 6 ft (1.83 m) shoulder in each direction. Figure 6.51 is

an artist's rendering showing the precast V-piers with the 7 ft (2m) deep box girder segments.

In the preliminary design stage three methods of segmental construction were considered: balanced cantilever, span-by-span, and progressive placement. The progressive placement method was discarded because it was felt (at the time) to be too new for acceptance in U.S. practice. It was later introduced on the Linn Cove Viaduct in North Carolina (see Section 6.3.2).

This is the first use of a precast span-by-span method in the United States. The segments are transported from the casting yard to their location in the structure by barge. The segments are then placed with a barge crane on an erection truss, which is supported by a steel grillage at the V-piers. Each span has a 6 in. closure pour after all the segments have been placed on the erection truss and properly aligned. The essential operations are indicated in Figure 6.52.

Segment weight is approximately 65 tons (59 mt). Each segment is placed on the erection truss on a three-point support and brought into its final position. It takes approximately four to six hours

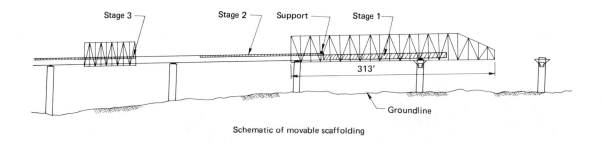

Schematic of movable scaffolding

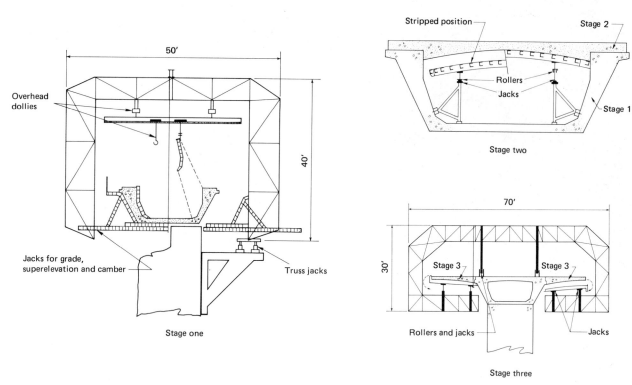

Stage one

Stage two

Stage three

FIGURE 6.42. Denny Creek Bridge, schematic of construction stages, from reference 9 (courtesy of the Portland Cement Association).

FIGURE 6.43. Denny Creek Bridge, view of launching truss.

FIGURE 6.44. Denny Creek Bridge, view of landing wings at piers (courtesy of J. L. Vatshell, Washington DOT).

309

FIGURE 6.45. Denny Creek Bridge, close-up view of landing wing (courtesy of J. L. Vatshell, Washington DOT).

FIGURE 6.46. Denny Creek Bridge, view of outside steel forms (courtesy of J. L. Vatshell, Washington DOT).

FIGURE 6.47. Denny Creek Bridge, view of interior working area between trusses (courtesy of Herb Schell, FHWA Region 10).

FIGURE 6.48. Denny Creek Bridge, insulation on exterior steel forms with installed heat cables (courtesy of Herb Schell, FHWA Region 10).

to place the segments required for one span. The contractor has placed as many as three spans per week for a total of 354 ft (108 m) of completed superstructure per week and has averaged 2.25 spans per week.

Another major deviation from United States practice in this project was the use of external prestressing tendons (located inside the box girder cell). This requires that the tendons be considered as unbonded for ultimate-strength analysis. Placing the tendons inside the box girder void allows the web thickness to be minimized. Tendon geometry is controlled by deviation blocks cast monolithically with the segments at the proper location in the span, Figure 6.53. These blocks perform the same function as hold-down devices in a pretensioning bed. The tendon ducts between deviation blocks or anchorage locations or both are composed of polyethylene pipe, which is then grout-injected upon completion of stressing operations—a corrosion protection system similar to that used for the cable stays on some cable-stay bridges.[10,11]

FIGURE 6.49. Denny Creek Bridge, view of metal form used for stage-two construction (courtesy of J. L. Vatshell, Washington DOT).

FIGURE 6.51. Long Key Bridge, artist's rendering.

The external tendons overlap at the pier segment to develop continuity. The bridge is continuous between expansion joints for eight spans, 944 ft (288 m). After the closure pour reaches the required strength, the post-tensioning is accomplished and the span is complete. A 30 in. (760 mm) diameter waterline is installed inside the void of the box girder. The erection truss is then lowered and moved away from the completed span. The erection truss is handled at a one-point pick-up location by a C-shaped lifting hook, Figure 6.52. The truss is supported against the barge crane and moved parallel to the new bridge until it

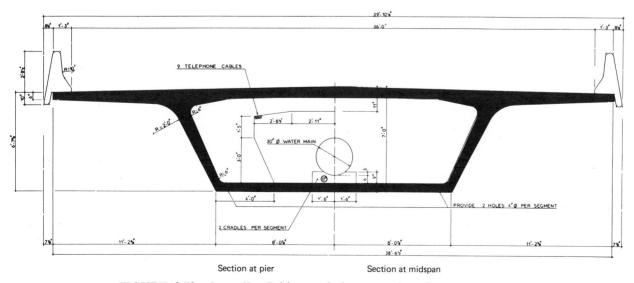

Section at pier   Section at midspan

FIGURE 6.50. Long Key Bridge, typical cross section of superstructure.

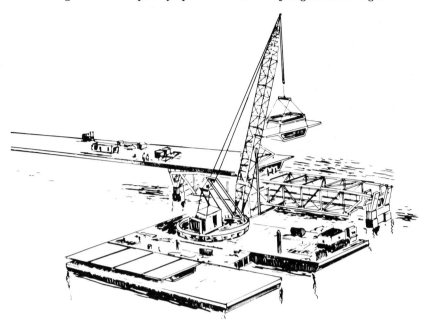

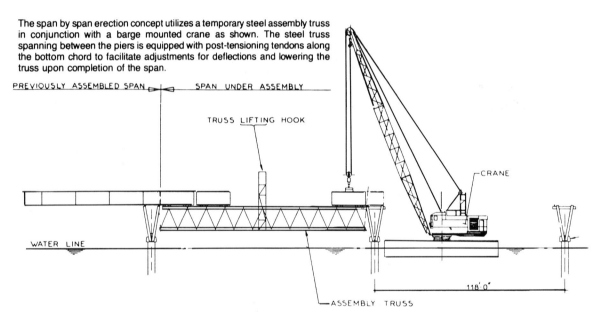

The span by span erection concept utilizes a temporary steel assembly truss in conjunction with a barge mounted crane as shown. The steel truss spanning between the piers is equipped with post-tensioning tendons along the bottom chord to facilitate adjustments for deflections and lowering the truss upon completion of the span.

FIGURE 6.52.   Long Key Bridge, span-by-span erection scheme.

reaches the position for a new span, and the cycle is repeated.

6.5.2   *SEVEN MILE BRIDGE, U.S.A.*

The Seven Mile Bridge, Figure 6.54, in the Florida Keys carries U.S. Highway 1 across Seven Mile Channel and Moser Channel from Knights Key west and southwest across Pigeon Key to Little Duck Key.

The existing structure consists of 209 masonry arch spans, 300 spans of steel girders resting on masonry piers, and a swing span over Moser Channel. The spans range in length from 42 ft 7½ in. (13 m) to 47 ft 4½ in. (14.4 m) for the masonry arches and from 59 ft 9 in. (18.2 m) to 80 ft (24.4 m) for the steel girders resting on masonry piers, which along with the 256 ft 10 in. (78.3 m) swing span, produce a total bridge length of 35,716 ft 3 in. (10,886 m).

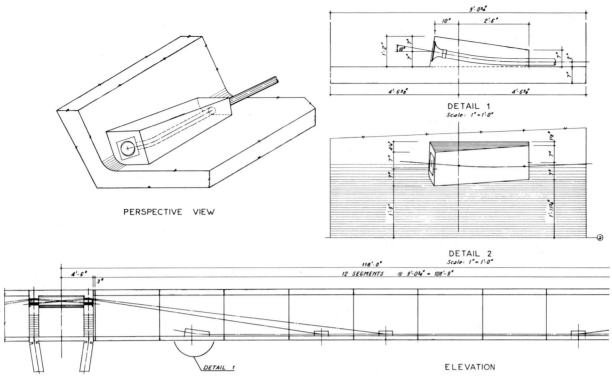

PERSPECTIVE VIEW

DETAIL 1
Scale: 1" = 1'-0"

DETAIL 2
Scale: 1" = 1'-0"

ELEVATION

FIGURE 6.53. Long Key Bridge, typical tendon layout.

FIGURE 6.54. Seven Mile Bridge, artist's rendering.

The new bridge, presently under construction, is located to the south of the existing bridge. It is a precast segmental box girder constructed by the span-by-span method with 264 spans at 135 ft (41.15 m), a west-end span of 81 ft 7½ in. (24.88 m), and an east-end span of 141 ft 9 in. (43.2 m) for a total length of 35,863 ft 4½ in. (10,931 m). The roadway requirements are the same as for the Long Key Bridge and the cross section is almost identical, Figure 6.50. Seven Mile Bridge crosses the Intracoastal Waterway with 65 ft (19.8 m) vertical clearance, and its alignment has both vertical and horizontal curvature.

The consultants, Figg and Muller Engineers, Inc., used the same concepts as had been used for the Long Key Bridge, except they omitted the V-pier alternative in favor of a rectangular hollow box-pier scheme that is precast in segments and post-tensioned vertically to the foundation system.

As mentioned in Section 1.9.3, the contractor elected to alter the construction scheme in this bridge from that of the Long Key Bridge by suspending the segments from an overhead truss rather than placing them on an underslung truss. The essential operations for construction of a typical span are as follows:

1. Transportation of all segments by barge to the erection site.
2. Assembly of all segments in a span (with the exception of the pier segment) on a structural steel frame supported by a barge.
3. Placing the pier segment on the pier adjacent to the previously completed portion of the deck with the overhead truss working in cantilever.
4. Launching the overhead truss onto this newly placed pier segment.

5. Lifting in place the entire assembly of typical segments with four winches supported by the truss.

6. Post-tensioning the entire span after the closure joint has been poured between the finished span and the new span.

7. Launching the overhead truss to repeat a new cycle of operations.

After a period of adjustment, the method has allowed a speed of construction equal to that for the assembly truss scheme used for the Long Key Bridge. One complete span may be constructed in one day, and as many as six 135 ft spans have been placed in a single week. Figure 6.55 shows the assembly of segments being erected in a typical span.

6.6 Design Aspects of Segmental Progressive Construction

6.6.1 GENERAL

The use of temporary stays to carry the weight of segments during construction induces only a normal compression load in the deck and a very limited amount of bending. Consequently, the static scheme of the structure during construction is very close to that of the finished structure. This is a significant advantage over the conventional cantilever construction scheme, where continuity of the successive cantilever arms results in two static schemes significantly different between construction and service.

Because of this similarity of static scheme throughout erection and service, it is expected that the layout of prestress tendons found in cast-in-place structures or in span-by-span construction

should be applicable to progressive construction, with the added advantage that the tendons can be regularly stressed and anchored at the successive joints between segments in a simple manner.

On the other hand, progressive construction differs in several aspects such as pier design and deflection control during construction, calling for a more detailed examination.

6.6.2 REACTIONS ON PIERS DURING CONSTRUCTION

Construction of a typical span proceeds in two stages, as shown in Figure 6.56: (1) pure cantilever erection, of a length a from the pier, and (2) construction with temporary stays on the remaining length $(L - a)$. Length a should be selected (within the nearest number of segments being placed) such as to keep the girder load moments over the pier within allowable limits.

Assuming that this moment is of exactly the same magnitude as the fixed end moment of a typical span under the same unit load W, one may write:

$$\frac{Wa^2}{2} = \frac{WL^2}{12}$$

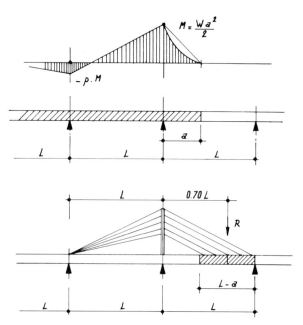

FIGURE 6.55. Seven Mile Bridge, erection of a typical span.

FIGURE 6.56. Progressive construction, deck reactions on piers.

for a constant-depth girder, which is the general case for progressive construction. Thus:

$$a = 0.408L \simeq \underline{0.40\,L}$$

For $a = 0.40L$ the moment over the pier is equal to $M = 0.08WL^2$. The moment over the preceding pier, for a structure with a large number of identical spans, is equal to $0.268M$. Therefore, the reaction over the pier at the end of this first stage of construction can be easily computed as:

$$R = \underline{0.40WL} + 1.268 \times 0.08WL = \underline{0.50WL}$$

During the second construction stage the weight of the remaining part of the span is supported by the temporary stays, which are anchored in the rear span as close as possible to the previous pier so as not to induce undesirable variations of moments in the last completed span. Consequently, the weight of that part of the span induces in the pier a reaction equal to:

$$0.6WL + \frac{1.70}{1.00} = \underline{1.02WL}$$

The total reaction during construction applied to the pier is thus:

$$R = 0.50WL + 1.02WL = \underline{1.62WL}$$

as opposed to $R = WL$ for cast-in-place or span-by-span construction. This temporary increase of girder load reaction of 62% will eventually vanish when construction proceeds. It is important to verify how critical this pier temporary overload may be for the design of the substructure. Taking the example of a 150 to 200 ft span, the average loads are as follows for a 40 ft wide bridge designed for three lanes of traffic:

Girder load	8.0 ksf
Superimposed load	1.5 ksf
Equivalent live load including impact	2.6 ksf

The maximum reaction during construction compares with that after completion as follows (values given are the ratio between reaction and span length):

1. During construction, $1.62 \times 8.0 = $ <u>13 ksf</u>
2. Completed structure:
   a. Girder load   8.0
   b. Superimposed load   1.5
   c. Live load, including provision for continuity

over the support
(15%), $2.6 \times 1.15 = $ <u>3.0</u>

<u>12.5 ksf</u>

The difference is small and usually more than offset by the fact that horizontal loads during construction are smaller than during service.

6.6.3 *TENSIONS IN STAYS AND DEFLECTION CONTROL DURING CONSTRUCTION*

As shown previously, progressive construction of a typical span entails two successive stages:

Cantilever construction on a length a

Temporary suspension by stays on the remaining part of the span $(L - a)$

This second stage induces small deflections and rotation, provided that the vertical component of the stay loads balances the total deck weight. On the other hand, the first-stage construction not only creates substantial deflections but also changes the geometric position of the entire span, as may be seen in Figure 6.57.

The weight (Wa) of the deck section produces:

A rotation of the previous span, ω_1, which will project at the following pier and create a vertical deflection, y_1

a deflection of the cantilever proper, y_2

a rotation at the end of the cantilever, ω_2, which will project again at the following pier into a deflection $\omega_2 (L - a)$

Altogether the total deflection is:

$$y = \frac{Wa^2}{24EI} (2L^2 \sqrt{3} + 4aL - a^2)$$

If we let $u = a/L$, the deflection can then be written as:

$$y = \frac{WL^4}{24EI} u^2 (2\sqrt{3} + 4u - u^2)$$

With $u = 0.4$ as assumed before, the total deflection is:

$$y = 0.0327 \frac{WL^4}{EI}$$

where $W = $ unit deck load,
         $L \;= $ span length,

E = concrete modulus,

I = section inertia.

A simple parametric analysis will reveal the importance of this problem. If $\bar{w}$ is the specific gravity of concrete and A the cross-sectional area, then $W = \bar{w}A$. It was shown in Chapter 4 that the efficiency factor of a box section is:

$$\rho = \frac{I}{Ac_1c_2} = 0.60 \text{ to } 0.63$$

If the section is symmetrical, $c_1 = c_2 = 0.5\,h$ (h = section depth), and $I = 0.157\,Ah^2$ max. If $c_1 = 0.33\,h$ and $c_2 = 0.67h$, which is the practical dissymmetry of a box section, $I = 0.133Ah^2$ min. For all practical purposes, assume $I = 0.14Ah^2$. The deflection then becomes:

$$Ey = 0.23\,\bar{w}L^2\left(\frac{L}{h}\right)^2$$

Because the construction proceeds rapidly, E should be taken for short-duration loading; that is, $E = 800,000$ ksf; the specific gravity of concrete is $\bar{w} = 0.15$ kcf. The slenderness ratio L/h varies between 18 and 22. Results are shown in Figure 6.58.

Construction of a 200 ft span, for example, with a slenderness ratio of 20 will be accompanied by a deflection under girder load (without prestress) at the next pier of 8.3 inches. The construction method is therefore very sensitive to concrete deflections, which are magnified by the great lever arm of the first-stage construction of the span projecting its intrinsic deformation to the following pier.

Fortunately, prestress will give a helping hand and contribute to substantially decreasing the girder load deflection. The minimum prestress required at this stage is to balance the tensile stresses induced by the girder load moments. With the same notations as above, one may compute the prestress force and the corresponding moment for three positions of the neutral axis:

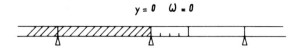

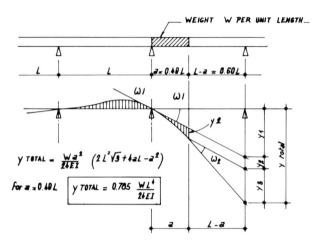

FIGURE 6.57. Progressive construction, deformations.

For an efficiency factor $\rho = 0.65$ the corresponding values would be:

0.58	0.47	0.39

The prestress will therefore reduce the deflections by the same amount—that is, approximately half the total girder load deflections. The resultant deflection (girder load + prestress) still remains very significant as soon as the span length is above 150 ft. These deflections must be taken into full account to compute the camber diagram (for segment precasting).

The next important point to consider here is the second-stage construction of a typical span when the remaining part of the girder is suspended from the temporary stays. The concrete girder and the group of stays form an elastic system that supports the applied loads: girder load for the segments already in place, swivel crane and new segment

	$c_1/h = 0.5$ $c_2/h = 0.5$	$c_1/h = 0.4$ $c_2/h = 0.6$	$c_1/h = 0.33$ $c_2/h = 0.67$
Efficiency factor	$\rho = 0.60$	$\rho = 0.60$	$\rho = 0.60$
Distance from centroid of prestress to top fiber	$d = 0.05h$	$d = 0.05h$	$d = 0.05h$
Eccentricity of prestress	$e = 0.45h$	$e = 0.35h$	$e = 0.28h$
Lower central core	$r^2/c_1 = 0.30h$	$r^2/c_1 = 0.36h$	$r^2/c_1 = 0.40h$
Lever arm of prestress	$0.75h$	$0.71h$	$0.68h$
Prestress moment (ratio of girder load moment)	$\dfrac{0.45}{0.75} = 0.60$	$\dfrac{0.35}{0.71} = 0.49$	$\dfrac{0.28}{0.68} = 0.41$

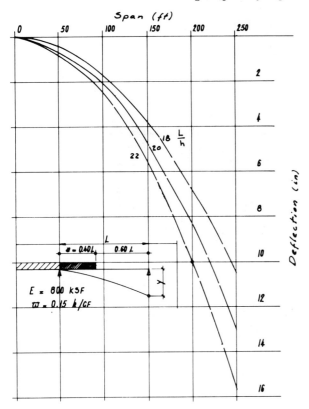

FIGURE 6.58. Progressive construction, deflections.

traveling over the bridge with the trailer and tractor. Two examples have been considered to show the relative response of the various components of this elastic system toward the application of a load.

1. *108 ft (33m) span* This was one typical span of the Rombas Viaduct. The span has been assumed to be completed except for the pier segment over the next pier. For this construction stage, the swivel crane and the new segment apply to the stayed cantilever a load of 88 tons (80 mt). In view of the great stiffness of the concrete girder compared to the group of stays, the total moment induced by the load remains almost entirely in the concrete girder and there is only a small spontaneous increase of the stay loads, as shown in Figure 6.59. The magnitude of temporary prestress in the deck must be designed accordingly to keep all joints under compression for all intermediate loading cases.

2. *260 ft (80 m) span* This example is taken from a recent design for a large project in Europe

where progressive construction was contemplated for a viaduct with a large number of identical 260 ft (80 m) spans all made up of 26 segments 10 ft (3 m) long. Figures 6.60 and 6.61 show the distribution of moments between concrete girder and temporary stays at three successive stages of segment placing: segments 15, 20, and 25, respectively. The first nine segments are placed in cantilever; the following 15 segments are suspended from temporary stays, while the last typical segment and the adjacent pier segment are placed without stays.

The proportion of the load (and corresponding moment) taken by the stays increases as the cantilever length increases and, when the last segment is placed, more than half the load is supported by the stays. For very-long-span stayed bridges, this distribution of load between stays and concrete girder reaches the situation where the load is almost entirely supported by the stays and the concrete girder is subjected only to an axial force, except in the area of the longest stays.

The consideration of distribution of loads and moments between stays and concrete girder has an important aspect during construction—that is, the accuracy of the tension in the stays and consequences of an accidental deviation between computed values of stressing loads in the stays and their actual values in the field. For example, take the simple case of a span L with 40% built in pure cantilever and the remaining 60% suspended by stays (see Figure 6.56). The moment over the pier due to the second-stage construction load is $M = 0.42WL^2$. Assume that an accidental deviation took place of 5% between the design loads for the stays and the actual values obtained in the field (owing to friction in the jacks, inaccuracy in the pressure gauges, and so on). As a result, an additional moment will appear over the pier of $\Delta M = \frac{1}{20} 0.42WL^2 = \underline{0.021WL^2}$. The corresponding tensile stress at the top fiber (assuming the error in stay loads was to reduce the theoretical values by 5%) can be easily computed by:

$$\Delta f = \Delta M \frac{c_1}{I} = \frac{0.021\overline{w}AL^2c_1}{A\rho c_1 c_2}$$

$$= \frac{0.021\overline{w}L^2}{\rho c_2}$$

With $\overline{w} = 0.15$ kcf, $\rho = 0.60$, and $c_2 = 0.60h$:

$$\Delta f = 0.0088 \frac{L^2}{h}$$

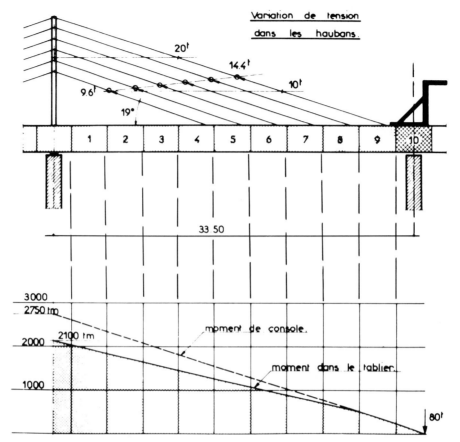

FIGURE 6.59.   Progressive construction, increase of stay loading.

The stress in ksf for $L/h = 20$ (slenderness ratio) is the following for several span lengths:

L (ft)	100	150	200	250
$\Delta f = 0.175L$ (ksf)	18	26	35	44

This stress is not critical for short spans but may become significant for long ones. The simple derivation given above shows that control of the stay-tensioning operations at the site should always be on the safe side with due allowance for inaccuracy.

A deviation in the tension of the stays will also affect the deflections during construction. Without the presence of the stays the total deflection over the next pier due to the load on the length $(L - a)$ would be:

$$y = \frac{WL^4}{24EI}(3 + 2\sqrt{3} - 2u^2\sqrt{3} - 4u^3 + u^4)$$

which gives for $u = 0.4$ as before:

$$y = 0.2366 \frac{WL^4}{EI}$$

Assume that the inaccuracy of the stay loads leaves in the concrete girder 5% of its own weight to be carried by bending; the resulting deflection over the pier would be:

$$y = 0.0118 \frac{WL^4}{EI}$$

This value should be compared to the effect of the first-stage construction, which was previously given as:

$$y = 0.0327 \frac{WL^4}{EI}$$

In summary, a 5% deviation of the stay tension loads will increase the cantilever deflection due to girder load by 36%. Considering the beneficial effect of prestressing for the latter, we see that approximately 7% deviation of the stay load produces the same deflection as the first-stage construction loads including prestressing. This shows that the deflections are important, particularly for long spans built in progressive construction, but that proper deflection control is an excellent tool to

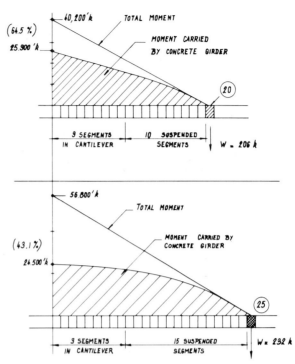

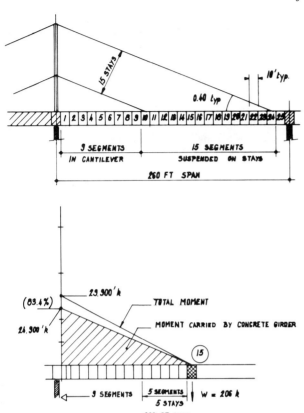

FIGURE 6.61. Progressive construction, distribution of moment between stays and girder.

FIGURE 6.60. Progressive construction, distribution of moment between stays and girder.

verify that stresses in the concrete girder are always kept within allowable limits.

6.6.4 LAYOUT OF TENDONS FOR PROGRESSIVE CONSTRUCTION

Because the static scheme at the end of each construction step is identical to that of a cast-in-place structure, the permanent tendons can be installed in the structure immediately, without the transition situations required by other construction methodologies such as incremental launching.

A typical prestress layout for progressive construction will thus include:

A first family of tendons located in the top flange over the various piers, with anchors symmetrically located in blisters, the purpose of which is to resist negative moments over the supports.

A second family of tendons located along the span in the bottom flange and also anchored in blisters inside the box section. Usually the top and bottom blisters are joined to a web rib, allowing temporary prestress bars to be anchored during segment placing.

Possibly a third family of tendons made of internal stays with a draped profile and anchored over the piers in the diaphragm, the purpose of which is to supplement both other families while reducing the net shear stresses in the webs because of the vertical component of prestress.

References

1. H. Wittfoht, "Prestressed Concrete Bridge Construction with Stepping Formwork Equipment," First International Symposium Concrete Bridge Design, Paper SP 23–28, ACI Publication SP-23, American Concrete Institute, Detroit, 1969.

2. H. Wittfoht, "Die Verwendung von Vorschbrüstungen biem Brückenbau" (The Use of Traveling Formwork in Bridge Construction), International Association Bridge and Structural Engineering, Ninth Congress, Amsterdam, May 8–13, 1972.

3. H. Thul, "Spannbeton im Brückenbau," *Zement und Beton*, Heft 42, Dezember 1968.

4. Man-Chung Tang, "Recent Development of Construction Techniques in Concrete Bridges," Transportation Research Record 665, Bridge Engineering, Vol. 2, *Proceedings of the Transportation Research Board Conference*, September 25–27, 1978, St. Louis, Mo., National Academy of Sciences, Washington, D.C.

5. U. Finsterwalder and H. Schambeck, "Die Elztal-brücke," *Der Bauingenieur*, Heft 6, June 1966, and Heft 1, January 1967.

6. H. Thul, "Brückenbau," *Beton- und Stahlbetonbau*, Heft 5, May 1966.

7. Anon., "Bau der Loisachbrücke bei Ohlstadt," *Dywidag-Berichte 1971-3*, Dyckerhoff & Widmann, AG, Munich.

8. Anon., "Bauausführung der Autobahnbrücke über die Loisach bei Ohlstadt," *Dywidag-Berichte 1972-5*, Dyckerhoff & Widmann, AG, Munich.

9. Anon., "Denny Creek-Franklin Falls Viaduct, Washington," Bridge Report SR 202.01 E, Portland Cement Association, Skokie, Ill., 1978.

10. Anon., "Florida's Long Key Bridge to Utilize Precast Segmental Box Girder Span-by-Span Construction," Bridge Report, Post Tensioning Institute, Phoenix, Arizona, January 1979.

11. Walter Podolny, Jr., "An Overview of Precast Prestressed Segmental Bridges," *Journal of the Prestressed Concrete Institute*, Vol. 24, No. 1, January–February 1979.

7

Incrementally Launched Bridges

7.1 Introduction

The concept of incrementally launched segmental prestressed concrete bridges was described in Section 1.9.5. This chapter will describe the implementation of this innovative concept in several representative projects.

Since the implementation of the incremental launching technique on the Rio Caroni Bridge, some eighty bridge superstructures have been constructed by this method through 1976, with gradual refinements and improvements in the method.[1] By concentrating the casting of segments behind an abutment with a temporary shelter, if required, this method can provide the same quality control procedures and quality of concrete that can be achieved in a concrete precasting plant. It minimizes temporary falsework, extensive forming, and other temporary expedients required during construction by the conventional cast-in-place on falsework method. Basically the method entails incremental fabrication of the superstructure at a stationary location, longitudinal movement of the fabricated segment an incremental

length, and casting of a new segment onto the one previously cast. In other words, the procedure can be considered as a horizontal slip-form technique, except that the fabrication and casting occur at a stationary location. Stringent dimensional control, however, is an absolute necessity at the stationary casting site, since errors are very difficult to correct and result in additional costs in launching.[1]

Straight superstructures are the easiest to accommodate; however, curvature (either vertical or horizontal) can be accomplished if a constant rate of curvature is maintained. If the grade of the structure is on an incline, it is preferred to launch the structure, wherever possible, downward. Where the fall is 2%, the superstructure has to be pushed or held back, depending upon the coefficient of friction. Where the fall is in excess of 4%, special provisions are required to prevent a "runaway" superstructure during launching.[1] To the authors' knowledge, this situation has never occurred. Piers, either temporary or permanent, should be designed to resist the lateral force produced by the launching operation. A friction force varying from 4 to 7% has been considered for design purposes, although values of only 2 to $3\frac{1}{2}$% have been observed in the field.

At present, it is felt that this system can be used for superstructures up to 2000 ft (610 m) in length; for longer structures incremental launching is accomplished from both abutments toward the center of the structure. The technique has been applied for spans up to 200 ft (60 m) without the use of temporary supporting bents and for spans up to 330 ft (100 m) with such bents. Girders usually have a depth-to-span ratio ranging from one-twelfth to one-sixteenth of the longest span and are of a constant depth. The launching nose has a length of approximately 60% of the longest span.

The principal advantages of the incremental launching method are the following[2]:

1. No falsework is required for the construction of the superstructure other than possibly falsework bents to reduce span length during construction. In this manner cantilever stresses during launching can be maintained within allowable limits. If falsework bents should prove to be impractical, then a system of temporary stays can be used as indicated in Figure 1.63. Obviously, depending on site conditions, any or all combinations of temporary bents, launching nose, and temporary stays may be used, the point being that conventional use of falsework is greatly minimized. This is particularly interesting for projects in urban areas or spanning over water, highways, or railroads.

2. Depending on the size of the project there can be a substantial reduction in form investment. Because casting of the segments is centralized at a location behind the abutment, the economic advantages of mass production and a precasting plant operation can be duplicated.

3. The method eliminates transportation costs of segments cast at a fixed plant and transported to the site.

4. It eliminates heavy cranes or launching trusses and associated erection costs.

5. It eliminates epoxy joints. Since epoxy is not involved, construction can continue at lower temperatures.

6. Camber control and other geometry controls are easily obtained.

Disadvantages are as follows:

1. As mentioned in Section 1.9.5, bridge alignment for this type of construction must be either straight or curved; however, curvature, either vertical or horizontal, must be of a constant radius.

2. As mentioned above, strict dimensional control during casting is required. Any mistakes in casting are difficult and expensive to correct, especially if they are not discovered until after some length of bridge has been launched.

3. The superstructure must be of a constant section and depth. This is a disadvantage in long spans, where a variable-depth section would provide a better economy of materials.

4. Considerable area is required behind the abutment(s) for casting the segments. In some project sites this may not be feasible.

In the present state of the art of incrementally launched bridges there appear to be basically two methods of construction, which we shall call *continuous casting* and *balanced casting*. They are different in mode of execution and in their areas of utilization. The continuous casting method is somewhat analogous to the span-by-span method, and balanced casting is similar to the cantilever method.

The continuous casting method is generally used for long viaduct-type structures with numerous equal (or nearly equal) spans. Its principal characteristics are the following:

1. Entire spans, or portions of spans, are concreted in fixed forms. The forms are reused, as in the span-by-span method, except that the forms are fixed instead of mobile and are moved from span to span. Subsequent spans (or portions of a span) are cast and joined to the one previously cast, and the superstructure is progressively launched.

2. Usually the casting area behind the abutment is long enough to accommodate either a span length plus launching-nose length or some multiple of span segment length plus launching-nose length.

3. Operations involve successive concreting and launching. The principal phases are: forming; placing of reinforcing and tendons; concreting and curing; tensioning and launching.

4. The two types of superstructure cross section used have been box girder and double T.

5. Longitudinal prestressing consists of two families of tendons: tendons concentrically placed and tensioned before launching, and tendons placed and tensioned after launch-

ing—that is, negative-moment tendons over the supports and positive-moment tendons in the bottom of the section in the central portion of the span.

The balanced casting method is used for smaller projects up to a total length of 650 ft (200 m). It is used for symmetric three-span structures where the central span is twice the end span. Its principal characteristics are:

1. Concreting of segments is accomplished symmetrically with respect to a temporary support located in the embankment behind the abutments. This method is similar to the balanced cantilever except that the forms are supported on the embankment fill.

2. Two areas of casting are required, one behind each abutment. The half-superstructures are constructed at opposite ends of the project. The distance between the abutment and the axis of the temporary massive support is generally slightly less than one-fourth the length of the project.

3. After the two half-superstructures have been concreted on the access fill, the two halves are launched over the piers and joined at midspan of the central span by a closure pour, which usually has a length of 3 ft (1 m).

4. Longitudinal prestressing consists of three families: cantilever tendons for each segment, located in the upper portion of the cross section and stressed before launching; continuity tendons, tensioned after closure and situated in the lower flange; and provisional tendons, located in the lower flange, tensioned before launching, and opposing the cantilever tendons.

There are two methods of launching. The method used on the Rio Caroni Bridge, Figure 1.67, has the jacks bearing on an abutment face and pulling on a steel rod, which is attached by launching shoes to the last segment cast. The second, and more current, method is essentially a lift-and-push operation using a combination of horizontal and vertical jacks, Figure 7.1. The vertical jacks slide on teflon and stainless steel plates. Friction elements at the top of the jacks engage the superstructure. The vertical jacks lift the superstructure approximately $\frac{3}{16}$ in. (5 mm) for launching. The horizontal jacks then move the superstructure longitudinally. After the superstructure has been pushed the length of the hor-

FIGURE 7.1. Incremental launching—jacking mechanism (courtesy of Prof. Fritz Leonhardt).

izontal jack stroke, the vertical jacks are lowered and the horizontal jacks retracted to restart the cycle.[1] Figure 7.2 is a schematic depiction of this cycle.

To allow the superstructure to move forward, special temporary sliding bearings of reinforced rubber pads coated with teflon, which slide on chrome-nickel steel plates, are provided at the permanent piers and temporary bents, Figures 7.3 and 7.4. A sequence of operations showing the bearing-pad movement on the temporary bearing is depicted in Figure 7.5. A temporary bearing with a lateral guide bearing is shown in Figure 7.6.

7.2 *Rio Caroni, Venezuela*

The design for this structure was proposed by consulting engineers Dr. Fritz Leonhardt and Willi Baur of the firm Leonhardt and Andra, Stuttgart, West Germany, in an international competition. Design and planning occurred in 1961 and construction in 1962 and 1963. This structure, Figure 7.7, consists of a two-lane bridge with end spans of 157.5 ft (48 m) and four interior spans of 315 ft (96 m), for a total length of 1575 ft (480 m).[1] The site provided some formidable construction problems. The Rio Caroni River during flood stage reaches a depth of 40 ft (12 m) with velocities of 13 to 16 ft/sec (4 to 5 m/sec), thus eliminating the consideration of a cast-in-place concrete superstructure on falsework. Balanced cantilever segmental construction was considered; however, the interruptions during high-water periods would require an extensive construction period with attendant high costs.[3]

The proposed method consisted of assembling and prestressing the entire length of bridge on

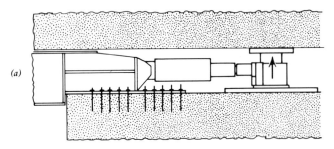

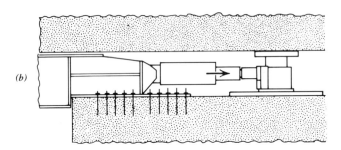

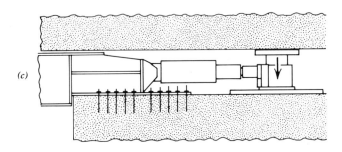

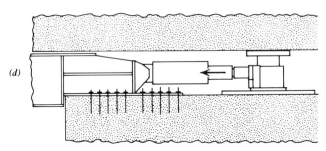

FIGURE 7.2. Schematic of launching jack operation. (*a*) Lift. (*b*) Push. (*c*) Lower. (*d*) Retract.

land adjacent to the bridge site, using precast segments, and launching in a longitudinal direction, over the piers, into final position. Temporary piers were used at midspan of each interior span to produce ten equal spans of 157.5 ft (48 m) during the launching of the superstructure. Accommodation of on-site assembly of the total superstructure required a 1600 ft (500 m) long fabrication bed to the rear of one abutment, which was partly excavated in rock and had to be backfilled and compacted upon completion of the project. At the far end of

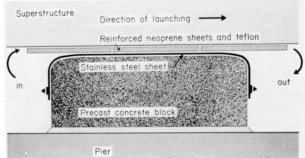

FIGURE 7.3. Incremental launching—longitudinal section of launching bearing, from reference 3 (courtesy of the American Concrete Institute).

FIGURE 7.4. Launching bearing, Wabash River Bridge, Indiana.

this fabrication bed stationary steel forms were installed to cast the precast box segments, which were 18 ft 4 in. (5.6 m) high and cast in 30 ft (9.2 m) lengths.

After the precast segments attained sufficient strength they were stripped from the form and positioned in the fabrication bed to correspond with their location in the final structure. The segments were moved from the form on wooden rails accurately positioned in the assembly bed, employing formica sheets and a petroleum-base lubricant between the bottom of the segment and the top of the wood rails, Figure 7.8. A space of 1 ft 4 in. (40 cm) was left between the precast segments for an in situ joint. Accurate positioning of the segments in the assembly bed was required before casting of the joints. To avoid shrinkage damage, the joints were cast during the second half of the night so that the temperature expansion of the precast segments during the heat of the day would compensate for the shrinkage in the cast-in-place joint.[3]

After the joints were cast, concentric prestressing located inside the box and passing through openings in the web stiffening ribs, Figure 7.9, was prestressed with a force of 5000 tons in one opera-

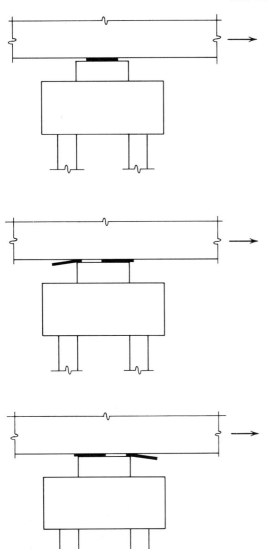

FIGURE 7.5. Temporary sliding bearing, sequence of operations.

FIGURE 7.6. Incremental launching—temporary bearing and lateral guide bearing (courtesy of Prof. Fritz Leonhardt).

FIGURE 7.7. Completed Rio Caroni Bridge, from reference 3 (courtesy of the American Concrete Institute).

FIGURE 7.8. Precast segments in assembly bed (courtesy of Arvid Grant).

tion. The prestress tendons were continuous around a large half-round concrete block at one end of the structure, Figure 7.10. This block reacted against a number of jacks and a 10 ft (3 m) thick concrete bulkhead wall. By activating the jacks between the block and the bulkhead and causing a movement of 9 ft (2.8 m) in the stress block, the initial prestress force was induced into the tendons. The prestressing tendons were not attached to the webs. To reduce the hazard of any accidental elastic instability condition, temporary steel bracing frames were installed at 60 ft (20 m) intervals.[3] The 33 ft 10 in. (10.3 m) top flange of the box girder section was transversely prestressed, Figure 7.9.

Upon completion of the prestressing operations the superstructure was ready for launching over the temporary and permanent piers to its final position. To maintain acceptable levels of concrete stresses, as the girder was launched over the 157.5 ft (48 m) spans, a 56 ft (17 m) tapered structural steel launching nose was attached to the leading

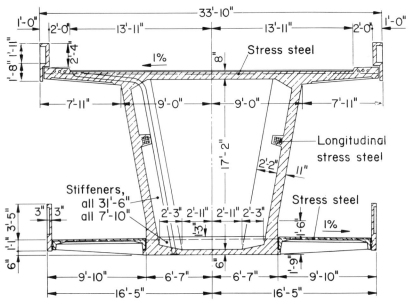

FIGURE 7.9. Rio Caroni, girder cross section, from reference 3 (courtesy of the American Concrete Institute).

FIGURE 7.10. Rio Caroni, prestressing block (courtesy of Arvid Grant).

FIGURE 7.11. Rio Caroni, launching nose, from reference 3 (courtesy of the American Concrete Institute).

end of the superstructure, Figure 7.11. Two double jacks with a total capacity of 600 tons, mounted against the bridge abutment and pulling on steel rods fastened to the girder, provided the horizontal force required for the longitudinal launching movement. To accommodate movement over the piers, two sliding bearings were provided at each temporary and permanent pier top. These bearings consisted of chrome, polished steel plates which supported teflon covered bridge bearings which were placed in an inverted position such that they bore against the underside of the girder and slid on the steel plates. After a launching movement of 3 ft (96 cm) in the longitudinal direction

the operation was halted to allow the entire superstructure to be jacked vertically, simultaneously at all piers. The teflon plates were then moved back to their original position (the one they occupied when the launching operation started) and rotated 180 degrees, with respect to a vertical axis, to compensate for any one-directional movement of the teflon coating. Longitudinal launching movement occurred at a rate of $2\frac{3}{8}$ in./min (6 cm/min); thus, one 3 ft (6 cm) increment of movement took 16 minutes. A total cycle of operation, after subsequent synchronization, which included the simultaneous jacking at 22 locations and repositioning of 22 teflon bearings, required 30 minutes for each 3 ft (96 cm) of movement. In this manner, a daily movement of 63 ft (19.2 m) could be accomplished. The required initial jacking force for launching was 220 tons; this gradually increased to 400 tons for the total girder weight of 10,000 tons, which indicates a friction of 2 to 4%.[3]

After the launching operation was completed, the initial concentric prestressing tendon profile was changed to accommodate the loading condition in the superstructure after temporary piers were removed. To accomplish the change in tendon profile, special U-shaped rods were installed so that they projected upward through the top flange or downward through the bottom flange, the tendons being cradled in the U rods. The rods were then jacked simultaneously at 24 points upward or downward, depending on their location. During this operation the half-round stress block, Figure 7.10, was gradually released such that upon final positioning of the tendons it had retracted 8 ft 6 in. (2.6 m). After the tendons had been relocated, they were attached to the web and concreted for corrosion protection.[3]

The procedure used for the construction of the Rio Caroni Bridge, although technically adequate, is prohibitively expensive. The methodology has since been refined such that segments are cast directly behind the abutment in lengths of 33 to 100 ft (10 to 30 m) and incrementally launched after curing of the last segment cast.[1]

7.3   Val Restel Viaduct, Italy

Because of rugged mountain terrain the alignment of a 1050 ft (320 m) portion of this viaduct re-

quired a sharp horizontal curvature of 492 ft (150 m) radius, and a vertical curvature of approximately 8860 ft (2700 m) radius, Figure 7.12. Maximum pier height is 212 ft (64.61 m). Site conditions and alignment precluded construction by the balanced cantilever method or conventional cast-in-place on falsework, leading to the decision to construct by the incremental launching method.

The curved 1050 ft (320 m) length of this viaduct consists of 52.5 ft (16 m) long segments, which were fabricated in an enclosed shed behind an abutment. The bottom flange and bottom stubs of the webs of the first segments were cast first, Figure 7.13a, b, in a 52.5 ft (16 m) length, and approximately 118 ft (36 m) behind the first abutment. After curing and stressing of the partial segment it was jacked forward an increment of 52.5 ft (16 m) toward the abutment, where the balance of the section was cast, Figure 7.13a, c. At the same time the formwork vacated by the first-segment bottom flange was reused for the casting of the bottom flange of the second segment, monolithically with the previous segment. After launching another 52.5 ft (16 m) increment the cycle was repeated until the superstructure was completed.[4]

Placement of the bottom flange mild steel reinforcement is shown in Figure 7.14, with the web forms in the background. The side forms for the webs and underside of the top flange cantilever, and the hydraulic jacking arrangement for stripping, are illustrated in Figure 7.15. Reinforcement in the top flange is shown in Figure 7.16 and the completed top flange with the following segment in the background in Figure 7.17. The completed segment with rails in place as it emerges from the casting shed is shown in Figure 1.61.

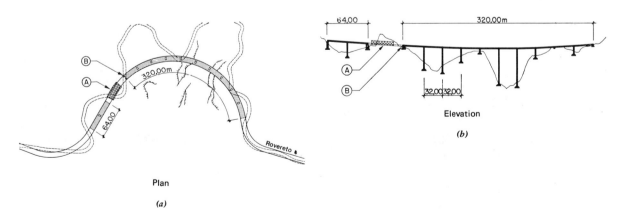

FIGURE 7.12.   Plan (*a*) and longitudinal profile (*b*) of the Val Restel Viaduct, showing: A, shed for the construction of the deck segments; B, hydraulic equipment used for launching. From reference 4.

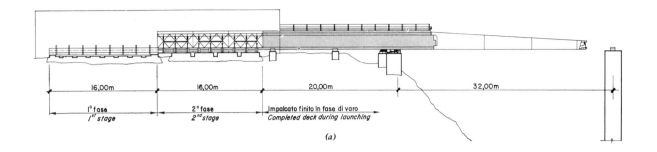

16,00m   16,00m   20,00m   32,00m

1ª fase / 1st stage   2ª fase / 2nd stage   Impalcato finito in fase di varo / Completed deck during launching

(a)

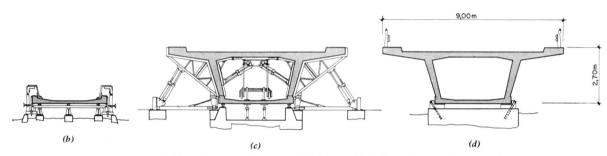

(b)   *(c)*   *(d)*

FIGURE 7.13. Construction stages Val Restel Viaduct, from reference 4.

FIGURE 7.14. Val Restel, placement of bottom flange reinforcement, from reference 4.

FIGURE 7.16. Val Restel, top flange reinforcement, from reference 4.

FIGURE 7.15. Val Restel, side form stripping mechanism, from reference 4.

FIGURE 7.17. Val Restel, completed top flange, with reinforcement for next segment in background, from reference 4.

The superstructure cross section is shown in Figure 7.18*a*. Width of the segment is 29.5 ft (9.0 m). Total depth of segment is 8.13 ft (2.48 m), for a depth-to-span ratio of 1/13. The top flange has a thickness of 9.8 in. (250 mm) and the bottom flange a thickness of 5.9 in. (150 mm). Figure 7.18*b* is a longitudinal section of the superstructure showing a layout of the second-stage prestressing tendons required after launching to accommodate loads on the final structure. Figures 7.19 and 7.20 show the interior anchorage blocks for the second-stage prestressing before and after concreting, respectively.

A complete cycle of fabricating and launching a 52.5 ft (16 m) segment was accomplished in four nine-hour working days. Actual launching time for one segment was 60 to 65 minutes.[4] Figures 7.21 and 7.22 show the launching nose approaching and landing on a pier. Views of the completed structure are shown in Figures 7.23 and 7.24. Construction of this bridge was accomplished in ten months, from January 1972 through October 1972.

7.4 Ravensbosch Valley Bridge, Holland

The 1378 ft (420 m) long Ravensbosch Valley Bridge near Valkenburg represents the first bridge in Holland built by the incremental launching method of segmental construction, Figure 7.25. This dual structure has end spans of 137.8 ft (42 m) and six interior spans of 183.73 ft (56 m). Hollow rectangular piers vary in height from 21 ft (6.5 m) to 77 ft (23.5 m) and have exterior dimensions

of 6 ft (1.8 m) by 19 ft (5.8 m) with wall thickness of 1.3 ft (0.4 m), Figure 7.26.

The superstructure consists of two single-cell trapezoidal box girders connected at the interior upper flange tips by a 8.3 ft (2.5 m) slab and prestressed transversely, Figures 7.26 and 7.27. Each box has a width of 56.8 ft (17.32 m) and a constant depth of 10.8 ft (3.3 m) for a depth-to-span ratio of 1/17. The top flange has a thickness of 9.8 in. (250 mm) and the bottom flange a thickness of 7.9 in. (200 mm). Top flange cantilever is 13 ft (4.01 m).

Each dual structure consists of 22 segments approximately 62 ft 4 in. (19 m) in length. The con-

FIGURE 7.19. Val Restel, second-stage prestressing anchorage block before concreting, from reference 4.

FIGURE 7.20. Val Restel, second-stage prestressing anchorage block after concreting, from reference 4.

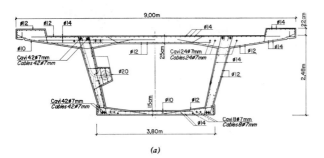

(a)

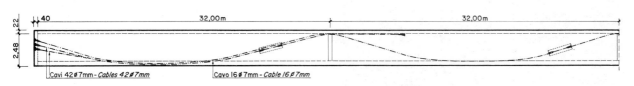

(b)

FIGURE 7.18. Val Restel. (*a*) Cross section of deck. (*b*) Longitudinal section of deck. From reference 4.

FIGURE 7.21. Val Restel, launching nose approaching pier, from reference 4.

FIGURE 7.22. Val Restel, launching nose landing on pier, from reference 4.

FIGURE 7.23. Val Restel, view of incrementally launched curved viaduct after launching, from reference 4.

FIGURE 7.24. Val Restel, completed Viaduct, from reference 4.

FIGURE 7.25. Ravensbosch Valley Bridge, general view (courtesy of Brice Bender, BVN/STS).

struction of the superstructure was based upon a cycle of one segment per week.

To accommodate bending moments during launching operations a 52.5 ft (16 m) long launching nose was used, Figure 7.28, in conjunction with a concentric first-stage prestressing consisting of 26 $1\frac{1}{4}$ in. (32 mm) diameter Dywidag bars per box girder. In addition, temporary piers were used at midspan, Figure 7.28. During launching, friction amounted to 2 to 4%, equivalent to a maximum pushing force of 430 tons for a completed box girder.

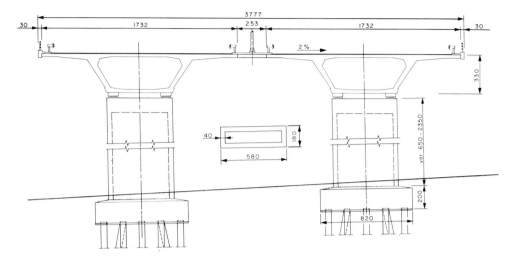

FIGURE 7.26. Ravensbosch Valley Bridge, dual structure cross section (courtesy of Brice Bender, BVN/STS).

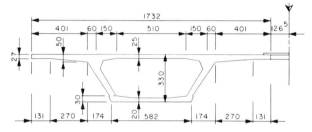

FIGURE 7.27. Ravensbosch Valley Bridge, girder cross section (courtesy of Brice Bender, BVN/STS).

FIGURE 7.28. Ravensbosch Valley Bridge, view of launching nose (courtesy of Brice Bender, BVN/STS).

After completion of the launching, second-stage prestressing following a parabolic profile and consisting of 12-0.62 in. (16 mm) diameter strands was installed and stressed. This structure was completed in 1975.

7.5 Olifant's River Bridge, South Africa

This railroad structure, upon completion, held the world's record for the longest bridge accomplished by incremental launching. It has a total length of 3395 ft (1035 m), consisting of 23 equal spans of 147.6 ft (45 m). The final structural arrangement consists of 11 continuous spans on each side fixed at the abutment and one simply supported center span—that is, an expansion joint on either side of the center span. With this structural arrangement the braking force of the trains (transporting iron ore) is transmitted to the abutments (10% of live load). In this manner the flexible piers can be used, resulting in an economy in the foundations by comparison with the classical solution, where the longitudinal force is transmitted through the piers to the foundations.

All 23 spans were incrementally launched as 23 continuous spans from one abutment, Figure 7.29. During launching the two expansion joints were made temporarily continuous by temporary prestressing. The joints were released after the structure was in place and before it was rested on its permanent bearings. A launching nose, 59 ft (18 m) long, was prestressed to the first segment to maintain the cantilever stresses, during launching, in the concrete within allowable limits. The tip of

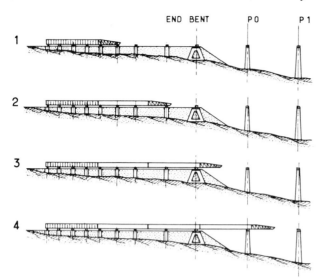

FIGURE 7.29. Olifant's River Bridge, incremental launching arrangement.

the launching nose had a jacking arrangement to accommodate deflection of the nose as it approached the pier.

In cross section, Figure 7.30, the superstructure is a constant-depth rectangular single-cell box girder. Depth is 12.5 ft (3.80 m); the top flange is 18 ft (5.50 m) wide and the bottom flange 10 ft (3.10 m) wide. The webs and flanges are of a constant thickness throughout the structure. Web thickness is 13.75 in. (0.35 m) and contains vertical bar prestressing tendons to carry shear. Longitudinal prestressing is straight and contained in the flanges. Anchorage blocks for the longitudinal tendons are continuous across the width of both flanges (interior buttresses) to assure a more favorable distribution throughout the section. There are no diaphragms at the piers; the interior corner fillets are such as to permit the effect of torsion to be accommodated by a transverse box frame.

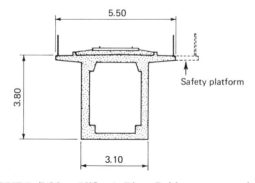

FIGURE 7.30. Olifant's River Bridge, cross section.

Construction of the superstructure was accomplished in nine months. Segments were span length, with the theoretical cycle per span of ten hours attained in the tenth operation and gradually reduced to seven hours at the conclusion of casting operations. Reinforcing cages were prefabricated in templates at the side of the forms. A cycle of operations consisted of the following:

Cleaning and adjustment of forms

Placement of reinforcing and tendons for the lower flange and webs

Concreting of this first phase

Placement of reinforcing and tendons for the upper flange

Concreting of this phase

Tensioning of tendons in second phase of previous span cast

Tensioning of tendons in first phase of span in forms

Stripping of forms

Launching

After launching, and before placing the structure on its final bearings, it was necessary to adjust the joints within $\frac{3}{8}$ in. (10 mm). The principal difficulties in accomplishing this operation were:

Temperature differential between night and day, which produced a variation in length of the superstructure of 9.8 in. (250 mm)

Age of concrete at time of adjustment, which varied from nine months to ten hours

Jacking operations, which could not retract the structure in case of an error in pushing forward

The solution of the temperature problem was to quickly accomplish the adjustment early in the morning. Because of the constant temperature during the night the temperature of the superstructure was known, and its length was determinable in spite of the thermal inertia of the concrete.

The superstructure was then jacked into its theoretical position on the abutment and firmly maintained by a system of blockage. The temporary tendons that had fixed the first joint were released and jacks were placed into the joint to push the remaining 12 spans and place the central simple span in its exact position. The second joint was then opened, and jacks at the other abutment positioned the last 11-span portion of the super-structure.

When the superstructure had thus been placed in position, it was jacked up off the piers, and the temporary sliding bearings were replaced by the permanent bearings.

7.6 Various Bridges in France

7.6.1 LUC VIADUCT

This is a dual structure 912 ft (278 m) long on a curve of a 3280 ft (1000 m) radius. The super-structure was constructed by incremental launch-ing of complete spans on sliding bearings. Resis-tance of the structure to its dead load during launching was accommodated by a temporary cable-stay system in which the tension was adjusted as construction proceeded, Figure 7.31. No supplementary prestressing was provided during the launching phases. A 26 ft (8 m) launching nose was provided at the leading end in order to reduce the weight of the cantilevered structure.

It is a continuous structure supported on neo-prene bearings and has a double-T cross section, as indicated in Figure 7.32. Roadway width is 46 ft (14.0 m), and depth of superstructure is a constant 10.3 ft (3.15 m). Spans are 133.5 ft (40.7 m).

7.6.2 CREIL VIADUCT

This structure consists of eight continuous spans having a total length of 1102 ft (336 m), crossing a railroad and the Oise River. The project is of inter-est in that it was launched from both abutments without the use of a launching nose or a temporary cable-stay system. However, temporary bents were used to control the cantilever stresses. In cross sec-tion the superstructure is a single-cell box, Figure 7.33.

Segments for each of the two half-super structures were from 65.6 to 98.4 ft (20 to 30 m) in length. A launching was effected upon com-pletion of each segment. After the two half-superstructures had been launched to their final position, a closure pour of 3.3 ft (1 m) in length was consummated to provide continuity.

Longitudinal prestress consists of six sets:

Cantilever tendons, tensioned before launching, located in the top flange and anchored in fillets at the intersection with the web

Concentric tendons from one end to the other of each half-superstructure, coupled together at each phase of concreting of segments

Straight, short tendons in the top flange over the piers and in the bottom flange, centered in the span and tensioned after launching

Continuity tendons, tensioned after launching, situated in webs and anchoring at the upper flange

Short parabolic tendons, located in the webs and anchoring in the top flange, tensioned after launching

Temporary tendons in the upper flange, having the same effect as the cantilever tendons

7.6.3 OLI VIADUCT

This viaduct spans the valley of Oli in 15 spans of 134.5 ft (41 m) for a total length of 2017 ft (615 m) at a height of 197 ft (60 m). The structure has a grade of 5.355% and a horizontal curve with a radius of 6700 ft (2046 m). Total weight of the superstructure is 16,500 tons (15,000 mt).

Incremental launching in this structure, rather than pushing the superstructure out over the piers, was accomplished by a restrained lowering down the grade. The force required in braking the structure was approximately 660 tons (600 mt) as compared to the estimated force of 1540 tons (1400 mt) to push the structure uphill.

In its final configuration, because it was difficult to accommodate horizontal forces due to braking and seismic effects in the tall flexible piers, the superstructure is anchored in the terrain in the area of the abutments by a tie of a large stiffness. All of this longitudinal global force is accommo-dated in the large stiff tie, the abutments, and the relatively short stiff piers in each bank. A central joint divides the structure into two independent structures.

Upon completion of launching and before plac-ing the superstructure on its permanent bearings, it was necessary to "unlock" the joint that held the two half-superstructures together during con-struction and to adjust its position within approxi-mately $\frac{3}{8}$ in. (10 mm). This operation was con-ducted as follows:

The superstructure was restrained at the upper abutment until the distance between its theoretical position and the end of the lower abutment was approximately 8 in. (200 mm).

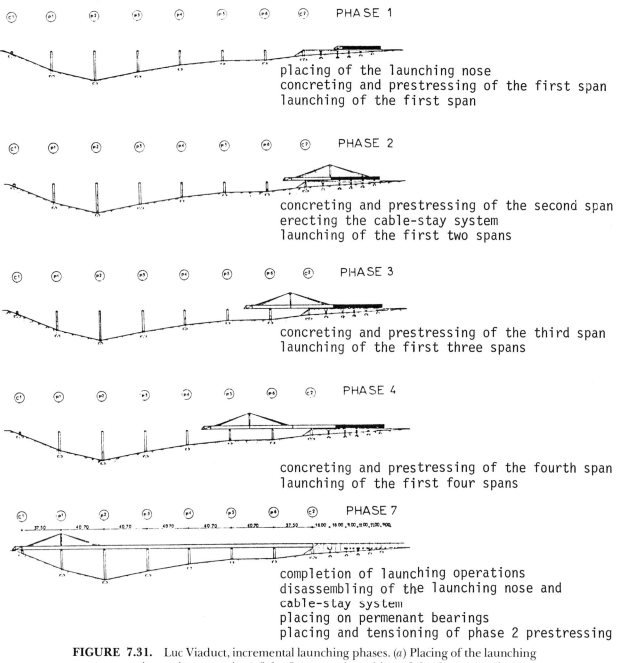

PHASE 1

placing of the launching nose
concreting and prestressing of the first span
launching of the first span

PHASE 2

concreting and prestressing of the second span
erecting the cable-stay system
launching of the first two spans

PHASE 3

concreting and prestressing of the third span
launching of the first three spans

PHASE 4

concreting and prestressing of the fourth span
launching of the first four spans

PHASE 7

completion of launching operations
disassembling of the launching nose and
cable-stay system
placing on permanent bearings
placing and tensioning of phase 2 prestressing

FIGURE 7.31. Luc Viaduct, incremental launching phases. (*a*) Placing of the launching nose, concreting and prestressing of the first span, launching of the first span. (*b*) Concreting and prestressing of the second span, erecting of the cable-stay system, launching of the first two spans. (*c*) Concreting and prestressing of the third span, launching of the first three spans. (*d*) Concreting and Prestressing of the fourth span, launching of the first four spans. (*e*) Completion of launching operations, disassembling of the launching nose and cable-stay system, placing on permanent bearings, placing and tensioning of phase-two prestressing.

The temporary tendons connecting the two half-superstructures were successively detensioned. However, two temporary tendons restrained the lower half-superstructure. The upper half-superstructure was fixed to the upper abutment by a system of prestress bars and complementary reinforcement installed in the upper abutment.

The two temporary tendons restraining the lower half-superstructure were detensioned in increments, allowing the lower half-superstructure to

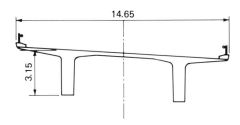

FIGURE 7.32. Luc Viaduct, cross section.

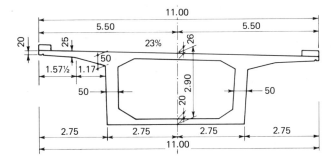

FIGURE 7.33. Creil Viaduct, cross section.

descend to a blocking system in the lower abutment. Fixing of the lower half-superstructure to the lower abutment was then accomplished.

The superstructure was positioned on its final bearings.

7.7 Wabash River Bridge, U.S.A.

This structure, the first incrementally launched segmental bridge constructed in the United States, carries two lanes of U.S. 136 over the Wabash River near Covington, Indiana. It is a six-span structure with end spans of 93 ft 6 in. (28.5 m) and four interior spans of 187 ft (57 m), Figure 7.34.

Roadway width is 44 ft (13.4 m). Pier heights are approximately 40 ft (12 m); average river depth is 11 ft (3.35 m) with low water at 8 ft (2.4 m) and high water at 24 ft (7.3 m). The superstructure is a two-cell box girder with a constant depth of 8 ft (2.4 m). The project was awarded in September of 1976 with a completion date of October 1978. The entire superstructure was completed in November of 1977.

Original design plans prepared by American Consulting Engineers, Inc., of Indianapolis for the State Highway Commission called for a precast segmental balanced cantilever design; however, the bid documents permitted alternative methods of constructing the superstructure. The successful contractor, a joint venture of Weddle Bros. Con-

struction Co., Inc., and the Ralph Rodgers Construction Co., both of Bloomington, Indiana, investigated three alternatives for the superstructure construction. These alternates included cast-in-place segments supported on falsework, incremental launching, and the cast-in-place segmental balanced cantilever method. Incremental launching was the successful method and reportedly saved $100,000 over the other precast segmental method.[5] The V.S.L. Corporation of Las Gatos, California, was the subcontractor for prestressing and launching.

A 140 ft (42.7 m) casting bed was located behind the west abutment of the bridge and could accommodate three 46 ft 9 in. (14.25 m) segments. The forms for casting were supported on I beams, which were supported on steel piling to provide a solid foundation and prevent any settlement of the casting bed, Figure 7.35. The bottom third of the two-cell box superstructure was cast at the most westerly end of the casting bed, Figure 7.35. It was then advanced 46 ft 9 in. (14.25 m), where forms for the balance of the section were positioned, mild steel reinforcement and prestressing tendons placed, and the balance of the segment cast, Figure 7.36. After the segment had been poured and cured, the 20-ton jacks that held the forms in position, Figure 7.37, were released to break the bond and remove the forms. The large metal forms stayed in place and were simply swung in and out as needed. The segment was then advanced to the forward third of the casting bed for surface finishing by a conventional Bidwell screed, Figure 7.38, before launching over the abutment. In this manner a production-line methodology was maintained. Three segments were always in various stages of fabrication, with reinforcement and prestressing tendons continuous between segments.

The first-stage pour required approximately 53 yd³ (40.5 m³) and the second pour required from 101 to 130 yd³ (77.2 to 99.4 m³). It took approximately four hours for each pour. Twenty-eight-day design strength was 4800 psi (3.37 kg/mm²), and 6000 to 7000 psi concrete strengths were actually attained (4.2 to 4.9 kg/mm²). A 3500 psi (2.46 kg/mm²) strength was required before stressing, and this was normally achieved in 24 to 30 hours. As segments were completed, each was stressed to its predecessor by first-stage prestressing consisting of eight tendons of twelve ½ in. (12.7 mm) diameter 27 ksi (190 kg/mm²) strands, Figure 7.39. Initially the contractor was able to complete one cycle of segment fabrication and launching in two weeks;

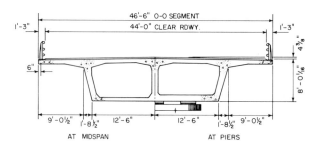

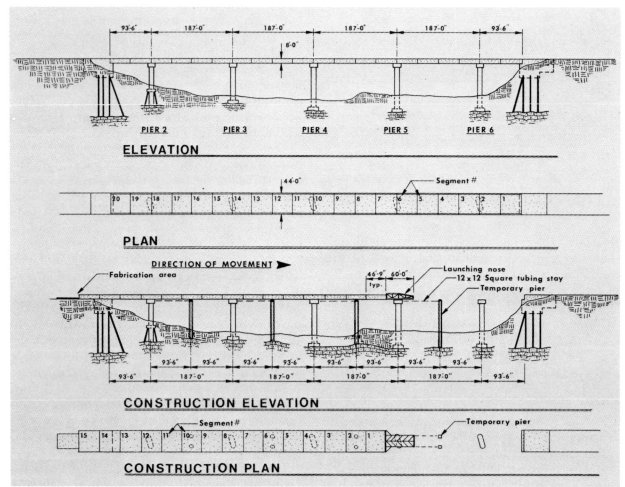

FIGURE 7.34. Wabash River Bridge: cross section of girder, from reference 6; construction details, from reference 2.

however, as experience was gained, two cycles per week were attained.

To accommodate the launching stresses a 56 ft (17 m) launching nose was attached to the lead segment, Figures 7.34 and 7.40. In addition, the four interior spans had temporary steel bents at midspan, Figures 7.34 and 7.41. In this manner the total structure length was divided into ten equal spans of 93 ft 6 in. (28.5 m) during the launching procedure.

Because of the longitudinal force on the piers during launching, the permanent piers were tied back to the abutment with four prestressing strands each. These strands were stressed to 96 kips (43,545 kg) before launching commenced. Each temporary pier was tied back to the preced-

FIGURE 7.35. Wabash River Bridge, casting-bed support.

FIGURE 7.37. Wabash River Bridge, side form jacks.

FIGURE 7.36. Wabash River Bridge, casting bed.

FIGURE 7.38. Wabash River Bridge, surface finishing top flange.

FIGURE 7.39. Wabash River Bridge, first-stage prestressing.

FIGURE 7.40. Wabash River Bridge, launching nose.

FIGURE 7.41. Wabash River Bridge, temporary steel bent.

ing permanent pier by two stays of 10 in. by 10 in. (254 mm by 254 mm) structural steel tubing, Figures 7.34 and 7.42.

The jacking procedure during launching used the two-jack system (one vertical and one horizontal) and teflon pads, as described in Figure 7.2. The vertical jacks had a 2 in. (50 mm) stroke and the

horizontal jacks an 18 in. (457 mm) stroke. The vertical jacks lifted the superstructure about $\frac{1}{2}$ in. (13 mm) and the horizontal jack pushed it forward 17 in. (432 mm). Each jacking cycle required about five minutes, and the entire launching of a 46 ft 9 in. (14.25 m) segment required about three hours.

Temporary bearings, Figure 7.4, were located at each temporary bent and permanent pier. During the launching operation workmen were stationed at each bearing location to insert the teflon pads as the superstructure slid over the bearings. To maintain lateral alignment of the superstructure, lateral guide bearings, Figure 7.43, were also located at each temporary bearing and also used teflon pads. Workmen would tighten bolts on one side of the superstructure and loosen them on the opposite side to push the superstructure laterally. Final positioning of the superstructure on the east abutment was within $\frac{1}{32}$ in. (0.8 mm) of its prescribed location.

7.8 Other Notable Structures

7.8.1 MÜHLBACHTALBRÜCKE, GERMANY

Another example of this type of construction is the Mühlbachtalbrücke about 30 miles (50 km) southwest of Stuttgart, West Germany, Figure 7.44. This structure has an overall length of 1903 ft (580 m) with 141 ft (43 m) spans. The far-side trapezoidal box girder is shown in Figure 7.44 completed from abutment to abutment; the near-side trapezoidal box girder has been launched from the left abutment and the launching nose has reached the first pier. A general view of the structure is presented in Figure 7.45.

FIGURE 7.42. Wabash River Bridge, structural steel tubing tie.

FIGURE 7.43. Wabash River Bridge, lateral guide bearing.

FIGURE 7.44. Mühlbachtalbrücke, aerial view.

FIGURE 7.45. Mühlbachtalbrücke, general view.

Some idea of the size of the box girder may be obtained from Figure 7.46, showing the interior of the formwork at the rear of the abutment. First-stage prestressing tendon anchorage at the top of the web may be seen in Figure 7.47. The anchorage block for the second-stage prestressing is located inside the completed box, Figure 7.48.

FIGURE 7.46. Mühlbachtalbrücke, segment in stationary forms.

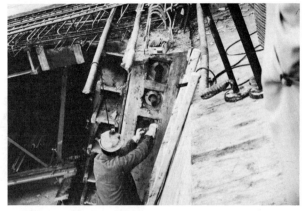

FIGURE 7.47. Mühlbachtalbrücke, first-stage prestressing tendon anchorage.

FIGURE 7.48. Mühlbachtalbrücke, second-stage prestressing anchorage block.

7.8.2 *SHEPHERDS HOUSE BRIDGE, ENGLAND*

The Shepherds House Bridge is the first incrementally launched bridge constructed in England. This highway structure crosses four railroad tracks at Sonning Cutting, near Reading, about 30 miles (48 km) west of London. The new structure contrasts sharply with an existing brick arch structure built in 1838 by Brunel, a famous English engineer. The existing structure consists of three circular brick arches supported on tall brick piers with the abutments founded in the sides of the cutting.[7] A general plan showing the existing bridge, railroad tracks, and alignment of the new structure is presented in Figure 7.49.[8]

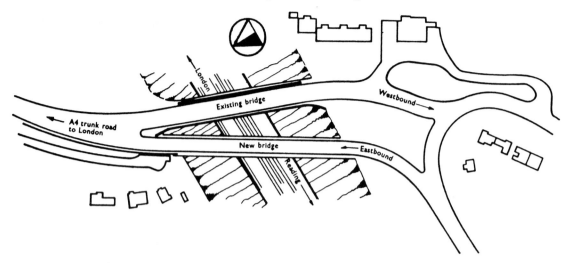

FIGURE 7.49. Shepherds House Bridge, general plan, from reference 8 (courtesy of Institution of Civil Engineers).

In 1971 the north abutment settled and the existing bridge was temporarily closed for repairs. In March of 1972, because the life expectancy of the existing structure was in question and because it did not comply with current highway standards, the Ministry of Transport instructed consulting engineers, Bullen and Partners, to prepare a study to determine the type and method of construction for a new structure. The new bridge provides a dualing of the existing road, and in the future the existing bridge will be replaced by a parallel structure.

Because British Rail was engaged in extensive maintenance and upgrading of the tracks prior to introduction of high-speed trains, there would be severe limitations on track possession. Further, it was dictated that piers between tracks were to be avoided and that foundations on the north slope of the cutting were not to disturb the foundations of the existing bridge abutment. Construction working area was restricted because traffic was to be maintained on a residential street at one end and a trunk road at the other end. Soil conditions required that any temporary conditions that would load or disturb the slopes was to be avoided, thus requiring pile foundations with the pile caps at the surface to avoid extensive excavation in the slopes.[8]

The consultants initially studied five possible schemes for construction of a bridge. Schemes using cast-in-place construction on falsework had earlier been rejected.

An incremental launching scheme was recommended, even though there were no accurate cost data for construction in the U.K. The consultants concluded that this scheme, although of shorter length than customary for this type of construction, would solve the problems of restricted working space and interference with residential streets and would require the least track downtime.

The west elevation of the bridge is shown in Figure 7.50. Span lengths, determined by track location, are 75.5 ft (23 m), 121.4 ft (37 m), and 82 ft (25 m). The bridge is fixed at the south abutment with an expansion joint at the north abutment. The casting bed for the production of 31.5 ft (9.6 m) segments was located to the rear of the south abutment. The south abutment was located to provide maximum work space for the casting bed and to clear a large number of Post Office communication cables. Interior piers b and c were designed to withstand the friction forces exerted during launching operations. In addition, pier c, located close to the railroad tracks, was subject to damage or complete demolishment in the event of a derailment. Therefore, the superstructure was designed to withstand the removal of pier c by an accident. Six untensioned but anchored Macalloy tendons in certain segments were added so as to preclude ultimate collapse with no live load on the bridge and pier c removed.[7,8]

Normally, in this type of construction, the casting bed is of sufficient length to accommodate at least two and sometimes three segment lengths, such that the bottom flange may be cast separately in advance of the webs and top flange. In this project, with restricted space for the casting bed, it was decided to cast one complete segment in one pour.

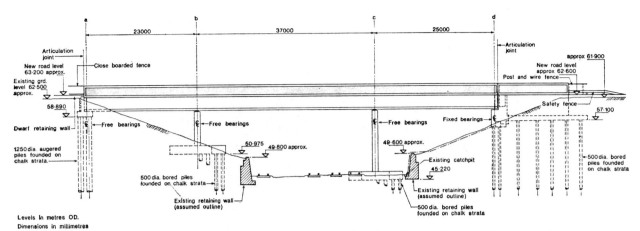

FIGURE 7.50. Shepherds House Bridge, west elevation, from reference 7 (courtesy of The Concrete Society, London).

A maximum of three weeks was allowed for construction and launching of a segment. This time was later reduced to two weeks except for those segments with a diaphragm.[7] A typical cross section of the box girder segment is shown in Figure 7.51.

The launching sequence is shown in Figure 7.52. The steel launching truss nose was first erected using a temporary intermediate support. The first segment was cast against the launching nose and post-tensioned by Macalloy bars, some of which were used to connect the launching nose to the first segment. The launching nose, in position, before the launching of the first segment is shown in Figure 7.53. After the first segment had been launched forward, the next segment was cast and post-tensioned to the previous one. This procedure was repeated until the completed bridge was launched to the north abutment. The launching nose passing over pier c is shown in Figure 7.54. Arrival of the launching nose at pier b is shown in Figure 7.55. The launching nose was removed after the concrete superstructure arrived at pier b, Figure 7.56.

The superstructure was launched over temporary bearings, which consisted of high-grade concrete pads with a $\frac{1}{32}$ in. (1 mm) thick stainless steel plate clamped and tensioned across the top surface. Lateral guide bearings were also provided to keep the superstructure on line. Upon completion of launching the superstructure was jacked in a predetermined sequence and the temporary bearings were replaced with permanent bearings.[8]

The jacking force for launching was provided by two jacks pulling on a set of nine 0.6 in. (15 mm)

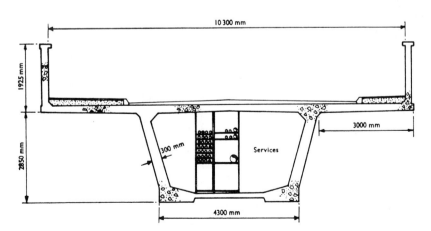

FIGURE 7.51. Shepherds House Bridge, girder cross section, from reference 8 (courtesy of The Institution of Civil Engineers).

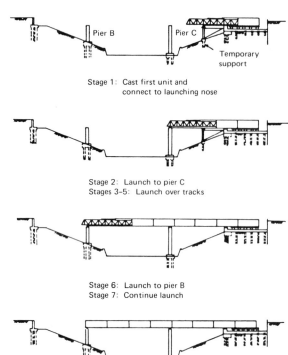

Stage 1: Cast first unit and
connect to launching nose

Stage 2: Launch to pier C
Stages 3–5: Launch over tracks

Stage 6: Launch to pier B
Stage 7: Continue launch

Stage 8: Reach pier B and remove nose
Stages 9 and 10: Complete launch

FIGURE 7.52. Shepherds House Bridge, sequence of incremental launching, from reference 8 (courtesy of The Institution of Civil Engineers).

FIGURE 7.53. Shepherds House Bridge, launching nose in position before launching, from reference 7 (courtesy of The Concrete Society, London).

FIGURE 7.54. Shepherds House Bridge, launching nose passing over pier c, from reference 7 (courtesy of The Concrete Society, London).

FIGURE 7.55. Shepherds House Bridge, launching nose at pier b, from reference 7 (courtesy of The Concrete Society, London).

FIGURE 7.56. Shepherds House Bridge, superstructure launched to pier b and launching nose removed, from reference 7 (courtesy of The Concrete Society, London).

diameter cables passing under the casting bed and anchored to the front of the abutment. The load was applied to a fabricated bracket secured to the rear of the segment by bolts coupling with the projecting ends of the Macalloy bar tendons in the top and bottom flanges of the segment, Figure 7.57. The two jacks were operated in tandem by a single pump. This system required 30 seconds for jacking and 30 seconds for retracting for each 10 in. (254 mm) stroke.[8]

FIGURE 7.57. Shepherds House Bridge, segment being launched from formwork, from reference 7 (courtesy of The Concrete Society, London).

7.9   Design of Incrementally Launched Bridges

7.9.1   BRIDGE ALIGNMENT REQUIREMENTS

The designer must always remember that in order to construct incrementally launched bridges, the horizontal and vertical alignment must be either straight or constantly curved or twisted. This is generally not the case, as road planners are not bridge builders. As a matter of fact, it is the soffit of the bridge deck that has to be designed with a constant radius of curvature; the transverse cantilever of the deck flange can be varied to accommodate possible small deviations.

7.9.2   TYPE, SHAPE AND DIMENSIONS OF SUPERSTRUCTURE

This method of construction requires a cross section with a constant depth, since the designer has to insure the resistance of the superstructure, under its own weight, at all sections as the launching proceeds. Economic considerations dictate a constant moment of inertia.

Two types of cross section have been used to date: the box girder and the double T. The box girder provides a better stiffness and resistance to torsion and at the same time an easier placement of the prestressing tendons in the cross section. The depth of the box is usually one-twelfth to one-sixteenth of the longest span, the first value applying to larger and the second to smaller spans. Table 7.1 summarizes the characteristics of several incrementally launched bridges.

The dimensions for typical cross sections presented in Section 4.5.4 remain valid for the web thickness, but the top flange and bottom flange thickness may have to be increased, depending on the type of prestressing layout adopted (see Section 7.9.4).

7.9.3   SPAN ARRANGEMENT AND RELATED PRINCIPLE OF CONSTRUCTION

The constant-depth requirement limits the economical use of this construction method to spans not longer than 160 to 200 ft (50 to 60 m). It is advantageous if all the spans are equal in length. However, much longer spans have been built by utilizing special techniques in conjunction with the basic principle of incremental launching.

A three-span construction may be launched from both sides. In this way the center span can be twice the length of the edge spans without increase of the stresses in the deck. The span configuration then becomes: $L—2L—L$ (see Figure 7.58). Champigny Bridge near Paris was the first structure of this type. Longer bridges are often launched from one side only (the record length is that of Olifant's River Bridge in South Africa, in excess of 3300 ft). Auxiliary temporary devices are used to reduce the bending moments in the front portion of the deck (launching nose or tower stays)

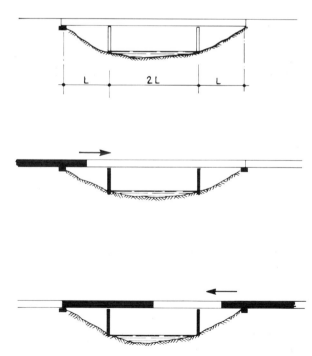

FIGURE 7.58.   Three-span symmetrical incrementally launched bridge.

TABLE 7.1. Characteristics of Incrementally Launched Bridges

Name	Year	Cross Section	Typical Span (ft)	Total Length (ft)	Launched Weight (t)	Vertical Curve	Horizontal Curve
Nuel Viaduct, France	1976	41' / 10'	135	807	6,000	Slope 6%	$R = 2,460$ ft
Borriglione Viaduct, France	1976	41' / 10'	135	807	6,000	Slope 5.5%	$R = 2,460$ ft
Kimonkro Bridge, Ivory Coast	1978	31.3' / 8.5'	118	709	3,600		Straight
Tet Viaduct, France		39' / 8'	141	660			
Luc Viaduct, France		48'	135	915	7,900	Slope 3.8%	Straight
Paillon Bridge, France	1976	34'	135	1,151		Slope 1.3%	Curve
Oli Viaduct, France	1976	40.5' / 10'	135	2,018	15,000	Slope 5.85%	$R = 6,712$ ft
Marolles Bridge, France	1972	29.5' / 8'	131	345			
Creil Bridge, France	1978	36' / 9.5'	194	1,102			

344

TABLE 7.1. *(Continued)*

Name	Year	Cross Section	Typical Span (ft)	Total Length (ft)	Launched Weight (t)	Vertical Curve	Horizontal Curve
Gronachtal Bridge, Germany	1978	46.3' / 11' / 17.5'	262	1,732	13,000	Slope 0.7%	$R = 7,217$ ft
Var Viaduct, France	1976	32' / 8.5'	138	1,107	9,700		Straight
Inn Bridge, Kufstein, Germany	1965	18'	335	1,476			
Koches Valley Bridge, Germany		13'	169	1,562			
Querlin Guen Bridge, Germany		10'	138	1,398			
Abeou Aqueduct, France	1967	19' / 19'	108	469			
Ingolstadt Bridge, Danube Bridge, Germany	1978	62' / 11' to 14'	6 spans 197 to 377	2 × 1,246			

as previously indicated in some of the examples described in this chapter.

When the spans become too large, intermediate temporary bents are used. This was done for the first bridge over the Caroni River in Venezuela. The record span length for incrementally launched bridges was obtained by a structure over the Danube River designed by Prof. Leonhardt, the originator of the method, Figure 7.59. The cost of the temporary bents depends greatly on the foundation conditions; it may be prohibitive if the bent height is greater than 100 ft (30 m) and soil conditions require deep piling.

For very long bridges, intermediate expansion joints are needed, much the same as for cantilever bridges. The expansion joints are temporarily fixed by prestressing during launching and are released at the end of construction to allow for thermal expansion in the structure during service. A very ingenious variation of this principle was de-

FIGURE 7.59. Danube River Bridge, Austria.

veloped for the Basra Bridge in Iraq, where a concrete swing span was launched together with the approach spans as a single unit and later arranged to serve its purpose as a movable bridge over the navigation channel, Figure 7.60.

7.9.4 DESIGN OF LONGITUDINAL MEMBERS FOR FLEXURE AND TENDON PROFILE

During launching, the superstructure is subjected to continually alternating bending moments, so that any one section is subjected to a continual variation of bending moments, both positive and negative, as shown in Figures 7.61 and 7.62. These bending moments are balanced by internal uniform axial prestressing.

In the final stage, additional tendons are required to supplement the uniform axial prestressing in order to carry the service loads. Conventional solutions are applied to this problem, and in the present discussion we need only enlarge upon the specific problem of the axial prestressing. For this prestressing, tendons are so arranged that the compressive stresses are the same over the entire cross-sectional area. The required tendons are placed in the top and bottom flanges of the box section. They are usually straight, tensioned before launching, so couplers are needed at each joint between successive segments.

Segment length may vary from 50 ft (15 m) to 100 ft (30 m). As noted in our discussion of the progressive construction method, there are limitations to the deck's capacity to carry its own weight during launching when the front part is in cantilever beyond a typical pier. To keep bending moments and stresses within allowable values, it is usually necessary to use a launching nose, a light steel member placed in front of the concrete structure to allow support from the next pier, rather than launching the concrete deck all the way with no support. Numerical values are given in Figures 7.61 and 7.62 for the critical maximum positive and negative moments during launching.

Assuming the unit weight of the launching nose to be 10% of the weight of the concrete deck (a value somewhat lower than average), the critical

FIGURE 7.60. Basra Bridge, Iraq.

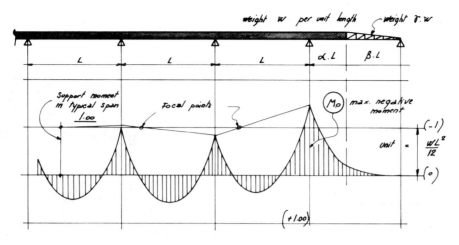

FIGURE 7.61. Critical negative moments during launching with nose. $M_0 = (WL^2/12)[6\alpha^2 + 6\gamma(1 - \alpha^2)]$. Multiplier: $WL^2/12$. For $\gamma = 0.10$:

α	β	M_0
0.20	0.80	0.82
0.30	0.70	1.09
0.40	0.60	1.46
0.50	0.50	1.95
1.00	0.00	6.00

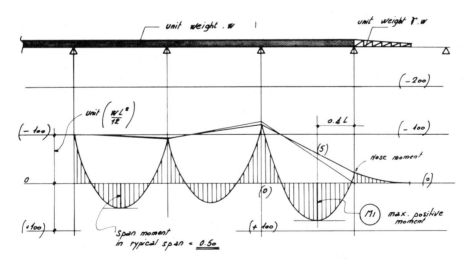

FIGURE 7.62. Critical positive moment during launching with nose. $M_1 = (WL^2/12)(0.933 - 2.96\gamma\beta^2)$. Multiplier $= WL^2/12$. For $\gamma = 0.10$:

α	β	M_1
0.20	0.80	0.74
0.30	0.70	0.79
0.40	0.60	0.83
0.50	0.50	0.86
1.00	0.00	0.93

moments are as follows for various lengths of the launching nose:

Nose Length, Percent of Typical Span	Maximum Moments		M_0/M_1
	Support (M_0)	Span (M_1)	
50	1.95	0.86	2.27
60	1.46	0.83	1.76
70	1.09	0.79	1.38
80	0.82	0.74	1.11

Moment factor is $WL^2/12$

(W = weight of concrete per unit length and L = span length)

Technologically, the uniform axial prestress may be installed in the superstructure in several different ways:

1. Straight tendons running through the top and bottom flange of each segment, joined by couplers at the joints between segments.
2. Straight tendons running through the top and bottom flanges, anchored in block-outs inside the box girder, Figure 7.63.
3. Temporary curved tendons may be used to balance the final continuity tendons during construction. These tendons are outside the concrete section between supports, Figure 7.64. This method has been used for several large projects.

Figure 7.65 shows the Sathorn Bridge in Bangkok, Thailand, with the temporary tendons installed

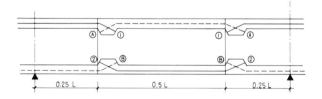

FIGURE 7.63. Lapped prestressing tendons.

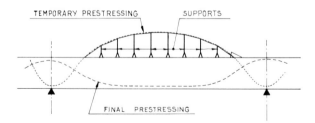

FIGURE 7.64. Temporary external prestressing system.

FIGURE 7.65. Sathorn Bridge, Thailand.

above the concrete deck with steel deviation saddles at intermediate joints.

The three solutions above have their relative merits and disadvantages:

1. The first solution may require local thickening of the concrete flanges for placement of the couplers. However, it is often preferred to increase the thickness of the flanges over the entire bridge length to simplify casting of the segments. Axial prestressing tendons are permanent and cannot be removed. They must be incorporated in the final prestressing layout. The joints between segments have to be carefully designed, owing to the presence of couplers and concrete voids that may significantly weaken the section.

2. The main advantage of the second solution pertains to the removal and reuse of those tendons not required in the final prestressing layout. However, the cost and difficulty of providing a large number of block-outs offsets a significant part of the advantage of removing the temporary tendons. In order to obtain a satisfactory shear resistance from the webs, particularly during launching with alternating shear and bending stresses, the configuration of the box section and location of the upper and lower blisters must be carefully considered. This problem was mentioned in Chapter 4 as presenting potential difficulties. A satisfactory solution is shown in Figure 7.66, where upper and lower blisters are not in the same vertical plane. A sufficient amount of vertical prestress will insure the resistance of webs against shear during all construction stages.

3. The third solution is theoretically a satisfactory one, allowing the permanent prestress to be installed during construction and the temporary prestress to be designed only to counteract the un-

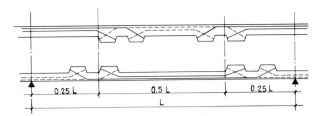

FIGURE 7.66. Offset lapped prestressing tendons.

desired effects of the former during moment reversals created by the successive launching stages. In practice, installation of the tendons passing from the inside to the outside of the box section is not particularly simple. An attempt should be made to reuse these temporary tendons to reduce the investment in nonproductive materials.

A comparative analysis between the first two methods of temporary prestressing has been made for a typical railway bridge. Solution 2 requires 19% more conventional reinforcement than solution 1 because of the many blisters and more elaborate tendon layout. The total cost of materials (concrete prestress and reinforcement) is 9% higher for solution 2 than for solution 1. These results may be significantly different for highway bridges, where the ratio between girder load and superimposed dead and live loads is very different.

7.9.5 CASTING AREA AND LAUNCHING METHODS

The precasting area is located behind one abutment and has a length usually equal to that of two or three segments. There are two different launching methods:

1. The launching force is transmitted from the jacks bearing against the abutment face to the bridge by pulling tendons or steel rods anchored in the bridge soffit.
2. A launching device consisting of horizontal and vertical jacks is placed over the abutment. The vertical jack rests on a sliding surface and has a special friction gripping element at the top. The vertical jack lifts the superstructure for launching, and the horizontal jack pushes it horizontally.

The designer should be concerned with the following items:

The first launching method applies high local forces to the concrete soffit where the pulling device is anchored. Careful design of the passive

reinforcement must be made in an area already densely prestressed.

The second launching method requires sufficient vertical reaction on the vertical jack. This could be critical at the end of launching, when the required launching force reaches its maximum with a corresponding small vertical reaction.

A very precise geometry control is required during launching. The possibility of foundation settlement must be considered in the design. Whichever launching method is used, after completion of the launching procedure the deck must be raised successively at each pier so that the permanent bearings may be installed. This phase also calls for careful analysis.

7.9.6 LAUNCHING NOSE AND TEMPORARY STAYS

The large cantilever moments occurring in the front part of the superstructure that is being launched from pier to pier inevitably call for special provisions to keep the bending stresses and the temporary prestress within allowable and economically acceptable limits. Two methods have been used together and separately, as previously mentioned:

Launching nose: A steel member made either of plate girders or of trusses is temporarily prestressed into the end diaphragm of the concrete bridge, which is the front section of the deck during launching.

Tower and stays: This method was described in Chapter 6 for progressive construction. Its application to incremental launching, however, needs a special approach, because the relative position of the tower and the stays changes constantly with regard to the permanent piers.

The advantage of the launching nose to reduce cantilever moments in the concrete superstructure was discussed in Section 7.9.4. It is important not only to select the proper dimensions of the launching nose but also to take into proper account the actual flexibility of the steel nose in comparison to that of the concrete span. This relative flexibility may be characterized by the following dimensionless coefficient:

$$K = \frac{E_s I_s}{E_c I_c}$$

where E_s and E_c refer to steel and concrete moduli, and I_s and I_c are the moments of inertia of the steel nose and concrete superstructure. Figure 7.67 presents the results of a study analyzing the variation of the maximum support moment in the concrete deck for different launching stages with the relative stiffness K. This chart confirms the obvious fact that a flexible nose has only a limited efficiency in reducing the moments in the concrete deck. The following table gives the characteristics of several structures using a launching nose and serves as a reference for preliminary investigations of the optimum launching method.

Bridge	Launching Nose Length [ft (m)]	Weight of Launching Nose (tons)	Stays
Wabash River	56 (17)	30	No
Oli River	59 (18)	36	Yes
Saone	93.5 (28.5)	65	No
Roche	124.5 (38)	90	No

For longer spans the launching nose is not necessarily the optimum solution, while temporary bents may also be expensive. A tower-and-stay system has been successfully used either alone or in conjunction with a launching nose to reduce the cantilever moments in the front part of the superstructure.

To allow the method to be effective in all launching stages, it is necessary to constantly control the reaction of the tower applied to the concrete deck. When the tower is above one pier, it is totally efficient. When launching has proceeded for another half-span length, the tower and stays produce additional positive moments at midspan, exactly contrary to the desired effect. For this reason the tower may be equipped with jacks between the concrete deck and the tower legs, and the tower reaction may be constantly adjusted to optimize the stresses in the concrete superstructure. Figure 7.68 shows a device being successfully used for the first time in the construction of the Boivre Viaduct, near Poitiers, France.

7.9.7 PIERS AND FOUNDATIONS

The loads applied to the piers and foundations during the incremental launching procedure are very different from those appearing during service. The static configuration of the piers is also

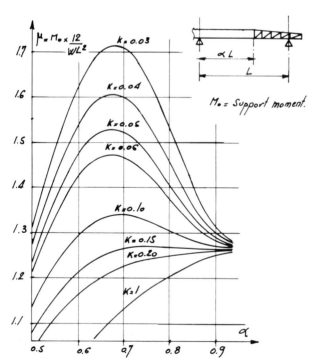

FIGURE 7.67. Variation of the maximum support moment.

FIGURE 7.68. Boivre Viaduct, near Poitiers, France.

different. During construction, the bridge slides over the pier tops and the buckling length of the pier is larger than that during service. The horizontal force applied to the pier top is also higher than during service, thus requiring a close study of this construction phase.

Loads Acting on the Piers The various systems of horizontal forces that may act on the piers depend on the following:

Longitudinal profile of the superstructure

Direction of launching

Friction coefficient of sliding bearings

Notation:

θ = angle of bridge superstructure with respect to the horizontal; $\tan \theta = r$

ϕ = angle of friction of sliding bearings; $\tan \phi = \rho$

R = total reaction of the superstructure on the pier: vertical and horizontal components V and H, normal and tangential components N and T

The following four cases will be considered (see Figure 7.69):

1. $\theta > \phi$, *upward launching:* Sliding starts on the bearings when the inclination of the reaction R with respect to the vertical is:

$$\alpha = \theta + \phi, \qquad H = V \tan (\theta + \phi)$$

For small values of θ and ϕ:

$$H = (r + \rho)V$$

2. $\theta > \phi$, *downward launching:* Sliding starts when $\alpha = \theta - \phi$. The horizontal force on the pier acts in the direction opposite to that of movement with a value:

$$H = V \tan (\theta - \phi)$$

For small values of the angles:

$$H = (r - \rho)V$$

Because ρ varies with environmental conditions (cleanness of the plates in particular), the launching equipment and the pier will be designed for $H = rV$. The downward movement of the bridge is controlled by a restraining jacking force:

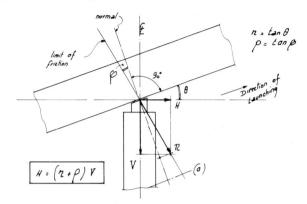

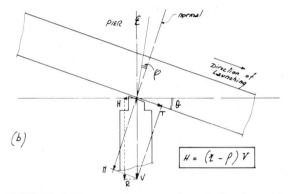

FIGURE 7.69. Reactions on piers during launching. (*a*) upward launching. (*b*) downward launching.

$$F = N(\tan \theta - \tan \phi) \quad \text{or} \quad F = N(r - \rho)$$

For the same reasons as above, the safe value of F is equal to Nr.

3. $\theta < \phi$, *upward launching:* As above, the horizontal load applied to the pier is:

$$H = (r + \rho)V$$

4. $\theta < \phi$, *downward launching:* In this case the horizontal load on the pier is applied in the direction of the movement with a value of:

$$H = (r - \rho)V$$

Because of the possible variation in the angle of friction, it is safer to provide a braking system to control the movement of the bridge.

Pier Cap Detailing The pier caps must be carefully detailed in order to provide room for the following devices:

Temporary sliding bearings

Vertical jacks to lift the bridge after launching to install the permanent bearings

Horizontal guiding devices during launching

Adjusting jacks for correction of the relative displacements between piers and deck

Moreover, to reduce the pier bending moments induced by launching, the sliding bearings are often eccentric. However, it is possible to reduce or balance this horizontal force by installing ties anchored in the ground. If the piers are very high, the horizontal force can be eliminated by using jacking equipment directly installed on the piers.

7.10   Demolition of a Structure by Incremental Launching

We close this chapter with an unusual application showing the interesting potential of incremental launching. An overpass structure over the A-1 motorway north of Paris needed to be demolished for replacement by another structure as part of a highway relocation program. The limited headroom between the existing bridge soffit and the clearance diagram, together with the considerable traffic on the major motorway providing permanent access from Paris to Charles de Gaulle Airport, made all conventional methods of demolition extremely difficult and unadapted.

A very simple scheme was devised whereby the deck was launched away from the traffic onto the approach embankment to be conventionally demolished at leisure. The dimensions of the bridge

and the principle of the method are shown in Figure 7.70. The 900-ton structure had a width of 26 ft and the following spans: 46, 55, 55, 46 ft.

The existing reinforcing did not provide the necessary strength to resist superstructure dead load during launching. Therefore, a rear launching-out tail 26 ft long was installed at the end opposite the direction of launching, while exterior post-tensioning tendons were placed above the deck to strengthen the structure.

The bridge was lifted off its bearings 7 in. to install sliding bearings and lateral guiding devices in preparation for the operation. The whole operation was performed in $5\frac{1}{2}$ weeks as follows:

Design and preparation of the contract	2
Mobilization and purchase of equipment	2
Launching	$1\frac{1}{2}$
	$5\frac{1}{2}$

Traffic was interrupted for only four nights between 10 P.M. and 6 A.M. The operation turned out to be a complete success in spite of its originality.

References

1. Willi Baur, "Bridge Erection by Launching Is Fast, Safe, and Efficient," *Civil Engineering—ASCE*, Vol. 47, No. 3, March 1977.

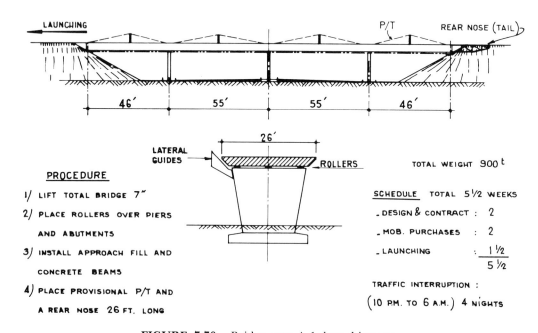

FIGURE 7.70.   Bridge over A-1, launching out.

2. Anon., "First Incrementally Launched Post-Tensioned Box Girder Bridge to Be Built in the United States," Bridge Report, December 1976, Post-Tensioning Institute, Phoenix, Ariz.

3. Arvid Grant, "Incremental Launching of Concrete Structures," *Journal of the American Concrete Institute*, Vol. 72, No. 8, August 1975.

4. Anon., "Val Restel Viaduct for the Provincial Road No. 89 Near Rovereto, Trento," *Prestressed Concrete Structures in Italy 1970/1974*, Associazione Italiana Cemento Armato E Precompresso (AICAP) and Associazione Italiana Econonica Del Cemento (AITEC), Rome 1974.

5. Anon., "Segmental Box Girder Bridges Make the Big Time in U.S.," *Engineering News-Record*, March 2, 1978.

6. Anon., "Wabash River Bridge, Covington, Indiana," Portland Cement Association, Bridge Report, SR201.01E, 1978, Skokie, Ill.

7. M. Maddison, "Crossing the Cutting with Segments at Sonning," *Concrete, The Journal of the Concrete Society (London)*, Vol. 12, No. 2, February 1978.

8. K. H. Best, R. H. Kingston, and M. J. Whatley, "Incremental Launching at Shepherds House Bridge," *Proceedings, Institution of Civil Engineers*, Vol. 64, Part I, February 1978.

8

Concrete Segmental Arches, Rigid Frames, and Truss Bridges

8.1 Introduction

An arch bridge, in a proper setting, is an elegant and graceful structure with aesthetic appeal. Instinctively, a layman relates to an arch bridge as a form that follows its function. Long before prestressed concrete was developed as a technology, concrete arches were used for long spans, taking advantage of the compressive stress induced by gravitational forces into a curved member much as earlier generations of builders had done with masonry arches.

Three bridges designed and built by Eugene Freyssinet between 1907 and 1910 in central France were to become a major landmark in the development of concrete structures. In the Veurdre Bridge, Figure 8.1, the three hinged reinforced concrete arches had a clear span of 238 ft (72.50 m) and an unusual rise-to-span ratio of 1/15 dictated by the topography of the site and the sudden floods of the Allier River. The venture was an unqualified success both during load testing and after opening to traffic. As Freyssinet wrote in his memoirs:

Load testing was a triumph. On the right bank, a hill overlooking the bridge site was occupied by several thousand spectators who had taken their place already at dawn to watch the failure of the bridge predicted by a local newspaper sold to some unhappy competitor. These hopes were deceived, and we had a continuous lane of heavy steam rollers traveling the bridge back and forth quite unable to produce anything more than the computed elastic deflections.

Between 1907 and 1911, however, fears developed in Freyssinet's mind. It seemed that the hand rails, which had been properly aligned at the time of the load test, were showing some convexity toward the sky at the nodes of the crown hinges. By the spring of 1911 the crown had moved downward as much as 5 in. (0.13 m), and correspondingly the springings had raised appreciably. Without telling anyone, Freyssinet mobilized a team of four devoted men and placed hydraulic rams at the arch crowns to raise the bridge spans to their original profile; he then replaced the hinge by a rigid concrete connection between the two abutting half-arches. This near-disaster was the

354

FIGURE 8.1. Veurdre Bridge.

first consequence seen in a structure of a phenomenon theretofore completely ignored: long-term concrete creep.

Other beautiful concrete arches were also constructed in the same period. The Villeneuve Bridge over the Lot River in southwestern France, Figure 8.2, is an interesting example. The twin arch ribs are of plain concrete with a clear span of 316 ft (96 m) and a rise of 47 ft 4 in. (14.5 m). Each rib has a solid section 10 ft (3 m) wide and 4 ft 9 in. (1.45 m) deep built in at both ends into the concrete abutments. The reinforced concrete deck rests upon the arch ribs through a series of thin spandrel columns, faced with red brick.

Construction began shortly before World War I and was interrupted for four years, fortunately not before the concrete arch ribs could be cast on a wooden falsework, Figure 8.3. Immediately upon completion, hydraulic rams were used at the midspan section to lift the concrete arches off the falsework and actively create the compressive stress in them, a technique from Freyssinet's fertile mind that already contained the germ of the idea of prestressing.

The bridge was completed in 1919 and kept the world's record for long-span concrete structures for several years. The photograph appearing in Figure 8.2 was taken by one of the authors in the summer of 1980; it shows that beautiful structure in a remarkable state after sixty years of continuous operation under constant urban traffic.

Another Freyssinet design, the Tonneins Bridge over the Garonne River, was built at the same time, and he considered it to be one of his nicest bridge structures, Figure 8.4.

The Plougastel Bridge in Brittany, Figure 1.38, reached for longer spans with concrete arches. For the first time a box section was employed, calling on an ingenious method of construction in which a wooden falsework was floated into position and reused several times for the various arch ribs. Dimensions of the structure and typical details of the arches are shown in Figure 8.5, which is a facsimile of a document published in 1930.

The three arches have a span length of 611 ft (186.40 m) and carry a single-track railroad and a two-lane highway. The reinforced concrete trussed double deck accommodates the train track on its lower level and the highway on the upper. Near the arch crown in each span, the train passes through the arch rib.

The arch ribs were only slightly reinforced and the quantity of steel was 39 lb/yd³ (23 kg/m³), in spite of the relatively thin walls used for the box section.

The three arch ribs were constructed one after the other on a temporary wooden arch built on shore and floated into position for each of the three concrete arches, Figures 8.6 and 8.7. This wooden arch was 490 ft (150 m) long and weighed 550 tons (500 mt), including the two reinforced concrete end sections, which allowed the thrust created by the concrete arch ribs to be transferred

FIGURE 8.2. Villeneuve Bridge over the Lot River.

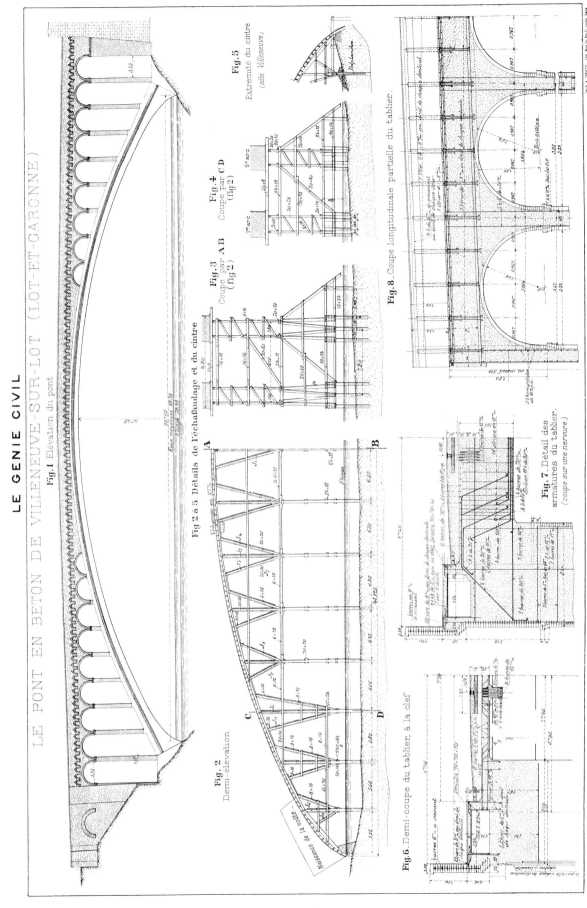

FIGURE 8.3. Villeneuve Bridge, timber falsework details.

FIGURE 8.4. Tonneins Bridge over the Garonne River, France.

to the arch springings completed earlier on the foundation caissons.

Two barges and a temporary steel tie slightly above the water level, with the help of the large tidal range, allowed the transfer of this falsework from the construction area to the three positions of use and its final return after completion of the concrete structure.

As this outstanding undertaking neared completion in 1930 after five years of uninterrupted effort, Freyssinet expressed his thoughts as follows:

In Brittany light is like a fairy who constantly plays at covering nature with [many] changing coats, now of lead, now of silver or of pearls, or of something immaterial and radiant.

Toward the evening of the load testing of the bridge, she had spread her most sumptuous treasures on the roadstead and each line of the work, changed into a long rosary of unreal light, added another touch of beauty to the marvellous whole, proving in this way that the Fairy of the Roadstead had already adopted the child that men had imposed on her and had known how to weave for him garments magnificent enough to hide all the imperfections of the work.

8.2 Segmental Precast Bridges over the Marne River, France

Located some 30 miles (50 km) east of Paris, the Luzancy Bridge represents probably the first application of truly segmental construction as we

know it today. It incorporated so many innovations in a single structure that it would not be out of place in today's modern bridge technology.

The single-span structure, Figure 8.8, is a double-hinged arch with a distance between hinges of 180 ft (55 m) and a very tight clearance diagram for river navigation that allowed only 4 ft 3 in. (1.30 m) below the finished grade of the roadway. Consequently, not only is the bridge structure very shallow, 4.16 ft (1.27 m), at midspan, but the rise-to-span ratio of the arch is unusual: 1/23. The bridge consists of three parallel box sections made up of precast segments 8 ft (2.44 m) long, connected after placement in the structure by precast slab sections at both top and bottom flanges, Figure 8.9.

The bridge is prestressed in three directions:

The 4 in. (0.10 m) webs are vertically prestressed to resist shear.

The longitudinal box girders are then prestressed to connect the precast segments and resist bending. The negative-moment prestressing tendons at the top flange level over the arch springings are located in grooves provided at the top surface of the precast segment upper flange and are ultimately embedded in a 2 in. (50 mm) concrete topping. This dense, high-quality concrete pavement provides the sole protection for the high-tensile steel wires and also serves as the sole roadway wearing course. In spite of the excellent behavior of this structure after more than 34 years of operation, it would probably be difficult to envisage duplicating it today.

Transverse connection between the box girders and the connecting slabs is achieved by prestressing.

There was no conventional reinforcing steel in the bridge superstructure except in local areas, such as the Freyssinet concrete hinges at the arch springings. The erection was just as remarkable as the conception of the bridge. Each box girder consisted of 22 segments, which were cast in a central yard at the rate of one a day (little progress has been achieved after thirty years). Afterward they were carefully aligned on concrete blocks to take the profile of the finished structure with proper provision for camber. The $\frac{3}{4}$ in. (20 mm) wide joints were dry packed to allow segment assembly by prestressing. In fact, the 22 segments of each box girder were assembled at this stage in three units: two side units made up of three segments each, and the center unit incorporating the remaining 16

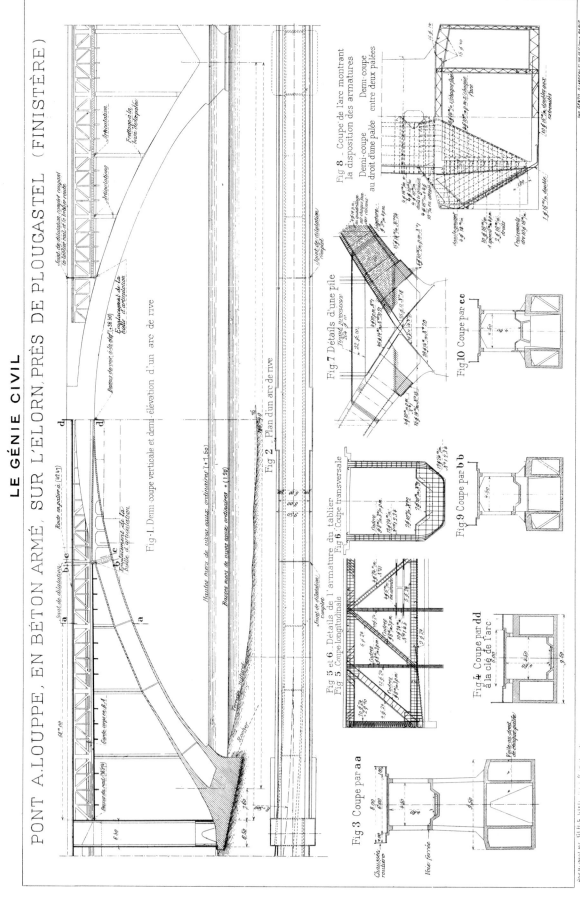

FIGURE 8.5. Plougastel Bridge, dimensions of the structure and details of the arches, a facsimile of a document published in 1930.

FIGURE 8.6. Plougastel Bridge, wooden falsework.

FIGURE 8.7. Plougastel Bridge, wooden falsework.

FIGURE 8.8. Luzancy Bridge.

segments with a length of 170 ft (52 m) and a maximum weight of 134 tons (122 mt). All three units were assembled on the bridge centerline immediately behind one abutment, while the delta-shaped sections representing the arch springings were cast in place over the abutment in their final location in the structure.

A special aerial cableway made up of two steel towers resting on both banks and properly anchored to the rear, a system of suspended winches, and a unique elliptical drum allowed the transfer of the precast girder units from their assembly po-

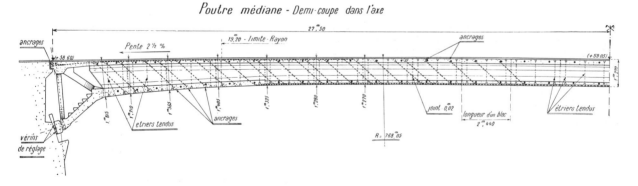

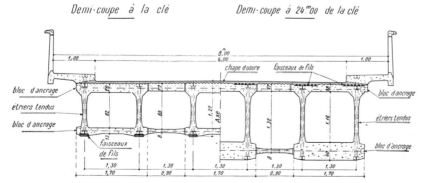

FIGURE 8.9. Luzancy Bridge, concrete dimensions.

sition on the banks to their final location in the structure. In spite of a seemingly involved concept, the operations were carried out safely and rapidly; a center beam was placed in only eight hours and a complete arch including all preparatory and finishing operations was assembled in 120 hours, Figure 8.10.

Another interesting feature of this structure was the incorporation at both arch springings of Freyssinet flat jacks and reinforced concrete wedges between the arch inclined legs and the abutment sills, to adjust and control the arch thrust and the bending moments at midspan.

The bridge was opened to traffic in May 1946 after successfully proving its structural adequacy through a comprehensive series of static and dynamic load tests, following a custom still in use today in several European countries. Figure 8.11 gives a view of the finished structure.

This first precast segmental arch bridge was followed a few years later by a series of five other structures, all of the same type and in the same geographical area, the valley of the Marne River,

FIGURE 8.10. Luzancy Bridge, erection of central section.

FIGURE 8.11. Luzancy Bridge, view showing flat arch rise.

FIGURE 8.12. One of the five Marne River Bridges: Esbly, Anet, Changis, Trilbardou, and Ussy.

Figure 8.12, at the following locations: Esbly, Anet, Changis, Trilbardou, and Ussy. All five bridges have the geometric dimensions shown in Figure 8.13:

Distance between hinges: 243 ft (74 m)

Rise of the central axis at the crown over the abutment hinge: 16.3 ft (4.96 m)

Depth at crown: 2.82 ft (0.86 m)

Deck width: 27.5 ft (8.40 m)

The deck structure is made up of six precast girders, each consisting of:

Two precast delta-shaped sections at the springings

Thirty-two precast segments 6.8 ft (2.07 m) long and weighing from 2 to 4.2 tons (1.8 to 3.8 mt).

The same design and construction principles used at the Luzancy Bridge were repeated for this series of five bridges, except for some improvements commensurate to the experience gained from the first structure and taking into account the importance of the project. Precasting of the 960 segments was achieved in a factory completely enclosed and using the most modern concrete manufacturing techniques of that period.

Each segment was fabricated in two stages in heavy steel forms. Top and bottom flanges were cast first, with high-strength steel stirrups embedded in both units. After strength was achieved, a set of steel forms equipped with jacks was placed between the flanges, which were jacked apart to stress the web pretensioned stirrups. Then the web was cast between the flanges. There was no need for any conventional reinforcing steel in the precast segments.

The concrete was vibrated with high-frequency external vibrators, then compressed for maximum

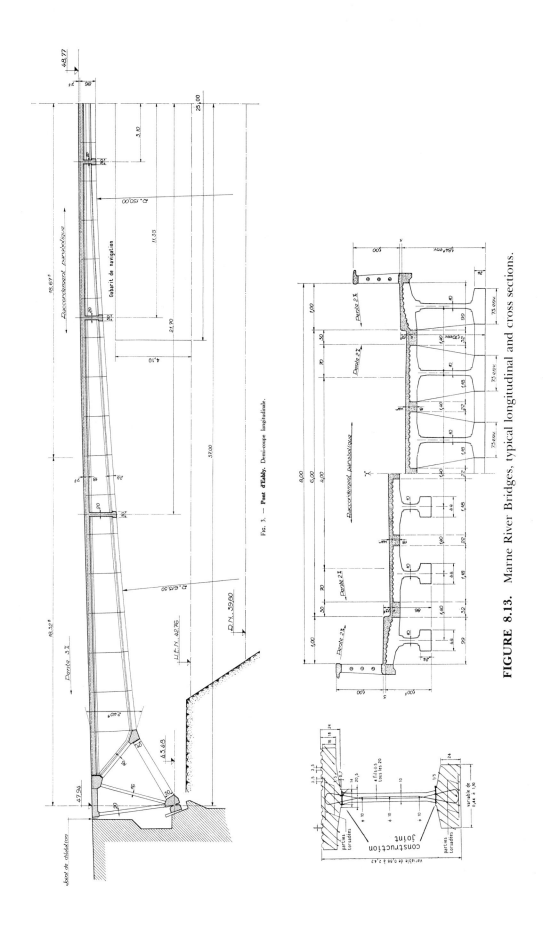

Fig. 3. — **Pont d'Eably.** Demi-coupe longitudinale.

FIGURE 8.13. Marne River Bridges, typical longitudinal and cross sections.

361

compaction and steam cured for a fast reuse of the forms. The equivalent 28-day cylinder strength was in excess of 6500 psi.

Near the precast factory, an assembly yard allowed the segments to be carefully aligned and assembled by temporary prestressing into sections, which were transferred into barges to be floated to the various bridge sites. Each longitudinal girder was thus made up of six sections:

The two delta springing sections

Two intermediate five-segment sections

Two center ten-segment sections

Handling of these various sections was performed by the Luzancy cableway properly rearranged for the purpose.

The stability of the side sections, at both ends, was obtained by temporary cantilever cables anchored in the abutments, while the two center sections were suspended to the cableway until casting of the wet joints was completed and longitudinal prestressing installed to allow the arches to support their own weight. Figures 8.14 through 8.16 show the various sequences of the arch construction, while one of the finished bridges is shown in Figure 8.17.

The quantities of materials for the superstructure were very low, considering the span length and the slenderness of the structure:

Precast concrete: 353 yd³ (270 m³)

Reinforcing steel: 13.2 tons (12 mt)

Prestressing steel: 13.2 tons (12 mt)

For a deck area of 6540 ft², the quantities per square foot were:

FIGURE 8.14. Marne River Bridges, erected end section.

FIGURE 8.15. Marne River Bridges, erection of central section.

FIGURE 8.16. Marne River Bridges, erection of central section.

Precast concrete: 1.46 ft³/ft²

Reinforcing steel: 4.0 lb/ft²

Prestressing steel: 4.0 lb/ft²

As in the Luzancy Bridge, the high-density concrete placed over the exposed longitudinal prestressing tendons was also used for the roadway

FIGURE 8.17. Marne River Bridges, completed structure.

FIGURE 8.19. Caracas Viaducts, Bridges 2 and 3.

wearing course. The behavior of these bridges has been excellent for thirty years.

8.3 Caracas Viaducts, Venezuela

In Venezuela in 1952 a highway was being constructed between Caracas and La Guaira airport. Alignment of this highway necessitated crossing a gorge at three locations with relatively large bridges. These structures were designed and constructed under the direction of Eugene Freyssinet.[1]

Although the three bridges are similar in appearance, Figures 8.18 and 8.19, they vary in

FIGURE 8.18. Caracas Viaducts, Bridge 1.

length as shown in Table 8.1.[2] Preliminary investigations indicated that adequate soil material would probably be found irregularly at great depths. Construction of abutments to resist large bending moments under these conditions would be difficult if not impossible. The decision was therefore made that the abutments would resist only the centered thrust of the arches and that the bending moments applied to the abutment would be reduced, as far as practical, to zero. This required that hinges be located as near as possible to the points of origin of the arches. Because of consideration of long-term creep deformation on buckling of the arch and possible consequences of abutment displacement as might be caused by an earthquake, the decision was made to eliminate a crown hinge, thus resulting in two hinged arches.[1]

Although the bridges vary considerably in dimensions, they are quite similar in appearance. Because of the valley profile, it was possible to use the same basic design for all three structures. All were designed for AASHO H20-44 loading. Wherever possible, the elements were standardized in order to minimize design and maximize precasting and prefabrication.

Pilasters were placed at each end of the arch in Bridge 1 so as to avoid an unpleasant appearance of a change without transition from the main structure to the approach viaducts.

TABLE 8.1. Caracas Viaduct Arches

Bridge	Total Length	Height from Bed of Gorge	Main Span
1	1013 ft (308.8 m)	230 ft (70.1 m)	498 ft (151.8 m)
2	830 ft (253 m)	240 ft (73.2 m)	478 ft (145.7 m)
3	700 ft (213.4 m)	170 ft (51.8 m)	453 ft (138.1 m)

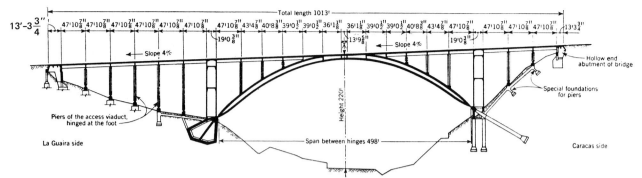

FIGURE 8.20. Caracas Viaducts, elevation of Bridge 1, from reference 1 (courtesy of Civil Engineering-ASCE).

An elevation of Bridge 1, Figure 8.20, shows the principal dimensions and foundations of the arch. The three bridges have identical cross sections, Figure 8.21. The poured-in-place concrete deck topping varies in thickness from 2 in. (50 mm) at the edges to $7\frac{1}{2}$ in. (190 mm) at the center to provide a transverse slope of 1.5% for drainage. Each deck span, except at the crown, consists of eight precast prestressed I girders. Variations in span length of the deck girders are accommodated by adding or removing standard form units. Identical transversely prestressed precast stay-in-place deck slabs span transversely between the deck girders. Continuity of the deck girders is accomplished by longitudinal tendons placed in a groove in the top of the top flange of the girders.[2]

Approach piers and spandrel columns over the arches consist of three I-shaped columns of a standard cross section shown in Figure 8.21. A five-segment precast cap beam on the columns re-

ceives the eight deck I girders. A perspective of the deck over the piers is shown in Figure 8.22. The precast deck girders, cap beams, and slab are supported on the cast-in-place piers, and the whole assembly is prestressed vertically, transversely, and longitudinally.

The center span consists of three parallel double-hinged arch ribs 27 ft 6 in. (8.4 m) on center, Figure 8.21. Each arch rib is a box with a width of 10 ft 6 in. (3.2 m) and a slightly varying depth from 9 ft 6 in. (2.9 m) to 10 ft (3.05 m) at the supporting points of the deck. To provide increased capacity to resist end moments developed by horizontal loads, the width of the ribs is increased to 17 ft (5.18 m) at the spring lines. The 5 in. by 5 in. (127 mm x 127 mm) fillets provided at each inside corner of the box are to reduce the concentration of torsion stresses. Thickness of the bottom flange of the box rib was kept to a minimum to reduce weight on the falsework. The

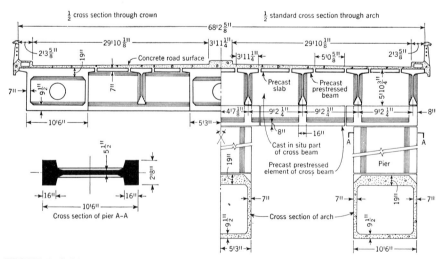

FIGURE 8.21. Caracas Viaducts, typical cross section, from reference 1 (courtesy of Civil Engineering-ASCE).

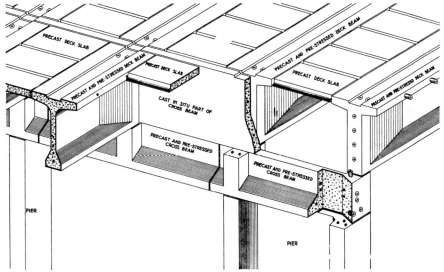

FIGURE 8.22. Caracas Viaducts, perspective of deck over piers, from reference 1 (courtesy of Civil Engineering-ASCE).

thicker top flange provides the box rib with the required area and moment of inertia for resisting thrust and live-load moments.

Design of these structures considered a design wind pressure of 50 psf (2.4 kN/m²). The arch ribs carry part of the wind pressure to which they are directly subjected; the remainder is transmitted to the deck structure by bending of the spandrel columns and the connection of the arch rib to the deck at the crown. The arches were assumed to be transversely fixed in the foundations, the end moment developed in the springings resulting in a slight transverse displacement of the pressure line.[2]

Thus, the deck structure was chosen as the principal member to resist wind loads, requiring the exclusion of all joints in the deck from abutment to abutment. The condition of deck continuity led to the attachment of the deck to the arch on both sides of the arch crown. This was accomplished by prestressing the continuous cables provided over the top flange of the girders and anchoring them into the arch. Six girders were connected to the arch in this manner; the two intermediate girders that do not rest directly on the arch were lengthened to the crown, Figure 8.21.[2]

During construction, an open joint was provided at the crown. In this joint Freyssinet flat jacks staggered with concrete wedges were inserted, acting as a hinge for the arches to adjust the pressure line during different phases of construction.

Expansion and contraction of the deck due to temperature, creep, and shrinkage take place over

an approximate length of 1000 ft (305 m), developing approximately symmetrically on both sides of the arch crown. Free movement of the deck structure over the pilasters was accommodated by providing two concrete rockers over each transverse wall of a pilaster. The rockers consisted of a 3 ft 6 in. (1.07 m) high continuous wall throughout the width of the bridge with a continuous Freyssinet-type concrete hinge at both the top and bottom. Approach piers were fixed in the deck at the top and hinged at their footings. Because of their height, these piers have sufficient flexibility to allow movement of the deck without developing appreciable bending moments, the exception being the short stiff piers next to the abutment, which were hinged both top and bottom.[2]

We shall describe the construction procedure for the superstructure of Bridge 1, which was also used for the other two bridges. Because the cableway did not have the capacity to transport the deck girders across the canyon, precasting operations were established at both ends of the bridge. During construction of the foundations, precasting operations were started at both sites at either end of the bridge.

When the foundations for the approach piers were completed, the cableway transported and positioned the precast Freyssinet pier hinges to their respective locations, where they were grouted to their respective foundations. Pouring of the piers then commenced, using special steel forms attached to the hinge blocks. Two sets of forms were used in leap-frog fashion to maintain a pouring rate of 5 ft (1.52 m) per day. Because of the hinge at the base of each pier column, the piers required temporary support until the deck girders could be placed. The first 25 ft (7.62 m) lift of each column in each pier was supported by a light steel scaffolding that surrounded each column; the scaffoldings, in turn, were braced together. Succeeding 25 ft (7.62 m) lifts were braced to the previous lift by light timber trusses. As the columns in the piers rose, steel reinforcement was placed; at the same time, holes for vertical prestressing tendons were cast in the concrete by the insertion of $1\frac{1}{2}$ in. (38 mm) steel tubes, which were withdrawn $1\frac{1}{2}$ hours after concrete placement.[3]

Upon completion of the three columns of an approach pier, precast segments of the cap beam were placed atop the columns and prestressed vertically to them as indicated in Figure 8.22. The two intermediate cap beam segments were placed by the cableway and temporarily held in position by steel brackets. Four prestressing tendons were then placed through the cap beam segments and the four vertical $1\frac{1}{2}$ in. (38 mm) joints between the segments were packed with a rich mortar. After eight to ten hours the longitudinal tendons in the cap beam were stressed and anchored to complete a pier bent, which was then ready to receive the deck girders and slabs. The 137 ft (41.75 m) high pilasters at each end of the arch are four-celled hollow boxes 20 by 80 ft (6.1 x 24.4 m) in plan with all walls $4\frac{3}{4}$ in. (120.65 mm) thick. They were constructed in lifts with special steel forms that were leap-frogged. Ten vertical prestressing tendons anchored into the foundation provided stability against wind forces.[3]

Upon completion of the abutments and the first approach piers, erection of the bridge deck girders and slabs commenced. It was accomplished with a 126 ft (38.4 m) long structural steel lattice girder gantry, 60 ft (18.3 m) of which extended as a cantilever. One 48 ft (14.6 m) span, consisting of eight precast beams and 112 precast slabs, required nine working days and a crew of 16 men. When the approach viaduct decks were in place, they were prestressed longitudinally by prestressing tendons placed in the grooves of the top flange of the deck girders, which were anchored at one end into the abutment and at the other end over the arch pilasters.

The three arch ribs of the main span were cast in place on a light wooden falsework, which was reused almost in its entirety for the two other bridges. Basically, the system adopted was to erect the timber formwork for casting the arch ribs by the cantilever method, this formwork being placed by the overhead cableway and held in place by a system of cable stays. Thus, the arch rib was essentially constructed to the quarter-points. The center half-span formwork was constructed as a light wooden trussed arch assembled at the bottom of the canyon and winched into position from the ends of the quarter-span cantilevers. The timber falsework truss was wedged against the concrete arch ribs already erected. It acted as an arch under the weight of the bottom flange concrete, transmitting its thrust to the cantilevered arch sections previously erected. Later the timber falsework acted composite with the hardened bottom flange concrete to support the webs and top flange of the hollowbox arch ribs when they were placed.[1]

The following discussion describes the erection sequence of the center-span arch ribs.[3] The first falsework unit in the quarter-span for each arch rib consisted of a timber platform 31 ft (9.45 m) in length with a width of 27 ft 8 in. (8.43 m) at the spring line and a width of 17 ft 2 in. (5.23 m) at the opposite end, Figure 8.23 (Phase 1). This platform was constructed of 3 x 10 in. (76.2 x 254 mm) timbers on edge at $10\frac{1}{2}$ in. (267 mm) centers covered on the upper face with $\frac{1}{2}$ in. (12.7 mm) thick plywood. It provided the form for the bottom of the arch rib. For the first section of the quarter-span, three of these units (one for each rib) were placed by the cableway, supported by cable stays A and B, and their position adjusted by hydraulic jacks at the ends of the anchor cable stays. Next four precast Freyssinet hinge blocks were positioned at the spring line and assembled into one hinge block by prestressing them together. Forms were then erected on the falsework for the webs of the arch rib, and placement of concrete commenced, Figure 8.23 (Phase 2). As the weight of each increment of concrete came onto the forms, the cable stays elongated and the geometry of the arch-rib soffit had to be carefully adjusted by the hydraulic jacks.

Upon completion of the concreting for the first section of the quarter-span, falsework section 2 was attached to it and supported by two more cable stays, C and D. After geometry adjustment, concreting continued, Figures 8.23 (Phase 3) and 8.24. As a result of the position of the cable stays and the concreting sequence, angular deformations were possible between falsework sections 1 and 2. Therefore, a temporary concrete hinge was placed in the lower flange of the arch rib, which would allow angular deformation but transmit the thrust to maintain equilibrium. When the concreting of

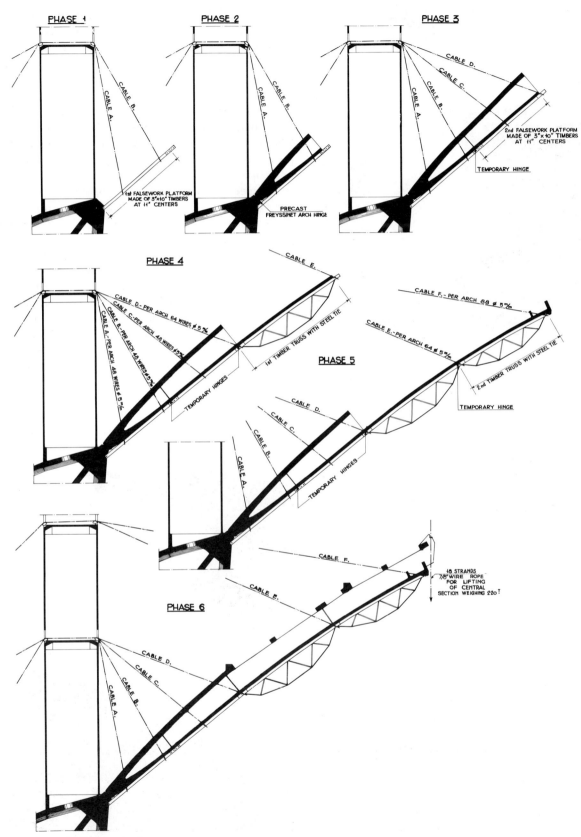

FIGURE 8.23. Caracas Viaducts, erection and construction sequence, from reference 3 (courtesy of Civil Engineering-ASCE).

FIGURE 8.24. Caracas Viaducts, construction of arch springings on suspended scaffolding.

the second portion of arch rib was completed and geometry adjustment made, the temporary hinge was blocked and the two sections were prestressed together. In the same manner, temporary hinges were used for the remaining sections of the quarter-span arch rib and at each end of the central half-span arch section.

The first two sections of arch rib thus became a continuous member supported at the outer end by cable stays, and during construction of the rest of the arch its geometric position was adjusted by cable stay D.

The next operation was the erection of the third falsework unit consisting of a trusswork. Its weight was such that it could not be accommodated by the cableway. Therefore, it was assembled at the bottom of the canyon below its position in the arch. The outer end was lifted by the cableway and the inner end by a winch located at the end of the previously concreted section of the arch. Stay cables E passing over the pilaster were attached, and the bottom flange of the new arch rib section was cast, Figures 8.23 (Phase 4) and 8.25.

In like manner the next section of trussed falsework was positioned and supported by cable stay F. Next, concrete for the bottom flange of the rib was placed, including small concrete brackets

which protruded below the bottom flange to take the thrust of the 267 ft (81.4 m) central falsework after its positioning, Figure 8.23 (Phase 5).

In the last phase of the quarter-span concreting, the vertical webs were formed and concreted, as well as a few narrow strips across the top to provide stiffness to the arch-rib members, which at this stage had a U-shaped cross section, Figure 8.23 (Phase 6). The anchor stay cables were again adjusted to bring the 125 ft (38 m) quarter-span into its proper position.

The central 267 ft (81.4 m) falsework span had been assembled at the bottom of the canyon below its final position in the arch, Figure 8.26. The ends of the timber falsework arches were tied together by steel cables acting as ties to keep the arch falsework rigid. The whole central falsework was hoisted into position by winches located at the ends of the cantilevered quarter-span units, Figure 8.27.

Once the central falsework was in place and the location of the crown exactly positioned, cement mortar was packed in the gap between the ends of the central falsework and the quarter-span falsework, and extra-flat sand boxes were embedded in the joint for subsequent stripping of the central falsework.

After two days, the steel tie cables on the central falsework were released and the winches support-

FIGURE 8.25. Caracas Viaducts, lifting one wooden truss.

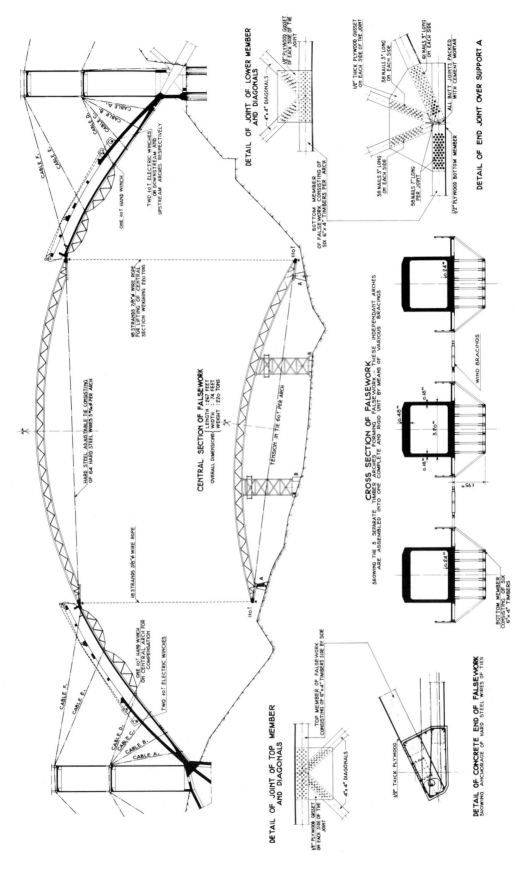

FIGURE 8.26. Caracas Viaducts, erection of center portion of arch falsework.

369

FIGURE 8.27. Caracas Viaducts, lifting center falsework.

ing the section were loosened. At this point the combination of the central trussed falsework and the concreted quarter-span units acted as a complete arch from abutment to abutment.

Next, the bottom flanges of the arch ribs were concreted, in a previously arranged sequence, up to the crown on each side, and temporary crown hinge blocks were placed. The other temporary hinges between elements of the quarter span were blocked and the cable stays up to stay D removed. The combination of timber falsework and partly built concrete arch ribs continued to be held in position by stays D, E, and F, with a temporary hinge at F only.

The vertical webs of the arch ribs over the central section were then concreted up to the crown hinge; cable stay D was released; crown concrete was completed; the remaining construction joints were tied with prestressing tendons; and the last cable stays E and F were released. At this point the

concrete arch ribs, less the top flange over the center 260 ft (79.25 m) section, carried themselves as well as the dead load of the entire falsework.

Next, the cement joints at the ends of the falsework were destroyed, sand boxes emptied, and, after the steel cable ties had been retightened, the central section of falsework was lowered, Figure 8.28. Falsework elements in the quarter-spans were lowered by hand winches.

Spandrel columns were constructed next. Then, following a carefully worked out sequence, the top flanges of arch ribs over the central section were concreted. Upon completion of the arch ribs the deck beams and slabs were placed, in the manner previously described for the approach viaducts, in a symmetrical and simultaneous manner on both sides of the crown. After the deck had been prestressed transversely, it was prestressed longitudinally in the same manner as the approach viaducts. Finished Viaduct 1 is shown in Figure 8.29.

In 1973, twenty-one years after the construction of these arches, they were reevaluated to see how they would now be designed and constructed. Figures 8.30 and 8.31 compare the actual project constructed in 1952 with the structure as it would have been designed in 1970 (two boxes) and in 1973 (single box). The three-arch-rib and eight-beam superstructure would be replaced by a variable-depth box section (cantilever construction using precast segments) supported on slip-formed piers.

The arch remains an appealing and aesthetic structure and might still prove to be competitive; but perhaps the construction technique suggested in the Neckarburg Bridge (Section 8.5.2) might be more appropriate today, either cast in place or precast.

FIGURE 8.28. Caracas Viaducts, lowering center falsework.

FIGURE 8.29. Caracas Viaducts, finished Viaduct 1.

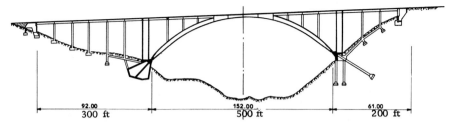

As constructed in 1952

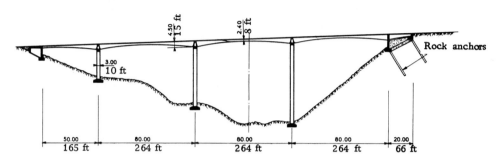

Rock anchors

Possible alternative in 1973

FIGURE 8.30. Caracas Viaducts, comparison of longitudinal sections.

8.4 Gladesville Bridge, Australia

This precast segmental arch bridge, completed in 1964, spans the Parramatta River between Gladesville and Drummoyne and serves a large section of the northern area of the Sydney Metropolis, Figure 8.32.

After award of contract the contractors submitted an alternative design. They proposed that the arch be built on fixed falsework, whereas in the original design part of the arch was to be built on floating falsework and towed into position. The original design called for an arch span of 910 ft (277.4 m). The alternate design increased the clear span of the arch to 1000 ft (305 m) and eliminated the necessity for deep-water excavation for the arch foundations on the Gladesville, or northern, side of the river.[4]

Total bridge length between abutments is 1901 ft 6 in. (579.6 m). The 1000 ft (305 m) clear span arch consists of four arch ribs, Figure 8.33, supported on massive concrete blocks, known as "thrust blocks," founded on sandstone on each side of the river. Roadway width is 72 ft (22 m) with 6 ft (1.8 m) wide sidewalks on each side. The roadway has a grade of 6% at each end, and the grades are connected by a vertical curve 300 ft (91.4 m) in length over the center portion of the structure. The arch has a maximum clearance, at the crown,

of 134 ft (40.8 m) above the water and not less than 120 ft (36.6 m) above water level for a width of 200 ft (61 m) in the center of the river.

Construction of the bridge involved the following main operations[4]:

1. Excavation for foundation of:
    a. Arch thrust blocks on each side of the river at the shoreline and partly below water.
    b. Abutments at the ends of the bridge.
    c. Shore pier columns of the approach spans on each side of the river.
2. Concreting of the arch thrust blocks, the abutments and columns.
3. Driving of falsework piles in the river and erection of steel falsework to support the hollow concrete blocks and diaphragms forming each of the four arch ribs.
4. Casting of the box-section segments of the arch and diaphragms and the erection of the four arch ribs one at a time.
5. Jacking each rib to raise and lift it off the falsework.
6. Casting of concrete deck beams on each side of the river.
7. Erection of the deck beams to form the roadway over the arch.
8. Paving of the concrete roadway and final completion of the structure.

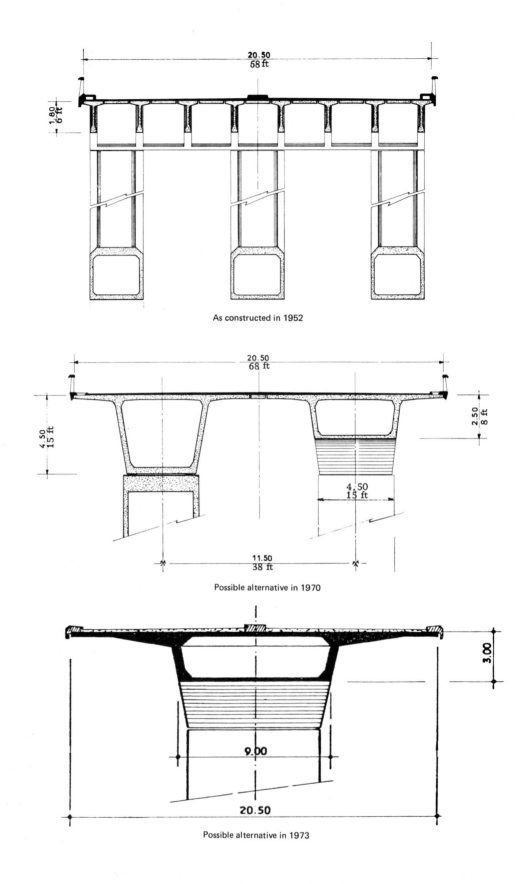

FIGURE 8.31. Caracas Viaducts, comparison of cross sections.

FIGURE 8.32. Gladesville Bridge, aerial view, from reference 4.

FIGURE 8.34. Gladesville Bridge, arch rib falsework and positioning of arch rib segment, from reference 4.

The roadway deck is supported on pairs of pre-stressed concrete columns, Figure 8.33. The wall thickness is 2 ft (0.6 m), except in the tall columns above the arch foundation where the wall thickness is increased by 6 in. (152 mm). At the top of each pair of columns there is a reinforced concrete cap beam to support the deck girders.

During construction it was necessary to provide falsework to support the box segments and diaphragms that make up each of the four arch ribs in the arch. The falsework was made up of steel tubular columns on steel tubular pile trestles carrying spans of steel beams 60 ft (18.3 m) long and a steel truss span of 220 ft (67 m) over a navigation opening in the Gladesville (northern) half of the falsework. These falsework units were tied together and anchored at each end to the thrust blocks, Figure 8.34. Piling was taken down to rock in the river bed.

Steel columns, braced together, formed a tower extending transversely the full width of the bridge at the center of the falsework. Transverse mem-

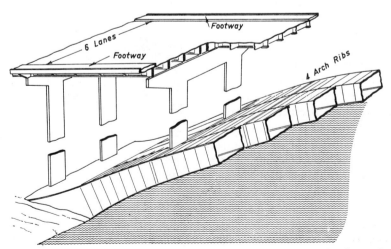

FIGURE 8.33. Gladesville Bridge, schematic of four arch ribs, columns, and deck, from reference 4.

bers, extending the full width of the bridge, above the waterline connected the pile trestles, Figure 8.34. The balance of the falsework was of sufficient width to support one arch rib. Upon completion of erection of an arch rib, the falsework was moved transversely on rails on the transverse members of the pile trestle to a position to enable erection of the adjacent arch rib, until all arch ribs were erected.

Equipment installed on the central tower lifted the arch box segments and diaphragms from water level and positioned them. The tower also served as a lateral bent to stabilize the individual arch ribs after they were self-supporting and until they were tied together.[4]

The hollow-box segments and diaphragms were cast 3 miles (4.8 km) downstream from the bridge site. The casting yard was laid out to accommodate the manufacture of one arch rib at a time. Each arch rib consists of 108 box segments and 19 diaphragms. Each arch-rib box segment is 20 ft (6 m) wide, with depths decreasing from 23 ft (7 m) at the thrust block to 14 ft (4.3 m) at the crown of the arch, measured at right angles to the axis of the arch. The length of the box segments along the arch varies from 7 ft 9 in. (2.36 m) to 9 ft 3 in. (2.82 m). After the box units were manufactured, they were loaded on barges and transported to the bridge site. The box segments and diaphragms were lifted from the barges to the crown of the arch falsework and winched down to their proper position, Figure 8.34. Diaphragms are spaced at intervals of 50 ft (15.24 m), serving not only to support the slender columns that support the roadway above but also to tie the four arch ribs together.

When the units were located in position on the falsework, a 3 in. (76 mm) joint between the precast segments was cast in place. At two points in each rib, four layers of Freyssinet flat-jacks were inserted, with 56 jacks in each layer. The rib was then jacked longitudinally by inflating the jacks with oil one layer at a time, the oil being replaced by grout and allowed to set before the next layer was inflated. Inflation of the jacks increased the distance between the edges of the segments adjacent to the jacks and thus the overall length of the arch along its centerline. In this manner a camber was induced into the arch rib, causing it to lift off the supporting falsework. The falsework was then shifted laterally into position to support the adjacent arch rib and repeat the cycle. Figure 8.35 is a view of the completed four arch ribs, and Figure 8.36 shows the completed bridge.

FIGURE 8.35. Gladesville Bridge, completed four arch ribs, from reference 4.

8.5   Arches Built in Cantilever

Until the appearance of the concrete cable-stay bridge starting in 1962 (see Chapter 9), long-span concrete bridges were the domain of the arch type of structure. Until 1977, with the completion of the Brotonne Cable-Stay Bridge in France with a span of 1050 ft (320 m), the record length for a concrete bridge had always been held by an arch-type bridge. When the Kirk Bridges in Yugoslavia were completed in 1980, the larger arch with a span of 1280 ft (390 m) once again regained for the arch the record of longest concrete span.

FIGURE 8.36. Gladesville Bridge, view of completed bridge.

Here is a brief chronology of record concrete arch spans up to 1964:

1930, Plougastel Bridge, France: three spans of 611.5 ft (186.40 m)

1939, Rio Esla, Spain: 631 ft (192.4 m) span

1943, Sandö, Sweden: 866 ft (264 m) span

1963, Arrabida, Portugal: 886 ft (270 m) span

1964, Iguacu, River Parana, Brazil: 951 ft (290 m) span

1964, Gladesville, Sydney, Australia: 1000 ft (305 m) span

The concrete arch bridge does not enjoy the favor it once did. Modern methods of bridge construction utilizing prestressing, cable stays, and segmental construction have all but eliminated it from contention as a economical bridge type. However, with the application of these modern methods to the older form, and given the proper site conditions, concrete arches may regain some of their lost popularity.

8.5.1 REVIEW OF CONCEPT; SUMMARY OF STRUCTURES WITH TEMPORARY STAYS

The use of temporary stays to facilitate the construction of arch bridges began, perhaps, with the Plougastel Bridge. Temporary prestress tendons were used to provide stability to the short arch cantilever sections emanating from the arch foundations (see Figure 8.5). Prestressing tendons were used to support the falsework of the Rio Esla Bridge and were incorporated into the structure. However, the more novel method, which is the birth of today's technology, was employed in the construction of the Saint Clair Viaduct at Lyon, France, by M. Esquillan. The stability of precast segments was obtained by the use of temporary stays.

In the construction of the Caracas Viaduct, Freyssinet extended this concept by using temporary stays to support the falsework and construct a much longer cantilever section of the arch. This same stay system was then used to accommodate the forces produced by lifting the center arch section falsework (see Section 8.3). This concept was partially recaptured for the construction of the Iguacu Bridge in Brazil, where the falsework of the central portion of the arch was supported by temporary stays.

The first arch bridge to be constructed using the concept of supporting segmental sections of the

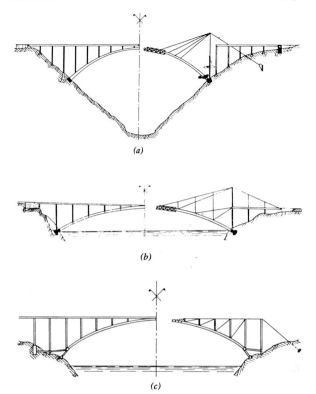

FIGURE 8.37. Concrete arches built in cantilever with temporary stays. (*a*) With stays and pylons. (*b*) With stays, spandrel columns, and pylons. (*c*) With spandrel columns, tie diagonals and stays.

arch by temporary stays is the Sibenik Bridge in Yugoslavia. Falsework for an approximate length of 88.6 ft (27 m) was supported on Bailey trusses, which were in turn supported by temporary stays, Figure 8.37*b*, consisting of a combination of cables and structural steel rolled shapes. This arch was constructed in nine sections, four on each side and the central closure section. A modification of this concept was used for a second Yugoslav bridge at Pag with a 634 ft (193.2 m) span constructed in seven sections. A further modification was used for the Van Staden Bridge in South Africa, Figure 8.37*a*, with a span of 656 ft (200 m).

A somewhat different concept is where, with the assistance of spandrel columns, the stays act as temporary diagonals during construction, Figure 8.37*c*. In this manner, the structure is built as a variable-depth Pratt truss. This concept was used for the Kirk Bridges in Yugoslavia. In some instances these temporary diagonal stays may be incorporated into permanent diagonals such that in the final configuration the structure is a truss and not an arch (see Section 8.7.3).

In summarizing the construction methods using temporary cable stays, we find two basic categories:

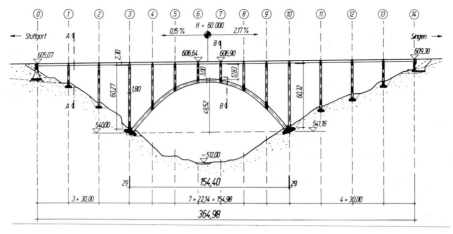

Longitudinal section

(a)

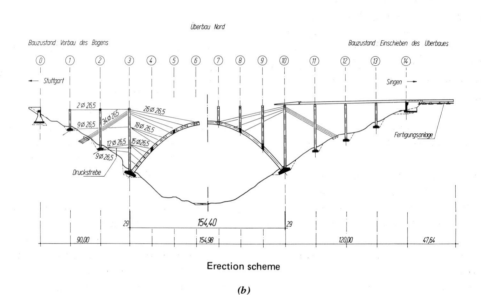

Erection scheme

(b)

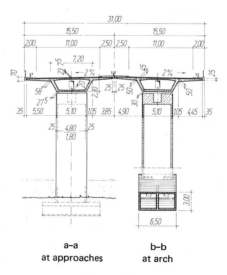

a–a
at approaches

b–b
at arch

Cross–sections

(c)

Where the arch is supported directly by the temporary stays

Where the temporary stays act as diagonals of a Pratt truss during construction

Characteristics of the arch bridges using this concept of temporary stays during construction are presented in Table 8.2.

8.5.2   NECKARBURG BRIDGE, GERMANY

This unique and contemporary arch-supported structure, some 50 miles (80 km) southwest of Stuttgart, crosses the Neckar River near Rottweil, Germany. It is a part of the federal expressway A-81 from Stuttgart to the west of Bodensee with a connection to Zurich, Switzerland.

The original scheme proposed by German authorities consisted of a steel girder structure supported on tall piers. Designer-contractor Ed. Zublin, Stuttgart, developed an alternative design consisting of twin concrete arches to support the roadway. The proposal was to construct the arches segmentally by the cantilever method and construct the twin single-cell trapezoidal box girders for the roadway by the incremental launching technique (see Chapter 7). The Austrian method called the Mayreder system was used to construct the arches without scaffolding.[5,6]

The roadway of this 1197 ft (364.98 m) long structure is approximately 310 ft (94.7 m) above the Neckar River, Figure 8.38. The 507 ft (154.4 m) arch span, Figure 8.39, has a rise of 164 ft (49.85 m). Total roadway width is 102 ft (31.0 m). The

FIGURE 8.40. Neckarburg Bridge, arch just before closure (courtesy of Willhelm Zellner).

structure is constructed as two independent parallel structures with a 1.8 ft (0.54 m) gap in the median. Roadway spans are 98 ft (30 m) in the approach sections and 72.6 ft (22.14 m) over the arch.

Each independent arch rib is a two-cell box. The arch ribs were constructed in symmetrical halves, Figure 8.40. The curved formwork was 43 ft (13.1 m) long, the first 23.3 ft (7.1 m) of the form clamped to the previously constructed arch segment and the remaining 19.7 ft (6 m) remained to cast the next segment increment. The first 23.3 ft (7.1 m) of arch segment at the arch foundation was constructed by conventional forming methods. There are 14 segments on each side of an arch rib and a closure segment at the crown of each arch. The exterior dimensions of each two-cell arch rib are 21.3 ft (6.5 m) wide by 9.8 ft (3.0 m) deep. Exterior webs vary in thickness from 10 to 11 in. (260 to 280 mm), and the interior web is 6.3 in. (160 mm) thick. The arch rib was cast in two operations —first the bottom flange and second the webs and top flanges.[5]

Piers supported by the arch or independent foundations are of a constant section and slip-formed by conventional methods. Sliding bearings are used at the abutments and the short stiff piers 1 and 13. The remaining piers are hinged to the superstructure deck such that the elastic piers can follow the superstructure movement.[5,6]

During construction, as each half-rib was cantilevered out from its foundation, it was supported by a temporary system of Dywidag bar stays, Figures 8.38, 8.41, and 8.42. After completion of the arch, the temporary stays were removed, except those required to stabilize the arch during the incremental launching of the superstructure deck. Dywidag bar stays were anchored either to a pier foundation or to Dywidag rock anchors in the side of the valley.[5]

FIGURE 8.39. Neckarburg Bridge, completed arch (courtesy of Willhelm Zellner).

TABLE 8.2 Characteristics of Arch Bridges Constructed with Cable Stays

Name	Country	Year of Construction	Span, ft. (m)	Stay Method	Arch Construction	Arch Type	Deck Type	Static Arch Scheme	Remarks
Sibenik	Yugoslavia	1964–66	807 (246)	Four stays formed from rolled steel shapes and cables, supporting directly the arch with an auxilliary pylon	Nine sections on falsework of 88.6 and 95 ft (27 and 29 m)	Three-cell rectangular box	Simple precast girders of 76.4 ft (23.30 m) span made continuous	Possibility of correcting the thrust at the crown by a battery of hydraulic jacks	
Pag	Yugoslavia	1966–67	634 (193.2)	Three stays formed from rolled steel shapes and cables, auxiliary pylon, the longer stay being additionally supported on columns	Seven sections on falsework	Three-cell rectangular box	Simple precast girders of 76.4 ft (23.30 m) span made continuous	Possibility of correcting the thrust at the crown by a battery of hydraulic jacks	
Van Staden	South Africa	About 1970	656 (200)	Four stays, relocated gradually as construction proceeds, supported from a temporary pylon	Segments 19.6 ft (20 m) long	Three-cell rectangular box	Simple precast girders of 55 ft (16.8 m) span made continuous	Fixed	
Niesenbachbrücke	Austria	1973	394 (120)	Multiple stays supporting the arch directly with the aid of an auxiliary pylon	Mobile forms permitting the successive construction of 21 ft (6.5 m) long segments	Two parallel two-cell boxes	Continuous double-T span of 65.6 ft (20 m)	Fixed	Horizontal curvature of deck is R = 1092 ft (332.8 m)
Hokawazu	Japan	1973–74	558 (170)	Five stays used as temporary diagonals	Formwork partially supported by a stay for the first section between the abutment and the first spandrel column. Afterward, construction by successive cantilevers by segments of 11 ft (3.4 m) length.	Rectangular two-cell box. Near the springings, the width increases linearly from 26 to 52 ft (8 to 16 m) to improve the lateral stability	Hollow slab of 2 ft (0.60 m) thickness; 50 ft (15 m) continuous spans constructed in a span-by-span movable falsework	Hinged at the two springings of the arch	

Krummbachbrücke	Switzerland	1976–77	407 (124)	Multiple stays supporting the arch directly from an auxiliary pylon	Constructed in segments of 20.5 ft (6.25 m) length	Two parallel arches, diaphragm at the columns. Each arch is a solid rectangular rib 3.6 × 6.6 ft (1.1 × 2.0 m)	Double T with continuous spans varying between 32.8 and 65.6 ft (10 to 20 m)	Fixed	The deck is situated clearly above the arch, permitting the stays to support the arch directly without an auxiliary pylon
Neckarburg	Germany	1977	507 (154.4)	Multiple stays supporting the arch directly	Constructed of successive segments 19.7 ft (6.0 m) in length	Two parallel arches, each consisting of a rectangular two-cell box	Two single-cell boxes with spans of 72.6 ft (22.4 m) constructed by incremental launching	Fixed	Railroad bridge
Schwarzwasserbrücke	Switzerland	1977–79	374 (114)	Multiple stays directly supporting the arch with the assistance of auxiliary pylons	Successive cantilever segments 16.4 to 17.7 ft (5 to 5.4 m) in length	Rectangular slab	Continuous double T	Fixed	
Akayagawa	Japan	1978	413 (126)	Temporary stays used as diagonals of a Pratt truss	Constructed with mobile forms such that a complete panel was cast, including the arch, the column, and the deck	Arch consists of a rectangular thin slab between two columns	Two-cell box	Fixed	Railroad bridge
Kirk Bridge (smaller arch)	Yugoslavia	1978	800 (244)	Stays used as diagonals of a Pratt truss	Precast cantilever segments, assembled with cast-in-place joints, segments 16.4 ft (5 m) long	Rectangular three-cell box	Precast girders of 93.5 ft (28.5 m) span made continuous	Fixed; possibility of correcting the thrust at the crown by a battery of hydraulic jacks	
Kirk Bridge (larger arch)	Yugoslavia	1979	1280 (390)	(Same technique as smaller arch above)	(Same technique as smaller arch above)	Rectangular three-cell box	Precast girders of 110 ft (33.5 m) span made continuous	(Same as above, for smaller arch)	

FIGURE 8.41. Neckarburg Bridge, temporary Dywidag bar stays supporting cantilevered arch rib (courtesy of Willhelm Zellner).

FIGURE 8.42. Neckarburg Bridge, temporary Dywidag bar stays supporting cantilevered arch rib (courtesy of Willhelm Zellner).

The trapezoidal box girders of the superstructure deck were constructed behind the Singen abutment and incrementally launched "downhill" toward the Stuttgart abutment, Figure 8.43. A close-up of the launching nose is shown in Figure 8.44. Overall girder width is 48.8 ft (14.9 m) with a constant depth of 7.5 ft (2.3 m). Girder segments were cast in lengths of 65.6 ft (20 m). The lift and push combination of hydraulic jacks (see Chapter 7) launched the girder in 10 in. (0.25 m) increments. To maintain deformations of the arch and

FIGURE 8.43. Neckarburg Bridge, launching of deck girder.

FIGURE 8.44. Neckarburg Bridge, close-up of launching nose.

piers, resulting from the horizontal forces of the incremental launching operations, within allowable limits, the tops of the piers were tied back to the abutments and the arch was tied back by the temporary stays used during the arch construction. An innovation introduced by Zublin on this project was the use of bearings for the incremental launching that remained as permanent bearings. Prior procedure had employed a system of temporary bearings for the incremental launching and then a transfer to permanent bearings.[5]

8.5.3 NIESENBACK BRIDGE, AUSTRIA

This is a two-rib arch structure utilizing the free cantilever construction method for each half-arch, Figure 8.45. The arch has a span of 394 ft (120 m) with a rise of 123 ft (37.5 m). Each arch rib is a two-cell box with exterior dimensions of 16.4 ft (5 m) wide by 8.2 ft (2.5 m) deep. The roadway consists of a concrete slab and girder system with an overall width of 57.7 ft (17.6 m). Although the longitudinal axis of the arch is in a straight line, the

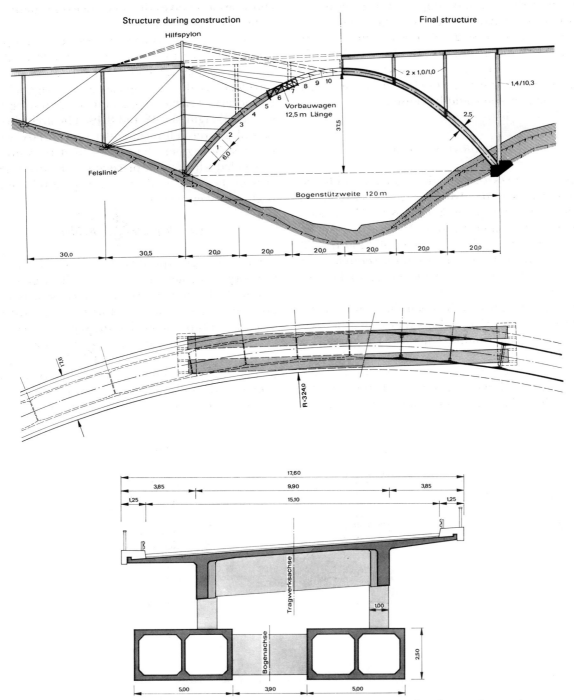

FIGURE 8.45. Niesenback Bridge, elevation, plan, and cross section, from reference 7.

roadway it supports has a centerline radius, in plan, of 1092 ft (332.8 m).

The curved roadway structure has spans of 65.6 ft (20 m) over the arch and is supported by two 3.3 ft (1.0 m) square piers, one on each arch rib. At the arch foundations, roadway support is by a wall pier with dimensions of 4.6 ft (1.4 m) by 33.8 ft (10.3 m).

Each two-cell box arch rib is constructed by the cantilever method, using a 41 ft (12.5 m) long traveling form. The form clamps to the preceding construction such that a 19.7 ft (6.0 m) segment can be cast. A crew of seven men was able to cast a segment on a weekly cycle.

To keep moments in the cantilevering arch to a minimum during construction, the cantilevered portion of the arch was supported by a system of Dywidag bar stays, Figure 8.45. Stay stresses are monitored at each stage of construction to maintain a nearly moment-free condition in the arch. Dywidag bars used in the stays were 1 in. (26.5 mm) diameter and were used because they were easily coupled and could be reused.[7]

8.5.4   KIRK BRIDGES, YUGOSLAVIA

These structures connect the mainland with the Island of Kirk in the Adriatic Sea. In between is a small rocky outcropping known as St. Mark, such that from the mainland to St. Mark is the world's longest concrete arch with a span of 1280 ft (390 m) and from St. Mark to Kirk is the seventh longest concrete arch with a span of 800 ft (244 m), Figures 1.40 and 8.46.

Because the distance between the shores of the mainland and St. Mark is 1509 ft (460 m), the arch support is partially founded in the sea, Figure 8.47. The arch reaction of approximately 15,400 tons (14,000 mt) is accommodated by the inclined pier in the sea, which takes 9900 tons (9000 mt) to the rock, while the nearly horizontal box structure

above sea level takes the other reaction component of 6600 tons (6000 mt).

A system of temporary stays was used to support the arch as it was progressively cantilevered out from the springings, Figure 8.48. These temporary stays were used as the top chord and diagonals of a temporary variable-depth Pratt truss during construction, Figures 8.48 and 8.49. The arch rib consists of a three-cell rectangular precast box, which was cast in segment lengths of 16.4 ft (5 m) and assembled with cast-in-place joints, Figure 8.48. A view of the completed arch with spandrel columns is given in Figure 8.50.

8.6   Rigid-Frame Bridges

Another bridge type that lends itself to the contemporary segmental concept is the rigid-frame bridge. Unfortunately, segmental construction has not often been applied to this type of structure. The reason is probably that the segmental concept is associated with the conventional girder type bridge, and designers have given little consideration to applying this method to the rigid-frame bridge. Hopefully, the few examples that follow will stimulate thinking about this type of structure.

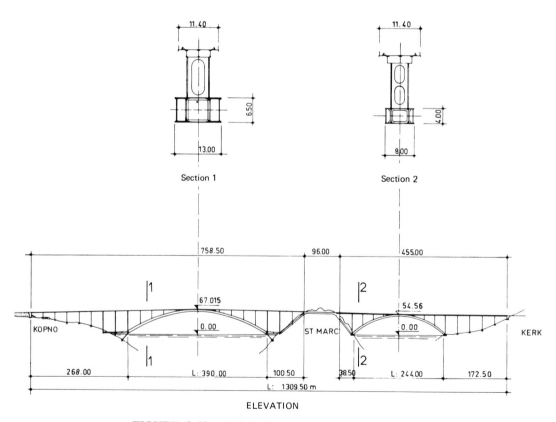

FIGURE 8.46.   Kirk Bridges, elevation and sections.

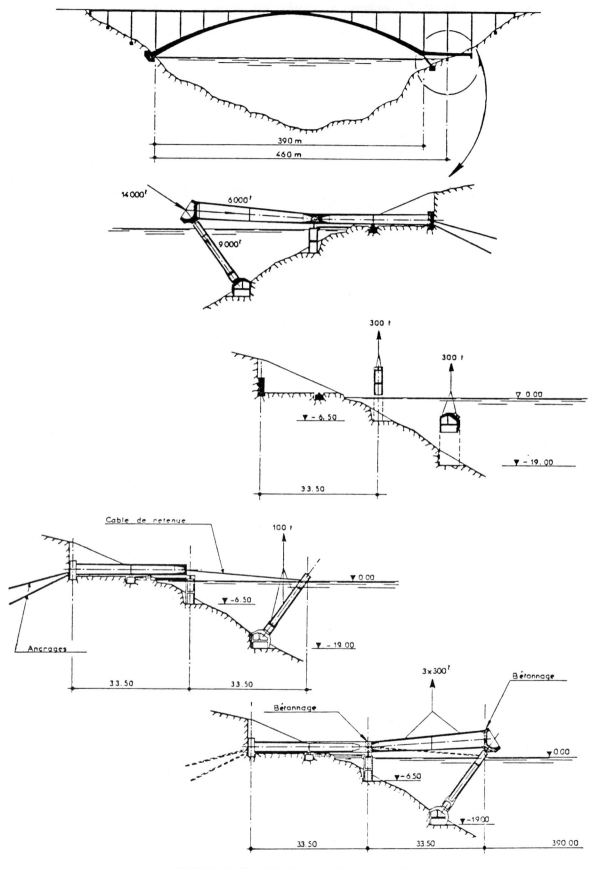

FIGURE 8.47. Kirk Bridge, foundation detail.

FIGURE 8.48. Kirk Bridge, erection of first arch section.

FIGURE 8.50. Kirk Bridge, completed arch.

FIGURE 8.49. Kirk Bridge, erection approaching crown.

FIGURE 8.51. Saint Michael Bridge, view of the completed structure.

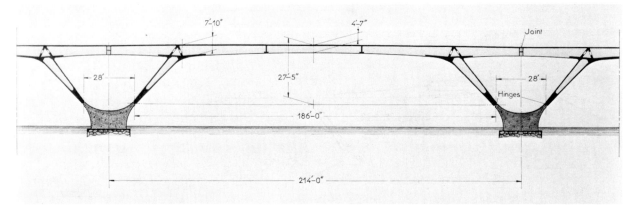

FIGURE 8.52. Saint Michael Bridge, partial longitudinal section.

8.6.1 *SAINT MICHEL BRIDGE IN TOULOUSE, FRANCE*

This beautiful structure, Figure 8.51, appears as a succession of arches with inclined legs, crossing the two branches of the Garonne River in the southern city of Toulouse, France. Typical dimensions of a rigid frame are presented in Figures 8.52 and 8.53.

Because the bridge replaced an obsolete structure resting on masonry piers, it was possible to construct the inclined legs on suspended scaffolding using temporary ties anchored to the masonry piers before they were demolished, Figure 8.54. The longitudinal girders were cast in place between the legs to complete the rigid frame. Over each pier an expansion joint with laminated bearings is provided in the roadway slab, Figure 8.54.

Another view of the finished bridge is presented in Figure 8.55.

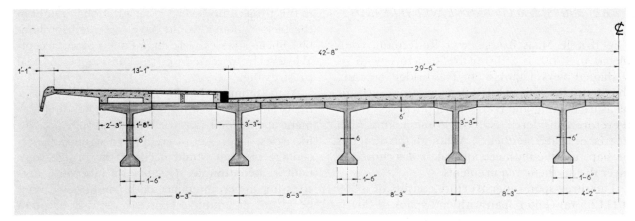

FIGURE 8.53. Saint Michael Bridge, typical section.

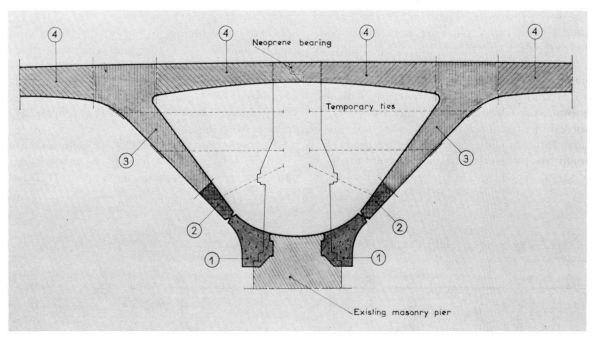

FIGURE 8.54. Saint Michael Bridge, construction sequence at typical pier.

FIGURE 8.55. Saint Michael Bridge, finished structure.

FIGURE 8.56. Briesle Maas Bridge, general view.

8.6.2 *BRIESLE MAAS BRIDGE, NETHERLANDS*

The Briesle Maas Bridge near Rotterdam, completed in 1969, is a distinctive structure with its V-shaped piers, Figure 8.56. This bridge, crossing the Meuse River, is situated in an area reserved for pleasure boating and recreational purposes. It was therefore considered essential to maintain a high degree of bridge aesthetics. Although the design is perhaps not the most economical, it was chosen to meet the aesthetic requirements.

The three-span superstructure consists of a 369 ft (112.5 m) center span with end spans of 264 ft (80.5 m). Transversely, the superstructure consists of three precast single-cell boxes, joined at their flange tips by a longitudinal closure pour and transversely prestressed, Figure 8.57. The hollow inclined legs of the V piers are structurally connected to the deck structure by post-tensioning, and the V pier is supported at its base through neoprene bearing pads on the pile cap foundation, Figures 8.58 and 8.59. The superstructure, with the exception of a few cast-in-place closure joints, is composed of precast segments.

Shear forces, mainly concentrated in the webs, normally are transferred to piers or columns by a diaphragm. Prefabrication prevented this solution

in this project, however, as the additional weight in the pier segments would have increased intolerably. Shear stresses were maintained at an acceptable level by increased web thickness and by triaxial prestressing.

At the moment that the midspan closure pour of the center span is consummated, the bending moment at this joint is zero. With time this moment increases, as a result of creep, to a significant percentage of what would occur if the bridge were built as a continuous structure on falsework. Prestressing to accommodate both conditions cannot be given maximum eccentricity, and it becomes both difficult to execute and expensive. A considerable amount of prestressing was saved by eliminating the condition of zero stress at closure and therefore preventing creep. This was accomplished by inducing an upward reaction under segments 7 and 72, Figure 8.59, after joint closure. Simultaneously with the increase of these reaction forces, prestressing tendons in the central span were stressed. Upon completion of the end spans the induced forces were released automatically by prestressing the end spans.

Segments were produced at an existing casting yard 68 miles (110 km) from the bridge site. A long-line precasting bed (see Figure 11.37) was

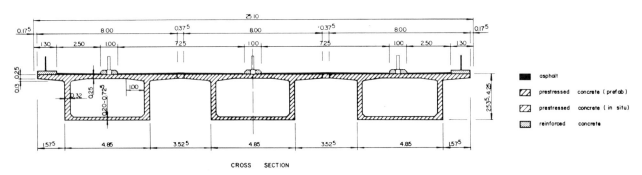

FIGURE 8.57. Briesle Maas Bridge, transverse cross section.

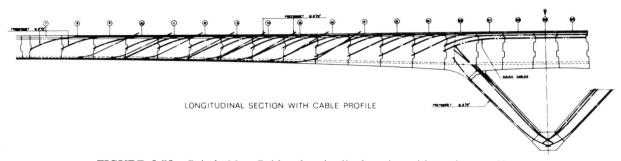

FIGURE 8.58. Briesle Maas Bridge, longitudinal section with tendon profile.

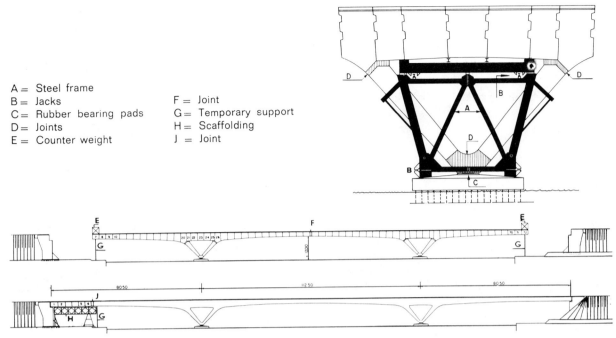

A = Steel frame
B = Jacks
C = Rubber bearing pads
D = Joints
E = Counter weight

F = Joint
G = Temporary support
H = Scaffolding
J = Joint

FIGURE 8.59. Briesle Maas Bridge, erection sequence.

used with a length equal to a half-span—that is, one cantilever. Three sets of segment forms were employed to cast a total of 234 segments, averaging 78 reuses. Segments were transported to the bridge site by barge.

The various stages of erection are indicated in Figure 8.59. A special structural steel frame was used to position the inclined precast hollow-box legs of the piers and to support the seven precast roadway girder segments before casting the joints at the corners of the delta pier portion of the structure. This frame was also utilized to balance the pier during erection of the remainder of the roadway girder segments and to adjust, by means of jacks, the loads in the inclined legs of the pier during various stages of erection.

Upon completion of the balanced cantilever erection about both piers, temporary supports were placed under segments 7 and 72 (the extreme end segments of the partially completed end spans) so that the temporary steel frames under the piers could be removed. At this point both halves of the structure were in an unstable equilibrium condition, therefore, counterweights were placed over the supported segments, Figure 8.59, to prevent the half-structures from toppling over.

Jacks atop the temporary supports were used to adjust the position of the bridge halves with respect to one another and to induce the upward vertical reaction forces previously discussed. Also, differences in elevation between the three box girders

were adjusted by these jacks. After casting the center-span closure joint and stressing in the center span, the remaining segments in the end spans were placed on falsework, Figure 8.60; closure joints were cast; and longitudinal and transverse prestressing was completed.

All segments in the balanced cantilever portion of the structure were placed by a floating crane. Because of the crane's small reach, it could not place the last five segments needed to complete the end span. Therefore, it placed them on a small dolly installed on top of the falsework, which would roll them into their final positions. To avoid dismantling the falsework after completing one girder and reinstalling it under the next, it was constructed so that it could be lowered and moved transversely into position, Figure 8.60.

A close-up of the piers of the finished structure is shown in Figure 8.61.

8.6.3 *BONHOMME BRIDGE, FRANCE*

The Bonhomme Bridge over the Blavet River in Brittany, France, was designed and built between 1972 and 1974, Figure 8.62. This three-span slant-leg portal-frame bridge has a center span of 481 ft (146.7 m) and end spans of 223 ft (67.95 m), Figure 8.63. The span between the foundations of the slant legs is 611 ft (186.25 m). A tubular steel framework was used to support the slant legs temporarily until closure at midspan, Figures 8.64 and

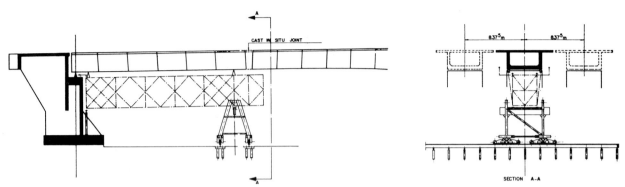

FIGURE 8.60.   Briesle Maas Bridge, erection falsework for last five segments in the end span.

FIGURE 8.61.   Briesle Maas Bridge, close-up view of V piers.

8.65. This structure was built by the cast-in-place balanced cantilever method.

For adjusting the geometry of the bridge, flat jacks were placed under the legs and at midspan. A detail of the adjusting jacks placed on top of the temporary support is shown in Figure 8.66. Flat jacks and sand boxes were used both to adjust the geometry of the bridge before closure was achieved at midspan and later to release the energy stored in the legs of the temporary supports, which were loaded with the full weight of the bridge.

FIGURE 8.62.   Bonhomme Bridge over Blavet River.

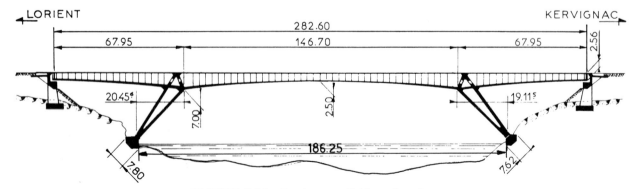

FIGURE 8.63.   Bonhomme Bridge, elevation.

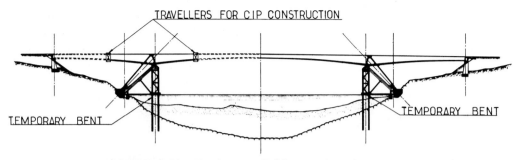

FIGURE 8.64. Bonhomme Bridge, construction stages.

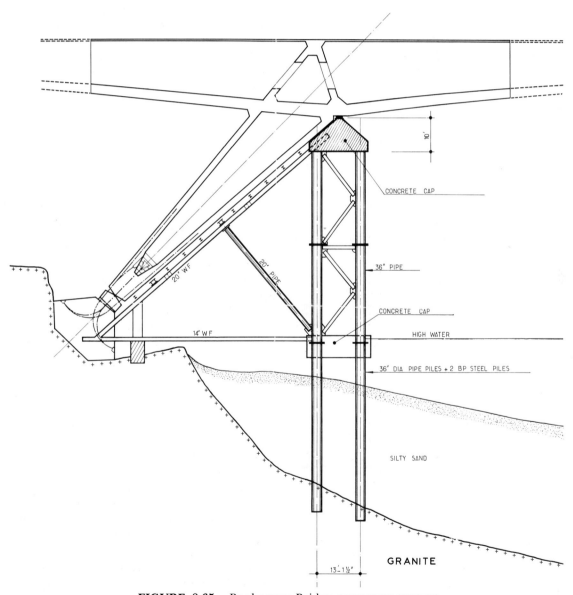

FIGURE 8.65. Bonhomme Bridge, temporary support.

389

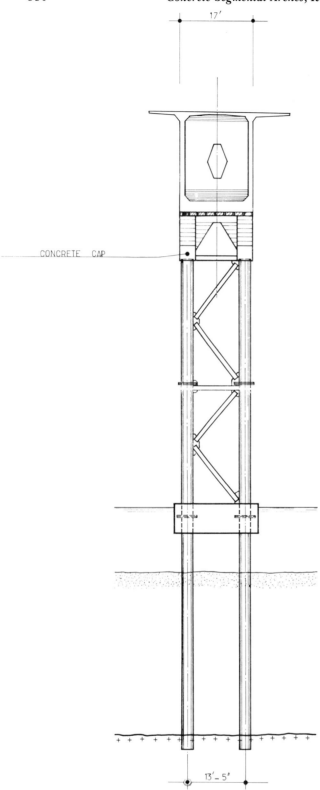

17'

CONCRETE CAP

13' – 5'

FIGURE 8.65. *(Continued)*

The scheme is a very satisfactory one in terms of both the aesthetics of the finished structure and simplicity of construction. However, it may be used only when site conditions allow the foundations of the temporary supports to be established safely at a reasonable cost. Figure 8.67 shows the temporary supports during the balanced cantilever construction of the bridge.

8.6.4 MOTORWAY OVERPASSES IN THE MIDDLE EAST

The use of precast segmental construction for the Alpine Motorways in southern France was described in Section 3.15. It was shown how mass production could be applied to the construction of a large number of similar overpasses.

This experience was repeated recently in a middle eastern country for the construction of 17 overpass structures over an existing freeway, Figure 8.68. To minimize disturbance of freeway traffic, it was felt that a three-span rigid-frame structure with inclined legs would be an attractive solution.

Dimensions are shown in Figures 8.69 and 8.70. The total deck length of 252 ft 3 in. (77 m) is divided into 32 precast segments for each of the twin box girders. Deck width of the overpasses is either 36 ft (11 m) or 46 ft (14 m). The same box section is used for all structures, and the cast-in-place longitudinal closure strip varies as required.

The slant legs are precast in the same plant where the deck segments are produced. The typical erection sequence is shown in Figure 8.71. A temporary bent founded at the edge line of the new freeway is used to place and adjust the precast legs on either side of the bridge. Segments are placed in balanced cantilever from the special segment located atop the slant legs. A light temporary bent in the short side spans is used to reduce the bending moment in the slant legs during construction.

After completion of the deck and removal of all temporary supports, the structure is in effect a two-hinged arch with vertical restraints at both ends. The bridges were analyzed for earthquake and large thermal variation loads (seasonal variation of 120°F and temperature gradient between top and bottom flange of 18°F).

Figure 8.72 shows a detailed view of the inclined legs and the temporary support during construction.

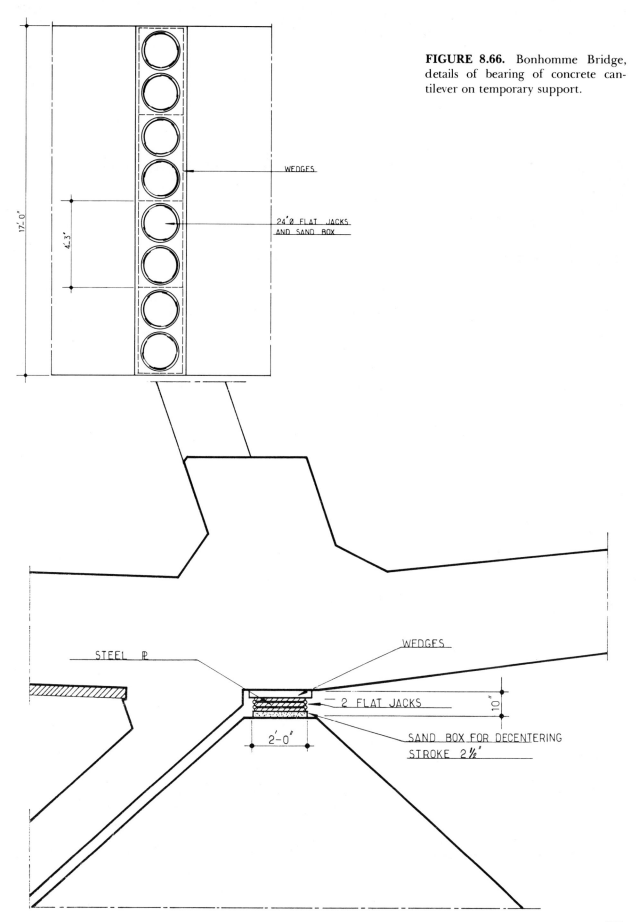

WEDGES

24'Ø FLAT JACKS AND SAND BOX

17'-0"

4'-3"

STEEL ℙ

WEDGES

2 FLAT JACKS

SAND BOX FOR DECENTERING STROKE 2½"

2'-0"

10"

FIGURE 8.66. Bonhomme Bridge, details of bearing of concrete cantilever on temporary support.

FIGURE 8.67. Bonhomme Bridge, during cantilever construction.

FIGURE 8.68. Motorway Overpass Frames, general view.

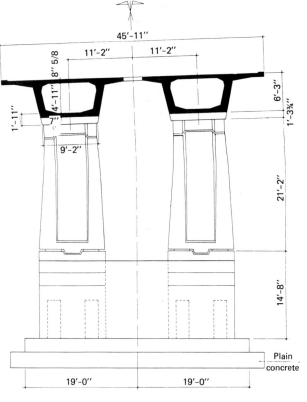

FIGURE 8.70. Motorway Overpass Frames, cross section and elevation of inclined legs.

8.7.1 *RETROSPECT ON CONCEPTS FOR CONCRETE TRUSS BRIDGES*

Trusses were used in all long-span cantilever steel bridges, and it was logical to conceive of the application of this type of structure to prestressed concrete. An interesting example of such an approach is presented in Figure 8.73, in which an original sketch made in 1948 by Eugene Freyssinet for the design of a precast prestressed concrete truss is reproduced. The studies were applied to two specific examples:

8.7   *Truss Bridges*

As with rigid frames, segmental construction has seldom been applied to truss bridges. Once again the designer must realize that the principles of segmental construction, together with imagination, can be applied to bridge structures other than the conventional girder bridge.

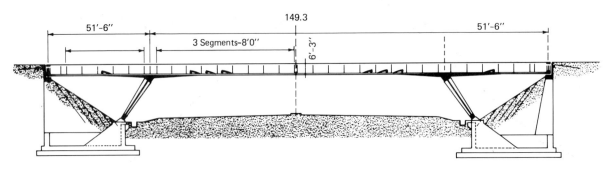

FIGURE 8.69.   Motorway Overpass Frames, longitudinal section.

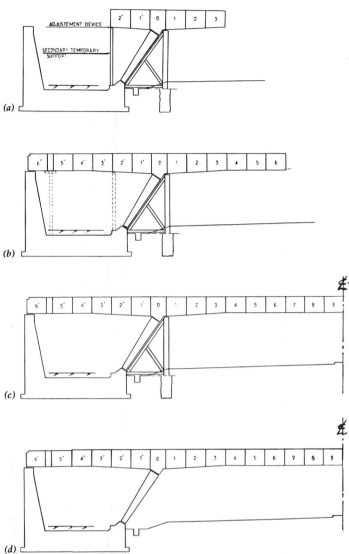

FIGURE 8.71. Motorway Overpass Frames, erection sequence.
(*a*) Stage 1. (*b*) Stage 2. (*c*) Stage 3. (*d*) Stage 4.

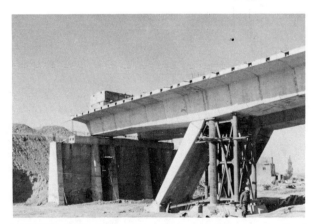

FIGURE 8.72. Motorway Overpass Frames, detail of inclined leg and temporary support.

A bridge over the Hanach River near Algiers, Algeria, with a clear span of 400 ft (123 m), Figures 8.74 and 8.75.

A major crossing of the Rhine River at Pfaffendorf, Germany, with a main span of 600 ft (180 m)

These studies were very encouraging from the viewpoints of both economy of materials and simplicity of construction. The deck was to be entirely precast, with members assembled by prestressing. Construction would proceed in balanced cantilever from the main piers until reaching midspan closure, where adjustment of the deck geometry and loads in the members was provided by jacks.

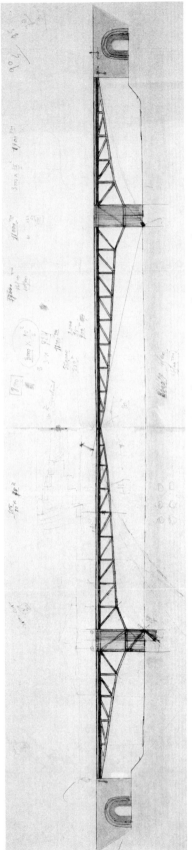

FIGURE 8.73. Original sketch of E. Freyssinet for a concept of prestressed precast concrete truss (1948).

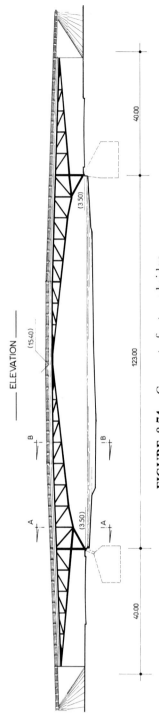

ELEVATION

(15.40)

(3.50)

(3.50)

B

B

A

A

40.00

12300

40.00

FIGURE 8.74. Concept of a truss bridge.

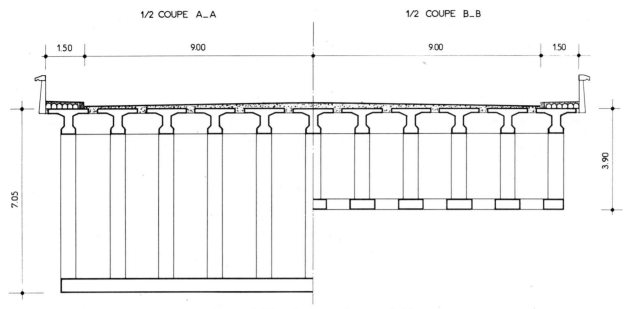

FIGURE 8.75. Concept of a truss bridge.

The use of I girders at 7 ft (2 m) spacing for the precast deck would not be considered today as the optimum design. One of the authors, who was involved in the studies with E. Freyssinet, remembers also that many technological problems such as the connection details between diagonals and chords were not completely solved.

Neither of these two designs reached the construction stage, and the concept was rapidly forgotten before its potential could be objectively ascertained.

Oddly enough, the designers of steel structures followed a similar path. Abandoning prematurely the concept of truss structures, which had allowed such outstanding structures as the Firth of Forth Bridge to be built all over the world, they turned to web girder structures and closed box sections with all the critical problems they entailed, such as elastic stability. Perhaps it is time to reassess some major design approaches in both steel and concrete for very long spans.

8.7.2 MANGFALL BRIDGE, AUSTRIA

The Mangfallbrücke in Austria, Figure 8.76, on the autobahn between Munich and Salzburg was constructed in 1959. This structure is perhaps best described as a large box girder with the webs being a trusswork. Total length is 945 ft (288 m) from abutment to abutment; the center span is 354 ft (108 m) with side spans of 295.5 ft (90 m). It was constructed as cast-in-place segmental using the free cantilever method. However, it was not bal-

anced cantilever, as construction started at one abutment and proceeded to the opposite abutment by progressive placement. Temporary intermediate piers were used as required to reduce the cantilever stresses.

Figure 8.77 shows an interior view. The lower flange is used as a walkway for pedestrians and for bicycles. The railing in the center surrounds an opening in the bottom flange where stress conditions do not require the concrete area. Figure 8.78 is an interior view looking through one of the floor openings, and Figure 8.79 is another interior view.

8.7.3 RIP BRIDGE, AUSTRALIA

The recently completed Rip Bridge, Figure 8.80, north of Sydney, Australia, has a center span of

FIGURE 8.76. Mangfallbrücke, general view.

FIGURE 8.77. Mangfallbrücke, interior view showing trusswork.

FIGURE 8.80. Rip Bridge, general view.

FIGURE 8.78. Mangfallbrücke, interior view looking through floor opening.

FIGURE 8.79. Mangfallbrücke, general interior view.

600 ft (182.88 m). The identical cantilever trusses, which sit symmetrically on either side of the crossing, reach out 240 ft (73.56 m) toward each other to support a 122 ft (37 m) drop-in simple span at their extremities, Figure 8.81.

The erection scheme is illustrated in Figure 8.82. Note that cable stays were used as diagonal members during construction to support the arch segments. Temporary falsework bents were used at each panel point of the truss on the landward side of the main piers. Precast concrete elements were delivered from a precasting plant some 80 miles (130 km) from the site.

Each panel of the lower chords of the truss was assembled from five precast I-shaped elements with a 1 ft (0.3 m) longitudinal pour strip between the flange tips. Similarly, the upper chord was assembled from five rectangular two-cell precast members. Erection of one of the lower chord members is shown in Figure 8.83. The exterior two I-shaped lower chord members are supported by the diagonal stays, while the interior three elements of the lower chord are supported by a transverse beam arrangement from the exterior two during construction.

Each diagonal member was assembled from longitudinally split halves, which, when brought together, encase the diagonal prestress tendon stays, incorporating them into the structure by concrete poured in place between the two halves. The upper chord or deck members are erected after the vertical members along with temporary falsework to support the deck panels, while the cast-in-place concrete is placed between the deck elements and transversely prestressed.

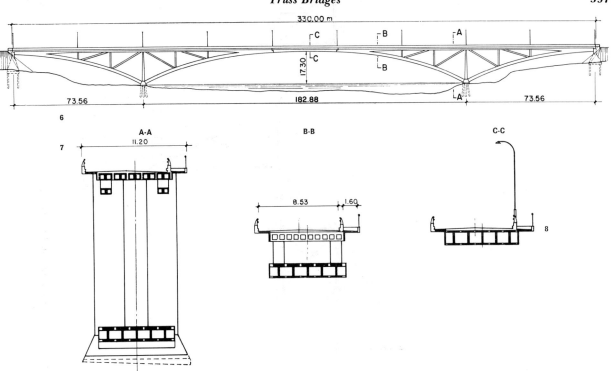

FIGURE 8.81. Rip Bridge, elevation and cross sections.

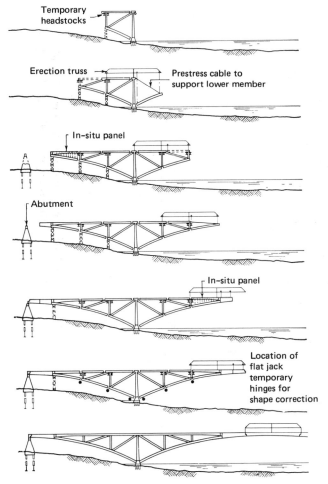

FIGURE 8.83. Rip Bridge, erection of lower chord.

The deck performs as a prestressed concrete tension member. As construction proceeds, additional prestress is progressively added to ensure that the deck remains in compression.

8.7.4 CONCEPT FOR A CROSSING OF THE ENGLISH CHANNEL

Certain projects for crossings, such as of the English Channel between France and Great Britain, the Straits of Messina, and even the Straits of Gibraltar, have exerted a powerful fascination on the minds of the great engineers of this century.

FIGURE 8.82. Rip Bridge, erection sequence.

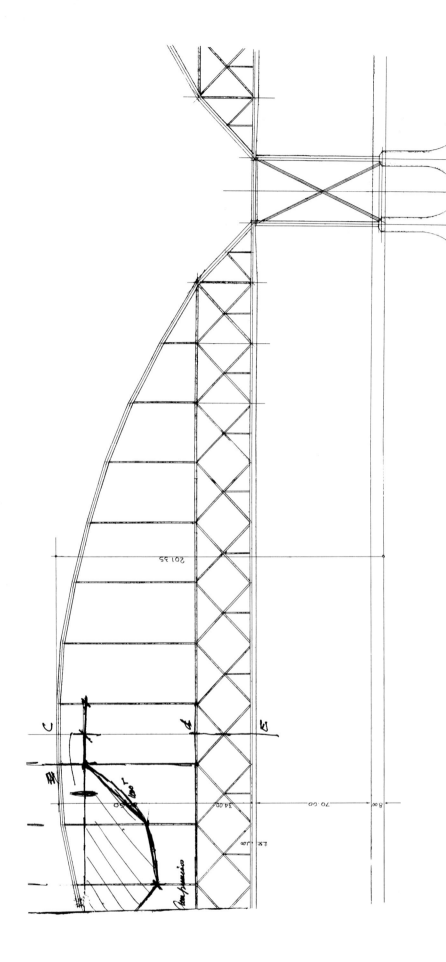

FIGURE 8.84. Freyssinet's concept of preconfined concrete arch crossing the English Channel with a series of 2000 ft (612 m) spans.

Eugene Freyssinet was no exception, and he spent the last years of his long professional career studying the crossing of the English Channel with a series of 2000 ft (612 m) long prestressed concrete spans. The many worthwhile ideas contained in this concept are not likely to be developed soon, or even by the turn of the century.

Figure 8.84 presents an elevation of a typical 2000 ft (612 m) span, which was contemplated as a prestressed concrete composite truss. Major members of the truss were not of conventional prestressed concrete, because such high stresses had to be accepted to keep the weight of the span within acceptable limits. A new material to be used for that purpose had occupied Freyssinet's mind for several years and had even been laboratory tested for confirmation of the concept. When a concrete member is completely confined in an envelope that creates permanently biaxial transverse compressive stress, it will resist safely much higher stress than if subjected to a monoaxial stress or reinforced conventionally with untensioned transverse reinforcing (such as spirals in a circular column).

From a technological point of view, the permanent active restraint creating the biaxial transverse compression is easily achieved in a member that has a circular cross section by confining it in a high-strength steel pipe or within a continuous spiral of prestressing steel wires, which are prestressed at the time the concrete is cast.

This material, which could be called "pre-confined concrete," has extraordinary properties such as total absence of brittleness and a capability to sustain several times as much longitudinal compressive stress as a reinforced concrete member without excessive strains, provided it is initially loaded to offset the initial strain.

Such a project and such a material could not be developed in a short period of time. They are mentioned here at the close of this chapter as a conceptual heritage, which it is our duty to make functional.

References

1. E. Freyssinet, "Largest Concrete Spans of the Americas—Three Monumental Bridges Built in Venezuela," *Civil Engineering–ASCE,* March 1953.

2. Jean Muller, "Largest Concrete Spans of the Americas—How the Three Bridges Were Designed," *Civil Engineering—ASCE,* March 1953.

3. Robert Shama, "Largest Concrete Spans of the Americas—How They Were Built," *Civil Engineering—ASCE,* March 1953.

4. Anon., "New Bridge over Parramatta River at Gladesville," *Main Roads,* Journal of the Department of Main Roads, New South Wales, December 1964.

5. Anon., "Talbrücke Rottweil-Neckarburg," *Zublin-Rundschau,* Heft 7/8, Dezember 1976, Stuttgart, Germany.

6. "Arch Slipformer Shuns Ground Support to Cross Valley," *Engineering News-Record,* June 1, 1978.

7. Anon., "Niesenbachbrücke, Bogen im Freien Vorbau," Austria 1970–74, FIP Congress 1974, New York.

9

Concrete Segmental Cable-Stayed Bridges

9.1 Introduction

The concept of supporting a beam or bridge by inclined cable stays is not new, and the historical evolution of this type of structure has been discussed in the literature.[1-6] Although the modern renaissance of cable-stayed bridges is said to have begun in 1955, with steel as the favored material, in the last two decades a number of cable-stayed bridges have been constructed using a reinforced or prestressed concrete deck system. In recent years several concrete cable-stayed bridges have been built in the long-span range. In at least four current projects, alternative designs in concrete and steel have been prepared for competitive bidding. Cable-stayed bridges are extending the competitive span range of concrete bridge construction to dimensions that had previously been considered impossible and reserved for structural steel. To date, approximately 21 concrete cable-stayed bridges have been constructed, and others are either in design or under construction. A tabular summary of concrete cable-stayed bridges is presented in Tables 9.1 and 9.2.

9.1.1 HISTORICAL REVIEW

Since the beginning of the cable-stay renaissance in 1955, whether for technical or other reasons, structural steel has been the preferred construction material. In 1957, however, considerable excitement was generated when Prof. Riccardo Morandi's prize-winning design of a prestressed concrete 1312 ft (400 m) center span cable-stayed bridge for the Lake Maracaibo crossing was announced. Regrettably the Lake Maracaibo Bridge was not constructed as originally conceived. The modified structure, built in 1962, is generally considered to be the first modern cable-stayed bridge. However, the Lake Maracaibo Bridge was preceded by two little-known concrete cable-stayed structures.

The first concrete structure to use cable stays was the Tempul Aqueduct crossing the Guadalete River in Spain.[7] Designed by the famous Spanish engineer, Prof. Torroja, who has introduced many original concepts in prestressed concrete, this structure has a classical three-span symmetrical cable-stayed bridge configuration with two pylons.

TABLE 9.1. Concrete Cable-Stayed Bridges—General Data

	Bridge	Location	Type	Spans (ft)[d]	Year Completed
1	Tempul	Guadalete River, Spain	Aqueduct	66–198–66	1925
2	Benton City	Yakima River, Wash., U.S.A.	Highway	2@57.5–170–2@57.5	1957
3	Lake Maracaibo	Venezuela	Highway	525–5@771–525	1962
4	Dnieper River	Kiev, U.S.S.R.	Highway	216.5–472–216.5	1963
5	Canal du Centre	Obourg, Belgium	Pedestrian	2@220	1966
6	Polcevera Viaduct	Genoa, Italy	Highway	282–664–689–460	1967
7	Magliana	Rome, Italy	Highway	476–176	1967
8	Danish Great Belt[a]	Denmark	Highway & rail	multispans 1132	Delayed by funding
9	Danish Great Belt[b]	Denmark	Highway & rail	multispans 1148	Delayed by funding
10	Pretoria	Pretoria, S. Africa	Pipe	2@93	1968
11	Barwon River	Geelong, Australia	Pedestrian	180–270–180	1969
12	Mount Street	Perth, Australia	Pedestrian	2@116.8	1969
13	Wadi Kuf	Libya	Highway	320–925–320	1971
14	Richard Foyle	Londonderry, N. Ireland	Highway	230–689	Project abandoned
15	Mainbrücke	Hoechst, West Germany	Highway & rail	485.6–308	1972
16	Chaco/Corrientes	Parana River, Argentina	Highway	537–803.8–537	1973
17	River Waal	Tiel, Holland	Highway	312–876–312	1974
18	Barranquilla	Barranquilla, Columbia	Highway	228–459–228	1974
19	Danube Canal	Vienna, Austria	Highway	182.7–390–182.7	1974
20	Kwang Fu	Taiwan	Highway	220–440–440–220	1977
21	Pont de Brotonne	Normandy, France	Highway	471–1050–471	1977
22	Carpineto	Province Poetenza, Italy	Highway	100–594–100	1977
23	Pasco-Kennewick	State of Wash., U.S.A.	Highway	406.5–981–406.5	1978
24	M-25 Overpass	Chertsey, England	Rail	2@180.5	1978
25	Ruck-A-Chucky[c]	Auburn, California, U.S.A.	Highway	1300	Design completed
26	Dame Point[c]	Jacksonville, Florida, U.S.A.	Highway	650–1300–650	Design completed
27	East Huntington[c]	East Huntington, W.Va., U.S.A.	Highway	158–300–900–608	Under construction
28	Weirton-Steubenville[c]	Weirton, W.Va., U.S.A.	Highway	820–688	In design

[a] Design by White Young and Partners.
[b] Design by Ulrich Finsterwalder.
[c] Alternative design with structural steel.
1 ft = 0.305 m.

The stays were introduced to replace two piers that were found to be too difficult to construct in deep water. Thus, the stays were introduced to provide intermediate support in the main span.

On July 5, 1957, a stayed structure crossing the Yakima River at Benton City, Washington, was opened to traffic. Designed by Homer M. Hadley, the structure has a total length of 400 ft (122 m) with a center span of 170 ft (51.9 m) flanked on each side by two continuous spans of 57.5 ft (17.53 m) each. A 60 ft (18.3 m) central drop-in span of 33 in. (0.84 m) deep steel beams is supported by transverse concrete beams, supported in turn by structural steel wide-flange stays. Continuous longitudinal concrete beams comprise the remainder of the structure and receive support at their extremity, in the center span, from the transverse concrete beams and steel stays.[4,8]

In the more than half-century that has elapsed since Torroja's Tempul Aqueduct, 21 cable-stayed bridges have been constructed (Table 9.1). Thirteen, or 62%, of these structures have been constructed in the past decade. In the last five years nine have been completed, representing 43% of the total. Within the last three years the span of 1000 ft (300 m) has been exceeded, and a current design contemplates a span of 1300 ft (400 m). It has taken almost a quarter-century to reach a span contemplated by Prof. Morandi in his original design concept for the Lake Maracaibo Bridge. Be that as it may, it is obvious from the statistics that in recent years the concrete cable-stayed bridge has been accepted as a viable structure.

9.1.2 ADVANTAGES OF CONCRETE CABLE-STAYED BRIDGES

As engineers, we are aware that no particular concept or bridge type can suit all environments, considerations, problems, or site conditions. The selection of the proper type for a given site and set of circumstances must take into account many parameters. The choice of material, in addition to

TABLE 9.2. Concrete Cable-Stayed Bridges—Dimensional Parameters

Bridge	Stay Planes	No. Stays	Stay Arrangement	Pylon Height Above Deck (ft)	Pylon Height-to-Span Ratio[c]	Deck Width (ft)	Girder Depth (ft)	Span-to-Depth Ratio[c]	Girder Construction Type[d]
1 Tempul	2	1	—	14.1	0.07	—	6.9	28.7	CIP
2 Benton City	2	1	—	—	—	—	3.25	52.3	CIP
3 Lake Maracaibo	2	1	—	139.4	0.18	57	16.4	46.7	CIP/PC d-i-s
4 Dnieper River	2	3	Radiating	95	0.20	—	4.8	98.75	PC
5 Canal du Centre	2	4	Radiating	65.6	0.30	5.87	1.94	113	PC
6 Polcevera Viaduct	2	1	—	148	0.21	59	15	46	CIP/PC d-i-s
7 Magliana	2	1	—	111.5	0.23	79	9.8–13.2	36	CIP/PC d-i-s
8 Danish Great Belt[a]	3	2	Radiating	—	—	51.75[f]	23.5	48	PC segments
9 Danish Great Belt[b]	2	16	Harp	315	0.27	46	2.95	390	CIP segments
10 Pretoria	2	2	Radiating	41	0.44	15.8	3	31	CIP
11 Barwon River	2	2	Fan	43	0.16	6	7	38.5	CIP
12 Mount Street	1	2	—	49	0.42	15.75	2	58.4	CIP
13 Wadi Kuf	2	1	—	177.5	0.19	42.5	11.5–23	70	CIP/PC d-i-s
14 River Foyle	1	2	Harp	360	0.52	98	11.5	60	PC segments
15 Mainbrücke	2	13	Harp	172	0.38	101.5	8.5	57	CIP
16 Chaco/Corrientes	2	2	Radiating	155	0.19	47	11.5	70	PC/CIP d-i-s
17 River Waal	2	2	Radiating	151.8	0.17	101	11.5	76	PC and CIP
18 Barranquilla	2	1	—	—	—	37	10	46	CIP segments
19 Danube Canal	2	1	—	52.5	0.15	51.8	9.2	42.5	PC and CIP
20 Kwang Fu	2	2	Radiating	—	—	67	—	—	PC
21 Pont de Brotonne	1	21	Fan	231	0.22	63	12.5	84	PC and CIP
22 Carpineto	2	1	—	94.75	0.16	41.3[f]	11.5	52	CIP
23 Pasco-Kennewick	2	18	Radiating	220	0.22	79.8	7	140	PC segments
24 M-25 Overpass	2	2	Fan	71	0.39	39	9	20	CIP
25 Ruck-A-Chucky	2	20	[e]	—	—	54	8.5	153	PC segments
26 Dame Point	2	21	Harp	302	0.23	105.75	5–6	260	CIP and PC
27 East Huntington	2	15/16	Radiating	279.4	0.31	41	5	180	Composite
28 Weirton-Steubenville	2	24	Radiating	333.2	0.41	103.5	8.5	96.5	Composite

[a] Design by White Young and Partners.
[b] Design by Ulrich Finsterwalder.
[c] See Table 9.1 for major span dimensions.
[d] CIP = cast-in-place, PC = precast, d-i-s = drop-in-span.
[e] Form hyperbolic paraboloid in space.
[f] Per single-cell box.
1 ft = 0.305 m.

material properties, depends on availability and the prevailing economics at a particular time as well as the specific location of the site. The process of weighting and evaluating these parameters for various types of bridges under consideration is certainly more an art than a science.

In evaluating a concrete cable-stayed bridge, the designer should be aware of the following advantages:

1. The main girder can be very shallow with respect to the span. Span-to-girder-depth ratios vary from 45 to 100. With proper aerodynamic streamlining and multistays the deck structure can be slim, having span-to-depth ratios of 150 to 400, and not convey a massive visual impression.

2. Concrete deck structures, by virtue of their mass and because concrete has inherently favorable damping characteristics, are not as susceptible to aerodynamic vibrations.

3. The horizontal component of cable-stay force, which causes compression with bending in the deck structure, favors a concrete deck structure. The stay forces produce a prestress force in the concrete, and concrete is at its best in compression.

4. The amount of steel required in the stays is comparatively small. A proper choice of height of pylon with respect to span can yield an optimum solution.[9]

5. Live-load deflections are small because of the live-load-to-dead-load ratio, and therefore

concrete cable-stayed bridges are applicable to railroad or mass-transit loadings.

6. Erection of the superstructure and cable stays is relatively easy with today's technology of prestressing, prefabrication, and segmental cantilever construction.

9.1.3 STRUCTURAL STYLE AND ARRANGEMENT

Many of the concrete cable-stayed bridges have been designed by Morandi or have been strongly influenced by his style. Commencing with the Lake Maracaibo Bridge, of the 12 bridges constructed, excluding pedestrian and pipe bridges (see Table 9.1), six have been designed by Morandi, Figures 9.1 through 9.6. A third prize winner in the 1967 Danish Great Belt Bridge Competition was the Morandi-style design proposed by the English consulting firm of White Young and Partners, Figure 9.7. The Chaco/Corrientes Bridge, Figure 9.8, very much resembles the Morandi style.

FIGURE 9.3. Magliana Viaduct (courtesy of L'Industria Italiana del Cemento).

FIGURE 9.4. Wadi Kuf Bridge, general construction view (courtesy of Prof. R. Morandi).

FIGURE 9.1. Lake Maracaibo Bridge, general view, from reference 11 (courtesy of Julius Berger-Bauboag Aktiengesellschaft).

FIGURE 9.2. Polcevera Creek Bridge, general view.

FIGURE 9.5. Barranquilla Bridge (courtesy of L. A. Garrido).

FIGURE 9.6. Carpineto Viaduct (courtesy of L'Industria Italiana del Cemento).

FIGURE 9.7. Danish Great Belt Bridge, artist's rendering (courtesy of White Young and Partners).

FIGURE 9.8. Chaco/Corrientes Bridge, general view, from reference 13 (courtesy of Normer Gray).

These structures, with the exception of the Magliana, Barranquilla, and Carpineto bridges, are typified by the A-frame pylon positioned in the plane of the stays and an auxiliary X frame or inclined struts to support the deck structure at the pylon. They are statically determinate systems so as to preclude any possible damage from differential settlements of the bridge piers and pylons or from light seismic shocks.

A simple schematic of the structural scheme is shown in Figure 9.9, which consists of a series of independent balanced systems, each carried by an individual pier and pylon. These systems are then connected by drop-in girders, which are simple span girders spanning between independent systems.[10] The cantilever girder is supported at two points (C and D) by a pier system and elastically supported at two points (B and E) by the cable stays, thus producing a three-span girder with cantilevers on each side. The stays are supported by a pylon portal frame that is independent of the pier system supporting the girder.

Another entry in the 1967 Danish Great Belt Competition by Ulrich Finsterwalder, of the German firm Dyckerhoff & Widmann, deviated from the Morandi style and was awarded a second prize. Finsterwalder's design proposed a multiple-span, multistay system using Dywidag bars for the stays, Figure 9.10. The deck was envisioned as being constructed by the cast-in-place balanced cantilever

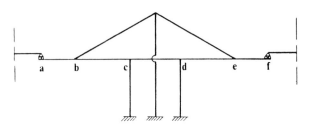

FIGURE 9.9. Schematic of Morandi-style structural scheme, from reference 10 (courtesy of the American Concrete Institute).

FIGURE 9.10. Danish Great Belt Bridge, artist's rendering (courtesy of Ulrich Finsterwalder).

segmental method, each segment being supported by a set of stays. This concept was later to be consummated in the Main Bridge and in the design of the Dame Point Bridge.

The choice of geometrical configuration and number of stays in a cable-stayed bridge system is subject to a wide variety of considerations. If cable stays are few, they result in large stay forces, which require massive anchorage systems. A relatively deep girder is required to span the large distance between stays, producing span-to-depth ratios varying from 45 to 100 (see Table 9.2). Depending upon the location of the longitudinal main girders with respect to the cable-stay planes, large transverse cross girders may be required to transfer the stay force to the main girder.

A large number of cable stays, approaching a continuous supporting elastic media, simplifies the anchorage and distribution of forces to the girder and permits the use of a shallower girder, with span-to-depth ratio varying from 150 to 400 (see Table 9.2). The construction of the deck can be erected roadway-width by free cantilever methods from stay to stay without auxiliary methods or stays. If the depth of the roadway girder can be kept at a minimum, the deck becomes, more or less, the bottom chord of a large cantilevering truss; it needs almost no bending stiffness because the inclined stays do not allow any large deflections under concentrated loads.[6]

In the 55 years since Torroja's Tempul Aqueduct the concrete cable-stayed bridge has evolved from basically a statically determinate structure with one stay on each side of the pylon to a highly indeterminate system with multistays. As demonstrated by the Danish Great Belt Bridge Competition, the Pasco-Kennewick Bridge, and the Pont de Brotonne, spans of approximately 1000 ft (300 m) are practical and have been accomplished. The practicality of spans of 1300 ft (400 m) is demonstrated by the Dame Point Bridge, and spans approaching 1600 ft (500 m) are considered technically feasible. Leonhardt[6] has projected that with an aerodynamically shaped composite concrete and steel deck a span of 2300 ft (1500 m) can be achieved. With today's technology of prefabrication, prestressing, and segmental cantilever construction, it is obvious that cable-stayed bridges are extending the competitive span range of concrete bridges to dimensions that had previously been considered impossible and into a range that had previously been the domain of structural steel. This technological means exist; they only require implementation.

9.2 Lake Maracaibo Bridge, Venezuela

This bridge, Figure 9.1, has a total length of 5.4 miles (8.7 km). Five main navigation openings consist of prestressed concrete cable-stayed structures with suspended spans totaling 771 ft (235 m). The cantilever span is supported on four parallel X frames, while the cable stays are supported on two A frames with a portal member at the top. There is no connection anywhere between the X and A frames, Figure 9.11. The continuous cantilever girder is a three-cell box girder 16.4 ft deep by 46.7 ft wide (5 m by 14.22 m). An axial prestress force is induced into the girder as a result of the horizontal component of cable force, thus, for the most part, only conventional reinforcement is required. Additional prestress tendons are required for negative moment above the X-frame support and the transverse cable-stay anchorage beams.[11]

The pier cap consists of the three-cell box girder with the X frames continued up into the girder to act as transverse diaphragms, Figures 9.12 and 9.13. After completion of the pier, service girders were raised into position to be used in the construction of the cantilever arm. Owing to the additional moment, produced during this construction stage by the service girder and weight of the cantilever arm, additional concentric prestressing was required in the pier cap, Figure 9.13. To avoid overstressing of the X frames during this operation, temporary horizontal ties were installed and tensioned by hydraulic jacks, Figures 9.13 and 9.14.

FIGURE 9.11. Lake Maracaibo Bridge, pier cap with X frames, from reference 11 (courtesy of Julius Berger-Bauboag Aktiengesellschaft).

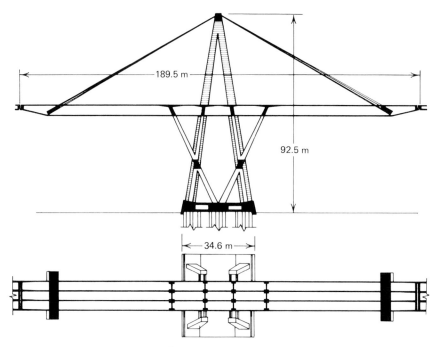

FIGURE 9.12. Lake Maracaibo Bridge, main span tower and X-frames, from reference 11 (courtesy of Julius Berger-Bauboag Aktiengesellschaft).

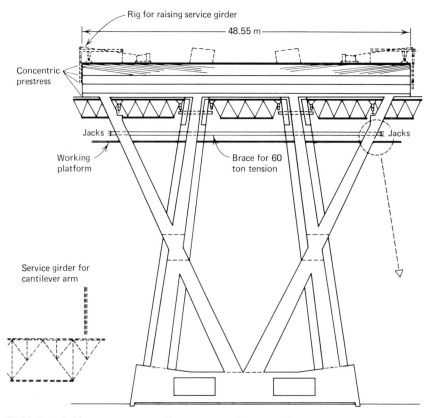

FIGURE 9.13. Lake Maracaibo Bridge, pier cap of a main span and service girder, from reference 11 (courtesy of Julius Berger-Bauboag Aktiengesellschaft).

FIGURE 9.14. Lake Maracaibo Bridge, brace members bear against X frames after being tensioned by hydraulic jacks, from reference 11 (courtesy of Julius Berger-Bauboag Aktiengesellschaft).

FIGURE 9.15. Lake Maracaibo Bridge, placing service girder for forming cantilever girders, from reference 11 (courtesy of Julius Berger-Bauboag Aktiengesellschaft).

In the construction of the cantilever arms, special steel trusses (service girders) were used for formwork. They were supported at one end by the completed pier cap and at the other end by auxiliary piers and foundations, as shown in Figure 9.15.

The anchorages for the cable stays are located in a 73.8 ft (22.5 m) long prestressed inclined transverse girder. The reinforcing cages for these members were fabricated on shore in a position corresponding to the inclination of the stays. They weighed 60 tons and contained 70 prestressing tendons, Figure 9.16. The cable stays are housed in thick-walled steel pipes, Figure 9.17, which were welded to steel plates at their extremities and were encased in the anchorage beam. A special steel spreader beam was used to erect the fabricated cage in its proper orientation. The suspended spans are composed of four prestressed T sections.

9.3 Wadi Kuf Bridge, Libya

The Wadi Kuf Bridge in Libya, designed by Prof. Morandi, consists of two independent balanced

FIGURE 9.16. Lake Maracaibo Bridge, fabrication of anchorage beam, from reference 11 (courtesy of Julius Berger-Bauboag Aktiengesellschaft).

FIGURE 9.17. Lake Maracaibo Bridge, housing for cable stays, from reference 11 (courtesy of Julius Berger-Bauboag Aktiengesellschaft).

cable-stay systems having their ends anchored to the abutment by a short hinge strut. The cable-stay systems are connected by a simply supported drop-in span, Figure 9.4.

This structure consists of only three spans. The center span is 925 ft (280 m) long and the two end spans are each 320 ft (97.5 m), for a total length of 1565 ft (475 m). The simply supported drop-in center portion of the main span consists of three double-T beams 180 ft (55 m) in length; each beam weighs approximately 220 tons (200 mt).[12]

The A-frame towers are 459 ft and 400 ft (140 and 122 m) high and the roadway deck is 597 (182 m) above the lowest point of the valley beneath the structure.[12] The superstructure is a single-cell box girder that varies from 13 ft (4.0 m) to 23 ft (7.0 m) at the pylons. The single-cell box is 24 ft (7.4 m) wide and with cantilever flanges forms a 42.7 ft (13 m) deck.

The contractor made good use of traveling forms to construct the box girder and deck, using the balanced cantilever technique to build on both sides of the pylons at the same time. Traveling forms were used because extreme height and difficult terrain made other conventional construction methods impossible or too costly. The deck was constructed by progressive cast-in-place segments, attached to the previously completed segments by means of temporary prestress ties and subsequent permanent post-tensioning Dywidag bars. The procedure adopted required temporary cable stays to support the cantilever arms during the construction sequence as the superstructure progressed in both directions from the pylon. When the superstructure extended sufficiently, the permanent stays were installed, and the structure was completed in the same manner.

9.4   Chaco/Corrientes Bridge, Argentina

The Chaco/Corrientes Bridge (also referred to as the General Manuel Belgrano Bridge) crosses the Parana River between the provinces of Chaco and Corrientes in northeast Argentina and is an important link in one of the highways between Brazil and Argentina, Figure 9.8. It has a center navigation span of 803 ft 10 in. (245 m), side spans of 537 ft (163.7 m), and a number of 271 ft (82.6 m) approach spans on both the Chaco and Corrientes sides of the river. The vertical clearance in the main spans above flood level is 115 ft (35 m).[13,14]

The superstructure of this bridge consists of two cast-in-place concrete A-frame pylons, which support a deck of precast segmental post-tensioned concrete. The pylons are flanked by concrete struts, which reduce the unsupported length of the deck, Figure 9.18. Although the pier cap section of the deck (between inclined struts) is cast in place, the cantilever portion consists of precast segments. The drop-in spans are cast in place.

The deck structure consists of two longitudinal hollow boxes 8 ft 2½ in. (2.5 m) wide and with a constant depth of 11 ft 6 in. (3.5 m), which support precast roadway deck elements, Figure 9.19. The precast girder elements were match-cast on the river bank in lengths of 13 ft 1½ in. (4.0 m), with the exception of shorter units at the point of stay attachment, which contain an inclined transverse anchorage beam, Figure 9.20. Units were cast by the long-line method on a concrete foundation with the proper camber built in. Each unit was cast with three alignment keys, one in each web and one in the top flange. The units were erected as balanced cantilevers with respect to the pylon to minimize erection stresses. After a unit was hoisted, an epoxy joint material was placed over all of the butting area; then the unit was placed against the already erected unit and tensioned.[13]

To eliminate the need for falsework, the inclined struts and pylon legs were supported by horizontal ties at successive levels as construction proceeded, Figure 9.21. The legs were poured in segments by cantilevering the formwork from previously constructed segments. When deck level was reached, the girder section between the extremities of the inclined ties was cast on formwork. To further stiffen the pylon structure, a slab was cast between box girders at the level of the girder bottom flanges. This slab is within the limits of the cast-in-place box girders and inclined struts and serves as an additional element to accept the horizontal thrust from the cable stays. The upper portion of the pylon was

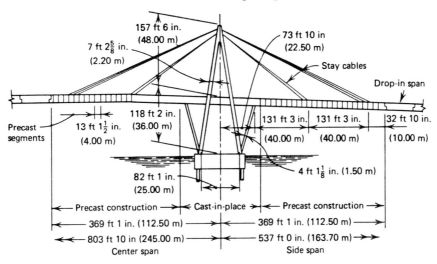

FIGURE 9.18. Chaco/Corrientes Bridge, longitudinal geometry, from reference 14 (courtesy of Civil Engineering-ASCE).

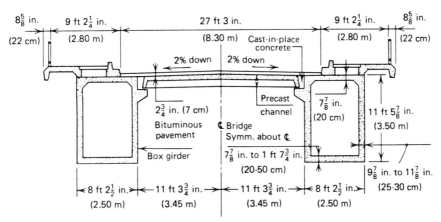

FIGURE 9.19. Chaco/Corrientes Bridge, deck cross section, from reference 14 (courtesy of Civil Engineering-ASCE).

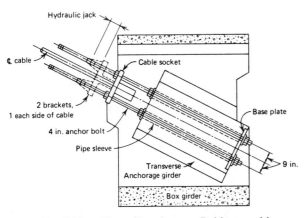

FIGURE 9.20. Chaco/Corrientes Bridge, cable anchorage at girder, from reference 14 (courtesy of Civil Engineering-ASCE).

then completed, using horizontal struts to brace the legs until they were connected at the apex, Figure 9.21.[13,14]

The precast box girder units, with the exception of those at the cable-stay anchorage, were cast 13 ft 1½ in. (4 m) in length by the long-line, match-cast procedure. The soffit bed of the casting form had the required camber built in. Alignment keys were cast into both webs and the top flange. Match casting and alignment keys were required to ensure a precise fit during erection. Each 44 ton (40 mt) unit was transported by barge to the construction site and erected by a traveling crane operating on the erected portion of the deck. Since each box was lifted by a balance beam, four heavy vertical bolts had to be cast into the top flange of each box. The lifting crane at deck level allowed longitudinal

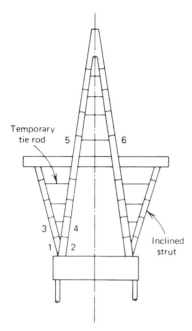

FIGURE 9.21. Chaco/Corrientes Bridge, erection sequence of pylon, from reference 14 (courtesy of Civil Engineering-ASCE).

movement of the suspended box. Upon erection to the proper elevation, the unit was held to within 6 in. (150 mm) of the mating unit while epoxy joint material was applied. Bearing surfaces of the unit were sand-blasted and water-soaked before erection. The water film was removed before erection and application of the epoxy joint material. The traveling deck crane held the unit in position against its mating unit until it could be post-tensioned into position. The crane was slacked off without waiting for the joint material to cure.[13,14]

To minimize overturning forces and stresses in the pylon, it was necessary to erect the precast box units by a balanced cantilever method on both sides of the centerline of the pylon. The erection schedule demanded simultaneous erection at each pylon, although the pylons are independent of each other. When four precast box units were erected in the cantilever on each side of the pylon, temporary stays were installed from the top of the pylon to their respective connections at deck level. After installation of the temporary stays, cantilever erection proceeded to the positions of the permanent stays, and the procedure was repeated to completion of the installation of the precast box units.[13]

The erection sequence may be outlined as follows:

1. Erect precast boxes and post-tension successively.

2. Erect diaphragms between lines of boxes and post-tension.

3. Place temporary and permanent stays as erection proceeds.

4. Remove temporary stays.

5. Remove temporary post-tensioning in the cantilever sections.

6. Place precast deck slabs between box girders.

7. Concrete the three 65 ft 8 in. (20 m) drop-in spans.

8. Place asphalt pavement, curbs, and railings.

9.5   Mainbrücke, Germany

The Main Bridge near Hoechst, a suburb of Frankfort, constructed in 1971 is a prestressed, cast-in-place, segmental, cable-stayed structure that connects the Fabwerke Hoechst's chemical industrial complex on both sides of the River Main in West Germany, Figure 9.22. It carries two three-lane roads separated by a railway track and pipelines. This structure, a successor to Finsterwalder's Danish Great Belt Bridge proposal, represents the first practical application of the Dywidag bar stay.[15]

The bridge spans the river at a skew of 70° from the high northern bank to the southern bank, which is 23 ft (7 m) lower. The center navigation span is 486 ft (148.23 m) with a northern approach span of 86 ft (26.17m) and southern approach spans of 55, 84, 95, and 129 ft (16.91, 25.65, 29, and 39.35 m), Figure 9.23.

Railroad track and pipelines are in the median between the two cantilever pylon shafts and are supported on an 8.7 ft (2.66 m) deep torsionally stiff box girder, Figure 9.24. The centerline of the

FIGURE 9.22. Mainbrücke, from reference 16.

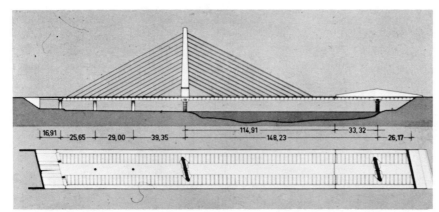

FIGURE 9.23. Mainbrücke, elevation and plan, from reference 16.

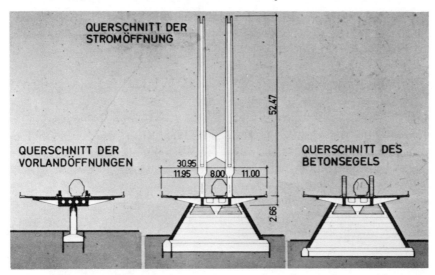

FIGURE 9.24. Mainbrücke, cross sections, from reference 16.

longitudinal webs of the box girder coincides with the centerline of the individual cantilever pylons, and they are 26.25 ft (8 m) apart. Transverse cross beams at 9.8 ft (3 m) centers form diaphragms for the box and cantilevers, which extend 39 ft (11.95 m) on one side and 36 ft (11 m) on the other side of the central box to support the two roadways, Figure 9.25.

The cross section of the towers consists of an anchoring web in the center, sandwiched by two flatplate flange elements, Figure 9.26. In a transverse elevation of the pylons, the width of the pylon increases from the top to just below the transverse strut, where it decreases to accommodate clearance requirements for both modes of traffic, Figure 9.26. The stay cables (Dywidag bars) are in pairs, horizontal to each other in the main span and vertical in the side span, thus simplifying the anchorage detail at the pylon, Figure 9.26.[16]

FIGURE 9.25. Mainbrücke, view of deck at pylon (courtesy of Richard Heinen).

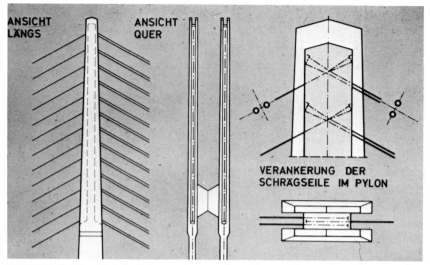

FIGURE 9.26. Mainbrücke, pylon and cable configuration, from reference 16.

Construction of the bridge superstructure was by the cast-in-place segmental method, Figure 9.27. Segments in the river span were 20.7 ft (6.3 m) in length, corresponding to the spacing of the stays. Segments in the anchor span were 19 ft (5.8 m) in length. Segments in the anchor span were concreted before the corresponding segment in the river span to maintain stability. The pylon segments were associated with the superstructure segments, and each pylon segment was slip-formed.

Figure 9.28 shows the partially completed structure and the falsework necessary to install the stays. Each stay is composed of twenty-five 16 mm (⅝ in.) diameter Dywidag bars encased in a metal duct, which is grouted for corrosion protection similar to post-tensioned prestressed concrete construction.

9.6 Tiel Bridge, The Netherlands

The Tiel Bridge,[17] Figures 9.29 and 9.30, crosses the Waal River, which, together with the Maas and the Rhine, flowing east to west, divides the

FIGURE 9.27. Mainbrücke, casting of deck segments (courtesy of Dyckerhoff & Widmann).

FIGURE 9.28. Mainbrücke, partially completed structure (courtesy of Richard Heinen).

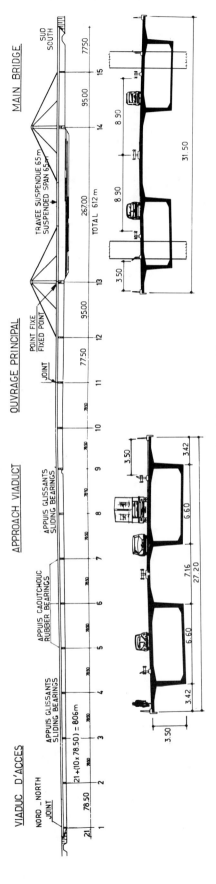

FIGURE 9.29. Tiel Bridge, general layout.

413

FIGURE 9.30. Tiel Bridge, main spans.

Netherlands into northern and southern parts. This structure provides a needed traffic link between the town of Tiel and the south of the country and is a major north-south route.

The structure has an overall length of 4656 ft (1419 m) and consists of a 2644 ft (806 m) curved viaduct on a 19,685 ft (6000 m) radius, which includes ten continuous 258 ft (78.5 m) long spans and a 2008 ft (612 m) straight main structure comprising three stayed spans of 312, 876, and 312 ft (95, 267, and 95 m) and two 254 ft (77.5 m) side spans.

The cross section consists of two precast concrete boxes, each supporting two vehicular and one bicycle lane. The total width of the superstructure, which is 89 ft (27.2 m) in the access viaduct, Figure 9.31, is enlarged to 103 ft (31.5 m) over the main structure so as to accommodate the pylon supporting the stays.

The structure crosses not only the Waal River but also a flood plain, which is under water during the winter months. Navigation requirements dictate a horizontal clearance of 853 ft (260 m) and a vertical clearance of 30 ft (9.1 m).

FIGURE 9.31. Tiel Bridge, approach viaduct.

The ten-span 2648 ft (806 m) long access viaduct is continuous over its entire length. The superstructure is supported on the piers by sliding teflon bearings, except at the three center piers where it is supported on neoprene bearings, having a thickness such that they fix the viaduct at these piers. Expansion joints are located at piers 1 and 11. The superstructure in the access viaduct consists of two precast rectangular boxes of a constant depth of 11.5 ft (3.5 m) and width of 21 ft 8 in. (6.6 m). The top flange including cantilever overhangs has a width of 44 ft (13.44 m). The overall width of the approach viaduct deck is 89 ft 3 in. (27.2 m), including a longitudinal pour strip. The viaduct was constructed by the precast balanced cantilever method with cast-in-place closure pours at the midspans. To accommodate the cantilever compressive stresses in the bottom flange over the piers, the thickness of the bottom flange is linearly increased from a minimum of 8 in. (200 mm) to 24 in. (600 mm) over a length of 33 ft (10 m) on each side of the pier. Each pier segment contains a diaphragm.

Because of the potential flooding of the river from April through December and the consequent loss or damage of falsework and loss of time, it was decided to build the access viaduct utilizing precast segments in the balanced or "free" cantilever construction. The segments could be cast during flooding and placed in storage. Erection of the segments, which would take less time than the casting, could be accomplished after the flood had subsided.

The precast segments, weighing 132 tons (120 mt), were cast in movable forms on a casting bed having the length of one span (by the long-line method, see Section 11.6.2). Segments were stored by and parallel to the casting bed and handled by a 130 ft (40 m) span gantry crane, Figure 9.32. They were transported to the site (access viaduct abutment) by means of a 132 ton (120 mt) capacity trolley and then placed in the structure by the same gantry crane used in the precasting yard for handling, Figure 9.33. The trolley was used to transport the segments because the gantry was usually engaged in the precasting yard or in placing segments in the viaduct. The gantry crane was such that it spanned over the twin boxes in the superstructure and the trolleyway used to transport the segments.

Segment joints are of the epoxy-bonded type (see Section 11.5). Cantilever imbalance is accommodated by a temporary support adjacent to the pier, Figure 9.33. Five temporary prestress bars

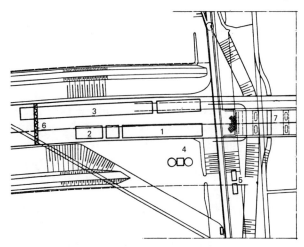

FIGURE 9.32. Precasting plant. (1) Casting bed, (2) re-bar storage, (3) segment storage, (4) concrete batch plant, (5) office, (6) gantry crane, (7) bridge approach.

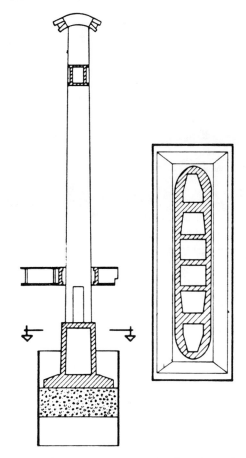

FIGURE 9.34. Free passage of pylon through deck.

are used as provisional prestressing to hold the segments in position until permanent prestress tendons can be threaded into the ducts and stressed.

The symmetrical box girder main structure consists of a 254 ft (77.5 m) side span, a 312 ft (95 m) side stayed span, and a 331 ft (101 m) section of stayed center span cantilevering toward the center of the bridge. The center section between the stayed cantilever ends is made up of four 213 ft (65 m) suspended lightweight concrete girders.

Two alternatives were considered for the cable-stay pylons: a single pylon located on the longitudinal centerline of the bridge or a portal-type pylon. To simplify the project, the portal-type pylon was selected. The portal pylon is fixed to the pier and passes freely through the superstructure, Figure 9.34. The superstructure is fixed at the pylon piers except for rotation. It is allowed to move longitudinally at succeeding piers.

Two alternatives were also considered for the stay system: a multiple stay system supporting the deck almost continuously and a system consisting of a few large stays. As prestressed concrete stays had been selected, the second solution became somewhat mandatory. Construction of prestressed

concrete stays is a costly operation requiring extensive high scaffolding, Figure 9.35; thus it is advantageous to reduce the number of stays.

The short stays of the bridge have a slope of 1:1 and the long stays a slope of 1:2. Their points of anchorage to the deck are respectively at 156 ft (47.5 m) and 312 ft (95 m) on both sides of a pylon. The long stays have a cross section of 3 by 3.3 ft (0.9 by 1.0 m) and are prestressed by 36 tendons on the bank side and by 40 tendons on the river side, because of the larger load on that side, Figure 9.36a. The effect of the different loads on the stays introduces a flexural moment into the pylon. The short stays have a cross section of 2.13 by 3.3 ft (0.65 by 1.0 m) and are prestressed by 16 tendons

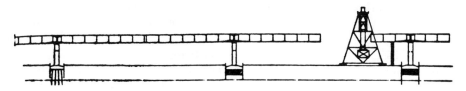

FIGURE 9.33. Placing of segments by gantry crane.

FIGURE 9.35. Falsework for stay construction.

on the bank side and 20 tendons on the river side, Figure 9.36*b*.

The concrete of the stays has a 28-day strength of approximately 8700 psi (60 MPa). Its function is not only to protect the tendons, but also to increase the rigidity of the stays, which is four times that of the tendons alone.

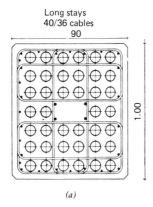

Long stays
40/36 cables
90

1.00

(a)

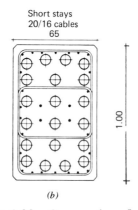

Short stays
20/16 cables
65

1.00

(b)

FIGURE 9.36. Cross section of stays.

Three loading conditions were considered for the stays from a statics point of view:

1. For the self-weight of the stays and dead load of the superstructure, the deck is considered as supported on nonyielding supports, which are the stay anchorage points, and the load in the stays results from the reactions at these points.

2. For design live load, the deck is considered as supported on yielding supports, the rigidity of which is determined by the rigidity of the prestressed stays.

3. The prestress of the stays was calculated with a safety factor against cracking of 1.1 for dead load and 1.3 for live load, without allowing any tension in the concrete. The ultimate load safety factor is 1.8. For the load condition between cracking and collapse the stay rigidity is reduced to the rigidity of the tendons alone. Their excessive elongation, in case they yielded, would lead to an excessive deflection of the box girder and a premature collapse before the proposed safety limit. Therefore, it was necessary to reduce the initial stress of the tendons to 40 to 45% of their ultimate strength in order to keep them in the elastic range up to ultimate load determined by the safety factor of the structure as a whole.

The sag of the long stay is 2.3 ft (0.70 m) in a length of 328 ft (100 m) under dead load. Under live load the sag is reduced to 1.8 ft (0.55 m). The cross section of the stays at their extremities is increased slightly to resist bending stresses. These stresses were calculated by the method of finite differences.

In the longitudinal direction the girders are prestressed primarily by the horizontal components of the stay forces. The unstayed end spans are prestressed with 54 tendons. In the other spans additional prestressing is provided by 10 tendons that overlap each other at the supports. These tendons were required until such time as the stay forces were applied and, at completion, to provide safety against cracking and collapse. The deck slab is prestressed transversely by tendons spaced at 12 to 17 in. (0.30 to 0.44 m).

The suspended 213 ft (65 m) span is composed of four precast lightweight concrete girders with a 6500 psi (45 MPa) concrete. The cast-in-place deck slab is increased from a thickness of 9.8 in. (250 mm) in the box girders to 12.6 in. (320 mm), owing to the smaller restraint of the slab in the one web girders.

The following restraints and conditions were considered in the determination of the construction procedure for the main spans of the structure:

1. The exclusion of falsework from the river because of navigation requirements.
2. The potential for flooding.
3. The presence of the precasting plant on the north bank.
4. The possibility of adjusting the attachment points of the stay to the deck.

Construction was executed in increments limited by the attachment points of the stays to the deck. The stays were prestressed progressively, by increasing the number of stressed tendons as the load in the stays increased. However, during certain construction phases when the load in the stays decreased, some of the tendons were detensioned or slacked off.

Using the north side (access viaduct side) as an example, the construction was divided into the following phases, Figure 9.37:

Phase 1: *Construction of the outer spans—that is, the stay-supported side span and flanking span*

    a. Superstructure from pier 11 to pier 12 and a 72 ft (22 m) cantilever into the next span

    b. Extension up to temporary support 12A

    c. Extension up to pier 13 with a 26 ft (8 m) cantilever into the center span; simultaneous construction of the pylon

Phase 2: *Construction of the first section over the river and the short forestay.*

Phase 3: *Construction of the second section over the river and the long forestay.*

The external spans on the north side were constructed on falsework during the dry season. Utilizing the precast plant on the north side, precast segments 16.7 ft (5.10 m) long weighing 132 tons (120 mt) were assembled on the falsework. Segments were joined by $\frac{1}{4}$ in. (5 mm) cast-in-place joints. Placing of the segments was carried out by the same gantry crane as for the access viaduct. On the south bank, where there was no precasting plant, the external spans were cast in place on falsework.

The cantilever river spans were built on 157 ft (48 m) long steel falsework, consisting of four 10 ft

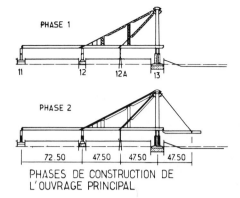

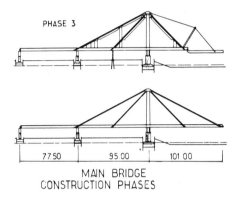

FIGURE 9.37. Main bridge construction phases.

(3 m) deep girders on 23 ft (7.10 m) centers. This falsework was suspended at one end by prestressing strands from the top of the pylons. At the lower end, the temporary support strands were anchored in a cross beam that supported the steel falsework by four 350 ton (315 mt) jacks. The 3 ft (1.0 m) stroke of the jacks allowed adjustment of the level of the suspension points, and the jacks were used also to release the temporary prestress suspension strands when the final stays were installed. At the opposite end, the steel falsework was hinged. The horizontal force component on these hinges was transmitted directly to the completed part of the deck, and the vertical component was taken by 1 in. (26 mm) bars.

In Phase 3, the temporary stays were deflected by means of 95 ft (29 m) booms. This provided the advantage of maintaining the angles at the lower connection equal to that of Phase 2 and keeping approximately the same force level in the temporary stay.

The falsework used in Phases 2 and 3 was carried on a barge; it was positioned by two derricks located on the completed part of the deck and by a floating crane. After the box girders were cast, the level of the falsework was adjusted, the last joint was cast, and the concrete was prestressed. The next steps were constructing the stays, prestressing them, releasing the temporary stays, and removing the falsework.

In order to reduce creep and shrinkage, the stays were made of 17 ft (5.15 m) long segments with protruding reinforcement and 16 in. (0.4 m) cast-in-place joints. The building of the falsework for the stays and the handling of the precast segments were carried out with the help of a 16 ton (15 mt) tower crane 213 ft (65 m) high, running on the deck.

The precast 213 ft (65 m) suspended span girders weighed 468 tons (425 mt) and were transported by barge.

9.7 *Pasco-Kennewick Bridge, U.S.A.*

The first cable-stayed bridge with a segmental concrete superstructure to be constructed in the United States is the Pasco-Kennewick Intercity Bridge crossing the Columbia River in the state of Washington, Figure 9.38. Construction began in August 1975 and was completed in May 1978. The overall length of this structure is 2503 ft (763 m). The center cable-stayed span is 981 ft (299 m), and the stayed flanking spans are 406.5 ft (124 m). The Pasco approach is a single span of 126 ft (38.4 m),

FIGURE 9.38. Pasco-Kennewick Intercity Bridge (courtesy of Arvid Grant).

while the Kennewick approach is one span at 124 ft (37.8 m) and three spans at 148 ft (45.1 m).[4,15,18,19]

The girder is continuous without expansion joints from abutment to abutment, being fixed at the Pasco (north) end and having an expansion joint at the Kennewick (south) abutment. The concrete bridge girder is of uniform cross section, of constant 7 ft (2 m) depth along its entire length and 79 ft 10 in. (24.3 m) width. The shallow girder and the long main spans are necessary in order to reduce roadway grades to a minimum, to provide the greatest possible navigation clearance below, and to reduce the number of piers in the 70 ft (21.3 m) deep river.

The bridge is not symmetrical. The Pasco pylon is approximately 6 ft (1.8 m) shorter than the Kennewick pylon, and the girder has a 2000 ft (610 m) vertical curve that is not symmetrical with the main span. Therefore, the cable-stay pairs are not of equal length, the longest being 506.43 ft (154 m).[19]

There is no attachment of the girder at the pylons, except for vertical neoprene-teflon bearings to accommodate transverse loads. The girder is supported only by the stay cables. There are, of course, vertical bearings at the approach piers and abutments. It is estimated that the natural frequency of the girder, where it will respond to dynamic acceleration (i.e., earthquake), is 2 cycles per second. If the situation occurs where the longitudinal acceleration exceeds this value, the vertical restraint at the Pasco (north) abutment is designed to fail in direct shear, thus changing the structure frequency to 0.1 cycles per second, which renders the system insensitive to dynamic excitation. The three main spans were assembled from precast, prestressed concrete segments, while the approach spans were cast in place on falsework, Figures 9.39 and 9.40.

Deck segments were precast about 2 miles (3.2 km) downstream from the bridge site. Each segment weighs about 300 tons (272 mt) and is 27 ft (8.2 m) long, Figure 9.41. The segment has an 8 in. (0.2 m) thick roadway slab, supported by 9 in. (0.22 m) thick transverse beams on 9 ft (2.7 m) centers, and is joined along the exterior girder edges by a triangular box which serves the function of cable anchorage stress distribution through the girder body, Figure 9.42.[6] Each match-cast segment required approximately 145 yd³ (111m³) of concrete, continuously placed in a previously adopted sequence within six hours. After initial curing in the forms, the girder segments were wet cured for two weeks in the storage yard, air cured for an additional six months, prestressed transversely,

FIGURE 9.39. Pasco-Kennewick Intercity Bridge, precast segments in main spans (courtesy of Arvid Grant).

FIGURE 9.40. Pasco-Kennewick Intercity Bridge, approach spans cast in place on falsework (courtesy of Walter Bryant, FHWA Region 10).

FIGURE 9.41. Pasco-Kennewick Intercity Bridge, precast segments in casting yard (courtesy of Arvid Grant).

cleaned, repaired, completed, loaded on a barge, and transported to the structure site for installation in their final location. For possible unpredicted developments a shimming process was held in reserve for maintaining the assembled girder geometry correctness, but it was not used. There are no shims in the segmentally assembled, epoxy-joined prestressed concrete girder.[15,18,19] The sections were barged directly beneath their place in the bridge and hoisted into position, Figure 9.43. Fifty-eight precast bridge girder segments were required for the project.

The stays are arranged in two parallel planes with 72 stays in each plane—that is, 18 stays on each side of a pylon in each plane. They are held at each pylon top, 180 ft (55 m) above the bridge roadway, in a steel weldment, Figure 9.44. Stay anchorages in the bridge deck are spaced at 27 ft (8.2 m) to correspond with the segment length. The stays are composed of $\frac{1}{4}$ in. (6 mm) diameter parallel high-strength steel wires of the BBR type. The prefabricated stays, manufactured by The Prescon Corporation, arrived on the job site on reels, Figure 9.45, and contained from 73 to 283 wires, depending upon their location in the structure. They were covered with a $\frac{3}{8}$ in. (10 mm) thick polyethylene pipe, and after installation and final adjustment were protected against corrosion by pressure-injected cement grout. The outside diameter of the pipe covering varies from 5 to 7 in. (0.12 to 0.17 m). Design stress level for the stays is 109 ksi (751.5 MPa). Stay anchorages are of the epoxy-steel ball (HiAmp) fatigue type produced by The Prescon Corporation.

This structure was designed by Arvid Grant and Associates, Inc., of Olympia, Washington, in professional collaboration with Leonhardt and Andra of Stuttgart, Germany.

9.8 Brotonne Bridge, France

The Pont de Brotonne, designed and built by Campenon Bernard of Paris, crosses the Seine River downstream from Rouen in France. Because of increased navigation traffic in the area, a second crossing over the Seine River was urgently needed between the two harbors of Le Havre and Rouen. The first one, the steel suspension bridge of Tancarville, was opened to traffic in 1959. The second, the Brotonne Bridge, the world's largest cable-stayed prestressed concrete bridge, was opened to traffic in June 1977.[20] A model of the structure is

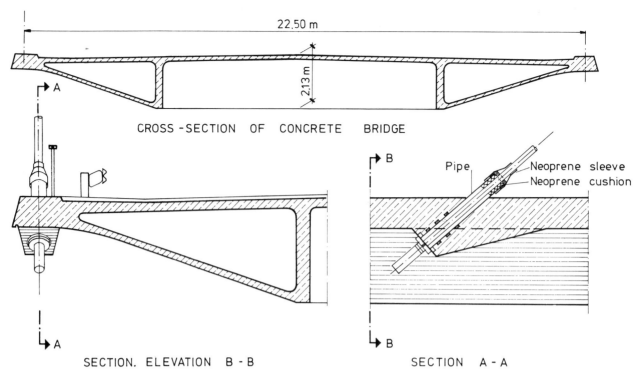

22,50 m

2.13 m

CROSS -SECTION OF CONCRETE BRIDGE

Pipe

Neoprene sleeve
Neoprene cushion

SECTION. ELEVATION B - B

SECTION A - A

FIGURE 9.42. Pasco-Kennewick Intercity Bridge, cross section and anchorage of stay cables (courtesy of Prof. Fritz Leonhardt).

FIGURE 9.43. Pasco-Kennewick Intercity Bridge, erection of precast segments from barge (courtesy of Arvid Grant).

FIGURE 9.44. Pasco-Kennewick Intercity Bridge, pylon and stay attachment steel weldment at top (courtesy of Arvid Grant).

FIGURE 9.45. Pasco-Kennewick Intercity Bridge, prefabricated cable stay on reel.

FIGURE 9.47. Artist's rendering of the Pont de Brotonne.

shown in Figure 9.46 and the general layout in Figures 9.47 and 9.48. The box girder carries four lanes and replaces ferry service between two major highways that run north and south of the Seine. Because large ships use this section of the river to approach the inland port of Rouen 22 miles (35 km) to the east, vertical navigation clearance is 164 ft (50 m) above water level, which results in a 6.5% grade for its longer approach.[15,21]

Total length of structure is 4194 ft (1,278.4 m), consisting of the main bridge and two approach viaducts. The main crossing has a span of 1050 ft (320 m). On the right bank, the transition between the main span and the ground is quite short because of a favorable topography where limestone strata slope upward to a relatively steep cliff. On the left bank, the terrain is flat and occupied by meadows. With an allowable maximum grade of 6.5% and a maximum height of fill of 50 ft (15 m), a nine-span viaduct was required to reach the main bridge. In a structural sense, the bridge is divided into two sections separated by an expansion joint at a point of contraflexure in the left-bank viaduct span adjacent to the cable-stayed side span, Figure 9.48.[20]

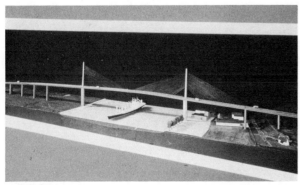

FIGURE 9.46. Model of the Pont de Brotonne.

The prestressed segmental concrete deck consists of a single-cell trapezoidal box girder with interior stiffening struts, Figures 9.49 and 9.50. In the approach spans, web thickness is increased from 8 in. (200 mm) to 16 in. (400 mm) near the piers, and the bottom flange thickness is increased to a maximum thickness of 17 in. (430 mm). The only portion of the segment that was precast is its sloping webs, Figure 9.51, which were precast at the site. The other portions of the cross section, including top and bottom flanges, interior stiffening struts, and cable-stay anchorages (in the main structure only), were cast in place. Each segment is 9.8 ft (3 m) long.

Extensive use of prestressing was made in the deck to provide adequate strength to this light structure. To resist the extreme shear stresses it was decided to place vertical prestressing in the webs. Pretensioned units were stressed on a casting bed, Figure 9.52, and equipped with specially designed button heads, thus producing a combination of pretensioning and anchorage plates. This system has the advantage of ensuring a perfect centering of the prestressing force together with a very rapid transfer of this force at both ends. Intensive rupture tests proved that an extremely high resistance to shear was created by this system.[20]

Finally, prestressing was also used as follows, Figure 9.53:[20]

1. Transversely in the top flange to provide flexural strength to the thin 8 in. (200 mm) slab.
2. In the inclined internal stiffeners, to accommodate tensile forces created by the transfer of loads from the box girder to the stays.

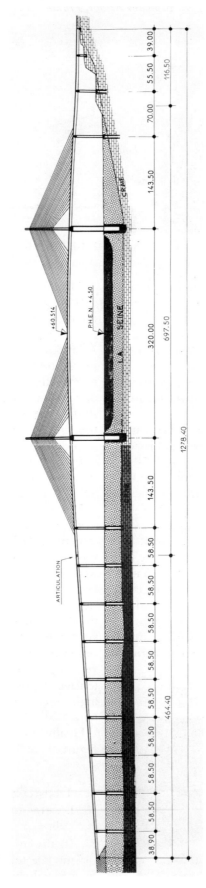

FIGURE 9.48. General layout of Brotonne Bridge.

422

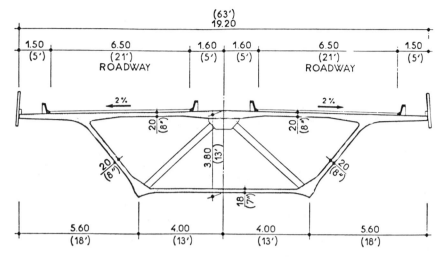

FIGURE 9.49. Cross section of Brotonne Bridge.

FIGURE 9.50. Interior view of deck, Brotonne Bridge.

FIGURE 9.51. Precast webs, Brotonne Bridge.

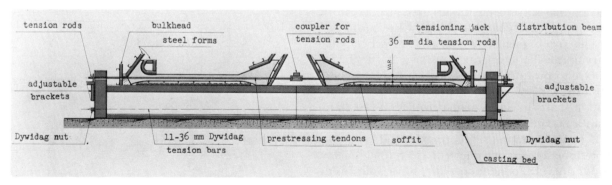

FIGURE 9.52. Casting bed for pretensioned webs.

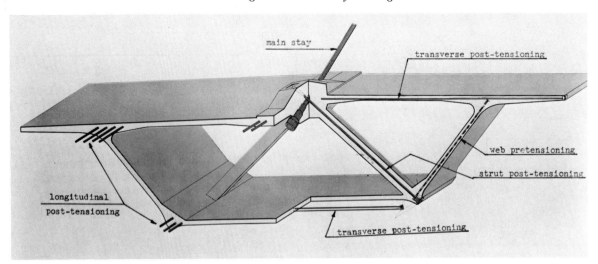

FIGURE 9.53. Various prestressing systems in the box girder.

3. Transversely in the bottom flange, to counteract tensile forces created by the stiffeners.

4. Longitudinally near the center of the main span, to allow for a reasonable margin of the order of 300 psi (2 MPa) of compressive stress in view of creep and secondary tensile stresses.

Before erection of the superstructure, the bridge's 12 approach piers were slip-formed, nine on the left bank and three on the right. The pier shafts have an octagonal curvilinear cross section inscribed inside a 13 by 29 ft (4.0 by 8.75 m) rectangle, Figure 9.54. The same section was used for all the approach-span piers, whose height varied from 40 to 160 ft (12 to 49 m). The shape of the piers did not substantially increase costs but did increase the aesthetic appeal of the piers. The piers bear through a reinforced concrete footing on four rectangular slurry trench walls used as piles with a maximum length of 60 ft (18 m), Figure 5.17.

The pylon pier shafts also have an octagonal curvilinear shape inscribed inside a 30 ft (9.2 m) square to produce equal bending resistance about both principal axes. They are supported on foundation shafts having a diameter of 35 ft (10.86 m) with a maximum wall thickness of 6 ft 8 in. (2.03 m). The foundation shafts transfer the loads to a limestone stratum at a depth of 115 ft (35 m) below ground level. Foundation shafts were built inside a circular slurry trench wall, which was used as a cofferdam for dewatering.[20]

When slip-forming of the piers reached deck level, the piers were prestressed to their foundation so as to stabilize them for erection of the deck segments. As the precast deck units were erected,

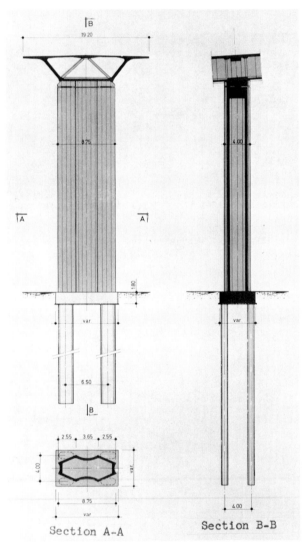

FIGURE 9.54. Pier and foundation of approach spans.

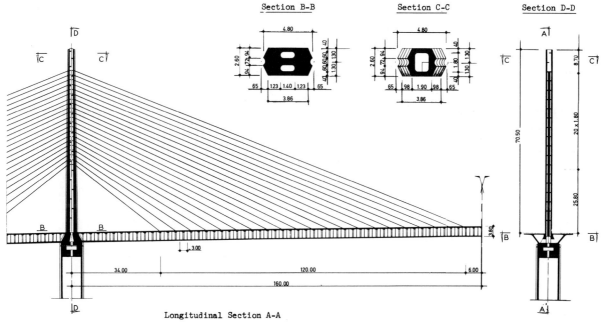

FIGURE 9.55. Half center span and pylon.

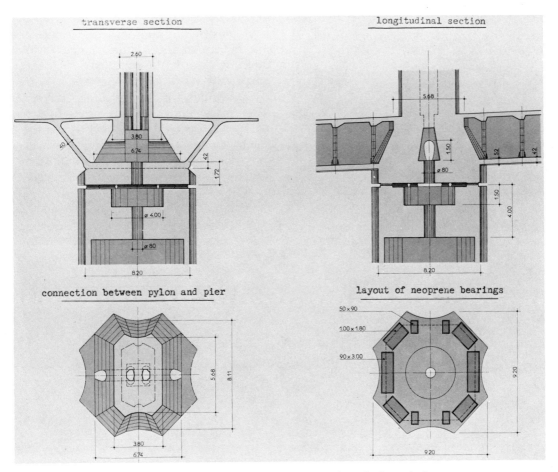

FIGURE 9.56. Connection between pylon, deck, and pier.

425

the pylon was constructed by conventional methods.

Two single-shaft pylons carry a system of 21 stays located on the longitudinal axis of the structure, Figure 9.55. The reinforced concrete pylons required limited cross-sectional dimensions to preclude an unnecessary increase of the deck width while providing sufficient dimension to accommodate bending stresses from a transverse wind direction. Total pylon height above the deck is 231 ft (70.5 m). Construction of the pylon required leapfrog forms with 10 ft (3 m) lifts. An interesting feature is the total fixity of the pylon with the box girder deck. Because the bending capacity of the pylon pier and foundation had to be such as to accommodate unsymmetrical loads due to the cantilever construction, a decision was made to take advantage of this requirement in the final structure to reduce the effect of live load in the deck. Therefore, the pylon was constructed integral with the deck at its base, both pylon and deck being separated from the pier by a ring of neoprene bearings, Figure 9.56.[20]

FIGURE 9.57. Cable-stay anchorage.

All deck loads are carried to the pylon piers by 21 stays on each pylon. Each stay consists of 39 to 60-0.6 in. (15 mm) strands encased in a steel pipe, which is grouted after final tensioning. Stay length varies from 275 to 1115 ft (84 to 340 m). Anchorage spacing of the stays at deck level is every 19.7 ft (6 m), every other segment, where the inclined stiffeners in the deck segments converge, Figures 9.53 and 9.57. A special deck anchorage block was designed to accommodate the variable number of strands in the stay as well as to allow full adjustment of the tension in the stays by a simple anchoring nut, Figure 9.58. The anchorage of the stays is such that it is possible at any time during the life of the structure to either readjust the tension in the stay or replace it without interrupting traffic on the bridge. Permanent jacks are incorporated into the anchorage, Figure 9.59, such that by tensioning the stay the adjusting nut can be slacked off. Stays are continuous through the pylon where they transfer load to the pylon by a steel saddle. The pipe wall thickness is increased near the anchorage points and near the pylon so as to improve fatigue resistance of the stays with regard to bending reversals.[20]

In constructing the deck girder, the operation was to extend the bottom flange form from a traveling form at the completed segment, placing the precast web units that form the basic shape and act as a guide for the remaining traveling form. After placement of the precast webs the interior steel form was jacked forward to cast the bottom flange struts and the top flange. Tower cranes at the pylon placed, as far as they could reach in both directions, the precast webs, Figure 9.60. Beyond the range of the tower cranes, gantry cranes running on rails on the top flange and extending 9.8 ft

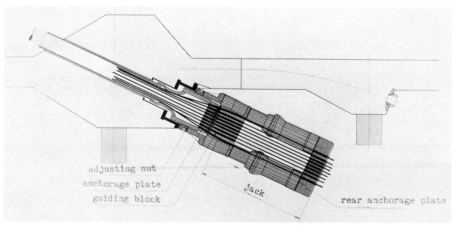

FIGURE 9.58. Jacking of stay.

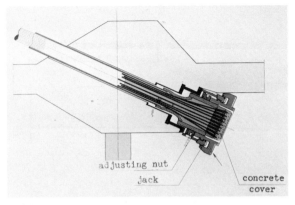

FIGURE 9.59. Permanent stay anchorage.

FIGURE 9.61. Start of main span construction, from reference 20.

FIGURE 9.60. Main pier, pylon, and deck during construction, from reference 20.

FIGURE 9.62. Before closure of main span, from reference 20.

FIGURE 9.63. Aerial view of the Brotonne Bridge, from reference 20.

(3 m) beyond the end of the completed section were used to place new elements.

The structure is shown at the start of main span construction in Figure 9.61, before closure of the main span in Figure 9.62, and completed in Figure 9.63.[20]

9.9 Danube Canal Bridge, Austria

This structure is located on the West Motorway (Vienna Airport Motorway) and crosses the Danube Canal at a skew of 45°. It has a 390 ft (119 m) center span and 182.7 ft (55.7 m) side spans,

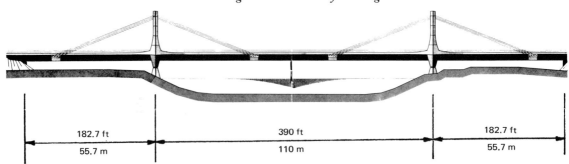

182.7 ft   390 ft   182.7 ft
55.7 m   110 m   55.7 m

FIGURE 9.64.   Elevation of the Danube Canal Bridge.

Figure 9.64. It is unique because of its construction technique. Because construction was not allowed to interfere with navigation on the canal, the structure was built in two 360.8 ft (110 m) halves on each bank and parallel to the canal, Figure 9.65. Upon completion the two halves were rotated into

FIGURE 9.65.   Construction of half-bridge on bank of canal.

final position and a cast-in-place closure joint was made, Figures 9.66 through 9.69. In other words, each half was constructed as a one-time swing span.

The bridge superstructure is a 51.8 ft (15.8 m) wide trapezoidal three-cell box girder, Figure 9.70. The central box was cast in 25 ft (7.6 m) long segments on falsework, Figure 9.71. After the precast inclined web segments were placed, Figure 9.72, the top slab was cast.

Each half-structure has two cantilever pylons fixed in a heavily prestressed trapezoidal crosshead protruding under the deck with a two-point bearing on the pier, Figure 9.73. At the deck level the stays attach to steel brackets connected to prestressed crossbeams, Figures 9.74 and 9.75.

Each stay consists of eight cables, two horizontal by four vertical. At the top of the pylons each cable is seated in a cast-iron saddle. The cable saddles are stacked four high, Figure 9.76, and are fixed to each other as well as to those in the adjacent plane. The cables were first laid out on the deck, fixed to a saddle, and then lifted by a crane for placement at the top of the pylon. The cables were then pulled

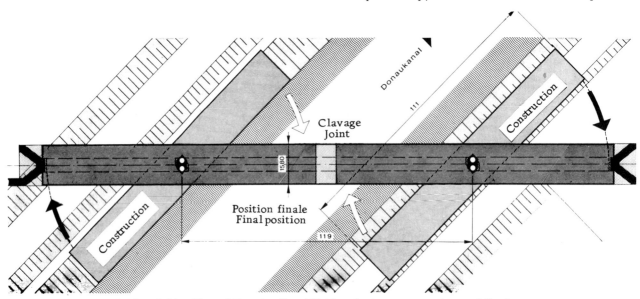

FIGURE 9.66.   Plan of Danube Canal Bridge during construction and final state.

FIGURE 9.67. Danube Canal Bridge during rotation.

FIGURE 9.69. Closure joint, Danube Canal Bridge.

FIGURE 9.68. Danube Canal Bridge during rotation.

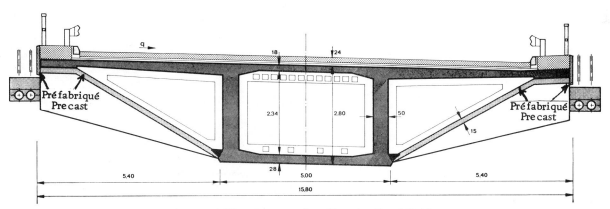

FIGURE 9.70. Cross section, Danube Canal Bridge.

at each extremity by a winch rope to their attachment point at the deck level.

During rotation of the two half-bridges, the deck and pylon sat on a bearing consisting of five epoxy-glued circular steel plates. The top plate was coated with teflon, sitting in turn on a reinforced concrete block that sat on a sand box. After rota-

tion the structure was lowered to permanent bearings by emptying the sand box.

At the canal-bank end the deck had a concrete wall on its underside, bearing on a circular concrete sliding track, Figure 9.77. The bearing between the wall and the track was effected by two concrete blocks clad with steel plates, under which

FIGURE 9.71. Construction on bank, Danube Canal Bridge.

FIGURE 9.72. Precast webs, Danube Canal Bridge.

FIGURE 9.73. Trapezoidal crosshead, Danube Canal Bridge.

teflon-coated neoprene pads were introduced during the rotation movement (similar to the incremental launching method). The pivoting was accomplished by means of a jack pulling on a cable anchored in a block located near the sliding-track end.

After rotation the two halves of the structure were connected by a cast-in-place closure joint, and continuity tendons were placed and stressed.[22] The final structure is shown in Figure 9.78.

9.10 Notable Examples of Concepts

9.10.1 PROPOSED GREAT BELT BRIDGE, DENMARK

The competition for a suitable bridge design in Denmark produced many new concepts and architectural styles. The design requirements specified three lanes for vehicular traffic in each direction and a single railway line in each direction.

FIGURE 9.74. Jacking of stays, Danube Canal Bridge.

The rail traffic was based on speeds of 100 mph (161 km/hr).[23] Navigational requirements stipulated that the bridge deck be 220 ft (67 m) above water level, and the clear width of the channel was to be 1130 ft (345 m).

A third prize winner in this competition was the Morandi-style design proposed by the English consulting firm of White Young and Partners, Figure

FIGURE 9.75. Cable-stay attachment, Danube Canal Bridge.

FIGURE 9.77. Circular concrete sliding track, Danube Canal Bridge.

FIGURE 9.76. Stay saddles at pylon, Danube Canal Bridge.

FIGURE 9.78. Completed Danube Canal Bridge.

9.7. This design embodied the principles of a cable-stayed bridge combined with conventional approaches of girders and piers with normal spans.

The principal feature of this bridge design is the three-plane alignment of cable stays. This feature may become more important in urban areas, where trends in the future may dictate multimodal transportation requirements and an increase in the number of automobile traffic lanes. The deck consists of two parallel single-cell prestressed concrete box girder segments, Figure 9.79. The rail traffic is supported within the box on the bottom flange and the road traffic is carried on the surface of the top flange.

The box girder contemplated a depth of 23.5 ft (7.2 m) and width of 27.75 ft (8.45 m) with the top flange cantilevered out 12 ft (3.7 m) on each side. The piers and towers were to be cast-in-place construction to support the deck segments, which were to be precast at various locations on shore and floated to the bridge site for erection. The maximum weight of a single box segment was estimated at 2200 tons (2000 mt). All segments of the superstructure were to be of reinforced and prestressed concrete.

Up to this point in time, when the competition for this structure was conducted, all the concrete cable-stayed bridges had been either designed by

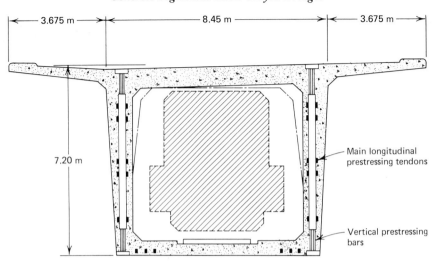

FIGURE 9.79. Danish Great Belt Bridge, section through deck beam at expansion and construction joint, from reference 23.

Morandi (Lake Maracaibo, Wadi Kuf, and so on) or strongly influenced by his style (Chaco/ Corrientes). They were typified, for the most part, by the transverse A-frame pylon with auxiliary X-frame support for the girder. However, an entry in the Danish Great Belt Competition by Ulrich Finsterwalder of the German firm of Dyckerhoff & Widmann deviated from this style and was awarded a second prize.

Finsterwalder proposed a multiple span, multistay system using Dywidag bars for the stays, Figure 9.10. This proposal contemplated a spacing between pylons of 1148 ft (350 m) and a spacing of the stays at deck level of 32.8 ft (10 m). Pylon height above water level was 520 ft (158.5 m). In a transverse cross section the deck was 146 (44.5 m) wide with two centrally located vertical stay planes 39 ft 4 in. (12 m) apart to accommodate the two rail traffic lanes, and three automobile traffic lanes in each direction outboard of the stay planes, Figure 9.80.

The solid concrete deck had a thickness of 3 ft (0.9 m) in the transverse center portion, under the rail traffic, and tapered to a 1.3 ft (0.4 m) thickness

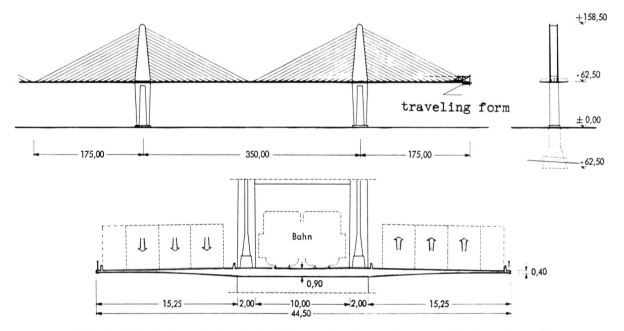

FIGURE 9.80. Danish Great Belt Bridge, elevation and cross section (courtesy of Dyckerhoff & Widmann).

at the edges. The deck was to be constructed by the cast-in-place balanced cantilever segmental method, each segment being supported by a set of stays.

9.10.2 PROPOSED DAME POINT BRIDGE, U.S.A.

The proposed Dame Point Bridge over the St. Johns River in Jacksonville, Florida, as designed by the firm of Howard Needles Tammen & Bergendoff, is a cable-stayed structure with a concrete and a steel alternative. An artist's rendering of the concrete cable-stayed bridge alternative is shown in Figure 9.81. Navigation requirements dictate a 1250 ft (381 m) minimum horizontal opening and a vertical clearance of 152 ft (46.3 m) above mean high water at the centerline of the clear opening. The proposed concrete cable-stayed main structure will have a 1300 ft (396 m) central

span with 650 ft (198 m) flanking spans. The layout of the main structure is shown in Figure 9.82.[24]

Structural arrangement of the bridge deck is shown in Figure 9.83. The bridge deck, which will carry three lanes of traffic in each direction, will span between longitudinal edge girders on each side. The longitudinal edge girder is in turn supported by a vertical plane of stays arranged in a harp configuration. The concrete deck and edge girders take local and overall bending from dead and live load in addition to the horizontal thrust from the stays.[25] The stay cables are anchored in massive vertical concrete pylons, two at each main pier, which carry all loads to the foundations, Figure 9.84.

In the center span, at each edge of the deck, the stays are in a single plane spaced 30 in. (0.76 m) vertically, Figures 9.84 and 9.85. Stays in the side spans, along each edge, are in two planes spaced 30 in. (0.76 m) transversely. Spacing of pairs of stays along the edge beam is approximately 30 ft (9.1 m). Preliminary design contemplates 7 to 9 Dywidag bars per stay, 1¼ in. (31.75 mm) in diameter, the number of bars per stay being a function of stress in the stay. The Dywidag bars are to be encased in a metal duct. During erection the fabricated length of duct is left uncoupled. After final adjustment the lengths of duct are coupled and pressure-grouted. Thus, the steel encasing tube will then be composite for live load and secondary dead load.[25]

Construction proceeds by conventional methods from the top of the pier bases at elevation 15.0 ft (4.6 m) to the level of the roadway at elevation 144.6 ft (44 m). At this point, a fixed formtable is secured and the first elements of the pylon and edge girders are cast. Erection of the deck is by the

FIGURE 9.81. Dame Point Bridge, artist's rendering (courtesy of Howard Needles Tammen & Bergendoff).

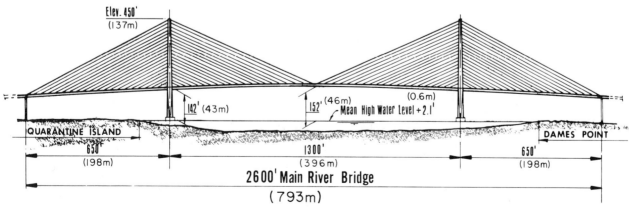

FIGURE 9.82. Dame Point Bridge, concrete cable-stayed alternative, from reference 24 (courtesy of Howard Needles Tammen & Bergendoff).

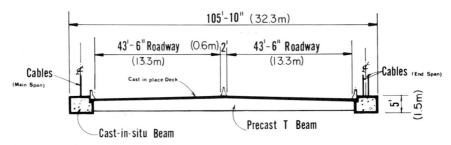

FIGURE 9.83. Dame Point Bridge, structural arrangement of bridge deck, from reference 24 (courtesy of Howard Needles Tammen & Bergendoff).

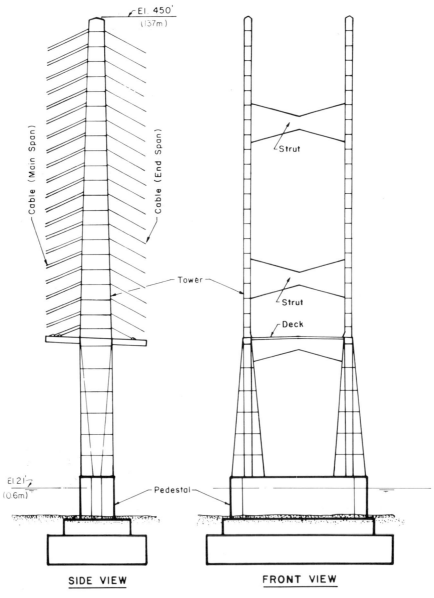

FIGURE 9.84. Dame Point Bridge, pylon arrangment, from reference 24 (courtesy of Howard Needles Tammen & Bergendoff).

PLATE 17

ISOMETRIC VIEW OF ERECTION SEQUENCE

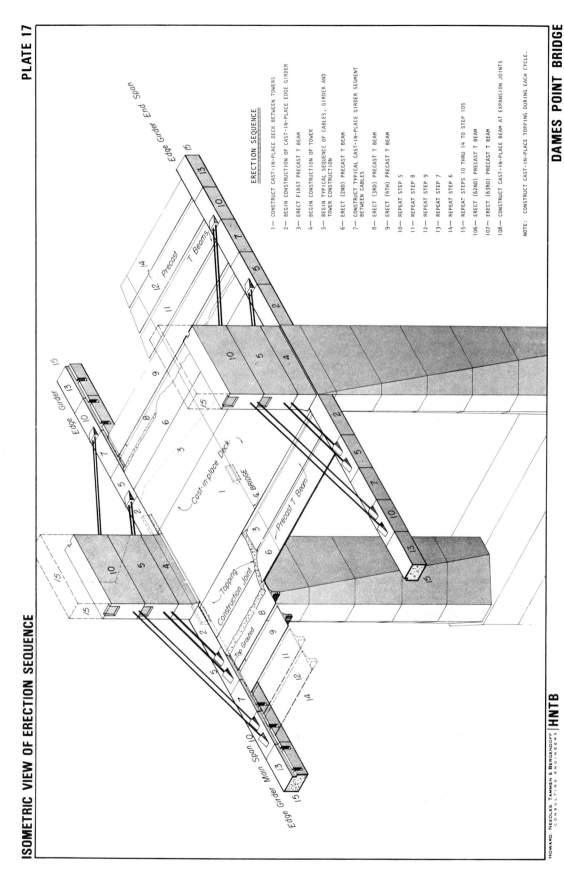

ERECTION SEQUENCE

1— CONSTRUCT CAST-IN-PLACE DECK BETWEEN TOWERS
2— BEGIN CONSTRUCTION OF CAST-IN-PLACE EDGE GIRDER
3— ERECT FIRST PRECAST T BEAM
4— BEGIN CONSTRUCTION OF TOWER
5— BEGIN TYPICAL SEQUENCE OF CABLES, GIRDER AND TOWER CONSTRUCTION
6— ERECT (2ND) PRECAST T BEAM
7— CONSTRUCT TYPICAL CAST-IN-PLACE GIRDER SEGMENT BETWEEN CABLES
8— ERECT (3RD) PRECAST T BEAM
9— ERECT (4TH) PRECAST T BEAM
10— REPEAT STEP 5
11— REPEAT STEP 8
12— REPEAT STEP 9
13— REPEAT STEP 7
14— REPEAT STEP 6
15— REPEAT STEPS 10 THRU 14 TO STEP 105
106— ERECT (62ND) PRECAST T BEAM
107— ERECT (63RD) PRECAST T BEAM
108— CONSTRUCT CAST-IN-PLACE BEAM AT EXPANSION JOINTS

NOTE: CONSTRUCT CAST-IN-PLACE TOPPING DURING EACH CYCLE.

DAMES POINT BRIDGE

HOWARD NEEDLES, TAMMEN & BERGENDOFF | **HNTB**
CONSULTING ENGINEERS

FIGURE 9.85. Dame Point Bridge, superstructure configuration, from reference 25 (courtesy of Howard Needles Tammen & Bergendoff).

balanced cantilever method. Two pairs of traveling forms are then used for sequential casting of 17.5 ft (5.3 m) lengths of edge girders on each side of the pylon. The bridge deck consists of single-T precast floor beams spanning between longitudinal edge girders and a cast-in-place topping. The precast T's are pretensioned for erection loads. After erection the entire deck is post-tensioned to provide positive precompression between edge girders under all conditions of loading, Figure 9.85.[24,25]

A hinge expansion joint is provided at the centerline of the main span to allow for changes of superstructure length due to temperature, creep, and shrinkage. Similar joints are provided at the end piers, and link connections are used to prevent vertical movement of the superstructure.

9.10.3   PROPOSED RUCK-A-CHUCKY BRIDGE, U.S.A.

The site for the proposed Ruck-A-Chucky Bridge designed by T. Y. Lin International, Figure 9.86, is approximately 10 miles (16 km) north of the proposed Auburn Dam and about 35 miles (56 km) northeast of Sacramento, California, crossing the middle fork of the American River. The river at this location is about 30 ft (9 m) deep and 100 ft (30.5 m) wide; however, upon impounding of the water behind the proposed dam, the river will become 450 ft (137 m) deep and 1100 ft (335 m) wide.[26]

In order to provide a 50 ft (15 m) vertical clearance above high reservoir water level, a bridge length of 1300 ft (396 m) will be required between the hillsides, which rise at a 40° angle from the horizontal. Two existing roads parallel the canyon faces; a straight bridge across the river would require extensive cuts into the rock faces of the canyon to provide the necessary turning radius at the bridge approaches. This would be not only expensive but would also be damaging to the environment. Conventional piers in the river provide prohibitive design constraints, not only because of the 450 ft (137 m) water depth, but also because of the seismicity of the area. The hydroseismic (seiche effect) forces provide a formidable design load.

After extensive studies, the proposed final solution was that of a hanging arc, Figures 9.87 and 9.88. The geometric configuration of this structure is such that the stays are tensioned to control the stresses and strains, in order to balance all the dead load with zero deflection; the curved girder carries the traffic and absorbs the horizontal component of the stays as axial compression. The stays are anchored on the slope according to the design formation to control the line of pressure in the girder. Thus, an ideal stress condition is achieved with almost no bending or torsional moments. After numerous studies and trade-offs a final radius of curvature was selected at 1500 ft (457 m).[26]

Two alternative designs have been prepared for this structure, one with a steel box girder and one with a lightweight concrete box girder. The concrete box girder, Figure 9.89, is fixed at the abutments and has no hinges or expansion joints in the 1300 ft (396 m) span. Depth of this box girder is 8.5 ft (2.6 m), so as to provide vertical stiffness and to distribute live load and construction loads on the deck to a sufficient number of adjoining cables. Stay anchorage at the girder is at 30 ft (9 m) intervals, based on construction and aesthetic considerations.[26]

FIGURE 9.86.   Ruck-A-Chucky Bridge, artist's rendering (courtesy of T. Y. Lin).

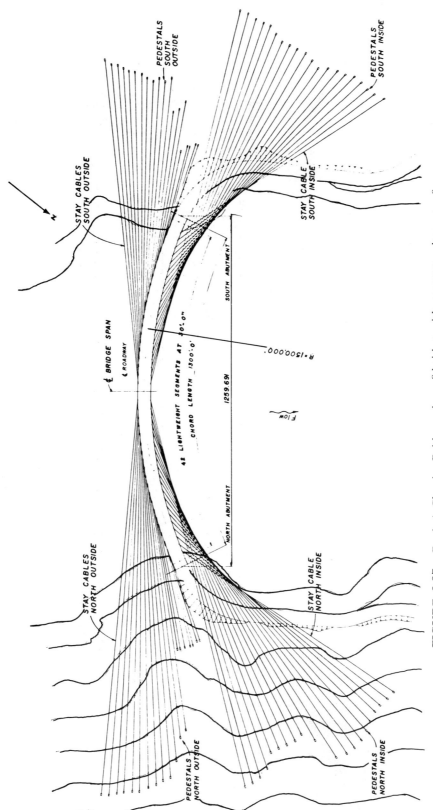

FIGURE 9.87. Ruck-A-Chucky Bridge, plan of bridge with concrete alternate, from reference 26.

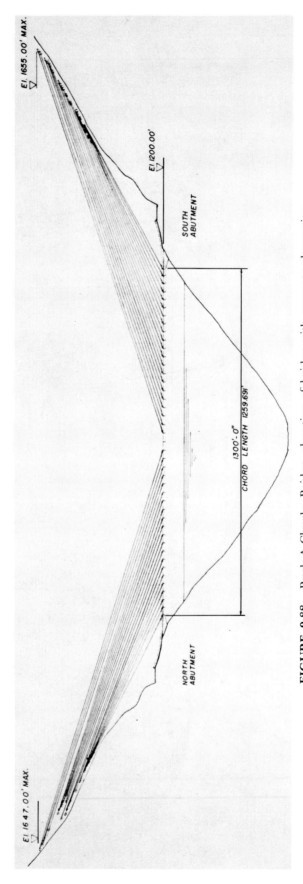

FIGURE 9.88. Ruck-A-Chucky Bridge, elevation of bridge with concrete alternative, from reference 26.

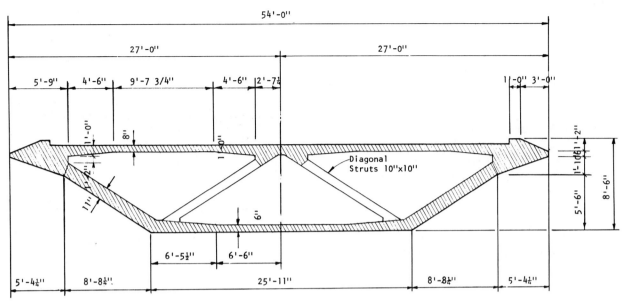

FIGURE 9.89. Ruck-A-Chucky Bridge, cross section of concrete box girder alternative, from reference 26.

References

1. A. Feige, "The Evolution of German Cable-Stayed Bridges—An Overall Survey," *Acier-Stahl-Steel,* No. 12, December 1966 (reprinted in *AISC Engineering Journal,* July 1967).

2. H. Thul, "Cable-Stayed Bridges in Germany," *Proceedings, Conference on Structural Steelwork, Institution of Civil Engineers, September 26 to 28, 1966, London.*

3. W. Podolny, Jr., and J. F. Fleming, "Historical Development of Cable-Stayed Bridges," *Journal of the Structural Division, ASCE,* Vol. 98, No. ST9, September 1972.

4. W. Podolny, Jr., and J. B. Scalzi, "Construction and Design of Cable-Stayed Bridges," John Wiley & Sons, Inc., New York, 1976.

5. M. S. Troitsky, "Cable-Stayed Bridges—Theory and Design," Crosby Lockwood Staples, London, 1977.

6. F. Leonhardt, "Latest Developments of Cable-Stayed Bridges for Long Spans," *Saetryk af Bygoningsstatiske Meddelelser,* Vol. 45, No. 4, 1974 Denmark).

7. E. Torroja, *Philosophy of Structures,* English version by J. J. Polivka and Milos Polivka, University of California Press, Berkeley and Los Angeles, 1958.

8. H. M. Hadley, "Tied-Cantilever Bridge—Pioneer Structure in U.S.," *Civil Engineering, ASCE,* January 1958.

9. F. Leonhardt and W. Zellner, "Vergleiche zwischen Hängbrücken und Schrägkabelbrücken für Spannweiten über 600 m," *International Association for Bridge and Structural Engineering,* Vol. 32, 1972.

10. R. Morandi, "Some Types of Tied Bridges in Prestressed Concrete," First International Symposium, Concrete Bridge Design, ACI Publication SP23, Paper 23-25, American Concrete Institute, Detroit, 1969.

11. Anon., *The Bridge Spanning Lake Maracaibo in Venezuela,* Wiesbaden, Berlin, Bauverlag GmbH., 1963.

12. Anon., "Longest Concrete Cable-Stayed Span Cantilevered over Tough Terrain," *Engineering News-Record,* July 15, 1971.

13. N. Gray, "Chaco/Corrientes Bridge in Argentina," *Municipal Engineers Journal,* Paper No. 380, Vol. 59, Fourth Quarter, 1973.

14. H. B. Rothman, and F. K. Chang, "Longest Precast-Concrete Box-Girder Bridge in Western Hemisphere," *Civil Engineering, ASCE,* March 1974.

15. W. Podolny, Jr., "Concrete Cable-Stayed Bridges," Transportation Research Record 665, Bridge Engineering, Vol. 2, *Proceedings, Transportation Research Board Conference, September 25–27, 1978, St. Louis, Mo.,* National Academy of Sciences, Washington, D.C.

16. H. Schambeck, "The Construction of the Main Bridge-Hoechst to the Design of the 365 m Span Rhein Bridge Dusseldorf-Flehe," Cable-Stayed Bridges, Structural Engineering Series No. 4, June 1978, Bridge Division, Federal Highway Administration, Washington, D.C.

17. Anon., "Tiel Bridge," *Freyssinet International, STUP Bulletin,* March-April 1973.

18. Arvid Grant, "Pasco-Kennewick Bridge—The

Longest Cable-Stayed Bridge in North America," *Civil Engineering, ASCE,* Vol. 47, No. 8, August 1977.

19. Arvid Grant, "Intercity Bridge: A Concrete Ribbon over the Columbia River, Washington," Cable-Stayed Bridges, Structural Engineering Series No. 4, June 1978, Bridge Division, Federal Highway Administration, Washington, D.C.

20. C. Lenglet, "Brotonne Bridge: Longest Prestressed Concrete Cable Stayed Bridge," Cable-Stayed Bridges, Structural Engineering Series No. 4, June 1978, Bridge Division, Federal Highway Administration, Washington, D.C.

21. Anon., "Cable-Stayed Bridge Goes to a Record with Hybrid Girder Design," *Engineering News-Record,* October 28, 1976.

22. Anon., "The Danube Canal Bridge (Austria),"

Freyssinet International, STUP Bulletin, May–June, 1975.

23. Anon., "Morandi-Style Design Allows Constant Suspended Spans," *Consulting Engineer* (London), March 1967.

24. H. J. Graham, "Dame Point Bridge," Cable-Stayed Bridges, Structural Engineering Series No. 4, June 1978, Bridge Division, Federal Highway Administration, Washington, D.C.

25. Anon., "Dame Point Bridge," Design Report, Howard Needles Tammen & Bergendoff, November 1976.

26. T. Y. Lin, Y. C. Yang, H. K. Lu, and C. M. Redfield, "Design of Ruck-A-Chucky Bridge," Cable-Stayed Bridges, Structural Engineering Series No. 4, June 1978, Bridge Division, Federal Highway Administration, Washington, D.C.

10

Segmental Railway Bridges

10.1 Introduction to Particular Aspects of Railway Bridges and Field of Application

Construction of segmental post-tensioned bridges for railway structures started in France in 1952 with a bridge crossing the Rhone River at La Voulte, Figure 10.1. It has been used extensively since that time in many countries. Precast segmental construction was introduced in railway structures in France with the Marne la Vallee Viaduct and in Japan with the Kakogawa Bridge, while incremental launching was adopted for several large railway crossings including the world's longest bridge of this type: the Olifant's River Bridge in South Africa (see Section 7.5).

The major characteristic distinguishing railway bridges from highway bridges is the magnitude and application of loading. Live loading on a railway structure is two to four times larger than that applied to a highway bridge of comparable size. Every time a train crosses a railway bridge, the actual load applied to the structure is much closer to design live load than for a highway bridge, where even dense truck traffic usually represents only a moderate proportion of the design load. Fatigue and durability of railway structures, therefore, are essential problems and need careful consideration, particularly in view of the fact that maintenance and repair of railway structures under permanent

FIGURE 10.1. La Voulte Bridge, view of the completed structure.

441

traffic is a very critical operation that can lead to unacceptable disturbance in a railway network.

10.2 La Voulte Bridge over the Rhone River, France

This first segmental prestressed concrete railway bridge is a notable structure and a landmark in the development of prestressed concrete. Constructed in 1952, it carries one railway track over the Rhone River near la Voulte, 80 miles (128 km) south of Lyons, in the southeastern part of France.

The structure has five spans, each 164 ft (50 m) long. Each pier is made up of two inclined legs, and each span is an independent frame supported by an inclined leg at each end. Between the inclined legs on each pier, the deck is supported by a small beam resting on simple bearings.

Construction proceeded using the cantilever scheme, with poured-in-place segments. The form travelers were supported by a temporary steel truss bridge, Figure 10.2. The cantilevers were built symmetrically in one span, the unbalanced moments being taken care of by temporary post-tensioning connecting the two inclined legs and the independent beam on one pier. The segments were 9 ft (2.75 m) long. The bending moments of each completed frame were adjusted by jacks placed at midspan and by continuity post-tensioning tendons, Figure 10.3.

10.3 Morand Bridge in Lyons, France

This structure is a combined highway and mass-transit bridge over the Rhone River in Lyons,

FIGURE 10.3. La Voulte Bridge, cantilever deck construction in progress.

France's third largest city. It is a three-span continuous structure with span lengths of 160, 292, and 160 ft (49, 89, and 49 m), resting on two river piers and two end abutments, which allow the transition of highway and railway traffic on both banks. The deck is made up of two parallel box girders carrying at the upper level three lanes of highway traffic including sidewalks. Inside each box girder is a railway track for the mass-transit system, Figure 10.4.

This final scheme proved to be significantly less expensive and more efficient in terms of the layout of the railway system than did the initial proposal, which contemplated a submerged tunnel for the railway crossing and a separate bridge for the highway traffic.

Dimensions of the structure in cross section are shown in Figure 10.5. The railway clearance of 13 ft 5 in. (4.12 m), including ballast and rail, calls for a 15 ft (4.56 m) structural height in excess of the normal requirements for a maximum span length of 292 ft (89 m). A constant-depth girder could thus be maintained throughout the river crossing except in the vicinity of the river piers, where short straight haunches allow the depth to be increased to 22 ft 7 in. (6.90 m). Over the piers a strong transverse diaphragm connects the two box girders, and the additional height over the pier allows the continuity of the diaphragm over the height of the haunch while the full clearance of the trains is maintained inside the box girders.

The deck was built in balanced cantilever with 10 ft (3.0 m) long cast-in-place segments using one pair of travelers on a typical one-week cycle, Figures 10.6 and 10.7.

Typical quantities of materials are as follows for the deck alone:

FIGURE 10.2. La Voulte Bridge, aerial view of the deck under construction.

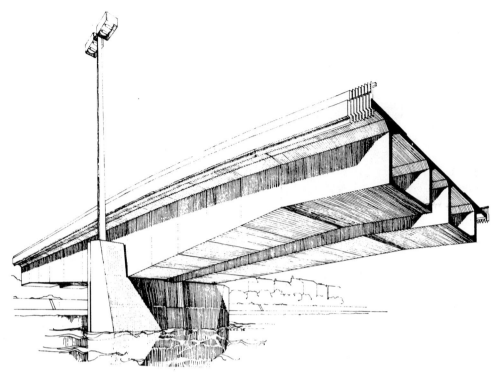

FIGURE 10.4.   Morand Bridge, perspective view of the structure.

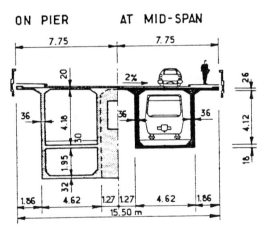

FIGURE 10.5.   Morand Bridge, typical cross section.

FIGURE 10.6.   Morand Bridge, construction of the superstructure.

Deck area	31,200 ft²	2,900 m²
Concrete	3,100 yd³	2,400 m³
Reinforcing steel	618,000 lb	280,000 kg
Prestressing steel (longitudinal and transverse)	256,000 lb	116,000 kg

Both concrete and reinforcing steel quantities far exceed those required for a typical highway because of the very important increase of loads due to the railway lines in the box girders.

The structure was completed and opened to traffic in 1977.

FIGURE 10.7. Morand Bridge, construction of superstructure. Note pier segment for second parallel box girder.

10.4   *Cergy-Pontoise Bridge near Paris, France*

A new railway line was completed in 1977 between Paris and the new satellite town of Cergy-Pontoise. A major prestressed concrete structure carries this line over several obstacles, including an interchange between two expressways (A-86 and A-14) and two branches of the Seine River.

The trestle structures have a solid slab deck with spans varying between 65 ft (20 m) and 117 ft (35.60 m). Typical dimensions of the two main bridges over the Seine are shown in Figure 10.8. A single box carries the twin tracks, with the depth varying between 13.6 ft (4.15 m) and 17.9 ft (5.45 m) for the maximum span length of 280 ft (85 m) as shown in Figures 10.9 and 10.10. The segmental deck was cast in place, with travelers working in the conventional balanced cantilever fashion.

10.5   *Marne la Vallee and Torcy Bridges for the New Express Line near Paris, France*

The extension of the Paris mass-transit system in the highly populated southeastern suburbs was the occasion for building a long elevated segmental prestressed concrete railway structure in a sensitive urban environment, Figure 10.11. This structure, located in the city of Marne la Vallee, includes a bridge over the Marne River and a long viaduct carrying two parallel railway tracks. Near the transition between the river bridge and the viaduct a passenger station is carried by the bridge structure.

Three major considerations guided the choice of the structure:

Maintain maximum clearance at ground level, not only to reduce the visual disturbance to the neighboring population, but also to allow all piers of the new structure to be fully compatible with the layout of all existing and future roads.

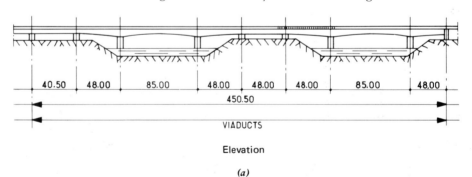

Elevation

(a)

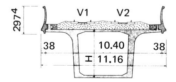

Typical cross section

(b)

FIGURE 10.8.   Cergy-Pontoise Bridge, dimensions. (*a*) Elevation. (*b*) Typical cross section.

FIGURE 10.9. Cergy-Pontoise Bridge, cantilever construction.

FIGURE 10.11. Marne la Vallee Bridge, aerial view of the completed structure.

FIGURE 10.10. Cergy-Pontoise Bridge, main span closure.

FIGURE 10.12. Marne la Vallee Bridge, view of finished structure from ground level.

Produce a structure that is aesthetically pleasing when seen constantly from nearby.

Protect the neighboring population from unacceptable noise aggression.

Basically, the structure is a single box of constant depth built of precast segments assembled by prestress into a continuous beam; the beam rests upon vertical piers provided with an architectural shape and regularly distributed at distances of 90 ft (27 m) to 120 ft (36 m), Figure 10.12.

Both parallel tracks are laid on the transversely prestressed deck slab of the box girder and on a crushed-stone bed retained sideways by three continuous reinforced concrete walls. A central noise barrier separates the two opposite tracks and prevents the noise of a train riding one track to travel across to the other. At the edge of the concrete box girder, precast concrete panels manufactured with special white cement improve the appearance of the structure while providing the outside sound barriers.

In plan, the structure is laid out on a curve with a minimum radius of curvature of 1640 ft (500 m), Figure 10.11. Characteristic dimensions of the Marne la Vallee Viaduct are shown in Figures 10.13 and 10.14 and are summarized as follows:

1. Bridge over the Marne River:
    a. Total length, 528 ft (161 m).
    b. Three-span continuous bridge with spans of 157, 246, and 125 ft (48, 75, and 38 m).
    c. Cross section: constant-depth box section with depth of 12.8 ft (3.90 m), web thickness varying from 20 to 35 in. (0.50 to 0.90 m) and bottom flange thickness from 7 in. (0.18 m) at midspan to 51 in. (1.30 m) over the river piers. Length of precast segments 5.6 ft (1.71 m).
    d. Two river piers are founded on large-diameter bored piles and support the superstructure through special teflon bearings.

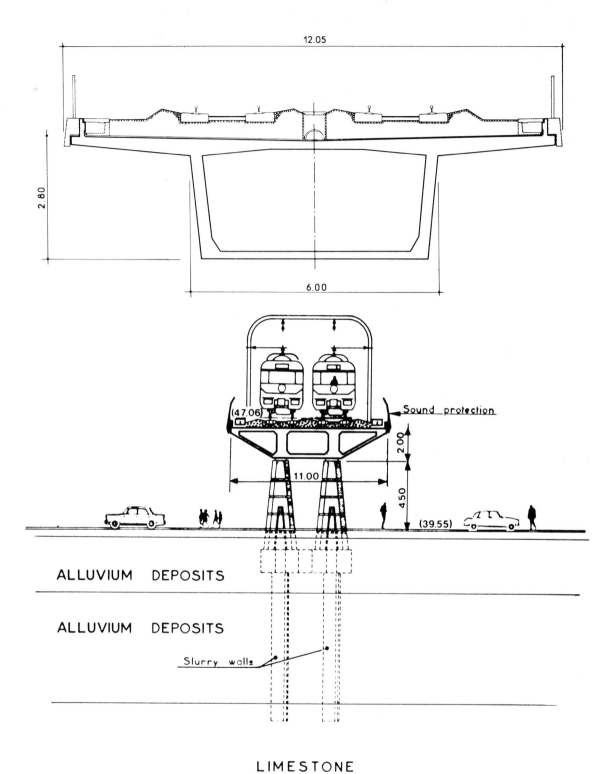

FIGURE 10.13. Marne la Vallee Bridge, typical sections of deck and piers.

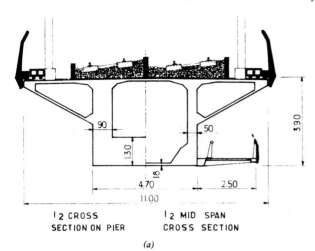

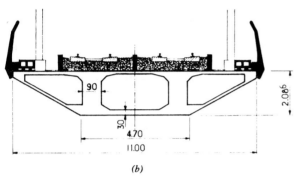

FIGURE 10.14. Marne la Vallee and Torcy Viaduct, typical deck sections. (*a*) Marne la Vallee trestle and Torcy Viaduct cross section. (*b*) Marne la Vallee Bridge over the Marne River.

2. Elevated viaduct:

a. Total length, 4482 ft (1367 m).

b. The viaduct is divided into 11 sections separated by expansion joints, allowing compatibility of thermal stress between the continuous welded rails and the concrete superstructure. The typical section is 412 ft (126 m) long with four spans of 88, 118, 118, and 88 ft (27, 36, 36, and 27 m).

c. The two south viaduct sections adjacent to the main river crossing carry the passenger station and have shorter spans 69 and 92 ft (21 and 28 m).

d. Typical cross section is a single box carrying the two tracks with two main vertical webs 35 in. (0.90 m) thick and two sharply inclined facia webs used essentially for architectural purposes to reduce the apparent structural depth of the box and focus the eye on the high parapet wall.

e. Average length of precast segments 7.5 ft (2.30 m).

f. All bearings in the viaduct are standard laminated elastomeric pads.

g. Piers are made of twin columns located under the webs of the box girder and connected at ground level by a common footing, which transfers the loads to deep slurry trenched walls anchored in limestone. The number and position of these bearing walls under each pier has been determined in relation to the magnitude of the transverse and longitudinal horizontal loads transferred by the superstructure, particularly in the curved portion of the viaduct.

The entire project was predicated on the use of precast segments with match casting and epoxy joints. A precasting yard on the south bank of the Marne, using four casting machines, produced the 690 segments with a maximum weight of 60 tons (55 mt) in eleven months. Segments were transported with a tire-mounted self-propelled carrier over the finished portion of the deck and placed in the structure with a launching gantry, Figure 10.15, in balanced cantilever. The gantry used on that project was that designed and built earlier for the B-3 Viaducts project.

The gantry allowed all operations to be performed from the top in complete independence from the ground and all its related constraints. Placing of all segments was performed in a period of nine months between March and December of 1976, including the three spans of the main bridge and the forty-four spans of the viaduct. The entire project was completed in 24 months (including preparation of the final design), for a total deck area of 190,000 ft² (17,600 m²). Figure 10.16 shows

FIGURE 10.15. Marne la Vallee Bridge, precast segments placed with the launching gantry.

FIGURE 10.16.   Marne la Vallee Bridge, crossing the Marne River and elevated passenger station.

FIGURE 10.17.   Marne la Vallee Bridge, aerial view of the river crossing, a passenger station, and the elevated viaduct.

the northern span of the river crossing and the elevated passenger station. Figure 10.17 is an aerial view of the overall project.

In view of the success of this first application of segmental construction in urban railway elevated structures, the Paris Mass-Transit Authority decided to extend the same concept to construct another large structure a few miles eastward: the Torcy Viaduct. Fortunately, the precasting yard for the first bridge was still available and all segments could be manufactured there and trucked to the second bridge site, Figure 10.18.

Dimensions of this new bridge are as follows:

Cross section: exactly the same as for the Marne la Vallee elevated viaduct.

Distribution of spans: 17 spans with typical span length of 115 ft (35 m).

FIGURE 10.18.   Torcy Viaduct, segment transportation from Marne la Vallee to Torcy.

The total length of 1870 ft (570 m) is divided into three separate sections: one four-span unit, one nine-span unit, and one four-span unit.

Precast segments were placed in the structure with an overhead launching gantry of a type slightly different from the one used previously, although calling on the same sequence of movements. Two parallel longitudinal trusses make the track for a transverse overhead portal crane carrying and placing the segments between the trusses. Figures 10.19 and 10.20 show the general view of the gantry and the detail of one segment placing. The overall view of the finished bridge appears in Figure 10.21.

FIGURE 10.19.   Torcy Viaduct, precast segment placing with launching gantry.

FIGURE 10.20. Torcy Viaduct, detail of segment handling between twin trusses of launching gantry.

FIGURE 10.21. Torcy Viaduct, view of the completed structure.

10.6 Clichy Railway Bridge near Paris, France

At about the same time the two structures described above were built, a large and innovative railway bridge was constructed in the northeastern suburb of Paris for another extension of the reno-vated metro. It crosses the Seine River adjacent to a new highway bridge between the cities of Clichy and Asnieres, as shown in Figure 10.22. Layout and principal dimensions appear in Figures 10.23 and 10.24.

The prestressed concrete segmental structure is 1350 ft (412 m) long with a 280 ft (85 m) main span over the river with a deck of variable depth. The river piers of the two railway and highway bridges match exactly to minimize water flow and barge traffic disturbance. A provision is made for a second future highway bridge at the other side of the railway bridge, as seen clearly in Figure 10.25*a*.

The restricted transverse clearances between the three structures and their corresponding traffic explains the special shape of the piers for the center railway bridge, which was carefully studied architecturally to enhance the appearance of the project. Foundations were very close to one another but could be maintained structurally independent to better control settlement and avoid vibration interference between bridges and in the ground.

To carry the two railway tracks, the deck has a typical cross section consisting of three precast webs connected by a bottom slab, which forms essentially the compression flange over the piers, and an intermediate slab, which receives the ballast, Figures 10.25*b* and 10.26. The depression thus realized between the web top flange and the tracks has several advantages, including providing full safety against derailing on one track and reducing the noise level.

Construction of the superstructure included match casting of all webs in a yard near the project site. The webs were placed in balanced cantilever with a light portal crane carried by the finished

FIGURE 10.22. Clichy Railway Bridge, view of the completed structure.

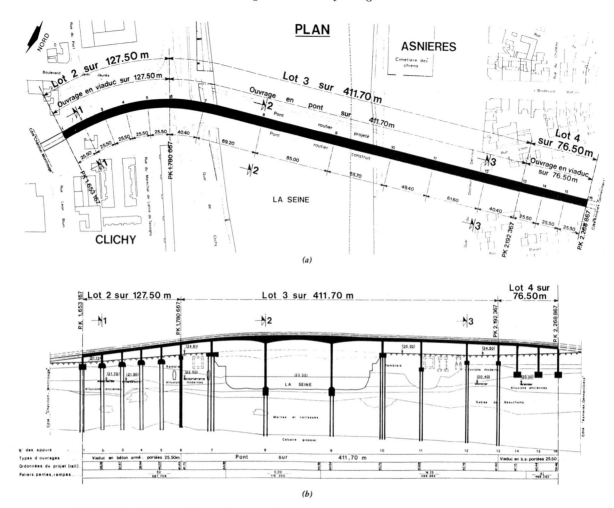

FIGURE 10.23. Clichy Railway Bridge, layout and elevation of the structure. (*a*) Plan view. (*b*) Elevation.

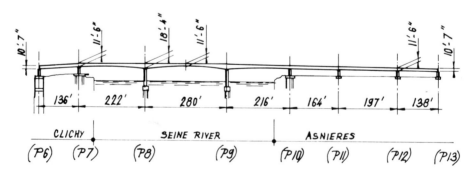

FIGURE 10.24. Clichy Railway Bridge, main dimensions of segmental structure.

portion of the deck, Figure 10.27. Maximum weight of precast webs was 19 tons (17 mt), whereas segments that included the full three-web box (or even a more conventional single box for the equivalent span length) would have weighed in excess of 66 tons (60 mt). After assembly of precast webs with longitudinal post-tensioning, the two twin slab sections were poured in place between the webs in balanced cantilever on very simple travelers. Web segments were 7.3 ft (2.22 m) long for the constant-depth part of the deck and 4.8 ft (1.48 m) for the variable-depth part. In fact, the slabs were cast in place between the three webs in two or three increments of that length respectively (a length of

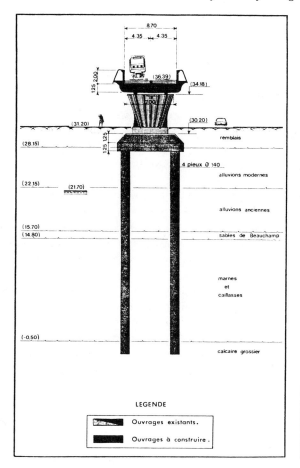

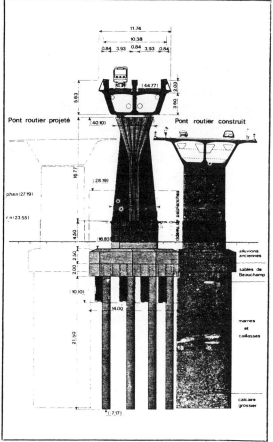

(a)

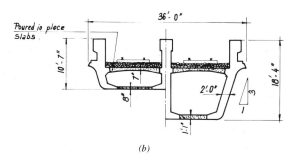

(b)

FIGURE 10.25. Clichy Railway Bridge, typical sections of piers and deck. (*a*) Elevation of land and river piers. (*b*) Dimensions of the deck cross section.

14.6 or 4.44 m) to reduce the number of site operations. A three-day cycle of operations could be constantly maintained, including some overtime work for the larger segments near the river piers. Overall, construction in cantilever of the total superstructure took one year between September 1977 and September 1978.

A special design aspect, specific to railway bridges, was the transfer of horizontal loads (in-

FIGURE 10.26. Clichy Railway Bridge, pier segment and cantilever construction.

duced through braking or starting of the trains over the bridge), to the piers and foundations. A single fixed bearing was provided over pier P6, the foundation of which was designed to transfer to

FIGURE 10.27. Clichy Railway Bridge, placing precast webs for cantilever construction.

the limestone stratum the total maximum horizontal load of 660 tons (600 mt) applied to the bridge. There are three pot bearings between the deck and the pier shaft, each capable of safely transferring half of the maximum horizontal load. Each bearing can thus be changed under traffic without reducing the capacity of the structure.

Special provisions were also included at the design stage, Figure 10.28, to allow additional prestressing to be incorporated in the structure should

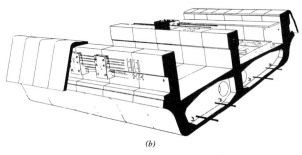

(b)

FIGURE 10.28. Clichy Railway Bridge. (a) View of adjacent highway and railway bridges crossing the Seine River. (b) Provisions for future additional prestress.

the need arise in the future. Two families of tendons could be added:

Above the lower slab in the two voids of the box section, anchors being provided in blisters already built in the structure.

Atop the center precast web and on the outside face of the two facia webs, anchor blocks and deviation saddles being prestressed by high-strength bolts to the precast webs.

The large precast architectural panels on both sides of the deck could be temporarily removed to allow this work of additional prestressing to be performed. Upon completion, all additional tendons would be fully protected and concealed behind the panels.

The new line has been open to traffic since May 1980, and the first months of operation confirm that the precautions taken to reduce noise and vibration disturbance through welded continuous rails and sound-barrier panels make such elevated structures an acceptable solution for mass-transit lines in urbanized areas.

10.7 Olifant's River Bridge, South Africa

This structure is part of a line carrying iron ore on special heavy trains 7500 ft (2300 m) long made up of 200 cars with a total weight of 19,000 tons (17,000 mt) to connect the Sishen mines to the harbour of Saldanha 110 miles north of Capetown. Olifant's River Viaduct is today the world's longest incrementally launched prestressed concrete structure (refer to Chapter 7) with a total length of 3400 ft (1035 m) and 23 spans of 148 ft (45 m), Figure 10.29.

Shown in cross section in Figure 10.29, the single box girder deck accommodates only one track on ballast. The equivalent uniform live load of the 33 ton (30 mt) axles is 7.1 kips/lineal ft (10.5 mt/lm), which is increased by an impact factor of 1.29.

The 23 spans are divided into two 11-span sections, each anchored to the end abutment, and one single transition span at the center. This scheme allows all horizontal loads to be transferred to the abutments. The maximum horizontal reaction including all thermal effects is in excess of 1200 tons (1100 mt). The piers, which vary between 80 ft (25 m) and 150 ft (55 m) in height, are extremely flexible and do not, therefore, have an important effect on the horizontal restraint of the structure, except during construction. The pier shafts have an I-

(a)

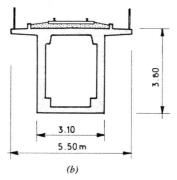

3.80

3.10

5.50 m

(b)

FIGURE 10.29. Olifant's River Viaduct. (*a*) General view of the structure. (*b*) Typical cross section.

shaped cross section with longitudinally tapered faces. Neoprene bearings are used for the piers near the abutments and teflon sliding bearings in the center of the structure.

The deck was entirely constructed behind one abutment (see schematic view in Figure 7.29) and incrementally launched in one direction. Construction time for the superstructure was nine months, with a theoretical cycle of 10 working days for a typical 148 ft (45 m) span realized after 10 spans; it was further reduced to seven days with two shifts toward the end of the project. The total weight of the superstructure of 14,500 tons (13,000 mt) called for two 200 ton jacks for the push-out operations in increments of 3.5 ft (1.00 m). A 60 ft (18 m) long launching nose was used in front of the first span to reduce the variation of bending stresses in the superstructure during the successive stages of construction, Figure 10.30. The bridge nearing completion is shown in Figure 10.31; it was opened to iron ore trains in 1976.

10.8 Incrementally Launched Railway Bridges for the High-Speed Line, Paris to Lyons, France

To meet increased competition by domestic airlines, the French National Railways decided to

FIGURE 10.30. Olifant's River Viaduct, launching nose reaching beyond a high pier.

build some new very-high-speed train lines (safe maximum speed of 200 mph or 320 km/hr) and started the construction of the first such line between Paris and Lyons, which included an entirely new structure over a distance of 250 miles (400 km) with proper connections to the existing metropolitan track and station system.

The new project required 400 bridges including nine large viaducts, such as the structure shown in Figure 10.32. A very comprehensive optimization study followed, and a set of guidelines and structural standards were prepared for the French National Railways by a team of engineers headed by one of the authors. Results of the preliminary investigations and of this optimization study can be summarized as follows:

1. Track alignment is chosen to keep the curvature in plan more than 10,500 ft (3200 m) and preferably more than 13,000 ft (4000 m). The

FIGURE 10.31. Olifant's River Viaduct, view of the structure nearing completion.

FIGURE 10.32. Railway Viaducts for Paris-Lyons high-speed line, view of the viaduct over the Saone River.

corresponding cross fall between rails is 7 in. (180 mm).

2. All rails are to be continuously welded and placed on a ballast bed with a minimum thickness of 14 in. (0.35 m).

3. Maximum rigidity of the structures is obtained by using a continuous box section with slenderness ratio of 1/14. The corresponding

maximum deflection under design load is therefore 1/2000 of the span, whereas conventional specifications for normal-speed lines allow up to 1/800.

4. Adopt as much as possible single box girder decks for the two parallel tracks with minimum web thickness of 14 in. (0.35 m) and a minimum top slab thickness of 10 in. (0.25 m).

5. The optimum span length is between 150 and 170 ft (45 to 50 m), which leaves the construction method open to various solutions (cantilever, span-by-span or incremental launching).

6. The horizontal loads should be transferred to one abutment equipped with a special fixed bearing, allowing all piers to be relieved of any appreciable longitudinal bending. A typical H-section was adopted as the most appropriate except for certain specific locations where a box section might be required.

Because many of the viaducts were located in environmentally sensitive areas, an overall architectural study was also conducted to establish a unity of appearance for all bridges in terms of the shapes of deck and piers, parapet or guard rails, abutments and approach fills.

Of the nine viaducts, two were finally constructed with conventional methods and the remaining seven were incrementally launched. This method proved economical in view of the moderate span lengths, the depth of the box section available, and especially because the superimposed dead and live loads were so much more important than for a highway bridge that the increased dead-load moments during construction were in proportion of much less significance.

Table 10.1 gives the essential characteristics of the seven segmental viaducts, including principal quantities of materials for the superstructure. Elevations of five bridges appear in Figure 10.33.

As an example of the construction method, some details are given for the bridge over the Saone River, where a launching nose 93 ft (28.50 m) long and weighing 71 tons (65 mt) was used in front of the first span to reduce the stress variations in the superstructure during launching, Figure 10.34.

The bridge superstructure was cast in successive increments in a fixed location behind the right bank abutment in the length of a half-span, Figure 10.35. A typical sequence of operations is shown schematically in Figure 10.36. Each superstructure section is in fact cast in two stages

Table 10.1. Characteristics of Segmental Viaducts on the Paris-Lyons High-Speed Line

Bridge Location and Span Lengths [ft (m)][a]	Bridge Layout	Dimensions of Deck [ft or in. (m)]							Pier Height [ft (m)]	Quantities of Deck			Year Completed
		Bridge Length	Total Width (ft) (m)	Height (ft) (m)	Box Width (ft) (m)	Web Thick. (in.)	Flange Thick. Top (in.)	Flange Thick. Bottom (in.)		Concr. [ft³/ft²] (m³/m²)	H.T. Steel [lb/yd³] (kg/m³)	Reinf. Steel [lb/yd³] (kg/m³)	
⑥ Saulieu 115 – 3 @ 144 – 115 (35 – 3 @ 44 – 35)	Long. grade: 1.3% Radius in plan: 20,000 ft (6000 m)	662 (202)	41.0 (12.50)	10.8 (3.30)	18.0 (5.50)	18/49 (0.45/1.25)	11 (0.275)	10 (0.25)	46/121 (14/37)	2.52 (0.77)	78 (46)	240 (140)	1978
② Serein 115 – 3 @ 144 – 115 (35 – 3 @ 44 – 35)	Long. grade: 0.95% Radius in plan: 26,000 ft (8000 m)	662 (202)	41.0 (12.50)	10.8 (3.30)	18.0 (5.50)	18/49 (0.45/1.25)	11 (0.275)	10 (0.25)	66/148 (20/45)	2.52 (0.77)	78 (46)	240 (140)	1979
⑦ Saone River 155 – 5 @ 164 – 137 (47.2 – 5 @ 50 – 41.8)	Circular profile in elevation: R = 130,000 ft (40,000 m)	1112 (339)	40.3 (12.30)	11.5 (3.51)	18.0 (5.50)	20 (0.50)	12.5 (0.32)	12.5 (0.32)	46 (14)	2.46 (0.75)	84 (50)	210 (125)	1979
④ Digoine 109 – 8 @ 144 – 109 (33.4 – 8 @ 44 – 33.4)	Long. grade: 2.5% Straight in plan	1370 (419)	39.0 (11.90)	10.8 (3.30)	18.0 (5.50)	24 (0.60)	12.5 (0.32)	14 (0.35)	43/105 (13/32)	2.30 (0.70)	84 (50)	250 (150)	1978
⑥ Roche 108 – 7 @ 149 – 108 (33.1 – 7 @ 45.5 – 33.1)	Long. grade: 3.5% Radius in plan: 10,600 ft (3250 m)	1260 (385)	39.0 (11.90)	10.8 (3.30)	18.0 (5.50)	24 (0.60)	12.5 (0.32)	14 (0.35)	43/115 (13/35)	2.30 (0.70)	84 (50)	250 (150)	1978
① Seine River 114 – 201 – 114 (34.8 – 61.4 – 34.8)	Long. grade: 0.55% Straight in plan	429 (131)	41.0 (12.50)	13.1 (4.00)	19.0 (5.80)	24/35 (0.60/0.90)	11 (0.28)	12/20 (0.30/0.50)	36 (11)	—	84 (50)	190 (110)	1980
⑤ Center Canal (length) 85 – 105 – 85 (26 – 32 – 27)	Long. grade: 0.2% Straight in plan	279 (85)	40.0 (12.10)	7.8 (2.37)	19.0 (5.80)	12 (0.30)	10 (0.25)	8 (0.20)	43 (13)	—	—	—	1978

[a]Structures are numbered with increasing numbers from Paris to Lyons.

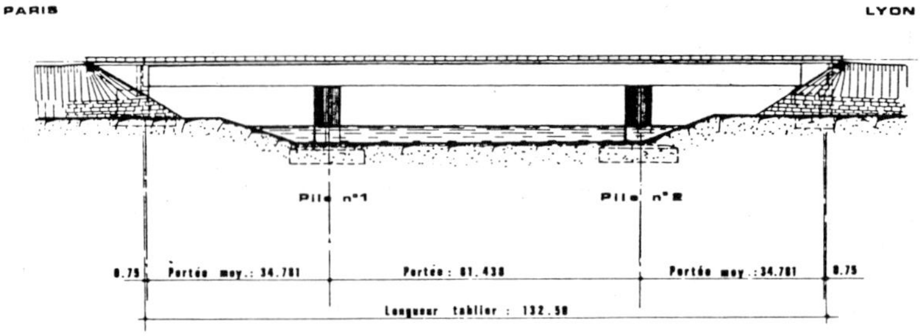

PARIS   LYON

Viaduc sur la Seine.

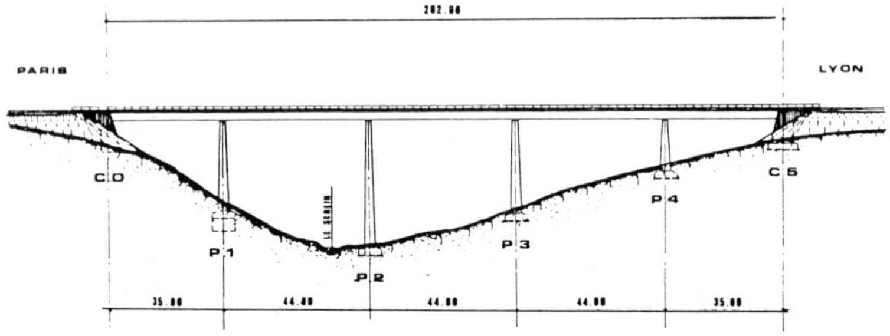

Viaduc du Serrein.

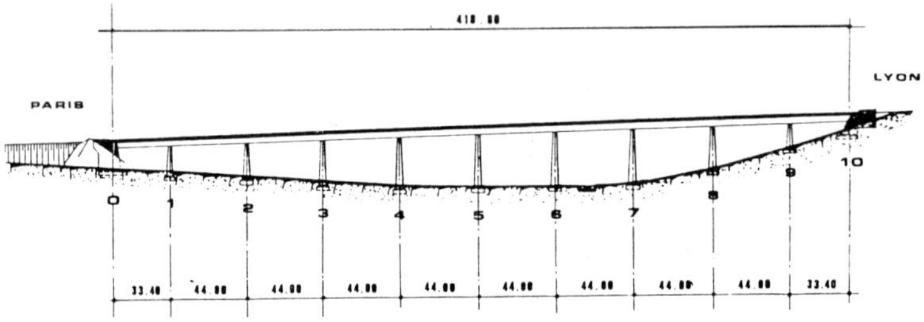

Viaduc de la Digoine.

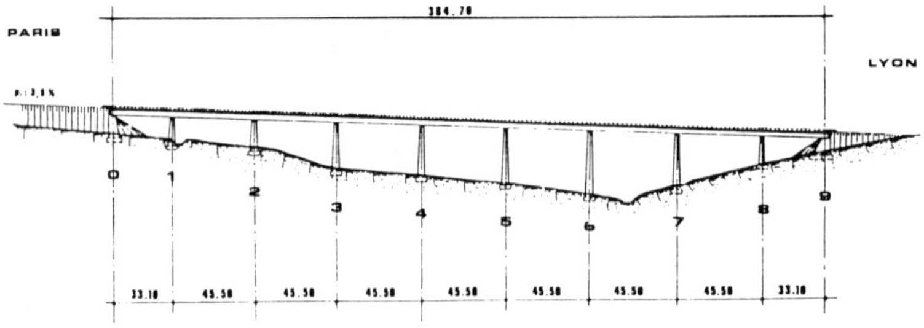

Viaduc de la Roche.

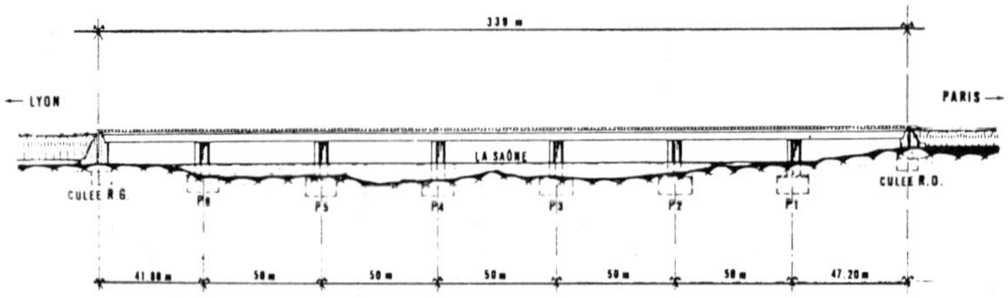

Viaduc sur la Saône.

FIGURE 10.33. Elevation of five segmental bridges for Paris-Lyons line.

456

FIGURE 10.34. Saone River Bridge, launching nose approaching pier.

FIGURE 10.35. Saone River Bridge, aerial view with casting yard in behind abutment in foreground.

(bottom slab during the first stage, webs and top slab during the second stage). The typical construction cycle allowed casting a half-span every week—that is, constructing two spans per month.

The launching operation proper called for a very efficient system, developed and perfected previously in Germany, including under each web of the box section:

One vertical jack with sliding plate

Two coupled horizontal jacks for actual launching, allowing movements in 3 ft increments

Typically, launching of an 80 ft section took three to three and a half hours, despite the large weight of the concrete superstructure, reaching 9000 tons (8000 mt) at the end of construction.

Figure 10.37 shows a completed structure, and Figure 10.38 shows another aspect of the construction of these seven viaducts.

10.9 Segmental Railway Bridges in Japan

Many railroad bridges have been built in Japan using the segmental construction technique. The sketches shown in Figures 10.39 through 10.42 depict the elevation and the cross section of the following cast-in-place segmental bridges:

Kyobashigawa Bridge

Natorigawa Bridge

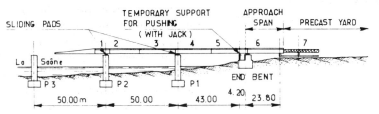

SITUATION DURING FABRICATION OF SEGMENT 7

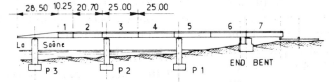

SITUATION AFTER PUSHING OF SEGMENT 7

GENERAL PRINCIPLE OF THE CONSTRUCTION METHOD BY PUSHING

FIGURE 10.36. Saone River Bridge, typical construction stages of incremental launching.

FIGURE 10.37. Saone River Bridge, view of the completed structure.

FIGURE 10.38. Digoine Bridge, incremental launching over high piers.

Kisogawa Bridge

Ashidagawa Bridge

Figure 10.43 shows the Kakogawa Bridge during construction. The superstructure is made of twin constant-depth box girders, one box girder carrying one railway track. The total length of the bridge is 1640 ft (500 m), with typical span length of 180 ft (55 m). Each box is 13 ft (4 m) wide and 11.5 ft (.3.50 m) deep. The precast segments were handled by a launching gantry and assembled by longitudinal post-tensioning tendons. The erection used the balanced cantilever system.

The most outstanding prestressed concrete railway structure, however, is the Akayagawa arch bridge shown in Figure 10.44. Total length is 980 ft (298 m) and the center arch span is 410 ft (126 m). The 13 ft (4.00 m) deep box girder carrying two railway tracks is continued throughout between abutments and rests over the center gorge on a very flat arch rib through ten spandrel columns. The respective proportions are such that the deck carries all bending moments and the arch rib carries the normal load induced by its curvature. The erection scheme was unique and called for cantilever construction starting from both sides.

A very strong back stay made up of a prestressed concrete member with a prestress force of 5300 tons (4800 mt) was installed diagonally between the top of the main transition piers between the arch structure and the approaches on one hand, and the foundation of the adjacent piers in the approach structures on the other hand.

While erection progressed, high-strength steel bars were placed diagonally between the vertical members, forming a temporary truss structure until the crown was reached from both ends. Control of tensioning of those steel bars was very critical and complicated. Finally, all steel bars and the two temporary back stays were removed after closure of the arch at midspan.

10.10   Special Design Aspects of Segmental Railway Bridges

10.10.1   MAGNITUDE OF VERTICAL LOADS

Most bridges carry tracks laid on ballast with a minimum thickness of 10 to 14 in. (0.25 to 0.35 m).

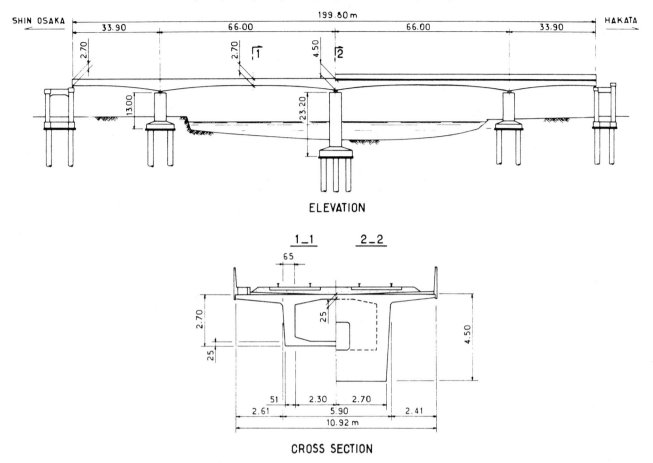

FIGURE 10.39. Hyobashigawa Bridge, Japan.

Live loading used in design of railway bridges varies between countries—Cooper loading for Anglo-Saxon countries, new UIC loading for most European countries—and also according to the nature of the structure: mass-transit lines are usually designed for much lighter loads than normal train lines. The heaviest loadings are for ore freight trains.

To exemplify the basic difference between a highway and a railway bridge, Figure 10.45 compares a typical 150 ft span and a 36 ft wide deck normally designed for three highway lanes of traffic or two railway tracks. The total superimposed dead and live load is 3.6 times greater for the railway bridge. In addition, the weight of ballast (representing 40% of the total load) must be considered as a live load to cover the cases where the ballast is removed from the deck or has not yet been placed on a new bridge.

10.10.2   HORIZONTAL FORCES

Railway bridges have to carry very important horizontal forces, between five and ten times the horizontal forces carried by a highway bridge of similar size. The standard current practice for long viaducts is to have a fixed bearing on one abutment if the bridge length is less than 1500 ft (450 m), and on both abutments and on intermediate special bents if it is greater. The order of magnitude of this horizontal force on the abutments carrying the fixed bearings is often 1000 tons for a two-track viaduct.

The various forces involved are described below:

Longitudinal Forces

Braking and acceleration forces

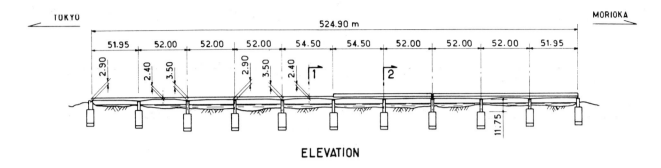

ELEVATION

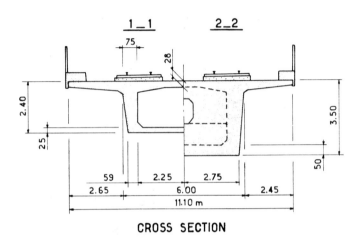

CROSS SECTION

FIGURE 10.40.   Natorigawa Bridge, Japan.

Forces due to box girder deformations: creep, shrinkage, and temperature variations

Loads induced by the length variations of long welded rails under temperature variations

Longitudinal component of wind forces

Braking and acceleration forces are one-seventh of the total weight of live loads, with a ceiling of 285 tons for braking and 53 tons for acceleration (French regulations).

Forces due to longitudinal deformations of the box girder vary because of creep, shrinkage, and temperature variations. The bearing displacements induce horizontal loads by distortion or friction.

Length variations of the long welded rails due to temperature variations create a horizontal force parallel to the rail. This force can be estimated at 50 tons per rail (length of rail more than 100 meters). For a two-track bridge it is $2 \times 2 \times 50 = 200$ tons.

Longitudinal component of wind forces are described in the AASHTO specifications for bridges.

Transverse Horizontal Forces   Centrifugal horizontal force can be very important for high-speed trains. For the 200 mph train from Paris to Lyons this force is more than 400 tons for some viaducts 1200 ft (380 m) long with two tracks and radius of curvature of 10,500 ft (3200 m). The lateral acceleration is more than 20% of that of gravity.

Transverse wind force is described in the AASHTO standards (50 lb/ft²).

10.10.3   BEARINGS

In order to gain complete control of these very large horizontal forces, the bearings are specially designed to take care of the vertical loads and rotation of the box girder and simultaneously to provide all possible horizontal restraints (fixed bearing, bearing free lengthwise or crosswise, or both).

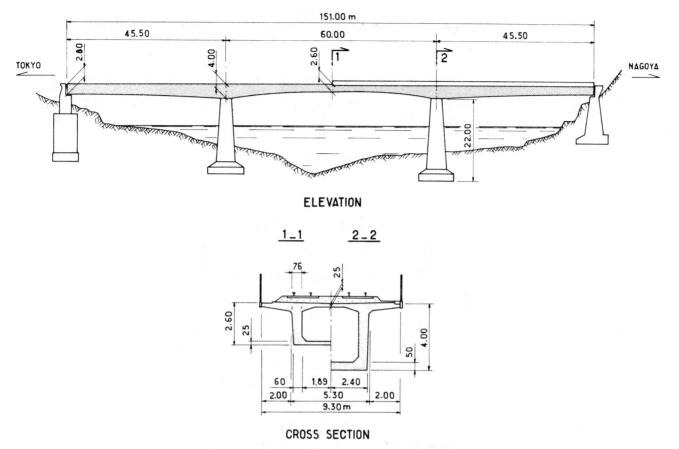

FIGURE 10.41. Kisogawa Bridge, Japan.

These bearings are specially manufactured for this type of structure, Figures 10.46 and 10.47. The sliding parts consist of a teflon-coated plate resting on a stainless steel plate, and the restraints are provided by steel keys.

10.10.4 STRAY CURRENTS

For structures carrying electrified railways there is some uncertainty about the long-term effect of stray currents generated near the power lines. In order to preclude electrolytic corrosion of reinforcing steel and prestressing steel, the following precautions are now taken in prestressed concrete structures:

The deck is electrically isolated from the ground, piers, and abutments by elastomeric plates.

The reinforcing and prestressing steel systems of the entire deck are interconnected by mild steel bars to equalize the electric potential. The dif-

ference of potential with the ground may be measured at regular intervals, and a permanent connection with the ground may be decided on as a result.

10.10.5 DURABILITY OF THE STRUCTURE

Because very difficult problems of train traffic would arise during repairs to these bridges, their durability needs special attention. The following provisions were established for the high-speed bridges between Paris and Lyons:

Under the worst service loads the concrete must remain under a 140 psi minimum compression.

For continuous bridges, the design shall be checked by weighing the dead-load vertical force on the bearings.

The stressing force of the post-tensioning tendons shall be less than 80% of the ultimate strength of the tendons.

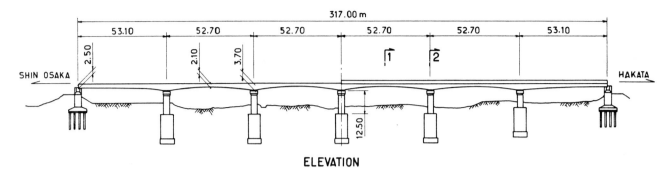

ELEVATION

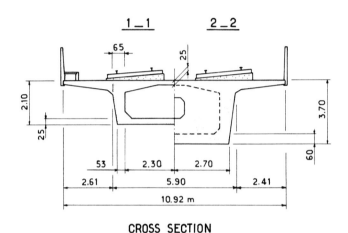

CROSS SECTION

FIGURE 10.42. Ashidagawa Bridge, Japan.

FIGURE 10.43. Kakogawa Railway Bridge, placing precast segments with launching gantry.

The ultimate strength of the structure should be capable of supporting the service loads increased by 30%, if 30% of the post-tensioning steel were missing.

Provisions shall be made for installing additional tendons while the structure is under traffic. The additional post-tensioning force shall be 15% of the designed force minimum.

It shall be possible to replace all the bearings.

10.10.6   CONCLUSION

This review of specific design problems of railway bridges should raise no doubts whatsoever about the advantages of prestressed concrete and segmental construction in this field. Prestressed concrete is the safest material known today to resist indefinitely the large variations of loads such as those applied to a railway bridge.

The problem of fatigue has been covered briefly in Chapter 4, and the results mentioned there apply particularly well to railway bridges. The main objective in the design and construction of prestressed concrete bridges should be to minimize and even eliminate concrete cracking, which is always a source of weakness in a structure subject to cyclic loading.

The use of the provisions laid down in Section 10.10.5 should result in practically crack-free structures with an expected life free of major maintenance.

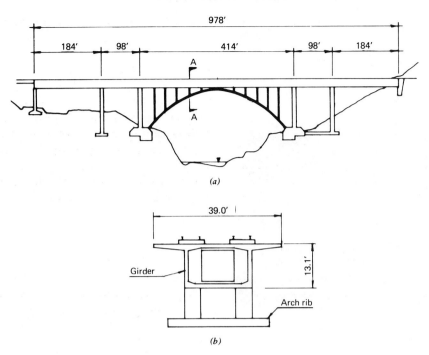

FIGURE 10.44. Akayagawa Railway Bridge, general dimensions. (*a*) Elevation. (*b*) Typical cross section A-A.

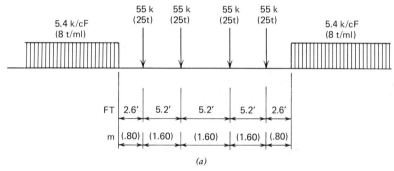

Description	Highway Bridge		Railway Bridge	
Span length	150 ft (45 m)		150 ft (45 m)	
Deck width	36 ft (11 m)		36 ft (11 m)	
Number of lanes or tracks	Three lanes		Two tracks	
Superimposed dead load:				
Ballast	—		6.5 kips/ft	
Curb, pavement, etc.	1.5 kips/ft		0.5 kips/ft	
Total S.L.		1.5 kips/ft		7.0 kips/ft
Live loads:				
Equivalent uniform load	2.4 kips/ft		6.8 kips/ft	
Impact factor	18%		30%	
Total L.L.		2.8 kips/ft		8.8 kips/ft
Total (S.L. + L.L.)		4.3 kips/ft		15.8 kips/ft

FIGURE 10.45. Vertical loading on railway bridges. (*a*) Typical UIC - track loading. (*b*) Comparison of superimposed dead and live loading on highway and railway bridges.

FIGURE 10.46. Detail of pot bearing with unidirectional horizontal movement.

FIGURE 10.47. Detail of fixed bearing.

10.11 Proposed Concepts for Future Segmental Railway Bridges

We should note that many types of structures described for highway bridges are equally appropriate for railway bridges: the structures described in this chapter were essentially girder or arch bridges built in cantilever or incrementally launched.

Today, many design projects are based on stayed bridges. As an example, Figure 10.48 shows a proposed crossing of the Caroni River in Venzuela for heavy iron ore freight trains.

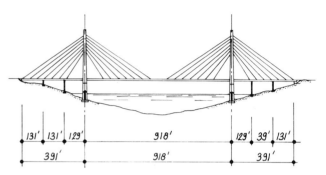

FIGURE 10.48. Proposed crossing of Rio Caroni for iron ore railway line.

11

Technology and Construction
of Segmental Bridges

11.1 Scope and Introduction

Certain problems are common to all types of segmental construction—for example, the selection and control of materials, prestressing operations, and choice of bearings, joints, and wearing surface. Other problems are specific to a particular construction method. The use of form travelers in cast-in-place cantilever construction and the casting and handling of segments in precast cantilever construction are two such examples. This chapter covers these various topics in the following order:

1. Problems common to all segmental bridges
2. Problems specific to cast-in-place cantilever construction
3. Problems specific to match-cast segmental bridges with particular emphasis on cantilever construction, which is the most widely used method.

In designing segmental bridges, it is important to pay attention to certain details at the time of conception, in order to keep the project as simple as possible and thereby achieve economy and effi-

465

ciency during construction. The following guidelines apply to both cast-in-place and precast construction:

1. Keep the length of the segments equal, and keep the segments straight even for curved structures (chord elements).

2. Maintain constant cross-section dimensions as much as possible. Variations of cross-section dimensions should be limited to change of depth of webs and thickness of bottom slab.

3. Corners should be beveled to facilitate casting.

4. Segment proportions (shear keys, for example) should be such as to allow easy form stripping.

5. Avoid as much as possible surface discontinuities on webs and flanges caused by anchor blocks, inserts, and so on.

6. Use a repetitive layout for tendons and anchors, if possible.

7. Minimize the number of diaphragms and stiffeners.

8. Avoid dowels passing through formwork, if possible.

11.2 Concrete and Formwork for Segmental Construction

11.2.1 CONCRETE DESIGN AND PROPERTIES

Uniform quality of concrete is essential for segmental construction. Procedures for obtaining high-quality concrete are covered in PCI and ACI publications.[1,2] Both normal weight and lightweight concrete can be made consistent and uniform by means of proper mix proportioning and production controls.

Ideal concrete will have a slump as low as practicable, notwithstanding the possible use of special placing equipment such as pumps, and a 28-day strength greater than the minimum specified by structural design. It is recommended that statistical methods be used to evaluate uniformity of concrete mixes.

The methods and procedures used to obtain the concrete characteristics required by the design may vary somewhat, depending on whether the segments are cast in the field or in a plant. The results will be affected by curing temperature and type of curing. Liquid or steam curing or electric heat curing may be used.

In temperate climates and where curing is carried out in an isothermal enclosure, only small additions of heat are required to maintain the curing temperature, full advantage being taken of the heat of hydration generated by the fresh concrete. In this case heat demand will be a function of the ambient temperature, more heat being required in winter and little or no additional heat during hot summer weather.

Where segment production rate is not critical, it may be possible to do without accelerated curing and simply use a normal curing period of a few days, during which the concrete is well protected against excessive temperature variations and all exposed surfaces are kept moist.

A sufficient number of trial mixes must be made to assure uniformity of strength and modulus of elasticity at all important phases of construction. Careful selection of aggregates, cement, admixtures, and water will improve strength and modulus of elasticity and will also reduce shrinkage and creep. Soft aggregates and poor sands must be avoided. Creep and shrinkage data for the concrete mixes should be determined by tests.

Corrosive admixtures such as calcium chloride should never be used, since they can have a detrimental effect on hardened concrete and can cause corrosion of reinforcement and prestressing steel. Water-reducing admixtures and also air-entraining admixtures that improve concrete resistance to environmental effects, such as de-icing salts and freeze and thaw actions, are highly desirable. Very careful control at the batching stage is required, however, since the advantages of air-entrained concrete cannot be relied upon unless the quantity of entrained air is within specified limits.

The cement, fine aggregate, coarse aggregate, water, and admixture should be combined to produce a homogeneous concrete mixture of a quality that will conform to the minimum field-test and structural design requirements. Care is necessary in proportioning concrete mixes to insure that they meet specified criteria. Reliable data on the potential of the mix in terms of strength gain, creep, and shrinkage performance should be developed to serve as the basis for improved design parameters.

Proper vibration should be used to permit the use of low-slump concrete and to allow for the optimum consolidation of the concrete.

11.2.2 CONCRETE HEAT CURING

An early concrete strength usually is required to reduce the cycle of operations and to maintain the efficiency of the special equipment used either in cast-in-place or in precast construction. Two methods may be used for this purpose, either separately or together: (a) preheating the fresh concrete, before placing it in the forms or in the casting machines, (b) heat curing the concrete after consolidation in the forms.

In the first case the concrete is preheated to about 85 to 90°F (30 to 35°C). This operation is achieved in several ways:

1. Steam heating the aggregates—a simple solution that presents the disadvantage of changing the aggregate water content

2. Heating the water—a solution that has limited efficiency, owing to the small proportion of water in comparison with the other components (water at 140°F raises the concrete temperature by only 20°F).

3. Direct heating of the concrete mix by injecting steam into the mixer itself—the best solution and the one most easily controlled.

To avoid heat loss, the forms are generally insulated and some source of radiant heat is installed inside the segment (radiators or infrared elements).

In the second case, the concrete is heated in its mold inside a container in which low-pressure steam is circulated. In this way it is relatively easy to obtain the strength required for prestressing operations [3500 to 4000 psi (25 to 28 MPa)] after one or two days, even in winter. If however, tensioning operations are to be performed earlier, after 24 hours for example, modifications must be made to the concrete in the anchorage zone.

Electrical resistances may be embedded in the concrete, or precast end-blocks may be used. Precast end-blocks were used notably for the Issy-les-Moulineaux, Clichy, and Gennevilliers Bridges. For the Gennevilliers Bridge, despite the exceptional dimensions of the box girder deck, two segments were cast each week through an early stressing of the prestress tendons.

In the case of precast segments, the accelerated curing of the concrete must attain two apparently contradictory objectives:

1. Accelerated curing to permit rapid stripping.

2. Final compressive strength as near as possible to that of the design concrete.

Several curing systems may be considered:

1. Conventional kilns.

2. Direct heating of forms with electric resistances.

3. Direct heating of forms with low-pressure steam.

The use of a conventional kiln entails several precautions. First, a constant temperature must be maintained in the kiln. Second, the segment sections of varying thickness are all heated to the same temperature, which may produce unacceptable local thermal gradients and cracking if heat curing is excessive. Finally, the heated segment may be subjected to a thermal shock when removed from the kiln, if the difference between the ambient temperature and the kiln temperature is greater than 60°F. However, kiln curing is a simple solution and is acceptable for long curing cycles—for example, of 10 to 14 hours.

Form heating by means of electrical resistances is perfectly adapted to long curing cycles. This system permits a wide range of adjustment per zone, varying the temperature between the thick and thin sections of the segment and thereby minimizing thermal gradients and eliminating the risk of permanent damage to the concrete at the beginning of its solidifying phase.

The heating of forms with low-pressure steam is preferable for short curing cycles lasting less than five hours, as it permits the distribution of a large quantity of calories over a short period, causing a rise in the internal temperature of the concrete of the order of 20 to 30°F (10 to 15°C) per hour. This system, however, requires a complex regulator to ensure an equal temperature in all the form panel enclosures, at all times during the treatment, whatever their thermal inertia and the external influences to which they are subjected, Figure 11.1.

FIGURE 11.1. Heat-curing control system (B-3 South Viaducts).

The different systems (kiln, electrical resistances, and low-pressure steam) have all been applied successfully to segmental bridges. The segments for the Choisy-le-Roi and Courbevoie bridges were kiln cured. Electric heating was adopted for the construction of the upstream and downstream bridges on the Paris Ring Road and the Blois Bridge, among others. Form heating using low-pressure steam was used for the Pierre Benite Bridges, the Oleron Viaduct, and the B-3 South Viaducts.

Whether forms are heated by electricity or by steam, it is relatively easy to produce a long curing cycle, and the desired final concrete strength is easily obtained. A short curing cycle, on the other hand, requires a great deal of caution and meticulous preliminary calculations. Particular attention must be given to:

1. Choosing a cement, the performance of which is adapted to the accelerated curing of concrete (preferred is artificial Portland cement with: $C_3A \leq 11\%$ and $C_3S/C_2S \geq 3$).
2. Consistently manufacturing concrete with a minimum water content and a maximum temperature of 95°F (35°C) at the time of pouring.
3. Using sufficiently rigid forms to resist the thermal expansion of the concrete in its plastic state while heating.

In order to avoid a drop in the long-term mechanical properties of the concrete, the temperature curve during the heat curing must necessarily include, see Figure 11.2:

An initial curing period of two to three hours, during which the concrete is kept at the ambient temperature

An increase in temperature at a low rate of less than 36°F (20°C) per hour

A period (depending upon the concrete strength to be attained) during which the temperature is held constant and below 150°F (65°C)

A period during which the concrete is cooled at a rate similar to that used for the temperature increase

The loss of strength in the long term will be greater:

If the initial curing period is short

If the temperature increase is rapid

If the maximum temperature is high

As an example, the short-cycle treatment used for the B-3 Viaduct segments was the following, see Figure 11.3:

Initial period of $1\frac{1}{2}$ hour at 95°F (35°C) (mixing temperature)

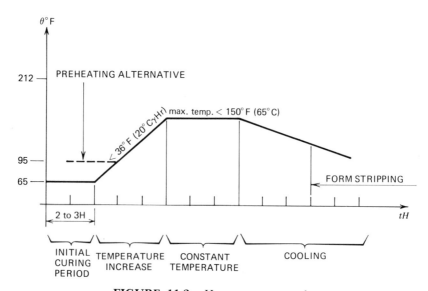

FIGURE 11.2. Heat-treatment cycle.

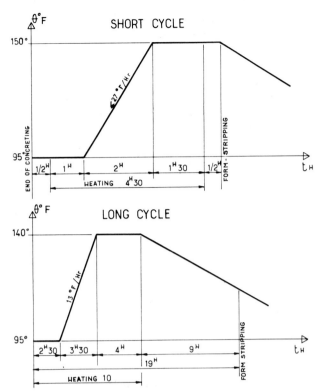

FIGURE 11.3. Example of short and long cycles.

Temperature increase of 27°F (15°C) per hour for 2 hours

A constant temperature of 150°F (65°C) for $1\frac{1}{2}$ hours

Figure 11.3 shows an example of long-cycle heat treatment, the Conflans Bridge, which had a total heat-treatment duration of 19 hours.

11.2.3 DIMENSIONAL TOLERANCES

Formwork that produces typical bridge box girder segments within the following tolerances is considered to be of good quality[3,4]:

Width of web	$\pm\frac{3}{8}$ in.	($\pm$10 mm)
Depth of bottom slab	$+\frac{1}{2}$ in. to 0 in.	(+10 mm to 0 mm)
Depth of top slab	$\pm\frac{1}{4}$ in.	($\pm$5 mm)
Overall depth of segment	$\pm\frac{1}{500}$ of depth with $\frac{1}{4}$ in. min.	(5 mm min.)
Overall width of segment	$\pm\frac{1}{2000}$ of width with $\frac{1}{4}$ in. min.	(5 mm min.)
Length of match-cast segment	$\pm\frac{1}{4}$ in.	($\pm$5 mm)
Diaphragm dimensions	$\pm\frac{3}{8}$ in.	($\pm$10 mm)

11.2.4 FORMWORK FOR SEGMENTAL CONSTRUCTION

Formwork along with its supports and foundations must be designed to safely support all loads that might be applied without undesired deformations or settlements. Soil stabilization of the foundation may be required.

Since economical production of cast-in-place or precast segments is based on repetitive use of the same forms as much as possible, the formwork must be sturdy and special attention must be given to construction details. Where formwork is to be assembled by persons other than the manufacturer or his representatives, particular care must be taken with erection details and assembly instructions. All elements of the formwork must be easy to handle.[1,2]

Formwork for structures of variable geometry will need to be relatively flexible in order to allow adaptation at the various joints. Both external and internal forms are usually retractable in order to leave a free working space for placing reinforcing steel and prestressing ducts.[3]

Special consideration must be given to those parts of the forms that have variable dimensions. To facilitate alignment or adjustment, special equipment such as turnbuckles, prefitted wedges, screws, or hydraulic jacks should be provided.

Tendon anchors and inserts must be designed in such a way that they remain rigidly in position during casting. Projecting anchorage blocks or other such irregularities should be detailed to permit easy form stripping.[3]

If accelerated steam curing with temperatures of the order of 130°F (55°C) is to be used, then the deformations of the forms caused by heating and cooling must be considered in order to prevent cracking of the young concrete.

In general, internal vibration using needle vibrators should always be applied. External vibrators, if used, must be attached at locations that will achieve maximum efficiency of consolidation and permit easy replacement in the case of a breakdown during casting operations. External vibration may lead to fatigue failure in welded joints, and regular inspection should be made to help prevent any sudden failure of this kind.[3]

Paste leakage through formwork joints must be prevented by suitable design of joint seals. Normally this can be achieved by using a flexible sealing material. This is particularly important at the joint face with the matching segment, where loss of cement paste can lead to poorly formed joint surfaces and subsequent spalling and loss of matching, requiring repair. Special attention must be given to the junction of tendon sheathing with the forms.[3,4] All form surfaces, especially welded joints in contact with the concrete, must be perfectly smooth and free from reentrant areas, pitting, or other discontinuities, which could entrap small volumes of concrete and lead to spalling during form stripping.[3]

11.3 Post-Tensioning Materials and Operations

11.3.1 GENERAL

Technical details relating to the different methods available are described in the various post-tensioning manuals[5,6] and in the specific documents issued by suppliers.

11.3.2 DUCTS

Ducts are used to form the holes or enclose the space in which the prestressing tendons are located. The ducts may be located inside or outside the concrete section.

Although in some instances the tendons are placed in the ducts before concreting (cast-in-place and span-by-span construction), post-tensioning tendons will normally be threaded into the ducts after erection of the segments. The duct cross section must, therefore, be adequate to allow proper threading; and in general it will be about $\frac{1}{4}$ in. (5 mm) larger in any direction than for ducts in which the tendons are placed before concreting.

The duct dimension must allow not only the installation of the tendons but also free passage of grout materials after stressing. The ratio or proportion of cross-sectional area of the duct with respect to the net area of prestressing steel should conform to appropriate specifications or codes.[4] A minimum value of 2 usually leads to satisfactory results.

Ducts must have sufficient grouting inlets, shut-off valves, and drains to allow proper grouting and to avoid accumulation of water during storage. Vent pipes should not be spaced more than approximately 400 ft (120 m) apart.[7] This spacing may have to be reduced, depending upon the expertise of the personnel performing the grouting.

Particular attention must be paid to the quality of duct connections at the joints between segments. At the joints, accurate placing is mandatory. The method of duct connection depends on the type of joint[3]:

Telescopic sleeves pushed over projecting ducts —wide joints

Screw-on type sleeves—wide joints

Internal rubber or plastic sleeves—match-cast joints

Gaskets or other special seals—match-cast joints

No special provisions: clean ducts with a torpedo after jointing to remove penetrated epoxy if any—match-cast joints

Connection tightness is essential in order to prevent penetration of joint material, water, or other liquids or solids into the ducts, which would introduce a risk of blockage, and also to prevent leakage at the joint during tendon grouting operations.[3]

11.3.3 TENDON ANCHORS

Tendon anchors usually consist of a bearing plate and an anchorage device either in combination or as separate units. Shape and dimensions of the anchors must conform with the applicable specifications, particularly insofar as bearing stresses are concerned.

Choice of anchor positions in the segments should take into account the following considerations[3]:

Tendon layout requirements and installation sequences.

Stresses generated around the anchors.

Ease of tendon threading and stressing.

Ease of formwork preparation, stripping and concrete placing.

Certain anchorage positions, such as the anchorage block on a thin slab shown in Figure 11.4, should be avoided. If this type of detail cannot be avoided, then particular care must be taken in design and construction of the zone concerned.[3]

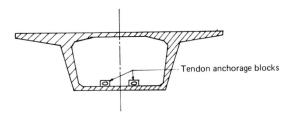

FIGURE 11.4. Anchorage block position to be avoided.

Bearing plates are usually embedded in the segment at the time of casting. In certain cases they are installed against the hardened surface of the concrete with a dry mortar bed or a suitable cushioning material such as asbestos cement or synthetic resin.

11.3.4 TENDON LAYOUT

This subject has been covered in Chapter 4 relating to design. The choice of tendon layout must be treated carefully, with special attention paid to the following factors:

Construction sequence with respect to tendon placing, segment casting (or erection), and other construction imperatives

Standardization and repetition of essential features, especially duct and anchor positions at joints (in order to facilitate formwork design)

Various loading conditions throughout the construction period and in service

When using large tendons, it is not advisable to use couplers or crossed splices, for reasons of congestion and formwork complication. Also, couplers and splices should not be located in areas where yielding may occur under ultimate load conditions.[3]

In order to limit friction losses, and to facilitate tendon threading, excessively curved tendons should be avoided if possible.

11.3.5 FRICTION LOSSES IN PRESTRESSING TENDONS

Segmental construction usually calls for prestressing tendons to be installed through a succession of short duct lengths coupled to one another at the joints between segments, these being at approximately 8 to 30 ft (2.5 to 10 m) intervals.

The friction factors (for curvature and wobble) usually accepted for long tendons in cast-in-place structures may not be realistic for this type of construction under ordinary working conditions and supervision. The actual results obtained in a segmental bridge built in Europe are given below by way of example for the benefit of future project designers.

Cantilever tendons were placed along a straight profile in the roadway slab and anchored either on the segment face or in a block-out inside the box girder. Continuity tendons were either anchored in a block-out at the bottom slab level or draped upward in the webs and anchored in the same block-out of the cantilever tendons. All tendons were made up of twelve 0.6 in. diameter strands. Soluble oil for reducing friction in the ducts was not allowed by the consultant. The calculations were carried out using the following values for curvature and wobble friction coefficients:

$$\mu = 0.20, \qquad K = 0.007/\text{ft} = 0.0021/\text{m}$$

The Young's modulus of the tendon samples tested in the factory or in the laboratory varied between 28,000 and 29,000 ksi, and the variation between various heats over the whole structure was very low. According to direct tests carried out on site, and a systematic analysis of all results of tendon elongations recorded during the stressing operation, the actual Young's modulus of a (twelve 0.6 in. diameter strand) tendon at first tensioning varied between 25,000 and 26,000 ksi, which is only 90% of the value recorded during factory and laboratory tests.

Figures 11.5 and 11.6 show values of the wobble friction coefficient K measured for all the tendons in the structure's 18 cantilevers. All the tendons are shown in Figure 11.5, while Figure 11.6 shows only those tendons in the spans without hinges, and separates the tendons anchored on the segment face from those anchored in block-outs (the tendons had the same layout except a rather severe curvature at the end). It is obvious that:

1. As construction proceeded and the quality of manufacture and supervision improved, the results got better.

2. At the beginning of the job, the effect of the curved ends of certain tendons was lost in the generally mediocre results. As these results got better (value of K equal to that used in calculation from cantilever 11 on), this effect became preponderant, counteracting that of the improved standard of work.

3. As the site staff became accustomed to the work and the effort and supervision dropped, the results became gradually worse (compare cantilevers 13 and 17, for example).

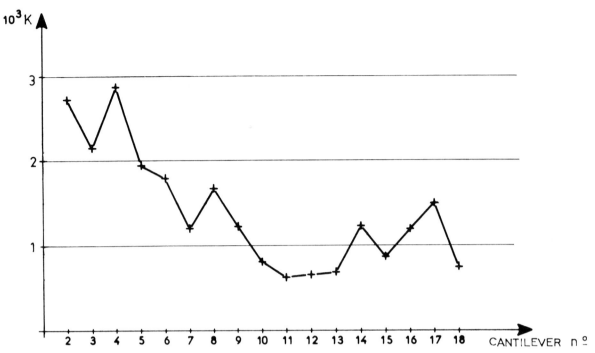

FIGURE 11.5. Prestressing in a cantilever bridge. Variation of wobble friction coefficient for cantilever tendons in each of the structure's 18 spans.

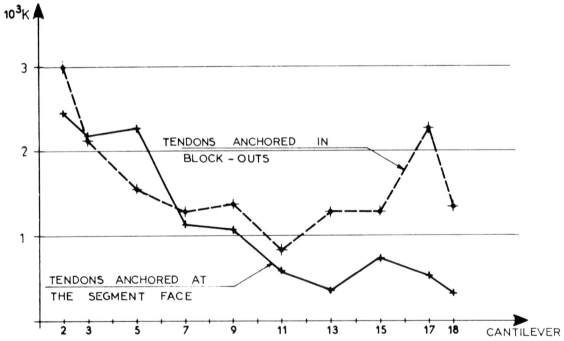

FIGURE 11.6. Prestressing in a cantilever bridge. Wobble friction coefficient for cantilever tendons in the 10 spans without hinges.

As an example, a straight tendon in the top slab fillet between slab and web was isolated. The wobble friction coefficient depends on the care exercised in fastening the duct to the reinforcing steel cage as the concrete is poured (when the tendon is in the slab rather than in the fillet, the accidental deviations are much smaller). For the first seven cantilevers (see Figure 11.7) the wobble coefficient

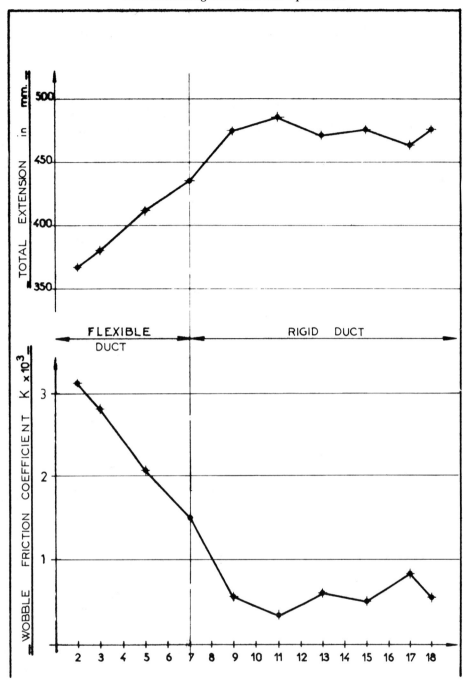

FIGURE 11.7.   Prestressing in a cantilever bridge. Wobble friction coefficient for a straight tendon located in the upper fillet.

reached up to six times the assumed value used in the calculations, and yet very careful construction will enable this assumed value to be reached or at least approached closely to obtain the desired prestress with little room for uncertainty.

The presence of hinged segments not only complicates the tendon profile and the construction phases, but introduces uncertainty about obtaining the required prestress force. Owing to the technical restrictions imposed by the consultant, the traditional prestress layout employed in earlier bridges could not be used. Consequently, long tendons stressed only at the opposite end had to be accepted. It was thought that a realistic value of the final force for each of the tendons (twelve 0.6 in. diameter strand) would be 350 kips (160 mt). It is fortunate that a direct check was made at the site, which revealed the actual initial load at transfer to be the following for the four tendons under consideration: 130 kips (60 mt), 210 kips (96 mt), 130 kips (60 mt), and 200 kips (90 mt). The average initial prestress load per tendon was therefore 170 kips (78 mt), and the probable final force would have been 150 kips (70 mt) as compared to the assumed value of 350 kips (160 mt). Fortunately, the situation could be easily corrected and remedial measures put into effect as follows:

1. The reinforcing steel and local prestressing tendons allowed for a certain margin of safety.
2. It was possible to restress two of the four cables in the first cantilever and then to change the profile and method of placing segments in order to stress all the tendons at both ends for the rest of the cantilevers.

The above results, quoted rigorously so as to illustrate several important aspects of friction losses, must not lead the reader to suppose that the safety of the structure was at any time compromised. The force in a tendon varies much more slowly than any changes in the friction coefficients for ordinary tendon profiles. For example, in a 270 ft (80 m)

tendon stressed at both ends, if the friction coefficients are multiplied by 4, the minimum force in the tendon is reduced by only 16%.

It is interesting to examine the results for the actual prestress obtained in cantilevers 2 and 3 (the ones having the worst results) shown in Figure 11.8 for each section, compared with the prestress used in the calculations. The lack of prestress, most marked at midspan, was compensated by additional tendons to bring the force back up to that required by the calculations in the first two spans. Afterward, the originally calculated prestress was always sufficient.

To summarize, the authors wish to underline the following points:

1. Bench tests should be performed on site to determine a realistic value of the modulus of elasticity of the tendons to be used to compute the theoretical tendon elongations.
2. Realistic values of curvature and wobble friction coefficients should be used in the design and further controlled on site. Direct friction tests should be made together with a statistical analysis of the measured elongations for all tendons.

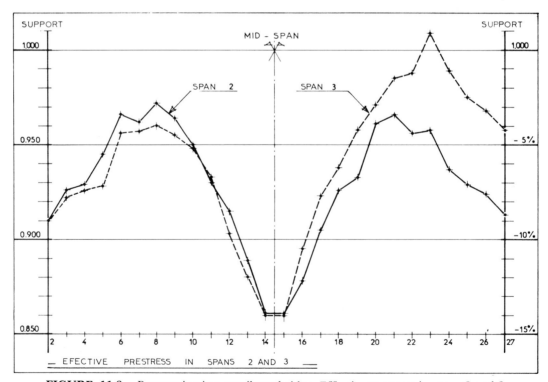

FIGURE 11.8. Prestressing in a cantilever bridge. Effective prestress in spans 2 and 3.

3. Provisions should be made at the design stage for additional prestress to compensate for any unexpected reduction in the design prestress force due to excessive friction. This may be done as follows:

a. By adding additional ducts over and above the number required by design calculations; if this method is used, the unused ducts at the end of construction must be grouted to prevent water from seeping inside and subsequently freezing with disastrous effects on the structure.

b. By using larger than required sizes for some of the ducts, so as to allow the use of larger-capacity tendons if required.

c. By providing anchor blocks and possible deviation saddles so as to allow the installation of external tendons located inside the box girder but outside the concrete section.

If the correct approach is taken at the conception stage, perfect control of this aspect of prestress may be obtained and very satisfactory structures can be built that give maintenance-free long-term performance.

11.3.6 GROUTING

As in conventional post-tensioned structures, segmental construction requires the grouting of prestressing tendons after tensioning to provide corrosion protection and to develop bond between the tendon and the surrounding concrete. Current recommendations and provisions of good practice are therefore applicable to segmental bridges. However, several important points need to be examined.

Grouting must not be carried out if the temperature in the ducts is less than 35°F (2°C) or if the surrounding concrete temperature is less than 32°F (2°C). This requirement virtually precludes grouting operations during the winter months in the northern and middle western United States, unless very special winter precautions are used. It is preferable to postpone all grouting operations until the following spring, even though some tendons may be left tensioned and ungrouted for a long period. Attention must then be given to corrosion protection of the high-tensile steel bars or strands. Satisfactory protection is obtained by sealing all tendon ducts at both ends after blowing out with cool compressed air. Hot air should not be used because it increases the moisture content of the air and reduces the natural corrosion protection.

Another important and sometimes acute problem relates to potential grout leakage at segment joints, which can lead to the passing of grout from one duct to another. For this reason ducts must be well connected and sealed at joints. To check the grout tightness of the joints and to avoid blockages, it is advisable to flush the ducts with water under pressure before grouting. Any leakage points thus detected may then be sealed. If communication is discovered between tendon ducts, the tendon groups affected should be grouted in one operation after threading and stressing of *all* the tendons involved.[3]

If couplers are being used (notably for single-bar tendons), precautions must be taken to limit the risk of grout blockage at the coupling points. Couplers must be housed in special enlarged enclosures with two essential features[3]:

1. Clear cross-sectional area for the passage of grout equal to or greater than that for the rest of the tendon.
2. Independent grout inlets and vent pipes.

11.3.7 UNBONDED TENDONS

Unbonded tendons may be used in segmental construction provided that the performance requirements of the post-tensioning steel are also met by the tendon anchorage, notably with respect to fatigue characteristics. In unbonded post-tensioning a corrosion protection system must be provided to guarantee at least the same degree of corrosion protection as for bonded tensioning. This may be achieved by enclosing the tendons in flexible ducts (such as polyethylene pipes) and by cement grouting after tensioning.

11.4 Segment Fabrication for Cast-in-Place Cantilever Construction

11.4.1 CONVENTIONAL TRAVELERS

The conventional form traveler supports the weight of fresh concrete of the new segment by means of longitudinal beams extending out in cantilever from the last segment in order to support the forms and service walkways.

Form Travelers with Top Main Beams (Figure 2.83) The longitudinal main beams or girders are usually located above the segment to be concreted, in line with the webs. The outside forms, the bottom forms, the work floor, and the service walkways are hung from the main beams with the help of cross beams. The inside forms are supported on a trolley, which travels inside the deck.

The main beams are anchored to the previous segment. In order to maintain stability during the pouring operation a counterweight is sometimes used to reduce the uplift forces applied to the concrete section. When the traveler is transported to its new position ready for the next segment, the counterweight keeps it in balance between two successive anchoring positions. The main beams that support the load due to concrete, forms, walkways, and so on are often subject to large deflections, which can give rise to transverse cracking along the joints between segments. These cracks appear at the upper face of the bottom slab and at the connection between web and top slab. This undesirable condition can be avoided by using a rigid structure; the weight of the traveler is increased together with the prestress required in the cantilevers. The form traveler used for the Oissel Bridge weighed 120 tons (110 mt) and may be considered as a heavy form traveler.

If the travelers are light, care must be taken to compensate deflections during concreting by adjusting jacks. This type of traveler weighs (excluding counterweight) a little less than half the maximum concrete segment weight. An example of a light form traveler is shown in Figure 11.9 for the Tourville Bridge. Each traveler weighs 33 tons (30 mt).

Form Travelers with Lateral Main Beams (Figure 11.10) Travelers with their main beams above the bridge deck present the disadvantage of hindering the construction operation concerning the upper part of the segment. For this reason certain form travelers have their main beams disposed laterally parallel to the outside webs, underneath the bridge deck. This solution leaves a clear working surface and allows easy access to all surfaces to be formed, reinforced, and concreted. In this way, the technology originally developed for precast segmental construction can be applied to cast-in-place cantilever methods, resulting in shorter construction cycles. The Moulin-les-Metz Bridge in eastern France, Figure 11.11, was constructed using this type of form traveler.

FIGURE 11.9. Tourville-la-Riviere Bridge form traveler.

11.4.2 *SELF-SUPPORTING MOBILE FORMWORK*

In the case of traditional form travelers, the resulting deflections seen during construction are almost entirely due to the main beams. The formwork as such usually acts only as a mold and does not support any part of the total load, even though it comprises very stiff walls.

In several recent bridges the traveler concept has been modified so as to use the rigid formwork as the weight-carrying member, thus producing a self-supporting rigid mold. Several advantages are gained with this concept:

Surveying control and correction of bridge deck geometry are easily obtained.

Cracking near the joints caused by the deflection of conventional travelers is completely eliminated.

The work area is maintained completely free and allows prefabricated reinforcing steel cages to be used as in precast segmental construction.

This type of mobile formwork was first used for constant-inertia bridge decks such as the Kennedy Bridge, Dijon, and the Canadians Interchange in Paris, Figure 11.12.

During the concreting operations, the mobile formwork is prestressed to the existing deck. The exact positioning of the formwork is obtained by

1_ CONCRETING PHASE

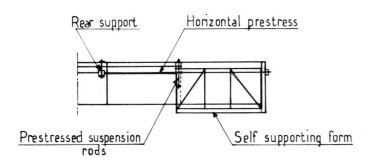

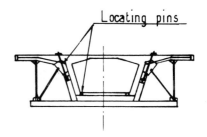

2_ LAUNCHING PHASE

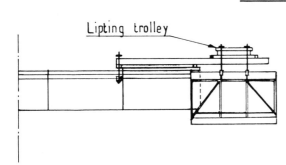

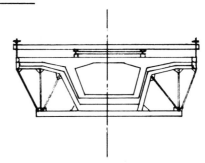

FIGURE 11.10.   Typical form traveler with lateral main beams.

FIGURE 11.11.   Moulins-les-Metz form traveler.

FIGURE 11.12.   Canadians Viaduct (Paris), view of form traveler in operation.

means of adjusting pins located at the rear in reservations provided in the previously poured segments. The formwork is transported to its new position, ready for the next segment, on an overhead trolley, which travels along short steel girders cantilevered out from the existing hardened concrete in line with the webs.

A further refinement was to use pretensioned reinforcing to add to the stability of the traveler while pouring the segment. Figure 11.13 shows the arrangement for the Canadians Viaduct in Paris, France. Monostrands located in the webs are provisionally anchored to the front of the traveler and embedded in the webs of the concrete segments to be incorporated in the reinforcement of the permanent structure.

The use of the self-supporting mobile formwork was later extended to variable-depth bridge decks

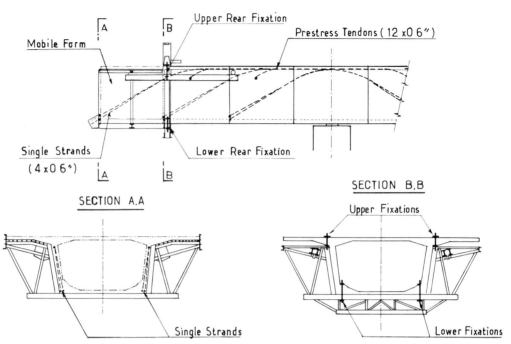

FIGURE 11.13. Canadians Viaduct (Paris), details of the self-supporting form traveler.

as well as three-web cross sections, as in the Clichy, Orleans, and Gennevilliers Bridges.

The structural members of the mobile formwork are therefore the side forms of the exterior face of the outside webs and the bottom forms of the underside of the bottom slab, both of which are stiffened transversely by front and rear frames braced together for additional rigidity, Figure 11.14. In this manner a rigid box is formed, which is prestressed to the existing deck. The change of section height is achieved by vertical displacement of the bottom forms, which are fastened to the front stiffening framework and bottom slab of the last segment.

The stability of the self-supporting mobile forms of the Gennevilliers Bridge was ensured by (Figure 11.15):

1. Two steel pins fixed to the top of the outside forms and matching imprints provided on the outside face of the previous segment, the connection being assured by high-strength bars going through each web.
2. Two steel pins fixed to the upper surface of the bottom forms and matching the corresponding imprints provided in the last segment bottom slab, again held by prestress bars.

The self-weight of the mobile forms and the fresh concrete creates an overturning moment, which is balanced by two forces F sustained by the previously described locating pins. Practically all the shear force is taken by the upper pins. Because of the large forces transmitted through the top pins to the concrete, precast concrete elements are used to avoid the transmission of high stresses to young concrete, Figure 11.16. These forces are transmitted by friction between pin and concrete, and this determines the necessary prestress force.

11.4.3 TWO-STAGE CASTING

The method of two-stage casting involves, first, the fabrication of the bottom slab and the webs together with a small part of the top slab in order to create a flange in which all or some of the cantilever tendons can be located. This operation, carried out using a conventional form traveler, produces either a U-shaped or a W-shaped section, depending on the number of webs, Figure 11.17. After the cantilever tendons are stressed the form traveler is moved to the next position, the top is poured using a mobile formwork of relatively simple design. This second stage usually follows the first with a minimum interval of two or three segments, and concrete can be placed in a simple pour over the length of several segments.

This method has the advantage of reducing the concrete volume to be supported by the form traveler, thus reducing the weight of the traveler.

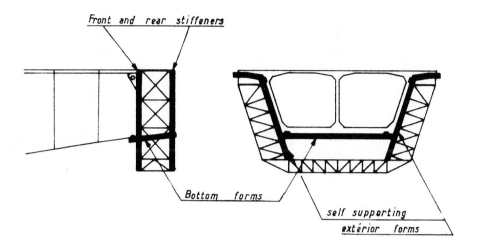

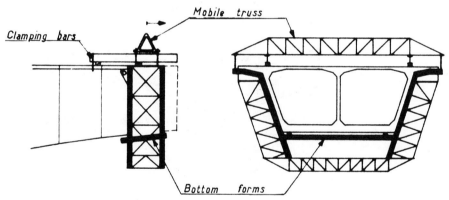

FIGURE 11.14. Self-supporting mobile forms for variable-depth bridge decks. (*a*) Concreting. (*b*) Moving forward.

In addition, the second stage is independent with respect to the first and so is no longer on the critical path of concreting operations.

The bridge decks of the Saint Isidore and Magnan Viaducts on the Nizza A-8 bypass were constructed using this method. All of the 130 ft (40 m) spans of the Saint Isidore Viaduct were completed for stage one only, including closure to the preceding span, before the second stage was completed, using mobile formwork which rolled along the bottom slab from one abutment to the other. As regards the Magnan Viaduct, the second stage followed the first with an interval of three seg-

ments, because of the long spans in this structure. The same procedure was used for the Clichy, Joinville, and Woippy Bridges, Figure 11.18.

11.4.4   COMBINATION OF PRECAST WEBS WITH CAST-IN-PLACE FLANGES

The preceding methods allowed a considerable reduction in the construction cycle. Two pairs of segments could thus be completed every week, corresponding to an average rate of construction of 7 to 10 ft (2 to 3 m) per working day.

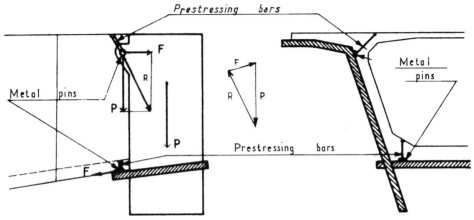

FIGURE 11.15.   Stability of the Gennevilliers Bridge self-supporting mobile forms.

PRECAST   JOINT

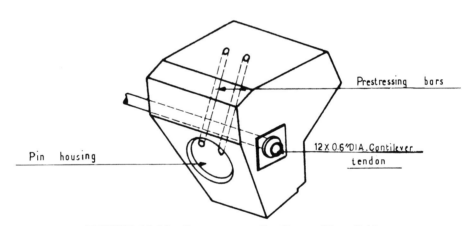

FIGURE 11.16.   Precast gusset for Gennevilliers Bridge.

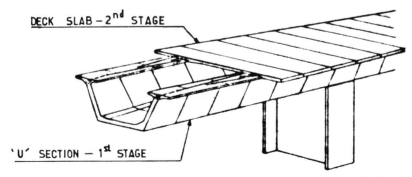

FIGURE 11.17.   Two-stage construction of a two-web bridge deck.

FIGURE 11.18. Woippy Viaduct, France. Detail of the self supporting form traveler and two-stage casting.

FIGURE 11.19. Brotonne Bridge, mobile form carrier.

The main obstacle preventing further reduction in the construction cycle and therefore a closer approach to the speed of precast segmental construction is the lack of strength of young concrete and the consequent interference with stressing operations. Apart from several other methods already discussed, the problem can be partially overcome by using precast end blocks or precast webs or both. This was first tried for the construction of the Brotonne Viaduct approach spans, Figure 11.19. The webs, which were rather thin and heavily inclined, were precast in pairs and pretensioned, Figure 11.20.

The deck was cantilevered out from the piers using 10 ft (3 m) long segments assembled in two phases. In the first phase, the precast webs weighing up to 18 tons (16 mt) were placed inside the form traveler, previously adjusted to the bridge profile including the desired camber. The webs were then prestressed to the preceding segment with provisional prestress bars, the joint being match-cast or cast in place. The second phase consisted of casting the rest of the segment inside the form traveler, which was now suspended from the newly stressed webs.

This procedure, which requires partial prefabrication of the segments using light casting equipment, enables a considerable simplification of the form traveling equipment, the limitation of total weight to 39 tons (35 mt), and a reduction in the construction cycle such as to produce, even for a cable-stayed bridge, as many as four segments per week for each pair of form travelers.

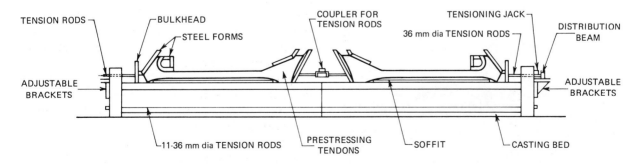

BED FOR PRETENSIONED WEBS

FIGURE 11.20. Brotonne Bridge, precasting of webs.

During construction of the Brotonne cable-stayed bridge, the precast webs were placed by tower crane traveling parallel to the bridge deck above the river banks and by an overhead gantry crane above the Seine River.

Another example of the use of precast webs is found in the Clichy Bridge carrying the metropolitan line over the Seine in the northwest of Paris. The bridge deck with a 280 ft (85 m) maximum span consists of a three-web box girder without cantilever flanges and with the deck supporting the live loads as low as possible in order to reduce the length of the access ramps to the structure. The 8 ft (2.5 m) long segments were also constructed in two stages, Figure 11.21.

The precast webs, with epoxy match-cast joints, are placed with the aid of a mobile handling system rolling along the webs of the previously placed segments. They are then prestressed to the existing structure before the top and bottom slabs are poured in place on the length of two segments.

11.4.5 *PRACTICAL PROBLEMS IN CAST-IN-PLACE CONSTRUCTION CAMBER CONTROL*

Before proceeding with the cantilever construction proper, a starting base must first be completed on the various piers. This first special segment, called a pier segment or a pier table, is generally constructed on a temporary platform anchored by

FIGURE 11.21. Precast web placing equipment for Clichy Bridge carrying the metropolitan line over the Seine River.

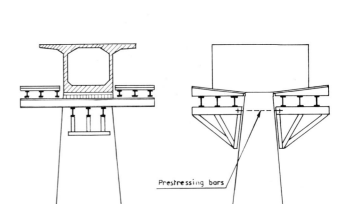

FIGURE 11.22. Construction of the pier segment for a cast-in-place cantilever deck.

prestressing the pier top, Figure 11.22. This special segment may either be given the minimum length to insure adequate connection to the pier for the stability of the future cantilever or else be of such length as to allow both travelers to be installed simultaneously, Figure 11.23.

Another important problem relates to the safety of the travelers during construction. Chapter 4 described the difficulties of ensuring pier safety in the event a form traveler fell during transfer from one position to the next. The difficulties would even be greater in the event of an accident during the casting operation. Consequently, all precautions must be taken both at the design stage and during construction to eliminate this potential hazard. The load-carrying members of the traveler must be carefully inspected and may even be load tested before use so as to practically eliminate the danger of structural failure.

The most critical areas are in the safety of the suspension rods and the transfer of the traveler reactions to the concrete. Preferably all suspension rods and anchor bars should be doubled. Also, the prestressing tendons must have an adequate margin of safety. Use of a single strand or a single bar in each web of the box should be avoided. Rather a multistrand tendon with individual anchors for each strand or two prestress bars should be used.

Worldwide use of cast-in-place cantilever construction has established an extremely good safety record, much better than that for cast-in-place construction on falsework. Accidents are very few and far between; however, designers and constructors must always be safety conscious.

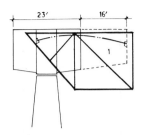

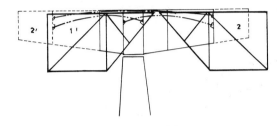

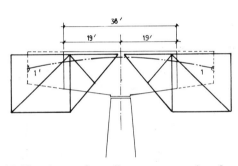

FIGURE 11.23. Start of cantilever construction from the pier segment. (*a*) Short pier segment — successive installation of travelers. (*b*) Long pier segment —simultaneous installation of travelers.

The most critical practical problem of cast-in-place construction is deflection control, particularly for long-span structures. There are five categories of deflections (or space geometrical movements of the structure) during construction and after completion:

1. Deflection of the travelers under the weight of the concrete segment. This value is given by the manufacturer or may be computed and checked at the site during the first operations.

2. Deflection of the concrete cantilever arms during construction. For each casting of a pair of segments, the weight of the concrete segments and the corresponding cantilever pre-

stress forces impose upon the cantilever a new deflection curve.

3. Deflections of the various cantilever arms after construction and after removal of the travelers before continuity is achieved with the other parts of the deck.

4. Short- and long-term deflections of the continuous structure, including the effect of superimposed dead loads (curbs, railings, pavements, utilities, and so on) and live loads.

5. Short- and long-term pier shortenings and foundation settlements.

Using the data available on concrete properties and foundation conditions, the designer should compute the various deflections mentioned under items 3, 4, and 5 above, assuming the bridge unloaded for foundation settlements and long-term concrete deflections and half the design live load for computation of the short-term concrete deflections.

The sum of the various deflection values obtained in the successive sections of the deck allows the construction of a camber diagram, which should be added to the theoretical longitudinal profile of the bridge to determine for each cantilever arm an adequate casting curve. This casting curve is the goal toward which construction proceeds during cantilever casting. The essential difficulty is that no absolute coordinates are available in a system where everything changes at each construction stage (transfer of traveler, concrete casting, or cantilever prestressing).

A very simple example may illustrate the solution of the problem of accommodating the deflections described under item 2 above. For simplicity, assume only a four-segment cantilever arm, for which a horizontal longitudinal profile is required, Figure 11.24.

As outlined in Chapter 4 and summarized briefly above, the designer analyzes the various deflection curves for each construction step (casting segment and precasting). The typical results are shown in Figure 11.24. The cumulative deflection curve is immediately obtained together with the camber diagram, Figure 11.25. The use of the camber diagram for determining the adequate deflection at each construction stage is simple; however, it is much less simple to use in a proper manner in the field, and experienced surveyors have often made mistakes.

When properly used, the camber diagram allows the determination at each joint, of offset values such as y_{1-2}, y_{2-3}, and y_{3-4} at each point, which will

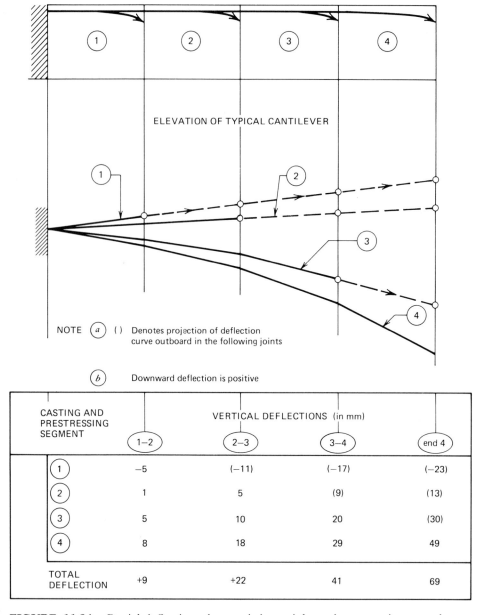

ELEVATION OF TYPICAL CANTILEVER

NOTE (*a*) ( ) Denotes projection of deflection curve outboard in the following joints

(*b*) Downward deflection is positive

CASTING AND PRESTRESSING SEGMENT	VERTICAL DEFLECTIONS (in mm)			
	(1–2)	(2–3)	(3–4)	(end 4)
1	−5	(−11)	(−17)	(−23)
2	1	5	(9)	(13)
3	5	10	20	(30)
4	8	18	29	49
TOTAL DEFLECTION	+9	+22	41	69

FIGURE 11.24. Partial deflections due to girder weight and prestressing at each construction stage.

bring the traveler in the proper position to realize the desired final geometry. The sketch and table in Figure 11.26 show how to use the camber diagram properly. It is very important to realize that at no construction stage does the profile of the cantilever coincide with either the final deflection curve or the camber diagram.

The natural tendency would be to build up the traveler to the required offset to make its nose fall exactly on the camber diagram. The results of this improper procedure are shown in detail in Figure 11.27. The bridge is built with an undesired double curvature, particularly undesirable toward the end of the cantilever. When the mistake is discovered, it is usually too late to put into effect any remedial measures, because the final shape of a cantilever depends essentially upon the accuracy of the geometry near the piers, where the deck is sub-

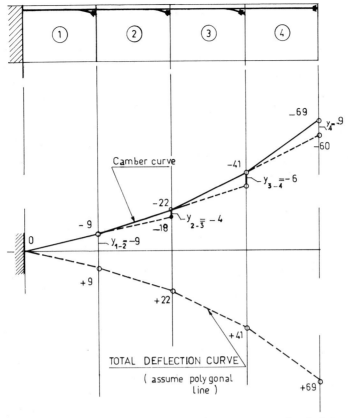

FIGURE 11.25. Cumulative deflection curve and choice of camber.

jected to the highest moments and where its deflections have the greatest effect at midspan.

11.5 Characteristics of Precast Segments and Match-Cast Epoxy Joints

Developed originally to allow a rapid and safe assembly of precast segments at the construction site, the technique of match casting was progressively refined as experience was gained. We shall describe the characteristics of segments in the early structures to further highlight the latest improvements and variations of the original concept.

11.5.1 FIRST-GENERATION SEGMENTS

In those early structures the epoxy resin played several important roles:

1. During assembly before hardening:
   a. To lubricate the mating surfaces while final positioning took place.
   b. To compensate for minor imperfections in the match-cast surfaces.

2. In the finished structure after hardening:
   a. To ensure the watertightness of the joints, especially in the top slab.
   b. To participate in the structural resistance by transmitting compression and shear forces. However, before hardening of the epoxy resin, the joints present no shear resistance whatsoever, because the epoxy behaves like a perfect lubricant. It was therefore necessary to provide shear keys in each web in order to ensure the shear-force transfer between segments. These keys, as well as those situated in the top slab, also allowed a very accurate assembly of one segment with respect to another.

During assembly of the deck, some sort of temporary fixation, either mechanical or by means of prestress bars, allowed the placing equipment (launching girder, crane, and so on) to be quickly

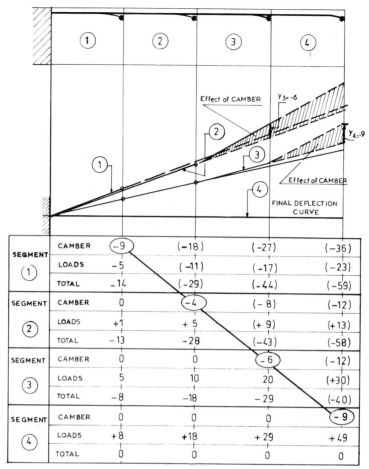

		①	②	③	④
SEGMENT ①	CAMBER	-9	(-18)	(-27)	(-36)
	LOADS	-5	(-11)	(-17)	(-23)
	TOTAL	-14	(-29)	(-44)	(-59)
SEGMENT ②	CAMBER	0	-4	(-8)	(-12)
	LOADS	+1	+5	(+9)	(+13)
	TOTAL	-13	-28	(-43)	(-58)
SEGMENT ③	CAMBER	0	0	-6	(-12)
	LOADS	5	10	20	(+30)
	TOTAL	-8	-18	-29	(-40)
SEGMENT ④	CAMBER	0	0	0	-9
	LOADS	+8	+18	+29	+49
	TOTAL	0	0	0	0

FIGURE 11.26. Follow-up of deflections with proper use of camber diagram.

unloaded without waiting for the cantilever tendons to be stressed.

Figure 11.28 shows how a typical first-generation segment can be assembled to the existing structure using a temporary apparatus located on the top and bottom slabs, which is used to create forces F_1 and F_2 which ensure the equilibrium of the new segment at the joint.

These two forces, combined with the weight W of the segment, give the resultant force R, which is inclined with respect to the joint. Because of the very small coefficient of friction of the epoxy, the shearing component of R produced by W can be balanced only by the vertical component of the reaction C, which exists normal to the bottom face of the web shear keys, Figure 11.28. The resultant R is composed, therefore, of the oblique reaction C supported by the shear keys and a horizontal reaction N, which is responsible for securing the joint.

The axial stress distribution at the joint cross section differs in this case from what would be obtained by ordinary calculations. It is obvious that N is smaller than F (the sum of forces F_1 and F_2). Let α be the angle of the key support faces with respect to the horizontal; then $F - N = W \tan \alpha$, and for a typical case of $\tan \alpha = 0.50, F - N = W/2$. Consider a segment weighing 50 tons (45 mt), temporarily assembled by a prestress force of 100 tons (90 mt) located in the top slab; the axial force reduction is 25 tons (23 mt)—that is, 25% of the total applied prestress force.

If the rate of erection of the precast segments is sufficient to ensure the positioning of four segments before the resin in the first joint has set, then the reduction in the effective axial force in this joint will be 100 tons (90 mt), which more or less corresponds to one tendon of twelve $\frac{1}{2}$ in. diameter strands. The same conclusion would be valid when the permanent prestressing was used to ensure the temporary stability of the cantilever.

In conclusion, it is recommended that this reduction of the effective prestress force be taken

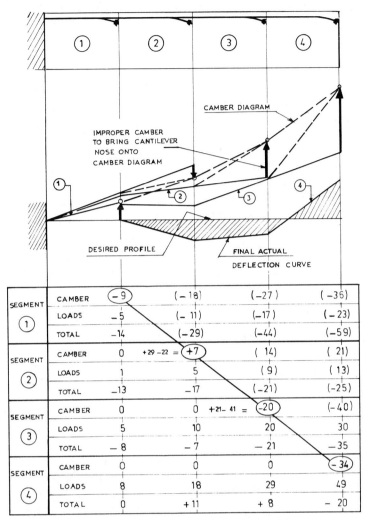

SEGMENT 1	CAMBER	(-9)	(-18)	(-27)	(-36)
	LOADS	-5	(-11)	(-17)	(-23)
	TOTAL	-14	(-29)	(-44)	(-59)
SEGMENT 2	CAMBER	0	+29 -22 = (+7)	(14)	(21)
	LOADS	1	5	(9)	(13)
	TOTAL	-13	-17	(-21)	(-25)
SEGMENT 3	CAMBER	0	0	+21 -41 = (-20)	(-40)
	LOADS	5	10	20	30
	TOTAL	-8	-7	-21	-35
SEGMENT 4	CAMBER	0	0	0	(-34)
	LOADS	8	18	29	49
	TOTAL	0	+11	+8	-20

FIGURE 11.27. Follow-up of deflections with improper use of camber diagram.

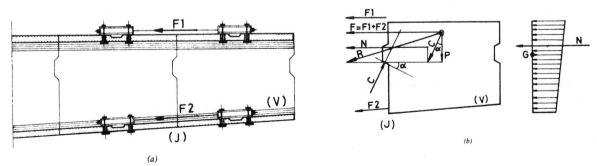

FIGURE 11.28. Temporary assembly. (*a*) Elevation of temporary assembly. (*b*) Joint equilibrium.

into account while verifying the cantilever resistance and stability. Failure to do so may result in temporary joint opening, which is undesirable although not dangerous for stability.

It is also preferable to choose the intensity and the point of application of the forces F_1 and F_2 such as to allow the axial force N to be as close as possible to the section centroidal axis, thus ensuring a nearly uniform axial stress distribution over the total height and hence a resin film of constant thickness.

Permanent Assembly: Structural Importance of Epoxy Resins　As regards the final prestress tendon profiles, it was shown in Chapter 4 how the resistance of the different cantilevers is ensured by a first group of tendons, known as cantilever tendons, which may be straight or curved in profile and anchored on the various segment faces. The stressing operations remain in the critical path of construction because a new pair of segments cannot be placed before the last pair has been stressed to the existing cantilever, Figure 11.29.

The second group of tendons joins the different cantilevers together and makes the structure continuous. They are anchored either in block-outs in the bottom slab or in the fillets at the junction between the top slab and the webs after upward deviation to top slab level.

The service shear forces that act upon the joints vary according to the type and characteristics of the structure. In variable-depth bridge decks with draped prestressing tendons the shear stress across the joints is usually low. In a long-span, constant-depth bridge deck with straight tendons, however, the shear stresses at the joints can exceed 600 psi (4 MPa), as was the case in several structures mentioned in Chapter 4. A bad choice, or improper use, of the epoxy resin can be a critical factor concerning the shear resistance of the joints, and for this reason joints of this type require strict quality control.

In general, the different types of epoxy resins available have final strengths substantially exceeding that of concrete, so they do not constitute a weak point in themselves. Several conditions must be satisfied, however, in order that the resin cure properly.

1. Mixing the constituents in their correct proportions.
2. Eliminating any solvents that have a fatal effect on the properties of the resin.
3. Avoiding any flexible additives, such as thiokol, that greatly increase the deformability of the epoxy.
4. Mixing and applying carefully.

With respect to the last point, the surfaces to be joined must be specially treated if the best results are to be obtained. Comparative tests have shown that sand blasting gives the most satisfactory results, the surfaces being kept clean, dry, and free from grease during placing. In damp or rainy weather alcohol is burnt on the joint surfaces to eliminate surface moisture. The water present in the concrete itself has no detrimental effect on the performance of the resin.

It has also been established that rapid placing of successive segments has a favorable effect on the properties of the resin. The additional compressive stress applied to an epoxy joint under polymerization when the next segment is prestressed improves the resin's ultimate mechanical properties.

Finally, note that in variable-height structures the joint detailing is such that the joint plane is not normal to the principal stress, especially at the bottom slab level. The epoxy joint is then subjected to shear forces that may be quite large and that can cause failure of the bottom slab in the event of nonpolymerization of the epoxy resin.

In addition to the precautions taken to ensure correct curing, one may provide against the risk of bad results by including shear keys in the bottom slab.

11.5.2　SECOND-GENERATION SEGMENTS

Although the characteristics and performance of the first structures built with match-cast joints are not in doubt, it seems a good idea to investigate new types of joints allowing the transmission of shear forces without relying on the strength of epoxy resins.

Second-generation segments do just this, being equipped with interlocking keys in the top and bottom slabs and in most of the height of the webs. This configuration of shear keys at regular intervals, which improves the behavior of joints by relieving the epoxy of its structural role, has the

FINAL SEGMENT ASSEMBLY

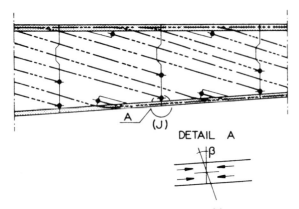

FIGURE 11.29.　Final segment assembly.

advantages of simplicity and safety. This type of segment has been used with success in several bridges, notably the Alpine Motorways, the Saint Andre de Cubzac Bridge, and the Sallingsund Bridge, and more recently in several structures in the United States such as the Long Key and Seven Mile bridges in Florida.

Ribs and Interior Anchorage Blocks Anchorage blocks (blisters) or stiffening ribs are currently used inside the segments for the final longitudinal prestress anchors. The tendons, ensuring the stability and resistance of the cantilever and placed progressively as construction proceeds, can be anchored away from the joint faces, thereby rendering the stressing operations and the segment-placing operations independent of one another. The ribs and anchorage blocks are generally used to house the temporary prestress that ensures the provisional stability of the cantilever, thus leaving the top slab completely free.

Bolted Ribs Despite the tensile strength of the epoxy resin at a glued joint, no tensile resistance is usually considered, as precast segmental structures are nearly always totally prestressed and so no tensile stresses can develop across the joint. However, we can further improve epoxied match-cast joints by giving them a certain resistance to tension by using bolted ribs, which ensure the continuity of the longitudinal reinforcing steel, Figure 11.30.

11.5.3 EPOXY FOR JOINTS

The structural importance of the thin layer of epoxy resin forming the joint between two adjacent precast segments was discussed in Section 11.5.1. We now take a closer look at the physical and mechanical properties of these resins and the various precautions to be taken to ensure satisfactory and consistent results.

Epoxy Types Epoxy resin glues are made up from two components: the epoxy resin and the hardener. Mixing these two components in the correct proportions gives a thermostable product with properties that depend upon the type of resin and hardener used. Three grades of epoxy resin are commonly used, depending upon the ambient temperature range under which the resin is to be applied:

40 to 60°F (5 to 15°C)	Fast-reacting epoxy
60 to 75°F (15 to 25°C)	Medium-fast-reacting epoxy
75 to 105°F (25 to 40°C)	Slow-reacting epoxy

1. *Color* The resin and the hardener must be of clearly contrasting colors thus avoiding any confusion. When properly mixed, the final product is to be a homogeneous gray color similar to that of concrete.

2. *Shelf life of components* Both components may be stored for up to one year, provided that the storage temperature is kept between 50 and 70°F (10 and 20°C). After three months' storage it is necessary to check that the epoxy resin shows no sign of becoming crystalline. If it does, then special treatment must be given to the resin, followed by tests, before use.

3. *Pot Life of the Mixed Glue* The pot life of an epoxy resin is a measure of the time interval between the mixing of the components together and the moment when the glue becomes no longer workable. The workability of the glue is determined by its internal temperature, depending upon the grade of epoxy resin employed. For a 10 lb (5 kg) mix used on site, mixed under isothermic conditions until an even color of mix is obtained, the following results are required:

Epoxy Grade	Workability Limit Temperature
5 to 15°C	40°C (104°F)
15 to 25°C	40°C (104°F)
25 to 40°C	55 to 60°C (131 to 140°F)

The pot life must be approximately:

	Ambient Temperature					
Epoxy Grade	41°F (5°C)	50°F (10°C)	59°F (15°C)	68°F (20°C)	86°F (30°C)	95°F (35°C)
5 to 15°C	40 min.	15 min.				
15 to 25°C			20 min.	15 min.		
25 to 40°C					25 min.	18 min.

BOLTED RIB JOINTS

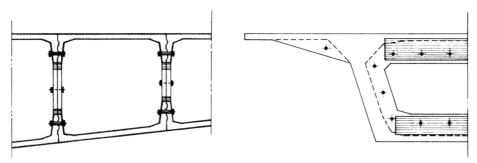

FIGURE 11.30. Bolted rib joints.

On site, each 10 lb (5 kg) mix of epoxy resin must be applied to the concrete surface within the pot-life period as specified above.

4. *Open Time of the Applied Epoxy Glue* The open time of the glue is defined as the period between its application to the concrete surface and the moment when it reaches its workability limit temperature. Because of the much greater heat dissipation from the thin layer [$\frac{3}{64}$ to $\frac{1}{8}$ in. (1 to 3 mm)] on the concrete surface, the applied glue takes much longer to reach the workability limit temperature than the mix in the pot.

The open time must never be less than one hour, regardless of the grade used. One measuring device used to determine open time is the Vicat's needle shown in Figure 11.31. A 1 mm layer of epoxy glue is spread onto a steel plate, and the stopwatch is started. The time lapsed before the needle will penetrate only 0.5 mm into the glue layer is defined as the open time.

5. *Thixotropy* This characteristic gives an indication of the epoxy resin's ability to be applied to vertical surfaces with relative ease and yet with subsequent running. Thixotropy may be measured using Daniel's gauge, Figure 11.32. The gauge is placed on a level surface with the gutter section horizontal. The gutter is then filled with freshly mixed resin and hardener and abruptly turned to the upright position, as shown in the diagram. The flow time relationship is recorded. The test should be carried out at the maximum temperature for which the resin is specified. A resin that flows less than 30 mm in 10 minutes is suitable for application to vertical concrete surfaces. Other testing methods are available such as the sag flow apparatus according to ASTM D2730-68.

Other characteristics of the epoxy glue that may be tested on site are:

The angle of internal friction: The ease with which the excess resin may be squeezed out of the joint when subject to uniform pressure.

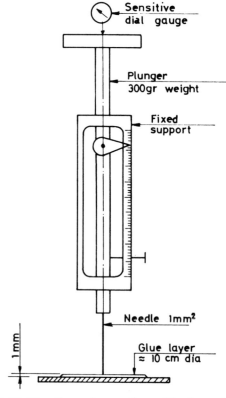

FIGURE 11.31. Open-time testing—Vicat's needle.

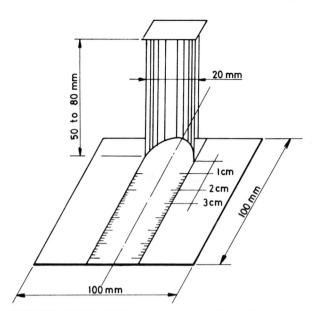

FIGURE 11.32. Thixotropy testing—Daniel's gauge.

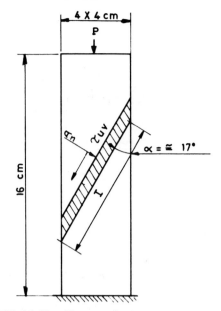

FIGURE 11.33. Shear-resistance test.

Shrinkage: Must be practically nil.

Water absorption rate and solubility in water: Maximum permissible true water absorption—12%. Maximum permissible quantity of epoxy soluble in water at 25°C (77°F)—4%.

Heat resistance: Minimum required value according to Mostens (DIN 53458) on week-old 10 × 15 × 120 mm test rods is 50°C (122°F).

Mechanical properties

1. *Shear resistance* The shear resistance of the mixed epoxy glue is determined on rectangular concrete test specimens with the following dimensions: 1.6 × 1.6 × 6.3 in. (4 × 4 × 16 cm) with a resin interface at 17° to the vertical, Figure 11.33. The concrete test pieces are made from a high-quality concrete comparable to that used in precast segment manufacture and are cured under water seven days from time of casting.

After removal from the water the pieces are dab-dried and the surfaces to be assembled are prepared by shot blasting, wire brushing, or other similar methods to remove laitance. The test pieces are then resubmerged in water for three hours, after which they are removed and dabbed dry with a clean cloth. The resin is then applied in a layer of $\frac{5}{64}$ in. (2 mm) on one surface and the test beam clamped in an assembly that maintains a normal pressure on the interface of 21 psi (0.15 MPa). The assembly is stored for seven days at a temperature representative of the desired working conditions, and then the test is carried out. The minimum ac-

ceptable ultimate shear stress at the interface is 1400 psi (10 MPa).

2. *Shear Modulus* The instantaneous shear modulus (C_i) must be greater than 220,000 psi (1500 MPa) at:

15°C (59°F) for grade 5 to 15°C

25°C (77°F) for grade 15 to 25°C

40°C (104°F) for grade 25 to 40°C

The long-term shear modulus must be greater than 14,500 psi (1000 MPa) after 28 days at the same temperatures as above. Solid cylindrical test pieces are used for measuring these values in conjunction with the easily made test apparatus shown in Figure 11.34.

Certain epoxy resins show an excessive sensitivity to high temperatures that makes them unacceptable in warm climates. Figure 11.35 shows comparative results of ten different resins tested for the Rio Nitcroi Bridge. It is obvious that a product that becomes practically plastic with no shear modulus at 60°C is completely unacceptable.

3. *Tensile Bending Strength* A three-point bending test is carried out on a pair of glued concrete cubes with a compressive strength of 5700 psi (400 kg/cm²), Figure 11.36. The faces to be glued are shot blasted, or bush hammered, so as to remove laitance. The cubes are then submerged in water for 72 hours. When taken out of the water the surfaces to be glued are dried simply by dabbing with a clean cloth. Immediately after the dab

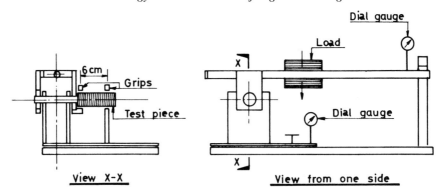

FIGURE 11.34. Shear-modulus test.

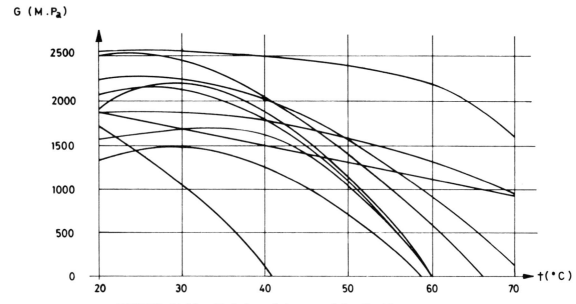

FIGURE 11.35. Variation of shear modulus G with temperature.

drying the glue is applied in a layer of $\frac{1}{16}$ in. (1.5 mm) to one of the prepared faces. The corresponding face of the other cube is placed against the glue layer, and the two cubes are clamped together with a clamping force of 300 lb (150 kg). The assembly is then wrapped in a damp cloth, which must be kept wet until the three-point bending test is carried out.

4. *Compressive Strength* The compressive strength is determined according to DIN 1164 on 4 cm (1½ in.) cubes of cured epoxy glue. After 24 hours (from the time of preparing the samples) at the maximum temperatures for each grade the compressive strength must be not less than 12,000 psi (80 MPa). The loading rate is to be approximately 3600 psi (25 MPa) per minute.

5. *Elastic modulus in compression* The instantaneous modulus (E_i) is determined on cubes of pure epoxy after curing for seven days at the maximum group temperature. These cubes are the same size as those used for the compressive-strength determinations. The modulus must not be less than 1,140,000 psi (7850 MPa)

Practical Use of Epoxy in Match-Cast Joints In regard to the use of the resin, the two components should be mixed carefully and quickly as near as possible to the surfaces to be coated. Under no circumstances should oil or grease be allowed to come into contact with surfaces that are to be glued. Most standard demolding agents are suitable for use, but care should be taken to ensure that no oil-based demolders are used. Exposure to weather during the storage period is often sufficient to remove the demolding agent. For best results, surface laitance should be removed by shot blasting or bush hammering. This treatment is normally carried out in the storage yard. With the use of multiple keys, the structural role of the

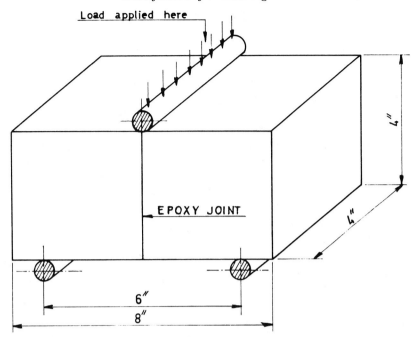

FIGURE 11.36. Tensile bending-strength test.

epoxy is considerably reduced and a special preparation of the surface is not a mandatory feature.

Immediately before the glue is applied, the surfaces are to be cleaned to remove traces of dirt, grease or oil, and dust.

Under normal climatic conditions it will not always be possible to avoid dampness on the surfaces to be glued. If the surfaces do show signs of moisture, they must be dab dried with a clean cloth, and no gluing may proceed until all free water has been eliminated.

The thickness of the glue layer should be about $\frac{1}{16}$ in. (1.5 mm). As soon as possible after the resin has been applied, the surfaces must be brought together. Pressure must be applied before the open time of the epoxy resin expires. The pressure applied by either temporary or final prestress should not be less than 30 psi (0.2 MPa).

11.6 Manufacture of Precast Segments

11.6.1 INTRODUCTION

The various methods used until now for precasting segments fall into two basic categories:

1. Long-line casting, where all segments to make up either half or a full cantilever are manufactured on a fixed bed with the formwork moving along the bed for the successive casting operations.

2. Short-line casting (with either horizontal or vertical casting), where segments are manufactured in a step-by-step procedure with the forms maintained at a stationary position.

For match-cast joint structures, the accuracy of the segment geometry is an absolute priority. Adequate surveying methods and equipment must be used to ensure an accurate follow-up of the geometry and an independent verification of all measurements and adjustments.

Immediately after the manufacture of a segment the as-cast geometry should be controlled and compared to the theoretical geometry to allow any necessary adjustment to be incorporated in subsequent casting operations. This aspect of match casting is particularly important for the short-line method and will be covered later in this chapter.

11.6.2 LONG-LINE CASTING

In this method all the segments are cast, in their correct relative position, on a casting bed that exactly reproduces the profile of the structure with allowance for camber. One or more formwork units travel along this line and are guided by a preadjusted soffit. With this method the joint surfaces are invariably cast in a vertical position.

Figure 11.37 shows the casting sequence.[3] The pier segment (3) is cast first, then the segments on either side of the pier segment (1) and (2). If a pair of forms is used, then the symmetrical segments on each side of the pier segment can be cast simultaneously, thus saving casting time. As segment casting progresses, the initial segments may be removed for storage, leaving the center portion of the casting bed free. If enough forms are available, then the casting of a second pair of cantilevers may proceed even though the first pair is not completely cast.

Figure 11.38 shows the typical cross section of a long-line casting bed with the formwork in operation. The method was initially developed for constant-depth box girders (Choisy-le-Roi and Courbevoie Bridges). It was later extended to the case of variable-depth decks such as the Oleron Viaduct (the two sketches of Figures 11.37 and 11.38 refer to this structure) and also adopted in other countries (Hartel Bridge in Holland).

The important advantages of the long-line casting method are:

It is easy to set out and control the deck geometry.

After form stripping, it is not necessary to immediately transfer the segments to the storage area in order to continue casting.

The disadvantages are:

Substantial space may be required. The minimum length is usually slightly more than half the length of the longest span of the structure, but it depends upon the geometry and the symmetry of the structure.

The casting bed must be built on a firm foundation that will not settle or deflect under the weight of the segments. If the structure is curved, the long line must accommodate this curvature.

All equipment necessary for casting, curing, and so on must be mobile.

11.6.3 SHORT-LINE HORIZONTAL CASTING

The short-line casting method requires all segments to be cast in the same place, using stationary forms, and against the previously cast segment in order to obtain a match-cast joint. After casting and initial curing, the previously cast segment is

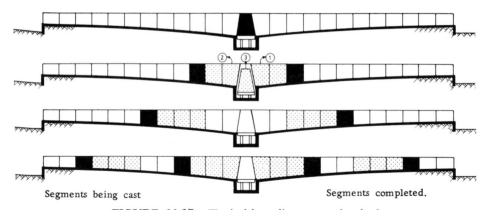

Segments being cast   Segments completed.

FIGURE 11.37. Typical long-line precasting bed.

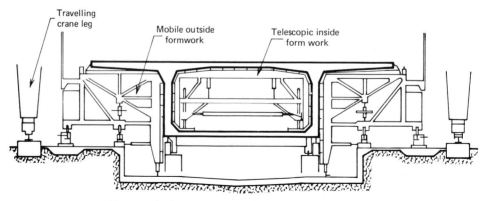

FIGURE 11.38. Typical cross section of long-line casting bed with formwork.

removed for storage and the freshly cast segment is moved into its place. The casting cycle is then repeated. This operation is illustrated in Figures 11.39 and 11.40.[3,4]

It is important that the reader fully comprehend the principle of the method insofar as building a deck of a given geometry is concerned. When a straight box is desired, Figure 11.41, the match marking mate segment $(n - 1)$ is moved from the casting position to the match-cast position along a straight line, and this is usually verified by taking measurements on four elevation bolts (a) embedded in the concrete roadway slab and two alignment stirrups (b) located along the box centerline. A pure translation of each segment between the cast and match-cast positions therefore results in the construction of a perfectly straight bridge (both in elevation and in plan view), within the accuracy of the measurements made at the casting site.

To obtain a bridge with a vertical curve, the match-cast segment $(n - 1)$ must first be translated from its original position and then give a small rotation in the vertical plane (angle α shown in Figure 11.42). Usually the bulkhead is left in a fixed position, and all segments have in elevation the shape of a rectangular trapezoid with the tapered face along the match-catch segment. It is therefore only necessary to adjust the soffit of the cast segment during the adjustment operations.

A curve in the horizontal plane is obtained in the same fashion, Figure 11.43, by first moving the match-cast segment $(n - 1)$ to its position by a pure translation followed by a rotation of a small angle β in plan to realize the desired curvature.

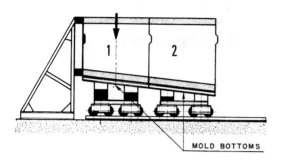

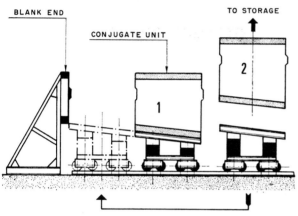

FIGURE 11.39. Typical short-line precasting operation.

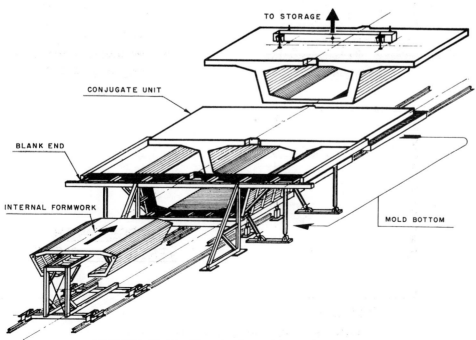

FIGURE 11.40. Formwork used in casting segments.

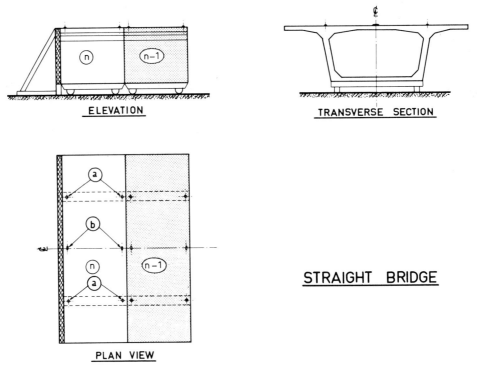

ELEVATION

TRANSVERSE SECTION

PLAN VIEW

STRAIGHT BRIDGE

FIGURE 11.41. Straight bridge.

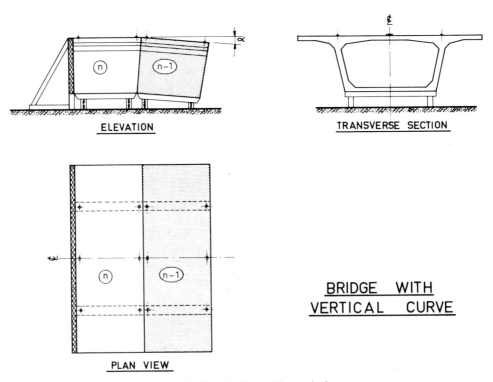

ELEVATION

TRANSVERSE SECTION

PLAN VIEW

BRIDGE WITH
VERTICAL CURVE

FIGURE 11.42. Bridge with vertical curve.

496

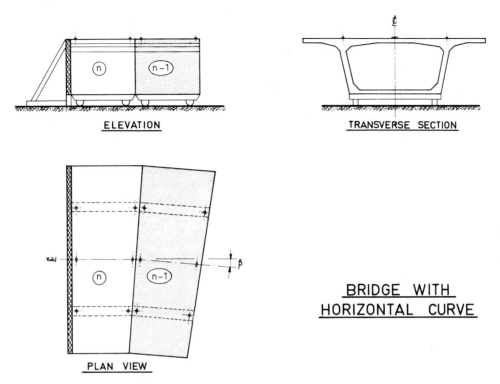

ELEVATION

TRANSVERSE SECTION

BRIDGE WITH
HORIZONTAL CURVE

PLAN VIEW

FIGURE 11.43.   Bridge with horizontal curve.

Change in the superelevation of the bridge may also be achieved with a short-line casting; however, the principle is a little more difficult to properly grasp, Figures 11.44 and 11.45. A constant transverse fall of the bridge does not need to be repeated in the casting machine. Segments may be cast with soffit and roadway slab both horizontal and placed at their proper attitude in the bridge by offsetting the bearing elevation under the webs to obtain the desired cross fall. Only a variable superelevation must be accounted for in the casting operation, and this is the normal case in bridges with reverse curves and in transition areas between curves and straight alignments. In such a case match-cast segment $(n - 1)$ needs to be rotated by a small angle such as γ around the bridge centerline. Because the bridge geometry is usually defined at roadway level and not at soffit level, the rotation given to the match-cast segment results in a slight horizontal displacement of the soffit in the casting machine, which must be accounted for. Also all surfaces of the box segment (top slab, soffit, and webs) are no longer true planes but are slightly warped. To allow the formwork panels to adjust to this change of shape, it is absolutely mandatory to eliminate all restraints such as closed torsionally stiff members.

The basic advantages of the short-line casting method are therefore the relatively small space required and the fact that all equipment and formwork remain at a stationary position. The mobility of equipment necessary for the long-line method is no longer needed. Also, horizontal and vertical curves as well as variable superelevation are obtained with short-line casting without the major change in soffit configuration that would be required in the long-line casting method. However, success will depend upon the accuracy of adjustment of the match-cast segments, and precise survey and control procedures must be initiated (Section 11.6.5). This last aspect represents the major potential disadvantage as a direct consequence of the intrinsic potential of the method.

11.6.4   SHORT-LINE VERTICAL CASTING

Normally, for both the long- and short-line methods, the segments are cast in a horizontal position. A variation in the short-line method is that used for the Alpine Motorways near Lyons, France, where the segments were cast in a vertical position (cast on end) as shown in Figure 3.100. The procedure is as follows: after the first segment is cast, the forms are removed and moved upward

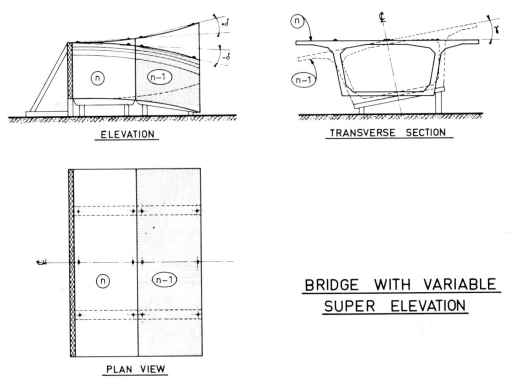

FIGURE 11.44. Short-line casting—bridge with variable superelevation.

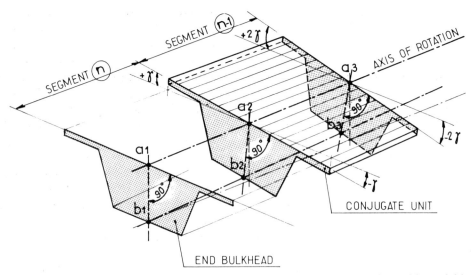

FIGURE 11.45. Short-line casting—isometric view of segment casting with variable superelevation.

so that each succeeding segment can be cast above the previous one. After a segment is cast and cured, the segment beneath it is transferred to storage and the one removed from the forms is moved down, to rest on the floor. The advantages claimed for vertical match casting include easier placing and vibration of the concrete. However, special handling equipment and procedures are required to rotate the segment from the vertical to its final horizontal position.

11.6.5 GEOMETRY AND SURVEY CONTROL

Segment Precasting in a Casting Machine

The principles described in this section apply to short-line horizontal casting but may be easily extended to vertical casting. The apparatus used to form the concrete segment is usually referred to as a casting machine and is made up essentially of five components:

1. The bulkhead that forms the front section of the segment.
2. The match-cast segment, properly coated at the front end section with a suitable demolding agent and used to form the back end section of the newly cast segment.
3. The mold bottom (or soffit).
4. The side forms, properly hinged for stripping and firmly sealed to the bulkhead and the match-cast segment during casting. The inside forms, which pivot and retract for stripping.
5. The inside forms, which pivot and retract for stripping.

The relationship between an individual segment and the finished structure is established by means of three different systems of reference:

1. *The final system of reference,* which is the reference for the finished geometry of the structure. In this system each segment is described by its basic geometry.
2. *The auxiliary system of reference,* which corresponds to the precasting machine and is attached thereto.
3. *The elementary reference system,* which is attached to each segment and would be the equivalent of intrinsic coordinates in space geometry.

The principle of the precasting method is as follows. During the casting of segment A (segment B being in the match-cast position) the elementary reference system of A is identical with the auxiliary reference system, that of the casting machine.

To position B with respect to A becomes simply a matter of positioning B with respect to the precasting machine. It is the task of the design office to provide the theoretical geometric information necessary for positioning. The values are computed from the basic geometry with the addition of the relevant compensatory values for deflections. The definitions of these reference systems are presented below.

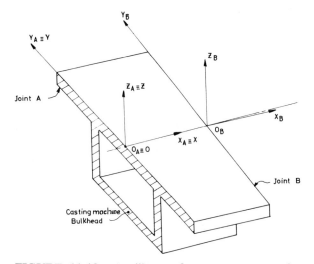

FIGURE 11.46. Auxiliary reference system (casting-machine reference).

The auxiliary reference system refers to the casting machine and is defined in Figure 11.46. The plane of the bulkhead is perfectly vertical. The upper edge of the bulkhead is a horizontal in this plane except when segments do not have planar top surfaces. The x, y and z axes refer to the casting-machine reference system, whereas x_A, y_A, and z_A refer to the elementary system of reference. The elementary system of reference is materialized on each segment in the following manner:

1. *The x_a axis:* This axis is represented by marks (such as saw cuts) made on two steel stirrups anchored in the top slab as near as possible to the joints.
2. *The origin o_a:* The origin o_a is located at the point where the x_a axis intersects the plane of the joint at the bulkhead.
3. *The plane x_a, o_a, y_a:* This plane may be defined by three fixed leveling points, the position of each point with respect to the plane x, o, y being arbitrary but invariable. For practical reasons, four leveling points are used and materialized by bolts anchored in the top surface of the segment above the webs and as close as possible to the joints.

Now that the elementary system of reference has been established (all measurements and readings being made while the segment is in the casting machine before the forms are removed), the segment can be positioned with respect to the auxiliary reference system, so that it can be placed in the correct countercasting position according to the calculations supplied by the design office.

In order to correctly position the countercasting segment, information is needed about the final geometry of the structure. The overall geometry of a bridge structure is normally defined by the geometry of the roadway. From this roadway geometry it is necessary to determine the geometry of the concrete structure itself.

The longitudinal reference line to which all the necessary parameters are related is known as the *box girder line (BGL)*. This line may coincide with the top concrete surface of the box girder, but it may also be a fictitious line of reference if the box girder top slab shape is not regular.

The box girder line is usually described using two curves, Figure 11.47:

One curve (σ) in a horizontal plane, which gives y as a function of x for each point where the box girder line intersects a joint plane between segments and also the center points of supports (abutments or piers); this curve is simply the projection of the true space box girder line onto a horizontal plane and is sometimes referred to as the "bgl" (small letters).

One curve (s) in a developed vertical plane giving z as a function of σ for the same points mentioned above. This s curve is the real box girder line, BGL.

To complete the definition of the segment position in space—at each joint line and at support centers—we must define the transverse slope of the theoretical extrados line.

It is important for both the bgl and the BGL to calculate the σ and s parameters, respectively, in order to obtain an accurate determination of projected and real span lengths.

The calculations and structural drawings refer to nominal segment lengths and span lengths. Usually these lengths refer to the projection on a horizontal plane and follow the curvilinear abscissas. The segment lengths chosen on this basis may be retained, but in calculating the real lengths of cast-in-place closure joints and three-dimensional s curve must be used.

Because of the way a casting machine works, the segment joint at the bulkhead end is invariably perpendicular to the axis of the segment. Therefore, in plan view, the segments are generally of trapezoidal shape, except for segments over the piers which are rectangular in order to provide a constant starting point for each cantilever, Figure 11.48.

Segment Casting Parameters

All measurements on a segment are made when the segment is still in the casting machine. Readings must be taken when the concrete has hardened and before formwork stripping, Figure 11.49. Horizontal alignment readings give the distance of the segment axes as marked on the stirrups from the casting-machine reference line. Longitudinal profile level readings are given by the four bolt elevations relative to the horizontal reference plane.

Readings must be taken on the segment just cast and also on the match-cast segment. Corrections are applied to allow for the geometric defects in the preceding segment, Figure 11.50, and are used as "theoretical values for adjustment."

Survey Control During Precasting Operations

The surveyor in charge of the operations must complete a data sheet for each segment containing essentially:

1. Theoretical basic data supplied by the design office, allowing the preparation of the horizontal alignment and the two parallel bolt lines.
2. Corrected values defined either graphically or by computer.
3. Survey control readings.
4. Linear measurements on the segments.
5. Schematic representation of the segment to rapidly verify the relative positions of the segment axes.
6. A level check to pick up any gross error in level readings on the same segment.
7. Comments on the casting operations.

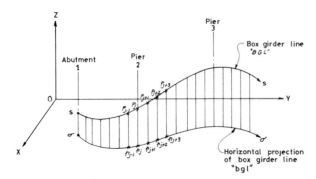

FIGURE 11.47. Box girder line curves.

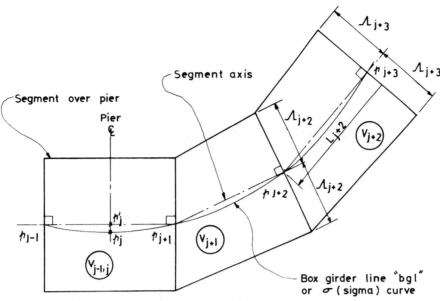

FIGURE 11.48. Short-line casting—position of segment joints in plan view.

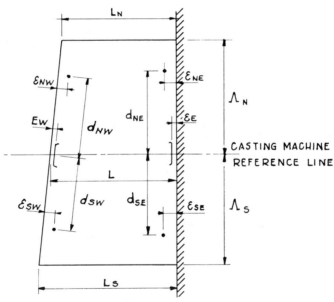

FIGURE 11.49. Casting-machine orientation and segment measurements.

As an example, Figure 11.51 shows the typical survey control made on the first four segments of a typical cantilever. Control of alignment and levels may be followed graphically or numerically by computer, using the basic geometric data obtained in the casting machine and shown in Figure 11.52.

In order to avoid any significant deviation from the theoretical geometry, it is necessary to provide for corrections when casting the next segment. Figure 11.53 shows how this would be done for the plan alignment. Similar corrections are made for the longitudinal profile on the two parallel bolt lines. It is essential not only to follow carefully the trajectory of the two bolt lines separately but also to check for <u>each</u> segment that the superelevation (given by the crosswise difference in level between

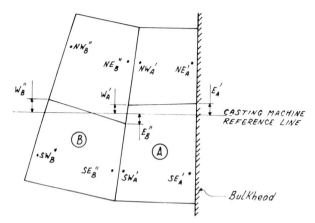

FIGURE 11.50. Plan view of casting operation—readings using survey instruments.

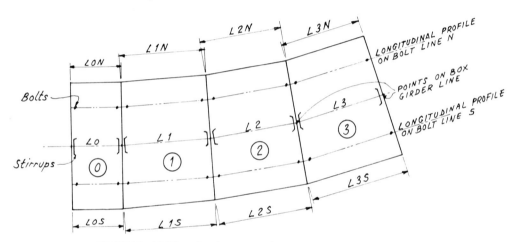

FIGURE 11.51. Casting operation—typical survey control.

the two bolt lines) varies regularly according to the theoretical geometry. Failure to do so has resulted in important geometric imperfections on certain projects.

Survey Control During Construction

The nature of match-cast segmental construction is such that the structure is really "built" in the precasting yard. Although corrections can be made in the field, such corrections are undesirable and always a source of additional expense and delays. Close control of precasting is far more efficient. It is nevertheless important to check the evolution of the structural geometry during segment placing:

1. To compare actual deflections with computed values,

2. To ensure that no major errors have escaped the control in the precast yard or factory.

Such checks at the site should include:

1. Pier positions, height and in plan.
2. Bearing positions, level and orientation.
3. Pier segments, level and orientation.
4. Cantilevers proper, every third segment, including levels, superelevation, and orientation.
5. Overall geometry of the structure after continuity is achieved between the individual cantilevers.

Conclusion

The principles of geometry and survey control are more complicated to explain than to use, once the

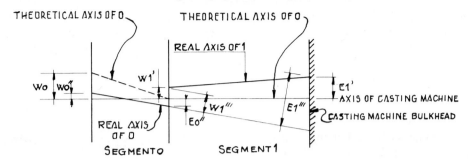

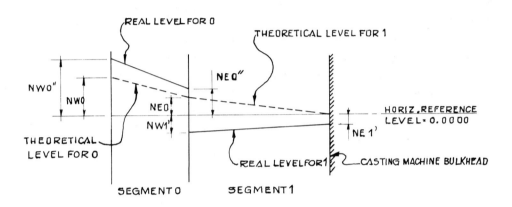

FIGURE 11.52. Survey control—horizontal alignment and longitudinal profile results. (*a*) Horizontal alignment. (*b*) Longitudinal profile.

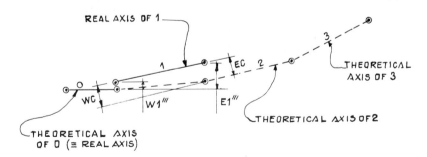

FIGURE 11.53. Typical alignment corrections during casting operations.

basic principles of a casting machine are thoroughly understood. The short-line method has great potential to construct segments for bridges, even those with very complicated trajectories, rapidly and economically. Outstanding examples are the Chillon and St. Cloud Viaducts in Europe and Linn Cove Viaduct in the United States. At Saint Cloud, 120- to 140-ton segments were cast on a one-day cycle, and the final geometry of the bridge was obtained with no on-site adjustment.

On the other hand, a loose approach to geometry control at the casting yard may lead to serious difficulties at the project site.

11.6.6 PRECASTING YARD AND FACTORIES

The precasting operations are usually carried out in a yard or even a factory if the size of the project allows the corresponding investment. All operations, such as:

Preparation of the reinforcing steel cages and ducts for post-tensioning tendons

Manufacture of concrete

Manufacture of segments including heat curing

Storage of segments including finishing and quality control are performed in a repetitive fashion under factory conditions.

As an example of typical precasting-yard layouts, Figures 11.54 and 11.55 show views of:

The Saint Cloud Viaduct precasting yard with short-line casting

The Oleron Viaduct precasting yard with long-line casting

The typical precasting cycle (with either the long-line or the short-line method) is of one segment per formwork per day with a one-day work shift, concrete hardening taking place during the night (at least 14 hours between the completion of concrete placing in the evening and the stripping of forms the next morning). Shorter construction cycles may be obtained by reducing the time of concrete hardening, but quality may decline if all the operations are not kept under very strict control.

Heat curing of the concrete to reduce the construction cycle and accelerate the rotation of the casting machines is perfectly acceptable. Its improper use, however, may alter the accuracy of joint matching between segments, as shown in Figure 11.56. This effect would be particularly significant for wide but short segments.

Typical segments usually have the following dimensions:

Width	30 to 40 ft (9 to 12 m)
Length	10 to 12 ft (3 to 3.6 m)
Ratio width/length	3 to 3.5

In the case of wide decks or long spans, where the segment length is reduced to reduce the unit weight, the usual geometric proportions may vary considerably; such is the case for two notable structures:

St. Cloud	width 70 ft, length 7 ft, ratio 10
St. Andre de Cubzac	width 58 ft, length 5.8 ft, ratio 10

For such segments, heat curing is more likely to create small changes in the segment shape, which may build up progressively and so alter the effectiveness of joint matching. This is due to the development of a temperature gradient in the match-cast segment, which is in contact on one side with the newly cast heated segment and on the other side with the lower outside temperature.

The problem may be completely eliminated by always heat curing both segments simultaneously so as to avoid any temperature gradient. Experience has proved the method totally efficient.

When the project involving segment precasting is of sufficient magnitude or where climatic conditions are adverse, precasting factories are a logical extrapolation from the short-line method performed in an open precasting yard. Segment manufacture takes place in a completely enclosed building with a better use of personnel and a more consistent quality of products.

An interesting example is afforded by the B-3 South Viaducts, requiring production of 2200 precast segments weighing between 28 and 58 tons (25 to 53 mt). The precasting site was installed close to the project and included four main areas:

1. An assembly workshop, where the reinforcing steel cages were prepared and the prestressing ducts positioned. The finished cages were handled by a 5 ton tower crane.

2. A concrete mixing plant.

3. A precasting factory where the segments were cast and cured.

4. A storage area where the finished segments were left to cure adequately. These segments were handled by a traveling portal crane.

The precasting factory was equipped with four precasting machines, all of which were entirely protected from the outside environment. Two machines were reserved for the manufacture of 15 to 20 ft (4.5 to 6 m) segments and two for the 20 to

PRECASTING YARD

Scale 1/500

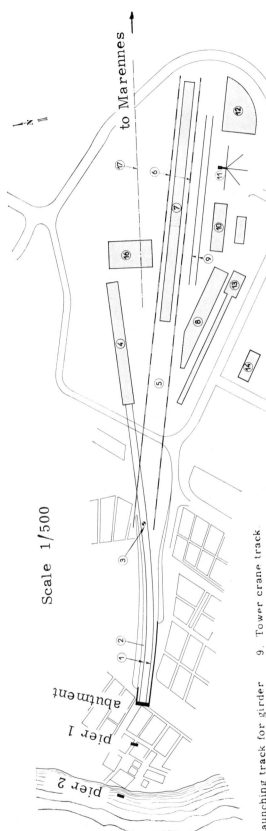

1. Launching track for girder and trolley.
2. Access ramp.
3. Loading point for segments
4. Launching girder assembly zone.
5. Segment storage.
6. Travelling crane track.
7. Mould bottom
8. Prestressing steel storage.
9. Tower crane track.
10. Reinforcement assembly.
11. Concrete plant.
12. Precast elements.
13. Prestress tendon manufacture.
14. Offices.
15. General Services.
16. Toll gate position
17. Future carriageway alignment.

FIGURE 11.54. St. Cloud Viaduct, precasting yard layout. (1) Launching track for girder and trolley. (2) Access ramp. (3) Loading point for segments. (4) Launching-girder assembly zone. (5) Segment storage. (6) Traveling crane track. (7) Mold bottom. (8) Prestressing steel storage. (9) Tower crane track. (10) Reinforcement assembly. (11) Concrete plant. (12) Precast elements. (13) Prestress tendon manufacture. (14) Offices. (15) General services. (16) Toll gate position. (17) Future carriageway alignment.

505

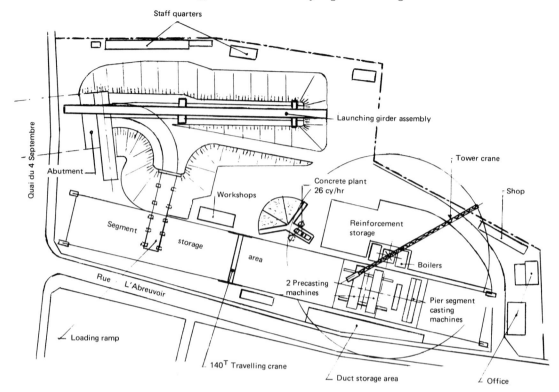

FIGURE 11.55. Oleron Viaduct, precasting yard layout.

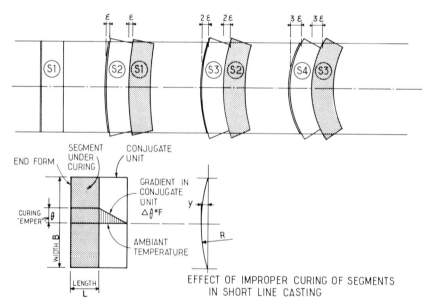

FIGURE 11.56. Effect of improper curing of segments in short-line casting.

31 ft. (6 to 9.5 m) segments, Figures 11.57 and 11.58. Each casting machine was made up of a mobile form, an end form or bulkhead, two hinged outside forms, and a telescopic inside form, Figure 11.59. Handling of concrete and reinforcing steel inside the factory was performed by two 10 ton travel cranes.

The production of the different segments involved the following operations:

1. Assembly of the steel cages in a template.
2. Steel-cage storage.
3. Final steel-cage preparation and duct installation.

FIGURE 11.57. B-3 South Viaducts, inside view of the precasting factory.

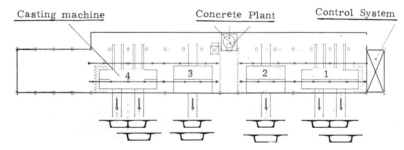

FIGURE 11.58. B-3 South Viaducts, plan view of the precasting factory.

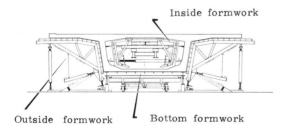

FIGURE 11.59. B-3 South Viaducts, detail of a casting machine.

4. Positioning of steel cage inside the formwork.
5. Adjustment of casting machine, including alignment of match-cast segment and sealing of all form panels.
6. Concrete casting and finishing.
7. Steam curing.
8. Formwork stripping, followed by transfer of the match-cast segment to the storage yard and

of the newly cast segment to the match-cast position by means of an independent motorized trolley.

11.7 Handling and Temporary Assembly of Precast Segments

In either long- or short-line casting, segments cannot be handled before the concrete has reached a sufficient strength to prevent:

Spalling of edges and keys

Cracking of the parts of the segment subjected to appreciable bending stresses due to self-weight

Inelastic deformations that would ultimately impair proper matching of the segments

Critical sections in a typical single-cell box segment are, Figure 11.60:

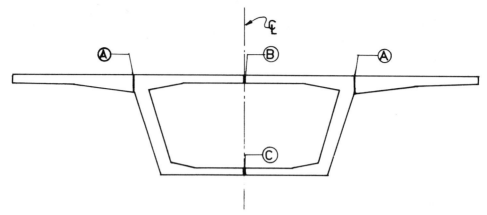

FIGURE 11.60.   Critical sections in a typical segment at time of formwork stripping.

Section A where the side cantilevers are attached to the webs

Sections B and C at midspan of the top and bottom slab

Section A is almost always the most critical. Section B is usually subjected to moderate tensile stress because the top slab is built-in on the web when the inner formwork is stripped. Section C is critical only on long-line casting when the casting bed does not have a continuous soffit and when the span of the bottom slab is larger than 16 to 20 ft (5 to 6 m).

Experience has shown that at the time of form stripping and before any handling of the segment is allowed, the tensile cracking strength of the concrete should be at least equal to the bending stress due to the segment weight in the most critical sections (A, B, and C). Practically, the corresponding compressive strength is:

$$f'_{ci} = 3000 \text{ to } 4000 \text{ psi } (21 \text{ to } 28 \text{ MPa})$$

In the casting yard, segments are usually handled by a portal crane traveling on rails or on steering wheels for added mobility. A typical portal crane in the Oleron Viaduct precasting yard is shown in Figure 11.61.

Proper handling of the segment requires proper pick-up points to keep the stresses in the section within the allowable limits. A typical example of handling three different shapes of box girders is shown in Figure 11.62.

For the conventional single box, inserts or through holes are provided near the web in the roadway slab, allowing lifting to be accomplished by a simple spreader beam.

FIGURE 11.61.   Oleron Viaduct, portal crane in precasting yard.

For the twin-box, three-web section, a four-point pick-up is usually necessary to eliminate excessive transverse bending of the top and bottom slab. A triple spreader-beam arrangement allows the load transfer from the four pick-up points to the single lifting hook.

For a triple-box, four-web section (such as used in the Saint Cloud Bridge), temporary ties are provided in the outer cells to transfer the reaction of the outside webs to the center webs. A simple spreader beam is then sufficient to lift the segment.

Segments must be stored in a manner designed to eliminate warping or secondary stresses. Concrete beams installed at ground level provide a good bearing for the segments, which must be supported under the web or very close thereto. If stacking is required to save storage space, precautions must be taken to transfer weight from the

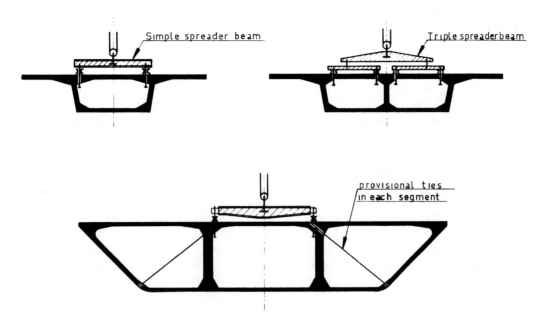

FIGURE 11.62. Handling precast segments. (*a*) Two-web segment. (*b*) Three-web segment. (*c*) Four-web segment.

upper to the lower layers of segments without excessive bending of the slab.

11.8 Placing Precast Segments

Transportation and placement of segments may be performed by one of several methods, depending on the site location and the general characteristics of the structure. These methods can be divided into three main categories:

1. Transportation by land or water and placement by an independent lifting apparatus.
2. Transportation by land or water and placement with the help of a beam and winch carried by the bridge deck itself.
3. Transportation by land, water, or along the bridge deck already constructed and placement with the help of a launching girder.

There are methods that fall into none of these categories, such as the use of a cableway, but their use is limited.

11.8.1 INDEPENDENT LIFTING EQUIPMENT

This method, where feasible, is the simplest and least expensive. It was used for the Choisy-le-Roi, Courbevoie, Juvisy, and Conflans bridges, where the navigable stretch of water lent itself to the use

of a barge-mounted crane, ensuring the collection of segments from the precasting site and their positioning in the final structure. A terrestrial crane was employed for the Gardon, Bourg-Saint Andéol, and Bonpas Bridges. The same crane, maneuvering either on land or over water (on a barge), assured the positioning of all the segments used to construct the upstream and downstream bridges of the Paris Ring Road.

When site conditions are suitable, the same lifting crane may be used both to serve the precasting yard and to transport the segments to their final position in the structure (Hartel Bridge, Holland). This principle was enlarged successfully during the construction of the bridges over the Loire River at Tours (Motorway Bridge and Mirabeau Bridge), where the segments were placed with the aid of a mobile portal frame. The portal frame is placed astride the bridge deck and moves along a track supported by two bailey bridges, one either side of the structure. The track length is approximately twice that of the typical span, and the track itself is moved forward progressively as construction proceeds. The bailey bridges are supported on temporary piers driven into the river bed. The segments are first brought to the bridge deck and then taken by the mobile portal frame, which transports them to their final position in the finished structure, Figure 1.47.

Where a mobile truck or crawler crane is used for placement, there are often difficulties in the positioning of the key segments at midspan, because the finished structure on either side of the key segment prevents the crane from maneuvering properly and hinders the positioning of the segment, which may be carried out only from the side of the structure. For the B-3 Motorway Bridges a special apparatus was designed to place those segments in the cantilever arm to be constructed in the direction of the completed structure, Figure 3.95. Two longitudinal girders are braced together and rested on the pier head of the cantilever to be constructed at the front, and on the existing structure at the rear. The apparatus consists of a mobile winch-trolley, ensuring the hoisting and positioning of the segments, and an advancing trolley situated at the rear and equipped with a translation motor. The front and rear supports are conceived in such a manner as to transmit the vertical loads through the segment webs.

The segments on the other side of the cantilever are easily placed by the mobile crane. This beam may easily be used to ensure cantilever stability during construction when the piers are not sufficiently rigid to support unsymmetrical loading. The cantilever is rigidly fixed to the girders by clamping bars capable of resisting both tension and compression. The crane and the girders, used together, will allow a 130 ft (40 m) span to be erected in four working days.

Placement of segments with a mobile crane has found another application in the construction of small-span structures such as three-span motorway overpasses (see the discussion of the Alpine Motorway, Section 3.15, and Figure 3.103). The segments are precast in a central factory, transported to the various sites by road and positioned by a mobile crane according to the erection scheme, which consists essentially of the following:

Two temporary adjustable props, easily dismountable, placed at the one-fourth and three-fourths points of the central span.

Temporary supports with jacks allowing cantilever construction

Temporary prestress to tie the segments together before stressing the final prestress

Elimination of the classic cast-in-place closure joint by direct junction of the two cantilever arms face to face.

Final prestress by continuous tendons instead of cantilever-type layout.

The total construction time for such an overpass, including the piers, usually does not exceed two weeks, of which less than one week is spent on the bridge superstructure itself. This method has been used with great success for the Rhone-Alps motorway overpasses, with spans varying between 60 ft (18 m) and 100 ft (30 m).

11.8.2   *THE BEAM-AND-WINCH METHOD*

The beam-and-winch method of placing precast segments was conceived for the construction of the Pierre-Benite Bridges over the Rhone River. This construction method requires a fairly simple apparatus rolling along the already constructed part of the cantilever and ensuring the lifting, translation, and positioning of all the segments. The apparatus is shown diagrammatically in Figure 11.63. It consists of the lifting gear B carried by the trolley C rolling along the bridge deck on tracks D. The segment A is brought, by land or water, beneath the pier in question, where it is lifted by the equipment. It is then transported to two launching beams E that cantilever out from the bridge deck, upon which it continues to advance until reaching its final position, whereupon it is lifted to its final level next to the previous segment, Figure 11.64. This system can, of course, be simplified if the segment can be brought by some independent means to a location vertically below its final position in the structure.

As originally conceived, this system was not completely independent; another construction procedure was required to erect the pier segment. The pier segment was cast in place in the Pierre-Benite Bridges. It was precast and placed by a crane for the Ampel Bridge in Holland and by a floating barge crane for the Bayonne Bridge over the river Adour. This weakness was eliminated in the construction of the Saint-Andre-de-Cubzac Bridge. For this structure, the pier segments, which form the starting point for each cantilever, were placed by the same equipment that placed the typical span segments, Figure 3.72. The equipment was hung, with the help of cables, to an auxiliary mast fixed to a lateral pier face. The pier segment was brought in from the opposite side, lifted and placed by the mobile equipment's winches. In the same position the following segment was located and the auxiliary mast removed, Figure 3.73. At this point it was a simple matter to reposition the mobile lifting equipment in order to place the typical span segments, Figure 3.70.

PLACING SEGMENTS NEAR RIGHT BANK

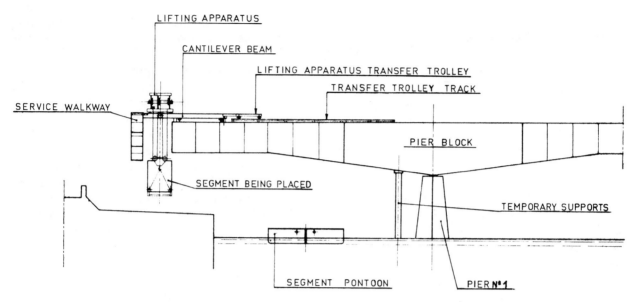

FIGURE 11.63. Paris Downstream Bridge, placing apparatus.

FIGURE 11.64. Paris Downstream Bridge, positioning a segment.

11.8.3 LAUNCHING GIRDERS

This last method, by far the most elegant, uses a launching girder above the bridge deck to bring the segments to their position in the structure. Employed for the first time during construction of the Oleron Viaduct in France, this method has now been successfully used for many different bridges throughout the world. We shall now look at the most important structures constructed by this method to see how the launching girder has evolved and how the original concept has been modified.

Launching Girders Slightly Longer Than the Span Length

We first consider the construction method of the Oleron Viaduct Bridge superstructure, Figure 3.32. The segments were brought along the top slab until they reached the launching girder, then lifted by the latter, transported to their final position, lowered so as to come into contact with the previous segment erected, and prestressed to the cantilever. The launching girder itself, slightly longer than the span length, was made up of a steel trellis beam with an entirely welded rectangular section weighing 124 tons (113 mt) and measuring 312 ft (95 m). The maximum span length of the bridge was 260 ft (79 m).

The launching-girder system consists of two fixed supports, called tunnel legs, allowing the segments to pass between them, one at the rear of the girder and the other at the center. At the front end is a mobile prop enabling the girder to find support on the next pier. The bottom chords of the girder are used for the rolling track that supports the segment trolley, which can move the segment horizontally and vertically and rotate it a quar-

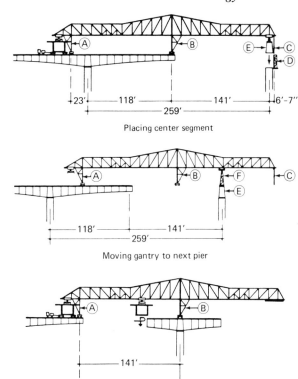

FIGURE 11.65. Oleron Viaduct, launching-girder operations. (A) Rear support, (B) center support, (C) temporary front prop, (D) prop support, (E) pier segment, (F) temporary support.

ter-turn. Three phases are clearly distinguishable in the construction of a cantilever, Figure 11.65:

Phase 1: Placing the pier segment
The launching girder rests on three supports—the rear support, the center support near the end of the newly constructed cantilever, and the front prop, which is attached to the front of the next pier with the help of a temporary prop support.

Phase 2: Moving the launching girder forward
The girder rolls along on the rear support and the segment trolley, which is rigidly attached to a metal framework known as the temporary translation support, which is fixed to the pier segment. The rear and central supports are equipped with bogies and roll along a track fixed to the bridge deck while the girder is being moved forward.

Phase 3: Placing typical segments
The launching girder rests on two supports, the central support anchored to the pier segment and the rear support tied with prestressing bars to the end of the previously constructed cantilever.

A support adjustment was carried out with the help of hydraulic jacks when the girder was resting on the rear and central supports and the temporary front prop, before installing the pier segment. The purpose of this adjustment was to obtain the optimal distribution of the launching girder self-weight among the three supports. While the front prop is being installed, the central support rests on the end of the previous cantilever in the same position in which the rear support will be during the erection of the typical segments. In this phase the launching girder rests on two supports and is therefore statically determinate; nothing can be done to change the rear-support reaction. While the pier segment is being placed, however, the girder is resting on three supports and is statically indeterminate. It is therefore necessary to ensure that the reaction at the central support is less than or equal to that which will be produced by the rear support during the next construction stage, including the weight of the trolley and the tractor placed in the near vicinity. Several other structures have been built with launching girders of the same generation as the one used for the Oleron Viaduct.

The Chillon Viaduct, Figures 3.43, 11.66, and 11.67, along the bank of Lake Leman used a 400 ft (122 m) launching girder weighing 253 tons (230 mt). The maximum span length was 341 ft (104 m). The launching girder, of constant rectangular section, was of the suspension type, being suspended at the one-quarter points by cable stays anchored at the central mast, which extended above the level of the launching girder. The supports were hydraulically adjustable, allowing the girder to cope with different angles of superelevation, Figure

FIGURE 11.66. Chillon Viaduct, launching-girder in operation.

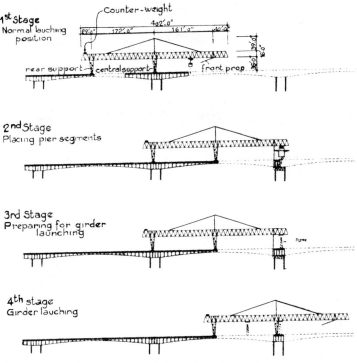

FIGURE 11.67. Chillon Viaduct, launching-girder movements.

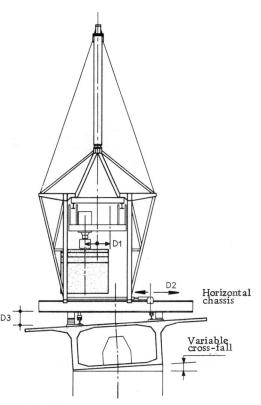

FIGURE 11.68. Chillon Viaduct, launching-girder adjustments.

11.68. The launching girder included three means of adjustment:

Adjustment D1: Lateral movement of the trolley in order to place eccentric segments

Adjustment D2: Lateral translation of the central support in order to cope with horizontal curvature of the structure

Adjustment D3: Vertical adjustment of bogies to take up the superelevation and so keep the central support vertical.

In order to follow the horizontal curves the launching girder rotated about the rear support while moving sideways across the central support, Figure 11.69. The mobile temporary front prop was conceived in the same way as the other supports so as to allow the passage of the first segments to either side of the pier segment.

The Blois Bridge on the Loire River in France had a 367 ft (112 m) long launching girder weighing 135 tons (123 mt), Figure 11.70. The maximum span length was 300 ft (91 m). The launching girder, of constant triangular section, could be dismantled and transported by road. All of the girder components were assembled with high-strength bolts, ensuring the transmission of

CONSTRUCTION OF HORIZONTAL CURVE   (STAGE 1.)

CONSTRUCTION OF HORIZONTAL CURVE   (STAGE 2)

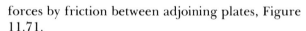

FIGURE 11.69. Chillon Viaduct, curved span construction.

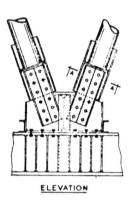

ELEVATION

SECTION A

FIGURE 11.70. Blois Bridge, launching girder.

FIGURE 11.71. Blois Bridge, launching-girder assembly detail.

forces by friction between adjoining plates, Figure 11.71.

The use of a very light structural steel framework carried with it the risk of large deflections. These were reduced and controlled by two sets of cable stays, passive and prestressed, which came successively into play during maneuvering of a segment (upper passive stays) and during the launching-girder advancement (lower prestressed stays). This launching girder was later used for the erection of two other structures: the Aramon Bridge on the Rhone River, Figure 11.72, and the 2950 ft (900 m) long Seudre Viaduct.

The Saint Cloud Bridge on the Seine, Figure 3.78, is a recent example of the use of a large launching girder. The girder could place segments weighing up to 143 tons (130 mt) in spans of up to 335 ft (102 m) with a minimal radius of curvature in plan of 1080 ft (330 m), Figure 3.79. The weight of the launching girder was 260 tons (235 mt) and its total length was equal to 400 ft (122 m).

The adjustments adopted were similar to those used for the Oleron, Blois, and Chillon bridges. The launching girder, which used upper passive stays and lower prestressed stays, was constructed

FIGURE 11.72. Aramon Bridge over the Rhone River.

with a constant triangular section made up of individual elements assembled by prestressing. This launching girder is notable, apart from its assembly by prestress, for its ability to follow extremely tight curves. The movements used for the Chillon Viaduct were, of course, used for this purpose. However, in the Saint Cloud Bridge it was necessary also for the launching girder to take up several intermediate positions during the erection of a given cantilever so as to bring each segment to its final position in the structure. The total lateral translation reached 19.7 ft (6 m) at its maximum. Construction speed of the bridge deck was 130 ft (40 m) per week, including all launching-girder maneuvers. Two other structures erected with the help of the Saint Cloud launching girder were the Angers Bridge and the Sallingsund Viaduct.

The launching girder used for the Alpine Motorway network was conceived for spans and segment weights of more modest dimensions; it is typical of lightweight universal equipment that can be easily dismantled for reuse in another structure, Figure 11.73. This girder allowed the handling of segments weighing up to 55 tons (50 mt) over spans up to 200 ft (60 m).

Reflecting on the launching girders mentioned above, we note that their evolution centers on two major characteristics: the structural conception of the girder and the assembly method (connection types, number of elements, and so on).

Launching girders tend more and more to be of the lightweight type, relying on exterior forces to cope with different loadings. These exterior forces are provided by the external active cable stays, which allow the structure to be placed in a condition ensuring a favorable behavior under a given loading. This approach to launching-girder design provides more optimal use of materials than did the first-generation girders of variable cross section.

Another advantage of a constant cross section is that it facilitates the construction of standard sec-

tions that can be interchanged and assembled on site. In this way the girder length can be varied according to the span length and the weight of the segments. Connections are made with tensioned bolts, Figure 11.74, which reduce considerably the number required and consequently the time needed to assemble or dismantle the structure. These connections have recently replaced those made with high-strength bolts and fishplates, notable on such structures as the Deventer Bridge and the B-3 Viaducts.

Means of erection adjustments also have improved, tending to reduce the forces applied to the deck itself by ensuring that the girder supports are located over the piers or at least in the very near vicinity.

This natural evolution leads us toward a new type of launching girder, one whose total length is slightly greater than twice the typical span length, allowing the simultaneous placing of the typical segments of cantilever N and the pier segment of cantilever $N + 1$.

Launching Girders Slightly Longer Than Twice the Typical Span

The first launching girders of this type were used on the following bridges: Rio Niteroi in Brazil; Deventer in Holland, Figure 3.50; and B-3 South Viaducts in the eastern suburbs of Paris, Figure 3.93.

The Rio Niteroi Bridge (Section 3.8), linking the city of Rio de Janeiro with Niteroi, consists of 10 miles (16 km) of bridge deck constructed by four identical launching girders, Figures 3.55 and 3.56. Each 545 ft (166 m) long girder could be completely dismantled. The constant triangular sec-

FIGURE 11.73. Alpine Motorway launching girder.

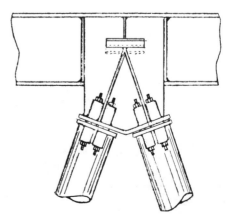

FIGURE 11.74. Prestressed connections.

tion, weighing 440 tons (400 mt), could cope with spans of up to 260 ft (80 m). The connections were identical in principle to those used for the Blois girder. Each installation was equipped with three supports of nontunnel type, one fixed and the other two retractable.

The erection sequence was as follows, Figure 1.51:

Phase 1:   Segment placing
The girder rests on three supports, each one over a pier. Two segments are erected simultaneously, one on either side of the double cantilever under construction. The pier segment of the next cantilever is also placed with the launching girder in this position.

Phase 2:   Moving the launching girder forward
The girder rolls on two temporary translation supports, one placed above the pier of the finished cantilever and the other above the pier of the cantilever to be constructed. These temporary supports are attached to the trolleys; the launching girder is lifted, thus freeing the permanent supports; and the trolleys are engaged, enabling the translation of the launching girder to a position to erect the next cantilever. The temporary translation supports are equipped with a mechanism allowing transverse movements, as the structure includes a certain amount of horizontal curvature.

The Rio Niteroi girder was equipped with three sets of active stays: lateral stays, central stays, and launching stays. The lateral stays, positioned on the underside of the two spans and constantly under tension, ensure the resistance of the girder while the load (segment) passes near midspan. The central stays strengthen the girder in the vicinity of the central support. The launching stays, under tension while maneuvering the girder, transfer the front and rear reactions to the central support.

Owing to the length of the bridge and the presence of a large stretch of water beneath the structure, the segments were brought to the launching girder on barges. The cantilever stability of the bridge was assured by the launching girder itself, and ties and props were positioned as construction proceeded.

The launching girder used for the Deventer Bridge in Holland, Figures 3.49 and 3.50, were also capable of being entirely dismantled and of triangular section. Its total length was 512 ft (156 m) for a weight of 198 tons (180 mt). The maximum span length was 243 ft (74 m).

Assembly of the launching-girder elements was consummated by prestress bars normal to the joints. It was supported by the fixed supports, of which the rear and the central allowed the passage of a segment, and two sets of cable stays: central stays and launching stays. The translation operations were identical to those of the Rio Niteroi Bridge, even though only one segment could be lowered into place at a time.

What was peculiar about this launching girder was its ability to raise itself to its working level by its own means, and this from the ground level where it was assembled. This was made possible by the central suspension mast, which acted as a lifting jack.

In the case of the B-3 South Viaducts, Figure 3.92, the constantly varying structure supported by 200 piers, crossing five railway tracks, the Ourcq Canal, and several urban roadways, was mastered by a highly mechanized launching girder. The simultaneous placing of two segments of the same cantilever, each weighing between 33 and 55 tons (30 and 50 mt) either side of the pier, is controlled by a radio-controlled servo mechanism that synchronizes the loading at each end of the girder. Again the length of the launching girder was slightly greater than twice the typical span length,

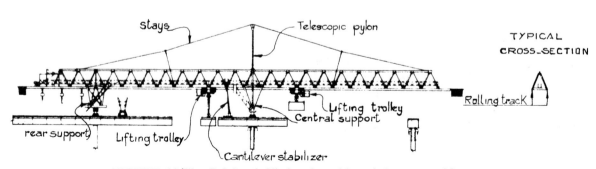

FIGURE 11.75.   B-3 South Viaduct launching girder, general layout.

FIGURE 11.76. B-3 South Viaduct, segment transport tractor.

which varied between 100 and 164 ft (30 and 50 m), Figure 11.75. The girder support reactions were thus applied in the region of the piers, and the cantilever stability was ensured by the launching girder itself. This stabilizing device can be seen to the left of the central support in Figure 11.75.

The segments were supplied by a special eight-wheeled tractor moving along the top slab, Figure 11.76. A special device used to unload and store the segments brought by the tractor freed the latter and removed the supply of segments from the erection critical path. The cycle of segment placement and girder advancement is represented in Figure 3.93. The next pier segment was placed during the same phase as the typical segments. About two spans were constructed each week—

that is, between four and six segments per day. The average construction speed, including launching-girder maneuvers, was therefore 200 ft (60 m) per week.

The B-3 launching girder was recently reused for the Marne-la-Vallee Viaduct, which carries high-speed suburban rail for the Paris transport authority.

References

1. Anon., *Manual for Quality Control for Plants and Production of Precast Prestressed Concrete Products*, MNL-116-70, Prestressed Concrete Institute, Chicago, 1970.

2. Anon., *ACI Manual of Concrete Practice*, Part I, American Concrete Institute, Detroit, 1973.

3. "Proposed Recommendations for Segmental Construction in Prestressed Concrete," FIP Commission—Prefabrication, 3d Draft, September 1977.

4. "Recommended Practice for Segmental Construction in Prestressed Concrete," Report by Committee on Segmental Construction, *Journal of the Prestressed Concrete Institute*, Vol. 20, No. 2, March–April 1975.

5. Anon., *PCI Post-Tensioning Manual*, Prestressed Concrete Institute, Chicago, 1972.

6. Anon., *PTI Post-Tensioning Manual*, Post-Tensioning Institute, Phoenix, Arizona, 1976.

7. T. J. Bezouska, *Field Inspection of Grouted Post-Tensioning Tendons*, Post-Tensioning Institute, Phoenix, Arizona, March 1977.

12

Economics and Contractual Aspects
Of Segmental Construction

12.1 Bidding Procedures

A bridge design should on principle be economical and as a practical matter must fall within budgetary restrictions of a particular project. The economic "moment of truth" for a given bridge design occurs when bids are received and evaluated.

In a basically stable economy where material and labor costs are predictable within relatively small fluctuations, the selection of structure type and materials is relatively straightforward. This situation prevails when the time required for the design is relatively short and thus is not affected by economic cycles, or, if the design time is relatively long, the economic cycles are mild. In an inflationary economy there is no economic stability, and designers are hard put to make rational choices, as they have no control over economic parameters that can influence their design decisions. In short, the problem is whether economic assumptions made during the course of design are valid at the time of bidding.

Obviously, the design and the bidding (tendering) of a project are closely related. Contractual bidding procedures vary from country to country, and current economic pressures are leading to changes in these procedures. The various bidding methods used in various countries can be broadly categorized (with some possible variations) as follows: (1) single design, (2) design and build, (3) value engineering, and (4) alternate designs.

12.1.1 SINGLE DESIGN

Heretofore, single design was the major method used in North America and Great Britain. In this method, in general, design drawings prepared for bid are very detailed, to the extent that even the length and other dimensions of every reinforcing bar may be given. The bidding period is followed by a tight construction schedule. The contractor bids and executes the project in strict accordance with the bidding documents. No variation from the documents is allowed unless an error in design is

518

discovered, or a specific detail proves impractical to consummate, or geological perturbations are discovered that differ from what was assumed in design and delineated in the contract documents. These changes are authorized by a change order, and if there is an increase in cost the contractor is paid an "extra."

This system worked well for many years when the economy was fairly stable and predictable and when economic changes were gradual over an extended period. Its disadvantage is its lack of flexibility to accommodate an inflationary economy, sudden price changes in materials, a rapidly advancing technology, and the current emergence of specialty contractors with unique equipment or skills, proprietary designs, and patented construction methods. Its biggest advantages are ease in administering the contract and absolute control over the final design.

12.1.2 DESIGN AND BUILD

In some European countries, by contrast, bid documents are prepared with the intention that the contractor will prepare and submit his own detailed design for the project. Thus, bid plans will be more general and, for a bridge, may show only span lengths, profile, and typical sections. The contractor may then refine the original design or submit an alternate design of his own choice, the responsibility for producing the final design and details being his rather than the engineer's. This procedure allows the contractor to use any special equipment or technique he may have at his disposal. For example, a cast-in-place concrete box may be substituted for a steel superstructure where the contractor has special know-how in concrete construction, or the change may be less drastic and involve only a reduction in the number of webs in a box girder.

Verification of the adequacy of the contractor's final design is generally carried out by a "proof engineer" who is retained by the owner or is on the owner's engineering staff. In order to minimize disagreements between the contractor and the proof engineer, European codes have been made very specific. As a result, European contractors usually maintain large in-house engineering staffs, although they may also use outside consultants. The outcome apparently is a savings in construction cost, achieved by the investment of more design time and effort than in the single-design method.

The advantage of the design-and-build method is that in an atmosphere of engineering competition, innovative designs and construction practices advance very rapidly. The state of the art of designing and constructing bridges advances in response to the need for greater productivity. The disadvantage is the lack of control over the selection of the type of structure and its design. There is some concern, too, that quality of construction may suffer as a consequence of overemphasis on productivity and initial cost. However, the contractor is usually required to produce a bond and guarantee his work over some period of time, and any defects that surface during this period have to be repaired at his expense. Whether such a system could be adopted in the United States is debatable.

12.1.3 VALUE ENGINEERING

Value engineering is defined by the Society of American Value Engineering as "the systematic application of recognized techniques which identify the function of a product or service, establish a value for that function, and provide the necessary function reliability at the lowest overall cost. In all instances the required function should be achieved at the lowest possible life-cycle cost consistent with requirements for performance, maintainability, safety, and esthetics."[1]

In 1962 the concept of value engineering became mandatory in all U.S. Department of Defense armed services procurement regulations (ASPR). Before this time value engineering had been applied to materials, equipment, and systems. The advent of ASPR provisions introduced value engineering concepts to two of the largest construction agencies in the United States—the U.S. Army Corps of Engineers and the U.S. Navy Bureau of Yards and Docks. Soon thereafter the U.S. Bureau of Reclamation and the General Services Administration (GSA) adopted and inserted value engineering clauses in their construction contracts, and the U.S. Department of Transportation established a value engineering incentive clause to be used by its agencies.

Several value engineering clauses (or incentive clauses) are in use today by many agencies. In general, they all have the following features[1]:

1. A paragraph that defines the requirements of a proposal: (a) it must require a change to the contract and (b) it must reduce the cost of the contract without impairing essential functions.

2. A "documentation" paragraph that itemizes the information the contractor should furnish with each proposal. It should be comprehensive enough to ensure quick and accurate evaluations, detailed enough to reflect the contractor's confidence in its practicability, and refined to the point where implementation will not cause undue delay in construction operations. Careful development of this paragraph and meticulous adherence to its requirements will preclude scatter-shot proposals by the contractor and burdensome review by the agency.

3. A paragraph on "submission." This paragraph details the procedure for submittal.

4. A paragraph on "acceptance," which outlines the right of the agency to accept or reject all proposals, the notification a contractor may expect to receive, and appropriate reference to proprietary rights of accepted proposals.

5. A paragraph on "sharing," which contains the formula for determining the contract price adjustment if the proposal is accepted and sets forth the percentage of savings a contractor may expect to receive.

As generally practiced by highway agencies in the United States, a value engineering proposal must indicate a "substantial" cost savings. This is to preclude minor changes such that the cost of processing offsets the savings to be gained. Some other reasons for which a value engineering proposal may be denied are as follows:

Technical noncompliance.

Delay in construction such that the cost savings would be substantially nullified.

Proposed change would require resubmission of the project for any number of various permits, such as environmental impact statement, wetlands permit, and navigation requirements. Resubmission would in all probability delay construction and nullify any cost savings.

Savings resulting from a value engineering proposal are generally shared equally by the agency and the contractor, after an allowance for the contractor's development cost, the agency's cost in processing the proposal, or both. As practiced in the United States, all contractors must bid on the design contained in the bid documents, and only the low bidder on the base bid is allowed to submit a value engineering proposal. This is, of course, value engineering's biggest disadvantage. Any number of contractors may have more cost-effective proposals that they are not allowed to submit because they were not low bidder on the base bid. Its advantage is that to some degree it allows contractor innovation to be introduced.

12.1.4 ALTERNATE DESIGNS

Alternate designs, as it is developing in the United States, basically is an attempt to produce a hybrid system consisting of the best elements of the single-design and the design-and-build methods. It attempts to accomplish the following:

Retain for the authorizing agency control over the "type selection" of the structure and its design

Provide increased competition between materials (structural steel versus concrete or prestressing strand versus bars) or construction procedures (cast-in-place versus precast segmental or balanced cantilever versus incremental launching, and so on)

Provide contractor flexibility (construction procedures, methods, and/or expertise)

This method has developed, with encouragement from the Federal Highway Administration, as an anti-inflationary measure to combat dramatic increases in highway construction costs. A technical Advisory[2] published by the Federal Highway Administration states:

Because of fluctuating economic conditions, it is felt that on multiple repetitive spans, long spans or major bridges, or where there is an extended period of design from conception of the project to a release for bids, there can be no assurance of price stability for a particular material or construction methodology. With alternate designs, no matter how the economy changes, more designs are available at the time of bidding that are likely to be suited to the prevailing economic conditions.

General recommendations regarding alternate designs from the same document[2] are as follows:

1. To receive the most economical construction between basic structural materials, consistent with geographic, environmental, ecological or other site restrictions, there should be maximum opportunity for competition between structural steel and concrete.

2. Within environmental, aesthetic, site, and other constraints, the plans and bid documents should show or otherwise indicate what alternative types of structures will be allowed or considered. The contractor should be allowed the option to bid any designated alternative design that is consistent with the contractor's expertise, available equipment, and so on.

3. Bid documents and the contract plans should clearly indicate the design criteria and what type of alternative designs and/or contractor options will be acceptable. Determination of practical and economical alternatives and/or contractor options should be developed in the preliminary design.

4. Bid documents should be considered as "open" documents in regard to construction method, erection systems, and prestressing systems.

5. Consistent design criteria should be used for alternatives; for example, if load factor design is used, it should be used for all alternatives.

6. Span lengths should be identified on the contract plans. However, other than where pier locations are constrained by physical and geological conditions at the site, consideration should be given to allowing a tolerance in pier location to avoid placing a particular alternative at an economic disadvantage. For example, in a typical three-span structure, the side span should be approximately 80 percent of the center span for structural steel, 70 percent for conventional cast-in-place concrete on falsework, and 65 to 70 percent in segmental balanced cantilever construction.

7. To avoid an economic disadvantage to a particular superstructure alternative, alternative substructure designs may be required. Limitations on the substructure, such as allowable axial load and moment, should be clearly identified on the contract plans.

8. Where specific design requirements are not covered by the American Association of State Highway and Transportation Officials (AASHTO) Bridge Specifications, the contractor should be allowed to use other recognized codes and standards where applicable. However, the alternative design should document where these provisions are to be used, why the AASHTO requirements do not apply, and which articles of the substituted code or standard are to be used. Such provisions should be subject to approval by the engineer and appropriate agencies.

9. Prebid conferences are to be encouraged as a means of communication between the engineer, highway agencies, and contractors.

10. In order to allow a contractor adequate time to investigate the various alternatives and prepare plans, it is recommended that the advertising time be commensurate with the size and complexity of the project with a minimum of 60 days.

11. In order to allow adequate review and checking of the low bidder's proposal, award of contract should be extended commensurate with the size of project.

Specific recommendations[2] regarding prestressed concrete alternates are as follows:

1. To increase the competition in post-tensioned concrete construction, it is recommended that plans and other bid documents allow conventional cast-in-place on falsework, precast prestressed span units, and segmental construction or combinations thereof.

2. Segmental construction should allow the following at the contractor's option:
   a. Precast or cast-in-place segmental construction.
   b. Any of the post-tensioning systems—that is, strand, wire, or bars or combinations thereof.
   c. Any of the following construction methods: balanced cantilever, span-by-span, progressive placing, incremental launching, or combinations thereof.
   d. Exterior dimensions of the cross section should be fixed. At the contractor's option, the thickness of webs and flanges may be varied to accommodate proposed construction and erection methods and post-tensioning systems, providing that any changes in the dead weight, shear, and so on are accommodated in the design.

3. The contract plans should indicate the *maximum* and *minimun* final prestressing force (P_f) and moment ($P_f \times e$) required, after all losses, for the final condition of the structure —that is, dead, live, impact, and all superimposed loads. Any increase in prestressing force

requirements as a result of the method of construction, erection, or type of tendon system should be evaluated at the shop drawing stage.

4. Changes in eccentricity of prestress should be accompanied with appropriate changes in prestress force to produce the same minimum compressive stress due to prestress.

5. The minimum prestress force should be such that under any loading condition, both during and after construction, stresses will be within allowable limits. Consideration should be given to secondary moments due to prestress, redistributed moments due to creep, and stresses resulting from thermal gradient (between the top and bottom of the girder and between the inside and outside of webs).

6. Contractor revisions to contract plans, with supporting calculations, should be submitted to the engineer for approval.

12.1.5 SUMMARY REMARKS ON BIDDING PROCEDURES

All of the bidding procedures described above have one thing in common: they all attempt to produce the lowest initial cost by competition in construction and/or design. All of the last three approaches (design-and-build, value engineering, and alternate designs) require decisions based on comparisons of basic structural materials, structure types, construction methods, and so on. This implies that the basic premise in the selection process is equivalency—comparable service, performance, and life-cycle cost of the facility.

Life-cycle costs refer not only to initial cost, but also to maintenance and any rehabilitation costs during the life of the structure. True cost of the project must be considered. What may be initially least expensive may in the long run, when future costs are accounted for, be actually most expensive. Some newer structure types and designs are at the fringe of the state of the art and have only been used in the United States within the last decade or less. Thus, an adequate background of experience is unavailable to evaluate life-cycle costs. The estimation of life-cycle costs may be difficult in many cases, such as for new and progressive bridge designs. Functionally, alternative structures are designed to the same criteria. Only years of operational experience can provide the data base for reasonably estimating life-cycle costs and thereby true equivalency in design insofar as cost is in-

volved. However, the problem of adequacy of data does not diminish the importance of the question and the need to attempt to answer it.

Another anti-inflationary measure used in recent years is that of stage construction. This concept may take one of two forms. Major structures, because of their size, lend themselves to stage construction—that is, separate substructure and superstructure contracts. Usually several years will elapse between bidding and awarding of the substructure contract and the superstructure contract. The economic superstructure span range for different alternative types and materials is a variable. In this form of stage construction the substructure is let first; thus the spans for the superstructure design become fixed. This may or may not impose an economic disadvantage to specific superstructure alternates. The substructure must be designed for the largest self-weight superstructure alternative, which may or may not be the successful superstructure alternative. It appears that this form of stage construction may be to some extent self-canceling or counterproductive to cost savings. With a total alternative design package, the substructure (foundation, piers, span arrangement) can also have alternatives commensurate with the superstructure alternatives.

The other form of stage construction concerns a large project, containing many bridges, that is subdivided for bidding purposes into a number of smaller projects. Its primary purpose is to encourage small contractors by providing projects of manageable size, thus increasing competition. However, certain construction techniques, by virtue of the investment in sophisticated casting or erection equipment, require a certain volume of work to amortize the equipment and be competitive. Depending upon the size of the subdivided contract, this form of stage construction in some instances may also become counterproductive.

The value engineering concept can be divided into two major areas of application: during design and during construction. Value engineering procedures in the design stage may result in very specific recommendations based on a certain set of assumptions at a particular point in time for the design. If conditions change during the interval between the design decision and the actual construction, which can be several years, conditions on which the assumptions were based may have changed. Such changes could make the original value engineering decision incorrect. The alternative design concept, on the other hand, does not make all such specific design decisions at an early stage but retains some options in order to allow a later response to changed conditions. Therefore, there is an apparent incompatibility between the application of value engineering principles in the design stage and the concept of alternative designs for bidding purposes. However, the concept of value engineering is a powerful tool and can be made compatible with the concept of alternative designs if its principles are used to determine whether a given project should require alternative designs and, if so, what structure types should be considered as equivalent alternates.

12.2 Examples of Some Interesting Biddings and Costs

12.2.1 PINE VALLEY CREEK BRIDGE, CALIFORNIA

The Pine Valley Creek Bridge (Section 2.7) was the first segmental bridge in the United States to incorporate the concept of value engineering (cost-reduction incentive proposal) in the bidding documents. The original design assumed cast-in-place balanced cantilever construction with the prestressing force (P_f) and moment ($P_f \times e$) based on strand capabilities.

Project plans developed by CALTRANS required construction of the cantilevered sections at piers 3 and 4 before those at piers 2 and 5 (refer to Figure 2.40). Because of rigid specification requirements for the protection of the valley slopes,

the contractor was faced with a difficult and costly erection procedure. At least one cableway spanning the entire valley would have been required to transport men and material to appropriate locations during the construction procedure. Complete site installations on both sides of the valley would have been required, which were accessible only with a great deal of difficulty.

The superstructure design alternative submitted under this proposal employed the Dywidag system, which included the following: (1) use of the threaded-bar system especially suited to segmental construction, (2) increased prestress-force eccentricities, since most longitudinal prestressing bars could be placed and anchored in the slab, (3) diagonal prestressing in the webs to cater to the shear stresses, and (4) a modification in construction sequence so as to work from piers 5, 4, 3, and 2, Figure 2.44.

Changes proposed under the value engineering clause are summarizied in Table 12.1. Total savings as a consequence amounted to $382,000.[3]

12.2.2 VAIL PASS BRIDGES, COLORADO

The Vail Pass structures are part of Interstate I-70 near Vail, Colorado, in an environmentally sensitive area. Environmental considerations played a dominant role in the selection of the bridge types and the design thereof. Another factor considered was the relatively short construction season at the high elevations of the sites.

TABLE 12.1. Pine Valley Creek Bridge, Value Engineering Proposal

	Original	CRIP	Savings estimated
Construction sequence	Long cantilevers before short to minimize creep Δs	Reverse to facilitate constr. from abutment	$ 88,000
Structural system	Cantilever for D.L., continuous for L.L. + added D.L.	Continuous for all loads	
	No Redistribution	Full redistribution	
Concrete stresses:			
Construction	$0.4f'_c$	$0.55f'_c$	
Tension	0	$3\sqrt{f'_c}$	$228,000
Concrete shear	"63" ACI, mild steel	Principal stresses diagonal prestress	22,000
Slab designs	AASHTO loads, method and distribution reinf.	AASHTO loads with "Homberg" graphs, no distribution reinf.	22,000
Hinge	Two diaphragms	No diaphragms	22,000
			$382,000

Of the 21 bridge structures in this project, 17 were designed and bid on the basis of alternative designs. One alternative design considered trapezoidal steel box girders composite with a concrete roadway flange. The other alternative design was for precast concrete segmental box girder design, with the Federal Highway Administration requiring that the contractor be given the option of cast-in-place segmental construction.

At two locations, the site constraints were such that they were bid without alternatives as steel box girders. Two other locations required 80 ft (24 m) long simple-span underpass structures to provide for wildlife migration. These structures were built of cast-in-place concrete box girder construction. The remaining 17 structures were completely designed and detailed for the two alternatives, one in structural steel and the other in precast concrete segmental (with a contractor option of providing a cast-in-place segmental design). Spans varied in number from two to five and in length from 30 to 260 ft (9 to 79 m).

Table 12.2 tabulates the five contracts that involved the 17 bridges bid on the basis of alternative designs and lists them in the order in which they were bid.[4] Approximately a year elapsed between the letting of the first and last contracts. Although considerable differences in bid prices are shown in individual projects, for the total project there is less than $80,000 difference out of an approximate total cost of $17 million, or less than 0.5% dif-

ference in bid prices for the alternatives. Precast segmental was the low bid on project 1 and cast-in-place segmental was the low bid on project 4. Based upon length (width was constant), the segmental concept was successful in approximately 60% of the total project.

The consultants, International Engineering Company, Inc., estimated that the additional cost to produce alternative designs was about 2.5% of construction cost. It is difficult to estimate what savings were achieved by bidding alternative designs rather than a single design; however, overall savings of 7 to 10% of the construction costs are not unreasonable.[4]

12.2.3 LONG KEY BRIDGE, FLORIDA

The Long Key Bridge in the Florida Keys was bid utilizing the concept of alternate designs. Four complete sets of contract plans were prepared for the alternative construction schemes indicated in Table 12.3. Plans for the AASHTO precast, pretensioned I girders were prepared by the Florida Department of Transportation. Plans for the three basic precast segmental schemes were prepared by the state's consultant, Figg and Muller Engineers, Inc.

In the preliminary design stage three methods of segmental construction were considered for this project: balanced cantilever, span-by-span, and progressive placing. The progressive placing

TABLE 12.2. Results of Alternative Bids, Vail Pass Bridges

Proj. No.	Bridge No.	No. Spans	Length (ft)	Total Length (ft)	Low Steel Bid	Cost/Ft², Steel	Low Concrete Bid	Cost/Ft², Concrete
1	F-11-AX	4	727					
	F-11-AW	5	880					
	F-11-AV	4	690					
	F-11-AU	4	668	2965	$5,992,155	$48.12	$5,527,318	$44.39
2	F-12-AK	3	220					
	F-12-AM	2	240					
	F-12-AN	3	350					
	F-12-AO	3	368					
	F-12-AP	3	600	1778	$3,777,549	$50.59	$4,111,170	$55.05
3	F-11-AP	3	310					
	F-11-AO	2	222	532	$994,347	$44.50	$1,053,364	$47.14
4	F-11-AN	4	740					
	F-11-AM	4	744					
	F-11-AL	4	514					
	F-11-AK	3	450	2448	$4,257,771	$41.41	$4,108,057	$39.96
5	F-12-AT	4	726					
	F-12-AS	4	726	1452	$2,298,409	$37.69	$2,598,938	$42.62
Totals				9175	$17,320,231	$44.95	$17,398,847	$45.15

TABLE 12.3. Long Key Bridge, Alternatives

Superstructure	Substructure	
	Precast Piles	Drilled Shafts
Precast girders, AASHTO	A	B
Segmental:		
Span by span, V piers	C	D
Span by span, vertical piers	E	F
Cantilever, vertical piers	G	H
First option, slab reinforcing	R/C epoxy coated	
	Pretensioning	
Second option, barrier curbs	Cast-in-place conventional	
	Precast (never integral)	

method was discarded because it was felt to be (at the time) too new for acceptance in U.S. practice. It was later introduced on the Linn Cove Bridge in North Carolina. The basic difference in the two span-by-span alternatives for the Long Key Bridge is in the pier configuration: V piers or vertical piers.

Aside from the construction alternatives and pier types, the contractor was offered the option on all segmental alternatives of transversely reinforcing the top flange either with epoxy-coated conventional reinforcing steel or by transversely pretensioning with $\frac{1}{2}$ in. (12.7 mm) diameter strand. Further, he had the option on all segmental alternatives of either precasting or casting in place the traffic barriers.

The contractor also had the option of casting the segments rightside up or upside down. Casting the segments upside down was intended to facilitate transversely pretensioning the top flange. However, since no waterproof membrane or wearing surface was specified, the top flange surface of the deck was required to have a grooved or tined surface for skid resistance. If the segment were cast upside down, then, the form would be required to produce the desired texture. Specifications were left open such that strand or bar prestressing tendons could be bid. All conventional steel reinforcement was required to be epoxy coated in all alternatives.

The eight basic alternatives for this project produced bids from eight contractors, as indicated in Table 12.4. Note that there were six bids for the span-by-span method, one for the balanced cantilever method, and one for the precast pretensioned AASHTO I girders.

The low bid in precast segmental was $2.6 million less than the AASHTO I-girder bid. Low bid was for the span-by-span alternative with precast V

TABLE 12.4. Long Key Bridge, Bid Tabulation

Bid Rank	Alternative Chosen	Relative Bid
1	D	1.0000
2	F	1.0225
3	F	1.0539
4	F	1.0963
5	B	1.1731
6	F	1.1844
7	F	1.2557
8	H	1.3063

piers and drilled shaft foundations. The contractor elected to precast the segments near the project site and cast the segments rightside up, using transverse prestressing in the top flange. He slip-formed the cast-in-place barriers after segment erection. Further, he elected to move the scaffolding trusswork from span to span by using a barge-mounted crane as opposed to having the falsework trusses mounted on barges.

Table 12.5 presents a cost analysis of the low bid as compared with the AASHTO pretensioned I-girder alternative.[5]

TABLE 12.5. Long Key Bridge, Cost Analysis of the Low Bid and the AASHTO I-Girder Bid

	Span-by-Span Segmental	Precast AASHTO I Girder
Total cost[a]	$26.63/ft²	$30.95/ft²
Superstructure cost	$21.43/ft²	$23.59/ft²
Substructure cost	$ 5.20/ft²	$ 7.36/ft²
Segments erected	$19.16/ft²	
Total bid	$15,307,375.91	$17,956,538.75
Total area	468,301 ft²	470,277 ft²

[a]The mobilization bid items were proportioned to the structural items in all cases. The Florida Department of Transportation estimate was $14,550,000.

TABLE 12.6. Seven Mile Bridge, Alternatives

Superstructure	Substructure	
	Precast Piles	Drilled Shafts
Precast AASHTO I-girders	A	B
Segmental:		
Span-by-span, vertical piers	C	D
Cantilever, vertical piers	E	F
First option, slab reinforcing	R/C epoxy coated	
	Pretensioning	
Second option, barrier curbs	Cast-in-place conventional	
	Precast (never integral)	
Third option, box piers	Cast-in-place conventional	
	Precast	

12.2.4 SEVEN MILE BRIDGE, FLORIDA

Seven Mile Bridge in the Florida Keys had the same basic alternatives as Long Key Bridge, except that the span-by-span with V piers was eliminated and the contractor had the further option for the vertical piers of casting in place conventionally or precasting, Table 12.6.

Six bids were received, with all bidders selecting alternative D, Table 12.7. Low bid was $44,986,942.31. There were no bids for the AASHTO I-girders. The low bidder optioned to reinforce the top slab with conventional reinforcement, epoxy coated; to cast the barrier curb in place; and to precast segmental box piers. The low bid included $5,128,600 for waterline, roadway approaches, and navigational requirements. Analysis of the bid items revealed a superstructure cost of $23.22/ft^2 and a substructure cost of $5.68/ft^2, resulting in a $28.90/ft^2 total cost. The Florida Department of Transportation estimate was $52 million ($7 million higher than the low bid).

12.2.5 ZILWAUKEE BRIDGE, MICHIGAN

This structure was designed with alternatives of steel plate girders and precast segmental concrete box girder. Bids were first taken in November 1978, Table 12.8. The engineer's estimate for the concrete alternative was $60,609,614.30 and for the steel alternative $71,316,854.90. On the basis that the low bid of $80,999,445.50 was 33% higher than the estimate, the bids were rejected.

The design underwent revision, and the bid documents allowed the contractor to make design and prestressing system changes under a "cost reduction incentive," and an escalation clause was introduced. The project was rebid in August 1979 (nine months later), Table 12.9. The engineer's estimate was $71,645,661.50 for the concrete alternative and $71,965,516.70 for the steel alternative. The low bid of $76,787,252.65 was 7% over the estimate—5% below the previous low bid. By rebidding the project (after nine months of inflation) a savings of $4.2 million was achieved.

TABLE 12.7. Seven Mile Bridge, Bid Tabulation

Bid Rank	Alternative Chosen	Relative Bid
1	D	1.0000
2	D	1.0214
3	D	1.0768
4	D	1.1404
5	D	1.2297
6	D	1.2556

TABLE 12.8. Zilwaukee Bridge, Ranking of First Bids

Bid Rank	Relative Bid	Alternative
1	1.0000	Concrete
2	1.0115	Concrete
3	1.0562	Steel
4	1.0816	Concrete
5	1.1071	Steel
6	1.1375	Steel

TABLE 12.9. Zilwaukee Bridge, Ranking of Second Bids

Bid Rank	Relative Bid	Alternative
1	1.0000	Concrete
2	1.0798	Concrete
3	1.0829	Concrete
4	1.1231	Steel
5	1.1501	Steel

12.2.6 CLINE AVENUE BRIDGE, INDIANA

The Cline Avenue bid documents were very liberal toward redesign, with the bidder only having to inform the state of the intention to redesign at bid opening. As designed, the plans and specifications provided the option of a steel plate girder or precast segmental box girder structure. The structure was redesigned as cast-in-place on falsework, prestressed concrete box girder, except for the main channel spans which are cast-in-place segmental. The steel option was a composite load factor design. The low concrete bid was for $53,545,770.55 with the engineer's estimate being $53,560,259.78. Relative bids are listed in Table 12.10.

12.2.7 NAPA RIVER BRIDGE, CALIFORNIA

The Napa River Bridge (Section 2.11) is another example of the use of alternative designs. For this project, because the lower structure height made falsework feasible, bid documents were prepared for three alternative schemes:

A: Conventional continuous cast-in-place box girder bridge

B: Trapezoidal continuous structural steel box girder bridge

C: Cantilever prestressed segmental concrete bridge with either precast or cast-in-place segments, and erection either by the balanced cantilever method or on falsework

Because of poor foundation material and a readily available aggregate supply, all alternatives used lightweight concrete in their superstructures.

TABLE 12.10. Cline Avenue Bridge, Ranking of Bids

Bid Rank	Relative Bid	Alternative
1	1.0000	Concrete
2	1.0252	Steel
3	1.0596	Steel

Alternative C used a transverse prestressed deck in order to reduce the number of girders. Strong competition was expected from the steel industry, as this site is readily accessible by water from the yards of two major fabricators. However, the low bidder, G. F. Atkinson Company, selected alternative C and cast the bridge generally in half-span segments on falsework to the ground as a series of balanced T's. About 60 ft (18 m) of the 250 ft (76 m) span over the navigation channel was constructed in three segments on falsework suspended from the cantilevered boxes on each side.[6]

There were six other bidders, of which only one bid the steel alternative and none bid alternative A. Relative bids are listed in Table 12.11. The first six bids were for alternative C, and the last and highest was for alternative B.

12.2.8 RED RIVER BRIDGE, ARKANSAS

This is a seven-span structure with five interior spans of 210 ft (64 m), end spans of 135 ft (41 m), and a roadway width of 32 ft (9.75 m). Estimated cost was $3.3 million. Eight bids were received, six in structural steel and two for concrete segmental. Bids ranged from $3.22 to $4.89 million. The concrete segmental was completely open as to the method of construction (both concrete bids were based on the incremental launching method). Relative bids are listed in Table 12.12.

TABLE 12.11. Napa River Bridge, Ranking of Bids

Bid Rank	Relative Bid
1	1.0000
2	1.0928
3	1.1218
4	1.1837
5	1.2765
6	1.4305
7	1.5210

TABLE 12.12. Red River Bridge, Ranking of Bids

Bid Rank	Relative Bid	Alternative
1	1.0000	Steel
2	1.1437	Steel
3	1.2685	Steel
4	1.2800	Steel
5	1.3099	Concrete
6	1.3229	Concrete
7	1.4267	Steel
8	1.5175	Steel

Structural steel prices varied from a low of $0.65/lb to a high of $0.93/lb with an average of $0.78/lb. Structural steel prices in Arkansas for this type of construction had previously been in the range of $0.80 to $0.85/lb. The low bid price of $0.65/lb represents a reduction of approximately 19 to 23%. All steel prices were for domestic steel.

Note that the bid prices included the demolition of the existing bridge. If this item were deleted, the bidding would be rearranged as indicated in Table 12.13.

The lump-sum price for the concrete superstructure was, for the low concrete bidder, $31.37/ft², which compares favorably with the Keys bridges in Florida. However, this price was not competitive. Undoubtedly there are numerous reasons why. One may be that there was no precasting plant within sufficient distance of the site, and thus the cost of shipping the segments may have been prohibitive. The project was not large enough to attract contractors with the expertise to set up a precasting operation at the site. The two concrete segmental bids received were based on incremental launching, and evidently the project was not large enough to adequately amortize the cost of the casting bed and launching equipment on this project to make the method competitive.

12.2.9 NORTH MAIN STREET VIADUCT, OHIO

The low bid on this project was $25,715,733.00, as compared with the engineer's estimate of $29,200,000. Probably a major reason why the low bid was 12% under the engineer's estimate was the competition offered by the two plan alternative designs in concrete and structural steel, resulting in a minimum savings of at least $3,500,000. The competitive situation was further enhanced by allowing bidders to propose additional optional designs. Although no additional steel optional designs were submitted, three optional concrete redesigns were bid.

As designed, the plans and specifications provided the option of a steel plate girder or precast segmental box girder structure. Bid documents were quite liberal for redesign but required quite a bit of detail with the bid documents. The winning bid was steel girders, as designed, priced at about $87/ft² without one abutment, which was to be constructed under another contract.

The steel girders were a noncomposite, working-stress design. The approximately 15 million pounds of A588 structural steel was bid at $0.75/lb. It should be noted that additional savings in steel could have been accomplished with a composite design. Table 12.14 is a relative summary of the eight bids.

Note that the low concrete bid was only 3.7% above the low bid, which indicates the competitiveness.

12.2.10 SUMMARY OF CALIFORNIA'S EXPERIENCE

California's experience with a cost reduction incentive proposal (CRIP) (value engineering) and alternative designs for projects involving segmental construction is summarized in Table 12.15.[6]

12.3 Increase in Efficiency in Concrete Bridges

As stated in previous chapters, prestressed concrete segmental bridges have extended the practical and competitive economic span range of concrete bridges. An interesting comparative exercise is to look back at bridges built in the past and evaluate them in the light of present-day developments.

TABLE 12.13. Red River Bridge, Reranking of Bids

Bid Rank[a]	Relative Bid	Alternative
1	1.0000	Steel
4	1.1147	Steel
2	1.1620	Steel
8	1.2841	Steel
3	1.3379	Steel
5	1.3919	Concrete
6	1.4054	Concrete
7	1.5276	Steel

[a]Ranking corresponds with that presented in Table 12.12.

TABLE 12.14. North Main Street Viaduct, Ranking of Bids

Bid Rank	Relative Bid	Alternative
1	1.0000	Steel alternative as per plan
2	1.0370	Redesign concrete alternative
3	1.0401	Steel alternative as per plan
4	1.0579	Concrete alternative as per plan
5	1.0884	Steel alternative as per plan
6	1.1128	Steel alternative as per plan
7	1.1508	Redesign concrete alternative
8	1.4099	Redesign concrete alternative

TABLE 12.15.   Summary of California's Segmental Prestressed Bridge Experience

Date Bid	Bridge	Length/Max. Span (ft)	Cost—Bridge Work Only	Design Alternatives Provided	Remarks
2/72	Pine Valley Creek	1700/450	$14.2 M = $69/ft²	A. Cantilever prestressed concrete segmental box girder with either: 1. Prestressed rock anchor footings[a] 2. Mined rock shaft foundation	CRIP by contractor revised superstructure design and construction sequence. Savings to state, $191,000.
9/72	Stanislaus River at New Melones	2250/550	$12.0 M = $127/ft² (incl. prov. for future widening)	A. Cantilever prestressed concrete segmental box girder B. Structural steel box girder[a] Both with either: 1. Prestressed rock anchor footings 2. Mined shaft foundations[a]	Seven contractors bid steel and two bid concrete 1.6% separated low steel and low concrete.
5/73	Eel River Br. and Overhead	1387/310	$5.0 M = $37/ft²	A. Conventional twin two-cell cast-in-place prestressed concrete box girders	CRIP modified design to segmental single-cell boxes. Max. falsework height 92 ft ±. Savings to state, $112,824.
11/74	Napa River at Napa	2230/250	$8.9 M = $54/ft²	A. Conventional six-cell cast-in-place prestressed box girder B. Structural steel box girder C. Cantilever prestressed concrete segmental two-cell box girder[a]	Six of seven bidders chose C. Falsework heights varied from 64 to 132 ft.
9/75	Colorado River at Yuma	2750/220	7.4 M = $34/ft²	A. Segmental prestressed concrete single cell box with criteria provided to convert to cantilever	Cantilever construction considered by contractor but not used because contractor owned adequate supply of falsework. Max. falsework height 70 ft ±.
12/76	Guadalupe River at San Jose	1009/155	$2.6 M = $28/ft²	A. Conventional seven-cell prestressed concrete box[a] B. A four-cell prestressed box designed for segmental construction	Maximum falsework height 40 ft over a seasonally dry river. Contractor inexperienced in segmental construction.
5/76	San Joaquin River at Antioch	9404/460	$33.4 M = $79/ft²	A. Prestressed concrete with three main spans designed for cantilever segmental construction and 20 300 ft approach spans designed for segmental construction with provisions to modify to cantilever B. Structural steel welded plate girders (unpainted A-588) with 29 200 ft approach spans[a] C. Same as A with 200 ft approach spans	All five bidders chose steel. Lower-than-anticipated (foreign) steel prices prevailed.

TABLE 12.15. (*Continued*)

Date Bid	Bridge	Length/Max. Span (ft)	Cost—Bridge Work Only	Design Alternatives Provided	Remarks
1/78	San Francisco Bay at Dumbarton (approach spans)	4650/150	$24.3 M = $59/ft²	A. Precast delta girders[a] B. Twin single-cell prestressed box girders designed for segmental construction with criteria for redesign for cantilevering or launching C. Structural steel box girder	Much bidder interest in all choices during prebid stage. Final results: seven chose A, one chose C. Some uncertainties about criteria provided in B.

[a]Selected by low bidder.

12.3.1 REDESIGN OF CARACAS VIADUCTS, VENEZUELA

The Caracas Viaducts in Venezuela (Chapter 8) were completed in 1952, approximately thirty years ago. If these viaducts were built today, the chosen structure would probably be very different from that chosen at the time after exhaustive feasibility studies. In 1973 these structures were reevaluated in terms of the more conventional balanced cantilever method of girder construction. Figures 8.30 and 8.31 compare the actual project constructed in 1952 with possible alternative designs in 1973 and 1975. The three-arch-rib and eight-beam superstructure would be replaced by a variable-depth twin box section (cantilever construction using precast segments) supported on slip-formed piers.

Today, with the same span arrangement considered in 1973, possible alternatives might be a single two-cell box similar to that used in the Kipapa Stream Bridge, or a ribbed single-cell box as in the Vejle Fjord Bridge, Figures 4.24 and 4.22, respectively. This approach would require only single shaft piers.

12.3.2 COMPARISON BETWEEN TANCARVILLE AND BROTONNE BRIDGES, FRANCE

Progress is made slowly through accumulated experience, and it is worthwhile to look back periodically and try to measure such progress. With this in mind, and as a conclusion to this chapter, a comparison is offered between two similar concrete structures separated in time by seventeen years.

As mentioned in Section 9.8, the Seine River between the maritime inland harbor of Rouen and the English Channel is now crossed twice by two outstanding structures:

Tancarville Bridge designed in 1956 incorporating a 2000 ft (610 m) span steel suspension bridge

Brotonne Bridge designed in 1973 incorporating a 1050 ft (320 m) span concrete stayed bridge

These two structures are only 20 miles (32 km) apart and are located in very similar surroundings topographically and geotechnically (see Figures 12.1 and 12.2).

On the left bank, a flat expanse of meadows and fields requires a long approach viaduct to reach the desired altitude of the main crossing above the navigation channel, while a deep formation of soft soil overlying the load-bearing strata requires deep pile foundations. On the right bank, the limestone cliff extends close to the river bank and calls for only a short transition between the main river span and the approach highway. The comparison presented here pertains only to the left-bank approach viaduct of each structure, although interesting comments could be made also on the relative characteristics of their other parts.

The Tancarville approach viaduct has eight 164 ft (50 m) spans, having five 140 ton (127 mt), 10 ft

FIGURE 12.1. Tancarville Bridge, aerial view from the southwest showing left bank approach viaduct.

FIGURE 12.2. Brotonne Bridge, aerial view from the southwest showing left bank approach viaduct.

(3 m) deep precast girders in each span, Figures 12.3 and 12.4. Piers are founded on precast concrete piles and were cast in place with a box section. When the design was prepared, it represented the most advanced technology in terms of use of materials. The elastic stability of these very long, slender precast girders was even the occasion of interesting innovative studies. Construction methods were also far from conventional.

All girders were prefabricated in a yard located at the original ground level. Moving and lifting operations for one girder (see Figure 12.5) included:

Placing girder on dollies, moving in two perpendicular directions to bring it at the foot of the supporting piers

Hoisting girder along the piers with special steel rigs, Figure 12.6

Placing girder on top of the pier with the rotating arm of the special rig, Figure 12.7

Transverse displacement of girder to its final position

Suspension of the girder at both ends was achieved by the means of special cantilevers to provide the highest safety against lateral buckling during lifting operations of such slender girders, Figure 12.8. The project was carried out smoothly and completed successfully a long time ahead of the other contracts for the entire crossing.

Fifteen years later, the same problem of safely and economically building an aesthetically pleasing

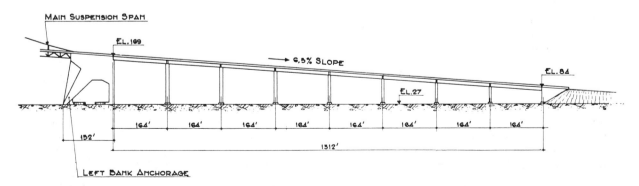

FIGURE 12.3. Tancarville Bridge, elevation of approach spans.

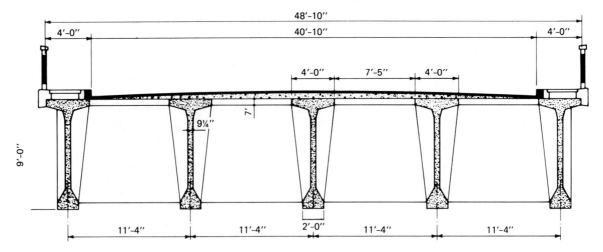

FIGURE 12.4.   Tancarville Bridge, typical cross section of approach spans.

FIGURE 12.5.   Tancarville Bridge, lifting one precast girder for the approach spans.

approach viaduct for the Brotonne crossing was solved with very different methods, both of design and construction. The light single box section selected for the stayed structure was also used for the approach spans. Precast piles were replaced in the foundations by cast-in-place slurry load-bearing walls. Box piers were slip-formed instead of incrementally cast in successive lifts. The superstructure was cast in place in balanced cantilever with travelers, Figure 12.9. Today precast segments would probably be preferred, although the characteristics of the deck would remain substantially unchanged.

A comparison between quantities of materials per square foot of deck appears in Table 12.16. The savings in concrete volume of Brotonne over

TABLE 12.16.   Cost Comparison Between Tancarville and Brotonne Approach Viaducts

	Tancarville, 1956 (Adjusted 1973)	Brotonne, 1973
1. *Quantities* (per ft²) (super- and substructure)		
Concrete (yd³)	0.14	0.11
Reinforcing steel (lb)	11	14
Prestressing steel (lb)	6.4	3.1
2. *Labor* (hr/ft²)	4.1	1.6
3. *Cost* ($/ft²)		
Labor	14.20	5.60
Materials	6.90	6.30
Equipment, plant, and job overhead	15.70	5.00
Subcontracts	3.70	4.20
Design, overhead and fee	12.90	4.20
4. *Total*	$53.40	$25.30

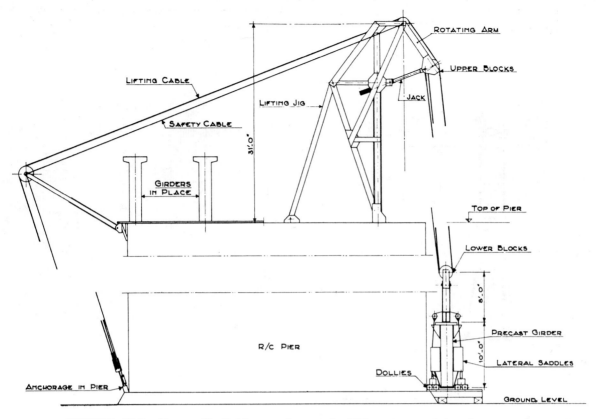

FIGURE 12.6. Tancarville Bridge, equipment for lifting precast girders in approach spans.

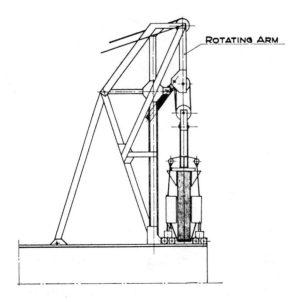

PLACING GIRDER ON PIER

FIGURE 12.7. Placing precast girder over pier cap.

Tancarville is justified only by the fact that minimum weight was vital for the concrete stayed bridge and was maintained in the approach spans. Weight of prestressing steel is approximately half because the deck is continuous at Brotonne and the box section is more efficient than the I-girder section.

More important, however, is the comparison of costs and the components thereof, Table 12.16 and Figure 12.10. One is struck by the total labor requirements for both sub- and superstructure:

Tancarville   4.1 hr/ft²
Brotonne   1.6 hr/ft²

In the 15 years that elapsed between the two projects, the combination of design improvements and more efficient construction methods allowed the labor to be divided by 2.5.

A similar trend has been observed in other fields. For example, a complete survey of all hydroelectric

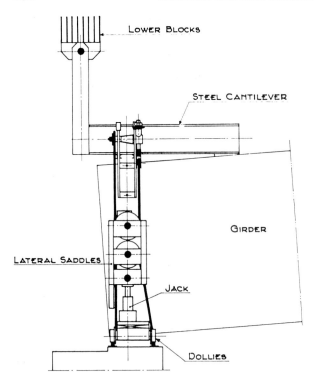

DETAIL OF GIRDER SUSPENSION

FIGURE 12.8. Lifting device at precast girder ends.

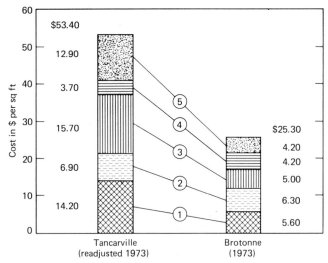

FIGURE 12.10. Cost comparison between Tancarville and Brotonne approach viaducts. (5) Design overhead and fee, (4) subcontracts, (3) equipment, plant, and site overhead, (2) materials, (1) labor.

FIGURE 12.9. Brotonne Bridge, cantilever construction of superstructure of approach spans.

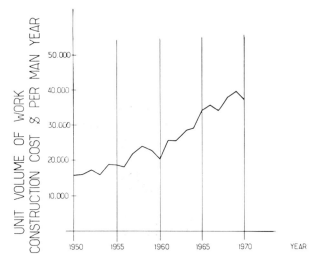

FIGURE 12.11. Increase of productivity on power projects in France.

projects carried out by French Electricity between 1950 and 1970 showed that the annual value of investment for each worker was multiplied by 2 without allowance for inflation and by 3 including inflation, Figure 12.11. Costwise the true gain would be somewhat less significant, because labor

rates have constantly increased faster than material rates.

The comparison between other items of the cost breakdown of Tancarville and Brotonne is equally instructive. Material costs are almost equal, including the value of subcontracts (pile foundations and roadway work in both projects). The essential differences are seen in the two following areas:

Equipment, plant, and job overheads: reduced from $15.70 at Tancarville to $5 at Brotonne. This difference is due essentially to increased efficiency in management but also to a climate of fierce competition.

Design, overheads and fees: reduced from $12.90 for Tancarville to $4.20 for Brotonne. The same two reasons explain this drastic reduction, which also reflects the change in the overall operation of large construction companies during the last twenty years from family-owned or controlled craftsmen such as building contractors to modern management industrial companies.

When Eugene Freyssinet designed his Plougastel Bridge masterpiece (see Chapter 8), he was personally involved in the project for more than three years and probably involved in little else. One generation later, an experienced engineer would have to control or at least participate in many different projects during the same period.

In summary, the comparison of costs between Tancarville and Brotonne approach viaducts with prices of both projects reduced to 1973 levels is:

Tancarville $53.40/ft²
Brotonne $25.30/ft²

Both projects were bid completely on a design-and-build basis and awarded to the lowest bidder. The above costs are a true picture of the technology and of the level of prices for the two respective periods.

To estimate both projects at the level of today's prices (1980) it would be necessary to multiply the labor rates by 2.3 and the materials and equipment rates by 1.7.

References

1. "Guidelines for Value Engineering (VE)," prepared by Task Force 19, Subcommittee on New Highway Materials, AASHTO-AGC-ARTBA Joint Cooperative Committee.
2. "Alternate Bridge Designs," FHWA Technical Advisory T5140.12, December 4, 1979, Federal Highway Administration, Washington, D.C.
3. Richard A. Dokken, "CALTRANS Experience in Segmental Bridge Design," *Bridge Notes,* Division of Structures, Department of Transportation, State of California, Vol. XVII, No. 1, March 1975.
4. A. B. Milhollin, and C. L. Benson, "Structure Design and Construction on the Vail Pass Project," Transportation Research Record 717, Transportation Research Board, National Academy of Sciences, Washington, D.C., 1979.
5. James M. Barker, "North American State of the Art Current Practices," *Prestressed Concrete Segmental Bridges,* Structural Engineering Series No. 6, Federal Highway Administration, Washington, D.C., August 1979.
6. Donald W. Alden, "California's Experience with Cost Saving Contracting Techniques," *Prestressed Concrete Segmental Bridges,* Structural Engineering Series No. 6, Federal Highway Administration, Washington, D.C., August 1979.

13

Future Trends and Developments

13.1 Introduction

As observed in previous chapters, prestressed concrete segmental bridges have extended the practical and competitive economic span range of concrete bridges. The Bendorf Bridge in Germany (Section 2.2) constructed in 1964 with a navigation span of 682 ft (208 m) was a monumental achievement. Because of economic differences between Europe and the United States (primarily the ratio of labor cost to material cost) it was not until the early 1970s with the JFK Memorial Causeway (Section 3.10) with a span of 200 ft (61 m) and shortly therafter the Pine Valley Creek Bridge (Section 2.7) with a span of 450 ft (137 m) that segmental construction was introduced in the United States. Today these spans are somewhat commonplace when one considers the Three Sisters Bridge (Section 1.10), the Koror-Babelthuap Bridge (Section 2.12), and the Houston Ship Channel Bridge (Section 2.14), with spans of 750 ft (229 m), 790 ft (241 m), and 750 ft (229 m), respectively. When combined with the cable-stay concept, spans increase to 981 ft (299 m) for the Pasco-Kennewick Bridge, 1050 ft (320 m) for the Brotonne Bridge, and 1300 ft (396 m) for the Dame Point and Ruck-A-Chucky Bridges.

In earlier years these spans for concrete bridges would have been considered incomprehensible and certainly not economical. The fact that they have become achievable, only within the last decade, stands as a testimonial to rapid technological advances and to the courage and vision of those engineers who participated in this development.

In the United States as of November 1980, 19 segmental bridges had been completed and there were 16 under construction, 22 in design, and 29 under study—a total of 86 bridges. We may conclude that segmental prestressed concrete construction is a viable concept for highway bridges and that there are no known major problems to inhibit its use. What, then, is the potential for segmental bridge construction in the 1980s? This chapter will look at this potential in terms of new or improved materials, potential application in bridge decks, piers, and substructure, and application to existing or new bridge superstructure types.

13.2 Materials

During the nineteenth century timber, stone, and masonry were the common materials for bridge construction. Then iron, steel, concrete, and reinforced concrete emerged successively as favorite materials, culminating in the twentieth century with prestressed concrete. The present materials used in bridge construction have some or all of the following disadvantages: weight, cost, or inherent weaknesses in one form or another. In the recent past, development of improved bridge systems has evolved primarily by more exact methods of calculation made feasible by the electronic computer or by innovative bridge systems such as the cable-stayed and segmental types of bridges. Intensive development of the materials themselves has barely begun.

13.2.1 PRESTRESSING TENDONS

Until recently, corrosion of prestressing tendons has caused few problems and little concern. However, with the advent of segmental construction and transverse prestressing on the top flange, an increasing concern has been expressed about the potential deterioration of the tendons resulting from their closeness to the deck surface and exposure to the action of de-icing chemicals. Current methods of alleviating this concern are the use of polyethylene ducts or the possibility of epoxy coating the duct, epoxy coating post-tensioning bar tendons, and possibly epoxy coating the prestressing strand. A research effort is required to determine the production feasibility and cost; the effect, if any, that nonmetallic coatings might have on the bond of strand to concrete; and the compatibility of strains between the coating and the tendon. Another potential method uses individual unbonded strands with successive coatings of teflon, a corrosion inhibitor, and polypropylene, Figure 13.1.

An old idea that may need to be resurrected is that of using glass fibers for prestressing. This material was being investigated in the 1950s,[1] but for either technical or economic reasons it never reached fruition. There were problems of chemical reaction of the glass fibers with the cement; however, Owens-Corning Fiberglass Corp. has developed a coating for glass fibers for fiber-reinforced concrete. Perhaps this coating could be used for a glass fiber prestressing strand. An ultimate strength of 400 ksi (2758 MPa) and a low modulus of elasticity ranging from 6000 to 10,000 psi (41 to 69 MPa) might be expected. The high strength and low modulus would indicate a low percentage of prestress losses—a decided advantage. The high strength would produce, for a given required prestress force, fewer or smaller tendons, thus reducing congestion. Smaller tendon sizes would reduce web thickness, thus reducing dead weight and prestress force requirements, and so on. Obviously, suitable end anchorages would have to be developed.

13.2.2 HIGH-STRENGTH CONCRETE

Early prestressed concrete designs were based on 3000 psi (20.7 MPa) strength concrete. As knowledge of concrete properties and quality control increased, it became more feasible to use a 6000 psi (41.4 MPa) strength concrete for many prestressed concrete structures. In the Pacific Northwest an 8000 psi (55.2 MPa) strength is readily and routinely available. Use of such concrete has permitted the design of longer-span, lighter-weight concrete structures.

Within the past few years it has been found that strengths of 10,000 psi (68.9 MPa) and higher can be obtained where special attention is given to (1) selecting the constituent materials, (2) proportioning the concrete mix, and (3) handling, placing, and curing the concrete.

It has recently been demonstrated that the application of ultrahigh-strength concrete is not only practical but also economically feasible. High-strength concrete, 9000 to 11,000 psi (62 to 75.8 MPa), has been used in the columns of five high-rise buildings in Chicago. The concrete was produced in a local ready-mix plant and trucked to the

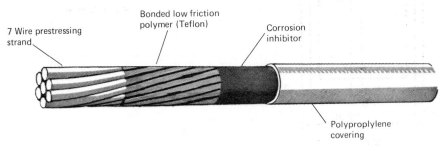

FIGURE 13.1. Corrosion-resistant strand tendon.

project site. An economic study for a short tied column indicated that the cost per foot varied with the concrete strength and steel percentage as follows: $15.50 for 9000 psi (62 MPa) concrete and 1% steel compared to $39 for 4000 psi (27.6 MPa) concrete and 8% steel.

Over the past five to ten years considerable research has been conducted on high-strength concrete, dealing primarily with selecting materials, developing concrete mix design criteria, and determining basic physical properties of the concretes. Very little, if anything, has been done regarding the implementation of high-strength concretes, especially in bridge structures.

In an interim report,[2] "Applications of High Strength Concrete for Highway Bridges," prepared by Concrete Technology Corporation for the Federal Highway Administration, a segmental bridge segment at a pier was redesigned with high-strength concrete. The purpose was to determine to what extent the thickness of the lower flange could be reduced, and in turn what effect this reduction would have on the overall moments.

For purposes of this study, the Shubenacadie Bridge in Nova Scotia (Section 2.15.4) was selected as a design example. Overall dimensions of the bridge are shown in Figure 13.2. It has a 700 ft

(213.4 m) main span and 372 (113.4 m) side spans. The bridge was constructed with a 5000 psi (34.5 MPa) concrete strength and used $1\frac{1}{4}$ in. (32 mm) diameter Dywidag bars for post-tensioning. For the analysis, the top flange was assumed to be uniform and $11\frac{1}{2}$ in. (292 mm) thick. The bottom flange was assumed to taper uniformly from its thickest point at the support piers to 6 in. (152 mm) at midspan. The centroid of the prestressing force was assumed to be located $5\frac{3}{4}$ in. (146 mm) below the top of the section—that is, centered in the top flange. AASHTO HS 20-44 was used for loading, as in the actual bridge.

Prestress force was provided by $1\frac{1}{4}$ in. (32 mm) diameter Dywidag bars with a minimum yield stress of 150 ksi (1034 MPa). These bars were assumed to provide 104 kips (0.46 MN) of final prestress force each. This assumes a jacking force of 70% of the minimum yield strength and 20 ksi (137.9 MPa) losses. Maximum allowable compressive stress in the concrete was assumed to be $0.4f'_c$, and an allowable tensile stress was assumed to be zero.

Significant benefits were found in the use of high-strength concrete to reduce the thickness of the lower flange. As shown in Figure 13.3, the total flexural prestress demand is reduced by approxi-

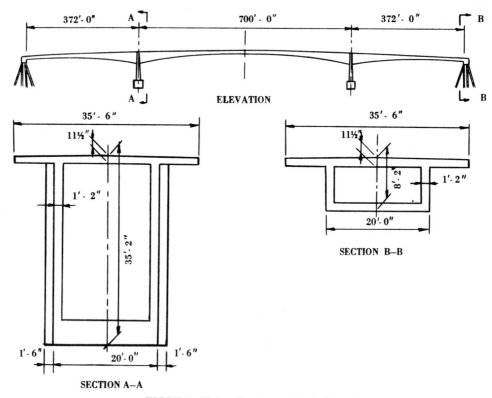

FIGURE 13.2. Shubenacadie Bridge.

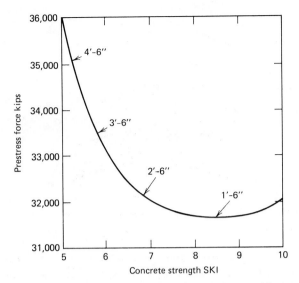

FIGURE 13.3. Variation of prestress force with concrete strength—Shubenacadie Bridge.

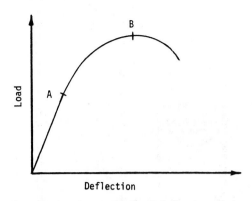

FIGURE 13.4. Schematic load-deflection diagram.

mately 10% as a result of the reduced dead load. The optimum lower flange thickness is about 1 ft 8 in. (508 mm), obtained at 8 ksi (55 MPa) concrete strength.

13.2.3 FIBER-REINFORCED CONCRETE

A relatively new material that has not yet seen much application in structures is fiber-reinforced concrete. Fibers have been used to reinforce brittle materials since ancient times; straws were used to reinforce sun-baked bricks, horsehair was used to reinforce plaster, and more recently various fibers have been used to reinforce Portland cement.[3] A state-of-the-art report[4] prepared by ACI Committee 544 defined fiber-reinforced concrete as "concrete made of hydraulic cements containing fine or fine and coarse aggregates and discontinuous discrete fibers."

Several types of fibers along with several of their properties are listed in Table 13.1.[3,4] As can be seen, fibers have been produced from steel, plastic, glass, and natural materials in various shapes and sizes.

Two stages of behavior in the load-deformation curve have been generally observed when fiber-reinforced concrete specimens are loaded in flexure. The load-deformation curve may be considered as approximately linear up to point *A* in Figure 13.4. Beyond this point the curve is significantly nonlinear, reaching a maximum at point *B*. The load or stress corresponding to point *A* has been called *first-crack strength, elastic limit,* or *proportional limit,* while the stress corresponding to point *B* has been termed the *ultimate strength.*

Two theories have been suggested for predicting the first-crack strength of fiber-reinforced concrete: the *spacing concept* and the *composite-materials concept.* The spacing concept attempts to explain or determine the first-crack strength by a crack-arrest mechanism derived from the field of fracture mechanics. The basic mechanism that controls the

TABLE 13.1. Typical Properties of Fibers

Type of Fiber	Tensile Strength (ksi)	Young's Modulus (10^3 ksi)	Ultimate Elongation (%)	Specific Gravity
Acrylic	30–60	0.3	25–45	1.1
Asbestos	80–140	12–20	0.6	3.2
Cotton	60–100	0.7	3–10	1.5
Glass	150–550	10	1.5–3.5	2.5
Nylon (high tenacity)	110–120	0.6	16–20	1.1
Polyester (high tenacity)	105–125	1.2	11–13	1.4
Polyethylene	100	0.02–0.06	10	0.95
Rayon (high tenacity)	60–90	1.0	10–25	1.5
Rock wool (Scandinavian)	70–110	10–17	0.6	2.7
Steel	40–600	29	0.5–35	7.8

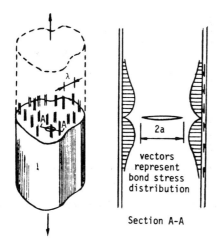

FIGURE 13.5.   Schematic of arrest mechanism.

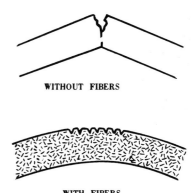

FIGURE 13.6.   Idealized crack-arrest mechanism in bending.

first-crack strength depends primarily on the spacing of the fibers.[5]

The crack-arrest mechanism for fiber-reinforced concrete, as presented by Romualdi and Batson,[6] can best be described with the aid of Figure 13.5, which represents a mass of concrete in tension. The reinforcement consists of a rectangular array of rods at a spacing λ and located parallel to the direction of tension stress. At some interior location an internal flaw exists in the form of a flat disk-shaped crack.

The basic rationale is illustrated by section *A-A*, which is a side view of an internal crack between two fibers. In the presence of a gross stress the extensional strains in the vicinity of the crack tip, by virtue of the stress concentration, are larger than the average strains. These strains, however, are resisted by the stiffer fiber, and there is created a set of bond forces (assuming that the bond between the mortar and the steel is intact) that act to reduce the magnitude of stresses at the crack tip. Under proper conditions of fiber spacing and diameter, an internal flaw could be prevented from propagating to join up with other flaws into microcracks which then join with other microcracks to form macrocracks. The basic philosophy is that if the internal flaws can be locally restrained or retarded from extending into adjacent material, thereby restraining crack propagation, the tensile-strength characteristic of the concrete is improved.

The crack-arrest mechanism in bending may be idealized as indicated in Figure 13.6. When a critical strain is reached, the beam cracks; unlike the nonreinforced beam, however, the cracks do not propagate through the beam but are arrested by the fibers that span the cracks.

The composite-materials concept hypothesizes that the properties of fiber-reinforced concrete, including the first-crack strength, can be predicted from the individual properties of matrix and fibers. It assumes that fiber-reinforced concrete can be analyzed as conventional reinforced concrete, the main difference being that the reinforcement is shorter, thinner, and randomly distributed.

Table 13.2 summarizes the improvement of the properties of a steel-fiber-reinforced concrete as compared to plain concrete.[3]

13.2.4   POLYMER CONCRETE

Concrete produced with Portland cement and air-entraining agents can contain approximately 13% voids, which are interconnected and distributed throughout the mass. When this concrete is heated to drive out the chemically unbonded moisture and

TABLE 13.2.   Concrete Reinforced with U.S.S. Fibercon Steel Fiber

Properties	Approx. Improvement over Plain Concrete
Compression	10–30%
Flexural modulus of rupture	70–300%
Tensile strength	50–300%
Impact strength	150–1000%
Crack and spall resistance	70–300%
Fatigue strength to 2 million cycles	100%
Abrasion	30%
Shear and torsional strength	50–300%
Corrosion resistance	Good as or better
Freeze-thaw	Good as or better
Conductivity (thermal and electrical)	Conducts both

TABLE 13.3. Summary of Properties of Concrete-Polymer Material

Property	Concrete Control Specimen (Type II Cement)	Concrete with up to 6.7 Weight % Loading of Polymethyl Methacrylate, Co-60 Gamma Radiation Polymerized
Compressive strength (psi)	5,267	20,255
Tensile strength (psi)	416	1,627
Modulus of elasticity (psi)	3.5×10^6	6.3×10^6
Modulus of rupture (psi)	739	2,637
Flexural modulus of elasticity (psi)	4.3×10^6	6.2×10^6
Coefficient of expansion (in./in. °F)	4.02×10^{-6}	5.36×10^{-6}
Thermal conductivity at 73°F (23°C) (BTU/ft-hr-°F)	1.332	1.306
Water permeability (ft/yr)	6.2×10^{-4}	0
Water absorption (%)	5.3	0.29
Freeze-thaw durability:		
Number of cycles	590	2,420
Percent weight loss	26.5	0.5
Hardness—impact ("L" hammer)	32.0	55.3
Corrosion by 15% HCl (84-day exposure), % weight loss	10.4	3.6
Corrosion by sulphates (300-day exposure), % expansion	0.144	0
Corrosion by distilled water	Severe attack	No attack

then impregnated with a chemical monomer, such as methyl methacrylate (MMA), and irradiated with gamma rays, some startling changes in its properties are produced, Table 13.3.[7] Tensile and compressive strength are almost quadrupled. Modulus of elasticity is increased by a factor of 1.8 and modulus of rupture by more than 3.5. A compressive stress-strain curve for this material shows complete linearity up to more than 75% of failure load, Figure 13.7.[7]

Thus far, research with this material has aimed toward its application in bridge decks. Problems in polymerizing large units such as bridge segments have yet to be solved. Practical resolution of these problems could offer a tremendous advantage for concrete structures.

13.2.5 COMPOSITE CONCRETE MATERIALS

Assuming that the materials previously discussed can be developed to a point of practical usage, what improvement in properties might be expected if these materials were combined? Sukiewicz and Virola[8] have presented flexural-load-versus-deflection data for concrete and composite materials, Table

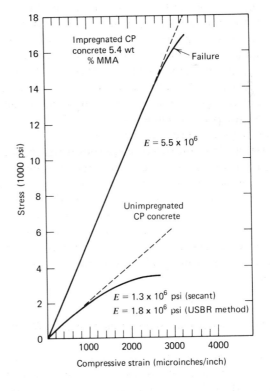

FIGURE 13.7. Compressive stress-strain curve for MMA-impregnated concrete.

TABLE 13.4.   Relative Load Versus Relative Deflection

	Approx. Relative Max. Load	Approx. Relative Midspan Deflection at Max. Load
Plain concrete	5	5
Steel-fiber reinforced	18	20
Polymer impregnated	20	13
Polymer impregnated and steel-fiber reinforced	100	105

13.4. It is obvious that a vast improvement in behavior and toughness can be expected.

13.2.6 *MATERIAL LIMITATIONS*

With improved material properties, not only would structures become lighter but also the depth of superstructure and thickness of individual elements would be reduced. There are some practical limitations, however, as to how much the thickness of a web, for example, may be reduced. The practical limitations of placing the concrete in the forms and of congestion of supplemental reinforcement and prestressing tendons must still be considered. To some extent this could be alleviated by the use of external tendons, as implemented in the Long Key Bridge in Florida, Figure 6.53. This also has the advantage of reducing the complexity of fabrication for precast segments.

Perhaps a more important limitation in using materials with improved properties is that at some point in the design, stress no longer becomes the controlling criterion. Deformations, both global and local, may govern. Because of the reduced section required from a strength point of view, there may be more concern not only with flexibility of the structure in a global sense but also with the possibility of web buckling and limberness of the deck slab.

13.3 *Segmental Application to Bridge Decks*

To date, there has been very little use of precasting, prestressing, and segmental construction for bridge decks. Transverse prestressing has been used in the top flange of large, cast-in-place on falsework, concrete box girders. Lately, transverse prestressing has been used to a greater extent in the construction of segmental bridges—to provide greater load capacity and load distribution for large overhanging flanges and between adjacent single-cell box girders.

Although a few bridge designs have included transverse prestressing, much greater use could be made of it for more economical bridge structures. For replacement of the decks on existing bridges, precast prestressed concrete segmental construction offers great advantages, only some of which can be associated with identifiable costs.

As with the segmental box girder, a full-depth segmental panel bridge deck may be precast in short segment lengths longitudinally and may be full deck width or partial deck width, Figure 13.8, depending on the width of deck required for a particular application. Also, in addition to the transverse prestressing, segmental bridge decks may be conceived as having expoxied transverse joints and longitudinal prestressing.

A transversely prestressed segmental full-depth panel bridge deck, Figure 13.9, has been proposed by T. Y. Lin International as an alternative design for SR 182, Columbia River Replacement Bridge, in the state of Washington. This proposal has the following features:

1. Precast full-depth panels of lightweight concrete to reduce dead load.

2. Transverse prestressing to achieve large cantilever overhangs and thus economies in the superstructure.

3. Attachment of the panels to the superstructure with shear studs in block-outs of the panel to achieve composite action with the superstructure.

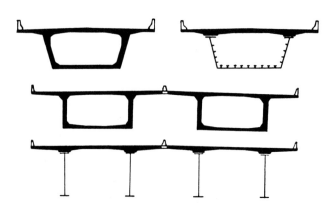

FIGURE 13.8.   Deck configurations.

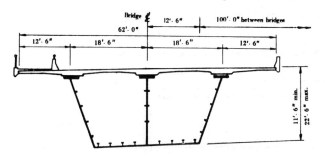

FIGURE 13.9. SR-182 Columbia River Bridge.

4. Longitudinal prestressing of the deck to maintain a compression across the transverse joints.

Another segmental method of constructing a bridge deck is a transfer of technology from the incremental launching of segmental box-girder bridges.[9,10,11] This methodology, as applied to bridge decks, has been pioneered in Switzerland and consists of the following operations:

1. The casting of a convenient segment length of bridge deck behind an abutment, Figure 13.10, or at midlength of the bridge, Figure 13.11, whichever is more convenient. Segment length is normally 65 to 80 ft (20 to 25 m).
2. The jacking forward of the segment, Figure 13.12, onto the flanges of the steel superstructure, Figure 13.13, thus freeing the casting bed.
3. Preparing the casting bed for concreting the next segment.
4. Repeating the cycle until completion of the bridge deck.

The finished deck, therefore, consists of segments that have been incrementally cast and longitudinally launched. As in conventional structures the deck is attached to the superstructure and

made to act compositely by means of shear-transfer devices placed at regular intervals through blockouts cast into the deck.

To date, the incremental launching method has been implemented for the construction of ten bridge decks in Switzerland.[10,11]

13.4 Segmental Bridge Piers and Substructures

Piers do not have to be massive solid cross sections; a tubular cross section may be more effective and more economical. In the United States it is generally felt to be more economical to cast a solid pier. However, for tall piers the economics of solid-pier casting should be evaluated against the cost of the additional dead load the pier is supporting and transferring to the foundations. It may be desirable to precast the pier as tubular segments that are prestressed vertically to each other as well as the foundation.

In the Vail Pass Bridge structures the piers were constructed of diamond-shaped segments, stacked vertically and post-tensioned to the foundations, Figure 13.14. Footings were cast in place with ducts to allow the placing of prestressing tendons.

Other examples of segmental application to piers and substructure, previously discussed, are:

1. Linn Cove Viaduct, Section 6.3.2, Figure 6.17
2. I-205 Columbia River Bridge, Section 5.4.3, Figures 5.25 and 5.26
3. Sallingsund Bridge, Section 5.4.2, Figures 5.20 and 5.21

The Long Key Bridge, Section 6.5.1, used precast V piers; and the Seven Mile Bridge, Section 6.5.2, used precast segments stacked vertically. It is to be hoped that these concepts will be refined and utilized for future structures where applicable.

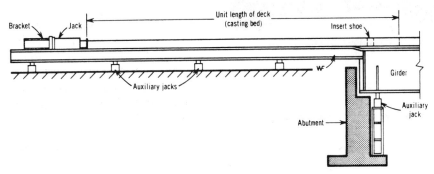

FIGURE 13.10. Incremental launching, behind abutment, from reference 10 (courtesy of American Society of Civil Engineers).

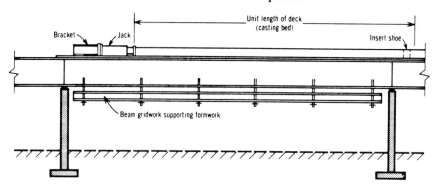

FIGURE 13.11. Incremental launching, midlength of bridge, from reference 10 (courtesy of American Society of Civil Engineers).

FIGURE 13.12. Incremental launching, jacking of deck slab.

FIGURE 13.13. Incremental launching, deck on superstructure.

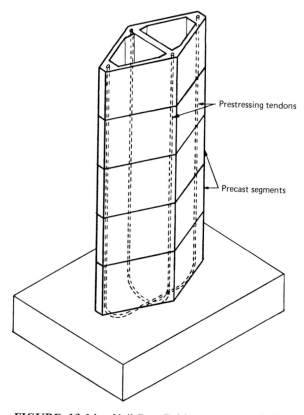

FIGURE 13.14. Vail Pass Bridges, segmental pier.

13.5 Application to Existing or New Bridge Types

With the exception of the Pasco-Kennewick and Dame Point cable-stayed bridges, the implementation of the concept of segmentally constructed bridges in the United States has been limited to the girder type of bridge. In other parts of the world,

the segmental concept has been applied not only to the cable-stayed bridge, but also to rigid frames, arches, trusses, and to a limited extent to overpass structures. Segmental construction is versatile and should not be stereotyped to girder bridges only; it can be applied to other types of bridge construction.

13.5.1 OVERPASS STRUCTURES

The main application of prestressed concrete segmental bridge construction has been to the long or intermediate span range and to viaducts. However, this method of construction has been applied to highway overpass structures, proving its versatility. Examples of overpass structures previously presented are:

1. Rhone-Alps Motorway, Section 3.15
2. Motorway Overpasses in the Middle East, Section 8.6.4

The Federal Highway Administration (FHWA) in cooperation with the American Association of Highway and Transportation Officials (AASHTO) is embarking on a study of the feasibility of standard sections for segmental box girder bridges. If feasible, standardization of sections, especially for overpass bridges, could provide additional economy for bridge construction.

An important and costly problem in building overpass structures over heavily traveled highways and freeways is that of traffic control during construction. An idea that might minimize this problem can be borrowed from the construction procedure for the Vienna Motorway cable-stayed segmental bridge. Because construction was not allowed to interfere with navigation on the canal, the structure was built in two 364 ft (111 m) halves on each bank and parallel to the canal. Upon completion, the two girder halves were swung into final position, Figure 9.66, and a cast-in-place closure joint was made. In other words, each half is constructed as a one-time swing span. This concept was considered for a long skewed overpass in Illinois, but the contractor elected a more conventional procedure.

13.5.2 ARCHES, TRUSSES, RIGID FRAMES

The adaptation of segmental concepts to arches, trusses, and rigid frames has yet to be implemented on the North American Continent. As indicated in Chapter 8, there are ample examples to indicate that segmental technology can be used for these types of structures. As previously noted and adequately illustrated, segmental construction should not be stereotyped to girder bridges only.

13.5.3 WICHERT TRUSS

The resurrection of the Wichert truss principle,[12] Figure 13.15, might yield economies in segmental cantilever construction. This type was developed for structural steel trusses and has the curious property of providing a fixing moment while remaining statically determinate. The fixing moment is provided as a function of the geometry of the

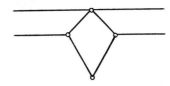

FIGURE 13.15. Wichert truss principle.

quadrilateral support, any desired degree of fixing moment being obtained by arranging the geometry of that quadrilateral, with the structure remaining determinate. Consequently there is no danger of complications from settlement of supports or parasitic moments caused by prestressing.

The Wichert truss principle has, among others, the following advantages:

1. Economy of girder material
2. Economy of foundations
3. Elimination of intermediate hinges
4. Stresses unaffected by temperature difference between chords or flanges

The Smithy Wood Footbridge, Figure 13.16, in the United Kingdom is one of three footbridges constructed in about 1970 over the M-1 Motorway using the principle of the Wichert Truss.

13.5.4 STRESS RIBBON BRIDGES

Another new type of bridge, introduced relatively recently, is the Spannbandbrücke or stress ribbon bridge.[13,14] Its origin is obscure and can be traced back to early societies. Basically the early versions consisted of wood planking supported directly on main catenary cables. It is still used in certain parts of the world, Figure 13.17.

The first modern attempt at the implementation of this concept was in 1958, when Ulrich Finsterwalder unsuccessfully entered the concept in the Bosporus Bridge competition, Figure 13.18, and again in 1961 for the Zoo Bridge at Cologne. The first successful construction of a stress ribbon structure was in 1963 and 1964 in Switzerland for a conveyor-belt bridge at the Holderbank-Wildeck Cement Works, with a span of 710 ft (216.4 m). The Freiburg, Germany, footbridge, Figure 13.19, constructed in 1969 and 1970 has an overall length of 448 ft (136.5 m) with a center span of 130 ft (39.5 m). Notice that the tops of the piers, in effect, form a large-radius saddle for the catenary cables. The deck has a width of 14.4 ft (4.40 m) and a thickness of 10 in. (0.25 m). In 1971 the Rhone Genf-Lignon stress ribbon bridge, Figure 13.20,

FIGURE 13.16.   Smithy Wood Footbridge.

FIGURE 13.17.   Early stress ribbon bridge in the Orient.

FIGURE 13.19.   Freiburg Stress Ribbon Footbridge.

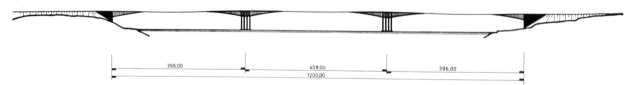

396,00	408,00	396,00
	1200,00	

FIGURE 13.18.   Stress ribbon concept for the Bosporus Bridge.

was constructed with a single span of 446 ft (136 m) and a width of 10.2 ft (3.10 m).

This type of structure has used prefabricated transverse and longitudinal prestressed precast segments supported on the main catenary cables. Wind-tunnel tests have indicated that a stress ribbon bridge is safe against torsional oscillation.[15] It can have a relatively flat sag, such that the grade at the abutments and piers can be kept at approximately 4%. Its largest disadvantage is the large abutments required to sustain the large tensile force in the main cables.

FIGURE 13.20. Rhone Genf-Lignon Stress Ribbon Bridge.

13.5.5 SPACE FRAME BRIDGES

In 1980, one of the authors served in an advisory capacity to the Kuwait Ministry of Public Works to evaluate responses to a request for proposals for the Bubiyan Bridge Project. An interesting proposal was submitted by Bouygues, a French firm. This proposal consisted of a three-dimensional truss or space frame concept, Figures 13.21 through 13.23.

The concept of prestressed concrete trusses is not a new one. Concrete trusses have been used in building construction and in bridges (Chapter 8) in various projects throughout the world. For example:

1. The Mangfall Bridge in Austria (Section 8.7.2) is a three-span, cast-in-place, prestressed concrete structure. It may be described simply as a box girder consisting of solid top and bottom flanges connected by two vertical webs, which are trusses.

2. The Rip Bridge in Australia (Section 8.7.3), just north of Sydney, is a three-span cantilever arch-truss structure. The upper chord (roadway slab), diagonal and vertical truss members, and lower chord are composed of precast elements, which are made integral by cast-in-place concrete and post-tensioning.

3. At least three prestressed concrete cantilever arch-truss bridges have been constructed in Yugoslavia, including the Kirk Bridge (Section 8.5.4), which presently holds the record for the longest concrete arch in the world, a 1280 ft (390 m) span.

4. Other prestressed concrete truss bridges have been constructed in France, the U.S.S.R., and Japan.

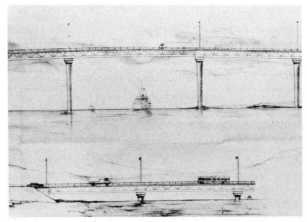

FIGURE 13.21. Elevations of Bubiyan Bridge Proposal prepared by Bouygues, Paris.

FIGURE 13.22. Isometric of Bubiyan Bridge Proposal prepared by Bouygues, Paris.

FIGURE 13.23. Construction-stage model of Bubiyan Bridge Proposal.

All the structures mentioned above have one thing in common: the prestressed concrete trusses are all oriented in a vertical plane. The concept is the same as in conventional truss bridges constructed of structural steel members.

The three-dimensional truss concept presented for the Bubiyan Bridge is essentially a multitriangular-cell concrete box girder wherein the longitudinal solid webs are replaced by an open lattice system of trusses. Because the lattice truss webs are oriented in an inclined plane, as opposed to a vertical plane, adjacent trusses have common node points (intersection of diagonal and vertical truss members with the flanges). This spatial geometry then forms in the transverse direction another system of trusses. Thus, the flanges are connected by a system of inclined orthogonal trusses (a system of mutually perpendicular trusses), Figure 13.24. Because the trusses are inclined to each other, with the diagonal and vertical members intersecting at common node points, they form a space frame composed of interconnecting pyramids. Thus, the structural behavior of the bridge with regard to distribution of load resembles that of a two-way slab in building construction.

This structural concept is new in regard to its application to a bridge structure. However, the concept of a space frame truss has been previously applied to roof structures for large column-free sport facilities, auditoriums, civic centers, and the like. These space structures have been constructed primarily of metallic (steel or aluminum) tubular sections. There is no reason to believe that with the current state of the art in prestressed concrete, segmental construction and existing concrete truss construction, a prestressed concrete space frame concept cannot be consummated—in particular for a bridge structure.

The advantage of this concept is that as a result of the "openness" of the trellis framework of trusses the dead or self-weight of the superstructure is much less than that of conventional prestressed concrete construction. This comparative reduction in weight of the superstructure reduces the dead load to be transmitted to the substructure and thus reduces the mass of the substructure, with resulting economies. Further, there is an advantage in the manner the load is distributed throughout the structure. That is to say, there are many load paths. In the unforeseen event of a member failure, the load would redistribute by seeking an alternative load path. Therefore, there is a greater degree of redundancy, which means that there is greater safety from a collapse failure. Or, in other words, by virtue of the spatial geometry there is an inherent reserve capacity.

In all other respects the fabrication and erection of the superstructure is consistent with state-of-the-art conventional prestressed, precast segmental construction, including the external prestressing. Although the concept of a space frame structure is new to bridge construction, its newness is only in assembling existing concepts into a single concept.

13.6   Summary

The last decade has seen considerable changes in bridge design and construction, many of which have been evolving since the 1950s. As we move into the 1980s, we must remain aware of change. Research already underway on inproved materials may have dramatic impact in the indusry. Applications of new systems to existing bridge types are being attempted along with new and improved types of bridge structures. Many of the improved materials and new concepts will reach practical application; others will be abandoned for technical or economic reasons. Unforeseen improvements in materials and new types of bridge structures are certain to evolve in the next decade, which promises to be one of excitement and challenge.

As engineers whose basic responsibility is the betterment of mankind, we must be constantly open to new concepts and ideas that will technically and economically improve the structures we attempt to build. However, at the same time we must anticipate a new generation of problems that changes in methodology are certain to bring. Of

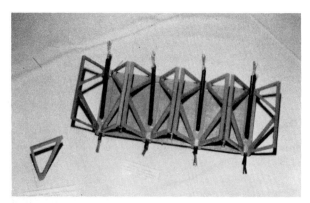

FIGURE 13.24. Model of typical segment with top flange removed (note external post-tensioning tendons), Bubiyan Bridge Proposal.

prime importance, we must not fall into a trap of oversophistication in design at the expense of simplicity and thus economy in construction.

As we strive for longer spans and improved means of constructing bridges, it would be well to remember the words of F. Stüssi, an eminent Swiss engineer:

The problem of Long Spans has always fascinated the specialist as well as the layman. The realization of a bridge with a length of span hitherto unattained not only requires great technical knowledge and capability, but also intuition and creative courage; it signifies a victory over the forces of nature and progress in the battle against human insufficiency.

This philosophy applies not only to the achievement of longer spans, but also to the changing technology of the future.

References

1. I. A. Rubinsky and A. Rubinsky, "A Preliminary Investigation of the Use of Fiberglass for Prestressed Concrete," *Magazine of Concrete Research*, September 1954.

2. James E. Carpenter, "Applications of High Strength Concrete for Highway Bridges," Interim Report, July 1979, Concrete Technology Corporation, Contract No. DOT-FH-11-9510 (unpublished report).

3. W. Podolny, Jr., "Properties of Fiber-Reinforced Concrete," *Highway Focus*, Vol. 4, No. 5, October 1972, Federal Highway Administration, Washington, D.C.

4. "State-of-the-Art Report on Fiber Reinforced Concrete," Reported by ACI Committee 544, *Journal of the American Concrete Institute*, November 1973.

5. J. P. Romualdi and G. B. Batson, "Mechanics of Crack Arrest in Concrete," *Proceedings of the ASCE*, Vol. 89, No. EM 3, June 1963.

6. J. P. Romualdi and G. B. Batson, "Behavior of Reinforced Concrete Beams with Closely Spaced Reinforcement," *Journal of the American Concrete Institute*, Vol. 60, Title No. 60-40, June 1963.

7. "Polymer Concrete," *FIP Notes*, 38 January/February 1972, Federation Internationale de la Precontrainte.

8. Jan Sulkiewicz and Juhani Virola, "Future Aspects of Bridge Construction," *International Civil Engineering Monthly*, Vol. III, No. 2, 1974 (Jerusalem).

9. G. H. Beguin, "Vergundbrücken—Ausführungsprobleme beim Fahrbahn platten—Schiebeverfahren, *Der Stahlbaum*, Heft 12, Dezember 1975.

10. G. H. Beguin, "Composite Bridge Decking by Stage-Deck Jacking," *Journal of the Structural Division, ASCE*, Vol. 104, No. ST 1, January 1978.

11. Rene Ryser, Discussion of "Composite Bridge Decking by Stage-Deck Jacking," *Journal of the Structural Division, ASCE*, Vol. 104, No. ST 10, October 1978.

12. D. B. Steinman, *The Wichert Truss*, Van Nostrand-Reinhold, New York, 1932.

13. Rene Walther, "Stressed Ribbon Bridges," *International Civil Engineering Monthly*, Vol. II, No. 1, 1971/1972 (Jerusalem).

14. Heinz Nehse, "Spannbandbrücken," in *Festschrift Ulrich Finsterwalder 50 Jahre für Dywidag, Dyckerhoff & Widmann, A.G.*, Munich, 1973.

15. Ulrich Finsterwalder, "Free-Cantilever Construction of Prestressed Concrete Bridges and Mushroom-Shaped Bridges," *First International Symposium, Concrete Bridge Design*, American Concrete Institute Publication SP-23, Detroit, 1969.

Index of Bridges

Index of Personal Names

Index of Firms and Organizations

Index of Subjects